THE GAY AND LESBIAN
Literary Heritage

THE GAY AND LESBIAN
Literary Heritage

A READER'S COMPANION TO THE
WRITERS AND THEIR WORKS,
FROM ANTIQUITY TO THE PRESENT

Edited by Claude J. Summers

BLOOMSBURY

First published 1995 by Henry Holt and Company, Inc.
115 West 18th Street, New York, New York 10011

This edition published 1997 by Bloomsbury Publishing Plc,
38 Soho Square, London W1V 5DF

The moral right of the author has been asserted.

A copy of the CIP record for this book
is available on request from the British Library

Printed in the United States of America

ISBN 0 7475 3295 8

10 9 8 7 6 5 4 3 2 1

For Ted, again.

Still crazy after all these years.

Contents

Acknowledgments

A collaborative project of the scope of *The Gay and Lesbian Literary Heritage* necessarily depends on the kindness and cooperation of numerous individuals, including most obviously the contributors. I am particularly grateful to the individuals who offered advice and made suggestions on topics and authors and contributors, especially David Bergman, Gregory Bredbeck, Margaret Breen, Joseph Cady, Douglas Chambers, Louis Crompton, Raymond-Jean Frontain, Anne Herrmann, Karla Jay, Simon Karlinsky, Kevin Kopelson, Sharon Malinowski, Robert Martin, Toni McNaron, Edmund Miller, Emmanuel Nelson, Lawrence Normand, William A. Percy, Oktor Skjaervo, Bruce Smith, Donald Stone, Martha Vicinus, Ann Wadsworth, Gregory Woods, G. Patton Wright, and Randal Woodland. I need also express gratitude to the staff of the computing center at the University of Michigan-Dearborn and to the secretarial staff in the Department of Humanities and the College of Arts, Sciences, and Letters. The enthusiasm and efficiency of Elizabeth Frost Knappman and the staff of New England Publishing Associates, Inc. have been crucial to the success of this project. For encouragement and moral support, I am especially grateful to my friends Terry Kihara, Michael Twomey, Neil Flax, Francisco Soto, Mark Albano, Dorothy Lee, Emily Spinelli, Cel Walby, and, of course, Ted-Larry Pebworth, to whom this volume is dedicated.

Claude J. Summers

Introduction

The Gay and Lesbian Literary Heritage is a reader's companion to a remarkable range of literature and authors. It provides overviews of the gay and lesbian presence in a variety of literatures and historical periods, in-depth critical essays on major gay and lesbian writers in world literature, and briefer treatments of other topics and figures important in appreciating the rich and varied gay and lesbian literary traditions. The more than 350 essays gathered here attest to the pervasiveness of homoeroticism in literature, from ancient times to the present, as well as to the recurrent preoccupation of gay and lesbian literature with certain themes and motifs, such as self-realization, erotic longing, alienation from society, and the celebration of beauty and forbidden pleasures. They are also witness to the historical and continuing attempts to suppress and silence homoerotic expression and to the (sometimes heroic) persistence of gay and lesbian writers in making their voices heard, often in difficult and dangerous circumstances. Given the nature of homosexuality—both historically and currently—as a controversial subject, this book cannot help partaking of a specific cultural (and political) agenda, the recovery and consolidation of a perpetually threatened legacy of same-sex love in literature and life.

The literary representation of homosexuality is a crucially important topic for gay men and lesbians. The vital role that literature plays in the lives of many homosexuals is due not only to the fact that an awareness of sexual difference may encourage the introspection that leads to enhanced literacy and to artistic creation, but also to the peculiar relationship of contemporary gay men and lesbians to their society. Homosexuals differ significantly from ethnic, national, and religious minorities, who may face discrimination and disdain, but who develop within their families important systems of support and nurturance. By contrast, most lesbians and gay men grow up in families in which their sexual orientation is concealed, ignored, or condemned. They often come to a realization of their gayness with little or no understanding of homosexuality beyond the negative stereotypes that pervade contemporary society, and they usually feel isolated and frightened at the very time they most need reassurance and encouragement. Not surprisingly, a staple of the gay and lesbian "coming out" story is the trip to the local library, where the young homosexual, desperate for the most basic information, is usually utterly confused or bitterly disappointed by what he or she discovers, for even now our society does not make it easy for young people to find accurate information about homosexuality. Only later is the homosexual's radical loneliness assuaged by the discovery of a large and varied literary and cultural heritage, one that speaks directly to the experience of contemporary Western men and women but that also reflects other forms of same-sex love and desire in different times and places.

This volume is at once a documentation and reclamation of that heritage and also a contribution to it. It participates in a long endeavor by gay men and lesbians to recover their social and literary history. For centuries, educated and literate homosexuals living in eras that condemned homosexuality have looked to other ages and other societies in order to find cultural permission for homosexual behavior, to experience some relief from the incessant attacks on their self-esteem, and to penetrate the barriers of censorship that precluded open discussion of the love that dared not speak its name. Such attempts range from the ubiquitous lists of famous homosexuals in history to more elaborate and sophisticated historical research, such as that of Jeremy Bentham in the eighteenth century and of Edward Carpenter and John Addington Symonds at the end of the nineteenth century, as well as the recurrent attempts by gay and lesbian writers to discover traditions and languages through which to express themselves. Too often, however, attempts to document the gay and lesbian cultural legacy paid little attention to historical differences and tended to make few distinctions between different kinds of homosexualities, equating the emergent homosexual of the nineteenth century with the ancient Greek pederast, the medieval sodomite, and the North American *berdache,* for example, as though all four phenomena were merely minor variations on the same pattern.

The Gay and Lesbian Literary Heritage is, of course, motivated by the identical impulse to understand the past and to recover the (often suppressed or disguised) artistic expressions of same-sex love that propelled earlier projects. But as the beneficiary of a more open climate and a recent explosion of knowledge about homosexuality in history, it is in a far better position than they were to discover a usable past. The new understanding of sexuality in history and culture that emerged in the 1980s and 1990s constitutes one of the major intellectual achievements of the last quarter of the twentieth century. The efflorescence of gay and lesbian studies within North American and European universities has, in fact, enabled this particular enterprise. Without the gay and lesbian studies movement, this volume would not have been possible. In entering the academic mainstream, gay and lesbian studies have enlarged our understanding of the meaning of being gay and lesbian, both in our own culture and in other times and places. They have challenged naïve, uninformed, and prejudiced views, and, perhaps most important, have discovered and recovered significant texts and authors. Gay and lesbian studies have also claimed mainstream literature, revealing the pertinence and centrality of (frequently disguised) same-sex relationships in canonical texts.

But although gay and lesbian studies have enriched the academic study of history and literature, they still tend to be ghettoized in elite universities, often in women's studies programs that are themselves frequently isolated. Meanwhile, standard literary anthologies and histories continue all too often to omit or discount gay and lesbian texts and subtexts, fail to supply relevant biographical information about gay and lesbian writers, and foster the grievously mistaken impression that the world literary traditions are almost exclusively heterosexual. *The Gay and Lesbian Literary Heritage* aims to redress these deficiencies. It

seeks to place portrayals of same-sex desire in historical context, to provide accurate biographical information about writers who have contributed to gay and lesbian literary traditions, and to explore important questions about the presence of homoeroticism in world literature. How has homosexual literature been shaped by the religious and cultural strictures against homosexuality? How does the homosexuality of an author affect his or her work even when that work has nothing specifically to do with homosexuality? How does one decipher the "coding" of literature in which the homosexual import is disguised? Is there such a thing as a gay sensibility? Are some literary genres and movements more amenable to homoeroticism than others? What are the connections between gay male literature and lesbian literature? Do gay and lesbian readers respond to ostensibly "straight" literature differently from heterosexual readers? What is the connection between lesbians and amazons? Why is St. Sebastian an icon of gay male artists? These are some of the questions asked and variously answered in this book.

The Gay and Lesbian Literary Heritage testifies to the unique power of literature to express desire and signify sexual difference. More than any other kind of discourse, imaginative literature provides access to the subjectivity and complexity of sexuality by depicting the psychological nuances and ambivalences of desire and its frustration or fulfillment from the inside as well as the outside, and does so with the concreteness and specificity of lived experience. For example, at a crucial point in his coming to terms with his sexuality, the eponymous hero of E. M. Forster's novel *Maurice* thinks of himself as wandering "beyond the barrier . . . the wrong words on his lips and the wrong desires in his heart, and his arms full of air," while in Whitman's "When I Heard at the Close of the Day," the poet defines happiness not in terms of "plaudits in the capitol" but in the joy of communion with his lover, a fulfillment that nature itself seems to ratify:

> And when I thought how my dear friend my
>   lover was on his way coming, O then I was
>   happy,
> O then each breath tasted sweeter, and all that
>   day my food nourish'd me more, and the
>   beautiful day pass'd well,
> And the next came with equal joy, and with
>   the next at evening came my friend,
> And that night while all was still I heard the
>   waters roll slowly continually up the shores,
> I heard the hissing rustle of the liquid and
>   sands as directed to me whispering to
>   congratulate me,

For the one I love most lay sleeping by me
    under the same covers in the cool night,
In the stillness in the autumn moonbeams his
    face was inclined towards me,
And his arm lay lightly around my breast—
    and that night I was happy.

Forster's powerful images of isolation and emptiness capture the emotion of alienation with an intensity and immediacy of feeling that no psychological treatise could describe, just as no sociological study could explain the heightened contentment that Whitman conveys. Nor could a clinical description approach the lightening-bolt accuracy of Muriel Rukeyser's account of the pain of the closet in "The Poem as Mask":

When I wrote of the women in their dances
    and wildness, it was a mask,
on their mountain, god-hunting, singing
    in orgy,
it was a mask; when I wrote of the god,
fragmented, exiled from himself, his life, the
    love gone down with song,
it was myself, split open, unable to speak, in
    exile from myself.

Imaginative literature, quite simply, captures human experience with a vividness that other kinds of discourse cannot.

Literature, however, is not merely a creation of particular perspectives by isolated artists; it is at once a reflection and an expression of social attitudes and individual sensibilities. As a complex interaction between artist and circumstance, and text and context, imaginative literature provides a rich record of historical lore. Hence, to study gay and lesbian literature is also to come to understand both the varying insights of particular authors and the changing historical conditions under which lesbians and gay men have lived and written. Insofar as literature documents—or challenges—its period's sexual beliefs and prohibitions, it is an extraordinarily valuable resource for charting the outlines of sexual ideology at any particular time.

Many readers may wonder whether a heritage that includes individuals as dissimilar as Sappho, Mehemmid Ghazali, William Shakespeare, Aphra Behn, Stefan George, Christina Rossetti, Gertrude Stein, Sophia Parnok, James Baldwin, Yukio Mishima, and Jack Kerouac is coherent enough to be useful. Indeed, the variety—or dissimilarity one from the other—of figures discussed in this volume is striking, both in terms of individual sensibilities and of different historical positions. This ought not to be surprising, however, since one of the central tenets of

gay and lesbian studies is the wide diversity of gay men and lesbians, a principle that this book amply verifies. The resistance of gay men and lesbians to reductive stereotyping is a very important aspect of the literary heritage. Homosexuals are far too diverse to share a single sensibility, and the manifestations of homosexuality are too various to permit sweeping generalizations. Different individuals are affected differently by particular characteristics, and those characteristics are assigned different meanings in different societies. Even the identifiable homosexual styles—such as, for example, camp—that emerge from time to time are clearly the product of cultural and subcultural influences and are never universally shared by all homosexuals. As this volume demonstrates, there are in fact many gay and lesbian literary traditions, often co-existing with one another. It is not in their coherent unity—though many connections and continuities are apparent—but in their diversity and multiplicity that these traditions constitute a valuable heritage.

The literary study of homosexuality must inevitably confront a variety of vexed issues, including basic conceptual questions of definition and identity. Who, exactly, is a homosexual? What constitutes sexual identity? To what extent is sexuality the product of broadly defined social forces? To what degree do sexual object choices manifest a biological or psychological essence within the desiring individual? These questions are not only problematic for the historical study of homosexuality, but they also reflect current controversies about contemporary and historical sexual roles and categories, and they resist glib answers. Although contemporary North Americans and Western Europeans typically think in terms of a dichotomy between homosexuality and heterosexuality, and between the homosexual and the heterosexual, with vague compartments for bisexuality and bisexuals, such a conception is a historically contingent cultural construct, more revealing of our own age's sexual ideology than of actual erotic practices even today. The range of human sexual response is considerably less restricted than these artificial classifications suggest, and different ages and cultures have interpreted (and regulated) sexual behavior differently.

Because human sexual behavior and emotions are fluid and various rather than static or exclusive, the sexologist Alfred Kinsey and others have argued that the terms *homosexual* and *heterosexual* should more properly be used as adjectives rather than nouns, referring to acts and emotions but not to people. Moreover, the conception of homosexuality and heterosexuality as essential and exclusive categories has historically operated as a form of social control, defining the person who responds erotically to individuals of his or her own sex as the "Other," or, more particularly, as *queer* or *unnatural*. But though it may be tempting to conclude that there are no such entities as homosexuals or heterosexuals, this view, which so attractively stresses the commonality of human beings and minimizes the significance of sexual object choices, poses its own dangers. Human sexuality is simply not as plastic as some theorists assert, and to deny the existence of homosexuals, bisexuals, and heterosexuals—or the pertinence of such categories—is to deny the genuineness of the personal identities and forms of erotic life that exist today. It is, indeed, to engage in a process of denial and erasure, rendering invisible a group that has had to struggle for recognition and visibility. For most people in the West today, sexual orientation is not merely a matter of choice or preference but a classification that reflects a deep-seated internal, as well as social, reality. However arbitrary, subjective, inexact, and culture-bound the labels may be, they are impossible to escape and affect individuals—especially those in the minority categories—in profound and manifold ways.

The most painful and destructive injustice visited upon gay men and lesbians has been their separation from the normal and the natural, their stigmatization as *queer*. Yet the internalization of this stigma has also been their greatest strength and, indeed, the core of their identity in societies that regularly assign individuals to ostensibly exclusive categories of sexual desire. The consciousness of difference both spurred and made possible the recent creation of a homosexual minority—a gay and lesbian community—in the Western democracies, a process that involved transforming the conception of homosexuality from a "social problem" and personal failing to an individual and collective identity. Quite apart from the fact that it facilitates identity politics, however, an acceptance of otherness is also often personally empowering. Fostering qualities of introspection and encouraging social analysis, it enables people who feel excluded from some of the core assumptions and rituals of their society to evaluate themselves and their society from an ambiguous and often revealing perspective. The reluctance to surrender the sense of difference, what E. M. Forster detected in the modern Greek poet C. P. Cavafy as the sensation of standing "at a slight angle to the universe," may account in part for the hostility of many gay men and lesbians to theoretical explanations of sexuality that translate the vividness of individual experience into ill-defined social phenomena and reduce sexual identity to a product of impersonal historical forces.

Homoerotic desire and behavior have been documented in every conceivable kind of society. What varies are the meanings that they are accorded from era to era and place to place. In some societies, homosexuality is tolerated and even institutionalized, whereas in others it is vilified and persecuted. In every society, there are undoubtedly individuals who are predominantly attracted to members of their own sex, but the extent to which that sexual attraction functions as a defining characteristic of these individuals' personal and social identities varies considerably from culture to culture. For example, even today the so-called Mediterranean homosexuality (which predominates in Latin America, the Balkans, and the Islamic countries of the Mediterranean, as well as in the Latin countries of Europe) differs significantly from the Western European and North American pattern. Mediterranean homosexuality is characterized by a sharp dichotomy between active and passive partners, with only the passive partner in sexual relations ascribed a homosexual identity (and stigmatized), while the homosexuality predominant in North America and industrialized Europe emphasizes egalitarian relationships in which sexual roles are not rigidly polarized. And whereas the contemporary Western European and North American version of homosexuality is conceived in sharp opposition to heterosexuality, that is not so in many Asian societies, where homosexuality is accommodated within the paramount cultural obligations of heterosexual marriage and reproduction. Thus, any transhistorical and transcultural exploration of the gay and lesbian literary heritage must guard against the risk of anachronism, of inappropriately imposing contemporary culture-bound conceptions of homosexuality on earlier ages and different societies. Sexual categories are always historically and culturally specific rather than universal and invariant.

On the other hand, however, the recognition of cultural specificity in regard to sexual attitudes need not estrange the past or obscure connections and continuities between historical periods and between sexual ideologies. For instance, modern North American and Western European male homosexuality, which is predominantly androphiliac (that is, between adults) and socially disdained, is in many crucial respects quite different from ancient Greek male homosexuality, which was predominantly—though by no means exclusively—pederastic and incorporated a socially valorized educational function; but awareness of those differences does not obviate the similarities that link the two distinct historical constructs. Neither does the acknowledgment of the distinctions between ancient Greek homosexuality and modern homosexuality entail the dismissal of the enormous influence that classical Greek attitudes toward same-sex love exerted on the formation of modern Western attitudes toward homosexuality. For many individuals in the early modern and modern eras, ancient Greek literature and philosophy helped counter the negative attitudes toward same-sex eroticism fostered by Christian culture. Ancient Greek literature has provided readers and writers of subsequent centuries a pantheon of heroes, a catalogue of images, and a set of references by which homosexual desire could be encoded into their own literatures and through which they could interpret their own experiences. Thus, though well aware of the differences between modern homosexuality and ancient Greek love, we may still claim Greek classics of homoeroticism as important elements in the gay and lesbian literary heritage.

Nor should our sensitivity to the cultural specificity of sexual attitudes cause us to rob individual authors of individual perspectives or to condescend toward the past. All writers exist in relation to their time and must necessarily write from within their world views, or, as philosopher Michel Foucault would say, the *epistemes* of their ages. But the fact that writers and other artists are embedded in their cultures does not mean that they lack agency and individuality. Artists tend to be more independent than their contemporaries, not less; and although they may express the tendencies and suppositions of their societies, they also frequently challenge them, even if those challenges are themselves facilitated and contained by societal beliefs. Hence, it is a mistake to assume that writers in earlier ages, before the general emergence of a modern homosexual identity, could not share important aspects of that consciousness, including a subjective awareness of difference and a sense of alienation from society. One of the rewards of studying the gay and lesbian literary heritage is, in fact, the discovery of homosexual subjectivity in the past and of the affinities as well as differences between earlier and later homosexualities.

For all its considerable heft, *The Gay and Lesbian Literary Heritage* has no pretensions to comprehensiveness. There are some notable omissions of topics and authors, due variously to lack of space, an absence of available information and research, or a difficulty in finding qualified contributors. Among essays that would be desirable, for example, are overviews of Scandinavian and eastern European literatures, as well as entries on numerous authors for whom no room could be found. Moreover, the *Heritage* is undoubtedly biased in favor of English and American literary traditions, even as it also provides a great deal of information about other traditions and cultures. The point that needs emphasis, however, is that this companion is an important beginning, not an end. It introduces readers to a wealth of literature, making accessible the fruits of the intense study that has recently been focused on gay and lesbian literature. It aspires to be a valuable companion to readers interested in the literary representation of homoeroticism from ancient times to the present.

How to Use *The Gay and Lesbian Literary Heritage*

In a famous formulation, Sir Francis Bacon divided books into three types. "Some books are to be tasted, others to be swallowed, and some few to be chewed and digested: that is, some books are to be read only in parts; others to be read, but cursorily; and some few to be read wholly and with diligence and attention." This book aspires to all three categories. We certainly hope that it will be inviting and rewarding enough to entice readers into diligent and attentive study. At the same time, however, we hope that the book will also invite browsers, who will dip into it repeatedly over time for pleasure and enlightenment. In addition, we hope that it will also serve as a valuable reference tool for readers who need to find particular information quickly.

The essays in the *Heritage* are presented alphabetically, an arrangement that should encourage browsing. They are generally of three types: overviews of national or ethnic literatures, essays on topics or movements of particular significance for gay and lesbian literature, and essays on individual authors, not all of them gay or lesbian. The overviews of national literatures sometimes comprise several essays. For example, the entry on ENGLISH LITERATURE includes distinct essays on the following periods: Medieval, Renaissance, Restoration and Eighteenth Century, Romanticism, Nineteenth Century, and Twentieth Century. Similarly, the entries on AMERICAN LITERATURE, FRENCH LITERATURE, GERMAN LITERATURE, and GREEK LITERATURE include essays on particular periods, with twentieth-century American literature being further divided into essays on Gay Male Literature, 1900–1969; Lesbian Literature, 1900–1969; Gay Male Post-Stonewall Literature; and Lesbian Post-Stonewall Literature.

Topic entries also sometimes include multiple essays, as, for example, the entry for POETRY, which is subdivided into separate essays on Gay Male Poetry and Lesbian Poetry, or the entry for DRAMATIC LITERATURE, which consists of separate essays on Modern Drama and Contemporary Drama, or the entry for AFRICAN-AMERICAN LITERATURE, which includes separate essays on African-American Gay Male Literature and African-American Lesbian Literature.

The author entries range from brief accounts to in-depth critical analyses of major figures like Sappho, Plato, William Shakespeare, Walt Whitman, Emily Dickinson, Marcel Proust, or Virginia Woolf. The most important criterion in determining whether an author was assigned an entry is the author's contribution to gay and lesbian literary traditions, regardless of his or her own sexual orientation. The lack of an individual entry for an author does not, however, mean that the author is not significant to the gay and lesbian heritage or not discussed in the volume. For example, there are no entries for Wolfgang von Goethe, Jo Sinclair, Kate Millet, Tony Kushner, Michael Nava, or Samuel Delany, but each receives detailed discussion: Goethe in GERMAN AND AUSTRIAN LITERATURE: BEFORE THE NINETEENTH CENTURY, Sinclair in JEWISH AMERICAN LITERATURE, Millett in AMERICAN LITERATURE: LESBIAN POST-STONEWALL, Kushner in the essays on DRAMATIC LITERATURE: CONTEMPORARY DRAMA and AIDS LITERATURE, Nava in MYSTERY FICTION, GAY MALE, and Delany in the entry on SCIENCE FICTION. Discussions of authors who are not accorded individual author entries can most conveniently be found via the Index.

The frequent cross-references should be helpful for readers interested in related topics or in finding further discussions of particular authors. The *Heritage* employs two systems of cross-references. The first time an author who is the subject of an entry elsewhere in the volume is mentioned, his or her name is given in small caps, indicating that more information about that particular author can be found in his or her own entry. The same is true for topics or literary movements that are referred to in essays. In addition, readers are often urged to "see also" other entries.

Each entry is followed by a brief bibliography. With some exceptions, the bibliographies emphasize secondary rather than primary material, pointing the reader to other studies of the topic or author. In the bibliographies, individual items are separated by bullets; the long dash indicates that a particular item is by the same author as that of the item immediately preceding it.

Finally, the Index should be of help in maneuvering through this large volume. Some writers, such as Sappho, Oscar Wilde, and Radclyffe Hall, are discussed in several entries in addition to their own author entries, whereas others who have no individual author entries are discussed in the overviews or topic essays. Please consult the Index to find such discussions.

Ackerley, J. R.
(1896–1967)

From 1935 until 1959, Joe Randolph Ackerley edited *The Listener*, BBC's weekly literature and arts journal, so skillfully and so eclectically, that he came to be recognized as "one of the most brilliant editors of his generation." Under his editorship, the journal counted not only E. M. FORSTER, VIRGINIA WOOLF, Herbert Read, and Clive Bell among its regular contributors, but also such new talents as W. H. AUDEN, CHRISTOPHER ISHERWOOD, and STEPHEN SPENDER. Spender commented that Ackerley "cared immensely about what books were reviewed—and by whom—and what poems he published. He encouraged young writers."

Ackerley's output as a writer himself was small: one play, one novel, three autobiographical works, and a handful of poems. Their candor, frankness, and honesty often upset readers and friends alike, so much so that Forster once said, "I wish I could give him a good smack." Ackerley's aesthetic, however, was far closer to the aims of the socially conscious 1930s and 1940s than to modernist detachment. Late in life, he explained his assumptions to Spender thus: "to speak the truth, I think that people *ought* to be upset, and if I had a paper I would upset them all the time. I think that life is so important and, in its workings, so upsetting that nobody should be spared."

When Ackerley died in 1967, readers knew him for *The Prisoners of War* (1923), a psychological drama based on his own experiences as a German prisoner of war that critiques the British officer class and code and maturely treats homosexual themes and ties, and perhaps for *Hindoo Holiday* (1932), a journal of his months in India while private secretary to a maharajah. In addition, his two "dog books," *My Dog Tulip* (1956) and *We Think the World of You* (1960), had their champions and demonstrated that Ackerley found his much longed-for Ideal Friend among animals, rather than men.

The posthumous publication of *My Father and Myself* (1968), however, necessitated a complete reconsideration of Ackerley's significance. The book—simultaneously a coming-out story; a meditation on masculinity, paternity, and sonship; a chronicle of a Victorian family coping with the twentieth century; and a record of mutual deceptions—certainly merits TRUMAN CAPOTE's comment that it is "the most original autobiography I have ever read" and Diana Trilling's judgment that it is "the simplest, most directly personal report of what it is like to be a homosexual that . . . has yet been published."

Ackerley tells of the familiar sexual temptations in the British public school, his wartime adventures in "Boom Ravine," his unsuccessful attempts to create direction in his writing, and his quest for an Ideal Friend. He richly details his attractions to lower- and working-class men and uniformed men and describes the general gay milieu of the 1920s and 1930s. Epiphany came with his father's death in 1929 when Ackerley read two letters, dating from 1920 and 1927, in which his father told his son of a "secret family"—his long-time mistress, three daughters, and a comfortable home in Castelnau. Up to this point, Ackerley felt that his father, a prosperous fruit importer, had a life complete in "the steady regularity of its domestic rhythms" and was more than a little puzzled by and even contemptuous of his homosexual son. With coincidences that art often denies itself, life in a Hammersmith flat confronts Ackerley with a portrait of Count James Francis de Gallatin, who, evidence suggests, may well have been his father's lover when his father was a member of the Household Cavalry. A somewhat melancholy tone informs *My Father and Myself*, because of Ackerley's regret over his lack of communication with his father, created largely by social convention, British reticence, and his own uncertainties over the standing of the homosexual in British society. (See also DRAMATIC LITERATURE: MODERN DRAMA and ENGLISH LITERATURE: TWENTIETH CENTURY.)

—*David Leon Higdon*

BIBLIOGRAPHY

Parker, Peter. *Ackerley: A Life of J. R. Ackerley*. New York: Farrar, Straus and Giroux, 1989.

Aesthetism

At once a theory of art and an approach to living, aestheticism emphasizes the absolute autonomy of works of art, their total preeminence over other aspects of life, and their independence of moral and social conditions. The aestheticist movement took on extraordinary force at the end of the nineteenth century, primarily in France and England but also in Italy, Germany, and to a lesser extent, the United States. In histories of the movement, aestheticism is often conflated with the French *l'art pour l'art* movement, literary decadence, and *fin-de-siècle* dandyism. Historically, it has been linked to homosexuality, not only because of the implications of its principles, but also because of the personal sexual tastes of some of its key adherents. Among its more important propagandists were, in France, Théophile Gautier, CHARLES BAUDELAIRE, J. K. HUYSMANS, PAUL VERLAINE, Count Robert de Montesquiou, Claude Debussy, ARTHUR RIMBAUD, Stephane Mallarmé, JEAN COCTEAU, and MARCEL PROUST and, in England, ALGERNON SWINBURNE, George Moore, WALTER PATER, Lionel Johnson, Arthur Symons, William Butler Yeats, James McNeill Whistler, JOHN ADDINGTON SYMONDS, Edmund Gosse, and OSCAR WILDE, as well as members of the Pre-Raphaelite circle of painters and such BLOOMSBURY figures as the art critic Roger Fry. Others whose work suggests ties to aestheticism were Gabriele d'Annuzio, Gustav Klimt, Rainer Maria Rilke, Serge Diaghilev, and HENRY JAMES, particularly the James of the novelist's late phase and the critical prefaces. The variety of such an inventory should help indicate how troublesome is any attempt to define aestheticism as, strictly speaking, a homosexual enterprise. Yet there is little question that the arguments of the aestheticist movement were frequently thinly veiled attempts by *fin-de-siècle* homosexuals, particularly those educated at Oxford and Cambridge, at justifying relations between members of the same sex.

The philosophical premises of aestheticism originate in the German philosophical tradition represented by Kant, Schelling, Goethe, and Schiller. Kant's claim concerning works of art—that they are disinterested, "pure," and that they bespeak a second nature through human agency—might be understood as supplying an intellectual basis for homosexual relations, particularly if one chooses to conceive of "second nature" in erotic terms. Kant's view of art as "purposiveness without purpose," moreover, could be willfully construed as suggesting that procreative sexuality is inessential. Kierkegaard's negative diagnosis of aesthetic man in his *Either/Or* (1864) contrasted the man of aesthetic commitments with ethical man because of the former's absorption in a series of moods to which he completely surrenders himself. In a rebuttal of Pater before Paterian aesthetics, Kierkegaard criticized aesthetic man because of his refusal to assume a single, coherent personality. Without ever alluding to homosexuality, Kantian and Kierkegaardian ideas thus gave a certain philosophical foundation to a life devoted to "amoral" impulses. The schism between moral austerity and aestheticist principle identified by Kierkegaard was one that homosexual artists frequently chose as the very subject of their treatment of aestheticism.

Théophile Gautier (1811–1872), dance, theater, and art critic, offered the first full defense of the aestheticist credo in his celebrated preface to his novel *Mademoiselle de Maupin* (1835), where the author, in expressing his ire at the pervasive utilitarianism of Parisian literary critics, insists on the all-determining importance of beauty. The novel itself enacts the argument of the preface through the astonishing narrative of a man who, along with his mistress, believes he has fallen in love with a ravishing boy by the name of Silvio; in fact, they have become infatuated with Mademoiselle de Maupin. Before they realize their mistake, however, the hero worries that he may love men. Gautier's Shakespearean comedy of manners presents an argument for aestheticism in such a way that the philosophy of *l'art pour l'art* is inextricably entangled with questions of sexual preference. Beauty, the novel strongly intimates, can be loved independently of a particular sex. Furthermore, according to the reasoning of *Mademoiselle de Maupin,* a true connoisseurship of the beautiful must be indulged without an allegiance to conventional morality. In a number of Gautier's pronouncements in the novel—"There is something great and fine in loving a statue," for example, or "The impossible has always pleased me"—one glimpses aestheticism's debt to Romanticism in its concern with an exaggerated individualism and an exalted subjectivity.

The sexual ambiguity of so much aestheticist ideology often appears to be a cagey avowal of elitist homoerotics, which, like aestheticism, proclaimed that what was "unnatural" was more beautiful and therefore preferable to that which was found in mundane nature. In a controversial 1893 article in *Harper's* magazine entitled "The Decadent Movement in Literature," the critic Arthur

Symons expressed his fondness for decadent aesthetics as a "new and interesting and beautiful disease," a view contemporaneously articulated, albeit in sterner scientific terms, by medical science in its discussion of homosexual "illness." A seminal aestheticist text of the period was J. K. Huysmans's *À Rebours* (1884), published in English as *Against the Grain* although often translated inaccurately (but more suggestively) as *Against Nature,* a book that transfixed Oscar Wilde. In its account of the dandiacal erotic practices of Duc Jean Floressas des Esseintes, the author established a link between aestheticism and decadent behavior. One striking passage in the novel—one that especially fascinated Wilde—is Des Esseintes's recollection of a homosexual exploit. Des Esseintes remarks that the event, having been homosexual, was different from all of his other exploits. Des Esseintes's seeming conversion to Catholicism in the book's concluding pages is less a rejection of aestheticist principles than an apotheosis of aestheticist belief, providing the hero with yet another avenue for the expression of his obsession with the rituals of self-devotion and the steady accumulation of ecclesiastical *objets d'art.* One of the models for Huysmans's anti-hero was Robert de Montesquiou, who was also the prototype for Proust's Baron de Charlus. Chaste yet forever in the company of charming young men, aristocratic, haughty, and elegant, Montesquiou's sexual identity, so opaque yet charismatic, embodied many of the contradictions of aestheticism's sexual politics. Possibly a model for Wilde's Dorian Gray, Montesquiou waged a crusade on behalf of beauty yet was known for personal acts of extraordinary viciousness. Perhaps his most fitting symbol (which can be found among Des Esseintes's collectibles in *À Rebours*) was his jewel-encrusted tortoise, which in Huysmans's novel has died as a result of its heavy burden of brilliant baubles.

In England, Swinburne, Symonds, and Pater established a tradition of English aestheticism that threatened the Victorian belief, expressed most forcefully by Matthew Arnold, in art's requisite ethical and social dimension. At a time when nineteenth-century social thinkers were establishing medical models for an understanding of same-sex behavior, these writers looked back to Greek and Renaissance civilizations for alternative historical examples of homosexual affection that had been tolerated and even encouraged. In extolling earlier periods of high creative achievement, English aesthetes insisted that artists of genius by definition defied ordinary categories of correct masculine and feminine behavior, implying that all moral distinction must be subsumed to the search for the beautiful. Swinburne declared that "great poets are bisexual, male and female at once," and in his poem "Anactoria" (1866), he presented a dramatic monologue in the voice of SAPPHO, in which the Greek poet declares that: "There are those who say an array of horsemen, and others of marching men, and others of ships, is the most beautiful thing on the dark earth / But I say it is whatever one loves." In the chapter "The Genius of Greek Art" in volume two of his *Studies of the Greek Poets* (1875), Symonds celebrates a return to an eroticized ideal of aesthetics as a guide to proper moral conduct. Symonds's posthumously published memoirs revealed the anguish of his life as a married homosexual, but during his lifetime he expressed his feelings toward other men through an exploration of the Greeks and their Renaissance devotees as precursors of aestheticism.

In his novel *Marius the Epicurean* (1885), Pater, a long-time bachelor and professor at Oxford, sketched a portrait of a susceptible aesthete who is drawn to a series of cults, among them Cyrenaicism, whose credo "from time to time breaks beyond the limits of the actual moral order, perhaps not without some pleasurable excitement in so bold a venture." Pater created a storm of dissent with his notorious "Conclusion" to *Studies in the History of the Renaissance* (1873), in which he urged his readers—in the chapter's most frequently quoted clause—"to burn always with this hard gem-like flame" and to discover happiness in the avid pursuit of sensations raised to the pitch of "poetic passion, the desire of beauty, the love of art for art's sake." Pater chose to excise the "Conclusion" from the book's second edition but brazenly reinserted it in the third edition. That Pater's initial audience was potentially impressionable young Oxford students augmented the *Renaissance*'s reputation as a piece of pederastic propaganda. The novelist George Eliot, for one, declared that *Studies in the History of the Renaissance* "seems to me quite poisonous in its false principles and criticism and false conception of life." Pater's sway over writers of the 1890s, however, was incalculable.

Although Wilde downplayed Pater's influence on his work, Pater, Gautier, and Huysmans were of collective importance in helping determine Wilde's special brand of aestheticism. Although Wilde is generally considered to be the *fin-de-siècle* aesthete *par excellence,* looked at as a whole his writings on aestheticism reveal a far more complex and even critical attitude toward a life devoted to artistic sensation. *The Picture of Dorian Gray* (1891), in portraying the cruelty and disintegration of a young aesthete, is scarcely a defense of aestheticism; as Wilde's biographer Richard Ellmann noted, the aestheticist aphorisms that make up the preface function in dialectical relation to the main body of the book, which rapidly changes from breezy salon novel into dark cautionary tale. The true Wildean aesthete in *Dorian Gray* is Lord Henry, who, though married, is smitten with Dorian and attempts to lure him into a life devoted to art and hedonism. Dorian's descent into crime is thus an allegory of how Lord Henry's aestheticist axioms, taken to extremes, negate life, even one devoted to art.

Wilde's epigrammatic essays, particularly "The Decay of Lying" (1888), do, however, provide a coherent rationalization for aestheticism. Here Wilde claims that "All art is entirely useless" and "Nothing that actually occurs is of the smallest importance." Identifying two basic energies of art, Wilde asserts that artistic works exist in isolation from experience and that art is drenched in images, a recapitulation of Baudelaire's belief in an art composed of a "forest of symbols." Most important, Wilde insists that just as form determined content, art dictates life. It was not, Wilde claimed, a given age that shapes art (as the literary historian Hippolite Taine had asserted) but art that shapes a given age. "The nineteenth-century, as we know it," Wilde declares, "is largely an invention of Balzac," an idea polished into comic paradox in the playwright's remark that London had become foggy only after Turner had painted his misty London cityscapes. Wilde's continual stress on the value of artifice and the insincere can be read not only as a defense of the "unnatural vice" of homosexuality but as a sophisticated appreciation of the way in which sexuality is neither unified, static, nor constant, but contextual. In an era when the homosexual was "invented" by medical sexology as a separate species from the heterosexual, Wilde's aestheticism offered the retort that sexuality, like taste, was simply a heightened sensitivity to the beautiful.

Beginning with Gilbert and Sullivan's *Patience* (1881), Wildean aestheticism was the target of satire. Wilde is lampooned as the effeminate aesthete Reginald Bunthorne in an operetta whose popularity led Max Beerbohm to declare that it helped prolong the aestheticist movement after its heyday. More catastrophically for Wilde, Robert Hichens's *The Green Carnation* (1894), with innumerable sexual double entendres, underlined the connections between aestheticism and same-sex erotics. Hichens spoofed the playwright and his lover Lord Alfred Douglas ("Bosie") as Mr. Amarinth and Lord Reggie, master wit and his slavishly imitative friend, leaving no doubt about Douglas's sexuality when he depicts Lord Reggie chasing a boy. Although undoubtedly intended as an affectionate satire (Wilde himself expressed admiration for the book), *The Green Carnation* strongly confirmed Lord Queensbury's charges concerning Wilde's indecent sexual influence over his son, thus helping doom the playwright as a reckless corrupter of youth during Wilde's legal imbroglio. It is perhaps an irony of the English aestheticist movement that its chief proponent, Wilde, and the author of a damning parody of aestheticism, Hichens, were both men of homosexual inclinations.

Henry James's unresolved attitude toward the aestheticist movement was in part a reaction to the implied and actual homosexuality of Pater, Symonds, and Wilde, which James undoubtedly found personally threatening. James's first novel, *Roderick Hudson* (1876), was partly an exploration of the meaning of aestheticism for its painter-hero, but perhaps James's greatest fictional meditation on the subject is one of his finest short stories, "The Author of Beltraffio" (1884), which was modeled on Symonds's relationship with his wife, though James later explained that he was unaware of Symonds's homosexuality at the time of the tale's composition. Having heard from Edmund Gosse that Symonds's wife intensely disliked her husband's writings on art, James conjured up the character of Mark Ambient, whose works herald the gospel of aestheticism. One afternoon, while visited by the narrator, an admiring acolyte, Ambient's wife locks their sickly son into her bedroom. Before James's narrative is over, the child has mysteriously died, a casualty of its parents' unspoken dispute over Ambient's excessive devotion to an art devoid of moral purpose. Aestheticism, "The Author of Beltraffio" suggests, is too dangerous for the cultivation of children; it begets moral chaos. In *The Tragic Muse* (1890), however, James refused to demonize Wilde in a figure based on the playwright, Gabriel Nash. "I drift, I float," announces the charming Nash when asked where he can be reached. "Where there's anything to feel, I try to be there!" Lightly satiric, a study in the harmlessness of aestheticism, the novel indicates that James was not wholly hostile to the aestheticist enterprise. Moreover, as a man to whom nothing was allowed to happen so that the discipline of art might dominate him absolutely, James established his own unique and enduring aestheticist doctrine.

In its self-conscious disengagement from the claims of the so-called world, homosexually inflected aestheticism was often less a defense of homosexual relations per se than a concerted effort at retreating from all convention, including compulsory heterosexual relations. With the achievements of such would-be heirs to aestheticism as ELIOT, Pound, and Stevens, literary aestheticism lost much of its homoerotic impetus. A good deal of the opposition deployed against homosexual aestheticism in the post-1890s epoch originated with homosexual artists themselves; E. M. FORSTER's stinging portrayal of Cecil Vyse in his 1908 *Room with a View* (a portrait based on Pater) and WILLA CATHER's poignant depiction of a doomed adolescent aesthete in her 1905 story "Paul's Case" (possibly composed from her ambivalence concerning the Wilde trials) intimated that homosexual aestheticism was a callow retreat from a full engagement with life, however understandable the aestheticist impulse was as a reaction to a homophobic culture. But if aestheticism as a cultural force has waned, the movement's appeal for so many homosexually identified men at the turn of the century has survived in our own time in the received wisdom that homosexuality and thoroughgoing artistic accomplishment are inseparably entwined.

—Richard Kaye

BIBLIOGRAPHY

Dellamora, Richard. *Masculine Desire: The Sexual Politics of Victorian Aestheticism.* Chapel Hill: University of North Carolina Press, 1990. ■ Dowling, Linda. *Language and Decadence in the Victorian Fin de Siècle.* Princeton: Princeton University Press, 1986. ■ Ellmann, Richard. *Oscar Wilde.* New York: Random House, 1986. ■ Showalter, Elaine. *Sexual Anarchy: Gender and Culture at the Fin de Siècle.* New York: Viking Press, 1991. ■ Stevenson, Lionel. *The Pre-Raphaelite Poets.* New York: W.W. Norton, 1974. ■ Summers, Claude. *Gay Fictions: Wilde to Stonewall.* New York: Continuum, 1990.

African Literatures

The elusive yet universal force of sexuality appears in virtually all genres of literature, with its definition and expression determined by the interwoven threads of cultural mores and traditions, historical experiences unique to each land and century, and the intent of individual authors. The massive twentieth-century explosion of literature by African authors using Western literary forms offers an opportunity for the exploration of sexual attitudes. Any attempt to understand the treatment of homosexuality as a theme in modern African plays, poetry, and novels must take into account traditional views on same-sex relationships, the influence of the imported religions of Christianity and Islam, and the political and legal conditions faced by the authors, especially the legacy of colonialism.

Contrary to the claims of some scholarship, homosexuality was not an unknown behavior over much of the African continent before colonialism. The range of local opinion on the topic, however, varied considerably. In his landmark 1988 work *The Construction of Homosexuality,* David Greenberg proposed a four-part classification to bring order to the descriptions of homosexual behavior recorded for various cultures across the centuries. Robert Baum's 1993 application of this analytic framework to published ethnographic data on fifty African cultures verified the presence of three types of homosexual behavior in traditional African societies, namely, transgenerational, transgenderal, and egalitarian relationships. Available data indicate that the transgenerational and transgenderal patterns of homosexual behaviors are of great significance in many traditional African belief systems. Their function is involved with the proper maturation of children into full adulthood and the achievement and transfer of certain types of spiritual and religious authority. In an interesting parallel to the North American *berdache* tradition, some societies also recognize the existence of an intermediate gender considered sacred and with powers beyond the ordinary. Egalitarian homosexuality covers the familiar category of adolescent sexual exploration between members of the same gender, which is viewed as natural and acceptable for that stage of life but not usually sanctioned in adulthood. The lack of extensive and reliable data on homosexuality in African cultures in the literature of anthropology is due to factors ranging from a true absence of the phenomenon in the culture under study to informant awareness of the disapproval with which the researcher's culture viewed same-gender relationships.

Although Christianity had been introduced to the cities of the Roman province of Libya by the second century C.E., its influence in sub-Saharan Africa (outside the Coptic faith of Egypt and the monophysite church of Ethiopia) was limited prior to the late fifteenth century. The Portuguese mission to the Kingdom of Kongo in 1486 had as one of its objectives the spreading of the faith and served as the forerunner of some three centuries of evangelization by various denominations. Success in transplanting specific mores and codes of conduct varied with the zeal of individual workers and the degree of cultural sensitivity they possessed. A common goal of all evangelizing was the provision of basic education, including literacy, as a means of inculcating Christian values and standards of behavior, including prohibitions against homosexuality. Christian educational institutions (perceived as both beneficial and imperialistic) profoundly influenced African literature in many areas of the continent.

The coming of Islam to Africa occurred as part of the initial wave of conversion sent forth by the heirs of the Prophet Muhammad in the seventh century. The swift acceptance of Islam by many cultures had less to do with specific dogma and more with its willingness to be flexible on such matters as polygamy. Its adoption was most pronounced in West and North Africa although the trading cities of the Indian Ocean coast such as Mombasa and Malindi also had connections to the Muslim world. With the advent of Islam in Africa, local mosques served as sources of education alongside established bodies of folklore and animistic beliefs. Emphasis was placed on learning Arabic, the original language of the Holy Koran, as translation of the scriptures into local vernaculars was forbidden. Thus, as Islam spread, the idea of written literature was disseminated across much of Africa.

A basic tenet of the new faith was submission of each individual's will to the will of God as codified in the body of Islamic law called the Shari'ah, "the path." In this frame of reference, sexuality is viewed as a natural and positive drive present in all human beings, with heterosexual marriage regarded as a foretaste of the eternal joys of Paradise. As a type of sexual activity occurring outside the licensed boundaries of marriage, homosexuality is classed as a form of adultery, a revolt against the divinely established order, and a source of darkness and disruption. Its practice is explicitly condemned in the two most fundamental documents of Islam: the Koran, the word of God as revealed to the Prophet, and the Hadith, a collection of deeds and sayings attributed to him and used as a source of precedent. Although the punishments of one hundred lashes and death by stoning are mandated for homosexual acts by unmarried and married persons, respectively, a chief aim of the Shari'ah is the discouragement of unacceptable behavior, rather than any desire to carry out the full letter of the written law. This emphasis on preserving the divinely ordered social plan effectively isolated homosexuality as a practice known to occur but seldom publicly recognized.

A review of African laws pertaining to homosexuality compiled as part of the Second ILGA Pink Book, a compilation of the legal and social restrictions imposed on gay and lesbian people worldwide issued by the International Lesbian and Gay Association in 1988, reveals several judicial approaches. The practice may be flatly stated not to exist in the country, as in the case of Congo; to be present but to receive no public attention, as in Cameroon; or to be considered not illegal, but socially taboo, as in Senegal. By far the most common report was either that no information was available or that same-gender sexual relations were explicitly prohibited in the national penal codes and subject to a variety of punishments ranging from the payment of fines and jail sentences to the death penalty. The ILGA summary notes that where such sanctions do exist, almost all apply exclusively to men. The prohibitions are a consequence of the transfer of European legal codes to colonial venues, which accounts in part for the strictly condemnatory attitude taken by some former British possessions such as Nigeria and Kenya in contrast to a more relaxed approach where the French Code Napoleon (which makes no mention of consensual homosexual relations between adults) served as the judicial model.

Contemporary African writing of all genres is inextricably rooted in the experience of colonial rule, which in some regions of the continent lasted up to three centuries. A key tenet of imperialist ideology was to view indigenous cultures and peoples as possessing no values of their own worth perpetuating, thus rendering them prime candidates for the civilizing mission of Europeans. Perhaps most familiarly phrased as "the White Man's Burden," this belief led to the foundation of school systems on the Western model to replace traditional initiation practices by tribal elders and to train civil service personnel for colonial bureaucracies. These same classrooms also served as the wombs of a new literature born of the transfer of European literary forms to the African imagination. The first products of this new literature were devoted to the affirmation and validation of a unique and valuable African identity and the articulation of grievances and complaints against the established order. Much of this writing appeared originally in school literary magazines, but the more highly political poems and essays were often circulated surreptitiously.

On the achievement of political independence by most African colonial possessions and territories in the decades following World War II, the focus of African literary output shifted. Whereas initially its purpose had been to serve as a voice for the oppressed masses who could not state their demands, African literature began to explore the tumultuous minds and hearts of the newly liberated. The novel of manners became popular as a vehicle for social commentary and criticism, subjecting all aspects of the collision between the forces of modernization and tradition to examination and reflection. Among those aspects of traditional life most heavily affected by modernization were sexuality and its permissible expressions, as well as the roles of men and women in a world lacking clearly defined and enforced boundaries. Hence, sexual and gender roles became acceptable, if necessarily controversial, subjects in the new literature. It is within this uncertain landscape that homosexuality first makes its appearance in the pages of contemporary African writing.

It must be frankly admitted that the exploration of the presence of homosexuality in African literature is as yet in its infancy. The primary research in this area is a 1983 survey by Daniel Vignal, at the time a member of the faculty of the Department of French at Ahmadu Bello University in Nigeria. Published in the journal *Peuples Noirs, Peuples Africains* as an article entitled "L'homophilie dans le roman negro-africain d'expression anglaise et francaise," it examined African literature in both English and French for its use of homosexual themes. Vignal's list of relevant works ranges in date from 1960 to the early 1980s and includes some twenty-three novels and one short story from authors representing Cameroon, the Central African Republic, the Congo, Ghana, the Ivory Coast, Kenya, Mali, Guinea, Nigeria, Senegal, Sierra Leone, Uganda, and Zaire. Among the volumes included are such widely read creations as Ayi Kwei Armah's *Two Thousand Seasons* (1973), Kofi Awoonor's *This Earth, My Brother* (1971), Wole Soyinka's *The Interpreters* (1973), and Yulisa Amadu Maddy's *No Past, No Present, No Future* (1973). Following a lengthy and detailed documentation of the varied depictions and literary uses of homosexuality, Vignal observes that "for the majority . . . homophilia is exclusively introduced by colonialists or their descendants; by outsiders of all kinds; Arabs, English, French, Métis and so on. It is difficult for them to conceive that homophilia might be the act of a black African."

In 1989, a more comprehensive survey based on Vignal's initial conclusions was conducted by Chris Dunton, which confirmed the patterns observed in the earlier research and extended the range of homosexual behaviors considered to include such practices as masturbation, pedophilia, and lesbianism. Rather than attempting to replicate Vignal's encompassing approach, Dunton focused his attention on the manner in which homosexuality was used as a plot device, "how the treatment of homosexuality provides a . . . reference point . . . which helps reveal the general thematic concerns and . . . larger narrative strategy of the text." Novels examined by Dunton include Yambo Ouologuem's *Bound To Violence* (1971), Maddy's *Our Sister Killjoy* (1977), Mariama Ba's *Scarlet Song* (1985), Armah's *Why Are We So Blest?* (1972), and Soyinka's *The Interpreters.*

Most recently, Gregory Woods has extended the analysis begun by Vignal and Dunton to the field of poetry with his 1994 article "Poems of Black African Manhood." Among the poets and works utilizing homosexual imagery noted by Woods are South Africa's Dennis Brutus, whose prison poems in *Letters To Martha* (1968) speak of the "love, strange love" between men in the prisons of apartheid; Taban lo Liyong's "The Marriage of Black and White," whose narrator prefers "the woman who does not answer when Sappho calls the tune"; Okot p'Bitek's *Song of Lawino* (1966) with its complaint that Westernized African men are behaving "like a woman trying to please her husband"; and Christopher Okigbo, who in *Limits V* refers to the male bond between GILGAMESH, the mythical king of Uruk, and "his companion and second self" Enkidu.

Most novelistic depictions of homosexuality are negative. In *Two Thousand Seasons,* Armah portrays homosexuality as a practice of the Muslim destroyers from the desert who began the first seasons of enslavement, and of one of the kings of Anoa, Jonto, whose practices with young boys are ended only when he is poisoned. In *This Earth, My Brother,* Awoonor names homosexuals as one of the categories of people who are sent to Africa as part of the colonial civil administration. Mariama Ba's scathing examination of the problems of women facing both sexist attitudes and colonialism, *Scarlet Song* (1985), presents homosexuality as an unsatisfactory future for a child. Yaye Khady, one of the principal characters, observes with pity a fifteen-year-old boy who prefers the company of girls and adopts female behavior and tasks. She reflects on his future as a *gor-djiguene,* "a pansy destined to spend his life at the feet of a courtesan, doing all her dirty work," such as keeping the accounts, soliciting lovers for his mistress, and "sometimes it might happen that the clients would fancy him rather than his mistress." A similar figure appears later in the work at Ousmane's wedding to Ouleymatou, where he is described as "one of those persons of ambiguous sex."

The most completely realized homosexual character yet found in contemporary African literature comes from *No Past, No Present, No Future* (1973) by Yulisa Amadu Maddy of Sierra Leone. The plot of this novel follows the fate of three African men who leave their nation for life in Europe, each seeking to escape the limitations of their own natures. The homosexuality of one of them, Joe Bengoh, is traced from his earliest experiences with a mission priest to realization of himself in the cosmopolitan gay world with a white lover. Maddy also utilizes the common Western stereotype of the theater as an accepting environment for gay men by having Joe unsuccessfully major in drama and attempt an acting career. A particularly powerful aspect of this novel is its frank exploration of the prejudice directed against Joe by his two erstwhile friends, whose rejection is based on their adoption of the view of homosexuality as sick and morally inferior to their own self-destructive behaviors. In the end, however, Joe is the only one of the three whose acknowledgment of his true self does not destroy him. Another of Maddy's novels, *Our Sister Killjoy,* is unusual for its open discussion of lesbianism.

One of the chief difficulties in carrying out a study of homosexuality in African literature is the virtually total absence of investigations of the African historical record by practitioners of the emerging discipline of gay and lesbian studies. A major exception is T. Dunbar Moodie's 1988 review of same-sex pairings among migrant laborers in the Witwatersrand gold fields of South Africa. Based on interviews by Vivienne Ndatshe and British Sibuyi with Mpondo and Tsonga veterans of the mines, Moody documents the institution of the *tinkonkana*, "the wives of the mine," younger men who entered into sexual relationships with older miners for the duration of their contracts. The miners' memories of this bond created to cope with the artificial world of the labor compounds date chiefly from the 1930s and 1940s. It is noteworthy that the classic novel of South African literature dealing with conditions on the Rand, Peter Abrahams's *Mine Boy* (1955), makes no mention of this system of relationships, which was governed by a code of law known as the *mteto ka Sokisi*, focusing rather on the inequities of the apartheid system. In part, this silence can be explained by the gradual changes on the Rand itself over a period of decades, which made such a network of tacitly acknowledged same-sex relationships no longer viable. The tradition does appear in the poem "Amagoduka at Glencoe Station" by Oswald Mtshali, where workers bound for the mines speak of living "in compounds where young men are pampered into partners for older men."

The literature spawned by the AIDS pandemic in the United States gay community through such catalytic works as LARRY KRAMER's play *The Normal Heart* (1985) has, as yet, no parallel in contemporary African writing. This is due chiefly to the manner of expression of the disease, which, transmitted almost exclusively through heterosexual intercourse, has substantially reduced the population of many provinces and struck at the heart of the African extended family support network. The absence of AIDS as a theme in African writing may also be attributed to the deaths of members of the educated elites who might otherwise have served as creators.

In Africa generally, sexual expression is considered a spectrum of activity spanning an individual's entire life rather than the hallmark of distinct and separate lifestyles or identities, as is the case in the West. In African literature, many writers, such as Armah and Soyinka, continue to place homosexuality as entirely an activity of European or American expatriates within more general considerations of recent African history as cultural trauma. The alienness of the concept of a separate class of beings known as "homosexuals" to the African frame of reference is perhaps most baldly stated by the grandmother in Maddy's play *Big Berrin* (1984). On being informed that a certain person is a homosexual, she inquires "Homosexuality? Wheyting be dat?" With the rise of gay and lesbian activism on the continent, this question may in time be given an African answer.

—*Robert B. Marks Ridinger*

BIBLIOGRAPHY

Baum, Robert M. "Homosexuality and the Traditional Religions of the Americas and Africa." *Homosexuality and World Religions.* Arlene Swindler, ed. Valley Forge, Pa.: Trinity Press International, 1993. 1–46. ■ Dunton, Chris. "'Wheyting Be Dat?': The Treatment of Homosexuality in African Literature." *Research in African Literatures* 20 (1989): 422–448. ■ Moodie, T. Dunbar. "Migrancy and Male Sexuality on the South African Gold Mines." *Hidden from History: Reclaiming the Gay and Lesbian Past.* Martin Duberman, Martha Vicinus, and George Chauncey, Jr., eds. New-York: Penguin, 1990. 411–425. ■ Vignal, Daniel. "L'Homophilie dans le roman negro-african d'expression anglaise et francaise." *Peuples Noirs, Peuples Africains* 33 (May–June 1983): 63–81. ■ Woods, Gregory. "Poems of African Manhood." *Perversions* 1.1 (1994).

AFRICAN-AMERICAN LITERATURE

African-American Literature, Gay Male

The African-American gay male tradition in literature—though it has yet to receive adequate scholarly attention—consists of a substantial body of texts, spans a period of nearly seven decades, and includes some of the most gifted writers of the twentieth century. It is a rich and vibrant tradition; its vitality emerges at least in part from the complexities of the black gay lives that it articulates and affirms. It is an intensely political tradition that offers relentless and simultaneous challenges to black as well as white homophobia, to straight as well as queer racism. Yet its concerns extend far beyond social protest to engage a wide variety of issues that range from quintessentially African-American themes to universally human ones. Begun on a modest scale by a pioneering coterie of writers in Harlem during the 1920s, the gay male tradition in African-American literature was vastly strengthened by JAMES BALDWIN during the 1950s and 1960s. And since the mid-1980s, a host of talented artists have emerged to generate a veritable renaissance in black gay writing.

The HARLEM RENAISSANCE of the 1920s, celebrated as a most significant event in the African-American intellectual tradition, was also a crucial moment in gay literary history. Many of its central protagonists—such as Alain Locke, LANGSTON HUGHES, Wallace Thurman, COUNTEE CULLEN, Claude McKay, and Richard Bruce Nugent— were either gay or bisexual. Locke, a professor at Howard University and one of the most distinguished scholars of the era, was an older gay man who became a mentor to many of the Harlem-based young male artists of the day. His intellectual presence and personal friendship—coupled with the fact that Nugent, Cullen, McKay, and others were at least peripherally involved in the then thriving gay and lesbian community of Harlem—perhaps encouraged them to explore, though discreetly, the subject of homosexuality in their works.

Richard Bruce Nugent's "Sadhji," a short story included in Locke's *The New Negro* (1925), is arguably the first gay text published by an African-American male. But it is his thinly disguised autobiographical narrative titled "Smoke, Lilies and Jade" (1926) that remains the most defiantly explicit gay text produced during the Harlem Renaissance. Unapologetic in its rhapsodic celebration of male beauty, it first appeared in *Fire!!*—an avant-garde journal published by the Harlem literati with the explicit intention of shocking the conservative black bourgeois readership. Nugent, unperturbed by the notoriety that his text earned him, continued to engage gay themes in many of his subsequent works.

Some of the other writers of the Harlem Renaissance, however, were more cautious than Nugent. Novelists such as Wallace Thurman and Claude McKay, both of whom were bisexual, introduced gay themes in their works though neither treated the subject with Nugent's exceptional candor. Thurman's first novel, *Blacker the Berry* (1929), a poignant ex-

ploration of the psychology of the oppressed, has an unsympathetic bisexual male character. His second novel, *Infants of the Spring* (1933), a hilarious satire on the Harlem Renaissance and its major figures, has an important bisexual male character, and the friendship between two other male characters in the novel has obvious homoerotic qualities. Similar homoerotic male bonding is a feature of McKay's *Banjo* (1929). And his *Home to Harlem* (1928), a sensational portrayal of Harlem life in the Jazz Age, has a minor black male character.

Langston Hughes and Countee Cullen tend to be even more cautious. Hughes, in fact, appears to have taken extraordinary measures to conceal his bisexuality; perceptive (gay) readers, however, may easily sense the homoerotic undertones in poems such as "Young Sailor" and "Cafe: 3 A.M." as well as in the elaborate sexual silences that mark his major autobiographical works such as *The Big Sea* (1940) and *I Wonder as I Wander* (1956). Like Hughes, Cullen too prefers to reveal his gay self only through coded language, as in poems such as "The Black Christ," "Tableau," "Every Lover," and "Song in Spite of Myself," among others.

The relative sexual reticence of the Harlem writers, however, has to be understood in the larger cultural contexts in which they lived and created art. Unlike their white peers who had the luxury of living in a society that viewed their whiteness as normative, the black artists had to confront in their daily lives as well as in their imaginative works the painfully problematic implications of their racial identity. The issue of race, therefore, was a politically necessary and personally compelling concern for all the writers of the Harlem Renaissance. Their art reflects this preoccupation. The demands of their audiences further complicated their predicament: Both black and white readers expected the writers to foreground the race-specific aspects of the African-American experience. And the economics of the literary marketplace and the tenuousness of the black writer's position in the United States during the 1920s denied them the level of artistic freedom and personal autonomy necessary for forthright explorations of unconventional sexualities. Therefore, it is indeed remarkable that several gay and bisexual writers of the Harlem Renaissance, despite numerous daunting obstacles, managed to project discreetly into their art their private sexual concerns. The gay ambience that they helped generate did in fact succeed in providing a mildly subversive shape to the sexual and racial politics inscribed in the literature of the Harlem Renaissance.

James Baldwin emerged on the American literary scene almost a generation after the collapse of the

Harlem Renaissance. His entry marks a nodal point in the development of the African-American gay male literary tradition. An outsider in every sense of the term, Baldwin was poor, black, gay, and extraordinarily gifted. He launched from his marginal location an articulate and sustained attack on the dominant cultural fictions of race and sexuality. Intellectually daring and fiercely eloquent, he became one of the most celebrated writers of his time. Although he occupies an important place in African-American as well as gay American literatures, the significance of his life and work in the specific context of the black gay male literary tradition is immeasurable. He continues to be its defining figure.

"The Preservation of Innocence" (1949), an essay that Baldwin published in *Zero,* a Moroccan journal, within months after his arrival in Paris, is an early signal of his personal willingness to engage the topic of homosexuality in a public forum. "Outing," a short story he published in 1951, is his first tentative attempt to approach the topic in fiction; the story is a gracefully subtle portrayal of adolescent homosexual awakening. In his first major work of fiction, *Go Tell It on the Mountain* (1953), Baldwin explores the adolescent consciousness on a more elaborate scale, and here he presents the youthful protagonist's emerging homosexual awareness as a subtle but integral part of his quest for personal identity.

By the mid-1950s Baldwin had earned his reputation as an important African-American writer; his readers and critics had come to expect in his works incisive analyses of the black experience. But in 1956 he disappointed a good many of them by publishing *Giovanni's Room,* a novel with an all-white cast that poignantly documented the consequences of internalized homophobia through its young protagonist's unwillingness to accept his gayness. For a young black writer to publish such an openly gay narrative in the mid-1950s was an enormously risky endeavor: The political climate in the United States was hardly ready for such honesty, and there was a very real possibility that the publication of such a novel might permanently damage his career. That Baldwin took such a risk is a testament to his immense personal courage and artistic integrity. He survived the controversy generated by *Giovanni's Room* and, in that process, earned his preeminent place in the gay American literary tradition. More important, its publication liberated Baldwin from the closet and enabled him to treat gay and bisexual themes even more vigorously and explicitly in three of his subsequent major works of fiction: *Another Country* (1962), *Tell Me How Long the Train's Been Gone* (1968), and *Just Above My Head* (1979). And through such works he

helped create the necessary space for a new generation of talented young black gay writers who followed him.

Even though Baldwin's influence on the current generation of African-American gay writers is a vital and enduring one, a number of other cultural factors have also helped nurture the new artists. The civil rights movement, the feminist movement, the Stonewall Riots, the predominantly white-led and often racially insensitive gay liberation movement, and the emergence of a confident black gay and lesbian middle-class gave impetus to the growth of political activism among black gay men and lesbians during the 1970s and 1980s. The new personal and political consciousness led to the establishment of many black gay and lesbian organizations, to the publication of several specialized journals (though many were short-lived), and to the articulation of a specifically black gay and lesbian cultural agenda.

These developments inevitably affected black gay literary creativity. Initially black gay artists, rejected by straight- as well as gay-owned presses, published their works largely in black gay journals and in privately printed chapbooks. This practice still continues on a significant scale. However, given the recent phenomenon of many publishers' relative openness to gay material in general, some black gay writers, at least since the mid-1980s, have been reasonably successful in placing their manuscripts with major trade publishers and, on rare occasions, even with prestigious university presses. Further, the growing interest of nonblack gay readers in black gay texts—as the commercial success of recent works by Essex Hemphill and Assoto Saint clearly suggests—has given additional stimulus to the production, publication, and circulation of black gay literature.

The literary styles of the post-Baldwin generation of black gay writers differ widely; they range from the innovative science fiction of SAMUEL DELANY to the rich magic-realist narratives of Randall Kenan; from the revisionist Southern gothicism of Melvin Dixon to the campy elegance of Larry Duplechan; from the densely allusive academic poetry of Carl Phillips to the aggressive agit-prop lyrics of Essex Hemphill. They engage a variety of themes as well: from the more private concerns of identity, love, family, and relationships to the larger political issues of racist violence and homophobic repression. Although it is risky to make any sweeping generalizations about this diverse body of literature, it is possible to identify at least four major themes that dominate the works of contemporary black gay male writers: the complex relationship between the individual black gay self and the larger African-American community, the devastating consequences of racism, the pain and the possibilities of interracial love, and the tragedy of AIDS.

The relationship between the individual black self and the black community—a frequent theme in African-American literature in general—surfaces insistently in the works of many contemporary black gay male writers. Since a strong and enabling sense of racial self is necessary to cope with the psychological assaults of white racism, the black gay male protagonist can rarely afford to disconnect himself completely from the black community and seek total assimilation into the predominantly white gay community. But the black community, with its heterosexist values, is often not prepared to accommodate his sexuality unproblematically. The tension that arises from these conflicting sources of black gay identity, therefore, constitutes one of the central features of black gay literature. Joseph Beam's defiant declaration in his introduction to the ground-breaking anthology, *In the Life* (1986), clearly reveals the potential drama inherent in this tension: "We are coming home with our heads held up high." Similarly, Gordon Heath's autobiographical *Deep Are the Roots* (1992), poignantly illustrates the narrator's determined struggle to claim his racial as well as sexual birthrights. Even when a protagonist fails in his struggle to harmonize his conflicting subjectivities—young Horace in Randall Kenan's *A Visitation of Spirits* (1989), for example, commits suicide—the individual failure is also presented as a violent indictment of the community's inhumane rigidity.

Racism is another central concern in the works of virtually every contemporary black gay artist. Writers who are anthologized in *Other Countries* (1988), *In the Life* (1986), *Brother to Brother* (1991), *The Road Before Us* (1991), and *Here to Dare* (1992) not only challenge American racism in general but also vigorously expose the racism of white gay communities. Some writers, such as Randall Kenan and Steven Corbin, offer broad historical perspectives on racism; others, such as Essex Hemphill, Craig Harris, and Assoto Saint, bear painfully personal testimony to racial injury. Even in the works of Larry Duplechan— someone who argues that his gay self is significantly more important to him than his racial self—there is considerable concern with racism and its maiming effects.

Despite the preoccupation with racism—or, perhaps, precisely because of it—interracial love is a recurrent theme in recent African-American gay literature. There are, of course, many writers who focus only on intraracial gay relationships and celebrate the black male body as a site of pleasure, but there are others who, with remarkable honesty, reveal their colonized sexual imaginations. Robert Westley, for example, goes looking for "the last big-dick/White boy" ("The Pub" in *Here to Dare*), while Thom Beam writes a plaintive "Love Song for White Boys Who Don't Know Who I Am" (in *The Road Before Us*). Reginald Shepard's "On Not Being White" (in *In the Life*) is an exquisitely painful statement on colonial desire, just as Essex Hemphill's "Heavy Breathing" (in *Ceremonies* [1992]) reveals his erotic longing for a white gay man who studiously rejects black partners. Assoto Saint's autobiographical *Stations* (1989) is a paean to enduring interracial love. Likewise, Canaan Parker's *The Color of Trees* (1992), set on the campus of an elite prep school in New England, affirms the possibility of love that transcends cultural and class differences. But other writers sound far less sanguine about the durability of cross-racial connections. Duplechan's *Eight Days in a Week* (1985), for example, deals with the relationship between Johnnie Ray, who is black, and Keith, who is white. Their relationship ultimately fails: Their racial difference, which is the basis of their desire for each other, ironically proves to be too disruptive. More disturbing, Corbin's *Fragments That Remain* (1993) and Dixon's *Vanishing Rooms* (1991) suggest that a white man, even when he is very much in love with a black man, can remain fundamentally racist.

AIDS is yet another dominant concern of contemporary African-American gay writers. Without referring to AIDS by name, Delany examines in *Flight from Neveryon* (1985) the distressing impact of the plague on the collective psyche of a frightened population. Duplechan, in *Tangled Up in Blue* (1989), explores the insidious effects AIDS has on individuals and on relationships by focusing on Maggie and Daniel Sullivan, a straight couple, and Crockett, their gay friend. But even more compelling because of their emotional immediacy are the numerous testimonial narratives and poems—by writers such as David Frechette, Assoto Saint, Bobby Smith, Donald Woods, and many others—that bear witness to illness and death, mourn the loss of friends and lovers, and memorialize the many thousands gone.

Some of the most talented black gay writers of the post–Baldwin generation, including Melvin Dixon, Craig Harris, and Joseph Beam, among others, have already died of AIDS-related illnesses. Still others— such as Essex Hemphill, Assoto Saint, and Steven Corbin—are fighting personal battles against the infection. Contemporary black gay writing, therefore, reflects a mounting sense of emergency while it continues to give voice and visibility to black gay men living through these treacherous times. (See also AIDS LITERATURE.)

—*Emmanuel S. Nelson*

BIBLIOGRAPHY

Beam, Joseph, ed. *In the Life: A Black Gay Anthology.* Boston: Alyson, 1986. ■ Corbin, Steven. *Fragments That Remain.* Boston: Alyson, 1993. ■ Flannigan-Saint-Aubin, Arthur. "'Black Gay Male' Discourse: Reading Race and Sexuality Between the Lines." *Journal of the History of Sexuality* 3.3 (Spring 1993): 468–490. ■ Heath, Gordon. *Deep Are the Roots: Memoirs of a Black Expatriate.* Amherst: University of Massachusetts Press, 1992. ■ Hemphill, Essex, ed. *Brother to Brother: New Writings by Black Gay Men.* Boston: Alyson, 1991. ■ Nelson, Emmanuel, ed. *Contemporary Gay American Novelists: A Bio-Bibliographical Critical Sourcebook.* Westport, Conn.: Greenwood Press, 1993. ■ ———, ed. *Critical Essays: Gay and Lesbian Writers of Color.* New York: Haworth Press, 1993. ■ *Other Countries: Black Gay Voices.* New York: Other Countries Collective, 1988. ■ Phillips, Carl. *In the Blood.* Boston: Northeastern University Press, 1992. ■ Saint, Assoto, ed. *Here to Dare: 10 Gay Black Poets.* New York: Galiens Press, 1992. ■ ———, ed. *The Road Before Us: 100 Gay Black Poets.* New York: Galiens Press, 1991. ■ Stanford, Adrian. *Black and Queer.* Boston: Good Gay Press, 1977.

African-American Literature, Lesbian

Located at the juncture of several divergent literary traditions, African-American lesbian writing represents a provocative intervention into previous conceptions of lesbian, African-American, and canonical U.S. literature. Yet this tradition rarely included open affirmations of women's same-sex desire until the 1970s. Thus in her groundbreaking 1977 essay, "Toward a Black Feminist Criticism," Barbara Smith implies that the "massive silence" surrounding writings by black women and black lesbians has prevented readers from recognizing the unique contributions these writers make to twentieth-century literature. Smith's essay, which itself represents a significant challenge to previous conceptions of literary scholarship, can be described as one of the first steps in the invention of an identifiable African-American literary tradition, a tradition that has made remarkable progress in recent years. Indeed, Smith's desire to construct a positive, self-affirming history and tradition of black lesbian artists has played a significant role in shaping African-American lesbian literature and criticism. The 1980s and 1990s have seen a proliferation of writings by and about African-American lesbians, ranging from the inclusion of lesbian and bisexual characters in mainstream, heterosexually identified popular fiction by Gloria Naylor, Ntozake Shange, and ALICE WALKER to erotic celebrations of same-sex passion in poetry and prose by openly lesbian writers, such as AUDRE LORDE, Becky Birtha, Cheryl Clarke, and Cherry Muhanji. Like Smith, these fiction writers and poets develop self-naming processes that simultaneously invent and reflect their black lesbian identities. They combine self-expression with culturally specific metaphors and create positive images of black lesbian identity that replace their historic and aesthetic erasure with a continuum of female bonding.

Although African-American lesbian literature could be said to have its beginnings in the lesbian, gay, and bisexual culture that flourished during the Harlem Renaissance of the 1920s and early 1930s, black lesbians' self-naming process occurred only in an ambivalent, highly codified fashion. The increased sexual freedom and openness that made it possible for black gay and bisexual male writers like Richard Bruce Nugent, Wallace Thurman, and Claude McKay to produce gay-identified texts had a less obvious impact on women. Although a number of lesbian and bisexual blues singers—including Bessie Smith, Ma Rainey, Josephine Baker, and Ethel Waters—attained a level of sexual openness in their music, these women generally hid their same-sex relationships behind a public guise of heterosexuality. Only rarely did their lyrics even allude to their sexual desire for other women, and generally all such allusions were tinged with an ambivalence suggesting an elusive sexuality. In "Prove It on Me Blues," for instance, Ma Rainey simultaneously celebrates and denies her sexual preference by daring her listeners to "prove it" on her.

This ambivalence is even more pronounced in texts by middle-class Harlem Renaissance lesbian and bisexual women writers. In addition to the sexism that made it difficult for early twentieth-century women of any color to adopt openly lesbian lifestyles and identities, the highly sexualized images of black women that developed during slavery to justify the institutionalized rape of enslaved women made it even less likely that African-American bisexual and lesbian writers would risk inadvertently confirming these stereotypes by depicting their sexuality in print. The writings of Alice Dunbar-Nelson, Angelina Weld Grimké, and NELLA LARSEN illustrate the effects of this culturally imposed self-silencing. Although Gloria Hull has uncovered journal evidence indicating that Alice Dunbar-Nelson was romantically involved with both women and men and that Angelina Weld Grimké had at least one woman lover, these signs of bisexual and lesbian desire appear only in highly veiled form in Dunbar-Nelson's and Grimké's published works. A similar type of sexual encoding can be found in Nella Larsen's *Passing* (1929). Ostensibly an exploration of racial passing, this novella can also be read as an account of the growing sexual attraction between its two protagonists, Irene Redfield and Clare Kendry. As Debra McDowell notes in her 1986 introduction to *Passing,* the title has more than one meaning: Just as Clare Kendry passes as white, *Passing* itself passes as heterosexual, hiding its homoerotic subtext beneath the more obvious racialized theme.

Writings by and about African-American lesbians have made significant progress since the early 1900s, when Angelina Weld Grimké and others were compelled to bury their sexualities beneath a facade of Victorian propriety. Influenced by the black power, gay liberation, and feminist movements of the 1960s and 1970s, several self-identified black lesbians began publishing works with lesbian characters and themes. These early publications—which included Pat Parker's *Movement in Black* (1969), Anita Cornwell's journalistic essays published during the early 1970s, Audre Lorde's *From a Land Where Other People Live* (1973) and *New York Head Shop and Museum* (1974), and ANN ALLEN SHOCKLEY's *Loving Her* (1974)–encompass a remarkable variety of thematic, stylistic, and generic concerns, thus indicating the multiple directions later African-American lesbian literature would take. This variety is especially evident in Parker's and Lorde's poetry. Although both writers incorporate autobiographical experience into their work and explore a wide range of social issues, including racism, sexism, and homophobia, their styles are quite distinctive. Whereas Parker generally uses black English, concrete images, accessible language, and a conversational tone to convey her highly political themes, Lorde's early poetry is more formal; she develops complex metaphors that connect her personal experiences with an intricate web of local, national, and international events. As she integrates her aesthetics with self-discovery and social protest, Lorde creates highly polished lyrical verse.

As the first openly black lesbian novel published in the United States, Ann Allen Shockley's *Loving Her* made a significant contribution to the emerging field of African-American lesbian literature. This groundbreaking novel—which recounts the story of Renay, a young black female musician who, after falling in love with a financially independent white woman, leaves an abusive relationship with an alcoholic husband—contains a number of themes explored in later African-American lesbian literature, including the awakening of lesbian desire; lesbianism as an empowering form of self-love; racism among white lesbians; homophobia and sexism in black communities; butch–femme roles; and interracial relationships. Yet *Loving Her* occupies a paradoxical place within the emerging field of African-American lesbian literature, for its depiction of Renay's relationship with her white, upper-class lover has been criticized for its visionary, depoliticized perspective. Still, Shockley's novel makes several provocative interventions into the lesbian literature of the 1970s, which focused primarily on issues relevant to middle- and upper-class Euro-American women. To begin with, by introducing black lesbian issues to a wide, multicultural readership, *Loving Her* served as a necessary corrective to earlier conceptions of U.S. lesbian fiction. Unlike many Euro-American lesbian novels and short stories—which often focus almost exclusively on issues related to gender and sexuality—*Loving Her* explores the intersections of sexuality, ethnicity, gender, and class. One of the most intriguing yet rarely discussed effects of this multifaceted exploration can be seen in Shockley's depiction of the interconnections between black and white ethnic identities. As her light-skinned protagonist speculates on the mixture of European and African ancestry that accounts for her own coloring, Shockley challenges both the color prejudice within some black communities and commonly accepted beliefs concerning racial purity, miscegenation, and the binary opposition between black and white identities. Significantly, these themes are explored in more detail in later African-American lesbian writings by Audre Lorde, Becky Birtha, Cherry Muhanji, and others.

The publication by mainstream presses of several works with explicitly lesbian and bisexual elements—including Gloria Naylor's critique of black communities' homophobia in *The Women of Brewster Place* (1982), Ntozake Shange's positive representations of black lesbians in *Sassafrass, Cypress, and Indigo* (1982), and Alice Walker's depiction of women's sexual and emotional love for each other in *The Color Purple* (1982)—signaled another important development in African-American lesbian literature. Although these novels do not deal exclusively with lesbian and bisexual characters and themes, they complicate simplistic notions of African-American lesbian literature in several ways. First, by declining to identify as lesbian, Naylor, Walker, and Shange challenge the commonly accepted belief in a one-to-one correspondence between a writer's personal identity and the material she explores, thus opening the way for nonlesbian writers, readers, and critics to examine issues related to women's same-sex desire. Second, by depicting a spectrum of female sexualities and a variety of woman-identified relationships, they compel readers to reexamine restrictive, stereotypical images of black womanhood and lesbian identity.

The publication of these critically acclaimed novels indicates a growing acceptance of black lesbian themes among a wide readership; however, this acceptance did not extend to lesbian-centered texts, especially when written by openly identified black lesbian-feminists. Audre Lorde's *Zami: A New Spelling of My Name,* also published in 1982, and Barbara Smith's *Home Girls: A Black Feminist Anthology,* published the following year, were not picked up by mainstream U.S. presses. Both the erotic celebrations of lesbian sexuality in Lorde's autobiographical novel and the lesbian-affirmative perspectives in many of the pieces collected in Smith's anthology significantly challenge the stereotypes concerning black women by creating a continuum of heterosexual, bisexual, and homosexual women loving women. Although these texts are highly regarded in feminist scholarship, they are rarely included in discussions of African-American or canonical U.S. literature.

Despite this continuing resistance to lesbian-centered African-American texts, the 1980s and 1990s have seen a proliferation of writings by and about black lesbians, extending from openly erotic celebrations of same-sex passion, to imaginative revisions of history, to lyrical yet highly political essays indicting the homophobia and sexism both in black communities and in the dominant U.S. culture. It is, of course, impossible to arrive at definitive statements concerning such a diverse body of writings; however, several recurring themes could be said to characterize African-American lesbian literature, including the use of revisionist mythmaking to invent culturally specific mythic, historic, and linguistic images that revise previous conceptions of lesbian identity; explorations of interracial relationships; and the creation of Afrocentric feminist perspectives that expand existing definitions of mainstream U.S. feminism. Coupled with an emphasis on honesty and direct speech, these trends illustrate the complex self-naming processes that make twentieth-century African-American lesbian literature such a vital, fast-growing field of study.

One of the most important devices found in African-American lesbian literature is the use of revisionist mythmaking to create an empowering African-based womanist tradition that affirms lesbian identity. Audre Lorde's work provides a useful illustration of this process. Like a number of other twentieth-century North American women writers, she replaces the Judeo-Christian male God and other patriarchal myths that depict women as subordinate to men with positive images of female identity. However, unlike those revisionist mythmakers who rely almost exclusively on the Greco-Roman mythic tradition and thus inadvertently reinforce Eurocentric concepts of womanhood, Lorde does not. By incorporating West African female creatrix figures like Mawulisa, Yemanja, and Seboulisa into her poetry, fiction, and prose, she invents culturally specific images of lesbian identity. In *The Black Unicorn*—her 1978 collection of poetry thematically unified by its references to West African orisha, or spiritual forces—she identifies her voice with Seboulisa's, both to underscore her personal ties with Africa and to establish her place in a transhistorical, cross-cultural community of African women. Again in *Zami: A New Spelling of My Name,* she uses references to Carriacou, her mother's West Indian homeland, and identifies herself with Afrekete, a highly sexualized trickster figure. By so doing, she creates a culturally specific tradition of female bonding that includes both sexual and nonsexual relationships between women. This use of revisionist myth serves several interrelated purposes. First, by associating herself with eroticized West African mythic symbols, Lorde naturalizes her sexuality and connects it with a long-standing Afrocentric tradition, thus challenging the homophobic accusations of cultural betrayal found in some African-American communities. Second, by replacing conventional Greco-Roman mythic images with those of West Africa, she simultaneously critiques U.S. feminists' ethnocentric concepts of womanhood and provides Western readers with alternative models of female identity.

Like Lorde, Cheryl Clarke, Ann Allen Shockley, and other self-identified black women writers also use revisionary tactics to create positive, Afrocentric images of lesbian identity. By incorporating culturally specific references to historic and mythic figures into their poetry and fiction, these poets and novelists invent self-empowering authentic black female cultural traditions. For instance, in *Living as a Lesbian* (1986) and *Humid Pitch* (1989), Clarke borrows lyrics and lifestyles popularized by the blues tradition and creates erotic poems exploring physical lust, unfulfilled desire, and passionate sexual encounters. In *Say Jesus and Come to Me* (1987), Ann Allen Shockley draws on the southern tradition of gospel music and revival meetings to expose the heterosexism, homophobia, and misogyny in patriarchal forms of Christianity. In *The Gilda Stories,* a short-story cycle depicting 200 years in the life of a black lesbian vampire, Jewelle Gomez associates her protagonist with a long tradition of African women and alludes to culturally specific historical and mythic figures, including enslaved women, Alice Dunbar-Nelson, and conjure women. As she retells history from a black lesbian-feminist perspective, Gomez explores the many forms of individual and collective resistance black women have developed. Like Gomez, JUNE JORDAN revises conventional accounts of U.S. history and creates a long tradition of powerful foremothers. In a number of poems collected in *Naming Our Destiny* (1989), she simultaneously reconstructs and celebrates the lives of Phillis Wheatley, Sojourner Truth, Fannie Lou Hamer, Winnie Mandela, and other black women whose accomplishments have been almost entirely ignored in standard historical records.

These revisionary perspectives on history and myth enable Lorde, Clarke, Shockley, and other self-identified African-American lesbians to replace ethnocentric concepts of womanhood with culture-based models of female identity, thus creating feminine, Afrocentric voices and collective identities that affirm black women's power. Significantly, this affirmation of black womanhood occurs simultaneously with attempts to establish various types of cross-cultural alliances, including friendships, political coalitions, and romantic, sexualized relationships. Lorde's essays and speeches collected in *Sister Outsider* (1984) illustrate this willingness to create multiethnic communities. Indeed, both her desire to develop cross-cultural bonds and her ability to negotiate between diverse types of women have provided readers of all ethnic backgrounds with an invaluable model. By naming herself as "sister outsider" and thus emphasizing her membership in a number of apparently disparate groups, Lorde enacts a double movement enabling her both to reclaim her place in a community of black women and to establish new ties with others. As she affirms the various components of her identity—black, female, lesbian, mother, daughter, feminist—she creates a holistic Afrocentric perspective expansive enough to encompass the many differences between herself and others. Thus in her often-quoted "Open Letter to Mary Daly" (in *Sister Outsider*), Lorde challenges Daly and other Euro-American women to recognize their own ties to an empowering African mythic tradition, or to what she calls "the Black mother in us all." Unlike the stereotypical black matriarch, Lorde's "Black mother" represents an inner-directed principle of excellence enabling women of all ethnic backgrounds to develop new forms of interconnectedness.

Often, these explorations of cross-cultural connections include a visionary dimension. For example, in *Loving Her* and in many of the stories collected in *The Black and White of It,* Shockley implies that African-American lesbians can develop positive, self-affirming sexual relationships with women from other cultural and class backgrounds. Similarly, Becky Birtha opens her 1991 collection of poetry, *The Forbidden Poems,* with an affirmation of her multiethnic heritage. By reclaiming her Irish, West African, Cherokee, and Choctaw ancestry, she rejects monolithic notions of black female identity and establishes alliances with diverse groups of women. Like Lorde and Shockley, Birtha attempts to develop multiethnic communities that do not negate the culturally specific dimensions of her African-American identity. Thus in her collections of short stories—*For Nights Like This One: Stories of Loving Women* (1983) and *Lovers' Choice* (1987)—Birtha emphasizes both the similarities and the differences between lesbians of African and European descent. June Jordan takes this desire to establish complex collective identities even further, and in both her poetry and her political essays, she negotiates between diverse groups, including gay men of all colors, women of the African diaspora, unemployed black men, and Palestinian refugees.

Although "lesbian" and "feminist" are not interchangeable terms, a number of self-identified black lesbian writers have closely associated their lesbianism with their feminism. This association is transformational, for by drawing on their experiential knowledge of the interlocking forms of oppression in U.S. culture, they expand previous definitions of feminism. Anita Cornwell, for example, describes the invisibility she experienced during the early stages of the contemporary women's movement and challenges Euro-American feminists to incorporate an analysis of racism into their work. Writings by Pat Parker, Audre Lorde, Barbara Smith, Cheryl Clarke, and many others both confirm and broaden this critique. In their poetry, fiction, and prose, they maintain that feminists' exclusive emphasis on gender-based oppression overlooks the ways racism, classism, and heterosexism complicate women's experiences of sexism. By reminding their readers that although all women might be oppressed, the specific forms of oppression they experience vary cross culturally, this challenge has significantly altered the direction of U.S. feminist theory and activism in the 1990s.

This alteration of feminist theory and praxis reflects the transformational perspective found throughout twentieth-century African-American lesbian poetry, fiction, and prose. By developing Afrocentric feminist perspectives that validate self-affirming, woman-identified speech, black lesbian literature successfully challenges Eurocentric, patriarchal constructions of female and ethnic identities. As they depict their complex self-naming processes, African-American lesbian writers simultaneously redefine female identity and develop innovative models for cross-cultural communities.

—*AnnLouise Keating*

BIBLIOGRAPHY

Cornwell, Anita. *Black Lesbian in White America*. Tallahassee, Fla.: Naiad Press, 1983. ■ Hull, Gloria. *Color, Sex, and Poetry: Three Women Writers of the Harlem Renaissance*. Bloomington: Indiana University Press, 1987. ■ Jordan, June. *Civil Wars*. Boston: Beacon Press, 1981 ■ ———. *On Call: Political Essays*. Boston: South End Press, 1987. ■ ———. *Technical Difficulties: African-American Notes on the State of the Union*. New York: Pantheon, 1992. ■ Smith, Barbara, ed. *Home Girls: A Black Feminist Anthology*. New York: Kitchen Table, Women of Color, 1983. ■ ———. "Toward a Black Feminist Criticism." 1977. *The New Feminist Criticism: Essays on Women, Literature, Theory*. Elaine Showalter, ed. New York: Pantheon, 1985. ■ ———. "The Truth that Never Hurts: Black Lesbians in Fiction in the 1980s." *Feminisms*. Robyn R. Warhol and Diane Proce Herndl, eds. New Brunswick: Rutgers University Press, 1991. 690–712.

AIDS Literature

Since its appearance in America in 1980, AIDS has shifted from a largely "unspeakable" and "untouchable" phenomenon—because of its first association with a gay male population already stigmatized in those terms—to a semi-acknowledged and still dismaying reality. Certain sectors of society now regularly "touch" and "speak" about AIDS, whereas the larger population remains generally ignorant of or indifferent to the disease and frustrated activists and practitioners see no cure in sight. This tension was captured in microcosm on World AIDS Day 1993, when, on the one hand, the U.S. Postal Service issued a red-ribbon AIDS stamp and, on the other, President Clinton cited in a speech the recent stirring *New York Times Magazine* essay "Whatever Happened to AIDS?" by the late journalist and person with AIDS Jeffrey Schmalz, conceding that AIDS is "receding in the public consciousness as a thing to be passionate about."

A striking amount of AIDS literature has been written in the relatively short span of the epidemic. In the United States and much of the West, this literature has also largely been a gay literature. This fact has reflected partly the epidemiology of the disease since at first gay or bisexual men constituted almost all American AIDS cases, and in December 1993 they still made up approximately 60 percent of the diagnoses reported to the Centers for Disease Control; partly the preexistence of a politicized gay literature available to embrace the issue; and partly the already outcast status of gay men, who had nothing left to lose in taking up the stigmatized subject. Though infectivity is rising proportionately faster now in other CDC-defined risk groups, such as heterosexual women and IV-drug users, those groups have as yet produced only a scattering of their own AIDS writing.

Even in its apparently most private examples, AIDS literature has inevitably been a social literature. Common to all of it has been some desire to "speak" the "unspeakableness" of AIDS and to bring the detached majority audience in closer "touch" with the subject. Some authors have practiced an immersiveness whose priority is to expose readers as closely as possible to the emergency of the epidemic and the suffering of affected individuals. In its rawest examples, this kind of literature mimics a frontal assault on the majority society's denial by thrusting readers into a direct, unrelieved, imaginative encounter with the devastation of AIDS. At the same time, AIDS literature has also had a counterimmersive strain that reflects marked conflict about sustained "touch" with the subject. In this typically ironic mode, the characters are often in kinds of denial, whether persons with AIDS (PWAs) themselves or survivors or bystanders, and an immersive incident or realization is countered by some distancing device such as CAMP wit, broad humor, or a shift to another subject that ultimately shields the audience from too jarring a confrontation with AIDS. This protective framing may provide a temporary release from distress, but it also risks cooperating with the larger cultural denial of AIDS since it does nothing to dislodge readers from it.

Though some AIDS writing had appeared earlier, it was not until 1985 that AIDS became a widely acknowledged American literary subject, with the success of two New York plays, William M. Hoffman's *As Is* and LARRY KRAMER's *The Normal Heart*. Each vividly "spoke" the emergency of AIDS to audiences that had typically seen no artistic demonstration of it before. Hoffman combined the poignant tale of a person with AIDS and his lover with fuguelike choruses of other affected people, whereas Kramer offered a high-decibel chronicle of early AIDS activism augmented by graphic didactic sets. In 1985 also appeared the pioneering "The Tale of Plagues and Carnivals," Part III of *Flight from Neveryon* by the gay African-American science-fiction writer Samuel R. Delany. Delany intertwines reflections about the mounting AIDS crisis in New York between 1982 and

1984 (including a rare depiction of AIDS among street people) with a narrative about a similar plague in his fantasy realm. An early portrait of AIDS among African Americans by a black gay author, about a man who is shunned by his lover's family at his lover's funeral, is the story "Cut Off from Among Their People" by Craig G. Harris (d. 1991), which appeared in *In the Life: A Black Gay Anthology* (1986), edited by Joseph Beam (d. 1988).

Appearing in France in 1987 was the intense *Corps à Corps* (trans. *Mortal Embrace,* 1988) by Emmanuel Dreuilhe (d. 1988). Based on Dreuilhe's diary during the preceding three years in New York, this "News from the Front" is pervaded with martial metaphors that occasionally obscure the specificity of the author's experience of AIDS while attesting to its severity. The success in the same year of *And the Band Played On,* the impassioned chronicle by RANDY SHILTS (d. 1994) of the widespread national inaction about AIDS between 1980 and 1985, gave added momentum to AIDS literature. Appearing in 1988 were two groundbreaking classics by PAUL MONETTE (d. 1995)—*Love Alone: Eighteen Elegies for Rog,* a book of poems, and *Borrowed Time,* a prose memoir—that chart the suffering and death of Monette's lover Roger Horwitz from AIDS in 1985–1986, encompassing at the same time the struggles of affected friends and of the concerned gay community nationwide. *Love Alone* is the supreme work of immersive AIDS writing so far. It thrusts the horrors of AIDS in the reader's face. Monette embodies his and Rog's harrowing experience in an equally harrowing style, relentlessly withdrawing secure ground from under the reader's feet by a constant shifting of reference, focus, and tone and by stripping each poem of the traditionally stabilizing markers of stanza breaks, punctuation, and end-stopped lines. Another immersive 1988 work is the documentarylike *Someone Was Here: Profiles in the AIDS Epidemic* by George Whitmore (d. 1989), which reports on a middle-class white gay male PWA in New York City, a working-class Chicano gay male PWA in rural Colorado, and the AIDS service at Lincoln Hospital in the South Bronx, whose patients are overwhelmingly poor, African American or Hispanic, heterosexual IV-drug users. Whitmore's remains the only detailed portrait of the latter group in AIDS literature so far.

Three 1988 books by acclaimed gay male writers signal the force of counterimmersiveness in this literature as well. Slight touches appear in *Second Son* by ROBERT FERRO (d. 1988), the most distinguished American AIDS novel to that point. Ferro occasionally deflects the reader's attention from the moving love story of two men with AIDS, Mark and Bill, with Mark's family tensions and his camp correspondence with his friend Matthew. The stories in the pioneering collection *The Darker Proof*—four by the British writer ADAM MARS-JONES and three by the American novelist EDMUND WHITE—all concern AIDS in some way, yet all seem preoccupied by a fear of getting "more-ish" about the subject. The central characters—three PWAS, four surviving lovers, friends, or caretakers—are highly "defended" and, though some are occasionally "pierced" by their experiences of AIDS, most continue to function with "clenched teeth." Moving tributes to dead or imperiled friends dot ANDREW HOLLERAN's essay collection, *Ground Zero,* but most of the pieces concern Holleran's own "depression" at AIDS and his difficulty in writing about the epidemic as an author whose predominant modes have been doomed romanticism and camp wit.

In 1989, Larry Kramer issued *Reports from the Holocaust: The Making of an AIDS Activist,* his historically valuable, Cassandra-like "collected diatribes" about AIDS from 1981 to 1988, plus an essay paralleling gay oppression under AIDS with the Nazi genocide against the Jews. Another signal 1989 collection is *Poets for Life: Seventy-Six Poets Respond to AIDS,* edited by Michael Klein, which includes work by gay and heterosexual poets, people with AIDS, and loved ones and caretakers. Among its many notable contributions are work by groups that have been underrepresented in AIDS literature: a gay African-American writer—Melvin Dixon (d. 1992)—and several lesbian authors, including Marilyn Hacker and ADRIENNE RICH. The anthology includes a rare portrait of woman-to-woman AIDS, Carol Ebbecke's "Good Timing," and the moving "Memoir" by Honor Moore and "White Balloon" by Maureen Seaton. Appearing in Italy in 1989 was *Camere Separate* (trans. *Separate Rooms,* 1992) by Pier Vittorio Tondelli (d. 1991), a novel of "deep and sacred mourning" that reviews the love affair of the young Leo and Thomas and traces the quest of the intensely self-examining and chronically "separate" Leo to "become available" to experience again after Thomas's death from AIDS.

Two celebrated 1989 novels illustrate the continuing conflicts in AIDS literature about close "touch" with the subject. David B. Feinberg's *Eighty-Sixed,* a problematic attempt to write AIDS comedy, chronicles the adventures of a panicked seronegative New York gay "clone," B. J., and relegates actual AIDS to a secondary character with whom B. J. had a one-night stand and whom he is pressured into helping ("I don't want to touch Bob"). John Weir's *The Irreversible Decline of Eddie Socket* does have a person with AIDS as a main character; and in the "blank generation" Eddie, who even in his illness cannot stop living "in quotes" from movies and television, it gives a painful picture of a life wasted in reactive irony. Yet, though some breaks from flipness occur, the book often stays stuck in distancing irony itself through its cool third-person narrator and other "blocked" characters who live in their own "as if" ways.

The most pointed gay American AIDS fiction of 1990 appeared in *The Body and Its Dangers* by Alan Barnett (d. 1991); four of the collection's six stories concern AIDS. Its centerpiece, "The *Times* As It Knows Us," counterpoints the media's stereotypical depiction of gay men under AIDS with the more complicated behavior of a Fire Island household during a weekend AIDS crisis. Notable American AIDS drama also appeared in 1990. Terrence McNally's teleplay *André's Mother* movingly documented a surviving lover's mourning and his rapprochement with his dead lover's mother. In their musical *Falsettoland*, which enjoyed a successful Off-Broadway run, William Finn and James Lapine brought the characters from their earlier *March of the Falsettos* (1981) into the age of AIDS and its painful losses. Published in France in 1990 was *A L'ami Qui Ne M'a Pas Sauvé La Vie* (trans. *To the Friend Who Did Not Save My Life*, 1991) by Hervé Guibert (d. 1992). The autobiographical novel focuses on a young writer who obsessively confronts the "calamity" of his disease and at the same time seeks the "salvation" of a miracle vaccine promised by an American friend who never delivers. In sketching AIDS in the narrator's friends as well, the book created an extra stir for its portrait of the philosopher MICHEL FOUCAULT as the stricken Muzil.

The most vehement AIDS writing of 1991 was the collection *Close to the Knives: A Memoir of Disintegration* by the AIDS-activist painter David Wojnarowicz (d. 1992), which includes "Postcards from America: X Rays from Hell," the blistering essay that sparked opposition from Jesse Helms and the National Endowment for the Arts when it introduced the catalogue of the 1989 New York AIDS art show *Witnesses: Against Our Vanishing*. As piercing in their quiet realism are the last two chapters of Paul Gervais's *Extraordinary People* (1991), a novel in the form of linked short stories about two dissimilar homosexual brothers and their family. The narrator and his lover return to Boston to be with his older brother and his lover as his brother dies of AIDS and then face the emotional aftermath back in their expatriate home in Italy. The most extensive African-American AIDS writing to that point appeared in *Brother to Brother: New Writings by Black Gay Men* (1991), edited by Essex Hemphill and conceived by Joseph Beam. More than a quarter of the book concerns AIDS, from stirring poems by Melvin Dixon, David Frechette (d. 1991), and Craig G. Harris, to unembellished autobiography like "*The Scarlet Letter,* Revisited" by Walter Rico Burrell (d. 1990), to an interview and poem by Marlon Riggs (d. 1994) about his film *Tongues Untied*. A rare 1991 volume is Rachel Hadas's *Unending Dialogue: Voices from an AIDS Poetry Workshop*, which includes forty-five poems by the eight members of a poetry workshop the author led at New York's Gay Men's Health Crisis from 1989 to 1991. It features particularly skillful work by Charles Barber ("Thirteen Things About a Catheter"), Glenn Philip Kramer ("Pantoum for Dark Mornings"), Glenn Besco ("Vernon Weidner Visits in a Dream"), and Dan Conner ("Retinitis").

In recounting the harrowing AIDS deaths of Hugo and most of his friends in *A Matter of Life and Sex* (1991), Oscar Moore assaults the British tolerance of "solitary suffering" with AIDS as well as the general British "embarrassment" at "too much" expressiveness. Yet Moore seems implicated in the same universe himself (and risks distancing readers) in featuring as his protagonist an emotionally constricted sex- and drug-addicted "nice" boy ("Hugo enjoyed appearing detached") reacting against his suburban and Cambridge milieus by plunging "into low-man's land." David B. Feinberg's even more acclaimed *Spontaneous Combustion* (1991) is a sequel to his *Eighty-Sixed*. Now B. J. is HIV-positive, and the tensions in writing AIDS comedy are even more acute, with Feinberg alternately collaring the audience with blunt statements of suffering—"The course of the illness left one raw. Nothing was left but tension and anger"—and placating it with arch remarks: "Why couldn't I have leukemia or some other more socially acceptable malady?"

Two 1992 American AIDS dramas received widespread critical praise. Winning the Tony Award for best book of a musical, William Finn and James Lapine united their earlier *March of the Falsettos* and *Falsettoland* into *Falsettos* and made Whizzer's AIDS death even more wrenching by juxtaposition to the lovers' original romance. Larry Kramer's *The Destiny of Me*, which had a successful Off-Broadway run, continued the story of Ned Weeks from *The Normal Heart*, with Ned now an AIDS patient at the National Institutes of Health having flashback conversations with his younger self and family. A third of THOM GUNN's *The Man with Night Sweats* (1992) concerns AIDS, with especially noteworthy, rending elegies for lost friends (for example, "Lament," "The J Car"). *Was* (1992), by the Canadian-born Geoff Ryman, contains one of the most vivid and moving depictions of AIDS in fiction, in the story of the stricken actor Jonathan, one of several figures involved variously with *The Wizard of Oz* whose lives Ryman intertwines in the novel. In contrast, Adam Mars-Jones's

Monopolies of Loss (1992)—which reprints his four stories from *The Darker Proof* and adds five new pieces—largely confirms the point he makes in the book's introduction about the "detachment" of his artistic approach to AIDS. AIDS is a dominant concern in only two of the new stories, and in the one that comes closest to "facing things" about the epidemic, the sometimes very poignant "The Changes of Those Terrible Years," Mars-Jones has the man who turned his home into an AIDS hospice finally close it down.

The most sustained and affecting gay American AIDS fiction of 1993 was Jameson Currier's collection *Dancing on the Moon: Short Stories About AIDS*. At the hearts of most of these "simple," realistic stories are acts of "passionate" caretaking that demonstrate how the lives of gay men under AIDS, their friends, and families "keep interweaving" and that unembarrassedly convey "the unbearable sorrow which had punctured their souls." In his moving *Scissors, Paper, Rock* of the same year, a collection of linked short stories in the form of a novel, Fenton Johnson also uses traditional realism to "name the unspeakable death" of a young gay man with AIDS who returns to his working-class Kentucky family to die and whose story takes up half of the book. The landmark *Sojourner: Black Gay Voices in the Age of AIDS* (1993), the first anthology devoted entirely to African-American AIDS writing, follows the sample in the earlier *Brother to Brother* in maintaining that literature's testifying, "kicking and screaming" tradition, with a range of outspoken materials covering interviews, personal essays, fiction, and some vivid poems: for example, Marvin K. White's "Last Rights," Rodney McCoy, Jr.'s "Confessions of an HIV Health Educator," Harold McNeil Robinson's "The Vale of Kashmir," and B. Michael Hunter's "Untitled News."

Several other 1993 works about AIDS reflect in differing ways the current national tension about "speaking" and "touching" AIDS. The most blatantly counterimmersive is Paul Rudnick's highly praised play *Jeffrey,* where occasional spirited testimony about AIDS is engulfed by burlesque or camp humor ("It's still our party," says Darius's ghost). The audience is ultimately allowed the self-exonerating experience of feeling it is encountering AIDS while actually being largely diverted from it. *Jeffrey*'s commercial and critical success indicates how powerful the need to evade AIDS remains in our society. Other 1993 works about AIDS seem to have immersive aims but are also instilled with elements that distance the subject. In the painful death of the narrator's lover, Jasper, as well as in its unusual amount of technical medical information, Christopher Coe's *Such Times* seems to want to impress readers with AIDS' "waves of dying," yet the characters' often heartless "pansy bitch" personae give the book a distant and chilly texture. In

James Robert Baker's outwardly gritty *Tim and Pete,* an "over the edge" Southern California sexual picaresque, violent rage toward reactionary national responses to AIDS (at the end, a gang of drugged-out "postmodern" terrorist gay men with AIDS is on its way to machine-gun the convention of the right-wing "American Values Foundation") is offset by varieties of alienating thoughtlessness, from the terrorists' "moral insanity" to the title pair's pop-entertainment derivativeness to reliances on contrived plot devices and soap opera romance conventions.

Even the two most acclaimed 1993 works about AIDS—Tony Kushner's two-part *Angels in America: Millennium Approaches* and *Perestroika* and Dale Peck's *Martin and John*—have, along with their obvious distinction, some overlooked concessive implications. *Angels in America* won the Pulitzer Prize and Tony Award for best play (both parts), but more time is needed to tell whether the praise lavished on it reflects its merit or chiefly critics' guilt at having overlooked earlier AIDS art. In the stories of Prior, Louis, Joe, Belize, and Roy Cohn, *Angels in America* has brought AIDS and American gay male life before more mainstream viewers than any other work of AIDS writing. Yet the play also regularly shifts focus to another subject, heterosexual women (whom it ironically makes Mormons, one of the most homophobic religions), and also relies heavily on spectacle and a supernatural context (which it then ultimately tries to frame ambiguously). Each of these elements implies an audience (and world) that doesn't want to "touch" AIDS too frontally, plainly, or entirely, and, no matter what Kushner's intention, gives the play an evasive dimension. Relatedly, though we learn at the end of the consciously "decentered" *Martin and John* that the book's various "Martin" and "John" stories are the narrator's way of finding something "to grab on to" after the "real" Martin's death from AIDS, and though some of the scenes of AIDS suffering are harrowing, the actual subject of AIDS does not enter the book until almost halfway through. Moreover, most of the stories do not concern AIDS though several concern subjects as unnerving in their own terms as degenerative illness, child abuse, and homophobic hatred and violence.

Other selected works of gay AIDS literature also deserve mention: Paul Reed's *Facing It* (1984), the first gay American AIDS novel; *Night Sweat* (1984) by Robert Chesley (d. 1990), the first American AIDS play (published in his 1990 collection, *Hard Plays, Stiff Parts*); the last three volumes of ARMISTEAD MAUPIN's *Tales of the City* series, *Babycakes* (1984), *Significant Others* (1987), and *Sure of You* (1989), where AIDS becomes an ever more prominent subject; the four to six stories about AIDS in each of the *Men on Men: Best New Gay Fiction* collections (1986,

1988, 1990, 1992); HARVEY FIERSTEIN's *Safe Sex* (1987), three one-acts; the moving AIDS-related poems that dot Mark Doty's books, *Turtle, Swan* (1987), *Bethlehem in Broad Daylight* (1991), and the National Book Critics' Circle Award–winning *My Alexandria* (1993); Christopher Davis's *Valley of the Shadow* (1988), about a wealthy young New York man and his ex-lover as they die from AIDS; Richard Greenberg's play *Eastern Standard* (1988), which features a gay man with AIDS among its main characters; *Zero Positive* (1988) by Harry Kondoleon (d. 1994), which mixes AIDS among homosexual and heterosexual New Yorkers with other subjects (published in M. Elizabeth Osborn's 1990 anthology, *The Way We Live Now: American Plays & the AIDS Crisis*); Larry Kramer's play *Just Say No* (1988), a delirious skewering of the Reagan and Koch administrations in which government inaction on AIDS is one of several targets; Joel Redon's *Bloodstream* (1988), a brooding autobiographical novel in which a young gay man with AIDS returns to his Oregon family; Christopher Bram's *In Memory of Angel Clare* (1989), about the surviving lover and friends of a New York filmmaker who died of AIDS; the autobiographical *Les Nuits Fauves* ([1989]; trans. *Savage Nights,* 1993) by Cyril Collard (d. 1993), the basis for the 1992 film about an HIV-positive bisexual French filmmaker; the black gay author Larry Duplechan's engaging *Tangled Up in Blue* (1989), in which an HIV-positive gay man, his bisexual ex-lover, and his ex-lover's wife deal with the effects of AIDS on their relationships in 1985 Los Angeles; Gary Indiana's *Horse Crazy* (1989), where AIDS figures occasionally as a writer obsessively pursues a beautiful, manipulative addict, and his *Gone Tomorrow* (1993), which in its last third documents the AIDS deaths and suicides of several members of an international film crew; *These Waves of Dying Friends* (1989) by Michael Lynch (d. 1991), poems by a Toronto-based American AIDS-activist and academic; *Personal Dispatches: Writers Confront AIDS* (1989), edited by John Preston (d. 1994), a diverse collection of stirring essays by gay and lesbian authors; Ron Schreiber's *John* (1989), poems chronicling the sickness and death from AIDS of the author's lover; Michael Cunningham's much-praised *A Home at the End of the World* (1990), which incorpo-

rates a person with AIDS in its final sections; Paul Monette's more popularly written novels: *Afterlife* (1990), about three gay male "AIDS widowers" in Los Angeles, and *Halfway Home* (1991), in which a gay male PWA and his heterosexual brother reconcile; lesbian novelist SARAH SCHULMAN's *People in Trouble* (1990), where an East Village lesbian and her bisexual lover negotiate their relationship against a background of AIDS activism; Hervé Guibert's *Le Protocole Compassionel* ([1991]; trans. *The Compassion Protocol,* 1993), *L'Homme au Chapeau Rouge* ([1992]; trans. *The Man in the Red Hat,* 1993), *Le Paradis* (1992) and *Cytomégalovirus: Journal d'Hospitalisation* (1992), sequels to his *To the Friend Who Did Not Save My Life; Boys Like Us* (1991) and *Sweetheart* (1992) by Peter McGehee (d. 1991), two semicomic, semisorrowful novels tracing a group of gay male Toronto friends during the epidemic, and *Labour of Love* (1993), a further sequel by McGehee's lover, Doug Wilson (d. 1992), based on McGehee's notes; Joseph Caldwell's *The Uncle from Rome* (1992), in which a visiting American opera singer becomes entangled with several Italians, including a transvestite prostitute threatened by AIDS, and is finally able to grieve for his American ex-lover who died of the disease; the collection *Fidelities* (1992) by RICHARD HALL (d. 1992), which has four AIDS-related stories ("The Jilting of Tim Weatherall," "The Cannibals," "Manhattan Transfer," and "Being a Baroness"); and *One Boy at War* (1993) by Paul A. Sergios (d. 1994), which includes the author's experiences as a PWA in what is chiefly a report about AIDS treatments and the alternative AIDS-drug underground.

—*Joseph Cady*

BIBLIOGRAPHY

Crimp, Douglas, ed. *AIDS: Cultural Analysis/Cultural Activism.* Cambridge, Mass.: MIT Press, 1988. ■ Miller, James, ed. *Fluid Exchanges: Artists and Critics in the AIDS Crisis.* Toronto: University of Toronto Press, 1992. ■ Murphy, Timothy F., and Suzanne Poirier, eds. *Writing AIDS: Gay Literature, Language, and Analysis.* New York: Columbia University Press, 1993. ■ Nelson, Emmanuel S., ed. *AIDS: The Literary Response.* Boston: Twayne Publishers, 1992. ■ Pastore, Judith Laurence, ed. *Confronting AIDS Through Literature: The Responsibilities of Representation.* Urbana: University of Illinois Press, 1993.

Albee, Edward
(*b.* 1928)

Edward Albee holds a problematic position in the histories of American drama and of gay drama. For a handful of years, he seemed to be the heir to the late Eugene O'Neill and to Arthur Miller and TENNESSEE WILLIAMS, who had, by the early 1960s, lost their winning streaks. However, Albee was something of a has-been by the mid-1960s. Unlike his predecessors, Albee had his early success Off-Broadway with a series of one-act plays, *The Zoo Story* (1958), *The American Dream* (1960), and *The Death of Bessie Smith* (1961). His first full-length play was the controversial three-and-a-half-hour *Who's Afraid of Virginia Woolf?* (1963), his one Broadway hit. During the ensuing years, Albee alternated increasingly arid original plays with adaptations of stories and novels by contemporaries like CARSON MCCULLERS (*The Ballad of the Sad Cafe*, 1964) and JAMES PURDY (*Malcolm* [1966]). By 1970, Albee was a forgotten playwright whose later plays, *The Lady from Dubuque* (1980), *Lolita* (1981), and *The Man Who Had Three Arms* (1983), hold places only in the pantheon of major Broadway disasters.

Albee's place in the history of gay drama is as ambiguous. His early Off-Broadway work was, for its time, daring in its mention of homosexuality and its implied homoeroticism. *The Zoo Story* is a Central Park confrontation between Peter, an ineffectual wealthy man, and Jerry, a countercultural figure intent on telling his life story and driving someone to kill him. Jerry's world is the zoo of the title, a brutal universe in which God is "a colored queen in a kimono," indifferently filing his nails. Here, as elsewhere in Albee, love and violence are conjoined: Loving is the ultimate act of violence, violence is the most effective expression of love. The American dream is a scantily clad, beautiful but heartless male hustler. Yet Albee's homosexuality and the gay subtext of his early work came to haunt him. Some heterosexist critics, angered by Albee's scathing picture of modern marriage in *Who's Afraid of Virginia Woolf?*, insisted that George and Martha, the feuding central couple in the play, had to be a crypto-gay couple (by this logic *The Taming of a Shrew* is a crypto-gay play) or that the play was an act of homo-sexual spite. By this time, leading New York critics were becoming increasingly hostile toward the more openly gay work of Williams, WILLIAM INGE, and Albee. When Albee's allegorical *Tiny Alice*, in which a cardinal and a lawyer are bickering ex-lovers, opened in 1964, critics attacked furiously. Philip Roth, chronicler of heterosexual neuroses, lambasted the play's "ghastly pansy rhetoric." Indeed, the most famous production of *Tiny Alice*, by William Ball at the American Conservatory Theatre in San Francisco, turned Albee's obtuse religious allegory into a homoerotic camp extravaganza.

It is true that Albee's only theatrically vital women have more than a touch of the drag queen about them and that there is always a hint of the homoerotic about his male–male confrontations. Conventional heterosexual marriage, which is always depicted as infertile, and heterosexual all-American boy-men are his favorite targets. However, Albee saw himself as a satirist of the American condition and not a dramatist of the gay community. As a playwright who staked his success on Broadway in the 1960s and 1970s, he had no choice. However, his critics, though seldom fair, were partly right: It is impossible to ignore the far from gay homosexuality in Albee's plays.

—*John M. Clum*

BIBLIOGRAPHY

Albee, Edward. *Selected Plays of Edward Albee*. Garden City, N.Y.: Doubleday, 1987. ■ Bigsby, C. W. E., ed. *Edward Albee, A Collection of Critical Essays*. Englewood Cliffs, N.J.: Prentice-Hall, 1987. ■ ———. *A Critical Introduction to Twentieth-Century American Drama, II: Williams, Miller, Albee*. Cambridge: Cambridge, 1982. ■ Clum, John M. *Acting Gay: Male Homosexuality in Modern Drama*. New York: Columbia, 1992. ■ Sarotte, Georges-Michel. *Like a Brother, Like a Lover: Male Homosexuality in the American Novel and Theatre from Herman Melville to James Baldwin*. Garden City, N.Y.: Doubleday, 1978.

Allen, Paula Gunn
(*b.* 1939)

Paula Gunn Allen was born on the Cubero Spanish-Mexican land grant in New Mexico to a Laguna-Sioux-Scottish mother and a Lebanese-American father. After attending several colleges in New Mexico and Colorado, she received a B.A. in English from the University of Oregon in 1966 and an M.F.A. in creative writing two years later. During this time, she married, became a mother, and divorced. She then went to the University of New Mexico in Albu-querque, and in 1975 completed a Ph.D. in American Studies with an emphasis in Native-American Studies. By the early 1980s, Allen had achieved significant recognition as a Native-American poet, literary scholar, and spokesperson. Her introduction to *The Sacred Hoop: Recovering the Feminine in American Indian Traditions* (1986) indicates an important shift in her career, for in it she comes out as a lesbian. Allen has received a number of awards, including a National

Endowment for the Arts Creative Writing Fellowship (1978), a post-doctoral fellowship at the University of California, Los Angeles (1980–1981), and a post-doctoral research grant from the Ford Foundation (1984–1985). She has taught English and Native-American Studies at the University of New Mexico, Stanford University, the University of California, Berkeley, and the University of California, Los Angeles.

Allen's culturally mixed heritage greatly influences her work as a poet, fiction writer, and literary scholar. In both her creative and critical writings, she reinterprets the historic and mythic beliefs of indigenous North American peoples from a twentieth-century lesbian-feminist perspective and develops a highly distinctive, woman-focused, nonheterosexist tradition. By incorporating Native-American accounts of a cosmic feminine power into her poetry, she connects the past with the present and creates a complex pattern of continuity, regeneration, and change that affirms her gynecentric spirit-based overview. In "Some Like Indians Endure," for example, she associates lesbians with Native Americans in order to underscore the importance of maintaining a self-empowering visionary belief in the interconnectedness of all things. Relatedly, her novel, *The Woman Who Owned the Shadows* (1983), explores the cultural, sexual, and spiritual fragmentation experienced by those who have become disconnected from this overarching life force.

Allen has played a pivotal role in redefining scholarly views of traditional and contemporary Native-American sexualities. In "*Hwame, Koshkalaka,* and the Rest: Lesbians in American Indian Cultures" and several other essays collected in *The Sacred Hoop,* she argues that European colonizers and Western-trained ethnographers erased or otherwise distorted evidence of same-sex relationships in tribal cultures. Her unique mythic system, described in *The Sacred Hoop* and *Grandmothers of the Light* (1991), represents an innovative departure from the heterosexual bias found in most mythologies. By incorporating aspects of Keres, Navajo, and other Native-American theologies into her revisionist myths, she distinguishes between (hetero)sexual biological reproduction and other forms of creativity. Allen's work as an editor and literary scholar, along with her willingness to identify herself as lesbian in print, has enabled her to make important contributions to the careers of other lesbian and gay American-Indian writers. (See also NATIVE NORTH AMERICAN LITERATURE.)

—*AnnLouise Keating*

BIBLIOGRAPHY

Hanson, Elizabeth I. *Paula Gunn Allen.* Boise State University Western Writer Series. Boise: Boise State University, 1990. ■ Jahner, Elaine. "A Laddered, Rain-Bearing Rug: Paula Gunn Allen's Poetry." *Women and Western American Literature.* Susan Rosowski and Helen Stauffer, eds. Troy, N.Y.: Whitston Press, 1982. 311–325. ■ Keating, AnnLouise. "Myth Smashing, Myth Making: (Re)Visionary Techniques in the Works of Paula Gunn Allen, Gloria Anzaldúa, and Audre Lorde." *Journal of Homosexuality* 26 (1993): 73–95. ■ ———. "Reading 'Through the Eyes of the Other': Self, Identity, and the *Other* in the Works of Paula Gunn Allen, Gloria Anzaldúa, and Audre Lorde." *Readerly/Writerly Texts: Essays on Literature, Literary/Textual Criticism, and Pedagogy* 1 (1993): 139–165.

Allison, Dorothy E.
(*b.* 1949)

Dorothy Allison was born in 1949 in Greenville, South Carolina, the setting for her first collection of short stories, *Trash* (1988), and her highly acclaimed novel, *Bastard Out of Carolina* (1992). She was graduated from Florida Presbyterian College in 1971 and subsequently earned her M.A. in anthropology at the New School for Social Research. *The Women Who Hate Me,* a volume of poetry, appeared in 1983; it was expanded and reissued in 1991. *Trash* won two Lambda Literary Awards, for Best Small Press Book and Best Lesbian Book, in 1989. *Bastard Out of Carolina* was a finalist for the National Book Award in 1992.

In the preface to *Trash,* Allison describes her stories as a "shout of life against death, of shape and substance against silence and confusion. Writing . . . is the only way I know to make sure of my ongoing decision to live, to set moment to moment a small piece of stubbornness against an ocean of ignorance and obliteration." Indeed, the voice in Allison's fiction, the palpable expression of this motive, is its strongest feature. The stories in *Trash,* variously focused on the disasters of family, on religion, poverty, physical violence, and sexuality, achieve their unity through the first-person voice and the "sheer avidity," as Roz Kaveney has observed, with which it recalls "even the most terrible experiences." The voice in *Bastard Out of Carolina* is that of its adolescent narrator, Ruth Anne Boatwright, called Bone, whose earliest record is drawn from Allison's life. (Had the novel been wholly autobiographical, Allison noted in *The New York Times,* "it would have been a lot meaner.") Bone observes with wit and painful clarity the life of her working-class Southern family: hard-drinking uncles, feisty aunts, a mother who disappears into her own exhaustion, and, terrifyingly, a stepfather who abuses the child to punish her "for the fact of my life, who I was in his eyes and mine." The intricacies of family love, at once supportive and treacherous, emerge from Bone's perspective as concretely as hunger. At the novel's mysterious conclusion, Bone herself emerges as a force of will, who lives, finally, by acknowledging the truth her story teaches: that "we do terrible things to the ones we love sometimes."

Bastard Out of Carolina, Allison maintains, "is not about growing up queer successfully." Here, and elsewhere, she has resisted pressure to write either the didactic illustration of lesbian experience, or what she calls the "romantic solution" story. "I don't believe that story," she tells Amber Hollibaugh, "so I can't write it and it seems to me to be a very small thing to do with a book." Allison takes as her "purpose in life" to "write books in which lesbians live." Against the context her fiction creates, that verb takes on the resonance of triumph. As such, Allison's fiction forges a subtle politics of identity, expressed as forcefully in her writing as in the "damn sure truth" of her life: "If I wasn't queer," she says, "I wouldn't be a writer. I would probably be dead."

—*Ann E. Imbrie*

BIBLIOGRAPHY

Brady, Anne Vaccaro. "Interview." *Ms Magazine* (November–December, 1993): 149. ■ Drabelle, Dennis. "No Friends of Dorothy." *The Advocate* (March 9, 1993): 66–67. ■ Garrett, George. "'No Wonder People Got Crazy as They Grew Up." *New York Times Book Review* (July 5, 1992): 3. ■ Hawthorne, Mary. "Born of Ignorance." *Times Literary Supplement* (August 14, 1992): 18. ■ Hollibaugh, Amber. "In the House of Childhood." *Women's Review of Books* 9. 10–11 (July 1992): 15. ■ ———. "Telling a Mean Story: Amber Hollibaugh Interviews Dorothy Allison." *Women's Review of Books* 9. 10–11 (July 1992): 16–17. ■ Kaveney, Roz. "Subcultural Strengths." *Times Literary Supplement* (March 8, 1991): 18.

Alther, Lisa
(*b.* 1944)

Born July 23, 1944, in Tennessee, Lisa Alther had a privileged upbringing as the daughter of a surgeon. Educated at Wellesley College in the 1960s, Alther experienced firsthand the tumultuous events that were to be portrayed so vividly in her best-known novel, *Kinflicks* (1976).

This satirical novel, Alther's first, met with tremendous popular success, shooting to the top of the best-seller list. Ginny Babcock, the book's heroine, leaves her Tennessee home to attend Worthley College, an elite women's college in the East, where she meets Eddie, a fiery young radical lesbian. In order to sort out their new priorities, Ginny and Eddie leave college, live in Boston, and, finally, move to a lesbian communal farm in Vermont. Life on the farm is hectic and hilarious since none of the residents have any extensive knowledge of farming. But lesbianism is only one phase in Ginny's constantly changing life: Next, she tries marriage to a man, and at the conclusion of the novel, she leaves her husband to return to the South to minister to her dying mother. This novel is memorable for its depiction of lesbian feminism and separatist politics in the 1960s and for presenting lesbianism as a desirable way of relating to other women.

Alther's other novels also focus on the dynamics of lesbian interactions. *Original Sins* (1981) shows one of its central characters, Emily, coming to recognize her lesbianism against the background of the women's rights struggle and the civil rights movement. *Other Women* (1984) explores the relationship between Caroline Kelley and her lover, charting the changes in it as Caroline undergoes psychotherapy. She struggles to understand her relationship to her therapist and her parents, as well as the seemingly random and awful happenings in the world. This novel depicts the often ludicrous behavior of both heterosexuals and homosexuals, without suggesting that one group is superior to the other.

Bedrock (1990), like many of Alther's novels, shows how difficult it is to define who is a lesbian and who is not. Clea Shawn is married and has children, yet she has a friendship with another woman, Elke, which is described as a "charged connection" compared to the "more comfortable old-shoe camaraderie each shared with her husband." Neither of these women is explicitly identified as lesbian, and Elke even wonders, "Like the tree falling in the woods with no one to hear it, if you didn't act on your attraction to women, were you nevertheless a lesbian?" Alther provides no clear answer to this question but does show lesbian relationships as one of the many ways in which women try to communicate with each other.

In Alther's fictional world, lesbianism is a fluctuating force, which is as tenuous as all other forms of relationships in a universe that frequently appears frighteningly absurd. Alther points out that any form of relationship between humans, including lesbianism, deserves our understanding and sympathy since, as the Cheshire Cat observes in *Alice in Wonderland*, "we're all mad here."

—*Sherrie A. Inness*

BIBLIOGRAPHY

Heller, Zoe. "Journey to Herself." *New Statesman & Society* (August 17, 1990): 36–37. ■ Montrose, David. "Imperfections of the Art and of the Life." *Times Literary Supplement* (August 17, 1990): 868.

Amazons

In ancient Greek legends, the Amazons were fierce warrior women, living in their own country ruled by a queen (or pair of queens). Said to have descended from the war god Ares, they worshipped Artemis. They shunned men, except for ritual mating in the spring. Only Amazons who had killed in battle were allowed to mate. They were variously alleged to kill male offspring, to return them to their fathers, or to mutilate and enslave them. Although some sources, like Diodorus Siculus, place them in North Africa, in Herodotus, Aeschylus, and other Greek texts, the Amazons inhabit the area around the Black Sea, and some attribute to them control over much of Asia. Amazons represent a border between (patriarchal) Greek civilization and barbarian savagery. Vase paintings c. 575 B.C. portray the battle between Amazons and Heracles, whose ninth labor was to capture the girdle of the Amazon queen. The Amazon queen has no horse and is shown with both breasts. The tradition that Amazons removed one breast in order to use the bow or javelin more easily appeared much later. Following the Athenian defeat of Persian invaders in 490 B.C., images center on Theseus, legendary founder of Athens, who had captured and married the queen of the Amazons, Hippolyta (or sometimes Antiope). The outraged Amazons invaded Athens but were defeated by Theseus. In another Greek myth, the Amazon Penthesilea brought her army of women to the aid of Troy. She was slain by Achilles after a fierce battle. Some versions portray Achilles (or his son) removing her helmet and falling in love with her beauty.

For the Greeks, Amazons represented the chaos and disorder of women not subservient to men. In some versions, their nation originated in revolt by married women who slew their husbands. The Romans, who traced their own mythic roots to Troy, had a more positive view of Amazons and included them in many works, including some by VIRGIL, Seneca, and Ovid.

Numerous scholars have tackled the question of the historical existence of Amazons. Many theories have been proposed, but there is no conclusive proof. Some modern feminist scholars believe Amazon legends arose from Greek contact with more egalitarian or matriarchal societies.

Regardless of whether they actually existed, the Amazons have inspired many writers since classical times. However, until the twentieth century, Amazon characters were not associated with lesbianism. The development of the literature tended rather to make Amazons more heterosexual than they were originally. Around the twelfth century, Amazon figures appeared in works such as Benoît de Sainte-Maure's *Roman de Troie* as chivalrous female knights who often fall in love with men. In Christine de Pizan's *The Book of the City of Ladies* (1405), Amazons are examples of female power and intelligence. Amazon characters (especially Hippolyta, married to Theseus) were extremely popular in the fourteenth through the sixteenth centuries, appearing in works by Boccaccio, CHAUCER, SHAKESPEARE, Spenser, and numerous other authors. The motif reached a height of popularity in the Elizabethan period, with Elizabeth herself sometimes compared to an Amazon queen. A few major writers of the seventeenth century also treated the theme. In most works, however, the Amazon characters are either chaste virgins or heterosexual lovers.

Christopher Columbus, relying on Marco Polo's travel accounts, thought he would find an Amazon island off the coast of China. He sought it as proof that he had found Asia, and in 1493, he claimed to have found an island of armored women archers, rumored to possess a nearby island filled with gold. The Amazon river was so named because its Spanish explorers encountered women archers fighting alongside men. The legend of Queen Califia and her golden-armored warriors grew out of the Spanish quest for the fabled Amazons, and California was named for her.

The first open literary association of Amazons and lesbians came in the person of NATALIE CLIFFORD BARNEY (1876–1972), a wealthy American who founded a remarkable lesbian circle in Paris. Nicknamed the Amazon, she wrote two books entitled *Pensées d'une amazone* (1920) and *Nouvelles pensées de l'amazone* (1939). Barney and her lover, poet RENÉE VIVIEN, deliberately set out to recreate a lesbian society based on their reading of SAPPHO. Barney's salon included such lesbian artists as Romaine Brooks, RADCLYFFE HALL, DJUNA BARNES, Lucie Delarue-Mardrus, Isadora Duncan, CO-LETTE, GERTRUDE STEIN, Rachilde, Mina Loy, and Elizabeth de Gramont. Barnes's *Ladies Almanack* (1928) is about Barney's circle, and she was the model for a character in Hall's *The Well of Loneliness* (1928).

Despite Barney's equation of Amazons with lesbians and Helen Diner's effort to reclaim Amazons as feminist models (*Mothers and Amazons,* 1930), the literary image of the Amazon had become in the early decades of this century a heterosexual formula of the beautiful, man-hating woman who abandons her ways when she meets the "right" man. Katherine Hepburn starred in the first Broadway play using this theme, *The Warrior's Husband* (1931), later revived as a musical by Rodgers and Hart, *By Jupiter* (1942). The comic book character Wonder Woman is an Amazon princess who leaves Paradise Island to help battle America's enemies. Such treatments have no lesbian content.

Amazons were definitively linked with lesbians by the advent of lesbian feminism in the late 1960s. MONIQUE WITTIG's *Les Guérillères* (1969) is an Amazonian utopia set within a brilliant deconstruction of male cultural discourse. Wittig's entire oeuvre represents a world in which lesbians lead a revolution against the very concept of gender, and her novels and essays are among the most important explorations of lesbian theory today. Amazons appealed to lesbians not only because of the warrior image (the two-headed axe or labrys associated with Amazons became a lesbian symbol), but also because Amazons lived without men. Titles of lesbian works like *Amazon Expedition: A Lesbian/Feminist Anthology,* edited by Phyllis Birkby and others (1973), *Amazon Poetry,* edited by Elly Bulkin and Joan Larkin (1975), and Ti-Grace Atkinson's *Amazon Odyssey* (1974) reflect these associations. Noretta Koértge's novel *Valley of the Amazons* (1984) satirizes the most extreme separatist positions.

Though Amazons inspired "mainstream" fiction, most images appeared in SCIENCE FICTION and utopian literature. JOANNA RUSS's influential *The Female Man* (1975) contrasts our sexist world with an all-lesbian world. Numerous other novels show Amazonlike lesbians, either in all-female worlds or, more often, as women in revolt against oppressively sexist worlds. Examples of the latter include Suzy McKee Charnas's *Motherlines* (1978) and Marion Zimmer Bradley's "Society of Free Amazons" within her popular "Darkover" novels. Although most of these treatments occurred in the 1970s and early 1980s, the theme continues to inspire writers.

—*Diane Griffin Crowder*

BIBLIOGRAPHY

Jay, Karla. *The Amazon and the Page: Natalie Clifford Barney and Renée Vivien.* Bloomington: Indiana University Press, 1988. ■ Kleinbaum, Abby Wettan. *The War Against the Amazons.* New York: McGraw-Hill, 1983. ■ Monaghan, Patricia. *The Book of Goddesses and Heroines.* New York: E.P. Dutton, 1990. ■ Salmonson, Jessica A. *The Encyclopedia of Amazons: Women Warriors from Antiquity to the Modern Era.* New York: Paragon House, 1991. ■ Samuel, Pierre. *Amazones, guerrières et gaillardes.* Brussels: Editions complexe—Presses universitaires de Grenoble, 1975. ■ Sobol, Donald J. *The Amazons of Greek Mythology.* London: Thomas Yoseloff, 1972. ■ Taufer, Alison. "The Only Good Amazon is a Converted Amazon: The Woman Warrior and Christianity in the *Amadis Cycle.*" *Playing with Gender: A Renaissance Pursuit,* Jean R. Brink et al., eds. Urbana: University of Illinois Press, 1991. 35–51. ■ Tyrell, William Blake. *Amazons: A Study in Athenian Mythmaking.* Baltimore: Johns Hopkins University Press, 1984. ■ Walker, Barbara G. *The Woman's Encyclopedia of Myths and Secrets.* San Francisco: Harper & Row, 1983.

AMERICAN LITERATURE

American Literature: Colonial

Knowledge of what we might now call homosexuality in early British America comes to us—through court documents, letters, sermons, travel narratives—in the frequently reticent languages of sodomy and love, of act and affect. What we (often rightly) interpret as a reluctance in these texts to name or specify sanctioned behaviors is, in many cases, an effect of a need to read these texts in a certain way, to find in them evidence of connection to contemporary behavior and identity. There are in fact many texts—ranging in tone from scandalized to exuberant—that engage in frank descriptions of what was done and what was felt by these earlier Americans. The reasons for that frankness (and that scandal and exuberance) are perhaps what is underarticulated.

In the British colonies, certain kinds of nonprocreative sexual activity were not only recognized, but common enough to warrant the severest sanctions. Many courts shied away from describing fully such acts, even as they pronounced their terrible sentences. Others were more forthcoming. For example, the *Minutes of the Council and General Court of Colonial Virginia* record the 1625 testimony against Richard Cornish, which accuses him of luring another man (here, the "examinee") into his bed:

> Cornish went into the bed to him, and there lay upon him, and kissed him and hugged him, saying that he would love this examinee if he would now and then come and lay with him, and so by force he turned this examinee upon his belly, and so did put this examinee to pain in the fundament, and did wet him, and after did call for a napkin which this examinee did bring unto him. . . .

This kind of elaboration, however, is more often reserved for the ways in which crimes "not to be named" were dealt with. Though he "forbear[s] particulars" in his description of a case of "buggery" (bestiality) and certain "sodomitical attempts," William Bradford's account, in *Of Plymouth Plantation* (first published in 1856), of the resulting 1642 execution is served up in grotesque detail:

> first the mare and then the cow and the rest of the lesser cattle were killed before his face, according to the law, Leviticus xx.15; and then he himself was executed. The cattle were all cast into a great and large pit that was digged of purpose for them, and no use made of any part of them.

Such appeals to biblical authority were of course common (and may help explain the near absence of references to sexual activity between women in colonial texts). This is true with respect to tropes for friendship as well as to legal and ecclesiastical sanctions. The story of David and Jonathan, for instance, is a locus classicus for the discourse of love in Puritan texts like John Winthrop's 1630 sermon, *A Model of Christian Charity*. Social, spiritual, and affectional bonds seem to blur together in such texts, making the language of love, like the language of sodomy, difficult to read if we are reading for evidence of sexualities akin to our own.

This is true of more clearly secular texts as well. In his *General History of Virginia* (1624), for example, John Smith describes some curious trading practices in which members of his company barter with some sailors for food, using "Saxefras, furres, or love" as currency. Despite the general randiness of sailors in narratives by Smith and others (Bradford describes, with unchristian relish, the death from illness of "a proud and very profane young man, one of the seamen, of a lusty, able body, which made him the more haughty"), "love" here may not refer to sexual favors. Yet it seems even less likely that strong affectional ties are indicated.

Such ties, however, are very much the subject of the letter—reproduced in *The Saltonstall Papers, 1607–1815* (1972–1974)—Richard Saltonstall, Jr., wrote to his friend John Winthrop, Jr., on June 22, 1632:

> My dear brother, I am every way bound unto you; and for ever: and it is my rejoicing that I am bound unto you for your love; in the bond of love. I remember your unfayned love; in much love; and I love you againe; and I confesse my selfe indebted to you for your love, and will labour to requite your love, with love. And now (my deare brother,) although I want time to express my love, in this letter; yet (you know) I love you never the lesse for that; and therfore judge not of my love, by my letter: but of my letter by my love.

Saltonstall's exuberance here (at age twenty-two) may have more to do with letters than with love, though the injunction with which this passage ends wittily reveals a Puritan's awareness of the extent to which language conditions social bonds. Whatever delights the letter may have held for young Winthrop, it is Saltonstall's rhetorical flourish that strikes us most forcibly, and it is to his language—his "letter"—that we must appeal for any conclusions we might form.

Almost 150 years after Saltonstall addressed his love to his friend, Alexander Hamilton (also at age twenty-two) did the same in a letter to John Laurens: "Cold in my professions, warm in my friendships, I wish, my Dear Laurens, it might be in my power, by action rather than words, to convince you that I love you."

From 1779 to 1782, Hamilton and Laurens developed an affectional language in a series of letters—reproduced in *The Papers of Alexander Hamilton* (1961)—that are almost too easy to read as the record of an affair. The words that, for Hamilton, take the place of actions assume, in one way of reading, the status of actions themselves. Yet conclusions about the nature of Hamilton's relationship with Laurens, or Saltonstall's with Winthrop, are ultimately less interesting than the claims we make on the texts of these lives as part of a heritage more or less our own.
— *Max Cavitch*

BIBLIOGRAPHY

Goldberg, Jonathan. *Sodometries: Renaissance Texts, Modern Sexualities.* Stanford: Stanford University Press, 1992. ■ Hughes, Walter. "'Meat Out of the Eater': Panic and Desire in American Puritan Poetry." *Engendering Men: The Question of Male Feminist Criticism.* Joseph A. Boone and Michael Cadden, eds. New York: Routledge, 1990. 102–121. ■ Katz, Jonathan. "The Age of Sodomitical Sin, 1607-1740." *Reclaiming Sodom.* Jonathan Goldberg, ed. New York: Routledge, 1994. 43–58. ■ ———. *Gay American History.* New York: Harper & Collins, 1976. ■ Oaks, Robert. "'Things Fearful to Name': Sodomy and Buggery in Seventeenth-Century New England." *Journal of Social History* 12 (1978): 268–281. Rpt. *The American Man.* Elizabeth H. Pleck and Joseph H. Pleck, eds. Englewood Cliffs, N.J.: Prentice-Hall, 1980. 53–76. ■ Warner, Michael. "New English Sodom." *American Literature* 64 (1992): 19–47.

American Literature: Nineteenth Century

Although it would appear that a male homosexual subculture was well established and visible in London by the eighteenth century, there does not seem to have been a comparable development in America. Whether this is due to the relatively small size of urban centers in America, to the persistence of Puritan theology, or to the availability of free land in the West for men interested in other men, there is little evidence of a gay or lesbian subculture in America until the second half of the nineteenth century. Leslie Fiedler famously argued for the universality of male homosexuality in American literature, but he confused the categories of friendship, male bonding, and misogyny. As he himself suggested, the male couples he describes have a mythic rather than a real existence.

The Transcendentalists were the first group in America to explore the relations between persons of the same sex, and they did so through their understanding of Platonic philosophy and German Romanticism. Ralph Waldo Emerson, the best known of the group, had been infatuated with a classmate, Martin Gay, at Harvard. In his mature life, however, "his craving for friendship and love seldom found adequate satisfaction," as his biographer Stephen Whicher put it. Emerson's 1839 essay on friendship is troubled by the impossibility of realizing the ideal in flesh and blood. His concept of friendship was gendered male and seen as superior to heterosexual love. For Emerson, friendship is a "select and sacred relation which is a kind of absolute [that] leaves the language of love suspicious and common." Emerson's friend HENRY DAVID THOREAU also had difficulty rec-

onciling an abstract commitment to friendship with an aversion to the physical. In the same year that Emerson wrote his essay, Thoreau wrote his poem "Sympathy," apparently prompted by his love for the eleven-year-old Edmund Sewell. The poem draws on SHAKESPEARE's sonnets, as well as on MILTON's "Lycidas," while finding its consolation in the thought that the spirit of the love will survive even the disappearance of the object of love. Thoreau's diary for this period is filled with thoughts on friendship and the sense of a "secret." His reflections are deeply moving: "My friend is the apology for my life. In him are the spaces which my orbit traverses."

The most significant woman in the Concord circle, Margaret Fuller, also participated in the discourses of friendship although her approach was both more personal and more political. Emerson described Fuller's female friendships as "not unmingled with passion, . . . romantic sacrifice and ecstatic fusion." Fuller sought to locate her own friendships in a literary and cultural tradition, evoking for instance the relationship between Mme. de Stael and Mme. Récamier. Fuller's major work, *Woman in the Nineteenth Century* (1845), is quite discreet on the subject of female friendship although she does insist on a fundamental androgyny: "There is no wholly masculine man, no purely feminine woman." Fuller is clearly anxious in her response to the cross-dressing, cigar-smoking George Sand. The Frenchwoman is "rich in genius" but "would trample on every graceful decorum." Still, she was the person Fuller insisted on seeing first when she traveled to Europe. Fuller's greatest tribute to her commitment to female friendship is her translation of the letters between Bettina von Arnim and Karoline von Günderode, German romantic friends who were separated by the suicide of Günderode. Such a friendship offered to Fuller the possibility of a relation of equals and the expression of a deep desire to escape from the limitations of the "feminine."

For many writers of the mid-nineteenth century, it seemed necessary to locate the desired partner of the same sex in a distant, exotic setting. Reports of the sensuality of the South Seas had been frequent since their "discovery" by Europeans. Richard Henry Dana recorded his experiences in Hawaii in his popular *Two Years Before the Mast* (1840), which was to influence HERMAN MELVILLE (and later CHARLES WARREN STODDARD) significantly. Dana's friendships with the English sailors fit quite well into a tradition of the handsome noble sailor (as in the works of Frederick Marryat). His friendship with Hope, his Hawaiian special friend (*aikane*), introduces the text's cross-cultural theme of self-exploration. Despite the abuse he receives, and the fact that he is dying of syphilis presumably contracted from a Western sailor, Hope remains civil, and Dana attempts to counteract the captain's racism by procuring medicine for him. Dana's journey to such a world is a kind of delayed adulthood, represented by the America to which he returns "in a state of indifference."

Melville carried the theme further in his exploration of the South Seas in *Typee* (1846). Abandoning ship meant fleeing paternal and patriarchal authority. Melville brought to his experiences a taste trained by Western classicism, and so he can see Marnoo as a "Polynesian Apollo" even though he is put off by the Polynesians' tattooed bodies. Some of Melville's contemporaries, such as Bayard Taylor, sought out even more remote locales for the exploration of male eroticism.

Taylor, like so many Americans of the mid-nineteenth century, was deeply influenced by Goethe, and imitated Goethe's "Orientalizing" poems of the *Westöstlicher Divan* (1819). The adoption of a Persian model permitted the exploration of erotic poems addressed to a boy, such as Taylor's "To a Persian Boy" (1851), with its celebration of "the rich, voluptuous soul of Eastern land" in "the wonder of thy beauty." The journey east was a voyage of self-discovery in a world where gender and desire were regulated differently. It could lead to self-recognition, or coming out, as Taylor intimates in "L'Envoi" (1855):

> I found among those Children of the Sun,
> The cipher of my nature,—the release
> Of baffled powers, which else had never won
> That free fulfillment, whose reward is peace.

Taylor's 1870 novel *Joseph and His Friend* marks his attempt to shift from the Oriental lyric to American prose. It is quite explicit in its adoption of a political stance toward homosexuality. The young Joseph Aster has grown up sensitive and isolated, taught to reject his body. On the train returning from his engagement, he meets Philip Held, with whom he falls in love and who explains to him "the needs" that are often unfulfilled in conventional society. Philip argues for the "rights" of those "who cannot shape themselves according to the common-place pattern of society." The two young men go off to California in search of the Happy Valley, the place where they can realize their love.

Like so many homosexuals of this period, Taylor felt a considerable debt to WALT WHITMAN. Although Whitman's first edition of *Leaves of Grass* in 1855 included scenes of apparently homosexual desire and sexuality, the publication of the "Calamus" poems in the 1860 edition made Whitman into a beacon for many gay men who felt touched by his exploration of the consequences of his homosexuality. Taylor wrote to Whitman in 1866, praising Whitman's treatment of "that tender and noble love of man for man" and his "unwearied, affectionate practical fraternity." Charles Warren Stoddard was another of Whitman's admirers, like Taylor sending the older poet a copy of one of his books and seeking confirmation of the sexual themes. Although Whitman did not answer Stoddard's first letter and book, he did reply in 1869, sending a photograph, asserting that "those tender & primitive personal relations away off there in the Pacific Islands . . . touched me deeply." Although Stoddard clearly wanted Whitman's approval, there were many obstacles to any connection between them. Stoddard's search for the exotic would lead him finally to the Roman Catholic Church, haven for so many homosexual aesthetes in the second half of the nineteenth century.

If Taylor and Stoddard could feel affirmed in their sexual identities by Whitman's example, the young HENRY JAMES reacted very differently. James's 1865 review of *Drum-Taps* is extraordinarily, overdeterminedly hostile. Whitman's work is called by James "monstrous because it pretends to persuade the soul while it slights the intellect; because it pretends to gratify the feelings while it outrages the taste." Thirty-three years later, James, no longer quite so fastidious, had little but praise for Whitman's letters to Peter Doyle, which he termed "positively delightful." Whitman's "queerness" was, James now sees, perfectly American, and this record of his love for the working-class Doyle is "the beauty of the natural . . . the beauty of the particular nature . . . the personal passion."

By the 1890s, James found himself often in the throes of homosexual passion (whether requited or not), notably with Jonathan Sturges and Morton Fullerton. He was close to important homosexual circles in England through his friendship with Edmund Gosse. At the same time, the OSCAR WILDE trial in 1895 served as a warning of the possible consequences of exposure. James kept a safe distance from the disgraced Wilde. In an early work, *Roderick Hudson* (1875), James had portrayed passionate male friendship, celebrating the love of Rowland Mallet for his protégé Roderick. Their affectionate companionship offers a "high felicity" experienced in the sexually charged atmosphere of Venice. In his later novels, until the 1890s, James played down homosexual imagery. When he returned to the subject, he once again wrote of the dangers of the guardian or tutor. In "The Pupil" (1891), the tutor refuses his pupil's offer of a life together and thus causes his death, whereas in "The Turn of the Screw" (1898), little Miles is tormented by the vigilance of the governess and the ghost of the dead tutor. A complex treatment of the matter is offered in "The Author of 'Beltraffio'" (1884), based on JOHN ADDINGTON SYMONDS, a text that is anxious about the possession of a child's soul and at the same time critical of a moralistic wife who, like the governess in "The Turn of the Screw," does more harm out of a desire to keep the child "pure" than anyone else.

The misuse of power in the name of freedom is the subject also of James's novel of women's rights, *The Bostonians* (1886). Olive Chancellor arranges to "buy" the attractive and talented Verena Tarrant away from her father, and then replaces Tarrant as a mesmeric force seeking to make Verena into a spokeswoman for Olive's ideology and preserving her from marriage. Challenged by her cousin Basil Ransom for control of Verena, Olive, who believes in the power of free choice and is portrayed as a latter-day Transcendentalist, abandons her principles to fight for the young woman. Verena eventually chooses romantic love and domesticity as offered by Basil, leaving Olive alone to face the crowd of activists. Although the novel ends in marriage, James ironically undercuts the ending by commenting that Verena's tears "were not the last she was destined to shed." Some of the impetus for the book came from James's observation of his sister Alice and her friend Katharine Loring, who shared a life from 1879 until Alice's death from cancer in 1892.

James's circle included more open homosexuals, such as HOWARD OVERING STURGIS, American expatriate, who wrote *Tim* (1891), a school novel about the love of a frail boy for an unfeeling older boy. The two are united only at the moment of death, when the extent of Tim's love can be acknowledged. Sturgis's cousin was GEORGE SANTAYANA, poet and philosopher, who wrote a series of sonnets celebrating his love for Warwick Potter, a friend who died young. Like his contemporary in England, A. E. HOUSMAN, Santayana celebrated the purity of the dead, who are preserved from time and loss.

Male friendships of the period were nurtured in schools and universities. Thomas Wentworth Higginson, later EMILY DICKINSON's mentor, remembered his love for William Henry Hurlbut whom he had known as a student at Harvard in the 1840s. As Higginson put it, "for him my love had no bounds." Hurlbut was apparently also the model for Theodore Winthrop's *Cecil Dreeme* (1862), in which the eponymous hero is revealed at the end to be a woman dressed as a man. Although this sudden revelation enables a "happy ending" in heterosexual terms, it is hardly greeted with enthusiasm in the text. Byng's love for Dreeme is clearly located in a homosexual tradition by his comment that "him I love with a love passing the love of women." In another novel, *John Brent* (1862), Winthrop uses a Western setting for a text that celebrates the joining of nature and culture, the softness of youth with the hardness of masculinity. As in *Cecil Dreeme,* male friendship is the privileged site of affection: "I have known no more perfect union than that one friendship."

As women's lives were largely confined to the home, so their affections developed in a domestic setting. Emily Dickinson's intense romantic friendships for Kate Anthon and Sue Gilbert existed alongside her heterosexual desires, with no apparent sense of conflict. In 1852, Dickinson wrote to Sue Gilbert, "will you be my own again and kiss me as you used to? . . . I feel that now I must have you—that the expectation once more to see your face again, makes me feel hot and feverish, and my heart beats so fast." Recent studies of Dickinson have stressed the role of the poems as tokens of love and desire, and have called attention to the concern with detail and small objects as a sign of clitoral imagery. Even a well-known poem such as "I taste a liquor never brewed" yields a very different meaning, and a very different poet, if read in terms of sexuality. In public, at least, American women did not express sexual desires directly but through passionate long-lasting friendships, often called Boston marriages. Since such friendships were imagined to be lacking in sexuality, emotional expression knew no limits. Many women shared lives over many years and were widely accepted in the community. One of the most striking of such relationships was that between Annie Fields and SARAH ORNE

JEWETT. Fields's husband died in 1881, after which Fields and Jewett lived together most of the year except for a few months when Jewett retired to Maine to write. Jewett's work, although probably written without any awareness of a category such as "lesbian," celebrates female community and women's friendships. Her story, "Martha's Lady" (1895) concerns a brief but intense friendship between a young woman and a young maidservant. The woman marries and leaves Martha behind, waiting faithfully for her return. When that return takes place, both the women are old, but their affection is restored, as Helena realizes what her friendship has meant to Martha. The need to accept the marriage of one of the partners was a repeated theme of Jewett's stories of female friendship, but she constantly sought ways to preserve that friendship, so much more powerful for her than the marriage tie. Jewett's great admirer and literary follower was WILLA CATHER although Cather did not feel free to be as open in her treatment of same-sex relations as Jewett had been. In fact, Jewett wrote to Cather in 1908 gently chastising Cather for writing in "masquerade," when, according to Jewett, "a woman could love her in the same way." Jewett's response is now usually attributed to her innocence of later models of homosexuality that made Cather so cagey; whatever the validity of that, it testifies also to her commitment to love between women, regardless of what it is called.

—*Robert K. Martin*

BIBLIOGRAPHY

Austen, Roger. *Genteel Pagan. The Double Life of Charles Warren Stoddard.* John W. Crowley, ed. Amherst: University of Massachusetts Press, 1991. ■ Faderman, Lillian. *Surpassing the Love of Men. Romantic Friendship and Love between Women from the Renaissance to the Present.* New York: Morrow, 1981. ■ Martin, Robert K. *The Homosexual Tradition in American Poetry.* Austin: University of Texas Press, 1979. ■ ———. "Bayard Taylor's Valley of Bliss: Pastoral and the Search for Form." *Markham Review* (Fall 1979): 13–17. ■ ———. "Knights-Errant and Gothic Seducers: The Representation of Male Friendship in Mid-Nineteenth-Century America." *Hidden from History. Reclaiming the Gay and Lesbian Past.* Martin Duberman, Martha Vicinus, and George Chauncey, Jr., eds. New York: New American Library, 1989. ■ Savoy, Eric. "Reading Gay America: Walt Whitman, Henry James, and the Politics of Reception." *The Continuing Presence of Walt Whitman.* Robert K. Martin, ed. Iowa City: University of Iowa Press, 1992. 3–15.

American Literature: Gay Male, 1900–1969

Long before the 1969 Stonewall riots and the launching of the contemporary gay liberation movement, twentieth-century gay and bisexual male American writers had produced notable literature about the subject. There was frank and affirmative gay male American writing from the century's start, but it was usually published abroad or by marginal presses or remained private and unpublished. As the century advanced, there were marked increases in both the amount of frank gay male American writing and the amount of it issued by mainstream publishers. This pattern became unmistakable in the 1940s, when, among other firsts, books clearly concerned with homosexuality became best-sellers. A relative burst in published gay male American writing then followed in the 1950s, and this was in turn followed by what in context amounted to a flood of work in the pre-Stonewall 1960s. But this increased public depiction of homosexuality was usually tinged with misery, when it was not totally bleak. It was as if gay male writers in these years were subject to a rule of concessiveness (either explicit or tacit), in which the price of greater public access was the confirming of homosexual stereotypes. None of these patterns was seamless, however—for example, some relatively positive portrayals emerged from mainstream publishers early in the century, and some stereotypical ones appeared from independent presses; in addition, some amazingly positive depictions appeared in the decades just before Stonewall.

At least three general points need to be underscored about this remarkable body of material. First, it adds to the growing knowledge that, despite its epochal quality, Stonewall was not a self-generated event—it was preceded not only by earlier homosexual political organizing but by a mounting body of persistent gay male American writing. Second, it implies that one of the greatest fears of the widespread reading public (and, by extension, of the society at large) was the prospect of encountering a nonstereotypical homosexual whose lot was no more restricted and troubled than an average heterosexual's. Third, though a few works within it received marked publicity, as a consistent and purposeful whole this body of writing was invisible to the general public, and as in every other potentially enabling aspect of their experience, gay readers and writers during this period had to be self-relying and self-inventing in finding and learning from this literature. Because of homosexuality's continuing official "unspeakableness" for most of the century, no public commentator before Stonewall studied and organized this material into a discussible entity from which gay readers might have benefited.

The frankest and most affirmative gay male American work in the century's first decade was *Imre: A Memorandum* (1906), a little-known melodramatic novel by the equally little-known EDWARD I. PRIME-STEVENSON (1868–1942), an expatriate who wrote as "Xavier Mayne." In *Imre,* which is structured as a "memorandum" sent to the author by a British friend, Oswald pursues Imre, a Hungarian soldier, while summering in his country, and the book ends with Imre's reciprocating Oswald's love: "I love thee as thou lovest me. I have found the friendship which is love, the love which is friendship." *Imre* reflects an interest in gay history as well—the two men have a long conversation about great earlier homosexuals. Two years later, Stevenson expanded on this concern with *The Intersexes: A History of Similisexualism as a Problem in Social Life* (1908), a 641-page discussion of earlier homosexual figures and of sexologists and recent homosexual liberation pioneers, like Karl Heinrich Ulrichs, JOHN ADDINGTON SYMONDS, and EDWARD CARPENTER. Both books show the constraints of their time. Issued pseudonymously, they were published privately, abroad (in Italy), and in small printings.

Other noteworthy, if less blunt, work of this decade included the most nearly frank, accepting, and political homosexual fiction by HENRY JAMES (1843–1916), his 1900 story "The Great Good Place." In this coded tale, a harried bachelor novelist, based on James himself, falls asleep and imagines an all-male "cloister" of "brothers" who "recognise each other as such," a "scene of . . . new consciousness" that is dubbed "The Great Good Place," as well as "liberty-hall" and the site of "The Great Want Met." "The Great Good Place," whose last sentence is "It *was* all right," may be the closest James came to defiance of the recent WILDE scandal and reflects the more open homosexual desire he let himself show in later life, as in his attachments to Hedrick Andersen, Jocelyn Persse, and Hugh Walpole. Three years later, CHARLES WARREN STODDARD (1843–1909), who also worked chiefly in the nineteenth century, published his little-known autobiographical San Francisco novel, *For the Pleasure of His Company: An Affair of the Misty City* (1903). Occasional homosexual allusions dot this diffuse book, which is chiefly concerned with the career woes of a young writer, Paul Clitheroe. Paul's closest relationships are with two men (one of whom tells

him, "I love you better than any fellow I ever met. You understand me," while the other "encircles him in the warm manly pressure of his arms"), and the novel ends with Paul jumping ship to join "three naked islander chiefs" who happen by in a boat. Paul also discusses "girl-boys" with a female friend. Stoddard is somewhat more overt in his 1904 *The Island of Tranquil Delights,* a collection of South-Sea tales resembling his earliest work. In "Kane-Aloha," he is "touched to the quick" by the title youth and hopes the story will give "pleasure to the careful student of the Unnatural History of Civilization."

The most venturesome American gay male publication of the teens was *Bertram Cope's Year* (1919), by Henry Blake Fuller (1857–1929), best known for his realistic Chicago fiction of the 1890s. Following Fuller's more frank and daring portrait of homosexuality in his 1896 one-act play "At Saint Judas's," *Bertram Cope's Year* focuses on the young college instructor Cope as he is pursued by several characters, including some women, an older man, Basil Randolph, and a school friend, Arthur Lemoyne, who comes to live with Cope in mid-year. Randolph's attraction to Cope is nearly transparent (he imagines Cope sharing his apartment as "a young knight, escaped from some 'Belle Dame sans Merci'"), as is the homosexuality of the Bertram–Arthur relationship ("Lemoyne, softening, pressed his hand on Cope's own"). But Fuller later wrote that he had had to be "careful" in *Bertram Cope's Year,* and in that spirit he casts a final uncertainty over the characters' feelings. Still, *Bertram Cope's Year* was rejected by every publisher and had to be issued privately at Fuller's own expense, and the book went almost unnoticed, with only one critic remarking that Fuller had "essay[ed] a delicate theme." As the first published novel by a nationally known American writer to deal near frankly and exclusively with homosexuality, *Bertram Cope's Year* deserves greater exposure and discussion. HART CRANE (1899–1932) published some early poems with strong homosexual implication in this decade—for example, "C33" (1916), a homage to Oscar Wilde named after Wilde's prison identification number, and "Modern Craft" (1918), where Crane cites his "modern love . . . charred at the stake in younger times." Crane also "came out" as homosexual in a December 27, 1919, letter to the critic Gorham Munson.

The frankest, most extensive, and most revealing American gay male writing of the 1920s did not reach public view until the 1970s. This is the correspondence between the critic F. O. MATTHIESSEN (1902–1950) and his lover, the painter Russell Cheney (1881–1945), begun shortly after they met in 1924 and continuing for twenty-one years. With half of its 3,000 letters clustered in the 1920s, the Matthiessen-Cheney correspondence offers a unique and moving portrait of two gay men trying to understand themselves positively as homosexual and to create a devoted relationship without public models and support. A selection appeared as *Rat & the Devil* (the two men's nicknames for each other) in 1978, but the majority remain unpublished and would be a treasury of information for readers of gay history. Hart Crane's letters of the 1920s continue to contain frank homosexual statements; these have been published posthumously, but only in part. Crane's first book, *White Buildings,* appeared in 1926, but its homosexual content is veiled—for example, the six-part "Voyages" is for his lover, Emil Opffer, but the gender of the beloved "you" is not specified. Crane's frankest gay poem of this decade, the 1920 "Episode of Hands" (in which "the two men smiled into each other's eyes") was not published until 1948.

Two authors provided the most candid published American gay male writing of the 1920s. Robert McAlmon (1896–1956) dealt with homosexuality in much of his work of these years—for example, there are homosexual personae in two of his poetry collections, *Explorations* (1921) and *The Portrait of a Generation* (1926); homosexuality is clearly implied in his portrait of Marsden Hartley as the character Brander Ogden in his roman à clef *Post-Adolescence* (1923); and his story "One More to Set Her Up," from *A Companion Volume* (1923), may be the first frank portrait of a "fag hag" in American fiction. McAlmon's most extended homosexual work, his 1925 collection *Distinguished Air (Grim Fairy Tales),* focuses on gay and lesbian characters in post-war Berlin and includes the first gay and lesbian bar scenes in American fiction. McAlmon separates himself from his homosexual characters, however, and their fate is usually portrayed as despairing. Furthermore, all McAlmon's work was published abroad and by small presses, chiefly by his own pioneering Contact Press. At least equally startling is the little-known *The Western Shore* (1925) by the forgotten Clarkson Crane (1894–1971). In this novel about Berkeley in 1919, one chief character is a homosexual English instructor, Philip Burton, who is presented remarkably frankly for the period—for example, characters speculate openly about Burton's "tendencies in love" and whether he is "queer." Burton is strongly drawn to a freshman, Milton Granger, who Crane suggests is also homosexual. Most notably, Burton is not dealt a tragic fate, and the novel had a mainstream publisher, Harcourt, Brace. More needs to be known about the author and reception of this risky work. Another

pathbreaking work of this decade is the 1926 story "Smoke, Lilies and Jade" by Bruce Nugent (b. 1906), the first frank portrait of black gay male experience in American writing. Nugent published the story under a pseudonym, however (in the short-lived Harlem Renaissance journal *Fire!!*), and ultimately makes his protagonist bisexual.

CARL VAN VECHTEN (1880–1964) also did much of his writing in the 1920s. Van Vechten's flamboyant work is often read homosexually, but it typically only teases the reader with the subject. For example, in *The Blind Bow-Boy* (1923) the hero is called a "sissy" as a child, and the motto on another male character's stationery is "A thing of beauty is a boy for ever," but both are presented as manifestly heterosexual. However, Van Vechten's letters, which have only been published in part and which include correspondence with many fellow homosexuals, are more frank, as when he joked with LANGSTON HUGHES in 1964 that "you and I have been through so many new Negroes that we are a little tired of it all." COUNTEE CULLEN (1903–1946) and Langston Hughes (1902–1967) also began publishing in the 1920s, but mostly kept their homosexuality out of their work, with exceptions like Cullen's "Tableau" (from *Color,* 1925), which can also be read as paean to interracial brotherhood, and Hughes's "Café: 3 A.M." (from *Montage of a Dream Deferred,* 1951), a portrait of a raid on a gay bar.

In the 1930s, frank private gay male American writing persisted and increased. Glenway Wescott (1901–1987) only hinted at his homosexuality in his best-selling fiction of the 1920s (for example, the story "Adolescence" in his 1928 *Good-Bye Wisconsin*), but in 1937 he began a journal that focuses extensively on his relationships with lovers and fellow homosexual artists (for example, Monroe Wheeler, George Platt Lynes, Paul Cadmus). Continuing through the 1950s and published in 1990 as *Continual Lessons,* Wescott's journal offers an invaluable portrait of pre-Stonewall American gay male cultural life. In 1933, Donald Vining (b. 1917) started a journal, which he began publishing in 1979 under the title of *A Gay Diary.* (Four volumes, covering the years until 1975, have appeared so far.) Less self-reflective than Wescott's, Vining's diary is nonetheless a goldmine of information about earlier American gay male social life, especially during World War II and the immediate post-war years.

Homosexuality came more clearly into view in the poems of Marsden Hartley (1877–1943) in the 1930s, but this work, too, remained private at the time, not reaching print until after Hartley's death. Among Hartley's noteworthy homoerotic works are his "Gay World" of the early 1930s (published in his 1945

Selected Poems), where he plays on the "innocent" public meaning of "gay" to make what knowing readers would recognize as a homosexual statement ("It's a gay world after all; I knew it"); "K. von F.—1914—Arras-Bouquoi," his late 1930s elegy for his German lover, Karl von Freyberg, killed in World War I (not published until 1987); and "Cleophas and His Own" and "Three Loving Men" (first published in 1982 and 1987), prose and poetry memorials to Alty and Donny Mason, who drowned off Nova Scotia in 1936 while Hartley was living with their family ("I alone am loving / two consummate men / who will not come again"). Hartley's letters, which include frank correspondence with fellow homosexuals like Robert McAlmon and Charles Demuth, ought to be published. Other frank but unpublished work of these years are the eight autobiographical "Johnson" stories that PAUL GOODMAN (1911–1972) wrote in 1932–1933, in which the title character is technically bisexual but where the plainest eroticism is homosexual; the majority did not see print until 1976.

In a major shift, however, in the 1930s frank private gay male American writing is matched by published work for the first time, a change epitomized by two 1933 novels, *The Young and Evil* by Charles Henri Ford (b. 1910) and Parker Tyler (1904–1974) and *Better Angel* by the playwright Forman Brown (b. 1900), who issued the book under the pseudonym "Richard Meeker." A roman à clef about the authors' experiences in New York in 1930–1931, *The Young and Evil* echoes Joyce, GERTRUDE STEIN, and DJUNA BARNES in its stream-of-consciousness presentation of Julian (Ford) and Karel (Tyler)'s adventures and of the city's homosexual subculture (for example, Greenwich Village gay bars, a drag ball in Harlem, a beating and arrest for cruising on Riverside Drive). Vivid and direct, *The Young and Evil* implicitly endorses a "feminine" and depressive picture of male homosexuality, however ("You homos . . . got your eyes fixed on the male symbol. . . . You couldn't fall in love with each other"). *Better Angel,* which takes its title from SHAKESPEARE's sonnet 144, is *The Young and Evil*'s complement. Less artfully written, it traces the development of Kurt Grey from a lonely and "sensitive" adolescent "set apart from his companions" to a young and successful composer and music teacher involved passionately and happily with another man, David. With many didactic passages designed to hearten an assumed audience of homosexual readers ("He longed to spread abroad the injustice of it, as a zealot and reformer. . . . Somewhere there must be an honest picture of it all"), *The Better Angel* can nonetheless allow Kurt and David no more than a "secret" relationship, and one achieved only in opposition to any homosexual subculture, which it sees as a "flayed and slightly nauseous society of 'les hommes-femmes.'"

The publication histories of both novels show the limits frank homosexual writing still faced in America. *The Young and Evil* had to be published abroad (in Paris), by an alternative press (Obelisk), and British and American customs refused to allow copies into the countries. (A 1960 Olympia Press reprint did make its way into the United States.) *Better Angel* found an American publisher, but a marginal one sometimes associated with pulp fiction (Greenberg), and though it went through two printings and thus seems to have found an audience, little is known about its reception, and it soon disappeared from sight. Other forthright published homosexual work of this decade included some early poems of Paul Goodman, though they appeared in pamphlets he issued himself—for example, "Epode. The New Bus Terminal" (1934), "Ballade to Jean Cocteau" (1937), and "For My Birthday, 1939" (1939).

More bracketed or indirect gay male writing also appeared in the 1930s, and from mainstream publishers. The 1932 *Infants of the Spring* by Wallace Thurman (1902–1933) is the most extended portrait of homosexuality in fiction by a gay male African-American writer before JAMES BALDWIN. In this roman à clef satire of the Harlem Renaissance, homosexuality is only suggested in the central story of the writer Raymond (who sleeps in the same bed with his white European friend, Steve), but is almost blatant in several secondary strands—for example, a "fanciful aggregation of Greenwich Village uranians" attends a Harlem rent party; black homosexual writers like Alain Locke, Countee Cullen, and Langston Hughes make camouflaged cameo appearances; and one character, Paul Arbian, specializes in drawings of phalluses and ends a suicide in the Greenwich Village apartment of a "slender fluttering white youth." One section of *Flesh Is Heir* (1932), an early episodic novel by Lincoln Kirstein (b. 1907), frankly depicts a set of European homosexuals who flock around a wealthy heterosexual woman in London and Paris, and in another section Diaghilev and his "curious reputation" figure. Kirstein dissociates his autobiographical hero from the subject, however. In his best-selling *The Last Puritan* (1935), GEORGE SANTAYANA (1863–1952) insinuates suggestions of homosexuality in the nude swimming scene between Oliver Alden and Jim Darnley ("What a chest, and what arms!"), and Darnley speaks at length about being drummed out of the English Navy for "immorality" with other sailors. Hart Crane obliquely evokes homosexuality in sections of *The Bridge* (1930)—for example, in his union with WHITMAN in "Cape Hatteras" and in the "The Harbor Dawn"'s unindividuated love scene, which biographers have traced to an encounter with another man in New York. Other work of this time published in Crane's posthumous *Collected Poems* (1933) is more nearly frank—for example, "The Visible The Untrue" (another poem to Emil Opffer), "Reply," and "Reliquary."

The momentum evident in the 1920s and 1930s culminated in some notable firsts in American gay male writing of the 1940s. Three books importantly concerned with homosexuality, all published by mainstream houses, won critical notice and also became best-sellers. *The Gallery* (1947), the first novel by JOHN HORNE BURNS (1916–1953), was chosen the best war book of the year by *Saturday Review*. Among the "portraits" that punctuate the narrative is one called "Momma" depicting a soldiers' gay bar in Naples. Though not the first gay bar scene in American gay male writing, "Momma" has a heterogeneous cast of characters and explicit political commentary ("a minority should be let alone"), innovations partly undercut by Burns' ending the section with a brawl and a raid. In *Other Voices, Other Rooms* (1948), the sensational best-selling first novel by TRUMAN CAPOTE (1924–1984), homosexuality is a prominent strand in the action, in the transvestite Cousin Randolph and, implicitly, in the decision of the adolescent hero, Joel, to stay with him. *The City and the Pillar* (1948) by GORE VIDAL (b. 1925) was the most talked-about American gay male text of the 1940s. Most readers, ignorant of the earlier works discussed above, saw *The City and the Pillar* as the first exclusively homosexual American novel. But its real distinctions were its choice of a handsome athlete with the prototypical "all-American boy" name of Jim Willard as its homosexual protagonist and its unshocked way of documenting his growing self-awareness and education in a widespread and varied male homosexual world, an education that ends, however, in Jim's literal murder of his adolescent fantasy, the heterosexual Bob, and in a future as an outlaw and nomad. Immediately controversial, and penalizing Vidal professionally for several years, *The City and the Pillar* quickly made *The New York Times* best-seller list, at the same time that the paper refused to carry advertising for the book. "The Homosexual in Society," an essay by ROBERT DUNCAN (1919–1988) in the August 1944 issue of *Politics*, is another landmark of the decade in its own different terms. It is the first unequivocal "coming out" by an American writer. Identifying himself frankly as gay, Duncan calls for organization by homosexuals as a historically persecuted group, though not based on what he sees as the "self-ridicule" and cold-heartedness of traditional CAMP culture.

In addition, these landmarks were surrounded by other pointed gay portrayals in the course of the decade. Paul Goodman continued publishing homosexual poems in journals and pamphlets—for example, "A Meeting" (1941), "The Cyclist" (1946), "Lines" (1947), and "Classical Quatrain" (1949). "A Ceremonial," in Goodman's first collection of stories, *The Facts of Life* (1945), contains a homosexual relationship, and the narrator of the title novella in his second collection, *The Break-Up of Our Camp* (1949), is behaviorally bisexual though more ardent about other males ("My homosexuality revived hot"). In two books of war lyrics, the now-forgotten Dunstan Thompson (1918–1975) made his homosexuality as manifest as he could given his intricate and dense style—the 1943 *Poems*, where "gay" is used wittily throughout (for example, "Images of Disaster"), and the 1947 *Lament for the Sleepwalker* (for example, "This Tall Horseman, My Young Man of Mars," "In All the Argosy of Your Bright Hair," "Nor Mars His Sword," "The Everlasting Gunman"). In 1946, Charles Jackson (1903–1968) published *The Fall of Valor*, a widely reviewed novel entirely concerned with a repressed middle-aged literature teacher's growing awareness of his homosexuality, an awareness that ends in violence and the possible disintegration of his marriage. Nothing has been written about the married Jackson's sexuality, but the emotional tension achieved in the book seems unlikely to have been the work of an outsider. Robert Duncan's first book, *Heavenly City, Earthly City* (1947), contains several poems referring to a male lover—for example, "Treesbank Poems," "An Apollonian Elegy," and the title poem. TENNESSEE WILLIAMS (1914– 1983) alluded briefly to homosexuality in his early plays (for example, Blanche's suicidal husband in the 1947 *A Streetcar Named Desire*), but in his first collection of stories, *One Arm* (1948), the subject dominates two, "One Arm" and "Desire and the Black Masseur," where it is associated with prostitution and murder, and is a frank issue in two others, "The Angel in the Alcove" and "The Night of the Iguana."

Indirect, coded, or otherwise buffered gay male writing continued in the 1940s as well. Edwin Denby (1903–1983), best-known for his dance criticism, included pieces suggestive of his homosexuality in his first book of poems, *In Public, In Private* (1948)—for example, "The Subway" and "Groups and Series." In the first two volumes of his autobiography, *Persons and Places: The Background of My Life* (1944) and *The Middle Span* (1947), Santayana describes his male friendships in rhapsodic terms ("In him I tasted two of the sweets of friendship, which have regaled me since in many a 'nice fellow.' . . . Strange enchantment!"). John Horne Burns's second novel, *Lucifer With a Book* (1949), with an epigraph from the *Inferno* canto about the sodomites, frankly describes homosexuality among its prep school faculty and students, and a strong attraction is implied between the main character and his favorite student, though the teacher is finally portrayed as heterosexual.

American gay male writing of the 1950s contains even more landmarks. The subject was probably given the widest exposure by two well-known works of 1956, *Giovanni's Room* by James Baldwin (1924–1987) and *Howl* by ALLEN GINSBERG (b. 1926). Indebted to GIDE and echoing the Old Testament model in the names of its lovers, David and Giovanni, Baldwin's much-discussed novel was issued by a mainstream publisher and surpasses *The City and the Pillar* in not only focusing on an "all-American" male's homosexual self-discovery but in intimately portraying a homosexual relationship; the relationship ends, however, with one lover an executed murderer and the other doomed to despondent wandering. *Howl,* from a small press, became one of the decade's most influential books of poetry, partly for its role in defining the BEAT GENERATION and partly for its 1957 obscenity trial. Frank homosexuality appears in the long title poem ("hipsters . . . who let themselves be fucked in the ass . . . and screamed for joy"), in "A Supermarket in California" ("I saw you Walt Whitman, . . . eyeing the grocery boys"), and in "America" ("I'm putting my queer shoulder to the wheel").

In addition, from what we know about a self-conscious gay male readership at this time, two authors of the early 1950s seem to have struck a special chord with it, James Barr (the pseudonym of James Fugaté, b. ?) and Fritz Peters (Arthur Anderson Peters, 1913–1979). Barr's popular *Quatrefoil* (1950) was published by the same marginal press as *Better Angel* (Greenberg) and, like it, seems consciously designed to hearten a male homosexual audience as it programatically portrays the developing homosexual self-awareness and self-acceptance of the young naval officer Phillip Froelich under the tutelage of his older lover and fellow officer, Tim Danelaw; Barr kills Tim off in an accident at the end, however, before the two men's relationship can develop. Barr followed *Quatrefoil* in 1951 with a book of stories, *Derricks* (also from Greenberg), each of which frankly concerns homosexuality. Peters's well-written and widely reviewed *Finistère* (1951) had a mainstream publisher (Farrar, Straus) and frankly depicts homosexual characters, relationships, and subcultures as it acutely traces the love affair between young Matthew Cameron and his boarding-school athletics teacher Michel Garnier against a background of family tensions that ultimately leads to Matthew's suicide. Another standout of the 1950s was the now-forgotten *Sam* (1959), by Lonnie Coleman (1920–1982), a novelist best-known for his later, popular "Beulah Land" trilogy. *Sam* totally accepts the homosexuality of its title character, a New York publisher, and shows him functioning openly and successfully with professional and social friends while it also candidly depicts a range of gay characters and contexts (for example, bars and baths). Complexities are skimmed over in the rush toward a happy ending (ditched by Walter, an opportunistic actor, Sam soon finds true love with Richard, a surgeon), but in its utter frankness and positiveness about homosexuality, *Sam* is astounding for its time, and more needs to be known about its publication (by an established publisher, David McKay) and reception.

These were but parts, however, of a notable American gay male literature that persisted through the 1950s and constituted a relative burst of expressiveness, approximately doubling in volume the output of the 1940s. This body includes both the melodramatic pulp novels of Jay Little (pseudonym of Clarence L. Miller), which were written for a specifically gay audience, and the work of authors who incorporated gay themes in mainstream fiction and poetry. Homosexuality figures centrally in two searing stories in *The Delicate Prey* (1950), the first collection by PAUL BOWLES (b. 1910)—"Pages from Cold Point" and "The Echo." Like his short fiction, Paul Goodman's 1951 novel, *Parents' Day,* has a technically bisexual protagonist who seems more ardently homosexual, a teacher who loses his job at a progressive boarding school after admitting to sex with his male students. W. H. AUDEN (1907–1963), an American citizen since 1946, became more open about his homosexuality in his later poetry, as in his campy "The Love Feast," from his 1951 *Nones*. A major lesbian character, Eunice Goode, appears in Paul Bowles's second novel, *Let It Come Down* (1952). Under the pen name of William Lee, WILLIAM S. BURROUGHS (b. 1914) published his first book, the autobiographical *Junky,* in 1953, as a pulp paperback. This novel of addiction is dotted with "fruits" and "queers," and its ambivalent married narrator has occasional homosexual sex while protesting his "horror" at "fags." At the same time, Burroughs wrote the blunter, fragmented, *Queer,* which remained unpublished until 1985.

CHRISTOPHER ISHERWOOD (1904–1986), who became an American citizen in 1946, deals with homosexuality more frankly and fully than ever before in *The World in the Evening* (1954), chiefly in the secondary characters Michael Drummond and the couple Charles Kennedy and Bob Wood, to whom he furthermore gives relatively happy endings. *The World in the Evening* also has notable gay political commentary (Bob, a Quaker, refuses to be a conscientious objector in World War II because he realizes that "I'd fight till I dropped . . . if they declared war on the queers") and the first exposition of the term *camp* in mainstream writing. Tennessee Williams evokes homosexuality more fully in some plays of the 1950s, though keeping it in the background and off-stage (*Cat on a Hot Tin Roof* [1955], *Suddenly Last Summer* [1958]), while he continues to portray it openly in his stories—for example, "Two on a Party," "Hard Candy," and "The Mysteries of the Joy Rio" in *Hard Candy* (1954). Before *Sam*, Lonnie Coleman included a frank and happy homosexual tale in his *Ship's Company* (1955), a composite of vignettes about the crew of the aptly named U.S.S. *Nellie Crocker* during World War II. In "The Theban Warriors," Montgomery, a blatantly swish sailor who is also a championship boxer, woos and wins his shipmate Barney. Paul Goodman again published some homosexual poems in pamphlets during the decade: "Lloyd (September 9, 1941)" (1955) and "Solstice" (1958).

Three stories in Gore Vidal's *A Thirsty Evil* (1956) openly concern homosexuality—"Three Stratagems," "The Zenner Trophy," and "Pages from an Abandoned Journal." In his first novel, *Jamie Is My Heart's Desire* (1956), Alfred Chester (1929–1971) implies "queer feelings" between the mysterious figures Mark and Jamie. In Edwin Denby's second book, *Mediterranean Cities* (1956), "Villa Adriana" and "Segesta" allude to homosexuality. JOHN CHEEVER (1912–1982), whose homosexual affairs were revealed in posthumously published memoirs, letters, and diaries, included a chapter on "the unsavory or homosexual part of our tale, [which] any disinterested reader is encouraged to skip" in his prize-winning first novel, *The Wapshot Chronicle* (1957). In his second book of poems, *Meditations in an Emergency* (1957), FRANK O'HARA (1926–1966) starts to portray his homosexuality more directly, as in the title poem, "Ode," and the moving "To the Harbormaster." JACK SPICER (1925–1965) was openly gay throughout his career, but when he deals with the subject at all in his largely surrealistic work it is usually allusively—for example, his first book, *After Lorca* (1957) contains mock letters to FEDERICO GARCIA LORCA and loose translations of his poems. In *Color of Darkness* (1957), the first collection by JAMES PURDY (b. 1923), homosexuality figures centrally in one story, "Man and Wife," and secondarily or implicitly in two others, "63: Dream Palace" and "You May Safely Gaze."

The Hotel Wentley Poems (1958), the first book by John Wieners (b. 1934), contains two frankly gay pieces—"A poem for cock suckers" and the love poem "A poem for the old man." JONATHAN WILLIAMS (b. 1929) included gay content in his witty, objectivist work even early in his career—for example, "The Chameleon" in *The Empire Finals at Verona* (1959). Paul Bowles's second collection, *The Hours After Noon* (1959), contains the autobiographical "The Frozen Fields," in which he forecasts his own homosexuality in the young protagonist's reaction to two older homosexual characters. Mr. Cox, the astrologer who launches the young hero on his worldly education in James Purdy's arch first novel, *Malcolm* (1959), is identified as "a pederast." In Paul Goodman's long novel/romance *The Empire City* (1959), characters have homosexual experiences, though usually as part of an overall bisexuality, and at one point Goodman casts the god Eros as a gay street hustler. In William S. Burroughs's *Naked Lunch* (1959), homosexual sex predominates among the novel's phantasmagoric polysexuality, the Divisionist party in Interzone is all-homosexual, and the "Benway" and "Examination" sections satirize medicine's complicity in the social control of homosexuality.

The most notable gay male literary landmarks of the 1960s reached especially large audiences, or were breakthroughs in their authors' works, or made considerable strides in the representation of gay men. James Baldwin's best-selling *Another Country* (1962), has a homosexual, the actor Eric, among its major characters and gives him one of the novel's happier endings, concluding the book with a reunion between male lovers; at the same time, Baldwin makes Eric more "acceptable" by providing him with an affair with a woman as well. Another much-discussed best-seller, the exposé-like *City of Night* (1963) by JOHN RECHY (b. 1934), portrays a wide canvas of homosexual American men as it chronicles the cross-country encounters of its "youngman" hustler narrator, who maintains that he himself is not homosexual. In *A Single Man* (1964), Christopher Isherwood makes a clearly identified gay man the central character of one of his novels for the first time and forces the audience to spend the book's entire single day in his presence, as he fantasizes about organizing a group of gay terrorists and struggles to deal with the death of his lover. *Totempole* (1965), the highly praised first novel by Sanford Friedman (b. 1928), was issued by a mainstream publisher and is the first fully developed gay male American *bildungsroman,* going beyond precedents like *Better Angel* to trace in extensive detail, from childhood to young manhood, the developing homosexual awareness of its protagonist, Stephen Wolfe, and giving him a comparatively happy ending through his army love affair with a North

Korean doctor prisoner. Near the end of the decade, *The Boys in the Band* (1968) by Mart Crowley (b. 1935), the long-running Off-Broadway play, made theater history by focusing its (and the audience's) entire attention on a group of New York gay men at a birthday party.

These works were surrounded, however, by a relative mass of other gay male writing in the decade, whose year-by-year persistence has, in context, the look of a flood (almost doubling, for instance, the already formidable output of the 1950s). Jerry, one of the two characters in *The Zoo Story* (1960), the first play by EDWARD ALBEE (b. 1928), proclaims that he was "queer" when he was fifteen and dots his monologues with homosexual references. There is no overt sexuality in the best-selling *A Separate Peace* (1960) by John Knowles (b. 1926), but, commenting on the relationship of the main characters in a 1972 interview, the author admitted, "Finny and Gene were in love." A homosexual couple, Willard Baker and Vernon Miller, are important characters in James Purdy's *The Nephew* (1960). Paul Goodman's third short story collection, *Our Visit to Niagara* (1960), includes two pieces with homosexual content or implication, "A Statue of Goldsmith" and the lyric "Adam." Robert Duncan's books of the 1960s continue to have frank homosexual poems—for example, "This Place Rumord to Have Been Sodom" in *The Opening of the Field* (1960); "Night Scenes" and the lovely "Sonnet 1" ("Now there is a Love of which Dante does not speak unkindly") from *Roots and Branches* (1964); and, from *Bending the Bow* (1968), "Sonnet 4," "The Currents, *Passages* 16," and the breathtaking "The Torso, *Passages* 18" ("For my Other is not a woman but a man"). In his later books, Robert Francis (1901–1987) included poems more suggestive of his homosexuality, like "Boy Riding Forward Backward" and "Farm Boy After Summer" in *The Orb Weaver* (1960) and "Time and the Sergeant" in *Come Out into the Sun* (1965). Harold Norse (b. 1916) depicted frank homosexual situations in some work of the 1960s such as "Lot at Home" in his *The Roman Sonnets of G. G. Belli* (1960); "The Search (After Catullus)" and "Victor Emmanuel Monument (Rome)" in *The Dancing Beasts* (1962); and the title poem in *Karma Circuit* (1966). Jonathan Williams's books of the 1960s continued to have frank gay references—for example, "Finger Exercises" from *Amen/Huzza/Selah* (1960); "Dangerous Calamus Emotions" from *Elegies and Celebrations* (1962); "'Always the Deathless Musick'" and "The Honey Lamb" from *Jammin' the Greek Scene* (1969).

Frank gay love poems and social commentary persist in Allen Ginsberg's books of the 1960s, including "Message" (*Kaddish*, 1961); "In Society" (*Empty Mirror*, 1961); "The Green Automobile" and "Malest Cornifici Tuo Catullo" (*Reality Sandwiches*, 1963); "Why Is God Love, Jack?" "Message II," "Chances 'R'," and "City Midnight Junk Sounds," his moving elegy for Frank O'Hara (*Planet News*, 1968). THOM GUNN (b. 1929) has made his home in America since 1960 and in some of his work of the 1960s implicitly depicts situations that could only be homosexual—for example, the cruising and sex scenes in "The Feel of Hands" and the two "Modes of Pleasure" poems from *My Sad Captains* (1961). The explicit sex in William S. Burroughs's hallucinogenic Nova trilogy of the early 1960s—*The Soft Machine* (1961), *The Ticket That Exploded* (1962), and *Nova Express* (1964)—is almost entirely homosexual. In his autobiographical *Down There on a Visit* (1962), Christopher Isherwood presents frank homosexual characters like Ambrose, who fantasizes about establishing an all-gay commonwealth on his Greek island, while hedging about his own sexuality and that of the campy but officially bisexual Paul. Paul Goodman's first collected poems, *The Lordly Hudson* (1962), issued by a mainstream publisher, prints several new, frank gay poems—for example, "March Equinox," "Ballade of the Moment Before," "Moments I Had of Glad Delight," "Buddha," "Commerce (Manner of Wordsworth)," "I love you Donny." The narrator of Goodman's autobiographical *Making Do* (1963) is a married bisexual intellectual, but the central relationship of the novel is his affair with a male student, Terry (also presented as bisexual), and identified homosexual characters also appear (the worker Harold).

Blunt homosexual scenes occur in *The Messenger* (1963), the autobiographical first novel by Charles Wright (b. 1932), but the African-American narrator, who hustles part-time with both men and women, is portrayed as basically heterosexual. EDWARD FIELD (b. 1924) included his wonderful "sissy" poems, "Unwanted" and "The Sleeper," in his prize-winning first book, *Stand Up, Friend, with Me* (1963). John Wieners's second book, *The Ace of Pentacles* (1964), contains several more frank gay poems, such as "Strange," "Act #2," and "Sonnet." In James Purdy's scathing *Cabot Wright Begins* (1964), one of the few moments of tenderness is a one-night stand between two married men, Bernie Gladhart and Winters Hart. The bulk of *Stations* (1964) by Burt Blechman (b. 1932) seems to concern a gay man who cruises the New York subway johns for sex, but the heavily symbolized and frenzied narrative makes a clear picture of the situation impossible. Three stories in Alfred Chester's collection *Behold Goliath* (1964) are frankly homosexual: "From the Phoenix," "Ismael," and the piercing "In Praise of Vespasian." In 1964, the Caffe Cino, a pioneering New York outpost for gay theater in what later would become Off-Off Broadway, produced *The Madness of Lady Bright,* an early one-act by LANFORD WILSON (b. 1938), which depicts the breakdown of an aging, isolated, "bitchy queen." In the same year, the Cino also produced *The Haunted Host,* the first play by ROBERT PATRICK (b. 1937), in which a "high queen" gay writer exorcises his dead lover's ghost. Also premiering in 1964 was the first play by Terrence McNally (b. 1939), *And Things That Go Bump in the Night,* where a frankly presented homosexual character and encounter are crucial to the unraveling of the play's demented, hermetic family. In *Rhymes of a PFC* (1964), about his World War II experiences, Lincoln Kirstein invokes one of the oldest conventions in male homosexual writing and uses the military situation to paint several frank and affectionate homosexual portraits, including "Gloria," "Fixer," "Charlie Boy," and "Das Schloss." Homosexuality recurs as a subject in Frank O'Hara's books of the 1960s, especially in the more private of his *Lunch Poems* (1964) and throughout his last book, *Love Poems (Tentative Title)* (1965), where all the poems concern his lover, Vincent Warren, though only a few, such as the beautiful "Having a Coke with You" and "Poem 'A la recherche de Gertrude Stein,'" specify the "you" as male.

An affair in Rome between a married American and a young Italian bisexual hustler is the core of *Two People* (1965) by DONALD WINDHAM (b. 1920), which was published by a mainstream publisher (Coward-McAnn) and with glowing blurbs by E. M. FORSTER, Truman Capote, and Tennessee Williams. W. H. Auden's "The Common Life," the final poem in the "Thanksgiving for a Habitat" sequence from his *About the House* (1965), commemorates his twenty-four-year relationship with Chester Kallman. Homosexuality is almost the entire sexuality in Paul Goodman's *Five Years: Thoughts During a Useless Time* (1966), a selection from his journals from 1955 to 1960. In his *Paris Diary* (1966), which covers the years from 1951 to 1955, NED ROREM (b. 1923) makes transparent allusions to homosexuality and details an intense love affair with "P.," whereas his *New York Diary* (1967), which proceeds to 1961, is even franker and fuller, with a thirty-three-page love letter to a male lover included in the book. *Hawkweed* (1967), Paul Goodman's second collection of poems from a mainstream publisher, prints a score more new, frank gay pieces, including the daring "Lines (His cock is big and red when I am there)" and the beautiful love poems "Haverford" and "Long Lines (I opened with my key, to my astonished joy)." James Purdy's gothic *Eustace*

Chisolm and the Works (1967) almost entirely involves homosexuality, with its focus on the intense, blocked, and ultimately murderous loves of Amos, Daniel, Stadger, and Reuben Masterson. One of the brothers in Christopher Isherwood's *A Meeting by the River* (1967) is a married bisexual who seems more passionate about his male lover but who eventually renounces him for the "easier" world of wife and children.

The ex-hustler in John Rechy's *Numbers* (1967) struggles against admitting his own homosexuality by vowing to make thirty men approach him for sex within ten days in Los Angeles's Griffith Park. Male homosexual characters and couples pervade Alfred Chester's hallucinogenic roman à clef, *The Exquisite Corpse* (1967). Edward Field's second book, *Variety Photoplays* (1967), contains his witty "Giant Pacific Octopus," a transparent gay love poem. James Baldwin deals with homosexuality among African Americans for the first time in *Tell Me How Long the Train's Been Gone* (1968), through the love affair between the actor-narrator Leo Proudhammer and the younger, more militant Christopher, both presented as bisexual. In his best-selling *Myra Breckenridge* (1968), Gore Vidal skewers conventional American sexuality by making the preoperative Myra a gay male and having the super-masculine Rusty turn homosexual after Myra rapes him with a dildo. In *The Missolonghi Manuscript* (1968), which purports to be a journal of BYRON's last year, Frederick Prokosch (b. 1906) depicts homosexuality more straightforwardly than ever before, going beyond the implied homoeroticism of his popular male-bonding adventure novels of the 1930s (such as *The Asiatics* [1935] and *The Seven Who Fled* [1937]) to portray Byron's homosexual affairs completely frankly. Among the pieces printed for the first time in Paul Goodman's collected stories, *Adam and His Works* (1968), are two with homosexual content, "The Old Knight" and "Martin." In *Keep the River on Your Right* (1969), about his life with the cannibal Akaramas in the Peruvian jungle, Tobias Schneebaum (b. 1921) frankly portrays the homosexuality of Manolo, the lay missionary, and clearly implies his own in his feelings for the men of his tribe.

The remarkable achievement of twentieth-century American gay male writing before Stonewall might at first appear to be offset by the fact that much of it seems concessive. For example, in their association of homosexuality with violence, suicide, murder, or other kinds of pathetic death or at best with lives of freakishness or isolation, many works in the post-World War II outpouring of published gay male writing seem to confirm Mart Crowley's famous line in

The Boys in the Band, "Show me a happy homosexual, and I'll show you a gay corpse." Even some positive portrayals surround the subject with distracting reassurances, like the bisexuality in Baldwin's and Goodman's work. Three points need to be made about this pattern, however. First, it was not total, as indicated by the work of Clarkson Crane in the 1920s, Forman Brown ("Richard Meeker") in the 1930s, and Duncan, Thompson, O'Hara, Isherwood, Coleman, Kirstein, and Friedman in the post-war period. Second, it may chiefly represent a marketplace compromise authors felt they had to make to get their work published. Third, even when writers might have shared some of these materials' depression about homosexuality, that could not have represented the whole or the core of their feelings. If twentieth-century American gay male writers before Stonewall had been thoroughly concessive, there would not have been any published gay male writing then at all, for they would have conceded to the long-standing stigma of homosexuality's "unspeakableness" and remained publicly silent. Since the very act of a gay writer's picking up the pen to write about the subject thus inherently contests stereotype, some degree of an opposing positive apprehension about homosexuality is contained even in this material's bleakest portrayals. The same point is, of course, implied by the fact that, during years when homosexuality was still largely invisible in society and chiefly vilified when it was spoken of at all, these writers persisted in writing about the subject and in mounting numbers.

Finally, it should be noted that the dimensions of the twentieth-century American gay male literary situation before Stonewall surpass even this survey. For reasons of space, I have had to exclude earlier gay male writers who were largely discreet about their homosexuality in their work, like Francis Grierson (1848–1927), Logan Pearsall Smith (1865–1946), Witter Bynner (1881–1968), and Thornton Wilder (1897–1975), and writers mentioned in earlier surveys of gay fiction whose works were unavailable to me or whose overall picture was unclear (for example, the 1933 Goldie by "Kennilworth Bruce," Hubert Creekmore's 1948 The Welcome, Thomas Hal Phillips's 1949 The Bitterweed Path, the 1949 Stranger in the Land by "Ward Thomas" [Edward T. McNamara]), and distinguished contemporaries whose homosexuality only became more evident in their work after Stonewall, like James Schuyler (1923–1991), JAMES MERRILL (b. 1926), and RICHARD HOWARD (b. 1929).

—Joseph Cady

BIBLIOGRAPHY

Austen, Roger. Playing the Game: The Homosexual Novel in America. Indianapolis: Bobbs-Merrill, 1977. ■ Bergman, David. Gaiety Transfigured: Gay Self-Representation in American Literature. Madison: University of Wisconsin Press, 1991. ■ Levin, James. The Gay Novel in America. New York: Garland, 1991. ■ Martin, Robert K. The Homosexual Tradition in American Poetry. Austin: University of Texas Press, 1979. ■ Sarotte, Georges-Michel. Like a Brother, Like a Lover: Male Homosexuality in the American Novel and Theatre from Herman Melville to James Baldwin. Garden City, N.Y.: Anchor/Doubleday, 1978. ■ Summers, Claude J. Gay Fictions: Wilde to Stonewall. New York: Continuum, 1990. ■ Woods, Gregory. Articulate Flesh: Male Homoeroticism and Modern Poetry. New Haven, Conn.: Yale University Press, 1987. ■ Yingling, Thomas E. Hart Crane and the Homosexual Text. Chicago: University of Chicago Press, 1990.

American Literature: Lesbian, 1900–1969

Lesbian literature throughout the first two-thirds of the twentieth century has exploited the "outlaw" status of the lesbian. We can trace this phenomenon from early experiments with narrative (SARAH ORNE JEWETT's The Country of the Pointed Firs), to modernist questionings of genre and technique (DJUNA BARNES's Nightwood, GERTRUDE STEIN's Lifting Belly, and H.D. [HILDA DOOLITTLE]'s posthumously published Paint It Today), to the literatures of affirmation and political activism written and supported by lesbian publishers Barbara Grier, JUDY GRAHN, and the Daughters of Bilitis. Thus, as Bonnie Zimmerman observes, lesbian critics and critics of lesbian texts often pose questions about identity and literary creativity: "How, for example, does the lesbian's sense of outlaw status affect her literary vision? Might lesbian writing, because of the lesbian's position on the boundaries, be characterized by a particular sense of freedom and flexibility or, rather, by images of violently imposed barriers, the closet? Or, in fact, is there a dialectic between freedom and imprisonment that is unique to lesbian writing?" The year 1900 marks the fin-de-siècle, as the turn from the nineteenth century to the twentieth witnessed the pathologizing of homosexuality by the medical profession, while 1969 heralds the Stonewall rebellion, widely received as the originary moment of the gay and lesbian liberation movements. Though Stonewall is certainly a marker for lesbians, the formation of lesbian presses and periodicals that emerged during the period from the 1940s through the 1970s was as much a result of the women's liberation movement as of that monumental event of gay liberation. Stonewall, of course, bolstered a lesbian literary movement well underway and, by making gay and lesbian worlds more visible, provided a desperately needed antidote to the homophobia expressed by some of the women's movement's key leaders (such as Betty Friedan).

Concomitant with the repression of the lesbian within feminist struggles for liberation are debates over what and who count as lesbian and when a situation or character is lesbian. As Catharine Stimpson and other lesbian critics, theorists, and writers have reminded us, *lesbian* is still a term to which one attaches oneself at great risk. To be unambiguously visible as lesbian is to challenge the conventions of heterosexual patriarchy on which legal and social orders rest, and therefore position oneself to be received as threatening, menacing, disruptive to the foundations of culture and society. Thus many lesbian writers have deftly encoded expressions of lesbian desire and portrayals of lesbian figures; constricted by literary traditions, they have turned to experimental forms as they attempted to create literature whose very subject matter is new and revolutionary simply because of the fact that lesbian love has been denied as a vital reality of the human heart.

Whatever form it assumes—poetry, prose fiction, political treatise, autobiography, biography, history, criticism, theory—lesbian literature, as MONIQUE WITTIG has argued and Marilyn Farwell reiterated, occupies a "space which is 'not-woman,' which is not dependent on the categorization of difference that resides in the dualisms of man and woman. . . . *Lesbian* is a word that denotes, then, a new positioning of female desire, of the lover and the beloved, of the subject and object." This extends even to familiar roles like that of "butch" and "femme" in lesbian pulp fiction, too quickly dismissed by some as a failure of lesbian imagination. As Elizabeth Meese, drawing on the analyses of Judith Roof and Joan Nestle, observes, "Butch-femme relationships are complex erotic statements, not phony heterosexual replicas"; for example, refusing "analogy to the heterosexual gender roles of masculine and feminine," the butch lesbian creates "an original style to signal to other women what she [is] capable of doing—taking erotic responsibility."

Zami, AUDRE LORDE's biomythography, describes 1950s Greenwich Village lesbians passing around pulp paperbacks that proliferated during this period such as *The Price of Salt* (1952) by Claire Morgan [PATRICIA HIGHSMITH] and *Odd Girl Out* (1957) and *Women in the Shadows* (1959) by ANN BANNON. Literature that promised entry into an outcast world of "twilight" love, these novels were, as Lillian Faderman remarks, "generally cautionary tales: 'moral' literature that warned females that lesbianism was sick or evil and that if a woman dared to love another woman she would end up lonely and suicidal." Yet many lesbians avidly read these novels that "could be picked up at newsstands and corner drugstores, even in small towns" because they "helped spread the word about lesbian lifestyles" and offered public images of lesbian "romance and charged eroticism." By the late 1960s, lesbian literature had been tremendously emboldened by the gay and women's liberation movements and, in contrast to these tales of the outcast, offered more and more stories of a proud and affirmative community bent on changing public discourse and conventional society's reception of lesbian life.

The best known literary lesbian of the twentieth century is of course Stephen Gordon, the hero of British writer RADCLYFFE HALL's *The Well of Loneliness* (1928). Hall's widely publicized obscenity trial evinced a bigoted general attitude of scorn for lesbians that had a chilling effect on many American lesbian and bisexual writers, especially expatriates like H.D. Though H.D. was writing explicitly lesbian fiction, none of it was published until after her death. Unpublished until 1992 in "The Cutting Edge: Lesbian Life and Literature" series, *Paint It Today* serves as "the repressed political unconscious of her *Asphodel* and *Madrigal*," "countering an androcentric social construction of desire" by proposing a "lesbian matrix of sister-love." This daring probing of myths of psychology has been overshadowed by H.D.'s more conventionally palatable *Tribute to Freud*, in print since 1956. Similarly, *Lifting Belly* (1953), Gertrude Stein's delicious celebration of lesbian sexuality was not published until after her death, while *Tender Buttons* (1914), her experimental poems collected under the cunningly titled pun on tend-her-buttons, was published but subjected to ruthless critical ridicule. As Stimpson points out, when Hall "represents the lesbian as scandal and the lesbian as woman-who-is-man," she is "making an implicit, perhaps unconscious pact with her culture" as the "lesbian writer who rejects both silence and excessive coding" and claims her "right to write for the public in exchange for adopting the narrative of damnation." A 1939 novel such as DIANA FREDERICS's *Diana*, which presents a "kind of lesbian chauvinism" ("a stupid girl would probably never ascertain her abnormality if she were potentially homosexual. . . . No woman could adjust herself to lesbianism without developing exceptional qualities of courage") is quite the exception in its championing of lesbian life and desire, even as it plainly acknowledges the larger culture's homophobic suppressions.

Yet Shari Benstock contends that if the "critics who confer canonization" took seriously Blanche Wiesen Cook's claim that VIRGINIA WOOLF's "imagination was fueled by Sapphic erotic power," then "they would be forced to redefine modernism in ways that acknowledge its Sapphic elements." If this "erotic power were theorized as Sapphic modernism," not only for Woolf but for Djuna Barnes, H.D., and Stein, "it could profoundly change not only our notions about modernist art, but also redefine the erotic in relation to the creative sources for all art." Understanding lesbian literary experimentation and its challenges to aesthetic, cultural, and historic concepts will, therefore, remap literary history and reconfigure its intellectual values, including that invested in the "Author."

Three traditions of literary history have particularly hindered our appreciation of lesbian literary collaborations: tradition of the autonomous male genius producing works of classic literature; women's symbolic function for men as a passive female muse; and the correlation between creative production and procreative reproduction. This conventional symbology linking heterosexual desire and poetic inspiration has made collaborations between women writers alien to literary history. Various female collaborations remain insufficiently examined: the "Boston marriage" of Sarah Orne Jewett and Annie Fields that proved a mainstay for the former's literary production; WILLA CATHER's forty-year partnership with Edith Lewis that provided the writer with the stability and freedom necessary to create; ELIZABETH BISHOP's founding of a literary magazine at Vassar with Mary McCarthy, whose best-selling novel *The Group* (1963) "showed that lesbianism could be an acceptable, even admirable subject," as well as Bishop's long relationships with Lota Costellat de Macedo Soares and Alice Methfessel; and, as Sandra Gilbert and Susan Gubar explore in "'She Meant What I Said': Lesbian Double Talk," the collaborative lesbian literary relationships like those between RENEE VIVIEN and NATALIE BARNEY, H.D. and Bryher, and Stein and Toklas are striking markers of the endeavors of expatriate American and British women writers in the early twentieth century.

Relationships with audience are also vital considerations begging for more thorough scrutiny. Analyzing Barnes's work, Benstock argues that *Nightwood* (1936), with which general audiences tend to be more familiar, and *Ladies Almanack* (1928) are addressed to two markedly different audiences and that it is crucial for readers to be aware of that in order to understand the very different kinds of cultural work the two are doing. While "*Nightwood* carefully conceals the psychosexual premises on which it establishes its social-cultural critique, *Ladies Almanack* reveals Barnes's enormous ambivalence about the sexual and social privilege it satirizes," that of a "small and select audience of lesbians well known to Barnes (members of Natalie Clifford Barney's salon). . . . *Nightwood* invokes the underside of high modernism while *Ladies Almanack* is addressed to the women who are themselves the subjects of its satire." Misunderstanding audience and intention has contributed to the dismissal of lesbian literature as a narrow "special interest" and to the refusal to recognize lesbian eroticism as an important wellspring for artistic movements.

This question of audience, or of insufficient consideration of audience, has also resulted in dismissals of poetry like that by Angelina Weld Grimké as "too conventional." African-American and probably lesbian, Grimké was confronted with at least three formidable cultural biases (those toward women, blacks, and homosexuals), and thus her apparently timid adherence to form and meter might be seen as a strategy for acceptable expression of unacceptable desires. In *Color, Sex, & Poetry: Three Women Writers of the Harlem Renaissance*, Gloria Hull examines how "Grimke handled in her public art what seem to be woman-to-woman romantic situations" by eschewing "third-person pronouns and the usual tendency most readers have . . . to image the other in a love poem as being opposite in sex from the poem's known author." Hull also recovers Alice Dunbar-Nelson's lesbian attractions and the fact that the few of her poems on this subject that have survived *and* been made available reveal "the existence and operation of an active black lesbian network" in the 1920s. Also significant in this period are the vibrant songs performed by blues artists Bessie Jackson and Bessie Smith, which, as Elly Bulkin observes, provide "a rich source of lesbian expression." Jackson performed "B.D. Blues (Bull Dagger Blues)" during her career (1923–1935), while Bessie Smith sang several songs with explicitly lesbian lyrics. Perhaps ironically, lower class status may well have enabled these women to be more daring in lesbian expression than the economically privileged Grimké. Chris Albertson's biography of the blues singer, *Bessie* (Smith), quotes the unequivocal "The Boy in the Boat" (1930): "When you see two women walking hand in hand, / Just look 'em over and try to understand: / They'll go to those parties—have the lights down low—/ Only those parties where women can go. / You think I'm lying—just ask Tack Ann—/ Took many a broad from many a man."

In fact, women outside culturally advantaged circles (academe, elite literary cliques) have been largely responsible for lesbian literary movements in the twentieth century, and influential publications have emerged from middle-class America. *The Ladder*, the newsletter of America's first lesbian emancipation group, the Daughters of Bilitis, and *Vice Versa* both sought assimilation for lesbians into the mainstream. Not surprisingly, then, authors often used pseudonyms like Lisa Ben (anagram of L-E-S-B-I-A-N) or Laurajean Ermayne. It is crucial for lesbian readers, writers, historians, and critics to be aware of this for, as in the case of Ermayne, "she" has been married to the same woman for forty-one years, has spent a lifetime writing about assorted monsters, goblins, ghouls, politicians, wizards, witches, warlocks, and is actually Forrest J. Ackerman, editor of *Famous Monsters of Filmland* magazine, who wrote as a lesbian because he does not believe in "discrimination against gays-blacks-browns-yellows-red-polkadots-Jews." For us to know that an admittedly eccentric but nevertheless sexually "straight" man was writing for a lesbian magazine in the late 1940s, not for self-titillation but for lesbian and gay liberation, is of vital importance. Our allies and supporters have been more numerous than the keepers of society's conventional and repressive editorial practices would have us believe.

The trajectory of lesbian literature for the first two-thirds of the twentieth century can be described as a movement from encrypted strategies for expressions of the love that dare not speak its name to overtly political celebrations of woman-for-woman passion that, by the late 1960s, refuses to be denied, denigrated, or expunged. (See also BUTCH/FEMME and JOURNALISM AND PUBLISHING.)

—*Martha Nell Smith*

BIBLIOGRAPHY

Benstock, Shari. *Women of the Left Bank: Paris, 1900–1940.* Austin: University of Texas Press, 1986. ■ Cruikshank, Margaret, ed. *Lesbian Studies: Present and Future.* Old Westbury, N.Y.: The Feminist Press, 1982. ■ Faderman, Lillian. *Odd Girls and Twilight Lovers: A History of Lesbian Life in Twentieth-Century America.* New York: Columbia University Press, 1991. ■ Friedman, Ellen G., and Miriam Fuchs, eds. *Breaking the Sequence: Women's Experimental Fiction.* Princeton: Princeton University Press, 1989. ■ Friedman, Susan Stanford. *Penelope's Web: Gender, Modernity, H.D.'s Fiction.* Cambridge: Cambridge University Press, 1990. ■ Gilbert, Sandra M. and Susan Gubar. "She Meant What I Said." *Sexchanges,* Vol. 2, *No Man's Land: The Place of the Woman Writer in the Twentieth Century.* New Haven: Yale University Press, 1989. 215–57. ■ Hull, Gloria T. *Color, Sex, & Poetry: Three Women Writers of the Harlem Renaissance.* Bloomington: Indiana University Press, 1987. ■ Jay, Karla, and Joanne Glasgow, eds. *Lesbian Texts and Contexts: Radical Revisions.* New York: New York University Press, 1990. ■ Meese, Elizabeth. *(Sem)erotics: theorizing lesbian: writing.* New York: New York University Press, 1992. ■ Stimpson, Catharine R. "Zero Degree Deviancy: The Lesbian Novel in English." *Writing and Sexual Difference.* Elizabeth Abel, ed. Chicago: University of Chicago Press, 1982. 243–59. ■ Whitlock, Gillian. "'Everything is Out of Place': Radclyffe Hall and the Lesbian Literary Tradition." *Feminist Studies* 13 (1987): 555–582. ■ Zimmerman, Bonnie. "What Has Never Been: An Overview of Lesbian Feminist Literary Criticism." *Feminist Studies* 7.3 (1981): 451–475.

American Literature: Gay Male, Post-Stonewall

In the years directly after the 1969 Stonewall Riots, a number of books—more journalism than literature—appeared that mixed autobiography with reflections on the political and cultural changes gays were experiencing. The most noteworthy were John Murphy's *Homosexual Liberation: A Personal View* (1971), Donn Teal's *The Gay Militants* (1971), and Arthur Bell's *Dancing the Gay Lib Blues: A Year in the Homosexual Liberation Movement* (1972). Each of these books suggests how important literature was to the authors' senses of what it means to be gay. Indeed, Bell writes how an important leader in the Gay Activists Alliance, the largest gay liberation organization of the time, missed the first meeting so that he could hear ALLEN GINSBERG read his poetry. If novelists and poets did not immediately respond to political changes, it was not because they were unaffected or uninterested in them, but rather because in many ways they had anticipated the views that were taking political shape. Nevertheless, gay critics at the time were frustrated by the range of American gay male fiction even as they applauded the breadth of American gay male poetry.

Before Stonewall, novels that contained gay characters and themes existed in one of four categories. The first two categories contain novels primarily or ostensibly written for straight readers. In those novels, gay characters and themes played minor roles in works whose main concerns and characters are heterosexual, or they were sentimental and sensational novels in which gay characters lived lonely, tragic lives that ended in murder or suicide. Heterosexual critics allowed for a small number of highly literary—particularly foreign—works to contain gay subjects; ANDRÉ GIDE, JEAN GENET, MARCEL PROUST, and THOMAS MANN could have overt gay subject matter. But the only novels clearly written for gay readers were by definition pornography. In *Homosexual Liberation,* John Murphy complained that he found that "the choice of books dealing with *his* sexual concerns are limited to a few serious 'classics,' some sensational popular novels, and pornography."

Nevertheless, in the immediate years before Stonewall, a number of books were published that lay out a new direction for gay writers. Of greatest importance were CHRISTOPHER ISHERWOOD's *A Single Man* (1964), JOHN RECHY's *City of Night* (1963), and WILLIAM S. BURROUGHS's *Naked Lunch* (1959). These are very different books in style, technique, and point of view, but they maintain a gay perspective by not explaining, but assuming a knowledge of gay experience; they also avoid sentimentality. Of these books, Isherwood's *A Single Man* was the most important since its gracefully lean prose assumed the reader would take on the perspective of its unremarkable, middle-aged, middle-class narrator and because Isherwood had already established an international literary reputation. *A Single Man* avoided the demonology, special pleading, and sensationalism of other gay novels.

But there were other fiction writers whose works avoided easy classification. Among the most prominent were JAMES PURDY, Sanford Friedman, Hubert Selby, Alfred Chester, and GORE VIDAL. Yet pre-Stonewall gay works did not represent a gay literary movement. They were published as individual volumes, not as part of a continuous gay list or publishing focus. No literary publisher—large or small—published a line of gay books before the 1970s.

The emergence of a distinctive gay literary movement was built on the development of gay newspapers, magazines, and quarterlies. In addition, throughout the 1970s, gay bookstores began appearing across the United States. It is important to distinguish between gay bookstores whose chief purpose was to serve the political, social, and reading needs of the gay community and the legion of "dirty" bookstores where gay readers found gay-related materials and illicit sexual encounters. The Oscar Wilde Bookshop in New York opened in 1967 with only about twenty-five titles, since the owner refused to sell pornography. When Lambda Rising opened in Washington, D.C., in 1974, it carried some three hundred titles, some of which were erotica. Today, Lambda Rising operates stores in three states, runs a mail order department, and publishes *The Lambda Book Report,* the most widely distributed journal focused exclusively on gay and lesbian books. A Different Light, another chain of gay bookstores, now has operations on both coasts. Nearly every large American city now has at least one gay and lesbian bookstore.

Gay literary journals provided an important opportunity for young gay writers (and older ones as well) to find readers and practice their art. In 1970, *Gay Sunshine* began publishing as a radical newspaper from Berkeley, California. By 1973, it turned into a literary and cultural journal. It was joined later in the 1970s by *Fag Rag* out of Boston and *Mouth of the Dragon* in New York, as well as other smaller journals. Finally, in May 1976, *Christopher Street* appeared and for many years was the premiere venue for gay short fiction, essays, and poetry. Today, small press publishing has fragmented into a number of different regional and aesthetic movements, some like *BLK* serving gay black writers and readers, others like *RFD* growing out of alternative, communal, and rural experiences, and still others like *The James White Review* catering to a more mainstream readership.

One of the major outcomes of the appearance of gay literary magazines is that they sparked the growth of gay short fiction, which had been very difficult to place. Many writers dedicated themselves to the form, including RICHARD HALL, Allen Barnett, and Lev Raphael. The importance of the short story has been further elevated by a series of anthologies, most notably *Men on Men: Best Gay Short Fiction,* which went through four volumes under the editorship of George Stambolian. Begun in 1986, *Men on Men* was never intended to become a series, but its popularity has led to a new volume every other year.

Parallel to the development of gay literary journals was the development of gay small presses. In 1975, Gay Sunshine Press published its first book. In New York, Felice Picano founded The Sea Horse Press in 1977, the same year that Larry Mitchell began Calamus Press. In 1980, Sasha Alyson founded Alyson Publications in Boston. In addition, Crossing Press and Jargon Society as well as Grey Fox Press regularly published gay works. Many of the gay writers who were finally published by New York trade publishers began their careers in small gay presses. (See also JOURNALISM AND PUBLISHING.)

A watershed year for the gay literary movement was 1978, nearly a decade after the Stonewall Riots. In that year, LARRY KRAMER published *Faggots,* EDMUND WHITE published *Nocturnes for the King of Naples,* and ANDREW HOLLERAN published *Dancer from the Dance.* The three books—published by three different commercial or "trade" publishers—met with critical and financial success. They were widely reviewed and available in most bookstores—even those that would not ordinarily carry gay books. The simultaneous publication of three successful gay books meant that trade publishers and bookstores could no longer ignore gay works, and from that time, gay books have become a permanent part of many of the leading publishing houses. Three editors should be mentioned: Bill Whitehead at Dutton and later at Random House cultivated many of the early important gay writers, as Michael Denneny at St. Martin's Press and Arnold Dolin at NAL/Dutton continue to do today.

Faggots, Dancer from the Dance, and *Nocturnes* contain many similarities. All three are set in a predominantly white, cosmopolitan social milieu. *Dancer* and *Faggots* end on Fire Island, the long-established gay beach resort on the south shore of New York's Long Island. All three concern the lives of those Holleran refers to as "doomed queens," gay men who live in an exclusively gay neighborhood, have exclusively gay associates, spend their afternoons at the gym and their nights either at the bathhouses or dance bars, and who manage somehow through marginal jobs, trust funds, or the kindness of strangers to live lives of drugs, dancing, physical beauty, and sex. The novels are about the rich and their various hangers-on and are not far removed in that respect from the literary worlds of F. Scott Fitzgerald and ERNEST HEMINGWAY and, in Kramer's case, Nathaniel West. Like the fiction of Hemingway, Fitzgerald, and West, the works of Holleran, Kramer, and White are filled with the sense both of apocalyptic doom and moral condemnation, which in *Dancer from the Dance* and *Nocturnes for the King of Naples* is offset by lyric tenderness and aesthetic delight. No such compensations blunt the devastating satire of Kramer's *Faggots*.

In 1978, all three authors—Kramer, White, and Holleran—were living in New York. White and Holleran became members of what was dubbed THE VIOLET QUILL CLUB, the first important gay literary coterie. The Violet Quill, which formally lasted only about a year from March 1980 until March 1981, grew out of the friendships that the various members had formed, and the group was recognized even before its quasi-formal meetings began. Andrew Holleran was a longtime friend of ROBERT FERRO and Michael Grumley, lovers for nearly twenty years, whom Holleran met when all three were students at the Iowa Writers' Workshop. In addition to *Dancer from the Dance,* Holleran is the author of *Nights in Aruba* (1983) and a collection of essays about AIDS, *Ground Zero* (1988). Robert Ferro, after producing the little known and highly mysterious novella *The Others* (1977), wrote a series of critically acclaimed and popular novels, including *The Family of Max*

Desir (1984), *Blue Star* (1985), and *Second Son* (1988), the latter arguably the first novel about AIDS. These novels—which are a mixture of the autobiographical and the utterly fantastic—often center on a gay man's struggles with his close-knit but highly conflicted family. Michael Grumley published a number of nonfiction works, including an early book on sadomasochism, *Hard Corps* (1977). His sole novel, *Life Drawings* (1991), was published posthumously. Two other members of the Violet Quill—George Whitmore and Christopher Cox—had been lovers of Edmund White. White has produced a large body of both fiction and nonfiction. He first received popular recognition for *The Joy of Gay Sex* (1977), which he coauthored, and for *States of Desire: Travels in Gay America* (1980). But his critical reputation is based on his novels, which along with *Nocturnes for the King of Naples* include *Forgetting Elena* (1973), *Caracole* (1985), and the first two volumes of a promised trilogy, *A Boy's Own Story* (1982) and *The Beautiful Room Is Empty* (1988). Cox published little in his lifetime, but he was an editor who served under Bill Whitehead. The last member of the Violet Quill was in fact its most commercially successful member, Felice Picano, author of the psychological thriller *Eyes* (1976) and founder of Sea Horse Press. Among Picano's many other works are the novels *Late in the Season* (1981) and *The Lure* (1978) and two fictionalized memoirs, *Ambidextrous* (1985) and *The Men Who Loved Me* (1989). Of the seven members of the Violet Quill, only three are alive at this writing. The rest died of AIDS-related complications.

Although the Violet Quill was formed out of friendship and came to an end when those friendships dissolved, it emerged out of real need. The writers wanted criticism of their works-in-progress and felt that they could not get useful feedback from heterosexual readers who would still be grappling with the unfamiliar subject matter. Although no formal charter was ever written for the Violet Quill, the members shared several concerns: a desire to write works that reflected their gay experiences and specifically autobiographical fiction; a desire to write for gay readers without having to explain their point of view to shocked and unfamiliar heterosexual readers; and to write, to paraphrase William Wordsworth, in a selection of the language really used by gay men.

George Whitmore began his career as a playwright and poet. His novel *Nebraska* (1977) is a haunting story of a young man's discovery that his uncle has been lobotomized by his family as a treatment to "cure" homosexuality. His last book, *Someone Was Here: Profiles in the AIDS Epidemic* (1988), is one of the first works to give the human dimension of AIDS.

He wrote a fictionalized version of his sex therapy with Charles Silverstein (coauthor with Edmund White of *The Joy of Gay Sex* and with Felice Picano of *The New Joy of Gay Sex*) for *Christopher Street*. The expanded version of these articles was published as *The Confessions of Danny Slocum* (1980), and the novel in some ways epitomizes the concerns of the Violet Quill. Danny suffers from secondary impotence—he is slow to ejaculate. Virgil, the psychiatrist, pairs Danny with Joe, who suffers from the same problem, and Virgil gives them a series of exercises to make them more sexually responsive and comfortable. Danny and Joe develop a relationship that is at once extraordinarily intimate, highly sexual, and utterly unromantic. In this odd way, Whitmore explores alternative relations between men, relationships nowhere to be found in heterosexual novels. Indeed, what is striking about all the novels of the Violet Quill is their rendering of gay friendships—sometimes sexualized friendships, more often nonsexual.

Several gay fiction writers are associated with the West Coast and the so-called New Narrative Movement, particularly Dennis Cooper and Robert Glück, although Cooper lived in New York for many years and both authors were published by Felice Picano's Sea Horse Press. Cooper's work is characterized by his concern for disengaged young men whose violence is recorded with a punky sangfroid. Glück's more philosophical work involves meditations on everyday life that reveal its mystery and depth. Both have written prose and poetry. Cooper is the more prolific. His major works include three novels: *Frisk* (1991), *Closer* (1989), and *Safe* (1984) and a collection of short stories, *Wrong* (1992). Glück has published one novel, *Jack the Modernist* (1985), and a volume of short stories, *Elements of a Coffee Service* (1982), as well as several volumes of poems. No discussion of West Coast writing would be complete without mentioning ARMISTEAD MAUPIN, whose *Tales of the City* volumes have been the most popular works of the post-Stonewall generation, perhaps because of their literary limitations. Begun in 1976 as a series of articles in the *San Francisco Chronicle, Tales of the City* tells the story of a closely knit group of eccentric, but lovable, people living on Barbary Lane.

A writer who bridges both coasts is PAUL MONETTE, whose poems and novels are overshadowed by his two remarkable works of autobiography, *Borrowed Time* (1988) and *Becoming a Man* (1992), the latter of which won the National Book Award. These memoirs record his life from his sexual awakening through his lover's death from AIDS. His novels *Afterlife* (1990) and *Halfway Home* (1991) also dramatize living with AIDS.

A number of important writers have emerged since the Violet Quill and the New Narrative writers—authors who have emerged in the face of AIDS. Any list is only partial. Among the finest was Allen Barnett, who died of the disease about a year after the appearance of his only volume, *The Body and Its Dangers* (1990). Peter McGehee also died early in his promising career. The black novelist, poet, and scholar Melvin Dixon, who recently died of AIDS, wrote two fine novels, *Trouble the Waters* (1989) and *Vanishing Rooms* (1991), before his death. Another black writer of distinction is Randall Kenan, whose novel *A Visitation of Spirits* (1989) and collection of interlocking short stories *Let The Dead Bury Their Dead* (1992) record the lives of the blacks of Tims Creek, North Carolina, in sometimes magic ways. Harlan Greene's two novels, *Why We Never Danced the Charleston* (1984) and *What the Dead Remember* (1991), chronicle the white South around Charleston. Another Southern writer, Allen Gurganus is the best-selling author of *The Oldest Living Confederate Widow Tells All* (1989) and the volume of short stories *White People* (1991). Stephen McCauley's two novels of the bittersweet lives of young men struggling to escape adulthood, *The Object of My Affection* (1987) and *The Easy Way Out* (1991), have established him as a writer of enormous potential and craft, while Michael Cunningham's *Home at the End of the World* (1990), about young men trying to establish a family undermined by the horrors of AIDS, has received a great deal of notice. Joe Keenan has made a reputation for himself as a comic novelist with *Blue Heaven* (1988) and *Putting on the Ritz* (1991). David B. Feinberg's mordant humor can be found in his novel, *Eighty-Sixed* (1989), and his collection of short stories, *Spontaneous Combustion* (1991), both dealing with AIDS. Ethan Mordden has acquired a following for his comic works. Matthew Stadler wrote the delicate and haunting *Landscape: Memory* (1990), set in turn-of-the-century San Francisco.

Perhaps no gay writer of the post-AIDS generation has gotten more attention than DAVID LEAVITT, whose novels *The Lost Language of Cranes* (1986), which has subsequently been made into a television movie, and *Equal Affections* (1989) followed the success of his first volume of short stories, *Family Dancing* (1985). Leavitt's work adds to the typical *New Yorker* short story of understated upper-middle-class suburban life the theme of homosexuality, a theme that has always been implicit in this subgenre.

The situation for poetry after the Stonewall Riots was very different, as mentioned earlier. Several important poets had written works with explicitly gay content before Stonewall, and the issue of how autobiographical a work should be was not as problematic for poets, who work from a long tradition of highly personal lyrics, as it was for fiction writers. Consequently, poets did not have the same problems establishing a network and distribution system that fiction writers had.

It is easy to speculate as to why poetry had an easier time of articulating gay experience than had prose. In the first place, the highly metaphorical nature of poetry insulates poetic disclosure. Also, because poetry has a smaller, better-educated cadre of readers than does prose, it met with a more sophisticated and less-shockable readership, and therefore poets felt freer to address homosexual material. In addition, the tradition of lyric poetry in general permitted writers to deal with more explicit sexual material. Because of WALT WHITMAN, gay American writers have from the outset found poetry a congenial medium for expressing their thoughts. Moreover, the confessional poets of the late 1950s and 1960s—Robert Lowell, Sylvia Plath, Anne Sexton, for example—had so prepared readers for "shocking" material about suicide, drugs, and other forms of unauthorized sexual behavior, that homosexuality seemed not particularly unusual. Finally, Allen Ginsberg's candid and popular works, particularly *Howl* (1955), set the stage for other poets to be equally candid.

Gay American poets can be roughly—but only roughly— divided into two camps: formalists and free verse writers. There is a strongly formalist element to some gay poetry, particularly that influenced by W. H. AUDEN, the great Anglo-American poet, who taught by example several generations of Americans. Erudite, witty, and controlled, Auden's poetry could dig into the unseemly parts of the human psyche and reveal the sexual—often homosexual—basis of affection. As RICHARD HOWARD said in an elegy addressed to Auden: "After you, because of you, / all songs are possible."

Perhaps the most important poet to follow in Auden's footsteps has been JAMES MERRILL, in whose epic *The Changing Light at Sandover* (1982) Auden plays a major role. In *The Changing Light at Sandover,* Merrill and his longtime lover David Jackson come in contact, while playing with a Ouija board, with several voices from the dead. In the first volume, *The Book of Ephraim* (1976), the controlling voice is one of the Emperor Tiberius's minions. In *Mirabell* (1978), the speaker becomes a peacock. But in the final version, the controlling voice is Auden, who reveals the lessons of the cosmos to his two old friends. Part of the cosmology of *The Changing Light at Sandover* is that gay people—rather than being sinners condemned to one of the pleasanter circles of Hell, as they are in DANTE—are the more spiritually

advanced sexual group, able to love without the obsession of bodily reproduction. Merrill has published more than a dozen books of poems, two novels, plays, and criticism.

Richard Howard is also a poet and translator who, as the preceding quotation indicates, has been empowered by Auden's example. Howard also draws from the entire body of gay poetry to make up his voice or voices. *Two-Part Inventions* (1974), his remarkable series of dialogues, contains the imagined and imaginary conversations of Oscar Wilde and Walt Whitman ("Wild Flowers"); Edith Wharton and Mr. Roseman, who discover on the way to the cemetery that they shared the same lover ("Lesson of the Master"); and Rodin and an unknown railway traveler, who reveal their mutual pederastic desires ("Contra Naturam"). Other poets following in the same line include DARYL HINE, William Meredith, and J. D. McClatchy. Wayne Koestenbaum and David Bergman are two younger poets in this tradition.

Free verse writers are a diverse lot. In San Francisco, a number of poets gathered around ROBERT DUNCAN and Allen Ginsberg. Duncan's extremely hermetic poetry has had a more limited influence than Ginsberg's, but it has exerted a major force on those who have come under its spell. THOM GUNN is an interesting example of an expatriate Englishman who has made his home in the Bay Area since the 1950s. In his tightly controlled, formal verse, he recalls Auden. But his poems that articulate the effects of LSD recall Duncan. His most recent book, *The Man with Night Sweats* (1992), is one of the most impressive works to be inspired by AIDS. John Wieners, JACK SPICER, Robin Blaser, and James Broughton also were part of this San Francisco circle of poets.

Beginning in the 1950s, a group of poets formed a network that has been dubbed the New York School. Of the four leading members, three—JOHN ASHBERY, FRANK O'HARA, and James Schuyler—are or were gay. O'Hara's work is often playfully campy and lyrically soulful, conveying the giddy delight of new love or the sadness of emotional loss. Killed at an early age on the beach at Fire Island by an illegal dune buggy, O'Hara's work has been brought together in a massive *Collected Poems* (1971). Schuyler, who suffered from manic-depression and titled one book *The Crystal Lithium* (1972), wrote either short, delicate poems of a melancholic tone or long, exuberant odes to joy. His major books include *Hymn to Life* (1974), *The Morning of the Poem* (1980), and *A Few Days* (1985). Ashbery, perhaps the most celebrated poet of the last two decades, rarely speaks explicitly of homosexuality, but its trace can be felt in many of his enigmatic poems.

Contemporary black poets have had a rich tradition to build on since many of the major figures of the HARLEM RENAISSANCE were gay. Perhaps the two most important African-American gay poets are Essex Hemphill, whose works are featured in the controversial film *Tongues Untied,* and Assoto Saint. Both have been important anthologists. Hemphill, carrying on the work of Joseph Beam, edited *Brother to Brother* (1991), and Saint has edited *The Road Before Us: 100 Black Poets* (1991) and *Here to Dare: 10 Black Poets* (1992). Because black writers do not have the same access to publishing as do white writers, and black gay poets have even less, Assoto Saint established his own publishing house, Galiens Press. Both Hemphill and Saint are HIV-positive, and they have been eloquent AIDS activists.

Two of the finest gay poets—EDWARD FIELD and Alfred Corn—do not fall into any simple grouping. Field is a poet who has attempted to strip his work of all the artifice he can while still keeping the words resonant with emotion. His poems of plain speaking are often both hilarious and moving. Tender and self-mocking, he extends his love to baby seals, roaches, tulips, and sharks as well as to people of all stripes and nationalities. His sense of absurdity and honesty keep these poems from the sentimentality they invite at every turn. *Variety Photoplay* (1967) is often a campy retelling of Hollywood films. *A Full Heart* (1977) is a richly evocative collection centered on gay

life. *Counting Myself Lucky* (1992) brings together the best of his work over three decades. Alfred Corn tries to combine the ordinary language and American subject matter of William Carlos Williams with the more refined tone and formal invention of James Merrill. *A Call in the Midst of the Crowd* (1978) gives a panoramic view of New York City, whereas *Autobiographies* (1993) gives a panorama of his life and the lives of others. *The Various Light* (1980) and *The West Door* (1988) are more delicately local assays. Also notable are such younger poets as Henri Cole, Kenny Fries, Walter Holland, and Mark Doty.

It is impossible, then, to summarize the direction of gay poetry and fiction. The healthiest sign is its present remarkable diversity, even as it comes to grips with the devastations caused by AIDS. There is no approved style or required point of view. No genius has come to top all the others. If writers from the two coasts dominate the list, they do not crowd out the remarkable talents that appear throughout the nation. The greatest threat to gay writing seems to be the dream of the crossover bestseller, the belief that one cannot succeed as "merely" a gay writer, even though over and over again it has been the intimate connection between authors and their imagined gay audiences that has produced such penetrating, demanding, and challenging work to date.

—*David Bergman*

American Literature: Lesbian, Post-Stonewall

Politics is implicit in much of the lesbian literature that emerged in the years immediately following Stonewall. The "new," reactivated, women's movement had as much to do with the tone and character of lesbian writing during these years as the developing (largely male) gay liberation movement.

Kate Millett was an early fighter at the barricades, and her experience was a bellwether. Although her *Sexual Politics* (1970) was not explicitly lesbian in content, her indictment of the patriarchal system and her blueprint for change led the wave of new aggressive feminism, and this work, against all probability, became a best seller. However, under pressure from several lesbian groups to reveal her own bisexuality, she did, and the sales of *Sexual Politics* fell off almost immediately. Millett returned in 1974 with *Flying,* a rambling but vivid account of the entire affair, as well as of her politics, her professional life, and her strug-

gles with her sexuality. Millett's experience with *Sexual Politics* helped draw the battle lines between radical lesbian groups and more moderate feminist groups (which then included the National Organization for Women), and certainly between what remained of mainstream 1960s political activists (largely straight, white, and male) and the emerging body of new feminists—such as Charlotte Bunch, Julia Penelope, Robin Morgan, Karla Jay, Barbara Smith, and Martha Shelley—who challenged many of the concepts that had been fundamental to the politics of the 1960s.

As one might expect, lesbian literature from this period of rapid change reflects confusion, elation, and rage. Two important works that attempted to identify the issues of these early years were Sidney Abbott and Barbara Love's *Sappho Was a Right-On Woman* (1972), and Del Martin and Phyllis Lyon's *Les-*

bian/Woman (1972). Both defined the profound injustices of the status quo and attempted with courage and understanding to give fledgling lesbian-feminists a shove out of the nest and a glimpse of what a different future could hold. These were books that were desperately needed, and in the early 1970s they fell like rain onto parched earth. Lesbian/Woman has become a classic and was reprinted as recently as 1991.

ISABEL MILLER's Patience and Sarah, a novel that also rode the cusp into the early 1970s, carried with it some of the softness and brave-new-world, just-the-two-of-us attitude that challenged the conventional characterization of fictional lesbians as sordid, suicidal creatures of the night, a view predominant in lesbian literature of the pre-Stonewall years, when "lesbian fiction"—even for many lesbians—meant either ANN BANNON or RADCLYFFE HALL. Miller, who first published her novel privately as A Place For Us in 1969, reissued the work by a major press as Patience and Sarah in 1973. This sweet love story does not shirk from taking on issues of gender roles and sexuality between women in frontier America, and although the story reaches a happy conclusion, the protagonists must contend with many of the same issues of oppression that challenged their modern sisters in the early 1970s.

In the late 1960s and early 1970s, there were also the calm, reflective novels of JANE RULE, whose best-known work, Desert of the Heart, was published in 1965, before Stonewall; and the cautious ventures of MAY SARTON, who published two novels with discreet lesbian themes before Stonewall (The Small Room [1961] and Mrs. Stevens Hears the Mermaids Singing [1965]). Sarton's journals, however, with their oblique female reference points, always seemed to have more of a lesbian sensibility. Both writers now have a large body of work with lesbian themes, and neither has strayed far from the intelligent, reflective fictional characters with whom they obviously feel most comfortable. Both writers have also written about the lives and emotions of older lesbians with great insight, and Rule published Lesbian Images, a collection of essays on lesbian writers, in 1975.

But the times were changing. Jill Johnston, BERTHA HARRIS, and RITA MAE BROWN, like a trio of stampeding horses, brought Lesbian Nation into the 1970s with an infusion of energy that matched the increasingly dynamic rhetoric of the lesbian-feminist community. Jill Johnston in Lesbian Nation (1973) named the territory and defined the turf, Bertha Harris in Confessions of Cherubino (1972) and Lover (1976) brilliantly decorated the landscape, and Rita Mae Brown in Rubyfruit Jungle (1977) wreaked hysterical mayhem over the terrain. Lesbian Nation, which evolved out of a series of outrageous pieces Johnston wrote for the Village Voice, describes the growth of her political consciousness in exhaustive and sometimes bizarre detail. Forthright and often very funny ("All women are lesbians except those who don't know it"), Lesbian Nation is a mix of intense political theory, journal entries, descriptions of sexual escapades, and movement gossip that twenty-odd years later still has the capacity to enlighten and entertain. Johnston continued her analysis in a somewhat calmer state of mind with Gullibles Travels in 1973.

Harris, who remains the most stylistically innovative writer to emerge after Stonewall—and who could be viewed as the spiritual heir of JANE BOWLES—brought wit and a keen aesthetic sensibility to her fictional ruminations on the nature of love and the lover. Desire and separation are the concerns in Cherubino; transcendence and metamorphosis in Lover. (A 1993 reprint of Lover contains a lengthy introduction by the author describing the personal milieu in which the novel was created and also provides an insider's look at the sturm und drang of sexual politics in New York during the early 1970s.) Rita Mae Brown's Rubyfruit Jungle, the quintessential coming-out story, widely—and usually unsuccessfully—imitated during the late 1970s and 1980s, tells of the emancipation of Molly Bolt, her funky, in-your-face protagonist. Molly's buoyant semiautobiographical adventures as a dyke banished forever the "women in the shadows" lesbian heroines of the pre-Stonewall era. Brown, too, has continued with more mainstream writing such as Six of One (1978) and In Her Day (1988).

In the early years after Stonewall, some lesbian writers also began to imagine a perfect matriarchal society in which women claimed the power that had always been denied them. June Arnold, founder of Daughters, Inc., one of the earliest lesbian-feminist presses, wrote The Cook and the Carpenter (1973) and Sister Gin (1975), both of which deal in different ways with issues relating to women living communally and with problems inherent in the conflict of the personal and the political. Sister Gin was unique at the time in its depiction of the older lesbian as independent, humorous, and as politically and sexually active as her younger sisters. Inez, the protagonist of ELANA DYKEWOMON's Riverfinger Woman (1974), although she was born sooner, could be Molly Bolt's younger sister. JOANNA RUSS in The Female Man (1975) carries communality into utopia, and her On Strike Against God, which was issued at the end of the decade (1980), is an inventive coming-out story, foreshadowing her SCIENCE-FICTION AND FANTASY writ-

ings that were to come. Sally Gearhart's *The Wanderground* (1978) presents a powerful vision of a struggling society of women and is one of the earliest works to incorporate ecological themes with political ones.

During the 1970s, it became clear that only a very small percentage of lesbian writing was found acceptable by mainstream publishing houses. In reaction to this situation, several small women's presses sprang up in an attempt to get more lesbian writing into print. A number of them, such as Daughters Inc., Diana, Persephone, Amazon, and the Women's Press Collective saw to it that writers such as Rita Mae Brown, Sharon Isabell (author of *Yesterday's Lessons*, 1974), and Sally Gearhart reached print. Moreover, writers such as Bertha Harris and later Jane Rule often chose to have their works reprinted by these smaller women's presses. Harris, in her introduction to the 1993 edition of *Lover*, recalls the harrowing rise and fall of June Arnold and Daughters Inc., a tale that clearly shows the enormous toll that was taken on all the women who were involved in these publishing ventures. As presses such as Daughters and Diana fell, however, and factionalism within the lesbian and feminist community became more of an issue, new presses such as Seal, Crossing, Naiad, Firebrand, Spinsters, and others rose in the 1980s to carry on. In 1981, AUDRE LORDE, with Barbara Smith, CHERRÍE MORAGA, and others, cofounded Kitchen Table/Women of Color Press.

The problem of why lesbian presses have been necessary, or felt to be necessary, is an interesting one since there is no exact counterpart for gay male writers. The answer is probably political; lesbian-feminist writers had their own agenda, which did not for a long while include the general public. Mainstream publishers did not believe the market would support the politically and sexually explicit work that was coming out of the lesbian-feminist community, and so presses were started up that did. Women's presses also, at least in theory, gave writers more control over how their work was produced. During this period, some gay male writers slipped quietly into the mainstream, and many of their writings have come to be popular with both gay and straight audiences, a phenomenon that has occurred only on a small scale among lesbian writers. Writers such as Great Britain's JEANETTE WINTERSON, who has a general lesbian focus to her work but incorporates this focus into intriguing novels of ideas, have found larger audiences, but few American lesbian writers of fiction other than Bertha Harris, Audre Lorde, and perhaps the stylish Carole Maso (author of *Ghost Dance* [1986] and *The American Woman in the Chinese Hat* [1994]) have been able to escape the strictures of lesbian political and cultural

expectancy and enlarge their vision. Instead it has been left to authors such as ALICE WALKER, Lois Gould, and more recently Kathryn Davis (in *The Girl Who Trod on a Loaf* [1993]), who do not identify themselves primarily as lesbians, to include important lesbian characters and situations in work directed to a mainstream audience. (See also JOURNALISM AND PUBLISHING.)

The lesbian community has never lacked first-class poets, and their output during the 1970s was astonishingly rich. In this one decade OLGA BROUMAS won the Yale Younger Poets Award for *Beginning With O* (1977); JUDY GRAHN published *Edward the Dyke* (1971), the groundbreaking *A Woman is Talking to Death* (1974), and *The Work of a Common Woman* (1978); Susan Griffin's *Like the Iris of an Eye* (1976) appeared; Joan Larkin published *Housework* (1975); Audre Lorde issued her third book, *From a Land Where Other People Live* (1973), which was nominated for a National Book Award, and her fourth, *Our Dead Behind Us* (1976); Pat Parker's *Child of Myself* (1972), *Pit Stop* (1973), and *Womanslaughter* (1978) were released; JUNE JORDAN published *Things That I Do in the Dark* (1977) and other works; Robin Becker added *Personal Effects* (1976); and ADRIENNE RICH published *The Dream of a Common Language* (1978), which included "Twenty-One Love Poems," and *On Lies, Secrets and Silence* (essays, 1979)— among many other works. This list is one to reckon with, and it is only a partial one. Of older lesbian poets, MAY SWENSON, ELIZABETH BISHOP, and May Sarton were still actively writing, but not generally about overtly lesbian subjects, though Brett Millier's *Elizabeth Bishop: Life and the Memory of It* (1992) prints a wonderful, previously unpublished love poem by Bishop. Entitled "It is marvelous to wake up together," the poem was found among Bishop's papers after her death, and written while she was living with a female lover in Key West.

Much lesbian poetry first saw the light of day in the pages of the many women's journals that proliferated during the late 1970s and through the 1980s. *Heresies, Conditions, Sinister Wisdom, Amazon Quarterly, off our backs, Dark Horse,* and *Focus* make up only a short list of some of the publications that were absolutely vital to the process of "getting the words out" to lesbians, not only in urban centers, but in parts of the country that offered little, if any, community support for the lesbian trying to make sense of her life and the different types of personal struggle that at once bound the lesbian community together and were beginning to cause growing disquiet in the ranks. *Conditions* was of consistently high quality, due largely to its multicultural editorial policies; *Conditions Five: The Black Women's Issue* (1980) remains a high-water mark of women's journalism.

Adrienne Rich and Audre Lorde emerged as the most articulate voices of radical change during the late 1970s and 1980s. Although poetry was their central discipline, they were formidable verbal opponents of oppression in all its forms and embraced the common battles of all women. Rich's books of poetry in the 1980s include *A Wild Patience Has Taken Me This Far* (1981) and *Your Native Land, Your Life* (1986); she also published *Blood, Bread, and Poetry,* a collection of essays, in 1986. Rich, whose poetry at the beginning of her career was intensely lyrical, took on a harder edge as her political involvements began to inhabit her work with more fury, but her essays grew increasingly more profound, with a lyrical quality of their own.

Lorde's work is full of anger tempered by compassion and good humor; it embraces all and transcends all with dignity and forthrightness. Her books published during the 1980s include *The Cancer Journals* (1980), *Sister Outsider* (essays and speeches, 1984), and *Our Dead Behind Us* (poetry, 1986). Perhaps her most intriguing work, however, is her autobiographical novel *Zami: A New Spelling of My Name* (1984), which she called a "bio-mythography." Here, in a "fever of wanting to be whole," she recreates the mythic world of her African and West Indian ancestry, and in recreating herself, moves toward an authentic mythology for all black women.

Black lesbian writers produced a rich and varied body of work in the 1980s. ANN ALLEN SHOCKLEY, for example, in *Loving Her* (1987), contributed one of the first successful novels with an interracial lesbian relationship as its central focus. *Say Jesus and Come to Me,* also published in 1987, draws a strong picture of a vital and cohesive black lesbian community. The work of Jewelle Gomez (*The Gilda Stories* [1991]) is founded in an observant lyricism and a profound sense of passion and social conscience. Becky Birtha's *For Nights Like This One* came out in 1983 and *Lover's Choice* in 1987.

The focus of much lesbian writing shifted around the beginning of the 1980s to a concern with the politics of entitlement and away from the 1970s debates about transcendent solutions to common problems. The field sometimes turned into a range war among groups of extremely competent writers, many of whom seemed to be justifiably furious. There developed a literature for nearly every lesbian group with an ax to grind, and the best of it challenged readers to incorporate every woman's experience into her own. Besides collections of writings by lesbians from diverse ethnic backgrounds, there were novels

with sadomasochistic themes; butch–femme stories, which had been trashed in the 1970s, resurfaced; lesbian erotica attracted a certain audience; and there was a concentration of novels concerned with lesbian science fiction, lesbian mothers, older lesbians, lesbian–lesbian abuse, and of course, the romances and detective stories that now, in the mid-1990s, constitute an odd majority of titles on most women's bookstore fiction shelves.

Bonnie Zimmerman, in her excellent survey of lesbian fiction, *The Safe Sea of Women* (1990), accurately observes that as the uniformity and the sense of common struggle that characterized lesbian writing of the 1970s began to break down in the early 1980s, writers began to concentrate on the politics of difference. "Eventually," she writes, "in place of Lesbian Nation, we had microscopic rooms containing one or two women apiece." And Audre Lorde, who had a knack for hitting the nail on the head, wrote in the Epilogue to *Zami:* "In . . . growing, we came to separation, that place where work begins." Meanwhile, in a speech at Berkeley in 1979, activist Charlotte Bunch called the lesbian-feminist subculture a "ghetto," and urged lesbians to "get out of the ghetto and into the mainstream." Although there were doubts among writers about whether either of these solutions was an acceptable answer to the problem of factionalism, the "mainstream" was simply not an option available for most lesbian writers. Therefore, Lorde's call for splitting off was not necessarily seen as a negative step; it was instead a clear call to create a mature body of lesbian literature, complex in its makeup and multicultural in its appeal. PAULA GUNN ALLEN, in her introduction to *Spider Woman's Granddaughters* (1989), observed that "For Indians, relationships are based on commonalties of consciousness, reflected in thought and behavior." For many minority lesbians, however, the commonality of consciousness that had united them in the 1970s was being fractured by conflict in the 1980s.

Of the works that began to emerge from ethnically and racially diverse lesbian groups in the 1980s, perhaps the one that set the tone was *This Bridge Called My Back: Writings By Radical Women of Color* (1981), edited by Cherríe Moraga and GLORIA ANZALDÚA. This anthology of essays, fiction, and poetry eloquently articulates the general sense of anger and frustration experienced by Chicana, black, and other lesbians of color. Anzaldúa went on to write *Borderlands/La Frontera: The New Mestiza* (1987), which in prose, poetry, and lyric memoir explores the spiritual and physical boundaries of her life. Moraga, Chicana poet, playwright, and essayist, produced a number of other works, including *Loving in the War*

Years (*Lo Que Nunca Pasó Por Sus Labios* [1983]), an autobiographical narrative in which she describes her search for cultural identity.

Native-American Paula Gunn Allen also searches for her place in the ritual traditions of her people. Her works, especially her novel *The Woman Who Owned the Shadows* (1983) and her volume of essays *The Sacred Hoop: Recovering the Feminine in American Indian Tradition* (1986), illuminate her struggle to achieve a whole personal and political identity, an identity denied her and many other lesbians of color and diverse ethnic heritage by a society that oppressed them as women, as lesbians, and as members of minority cultures. The core of much of the writing of Chicana, Latina, Native-American, black, Asian, Jewish, and other minority lesbians was formed by the intensity of these concerns.

Willyce Kim is probably the best known of Asian-American lesbian writers, although her novels *Dancer Dawkins and the California Kid* (1985) and *Dead Heat* (1988) have neither a clearly lesbian nor Asian-American focus. Michelle Cliff in her novels *Abeng* (1984) and *No Telephone to Heaven* (1987) explores her Jamaican heritage and the racism of that society. Adrienne Rich points out that writers such as Cliff, Moraga, Anzaldúa, Allen, and Lorde are determined that women of color should have their *own* written history, in their own voices, not one incorporated into a more general literary tradition focused on white women, or on white or black men ("Resisting Amnesia," 1983). This determination is even stronger when the writer is also a lesbian.

In 1982, Evelyn Torton Beck edited *Nice Jewish Girls: A Lesbian Anthology,* the first collection of its kind. SARAH SCHULMAN, Ruth Geller, Alice Bloch, and Lesléa Newman are novelists whose Jewish heritage is implicit in their characters and their points of view although often political and religious issues are not the primary focus of their works. Schulman, who began with the street-smart *Sophie Horowitz Story* (1984), continued with the darker and more mature *After Delores* (1988) and *Empathy* (1992). Newman, who has the distinction of having published the first (and perhaps only) lesbian novel dealing with bulimia and coming out (*Good Enough to Eat* [1986]), also wrote the important *Heather Has Two Mommies* (1989), a children's book set in a lesbian household, which was controversial enough to land Newman on the "Phil Donahue Show" and on the front page of the *New York Times*. There is a strong Jewish sensibility in Newman's work, especially in her most recent novel, *In Every Laugh a Tear* (1992). Alice Bloch in *The Law of Return* (1983) concerns herself with the search for home, a common theme among Jewish lesbian writers.

Among Jewish lesbian poets, Polish-born Irena Klepfisz, author of *Keeper of Accounts* (1982) and *Different Enclosures* (1985), deals movingly with women and the Holocaust.

Other fiction published during the 1980s took some odd turns. The phenomenon of the lesbian detective story took hold and flourished, almost to the point of inundation. Although most of these works have conventional plots and formulaic story lines, some of them are fun to read, and the view might be taken that any work that furthers "popular lesbian fiction"—a term that was once an oxymoron—is valuable. The detective novels of Mary Wings are particularly inventive (*She Came Too Late* [1987], *She Came in a Flash* [1988], and *Divine Victim* [1992]), and Katherine Forrest's *Amateur City* (1984) and *Murder at the Nightwood Bar* (1987) have become classics of the genre. Camarin Grae has also written a number of popular detective tales (*Slick* [1990]), and Shelley Smith added a lesbian spy novel (*The Pearls* [1987]).

As if the 1980s were the 1940s, the romance novel followed the detective story onto the lesbian popularity charts of the decade. Katherine Forrest championed this genre as well, and her *Curious Wine* (1983) remains the classic contemporary tale of girl meets girl. The lesbian romantic novel, a child of the coming-out tales of the 1970s, has also settled into a somewhat formulaic groove, but is produced by a number of competent writers, including Paula Christian (*The Cruise* [1982] and other works), Sarah Aldrich (*Flight of Angels* [1992], *Keep to Me, Stranger* [1989]), and Lee Lynch (*Toothpick House* [1983]). The lesbian detective story and the lesbian romance have been greatly aided by the Naiad Press, a stalwart publishing house that has, under the direction of pioneer lesbian publisher Barbara Grier, furthered the cause of reasonably priced, popular lesbian fiction.

Lesbian romantic novels of a more complex sort were produced by Kathleen Fleming, whose *Lovers in the Present Afternoon* (1984) is a well-crafted story that deals not only with lesbian love, but also with the sometimes unpleasant realities of living with that love in a contemporary world. The characters in Nancy Toder's *Choices* (1980) wrestle with the issue of "what has made me a lesbian?" Noretta Koertge in *Who Was That Masked Woman?* (1981) struggles with her own lesbian identity and in *Valley of the Amazons* (1984) expands that struggle into a search for a true lesbian community. Another 1980s lesbian love story (although it was published late in 1979) is DORIS GRUMBACH's *Chamber Music*. The last third of this restrained and beautifully written novel, based loosely on the lives of composer Edward MacDowell and his wife Marian (who later founded the Mac-Dowell Colony), describes the love affair that develops after the husband's death (from syphilis, which he contracted from another man) between the widow and his nurse.

Restrained is not the word for some of the fiction with sadomasochistic themes and some of the lesbian erotica (written by women for women) that emerged in the 1980s. Lesbian writers are still feeling their way when it comes to writing about sex, and in fact whether it is the "melting" kind (as in Forrest's *Curious Wine*) or the ropes and hot wax of *Coming to Power: Writings and Graphics on Lesbian S/M* (2d ed. published in 1982 by Samois, a lesbian S/M group), the writing is often unconvincing. The subject is (not surprisingly) politically charged, and Pat Califia has been an articulate (and often lonely) voice arguing for complete sexual freedom. Her essays and short stories blatantly challenge the large numbers of lesbians clamoring for her head, but fortunately she has a sense of humor, as evidenced in her *Macho Sluts* (1988). Among lesbians writing erotica for other lesbians, Robbi Sommers (*Pleasures* [1989], *Kiss and Tell* [1991]) seems to have no trouble finding unique ways for her heroines to get it on, and Tee Corinne (*Dreams of the Woman Who Loved Sex* [1987]) writes elegantly and explicitly of sexual encounters between women. Susie Bright has also written a number of books of erotica for lesbians.

The BUTCH-FEMME issue lay dormant at the feet of feminism for many years, but in the 1980s and early 1990s, it resurfaced as writers began to reexplore the various ways of "being" lesbian. Much of this interest was stimulated by a curiosity about segments of a lesbian past that writers such as Joan Nestle, one of the founders of the Lesbian Herstory Archives and editor of *The Persistent Desire: A Butch/Femme Reader* (1992), were beginning to discuss. Novelists such as Lee Lynch (*The Swashbuckler* [1985]) and Leslie Feinberg (*Stone Butch Blues* [1993]) incorporate butches and femmes naturally into their work, and social historians Elizabeth Kennedy and Madeline Davis devote an entire book to the butch–femme community of Buffalo, New York, in *Boots of Leather, Slippers of Gold* (1993).

As the 1990s began, it seemed that some of the lines that had divided the lesbian literary community during the 1980s were beginning to soften. Although problems remained, there was at least a conciliatory feeling among those lesbians who were committed to fully integrating their sexual orientation into their larger work. Among novelists of the 1990s, Jenifer Levin (*The Sea of Light* [1993]) and LISA ALTHER (*Bedrock* [1990]) both continue to create lesbian char-acters whose sexual orientation, although an integral component of their personalities, is not particularly an issue. Helen Elaine Lee's recent multigenerational saga of an African-American family, *The Serpent's Gift* (1994), deftly incorporates a lesbian story within the African-American experience. On the other hand, the novels of Blanche McCrary Boyd (*Revolution of Little Girls* [1991]) and DOROTHY ALLISON (*Trash* [1989], *Bastard Out of Carolina* [1993]) are sometimes chastised for "not being lesbian enough." This criticism, however, might be viewed as a positive symptom of the shifting, broadening focus of lesbian fiction in general. The novels of Jane DeLynn, such as *Don Juan in the Village* (1980), are sometimes difficult to characterize but are always entertaining.

Of lesbian poets, the most outstanding are Marilyn Hacker and Mary Oliver. Hacker's *Love, Death, and the Changing of the Seasons* won the National Book Award for Poetry in 1986; her *Going Back to the River* appeared in 1990. Oliver, whose *American Primitive* won the Pulitzer Prize for Poetry in 1984, quietly added the National Book Award for Poetry to her shelf in 1992 for *New and Selected Poems*. Both of these poets continue to produce work of expanding vision.

Although women in the lesbian community have not been struck nearly as severely as their gay brothers by the AIDS pandemic, they have suffered their share of devastating losses. And although lesbians have also experienced some of the social backlash from the epidemic and many are vitally involved in AIDS-related causes, they have, oddly, written very little about it. Bonnie Zimmerman suggests that this has much to say about the general mood of the community today; lesbians—in this case, at least—are accommodating themselves to loss and compromise and are more inclined to act than to write about it. In many ways, the struggle against AIDS has brought gay men and lesbians alike back to 1969, where the fight began. Now, however, through our writing, we have come to know the depth of our strength, and this battle too is one we are now prepared to win. (See also AFRICAN-AMERICAN LITERATURE, LESBIAN; ASIAN AMERICAN LITERATURE; JEWISH AMERICAN LITERATURE; JOURNALISM AND PUBLISHING; LATINA LESBIAN LITERATURE; and NATIVE NORTH AMERICAN LITERATURE.)

—*Ann Wadsworth*

BIBLIOGRAPHY

Castle, Terry. *The Apparitional Lesbian: Female Homosexuality and Modern Culture.* New York: Columbia University Press, 1993. ■ Grahn, Judy. *Another Mother Tongue: Gay Words, Gay Worlds.* Boston: Beacon Press, 1984. ■ ———. *The Highest Apple: Sappho and the Lesbian Poetic Tradition.* San Francisco, Calif.: Spinsters, Ink., 1985. ■ Grier, Barbara, ed. *The Lesbian in Literature*. 3d ed. Tallahassee, Fla.: Naiad Press, 1981. ■ Harris, Bertha. "What We Mean To Say: Notes Toward Defining the Nature of Lesbian Literature." *Heresies* 3 (1977): 5–8. ■ Jay, Karla and Joanne Glasgow, eds. *Lesbian Texts and Contexts: Radical Revisions*. New York: New York University Press, 1990. ■ Lorde, Audre. *Sister Outsider: Essays and Speeches*. Trumansburg, N.Y.: Crossing Press, 1984. ■ Munt, Sally, ed. *New Les-* *bian Criticism: Literary and Cultural Readings*. New York: Columbia University Press, 1992. ■ Potter, Clare, ed. *The Lesbian Periodicals Index*. Tallahassee, Fla.: Naiad Press, 1986. ■ Rich, Adrienne. *Blood, Bread, and Poetry: Selected Prose, 1979–1985*. New York: W.W. Norton, 1986. ■ Zimmerman, Bonnie. *The Safe Sea of Women: Lesbian Fiction, 1969–1989*. Boston: Beacon Press, 1990.

American Writers on the Left

The topic of gay, lesbian, and bisexual "Writers on the Left" in mid-twentieth-century U.S. literature is potentially a large and rich field for inquiry although scholarship still remains in its infancy. Research is complicated by the combined effects of modern anticommunism and homophobia. In *Odd Girls and Twilight Lovers,* Lillian Faderman documents how homosexuals became special targets of persecution along with leftists during the Cold War years. Thus, many writers learned to obscure both their sexual orientation and their political identity in memoirs, interviews, and autobiographical statements. This habit of mind continued even after the cultural climate of the country liberalized in the 1960s.

The expression "Writers on the Left" derives from Daniel Aaron's famous 1961 book by that name. The category traditionally refers to creative writers and literary critics drawn to Marxist-oriented parties and social movements between the Russian Revolution of 1917 and the appearance of a New Left in the early 1960s. For the most part, such writers were variously associated with Communism, although some important ones, such as the famous gay film critic Parker Tyler (1904–1974) and the bisexual poet John Brooks Wheelwright (1897–1940), were drawn to Trotskyism. The Communist party was officially closed to homosexuals, but many rank and file activists, prominent fellow travelers, and even some national party leaders, such as Elizabeth Gurley Flynn (1890–1964), had same-sex relationships.

Few gay, lesbian, and bisexual writers of this generation chose to publicly state their sexual orientation; several even had long-term heterosexual marriages. A homosexual identity is rarely claimed in their creative or critical writing; on the contrary, a number of left-wing writers known to have same-sex relations depicted homosexuals negatively in their fiction and drama. Thus, it is difficult to document sexual orientation and hard to find the appropriate terminology to describe writers, most of whom might have denied that they had same-sex relations or at least declined to accept the identifications used today.

Labels are also problematic because some gay, lesbian, and bisexual writers may suspect that their literary output will be classified and judged by sexual orientation alone. Such a concern parallels that of many left-wing writers who refuse to accept political designations such as "Communist" out of fear that they, too, will be simplistically labeled and dismissed. Thus, although many writers were, in fact, pro-Communist and had same-sex relationships, few would accept characterization as "Gay Communist writers" or "Lesbian Communist writers."

The apprehension of gay, lesbian, and bisexual Marxist writers that information about their sexuality and politics may be used to discredit or oversimplify their lives and works is well-founded. An example of a left-wing writer whose sexuality was employed for dramatically different purposes when her sexual orientation (which she tried to hide) and politics became a matter of public record is Josephine Herbst (1892–1969). Her most highly regarded work is a trilogy of novels based on the saga of the Trexler family, *Pity Is not Enough* (1933), *The Executioner Waits* (1934), and *Rope of Gold* (1939), although she published significant journalism, biography, and fiction from the 1920s through the 1960s.

Herbst had been omitted, like most radical women writers, from biographical consideration in all the pioneering studies of the Literary Left, but the posthumous discovery of a packet of letters that she wished to have destroyed caused her to become the subject of Elinor Langer's *Josephine Herbst: The Story She Could Never Tell* (1984). This is a fascinating biography that, among other things, candidly describes Herbst's lesbian relationships with the radical muralist Marion Greenwood and other women. Since no evidence of official Communist party membership for Herbst could be found, Langer chooses to depict Herbst as an independent-minded but loyal fellow traveler. Herbst's sexuality is discussed from the perspective of the concerns of contemporary feminists; it is marked by a frustration and lack of satisfaction due to the sexism of the Left as well as the dominant culture.

In contrast, a more recent study, Stephen Koch's *Double Lives* (1993), uses mostly the same sources to denounce Herbst as a political and sexual degenerate. She is depicted as a Soviet agent whose sexual hedonism leads to her being seduced into a lesbian affair that ruins her marriage. Neither book treats seriously Herbst's art, where one might possibly glean greater insight into her motives, character, and personality.

However, a recent work of Marxist-feminist theory, Paula Rabinowitz's *Labor and Desire* (1991), considers *Rope of Gold* in light of the affair with Greenwood, which the novelist fictionalizes as a heterosexual relationship between the heroine, Victoria Chance, and a rarely seen German revolutionary in exile, Kurt Becher. Rabinowitz suggests that, though social pressure may have caused Herbst to transform her lesbian lover into a man in this autobiographical novel, the treatment of the character Becher as nearly always offstage, "hidden from view," "repressed in the text," and "felt as a presence primarily in his absence," links him to Herbst's feelings about the repression of lesbianism in our culture.

The case of Herbst creates a dilemma for scholars. If one frankly describes the politics and sexual orientation of writers, there is the danger of abuse by anticommunists, homophobics, and others who tend to oversimplify. If one demurs, then the actual record of political commitment among writers with same-sex relations remains obscure and unwritten. Fortunately, three recent books on gays and the Left have set a high standard for an open and intelligent discussion of the strong connections between left-wing politics and homosexuality. Eric A. Gordon's *Mark the Music* (1989) is a superbly researched study of the life and work of composer Mark Blitzstein (1905–1964) that is explicit about his period of Communist party membership and gayness. Harold Norse's *Memoirs of a Bastard Angel: A Fifty Year Literary and Erotic Odyssey* (1989) contains information about gay left-wing poets and faculty at Brooklyn College in the late 1930s although the identities of several individuals are masked by the use of pseudonyms. Stuart Timmons's *The Trouble with Harry Hay* (1990) explains how Hay's twelve years in the Communist party, to which he was recruited by the gay and Communist actor Will Geer, led to his founding in 1950 of the Mattachine Society, regarded by many as the most significant forerunner of the contemporary gay movement.

The biographical scholarship about the radical politics of other gay, lesbian, or bisexual writers is uneven, usually relying on the writer's own testimony. For example, novelist PAUL BOWLES (b. 1910) wrote in *Without Stopping* (1972) that he and fiction writer JANE BOWLES (1917–1973) held membership in the Communist party in the late 1930s. African-American poet AUDRE LORDE (1934–1992) acknowledged that she was a member of the Communist youth group, the Labor Youth League, in the 1950s. African-American poet COUNTEE CULLEN (1903–1946) held Communist party membership briefly in the early 1930s. Recent research by Professor Alan Filreis of the University of Pennsylvania indicates that the poet and pioneer filmmaker Willard Maas (1911–1971) held membership in the Communist party and had many same-sex relations although he was also married twice.

Other writers who had same-sex relations were close to the Communist movement but never acknowledged Party membership. Playwright LORRAINE HANSBERRY (1930–1965) was certainly pro-Communist and possibly a member of Communist organizations. Ella Winter (1898–1980), a famous fellow traveler in cultural circles, had love affairs with women. She was married to radical muckraking journalist Lincoln Steffens and then left-wing Hollywood humorist Donald Ogden Stewart. She wrote favorably about the personal life of citizens under Communism in books such as *Red Virtue: Human Relationships in the Soviet Union* (1933). MURIEL RUKEYSER (1913–1980), a poet, novelist, translator, and biographer, was active on the Left throughout her life.

The poet and translator Robert Friend (b. 1913) emigrated to Israel in 1951 when the House Un-American Activities Committee threatened to revoke his passport. Like Harold Norse (b. 1916), Friend attended Brooklyn College where he was associated with the Left, and, also like Norse, eventually addressed his sexual orientation in his later writings. Another gay poet with a background in the Brooklyn College Left is Chester Kallman (1921–1975), who was the companion of W. H. AUDEN for thirty-four years; in fact, he and Auden met at an April 6, 1939, gathering of the Communist-led League of American Writers.

William Rollins, Jr. (1898–1950) was an important left-wing novelist in the 1930s whose homosexuality was known to his friends even though he never acknowledged his sexual orientation. Rollins came from a comfortable Boston family and, after joining the American Ambulance Service in World War I, was part of the expatriate circle around ERNEST HEMINGWAY and Harold Loeb. According to the memoir *An Ethnic at Large* (1978), by his friend and fellow novelist Jerre Mangione, Rollins was a devoted Marxist "convinced that only through socialism could democracy be achieved for all Americans, and that only the Communists had the leadership to bring about the necessary changes." On the other hand, Rollins "could not relinquish his individuality to submit to the discipline of the Communist Party any more than he could resist exercising his sense of humor."

Rollins contributed to the Communist-sponsored cultural journal *New Masses*, and his 1934 novel, *The Shadow Before*, was highly regarded by left-wing writers and critics. Although the story concerns a Massachusetts textile strike, many of the events are borrowed from the famous 1929 strike in Gastonia, North Carolina, and Rollins is frequently discussed in scholarship about the six "Gastonia Novels." The work was praised at length by John Dos Passos in the April 4, 1934, issue of *The New Republic* for its extraordinary characterization and use of language, and was often cited in Marxist literary discussions of the day for its experimental techniques. Sexual themes with Freudian overtones are omnipresent in the novel as well. Among the factory workers, there is a homosexual Swedish youth, Olsen, who is portrayed unsympathetically even though he is savagely beaten after he reveals his desire for Doucet, a heavy-drinking Frenchman.

Rollins began as a pulp detective writer for *Black Mask*, and his early books include two mystery novels, *Midnight Treasure* (1929) and *Murder at Cyprus Hall* (1933), the latter published under the pseudonym O'Connor Stacy. In 1930, he published *The Obelisk*, a novel of adolescence somewhat influenced by Joyce. In 1938, he sought to blend his politics and talent for producing popular fiction in a novel of the Spanish Civil War, *The Wall of Men*, issued in paperback by the new Modern Age publishing house. In a March 8, 1938, review in the *New Masses*, the African-American Marxist novelist Richard Wright observed that "*The Wall of Men* may be the beginning of a popular mass pulp fiction in America, a brand which can be read with pleasure by workers, without the danger of their becoming duped or misled." Before his death at age fifty-two, Rollins returned to mystery fiction with *The Ring and the Lamp* (1947).

It is likely that many other writers were like bisexual novelist JOHN CHEEVER (1912–1982). According to the 1988 biography by Scott Donaldson, Cheever sympathized with the Communist-led Left in the 1930s, but, in order to protect his career, refused to sign any manifestos or join organizations.

Several major literary critics were homosexuals and closely associated with the Left. F. O. MATTHIESSEN (1902–1950) was an eminent Harvard professor and author of *Sarah Orne Jewett* (1929), *The Achievement of T.S. Eliot* (1935), *American Renaissance* (1941), *Henry James: The Major Phase* (1944), *The James Family* (1947), *From the Heart of Europe* (1948), and *Theodore Dreiser* (1951). Although a Christian, he frequently supported causes championed by the Communist party and was chosen to second the nomination of Henry Wallace for president on the Progressive party ticket in 1946. Matthiessen's suicide, by jumping off the twelfth-floor ledge of Boston's Hotel Manger, is generally attributed to a combination of despair over the Cold War and the death in 1945 of his long-time lover, the painter Russell Cheney.

Another important scholar of U.S. literature, Newton Arvin (1900–1963), was strongly pro-Communist in the 1930s although he never joined the party. He wrote major books on *Hawthorne* (1929), *Whitman* (1938), *Herman Melville* (1950), and *Longfellow* (1963). Although Arvin tried to conceal his homosexuality, it was well known to his friends. Arvin was eased out of his job at Smith College in 1960 after the police raided his home and discovered homoerotic photographs.

In addition to Lorde, Cullen, and Hansberry, many African-American leftists had same-sex relationships. The poet and novelist Claude McKay (1890–1948) was on the editorial board of the revolutionary magazine *Liberator*, and close to the Communist movement throughout the 1920s. Alain Locke (1886–1954), the first black Rhodes Scholar and a professor of philosophy at Howard University who published *The New Negro* (1925) heralding the HARLEM RENAISSANCE, was a fellow traveler at times. The poet Robert Hayden (1913–1981), who seemed tormented by his homosexual urges, was a member of the Communist-led John Reed Club of Detroit. The novelist JAMES BALDWIN (1924–1987) was a devoted fellow traveler of the Communist party in his high school years. The poet and dramatist Owen Dodson (1914–1983) appeared frequently in left-wing magazines. Novelist Dorothy West (b. 1909) and short story writer Marion Minus (1913–1973) also had left-wing associations in the mid-1930s.

LANGSTON HUGHES (1902–1967), a major black poet, playwright, novelist, and autobiographer, collaborated closely with the Communist party throughout the 1930s. He published in the *New Masses*, wrote a pamphlet praising the Soviet Union's treatment of its darker nationalities, produced a poem to honor the 1934 convention of the Communist party, and was elected president of the Communist-led League of Struggle for Negro Rights. He served as a correspondent during the Spanish Civil War, and his 1938 collection of poems, *A New Song*, was published with an introduction by the famous Communist novelist Mike Gold, known for his gay-baiting attack on the closeted gay writer Thornton Wilder in the October 22, 1930, issue of *The New Republic*. Although

Hughes drifted away from the Communist party in the 1940s, he supported the Progressive party presidential campaign in 1948 and condemned the prosecution of Communist leaders under the Smith Act in 1949. Following a 1953 subpoena to appear before the House Committee on Un-American Activities, Hughes distanced himself from the Left until the 1960s. Although dozens of poems attest to his revolutionary convictions, only a few, such as the enigmatic "Impasse" (in *The Panther and the Lash,* 1967), seem to reflect on his sexual orientation.

Among the most misunderstood African-American writers is Willard Motley (1912–1965), author of the best-selling *Knock on Any Door* (1947) and three other novels. According to research I personally conducted among his friends and relatives, Motley studied Marxism and politically collaborated during the 1940s with both Communists and Trotskyists. However, references to his homosexuality and radical associations are absent from extant scholarship, which is also inaccurate about the identities of his parents and other relatives. In *Knock on Any Door,* the young, tough-guy Italian-American protagonist Nick Romano is depicted as having sexual relations with men, ostensibly for money. However, one of these men, Owen, falls in love with Romano and, although he is depicted as weak and dependent, Owen turns out to be a loyal friend to the doomed hero.

Another left-wing writer of color was Lynn Riggs (1899–1954), a poet and dramatist who was part Cherokee from Oklahoma. According to the memoir, *A Very Good Land to Fall With* (1987) by his friend John Sanford, who was a novelist and Communist, Riggs sought admission to the Communist party during World War II but was discouraged by party leaders in Los Angeles because of his homosexuality. Riggs was most famous for *Green Grow the Lilacs* (1931), but his play about Native-American identity, *Cherokee Night* (1936), may also indirectly express frustrations he felt in the face of homophobia.

Although there is abundant evidence that many gay, lesbian, and bisexual writers found a place for themselves in the front ranks of the Literary Left, it is unlikely that a single explanation can account for the motives of a group so diverse in other respects. Among the questions that need to be addressed by scholars is whether homosexuals were drawn to Communist and Trotskyist organizations because of, or in spite of, their sexual orientations. Along these same lines, the similarities and differences of the socially imposed secrecy about Communist and homosexual identity need to be studied.

Unfortunately, the absence of a substantial body of fiction, poetry, and criticism of the era of the 1930s through the 1950s that simultaneously and candidly addresses left-wing as well as gay, lesbian, and bisexual themes has been an obstacle to the development of an effective method of literary analysis. Most disconcerting is the appearance of unattractive homosexual characters in works such as those cited by Motley and Rollins. Scholars need to investigate the range of motivations for such depictions. It may turn out that some of these representations are coded in complex ways so as to subvert the stereotypes they appear to reproduce. Moreover, there may be places in the texts, not obvious in a first reading, that are the sites of additional, alternative, or coded dramatizations of sexual themes.

Today, there is a major revival of interest among scholars in the history and culture of the U.S. Left. So far, the focus has been on rank-and-file agency viewed through the categories of gender, race, and ethnicity. It is likely that new books, dissertations, and articles will soon appear that will also address the kinds of issues I have raised, as well as other new perspectives about gay, lesbian, and bisexual writers on the Left.

—*Alan Wald*

BIBLIOGRAPHY

Aaron, Daniel. *Writers on the Left: Episodes in American Literary Communism.* With a New Preface by Alan M. Wald. New York: Columbia University Press, 1992. ■ Baxandall, Rosalyn. "Elizabeth Gurley Flynn." *The American Radical.* Mary Jo Buhle et al., eds. New York: Routledge, 1994. 129–132. ■ Bergman, David. *Gaiety Transfigured: Gay Self-Representation in American Literature.* Madison: University of Wisconsin Press, 1991. ■ Cooper, Wayne F. *Claude McKay: Rebel Sojourner in the Harlem Renaissance.* Baton Rouge: Louisiana State University Press, 1987. ■ Donaldson, Scott. *John Cheever: A Biography.* New York: Random House, 1988. ■ Duggan, Lisa. "Audre Lorde." *The American Radical.* Mary Jo Buhle et al., eds. New York: Routledge, 1994. 353–359. ■ Fabre, Michel. *Black American Writers in France, 1840–1980.* Urbana: University of Illinois Press, 1991. ■ Faderman, Lillian. *Odd Girls and Twilight Lovers: A History of Lesbian Life in Twentieth-Century America.* New York: Columbia University Press, 1991. ■ Gordon, Eric A. *Mark the Music: The Life and Work of Mark Blitzstein.* New York: St. Martin's, 1989. ■ Hatch, James V. *Sorrow Is the Only Faithful One: The Life of Owen Dodson.* Urbana: University of Illinois Press, 1993. ■ Koch, Stephen. *Double Lives.* New York: Free Press, 1994. ■ Langer, Elinor. *Josephine Herbst: The Story She Could Never Tell.* Boston: Little, Brown, 1984. ■ Mangione, Jerre. *An Ethnic at Large.* New York: G.P. Putnam's Sons, 1978. ■ Norse, Harold. *Memoirs of a Bastard Angel.* New York: Morrow, 1989. ■ Rabinowitz, Paula. *Labor and Desire: Women's Revolutionary Fiction in Depression America.* Chapel Hill: University of North Carolina Press, 1991. ■ Sanford, John. *A Very Good Land to Fall With.* Santa Barbara, Calif.: Black Sparrow Press, 1987. ■ Timmons, Stuart. *The Trouble with Harry Hay.* Boston: Alyson, 1990. ■ Tucker, Martin. *Literary Exile in the Twentieth Century.* Westport, Conn.: Greenwood, 1991. ■ Wald, Alan M. *The Revolutionary Imagination: The Poetry and Politics of John Wheelwright and Sherry Mangan.* Chapel Hill: University of North Carolina Press, 1983.

Anzaldúa, Gloria
(b. 1942)

Gloria Anzaldúa was born and raised in a South Texas ranching environment. She pursued her formal education at Pan American University, the University of Texas, and the University of California, Santa Cruz. She currently resides in Santa Cruz, where she works on the editorial boards of journals and is a much-sought-after teacher and public speaker as well as a prolific writer.

In 1981, Persephone Press published the first edition of *This Bridge Called My Back: Writings by Radical Women of Color,* edited by Anzaldúa and CHERRÍE MORAGA. *This Bridge* was soon recognized as a landmark event in feminist publishing. It was the first articulation in a collective, systematic, and widely publicized form of the voices of feminists of color in the United States and their critiques of the racism and classism that had characterized much canonized feminist thinking and writing of the 1970s and 1980s. A no less remarkable characteristic of *This Bridge* was its full engagement with lesbian concerns and voices, and the non-tokenistic presence of lesbian writers in all sections of the book. Both of the volume's editors identify as lesbians as well as Chicanas.

Almost ten years after the first publication of *This Bridge,* Anzaldúa edited a follow-up collection, *Making Face, Making Soul/Haciendo Caras: Creative and Critical Perspectives by Women of Color* (1990). This anthology, while continuing the critiques and proclamations of *This Bridge,* also takes some of that work as given in order to focus instead on the complexity of identifications, self-identifications, and differences between and among women of color.

Anzaldúa's own writing includes numerous published short stories, poems, talks, essays, and texts that combine and confound these genre categories, including the book *Borderlands/La Frontera: The New Mestiza* (1987). Her work insistently refuses to prioritize any one component of her identity. This no doubt accounts for the relative marginalization of Anzaldúa's work, even today. Although Anzaldúa has won literary awards and is increasingly taught in Women's Studies classes, she continues to remain absent from the pages—and even the indexes—of most books of Chicano and Chicana criticism and from the syllabi of fashionable seminars in Lesbian and Gay Studies and Queer Theory in academic institutions (even though she used the term *queer* in *Borderlands/La Frontera* several years before it regained its current popularity in academic and activist circles).

But it is precisely Anzaldúa's multiple and enigmatic self-positioning and social relegation in and outside identities, canons, and institutions that offer the greatest challenge to queer theorists and activists, and to critics of lesbian and gay literatures. She writes of the borderlands between the United States and Mexico, between and within cultures, genders, genres, languages, and the self,

> The prohibited and forbidden are its inhabitants. *Los atravesados* live here: the squint-eyed, the perverse, the queer, the troublesome, the mongrel, the mulatto, the half-breed, the half dead; in short, those who cross over, pass over, or go through the confines of the "normal."

Anzaldúa contests liberal pluralist delineations of lesbian and gay subjectivity merely in terms of identity or lifestyle, instead positing a politicized queerness that reclaims the revolutionary roots of gay liberation in its radical interconnectedness with all struggles against oppression. Her work demonstrates that if "queer" is not to become a category that normalizes middle-class white maleness, working-class queers, female queers, and queers of color must determine any queer agenda. (See also LATINA LESBIAN LITERATURE.)

—*Ian Barnard*

BIBLIOGRAPHY

Alarcón, Norma. "Chicana Feminism: In the Tracks of the 'Native Woman.'" *Cultural Studies* 4.3 (1990): 248–256. ■ Andrist, Debra D. "La Semiótica de la Chicana: La Escritura de Gloria Anzaldúa." *Mujer y Literatura Mexicana y Chicana: Culturas en Contacto,* 2. Aralia López González, Amelia Malagamba, and Elena Urrutia, eds. Tijuana: El Colegio de la Frontera Norte, 1990. 243–247. ■ Baldwin, Elizabeth. Interview with Anzaldúa. *Matrix* (May 1988): 1–33. ■ Freedman, Diane P. "Writing in the Borderlands: The Poetic Prose of Gloria Anzaldúa and Susan Griffin." *Constructing and Reconstructing Gender: The Links Among Communication, Language, and Gender.* Linda A. M. Perry, Lynn H. Turner, and Helen M. Sterk, eds. Albany: SUNY Press, 1992. 211–217. ■ Saldívar-Hull, Sonia. "Feminism on the Border: From Gender Politics to Geopolitics." *Criticism in the Borderlands: Studies in Chicano Literature, Culture, and Ideology.* Héctor Calderón and José David Saldívar, eds. Durham: Duke University Press, 1991. 203–220. ■ Smith, Sidonie. "The Autobiographical Manifesto: Identities, Temporalities, Politics." *Autobiography and Questions of Gender.* Shirley Neuman, ed. London: Frank Cass, 1991. 186–212. ■ Torres, Héctor A. "Gloria Anzaldúa." *Dictionary of Literary Biography, Volume 122: Chicano Writers.* 2nd series. Francisco A. Lomelí and Carl R. Shipley, eds. Detroit: Brucolli-Gale, 1992. 8–17.

Arenas, Reinaldo
(1943–1990)

Born on July 16, 1943, in the rural poverty of the Cuban countryside, Arenas's childhood can only be described as wretched and harsh. One of his first memories was of eating dirt because of a scarcity of food. As an idealistic teenager, he joined the revolutionary forces of Fidel Castro and fought against the dictatorial government of Fulgencio Batista. Two years after the triumph of the Revolution, he moved to Havana where his literary career officially began. In 1967, at the age of twenty-two, he published his first novel, *Celestino antes del alba* (*Singing from the Well*), the story of a child, persecuted by his family as well as by the impoverished conditions of his rural existence, who must rely on his imagination to survive. Shortly after its publication in a limited print run of 2,000 copies, Arenas's novel, a free-flowing narrative that undermines the realistic mode of writing, fell out of favor with the revolutionary cultural policymakers who demanded a literature that clearly contributed to a revolutionary consciousness.

In the mid-1960s, when the Castro regime openly persecuted homosexuals, Arenas turned away from the Revolution. His dissatisfaction with the government deepened when his writings—transgressive, unconventional, and supportive of the individual's right to self-expression—were declared "antirevolutionary" and censored. Soon afterward, Arenas was no longer permitted to publish on the island. Defiant, he secretly sent his manuscripts abroad, where they were immediately published, an act that infuriated the regime, which on various occasions confiscated and destroyed his work and ultimately branded him a nonperson in Cuba. While his novels were being read and praised in Europe and Latin America for their intelligence and wit, Arenas was reduced to living a somewhat picaresque life in Havana, moving constantly and working at odd jobs simply to survive. Finally in 1980, as a result of a bureaucratic blunder, he managed to escape from the island through the Mariel exodus.

After his arrival in the United States, Arenas settled in New York City. Having been censored in Cuba for so long, the author, as if intoxicated with his newly found freedom, began to write prodigiously: novels, short stories, poetry, dramatic pieces, essays, newspaper articles. For him, writing was both a liberating act of self-expression and an act of fury in which he challenged, undermined, and subverted all types of ideological dogmatism, all forms of absolute "truths."

On December 7, 1990, suffering from AIDS and too sick to continue writing, Arenas committed suicide. In a moving farewell letter sent to the Miami Spanish newspaper *Diario las Américas,* the writer made it quite clear that his decision to take his life should not be interpreted or construed as defeat. "My message is not a message of failure," he declared, "but rather one of struggle and hope. Cuba will be free, I already am." These final words reveal the self-determination and indomitable spirit of this gifted writer and political activist.

Like many Latin American writers who find it impossible to separate their literary careers from the sociopolitical realities of their countries, Arenas was an outspoken critic of Fidel Castro's regime. But Arenas's criticism of the Cuban Revolution was much more than an attack on communism; it was an angry cry against a system under which he, like many others, had been persecuted for being homosexual.

Although there are implicit and explicit homosexual characters, episodes, and scenes in practically every text that Arenas wrote, it is in *Otra vez el mar* (*Farewell to the Sea*, 1982), *Arturo, la estrella más brillante* ("The Brightest Star," 1984), *Viaje a La Habana* (*Trip to Havana*, 1990), *El color del verano* (*The Color of Summer*, 1991), and *Antes que anochezca* (*Before Night Falls*, 1992), the author's autobiography, where the reader finds the greatest explicitness in the depiction of gay characters and homosexual desire. Arenas's representation of homosexuality cannot be considered "positive" in the way that much of contemporary Anglo-American gay literature strives to celebrate homosexual identity and represent ideal gay relationships based on mutual respect and equality. Nonetheless, if one carefully examines Arenas's entire *oeuvre,* one finds an argumentative center that persistently resurfaces, supporting the rights of all individuals, regardless of their sexual orientation.

"The Brightest Star," a fictitious account of one man's experience in the notorious forced labor camps in which homosexuals were interned in the mid-1960s, is of particular interest. The story is a moving defense of the individual's right to dream, to rise above the oppression that threatens his or her experience. As a study of oppression, "The Brightest Star" is a companion piece to Arenas's earlier *La Vieja Rosa* (1980), with which it has been published in translation as *Old Rosa: A Novel in Two Stories.* Like his work generally, these two stories defend the individual's imaginative capabilities and right to self-expression in a world beset by ignorance, intolerance, and persecution.

The last text Arenas wrote before his death was *Antes que anochezca* (*Before Night Falls*), his autobiography. Central to this memoir is the sexual and political repression the author had to endure in Cuba. Far from being a traditional autobiography, *Antes que anochezca* utilizes a combination of historical facts and delirious and exaggerated fiction. Curiously, this mixing of fact and fiction in no way diminishes the strength of the testimony. Arenas does not limit himself to simply declaring his homosexuality, but rather graphically presents his sexual escapades, going beyond what many readers would consider "good taste." Arenas was quite aware of the hypocrisy and homophobia of his Hispanic audience, but rather than making concessions, allowing himself to be closeted by bigotry disguised as "good taste," he expressed his experiences honestly, to the point of possibly alienating certain readers. In 1992 in his review of the autobiography, Mario Vargas Llosa observed: "This is one of the most moving testimonies that has ever been written in our language about oppression and rebellion, but few will dare to acknowledge this fact since the book, although one reads it with an uncontrollable appetite, has the perverse power of leaving its readers uncomfortable" (my translation).

"Autoepitafio" ("Self-Epitaph"), one of the writer's last poems, splendidly captures Arenas's spirit of irreverence, pathos, and irony. The poetic voice, speaking in the third person, recounts the poet's instructions of what to do with his body after death: "He arranged for his ashes to be scattered into the sea / where they would flow forever. / Not having given up his habit of dreaming, / he awaits a young man to dive into his waters" (*Voluntad de vivir manifestán-dose*, my translation).

—Francisco Soto

BIBLIOGRAPHY

Béjar, Eduardo C. *La textualidad de Reinaldo Arenas*. Madrid: Editorial Playor, 1987. ■ Foster, David William. "Critical Monographs, Dissertations, and Critical Essays about Reinaldo Arenas." *Cuban Literature: A Research Guide*. New York: Garland Publishing, 1985: 89–91. ■ ———. *Gay and Lesbian Themes in Latin American Literature*. Austin: University of Texas Press, 1991: 66–72. ■ Hernández-Miyares, Julio, and Perla Rozencvaig, eds. *Reinaldo Arenas: alucinaciones, fantasía y realidad*. Glenview, Ill.: Scott, Foresman, 1990. ■ Rozencvaig, Perla. *Reinaldo Arenas: narrativa de transgresión*. México: Editorial Oasis, 1986. ■ Schwartz, Kessel. "Homosexuality and the Fiction of Reinaldo Arenas." *Journal of Evolutionary Psychology* 5, no. 1–2 (March 1984): 12–20. ■ Soto, Francisco. "*Celestino antes del alba*: escritura subversiva/sexualidad transgresiva." *Revista Iberoamericana* 57, no. 154 (enero–marzo 1991): 345–354.———. *Conversación con Reinaldo Arenas*. Madrid: Editorial Betania, 1990. ■ ———. "Reinaldo Arenas's Literary Legacy." *Christopher Street Magazine* 156 (May 1991): 12–16. ■ ———. *Reinaldo Arenas: The Pentagonía*. Gainesville: University Press of Florida, 1994. ■ Valero, Roberto. *El desamparado humor de Reinaldo Arenas*. North Miami: Hallmark, 1991. ■ Vargas Llosa, Mario. "Pájaro tropical." *El País*, lunes 15 de junio de 1992: 15–16.

Ashbery, John
(*b.* 1927)

John Ashbery was born in 1927 near Rochester, New York. He is the author of more than fifteen books of poems, beginning with *Turandot and Other Poems* in 1953, and is considered one of the leading contemporary American poets. His works range in length from two-line poems and haiku to the book-length *Flow Chart* (1991).

Ashbery is a disconcerting poet to read. He produces poems that look like poems, yet do not live up to our expectations of poems and how they create meaning. His poems follow the action of his mind and so always are in danger of being solipsistic, yet they are also clearly engaged in a discourse with the reader.

Ashbery is often referred to as a philosophical poet. He is clearly concerned with the nature of language and its connection to thought. He is also concerned more specifically with the nature of poetry and its boundaries in the second half of the twentieth century, as well as with the relationship between poet and reader.

Although Ashbery's poems often have the feel of autobiography, he does not include his own life in his poetry in a recognizable way. His claim to being a gay poet depends more on his friendship with FRANK O'HARA and his inclusion in O'Hara's poems than it does on anything in his own writing. For example, Ashbery appears as a character in O'Hara's "At the Old Place," under the names "Ashes," "J.A.," and "John." In a memorable section of this poem celebrating a seedy gay bar, O'Hara dances with Ashbery: "Wrapped in Ashes' arms I glide. / (It's heaven!)."

The critic and poet RICHARD HOWARD makes a distinction between "homosexual writers" and "writers who are homosexual." Although most Ashbery criticism places him in the latter category, ignoring questions of sexual preference either in his life or the poems, there have been a few attempts to read Ashbery as a gay poet. One approach is to try to assign a specific biographical meaning to Ashbery's fluid self(?)-descriptions. Helen Vendler has identified a passage in *Flow Chart* as referring to Ashbery's adolescent difficulties with being gay, but this reading, like all readings of Ashbery, can be only probably, not certainly, true. Another approach is to use psychoanalytic tools to discover the meaning beneath the surface of the text. For example, David Bergman, in a Freudian reading of Ashbery, has seen "egolessness" as a sign of homosexual writing in general and of Ashbery's in particular.

Since Ashbery intends to frustrate all labeling projects, in making our estimate of him as a gay poet we come up against our own understanding of what we expect from a gay poet. Despite the lack of explicit gay content, his work shares concerns with other late twentieth-century gay writing. Ashbery probes the nature of identity, how a person constructs his own identity and that of others, and the degree to which that identity depends on the culture around us. He also adopts an attitude similar to CAMP. His ironic mocking of the culture he lives in betrays his passion for that culture.

—*Terrence Johnson*

BIBLIOGRAPHY

Berger, Charles. "The Vision in the Form of a Task." *Beyond Amazement: New Essays on John Ashbery.* David Lehman, ed. Ithaca, N.Y.: Cornell University Press, 1980. 163–208. ■ Bergman, David. *Gaiety Transfigured: Gay Self-Representation in American Literature.* Madison: University of Wisconsin Press, 1991. ■ Bloom, Harold, ed. *Modern Critical Views: John Ashbery.* New York: Chelsea House, 1985. ■ Howard, Richard. *Alone with America: Essays on the Art of Poetry in the United States Since 1950.* New York: Atheneum, 1980. ■ Vendler, Helen. "A Steely Glitter Chasing Shadows." *The New Yorker* (August 3, 1992): 73–76.

Asian American Literature

The names "Asian" and "Pacific (Islander)" are often yoked together to emphasize the shared concerns of Asians, Asian Americans, and Pacific Islanders. Asian and Asian American groups have been comparatively more visible in recent mainstream media than Pacific Islanders, whose colonial histories remain relatively obscure. This entry will focus on Asian American artists, many of whom choose to name themselves "Asian/Pacific gays and lesbians."

Asian/Pacific gays and lesbians share problems of invisibility specific to histories fraught with Orientalist stereotypes. To compound this situation, racialized and gendered stereotypes pervasive in heterosexual communities return to disfigure representations of Asian/Pacific homosexualities. For Asian/Pacific gays, Hollywood images of asexual Charlie Chans and emasculated Fu Manchus recirculate within gay communities where Asian/Pacific men find themselves repositioned as Cio-Cio-San from Puccini's *Madama Butterfly.* Similarly, Asian/Pacific women's bodies are disfigured by racist constructions of "slanted cunts," while stereotypes of Suzy Wong and geisha girls configure the Asian/Pacific lesbian as a submissive, exotic object of lesbian desire or as solely an object of male desire and thus irrevocably heterosexual. Although these problems of representation demand an interrogation of desires based on racial stereotypes, what is urgently needed is the recognition that Asian/Pacific gays and lesbians voice richly multiple and diverse identities.

"I am an Oriental," explains a disrobed Song to the investigating judge in David Henry Hwang's *M. Butterfly,* "[a]nd being an Oriental, I could never be completely a man." Hwang's 1988 Tony Award-winning drama explores one of the greatest concerns for gay Asian/Pacific artists: the pervasive racialized stereotype of the Asian/Pacific man as an emasculated sissy, what writer Frank Chin has broadly labeled the "Charlie Chan Sex Syndrome." Gay filmmaker and critic Richard Fung further adds that "the Asian man is defined by a striking absence down there. And if Asian men have no sexuality, how can we have homosexuality?" Yet homosexuality certainly persists within the field of Asian American literature, significantly informing many of its anxieties over issues of masculinity and paternity.

Two of the earliest Asian American gay-themed stories can be found in the groundbreaking Asian American anthologies *Aiiieeeee!* (1974) and *The Big Aiiieeeee!* (1991), respectively. Wallace Lin's (a.k.a. Russell Leong) "Rough Notes for Mantos" (1974) is about a racially and sexually displaced Asian American man who copes with both the loss of his would-be lover and his inability to accept the heterosexual imperatives of his demanding father. Lonny Kaneko's "The Shoyu Kid" (1976) recounts the molestation of a young Japanese American boy by a white soldier in a World War II internment camp. Highlighting the intersection of racism and homosexuality, Kaneko's story calls for a revisioning of American history and a reclaiming of sexual autonomy.

In the tide of concerted gay activism around AIDS, the late 1980s and early 1990s have witnessed an increased representation of Asian/Pacific gays in mainstream publications by well-known but straight-identified writers such as Jessica Hagedorn and David Wong Louie. Concomitantly, there has also been a proliferation of works by queer Asian/Pacific artists who explicitly address their own concerns and desires, while contesting the absence of their images within the commercial and political sectors of mainstream gay artistic circles. Artists such as Norman Wong, Han Ong, and Dwight Okita have written and produced notable stories, dramas, and poetry. For instance, Wong's eponymous story from his collection *Cultural Revolution* (forthcoming) narrates the dilemmas of a young Chinese American man who accompanies his father on a visit to their ancestral village in China. The story probes issues of cultural and sexual alienation as the protagonist becomes sexually involved with a white history student who seems to know more about China than he does.

Contemporary issues raised by Asian/Pacific gay artists in *The Asian Pacific American (APA) Journal*'s special issue "Witness Aloud: Lesbian, Gay and Bisexual Asian/Pacific American Writings" (Spring/Summer 1993) and the "Smut" issue of *The Lavender Godzilla* (Fall 1992) include the negotiation and reconciliation of a gay identity within racialized communities often marked by cultural homophobia and gay communities often tainted by overt racism. Lawrence Chua's "Love in a Cold Climate" plays out the ambivalences of internalized homophobia and the difficulty of naming gay love. Martin F. Manalansan's "Your Cio-Cio-San" explores the controversial topics of cross-racial dating and "Rice Queens"—gay white males attracted to Asians through their racist fantasies of a submissive and feminized gay Asian "bottom." Another related problem raised by Quentin Lee's "The Sailor & the Thai Boys" is the often radical class disparities between Rice Queens and their Asian/Pacific lovers. These inequities introduce the specter of prostitution, literal and figurative. Looking at class relations from a different perspective, John Silva's "The Romantic Banquero" examines economic and sexual privilege mapped along international lines between a boatman and a Filipino expatriate vacationing in the Philippines. An additional form of domination is revealed by John Albert Manzon's "Willi": domestic violence.

The gay community has largely considered it inconceivable for Asian/Pacific men—all stereotyped as "bottoms"—to date one another. Nevertheless, a current debate fueled by works such as Justin Chin's "Bite" revolves around the topic of "Sticky Rice," gay Asian/Pacific men who do date one another. This situation has created a dialogue around the problems of cross-racial dating *between* gays from different Asian/Pacific ethnic groups as well as dating between immigrant and American-born Asian/Pacific gays.

The devastating effects of AIDS has demanded a personal as well as a collective response from the gay Asian/Pacific community. Dwight Okita's poem "Where the Boys Were," in his collection *Crossing with the Light* (1992), examines this issue with striking visceral beauty: "When they look at my life / like a charcoal sketch / ripped from a pad, tell them / I wasn't done. / That there was color to be added — / oranges, pinks, greys." In addition, *Vox Angelica* (1992), a collection of poetry by Timothy Liu, also ponders the exigencies of AIDS, while quilting together other concerns such as pornography and political agency. Several performance art pieces have been produced not only to educate but also to instill a sense of responsibility and empowerment within the Asian/Pacific community regarding issues around HIV. For example, the "Love Like This Theatre" of San Francisco's Asian AIDS Project recently toured the United States and Asia with their performance of director Vince Sales's *Dates,* a series of tableaus organized around three gay Asian friends grappling with issues of intimacy in the face of AIDS.

Like their gay counterparts, Asian/Pacific lesbians have been writing and speaking long before their narratives were published. Living at the intersections of often mutually exclusive heterosexual Asian American communities and European American feminist and lesbian communities, however, has frequently put the Asian/Pacific lesbian in the position of having to "prove" she is possible. When white lesbians look at her in a bar, Alice Hom wonders, "Maybe they are surprised to see me because Asian/Pacific women stereotypes are so ingrained in the heterosexual context that Asian lesbians do not even come to mind." Nevertheless, Asian/Pacific lesbians contest these erasures of their sexual identities by representing their lesbian desires.

"I, splinter trees / with the roar / of my voice," writes Willyce Kim in *Under the Rolling Sky* (1976), her third book of poetry. Although lesbian-themed works, such as Margaret Chinen's play *All, All Alone* (1947), have been published since the 1940s, Kim is recognized as the first Asian/Pacific lesbian to publish a collection of poetry, *Curtains of Light* (1971); she is also the first to publish a novel, *Dancer Dawkins and the California Kid* (1985). Challenging the racialized, gendered, and sexualized conventions of the Western, Kim introduces new terms for a Korean American lesbian Western. In "Poem for Zahava," Kim writes, "we could: / roll five joints with either hand, / rescue ten women with a smile, / and kick the shins out of any man."

Other early writers, Barbara Noda, Kitty Tsui, Merle Woo, and Canyon Sam wrote to revise dominant versions of history. For instance, in *Strawberries* (1979), Noda limns one critical strategy in Asian/Pacific lesbian narratives: to figure forth her own Japanese American lesbian body through inscribing desire and personal history upon the mirror of her lover's body. Noda writes upon that body both the sweetness of its forbidden fruit and her father's bitterness as a seasonal fruit picker in the difficult years following internment during World War II. In a similar vein, Tsui re-envisions a myth of origins more specific to her than European genealogies tracing lesbian desire to SAPPHO. In her short story, "Why the Milky Way is Milky" (1982), republished in Irene Zahava's *Lesbian Love Stories,* Tsui writes a Chinese lesbian myth of origins that revises the heterosexual Chinese legend of Spinning Girl and Shepherd Boy. For Woo, writing history in *Yellow Woman Speaks* (1986) engages her own particular struggles for minority rights in her antidiscrimination suit against the University of California, Berkeley in 1982. Looking back on the history behind Asian/Pacific lesbian communities, Sam contrasts the collective Asian/Pacific lesbian activism of the 1980s with the isolation and loneliness she felt in the 1970s. Published in Zahava's *Lesbian Love Stories,* "Sapphire" (1989) recalls her momentous first meeting with another Asian/Pacific lesbian.

Concerns over the necessity of forming coalitions converged in the first Asian/Pacific lesbian anthology, *Between the Lines: An Anthology by Pacific/Asian Lesbians of Santa Cruz, California* (1987). Writings by A. Kaweah Lemeshewsky, Alison Kim, Anu, and Cristy Chung chart the difficulties of forging alliances across racial and ethnic differences, geographical boundaries, and divisions between lesbian, bisexual, and straight women. The anthology also features excerpts from Alison Kim's compilation of the earliest Asian/Pacific lesbian bibliography. The call for international coalitions has, in turn, emphasized the importance of alliances between lesbians of color. Chea Villanueva's epistolary novels *Girlfriends* (1987) and

Chinagirls (1991) follow street-smart African American, Korean American, Chinese American, Filipina American, and racially mixed lesbians whose bonds see them through both dangerous and raunchy escapades.

Most recently, *The APA Journal*'s "Witness Aloud" issue (Spring/Summer 1993) stitches together an impressive array of Asian/Pacific lesbian voices. The title of Indigo Chih-Lien Som's poem "Just once before I die I want someone to make love to me in Cantonese" calls for the need to name desires with a language of one's own. Similarly, Donna Tanigawa reclaims Hawaii's multiracial pidgin in "Pau Trying Fo' Be Like One Haole Dyke" in order to contest the "standards" set by English and the white lesbian body. As Anu's poem "Silence of Home" illustrates, however, the Indian voices associated with home bring pain as well as pleasure. In other works, words take on different meanings when situated against the body of a lover. Meditating on the meaning of "Passion," Elsa E'der writes of conflicting desires for a lover who has survived sexual abuse. Sharing similar concerns with Asian/Pacific gays, Margaret Mihee Choe's "*Chamwe* at the Club" confronts the internalized racism that makes it difficult for Asian/Pacific lesbians to date one another.

On both the East and West coasts, Asian/Pacific gay and lesbian organizations make visible their constituencies through newsletters featuring poetry, short stories, and autobiographical narratives. San Francisco's Gay Asian Pacific Alliance (GAPA) started publishing the *The Lavender Godzilla* in 1987, a monthly newsletter producing literary supplements three times a year. In New York, the Asian Lesbians of the East Coast (ALOEC) began publishing the *ALOEC Newsletter* in 1984, and a year later, in San Francisco, the Asian Pacifica Sisters (APS) put out its first newsletter, *Phoenix Rising*. These newsletters provide a forum for Asian/Pacific gays and lesbians to discuss issues close to home: domestic violence, AIDS in their communities, safe sex, possibilities for coalition, the politics of publishing.

Gay and lesbian Asian/Pacific artistic creativity blossoms in video and film, media more accessible to marginalized peoples, perhaps, than mainstream commercial publishing. Both the 1993 New York and San Francisco Gay and Lesbian Film Festivals featured videos by queer Asian/Pacific artists Pablo Bautista, Quentin Lee, and Ming-Yuen S. Ma. In addition, films by Greg Araki (*The Living End*) and Rico Martinez (*Glamazon*) recently premiered with notable acclaim. Many of these works are available on videotape from the National Asian American Telecommunications Association (NAATA), which also distributes lesbian films, including Ann Moriyasu's *Issei Wahine* and Eileen Lee and Marilyn Abbink's *Women of Gold*.

Productions by these talented artists, as well as many others, attest to the ways Asian/Pacific gays and lesbians will continue to gain recognition for their different communities. In 1994, two additional collections brought together gay and lesbian writers: Jessica Hagedorn's *Charlie Chan is Dead: An Anthology of Contemporary Asian American Fiction* hosts a large gay and lesbian presence, and *Amerasia Journal* published a critical and literary issue entitled "New Dimensions, New Desires."

As Kitty Tsui reminds us in her poem "It's in the Name," we are "each with a name / each with a face / blood, bone, breath."

—*David L. Eng and Candace Fujikane*

BIBLIOGRAPHY

Asian Lesbians of the East Coast. ALOEC Newsletter. P.O. Box 850, New York, NY 10002. ■ Asian Pacifica Sisters (APS). *Phoenix Rising.* P.O. Box 170596, San Francisco, CA 94117. ■ Chin, Curtis, Gayatri Gopinath, Joo-Hyun Kang, and Alvin Realuyo, eds. *Witness Aloud: Lesbian, Gay and Bisexual Asian/Pacific American Writings. The Asian/Pacific American Journal* 2:1 (Spring/Summer 1993). ■ Chinen, Margaret. *All, All Alone. College Plays.* Honolulu: University of Hawaii Department of English, 1947–1948. ■ Chung, C., A. Kim, and A. K. Lemeshewsky, eds. *Between the Lines: An Anthology by Pacific/Asian Lesbians of Santa Cruz, California.* Santa Cruz, Calif.: Dancing Bird Press, 1987. ■ Fung, Richard. "Looking for My Penis: The Eroticized Asian in Gay Video Porn." *How Do I Look? Queer Film and Video.* Bad Object Choices, ed. Seattle: Bay Press, 1991. ■ Gay Asian Pacific Alliance (GAPA). *Lavender Godzilla Newsletter.* P.O. Box 421884, San Francisco, CA 94142-1884. ■ Hagedorn, Jessica, ed. *Charlie Chan is Dead: An Anthology of Contemporary Asian American Fiction.* New York: Penguin, 1994. ■ Hagedorn, Jessica. *Danger and Beauty.* New York: Penguin, 1993. ■ Hom, Alice. "In the Mind of An/Other." *Amerasia Journal* 17:2 (1991): 51–54. ■ Hwang, David Henry. *M. Butterfly.* New York: Plume, 1988. ■ Kaneko, Lonny. "The Shoyu Kid." *The Big Aiiieeee! An Anthology of Chinese American and Japanese American Literature.* Jeffery Paul Chan, Frank Chin, Lawson Inada, and Shawn Wong, eds. New York: Meridian, 1991. ■ Kim, Willyce. *Curtains of Light.* Self-published, 1971. ■ ———. *Dancer Dawkins and the California Kid.* Boston: Alyson, 1985. ■ ———. *Dead Heat.* Boston: Alyson, 1988. ■ ———. *Eating Artichokes.* Oakland: Women's Press Collective, 1972. ■ ———. *Under the Rolling Sky.* N.p.: Maud Gonne Press, 1976. ■ Leong, Russell. *In the Country of Dreams and Dust.* Albuquerque, N.Mex.: West End Press, 1993. ■ Leong, Russell, ed. "New Dimensions, New Desires." Special queer issue of the *Amerasia Journal* 20:1 (Spring 1994). ■ Lim, Paul Stephen. *Homerica: A Trilogy on Sexual Liberation.* Louisville, Ky.: Aran Press, 1985. ■ Lin, Wallace (a.k.a. Russell Leong). "Rough Notes for Mantos." *Aiiieeeee! An Anthology of Asian American Writers.* Jeffery Paul Chan, Frank Chin, Lawson Fusao Inada, and Shawn Wong, eds. New York: Anchor, 1974. ■ Liu, Timothy. *Vox Angelica.* Cambridge, Mass.: alicejamesbooks, 1992. ■ Louie, David Wong. "Pangs of Love." *Pangs of Love.* New York: Knopf, 1991. ■ National Asian American Telecommunications Association (NAATA). 346 Ninth Street, Second Floor, San Francisco, CA 94103. ■ Noda, Barbara. *Strawberries.* Berkeley: Shameless Hussy Press, 1979. ■ Okita, Dwight. *Crossing with the Light.* Chicago: Tia Chucha Press, 1992. ■ Tsui, Kitty. *Words of a Woman Who Breathes Fire.* San Francisco: Spinsters, 1983. ■ Villanueva, Chea. *Chinagirls.* N.p.: Lezzies on the Move Productions, 1991. ■ ———. *Girlfriends.* New York: Outlaw Press, 1987. ■ Wong, Norman. *Cultural Revolution.* New York: Persea Press, 1994. ■ Woo, Merle. *Yellow Woman Speaks.* Seattle: Radical Women Publications, 1986. ■ Zahava, Irene, ed. *Lesbian Love Stories.* Freedom, Calif.: Crossing Press, 1989.

§ *Auden, W. H.*
(1907–1973)

Described by Edward Mendelson as "the most inclusive poet of the twentieth century, its most technically skilled, and its most truthful," Auden is the first major poet to incorporate modern psychological insights and paradigms as a natural element of his work and thought. The foremost religious poet of his age, the most variously learned, and the one most preoccupied with existentialism, Auden is also an important love poet. Although particularly concerned with the relationship of Eros and Agape and characteristically practicing a "poetry of reticence," Auden celebrates erotic love as a significant element in his geography of the heart.

Born into an upper-middle-class professional family in York in 1907 and educated at Christ Church College, Oxford, from which he received his B.A. in 1928, Wystan Hugh Auden was the third son of a physician and a nurse, from whom he imbibed scientific, religious, and musical interests and a love of the Norse sagas. Following his graduation, he spent a year in Berlin, where he enjoyed the city's homosexual demimonde and absorbed German culture. He returned to teach in public schools in Scotland and England from 1930 to 1935. In 1938, he married Erika Mann, daughter of the German novelist THOMAS MANN, in order to enable her to obtain a British visa and escape Nazi Germany; the marriage was not consummated. In January 1939, disillusioned with the left-wing politics they had embraced, Auden and his friend and frequent collaborator, CHRISTO-

PHER ISHERWOOD, emigrated to the United States. Settling in New York City, Auden soon fell in love with a precocious eighteen-year-old from Brooklyn, Chester Kallman, with whom he maintained a relationship for the rest of his life, sharing apartments in New York and, later, summer residences in first Ischia and then Austria. Auden died in Vienna on September 29, 1973.

Auden dominated the British literary scene of the 1930s, quickly emerging as the leading voice of his generation. With the publication of *The Orators* (1932) and the enlarged edition of *Poems* (1933), Auden became, by his mid-twenties, firmly established as an important literary presence, the leader of the "Auden Gang" that included Isherwood, STEPHEN SPENDER, C. Day Lewis, and Louis MacNeice. Auden's early poetry breathed an air of revolutionary freshness. In language at once exotic and earthy, alternately banal and elegant, colloquial yet faintly archaic, Auden's verse diagnosed psychic disturbances with an extraordinary resonance. Although most of his early poems have their origins in his personal anxieties, especially those related to his homosexuality and his search for psychic healing, they seemed to voice the fears and uncertainties of his entire generation.

Auden may have initially regarded his gayness as a psychic wound, but he came to see it as a liberating force. In the prose poem "Letter to a Wound" (1932), he writes,

> Thanks to you, I have come to see a profound significance in relations I never dreamt of considering before, an old lady's affection for a small dog, the Waterhouses and their retriever, the curious bond between Offal and Snig, the partners in the hardware shop on the front. Even the close-ups in the films no longer disgust nor amuse me. On the contrary, they sometimes make me cry; knowing you has made me understand.

Auden's acceptance of his gayness thus leads him to new insight into the universal impulse to love and enlarges his understanding of all kinds of relationships. At the same time, however, Auden is acutely aware of the limitations of eroticism. His earliest love poems complain of his lack of sexual success, but his poems from the later 1930s such as "May with its light behaving" lament an emotional isolation that accompanies physical intimacy. In the poem beginning "Easily, my dear, you move," erotic love and feverish political activity are both depicted as expressions of vanity and the desire for power. Auden finally reaches the conclusion that Eros and Agape are interdependent.

Auden's recognition of the interdependence of Eros and Agape is at the heart of perhaps the greatest love poem of the century, the grave and tender "Lullaby" (["Lay your sleeping head"] 1937), which moves so nimbly and with such grace among abstractions evoked so subtly that it may well be regarded as the premiere example of the poet's intellectual lyricism. The luminous moment of fulfillment that the poem celebrates is placed in a context of mutability and decay that poignantly underlines the fragility of a love endangered from within by guilt, promiscuity, and betrayal, and from without by the "pedantic boring cry" of homophobic "fashionable madmen."

Auden's marriage to Kallman was not to prove entirely happy (primarily due to Kallman's promiscuity), but it provided the poet with loving companionship and helped seal the permanence of his self-exile. Auden's first flush of passion for Kallman immediately inspired several poems of fulfilled erotic love, including "The Prophets," "Like a Vocation," "The Riddle," "Law Like Love," and "Heavy Date," in which he tells his lover, "I have / Found myself in you." Kallman introduced Auden to opera, an interest that would shape the curve of his career. The partners collaborated on several original libretti, including one for Stravinsky's *The Rake's Progress* (1951), and on translating others.

Auden movingly celebrates his relationship with Kallman in "The Common Life" (1965), which tellingly declares that "every home should be a fortress." Also among Auden's late poems is "Glad," a light but deeply felt account of his relationship with a male hustler, "for a decade now / My bed-visitor, / An unexpected blessing / In a lucky life." In "Since," a poem probably inspired by his relationship with Kallman, Auden suddenly remembers an August noon thirty years ago and "You as then you were." He juxtaposes the memory of his youthful love-making with an account of the failures of Eros and Agape in the world since then and finds sustenance in the memory: "round your image / there is no fog, and the Earth / can still astonish." In a remarkable conclusion that bravely faces the issue of aging with unsentimental wit, he concludes, "I at least can learn / to live with obesity / and a little fame." A stunning achievement, "Since" validates the vision of Eros as a life-sustaining experience that can compensate at least in part even for the inevitable failures of Agape.

Auden's homosexuality is also expressed throughout his canon in the camp wit that discerns defensive fun in serious fear, as in the limerick "The Aesthetic Point of View" (1960). Moreover, the humorous self-revelations of the "Shorts" (1960), the "Marginalia" (1969), or "Profile" (1969), as well as the bawdy verse—such as "A Day for a Lay"—circulated among friends, helped establish for Auden a persona that has been particularly influential on younger gay poets, such as JAMES MERRILL, RICHARD HOWARD, and Howard Moss. In Merrill's series of adventures with the Ouija board, for example, Auden is a ghostly presence, the embodiment of a homosexual artistic sensibility. (See also ENGLISH LITERATURE: TWENTIETH CENTURY.)

—*Claude J. Summers*

BIBLIOGRAPHY

Callan, Edward. *Auden: A Carnival of Intellect.* New York: Oxford University Press, 1983. ■ Carpenter, Humphrey. *W.H. Auden: A Biography.* London: Allen & Unwin, 1981. ■ Farnin, Dorothy J. *Auden in Love.* New York: Simon & Schuster, 1984. ■ Mendelson, Edward. *Early Auden.* New York: Viking, 1981. ■ Spender, Stephen, ed. *W.H. Auden: A Tribute.* New York: Macmillan, 1975. ■ Summers, Claude J. "American Auden." *Columbia History of American Poetry.* Jay Parini, ed. New York: Columbia University Press, 1993. ■ ———. "'And the Earth Can Still Astonish': W.H. Auden and the Landscape of Eros." *The Windless Orchard* 32 (1978): 27–36. ■ Wright, George T. *W.H. Auden.* Rev. ed. Boston: Twayne Publishers, 1981.

Augustine of Hippo
(354–430)

Augustine was born in Thagaste, Numidia (now Algeria), to a Romanized family of Berber origins. Much of his youth and early adulthood was dominated by his mother, Monica, a pious and spirited Christian. Having received a traditional literary education, he embarked on the career of a Roman rhetorician. At about nineteen, he was converted to the "love of wisdom" by reading Cicero's *Hortensius.* Henceforth the promotion of a career would be balanced by intellectual and spiritual pursuits. Being repelled by the Bible's apparent "barbarity," Augustine drifted into Manichaeism. After nine years' involvement with this religion, he became disillusioned with its truth-claims. He traveled to Rome and, after a brief liaison with academic skepticism, was appointed imperial rhetorician at Milan. There he was introduced to Bishop Ambrose, a man whose spiritual intensity was matched only by his political ability. Ambrose's allegorical method of interpretation largely reconciled Augustine to the Christian Scriptures. In addition, he became deeply influenced by the philosophy of Plotinus and Porphyry, and also began an attentive reading of St. Paul's letters. It was in this intellectual-religious context that Augustine committed himself to Christianity. Although he proposed to himself an ideal of the Christian life conceived in terms of retirement, prayer, and study, and even established a monastic community at Thagaste, in 391 Augustine was press-ganged into the priesthood at Hippo Regius on the North African coast. Within five years, he was made Bishop. His experience in pastoral ministry, as well as his conflicts with the Donatists, appear to have extinguished the humanism of his youth. His later writings are grimly pessimistic. Augustine's influence on the Western church has been incalculable, especially during the Middle Ages and the Reformation.

Augustine's condemnation of homosexuality should be evaluated within the larger context of his general hostility to all forms of nonprocreative sexuality, including heterosexual eroticism, which he finds almost as, if not equally, reprehensible. "Passive" homosexuality receives special censure on misogynistic grounds: Men should not degrade their bodies by using them as women do. He rarely, if ever, conceives of natural libido in a favorable sense. In his youth, Augustine may have shared the easy bisexuality common in the ancient Mediterranean, as is suggested in *Confessions* 3.1. Again, as was common in his culture, his same-sex friendships appear to have played a more important role in his emotional and personal life than his relationships with women, except his mother. He denied the heterosexual companionate marriage, arguing that, if marriage were intended for companionship, men would marry other men. Augustine's lamentation for the death of an unnamed friend (*Confessions* 4:4–6) is among the most moving examples of this sort of writing to be found in antiquity. Although it is debatable to what extent, if any, these passionate friendships were homoerotic, they express a sensibility that today is probably to be found, at least in Western industrial societies, only among gay men.

—*Brad Walton*

BIBLIOGRAPHY

Boswell, John. *Christianity, Social Tolerance, and Homosexuality.* Chicago: University of Chicago Press, 1980. ■ Brown, Peter. *Augustine of Hippo.* London: Faber and Faber, 1967. ■ Chadwick, Henry. *Augustine.* Oxford: Oxford University Press, 1986.

Australian and New Zealand Literatures

Until the late twentieth century, homosexuality was forbidden throughout the Pacific colonies of Britain. Nonetheless, the Australian penal colonies and the whaling and sealing crews around New Zealand's shores encouraged the practice, as did the exclusive "public" (that is, private) school, the army, the university sports team, and other nation-building institutions within which homosexuality could have a fugitive existence. A discreet literature used these contexts to tell stories in which homosexuality occupied subtextual levels. Although the desires they treated could only be suggested, the stories may have somewhat reassured those who could identify the impulses they recorded, while readers who wished to could ignore any sexual resonance.

Some Australian novels now have the status of homosexual classics. Kenneth "Seaforth" Mackenzie's *The Young Desire It* (1937) is a public school story. Mr. Penworth, a teacher fresh from Oxford, becomes infatuated with the adolescent Charles and attempts to seduce him. Charles responds to Penworth's kind attentions but draws away as he realizes what Penworth really wants of him. He falls in love with a girl he meets near his mother's farm and, faced with a choice, rejects Penworth for Margaret. This is a significant novel for the way it reveals gaps between sex and gender. Within the larger society, Penworth is masculine in gender as well as male in sex, adding the schoolmaster's authority to his influence over Charles; however, his Englishness, youthfulness, and profession of the Classics modify this masculinity. Charles, on the other hand, feminized by masters and students as a "pretty" boy, falls in love with a female and brings gender in line with sex. It seems anachronistic, given the explicitness of scenes between Penworth and Charles, that *The Young Desire It* won an Australian award, particularly since Mackenzie treats Penworth with sympathy. Perhaps readers, well aware of the homoeroticism endemic in elite schools, applauded Charles's unequivocal choice of Margaret over Penworth.

Besides schoolyard and institutional dormitory, the army is a milieu that has permitted limited expression of homosexual bonds within its homosocial society. Randolph Stow's *The Merry-Go-Round in the Sea* (1965) testifies to this. Rick Maplestead, blond inheritor of wealthy grazier blood, is the potential homosexual of this novel. Leaving to fight in Southeast Asia in 1941, he seems "normal": handsome, physically admirable, brave. But through the eyes of his young cousin Rob, who has worshipped him, the reader watches Rick's masculinity disintegrate. Imprisoned in Japanese camps, he establishes tender bonds with his fellow prisoners, especially with working-class Hughie. In fact, as war ends, Rick and Hughie seem to plan their return as a "couple." Set adrift when Hughie marries into suburban normality, Rick finds a girlfriend but cannot bring himself to marry. "I wish I could go with you," he tells Hughie; the latter's response is, "boys grow up, and they marry girls." Whether Rick will seek homosexual satisfactions is not clear, but the novel destabilizes the myth of normative heterosexuality. As in *The Young Desire It,* sex–gender alignment is shaken, given Stow's exposure of vulnerability in the ideally masculinized Rick and the heterosexual disillusionment of his cousin.

The private school and the army have continued to provide opportunities for the exploration of homosexual nuances within all-male institutions. Hal Porter's story "The Dream" (1962) adds collective resonance to the situation Mackenzie dealt with, while also sexualizing it in surrealistic tones. As for homosexuality in the army, in *Fairyland* (1990) Sumner Locke Elliott presents the consummation of the love between an Australian officer and a private in terms that are serious and lyrical. Robert Dessaix's recent *Australian Gay and Lesbian Writing: An Anthology* (1993) includes these two items in its generous selection.

Another novel, David Malouf's *Johnno* (1975), elegizes the unspoken love between two men during the 1950s and 1960s, when strong male–male ties could find alibis that permitted the limited exchange of devotion. As Dante looks back on his relationship with Johnno, after the latter's death, he recognizes how he refused to acknowledge the more-than-emotional investments of the friendship. Where he once characterized Johnno as a heterosexual rebel, Dante now sees him as dependently in love with him. Acknowledging his own sexual confusions, and realizing that he will not marry, he comes to see his affiliations with the dead Johnno in reconstructing their enigmatic relationship. In shock, he rereads one of Johnno's letters: "I've spent years writing letters to you and you never answer, even when you write back. I've loved you—and you've never given a fuck for me, except as a character in one of your funny stories. Now for Christ sake write to me!" But Dante never responded to this plea. David Malouf has written little explicitly gay fiction, but exploration of unspoken bonds between men animates much of his fiction and poetry, including his war novel *The Great World* (1990).

PATRICK WHITE, Australia's greatest writer at the time of his death in 1990, produced novels appearing to say nothing about the gay world before startling his audiences with *The Twyborn Affair* (1979), which thematizes the transgression of gender lines; and he followed this up with a "self-portrait" (*Flaws in the Glass,* 1981) in which he "came out." Although White's belated announcement may have owed something to the libertarianism of the 1960s, his gesture almost certainly paved the way for the frank literary development of gay and lesbian themes that has marked Australia in the last decade and a half. Among the novels of this period that present gay situations directly and thematize diverse aspects of gay experience are Simon Payne's *The Beat* (1984), Nigel Krauth's *JF Was Here* (1990), Benedict Ciantar's *Distractions* (1991), and Dennis Altman's *The Comfort of Men* (1993). Tony Page, Peter Rose, and David Herkt are writers who have participated in a similar explosion in poetry. The time when homosexuality could be treated only in thickly veiled terms is gone in Australia, and that country now occupies a leading place in the literary production of gay and lesbian experience.

Lacking Australia's longer history, larger population base, and wealthier grazier society, New Zealand has produced a smaller and safer literature. Its puritanism saw homosexuality in a more luridly abhorrent light than was the case in Australia. Some New Zealand critics still dismiss those writers generally known to have harbored homosexual impulses with the code word "effete." Such is the case with Walter D'Arcy Cresswell (1896–1960). An eccentric poet, Cresswell is hardly a New Zealand William McGonagall (as one historian calls him) even though his verse used unconventional forms and archaic diction. Cresswell's low reputation has more to do with his endorsement of WALT WHITMAN, along with valorization of classical Greek masculine ideals and the biblical love that "surpasses the love of women." Cresswell dared to criticize the rigid alignment of sex and gender: "In New Zealand the feminine and sentimental are supposedly confined to the sex in which these attributes are thought to be most becoming—so are the masculine and insensitive" (*Margaret McMillan,* 1948). Even though his work advances homoeroticism rather than homosexuality, a homophobic critical establishment has relegated him to the margins.

The homosexuality of James Courage (1903–1963) is more explicit though not in his best-known novel, *The Young Have Secrets* (1954). That title echoes Mackenzie's *The Young Desire It.* Where adolescent Charles is desiring, Courage's prepubescent Walter is

burdened with secrets. He, too, is separated from his sheep-station family, at school in the city, and under a repressive regime. Boarding at the home of a schoolmaster, he acquires the secrets of pinched New Zealand society. Although there is no direct suggestion that Walter will grow up homosexual, his male bonds are privileged, as are his pupil–mentor relationships; and unmarried Mark is clearly not heterosexual, finding refuge from suburban colonial society as a lighthousekeeper. Courage wrote more explicit novels; a reviewer dismissed *A Way of Love* (1959) on grounds that a novelist could not treat homosexuality on the same level as heterosexuality because the latter is "natural" whereas homosexuality is "unnatural." Courage's mentions of PLATO, GIDE, and PROUST are sneered at; evidently, critical homophobia seeks to exclude homosexuality from literature. In the early fiction of FRANK SARGESON (1903–1982), for example, extraordinary investment in relationships between males is accounted for as a variant of Australian "mateship." Although English readers of homosexual sympathy, like WILLIAM PLOMER and John Lehmann, acclaimed Sargeson's work for its nuances of sex and gender, New Zealanders saw his stories as triumphs of realism. One critic explained away the lesbianism of the main character of "I For One" (1952) as the "self-inflicted repressions of a genteel society." In his later work, specifically in the story "A Game of Hide and Seek" (1972), Sargeson raised differences in sexual preference directly, highlighting them in an overwrought, campy style. The critical establishment, still deprecating homosexual nuances, insisted on reading Sargeson's handling of the gay male in society as a presentation of the "humiliations and the instability of the homosexual's life, the pathetic concern of the aging pansy for his looks," and so on. But as writers continue to foreground gay characters and experience, Sargeson's work will be revalued in fresh contexts.

The surest sign that New Zealand's literary disposition about gay issues is about to change comes from the publication of Peter Wells's stories, *Dangerous Desires* (1991), which won the Reed fiction award. This volume confronts homosexual desire directly, as several recent Australian titles have. The work is contextualized within the AIDS issue since three stories deal with the friendship between two gay men as one of them discovers he has AIDS and faces his death. But this mordant context is relieved by stories portraying homosexual desire through a variety of situations and in the somewhat "campy" styles that have proved so subversive to New Zealand's critical establishment. *Dangerous Desires* is a landmark in New Zealand writing.

If femininity itself had to be kept in its place in the Pacific's colonial formations, it is hardly surprising that feminism and lesbianism were slow to emerge as personal and cultural possibilities. In Australia, from the gender subversion of Henry Handel Richardson (1870–1946) to contemporary, explicitly lesbian fiction, the archetypal woman's story is about gaining freedom from the confines of the oppressively male sheep station on the one hand and, on the other, the oppressively genteel girls' school. This paradigmatic quest has begun to produce a literature that enlists language in exploring women's freedom. Lesbian women, whose "bodies were being inscribed with the language of Law and Culture," who "were becoming gendered subjects, forever doomed to stereotypes" (Sue Chin, in *The Exploding Frangipani,* 1990), are escaping with a vengeance. Four novels from the past two decades have established lesbianism as material for literary production in Australia. The experiences they transform move in from the margins to occupy the center.

In its immediacy and authenticity, Elizabeth Riley's novel of personal growth and education, *All That False Instruction* (1975), advanced significant possibilities for an explicitly lesbian Australian literature. Written in first-person confessional mode, it charts the early life of Maureen in the mean environment of New South Wales during the 1940s, 1950s, and 1960s. Maureen's detailed portrait of her emerging sexuality is also an analysis of her environment: parents and brother, schooling, university life in Sydney, friends, and lovers. Cruelty, intolerance, exclusion, and rejection continuously threaten to extinguish her spirit, but by the time she leaves Australia, Maureen has attained a strong sense of herself, her desires and powers. *All That False Instruction* is as courageous in its expressivity as Maureen was in her self-exploration, and it was ahead of its time in its analysis of patriarchal heterosexuality. The novel is flawed in its repetitiveness (each of Maureen's relationships seeming to repeat its predecessor) and in its implication that lesbianism is basically a female response to patriarchal relations. Yet within its scope, this novel foregrounds analysis, advocates choice, and witnesses to its protagonist's courage in the face of social repression.

Beverley Farmer's *Alone* (1980) is a short novel that reads like a prose poem. At less than half the length of Riley's novel, it is as if Farmer had taken Maureen's first lesbian affair and rendered it a final private tragedy. Shirley I. Nunn (S.I.N.) prepares to commit suicide on her eighteenth birthday, after her lover Catherine has rejected her. Shirley's connection with the world is limited to this one relationship and to the intense writing she does. In fact, she has no other language with which to deal with her betrayal than poetic texts: ELIOT's *The Waste Land,* BAUDELAIRE's *Fleurs du Mal,* RIMBAUD's poems. Feeling the same disgust as Maureen for family, men obsessed by their sexual needs, and suburban Australia in the 1950s, Shirley cannot stir beyond the grip of

solitude and self-disgust caused by rejection. Indeed, as her literary web distances the nunlike Shirley from emotion and sexuality, it infuses her existence with irony—absurdity, even—and makes unthinkable any outcome other than melodramatic self-destruction. Susan Hawthorne's *The Falling Woman* (1992) shares much with the narratives of Farmer and Riley in its presentation of rural childhood, boarding school life, and self-discovery as lesbian. The story of the developing relationship between Stella and Olga during a trip into the desert is interspersed with flashbacks to Stella's childhood and adolescence. Italicized voices, representing Stella's rich inner life, also interrupt the narrative, to resonate beyond Stella herself and to suggest how myth—particularly aboriginal myth—can inform the development of lesbian self-understanding and articulation. Stella's quest for identity and relationship is complicated by her epilepsy, which can be read as a suggestive metaphor for female and lesbian experience. Despite its title, this is a warm novel that privileges affirmation over anger, future potential over past tragedy.

Like Hawthorne, Finola Moorhead seeks alternative forms of female knowledge, through astronomy and astrology, magic, mathematics, myth. These, as well as "Women & their anarchy. Action & intelligence. Inquiry & relationship. Sex and caring" (*A Handwritten Modern Classic,* 1977), are the subjects of *Remember the Tarantella,* Moorhead's 1987 novel. Novelist Christina Stead had remarked that a novel without men would be almost impossible to write, and it was this challenge Moorhead took up. Twenty-six women (as there are twenty-six alphabet letters), most of them lesbian, are characters. Their lives intersect and intertwine. As individuals, they strive to construct identity through action, reflection, and relationship; as a collective, they explore possibilities for solidarity and community. Since dance is one situation that can combine individual expression with community celebration, Moorhead recuperates the tarantella—once associated with reaction to a deadly snake bite—as a joyous female rite, an answer to Dionysian revel. As the women travel throughout Australia and the world, in and out of relationships, caught in private and political webs, they participate in "dances" that prefigure the ecstasy of a tarantella of full lesbian affirmation. Moorhead's open-ended novel explores an amazing range of female experience, employing realism, symbolism, and magic while resisting the temptation to wish-fulfillment and closure.

Sydney writer Mary Fallon's award-winning novel, *Working Hot* (1989), is important for its interrogation of conventional representations of femininity and female sexuality within a lesbian context; part of its project of subversion is accomplished by an inventive formal hybridity that encompasses verse narrative, monologue, play scripts, and opera libretto as well as prose narrative.

The development of the lesbian novel in Australia in the last two decades is a phenomenon that has not yet been matched in New Zealand, though Renée is a prolific published New Zealand lesbian writer. Her writing is varied and direct. Besides a number of plays, she has produced three books of fiction: the story collection *Finding Ruth* (1987), and the novels *Willy Nilly* (1990) and *Daisy and Lily* (1993). Beryl Fletcher's two feminist novels (*The Word Burners,* 1991; *The Iron Mouth,* 1993) consider lesbian issues and impulses explicitly, as an important aspect of female textuality in its New Zealand context. However, in both countries—distinct societies, with differing histories and contemporary realities—women writers use the story form to explore issues of self, body, voice, and lesbian revision. Although the short story has tended to be a realist form, some lesbian writers have found it amenable to fantasy, to expression of vivid constructive (and destructive) dreaming; furthermore, it has favored a new kind of focus on language itself, on language's innate capacity for deconstruction and reformulation, for challenging language as patriarchal property.

The Exploding Frangipani (edited by Cathie Dunsford and Susan Hawthorne) and *Subversive Acts* (edited by Cathie Dunsford) are two recent story anthologies that include a number of Australian and New Zealand feminist and lesbian writers, revealing the intense and widespread energy in a new writing of sex and gender. From Australia, Thalia, Sandy Jeffs, Sue Chin, Susan Hawthorne, Jenny Pausacker, and Susan Hampton are representative of this innovative work, whereas in New Zealand Susan Sayer, Nancy Stone, Julie Glamuzina, Louise Simone, and Sandy Hall are active writers. There are three important aspects to this lesbian-feminist work as demonstrated in these two anthologies. First, *Subversive Acts,* a New Zealand anthology that includes both lesbian and feminist (heterosexual) work, emphasizes the continuities within women's experience, whether it be heterosexual or lesbian. Second, *The Exploding Frangipani,* an anthology of Australian and New Zealand lesbian writing, emphasizes the continuities in

experience between the two distinct yet related societies. Third, both collections include the work of Native writers: the Australian aborigine Eva Johnson, and New Zealand Maori Marewa P. Glover and Ngahuia Te Awekotuku. All three aspects underline something significant about lesbian writing: that it is prepared to transgress boundaries, to search for inclusive experience, to make creative alliances.

In all this writing—gay or lesbian, from Australia or New Zealand—exploration and revision of sex and gender traditions take place within the dismantling of a crippling, colonial past that was strenuously patriarchal. Such revision seeks to end the repression of women, lesbians, and gays that many, until recently, would take for granted.

—*Patrick Holland*

BIBLIOGRAPHY

Cresswell, Walter D'Arcy. *The Poet's Progress.* London: Faber, 1930. ■ ———. *Margaret McMillan.* London: Hutchinson, 1948. ■ Courage, James. *The Young Have Secrets.* London: Jonathan Cape, 1954. ■ ———. *A Way of Love.* London: Jonathan Cape, 1959. ■ Dessaix, Robert. *Anthology of Australian Gay and Lesbian Writing.* Melbourne: Oxford University Press, 1993. ■ Dunsford, Cathie, ed. *Subversive Acts: New Writing by New Zealand Women.* Auckland, NZ: Penguin, 1991. ■ Dunsford, Cathie, and Susan Hawthorne, eds. *The Exploding Frangipani: Lesbian Writing from Australia & New Zealand.* Auckland, NZ: New Women's Press, 1990. ■ Farmer, Beverley. *Alone.* Carlton South, Victoria: Sisters Publishing, 1980. ■ Hampton, Susan. *Surly Girls.* Sydney, NSW: Angus & Robertson, 1989. ■ Hawthorne, Susan. *The Falling Woman.* North Melbourne, Victoria: Spinifex Press, 1992. ■ Mackenzie, Kenneth "Seaforth." *The Young Desire It.* Sydney, NSW: Angus & Robertson, 1972. [First published 1937] ■ Malouf, David. *Johnno.* St. Lucia, Queensland: University of Queensland Press, 1975. ■ Moorhead, Finola. *A Handwritten Modern Classic.* Fitzroy, NSW: Sybylla Co-operative, 1977. ■ ———. *Remember the Tarantella.* Sydney, NSW: Primavera Press, 1987. ■ Riley, Elizabeth. *All That False Instruction.* London: Angus & Robertson, 1975. ■ Sargeson, Frank. *Man of England Now.* London: Martin Brian and O'Keefe, 1972. [Includes "I For One" and "A Game of Hide and Seek"] ■ ———. *The Stories of Frank Sargeson.* Auckland, NZ: Longman Paul, 1973. ■ Stow, Randolph. *The Merry-Go-Round in the Sea.* Harmondsworth: Penguin, 1968. [First published 1965] ■ Wells, Peter. *Dangerous Desires.* Auckland, NZ: Reed Publishing, 1991. [Pacific Writers Series] ■ White, Patrick. *The Twyborn Affair.* New York: Viking, 1979. ■ ———. *Flaws in the Glass: A Self-Portrait.* New York: Viking, 1981.

Azaña, Manuel
(1880–1940)

Manuel Azaña Díaz was born in Alcal de Henares, Spain, in 1880, and died in exile in 1940. He was one of the leading political figures on the left and held a number of government positions, including that of president of the Popular Front government that came to power in 1935. It was this government that was opposed by a coalition of army generals, Catholics, fascists, and monarchists who rebelled and plunged Spain into its bloody three-year Civil War. In 1939, Azaña crossed the border into France, never to return to Spain.

Azaña was a great lover of art, music, and literature, and a voracious reader. A number of his written works are political. His imprisonment in Barcelona by the right-wing government in 1934 became the material for his work *Mi rebelión en Barcelona* (*My Rebellion in Barcelona,* 1935). His book *La velada en Benicarló* (*Vigil in Benicarló,* 1939) is a dialogued novel in which an odd mix of people spend the night together commenting on the significance of the Spanish Civil War from their different perspectives. Besides strictly political works, he published works of fiction: *El jardín de los frailes* (*Garden of the Monks,* 1927) and *Fresdeval,* an unfinished work that was published posthumously; a play, *La corona* (*The Crown,* 1933); and some literary criticism. He is also known as an accomplished translator. He and a close friend edited *La pluma,* a literary journal. His personal contributions to the journal have been gathered in the volume *Plumas y palabras* (*Pens and Words,* 1930).

Azaña's political and moral cause was freedom. He was also strongly repulsed by violence, as is witnessed in his commentaries in *La velada en Benicarló.* He believed all Spanish institutions needed to be liberalized if Spain was to become a truly free and modern society. One of his most ardent battles, and the one that probably gained him the greatest number of enemies, was against the narrowness, hypocrisy, and dominance of the Catholic Church in Spain. His first novel, *El jardín de los frailes,* catalogues some of his hostilities toward this institution. Despite this animosity, Azaña was married in the church in 1929 to Dolores de Rivas Cherif—a woman twenty-two years younger than he, the sister of his close friend and collaborator, Cipriano. They had no children.

A difficulty arises in assessing Azaña because of his personality. He was known to be so shy that he remained a mystery even to his closest friends. In his semiautobiographical work, *El jardín de los frailes,* he describes himself as a lonely and solitary figure. Friends and biographers have also mentioned his hypersensitivity and his pride as further obstacles to truly knowing the man. References to a possible "secret life" are recorded in a novel written by Daniel de Bois-Juzan entitled *Celui qui fut Pedro Muñoz* (*The Late Pedro Muñoz*). Muñoz is a thinly disguised Azaña, president of the Republic of Turdénie, which is recognizably the Spanish Republic. Curiously, the novel vanished from bookstores almost immediately after being released in 1949.

Although never referring to his own personal life, Azaña did write about the romantic adventures of a nineteenth-century Spanish author (*Valera en Italia: Amores, política y literatura*), in whom Azaña admired the cautious maintenance of his private life, as well as his aversion to traditional Spanish society.

Sexuality does not appear in any of Azaña's works. Although he chronicles his growing political awareness and his absolute commitment to liberal freedom and revolutionary reforms, as well as sarcastically mocking the malignant influence of the Church on the minds of the people, he also staunchly defends the privacy of personal life.

—*María Dolores Costa*

BIBLIOGRAPHY

Agnado, Emiliano. *Don Manuel Azaña Díaz.* Madrid: Editorial Nauta, 1972. ■ Bois-Juzan, Daniel de. *Celui qui fut Pedro Muñoz.* Paris: Amiot-Dumont, 1949. ■ Casares, Francisco. *Azaña y ellos.* Granada: Editorial Prieto, 1938. ■ Espinalt, Carlos M. *Estudi de Manuel Azaña.* Barcelona: Rafael Salvá, 1971. ■ Giménez Caballero, Ernesto. *Manuel Azaña: Profecías españolas.* Madrid: Editorial Gaceta Literaria, 1932. ■ Góngora Echenique, Manuel. *Ideario de Manuel Azaña.* Valencia: Pacual Quiles, 1936. ■ Marichal, Juan. *La vocación de Manuel Azaña.* Madrid: Edicusa, 1968. ■ Mola, Emiliano. *El pasado: Azaña y el porvenir.* Madrid: Editorial Bregua, 1934. ■ Rivas-Cherif, Cipriano de. *Retrato de un desconocido: Vida de Manuel Azaña.* México: Editorial Oasis, 1961. ■ Sedwick, Frank. *The Tragedy of Manuel Azaña.* Columbus: Ohio State University Press, 1963. ■ Villanueva, Francisco. *Azaña: El gobierno.* México: Editorial Moderna, 1941.

Bacon, Sir Francis
(1561–1626)

Sir Francis Bacon, the philosopher who "took all knowledge for his province" and the lawyer-politician who became JAMES I's Lord Chancellor, went through the heterosexual marriage required of an ambitious Renaissance public man. In addition, reflecting the needs of an era so grateful for secure royal succession that it maintained comparative silence about the homosexuality of its own king, Bacon condemned homosexuality in his more magisterial, philosophical work. For example, in his *New*

Atlantis (written 1610, published 1627), Bacon declared that his utopian land of Bensalem had "no touch" of "masculine love" (a Renaissance term for male homosexuality).

However, Bacon subversively inserts homosexual innuendo elsewhere in his writings. In his suggestively titled *The Masculine Birth of Time,* an unfinished critique of prevailing philosophical and educational traditions composed around 1603 and left unpublished, the older male speaker instructs a younger man, pleading, "My dear, dear boy . . . from my inmost heart . . . give yourself to me so that I may . . . secure [you] an increase beyond all . . . ordinary marriages." Bacon also provocatively suggests his homosexuality in some of his *Essays* (third and final edition, 1625): negatively in "Of Love," where he can stir himself to give only three examples from history and which he calls a "passion . . . great spirits . . . keep out" (when used as a noun classifying desire, "love" referred only to male–female attraction in the Renaissance and thus was the age's de facto language for "heterosexuality"); in "Of Marriage and the Single Life," where he praises "unmarried and childless men" as the "best friends, best masters, best servants" and as sources of "the best works, . . . of greatest merit for the public"; in "Of Friendship," the longest essay, where he conforms to the tradition in earlier male and female homosexual writing of using "friendship" terminology to imply same-sex romantic attachment ("wives, sons, nephews [can] not supply the comfort of friendship"); and, most daringly, in "Of Beauty," where he discusses examples of "beautiful men" only.

Bacon is also one of the few homosexual writers from periods as distant as the Renaissance for whom there is contemporary testimony about his sexuality. On April 17, 1593, Bacon's mother wrote to his brother Anthony castigating Bacon for keeping a "bloody Percy . . . as a coach companion and bed companion." Since the nonsexual same-sex sharing of beds was common in the period, "bed companion" here need not imply eroticism. But "coach" language was commonly used to signify a sexual connection (coaches were one of the few places that provided privacy for a sexual liaison), so Lady Bacon's reference to "coach companion" gives her entire comment a sexual cast. Additionally, the chronicler John Aubrey declares in his *Brief Lives* (composed 1665–1690) that Bacon "was a pederast." (Technically meaning "love of youths," "pederasty" was often used in the age to denote a more generic "homosexuality," as indicated by "E. K.")'s use of it when discussing the Colin–Hobbinol peer-relationship in Spenser's 1579 *The Shepherd's Calendar.*) And although Bacon married, he did so late (at the age of forty-five), and his marriage was childless.

—*Joseph Cady*

BIBLIOGRAPHY

Aubrey, John. *Aubrey's Brief Lives.* Oliver Lawson Dick, ed. Ann Arbor: University of Michigan Press, 1957. ■ Bacon, Francis. *The Works of Francis Bacon.* James Spedding, Robert Leslie Ellis, and Douglas Denon Heath, eds. 7 vols. London: Longman, 1857–1859. ■ Cady, Joseph. "'Masculine Love,' Renaissance Writing, and the 'New Invention' of Homosexuality." *Homosexuality in Renaissance and Enlightenment England: Literary Representations in Historical Context.* Claude J. Summers, ed. New York: Haworth Press, 1992. ■ ———. "Renaissance Awareness and Language for Heterosexuality: 'Love' and 'Feminine Love'." *Renaissance Discourses of Desire.* Claude J. Summers and Ted-Larry Pebworth, eds. Columbia: University of Missouri Press, 1993. ■ duMaurier, Daphne. *Golden Lads: Sir Francis Bacon, Anthony Bacon and their Friends.* Garden City, N.Y.: Doubleday, 1975. ■ Farrington, Benjamin. *The Philosophy of Francis Bacon.* Chicago: University of Chicago Press, 1966. ■ Spedding, James, ed. *The Letters and the Life of Francis Bacon.* 7 vols. London: Longman, 1861–1874.

Baldwin, James
(1924–1987)

The circumstances of James Arthur Baldwin's birth were unremarkable: He was born on August 2, 1924, at Harlem Hospital in New York City to a poor, unmarried, twenty-year-old woman named Emma Berdis Jones. But his death sixty-three years later on December 1, 1987, at his home in southern France was an event reported on the front pages of newspapers around the world. Indeed, his journey from a difficult childhood in Harlem to his eventual status as a legendary artist with a large and loyal international audience constitutes one of the most compelling American life stories of the twentieth century.

Baldwin's early years were deeply troubled. At home, he was terrorized by an abusive father; outside the home, he was taunted by his peers because of his diminutive stature and effeminate mannerisms. As an adolescent, he sought refuge in the church, and after an emotionally charged spiritual conversion, he became at age fourteen a minister who regularly preached at evangelical churches in and near Harlem. As a young adult, he held a variety of odd jobs: He was at times a railroad construction worker, waiter, busboy, and elevator operator. It was during this time that he began to write seriously, beginning with book reviews and essays.

During his young adulthood, he also became fully aware of the implications of being black in America. Everyday exposure to racism left him deeply wounded. His increasing consciousness of his homosexuality added to his pain and confusion. To escape what he felt was impending madness, he left for Paris in 1948 with forty dollars in his pocket and no knowledge of French. In France, where he would spend the better part of his remaining years, he became a professional writer.

A prolific artist, Baldwin published twenty-two books during a career that lasted nearly forty years; he wrote formal essays, fiction, drama, and poetry. In his early collections of elegantly written essays—such as *Notes of a Native Son* (1955) and *Nobody Knows My Name* (1961)—he combined autobiography with trenchant cultural analysis to create brilliant critiques of American race relations. In *The Fire Next Time* (1963), Baldwin's most famous nonfiction work, he relentlessly challenged the logic of white racism and proposed a redemptive journey away from racial apocalypse. In his more controversial texts—such as *Blues for Mister Charlie* (1964) and *The Evidence of Things Not Seen* (1985)—he insistently explored the interconnections between sexual insecurities and racial hostilities. Though he was an angry prophet, behind his rhetoric of racial outrage lurks a poignant and reassuring message of reconciliation, forgiveness, and love.

To understand Baldwin's significance for the gay literary heritage, one must begin with Baldwin's little-known essay titled "The Preservation of Innocence." He published it in *Zero,* an obscure and now defunct Moroccan journal, in the summer of 1949; it did not appear in print in the United States until 1989, when it was published in *Out/Look* with a foreword by Melvin Dixon. In this early essay—one of very few nonfiction narratives in which Baldwin explicitly engages the subject of homosexuality—he defends the naturalness and legitimacy of homosexual desire and suggests that homophobia is a consequence of heterosexual panic. Hostility toward homosexuals, like racially motivated hostility, signals a radical failure of imagination and an inability to acknowledge the fullness of one's own humanity. These early insights anticipate his subsequent treatment of gay and bisexual themes in his fiction.

"Outing," a short story published in 1951, is Baldwin's first fictional text that thematizes homoeroticism. A story of sexual awakening, it centers on two adolescent boys, Johnny Grimes and David Jackson, who spend much of a day together on a church picnic. As the day progresses, Johnny becomes increasingly conscious of his sexual feelings for David—feelings that excite as well as terrify him. The narrative ends on a hauntingly ambivalent note, as Johnny gains a heightened awareness of his emerging sexuality that holds new possibilities as well as perils.

Baldwin develops this theme of adolescent homosexual awakening more elaborately in his first and perhaps his best novel, *Go Tell It on the Mountain* (1953). Though arguably a record of Baldwin's own attempt to come to terms with his inheritance, *Go Tell* is much more than merely autobiographical. Imbued with an epic sense of history and resonant with elaborate biblical imagery, it is a universal story of initiation, of coming of age, of a young man's struggle to forge an autonomous identity in opposition to surrounding authority figures. While the main plot of the narrative defines the familial and racial histories that shape the identity of the fourteen-year-old protagonist, John Grimes, its subplot tracks the evolution of his sexual self. As John is increasingly drawn to Elisha, his seventeen-year-old Sunday school teacher, his barely articulated feelings of excitement and fear reveal his private struggle with his budding sexuality. Few novels in American literature provide a more subtle and graceful insight into adolescent gay consciousness.

This theme of sexual identity dominates Baldwin's second novel, *Giovanni's Room* (1956). Its all-white cast of characters and its candid treatment of homosexual romance disappointed many of Baldwin's readers, yet *Giovanni's Room* eventually helped secure Baldwin's central place in gay American literature. A lyrical novel of remembrance and atonement, *Giovanni's Room* focuses on David, a young American in Paris. There he falls in love with Giovanni, a handsome Italian. But David, unable to accept his own gay self, abandons Giovanni, who helplessly seeks refuge in the Parisian sexual underworld. In a rather sensational turn of events, Giovanni murders Guillaume, an employer who humiliates and exploits him; soon he is caught, tried, found guilty, and sentenced to death. The narrative begins on the eve of his execution and, in an extended flashback, David reconstructs his relationship with Giovanni and his own role in contributing to Giovanni's current plight. In David's recollections, Baldwin forcefully dramatizes the central dilemma of the protagonist: He is caught between cultural expectations of heterosexual conduct, which he himself has internalized, and his private sexual desire for other men. David fails to resolve the dilemma; because he is unwilling to accept his sexuality honestly, he is unable to live and love authentically.

Another Country, Baldwin's controversial bestseller, was published in 1962. A complex narrative, it explicitly combines racial and sexual protests. Its setting is mostly New York City; its plot is structured around the lives of eight racially, regionally, socio-economically, and sexually diverse characters. This multicultural cast constitutes a microcosmic America; the conflicts among them, therefore, become emblematic of larger crises in American society. But even as the novel projects a nightmarish vision of contemporary life, it extols the possibility of redemption through love. And for a pre-Stonewall novel, its treatment of homosexuality is remarkably sophisticated. Here homosexuality does not cause panic or produce guilt. True, it leads to suffering, as it does in the case of Eric—a gay Southern white male character who plays the most healing role in the novel—but in Baldwin's theology, suffering can lead to redemptive self-knowledge, to a more humane understanding of the self and the Other. Gayness, Baldwin suggests, has redemptive potential and can indeed be a valid basis to imagine and build a bold new world.

The idea that homosexuality may hold redemptive possibilities is articulated even more forthrightly in Baldwin's next novel, *Tell Me How Long the Train's Been Gone* (1968). It is the story of Leo Proudhammer, a bisexual, thirty-nine-year-old, highly successful black actor. While recuperating in a San Francisco hospital from a massive heart attack, Leo looks back at his life and imaginatively charts his journey from a bleak childhood in Harlem to his present status as a phenomenally successful artist. He seeks through his recollections a pattern that would grant at least a semblance of order to his anarchic life. In his memory of his gay relationship with Christopher, a young black militant committed to revolutionary change, Leo ultimately recognizes the central justification for his life. Here, as in *Another Country,* Baldwin casts the homosexual in a redemptive role. Christopher's name itself, for example, suggests his role as a racial savior. But Christopher is also comfortably and confidently gay. Thus by combining black militancy and gay sexuality in Christopher, Baldwin suggests that there is no fundamental conflict between the two traits. Such a suggestion may be at least in part a calculated response by Baldwin to the viciously hostile reaction his earlier gay-themed novels elicited from angry black militants who were uncomfortable with the increasingly visible role of Baldwin—an openly gay black man—in the civil rights movement.

There is in Baldwin's next novel, *If Beale Street Could Talk* (1974), a conspicuous absence of gay themes. But in his sixth and final novel, *Just Above My Head* (1979), the focus is on the life of Arthur Montana, a recently deceased black gay gospel singer, as seen through the eyes of his surviving brother, Hall Montana. A lengthy narrative, *Just Above My Head* is Hall's love song for his brother, an attempt to understand his troubled life and lonely death. Gay sexuality, as in *Another Country* and *Go Tell,* is one of the major themes in the novel; however, in contrast to those earlier works, here Baldwin treats it less self-consciously and less polemically. The gay theme, in fact, is more smoothly integrated into the narrative, and it is presented as an essentially unsensational, though problematic, aspect of Arthur's search for identity, meaning, and love.

Baldwin is a pioneering figure in twentieth-century literature. As a black gay writer in a culture that privileges those who are white and straight, he offered in his work a sustained and articulate challenge to the dominant discourses of American racism and mandatory heterosexuality. As an African-American writer, he ranks among the finest. As a gay writer, he occupies a preeminent place. Long before the Stonewall Riots of 1969 helped liberate the gay literary imagination in the United States, he boldly made his sexuality a vital part of his artistic vision. Even more important, by insisting on honest and open explorations of gay and bisexual themes in his fiction, he made a sharp break from the established African-American literary conventions. Through such a radical departure from tradition, he helped create the space for a generation of young African-American gay writers who succeeded him. (See also AFRICAN-AMERICAN GAY MALE LITERATURE and NOVEL: GAY MALE.)

—*Emmanuel S. Nelson*

BIBLIOGRAPHY

Adams, Stephen. *The Homosexual as Hero in Contemporary Fiction.* London: Vision Press, 1980. ■ Bergman, David. *Gaiety Transfigured: Gay Self-Representation in American Literature.* Madison: University of Wisconsin Press, 1991. ■ Bigsby, C. W. E. "The Divided Mind of James Baldwin." *Journal of American Studies* 14 (1980): 325–342. ■ Bloom, Harold, ed. *James Baldwin.* New York: Chelsea House, 1986. ■ Campbell, James. *Talking at the Gates: A Life of James Baldwin.* New York: Viking, 1991. ■ Cederstrom, Lorelei. "Love, Race and Sex in the Novels of James Baldwin." *Mosaic* 17.2 (1984): 175–188. ■ Cohen, William A. "Liberalism, Libido, Liberation: Baldwin's *Another Country.*" *Genders* 12 (Winter 1991): 1–21. ■ Giles, James R. "Religious Alienation and 'Homosexual Consciousness' in *City of Night* and *Go Tell It on the Mountain.*" *College English* 36 (November 1974): 369–380. ■ Harris, Trudier. *Black Women in the Fiction of James Baldwin.* Knoxville: University of Tennessee Press, 1985. ■ Kinnamon, Kenneth, ed. *James Baldwin: A Collection of Critical Essays.* Englewood Cliffs, N.J.: Prentice Hall, 1974. ■ Lowenstein, Andrea. "James Baldwin and His Critics." *Gay Community News* 9 February 1980: 11–12, 17. ■ Macebuh, Stanley. *James Baldwin: A Critical Study.* New York: The Third Press, 1973. ■ Nelson, Emmanuel S. "James Baldwin." *Contemporary Gay American Novelists: A Bio-Bibliographical Critical Sourcebook.* Emmanuel S. Nelson, ed. Westport, Conn.: Greenwood Press, 1993. 6–24. ■ ———. "James Baldwin's Vision of Otherness and Community." *MELUS* 10.2 (1983): 27–31. ■ Sarotte, Georges-Michel. *Like a Brother, Like a Lover: Male Homosexuality in the American Novel and Theatre from Herman Melville to James Baldwin.* Garden City, N.Y.: Anchor Press/Doubleday, 1978. ■ Summers, Claude J. *Gay Fictions: Wilde to Stonewall.* New York: Continuum, 1990. ■ Trope, Quincey, ed. *James Baldwin: The Legacy.* New York: Simon & Schuster, 1989.

Balzac, Honoré de
(1799–1850)

Although Balzac was trained in the law, he turned his back on a conventional career as soon as his legal studies had been completed (1819) and promptly began to write fiction. In the hope of accumulating enough wealth to finance his writing, he undertook various business ventures and speculated extensively. These actions resulted not in independence but in mountainous debts from which neither the assistance of adoring women nor the output of his febrile imagination could free him. Balzac's more than ninety novels display an acute grasp of the inner workings of society and have earned him an undisputed place among the masters of French nineteenth-century fiction.

In 1834, Balzac began to organize his novels into a systematic whole. They appeared in that form between 1842 and 1848 under the collective title *La Comédie humaine* (*The Human Comedy*). Balzac intended the *Comédie* to be a comprehensive investigation into human behavior, touching on varied environments (such as the provinces and Paris) and on specific conditions (military life, political life). Although uneven in quality and scope, the result presents such a dazzling mixture of melodrama and insight, sociological detail and romantic portraits of all-consuming passion and ambition that HENRY JAMES declared Balzac to be "the first and foremost member of his craft."

Homosexuality surfaces only rarely in the *Comédie humaine,* but nevertheless Balzac endows its portrait with some of his most provocative material. In, for example, *La Fille aux yeux d'or* (*The Girl with the Golden Eyes*) (1834–1835), a lesbian relationship between Paquita Valdès and the Marquise de San-Réal turns tragic when Paquita introduces into their bed Henri de Marsay, a man and the Marquise's half-brother. De Marsay determines to kill Paquita on learning of her lesbianism, but the Marquise prevents him so that she can commit the act herself. The ambiguous—indeed androgynous—nature of love (Paquita may come to prefer Henri to her lover; yet she is drawn to him through his resemblance to the Marquise) and the ambiguity of gender (whereas the male hero resolves to avenge his honor, his feminine half-sister accomplishes the act) are but some of the issues Balzac raises with this novel.

Balzac's account of the life of Jacques Collin (alias Vautrin, alias Abbé Carlos Herrera) embraces *Le Père Goriot* (*Father Goriot*) (1834–1835), *Illusions perdues* (*Lost Illusions*) (1837–1843), and *Splendeurs et misères des courtisanes* (*Highs and Lows of Harlots*) (1838–1847). It introduces the reader to the homosexual *mores* of Paris prisons and to a master criminal who by the scope of his powers and creative ambition has long been recognized as the character in the *Comédie* most reminiscent of its author.

That Collin's relationship with fellow convict Théodore Calvi and with Lucien de Rubempré is pederastic, critic Philippe Berthier has demonstrated beyond any doubt, but Balzac also makes the bond Mephistophelean and paternal, ruthless and loving. He establishes the criminality—legal as well as sexual—that places Collin outside the realm of "acceptable" behavior only to accentuate a grandeur and humanity by which Collin outstrips the corruption of his right-minded contemporaries. Indeed, when we last see Collin, he has just retired as head of the Sûreté (police)!

Does Collin mirror Balzac as writer and lover? Despite Balzac's well-documented adventures with numerous women, the memoirs of one contemporary, Philarète Chasles, implied the existence of homosexual feelings in Balzac, and Balzac's own letters occasionally betray strong emotional ties with various younger men whose careers he tried to advance. We may never know with certainty whether Jacques Collin represents a side of Balzac to which the writer allowed full satisfaction only in fiction, but the possibility provides yet one more reason to place him among Balzac's most remarkable creations. (See also FRENCH LITERATURE: NINETEENTH CENTURY.)

—*Donald Stone*

BIBLIOGRAPHY

Berthier, Philippe. "Balzac et Sodome." *L'Année balzac-ienne.* (1979): 147–177. ∎ Courtivron, Isabelle de. "Weak Men and Fatal Women: The Sand Image." *Homosexualities and French Literature.* George Stambolian and Elaine Marks, eds. Ithaca, N.Y.: Cornell University Press, 1978. 210–227. ∎ Hunt, Herbert J. *Balzac's Comédie Humaine.* New York: Oxford University Press, 1964.

Bannon, Ann
(b. 1932)

Along with Valerie Taylor and Paula Christian, Ann Thayer, who adopted the pseudonym Ann Bannon, wrote lesbian pulp novels in the late 1950s and early 1960s. When first published, Bannon's five novels, which form an interlinked series, achieved considerable popularity; they were even translated into other languages. Their appeal lies in their plausible descriptions of lesbian life in New York City; as critic Diane Hamer comments, Bannon's novels "read like a travelogue or tourist guide of Greenwich Village and its homosexual bars."

It was Thayer's own liminal position, existing between the heterosexual and homosexual communities, that made her such a perceptive commentator about the difficulties of pursuing a lesbian lifestyle in the 1950s. Thayer began to lead a double life at an early age. She was conventionally married yet slipped away on the weekends to experience the gay night life of Greenwich Village. Valuing her privacy and not wishing to be connected with lesbian pulps, she dropped from sight after her books were published. Only in 1980, when her books were republished by Naiad Press, did she acknowledge authorship.

Although written last, *Beebo Brinker* (1962) is actually the first novel in Bannon's sequence, chronologically. The novel introduces young Beebo, fresh from the Midwest, who comes out as a lesbian in the Greenwich Village gay culture. Beebo, the stereotypical butch, is a central figure in Bannon's other novels, as well. Apart from its depiction of Beebo, this novel is also notable for its accurate account of the social pressures that confronted lesbians in this period.

Odd Girl Out (1957) centers on the growth of a lesbian relationship between two college students. Shy, sheltered Laura is at first horrified to discover her feelings toward Beth since she assumes that lesbians are "great strong creatures in slacks with brush cuts and deep voices." Here, Bannon uses her fiction to explode lesbian stereotypes. By the end of the story, Laura accepts her lesbianism, but Beth flees into the safety of marriage to a man. Such a conclusion seems at first glance to endorse the benefits of heterosexual marriage, but for Bannon denying one's lesbianism can lead only to dissatisfaction, and the marriage fails.

I Am a Woman (1959) revolves around Laura's attempt to establish her lesbian identity and find love after she has left college. Bannon is particularly good at portraying how Laura manages to move from a heterosexual environment, such as the office where she works, to the lesbian bars where she meets Beebo. Despite the novel's rather pat conclusion—the two women kiss and declare their love—*I Am a Woman* provides a sensitive study of the Greenwich Village homosexual community of the late 1950s.

The bleakest of Bannon's novels is *Woman in the Shadows* (1959). Beebo, now an alcoholic, antagonizes Laura and they have fights, often ending in physical confrontations. To escape her embattled relationship with Beebo, Laura has an affair, but it ends bitterly. At the book's conclusion, Laura has left Beebo and, rather implausibly, has married Jack, a gay man, and become artificially inseminated.

Journey to a Woman (1960) recounts Beth's story of fleeing her unhappy marriage in order to search for Laura. Even though Beth leaves her husband and children, Bannon portrays this not as negative, but as necessary in order for Beth to find her true identity. Although at the end of the novel, Beth has found happiness with Beebo, her new lover, other lesbians are not as fortunate. Vega, for instance, rejects her lesbianism, which drives her to insanity. In this fashion, Bannon reverses the then common assumption that lesbianism itself was a form of insanity. As do all of her novels, *Journey to a Woman* criticizes how heterosexual society views homosexuality, a pertinent reason for still studying Bannon's texts. Bannon's novels, as well as other lesbian pulps, provide an important record of lesbian life in a period when few women dared speak about homosexuality.

—*Sherrie A. Inness*

BIBLIOGRAPHY

Barale, Michele Aina. "When Jack Blinks: Si(gh)ting Gay Desire in Ann Bannon's Beebo Brinker." *Feminist Studies* 18.3 (Fall

1992): 533–549. ■ Benns, Susanna. "Sappho in Soft Cover: Notes on Lesbian Pulp." *Fireworks: The Best of Fireweed.* Makeda Silvera, ed. Toronto: Women's Press, 1986. 60–68. ■ Hamer, Diane. "'I Am a Woman': Ann Bannon and the Writing of Lesbian Identity in the 1950s." *Lesbian and Gay Writing: An Anthology of Critical Essays.* Mark Lilly, ed. Philadelphia: Temple University Press, 1990. 47–75. ■ Tilchen, Maida. "Ann Bannon: The Mystery Solved!" *Gay Community News* 8 (January 1983): 8–12. ■ Walters, Suzanna. "As Her Hand Crept Slowly Up Her Thigh: Ann Bannon and the Politics of Pulp." *Social Text* 23 (1989): 83–101. ■ Weir, Angela and Elizabeth Wilson. "The Greyhound Bus Station in the Evolution of Lesbian Popular Culture." *New Lesbian Criticism: Literary and Cultural Readings.* Sally Munt, ed. New York: Columbia University Press, 1992. 95–113. ■ Zimmerman, Bonnie. *The Safe Sea of Women: Lesbian Fiction, 1969-1989.* Boston: Beacon, 1990.

Barnes, Djuna
(1892–1982)

Djuna Barnes was born on June 12, 1892, in Cornwall-on-Hudson, New York, the daughter of an Englishwoman, Elizabeth Chappell, and an unsuccessful American writer, Wald Barnes. "Barnes" is the birth name of her paternal grandmother, Zadel Barnes Gustafson, a feminist writer, spiritualist, and journalist who helped educate her and who inspired the character Sophia in her semi-autobiographical novel *Ryder* (1928). The complex network of family relationships produced by her father's bigamy and the experience of being "given" in marriage in 1909 to her father's second wife's brother influence both *Ryder* and the later family drama *The Antiphon* (1958).

Barnes left home almost immediately after the marriage and around 1912 arrived in Greenwich Village where she supported herself by writing feature stories and local color sketches for several New York dailies. In a few of the sketches, using what MONIQUE WITTIG has characterized as her "out-of-the-corner-of-the-eye perception," Barnes captures the same-sex desire encoded in the accoutrements and cultivated eccentricities of the Villagers. A number of the articles she wrote for *Vanity Fair* and other magazines over the next twenty years verge on a CAMP sensibility; among the titles are "How the Woman in Love Should Dress" and "What is Good Form in Dying? In Which a Dozen Dainty Deaths Are Suggested for Daring Damsels."

During the 1910s, Barnes had several affairs with men and may have been involved sexually with women. The lesbian subtexts of her poetry and short stories of the period, particularly *The Book of Repulsive Women: 8 Rhythms and 5 Drawings* (1915) and "Paprika Johnson" (1915), suggest such involvement. And she clearly felt a profound love for the poet Mary Pyne who died in 1919 and to whom she dedicated a cycle of poems in *A Book* (1923).

In 1920, Barnes moved to Paris where she lived for most of the decade with her lover, the sculptress and silverpoint artist Thelma Wood. In Paris, Barnes found both an international writing community and a dynamic lesbian community. *Ladies Almanack* (1928), which she printed and sold privately, is a playful satire of this community and the first text in which Barnes's lesbian imagination directs her literary project. The digressions on philosophy, Christianity, sexology, and other discourses of social regulation are held together loosely by the story of Dame Musset's (NATALIE BARNEY's) quest to rescue damsels in various degrees of sexual distress. Barnes subtly mocks the aristocratic pretensions of Barney and her entourage in the same way she had mocked the Villagers' leisured preoccupation with the latest *cause célèbre* in her New York journalism. In both cases, she speaks from the position of a working woman with limited access to the privilege of the community of which she is a part.

A few critics have read *Ladies Almanack* as an attack on Barney and suggested that Barnes's anatomy of the lesbian body never really frees itself from heterosexist representations. Barnes's strategy of subversively repeating those representations in order to expose their consequences in the lives of women inevitably runs the risk of such a reading. In her comments on *The Book of Repulsive Women*, Quebec writer NICOLE BROSSARD recognizes the productive contradictions of Barnes's strategy of subversive repetition: Are the women repulsive in their resignation to their role as "still-lifes," she asks along with Barnes, or are they repulsive because they carry on their lips truths that confront the patriarchal lie at work in their faces and in their flesh?

In 1931, after her break with Wood, Barnes left Paris and spent several years in England. There, at Peggy Guggenheim's rented country manor, Hayford Hall, in the company of writers Emily Coleman and Antonia White, and critic John Ferrar Holms, she wrote her best-known work, *Nightwood* (1936). The novel dramatizes Barnes's need to write about her love for Wood in a number of ways, notably in Nora

Flood's struggle to tell her story to the aging transvestite, Doctor Matthew O'Connor, and in her obsessive letter writing to her former lover, Robin Vote. Robin, a character whose constant movement thwarts the attempts of other characters to possess her, is a figure of desire. Barnes withholds any stable representation of Robin, leaving the configurations of desire as open as possible. In the words of the novel, Robin is moving toward "something not yet in history." Matthew compares Robin to the androgynous princes and princesses of fairy tales who are "neither one and half the other." This metaphor not only uncovers lesbian subtexts hidden in Western culture but also disturbs the binary models of gender that inform the theories of sexologists from Magnus Hirschfeld to Havelock Ellis.

Barnes's style in *Nightwood* emerges from Symbolist and Decadent aesthetics. The text's elaborately worked surface, its string of nonevents, its endless detailing of decor and costume, and its cast of exuberant "degenerates" take the practices and preoccupations of these movements to an extreme. The text, like its writer, is overwrought. The surplus of detail and ornament signals the difficulty of bringing a sexual relationship between two women to literary representation. At the same time, the novel's exclusive focus on sexually and socially marginalized figures makes their experience the rule rather than the exception; without apologies, the sideshow becomes the main act. Lillian Faderman and others have expressed concern that *Nightwood* simply reproduces images of lesbians drawn by male Symbolists and Decadents. However, read in the light of Barnes's own analysis in *Ladies Almanack,* the tragedy and despair of her lesbian characters are not the result of a pathological condition. Rather they are the lived effects of compulsory heterosexuality and of the will to control a character such as Robin.

Barnes returned to New York in 1939 where she lived, chronically ill and relatively poor, until her death in 1982. She grew increasingly resistant to lesbian interest in her work and its place in a tradition of lesbian writing. "I am not a lesbian," she insisted in the 1970s, "I just loved Thelma." However, given that in 1936, she had been able to write, "Please do not think of it—I was not offended in the least to be thought lesbian—it's simply that I'm very reticent about my personal life," her later denial may say more about differences in what it means to identify oneself as lesbian at different historical moments than about Barnes's sexuality. Wittig suggests that Barnes "dreaded that lesbians should make her *their* writer, and that by doing this they should reduce her work to one dimension." She wanted to be remembered for *Nightwood* and *The Antiphon* rather than for *The Book of Repulsive Women* or *Ladies Almanack,* works she was happy to see out of print. Nevertheless, a number of contemporary lesbian writers and theorists—among them Nicole Brossard, Michèle Causse (French translator of *Ladies Almanack*), Teresa de Lauretis, Elizabeth Meese, and Wittig—have found in Barnes's work an important example of how to make the effects of the heterosexual contract visible and, at the same time, to allow lesbians new forms of self-representation in society and culture.

—Lianne Moyes

BIBLIOGRAPHY

Benstock, Shari. *Women of the Left Bank: Paris, 1900-1940.* Austin: University of Texas Press, 1986. ▪ Broe, Mary Lynn. "Djuna Barnes." *The Gender of Modernism.* Bonnie Kime Scott, ed. Bloomington: Indiana University Press, 1990. 1–45. ▪ ———, ed. *Silence and Power: A Reevaluation of Djuna Barnes.* Carbondale: Southern Illinois University Press, 1991. ▪ Brossard, Nicole. "Djuna Barnes: De Profil Moderne." *Mon héroïne.* Montréal: Remue-ménage, 1981. 189–214. ▪ Faderman, Lillian. *Surpassing the Love of Men: Romantic Friendship and Love Between Women from the Renaissance to the Present.* New York: William Morrow, 1981. ▪ Field, Andrew. *Djuna: The Life and Times of Djuna Barnes.* New York: G.P. Putnam's Sons, 1983. ▪ Lanser, Susan Sniader. "Introduction." *Ladies Almanack.* New York: New York University Press, 1992. xv–li. ▪ Meese, Elizabeth. *(sem)erotics theorizing lesbian: writing.* New York: New York University Press, 1992. ▪ O'Neal, Hank. *"Life is painful, nasty and short—in my case it has only been painful and nasty": An informal memoir.* New York: Paragon House, 1990. ▪ Wittig, Monique. *The Straight Mind and Other Essays.* Boston: Beacon, 1992.

Barney, Natalie Clifford
(1876–1972)

Natalie Clifford Barney was born in Dayton, Ohio, on October 31, 1876; she grew up in Cincinnati and Washington, D.C. Her father, Albert Clifford Barney, inherited a railroad fortune, and when the family lived in Washington, Natalie moved in the highest social and diplomatic circles. The rigid protocol of high society bored her, however, and she was eager to pursue her own adventures in an atmosphere more conducive to sexual, and especially lesbian, expression. As a child, she had visited Europe many times, and when she was twenty-four she settled permanently in Paris.

Famous for her operatic love affairs—most notably with the poet RENÉE VIVIEN and the painter Romaine Brooks—and her philosophical commitment to flirtation and nonmonogamy, Natalie Barney met her last lover on a park bench on the Avenue des Anglais in Nice, in 1956, at the age of seventy-nine. Her life and temperament have provided inspiration for many literary portraits, including those of Flossie in Liane de Pougy's *Idylle sapphique* (*Sapphic Idyll*, 1901), Miss Flossie in COLETTE's *Claudine s'en va* (*Claudine and Annie*, 1903), Valerie Seymour in RADCLYFFE HALL's *The Well of Loneliness* (1928), and Laurette in Lucie Delarue Mardrus's *L'Ange et les pervers* (*The Angel and the Perverts*, 1930). Though these characters are quite different one from another, they share a strong lesbian identity, generosity of spirit, and the ability to laugh at themselves. René de Gourmont, the French writer and literary critic, struck up a close friendship with Natalie Barney after reading her *Eparpillements* (*Scatterings*, 1930). He published two collections of the letters he had written her, *Lettres à l'amazone* (1914) and *Lettres intimes à l'amazone* (1926); thus she became known in French literary circles as "the AMAZON."

Barney was not merely the muse of other writers, but a poet, memoirist, and epigrammatist in her own right. Her first collection of poetry, *Quelques portraits-sonnets de femmes*, celebrating many of her lovers, was published in 1900. Although her poetry and plays are mostly works of juvenilia or old-fashioned exercises in nineteenth-century French verse style, her memoirs and portraits such as *Aventures de l'espirit* (*Adventures of the Mind*, 1929), and *Souvenirs Indiscrets* (*Indiscreet Memoirs,* 1960) are vivid, perceptive pieces that describe many of the gays and lesbians who frequented the literary salon she held in Paris for fifty years: Colette, ANDRÉ GIDE, Lucie Delarue Mardrus, GERTRUDE STEIN, DJUNA BARNES, Romaine Brooks, OSCAR WILDE, MARCEL PROUST. She comments on the gay lifestyles of the period, producing a spirited defense of homosexuality with the same unabashed openness and enthusiasm with which she lived her life. It is, however, the epigrams—*Eparpillements, Pensées d'une amazone* (*Thoughts of an Amazon,* 1920) and *Nouvelles pensées d'une amazone* (*More Thoughts of an Amazon,* 1939)—that show a real literary merit and a rare talent for beautifully turned, perfectly aimed verbal barbs and ironic comment.

Natalie Barney died on February 2, 1972, at the age of ninety-five in the same house at 20 rue Jacob where she had lived and run her salon for more than fifty years. It was not, however, until 1992 with the publication of *A Perilous Advantage* and *Adventures of the Mind* that her work became available to English-speaking readers.

—*Anna Livia*

BIBLIOGRAPHY

Causse, Michele and Berthe Cleyrergues. *Berthe ou un demisiècle auprès de l'amazone.* Paris: Editions Tierce, 1980. ■ Colette. *Claudine s'en va.* Paris: Ollendorf, 1903. ■ Gourmont, René de. *Lettres à l'amazone.* Paris: Cres, 1914. ■ ———. *Lettres intimes à l'amazone.* Paris: La Centaine, 1926. ■ Hall, Radcliffe. *The Well of Loneliness.* New York: Covici-Friede, 1928. ■ Jay, Karla. *The Amazon and the Page.* Bloomington: Indiana University Press, 1988. ■ Mardrus, Lucie Delarue. *L'Ange et les pervers.* Paris: Ferenczi, 1930; trans. as *The Angel and the Perverts* by Anna Livia. New York: New York University Press, forthcoming. ■ Pougy, Liane de. *Idylle Sapphique.* Paris: Plume, 1901. ■ Wickes, George. *The Amazon of Letters: The Life and Loves of Natalie Barney.* New York: Putnam, 1976.

Barnfield, Richard
(1574–1627)

Born in Norbury, Staffordshire, Richard Barnfield lived most of his life in the English countryside. After taking a degree at Oxford in 1591, he spent a few years in London but left the city by 1606 to settle near the town of Darlaston. Between 1594 and 1598, he published four volumes of poetry. For the last twenty-two years of his life, he lived quietly, writing no poetry after the age of twenty-four. He married. His will mentions both a son (Robert) and a granddaughter (Jane). The first biographical material on Barnfield is dated 1813, almost two centuries after his death.

Barnfield's reputation as a homoerotic poet rests on two of his volumes: *The Affectionate Shepheard* (1594) and *Cynthia, with Certaine Sonnets* (1595). The title poem of the earlier book concerns a shepherd named Daphnis who loves a boy named Ganymede. Offering the boy unlimited pastoral delights, Daphnis finds his love unreturned because Ganymede is interested in Guendolen. The poem is a thinly disguised attack on Penelope Devereux, the woman Sir Philip Sidney immortalized in *Astrophil and Stella,* and there is evidence in the poem that Daphnis himself is Barnfield and Ganymede is Sir Charles Blount, whom Barnfield may have known at Oxford.

In the preface to *Cynthia, with Certaine Sonnets,* Barnfield defends Daphnis's homoerotic love and explains that he was attempting in *The Affectionate Shepheard* to imitate VIRGIL's second eclogue. Some critics believe that Barnfield was thus trying to explain away the homoeroticism of the shepherd for the boy, but such critics have to contend with the homoerotic sonnets that are printed in the *Cynthia* book. They are, if anything, even more insistent in purpose and frustrated in tone than the earlier Daphnis pastoral. Within the twenty sonnets, not once does the boy give any indication that he is interested in the narrator. The poems are within the traditional sonnet mode of unattainable love that reaches back to Petrarch and are symptomatic of the problems involved in identifying homosexual behavior within a specific historical context.

Contemporary reaction to Barnfield's poetry began one year after the publication of *The Affectionate Shepheard* with a notice by Henry Chettle that the poem was receiving praise. Then Francis Meres in 1598 named Barnfield alongside Spenser and Sidney as among the best writers of pastoral. Early nineteenth-century critics disdained the verses as perverse, and since that time, Barnfield has ridden the rocky road of critical whim. Even at the end of the twentieth century, critics are still misreading the Barnfield poems and finding them distasteful. For example, the

only book-length study of the poet, *Richard Barnfield, Colin's Child,* by Harry Morris, refers repeatedly to Barnfield's homoeroticism as "unnatural." One excellent assessment of Barnfield, however, was done by Montague Summers, who in his preface to the 1936 edition of Barnfield's poems set Barnfield within a context of homoerotic pastoral verse going back to the classics. Among modern critics, Gregory Bredbeck has championed Barnfield as having a special Renaissance voice able both to make sense of sodomy and to disavow it. Bruce Smith, on the other hand, finds Barnfield's lyrics campy and pornographic experiments with self-absorption in what Smith calls "the soft side" of pastoral poetry. Klawitter's 1990 edition of the poems contains extensive notes for the poems and an introduction appreciative of Barnfield's talents.

—*George Klawitter*

BIBLIOGRAPHY

Barnfield, Richard. *The Complete Poems.* George Klawitter, ed. Selinsgrove, Pa.: Susquehanna University Press, 1990. ■ Bredbeck, Gregory W. *Sodomy and Interpretation: Marlowe to Milton.* Ithaca, N.Y.: Cornell University Press, 1991. ■ ———. "Tradition and the Individual Sodomite: Barnfield, Shakespeare, and Subjective Desire." *Homosexuality in Renaissance and Enlightenment England.* Claude Summers, ed. New York: The Haworth Press, 1992. 41–68. ■ Giantvalley, Scott. "Barnfield, Drayton, and Marlowe: Homoeroticism and Homosexuality in Elizabethan Literature." *Pacific Coast Philology* 16 (1981): 9–24. ■ Morris, Harry. *Richard Barnfield, Colin's Child.* Tampa: Florida State University Studies (no. 38), 1963. ■ Smith, Bruce R. *Homosexual Desire in Shakespeare's England.* Chicago: University of Chicago Press, 1991. ■ Summers, Claude. "Homosexuality and Renaissance Literature, or the Anxieties of Anachronism." *South Central Review* 9 (1992): 2–23.

Barthes, Roland
(1915–1980)

Like ANDRÉ GIDE and MARCEL PROUST, two of his favorite writers, Roland Barthes, a semiotician many "queer theorists" find inspiring, occupied an extremely marginal position in French society. He was Protestant. (France is predominantly Catholic.) He was left-handed. (France is, of course, predominantly right-handed.) He was *déclassé.* (Barthes's father, a naval officer, died in World War I, and his mother had to work as a bookbinder.) He was consumptive. (Barthes spent several years in sanatoria.) And he was expatriate. (Barthes spent the 1950s in the Middle East and Eastern Europe, working for cultural services.) Barthes also occupied a marginal position within the French academy. Having

failed to sit the *agrégation* exam that would have led to an orthodox career, but having already published extensively, he was forty-four when he began teaching at the École Pratique des Hautes Études, a lackluster post, and sixty when he was elected to a chair in the Collège de France, a prestigious one. If a single factor, however, can be said to have alienated Barthes from the bourgeois culture he came to distrust and felt compelled to demystify—a deterministic approach Barthes himself rejected—it would be his "perverse" sexuality. Like Proust, if not like Gide, who saw himself as a pederast, Barthes was homosexual. And like *Remembrance of Things Past,* a work in which everyone *except* the narrator (who may or may not be named "Marcel") turns out to be gay, Barthes's critical texts—including ones that concern "text"—are best understood in relation to this sexual marginality.

Barthes preferred the notion of "text," which posits writing as open and derivative, to that of "work," which posits it as closed and sui generis. In fact, texts are so open—to playful ("ludic") interpretation and abysmal contextualization—as to be completely meaningless in any conventional sense of the word. Barthes, however, has an unconventional—and appreciative—sense of meaninglessness. He sees meaninglessness, or "exemption from meaning," as a way of displacing conventional wisdom and dominant ideology. "What is difficult," Barthes writes, "is not to liberate sexuality according to a more or less libertarian project but to release it from meaning, including from transgression as meaning." Meaningless text, for example, displaces the conventional stereotypes (such as sexual "inversion") that pertain to gay male identity. Because Barthes sees homosexuality, and for that matter any transgressive and eccentric "perversion," as unclassifiable, he takes the classification "inversion" to be inaccurate—a notion that will come as a surprise to gays and lesbians who see themselves as "inverts," but that, contrary to popular belief and to conventional critical wisdom, came as no surprise to Proust.

If he had to characterize—to "predicate"—gays and lesbians, Barthes might have chosen the term *noninvert*. Noninvert has two advantages: It is both imprecise and paradoxical. Like OSCAR WILDE, whom he does not appear to have read attentively, Barthes conceives of truth as antithetical: "A *Doxa* (a popular opinion) is posited, intolerable; to free myself of it, I postulate a paradox; then this paradox turns bad, becomes a new concretion, itself becomes a new *Doxa*, and I must seek for a new paradox." He also conceives of truth as orgasmic: "Paradox is an ecstasy, then a loss—one of the most intense." (Like Wilde, Barthes tends to think in terms of bodily pleasure.) Unfortunately, paradoxical formulae are not quite meaningless because, as Barthes himself realizes, "both sides of the paradigm [*doxa/paradoxa*] are glued together in [a] complicitous fashion." Noninvert, when all is said and done, means non*invert*.

Oddly enough, Barthes doesn't reject *every* gay male stereotype in an attempt to exempt (homo)sexuality from meaning. Barthes rejects sexual inversion, but embraces "tricking" and "cruising," activities that he claims represent true sexual liberation. (Not that they did so for Barthes himself; his autobiographical texts suggest he had an unhappy love life.) People who "trick," he writes, neither "are" nor "aren't" homosexual. They refuse "to proclaim [themselves] something . . . at the behest of a vengeful Other, to enter into his discourse, to argue with him, to seek from him a scrap of identity." Rather, they are "*nothing*, or, more precisely, [they are] *something* [that is] provisional, revocable, insignificant." People who "cruise" avoid repetition and therefore evade stereotypology: Whereas repetition is a "baleful" theme for Barthes ("stereotype, the same old thing, naturalness as repetition"), cruising, he writes, is "anti-natural, anti-repetition." It may be that Barthes is simply "protecting" his sexuality here (something he feels all writers do), or at least the macho ("phallocentric") part of his sexuality because whereas sexual inversion feminizes gay men, cruising for tricks is a rather manly (and purportedly desirable) thing to do.

Barthes sees tricking and cruising as senseless in another sense as well. The trick, he writes, "is homogenous to the amorous progression; it is a virtual love, deliberately stopped short on each side, by contract." Likewise, men cruise with "the invincible idea that one will find *someone with whom to be in love*." Some gays (who cruise for sex, not love) will find these descriptions unrealistic. Barthes, however, feels that sentimentality, in an age such as ours in which love doesn't make too much sense, is essentially—and even nonparadoxically—insignificant. He finds that love is now "perverse" (meaningless) enough to liberate sexuality beyond any possibility of recuperation; and in a thorough estrangement of the category states that the sentimentality of love has an "alien," and therefore radically transgressive, strength that sexual freedom fighters would do well to deploy. The reintroduction into sexuality of even "*a touch of sentimentality*," he writes, would be "the *ultimate* transgression . . . the transgression of transgression itself . . . [the return of] *love . . . but in another place*."

Although many theorists support this ludic and loving project, others find it ineffective. They find Barthes far too utopian and apolitical, and believe that true sexual liberation will depend upon "materialist" (Marxist) scholarship. Barthes, however, sees Marxism as ideological, and hence both problematic (part of a futile "war of meanings") and counterrevolutionary. This is why he promulgates—and politicizes—the idea of "semioclasm." According to Barthes, "it is Western discourse as such"—discourse that marginalizes and stereotypes gays and lesbians—"that we must now try to break apart."

—*Kevin Kopelson*

BIBLIOGRAPHY

Beaver, Harold. "Homosexual Signs (In Memory of Roland Barthes)." *Critical Inquiry* 8 (1981): 99–120. ■ Bredbeck, Gregory. "B/O—Barthes's Text/O'Hara's Trick." *PMLA* 108.2

(March 1993): 268–282. ■ Culler, Jonathan. *Roland Barthes.* New York: Oxford University Press, 1983. ■ Heath, Stephen. "Barthes on Love." *Substance* 37–38 (1983): 100–106. ■ Kopelson, Kevin. *Love's Litany: The Writing of Modern Homoerotics.* Stanford: Stanford University Press, 1994. ■ ———. "Wilde, Barthes, and the Orgasmics of Truth." *Genders* 7 (March 1990): 22–31. ■ Kritzman, Lawrence D. "The Discourse of Desire and the Question of Gender." *Signs in Culture: Roland Barthes Today.* Steven Ungar and Betty R. McGraw, eds. Iowa City: University of Iowa Press, 1989. ■ Lavers, Annette. *Roland Barthes: Structuralism and After.* London: Methuen, 1982. ■ Miller, D. A. *Bringing Out Roland Barthes.* Berkeley: University of California Press, 1992. ■ Moriarty, Michael. *Roland Barthes.* Stanford: Stanford University Press, 1991. ■ Morton, Donald. "The Politics of Queer Theory in the (Post) Modern Moment." *Genders* 17 (Fall 1993): 121–150. ■ Schor, Naomi. "Dreaming Dissymentry: Barthes, Foucault, and Sexual Difference." *Coming to Terms: Feminism, Theory, Politics.* Elizabeth Weed, ed. New York; Routledge, 1989. 47–58. ■ Stanton, Domna. "The Mater of the Text: Barthesian Displacement and Its Limits." *L'Esprit Créature* 25.2 (Summer 1985): 57–72. ■ Ungar, Steven. *Roland Barthes: The Professor of Desire.* Lincoln: University of Nebraska Press, 1983.

Bartlett, Neil
(b. 1958)

Neil Bartlett was born in England in 1958, and is a theater director, performer, writer, and translator. He is now director of the Lyric Theatre, Hammersmith, London. As a performance artist, he devised and acted in *Sarrasine,* a work of musical theater from BALZAC's story, and *A Vision of Love Revealed in Sleep* (1989), inspired by the life of the Pre-Raphaelite artist Simeon Solomon, who persisted in painting and loving boys despite poverty and neglect following his arrest for having sex with a man. Drawing on Solomon's 1871 prose poem of the same name, the latter show, which was a solo performance by Bartlett, dramatizes a young man's journey from fear to revelation guided by allegorical figures of his soul. Bartlett has said that the show's "central images of an isolated, naked, shaved, haunted and very sexual male body were all derived from Solomon's paintings." In his performance pieces, he seeks to create a gay theater that utilizes gay images and language, not just characters. A concern with theater language is also evident in his translations of French classic plays by Racine and Molière. He is drawn to the strict verse forms, grand speech, and popular idioms of these apparently remote plays as ways of expressing and analyzing extreme emotions.

In the book *Who Was That Man? A Present for Mr. Oscar Wilde* (1988), Bartlett uses autobiography, reflection, fantasy, and imaginative recreation in order to think about WILDE's writing and life in late nineteenth-century London. He searches for traces of lives almost lost from sight, looking with a scholarly passion for clues in literary texts, especially Wilde's works, but also police reports, newspapers, dictionaries, and medical books, in order to reimagine gay lives in nineteenth-century London, and what they share with his life in the 1980s. What emerges is evidence of a gay subculture twenty years before the Wilde trial, and, more generally, a questioning of the processes of invention and creativity by which gay selves and history have been made.

The novel *Ready to Catch Him Should He Fall* (1990) concerns archetypal figures, Boy, O (the Older Man), Father, and Madame, who runs the Bar where the action is centered. The story follows Boy's first appearance in the Bar, his meeting, courtship, and marriage with O, and the couple's taking care of Father until his death. Although the characters and the action are virtually allegorical, the setting suggests an imaginary city like contemporary London, while time-shifts to other periods give a sense of gay history and culture permeating the present. The narrative sometimes becomes theatrical performance or moments of fantasy, which are reworkings from Wilde, FREDERICK ROLFE, or JEAN GENET, or echoes from films or musicals. Bartlett said that the novel represents the standard narrative of romance—attraction, courtship, marriage, child. Its major reworkings are of the rituals of *The Book of Common Prayer* into equivalent gay ceremonies. Bartlett's work always involves "reinventing the past as a way of articulating the present," and finding artistic forms and language that are vivid, passionate, and intelligent.

—*Lawrence Normand*

BIBLIOGRAPHY

Burton, Peter. "Neil Bartlett." *Talking To . . .* Exeter: Third House, 1991. 1–8.

Baudelaire, Charles
(1821–1867)

A central figure in nineteenth-century French literature, Charles Baudelaire was born on April 9, 1821, in Paris, and died on August 31, 1867. Two collections of Baudelaire's poetry continue to intrigue and influence writers: *Les Fleurs Du Mal* (*Flowers of Evil*, 1867) and *Le Speel De Paris* (*Paris Spleen*, 1869). In the latter collection, published posthumously, he essentially invented the "prose poem."

Had he written only poetry, Baudelaire's reputation would be secure; however, he is also an important art and literary critic. His defense of painters not recognized by the artistic establishment of his time, especially the Impressionists, helped gain them an audience and respect. Likewise, his translations of Poe's work established Poe in France as a major literary talent.

Speculation continues about his personal life. Some early writers suggested that he died a virgin; many others now believe that he died of syphilis acquired in 1841. He had complicated relations with Jeanne Duvall, a prostitute; Madame Sabatier, a courtesan for the wealthy and socially prominent; and Marie Daubrun, an actress. The poems Duvall inspired portray her as both the apex of beauty and the nadir of evil.

Lesbianism fascinated Baudelaire. He even considered naming his first book of poems *Les Lesbiennes*. "Lesbos," from *Les Fleurs Du Mal,* celebrates lesbian love and evokes SAPPHO, who is described as both "mannish" and "beautiful." Further, the speaker challenges the authorities who would "dare" judge those who inhabit Lesbos. Even the gods would not dare to judge these women, he asserts. Two other poems called "Femmes damnees" also explore lesbianism. Here the lovers, with their disordered souls, must suffer in a world wound tight with rules. The bourgeois considers such women demonic; that alone makes them fascinating to Baudelaire. Male homosexuality does not receive this kind of direct treatment; gay men can find no equivalent "Lesbos" in his work.

Baudelaire's best poetry evokes both sensuality and sensuousness. For him, the world is never rational; our attempt to build systems out of chaos leads to madness. Many of his poems target the middle class with its fatuous love of respectability. The more they demand laws to restrict behavior, the sillier and more hypocritical they appear. His solution to middle-class boredom? Shake it off by becoming drunk—on wine, virtue, or poetry—as he suggests in "Intoxication," a poem from *Le Spleen De Paris.*

Baudelaire's poetry has deep roots in Romanticism, but it is often bleak and ultimately urban. The city, Paris, replaces the countryside as the principal roost of poetry. Baudelaire prefers the city's hothouse flowers to the real ones found in the country. The lesbians in his work may be associated with distant island-havens such as "Lesbos," but they are Parisians. What he romanticizes is their outlaw status, their preference for sensuality over respectability.

The French Symboliste writers, including RIMBAUD and VERLAINE, followed Baudelaire and continued to examine and highlight the themes and issues that surface in his poetry. Baudelaire was among the first French poets to include lesbians as subjects. By doing so, he did much to widen the scope of what is acceptable content in poetry. (See also FRENCH LITERATURE: NINETEENTH CENTURY.)

—*Kenneth Pobo*

BIBLIOGRAPHY

Carter, A. E. *Charles Baudelaire.* Boston: G.K. Hall, 1987. ■ Peyre, Henri, ed. *Baudelaire: A Collection of Critical Essays.* Englewood Cliffs, N.J.: Prentice-Hall, 1962. ■ Raser, Timothy. "Language and the Erotic in Two Poems by Baudelaire." *Romantic Review* 79 (1988): 443–451. ■ Sieburth, Richard. "Poetry and Obscenity: Baudelaire and Swinburne." *Comparative Literature* 36 (1984): 343–353. ■ Van Nortwick, Thomas. "Flores Mali: Catullus and Baudelaire." *Kenyon Review* 11:1 (1989): 67–77.

Beach, Sylvia
(1887–1962)

Sylvia Beach was born Nancy Woodbridge Beach to Sylvester Woodbridge Beach, a Presbyterian minister in Bridgeton, New Jersey, and his wife, Eleanor Orbison. Nancy changed her name to Sylvia when she was a teenager. At the birth of a third daughter, her mother stopped sleeping with her father and devoted her life to art and to the interests of her three daughters. Eventually, Sylvia fled the parsonage in Princeton for a career in Paris, where she lived during her impressionable teenage years, when her father had been an assistant pastor at the American Church. After traveling in Italy and Spain, and serving after World War I with the Red Cross in Serbia, she settled permanently there and founded the bookshop, Shakespeare and Company (1919–1941), a literary center for American expatriates. As its proprietor, she first published James Joyce's controversial novel *Ulysses*, which had been banned elsewhere because it was considered obscene.

Beach opened this first English-language lending library and bookshop in Paris on the Left Bank with the encouragement of her friend and lover, Adrienne Monnier, who owned La Maison des Amis des Livres. In 1921, Beach moved from her tiny shop at 8, rue Dupuytren to 12, rue de l'Odéon, across the street from Monnier's French bookshop. For two decades, they dominated French-Anglo-Irish-American literary relations. Shakespeare and Company distributed a dozen expatriate little reviews, found publishers and translators, and offered readings by such literary figures as T. S. ELIOT, Paul Valery, ANDRÉ GIDE, and André Maurois. It was a clubhouse, bank, library, post office, publishing company, and confessional for two decades between the world wars.

Beach's greatest achievement was to publish a score of editions of James Joyce's *Ulysses* when it was available nowhere else in the world. She also published his *Pomes Penyeach* (1927) and *Our Examagination Round His Factification for Incamination of Work in Progress* (1929), essays analyzing *Finnegans Wake,* yet to be published.

Although Beach's name is connected to ERNEST HEMINGWAY, whom she called "my best customer," Robert McAlmon, and Ezra Pound as well as GERTRUDE STEIN and NATALIE BARNEY, her closest associations were with the French. And her most intimate relations were with women. There is no evidence that she was ever romantically involved with men. She had long friendships with a number of women, including the writer Bryher (Winifred Ellerman, HILDA DOOLITTLE's friend), but the love of her life was Monnier, with whom she lived from 1920 until 1936, when Monnier began a brief affair with another woman. Although from that time on Beach lived alone, the two women continued a devoted friendship, dining together every evening until Monnier's death in 1955.

The loyalty of her women friends was prodigious. Bryher financed the operation of Shakespeare and Company in the 1930s when the shop doors would have closed for lack of money. Monnier and Beach translated essays and poetry, including T. S. Eliot's "The Love Song of J. Alfred Prufrock," the first poem by Eliot completely translated into French. Beach assisted Monnier in editing her magazine *Navire d'argent,* and participated, with her, in editing Marguerite Caetani's *Commerce,* an international literary review.

Out of a sense of privacy bred in the parsonage, Beach did not talk openly of her love relationship with Monnier. In fact, both women were discreet, though not secretive, about their sexual relationship. Yet the example of their loyal and loving relationship speaks for itself. The strength of their union, their willingness to share difficult work, and the historical timing of their bookshops placed them in a position to influence the course of modern literature on two continents.

—*Noel Riley Fitch*

BIBLIOGRAPHY

Beach, Sylvia. *Shakespeare and Company.* New York: Harcourt Brace, 1959. ■ ———. Sylvia Beach Papers. Firestone Library. Princeton University, New Jersey. ■ Benstock, Shari. *Women of the Left Bank: Paris, 1900–1940.* Austin: University of Texas Press, 1986. ■ Fitch, Noel Riley. "The Elusive 'Seamless Whole': A Biography Treats (or Fails to Treat) Lesbianism." *Lesbian Texts and Contexts: Radical Revisions.* Karla Jay and Joanne Glasgow, eds. New York: University Press, 1990: 59–69. ■ ———. *Sylvia Beach and the Lost Generation: A History of Literary Paris in the Twenties and Thirties.* New York: W.W. Norton, 1983. ■ Ford, Hugh. *Published in Paris: American and British Writers, Printers, and Publishers in Paris, 1920–1939.* New York: Macmillan, 1975. ■ Joyce, James. *James Joyce's Letters to Sylvia Beach.* Melissa Banta and Oscar A Silverman, eds. Bloomingdale: Indiana University Press, 1987. ■ Monnier, Adrienne. *The Very Rich Hours of Adrienne Monnier.* Trans. Richard McDougall. New York: Scribners, 1976. ■ "Memorial Edition to Sylvia Beach." *Mercure* 349 (Aug.–Sept. 1963).

Beat Generation

Like the "Lost Generation" of the 1920s, the American "Beat Generation" of the 1950s names both a literary current and a broader cultural phenomenon or mood. Rejecting the conformism and stress on "normality" of the Truman and Eisenhower years, the Beats emphasized an openness to varieties of experience beyond the limits of middle-class society; they explored the cultural "underground" of bebop jazz, drug use, "polymorphous perverse" sexuality, and non-Western religions. The central Beat writers—WILLIAM BURROUGHS, ALLEN GINSBERG, and JACK KEROUAC—were gay or bisexual. So were several minor Beat literary figures, including Neal Cassady, Herbert Huncke, Peter Orlovsky, and Carl Solomon. This loose network of friends became nationally famous thanks to Allen Ginsberg's *Howl and Other Poems* (1956) and the obscenity trial that followed its publication. This publicity opened the way for the appearance of Kerouac's *On the Road* (1957) and Burroughs's *Naked Lunch* (1959) after years when no commercial publisher would consider them. By the late 1950s, the term *beatniks* (coined by a disapproving journalist) entered common usage to describe the subculture of bohemians inspired by the Beat writers.

The original Beat cohort formed in the late 1940s; it consisted of a group of writers, young and for the most part unpublished, living in New York and San Francisco. Besides their enthusiasm for jazz and drugs, the group around Burroughs, Ginsberg, and Kerouac shared an interest in literary experimentation. Their work stressed spontaneous and uncensored writing, often based on their own experiences among small-time criminals and drifters. Although explicitly rejecting what they saw as a domestication of the modernist *avant garde* by the New Critics and other academics, the Beats had a strong sense of working in a literary tradition of demotic and colloquial expression, ranging from Archilochus to Villon, WHITMAN, and Celine. A complex pattern of sexual relations emerged among the men—which, in a rather self-consciously literary fashion, they sometimes regarded as resembling the affair of RIMBAUD and VERLAINE. Like Rimbaud, they endorsed "the systematic derangement of the senses"—through intoxicants, meditation, and other forms of intense experience ("kicks")—as a means to reach states of expanded awareness.

Kerouac, who coined the expression *Beat,* insisted that it meant not simply "beat down" or exhausted, but also "beatific." And indeed, when writing about their pursuit of extreme experience, Kerouac and Ginsberg sometimes employed a mystical vocabulary—drawing on imagery of divine madness, the wise fool, and the holy sinner. Besides encouraging a sympathetic (if often sentimental) treatment of the lower depths of society, such religious language permitted the Beats to practice the jeremiad: a prophetic denunciation of the soul-less, bureaucratized, and consumerist ethos of Cold War society.

This embrace of marginality and denunciation of "square" conformity emerged primarily from an interest in African-American culture, particularly jazz. But it also extended to homosexuals—or at least to gay men since Beat writing showed little awareness of lesbians. There was some contact between Beat circles and gay literary figures such as FRANK O'HARA, ROBERT DUNCAN, PAUL BOWLES, and JOHN RECHY. Though the sexual preference of Jack Kerouac and Neal Cassady was primarily heterosexual, their writings acknowledged that they had had other sorts of encounters as well. Hubert Selby's Beat-influenced novel, *Last Exit to Brooklyn*, included a powerful and sympathetic portrait of a drag queen. And Seymour Krim, an essayist associated with the Beats, wrote "The Revolt of the Homosexual" (1958), an imaginary conversation between a defensive "straight guy" and an outspoken homosexual man. Even though Krim was himself heterosexual, the dialogue is unambiguously pro-gay rights: Every prejudiced remark uttered by the "straight guy" in the exchange is answered decisively.

But perhaps the most profound impact of Beat writing came, not through such programmatic endorsements of gay rights (significant though that was), but rather through its insistence that the writer should refuse inhibition and self-censorship. Or as Kerouac put it, in his aesthetic credo: "Believe in the holy contour of life. Struggle to sketch the flow that exists intact in the mind. . . . No fear or shame in the dignity of yr experience, language & knowledge." This did not always yield great literature, of course. Inspired by the Beat example, countless writers charted "the flow that exists intact in the mind"—which turned out, often enough, to sound like an imitation of Kerouac, Ginsberg, or Burroughs. Yet the Beats represented a struggle to accept the facts of experience and identity, and to convey them in literature, which considerably broadened the universe of public discourse in the post-World War II era.

A very large biographical, critical, and memoiristic literature has grown up around the major Beat writers. Gerald Nicosia's book on Jack Kerouac discusses in considerable detail the sexual relations within the group—which are also recorded in various collections of letters among Kerouac, Ginsberg, Burroughs, Orlovsky, and Cassady. Ann Charters's *Portable Beat Reader* offers an extremely intelligent and deeply informed selection of poetry, fiction, and essays by more than three dozen writers in and around Beat circles—including work by important figures such as Diane Di Prima, Bob Kaufmann, and LeRoi Jones, who do not fit the Beats' primarily white, male profile. A cycle of stories about the bohemia created in the wake of the Beats' emergence, Ed Sanders's *Tales of Beatnik Glory* has little to say about the movement's impact on pre-Stonewall gay life. Even so, it can be recommended as a humorous fictional treatment of that American countercultural species, the beatnik, circa 1962.

—Scott McLemee

BIBLIOGRAPHY

Charters, Ann, ed. *The Portable Beat Reader*. New York: Viking, 1992. ■ French, Warren. *The San Francisco Poetry Renaissance, 1955–60*. Boston: Twayne Publishers, 1991. ■ George, Paul S. and Jerold M. Starr. "Beat Politics: New Left and Hippie Beginnings in the Postwar Counterculture." *Cultural Politics: Radical Movements in Modern History*. Jerold M. Starr, ed. New York: Praeger, 1985. 189–233. ■ Krim, Seymour. "The Revolt of the Homosexual." *Views of a Nearsighted Cannoneer*. New York: E. P. Dutton, 1968. ■ Nicosia, Gerald. *Memory Babe: A Critical Biography of Jack Kerouac*. New York: Grove Press, 1983. ■ Sanders, Ed. *Tales of Beatnik Glory: Volumes I and II*. New York: Citadel Underground, 1990. ■ Stimpson, Catherine R. "The Beat Generation and the Trials of Homosexual Liberation." *Salmagundi* 58–59 (1982–1983): 373–392. ■ Tytell, John. *Naked Angels: The Lives and Literature of the Beat Generation*. New York: McGraw-Hill, 1976.

Beckford, William
(1760–1844)

William Beckford was born to an extremely wealthy and powerful family. His father was alderman and lord mayor of London, and his mother, connected by marriage to the dukes of Hamilton, was a stern and unrelenting Calvinist. Beckford's father died when he was ten, and his mother decided that it would be best not to risk sending her delicate son away to school. She hired a series of tutors and monitored his education herself. Beckford early on displayed an interest in art and music, and especially in the exotic Oriental arts of the Arab world. As he entered adolescence, he was lucky that one of his series of tutors was Alexander Cozens, whose own fascination with Eastern lore encouraged Beckford's own.

At the same time that Beckford's aesthetic taste began to develop, so did his devotion to emotional self-indulgence. Chief among his emotional attachments was a young cousin, William Courtenay, known as "Kitty" to family and friends, who responded to Beckford's attentions with adolescent devotion.

For years, Beckford poured out his soul in a series of epistolary endearments to Courtenay that were as extreme as they were indiscreet. These letters, almost inevitably, fell into the hands of Courtenay's reactionary and powerful uncle Lord Loughborough, a chief justice. Although, Loughborough could not catch Beckford and Courtenay *in flagrante dilectu,* he let out a rumor that he had, and he advertised the scandal in the morning newspapers from October through December 1784.

The result of this newspaper campaign was the utter ruin of Beckford's reputation. He lived as an exile in his own estate at Fonthill, and he traveled freely on the continent. But he was never again received in polite society. He lived until 1844, for sixty years an outcast.

In his travels, he met various men who befriended him and boys whom he loved. Some stayed close to him throughout his life, and a few earned his sincere devotion. But society meant too much to him not for him to feel the blow of his disgrace, and the frantic building that went on at his estate, which began with a wall around the entire property and ended with his massive gothic Fonthill Abbey with its huge central tower, might be understood as his attempt to deal with his status as an outcast.

Beckford wrote one novel that is still read with wonder, *Vathek* (1786), which appeared in an unauthorized translation of the original French in which he wrote it. It tells the story of Vathek the ninth Caliph of Abassides, who, goaded on by a wicked mother, indulges his appetites in a fantasy of sensual power. His companions in wickedness are the lovely Nouronihar and the child Gulchenrouz, who remains pure. It is easy to see Beckford's personal life in this tale and to understand his celebration of Gulchenrouz at its close as a clear articulation of pederastic love. At the same time, it is important to understand it also as a consideration of the pleasures of the flesh and a protest that they cannot be enjoyed without cost. In a sequel to *Vathek,* which he never published, Beckford planned a series of episodes that explored various forms of aberrant sexual behavior. (See also ENGLISH LITERATURE: ROMANTICISM, ENGLISH LITERATURE: NINETEENTH CENTURY, GOTHICISM, and TRAVEL LITERATURE.)

—George E. Haggerty

BIBLIOGRAPHY

Alexander, Boyd. *England's Wealthiest Son: A Study of William Beckford*. London: Centaur Press, 1962. ■ Chapman, Guy. *Beckford*. London: Jonathan Cape, 1937. ■ Crompton, Louis. *Byron and Greek Love: Homophobia in Nineteenth-Century England*. Berkeley: University of California Press, 1985. ■ Fothergill, Brian. *Beckford at Fonthill*. London: Faber & Faber, 1979. ■ Haggerty, George E. "Literature and Homosexuality in the Late Eighteenth Century: Walpole, Beckford, and Lewis." *Studies in the Novel* 18 (1986): 341–352.

Behn, Aphra
(ca 1640–1689)

Aphra Behn, known to her contemporaries as a "scandal" for both her writings and her flamboyant personal life, was one of the most influential dramatists of the late seventeenth century. Today, she is better known as a poet and novelist than playwright, and her extraordinary biography remains intriguing. Her birth name and parentage is a mystery. She was probably born in Wye, in 1640. Speculations about her early life include the possibility of several sets of parents. A biographical essay by "One of the Fair Sex" affixed to the collection of *The Histories and Novels of the Late Ingenious Mrs. Behn* (1696), maintains that Aphra was the daughter of Mr. and Mrs. John Johnson of Canterbury, whom Aphra accompanied, along with a young boy supposed to be her brother, on a voyage to the West Indies in 1663. Johnson, who was to have had an official appointment, died on the way. The mother and two children lived for a while in Surinam, then a Dutch possession, and Behn's most famous novel, *Oronooko or The Royal Slave* (1688), is based on her experiences there.

Upon Behn's return to England in 1664, she met and might have married a Dutch merchant whose name she took. Soon after, in 1665, he died, leaving Aphra without financial support. Perhaps because of her association through him with the Dutch and her knowledge of the language from her trip to Surinam, she was appointed an intelligence gatherer for King Charles II, who was to pay her expenses for a trip to Antwerp as his spy. The King, however, did not pay, and Behn's requests for money for her trip home were not answered. In December 1666, she was forced to borrow from a friend for passage back to England. Charles refused to reimburse her, and in 1668, Behn was put in debtor's prison. After her release, Behn determined never to depend on anyone else for money again, and she earned her living first in the theater and then as a novelist until her death on April 16, 1689. Behn was one of the period's foremost writers, with over twenty published plays produced on the London stage.

Claimed by VITA SACKVILLE-WEST to be the first woman in England to earn her living by writing, Behn was a dramatist when women were just being permitted to act on the English stage, and when no other woman was known as a playwright. She is also now acknowledged to be the first English novelist, as her two-volume book, *Love Letters Between a Nobleman and His Sister* (1682–1685), appeared in serial form years before the book traditionally cited as the first English novel, *Pamela or Virtue Rewarded* by Samuel Richardson, was published in 1740.

Behn's close association with royalty, especially her friendship with the King's mistress, Nell Gwyn, and her long-standing liaison with John Hoyle, whose affairs with other men were notorious, made Behn a prime subject for court and theater gossip. Widowed early, she refused to remarry and declared that she would not have been criticized so strongly if she had been a man. In a century when female behavior was socially circumscribed, the scandal of Behn's activities was not so much what she did, but the public way in which she did it, and the very public way she wrote about herself and her friends. Many of her poems document her relationships with other women, some are standard heterosexual romances, and others are clever and unusual treatments of taboo subjects such as rape, impotence, and male homosexuality. The majority of Behn's poetry was published in two collections that also include longer narrative works combining prose and poems. Most of her poems, however, are short lyric verses that reflect the customary English use of classical, pastoral, courtly, and musical modes, as well as the more recent satirical wit of her contemporaries. They also express her own unconventional attitudes.

Just as Behn was notorious for presenting sensational subjects on stage despite societal taboos, she achieved a reputation for unusually explicit accounts of erotic and sexual episodes in her poems. Many of these celebrated gay male and lesbian relationships. In recognition of her homoerotic predilection as well as her poetic achievement, Behn was heralded as a successor of SAPPHO of Lesbos by her admirers in a series of introductory poems that preface the collections of her works. She was also compared to her predecessor, the poet KATHERINE PHILIPS, who wrote poems about her own romantic liaisons with other women. Known as "The Incomparable Astrea," a complimentary title based on the code name she had used when she was Charles II's spy, Behn only subtly masked the true identities of her associates in her poetry, frequently employing some classical or pastoral disguise; and sometimes she outspokenly used their true names. Behn's poetry, therefore, was, in a sense, less public than her plays or her prose fiction since it depended, in many cases, on the enlightened audience's recognition of her topics for full comprehension of both the expression and implications of her verse. Such poetic technique involved a skill and craft that earned her the compliments of her cohorts as one who, despite her female form, had a male intelligence and masculine powers of reason. Since the term *androgyne* implied not only a female with male characteristics of reason, but one with a presumptively male attraction to other women, this high praise was a tacit recognition of Behn's sexual identity as well as a compliment to her verse.

In *Poems upon Several Occasions* (1684), the portrayal of many relationships is in the traditional pastoral mode, and several poems present the classical concept of the androgyne or hermaphrodite as the basis for same-sex eroticism. In the poem "*A Farewel to Celladon, On his Going into Ireland*," an intimate male friendship is elevated over politics and commerce. These verses ask Celladon why he bothers with boring government business ("To Toyl, be Dull, and to be Great"), when he knows that success will not bring happiness. It is more important, the speaker advises him, to enjoy the company of his close friend, Damon, to whom Celladon is "by Sacred Friendship ty'd," and from whom "Love nor Fate can nere divide" him. In other poems as well, there is a precedence of close personal relationships over public enterprise. Among these is one section, "Mr. Ed. Bed.," in "our Cabal," a long poem describing Behn's social circle in which "Friendship" that is "Too amorous for a Swain to a Swain" describes the relationship between Philander and Lycidas in conventionally androgynous terms, with clear overtones of sexuality. Philander, she writes, "nere paid / A Sigh or Tear to any Maid . . . / But all the Love he ever knew, / On Lycidas he does bestow."

Homoeroticism is standard in Behn's verse, either in descriptions such as these of male-to-male relationships or in depictions of her own attractions to women. Behn was married and widowed early, and as a mature woman, her primary publicly acknowledged relationship was with a gay male, John Hoyle, himself the subject of much scandal. Behn was known to have had male lovers throughout her lifetime, most notably the man allegorized as "Amyntas" in her verses, but she also writes explicitly of the love of women for each other. Just as the emotional and physical closeness of males is justified by their androgynous qualities, so, for women, hermaphroditic characteristics transcend conventional boundaries by allowing the enjoyment of female and male qualities in the lovers.

The breaking of boundaries in poetry, as in her life, caused Behn to be criticized as well as admired publicly. Her best known poem, "The Disappointment," finely illustrates Behn's ability to portray scandalous material in a somewhat acceptable form. The poem is usually read as a depiction of the frustrations of impotence: Cloris, having been aroused by Lysander, flees from him in shame, and the lovers are both disappointed by Lysander's inability to consummate their relationship. But the text has another interpretation that illustrates Behn's ability to layer diverse meanings in her poems. In this reading, the poem presents a woman's point of view on how rape may be disguised as courtship. For Cloris, defloration is a fate worse than death, and she will not endure dishonor even for one she loves. When Lysander continues to force her "without Respect," she lies "half dead" and shows "no signs of life" but breathing. Traditionally, her passion and breathlessness have been read as sexual arousal, but they might just as easily be read as signs of her struggle to escape Lysander, which exhausts her. As soon as her struggle ends, he is "unable to perform." When Cloris is unconscious, Lysander tries self-stimulation, ostensibly to continue the attack. Upon awakening, Cloris is unsympathetic, and takes the first opportunity she has to run away. Lysander's rage, which is more that of a thwarted assailant than an embarrassed lover, is greater than mere disappointment—he rants at the gods and the universe for his impotence and accuses Cloris of witchcraft.

In contrast, the joys of love are presented in such other poems as "Song: The Willing Mistriss," which describes how the female speaker becomes so aroused by the excellent courtship of her lover that she is "willing to receive / That which I dare not name." After three verses describing their lovemaking, she concludes with the coy suggestion, "Ah who can guess the rest?"

Behn writes as the champion of women who allies herself openly with women against men in the war conventionally called love. She tells her friend Carola, "Lady Morland at Tunbridge," that even though they are rivals for Behn's lover, when Behn saw Lady Morland, she grew to admire and love her. Because of that, Behn warns, beware of taking my lover as your own—he is experienced and can slip the chains of love. You deserve a virgin, she says, someone who has never loved before, who has eyes only for you, and has a "soul as Great as you are Fair."

Women uniting to oppose a faithless male lover is the theme of Behn's entertainment, "Selinda and Cloris," in which the title characters befriend each other in order to deal with betrayal. First Selinda is warned by Cloris about Alexis, who was untrue to her. Selinda's response is to ally herself with the other woman and vow that Alexis will not conquer her as he did Cloris. The women praise each other's generosity and intelligence, agreeing to be good friends. The reciprocal relationship between the women includes both physical and intellectual attraction, friendship, and sexuality. Cloris "will sing, in every Grove, / The Greatness of your Mind," to which Selinda responds, "And I your Love." They trade verses and sing together just as traditional pastoral speakers do. In this case, however, in addition to being poets, lovers, singers, and shepherds, the speakers are also, untraditionally, female. The celebration of their mutual joy is a variant on the conventional wedding masque of Hymen, and presents in song and dance a formal poetic drama that emphasizes the eroticism of the women's relationship.

The bonding of women in female friendship is most clearly stated by Behn in her explicitly lesbian love poem, "*To the fair* Clarinda, *who made Love to me, imagin'd more than Woman.*" This is the last of the poems appended to *Lycidus* (1697), and in it Behn shows how important to her were those androgynous qualities for which she herself was praised. Just as she was commended in the dedicatory verses of her *Poems* for having "A Female Sweetness and a Manly Grace," Behn asserts the unity of "masculine" and "feminine" characteristics in her "beloved youth." She cleverly argues that she "loves" only the "masculine" part of Clarinda and to the "feminine" gives merely friendship. Since Clarinda's perfection manifests the idealized Platonic form, loving her cannot and should not be resisted. Further, since that by which society defines sex is not found in the female form, that is, women do not have the necessary physical equipment to consummate what is, in a phallocentric culture, considered "the sex act," love between women is, by definition, "innocent," and therefore not subject to censure. Clarinda is a hermaphrodite, a "beauteous Wonder of a different kind, / Soft *Cloris* with the dear *Alexis* join'd." Clarinda is not a passive fair maiden, but one who, the title states, "made Love" to the speaker and, therefore, may also be seen as the initiator of their sexual activity. The reciprocity of their eroticism sug-

gests the mutuality of some lesbian relationships that reject the domination and subordination patterns of traditional heterosexual roles. As the poem ends, Behn, in a witty pun, asserts the multigendered sexuality of both Clarinda and the speaker: "we the noblest Passions do extend / The Love to *Hermes, Aphrodite* the Friend."

Through the centuries, there has been interest in at least some of Behn's works. Her later reputation has been enhanced by her prominence as a model for women writers as noted in Sackville-West's early biography (1927) and VIRGINIA WOOLF's memorializing of Behn in *A Room Of One's Own* (1929). Contemporary readers may recognize even more of the multi-layered messages in Aphra Behn's homoerotic works that place her foremost in gay and lesbian literary history.

—*Arlene M. Stiebel*

BIBLIOGRAPHY

Cameron, W. J. *New Light on Aphra Behn.* Auckland, New Zealand: University of Auckland, 1961. ■ Duffy, Maureen. *The Passionate Shepherdess.* London: Cape, 1977. ■ Goreau, Angeline. *Reconstructing Aphra.* New York: Dial Press, 1980. ■ Greer, Germaine. *The Uncollected Verse of Aphra Behn.* Essex, England: Stump Cross, 1989. ■ Link, Frederick M. *Aphra Behn.* New York: Twayne Publishers, 1968. ■ Mermin, Dorothy. "Women Becoming Poets: Katherine Philips, Aphra Behn, Anne Finch." *ELH* 57.2 (1990): 335–356. ■ O'Donnell, Mary Ann. *Aphra Behn: Annotated Bibliography of Primary and Secondary Sources.* New York: Garland, 1986. ■ Sackville-West, Vita. *Aphra Behn, The Incomparable Astrea.* London: Howe, 1927; New York: Viking, 1928. ■ Stiebel, Arlene. "Not Since Sappho: The Erotic in Poems of Katherine Philips and Aphra Behn." *Homosexuality in Renaissance and Enlightenment England.* Claude J. Summers, ed. Binghamton, N.Y.: Haworth, 1992. 153–171. ■ ———. "Subversive Sexuality: Masking the Erotic in Poems by Katherine Philips and Aphra Behn." *Renaissance Discourses of Desire.* Claude J. Summers and Ted-Larry Pebworth, eds. Columbia: University of Missouri Press, 1993. 223–236. ■ Summers, Montague, ed. *The Works of Aphra Behn.* London, 1915. ■ Woodcock, George. *The Incomparable Aphra.* London: Boardman, 1948.

Benson, E. F.

(1867–1940)

Born in 1867 to Edward White Benson, Headmaster of Wellington College, later Bishop of Truro, then Archbishop of Canterbury, and Mary Sidgwick, whom W. E. Gladstone once called "the cleverest woman in Europe," Edward Frederick Benson enjoyed a privileged upbringing within his elite

Victorian family and, like his siblings, fell easily into prolific writing. By the time of his death in 1940, he had written over one hundred books: tales of the supernatural, books on winter sports (he excelled at figure skating), biographies, autobiographies, but most of all novels, all of them enriched by his tenacious memory, his satiric wit, and his anecdotal charm. His autobiographical volumes—*Our Family Affairs* (1920), *As We Were: A Victorian Peep-Show* (1930), and *Final Edition* (1940)—remain excellent introductions to the Victorian and Edwardian worlds and effectively convey what protective coloration a gay man in these worlds had to adapt.

None of the Benson siblings married; three of them experienced periods of destructive depression; all of them at one time or another had same-sex relationships; and encouraged by their parents, they all wrote voluminously. The eldest, Arthur Christopher (1862–1925), is remembered for his poem "Land of Hope and Glory" and a five-million-word diary; Robert Hùgh (1871–1914), the youngest, became a Catholic priest and apologist, writing moral puzzle novels as well as melodramatic novels such as *Come Rack! Come Rope!* Benson knew that his brothers considered his "works and days . . . both dilettante and frivolous" because he committed himself to the social rather than to the academic or the theological world. After taking a double first at Cambridge, he worked for the British School of Archaeology in Greece and Egypt from 1892 until 1897, then returned to London. His life settled into the easy rounds of Addington (the family home) for holidays, Capri in the summer, Switzerland for winter sports, and eventually Rye, where he had acquired Lamb House, HENRY JAMES's home, and where he became the town's 645th mayor.

Success came quickly and easily for Benson, and he later regretted this. In *Final Edition,* he notes: "I saw now what a disaster that first success [*Dodo*] had been, for, backed by such critical encouragement, it made me think that all I had to do was to keep up my interest in life and dash off stories with ease and enjoyment." He tended to exploit characters through sequels if they were popular when first introduced. *Dodo* (1893) was joined by *Dodo's Daughter* (1913), *Dodo the Second* (1914), and *Dodo Wonders* (1921). Once Mrs. Emmeline Lucas, better known as La Lucia, came into existence, Benson quickly expanded her adventures in *Queen Lucia* (1920), *Miss Mapp* (1922), *Lucia in London* (1929), *Mapp and Lucia* (1931), *Lucia's Progress* (1935), and *Troubles for Lucia* (1939). The Lucia books have become cult classics, especially among gay readers, who delight in their campy exaggerations, social jealousies, and gentle but not altogether affectionate social satire.

Benson's reputation faded quickly after his death, until the BBC adaptation of the Lucia books restored him to prominence. One reads his books now with regret—regret that he did not write more openly and more tellingly about his own sexuality and the richly varied homosexual world that he knew and in which he participated. He wrote, though, with a fiercely guarded privacy and a keenly honed Victorian reticence. Homoeroticism, though, especially informs his university novels, such as *The Babe, B.A.* (1896), *David Blaize* (1916), *David Blaize and the Blue Door* (1918), and *David of King's* (1924), as well as the unusual *Raven's Brood* (1934); and he did write a biography of Alcibiades, the uninhibitedly bisexual Greek renowned for his physical beauty and his relationship with Socrates.

—*David Leon Higdon*

BIBLIOGRAPHY

Askwith, Betty. *Two Victorian Families*. London: Chatto & Windus, 1973. ■ Williams, David. *Genesis and Exodus: A Portrait of the Benson Family*. London: Hamish Hamilton, 1979.

Bentham, Jeremy
(1748–1832)

Jeremy Bentham, English philosopher, jurist, economist, and political scientist, was the leader of the so-called utilitarian school of ethics that held that the aim of legislation should be the "greatest happiness of the greatest number." Bentham was the most notable law reformer the English-speaking world has ever produced; in this role, his influence extended not only to Britain and the United States but also to France, Spain, and Latin America. Several of the emerging republics of South and Central America consulted him in drawing up their constitutions and law codes. In the Hispanic world, he was hailed as "el legislador del mundo." Madame de Staël, a French observer with a wide knowledge of European politics and literature, thought her age should be known not as the age of Bonaparte or BYRON, but as the age of Bentham. His international reputation was established by his *Principles of Morals and Legislation*, which appeared in the fateful year of 1789. Napoleon, for whom law reform was an issue of prime concern, called it a "work of genius."

Bentham, however, wrote far more than he published. The survey of his career that appeared in the

Dictionary of National Biography in 1885 noted that a vast number of treatises, complete or unfinished, existed in manuscript at the time of his death, and conjectured that "owing to the almost insuperable difficulties in deciphering Bentham's handwriting in the later years, much of it has perhaps never been read." Among these all but illegible papers were hundreds of pages, written at intervals over half a century, which make a contribution to what we would today call "gay studies." Bentham did not dare to publish any of them during his lifetime. Though a fragment of twenty-two pages appeared in print in 1931, no comprehensive account of the scope and significance of this impressive body of materials was published until 1985.

Bentham's primary interest in homosexuality arose in connection with law reform. In his day, men convicted under the English "buggery" statute were regularly hanged, a punishment public opinion enthusiastically applauded in England long after executions had ceased in the rest of Europe. Nor was this harsh policy challenged anywhere in the public press or legal scholarship. Bentham's task as reformer was made difficult not just by the force of English prejudice, but also by the absolute taboo on public discussion of homosexuality. In law books and in parliamentary debate, homosexual behavior was referred to stereotypically by the Latin formula, "peccatum illud horribile, inter Christianos non nominandum"—"that horrible crime not to be named among Christians." Bentham candidly admits in his notes the extreme fear he felt at the idea of making public his liberal opinions on the subject.

In order to counter British hostility, Bentham appealed to classical history and literature and to contemporary anthropological knowledge. The sketchy nature of his information shows how lacking scholarly sources were in his day. Bentham's work was a truly pioneering effort. Though he had been an outstanding student of Greek and Latin at Westminster School, his knowledge of classical texts bearing on homosexuality was limited largely to Thucydides' *History,* Xenophon's *Symposium and Anabasis,* PLUTARCH's *Lives,* Suetonius, Cicero's speeches, and Pliny's letters. He was, moreover, aware of the homoerotic poetry of CATULLUS, HORACE, and VIRGIL. He cites especially Virgil's Corydon eclogue and, interestingly, in light of Byron's contemporary response, singles out the Nisus and Euryalus story in the *Aeneid* as evidence that the Romans condoned male love. Astonishingly, he seems ignorant of PLATO's *Symposium* and *Phaedrus,* a circumstance that demonstrates how much Plato was neglected by students of the classics in Bentham's day. Among the unpublished notes for 1774 is a brief, curious literary *jeu d'esprit,* which combines the satirical style of Swift with much imaginative fantasy, bearing the odd title, "Castrations to Mr. B, from the Daemon of Socrates." It makes the point that though Socrates declined to be seduced by Alcibiades, such relations were commonly accepted in his society. The portrayal of Socrates draws on Xenophon rather than Plato.

Bentham seems to have been quite isolated in arguing for a tolerant attitude to homosexuality. He complains that in England "nothing less than the heart's blood of the victims marked out for slaughter" could appease popular hatred; he describes the face of a judge who had just sentenced two men to hang as glistening with "delight and exultation." Despite this fierce national animus and the lack of support for his liberal views, Bentham returned repeatedly to the subject throughout fifty years. In the end, he wrote over five hundred pages, mainly in five different periods—1774, 1785, 1814, 1816–1818, and 1824. This is astonishing when we realize that no essay on homosexuality appeared in English until JOHN ADDINGTON SYMONDS printed ten copies of his *A Problem in Greek Ethics* for private use in 1883. We may appreciate the difficulties scholars who attempted to enlighten the public faced when we recall that the first book on the topic published in England, Havelock Ellis's *Sexual Inversion,* was suppressed by the courts as obscene in 1898.

The twenty-five pages of miscellaneous fragments Bentham wrote in 1774 take note of the intensity of English antihomosexual sentiment and contrast this with the tolerance of ancient Greece and Rome. In 1785, Bentham prepared a formal essay in a polished and coherent style, apparently meant for circulation. It is not clear what prompted this unique effort. Under the stimulus of treatises by Cesare Beccaria, Montesquieu, and Voltaire, law reform had received a powerful stimulus in Europe. Nevertheless, in some rough manuscript notes preceding his essay, Bentham expresses his private anxiety about writing on this topic and dramatically reveals the distance of his perceptions from his countrymen's. "On this subject," he writes, "a man may indulge his spleen without control. Cruelty and intolerance, the most odious and mischievous passions in human nature, screen themselves behind a mask of virtue." Perhaps Bentham prepared the essay for circulation among his French disciples since it seems especially to address continental opinion. We do not know if it helped persuade members of the French Constituent Assembly to decriminalize sodomy (hitherto a capital crime) in the revolutionary *Code Pénal* of 1791. Voltaire and Montesquieu had both opposed the death penalty for sodomy but had seen social dangers in its practice. Voltaire speculated that it was a threat to population, Montesquieu feared its effeminizing influence might weaken a nation's military strength. In reply, Bentham gives instances of tolerant societies that suffered from overpopulation, and cites Julius Caesar and such Greek generals as Agesilaus, Xenophon, Themistocles, Aristides, Alcibiades, and Alexander as instances of bisexual men whose military prowess was remarkable.

Bentham regarded prejudice against homosexuals simply as an irrational hatred and antipathy. It is one of the distinctions of his later writings (from 1814 on) that he identifies what we now call homophobia and directs his efforts to analyzing it. In Bentham's view, it was this negative bias that needed explanation, not the phenomenon of same-sex desire. He finds its origin in religious asceticism inspired by the superstitious fear of a vengeful deity and in the desire of men who lead profligate lives to gain a reputation for virtue by damning a sin they are not inclined to. He excoriates the contemporary press for intensifying popular prejudice by an unvaried tone of vituperation that made rational debate impossible. With respect to contemporary literature, Bentham takes to task Henry Fielding, Tobias Smollett, and certain French and German novelists for introducing homophobic episodes in their fiction. But Bentham does not stop at countering negative attitudes toward homosexuality. Utilitarian ethics held that pleasure was good and pain bad. Its aim was to maximize the former and minimize the latter. In reviewing varieties of unorthodox sexual conduct, Bentham argues for the "beneficial effects of certain of these modes of enjoyment," that is, homosexuality. In his view, this was a harmless and pleasurable form of sexual behavior that did not have bad consequences such as unwanted pregnancies, abortion, infanticide, and female prostitution.

Of special interest is a detailed proposal Bentham wrote out in the form of a prospectus addressed to WILLIAM BECKFORD in 1817. Beckford, the wealthiest man in England and the author of a famous romance, had been wholly ostracized by English society for some three decades on account of a homosexual scandal. Bentham, who had known Beckford slightly before his disgrace, seems to be suggesting that they collaborate on a book. The work was to be a defense of homosexuality that would appeal to utilitarian values as against "gloomy and antisocial" ideals derived from Calvinist religion. It was to have three chapters devoted to literary and historical topics—perhaps Bentham thought that Beckford as a literary man could help him here. What inspired Bentham to contemplate this approach to the millionaire recluse is unknown; presumably Beckford never saw the document, since it breaks off unfinished.

The title Bentham proposed for their joint effort had a startling ring; he suggested calling it "Not Paul but Jesus." Though the collaboration never took place, Bentham pressed ahead in the next two years with a sketch for a book that would critically analyze biblical attitudes toward homosexuality.

This pioneering work in biblical studies adumbrated Derrick Sherwin Bailey's *Homosexuality and the Western Christian Tradition,* which appeared in 1955. Bentham argued that the threatened outrage at Sodom did not involve consensual sex, but was rather a mass rape violative of eastern traditions of hospitality. He noted that none of the Old Testament prophets who mentioned Sodom associates the city with homosexuality, nor does Jesus do so in the gospels. Pointedly, he contrasts Paul's vehement denunciation of homosexuality with Jesus' silence on the subject. Bentham's radicalism leads him to interpret the story of David and Jonathan as a homosexual romance akin to that of Aristogiton and Harmodius or Nisus and Euryalus, and more daringly, to argue that the bond between Jesus and John "the beloved disciple" was of the same sort. Bentham did publish a book entitled *Not Paul but Jesus* in 1823 under a pseudonym; however, though this work challenged Paul's claim to set himself up as a spokesman for Jesus and Christianity, it did not incorporate that part of Bentham's notes that touched on the dangerous topic of homosexuality.

A noteworthy feature of Bentham's writings on homosexuality is his effort to find a vocabulary that did not itself automatically incorporate pejorative or condemnatory judgments. In this enterprise, he preceded by more than fifty years the German, French, and Italian sexologists of the late nineteenth century who first developed a scientific nomenclature for sexual behavior free from traditional theological and legal connotations. Bentham was keenly aware of the harm that could be done by negative language: "It is by the power of names, of signs originally arbitrary and insignificant, that the course of imagination has in great measure been guided." He has of course no word that is exactly equivalent to the modern term *homosexual.* He often employs "paederast," sometimes in its original sense of a lover of boys, but often also to mean an adult male who is sexually involved with another man, as in modern French usage; in this latter sense, it approximates closely to "homosexual." In his early notes, and in his "Essay on Paederasty" of 1785, Bentham occasionally uses stereotyped contemporary expressions—for instance, referring to homosexuality as "this perverted taste." Later, he consciously repudiates such loaded terms and invents ingenious alternatives to signify same-sex desire and behavior; these include such expressions as "the improlific appetite" and (in reference to Greek tradition) "the Attic mode."

—*Louis Crompton*

BIBLIOGRAPHY

Bentham, Jeremy. "Bentham on Sex." *Theory of Legislation.* C. K. Ogden, ed. London: Kegan Paul, Trench, Trubner, 1931. 476–497. ∎ ———. "Essay on Paederasty." L. Crompton, ed. *Journal of Homosexuality* 3(1978): 383–405, 4(1978): 91–107. ∎ Boralevi, Lea Campos. *Bentham and the Oppressed.* New York: W. de Gruyter, 1984. ∎ Crompton, Louis. *Byron and Greek Love: Homophobia in 19th-Century England.* Berkeley: University of California Press, 1985.

The Bible

Perhaps no other book has been more influential—for better or worse—in determining the construction of gay and lesbian identity in the modern world, as well as social attitudes toward homosexuality, than the Bible. The story of Sodom and Gomorrah, for example, has given the name to "sodomy," and Levitical and Pauline imprecations have supplied the language used to legislate against many same-sex behaviors. At the same time, however, the Samuel narrative has provided one of the most influential models of male beauty, and the relationships of David and Jonathan, of Jesus and John the Beloved Disciple, and of Ruth and Naomi have authorized same-sex relationships. Indeed, the Bible has proved to be one of the richest and most creative sources of challenge to the gay and lesbian literary imagination, as well as one of the most powerful tools of self-validation.

Sexual World of Ancient Israel

The world of ancient Israel was deeply charged sexually. Early biblical narratives, designed to reassure readers or listeners of the beleaguered tribe's survival in a politically inhospitable climate, concentrate on miraculous propagation; Genesis, for example, deals not simply with the creation or genesis of the cosmos, but with the act of sexual generation as well. Barren or seemingly unmarriable women are repeatedly blessed with remarkable issue, often under dramatic circumstances. Widowed Tamar, for example, disguises herself as a prostitute in order to become pregnant by one of her late husband's reluctant male relatives (Gen. 38); Lot's daughters get him drunk so that they may seduce him and become pregnant (Gen. 19:30–38); and in a daring plan to force Boaz to propose to her, Ruth is so bold as to "uncover" her kinsman's feet as he lies sleeping on the threshing room floor at harvest time (Ruth 3:4–7). Hannah prays so fervently to be made fertile that she is rebuked by the priest for coming to the temple intoxicated (1 Sam. 1:12–16); and sisters Rachel and Leah frantically compete to see who can become pregnant the most often by their joint husband, Jacob (Gen. 29–30). So important is it for a family or a tribal line to continue that the leaders of Israel encourage the Benjaminites to abduct the virgins of another tribe after they are punished for the fatal rape of a Levite's concubine by having their own women taken from them (Judg. 21). Life must go on in the biblical world, no matter the cost to what modern readers might consider normative sexual morality.

This concern with the issues of survival and generation is responsible for the Old Testament's seemingly contradictory attitudes toward male and female homosexuality. As Jane Rule points out, "a people continually threatened with extinction must be concerned with producing as many strong and healthy children as possible," making the "spilling of seed" in male homosexual practice "wasteful and dangerous." A woman's sins, conversely, "are the sins of the field, remaining barren or accepting seed foreign to her designated crop." Thus, as long as she bore children to a Jewish male who had been circumcised, and did not confuse his line by committing adultery, a woman might seek emotional and perhaps even sexual fulfillment with another woman without alarming her culture; significantly, there is no direct prohibition placed on female homosexual acts in the Hebrew Testament. On the other hand, it is only when bonding with another male provides the beleaguered hero with the physical and emotional support essential to his survival—as in the cases of David and Jonathan, and of Jesus and John the Beloved Disciple—that a male homoerotic relationship is promoted as a model for others to follow.

This survivalist instinct seems also to have led the Israelites to figure their covenant with Yahweh as a heterosexual marriage relationship. The original covenant that Yahweh makes with Abraham equates devotion with propagation, Yahweh promising not only to make Abraham "exceeding fruitful," but guaranteeing to him "and to thy seed after thee, the land wherein thou art a stranger, all the land of Canaan," if he will "circumcise the flesh of [his] foreskin," male circumcision being the "token" of their covenant (Gen. 17:8–11). The covenant is recast in more explicitly heterosexual terms in Hosea, however: "And I will betroth thee unto me for ever . . . and thou shalt know the Lord" (2:19–20). Here Israel becomes a woman whose fertility depends on the extraordinarily potent lovemaking of her husband; in their worship of the carved images of foreign gods, Israel and her sister nation Judah are seen as harlots who left their loving husband and "defiled the land" by committing adultery "with stones and with stocks" (Jer. 3:6–9). The agony of the Lord in Hosea as an unrequited lover, refusing to throw off his adulterous wife, always willing to take her back, is one of the most powerful images in Hebrew scriptures, especially when read in the context of the sensual, celebratory lyric exuberance of The Song of Songs, traditionally interpreted to figure the marriage relationship between Yahweh and His chosen people. Nonreproductive homosexual sex, which assumes the basic equality of the lovers, could not answer the psychic needs of the ancient Israelites who—threatened by enemies of superior size on every border—were desperate for the protective reassurance that a hierarchical, heterosexual trope imaginatively provided.

Finally, the Hebrew attitude toward male homosexual activity was complicated by its association with idolatry. The native Canaanites valued the communities of men and boys who lived at the temple and at local shrines that were marked by stone pillars or columns presumably phallic in shape; intercourse with a *kadesh* (a temple prostitute) seems to have been perceived as a way of ritually enhancing both the individual's fertility and the tribe's power. (The judge Samuel, in fact, may have functioned early in life as a temple prostitute.) The communities of *kadeshim* were dissipated by the seventh-century B.C.E. prophetic movement that attempted to purify Judaism of foreign influences that threatened cultic purity. Deuteronomy 23:17–18, for example, strictly enjoins that "there shall be no whore of the daughters of Israel, nor a sodomite [*kadesh*] of the sons of Israel. Thou shalt not bring the hire of a whore, or the price of a dog [male prostitute] into the house of the Lord thy God for any vow: for even both these are abomination unto the Lord thy God." Likewise, 1 Kings 14:23–24 links "sodomites" with the worship of false idols "on every high hill, and under every green tree." Josiah's breaking "down the houses of the sodomites, that were by the house of the Lord" (2 Kings 23:7) indicates the tension that persisted over the coexistence of the two institutions despite Asa's earlier attempt to drive "the sodomites out of the land, and remove . . . all the idols that his fathers had made" (1 Kings 15:12; see also 22:46).

The opprobrium heaped on homosexual behavior in the Levitical "Holiness Code," then, reflects not a disparagement of homosexuality or of homosexual persons per se, but of idolatrous religious practices. It must have been especially offensive to the Israelite elders that the Canaanite cult prostitutes, who presumably were uncircumcised, should threaten the divine covenant by encouraging the practice of idolatry in a sexually sullying way. Thus, "if a man also lie with mankind, as he lieth with a woman, both of them shall have committed an abomination," Leviticus 20:13 unflinchingly threatens, "they shall surely be put to death." This obsession with cultic purity was extended by St. Paul into the Christian era. His concern for the holiness—and reputation—of the founding Christian churches led him to concentrate in particular on the sexual practices of early Christian communities, many of which took Christ's commandment to love one another quite literally. Paul seems to have been particularly troubled by the number of men in the early Christian communities who engaged passively in homosexual acts. The "abusers of themselves with mankind" (1 Cor. 6:9–10; see also 1 Tim. 1:9–10), as Paul termed them, leave "the natural use of the woman" to "burn in lust one toward another." But, Paul assures his followers, they have been given up by God to "uncleanness," "vile affections," and "a reprobate mind" (Rom. 1:26–27) and are to be excluded from the Christian community. (Some readers take Paul's vague complaint that even the women of the ungodly "did change the natural use into that which is against nature" to refer to lesbian activity, which would make Romans 1:26 the only biblical imprecation against female homosexuality.) His reiterated concern over homosexual practices, however, suggests how common they must have been.

Conservative social critics charge that any restoration of a historical context that mitigates, if not entirely erases, biblical imprecations against homosexuality is but special pleading and so is culturally and intellectually suspect. The danger of decontextualizing such influential biblical teaching, however, is illustrated by the interpretive history of the Sodom narrative (Gen. 19:1–11). The story seems originally to have been intended as an object lesson about hospitality. Lot takes home as his guests two male visitors to the city whom he must defend later that evening against a crowd that demands he send them outside "that we may know them." Lot offers his virgin daughters instead, is rudely rebuffed, and is saved from violence himself only when the visitors reveal themselves as angels and strike the men of Sodom blind. The episode is similar to Zeus's testing the hospitality of Lycaon in Book 1 of Ovid's *Meta-*

morphoses and to Odysseus's defending himself from the uncivil Cyclops in Homer's *The Odyssey* (Book 9) as the beleaguered hero makes his way home from the Trojan War. Such tales remind a seafaring people like the early Greeks, or a nomadic people like the early Israelites, who were forced to depend on the hospitality of indigenous peoples for their own survival, of the reciprocal responsibilities of host and guest.

Significantly, no other biblical reference to Sodom assumes homosexuality to have been the sin for which the "cities of the plain" were punished. Rather, early rabbinic and patristic commentary on the story assumes that the Sodomites, a proverbially wealthy community, wantonly abused the power accorded them by their wealth, their attempted sexual abuse of defenseless strangers being part of a larger pattern of their inhumane treatment of persons less fortunate than they. Their blinding by the visiting angels was, consequently, an appropriate punishment for having allowed themselves to become "blinded" by materialistic pride to the law of God and of becoming a law unto themselves; likewise, the sterility visited on their once-great cities is a reminder to live humbly in service to the poor rather than luxuriate in sexual self-indulgence. Such a reading of the text is supported by the fact that it is not the single episode with the handsome guests of Lot that dooms the people of Sodom; rather, as verses 20–21 make clear, Yahweh had already decided to destroy them and sent the angels to Sodom as *agents provocateurs*. Curiously, for those who want to read the Sodom episode and the parallel story in Judges 19 as evidence of God's prohibiting homosexual behavior, characters in both narratives volunteer to substitute the heterosexual rape of their virgin daughter or bondswoman for the homosexual rape of a visitor, a critical challenge to "normative" sexual morality.

Once Philo Judaeus (around 50 C.E.) associated the "sin of Sodom" exclusively with homosexuality, however, a curious transformation of the interpretive tradition began. "Burning with insane love for boys," as Clement of Alexandria puts it, came increasingly to be seen, first, as *one* of the many instances of sexual excess to which the Sodomites' love of sensual luxury brought them, but eventually as their *sole* crime. Even as late as the mid-seventeenth century, JOHN MILTON recorded in his commonplace book plans for a drama called "Sodom" in which "each evening everyone with mistress or Ganymede [walked] gitterning along the streets"; he clearly still assumed biblical Sodom to have been the site of both heterosexual and homosexual license. But after the shift in Western attitudes toward homosexuality that John Boswell demonstrates as taking place between 1150 and 1350, such

even-tempered approaches as Milton's became very rare.

Thus, the destruction of the biblical cities by fire justified for England's most influential jurist, William Blackstone, the punishment accorded sodomites in England by a 1533 statute. In his famous *Commentaries* (1765–1769) on the law, Blackstone asserts that both "the voice of nature and of reason, and the express law of God" determine sodomy to be a capital offense: "Of which we have a signal instance . . . by the destruction of two cities by fire from heaven. . . . And our ancient law in some degree imitated this punishment, by commanding such miscreants to be burnt to death." By the late seventeenth century, the noun *sodomite* came to indicate not simply an individual who engaged in anal intercourse but an identifiable sexual orientation; George Lesley's *Fire and Brimstone: Or, The Destruction of Sodom* (1684) is not only a dramatic diatribe against "buggary," but one of the first English-language tracts to identify as a discrete personality type men whose sexual engagements are exclusively with members of their own sex.

Biblical Authorizations of the Homoerotic

If Pauline and Levitical legal proscriptions, and narratives like that of Sodom and Gomorah, have provided the basis for the repression of homosexuality, three sets of biblical characters have offered models for homosexual love, strongly influencing its literary representation.

David. The narrator of The First Book of Samuel emphasizes the special relationship that existed between Jonathan, the son of King Saul, and David, the harp-playing shepherd turned soldier and fugitive, who is described as being "ruddy, and withal of a beautiful countenance, and goodly to look to" (1 Sam. 16:12). "The soul of Jonathan was knit with the soul of David," the narrator records, "and Jonathan loved him as his own soul" (1 Sam. 18:1). Later, when Saul's murderous jealousy causes his young rival to flee the court, the two friends suffer a poignant parting at which "they kissed one another, and wept one with another, until David exceeded" (1 Sam. 20:41). Jonathan's death alongside his father in battle with the Philistines occasions from David this powerful lament: "The beauty of Israel is slain upon the high places; how are the mighty fallen! . . . I am very distressed for thee, my brother Jonathan; very pleasant hast thou been unto me: thy love was wonderful, passing the love of women" (2 Sam. 1:19–26).

Not surprisingly, the David story—unparalleled in the Bible for its depiction of male love so lavish that it becomes "excessive" (to adapt the telling word employed by the King James translator)—has inspired several of the best developed Western homoerotic literary traditions. First, the David story has proved the most influential biblical justification for the description of sensuous male beauty. The lush description of David in the flush of early adulthood in lines 57–72 of Michael Drayton's "David and Goliah" (1630), for example, seems better fitted to an Ovidian celebration of sexual amorphousness than to a biblically inspired brief epic. Likewise, FREDERICK ROLFE, the self-styled Baron Corvo (1860–1913), cited the Bible's description of David as the statement of his erotic ideal: "a large boy of sixteen to eighteen years clothed with 'most lovely pads of muscular sweet flesh,' whose skin was of a 'rosy satin fineness and softness.' Such a boy was at his prime before 'some great fat slow cow of a girl' had an opportunity to 'open herself wide and lie quite still & drain him dry,' before he had got 'hard and hairy' with a moustache, 'brushes in his milky armpits' and 'brooms on his splendid young thighs.'"

Rolfe's ideal approaches that of the Greek ephebe, and David—to judge from how he was frequently represented in Renaissance art—was the primary biblical justification for the Christian artist's sculpturally reclaiming that figure. Two statues in particular have seized the gay imagination. Donatello's bronze David (around 1430–1440) might have modeled for Rolfe's fantasy; indeed, in "The Giant on Giant-Killing" (*Fellow Feelings*, 1976), RICHARD HOWARD pays "Homage to the bronze *David* of Donatello," asserting that the legendary giant was felled not by the stones launched from the boy's slingshot, but by the sight of his magnificent beauty ("No need for a stone! My eyes / were my only enemy"); any adult male viewer of Donatello's rendering of post-pubescent male beauty risks, by extension, suffering the same fate.

Even more significant has been MICHELANGELO's seventeen-foot-tall sculpture of David in white marble (executed 1501–1504), epic in proportion yet incandescent in hue. As Harold Norse notes in "Meditations of the Guard at the Belle Arti Academy" (*Carniverous Saint*, 1977), the statue is "read" differently by gay viewers than by heterosexual ones. In his "Unfinished Sculpture" (*The Young Sailor and Other Poems*, 1986), LUIS CERNUDA tries to imagine the relationship that existed between Michelangelo and his model that resulted in David's features being so lovingly drawn; the creation of the statue, the poem suggests, must have involved the model-speaker's being called to life in a love relationship with the sculptor simultaneous with the statue's form emerging from the block of stone.

So powerful is Michelangelo's image, in fact, that it has become the Western world's most pervasive symbol of male beauty and one of the staples of gay popular culture. Art critic Michael Bronski's recollection of the reproductions of Michelangelo's *David* that were displayed in many gay men's homes in the 1950s suggests how completely the image has been claimed by the gay community. "The *David*s [sic] were not just erotically pleasing pieces of inexpensive art," he writes; "they were also signals to visitors in the know that the homeowners were homosexual, functioning as a kind of aesthetic Morse code of sexual identity." That code operates even more effectively when signaling an invitation to engage in male eros. In Alan Hollinghurst's *The Swimming-Pool Library* (1988), the protagonist enters a theater whose front window had been "painted over white but with a stencil of Michelangelo's David stuck in the middle," an indication that homosexual activity was allowed on the premises; and, at one point in the late 1970s, Manhattan's David Cinema, a pornographic movie house, screened a film titled *Michael, Angelo and David*. So completely has the gay community identified with the erotic element of Michelangelo's *David* that its image was used to market a brand of amyl nitrate in the late 1970s and early 1980s, and verbal reference to the statue has served as effective a purpose as its visual reproduction. Writing of his first visit to post-war Italy, for example, TENNESSEE WILLIAMS assessed the local "talent" for a friend in the United States, noting that "I have not been to bed with [Michelangelo's] David but with any number of his more delicate creations."

Richard Howard's intimation that Goliath was defeated, not by David's tactical prowess, but by the sight of his beauty represents a second major use of the David narrative in gay literature: as a means of exploring the psychology of homosexual relations. Three relations in particular—with Goliath, with Saul, and with Jonathan—have invited scrutiny. The Bible's emphasis on the visual element in Goliath's encounter with David—"And when the Philistine looked about, and saw David, he disdained him: for he was a youth and ruddy, and of fair countenance" (1 Sam. 17:42)—led Drayton to describe how David's locks of hair, tossed by the breeze, "did with such pleasure move, / As they had been provocative for love" ("David and Goliah," 713–714). In *Davideis* (1656), Abraham Cowley summarizes the visual transaction with the curt but expressive "as he [Goliath] saw, he *lov'd*" (2:28–41). Donatello's statue significantly depicts on Goliath's helmet a scene of the Triumph of Love, the helmet's plume rising erotically up the inside of the naked boy's thigh toward his buttocks, suggesting iconographically that Goliath was killed by his desire for the beautiful boy.

Similarly, several writers who examine the reason for King Saul's obsessive persecution of young David conclude that David is so beautiful he leaves the older man sick with love. In both ANDRÉ GIDE's *Saul* (1896) and Michael Mason's story of the same title (reprinted in Stephen Wright's anthology, *Different,* 1974), sexual frustration and fear of his own homosexual longing are responsible for Saul's alternating feelings of love and hate for the boy. And though HERMAN MELVILLE allows the title character in *Clarel* (1876) to wonder about the possibility of enjoying a bond such "as David sings in strain / That dirges beauteous Jonathan, / Passing the love of woman fond," he suggests in *Billy Budd* (written in 1891) that Claggart's jealousy of Billy's "significant personal beauty" partook "of that streak of apprehensive jealousy that marred Saul's visage perturbedly brooding on the comely young David," thus raising the possibility that Claggart's designs on Billy are sexual.

But the most famous—and influential—of David's relationships is that with Jonathan. The legendary friendship between the two necessitated their inclusion—along with Damon and Pythias, Hercules and Hylas, Achilles and Patroclus, and Pylades and Orestes—on every list of male couples whose relationship is to be exalted. But as Cowley's praise of the friendship between David and Jonathan in the extraordinary "digression concerning the nature of Love" in *Davideis* suggests, it is difficult to specify the nature of the passion that animated that friendship. Poetic renderings of David's lament for Jonathan seem particularly suited for expressing homoerotics under the guise of imitating the biblical praise of friendship. Thus, Peter Abelard (1079–1142) could extend the biblical verses to 110 lines in which grief-stricken David protests "to outlive you / Is to die at every moment: Half a soul is not / Enough for life" (trans. Thomas Stehling), without risking ecclesiastical censure, while German poet Rainer Maria Rilke (1875–1926) could write a highly eroticized "Klage um Jonathan" ("Lament for Jonathan"). In *David: A Play* (1926), D. H. LAWRENCE uses the biblical relationship to signal the erotically charged but supposedly nongenital "blood-brotherhood" he hoped to share with another man. But in *Giovanni's Room* (1956) JAMES BALDWIN uses the biblical relationship as a foil to the failed homosexual love relationship between David, an uptight American who cannot accept his homosexuality, and Giovanni (Italian for Jonathan), the younger man whose loss David must spend the remainder of his life lamenting. A verse from 2 Samuel 1 provides an ironic text for the chaplain's sermon in Michael Campbell's tragicomic portrait of boarding school love, *Lord Dismiss Us* (1967).

So provocative are the details of the Bible's description of David's relationship with Jonathan that allusion to it becomes a discreet way of suggesting homosexuality in a literary climate inhospitable to more explicit assertion. At his trial, OSCAR WILDE described "the love that dare not speak its name" as "the noblest form of affection" that can exist between two men. "There is nothing unnatural about it," he asserted. "It is intellectual, and it repeatedly exists between an elder and a younger man, when the elder man has intellect, and the younger man has all the joy, hope and glamour of life before him." One example that he gives for such a love is the relationship of David and Jonathan.

Likewise, in "Twin Love" (1871) Bayard Taylor suggestively names the two boys who are "as unhappy as separated lovers" when living apart David and Jonathan. (Taylor's earlier collection of poems, *Poet's Journal* [1862], describes a relationship between two brothers likewise called David and Jonathan.) In Theodore Winthrop's *Cecil Dreeme* (1861), narrator Robert Byng consciously evokes the Bible's description of David's love for Jonathan when he says of his relationship with the title character: "His friendship I deemed more precious than the love of women," and "him I love with a love passing the love of women." (Since Cecil is revealed finally to be a woman in disguise, such statements are ironic. Winthrop is able to raise the specter of homosexuality but lay it to rest without offending his more conservative readers.) Ralph Waldo Emerson submerged his homoerotic attraction to Marvin Gay by creating in his journal the fiction of an author named "Froedmer" and a play called *The Friends,* which contains pointed allusions to love passing the love of women. Arna Bontemps's auditors presumably did not fail to understand what was intended by his description of poet COUNTEE CULLEN and Harlem schoolteacher Harold Jackson as the "Jonathan and David of the Harlem Renaissance." E. M. FORSTER alludes to the homosexual possibilities of Philip and Gino's relationship in *Where Angels Fear to Tread* (1905) by suggesting that they might "become as David and Jonathan." And William Faulkner is able to suggest the homoerotic attraction of Charles Bon for Henry Sutpen by framing *Absalom, Absalom!* (1936) with the biblical narrative.

Conservative writers have been equally assiduous in attempting to contain the homoerotic resonance of the biblical relationship. Writing little more than a century after the last of the David story in the Books of Kings had been composed and recorded, for example, the compilers of the biblical Books of Chronicles deleted the episodes of David's affection for Jonathan (as well as mention of any other instance of his emotionally exuberant behavior) in order to fashion a David who might more easily serve as an example of the decorous moral ideal to which successive rulers should aspire. Likewise, in *The Jewish Antiquities* (early first century C.E.), Josephus deleted the passage describing Jonathan's stripping off his princely garments as a token of his devotion to the handsome shepherd-commoner, in its place adding parenthetically—just after describing Jonathan's amazement at Saul's outburst against David—that Jonathan "revered him for his virtue," thus deflecting his father's charge that Jonathan's affection for Saul's enemy called his legitimacy into doubt (1 Sam. 20:30). Josephus also replaced David's sublime elegy for Jonathan with the prosaic explanation that David's "grief was made heavier by the thought of Saul's son Jonathan who had been his most faithful friend and had been responsible for saving his life." More recently, in *God Knows* (1984), Joseph Heller has David reason that "most likely it was that line about Jonathan, love, and women near the end of my famous elegy that is more to blame than anything else for the malicious gossip about the two of us," protesting finally that "I am David the King, not Oscar Wilde."

Richard Howard's retelling the story of David's defeat of Goliath from the giant's point of view, however, offers an apt model for gay reclamation of an important cultural tradition. Howard's poem allows a voice to be heard that the Bible does not permit to speak and that orthodox tradition attempts to still.

Ruth. Ruth's refusal to desert her mother-in-law Naomi during her worst distress—and particularly her oath that "wither thou goest, I will go: and where thou lodgest, I will lodge: thy people shall be my people, and thy God my God" (Ruth 1:16)—makes The Book of Ruth the biblical narrative most immediately available to lesbian interpretation. Jeannette Foster, for example, reads the Ruth narrative as "a masterly portrait of a somewhat passive young woman, twice playing the heterosexual role with success, but dominated by another love at least as compelling as that for the men she successively married"—first Naomi's son and then her kinsman Boaz. Indeed, concludes Foster, The Book of Ruth is so touching *because* of its subtle depiction of a "devotion" seemingly "unconscious of its own deeper significance."

Ruth's promise of fidelity to Naomi has had a particular resonance in lesbian writing. In Helen Anderson's *Pity for Women* (1937), for example, protagonists Ann and Judith recite Ruth's words while attempting to ceremonialize their union. The thematic center of ISABEL MILLER's *Patience and Sarah* (1969), perhaps the first self-consciously lesbian-feminist American novel to have commercial success, is the painting that Patience, an artist, makes for their home. She "painted Boaz and Ruth and Naomi, Boaz distant, very small, his back turned, leaving. I call it, 'Where Thou Lodgest, I Will Lodge.'" Patience is at first concerned that, despite the camouflage offered by a biblical subject, visitors might be upset by the passion of the two women's embrace depicted in the scene. Her conclusion to proceed with the painting anyway both reenacts the courage of the biblical women to persevere together and dramatizes the inspiration that that courage has been to lesbian lovers and artists.

Jesus and the Beloved Disciple. Identification of John as the disciple who would "lean . . . on Jesus' bosom, whom Jesus loved" (John 13:23; see also 21:20) inspired an important medieval homoerotic tradition. In his twelfth-century treatise *De speculo caritas,* for example, Aelred of Rievaulx defends those occasions when "some are joined to us more intimately and passionately than others in the lovely bond of spiritual friendship" by asserting that Jesus himself had forestalled criticism that such special relationships were "improper" by allowing "one, not all, to recline on his breast as a sign of his special love." Likewise, in *De Amicitia Spirituali,* Aelred contrasts John with Peter, emphasizing that "to Peter he gave the keys of his kingdom; to John he revealed the secrets of his heart. . . . [Peter] was exposed to action, John was reserved for love." Depictions of John as an ephebe resting his head on the chest of a bearded Jesus were popular in medieval art; such statues were often situated at the entrance to monasteries.

Fourteenth-century attempts to spiritualize the Ganymede story led to the conflation of John, thought to have been spiritually ravished with the gift of eagle-sighted prophecy, with the beautiful young shepherd whom Zeus/Jupiter took the form of an eagle to ravish sexually and abduct to heaven. James Saslow summarizes the features of the comparison made in works like the fourteenth-century *Ovidius moralizatus:* "As Jupiter symbolizes the Christian godhead, so the eagle who transports Ganymede into heavenly realms prefigures the attribute of John, the pure young disciple especially beloved of Jesus, who received a similar *furor divinus* from the eagle who inspired his apocalyptic visions and writing." The association of John with Ganymede permitted the presentation of homoerotic images under the guise of pious inspiration. In 1533, for example, fellow painter Sebastiano del Piombo suggested to Michelangelo that in the vault of the Medici Chapel's lantern he should paint a Ganymede with "a halo so that he would look like St. John of the Apocalypse when he was carried to heaven."

The Bible's ambivalence regarding John and Jesus's relationship has been adopted by later writers for varied effect. On the one hand, George Herbert simply asserts a typological similarity when, speaking in "The Church-Porch" of divine models for love and friendship, he notes that "David had his Jonathan, Christ his John," or meditates in *Lucus* 24 on John 21:20. On the other, KING JAMES I shrewdly neutralized in Parliament charges made against his relationship with George Villiers, Duke of Buckingham, by noting that "Christ had his John and I have my Steenie," thus leaving his critics unable to assert that there was anything improper about the king's relationship without suggesting that the relationship between Jesus and John was sexual as well. In 1817, JEREMY BENTHAM considered not only whether Jesus and John might have been sexually involved, but if the young man present at Jesus' arrest who eventually flees the garden naked (Mark 14:50–52) might not have been a homosexual temple prostitute who proved more loyal to Jesus than the disciples.

Other biblical identities have proved influential as well. The description of Absalom, David's son, as beautiful and having especially luxurious hair, set the medieval standard for male beauty so lavish that it proves effeminate. Likewise, the description of the Bridegroom in The Song of Songs has licensed poetic cataloging of the features of erotic male beauty; William Alan Robinson's "Song of Gabriel" (*Gay Literature,* Winter 1976), for example, puts in a male speaker's mouth the biblical Bride's praise of her lover's body and description of their lovemaking, not only deallegorizing traditional religious interpretations of an erotically charged text, but effectively challenging objections to homosexual love on religious grounds by dramatizing gay love as an act of emotional surety and religious faith. And, as the epigraph to the "Three Night Watchmen" chapter of Dale Peck's *Martin and John* (1993), Song 3:1–3 functions as a haunting refrain to a tale of desire and loss.

Subversions of Biblical Antihomoeroticism

The most telling challenge offered gay and lesbian writers by the Bible has been to reclaim the very passages that seem to censor homosexual love. Few writers in this category have not intended deliberately to shock the orthodox, as when CHRISTOPHER MARLOWE supposedly claimed "that St. John the Evangelist was bedfellow to Christ and leaned always in his bosom, that he used him as the sinners of Sodoma." The challenges they offer to the social construction of homosexual identity have placed them among the most controversial of Western literary texts.

Sodom. If for the readers of DANTE's *Inferno* Sodom has traditionally been the site of sexual and spiritual sterility, for countless others it has licensed contestation of Western sexual norms. Few moralists have, like Jeremy Bentham, been willing to question directly whether sodomy proved "a sufficient warrant" for so drastic an act as "God's burning Sodom." Most, like GORE VIDAL in *The City and the Pillar* (1948), rather, have used the Sodom narrative to question whether it is not preferable to be "damned" than to be "saved."

On the simplest level, recounting the Sodom story offers the titillating pleasure of considering what excesses might have warranted their destruction. In MARCEL PROUST's *Cities of the Plain* (*Sodom et Gomorrhe,* 1922), the narrator does not doubt homosexuals to be "a race accursed, because [their] ideal of beauty and [their] nourishment of desire also embody a source of shame and a fear of punishment." But this does not stop him from enjoying the voyeuristic pleasure of spying on the Baron de Charlus as he effects a gay liaison, on Albertine as she dances with Andrée, or from detailing the goings-on at Jupien's male brothel. The reader is similarly entrapped by the voyeuristic pleasure of Proust's text: nonreproductive sexuality comes to represent a license that fascinates and transfixes the reader's gaze but, unlike Lot's wife, the reader does not turn into a post of salt for looking.

Even more unsettling of normative sexual morality are eighteenth-century attempts to reclaim Sodom as a site of radical integrity. Responding to fourteenth-century scholasticism's labeling of sodomy as "unnatural" and the argument of moralists like Blackstone that "the voice of nature and reason" condemns sodomy, the libertine naturalists of the Englightenment celebrated the irrational by showing how artificial social constructions of the "natural" actually are. In *Sodom, or The Quintessence of Debauchery* (attributed to JOHN WILMOT, EARL OF ROCHESTER), the king of a licentious realm outlaws vaginal intercourse and makes sodomy the order of the day, encouraging all "to break all former vows / And do what love and nature disallows." Although the members of his court eventually rebel and force Bolloxion to rescind his decree, Rochester opens discussion of the pleasures of anal versus vaginal intercourse, making riotously satiric argument in favor of the former and proving how arbitrary manufactured restraints like Blackstone's laws are.

The most famous appropriation of the Sodom myth is that by the MARQUIS DE SADE, whose *120 Days of Sodom*—written in 1785 while he was imprisoned in the Bastille—attempts deliberately to "outrage the laws of both Nature and religion." Four men of the highest society secret themselves in an unnamed chateau for an extended period during which "everything of the lewdest invented in Sodom and Gomorrah was executed" on forty-two victims of their lust. Sade structures his narrative according to the 150 "simple," "complex," "criminal," and "murderous" passions that are recounted and acted out, his purpose being to "unveil" the nature that society would keep hidden.

Sade has been particularly influential for modern "speakers of truth" who defy the empty value systems and petrified structures of authority that attempt to control individual behavior, supposedly for the good of society, but actually to perpetuate a corrupt status quo. "Everything which other men take as obvious and accept, for me are abstrusely and painfully open to question," Italian poet and filmmaker PIER PAOLO PASOLINI acknowledged early in life. His *Salo* (1975) appropriates Sade's *Sodom* as an analogy for the political fascism that Italy suffered under as he was growing up, and for the even more insidious fascist control that the Roman Catholic Church and the ruling Christian Democratic Party exerted on every aspect of post-war Italian life. Paul Russell's *The Boys of Life* (1991) has appropriated, in turn, the details of Pasolini's aesthetic, his controversial life, and especially his violent death to tell the story of filmmaker Carlos Reichart's affair with teenaged Tony Blair, whom he casts in a number of disturbing films, among them *The Gospel According to Sodom,* in which Tony plays an angel whose arrival in the biblical city provokes a disturbing sexual apocalypse. Reichart's determination to break through every sexual and artistic boundary in the search for a brutal, naked truth is as much Pasolini's as Sade's.

As the litany of forbidden words in the song "Sodomy" from the 1968 rock musical *Hair* is intended dramatically to enact, a speaker's appropriation of what has been condemned socially can be both psychologically and culturally empowering. By reversing the poles of what are assumed to be good and evil, the writers of some of Western literature's most troubling social commentary have been able to question the values that many people take for granted, particularly in terms of society's control of individual sexual identity.

Paul. Paul, not Jesus, extended the Levitical attitudes toward homosexual acts into the Christian era. Contrasting Paul's fear and distrust of pleasure with Jesus' acceptance of the sexually marginal, Jeremy Bentham noted that "Jesus was one person, Paul was another. The religion of Jesus was one thing, the religion of Paul another; where Jesus had been silent, Paul was vehement." (Bentham unfortunately never completed his work, which was to have been a contrast of homoerotic love as justified by Jesus' teachings and example, with the homophobic influence of Paul.) Some pastoral counselors, familiar with the psychology of the homophobe whose vehemence masks his own homoerotic feelings, have seen in Paul's epistles evidence of a psychosexual disorder. In Gore Vidal's *Live from Golgotha* (1992), the narrator—a fifteen-year-old, well-endowed Greek boy who would enter the church calendar as Saint Timothy—complains of Paul's "double standard": "officially, he hated sex inside and outside of wedlock on the ground that it made you unclean in the eyes of God," but Paul himself never stopped "fussing around with my [Timothy's] bod," or with that of any other attractive younger male.

Vidal is not alone in thinking that biblical Paul protests too much. In "St. Paul and All That" and "Those Who Are Dreaming, A Play About St. Paul," FRANK O'HARA plays on a lover's middle name (Paul) to mock his fear of having his homosexuality revealed to his parents by being named in O'Hara's autobiographically explicit poems. Identification of his self-conscious lover with his biblical namesake comments on the self-repression of closeted homosexuals, whether in biblical or modern times. With more angry intent, Pasolini was planning at the time of his death to make a film suggesting that the "spirit" that infused biblical Paul was phallic. Pasolini, of course, courted public resistance to his films, which in this case would undoubtedly have proved phenomenal. Significantly, one of only two weekly columns during Pasolini's long association with the *Corriere della Sera,* Italy's most distinguished newspaper, that the paper refused to print is that in which he lambasted the self-hating homosexuality of St. Paul.

Conclusion

Two conclusions may be drawn regarding the Bible's place within the gay and lesbian literary heritage.

First, it is surprising that the Bible has not inspired more significant lesbian attention. For example, the narratives of Deborah, the only female judge of Israel, and of Jael and Judith, who adroitly save their people when the male leaders of the community prove unequal to the task, offer significant models of the self-empowering woman; yet the lesbian literary imagination has been more fully engaged by the legendary Greek AMAZONS. Likewise, although The Song of Songs licenses the erotic description of female anatomy, it has been almost exclusively appropriated by male writers in a heterosexual context; lesbian poets have found in the poems of SAPPHO more productive lyric models. The problem of invisibility that has historically excluded female same-sex activity from legal consideration seems to operate even in terms of the biblical literary tradition: Although Sodom's sister city Gomorrah has often been interpreted (as in Proust's *Cities of the Plain*) to signify lesbianism, there is no lesbian interpretive tradition corresponding to the incredibly rich one surrounding Sodom. The homoerotic literary traditions that issue from the Bible are predominantly male.

Second, the Bible significantly refers to certain acts, not to persons of one orientation or another; as John McNeill concludes, what is referred to in the Bible under the rubric of homosexuality is neither the same "reality as we have today" nor predicated on "the same understanding of that reality as we have today." Further, it can be seriously questioned whether what is understood today as the true homosexual and his or her activity is ever the object of explicit moral condemnation in Scripture." For this reason, a survey of interpretive strategies as applied to the Bible proves in part to be a history of social attitudes toward homosexuality.

But whether the Bible is seen as promoting the acceptance or the repression of homosexuality, its most important function historically has been to place homosexuality into discourse and, by its ambivalence and seemingly conflicting traditions, to keep it under discussion.

—*Raymond-Jean Frontain*

BIBLIOGRAPHY

Bailey, Derrick Sherwin. *Homosexuality and the Western Christian Tradition*. 1955. Rpt. Hamden, Conn.: Archon Books, 1975. ■ Boswell, John. *Christianity, Social Tolerance, and Homosexuality: Gay People in Western Europe from the Beginning of the Christian Era to the Fourteenth Century*. Chicago: University of Chicago Press, 1980. ■ Bredbeck, Gregory W. *Sodomy and Interpretation: Marlowe to Milton*. Ithaca, N.Y.: Cornell University Press, 1991. ■ Cole, William Graham. "Homosexuality in the Bible." *Sex and Love in the Bible*. New York: Association Press, 1959. 342–372. ■ Crompton, Louis. *Byron and Greek Love: Homophobia in 19th-Century England*. Berkeley: University of California Press, 1985. ■ Foster, Jeannette. *Sex Variant Women in Literature*. 2nd ed. Baltimore: Diana Press, 1975. ■ Frontain, Raymond-Jean. "'Ruddy and goodly to look at withal': Drayton, Cowley, and the Biblical Model for Renaissance Hom[m]osexuality." *Cahiers Elisabethains* 36 (Oct. 1989): 11–24. ■ Goldberg, Jonathan, ed. *Reclaiming Sodom*. New York: Routledge, 1994. ■ Hallam, Paul. *The Book of Sodom*. New York: Verso, 1993. ■ Horner, Tom. *Jonathan Loved David: Homosexuality in Biblical Times*. Philadelphia: Westminster Press, 1978. ■ Jeffrey, David L., ed. *A Dictionary of Biblical Tradition in English Literature*. Grand Rapids, Mich.: Eerdmans, 1992. ■ Kay, Richard. *Dante's Swift and Strong: Essays on Inferno XV*. Lawrence: Regents Press of Kansas, 1978. ■ McNeill, John J. *The Church and the Homosexual*. Kansas City: Sheed Andrews and McNeel, 1976. ■ Pebworth, Ted-Larry. "Cowley's *Davideis* and the Exaltation of Friendship." *The David Myth in Western Literature*. Raymond-Jean Frontain and Jan Wojcik, eds. West Lafayette, Ind.: Purdue University Press, 1980. 96–104. ■ Rule, Jane. *Lesbian Images*. Garden City, N.Y.: Doubleday, 1975. ■ Sakenfeld, Katharine Doob. "Loyalty and Love: The Language of Human Interconnections in the Hebrew Bible." *Michigan Quarterly Review* 22 (Summer 1983): 190–204. ■ Saslow, James M. *Ganymede in the Renaissance: Homosexuality in Art and Society*. New Haven: Yale University Press, 1986.

Bisexual Literature

Although experiences that can be termed "bisexual" appear in works throughout literary history, they are rarely discussed from that perspective. Instead, explicit scenes or implicit evidence of erotic activity in which a single character is involved with members of both the same and other sex is usually considered as evidence indicating a primary sexual orientation that is either hetero- or homosexual. The continued reliance in modern Anglo-American and European culture upon binary systems of classification and identification has meant the practical erasure of bisexuality, as such, from most works of literary and cultural analysis. But life in all its nonbinary complexity and as it is reflected in literary works continues to subvert such reductiveness. An overview of relevant theories of bisexuality and its pervasiveness in literature challenges us to recognize the continuing importance of a specifically bisexual literary heritage, one that both converges with and diverges from the lesbian and gay literary heritage.

Beginning with Freud, bisexuality has been acknowledged but heavily stigmatized by many psychological and social theorists. In *Three Essays on the Theory of Sexuality* (1905), Freud asserts that bisexuality is, in fact, a natural state for infants and discusses at length young children's "polymorphous perversity" as they invite and enjoy all pleasurable tactile sensations. But the use of the word *perversity* is key here, for Freud argues that bisexuality is an inherently infantile, regressive state, one that is invariably abandoned as psychological maturation proceeds. As David T. Evans explores in *Sexual Citizenship* (1993), Freud never really accepts the possibility of bisexuality existing among adults, implying instead that sexual orientation is primarily heterosexual (which is preferable) or homosexual (which is itself regressive), with other anomalous experiences placed for the most part under the heading "contingent" and dismissed as such. Implicit in Freud's schema is a judgment found in much succeeding analysis, from Richard von Krafft-Ebing through Irene Fast, that bisexuals do not actually exist, that those who claim to be bisexual are being dishonest about their true orientation, and that such fence-sitting is simply childish. Of course, this general condemnation has not gone uncontested, for even Freud and his numerous devotees affirm that bisexuality is a natural state, even if "normal" progression toward maturity requires its abandonment. But what, one might ask, is "normal"? Constructions of normality are invariably suspect, for they are always historically and culturally specific, determined by ideology and tradition. Wilhelm Stekel, a contemporary of Freud, argued in *Bisexual Love* (1922) that both heterosexuality and homosexuality require repression and sublimation of natural urges; this often leads to neurosis in adults. Recent theorists, such as Fred Klein, author of *The Bisexual Option* (1978), have expanded upon such commentary to validate bisexuality as a legitimate sexual orientation, one that Klein even argues is psychologically healthier than others because it gives freest reign to innate desires for intimacy. Polymorphous perversity has been reclaimed without stigma, as numerous bisexuals, writing in volumes such as *Bisexuality: A Reader and Sourcebook* (1990), *Bi Any Other Name: Bisexual People Speak Out* (1991), and *Closer to Home: Bisexuality and Feminism* (1992), have looked to each other and to literature for support and validation.

It is not surprising that many find clearest evidence of positive, fulfilling possibilities for bisexual existence among classical writers, whose texts reflect designations and classifications radically different from our own. As Eva Cantarella has explored in *Bisexuality in the Ancient World* (1992), bisexual activity existed among both the ancient Greeks and Romans, among both men and women. She finds overwhelming evidence of a general accommodation of mixed heterosexual and homosexual encounters for men in works by Homer, Anacreon, and Pindar among the Greeks, and PLUTARCH, Cicero, and CATULLUS, among the Romans. This is not to say that binarism was nonexistent among these groups, but that instead of classifying people as heterosexual or homosexual, the Greeks and Romans tended to divide individuals into active and passive sexual groups, regardless of the biological sex of a given erotic object choice.

Nevertheless, the profound sexism of ancient Greek and Roman society did severely limit the possibilities for expressions of lesbian or bisexual love by women. Although PETRONIUS's *Satyricon* (first century A.D.) includes vague references to bisexuality among women, the life and work of SAPPHO represents the one notable exception to a general silence on the issue. In fact, her love poetry directed toward other women as well as clear erotic involvement with men make her the paradigmatic strong-willed, healthy bisexual for theorist Janet Bode, who argues forcefully in *View from Another Closet: Exploring Bisexuality in Women* (1976) that Sappho has been erroneously appropriated as simplistically "lesbian" when in fact her poetry clearly mentions sexual attraction toward men and the value of heterosexual marriage. Bode and Cantarella find that the post-Freudian impetus toward reductive classification of sexual orientations has meant the suppression of important information about classical writers whose complex works challenge our overly narrow notions of IDENTITY. (See also GREEK LITERATURE, ANCIENT and ROMAN LITERATURE.)

And such complexity is not confined to the classical period alone. The "homosexuality" that John Boswell analyzes in his overview of the late classical and medieval ages, *Christianity, Social Tolerance, and Homosexuality* (1980), is as easily described as "bisexuality" since, as he aptly points out, references to sexual contact between men were often contextualized in descriptions of numerous other forms of erotic pleasure and social transgression. Although same-sex erotic activity was often singled out as particularly disturbing to church and political power structures, nowhere is it binarily categorized as indicative of an identity that excluded attraction to members of the other sex. This also helps account for the polymorphous eroticism of the Renaissance: the glorification of both male and female beauty in the art of MICHELANGELO and Raphael, as well as the explicit bisexual tensions in the works of SHAKESPEARE and MARLOWE. In the former's sonnets, especially in early ones such as numbers 20 and 42, the speaker seems caught in erotic triangles that are not reducible to simple designations of hetero- or homosexuality. Similarly, Marlowe celebrates the erotic beauty of both sexes in his poem "Hero and Leander," even as his Edward II in the play of the same name is married to and has fathered a child by a woman, but is shown to be in love with a man.

Lillian Faderman in *Surpassing the Love of Men* (1981) traces similar expressions of polymorphous sexuality by women during the sixteenth and seventeenth centuries. The French novelist Madame de La Fayette, the lover of La Rochefoucauld, was also passionately attached to a woman, Madame de Sévigné. KATHERINE PHILIPS, a popular poet from England in the seventeenth century, wrote love poetry to women, but evidence suggests that she was also happily married and certainly came to her husband's defense in public. In both cases it might be possible to identify a "preference" for such writers (La Fayette could be seen as primarily attracted to men and Philips to women), but bisexual readers and critics would question whether preference alone is enough to place a person within a narrowly defined sexual identity that was only theorized as such during the late nineteenth century.

And it is in the eighteenth and nineteenth centuries that we find not only the continuing presence of bisexuality, but also a sharpening homophobia and growing social need for narrow definitions of sexual identity. These slow changes clearly relate to the burgeoning social contestation of gender and class roles that historians Thomas Laqueur and David Greenberg have traced. Such conflict is also reflected in the life and works of the Romantic poet LORD BYRON, who stands as one of the preeminent figures in the history of bisexuality. His numerous affairs with both men and women, his tortured sense of isolation, and his portrayal of nonstandard forms of erotic attraction throughout his poetry make him seem the transgressor *par excellence*. But Byron's polymorphous eroticism was not met with full social acceptance as it might have been during the classical era. In *Byron and Greek Love* (1985) Louis Crompton argues forcefully that Byron was self-aware in his bisexuality and acted often on his attraction to members of both sexes, but was finally punished and exiled because of deepening fears of social instability. Such tensions concerning Byron's diverse and unpopular sexual desires produced uneven representations in his works; *Don Juan* (1819–1824) clearly recounts the hero's erotic adventures with women, but contains little homoeroticism, only a muted defense of classical writers of homoerotic verses. *Childe Harold* (1812–1818) too foregrounds heterosexual passions, even as it contains poignant but veiled references to the death of one of Byron's own loves, John Edleston. Byron actively mocks sexual conventions, though he also seems constrained by them in that he is explicit only in his portrayal of heterosexual desire, though that desire itself is often quite transgressive. Such a mixture of lustiness and restraint in Byron's works, as well as the chaos and pathos of his life, serve to illustrate both the changing contexts in which bisexuality was perceived and understood, and the difficulties shared by bisexuals and homosexuals during repressive eras.

But if bisexuality was muted in certain "high cultural" literary expressions from this era, it was still graphically portrayed in nineteenth-century pornography. In anonymous erotic novels such as *The Adventures of a Schoolboy* (1866) and *My Secret Life* (1888), and the stories published in the scandalous periodical *The Pearl* (1879–1880), bodies fuse socially and erotically with little attention paid to class or biological sex. Victorian pornography is filled with vignettes in which men and women alternate sexual encounters with members of the same and other sex. Erotic threesomes and foursomes engage in relatively uninhibited perversity as identity seems primarily constructed around libertinism rather than a narrow definition of sexual object choice. Although there is some indication in *The Adventures of a Schoolboy* that bisexuality is an inherently immature state, the opposite is true for *My Secret Life*, where the narrator explores increasingly transgressive forms of erotic behavior as he grows older. Little stigma is attached to such activity beyond that of living and loving counterculturally, of being fully sexual, rather than homo- or heterosexual. (See also EROTICA AND PORNOGRAPHY.)

And despite a tightening web of social discourses on sexuality during this period, erotic diversity was not confined to English pornography; continental and American works from many genres also demonstrate some rebellious expressions of bisexual desire. In French literature of the era, one finds not only gender transgression, in the life and work of George Sand, for example, but also transgressive sexuality. Théophile Gautier's title character in *Mademoiselle de Maupin* (1835) is explicitly bisexual, jumping from bed to bed with an abandon that many contemporary critics found scandalous. Similarly, the poet PAUL VERLAINE was well-known for his bisexual love affairs; indeed, his poetry portrays both heterosexual and homosexual erotic activity, including lesbian relationships. Across the Atlantic, the same polymorphous eroticism is evident in the works of WALT WHITMAN, whose poetry celebrates the physical beauty of both men and women; even those poems most often appropriated as singularly "gay," such as the "Calamus" series, do not focus solely on attraction between men. This clearly links his writings to those of EMILY DICKINSON, whose poetry also reveals an ambiguous sexuality, as Camille Paglia has explored at length in her controversial study *Sexual Personae* (1990). Such fluidity stands in sharp contrast to the image we have of the entire nineteenth century as a time of static prudishness and anxious demarcation of rigid social and sexual boundaries.

But such an image is not wholly unwarranted, for even as key works from early- and mid-century seem to indicate a continuing free play that may appear unusual today, we can also locate during this time the origins of certain narrow classifications that would work to foreclose erotic options, both in literature and, no doubt, in some individuals' lives. In the work of sexologists and psychologists such as Freud, Krafft-Ebing, Karl Heinrich Ulrichs, Havelock Ellis, and EDWARD CARPENTER, all of whom began their inquiries during the last decades of the nineteenth century, we find a medical colonization of sexuality and a general move toward the pathologization of same-sex desire. As MICHEL FOUCAULT has charted in volume one of *The History of Sexuality* (1978), the rise of a medical/psychological discourse on sexual orientation clearly formed a means for social control. Of course, such categorization and valuation also brought homosexuality into discourse, thereby providing an avenue for countering as well as enforcing social rules. But unlike homosexuality, bisexuality was practically erased from discourse; while the "homosexual" was often castigated, the "bisexual" was not even a legitimate "type" and therefore disappeared from much of literature except as a figure in transition. Nowhere is this transition more usefully represented than in the works of OSCAR WILDE. Wilde himself is most accurately termed a "bisexual" since he engaged in both heterosexual and homosexual activity. And certainly *The Picture of Dorian Gray* (1891) remains one of the most polymorphously perverse texts ever written, as desire seems to flow between, in, and around all the characters regardless of their biological sex. But another work attributed to Wilde, *Teleny,* demonstrates a far less fluid eroticism. Unlike pornographic works from earlier in the century, *Teleny,* written in the 1890s, portrays a clear pattern of sexual identification through binary opposition. Although sexual encounters between men and women are described in the novel, they are rendered horrific and "unnatural," given the specific sexual orientation of the main character Des Grieux, who comes to define himself against heterosexuality. No longer was libertinism an identity encompassing numerous forms of nonprocreational sex; instead, as Foucault argues, the homosexual was a "type" created through a process of exclusion and a careful delimitation of desire.

Thus numerous works from the early twentieth century revolve around this notion of a "true" identity, one that is either hetero- or homosexual. Although both E. M. FORSTER's *Maurice* (written 1914) and RADCLYFFE HALL's *The Well of Loneliness* (1928) portray characters who appear bisexual, they are not allowed to occupy that "in between" space without derision. Both novels attempt to portray the naturalness of homosexual desire (in obvious response to the discourses of medicine and psychology that argued the opposite), but they do so by casting the bisexual as untrue to himself or herself, unwilling to take the brave step of acknowledging a fundamental homosexual identity. Thus Clive in *Maurice* and Mary in *The Well of Loneliness* are portrayed as cowards, doomed to unhappiness because of their equivocation. Individuals who historically would have been celebrated for their ability to respond to both sexes came to be considered the truly unnatural ones, out of place and inconvenient in a literary and social war between homosexuals and their heterosexual oppressors.

This is not to say that bisexuality disappeared completely in terms of writers' lived experiences. VIRGINIA WOOLF was clearly bisexual, as was the imagist poet H.D. But even Woolf, who explores gender transgression in such radical ways in *Orlando* (1928) (whose hero/heroine changes biological sex), never celebrates bisexuality in her works as a unified identity. At best, bisexuality is present in early twentieth-century, Anglo-American literature as a tortured, tense state, such as that indicated in many of D. H. LAWRENCE's novels, where emotional commitments to both sexes are possible only if expressions of physical intimacy between members of the same sex are severely limited. Even more typical of the middle years of the century is the representation of bisexuality in EVELYN WAUGH's *Brideshead Revisited* (1945); though possibly bisexual himself, Waugh portrays it as a phase through which, at best, one passes on the way to a firm identity (which in the case of *Brideshead* means a healthy heterosexuality and pathological homosexuality). The same idea is echoed later in JAMES BALDWIN's *Giovanni's Room* (1956), where bisexuality is portrayed as a phase that, if not moved beyond, becomes unstable and leads to personal disaster.

But the rich complexity of human emotional response and the diversity of human desires cannot be so easily suppressed and dismissed. GORE VIDAL, in his afterward to *The City and the Pillar* (1948), reclaims bisexuality as the most "natural" human state. So too did the French novelist COLETTE, who both in her life and literary works celebrated bisexual eroticism. In the "Claudine" novels and later works, Colette portrays the many quandaries faced by a woman attracted to members of both sexes, ones that Colette herself encountered in her marriages to men and affairs with other women. Colette's novels from the early part of the twentieth century anticipate the portrayals of relatively healthy bisexuality that would only become common many decades later, after the gay and lesbian rights movements had gained a sense of legitimacy and rigid rules for self-identification began to erode.

In the years since the 1969 Stonewall uprising and the publication of the Kinsey sex surveys (in which bisexual activity was found to be very common), many more positive and complex portrayals of bisexuality have appeared in print. URSULA K. LE GUIN's celebrated science fiction novel *The Left Hand of Darkness* (1969) remains a remarkable exploration of sexual diversity, describing an alien people who can change biological sex as reproductive cycles demand. They have the natural, innate potential to respond to each other with enormous sexual freedom. Similarly utopian in its vision of future erotic liberation is Marge Piercy's *Woman on the Edge of Time* (1976), which portrays a human society in which bisexuality is the norm and where narrow gender roles and definitions of sexual orientation have been abandoned as unnecessary historical constructs. Bisexuality also plays a key part in the protagonist's growth toward fulfillment in ALICE WALKER's celebrated novel *The Color Purple* (1982), where erotic bonding between women is shown not only to be compatible with heterosexual desires, but even necessary for women's political strength and security. Lastly, important non-fictional discussions of bisexuality appear in the works of the French feminist theorist HÉLÈNE CIXOUS and those of the American literary and cultural critic Kate Millett, both of whom decry the oppressiveness of binary constructions of identity.

Numerous works by male writers of the mid- to late-twentieth century are equally "bi-positive." PAUL BOWLES's short stories, set in North Africa, explore the relative freedom allowed for bisexual men by some modern Arab cultures, even as they dramatize the harsh and unrelenting sexism of the same societies. A similar double-standard is explored in Norman Mailer's *Ancient Evenings* (1983), which brings to life Egypt during the reign of the pharaohs and takes as one of its basic assumptions the bisexuality of its male characters. Tom Spanbauer's *The Man Who Fell in Love With the Moon* (1991) explores bisexuality in yet another non-Western culture, that of the Native Americans; this first-person narrative is told from the perspective of a berdache, a biologically male, though transgendered, individual whose sexual ambiguity meets with relentless hostility from conservative Christian settlers on the American frontier. And finally, similar internal and external tensions confront bisexual characters in the works of DAVID LEAVITT and the poet Gavin Dillard, both of whom portray bisexuality as a natural state for some people, even as social and interrelational forces continue to urge, and sometimes force, individuals to choose between hetero- and homosexual identities.

But at the very least, the discourse on sexuality has rewidened since the mid-twentieth century so that validation for bisexuals is no longer impossible to locate in literature and social movements. Conceptualizations in the 1990s of a broad notion of a "queer" identity, one that embraces gays, lesbians, bisexuals, transgendered individuals, and even transgressive heterosexuals, have been welcomed by many in the subsumed communities, even as others have resisted any revision in the narrower, binarized notions of identity that have proved to be politically efficacious in the past. But simplistic designations of all human beings as fundamentally heterosexual or homosexual are clearly as oppressive toward some people as institutionalized homophobia has been toward gays and lesbians. Whether or not bisexuality is a natural state for all women and men, it is certainly so for some, as history and literature repeatedly bear out. And in recognizing the unique interests of the bisexual community, as well as the numerous ways such interests intersect with those of the gay and lesbian communities, we can come to a better understanding of social history and the rich heritage of literary traditions and representations that counter heterosexism and challenge the narrow, tradition-bound, and oppressive categories through which society identifies and thereby judges people.

—Donald E. Hall

BIBLIOGRAPHY

Bode, Janet. *View from Another Closet: Exploring Bisexuality in Women.* New York: Hawthorn, 1976. ■ Boswell, John. *Christianity, Social Tolerance, and Homosexuality.* Chicago: University of Chicago Press, 1980. ■ Cantarella, Eva. *Bisexuality in the Ancient World.* Trans. Cormac O'Cuilleanain. New Haven: Yale University Press, 1992. ■ Cixous, Hélène and Catherine Clement. *The New Born Woman.* Trans. Betsy Wing. Minneapolis: University of Minnesota Press, 1986. ■ Crompton, Louis. *Byron and Greek Love.* Berkeley: University of California Press, 1985. ■ Evans, David. *Sexual Citizenship: The Material Construction of Sexualities.* London: Routledge, 1993. ■ Faderman, Lillian. *Surpassing the Love of Men: Romantic Friendship and Love Between Women from the Renaissance to the Present.* New York: Morrow, 1981. ■ Foucault, Michel. *The History of Sexuality.* Vol. I. Trans. Robert Hurley. New York: Random, 1978. ■ Freud, Sigmund. *Three Essays on the Theory of Sexuality.* 1905. Trans. James Strachey. New York: Basic, 1962. ■ Gay, Peter. *The Tender Passion.* Vol. II of *The Bourgeois Experience: Victoria to Freud.* New York: Oxford University Press, 1986. ■ Geller, Thomas, ed. *Bisexuality: A Reader and Sourcebook.* Ojai, Calif.: Times Change Press, 1990. ■ Greenberg, David E. *The Construction of Homosexuality.* Chicago: University of Chicago Press, 1988. ■ Hutchins, Loraine and Lani Kaahumanu, eds. *Bi Any Other Name: Bisexual People Speak Out.* Boston: Alyson, 1991. ■ Klein, Fred. *The Bisexual Option.* New York: Arbor House, 1978. ■ Laqueur, Thomas. *Making Sex: Body and Gender from the Greeks to Freud.* Cambridge, Mass.: Harvard University Press, 1990. ■ Lottman, Herbert. *Colette: A Life.* Boston: Little, Brown, 1991. ■ Millett, Kate. *Flying.* New York: Knopf, 1974. ■ Paglia, Camille. *Sexual Personae: Art and Decadence from Nefertiti to Emily Dickinson.* New York: Vintage, 1991. ■ Weise, Elizabeth, ed. *Closer to Home: Bisexuality and Feminism.* Seattle: Seal Press, 1992.

Bishop, Elizabeth
(1911–1979)

Elizabeth Bishop was born on February 8, 1911, in Worcester, Massachusetts, the only child of Gertrude May Boomer Bishop of Great Village, Nova Scotia, and William T. Bishop, eldest son of a wealthy Worcester family. When Elizabeth was eight months old, her father died of Bright's Disease. Her mother, stricken by the shock of his death, over the next five years was intermittently hospitalized for nervous breakdowns, until she was committed in 1916 to a public sanitarium in Dartmouth, Nova Scotia, where she remained until her death in 1934. Elizabeth was cared for by her mother's parents in Great Village in 1917, when her paternal grandparents, believing that she would benefit from the material and social privileges they could offer, brought her to live with them in Worcester. The stress of her sudden displacement from congenial village life to the isolation and cold propriety of the Bishop house caused Elizabeth to develop severe asthma, eczema, and bronchitis, and after only nine months she was taken in by her mother's sister, Maude, who lived in a south Boston tenement. Maude's care, along with summer visits to Nova Scotia, considerably improved Elizabeth's health though she had little formal education until high school because of her illnesses, and she suffered from chronic asthma for the rest of her life.

After attending the Walnut Hill boarding school in Natick, Massachusetts, from 1927 to 1930, she matriculated at Vassar College, where she majored in English. While at Vassar, she discovered the poetry of Marianne Moore, and in the spring of her senior year she met Moore, who became her close friend and mentor, a relationship Bishop later documented in her essay, "Efforts of Affection." After graduation in 1934, Bishop lived off an inheritance from her father's estate and traveled so incessantly that she rarely stayed in the same place for more than a few months. Between 1935 and 1937, she made two trips to Europe; when in the United States, she lived in New York City boarding hotels, a cottage on the Massachusetts coast, and with friends in Florida. In 1938, she bought a house in Key West, but still spent time in New York, and from April to December 1942, she visited Mexico with a Key West lover, Marjorie Stevens. After their return, Bishop rented her house and moved in with Marjorie, yet periodically retreated to New York over the next several years.

Neither Marjorie's devotion nor the publication of *North and South* in 1946 could assuage the depression and alcoholism from which Bishop suffered—nor could trips to Nova Scotia in August 1946 and in the summer of 1947. Having sold the house and ended her relationship with Marjorie, during the next two years, Bishop spent time in New York, Maine, Key West, and Haiti and was hospitalized for depression in the summer of 1949. In September 1949, she moved to Washington, D.C., to serve as poetry consultant to the Library of Congress—a position secured for her by her new friend Robert Lowell. After her year-long tenure, she went to the Yaddo writer's colony in October 1950 where, except for a Christmas hospitalization for alcohol-related problems, she stayed until March 1951, when she learned that, on Moore's recommendation, she had won a Lucy Martin Donnelly Travelling Fellowship from Bryn Mawr College.

The trip that Bishop embarked on with her prize money changed her life. Intending to travel around the world, she sailed for Rio de Janeiro in November 1951, but after her arrival had a severe allergic reaction to the fruit of the cashew. She was nursed back to health by a Brazilian friend, Lota de Macedo Soares, who soon became her lover. Bishop's initial postponement of her trip turned into a sixteen-year stay with Lota, who, wealthy, energetic, and nurturing, provided the emotional security she craved and helped her control her alcoholism. Brazil also appealed to Bishop because there she could live more openly as a lesbian than in the United States, escape the U.S. literary milieu that she dreaded, and re-experience village life at Lota's house in Petrópolis and, later, in the eighteenth-century house that she purchased and renovated for herself in Ouro Prêto.

Bishop was quite productive during her years with Lota. *A Cold Spring*, which contains her great landscape poems and a number of lesbian love poems, was published in 1955 along with a reissue of her first book as *Poems: North and South—A Cold Spring;* the volume won the Pulitzer Prize in 1956. She translated *Minha Vida de Menina*, the diary of an adolescent girl who lived in Diamantina, a Brazilian diamond mining village, in the 1890s; the book appeared in 1957 as *The Diary of "Helena Morley."* As Brett Millier observes, "Bishop's access to the child-consciousness of Helena helped give her access to her own," for in poems such as "Manners," "Sestina," and "First Death in Nova Scotia" and prose such as "The Country Mouse," "Gwendolyn," and "In the Village," she adopts a child's-eye view of the world and writes about her childhood with devastating clarity. These poems and "In the Village" were collected in *Questions of Travel* (1965), a book dedicated to Lota in which Bishop also included poems about Brazil that consider the country's conquest by Portugal, the complexities of its race and class divisions, and the sheer magic of its tropical landscapes. The poems from her first three books, along with additional poems about her life in Brazil, translations from Brazilian poets, and several uncollected poems from the 1930s, were published as *The Complete Poems* (1969), which won the National Book Award in 1970.

But by 1970 Bishop's life had changed dramatically, for Lota, emotionally exhausted from a government post as overseer of the development of a large public park in Rio de Janeiro, committed suicide in September 1967. Although over the next several years Bishop tried, on and off, to live in Ouro Prêto, she found that ordinary financial transactions and the complex house renovations were difficult to manage without Lota to intercede for her with the Brazilians. Moreover, her alcoholism had worsened; and a new lover, a young woman with whom she had lived in San Francisco from January 1968 until May 1969, suffered a nervous breakdown in April 1970 after an eleven-month stay with Bishop in Ouro Prêto.

In September 1970, Bishop returned to make her permanent home in the United States. Until her death on October 6, 1979, from a cerebral aneurysm, she taught at Harvard and also briefly at the University of Washington and New York University. With her new lover, Alice Methfessel, who helped sustain her during these years, she traveled to the Galápagos Islands, Machu Picchu, Scandinavia, Nova Scotia, and Greece, and spent summers in Maine. In 1976, she published *Geography III,* which, although it contained only nine new poems, won the National Book Critics Circle Award in 1977. Also in 1976 she became the first woman to win the prestigious Books Abroad/Neustadt International Prize for Literature.

Widely acknowledged as one of the finest twentieth-century American poets, Bishop has long been known as "a poet's poet" because of her seemingly effortless mastery of form. She often adopts a supple yet relaxed iambic pentameter, and her rhymes are both innovative and understated. She initially learned her craft from an eclectic mix of writers she had discovered on her own—George Herbert, GERARD MANLEY HOPKINS, and modern poets from Harriet Monroe's anthology—as well as the hymns she loved. Moore's influence fostered her attention to descriptive details, and her reading of French surrealists colored many of the poems in *North and South*. Finally, her friendship with Lowell inspired her to move toward a more open treatment of experience in her poetry and prose, as opposed to the fascinating but oblique self-allegories of poems such as "The Man-Moth," "The Imaginary Iceberg," and "The Unbeliever" and stories such as "In Prison" and "The Sea and Its Shore."

Nevertheless, suspicious of the sentimentality and self-aggrandizement that she saw in much confessional poetry, and, like many gay poets of her generation, equally suspicious of overtly proclaiming her sexuality, Bishop couched her experience in redactions of familiar narratives ("The Prodigal"; "Crusoe in England"), descriptions of ordinary scenes and objects ("The Bight"; "Poem"), and mundane settings such as a dentist's waiting room ("In the Waiting Room") and a bus ride ("The Moose"). Throughout her career, as ADRIENNE RICH argues, "the themes of outsiderhood and marginality in her work, as well as its encodings as obscurities, [are connected with] a lesbian identity." Thus, although metaphors of imprisonment, self-division, and doubling prevail, the poems often offer resolution in spite of doubt. "The Gentleman of Shalott," for example, a half-man whose mirror reflection makes up the whole, finds his uncertainty "exhilarating," and decides that "half is enough." In "The Weed," inspired by Herbert's "Love Unknown," a weed sprouts from the prone speaker's heart and divides it. These and other poems from *North and South* chart Bishop's meditations on her sexuality and her consciousness that in American poetry and culture, lesbian love is a love unknown. The book closes with "Anaphora," a poem she later dedicated to Marjorie, whose verbal doublings culminate in "endless / endless assent." Such a pattern, which begins with doubt and self-division but ends with a strong affirmation, characterizes Bishop's anatomy of lesbian identity. The inverted mirror world of "Insomnia," the broken cage of "Rain Towards Morning," and the dividing caesuras of "O Breath" suggest the tension between passion and reticence from which, in her last poem, "Sonnet," the divided creature joyfully breaks, free to be gay.

—*Meg Schoerke*

BIBLIOGRAPHY

Costello, Bonnie. *Elizabeth Bishop: Questions of Mastery.* Cambridge, Mass.: Harvard University Press, 1991. ■ Goldensohn, Lorrie. *Elizabeth Bishop: The Biography of a Poetry.* New York: Columbia University Press, 1992. ■ Harrison, Victoria. *Elizabeth Bishop's Poetics of Intimacy.* Cambridge: Cambridge University Press, 1993. ■ Kalstone, David. *Becoming a Poet: Elizabeth Bishop with Marianne Moore and Robert Lowell.* Robert Hemenway, ed. New York: Farrar, Straus, and Giroux, 1989. ■ Merrin, Jeredith. *An Enabling Humility: Marianne Moore, Elizabeth Bishop, and the Uses of Tradition.* New Brunswick: Rutgers University Press, 1990. ■ Millier, Brett. *Elizabeth*

Bishop: *Life and the Memory of It.* Berkeley: University of California Press, 1993. ■ Parker, Robert Dale. *The Unbeliever: The Poetry of Elizabeth Bishop.* Urbana: University of Illinois Press, 1988. ■ Rich, Adrienne. "The Eye of the Outsider: Elizabeth Bishop's *Complete Poems, 1927–1979.*" *Blood, Bread, and Poetry: Selected Prose 1979–1985.* New York: W. W. Norton, 1986. ■ Schwartz, Lloyd, and Sybil P. Estess, eds. *Elizabeth Bishop and Her Art.* Ann Arbor: University of Michigan Press, 1983. ■ Stevenson, Anne. *Elizabeth Bishop.* New York: Twayne Publishers, 1966. ■ Travisano, Thomas J. *Elizabeth Bishop: Her Artistic Development.* Charlottesville: University Press of Virginia, 1988.

Blais, Marie-Claire

(b. 1939)

Marie-Claire Blais was born into a working-class family in Québec City on October 5, 1939. She was sent to a convent for her early education but left when she was fifteen at her parents' insistence to go to secretarial school. She did, however, attend courses in French literature at the University of Laval and published her first novel, *La Belle Bête,* when she was nineteen, a feat that inevitably caused her to be compared with another young woman writing in French, Françoise Sagan.

The comparison was a superficial one since the two writers are linked only by precocity and language. Blais has gone on to be an immensely prolific presence on both the Québec and the international French literary scene. Her earlier novels, *La belle bête* (translated as *Mad Shadows*), *Tête blanche* (1960), *Une saison dans la vie d'Emmanuel* (1965), and *Manuscrits de Pauline Archange* (1968), are lyrical and intense depictions of brutalized, tormented, and victimized young protagonists who inhabit a world that can increasingly be identified with the Gothic, repressive Québec in the years before *la révolution tranquille* of the early 1960s.

Her fiction generated a storm of controversy, and it was in part to escape both her celebrity and her notoriety that Blais went to the United States in 1963. There Edmund Wilson introduced her to the painter, Mary Meigs, with whom she subsequently became lovers. Blais went to live with Meigs at Wellfleet on Cape Cod, where she became acquainted with the literary and artistic circle of which Wilson was a prominent member. As Meigs eloquently documents it in her autobiography, *Lily Briscoe,* this must have been a painful period, for the then-closeted Blais had to endure the unacknowledged heterosexist and cultural colonialism of an intimidating group of famous Americans, all the while attempting to work out an ultimately doomed three-way relationship with Meigs's lover of fourteen years, Barbara Deming. In the end, Blais and Meigs left the Cape for Brittany, only to become involved in a destructive triangular relationship with a French woman novelist. (All three have recorded their versions of the event: Meigs in *The Medusa Head* and Blais in *Une liaison parisienne,* in which the protagonist is male, and the whole relationship can be subject to a political interpretation as representative of French cultural arrogance toward its former colony.)

Although Blais's fiction had always included homosexual references and her novel *Le Loup* (1972; translated as *The Wolf,* 1974) featured a gay male protagonist, it was not until 1978, in *Les Nuits de l'Underground,* set in part in the legendary and now-defunct Montréal lesbian bar, Madame Arthur, that Blais unequivocally turns her attention to lesbian life. The book is, as Blais herself has said, a more honest version of *Une liaison parisienne,* one in which lesbian passion is at once lyrical, mystical, and liberating. Her most recent novel, *L'ange de la solitude* (1990), which has yet to appear in English, is a visionary account of a literary commune composed of young lesbians affected by the death, at twenty, of one of their members.

Blais remains enormously productive and, despite a certain reluctance among critics and the establishment altogether to accept the gay and lesbian content of her fiction, she continues to enjoy public acclaim. She has received, among many other prizes, the Canadian Governor General's award (twice), the Prix France-Québec, the Prix Medicis, the Prix Académie française, and recently, the singular honor of being elected to the Belgian Académie française. She returned to North America in 1978 and now divides her time between Kingsbury, Québec, and Key West, Florida. (See also QUÉBÉCOIS LITERATURE.)

—*Yvonne Mathews Klein*

BIBLIOGRAPHY

Kraft, James. "Fiction as Autobiography in Québec: Notes on Pierre Vallières and Marie-Claire Blais." *Novel* 6 (Autumn 1972): 73–78. ■ Meigs, Mary. *Lily Briscoe: A Self-Portrait.* Vancouver: Talonbooks, 1981) ■ ———. *The Medusa Head.* Vancouver: Talonbooks, 1983. ■ Stratford, Philip. *Marie-Claire Blais.* Toronto: Forum House, 1971. ■ Wilson, Edmund. *O Canada: An American's Notes on Canadian Culture.* New York: 1965.

Bloomsbury

Seeking to explain the phenomenal popularity in the 1970s of biographical studies of those artists and intellectuals associated with Bloomsbury, the literary critic Elizabeth Hardwick pinpointed its "gay liberation, its serious high CAMP." Whether one considers Bloomsbury as a self-infatuated coterie, a forward-thinking commune, a circle of "New Athenians," or a mean-spirited mob, Bloomsbury's open acceptance of erotic license and its hostility toward social convention lend it considerable interest in the history of homosexuality among the English upper classes.

The novelist E. M. FORSTER called Bloomsbury the "only genuine *movement* in English civilization." Its name was taken from the London neighborhood encompassing Gordon and Fitzroy Squares, where the sisters Virginia and Vanessa Stephen established residence after the death of their father, Leslie, in 1904. Those avowedly homosexual figures associated with Bloomsbury, notably Forster, the biographer LYTTON STRACHEY, the economist John Maynard Keynes, and the painter Duncan Grant, found exuberant advocates in their fellow-traveling Bloomsbury friends VIRGINIA WOOLF, Vanessa Bell, Virginia's husband, Leonard Woolf, the art critics Clive Bell and Roger Fry, the painter Dora Carrington, and the hostess Ottoline Morell, whose estate Garsington was a Bloomsbury outpost of amorous badinage, infatuation, and gossip, much of it homosexual in character. "Sex permeated our conversation," recalled Virginia Woolf before the London Memoir Club in 1922. "The word bugger was never far from our lips."

Undoubtedly the most flamboyant of the "Bloomsbuggers," as the homosexual members of Bloomsbury were called, was Giles Lytton Strachey (1880–1932), son of a distinguished soldier and Indian administrator. While a student at Trinity College, Cambridge, Strachey met Keynes and Leonard Woolf and later went on to head the Apostles, Cambridge's exclusive intellectual society to which also belonged several other figures associated with Bloomsbury, including Forster, Leonard Woolf, and Keynes. Strachey's classic *Eminent Victorians* (1918) was in some ways Bloomsbury's definitive text, a withering attack on the Victorian era's earnest promotion of self-improvement, chauvinism, and hypocrisy. Skewering Cardinal Manning as a Machiavellian careerist, Florence Nightingale as a manipulative neurotic, the educator Dr. Arnold as a middle-brow prig, and Gen-

eral Gordon as an imperialist crank, Strachey targeted a whole system of repressive values left over from the previous era. *Eminent Victorians,* along with Strachey's *Queen Victoria* (1921) and *Elizabeth and Essex: A Tragic History* (1928), was among the earliest biographical works to employ Freudian analytical techniques. (Strachey's brother James was the first English translator of Freud.) Lytton's fondness for comic biographical detail—Cardinal Wiseman's Irish servant respectfully referring to the heavy-set cardinal as "your immense," Florence Nightingale employing soldiers' wives to clean her laundry during the Crimean War—made Strachey the architect of an altogether new literary genre: camp biography. Indeed, Strachey was the true heir of OSCAR WILDE in the irreverent brio of his wit, captured in Strachey's celebrated retort to an officer who, confronted with the writer's pacifist objections to joining the army, demanded to know what he would do if a Hun attempted to rape his sister. "I would," Strachey responded coolly, "insert my own body between them." Asked by a woman during the war years why he was not fighting for civilization, he answered, "I *am,* Madam, the civilization for which they are fighting."

Although none of Strachey's published work addressed homosexual issues, his correspondence is a testament to the ardor that Strachey lavished on the young men with whom he was continually, guiltlessly smitten. "His face is outspoken," Strachey wrote of Duncan Grant, "bold and not just rough. It's the full, aquiline type, with frank grey-blue eyes and incomparably lascivious lips." His brief account of Bloomsbury life, reminiscent of Virginia Woolf's free-associative fiction, captured Bloomsbury's quality of pastoral homoeroticism: "Perhaps it was because of the easy goingness of the place and the quantities of food, or was it because . . . and then the vision of that young postman with the fair hair and the lovely country complexion who had said 'Good evening, sir', as he passed on his bicycle, flashed upon me." Strachey's *Ermyntrude and Esmeralda* (composed in 1913 but published in 1969), a semipornographic epistolary novel written as an exchange of letters between two naive seventeen-year-old girls, is a send-up of, among other matters, sodomy among the middle classes. Strachey, with his rationalist attitude toward homosexual sex and his tone of ironic detachment, was the most characteristic Bloomsbury figure. He could inspire, however, keen contempt among outsiders. The novelist VITA SACKVILLE-WEST loathed him, while the poet Rupert Brooke described a meeting with Strachey as a "most unbearably sickening disgusting blinding nightmare."

The bearded, wiry, and bespectacled Strachey conducted several homosexual love affairs, among them a relationship in the winter of 1905–1906 with his cousin Duncan Grant. Grant's sexual charisma was famously overwhelming. "Anyone could fall in love with Duncan if he wanted to," noted Keynes. (A common quip had it that Bloomsbury could be defined as a congeries of men and women in love with Grant.) "I have fallen in love hopelessly and ultimately," Strachey wrote to Clive Bell after beginning his affair with Grant. "I have experienced too much ecstasy." Soon, however, the affair fizzled, for not only was Grant distressed by Strachey's unchecked enthusiasm, he had recently begun a relationship with Harold Hobhouse, and subsequently, with John Keynes, a romantic involvement that lasted from 1908 to 1912. The still-smitten Strachey, meanwhile, continued to correspond with Keynes over his love for Grant. "He's a *genius*—a colossal portent of fire and glory," gushed Strachey to Keynes of the painter. On learning of Grant's affair with Keynes, Strachey was at first crushed and then attempted, in typical Bloomsbury fashion, to put a cheerful face on what conventional society would have deemed an impossible situation. "If you were here just now I should probably kiss you," he told Keynes, "except that Duncan would be jealous, which would never do!" The friendship between Grant and Keynes endured until Keynes's death in 1946.

One of Strachey's strongest emotional attachments was to Dora Carrington, who, though aware of his taste in men, idealized Strachey for some seventeen years even as she conducted an affair with the Russian-Jewish emigré painter Mark Gertler. "When one realizes it is there—a part of them [homosexuals] and a small part—it is worthwhile overlooking it for anything bigger and more valuable," she wrote. On Strachey's death, Carrington committed suicide, claiming she could not survive without her lifelong confidant. The Strachey–Carrington–Gertler triangle served as a defining myth of Bloomsbury's appeal as an enlightened, close-knit enclave open to same-sex *amours*. Carrington's death and Gertler's subsequent suicide before the Second World War lend the affair a pathos that undermines Bloomsbury's reputation as a place of endless light-hearted mischief, much as did Virginia Woolf's suicide shortly after the outbreak of World War II.

Woolf's attenuated affair with Vita Sackville-West, wife of British MP Harold Nicolson, was a notable romantic escapade in Bloomsbury's history. "Am I in love with her?" wondered Woolf in her diary, "But what is love?" Sackville-West wrote to Nicolson, "Oh my dear, what an enchanting person Virginia is! How she weaves magic into life." An outsider to Bloomsbury, Vita became the inspiration for the heroine of Woolf's novel *Orlando* (1928), the story of a time traveler who changes sexes through different historical epochs. Woolf remained giddily taken up with the homosexual antics of her fellow Bloomsburies, a fascination that began as an ingenue's awakening to the preponderance of homosexual males in her circle. "I knew there were buggers in PLATO's Greece," Virginia wrote, "but it never occurred to me that there were buggers even now in the Stephen sitting-room in Gordon Square." To the extent that Woolf held an interest in homosexual literary themes, that interest was subsumed under the novelist's promotion of an "androgynous" creative outlook as an escape from the suffocating binaries of masculine and feminine. Other Bloomsburies were similarly absorbed with the subject of androgyny. At Cambridge, Duncan and Vanessa had decorated Keynes's rooms with a series of alternating panels depicting androgynous male and female types.

Equal in stature to Virginia Woolf and Forster, John Maynard Keynes saw enormous fame outside Gordon Square as the architect of one of the twentieth century's most influential economic theories. Strachey, like other members of the Bloomsbury set, considered Keynes a Bloomsbury anomaly in his insufficiently evolved aesthetic sense. (Virginia complained that Keynes's *Economic Consequences of the Peace* "goes on influencing the world, although it is lacking in artistic worth," a remark that may have been generated by Keynes's once having suggested to Woolf that she limit her writing to nonfiction.) Keynes's marriage to the Russian ballerina Lydia Lopokova in 1925 struck many Bloomsburies as a betrayal of personal allegiances. Yet of all the "Bloomsbuggers," Keynes was the least susceptible to effete malice. In his memoirs, he hazarded that "We [members of Bloomsbury] had no respect for traditional wisdom or the restraint of custom. . . . It did not occur to any of us to respect the extraordinary accomplishment of our predecessors in the ordering of life (as it now seems to me to have been) or the elaborate framework they had devised to protect this order."

Despite the close attention devoted to homosexual affairs by Bloomsbury and its inspired attacks on middle-class morality, its followers contributed few theoretical or creative insights to questions concerning same-sex eros, though Forster, who claimed he was not an authentic member of the Bloomsbury set, could write powerfully on homosexual themes. While pacifist in outlook, Bloomsbury harbored no politically activist impulses of the kind that animated the contemporaneous Fabians and that might have given their self-confident advocacy of bisexuality resonance beyond the self-preening confines of Gordon Square. Although Leonard Woolf was a socialist and Virginia's *Three Guineas* became a landmark of feminist thought, Bloomsbury was too remorselessly and independently skeptical to embrace a "homosexual cause"—or, for that matter, any cause.

The group's intellectual affiliations partly stemmed from the philosopher G. E. Moore's *Principia Ethica*, an influential text for the youthful Strachey, Bell, Forster, and Keynes as students at Cambridge. In a passage that could have constituted Bloomsbury's credo, Moore asserted that "by far the most valuable things which we can know or imagine" are "certain states of consciousness, which may be roughly described as the pleasures of human intercourse and the enjoyment of beautiful objects." The Fabian thinker Beatrice Webb called Moore's book "a metaphysical justification for doing what you like and what other people disapprove of." Webb's criticism reveals the fissures between the activism of Fabian socialism and the hedonism of Bloomsbury philosophy, suggesting, too, why Bloomsbury retains the reputation of a largely apolitical Edwardian idyll. With the exception of Virginia, Bloomsbury was more anti-Victorian than promodernist, its followers more the heirs to Paterian AESTHETICISM than participants in the unfolding modernist awakening inspired by Joyce, LAWRENCE, ELIOT, and STEIN. Moreover, Bloomsbury grew to distrust any hint of sincerity or philosophical utilitarianism. "Were all truths equally good to pursue and contemplate?" asked Keynes in his recollection of Bloomsbury before the Memoir Club. "We were disposed to repudiate very strongly the idea that useful knowledge could be preferable to useless knowledge."

Enemies of Bloomsbury usually cast it as a site of homosexual self-indulgence and self-preening snobbery. The writer Wyndham Lewis called Duncan Grant "A little fairy-like individual who would have received no attention in any country except England." D. H. Lawrence, who inserted a portrait of Duncan into *Lady Chatterley's Lover* as a "dark-skinned taciturn Hamlet of a fellow," complained that Bloomsbury members "talk endlessly, but endlessly—and never, never a good thing said. They are cased each in a hard little shell of his own and out of this they talk words." Taking an instant dislike to David Garnett's friend, the emphatically homosexual Francis Birrell, Lawrence wrote to Garnett, "You must leave these friends, these beetles, Birrell and Duncan Grant are done forever." Lawrence's own insecurities as a working-class artist with homosexual inclinations, a graduate of Nottingham University and not Cambridge, undoubtedly fed his disgust. Bloomsbury paid him and other critics little mind, however. Garnett would later take Grant as a lover, and, in an astonishing development, Vanessa Bell's and Grant's out-of-wedlock child, Angelica, became at age twenty-three Garnett's wife. Perhaps the most devastating critique of Bloomsbury came from Angelica Garnett. In 1984, she published a memoir, *Deceived with Kindness: A Bloomsbury Childhood,* in which she detailed her shock at discovering as an adult the identity of her real father and her realization that her husband had been her father's lover. The book's note of mournful betrayal in the face of what Garnett termed Bloomsbury's "precarious paradise" of damaging ambiguities provided a sobering coda to what had become the much-burnished myth of 46 Gordon Square.

A sun-dappled Brook Farm for bisexual transcendentalists, Bloomsbury stands as an alluring if rarefied instance in the history of personal relations.

—*Richard Kaye*

BIBLIOGRAPHY

Bell, Quentin. *Virginia Woolf.* 2 vols. New York: Harcourt Brace Jovanovich, 1968, 1972. ■ Edel, Leon. *Bloomsbury: A House of Lions.* New York: Lippincott, 1979. ■ Gadd, David. *The Loving Friends: A Portrait of Bloomsbury.* New York: Harcourt Brace Jovanovich, 1974. ■ Garnett, Angelica. *Deceived with Kindness: A Bloomsbury Childhood.* New York: Harcourt Brace Jovanovich, 1987. ■ Holroyd, Michael. *Lytton Strachey: A Biography.* New York: Penguin, 1971. ■ Rosenbaum, S. P., ed. *The Bloomsbury Group: A Collection of Memoirs, Commentary and Criticism.* Toronto: University of Toronto Press, 1975. ■ Skidelsky, Robert. *John Maynard Keynes: Volume 1, Hopes Betrayed, 1883-1920.* New York: Penguin, 1986. ■ ———. *John Maynard Keynes: Volume II, The Economist as Saviour, 1920–1937.* New York: Penguin, 1994.

Bowen, Elizabeth
(1899–1973)

Elizabeth Dorothea Cole Bowen was born on June 7, 1899, in Dublin. According to her biographer, Victoria Glendinning, Bowen came from a long line of Bowens, originally Welsh, who settled in County Cork, Ireland. Elizabeth Bowen inherited the family country house, Bowen's Court, the names of her ancestors, and an Anglo-Irish heritage that would mark her life and work. By the time she died on February 22, 1973, Bowen had led an exciting life and one important to modern literature: She wrote ten novels, several volumes of short stories, and countless reviews, articles, and other journalism.

Glendinning reports that Bowen originally set out to be a painter but discovered fairly early on that her gift was in writing. Her marriage to Alan Cameron in 1923 helped that end since he provided both material and emotional support; Bowen's mother had died when Bowen was young, and her father was emotionally unstable. Perhaps because of the unusual circumstances of her girlhood and marriage—Glendinning quotes an anonymous lover who believes he took Bowen's virginity *after* her marriage—Bowen was very nonjudgmental of romantic relationships of all kinds, her own and others. As Glendinning says, Bowen's friends and associates included a number of homosexual men and women, largely literary, and Bowen seems to have prided herself on her own sophistication in accepting such people and their arrangements with little thought to the conventional morality of the day. One might add that she thought equally little of that morality applied to heterosexual arrangements as well; the varied sexual identities or lack thereof of her characters is a significant part of Bowen's work.

Glendinning reports on Bowen's attractiveness to other women and lesbians, and offers an interpretation of MAY SARTON's brief romantic encounter and long friendship with Bowen, recorded by Sarton in *A World of Light*. If Bowen herself was almost exclusively heterosexual in her personal life, her vast quantity of fiction is sprinkled with people and relationships, usually coded, of either clear or ambiguous homosexuality. For example, the novelist St. Quentin in Bowen's best-known novel, *The Death of the Heart* (1938), is seen easily as homosexual in the HENRY JAMES-dispassionate-homosexual-man mode. Similarly, Naomi in *The House in Paris* (1935) appears to be far more erotically attached to the friend Karen, who steals her fiancé, Max, than she does to

Max himself. In *The Little Girls* (1964), one character outright asks another, Clare, if she is lesbian; the question is never really answered, though Clare certainly appears to be. Other Bowen novels also feature male and female characters who exhibit behaviors associated with homosexuality, but these behaviors are so coded that their definite identification as homosexual is difficult; consider the relationships between older and younger women in *The Hotel* (1927), *The Last September* (1929), and *The Death of the Heart* (1938), to name but three.

The question is complicated by the ambiguity of these relationships: How much of an erotic spark do they contain? They may certainly be interpreted as having homosocial and homoerotic overtones, even if such relationships were never consummated. Homoerotic pairings are also found in some of the stories published in *The Collected Stories of Elizabeth Bowen* (1984). For example, "The Apple Tree" is a notable example of an older woman saving, with more than casual interest, the emotional life of a younger one. Another story, "The Demon Lover," might be read as a woman's running away from heterosexuality. Although homosexuality is but one of many elements in Bowen's canon, it makes her fictive world complete. Bowen's fiction was far ahead of its time and place in showing a range of homosexualities, and that element of her work merits far more attention than it has received to date.

—*Thomas Dukes*

BIBLIOGRAPHY

Austin, Allen. *Elizabeth Bowen.* New York: Twayne Publishers, 1971. ■ Brooke, Jocelyn. *Elizabeth Bowen.* London: British Council, 1972. ■ Glendinning, Victoria. *Elizabeth Bowen.* New York: Avon, 1977. ■ Heath, William. *Elizabeth Bowen.* Madison: University of Wisconsin, 1961. ■ Jordan, Heather Bryant. *How Will the Heart Endure: Elizabeth Bowen and the Landscape of War.* Ann Arbor: University of Michigan, 1992. ■ Kenney, Edwin J. *Elizabeth Bowen.* Lewisburg, Pa.: Bucknell, 1974. ■ Lee, Hermione. *Elizabeth Bowen: An Estimation.* London: Vision, 1981. ■ Rule, Jane. *Lesbian Images.* Garden City, N.Y.: Doubleday, 1975. ■ Sarton, May. *A World of Light.* New York: Norton, 1976.

Bowles, Jane Auer
(1917–1973)

Bowles, born in New York City on February 22, 1917, spent her life examining lesbian identity with an honest and sardonic wit. In 1934, on a ship returning from Switzerland, Bowles met the French author Celine, whose work she had been

studying, and she suddenly decided that "I am a writer." Her first novel, *La Phaeton Hypocrite,* a parody of the Phaeton myth, was privately printed. Although admired by her mother, Bowles regarded the novel, no copy of which survives, as a childish exercise. Bowles's adventures in the lesbian and gay bars of Greenwich Village, and her open pursuit of women lovers, caused her mother and her family consternation. In 1937, she was introduced to the novelist and composer Paul Bowles—himself a homosexual—and agreed to marry him. The two soon recognized that their marriage would succeed only as a platonic friendship; both continued their homosexual liaisons. Bowles claimed that her novel, *Two Serious Ladies* (1943), was heavily indebted to Paul's editorial advice; and her biographer, Millicent Dillon, stresses that Jane relied on Paul's calm and rather detached sensibility in order to cope with the exigencies of life. At her death on May 4, 1973, Bowles was working on two novels, *Out in the World* and *Going to Massachusetts,* which feature women who have chosen to isolate themselves. Bowles also maintained a lively correspondence with her lovers, friends, and husband; these letters are collected and edited by Dillon in *Out in the World: Selected Letters of Jane Bowles 1935–1970* (1985).

Bowles's writing is existentialist but with a unique lesbian sensibility. Like those of DJUNA BARNES, her characters speak in curiously formal yet mocking tones. The puppet play, *A Quarreling Pair* (1945), is a fine example of Bowles's unique blend of existentialist dramaturgy, irony, and lesbian sensibility. Two middle-aged sisters, Harriet and Rhoda, sit in separate rooms and quarrel endlessly about trivial tasks, the futility of life, and their inextricable bond. Dillon suggests that the play is a transcription of Bowles's relationship with Helvictia Perkins, but it perhaps better reflects Jane's marriage of convenience.

Bowles's family and her lover, Helvictia Perkins, rejected her first novel, *Two Serious Ladies,* as too obviously lesbian, but despite recognition that the novel's main theme is women's sexuality, the novel's lesbian content has yet to be seriously considered. The two protagonists, Christina Goering and Mrs. Copperfield, seek salvation in a world that Bowles depicts as fragmented and threatening. From her childish religious obsessions to her adult pursuit of hopeless heterosexual love affairs, Goering seeks redemption from a self she believes is flawed by inherent sin. Her childhood friend, the more complacent Mrs. Copperfield, suddenly leaves her husband when she meets Pacifica, a prostitute who initiates her into the sensual pleasures of lesbian sex. Ironically, it is Mrs. Copperfield who finds the serenity that Goering desperately longs for.

Bowles's play *In the Summer House* was produced in Ann Arbor and then moved to Broadway in 1953. Remarkable for its strong women's roles, it was not the financial and critical success that Bowles desired.

The play opens with Gertrude Eastman's long monologue in which she bemoans the hypocrisies of the world and berates her daughter Molly, whose reclusive nature Gertrude regards as pathologically antisocial. Molly's belief that she alone possesses her mother's affection is upset by the arrival of two rivals, the ingenuous Vivian and Mr. Solares. Mr. Solares seduces Gertrude with displays of his wealth, and Vivian charms Gertrude with her clever comments. Feeling betrayed by her mother, Molly pushes Vivian off a cliff, but her action only reveals the hollowness of the Eastman home. By allowing Molly to dream endlessly in the ivy-covered summerhouse, Gertrude has trapped Molly in childhood. Molly's passion disconcerts Gertrude, who flees into a marriage with Mr. Solares. Abandoned, Molly tries to recreate the safety of the Eastman home by marrying the equally innocent Lionel. Gertrude finds Solares's affection superficial, and she returns to Molly. The play concludes on an ambiguous note, for now Gertrude and not Molly is the seeker after absolute love.

Men are either ineffectual or disruptive forces in Bowles's shorter fiction, which is collected in *My Sister's Hand in Mine: An Expanded Edition of the Collected Works of Jane Bowles* (1978). Following Paul's advice, Jane removed "A Guatemalan Idyll" from the original manuscript of *Two Serious Ladies.* Once again the search for peace of mind highlights this tale of Mrs. Ramirez and her two daughters who are vacationing in a Guatemalan pension. Mrs. Ramirez seduces a male American traveler who has mistakenly wandered into the hostel, but she regards his eventual departure with dispassion. Mrs. Ramirez's young daughter, Lilina, believes that the possession of a snake owned by a local boy, Ramon, will provide her with omniscient power. After bargaining with Ramon's mother, Lilina is forced to recognize the futility of seeking salvation through the possession of another being. The snake is crushed by a passing cart, and Lilina expresses only contempt for Ramon's anguish. In "A Day in the Country," two lesbian prostitutes toy with two unwitting Mexican businessmen whose attempts to romanticize the women are juxtaposed to the women's more calculated seduction. "Plain Pleasures" and "A Stick of Green Candy" feature men as catalysts of destruction. In "Plain Pleasures," the widowed Mrs. Perry agrees to meet her neighbor, Mr. Drake, for dinner but, once seated, she mocks his romanticism and rejects his marriage proposal. She runs upstairs and, sitting in the vacant bedroom, recognizes the essential absurdity of existence. Her rape by the lecherous restaurant owner and the loss of Mr. Drake's friendship cannot diminish her insight. "A Green Stick of Candy" concerns prepubescent Mary, who has her sense of self destroyed when a boy violates her clay pit where she has constructed a world. In this clay pit, she is a general, but she perceives herself as a weaker figure when her father ignores her loss.

Another set of stories explore lesbian space. In "Everything is Nice" and "East Side: North Africa," Bowles describes the games played by the women in the Moroccan markets. Writing of her relationship with Cherfia—a Moroccan lesbian who was both her lover and longtime companion—Bowles finds pleasure in these dramas of misunderstandings as she celebrates the homosocial world of Morocco. "Camp Cataract" describes the longings of Sadie, who seeks an unconditional love with her sister Harriet, who has rejected her. Obsessed with Harriet, Sadie follows her to the retreat where Harriet has sought solitude. At the camp's waterfall, Sadie undergoes the author's signature revelation scene: She recognizes herself and Harriet as one and as nothing and then commits suicide as a sacrifice to Harriet.

Bowles's recording of her particular vision of the world was halted only when she grew too blind to write. In her obituary in *The New York Times*, JOHN ASHBERY proclaimed her to be "one of the finest writers of fiction" despite her lack of recognition by the literary establishment—an evaluation that she would no doubt have considered suitably ironic.

—Amy Gilley

BIBLIOGRAPHY

Bassett, Mark T. "Imagination, Control and Betrayal in Jane Bowles' 'A Stick of Green Candy'." *Studies in Short Fiction*, 24:1 (1987): 25–29. ■ Dillon, Millicent. *A Little Original Sin: The Life and Works of Jane Bowles*. New York: Holt, 1981. ■ ———. "Jane Bowles: Experiment as Character." *Breaking the Sequence: Women's Experimental Fiction*. Princeton: Princeton University Press, 1989. 140–147. ■ Lakritz, Andrew M. "Jane Bowles's Other World." *Old Maids to Radical Spinsters: Unmarried Women in the Twentieth Century Novel*. Laura L. Doan, ed. Urbana: University of Illinois Press, 1991. 213–214. ■ Lougy, Robert. "The World and Art of Jane Bowles (1917–1973)." *CEA Critic*. 49: 2–4 (1986–1987): 157–173.

Bowles, Paul
(*b.* 1910)

Paul Bowles was born in New York on December 30, 1910. His father was a dentist who exhibited little warmth for his son; an inflexible man, he evoked responses of passive resistance and secrecy, characteristics that would mark Paul's life and writing. As a boy, Bowles had few friends and took refuge in fantasy writing. He matriculated at the University of Virginia, but academic life did not interest him, and he left for Paris abruptly in 1929. Although he soon returned to New York, from 1931 onward he would spend most of his life outside the United States.

Bowles's literary reputation rests on his novels, but until he was thirty-five he showed more interest in musical composition and poetry. Aaron Copland was a mentor, and in France, he intrigued GERTRUDE STEIN, though she thought he was no poet. But Bowles was gifted in a number of fields, and increasingly he spread his skills over several: music for plays and films, short stories, autobiography, travel writing, and translations.

In childhood, Bowles was fond of a homosexual uncle. During one stay-over with him, he happened to enter a room where men were dancing intimately together. His uncle's anger at his nephew hurt Bowles, who had not been alarmed at this sight, and the incident suggests Bowles's attitude to different sexual behavior: He liked to examine sexuality from a dis-

passionate perspective for its psychological suggestiveness. Such is the case in his most explicitly homosexual story, "Pages from Cold Point" (1947), in which a boy tries to seduce his father.

"Pages from Cold Point" marked a turning point in Bowles's life. In 1938, he had married Jane Auer, and in 1947, they went to live in Tangier. JANE BOWLES had published *Two Serious Ladies,* and explored gay relationships in both her life and in her fiction. Paul Bowles explored the psychological dimensions of relationships less directly, and many readers prefer to interpret his ground-breaking novel *The Sheltering Sky* (1949) in existentialist terms, even though it deals centrally with the extraordinary dynamic of his relationship with Jane—a dynamic to which the homosexuality of both is relevant.

With the arrival of the Bowleses, the Tangier cult developed rapidly. American writers and artists of the BEAT GENERATION—WILLIAM BURROUGHS, ALLEN GINSBERG, Gregory Corso, TENNESSEE WILLIAMS, TRUMAN CAPOTE, and others—visited and socialized; the ambience of Tangier, as well as its toleration of experiments in drug use and sexual expression proved liberating and stimulating. Jane Bowles, always on the edge of sexual scandal, died in 1973. Paul Bowles, though he continued to attract interesting figures and, in his discreet way, a cult following, was very stable, and has continued to produce a stream of work. His translation work started with the Sartre classic *No Exit* (1958) but became more significant with his translation of previously unknown works by Moroccan writers Mohammed Mrabet, Mohamed Choukri and, subsequently, others. Bowles's self-containment is signaled in his response to Christopher Sawyer-Laucanno's biography, which he has attacked as being based on the testimony of "certain mischievous gossips." It should, however, be noted that several other texts about Tangier, its status as a cult-site, and Paul and Jane Bowles are even more "gossipy."

—*Patrick Holland*

BIBLIOGRAPHY

Finlayson, Iain. *Tangier: City of the Dream.* London: Harper Collins, 1992. ■ Green, Michelle. *The Dream at the End of the World: Paul Bowles and the Literary Renegades in Tangier.* New York: Harper Collins, 1991. ■ Sawyer-Laucanno, Christopher. *Paul Bowles: An Invisible Spectator.* New York: The Ecco Press, 1990.

Brecht, Bertolt
(1898–1956)

Born in 1896, Bertolt (Eugene Berthold) Brecht became Germany's most celebrated and influential dramatist of the twentieth century. His depictions of homosexual desire are found only in a few of his earliest writings. In these works, homosexuality is often cloaked in ambiguity and almost always is tied to issues of power struggle, manipulation, and sadomasochism.

As Eric Bentley has stated: "Brecht is not the poet of Gay Liberation." Only in the early short story "Bargan läßt es sein" ("Bargan Gives Up" [1921]) and the poem "Ballade vor der Freundschaft" ("Ballad of Friendship" [1920]) do homosexual relationships in works by Brecht survive more or less intact. Nevertheless, it is significant that Brecht, as one of the most influential figures in twentieth-century literature and theater, chose to portray same-sex desire in several literary works.

One example is *Leben Eduards des Zweiten von England,* the adaptation of CHRISTOPHER MARLOWE's *Edward II* that Brecht undertook in 1923 in collaboration with Lion Feuchtwanger. Performed and published in 1924, the play's dramatic action concerns Edward's overthrow, a plot prompted by what is perceived as a socially disruptive sexual relationship, the monarch's physical and emotional infatuation with Gaveston, in Brecht's version an attractive butcher's son on whom the King lavishes his affections, sexual favors, and wealth. Edward refuses to relinquish his favorite even at the risk of the throne being forcibly wrested from him by his enemies. Edward loses Gaveston, the throne, and eventually, his life but gains in the process spiritual transcendence and the status of tragic hero.

Young Brecht was an avid reader and became enthralled with the works of ARTHUR RIMBAUD. He was also intrigued by Rimbaud's tempestuous relationship with PAUL VERLAINE. The plays *Baal* and *Im Dickicht der Städte (In the Jungle of Cities)* both bear influences of Rimbaud's poetic discourse and the Rimbaud–Verlaine liaison.

Baal, begun in 1918 and published in 1922, comprises twenty-two scenes that depict Baal's shameless, voracious pursuit of total pleasure and sensual self-fulfillment. Baal is lecherous, gluttonous, adulterous, and hedonistic, yet it is his companionship with Ekart, an itinerant composer, in the wilderness that fills a major portion of the dramatic action. Their complex love–hate relationship, by turns erotic, nurturing, violent, and indifferent, comes to an abrupt end when Baal, provoked into a jealous rage, murders Ekart in a tavern.

Similar passionate extremes characterize the prolonged, seemingly unmotivated battle that occurs in *Im Dickicht der Städte* between Shlink, a Malayan timber merchant, and George Garga, an impoverished clerk at a lending library who cryptically quotes Rimbaud. The play, which Brecht began writing in 1921 but was not performed and published until 1927, contains no overt scenes of homosexual love. A homoerotic tension, however, must be viewed as underlying the two rivals' revenge and humiliation tactics and their quest for control of not only each other's destinies and financial resources but also Garga's family and girlfriend. The attractiveness of their chaotic conflict and the desire it has produced are finally acknowledged by both, overtly by Shlink prior to his death and obliquely by Garga afterward.

These early writings have led to questions about Brecht's own sexual orientation. Although his heterosexual exploits are well documented by biographers, memoirists, and by Brecht himself in his diaries, the playwright's possible gayness remains speculative. Brechtian scholar Erika Munk has asserted that Brecht "preferred male company" during his late teens and early twenties and has suggested that Brecht's "bisexuality is not reasonably in doubt."

—*Jay Scott Chipman*

BIBLIOGRAPHY

Bentley, Eric. *The Brecht Chronicles*. London: Eyre Methuen, 1981. ■ Case, Sue-Ellen. "Brecht and Women: Homosexuality and the Mother." *Brecht: Women and Politics*. Detroit: Wayne State University Press, 1985. 131–145. ■ Munk, Erika. "Alas or Thank God: The Private Dialectic of Bertolt Brecht." *Brecht: Women and Politics*. Detroit: Wayne State University Press, 1985. 245–254.

Brophy, Brigid
(b. 1929)

Brigid Brophy was born in London, June 12, 1929, the daughter of the novelist John Brophy and Charis Grundy, the American-born daughter of the Bishop ("Angel") of Liverpool of the apocalyptic and now-defunct Irvingite sect. She was educated at St. Paul's Girls' School, London, and, in 1947, was admitted to St. Hugh's College, Oxford, on scholarship. In her second year at Oxford, she was "sent down" for "unspecified offences," which have been variously rumored to be drunkenness in chapel or lesbianism. After her expulsion, she worked as a secretary to a pornographer, among other odd jobs, in London and began to write fiction. In 1953, she published *The Crown Princess and Other Stories,* a collection of short works, and *Hackenfeller's Ape,* a novel indicative of her ongoing interest in animal rights. Both works brought her favorable critical attention, the latter winning the Cheltenham Literary Festival prize for best first novel.

In 1954, Brophy married Michael Levey, art historian and author of *The Case of Walter Pater.* During the 1960s, their unconventional marriage, informed by Brophy's boldly outspoken views favoring bisexuality and opposing monogamy and institutional heterosexuality, was a *cause célèbre* in the British press and literary circles. Her social and sexual concerns, outlined in essays in *Don't Never Forget* (1963) and *Baroque 'n' Roll and Other Essays* (1986), are among the recurring themes of Brophy's fiction. Her semi-autobiographical second novel, *The King of a Rainy Country* (1956), explores the nexus of heterosexuality and homoerotic desire against the backdrop of Wolfgang Amadeus Mozart's opera *Le Nozze di Figaro.* In this picaresque tale, a youthful and not-quite-straight pair, Susan and Neale, travel across Europe in search of Cynthia, Susan's long-lost love from her schoolgirl days. Throughout the early 1960s, Brophy employed the comedy of manners as her favored mode for exploring social and sexual mores. From a cool, detached perspective, *Flesh* (1962) traces the develop-

ment of a hedonist. In *The Snow Ball* (1963), she returns to Mozartean sources, examining the sexual psychology of the opera *Don Giovanni* in the context of a New Year's Eve costume party in contemporary London. *The Finishing Touch* (1963), a tale of romantic misadventures in a lesbian-run girls school on the French Riviera, pays homage to the novels of RONALD FIRBANK, another of Brophy's icons. Her most ambitious work, *In Transit* (1969), is a free-associative narrative set in the international terminal of an airport. While the text explores through puns and allusions many of Brophy's favorite themes (for example, opera, pornography, rationalism, varieties of sexuality), protagonist Patrick/Patricia loses knowledge of language, hence the linguistic means of differentiating sex and gender and, consequently, his/her own distinctive sex or gender. *A Palace without Chairs* (1978), her last novel, is a modern-day fairy tale set in an imaginary Eastern European socialist monarchy and relates the tragicomic woes of its impecunious royal family, including the lesbian Archduchess Heather who, through a series of disasters, unwittingly and unwillingly inherits the throne.

In addition to her novels, Brophy has published several volumes of essays, short stories, and literary criticism, as well as authoritative critical biographies of Mozart, Firbank, and painter Aubrey Beardsley. She is founder, with novelist MAUREEN DUFFY, of Writers Action Group, which successfully campaigned throughout the 1970s for parliamentary approval of the Public Lending Right, by which writers are guaranteed remuneration for public use of their works. Since 1984, Brophy has been afflicted with multiple sclerosis, and she and her work have, to some extent, faded from public notice. Recent reprints of her novels and renewed critical interest, however, are beginning to reverse this neglect of one of the 1960s' most daring voices of sexuality difference.

—*Patricia Juliana Smith*

BIBLIOGRAPHY

Brophy, Brigid. *Baroque 'n' Roll and Other Essays*. London: Hamish Hamilton, 1986. ■ ———. *The Crown Princess and Other Stories*. London: Collins, 1953. ■ ———. *Don't Never Forget: Collected Views and Reviews*. London: Cape, 1963. ■ ———. *The Finishing Touch*. London: Secker & Warburg, 1963. ■ ———. *Flesh*. London: Secker & Warburg, 1962. ■ ———. *Hackenfeller's Ape*. London: Hart Davis, 1953. ■ ———. *In Transit*. London: Macdonald, 1969. ■ ———. *The King of a Rainy Country*. London: Secker & Warburg, 1956. ■ ———. *A Palace without Chairs*. London: Hamish Hamilton, 1978. ■ ———. *Prancing Novelist: A Defence of Fiction in the Form of a Critical Biography in Praise of Ronald Firbank*. London: Macmillan, 1963.

Brossard, Nicole
(*b.* 1943)

Brossard's native Montréal figures in her work as a site of writing and renewal. She was born into a prestigious family that included a supreme court judge and into a repressive culture controlled by the Catholic Church. She credits her personal independence to a breech birth, to a family tradition of high ideals and liberal ideas, and to her suffragist paternal grandmother. The timely demise in 1959 of the conservative prime minister, Maurice Duplessis, was a liberating event for Québec and for Brossard. A philosopher at fifteen, she resembled the heroine of *Mauve Desert* (*Le Désert mauve*, 1987): "Very young, I was already crying over humanity. With every new year I could see it dissolving in hope and in violence."

After a fashionable high school in English-speaking Westmount, she worked two years as a secretary, which her family felt would secure her future. With her savings, she went to Europe and then to the Université de Montréal. There she met poets, artists, and political activists; she discovered Québécois literature, jazz, and journalism. In 1965, she published her first volume of poetry and cofounded the experimental literary journal, *La Barre Du Jour*. In 1966, she married and published a second book of poems. With her husband, she demonstrated against the Vietnam War and for Québécois independence. After graduation from the university, she taught high school for two years, publishing her first work of fiction, *Turn of a Pang* (*Sold-out*, 1973), with a grant from the Canada Arts Council. In 1972, she met a young gym teacher, Germaine, and the next summer they left for six weeks in Greece, where they became lovers. Seized with an unquenchable thirst for feminist texts, she also found herself pregnant. Her body and her thoughts were transformed simultaneously. By the time her daughter was born in 1974, Brossard was a radical feminist and a lesbian in love. The problem was how to reinvent her life so that it would correspond to her revised values and her desire. As she later explained in an interview, she "would have to venture, body and soul, into a semantic field strewn with countless mines, some already exploded in the form of everyday sexism, others, even more terrifying, the buried mines of misogyny." Along with the terror was a surge of energy, a communal sense of urgency shared with women of many backgrounds, and a perception that "normal," heterosexual lives now seemed incongruous or even surreal.

A guiding spirit of a generation determined to be "resolutely modern," Brossard's unconventional praxis stood her in good stead as she addressed the problems of creating a space in language—the inherited system of codes and symbols—for a revised subjectivity and a refurbished imagination that could accommodate the desire of women. Beginning with *These Our Mothers or The Exploding Chapter* (*L'Amèr*, 1977), she creates texts that are radical in their approach to gender and sexuality while continuing to transgress literary conventions. Initiating young girls to the male is like a "current practice of lobotomy," she observes. She reads the institution of motherhood as forced reproduction, stating she has "killed [her] womb." She declares war against heterosexist ideas and patriarchal institutions. *These Our Mothers* is the first work she qualifies as "fiction theory." The next two volumes in her lesbian trilogy, *Lovhers* (*Amantes*) and *Surfaces of Sense* (*Le Sens apparent*, 1980), continue to deconstruct phallogocentrism and open a space for lesbian desire.

In 1978, Brossard met Marisa, the woman of her life, and celebrated her love in *Lovhers* and in *Picture Theory* (1982), her most ambitious work. Always an explorer, she uses figures that suggest the indeterminacy and multidimensionality of quantum physics and laser optics, vertigo, the spiral, cortex (corps-texte), the hologram, the horizon. *Picture Theory* is Brossard's answer to Joyce and Wittgenstein. Here she raises epistemological questions in what she describes as her "desire to unravel the great patriarchal enigma," setting language adrift in an effort to capture the "subliminal" or "generic" woman. She uses holography to figure "mental space for a contemporary vision," working with "potential" forms to "conquer reality, make it plausible." Negotiating between fiction and reality, in *Picture Theory* she invents "border crossers, radical city dwellers"; her "synchronous women" will "modify the horizon," using "the science of energy."

The death of Brossard's father in 1982 occasioned an uncharacteristic anguish over her writing. She wrote poetry and pondered translation—issues raised by the dual-language, post-colonial context of Québec, by work with her translators, and by her collaboration with Daphne Marlatt. Eventually, *Mauve Desert* resulted, representing the "postmodern condition," set in the "indescribable," hyperreal, and unforgiving Southwestern landscape with its bombs and fragile motels, where no window frames the blinding play of light. Like Escher's hand drawing itself drawing, the text is a self-translation. The hyped-up young narrator criss-crosses the desert at breakneck speed in her mother's Meteor, trying to understand, to "bend reality toward the light," while the translator tries to slip between the words. Translation, like writing, opens up a quantum field of inquiry into words, syntax, grammar, and the production of meaning.

Brossard's fiction foregrounds writing and bookmaking, playing with typography, problematizing literary conventions, interfacing visual images, creating books within books. Like an explorer, she investigates "surfaces of meaning," black marks on the white page, sometimes figured as skin or screen. She creates "virtual" texts that resemble holographic images, with narrative elements continuously displaced. Brossard's writing is fueled by a utopian energy that has its source in the lesbian body. Relieved of gravity (in both senses) the island-continent of lesbian desire has "aerial roots." Brossard explodes generic boundaries, working as she does in interrelated cycles of poetry, theory, and fiction. With modernist lesbian writers GERTRUDE STEIN and DJUNA BARNES as models, she combines a formalist approach to textuality with

a feminist consciousness, working always "in the light of a woman's gaze."

Theoretical essays in *The Aerial Letter* (*La Lettre aérienne,* 1985) have engaged two generations of feminist readers. "Writing in the feminine" for Brossard taps into an erotic substratum that is necessarily creative despite the nightmares, a symbolic code that forces women to stutter, and the daily violence of women's lives. Although Woman, a projection of phallic desire and will to power, lies "suspended over our heads like a threat of extinction," to intervene through writing is to create an alternative reality. As she remarks in *These Our Mothers,* "To write *I am a woman* is full of consequences." (See also QUÉBÉCOIS LITERATURE.)

—*Alice A. Parker*

BIBLIOGRAPHY

Dupré, Louise. *Stratégies du vertige. Trois poètes: Nicole Brossard, Madeleine Gagnon, France Théoret.* Montréal: Remue-Ménage, 1989. ■ Forsyth, Louise. "Beyond the Myths and Fictions of Traditionalism and Nationalism: The Political in the Work of Nicole Brossard." *Traditionalism, Nationalism and Feminism: Women Writers of Québec.* Paula Gilbert Lewis, ed. Westport, Conn.: Greenwood Press, 1985. 157–172. ■ Godard, Barbara. "L'Amèr or the Exploding Chapter: Nicole Brossard at the Site of Feminist Deconstruction." *Atlantis* 9.2 (Spring 1984): 23–43. ■ Gould, Karen. *Writing in the Feminine: Feminism and Experimental Writing in Québec.* Carbondale, Ill.: Southern Illinois University Press, 1990. ■ Parker, Alice. "The Mauve Horizon of Nicole Brossard." *Québec Studies* 10 (Spring/Summer 1990): 107–119. ■ ———. "Nicole Brossard: A Differential Equation of Lesbian Love." *Lesbian Texts and Contexts: Radical Revisions.* Karla Jay and Joanne Glasgow, eds. New York: New York University Press, 1990. 304–329. ■ Servin, Henri. "*Le Désert mauve* de Nicole Brossard ou l'indicible référent." *Québec Studies* 13 (Fall 1991 / Winter 1992): 55–63. ■ *Traces: Ecriture de Nicole Brossard.* Colloquium Proceedings. *La Nouvelle Barre du jour* 118–119 (September 1982). ■ Weir, Lorraine. "From Picture to Hologram: Nicole Brossard's Grammar of Utopia." *A Mazing Space: Writing Canadian Women Writing.* Shirley Neuman and Smaro Kamboureli, eds. Edmonton: Longspoon/NeWest, 1986.

Broumas, Olga
(*b.* 1949)

Born in Syros, Greece, Olga Broumas moved to the United States as a young woman and attended the University of Pennsylvania (B.A. in architecture, 1970) and the University of Oregon (M.F.A. in creative writing, 1973). Her fellowships have included a Guggenheim (1981) and a grant from the National Endowment for the Arts (1978). Broumas

has taught at many colleges and universities, taking time out in the 1980s to learn to play jazz saxophone and to develop and practice bodywork skills as a tool for healing and self-expression.

Broumas's first work published in North America was *Caritas* (1976), an unbound collection of five broadsides declaring one woman's love for another.

She chose the Greek word for her title because "none of the available English words signifying affection are free from either negative heterosexist connotations, or limitations of meaning so severe or so totally genital as to render them useless as names for our womanly songs of praise."

In 1976, the poet and literary critic Stanley Kunitz chose *Beginning with O* as the seventy-second winner of the Yale Younger Poets Prize. In his introduction to the volume, Kunitz said, "This is a book of letting go, of wild avowals, unabashed eroticism; . . . Broumas aspires to be an archaeologist of 'the speechless zones of the brain,' to grope her way back to the language of the ancestral mothers." This volume most clearly identifies Broumas with the development of lesbian culture in the twentieth century. Openly erotic toward her women lovers, the poet creates a rich world full of ancient Greek echoes juxtaposed to the immediacy of late twentieth-century idiom. Always informed by a distinct musicality, these poems progress from a rewriting of several Greek myths about goddesses to a central section devoted to her former husband to a final group in which she celebrates her lesbian ecstasy and explores the tangled matrix of mother–daughter bonds. Even when she limns her erotic passion for women, Broumas insists on placing that love within the material context in which she lives. The result is a poetry that is simultaneously politically brash, antiromantic and yet strikingly lyri-cal. This electrifying volume also establishes the textured relationship between lesbian love-making and language through the use of "tongue" in both its anatomical and linguistic context. Broumas defines lesbianism as an epistemological as well as a carnal enterprise. She goes so far as to assert that "braille / is a tongue for lovers" and to flaunt her lesbian affection by taking what she calls "unspeakable / liberties as / we cross the street, kissing / against the light."

Although subsequent volumes lack the laserlike focus on lesbian love, and her subject matter has become more diffuse, Broumas has continued to combine lyricism with a keen political edge. Whether she is thinking about the endangered environment, musing on her latest massage client, or once again singing the pleasures of her own and her lover's body, Olga Broumas writes athletic poetry that has the capacity to move and educate readers. In addition to her own poetry, she has translated from the Greek two volumes by the Nobel Laureate, Odysseas Elytis.

—*Toni A. H. McNaron*

BIBLIOGRAPHY

Broumas, Olga. *Beginning with O*. New Haven: Yale University Press, 1977. ■ ———. *Caritas*. Eugene, Ore.: Jackrabbit Press, 1976. ■ ———. *Pastoral Jazz*. Port Townsend, Wash.: Copper Canyon Press, 1983. ■ ———. *Perpetua*. Port Townsend, Wash.: Copper Canyon Press, 1989. ■ ———. *Soie Sauvage*. Port Townsend, Wash.: Copper Canyon Press, 1979.

Brown, Rita Mae
(*b*. 1944)

Rita Mae Brown was born on November 28, 1944, in Hanover, Pennsylvania, to an unwed mother who turned her over to an orphanage. She was then given into the care of Ralph and Julia Ellen Brown of York, Pennsylvania, who eventually became her adopted parents. When Brown was eleven, the family moved to Florida, where they remained throughout the rest of her childhood. She eventually enrolled in the University of Florida in Gainesville, where she campaigned for civil rights and greater racial integration. This outspokenness was responsible for her expulsion from the university in 1964.

Brown then hitchhiked to New York City and lived for a brief time in Greenwich Village in an abandoned car. She struggled in poverty for a while but continued to write and remain politically active. She was an early member of the National Organization for Women but was expelled for insisting that the group give more recognition to its lesbian constituents. Brown attended New York University, where she earned a B.A. in English and the classics. In 1973, she received a Ph.D. from the Institute for Policy Studies in Washington D.C. While attending NYU, Brown published two collections of feminist poetry: *The Hand That Cradles the Rock* (1971) and *Songs to a Handsome Woman* (1973). The year 1973 was extremely important for her because it was also the year her lesbian classic, *Rubyfruit Jungle*, was published. The book launched her career as a novelist.

Throughout the remainder of the 1970s, Brown continued to pen novels (*In Her Day*, 1976; *Six of One*, 1978) and published an anthology of her political essays (*A Plain Brown Rapper*, 1976). During this period, Brown also met and began a relationship with tennis star Martina Navratilova. The two moved in together in 1979, and their relationship became part of the inspiration for Brown's novel *Sudden Death* (1983), which looks at life within the women's tennis circuit.

In 1981, Brown's relationship with Navratilova ended, and she headed to California to begin writing for television. She has continued to write for television periodically, including coauthoring the script of "My Two Loves," a 1986 television movie dealing with lesbian subject matter. Also in 1986, Brown stepped out from behind the typewriter to narrate the documentary "Before Stonewall." The 1980s also saw the publication of several more novels (*Southern Discomfort,* 1982; *High Hearts,* 1986; *Bingo,* 1988) and a writer's manual (*Starting From Scratch,* 1988).

After taking a hiatus to write two mystery novels "with" her cat, Sneaky Pie (*Wish You Were Here,* 1990; *Rest in Pieces,* 1992), Brown has returned to lesbian subject matter in her latest book, *Venus Envy* (1993), which is the story of a woman who comes out to friends and family because she believes she has terminal cancer but then discovers she has been misdiagnosed.

Even though she has had a long and varied career, Brown is still best known for her semiautobiographical, picaresque novel, *Rubyfruit Jungle,* in which she introduces the headstrong young lesbian, Molly Bolt. Molly feels no need to apologize for her lesbianism and storms through society with her openness and honesty, refusing to conform to the expectations of either the dominant heterosexual society or the New York lesbian subculture. The novel espouses a doctrine of radical individualism that runs counter to much post-Stonewall lesbian literature that emphasizes communitarianism. *Rubyfruit* has sold millions of copies, and is one of the best-selling gay–lesbian books of all time. A prolific and commercially successful writer, Brown articulates a lesbian voice that resists neat categorization: nonetheless, a voice that began the tradition of the lesbian picara, the proud lesbian "hero." (See also NOVEL: LESBIAN.)

—*Beth A. Kattelman*

BIBLIOGRAPHY

Faderman, Lillian. *Surpassing the Love of Men: Romantic Friendship and Love Between Women from the Renaissance to the Present.* New York: William Morrow, 1981. ■ Marchino, Lois. "Rita Mae Brown." *American Women Writers: A Critical Reference Guide from Colonial Times to the Present.* Lina Mainiero, ed. Vol. 1 of 4. New York: Frederick Ungar, 1979. 257–258. ■ Roof, Judith. *A Lure of Knowledge: Lesbian Sexuality and Theory.* New York: Columbia University Press, 1991. ■ Rule, Jane. *Lesbian Images.* Garden City, N.Y.: Doubleday, 1975. ■ Wolf, Susan J. and Julia Penelope, eds. *Sexual Practice, Textual Theory: Lesbian Cultural Criticism.* Cambridge: Blackwell, 1993. ■ Zimmerman, Bonnie. *The Safe Sea of Women: Lesbian Fiction 1969-1989.* Boston: Beacon, 1990.

Burns, John Horne
(1916–1953)

John Horne Burns was born October 7, 1916, in Andover, Massachusetts, the eldest of seven children in a prominent Irish Catholic family. He was educated at the Sisters of Notre Dame convent school and then Andover Academy, where he pursued musical, rather than literary, endeavors. Burns spent the next four years at Harvard as a loner, studying English literature and finding comfort in music. His 1937 Phi Beta Kappa graduation resulted in a teaching post at the Loomis School in Windsor, Connecticut. Entering the infantry as a private in 1942, he served in military intelligence in Casablanca and Algiers until Pentagon officials sent him to the Adjutant General's School in Washington, D.C., when his knowledge of Italian became known. Subsequently commissioned a second lieutenant, he spent the remainder of the war censoring prisoner-of-war mail in Africa and Italy.

War service provoked in Burns a skepticism about America's class-coded, heterosexist morality, as well as its ethnocentrism and marketplace mentality. He returned to the Loomis School after his 1946 army discharge, but he lasted there only a year. The cornerstone of Burns's literary reputation, his first novel, *The Gallery,* was published in the summer of 1947. His second novel, *Lucifer with a Book,* appeared in 1949, but received little praise, and he wrote travel pieces for *Holiday* magazine to survive. Disheartened by the critical reception of his novel, he retreated to Italy, where he began his last published work, *A Cry of Children* (1952). When this work also received negative press, he wrote a fourth novel, never published because Burns died before making the extensive revisions required for its publication. After a sailing trip, he lapsed into a coma and died from a cerebral hemorrhage on August 11, 1953. Rumors circulating at the time suggested suicide because of Burns's frustrated writing career and the ending of a tempestuous relationship with an Italian doctor. Initially buried in Rome, his remains were disinterred and reburied in Boston.

As recorded by his contemporary, GORE VIDAL, Burns reportedly said that to be a good writer, one must be homosexual, perhaps because his or her marginalized status provides the gay or lesbian author with an objectivity not attainable within mainstream culture. Certainly the type of critique that such marginalization can engender is apparent in Burns's novels and constitutes his contribution to the gay and lesbian literary tradition. *The Gallery*, a series of vignettes centered on the Galleria Umberto in Naples, Italy, comments on the social and sexual mores of the American way of life, represented by the escapades of various American service personnel unleashed on the recently liberated Old World. Similarly, the autobiographical *Lucifer with a Book* scrutinizes the incubator for such value systems, the private school, as Burns tells the story of a battle-scarred history teacher who, although heterosexual, cannot willingly contribute to the "brainwashing" of the next generation he teaches. And his last novel, *A Cry of Children*, chronicles concert pianist David Murray's search for meaning and connection within America's stifling conceptions of motherhood, heterosexual courtship, and religious practices.

Although he primarily focuses on heterosexual characters and situations, in none of Burns's work is some consideration of homosexuality absent. *The Gallery*, for example, presents a memorable portrayal of a Neapolitan gay bar and the wide spectrum of international patrons, both high- and low-born, who frequent it. And in *Lucifer with a Book*, Burns reveals the coterie of young homosexuals who form the underground social structure of the school whose other secrets he lays bare. Had he survived, he may have lived up to his early reputation as among the best of up-and-coming post-war writers. Unfortunately, post-war America had little patience with Burns's critique of a way of life affirmed by victory abroad.

—*Mark A. Graves*

BIBLIOGRAPHY

Aldridge, John W. *After the Lost Generation: A Critical Study of the Writers of Two Wars.* New York: McGraw-Hill, 1951. ■ Byrd, David. "John Horne Burns." *Dictionary of Literary Bibiography.* 1985 yearbook. Jean W. Ross, ed. Detroit: Gale. 338–343. ■ Brophy, Bridget. "John Horne Burns." *Don't Never Forget: Collected Views and Reviews.* New York: Holt, Rinehart and Winston, 1966. 192–202. ■ Mitzel, John. *John Horne Burns: An Appreciative Biography.* Dorchester, Mass.: Manifest Destiny, 1974. ■ Smith, Harrison. "Thirteen Adventurers: A Study of a Year of First Novelists, 1947." *The Saturday Review of Literature* (February 14, 1948): 6–8+. ■ Vidal, Gore. "John Horne Burns." *Homage to Daniel Shays, Collected Essays 1952-1972.* New York: Random House, 1972. 181–185.

Burroughs, William S.
(b. 1914)

In his novels as in his life, William S. Burroughs has long been an outlaw and a provocateur. Beginning with *Naked Lunch* (1959), his fiction has been distinguished by violently hallucinatory images, rendered in prose that brilliantly mimics the speech of criminals, redneck sheriffs, bureaucrats, political extremists, and hipsters. A series of later writings applies collage techniques to the novel form. Burroughs has always incorporated transgressive sexual imagery and situations into his writing. In this, he has gone far beyond the acknowledgment, in the 1950s, of his own homosexuality. His novels contain representations of such practices as autoerotic asphyxiation and sadomasochism. Primarily a satirist, Burroughs treats both sexuality and language as manifestations of social power—and as sites of conflict.

Born in St. Louis, Missouri, to a wealthy family, William Burroughs studied English, medicine, and anthropology at Harvard and the University of Vienna before becoming addicted to narcotics in the mid-1940s. Following an arrest for heroin and marijuana possession, he fled to Mexico. There, in 1951, he accidentally shot his wife, Joan Burroughs, during a drunken imitation of William Tell. He spent much of the 1950s recovering from heroin addiction and brooding over the act of violence that ended his companion's life.

Life in the underworld of addicts and petty criminals is the basis of his first published novel, *Junkie* (1953), written in a "hardboiled" style and published under the pseudonym of "Bill Lee" (his mother's maiden name). During this period, Burroughs started another novel, in the same stylistic vein, describing the gay demimonde; this unfinished manuscript was published, much later, as *Queer* (1985).

With *Naked Lunch* (1959), Burroughs abandoned the naturalistic depiction of "outsider" subcultures and began to write in a surrealistic and bitterly satirical mode. This novel incorporated characters and scenarios Burroughs had created while improvising skits to amuse his friends (including ALLEN GINSBERG and JACK KEROUAC, fellow members of the BEAT GENERATION literary group). Often highly scatological, laced with the argot of various underworlds Burroughs had encountered in his travels, the paranoiac and hallucinatory scenes in *Naked Lunch* treated addiction as a complex metaphor for all varieties of domination and control. The novel was subject to a number of court cases for obscenity.

In a trilogy of novels—*The Soft Machine* (1961), *The Ticket That Exploded* (1962), and *Nova Express* (1964)—Burroughs developed an elaborate mythology of addiction, involving intergalactic conspiracies and secret agencies at war to control the drug trade. These books scrambled narrative and character, fracturing syntax and the arrangement of text on the printed page; they sought to break up the reader's habits of perception in order to permit a "return of the repressed" into the literary work.

Burroughs has often drawn on the paraliterature of "pulp" or genre fiction—such as detective novels, science fiction, spy thrillers, and westerns—but the conventions of these genres are violently distorted in his hands. Influenced by dissident psychoanalytic theorist Wilhelm Reich, Burroughs focuses on sexual repression as the fundamental element of social control. Works of genre literature usually conform to the stereotypes of the dominant culture, including, typically, homophobia. By incorporating the "deviant" perspectives of the drug addict or the sexual outlaw into novels with "pulp" qualities, Burroughs produces fiction that, if never "political" in any ordinary sense, is certainly subversive. For instance, *The Wild Boys* (1971) fuses pornographic scenes into its science-fiction treatment of a band of homosexual terrorists rampaging through the near future.

Combining pop-culture materials with avant garde experiments, Burroughs's writings were an early instance of post-modernism, especially in their fragmentary quality, which dispenses with linear narrative and realistic character portraiture. And with his conception of language itself as a force beyond conscious control, Burroughs likewise anticipated such post-structuralist thinkers as MICHEL FOUCAULT and Jacques Derrida. To emphasize this sense of discourse as a power strangely alien to human will, Burroughs once wrote, "Language is a virus from outer space." This imagery was refigured in the uncannily prophetic novel *Cities of the Red Night* (1981), where a virally transmitted disease induces sexual delirium and violent death.

The best overview of Burroughs's cultural politics and rather eccentric cosmology may be found in a set of interviews, *The Job* (1970), whereas *The Adding Machine* (1986) gathers various essays on sex, addiction, and writing. *The Burroughs File* (1984) collects fictional texts and short autobiographical works originally published as pamphlets or in the underground press. With *The Place of Dead Roads* (1983) and *The Western Lands* (1987), Burroughs approached the end of his career as a novelist.

During the 1980s, Burroughs began performing with some regularity in films and on television, and several recordings have been made of the writer reading portions of his work. David Cronenberg's film adaptation of *Naked Lunch* (1992) treated the novel as a story of the author's literary and sexual self-discovery. Burroughs's work has been influential for several generations of novelists, poets, performance artists, and feminist and queer theorists. (See also SCIENCE FICTION AND FANTASY.)

—*Scott McLemee*

BIBLIOGRAPHY

Goodman, Michael B. *Contemporary Literary Censorship: The Case History of Burroughs' Naked Lunch.* Metuchen, N.J.: Scarecrow Press, 1981. ■ ———. *William S. Burroughs: A Reference Guide.* New York: Garland, 1990. ■ Johnston, Allan. "The Burroughs Biopathy: William S. Burroughs's *Junky* and *Naked Lunch* and Reichian Theory." *Review of Contemporary Fiction* 4.1 (1984): 107–120. ■ Lydenberg, Robin. *Word Cultures: Radical Theory and Practice in William S. Burroughs' Fiction.* Urbana: University of Illinois Press, 1987. ■ Morgan, Ted. *Literary Outlaw: The Life and Times of William S. Burroughs.* New York: Henry Holt, 1988. ■ Skau, Michael. "The Central Verbal System: The Prose of William Burroughs." *Style* 15.4 (1981): 401–414. ■ Zarbrugg, Nicholas. "Burroughs, Barthes, and the Limits of Intertextuality." *Review of Contemporary Fiction* 4.1 (1984): 86–107.

Butch-Femme Relations

It is impossible to understand twentieth-century lesbian literature without recognizing the significance of butch-femme relationships, both in reality and in literature, throughout the century. Whether we think of the great modernist writer GERTRUDE STEIN and her relationship with Alice B. Toklas, or WILLA CATHER's years with Isabelle McClung and then her forty years with Edith Lewis, or RADCLYFFE HALL's relationship with Lady Una Troubridge, we find authors who have, to one extent or another, used butch-femme relationships as a way to configure their lives. Thus, their complex understandings of butch and femme roles need to be untangled in order to understand their lives as well as their literary works. Moreover, since butch-femme identities have played a prominent role in lesbian experience throughout this century, no lesbian writer should be studied without considering how she has been influenced by such roles.

First of all, it is necessary to define what "butch" and "femme" mean, which is a complex task since many possible interpretations exist, and it is difficult to find consensus; as Elizabeth Lapovsky Kennedy and Madeline Davis comment in their recent study, *Boots of Leather, Slippers of Gold: The History of a Lesbian Community* (1993), "all language for talking about butches and fems is inadequate." A simple definition is that butch and femme lesbians adopt roles that have been traditionally associated with men and women, with butches assuming masculine identities and femmes assuming feminine ones. For instance, a butch might wear men's clothing and be sexually aggressive, whereas a femme would adopt feminine clothing and be sexually passive. We must recognize the limitations of such a definition, however, since it fails to take into account the many changes in butch-femme roles that have occurred in the last century, particularly in the 1980s when lesbian sexual radicals altered butch-femme roles dramatically. Despite changes, however, butch-femme roles have had a prominent place in the lesbian community for over fifty years. Their popularity has risen and fallen in different periods. For instance, during the 1940s and 1950s, butch and femme roles were accepted by a large number of lesbians as a model for lesbian unions. By the 1970s, butch-femme roles had fallen out of favor and were widely perceived by lesbian feminists as oppressive. Through their writing, many lesbian authors have sought to understand the historical changes in butch-femme relationships. For those interested in more information about the historical changes in butch-femme roles, there is excellent historical material by scholars such as Vern and Bonnie Bullough, Madeline Davis and Elizabeth Lapovsky Kennedy, Lillian Faderman, and Joan Nestle.

Relationships that appear to be based on male-female roles have not been limited to the twentieth century, of course. Reflecting on the nineteenth century, we have only to think of MARIE CORELLI, the English author, and Bertha Vyver; or ALICE FRENCH, the American writer, and Jane Crawford; or Rosa Bonheur, the French artist, and Nathalie Micas—all women couples in which one woman adopted the more feminine role while the other adopted the more masculine. We must be cautious about categorizing such relationships as "butch-femme," however, since they are situated in a different historical period, where our terminology may have only limited application.

Although it is inappropriate to say that butch-femme roles existed in the early nineteenth century, we can state with more assurance that recognizable butch-femme roles have been around since at least the 1890s when, as historian Lillian Faderman points out, women dressed in tuxedos would attend homosexual balls in order to waltz with more conventional-appearing feminine women. Further, in this historical period sexologists, such as Richard von Krafft-Ebing and Havelock Ellis, began to stress that the female "invert," as they named the lesbian, was typically masculine but often had relationships with feminine women. It was not until the 1920s, however, that an urban, working-class lesbian culture appeared in which butch and femme roles were clearly evident. In the 1920s as well, butch and femme roles began to appear with increasing frequency in literature. Sometimes, these roles were used in books and stories by heterosexual writers as signs of everything that was "abnormal" and "unhealthy" about lesbianism. One of the most memorable of such works is D. H. LAWRENCE's story "The Fox" (1920). In this story, two women, Banford and March, try to earn a livelihood from a small farm. Although Lawrence never explicitly identifies their relationship as lesbian, it is almost impossible to avoid the assumption. Banford's and March's farm is remarkably unsuccessful; even their chickens are sterile, reflecting what Lawrence perceived as the sterility of such a relationship. Only after Banford, who plays the "man about the place," is killed by a falling tree, is March "saved" in order to start a relationship with a wandering soldier who has stopped by the farm.

The first book by a lesbian author with a lesbian heroine who could be identified explicitly as butch appeared in 1928 with the publication of *The Well of Loneliness* by Radclyffe Hall. Unlike Hall's contemporaries Gertrude Stein and Willa Cather, who depicted their personal relationships only obliquely, Hall wished to write about lesbianism openly although she was aware that her own lesbian relationships would be held up to public scrutiny. Hall's work is not only the best-selling lesbian novel of all time, but it also surely presents the most famous image of a butch lesbian in the protagonist, Stephen Gordon, a wealthy Englishwoman who is rejected by her family because of her lesbianism. Born "a narrow-hipped, wide-shouldered little tadpole of a baby," Stephen is easily identified as butch, marked by "the curious suggestion of strength in her movements, the long line of her limbs—she was tall for her age—and the pose of her head on her over-broad shoulders." Although it was at first banned as obscene, Hall's book about Stephen Gordon's coming of age as a lesbian has gone on to influence countless readers, both homosexual and heterosexual. For decades, Hall's handsome, androgynous heroine served as a model for butches to emulate. *The Well* might seem dated to modern readers because of its insistence that "real" lesbians are born and not a product of their cultural influences, yet we must not forget the tremendous impact this book has had on countless readers for over half a century as the best-known account by a lesbian about lesbian life. It certainly has influenced many readers to understand butch-femme relationships, as depicted by Stephen and her lover, Mary, as the typical form for lesbian unions.

In the 1950s, as lesbian historian Lillian Faderman points out, butch-femme roles became even stricter than they had been in previous decades. A heterogenderal pattern for relationships seemed the only conceivable model to many gay men and women of this period. Given the predominance of butch-femme roles and the often unquestioning assumption that all lesbians were butches or femmes, it is hardly surprising that much of the literature of this period dwells on the importance of butch-femme relationships. Hundreds of cheap paperbacks with sensational titles were produced in the 1950s and 1960s for both heterosexual and homosexual readers. ANN BANNON's Beebo Brinker books, which were reissued by Naiad Press in the early 1980s, are some of the most perceptive accounts of the difficulties facing lesbians in this period. In *Women in the Shadows* (1959), *Beebo Brinker* (1962), and other novels, Bannon depicts a world in which butch-femme relationships are essential, yet often can lead to conflict. Even Beebo Brinker, the handsome, self-assured butch who first appears in the novel bearing the same name, cannot remain unaffected by the society around her that considers butch women to be unattractive and unnatural. Unable to fit into typical "feminine" jobs, Beebo ends up working as an elevator operator for ten years because it is one of the few positions that will allow her to wear pants. Even Laura, Beebo's lover, is "ashamed to go anywhere out of Greenwich Village with her . . . Beebo, nearly six feet of her, with her hair cropped short and her strange clothes and her gruff voice." The butch lesbian, whether Stephen Gordon or Beebo Brinker, is an eternal exile from heterosexual society,

which is one of the reasons she is such a recurring figure in lesbian literature; she represents not only her alienation, but also the alienation of the entire lesbian community from heterosexual norms.

Like Beebo and Stephen, Christopher Hamilton in Randy Salem's novel *Chris* (1959), is a butch lesbian who fails to blend into heterosexual society: "Lean and firm, built like a young boy, she did not look like a thirty-year-old woman. She was all things beautiful, graceful and desirable." But whereas Beebo is unsuccessful at her career, Chris is highly successful as a marine biologist and deep-sea diver. Although Chris's life is certainly not free of anxiety (she has a drinking problem and a beautiful but cold girlfriend), she is still portrayed as a heroine with whom the audience can identify, particularly when she gives up her demanding and deceitful girlfriend in order to follow her own career aspirations. For a lesbian audience, Chris, like Beebo, is portrayed as a potentially desirable role model, explaining some of the allure early pulp novels had for lesbian readers.

Compared with the very evident butch-femme roles of Bannon's or Salem's books, the butch-femme relationships in Valerie Taylor's lesbian pulp novels of the 1960s are typically less apparent. For instance, in Taylor's novel *A World Without Men* (1963), the main lesbian characters, the lovers Erika and Kate, fit into butch and femme roles, respectively, yet their roles are not nearly so clearly demarcated as are the roles of Beebo and Laura. Although she is "a girl who looked like a boy," Erika still is more responsible for domestic chores than is Kate. And both women are horrified by the blatant butch-femme roles of a couple they pass. Whether in Bannon's or Taylor's books or the hundreds of other lesbian pulp novels that were produced in the 1950s and early 1960s, butch and femme roles were explored in myriad ways, yet only rarely were they questioned; most writers simply assumed that they were the "natural" way to divide the lesbian community.

Although most of the lesbian pulp writers focused on contemporary lesbian experiences, other writers sought to create a lesbian past. The necessity of narrating a lesbian past is an important issue in ISABEL MILLER's novel, *Patience and Sarah,* first published as *A Place for Us* in 1969, a text that examines the lives of two lesbians in early nineteenth-century New England. Along with *The Well of Loneliness,* Miller's novel is one of the literary works most frequently cited by lesbian readers for its prominent butch-femme couple. Sarah, a young woman who wears men's clothing, cuts her hair short, performs tasks commonly associated with males, travels around the countryside masquerading as a man, and complacently announces that she is "Pa's boy," falls in love with Patience, who engages in more traditionally feminine activities, such as needlework, and has a more stereotypical female appearance. When faced with the hostile reactions of others toward their relationship, Patience and Sarah set out for rural New York to begin a farm. As in many lesbian novels, a butch-femme relationship is portrayed very positively. Patience and Sarah, rather than merely mimicking male-female roles, however, actively seek to create their own identities. For them, their relationship offers an escape from the often stultifying traditional roles available to heterosexual farm women in the early 1800s. In addition, this novel attempts to build up a lesbian history of "what might have been," an activity that is particularly important for the lesbian novelist, given the scarcity of materials available about lesbians in the past.

Unlike *Patience and Sarah* and the many other lesbian novels and short stories that discussed butch-femme relationships as a central experience in lesbian life, many literary works written by lesbians in the late 1960s and early 1970s turned away or even rejected completely the butch-femme couple. Instead, lesbian writers, influenced by the feminist movement, sought to escape the widespread assumption that all lesbians were either butch or femme. *Rubyfruit Jungle* (1973) by RITA MAE BROWN is only the best known of many literary texts that focus on lesbians who give little attention to which lesbians identify as butch, femme, or neither.

After the rejection of butch-femme roles by many lesbians in the 1970s, there was a renewed interest in such roles in the 1980s, an interest reflected in the literature of the period. Authors tried to portray butch-femme roles in ways that were affirming, rather than negative. For example, in her fiction Lee Lynch portrays butch-femme relationships as enjoyable and exuberant. In books such as *The Swashbuckler* (1985), *Old Dyke Tales* (1984), and *Toothpick House* (1983), Lynch frequently focuses on butch-femme roles and relationships in working-class communities. She has a special fondness for depicting the struggles that working-class butch lesbians confront. For instance, Annie Heaphy, the main character of *Toothpick House* who drives a cab, must struggle with how to combine her socioeconomic background with her developing interest in the feminist movement, where her butch attitude and class background at first make her feel unaccepted. In *The Swashbuckler*, Frenchy prides herself on the fact that she walks like a butch and considers herself a bulldyke, yet she must confront the daily reality of dressing in her "straight clothes" for her weekly work as a cashier at a grocery store.

Like the literary work of many lesbian writers, Lynch's novels and short stories try to grapple with how lesbians manage to bring the different parts of their lives together as they strive to survive in both heterosexual and homosexual environments.

Pat Suncircle's short story "Mariam" (1981), like Lynch's fiction, explores the problems confronting butch women who do not blend into heterosexual society. In this story, Mariam is a black woman who is "enfolded in butch like a bat inside its wings and upside down." Despite the stares and double-takes that people give her, Mariam retains her leather vest and coat, cowboy boots, and swaggering walk, even when her friend Phoebe, a much less obvious butch, becomes uncomfortable. Phoebe slowly learns that Mariam, rather than someone to be embarrassed by, is someone to admire and respect for her "graceful, proud lumberjack" walk and her unbending pride in her own identity. As Phoebe realizes, loving Mariam "is to be unable to lie." Mariam, like Stephen Gordon, is unwilling to give up her self-image in order to find acceptance in the heterosexual world. It is exactly this refusal that establishes her as a heroine for other lesbians.

For well over half a century, lesbian writers have included butch and femme roles in their own personal lives or have struggled to write about such roles in a way that insightfully explores the complexities of such multifaceted identities. By writing about these roles and by proclaiming them as viable alternatives for women, lesbian writers have made an invaluable contribution in showing readers that butch-femme relationships were not the "warped, perverted" relationships that mainstream heterosexual society proclaimed them to be.

—*Sherrie A. Inness*

BIBLIOGRAPHY

Ardill, Susan, and Sue O'Sullivan. "Butch/Femme Obsessions." *Feminist Review* 34 (Spring 1990): 79–85. ■ Case, Sue-Ellen. "Towards a Butch-Femme Aesthetic." *Discourse* 11 (Winter 1988–1989): 55–73. ■ Faderman, Lillian. *Odd Girls and Twilight Lovers: A History of Lesbian Life in Twentieth-Century America.* New York: Columbia University Press, 1991. ■ ———. "The Return of Butch and Femme: A Phenomenon in Lesbian Sexuality of the 1980s and 1990s." *Journal of the History of Sexuality* 2 (1992): 578–596. ■ "Femme and Butch: A Readers' Forum." *Lesbian Ethics* 2 (Fall 1986): 86–104. ■ Hollibaugh, Amber, and Cherrie Moraga. "What We're Rollin Around in Bed With: Sexual Silences in Feminism." *Powers of Desire: The Politics of Sexuality.* Ann Snitow, Christine Stansell, and Sharon Thompson, eds. New York: Monthly Review Press, 1983. 394–405. ■ Jeffreys, Sheila. "Butch & Femme: Now and Then." *Not a Passing Phase: Reclaiming Lesbians in History 1840-1985.* Lesbian History Group, ed. London: Women's Press, 1989. 158–187. ■ Kennedy, Elizabeth Lapovsky, and Madeline Davis. *Boots of Leather, Slippers of Gold: The History of a*

Lesbian Community. New York: Routledge, 1993. ■ Loulan, JoAnn. *The Lesbian Erotic Dance: Butch, Femme, Androgyny, and Other Rhythms.* San Francisco: Spinsters, 1990. ■ Nestle, Joan. "The Fem Question." *Pleasure and Danger: Exploring Female Sexuality.* Carole S. Vance, ed. Boston: Routledge, 1984.

232–241. ■ ——, ed. *The Persistent Desire: A Femme–Butch Reader.* Boston: Alyson, 1992. ■ Rubin, Gayle. "Of Catamites and Kings: Reflections on Butch, Gender, and Boundaries." *The Persistent Desire: A Femme–Butch Reader.* Joan Nestle, ed. Boston: Alyson, 1992. 466–482.

Butler, Lady Eleanor (1739–1829) and Sarah Ponsonby (1755–1831)

Best known as the Ladies of Llangollen, after the Welsh village where they lived in "delicious Retirement," Lady Eleanor Butler and Sarah Ponsonby were daughters of the Anglo-Irish Ascendency who eloped together in 1778. Ponsonby, sixteen years Butler's junior, lost both parents in early childhood and her stepmother when she was thirteen. Given into the care of her father's cousin Lady Betty Fownes, she was sent to Miss Parke's boarding school in Kilkenny. There, in 1768, she met Butler, youngest daughter in a Catholic branch of an ancient and noble family of Kilkenny. Educated in an English Benedictine convent in France, Butler became Ponsonby's intellectual mentor and intimate friend. After Ponsonby left Miss Parke's in 1773, the two women entered upon a secret correspondence and determined to live together.

Butler and Ponsonby's first elopement failed; they were discovered, returned, and separated by their two families. Eleanor was urged to a convent, whereas Sarah, it was hoped, would be married. When both women resisted these pressures and Sarah threatened to make public the attentions of her guardian's husband, the families relented and the women fled to Wales. They took a cottage, which they named Plas Newydd, and there settled for the rest of their long lives.

The Ladies' pastoral retreat drew many prominent visitors, including Edmund Burke, William Wordsworth, ANNA SEWARD, and Stéphanie de Genlis. Their mutual attachment, and their life of shared reading, writing, walking, and gardening, were celebrated and mythologized in such contemporary writings as Seward's "Llangollen Vale" and Wordsworth's "Sonnet Composed at Plas Newydd." The women shared bed, board, books, income, and daily walks; dressed similarly in men's waistcoats and women's skirts; signed their correspondence jointly; named one of their dogs Sappho; and refused to spend even one night away from home. Butler's journals refer to Ponsonby as "my Beloved" and "my sweet love," describe physical attentions bestowed for headaches and illnesses, and express the couple's longings, when visitors were too plentiful, to be alone again.

There has been considerable debate about whether Butler and Ponsonby's union should be labeled "lesbian." During their lifetime, implications of homosexuality circulated occasionally in the press and among visitors, although their upperclass status and connections undoubtedly protected them. Their homophobic neighbor Hester Thrale Piozzi suspected them of Sapphism; Genlis considered them imprudent victims of an excessive sensibility. Anne Lister, the Yorkshire woman who recorded her own homosexual activities in coded diaries, wrote after visiting Llangollen in 1822, "I cannot help thinking that surely it was not Platonic. Heaven forgive me, but I look within myself & doubt."

Whether the Ladies of Llangollen have been regarded as celibate or sexual, their relationship has emblematized ROMANTIC FRIENDSHIP for over two centuries. Deeply immersed in the literary culture of their day as readers, conversationalists, and occasional writers, they have also remained literary subjects. COLETTE speculates about them in *The Pure and the Impure* (1928), Constance Stallard dramatizes their relationship in "The Ladies of Llangollen" (1955), and novels by DORIS GRUMBACH (*The Ladies*, 1984) and Morgan Graham (*These Lovers Fled Away*, 1988) imagine their life. Elizabeth Mavor's 1971 biography remains the major resource for scholars; Mavor's selection from Butler's and Ponsonby's private writings is also a valuable textual source. (See also ENGLISH LITERATURE: ROMANTICISM.)

—*Susan S. Lanser*

BIBLIOGRAPHY

Bell, Eva Mary Hamilton, ed. *The Hamwood Papers of the Ladies of Llangollen and Caroline Hamilton.* London: Macmillan, 1930. ■ Butler, Eleanor. *Life with the Ladies of Llangollen* [rpt. as *A Year with the Ladies of Llangollen*]. Elizabeth Mavor, ed. Harmondsworth: Viking, 1984. ■ Colette. *The Pure and the Impure.* Trans. Herma Briffault. New York: Farrar Straus, 1967.

■ Gordon, Mary Louisa. *Chase of the Wild Goose: The Story of Lady Eleanor Butler and Miss Sarah Ponsonby, Known as the Ladies of Llangollen*. London: Hogarth Press, 1936; rpt. New York: Arno Press, 1975. ■ Mavor, Elizabeth. *The Ladies of Llangollen: A Study in Romantic Friendship*. London: Michael Joseph 1971; Penguin, 1973. ■ Prichard, John. *An Account of the Ladies of Llangollen*. Llangollen: Hugh Jones, 1887. ■ Seward, Anna. *Llangollen Vale*. 1796; rpt. Oxford: Woodstock Books, 1994. ■ Stallard, C. L. *Seven Plays*. London: Mitre Press, 1955.

Butler, Samuel
(1835–1902)

Samuel Butler was born on December 4, 1835, at Langar Rectory near Bingham, Nottinghamshire, England. He was both the son and grandson of Anglican clergy. He received his education at Shrewsbury School and St. John's College, Cambridge, where he earned a degree in 1858. Although Samuel and his family had made plans for him to enter the ministry, he began to have doubts about his religion and ordination. After Cambridge, he worked briefly among the poor in London as a lay minister while trying to decide his future. In 1860, he emigrated to New Zealand and became a successful sheep rancher while publishing articles in the local press. Four years later, he returned to England, where he studied to become a painter and continued his writing.

Much of Butler's work concerns his two primary interests, religion and evolution. He was particularly intrigued by the writings of Charles Darwin, an interest reflected in the extremely successful *Erewhon* (1872), a utopian vision of the future and parody of Victorian England, as well as in *The Fairhaven* (1875), a satire on Christianity and rationalism. Butler completed many other essays, nonfiction works, and another novel, *Erewhon Revisited* (1901), but it was his autobiographical novel, *The Way of All Flesh* (published posthumously in 1903), that most fully revealed Butler's moral beliefs while blasting the images of the Victorian family, religion, and society.

Butler's life and writings are strongly male-identified with intense homoerotic overtones. He was a lifelong bachelor who had several intense relationships with men, especially with Charles Paine Pauli. They met in New Zealand in 1861 and returned to England together in 1864. Butler supported Pauli financially for the next thirty years, only to learn on Pauli's death that he had amassed a fortune, excluded Butler from his will, and had been supported by two other men during the years of Butler's support. Henry Festing Jones, Butler's companion and biographer, also recalls the writer's love for another young man, the Swiss Hans Faesch, whose early death prompted Butler's emotional poem, "In Memoriam H.R.F."

(1895), and his wearing a lock of Faesch's hair in a pendant. Although some critics have suggested that this friendship indicated Butler's intense longing for a son, Jones notes that the poem's publication caused Butler to be concerned that he might be regarded as another OSCAR WILDE, whose trials caused a wave of antihomosexual feeling in English society in 1895 and afterward.

Butler's predilection for intense male friendships is expressed through the characters of Ernest Pontifex, Towneley, Pryor, and Overton in *The Way of All Flesh*. Throughout the novel, Ernest Pontifex struggles against his feelings for other men. After his ordination, he encounters the curate Pryor, and realizes that he is not alone in his sentiments. Determined to marry in the hopes that marriage will alleviate the problem, his marriage turns out to be a fraud, much to his relief. The character of Overton, who represents Butler as an older man, repeatedly mentions his dislike of women, marriage, and the dissolution of male friendship because of marriage. *The Way of All Flesh* was to have a profound influence on E. M. FORSTER, whose *The Longest Journey* (1907) expresses some of the same sentiments regarding marriage.

Butler's other writings include *The Authoress of the Odyssey* (1897), in which he posits the idea that the *Odyssey* was written by a woman; and *Shakespeare's Sonnets Reconsidered* (1899), which contends that SHAKESPEARE had become infatuated with a younger man who duped and betrayed him, a thesis that parallels his own sad relationship with Pauli.

Butler died in 1902 after a prolonged illness, attended by his devoted manservant, Alfred Catie, and his companion, Henry Festing Jones.

—*Catherine Geddis*

BIBLIOGRAPHY

Cole, G. D. H. *Samuel Butler*. London: Morrison & Gibb, 1948. ■ Henderson, Philip. *Samuel Butler: The Incarnate Bachelor*. Bloomington: Indiana University Press, 1954. ■ Holt, Lee. *Samuel Butler*. Boston: Twayne Publishers, 1989. ■ Jeffers, Thomas. *Samuel Butler Revalued*. University Park: Pennsylvania

State University Press, 1981. ■ Muggeridge, Malcolm. *The Earnest Atheist, A Study of Samuel Butler.* New York: G.P. Putnam, 1937. ■ Raby, Peter. *Samuel Butler—A Biography.* London:

Hogarth Press, 1991. ■ Stuart, Ross. "Samuel Butler and Charles Paine Pauli: A Friendship Reconsidered." *English Literature in Transition* 28 (1985): 144–161.

Byron, George Gordon, Lord
(1788–1824)

No poet has ever fascinated his contemporaries to the same extent as Byron. His poetry enjoyed an immediate popularity inconceivable in our own day. What his contemporaries called a "Byronomania" was ignited by his aristocratic glamour, his personal beauty, and his literary persona, which mixed proud disdain with tantalizing hints of guilty secrets. His love affairs with women and the rumors attending the breakup of his marriage increased the notoriety that was always half of his fame. To the nineteenth century, he was the archetypal nobleman-rake, poète maudit, and, after his death in Greece, heroic liberator. His influence on other writers in Europe and the Americas and beyond was enormous; his narrative and descriptive poetry was also a major source of inspiration to painters, and to musicians like Berlioz, Rossini, Schumann, and Tchaikovsky.

What was not understood in Byron's own century (except by a tiny circle of his associates) was that Byron was bisexual. During at least three periods of his life, homosexual interests predominated over his numerous heterosexual involvements. This side of Byron's nature, however, did not become general knowledge among scholars until the publication of biographical studies by G. Wilson Knight and Leslie Marchand in 1957.

The taboo against homosexuality in England and the punitive measures against it (including frequent executions) reached their zenith in Byron's lifetime. Despite this hostility to same-sex love, there was at the same time a notable cult of romantic friendships among boys at English private schools, well attested by such writers as Benjamin Disraeli, Leigh Hunt, and Percy Bysshe Shelley. Inspired by this literary tradition and his own strong personal inclinations, Byron wrote a significant number of poems in this genre based on his feelings for younger boys at Harrow school. These appear in two collections, *Fugitive Pieces* (1806) and *Poems on Various Occasions* (1807), which Byron printed privately while he was at Cambridge. In "Childish Recollections," he himself expresses puzzlement at the strength of these attachments. They may well have had a sexual element. Lady Caroline Lamb,

in revelations she made to Byron's wife, claimed that Byron confessed to her that he had had "unnatural" connections with his schoolfellows.

In 1807, Byron published *Hours of Idleness,* in which he reprinted some of these early friendship poems, but suppressed "The Cornelian," the most personal and revealing of them. Two years earlier, he had met and fallen in love with John Edleston, a young chorister at Trinity College. "The Cornelian" records an emotional moment in their love affair. In "To Thyrza," a poem in which he pretends to be writing about a woman, Byron laid emphasis on the clandestine nature of their love: "Ours too the glance none saw beside / The smile none else might understand." He implies that he was sexually attracted to "Thyrza" but that the relation remained chaste. Byron, who boasted he had spent thirteen years studying Greek and Latin, found support for the homosexual element in his own makeup in classical literature. He translated one of CATULLUS's love poems to Juventius (retitling it "To Ellen"), was well aware of HORACE's bisexuality and VIRGIL's Corydon eclogue, and published a translation of "The Episode of Nisus and Euryalus" from the *Aeneid.*

After graduating from Cambridge, Byron made his first voyage to Greece. His letters to his Cambridge friends Charles Skinner Matthews and John Cam Hobhouse, which employ Latin codes based on PETRONIUS and Horace (first deciphered by Marchand in 1957), show that he had numerous homosexual experiences there. Though later tradition focused on his flirtation with Theresa Macri, the "Maid of Athens," Byron was in fact more intrigued by the schoolboys in a local convent where he took up lodgings. His main involvements were with an effeminate youth named Eustathius Giorgiu and with the more robust Nicolo Giraud, whom he made his heir on returning to England. While abroad, Byron received coded letters from his friend Matthews giving many details about homosexual scandals in England, including hangings and pilloryings. These reveal that Byron, Hobhouse, and Matthews formed a circle with shared interests at Cambridge and were keenly aware of the harsh sanctions visited upon homosexuals in England in their day. On his return to England, Byron was devastated to learn of Edleston's death, and wrote a series of elegies, the so-called "Thyrza" poems, in which he affected to be mourning a female lover. These include "To Thyrza," "Away, away, ye notes of woe!" "One struggle more and I am free," "And thou art dead, as young and fair," and "On a cornelian heart which was broken." The first three elegies were added to the first edition of *Childe Harold's Pilgrimage* in 1812. They aroused considerable interest because of their obviously personal nature and inspired much speculation about Thyrza's identity, which Byron kept mysteriously secret.

Byron had also written a stanza for inclusion in *Childe Harold* reflecting on the dire fate of WILLIAM BECKFORD, whose home in exile Byron had visited at Cintra in Portugal. It addressed Beckford as "Unhappy Vathek!" after the hero of his romance. Like Byron a famous author with aristocratic connections, and in addition, the wealthiest man in England and an accomplished musician and connoisseur, Beckford had been ostracized by English society for many years because of his rumored homosexuality. Byron's letters from Greece reveal that he himself had planned to live abroad; they show a paranoia exacerbated, no doubt, by his awareness that Beckford's fate might be his own. But the enormous success of *Childe Harold*, which made Byron famous overnight, changed his plans. It catapulted him to the heights of English society, and led to a series of widely publicized love affairs with fashionable women. The most important of these was Lady Caroline Lamb, who visited his apartments disguised in the uniform of her page boys. But Caroline's jealousy and flamboyant behavior soon alienated Byron and he sought to break with her. Unfortunately, he had told her something of his homosexual affairs and this gave her a powerful instrument for blackmail. On one occasion, with typical histrionic extravagance, she left an ominous warning ("Remember me!") in a copy of Beckford's *Vathek* in Byron's rooms.

Complicating an already difficult situation, Byron now embarked on an incestuous affair with his married half-sister, Augusta Leigh. To extricate himself from these imbroglios, Byron proposed marriage to Annabella Milbanke, an aristocratic heiress of a decidedly moralistic turn. The marriage was spectacularly unhappy, and after a year the hurt and baffled Annabella, whom Byron had scandalized by defending the sexual habits of the Turks and Greeks, sought a separation. Byron's fame made this event an international scandal of the first dimension, and speculation on Lady Byron's reasons for leaving her husband was rife on two continents. Lady Caroline now spread stories about Byron's homosexuality and incest throughout London. Though incest was scandalous enough, the accusation of sodomy was far more damning. Bryon was publicly insulted and ostracized, the situation becoming so intolerable that within a few weeks he left England for good in an extremely bitter mood.

During these troubles, Byron wrote his highly popular Turkish tales. These extremely romantic verse narratives, published in 1813 and 1814, drew on his knowledge of the orient and feature typical "Byronic heroes," that is, proud desperadoes who are contemptuous of society but haunted by unnamable crimes. *The Bride of Abydos* hints at incest, and *Lara* at homosexuality in the person of a page who is devoted to Lara but who turns out to be a girl. In this, *Lara* parallels an unpublished episode from *Vathek* where a page also undergoes a similar change of gender. (In Beckford's tale, the master's preference for his page is unabashedly pederastic, but Byron does not go so far.)

Byron faced snubs from English residents and visitors during his sojourn in Switzerland and finally settled in Venice where there was no English colony. There, in 1819, he began his satirical masterpiece, *Don Juan*. In the first canto, Byron ridicules English prudery, playing on the paradox that though English schoolboys were supposed to be shielded from any knowledge of sex, and especially of homosexuality, the standard curriculum was based on poets like SAPPHO, Anacreon, Catullus, and Virgil, who freely treated such themes. In Italy, Byron also wrote an autobiography that was destroyed after his death by his literary executors. Apparently this did not deal with any of his homosexual experiences—Byron would hardly have been so indiscreet as to have included such details. It is possible, however, that a mysterious "love of loves" he is known to have mentioned in the manuscript referred to Edleston. Byron also wrote some supplementary private biographical notes under the title "Detached Thoughts." There he speaks of a "violent, though *pure* love" he experienced at Cambridge—a veiled reference to his love for the choirboy. He lends credence to the idea that his bisexuality was one source of the anguished guilt felt by the Byronic hero when he remarks a few lines later, "If I could explain at length the *real* causes which have contributed to this . . . melancholy of mine which hath made me a bye-word—nobody would wonder." But he admits that this would cause "much mischief" and breaks off, as he puts it, to avoid "paralyzing posterity."

During his years in Italy, we have no evidence that Byron's bisexuality manifested itself apart from Shelley's mysterious remark that Byron "associated with wretches" who avowed practices unnamed in England. After a highly promiscuous period, during which he had relations with women of all social classes, Byron settled down to comparative domesticity with Teresa Guiccioli, the estranged wife of an Italian count. This period of his life ended when the London Committee for Greek independence was formed in 1823. Byron's account of his travels in Greece in *Childe Harold's Pilgrimage* had helped fire interest in the cause of Greek freedom. Enthusiasm for Greek art in this period of the "Greek Revival" had been earlier aroused by the writings of the German critic JOHANN JOACHIM WINCKELMANN, whose warm regard for Greek sculpture undoubtedly owed something to his own homoerotic nature. Shelley shared Winckelmann's admiration for androgynous Greek male beauty, but whether Shelley's preference is simply aesthetic or tinged by an unconscious erotic response is difficult to determine. Byron's poetry directly echoes famous passages from Winckelmann. It also shows an awareness of the heroic traditions of Greek love. In *Childe Harold,* Byron celebrates the heroism of Harmodius, and in his notes to the poem, speaks of Antinous as one "whose death was as noble as his life was infamous." Byron was apparently aware of the story that Antinous had sacrificed his life for his lover, the emperor Hadrian. But under the homophobic conventions of the day, Byron could refer to male love affairs in a published work only if he appeared to condemn them.

Whether Byron anticipated further adventures with boys in Greece when he landed on the island of Cephalonia in August of 1823 is impossible to say. The last months of his life, however, saw him embroiled in just such an affair. On Cephalonia, he gave aid to a Greek widow who was a refugee from the war; later her fifteen-year-old son Lukas joined her there, and Byron fell desperately in love with him. This important episode was not freely discussed by Byron biographers until the mid-twentieth century. The story may be pieced together from Byron's letters and from a series of three remarkable love poems, the last poems he wrote. Byron took Lukas into his suite as a page, gave him a splendid uniform and command of a troop of thirty soldiers. On the voyage from Cephalonia to Missolonghi, Byron was afraid Turkish sailors might take Lukas prisoner. On a second voyage, he was apprehensive for his safety during a threatened shipwreck. When Lukas contracted a fever in Missolonghi, Byron nursed him and gave him his own bed. He was, however, irritated by Lukas's continual demands for money and luxuries. Lukas, unlike the boys of Byron's earlier Greek visit, did not reciprocate Byron's ardor and seems to have exploited the relationship to his own advantage. The cycle of poems in which Byron expresses his feelings about Lukas

begins with "On This Day I Complete My Thirty Sixth Year." These stanzas became widely known shortly after Byron's death and were regarded for many years as his final poetic testament. They begin with Byron's declaration that he is in love with someone who does not love him. However, he pledges to "tread these reviving passions down" and devote himself to the heroic struggle for Greek freedom, anticipating death on the battlefield. The poem should have raised questions since Teresa's devotion to Byron was undoubted, and there was patently no other woman in his life. Certainly Byron's friends in Missolonghi were quite aware of his devotion to Lukas and were very uneasy about the complexion that might be placed on what one of them called this "mischievous topic."

For sixty years, "On This Day" was thought to be Byron's last poem. But John Cam Hobhouse had, in fact, preserved two later poems, which were not published until after his death in 1887. In "Last Words On Greece," a single stanza in the form of a truncated sonnet, Byron abandons the resolution of "On This Day." He declares that the fate of Greece and his own fame mean nothing to him when compared to the "maddening fascination" that has enthralled him. "Love and Death" is explicitly autobiographical in a very detailed way. Byron enumerates the occasions in which Lukas's welfare had caused him worry: the threatened capture and shipwreck, an earthquake when he had been concerned for Lukas's safety, the boy's illness. The poem ends with Byron's despairing admission that Lukas does not and cannot love him "though it be my lot / To strongly—wrongly—vainly—love thee still." We may wonder why so minutely autobiographical a poem was not read as an avowal of love for Lukas until seventy years after its appearance in print. The reason was that Hobhouse had left a note, purportedly by Byron himself, which was published with the poem in 1887, to the effect that it referred "to no one in particular" and was "a mere poetical Scherzo." Nevertheless, the overwhelming evidence of Byron's letters proves that Lukas is referred to in each of the six stanzas. The episode makes a poignant coda to the story of Byron's life and loves.

When news of Byron's death at Missolonghi reached London, Hobhouse (who had not read it) insisted that the pages of Byron's unpublished memoirs be burned; he was able to persuade John Murray, Byron's publisher, and Thomas Moore, to whom Byron had entrusted the manuscript, to do this against their better judgment. As we have indicated, it is unlikely Byron gave any clear hints about his sexual orientation in this work. However, within a decade of his death, some as yet unidentified poet wrote a pseudo-autobiography that was surprisingly accurate on Byron's homosexual affairs. This mysterious document was a poem in rhymed couplets that bore the title *Don Leon, A Poem by Lord Byron, Author of Childe Harold, Don Juan &c., &c., And Forming Part of the Private Journal of His Lordship, Supposed to have been Entirely Destroyed by Thos. Moore.* Though not by Byron, *Don Leon* can hardly be called an attempt at forgery. No one had imagined Byron's memoirs were in verse instead of prose, and the poem made allusions to many incidents that any contemporary reader would immediately have recognized as taking place after Byron's death.

Don Leon is of interest to Byron studies because it gives accurate details of Byron's love for John Edleston (without the author's realizing, however, that the Thyrza elegies mourned him) and of his consummated affair in Greece with Nicolo Giraud, a part of Byron's life on which the Leon poet seems especially well informed. It also presents, in a sensitive and insightful fashion, a psychological portrayal of the adolescent Byron's awakening awareness of his interest in other boys. Nevertheless, the main impetus behind the poem and its real raison d'être was to protest the continued hanging of homosexuals in England in the years following Byron's death. Such executions had been common during Byron's lifetime, averaging about two a year. But in 1832, despite passage of the Reform Bill and the extensive law reforms introduced by the new liberal parliament, there was no change in the law that made homosexual acts capital offenses, and the statute was still enforced in its full rigor. Consequently, the poem opens with a strong protest against a sentence of death, which the notes identify as that pronounced on Captain Henry Nicholls in August 1833.

The poem describes at length several parliamentary careers ended by arrests or exile. It describes the arrest of Byron's friend William Bankes in June 1833, whose case is represented as unresolved. Since Bankes was in fact acquitted at a well-publicized trial in December of the same year, it would appear that most of the poem was written before then though there are some references to events that took place two years later. The fifty pages of notes refer principally to arrests between 1833 and 1859 and appear to have been repeatedly revised. We know that the poem was printed sometime before 1853 since a query about it appeared in *Notes and Queries* that year. However, no copies of this first edition have come to light; the earliest extant copies are from a printing by William Dugdale in 1866. In 1930, the Fortune Press reprinted *Don Leon,* but the edition was ordered destroyed by the British courts on the grounds that the work was obscene. The poem is forceful satire in the style of Byron's own *The Curse of Minerva,* with many striking passages. It makes an impassioned and eloquent plea for law reform, despite its odd use of contemporary homophobic language. All in all, *Don Leon* may justly be described as one of the most remarkable documents in gay literary history to appear between the end of the classical period and the twentieth century. (See also JEREMY BENTHAM and ENGLISH LITERATURE: ROMANTICISM.)

—*Louis Crompton*

BIBLIOGRAPHY

Byron, George Gordon, Lord. *The Complete Poetical Works.* J. J. McGann, ed. 7 vols. Oxford: Clarendon Press, 1980–1992. ■ ———. *Byron's Letters and Journals.* L. Marchand, ed. 12 vols. Cambridge: Harvard University Press, 1973–1982. ■ Crompton, Louis. *Byron and Greek Love: Homophobia in 19th-Century England.* Berkeley: University of California Press, 1985. ■ *Don Leon. A Homosexual Emancipation Miscellany c. 1835–1952.* New York: Arno Press, 1975. 1–107. ■ Knight, G. Wilson. *Lord Byron's Marriage: The Evidence of Asterisks.* London: Routledge and K. Paul, 1957. ■ Marchand, Leslie. *Byron: A Biography.* 3 vols. New York: Knopf, 1957. ■ Moore, Doris Langley. "Appendix 2: Byron's Sexual Ambivalence." *Lord Byron: Accounts Rendered.* London: John Murray, 1974. 437–459.

Camp

One of the few things that writers about camp agree on is that it cannot be adequately defined. CHRISTOPHER ISHERWOOD, the Anglo-American novelist who was the first person to discuss camp, wrote in *The World in the Evening* (1956), "it's terribly hard to define. You have to meditate on it and feel it intuitively, like Laotse's *Tao.*" Charles Ludlam, the playwright and actor and master of theatrical camp, simply stated "I don't think camp can be defined," and SUSAN SONTAG argued that "to talk about Camp is . . . to betray it." Every student of camp must contend with its indefinability, its elusiveness, and its changeability.

Even the origins of the word *camp* are shrouded in mystery. Bruce Rodgers in *Gay Talk* (1972) argues that camp's origins are in sixteenth-century English theatrical slang for a male actor dressed as a woman, and refers to the French word for countryside, *campagne,* since French strolling players often dressed as women in the country. Others see the origin as related to the French verb *camper,* to pose. Whatever its origins, the term seems to be quite old and related to theater.

Camp can refer to either a style of performance or a mode of perception. For example, a person may regard an object that was not intended to be seen as camp as campy. Such narrative ballets as *Swan Lake* or *Giselle* have been viewed as camp although their choreographers had no such intentions. In such works, camp is in the eye of the beholder. However, other artists have intended their works to be campy— the English novelist RONALD FIRBANK and the American playwright Tony Kushner are two examples. But not all objects can be transformed by perception into camp, and not everyone in an audience will see camp even in the campiest performance. The camp effect requires a fit between performance and perception, between object and audience.

To understand this fit, we must understand the historical forces that made camp both possible and necessary. Camp emerged seemingly with the first evidence of a gay subculture, and camp is a way of coping with a hostile dominant culture. Many subcultures have developed stylistic manners to cope with oppression. Jewish "gallows humor" and the street language of urban blacks are two examples. These subcultural modes function in at least two ways: First, they help cement solidarity between members of the subculture as any "secret" language helps bind those who share the "secret." Second, they help members of the subculture communicate with one another in the presence of those from outside the subculture. Camp protects members of the gay and lesbian communities in situations in which they are at risk of being identified, stigmatized, and possibly abused. Of course, one might say that camp also helps ghettoize the gay community by isolating it, and insofar as camp has helped reinforce gay IDENTITY, one might criticize camp for also reinforcing the binarisms of gay–straight that are part of the language of heterosexism. Philip Core subtitled his book on camp, *The Lie That Tells the Truth* (1984); camp seems elusive because it is built on a paradoxical relationship between performance and message. But one might also say that camp is the truth that tells a lie by suggesting that there is a separate gay or lesbian identity and by reinforcing that reified category.

A good example of how one homosexual signals his homosexuality to another can be found in HENRY JAMES's letter to JOHN ADDINGTON SYMONDS. At the time of James's correspondence, homosexual activity was a felony, punishable with many years of hard labor. Letters could and were used as evidence in courts of law. Thus, James, the American novelist, wrote Symonds, the English poet and historian, very cautiously. His letter could pass as merely a "friendly note" to an unsuspecting postal inspector who might come across it, but a gay reader would recognize its excessiveness as camp, and its author as a homosexual signaling his sexuality to another homosexual. James reminds Symonds that he sent Symonds his article on Venice. (Venice, it should be noted, is a city especially associated with the homosexual underworld.)

> I sent [my article] to you because it was a constructive way of expressing the good will I felt for you in consequence of what you had written about the land of Italy—and of intimating to you, somewhat dumbly, that I am a sympathetic reader. I nourish for the said Italy an unspeakably tender passion, and your pages always seemed to say to me that you were one of the small number of people who love it as much as I do . . . for it seemed to me that the victims of a common passion should exchange a look.

James wants to indicate "somewhat dumbly" that they share "A common passion." That "unspeakably tender passion" is best "exchanged" not with explicit statements but with "a look." Their taste for Italy is not to be compared to the mass enjoyment of the country. Their "love" is shared by only a "small number of people," who are "victims" of this "common passion." The excessiveness and the encoding of such key terms as "unspeakable passion" and "victims of a common passion" intimate that this passage is more than just about the fact that they both like Italy.

One may find the same style used in literature of the time. In *The Green Carnation* (1894), published a year before OSCAR WILDE's first trial, Robert Hichens produced an admiring but campy portrait of the playwright, poet, and essayist. Mr. Amarinth, Wilde's name in the novel, first appears proposing that operas should be performed not in the evening, but in the middle of the day. Lady Locke, a woman with a "sensible" face, argues, "But surely it would spoil one for the rest of the day. . . . One would be fit for nothing afterwards." Amarinth replies:

Quite so. . . . That would be the object of the performance, to unfit one for the duties of the day. How beautiful! What a glorious sight it would be to see a great audience flocking out into the orange-coloured sunshine, each unit of which was thoroughly unfitted for any duties whatsoever. It makes me perpetually sorrowful in London to meet people doing their duty. I find them everywhere. It is impossible to escape from them. A sense of duty is like some horrible disease. It destroys the tissues of the mind, as certain complaints destroy the tissues of the body. The catechism has a great deal to answer for.

This language, which is both effusive and inverted, suggests that camp coding was a pervasive element in homosexual literate culture. "Doing one's duty," the euphemism of performing the conventional masculine tasks of marrying, siring children, and earning money or assuming social responsibilities—the principles of decent English society—is stood on its head. Camp often performs this sort of inversion of hierarchy. However, whereas James's camp helped protect him from prosecution, Wilde's had no such efficacy and, indeed, may have actually contributed to the vehemence with which he was eventually prosecuted.

Esther Newton in her pioneering study of drag artists identifies three elements of camp: *incongruity, theatricality,* and *humor.* These qualities do not define camp, but they are always present in camp.

Camp, according to Newton and others, "depends on the perception or creation of incongruous juxtapositions." For the drag artist, the incongruity begins with a man dressing in woman's clothing. But camp can embrace many different reversals of polarities: an effeminate boy in macho dress, a lower-class person affecting the manner of the upper classes, the old in the shape of the new or the new in the shape of the old. Camp objects often have their purpose disguised by being made to look like something less utilitarian: the lamp made to look like a flowering plant, the stapler in the shape of a frog, the seafood restaurant in the shape of a Spanish galleon, all are potentially campy. (As the last example shows, people are not always aware that they camp.)

Camp incongruity often takes the form of inversion, standing concepts on their head. The serious is taken for the humorous, whereas the humorous is taken seriously. In John Waters's camp classic *Pink Flamingoes* (1973), for example, Divine is outraged when other people challenge her claim to be called "the filthiest woman in the world." In this world turned upside down, filth is an honor bestowed on the lucky few. At the movie's conclusion, Divine eats a dog turd to prove—if there were any question—that she is the queen of filth.

One of the central inversions performed by camp is to place aesthetic concerns above ethical concerns. Oscar Wilde, the greatest exponent of a certain form of camp sensibility, in his set of aphorisms "Phrases and Philosophies for the Young," wrote: "Dullness is the coming of age of seriousness. In all unimportant matters, style, not sincerity, is the essential. In all important matters, style, not sincerity, is the essential." Or as he says in another aphorism, "One should either be a work of art, or wear a work of art." Ethical considerations—particularly pious, moralistic, and rigid ethical considerations—must give way to beauty and style.

Because camp likes to stand the world on its head, it is comparable to Mikhail Bakhtin's notion of the *carnivalesque,* a style noted for its "gay relativity" and its "mocking and deriding" tone. The carnivalesque, like camp, is characterized by a licensed release of anarchic forces that tend to invert standard social hierarchies. But the carnivalesque ultimately celebrates the fertility of this released energy and its reproductive potential. Bakhtin conceives of the carnivalesque as a condition that releases the natural energies society has smothered, restrained, and suppressed. The carnivalesque celebrates a Dionysian unselfconsciousness. Camp, however, is extremely self-conscious; it does not celebrate the natural, but the artificial. So although camp and the carnivalesque may share many similarities, they also differ in very important ways.

If camp can be said to invert hierarchies, it also erects others. One of the most important is the distinction between High and Low Camp. High Camp usually refers to the camping of socially respected performances and objects. NOEL COWARD comedies are High Camp, but the television series "Batman" is Low Camp because live theater is generally valued above television. A lava lamp is Low Camp, but an *art nouveau* candelabra in the shape of wisteria vines is probably High Camp because it is so much more valuable. Grand opera is High Camp, but soap operas are Low Camp. Literary camp is usually High Camp.

Camp also has to be performative, even when the performer is unaware of how campy the performance is. The restaurateur, for example, who designed his eatery in the style of a Spanish galleon, knew he was creating a stage set, that he was engaged in a performance, but he probably took that performance seriously. The restaurant becomes campy for those who cannot take the effect as other than humorous, as missing the mark, as overly self-conscious and exaggerated. Adam West, the actor who played Batman on the short-lived television series, was disturbed by people who regarded his performance as campy. He wanted to be taken seriously as a satiric performer. Perhaps because he is not as good an actor as he imagines himself to be, the performance failed to be convincing as satire. But as much as it failed as satire, it succeeded as camp—as uncovering the incongruousness of the desire for heroism in modern society. Camp is marked by its self-conscious artificiality, and many performances that are intended as "serious" performances fail because they become self-consciously artificial. Such "bad" acting is always a prime target of camp perception, and camp performers frequently transform "bad" acting into an art. For example, the drag queen—as opposed to the female impersonator—rarely intends to be taken seriously as a woman; from the outset, the drag artist intends us to see the self-conscious artificiality of the performance. The camp performance, unlike the standard theatrical event, demands not the suspension of disbelief, but the intense awareness of artificiality. The great camp performers—like Mae West—never hide that they are acting, but brilliantly play on their artificiality.

Theater is never unstylized. All forms of art demand both stylization and exaggeration. But there are kinds of stylizations and exaggeration that do not draw attention to themselves and that audiences have been conditioned to overlook or see as "natural." Camp is so highly stylized and exaggerated that its artificiality cannot be overlooked. We might say that a performance that was not meant to be camp becomes camp when we cannot forget about its artificiality and stylization. Greta Garbo, one of the great screen actresses, has become one of the great camp performers although it is quite clear that she never intended to be campy (except perhaps in the comedy *Ninotchka* [1939]). Yet because gay audiences are constantly aware of her artifice, her extraordinary powers of stylization, her theatricality is now often viewed as campy. "I have always been overwhelmed by the feeling," Parker Tyler wrote in his groundbreaking study *Screening the Sexes* (1972), "that within [Garbo's] woman's shape, behind all her beauty and feminine postures, a man has hid himself and walked around with her." Garbo has not only inverted the sex roles, but has made Tyler self-conscious of them and of their theatricality.

Sometimes the self-conscious artificiality of camp performances help protect gay people. Liberace, for example, seemed to be acting the part of the most flamboyant homosexual with his bejeweled clothes, fingers, and cars, his glittering candelabra, and his piano-shaped swimming pools. He so flamboyantly played the homosexual that some people believed he could not possibly be a homosexual. Liberace is not alone in using such a strategy: Peewee Herman is another example.

When does stylization become so exaggerated that it becomes funny, and when is stylization to be taken seriously? The line that separates the unfunny rituals of the church from the hilarious rituals of the Marx Brothers is often a very thin one.

Some very sophisticated artists like to hover above this line so that an audience cannot determine whether to take them seriously. For example, Charles Ludlam wrote and performed the title role in his play *Galas* (1983), a reworking of the life of the opera star Maria Callas, a highly stylized but serious performer. In the climactic scene, Galas commits suicide dressed as Madame Butterfly. Ludlam was able to bring much of his audience to the brink of tears even as they were rolling in the aisles. High Camp often straddles that line between the serious use of the ridiculous and ridicule of the serious. Tony Kushner in the climactic scene of Part I of *Angels in America* (1993), has Prior, a man dying of AIDS, remark on the arrival of his guardian angel, who descends in a fiery burst of theatrical lightning, "How Steven Spielberg!" The line both deflates and problematizes the notions of spiritual salvation. Such a campy remark at the crucial moment of the play deepens the ambiguity of the action and keeps the play from providing simple answers to the problems of AIDS and national purpose by undercutting the sanctimoniousness of the angel's arrival, yet because it is so campy, the remark cannot be taken with entire seriousness. Camp has the power to open up dimension after dimension of ambiguity and undecidability.

Camp then is funny, but it is not only amusing. It frequently has a serious point behind its surface of frivolity. Indeed, one of the powerful aspects of camp humor is the uncertainty of whether one should laugh at it—is it really funny? Susan Sontag says that camp can be defined at least in part as "failed seriousness." But if camp fails as seriousness, it often fails at humor as well, or it is a humor that has a dark side. The great objects of campiness—grand opera, narrative ballets, films noire—are often tales of murder, madness, and social mayhem. Only a camp sensibility could find in the film *Whatever Happened to Baby Jane?* (1962), the psychological horror story of an insane former child actress tormenting her crippled sister, an endless supply of humor and amusement.

Emphasis has been given to camp in theater, film, and television because camp is essentially theatrical. But camp can be found in most forms of art and in poetry and fiction, as well as in drama. In *Frivolity Unbounded* (1990), Robert F. Kiernan identifies what he calls the camp novel; its masters are Thomas Love Peacock, Max Beerbohm, Ronald Firbank, E. F. BENSON, P. G. Wodehouse, and IVY COMPTON-BURNETT. The action of the camp novel is fantastically unreal, the tone is light, and the novels tend to be filled with dialogue that is both witty and absurd. In Firbank's novel *The Flower Beneath the Foot* (1924), the King and Queen of Pisuerga wish their son to marry a princess of another kingdom although he is in love with Mademoiselle de Nazianzi. At one point, the Queen remarks to Prince Yousef:

> "How spent you look, my boy .... Those eyes ... "
> His weariness grimaced.
> "They've been rubbing in Elsie!" he said.
> "Who?"
> "'Vaseline' and 'Nanny-goat'!"
> "Well?"
> "Nothing will shake me."
> "What are your objections?"
> "She's so extraordinarily uninteresting!"
> "Oh, Yousef!" his mother faltered: "*Do you wish to break my heart?*"
> "We had always thought you too lacking in initiative," King William said (tucking a few long hairs back into his nose), "to marry against our wishes."
> "They say she walks too wonderfully," the Queen courageously pursued.
> "What? Well?"
> "Yes."
> "And can handle a horse as few others can!"

This conversation between parents and their child about a prospective wife is commonplace enough in literature and life, but Firbank makes it into an utterly bizarre and humorous discussion, at once too passionate and too matter-of-fact. Kiernan's examples are all British and with one exception all male. But the camp novel has had several women practitioners as well, including JANE BOWLES, Muriel Spark, and Blanche Boyd. Today, the form is carried on most notably by James McCourt in America and PATRICK GALE in England.

Camp has become an important part of modern poetry as well. Karl Keller identified what he considered "camp" elements in WALT WHITMAN's poems, but only in poems in the second half of the twentieth century does camp have an unmistakable presence. W. H. AUDEN, for example, hits that note in "In Praise of Limestone" when he discusses the kinds of friends who go "to the bad."

> [T]o become a pimp
> Or deal in fake jewellery or ruin a fine tenor
>   voice
> For effects that bring down the house, could
>   happen to all
> But the best and worst of us ...

Auden's list of common excesses is incongruous, stylized, and very funny. JAMES MERRILL in "The Book of Ephraim," part of his long poem *The Changing Light at Sandover,* is often campy, and Ephraim's gossipy, witty, homosexual voice is one of the delights of the poem. Auden and Merrill represent the High Camp side of modern poetry, but Low Camp also has its adherents. In his celebration of roaches ("they are among the brightest / and most attractive of small creatures"), or of a Giant Pacific Octopus, or in his retellings of old Hollywood movies, EDWARD FIELD uses camp as one of his distinguishing features, and it gives his voice a range and subtlety that seems almost impossible given the plainness of his subjects and the unpretentiousness of his manner.

Because camp is so intimately involved with the intersection of social hierarchy and gender roles, its political and ethical proprieties have often been questioned both inside and outside the gay and lesbian community. Low Camp has been especially vulnerable to attack, particularly Low Camp as exemplified by the drag queen. Gay men have viewed the drag queen as reinforcing the homophobic stereotype of the gay man as effeminate. Feminists, both lesbian and heterosexual, have viewed the drag queen as ridiculing women and as reinforcing misogynistic stereotypes.

Andrew Ross believes that camp reconciles people to their powerlessness, that it is compensation for failure and a sort of nostalgia for the good old days. Consequently, for Ross, camp is part of the problem of mass culture that tries to keep the populace from becoming aware of its oppression; it is part of the controlling mechanism of late capitalism. Ross points to the way Victorian melodrama becomes camp only because it is now powerless to hold us in its grip. Similarly, *Whatever Happened to Baby Jane?* is not only *about* two faded film stars, but was performed *by* two faded film stars, Bette Davis and Joan Crawford. For Ross, camp is the opiate of the homosexual masses, a way of keeping queer people happy with what they have.

For Judith Butler, however, camp is at the heart of a radical program for transforming consciousness. Because of its capacity to stand received ideas on their head, by inverting notions, and by emphasizing the "unnaturalness" of what the dominant society believes to be "natural," camp has a central part to play in sexual politics. Of greatest interest to Butler is that camp, as epitomized by the drag queen, shows that gender is "performative"; in other words, people are not born masculine or feminine but perform "masculinity" and "femininity." By upsetting notions of the naturalness of gender, camp frees us to perform in whatever way we like.

Evidence can be found on both sides of the argument. One might point to the fact that the Stonewall Riots, that defining moment of gay history, was started not by middle-class gay men but by street hustlers and drag queens—the segment of the gay population that was most conscious of the performativity of gender. However, one can also point to the fact that homophobic men are now wearing earrings and sporting ponytails. Such seemingly gender-bending practices have apparently had no effect on their consciousness. The truth lies somewhere, it seems, between these two versions of camp's power. Although it has helped gay men and women to survive in a homophobic society and to reinforce their feelings of a gay community, it has also reconciled them to their oppression and made them feel that such oppression is "natural" or at least "unavoidable." (See also HUMOR.)

—*David Bergman*

BIBLIOGRAPHY

Bakhtin, Mikhail. *Rabelais and His World*. Cambridge, Mass.: MIT Press, 1968. ■ Bergman, David, ed. *Camp Grounds: Style and Homosexuality*. Amherst, Mass.: University of Massachusetts Press, 1993. ■ Booth, Mark. *Camp*. New York: Quartet, 1983. ■ Bronski, Michael. *Culture Clash: The Making of Gay Sensibility*. Boston: South End Press, 1984. ■ Butler, Judith. *Gender Trouble: Feminism and the Subversion of Identity*. New York: Routledge, 1990. ■ Core, Philip. *Camp: The Lie That Tells the Truth*. New York: Delilah Books, 1984. ■ Dyer, Richard, ed. *Gays and Film*. London: British Film Institute, 1977. ■ ———. *Now You See It: Studies on Lesbian and Gay Film*. London: Routledge, 1990. ■ James, Henry. *Letters*. Leon Edel, ed. Vol 3. Cambridge, Mass.: Harvard University Press, 1984. ■ Kiernan, Robert F. *Frivolity Unbounded: Six Masters of the Camp Novel*. New York: Continuum, 1990. ■ Ludlam, Charles. "Camp." *Ridiculous Theatre—Scourge of Folly: The Essays and Opinions of Charles Ludlam*. Steven Samuels, ed. New York: Theatre Communications Group, 1992. ■ Melly, George. *Revolt into Style: The Pop Arts in Britain*. London: Allen Lane, 1970. ■ Newton, Esther. *Mother Camp: The Female Impersonator in America*. Chicago: University of Chicago Press, 1979. ■ Rodgers, Bruce. *Gay Talk: A Dictionary of Gay Slang*. New York: Paragon Books, 1972. ■ Ross, Andrew. "Uses of Camp." *The Yale Journal of Criticism* 2, no. 2 (1988): 1–24. ■ Russo, Vito. *The Celluloid Closet: Homosexuality and the Movies*. New York: Harper and Row, 1981. ■ Sontag, Susan. "Notes on Camp." *Against Interpretation and Other Essays*. New York: Dell, 1966. ■ Tyler, Parker. *Screening the Sexes: Homosexuality in the Movies*. New York: Holt, Rinehart and Winston, 1972. ■ Wilde, Oscar. *The Artist as Critic: The Critical Writing of Oscar Wilde*. Richard Ellmann, ed. New York: Random House, 1968.

Canadian Literature in English

Canadian gay literature is almost a contradiction in terms. Frequently written by authors born in the United States and published there as well, it is difficult to distinguish from writing in more dominant English-speaking cultures. Caught between the traditionally overwhelming influence of British culture and, more recently, the powerful stranglehold of American literature, the Canadian voice (gay or straight) is hard to hear. Marginalized, outnumbered, and patronized (when it is not simply neglected), this voice is often, not surprisingly, ironic. Even within the Library of Congress classification system, Canadian literature has an ambiguous place. In some libraries, it is still "PR," that is, a subspecies of Commonwealth Literature; and in others it is now "PS," that is, a subspecies of American. To be a Canadian writer of any kind, in other words, is to be "queer" in a world where the definitions are made elsewhere.

Like the mainstream heterosexual literature of Canadian culture, Anglophone gay literature is also extremely balkanized, with the result that what is published by a small press in British Columbia or Saskatchewan is often unknown in Toronto, let alone in Halifax. Nonetheless, this literature would not exist at all were it not for these same small presses: from Blewointment, New Star, Arsenal Pulp, and Talonbooks in British Columbia, to Stumblejumper in Regina, Blizzard in Winnipeg, Catalyst, Coach House, and Women's Press in Toronto to Gynergy in Charlottetown.

Of the three major cities (Toronto, Montréal, and Vancouver), Toronto (the largest) has produced the greatest amount of work. Thanks largely to the influential run of the now-defunct gay newspaper, *The Body Politic* (1971–1987), Toronto has also appropriated the national Anglophone voice. Perhaps there is poetic justice in this development in that OSCAR WILDE's constant friend, Robbie Ross, came from Toronto. In the absence of any Anglophone hero equivalent to the Québécois writer Emile Nelligan, Robbie Ross might be thought of as a kind of inspiring genius of Anglo-Canadian gay literature. Although no Canadian writer has ever taken up his story, Jim Bartley's interesting play *Stephen and Mr. Wilde* (1993) does at least deal with Wilde's famous visit to Canada in 1882. Another early chapter in the history of Anglo-Canadian gay literature centers on WALT WHITMAN's visit to Canada in the following year. The influence of Whitman's visit was the subject of a gay conference in Toronto in 1980 and became the subject of the film *Beautiful Dreamers* (1989), directed by John Kent Harrison.

Such conferences as this one and the "Doing It" conference two years later have served to put gay literature on the map in Canada in a way that is very un-American. Canadian gay and lesbian writing speaks to that element in the national soul that is looking for an identity, as if it summarized articulately the national quest for definition. MICHEL TREMBLAY, who wrote the libretto for an opera about Nelligan, wrote *Hosanna*, a 1967 play about a drag queen's leather fantasies, that was read in Canada as an allegory of Francophone–Anglophone relations before it was recognized as a gay play. This concern for finding a distinctively Canadian identity, explored by such heterosexual critics as Northrop Frye and Margaret Atwood, may well explain the solidarity of many heterosexuals with many gay issues in Canada, not least censorship and personal freedom.

Canadian gay literature only began to appear in the 1960s. The first gay-identified book of poetry published in Canada was E. A. Lacey's *Forms of Loss* (1965). Like his gay Canadian poetic contemporary, DARYL HINE, however, Lacey has spent most of his writing career abroad, a situation understandable in the generally homophobic climate of the 1950s and early 1960s. Given that Canada's "Stonewall," if it can be said to have had one, was the Toronto "riot" in response to the police raids on the baths in 1981, it is not surprising that the emergence of a widespread gay and lesbian literature is a relatively recent phenomenon. Nor is it surprising, given the late development of gay and lesbian literature, that one of the best gay Canadian short stories, "The Turkey Season," is by the straight writer, Alice Munro, or that the most powerful piece of Canadian homoeroticism is in the first chapter of *The English Patient* (1992) by the straight novelist Michael Ondaatje.

Although Canada has produced a gay painter of unquestionable international distinction, Attila Rich-ard Lukacs, it has yet to produce the equivalent Anglophone writer. The best-known gay writer in Canada, Timothy Findley, has not until recently dealt openly with gay subjects in his fiction. Findley's early novels have, admittedly, the fey quality of TRUMAN CAPOTE, a feyness that is evident in the work of many subsequent gay Canadian writers in all genres. If there is nothing particularly Canadian about the distinction between soulful winsomeness on the one hand and sexual realism on the other, nonetheless, a great deal of Anglophone gay writing in Canada seems to fall into one "camp" or the other.

Certainly, realism characterizes the first gay Canadian play, John Herbert's *Fortune and Men's Eyes,* and Scott Symons's graphic novel *Place d'Armes,* both published in 1967, the *wunderjahr* of the Canadian centennial. The no-holds-barred quality of Symons's novel, like the hard-edged prison reality of Herbert's play, announced unmistakably a new subject and a new audience. Both works were *succès de scandal* at the time. A significant contribution to Anglophone gay drama was the work of Michel Tremblay, especially after the first production of *Hosanna* in 1967. English translations of many of Tremblay's plays have been produced and directed by the influential gay director, Bill Glassco, and they have now achieved a respectable place within the repertoire of the leading theater in the country, the Stratford Festival.

Drama is probably the easiest of the genres to identify and deal with in Canadian Anglophone gay writing. Thanks to the critical work of Robert Wallace, there are both a recent anthology of plays by gay men (*Making, Out,* 1993) and a number of articles and interviews on gay theater in English. The Fall 1976 issue of *Canadian Theatre Review,* edited by Wallace, is a benchmark in gay Canadian drama and contains Ken Gass's *The Boy Bishop.*

Written by a playwright who is not gay identified, *The Boy Bishop* nonetheless contains what Gass calls "fragments of oneself" that include homosexuality. Certainly the Boy of the title is very homoerotic, and his speech about a future free of prejudice where "the world will discover more colours" is of a piece with much post-Stonewall literature. It is also a sort of allegory, however, of the French–English problem that was vexing the country as a whole at that time. And, in spite of the play's indebtedness to much Anglo-Canadian theater of the period, it also employs a liturgical kind of performance that is more characteristic of the Francophone tradition.

The Boy Bishop is one of a number of gay plays, written by gay or bisexual men, that were produced in a largely heterosexual Anglo-Canadian theater in the early 1970s. All of them contain gay themes or characters or situations, but what many have in common is a preliberation bleakness: Tom Hendry's *How Are Things With the Walking Wounded?* (1970) and *The Missionary Position* (1971); Louis Del Grande's *So Who's Goldberg?* (1975); Larry Fineberg's *Hope* (1972) and *Human Remains* (1975); Michael Hollingsworth's *Strawberry Fields* (1972); Larry Kardish's *Brussel Sprouts* (1972); Martin Kinch's *Me?* (1973); and John Palmer's *A Touch of God in the Golden Age* (1971) and *The End* (1972).

As founder of the Manitoba Theatre Centre, Toronto Free Theatre, and the influential publishing house Playwright's Co-op, which has published a number of gay authors, Tom Hendry brings a high profile to the relatively few gay plays he has written. *The Walking Wounded,* however, is both uneven and very talky. Hendry's plays have the advantage of comprehensible narrative and credible dialogue, but their manner is strongly derivative from Terence Rattigan and NOEL COWARD. Of the rest, however, only Del Grande's Pinteresque play, *So Who's Goldberg?,* betrays more than clichéd characterization or situation. Where Hollingsworth is grimly Beckettian, Kardish and Fineberg drift off into a Goreyesque fantasy world where the chief action consists of talking. Kinch's *Me?* and Palmer's *A Touch of God* both treat the impossibility of love, but though Palmer's play is more persuasive, its surreal "no exit" quality is a long way from gay liberation.

Even Palmer's nearly contemporary play, *The End,* though often funny, betrays hasty creation in its frenzied dialogue and characterization. Palmer, who bridges the gap between the two generations of Anglo-Canadian gay theater, points to the establishment of the Canadian Charter of Rights and Freedoms (1982) as the moment when Canadian society "embarked on a complete change in how it operates and how it views itself" and hence made real gay theater possible. Others point to the 1969 same-sex amendment of the federal criminal law or the inclusion of sexual orientation in the human rights codes of many of the provinces in the 1980s as equally significant. The gradual impact of the AIDS crisis and the organizations formed to fight it constitutes another significant watershed. Whatever the reason, the 1980s was a decisive decade in Anglophone gay Canada.

Most of the plays of the early 1970s are in the realist mode with surrealist touches. Palmer's more recent *A Day at the Beach* (1987) was written in the wake of what one of his characters calls "the holocaust," that is, AIDS. In each half of this two-part play, gay and straight characters, respectively, confront love, definition, and acceptance in a way that is far less simply zany than in many of the play's predecessors.

Of all the theatrical developments in the 1980s, however, the establishment of the Buddies in Bad Times Theatre in Toronto and the various festivals associated with it was probably the most substantial. Publicly supported and given its own theater by the City of Toronto, Buddies has been enormously successful both within and outside the gay community and has had a considerable influence on mainstream theater. Since its inception, Buddies has provided a venue for new gay plays, not least by its founder, Sky Gilbert. Gilbert's extensive repertoire is impressive, especially his early AIDS play, *The Dressing Gown* (1984). But Gilbert's plays, like many produced at Buddies, are frequently the plays of one idea—a gay historical situation or character (CAVAFY, PASOLINI, Capote)—or dress-up spectaculars of the sort parodied in Peter McGehee's novel, *Boys Like Us* (1991).

Audrey Butler, herself the author of plays first produced at Buddies, has observed that "an author is only as good as her rewrites": a sentiment that one wishes were more widely believed at Buddies. In Gilbert's play, *Capote at Yaddo* (1990), for example, supposedly literary characters utter such phrases as "with Newton and I" and "you who holds": an apparently deliberate carelessness. Cute and clever are no substitute for intelligence and craft, and the four Toronto plays that are included in *Making, Out* suffer from the same post-modern cleverness that the comma in the anthology title suggests. Only in David Demchuk's *Touch* (1986) does one find credible (not pastiche) characterization. Ken Garnhum's *Beuys Buoys Boys* (1989) is a performance piece that does not read well as a text. Its title suggests what it shares with the work of another Maritime playwright, Daniel MacIvor's *2-2-Tango* (1990): a "neat" idea that seems unsubstantial.

Like MacIvor, Audrey Butler is also from Cape Breton, but she has drawn on the strengths of local character and narrative to create, especially in *Black Friday?* (published in *Radical Perversions,* 1990), a play that deals credibly and movingly both with lesbian coming out and with its place in working-class culture and its history. The working class also gets refreshing treatment in David Tipe's *Just Us Indians* (1983), set in downtown Toronto. "We're the garbage they leave behind because it won't fit in the cans," says one of his characters, touching more potently on the relation between subcultures than any amount of fashionable theory. Leaving home is also the theme of much Canadian heterosexual drama, but it has a special poignancy in Butler's consistent attention to the creation of new families that are not simply suburban facsimiles. Butler is now associated with the main producer of lesbian drama, Nightwood Theatre in Toronto, where Ann-Marie Macdonald's *Goodnight Desdemona (Good Morning Juliet)* (1990) also played. Although more popular than Butler's play, *Goodnight Desdemona* has too much of Tom Stoppard's literary cleverness to be continuously enjoyable.

There are two powerful plays in *Making, Out,* both of them very much post-AIDS dramas: Harry Rintoul's *Brave Hearts* (1991) and Colin Thomas's *Flesh and Blood* (1991). Although both works have their defects, each is moving and confronts with a tough irony both real pain and the nature of relationships in a post-AIDS era. *Flesh and Blood* shares with Brad Fraser's *Unidentified Human Remains and the True Nature of Love* (1988) a cast that includes gay and straight characters. Fraser's play, set in Alberta, is also a clever examination of the fictions of monstrosity and the banality of evil. Widely popular, it has become the most successful gay Anglo-Canadian play, having been both performed in London and New York and filmed by a well-known Canadian director, Denys Arcand.

There are at least two gay first-nation playwrights in Canada, Thomson Highway and Daniel David Moses, but neither has written about gay subjects in a manner that is recognizable in conventional gay Anglophone culture. Highway, who includes Cree and Ojibway speeches in his dialogue, is the better known of the two, not least for such moving collaborations with his late brother, the dancer René Highway, as *The Sage, the Dancer and the Fool* (1984), a danced play about native mythologies and sexual selves. The closest one comes to gay material in Highway's very successful plays, *The Rez Sisters* (1986) and *Dry Lips Oughta Move to Kapuskasing* (1989), however, is the sexually indeterminate mythological figure, Nanabush, who governs the action.

The problem of gay-identified authors is even more problematic in lesbian writers: an aspect of "*écriture au feminin*" that is especially evident in Canadian literature. An intelligent treatment of this issue appears in the essays of the Montreal fiction writer and journalist Gail Scott, called *Spaces Like Stairs* (1987). There is no male equivalent of the movable line between feminist and lesbian, nor is the difference in color so markedly political in male writers, with the possible exception of Ian Rashid's poetry collection, *Black Markets / White Boyfriends* (1991). Terry Castle has recently complained of "gal-pal" miscellanies in which any female writing about or for or out of lesbian experience can be included, whereas male writers on the subject are excluded. That male authors are excluded, however, does not make the work of identifying what is truly lesbian writing any the easier.

The case of Dorothy Livesay, a distinguished Canadian poet, is a good example. Widowed and having had an affair with a younger man, she refuses to be merely "feminine" or to identify herself with any school or party. Nonetheless, her poems about lesbian experience in *The Phases of Love* (1983) qualify her for inclusion in any consideration of lesbian writers. "You must let your mouth go / you must drown in me" (from her "Dawnings") is undeniably powerful, as powerful as another west-coast (though originally Australian and married) poet, Daphne Marlatt. Marlatt describes herself as a poet of "open form," where the line may be like a wave in water, and as an antirationalist who, like the great gay poet ROBERT DUNCAN, seeks "to recreate the imaginary/sensory language of the Mother." "Desire floods in / your look i meet / and met, flushed, hear / the singing sound of my blood / rising to it," she writes, moving increasingly toward a poetry that is a sort of compacted and intensified prose.

A turning point in both women's and lesbian poetry in Canada was the anthology *Women and Words* (1984), edited by the West Coast Collective. Livesay and Marlatt are included in it, as well as another (now) western poet, Betsy Warland, who was the collection's coordinator. Warland has also been very active in encouraging women's writing; she founded the Women's Writing Collective in 1975. Like Marlatt, Warland is included in another influential anthology, *SP/ELLES* (1986), where she writes of positioning herself against the "universalism" of imperial male discourse in the interests of what she calls "multi-versality," transversing and transcendence. A fine elegist of desire, she thus avoids sentimentality by looking through different eyes and finding new narratives. She and Marlatt, in their cooperative writing, exemplify a trend that is noticeable in the work of Canadian lesbians: *All Names are Spoken* (1992), by Tamai Kobahashi and Mona Oikawa, for instance.

In the poetry of Gwen Hauser, lament for the loss of Amerindian and classical goddesses is connected with her recognition that lesbian writing involves unmaking the language of men, syntactically as well as imagistically. That she does so in a poetic much influenced by a gay male poet, bill bissett, is consonant with her nice sense of irony. Irony, however, is much more evident in the work of the Toronto poet Christine Donald, one of the two Canadian poets to be anthologized in *Gay and Lesbian Poetry of Our Time*. She brings a sharpness of eye and tongue to bear on cognition, the failings of the body, and the difficulties of language: "Under the closed eyelid / the tired mind races; in the still body / pain streaks through the belly." Of contemporary lesbian poets, Dionne Brand is probably the best known. Film director, author of a work of nonfiction, short stories, and six collections of poems, her 1990 collection *No Language is Neutral* is a classic.

In spite of the pioneering bibliographical work by the gay poet Ian Young, gay Anglo-Canadian poetry is much more difficult to trace than drama. Poetry, unlike drama or even fiction, also suffers from having more aspirants than achievers, and there is much in the history of it since the 1960s (gay and straight) that is beneath consideration. Of the achievers, clearly the most distinguished is Douglas LePan, a Toronto poet who came out very late in life with the collection of poems *Far Voyages* (1990). Largely elegies for a dead young lover, these poems are also a celebration of the reawakening to poetry that that love brought him: "Golden mouth to golden mouth. Our mouths / as they searched out each other. / By putting your lips to mine / you have brought me back from the drowse of exile."

The trail of Anglo-Canadian gay poetry, however, was blazed by another Toronto poet, Edward Lacey, and by Daryl Hine (from Vancouver), and later extended and elaborated by Ian Young's two anthologies, *The Male Muse* (1975) and *The Son of the Male Muse* (1983), both of which included Canadian poets. Whereas Young, especially in *Common-Or-Garden Gods* (1976), is refreshingly physical in his celebration of the male body, Lacey and Hine share with LePan the more "Canadian" sense of deference and *déférence*: gentility and the unspoken. Hine writes of "the educated ghost / Within me," but he is not able entirely to escape it or his Francophile *moeurs*. His poem, "Point Grey," about encounters with nude men on the beach, seems indebted to THOM GUNN, but he is left with the bloodless reflection: "A beauty of sorts is nearly always within reach." Lacey, who has spent much of his life in Central and South America is more candid about a preliberation culture: "snow is our rule of churches, work and laws, / our reticence, our loneliness, our pause, / the emptiness we live in. This is snow." Nonetheless, he is not constrained, as Hine often is, by the traditional forms his poems often take, and his risks are sometimes full of juicy joy. "'Wanna get sucked off?' he said," is better than prosy melancholy.

The other distinguished poet is another Vancouver writer, bill bissett. His bibliography extends to more than a hundred titles (*inkorrect thots,* 1992, is his latest), but many of his poems would pass as heterosexual. Influenced by sound poetry and a member of the influential group of poets, The Four Horsemen, bissett is also indebted to Ferlinghetti and cummings and mantra. His gay poems float like typographical exhalations, sound-bites on the page, full of passion: "my tongue in his / ear our heds so / togethr our hair

/ shaking thru th / waves th / waves th / moshun / uv / yuunyun." Stan Persky, another Vancouver writer who understands the liturgical power of repetition as bissett does, also understands irony: "After lots of swans the desire for swans dies," he writes in his interesting collection *Wrestling the Angel* (1976). Like Michael Lynch, whose poem "Cry" (from *These Waves of Dying Friends,* 1989) is inscribed on the AIDS memorial in Toronto, Persky is an American expatriate who has had a more profound effect on gay writing and culture in Canada through journalism. Lynch's pieces in *The Body Politic,* for example, are classics, and some of them are anthologized in the important collection, *Flaunting It!* (1982). Like the establishment of a Canadian Gay Archives in Toronto, a number of publicly funded conferences on lesbian and gay studies, and the establishment of gay and lesbian courses in several universities, journalism has played a large part in establishing the Canadian lesbian and gay community as a powerful force. Early in its career, *The Body Politic* set a high standard of critical writing. Several of its prominent writers are regular contributors to *The Globe and Mail,* Canada's "national" newspaper, which now frequently publishes essays and reviews on lesbian and gay themes.

It is impossible to canvas all the distinguished gay critical material produced by Canadians in the last three decades, but such a survey would have to include Marion Foster and Kent Murray's *A Not So Gay World* (1972), Persky's *Buddy's: Meditations on Desire* (1989), Brian Pronger's study of gays in sports, *The Arena of Masculinity* (1990), Robert Martin's *The Homosexual Tradition in American Poetry* (1989), Richard Dellamora's *Masculine Desire: The Sexual Politics of Victorian Aestheticism* (1990), Edgar Friedenberg's *Deference to Authority* (1980), Robin Wood's *Hollywood from Vietnam to Reagan* (1986), and Geoff Mains's *Urban Aboriginals: A Celebration of Leathersexuality* (1984).

The relation between the arts has also prompted some very interesting Anglo-Canadian gay and lesbian writing. *Fluid Exchanges* (1992), an anthology of writing about AIDS based on the traveling exhibition of AIDS posters organized by James Miller, is a case in point. So too is Richard Fung's essay, "Looking for My Penis: The Eroticized Asian in Video Porn," that appeared in the anthology *How Do I Look? Queer Film and Video* (1991). Another example of this important interchange is *Sight Specific,* the catalogue of a Toronto exhibition on the relation between lesbian sexual practices and images that was contributed to equally by lesbian artists and writers. So too is the lesbian painter Mary Meigs's well-written autobiographical fiction, *Lily Briscoe: A Self Portrait* (1981).

Graham Jackson's *The Secret Lore of Gardening* (1991), a book on male intimacy, would not find itself in such company. In spite of a rather silly scheme to account for kinds of behavior, however, a great deal of very interesting material about the history of homosexuality is assembled in it. Jackson's earlier piece, "The Theatre of Implication," from Ian Young's important bibliography, *The Male Homosexual in Literature* (1982), is also a seminal essay. Jackson is primarily a fiction writer in a rather old-fashioned symbolic mode. One of his "gothic" stories, "The Apothecary Jar," has an air of THOMAS MANN (the suppression and evasion of sex and its association with death), but his intensely self-occupied characters are also indebted to VIRGINIA WOOLF.

Will Aitken's fiction comes from a tougher school. His first novel, *Terre Haute* (1989), is a savage autobiographical account of growing up in Indiana that nonetheless contains some extraordinary passages of passion. An index of the problem of defining what is *Canadian* gay literature, however, is that *Terre Haute* was not acquired by the largest library in the country, though Aitken's recent powerful novel about incest and child abuse, *A Visit Home* (1993), has been. Altogether more amiable and easier reading are the mysteries of another gay Montréal writer, Edward Phillips. Phillips's first novel, *Sunday's Child* (1981), has led to a series of entertaining novels in the same manner, in which a set of gay and straight characters inhabit the closeted world of English-speaking Montréal. Mystery writing has not been a male preserve, however. Both Eve Zaremba (*A Reason to Kill*, 1978; *Uneasy Lies*, 1990) and Marion Foster (*Victims*, 1985; *The Monarchs are Flying*, 1987; *Legal Tender*, 1992) have written lively works in this genre from a lesbian perspective.

Author of three collections of short stories, *Beyond Happiness* (1985), *The I.Q. Zoo* (1991), and *Sweetheart* (1992), the late expatriate American writer, Peter McGehee, is now best known for his novel, *Boys Like Us* (1991). An odd mixture of the AIDS-afflicted community of Toronto and a sit-com version of Arkansas, McGehee's novel is good on witty narrative, but his characters are less than fully realized. Sounding like ARMISTEAD MAUPIN caricatures, they give the novel a strangely ventriloquist air as if (like many contemporary movies) filmed in Canada but really about the United States. Wit is also a feature of David Carpenter's earlier novel, *Jewels* (1985), a strange farrago of romance, whodunit, shabby subculture, and the academy. Not without its grotesques, it nonetheless makes a good story, and the gay worlds of Saskatoon and Victoria are a well-realized part of the fiction.

David Watmough's autobiographical collection of short stories, *Ashes for Easter* (1972), is largely set in England. Located in a time long before gay liberation, Watmough's stories inhabit a bleak 1940s and 1950s world of self-pity, oddly glossed over with an incongruously erudite diction that he has not entirely shaken in his later work. There is something of Watmough's social-realist misery in *Dog Years* (1991), a novel by another Vancouver author, Dennis Denisoff. Overshadowed as it is by AIDS and set largely in Soviet Ukraine, its autobiographical manner is more powerful. Denisoff also has a strong sense of the potency of language and culture as metaphors for gay exile. He also has a nicely ironic way with words. "My erogenous zones," his persona writes, "have always been on other people's bodies."

Denisoff's collection, *Queeries* (1993), is the first anthology of Anglo-Canadian gay male prose. Fortunately there have been several collections of lesbian fiction, including *Piece of My Heart* (fiction by lesbians of color anthologized by Makeda Silvera, 1991) and most recently *Getting Wet: Tales of Lesbian Seduction* (1992). Edited by two lesbians of color, Carol Allain and Rosamund Elwin, the latter volume continues the tradition that Elwin has encouraged through the Lesbian Writing and Publishing Collective that created another anthology, *Dykewords*. *Getting Wet* and another collection, *By Word of Mouth*, raise the issue of pornography, an issue that has often divided lesbian communities but in Canada has elicited strong lesbian support for erotic writing by women for women. Alongside some pretty torrid sex, *Getting Wet* contains the diction of the old pulp romances of preliberation days: "we had feasted to our hearts' fulness on each other." In so doing, it raises again the question of just what lesbian "literature" is, a question suggested also by the recent National Film Board production *Forbidden Love* (directed by Aerlyn Weissman and Lynne Fernie, 1992), where a piece of pulp fiction comes to life.

Periodicals are also a major source of gay and lesbian writing. Candis Graham, whose collection of short stories, *Imperfect Moments*, has recently appeared, for example, has previously published not only in *Women and Words* but in three other collections of lesbian stories: *Dykeversions* (1986), *By Word of Mouth* (1989), and *Tide Lines* (1991) as well as in the papers *Rites* and *Common Lives / Lesbian Lives*. (One might also add the feminist magazine *Fireweed* as a place where lesbian fiction frequently appears.) Graham's stories have the sort of amiable domesticity often associated with lesbian life; indeed, they are usually situated in the redefinition of "family." This is also a subject of many of the novels of

JANE RULE, another American expatriate. As the first major gay or lesbian novelist to publish in Canada, Rule still has the highest profile. Like her first novel, *Desert of the Heart* (1964), *This is Not for You* (1970) is centered in the relation of two women. Whereas the women in the first novel break through convention, the couple in the second do not. *Against the Season* (1972) introduces the same wide range of characters as recur in what is probably her best-known novel, *The Young in One Another's Arms* (1977), a novel in which the residents (gay and straight) of a rooming house become a "family" in order to fight a developer. In all of her work—and she has a large canon of short stories as well as subsequent novels—her concern has been to present lesbians and gays as "not heroic or saintly but real." This unsentimental clarity has also given her critical writing distinction, both in the pieces that appeared in *The Body Politic*, and have since been collected as *A Hot-Eyed Moderate* (1986), and in her influential earlier work, *Lesbian Images* (1975).

The advent of lesbian and gay literature in Canada has not gone unopposed by traditional forces of "morality," with the absurd result that publications supported by arts councils have sometimes been the subject of police action. The battle against Customs officers and police pornography squads eager to seize even the novels of Jane Rule has largely been carried on in Canada by such important bookstores as Glad Day in Toronto and Little Sisters in Vancouver but not without the active support of straight librarians and bookstores. What is remarkable is the vibrancy of gay culture generally, and gay writing in particular, in a country whose population is less than California's. Both Vancouver and Toronto have strong gay and lesbian publishing houses and theaters that would be the envy of much larger cities in the English-speaking world.

—*Douglas Chambers*

BIBLIOGRAPHY

A Not So Gay World. Marion Foster and Kent Murray, eds. Toronto: McClelland & Stewart, 1972. ■ *By Word of Mouth: Lesbians Writing the Erotic.* Lee Fleming, ed. Charlottetown, P.E.I.: Gynergy Press, 1989. ■ *Canadian Theatre Review* 12 (Fall 1976). ■ Denisoff, Dennis, ed. *Queeries: An Anthology of Gay Male Prose.* Vancouver: Arsenal Pulp Press, 1993. ■ *Dykewords: An Anthology of Lesbian Writing.* Toronto: Women's Press, 1990. ■ *Flaunting It!* Ed Jackson and Stan Persky, eds. Vancouver: New Star Books, 1982. ■ *Fluid Exchanges: Artists and Critics on the AIDS Crisis.* James Miller, ed. Toronto: University of Toronto Press, 1992. ■ *Getting Wet: Tales of Lesbian Seduction.* Anthol. Carol Allain and Rosamund Elwin. Toronto: Women's Press, 1992. ■ *How Do I Look: Queer Film and Video.* Seattle: Bay Press, 1991. ■ *Piece of My Heart: A Lesbian of Colour Anthology.* Anthol. Makeda Silvera. Toronto: Sister Vision, 1991. ■ *Sight Specific: Lesbians and Representation.* Toronto: A Space Gallery, 1988. ■ *SP/ELLES: Poetry by Canadian Women.* Judith Fitzgerald, ed. Windsor, Ont.: Black Moss Press, 1986. ■ *Tide Lines: Stories of Change by Lesbians.* Lee Fleming, ed. Charlottetown, P.E.I.: Gynergy Press, 1991. ■ Wallace, Robert, ed. *Making, Out: Plays by Gay Men.* Toronto: Coach House Press, 1992. ■ *Women and Words: The Anthology.* West Coast Collective, ed. Madeira Park, B.C.: Harbour, 1984. ■ Young, Ian. *The Male Homosexual in Literature: A Bibliography.* Metuchen, N.J.: Scarecrow, 1975. ■ ——, ed. *The Male Muse: A Gay Anthology.* Trumansburg, N.Y.: Crossing Press, 1975. ■ ——, ed. *The Son of the Male Muse: New Gay Poetry.* Trumansburg, N.Y.: Crossing Press, 1983.

Capote, Truman
(1924–1984)

Truman Capote was born Truman Steckfus Persons on September 30, 1924, in New Orleans. As his biographer, Gerald Clarke, reports, Capote's parents were mismatched, and Capote began a childhood in Monroeville, Alabama, with a batch of eccentric relatives he would later immortalize in his writing. His story "Miriam," published in *Mademoiselle* in 1945, launched Capote, whose reputation was further enhanced by the publication of "A Tree of Night" in *Harper's Bazaar* that same year. Capote's career after that was one of triumph and sorrow, with many feeling that he peaked with *In Cold Blood*, published as a book in 1966 after publication in *The New Yorker*. Although Capote did produce some good writing in the following years, alcoholism and other problems ruined both his art and life, and he died on August 25, 1984, just before turning sixty.

Capote's writing, especially his fiction and more direct autobiographical work, helped establish what might be called the quintessential homosexual writing style of the period, with clear links to the work of TENNESSEE WILLIAMS, for example. That style was at once closeted, in that it seldom dealt with overt homosexuality, and uncloseted, because its code for homosexual interpretations was so easily seen though. The basis for that style can be found in the emphasis on his southern background in such works as his first novel, *Other Voices, Other Rooms* (1948), *The Grass*

Harp (1951), *A Christmas Memory* (1966), and others; his attention to older women characters; his defining through his works what passed for a certain kind of "sensitivity" at the time (for example, the primacy given to feelings and emotions over action); and finally, his own effeminate, southern manner on television talk shows of the 1960s and 1970s, characterized by his wit, barbs, and outright insults before alcohol befuddled what was once a wonderful mind.

Perhaps the clearest example of Capote's homosexual sensibility is in *Breakfast at Tiffany's* (1958). As Clarke points out, the novel's heroine, Holly Golightly, was an amalgamation of the quirky, beautiful, socially ambitious women that Capote knew and idolized. With her wretched background followed by a progress to New York, Holly's life seemed also to reflect the desires of many homosexual men to escape to the big city for freedom. Yet she was undeniably a woman, not a disguised drag queen, à la Auntie Mame. Capote's ability to turn the oppressively inaccurate assumptions about gay men into art is but one area in which he has been seriously underappreciated. Capote's women characters are not gay men's fantasies about being women. Rather, Capote shows where the concerns and emotional needs of women and gay men intersect.

Capote was also involved to varying degrees in film, most successfully with his screenplay for *The Innocents,* as well as the musical theater, with the failure *House of Flowers.* (*Breakfast at Tiffany's* was adapted by others for the musical stage, becoming one of the most fabled disasters in Broadway history.) His finest work of journalism is *The Muses Are Heard* (1956), an account of a largely black company touring the Soviet Union with *Porgy and Bess.* As Clarke claims, the book reflects Capote's bitchy, lunchtime conversation mode at its best; the book is a perfect blending of a certain kind of gay sensibility with the reporting of a major cultural event that is not without humor.

After *In Cold Blood,* Capote's writing declined in quality as his notoriety increased. Most disastrously for him and his art was the publication in *Esquire* of a section from his unfinished novel *Answered Prayers,* in which he turned on all the friends who had helped make him and whom he had helped make. What we have of the novel is misogynistic, mean-spirited, and cruel; Capote became in life and prose the caricature that homophobic critics had unfairly labeled him before. The years prior to his death were unfortunate in the extreme, artistically and personally, as he destroyed what he had built for himself and his art.

Because Capote made himself a subject of much of his own writing, and sold that self through television as much as if not more than in his prose, his life deserves as much attention as his writing. Gerald Clarke's superb biography, *Capote,* shows how homophobia and being homosexual shaped Capote and his work. As "obvious" as any homosexual can be, Capote struggled all of his life to find a place for himself in the world, battling homophobia from childhood through his most famous years. His writing reflects clearly his attempts to understand and contain the hostile world in which he found himself. As Clarke makes clear, Capote used *on purpose* his persona as a nonthreatening homosexual to charm the people of Kansas, and the killers themselves, to get material for *In Cold Blood.* For his time, Capote was a cultural icon of homosexuality, if by no means the only one or the only famous one, and of a certain kind of homosexual who might be called a cultural darling. Clearly, the tragedy of Capote's later life and his failure to produce any major, substantial work after *In Cold Blood* came from his anger at the role he and his well-placed friends had established for him. That he had embraced that role—possibly he felt it was the only one he could have—in no way lessened his self-hatred. The fury absent from any of the early autobiographical novels or stories exploded finally in *Answered Prayers* (and in his television interviews): The result was his destruction. Thus, Capote's own life stands as a work as interesting and informative as any he wrote, indicated in some measure by Jay Presson Allen's play, *Tru* (1990), which gave Broadway star Robert Morse a triumphant role as Capote.

Capote is a writer of importance, but the greatness in art that he sought eluded him. He might have become the major social critic of his generation—a kind of HENRY JAMES of the 1950s and 1960s—if he had not self-destructed. Yet Capote's triumph over homophobia so that he could have a life and produce major writing took an enormous amount of strength. When an understanding of his life is combined with the careful appreciation of his work that is yet to come, Capote will no doubt emerge as a hero of gay liberation in the middle years of this century as well as a fine writer of a certain kind of gay literature whose value we are in danger of slighting.

—*Thomas Dukes*

BIBLIOGRAPHY

Allen, Jay Presson. *Tru.* Unpublished play. 1990. ■ Clarke, Gerald. *Capote.* New York: Ballantine, 1988. ■ Garson, Helen. *Truman Capote.* New York: Ungar, 1980. ■ ———. *Truman Capote.* Boston: Twayne Publishers, 1981. ■ Nance, William L. *The Worlds of Truman Capote.* New York: Stein and Day, 1970. ■ Reed, Terry. *Truman Capote.* New York: Twayne Publishers, 1981.

Carpenter, Edward
(1844–1929)

Edward Carpenter was born in England in 1844. His family was of the upwardly situated middle class, and his father, Charles, a former naval commander, earned a living as a lawyer and through investments in American and British railways. His mother, Sophia, patterned herself after the stereotypical vision of the placid Victorian housewife and spent her time tending to Edward and his six sisters. In 1881, she passed away, and Charles died a year later. Carpenter died at Guildford in 1929. These rather typical details do not foreshadow the role Carpenter was to build for himself in Britain, for by the time of his death, he was to be thought of as one of the great socialist visionaries of England and a champion of both women's and homosexuals' liberation.

Carpenter's life began to follow the course prescribed by his privileged station. He was educated at Oxford and Cambridge, and in 1868, began a career as a lecturer at Trinity Hall, Cambridge. During his second year, he was elected a clerical fellow and ordained a deacon. Carpenter's family had raised him in the relatively liberal doctrines of the Broad Church, and he soon found himself in conflict with the tenets of Anglicanism he was expected to uphold. By 1871, this conflict had led to physical debilitation, and after a brief leave of absence, he resigned his church roles and functioned solely as a lecturer. During this period, Carpenter formed a romantic attachment to Andrew Beck, but Beck ultimately denied the attachment and rebuked Carpenter so that he could marry and pursue an academic career as Master of Trinity Hall.

The aftermath of this breakup seems to have affected Carpenter profoundly, for it is during this period that he began to strongly identify with WALT WHITMAN and to pattern his own poetry around Whitman's liberational male body in *Calamus*. Also during this period, Carpenter began to systematically embrace the British socialist vision that hitherto had been only a sporadic theme in his thinking. The despair resulting from the breakup might also have motivated his joining the University Extension movement in Sheffield, certainly the deciding event in his development as a socialist.

The University Extension program in England was started by James Stuart of Cambridge in response to pressures from women demanding access to education. More conservative English academics saw a twofold purpose in establishing an extension university in Sheffield: First, it would help indoctrinate the more remote areas of England into the Cambridge class system; second, it would meet the demand for women's higher education while preserving the masculine sanctity of Cambridge itself. Stuart, however, saw these rather oppressive motives as an opportunity to attempt to forge an educational institution that would give equal access to all classes and both genders. This democratic vision attracted Carpenter, but certainly the opportunity to escape the presence of his former lover also strengthened his resolve. By 1877, Carpenter was firmly ensconced as a key player within the extension program and its socialist goals.

Following the death of his parents in 1880 and 1881, Carpenter resigned his teaching duties and devoted himself to full-time study at Millthorpe, a retreat he bought in the Sheffield countryside. He began what was to become a key part of his theoretical vision, a systematic study of Eastern religions and particularly of the *Bhagavad-Gita*. He also completed his epic poem cycle, *Towards Democracy*. Through his involvement with such groups as the Progressive Association, the Fellowship of the New Life, the Fabians, and the Social Democratic Federation (SDF), he met important political and social theorists such as William Morris, Havelock Ellis, and Olive Schreiner, one of the leading socialist feminists of the time. In 1884, William Morris broke alliance with the SDF and formed the Socialist League, and Carpenter followed suit. The development was crucial for Carpenter, for the League viewed the task of socialism to be the creation of a new inner consciousness for all people. This mingling of politics and spirituality enabled Carpenter to synthesize his own religious past, his current embrace of Eastern mysticism, and his strong allegiance to social reform into a unique vision that might be best termed mystic socialism.

The events of Carpenter's life, including details of his travels in the East, have been reliably and fluently set down by Sheila Rowbotham in *Socialism and the New Life*. Perhaps the most significant event in Carpenter's life, however, happened in 1891, when returning from a journey to India, he met George Merrill. Prior to this meeting, Carpenter had been in a relationship with George Adams, who with his wife, Lucy, lived in Millthorpe from 1893 to 1898. By 1898, it was apparent to Carpenter that he wanted to live his life with Merrill, and the resulting acrimony between him and Adams destroyed their friendship. Merrill had been raised in the slums of Sheffield and had no formal education. The attachment between the two men was undoubtedly one of real affection, but it also enabled Carpenter to achieve one of his long-standing goals in life: the realization of a bond between men that refused to be hindered by the rigid class divisions of English society. Indeed, the love of Carpenter and Merrill probably formed the motivation for E. M. FORSTER's representation of the love between Maurice Hall and the gamekeeper Scudder in *Maurice*, a novel that Forster recollects being created in his imagination the moment Carpenter touched him lightly just above his buttocks.

Carpenter's own writings tell a great deal about his life and the subtleties of passion that continually motivated and conflicted it. His first major work—and his only purely literary work—*Towards Democracy* (1883) is, in its final form, a collection of almost three hundred lyric poems divided into four sections. Although the bulk of the poems were written in 1883, Carpenter continued to add poems to the collection until at least 1902. The poems clearly foreshadow the combination of mysticism and socialism that fascinated Carpenter later in life and also show the obvious influence of Walt Whitman on Carpenter's young academic mind. The third poem from the first edition, for example, states, "I conceive a millennium on earth—a millennium not of riches, nor of mechanical facilities, nor of intellectual facilities, nor absolutely of immunity from disease, nor absolutely of immunity from pain; but a time when men and women all over the earth shall ascend and enter into relation with their bodies—shall attain freedom and joy." The stress on both men and women looks forward to his work in the feminist movement and suggests the extent to which the presence of six sisters and a strong mother must have influenced his thinking. Carpenter also published an autobiography, *My Days and Dreams* (1916), that intersperses bits of his theories with moments from his life.

Carpenter's reputation, however, rests largely on three important radical tracts dealing with issues of sex and gender relations in society, *Love's Coming-of-Age* (1896), *The Intermediate Sex* (1906), and *Intermediate Types Among Primitive Folks* (1914). *Love's Coming-of-Age* is a collection of three pamphlets, "Sex-love: and its Place in a Free Society," "Woman: and her Place in a Free Society," and "Marriage in a Free Society," which were published by the Labour Press in Manchester in 1894. A fourth pamphlet entitled "Homogenic Love: and its place in a Free Society" was not reprinted in the volume due to public hysteria following the trial of OSCAR WILDE in 1895 and did not appear until 1906. The first of these pamphlets, "Sex-love," argues that in industrial soci-

eties sex has become divorced from biological or natural need and instead is used to alienate men and women from their own bodies. It further argues that by purifying the sex–love passion, society can instill a new type of individualism that will lead to liberation and democracy. The second pamphlet, "Woman," is broken into three segments in the book, but its basic argument is that the disempowerment of woman in society results from a sort of elaborate reconfiguration of feudal relations that attempt to keep woman as a serf in relationship to man, the master. The final pamphlet on marriage argues that this particular social configuration is designed, again, to maintain a set of feudal relations between men and women, and that true economic liberation will happen only through an abolishment of it.

The Intermediate Sex comprises Carpenter's pamphlet on homogenic love, as well as a number of essays he wrote on homosexuality for liberal British journals between 1897 and 1899. The book is divided into four essays. The introduction and the first essay, "The Intermediate Sex," argue that through both social and natural evolution, sex has outgrown its simple biological purposes, and that increased instances of "uranism"—Carpenter's term for homosexuality—represent the evolution of a distinctive third sex designed to lead society into a new set of social relations. The second essay, "The Homogenic Attachment," is a survey of the history of homosexuality and of the current theorists of homosexuality, including Krafft-Ebing, Moll, Ulrichs, Ellis, and SYMONDS. It ends with a tribute to Whitman's democratic visions of "calamitic" love and suggests this as an alternative means of explaining the place of the Uranist in society. The final two essays, "Affection in Education" and "The Place of the Uranian in Society," discuss how to structure various social institutions around the concept of democratic male bonding derived from Whitman's writings.

The Intermediate Types Among Primitive Folk comprises two separate essays. The first, "The Intermediate in the Service of Religion," originally appeared as "On the Connection between Homosexuality and Divination" in the *American Journal of Religious Psychology* in 1911. In 1914, Carpenter added a second essay, "The Intermediate as Warrior," and the book was published. The book begins with a brief transcultural and transhistorical explanation of "the intermediate type" in a number of older, non-European cultures. The primary emphasis of both essays derives from the increased effects of Eastern philosophy and religion on Carpenter, for each essay attempts to demonstrate that Uranists in all cultures other than repressive industrial ones occupy spaces of spiritual

and social divination and protection designed to advance the evolution of a culture beyond the basic demands of biology and the environment.

Even though Carpenter's writings have been reissued in affordable and dependable editions from London's Gay Men's Press, he remains one of the most underexamined figures in the history of gay writing. One reason for this is that his mystical orientation, transhistorical sensibility, and eurocentrism initially seem to make him incompatible with current views of sex and sexuality. Yet if these traits are bracketed as the effects of the moment in which he wrote, a level of amazing cognizance and foresight appears. The influence of the feminist movement on Carpenter's work resulted in a theorization that views all sex and gender relations as effects of capitalism, a view that is entirely congruent with current Marxist and social-constructionist views. Moreover, his centrality within his own culture led to significant influences on authors such as E. M. Forster and D. H. LAWRENCE; the current neglect of Carpenter results in a decontextualization of these and other writers' thinking. It is to be hoped that as gay and lesbian studies continue to expand, the place of Carpenter as a social and sexual theorist will be more fully recovered. (See also ENGLISH LITERATURE: TWENTIETH CENTURY and POETRY, GAY MALE.)

—*Gregory W. Bredbeck*

BIBLIOGRAPHY

A Bibliography of Edward Carpenter. Sheffield: Sheffield City Libraries, 1949. ■ Carpenter, Edward. *Selected Writings, Volume I: Sex*. London: Gay Men's Press, 1984. ■ ———. *Towards Democracy*. London: Gay Men's Press, 1985. ■ Jones, Gareth Stedman. *Outcast London*. Oxford: Clarendon Press, 1971. ■ Pierson, Stanley. *Marxism and the Origins of British Socialism: The Struggle for a New Consciousness*. Ithaca, N.Y.: Cornell University Press, 1973. ■ Rowbotham, Sheila and Jeffrey Weeks. *Socialism and the New Life: The Personal and Sexual Politics of Edward Carpenter and Havelock Ellis*. London: Pluto Press, 1977. ■ Weeks, Jeffrey. *Sex, Politics and Society: The Regulation of Sexuality Since 1800*. London: Longman, 1981.

Cather, Willa
(1873–1947)

In 1922, Willa Cather declared that the power and quality of art arise from "the inexplicable presence of the thing not named," from "whatever is felt upon the page without being specifically named there." For decades, this remark in "The Novel Demeuble" was interpreted strictly in aesthetic terms as a statement of Cather's commitment to classical principles of starkness and simplification in art. Recently, however, the psychosexual implications of "the thing not named" have moved into the foreground, as biographers and critics have begun to grapple with how Cather's lesbianism, a fact of her life long ignored or denied, may have shaped both the form and the content of her writing. Nebraska's first lady of letters—the award-winning author of twelve novels and several collections of short fiction—who shared her life for nearly forty years with Edith Lewis, has thus been liberated from the stereotypes of the celibate artist or the sexless spinster whose reticence on the subject of heterosexuality was generally viewed as a sign of repression. The belated recognition of Cather's sexual identity has created a provocative new context for understanding her life and work and established her important place in gay and lesbian literary history.

Born in Back Creek, Virginia, on December 7, 1873, Willa Cather was the first of seven children. Her family moved when she was nine to the prairie country of Nebraska whose settlement she would immortalize in *O Pioneers!* (1913) and *My Antonia* (1918; rev. 1926). The wide open spaces of the prairie were socially and psychologically congenial to Cather, affording her the freedom needed for an unconventional adolescence. Red Cloud, the town her family moved to in 1884, could be confining and parochial, but family, friends, and neighbors encouraged Cather's love of books and theater, nurtured her ambitions (she first aspired to be a doctor), and most surprisingly, (reluctantly) tolerated her four-year masquerade as "William Cather." Begun when she was fourteen, Cather's elaborate and public episode of male impersonation is documented in studio photographs that show her sporting crewcuts and dressed in masculine attire. Letters from this period, including passionate epistles to another woman, are written over William's signature. She sustained the performance even after she moved to Lincoln to begin studying at the University of Nebraska. Biographer Sharon O'Brien has recently analyzed "William" as Cather's "first major work of fiction, a text in which she was both author and character." "He" was also, of course, a brave rejection of her culture's constraining ideology of femininity, an effort to fashion a self that was powerful, autonomous, and heroic rather than weak, dependent, and passive. Finally, "William" was a mask Cather could hide behind, a persona she could adapt for the purpose of articulating feelings that, by the 1890s, had been defined as signs of deviance. It is manifestly unfair, "William" laments in a letter to college crush Louise Pound, that feminine friendship should be unnatural. "William" was the first of many masks Cather would devise to camouflage or naturalize her "unnatural" passions.

Early in her college career, Cather's ambitions shifted from medicine to writing, and she began publishing in earnest, in campus publications and the local papers in Lincoln. Her columns on the arts and reviews of books, theater, and opera evince both critical acumen and youthful bravado, as, for example, when she confidently declares that Mark Twain is "neither a scholar, a reader or a man of letters and very little of a gentleman." For years after graduation, the need to support herself financially prevented Cather from devoting herself full time to the writing of fiction, so she worked in journalism in Lincoln, Pittsburgh (where she also taught Latin and English in high school), and New York until 1912, ending this phase of her career as managing editor of the immensely successful muckraking magazine, McClure's.

One fortuitous benefit of her work for McClure's was that in 1908, while in Boston doing research on the life of Mary Baker Eddy, she met Annie Fields, widow of the publisher James T. Fields, and SARAH ORNE JEWETT, a New England writer whose work she admired. In Fields's gracious Charles Street home, which Jewett shared for the several months of every year she spent in Boston, Cather made many valuable discoveries. She saw in the women's lives a model of the kind of female domestic partnership she was then establishing with Edith Lewis, though the older women's "Boston marriage" enjoyed a degree of acceptance that her own relationship would never attain as modern notions of sexuality and deviance took hold. She gained, through Fields's lively conversation and the rich sense of history her house contained, a vivid connection to America's literary and cultural past. Most important, she found in Jewett a successful woman writer who cared deeply about Cather's future. Though they knew each other only for the last sixteen months of Jewett's life and her health was fragile, Jewett generously mentored Cather, reading and commenting on her work, advising her in a letter to leave journalism and "find [her] own quiet centre of life" so that her talent might mature. Jewett's attention came at a propitious moment since Cather was feeling depleted by the demands of her job and concerned that she was making little progress as an artist, having published only one volume of poetry,

April Twilights (1903), and one collection of short stories, The Troll Garden (1905). When finally she took Jewett's advice and left McClure's, Cather produced her first two novels, Alexander's Bridge (1912) and O Pioneers!, in quick succession. She acknowledged her debt to the author of The Country of the Pointed Firs (1896) in the dedication to the second book: "To the memory of Sarah Orne Jewett in whose beautiful and delicate work there is the perfection that endures."

Once freed from the distractions of journalism, Cather achieved in her own work a perfection that has proved equally enduring. During her lifetime, she enjoyed both popular and critical success, earning a Pulitzer Prize for her novel of World War I, One of Ours (1922). However, no single critical label seems adequate for describing the elusive yet undeniable power of Cather's fiction. For her close attention to the rigors of pioneer life, she has been described as a realist. For her use of symbols and celebration of the transcendent value of art, she has been termed a romantic. For her faithful depictions of Nebraska and the American Southwest, she has been called a regionalist. For her restless experimentation with the form of the novel, she has lately been claimed as a modernist. She has been embraced as a feminist and rebuked as a misogynist. Clearly, the "perfection" of Cather's work is neither simple nor uncontroversial.

Cather is difficult to pin down because the range of her interests was wide and the shape of her career complex. Her early novels focused primarily on powerful, memorable heroines who dare to take control of their lives and of the less powerful male figures who surround them. In O Pioneers!, Alexandra Bergson has both the will and the intelligence necessary to succeed as a prairie farmer, whereas her dull brothers Lou and Oscar can do little more than follow orders. In The Song of the Lark (1915), Thea Kronborg is aided by a series of male teachers and admirers, each of whom is marked by some personal failure or disappointment, on her way to becoming an internationally famous opera singer. In My Antonia, the eponymous heroine is a Bohemian immigrant who revels in working "like mans" but winds up producing a huge brood of children. Her vitality and her fecundity earn for Antonia awe tinged with ambivalence from the childless male narrator who compulsively remembers her. In the end, Jim Burden describes Antonia as "battered but not diminished" by her difficult life and pays tribute to her accomplishments by comparing her to "the founders of early races."

Jim Burden is a sign, however, of the puzzling shifts Cather's fiction would take in the 1920s since, in the wake of World War I, she seems to have grown increasingly pessimistic about women's power in a culture that remained stubbornly masculinist. In *My Antonia,* the male narrator creates and appropriates the female character, for he possesses a linguistic authority the immigrant woman clearly lacks. Jim may be a mask for Cather's lesbian desires, but he is also a means of exploring gender's role in shaping perception and interpretation. Throughout the 1920s—Cather's most productive decade—such questions would haunt all of her major works, creating fissures and tensions that are absent or less apparent in most of the earlier novels. During this brilliant, disturbing middle phase of her career as a novelist, Cather's female characters are either large and dangerous (as, for example, are Marian Forrester in *A Lost Lady* [1923] and Myra Henshawe in *My Mortal Enemy* [1926]) or small and powerless (as are Lillian St. Peter in *The Professor's House* [1925] and all the women who hover in the background of *Death Comes for the Archbishop* [1927]). Male characters are in thrall to or flight from women who are duplicitous, vulgar, grasping, or destructive. This pattern culminates in the celebrations of male relationships and male worlds that are central to both *The Professor's House* and *Archbishop.*

Cather's marginalization of female characters may be, as some readers have suggested, a rejection of the feminine that signals internalized misogyny or homophobia, but it may also be a complex interrogation of the gender troubles that characterized post–World War I America. In particular, as a woman writing at a moment when the nation's "official" literary identity was being formulated in increasingly narrow and masculine terms—in works of criticism like D. H. LAWRENCE's influential *Studies in Classic American Literature* (1923), which completely ignored literature by women—Cather had to have been anxious about her own and other women's cultural authority. She seems to have sensed that the tide of American literary history was shifting against her, as Lawrence set the stage for the canonization of Hawthorne and MELVILLE in part by lashing out at America's New Women as "subtly diabolic." All the less likable or powerful female figures who crop up in her fiction of the 1920s may be viewed as signs of this anxiety, but none is more poignant or fascinating than Mother Eve, the Indian mummy discovered in *The Professor's House* with her mouth frozen open "as if she were screaming." As an emblem of the female voice, Mother Eve's "scream"—silent, eternal, indecipherable—indicates how far Cather had moved from the optimism that had issued in Thea Kronborg's commanding soprano.

In 1925, Cather sought to intervene in the sexual politics of American literary history by formulating an alternative to the Lawrentian model in her preface to *The Best Stories of Sarah Orne Jewett,* a volume she edited for Houghton Mifflin. There, she pays eloquent tribute to her mentor's "gift of sympathy," her form and technique ("the design is the story and the story is the design"), and her favorite materials ("Miss Jewett wrote of the people who grew out of the soil and the life of the country near her heart, not about exceptional individuals at war with their environment"). She also sketches out a mini-canon of American fiction by identifying *The Country of the Pointed Firs, The Scarlet Letter,* and *Huckleberry Finn* as "three American books which have the possibility of a long, long life." Cather's choices, aside from reflecting a significant change in her judgment of Twain, argue for inclusivity and diversity in the discussion of American masterpieces that Lawrence's book had helped ignite. In promoting Jewett as a writer of the first rank, she in effect promotes herself, seeking to secure both her and her foremother's place in history by establishing a favorable climate of reception for nondramatic narratives lacking in heroic "individuals at war with their environment." In making the case for *Pointed Firs,* she implicitly makes one for her own austere masterpiece, *Death Comes for the Archbishop,* which was in the planning stages as she prepared the Jewett volume.

Cather lived for twenty years after the publication of *Archbishop,* but she would not sustain the level of productivity or success she enjoyed in the 1920s. During the 1930s, she was devastated by personal losses (the deaths of her mother, a brother, and her beloved Isabelle McClung), pained by the suffering the Depression created for many of her friends, and embittered by attacks from leftist critics who accused her of nostalgia and escapism. She would publish three more novels—*Shadows on the Rock* (1931), *Lucy Gayheart* (1935), and *Sapphira and the Slavegirl* (1940)—and a collection of short stories, all generally well received, yet she seems to have felt that her earlier concerns about literary history were justified by her apparent rejection by a younger generation of readers. She retreated during these years into despair over the course of world events—a despair that would deepen with the advent of World War II—and an obsessive desire to protect her privacy. Perhaps fearing exposure of her lesbianism, Cather went on a rampage near the end of her life, destroying all the personal letters in her possession, asking friends to destroy any they had, and finally stipulating in her will that quotation from and republication of any surviving letters be forbidden. The author's actions resulted in inestimable losses to Cather studies and to gay and lesbian history, as silence creates ambiguity and forces speculation about how Cather experienced her sexuality in the transitional moments of the modern era. Nevertheless, her extraordinary career amply demonstrates what matters most— that is, that the maverick "William" Cather transformed "her"self into one of the twentieth century's premier literary artists.

—Marilee Lindemann

BIBLIOGRAPHY

Adams, Timothy Dow. "My Gay Antonia: The Politics of Willa Cather's Lesbianism." *Historical, Literary, and Erotic Aspects of Lesbianism.* Monika Kehoe, ed. New York: Harrington Park Press, 1986. 89–98. ■ Carlin, Deborah. *Cather, Canon, and the Politics of Reading.* Amherst: University of Massachusetts Press, 1992. ■ Fetterley, Judith. "*My Antonia,* Jim Burden, and the Dilemma of the Lesbian Writer." *Lesbian Texts and Contexts: Radical Revisions.* Karla Jay and Joanne Glasgow, eds. New York: New York University Press, 1990. 145–163. ■ Fryer, Judith. *Felicitous Space: The Imaginative Structures of Edith Wharton and Willa Cather.* Chapel Hill: University of North Carolina Press, 1986. ■ Gilbert, Sandra M. and Susan Gubar. "Lighting Out for the Territories: Willa Cather's Lost Horizons." *Sexchanges,* vol. 2 of *No Man's Land: The Place of the Woman Writer in the Twentieth Century.* New Haven, Conn.: Yale University Press, 1989. 169–212. ■ Irving, Katrina. "Displacing Homosexuality: The Use of Ethnicity in Willa Cather's *My Antonia.*" *Modern Fiction Studies* 36 (Spring 1990): 91–102. ■ Lewis, Edith. *Willa Cather Living: A Personal Record.* New York: Knopf, 1953. ■ Murphy, John J., ed. *Critical Essays on Willa Cather.* Boston: G.K. Hall, 1984. ■ O'Brien, Sharon. *Willa Cather: The Emerging Voice.* New York: Oxford University Press, 1987. ■ Russ, Joanna. "To Write 'Like a Woman': Transformations of Identity in the Work of Willa Cather." *Historical, Literary, and Erotic Aspects of Lesbianism.* Monika Kehoe, ed. New York: Harrington Park Press, 1986. 77–87. ■ Sedgwick, Eve. "Across Gender, Across Sexuality: Willa Cather and Others." *South Atlantic Quarterly* 88.1 (Winter 1989): 53–72. ■ Summers, Claude J. "'A Losing Game in the End': Aestheticism and Homosexuality in Cather's 'Paul's Case.'" *Modern Fiction Studies* 36 (Spring 1990): 103–119. ■ Woodress, James. *Willa Cather: A Literary Life.* Lincoln: University of Nebraska Press, 1987.

Catullus

(*ca* 85–*ca* 55 B.C.)

About the life of Gaius Valerius Catullus, we know very little. His family belonged to the ruling elite of Verona, where he was born, and his father seems to have been on good terms with Julius Caesar. Catullus's early adulthood was spent among leisured and aristocratic circles at Rome. There he and his friends, who were writers, advocates, and politicians, seem to have formed a sophisticated, witty, and cultured social set. He fell in love with a woman whom he calls "Lesbia" and whom later writers identified as Clodia, the wife of Q. Metellus Celer and the sister of Clodius Pulcher. There is a hostile description of her in Cicero's oration *Pro Caelio.* The course of the affair with Lesbia was painful and disappointing for Catullus, whose affections were eventually alienated. About the year 57, he accompanied the propraetor Memmius to Bithynia and probably visited the tomb of his brother, who had died near Troy. His last datable poem, number 11, refers to events that took place in 55. Catullus is believed to have died shortly thereafter.

Poets of Catullus's generation, normally referred to as "neoterics" and influenced by the Alexandrian Greeks, notably Callimachus, rejected the historical epic and emphasized the short, witty "personal" poem. Metrical variety, formal perfection, erudition, elegance, playfulness, and brevity were their principal literary values, and Catullus reflects most if not all of these ideals. Perhaps most significant, Catullus and his associates rejected the impersonality of epic poetry and made their own sensibility an important aspect of their writing.

Homoerotic themes of various kinds appear in Catullus's work. Several describe his own homosexual adventures. Four love poems (24, 48, 81, and 99) are addressed to an aristocratic adolescent male, Juventius, and delineate a tender but ultimately unrequited passion. In 21, he makes jealous threats against Aurelius, who flirts with his "boy." In 15, he ironically entrusts his darling to the care of the same Aurelius, again with threats. In 56, Catullus wittily describes a more casual sexual encounter with a youth who is also having an affair with one of his own female paramours.

A number of poems reflect other attitudes to homosexual activity. In 61, an epithalamium or marriage poem, Catullus describes how the bridegroom, now entering respectable married life, must give up his male lover. In some poems (16, 28), sexual activities such as pedication and irrumation represent domination, vengeance, or machismo. "Passive" homosexuality, fellatio, and effeminacy, which Catullus often invests with economic as well as moral associations (25, 33, 80, 112), are ridiculed.

Finally, some poems (such as 9, 30, and 50) reflect the passionate character of same-sex friendship in antiquity. The degree to which such poems are homoerotic is debatable. Some of them, however, are likely to be read by modern readers as love poems. (See also POETRY, GAY MALE and ROMAN LITERATURE.)

—*Brad Walton*

BIBLIOGRAPHY

Martin, Charles. *Catullus.* New Haven: Yale University Press, 1992. ■ Quinn, Kenneth, ed. *Approaches to Catullus.* New York: Barnes and Noble, 1972. ■ ———. *The Catullan Revolution.* Melbourne: Melbourne University Press, 1959. ■ Ross, David O. *Style and Tradition in Catullus.* Cambridge, Mass.: Harvard University Press, 1969. ■ Wheeler, A. L. *Catullus and the Traditions of Ancient Poetry.* Berkeley: 1964. ■ Wiseman, T. P. *Catullus and His World.* Cambridge: Cambridge University Press, 1985.

Cavafy, C. P.
(1863–1933)

Constantine P. Cavafy, now regarded as one of the greatest poets to have written in modern Greek, although recognized in his home city during his lifetime, has earned most of his fame since his death. Born into a family of rich Greek merchants in Alexandria, he had an outwardly uneventful life. In 1872, two years after his father's death depleted the family fortune, he went to England with part of his family and remained there between the ages of nine and sixteen. They returned to Alexandria, but events leading to the bombardment of the city by the British drove them to Constantinople in 1882, where Cavafy remained until 1885, when he went back to the city of his birth and gained employment in the civil service. He seldom left it for the rest of his life, although there were trips to France and England in 1897 and to Greece in 1901, 1903, and 1932.

Cavafy may have had his first gay experiences in Constantinople, but the details of his sexual life remain vague despite the critical attention devoted to him. He had no long-term companions, and if his erotic poems reflect his actual experiences, most of his sexual encounters must have been fleeting ones. Cavafy's mother died in 1899, and in 1907, he moved from the family home with one of his brothers, Paul, to an apartment in the Rue Lepsius. Later he lived alone. In this rather seedy location, Cavafy entertained guests and took part in Alexandrian literary life. Indeed, in LAWRENCE DURRELL's novel series *The Alexandria Quartet,* he is considered the presiding poet of the city. In 1922, Cavafy, who had made money on the stock exchange and been granted a pension, retired from the Ministry of Irrigation, where he had worked since 1889. He died of cancer of the throat in 1933.

The canon of 154 short poems that Cavafy wanted preserved was published in 1935, two years after his death; this body of work was composed over the years 1896 to 1933. During his lifetime, he published some poetry in periodicals and made little booklets and broadsheets of other poems for distribution to his circle of friends. In addition, there is a set of thirty-three uncollected early poems from the years 1884 to 1896 and sixty-three other poems that were unpublished in Cavafy's lifetime. These supplementary poems can be found in the revised edition of Rae Dalven's translation (1976), the largest collection in English. Cavafy was a shrewd judge of his own work, and this large body outside the canon adds little to his reputation.

The poetry of Cavafy in one sense constitutes a coming-out story, although its lack of detail keeps it from falling into the category of confessional poetry. In his twenties and thirties, Cavafy tried his hand, unsuccessfully, at heterosexual love poems, but when he was forty years old, he began to be more comfortable with same-sex themes and produced a body of about fifty poems that has made him a significant inspiration for gay and bisexual writers. E. M. FORSTER, who met him during World War I while working for the Red Cross in Alexandria, introduced his work to the broader European public, and since then Cavafy has been discussed in essays by such writers as W. H. AUDEN and MARGUERITE YOURCENAR. His poetry has been translated by STEPHEN SPENDER, Kimon Friar, Edouard Roditi, and JAMES MERRILL. It has also inspired etchings by David Hockney (1966) and photographs of male nudes by Duane Michals (1978).

Although Cavafy avoids both rhyme and metaphor, he is not considered an easy poet to translate, partially because of his mixture of old and new word forms. Cavafy's 154 canonical poems are available in translations by John Mavrogordato (1951), Rae Dalven (1st ed. 1961), Edmund Keeley and Philip Sherrard (1975), and Memas Kolaitis (1988), and sizable selections have been issued by Kimon Friar (1973) and George Khairallah (1979). Of these, only the 1975 edition of Keeley/Sherrard is bilingual, and the 1993 reissue of it dispenses with the Greek originals, revises the translations, and abbreviates the notes. Peter Bien analyzes the work of many of these translators, noting that Khairallah's version is the most explicit sexually.

Cavafy's poems fall into three major categories: historical, philosophical, and erotic. However, there is much overlapping; some of the historical poems are erotic and vice versa. To the general public, the historical poems, particularly those related to the Hellenistic world of which Alexandria was the capital, constitute Cavafy's chief claim to fame. For these readers, his greatest poems are "The City" (written 1894), "Waiting for the Barbarians" (1898), "The God Abandons Antony" (1910), and "Ithaka" (1910). Deliberately rejecting Classical Greece in favor of a decadent Hellenism, Cavafy was especially inspired by the last days of the Ptolemies, Cleopatra, and her lover Marc Antony. These poems breathe an air of resignation and evince detachment from ideology and great historical events even as they also imply a kind of nostalgic pessimism. Cavafy's distinctive voice is implicated in his persistent sense of "outsiderness." Forster described him as conveying a sensation of standing "at a slight angle to the universe."

Gay male readers have had a particular interest in Cavafy's erotic poetry, which constitutes a considerable fraction of his canon. In the early poem "Candles" (written 1893), Cavafy expresses his fear that the days to come are now falling behind him like a gloomy line of burnt-out candles. The reader is allowed much latitude in interpretation, but one can see here a fear of losing the opportunity to live life to the fullest, perhaps through sexual repression. In "Walls" (1896), the poet complains that he has allowed walls to be built up around him, cutting him off from the outside world. The scenario for the poem is vague, but it can be read as representing Cavafy's complicity in allowing himself to repress his sensual side. "The Windows" (1897) presents the poet wandering around, hoping to find windows to his closed room, at the same time fearing that light may prove another tyranny.

Cavafy made a breakthrough in five poems from the period late 1893 to early 1904 that he chose not to publish. Although he does not give the gender of the beloved or sex partner (and this remains the case in much of his erotic poetry), the situations can be easily read in a gay male context. In "September, 1903," the poet is sad that he cannot raise up the courage to approach the dreamlike body of the one he desires. "December, 1903" notes that he cannot speak of his love; all he can acknowledge is that his beloved permeates his manner of speaking. In "January, 1904," the poet tries to remember his beloved but fails. This is just one of many poems in which the memory of the beloved seems at least as important as being with him. "On the Stairs" recounts a brief meeting between the poet and a man he could have picked up as they passed on the stairs of a house of ill fame. Neither was satisfied by the casual pleasures of the establishment, but neither had the courage to seek out the tenderness of the other. The poet of "At the Theater" comments on the beauty of the youth he sees during a performance, and he is just one of many handsome young men who populate Cavafy's erotic poetry. In "Growing in Spirit," written in June 1903, the poet had already declared that in order to develop emotionally one must pass beyond laws and customs. Such a person will learn from sensual pleasures and not grow timid before the destructive acts that tear half one's house down in order to build for the future.

In their notes to the unpublished poems selected for translation in *Passions and Ancient Days,* Keeley and Savidis quote from a note in English of November 25, 1903, first published in the primarily Greek-language volume, *Anekdota Peza* (*Unpublished Prose*), in which Cavafy indicates his love for A. M., or Alexander Mavroudis, a minor Athenian poet who later moved to Paris, where he became a playwright under the pen name of Alex Madis. Apparently, Cavafy fell in love with him "perhaps without telling" on his trip to Athens in 1903. The two-paragraph note associates "September, 1903" and "December, 1903" with his feelings for Mavroudis, mentions two other men he loved only as "Sul." and "Bra.," and connects the poems "Windows" and "Walls" to his romantic longings.

The twenty-one erotic poems of 1904 to 1915, which were published privately from 1912 to 1918, and then made available to the wider public in the first edition of the canonical poems, edited by Singopoulos in 1935, present sexual encounters that are sometimes fulfilling and sometimes unhappy. In "Come Back" (written 1904), the poet asks his beloved to return and take hold of him. "I Went" (1905) shows the speaker going to the world of forbidden pleasures. "One Night" (1907) juxtaposes the cheapness of a sordid room with the fleeting, intoxicating passion the poet experienced there. The later poem "Understanding" (1915) can also be related to this series. The poet looks back at the sensual life of his younger days and resists the temptation to regret his dissolute youth since in his loose living his work as a poet was founded. Cavafy's later erotic poetry continues to play variations on these same themes; it does not move in striking new directions. But the noncanonical "The

Bandaged Shoulder" (1919) is unique in its explicitness. The poet takes the bloody rag of a wounded soldier to his lips, for the blood confirms his love for the injured man. The voyeuristic "Days of 1908" (pub. 1932), the last erotic poem, is notable for the poet's evocation of the memory of a beautiful young man whom he watched strip naked for bathing. In many of the poems, the difference in ages between lover and beloved is pronounced. None of the poems concerns a mutual love or a committed partnership.

Cavafy's corpus of erotic poems was not widely known in English-speaking countries until Mavrogordato published the first complete translation of the canonical poems in 1951. Because Cavafy wrote in Greek, he is too often omitted from surveys of twentieth-century gay male literature. But such an omission is particularly unfortunate since Cavafy has written some of the greatest homoerotic poetry of all time. Although some of the poems indicate guilty feelings about sex and others portray a world of one-night stands in seedy quarters, the overall tone of the entire canon is one of acceptance of gay male sexuality and a recognition that personal and artistic creativity can spring from what the bourgeois world may consider decadent or unrewarding encounters. (See also GREEK LITERATURE, MODERN.)

—*Peter G. Christensen*

BIBLIOGRAPHY

Alexiou, Margaret. "Eroticism and Poetry." *Journal of the Hellenic Diaspora* [Special Cavafy issue] 10.1–2 (Spring–Summer 1983): 45–65. ■ Beaton, Roderick. "Cavafy and Proust." *Grand Street* 6.2 (Winter 1987): 127–141. ■ Bien, Peter. "Cavafy's Homosexuality and His Reputation Outside Greece." *Journal of Modern Greek Studies* 8.2 (Oct. 1990): 197–211. ■ Forster, E. M. "The Poetry of C. P. Cavafy." *Pharos and Pharillon.* Richmond: Surrey: Hogarth Press, 1923. 110–117. ■ Friar, Kimon. "Cavafis and His Translators into English." *Journal of the Hellenic Diaspora* 5 (Spring 1978): 17–40. ■ Harvey, Denise, ed. *The Mind and Art of C. P. Cavafy: Essays on His Life and Work.* Athens: Denise Harvey & Co., 1983. ■ Jusdanis, Gregory. *The Poetics of Cavafy: Textuality, Eroticism, History.* Princeton: Princeton University Press, 1987. ■ Kapre-Karka, K. *Love and the Symbolic Journey in the Poetry of Cavafy, Eliot, and Seferis: An Interpretation with Detailed Poem-by-Poem Analysis.* New York: Pella, 1982. ■ Keeley, Edmund. *Cavafy's Alexandria: Study of a Myth in Progress.* Cambridge, Mass.: Harvard University Press, 1976. ■ Liddell, Robert. *Cavafy: A Critical Biography.* London: Duckworth, 1974. ■ Lilly, Mark. "The Poems of Constantine Cavafy." *Gay Men's Literature in the Twentieth Century.* London: Macmillan, 1993. 33–52. ■ Michals, Duane. *Homage to Cavafy.* Danbury, N.H.: Addison House, 1978. ■ Pinchin, Jane Lagoudis. *Alexandria Still: Forster, Durrell, and Cavafy.* Princeton: Princeton University Press, 1977. ■ Robinson, Christopher. *C. P. Cavafy.* Bristol: Bristol Classical Press, 1988. ■ Yourcenar, Marguerite. "A Critical Introduction to Cavafy." *"The Dark Brain of Piranesi" and Other Essays.* Trans. Richard Howard. New York: Farrar, Straus, Giroux, 1984. 154–198.

Censorship

Traditional culture has typically tried to render homosexuality totally silent, as reflected in the long-standing stigma of homosexuality's "unspeakableness." The most famous expression of this notion in gay history is probably OSCAR WILDE's reference to same-sex love as "the love that dare not speak its name" in the first of his 1895 trials, a phrase he took from Lord Alfred Douglas's 1894 poem, "Two Loves." But the claim has a long and continuing life. In the post-classical West, it was first voiced, as far we know now, in the twelfth century, in Peter Cantor's tract, "On Sodomy," where he denounces "intercourse of men with men and women with women" as "ignominious and unspeakable," and it continues into the present, as reflected in the "don't ask, don't tell" policy recently adopted toward gays in the American military. One chief expression of this stigma of homosexuality's total "unspeakableness" has been the censorship of homosexual writing, a censorship that has taken three main forms: government, institutional, or commercial censorship; censorship of homosexual content or of an author's homosexuality by later editors, translators, critics, or biographers; and self-censorship by homosexual writers themselves. Although censorship of heterosexual writing has also occurred, traditional culture's double standard about heterosexuality and homosexuality has applied here as everywhere else. For example, though *some* heterosexual representation (such as graphic sexual portrayals) has been declared obscene and unpublishable, traditionally *any* homosexual depiction, including plain statements of love, has been labeled iniquitous.

This subject has been unexplored until now, and space only permits mention of some highlights. But, from the present evidence, we find concerted instances of the second kind of censoring from at least the early Renaissance onward. Ficino's Latin translation and commentary on the *Symposium* (1469), at the start of the Renaissance rediscovery of PLATO, is one of the earliest records we have of censorship of homosexual writing by later editors, translators, critics, or biographers. Though accurately indicating the male–male nature of the love in the *Symposium,* Ficino completely spiritualized that love, erasing the eroticism in the Greek original. More blatantly, later in the Renaissance Michelangelo the Younger heterosexualized MICHELANGELO's romantic poems to other males when he prepared his grand-uncle's poems for their first collected edition in 1623, changing all the "he"'s to "she"'s and omitting other "incriminating" texts—for example, reducing from fifty to five the set of passionate memorial poems Michelangelo wrote about Checchino Bracci in 1544. An accurate version of Michelangelo's poems did not appear until Cesare Gausti's edition of 1863. At around the same time, in the "Love-Melancholy" section of his *Anatomy of Melancholy* (first three editions, 1621, 1624, 1628), Robert Burton rendered all of his examples of same-sex love in Latin, while leaving his surrounding discussion of male–female eroticism in English. A few years later, in 1640, John Benson performed the same operation on SHAKESPEARE as Michelangelo's grand-nephew had on him, heterosexualizing the *Sonnets* in the first collected edition of Shakespeare's poems. This falsified text remained the only available version of the *Sonnets* for 140 years.

The first English translations of Plato, Floyer Sydenham's of 1761–1767 and Thomas Taylor's of 1804, far surpassed Ficino's changes. For instance, Sydenham completely heterosexualized the text, making Plato's "army of lovers" an army of knights and ladies. As soon as the accurate text of Shakespeare's *Sonnets* was restored in the late eighteenth century, scholars systematically began to deny their homosexuality, a tradition that dominated Shakespeare criticism until the 1980s. For example, in 1799, George Chalmers claimed that Sonnet 20, the famous "Master Mistress" sonnet, "has no appearance of obscenity, if it be chastely examined, without listening to the suggestions of *platonism*." GERARD MANLEY HOPKINS's references to his attraction to Digby Mackworth Dolben and other men in his journal for 1865 were expurgated by the first editor of his *Journals and Papers;* a faithful text did not appear until 1989. In excluding almost all of Hopkins's early work from the first edition of Hopkins's poems, his executor Robert Bridges made special note of Hopkins's romantic 1865 poems about Dolben, writing in the margin of his autograph copy of "The Beginning of the End" that the first and third sonnets in that sequence "must *never* be printed"; they were not included until the third edition of 1948.

Along with the Shakespeare of the *Sonnets,* WALT WHITMAN is the other major writer in English who has experienced the most blatant heterosexualizing by later commentators. Starting not long after his death in 1892, with scholars like Emory Holloway leading the way and aided by Whitman's own disavowal, the tradition of critical denial of Whitman's homosexuality did not significantly lessen until the work of openly gay Whitman scholars from the late 1970s onward. TENNYSON's *In Memoriam A. H. H.* was read homosexually by several critics when it appeared in 1850, and when Hallam Tennyson published his biography of his father in 1897, he omitted all commentary that might have suggested homosexuality in him. For example, he deleted Benamin Jowett's remark, an allusion to Shakespeare's *Sonnets,* that "The love of the sonnets which he so strikingly expressed was a sort of sympathy with Hellenism." In the same year, after the first English publication of JOHN ADDINGTON SYMONDS's and Havelock Ellis's *Sexual Inversion,* Symonds's scandalized family had his name removed from all future editions. When the long letter Oscar Wilde wrote to Alfred Douglas from prison in early 1897 was first published under the title of *De Profundis* in 1905, the editor omitted all references to Douglas and their love affair; a full and accurate text did not appear until 1962. An especially painful example of a similar kind of censoring closer to the present is MAY SARTON's 1955 novel, *Faithful Are the Wounds,* a fictionalizing of the life and suicide of the critic F. O. MATTHIESSEN. Here, in what could be called a case of "compound closeting," a closeted lesbian writer "re-closets" an already camouflaged gay man by making no reference to Matthiessen's homosexuality and to the role that the death of his lover Russell Cheney played in his suicide, proposing instead that Matthiessen's stresses were all professional and political (the accepted public explanation at the time of his death in 1950).

Most homosexual writing before the early twentieth century could be thought of as in part an exercise in self-censorship. Reflecting the danger of open homosexual expression, earlier authors who published about their homosexuality typically had to write indirectly, and some avoided writing about the subject altogether. However, I limit my discussion here to more pointed forms of self-censorship in which homosexual authors withheld frank homosexual writing from publication or actually erased the homosexual content from their texts or publicly denied their homosexuality. Concerted instances of this kind of censorship also appear from at least the Renaissance onward. For example, Michelangelo the Younger may have felt justified in his later bowdlerizing by the fact that Michelangelo himself "de-homosexualized" some of his poems in draft, changing the addressee from male to female (for example, poems 230 and 246) or from male to unspecified gender (for example, poem 259). The most notable example of homosexual self-censorship in the eighteenth century is JEREMY BENTHAM's 1785 draft essay on "Paederasty," which he withheld from publication out of fear that "I should expose my personal interest so much to hazard as it must be . . . by the free discussion of a subject of this nature"; the essay did not appear until 1978. Bentham did the same with an even longer and unfinished set of writings defending same-sex sexuality that he composed between 1814 and 1818, the chief of which is a 309-page manuscript entitled "Not Paul but Jesus"; only a brief excerpt from these documents has ever been published.

As scholars have uncovered, BYRON's 1811–1812 "Thyrza" poems, addressed to a woman, are camouflaged memorials to the chorister John Edlestone, with whom Byron had fallen in love while at Cambridge and who had recently died from consumption. The best-known example of homosexual self-censorship in nineteenth-century American literature is Whitman's heterosexualizing of the text of "Once I Pass'd through a Populous City," from his 1860 *Children of Adam* collection—the "woman" who "passionately clung" to him in the poem's published version is a "man" in Whitman's manuscript. An even more blatant example of the same impulse in Whitman was his denial of his homosexuality in an 1890 letter to John Addington Symonds, who had been prodding him about the matter in correspondence since 1871, soon after first reading the transparently homosexual *Calamus* poems (1860). Whitman asserts that the "morbid inferences" Symonds was drawing from *Calamus* "are disavow'd by me & seem damnable. . . . That the calamus part has even allow'd the possibility of such construction as mention'd is terrible," and he ends by proclaiming his incontestable heterosexuality: "Tho' always unmarried, I have had six children."

Though uniquely courageous in broaching the subject of homosexuality in several of his published works, Symonds himself kept his most extended, frank discussions of homosexuality private, either by limiting them to private circulation or by withholding them from publication in his lifetime. For example, *A Problem in Greek Ethics,* Symonds's first extended defense of homosexuality, was first drafted in 1873, but only appeared in public print after his death, as "Appendix A" in the first edition of *Sexual Inversion.* Even more tellingly, Symonds left unpublished at the time of his death the pathbreaking *Memoirs* he wrote between 1889 and 1893, the first self-conscious ho-

mosexual autobiography known to us now; he left instructions for preservation of the manuscript, however, and it was finally published in 1984. After the critical dispute about his 1873 *Studies in the History of the Renaissance,* when he published a second edition in 1877 WALTER PATER omitted the especially controversial "Conclusion," where he had listed "the face of one's friend" as one possible source of "exquisite passion"; Pater restored the "Conclusion" in the third edition of 1888, however. A. E. HOUSMAN's two books of poems, his famous *A Shropshire Lad* (1896) and *Last Poems* (1922), contain some coded homosexual statements; at the same time, Housman left unpublished a number of frank manuscript poems about his unrequited love for Moses Jackson, his relationship with Jackson's brother Adalbert, and the Oscar Wilde trials. Housman left these to his executor, his brother Laurence, who was also homosexual, and they were published posthumously in the late 1930s.

GERTRUDE STEIN's frankest lesbian work is her first completed novel, *Q.E.D.* (1903), about a love triangle in which she was enmeshed with two other women medical students at Johns Hopkins. Stein "forgot" about the manuscript after completing it, but "rediscovered" it among her papers in 1932. *Q.E.D.* remained suppressed until after Stein's death, however; a slightly altered version appeared in 1950, and its full original text was not published until 1971. The best-known example of self-withholding by a twentieth-century homosexual writer is probably E. M. FORSTER's 1914 *Maurice,* which, as he indicates in his "Terminal Note," Forster felt was unpublishable at the time because of the legal situation for homosexuals in England then; *Maurice* was finally published in 1971, a year after Forster's death. When D. H. LAWRENCE published *Women in Love* in 1920, he omitted a "Prologue" he had written for the novel in 1916, in which Rupert Birkin's homosexuality is much more prominent than in the final version—for example, "It was for men that he felt the hot, flushing roused attraction which a man is supposed to feel for the other sex." The "Prologue" was finally printed, separately, in 1963.

The most famous sexual transposition in twentieth-century Western literature involves Albertine of MARCEL PROUST's *Remembrance of Things Past,* who first appears in Part II of the novel, *Within a Budding Grove* (1918). Unlike in simple pronoun substitutions, Albertine is not just a camouflaged male, nor should her relationship with the narrator be seen as a homosexual one in disguise. But Proust did tell ANDRÉ GIDE in 1921 that the Albertine strand of the *Remembrance* is a transposition of his homosexual experience, and scholars have noted the many emotional and factual parallels between Marcel's pursuit of Albertine and Proust's relationship with his chauffeur/secretary, Alfred Agostinelli; echoes of Proust's affair with the composer Reynaldo Hahn have also been cited. Among the papers Nigel Nicolson found carefully preserved after the death of his mother, VITA SACK-VILLE-WEST, is a frank autobiographical lesbian manuscript of 1920–1921, detailing her affair with Violet Trefusis and defending "the psychology of people like myself"; it appears as Parts I and III of Nicolson's 1973 *Portrait of a Marriage*. While only hinting at his homosexuality in his best-selling fiction (such as the story "Adolescence" in *Good-Bye Wisconsin* [1928]), Glenway Wescott kept a frank homosexual journal from 1937 until the 1950s. Focusing extensively on Wescott's relationships with lovers and fellow homosexual artists, including Monroe Wheeler, George Platt Lynes, and Paul Cadmus, the manuscript was not published until 1990, under the title *Continual Lessons*.

Gaps especially exist in our knowledge of earlier government, institutional, and commercial censorship of homosexual writing. Frank homosexual works may have been among the materials consigned to Savonarola's "Bonfires of Vanities" in the 1490s and to other public burnings of offensive materials in the Renaissance. We do know that in 1689 two British booksellers were convicted of obscenity for selling the Earl of ROCHESTER's *Sodom: or, The Quintessence of Debauchery* (first published in Antwerp in 1684), where the sodomy is almost entirely male–male. Additionally, JOHN CLELAND's *Memoirs of a Woman of Pleasure* or *Fanny Hill*, which has some frank homosexuality among its chiefly heterosexual adventures, was banned as obscene upon its publication in 1749. However, from our present knowledge, signs of a concerted tradition of government, institutional, or commercial censorship of homosexual writing do not appear in the West until approximately the mid-nineteenth century, almost 400 years after the traditions of editorial censorship and self-censorship among homosexual writers first become evident.

An arguable symbol of this turn is the 1857 conviction of CHARLES BAUDELAIRE and his publisher for an "outrage aux bonnes moeurs" with his *Les Fleurs du Mal*, resulting in a fine and the mandated removal of six poems from the book (a ban that was not officially lifted until 1949). Baudelaire seems to have been heterosexual, and only a few homosexual poems (all concerning lesbianism) appear amid the book's mainly heterosexual materials. But homosexuality seems to have been a chief issue in the book's prosecution since the ban involved a much larger proportion of homosexual than heterosexual pieces—three of the six proscribed poems involve frank lesbianism ("Lesbos" and "Damned Women") or the suggestion of bisexuality or hermaphroditism ("Jewels"). A related case of commercial censorship occurred in England in the next decade, of a book strongly influenced by Baudelaire, ALGERNON CHARLES SWINBURNE's 1866 *Poems and Ballads*. The publisher voluntarily withdrew *Poems and Ballads* from circulation a month after it appeared, in response to hostile reviewers and a campaign to indict it for obscenity led by a Christian Socialist spokesman; here the ire was directed almost entirely at the book's homosexual poems (again all involving lesbianism) and at those suggesting male bisexuality. However, Swinburne soon found another publisher (though one with a somewhat tainted reputation because of its sideline in erotica), and the demand for prosecution faded when leading literary figures would not support it.

Less lucky later in the century was Havelock Ellis, like Baudelaire a heterosexual with an interest in homosexuality (an interest intensified by the fact that his wife was a lesbian). In 1887, Ellis's publisher withdrew the volume of Marlowe he had edited for the Mermaid series of British dramatists because he had included as an appendix the famous "Baines Note," in which a contemporary informer reports Marlowe saying that "all they that love not tobacco and boys were fools." Of greater magnitude was the 1898 prosecution of a London bookseller for selling *Sexual Inversion*, labeled in the charge as "lewd, wicked, bawdy, scandalous, and obscene." Ellis himself was never indicted, and the bookseller got off with a fine and a promise never to "touch this filthy work again," but the scandal blocked Ellis from ever getting an English publisher for the rest of the *Studies in the Psychology of Sex*, which had to be published abroad. In 1915, D. H. Lawrence's *The Rainbow* was prosecuted for obscenity, chiefly because of its lesbian scenes, and the publisher cooperated with the police by allowing its remaining copies to be destroyed. The scandal made it difficult for Lawrence to find publishers for some time and no doubt influenced his decision to suppress his original "Prologue" to *Women in Love*. The best-known of these scandals in the twentieth-century is undoubtedly the 1928 English prosecution of RADCLYFFE HALL's *The Well of Loneliness*, whose publisher (though not author) was brought to trial under the Obscene Publications Act. Though many distinguished writers spoke in support of the book, conviction was won, and all the remaining copies were seized and burned. When *The Well of Loneliness* was issued in the United States the next year, its publisher was similarly charged and convicted. The conviction was overturned on appeal, however, and *The Well of Loneliness* was available in America from 1929 on; the book was not republished in Britain until 1949, when the government made no attempt to enforce the still-extant ban.

Homosexual materials were prominent in the rash of Nazi book burnings across Germany in the spring of 1933. Indeed, one of the first targets was Magnus Hirschfeld's Institute for Sexual Science in Berlin, which was looted and its library destroyed. In the same year, Charles Henri Ford and Parker Tyler's frankly gay novel, *The Young and Evil,* was published in Paris by the alternative Obelisk Press; when copies were shipped to England and the United States, they were seized by customs and refused entry. (An Olympia Press reprint did make its way into the United States in 1960.) The New York Society for the Suppression of Vice tried to have André Gide's autobiography *If It Die* declared obscene in 1936, concentrating on the book's homosexual passages and bringing suit against the Gotham Book Mart for selling it; the New York court declared that the book was not obscene, however. JEAN GENET's work also faced many censorship problems. In 1943, for example, the first publisher of *Our Lady of the Flowers* planned to issue the book without his imprint and even without Genet's name. In 1956, Genet was actually convicted of pornography for having published two works in 1948 that were "in contempt of morality," a poem called "The Galley" and the novel *Querelle.* By that time, however, both works were in print in the Gallimard edition of Genet's works; his eight months' sentence was suspended, and he seems not to have paid his 100,000 francs fine.

MARY RENAULT published *The Charioteer,* her frank novel of contemporary male homosexuality, in England in 1953, but her American publisher, William Morrow, refused to bring it out in the United States at the same time for fear of prosecution; the book was finally published in the United States six years later, by Pantheon. Copies of ALLEN GINSBERG's *Howl* (1956) were seized by San Francisco police at City Lights Bookstore in 1957, and the book was prosecuted as "indecent" under a California law. In a much-publicized trial, several prominent literary figures testified for the book, and the court ruled it not obscene. In the same year, a federal district court ruled that the early homophile magazine *One* was obscene and thus could not be sent through the mails. The ruling was upheld by an appellate court, but the United States Supreme Court reversed the decision in 1958. In 1963, JAMES BALDWIN's 1962 novel *Another Country,* with homosexuality prominent in its action, was banned as obscene by the New Orleans Public Library; after extensive litigation, it was restored to the shelves the next year. Originally published in Paris in 1959, WILLIAM S. BURROUGHS's *Naked Lunch,* whose sexuality is almost entirely homosexual, was seized by Boston police on its first American publication in 1962 and finally declared obscene by a Boston court in 1965; the Massachusetts Supreme Court reversed the ban on appeal in 1966, however. In 1976, on the basis of his privately circulated homosexual poems and letters, Gennady Trifonov, the only openly gay poet in the former Soviet Union, was sentenced to four years at hard labor under Article 121 of the Soviet criminal code, which prohibited homosexuality. Released in 1980, Trifonov was repeatedly denied an exit visa, and in 1986 was threatened with imprisonment again. He ultimately reversed himself painfully, publishing in 1989 what was in effect a turncoat article, in which he denounced Russian homosexual writing and other Russian homosexual authors (this despite the improved conditions at the time under Gorbachev).

In the West, progress has clearly been made for homosexuals since the start of the contemporary gay liberation movement in 1969, but instances of legal, institutional, or commercial censorship have nevertheless occurred since then. In 1977, a British jury convicted *Gay News* and its editor Denis Lemon for publishing, in June 1976, James Kirkup's poem "The Love That Dares to Speak its Name," in which a Roman soldier and Christ make love. The charge was for blasphemy rather than obscenity, but the issue was clearly the poem's frank homosexuality; the paper was fined 1,000 pounds and faced costs of 20,000 pounds, while its editor was fined 500 pounds and jailed for nine months. In the United States, the best-known recent government and institutional censorship has involved the visual and performing arts—for example, the Corcoran Gallery's cancellation of its Robert Mapplethorpe show in the summer of 1989; the National Endowment for the Arts' withdrawal of funds from the New York AIDS art show "Witnesses: Against Our Vanishing" in November 1989, partly because it included images of homosexual acts (reversed later in the month after opposition from the arts community); and the NEA's denial of grants in June 1990 to four performance artists known for the sexual content of their work, three of whom—Holly Hughes, John Fleck, and Tim Miller—were lesbian or gay. Commercial pressures have been put on American gay writing as well. For example, a few weeks before its May 1993 New York opening, the producer of Tony Kushner's eventual hit, *Angels in America,* asked him to remove the subtitle— "A Gay Fantasia on National Themes"—from the play, but relented when he refused.

In Canada, the February 1992 Supreme Court ruling that expanded the definition of obscenity to include words and images that degrade or exploit women and other groups has led to an explosion of censorship against gay and lesbian writing, chiefly through seizure of foreign materials by customs officials. About one quarter of the books sent from the United States to the largest gay and lesbian bookstore in Toronto have been regularly seized, and among the noted homosexual authors who have had works thus banned are JANE RULE, DAVID LEAVITT, Albert Innaurato, and Jean Genet.

At present, the censorship of homosexuality by later commentators survives chiefly in the academic world. Textbooks and anthologies, for example, often simply fail to mention the sexual orientation of gay and lesbian writers, even when that orientation is crucial to the literature being presented. More subtly, the "new-inventionist" movement that currently dominates gay studies, which argues that homosexuality is a relatively new historical invention and which denies the earlier existence of homosexuality and homosexuals, threatens to be a new form of censorship by stigmatizing scholarship that argues to the contrary and by excluding premodern materials from its curricula. The current movement to reshape "gay studies" as "queer studies" seems to involve a related silencing of homosexuality by deemphasizing it as a subject in favor of marginality of all kinds. Finally, with the greater self-respect made possible by the gay liberation movement and less material jeopardy because of legal changes self-censorship among Western homosexual authors has become rare, though a few distinguished authors who are gay or lesbian still dissociate themselves completely from the subject.

These patterns of censorship, and the larger insistence on homosexuality's "unspeakableness" that they express, carry important implications for the study of gay history. For example, in clearly indicating that traditional culture's preferred situation for homosexuality is silence, they caution against the current trend in the history of sexuality to link a culture's awareness of homosexuality to its possession of a precise language for homosexuality. On the contrary, this evidence suggests paradoxically that silence itself is traditional culture's first language for homosexuality and that a culture's lack of terminology for homosexuality can actually be a sign of that culture's

awareness of homosexuality. In addition, the apparent 400-year lag between the legal censorship and the other kinds of censorship discussed here cautions against giving too much weight to legal evidence in the study of gay history. Although "new inventionism" credits the first appearance of laws directed specifically at homosexuality in the late nineteenth century with a major role in "inventing" homosexuality, the evidence here suggests that legal targeting of homosexuality does not so much reflect the first "existence" or awareness of homosexuality in a culture as indicate that a culture's earlier and more diffuse means of controlling homosexuality are breaking down and need buttressing. The period when we first see a concerted tradition of legal censorship of homosexual writing emerging in the West, the mid-nineteenth century, is also the period when marked loosenings began to occur in the traditions of editorial censorship and self-censorship that the dominant culture had earlier counted on to keep homosexual writing silent.

—*Joseph Cady*

BIBLIOGRAPHY

Cady, Joseph. "'Masculine Love,' Renaissance Writing, and the 'New Invention' of Homosexuality." *Homosexuality in Renaissance and Enlightenment England: Literary Representations in Historical Context.* Claude J. Summers, ed. New York: Haworth Press, 1992. ■ Crompton, Louis. *Byron and Greek Love: Homophobia in 19th-Century England.* Berkeley: University of California Press, 1985. ■ Green, Jonathan. *Encyclopedia of Censorship.* New York: Facts on File, 1990. ■ Grosskurth, Phyllis. *Havelock Ellis.* New York: Knopf, 1980. ■ Haight, Anne Lyon and Chandler B. Grannis. *Banned Books, 387 BC to 1978 AD.* 4th ed. New York: Bowker, 1978. ■ Hurwitz, Leon. *Historical Dictionary of Censorship in the United States.* Westport, Conn.: Greenwood, 1985. ■ Martin, Robert Bernard. *Gerard Manley Hopkins: A Very Private Life.* New York: Putnam's, 1991. ■ Martin, Robert K. *The Homosexual Tradition in American Poetry.* Austin: University of Texas Press, 1979. ■ Ricks, Christopher. *Tennyson.* New York: Macmillan, 1972. ■ Rivers, J. E. *Proust and the Art of Love.* New York: Columbia University Press, 1980. ■ Rollins, Hyder E., ed. *A New Variorum Edition of Shakespeare: The Sonnets,* 2 vols. Philadelphia: Lippincott, 1944. ■ Saslow, James M. *The Poetry of Michelangelo: An Annotated Translation.* New Haven: Yale University Press, 1991. ■ White, Edmund. *Genet.* New York: Knopf, 1993.

Cernuda, Luis
(1902–1963)

Luis Cernuda was born in Seville, Spain, on September 21, 1902. He earned a law degree at the University of Seville, but he dedicated himself

professionally to literature. He became a literary critic and a professor. Something of a dandy, Cernuda always dressed in elegant clothes. He was a solitary figure, with a somewhat complex and acerbic personality. In earlier criticism of his work, much is made of this "difficult" personality though this characterization may have been in part a rejection of his homosexuality, which was never mentioned directly.

Cernuda is part of the much-praised Spanish "Generation of 1927." For a time, he was obscured by the more famous members of this movement, but recently his reputation as a poet has grown. He is now recognized as one of Spain's most important twentieth-century poets.

Cernuda's awakening to his own sexuality appears to have coincided with his interest in poetry. Through his poetry, he came to accept his homosexuality as an essential part of his being and even to document some of his love affairs. In his early years, surrealism was the means by which he could express his homosexuality directly, but not explicitly; the veils of surrealism enabled him to bypass his own internal inhibitions. Later in life, he would express his sexuality openly.

In his poems, Cernuda is preoccupied with love, which he views always in erotic terms. For Cernuda, desire and sexuality are life itself although social hypocrisy has forced us to deny this truth. The object of his love is often a mere creation of his desire, an erotic ideal. The poet becomes frustrated when his personal desires confront objective reality although he also senses that what makes the ideal valuable is that it remain unattainable. His romantic failures were seen by him as the result of social hostility toward homosexuality. The only way for desire to become reality would be to create a romantic ideal beyond society's reach.

Cernuda's poetry also speaks of a divided self. The conflict with society due to his homosexuality is translated into a conflict between the self and surrounding reality. Since ideal love is not to be found in another, but rather in the self, the search for love becomes a voyage of self-discovery. This search is particularly poignant for the homosexual, whose love is denied open expression within society. Cernuda believes that physical love can help us overcome our sense of isolation and breach the division between reality and desire.

Cernuda saw his homosexuality as a threat to society and accepted the role of the outsider who is justified in attacking those who have violently rejected him. As a young poet, Cernuda was politically committed against a society he found decrepit and deformed. His resentment in part stemmed from the repression he felt within his family and eventually led him to assume the role of exile and rebel. After the Spanish Civil War, Cernuda went into political exile, first in England, then in the United States, and finally, in Mexico. He died in Mexico in November 1963.

—*María Dolores Costa*

BIBLIOGRAPHY

Edkins, Anthony, and Derek Harris. *The Poetry of Luis Cernuda.* New York: New York University Press, 1971. ■ Jiménez-Fajardo, Salvador. *Luis Cernuda.* Boston: Twayne Publishers, 1978. ■ ———. *The Word and the Mirror: Critical Essays on the Poetry of Luis Cernuda.* London: Associated University Presses, 1989. ■ Polo, Milagros. "El erotismo en Cernuda, Alberti y Biedma." *Eros literaria: Actas del coloquio celebrado en la Facultad de Filología de la Universidad Complutense en diciembre de 1988.* Madrid: Universidad Complutense, 1989. 341–354. ■ Ramos Otero, Manuel. "La ética de la marginación en la poesía de Luis Cernuda." *Cupey* 1–2 (enero–diciembre): 16–29. ■ Silver, Philip. *"Et in Arcadia Ego": A Study of the Poetry of Luis Cernuda.* London: Tamesis Books, 1965. ■ Talens, Jenaro. *El espacio y las máscaras: Introducción a la lectura de Cernuda.* Barcelona: Editorial Anagrama, 1975.

Chambers, Jane
(1937–1983)

Jane Chambers was born Carolyn Jane Chambers in Columbia, South Carolina, on March 27, 1937. She spent her early years in Orlando, Florida, where she began her writing career with scripts for local public radio stations. In 1954, Chambers entered Rollins College in Winter Park, Florida, intent on becoming a playwright. This was a very frustrating time for her, however. As she told the *New York Times* in a 1981 interview, "When I went to college women were not allowed in the playwriting or directing courses unless there were seats left over after the men signed up." The frustration caused Chambers to leave Rollins in 1956 in order to study acting at California's Pasadena Playhouse for a season. The following year she moved to New York City.

Chambers stayed in New York for a brief time and then moved to Poland Spring, Maine, to work for TV station WMTW. In 1968, she returned to New York. Soon thereafter, Chambers, interested in completing her undergraduate degree, enrolled in Goddard College, Vermont. While at Goddard, she met Beth Allen, who was to become her lover, manager, and devoted lifelong companion.

Chambers completed her degree at Goddard in 1971. During this period, she also began to gain acceptance as a professional writer and to solidify her reputation as a playwright. In 1971, she received the Rosenthal Award for Poetry and a Connecticut Educational Television Award for her play *Christ in a Treehouse,* and in 1972, she was the recipient of a Eugene O'Neill Fellowship for her play *Tales of the Revolution and Other American Fables,* which was produced at the Eugene O'Neill Memorial Theatre in Connecticut. It was also during this time that Chambers began to work with the Women's Interart Center in New York City. She was instrumental in establishing the theater program at Interart, and the first piece produced at the Center was her *Random Violence* (1972). In the early 1970s, Chambers also wrote for the CBS-TV soap opera "Search for Tomorrow," for which she received a Writer's Guild of America Award in 1973.

In 1974 Playwrights Horizons in New York produced *A Late Snow.* The play, which portrays openly lesbian characters who spend two eventful days while stranded together during a snowfall, was to become one of Chambers's best known. It was one of the first plays to depict lesbians in a positive light and gained Chambers a reputation for being an important lesbian playwright.

In 1980, Chambers began working with The Glines, a New York company that focused on plays representing gay and lesbian experience. Chambers wrote *Last Summer at Bluefish Cove* for their First Gay American Arts Festival. The play centers on a character who has been diagnosed with terminal cancer and the impact this has on her and her lesbian friends who vacation together every summer. Chambers wrote *Bluefish Cove* after one of her own friends had died from cancer; it was to take on a very ironic tone, however, when Chambers herself was diagnosed with the disease in 1981.

Throughout the next two years, Chambers continued to write and went on to produce *My Blue Heaven*

for the Glines Second Gay American Arts Festival and *The Quintessential Image* for the Women's Theatre Conference in Minneapolis. In 1982, Chambers was a recipient of the Fund for Human Dignity award.

Chambers died on February 15, 1983, in her Greenport, Long Island, home. Beth Allen subsequently published a collection of her poetry as a memorial to her courage and spirit. The Women in Theatre Program of the Association for Theatre in Higher Education honored Chambers by creating the Jane Chambers Playwriting Award to encourage the writing of plays that reflect women's experience.

Chambers was one of the first playwrights to create openly lesbian characters who were comfortable with their own homosexuality. She believed that this would help eliminate homophobia. As Chambers told the *New York Times,* "As we become more comfortable with ourselves, the rest of the world will become comfortable with us." She opened the door for other playwrights who wished to write affirming plays about lesbians. (See also DRAMATIC LITERATURE: CONTEMPORARY DRAMA.)

—*Beth A. Kattelman*

BIBLIOGRAPHY

Feminist Companion to Literature in English: Women Writers from the Middle Ages to the Present. Virginia Blain, Patricia Clements, Isobel Grundy, eds. New Haven: Yale University Press, 1990. 192–193. ■ Gavin, Christy. *American Women Playwrights 1964–1989: A Research Guide and Annotated Bibliography.* New York: Garland Publishing, 1993. ■ Holden, Stephen. "Comedy of Self-Acceptance and a Portrait of Its Writer." *New York Times* 17 Aug. 1989, late ed.: C18. ■ Klein, Alvin. "Play's Theme: Lesbians Without Apology." *New York Times* 8 Feb. 1981: 21:15. ■ Landau, Penny M. "Jane Chambers: In Memoriam." *Women and Performance.* 1.2 (1984): 55–56. ■ ———. "Jane Chambers." *Notable Women in the American Theatre: A Biographical Dictionary.* Alice M. Robinson, Vera Mowry, and Milly S. Barranger, eds. New York: Greenwood Press, 1989. 117.

Chaucer, Geoffrey
(134?–1400)

Born into a family of wealthy London wine merchants in the early 1340s, Geoffrey Chaucer devoted his life to public service and to the writing of poetry. Despite his nonliterary commitments, Chaucer generated a substantial amount of poetry, not to mention scientific and religious treatises. By the end of his career, he had revised the French and Italian models on which much Middle

English literature, including his early work, heavily depended and had succeeded in using them to develop a native English tradition. It is for this reason that he was known to his followers as the father of English poetry. According to Chaucer's tombstone in Westminster Abbey, he died October 25, 1400.

To understand the relationship between Chaucer's writings and gay and lesbian literary history, it is necessary to know something about the late Middle Ages. In this period, though homosocial bonding (intense emotional friendships among people of the same sex) was considered a positive phenomenon, homosexual activity or sodomy (also known as the "crime against nature" or the "unnatural vice") and same-sex erotic desire were severely proscribed. In England, such homophobic attitudes, promulgated in particular by the Catholic Church, informed not only popular sentiment but also legislative attitudes: Although no secular law against sodomy was instituted there until the sixteenth century, two unofficial English legal treatises from the late thirteenth and early fourteenth centuries recommended that sodomites be put to death because of their nefarious deeds. This information does not mean that since sodomy was officially condemned there was no homosexual activity (there was, even among people we would today consider heterosexual) nor that homosexual desire was understood only in terms of sexual acts—some people evidently experienced it as meaning much more though the idea of something like a modern "gay" culture and sense of self had not yet fully developed. What it does mean, however, is that when sodomy and sodomites are represented in the period's literature, which generally reflects official moral and social doctrine on this issue, they are placed in a negative light.

In this respect, Chaucer's work differs little from that of other medieval English writers. Though most of his extant writings do not mention sodomy at all, his final but incomplete text, *The Canterbury Tales,* does. Written as a collection of stories told by late fourteenth-century English pilgrims en route to Canterbury Cathedral, *The Canterbury Tales* uses male homosexual relations and desire as a means to cast moral judgments on and to satirize characters in the text. (As in much medieval literature, homosexual issues concerning women are conspicuously absent.) "The General Prologue," the *Tales'* opening narrative, makes certain that its two most scurrilous male characters, the Summoner (who falsely summons people to ecclesiastical court and extorts them) and the Pardoner (who sells questionable indulgences and false relics), will be understood disapprovingly by portraying them as engaged in a homosexual relationship. Besides describing the Pardoner as a castrated, or even a female, horse—slang references probably indicating the passive recipient in anal intercourse and thus a male who disrupts medieval gender categories—the text notes that the Summoner sings the bass vocal part of a love song with the Pardoner. Though singing with another male friend could simply be a homosocial act, the words for the bass part are also a double entendre meaning erect penis and strongly

imply a sexual relationship in which, as medieval discussions of sodomy would have described it, the Summoner plays the active "male" role to the Pardoner's passive "female" one. Since only descriptions of the most evil characters are constructed through homosexual allusions, these negative representations cut two ways: Just as sodomy undermines these two unsavory pilgrims, the association of sodomy with them reinforces the proscription against the "unnatural vice."

Three of the tales following "The General Prologue" employ sodomy as a satirical means to disparage one's rivals and to gain advantage or control over others. In each story, the efficacy of this satire depends on—and strengthens—the medieval conception of homosexual activity as defamatory, immoral, and dishonorable. In the prologue to his tale, the Miller warns the Reeve, who has objected to the story, against prying into the private affairs of one's wife or of God. Since the term for private affairs is also a pun meaning genitalia, the Miller implies that improper spiritual inquiry is a metaphorical type of sodomy (prying into God's "privates") and thus successfully silences the Reeve. And in the tale proper, which is a parody of that told by the Knight, the Miller mocks his social better by transforming the homosocial bonds and rivalry between two of the Knight's noble characters, Palamon and Arcite, into the symbolic anal rape of the student Nicholas by the parish clerk Absolon. "The Summoner's Prologue and Tale" employs a similar type of parody, for the Summoner insinuates that it is his rival the Friar who is a sodomite, thus disparaging both the mendicant and his religious organization. The prologue transforms the traditional idea of friars residing under the Virgin's heavenly cloak in the afterlife and places them instead in the devil's infernal anus; moreover, the many phallic puns found in the tale and its description of the greedy friar groping around a sick man's anus in search of a reward uses sodomitical allusions to deflate further the Friar's social and spiritual standing. Finally, as a penitential tract, "The Parson's Tale" provides the concluding word on the subject of same-sex sexual relations. By characterizing sodomy as an unmentionably evil sin, it supplies theological justification to the proscriptive social, moral, and spiritual attitudes underwriting the uses of homosexual imagery and themes in the *Tales* as a whole.

Although the *Canterbury Tales* is periodically radical and frequently quite wonderful, the attitudes displayed toward homosexual activity and desire are in keeping with the homophobic traditional mores and values of its time. As such, however, Chaucer's poetry provides important literary evidence of the late medi-

eval roots of what would become modern homosexual oppression. (See also ENGLISH LITERATURE: MEDIEVAL.)
—*David Lorenzo Boyd*

BIBLIOGRAPHY

Boswell, John. *Christianity, Social Tolerance, and Homosexuality.* Chicago: University of Chicago Press, 1980. ■ Bowden, Muriel. *A Commentary on the General Prologue to The Canterbury Tales.* 2nd. ed. London: Souvenir Press, 1973. ■ Boyd, David Lorenzo. *Sodomy, Silence, and Social Control in Middle English Literature* (forthcoming). ■ Burger, Glenn. "Kissing the Pardoner." *PMLA* 107 (1992): 1143–1156. ■ Dinshaw, Caroline. *Straight is the Gate: The Heterosexual Subject of Medieval Narrative* (forthcoming). ■ Goodich, Michael. *The Unmentionable Vice.* Santa Barbara, Calif.: Ross-Erickson, 1979. ■ Greenberg, David R. *The Construction of Homosexuality.* Chicago: University of Chicago Press, 1988. ■ Hansen, Elaine. *Chaucer and the Fictions of Gender.* Philadelphia: University of Pennsylvania Press, 1992. ■ Mann, Jill. *Chaucer and Medieval Estates Satire.* Cambridge: Cambridge University Press, 1973. ■ McAlpine, Monica. "The Pardoner's Homosexuality and How it Matters." *PMLA* 95 (1980): 8–22.

Cheever, John
(1912–1982)

John William Cheever was born May 27, 1912, in Quincy, Massachusetts, the second son of Frederick Lincoln Cheever and Mary Devereaux Liley Cheever. Born to older parents, Cheever felt rejected and ignored as a child, and was haunted by the family story that his father had invited an abortionist to dinner during his mother's pregnancy: an incident Cheever included in both *The Wapshot Chronicle* (1957) and *Falconer* (1977). In 1926, Cheever's father lost his job as a salesman, and his mother opened a gift shop to support the family. Not only did these events heighten Cheever's feelings of neglect, but also led to his blaming his mother for "emasculating" his father. In 1930, Cheever published his first story, "Expelled" (based on his own expulsion from the prestigious prep school, Thayer Academy), in *The New Republic.* Cheever's relationship with his brother Fred deepened while they were on a walking tour of Germany in 1931. The brothers moved to Boston in 1932 and shared an apartment until Cheever felt their relationship was becoming too "incestuous." Fred helped Cheever support himself during these lean years even after Cheever moved to New York in 1934. On May 25, 1934, "Brooklyn Rooming House" appeared in *The New Yorker,* beginning Cheever's long association with the magazine. In 1941, Cheever married Mary Winternitz and remained married to her throughout his life despite his numerous affairs with partners of both sexes. Cheever's first book, *The Way Some People Live,* was published in 1943, the same year the first of his three children was born. Despite his own lack of a college education, Cheever taught for brief periods at Barnard, University of Iowa, and Boston College. An alcoholic for most of his life, Cheever was successfully treated in 1975 and spent the last seven years of his life sober. Throughout a long and distinguished career, Cheever was recognized with many awards and honors, including the National Book Award (1957), the Pulitzer Prize (1978), and the National Medal for Literature (1982). On June 18, 1982, he died of cancer and was later buried in Norwell, Massachusetts.

Prior to the publication of Cheever's selected short stories in 1978, he was regarded by most critics as a writer of formulaic stories in "*The New Yorker* style" that dealt exclusively with middle-class suburban American life. What *The Stories of John Cheever* revealed, however, was that Cheever had employed various forms and explored many subjects (including homosexuality) in his stories. This realization of the breadth of Cheever's work led to his recognition as a master of the short story.

The treatment of homosexuality in Cheever's work can be broken into two periods, each of which reflects Cheever's feelings toward his own bisexuality at the time. In Cheever's early work, homosexuality is treated ambivalently, stereotypically, and humorously. The first stories Cheever wrote that contained homosexual overtones are "Late Gathering" (1931) and "The Brothers" (1937). Each of these explores the close bond between two young men that not only parallels Cheever's relationship with his brother, but also reflects the ambivalence he felt toward it. In "Clancy in the Tower of Babel" (1953), Cheever dealt with homosexuality overtly for the first time. But his treatment is stereotypical; he portrays his homosexual characters as effeminate, hysterical, and tortured. In *The Wapshot Chronicle,* Cheever's comic treatment of Coverly Wapshot's doubts about his sexual orientation on being pursued by a male coworker only partially masks Cheever's own apprehension and ambivalence toward his bisexuality during the late 1950s.

As Cheever became more accepting of his sexual orientation, however, it was reflected in his work. In his breakthrough novel *Falconer,* Cheever invests homosexuality with redemptive and transforming powers. Ezekiel Farragut, who is imprisoned for murder, acquires the ability to love only after his affair with a fellow prisoner.

In "The Leaves, the Lion-Fish, and the Bear" (1974) and *Oh What A Paradise It Seems* (1982), Cheever depicts bisexual experiences free of guilt or remorse within the context of marriages, signaling his acceptance of his own bisexuality.

—*Carmine Esposito*

BIBLIOGRAPHY

Cheever, Susan. *Home Before Dark*. New York: Bantam, 1991. ■ Collins, Robert G., ed. *Critical Essays on John Cheever*. Boston: G.K. Hall, 1982. ■ Donaldson, Scott. *John Cheever: A Biography*. New York: Random House, 1988. ■ Waldeland, Lynne. *John Cheever*. Boston: Twayne Publishers, 1979.

Children's Literature

Gay- and lesbian-relevant themes and issues resonate throughout both classic and contemporary works of children's literature. Intense, even quasi-romantic, relationships between same-sex pairs are common in many texts from the nineteenth century, when the domain of children's literature first appeared as an entity separate from adult literature. Generations of children have enjoyed the warm homosociality of such novels written for a youthful audience as *Tom Brown's Schooldays* (1857) by Thomas Hughes and *Little Women* (1869) by Louisa May Alcott. Even many of the novels and poems appropriated from the ranks of adult reading material for use with children are charged with homosociality, even lesbian and gay eroticism. *The Adventures of Huckleberry Finn* (1884) by Mark Twain portrays an intense relationship between the protagonist, Huck, and the escaped slave, Jim, one that critic Leslie Fiedler has recognized as homoerotic. Similarly, *Goblin Market* (1862) by CHRISTINA ROSSETTI, which has appeared in several illustrated editions for children, contains passages that both explicitly and symbolically portray erotic contact between two sisters, Lizzie and Laura. That these works and others have raised relatively little controversy regarding such content can be partially attributed to the commonly accepted belief that homosexuality is a "phase" through which children and adolescents pass; all these texts end with a passage into adulthood that involves the breakup of a same-sex pair. Furthermore, childhood is traditionally seen as a time of innocence; in the past, representations of romantic love and eroticism were simply dismissed as irrelevant and invisible to children, as long as they remained relatively veiled or did not encompass the portrayal of an identity or lifestyle.

But lesbian and gay writers, critics, and activists have come to recognize how such veiling and tentativeness contribute to homophobia among heterosexuals and self-loathing among gays and lesbians. This awareness has dovetailed with a general trend as children's literature has become increasingly and explicitly politicized. In recent years, children's texts have been written to challenge directly sexist, racist, classist, ageist, and finally, heterosexist ideologies. Most of the homo-positive works for very young children, picture books, attempt to normalize lesbian and gay relationships by focusing on the experiences of happy families headed by two parents of the same sex. *Daddy's Roommate* (1990) by Michael Willhoite explores the love and support that can exist in a gay household from the perspective of a little boy who is happy to receive nurturing from both his Daddy and Frank, his father's lover. *Heather Has Two Mommies* (1989) by Leslea Newman not only validates the parenting skills of lesbians, but also answers the question "how" by explaining artificial insemination in elementary language. *Gloria Goes to Gay Pride* (1991), also by Leslea Newman, deals delicately with the issue of hatred, as Gloria, the daughter of two lesbians, encounters homophobic demonstrators at a gay pride parade. Finally, *The Generous Jefferson Bartleby Jones* (1991), by Forman Brown, celebrates the love present in one gay family by exploring the comic consequences for a boy who brags so often that two fathers are better than one, that his friends become jealous and borrow both of his dads. All these works have been the subject of intense debate as libraries and school districts struggle with parents and pressure groups that have attempted to ban these books and many others that recognize and applaud diversity among families and individuals.

This celebration of diversity is expanded upon in several recent books for older children and adolescents, ones that move beyond such simple validation and actually tackle the problems of growing up as a lesbian or gay individual in a homophobic society. One of the first books that dealt in a relatively honest way with this issue was *Ruby* by Rosa Guy, published in 1976. Although this novel ends with vague indications that the lesbian desires of its protagonist were just a phase, it does explore successfully the difficult terrain of urban poverty, violence, and homophobia in the African-American and Caribbean-American communities. Much less tentative in its approach to adolescent female homosexuality is *Annie on My Mind* by Nancy Garden (1982), which traces the development of a love affair between two high school students, Annie and Liza, who are finally forced to deny their sexual identity in public when a scandal erupts around their friendship with a lesbian teacher. Importantly, however, these characters never deny their identity to themselves. And even though it was written in 1982, this novel remains timely in its honest representation of homophobia among teenagers and in the school system.

Two works for adolescent boys stand out in similar ways for their validation of young gay male experience. *Reflections of a Rock Lobster* (1981) by Aaron Fricke is an honest, explicit autobiography written by a teenager for teenagers. Fricke's coming out story probes the isolation, self-hatred, and self-destructive behavior of a lonely young gay man who finally makes the courageous decision to live his life honestly. Fricke is best known for his legal campaign in the late 1970s for permission to bring a male date to his high school prom. His law suit garnered national attention and had both positive and negative personal consequences that are detailed in a sequel, *Sudden Strangers,* which Fricke co-authored with his father in 1991. Equally explicit and powerful, though a work of fiction, is Edmund White's *A Boy's Own Story* (1982), a novel that appeals to both an adolescent and adult audience. The young narrator details the process of coming to terms with his own sexuality by describing childhood events from the perspective of a boy who cannot reconcile the homosexual play and experimentation of other boys with their violent homophobia. A twist on this story is told in *Jack* (1989) by A. M. Homes, in which a young heterosexual adolescent boy must come to grips with the homosexuality of his father; though initially homophobic, Jack learns to accept his dad after being the mistaken target of homophobic abuse himself. All the works detailed here are appro-priate for high school students though most are not taught in schools because of their sexual content and hard, but honest, criticism of heterosexual parents, teachers, and young adults.

Thus children's literature is in a period of transition, moving toward more openly gay- and lesbian-positive representations and more explicitly political discussions. From early childhood through late adolescence, young readers can now find books that help them deal with a wide variety of gay- and lesbian-relevant topics. Two final stand-out examples of the ways children's literature changes to meet the needs of new audiences are MaryKate Jordan's fine work *Losing Uncle Tim* (1989) and Willhoite's very amusing *Uncle What-Is-It Is Coming To Visit!!* (1993). The former is a beautifully illustrated book for elementary school students on AIDS and grieving. The latter is a comic look at two children's fears about the impending visit of a gay uncle; they first envision a drag queen and then a leather queen breaking down the door of their house but finally meet their very tame Uncle Brett who talks to them about stereotypes. Thus new works appear on the bookshelves of stores and libraries every day that celebrate nontraditional families and social diversity. Although homoeroticism has long been a part of literature for children, it is only in recent years that lesbian and gay identities have been honestly portrayed. It is clear that the authors and illustrators today are contributing to what will continue to be a rich gay and lesbian heritage in literature for children. (See also YOUNG ADULT LITERATURE.)

—*Donald E. Hall*

BIBLIOGRAPHY

Faderman, Lillian. *Surpassing the Love of Men.* New York: Morrow, 1981. ■ Fiedler, Leslie. "Come Back to the Raft Ag'in, Huck Honey!" *The Collected Essays of Leslie Fiedler.* Vol. I. New York: Stein and Day, 1971. ■ Nodelman, Perry. *The Pleasures of Children's Literature.* New York: Longman, 1992. ■ Rudman, Masha Kabakow. *Children's Literature: An Issues Approach.* 2d ed. New York: Longman, 1984. ■ Wolf, Virginia L. "The Gay Family in Literature for Young People." *Children's Literature in Education* 20.1 (1989): 51–58.

Chinese Literature

During the first decade of this century, an anthology was published under the title of *The Cut Sleeve* (*Duanxiu pian*), edited by a man unknown except for his pseudonym, Ameng of Wu. The anthology gathered historical and literary sources on male homosexuality in China from the fifth century B.C.E. to the nineteenth century. Its title alluded to the story of Emperor Ai of the Han dynasty (first century

C.E.) and his favorite boy, Dong Xian. One day they were resting together; Dong Xian was asleep, with his head lying on the sleeve of the sovereign. The latter, wishing to get up but not wanting to disturb his beloved boy's sleep, cut off the sleeve. Ever since, "cut sleeve" (together with other expressions also referring to famous homoerotic passions of antiquity, such as "shared peach" and "longyang") entered the Chinese literary vocabulary to signify homosexuality. The recorded tradition of male homosexuality in China is a remarkably long and rich one, but it is with the emergence of vernacular fiction in the late sixteenth century, and with the related birth of erotica (particularly thriving in the first half of the seventeenth century), that homoeroticism becomes a prominent literary topic. A large part of homoerotic fiction in China is romantic in that it is concerned with the expression of emotions, particularly, of love. In Chinese erotica, unlike in the European tradition, love is not taboo; indeed, discourse on sexual pleasure is often carried on in tandem with discourse on feelings. It is in this context that male homosexuality finds its place. Female homosexuality is far less often encountered in Chinese fiction than the male variety although research in this area still waits to be done.

The Classified Brief History of Love (*Qing shi leilüe*)—a collection of stories on all the possible manifestations of love, published in the 1630s—included a chapter on male homosexual passions, which later constituted the bulk of *The Cut Sleeve*. The inclusion of homosexuality in this work indicates its acceptance as a legitimate form of love, an option by which a man might satisfy his sexual and emotional needs.

It is significant that the word most commonly used in the literature of this period to refer to male homosexuality is *nanse*, meaning literally "male beauty." The word is naturally opposed to the word *nüse*, meaning "female beauty." Now, given that grammatically the only possible subject of the expression "be fond of *nanse/nüse*" is a man, it is obvious that the grid of sexuality in Chinese society at this time is one in which the reference point is a male individual, men and women constituting the two possible directions of his desire. In this sense, such a notion of homosexuality very much resembles that of the Western Classical world, and in particular that of Republican Rome in that it lacks the educational aspect so central to the ancient Greek notion of homosexuality (and of that of samurais in Japan). In the Chinese sexual context, the main distinction to be made is between activity and passivity rather than between heterosexuality and homosexuality—activity being the sexual mode of adult men, passivity that of women and boys. A boy's ideal age was considered to fall between the sixteenth and

the seventeenth year, whereas at the age of nineteen or twenty a boy's decline was believed to begin. The criterion for a boy's ideal age seems to have remained unaltered into this century, as indicated by a chapter on male prostitution in a *Secret Shanghai Guidebook* published during the 1930s, whose author states that the male prostitutes' age ranged from fourteen to nineteen, unlike female courtesans, who could still enjoy popularity after the age of thirty.

As in Republican Rome, in China the passive homosexual was usually a servant or a professional entertainer or a prostitute who was also an actor since, generally speaking, to be sodomized was considered a shameful "loss of person" (*shi shen*) for a man. Seventeenth-century sources convey the image of a society in which a man could have a wife, concubines, and children and be at the same time fond of young men—and play with them a sexually active role—without feeling he was living a contradiction or offending morality. However, in order to be morally acceptable, his behavior had to be contained within certain boundaries. In particular, homosexuality could not be adopted as a total alternative to heterosexuality; such behavior would have clashed with the moral duty of reproduction, the first expression of filial piety, one of the cornerstones of Confucian morality.

Yet, in late imperial romantic fiction (roughly from the sixteenth to the nineteenth centuries), the Confucian, family-centered ethic is often rejected in favor of a romantic one in which the only real crime is the betrayal of the romantic oath. An example of the triumph of the romantic ethic in a homosexual context is the last story from the seventeenth-century collection *And Even the Stones Nodded* (*Shi dian tou*), in which two students fall in love and elope together to the mountains as holy hermits, thereby refusing to fulfill their duties as filial sons and as betrothed fiancés. Their families, thanks to a tip from a servant, find out where they are hiding and go to find them, taking along the two official fiancées. But when they arrive, the two young men have already ascended to Heaven. Two trees have grown on the burial mounds, their branches intertwining. The fiancées commit suicide, thereby blessing with their blood sacrifice a union already magically granted a cosmic confirmation. For the families the hunt is over. There is no other option but to kneel in awe.

Three specialized works of seventeenth-century erotica deal exclusively with male homosexuality. They survive in very rare exemplars and have only recently been available in photo-reprint editions. Two of them are by the same author, whom we know only by pseudonym, the West Lake-Crazed Master Moon-

Heart. His two collections, *Cap and Hairpins* (*Bian er chai*) and *Fragrant Stuff from the Court of Spring* (*Yichun xiangzhi*), each of which comprises four novellas, were published sometime between 1622 and 1646. The third collection, *The Forgotten Stories of Longyang* (*Longyang yishi*), by the pseudonymous Bamboo-Crazed Retired Gentleman, consists of twenty short stories and bears a preface dated 1632.

Cap and Hairpins represents an elaboration of the erotic discourse articulated in the *Classified Brief History of Love*. But in Master Moon-Heart's collection, homosexuality is upgraded from the status of one of the subcategories of love; it is worthy of its own subcategories. *Cap and Hairpins* is a gallery of exemplary sodomites; in correspondence with the four novellas, their perfection is seen in four romantic domains. As the title suggests, the collection deals with individuals who participate in both the masculine and the feminine worlds. The four romantic subdivisions are the conceptual playgrounds where ideas of female and male virtue meet. The heroes who wear—symbolically if not literally—both cap and hairpins are not so much the product of a mechanical replacement of virile virtues with feminine ones, as they are that of a new moral negotiation between the two. The protagonists of these novellas are, in fact, constructed through a transplanting of gendered moral values, so to speak; they are moral hybrids whose romantic originality is produced by setting, like a gemstone, female virtue in a male body and intelligence.

Almost without exception, the heroes of *Cap and Hairpins* are the sodomized boys, some of whom come from respectable families. The underlying thesis is that, although to be sodomized may generally represent for a boy a "loss of person," it ceases to have that effect when love intervenes. Master Moon-Heart thus projects a system of romantic morality onto the system of ordinary morality. An idea of sanctity through martyrdom underlies these plots. The final objective is didactic, in the sense that its rhetoric, while challenging the common parameters of judgment, aims to provide a broad education both sentimental (how to value love) and ethical (how to break preconceptions and broaden one's vision).

If one had to identify the main theme of the second of Master Moon-Heart's collections, *Fragrant Stuff from the Court of Spring*, it would be the ambiguity of passion—in this case, that between men. Love can be at once fire that causes destruction and fuel that is necessary for self-cultivation; love can be the instrument both of salvation and dissipation. The first story in the collection opens, in fact, with a poem and a discussion of love and its ambivalent nature. The lyric disdains those "youths plunged into dissipation" and who are obsessed with sex to the point of desiring a new "groom" every night.

All four novellas are about the consequences of losing control over the senses. In two of the stories, the protagonists succumb to sensuality, and their crime is naturally followed by their punishment. The other two protagonists are men who manage to repent at the very last moment. The redemption of Niu Jun, the protagonist of the last novella, comes as the culminating point of a process of self-knowledge that finally leads him away from the world of passion, as well as from Confucian learning, onto the Buddhist path of liberation. The story—which is probably Master Moon-Heart's best—is that of a revelation, whose instrument is a dream. The ugly Niu Jun, to whom love is denied, is given an erotic destiny in a dream in which he becomes beautiful and travels through fantastic realms, each of them corresponding to different sexualities. For him the dream performs the function of revealing the content of his desires. Male homosexuality features in this display as the most relevant discovery. His final resolution, once awakened from the dream, must be seen as springing from a double revelation—the direction of his desires as well as the emptiness of passion.

The title of the Bamboo-Crazed Retired Gentleman's collection, *The Forgotten Stories of Longyang*, evokes a classical story and a romantic standard. The Lord of Longyang was on a boat, fishing with his prince, when he began to cry. The prince asked him why he was weeping. The Lord replied that he had caught a fish, which had made him happy. But then, having caught a bigger fish, he had thrown away the other one. This had reminded him that, although he presently enjoyed the prince's favor, soon beautiful people will come to the Palace to compete for it, and he will be discarded, just like the fish. The tears of the Lord of Longyang apparently moved the prince, who proclaimed an edict that promised death for anybody who might recommend beauties to him.

The title of the collection thus links the work to a romantic tradition, to a seed of love planted two thousand years earlier. The tears of the Lord of Longyang are meant to induce in the reader a feeling of nostalgia for a golden age that contrasts with the present, which is a time when more often than not "longyang" means greedy boys who pretend to be pure and when betrayal is expected if more money is offered elsewhere. This collection is a mirror of the experience of the commercialization of male sex at the end of the Ming dynasty (1368–1644), a phenomenon that was frequently noted by both Chinese and Western writers at the time. European travelers to China in the sixteenth and seventeenth centuries never fail, in fact, to be scandalized by the lightness and ease with which homosexuality, and particularly male prostitution, appeared to be taken in the Central Kingdom.

The Forgotten Stories of Longyang leads us into a network of male seduction, all gravitating around male brothels. We learn about the unchallenged charm and skill of male entertainers from Suzhou; we learn about their patrons—the stingy merchants of Huizhou and the intolerably jealous men from Shaoxing; we learn of rich men who spend their fortunes on boys and of others who find riches by rescuing a beautiful boy, abandoned in a river by his lover's jealous wife. But throughout the twenty stories, the author's most urgent message appears to be a heartfelt complaint about aged prostitutes, who are already twenty years old, if not twenty-two, and still linger in boyhood. By refusing to wear a turban, the symbol of adulthood, they gravely damage the good reputation of male beauty.

The author delights in seeing old male harlots succumbing to the fierce competition of younger prostitutes. But aged boys do not invariably fail; there are several stories of successful ones. In the collection, men's passion for men is sometimes described as a congenital weakness though a perilous one to ignore. In one story, we are told of a merchant from Songjiang who has wasted away his patrimony on boys, until finally he is given a last chance by his father-in-law: money to make a textile deal in Suzhou. Before leaving, his wife advises him not to fall into the usual trap, suggesting that he could take a concubine instead: that would be a little more proper. The deal in Suzhou goes well and, excited by his success, the merchant meets a beautiful young man, whom he invites to come to Songjiang with him. Only when the boat has already landed does the man remember his wife's words; he decides to smuggle the boy into the house disguised as a concubine. Everything goes well until the curious wife licks a hole into the paper window and sees the concubine's body. Seminaked, the boy has to escape and, luckily, makes it back to Suzhou. But for the merchant the nostalgia is so strong that it brings sickness in his body and, consequently, failure to his business. The ailing man asks to see the boy one last time. The wife sends for him, and when the merchant sees him a miracle occurs: In a week, the man is up on his feet, and he and the boy make a joint venture and lots of money; they are blissful, and the wife is happy, too.

The point seems to be that obsessions, at least those of men, must be understood and encouraged since their repression may bring ruin to the person and, spreading like a contagious illness, to his entire household. Although the wife's idea suggests a hierarchy of propriety, in which having a male lover is less proper than having a concubine, in the end there is no moral disapproval of homosexuality: Everything is fine, so long as one encounters the right sodomite, a Lord of Longyang reborn. Then the house is blessed.

The stories of the Bamboo-Crazed Retired Gentleman never claim that they want to warn us or awaken us. There is no didactic intent here besides that of instructing about which boys are not worthy of being chased and why. In general, the author prefers sinners to angels, petty and old prostitutes to faithful companions. Unlike the author of *Cap and Hairpins,* rarely does the Bamboo-Crazed Retired Gentleman offer up heroes.

"Every respectable Chinese practices, has practiced or will practice pederasty," said a friend to J. J. Matignon, a French doctor who traveled in China at the turn of the century. In his book, *La Chine érmetique: superstitions, crime et misère* (Paris, 1936), Matignon listed homosexuality among the "crimes." As a scientist, he reported that the only real reproach Chinese public opinion made of homosexuality was that of having "a fateful influence on the eyesight." Beijing was still, at the beginning of this century, a most lively center of theater and, hence, of male prostitution. In this world of romantic meetings between young Beijing actors and their male patrons is set Chen Sen's novel *The Precious Mirror of Ranking Flowers* (*Pin hua baojian*), published during the 1840s. This work represents the culmination of a long literary tradition that jointly appreciated boy actors' beauty and their operatic skills.

Partially because of the Western influence on Chinese morality in the twentieth century, homosexuality has been the object of repression and persecution both under the Communist regime on the mainland and under the nationalist one of Taiwan. As a result, homosexuality virtually disappeared from Chinese literature. It finally reappeared in the writing of the Taiwanese novelist Pai Hsien-Yung, whose *Crystal Boys* (*Niezi,* tr. 1990) is one of the few contemporary Chinese novels to depict homosexuality openly. In contrast with earlier literature, however, this work portrays men forced by their society into the darkness of nights dense with frustration, stolen pleasure, and guilt.

—*Giovanni Vitiello*

BIBLIOGRAPHY

Hinsch, Bret. *Passions of the Cut Sleeve: The Male Homosexual Tradition in China.* Berkeley: University of California Press, 1990. ■ Vitiello, Giovanni. "The Dragon's Whim: Ming and Qing Homoerotic Tales from *The Cut Sleeve.*" *T'ong pao* 78 (1992): 341–372.

Cixous, Hélène
(b. 1937)

Hélène Cixous, an influential French feminist theorist and experimental novelist and dramatist, was born on June 5, 1937, in Oran, Algeria. Her father, a physician of mixed colonial-French and Sephardic Jewish background, died during her childhood, an early experience of loss that Cixous later explored in her writings. Cixous enjoyed a nurturing and creative bond with her mother, a Jewish woman of Austro-German origin. Although Cixous writes in French and teaches English literature, she considers German, her native maternal tongue, a richer and more embodied language than the more rationalistic discourse of French. In the colonial environment in which she was raised, Cixous felt displaced as female, Jewish, and nonnative Arab; accordingly, she became determined to free herself from the constrictions of the world into which she was born and to combat the encroachments of power on the individual. In her teens, Cixous began to study English literature, and shortly thereafter she emigrated to France to pursue her studies.

In the course of completing her doctorate, Cixous married, had two children, and was divorced. In 1968, she became professor of English literature and, in the aftermath of student uprisings, she was appointed to establish the experimental and politically controversial University of Paris VIII, which was to accommodate "nontraditional" students and provide an alternative to the more hierarchical French academic environment. In her published doctoral thesis, *The Exile of James Joyce* (1968), Cixous, like Joyce an "exiled" writer in France, praised Joyce's shrewd exposure of political and ideological manipulations as well as his conviction that language could transform mental structures. On the other hand, in an early indication of her revolt against the "death drive," Cixous critiqued Joyce's belief that one must metaphorically "kill" the mother, and therefore suffer guilt, in order to live. During this period, Cixous also began her prolific career as a creative writer, and her first novel, *Inside* (1969), won the prestigious Prix Médicis. *Inside* is an autobiographical text that, as the title suggests, explores the writer's "inside": an interior landscape that includes evocative meditations on the death of her father, the influence of her mother and grandmother, and her relationship with her brother. Here, as elsewhere in her writings, Cixous explores the multiple significations of her title: "inside" connotes for her, as a woman writer, a place of refuge and protection as well as a confining private domestic space to which women have been "exiled" from the public world of politics and history.

Cixous's critique of repression and social injustice, as well as her involvement in political causes that trivialized the concerns of women, led her to become a feminist. In *Nobody's Name* (1974), Cixous explores the relationships among the unified "phallic" or "masculinist" subject, narcissism, and death. As against the efforts of male writers such as Freud and Poe, for example, to place women in what she terms a "limited economy" dominated by an obsession with death, Cixous proposes an alternative "feminine" economy based on the "gift" and characterized by continuity, abundance, and the absence of fixed identities and categories. Although Cixous has been accused of being an "essentialist" who relates mental attributes to biological sex, and although she perceives women's knowledge as different from men's because of their position in culture and their capacity for motherhood, Cixous believes that women can partake in a "masculine" and men in a "feminine" economy.

In accordance with her deepening commitment to feminism, Cixous founded the Center for Research in Women's Studies in 1974 and, in the following year, published "The Laugh of the Medusa" (1975). In this article, Cixous analyzes a Freudian text on castration and argues that man, horrified by women's genitals, turns to "stone" and erects a symbolic "phallic" system to exclude women. Since oppositions are self-canceling, women should neither oppose nor support this system but rather laugh at it, for laughter not only dissolves ossified meanings but also affirms life and joyousness. By contrast, in her more "serious" theoretical article, "Sorties" (1975), Cixous sets forth her feminist epistemology by relating a series of hierarchical oppositions (for example, culture/nature, form/matter, speaking/writing, and head/heart) to the fundamental division between "man" and "woman." Cixous attacks the dialectical relation between these terms that, by privileging one term of a pair over another, creates a binary structure of unequal power marked by the constant threat of violence and chaos. Moreover, Cixous begins to explore the issue of sexuality by arguing that under this system of unequal binaries sexual difference is only tolerated when repressed or "closeted." As against Freud, she argues for the possibility of "bisexuality," understood not principally as a form of sexuality but as an embodied recognition of plurality and the coexistence of masculinity and femininity within individual subjects. In 1977, a crisis in Cixous's personal life led her to write *Angst* (1977), which not only chronicled the painful breakup of a love relationship but which also proved a definitive departure from what she later termed "the heterosexual scene." Even prior to this time, Cixous's growing awareness of the relationship between feminism and "sexuality difference" as well as the perceived need to refocus her energies on relations between women, led her to begin a series of creative collaborations with other women writers. With Catherine Clément, the author of the groundbreaking *Opera, or the Undoing of Women* (1979), Cixous wrote *The Newly Born Woman* (1975), whose title in French puns on "Là-je-nais" ("There I am being born") and La Genet, a female version of the famous twentieth-century French gay author, JEAN GENET. In this text, "born" of a collaboration between two women as well as the writings of a male homosexual author, Cixous and Clément argue that the desire for recognition should be replaced by that for alterity, which journeys toward the "other" and produces empathetic identification without the destructive fusion of opposites. Cixous exhorts women to break their complicit silence and write of their bodies and desires in a distinctive language she terms "feminine writing." This interest in a specifically female pleasure and language that has been denied to women is also central to *Coming to Writing* (1977), in which Cixous traces the origin of women's writing to the mother's voice and body.

In the following years, Cixous's work appeared principally under the imprint of the French feminist publishing house Des Femmes, where she enjoyed a close association with Antoinette Fouqué, the cofounder of the Movement for the Liberation of Women. Cixous's prose became more lyrical and erotic and less marked by ironic polemic as she turned her attention to relationships among women. Cixous not only continued her explorations of the relations between literature, opera, and painting, but also discovered an influential inspiration in the Brazilian author Clarice Lispector, whose surrealistic writings focus on women whose lives are inscrutable to the larger culture. Cixous's exploration of the creative potentials of female homoeroticism reaches its height in *The Book of Promethea* (1983). The action of this text, which combines philosophy and myth and is seductively ironic and erotic in tone, is divided among three characters: the narrator H, the subject "I," and the semimythic Promethea. H, in a manner reminiscent of but not identical with the author Cixous, describes herself as struggling for years to find in theoretical discourses the means to understand the world but has now concluded that they are all disappointing illusions. Promethea, as her name suggests, embodies the Promethean will to transgression, which enables her to produce erotic and creative fire. Promethea is not only the narrator's lover but also her inspiration: She constantly challenges H to risk more as a writer and lover. Promethea is a force of Dionysian transformation who embodies the virtues of innocence and simplicity along with the propensity for excess and violence that Cixous had earlier celebrated in Penthesilea, the Amazon of Homeric epic. The drama focuses on the conflict between a total identification that threatens the subject with annihilation and a separation that leads to unbearable grief, but the ironic distance of the text is maintained by humorous interludes in which Promethea suggests, for example, defrosting the refrigerator or cooking a meal. In this text, Cixous demonstrates that female creative powers are sustained and nourished by women's erotic and imaginative bonds with other women, both real and semimythical.

In recent years, Cixous has increasingly turned her attention to drama and history as well as to collaborations with the stage director Ariane Mnouchkine. Although Cixous cannot be termed a self-identified "lesbian" writer, this is principally because she, like other contemporary French literary theorists such as Luce Irigaray, Julia Kristeva, Jacques Derrida, ROLAND BARTHES, MICHEL FOUCAULT, and Gilles Deleuze have abandoned the concept of unified identity, as well as the opposition between heterosexuality and homosexuality, on which they argue such identities are grounded. Though Cixous is known in the United States principally for her feminist and theoretical writings, her lyrically erotic and experimental fictions celebrating female homoeroticism and feminist solidarity are now becoming increasingly well known thanks to the work of her fine translators.

—*Corinne Blackmer*

BIBLIOGRAPHY

Cixous, Hélène. *The Book of Promethea.* Trans. and Intro. Betsy Wing. Lincoln: University of Nebraska Press, 1991. ■ ———. *Coming to Writing and Other Essays.* Deborah Jenson, ed. Trans. Sarah Cornell, Deborah Jenson, Ann Liddle, and Susan Sellers. Cambridge: Harvard University Press, 1991. ■ ———. *Inside.* Trans. Carol Barko. New York: Schocken, 1986. ■ ———. "The Laugh of the Medusa." Trans. Keith Cohen and Paula Cohen. *Signs* 1 (Summer 1976): 875–899. ■ ———. *Readings: The Poetics of Blanchot, Joyce, Kleist, Kafka, Lispector and Tsvetayeva.* Ed., trans., and intro. Verena Andermatt Conley. Minneapolis: University of Minnesota Press, 1991. ■ Moi, Toril. *Sexual/Textual Politics.* London: Methuen, 1985. ■ Shiach, Morag. *Hélène Cixous: A Politics of Writing.* New York: Routledge, 1991.

Cleland, John
(1710–1789)

John Cleland is remembered for the one book he claims to have regretted writing, *Memoirs of a Woman of Pleasure* or *Fanny Hill* (1748–1749), the first (and probably the funniest and most humane) pornographic novel in English. Cleland's life is obscure. His father was a friend of Alexander Pope, his education was good, and he spent twelve years as a soldier and bureaucrat in India. On his return to England in 1741, he soon found himself in financial difficulty. He is said to have composed *The Memoirs of a Woman of Pleasure* while in Fleet Prison for debt. The Bishop of London attempted to suppress the *Memoirs*, probably because of the passages depicting sodomy, but charges were not pressed against Cleland, who published an expurgated version of the novel in 1750. Although he seems to have been promised a government pension, perhaps for propaganda work, this probably never materialized and the rest of his life was a financial struggle. He wrote novels, books on medicine and philology, and journalism without ever achieving a major success. He appears in James Boswell's *Journals* and elsewhere as an outspoken eccentric on the outskirts of the literary circles of eighteenth-century London.

Memoirs of a Woman of Pleasure is a novel in two parts told in the first person by Fanny Hill about her rise via prostitution from a poor orphan in the country to a rich, respectable, married woman. It is elegantly written and features an amazing series of ingenious euphemisms for sexual organs and acts. For example, the male member is a "nipple of love," semen is "my dear love's liquid emanation of himself" and the female genitalia are the "soft laboratory of love." The novel is a sexual fantasy in which women are endlessly compliant in satisfying male desire, in which all unattractive elements of sexuality and prostitution are avoided, and in which bourgeois morality is carefully balanced with a libertine philosophy claiming pleasure as the ultimate goal. Fanny loses her virginity to the man whom (after many sexual adventures) she will marry. Although heterosexual sex dominates the book, Fanny describes lesbians and male homosexuals, giving insight into the formation of these roles in the eighteenth century. Furthermore, as Nancy K. Miller and Donald H. Mengay have observed, the first-person narrator, Fanny, is Cleland himself doing a female impersonation. An apparently heterosexual text thus becomes a masterpiece of homoeroticism.

The Memoirs differs from most pornographic novels in the detail and coherency of its plot and in the development of its principal character, who undergoes an education in the novel, learning not only survival skills in the underworld of prostitution but also intellectual, emotional, and cultural skills that turn her into a devoted wife and mother, cultured upper-class lady, and sophisticated writer. However, her attitude toward same-sex relationships does not change. She learns about such relationships by experience among women at the beginning of the novel and by observation of men near the end. Although her judgments about such women are less harsh than those of the men, she thinks that "the bad of our own sex" (that is, women who seduce other women) can be as responsible for the downfall of women as men. Fanny's view of men who have sex with each other is much harsher; she describes them as "universally odious" and "absurd." She wants to turn the two young men she observes having sex over to the authorities (who would likely have hanged them), but is prevented from doing so by a fortunate fall from the stool she is using to spy on them. However, even if Fanny does not change her judgments, Cleland gives the reader enough information to change hers or his. Fanny's judgments on both men and women engaging in same-sex encounters never coincide with her actual observations. She describes having more sexual pleasure with women than she admits to. She thinks all sodomites are effeminate, but none of the men she describes fit that description.

The Memoirs gives us a glimpse into the manners and practices of eighteenth-century lesbians and gay men. How far Cleland knew these matters from first-hand experience is uncertain. In his later years, he was considered to be a sodomite, which may have been a political slander, a conjecture based on his writing of such matters in the *Memoirs*, or the true state of things.

—*Terrence Johnson*

BIBLIOGRAPHY

Cleland, John. *Fanny Hill, or Memoirs of a Woman of Pleasure.* Peter Wagner, ed. London: Penguin, 1985. ■ Epstein, William H. *John Cleland: Images of a Life.* New York: Columbia University Press, 1974. ■ Foxon, David. *Libertine Literature in England 1660-1745 With an Appendix on the Publication of John Cleland's* Memoirs of a Woman of Pleasure, *commonly called* Fanny Hill. New Hyde Park: University Books, 1965. ■ Kopelson, Kevin. "Seeing Sodomy: *Fanny Hill's* Blinding Vision." *Homosexuality in Renaissance and Enlightenment England: Literary Representations in Historical Context.* Claude Summers, ed. New York: Haworth Press, 1992. 173–183. ■ Mengay, Donald H. "The Sodomitical Muse: *Fanny Hill* and the Rhetoric of Crossdressing." *Homosexuality in Renaissance and Enlightenment England: Literary Representations in Historical Context.* Claude Summers, ed. New York: Haworth Press, 1992. 185–198. ■ Miller, Nancy K. "'I's' in Drag: The Sex of Recollection." *The Eighteenth Century* 22 (1981): 47–57. ■ Trumbach, Randolph. "Modern Prostitution and Gender in *Fanny Hill:* Libertine and Domesticated Fantasy." *Sexual Underworlds of the Enlightenment.* G. S. Rousseau and Roy Porter, eds. Chapel Hill: University of North Carolina Press, 1988. 69–85.

Cocteau, Jean
(1889–1963)

Born into a middle-class Parisian family on July 5, 1889, Jean Cocteau was only ten years old when his father died. Although an indifferent scholar, the boy took from the prestigious Lycée Condercet a haunting memory of a classmate, Pierre Dargelos, a "type of all that is not taught or learned or judged, of all that is not analyzed or punished . . . the first symbol of wild forces." After Dargelos died, Cocteau ran away to Marseille, where he lived among sailors and prostitutes. The image of Dargelos "as the shameless, untutored faun" appears in *The White Paper* (1928), Cocteau's celebration of homosexuality, as well as in his journal *Opium* (1930), the novel *Children of the Game* (1929), and the film *The Blood of the Poet* (1931).

Paris cafes, boulevards, theaters, salons, galleries, and lovers provided Cocteau a lifetime of education and entertainment, what the high-school dropout described as his "Sorbonne." The actor Edouard de Max, who played opposite Sarah Bernhardt, guided him through the Parisian scene (with the approval of Cocteau's mother) and helped the decadent youth publish his first three books of poems (*Alladin's Lamp,* 1909; *The Frivolous Prince,* 1910; and *Sophocles' Dance,* 1912).

The ballet brought him into contact with Nijinsky and Sergei Diaghilev, who in 1912 demanded of the youth: "Astonish me." Taking this advice to heart, Cocteau began an unending quest for the new. He wrote *Potomoc* (1913), a collection of drawings, poems, and meditations; attached himself to France's famous flyer Roland Garros, for whom he wrote a long poem, *The Cape of Good Hope* (1914); volunteered as an ambulance driver in 1914 at the outbreak of the Great War; and worked with Amedeo Modigliani, Guillaume Apollinaire, Max Jacob, Pablo Picasso, Igor Stravinsky, Erik Satie, and a host of other literary, artistic, and musical innovators.

Asked in the 1950s how he managed to be part of four avant-gardes, Cocteau answered, "I adhered not to the school but to the movement." His modernist works never failed to astonish. He wrote the scenario for the ballet *Parade* (1917), with sets by Picasso and music by Satie; a book on music, *The Rooster and the Harlequin* (1918); the pantomime *Do-Nothing Bar* (1920), performed by two famous clowns; and the play, *The Wedding on the Eiffel Tower* (1922), which combined dance, acrobatics, mime, drama, and music.

As a young man, Cocteau had sought collaborations with older men such as Edouard de Max or Igor Stravinsky but soon he found what he called his "enfants," a series of younger lovers and collaborators. The poet John Le Roy was perhaps the first. Cocteau arranged for the youth to read publicly in 1916; in 1918, he wrote ANDRÉ GIDE with news of his death: "Le Roy had become my pupil . . . I put into him what was wasted in me by a disorderly life. He was young, handsome, good, brave, full of genius, unaffected, everything Death likes."

In 1919, Cocteau met fifteen-year-old Raymond Radiguet; in a letter to the boy's father, he compared the youth to RIMBAUD. Radiguet demanded that Cocteau be more serious; Cocteau demanded that the boy be wilder. While living together, the two wrote four of the most celebrated novels of French post–World War I literature: Cocteau's *The Great Split* (1923) and *The Imposter* (1923) and Radiguet's *Devil in the Flesh* (1923) and *Count d'Orgel* (1924). Radiguet died of typhoid in 1923.

Some of Cocteau's ephebes were more predatory than talented. Maurice Sachs stripped Cocteau's apartment and left a bitter posthumous account of his master in *Witches' Sabbath* (1946) before he was killed by the Nazis. Jean Bourgoint (according to Glenway Wescott, "one of God's fools") became a monk who remembered Cocteau's "delicacy and temperance." Cocteau was living with Jean Desbordes in 1927 and wrote the preface to the latter's remarkable *J'Adore* (1928), which is essentially a two-hundred-page love letter to Cocteau. Desbordes declared, "I come everywhere, in gardens and on my own body; it is a carnal prayer. . . . I take love from everything." The young man became a Resistance leader and met a horrible death, his eyes reportedly plucked out by the Nazis. Cocteau inspired Sachs and Desbordes to write their most daring work; meanwhile, he himself wrote a homosexual reverie, *The White Paper*, which Sachs published.

In 1937, Jean Marais, a young actor, joined Cocteau, who spurred him to become a matinee idol of French cinema. Marais, who allowed himself to be molded in Cocteau's image, inspired the writer to become a filmmaker and scriptwriter. Cocteau later wrote a study of the actor whose own autobiography included Cocteau's poems for him.

Raymond Radiguet wrote, "Jean Cocteau will always be eighteen years old." In his sixties, Cocteau himself wrote, "everyone, one way or another, still treats me as if I were nineteen." He knew Freud through Marie Bonaparte, a first-generation psychoanalyst, but rejected the Freudian notions of sexual retardation and maturity. Cocteau offered an independent account of infantile sexuality, the Oedipus myth, homosexuality, dreams, and the unconscious. His *White Paper* celebrated "the love I have always had for boys," and concluded by rejecting Rimbaud's "Lo, we are come unto the age of assassins" for his own motto, "Love is to be reinvented." Oedipus could be supplanted by Orpheus the poet, and the word *poet* taken to its Greek root: *poienin,* "to create."

Greece provided Cocteau a magical realm of transcendence. In his youthful poems collected in *Sophocles' Dance* (1912), in his great dramas *Antigone* (1922), *Oedipus Rex* (1925), *The Infernal Machine* (1932), and *Bacchus* (1951), and in his extraordinary films *Orpheus* (1950) and *Testament of Orpheus* (1960), Cocteau reinterpreted the Greek myths in his own libidinal and liberating way. Like Freud, Cocteau drew on Frederick Nietzsche's *Birth of Tragedy;* however, unlike the Germans, he was more playful. He rejected the Freudian superego and even the ego and privileged the id. He constantly returned to the memories, fears, and experiences of childhood. In Cocteau's great novel *The Holy Terrors* (1929), later a film (1950), he declared, "Whatever the cost, the most important thing was to return to this reality of childhood: a grave, heroic, mysterious reality, implemented by humble details and the magic of which is most brutally disturbed by the queries of adults."

In his attempt to return to the magical realm, Cocteau smoked opium and wrote a classic of drug literature, *Opium*. He explained why he smoked: "All children possess the magic power of being able to change themselves into what they wish. Poets, in whom childhood is prolonged, suffer a great deal when they lose this power. This is undoubtedly one of the reasons which drives the poet to use opium." Perhaps he stopped smoking because the drug also put his sexuality to sleep.

In his drug recovery, Cocteau turned to Catholicism and received communion but fled the church after falling for a handsome monk. The poet was offended not only by the hypocrisy of the church's suppressed sexuality but also by its claims regarding art. In *Letter to Jacques Maritain* (1926), he wrote, "I shall learn that art is religion and will show the danger of religious art." Maritain responded that this was heresy.

During the German occupation of Paris, Cocteau was neither a collaborator nor a liberator. German censors prohibited performance of some of his works, and young Nazis assaulted him. Admiring neither the French nor German governments, Cocteau (like his mentor Edouard de Max) was an anarchist. In 1951, he wrote in his journal: "Many kings of France were assassinated. All were assassins." In a 1923 lecture, "Order Considered as Anarchy," he declared, "The conventions of scandal (Rimbaud would call it that 'old itch') still prevent people from admitting that, in the age in which we live, anarchy may reveal itself in the form of a dove." He earlier claimed that France's secret weapon "is her tradition of anarchy" found in her "underground elites—a vast hidden force with a spirit of contradiction that is the very basis of the spirit of creation."

Some of Cocteau's most famous dictums grew out of his anarchism. "One is either a judge or a defendant. The judge sits, the defendant stands," he declared and strove himself to live standing. Religious, political, and literary judges, whether Roman Catholic, Communist, or academic, repelled him because of their pretensions to absolute knowledge. To them, he proclaimed, "I am a lie that always tells the truth." He later explained, "I meant that every man is a lie because social life and the obligation to make contact burden him with masks. But every second I try to contradict this lie and through it to proclaim my truth."

Cocteau confronted the lies of heterosexuality and closetedness. He admired such lesbian and gay writers as PAUL VERLAINE, Arthur Rimbaud, OSCAR WILDE, MARCEL PROUST, COLETTE, André Gide, GERTRUDE STEIN, Raymond Roussell, JEAN GENET, and others. With Proust, Stein, Roussell, and Colette, he remained on familiar terms, but with Gide his relations were strained. Cocteau claimed that one of Gide's lovers used him to make Gide jealous. In addition, however, he may have recognized himself in Passavant, the evil homosexual who corrupts youths in Gide's novel *The Counterfeiters* (1926). In some sense, Cocteau's *White Paper* is a kind of response to Gide's *Corydon* (1911–1924). Whereas *Corydon* presents a homosexual narrator giving a heterosexual man a series of lectures, *White Paper,* in contrast, recounts a series of erotic and compelling images of sexual joy and pain. Cocteau celebrates and illustrates the wild love of sailors like the one with a "Born-to-Lose" (Pas de chance) tattoo. Stunned by the bitterness of Gide's journal comments, published at his death in 1951, Cocteau began his own journal *Past/Tense* in July of the same year and carefully avoided belittling Gide.

Cocteau also had problems in his relations with Jean Genet. He compared Genet to Rimbaud, but Genet never saw Cocteau as his Verlaine. The men met in 1943, after Cocteau had read portions of *Our Lady of the Flowers* and arranged to find a publisher. Later, Cocteau illustrated Genet's *Querelle* (1948) with erotic drawings of naked sailors buggering each other. He attended Genet's many trials, supported him in prison, and organized a successful campaign to win Genet a pardon when he faced possible life imprisonment as a habitual criminal. As a character witness, Cocteau swore under oath that Genet was "the greatest writer of the modern era." Cocteau resented the truth of that statement, and Genet resented being judged by Cocteau.

Cocteau's best criticism explains his own work and that of his friends. *Professional Secrets* (1922) and *The Difficulty of Being* (1947) resemble Nietzsche, whom both Genet and Cocteau emulated. Cocteau asserted that "Nietzsche never makes mistakes, except in *Zarathustra* when he becomes 'poetic.' To be poetic is the opposite of poetry." Cocteau perhaps makes similar mistakes in *The Rooster and the Harlequin,* an attack on Russian and German composers in favor of the French Six, Darius Milhaud, Georges Auric, Arthur Honegger, Germaine Tailleferre, Francis Poulenc, and Louis Durey. His attack here highlights one of his weaknesses and perhaps strengths, his complete Gallicism.

Cocteau's alleged frivolity might be charged to his immersion in the feminine. His father died in 1898, and he lived close to or with his mother until her death in 1943. He enjoyed the company of wealthy women like Coco Chanel, who often supported his work and his lovers. He played the little boy to figures such as his mother, Comtesse Anna de Noailles, Valentine Hugo, and Francine Weisweiller. He created powerful roles for women in his films and plays. Like many gay males, he loved actresses and women singers. A companion explained that women "formed part of the décor of his life." On the day that Edith Piaf died, he recorded a tribute to her, which was broadcast on French radio; he himself died later that day, October 11, 1963.

In celebrating the painter, Cocteau's *Ode to Picasso* (1919) celebrates the nine muses as each a separate aspect of creation or poetry. For Cocteau, genres did not separate but bound together his and others' work in the theater, the cinema, drawing, painting, music, dancing, and sexual relations. In bibliographies assembled in his later years, he catalogued his numerous works under various branches of poetry: Poetry itself; Poetry of the Novel; Critical Poetry; Poetry of the Theater; Graphics Poetry (including book illustrations); and Cinematographic Poetry.

Although he hated academies, Cocteau near the end of his life accepted their accolades: among them, an honorary degree from Oxford (1956) and membership in the Académie Royale de Belgique (1955), the Académie Française (1955), National Institute of Arts and Letters (New York, 1957), and the Légion d'Honneur (1961). The publication of his *Complete Works* (1946–1950) in ten volumes, though hardly complete, stamped him as a classic author. But the man himself, however much he reveled in celebrity, struggled continuously not to become monumental.

Today, Cocteau is best remembered for his cinema. Doubtless, this is more a commentary on our times than on Cocteau. He has been recognized as a pioneer in film and his films continue to inspire viewers and other filmmakers. In *Republic of Images: A History of French Filmmaking* (1992), Allan Williams writes, "Cocteau's films are arguably more significant as expressions of his personality and artistic vision than as contributions to film history. Though *in* the cinema's evolution, they are not *of* it." This comment could be said of all the genres he attempted. As Jean Genet remarked, "We deny Jean Cocteau the stupid title 'enchanter': we declare him 'enchanted.' He does not 'charm.' He is 'charmed.' He is not a wizard, he is bewitched." Cocteau relished such comments; he never wanted to be in the "in" crowd; he ever feared being killed by his own creations.

—*Charley Shively*

BIBLIOGRAPHY

Brown, Frederick. *An Impersonation of Angels: A Biography of Jean Cocteau.* New York: Viking, 1968. ■ Crowson, Lydia. *The Esthetic of Jean Cocteau.* Hanover, N.H.: University Press of New England, 1978. ■ Emboden, William A. *The Visual Art of Jean Cocteau.* New York: H.N. Abrams, 1989. ■ Evans, Arthur B. *Jean Cocteau and His Films of Orphic Identity.* Philadelphia: Art Alliance, 1977. ■ Fifield, William. *Jean Cocteau.* Columbia Essays on Modern Writers 70. New York: Columbia University Press, 1974. ■ Fowlie, Wallace. *Jean Cocteau: The History of a Poet's Age.* Bloomington: Indiana University Press, 1966. ■ Gilson, René. *Jean Cocteau: An Investigation into His Films and Philosophy.* Trans. Ciba Vaugh. New York: Crown, 1969. ■ Knapp, Betinna L. *Jean Cocteau.* Twayne's World Authors Series. Rev. Edition. New York: Twayne Publishers, 1989. ■ Peters, Arthur King. *Jean Cocteau and His World: An Illustrated Biography.* Foreword by Ned Rorem. New York: Vendome Press, 1986. ■ Saul, Julie, ed. *Jean Cocteau: The Mirror and the Mask: A Photobiography.* Boston: Godine, 1992. ■ Steegmuller, Francis. *Cocteau: A Biography.* Boston: Little Brown, 1970.

Colette
(1873–1954)

Colette is one of France's most beloved authors, a "national treasure" as one French reader has put it. This admiration is reserved for the Colette who in some sixty-odd books wrote magnificently and frankly about woman's condition. It does not generally extend to the Colette whose name invariably appears whenever lists of famous gay and lesbian authors are compiled. Colette's six-year liaison with the Marquise de Belboeuf, known as Missy, is dismissed as a phase and her other lesbian relationships are almost never mentioned in the admiring accounts of her life. *The Pure and the Impure* (1932, rev. 1941), which contains Colette's most explicit and extended writing on homosexuality, continues to baffle those who actually read it, and the strong lesbian subtext found throughout her *oeuvre* remains all but invisible even today.

Colette was born on January 28, 1873, in the Burgundian village of Saint-Sauveur-en-Puisaye. The house and garden, fields and forests, presided over by the major figure in her life, her mother Sido, constitute in her works a kind of earthly paradise, which a number of Colette's adult female characters seek futilely to regain. Colette's first experience with lesbian feelings, though she does not refer to it as such, occurred when she was about eleven and is briefly documented in her 1929 work *Sido*. The family was forced to leave Saint-Sauveur for financial reasons when Colette was seventeen; this was a major rupture in her life. At the age of twenty, she married the famous Paris critic, Henri Gauthier-Villars (known as Willy), who was thirteen years older than she and whose numerous published works were in fact written by ghost writers, among them a number of male homosexuals, and Colette herself. Married life with Willy was tumultuous and destructive: Colette almost died of a mysterious illness during the first year but was nursed back to health by Sido. She was forced to acknowledge, and even to entertain, Willy's mistresses. (Much later, she wrote about this period in *My Apprenticeships*, 1936.) Toward the end of the marriage, Colette was introduced to NATALIE CLIFFORD BARNEY's circle, and met Missy. Following her separation from Willy in 1906, Colette made her living as a professional dancer and mime (the subject of her 1911 novel *The Vagabond*). One of the most famous incidents of this period involved a performance at the Moulin Rouge of a pantomime in which the amateur Missy (who had taken a few lessons for this purpose) played the male role as the mysterious "Yssim" (no one was fooled) opposite Colette. As Colette arose from a sarcophagus, she and Missy acted out a love scene together: Their passionate kiss resulted in a near-riot among the protesting spectators.

Shortly after Sido died in 1912, Colette married Henri de Jouvenel and gave birth to a daughter, her only child. She divorced Jouvenel in 1924, and eleven years later, married Maurice Goudeket, sixteen years her junior. This marriage lasted until Colette's death at the age of eighty-one. Colette was the only woman to be given a state funeral in France's history. The Church refused a religious burial.

Colette's career as a writer began when Willy, short of funds, asked her to write about her schoolgirl experiences and to put something "spicy" in it. At first dismissing, then realizing the value of what she had written, he locked her in a room for four hours a day to write. The result was the wildly successful *Claudine* series, signed however by Willy and to which Colette was never able to have her name rightfully restored. The "spicy" elements Willy demanded include the lesbian headmistress in *Claudine at School* (1900) and an affair between Claudine and another woman arranged by Claudine's husband for his voyeuristic pleasure in *Claudine Married* (1902). After the *Claudine*'s, homosexuality is a recurrent, if not always recognized, theme in Colette's works. Among these, a sleepless erotic night (unquestionably with Missy) described in *Tendrils of the Vine* (1908) is additionally noteworthy because some editions change the gender of one of the participants, identifiable only through a single grammatical element, from female to male. An episode in *Sido* rarely mentioned in studies of Colette recounts the eleven-year-old Colette's notion of a first seduction and her "morbid" fascination with the breast of Sido's friend Adrienne, who as a game had exchanged babies with Sido and nursed the infant Colette. *My Apprenticeships*, in addition to describing Colette's acquaintance with Natalie Clifford Barney's circle, contains an obscure, all but unnoticed reference to writing one day about the "other slope" of her life. Given *My Apprenticeship*'s subtexts, there is every reason to expect that the "other slope" would be a lesbian text.

The Pure and the Impure, Colette's study of the spectrum of sexual behavior, is at once her most important and least understood work: She herself thought it would one day be considered her best book.

Four of the nine chapters deal exclusively with lesbians and one with male homosexuals. The title does not refer to conventional moral judgments of sexuality, but rather to excessive behavior (impure), which Colette condemns in heterosexuals and homosexuals alike, whereas purity, used only in conjunction with homosexuality, seems to signify completion, or wholeness. The first of the lesbian portraits focuses on Missy, known as La Chevalière in this work, who seeks in vain a "calm sentimental climate," in contrast to the "salacious" expectations of the lesbians surrounding her. RENÉE VIVIEN, who fears she will be killed by her imperious (female) "master" through what appears to be excessive sensual pleasure, and who dies from willful starvation and abuse of alcohol, is condemned by Colette for being consumed by her senses. La Lucienne is obsessed by the idea of being completely a man: Her illusion is shattered by the young blonde Loulou, who says she will not be with a man who can't "faire pipi" against a wall. Colette introduces her portrait of the Ladies of Llangollen (ELEANOR BUTLER AND SARAH PONSONBY) by exploring the effect that similarity between women has in lesbian relationships. Colette's approval is tempered by recognizing the dangers that threaten the lesbian couple on all sides. The Ladies, of Irish origin, withdraw to a Welsh village where, beyond reach of all, they lead a perfect life together for over fifty years. After claiming to defer to PROUST's monumental illumination of "Sodom" (but condemning his "misguided" representation of lesbianism), Colette then offers her own portrait of male homosexuals, admiring their virility and their rejection of other homosexuals who adopt female roles. She concludes The Pure and the Impure by revealing her conception of purity, significantly expressed in the context of a female couple.

Colette's work as a whole has always been acknowledged as some of the best writing on women we have. For a long time, however, her admirers were mainly outside the academy: Traditional critics patronizingly dismissed her "feminine sensibility" in matters of love and women's lives. Post-structuralist readings have done much to reveal a far more profound and complex writer. In the future, lesbian readings of Colette promise to unite the apparently scattered or, for the most part, invisible lesbian components of her *oeuvre,* demonstrating conclusively that in Colette, lesbianism is a major strategy for survival.

—*Ann Cothran*

BIBLIOGRAPHY

Benstock, Shari. *Women of the Left Bank: Paris, 1900-1940.* Austin: University of Texas Press, 1986. ■ Cottrell, Robert D. *Colette.* New York: Frederick Ungar, 1974. ■ Crosland, Margaret. *Colette: The Difficulty of Loving.* New York: Dell, 1973. ■ Dranch, Sherry A. "Reading Through the Veiled Text: Colette's *The Pure and the Impure.*" *Contemporary Literature* 24, no. 2 (1983): 176–189. ■ Eisinger, Erica and Mari McCarty, eds. *Colette: The Woman, the Writer.* University Park: Pennsylvania State University Press, 1981. ■ Jouve, Nicole Ward. *Colette.* Bloomington: Indiana University Press, 1987. ■ Lottman, Herbert. *Colette: A Life.* Boston: Little Brown, 1991. ■ Marks, Elaine. *Colette.* New Brunswick: Rutgers University Press, 1960. ■ Sarde, Michèle. *Colette: Free and Fettered.* Trans. Richard Miller. New York: Morrow, 1980. ■ Stambolian, George and Elaine Marks, eds. *Homosexualities and French Literature.* Ithaca, N.Y.: Cornell University Press, 1979.

Coming Out Stories

Coming out stories, both written and oral, have for many years been a staple of lesbian and gay culture building. No matter how sophisticated or theoretical we become, when groups of lesbians or gay men congregate, a usual suggestion is to share coming out stories. The coming out experience is so important that it tends to be the focus of a great deal of gay and lesbian literature, including novels and short stories. In recent years, several collections of lesbian coming out narratives have appeared to an eagerly awaiting readership. In 1980, two such collections were published: Margaret Cruikshank's *The Lesbian Path* and Julia Penelope Stanley and Susan Wolfe's *The Coming Out Stories.*

As the epigraph to her foreword for the second printing of *The Lesbian Path,* ADRIENNE RICH offers this quotation from Deena Metzger's *The Book of Hags.*

> The women gather their old flesh into sacks and carry it along the road. Under the bridges in the middle of the night, they tell stories to each other. Each secret told gains a year. "Why are you telling me this?" one asks. "So I won't die."

The sense of urgency in this passage underlies many of the oral tellings and written collectings of what an individual deems to be his or her coming out story. As members of a historically invisible minority, lesbians and gay men have routinely had difficulty positioning ourselves, partly because we have had no language with which to do so and partly because the larger culture has supplied no acceptable mirrors or images by which to fashion ourselves. The existence of coming out narratives between printed covers is a sign of existence both for those featured therein and for those who will read their accounts. Such narratives also provide mirrors in which people unsure of their sexual identity may recognize themselves, mirrors that have the capacity to enable newly emerging gay men and lesbians to acknowledge their sexuality sooner and with less confusion and pain than is likely the case in the absence of coming out stories.

Though most large cities in the United States have identifiable centers in which informational and social exchanges occur, much of the rest of the country continues to impose isolation on and exact silence from its lesbian and gay residents. Being able to obtain collections of stories, some of which will narrate exactly the situation in which the reader currently finds himself or herself, can mean the difference between feeling like a part of the world and falling into ever deeper despair and loneliness.

In literary terms, this genre is capable of simultaneity: If I tell others my particular story of awakening to my sexual orientation, that act is extremely individualistic, even unique; however, it also places me squarely in a community of others with equally individualistic and unique stories. Hence I assert my specialness at exactly the same moment as I identify with and affirm a group. Collections of coming out stories declare that lesbians and gay men are both alike and different from their sisters and brothers. This may be one of the most exciting aspects of these narratives, especially within the current cultural studies movement in which critical methodologies such as post-structuralism and deconstructionism argue that there may be no such thing as a unified self. Coming out stories may offer valuable insights into how to solve the dilemma of being absolutely sure of identity at the same time as being keenly aware of one's relativity to all others in one's class or group. This will make them a central element in any academic discourse about gay and lesbian studies and research.

Identifying characteristics of a coming out narrative would include some or all of the following: (1) Coming out stories recount the teller's initial recognition of themselves as "different" emotionally or sexually. (2) Coming out stories most often focus on a "first time" erotic or sexual experience with someone of the same sex. (3) Coming out stories are usually quite short, the shortest unit of shaped autobiographical writing. Like any good short story, these narratives have a single focus and a tight structure. They might be thought of as mini *romans à clef*. (4) Coming out stories are as varied in their details as they are numerous in their narrators. Commonality flows from the act of speaking, of giving language to the suppressed underlife, of bringing the "love that has no name" out of the darkness of bars and bedrooms into the light of gardens, offices, barracks, nurseries, and boardrooms. (5) Coming out stories involve a crucial naming of the self to the self as someone who loves a member of one's own sex, recognizing just how radical and dangerous such an act is in a virulently homophobic society. (6) Coming out stories empower their tellers on many levels in addition to the sensual. Indeed some such stories may not involve a sexual liaison at all, depending on the teller's particular circumstances. (7) Coming out stories defy the implicit and explicit demands of the dominant culture by refusing the injunction to hide or "pass" for heterosexual either to oneself or to those around one.

When Margaret Cruikshank published her anthology, she spoke in the introduction of its hardly being necessary in 1979 to prove that the lesbian community in North America was diverse. Yet she had not been able to make her initial collection reflect that diversity to the degree she had hoped. She called for subsequent publication of collections of coming out stories of lesbians of color, older lesbians, working class and poor lesbians. Many of these have appeared subsequently, along with anthologies grouped around such unforeseen themes as lesbians who once were nuns, gay men and lesbians over fifty, Asian-American lesbians, and gay men whose coming out has hinged on their finding themselves to be HIV-positive. It seems clear at this point in lesbian and gay history that we can continue producing collections of coming out narratives as long as we exist since our stories of self-recognition shift and multiply as our culture evolves. But since the very act of telling our stories is itself an act of personal and political disobedience, the one constant running through all coming out stories is the empowerment inherent in the articulation itself.

—*Toni A. H. McNaron*

BIBLIOGRAPHY

Adair, Nancy and Casey Adair, eds. *Word Is Out: Stories of Some of Our Lives*. New York: Dell, 1978. ■ Adelman, Marcy. *Long Time Passing: Lives of Older Lesbians*. Boston: Alyson, 1986. ■ Beck, Evelyn T. *Nice Jewish Girls: A Lesbian Anthology*. Watertown, Mass.: Persephone Press, 1982. ■ Cruikshank, Margaret, ed. *The Lesbian Path*. San Francisco: Grey Fox Press, 1980, 1985. ■ Curb, Rosemary and Nancy Manahan, eds. *Lesbian Nuns: Breaking Silence*. New York:

Warner, 1986. ■ Jay, Karla and Allen Young, eds. *After You're Out: Personal Experiences of Gay Men and Lesbian Women.* New York: Link Books, 1975. ■ Monette, Paul. *On Becoming a Man.* New York: Harcourt Brace, 1992 ■ Stanley, Julia P. and Susan J. Wolfe, eds. *The Coming Out Stories.* Watertown, Mass.: Persephone Press, 1980.

Compton-Burnett, I.
(1884–1969)

I[vy] Compton-Burnett was born June 5, 1884 (although she claimed 1892), earned a B.A. in Classics with second honors in 1906 from the Royal Holloway College of the University of London, was knighted in 1967, and died August 19, 1969. Compton-Burnett's method is to expose personal secrets between the lines of her novels-in-dialogue, but although she lived with her life companion—the writer, editor, and antiques expert Margaret Jourdain—from 1919 until Jourdain's death in 1951, no hint of this domestic arrangement surfaces in her fiction. All of Compton-Burnett's works are set in the traditional world of the English squirearchy before its genteel complacency was shattered by World War I.

Compton-Burnett's first novel, *Dolores* (1911), might better have been called *Dolores and Perdita* in light of the shift of focus in the middle from one character to the other. The passionate friendship of the two central characters in this novel shows more psychological presentation of love between women than anything in the later novels. Nevertheless, *Dolores* is not a successful novel. It is an imitation of George Eliot. Like much of Eliot, *Dolores* is badly proportioned, unselfconsciously proselytory, and extremely earnest, but its main weakness is a number of dull stretches where the author seems to get her characters talking and becomes unable to stop them even when they are saying nothing either to reveal their inner lives or to advance the plot. Compton-Burnett perhaps recognized these weaknesses since it was thirteen years before she again attempted fiction. She later disowned this novel, citing neither its structural weaknesses nor its lesbian subtext but instead the collaborative meddling of her brother.

When she did return to writing, in *Pastors and Masters* (1925), she produced an entirely different sort of novel, wisely scrapping the features inspired by Eliot and focusing centrally on the dialogue passages, in the tradition of Thomas Love Peacock and RONALD FIRBANK. This format allowed her to develop dialogue as a subtle medium for character revelation. She used this format throughout the rest of her career and developed it as a progressively more elliptical and subtle means of characterization as she went on.

Although there is nothing personal about the novels after *Dolores*, two novels are of particular interest because they include lesbian and gay characters. *More Women than Men* (1933) concerns the staff of a girls' school. Most of the staff are apparently homosexual, and the dynamics of their interrelationships are viewed with wry humor and detachment. The theme of the book is that affectional and power relationships of all kinds are always in flux. As a result, no character's homosexual identity is entirely permanent here, and it is perhaps even suggested that homosexual identity is eventually outgrown although only quite late in life by some people.

In *Two Worlds and Their Ways* (1949) Compton-Burnett again chronicles English public (that is, private) school life, this time using a boys' school as well as a girls'. The comedy is more brittle and epigrammatic than in the earlier work. And *Two Worlds and Their Ways* has an extremely complicated plot. Startling events succeed one another rapidly, creating parallels so elaborate that they generate comedy. As in *More Women than Men,* various homosexual couplings are implied, but these are even more obliquely suggested.

Though Susan Crecy describes Compton-Burnett as an indirect advocate of homosexuality by virtue of the devastating excoriation of family life in her novels, her homosexual characters are just as manipulative as her straight ones. Indeed, she is important for lesbian studies chiefly by virtue of treating her lesbian characters just like everyone else. Compton-Burnett's style is the subject of a parody by Richard Mallett.

—*Edmund Miller*

BIBLIOGRAPHY

Burkhart, Charles. *I. Compton-Burnett.* London: Gollancz, 1965. ■ Crecy, Susan. "Ivy Compton[-]Burnett: Family as Nightmare." *Lesbian and Gay Writing: An Anthology of Critical Essays.* Mark Lilly, ed. Philadelphia: Temple University Press, 1990. 13–22. ■ Grieg, Cecily. *Ivy Compton-Burnett: A Memoir.* London: Garnestone, 1972. ■ Grylls, R[osalie] Glynn [Lady Mander]. *Ivy Compton-Burnett.* London: Longman, 1971. ■ Mallett, Richard. *Literary Upshots; or, Split Reading.* London: Jonathan Cape, 1951. ■ Sprigge, Elizabeth. *The Life of Ivy Compton-Burnett.* New York: Braziller, 1973.

Corelli, Marie
(1855–1924)

Although she strove to conceal her origins through numerous fictions, Marie Corelli was born Mary (or Minnie) Mackay in Perth, Scotland, in 1855, the natural daughter of Dr. Charles Mackay, a minor literary figure who married her mother, a servant, in 1864. While in her twenties, she pursued a brief career as a concert pianist and assumed the fantastic, self-created persona of Marie Corelli, "a true Italian" descended from the seventeenth-century Venetian composer Arcangelo Corelli. Subsequently, she turned to the more lucrative venture of writing fiction. Her first novel, *A Romance of Two Worlds* (1886), combines science fiction and occultism in examining such disparate notions as out-of-body time travel, moral didacticism, and "personal electricity." After the moderate success of this initial venture, she produced, among other works, the best sellers *The Soul of Lilith* (1892), *Barabbas, a Dream of the World's Tragedy* (1893), and *The Sorrows of Satan* (1895). Initial sales of the latter work surpassed those of any English novel previously published, and, in all, fifteen of her nearly thirty novels had sales in excess of 100,000 copies. Her novels brought her extravagant wealth and fame; simultaneously, her melodramatic plots, purple prose, anachronistic and ill-informed use of antique or biblical settings and characters, and *idée fixes* (for example, Christian moralism, pseudo-science, and attacks on society women and the literary establishment) made her the target of critical ridicule, to which she publicly and self-righteously responded. As a result, Corelli was the most publicized British author of the 1890s, overshadowing even OSCAR WILDE. Her fame was ephemeral, however, and she fell from public popularity before her death, in 1924, in Stratford-upon-Avon.

Although Marie Corelli has been represented as a feminist or lesbian author, both definitions are highly problematic. Her novels, generally variations on the standard heterosexual romance plot, are frequently polemics against marriage and male dominance, and Corelli firmly believed in the essential spiritual superiority of women over the base carnality of men. She was an outspoken foe of women's suffrage, however, and denounced women with political and professional aspirations as both unwomanly and unladylike. From 1876 until her death, she lived with Bertha Vyver, who served as companion, confidant, housekeeper, and nurse. Corelli wore a ring Vyver had given her when both were young, and the entwined initials of the two women, who themselves appeared in public with their arms around each other, were carved into the mantelpiece of their home with the inscription *amor vincit*. Whether their relationship went beyond ROMANTIC FRIENDSHIP, however, is unclear. Corelli publicly inveighed against "sex feelings" and maintained a close friendship with Henry Labouchere, author of the amendment to the Criminal Law Act of 1885 by which Wilde was convicted and imprisoned. (Corelli proclaimed the she would have "that Douglas man [Wilde's lover Lord Alfred Douglas] soundly whipped.")

Ironically, Marie Corelli's most significant contribution to gay and lesbian culture is an unwitting one, that of a CAMP figure. In the early stages of their respective careers, Wilde derived amusement from the flamboyance of her writing (he wrote, "you certainly tell of marvellous things in a marvellous way") and advised her in the art of self-promotion. Additionally, the meddlesome and imperious Corelli, who was given to reciting imaginative historical "facts" and dispensing phrases in skewed French and Italian, provided E. F. BENSON, an occasional visitor to her home, with the perfect model for the protagonist of his Lucia novels.

Most of Corelli's novels are currently in print, their author having achieved something of a cult status since the 1960s. *The Romance of Two Worlds* remains a perennial favorite in occult bookstores.

—*Patricia Juliana Smith*

BIBLIOGRAPHY

Biglund, Eileen. *Marie Corelli: The Woman and the Legend.* London: Jarrolds, 1953. ■ Bullock, George. *Marie Corelli: The Life and Death of a Best-seller.* London: Constable, 1940. ■ Faderman, Lillian. *Surpassing the Love of Men: Romantic Friendship and Love Between Women from the Renaissance to the Present.* New York: William Morrow, 1981. ■ Masters, Brian. *Now Barabbas Was a Rotter: The Extraordinary Life of Marie Corelli.* London: Hamish Hamilton, 1978. ■ Vyver, Bertha. *Memoirs of Marie Corelli.* London: Alston Rivers, 1930.

Coward, Noël
(1899–1973)

Sir Noël Coward was the self-crowned laureate of his age. Born at the beginning of a new century, Coward always considered himself one of the most important writers of the twentieth century. His stylized manners and farcical sketches satirized Edwardian mores, while always respecting the dominant culture. Coward's partnership with actress Gertrude Lawrence was a formidable theatrical relationship that culminated in their production of Coward's *Private Lives* in 1930.

Although most of the dapper lovers in Coward's plays are heterosexual, Coward's homosexuality was an open secret for most of London society. Further, his plays "camp" up heterosexual romance. In *The Vortex* (1924), Coward's first major success, he deals with an aging mother, Florence, and her melancholic piano-playing son, Nicky. Trying to remain young and beautiful through her increasingly bored young lovers, Florence is a sympathetic woman, but a pathetic mother to her sensitive son. An allegory of the overripe Edwardian age, *The Vortex* builds on one of Coward's primary themes: the importance of rebellious youth in the comedy of manners.

The three plays for which Coward is best known, *Private Lives* (1930), *Design for Living* (1933), and *Blithe Spirit* (1941), are all plays about heterosexual couples, yet they partake in the language of CAMP that points toward Coward's predecessor, OSCAR WILDE. Coward's "romances" are pointedly weary of normative sexual relations; his couples are disenchanted with bourgeois sexual attitudes. In *Private Lives*, Amanda and Elyot are detached from their society—represented by the dull and "normal" Victor and Sybil. Normal sexuality is boring, passionless, and unattractive to the chic bohemian nature of Amanda and Elyot. Similarly, in *Design for Living*, the ménage à trois between Otto, Leo, and Gilda breaks down sexual barriers, complicating the whole notion of love and sexual attachment. *Blithe Spirit* ends with the liberating death of Charles Condomine's two wives. Their deaths relieve Charles of the burden of the women in his life. Charles declares, "now I'm free, Ruth dear, not only of Mother and Elvira and Mrs. Winthrop-Lewellen, but free of you too, and I should like to take this farewell opportunity of saying I'm enjoying it immensely." *Blithe Spirit* represents the ultimate freedom for the man of taste and distinction so important in Coward's drama.

Resolution in Coward is usually a form of escape from the responsibilities of everyday behavior. Coward's critique of daily life participates in his trademark camp sensibility and detachment from dominant norms. In *Private Lives*, Amanda and Elyot walk away from the bickering of Victor and Sybil, leaving the latter to discuss the pros and cons (mostly cons) of a heterosexual relationship. In *Design for Living*, Gilda finally abandons all three of the men in her life, leaving them to form their own homosocial bonds.

Coward's brand of camp was thoroughly modern and, underneath the shimmering surfaces, was uncompromising in its dissatisfaction with traditional sexual decorum. Coward's plays and sketches negate dominant sensibilities; they work against domestic values on the side of flamboyance, frivolity, and pleasure.

In his later career, Coward openly explored the closet that he felt limited his creative expression. This is seen implicitly in Uncle Bob in Coward's story "Pretty Polly" (1965), and explicitly in his presentation of Hugo Latymer in the play *Song at Twilight* (1966). In "Pretty Polly," a young niece admires her uncle for his bisexuality, his being "mysterious and a bachelor and leading a secret, sinful life in the exotic East." However, for Coward, there are problems with exiling one's sexuality in another culture and closeting one's sexuality in London in order to be a successful writer. In *Song at Twilight*, the novelist Hugo Latymer complains that even when the laws forbidding homosexuality no longer exist, "there will still be a stigma attached to 'the love that dare not speak its name' in the minds of millions of people for generations to come." Hugo, as Coward, goes on to defend his self-imposed closet, exclaiming, "My private inclinations are not the concern of my reading public. I have no urge to martyr my reputation for the sake of self-indulgent exhibitionism."

By the time of his death in Jamaica in 1973, Coward, a playwright, actor, screenwriter, producer, singer, songwriter, was more than a man with many talents: He had become the embodiment of a master showman. Always a comedian, Coward delighted audiences with his upper-crust English humor for over six decades. Noël Coward entertained troops during World War II, left England as a tax-exile in 1956, made a "comeback" in the 1960s, and was finally knighted in 1970. (See also DRAMATIC LITERATURE: MODERN DRAMA and ENGLISH LITERATURE: TWENTIETH CENTURY.)

—Amy Farmer

BIBLIOGRAPHY

Lahr, John. *Coward the Playwright*. London: Methuen, 1982. ■ Mander, Raymond and Joe Mitchenson. *Theatrical Companion to Coward: A Pictorial Record of the First Performances of the Theatrical Works of Coward*. New York: Macmillan, 1957. ■ Morley, Sheridan. *A Talent to Amuse: A Biography of Noel Coward*. Garden City, N.Y.: Doubleday, 1969. ■ Sinfield, Alan. "Private Lives/Public Theater: Noel Coward and the Politics of Homosexual Representation." *Representations* 36 (Fall 1991): 43–63.

Crane, Hart
(1899–1933)

Harold Hart Crane was born in Garrettsville, Ohio, on July 21, 1899, the only son of Grace Hart Crane, an intelligent, sensitive woman, and C. A. Crane, a success-driven businessman. The poet's childhood was materially secure but emotionally difficult. When Harold was five, the family moved to Warren, Ohio, where they lived until domestic conflicts drove Grace into a sanitarium and C. A. to Chicago; nine-year-old Harold was sent to his mother's parents in Cleveland. Grace returned in 1909, and C. A. later rejoined her at the Hart house, where they lived on uneasy terms until their divorce in 1916, the year that Harold, at seventeen, set off for New York City. He later confessed to Grace: "my youth has been a rather bloody battleground for yours and father's sex life and troubles." Still, he sympathized so strongly with her that in 1917 he chose to call himself "Hart." Although he eventually reconciled with his father, his relationship with his mother slowly deteriorated. He finally broke with her in 1928 after she threatened to tell C. A. about his homosexuality and tried to block a $5,000 inheritance left to him by his grandparents.

From 1916 to 1923, Hart shuttled between Cleveland—where he worked, unhappily, for his father as a candy salesman—and New York. During this time, he had his first love affairs with men, read widely, and wrote many of the lyrics collected in *White Buildings* (1926). In 1923, he moved permanently to New York, where he changed residences frequently and lived off occasional jobs writing advertising copy, money borrowed from friends, and small stipends from his parents. In 1926, a grant from a banker, Otto Kahn, allowed him to work on his long poem, *The Bridge*, for several months in New York and then, from May to October, at his grandparents' Caribbean plantation on the Isle of Pines, where he also wrote a number of fine lyrics. After his return to New York, he was distracted from *The Bridge* by Grace's financial and emotional troubles; her letters often prompted Crane's self-destructive drinking sprees. In 1927, he lived in Pasadena as a paid companion to a wealthy invalid and later moved to Hollywood to assist Grace, who was nursing her mother through a terminal illness; the nervous collapses Grace suffered whenever he wished to go out at night drove him to leave for New York City in May 1928, never to see her again. His grandmother died in September, and when he finally obtained his inheritance, he sailed in late December for Europe, where he met Harry Crosby, owner of the Black Sun Press, whose enthusiastic agreement to publish *The Bridge* inspired Crane to finish the poem after he returned to New York in 1929.

Crane's final years were marred by his alcoholism, inability to find work, and diminished poetic production. A Guggenheim Fellowship enabled him to spend his last year in Mexico, but, plagued by violent drinking bouts, grieved by the sudden death of his father in July 1932, and swept up in his first heterosexual love affair, he completed only one lyric, "The Broken Tower." During the early morning of April 27, 1933, on his journey back to New York by ship from Vera Cruz, Crane was badly beaten by sailors whom he had solicited for sex; at noon he returned to the stateroom he shared with his lover, bade her good-bye, went up to the deck, and leapt into the sea. According to Thomas Yingling, "Crane's self-destruction was a lethal combination of alcoholism, homosexual self-hatred, and the personal failures that both obsessions induced. . . . If his life became literally unlivable for him by 1933, part of the reason for that was that homosexuality was central to his life but was itself socially and psychically designed as an unlivable existence."

Crane was not strictly closeted; an open-hearted and voluble man, with his straight friends he made no secret of his homosexuality, and New York in the 1920s offered ample opportunities for gay life. Yingling argues that "Crane's generation stood precisely on that historical threshold when homosexuality began to be articulated as an identity through Western cultures, and Crane's is one of the first literary texts to provide literary representations grounded in that articulation." That the desire Crane expressed—and often cloaked—was homoerotic helps account for his dense style although, like many modern poets, he also found inspiration in the knotty paradoxes of JOHN DONNE and the luxurious surrealism of ARTHUR RIMBAUD. Unlike many moderns, however, Crane did not repudiate the Romantic tradition of Blake, Shelley, and Keats and, in particular, the American Orphic strain developed by Poe, WHITMAN, and MELVILLE. Like these Romantics, Crane strove to balance moments of ecstatic consciousness when spiritual transcendence seems within reach against the boundaries of human and material limitations. But for Crane, those moments were primarily sparked by homoerotic relationships, and the boundaries he encountered were society's strictures against homosexuality, for he tightly partitioned his life between the gay and straight worlds.

The lyrics from *White Buildings* are beautiful, compelling, and often opaque, for Crane so thickens his lines with tropes that he tests the limits of figurative language—particularly when he writes about sexual appetite as in "Paraphrase," "Possessions," "The Wine Menagerie," and "Recitative," and about joyful consummation in "Voyages," written for his lover Emil Opffer. The traditional forms that Crane prefers, however, such as his signature iambic pentameter quatrains, help ground his charged language. Just as in his life he sought to be both a homosexual adventurer and a man of letters, Crane wished in his writing to abandon himself to the flux of language while anchoring himself in the cadences of traditional forms. These obsessions are reflected throughout his poetry in his symbols of shifting sea and hurricane and the towers whose stability and completeness Crane often questions. His search for a poetic structure flexible enough to accommodate his restless vision found its fulcrum in *The Bridge*, where the Brooklyn Bridge, whose two broken towers contain and support the arcing cords that Crane compares to a lyre's strings, becomes the symbol with which he tries to span many oppositions: space and time, faith and doubt, the Old World and the New, primitive naturalism and modern industrialism, cultural and personal memory, high rhetoric and American demotic speech, pure and tainted manifestations of desire.

Since the poem's publication in 1930, many critics have complained that its varied lyrics and marked rhetorical shifts fail to cohere into a unified whole, in spite of Crane's links of recurring metaphors. But *spanning* oppositions doesn't require fusion; instead, their juxtaposition fuels the poem's startling energy and allows the bridge to symbolize both limitation and possibility. Crane's suspicion of heterosexual marriage, which he explored in "For the Marriage of Faustus and Helen" (1923), reveals itself in *The Bridge*'s emphasis on male communion. Although the men in the poem are sometimes inspired by virgin muses such as Mary and Pocahontas, the poem's intellectual and erotic energy swirls around groups and pairs of men. In the "Ave Maria" section, for example, the discoverer Columbus addresses his friends San Luis de Angel and Juan Perez and, later, Elohim, the plural manifestation of God; the pattern culminates in the poet's clasping of Whitman's hand in "Cape Hatteras." The male "hands of fire" extended throughout *The Bridge* offer the electric link between the risks and rewards of homoerotic desire by which Crane, in his life and work, was both dangerously seared and purified.

—Meg Schoerke

BIBLIOGRAPHY

Brown, Susan Jenkins. *Robber Rocks: Letters and Memoirs of Hart Crane, 1923–1932.* Middletown, Conn.: Wesleyan University Press, 1969. ■ Edelman, Lee. *Transmemberment of Song: Hart Crane's Anatomies of Rhetoric and Desire.* Stanford, Calif.: Stanford University Press, 1987. ■ Giles, Paul. *Hart Crane: The Contexts of the Bridge.* Cambridge: Cambridge University Press, 1986. ■ Lewis, Thomas S. W. *Letters of Hart Crane and His Family.* New York: Columbia University Press, 1986. ■ Martin, Robert K. *The Homosexual Tradition in Modern Poetry.* Austin: University of Texas Press, 1979. ■ Parkinson, Thomas. *Hart Crane and Yvor Winters: Their Literary Correspondence.* Berkeley: University of California Press, 1978. ■ Unterecker, John. *Voyager: A Life of Hart Crane.* New York: Farrar, Straus and Giroux, 1969. ■ Woods, Gregory. *Articulate Flesh: Male Homo-Eroticism and Modern Poetry.* New Haven, Conn.: Yale University Press, 1987. ■ Yingling, Thomas E. *Hart Crane and the Homosexual Text: New Thresholds, New Anatomies.* Chicago: University of Chicago Press, 1990.

Cross-Dressing

In literature, the gay male cross-dresser and the lesbian cross-dresser are often depicted quite differently. In representations of gay male cross-dressing, the drag queen—a gay man dressed in women's clothing—is usually conflated with the male-to-female transsexual, a man who has either completed or wants to begin a "sex change" operation. The medical change from a man to a woman is seen as a "cure" for the "problem" of cross-dressing. With lesbian cross-dressing, however, dressing as a man is seen as a way of claiming power in a society that limits the social mobility of women.

The spectacle of cross-dressing began in the late nineteenth and early twentieth century, when physicians and medical researchers like Richard von Krafft-Ebing coined terms—including "transvestite"—to classify people according to their sexuality. Naming not only established new categories, but, as Vern and Bonnie Bullough demonstrate in *Cross Dressing, Sex, and Gender,* it also fulfilled a need for the control of sexual behavior. The impetus behind the creation of these categories was historically specific, responsive to the growing presence of cross-dressers in public scandals of the day. The cross-dressers most familiar to the public were male prostitutes who, like the frequenters of London's "molly houses," dressed as women to advertise their profession. The association of sexuality and vestimentary advertising led physicians and medical researchers to the premise that cross-dressing was simply the *visualization* of homosexuality. The image of the gay male cross-dresser, or drag queen, has since become such a potent symbol of male homosexuality that the use of the term *cross-dressing* often omits female cross-dressers, or butches, entirely. Mainly this can be attributed to our patriarchal society's general erasure of women's sexualities and desires, but it also illustrates the significant difference gender makes in the representation of and attitude toward cross-dressing.

The drag queen is often depicted as crazy (naturally or drug-induced) and superficial. Georgette in Hubert Selby, Jr.'s *Last Exit to Brooklyn* (1964) is a typical example of the drag queen character. She is "a hip queer [who] took a pride in . . . the wearing of women's panties, lipstick, eye make-up (this including occasionally gold and silver—stardust—on the lids), long marcelled hair, manicured and polished fingernails, the wearing of women's clothes complete with padded bra, high heels and wig . . . and the occasional wearing of a menstrual napkin." Also typical is Miss Destiny in JOHN RECHY's *City of Night* (1963), "fluttering out of the shadows into the dimlights along the ledges like a giant firefly—flirting, calling out to everyone: 'Hello, darling, I love you—I love you too, dear—so very much—ummmm!'" Like most drag queen characters, Georgette and Miss Destiny are in love with butch men, are always depressed, and numb their pain with drugs and alcohol. Their colorful "queen speak" confirms Marjorie Garber's contention in *Vested Interests* that "the way cross-dressing works in . . . fiction is the way in which it concerns itself with language [which acts] as a hieroglyph of transvestic impersonation." Not only do the drag queens perform

in the text, their very words are part of their performance.

In Georgette, Selby emphasizes another trait repeatedly associated with drag queens: misogyny. To Georgette, women are nuisances or competitors, distracting the attention she should have from her men. Peter Ackroyd's "history" of transvestism and drag, *Dressing Up,* concurs with Selby that gay male drag "is misogynistic both in origin and in intent" and that it "parodies and mocks women." Ackroyd emphasizes the equation of *gay* drag with misogyny by defining the term *transvestism* as cross-dressing by *heterosexual* men, which is allegedly not misogynistic because "the contemporary male transvestite wishes to create at least the illusion of femininity [and that] for him, female clothes are a serious expression of [his] fetishistic or anarchic tendencies." To complete Ackroyd's logic, the gay male drag queen therefore wishes to become a woman, but this desire is not a "serious expression" like the (heterosexual) transvestite's; and it is this desire to become a woman that parodies and mocks real women. Ackroyd's misconception that drag queens are trying to be real women is not uncommon; it is an idea fueled by the general cultural anxiety induced whenever someone breaks gender codes. To "explain" drag queens by saying they want to be women solidifies our gender binarism—everyone is, or wants to be, either a *man* or a *woman*—and also confirms the innateness of heterosexuality.

Charles Wright's *The Messenger* (1963) illustrates the "womanliness" of the drag queen through the character of Claudia, "the Grand Duchess [who] often, after getting dolled up in female attire . . . cruises the street, rides the subways and buses, getting picked up by straight men who, after the shock subsides, often accompany him home." As in *Last Exit to Brooklyn* and *City of Night, The Messenger* shows that the drag queen is dedicated to passing as a woman in order to ensnare a "real" man. Yet the drag queen's life is riddled by the dilemma that causes her ubiquitous depression—she can never *really* be a woman. When *The Messenger*'s narrator, Charles, first visits her, "Claudia threw back his head and displayed the evil giveaway, his prominent Adam's apple."

The way to correct the reality of being male was already known by the time Wright's novel was published. The surgical treatment to "fix" those who "suffered from extreme transvestism," or people who felt they had been assigned the wrong gender at birth, even predated the medical term for the "condition," *transsexualism,* first used in a 1949 article by David O. Cauldwell. The term, however, rapidly became known with the public "cases" of male-to-female *transsexuals* like Christine Jorgenson, Jan Morris, and Renee Richards in the 1950s, 1970s, and 1980s. Not only did Jorgenson, Morris, and Richards become spokespeople for the transgendered community, their lives and surgeries became a new medically updated representation of the gay male body.

No fictional character is more emblematic of the association of transsexualism with drag and homosexuality than GORE VIDAL's Myra—originally Myron—Breckinridge. Vidal's *Myra Breckinridge* (1968) explains that Myron had the surgery because his "masculinity was, *at times,* intense, but the feminine aspects of his nature were the controlling ones." Although Myron's "death" and Myra's subsequent surgical "birth" are supposed to "cure" Myron of his effeminate homosexuality and make him into an "acceptably" effeminate heterosexual woman, the surgery has almost the opposite effect. Myra is aggressive, ambitious, abusive, and sadistic. She describes herself as "the new American woman who uses men the way they once used women." She even rapes a man with a strap-on dildo. But even being a superhuman transsexual, Myra still acts like a drag queen. Like Selby and Rechy, Vidal also uses "queen speak" to demonstrate Myra's theatricality and queenliness: "Myra Breckinridge is a dish, and never forget it, you motherfuckers, as the children say nowadays."

Myra Breckinridge represents a popular (mis)understanding of drag queens: transsexual surgery is the "natural" progression from, and "cure" for, drag. In literature, the male-to-female transsexual character is neatly defined by her surgery; her life and identity are divided into pre- or post-operation. Morris Meyer writes that central to the transsexual narrative is proof of, or the display of, her "newly-gendered," post-operation body. Such a display, or striptease, legitimates the surgery. It proves that the surgery can actually *make* a man into a woman. Whether literal striptease as in *Myra Breckinridge* where Myra "stands up and hikes up her dress and pulls down her goddam panties and shows us this scar where cock and balls should be," or figurative striptease as in *City of Night* when Miss Destiny's lover's family disinherits him once they "found out," finding, or finding what happened to, the penis is the most important action involving the transgendered character.

Bruce Benderson recreates this transsexual narrative for comic ends in his 1990 short story "Pretending To Say No," which chronicles a surprise visit by someone claiming to be Nancy Reagan. She comes to Carlos's apartment asking for red thread to fix a loose hem, and convinces everyone she really is the president's wife—until she asks to use the rest room. When she's in the rest room, everyone decides to spy on her: "what happened then was, instead of lifting the edge of her ass off the seat and wiping, the First Lady stood up. And when she did, it knocked us all on our ass, because the biggest cock you've ever seen flipped out the top of those panty hose." While Benderson replicates most of the typical characteristics of the drag queen character in his short story, including rampant drug and alcohol use, the "found out" narrative is there only for comedy. The person claiming to be Nancy Reagan is a drag queen named Brenda X. Her Nancy Reagan drag is just a joke, and, unlike with Miss Destiny, there are no severe consequences to be suffered by being "found out." In this way, Benderson subverts the narrative and image of the drag queen character even as he asserts it.

MANUEL PUIG's *Kiss of the Spider Woman* (1976) also invokes conventional drag queen narratives in order to subvert them. Set in a penitentiary in Buenos Aries, the novel focuses on the relationship between Valentín, a young Marxist activist, and Molina, an older drag queen, who share the same cell. Molina considers herself to be a woman: "As for my friends and myself, we're a hundred percent female. We don't go in for those little games—that's strictly for homos. We're normal women; we sleep with men." Like Georgette and Miss Destiny, Molina performs, passing the evenings in the cell recounting old films she has seen to Valentín. Like Myra, she also identifies with the famous and glamorous heroines of the films she retells, often relishing the details of the heroine's gown or hair. However, Molina escapes much of the grotesque exaggeration of the drag queen character. Her speech is not affected; *what* she says is not overshadowed by *how* she says it. Puig also prevents Molina from becoming a visual spectacle. Because *Kiss of the Spider Woman*'s narrative consists almost entirely of the dialogue between Molina and Valentín, there is no description of Molina's body. No wigs, no high heels. Only Molina's words.

Dialogue also liberates Arnold in HARVEY FIERSTEIN's 1983 play *Torch Song Trilogy* from drag conventions even while Fierstein uses them for comic ends. In many ways, Arnold is a representative drag queen, but unlike most such literary characters, Arnold does not have a feminine name, and he spends a great deal of the play *out* of drag. During the play, we witness Arnold work on relationship issues with his former lover Ed who comes to Arnold for support; we see Arnold find love with David, a younger man who is later killed; we see Arnold adopt a son; and we witness Arnold coming to terms both with his mother and with David's death. It is often argued that Arnold is the most "progressive" or "real" drag queen character in literature. But though *Torch Song Trilogy* is one of the few works that explores and presents the complexity of a drag queen's life, the reason we feel so comfortable with Arnold is that he embodies our society's middle-class aspirations. He is stable. He doesn't drink. He doesn't believe in casual sex. He is interested in establishing a family. But *Torch Song Trilogy* does not circumvent the striptease of drag queen narratives. Fierstein just makes it easier to locate Arnold's penis: He wears pants. This, too, is part of his stability. Yes, he *is* a drag queen, but we all know—and can see—that he's a man.

Timothy John Coldridge in Edward Swift's *Splendora* (1978) is a man, too; but this man returns to his east-Texas home town, the novel's namesake, "in her dress of white eyelet over mint green . . . [and] gold wire-rimmed glasses and Gibson-girl hair [that] were just the right touches for a country librarian still living in days gone by." As Miss Jessie Gatewood, Timothy John wreaks vengeance on the very town that ridiculed him as a child for being effeminate by reintegrating into the town and becoming the center of attention. Unlike Georgette and Miss Destiny, however, Miss Jessie does not flash Splendora with flamboyance. She earns the town's respect with her understated manner and style. She even finds a man, falling in love with Brother Leggett, the town pastor, who later confesses to her his homosexual desire.

Timothy John and Brother Leggett run off together, leaving Miss Jessie's dresses and house in flames, offering a rare "happy ending" for a drag queen character. But this ending is bought with the "suicide" of Miss Jessie, shortly after Timothy John "grows tired" of being her. In a sense, the "happy ending" is not intended for Miss Jessie at all: the tragic, unrequited drag queen dies in the fire. Drag conventions are also maintained with Timothy John's best friend, a sassy black drag queen named Magnolia, who makes all Miss Jessie's clothes and assists in "conceiving" her. In the end, *Splendora,* like *Torch Song Trilogy,* comforts with sensible, complex gay *men* who find happiness and just happen to be drag queens as well.

George C. Wolfe's 1987 play *The Colored Museum,* however, offers us no consolation in one of its "exhibits," "The Gospel According to Miss Roj." Wolfe invokes conventional drag queen attributes, but Miss Roj is not the blubbering Georgette, the domineering Myra, nor the hopelessly romantic Molina. Miss Roj, "dressed in striped patio pants, white go-go boots, a halter, and cat-shaped sunglasses [which she] wears as if it were high fashion," is a fierce black diva drag Snap Queen: "Snapping comes from another galaxy, as do all snap queens. That's right. I ain't just your regular oppressed American Negro. No-no-no!

I am an extraterrestrial. And I ain't talkin' none of that shit you seen in the movies! I have real power." Miss Roj is a shaman, our leader against the destruction of the world from a black gay bar called "The Bottomless Pit."

Although Miss Roj slurps rum and Cokes during her monologue, her warning is not just a drunken rant. She snaps her rage at exploitation and oppression. She snaps to indict our indifference to the inequalities of our lives. Despite the power of her message, however, being an "extra(gendered)terrestrial" only emphasizes Miss Roj's garish difference as exemplified by her body, a male body "degraded" to borrow Ackroyd's logic, by the desire to "become a woman." Ultimately, what Miss Roj models is her body, her "*posing*" as a woman, her figurative striptease.

The transsexual striptease and other conventions of drag queen narratives are enforced by the normalcy of masculinity. The normalcy of masculinity is also what makes lesbian cross-dressing *normal,* or hard to designate as cross-dressing. Women *do* "cross-dress" every day, wearing pants, suits, ties, and other traditionally male clothes, but women dressing as men is not the *performance* that men dressing as women is. In literature, *wearing* men's clothes is not the problem; the problem is what wearing them might *signify,* as ISABEL MILLER's *Patience and Sarah* (1969) demonstrates.

Set in 1816, Miller's novel explores the relationship between Patience White, a well-off single woman, and Sarah Dowling, infamous for her masculine appearance. Sarah first meets Patience when she delivers wood to her house "dressed just as her reputation claimed, in boots, breeches, jerkin, fur mittens, fur hat with a scarf tied over it to cover her ears." When Patience invites Sarah to dinner, her jealous sister-in-law Martha says "Then she can go home and put a dress on first . . . It's in the Bible. Not that *she'd* know that." The reaction to the relationship that develops between Patience and Sarah is similar at the Dowlings. When Sarah confides her affection for Patience to her sister Rachel, Rachel retorts "I used to worry about you. That no man would have you. I never thought to worry you'd think you *was* a man." Sarah's father, who had reared her to work like a man around the farm, beats her to attempt to dissuade her from eloping with Patience. But when Sarah decides to cut her hair short so that she can pass as a man, "nobody stopped me. They stood around and watched [as she cut], like watching a fist fight but not getting into it." Like Martha, they objected only to what passing as a man *signifies* because of her relationship with Patience.

Patience is the only one who has a problem with the way Sarah looks. When they initially plan to leave town together, Patience thinks, "Time enough later to teach her that it's better to be a real woman than an imitation man, and that when someone chooses a woman to go away with it's because a woman is what's preferred." She does eventually teach her; when they later leave together, Sarah does not keep her hair trimmed. Yet it is as a "man" that Sarah first travels, meeting a book salesman who teaches her to read. It is as a "man" that she betters herself, preparing herself for her trip with Patience; and even though Sarah eventually becomes a "woman" for Patience, her cross-dressing is never demeaned.

Even though the lesbian cross-dresser is not "degraded" for her desire to look like a man because of the advantages in becoming a man in a patriarchal society, she is not absolved from the stigma of the medical classifications. In 1886, Richard von Krafft-Ebing divided lesbians into four increasingly masculine categories, the most masculine, or "mannish lesbian," representing "the extreme grade of degenerative homosexuality." Yet the mannish lesbian's desire to cross-dress was not altogether criticized. The presumption behind Krafft-Ebing's classifications and other medical writing of the day was that being male *is* better. Esther Newton notes that for women gender reversal and the subsequent "gain" of masculinity have historically empowered lesbian, feminist women. Many women were inspired by famous mannish lesbians, including GERTRUDE STEIN and VITA SACKVILLE-WEST. But no one was more emblematic of the mannish lesbian than the cross-dressing protagonist of RADCLYFFE HALL's *The Well of Loneliness* (1928), Stephen Gordon.

Gordon's "cross-dressing" is not just vestimentary; it starts with her "narrow-hipped and wide shouldered" body, the source of her own "mannish" pride. Her androgynous body, however, is also the source of her alienation: "That night she stared at herself in the glass; and even as she did so, she hated her body with its muscular shoulders, its small compact breasts, and its slender flanks of an athlete. All her life she must drag this body of hers like a monstrous fetter imposed on her spirit." For Gordon, cross-dressing is not a masquerade; it is as congenital as "inversion" itself. Hall's argument for religious and social toleration and an end to homophobia rests on her presentation of homosexuality (and cross-dressing) as a congenital condition. But, as the novel's apt title indicates, her work is ultimately not a narrative of triumph.

VIRGINIA WOOLF's 1928 novel *Orlando* also has didactic aspirations although these aspirations are diluted by its satire. Subtitled "a biography," *Orlando* follows the life of its hero/heroine, from when he is sixteen in 1586 to her "thirty-sixth" year some three hundred forty-two years later in 1928. Unlike Sarah and Stephen, Orlando actually *changes* sex, but also unlike them, Orlando starts off as a boy. Woolf's satiric "transsexual" fantasy, however, is by no means *Myra Breckinridge;* Orlando's change is not a "cure" for anything and happens effortlessly: "He stretched himself. He rose. . . . he was a woman." The effortlessness of his/her transformation is central to Woolf's agenda in *Orlando:* "Different though the sexes are, they intermix. In every human being a vacillation from one sex to the other takes place, and often it is only the clothes that keep the male or female likeness, while underneath the sex is the very opposite of what it is above." Her intention here is further illuminated by her notes in *A Writer's Diary* that suggest "Vita [Sackville-West] should be Orlando, a young nobleman." Yet just because Orlando is based on a bisexual, cross-dressing woman whose life helped define the mythic mannish lesbian does not mean that Orlando lives a fulfilling life. Once a "woman," Orlando loses all control of her wealth and autonomy as a "man."

What are we to make of such a loss of power? Does *Orlando* sigh that ultimately men have social power and that nobody should ever want to be a woman because of women's social powerlessness? Or, since the novel is inspired by Sackville-West, are we to interpret Orlando the man as a cross-dressed Vita Sackville-West? Does the novel then prove that the cross-dressed lesbian should never divulge her real sex? Woolf never allows us close enough to the novel to decipher the answers. Despite *Orlando*'s playfulness, Woolf's novel is finally not too far from Hall's *The Well of Loneliness.*

Josephine Tey's mystery novel *To Love and Be Wise* (1951) also showcases a lesbian cross-dresser. Leslie Searle uses her cross-dressed identity as a famous American male photographer to revenge her cousin's death, who committed suicide while married to Walter Whitmore. Searle "kills" her male identity after a public fight with Whitmore to make it seem that Whitmore killed him. What is provocative about *To Love and Be Wise* is that despite Searle's criminal intent, her cross-dressing is never condemned. As with Gordon in *The Well of Loneliness,* cross-dressing is the logical conclusion for Searle's body. When Searle's plans are discovered by Inspector Grant, not only does he not press charges, but he becomes enamored of her, impressed by her cleverness. He compares her to a man in Gloucestershire who had worked for twenty years hauling coal, but, it was discovered after his death, was actually a woman. Grant resolves that "some are genuinely happier in men's things; but a great many do it from love of adventure, and a few from economic necessity."

Economic necessity and social mobility are recurrent issues in works concerned with lesbian cross-dressing and BUTCH-FEMME RELATIONSHIPS. Leslie Feinberg's 1993 novel *Stone Butch Blues* investigates the erotics of butch-femme relationships through its narrator, Jess Goldberg, who grows up in working-class Buffalo. Taunted by others because of her androgynous looks, beaten by her father, and raped by the high school football hero, she leaves home at fifteen in search of other people like herself, other "he-shes." Like Stephen Gordon and Leslie Searle, Jess was born with a masculine body and a masculine name. Like *The Well of Loneliness* and *To Love and Be Wise*, *Stone Butch Blues* chronicles the role the body plays in the heroine's life and how it shapes her identity.

Jess finds other "he-shes" and feels less isolated but believes the only way out of her situation is to *define* her gender the way her friend Grant has, with hormones and breast reduction surgery. She soon learns, however, that hormones and surgery are not the solution she wants. If anything, she is lonelier and more unsure afterward. The surgery and hormones change the only identity she ever knew as a "butch." She is no longer able to find a femme lesbian at the bars, and she frequently has to leave jobs, fearful that someone will discover that she is not really a man. Only when she moves to New York does she begin to find herself. As Inspector Grant resolves Lee Searle's cross-dressing with a "true story," so does Jess, when she stumbles across a headline in an old newspaper in the library, "Male Butler Discovered After Death To Be Woman": "Now I knew there was another woman in the world who had made the same complicated decision . . . I made." She also sees herself in her neighbor Ruth: "I could tell that womanhood had not come easily to her. It wasn't just her large Adam's apple or her broad, big-boned hands. It was the way she dropped her eyes and rushed away when I spoke to her." Like Stephen Gordon staring at herself in the mirror in *The Well of Loneliness*, Jess "saw herself." But the body Jess saw was not "a monstrous fetter" but another "he-she," one whom she loves. Through her relationship with Ruth, Jess finds the strength to be happy, to have hope.

Stone Butch Blues and *Patience and Sarah* both offer a rare pleasure: The cross-dresser gets his/her "woman"/"man" in the end. Both novels also offer endings wherein the cross-dressing characters transcend the "rules" of transgender romance that Carol Cooper argues "present a same-sex version of the male-dominant, female-submissive dynamic." Patience and Sarah, two "women," and Jess and Ruth, two "he-she's," subvert the conventional cross-dressing narratives they evoke.

Drag queen characters rarely have such luck. Save for *Torch Song Trilogy*'s Arnold who ekes out happiness and fulfillment in parenthood, and *Splendora*'s

Timothy John who finds love *sans* dress and wig, the only pleasure in the text for the gay male cross-dressed character is in the *performance*. Charles Henry Fuller's 1991 short story "The Jazz Singer" illustrates the pleasure of the performance with the story of Christopher, a young black man who retreats to the attic of his house, dons wig, nylons and open-toed heels to perform "The Jazz Singer." His father discovers him mid-performance, screams "take this shit off," and explains to Christopher, "There are things in this world a man can do and there are things a man would be better off dead than ever getting caught up in—especially a black man." Christopher does not flinch, however, as his father leaves the attic; he retreats into his performance, which "release[s him] from the confining roles of family misfit and neighborhood oddity."

The freedom that Christopher, Myra Breckinridge, Molina, and other gay male cross-dressed characters feel when performing "women" and the humble lives of Sarah or Jess as they pass as "men" in order to make a life for themselves and their loves illustrate the fundamental differences between the gay male and lesbian cross-dressed character. In literature, the gay male cross-dresser emulates the artifice of femininity. She strives to exaggerate the notion of femininity into a glamorous spectacle. She strives for the perfect pose. In contrast, the lesbian cross-dresser aims not to be noticed, to pass, to not be discovered until after death. He wants to live his life; she wants to live and relive that magic moment.

—*Seth Clark Silberman*

BIBLIOGRAPHY

Ackroyd, Peter. *Dressing Up: Transvestism and Drag: The History of an Obsession.* New York: Simon & Schuster, 1979. ■ Bullough, Vern L., and Bonnie Bullough. *Cross Dressing, Sex, and Gender.* Philadelphia: University of Pennsylvania Press, 1993. ■ Castelli, Elizabeth. "'I Will Make Mary Male': Pieties of the Body and Gender Transformation of Christian Women in Late Antiquity." *Body Guards: The Cultural Politics of Gender Ambiguity.* Julia Epstein and Kristina Straub, eds. New York: Routledge, 1991. ■ Cauldwell, David O. "Psychopathia transexualis." *Sexology* 16 (1949): 274–280. ■ Garber, Marjorie. *Vested Interests: Cross-Dressing & Cultural Anxiety.* New York: Routledge, 1992. ■ Meyer, Morris. "Unveiling the Word: Science and Narrative in Transsexual Striptease." *Gender As Performance.* Laurence Senelick, ed. Hanover: University Press of New England, 1992. ■ Murray, Sarah E. "Dragon Ladies, Draggin' Men: Some Reflections on Gender, Drag and Homosexual Communities." *Public Culture* 6.2 (Winter 1994): 343–363. ■ Nestle, Joan. *A Restricted Country.* Ithaca, N.Y.: Firebrand Books, 1987. ■ ———, ed. *The Persistent Desire: A Femme-Butch Reader.* Boston: Alyson Publications, 1992. ■ Newton, Esther. *Mother Camp: Female Impersonators in America.* Chicago: University of Chicago Press, 1972. ■ ———. "The Mythic Mannish Lesbian: Radclyffe Hall and the New Woman." *Signs* 9.4 (Summer 1984): 557–575.

Cullen, Countee
(1903–1946)

Countee Cullen, an African-American poet of the Harlem Renaissance, was heralded as the "poet laureate" of the period. Cullen's birthplace is difficult to ascertain but is generally agreed to have been Louisville, Kentucky. Countee Leroy Porter (the name he used until 1920) was born on May 30, 1903, and was raised by his grandmother, Mrs. Porter, who brought him to New York when he was nine. On her death, the orphaned Cullen seems to have been adopted (around 1918) by the pastor Frederick A. Cullen of Salem Methodist Episcopal Church in Harlem. Cullen was educated at the prestigious DeWitt Clinton High School (1922), graduated Phi Beta Kappa from New York University (1925), and completed an M.A. in literature from Harvard (1926).

Cullen was committed to a career as a poet from as early as his high school years; by the time he finished undergraduate school, he had published his first book of poetry, *Color* (1925). Given his short life, one is surprised at the immensity of Cullen's literary output. He penned five volumes of verse, edited an African-American poetry anthology, and published one adult novel and two storybooks for children. As a dramatist, Cullen collaborated with Arna Bontemps, Owen Dodson, and others writing plays for local production. A frequent contributor to *Crisis* and *Opportunity* magazines, Cullen wrote a regular column entitled "The Dark Tower" (1926–1928) for *Opportunity*. Just before his death in 1946, Cullen assembled what he considered to be his best poetry in a volume, *On These I Stand*, which was published posthumously in 1947.

Despite what Cullen admitted to LANGSTON HUGHES about wanting to be recognized as "a poet, not a Negro poet," he spent most of his life proving that a black poet could surely sing—and sing in a black voice. In fact, five of the seven volumes of poetry that bear Cullen's name have, in their very titles, a basis for racial themes that is borne out in the poetry itself. Yet, Cullen's poetry reveals a man who was torn between allegiances to his blackness and his vocation as a raceless poet.

Surely, Cullen's race created problems for his creative expression, but his sexuality posed even greater dangers. Although married to W. E. B. DuBois's daughter Yolande early in life and Ida Roberson only six years before his death, Cullen had a steady string of male lovers in the United States and France. Furthermore, Cullen was a premier member of a thriving gay coterie in Harlem. Cullen and most gays of the period were, understandably, closeted publicly. This closetedness worked to protect Cullen from certain discrimination while it also held a firm grip on his creative imagination. Although difficult to decipher, the influence of gayness on Cullen's literary imagination can be seen through the coded references to homosexuality in much of his poetry.

From his earliest attempts, Cullen developed a multifarious poetry that, on the surface, followed the British Romantic tradition. Cullen's break from these writers can be seen in his use of racial themes and in the complex integration of male–male relationships as a significant though veiled subject. In *Color*, for example, the poems "Tableau," "The Shroud of Color," "Fruit of the Flower," "For a Poet," and "Spring Reminiscence" can be classified as gay poems in which the speaker decries the oppression of those who are different. *Copper Sun* (1927), Cullen's next book of verse, has several thinly veiled gay poems, including "Uncle Jim," "Colors," and "More Than a Fool's Song."

"The Black Christ" (1929) was Cullen's attempt to write an epic poem on the subject of lynching. This 900-line piece exemplifies Cullen's brilliant poetic layering of racial and gay themes. The main character, Jim, can be viewed not only as the persecuted black who is falsely accused of rape, but also as the victim of heterosexism. When Jim is lynched at the end of the poem, Cullen puts him in the company of Lycidas, Patroclus, and Jonathan—all characters who have had long-standing associations with gay readings of their respective texts. In many ways, "The Black Christ" is key to gay rereadings of Cullen's poetry; for, in this text, we are alerted to the homosexual coding that marks the earlier poems as well as many in *The Medea and Some Poems* (1935). Understanding Cullen's poetry in the context of the gay closet in which it was written is the cornerstone on which to rebuild Cullen's reputation as a gay poet laureate and as the inaugurator of a black gay male poetic tradition. (See also THE HARLEM RENAISSANCE and AFRICAN-AMERICAN LITERATURE, GAY MALE.)

—*Alden Reimonenq*

BIBLIOGRAPHY

Avi-Ram, Amitai F. "The Unreadable Black Body: 'Conventional' Poetic Form in the Harlem Renaissance." *Genders* 7 (1990): 32–45. ■ Baker, Houston A. *Afro-American Poetics: Revisions of Harlem and the Black Aesthetic*. Madison:

University of Wisconsin Press, 1988. ■ Fabre, Michel. *From Harlem to Paris: Black American Writers in France, 1840-1980.* Urbana: University of Illinois Press, 1991. ■ Ferguson, Blanche. *Countee Cullen and the Negro Renaissance.* New York: Dodd, Mead, and Co., 1966. ■ Garber, Eric. "A Spectacle in Color: The Lesbian and Gay Subculture of Jazz Age Harlem." *Hidden from History: Reclaiming the Gay and Lesbian Past.* Martin Duberman, Martha Vicinus, and George Chauncey, Jr. eds. New York: New American Library, 1989. 318–331. ■ Lomax, Michael L. "Countee Cullen: A Key to the Puzzle." *The Harlem Renaissance Re-examined.* Victor A. Kramer, ed. New York: AMS Press, 1987. 213–222. ■ Perry, Margaret. *A Bio-Bibliog-raphy of Countee P. Cullen, 1903–1946.* Westport: Greenwood, 1971. ■ Reimonenq, Alden. "Countee Cullen's Uranian 'Soul Windows.'" *The Journal of Homosexuality* 26:2/3 (Fall 1993). ■ Shucard, Alan. *Countee Cullen.* Boston: Twayne Publishers, 1984. ■ Smylie, James H. "Countee Cullen's 'The Black Christ.'" *Theology Today* 38:2 (July 1981): 160–173. ■ Tuttleton, James W. "Countee Cullen at 'The Heights.'" *The Harlem Renaissance: Revaluations.* Amritjit Singh, William S. Shiver, and Stanley Brodwin, eds. New York: Garland Publishing, 1989. 101–137. ■ Wagner, Jean. *Black Poets of the United States.* Trans. Kenneth Douglas. Urbana: University of Illinois Press, 1973.

Dante Alighieri
(1265–1321)

Dante's *Divine Comedy* depicts sodomites, people whom we would now call "homosexuals," twice in the afterlife: those damned and eternally punished in Cantos 15 and 16 of *Inferno,* and those saved but still undergoing penitential purification in Canto 26 of *Purgatorio.*

Sodomy is punished in the deep seventh circle of Hell as a form of violence, according to VIRGIL in *Inferno* 11, and violence of the very worst kind—that committed against God. This sexual misconduct violates the godhead by means of "despising nature" (11.48), whose course is divinely ordained. Contempt of nature is expressed by precluding the proper end of sexual acts, which is reproduction. This idea is implicit in the environment of the sodomites, who must incessantly move under falling fire and over a sandy "plain that rejects all plants from its bed" (14.8–9). The hot, arid sand is an image of the infertility of intermale sexuality. The sin is thus conceived of as one against nature, and the judgment is the standard one of Catholic moral theology.

But the conception and categorization of the sin are drastically revised in *Purgatorio.* There sodomy is treated as a form of lust, the least serious of the seven capital sins expiated on the seven terraces of the mountain of Purgatory. The homosexually oriented souls move through the fire on the topmost terrace of the lustful, as do also, but in a counter direction, their opposite numbers, the heterosexually oriented souls, who had been located above them in Hell by a full five circles. Every other offense is more blameworthy than these two fleshly faults. In the seventh infernal circle, sodomites had been placed lower than all the incontinent sinners, but now they are promoted above all but the carnal wrongdoers, with whom they are on a par, and so they are now accounted less culpable than misers or spendthrifts or gluttons.

The schema of the capital sins in *Purgatorio* is crossed with another schema, that of "moderation," whereby excess becomes the determinant of sexual guilt. In Canto 17, Virgil, again, expounds universal moral truth and the coordinated tripartite scheme of the seven terraces in terms of love. Love is sinful when for an evil object or in being deficient or excessive when for a good object. The immoderate souls of the upper three levels lavish inordinate love on terrestrial goods, such as wealth or food or persons of either sex passionately desired. Sodomy is an excess of male erotic love for a male. It follows that if the sexual passion were tempered, rather than, say, extravagantly or compulsively or irresponsibly indulged, the practice of same-sex love would not be sinful at all. Never is sodomy in *Purgatorio* judged to be unnatural, nor can it be since the aptitude to love is "natural" to human creatures (17.90–93; 18.22–27), and sodomy is one of the kinds of love. In this canticle, Dante departs, radically and astonishingly, from the othodoxies of Catholic moral theology.

Moreover, Virgil himself, idolized by Dante and given so significant a role in the poem, as, for example, the voice of greatest moral authority until his disappearance in *Purgatorio* 30, was known in the Middle Ages to be a lover of boys.

Even in *Inferno,* Dante manifested an anomalous attitude toward homosexuality in condemning the sin but esteeming the sinners. This lenience is most dramatically revealed in the memorable encounter between the wayfarer through Hell and his revered old master Brunetto Latini. The meeting is so affectionate and poignant as to have prompted some commentators, most notably André Pézard and Richard Kay, to attempt to exonerate Brunetto from the scandal of sexual perversion. Among the arguments used to support their untenable theses is that no documentation outside the poem and its contingent exegesis confirms the imputation of homoeroticism to Brunetto. If so, we may have from the author of the *Inferno* the first—and the classic—instance of "outing."

The *Divine Comedy* does not recognize lesbian sodomy, but it does confound some gay historicist "theory" in so long ago recognizing as distinct personality types men who desire women and men who desire men. (See also PASTORAL.)

—*Joseph Pequigney*

BIBLIOGRAPHY

Boswell, John. *Christianity, Social Tolerance, and Homosexuality.* Chicago: University of Chicago Press, 1980. ∎ Comparetti, Domenico. *Vergil in the Middle Ages.* Trans. E. F. M. Beneke. Hamden, Conn.: Archon Books, 1966. ∎ Dall'Orto, Giovanni. "Dante Alighieri (1265–1321)." *Encyclopedia of Homosexuality.* Wayne R. Dynes, ed. 2 vols. New York: Garland, 1990. 1:294–296. ∎ Dante. *The Divine Comedy.* Ed. and trans. Charles S. Singleton. 6 vols. Princeton: Princeton University Press, 1970–1975. ∎ Harris, John. "Three Dante Notes (1: Brunetto the Sodomite . . .)." *Lectura Dantis: A forum for Dante research and interpretation* 2 (1988): 73–78. ∎ Kay, Richard. *Dante's Swift and Strong: Essays in "Inferno" XV.* Lawrence: The Regents Press of Kansas, 1978. ∎ Pequigney, Joseph. "Sodomy in Dante's *Inferno* and *Purgatorio.*" *Representations* 36 (1991): 22–42. ∎ ———, and Hubert Dreyfus. "Landscape and Guide: Dante's Modifying of Meaning in the *Inferno.*" *Italian Quarterly* 5–6 (1961–1962): 51–83. ∎ Pézard, André. *Dante sous la pluie de feu.* Paris: Vrin, 1950. ∎ Varanini, Giorgio. "Sodomiti." *Enciclopedia Dantesca.* Umberto Bosco, ed. 6 vols. Rome: Instituto della Enciclopedia Italiana, 1970–1978. 5:286–287.

Decadence

Decadence (from the Latin *de,* down, and *cadere,* to fall) has three related principal meanings. In its most general sense, the term refers to a society's decay, its fall from a position of strength and prosperity to a state of weakness and ruin. Decadence also refers to any ideological appreciation, and therefore support, of social decay. Whereas the first definition presents the term as an inevitable process signified by a society's relation to past societies, the second definition suggests that decadence is an individual approach to life and that social decay can be consciously perpetrated. During the nineteenth century, decadence acquired a third, closely related, aesthetic meaning that led to the formation of the Decadent Movement.

Although the term *decadence* entered European discourse in the Middle Ages, earlier formulations of the concept are apparent. These include the Indian notion of the Age of Kali and the Greek and Roman belief in a previous Golden Age from which their civilization had fallen. With the rise of Christianity, which both Voltaire (1694–1778) and Edward Gibbon (1737–1794) suggest was an inherent part of the Roman Empire's process of decay, decadence also became part of the concept of apocalypse, foreshadowing the end of the world.

During the modern era, images and legends of the decline of the Roman Empire formed the most popular conception of ancient decadence as an inevitable process of social transformation. Roman decadence is analyzed in, among other works, Charles-Louis le Secondat, Baron de La Brède et de Montesquieu's (1689–1755) *Considérations sur les causes de la grandeur des Romains et de leur décadence* (1734) and in Gibbon's *The History of the Decline and Fall of the Roman Empire* (1776–1788). Although Montesquieu presented the Roman fall as an unavoidable process, the decline is often seen to have been perpetrated by specific individuals, most notably the Roman emperor Nero (A.D. 37–68). Reported to have adopted Greek affectations and to have married a castrated male slave, Nero was a great fan of the writer PETRONIUS, who is most famous for his homoerotic novel *The Satyricon.* Viewed as an irresponsible and hedonistic ruler, Nero has often been seen to epitomize social decadence, even though he lived over 300 years before the major sacking of Rome by Alaric.

Closer to the time of the Decadent Movement, the works of the MARQUIS DE SADE also foreshadow the prominence that the concept of decadence as a lifestyle ideology gained during the nineteenth century. De Sade's appreciation of hedonistic nihilism and artificiality stand in stark contrast to Jean-Jacques Rousseau's (1712–1778) claims that the development of knowledge and culture promoted immorality, excess, and idleness. Another major thematic, as well as stylistic, influence on Decadent literature was the Gothic novel, and the writings of Edgar Allan Poe (1809–1849). Decrepit, isolated mansions; feeble, aristocratic lineages; and hypersensitive, refined bachelors are some of the stock elements of Decadent writing that can be traced to such writers as Poe and Ann Radcliffe (1764–1823). (See also GOTHICISM.)

In a sociopolitical vein, the Romantics' notion of individualism and their revolt against classical form and conservative morality helped formulate decadence into a self-conscious lifestyle choice that allowed individuals not only to accept but to celebrate preferences and tastes that were traditionally seen as deviant, immoral, and counterproductive. The strongest argument for a connection between Romanticism and a literary or aesthetic form of decadence during the first half of the nineteenth century was made by Désiré Nisard (1806–1888), in his antiromantic work *Etudes de moeurs et de critique sur les poètes latins de la décadence* (1834). Though focusing on late Roman poetry, the work succeeds in criticizing contemporary Romantic writing for its artificiality and deceptiveness, thus lending support to the frequent claim that the Decadent Movement represents the final phase of the Romantic era.

Even though the terms *Decadence* and AESTHETICISM have often been applied to late nineteenth-century literature interchangeably, not all Decadent literature is part of Aestheticism, just as not all Aesthetic literature can be called Decadent. Generally speaking, Aestheticism applies the concept of *l'art pour l'art* (art for art's sake) to art, whereas Decadence applies it to life and society, though Decadence also has other crucial defining characteristics, such as its interest in mind-altering drugs, the imagination, and physical and mental degeneration and alteration. However, even during the heyday of the Decadent Movement, the term *Decadent* was used to refer to both lifestyle and literature.

Decadent literature is writing that either describes aspects of a decadent lifestyle or reflects Decadence through the deformation and refinement of style, form, syntax, and language. Comparable tactics can be found in some nineteenth-century art, such as the paintings of Gustave Moreau (1826–1898) and the drawings of Felicien Rops (1833–1898) and Aubrey Beardsley (1872–1898). Most of the authors associated with the Decadent Movement are known for their writing rather than their lifestyles, just as a number of the Decadent authors who wrote about homosexuality or lesbianism were not overtly gay. A decadent approach to life and society was theoretically desirable, but it was rarely actually practiced by the authors. Some examples of writers who arguably lived decadent lives are the homosexual Count Eric Stenbock (1860–1895), in England, and PAUL VERLAINE (1844–1896) and ARTHUR RIMBAUD (1854–1891), in France, though their literature is not the clearest reflection of Decadence.

The general notion of decadence in the nineteenth century involved the claim that when a society reached its peak of prosperity, it would no longer have to concern itself with such things as subsistence or regeneration. Therefore, attention would shift from the communal to the individual, with individualism gaining greater import. During a period of social decay, society would be in a state of regression, but it would be marked by artistic genius. In 1876, Paul Bourget (1852–1935) argued that a period of decadence is superior to those epochs concerned with the livelihood of the community because of the "intensity of its geniuses" and its "daring artists." Théophile Gautier (1811–1872) similarly states that the style of decadence in literature and art reflects a civilization at the ultimate point of maturity as it attempts to communicate the most elusive remnants of its being, even while it pushes itself to neurosis, depravity, and madness. Gautier's 1868 "Notice" to CHARLES BAUDELAIRE's (1821–1867) *Les Fleurs du mal* (1857) depicts the Decadent Movement as the positive product of a period of decomposition. Baudelaire similarly correlates, in the first edition of *Les Fleurs du mal,* "the language of late Latin decadence" and "the modern poetic world."

The nineteenth-century Decadent Movement also reflects the sense of dehumanization and alienation that contemporary progress fostered primarily among members of western European society. Ironically, to signify humanity's position above the secular realm that produced the state of social discord that the Decadent authors were experiencing, they turned their praise to the artificial, itself often a product of the same process of mechanization. An appreciation of artifice, the argument goes, advertises humanity's freedom from, and superiority over, the secular realm. Since virtue was seen to belong to a higher realm, a logical correlation existed between the natural and evil, on the one hand, and the artificial and virtuous, on the other. The cult of the "unnatural" thus could be justified as a valorization of virtue.

In accord with the tenets of Aestheticism, the proponents of Decadence, disavowing any relation between art and the natural or secular, claimed that life should be viewed from an aesthetic perspective and that art need not serve any moral, political, or utilitarian purpose. Aesthetic strategies of representation that supported social values of morality, industry, perpetuity, and naturalness were challenged by an aesthetic valorization of immorality, indolence, decay, and unnaturalness. The nineteenth-century view of same-sex physical intercourse as unnatural, or "artificial," was a central reason for the affiliation of gay sex with the movement. The connection is especially clear in, for example, Jean Lombard's (1854–1891) novel *L'Agonie* (1888) and JORIS-KARL HUYSMANS's (1848–

1907) À rebours (1884). In addition, the valuation of an ideal, artificial world over conventional lifestyles, as well as the overt disavowal of moral values, was also a major reason for the affiliation of male homosexuality and lesbianism with Decadence.

Though the Decadent Movement was not clearly defined until the second half of the nineteenth century, Gautier, who was not wholly enamored of the term *decadence*, popularized the associated concept of *l'art pour l'art* and articulated some of the fundamental tenets of Decadence as early as 1836. In his defensive preface to *Mademoiselle de Maupin* (1835), which Mario Praz refers to as "the apologia of lesbian love" and "the Bible of Decadence," Gautier argues that only that which is useless can be truly beautiful and that morality is not a product of books. By implying that his text does not influence social morality but exists for its own useless sake, Gautier opened a space for Decadent art and for decadent social transgressions. Gautier's formulation of amoral art was admired by WALTER PATER, himself a central influence on the dominant version of Decadence that formed in England.

Mademoiselle de Maupin represents a number of decadent traits, principal among them being the transvestism and same-sex eroticism instigated through subterfugal cross-dressing, with the desire for a variety of sexual pleasures forming the principal narrative. The hero, D'Albert, wants to be a woman in order to experience new sensations, and the titular heroine ultimately makes love to both D'Albert and his mistress. While the gender ambiguities in Gautier's work allowed him to depict gay male and lesbian eroticism at a time when such representations were generally seen as illegal, they did so by defining sexuality through the Decadent aestheticization of the experience. Gautier's representations of homosexual and lesbian desire are followed by more overt depictions of homoeroticism in Verlaine's work and the praise for lesbianism in the writing of Baudelaire and Pierre Louÿs (1870–1925).

The same aesthetic control found in *Mademoiselle de Maupin* is presented in two other works by Gautier—*Fortunio* (1837), which foreshadows the writings of both Baudelaire and Huysmans, and *Une nuit de Cléopâtra* (1838). Unlike the titular heroine of *Mademoiselle de Maupin,* Gautier's Cleopatra is not in search of an ideal sexual experience but simply wants a distraction from her life of material excess. The heroine sees her carnal fling with a man, and his subsequent execution, as a purely aesthetic experience. Life becomes art and, of particular interest to readers who saw themselves as threatened for their sexual inclinations, the heroine is shown to be beyond the moral charges of society.

Baudelaire took Gautier's concept of otherworldly sexual desire one step further in his novella *La Fanfarlo* (1847), in which the hero of the work, rather than aestheticizing his experience, becomes attracted to his own mental perversity. Echoing the mentally deranged introspection of the antiheroes in works by Poe, the artistic fulfillment of the protagonist of *La Fanfarlo* is attained through a psychological self-aestheticization. Poe's Decadent writing was admired not only by Baudelaire, but also by ALGERNON SWINBURNE (1837–1909), OSCAR WILDE (1854–1900), and the Pre-Raphaelite painter and poet Dante Gabriel Rossetti (1828–1882). The self-alienating focus on one's mind as art that is found in *La Fanfarlo* stands in contrast to the external self-aestheticization of such dandies as Beau Brummel (1774–1840) and Oscar Wilde, the latter's approach implying a need for social interaction.

La Fanfarlo presents another important tactic in Decadent literature—the representation of narcissism, with its traditional implication of homosexuality and lesbianism. In preparation for a sexual interlude, the actress, Mademoiselle Fanfarlo, has Samuel Cramer (a self-portrait by Baudelaire) dress as Columbine, one of her roles. Baudelaire thus imagines himself having sex as a woman who is imagining having sex with herself. More complex and violent representations of narcissism can be found in Poe's short story "William Wilson" and Wilde's novel *The Picture of Dorian Gray*.

Another major element of Decadent writing, in both France and England, is the issue of religion, particularly Catholicism. A central paradox in Decadence is the fact that pure artifice, regardless of how much it is emulated, can never be attained. Ultimately, a decadent individual, whether real or fictional, must either see the Decadent program as a failure or proceed to a higher artifice that is defined as unattainable within the secular world—a spiritual artifice. This moment of crisis holds a pivotal position within the narrative of a central Decadent text—Huysmans's *À rebours*, which Arthur Symons (1865–1945) called "the breviary of the Decadence." Des Esseintes, the hero of Huysmans's novel, ultimately embraces the Church, foreshadowing the author's own turn to Catholicism. *À rebours* had a major effect on the Decadent Movement in France, England, and elsewhere. Its influence is most notable in Wilde's *The Picture of Dorian Gray,* in which Huysmans's text is indirectly referenced and often echoed. Though Dorian is too far gone, by the time he realizes the results of his decadence, to recant, Wilde succeeded in converting to Catholicism on his death bed.

Other French literature associated with the Decadent Movement includes Élémir Bourges's (1852–

1925) novel *Le Crépuscule des dieux* (1883), Catulle Mendès's (1842–1909) collection of short fiction *Lesbia* (1887) and his lesbian-themed *Méphistophéla* (1890), Stéphane Mallarmé's (1842–1898) symbolist work, and Jean Lorrain's (1856–1906) homoerotic writings. Lorrain's friendship with Wilde was a major link between the French and English Decadent Movements.

English Decadence, as an aesthetic approach, was less extravagant and less flaunting than its French counterpart. The term *decadent* was used in England as early as 1837, appearing in Thomas Carlyle's (1795–1881) *History of the French Revolution*. The major precursors of the English Decadents were Gautier, Baudelaire, Rossetti, and the Romantics, particularly John Keats (1795–1821). Although Rossetti was not fond of Aestheticism or artifice, many Aesthetes and Decadents appreciated his aesthetic tastes and the strong eroticism of his work. Swinburne, arguably the first English Decadent, was influenced by both de Sade and the *l'art pour l'art* movement. In 1862, he wrote an essay defending Baudelaire's work from an Aestheticist standpoint, thereby defining the concept for an English readership. A conflation of decadence and Aestheticism can be seen in his collection *Poems and Ballads* (1866), which was attacked for its sadism and satanism. Swinburne's aestheticized Decadent writing, in its accentuation of androgyny, also helped formulate the character of the fragile dandy, parodied in the journal *Punch* and in Max Beerbohm's (1872–1956) essay "No. 2, The Pines" (1920).

Another important text in the English Decadent Movement was Pater's *Studies in the History of the Renaissance* (1873), particularly its influential "Conclusion," with its claim that "art comes to you professing frankly to give nothing but the highest quality to your moments as they pass, and simply for those moments' sake." Pater's text also reinforced the Decadent penchant for corruption and the pleasures of vice, as in its essay on Leonardo da Vinci. Wilde, according to William Butler Yeats (1865–1939), referred to *The Renaissance* as "the very flower of decadence," whereas Symons wrote that Pater would follow Baudelaire in bettering nature.

Much of the English Decadent Movement's literature appeared in journals. The explicitly Decadent and homosexually themed journal, *The Chameleon,* appeared in England in 1894, with Wilde and LORD ALFRED DOUGLAS both contributing. The most famous Decadent journal was *The Yellow Book,* which ran from 1894 to 1897. One of its most popular articles was Beerbohm's essay "In Defense of Cosmetics," which, Beerbohm responded to critics, was a satire of the Decadent school. The art editor of the journal was Beardsley, who was the most talented of the *fin-de-siècle* Decadent artists and who often caricatured other Decadents and Aesthetes in his work, particularly Wilde. Beardsley's Decadent drawing is known not only for "the Beardsley curve" and his balanced imbalance (precursors of Art Nouveau techniques), but also for its depictions of lesbians and grotesquery, and its apparent revelry in the macabre and fetishistic. Beardsley's greatest literary work was the incomplete and highly erotic *The Story of Venus and Tannhauser,* which was published in the journal *The Savoy* and then, in expurgated version, on its own as *Under the Hill* (1897). Beardsley probably based his version of the narrative to some degree on the opera by Richard Wagner (1813–1883), whose work Beardsley admired and whom Nietzsche defined as a decadent artist. The Canadian decadent writer, John Glassco (1909–1981), wrote a completion to the narrative, published with Beardsley's text in 1959.

The Decadent Movement in England ended almost overnight, with the Wilde trials in 1895. During its peak in England, Decadence had become almost synonymous with symbolist writing. Symons's book *The Symbolist Movement in Literature* (1899) had originally been advertised as *The Decadent Movement in Literature*. He had also published an essay entitled "The Decadent Movement in Literature" in *Harper's New Monthly Magazine* in 1893. Symbolism, while echoing Decadence both in style and in its association of art with the realm of the mind and the imagination, minimized the seemingly perverse and immoral characteristics of the earlier movement.

Other notable examples of English Decadent literature include John Gray's (1866–1934) collection of poems *Silverpoints* (1893), Stenbock's *Studies of Death* (1893), Ernest Dowson's (1867–1900) collections *Verses* (1896) and *Decorations* (1899), and Wilde's play *Salomé* (1893). The supernatural fiction of VERNON LEE (Violet Paget, 1856–1935) also uses Decadent motifs. The English Decadents were often ridiculed, most notably in *Punch* and in Gilbert and Sullivan's play *Patience* (1881). By the last decade of the century, many of the Decadent authors became self-satirizing, or at least claimed to be.

Decadence also had an influence in Russia in the early twentieth century, rising within the Russian Symbolist Movement and being influenced primarily by French writing and the works of Poe. Fedor Sologub (1863–1927), whom Nikolai S. Gumilev (1886–1921) refers to as the only "absolutely consistent decadent" in Russian literature, had a strong interest in the macabre and in mental derangement, as well as in the character of the aesthete. Neither homosexuality nor lesbianism were central themes for any

Russian decadent writer, though MIKHAIL KUZMIN's (187?–1936) homosexual texts have characters modeled on aesthetes. Other European works that show the influence of Decadence include the writing of the Italian Gabriele D'Annunzio (1863–1938) and various plays, such as *Lulu,* by the German author Frank Wedekind (1864–1918). The Decadent and homoerotic work, *The House of the Vampire* (1907), was written in English by a German emigré to the United States, George Sylvester Viereck (1884–1962).

The most direct line of influence from Decadent literature is into Symbolism, with the movement also influencing, for example, Imagism and Surrealism, most notably in the work of ALFRED JARRY (1873–1907). Authors influenced by the movement include JEAN COCTEAU (1891–1963), ANDRÉ GIDE (1869–1951), JEAN GENET (1910–1986), H. G. Wells (1866–1946), and various members of the Rhymers' Club (1890–1895), such as Yeats and T. S. ELIOT (1888–1965).

—Dennis Denisoff

BIBLIOGRAPHY

Baudelaire, Charles. *Les Fleurs du mal.* Paris: Poulet-Malassis et de Broise, 1857. ■ Beckson, Karl, ed. *Aesthetes and Decadents of the 1890s: An Anthology of British Poetry and Prose.* New York: Random House, 1966. ■ Calinescu, Matei. *Faces of Modernity: Avant-garde, Decadence, Kitsch.* Bloomington: Indiana University Press, 1977. ■ Carter, A. E. *The Idea of Decadence in French Literature, 1830–1900.* Toronto: University of Toronto Press, 1958. ■ Charlesworth, Barbara. *Dark Passages: The Decadent Consciousness in Victorian Literature.* Madison: University of Wisconsin Press, 1965. ■ Croft-Cooke, Rupert. *Feasting with Panthers: A Consideration of Some Late Victorian Writers.* London: W. H. Allen, 1967. ■ d'Arch-Smith, Timothy. *Love in Earnest: Some Notes on the Lives and Writings of English 'Uranian' Poets from 1889 to 1930.* London: Routledge, 1970. ■ Dowling, Linda. *Aestheticism and Decadence: A Selective Annotated Bibliography.* New York: Garland, 1977. ■ Fletcher, Ian, ed. *Decadence and the 1890s.* New York: Holmes & Meier, 1980. ■ Gautier, Théophile. *Mademoiselle de Maupin.* 1835. Paris: Garnier freres, 1966. ■ Huysmans, Joris-Karl. *À rebours.* 1884. Paris: Fasquelle, 1968. ■ Pater, Walter. *Studies in the History of the Renaissance.* London: Macmillan, 1873. ■ Poe, Edgar Allan. *Collected Works of Edgar Allan Poe.* Thomas Ollive Mabbott, ed. Cambridge, Mass.: Harvard University Press, 1969. ■ Praz, Mario. *The Romantic Agony.* London: Oxford University Press, 1933. ■ Reade, Brian, ed. *Sexual Heretics: Male Homosexuality in English Literature from 1850 to 1900: An Anthology.* London: Routledge, 1970. ■ Showalter, Elaine. *Gender and Culture at the Fin-de-Siècle.* New York: Viking, 1990. ■ Stableford, Brian, ed. *The Dedalus Book of Decadence (Moral Ruins).* Cambridge: Dedalus, 1990. ■ Symons, Arthur. *The Symbolist Movement in Literature.* 1899. New York: Dutton, 1919. ■ Wilde, Oscar. *Complete Works of Oscar Wilde.* New York: Perennial Library, 1989.

Dickinson, Emily
(1830–1886)

Emily Dickinson's life has been traditionally viewed through her relationships with men—her father, her brother, her mentor, and the unidentified man she addressed as "Master" in three love letters and a number of poems. However, in the last decade, critics have begun to recognize the importance of her relationships with women. Dickinson sent many more of her 1,776 poems to women than to men, particularly to her sister-in-law Susan ("Sue") Gilbert Dickinson, who provided her with both a source of material and a faithful audience for a large portion of her writings. Because the poet's first editors were anxious to conceal the erotic implications and the literary significance of this relationship, they minimized Sue's role, but recent critics have shown her to have been crucial to Dickinson's life and work.

The poet was born December 10, 1830—200 years after the first Dickinson arrived in America—to one of Amherst, Massachusetts's leading families. Her grandfather helped found Amherst Academy, and her father and brother, both lawyers, served it as treasurer after it became Amherst College. Dickinson attended the academy for seven years and Mt. Holyoke Female Seminary for one, leaving early because she resisted its coercive religious environment and her parents wanted her at home. But they did not curtail her social life, as some have maintained: In her early twenties, the poet wrote wacky valentines to Amherst freshmen and uproarious letters to her brother Austin and her girlfriends recounting picnics, sugarings off, sledding parties, and a seemingly endless round of social calls. She spent nearly two months in 1855 visiting Washington and Philadelphia with her father and sister Lavinia, meeting "many sweet ladies and noble gentlemen."

But by age thirty, Dickinson would tell one correspondent, "I do not cross my Father's ground to any House or town," and inform another of her "custom" of "fleeing" when visitors arrived. Except for a few trips to Cambridge, Massachusetts, to have her eyes treated, the poet remained in Amherst for the rest of her life, seeing only her immediate family and a select group of children; in the years before she died, even her doctor had to examine her from another room.

Local gossips referred to Dickinson as "the Myth," expressing fascination at her "withdrawal," her habit of wearing only white, and her enigmatic notes accompanying gifts of food or flowers.

Those who knew her better accepted her reclusiveness, prizing her letters for the love and sympathy expressed in them, however elliptically. For all her reticence, Dickinson corresponded with a wide variety of relatives and friends: Sue; her nieces Louise and Frances Norcross; Elizabeth Holland and her husband, Josiah, an editor at *Scribner's;* Samuel Bowles, editor of a prominent local newspaper, and his wife, Mary; Thomas Wentworth Higginson, an editor at the *Atlantic* whom Dickinson adopted as her mentor; and the most popular woman poet of her day, Helen Hunt Jackson. Dickinson remained deeply involved in the lives of these people, readily celebrating their triumphs and mourning their losses, and leaving over a thousand letters, many of which contained poems.

Though Dickinson "published" her work to her correspondents throughout her life, she seems to have felt too ambivalent toward what she called "the Auction / Of the Mind" to pursue publication actively. In the early 1860s, she expressed enthusiasm about her literary prospects, writing Sue that she hoped to make her and Austin "proud—sometime—a great way off," and telling the Norcrosses, after alluding to her writing, that "every day life feels mightier, and what we have the power to be, more stupendous." But once she had solicited Higginson's view of her work in 1862 and he had suggested that she delay publishing, she insisted that she had never harbored any intention of seeing her poems into print. In the early 1880s, Jackson asked Dickinson if she might serve as her literary executor, and the publisher Thomas Niles offered to issue a book of her poems, but she politely ignored both requests. All told, only eight of her poems were published during her lifetime, most of them submitted without her permission by friends. But Dickinson did order her poems for her own purposes—and possibly for posterity—by sewing them into packets or "fascicles"; these were found by her sister Vinnie and edited by Higginson and her brother's lover, Mabel Loomis Todd.

When the poet's work was published four years after her death in 1886, reviewers expressed surprise that a seemingly eventless life could generate such passion. However, critics have since come to recognize that the less Dickinson interacted with others in person, the more intense her epistolary exchanges with them became. Her letters explaining why she could not see people suggest that she avoided those she loved because they affected her too powerfully. Yet she did not shy from acknowledging their power in writing: She told Elizabeth Holland once, "shame is so intrinsic

to a strong affection we must all experience Adam's reticence." After Samuel Bowles returned from a seven-month visit to Europe, Dickinson apologized for refusing to see him: "Did I not want to see you? Do not the Phebes want to come? They of little faith!" And when Sue returned from a two-week vacation, the poet wrote, "I cannot see you for a few days. You are too momentous. But remember it is idolatry and not indifference."

Dickinson was particularly cagey with Sue and Bowles because she was in love with each at various points, perhaps even with both at once during the late 1850s. Her relationship with Sue has barely been assessed, but critics have been scrutinizing the "Master" letters since the 1940s, trying to determine their addressee (many believe Bowles to have been he though the evidence is not conclusive). Regardless of whether he is the "Master," Bowles appears to have been an object of Dickinson's love from the late 1850s to the early 1860s. During these years, she sent him several poems alluding to their impending celestial marriage and the martyrdom with which she was currently earning it. Some of the poems she prefaced with remarks indicating they were addressed to him include the following: "Title divine — is mine! / The Wife — without the Sign! . . .," "Through the strait pass of suffering / The Martyrs — even — trod . . .," "Victory comes late / And is held low to freezing lips . . .," and "Speech is a prank of Parliament . . . ." Many of her letters to him from this period are so tenderly cryptic that they may as well be love poems, but after about 1864 she addressed him with more affection than ardor.

By contrast, Dickinson's passion for Sue extended from 1851 until her own death, and despite many vacillations in both women's feelings, Sue also remained her primary audience, receiving 267 poems, or nearly three times the amount sent to any other correspondent. The poet probably met Sue at Amherst Academy in the late 1840s. Judging from Dickinson's early letters, the two were close from the start, sharing their love of literature and nature, and their complaints about the steady round of housework. Both yearned for a more romantic existence, and the poet fantasized about establishing a haven with Sue, regarding her, by the mid-1850s, as some combination of a soul mate and ideal mother. She appears to have trusted Sue absolutely, divulging her hopes and fears about religion, marriage, her family, her own character, her visions of the future, and most of all, her passionate love for "Susie."

Sue does appear to have had similar tastes and temperament, and to have reciprocated Dickinson's love initially, but she apparently began to feel suffocated by the poet's demands for attention once she became engaged to Austin Dickinson. This event precipitated an inexplicable two-year gap in their correspondence, after which the poet approached Sue with a mixture of love and apprehension. Once Sue and Austin moved into a house next door to her in 1857 and the two women resumed corresponding, Dickinson began using poetry to mediate her expression of love and pain, developing the intimate but oblique, note-in-a-bottle voice characterizing many of her greatest poems. She wrote to Sue with a complex variety of intentions—to amuse her, to impress her, to woo her, to baffle her, to hurt her, to elicit guilt, to solicit criticism, or probably, most often, with some combination of these. Anxious to affirm her affection, yet keep her distance, the poet often addressed Sue as if she were a goddess, in notes such as these: "Susan's Idolator keeps a Shrine for Susan," or "Susan knows that she is a Siren — and that at a word from her, Emily would forfeit Righteousness."

Dickinson was clearly in love with her: Her letters to Sue beat with a passion surpassing even notions of friendship held by a less homophobic era. Caroll Smith-Rosenberg has shown that nineteenth-century women's friendships lent themselves to a wide range of expression, so that letters that raised no eyebrows then seem erotically charged to us. Even so, Dickinson's early descriptions of feeling hot and feverish at the thought of seeing "Susie," her insistence that Susie's absence "insanes" her, her designation of Sue as her "absent Lover," and her fantasies of holding her, kissing her, and looking into her eyes, as well as many remarks in later notes, suggest that, on the continuum where expressions of love and affection reside, Dickinson tips the scales toward homoeroticism.

Recent critics have opted for a wide range of terminology to describe the poet's relationship with Sue, some calling it a "ROMANTIC FRIENDSHIP," others outing her outright. The prevalence of both hetero- and homoerotic imagery in her writings suggests that Dickinson was bisexual, but did she regard herself as such? And, if she did, how are we to know? Some critics claim that she expresses guilt at having transgressed her own line between affection and homoerotic desire in some of her love letters to Sue. But could she have felt guilty if female homosexuality was not available to her as a concept? Smith-Rosenberg finds the theme of lesbianism in only one nineteenth-century literary genre, male French fiction, which would hardly have been accessible to the poet.

So when we analyze Dickinson's writings to Sue and other women, we need to entertain the possibility that the poet may not have acknowledged the homoerotic strain in her letters and poems. Some notes to women friends seem frankly erotic, but others seem more ambiguous. For instance, when Sue was out of town, she wrote:

> *It is sweet* to talk, dear Susie, with those whom God has given us, lest we should be alone — and you and I have *tasted it,* and found it *very sweet;* even as fragrant flowers, oe'r which the bee hums and lingers, and hums *more* for the lingering.

But she also sent Eudocia Flynt, a cousin to whom she was not particularly close, a rose accompanied by a poem ending with these lines, "Depths of Ruby, undrained — / Hid, Lip, for Thee, / Play it were a Humming Bird / And sipped just Me." Both writings seem to allude to female sexual pleasure, but the fact that the poet was in love with the first addressee and barely knew the second leads me to question whether we can draw any conclusions about her intentions in the passage to Sue.

But whether or not the poet recognized the erotic undercurrent in some of her writings to women, her fear of making herself too vulnerable to Sue is obvious. Torn between her desire to express her love and her need to protect herself, Dickinson used a variety of tactics for concealing her feelings. First, she sent Sue only a fraction of the hundreds of poems she wrote addressing the relationship, and when she did show them to her, she edited out some of the love evident in her private drafts. Second, in those poems she did send Sue she used metaphorically cryptic language likely to perplex her, placing the poet in a position of power. And third, she sent Sue some poems without framing them with a note, a salutation, or a closing, leaving her to guess whether to read them as communiqués or artifacts.

This tendency to send a poem without clarifying its rhetorical purpose reflects Dickinson's tendency to blur the distinction between letters and poems, though most editions of her work separate the two. A look at her manuscripts suggests that many of her writings might best be described as "letter-poems" because her prose gives way to poetry without a pronounced shift in tone, rhythm, or appearance. In letters, poems, and letter-poems, she uses the same imagery and literary techniques, the same rhythms (sections of some letters might be transcribed into three- and four-beat lines to read as poems), and the same oblique yet confiding voice. The poet's characteristic gesture, to Sue and other correspondents, was to offer precise analogies for her emotional state, without specifying the source of the pleasure or pain. She wanted to conceal the details of her passions but had a consuming need to disclose their intensity. One note to Sue reads in its entirety, "'For Brutus, as you know, was Caesar's

Angel,'" while another reads, "Great Hungers feed themselves, but little Hungers ail in vain." A third note acknowledges that both women appreciated such enigmas: "In a Life that stopped guessing, you and I should not feel at home."

The main way the poet kept Sue guessing was by using densely figurative language that might simultaneously intensify her expression of love, display mastery over her feelings, protect her pride, and baffle Sue. This language baffles critics also, but when we read difficult poems within the context of more accessible ones sharing their imagery, they become clearer. Dickinson uses several networks of imagery to depict her love for Sue, including two clustered around images of wealth and of nature's mystery. The first of these in particular reveals the extent to which the poet regarded Sue as her primary source of inspiration. Dickinson employs metaphors of wealth to depict Sue ("the Pearl — / That slipped my fingers through — / While just a Girl at school"); her love for Sue ("feelings so like gems, that I was sure I *gathered* them in whole baskets of pearls"); the poetic gifts she offers Sue ("I could bring You Jewels . . ."); the poetic trophies with which she hopes to triumph over Sue ("No matter — now — Sweet — / But when I'm Earl / Wont you wish you'd spoken / To that dull Girl? . . ."); and, ultimately, her writing ("I'll clutch — and clutch — / Next — One — Might be the golden touch . . .").

The link suggested by Dickinson's use of the same imagery to portray her love for Sue and her writing is made explicit in "It would never be Common . . . ." This poem recounts how, when the poet had her "drop — of India" (Sue is identified with India in two other poems) to write with and for, she "dealt of word of Gold / To every Creature" she met. But then,

> . . . suddenly — my Riches shrank —
> A Goblin — drank my Dew —
> My Palaces — dropped tenantless —
> Myself — was beggared — too. . . .
> I felt the Wilderness roll back
> Along my Golden lines. . . .

Once Sue became engaged to Austin and saw less of his sister, Dickinson felt as if she had been expelled from an Eden where poetic inspiration was "common." Nonetheless the poet remained devoted to Sue.

We might distinguish Dickinson's early and later views of Sue as naive versus informed idolatry. Conceding that she would never possess Sue completely, the poet compared her to Cleopatra, stressing her capacity to whet one's appetite for her without ever satisfying it. She conflates Cleopatra, Sue, and nature in her writing by using similar imagery to describe them: In "The tint I cannot take — / is best . . ." a sunset "swaggers on the eye / Like Cleopatra's Company," whereas in "Were nature mortal lady . . ." and "Like Some Old fashioned Miracle . . . ," nature is depicted as feminine and beguiling. But "What mystery pervades a well! . . ." most clearly associates nature's wiles with Sue's: One draft of the poem replaces "nature" with "Susan" in the line, "But nature is a Stranger yet." Like the well of the nature draft, Sue was unfathomable yet contained, domesticated, and familiar; and she *was* "a neighbor from another world / Residing in a jar," because Dickinson continually observed her comings and goings, from her bedroom facing Sue's house. Dickinson apparently never tired of watching her; a few years before her own death, she wrote Sue,

> To be Susan
> is Imagination,
> To have been
> Susan, a Dream —
> What depths
> of Domingo
> in that torrid
> Spirit!

Sue's role in the development of Dickinson's writing cannot be overemphasized: As a source of love and frustration, of literary camaraderie and competition, she provided the poet with both a source of material and an ideal reader. Sue's early friendship inspired her to express her love candidly in poems and letters, but her perceived defection forced Dickinson to resort to poetic language to communicate with her. No matter how strained their relationship, however, the poet continued writing to and for Sue, determined to keep her as an audience at any cost. As she wrote Sue in 1873, "We remind her we love her — Unimportant fact, though Dante didn't think so, nor Swift, nor Mirabeau." Functioning as the poet's love object, wellspring of pain, ideal reader, and literary rival, Sue was Dickinson's muse. She elicited from the poet a body of homoerotic love letters and poems as passionate and elusive as any in western literature.

—*Nancy Hurrelbrinck*

BIBLIOGRAPHY

Bennett, Paula. "'By a Mouth That Cannot Speak': Spectral Presence in Emily Dickinson's Letters." *Emily Dickinson Journal* 1. 2 (Winter 1992): 76–99. ■ ———. *Emily Dickinson: Woman Poet.* Iowa City: University of Iowa Press, 1991. ■ Faderman, Lillian. "Emily Dickinson's Letters to Sue Gilbert." *Massachusetts Review* 18 (Summer 1977): 197–225. ■ Farr, Judith. *The Passion of Emily Dickinson.* Cambridge, Mass.:

Harvard University Press, 1992. ■ Hart, Ellen Louise. "The Encoding of Homoerotic Desire: Emily Dickinson's Letters and Poems to Susan Dickinson, 1850-1886." *Tulsa Studies in Women's Literature* 9.2 (Fall 1990): 251–272. ■ Leyda, Jay. *The Years and Hours of Emily Dickinson.* 2 vols. New Haven, Conn.: Yale University Press, 1970. ■ Miller, Cristanne. *Emily Dickinson: A Poet's Grammar.* Cambridge, Mass.: Harvard University Press, 1987. ■ Pollak, Vivian. *Dickinson: The Anxiety of Gender.* Ithaca, N.Y.: Cornell University Press, 1984. ■ St. Armand, Barton Levi. *The Soul's Society: Emily Dickinson and Her Culture.* Cambridge: Cambridge University Press, 1984. ■ Sewall, Richard B. *The Life of Emily Dickinson.* New York: Farrar, Strauss, Giroux, 1974. ■ Smith, Martha Nell. *Rowing in Eden: Rereading Emily Dickinson.* Austin: University of Texas Press, 1992. ■ Smith-Rosenberg, Carroll. *Disorderly Conduct: Visions of Gender in Victorian America.* New York: Alfred A. Knopf, 1985.

Donne, John
(1572–1631)

John Donne ranks among the greatest poets in English literature. Founder of the so-called Metaphysical school, he helped revolutionize English poetry in the late sixteenth century by creating an intellectual, tough-minded verse characterized by "strong lines," colloquial language, natural rhythms, and surprising conceits. In Donne's poetry, an eccentric and often egocentric sensibility is explored and expressed in a unique voice and often in extreme terms. Donne's canon is large, comprising a great deal of prose as well as satires, love elegies, epigrams, epithalamions, epicedes and obsequies, verse letters, holy sonnets and other divine poems. His most famous grouping is the "Songs and Sonets," which includes most of his love lyrics. In "Songs and Sonets," idealistic and cynical attitudes toward love are juxtaposed, both within individual works and in the collection as a whole. Donne characteristically rejects neoplatonic asceticism, but he sometimes expresses disgust with carnality.

The witty and passionate Donne is justly recognized as the late Renaissance's supreme poet of heterosexual love. Known in his youth as a ladies' man, he caused a scandal in 1601 by secretly marrying the niece of his employer, Lord Keeper Egerton, an indiscretion that led to his dismissal and brief imprisonment and that ruined his prospects for a career in public service. He fathered twelve children and eventually took holy orders in the Church of England. When he died in 1631, he had become Dr. Donne, Dean of St. Paul's, and the most famous preacher in the land.

Donne's contribution to the gay and lesbian literary heritage resides principally in a series of verse letters that he wrote as a young man and in a remarkable dramatic monologue in a lesbian voice, "Sapho to Philaenis." Homosexuality recurs in his satires and his epigrams, though usually as an object of scorn or humor. In "The Jughler," for example, he playfully deconstructs the ambiguous Renaissance word *effeminate* to poke fun at the sodomite: "Thou call'st me

effeminat, for I love womens joyes; / I call not thee manly, though thou follow boyes." In the verse letters to "T.W." and in "Sapho to Philaenis," however, Donne takes homoeroticism seriously.

The four poems to "T.W." were probably written when Donne was eighteen years old and were likely addressed to Thomas Woodward, the sixteen-year-old brother of his friend and frequent correspondent Rowland Woodward. As George Klawitter has shown, the verse letters constitute a sequence that records, first, the poet's infatuation for his friend and, then, his severe disappointment when the youth fails to respond with a like ardor. The poems, including Woodward's response, are full of sexual puns and a highly charged homoeroticism.

"Sapho to Philaenis" is among the earliest positive portrayals of lesbian love in English. In it, the languishing Sapho celebrates the body of her absent lover as "a naturall *Paradise,* / In whose selfe, unmanur'd, all pleasure lies" (ll. 35–36). Donne challenges his culture's negative attitude toward homosexuality by figuring lesbianism as a utopian trope: "betweene us," Sapho tells Philaenis, "all sweetnesse may be had, / All, all that *Nature* yields, or *Art* can adde" (ll. 43–44). Indeed, as Janel Mueller observes, the poem "undertakes to imagine the pleasures, sustenance, and ideological implications by which lesbianism, as a mode of loving and being, resists patriarchal disposition and diminution of women."

—Claude J. Summers

BIBLIOGRAPHY

Empson, William. "'There Is No Penance Due to Innocence'—An Exchange on Donne." *New York Review of Books* 29.3 (March 4, 1982): 42–50. ■ Harvey, Elizabeth D. "Ventriloquizing Sappho: Ovid, Donne, and the Erotics of the Feminine Voice." *Criticism* 31.2 (1989): 115–138. ■ Holstun, James. "'Will you rent our ancient love asunder?': Lesbian Elegy in Donne, Marvell, and Milton." *ELH* 54 (1987): 835–867. ■ Klawitter, George. "Verse Letters to T.W. from John Donne: 'By You My Love Is Sent.'" *Homosexuality in Renaissance and Enlightenment England: Literary Representations in Historical Context.* Claude J. Summers, ed.

New York: Haworth, 1992. 85–102. ■ Mueller, Janel. "Lesbian Erotics: The Utopian Trope of Donne's 'Sapho to Philaenis.'" *Homosexuality in Renaissance and Enlightenment England: Literary Representations in Historical Context.* Claude J. Summers, ed. New York: Haworth, 1992. 103–134. ■ Revard, Stella P. "The Sapphic Voice in Donne's 'Sapho to Philaenis.'" *Renaissance Discourses of Desire.* Claude J. Summers and Ted-Larry Pebworth, eds. Columbia: University of Missouri Press, 1993. 63–76.

Doolittle, Hilda
(1886–1961)

H.D., born Hilda Doolittle on September 10, 1886, in Bethlehem, Pennsylvania, into a middle-class family of strong Moravian faith, was the fourth of six children and only daughter of Charles Leander Doolittle, professor of mathematics and astronomy at Lehigh University (then University of Pennsylvania), and Helen Wolle Doolittle, manager of a chaotic household that paid great deference to the father. She attended various private schools before she went off to Bryn Mawr for a year in 1905. Feeling an intellectual failure to her father and a social failure to her mother, the young H.D. left Bryn Mawr and looked for consolation in writing and reading Greek literature and in her engagement (disapproved of by the Doolittle family) to the upstart poet Ezra Pound, whom she had met in 1901. She also sought for a "sister," and in 1910 found Frances Josepha Gregg, a kindred spirit and her first female lover. What ensued was a painful romantic triangle between Hilda, Frances, and Ezra, the emotional intensity of which H.D. never fully left behind. In its aftermath, H.D. sailed for Europe with Gregg and Gregg's mother where she soon began in earnest her literary career.

Introduced into the literary avant-garde by Pound as "H.D., Imagiste," she wrote poetry in a style that was sparse, concrete, precise, and direct in its imagery. This style obeyed the "masculine" credos to pull poetry away from late Victorian, diffusive, sentimental, "feminine" writing. She stood out as a brilliant young writer of poetry undertaking radical innovations in language and rhythm in the name of MODERNISM. She met (and possibly had an affair with) Brigit Patmore, who in 1912 introduced her to Richard Aldington, free-lance writer and poet. H.D. said he was a man "who will make his way in the world, which I don't much like people to do." Their relationship ended after six years that included marriage, adultery, and the stillbirth of their child in 1915. When she left him, she began and quickly ended an affair with Cecil Gray, a musicologist briefly in her social circle, by whom she became pregnant.

H.D. had published at this point translations, her own *Sea Garden* (1916), and poems in little magazines and anthologies. Having read and admired the poet's work, a young woman who called herself Bryher (Annie Winifred Ellerman) sought her out, thus beginning their lifelong love and partnership. H.D. believed that Bryher saved her life when, soon after they met, Bryher helped nurse her through a dangerous influenza just before the birth of her daughter, Frances Perdita, in 1919. Although the passion of their affair eventually lightened, H.D. still gave to Bryher the intensity she brought to everything in her life. They lived, worked, and traveled together for the next twenty-six years, and corresponded closely when they were apart. Bryher married twice for appearances, appeasing her extremely wealthy and influential English family, and H.D. had intermittent affairs; but the two remained deeply committed to each other for the rest of their lives. H.D. never returned to live in the United States for any extended time; she divided her residence mostly between London and Switzerland, remaining a prolific and respected writer. After a stroke in June 1961, she died on September 27 at a Swiss clinic where Bryher cared for and comforted her.

During the modernist period, several lesbian writers produced and published works explicitly and implicitly exploring lesbian experience. H.D. kept her ties loose to these writers, who were mostly consolidated in Paris. Like them, however, she developed works that celebrated women's romantic relationships with each other. Her early poetry divulges her erotic attachments much more obliquely than her mostly autobiographical prose, which explores the complexity and depth of her feelings for women. Unfortunately, these prose novels were not published until after her death.

Three novels, composed in the 1920s, relate her creative, erotic, and emotional development as centered on passionate attachments to women, following many of the same events of her life while varying the details. As in RADCLYFFE HALL's *The Well of Loneliness* (1928) and DJUNA BARNES's *Nightwood* (1936), lesbianism is central to the plots and conflicts of *Paint It Today* (1921), *Asphodel* (1921–1922), and *HERmione* (1926–1927). Her poetry published at the time explores her often tormented heterosexual life; these manuscripts that she left unpublished disclose her homosexual life. For H.D., being out to the public was not only uncomfortable but risky. H.D. and Bryher downplayed their relationship by referring to themselves as "cousins." The books help make up what H.D. termed the "madrigal cycle" and follow her life from leaving Bryn Mawr feeling an academic failure through her intense love relationships with Pound and Gregg, her departure from the United States and the launch of her literary career, her subsequent marriage and its dissolution, to Perdita's birth and Bryher's entry into her life as caretaker and lover. The erotic female–female–male situations found in this work represent a scenario often repeated in her life.

As has been pointed out by critics, H.D.'s novels diverge from concurrent works and thought in the portrayal of female homosexuality. Bryher often considered herself a boy, and popular thought held that lesbians were males born with the wrong anatomical parts. But H.D. did not view her attraction for women as a result of mistaken identity or as a self-destructive compulsion. Gregg, H.D.'s first female lover, gets written into the texts as a complex character who has both devastating and restorative effects on H.D.'s life. Bryher figures into the narratives as a healing presence who allows for a supportive union of two autonomous and loving partners that H.D. did not feel attainable in a heterosexual world laden with inequalities.

H.D. wrote these novels at a time when she was feeling the constraint of having been labeled an imagist early on in her career and was searching for ways to loosen that stricture. The confessional prose that she penned, though not for the world to see immediately, is a scripting of her life with herself as creator/writer at the center. And in this process, she inquires into her imaginative and erotic selves, focusing particularly on the healing and generative power of female-oriented sexuality. She celebrates woman as writer and as desiring subject. Susan Stanford Friedman explains that *HERmione* is "A gynopoetic, a lesbian erotic, [that] displaces the male loop of textual desire." The central character refuses to be obliterated by a male desire to render her sexual, beautiful, and therefore passive for him and turns to a more spiritually

gratifying lesbian love. H.D. wrote this novel in highly stylized modernist prose, filled with interior stream-of-consciousness expression and nonlinear narratives.

H.D. recalls in these novels a yearning for a twin as a maternal replacement, a complementary figure to share and enhance her sense of self-worth. Having a partner so close to her own psyche meant walking a fine line between self-aggrandizement and self-annihilation. This tension gets echoed in poetry from the same period, here figured as matched arms in combat:

> It was not chastity that made me wild, but fear
> that my weapon, tempered in different heat,
> was over-matched by yours, and your hand
> skilled to yield death-blows, might break
>
> With the slightest turn–no ill will meant–
> my own lesser, yet still somewhat fine-wrought,
> fiery-tempered, delicate, over-passionate steel.
> ("Toward the Piraeus" 115–21)

In her later life and work, H.D.'s intense feelings for women shifted toward reverence for a somewhat remote mother or goddess figure necessary as a healing presence. H.D. wrote often of the renewal that an unconventional female energy could bring. H.D.'s inspiration was frequently derived from her passionate feelings for women, as she maintained strong women-centered paradigms throughout her writing. Directly and indirectly, her work expresses the complexity of homosexual desire and the calming and restorative power she felt in lesbian love.

—*Jennifer S. Wilson*

BIBLIOGRAPHY

Friedman, Susan Stanford. *Penelope's Web: Gender, Modernity, H.D.'s Fiction.* Cambridge: Cambridge University Press, 1990. ■ ——, and Rachel Blau Duplessis, eds. *Signets: Reading H.D.* Madison: University of Wisconsin Press, 1990. ■ Guest, Barbara. *HERself Defined: The Poet H.D. and Her World.* Glasgow: William Collins Sons, 1984. ■ Laity, Cassandra. "H.D. and A.C. Swinburne: Decadence and Modernist Women's Writing." *Feminist Studies* 15:3 (Fall 1989): 461–484. ■ ——. "Lesbian Romanticism: H.D.'s Fictional Representations of Frances Gregg and Bryher." Introduction to *Paint It Today* by H.D. Karla Jay, ed. New York: New York University Press, 1992. xvii–xlii.

Douglas, Alfred
(1870–1945)

Lord Alfred Bruce Douglas, universally known as Bosie, was born October 22, 1870, the third son of John Sholto Douglas, ninth Marquess of Queensbury, and Sibyl, née Montgomery. He is remembered today for his association with OSCAR WILDE and as a minor poet.

After a boyhood during which his parents separated, Douglas went up from Winchester to Magdalen College, Oxford, in 1889. He met Oscar Wilde through a mutual friend in early summer, 1891, and they became lovers the following spring. Douglas's beauty was "like a narcissus—white and gold," as Wilde told Robert Ross.

Most of Douglas's homoerotic poetry was written between 1893 and 1896 and appeared in undergraduate literary journals such as *The Spirit Lamp,* which he edited, and *The Chameleon,* or in small-circulation magazines like *The Artist.* Poems like "Hymn to Physical Beauty" (with a nod to Shelley), the sonnet "In an Aegean Port," and most famously "Two Loves," one of whom concludes the poem by sighing "I am the Love that dare not speak its name," are typical in their wistful tone. Some of these poems appeared in a French edition of Douglas's verse in 1896, but most were not republished until the *Sonnets* and *Lyrics* of 1935, and then, at least in the sonnet mentioned, with the homosexual content revised out.

In 1895, Douglas's father accused Oscar Wilde of "posing as a sodomite," whereupon Wilde (at Bosie's urging) sued him for libel. At the trial, Queensbury was found not guilty and a warrant was promptly issued for Wilde's arrest. His first trial resulted in a hung jury, but at the second Wilde was found guilty and sentenced to two years' hard labor.

Although Douglas and Wilde remained close until the latter's death in 1900, the scandal generated a sheaf of spiteful documents. In prison, Wilde wrote a long and bitter epistle later titled *De Profundis,* accusing Douglas of betraying their friendship. When the full text of *De Profundis* was made public in 1913, Douglas responded with *Oscar Wilde and Myself,* repudiating Wilde and his works.

Soon after Wilde's death, Douglas renounced his homosexuality; he married Olive Custance in 1902, and they had a son, Raymond. Douglas converted to Roman Catholicism in 1911, and he and his wife separated two years later. By his own account, Douglas remained celibate thereafter.

From 1907 to 1910, Douglas edited the journal *The Academy,* assisted by the obnoxious T. W. H. Crosland, who in fact, ghost-wrote most of *Oscar Wilde and Myself.* Douglas revived *The Academy* in 1920 and 1921 as *Plain English,* and the journal had a mild commercial success. Editorially, however, it was nonliterary and virulently antisemitic, simply a forum for Douglas's considerable collection of bigotries.

Douglas's intemperate expression of his views led to his arrest and conviction for writing and publishing a pamphlet libeling Winston Churchill. He spent six months in Wormwood Scrubs prison. There he turned again to poetry, but *his* prison writing, a sonnet sequence, was called *In Excelsis.*

Douglas spent the remaining twenty-one years of his life quietly, living in Hove or Brighton on allowances provided by his mother and wife. He produced his *Autobiography* during this time, several versions of his collected poems, occasional verse, and in 1940, his most judicious account of his life's central experience, *Oscar Wilde: A Summing Up.* He died on March 20, 1945, following a heart attack.

—*Michael N. Stanton*

BIBLIOGRAPHY

Croft-Cooke, Rupert. *Bosie: Lord Alfred Douglas, His Friends and Enemies.* New York: Bobbs-Merrill, 1963. ■ Douglas, Alfred. *The Autobiography of Lord Alfred Douglas.* 2nd edition. London: Martin Secker, 1931. ■ ———. *Collected Satires.* London: The Fortune Press, 1926. ■ ———. *The Complete Poems of Lord Alfred Douglas.* London: Martin Secker, 1928. ■ ———. *Lyrics.* London: Rich and Cowan, 1935. ■ ———. *Oscar Wilde: A Summing Up.* London: Duckworth, 1940. ■ ———. *Sonnets.* London: Rich and Cowan, 1935. ■ Ellmann, Richard. *Oscar Wilde.* New York: Knopf, 1988. ■ Hyde, H. Montgomery. *Lord Alfred Douglas.* New York: Dodd, Mead, 1985.

Douglas, Norman
(1868–1952)

Born in Thuringen, Vorarlberg, Austria, to a Scottish father, the manager of a cotton mill, and a Scottish-German mother, Douglas was educated first at Uppingham School (1881–1883) and then Karlsruhe Gymnasium (1883–1889). Although keenly interested in natural history, he entered the British Foreign Office (1893–1901) and was posted to St. Petersburg from 1894 to 1896. He purchased property on Capri, the Mediterranean island about which he would write eight books, and in 1898 married his cousin, Elizabeth Theobaldino FitzGibbon. They had two sons, but the marriage ended in 1904. Faced with financial reverses in 1907, Douglas existed in near and sometimes actual poverty for almost two decades as he and later his companion, Guiseppe Orioli, lived variously in Paris, St. Malo, Menton,

Florence, Lisbon, and London, before returning to Capri in 1946.

Douglas's first published work was an official report, *The Pumice Stone Industry of the Lipari Islands* (1895), which he felt contributed to the abolition of child labor, but his geographical and topographical travel books such as *Siren Land* (1911), about the Sorrentino peninsula, *Fountain in the Sand* (1912), about Tunisia, and *Old Calabria* (1915), first attracted attention. His travel books show a love of landscapes, a naturalist's eye glancing over the surroundings, an ear for anecdotes about the legends and people of the land, and loose, reflective meditations. From 1912 to 1914, Douglas was the assistant editor of *The English Review,* probably the most important prewar literary review in England, and met D. H. LAWRENCE, who would later depict Douglas as James Argyle in *Aaron's Rod* (1922). Douglas's *London Street Games* (1916) was labeled "a breathless catalogue" by one of its early reviewers and was praised for its remarkable knowledge of children. In later years, Douglas wrote several autobiographical works, including *Looking Back* (1933) and *Late Harvest* (1946).

Douglas earned epithets such as "pagan to the core" and "an unashamed connoisseur of pleasure"

with *South Wind* (1917), his only popular success. *South Wind* explores the pleasures of the hedonistic life. Set on the fictional island of Nepenthe (another depiction of Capri), *South Wind* tells the very loosely developed story of Thomas Heard, Bishop of Bambopo, during the season of the sirocco (south wind), which considerably affects the attitudes and behavior of the islanders. He encounters people holding various unorthodox views on moral and sexual questions, and Douglas develops the collision of opinions in "a series of Rabelaisian conversation pieces." Douglas said his plot involved making "murder palatable to a bishop" and described the work as "the result of my craving to escape from the wearisome actualities of life." The novel stands in a tradition of such works as Samuel Johnson's *Rasselas,* the MARQUIS DE SADE's *Justine,* Thomas Love Peacock's *Nightmare Abbey,* and W. H. Mallock's *The New Republic.*

—*David Leon Higdon*

BIBLIOGRAPHY

Greenlees, Ian. *Norman Douglas.* London: Longman's, Green, 1957. ■ Holloway, Mark. *Norman Douglas: A Biography.* London: Secker & Warburg, 1976.

DRAMATIC LITERATURE

Dramatic Literature: Modern Drama

Modern drama is usually defined as beginning with the realists, particularly Ibsen, in the 1870s. It is more difficult to say if or when modern drama ends and contemporary or post-modern drama begins. For gay and lesbian drama, one can say that the dividing line between modern and contemporary drama is the Stonewall Riots of 1969, which symbolized the change in lesbians and gay men from internalizing and acting on their society's negative attitude toward them and their insistence, supported by fellow homosexuals, in asserting their own worth and pride. Having somewhat arbitrarily established these parameters, one still has not defined gay and lesbian drama.

Dramas written by heterosexuals about gay and lesbian characters or relationships formed a subgenre in the first half of the century. BRECHT's first play, *Baal* (1918), featured a bisexual hero who cares far more for his friend and lover Eckard than for the scores of "bitches" he beds. His translation of MARLOWE's *Edward II* (1923), which trades Marlowe's mighty line for slangy verse, is more overt than Marlowe's 1594 original in establishing the sexual relationship of Edward and his minion, Piers Gaveston.

Lesbian and gay characters were more likely to appear in realistic problem plays, usually as "the problem" that had to be eliminated by the final curtain. Even these plays, which were hardly gay affirming, were often considered too immoral for production. *The Captive,* an American version of Edouard Bourdet's melodrama, *La Prisonnière* (1926), caused an outcry from the moral majority of the time, and Mae West's picture of gay life in the 1920s, *The Drag* (1927), was not allowed across the Hudson into New York City after its tryout in Bayonne, New Jersey.

The 1930s saw two critically acclaimed melodramas about lesbians and gay men, both sufficiently coded to allow production (the love that dared not speak its name could whisper cryptically). Mordaunt Shairp's *The Green Bay Tree,* which was produced in London and New York in 1933, depicts the corruption of a young man by his effete, domineering mentor. Although homosexuality is never mentioned and barely hinted at, there is no doubt about the nature of Dulcimer's hold over his protégé. In Shairp's play, the most ominous signs of homosexuality are expensive taste, bitchy wit, and—worst of all—a penchant for arranging flowers. The next year, Lillian Hellman's *The Children's Hour* presented a woman who, on realizing that her feelings for her best friend are, as destructive rumors have alleged, sexual, commits suicide. In an odd piece of dramaturgy that would be considered incompetent if the corpse in the next room were that of a heterosexual, characters go on about their business for the remaining fifteen minutes of the play as if the poor woman had not blown her brains out. After all, the poor lesbian did the only thing possible.

The 1950s gave Broadway the classic American melodrama of confused masculinity, Robert Anderson's *Tea and Sympathy* (1953), in which the sissy is heterosexual and the macho man is a latent homosexual. The noble housemaster's wife confronts her husband with his latent homosexuality and, at the final curtain, offers herself to the sensitive young man, who has been accused of being the unspeakable, to affirm his heterosexuality ("Years from now, when you talk about this, and you will, please be kind"). The Lord Chamberlain banned a London production even though homosexuality is never overtly mentioned.

Although these plays are *about* homosexuality, they really are not gay drama. Rather, the homosexual is the problem to be eliminated by the final curtain. Nor can the numerous works by homosexual authors that do not deal overtly with gay and lesbian characters and relationships be considered gay drama. Gay drama is drama by and about lesbians or gay men.

Virtually no drama by and about lesbians was produced during this period. Women playwrights were rare; openly lesbian playwrights virtually nonexistent. In America, lesbians found acceptance in various technical areas of theater but did not see their lives represented on stage.

During the modern period, overtly gay male characters were rare, in great part as a result of censorship laws. In England, until 1968 all plays presented in public theaters had to be approved by the office of the Lord Chamberlain. One of the taboos the Lord Chamberlain's office was most interested in safeguarding was homosexuality. In New York, the Wales Padlock Act was created to penalize any theater owner who allowed the presentation of homosexuality on his stage. Other cities had obscenity laws that could be invoked against any dramatic representation of a homosexual. Because of these legal sanctions, most representations of homosexuality were coded, as it is in TENNESSEE WILLIAMS's *A Streetcar Named Desire* (1947), which can be read as a play about the oppression of a sexually transgressive character by a white heterosexual male who has decided what and who will be allowed in his house literally and metaphorically. EDWARD ALBEE's early one-act plays, *The Sandbox* (1958), *The Zoo Story* (1959), and *The American Dream* (1961), and his 1964 full-length play, *Tiny Alice,* can be easily given gay readings. Homosexual playwrights enabled lesbians and gay men in the audience to endow the plays with gay readings, which were encoded in the text and in the erotics of the stage presentation; for one crucial aspect of gay male drama, closeted or uncloseted, is the presentation of the male as object of the audience's gaze and desire. From OSCAR WILDE's *Salome* (1895) to *A Streetcar Named Desire* and other plays by Williams to Edward Albee's *The American Dream* (1958), it is the male who is looked at and judged as sexual object in gay drama.

A few landmarks in modern gay drama openly present homosexual desire. Many of these early gay dramas were written by authors, most of whose famous work was in other genres but who were drawn to the erotics of theater to best represent homosexual desire.

ANDRÉ GIDE's *Saul,* written in 1896, may be the first modern gay drama. It was not published until 1906 and not produced until 1922 by Jacques Copeau at his famous Vieux Colombier. *Saul* justifies its pervasive homoeroticism through the authority of the Bible and the distance of history. We first see the Hebrew king with his favorite, the beautiful young cupbearer, Saki. King Saul has not slept with his wife since the conception of the supposed heir to the throne, the frail Jonathan. Saul is visited by demons who themselves offer homoerotic temptation to which the king succumbs. When the strong, beautiful David appears on the scene, Saul and Jonathan both fall in love with him. Saul shaves his beard so that he will look younger and more attractive to the young hero. Saul knows that he is "a man of desires" who loves David's strength and "the movement of his loins," but David adores Jonathan. Saul is paralyzed by prophecies that his son will not succeed him on the throne and discovers that David is God's chosen to be the next king. David, who dreads the thought of kingship, ultimately must accept the crown as he stands over the corpses of Saul and Jonathan. As in Christopher Marlowe's *Edward II* (1594), kingship means renouncing one's homoerotic desire. Saul's inability to fight the armies of Philistines at his gates and his succumbing to his demons are caused by his placing his desire before his duties as king. David dreads his inevitable kingship because of what he will have to give up to be king: his love for the frail Jonathan. At the end, David stands by the corpses of Saul and Jonathan. This tableau is emblematic of his victory over desire and passivity. All desire in *Saul* is homoerotic, yet that desire is at odds with heroic action or God's plan.

J. R. ACKERLEY's only play, *The Prisoners of War* (1925), is considered to be the first British play to deal openly with homosexual desire. Ackerley actually wrote the first draft of the play while he was interned in Switzerland in 1918 during World War I. It was produced by a private theater club in the summer of 1925 and, amazingly, was vetted by the Lord Chamberlain for a West End production.

Interned in a hotel in Mürren, Switzerland, with fellow wounded or ill officers, twenty-four-year-old Captain James Conrad is on the verge of a mental breakdown. Frustrated by inactivity, bored in this hermetic environment, he has lost the routine that enabled him to repress his homosexuality. As a result, he cannot hide or control his feelings for a callow young lieutenant. A gripping social and psychological study of young British gentlemen at odds outside their own society, *The Prisoners of War* also is unique in its candid presentation of repressed homosexuality in an all-male environment. One soldier remembers his childhood fascination with the Theban Band, the Spartan soldiers who fought alongside their lovers. When Conrad is accused of not appreciating "the fair sex," he answers, "The fair sex. Which one is that?" Whereas Conrad's unrequited infatuation is the last straw leading to his breakdown, another couple plan an idyllic postwar life together in Canada.

NOËL COWARD wrote only one full-length comedy in which homosexual desire is a motivating factor. *Design for Living* (1933), first presented in New York with Coward, Alfred Lunt, and Lynn Fontanne, chronicles the trials and tribulations of a peripatetic ménage à trois that travels, over the play's three acts, from Paris to London to New York City. The central character, Gilda, finds that she is in love with two

men, Otto and Leo, who were a couple before either of them became attracted to her. The only resolution for the conflicts, jealousies, and unhappiness of this equilateral triangle is for the three of them to live together. The butt of most of the play's jokes are the respectable people who cannot understand or approve of this "three sided erotic hotch-potch." Although many in the first audiences were somehow capable of overlooking the clear references to Otto and Leo's love for each other and see Coward's comedy as being only about the love of two men for the same woman, a post-Stonewall audience, particularly one who knows the private lives of the playwright and his two fellow actors, sees clearly all three sides of the triangle.

Modernism in drama comprises two parallel lines: realism, which remained dominant in English-speaking countries, and various strains of non- or anti-realistic theater (expressionism, futurism, surrealism, and so on), which had closer ties to the major schools of modern painting and sculpture. FEDERICO GARCIA LORCA clearly felt that the dramatic representation of homosexual desire would require a different form from the lyric realism he used for his tragedies of heterosexual repression. (Though clearly Lorca's series of dramas about women destroyed because of transgressive sexual desire were an expression of his own place as a homosexual in Spanish society.) His one extant openly gay play, the late, unfinished *The Audience* (its published English translation is inaccurately entitled *The Public*), was written in 1930–1931, but revised again shortly before his murder in 1936. One of Lorca's last social appearances was a private reading of *The Audience* for friends a month before he was arrested and executed, as much for his homosexuality as for his political sympathies. *The Audience* was one of a group of plays Lorca wrote under the rubric "Impossible Theater." Using surreal images and elaborate stage magic, and focusing on themes forbidden on the stage, like homosexuality, Lorca told friends he wrote these plays for the future. These plays remained in manuscript form during the poet's lifetime and all but *The Audience* were lost or destroyed.

In *The Audience,* a theatrical director is confronted by a series of bizarre dream images and transformations. In the fluid dream world of the play, characters switch costume, gender, and identity with startling rapidity. Though the play allows for a number of interpretations, a gay reading is inescapable. Throughout the play, men embrace and challenge one another to rip off the mask that forbids their love. The theater is the world of masks, including those of closeted homosexuals. The audience is the feared, judging world that would rip apart the true (homosexual) self. Yet, the play asserts that love and sexual desire know no boundaries of gender. Romeo and Juliet may be man and woman or, in performance, man and boy. SHAKESPEARE is regularly invoked as the creator of a world of gender fluidity: "If love is pure chance and Titania, Queen of the Fairies, fell in love with an ass, then, by the same reasoning, there wouldn't be anything extraordinary about Gonzalo drinking in the 'music hall' with a boy dressed in white sitting on his lap." *The Audience* is a call for a sexual revolution that would lead to the liberation of the human imagination and spirit.

Like his friend André Gide, Julien Green was better known for his novels and volumes of memoirs than for his plays. Born in Paris of American parents, Green studied at the University of Virginia before returning to Paris to begin a long, distinguished writing career. Though known as a French writer, Green's first and best-known play takes place in the American South, the home of his ancestors. *Sud* (*South*) was first produced in Paris in March, 1953, at the Théâtre de l'Athénée–Louis Jouvet. Green translated the play into English, and it was performed under the direction of the young Peter Hall at London's Arts Theatre Club in March, 1955, with the young Denholm Elliott in the leading role. The Lord Chamberlain banned public performance of the play, which meant it could be performed only by a private club, and a newspaper strike made proper publicity difficult. Word of mouth gave the production moderate success at the box office. A 1991 publication of an English translation makes the work accessible to readers.

South takes place on a plantation near Charleston during the twenty-four hours before the firing on Fort Sumter that will begin the Civil War. The central character is a Polish expatriate, Jan Wicziewsky, an officer with the Union Army stationed near Fort Sumter. Like his creator, Wicziewsky is a foreigner in his adopted land, a Catholic, and a homosexual. Stalking the plantation like a ghost, the melancholy Wicziewsky elicits violently mixed emotions from the women, who feel his indifference, and devotion from the men. Clearly Green had the economical, psychologically insightful tragedies of Racine in mind as he wrote *South*. While Racine's great tragedies focused on classical queens who were obsessed and ultimately destroyed by forbidden passions, so Green's play gives us a homosexual hero destroyed by a love he cannot express. The published edition of *South* has as its epigraph a quotation from Aristotle's definition of tragedy, "The purification of a dangerous passion by a violent liberation." The violent passion is Wicziewsky's love at first sight of the puritanical young Southern aristocrat, Erik MacClure. Realizing that his love can never be admitted or requited, Wicziewsky decides to "hurl myself against my fate as you hurl yourself against a stone wall." Jealous of MacClure's love for the young Angelina and furious that MacClure, like himself, lacks the courage to admit his love to his beloved, he goads MacClure into killing him in a duel. Wicziewsky would rather die than live with the anguish of a love that can never be expressed or returned. As Wicziewsky's corpse is brought into the main hall of the plantation, the guns firing on Fort Sumter can be heard in the distance. This personal tragedy will be followed by the national tragedy of the Civil War. As his classical forbears tied grand personal tragedies to the Trojan War, so Green ties his tragedy of male–male love to the Civil War. Actions in his play are fated though that fate is expressed in Christian terms.

Farceur JOE ORTON did more than any other British playwright to open the door to the closet that contained many of Britain's commercial playwrights and producers. Though Orton died young, his handful of plays, which are still revived regularly around the world, heralded the sexual revolution that would come shortly after his death. Orton was openly and unabashedly gay, but his plays contain no exclusively homosexual characters. Homosexual desire and homosexual acts are set within a framework of polymorphous perversity. In the horny world of Joe Orton's plays, everyone lusts after everyone regardless of gender or family relationship. This avoidance of homosexual identity within the omnisexual world of Orton's farces was probably more acceptable to London and New York audiences in the mid-1960s than the still taboo homosexual would have been.

The enormous success of Mart Crowley's *The Boys in the Band* (1968) was a turning point for gay drama. Strongly influenced by Edward Albee's closeted *Who's Afraid of Virginia Woolf?* in its extremes of camp comedy and melodrama and its focus on game playing, *The Boys in the Band* is the first commercial play to be set in a gay household. In a way, the play can be seen as a somewhat rotten slice of gay history in that it displays not only gay slang and manners of the period just before the Stonewall Rebellion, but it shows vividly the ways in which gay men suffered from internalized homophobia. There is no gay pride in Mart Crowley's play, only shame and self-hatred. Jealousy, bickering, alcoholism, and regret define the lives of these unhappy men, but at no point do they realize that the enemy is not themselves but the homophobia that shaped them.

By the time *The Boys in the Band* became a hit uptown, gay drama was already beginning to change. In Greenwich Village, at the Caffe Cino, where owner Joe Cino had been presenting plays since 1958, a group of young playwrights who had come to New York from various places around the United States began creating unashamedly gay theater for the adventurous audiences who frequented what became known as Off-Off-Broadway. Early plays by Doric Wilson, LANFORD WILSON (*The Madness of Lady Bright* [1964]) and ROBERT PATRICK (*The Haunted Host* [1964]) did not compromise to the prejudices of mainstream, predominantly heterosexual audiences but reflected the courage that would lead to Stonewall. The audience at Caffe Cino was predominantly gay, representing the split that would exist for decades to come between gay-positive theater written for gay audiences and mainstream gay representations that had to take into account the predominantly heterosexual audience before whom they would be performed. (See also DRAMATIC LITERATURE: CONTEMPORARY DRAMA and MUSICAL THEATER.)

—*John M. Clum*

BIBLIOGRAPHY

Clum, John M. *Acting Gay: Male Homosexuality in Modern Drama.* New York: Columbia, 1992. Revised paperback ed., 1993. ■ ———. "'Myself of Course': Self-Dramatization in J. R. Ackerley." *Theatre* (July 1993). ■ Curtin, Kaier. *We Can Always Call Them Bulgarians.* Boston: Alyson, 1987. ■ de-Jongh, Nicholas. *Not in Front of the Audience: Homosexuality on Stage.* London: Routledge, 1992. ■ Fowlie, Wallace. *Dionysus in Paris: A Guide to Contemporary French Theater.* London: V. Gollancz, 1961. ■ Lahr, John. *Prick Up Your Ears.* New York: Knopf, 1978. ■ Shepherd, Simon. *Because We're Queers: The Life and Crimes of Kenneth Halliwell and Joe Orton.* London: Gay Men's Press, 1989. ■ Stambolian, George and Elaine Marks, eds. *Homosexualities and French Literature.* Ithaca, N.Y.: Cornell University Press, 1979.

Dramatic Literature: Contemporary Drama

We define the starting point for contemporary lesbian and gay drama as the Stonewall Riots of June 1969, though in America the pioneers of openly gay drama were already working in venues like the Caffe Cino in Greenwich Village. Caffe Cino playwrights ROBERT PATRICK, Doric Wilson, and LANFORD WILSON were pioneers in establishing an American gay theater. Gay drama developed in two different types of venue: the small theaters geared toward the gay community, where Robert Patrick and Doric Wilson presented most of their work, and eventually, the mainstream commercial or subsidized theater, where Lanford Wilson achieved considerable success in the 1980s. Patrick and Doric Wilson were interested in holding a mirror up to their gay audiences to challenge them to seize power (Wilson) and to overcome their self-hatred and narcissism (Patrick). Both did this through sharply barbed satire. The performances of Wilson's *Street Theatre* (1981) at The Mineshaft, a Greenwich Village leather and sex bar, were prime examples of gay drama played in and for the gay community. *Street Theater* was a celebration of the Stonewall Riots and parodies a classic by a closeted homosexual (Thornton Wilder's *Our Town*) and the self-hating gay characters of *The Boys in the Band*. Though the Circle Repertory Company, which Lanford Wilson founded with director Marshall W. Mason, has become a major producer of gay drama, gay characters appear only occasionally in Wilson's post–Caffe Cino plays and are central only to his *5th of July* (1978), in which a gay, paraplegic Vietnam War veteran comes to terms with his past, present, and future.

During the 1960s in Greenwich Village theaters, Ronald Tavel was presenting apolitical CAMP extravaganzas filled with elaborate drag and parodies of flamboyant theatrical and film genres. One of Tavel's actors in the mid-1960s was the prodigiously talented, ambitious Charles Ludlam whom Tavel fired after the troupe presented one of Ludlam's plays in 1967. The next year Ludlam's Ridiculous Theater Company presented its first production, *When Queens Collide*. Ludlam's plays were not intended to be politically correct "gay drama" but transgressive "queer theater," which both emphasized the larger-than-life theatricality he loved and offered a vision that was decidedly antibourgeois. Ludlam's theater survived his death in 1987 and, under the direction of his lover, Everett Quinton, continues to this day. Many of Ludlam's plays have become regularly performed classics of gay drama though they lose something without his commanding presence as Hedda Gabler or Marguerite Gautier in his *Camille* (1973). Ludlam's *The Mystery of Irma Vep* (1984), in which two male actors portray all the male and female characters in a sendup of a Victorian "penny dreadful" has become one of the most popular plays in regional theater productions. The tradition of drag and camp developed by Tavel and Ludlam continues in the work of Charles Busch (*Vampire Lesbians of Sodom* [1985]) and groups like Bloolips and the lesbian troupe Split Britches.

Lesbian drama developed not only in lesbian spaces like the WOW theater in New York but also in women's theaters around the country. Although there have been some dramas by and about lesbians in small, gay-oriented theaters, little has been produced by major theaters or has been published. In her introduction to the 1987 collection, *Lesbian Plays,* Jill Davis wrote, "By comparison with the number of plays by gay men accessible in print and in Britain's larger theatres, lesbian theatre might be thought not to exist." The 25 percent or less representation of lesbian playwrights in major anthologies of gay and lesbian drama is a sign of the relative invisibility of lesbian playwrights in the commercial and subsidized theater. Lesbian playwrights have worked mostly within the networks of women's and gay theaters.

JANE CHAMBERS, the first major openly lesbian playwright, managed to create powerful dramas within the framework of dramatic realism. Chambers, by day a writer of soap operas, wrote a number of works that stand as classics of lesbian drama. In her plays, Chambers was more interested in the personal, emotional life of her characters than lesbian or feminist politics. Her strongest work, *A Late Snow* (1974), traps Ellie, a college professor, in her lakeside cottage during a snowstorm with four women who have been important to her at various stages of her life: her college friend and sometime lover who has accepted her lesbianism; her alcoholic, self-destructive former lover who won't give up on the possibility of reestablishing their relationship; her adoring young lover and protégée; and a famous writer with whom, at the final curtain, Ellie negotiates a new relationship. Within this conventional framework, Chambers, through her characters, explores the elements of a mature, reciprocal relationship. Ellie wants "a lover consumed by the greatest passion, a partner possessed of the greatest loyalty, a friend committed to the greatest love." She realizes that until now she has settled for one of three with each of the women in her life. Wanting it all, she starts over again. She also realizes that living in the closet is impossible: "I can't march. But I won't hide."

Chambers is unique in adhering to the conventions of dramatic realism. Though she wrote extremely well-crafted dramas, her work did not receive the exposure of her gay male counterparts. Other lesbian playwrights looked for freer, more ironically charged forms. Susan Miller's *Confessions of a Female Disorder* (1973) is a hilarious biography of a young woman from her first period until her realization that she is a lesbian and totally miscast in the married, country-club world in which she is trapped. Miller's use of funny choric characters to represent conventional masculine and feminine stereotypes, direct address to the audience, and actors playing multiple roles helps her audience see the universal implications of her character's battles with the agents of sexism and heterosexism. Holly Hughes's *The Well of Horniness*

(1983) is more fun than politics. In this mock radio broadcast, Hughes parodies the conventions and sound effects of radio melodrama to present a lesbian fantasy. Mysterious murders, a lesbian detective named Garnet McClit, and hundreds of double-entendres fill Hughes's script, which owes much to Theater of the Ridiculous. In recent years, lesbian writers and performers, influenced in part by the work of the many prominent feminist and lesbian theorists, have discarded the conventions and assumptions of realistic drama, seen by them as incompatible with feminism, for various forms of theatrical experimentation and performance art. The leading figures in contemporary lesbian theater are performance artists like Karen Finley and Holly Hughes.

British lesbian playwrights are more concerned with the social, economic, and political aspects of a lesbian's experience. Jane Kirby's *Twice Over* (1988) begins with the funeral of a middle-aged woman, Cora, who never acknowledged her loving relationship with her best friend, Maeve. Cora arranges for her diaries, the record of her love for Maeve, to fall into the hands of her teenage granddaughter, Evaki. Through Evaki, Maeve and Cora's family come to terms with the love that was central to Cora's life. The denouement is a replay of Cora's funeral as it should have been, with Maeve receiving the condolences of family and friends. *Twice Over* is a touching example of contemporary social realism, focusing on working-class characters and cross-generational relationships.

Unlike their lesbian compeers, gay men have maintained an investment in writing for mainstream theater partly because producers and theater companies have continued their historical preference toward male playwrights, gay or straight.

The few gay-positive plays that have appeared on the London stage in recent years are historical dramas rather than presentations of contemporary gay experience. The best of these is written by Martin Sherman, an American who lives in London. His *Bent* (1979) opened at the Royal Court Theatre with Ian McKellan; a Broadway production the following year featured Richard Gere. Beginning the morning after the Night of the Long Knives in 1934, *Bent* traces the growth of a young German man from self-hatred and a destructive life to his acceptance of love and affirmation in a Nazi prison camp. From its gay slang and camp humor to its famous scene of verbal sex, *Bent* is a celebration of gayness in the face of oppression. Its tenth-anniversary revival in London, again with McKellan, was akin to a religious experience for gay men, bristling under new laws forbidding positive portrayals of lesbians and gay men in government-supported theaters.

Peter Gill's *Mean Tears* (1987) is the best written play about contemporary gay experience in Britain. Eloquent and witty, it dramatizes the love a passionate intellectual has for a most unworthy object, a feckless bisexual. With surgical precision, Gill satirizes the mores and manners of young Britons, gay, straight, and bisexual, for whom sex is a simple transaction and commitment is impossible. Only the bookish gay central character demands more, but there seems to be no one who can offer the commitment he wants. *Mean Tears* is the only truly contemporary gay British drama to be produced by a major London theater. Most commercial British gay drama has been period pieces about famous and infamous gay and presumed gay men of the past: OSCAR WILDE, CONSTANTINE CAVAFY, Alan Turing, CHRISTOPHER MARLOWE, John Webster, EDWARD CARPENTER, Benjamin Britten, and Guy Burgess.

Sherman's work since *Bent* has achieved success on the West End. Gill's *Mean Tears* was produced at the Royal National Theatre. Most other gay drama, except for imports of American plays, has been produced in small fringe theaters in London and other cities. In the 1970s and 1980s, the center of gay theater in London was the Gay Sweatshop, a company devoted to presenting gay drama as a means of raising social consciousness. The group began in 1975 with a season of one-acts by British and American gay male dramatists presented as free lunchtime theater. By the next year, the company was devoted to the creation of gay and lesbian drama to be produced in London and on tour. Though some of the more powerful theaters reacted defiantly, much gay drama was squelched by Clause 28, passed by Parliament in 1988, which prohibited government money from being spent on any communication that promoted homosexuality positively, particularly homosexual relationships as alternatives to the nuclear family. The Oval House in South London and the Drill Hall Arts Centre in Bloomsbury continue to present lesbian and gay drama but without the coordination or creative energy of Gay Sweatshop. Only since the highly successful 1992 London production of Tony Kushner's *Angels in America, Part I: The Millennium Approaches,* has gay drama flourished even on the fringe.

By the late 1980s, a large proportion of North American drama was being written by openly gay playwrights. A variety of playwrights spread across Canada were writing works about the gay experience: the versatile Québécois MICHEL TREMBLAY, whose work reflects the nonrealistic explorations of postmodern European theater; Albertan Brad Fraser, whose *The Unidentified Nature and True Remains of Love* (1989) is similar to American Lanford Wilson's disruptions of time and place and explorations of the

relationship of sex and violence; and Torontan drag artist and playwright Sky Gilbert, whose theater pieces have been influenced by the gender bending and camp humor of Charles Ludlam and Charles Busch. This is not to suggest that Canadian drama is any more derivative than that of any other country but that Canadian dramatists draw on a wider range of British, European, and U.S. models than American playwrights do. (See also CANADIAN LITERATURE.)

In the 1990s, there is gay theater all over the United States. Theatre Rhinoceros in San Francisco, the Glines in New York City, OutProud and Actor's Express in Atlanta, and Manbites Dog Theater in Durham, North Carolina, are a few of the many theaters developing gay drama. Within the New York theater establishment, a majority of the most produced and published playwrights are gay even if they are not writing drama about gay characters. The explosion of gay drama is in part a result of demographics. Theater and gay culture have always been primarily urban phenomena, and the large urban gay communities have an investment in theater for a number of reasons, the principal one being the fact that, given the lack of representations of gay characters and problems on television or in film, theater becomes a crucial means of ratifying gayness. Given the demographics of urban centers, even heterosexual playwrights like David Henry Hwang (*M. Butterfly* [1988]) and John Guare (*Six Degrees of Separation* [1990]) have had their greatest commercial success with plays that focus on homosexual characters. It is a sign of the times for American theater when the most praised, honored, and talked about play in decades has the subtitle "A Gay Fantasia on American Themes."

A mini-history of American gay drama can be found in the works of Terrence McNally, who throughout the past three decades has managed to embrace gay characters and a gay vision successfully within mainstream New York theater. From the zany gay couples in his double bill, *Bad Habits* (1971), to the troubled heterosexuals dealing with their homophobia and fear of AIDS in *Lips Together, Teeth Apart* (1991), McNally has managed to assimilate gay and heterosexual experience. *The Ritz* (1974), which takes place in a New York gay bathhouse, managed a successful Broadway run and was made into a movie. Moving the doors and libido of classic French farce from the usual sleazy hotel to the baths, *The Ritz* is one of the few successful American farces in recent years. A fat, unhappy, middle-aged Italian-American finds that a contract has been put out on his life. When he asks a taxi driver to let him off at the place he is least likely to be found, he finds himself at the baths. All the possible complications of this situation are successfully mined without marginalizing anyone except the homophobe. In *The Ritz,* the gay bathhouse is the norm. *The Lisbon Traviata* (1985) dramatizes two dysfunctional gay men who escape from their personal failures into opera, particularly diva worship. When Stephen, the central character, learns that his lover, a young doctor, is leaving him for a less neurotic man, he turns the farewell into an opera, complete with death scene. Stephen's best friend, Mendy, self-imprisoned in his opulent apartment, lives only for his opera recordings. *Frankie and Johnnie in the Claire de Lune* (1987) is on the surface a heterosexual love story, but the names of the central characters are not the only hints that McNally wants his audience to see that the situation he presents is not gender-specific. His screenplay *Frankie and Johnnie* adds a gay counterpart to the heterosexual romance. *Lips Together, Teeth Apart* centers on two heterosexual couples. One woman has inherited a Fire Island house from her gay brother who just died of AIDS. She, her husband, her brother and his wife are frightened to use the swimming pool for fear they might become infected, and they are extremely uncomfortable about being in the middle of a gay society in which they are decidedly the minority. McNally's funny, bittersweet play shows that gay people hardly have a monopoly on insecurity and self-hatred, that the inadequacies gay people feel are part of being American, not part of being gay. *Lips Together, Teeth Apart* is among the few plays that dramatize powerfully the causes and effects of homophobia. McNally has also written the books for a number of musical comedies, most recently a musical adaptation of MANUEL PUIG's novel, *Kiss of the Spider Woman* (1992), about the relationship of two unlikely cellmates in a South American prison, a flamboyant homosexual hairdresser and a revolutionary.

HARVEY FIERSTEIN began his career as a drag artist and playwright in experimental venues Off-Off-Broadway. Three of his one-act plays were presented as *Torch Song Trilogy,* with Fierstein himself in the leading role, and moved successfully into the center of the New York theater district for a long run, a Tony Award for best Broadway play of 1981, and a film adaptation. *Torch Song Trilogy* is of considerable historical importance—a three-and-a-half-hour dramatization of the trials and tribulations of a tough, proud New York drag queen managed to become a mainstream success. Though the three plays that make up the trilogy are quite different in style, descending to sitcom in the third piece, "Widows and Children First," they offer a panorama of New York gay life just before AIDS: the backrooms, drag queens, and young hustlers; ambivalent bisexuals; homophobic families; and the tragedy of gay-bashing. In *Torch Song Trilogy* and the later trio of plays, *Safe Sex* (1987), Fierstein is strongest in the more experimental pieces, like "Fugue in a Nursery," a comic dramatization of a doomed weekend in the country with the central character, Arnold; his beautiful eighteen-year-old lover; his bisexual ex-lover, Ed; and Ed's too-well-meaning wife. Fierstein sets his series of misalliances in a stylized, giant bed and, as the title suggests, presents them in counterpoint to music played by a chamber ensemble. The bed, which dwarfs the characters, playfully emphasizes the various permutations of sexual desire that are bound to doom this weekend house party. He is weakest in the realistic final pieces of the trilogies, which present conflicts between the grieving Fierstein character and strong women who rob him of his right to mourn and refuse to validate his loving gay relationships. At their best, Fierstein's short plays are funny, insightful satires of the romantic dysfunctions of urban gay men in the age of gay liberation. They are also ardent pleas for assimilation and presage what will become a central gay concern in the 1990s, the right of lesbians and gay men to see their households, including their biological and adopted children, as legitimate, legally protected families.

Since *Torch Song Trilogy,* the majority of gay drama has centered on AIDS, the virus that has ironically both decimated and galvanized the gay community. Though AIDS dramas have been written in many countries by playwrights like Michel Tremblay (Québec), Copi (France), Colin Thomas (Canada), and Andy Kirby (England), it is the U.S. playwrights whose work has become known worldwide.

The central figure in AIDS drama is LARRY KRAMER, polemicist, AIDS activist, and playwright. Kramer's highly personal, passionate though problematic plays have become the object of much critical controversy. In both *The Normal Heart* (1985) and *The Destiny of Me* (1992), the central character, Ned Weeks, is a barely veiled version of the playwright; the other characters are as close to their real-life counterparts as the law allows. *The Normal Heart* chronicles gay politics in New York at the beginning of the AIDS pandemic. The play attacks gay men for continuing to see promiscuity as the center of gay political and personal agendas, even after the discovery of the AIDS virus, and lacerates the government, particularly the New York City government, for maliciously ignoring the devastation of the gay community. The passionate political scenes are set in counterpoint to the sentimental depiction of the loving relationship of Ned and an HIV-infected man. Ned and Felix become star-crossed lovers in a relationship doomed by AIDS, as Ned is expelled from the gay organizations he founded for telling his friends the truth about their self-destructive sex lives. Kramer sees his alter ego, Ned, simultaneously as Romeo and as Dr. Stockmann in Ibsen's *Enemy of the People*. There is always a contradictory combination of political activism and a sense of fate in Kramer's plays. In *The Destiny of Me* (1992), Ned Weeks, hospitalized himself, is cut off from the activist groups he founded. Alone in his room at the embattled National Institutes of Health, Ned relives his relationships with his parents, his beloved older brother, and his younger self. In this powerful but problematic play, the influence of Eugene O'Neill, which looms large, places a naturalistic determinism against the sense of self-creation and political activism Kramer seems to want to embrace.

Paul Rudnick, like Kramer, achieved early fortune, if not fame, in film. The lightness of his *Jeffrey* (1992) is the opposite of the *Sturm und Drang* of Kramer's plays. Rudnick manages to present gay life in New York City in the age of AIDS both hilariously and compassionately. *Jeffrey* is a rarity—an AIDS play without pathos. Jeffrey, a would-be actor but mostly waiter who has devoted much of his energies to the joyful pursuit of sex, decides that the only response to the angst of the AIDS era is to become celibate. Finally, on the advice of friends, counselors, frustrated admirers, and a horny priest who tells him, "There is only one real blasphemy—the refusal of joy," Jeffrey decides to embark on a passionate encounter with a gorgeous, HIV-positive man he has been running from throughout the play. Along the way, Jeffrey's travels take him through many of the institutions of contemporary gay life—gyms, self-help groups, sex clubs, and memorial services—all of which Rudnick treats to good-natured satire. With rave reviews from mainstream critics, *Jeffrey* has become, like *The Boys in the Band* and *Torch Song Trilogy*, a popular success with gay and straight audiences.

However, no drama in recent years, gay or straight, has received the attention and acclaim of Tony Kushner's epic *Angels in America* (1992). Commissioned by the Eureka Theater in San Francisco, Kushner's two-part, seven-hour "Gay Fantasia on American Themes" is the most comprehensive dramatic commentary on the moral, sexual, and spiritual state of America during and since the Reagan revolution.

Angels in America is structured like a Shakespearean romance. A seemingly stable world atomizes to be reconstructed and redeemed. Relationships are quickly brought to a crisis point. Destiny or coincidence causes unlikely collisions. Characters thought dead miraculously reappear. The real and the dream merge. Seemingly disparate actions are analogous. Comedy and tragedy alternate and, at times, coalesce.

Kushner takes the multiple plot lines of Shakespeare a step further by using a "split screen" method and playing analogous scenes simultaneously.

Angels in America focuses on four homosexual men who represent, in various ways, not only positive and negative possibilities for homosexuals, particularly the perils of the closet, but the moral and spiritual plight of America. The symbolic center is Roy Cohn, the powerful, ruthless, closeted, conservative who died of AIDS in 1986. For Cohn, one is defined by one's power, not one's sexuality, and power and gay identity are irreconcilable opposites. For him, the law is not an agent of order but an expression of the chaotic, dangerous universe. Kushner's Cohn is a moral monster, but his energy, both godlike and demonic, makes him an image of America itself.

Cohn's protégé is a young Mormon lawyer, Joseph Porter Pitt, who believes in the new order of the Reagan revolution (it is 1985) and the Jehovah-like fury and arbitrary power of Roy Cohn. Like Cohn, Joe cannot fit his homosexuality positively into that order. Since homosexuals do not exist in the Mormon faith, or in the Reagan revolution, Joe has tried his best to deny his sexuality and live within a loveless marriage, performing the "cheerful and strong" persona demanded of Mormons. But whereas the shameless Cohn can live his contradiction happily, Joe hates his dishonesty and sees himself only as "a shell." Joe leaves his unhappy, valium-addicted wife, Harper, and joins in a turbulent liaison with another self-hater, the literal and figurative "word processor," Louis Ironson. Louis has left his lover, Prior Walter, because he cannot deal with the gruesome reality of Prior's AIDS-related illnesses and impending death. He has failed "the hard law of love," and put his own needs and fears before those of his partner. Linked in their attraction and their self-hatred, Joe and Louis feel that they are doomed. Both have betrayed their commitments to lovers. They cannot go back, neither can they forgive themselves.

The dissolution of relationships and the various unmoorings of *Part I: The Millennium Approaches* seem to be the prelude to a revolution, the creation of a new order, heralded by the climactic appearance of an angel to the ailing Prior Walter. However, when *Part II: Perestroika* opens, Prior learns that the angel, instead, calls for stasis, death. Prior, however, wants "more life" and will, like Jacob, wrestle with the angel to get it. When Prior ascends the ladder to heaven to argue for his life, he finds that heaven is a simulacrum of San Francisco after the 1906 earthquake, ruled by squabbling, leaderless angels. *Perestroika* continues and develops a series of alliances and misalliances begun in *The Millennium Approaches*. The brief romance of Louis and Joe ends in a fight that gives Louis, at least, the punishment he wanted for abandoning Prior. Joe Pitt's stern mother, Hannah, becomes Prior's caregiver. Belize, the Black drag queen, becomes Roy Cohn's private nurse and guardian of his stash of AZT. But this conventional series of collisions and separations is punctuated by more mysterious interventions, more links between the historical and the spiritual.

The principal issue in *Angels in America* is not what stance heterosexuals should take toward gay people (the answer to that is obvious) or even the more complex question of what stance gay people should take toward heterosexual adversaries but what, in defining our community, do gay people do with homosexual adversaries like Roy Cohn or Joseph Porter Pitt. The answer comes from the key words in *Angels in America*: love, justice, blessing, and forgiveness.

Like the classics of Arthur Miller and TENNESSEE WILLIAMS, *Angels in America* manages to bring serious drama to the commercial theater. More important, this uncompromising, unabashedly gay play has become the most talked about mainstream dramatic work in New York and London (where it has been produced at the Royal National Theatre) in decades. Its critical and commercial success signifies the centrality of gay artists to the contemporary American theater. (See also DRAMATIC LITERATURE: MODERN DRAMA and MUSICAL THEATER.)

—*John M. Clum*

BIBLIOGRAPHY

Anthologies

Berman, Ed, ed. *Homosexual Acts: A Volume of Gay Plays.* London: Inter-Action Imprint, 1975. ■ Davis, Jill, ed., *Lesbian Plays.* 2 vols. London: Methuen, 1987, 1989. ■ ———. *Gay Plays: An International Anthology.* New York: Ubu Repertory Theatre Publications, 1989. ■ Helbing, Terry. *Gay and Lesbian Plays Today.* Portsmouth, N.H.: Heinemann, 1993. ■ Hoffman, William M. ed., *Gay Plays: The First Collection.* New York: Avon, 1979. ■ Osment, Philip, ed. *Gay Sweatshop: Four Plays and a Company.* London: Methuen, 1989. ■ Shewey, Don, ed., *Out Front: Contemporary Gay and Lesbian Plays.* New York: Grove Weidenfeld, 1988. ■ Wallace, Robert, ed., *Making, Out: Plays by Gay Men.* Toronto: Coach House Press, 1992. ■ Wilcox, Michael, ed., *Gay Plays.* 4 vols. London: Methuen, 1984, 1985, 1988, 1990.

Criticism

Case, Sue-Ellen, ed. *Performing Feminisms: Feminist Critical Theory and Theatre.* Baltimore: Johns Hopkins, 1989. ■ Clum, John M. *Acting Gay: Male Homosexuality in Modern Drama.* New York: Columbia, 1992. Revised paperback ed., 1994. ■ Curtin, Kaier. *We Can Always Call Them Bulgarians.* Boston: Alyson, 1987. ■ deJongh, Nicholas. *Not in Front of the Audience: Homosexuality on Stage.* London: Routledge, 1992. ■ Ludlam, Charles, *Ridiculous Theatre: Scourge of Human Folly: Essays and Opinions of Charles Ludlam.* Steven Samuels, ed. New York: Theatre Communications Group, 1992.

Thanks to Larry Kramer, Tony Kushner, and Paul Rudnick for giving me prepublication copies of their recent plays.

Duffy, Maureen
(b. 1933)

Maureen Duffy was born on October 21, 1933, in Worthing, Sussex, the daughter of Grace Wright and Cahia Duffy, an Irish laborer who left soon after her birth. Until the outbreak of World War II, when she was evacuated to Wiltshire, she was raised in London as part of her mother's extended family. Duffy, who began to write poetry and stories at an early age, was an exceptional and precocious child in a working-class environment shaped by the illegitimacy of her birth, extreme poverty, and a familial susceptibility to tuberculosis, which claimed the lives of many close relatives. Her mother, with whom she had a close and supportive relationship, nevertheless encouraged her daughter's literary and educational endeavors, enabling Duffy to attend various high schools for girls through scholarships awarded

her. In 1956, she received a Bachelor of Arts degree with honors from King's College, University of London, and taught in various South London schools for five years. During these years, she wrote poetry and several plays for stage and television. In 1961, Duffy was approached by publisher Graham Nicol to write a novel for Hutchinson's New Author Series. Although reluctant at first to change genres, she agreed at length and, in 1962, published the semi-autobiographical *That's How It Was.*

Mother–daughter love, the focal point of Duffy's first novel, is a recurring theme in her later work, particularly *The Love Child* (1971). It is, she implies, the relationship in which the roots of subsequent love of women by women often lie. Her purpose in this representation was "to show how a personality and a relationship that in the world's eyes were brave and fine could produce a psychological result which, also in the world's eyes . . . could be labelled sick or perverted and thought of as at best a great handicap." Her exploration of homosexuality became more explicit in *A Single Eye* (1964) in which Duffy's narrator, the unhappily married Mike, is configured in a variety of alternative sexual relationships. *The Microcosm* (1966), her best-known novel, presents the diverse lives and experiences of the clientele of a London lesbian bar through a pastiche of stories and literary styles, including the interpolated narrative of the eighteenth-century actress and cross-dresser Charlotte Charke. Although unique in its candid, nonmoralistic treatment of its subject, *The Microcosm* incurred the ire of certain lesbian critics and readers for its application of Freudian psychology, an experimental style that was considered "inaccessible," its representation and apparent acceptance of butch–femme roles, and its ultimate renunciation of lesbian separatism. In subsequent works, particularly her trilogy of London life (*Wounds* [1969], *Capital* [1975], and *Londoners: An Elegy* [1983]), *Change* (1987), and *Illuminations* (1992), she presents both lesbianism and male homosexuality as facets of a broader social and political panorama in which all forms of marginalization are interconnected. Duffy's concern with animal rights is manifested not only in her nonfiction work on the subject but also in *I Want to Go to Moscow* (1973), a sympathetically parodic thriller about a gang of upper middle-class antivivesectionists, and *Gor Saga* (1981), a futuristic tale in which the laboratory-created half-human, half-gorilla protagonist is reared as a human child and must attempt to live with self-respect and integrity in the brutal human world.

In addition to her novels, Duffy has published volumes of poetry, plays, a Freudian study of the erotic themes in literature, and a biography of Aphra Behn. She has been an activist for writers' causes and a leader in literary organizations, including the Writers Action Group, which she co-founded in 1972, and the Writers Guild of Great Britain, whose president she became in 1985.

Maureen Duffy's position as a lesbian writer is a paradoxical one. Although openly a lesbian and a leftist since the 1960s, she is much respected in mainstream British literary circles while she remains underappreciated and relatively unknown among many lesbian and gay readers. Many of her works are currently out of print, but the Virago reissue of *The Microcosm* in both Great Britain (1989) and the United States (1990) has renewed critical interest, and new editions of other works have appeared from time to time. Although her belief, expressed in *The Microcosm,* that "there are dozens of ways of being queer" may have been lost on much of her audience in the 1960s and 1970s, she may yet appeal to a new generation of "queer" readers.

—*Patricia Juliana Smith*

BIBLIOGRAPHY

Brimstone, Lyndie. "'Keepers of History': The Novels of Maureen Duffy." *Lesbian and Gay Writing: An Anthology of Critical Essays.* Mark Lilly, ed. London: Macmillan, 1990. 23–46. ■ Newman, Jenny. "Mary and the Monster: Mary Shelley's *Frankenstein* and Maureen Duffy's *Gor Saga*." *Where No Man Has Gone Before: Women and Science Fiction.* Lucie Armitt, ed. London: Routledge, 1991. 85–96. ■ Rule, Jane. *Lesbian Images.* New York: Doubleday, 1975. ■ Sizemore, Christine Wick. *A Female Vision of the City: London in the Novels of Five British Women.* Knoxville: University of Tennessee Press, 1989.

Duncan, Robert
(1919–1988)

Robert Duncan was born in Oakland, California, on January 7, 1919, to Edward and Marguerite Duncan. His mother died giving birth, and his father could not manage a small baby by himself while raising Robert's older brothers and sisters. At the age of seven months, Robert was adopted by Edwin and Minnehaha Symmes, who lived in Alameda, California, and belonged to a group called the Hermetic Brotherhood, an offshoot of Theosophy. An accident at the age of three left him with double vision. By the time he was eighteen, attending the University of California at Berkeley, he was in a relationship with a man. Adoption, double vision, hermetic philosophy, and homosexuality: these were the early forces that shaped Duncan's poetic practice.

After college, Duncan moved to New York City to begin his career as a writer. In August 1944, he published "The Homosexual in Society" in Dwight Macdonald's magazine *Politics.* In this article, Duncan called for openness regarding homosexuality, criticized homosexual writers who ghettoized themselves, and acknowledged his own homosexuality. The immediate consequence of this brave essay was that John Crowe Ransom refused to publish a previously accepted poem of Duncan's in *Kenyon Review*, thus initiating Duncan's exclusion from the mainstream of American poetry. Despite this rebuff from the literary establishment, the young poet persisted in writing. He became a leader of the San Francisco Renaissance as well as of the poets associated with Black Mountain College, where he taught in the 1950s. By the time of his death in 1988, Duncan was recognized as a significant American artist.

Duncan's understanding of homosexuality changed and grew throughout his career. His earliest poems, such as the *Bearskin* poems and "Among My Friends Love Is a Great Sorrow" (included in *Selected Poems*, 1993), reject gay men who develop a separate culture and regard themselves as different from or superior to "normal" society. At the same time, however, these poems show him longing for the companionship of gay men with values similar to his own. After 1951, when Duncan began his lifelong relationship with the artist Jess Collins, the "household" becomes a major theme in his work. The transition between these two visions of homosexual love is well depicted in "This Place Rumord to Have Been Sodom" from *The Opening of the Field* (1960). He first describes Sodom as "once / a city among men, a gathering together of spirit. / It was measured by the Lord and found wanting." However, by the end of the poem, he declares:

> In the Lord Whom the friends have named at
>   last Love
> the images and loves of the friends never die.
> This place rumord to have been Sodom is
>   blessd
> In the Lord's eyes.

Although Duncan has always been aware of the political consequences of homosexuality and has relished and celebrated the domestic pleasures of living with another man, for him the significance of being gay (as with all things) does not stop with the apparent.

"Within all daily love," he has written, "is another world sleeping or an otherness awake in which I am a sleeper" ("Correspondences" in *Letters,* 1958). In Duncan's love poetry, there is a constant interplay between "He," the Lord of Love, the ideal lover, and "you," the actual lover, the domestic companion. The theme of love so interacts with his other themes that any attempt to separate gay and nongay poems is meaningless. For example, in Duncan's last book, *Ground Work II: In the Dark* (1987), he does not mention homosexuality directly, but love, sexuality, and the "other," addressed as "You," circulate through these poems, bearing with them the meaning that Duncan has carefully given them throughout his career.

Duncan has, however, written a remarkable series of poems that deal directly with the love of men for other men. Many—such as "These Past Years: Passages 10"—celebrate his love for Jess Collins. "The Torso, Passages 18," on the other hand, is a more generalized love poem to all men, whereas "My Mother Would Be a Falconress" is an uncanny exploration of a delicate subject, the relationship of gay men to their mothers. In *Ground Work: Before the War* (1984), he includes a cycle of lyrics inspired by fellow poet THOM GUNN, "Poems from the Margins of Thom Gunn's *Moly*." In these poems, Duncan reviews his life as a lover of men. Finally, the lovely "Circulations of the Song," a meditation on the poems of Rumi, the Sufi poet, sums up Duncan's lifework by exploring the role love plays as a mediation between the world we can see and the world we cannot.

—*Terrence Johnson*

BIBLIOGRAPHY

Bertholf, Robert J., and Ian W. Reid, eds. *Robert Duncan: Scales of the Marvelous.* New York: New Directions, 1979. ■ Fass, Ekbert. *Young Robert Duncan: Portrait of the Poet as Homosexual in Society.* Santa Barbara, Calif.: Black Sparrow Press, 1983. ■ Gunn, Thom. *Shelf Life: Essays, Memoirs, and an Interview.* Ann Arbor: University of Michigan Press, 1993.

Durrell, Lawrence
(1912–1990)

Durrell was born on February 27, 1912, in Julundar, India, of an Irish mother and a British civil-engineer father. He attended the College of St. Joseph, Darjeeling, India, and St. Edmund's School, Canterbury, England. He chose not to qualify for Oxford or Cambridge. In 1935, the family moved to Corfu, Greece. From there, Durrell regularly visited London and Paris, where he met Henry Miller in 1937 after a two-year correspondence. Miller introduced him to T. S. ELIOT; and while he was in Paris in 1937 and 1938, Durrell, Miller, and Alfred Perlès formed an avant-garde literary magazine entitled *Booster* (renamed *Delta* in April 1938). Durrell's early life is reflected in his autobiographical poem "Cities, Plains, and People" (1943). Although Durrell was a heterosexual man who married many times, his art reflects an unusual degree of sexual liberation and incorporates characters of diverse sexualities.

A novelist, poet, translator, playwright, critic, and travel writer, Durrell is best known for *The Alexandria Quartet*, a series of four novels (*Justine* [1957], *Balthazar* [1958], *Mountolive* [1959], and *Clea* [1960]), which encompasses themes of sex, lust, and decadence in the twentieth century. Each of the novels is prefaced by an epigraph from the MARQUIS DE SADE, who is one of Durrell's artistic heroes. The novels titillate the reader with an exotic underworld of eroticism, including male homosexuality, lesbianism, incest, voyeurism, and prostitution. Even the mythical Tiresias, who has experienced both sexes, makes an appearance.

Durrell's *The Black Book* (1938) chronicles the events in the lives of the guests of the Hotel Regina, including the homosexual Tarquin and the prostitute Gracie. Another work, *Livia* (1978), contains a brothel scene with a promiscuous lesbian; in it, Blanford marries Livia and discovers that she has a black female lover named Thrush. *Monsieur* (1974) contains a black lesbian named Trash, but expands the kaleidoscope of sexuality to include ménage à trois, incest, transvestism, and bohemianism. Durrell also wrote a play in verse entitled *Sappho* (1959). His works reflect a love for the sensuous Mediterranean world, especially Alexandria and ancient Rome.

Durrell also translated the poetry of the modern Greek homosexual poet CONSTANTINE CAVAFY. In fact, the novelist has acknowledged Cavafy's profound influence on him, remarking that "I felt my way into the Alexandrian scene through him." Another influence was the symbolist homosexual poet ARTHUR RIMBAUD. Durrell—like Cavafy, GIDE, LAWRENCE, and PROUST—helped shape modern literature. His rococo literary style, ornate imagery, and exotic sensuality all contribute to the creation of a sophisticated literary world in which both male and female homosexuality are significant and recognized presences.

—*Clarence McClanahan*

BIBLIOGRAPHY

Morcos, Mona Louis. "Elements of the Autobiographical in *The Alexandria Quartet*." *Modern Fiction Studies* 13 (1967): 343–359. ■ Pinchin, Jane L. *Alexandria Still: Forster, Durrell, Cavafy*. Princeton: Princeton University Press, 1977. ■ Pine, Richard. *The Dandy and the Herald*. New York: St. Martin's, 1988. ■ Unterecker, John. *Lawrence Durrell*. New York: Columbia University Press, 1964. ■ Wickes, George, ed. *Lawrence Durrell and Henry Miller: A Private Correspondence*. New York: Dutton, 1963.

Dutch and Flemish Literature

Dutch is the language of twenty-one million people in The Netherlands and Flanders. Although the Dutch-speaking regions are small, the history of gay and lesbian literature in the Low Countries is rich and varied, reflecting the changing concepts of intimate relations between people of the same sex.

In the eighteenth and nineteenth centuries, accounts of sodomites and female transvestites appeared in newspapers, pamphlets, popular songs, stories, and plays. These accounts bear traces of distinct sexual and gender identities, but the sodomites and transvestites of this period were very different from modern gay men and lesbians. The same holds for the more or less "spiritual" male and female friendships of the day that were frequently celebrated in literature.

Betje Wolff (1738–1804) and Aagje Deken (1741–1804) were the most famous Dutch female romantic friends of the eighteenth century. Together, they wrote several successful epistolary novels, which gave moral and pedagogical advice to young women. In their letters and collections of "edifying poems" (*Stichtelijke Gedichten*), they praised the fruits of true, unselfish friendship, a relationship embedded in strong religious feelings. "Kindred spirits" like Wolff and Deken were criticized and ridiculed by male contemporaries not because of their same-sex relationship, but because of the fact that as "savantes," or learned women, they entered the male territory of scholarship and intellectualism. (See also ROMANTIC FRIENDSHIP, FEMALE.)

In the nineteenth century, a comparable friendship cult developed among students, who formed an all-male community. Johannes Kneppelhout (1814–1885) called this romantic comradeship "the real, pithy passion of youth" and expressed it in several stories, poems, and, especially, letters to his friends. In Kneppelhout's view, friendship meant more than fellowship between peers. His experiences as a teacher in a boarding school and his reading of PLATO's *Symposium* led to the conviction that friendship and education should go hand in hand. In an essay written in French, *L'éducation par l'amitié* (1835), he argues that an older friend must discover and stimulate the talents of his younger companion.

The well-to-do, dandylike Kneppelhout applied his ideas in his patronage of young artists like the violinist Jan de Graan. In *Een beroemde knaap* (*A Famous Boy* [1875]), Kneppelhout painted a warm portrait of his capricious protégé, who died at the early age of twenty-one years. His relationship with another yet unidentified boy, called Vischboer or perhaps of the profession of fish dealer (in Dutch "vischboer"), led to rumors of indecent practices. The gossip was never confirmed, but it inhibited Kneppelhout from initiating new intimate friendships with boys. He left the town of Leiden and retreated to a country estate in Oosterbeek.

The Flemish priest, teacher, and poet Guido Gezelle (1830–1899) also voiced strong feelings for some of his pupils. Gezelle expressed the "spiritual twofoldness" between master and student in some of his best poems. Gezelle's homoerotic feelings may have been platonic. Certainly, some of his admirers resist any suggestion that his feelings for his pupils were sexual. Nevertheless, his relationship with Eugène van Oye, whom he admired for his "angelic innocence" and whom he tried to comfort in his loneliness in the seminary, was deep indeed. It struck him as a tragedy when van Oye left the seminary in Roeselare in 1859. In his lamentation "To an Absent Friend," published in 1862, he called his loss greater than that of a mother missing her child.

It was not until 1892 that the word *homosexuality* was introduced in Dutch. In a period of some fifteen years, new concepts of same-sex relationships, like the biological idea of a "third sex," became widely known, existing alongside older theological and vernacular characterizations of individuals who engaged in same-sex behaviors. By the turn of the century, intimate friendship between two people of the same sex, especially between men, became highly suspicious. The two most important novelists who depicted homosexuality at this time, Louis Couperus and Jacob Israël de Haan, handled the new concepts in very different ways.

Couperus (1863–1923) is one of Holland's most famous writers. In his work, homoeroticism is a common theme, but never a central one. Couperus, who married his cousin, was a dandylike aesthete, who evinced strong interest in other men. Alongside "stocky," "big" men, modeled on some of his friends, he also depicted in his novels androgynous types, with

whom Couperus personally identified. His novel *Noodlot* (1890) was admired by OSCAR WILDE, who read the English translation (*Footsteps of Fate* [1891]). *Noodlot,* which sets a platonic friendship in a naturalistic context, tells the story of the androgynous dandy Bertie, who sponges on his well-built, earthy but weak-minded friend Frank. When Bertie learns that Frank is going to marry Eve, he succeeds in destroying their plans. To explain his action, he expresses passionate love for Frank. In a fit of anger, Frank kills Bertie, but many years later concludes that Bertie could not help himself. Eve agrees, and the story ends with the couple taking their own lives. Although many critics complained that Bertie's emotions were "unhealthy," the severest criticism was directed against the fatalistic philosophy that Couperus expressed in this novel.

Couperus, like many homosexuals in his day, was very drawn to the Mediterranean and to classic antiquity. His most outspoken "homosexual" novel is the three-volume *De berg van licht* (*Mountain of Light* [1905–1906]). In this complex work, Couperus experimented with the gender and sexual identity of the main character, the young priest-emperor Heliogabalus. In his psychological portrait of the third-century historical figure, Couperus not only used historical and literary sources, but also contemporary ideas about androgyny and theosophy. When the fourteen-year-old Heliogabalus becomes emperor, he fails in bringing together the eastern and western religions and customs. Neither does he succeed in developing both sides of his androgynous nature equally. His female side gets stronger and stronger, especially after marrying the muscular gladiator Hierocles. *De berg van licht* now is considered a high point in European fin-de-siècle decadent literature.

Another of Couperus's historical novels, *De komedianten* ([1917]; trans. as *The Comedians*), is set in Rome in the first century C.E. and tells the story of the adolescent twins Cecilius and Cecilianus. They are members of a traveling theater company, famous for its obscene plays and dances. The twins, portrayed as young rascals, are part of a motley crowd of actors, gladiators, whores, and gypsies, who all enjoy a playful and physical—often homoerotic—association. "This is finally," Couperus told a friend, "a story that I wrote only for my own pleasure and I think it is very charming."

The decadent classical context of Couperus's historical novels offered him an opportunity to describe homoeroticism more explicitly than was possible in a contemporary Dutch context. The reception of the novels of Jacob Israël De Haan (1881–1924) illustrates how furiously people could react to overtly homosexual characters in a contemporary, realistic setting.

De Haan was familiar with the new concepts of the inborn homosexual nature as described in Germany by Magnus Hirschfeld and in Holland by De Haan's friend, the writer and physician Arnold Aletrino. It is to Aletrino that De Haan dedicated his first novel, called *Pijpelijntjes* (Scenes from "De Pijp," a gray working-class district in Amsterdam). In this work, published in 1904, De Haan presents a homosexual relation as something that needs no explanation or apology. The two protagonists, Sam and Joop, with the nicknames and appearances of Aletrino and De Haan, live together as poor students. Sometimes they have sex together, sometimes Joop picks up a street boy for a one-night stand. The publication of *Pijpelijntjes* cost De Haan his friendship with Aletrino, who, together with De Haan's fiancée, bought almost the entire edition and destroyed it. De Haan lost his job as an editor and later also his teaching job. Nevertheless, the same year he published a rewritten version of his *Pijpelijntjes,* which was largely ignored, receiving only a few, negative reviews.

De Haan's second novel *Pathologieën; de ondergangen van Johan van Vere de With (Pathologies: The Destructions of Johan van Vere de With* [1908]) is a remarkable work of art in gay literary history. The protagonist of *Pathologieën* is a boy who realizes that he is attracted to other boys, comes to accept his feelings by reading unspecified scientific studies of homosexuality, and finds both happiness and disaster in a relationship with a sadistic artist. By means of a foreword by the Belgian writer Georges Eekhoud and several dedications (to the Danish writer Herman Bang, Wilde, and Eekhoud), De Haan expressly relates *Pathologieën* to a homosexual literary canon. He presents an image of homosexuality not yet common in the socio-historical or even the scientific literature. De Haan's hero experiences a process of consciousness-raising, rejection, acceptance, integration, and coming out. The process culminates in a modern homosexual IDENTITY, one not based on a male–female dichotomy or "third sex."

De Haan's novels were forgotten for almost seventy years. It was not until the mid-1970s that new editions of his prose became available. For a long time, De Haan was famous only for what his admirers called his "Jewish" poetry, although the homosexual content of his poems is as important as the Jewish. After becoming an orthodox Jew, De Haan in 1919 emigrated from Holland to Palestine. There he dissociated himself from the Zionist movement and in 1924 was murdered by extreme Zionists who spread the rumor that his death was a homosexual killing by Arabs.

Until the 1960s, homosexuality in literature was, almost by definition, associated with psychological and moral deficiencies, sin, crime, and feelings of guilt. With the introduction of clause 248bis in the Dutch criminal code in 1911, a discriminatory provision in Dutch law was enacted: The age of consent for same-sex behavior was set at twenty-one, whereas the age of consent for heterosexual behavior was set at sixteen. (Except for the period of Nazi occupation of the Netherlands, 1940–1945, no law prohibiting homosexuality itself was ever enacted in the modern era.) Only one year later, in 1912, the Scientific Humanitarian Committee (NWHK), the first Dutch homosexual emancipation organization, was founded. Among its other activities, the committee distributed several tendentious novels, which propagated the concept of the "third sex," an idea that presented homosexuality as a congenital, natural condition.

Until the 1930s, lesbian sexuality in Dutch literature was almost totally restricted to minor characters in novels written by male authors. Therefore, it is not surprising that the translation of RADCLYFFE HALL's *The Well of Loneliness* in 1928 was a very important event for many lesbian readers (the novel was reprinted twice the next year). *The Well* meant a recognition of their existence and offered possibilities for identification. Nevertheless, not everybody was convinced by the concept of the "manly woman" in Hall's novel. Indeed, *Terug naar het eiland (Back to the Island* [1937]), a novel by Josine Reuling (1899–1961), can be read as a commentary on Hall's bestseller. Reuling's hero, a Swedish girl called Brita, has much in common with Hall's Stephen Gordon, but unlike Stephen, Brita does not suffer from an identity and gender crisis. She rejects all theories about homosexuality, including third-sex and Freudian concepts. In one respect, Reuling's novel is very traditional: Brita's life is cut short prematurely when she is killed in a car crash.

Anna Blaman, pen name for Johanna Petronella Vrugt (1905–1960), not only was the most important lesbian writer in the 1950s, but also was Holland's major woman author of the era. As an intellectual, a public figure, and an independent woman who did not conceal her homosexuality, she was of great importance to Dutch lesbian emancipation. In her work, however, she expressed a pessimistic view of life, which partially was influenced by French Existentialism. Blaman's protagonists, including the lesbian Berthe in her best-known novel *Eenzaam Avontuur (Lonely Adventure* [1948]), experience the futility of human existence, an inadequacy in making contact and in knowing and understanding their partners. This existential loneliness is, in Blaman's view, typical of both heterosexual and homosexual individuals. The recent publication of her correspondence with other women, including

Marie-Louise Doudart de la Grée, author of tendentious lesbian novels, modifies Blaman's image as an unhappy, lonely, pessimistic intellectual.

Human solitariness is also a leading motif in the works of Dola de Jong (b. 1911). She was born in a conservative, Jewish family. A few days before the Germans occupied Holland, she broke off her career as a dancer and journalist and fled to Morocco and later to the United States. In 1946, she was granted American citizenship. She still lives in New York, where she has worked as novelist, literary agent, editor, and teacher of creative writing. In the United States, some of her books for young adults, as well as her novel about antisemitism, *The Field* (trans. of *En de akker is de wereld* [1946]), were successes. In 1954, De Jong published *De thuiswacht* (trans. as *The Tree and the Vine* in 1961). This novel about the friendship between Bea and the Stephen Gordon-like Erica, recounts a search for (sexual) identity. The confrontation with Erica's lesbian lifestyle awakens the narrator Bea. She becomes conscious of the instability of sexual identity, in her case a heterosexual one. As in almost all gay and lesbian literature published between 1910 and 1960, homosexuality is presented from the point of view of "the other," who usually only hints at the real nature of relationships.

Although in the 1950s, the image of lesbians became less stereotypical, the mannish lesbian continued to dominate Dutch literature. But in Blaman's later work, like the posthumously published novel *De Verliezers* (*The Losers* [1960]), the lesbian no longer "feels like a man." Carla Walschap and Andreas Burnier are responsible for a further radicalization of the lesbian image in Dutch literature. Walschap, one of the few Flemish writers to deal with lesbianism, presents in *De Eskimo en de roos* (*The Eskimo and the Rose* [1964]) a love affair between two women who are both thoroughly feminine. In Burnier's case, however, the representation of female homosexuality is more complex.

Andreas Burnier is the pen name that criminologist Catharina Dessaur (b. 1931) uses for her literary works. Analyzing the social position of lesbian women, she links lesbianism with feminism. In her first novels *Een tevreden lach* (*A Satisfied Smile* [1965]) and *Het jongensuur* (*The Boy's Hour* [1969]), lesbians experience the female body as a limitation, an obstacle to social progress and success. In both novels, we already find traces of Burnier's ideal of the androgynous existence, which transcends dichotomies like male-female, heterosexual-homosexual, rational-emotional, and physical-spiritual. *Het jongensuur* reveals a second determining factor in Burnier's works, namely, her experiences as a Jewish girl who went into hiding during World War II, stayed with many different families, and finally is uncertain of her Jewish identity.

Since the 1960s, homosexuality has been a subject in the works of major heterosexual Dutch and Flemish writers like Simon Vestdijk (1898–1971), Hugo Claus (b. 1929), and Harry Mulisch (b. 1927). At the same time, the most famous recent Dutch gay and lesbian writers have been accepted into mainstream literary circles. Indeed, several of them have received the P.C. Hooft-prize, the Dutch state prize for literature (Anna Blaman in 1957, GERARD REVE in 1968, Gerrit Komrij in 1993). In other words, homosexuality has become in many respects a literary subject like all other subjects. This development, supported by a liberal moral climate, has led to a great diversity in the literary expression of gay and lesbian lifestyles. In Flanders, this development has been slower in coming. In fact, in 1965, Belgian law, still based on the French Code Pénal, for the first time discriminated between the ages of consent for heterosexual and homosexual contacts. In the same period in Holland, several attempts were made to reverse this legal discrimination, which finally succeeded in 1971.

Gerard Reve, born in 1923 as Gerard Kornelis van het Reve, is Holland's best known, most popular, and most controversial gay writer. Coming from a communist and atheistic family, Reve later converted to the Roman Catholic church and expressed ideas that were perceived as conservative and controversial. His debut novel *De Avonden* (*The Evenings* [1947]) portrayed a disillusioned post-war generation. It contains some of Reve's dominant topics—(homo)sexuality, death, and religion—and the main characteristics of his literary style, which often is ironic and archaic and mixes the lofty with the trivial. *De Avonden* is now considered one of the milestones of twentieth-century Dutch literature.

In Reve's epistolary autobiographical books *Op weg naar het einde* (*On the Way to the End* [1963]) and *Nader tot U* (*Nearer to Thee* [1966]), homosexuality is an explicit theme, combined with Catholicism and sadomasochism. In the period of Reve's coming out—the mid-1960s—something like a "sexual revolution" took place in Holland. Reve, who also worked on the editorial staff of *Dialoog* (*Dialogue*), a liberationist gay and lesbian magazine (1965–1967), became the first Dutch gay celebrity. As he demonstrated in his work, it was no longer necessary to legitimate and explain homosexuality. Instead, Reve revealed himself as a great narrator of homosexual fantasies, which some critics thought to be rather pornographic. Reve's most recent novel, *Bezorgde Ouders* (*Parent's Worry* [1988]), incorporates all the major themes of his works, including "Revism," which refers to the act of seducing a beautiful boy with the intention to offer and sacrifice him in a sadistic way to one's own lover. Reve's novels and collections of letters command a large and diverse audience. Several of his novels have been adapted for the screen. Paul Verhoeven's *The Fourth Man* (1983), based on Reve's short novel *De Vierde Man* (1981), was internationally successful and became a gay cult movie in the United States.

Reve's contemporary Hans Warren (b. 1921) started his literary career as an art critic and poet. Together with his friend and partner Mario Molegraaf, he translated the collected poems of C. P. CAVAFY (1984). Warren achieved national fame with the publication of his *Geheime Dagboek* (*Secret Diary*). In the twelve volumes so far published, he gives a frank account of his awakening as a homosexual in the countryside, his tempestuous relations with his mostly North African lovers and with his wife, who gave birth to several children. He also explains his divorce and the start of a new life, first living alone, later with his lover Mario.

Ranked alongside Reve and Warren as one of Holland's most renowned gay writers is Gerrit Komrij (b. 1944). He has published an impressive body of work, including poetry, novels, plays, literary reviews, columns, translations, and essays. Komrij is both admired and feared because of his sardonic humor and biting pen. In *Verwoest Arcadië* (*Destroyed Arcadia* [1980]), he gives an autobiographical "reconstruction of a life amidst boys and books." His most recent publication is the libretto for Peter Schat's opera *Symposion* (1994), which dramatizes the last days in the life of Peter Ilyich Tchaikovsky.

Two Flemish writers, Eric de Kuyper (b. 1942) and Tom Lanoye (b. 1958), add new voices to Dutch gay writing, which in the 1960s and 1970s was dominated by authors born and raised in the Netherlands. Like Komrij, Kuyper would protest against being labeled a "gay writer." But both see homosexuality as a force that enables an artist to consider social phenomena from a different perspective. In his series of autobiographical novels, Kuyper investigates how fascination for arts and the male body come together in the fantasies and acts of his hero. In the matriarchal family, in which he is raised, he gets the opportunity to explore the world of ballet and film. Initially, he sees the male body only as an aesthetic object, but later, in his adolescent years, the discovery of bodybuilder magazines leads to new erotic, and therefore sinful and secret, meanings. The iconography of the male body is also an area for special attention in Kuyper's movies, like *Naughty Boys* and *Pink Ulysses,* and in his essays about film and film theory.

In *Kartonnen dozen* (*Cardboard Boxes* [1991]), Tom Lanoye gives an often hilarious account of "a trivial love and its consuming power." In the autobiographical story of a boy's friendship that was not allowed to become a love affair, Lanoye makes clear that a gay consciousness is determined by memories, images, dreams, fantasies, and ineffable feelings.

The same elements are used in the short novels of Willem Bijsterbosch. Comradeship is perhaps the keyword to characterize the relations between his protagonists, not only those between two boys or two elderly, eccentric women, but also between the younger and older generations. Bijsterbosch's heroes are mates or pals, who try to lead independent and spontaneous lives. Bijsterbosch creates an inviting fictional world by mixing elements of the picaresque and gothic novel with modern gay culture and romantic friendship.

The diversity of modern Dutch lesbian literature seems even greater than that of gay male literature, because it also includes black literature, lesbian romantic novels (by the "Writer's Squad" Dorcas), lesbian-feminist literature, and comic stories from the lesbian subculture (Sjuul Deckwitz). In novels like *Nergens, ergens* (*Nowhere, Somewhere* [1983]), Astrid Roemer (b. 1947), who was born in the former Dutch colony Surinam, tries to break through oppositions between black and white, lesbian and straight. Recently, Surinam–Dutch lesbian writing was augmented by *Vriendinnenvrouwen* (*Sisterwomen* [1994]), a novel by Joanna Werners, which gives a fragmented analysis of the discrimination against (lesbian) black women.

The poet Elly de Waard is "the uncrowned queen of the Dutch lesbians," and the leader of a group of young female poets called "The New Savages." The character of her poetry has developed from sober and reticent to ecstatic and explicitly lesbian. Her most recent collections of poems, *Eenzang* and *Eenzang: twee* (1991 and 1992), include works that give expression to the full range of lesbian love and sexuality.

Frans Kellendonk's *Mystiek lichaam* (*The Mystical Body* [1986]) is one of the few novels in Dutch and Flemish literature in which AIDS plays an important role. With this book, Kellendonk, who was born in 1951 and died of AIDS in 1990, caused a major uproar in the Dutch literary community. Many critics assumed a one-to-one relation between the philosophy expressed in this novel and Kellendonk's own views on social topics, and they accused him of anti-semitism and homophobia. *Mystiek lichaam* is a family saga about a father, his gay son Leendert, and his "silly" pregnant daughter Magda or "Prul." Despite her silliness, Prul's heterosexuality leads to procreation and is associated with life and nature, whereas

Leendert's homosexuality is sterile and associated with death (by an unnamed, "new disease") and artificiality. The portrayal of homosexuality in this novel is certainly not very encouraging to gay readers. Nevertheless, the doubts Kellendonk had about his own homosexuality, gay lifestyles, and gay liberation deserve literary expression. They challenge readers to redefine their own positions and roles in today's society.

—*Maurice van Lieshout*

BIBLIOGRAPHY

Dekker, Rudolf M., and Lotte C. van de Pol. *The Tradition of Female Transvestism in Early Modern Europe.* London: Macmillan, 1989. ■ Duyves, Mattias et al., eds. *Homojaarboek 2: Artikelen over emancipatie en homoseksualiteit.* Amsterdam: Van Gennep, 1983. ■ Hafkamp, H. "Homoseksualiteit in de Nederlandse Literatur." *Spiegel Historiael* 17.11 (1982): 584–593. ■ Hekma, Gert. "The Mystical Body: Frans Kellendonk and the Dutch Literary Response to AIDS." *AIDS: The Literary Response.* Emmanuel Nelson, ed. New York: Twayne Publishers, 1992. 88–94. ■ Lieshout, Maurice van. "The Context of Gay Writing and Reading." *Homosexuality, Which Homosexuality? International Conference on Gay and Lesbian Studies.* Dennis Altman et al., eds. Amsterdam and London: An Dekker and GMP, 1989. 113–126. ■ Veeger, Petra. "Tussen Blaman en Burnier. Het beeld van de lesbienne bij Nederlandse schrijfsters, 1940-1970." *Goed Verkeerd. Ein geschiedenis van homoseksuele mannen en lesbische vrouwen in Nederland.* Gert Hekma et al., eds. Amsterdam: Meulenhoff, 1989. 115–128. ■ Vermij, Lucie Th., ed. *Women Writers from the Netherlands and Flanders.* Amsterdam: International Feminist Book Fair Press, 1992.

Dykewomon, Elana
(b. 1949)

Elana Dykewomon was born Elana Nachman in New York City on October 11, 1949, to middle-class Jewish parents. Her father is a lawyer, her mother a librarian. The family moved to Puerto Rico when Elana was eight. She studied fine art at Reed College in Portland, Oregon, and received a B.F.A. in creative writing from the California Institute of Art.

At the age of twenty-one, she wrote her first novel, *Riverfinger Women,* published in 1974 by the pioneering women's press, Daughter's, Inc. One of her aims was to show the ordinary heroism of lesbian relations. Though the novel deals with sexual violence, sadism, humiliation, and prostitution, with sometimes searing directness, these typify heterosexual relationships, a sordid background against which the lesbian heroine stands out as a troubled seeker with a warm and comprehending heart. Written as an open text in which continual reference is made to the act of creation, and laced with documents of the 1970s—an army recruiting ad, letters from the "Women's Page" of a local newspaper—*Riverfinger Women* shows reality itself to be problematic and easily appropriated. As one of the first wave of lesbian novels with happy endings, *Riverfinger Women* has been extremely popular. The combination of lesbian content and hippie setting have assured its success.

With the publication of *They Will Know Me by My Teeth* (1976), Elana changed her surname to "Dykewoman," at once an expression of her strong commitment to the lesbian community and a way to keep herself "honest," since anyone reading the book would know the author was a lesbian. The stories and poems in the collection are written from within the lesbian community, addressing such issues as surgical breast reduction, masturbation, class, inventing creation myths, and mythic lesbian communities.

With her third book, *Fragments From Lesbos* (1981), published "for lesbians only," Elana began to spell her name "Dykewomon," to avoid etymological connection with men. Many of the poems are love poems, poems of the aching contentment of sex, but also the pleasures of solitude. It is a visual, sensuous collection describing the thoughts of a traveler, a cross-country driver as she considers the meteorological, the geographical, the material.

Some of Elana Dykewomon's most influential writing has taken the form of articles and poems that were copied and recopied by hand and machine before being published in anthologies and journals. "The real fat womon poems" and "Traveling Fat" deal movingly with fat oppression, making the radical connection between social sanction of stomach stapling in twentieth-century America and Chinese foot binding. "The Fourth Daughter's 400 Questions" has been widely used in lesbian seders and study groups.

Throughout her work, poetry or prose, novel or essay, the same themes recur: the lesbian as active, dynamic hero on center stage, a counter to the supposed heterosexual universal; the need for honesty, however difficult or painful; and a belief that breaking silence will strike a common chord in other women. In each genre, there walks the figure of the outsider: the Jew, the fat woman, the woman moving between communities.

In 1987, Elana became editor of *Sinister Wisdom*, a journal "for the Lesbian Imagination in the Arts and Politics." In her editorials and in her publishing decisions she continues to raise important issues and to let the voices of minority lesbians be heard.

—*Anna Livia*

BIBLIOGRAPHY

Dykewomon, Elana. "The Fourth Daughter's 400 Questions." *Nice Jewish Girls: A Lesbian Anthology.* Evelyn Torton Beck, ed. Boston: Beacon Press, 1982. ■ ———. *Fragments From Lesbos.* Langlois, Oreg.: Diaspora Distribution, 1981. ■ ———. (as Elana Nachman) *Riverfinger Women.* Plainfield, Vt.: Daughters, Inc., 1974; Tallahassee, Fla.: Naiad Press, 1992. ■ ———. (as Elana Dykewoman) *They Will Know Me by My Teeth.* Northampton, Miss.: Megaera Press, 1976. ■ ———. "Traveling Fat." *Shadow on a Tightrope.* Lisa Schoenfielder and Barb Weiser, eds. San Francisco: Aunt Lute, 1983. ■ Penelope, J. and Susan Wolfe. "Toward A Feminist Aesthetic." *Feminist Frontiers: Rethinking Sex, Gender and Society.* Laurel Richardson and Verta Taylor, eds. Reading, Mass.: Addison-Wesley, 1983. ■ Zimmerman, Bonnie. *The Safe Sea of Women–Lesbian Fiction 1969-1989.* Boston: Beacon Press, 1990.

Elegy

An elegy is a poetic response to the death of a greatly loved person. The typical elegy contains a lament and a celebration of the dead person and ends with the poet's finding consolation in the contemplation of something that is considered to be more important than the life or death of any one person. Most elegies are written by men about men and have a latent homoerotic tone and a blurring of the line between friendship and love. The homoeroticism of an elegy can often be seen in the way in which the poet departs from the traditional formulas.

The homoeroticism of the elegy is, in part, due to its classical sources. The elegiac tradition derives from classical laments such as Bion's "Lament for Adonis" and THEOCRITUS's "first Idyll" in Greek, and VIRGIL's "Fifth Eclogue" in Latin. These poems, and the others like them, concern the deaths of beautiful young men who—like Virgil's Daphnis—are often portrayed as shepherds from the mythical land of Arcadia. Some of these poems are openly homoerotic since, within certain limits, the classical world permitted male homosexuality.

The most famous English elegies were written approximately between 1500 and 1900, when homosexual acts were forbidden by the law and by the church. Nevertheless, laws against homosexual activity were selectively enforced: It seems that only sexual behavior that was seen as socially disruptive was likely to be punished. Furthermore, the distinction between friendship and romantic love—which has become important in the last century—appears often to have been impossible to make. There is usually no way to declare with certainty that a relationship between men was or was not sexual. The elegy, employing as it does a vocabulary and a form that any reader of classical poetry would recognize as connected to homoeroticism, tends to move back and forth on a continuum between love and friendship.

Among the earliest English elegies are those by Henry Howard, Earl of Surrey. In the decade ending in 1547, Surrey wrote elegies for his friend and brother-in-law the Duke of Richmond, his cousin and squire Thomas Clere, and the poet Sir Thomas Wyatt. Surrey's elegies for Richmond—"So crewell prison" and "When Windesor walles"—are particularly interesting. Although Surrey does not use the classical techniques or the Arcadian setting, he writes of his life with the dead man in a style that recalls his own love poetry and earlier love poetry in English. It is impossible to place the relationship between the two men on only one side of the imaginary line between love and friendship.

The elegies of JOHN MILTON, written about a century after Surrey's, are much more consciously classical. Milton's "Lycidas" (1638), with its use of classical names and settings, is very close in many respects to Virgil and Theocritus. The lesser-known "Epitaphium Damonis" (1638), which Milton wrote in Latin about his friend Charles Diodati, is more interesting than "Lycidas," considered strictly as an elegy. In "Epitaphium Damonis," Milton uses Virgil's life as well as his techniques. Milton wants, like Virgil, to move from pastoral poetry (like the elegy) to epic poetry, and in fact, the idea of composing an epic is Milton's consolation for Diodati's death. Pastoral poetry is seen as immature, whereas epic poetry is seen as mature. Elegiac poets often make a tacit comparison between poetry and human relationships, in which same-sex bonds are linked to adolescence and youth must give way to marriage and reproduction, which are linked to adulthood. Often, indeed, the idea of reproduction—usually expressed as the return of spring—is the consolation. In "Epitaphium Damonis," however, Milton does not mention his own marriage. Instead, he ends the poem by saying that Diodati will be rewarded for his earthly chastity with a marriage in heaven. This can be read as a defense against an anticipated accusation, especially since the final lines of the poem are a strongly erotic description of the heavenly marriage. The sexuality of this description represents the return of what has been repressed in this and other elegies. Here, as elsewhere in Milton's poetry, we see the poet dramatizing sexual temptation and using religion to defeat that temptation. What is remarkable here is that Milton simultaneously resists and gives in to the forbidden pleasures of sexuality.

In many elegies, the inevitability of the seasonal cycle is used to make the move from a homosexual to a heterosexual bond seem natural, so although love between a man and a woman can be connected to this cycle, a love between men or between women must exist outside it. This kind of love can be written only when it has been ended by death. After making this acknowledgment, the poet can move on to marriage. Milton, and most elegiac poets, could make this transition; THOMAS GRAY, writing about one hundred years after Milton, could not. In his most famous poem, "Elegy Written in a Country Church Yard" (1751), Gray calls attention to his separation from the sphere of marriage and familial ties by portraying himself as a solitary observer. Instead of mourning a man, Gray mourns a community, one from which he is cut off by inclination, education, and class. The life of the village is a life that Gray could never and would never live. He ends the poem with a description of his own grave, in which he stresses both his loneliness, in opposition to the closely knit rural community, and his anxiety about God's judgment, in opposition to the peace of the villagers who, he suggests, never had a chance to sin.

Gray had already written about these issues in "Sonnet on the Death of Richard West," a poem that was not published until after Gray's death. Richard West was a close friend, and perhaps lover, of Gray's who died suddenly when the two men were in their mid-twenties. The sonnet can be read as a passage from an elegy: It contains only the ending, the search for consolation. Gray complains of his inability to find consolation where elegiac poets usually find it—in the cycles of nature and, by analogy, in the thought of offspring. The poem employs images of rebirth and regeneration in order to emphasize the poet's separation from these phenomena. Gray says that his attempts to join the natural cycle are unsuccessful. For the typical elegiac movement from natural to human

(re)birth, Gray substitutes a contemplation of nature in which the poet is an outsider, which changes to a situation in which the propagation of the race is paralleled by Gray's mourning. His lament is his only child.

The most famous elegy of the nineteenth century is ALFRED TENNYSON's book-length *In Memoriam* (1850), written about his friend Arthur Hallam, who died when Tennyson was 24. In this poem, Tennyson moves from profound grief and an explicit rejection of consolation to a uniquely Victorian theological–philosophical excursus and, finally, to the resolution provided by marriage. It is significant, however, that the marriage at the end of the poem is not Tennyson's but his sister's. Tennyson himself did not marry until 1850, almost seventeen years after Hallam's death.

The characteristic quality of *In Memoriam* is excess; the length of the poem may itself be considered excessive, but what appears most excessive is Tennyson's emotion. The emotion may be perceived as excessive because *In Memoriam* was published at the very beginning of the existence of homosexuality as a fact that could not totally be ignored. Many of the early reviews of and letters about the poem reveal a certain uneasiness with the amount of affection Tennyson lavished on Hallam's memory. It was becoming increasingly difficult to give men who declared strong emotional attachments for other men the benefit of the doubt. Tennyson himself may well have been aware of this problem since he published *In Memoriam* anonymously in the year of his marriage.

The emergence in the second half of the nineteenth century of the homosexual as a recognizable category of person meant that fewer elegies like *In Memoriam* or "Sonnet on the Death of Richard West" were written or, at least, published. Nevertheless, some writers continued to use elegiac elements to express homoerotic sentiments. Poets like GERARD MANLEY HOPKINS and A. E. HOUSMAN took advantage of the idea that love for another man can be expressed only after the object of love is dead to write poems that celebrate the beauty of dead boys and men. In addition to using death in this way, the English poets separated themselves, at least in their poetry, from their own homoeroticism by mourning men of a different class. Hopkins's "Felix Randal" and Housman's *A Shropshire Lad* (1896) concern rural men whom the poets observe from a distance that is both social and spatial. In this, as in much else, they owe a great deal to Gray, in particular to his "Elegy" and also to his "Ode on a Distant Prospect of Eton College," in which the distance is spatial and temporal rather than social.

WALT WHITMAN wrote similar poetry, most notably in the "Drum Taps" section of *Leaves of Grass* (Whitman, of course, also celebrated living boys and men). Military conflict provides a place in which homoeroticism is expected, as Whitman found in the Civil War. The heightened sense of the fragility of male beauty and strength that war provides has given rise to a great deal of homoerotic poetry, perhaps most famously in the case of WILFRED OWEN, who was killed at the end of the First World War. Owen called his war poems elegies, which suggests that their lack of any consolatory passages can be seen as intentional, as if Owen were emphasizing that it is impossible to recover from the loss of so many loved men.

The absence of consolation is typical of elegiac poems in the twentieth century—with the exception of consciously classical and campy poems like FRANK O'HARA's elegies for James Dean. To some extent, this absence is due to the unwillingness of modernist and contemporary writers to use traditional poetic and philosophic formulas; more specifically, of course, writers who are openly gay do not see marriage as a solution to the loss of a loved one, and neither are they inclined to leave readers in doubt about whether the dead person was a friend or a lover. Sometimes even when the relation between the poet and the subject was friendship, as in ALLEN GINSBERG's "City Midnight Junk Strains" for Frank O'Hara, the poem tends to celebrate gay sexuality rather than to speculate about the afterlife.

Some recent poetry by lesbian and gay writers has used elements of the elegy. ADRIENNE RICH's "A Woman Dead in her Forties" simultaneously mourns a dead friend, acknowledges the hardships of women's lives, and celebrates various kinds of bonds between women. AUDRE LORDE's "Need: A Chorale of Black Women's Voices" is a complex and ambitious poem that speaks openly about the problems of black women in America and praises the strength shown in the face of this pain. These poems construct a specifically lesbian and feminist elegiac mode in opposition to the standard male elegy.

For most of the twentieth century, the elegy seemed to be outdated, like the ode. In the last decade, however, the AIDS pandemic has made the elegy relevant once again. As in war time, the fragility of human life is always apparent. Many poems about AIDS, like those collected by Rachel Hadas in *Unending Dialogue,* are elegiac; some poets, like PAUL MONETTE, call their poems elegies. Contemporary lesbian and gay poets, like their predecessors, have found that the elegy is always timely. (See also WAR LITERATURE.)

—*Stephen Guy-Bray*

BIBLIOGRAPHY

Bray, Alan. "Homosexuality and the Signs of Male Friendship in Elizabethan England." *History Workshop Journal* 29 (1990): 1–9. ■ Crewe, Jonathan. *Trials of Authorship.* Berkeley: University of California Press, 1990. ■ Dellamora, Richard. *Masculine Desire: The Sexual Politics of Victorian Aestheticism.* Chapel Hill: University of North Carolina Press, 1990. ■ Haggerty, George E. "'The Voice of Nature' in Gray's *Elegy.*" *Homosexuality in Renaissance and Enlightenment England.* Claude J. Summers, ed. New York: Haworth Press, 1992. 199–214. ■ Nunokawa, Jeff. "*In Memoriam* and the Extinction of the Homosexual." *English Literary History* 58 (1991): 427–438. ■ Sedgwick, Eve Kosofsky. *Between Men: English Literature and Male Homosocial Desire.* New York: Columbia University Press, 1985.

Eliot, T[homas] S[tearns]
(1888–1965)

Although Eliot liked to be thought of as the most impersonal of poets, looking at the world with a detached and objective eye, many personal elements in the poems deserve to be read with the poet's life in mind. Indeed, there may have been personal reasons for his "impersonality." Certainly, one of its effects was to give the impression that he had something to hide. A number of younger writers, including HART CRANE and Harold Norse, assumed he was homosexual.

At the emotional core of Eliot's poetry is his friendship with Jean Verdenal (1889–1915), a young Frenchman. All we know for certain is that the relationship took place in Paris in 1910 and 1911 while Eliot was studying at the Sorbonne and that Verdenal died in the Great War in 1915 at the age of 26. A month later, Eliot hurriedly married his first wife, Vivien. In 1917, he dedicated *Prufrock and Other Observations* to Verdenal's memory, over an epigraph from DANTE's *Purgatorio* that expresses "the measure of the love which warms me towards you."

This quotation comes from one of Eliot's two favorite segments of the *Divine Comedy,* both of which he kept returning to throughout his career: In *Inferno* XV, Dante meets Brunetto Latini among the sodomites (the "violent against nature"); and in *Purgatorio* XXVI, he meets Arnaut Daniel among more sodomites and "hermaphrodites."

Eliot's love for Verdenal is one of the central facts of *The Waste Land*. In particular, it is possible to identify the so-called Hyacinth girl of the poem's opening section with the poet's sentimental memory of "a friend coming across the Luxembourg Gardens in the late afternoon, waving a branch of lilac." This figure is then subsumed into the theme of death by water, which is in turn mixed with references to the trenches of the Great War. The poem's despair is expressed as both personal and philosophical loss in the crucial line, "He who was living is now dead."

The Waste Land is, in short, a funeral elegy. When John Peter wrote an essay to this effect in 1952, Eliot instructed his solicitors to intervene, and all traceable copies of the relevant issue of *Essays in Criticism* (II, 242–266) were destroyed. Peter reissued the essay, with additions, after Eliot's death.

One of Ezra Pound's self-appointed tasks as editor of the manuscript of *The Waste Land* was to tone down the poem's homoeroticism. For instance, he recommended the cutting of the poem "Saint Narcis-sus," that peculiar fusion of pagan and Christian imagery that now appears at the end of the *Complete Poems*. A number of familiar lines in the final draft of *The Waste Land* are toned-down versions of what appeared in the manuscript: "My friend, blood shaking my heart" was originally "My friend, my friend, beating in my heart"; "I have heard the key" was "friend, my friend I have heard the key"; and "your heart would have responded" was the more revealing "your heart responded."

For a brilliant account of the Eliot–Pound collaboration's homoerotic and homophobic tendencies, see Koestenbaum's *Double Talk*.

—*Gregory Woods*

BIBLIOGRAPHY

Koestenbaum, Wayne. *Double Talk: The Erotics of Male Literary Collaboration*. New York & London: Routledge, 1989. ■
Peter, John. "A New Interpretation of *The Waste Land*." *Essays in Criticism* 19:2 (April 1969): 140–175.

ENGLISH LITERATURE

English Literature: Medieval

The medieval English period covers almost a thousand years, stretching roughly from the fifth to the fifteenth century and witnessing the rise and fall of several different cultures. After the Romans withdrew their troops from Britain in the fifth century, aggressive tribes threatened the Celts, who had lived there under Roman rule. To protect themselves, the Celts invited Germanic troops to aid them against the onslaught. Not only did these troops secure Celtic lands, but they also decided to remain, and a Germanic onslaught began. Eventually these invaders overpowered the Celts (later known as the Welsh), and the Germanic (Anglo-Saxon or Old English) period began, lasting until the eleventh century when the Anglo-Saxons were in turn conquered by the Norman French (who themselves had a Germanic background). It is from this Anglo-Norman culture that Middle English society developed, reaching its height in the late fourteenth century and gradually giving way to the Early Modern period over the next hundred years. Hence medieval English literature varies culturally and linguistically, for it includes not only Old and Middle English texts but French, Welsh, and Latin ones as well.

To make clear the relationship between these writings and their representation of issues pertinent to gay and lesbian literary history (especially gay history since female homosexual issues do not appear explicitly in medieval English literature), it is helpful to know something about medieval European culture's "sexology." The Middle Ages placed a high value on homosocial bonding (intense emotional relationships between people of the same sex) and inherited much homoerotic literature from the classical past. But it generally frowned on homosexual practices and, for a complicated variety of reasons, censured such activities, especially passive homosexual anal intercourse, thought to disrupt gender difference by placing a man in a "female" role. Attitudes, informed in part by the Catholic Church, concerning the cause of same-sex sodomy varied widely: Some thinkers felt that homosexual desire was innate in specific people; others that it stemmed from an excess of general sexual desire and was therefore simply behavior in which anyone could potentially engage. Although it is difficult to know the extent to which the attitudes of dominant religious and social ideologies governed the actual sexual experience of common men and women, both these positions on sodomy ultimately condemned this "unmentionable vice" though the intensity of medieval homophobia waxed and waned throughout the period. Such proscription does not mean, however, that homosexual activity was understood by everyone to be a transgressive act: It has been argued that in twelfth-century intellectual circles, there occurred a resurgence of homoerotic values even though the idea of something akin to a modern "gay" subculture and subjective IDENTITY does not seem to have developed fully. Since all the different cultures inhabiting England had been Christianized during the medieval period—the Anglo-Saxons not until the late sixth century—their official view of homosexual desire and practice was heavily influenced by these disapproving attitudes. Hence, when sodomy and sodomites are found in medieval English literature, they are with few exceptions represented negatively and used to reinforce approved teachings on sexual behavior.

Though Celtic literature seems to be fairly silent on these issues, Anglo-Saxon vernacular and Latin writings do offer a few examples and contrast the value and strength of male bonding to homosexual activity. In *Beowulf,* for example, the love of the older Lord Hrothgar for the young warrior Beowulf is represented in terms that we would consider homoerotic today. After Beowulf destroys both the monstrous Grendel and Grendel's mother and prepares to return to his home, the poet describes Hrothgar's longing for the young man as a desire burning powerfully in the old warrior's blood. Even though it is possible that there is an erotic subtext to this description, its context is one of masculine social affection and friendship and is approved by the Christian narrator telling this story from the ancient past. This representation of such affection is not uncommon: In many texts, in fact, such a highly charged bond between a warrior and his lord is thought to be so powerful that its imagery is invoked frequently to describe heterosexual love.

But such same-sex affection contrasts markedly with the homosexual expression of such love. For example, in the description of Sodom and Gomorrah in the Anglo-Saxon poem *Genesis,* based on the biblical book of the same name, there is a clear denunciation of the Sodomites' desire to have sexual intercourse with two male angels as shameful and indecent. And one finds a similar case during this period in the Latin writings of the English scholar Alcuin. While residing at the court of Charlemagne, Alcuin wrote and exchanged with his students homoerotic poetry in the classical tradition. But while employing powerful homoerotic imagery to emphasize male love and friendship, Alcuin, nonetheless, as John Boswell discusses in *Christianity, Social Tolerance, and Homosexuality,* emphasizes, though certainly not as disapprovingly as the *Genesis* poet, that the physical expression of such passion should be avoided by scholars and clerics (who should, by the way, avoid heterosexual activity as well). What emerges from such writings is that though there might well be—at least as it appears to us—a fine line between the homosocial and the homoerotic, it is one that should not be crossed.

During the Anglo-Norman period, there was some positive homoerotic Latin verse written by English-born intellectuals, Hilary the Englishman and Serlo of Wilton, who followed the same classical tradition as Alcuin. Penning his verse to beautiful boys for whom he proclaims his devotion, Hilary employs the rhetoric of homosexual desire as he laments one youth's refusal to grant love or praises another's loveliness. Serlo records both the pleasure and the loss of his various loves, and much like Hilary, refers frequently to the famous mythical relationship of Ganymede and Jove. Despite the poets' overarching homoeroticism, however, it is difficult to judge whether the poems actually praise homosexual desire or, like many other such texts, use homoerotic rhetoric to represent homosocial feelings and desire (which might nonetheless contain homosexual elements).

Apart from these poems, however, the major Latin and Norman texts mentioning homosexual love and practices in the twelfth century are highly critical of both and mark an intensification of the fear and hatred surrounding alternative sexual practices for the remainder of the English Middle Ages. Alan of Lille's polemical *Plaint of Nature,* for example, goes so far as to suggest that homosexual activity is destroying the world and that Nature herself is upset at those who practice this unnatural vice. Sodomy, Alan claims, disrupts not only the natural heterosexual orientation of the world but also gender differences by transforming men (functioning as the recipient of another male's organ) into women. By invoking Nature to support his diatribe, Alan thus attempts to reinforce official teachings concerning sodomy by showing how they follow from the "natural" order of things. A similar invective against sodomy occurs in the anonymous Norman French *Eneas,* a retelling of Virgil's *Aeneid.* Connected to England through the country's close political and cultural situation as part of the Norman—and later, Angevin—empire until the very early thirteenth century, the poem represents Lavinia's mother dissuading her daughter from loving Eneas by falsely accusing the young hero of habitually committing sodomy, a filthy activity that, again, could destroy the world. Believing her mother at one point and continuing herself with the diatribe on Eneas' vice, Lavinia almost loses her affection for him, and her mother almost succeeds in controlling her. Both the *Plaint* and the *Eneas* illustrate the way that official culture reviled homosexual expression, but the Norman French text underscores a further, and perhaps even more important, point: that in a homophobic culture the accusation of sodomy can be used to suppress and control homosexual and heterosexual behavior alike.

After the breakup of the Angevin Empire in the thirteenth century and the gradual development of England as a distinct cultural, political, and linguistic entity, the fourteenth and fifteenth centuries saw a flowering of literature written in Middle English (modern English's precursor originating from a combination of Anglo-Saxon and Norman French). Though Middle English texts had first emerged in the twelfth century and much fourteenth-century literature in England was still written in French, the Middle English poetry of this late period nonetheless initiated a new era in England's literary history. But much like other English literatures, while condemning male homosexual relationships, it frequently places a high value on male homosocial ones. Poems such as the fourteenth-century Middle English rendition of the popular *Amis and Amiloun,* which praises the nonsexual love of two men for each other as superior to heterosexual love, provide a model of behavior for same-sex masculine devotion and friendship. Much like earlier medieval English literature, it seems that on a larger cultural level (though not declared explicitly in any specific texts), these writings attempted to police boundaries: to make certain that homosexual feelings and behavior do not cross over into the realm of homosocial relationships and to preserve heterosexual activity as an important marker of gender difference.

To demarcate these boundaries, late Middle English texts treating sodomy condemn it either explicitly or through opprobrious allusions and attempt to discourage homosexual love and sexual practices by invoking theological or social prohibitions that consider such desires and relations as transgressive. Like several other medieval texts, John Gower's *Confessio Amantis,* a long poem in which a lover's confession of his sins is used as a tool for supplying advice to readers, interprets the myth of Narcissus as a warning against homosexual love. Mistaking his image as female (disrupting gender categories) and falling in love with himself (a male falling in love with another male who is taken as a woman), Narcissus's desire, Gower tells his readers, is contrary to nature. Similar ideas emerge in the anonymous poem *Cleanness,* which, in its retelling of the story of Sodom and Gomorrah, discusses homosexual activity as a violation of proper masculine behavior, a turning away from natural law, and a pollution of the male body as God's vessel. The poem's disapproval is made clear on a thematic and linguistic level: In one passage, the choice of words describing sodomy imitate the act of spitting. And William Dunbar's *Dance of the Seven Deadly Sins* graphically singles out homosexual behavior as the kind of lecherous sin that will send mortals to hell: Each ugly and stinking man leads another man by the penis, which is later to be inserted into another male's anus. Since these texts situate their condemnation in contexts pointing out the ultimate destructive outcome of the "unnatural vice," they all play on the fear of punishment and suffering to control homosexual desire. Though certainly not as explicitly condemnatory, some selections from GEOFFREY CHAUCER's *The Canterbury Tales* could be included in this list as well.

For the most part, the history and texts of medieval English literature, though stunning in many ways, are not ones in which same-sex erotic behavior and desire—apart from their use for representing homosocial bonds—find much sympathy or affirmation. But for modern gay readers trying to understand the different cultural forces at the root of modern day homophobia and oppression, these writings are an invaluable starting point, for they underscore the way that earlier literature does not always question but rather frequently participates in policing cultural and theological sexual norms. And for lesbians attempting to understand why they have been silenced for much of the English tradition, it is with the silence of medieval English texts that they should begin.

—*David Lorenzo Boyd*

BIBLIOGRAPHY

Alan of Lille. *The Plaint of Nature.* Trans. James J. Sheridan. Toronto: Pontifical Institute of Mediaeval Studies, 1980. ■ *Amis and Amiloun.* MacEdward Leach, ed. Early English Text Society, O.S. 203. London: Humphrey Milford, Oxford University Press, 1937. ■ *Beowulf.* Trans. E. Talbot Donaldson. New York: Norton, 1966. ■ Boswell, John. *Christianity, Social Tol-*

erance, and Homosexuality. Chicago: University of Chicago Press, 1980. ■ Boyd, David Lorenzo. Sodomy, Silence, and Social Control in Middle English Literature (forthcoming). ■ Bullough, Vern L. and James Brundage, eds. Sexual Practices and the Medieval Church. Buffalo, N.Y.: Prometheus, 1982. ■ Chaucer, Geoffrey. The Canterbury Tales. The Riverside Chaucer. Larry D. Benson, ed. Boston: Houghton Mifflin, 1987. ■ Cleanness, in The Owl and the Nightingale; Cleanness; St. Erkenwald. Trans. Brian Stone. Harmondsworth: Penguin, 1971. ■ Cormier, Raymond J. One Heart One Mind: The Rebirth of Virgil's Hero in Medieval France. Biloxi, Miss.: University of Mississippi Press, 1973. ■ Dinshaw, Caroline. Straight is the Gate: The Heterosexual Subject of Medieval Narrative (forthcoming). ■ Dunbar, William. "Dance of the Seven Deadly Sins." Middle English Lyrics, 147–150. Maxwell S. Luria and Richard L. Hoffman, eds. New York: Norton, 1974. ■ Eneas. Trans. John A. Yunck. New York: Columbia University Press, 1974. ■ Genesis. Trans. Lawrence Mason. New York: Henry Holt, 1915. ■ Goodich, Michael. The Unmentionable Vice. Santa Barbara, Calif.: Ross-Erickson, 1979. ■ Gower, John. Confessio Amantis. Russell A. Peck, ed. Toronto: University of Toronto Press, in association with the Medieval Academy of America, 1980. ■ Greenberg, David R. The Construction of Homosexuality. Chicago: University of Chicago Press, 1988. ■ Medieval Latin Poems of Male Love and Friendship. Trans. Thomas Stehling. New York: Garland, 1984. ■ Pearsall, Derek. Old and Middle English Poetry. London: Routledge & Kegan Paul, 1977. ■ Ziolkowski, Jan. Alan of Lille's Grammar of Sex. Cambridge, Mass.: Medieval Academy of America, 1985.

English Literature: Renaissance

Homosexuality is writ large in the literature of the English Renaissance, but its inscription is only rarely direct and unambiguous. With the exception of a few crucially significant but atypical texts like WILLIAM SHAKESPEARE's Sonnets (1595?), CHRISTOPHER MARLOWE's Edward II (1593), RICHARD BARNFIELD's The Affectionate Shepherd (1594) and Certaine Sonnets (1595), or JOHN DONNE's remarkable dramatic monologue in a lesbian voice, "Sapho to Philaenis" (1613?), homoeroticism in the English Renaissance tends to be expressed implicitly rather than explicitly, seen from the outside rather than from the inside, and is nearly always shadowed by a penumbra of religious and social disapproval. The essential context in which male homoeroticism is textualized in the Renaissance is a pervasive homophobia tempered by a classical heritage of homoerotic literature and philosophy and a massively homosocial power structure whose institutions probably facilitated homosexual relations even as it condemned them. The statute making sodomy a capital offense was apparently enforced only against males and only in cases of rape, most often that of an underaged boy, but that law nevertheless effectively codified the period's official disapproval of homosexual contacts.

Although sodomy was defined as the sin not to be named among Christians, it was actually named quite often. There is, in fact, a considerable body of sodomitical literature in the Renaissance, that is, works in which same-sex sexual relations are construed in terms of the biblical prohibition that justified the destruction of the Cities of the Plain. In these texts, homosexuality is linked not only with other social and gender transgressions such as adultery and cross-dressing, but also with heresy, treason, and witchcraft. In the so-called Baines libel attributed to Christopher Marlowe, for example, the famous statements "That St John the Evangelist was bedfellow to Christ and leaned alwaies in his bosom, that he used him as the sinners of Sodoma" and "That all they that love not Tobacco & Boies were fooles" are tellingly interspersed with atheistic and seditious claims. In such texts, homosexuality is collapsed into a large category of undifferentiated vice and associated particularly with heresy and lèse-majesté.

Sodomitical discourse is found most pristinely in the moral and legal writings that denounce same-sex relations, such as the anonymous pamphlet describing the trial and execution of a seventeenth-century bishop, The Life and Death of John Atherton (1640), and in numerous sermons. But it can also be seen in satires that figure forth homoeroticism as the quintessence of debauchery. In such varied works as John Bale's Scriptorum Catalogus (1555–1559), John Marston's Certain Satyres (1598) and The Scourge of Villainie (1598), Donne's "Satire I" and "Metempsychosis" (1601), Michael Drayton's The Moon-Calf (1627), and some of Ben Jonson's Epigrammes (1616), homosexual desire is attacked as immoderate, ridiculous, symbolic of social decay, contrary to nature, and threatening to the political order. The virulence of the satires against sodomites may be evidence that there was at least a rudimentary homosexual subculture in London during the period. Most interesting in this regard are several diary entries and other manuscript accounts from the early years of the seventeenth century attacking King JAMES I and his relationships with his favorites, and depicting the Court as a center of homosexual activity.

Discourse about same-sex desire in the Renaissance is typically constrained by personal and cultural anxiety, as evidenced, for example, by the orthographical and linguistic peculiarities of Robert Burton's disquisition on homosexuality in his influential *Anatomy of Melancholy* (1621), which incorporates a large amount of curious (mis)information on the subject. Tellingly, the discussion of homosexuality is written in Latin and presented in a way that calls attention to itself: Burton's own sentences are presented in italics, whereas his quotations are printed in roman type, reversing the normal format of the rest of the book.

Lesbianism is almost invisible in the period. The cultural anxieties relating to female sexuality centered on heterosexual trangressions; nevertheless, the charge of lesbianism could be used to stigmatize women who violated social boundaries. Jonson, for example, hints at lesbianism in his attack on Cecilia Bulstrode for composing verse—in Jonson's view an unfeminine pursuit—in "An Epigram on the Court Pucell," a poem in which he coins the term *Tribade*. In addition, homophobic insults were frequently exchanged in the era's religious controversies. Indeed, sodomy was often considered a clerical vice, and the statute in which it was codified as a felony, 25 Henry VIII, chapter 6, was part of a whole panoply of legislation passed by the Reformation Parliament of 1533–1534 attacking the Roman Catholic Church. The scapegoating of homosexuals and the use of homophobia for political ends have long and ignoble histories.

Significantly, however, not all Renaissance discourse about homosexuality is either sodomitical or satiric. The revival of classical learning made available, at least to the educated, a rich body of literature in which homosexuality was constructed differently. The classical literature of homosexuality provided Renaissance writers and readers a pantheon of homosexual heroes, a catalogue of images, and a set of references by which homosexual desire could be encoded into their own literature and by which they could interpret their own experience. Admittedly, this classical heritage was never entirely secure. Translators of classical texts contained homoeroticism by directly countering it with Christian condemnation and by interpreting the works tendentiously, as in Philemon Holland's "Summarie" of PLUTARCH's "Of Love" that he prefaces to his 1603 translation or Thomas Heywood's disapproving representations of the Jupiter–Ganymede relationship in his *Pleasant Dialogues and Dramas* (1637), which are loose translations of LUCIAN's *Dialogues of the Gods*. And most of the many imitations or adaptations of homoerotic classical literature discreetly heterosexualized their sources, as in Jonson's famous lyric "To Celia," which is cobbled together from discrete passages of Philostratus's letters to a boy with whom he was infatuated. Moreover, the classical literature of homosexuality was subject to Christian culture's tendency to deny the physical. The works of Ovid no less than PLATO were Christianized. Even the myth of Ganymede, the most pervasive symbol of homosexuality in the era, could be interpreted—following Xenophon—as an allegory of spiritual ascent. Neoplatonic philosophers could celebrate passionate love between men but were careful to insist that it be purely spiritual. Still, despite the containment and denial to which it was subject, the classical legacy powerfully suggested to Renaissance writers and readers the possibility of alternatives to the sodomitical construction of homosexuality that dominated the period's legal and moral discourse.

In the poetry of the Renaissance, classical sources and allusions frequently served as a kind of excuse for homoeroticism, as it also did for much of the Neoplatonic philosophy of the time. Barnfield, for example, disingenuously cites the classical source of his Spenserean pastoral *The Affectionate Shepherd* as a license for its homoeroticism in his preface to *Cynthia, With Certain Sonnets, and the Legend of Cassandra.* "Some there were, that did interpret *The Affectionate Shepheard,* otherwise then (in truth) I meant, touching the subject thereof, to wit, the love of a Shepheard to a boy: a fault, the which I will not excuse, because I never made," he insists, and adds by way of justification: "Onely this, I will unshaddow my conceit: being nothing else, but an imitation of *Virgill,* in the second Eglogue of *Alexis.*" It is difficult to determine how much Barnfield's blithe self-confidence in the sufficiency of this lame explanation is simple naiveté and to what extent it is a brazen bluff designed to conceal deep-seated anxiety. Certainly, Barnfield was well aware of the moral transgression involved in the affectionate shepherd's love for Ganymede. "If it be sinne to love a Lovely Lad; / Oh then sinne I," the shepherd jauntily announces early in the poem. But Barnfield's appeal to classical precedence serves him well enough to allow him to proceed breezily to even more homoerotic poems in *Certaine Sonnets,* a collection whose protective veneer of classical imitation is far more tenuous than that which allegedly excuses *The Affectionate Shepherd.*

VIRGIL's second eclogue, which tells the story of the shepherd Corydon's unrequited love for Alexis, inspired not only *The Affectionate Shepherd* but several other poems of the period. Marlowe's "Come live with me, and be my love," for example, is a brilliant recital of the country pleasures with which Corydon attempts to woo Alexis. Imagining an idyllic, self-contained golden age far removed from the demands and constraints of Elizabethan society, the poem is charming and seductive. Yet what is most striking about it as an adaptation of the second eclogue is not that it contains homoerotic innuendoes but, quite to the contrary, that it suppresses the unapologetic homoeroticism of its source. Marlowe's nongendered representation of desire in this poem may query the universalizing assumptions of his age's dominant sexual ideology, but his suppression of the overt homoeroticism of Virgil's text also reveals the cultural anxieties surrounding homosexuality in the period.

Those cultural anxieties come to the fore in Edmund Spenser's *The Shepheardes Calendar* (1579), which rewrites Virgil's second eclogue with the Alexis character—Colin—as the protagonist, and reduces the Corydon figure—Hobbinol—to a minor role. When in the *Januarye* eclogue Colin announces his disdain for the "clownish gifts and curtsies" of lovesick Hobbinol—"Ah foolish *Hobbinol,* thy gyfts bene vayne: / *Colin* them giues to *Rosalind* againe"—the commentator E.K. (probably Spenser's close friend Gabriel Harvey) anxiously intrudes with a long note:

> In thys place seemeth to be some sauour of disorderly love, which the learned called paederastice: but it is gathered beside his [that is, Spenser's] meaning. For who hath red Plato his dialogue called Alcybiades, Xenophon and Maximus Tyrius of Socrates opinions, may easily perceive, that such loue is muche to be alowed and liked of, specially so meant, as Socrates vsed it: who sayth, that in deede he loued Alcybiades extremely, yet not Alcybiades person, but his soule, which is Alcybiades owne selfe. And so is paederastice much to be preferred before gynerastice, that is the loue which enflameth men with lust toward woman kind. But yet let no man thinke, that herein I stand with Lucian or hys devilish disciple Vnico Aretino, in defence of execrable and horrible sinnes of forbidden and vnlawful fleshinesse. Whose abominable errour is fully confuted of Perionius, and others.

Calling attention to the brief passage's "sauour of disorderly love" only to disavow it, E.K. first exposes and then attempts to conceal the scandal of Spenser's text. Hobbinol's apparently innocuous "clownish gifts and curtsies" require elaborate distancing from any association with sin and abomination. The disproportion between the text and the gloss is a measure of the danger that homosexuality represented to E.K. and to Renaissance culture generally. E.K.'s unstable assertions, retractions, and contradictory clarifications in the gloss illustrate the precarious balancing act that discourse about homoeroticism is forced to perform in a society that celebrated homosociality but resolutely condemned homosexuality.

Spenser also represents homosexual love in Book IV of *The Faerie Queene* (1590). Book IV is devoted to the Legend of Friendship, and there Spenser develops an ideal of companionate marriage by drawing on the egalitarian principles of the classical masculine friendship tradition. In Canto X, the protagonist Scudamor, in quest of virtuous Amoret, arrives at the temple of Venus. In the garden surrounding the temple, he notices thousands of lovers who "together by themselves did sport / Their spotlesse pleasures, and sweet loues content" (26.1–2). Also present in the amorous garden, but quite separate from these heterosexual lovers, are

> another sort
> Of louers lincked in true harts consent;
> Which loued not as these, for like intent,
> But on chast vertue grounded their desire,
> Farre from all fraud, or fayned blandishment;
> Which in their spirits kindling zealous fire,
> Braue thoughts and noble deedes did euermore
>   aspire. (26.3–9)

These masculine lovers include such classical, biblical, and medieval pairs as the following:

> Such were great *Hercules,* and *Hylas* deare;
> Trew *Ionathan,* and *Dauid* trustie tryde;
> Stout *Theseus,* and *Pirithous* his feare;
> *Pylades* and *Orestes* by his syde;
> Myld *Titus* and *Gesippus* without pryde;
> *Damon* and *Pythias* whom death could not
>   seuer. (27.1–6)

Scudamor is so attracted by these happy couples that he momentarily wishes he could join them. But instead of remaining with these male lovers, he reluctantly departs the garden to enter the temple of Venus, at the center of which is a statue of Hermaphroditus, "both male and female, both vnder one name" (41.7). There he discovers his long sought after Amoret.

The account of the masculine lovers in the garden of Venus incisively distinguishes those who love members of their own sex from those who love individuals of the opposite sex, clearly recognizing homoeroticism as a discrete sexuality. Moreover, it takes pains to represent the male lovers as nonsodomitical. Spenser does this by carefully linking his lovers with a tradition of masculine friendship that was frequently delibidinized to serve as an apologia for homosociality rather than homosexuality. Spenser's lovers ground their desire on the "chaste vertue" that inspires "Braue thoughts and noble deedes." Even though it undoubtedly derives from the homoerotic tradition of an army of lovers as described by Phaedrus in Plato's *Symposium,* the passionate love between men depicted here can plausibly be interpreted as nonphysical. At the same time, however, the palpable eroticism of the passage contradicts any narrow notion of chastity. After all, the lovers' happiness consists in their being able to "frankely there their loves desire possesse." Its spritualizing language may betray anxiety about same-sex eroticism, but the passage is nevertheless quite bold.

Even bolder is an episode in Marlowe's posthumously published *Hero and Leander* (1594). An Ovidian epyllion, *Hero and Leander* belongs to a genre that includes Francis Beaumont's *Salmacis and Hermaphroditus* (1602) and Shakespeare's *Venus and Adonis* (1593) and *The Rape of Lucrece* (1594) and in which male beauty is the focus of erotic attention (as it is also in works based on the biblical David, such as Abraham Cowley's *Davideis* [1656]). In Marlowe's poem, Leander's beauty is celebrated in a homoerotic blazon that lovingly details all of his bodily charms, including especially the shapeliness of his buttocks. But most defiant of all is the poem's farcical episode in which Neptune mistakes Leander for Ganymede and caresses and attempts to seduce him. Marlowe's joke is not only on the passionate god, but also on the naive youth, who can imagine only heterosexual desires. Moreover, the point of the episode, in addition to its titillation value and its foregrounding of the awkward heterosexual lovemaking of Hero and Leander, is to suggest the essential likeness of homosexual and heterosexual passion. The very playfulness of Marlowe's approach in this episode and throughout the epyllion destabilizes the seriousness of the dominant constructions of gender and sexuality in his age. For all its farcical humor, the poem is subversive and defiant.

Another important example of Renaissance homoerotic poetry is a series of four verse letters that the eighteen-year-old John Donne addressed to a younger male friend, "T.W.," probably Thomas Woodward, in 1590. George Klawitter has recently demonstrated that these poems constitute a sequence that records, first, Donne's infatuation for his friend and, then, his disappointment with the friend's failure to respond with a like ardor. These youthful verse letters poignantly voice Donne's desire for a physical and emotional relationship that in our own time would be labeled homosexual. These poems by the man who would become the late Renaissance's supreme poet of heterosexual love and who pillories stereotypical sodomites in his satires also offer concrete evidence of the fluidity of sexual and emotional response in Renaissance literature and life.

Donne's dramatic monologue in a lesbian voice, "Sapho to Philaenis," is particularly important as one of the few Renaissance works that represent lesbian desire frankly. Lesbian affectivity does appear in a late sixteenth-century Scots poem that survives in the Maitland Quarto, and was first printed in 1920, and in other accounts of female friendship; but Donne's poem is unique for its positive depiction of lesbian erotics. As Janel Mueller has noted, Donne's portrayal of lesbianism questions the conventions of Renaissance heterosexuality and establishes lesbianism as a master trope for utopian sexuality. The poem is also interesting for Donne's adoption of the Sapphic voice to define homoerotic love and to envision the return of a lost golden age of sexual freedom and equity in love.

The most significant lesbian voice in poetry of the English Renaissance is that of KATHERINE PHILIPS, who was known as "The English Sappho." More than half of her collected poems, which were published posthumously in 1664 and 1667, deal with her love for other women, addressed in pastoral names like "Lucasia" or "Rosania." In these works, Philips tactfully yet suggestively celebrates and defends ROMANTIC FRIENDSHIP between women. In "To My Excellent Lucasia, On Our Friendship," for example, the poet reassures her lover:

> No bridegroom's nor crown-conqueror's mirth
> To mine compar'd can be:
> They have but pieces of the earth,
> I've all the world in thee. (17–20)

Yet Philips insists that their love is "innocent." As Arlene Stiebel has argued, Philips uses standard literary conventions and references to an idealized classical friendship tradition to mask and diffuse the sexual reality inherent in the concrete, physical terminology that she employs. That is, the poems simultaneously cloak and reveal lesbian sexual desire. For all her respectable decorum, Philips is remarkably candid.

The great masterpiece of homoerotic poetry in the Renaissance (and, indeed, in English literature generally) is Shakespeare's *Sonnets,* published in a pirated edition in 1609 though the individual poems were probably written in the mid-1590s. The large majority of the poems—126 of 154—are concerned with the poet-speaker's obsession with a young man of surpassing physical beauty, if somewhat dubious character. The homosexual consciousness of the *Sonnets* is seen not merely in the celebrations of the young man's beauty, in the obsessiveness of the speaker's love, or even in his repeated attempts to define his relationship with the young man in terms of marriage, but also in his profound sense of otherness. The great sonnets of alienation and abnegation that give Shakespeare's sequence its distinctive aura of embattlement and despair articulate particularly well a homosexual subjectivity. This sense of difference is expressed forthrightly in the angry and defiant Sonnet 121, in which the speaker declares "I am that I am" and defends the naturalness of a sexuality that is decried and attacked by his culture. A highly complex, discomfitingly dark, richly ironic, and painfully intense record of obsessive love, the sequence plumbs depths of emotion that transcend sexual categories. Yet, by virtue of its inscription of a homosexual subjectivity, it has a particular importance in literary history and in gay literature.

The prose of the English Renaissance includes several romance narratives that feature homoerotic friendship, celebrations of androgynous male beauty, and transvestism that often facilitates mistaken identities. Robert Greene's *Menaphon* (1589), Sir Philip Sidney's *The Countess of Pembroke's Arcadia* (1593), and Thomas Lodge's *Rosalynde: Euphues Golden Legacie* (1590) all partake of these characteristics and depict homoerotic situations titillatingly. Sidney's work is especially significant for the depth of its portrayal of the friendship of Musidorus and Pyrocles though it (like the other works) sorts out all the sexual confusions and mistaken identities in a conventional conclusion that privileges heterosexual marriage. In these prose romances, homoerotic attraction seems to be a passion associated with the escapism of romance itself, a phase through which characters pass only to emerge into "mature" heterosexuality.

Another romance, Lady Mary Wroth's *Urania* (1621), deserves note for its account of a Duke "besotted on a young man," who viciously betrays him. The relationship depicted in this episode may be based, as Ellis Hanson has argued, on King James's infatuation for his ill-fated favorite Robert Carr. Herself an intimate of James's consort Queen Anne and a frequent visitor at Court, Wroth was in a good position to observe the king's affection for Carr. In any case, the episode in *Urania* is a fascinating story of obsessive love. Even after the young man in the story betrays him, the Duke cannot help loving him.

The prose works of SIR FRANCIS BACON are far more serious than the romances, but they are also revealing. Bacon hints at his homosexual attraction in his 1625 revisions and augmentations of his *Essayes,* especially "Of Friendship," which celebrates friendship at the expense of familial relationships; "Of Marriage and the Single Life," which tends to privilege singleness in comparison to the marital state; and "Of Beauty," which tellingly discusses only examples of male beauty. Yet in the "feast of the family" section of his utopian work about the land of Bensalem, *New Atlantis* (1610), Bacon exalts patriarchy and characterizes "masculine love" negatively. As Joseph Cady has written,

> it may have been at some emotional cost, or at least significant personal compromise, that Bacon—involved in a "late," childless, and pro forma marriage himself and attracted predominantly or exclusively to his own sex—composed this paean to marriage, the patriarchal family, and biological creation and depicted his ideal commonwealth as having absolutely "no touch" of "masculine love."

The English theater, with its transvestite tradition, was an especially important arena for the expression of erotic desires and aversions. The target of attacks by Puritans such as Phillip Stubbes who in his *Anatomie of Abuses* (1583) charged that stage plays incited viewers to "play the Sodomits, or worse," Renaissance theater depicted a surprisingly wide range of sexual possibilities. Those possibilities are apparent in Shakespeare's *As You Like It* (1598), for example, in which a boy actor plays a young woman, Rosalind, who disguises herself as Ganymede who pretends to be a woman and is wooed by both Orlando and Phebe and is herself deeply attached to her cousin Celia. Although the play's conclusion pairs off the characters in conventional heterosexual couples, that pairing is conspicuously arbitrary in a play that privileges subjectivity and stresses the importance of imagining alternatives. Indeed, Shakespeare's transvestite comedies, including *Twelfth Night* (1601), encourage the audience not merely to delight in mistaken identities, but also to value the liminal freedom that the plays indulge, especially the (temporary) release from oppressive social conventions. As Valerie Traub has emphasized, in Shakespeare's comedies homoeroticism—both male and female—"is constructed . . . as merely one more mode of desire."

Same-sex desire is also an important component in Shakespeare's other dramas. The relationship of Achilles and Patroclus in *Troilus and Cressida* (1602) is explicitly sexual; Thersites characterizes Patroclus as Achilles' "masculine whore." But the nonsexual bonding in such plays as *Coriolanus* (1606), *Love's Labor's Lost* (1594), and *The Two Noble Kinsmen* (1613) is also infused with romantic and erotic feeling, as are the more complicated relationships of Romeo and Mercutio in *Romeo and Juliet* (1594) and Othello and Iago in *Othello* (1604). The Shakespearean play that most poignantly depicts romantic friendship between males is *The Merchant of Venice* (1596), where the love of Antonio and Bassanio exists alongside Bassanio's need to marry. The dilemma of an older man who loves a younger one who may be attracted to a woman or who, at least, is expected to marry and reproduce is also explored in *Twelfth Night*, as well as in Shakespeare's sonnet sequence and in other poetry of the period. Indeed, the triangular relationship that exists between Antonio who loves Bassanio who loves Portia is fairly common in Renaissance homoerotic literature and reflects the fact that in the Renaissance sexual identity was not rigidly binarized—that is, homosexuality and heterosexuality were not seen as essential and exclusive categories to which all individuals were routinely and permanently assigned.

The Renaissance playwright who depicted homoeroticism most openly was not Shakespeare but Marlowe. Homoerotic incidents are featured in most of his plays, including *Dido, Queen of Carthage* (1587) and *The Massacre of Paris* (1592); but *Edward II*, his great tragedy of a man torn between his hereditary role as king and his love for another man, is his most radical exploration of homosexual love. Ending with the murder of the king by the assassin Lightborn, who thrusts a hot spit into the monarch's bowels, the play daringly inverts the Renaissance's sexual categories. The assassin and his employers are unmasked as truly sodomitical, whereas the apparent sodomite, the suffering king, is revealed as the bare, forked animal, unaccommodated man. In the work's revised economy of meaning, as crystallized in Lightborn's gruesome imitation of homosexual lovemaking, sodomy comes to signify not homosexuality but conspiracy, rape, and murder. The play is also noteworthy for linking the love of Edward and Gaveston with a catalogue of homosexual lovers culled from classical history and myth. By appealing to a classical past when homosexuality was not only not a grave offense, but even a mark of distinction, associated with mighty kings and great philosophers, Marlowe resists his age's dominant construction of homosexuality as sodomitical. (See also ELEGY.)

—*Claude J. Summers*

BIBLIOGRAPHY

Bray, Alan. *Homosexuality in Renaissance England*. London: Gay Men's Press, 1982. ■ Bredbeck, Gregory. *Sodomy and Interpretation: Marlowe to Milton*. Ithaca, N.Y.: Cornell University Press, 1991. ■ Goldberg, Jonathan. *Sodometries: Renaissance Texts, Modern Sexualities*. Stanford, Calif.: Stanford University Press, 1992. ■ ———. "Sodomy and Society: The Case of Christopher Marlowe." *Southwest Review* 69 (1984): 371–378. ■ Saslow, James. *Ganymede in the Renaissance: Homosexuality in Art and Society*. New Haven, Conn.: Yale University Press, 1986. ■ Schleiner, Winfried. "Burton's Use of *praeteritio* in Discussing Same-Sex Relationships." *Renaissance Discourses of Desire*. Claude J. Summers and Ted-Larry Pebworth, eds. Columbia: University of Missouri Press, 1993. 159–178. ■ ———. "'That Matter Which Ought Not To Be Heard Of': Homophobic Slurs in Renaissance Cultural Politics." *Journal of Homosexuality* 26.4 (1994): 41–75. ■ Smith, Bruce. *Homosexual Desire in Shakespeare's England*. Chicago: University of Chicago Press, 1991. ■ Summers, Claude J. "Homosexuality and Renaissance Literature, or the Anxieties of Anachronism." *South Central Review* 9.1 (Spring 1992): 2–23. ■ ———, ed. *Homosexuality in Renaissance and Enlightenment England: Literary Representations in Historical Context*. Binghamton, N.Y.: Haworth Press, 1992. ■ ———. "Marlowe and Constructions of Renaissance Homosexuality." *Canadienne Revue de Littérature Comparée* 21(1994): 27–44. ■ Traub, Valerie. *Desire and Anxiety: Circulations of Eroticism in Shakespearean Drama*. London: Routledge, 1992.

English Literature: Restoration and Eighteenth Century

Almost from the moment of his return from exile in France in 1660, King Charles II established the tone of his court, in town and country, based on personal pleasure and liberty. The drama, his favorite pastime, was reinstated as the main form of courtly entertainment, and sexual liberty was condoned in ways previously unknown. Although it was perfidious to speculate about the King's own sexuality, or even his anatomical body, the way he yoked priapism to divine authority was inescapable. Samuel Pepys the diarist idealized him for precisely this phallic reason and fantasized about his "massive shaft" and "mighty yard."

It was also perilous for playwrights to make sodomitical associations within the drama—depictions of beautiful men as well as their sexual liaisons—in part because the King himself was accused of engaging in overt sodomitical liaisons with the Duke of Buckingham. But interpretation of all these events involves a historical understanding of sodomy (the physical act of anal insertion) as distinct from our modern homosexuality (a psychological state of mind). Without such distinction, it is hard not to commit the sin of historical anachronism. For example, Pepys also records hearing a conversation in 1663 about "buggery," but did not know what buggery was: a remarkable stance for a court libertine like Pepys who claims to have "climaxed" in February 1668 while reading the anonymous, lurid *School of Venus* (translated into English in 1667).

A broad context is necessary to understand these complex sodomitical relations and the literature it produced. The Restoration was an age of transformation in philosophy and science, as well as a period of intense English nationalism and partisan politics. Imbroglio, intrigue, and scandal flourished, and though the libertinism of the court was overtly heterosexual, underneath resided what we today would call a tolerated bisexuality that had few parallels in prior European history. Pepys's London was a world of man–boy relations in which broadsides commonly called attention to relations with pages and "link boys vile." Homophobic broadsides decried these practices, and sermonists condemned them; still they thrived in town and at court.

It is a myth that Restoration bisexuality existed primarily in the form of male–female commensurability: that is, a man appearing with his (female) whore on one arm and his (male) catamite or "pathic" on the other. The issue is not the commensurability of *both* a male and female at the same time, but the interpretive problem of historical anachronism: studying the history of sexuality backward. Indeed, we must guard against the tendency to understand homosexuality through the eyes of its later versions in the nineteenth and twentieth centuries. The English Restoration (1660–1700) was populated with homosexual men in our modern sense, but they were neither portrayed on the stage as effeminate nor represented as flourishing in the homosexual subcultures that developed in the eighteenth century. The drama of the epoch portrays these arrangements more clearly than other literary forms. For example, in Sir George Etherege's *The Man of Mode* (1676) Medley's relation to Dorimant is indicated by their kissing, but despite Dorimant's interest in Medley's appearance, he has nothing in common with such effeminate fools as Lorenzo in APHRA BEHN's *The Amorous Prince* (1671), who pursues a girl dressed as a page boy, or Peacock in Edward Howard's *The Six Days Adventure* (1671), who embraces a link boy. Medley gossips with women but does not pursue them, nor should he as a figure representing the sodomite in love with Dorimant. Nemours in Nathaniel Lee's *The Princess of Cleve* (1689) is another character based on bisexual stereotypes; having consummated a sexual relationship with his young friend Bellamore, he allegedly retains his amorous interest in women.

In the drama, this bisexuality is portrayed as hierarchical by age (old–young) and social class (rich–poor) rather than as biologically predetermined, and its hierarchical status is further evident in the *disparity* of age between active and passive partners, especially the older man and younger boy, whether pageboy, linkboy, groom, or porter. Bisexuality flourished in the Restoration court and was abetted by the widespread practices of cross-dressing and transvestism that served to disguise erotic attachments. Cross-dressing was common at war as well as at home, on sea and land, in business and commerce where young women dressed as men to gain employment. These and other versions abound in the plays of the period.

JOHN WILMOT, THE EARL OF ROCHESTER (1647–1680), courtier and notorious libertine, epitomizes these trends. In real life, he was the extreme Restoration rake—a carefree aristocrat driven by lust and license—but his literary offensiveness and personal sexual recklessness brought him into disfavor even with the open-minded King. His poem called *Satyr against Mankind* (1675) intimates the degree of his vaunted misogyny and libertinism and his Sapphic vision of utopian male self-sufficiency. But it is his poetry, permeated with invocations of drunken revelry, sexual dissipation, and male separatism, and his involvement with the much disputed (and never staged) play *Sodom: or, The Quintessence of Debauchery,* which brilliantly demonstrates Restoration versions of bisexuality. Here androgynous boys are idealized as creatures of a "softer sex," often with the bodies of girls, but man–man relations—sexual relations between chronologically and economically similar men—are discouraged. In Rochester's works, more generally, the phallus (a force extending beyond the anatomic penis) is continually threatened by predatory females, who, even if not altogether ready to castrate the vital male organ, constantly attack it. Rochester's response entails a version of male separateness not entirely dissimilar from the radical gay and lesbian separatism of our time. And his "lewd boys" constitute a viable alternative to the "seductive females" represented as cunning, forbidding, and capable of emasculating the male.

Rochester's influence served to crystallize the image of the new self-styled sodomite as bisexual. But it was dangerous to stage his plays during periods of political upheaval (for example, in 1680 during the Popish Plot), and doubt remains about his personal view of the new versions of bisexuality. His rakes debate sodomy—as perhaps did the real-life rakes of the epoch—in new contexts related to their own vaunted libertinism, and often derogate its origins in what we post-moderns would term "gender preference." The denial sounds strange to our ears, but no matter how much the rakes profess to have developed a taste for sodomitical sex (that is, genitally considered), they are more often than not mute about their preference for males over females. In real life, sexual types were facilely jumbled together. John Hoyle was reported to have been sodomitical in the new, bisexual sense. He was Rochester's friend, as well as the chum of the female playwright Aphra Behn. On the surface, the three had little in common, yet they were associated in a number of biographical ways, including their mindset about the new bisexual sodomy.

On the stage, the dramatic "male bawd" also had close sodomitical affinities, especially insofar as metropolitan and court culture afforded him an opportunity for gain and exploitation. The bawd first appears in Etherege's *She Wou'd If She Cou'd* (1668) in the character of Sir Joslin Jolley and is developed in such familiar dramatic figures as Sir Jolly Jumble in Thomas Otway's *The Soldier's Fortune* (1681) and Coupler in Vanbrugh's *The Relapse* (1696). Both pursue brawny young men who are idealized as masculine and virile. Some actors with particularly attractive physiques specialized in sodomitical roles. They were often said to have entered into sodomitical relationships themselves, but whether this was a consequence of their public image or historical fact is hard to ascertain. The physically splendid Edward Kynaston was reputed to have been the favorite of the Duke of Buckingham; William Mountfort was alleged to have had romantic liaisons with Lord Chancellor Jeffries. Anthony Leigh was the best known of the sodomitical actors and made a fortune playing the leading roles, from Old Bellair in Etherege's *Man of Mode* to Chylas in Rochester's *Valentinian* (staged by 1684). Some sodomitical actors, James Nokes, for example, acquired their reputation by specializing in women's roles. Thomas Clark was adroit in playing young, beautiful men who were the object of older men's attentions. His career during the 1670s and 1680s coincided with the golden decades of bisexual representation on the stage, and he was especially praised for portraying a series of sodomitical characters in plays by Lee, John Dryden, and Rochester. These actors gradually shaped an English audience accustomed to sodomitical types. More specifically, however, sodomy entered serious drama through high heroic tragedy, such as Almazor in Dryden's *The Conquest of Granada* (1672) and in Lee's plays where erotically charged relationships between men figure prominently, as in the figures of Massinissa and Massina in *Sophonisba* (1675).

In these plays, male couples are often portrayed as "lovers" despite their concomitant retention of female lovers whom they marry. Such representative sodomitical "couples" are Alexander and Hephestion in Lee's *The Rival Queens* (1677), Anthony and Dorabella in Dryden's *All for Love* (1678), and two couples in Rochester's *Valentinian*. Lee, possibly homosexual himself and reputedly deranged, was especially adroit in the manipulation of sodomites on the stage without giving political offense, to such a degree that within Restoration dramatic history, he must be considered the master of homosexual representation. In other heroic plays, the love between men is merely homoerotic or homosocial without the slightest trace of genital intimacy. Moreover, students of the future will want to consider the degree to which men love other men in Otway's *Venice Preserv'd* (1682) and Lee's *Massacre of Paris* (1689) and *Caesar Borgia* (1680), a topic considered too politically sensitive by previous generations. The characters—Pierre and Jaffeir, the Duke and Ligneroles—are at least homoerotic and in a few cases (such as Ascanio, a "fine, effeminate Villain" in *Caesar Borgia*) actively sodomitical.

As the 1680s wore out, it was clear that sodomy had become a mainstay of English literature, especially on the stage, where it was always implicit that homosexuality was both flourishing and fashionable in English society at large. But both its pervasiveness and popularity remain riddled with factual quandaries, not least the degree to which its fashionability increased owing to King William III's notoriety as a sodomite. In this sense, the Stuart import of a Dutch Orangist king amounted to much more than a religious solution to a national problem.

It was perfidious, of course, to allude to the King's sexuality on the stage, but the ephemeral literature of the 1690s is permeated with references, to say nothing of benign allusions, to William and his catamites, and frank discussion of such a delicate matter could not have been conducted if its audiences had not already been shaped. Playwrights such as the now obscure Thomas Southerne and John Crowne, as well as the popular comic dramatists William Congreve and John Farquhar, all include varieties of sodomites in their plays. In Southerne's comedy *The Maid's Last Prayer* (1693), "Gayman" is the only figure who escapes without being labeled impotent or sexually compromised. Lord Malpert pimps for his wife by recruiting "Gayman" as her lover, and Malpert's friends Sir Symphony and Sir Foeminine Fanviles, are ridiculed for their degree of effeminacy. "Lovely" in Crowne's *The Married Beau* (1694) is married but "passionately fond" of, and sexually aroused by, his friend Polidor. Dorax in Dryden's *Don Sebastian, King of Portugal*

(1689) is obsessed with sodomy as a mode of behavior and state of human existence. Vainlove in Congreve's *The Old Bachelor* (1693) belongs to the litany of males of the 1690s who pursue women without erotic interest in catching them. In summary, Restoration drama displays a broad variety of homosexual male figures ranging from the genitally active braggadocio to the passively effeminate married man. It may be the richest treasure trove in English literature for its diversity of homosexual types.

However, no appraisal of the homosexuality of the English Restoration can be complete without discussion of its broad cults of CROSS-DRESSING that filled a number of socioeconomic purposes. On the stage, cross-dressing was used differently from how it had been in Elizabethan or Jacobean drama. Now, women were played by actresses who dressed as men primarily to display their legs; however, when men pursue other men on the stage, one of the parties is unfailingly played by a woman, as in Dryden's *Marriage a la Mode* (1673), where Doralice dresses as a boy and flirts with Palamede. But there are literally dozens of others. In Aphra Behn's *The Amorous Prince* (1671), Lorenzo tries to procure a page who is a woman in disguise. In Wycherley's classic *The Country Wife* (1675), Horner pursues Margery Pinchwife who is dressed as her younger brother. In Southerne's *Sir Antony Love* (1691), the Abbé pursues "Love," cast as a woman in disguise as a young man. Men cast as women, women as men: The point about fluid homosexual relationships is made explicitly through cross-dressing, but social types and social classes are also intentionally confused to locate the source of sodomitical affections.

Sodomitical arrangements based on real-life cross-dressing were equally diverse. For example, it is impossible to conceive of the historical "Beau Wilson"—Edward Wilson, an adolescent youth from Norfolk, who came to London in 1690 and was soon "kept" in sumptuous style by an admirer—as executing his dangerous amorous liaison with an anonymous nobleman, or noble woman, without the device of cross-dressing: The confusion enabled their nocturnal visitations. In *Love-Letters* (1723) an anonymous author wrote about their torrid affair a generation after it had supposedly occurred and emphasizes why Wilson entered his lover's house each night dressed as a *woman* and emerged the next morning in the garb of a *man*. But as the 1690s wore out, a backlash against these practices abetting gender ambiguity and sexual license gave way to severe moral rectitude and campaigns for change. Jeremy Collier spearheaded the reform of the stage, decrying its explicitly sexual material and claiming it was corrupting Britain's

youth. New societies for the reform of manners and propagation of Christian values arose seeking to quash the sexual liberty of previous decades. As a result, what had been above surface went below, and in just a decade or two, the attitude toward homosexuality in England assumed a meaner aspect: more stringent, less tolerant, legally severer than it had been for generations.

Few texts illuminate these transformations more clearly than the *Love Letters*. It is inconceivable that this small work of about forty pages could have been written a generation earlier—in the 1690s—when its historical plot is set. By the 1720s, the English novel and the social needs it fulfilled had begun to develop, its cultivation of diverse epistolary forms a subtle means of coping with the new stresses brought by urbanization to relations between the genders. Its "plot within the plot"—the story of Chloris and her amours—verges on pornography and narrates one of the earliest scenes of homosexual blackmail in literature. It is also a path-breaker in the developing novel itself and significant for the way it encodes literature and politics within a homosexual matrix. It can be read as political allegory, its versions of deviant sexuality the camouflage for diverse interest groups. Its author represents sentimental attachment purely in erotic terms, as in the nobleman's idealization of young Willy and his "ruby lips," and the mysterious plot compels the reader to wonder about the necessity for secrecy in all homoerotic liaisons. Some readers of 1723 must have pondered what all-male erotic attachments were if *de rigeur* they had to be represented through such extreme secrecy.

Secrecy, indeed, was the emblem of the early eighteenth-century homosexual—even the new commercial consumption promoted it. With secrecy in urban settings, new possibilities arose for a clandestine but economically viable homosexual subclass. The new consumer wealth enabled pleasure to become legitimized in ways it had previously been for the ruling class only and paved the way for the birth of leisure time. Leisure required amusement and mandated new forms of personal pleasure, as early Georgian homosexual men soon discovered. By the mid-eighteenth century, the homosexual male was no longer a social creature confined to courts, cities, or dramatic stages but roamed open spaces freely despite the need for secrecy, cruising and hunting, in pleasure grounds, parks, coffee and tea houses, at concerts and operas, masquerades and carnivals. Spas and watering holes attracted older, well-heeled homosexuals who had the cash to pay for younger men. The discerning human eye began to view the homosexual in new visual arrangements, especially in the light of his attire, gait, and manners. At the opera, introduced to England by 1730, eunuchs and castrati focused the viewer's attention; in the parks and green squares, men cruising other men proved less furtive than they thought; at the masquerade, the possibilities for disguise-within-revelation were paramount. The "London Spy"—a *nom de plume* Edward Ward took for himself as he surveyed the sights of "London Town"—claimed to see "sodomitical culture flourishing everywhere." Others penetrated the famed "molly houses," basements and crevices where men gathered for genital contact. But here secrecy was preserved at all costs in view of the severe legal consequences of detection.

Such proliferation of a homosexual type and its attendant repertoire of behavior was bound to elicit national opposition. Historically and culturally, repression has always resulted in subterfuge, and as England grew less tolerant of homosexuality than it had been in the Restoration, the "mollies" (one of the new names given to homosexual men) coped by developing an underground subculture providing economies, meeting places, living arrangements, covert signs of recognition, even rings to ensure professional preferment. Homosocial arrangements, as distinct from homosexual attachments, had always been a staple of upper-class life in England and continued to be, but not without the menace of exposure threatened by the new molly subculture. For example, the SCRIBLERIANS—the group of political writers and poets that included Alexander Pope, Jonathan Swift, John Gay, Thomas Parnell, John Arbuthnot, and Robert Harley, the Earl of Oxford—was homosocial in the extreme. But they wanted no filiation with "mollies," who were uniformly viewed as social pariahs. When the Earl of Stanhope, a powerful Whig politician who was also a publicly acknowledged sodomite, died in 1721, the opposition lost no opportunity to desecrate his name by linking it to lewd sodomitical preferment. He, rather than Sunderland, the Whig statesman despised by the new Prime Minister Robert Walpole, may be the mysterious "noble man" of the anonymous *Love Letters*.

By the 1730s, the old *bisexuality*, tolerated and cultivated, had clearly come under strain, if not disappeared altogether from public view. The new homosexuality was monolithically *male*: to be attracted to women was proof of outsider status and extremely dangerous. Secrecy flourished, caution heightened, and homosexual attachments formed at school endured for life, as HORACE WALPOLE and THOMAS GRAY found. Eventually, one lived in the daily chill of threats of exposure and blackmail, as Henry Fielding demonstrated in his novels and as any number of English homosexual aristocrats discovered, comforted only

when in the guaranteed safety of one's own homosexual group. Designation as a "sodomite" was now inexorably pejorative; what was clear by mid-century was that it now also inevitably led to radical public disgrace and the pillory. The public, rallied by new fundamentalist religions and developing fanatical sects, equated the slightest hint of sodomitical behavior with Satan, the Beast, the old Leviathan. The tolerant world of Charles II, and Rochester's Restoration stage, was now a nostalgic will-of-the-wisp: the pastoral memory of a bisexual Golden Age, incapable of being reified in Georgian London or ancien-regime Paris. When Lemuel Gulliver exhorts the Court of Brobdingnag about "this horrible Vice" at home—the sin of sodomy—he speaks for Everyman.

But despite its disrepute, at home the "vice" abounded, as the new literature demonstrated. Blending allegory, political satire, and social commentary, it often amounted to a sustained prose of attack, as in Thomas Gordon's *Conspirators* (1721). This stunning tract was composed as a "history of Cataline" and a commentary on the corruption of his age, but was in fact an exposé of the present, Walpolian administration. Dedicated "To the Right Honourable the Earl of S——d" (Lord Sunderland) because the author "cast his Eyes about for a Patriot and a Statesman, of your Lordship's shining Character," it was merely signed "Britannicus." The writer's invective is patent: "We live, *my Lord,* in an Age of Degeneracy and Corruption"; his call to action urgent, challenging "S—, like a second Cato, [to] persecute Corruption where-ever you find it." Homosexuality in all its newfangled forms is the target of the writer's debunking, especially the "effeminate Luxury" of Cataline's era for having "sunk into all the contrary Extremes of Vice, and Luxury, and every sort of Debauchery." But the author thinks modern sodomy worse than Roman because

the Entertainment, of which I am now speaking, was of a kind unknown before to the *Romans:* A Midnight Revel, where both Sexes met in strange Disguises; such as *Centaurs,* Satyrs, Sylvans, and the like; and convers'd with the utmost Freedom; without being suppos'd to know each other's Sex or Quality.

New forms of nocturnal revelry, especially masquerades and operas, are encouraging the new effeminate vice. As the author writes retrospectively, "the whole Stream of the People fell into this tempting [sodomitical] Debauchery." This is the sin of all-male sex: "the Men forgetting the Dignity of their Sex, and sunk into a Womanish Softness, like that Sex, were dress'd and adorn'd at the Looking-glass, and went out glittering with a Weight of Gold and Jewels." The Georgians who now practice sodomy are as debauched as the Romans: boys then and boys now remain the source. "*Ganymedes* were pamper'd and supported at a high Rate at his [Cataline's] Expence; and this propensity for Boys . . . gave them in this a Touch of his *own Taste,* but very slily avoiding to declare what his own particular views were."

From the 1720s forward, works like *Satan's Harvest Home: Reasons for the Growth of Sodomy in England* (1729) alerted the public to the allegedly new social menace. The developing novel was less monolithically pejorative than these didactic tracts. It was usually preoccupied with providing readers—as in Tobias Smollett's novels—with realistic descriptions of the new social type, first to elicit recognition and then to instill revulsion. In Daniel Defoe's novels of the 1720s, piracy is a trope for sodomy, the violence of pirates a metonymy for all-male ravishment, as in the transgressive milieu of Captain Singleton and Wilmot. Passing for "brothers" they link up, and in the *History of the Pirates* (1724), Defoe makes plain how nebulous are the borders between homoerotic and homosexual affinity. Even in his mythic version of contemporary economic reality, Defoe had imagined two men—Robinson Crusoe and Friday—stranded alone on a deserted south Pacific island. They engage in no genital contact, but the absence of women itself requires symbolic interpretation as a sign that something fundamental in human sexual relations has altered. Women also explored these new representations. In transgressive narratives, for example in the works of Aphra Behn, sodomitical relations loom large, as in her *Dutch Lovers* (1673), and the satirist and political writer Mrs. Delariviere Manley regularly displays women dressed as male pirates who venture out to sea. In Samuel Richardson's fiction, women are portrayed in such intimate homoerotic relationships (Clarissa Harlowe and Anna Howe, for example) as to prompt modern readers to wonder whether the origins of lesbianism as a psychological state of mind do not lie here rather than in the world of Havelock Ellis. And readers in our time of JOHN CLELAND's *Memoirs of a Woman of Pleasure* (1749), the pornographic novel we know as *Fanny Hill*, continue to claim that they cannot imagine this primal encodement of "Enlightenment sexuality" without its well-positioned scenes in which Cleland depicts two men engaging in torrid genital sex—so intrinsic are these sodomitical materials to the curious bourgeoise imagination at mid-century. But it was in the rough and tough homophobic milieu of satire—in black comedies such as Smollett's *Advice and Reproof*

(1746), *Roderick Random* (1747), and *Peregrine Pickle* (1751)—that all-male friendships were decried in their darkest silhouettes. *Humphry Clinker* (1771), for example, makes no bones about desecrating a certain "Captain C——, tall and raw-boned, hooknosed," whose "arch-leer" reveals his homosexual identity.' And in Laurence Sterne's *Sentimental Journey* (1768), the crowd's homophobia lies on the verge of erupting into fury when faced with Yorick's ambiguous sexuality. In general, the oversensitive sentimental man's sexuality was a thing to be denounced as "sodomitical." And the diaries, memoirs, and letters of the era offer a wider range of responses and representations, but here too ingrained homophobia threatens all human interaction. Charlotte Charke, the daughter of the poet laureate Colley Cibber, was perceived to be such a menace to society that she had to cross-dress and live in disguise from her real self, as a man, to get anywhere—her *Memoirs* (1755) read like an eighteenth-century version of life imitating art.

Life in British schools and colleges thrust same-sex relations into the public spotlight. The English school was, after all, an institution based on male bonding, where emotional attachments were formed that lasted a lifetime. Eton and Harrow, Oxford and Cambridge, produced figures like the "Quadruple Alliance"— Horace Walpole, Thomas Gray, Richard West, Thomas Mason—whose lives cannot be understood apart from their erotic schoolboy infatuations. In this system, social pressure rewarded immaturity by impeding emotional development in an atmosphere of pranks and jokes, so well captured in Smollett's *Peregrine Pickle* (1751). Flogging and sadomasochism flourished, as satires and novels depict; nocturnal revels, cross-dressing, and play-acting thrived despite denunciation. A Winchester schoolboy placed a huge phallic obelisk in his rooms that was worshipped by the other boys. The all-male colleges of Oxbridge carried these traditions forward, denying that they did so.

All through the persecutions and gender transformations of the period, the soldier was idealized as the embodiment of beautiful form within a shapely body. From youth, Englishmen had abundant opportunity to see each other nude: in school, on playing fields, at sea and in battle. As Richard Steele noted in *The Ephebe* (1721), a periodical, nude male bodies captured the male imagination. Others asked questions about the ancient Greeks: how they viewed male bodies and whether it was lawful to see them unclothed. It is hard to know when the military type— the clean-cut male with symmetrical body in uniform—was first idealized, but by the 1740s, it had been established, giving rise to a war literature not so different from our own. Street urchins represented the antithesis: Ragged, tattered, unkempt, undernourished, poverty stricken, marked with the pox or clap, they were ridiculed rather than idealized—asymmetrical creatures of a day, victims of a society riddled with internal contradiction.

Thomas Gray, the famous poet who lived as a recluse in a Cambridge college, met Victor de Bonstetten in London in 1767. Then twenty-one, the Swiss minor count was traveling north on the Grand Tour. (Gray was more than old enough to be his father.) Bonstetten was stunningly handsome, a military type, of smooth frame, clean-cut with cropped hair, ostentatiously military. Gray fell in love with him almost at first sight and whisked him up to Cambridge, where the two spent the better part of three months together. During this period, they exchanged no letters owing to their proximity. They saw each other every day and perhaps at night as well. A few months later, Bonstetten tired of Cambridge and perhaps tired of Gray as well. Within months, Gray was dead, perhaps of a broken heart. Thomas West, a gifted English lyric poet, had been the erotic flame of Gray's life, but Bonstetten did not linger far behind despite the discrepancy in age.

Others, like WILLIAM BECKFORD, idealized exotic, Eastern youths found further down the Adriatic: brown-skinned, brawny-armed, dark-lashed, speaking in non-Western tongues. Not the alpine soldier or Mediterranean sailor, but the sons of sultans and pashas were the idealized young Ganymedes here. These idealizations can be interpreted along the lines of national stereotypes and opposite attractions (north-south, east-west), but considerations of religion and the bourgeois family also played a part. The wealthy Beckford could afford to have anything he craved, including the sons of Eastern princes; he had less free will in his disgust for things domestic and familiar. But for every Beckford, there was a Gibbon. When Edward Gibbon, the historian and author of the *Decline and Fall of the Roman Empire* (1776), left England, more or less permanently for Lausanne, he "set up house" with Dyverden, a Vaudois, Calvinist, landed gentry man. Gibbon's letters home describing their first few weeks together are conceptualized along the lines of marriage and the family. Everything domestic and comfortable is shared in their Vaudois dwelling. Although Gibbon is not known to have been homosexual, his language of homosocial domesticity in this correspondence is extraordinary. It verges on the romantic when Gibbon professes that "Marriage to a woman" could not be better managed.

These aggressive, almost conquering, homosexual types had counterparts in the effete, delicate, nervous male. The Georgians themselves constituted a culture obsessed by all things "neurasthenic": nervous human anatomies, nervous societies, nervous governments. It was predictable they should construe the new, sensitive, often effeminate and aesthetic male in the light of his nervous anatomy and physiognomy. This is exactly what Mrs. Hester Thrale, the shrewd observer of English society, did when analyzing playwright Richard Cumberland's character. Passages of her *Diary* (1786) verge on modern psychoanalysis when she "reads" Cumberland's sexuality by "interpreting" his face, nerves, body. Thrale's conclusion was that he was representative of the new "neurasthenic type," in her view an epicene, narcissistic, possibly hysterical male. Medical theory of hysteria had undergone centuries of transformation by the time Thrale pronounced on Cumberland in the 1780s, including the view, adumbrated in the eighteenth century, that *males* could also be hysterical. Mrs. Thrale extended this posture, suggesting that clinically narcissistic neurasthenics like Cumberland also possessed different sexualities.

By the 1760s, a number of developments converged to sustain the view that sodomites were overrunning London, a view with parallels in our urban life. But the shrillest voices were not those demanding reforms in politics, education, and the arts, but in the lifestyles of the upper classes, whose dissipation, they claimed, filtered down. The year 1764 was particularly ominous: More than the usual number of arrests were made, and there was abundant gay bashing. It was also an election year in which candidates were smeared by the acerbic slogan that sodomy was a necessary *precondition* for election. For example, Charles Churchill, the poetic satirist, claimed in *The Times* (1764), while in a Swiftian mood of *reductio ad absurdam,* that homosexuals now controlled London; as proof, he offered the proliferation of all-male clubs. In fact, they had existed for some time, but Churchill's rhetoric attempted its point by absurd exaggeration. Sir Francis Dashwood's "Medmenham Monks" gathered clandestinely in deserted castles, decked out in medieval costume, performing satanic rites that included cross-dressed young males. The Hellfires and Beefstakes were less exotic but no less masculine. The Dilettanti, a private society of upper-crust connoisseurs, assembled to exhibit their collections of paintings and neoclassical "marbles"; their subtext exalted all things "Greek," presumably including Greek man–boy love. The Dandies and Macarronis passed themselves off as aesthetes and fashionable beaus; critics other than William Hogarth and Samuel Rowlandson discerned the homosocial basis of their association.

Even so, the stage never lay far from the tip of the civic imagination in responding to these new proliferations. By the 1770s, a theater milieu had developed within metropolitan culture that was *self-contained,* marking its difference from the Restoration stage world. The public considered its complacency scandalous, and some of our modern prejudice against theatrical persons derives from this early antipathy. Criticism mounted in diverse quarters: in hack poems such as William Jackson's *Sodom and Onan* (1776); in claims that plays still allegorized the sodomitical scandals of the gods mirrored in modern metropolitan society; and, of course, through direct attack on specific sodomites like Samuel Foote, actor and dramatist. He was no Adonis, but functioned as the center of a homosexual London network, and hurt himself by being seen in the constant company of Francis Delaval, a young man who possessed everything Foote lacked, especially family name, a face widely admired, position, and fortune. But whereas Delaval married the monstrously corpulent but wealthy Lady Isabella Pawlet, Foote remained single. Their intimacy bewildered the town and elicited malicious gossip—the inevitable conclusion, sodomitical debauchery. When Delaval's own plays were discovered to be permeated with sodomitical allusions, the criticism was said to have been well grounded.

Only a few voices resisted the allegations of social contamination and petitioned for toleration: Voltaire in Switzerland, Cesare Beccaria in Italy, and later, JEREMY BENTHAM in England. The scientists as yet ventured no theories—sodomy after all remained a sin against every branch of human society. Lockean associationism and Newtonian mechanism had virtually no effect on any secular conception of the sodomite, nor did the French *philosophes* tamper with it. The vast body of thought now classified as "European Enlightenment" commented on sodomy but pronounced nothing capable of changing its destiny. Lady Mary Wortley Montagu's sense of an emerging "third sex"—a kind of pre-Darwinian anticipation—was a witty construction intuitively articulated, without any knowledge of what the thing actually was. Nor did lawyers or medics have a clue. Doctors noted it and examined patients manifesting its symptoms, but discovered nothing anatomical beyond ulcerations on the sphincter affirming penetration. Not for another century would *homosexuality* become medicalized. A case in the Old Bailey dating from the 1720s suggests interest in the medical causes of sodomy, but not even these early Georgian "mad doctors" ventured views beyond the old saw that its frustrations could lead to insanity. I have not found a single case history written up by an eighteenth-century doctor.

If there was no "gay science," there nevertheless was plenty of "gay fiction": satirical, realistic, inciden-tal, and—after the 1780s—"Gothic." Connections between sodomy and Gothic sensibility remain difficult to pinpoint but exist nevertheless. The essence of the Gothic experience, in whatever form, is terror: moonlit moors, haunted castles, monsters, vampires, Frankensteins preying on human lambs. But which terror is most unspeakable? The reply supplied at the end of the eighteenth century was the perverse sexuality that could not be named. Only cannibalism—the devouring of raw, uncooked, human flesh—was worse, and it had not yet entered the Georgian imagination as it has ours. The point is not that diverse authors invented sodomitical outlaws, wolf men, vampires, and the like but that the sodomites themselves—Horace Walpole, Beckford, MATTHEW "MONK" LEWIS—invented and fantasized about this kind of Gothic fiction because it served as a metaphor for their own status as pariahs.

The Gothic fiction of the final decades of the century encompassed a large body of printed works, much of it, like Lewis's *The Monk* (1796), thriving on cross-dressing and the gender ambiguity of homosexual disguise. But even more so than Gothic sensibility, the French Revolution altered the fate of the European homosexual: his life, economy, social milieu, art—every aspect of his world. And the sense of homosexuality that literary figures such as Wordsworth and Coleridge, Shelley and BYRON, inherited was rather different from the one Beckford and Lewis—to name but two—knew. The alteration was fundamentally political, as Bentham insisted. In a new society overrun with political credos about man in relation to the state, the homosexual would become marginalized in ways never before conjured. No longer did his niche and function exist in a gray realm capable of subtle differentiation, as it had been for the era of Pepys and Rochester. He was now, like Cain in Byron's play of that name (1821), a villain and outlaw; a threat to the very concept of the state itself. As a consequence, he had to be marginalized because of the terror he exerted. The new novelists of the Regency and Victorian world—Anthony Trollope, William Makepeace Thackeray, Charles Dickens—saw to it that he was. (See also GOTHICISM and TRAVEL LITERATURE.)

—*George S. Rousseau*

BIBLIOGRAPHY

Aries, Phillipe, ed. *Sexualites occidentales.* Paris: Editions du Seuil, 1982. ■ Garber, Marjorie. *Vested Interests: Cross-Dressing and Cultural Anxiety.* New York: Routledge, 1991. ■ Gilbert, Arthur N. "Buggery and the British Navy, 1700–1861." *Journal of Social History* 10 (1977): 72–98. ■ Halsband, Robert. *Lord Hervey: Eighteenth-Century Courtier.* Oxford: Clarendon Press, 1973. ■ McGeary, Thomas. "'Warbling Eunuchs':

Opera, Gender, and Sexuality on the London Stage, 1705–1742." *Restoration and Eighteenth-Century Theatre Research* 7 (Summer 1992): 1–22. ■ Mayer, Hans. *Outsiders: A Study in Life and Letters.* Cambridge, Mass.: MIT Press, 1984. ■ Rousseau, G. S. *Perilous Enlightenment: Pre- and Post-modern Discourses: Sexual, Historical.* Manchester: Manchester University Press, 1990. ■ Tannahill, Reay. *Sex in History.* Slough, Berkshire: Hollen, 1980. ■ Trumbach, Randolph. "London's Sodomites: Homosexual Behavior and Western Culture in the 18th Century," *Journal of Social History* 11 (1977): 1–33. ■ Trumbach. "The Birth of the Queen: Sodomy and the Emergence of Gender Equality in Modern Culture, 1660–1750." *Hidden from History: Reclaiming the Gay and Lesbian Past.* Martin Duberman, Martha Vicinus, and George Chauncey, Jr., eds. New York: New American Library, 1989. 129–140. ■ Wagner, Peter. *Eros Revived: A Study of Eighteenth-Century Erotica.* London: Secker and Warburg, 1985. ■ Weber, Harold M. *The Restoration Rake-Hero: Transformations in Sexual Understanding in Seventeenth Century England.* Madison: University of Wisconsin Press, 1986.

English Literature: Romanticism

In the popular imagination, the term *romanticism* conjures up notions of intense, freewheeling emotionality, forceful individualism, and unrestrained lyrical expression, usually centered in love as an ultimate human value. The reality of the age (1785–1825) was rather different. If anything, this romantic ideal was generally a protest of lonely, unrealized desire against the increasing cultural restrictiveness with which a newly dominant, puritanical middle class asserted its power. At its core, in England at least, was a publicly sanctioned aversion to sexual transgressiveness of such extremity as to underscore the truth of Louis Crompton's argument that homophobia had reached its zenith in the British Isles in 1810. That was the year of the trial of the "Vere Street Coterie"—so-called to give an aura of dangerous subversion to the unassuming frequenters of the Swan in Vere Street, a molly-house (forerunner of the gay bar), who were apprehended one night in various states of impropriety and charged with capital crimes. The two caught in the act were hanged. Another six, convicted of the lesser charge of "attempted sodomy" (solicitation), were sentenced to the pillory. The procession of these latter men from Newgate Prison and their subjection to punishment on September 27, 1810, shut down central London for the day, drawing an abusive mob of between 30,000 and 50,000 spectators, who subjected the miscreants to such a barrage of offal, rotten fruit, dead animals, and hard missiles that they barely escaped with their lives. Although so hideous a legal public spectacle strains credulity, it points to an indisputable cultural pathology, one that explains why an open expression of homosexuality is out of the question in the literature of this age. In a climate in which the editor of the standard edition of SHAKESPEARE, George Steevens, could feel it his moral duty to bypass the sonnets, one might anticipate that even the mention of homosexuality would be rare, and then almost ritualistically deprecatory. It is indicative of the time that a widely read and cosmopolitan figure such as Samuel Taylor Coleridge, who in his twenties had a succession of intellectual crushes on men and who famously described a great mind as essentially androgynous, routinely scapegoats an actual homosexuality when setting moral limits for art: "Blest indeed is that state of society, in which the immediate purpose would be baffled by the perversion of the proper ultimate end; in which no charm of diction or imagery could exempt the Bathyllus even of an Anacreon, or the Alexis of VIRGIL [*Eclogue* 2], from disgust and aversion," he writes in his *Biographia Literaria*. Androgyny is just a trope, a figure of speech; homosexuality, paradoxically, is so real that it cannot even be named.

The Vere Street Coterie were without exception workers, artisans, and tradesmen. At the other end of the social scale, the persecution was no less severe, but there were options to escape the extremity of the laws. When the affair between WILLIAM BECKFORD and the adolescent Lord Courtenay became obvious to Courtenay's relations in 1785, Beckford, for all his enormous wealth, was forced to leave England. He settled in a luxurious villa in Cintra above Lisbon, where he continued as a social lion, however conspicuous the righteous snubbing of his visiting countrymen. Except for the infamous Dutch persecutions early in the eighteenth century, Europe, whatever private misgivings or clerical prescriptions obtained, was generally tolerant of homosexuality. In 1791, the new French penal code simply dropped it from the category of offenses, an omission sustained in its revisions as the Code Napoléon of 1801 and 1810. Throughout the nineteenth century, Paris, especially after Napoleon's fall, became the natural site for exile, from Lord Courtenay himself down to OSCAR WILDE. (It might be noted that Italy, conceived by the British as the center for this particular pestilence and where male hustling had long been something of an institution, likewise welcomed its share of English homosexual exiles throughout this time and, indeed, well into the twentieth century.) For the well-heeled, a distinct pattern developed. Arrested in incriminating circumstances, the miscreant (the code word commonly applied to homosexuals by the press) posted bond and immediately fled the country. This was the case with the celebrated incident of the Bishop of Clogher of 1822, a *cause célèbre* whipped into such dimensions by the press that it brought about the suicide of the Foreign Secretary and Tory leader of the House of Commons, Viscount Castlereagh, who was being blackmailed to keep his sodomy a secret. (It is perhaps fair to note that his widow denied the truth of the charge, and his biographers seem universally uncomfortable with it.) In this climate, it is worth remarking the bravery of William Beckford, who returned from Cintra and set himself up in palatial grandeur at Fonthill Abbey, where he lived with a retinue of fellow spirits and seems not to have worried too greatly about being systematically refused the notice of his respectable neighbors. Our knowledge of sexual norms and their transgression during this epoch is considerably indebted to his obsessive keeping of scrapbooks chronicling every prosecution for or scandalous insinuation of homosexual behavior, now part of the Beckford Papers in the Bodleian Library, Oxford.

Lesbianism in this period is harder to verify but was probably easier to live. Even while the legend of Sappho was wholly heterosexualized in England as in France, the romantic attachment of the Ladies of Llangollen, LADY ELEANOR BUTLER AND SARAH PONSONBY, was celebrated over a half century. Although sufficiently protective of their reputations that they threatened to sue over insinuations of a sexual liaison and although their cover was likewise sustained by their immediately dismissing an unmarried servant who became pregnant, their penchant for wearing male evening dress, the touching endearments of Lady Eleanor's journals, and the smallness of the bed they shared (still shown, even if in later reproduction, with straight faces by guides to their home Plas Newydd), allow one to surmise that behind a carefully preserved, necessarily impervious facade of good books, good works, and good behavior, the Ladies managed to live the inner romance of their legend. ANNA SEWARD, one of the poetic celebrants of that legend in the later eighteenth century ("Llangollen Vale," 1796), also left a distinguished body of love poetry in her poems of the 1770s to Honora Sneyd, a great beauty who became the wife of Richard Edgeworth (and mother-in-law of Maria), then died in 1780 of consumption. The conventions of female friendship allowed for an intensity of emotional attachment that was just as conventionally repressed among men: In the case of such women, though one cannot always be certain of an erotic extension, homosocial dynamics may strongly reveal themselves. An example is in Mary Wollstonecraft's *Mary, A Fiction* (1788), whose heroine as passionately envelops her consumptive friend Ann as she spurns her detested husband. Inasmuch as the conventional plot of novels about young women during this period ends with the transference of the commodified female from father's to young husband's arms, wherever the formulas are transgressed may be a site for staking a different claim for female identity. It is interesting, for instance, to rethink the centrality of Bath for the female novel from the perspective of the gossipy Hester Thrale, who in 1795 called it "a Cage of these unclean Birds," meaning, a center of lesbian activity. The one female circle of the late eighteenth century that was the subject of actual scandal was that surrounding HORACE WALPOLE at Strawberry Hill in Twickenham. Anne Damer, Walpole's heir and famous in her day as a sculptor, and his literary executor Mary Berry, who was her lover, were the luminaries of the Twickenham set of independent women. There was anonymous snickering in the press, but of course there were neither means for nor attempts at prosecution for female homosexuality. This is a circle whose achievements and activities merit much greater attention than they have received.

In respect to significant literary ramifications of homosexuality, much greater attention ought also to be paid to the theater of this time, writing for which, from the late 1760s into the Regency, seems to have been dominated by women and homosexual men. (Perhaps this is why it is all but totally ignored in literary history.) Isaac Bickerstaffe, who is credited with founding the English comic operetta, was publicly incriminated in 1772 and fled to Paris, where he lived for another thirty-five years. Samuel Foote, who dominated the comedy of the period, was broken professionally by a continuing insinuation of such intensity that it brought on a stroke from which he died in 1777. Although Richard Cumberland's very public conversion to ardent Methodism in the 1790s would seem to remove him from suspicion, the ever-attentive Hester Thrale snidely remarked on his effeminacy. In the Regency, the proclivities of George Colman the Younger were the subject of gossip, so much so that G. Wilson Knight, in inaugurating the modern concern with homosexual elements in BYRON, mistakenly attributed the notorious gay satire, *Don Leon,* to Colman. In one sense, Knight's intuition was telling: Byron's service in 1815 on the Committee for Drury Lane, vetting plays and overseeing the theater's long-term development, would have brought him back into contact with an alternative sexual life that his respectable marriage was designed to prohibit.

Homosexuality is such a reality to Byron's life and of such centrality to his poetry that it may be confidently asserted that only in recent years has either been sympathetically or even correctly "read." Yet it is hard to read what cannot be written, and it cannot be overemphasized how wholly written out of English Romantic culture was any overt expression concerning homosexual experience. The climate of censorship that pervades the years of the war with France (1793–1815), as well as the troubled decade afterward, extends far beyond political matters. So systematic is it that in a later time we must continually remind ourselves how preliminary to all authorial choices was the constriction of acceptable literary discourse. Even heterosexual passion is largely expurgated from English literature during this period, as can be witnessed by Thomas Moore's beginning his career in 1801 with a volume of traditional carpe diem verse and finding himself dogged by reviewers for years as a deleterious influence on British youth. The nice paradox of English Romanticism is how little "romance" it contains.

It is certainly telling that the two mainstream English authors of the age who were willing to write openly of homosexuality never published their remarks. Louis Crompton in different contexts has ably chronicled the lifelong interest of JEREMY BENTHAM in decriminalizing homosexuality, expressed in several unpublished manuscripts of prodigious length. Bentham appears to have felt that the public expression of these moderate views would have so raised an outcry against their author as to have set at risk his whole program of utilitarian values and so never dared bring them to print. In 1818, Shelley created the first unexpurgated, unregendered translation of PLATO's *Symposium* in English, and in projecting its publication began a preliminary "Discourse on the Manners of the Ancient Greeks Relative to the Subject of Love" that was meant to contextualize it so as to mitigate what he well construed as the moral offense implicit in such a publication. Surveying modern, heterosexualized treatments of classical Greek society by French and German novelists, Shelley laments the distortions sanctioned by European culture: "There is no book which shows the Greeks precisely as they were; they seem all written for children, with the caution that no practice or sentiment highly inconsistent with our present manners should be mentioned, lest those manners would receive outrage and violation." Although Louis Crompton, the only critic to look at this discourse from a modern gay perspective, considers it "distinctly marked by English anti-homosexual bias," he does not take into account the necessity Shelley must have felt, were he even capable of securing a publisher for his work, to accommodate as far as possible a reading public assumed to share a pervasive cultural hostility to such a translation of Plato. In any case, the issue of Shelley's sympathy or lack thereof may be thought academic since—tellingly—the full text of his "Discourse" was not published until 1949.

In a climate of homophobia so inveterate that the only open acknowledgments of alternate sexual behavior remain unpublished, where else does one look for understanding of its emotional or sexual dynamics, its cultural conditioning, its psychological costs? Covert expression, or gender displacement, are obvious ploys to writers of all sexual persuasions, but they are just as clearly interpretatively slippery, ever dependent on a particular reader's sense of nuance. A homoerotic interpretation of established authorial relations, such as Koestenbaum has attempted with the collaboration of Wordsworth and Coleridge, is likely to be construed by "straight" readers as special pleading and thus largely to be ignored. But on the other hand, the active willingness of almost all of his critics to participate in Byron's concealments, to hide behind his own cover, so to speak, is more than a little disconcerting. The circumstances in which *Manfred* (1817) was conceived—after hearing M. G. ("MONK") LEWIS, whom Byron himself identified as homosexual, translate the first part of Goethe's *Faust*— should have long ago been enough to allow a general recognition that the unnameable center of the drama is not sibling incest but transgressive and hopelessly divided sexuality. In fact, the recognition did come long ago, in 1902, but has never gained currency in mainstream criticism. Even further recessed within the obscure inner dynamics of Romantic culture is the characteristic phenomenon of the *doppelgänger,* the homosocialized double self. Its presence in so many of Byron's works may translate, depending on the period of his life, into either a fearful or exhilarating sense of multiple potentialities, probably most fully rooted in his sense of sexuality. But the double self figured forth in the writings of his friends Shelley (*Prometheus Unbound,* 1820) and Mary Shelley (*Frankenstein,* 1818) seems to have another, more directly ethical, import. And yet, as Eve Sedgwick has shown in her chapter on James Hogg's 1824 novel *Private Memoirs and Confessions of a Justified Sinner,* the homosocial dynamic impelling the good–evil *doppelgänger* still may mask a cultural homophobia of real significance.

The one genre in which displaced homosexual elements figure large is the gothic novel. The main male authors who created the conventions of gothic fiction in the later eighteenth century—Walpole, Beckford, and Lewis—were all (more or less) homosexual: Walpole may be thought to have been "iffily" so, as Sedgwick claims, or to have been afflicted late in life with what George Rousseau has termed "sexual fragility," but the attachments of his early years make his orientation plain enough. What this trio accomplished over the generation that spans the publication of Walpole's *Castle of Otranto* (1765) and Lewis's *The Monk* (1796) is succinctly articulated by Sedgwick: "The Gothic novel crystallized for English audiences the terms of a dialectic between male homosexuality and homophobia, in which homophobia appeared thematically in paranoid plots." As these comments suggest, the homosexual displacements of the gothic, once identified, are not easily celebrated as liberating. The gothic transgressor always gets his just deserts: for his "unrestrained passions and atrocious actions," we are told on the last page of the novel, the Caliph Vathek goes to a special place in hell, "a prey to grief without end and remorse without mitigation." Not only do we sense a ritualistic enactment of homosexual self-hatred in such paranoid fantasies, but the increasing misogyny of these gothic novels intensifies our awareness that the writers are participating in the cultural pathology they affect to be purging.

By no means on the same level of artistic achievement, John Polidori's *The Vampire* (1819) may nonetheless be thought an important document in this genre of homosexual paranoia. His contribution to the famous writing contest in Geneva that produced *Frankenstein, The Vampire* was actually begun by Byron, then taken over, in what appears a customary act of bonding with an older man, by Polidori. His suicide in 1820 has, in fact, been attributed to a despondency caused by the novella's being published as Byron's. The real terms are less romantic. Handsome, sexually repressed, and mentally unstable, Polidori seems never to have survived being dismissed by Byron as his personal physician over his erratic behavior. (Why Byron in 1816 had need of a "personal physician" as traveling companion is a question rather too seldom asked.) Whatever his psychological instabilities, however, it is the choice of subject matter that most deeply insinuates the homosexual displacement of *The Vampire*. Byron chose the subject after reciting to the entourage of young writers parts of Coleridge's just-published "Christabel," the one major poem of English Romanticism to be enveloped in a figurative homosexuality. There the innocent heroine accepts the witchlike Geraldine into her castle and then her bed, where through a sort of vampirelike experience, she is subjected to the woman's dark influence. That the homophobic Coleridge would picture lesbian experience as corrupting is by no means as culturally interesting as Byron's emphasis of the

passage and then the transference whereby the central figure, the vampire with an unpurgeable infection who craves a fraternity (in the Victorian period, of course, Bram Stoker would make it a sorority) of victims, is taken up by the two male writers. Having given over the subject to Polidori, Byron, in a second act of transference, recasts its terms into the enigmatic tragic hero, Manfred, whose love has destroyed its object, leaving him unfit to live or die. It is not surprising that such a trope should become encoded in these circumstances, for the homosexual as vampire is essentially the cultural condition enforced by the intense homophobia of the Romantic age in England.

One other extension of the literary transgressive strengthens, unfortunate as it may be, this link between the gothic and psychic self-destructiveness: the strange figure of Thomas Lovell Beddoes. The son of the great doctor Thomas Beddoes, who is known for his discovery of nitrous oxide (laughing gas) and as a friend of Wordsworth and Coleridge, Thomas Lovell left what he called "Cantland" after his graduation from Oxford in 1825 and, except for a few visits home, resided in Germany and Switzerland for the quarter century that ended with his suicide in Basel in 1849. A stormy radical but a medical prodigy, Beddoes seems always to have been accompanied by devoted young men about whom his editors and biographers are coyly reserved. His particular niche in English literature comes from his devotion to the macabre. His plays—*The Bride's Tragedy* (1822) and *Death's Jest-Book* (1825–1828)—are obsessed with wasting diseases, multiple deaths, and charnel houses. Here, too, the transgressive and the pathological seem directly related, and the displacement from homosexual self-loathing into an abiding sense of the monstrous enacts an extreme version of the paranoid gothic of earlier generations. In this psychic space, suicide seems all but inevitable.

It is this context, finally, against which one should read the particular odyssey of Byron as expressed in the overarching curve of his achievement. One is touched by the youthful "Thyrza" elegies (1811–1812) for the chorister John Edlestone, as much by the need to dissemble behind a female name as by their expression of authentic affection. One can read the bifurcation of the narrative voice in *Childe Harold's Pilgrimage* (1812–1818), or the unresolved contradictions of the various "Byronic heroes" of his early poems, as directly expressive of sexual uncertainty and ambivalent desire. His tragedies, particularly *Manfred* and *Sardanapalus* (1821), represent heroes who cannot exist within the culture that frames them and have only flamboyant rhetoric to hold on to. All these are recognizable embodiments of the unnameable object of disgust that is the homosexual in this age. Perhaps, indeed, given the paranoid displacements of the gothic tradition, they should even be admired for the acuity of their cultural understanding and the honesty of their attempts to find a means to an acceptance of the self without loathing. But nothing (except the incredible letters) quite prepares us for what Byron finally began to create in 1818, two years after his exile from England, a true poetic of transgressiveness that in *Beppo* (1818), in *Cain* (1821), and, most especially, in *Don Juan* (1819–1824), makes of it a way of life, virtually an ideology. In *Don Juan,* the tragic is turned inside-out into absurd comedy, and one's inability to fit in becomes the means by which one knows oneself most fully human. It is here (and, one is tempted to say, only here) that homosexuality and popular notions of Romanticism can be reconciled, as it is only here that English culture of the Romantic age can glimpse the psychic and sexual liberation that would take another two centuries to begin to effect. (See also ENGLISH LITERATURE: NINETEENTH CENTURY and GOTHICISM.)

—*Stuart Curran*

BIBLIOGRAPHY

Crompton, Louis. *Byron and Greek Love; Homophobia in 19th-century England.* Berkeley: University of California Press, 1985. ■ ——. "*Don Leon,* Byron, and Homosexual Law Reform." *Journal of Homosexuality* 8.3–4 (1983): 53–71. ■ ——, ed. "Jeremy Bentham's Essay on 'Paederesty' (1785)." *Journal of Homosexuality* 3 (1978): 389–405; 4 (1978): 91–107. ■ DeJean, Joan. *Fictions of Sappho, 1546–1937.* Chicago: University of Chicago Press, 1989. ■ Faderman, Lilian. *Surpassing the Love of Men: Romantic Friendship and Love between Women, from the Renaissance to the Present.* New York: Morrow, 1981. ■ Knight, G. Wilson. *Lord Byron's Marriage: The Evidence of Asterisks.* New York: Macmillan, 1957. ■ Koestenbaum, Wayne. *Double Talk: The Erotics of Male Literary Collaboration.* New York: Routledge, 1989. ■ Macdonald, D. L. *Poor Polidori.* Toronto: University of Toronto Press, 1991. ■ Norton, Rictor. *Mother Clap's Molly House: The Gay Subculture in England, 1700–1830.* London: Gay Men's Press, 1992. ■ Rousseau, G. S. "The sorrows of Priapus: anticlericalism, homosocial desire, and Richard Payne Knight." *Sexual Underworlds of the Enlightenment.* G. S. Rousseau and Roy Porter, eds. Chapel Hill: University of North Carolina Press, 1988. 101–53. ■ Sedgwick, Eve Kosofsky. *Between Men: English Literature and Male Homosocial Desire.* New York: Columbia University Press, 1985.

English Literature: Nineteenth Century

From its beginning, the nineteenth century in England had a purposeful homosexual literature. Like earlier and later homosexual writing, it was fettered by oppression, particularly by the long-standing cultural claim that same-sex desire was "unspeakable." As it did in previous eras, this ban on any public and positive expression of a homosexual orientation imposed two general patterns on nineteenth-century homosexual writing. It remained unpublished or was printed only for private circulation; or, when published publicly, its homosexual content was substantially camouflaged or buffered. Yet nineteenth-century English homosexual literature also departs from earlier homosexual writing in several significant ways. Most immediately, it is more abundant and persistent. The homosexual literature of the 140-year period that makes up the long eighteenth century in England was limited to the work of about fifteen men and women, whereas in the next hundred years at least sixty authors produced homosexual writing, if we count minor as well as major figures. In addition, earlier English homosexual writing occurred mainly in separate episodes or clusters, whereas nineteenth-century English homosexual writing proceeds uninterruptedly throughout the whole period. Furthermore, though the theme is not new to the nineteenth century, the age's homosexual writing seems better able to express the differing existential textures of homosexuality and heterosexuality—that is, the contrasts between homosexuality as a biologically nonprocreative love between "sames" and heterosexuality as a love between "differents" that is traditionally thought to be validated only by offspring.

Significant differences and changes also occur within nineteenth-century English homosexual literature. Based on current knowledge, there is considerably more male than female homosexual writing in the century, though the age's lesbian writing contains one of the era's frankest and most detailed homosexual documents. Furthermore, this literature as a whole does not have the steadily progressive development we usually associate with a tradition. Some of the century's homosexual writers recognized and were influenced by others, but, as mentioned, authors usually had to write indirectly and sometimes withheld their work from publication altogether. As a result, nineteenth-century English homosexual literature is a mixture of an incremental, linear tradition, in which authors build on others' examples, and a body of recurring essays, in which authors working independently restate the same motifs and concerns. Moreover, there are marked increases in both the amount and relative openness of English homosexual writing in the course of the century, with a relatively stable stream of writing for the first half of the century followed by significant, if not totally uniform, "bursts" occurring every decade from 1850 on. Despite these variations, nineteenth-century English homosexual literature conveys the overall impression of continuity and unity rather than of rupture and discrepancies. For example, from the very start of the century authors express a definite homosexual orientation and awareness, together with senses of homosexual oppression and of the more profound existential differences between homosexuality and heterosexuality. What changes during the century is not the existence of those awarenesses in themselves, but the relatively greater opportunities authors have to refine and voice them with a limited degree of frankness.

The early nineteenth century in England saw homophobic statements by cultural figures that echoed eighteenth-century spokespersons like the historian Edward Gibbon and that also expressed official public attitudes that remained static throughout the century. In 1803, Samuel Taylor Coleridge described male–male love as "that very worst of all possible vices" in defending SHAKESPEARE's *Sonnets* against a homosexual interpretation. Even Shelley, in his relatively more progressive "Discourse on the Manners of the Ancient Greeks Relative to the Subject of Love" (1818), referred to male–male "passion" as a subject "inconceivable to the imagination of a modern European" and one that "the laws of modern composition scarcely permit a modest writer to investigate." (Fittingly, the complete "Discourse" was not published until 1931, in a limited private edition, and not available to a general readership until 1949.) The most notorious homosexual scandal at this time was the 1810 Vere Street affair, in which several men were arrested at a London gay tavern and later savagely pilloried. As the work of H. Montgomery Hyde and Louis Crompton has shown, this was no isolated incident, but part of a pattern of blatant homosexual persecutions that continued for several decades. There were on average two hangings a year for male–male sodomy between 1806 and 1836, in contrast to one or two per decade during the second half of the eighteenth century. Other notorious homosexual scandals of these years were the 1822 arrest of the Bishop of Clogher and the 1833 and 1841 arrests of William Bankes, a Cambridge friend of BYRON and former member of Parliament.

Notwithstanding this homophobic climate, homosexual writing persisted during these years. The earliest authors in the nineteenth-century English homosexual literary tradition were carryovers from the late eighteenth century, where they had already done important homosexual work. For example, one of the most revealing homosexual documents early in the period is by WILLIAM BECKFORD (1759–1844), who had included homosexual implications in his famous oriental tales of the 1780s, *Vathek* and *Episodes of Vathek,* and who was the subject of a well-known homosexual scandal in 1784. This is Beckford's correspondence with Gregorio Franchi, a former employee who was also homosexual. Numbering over 1,100 items, only a small fraction of which have been published, Beckford's letters to Franchi show him with a clear sense of membership in a persecuted group. On July 11, 1810, he describes the Vere Street victims as "Poor sods! . . . What a pity not to have a balcony in Bow Street to see them pass, and worse still not to have a magic wand to transform into a triumph the sorry sequence of events." And commenting on a newspaper report about the hanging of "a poor honest sodomite" in letters of September and October 1816, he declares, "I should like to know what kind of deity they fancy they are placating with these shocking human sacrifices. . . . The stupid, hypocritical, bloodthirsty vermin! The day will come when their . . . stinking hypocrisies will be revealed to the eyes of all Europe." Another earlier figure, JEREMY BENTHAM (1748–1832), also addressed homosexual topics in work that could not then be published (and still has not been). Advancing on his 1785 "Paederasty" essay, between 1814 and 1818 Bentham drafted almost 500 manuscript pages defending same-sex sexuality against the prejudice of religion and the law. Similarly, LADY ELEANOR BUTLER (1739?–1829), who together with SARAH PONSONBY (1755?–1831) made up the lesbian couple known as the Ladies of Llangollen, continued her journal into the nineteenth century (only partly published to this day). Sections sprinkled with references to "my Better half" and "My Beloved" survive for 1807 and 1819.

The first exclusively nineteenth-century British author of homosexual writing was Byron (1788–1824), whose correspondence with Cambridge friends like Charles Skinner Matthews is suffused with homosexual awareness and whose homosexual writings cluster near the beginning and end of his overwhelmingly heterosexual public literary career. Byron employs and expands on two conventions from earlier homosexual writing that will also figure prominently later in the century—the language of "friendship" to describe homosexual attachment, which provided convenient protection while accurately expressing the greater potential for equality in same-sex romantic bonds; and a combination of the elegiac and military frameworks, where passionate same-sex statements can be made under the cover of a battle situation and can be further blunted for outsider readers by the fact that the beloved may die. Byron's early homosexual poems chiefly concern the Cambridge chorister John Edlestone, whose gift of a ring he commemorates in the 1806 poem "The Cornelian" and whom he memorializes after his death from consumption in the heterosexualized "Thyrza" series of 1811–1812, where he turns Edlestone into a woman. During the same years, Byron also published a revealing prose poem called "The Death of Calmar and Orla" (1807), about the exclusive attachment of two warriors, one of whom lives out his life alone after the other dies in battle. Byron's last poems also have a strong homosexual component, with their focus on his frustrated attraction to Loukas Chalandritsanos, who served as his page during the Greek campaign in which he died.

Some of the century's frankest and most extensive homosexual writing also appears in these early years and is also one of the few examples we now have of candid nineteenth-century English lesbian literature. These are the recently discovered journals of Anne Lister (1791–1840), a Yorkshire estate owner who from 1817 to 1840 kept a detailed coded account of her romantic and sexual relationships with other women locally and abroad, especially with her chief lover, Marianna Lawton, who eventually married. The two volumes of selections that have been published so far, from 1817 to 1826, are a gold mine of earlier modern lesbian language, communication, and consciousness. Here women talk of "Sapphic love," and Lister is emphatically aware of her same-sex orientation. She burns courtship verses sent to her by a man, she declares, so "that no trace of any man's admiration may remain. It is not meet for me. I love, & only love, the fairer sex & thus beloved by them in turn, my heart revolts from any other love than theirs." During these same years, strong homosexual suggestions sometimes appear in the lyrics and dramas of Thomas Lovell Beddoes (1803–1849), the Romantic poet and physician who lived most of his life abroad, where he committed suicide in January 1849, perhaps in distress at the course of his affair with a German actor, Konrad Degen. In "Dream-Pedlary" (1830) and "Threnody" (ca 1844–1848), Beddoes uses the elegy to express romantic male–male feeling, stating in the first that he wants to "Raise my loved longlost boy" and in the second that "The thought of him, who is no more, comes ringing / On my ear." Furthermore, in a May 1827 letter to his friend Thomas Forbes Kelsall, Beddoes interprets Shakespeare's *Sonnets* homosexually, as did several of the century's other gay male writers, calling them "deep & ardent expressions" in which Shakespeare "turned his heart inside out," revealing "the roots of a love, as firm & sacred as the foundations of the world."

The 1830s and 1840s were also the years of the Oxford Movement, which had insinuations about homosexuality directed at it, especially at its two fervently unmarried leaders, Hurrell Froude (1803–1836) and John Henry (later Cardinal) Newman (1801–1890). One commentator declared, "Of the mutually feminine attachment which bound Newman and Froude together, there is no need to say more." In his journal of the late 1820s Froude records his struggle against "vile affections" and, referring to an unnamed undergraduate private pupil, cautions himself "above all [to] watch and pray against being led out of the way by the fascination of his society." Newman's poems of the 1830s echo similar themes ("A Blight"), but also use well-known Biblical male pairs to make suggestive homosexual statements ("David and Jonathan" and especially "James and John," with its reference to a state where "man may one with man remain"). And in his "Separation of Friends," completed in 1836 after Froude's death from consumption, Newman uses the elegy form to express homosexual feeling, apotheosizing Froude as "dearest."

Additionally, it was apparently at this time (ca 1833) that one of the most militant homosexual documents of the era was written, the long poem "Don Leon," which purports to be Byron's own account of his homosexual life but which scholars agree is the work of another, still unidentified, author who nonetheless had to be an insider to the subject. "Don Leon" (which remained unpublished until 1866) is as much a plea for sodomy law reform and a defense of homosexuality in general as it is a record of Byron's male–male adventures—it mentions past and present homosexual scandals (Beckford, Bankes) and, continuing a common tradition among the century's gay writers, invokes Shakespeare's *Sonnets* as a homosexual text. "Don Leon" also clearly sees that homosexuality's biological nonprocreativeness sets it apart existentially and culturally from heterosexuality, describing it as a love that will "Produce no other blossoms than its own." Another revealing private homosexual document of this time is the ardent correspondence of the popular novelist Geraldine Jewsbury (1812–1880) with Jane Welsh Carlyle, which lasted from 1841, shortly after they met, until Mrs. Carlyle's death in 1866. (A selection of these letters from 1841 to 1852 was published in 1892;

Jewsbury destroyed all of Mrs. Carlyle's letters to her on her deathbed.) Apparently bisexual (she had similarly passionate correspondences with two men), Jewsbury speaks to Mrs. Carlyle in intense, and knowing, romantic terms—for example, on October 29, 1841, she declares, "I love you, my darling, more than I can express, more than I am conscious of myself. . . . I feel towards you much more like a lover than a female friend!"

Another of the century's frankest homosexual documents is also of this period. This is the recently published 1849–1850 diary of Edward Leeves (1790?–1870?), a well-to-do English expatriate in Venice about whom little else is known. The diary records Leeves's remorse at the death from cholera of Jack Brand, a trooper in the Royal Horse Guards Blues with whom he had an eight-week affair during a visit to England in the summer of 1849. Filled with frank romantic outpourings ("I told him how I loved him," "I . . . kissed the name on the cold stone which marks [his] last abode"), the diary also reflects the absolute jeopardy identifiable homosexuals faced during the period ("I try to think that his death has removed a great danger, . . . but it is no use"). It also suggests that the Royal Guards were a regular source of homosexual contacts at this time ("What a set of fellows these Blues are! . . . Bill Thompson—a rollicking Yorkshireman of prodigious gifts").

Except for Byron's work, British homosexual writing in the first half of the century could not have had any widespread impact on knowing readers since, as indicated, much of it remained unpublished or appeared from authors with relatively small audiences. That situation changed exactly in the middle of the century, with the appearance of the first nineteenth-century English literary work that evoked homosexuality forcefully for a widespread reading audience and that also served as a compelling landmark for the age's homosexual writers and readers. This was *In Memoriam A.H.H.* by ALFRED, LORD TENNYSON (1809–1892), the long poem of 1850 eulogizing his beloved Cambridge friend Arthur Henry Hallam that Tennyson began in 1833 after Hallam's sudden death. Including philosophical challenges to the period's new evolutionary science and Biblical scholarship amid what is predominantly a set of elegiac lyrics about Hallam, *In Memoriam* contains absolute romantic statements surpassing even the most emotional declarations permitted to same-sex friendships in the age. In sections 17, 103, and 129, Tennyson calls Hallam "all I love," "him I loved, and love / For ever," and "my lost desire." Others of its lines have been turned without strain into chestnuts of heterosexual love— for example, section 27's "'Tis better to have loved and lost / Than never to have loved at all." The poem even echoes traditional code terminology for homosexuality, as when Tennyson describes his feeling for Hallam in section 93 as "The wish too strong for words to name."

But two major protective features blunt *In Memoriam*'s homosexual content. The first is the elegiac situation, which customarily allowed greater same-sex emotional outpouring than in ordinary circumstances and where the fact that the praised loved one is dead gives anxious readers a way to avoid facing the romantic subject fully. Second, Tennyson gives the entire poem a heterosexual frame, ending it with a long "Epilogue" trumpeting the marriage of his youngest sister as symbolic of a restored cosmic order and faith (and forecasting his own long-delayed marriage, which finally took place two weeks after the poem's publication). These cloaking features were successful enough to make *In Memoriam* a Victorian best-seller (the Queen declared it her chief comfort after the Bible) and to generate a critical controversy that continues to the present. Nevertheless, *In Memoriam* became a widespread model and inspiration for later nineteenth-century homosexual and bisexual authors. In addition to being literally echoed in some cases, and not just in England but abroad (as in VERLAINE's 1888 elegy for his student lover, "Lucien Létinois"), *In Memoriam* helped generate the even greater use of elegiac situations in later nineteenth-century male homosexual writing and gave many the sense that more open homosexual speech could be ventured, though of course still hedged by safeguards.

Notable homosexual scandals continued in the second half of the century. Some, like the forced resignations of the Harrow headmaster Charles John Vaughan in 1859 and the Eton master William Johnson in 1872 and the arrest of the painter Simeon Solomon in 1873, were kept out of public view but were open secrets among the educated and upper classes and among writers and artists. Others, like Oscar Browning's dismissal from the Eton faculty in 1875, were mentioned in the press and the House of Commons, though charges were never specified. Still others, like the 1871 Bolton-Park trial and the 1884 and 1889 Dublin Castle and Cleveland Street scandals, were notorious, extensively discussed in the press, and ended in convictions, suicides, or flights to the continent. The best-known of these to modern audiences is undoubtedly OSCAR WILDE's prosecution and imprisonment in 1895, which, as can be seen, was not the first noted homosexual scandal of the century, but which publicized homosexuality nearly universally because of the widespread fame of the accused and new communication technologies. Meanwhile, when they were stated publicly at all, official cultural attitudes remained constant, as in W. E. H. Lecky's remark in his widely read *History of European Morals from Augustus to Charlemagne* (1869) that the "unnatural passion" of male–male love was "totally remote from all modern feelings."

Homosexual writing not only persisted but accelerated in these same decades, however. In the 1850s Tennyson's close friend Edward FitzGerald (1809–1883) published two works that to a knowing eye would have hinted strongly at his homosexuality. In his translation of Jamí's *Salámán and Abs l* (1856), an unmarried Shah produces a child without the aid of a woman. And in translating the Epicurean *Rubáiyát of Omar Khayyém* (1859), FitzGerald removed both the woman and the youth addressed in the original and left the sex of the beloved deliberately unidentified. Much more directly revealing of FitzGerald's homosexuality are his letters, particularly those about William Kenworthy Browne from the 1830s through 1850s and about "Posh" Fletcher and other sailors in the 1860s. The most open homosexual work of this decade was the 1858 *Ionica*, published anonymously by William Johnson (1823–1892), who changed his name to Cory after his dismissal from Eton. Cushioned by some heterosexual poems and by the classical or Medieval settings of most of the rest, *Ionica* contains several ardent expressions of male–male desire (for example, "Desiderato" and "A Separation," with its promise that "In brighter days to come / Such men as I would not lie dumb").

Inspired by *Ionica*, in 1861 JOHN ADDINGTON SYMONDS (1840–1893) began the succession of poems about other men that he peppered friends with in several privately printed volumes of the 1870s and 1880s and that occasionally appeared in his publicly distributed books as well. During these same years, Symonds also began the voluminous correspondence that is an invaluable source for his homosexuality, and his life was changed forever in 1865 when a homosexual Cambridge friend, F. W. H. Myers, introduced him to WHITMAN's work. CHRISTINA ROSSETTI (1830–1894) published *Goblin Market* in 1862, with at least three poems of strong lesbian implication: "My Dream," "The World," and especially the long title poem, where one sister, threatened with death from "suck[ing] fruit globes fair or red," is saved by another who, antidotally, has the goblins spread their fruits "against her mouth" and then begs her sister to "Hug me, kiss me, suck my juices / . . . Eat me, drink me, love me." Rossetti broke or rejected two engagements and maintained a lifelong attachment to her mother, sister, and religious communities of women, facts that, together with this material, suggest a lesbian aspect to her sexuality.

In 1864, Newman published his *Apologia Pro Vita Sua,* with its effusive closing dedication to the Rev. Ambrose St. John, who had apparently replaced Hurrell Froude in his feelings. Several of Newman's letters after St. John's sudden death in 1875 contain passionate statements, and on Newman's own death fifteen years later, the two men were buried at his request in the same grave. Between 1864 and 1866, the young religious enthusiast Digby Mackworth Dolben (1848–1867) wrote a group of love poems about his fellow Eton student Martin Le Marchant Gosselin that appeared, only in part and with some circumspection, in the first collection of his work in 1911. GERARD MANLEY HOPKINS (1844–1889) met Dolben at Oxford in 1865 and pursued him in a series of letters, while also obsessing about him in his diary and two poems, "Where art thou friend" and "The Beginning of the End." (In his autograph copy, Hopkins's editor, Robert Bridges, noted that the second of these "must *never* be printed"; it was not included until the third edition of 1948.)

In 1866, ALGERNON CHARLES SWINBURNE (1837–1909) published his controversial *Poems and Ballads,* which included three poems with frank lesbian content ("Anactoria," "Faustine," and "Sapphics") and two suggestive of male bisexuality ("Hermaphroditus" and "Fragoletta"). *Poems and Ballads* furthered the greater public "speakableness" of homosexuality during these years that *In Memoriam* started; in persistent demand, the book went through twelve editions in as many years. During this same period, Swinburne worked on his unfinished novel *Lesbia Brandon* (not published until 1952), where lesbianism is among the several "forbidden" sexual subjects. Critics usually describe Swinburne as a heterosexual masochist, but there is no record of his involvement with a woman beyond his brief 1867–1868 affair with Adah Isaacs Menken. On the basis of this evidence, plus his early championship of Whitman and his friendship with homosexual contemporaries like Simeon Solomon and George Powell (with whom he joked in an 1871 letter about "Dean Buggeridge [and] his work on the Cities of the Plain"), it seems likely that Swinburne's eroticism was at least bisexual.

In 1871, Simeon Solomon (1841–1905) published his only piece of writing, an allegorical prose poem called "A Vision of Love Revealed in Sleep," in which Love and all the attendant seraphim are male. In the same year, Symonds wrote his first letter to Whitman and began his extensive correspondence with Horatio Brown, a homosexual former student who became his literary executor. In 1873, Symonds first drafted, but left unpublished, *A Problem in Greek Ethics,* his first extended defense of homosexuality, based on his reading in the Greek classics. *Studies in the History of the Renaissance* by WALTER PATER (1839–1894), Hopkins's favorite Oxford tutor and another friend of Simeon Solomon, appeared in the same year. In this controversial exposition of "aesthetic criticism," Pater lists "the face of one's friend" as one possible source of "exquisite passion" in his "Conclusion." He also employs one of the commonest conventions in earlier homosexual writing, using a homosexual figure from earlier history or art to evoke the subject of homosexuality in the present. Pater's chapters on "The Poetry of Michelangelo" and "Leonardo da Vinci" (first issued as separate essays in 1871 and 1869) seem influenced in part by that motive, though he is not explicit about either's homosexuality. He is relatively more frank in his chapter on "Winckelmann" (first published in 1867), where he mentions the art historian's "affinity with Hellenism" and "romantic, fervid friendships with young men." *Narcissus and Other Poems,* an early volume by EDWARD CARPENTER (1844–1929) containing some discernible homosexual situations, was also published in 1873. In the next year, Carpenter wrote his first letter to Whitman.

In 1875, Symonds began his extensive correspondence with the scholar and essayist Edmund Gosse and in 1876 published his *Studies of the Greek Poets, Second Series,* where he broached the subject of homosexuality through his brief and qualified defense of Greek pederasty in the final chapter. It was that discussion that led Richard St. John Tyrwhitt to attack Symonds in an essay on "The Greek Spirit in Modern Literature" in the *Contemporary Review* the following year. This attack accuses Symonds of promoting "vices . . . which are not even named among us" and contributed to his loss of the Professorship of Poetry at Oxford. Similar insinuations had been made about Pater, in W. H. Mallock's satire of him as the effete "Mr. Rose" in his 1876 *The New Republic,* and when Pater issued a second edition of the *Renaissance* in 1877, he omitted his controversial "Conclusion." It was around this same time that the writer and reformer Edith Simcox (1844–1901) began her *Autobiography of a Shirt Maker,* a thinly disguised transcription of her private journal that focuses on the years 1876–1881 and on her passionate attachment at that time to George Eliot. Simcox describes George Eliot as "the love-passion of my life" and declares, "I am not the least attracted to any man; I only want to love you." The 175-page manuscript has never been published. In 1878, Symonds published his translation of MICHELANGELO's *Sonnets,* the first complete version in English and the first based on Gausti's accurate text of 1863, which corrected Michelangelo the Younger's heterosexualizing of the poems in his edition of 1623. Symonds does not trumpet the homosexuality of the sonnets, but he comes closer to divulging it than anyone had before by mentioning Michelangelo the Younger's altering of the poems about "masculine beauty" and by printing the sonnets to Tommaso Cavalieri in their true, male–male, form for the first time.

Also in 1878, Symonds published his first publicly distributed book of poems, *Many Moods,* which, cushioned by some heterosexual or sexually undifferentiated pieces, contains several ardent male–male texts about classical warrior-companions and famous classical and Biblical male pairs (for example, "Callicrates," "Love and Death," "The Lotos-Garland of Antinous," "The Meeting of David and Jonathan"). Hopkins had resumed writing poetry in 1875, after a nine-year silence, and in 1879, he wrote "The Bugler's First Communion," with its admiration for "mansex fine," and "The Handsome Heart," with its praise of his sacristan's "handsome face" as well as heart. In the same year, Edward Lear (1812–1888) wrote one of his two near-frank autobiographical poems, "How pleasant to know Mr. Lear!," where his mention that "Some think him . . . queer" could suggest his homosexuality. The same fact might be intuited from Lear's overriding concern with eccentrics in his earlier nonsense books, but the clearest evidence of Lear's attraction to other men is found in his letters and diaries of the 1850s, 1860s, and 1870s, particularly his references to Frank Lushington, Wilhelm Marstrand, and Hubert Congreve.

VERNON LEE, the nom de plume of Violet Paget (1856–1935), began publishing in 1880, with her *Studies of the Eighteenth Century in Italy,* but her works of the nineteenth century give little indication of her lesbianism. However, her letters and diaries of these years, which remain largely unpublished, reveal her intense attachments to other women, like Mary Robinson and Kit Anstruther-Thomson. In 1880, Hopkins wrote his elegiac "Felix Randal," praising the "hardy-handsome" farrier, and "Brothers," where the "love-laced" relationship between the two boys seems a projection of Hopkins's own homosexual feelings. In the same year, Symonds published his second publicly distributed book of poems, *New and Old,* which, along with the same buffers as in his first, contains a few daringly frank homosexual statements in the present ("The Ponte di Paradiso," "From Friend to Friend") and several filtered through classical Greek situations ("Leuké" and the majority in a section of "Poems on Greek Themes"). Two years later, Symonds's third such volume, *Animi Figura,* appeared. More abstract than his previous two, this contains a long guilt-ridden sonnet sequence called "L'Amour de L'Impossible," which concerns his homosexuality, as well as an insightful piece called "Paths of Life" contrasting marriage and "comradeship" and justifying the latter's "offspring . . . / Of thoughts and acts, an immaterial breed." Also in 1882, Hopkins wrote his famous letter to Bridges confessing, "I always knew in my heart Walt Whitman's mind to be more like my own than any other man's living." In the same year, Edith Simcox published her only work of fiction, *Episodes in the Lives of Men, Women, and Lovers.* All the book's love stories are of course heterosexual, but in *Autobiography of a Shirt Maker,* Simcox makes clear that they are transformations of her feelings for George Eliot and that the male lovers are based on herself.

In 1883, Symonds privately printed and distributed an expanded version of his 1873 *A Problem in Greek Ethics* and in the next year published his fourth book of poems, *Vagabunduli Libellus,* which evidences the greatest anxiety of any of his publicly distributed poetic works. Though containing a few short suggestive male–male poems (for example, "The Jodeller," "The Strolling Musician"), the book is dominated by a long camouflaging sonnet sequence called "Stella Maris," about an anguished affair that Symonds depicts as heterosexual. SAMUEL BUTLER (1835–1902) composed the bulk of *The Way of All Flesh* in 1883–1884 (the novel was posthumously published in 1903). His innuendo-filled depiction of the curate Pryer satirizes homosexuality among the mid-century Anglo-Catholic clergy and both reveals and clouds his own attraction to other men. In late 1884 and early 1885, Edward Lear completed his other near-frank autobiographical poem, "Incidents in the Life of My Uncle Arly," where the title character's "far too tight" shoes seem to represent the constraints Lear felt because of his homosexuality.

In 1885, Pater's novel, or philosophical romance, *Marius the Epicurean* appeared. The book is heavy with homosexual innuendo: At each stage Marius's education is advanced by contact with another man; Marius's relationships to his two chief "tutors" Flavian and Cornelius are described in the language of romantic love ("winning him now to an absolutely self-forgetting devotion"), and at the end, Marius sacrifices himself for another man. Sir Richard Burton (1821–1890) also published his daring essay on "Pederasty" in the same year as part of the "Terminal Essay" to his translation of *The Arabian Nights;* the first extensive published discussion of homosexuality in English, it created a great public outcry. Though proposing a preposterous "Sodatic Zone" theory of homosexuality, the essay is based in extensive research unlikely to have been pursued by an outsider. Burton was married, but rumors of homosexuality had followed him since his days in the Indian Army in the 1840s.

Between 1885 and 1888, Hopkins wrote several more poems with homosexual implications: "To what serves Mortal Beauty?" where all the examples of beauty are male; "(The Soldier)," where the figure of Christ falling on a soldier's neck and kissing it seems another projection of Hopkins's own desires; the "terrible sonnet" "I wake and feel the fell of dark," whose "dead letters sent / To dearest him that lives alas! away" recalls his attachment to Dolben; "Harry Ploughman," with its praise of "Amansstrength"; and "Epithalamion," where he is unable to complete a poem celebrating his brother's marriage and devotes the draft instead to the feelings of a man watching boys bathing ("Here he feasts: lovely all is!"). The year 1885 also saw the mysterious breach between A. E. HOUSMAN (1859–1936) and Moses Jackson, whom Housman had fallen in love with when they were both at Oxford and with whom he had shared a London flat for two years. Starting around this time, Housman drafted many of his frank manuscript poems about Jackson, which were not published until after his death: for example, "I promise nothing: friends will part," "The world goes none the lamer," "Shake hands, we shall never be friends, all's over," "Because I liked you better," "Oh were he and I together," "Ask me no more, for fear I should reply," "He would not stay for me; and who can wonder?"

In 1886 appeared *A Romance of Two Worlds,* the first book by the popular novelist MARIE CORELLI, the nom de plume of Mary Mackay (1855–1924), who lived with another woman, Bertha Vyver, all her life. Though biographers have made much of Corelli's apparent infatuation in middle age with the painter Arthur Severn, she wore a ring from Vyver all of her life and had constructed over a fireplace in their home a bas-relief representing their initials in a heart, above the inscription "Amor Vincit." The love affairs in Corelli's novels of course had to be heterosexual, but lesbianism is sometimes intimated, as in the closeness of the autobiographical heroine of *A Romance of Two Worlds* with another women, Zara. Pater issued a third edition of *The Renaissance* in 1888, restoring the controversial "Conclusion" he had cut in 1877. At around the same time, Oscar Wilde (1854–1900) began to evoke homosexuality more openly in his work. The charming and seemingly innocent fairy tale "The Happy Prince" (1888), which Wilde actually first wrote for some Cambridge undergraduates, depicts the devotion between the bejewelled statue of the Prince and a swallow, who had renounced a female reed to serve the Prince. They die together, after the prince has had the swallow distribute all the gems of his body to the poor and asks the swallow to "kiss me on the lips, for I love you." More nearly transparent was his story "The Portrait of Mr. W. H.," which appeared in its shorter form in *Blackwood's* in July 1889. (Wilde wrote an expanded and even franker version in the early 1890s, which was not published until 1921.) Here, in a text suffused with homosexual suggestiveness, Wilde blatantly pursues the homosexual interpretation of Shakespeare's *Sonnets* that, as we have seen, engaged earlier homosexual writers as well. "The Portrait of Mr. W. H." created a considerable stir and gave Wilde's enemies the first potent literary weapon they could use against him.

Long Ago, the first book of poems that Katherine Bradley (1846–1914) and Edith Cooper (1862–1913) issued under their pseudonym of MICHAEL FIELD, also appeared in 1889. A collection of sixty-eight lyrics spoken by SAPPHO and liberally modeled on the Sapphic fragments, *Long Ago* offers a predominantly heterosexual portrait of Sappho, yet injects some frankly and intensely lesbian poems into that picture. The lesbian couple EDITH SOMERVILLE (1858–1949) AND VIOLET MARTIN (1863–1915), who wrote under the pseudonym of Somerville and Ross and are best known for their *Irish R.M.* books, published their first novel in the same year. Somerville suggests the intensity of their attachment in her 1918 memoir of Ross, *Irish Memories,* but a franker picture appears in the unpublished papers both women left, including 116 diary volumes and thousands of letters. Also in 1889, Symonds began writing his pathbreaking *Memoirs,* the first self-conscious homosexual autobiography known to us now, which he finished just before his death in 1893 but which remained unpublished until 1984. In 1890, after fifteen years of friendship, Edmund Gosse (1849–1928) finally revealed his own homosexuality to Symonds, admitting in a February 24 letter, "I know of all you speak of." In 1891, Symonds completed and privately distributed his *A Problem in Modern Ethics,* a continuation of the defense of homosexuality he had begun in *A Problem in Greek Ethics,* this time focusing on later history and literature as well as on the new sexology and ending with a set of concrete proposals for legal reform.

In the same year, Wilde's *The Picture of Dorian Gray* was published in book form. In contrast to the somewhat franker magazine version (*Lippincott's,* June 1890), in the novel homosexuality is suggested rather than explicit, but the outcry about the book still centered on that issue and intensified Wilde's association with homosexuality in knowing eyes. In return for a copy sent by Wilde, the infatuated Lionel Johnson (1867–1902), who was Alfred Douglas's cousin, sent Wilde his Latin poem, "In Honorem Doriana Creatorisque Eius," praising the book's "apples of Sodom." Johnson's other notable homosexual poems

are angry and agonized. In 1892, having converted to Catholicism and turned against Wilde, Johnson directed a sonnet at him called "The Destroyer of a Soul" (presumably Douglas's, whom he had introduced to Wilde the previous June). In the following year, Johnson wrote what some consider his masterpiece, "The Dark Angel," rooted in anguish about his homosexuality.

In 1893, the year of his death, Symonds completed his *Memoirs* and published three books with homosexual content or implication. *In the Key of Blue,* a collection of essays, contains the frank reminiscence "Clifton and a Lad's Love." In his two-volume biography of Michelangelo, Symonds works to dismantle the myth of Michelangelo's attachment to Vittoria Colonna, while discussing in extensive detail Michelangelo's passionate poems and letters to Tommaso Cavalieri and other men. In *Walt Whitman, A Study,* Symonds acknowledges Whitman's August 1890 letter to him denying any homosexual meaning in *Calamus,* but insinuates that Whitman's work can nevertheless be read in those terms. Also in 1893, Michael Field (Katherine Bradley and Edith Cooper) published *Underneath the Bough,* a collection of five "books of songs" that, especially in the third book, contain some intense, autobiographical, lesbian love poems (for example, "It was deep April," "A girl," "Constancy"). In 1893, Housman wrote "A.J.J.," a romantic elegy for Adalbert Jackson, Moses Jackson's younger brother, who had shared their London flat and with whom Housman seems to have had an affair; the poem was not published until after Housman's death.

Pater meanwhile had continued to insinuate homosexual content into his writings—for example, in his 1892 imaginary portrait "Emerald Uthwart," with the "Hellenic fitness" of the title character and his "antique friendship" with his schoolmate and fellow-soldier, James Stokes; in "Apollo in Picardy" of the following year, with the implied attraction of Prior Saint-Jean to the "godlike, . . . rich, warm, white limbs" of the servant Apollyon and the echoing of the Apollo-Hyacinth story in Apollyon's relationship with the novice Hyacinthus; and in his praise of Greek male sculpture in his essay "The Age of Athletic Prizemen," published in February 1894, a few months before his death ("look into, look at the curves of, the blossomlike cavity of the opened mouth"). In 1894, appeared *Platonics: A Study,* a short novel by Ethel M. Arnold, who has been identified as a niece of Matthew Arnold but about whom little is known except that she lived for a time in Rome and worked as a translator of French literature. Evoking a traditional code term for homosexuality in its title, *Platonics* focuses on the lifelong closeness between two women who also had fleeting heterosexual attachments (one describes the other as "the solitary human being whom she loved"). This obscure novel, and its presently obscure author, merit more attention and study. In the same year, in the short-lived Oxford undergraduate magazine *The Chameleon,* Lord Alfred Douglas published his poem "Two Loves," which became notorious in the following year when Oscar Wilde quoted its description of homosexuality as "the love that dare not speak its name" in his defense in his first trial. Also in 1894, but expressing an opposite, affirmative attitude, Edward Carpenter published and circulated privately his *Homogenic Love and Its Place in a Free Society,* a daring liberationist essay that Carpenter had first delivered as a speech and that in general pattern and spirit follows Symonds's *A Problem in Modern Ethics.*

The year of the Wilde scandal, 1895, saw further notable manuscript work. Echoing Tennyson, Samuel Butler drafted "In Memoriam H. R. F." when the Swiss student Hans Faesch left London for home and followed it with several ardent letters. Housman wrote another poem about Adalbert Jackson, "He looked at me with eyes I thought," and, most significant, his "Oh who is that young sinner with the handcuffs on his wrists?," his angry response to the Wilde trials and to the perennial persecution of homosexuals; these did not see print until the late 1930s. In 1895–1896, FREDERICK WILLIAM ROLFE (1860–1913), better known by his pseudonym Baron Corvo, published in the *Yellow Book* the six pieces to which he would give the title *Stories Toto Told Me* when they were reissued in book form in 1898. Rolfe's description of Toto and his friends, based on a group of boys with whom he spent much of the summer of 1890 in the Italian countryside, is suffused with erotic feeling. In 1896, Housman's *A Shropshire Lad,* one of the period's most influential books of male homosexual writing, was published. Housman could of course only portray homosexuality indirectly in *A Shropshire Lad.* Nevertheless, he identifies his primary audience as "lads like me" in its final poem, "I hoed and trenched and weeded," and, fittingly, the book was read homosexually by contemporary gay male readers. For example, Wilde's friend and executor Robert Ross memorized poems from the book to recite to Wilde when visiting him in prison, and Housman sent Wilde an autographed copy upon his release.

In 1896 also appeared two pertinent publications by Goldsworthy Lowes Dickinson (1861–1932), one of E. M. FORSTER's favorite teachers at Cambridge and later the subject of a 1934 biography by him. The sequence of twenty-six sonnets in Dickinson's privately printed *Poems* concerns his feelings for Ferdinand Schiller, and his chapter on "Friendship" in his best-selling *The Greek View of Life* (which went through seventeen editions in his lifetime) is an almost open defense of male homosexuality. Symonds and Havelock Ellis's controversial study *Sexual Inversion* appeared first in a German translation of 1896 (where it had the title *Das Contrare Geschlechtsgefühl* or *Contrary Sexual Feeling*) and then in English in 1897. Symonds was dead by the time the book appeared, and the sections discussing homosexuality as pathology are Ellis's, not his. Still *Sexual Inversion* bore Symonds's mark in many ways: *A Problem in Greek Ethics* finally appeared publicly as Appendix A; Symonds supplied many of the case histories from the correspondence he had received in response to his earlier, privately circulated studies (Symonds himself is Case 17); and parts of *A Problem in Modern Ethics* are scattered throughout. Scandalized, Symonds's family insisted that his name be removed from all future editions.

Between January and March 1897, near the end of his prison term, Oscar Wilde wrote the long letter to Alfred Douglas that was later given the title *De Profundis* by Robert Ross and that was not published in its entirety until 1962. One of the most important documents in the history of homosexual writing, *De Profundis* is in part a male–male love letter and arose from an experience—state imprisonment—that was simply the ultimate expression of the homosexual's outsider, pariah status in Wilde's society. Also in 1897, a group of friends and former students published *Extracts from the Letters and Journals of William Cory,* a work that of course had to be circumspect about Cory's homosexuality and his Eton scandal, but that seems to assume an audience conversant with them. Among the subscribers listed in the front of the book is A. C. Benson (1862–1925), one of the three homosexual sons of the Archbishop of Canterbury and from 1915 Master of Magdalene College, Cambridge. Inspired by Cory's *Extracts,* Benson began his own diary in 1897 and continued it until his death. Filling 180 manuscript volumes, the diaries have never been published in anything near their entirety, though a discreet selection was made by Percy Lubbock in 1927, and they are the basis of a recent book by David Newsome. Benson's diaries may contain a wealth of information about English male homosexual writers and cultural figures in the late nineteenth and early twentieth centuries.

Wilde's letters after his release from prison are also important documents of nineteenth-century homosexual writing and parallel in several ways the Beckford letters to Franchi discussed earlier. For instance, Wilde's March 1898 letter to George Cecil Ives, a

British homosexual liberation pioneer and later a dominant figure in the British Society for the Study of Sex Psychology, recalls Beckford's remark about the Vere Street scandal: "Yes: I have no doubt we shall win, but the road is long, and red with monstrous martyrdoms. Nothing but the repeal of the Criminal Law Amendment Act would do any good." Also written around this time, and sparked by the Wilde scandal, is one of the earliest works of LYTTON STRACHEY (1880–1932), an unfinished piece called "Curious Manuscript" that purports to be the story of a married man hounded out of his country after losing a slander suit against a contemporary who had accused him of homosexual relations. "Why, I wish to know," the protagonist asks, "is it perfectly moral for me to copulate with a personage whose sexual organs are different from my own, and perfectly immoral for me to copulate with a personage whose sexual organs are not different?"; "Curious Manuscript" remained unpublished until 1972. Finally, at the very end of the century, we find a homosexual author once again declaring Shakespeare's *Sonnets* a homosexual text. In his 1899 *Shakespeare's Sonnets Reconsidered and in Part Rearranged,* Samuel Butler discusses the *Sonnets* as illustrative of "the love that passeth the love of women" and concludes that "the love of the English poet for Mr. W. H. was . . . more Greek than English."

Compared to homosexual writing in the immediately preceding eras, nineteenth-century English homosexual literature is more abundant, continuous, and, in its later years, relatively more frank. (For additional writers in the tradition I have not been able to mention here, see Brian Reade's 1970 anthology, *Sexual Heretics.*) Beyond those qualities, the most remarkable aspect of this literature is its challenge to the currently popular academic argument that homosexuality is a late nineteenth-century "invention." Its proponents arrive at this loosely defined notion by citing the large-scale social changes pertaining to same-sex sexuality that occurred in the late nineteenth century, particularly the first appearance of laws directed specifically against homosexuality rather than against a more generalized "sodomy" (though this in fact happened only in two countries, Germany in 1871 and England in 1885). These proponents also note the rise of sexological science and the coining of our modern terminology of "homosexuality" (though in fact a differentiating language for same-sex attraction had existed for centuries, such as the terms "masculine love" and "sapphic love" and words like "sodomy" and "pederasty" that had different technical meanings but in practice often designated homosexuality only).

In contrast, nineteenth-century English homosexual writing shows a clear sense of homosexual difference and a related sense of a distinct homosexual oppression existing among writers from the very start of the age. If we are meant to take the "new-inventionist" view of homosexuality strictly, homosexuality could not have emerged in England until the years 1885 to 1892 (the dates of the Labouchere Amendment criminalizing "gross indecency between males" separately for the first time and of the first English translation of Krafft-Ebing's *Psychopathia Sexualis,* the book that started the new widespread sexology). There is certainly more homosexual literature in the later 1800s in England, but, as evident here, there is significant earlier nineteenth-century homosexual writing as well, and the "bursts" in amount and relative frankness later in the age start well before 1885–1892.

The social changes cited by new-inventionists certainly affected the homosexual situation in many ways and may be crucial in the history of sexuality in other respects. But nineteenth-century English homosexual literature prompts us to look for the origins of modern homosexual consciousness and expressiveness less in the social-history factors currently favored by academics and more in a complex of both broader and more concrete elements. First, the increase in English homosexual writing right at the start of the nineteenth century identifies the years around 1800 as one of the most pivotal periods in homosexual history and suggests that the ideological revolutions of the Enlightenment and the Romantic Movement were crucial spurs to a relatively greater homosexual self-acceptance and expressiveness at that time. Among the key concepts of those movements that would have weakened the constraints on homosexuality and imparted a greater sense of possibility to homosexuals themselves were the new valuing of individual sensibility and of social and personal equality and the new "spiritualizing" or "de-materializing" of Nature, a "spiritualizing" that loosened the connection between Nature and the notion of physical production and instead legitimized as "natural" in themselves the exchange of passionate feelings and the forging of harmonious intimate bonds without any necessary material "result." These concepts would have accentuated and given more positive meaning to homosexuality's minority status, to the anatomical and gender-role "sameness" inherent in its relationships, and to its innate biological non-procreativeness. For instance, without the new "spiritualizing" of Nature, the "Don Leon" poet could probably not have so aggressively proclaimed homosexuality's "no other blossoms than its own" nor Symonds defended its "immaterial breed."

The other point suggested by nineteenth-century English homosexual literature is that homosexual writing itself was pivotal in the acceleration of modern homosexual consciousness and expressiveness. As mentioned, not all the writers in the era's homosexual literary tradition knew of one another's work. But, unconnected as they chiefly are to the large-scale social shifts emphasized by new-inventionists, the decade-by-decade "bursts" in homosexual literature in the second half of the century seem stimulated mainly by the breakthroughs in accessible homosexual writing in the years immediately preceding them—for example, by the models of Tennyson and Johnson/Cory in the 1850s, of Whitman and Swinburne in the 1860s, of Symonds and Pater in the 1870s, 1880s, and 1890s, and of Wilde in the 1890s (before as well as after his scandal)—as if available homosexual speech itself spurred progressively more homosexual speech in the age, The new-inventionist view of homosexual history assumes a "non-homosexuality," or, contradictorily, an "empty" homosexuality, until the phenomenon is created "top-down" by large-scale social changes. In contrast, the example of nineteenth-century English homosexual literature suggests more of an "inward-out" pattern to homosexual history. Its persistence, unity, and later quickening implies that homosexual consciousness is always latent in the distinct texture of individual homosexual experience (though perhaps with a special pointedness under heterosexual cultural domination) and only needs enabling conditions like the ones I have just sketched to know and declare itself.

—*Joseph Cady*

BIBLIOGRAPHY

Cady, Joseph. "'What Cannot Be': John Addington Symonds's *Memoirs* and Official Mappings of Victorian Homosexuality." *Victorian Newsletter* 81 (Spring 1992): 47–51. ■ Collis, Maurice. *Somerville and Ross.* London: Faber and Faber, 1968. ■ Croft-Cooke, Rupert. *Feasting with Panthers: A New Consideration of Some Late Victorian Writers.* London: W. H. Allen, 1967. ■ Crompton, Louis. *Byron and Greek Love: Homophobia in 19th-Century England.* Berkeley: University of California Press, 1985. ■ Dellamora, Richard. *Masculine Desire: The Sexual Politics of Victorian Aestheticism.* Chapel Hill: University of North Carolina Press, 1990. Ellmann, Richard. *Oscar Wilde.* New York: Knopf, 1988. ■ Faber, Geoffrey. *Oxford Apostles: A Character Study of the Oxford Movement.* London: Faber and Faber, 1933. ■ Faderman, Lillian. *Surpassing the Love of Men: Romantic Friendship and Love between Women from the Renaissance to the Present.* New York: Morrow, 1981. ■ Graves, Richard Perceval. *A. E. Housman: The Scholar-Poet.* New York: Scribner's, 1980. ■ Grosskurth, Phyllis. *The Woeful Victorian: A Biography of John Addington Symonds.* New York: Holt, Rinehart and Winston, 1964. ■ Gunn, Peter. *Vernon Lee. Violet Paget, 1856-1935.* London: Oxford University Press, 1964. ■ Hilliard, David. "Unenglish and Unmanly: Anglo-Catholicism and Homosexuality." *Victorian Studies* 25 (1982): 181–210. ■ Hyde, H. Montgomery. *The Love That Dared Not Speak Its Name: A Candid History of Homosexuality in Britain.* Boston: Little, Brown, 1970. ■ Martin, Robert Bernard. *Gerard Manley Hopkins: A Very Private Life.* New York: Putnam's, 1991. ■ ———. *Tennyson: The Unquiet Heart.* New York: Oxford University Press, 1980. ■ ———. *With Friends Possessed: A Life of Edward Fitzgerald.* New York: Atheneum, 1985. ■ McKenzie, K. A. *Edith Simcox and George Eliot.* London: Oxford University Press, 1961. ■ Masters, Brian. *Now Barabbas Was a Rotter: The Extraordinary Life of Marie Corelli.* London: Hamish Hamilton, 1978. ■ Mavor, Elizabeth. *The Ladies of Llangollen: A Study in Romantic Friendship.* New York: Penguin Books, 1973. ■ Newsome, David. *On the Edge of Paradise: A. C. Benson, the Diarist.* Chicago: University of Chicago Press, 1980. ■ Noakes, Vivien. *Edward Lear: The Life of a Wanderer.* Boston: Houghton Mifflin, 1969. ■ Reade, Brian, ed. *Sexual Heretics: Male Homosexuality in English Literature from 1850 to 1900.* New York: Coward-McCann, 1971. ■ Ricks, Christopher. *Tennyson.* New York: Macmillan, 1972. ■ Sedgwick, Eve K. *Between Men: English Literature and Male Homosocial Desire.* New York: Columbia University Press, 1985. ■ Sturgeon, Mary. *Michael Field.* London: George G. Harrap, 1922. Reprint. New York: Arno Press, 1975. ■ Weeks, Jeffrey. *Coming Out: Homosexual Politics in Britain, from the Nineteenth Century to the Present.* London: Quartet Books, 1977.

English Literature: Twentieth Century

In JEREMY BENTHAM's late eighteenth- and early-nineteenth century writings about homosexuality, Bentham weighs the pleasure of consensual homosexual relations against the pain or harm it causes the general public. Bentham concludes that, by causing no harm to others, homosexuality is justified by the pleasures of those who practice it. In the course of his justification, no stories about homosexuality's spiritual, psychological, cultural, political, and aesthetic virtues or vices are appealed to by Bentham, who finds such narratives to be burdensome and irrelevant to the calculus of pleasure, which alone warrants homosexuality's "right" to be free. For better or worse, however, at the turn of the nineteenth century into the twentieth, justifications of homosexuality (and condemnations as well) are caught up in elaborate stories about homosexuality's character and cultural impact. In the wake of OSCAR WILDE's trial, the rights of pleasure provide no court of appeal to homosexual men and women. Their sole recourse appears, first and foremost, to have been storytelling: narratives about homosexuality's legitimate place in biological, cultural, and political evolution. The storyteller who most fit the occasion is EDWARD CARPENTER (1844–1929).

Although Carpenter's work is intended to be read as psychology, sociology, and anthropology, it endures as a poetic fantasia on homosexual types and powers and as a repository of narratives about homosexuality that are, in relation to literary history, both dated and yet still influential. In *Love's Coming of Age* (1896–1911) and *The Intermediate Sex* (1896–1912), Carpenter denies the universality of patriarchal heterosexuality, and argues that, in contrast to homosexuality, Western heterosexual norms instance a historically arrested state of psychosexual evolution. Heterosexual conventions, especially when they are influenced by Judeo-Christian morality, are fixated on erotic, social, and economic possessiveness. They lag behind the progressive maturation whose vehicle is an alliance of feminism with the third, or intermediate, sex: homosexual men and women. Carpenter assigns to homosexual desire an innate egalitarianism and communitarianism, no matter where or when it appears in history. For, Carpenter argues, homosexuality invariably subverts the crudely binary structure that constitutes society as an order of gendered, racial, or economic oppositions. The intermediate sex develops cultural forms, especially in religious, political, and aesthetic realms, that are alternative to oppositional ones. Accordingly, Carpenter points to the cultural heroism, even the divinity, identified with intermediate types in cultures not stunted by Judeo-Christian censoriousness: prophets and priests, wizards and witches are mythic representations of the third sex. Moreover, he claims that in pre-Christian and non-Western cultures male–male and female–female comradeships exemplify consummate citizenship, the public virtues required by the state rather than the private virtues required by family values. Whether they are priests, soldiers, or aesthetes, Carpenter's homosexual men and women are the heroes and heroines of a heroic history of democratic progress. And all forms of intermediacy—whether personal or abstract—partake, for Carpenter, of the heroism of homosexuality.

The century's first strictly literary analogs of Carpenter's gay heroism in cultural life are to be found in the novels and the careers of FREDERICK ROLFE (pseud. Baron Corvo) (1860–1913) and RONALD FIRBANK (1886–1926). Rolfe's novels embody a will to renew both sacred and secular orders by means of heroic intermediate types: the shaman-like Englishman who becomes Pope in *Hadrian the Seventh* (1904) or the priestly satirist Nicholas Crabbe who loves a prototype of the third sex in *The Desire and Pursuit of the Whole* (1909; published posthumously). Although overtly critical of Carpenter's democratic bias, Rolfe's work repeats Carpenter's conviction that homoeroticism goes hand in hand with an exalted calling to redress the world's wrongs, at both personal and institutional levels. No less intransigent than Rolfe, and far more open and flamboyant, Firbank enacts his homosexuality as a high vocation (simultaneously exalted and comic), and as a posthumous marriage with Wilde, in a way that emphasizes "intermediate" transvestism, shamanistic mysticism, and, above all, exacting devotion to art. From *Vainglory* (1915), whose characters include a male composer and his male lover, to *The Princess Zoubaroff* (1920), a play about the founding of a lesbian convent, to *The Flower Beneath the Foot* (1923), which is pervaded by lesbian longings, to *Concerning the Eccentricities of Cardinal Pirelli* (1926), whose bisexual hero-prelate dies during a nude chase after his favorite choirboy, Firbank's novels couple the representation of homosexual desires and liaisons with a revolutionary address to the aesthetics of novelistic form. What James Joyce's Stephen Dedalus aspires to be in *A Portrait of the Artist as a Young Man* (1916)—a secular priest of art, transubstantiating reality into fiction—Firbank appears to realize in artistic practice. At the same time, in a way that repeats Carpenter's involvement of aesthetic intermediacy with egalitarian political impulses, Firbank's fiction dramatizes and protests imperialism's rule of global politics.

Two protestors against imperialism, from the same era as Rolfe and Firbank, supplement Carpenter's claims for the public dimensions of homosexual desire: Roger Casement (1864–1916) and T. E. LAWRENCE (1888–1935). Both figures are nonliterary writers; like Carpenter, however, their influence on literary culture is formative. Casement, an Irishman in the British foreign service knighted for his exposés of imperialist atrocities against natives in the Belgian Congo and in Brazil, became disgusted with England's postponement of Home Rule for Ireland. Invoking Ireland's neutrality during World War I, he enlisted German aid in support of the Irish Easter Rising (against England) of 1916. He was brought to trial in England and convicted as a traitor. His appeal of his conviction was quashed by the discovery and circulation of his secret diaries, describing his homosexual adventures on three continents. Casement was hanged, a martyr to Ireland and to homophobia. His supporters could not construe the compatibility of political integrity with homosexuality and promiscuity: They declared the diaries to be forgeries. Politically defeated, nevertheless, Casement lives on, arguably, in Joyce's celebrated allegory of Irish political self-division, *Finnegans Wake* (1924–1939), whose Irish hero is accused of homosexual no less than heterosexual promiscuity in public places, in circumstances made controversial by allegedly forged evidence of the hero's sin. A traitor to his country on behalf of an illicit, queerly alternative anti-imperialist nationhood, one that Carpenter might have approved, Casement joins the heterosexual Irish political leader and adulterer Charles Stewart Parnell as a primary inspiration for Joyce's influential fiction. Like Casement, T. E. Lawrence also betrays his imperialist home by taking the side, in World War I, of Arab nationalists seeking to be free of both Turkish and British domination. In Lawrence's memoir of his political career, *Seven Pillars of Wisdom* (1919–1922), British and Arab homosexual experience—including Lawrence's—is enlisted by Lawrence in order to formulate a "pathic ethics," that is, a mode of political action that undermines activism, militarism, and imperialism, and that suggests an unfixed, self-divided, intermediate sense of identity as a new political virtue and strategy. The literary and political impact of *Seven Pillars of Wisdom* is partly to be measured by its probable influence on E. M. FORSTER's composition of *A Passage to India* (1924) and on the politics and art of W. H. AUDEN (1907–1973) and CHRISTOPHER ISHERWOOD (1904–1986) in their youth.

Auden and Isherwood had mixed responses, however, to Lawrence's career. Harshly distrusting Lawrence's involvement of homosexuality with what they took to be self-dramatizing (and, after all, stubbornly imperialist) heroics, Auden and Isherwood suggest a younger generation's retreat from Carpenter's grand narratives about gay and lesbian political callings. The retreat first shows itself in the biographical and historical essays of LYTTON STRACHEY (1880–1932). Strachey's work implies a Benthamite approach to the apparent gravity of historical narrative scenarios. His *Eminent Victorians* (1917), which suggests that historical figures who are inspired by grandly conceived narratives about themselves suffer from a crazed self-denial of sensuous pleasure, includes a study of the repressed homosexual General Gordon. The study exhibits imperialism, as well as a mania for religious conversion, as symptoms of the repression of homosexual desire. In *Elizabeth and Essex* (1928), Strachey suggests that Essex's rebellion against Queen Eliza-

beth is motivated by Essex's hatred of her modernity, her shifting hermaphroditic or androgynous cast of mind and erotic nature, which projects itself as an antiheroic politics. In Essex, Strachey exhibits an ideological decisiveness that is equated with pre-modern patriarchy; in Elizabeth's undecided erotic role-playing, Strachey locates a mercurial alternative to Essex's patriarchal rigidity. Although Carpenter's intermediate type is preserved in Strachey's Elizabeth, intermediacy in Strachey's version becomes more ambiguous, as well as far more politically unreliable, than in Carpenter. In the light of Strachey's mistrust of grand historical projects and narratives, it is not surprising that he chose to be a conscientious objector during World War I, refusing to take ideological sides. His sense of the self-alienating effects of heroic historical vocations is complemented in two soldier-poets, both homosexual and both casualties of the war, Rupert Brooke (1887–1915) and WILFRED OWEN (1893–1918). In Owen's poems, an erotic pathos evoked by combat-weary and wounded male bodies becomes an antiheroic emblem for pacifism.

In the decade after World War I, a hitherto unprecedented representation of homosexual desire in literary writing includes striking portrayals of lesbians and a prominence of lesbian writers. The war itself, and the ideological deceptions pervading it, contributed to this development, first by creating new separate communities of men and women, then by inspiring attempts at a new honesty concerning historical and social order in all aspects, sexuality included. But pre-war feminism and aestheticism, and a prestigious circle of American expatriate lesbian writers living in Paris (DJUNA BARNES, NATALIE BARNEY, GERTRUDE STEIN, RENÉE VIVIEN) were no less contributory. The brilliant short story writer KATHERINE MANSFIELD (1888–1923), for whom Oscar Wilde was an ego ideal, initiated her career as a writer alongside personal experiments with lesbianism in the years 1906 to 1908. The heroine of *The Rainbow* (1915) by D. H. LAWRENCE has a passing but intense sexual passion for her schoolmistress. *Dusty Answer* (1927) by Rosamond Lehmann (b. 1903) varies the narrative of the heroine in *The Rainbow*: Here a liberated postwar lesbian undergraduate becomes an object of mixed desire and aversion for the novel's protagonist. *Vestal Fire* (1927) and *Extraordinary Women* (1928) by Compton Mackenzie (1883–1972) explore the need for a compensatory worldly success incited in homosexual men and women by the public condemnation of their desire. The latter novel shows the victory of one of its lesbian heroines, Rory, over censoriousness-induced competition for both love and public notoriety. But these writers and writings are only signs of lesbianism's new cultural and aesthetic prestige as expressed in the work of VITA SACKVILLE-WEST (1892–1962), VIRGINIA WOOLF (1881–1941), and RADCLYFFE HALL (1880–1943).

Sackville-West, married to the bisexual English diplomat Harold Nicolson (1887–1968), portrays in her novel *Challenge* (1924) her elopement, from her own marriage, with the novelist-to-be Violet Trefusis (1894–1972) although the novel transposes the lesbian relation into heterosexual terms. Sackville-West became the object of a passionate erotic attachment on the part of Virginia Woolf. Woolf, who in *Mrs. Dalloway* (1925) had already represented her heroine's adolescent sapphic love for a schoolgirl friend, reimagines Sackville-West's character and life in the experimental and surrealist novel *Orlando* (1928), about a man who lives for four centuries after he becomes a woman at the age of thirty. *Orlando* suggests the arbitrariness of gender divisions, of fixed erotic desires. And although *Orlando* once again figures Carpenter's intermediate type, Carpenter had claimed the type for biology, whereas *Orlando* suggests that biology itself is not nature, but artifice. The unnaturalness of homosexuality and sapphism is wittily averred by Woolf, on the grounds that no sexuality or gender is natural. In stark contrast to *Orlando*, Radclyffe Hall's *The Well of Loneliness*, which also appeared in 1928, maintains the innate, immobile fixity, hence the immovable nature and naturalness, of homosexuality. Because of Hall's detailed realism, which describes its heroine's erotic desires from the age of six, Hall's book suffered as *Orlando* did not: *The Well of Loneliness* was banned as obscene. The contrast between Hall's and Woolf's books, rooted in their differing addresses to nature, typifies a long-continuing debate about whether or not homosexuality is innate or is a sociocultural product. In Hall, the deep-rooted nature of homosexuality cries out to Stephen Gordon, the novel's heroine, for expressive representation in literary art and in polemic. But, consistent with Hall's differentiation of culture from nature, writing in *The Well of Loneliness* cannot bridge the gap between Stephen's culture and her erotic nature's longings. The demand that Stephen's kind of nature be represented, and have "the right to our existence," necessitates a committed self-sacrifice, a dark heroism of Carpenter-like proportions, that entails little pleasure and a guarantee of frustration. Nevertheless, nature in Hall must make its claims militantly. *Orlando*, in contrast, rises above the battle for nature's rights, or, rather, wins the battle by taking nature less in earnest, by indulging the pleasures of artifice, and by avoiding the strain of heroisms and narratives that attempt cultural redemption. Of

course, Woolf is militant too, in her feminist tracts *A Room of One's Own* (1929) (where, among other things, she asks for fiction writers to produce stories about women loving women) and *Three Guineas* (1939); but she maintains her fiction as another intermediate form: between polemic and pure fabrication.

Woolf's alliance with homoeroticism continues into the 1930s, especially in the best-seller *The Years* (1937), one of whose central figures is an emigré Polish homosexual and pacifist. Among other later flowerings of the lesbian writings and inspirations of the 1920s the most notable are *Dawn's Left Hand* (1931) by Dorothy Richardson (1873–1957), and the novels and poems of SYLVIA TOWNSEND WARNER (1893–1978). In *Dawn's Left Hand* (the tenth segment of Richardson's roman fleuve *Pilgrimage*), a shifting continuum between intense female friendships and homoerotic passion forms the intimacy between the novel's heroine Miriam and her suffragette and socialist friend Amabel. Just as Miriam is becoming the mistress of a married man—hence "the other woman" in a marital triangle—another other woman, Amabel, appears in her life. Taking the form of a mirror-image to whom Miriam is more passionately attached than to her male lover, Amabel repeats Carpenter's suggestion that heterosexual love is an immature or stunting development: The path of Miriam's growth lies through Amabel, not through the man. Sylvia Townsend Warner's first novel (and the first ever Book-of-the-Month Club selection) *Lolly Willowes* (1926) features a spinster heroine who becomes a witch and a companion to Satan in the name of feminism. The spinster-witch, as Carpenter had pointed out, is a lesbian prototype. Warner's next novel, *Mr. Fortune's Maggot* (1927), shows a missionary in the South Pacific lose his religion because of a baffled erotic attachment to a male islander. In 1931, Warner herself underwent a conversion to lesbianism, when she fell in love with the poet Valentine Ackland (d. 1969). In 1933, Warner and Ackland published a collaborative volume of poems, *Whether a Dove or Seagull*, and Warner's *Summer Will Show* (1936), a historical novel about love between two women caught up in the French revolution of 1848, is modeled on Warner's self-proclaimed marriage with Ackland. In later years, Warner's seventh novel, *The Flint Anchor* (1954), includes a study of the accepted practice of homosexuality by Dorset fishermen during the Regency period. Warner's biography in 1967 of T. H. White (1906–1964), the gay author whose revival of Arthurian romance in *The Sword and the Stone* (1939) and other books renews Carpenter's idea of male–male love as a benefit to the state, instances a convergence of lesbian biographer and gay male subject, whose shared ground in erotic and aesthetic realms is the borderland between realism and romance.

Among heterosexual fictions and literary essays about homosexuality originating in the 1920s, those by the artist-novelist-critic Wyndham Lewis (1886–1957) are most remarkable. They argue that homosexuality is not only "natural," but that it changes over time, varies according to its cultural milieu, and is of crucial political importance. In *The Lion and the Fox* (1926), a book-length critical study of SHAKESPEARE, Lewis presents the dramatist as a homosexual whose sexuality gave his poetic vision a peculiar advantage: creative skeptical distance from the Machiavellian agency that mesmerized Renaissance political practices. In effect transmuting T. E. Lawrence's pathic ethics into pathic aesthetics, Lewis argues that Shakespearian poetry owes part of its brilliance to transvestite inspirations: Shakespeare projects himself as Cleopatra to make love to his own Antony; Falstaff is a woman in drag. These inspirations, Lewis argues, valuably attack and undermine, even as they caress, masculine agency and function. Much as Lewis celebrates his gay Shakespeare, however, his attitudes toward homosexuality are self-divided. He fears that contemporary homosexuality will be fetishized and made into another form of class snobbery; he dislikes the alliance of feminism and homosexual rights movements. Yet Lewis, himself antipatriarchal, reluctantly admits sympathy with the alliance. In *The Art of Being Ruled* (1926), a book of cultural criticism, Lewis draws a political lesson from modern homosexuality, in a way that ties itself to *The Lion and the Fox:* He sees homosexual political aspirations bound to a form of spectatorship, both by virtue of homosexuals' rebelliousness and by the force of their exclusion from the "norm." The spectatorship is advantageous, however, Lewis argues; its distance from political action reveals the incoherence of democratic dogma and practice, and also teaches the public how spectatorial detachment can become the vengeance of the ruled over their repressive rulers. A passive politics, in Lewis's sight, can creatively counterbalance the heroic agency of men like Carpenter's shamans and warriors or women like Hall's Stephen.

Although it has been argued that the first part of this century's culture is dominated by attempts to keep homosexuality hidden, obviously the literary culture of the post-war years made homosexuality a matter of prominent public interest and controversy. But for every writer like Firbank and Hall, who wear their eros on their sleeves, an equal number of homosexual writers in the period maintain public silence about their sex lives, and dramatize homosexual themes indirectly, if at all. W. SOMERSET MAUGHAM (1874–

1965), the novelist and playwright whose plays dominate the English stage in the century's first third, omits mention of his homosexual loves in his 1938 memoir. E. M. Forster (1879–1970), author of five distinguished novels between 1905 and 1924, powerfully represents a frustrated homoerotic attachment, confused by class distinctions, between the two male protagonists of *The Longest Journey* (1907). But in 1914, Forster wrote and suppressed *Maurice*, a sexually explicit narrative of happy homosexual love (which was not published until 1971). The brilliant novelist IVY COMPTON-BURNETT (1884–1969) represents traditional family life exclusively in her work, in a style whose aesthetic impersonality seems far removed from the author's personal longtime relation, homophile if not homoerotic, with a female companion. The plays of NOËL COWARD (1899–1973) rivaled Maugham's in popularity, but Coward, an actor, composer, and entertainer as well as a writer, kept his homosexual life under wraps. Nevertheless, these writers express their suppressed love, after all, in a tendency to thematize persons and situations who oppose a cultural status quo depicted as shabby and tyrannical. Forster's novels exalt feminism and oppose imperialism. In such plays as *The Circle* (1921) and *The Constant Wife* (1926), Maugham subverts pieties about conventional marriage and about sexual ethics. Maugham's fiction sides with mystical renegades or victims of imperialism in a way that inflects the classic intermediate type and pathic suffering once more. Compton-Burnett's novels exhibit savagery as the heart of patriarchy and heterosexual family values as a form of horror. Coward comes closer to the subject of homosexuality than the others. *The Vortex* (1925) assigns to one of its minor figures, an elderly "male spinster," the role of an authoritative social critic; the play also suggests that unresolved homosexual panic causes the hero's drug addiction. *Post-Mortem* (1934), an indictment of the waste and hypocrisy of World War I, suggests the dignity of homoerotic love among soldiers. *Design for Living* (1936) bravely celebrates bisexual aspects of eros. Both Coward's and Maugham's plays, not incidentally, develop the forms and themes of Oscar Wilde's theater. In sum, given the content of these writers' works, the displacement of public utterance of their author's sexuality comes near to being an equally subversive mode of expression and self-exposure.

Because of the prominence in the culture at large of both open and covert representations of homosexuality, young men and women growing up and becoming writers during the first third of the century begin to consider their homosexual erotic lives as part of an increasingly established cultural tradition, no longer frighteningly unexampled. Consequently, the circle of poets, writers, and political activists emerging from Oxford around 1930, with Auden and Isherwood at their center, appear to take their homosexuality for granted—sufficiently at least to enable them, in a way that renews Bentham-like matter-of-factness about sexual desire and pleasure, to retreat from heroic figuring of homosexuality per se. Moreover, the impulse to subordinate homosexual desires and interests to arguably more comprehensive political ideologies—socialism, communism, liberalism, fascism—becomes strong among homosexual writers as World War II approaches. Auden's *The Ascent of F6* (1936), a verse play written with Isherwood, mocks the ambitions of a would-be hero whose character is based on T. E. Lawrence. Perhaps in line with suspicions of heroic claims made for a sexual orientation, Auden in the 1950s reintroduces Rolfe to readers by describing the ambition and ethical grandeur of Corvo's heroes, and of Corvo himself, as symptomatic of "the paranoid homosexual." Auden's intention to be beyond paranoia, to make no special historical or political case exclusively for homosexuality, results from a desire to find a common ground in poetry for the discussion of public issues in a way that makes the daily life and speech of all citizens, whatever their differences, the central measure of relevance. It is under the inspiration of political causes that are collective in the broadest meaning of the term, and not specific to an erotic "type," that Auden moves away from writing in the difficult, not-popular styles of modernist poetry, and toward poetic forms that, however elaborate, are part of a long tradition of public-minded plainness in verse.

Isherwood shares Auden's aim to merge the specificity of homosexual desire and experience with a general public concern, but he also vividly dissents from the aim. In the extraordinary memoir *Christopher and His Kind 1929–1939* (1976), Isherwood recounts his first decade as a writer in a way that connects his homosexuality to his particular history of conflicts with fascism and imperialism. England's enemy Germany, the agent of Isherwood's father's death in World War I, provided the post-war era with a homosexual mecca, thus impelling Isherwood to reside there, where he gathered material for the novels *The Last of Mr. Norris* (1935) and *Goodbye to Berlin* (1939). His German lovers, one in particular, inspired Isherwood to keep them out of the German army and war, and gave Isherwood's life a crucial antinationalist, antimilitarist determination. The general object of the determination is the idea of a sexual "kind," a queer international nation whose allegiance is to pacificism and to solidarity with "deviants" excluded from the life of citizens. In accordance with allegiance to this kind, on the eve of World War II, both Auden and Isherwood immigrated to America. Isherwood intended to became a conscientious objector; he found a motive for his decision in Eastern mysticism, partly because, under Western eyes, the latter had seemed a queer form of religion. Yet Isherwood's pacifism is not only a result of his homosexual position; it is partly the reflex of a personal and stylistic modesty, which means to show its solidarity with ordinary public democratic norms. And even as Isherwood insists on the specifically homosexual character of his history, he also insists on his right as a novelist to an artistic detachment from exclusive preoccupation with his own sexuality.

In their commitment to finding personal and social norms, Auden and Isherwood revise the epicene aspects of homosexual tradition: Wilde's brittleness, Firbank's high CAMP, Maugham's and Coward's glitter, are moderated by these later writers toward something stylistically and thematically more direct and spontaneous. Perhaps the most intense exponent of this antiartificial revision of the intermediate type is DENTON WELCH (1915–1948), artist, short-story writer, and novelist. Made irreversibly invalid by a motorcycle accident, Welch produced stories and novels ("When I Was Thirteen" and *In Youth Is Pleasure* [1944] are typical) whose homoeroticism is unequaled for their freshness and immediacy. Welch's pictures of young noncombatant men during World War II exhibit their subjects as anarchistic, impulsive, and probably gay. Always on the edge of extremes of despair and exhilaration, living under the constant threat of death, Welch's characters—both pathetic and strong—make the dizzy pleasure of disorientation an erotic end in itself; more than any other of Carpenter's heirs, Welch's protagonists let drop the high-minded narratives of homosexuality's cultural vocation. An equivalent representation of female experience, albeit subdued, accompanied by suggestions of lesbianism, is to be found in the novels and stories of ELIZABETH BOWEN (1899–1973). Two World War II stories about war-disoriented young women, "Mysterious Kôr" and "The Happy Autumn Fields," show Bowen's characteristic features: women finding passionate interrelations with each other via the elimination or marginalization of male intrusions on their intimacy.

The repetition of world conflict within a mere thirty years stimulated the connection of homosexuals with the passive endurance of extremity and, at the same time, with impulses to protest militantly the enlistment, on behalf of the state and the war effort, of gay and lesbian lives whose public importance and dignity had little place—outside literary culture—in peacetime. An example of the heterosexual world's cruelly mixed mode of simultaneously permitting and condemning homosexuality appears in the novel *Brideshead Revisited* (1945) by EVELYN WAUGH (1903–1966). One of the book's two heroes, the beautiful gay Sebastian Marchmain, is first idolized by the novelist and his narrator, then denounced and condemned for homosexuality and aestheticism. The cultural self-contradiction instanced by Waugh's narrative, long calling for correction, finds an answer, in the years following World War II, in the constitution by the Church of England's Moral Welfare Council of the Wolfenden Committee on homosexual offenses and prostitution. The Committee was to come to recommend de-criminalization of consensual homosexual relations in private, and to succeed with its recommendation—albeit not until 1967, when Parliament passed the reforming legislation.

During the long debate over the Committee's work and report, with the privacies of homosexual desire under aggressive public scrutiny, the temptation for homosexual writers to turn back in self-defense to heroic gay narratives was resisted—in spite of the occasion to do so presented by wearisome reiterations, in conservative quarters, of the need still to punish homosexual pleasure, and in spite of the tendency of even the Wolfenden Report's liberal supporters to express prejudice against the Report's subjects. As if presciently abreast of the self-deceptions and limitations of the Wolfenden committee's liberalism, the stories and novels of ANGUS WILSON (1913–1991) quizzically assess the shaky alliance between homosexuality and left-liberal ideologies. Tony, the wrinkled "pansy" of "Such Darling Dodos" (1950), and the bisexual novelist-hero of *Hemlock and After* (1952) both participate in protests against the managerial blindsidedness of liberal rational social planners. In later novels, Wilson depicts the failure of well-meaning left-liberal homosexuals themselves to make an impact on social and economic global conditions characterized by post-colonialism. In *No Laughing Matter* (1967) and *As If by Magic* (1973), homosexuality is one among many interests in a world governed by power struggles that transcend eros. In both novels, post-colonial natives derive some benefits from Wilson's gay figures, but they are not, as Carpenter might have hoped, redeemed by the latter. Wilson's matter-of-fact refusal to give homosexuals a mythological political aura, even in spite of the need to promote reform, is echoed on the stage in the matter-of-fact treatment of homosexuality in the later plays of Terence Rattigan (1911–1977): *Variations on a Theme* (1958); *Ross* (1960), a new study of T. E. Lawrence and the multiplicity of identity; and *Man and Boy* (1963).

Perhaps the most moving realism in the literary representation of homosexuality in this period is to be found outside fiction, in two memoirs: *My Father and Myself* (1968) by J. R. ACKERLEY (1896–1967) and *The Naked Civil Servant* (1968) by Quentin Crisp (b. 1908). Ackerley's book compares the author's homosexual life with his father's heterosexual life. Instead of merely justifying the former in terms of its erotic or political virtue, Ackerley shows how remarkably alike in instability, secrecy, pleasure, and frustration both the father's straight life and the son's gay life are. The father turns out, the son discovers, to have been a bigamist—and perhaps to have had in his youth a male lover. Just as the father deviates from his presumed sexual licitness, so the son, devoted to homosexuality, deviates from his deviation: Ackerley's greatest love is his female dog. Unlike both Carpenter and Bentham, Ackerley does not see erotic desire as particularly redemptive or as particularly satisfying. This concluding vision is liberating in itself, by virtue of its honesty, and of its Isherwood-influenced exactness and simplicity of style. Crisp's memoir, although written in the contrasting style of Wildean and Firbankian aphorisms, derives from convictions similar to Ackerley's. Known for flaunting an "outrageous" effeminacy in the 1920s and 1930s, Crisp mixes proud avowals of his life's erotic style with criticism of homosexual conventions: He finds camp undignified; he thinks intercourse a poor substitute for autoeroticism; he attacks gay bigotry against effeminate men. Above all, Crisp is struck by the irony of cultural history. In spite of decade-long parliamentary debates about them, "those who once inhabited the suburbs of human contempt"—homosexuals—"find that without changing their address they eventually live in the metropolis." And Crisp notes that, again in spite of censorious debates, by 1968 "the symbols which I had adopted forty years earlier to express my sexual type had become the uniform of all young people."

Two younger writers of the 1960s, the novelist BRIGID BROPHY (b. 1929) and the playwright JOE ORTON (1933–1967), exuberantly and fantastically complement the sober maturity of Ackerley and Crisp. Orton's *Entertaining Mr. Sloan* (1964), *Loot* (1966), and *What the Butler Saw* (1967) celebrate the Dionysian frenzy of amoral, polymorphously perverse sexualities. Brophy's *In Transit* (1969) revives the intermediate type, via *Orlando:* The novel's hero(ine) has no determinate gender, and the text's middle and end become "bitextual" inasmuch as the reader is furnished with alternative versions of the story, printed in double columns. Under the influence of "intermediate" inspirations, language and fiction are "in transit" to a new state of art and eros. Not surprisingly, and in a way that revives the heroic gay tradition, Brophy's next book after *In Transit* is her colossal reevaluation of Firbank, *Prancing Novelist* (1971), which along with *The Lion and the Fox* is one of the best critical studies in English of a gay writer.

The works and themes of Wilson and Brophy, along with *Christopher and His Kind,* remain paradigms of the last two decades' literary culture. During this time, homosexual men and women had to face on two fronts a new world war of sorts: first, the resurgence of religious, moral, and political conservatism in England since 1979, undermining both the modest legal gains of the Wolfenden legislation and the major literary-cultural achievements of homosexuality in the first three quarters of the century; second, the destruction of homosexual lives by the AIDS plague. Neither the call of heroic narrative nor of erotic pleasure easily withstands the new onslaught of cultural and biological suppression. Yet the literary work goes on, freshly reviving and revising the by now traditional motifs. *Oranges Are Not the Only Fruit* (1985) by JEANNETTE WINTERSON (b. 1959), echoing *Lolly Willowes,* intermingles realism and fairy-tale narrative as it presents a woman's lesbianism emerging from her domestic and religious compulsions. Forster's, Isherwood's, and Wilson's interest in the relation of homosexuality to post-colonial formations is taken up by PATRICK GALE (b. 1962) in the comedy of *Kansas in August* (1987), in which the gay hero Hilary loses his lover to his sister Henry, then is maneuvered into becoming the father of his Indian landlady's illegitimate granddaughter. The gay man thereby inherits, in a transformative way, the global political condition in which he now has only an equivocally advance guard status. A similar inheritance awaits the gay hero of Hanif Kureishi's *The Buddha of Suburbia* (1990), where a new breed of erotic and cultural possibilities emerges from three old histories: English, Indian, and gay. Retrospective meditations on English homosexual life's stories and pleasures, from Carpenter and Firbank to the present, are the substance of *The Swimming-Pool Library* (1988) by Alan Hollinghurst (b. 1954). Hollinghurst evokes both ancient and modern nonheroic compromises of homosexuality with racism and imperialism, with cultures that condemn as well as sustain homoeroticism, and with homosexuality's own capacity for erotic pleasure. The polish of Hollingsworth's narrator masks a dark pessimistic vision of modern homosexuality's relation to politics. A more optimistically intermediate point of view is recovered, surprisingly, in the AIDS stories *Monopolies of Loss* (1992) by Adam Mars-Jones (b. 1954). Although fully responsive to the horrors of AIDS, Mars-Jones's stories show the unsettling power of art's capacity to treat and transform mortality itself. Given the modern tradition that associates homosexuality with aestheticism, Mars-Jones's art becomes an implicit figure for homosexual reinventions of mortality.

The major English literary career of recent decades remains that of the poet THOM GUNN (b. 1929), whose life and work recapitulates many gay traditions since Carpenter. In his early years as a poet, Gunn pays homage to virile archetypes: ancient and contemporary versions of Carpenter's public-spirited homosexual Doric companions or samurai lovers. But although caught up in heightened poetic narratives of heroic gay masculinity, Gunn has simultaneously felt the influence of Auden's and Isherwood's less heroically inflected commitments to general public responsibility, no less than responsibility to one's homosexual kind. After repeating Auden's and Isherwood's emigration to the United States and (thereby also echoing Lawrence's and Casement's separation from the claims of a fatherland), Gunn's poetry has relaxed its tough homoeroticized masculinism and has rendered an apparently fixed homosexual eros into forms of flexible aesthetic play and lyric pleasure. The assault on play and pleasure by the impact of AIDS on Gunn's San Francisco community has inspired response from the poet in the poems in *The Man with Night Sweats* (1992). The book's meditations on the specificity of gay life's current involvement with death and art are mediated by the finely wrought Audenesque formality and generously public-minded tone of the poetry. Against the stress of mortality, Gunn recovers homosexual eros as the pleasure and dignity of an aesthetic counter-stress. The counter-stress, mingling pleasure and pain, perhaps is one of the latest variations of the intermediate type.

—*Robert L. Caserio*

BIBLIOGRAPHY

Boone, Joseph A., and Michael Cadden, eds. *Engendering Men.* New York: Routledge, 1990. ■ Brophy, Brigid. *Prancing Novelist.* New York: Barnes and Noble, 1973. ■ Committee on Homosexual Offenses and Prostitution. *The Wolfenden Report.* New York: Stein and Day, 1963. ■ Cunningham, Valentine. *British Writers of the Thirties.* Oxford: Oxford University Press, 1988. ■ Green, Martin. *Children of the Sun: A Narrative of "Decadence" in England after 1918.* New York: Basic Books, 1976. ■ Grey, Antony. *Quest for Justice.* London: Cassell, 1992. ■ Hobby, Elaine and Chris White, eds. *What Lesbians Do in Books.* London: Women's Press, 1991. ■ Meyers, Jeffrey. *Homosexuality and Literature, 1890-1930.* Montreal: McGill-Queen's University Press, 1977. ■ Shepherd, Simon. *Because We're Queers.* London: Gay Men's Press, 1989. ■ Silverman, Kaja. *Male Subjectivity at the Margins.* New York: Routledge, 1992. ■ Summers, Claude J. *Gay Fictions: Wilde to Stonewall.* New York: Continuum, 1990. ■ Woods, Gregory. *Articulate Flesh: Male Homo-eroticism and Modern Poetry.* 1987.

Erotica and Pornography

As a literary genre, pornography is writing that has sexual arousal as its primary objective. Erotica is such material with artistic pretensions. Thus, the descriptive term *pornography* implies a statement about intentionality and instrumentality without reference to merit, whereas the term *erotica* is evaluative and laudatory. In *Flesh and the Word*, John Preston more baldly says, "The only difference is that erotica is the stuff bought by rich people." Since current literary theory makes writing of every sort available to analysis, it has in effect done away with the distinction. To discuss the aesthetic effect of pornographic material is to accord it the status of erotica.

George Steiner has described as "fundamental to De Sade and much [heterosexual] pornographic art" the erroneous notion that "one can double one's ecstasy by engaging in *coitus* while being at the same time deftly sodomized." It is even more specifically the aim of gay pornography to perpetuate this myth since the interested reader will to some extent identify with all participants in a sexual encounter. The theme of the simultaneous orgasm is, in fact, the chief desideratum of much of the fantasy of modern gay fiction. To give pleasure while getting it, to have an orgasm while causing one, is taken as the great proof of the genuineness of the experience. But, as Steiner notes, it is really the sign of fantasy since real sex tends to fall somewhat short in intensity of the experiences chronicled in pornography. Of course, the ultimate simultaneity occurs when the reader participates along with the characters. On the other hand, as Philip Slater has noted, the ecstatic moment in the description of a sexual encounter is the entry, not the climax, and accordingly the most arousing pornography gives major attention to entry. On this point, the conventions of written pornography differ from those of video pornography, which tends to focus on orgasm. Historically, homoerotica has tended to emphasize some modes of sexuality out of proportion to their occurrence in life: pederasty in earlier times, sadomasochism in more modern. This is perhaps because pornography is about control of sex not simply about its occurrence. In an arena in which biological realities do not demarcate sexual roles, such themes empower the reader to experience the writer's mastery of the fantasy in a way that the flux of life often does not. The power dynamics of pornography allows readers to recognize and define the parameters of relationships.

The history of pornography in general is obscured by fashions in CENSORSHIP; the history of gay pornography, being doubly offensive to censors in many periods, has an even more obscure history. Five loosely defined periods may, nevertheless, be charted: classical, neoclassical, Victorian, modern, and post-Stonewall. Since pornography is defined by intentionality, until recently lesbian pornography has been difficult to distinguish from female-with-female material for a straight male audience and is dealt with separately.

Although classical Greek culture virtually institutionalizes pederasty, or more precisely ephebophilia rather than homosexuality in general or relationships between equal male partners, the culture certainly attached no stigma to homosexuality, and in evaluating literature made distinctions of form and style, not subject matter. As a result of these factors, a good deal of surviving Greek literature accepts or even celebrates homosexual relations of one kind or another, at least in passing. Unfortunately, the custodians of the surviving Greek texts in later ages had decided views on the appropriateness of various subject matters; a large amount of material that has disappeared was probably even more laudatory of ephebophilia and homosexuality and perhaps more explicit as well. The most explicit of overtly celebratory surviving works are lyrics in *The Greek Anthology*.

Since many more classical Latin manuscripts survive from antiquity and since these represent a more random selection of the material originally produced, it is not surprising to find a larger number of explicit works in Latin than in Greek. Although his more famous lyrics celebrate his mistress Lesbia, CATULLUS (87–54 B.C.) is one of several major Roman poets who write forthrightly of sexual encounters with boys. Martial (ca 40–ca 102) is another. And the surviving portion of *The Satyricon* of PETRONIUS (d. 66) describes similar activities. Indeed, forthrightness is a hallmark of Roman literature, and a historian like Suetonius (ca 69–ca 122) in *The Twelve Caesars* is pornographically explicit about the details of the homoerotic sadism practiced by a number of the early emperors.

The classical works of many non-Western cultures also include numerous ephebophiliac and sometimes pederastic episodes of frank eroticism. In China, for example, in an episode of *Jou Pu Tuan* ("The Carnal Prayer Mat," 1657) of Li Yü (1610–1680), the hero augments his own organ with a dog's penis and uses it to sodomize one of his servant boys. And in Japan, *The Great Mirror of Male Love* (1687) by IHARA SAIKAKU (1642–1693) sensualizes boys in a context of misogyny. Such material is especially common in Islamic societies. Poems celebrating the sexual attractions of boys, for example, form one of the major categories of the work of Abu Nuwas (ca 756–ca 810), one of the greatest of Arabic poets. The Persian poets Sa'di (ca 1215–ca 1292) and Hafiz (ca 1307–ca 1388) similarly eroticize boys. Indeed ephebophilia is so much an accepted part of classical Islamic civilization that it came to represent the norm of romantic involvement to the extent that many poets writing in Arabic and Persian used the mode of a love poem addressed to a boy even when they were not themselves inclined this way. In addition and in a different vein, by interpreting passionate male friendship as a vehicle of spiritual transcendence, the Persian mystic Rûmî ("The Man from Rûm," properly Jalal'l-Dîn [1207– 1273]) wrote perhaps the most erotic poetry of all Islamic literature. (See also MIDDLE EASTERN LITERATURE.)

As John Boswell has detailed, explicit celebration of pederasty was common throughout the European Middle Ages and Renaissance. The indiscriminate sexuality of classical civilizations that saw occasional sex between men and boys as an amusing change from sex between men and women continued to be chronicled in Renaissance pornography like *I piacevole ragionamenti* (*Diverting Dialogues* [1534–1536]) by Pietro Aretino (1492–1556). The first modern work with the celebration of pederasty as the primary focus is *L'Alcibiade fanciullo a scola* (*The Schoolboyish Alcibiades* [1651]) by Antonio Rocco (1576–1653). In the form of a Platonic dialogue describing the sexual education of a boy, this book satirizes Machiavelli's doctrine of expediency.

With the spread of printed books in the vernacular and the rise of the middle class, the situation in Europe began to change. These changes created a larger but less sophisticated reading public than had existed in the manuscript cultures of earlier periods. Sexual relations between men and boys were shunned as unnatural by these new readers to an extent that they had never been by previous aristocratic readers, and measures were taken to proscribe publications that offended the new sense of public decency. In addition, pornography in general became an identified—and stigmatized—genre, joining heresy, libel, and sedition for the first time as a censorable form of writing. Pornography went underground. As a result, a self-consciousness intruded in the prose style of pornography for the first time, giving it a distinctive literary character. Pornographic prose began to take on a hothouse lushness, as if the authors felt the need to sell their respectability by overwriting. In the cultures discussed so far, some authors wrote about sex explicitly, and some of these celebrated the love of boys, but all authors in each culture had existed in a single literary world. This unified intellectual climate rapidly ceased to exist with the rise of the middle class.

In England, with its early move away from agrarianism toward this middle-class respectability, the career of JOHN WILMOT EARL OF ROCHESTER (1641–1680) illustrates the growing tension. Although he retains his place as an author in the high culture, his pornographic play *Sodom,* in which a king makes "buggery" the preferred sexual activity at his court, is an underground work, excluded from collected editions and unrecognized in critical discussions until quite recently.

Fanny Hill (1748–1749) by JOHN CLELAND (1709–1789) represents a further stage of development. Although the first modern novels show a ribaldry and raciness the genre lost as the self-conscious respectability of the middle class grew, Cleland's sexual explicitness, despite or perhaps because of the fact that it is couched in the new florid pornographic style, kept *Fanny Hill* outside the pale of canonical literature from the beginning. It is in a sense the first underground novel. In addition, Donald Mengay shows how the rhetoric of *Fanny Hill* reveals it to be a homoerotic fantasy disguised as a heterosexual one. This deflection and also the suppression of the one explicit man-with-man sexual episode indicate the extent to which attitudes had already changed by the mid-eighteenth century. Although homosexual activity continued to be an occasional diversion of the upper classes and as such appeared up through modern times in such coterie works of aristocratic origin as *The 120 Days of Sodom* (composed ca 1785) by the MARQUIS DE SADE (1740–1814), the practice was no longer so much as alluded to in respectable literary works. Sade is, in fact, a transitional author in another sense since he complements the pederastic focus of the earlier periods with modern interest in the activities that now bear his name.

With the Victorian Era, several significant developments redirected Western homoerotica. A repetitious sameness came to characterize the prose of all pornographic descriptions, a sameness for which Steven Marcus has coined the term *pornotopia*. And there is a significant increase in the proportion of depictions of homosexuality that represent loving and equal relationships. Yet in the face of the stranglehold of middle-class morality on official public opinion, a frank merging of the interests of the upper and lower classes continued in the sex industry. Within the nether world, homosexual experiences had a surprising openness. In its sexual attitudes, the Victorian underground was as polymorphously perverse as classical antiquity. Open discussion of homosexuality was, however, severely restricted.

Yet many straight pornographic novels of the Victorian Era include without surprise or negative comment sexual encounters between (straight) men, with the implication that all men quite naturally on occasion desire other men. In *The Romance of Lust* (1873–1876), for example, protagonist Charlie Roberts is first introduced to sex by his uncle, and there are numerous scenes involving man-with-man sex interspersed throughout the novel. The principals participate in role-switching with a refreshing facility. In the pornographic world of carnality, anything is possible. In *The Power of Mesmerism* (1891), hypnotism is a magic force that licenses entry into this world of possibility. There are many instances when the protagonist Frank Etheridge uses his power to engage in sex with other men, and of course, he can never suffer any rebuff. Despite his absolute control of the sexual encounters (or perhaps because of this fact), he shows an admirable versatility. He is, however, primarily interested in releasing the lusts of his parents in an incestuous tangle.

Male homosexual encounters are also included in Victorian autobiographies like *My Life and Loves* (1926) by Frank Harris (1855–1931) and *My Secret Life* (1890). Unlike Victorian fictional heroes, the autobiographers are never quite comfortable with the implications of these occasional forays outside their usual sort of sexuality, but the works are important for showing that the frank bisexuality of numerous pornographic novels of the period is not simply fantasy but reflects actual activity. Even if the Walter who narrates *My Secret Life* is not transcribing his life with perfect accuracy, Harris is a real person who can be placed in the social fabric of the time, suggesting that modern Western polarized sexual identities were not yet the norm, at least for the upper and lower classes.

The Sins of the Cities of the Plain (1881) by Jack Saul (fl. 1881), with its surprisingly realistic depictions of rent boys and their patrons, is perhaps the first novel in English to focus primarily on man-with-man sexual relations. The poetry collection *White Stains* (1898) by Aleister Crowley (1875–1947) is the first work to illustrate what Brian Reade describes as the "brutal, burlesque approach to sexual intimacies and emotions . . . , [the] ribaldry" characteristic of modern attitudes. And *Teleny* in 1893 inaugurates the primary tradition of homoerotica in Europe. Perhaps owing a good deal of its influence to its frequent attribution to OSCAR WILDE (1854–1900), the work is apparently a

collaboration among members of the Wilde circle. It is also a real novel of adult experience in the sense that it has a plot that goes beyond the presentation of erotic encounters. One character takes his sexual experimentation too far when a wine bottle lubricated with pâté de foie gras breaks inside him while being used as a dildo. With great dignity, he winds up his affairs in the world and then kills himself rather than face the painful inevitability of slow death from internal damage. In addition, the main character, Camile Des Grieux, twice attempts to take his own life, and his beloved, René Teleny, actually succeeds in doing so. In fact, *Teleny* introduced the theme of suicide as a resolution to problems raised in gay-themed fiction. This served for many decades as a plot device to license the discussion of such problems. The tradition was continued and institutionalized in the pulp novels of the early modern period.

Although homosexuality is discussed openly but disparagingly in certain German works of the nineteenth century, the continuous history of modern, openly favorable treatment of homosexuality began in France with a relaxation of censorship during the Roaring Twenties, and a substantial amount of homoerotica appeared as part of this renaissance. The cumulative effect of French homoerotica of this period was to present a countercultural picture of a gay subculture. It thus polarized the world into gay and straight, doing so perhaps precisely because it focuses for the first time on man-with-man sex in the middle class. The openness of France spread gradually to other Western nations.

In works like *Our Lady of the Flowers* (1944) and *The Thief's Journal* (1948), JEAN GENÊT (1910–1986) was the breakthrough author who had brought explicit scenes of homosexual activity into the living rooms of middle-class society the world over by the end of this period. He did so by investing his use of obscene language and anatomical detail with a sense of existential determinism. The isolation of prison is redeemed in self-love, which is realized as self-abuse. The unsatisfactory nature of this masturbation in the womanless confines of prison generates erotic encounters between men. And the hopelessness of prison is redeemed by the spirituality of the resulting romanticized orgy. But by describing this etiology of homosexual activity, Genêt of course marks it as aberrant, occasional, apart from the real world. This explicit demarcation of homosexuality as an activity from a world apart—to a middle-class audience, a world of fantasy—is what legitimized him for high culture. The fact that he is a beautifully poetic writer probably helped. Just because he was not arousing for the general public who made him fashionable, he made it possible for explicit sexual material to be included in mainstream fiction, and it soon became apparent that this meant explicit heterosexual material as well as homosexual. The pornographic status of Genêt for homosexual readers is ambiguous. Despite his reiterated theme of the opportunistic nature of homosexual activity, he is in fact still arousing.

Because of a sudden imposition of press censorship in France and a number of important rulings liberalizing freedom of the press from the U.S. Supreme Court, the 1950s saw the locus of publication for erotic literature shift from Paris to Copenhagen, New York, and other American cities. Whereas the Parisian erotica had been largely the creation of Obelisk Press and its successor Olympia Press, American publication was from the beginning more diversified. In addition to Olympia, relocated in New York, numerous other publishers sprang up all over the country; the Guild Press in Washington was responsible for some of the most interesting gay titles. The paperback revolution also made it easier for new publishers and new writers to emerge. Although many works released under these circumstances were undoubtedly badly written as well as poorly bound and inadequately edited and proofread, the wide diversity gave some excellent writers opportunities to experiment. Although the vast majority of these pulp novels made unrealistic and inartistic use of the milieus they exploited, the occasional hot episode made the material useful for the intended purpose. There were many imitators of Genêt. Perhaps the best of these was JOHN RECHY (b. 1934) in City of Night (1963) and later works. While recreating the milieu of the hustler in vivid and realistic detail, Rechy's works are marked by an atmosphere of distaste or uncleanness that is darker and less celebratory than anything in Genêt and indicates the continuity of the legacy of guilt in homoerotica. Other American authors of the Genêt school like WILLIAM BURROUGHS (b. 1914) and Hubert Selby (b. 1926) tend to be as angst-laden as Rechy, as are many lesser writers, who tend to be less vivid as well. The angst licensed mainstream readers to appreciate these works, but it did not deeroticize them for homosexual readers (and perhaps not for heterosexual readers either).

But not all American authors followed this model. Casimir Dukahz (ca 1899–1988) in The Asbestos Diary (1966) creates the entirely different world of the "boysexual." With witty and wildly inventive word play, he evokes in a fashion appropriately episodic both the bittersweet transience of boyhood and all the adolescent silliness and surprise encountered by a man constantly available for the entertainment of boys. This subject matter, despite the obvious literary merit

of the treatment, has given Dukahz greater difficulty with censors than more explicit authors. Acolyte Press in the Netherlands, not without some difficulty, has reissued Dukahz's masterpiece and publishes such later works of his as Vice Versa (1976), Growing Old Disgracefully (1986), and Shakespeare's Boy (1991). Only the first of these matches the power of The Asbestos Diary, although they are all well written and amusing. Shakespeare's Boy is Dukahz's only attempt at traditional narrative.

The Loon trilogy by Richard Amory (fl. 1966–1974), consisting of Song of the Loon (1966), Song of Aaron (1967), and Listen, the Loon Sings (1968), inaugurates a stream of romanticism in gay male erotic fiction by uniting the rugged men-only adventure tale of Zane Grey (1872–1939) and explicit gay sexuality. Indeed Amory's books celebrate gay male sexuality as a solution to racial tensions as his cowboys and Indians happily get it on with one another. The books were so popular that there was even a 1969 soft-core film adaptation marketed to a more general audience than other gay erotic films of the time. Michael Perkins attributes equally to the lyricism of the Loon trilogy and to the campiness of the nonfiction work The Homosexual Handbook (1968) by Angelo d'Arcangelo (fl. 1968–1969) the breaking of the tradition of expiation through guilt that began with Teleny. Michael Bronski credits the 1967 Gay Whore by Jack Love (fl. 1967), but it was far less widely read than the other books in its day and has even evaded the bibliographer Ian Young. Yet, whoever was responsible, a mood of change was clearly already in the air in the late 1960s, a mood that culminated in the Stonewall Riots.

What Genêt, Dukahz, Amory, and even Rechy have in common in distinction from Victorian pornographers is that they redefine the duality of writers for whom gay sex and sex in general occur in a secret, stigmatized underground culture. Instead, each of these writers creates what is effectively a parallel universe in which gay sexuality is a perfectly natural state of affairs not answerable to mainstream society. And many lesser writers of this period adopt the same premise.

Several other writers who began working in this period are important historically because their later careers tell us something fundamental about changing public attitudes. Phil Andros, author of such books as Stud (1966) and San Francisco Hustler (1971), has since emerged as the gay mystery novelist Samuel Steward (1909–1993). The Steward novels create a wonderful sense of completeness in a world (Paris in the 1920s) in which gay sexuality is a natural and expected element of life. They are also amusing. But in the works he wrote as Andros, Steward is both more controlled as a stylist and more circumscribed in his picture of the world, probably because the world was a different place when he began writing these, a place in which gay sexuality was at ease only as liberating fantasy. His careful craftsmanship in this early work undoubtedly prepared Steward for his later career, and his current fame has led to the reprinting of the early material for a wider audience. Later Andros works include *Greek Ways* (1975). Although the books published under his own name do not include explicit sexual descriptions, Steward has argued for the legitimacy of pornography in *Chapters from an Autobiography* (1981) and described it simply as the straightforward way of writing about sex.

Similarly, James Colton, author of such works as *Lost on Twilight Road* (1964) and *Tongue and Cheek* (1969), is now the mystery writer JOSEPH HANSEN (b. 1923). The mainstream books depict a gay detective working in a real world (this time the contemporary one) in which his sexual identity is something taken for granted, but as with Steward, these books are no longer explicit. During his lifetime, Robin Maugham (1916–1981) had also revealed himself as the author of pornography, the 1967 David Griffin novel *The Wrong People*.

The rich development of lesbian and gay male literature of all kinds in the period since the Stonewall Riots is a phenomenon of our times. So much material is published that *The Lambda Book Report*, a review magazine devoted to gay books, can hardly keep up. Although there are still small publishers issuing poorly written, badly edited pulp novels (in fact, the quality of these has actually declined), in this climate of openness, more and more quality small presses are issuing well-written homoerotica. An important theorist of the new eroticism is Marco Vassi (1937–1989), who proposes in both essays and fiction a "fusion of mind and sex organs" in "metasexuality," arguing that "there is no real difference between what two men do in bed [and] what three women . . . do [or] a man and a woman."

One of the first major new gay male pornographers to emerge in the wake of the new openness is Larry Townsend (b. 1936). Although he does write novels, he is perhaps at his best and certainly at his most characteristic in *The Leatherman's Handbook* (1972). In this ostensibly nonfiction work, the tone is much darker than anything in Rechy but entirely without the apologia of the Genêt imitators. For Townsend, sex means cruelty and control. His pornographic vision is of the sort that Perkins has described as "assaultive." Though Townsend theorizes that sadomasochism is an exercise in trust, there is an edge of danger to the sex play unique to his powerful vision here and in his fiction.

Explicit, perverse, and perpetual man-with-man sex also distinguishes the *All* trilogy of Dirk Vanden (fl. 1969–1971): *I Want It All* (1969), *All or Nothing* (1970), and *All Is Well* (1971). Taking a sensual rather than an assaultive approach to the same milieu that Townsend treats, Vanden creates dream worlds of the subconscious as he explores coming to grips with sexual identity in the no-nonsense butch world of a fisting club. Despite the nature of the sex acts explored, Vanden always emphasizes the reassuring and caring nature of the personal dynamics. There is no pain or violence, or at least these represent immaturity to be ashamed of and outgrown. Bill Thorne, the hero of *All or Nothing,* for example, is dragged reluctantly into gang-banging a suspected queer at the beginning of the book, only to spend the rest of it searching for Brad Nelson, the man abused, to apologize and expiate his offense, which he finally does when he finds Nelson and experiences the joy of being fisted by him at an orgy. The message seems to be that real men come to accept, control, and like themselves by extending their sexual boundaries. Warren Miller, the hero of *I Want It All,* refuses to participate in the same gang-bang that begins *All or Nothing* and rescues Nelson. He then undergoes a career of self-discovery like Thorne's in the same time frame, eventually settling down in domesticity with Nelson.

John Preston (1945–1993) is a major new pornographer who has emerged more recently. In the popular *Mr. Benson* (1983), he expounds the correct leather slave mentality, emphasizing in particular the difference between going through the motions of dominance and submission and believing them to the extent that they take emotional hold. Despite many scenes of fisting, water sports, and savage beating, Preston manages to give a sweet romantic cast to his sadomasochism completely unlike Townsend's darkness, perhaps by adopting the had-I-but-known tone of Mary Roberts Rinehart (1876–1958). Preston, whose autobiography, *My Life as a Pornographer,* was published in 1993, has also written a series of mock-heroic action-adventure books about crime fighter Axel Kane and his faithful companion. And Preston has collected the stories of others in *Flesh and the Word* (1992) and the AIDS-conscious *Hot Living* (1985).

Indeed, despite all the activity, the novel is not particularly the vehicle of the new erotica. With mainstream novels like *Faggots* (1978) by LARRY KRAMER (b. 1935) and *Less than Zero* (1985) by Bret Easton Ellis (b. 1964) now often including more explicit and more extensive scenes of gay sexuality than many gay male pornographic novels did as recently as the late 1960s, it is perhaps no longer necessary to have a full-length narrative to justify short passages. The development and extensive growth of video pornography has undoubtedly also contributed to a movement away from the novel as the modal genre of written pornography. In the post-Stonewall era, quality homoerotic writing flourishes instead in shorter forms, the short story being especially well-suited to intense concentration on sexual experience. Issued together in a thin paperback, Preston's novellas *The Heir* (1980) and *The King* (1992) are an indication of this trend toward short forms alongside his popular anthologies and his own stories *Tales from the Dark Lord* (1992). His novel *The Arena* (1993) was originally a serial in *Stallion*, and *Mr. Benson* itself is, in fact, an expansion of a short story from *Drummer*. Moreover, the gay male erotic short story is now often the form in which new authors first make a mark.

Dozens of slick magazines now regularly print gay pornographic short stories. Available on public newsstands in all major cities in the United States and in many other countries, *Advocate Men, All Men, Blueboy, Drummer, Fresh Men, Friction, Honcho, Inches, In Touch, Jock, Male Insider, Mandate, Men, Numbers, Playguy, Stallion, Stroke, Torso, Uncut,* and similar monthly magazines are modeled after *Playboy* in the sense that they combine fiction (and sometimes nonfiction) of an openly sexual nature with photographic spreads of naked models. The difference is that the models are men, often with full erections, and that the fiction highlights explicit, detailed descriptions of sexual encounters between men. The growth in the number of such magazines published is not even so astonishing as the degree to which a high average standard has been maintained in the quality of the writing. Although Rupert Smith has suggested that the material from the 1970s and early 1980s was amateurish and that British gay pornography perhaps improved when it had to become less explicit in the wake of a censorship crackdown in the mid-1980s, American material has continued to be completely explicit, and excellent new writers appear all the time. When the Stonewall Riots precipitated the loosening of censorship restrictions, the American gay community had ready at hand a large number of authors willing and able to provide stimulating material with full artistic control.

Perhaps the best of the new writers is Aaron Travis (b. 1956). The works collected in *The Flesh Fables* (1990) typically unfold sharp psychological insights that make sense precisely because of the eroticism. He has described his "hyperthermal mode" of third-person melodramatic narrative in uncensored language as cinematic in two different ways: plotted explicitly like the *films noirs* of the 1940s and more generally cinematic in its immediacy and intensity. In the no-

vella *Crown of Thorns,* for example, the protagonist Eric is an American diplomat in Istanbul who becomes obsessed with a Turkish ship's stoker, losing his self-respect and finally his job in the process. There are parallels to *Death in Venice* (1913) by THOMAS MANN (1875–1955), but Travis is more immediate and vivid by virtue of his explicitness. In Travis's most famous story, a topman is mastered by the witchcraft of a "Blue Light" that first traps him, then dismembers him, and finally allows him to be entered like a woman. Travis's novel *Slaves of Empire* (1985) is an expansion of a story from *Drummer*. Other works include *Big Shots* (1993), which collects two powerful novellas, and *Beast of Burden* (1993), which collects short stories. Travis has recently begun publishing mystery novels under his own name, Steven Saylor.

John Rowberry (1948–1993), who has since become a critic and bibliographer of gay video porn, is perhaps less important as a storyteller in his own right than for encouraging writers like Travis and Preston when he was editor of *Drummer*. Though he certainly plunges right into all the mythic themes of homoerotica, the vision is always a little off. For example, in "The Mechanic," reprinted in *Lewd Conduct* (1993), the unnamed narrator's sudden abandonment of his past life raises questions that cry out for exploration in a much longer work. Far from allowing us to forget the narrator's unresolved past life, the story's orgy actually extends into real time the question of what is to become of his past.

A more consistent storyteller is Lars Eighner (b. 1948). His evocative interconnected stories of growing up with gay sex in Texas and Louisiana are collected in *Bayou Boy* (1985; the 1992 edition suppresses the ages of the boys). Eighner, remarkable for his realistic portrayal of a wide variety of different scenes, is also the author of *Lavender Blue: How to Write and Sell Gay Men's Erotica* (1987), and he has recently achieved fame with mainstream readers for the autobiographical description of his homeless life in the essay "On Dumpster Diving" from *Travels with Lizabeth* (1993).

Although he is also known for the experimental cinematic technique of his epic of San Francisco's Castro district, *Some Dance to Remember* (1990), Jack Fritscher (b. 1939) is known primarily as a writer of such short fiction as the stories of *Corporal in Charge of Taking Care of Captain O'Malley* (1984). Another interesting story writer is Leo Cardini (b. 1948), who recreates the lost way of life of the New York sex clubs in *Mineshaft Nights* (1990).

The stories collected by John Patrick (b. 1943) in such anthologies as *Unforgettable* (1994) are additional evidence of the vitality of the trend toward shorter forms. Patrick's own widely admired voyeuristic stream-of-consciousness novellas recounting life in the video porn industry have been collected in one volume as *Angel* (1991).

Less well-controlled than the fiction in the slick gay magazines and the anthologies are the sometimes even more exciting although often crudely written reminiscences of *S.T.H.* (*Straight to Hell*), periodically collected in book form by Boyd McDonald (1925–1993). The unashamed raunchiness of these nonprofessional writers often expresses a highly developed political consciousness, at least as nurtured by McDonald and framed by his social commentary. Fritscher began his career in pornography as editor of another such true-confessions magazine, *Man to Man*. Other amateur writers, constrained by copyright laws, circulate in a thriving underground gay pornographic stories about "Star Trek" characters and contribute to "gayzine" publications.

Of genuine lesbian pornography, there can be no history as such before 1969. Because straight men double their pleasure by fantasizing about two women at the same time, down the centuries there are innumerable scenes of woman-with-woman eroticism in straight pornography and even works focused on such material. But since women in general have preferred a romantic rather than a carnal view of sexuality, writings about women intended to arouse them to interest in other women are scarce and also not easy to identify amid the pseudonymity of most woman-with-woman historical pornography. Such historical material may have helped some lesbians of the past understand their own desires.

The lesbian pulp novels of the 1950s and 1960s certainly helped many women define themselves, but they are for the most part not explicit, and to the extent they are, their explicitness is not directed to women's sensibilities. Lisa Henderson describes the quality that defines the character of genuine lesbian eroticism as explicit material empowered by "framing." Woman-with-woman material genuinely intended for lesbians addresses the psychological issue of power and control by reassuring the reader that submissive acts are voluntary, not capitulatory, and that danger is only play. This character of lesbian pornography has undoubtedly emerged in part because of the problematic nature of pornography in general for many women.

Nevertheless, in the last decade, women have gone beyond the overt but not sexually explicit lesbianism of *Odd Girl Out* (1957) by ANN BANNON (b. 1932) and begun to write erotically about relationships with other women without the reticent romantic fantasy of *Challenge* (1924) by VITA SACKVILLE-WEST (1892–

1962) or *Orlando* (1928) by VIRGINIA WOOLF (1892–1941), without the apologia of a novel like *The Well of Loneliness* (1928) by RADCLYFFE HALL (1880–1943), and without the intention of stimulating the male reader of *Delta of Venus* (1969) by ANAÏS NIN (1903–1977). The breakthrough novel giving unapologetic lesbian subject matter mainstream respectability is *Rubyfruit Jungle* (1973) by RITA MAE BROWN (b. 1944). But although censorable by traditional standards and reassuring by modern ones, this is in no sense an arousing work.

The tendency among women is still toward a more romantic approach to sex, discrediting the insistent emphasis on sexual mechanics and visual detail that distinguishes gay male pornography today in particular and much pornography by and for men in general throughout history. The Naiad Press is committed to publishing such romantic lesbiana; this press has also made available to the general lesbian reading public *Lifting Belly,* the erotic but sometimes childish evocation of her domestic life that GERTRUDE STEIN (1874–1946) was not able to publish in her own lifetime.

Some major voices of a new lesbian eroticism have emerged. In light-hearted adventure novels like *Dancer Dawkins and the California Kid* (1985) and *Dead Heat* (1988), Willyce Kim (b. 1946) includes perhaps more story and less sex than is usual in male material, but as *The Feminist Bookstore News* suggests, her works "make clear the difference between merely describing lesbian relationships and delighting in them." In the immensely popular *Uncertain Companions* (1992) by Robbi Sommers (b. 1950), sensuality sweeps the heroine Veronica into a fantasy world where she becomes Feronia, the beloved of the moon goddess Devana. The mainstream lesbian mystery novelist Katherine V. Forrest (b. 1939) has written an erotic coming-out novel, *Curious Wine* (1983), as well. And she has collaborated on collecting the stories in *The Erotic Naiad* (1992). The writers in the 1991 anthology *Bushfire*, edited by Karen Barber, celebrate how much fun sex can be. Those in *Herotica* (1988) and its sequels, edited by Susie Bright (b. 1958), and *Woman in the Window* (1992), edited by Pamela Pratt (1958–1993), represent a variety of new voices. JoAnn Loulan (b. ca 1948) has written a number of sex guides. And there are even lesbian pornographic magazines, the most important of which is *On Our Backs*.

But the most striking index of the degree to which new possibilities are being explored by women is that some of the new work is sadomasochistic although with a very different feel from male-oriented material because, as Henderson notes, the authors are careful to imply the informed consent of all the characters. Perhaps the best of such works are the stories of

Macho Sluts (1988) by Pat Califia (b. 1954), the advice columnist of the gay news magazine *The Advocate* and also the author of man-with-man erotica. Sara Dunn describes the stories of *Macho Sluts* as moving "beyond the need to apologize." Califia herself describes the stories as liberating fantasies; apparent coercion is framed as fantasy controlled by the submissive partner. In the same vein, the novella *Bad Habits* (1991) by Lindsay Welsh (b. ca 1960) is distinguished by its balanced racial treatment. (See also SADOMASOCHISTIC LITERATURE.)

—*Edmund Miller*

BIBLIOGRAPHY

Boswell, John. *Christianity, Social Tolerance, and Homosexuality: Gay People in Western Europe from the Beginning of the Christian Era to the Fourteenth Century.* Chicago: University of Chicago Press, 1980. ■ Bright, Susie, ed. *Herotica: A Collection of Women's Erotic Fiction.* Burlingame, Ga.: Down There, 1988. ■ Bronski, Michael. "Classics from the Closet." *The Guide* 11.2 (February 1991): 118–121. ■ Dunn, Sara. "Voyages of the Valkyries: Recent Lesbian Pornographic Writing." *Feminist Review* 34 (1990): 161–170. ■ Eighner, Lars. *Lavender Blue: How to Write and Sell Gay Men's Erotica.* Intro. John Preston. Austin, Tex.: Liberty Imprint of Caliente (subsequently an imprint of Fire Island), 1987. ■ Marcus, Steven. *The Other Victorians: A Study of Sexuality in Mid-Nineteenth-Century England.* New York: Basic, 1966. ■ Mengay, Donald. "The Sodomitical Muse: *Fanny Hill* and the Rhetoric of Crossdressing." *Homosexuality in Renaissance and Enlightenment England: Literary Representations in Historical Context.* Claude J. Summers, ed. New York: Haworth, 1992. 185–198. ■ Munt, Sally, ed. *New Lesbian Criticism: Literary and Cultural Readings.* New York: Harvester, 1992. ■ Perkins, Michael. *The Secret Record: Modern Erotic Literature.* New York: William Morrow, 1976. ■ Preston, John. *My Life as a Pornographer and Other Indecent Acts.* New York: Richard Krasden Imprint of Masquerade, 1993. ■ Reade, Brian [Anthony], ed. *Sexual Heretics: Male Homosexuality in English Literature from 1850 to 1900.* New York: Coward-McCann, 1970. ■ Slater, Philip E[lliot]. *The Pursuit of Loneliness: American Culture at the Breaking Point.* Boston: Beacon, 1970. ■ Smith, Rupert. "One-Handed Reading." *Lesbian and Gay Writing: An Anthology of Critical Essays.* Mark Lilly, ed. Philadelphia: Temple University Press, 1990. 164–174. ■ Steiner, George. "Night Words: High Pornography and Human Privacy." *Perspectives on Pornography.* Douglas A. Hughes, ed. New York: St. Martin's, 1970. 96–108. ■ Steward, Samuel M. *Chapters from an Autobiography.* San Francisco: Grey Fox, 1981. ■ Vassi, Marco. *Metatext, Mirth, and Madness: Erotic Tales of the Absurdly Real.* Intro. Martin Shepard. New York: Penthouse, 1975.

Ethnography

Ethnography has become, in effect, the description of indigenous non-European peoples by Euro-Americans, in short, descriptions of so-called primitive people. Historically, ethnography has been a particularly attractive form of writing for homosexuals or those who wished to write about homosexuality. (To avoid anachronism and ethnocentrism in this article, the term *homosexuality* will refer to any sexual acts performed by persons of the same sex, and not merely to the form those acts took on in modern Euro-American culture.)

Before the twentieth century, writing about homosexuality in modern Europe came in one of two forms—pornography or studies of psychological or social pathology. Euro-Americans who had homosexual relations were considered either sick or criminals. Thus to talk of such people without stigmatization, authors had to move outside Euro-American culture, where they could write about homosexual relations as "primitive" rather than as "pathological."

In addition, ethnography was a way for writers to cloak themselves in the mantle of the scientific, which protected them from questions about their sexual orientation or political ideology. The scientific description of primitive homosexual relations could therefore counter the equally scientific—but more pejorative—work in social psychology and pathology.

Moreover, ethnography counters charges that homosexuality is "unnatural." The occurrence of homosexuality among so-called primitive peoples ("noble savages," as Rousseau called them) indicated that homosexuality was "natural." As Sir Richard Burton pointed out, homosexuality in the Americas "astonishes the anthropologist, who is apt to consider pederasty the growth of luxury and the especial product of great and civilized cities, unnecessary and therefore unknown to savagery."

Ethnography broke down other homophobic stereotypes such as the belief that homosexuals were weak and cowardly by describing homosexuality among tribal warriors and that homosexuals were ungodly by detailing the priestly roles of homosexuals in many cultures. However, ethnography did reinforce other stereotypes, such as that homosexuals were "artistic," "transvestites," "bestial," "corrupters of youth," and of "foreign origin."

Ethnography played on the erotic allure of the foreign. Homosexual relations have often been viewed as a "foreign" habit. Such terms in popular gay language as French and Greek sex for oral and anal intercourse derive from the English view that such practices must come from elsewhere. The term *buggery* derives from the belief that anal intercourse was a Bulgarian heresy. Insofar as foreign practices excite xenophobia, such references are negative. But the foreign also suggests attractive alternatives. Both heterosexual and homosexual Europeans often imagined—and sometimes lived on—tropical islands freed from the constraints of Euro-American prudery and sexual repression.

Ethnography with homosexual subject matter treated a number of different ethnic groups. The most important ethnic group treated by gay ethnographers was ancient Greeks. It is hard to underestimate the importance that ancient Greek pederasty had on the formation of modern concepts of homosexuality. Such nineteenth-century homosexual writers as JOHN ADDINGTON SYMONDS and EDWARD CARPENTER argued that since the Greeks are respected for the epitome of civilization, wisdom, and moral virtue, and the purest combination of the natural with the austerely rational, then homosexual behavior among the Greeks indicates that such practices are rational, natural, civilized, and moral. Symonds's book *A Problem of Greek Ethics* (1873) argued the importance of the Greek example. Carpenter's books *The Intermediate Sex* (1908) and *Intermediate Types Among Primitive Folk* (1914) were more popular and widely distributed. They discuss the Greeks as one among many other ethnic groups in which homosexuality was recognized and valued. Debate about how to interpret Greek sexual behavior still goes on, but the terms have changed. Whereas before K. J. Dover's *Greek Homosexuality* (1978), scholars still debated whether the Greeks valorized actual sexual activity and how frequently such behavior occurred, today the debate in such works as David M. Halperin's *One Hundred Years of Homosexuality* (1990), John J. Winkler's *The Constraints of Desire* (1990), and FOUCAULT's *The History of Sexuality* is how close Greek pederasty resembles modern homosexuality.

Yet another important Victorian work of ethnography is Sir Richard Burton's "Terminal Essay" to his edition of *The Arabian Nights* (1885). Burton believed that a "Sotadic Zone" circled the earth, stretching from the Mediterranean through the Near East, across India and Asia and throughout the Americas. Burton believed that homosexuality was "geographical and climatic, not racial." By blaming homosexuality on the weather, Burton removed it in part from the moral, racial, and biological arguments of the day.

More romantic versions of ethnography appeared. HERMAN MELVILLE's novels *Typee* (1846) and *Omoo*

(1847), were considered ethnography in their day. CHARLES WARREN STODDARD wrote highly romantic accounts of the Pacific Islanders, including *South-Sea Idyls* (1873) and *The Island of Tranquil Delights* (1904). J. R. ACKERLEY's *Hindoo Holiday* (1932) borrows from that tradition. Today, the American artist and anthropologist Tobias Schneebaum continues that tradition in such books as *Keep the River to Your Right* (1969) and *Where the Spirits Dwell* (1988).

It is important to distinguish between scholarly anthropology, early ethnography, and imaginative literature. Making such distinctions is most necessary in discussions of Native Americans. Spanish missionaries like Cieza de Leon gave lurid reports of sodomy and cannibalism among the natives. De Pauw, a French explorer, in his *Recherches Philosophiques sur les Américains* (1771) discusses transvestism in Mexico. These early accounts must be regarded with enormous skepticism. More reliable are recent anthropological studies such as Walter Williams's *The Spirit and the Flesh* (1986) and Will Roscoe's *The Zuni Man-Woman* (1991). But during the 1960s, Richard Amory wrote a series of pornographic books—beginning with *Song of the Loon* (1966)—which trades on the myth of the American West and the ethnographic studies of homosexuality among Native Americans. In such ways, ethnography surfaces into the popular imagination and popular literature.

One of the most positive and influential essays on homosexuality in the early twentieth century is Edward Westermarck's "Homosexual Love" in his *The Origin and Development of Moral Ideas* (1906). Westermarck's work is important among earlier work because it assumes that homophobia, rather than homosexuality, is what needs explanation. He asks how did the prohibitions against "sodomy" arise? His answer, after a look at ethnography, is that homophobia arose from the disgust many humans feel toward sexuality in general and from the need to control "unbelief, idolatry or heresy." He contends that as "people emancipated themselves from theological doctrines," they regard homosexuality with "somewhat greater leniency." Such tolerance is the proper response to "a powerful nonvolitional desire exercise[d] upon an agent's will."

—David Bergman

BIBLIOGRAPHY

Burton. Sir Richard. "Terminal Essay." *The Arabian Nights.* London: Privately printed, 1885. ∎ Carpenter, Edward. *The Intermediate Sex.* London: George Allen & Unwin, 1908. ∎ ———. *Intermediate Types Among Primitive Folk.* London: George Allen & Unwin, 1914. ∎ Westermarck, Edward. "Homosexual Love." *The Origin and Development of Moral Ideas.* London: Macmillan, 1906.

Feminist Literary Theory

Feminist literary theory is a complex, dynamic area of study that draws from a wide range of critical theories, including psychoanalysis, Marxism, cultural materialism, anthropology, and structuralism. Although feminist literary theory is often described simply as the use of feminist principles and techniques to analyze the textual constructions of gendered meaning, feminists' definitions of GENDER and of feminism have undergone a number of significant alterations since the early 1970s. By adopting already existing feminist insights and applying them in new ways, literary theorists transform them, thus creating an increasingly diversified field of study. Despite this diversity, most feminist literary theorists share several assumptions. To begin with, they generally agree that hierarchically ordered male–female gender relations impact on all aspects of human social existence, including apparently ungendered categories of thought, by establishing a series of binarisms—such as active/passive, presence/absence, and universal/particular—in which the "femininized" term occupies the devalued place. Because literary representations have concrete, material effects on people's lives, these non-symmetrical male–female binaries both illustrate and reinforce the oppression of real-life women. Like feminism, which critically analyzes and attempts to transform contemporary social systems, feminist literary theory entails a twofold movement encompassing both the critique of already existing sociolinguistic structures and the invention of alternative models of reading and writing.

In its earliest phases, this double movement focused almost exclusively on female-gendered issues; however, the increased participation of feminists of color, coupled with the rise of gender studies during the early 1980s, has expanded feminism's field of study considerably. Generally, feminist literary theory is divided into four stages or trends focusing in various ways on gender-based textual issues: (1) an analysis of representations of women in male-authored texts; (2) "gynocriticism," a term coined by Elaine Showalter that refers to the development of a uniquely female aesthetic and an alternative, women's literary tradition; (3) "gender studies," or an analysis of the ways all texts, including those written by men, are marked by gender; and (4) explorations of how racial, sexual, and class differences among women expand previous models of gendered reading and writing. It is, however, important to recognize that these stages are interconnected and overlapping; they represent tendencies often occurring simultaneously rather than discrete chronological stages. Thus, the rise in gender studies during the early 1980s developed concurrently with the recognition and analysis of the many ethnic, sexual, and class differences among women. Both trends represent expansions of already existing feminist insights: The analysis of the differences among women grew out of challenges by lesbian-feminists of all colors and heterosexual women of color, and gender studies developed out of the feminist insight that because gender is a relational term encompassing both women and men, theories of reading and writing are inscribed by both masculinity and femininity.

Although it is recognized that feminist theory has made significant contributions to the developing fields of lesbian, gay, and queer theory, the interrelationships among them are exceedingly complex. Whereas some theorists attempt to separate feminism from lesbian, gay, and queer studies, others do not. Gayle Rubin, for example, distinguishes between gender and sexuality and argues that because feminism is the "theory of gender oppression," it cannot account for the oppression of homosexuals and other sexual minorities. Thus in her influential 1984 essay, "Thinking Sex," she calls for the development of a new theoretical field capable of analyzing human sexualities. Eve Kosofsky Sedgwick makes a similar point in *Epistemology of the Closet* (1990), where she enacts a shift from feminist to "antihomophobic" theory. Citing Rubin's distinction between gender and sexuality, Sedgwick maintains that feminism's exclusive focus on gender-based issues obscures the distinctions between gender and sexuality as well as the complex dynamics inherent in the construction of gay male sexualities. For other theorists, however, an antihomophobic critical perspective is an essential aspect of feminism itself. For instance, in her groundbreaking 1977 essay, "Towards a Black Feminist Criticism," Barbara Smith emphasizes the importance of applying feminist-inspired analyses to lesbian texts by black women writers. She maintains that because issues concerning lesbianism and lesbian oppression emerged during the late 1960s and early 1970s from within the developing women's movement, writers' views of lesbianism are directly related to feminist issues. Similarly, in "What Has Never Been: An Overview of Lesbian Feminist Literary Criticism," Bonnie

Zimmerman challenges heterosexually identified feminists' reluctance to discuss lesbian-authored texts and maintains that feminist theory must play a pivotal role in constructing a lesbian literary tradition.

Despite these differing opinions, several interrelated principles and techniques of feminist theory clearly affect lesbian, gay, and queer studies. The most far-reaching contribution is, of course, feminists' analysis of the social construction of gender. By distinguishing between sex (that is, the biological differences between male and female) and gender (that is, the social, psychic, and cultural meanings imposed on these sex-based differences), feminists have denaturalized gender and demonstrated that masculinity and femininity are unstable categories that vary across cultural and historical periods. This sex–gender distinction has been further extended by lesbian, gay, and queer theory to encompass analyses of the intersections between gender and sexuality. As Rubin, Sedgwick, Judith Butler, Lee Edelman, and other recent theorists argue, sexuality—like gender itself—is a socially constructed category that has been shaped into heterosexual and homosexual identities that vary cross-culturally and historically. In addition to the pivotal role played by this sex–gender distinction, feminist theory has made a number of other significant contributions to the burgeoning fields of lesbian, gay, and queer studies, including the development of techniques to analyze the erasure of women and other socially marginalized groups from literary canons, the recognition that interlocking systems of oppression shape gendered identities differently, and arguments concerning the political implications of apparently personal issues.

Given feminism's early emphasis on woman-centered issues, it is not surprising that feminist literary theory has had a more extensive engagement with lesbian literature than with gay male writing. Indeed, as Smith's and Zimmerman's assertions suggest, often the challenges to feminist criticism have developed from within feminism itself and entail the use of feminist theory to critique existing feminist perspectives. In addition to expanding feminist theory significantly, these challenges have played an important role in developing a lesbian-specific theoretical field. For instance, in her influential 1980 essay, "Compulsory Heterosexuality and Lesbian Existence," ADRIENNE RICH draws on feminist critiques of patriarchal social structures developed by Dorothy Dinnerstein, Nancy Chodorow, and others yet expands them by suggesting that heterosexuality is a political institution that naturalizes women's social, economic, and psychological oppression. By exposing the heterosexist bias that

naturalizes male–female bonding in western cultures, Rich simultaneously builds on and critiques gynocritics' call for a separate, distinctly female literary tradition and an exclusively woman-identified relationship between writer, reader, and text, thus making possible a lesbian aesthetic. Similarly, in writings by Marilyn Farwell, Julia Penelope, Luce Irigaray, and HÉLÈNE CIXOUS, lesbian identity functions as a metaphor capable of breaking open the heterosexual male–female binary.

Yet as other lesbian-feminist theorists like Judith Roof, Teresa de Lauretis, and Elizabeth Meese have observed, these metaphoric uses of lesbian identity obscure lesbianism's sexually specific dimensions. Thus in *A Lure of Knowledge* (1991), Roof adapts feminist theories of reading and writing developed by Rich, Cixous, Irigaray, Patriancio Schweickart, Jonathan Culler, and Peggy Kamuf and argues that literary representations of lesbian sexuality function metaphorically to secure conventional, heterosexist definitions of female identity. Similarly, de Lauretis draws on already existing feminist critiques of heterosexist binary systems, as well as feminist-inspired analyses of the erasure of women and female desire, to examine the gaps and silences within existing representations of lesbian identity.

Despite its fairly recent emergence, gay male studies have benefited greatly from feminist literary theory. Indeed, by building on already existing feminist insights, gay male theory has made remarkable progress since the early 1980s. The recognition that male-authored texts are marked by gender, coupled with feminist critiques of the heterosexual matrix underlying Western literary and cultural forms, has provided scholars with a useful theoretical framework for the analysis of male homosexual and heterosexual identities. For instance, in *Between Men: English Literature and Male Homosocial Desire* (1985), Eve Sedgwick applies feminist insights concerning the gendered nature of all social relations to her analysis of the interconnections between male homophobia and the oppression of women. Drawing on Gayle Rubin's 1975 essay, "The Traffic in Women," Sedgwick reinterprets a number of canonical nineteenth-century literary texts to suggest that the exchange of women between men mediates yet conceals male homosocial bonding. In "Rebel Without a Closet" (1990), Christopher Castiglia modifies Sedgwick's model and applies it to popular culture films in which the homosexual, rather than homosocial, rivalry is more explicitly developed. He argues that by feminizing same-sex desire, recent filmic representations of gay male identity attempt to contain the growing AIDS-inspired fear of homosexuality. In *Homographesis*

(1994), Lee Edelman draws on Sedgwick's work, as well as on feminist analyses of sexual difference, to explore the invention of male identities in nineteenth- and twentieth-century literature and film.

Feminist literary theory has made a number of other important contributions to gay male studies. In "Engendering F.O.M: The Private Life of *American Renaissance*," Michael Cadden utilizes feminist insights concerning the interconnections between the private and public spheres to argue that sexuality plays an unrecognized role in the construction of literary canons. Like earlier feminists, Cadden simultaneously builds on and calls for alterations in currently existing theories. By demonstrating that F. O. MATTHIESSEN's attempt to separate his private life as a gay male from his public life as a scholar resulted in the construction of a highly masculinized literary tradition, Cadden emphasizes the importance of developing a politics of sexuality. In "Homo-Narcissism; Or, Heterosexuality," Michael Warner applies insights concerning gender domination developed by Simone de Beauvoir and other feminists to explore the inadequacies in psychoanalytic descriptions of male homosexuality as narcissism; and in "Redeeming the Phallus: Wallace Stevens, Frank Lentricchia, and the Politics of (Hetero)Sexuality," Edelman draws on earlier work by Elaine Showalter, Sandra Gilbert, and others to develop a gay reading practice.

In addition to these analyses of gender-specific representations of hetero- and homosexualities, theorists have built on feminism's explorations of the differences among women to examine the complex interconnections between various forms of oppression. As with lesbian-feminists' challenge to the homophobia in much feminist literary criticism, this realization developed from within feminism itself. In the late 1970s and early 1980s, AUDRE LORDE, CHERRÍE MORAGA, GLORIA ANZALDÚA, PAULA GUNN ALLEN, and other self-identified lesbians of color drew on existing feminist analyses of gender-based oppressions to argue that although all women are oppressed in Western cultures, the types of oppression they experience are not identical, for gender itself is variously inflected by ethnicity, sexuality, economic status, and other systems of difference. As an examination of recent work by Sedgwick, Gloria Anzaldúa, Judith Butler, and others indicates, this challenge to Euro-American feminists' ethnocentric conceptions of female identity has had a significant impact on the developing fields of lesbian, gay, and queer theory. In *Epistemology of the Closet*, Sedgwick builds on feminist explorations of differentially structured systems of oppressions, as well as arguments concerning the interconnections between personal and political issues, to analyze the growing homophobia triggered by AIDS. In *Bodies That Matter* (1993), Butler draws on feminist analyses of gendered ethnicities to explore the interconnections between appropriation and agency in twentieth-century literature and film; and in "To(o) Queer the Writer—Loca, escritora y chicana" (1991), Gloria Anzaldúa builds on already existing feminist analyses of the erasure of women to develop an inclusionary yet culture-specific theory of queer reading and writing.

As this brief overview indicates, feminist literary theory, which itself draws on and transforms many other theoretical perspectives, represents a tradition far too diverse to be summarized easily. Although the theoretical perspectives mentioned illustrate some of the ways feminist literary theory has influenced lesbian, gay, and queer studies, the connections between these quickly growing fields are far more numerous than this survey can indicate. Moreover, the dynamic interchange between feminist, lesbian, gay, and queer theorists has redefined feminism itself. This productive dialogue ensures that all four areas of study will continue changing, affecting each other in increasingly complex ways. (See also IDENTITY and LITERARY THEORY: GAY, LESBIAN, AND QUEER.)

—AnnLouise Keating

BIBLIOGRAPHY

Anzaldúa, Gloria. "To(o) Queer the Writer—Loca, escritora y chicana." *Inversions: Writing by Dykes, Queers, and Lesbians.* Betsy Warland, ed. Vancouver: Press Gang, 1991. ■ Boone, Joseph A., and Michael Cadden, eds. *Engendering Men: The Question of Male Feminist Criticism.* New York: Routledge, 1990. ■ Butler, Judith. *Bodies That Matter: On The Discursive Limits of "Sex."* New York: Routledge, 1993. ■ ———. *Gender Trouble: Feminism and the Subversion of Identity.* New York: Routledge, 1989. ■ Cixous, Hélène and Catherine Clément. *The Newly Born Woman.* Trans. Betsy Wing. Minneapolis: University of Minnesota Press, 1988. ■ de Lauretis, Teresa. "Sexual Indifference and Lesbian Representation." *Theatre Journal* 40 (1988): 155–177. ■ Edelman, Lee. *Homographesis: Essays in Gay Literary and Cultural Theory.* New York: Routledge, 1994. ■ Farwell, Marilyn R. "Toward a Definition of the Lesbian Literary Imagination." *Signs* 14 (1988): 100–118. ■ Meese, Elizabeth A. *(Sem)Erotics Theorizing Lesbian: Writing.* New York: New York University Press, 1992. ■ Rich, Adrienne. "Compulsory Heterosexuality and Lesbian Existence." *Signs* 5 (1980): 631–660. ■ Roof, Judith. *A Lure of Knowledge: Lesbian Sexuality and Theory.* New York: Columbia University Press, 1991. ■ Rubin, Gayle. "Thinking Sex: Notes for a Radical Theory of the Politics of Sexuality." *Pleasure and Danger: Exploring Female Sexuality.* Carole S. Vance, ed. 1984. New York: Pandora, 1992. 267–319. ■ ———. "The Traffic in Women: Notes on the 'Political Economy' of Sex." *Toward an Anthropology of Women.* Rayna R. Reiter, ed. New York: Monthly Review, 1975. 157–210. ■ Sedgwick, Eve Kosofsky. *Between Men: English Literature and Male Homosocial Desire.* New York: Columbia University Press, 1985. ■ ———. *Epistemology of the Closet.* Berkeley: University of

California Press, 1990. ■ ———. *Tendencies*. Chapel Hill: University of North Carolina Press, 1993. ■ Showalter, Elaine, ed. *Speaking of Gender*. New York: Routledge, 1989. ■ Smith, Barbara. "Toward a Black Feminist Criticism." 1977. *The New Feminist Criticism: Essays on Women, Literature, Theory.* Elaine Showalter, ed. New York: Pantheon, 1985.

Ferro, Robert
(1941–1988)

Robert Ferro was one of the original members of THE VIOLET QUILL, a group of seven gay writers who came together in New York City during the permissive post-Stonewall era to read, discuss, and criticize their work. Ferro's novels rely heavily on autobiography. Two of his mature works, *The Family of Max Desir* (1983) and *Second Son* (1988), center on artistic gay Italo-American young men, from the upper middle class, who travel to Italy to uncover their ethnic and sexual roots. Both protagonists, Max and Mark, find love and return home with their respective partners. Love of family, consistent with Italo-American tradition, is the motivating force in both novels. As the male couples attempt to find their places in the bosoms of the families they love, Ferro investigates the effects of gay mainstreaming. His protagonists reject the isolation and loss of tradition of ghettoization, but, at the same time, insist on uncompromising acceptance from their relations. The novels explore homosexual integration into the traditional family.

Ferro's is, in fact, a poetics of family values, where gay sons and their lovers participate in, contribute to, enrich, and diversify the family experience. Women and children adapt easily and welcome the new additions to their families, but the gay protagonists' fathers and brothers, challenged by the severe cultural strictures of Mediterranean machismo, are unable to totally embrace them. Inevitably this results in conflict that can only be partially resolved by mutual compromise.

Death is ever present in both these novels. Both protagonists suffer the loss of their mothers. *The Family of Max Desir,* in particular, chronicles in painful detail the mother's mortal deterioration. Matriarchal loss disrupts and weakens the fabric of the family. But in *Second Son,* Ferro fools death by transforming its very nature, making it a catalyst for a love that enriches life. The two lovers, Mark and Bill, are free to give and take completely from one another only because they are both fatally infected with AIDS, which is referred to in the text only as *It.*

The Blue Star (1985) is completely different from *Second Son* and *The Family of Max Desir.* This novel, actually two stories in one, concerns the lives of two friends, Peter Conrad and Chase Walker, who meet in a Florentine pensione and quickly become comrades in exploring the city's demimonde. Eventually Chase is induced to sire an heir for a bizarre, ancient Florentine family, whereas Peter falls in love with a faunlike Italian named Lorenzo, who is married with three children. Chase eventually accepts the responsibilities of his compromise. But Peter, like Max and Mark, will not live a life in the shadows as "the other man" and returns home, alone, to America.

Ferro is never comfortable with the logical reality he constructs for his works. In all three novels, he jolts narrative progress with forced intrusions of bizarre situations that sometimes run parallel to the main plot and at other times puncture its fabric at unbalanced intervals. These nonrealistic intrusions vary from the building of a secret underground Masonic Temple somewhere in Central Park to brief glimpses of voodoo and blond godlike explorers exploited by Amazonian Indians. In *Second Son,* Mark's friend writes to him about a secret, gay NASA, somewhere in Texas, offering seats on a spaceship bound for the planet Splendora, where gay vitality and sanity abound. Ferro reminds his readers that reality is never what it appears to be, and what seems bizarre to one person seems ordinary to another; calling something queer is but a frame of reference.

In 1988, Michael Grumley, Ferro's lover, died of AIDS; Ferro survived him by less than three months.

—*Joseph P. Consoli*

BIBLIOGRAPHY

Bergman, David. *Gaiety Transfigured: Gay Self-Representation in American Literature.* Madison: University of Wisconsin Press, 1991. ■ Dewey, Joseph. "Robert Ferro." *Contemporary Gay American Novelists: A Bio-Bibliographical Critical Sourcebook.* Emmanuel S. Nelson, ed. Westport, Conn.: Greenwood, 1992. 128–139. ■ ———. "Music for a Closing: Responses to AIDS in Three American Novels." *AIDS: The Literary Response.* Emmanuel S. Nelson, ed. New York: Twayne Publishers, 1992. 23–38.

Fichte, Hubert
(1935–1986)

Hubert Fichte, the first author to introduce homosexuality openly into German literature after World War II, was born on March 21, 1935, in Perleberg/Westpriegnitz. His Jewish father fled Germany before his birth, and his unwed Protestant mother reared him at her parents' home in Hamburg. In order to keep ahead of Nazi persecution, his mother hid him for a year (1942) in a Catholic orphanage in Upper Bavaria. At the age of eleven, Fichte began working as a child actor at some of the most important theaters in Hamburg. As an adolescent in high school, he met the Hamburg author and hormone researcher, Hans Henny Jahnn, whose complex character had a decisive impact on Fichte's intellectual development and sexual self-awareness. From his mid-teens to his late twenties, he studied French, worked as a shepherd in Provence, directed a camp for the poor in Paris, studied agriculture in Northern Germany and Sweden, and worked at a home for juvenile delinquents in Sweden. Already beginning to have some journalistic success with art and book reviews, he declared himself an independent author in 1963.

Although Fichte has entered German literary history as a "homosexual author," his person and work display a broad range of outsider positions: half-Jewish, illegitimate child, and bisexual. In his strongly autobiographical first four novels, *The Orphanage* (1965), *The Palette* (1968), *Detlev's Imitations* (1971), and *Attempt at Puberty* (1974), homosexuality is always present but only gradually becomes the defining factor. In *The Orphanage,* Fichte already portrays the six-year-old Detlev sexually experimenting with an older boy, but it is a relatively minor detail. Fichte's most successful novel, *The Palette,* is a vivid portrayal of Hamburg's underworld as it is embodied in the dive-bar after which the novel is named. This underworld is inhabited by junkies, bums, drunkards, hustlers, and fags. Although this is the novel that established Fichte's identity as a gay author, the gay existence that it describes is shared by all of society's semicriminal Others, and the sexual component is just one point on the spectrum. In *Detlev's Imitations,* the child actor Detlev first becomes aware of the taboo word *homosexual* from his mother; it invokes in him the image of Achilles and Patroclus as "Homersexuals." This is the first point in Fichte's work where homosexuality begins to have its own outsider identity. *Attempt at Puberty,* which has drawn the most critical acclaim, addresses homosexuality as the decisive stigma that accompanies the pubescent Detlev's transition into the adult Jäcki of *The Palette.*

When Fichte died on March 8, 1986, in Hamburg, he was still working on the nineteen-volume novel cycle, *The History of Sensitivity.* In these posthumously released novels, homosexuality figures as the means to become sensitive to other marginalized people, whether they be political prisoners in the Third World or African Americans in New York City. It is finally this voice of marginalization and nonidentification that unifies Fichte's work and finds its most universal expression in homosexuality.

—*Craig B. Palmer*

BIBLIOGRAPHY

Beckermann, Thomas, ed. *Hubert Fichte. Materialien zu Leben und Werk.* Frankfurt a.M.: Fischer, 1985. ■ Böhme, Hartmut, and Nikolaus Tiling, eds. *Leben, um eine Form der Darstellung zu erreichen. Studien zum Werk Hubert Fichtes.* Frankfurt a.M.: Fischer, 1991. ■ "Hubert Fichte." *Text + Kritik* 72 (1981). ■ Vollhaber, Tomas. *Das Nichts. Die Angst. Die Erfahrung. Untersuchung zur zeitgenössischen schwulen Literatur.* Berlin: Verlag rosa Winkel, 1987. ■ Wangenheim, Wolfgang von. *Hubert Fichte.* München: Beck/Verlag Edition Text + Kritik, 1980.

Field, Edward
(b. 1924)

Born in New York in 1924, Field's biography is told in his poetry. He portrays himself as an aging New York Jewish gay poet who likes plants, traveling, and popular culture and never got enough sex and companionship though he now gets more of the latter. The short version of his life is told in "Bio" (*Counting Myself Lucky,* 1992); the long version is the sum of all of his poems.

The critical discussion of Field centers on two issues, his diction and the confessional nature of his poetry. Field's diction is straightforward and "unpoetic." He does not seem to force the language into producing special effects, nor does he require his readers to have arcane knowledge. He was asked to do a children's book of translations of Eskimo poetry (*Eskimo Songs and Stories*, 1973) because, he explains in "Bio," "I was the only poet they could find, they said / whose poetry was understandable by ten-year-olds." Some readers find that this plainness produces immediacy and honesty, whereas others find it bland and clichéd. As for his honesty, Field seems to have no inhibitions regarding what he tells his readers. Some critics find this openness brave and engaging, an indication that Field regards his readers as friends. Others wish that Field were more reticent.

Field's development as a gay poet can be traced throughout his volumes. Apart from a sexually explicit version of the Ruth and Naomi story, which has not appeared in either of his collections of selected poems, and "Ode to Fidel Castro," there are few explicit references to homosexuality in his first book *Stand Up Friend With Me* (1963), which won the Lamont Poetry Selection for 1962. There are, however, two types of poems in this book in which homosexuality forms the obvious subtext. One is Field's animal poems. In "Donkeys," for example, the animals:

> do not own their bodies;
> And if they had their own way, I am sure
> That they would sit in a field of flowers
> Kissing each other, and maybe
> They would even invite us to join them.

The other homoerotic poems are about Sonny Hugg, a boyhood friend. In these poems ("Sonny Hugg Rides Again," "Sonny Hugg and the Porcupine," and "The Sleeper"), Field looks up to Sonny the athletic, aggressive boy who inexplicably likes Field. Sonny also has his vulnerable, sensitive side.

In *Variety Photoplays* (1967), Field uses popular culture, primarily films but also comics and other forms, as one of his principal sources of inspiration. In "Sweet Gwendolyn and the Countess" and "Nancy," there is lesbian material. The only explicitly gay male poem is "Graffiti," a story about a glory hole. But homoeroticism informs the wonderful "Giant Pacific Octopus," in which an octopus seen in a pet store becomes in Field's imagination a "boychik" with "the body of a greek god" who "will stay, one night or a lifetime, / for as long as god will let you have him."

In *A Full Heart* (1977), Field came out fully as a gay poet in genial poems that are of a piece with his other work. Field's gay manifesto is "The Two Orders of Love." In this poem, he sees homosexuality as as natural as heterosexuality and as necessary:

> Nature needs both to do its work
> and humankind, confusing two separate
>   orders of love
> makes rules allowing only one kind
> and defies the universe.

In "David's Dream," Field gives a typical self-deprecating portrait of himself as one who is "no fun. / I talk liberation / but my actions show otherwise." In "Street Instructions: At the Crotch," he portrays the sexually unrepressed person he would like to be.

New and Selected Poems (1987) contains fewer explicitly gay poems than the preceding volume, but by this time Field has established his persona as a gay man well enough that all of his poems read as meditations on life from a gay standpoint. *Counting Myself Lucky* (1992) also contains selections from his previous books as well as new poems. In this volume, growing older as a gay man becomes a primary concern.

Field's gay poems tend to fall into a few categories. The poems about sex are often wry and resigned, but sometimes playful and sexy, as, for example, "The Moving Man" in Winston Leyland's anthology *Angels of the Lyre* (1975). In addition, there are poems in praise of relationships and poems of regret about the suppression of his homosexuality when he was young, the cost of which is still coming home to him as he grows older, as is clear in "World Traveler." There are also a few political poems such as "Two Orders of Love" and "Oh, the Gingkos." In the latter, John Lindsay is described as a mayor no one liked, but who not only had trees planted in New York City, he also "stopped the police from raiding gay bars." Field's poetry is a pleasurable and valuable account of coming to terms with homosexuality in the literary world of New York in the second half of the twentieth century.

—*Terrence Johnson*

BIBLIOGRAPHY

Bergman, David. "Edward Field." *Dictionary of Literary Biography, Volume One Hundred Five, American Poets Since World War II: Second Series*. Detroit: Gale, 1991. 95–105. ■ Goldstein, Laurence. "The Spectacles of Edward Field." *Parnassus: Poetry in Review* 15 (1989): 240–255. ■ Howard, Richard. "Edward Field: 'His Body Comes Together Joyfully from All Directions.'" *Alone with America: Essays on the Art of Poetry in the United States Since 1950*. Enlarged Edition. New York: Atheneum, 1980. 143–157.

Field, Michael [Katherine Bradley *(1846–1914)* and Edith Cooper *(1862–1913)*]

Katherine Bradley and her niece Edith Cooper collaborated under the pseudonym "Michael Field" on a number of poetic dramas with historical and mythical subjects, one prose play, and eight volumes of verse. Sturge Moore has edited the women's journals and correspondence in *Works and Days* (1933).

As Mary Sturgeon, their biographer, relates, the women's being born into affluent Birmingham merchant families provided them access to the limited educational opportunities for the nineteenth-century British woman. In 1878, at University College at Bristol, where they advocated such causes as antivivisection and women's rights, they decided to live and write together. Sturgeon regards an untitled sonnet that they cowrote at this time, later published in *Underneath the Bough* (1893), a collection of their love lyrics to each other, as an exchange of marriage vows. Katherine would later record in the journals that, compared with the most famous literary couple of their day, Robert and Elizabeth Barrett Browning, she as "Michael" and Edith as her beloved "Henry" were more closely wedded.

Their early dramatic collaborations, especially *Callirrhoe* (1884) and *Brutus Ultor* (1886), which portrays Brutus as a champion of women's rights, received critical acclaim, attracting the attention of Arthur Symons, Robert Browning, and the young W. B. Yeats, who avidly read them when he was seeking models for his own poetic drama. Katherine admitted in an 1884 letter to Browning that the public was not ready to accept a passion for women's rights from women writers, thus the necessity for the pseudonym. What made the pseudonym even more necessary was their interest in portraying women's love for each other. For example, *Canute the Great* (1887) contains an explicit love scene between two women, while the poetry in *Long Ago* (1889), ostensibly in imitation of SAPPHO, celebrates lesbian love.

The women's work flourished in the 1890s. They presented Mary Stuart in *The Tragic Mary* (1890) as a politically exploited woman, an approach that OSCAR WILDE found much more human than SWINBURNE's treatment of the character. *Stephania, a Trialogue* (1892), an early example of symbolist drama in England, attacks the decadent notion of harlotry as aesthetic. *Attila, My Attila* (1896) examines, with what we would today term "black humor," what happens when an aggressive, patrician woman of the fifth century, like the "New Woman" of the 1890s, meets the Hun. *A Question of Memory* (1893), a departure from their usual approach of dealing with contemporary themes under the disguise of classical tragedy, and written in an innovative stream of consciousness prose, with a modern setting—the 1848 uprising in Hungary—ends with an intentionally shocking lovers' "triad." Two men and a woman decide to spend their lives together, an obvious correlative for their "Michael Field" relationship.

As a result of the negative reviews of this, their only publicly performed play, the women reverted to writing verse tragedies set in antiquity. On their conversion to Roman Catholicism in 1907, they began publishing volumes of devotional poetry. Both those claiming the women as homoerotic celebrants of women's expanding prerogatives and those championing them as Catholic mystics must understand what conversion to Roman Catholicism represented for them and for contemporaries like Oscar Wilde, LORD ALFRED DOUGLAS, Aubrey Beardsley, and others. The conversion was an embrace of antirational and mystical AESTHETICISM, a reaction against vulgar Victorian bourgeois values. That these women are so little known or read today measures the extent to which the values they rejected have prevailed.

—*David J. Moriarty*

BIBLIOGRAPHY

Maynard, Theodore. "The Drama of the Dramatists." *Carven from the Laurel Tree, Essays.* Oxford: B. H. Blackwell, 1918; rpt. Freeport, N.Y.: Books for Libraries Press, 1967. ■ Sturgeon, Mary. *Michael Field.* London: G. G. Harrap, 1922; rpt. Freeport, N.Y.: Arno Press, 1975. ■ ———. "Michael Field." *Studies in Contemporary Poets.* London: G. G. Harrap, 1920.

Fierstein, Harvey *(b. 1954)*

Harvey Forbes Fierstein was born on June 6, 1954, in Brooklyn. His parents were Irving Fierstein, a handkerchief manufacturer, and Jacqueline Harriet Gilbert Fierstein, a housewife. He was educated in the Brooklyn public schools and received a B.F.A. in art from the Pratt Institute in 1973. He appeared as a drag performer in various New York City area clubs in the early 1970s and made his first appearance in a more serious artistic venue playing an asthmatic lesbian in Andy Warhol's only play, *Pork,* in 1971. His earliest plays (*Freaky Pussy, Flatbush and Tosca,* and *Cannibals*—all unpublished) are set in the drag world of New York. In addition to his work as a playwright and a performer in the stage and film versions of his own plays, he has continued to act, appearing in the films *Garbo Talks* (1984), *The Harvest* (1993), and *Mrs. Doubtfire* (1993), in the successful New York revival of ROBERT PATRICK's *The Haunted Host* (1991), and on television episodes of "Miami Vice." He also provides the voice of a gay male secretary in "The Simpsons."

Fierstein is best known for his Broadway plays *Torch Song Trilogy* (1982) and *Safe Sex* (1987), his Off-Broadway show *Spookhouse* (1984), and his book for the award-winning Broadway musical *La Cage aux Folles* (1983). He won Tony awards for best play and for best actor in 1983 for *Torch Song Trilogy* and won again the next year for best book for a musical for *La Cage aux Folles.*

The early, experimental drag plays of Fierstein are reflected in "International Stud," the first part of *Torch Song Trilogy,* and in "Manny and Jake" and "Safe Sex" from *Safe Sex.* For many critics, these represent Fierstein's finest work. These uncompromising, lyrical portraits of gay men and their lives do not partake of dramatic realism or naturalism. In these plays, Fierstein depicts lives outside the boundaries of the mainstream by means of a dramaturgy that itself transgresses the boundaries of mainstream theater.

On the other hand, many critics have seen "Widows and Children First" from *Torch Song Trilogy* and "On Tidy Endings" from *Safe Sex* as failures precisely because they fit a traditional, "living room comedy" model that has for so long been used to present heterosexual romantic comedy. Some queer theorists have difficulty accepting portrayals of gay men's lives in terms that have so often been used to show how straight people live, and thus find Fierstein's work irrelevant. Furthermore, in their final acts both *Torch Song Trilogy* and *Safe Sex* depict gay marriages (each complete with a child) based overtly on heterosexual paradigms.

But perhaps Fierstein's greatest achievement is his ability to humanize drag queens, to portray them as characters worthy of an audience's understanding and sympathy, and not as the pathetic victims or exotic divas that they have so often been depicted. Thus Fierstein's choice to present these characters through the trappings of realism can be seen as a brave attempt to show drag performers as being as "realistic" as the characters who inhabit the plays that make up traditional Broadway comedic fare.

As a visible spokesperson for gay people, queer theater, and AIDS causes, Fierstein has achieved a celebrity that transcends the world of New York avant-garde theater. In his best pieces, Fierstein is one of the finest gay male playwrights working in the American theater today. (See also CROSS-DRESSING and DRAMATIC LITERATURE: CONTEMPORARY DRAMA.)

—D. S. Lawson

BIBLIOGRAPHY

Clum, John M. *Acting Gay: Male Homosexuality in Modern Drama.* New York: Columbia University Press, 1992. ■ Cohen, Jodi R. "Intersecting and Competing Discourses in Harvey Fierstein's *Tidy Endings.*" *Quarterly Journal of Speech* 77 (May 1991): 196–207. ■ de Jongh, Nicholas. *Not in Front of the Audience: Homosexuality on Stage.* London: Routledge, 1992. ■ Gross, Gregory D. "Coming Up for Air: Three AIDS Plays." *Journal of American Culture* 15 (Summer 1992): 63–67. ■ Nelson, Emmanuel S., ed. *AIDS: The Literary Response.* New York: Twayne Publishers, 1992. ■ Powers, Kim. "Fragments of a Trilogy: Harvey Fierstein's *Torch Song.*" *Theatre* 14.2 (Spring 1983): 63–67. ■ Scott, Jay. "Dignity in Drag." *Film Comment* 25 (January–February 1989): 9–12+.

Firbank, Ronald
(1886–1926)

Although his witty, high-camp, modernist fabulations mock the late-Victorian world of bourgeois materialism and "hearty" moral earnestness, Ronald Firbank, born Arthur Annesley Ronald Firbank in London in 1886, was himself the product of a "rags to riches" Victorian success story. Although his great-grandfather was an illiterate Durham coal miner, his grandfather acquired an immense fortune as a railway contractor, which enabled his father, Sir Thomas Firbank, to become a Member of Parliament. His mother, Lady Firbank, the daughter of an Irish clergyman, was an educated and cultivated woman who, with her husband, became a renowned collector of rare prints and porcelain. Until her death in 1924, Lady Firbank lent steadfast encouragement to her second son, which evidently helped sustain Firbank in a world he often regarded as malicious and self-serving, and which had become increasingly homophobic in outward demeanor since the prosecution of OSCAR WILDE for "indecent behavior" in 1895. Indeed, much of Firbank's work takes the form of a homage to Wilde and other *fin-de-siècle* aesthetes, inflected with a pervasive modernist irony and skepticism that, though eschewing propaganda and self-important "seriousness," evinces profound sympathy for blacks, lesbians, women, homosexuals, and other victims of early twentieth-century materialism and moral self-righteousness. Like his contemporary VIRGINIA WOOLF, Firbank constructed an elaborate mask of protective self-mythology designed to blur the distinction between the "Firbankian" legend and reality. Because of frequent childhood illnesses, Firbank developed the lifelong habit of traveling abroad to more favorable climates and cultures. His sudden disappearances and evasiveness contributed to the aura of mystery surrounding him. Educated privately for the most part in his youth, he subsequently attended Trinity Hall, Cambridge, which he left in June 1909, after six terms, without taking a degree. Already a published author and a fully formed personality by the time he entered Cambridge at the age of nineteen, Firbank took the further step of divorcing himself from English culture by converting, in 1907, to Catholicism, a religion whose ornate rituals, costumes, symbols, and pageantry provided him with a vehicle through which to express his homosexuality obliquely. His early sentimental story, "Odette d'Antrevernes," concerning a pious girl who prays for a vision of the Virgin Mary and instead encounters a destitute prostitute whom she dissuades from committing suicide, reveals his interest in sacred and profane love as well as his abiding sympathy for innocents victimized by circumstances beyond their control. Firbank visited Rome with the intention of taking holy orders; however, as he later revealed in a letter to Lord Berners, "The Church of Rome wouldn't have me, and so I mock her." Accordingly, his mature fiction is populated with a ribald gallery of homosexual choirboys, lesbian nuns, cross-dressing priests, salacious bishops, flagellants, and self-canonized saints.

Between his frequent travels abroad, Firbank resided in London and became a well-known figure in pre-war cafe society as well as in various dramatic and literary circles. The advent of World War I brought an end to his customary mode of living and was indirectly responsible for transforming Firbank into a serious literary artist. Evincing no interest in patriotic duties or war work, Firbank secluded himself for the duration of the war in Oxford, where he produced four novels in rapid succession. *Vainglory* (1915) concerns the ambitions of Mrs. Shamefoot to achieve immortality by having a stained glass window commemorating herself built at St. Dorothy's Cathedral. *Inclinations* (1916) tells the story of Miss Geraldine O'Brookomore ("authoress of *Six Strange Sisters, Those Gonzagas,* etc.") whose vision of an Arcadian lesbian romance is destroyed when the hostile Count Pastorelli ("not so pastoral as he sounds") marries her companion Miss Mabel Collins. *Caprice* (1917) follows the adventures of Miss Sarah Sinquier, the stage-struck daughter of a provincial clergyman, who, the morning after her successful debut in London as "An unfeminine Juliet . . . A decadent Juliet," accidentally falls to her death through a trapdoor while inspecting the empty theater. In the utopian world of *Valmouth* (1919), an imaginary health resort presided over by the black masseuse Mrs. Yajñavalkya, the characters engage in an intricate arabesque of secret amours and are eventually revealed to be gay, lesbian, or bisexual.

After the war, Firbank further developed the theme of gay–lesbian utopia in his one-act play, *The Princess Zoubaroff* (1920), which creates a pastoral "green world" of homosexual freedom and explores the advantages of social arrangements in which the sexes live apart. The happy, middle-aged Lord Orkish is Firbank's portrait of the Oscar Wilde who might have been had Wilde gone into exile rather than facing his persecutors in England. *Santal* (1921) explores the religious aspirations of a young Islamic boy. *The Flower Beneath the Foot* (1924), which includes a description of a party excavating "among the ruins of Chedorlahomor, a *faubourg* of Sodom," follows the adventures of Laura de Nazianzi, who achieves sainthood by renouncing heterosexual romance and joining the lesbian Convent of the Flaming Hood. *Sorrow in Sunlight* (1924), given the outrageous title *Prancing Nigger* in the American edition at the suggestion of Firbank's close friend CARL VAN VECHTEN, ascribes the typical social aspirations of the lower-middle-class English to Mrs. Almadou Mouth, who migrates with her black family to the local capital of an unnamed tropical isle so that she can get her daughters into society. His last and most explicitly gay work, *Concerning the Eccentricities of Cardinal Pirelli,* appeared in 1926, the same year as Firbank's early death at the age of forty. The book begins with the cardinal baptizing a police puppy named Crack, and ends when the naked cardinal ("elementary now as Adam himself") drops dead while pursuing a choirboy named Chicklet around his church. The posthumously published *The Artificial Princess* (1934) reworks Wilde's tragic play *Salome,* concerning the fatal encounter between Herodias's daughter and John the Baptist, as a comedy.

With the exception of *Prancing Nigger,* which enjoyed brisk sales in the United States, Firbank received no income from his literary works, which were published at his own expense and pointedly ignored by British critics unable either to gloss over or acknowledge his homosexual subject matter. By accusing him of "frivolity" Firbank's homophobic detractors have obscured recognition of his literary innovations, which place him in the company of other gay and lesbian modernists such as E. M. FORSTER, Virginia Woolf, MARCEL PROUST, EVELYN WAUGH, and GERTRUDE STEIN. No descriptive summary can begin to convey the rich allusiveness of his narratives, which abandon conventional plotting and chains of cause and effect and focus, rather, on the workings of an artistic consciousness through a series of interrelated conversations, animated tableaux, and symbols that constitute a veritable encyclopedia of gay and lesbian cultural reference. Excavating the homosexual meanings in everything from St. Sebastian to Egyptian statuettes, butterflies to orchids, and Priapus to Ganymede, his use of inverted word order, dashes, exclamation points, ellipses, and innuendo shows his characteristic "Sapphic" mode of presenting material in fragments in order to articulate the love that dares not speak its name. His description of Monsignor Parr in *Vainglory* as "something between a butterfly and a misanthrope, [who] was temperamental, when not otherwise . . . employed," gives some indication of his masterful use of indirection.

Committed to the preservation of gay and lesbian culture in an era of political backlash, as well as to the unfettered expression of his artistic self, Firbank himself may be fittingly characterized by the comment of Lady Parvula de Panzoust in *Valmouth* that "None but those whose courage is unquestionable can venture to be effeminate." He died on May 21, 1926, probably as a result of acute alcoholism and general debility. In a truly Firbankian scenario, he was accidentally buried in a Protestant cemetery, but—upon discovery of the error—was subsequently reinterred in the Catholic cemetery of San Lorenzo. (See also ENGLISH LITERATURE: TWENTIETH CENTURY.)

—*Corinne E. Blackmer*

BIBLIOGRAPHY

Benkovitz, Miriam J. *Ronald Firbank*. New York: Knopf, 1969. ■ Brooke, Jocelyn. *Ronald Firbank*. New York: Roy Publishers, 1951. ■ Brophy, Brigid. *Prancing Novelist: A Defense of Fiction in the Form of a Critical Biography in Praise of Ronald Firbank*. New York: Harper & Row, 1973. ■ Davies, Paul. "'The Power to Convey the Unuttered': Style and Sexuality in the Work of Ronald Firbank." *Lesbian and Gay Writing: An Anthology of Critical Essays*. Mark Lilly, ed. London: Macmillan Press, 1990. ■ Horder, Mervyn, ed. *Ronald Firbank: Memoirs and Critiques*. London: Duckworth, 1977.

Flanner, Janet
(1892–1978)

Janet Flanner was a novelist, translator, and journalist, best known for her fortnightly "Letter from Paris," which she wrote for the *New Yorker* from 1925 to 1975. She was born in Indianapolis, Indiana, on March 13, 1892. She matriculated at the University of Chicago in 1912, but left the university after two rocky years, worked for a time in a girls' reformatory, then in 1916 became a drama and art critic for the *Indianapolis Star*. Toward the end of World War I, Flanner, married to a man she did not love, moved to New York City where she became acquainted with Harold Ross and his wife, Jane Grant. They introduced her to the most profound and enduring love of her life, Solita Solano, drama editor for the *New York Tribune*.

In New York, Flanner explored her sexuality, participated in the suffrage movement and early feminist organizations, and moved in the circle of the Algonquin Round Table. As she began to find her own place among the strong and stimulating professional women of Greenwich Village and as her relationship with Solano intensified, the illusion of her marriage became increasingly difficult to maintain. When Solano was sent on assignment to Greece in 1921, Flanner went with her. By the time the two women settled in Paris in 1922, Flanner was divorced. Flanner lived almost all the rest of her life in France, returning to the United States only for the duration of World War II and again near the end of her life. She died on November 7, 1978, in New York City.

In Paris, Flanner knew virtually all the major figures of the literary expatriate community on the Left Bank. She regularly wrote to Jane Grant of Parisian personalities and cultural happenings. When Ross started the *New Yorker* in 1925, Grant encouraged him to include Flanner's letters as a regular feature. On October 10, 1925, Ross published the first "Letter from Paris," signing it "Genêt" without Flanner's knowledge. Her "Letters" had no journalistic model or precedent, but soon Flanner was developing and refining a new genre of analytic commentary that, as she described it in *Paris Was Yesterday* (1972), "instinctively leaned toward comments with a critical edge, indeed a double edge, if possible." Her instructions from Ross were to present to an American audience life as the French perceived it. He wanted the writing to be "precisely accurate, highly personal, colorful, and ocularly descriptive," the style that came to define the *New Yorker* itself.

Although none of Flanner's journalism or fiction develops in any real depth overt lesbian content or themes, she was a prominent figure in the lesbian community of expatriate Paris. She was a regular guest at NATALIE CLIFFORD BARNEY's famous lesbian salon, and she and Solano appear in DJUNA BARNES's satire of that community, *Ladies Almanack* (1928), as "Nip and Tuck," a pair of plucky journalists.

Although she wrote one novel, *The Cubical City* (1926), translated two novels for her friend COLETTE,

and published in dozens of journals, magazines, and newspapers, Flanner's position as a journalist set her apart from the other literary Americans in Paris. She considered herself only a "minor Left Banker" and admits that F. Scott Fitzgerald was "the only one of [her] writer friends who ever gave [her] the mutual identification of . . . having any literary sensibilities." She nonetheless won a National Book Award for *Paris Journal: 1944–1965* in 1966 and received an honorary Ph.D. from Smith College in 1958.

—*Carolyn Leste Law*

BIBLIOGRAPHY

Benstock, Shari. "From the Left Bank to the Upper East Side: Janet Flanner's Letter from Paris." *Women of the Left Bank: Paris, 1900–1940.* Austin: University of Texas Press, 1986. 99–140. ■ Rood, Karen. "Janet Flanner." *American Writers in Paris, 1920–1939. Dictionary of Literary Biography.* Vol. 4. Detroit: Gale, 1980. 151–161. ■ Wineapple, Brenda. *Genêt: A Biography of Janet Flanner.* New York: Ticknor & Fields, 1989.

Folklore

Folklore consists of traditional aspects of culture generally passed on by example or observation rather than in writing—jokes, stories, personal experience narratives, folk speech, songs, customs, various arts and crafts, and numerous other genres. These traditions serve as a way of organizing, explaining, and interpreting experience: People use folklore to entertain, to express their membership in a group, to show solidarity with their friends, to educate others, and to achieve many other ends. Authors often incorporate folklore into their works, but seldom in the form of recognizable texts. Rather they rely on such so-called minor genres as folk speech, accurate depictions of cultural groups and events, and such traditional communication strategies as HUMOR and double entendres to add a realistic texture to their writings.

Within the gay and lesbian subculture, one of the primary functions of folklore is to aid in acculturation. No one is brought up to be homosexual; lesbians and gay men must somehow learn to function successfully with other people of their own kind. Folklore helps them in this learning process, aiding in identifying and communicating with other homosexual people, fostering subcultural cohesion, and helping to cope with conflict.

The folk speech of lesbians and gay men, a relatively stable and extensive specialized language, is

called an argot. Through its use, homosexual people can communicate secretly with one another without conveying their sexual orientation to outsiders. Authors of lesbian and gay fiction sometimes use coding of this sort. GERTRUDE STEIN, for example, writes in "Miss Furr and Miss Skeene" (1922):

> They were regular in being gay, they learned
> little things that are things in being gay, they
> learned many little things that are things in
> being gay, they were gay every day, they were
> regular, they were gay, they were gay the same
> length of time every day, they were gay, they
> were quite regularly gay.

As Lillian Faderman observes, "The story is a play on the word 'gay,' which was not yet widely understood to mean homosexual—but those who had become a part of what was by this time a flourishing lesbian subculture would have discerned what Stein meant by her description of Georgine Skeene and Helen Furr." One must also wonder if *Georgine Skeene* is code for *Gertrude Stein* and Helen *Furr* code for Alice B. Toklas, whom Stein called *Pussy*.

Other authors have used a sort of open code to alert readers to characters' homosexuality before the characters attain such awareness themselves. In the openly lesbian novel *The Well of Loneliness* (1928), for example, RADCLYFFE HALL uses the word *queer* so frequently that it is almost intrusive: "[Stephen Gordon] was too young to know why the beauty of Morton [her ancestral estate] would bring a lump to her throat. . . . It was a queer feeling." And "She was shy to primness regarding certain subjects, and would actually blush if they happened to be mentioned. This would strike her companions as queer and absurd." Hall seems to be signaling Stephen's homosexuality to readers well before Stephen herself recognizes her lesbianism. To underscore the effect of such diction, Hall describes Stephen with stereotypes traditionally associated with lesbians: Even as an infant, she has a "masculine" body; Stephen's father gives her a typical boy's name; she is a tomboy; in childhood play, she pretends to be young male heroes; she is athletic; she longs to cut her hair short.

RITA MAE BROWN, in *Rubyfruit Jungle* (1973), like other contemporary authors, uses specifically gay and lesbian terms. For example, she writes, "Carolyn was dropping her beads, all right"; that is, she was revealing her homosexuality. In *Significant Others* (1987), ARMISTEAD MAUPIN uses the following phrases in the span of two pages: "She got some major dish out of Bette Midler" (great gossip); "That's cool. I'm a fag hag. I can handle it" (*fag hag* refers to a straight woman who chooses to spend much of her time with gay men; in this instance, however, the comment is made by a straight man, making it a sign of the closeness of his relationship with a gay character); "This is strictly brotherly. . . . Maybe even sisterly, for all I know" (a description of the relationship of two gay men). Use of the argot gives the novels a realistic texture that lesbians and gay men can appreciate.

Language is often a key to learning the culture. Sutherland, a gay character in ANDREW HOLLERAN's *Dancer from the Dance* (1978), serves as instructor for a young man relatively new to the gay subculture:

> "I find it a perfect *symbol* of the demise of America," said Sutherland in that low, throaty voice that always seemed breathlessly about to confide something undreamed of in your wildest dreams, "that dinge are the only people who take hats seriously!" . . .
>
> "Dinge?" said the boy in a cracked, earnest voice. . . .
>
> "Blacks, darling. *Schvartzers,* negroes."

Lesbians and gay men generally learn the folklore of their cultures in such casual ways. Since there are as yet no finishing schools for gay men and lesbians, they must learn appropriate ways of interacting with other homosexual people through informal means. This process of acculturation lies at the heart of the extensive body of gay and lesbian coming of age and coming out novels. (See also COMING OUT STORIES.)

Novels of this sort relate the struggles of gay men and lesbians as they come to terms with their homosexuality—whether they come out or are "brought out"—that is, guided by another person to recognize their own homosexuality. This rite of passage is possibly the quintessential experience of "out" lesbians and gay men. Indeed the coming out story is so much a part of homosexual culture that it constitutes a genre in its own right. Such stories, often related in gay and lesbian novels, are a type of personal experience narrative. In *Rubyfruit Jungle,* for example, Holly tells of being brought out:

> I'd been sleeping with guys since I was eighteen, but it took me four more years to get to women. . . . One night my roommate unblocked me. . . . She threw me in bed, really. I kicked and took a chunk out of her arm but that didn't last long. She wouldn't let go and I didn't want her to, secretly. Then I spent the next three weeks running away from her and telling her I didn't like it at all and I only gave in because I was tired of fighting. . . . She knew, and I didn't.

The roommate has not tried to "convert" Holly to homosexuality; rather she has recognized Holly's innate lesbianism and led her to awareness.

Like Holly's roommate, gay men and lesbians sometimes claim to have a sort of sixth sense, or "gaydar," that allows them to identify other homosexual people through nonverbal cues. The narrator of John Reid's *The Best Little Boy in the World* (1973), visiting a divorced man, has no problem decoding messages about sexuality:

> His $500-a-month (I'm guessing) one-bedroom apartment sent gay bleeps into my radar, bleeps that would probably not show up on a straight screen, like the tube of K-Y in the medicine chest or the Barbra Streisand albums among his record collection. I wondered: Could Esquire be gay? I remembered the time we had played handball on his membership at the New York Athletic Club . . . and what remarkable [sic] good shape he was in. I wondered why he had separated from his wife and why they had had no children.

The narrator's awareness of the use of K-Y jelly as a sexual lubricant and Streisand's immense popularity among gay men cause him to look for other clues to Esquire's sexual orientation: an apparent concern for remaining physically fit, unusual among heterosexual men of the period, and his marital and (non)parental status.

Humor is an important communication strategy in the lesbian and gay subculture. By inverting the symbols of the straight world, homosexual people can find humor in situations that would otherwise be painful to endure. Playing with heterosexual values, turning them around and using them against the oppressors, takes the sting out of the majority culture's weapons and underscores how silly stereotypes and homophobia are. Humor suffuses the argot, serving to express delight or hostility, to entertain or to insult. Noretta Koertge relies heavily on humor throughout *Valley of the Amazons* (1984):

> "Well, I said there were gay Christian alternatives. I told him about the Dignity meetings on Thursday night over at the rectory."
>
> What she hadn't mentioned to TJ and wouldn't discuss with Helen was the undignified atmosphere at those meetings. Father McCawley always drank too much wine and after the book report and formal discussion period he would turn raunchy and start talking about how he'd been down on his knees all night long.
>
> "Were you praying, Father," someone would shout.
>
> "No, but I sure had my mouth open," would come the reply.

Koertge layers stereotypes of gay men's preoccupation with sex with those of the lecherous nature of supposedly celibate priests who prey on rather than pray with their parishioners to question the value of religion and to suggest an incompatibility between homosexuality and Christianity. In a subsequent passage, she turns her wit to stereotypes of lesbians.

> The mike crackled. "Good evening, all you lovely dykes!" A roar of approval. "Kiss the womyn sitting next to you—" Giggles. "Go on." Confused hugs. "Did you check to see if she had grease under her fingernails?" Absolute shrieks. "Well, if she did, please send her right over to the Transport tent. Rubyfruit is having some ignition problems, but I'm sure if someone with a little knowhow will just twid-

dle with her plugs—she has *eight* of them you know." Laughter building to applause.

Beginning with the stereotype of lesbians as women who pursue "masculine" occupations, in this case automobile repair, Koertge creates the metaphor of lesbian woman as a powerful engine that simply needs the right woman to overcome her ignition problems—that is, to turn her over or to turn her on—perhaps by manipulating her sparkplug-nipples.

Sharing stories is a method of strengthening bonds and emphasizing the closeness of a relationship. Explaining esoteric aspects of gay or lesbian life to heterosexual friends can be an especially meaningful sign of trust. For example, in Maupin's *Tales of the City* (1978), Michael Tolliver, a gay character, signifies his intimacy with his straight friend Brian Hawkins by acceding to Brian's request for an explanation of cock rings. Michael concludes his explanation with a story:

> I used to know this guy . . . a very proper stockbroker, in fact . . . who wore one *all* the time. But he soon got cured of *that*. . . . He had to fly to Denver for a conference, and they caught him when he passed through the metal detector at the airport.

In illustrating a potential risk of wearing a cock ring, Michael relates a contemporary legend—a localized, supposedly true story set in the recent past. The teller usually asserts that the events actually happened to a friend of a friend. Legends are often cautionary tales. This one depicts the presumably humiliating public revelation of a man's use of sexual toys. The implicit warning is that sexual accouterments are best kept at home, behind closed doors.

Tony Fennelly uses another widely known legend from the gay male subculture as the basis of her mystery novel, *The Glory Hole Murders* (1985). Police Lieutenant Frank Washington, investigating a particularly gruesome murder, dryly lists the facts of the case:

> There are ten toilet booths. And each one has a hole in the wall. . . . The men signal one another from inside the booths and then have sexual contact through the holes. . . . After the deceased had put his penis through the hole, presumably in the hope of a relationship . . . some person or persons unknown thrust a long, thin object through it vertically. Sort of a giant hat pin.

Versions of this story about the risks of anonymous, semipublic sex have been circulating since the 1950s, if not earlier. The story warns that if one does not know who his partner is, he could be harmed or even killed.

Popular belief has long held that there is no such thing as a "happy homosexual." Conceding to this notion, authors often killed their primary gay and lesbian characters to make their books more palatable to publishers. This traditional plot strategy apparently originated with *Teleny* (1893), the pornographic novel attributed to the OSCAR WILDE circle, and with Alfred J. Cohen's *A Marriage Below Zero* (1899). Hall echoes the tradition in *The Well of Loneliness*. After suffering a life of poverty and illness, Barbara MacDonald dies; her lover, Jamie, then commits suicide. At the end of the novel, the feminine Mary Llewellyn is redeemed by Martin Hallam, leaving Stephen in despair. Although Stephen assumes the role of martyr, demanding of God "the right to our existence," one could take the message of the book to be that true lesbians are butch (masculine) and must suffer; femmes (feminine lesbians) are simply confused and can be saved. A similar situation concludes ANN BANNON's *Odd Girl Out* (1957), although with an interesting twist. The semibutch Beth is redeemed by Charlie Ayers; Laura, the femme, must suffer the loss of her love and run away to a new life.

One of the characters in Holleran's *Dancer from the Dance* comments on this traditional resolution of gay fiction: "You would have to make your novel very sad—the world demands that gay life . . . be ultimately sad. . . . They would demand it be ultimately violent and/or tragic." Through this character, Holleran demonstrates his familiarity with the tradition, signaling the reader that he may subsequently play with this plot device. Thus, near the end of the novel, Sutherland dies of a drug overdose, and the melancholy Malone is last seen swimming out to sea like Edna Pontellier in Kate Chopin's *The Awakening* (1899). Like Edna, Malone perhaps could not deal with the feelings that had awakened in him. On the other hand, Malone is reminiscent of many folk heroes who are presumed to live on, perhaps to return at a time when they are greatly needed, like King Arthur, Frederick Barbarossa, and Jesus Christ (or even John F. Kennedy and Elvis Presley): Rumored sightings of Malone occur long after his disappearance.

Just as Malone, Stephen Gordon, Holly, and many other gay and lesbian characters achieve enlightenment in literature, so do countless readers—men and women who feel an affinity with characters like themselves. The authors' incorporation of folklore into lesbian and gay literature helps readers make this connection. Traditional narratives, familiar language, and comfortable humor demonstrate an insider's awareness that makes these stories ring true.

—*Joseph P. Goodwin*

BIBLIOGRAPHY

Bergman, David. *Gaiety Transfigured: Gay Self-Representation in American Literature.* Madison: University of Wisconsin Press, 1991. ■ Browning, Jimmy D. "Maupin's Novels as Folk Artifacts." *New York Folklore* 19.1–2 (1993): 71–87. ■ Doty, Alexander. *Making Things Perfectly Queer: Interpreting Mass Culture.* Minneapolis: University of Minnesota, 1993. ■ Faderman, Lillian. "Lesbian Magazine Fiction in the Early Twentieth Century." *Journal of Popular Culture* 9 (1978): 800–817. ■ Goodwin, Joseph P. *More Man Than You'll Ever Be: Gay Folklore and Acculturation in Middle America.* Bloomington: Indiana University Press, 1989. ■ Radner, Joan N., and Susan S. Lanser. "Strategies of Coding in Women's Cultures." *Feminist Messages: Coding in Women's Folk Culture.* Joan Newlon Radner, ed. Urbana: University of Illinois Press, 1993.

Forster, E. M.
(1879–1970)

Although he always remained to some extent an Edwardian, E. M. Forster embodied more fully than any other imaginative writer of his generation a modern gay-liberation perspective. Born in London on New Year's Day 1879, the son of a promising architect who was to die within the infant's first year of life, Forster grew up cosseted by a host of female relatives. He became aware of his homosexuality in the climate of repression and self-consciousness that permeated English society in the aftermath of the WILDE scandal of 1895. As a student at King's College, Cambridge, where he matriculated in 1897, he fell in love with a fellow undergraduate, with whom he enjoyed kisses and embraces but probably not genital sexuality. Forster, in fact, was not to experience a fully satisfying sexual relationship of any duration until he was nearly forty, when he fell in love with an Egyptian tram conductor in Alexandria in 1919. His sexual frustration undoubtedly influenced his art almost as much as his homosexuality itself, accounting for the emphasis in his early work on the need for sexual fulfillment and wholeness of being.

Forster's homosexuality manifested itself in an erotic preference for foreigners and for men of the lower social classes. Reflecting an appreciation of the natural vitality he connected with working-class men and an ambivalence about his own overcivilized temperament, this preference helps account for his tendency to romanticize the lower classes and for his sensitivity to the injustices of the class system at home and to the effects of imperialism abroad. Perhaps because of his erotic preference for working-class men, Forster was also deeply affected by the belief that homosexuality could serve a positive social function by helping to bridge the barriers that separate the classes. This belief, which is reflected throughout Forster's fiction and surfaces most explicitly in *Maurice,* derives from the Whitmanesque ideal of comradeship as expressed in the early English gay liberation movement in writings by such "Uranian" leaders as EDWARD CARPENTER and JOHN ADDINGTON SYMONDS. Although Forster's affair with the tram conductor Mohammed el Adl was to end sadly, with Mohammed's premature death in 1922, Forster cemented a long-lasting relationship with a good-looking and intelligent police constable named Bob Buckingham in 1930. Their relationship survived even Bob's marriage in 1932 and continued until Forster's death at Coventry in the Buckinghams' home in 1970.

Forster's acute consciousness of gay oppression, as epitomized in the persecution of Wilde, haunted his imagination throughout his life, fueling his anger at social and political injustices of all kinds. When he was almost eighty-five years old, he noted in his diary, "how *annoyed* I am with Society for wasting my time by making homosexuality criminal. The subterfuges, the self-consciousness that might have been avoided." But notwithstanding his difficulties in making a sexual adjustment and despite recent attempts to characterize his attitude toward homosexuality as guilt-ridden and self-loathing, the fact is that Forster never felt shame for his sexual orientation. What he did feel were a sense of wariness and vulnerability and that sensation of standing "at a slight angle to the universe" that he detected in the poetry of C. P. CAVAFY. Forster's sensitivity to the pervasive homophobia of his age probably accounts for that tinge of sadness so characteristic of the Forsterian voice.

The posthumous publication of *Maurice* in 1971 and of *The Life to Come and Other Stories* in 1972, as well as the revelations of P. N. Furbank's scrupulously honest biography, caused a decided decline in Forster's reputation and led to a number of patently homophobic attacks on him and his work. The belatedness of the publication of Forster's explicitly gay fiction has also had a more insidious consequence: the tendency to isolate the posthumously published work from the justly celebrated novels and stories published in Forster's lifetime. Such a division is artificial, however, for despite important differences in dramatic situations and degrees of explicitness, the fiction embodies a consistent system of values centered on issues of self-realization, individualism, and responsiveness to life, nature, and the unseen. What June Perry Levine identifies as the predominant pattern of Forster's posthumous fiction—"the tame in pursuit of the savage, oscillating within a field of attraction and repulsion"—may be seen in all of his work.

Although it is presented discreetly, homoeroticism is a significant element in the five novels he published during his lifetime. The ironic comedy *Where Angels Fear to Tread* (1905), for example, traces the inchoate self-fashioning of the quintessential Forsterian protagonist, Philip Herriton, a painfully self-conscious and sexually repressed aesthete. As a result of his encounter with Italy, Philip matures to understand something of the complexity of life though he fails to recognize what Forster subtly informs the alert reader: that his real sexual attraction is not the intellectual response he develops for his Sawston neighbor Caroline Abbott but the physical passion he feels for Gino Carelli, the good-looking young Italian who functions in the novel as a kind of Pan figure, a symbol of natural sexuality and freedom from social restraints. Just as Philip's spiritual love for Caroline is a displacement of his sexual attraction for Gino, so in *The Longest Journey* (1907) Rickie Elliott's weak passion for his wife, Agnes, is aroused by his unconscious desire for Gerald Dawes, a brainless soldier who had mistreated him at school. The Pan figure in *The Longest Journey,* however, is not Dawes but Stephen Wonham, Rickie's illegitimate half-brother, who is the natural embodiment of the Greek spirit in the English countryside. As allied at the end of the novel with Ansell, an intellectual, homosexual Jew, Stephen represents the best hope for the future of England. A homosexual consciousness is more subtly present in *Howards End* (1910) and *A Passage to India* (1924), where the emotional center of each work resides in a same-sex (though nonsexual) relationship, that of Margaret and Helen Schlegel and Fielding and Aziz, respectively. Margaret's revolt when she overhears her husband and a physician debating whether Helen is "normal" is revealing: "How dare these men label her sister!" she exclaims, ". . . it seemed to Margaret that all Schlegels were threatened with her. Were they normal? What a question to ask! And it is always those who know nothing about human nature, who are bored by psychology and shocked by physiology, who ask it." Margaret's indignation here undoubtedly reflects Forster's own resentment at the persistent labeling of homosexuals as abnormal. The bond between Aziz and Fielding is not sexual but it is increasingly intimate, and Forster's masterpiece may be read as their love story.

Although the plot of *A Room with a View* (1908) makes it Forster's fullest celebration of heterosexual love, the novel is actually the product of the author's self-conscious attempt to discover a homosexual literary tradition; and it is suffused with homoeroticism and with the ideology of the late nineteenth-century homosexual emancipation movement. In an entry in his diary for New Year's Eve 1907, during a period when he was writing *A Room with a View,* Forster constructed a list of famous homosexual authors and artists, including A. E. HOUSMAN, WILLIAM SHAKESPEARE, John Addington Symonds, WALTER PATER, WALT WHITMAN, Edward Carpenter, SAMUEL BUTLER, H. S. Tuke, Luca Signorelli, and MICHELANGELO, all of whom are quoted in the novel or are otherwise influential on it. The point that needs emphasis is not that *A Room with a View* is a disguised homosexual love story with the protagonist Lucy Honeychurch actually a boy in drag but that the novel's celebration of "the holiness of direct desire" has homosexual as well as heterosexual application. Indeed, Forster's vision of a new Garden of Eden to be attained "when we no longer despise our bodies" emerges directly from the ideology of homosexual comradeship as developed by Whitman, Carpenter, and Symonds. The novel's search for a new chivalry based on sexual and social equality is firmly rooted in the early English homosexual emancipation movement.

Homosexual themes are also often implicit in the short stories that Forster published during his lifetime. The stories of *The Celestial Omnibus and Other Stories* (1911) and *The Eternal Moment and Other Stories* (1928) articulate the same social criticism that energizes the novels, but in them Forster does not so much analyze these social conditions as chronicle the breaking loose of characters from the imprisonment of social conventions. Forster's earliest tale, "The Story of a Panic," which resulted from a sudden revelation in 1902, is certainly susceptible to a gay reading, recounting as it does the epiphany of a fourteen-year-old English boy and his friendship with an older Italian youth. But the most revealing of Forster's published stories is "The Curate's Friend," written in 1907. A slight, fantastical tale of a young clergyman's transforming encounter with a Pan-like faun, the story on first reading appears hardly more than an anecdote; however, concealed beneath its comic veneer is an account of homosexual recognition and acceptance that is undoubtedly autobiographical. As a result of his encounter and self-acceptance, the protagonist rises beyond such concepts as guilt, sin, and conformity, yet he is also aware of the price society will exact should he reveal the source of his newfound happiness: "I might find myself an expense to the nation." The story thus illustrates the great value of honesty to oneself, even as it also acknowledges the necessity for discretion—even hypocrisy—in a repressive society. The story betrays Forster's awareness in 1907 of his own precarious position in a society that rewarded him as author of acclaimed novels but that was nevertheless prepared to punish him for the secret desires that animated his art.

Forster sometimes explained his failure to write novels during the final forty-six years of his life as a result of his inability to publish his works on homosexual subjects. This explanation begs a number of questions and should not be accepted at face value as the complete reason Forster abandoned the writing of novels at the height of his career, but it does indicate the importance he attached both to his sexual identity and to his gay fiction. He seems initially to have turned to gay subjects during difficult moments in writing on publishable subjects. In 1911, for example, soon after the triumph of *Howards End,* he expressed his overweening "Weariness of the only subject I both can and may treat—the love of men for women & vice versa," and abandoned a novel he was working on to compose homoerotic short stories. Similarly, he wrote *Maurice* when his attempts to write an Indian novel faltered after a few chapters. Although he knew that he could not publish it, he hoped that having completed his novel of homosexual love, his period of sterility would be over and he could return to publishable work, a hope that was not immediately realized.

Forster's decision to write *Maurice* was the direct result of a 1913 visit to Edward Carpenter at the home he shared with his working-class lover George Merrill in Derbyshire. The novelist had admired Carpenter as a pioneer in the early gay liberation movement for years and probably modeled Mr. Emerson in *A Room with a View* on him. Heartened by Carpenter and Merrill, Forster conceived his novel of homosexual passion in a flash of inspiration. He wrote the first draft quickly and with a sense of elation, guided by the conviction that "a happy ending was imperative." More than anything else, it was the happy ending that made *Maurice* unpublishable. Since homosexuality was illegal in England until 1967, the novel might have been construed as glorifying crime and hence could have been subject to prosecution. But even in manuscript, *Maurice* had a major literary influence as an important source for *Lady Chatterley's Lover* (1928), whose author, D. H. LAWRENCE, was among many of Forster's friends and associates to read the novel in typescript. (Ironically, when *Maurice* was published, some reviewers dismissed it as a homosexualized *Lady Chatterley's Lover*; more accurately, Lawrence's novel is a heterosexualized *Maurice*.) Forster tinkered with his manuscript often and made major revisions in 1920, 1932, and 1959. These revisions centered largely on increasing the prominence and credibility of Alec, who was initially a vague, romantic composite of the working-class men Forster admired from afar, and on making the ending more believable.

On its publication in 1971, *Maurice* was denigrated by reviewers and critics, who read it too narrowly as a sentimental apology for homosexuality. But the novel is not an apology at all. Rather, it is a convincing and affecting account of an ordinary young man's groping toward wholeness in a society that makes such growth very difficult. The eponymous hero moves painfully from conventionality to heroism. The "vast curve" of his life includes a progression from an alliance in which spirit educates spirit to one in which the flesh educates the spirit and develops "the sluggish heart and the slack mind against their will." He eventually rejects the life of respectability for a life of freedom and sacrifices a spurious safety for the struggle that "twists sentimentality into love." Forster's most concentrated novel, *Maurice* dramatizes in deeply felt human terms the most important recent conclusions of sexologists and psychologists— that homosexuality is a set of feelings, involving the connection and commitment one individual makes with another, and that such feelings predate sexual expression, sometimes by years—while placing this understanding in the concrete context of Edwardian England. The social setting is important, for the novel explores the impact of self-awareness on social attitudes. As always in Forster, individual growth is measured in terms of sharpened insight into the nature of convention and repression.

The first masterpiece of the early gay liberation movement, *Maurice* not only articulates the ideology of Uranianism but also mirrors a significant debate within the movement, enacting, as Robert K. Martin has demonstrated, a dialectic between the ideas and styles of Carpenter and Symonds. Both disciples of Whitman, the two men equally deserve credit as pioneers in sexual reform, but their styles were quite different, and *Maurice* pivots on the contrast between them. Symonds, who tended to be evasive and apologetic, implied the superiority of homosexuality to heterosexuality on the grounds that it was more spir-

itual; Carpenter, on the other hand, was more open and visionary, and insisted on the equality of the two emotions, considering neither to be more or less spiritual than the other. And while Symonds isolated homosexuality as a private experience and minimized physical passion, Carpenter discreetly acknowledged the physical and linked homosexual emancipation with feminism, labor reform, and social democracy. Rather than contrasting homosexuality and heterosexuality, *Maurice* juxtaposes these two conceptions of homosexuality.

Using a "double structure," the novel divides into two parallel sections, the action of each half mirroring the other with significant differences. The first half (Parts One and Two) is devoted to the relationship between Maurice and Clive, his Cambridge classmate who initiates him into an elitist homosexuality based on distrust of the body and on a bookish Hellenism. This part of the novel traces a false vision of "superior" homosexuality that is platonized and sublimated in the manner of Symonds. The second half of the novel (Parts Three and Four) is devoted to Maurice's alliance with Alec, the undergamekeeper on Clive's country estate. It tracks Maurice's salvation through a Carpenterian homosexuality that includes physical love and that leads Maurice to reject class barriers and social conventions. Maurice's relationship with Clive, who is probably based on Forster's first love, H. O. Meredith, is fascinating and beautifully detailed, but it is only a necessary preliminary to the fuller relationship he ultimately achieves with Alec. Maurice finally comes to embrace the political consequences of homosexuality and to adopt the radical perspective on society conferred by the outlaw status of the homosexual in 1913.

Appropriately, the most significant literary influence on Forster's novel is the work of Oscar Wilde, England's most famous homosexual outlaw. More specifically, Wilde's letter from Reading Gaol, *De Profundis*, informs *Maurice* at every turn. The frequent echoes of Wilde's letter serve to incorporate it into the very texture of Forster's novel and to establish Wilde's martyrdom as the historical reality that all considerations of the social and political consequences of homosexuality must confront. Wilde's insistence in *De Profundis* on the transcendent value of self-realization and on the redemptive potentiality of suffering shapes the development of Forster's protagonist. Moreover, Wilde's rejection of society and his expectation of solace in nature help explicate the retreat into the greenwood at the end of *Maurice*. Like Wilde, Forster has little faith in social reform. Hence, at the end of the novel Maurice and Alec must utterly reject society, whose injustices they perceive as a result of their homosexuality. But unlike Wilde's bitter pessimism, Forster's attitude is tempered by an optimistic belief in the value of personal relations. Maurice and Alec together accept England's air and sky as their birthright, facing the world unafraid, showing that "when two are gathered together majorities shall not triumph." Their escape into the greenwood thus simultaneously renders a summary judgment against society and endorses the possibility of the flesh's educating the spirit, even in the midst of repression. The communion of flesh and spirit finally achieved by Alec and Maurice promises help in a universe in which "man has been created to feel pain and loneliness without help from heaven."

What is most impressive about *Maurice* is its superb artistry. Full appreciation of its subtlety depends on the reader's engagement in a process of interpretation and reinterpretation. The book's "double structure" is complemented by an elusive narrative technique that combines the point of view of the focal character with frequent though cryptic authorial intrusions. The effect of this sophisticated technique is to force the reader to experience firsthand the protagonist's bewilderment and pain and exhilaration and muddle, thus contributing to the book's peculiar poignancy, as when Maurice envisions himself wandering "beyond the barrier . . . the wrong words on his lips and the wrong desires in his heart, and his arms full of air." Only later, on rereading the first section in light of the second, is the reader able to place the early events in context, thereby correcting his or her original responses. Much of the novel's pleasure resides in the subtle exposure of unexpected dimensions and unsuspected ironies. A book of haunting beauty, written in supple prose that is alternately spare, taut, lyrical, and impassioned, *Maurice* occupies an honored place in the gay literary heritage.

Although Forster published no more fiction after *The Eternal Moment and Other Stories* in 1928, he continued to write occasional stories, nearly all with homosexual themes. *The Life to Come and Other Stories* collects these gay fictions, as well as some early work that Forster did not publish during his lifetime. Some of the late stories, those written between 1922 and 1958, are among Forster's finest tales—ironic, witty, resonant, and angry. They express a healthy rage against a hypocritical society that denies the legitimacy of homosexual emotions and acts. Although they embody a vision consistent with that of the tales and novels published during Forster's lifetime, they differ significantly in their attitude toward sexuality. In these works, sexuality is at once more and less important than in the novels and stories Forster published. Sexuality is celebrated as an agent that expresses and intensifies love, and as a significant dimension of human identity, but it is also demystified as life-enhancing pleasure, valuable for its own sake.

The gay fictions of *The Life to Come* include three comic stories—"The Obelisk," "What Does It Matter? A Morality," and "The Classical Annex"—and Forster's only piece of historical fiction, "The Torque," as well as the haunting psychomachia, "Dr. Woolacott," and three superb works that rank among his greatest achievements, "The Life to Come," "Arthur Snatchfold," and "The Other Boat." The comic stories scorn the oppressive morality that inhibits personal growth and distorts social health. They attack the antisexual attitudes that, paradoxically, exaggerate the importance of sex and pervert true morality into moralistic prohibitions. These priapic stories celebrate recreational sex as a source of joy, accepting the pursuit of pleasure as a deeply human activity. At bottom anarchic, they emphasize the power of sex to humanize and invigorate both individuals and societies but pointedly refuse to justify sex in the name of love or refined emotions.

Forster's three most ambitious posthumously published tales merit special notice. "The Life to Come," which dates from 1922, concerns the devotion of a primitive tribal chief for an English missionary who betrays his love. The story, which weds satire and prophecy to tragedy and myth, is a fascinating parable that anticipates *A Passage to India* in its opposition of Eastern and Western values. As in the novel, Christianity is tested from an Eastern perspective and found to be narrow and small in its denial of the fullness of experience and in its refusal to take literally the doctrine of love that it professes. The tale satirizes Christian hypocrisy, exposes Christian complicity in imperialism as a failure of *agape* as well as of *Eros*, and suggests that the repression of Eros perverts the expression of *agape*.

"Arthur Snatchfold," written in 1928, pivots on a brief but fulfilling sexual exchange between a successful businessman and a young milkman, who is subsequently arrested and imprisoned for the dalliance. Despite the promise of a reduced sentence for identifying his partner, the milkman bravely refuses. The story, which raises interesting but deliberately unresolved questions about its morally ambivalent narrator, indicts a stupid and cruel society that criminalizes harmless pleasure and distances individuals and classes from each other.

The longest of Forster's gay stories is "The Other Boat," which was completed in 1958, when Forster was almost eighty years old. The tale recounts the struggle to fuse into wholeness the divided personality of Lionel March, a young army captain. The struggle comes to a crisis in his relationship with a sensuous, classless, effeminate youth named Cocoa, "a subtle, supple boy who belonged to no race and always got what he wanted." Lionel's search for wholeness is complicated by his confused identity and made especially difficult by the conflict between his secret love for Cocoa and his self-definition as a member of a racist society. The story's violent conclusion, in which Lionel murders Cocoa and then commits suicide, expresses the young officer's inability to face either a life led contrary to prevailing currents or one without tribal identity. Unlike Cocoa, he lacks the heroism to achieve wholeness. "The Other Boat" explores with profound insight the psychological effects of racism and homophobia.

In the final decades of his life, even as his reputation as a novelist grew with every novel that he did not write, Forster abandoned fiction and became a superb essayist, thoughtful critic and biographer, and a shrewd analyst of politics and culture. As a dogged defender of civil liberties, he protested the persecution of gay books and authors. For example, when RADCLYFFE HALL's lesbian novel *The Well of Loneliness* was prosecuted as obscene in 1928, he persuaded his BLOOMSBURY friends VIRGINIA WOOLF and LYTTON STRACHEY to join him in defending it though at the trial no expert testimony was permitted. As England's most thoughtful exponent of liberal humanism, Forster in his later years became a significant moral presence, a liberal conscience that countered the excesses of left and right alike. Especially for young gay writers in the 1930s like CHRISTOPHER ISHERWOOD, W. H. AUDEN, WILLIAM PLOMER, and J. R. ACKERLEY, he functioned as an uncle figure, a symbol of committed humanism and responsible intelligence. He summed up his beliefs in a series of memorable essays, most notably in "What I Believe" (1938), in which he announced his abiding faith in personal relations and individualism. He bravely asserted that "if I had to choose between betraying my country and betraying my friend, I hope I should have the guts to betray my country." In this credo, he also declared his belief in "an aristocracy of the sensitive, the considerate and the plucky," who, he asserted, "represent the true

human condition, the one permanent victory of our queer race over cruelty and chaos." Himself a member of this spiritual aristocracy, Forster deserves a special place in the gay and lesbian literary heritage. He was not only one of the finest English novelists of the twentieth century but also a tireless defender of humane values.

—*Claude J. Summers*

BIBLIOGRAPHY

Adams, Stephen D. *The Homosexual as Hero in Contemporary Fiction.* New York: Barnes & Noble, 1980. ■ Ebbatson, Roger. *The Evolutionary Self: Hardy, Forster, Lawrence.* Brighton, Sussex: Harvester Press, 1982. ■ Fletcher, John. "Forster's Self-erasure: *Maurice* and the Scene of Masculine Love." *Sexual Sameness: Textual Differences in Lesbian and Gay Writing.* London and New York: Routledge, 1992. 64–90. ■ Furbank, P. N. *E. M. Forster: A Life.* Volume One: *The Growth of the Novelist 1879–1914.* London: Secker and Warburg, 1977. Volume Two: *Polycrates' Ring 1914–1970.* London: Secker and Warburg, 1978. Rpt. 2 vols. in 1. New York: Harcourt, Brace, Jovanovich, 1978. ■ Herz, Judith Scherer. "From Myth to Scripture: An Approach to Forster's Later Short Fiction." *English Literature in Transition* 24 (1981): 206–212. ■ ———. *The Short Narratives of E. M. Forster.* London: Macmillan, 1988. ■ ———, and Robert K. Martin. *E. M. Forster: Centenary Revaluations.* Toronto: University of Toronto Press, 1982. ■ King, Dixie. "The Influence of Forster's *Maurice* on *Lady Chatterley's Lover.*" *Contemporary Literature* 23 (1982): 65–82. ■ Levine, June Perry. "The Tame in Pursuit of the Savage: The Posthumous Fiction of E. M. Forster." *Publications of the Modern Language Association* 99 (1984): 72–88. ■ Malek, James. "Persona, Shadow, and Society: A Reading of Forster's 'The Other Boat.'" *Studies in Short Fiction* 14 (1977): 21–27. ■ Martin, Robert K. "Edward Carpenter and the Double Structure of Maurice." *Journal of Homosexuality* 8.3–4 (1983): 35–46. Rpt. in *Literary Visions of Homosexuality.* Stuart Kellogg, ed. New York: Haworth Press, 1983. 35–46. ■ Page, Norman. *E. M. Forster's Posthumous Fiction.* English Literary Studies Monograph Series 10. Victoria, B.C.: University of Victoria, 1977. ■ Rahman, Tariq. "E. M. Forster and the Break Away from the Ephebophilic Literary Tradition." *Études Anglaises* 40 (1987): 267–278. ■ Summers, Claude J. *E. M. Forster.* New York: Ungar, 1983. ■ ———. *E. M. Forster: A Guide to Research.* New York: Garland, 1991. ■ ———. *Gay Fictions: Wilde to Stonewall.* New York: Continuum, 1990. ■ Wilde, Alan. *Art and Order: A Study of E. M. Forster.* New York: New York University Press, 1964. ■ ———, ed. *Critical Essays on E. M. Forster.* Boston: G. K. Hall, 1985. ■ ———. *Modernism, Postmodernism, and the Ironic Imagination.* Baltimore: Johns Hopkins University Press, 1981.

Foucault, Michel
(1926–1984)

One of the leading philosophers of the twentieth century, Michel Foucault has had an enormous influence on our understanding of the les-

bian and gay literary heritage and the cultural forces surrounding it. In his explorations of power and his examinations of the history of sexuality, Foucault traces the ways in which discourse shapes perception, focusing often on those individuals and practices considered marginal or abnormal, but finding in them keys to understanding the fragile and imperfect ways that power is deployed by the upper classes, the medical establishment, the scientific community, and the literary and political elite. In doing so, Foucault successfully challenges our notion of the "normal" and calls our attention to the historical contexts determining the narrow designations that restrict human freedom.

Born in Poitiers, France, on October 15, 1926, Paul-Michel Foucault grew up in the very atmosphere that he would later condemn, that of the stuffy, tradition-bound elite. His father's success as a surgeon, however, did allow Foucault a superb education. He distinguished himself in literature, history, and philosophy, and after moving to Paris in 1945, quickly became the protégé of Jean Hyppolite, a leading Hegelian philosopher and existentialist. Influenced as well by Jean-Paul Sartre, Martin Heidegger, and Louis Althusser, Foucault began to question the very bases of knowledge and perception. How do we know what we know? Why do we believe what we believe? In the fertile intellectual climate of post-World War II Paris, the brilliant young philosopher developed a fascination with the margins of normality and social acceptability. Foucault was an isolated, aloof student, and his behavior was often eccentric. He suffered a breakdown that culminated in a suicide attempt in 1948. The reason, it has been speculated, was his profound guilt as he became increasingly aware of his homosexuality. Clearly, however, Foucault's tortured sense of self and experience of marginalization also spurred some of his most groundbreaking and fascinating work.

From his doctoral thesis at the Sorbonne, later published as *Madness and Civilization* (1961), through later works, published while he held faculty posts at the University of Clermont-Ferrond and the College de France, Foucault probed the social relations that determine our usage of such simplistic, binary-based categories as the "sane and insane," the "ill and healthy," the "criminal and just," and the "proper and improper." Seeing such designations as serving the political and social interests of certain groups in European and Anglo-American society, Foucault also explored how such ways of structuring perception and belief are both maintained and disrupted. Throughout his works, Foucault concentrates on discourse, the field of language and representation, that forms the very foundation of consciousness and knowledge. In examining how discourses can vary from one segment of society to another and can evolve over time, Foucault works to undermine the smug, self-righteous pretensions of the cultural elite.

Foucault's most influential writings are also those most relevant to the gay and lesbian literary heritage. In *Discipline and Punish* (1975), Foucault examines the birth of the modern prison in the nineteenth century and uses the image of the panopticon, a model facility devised by JEREMY BENTHAM, as a metaphor to expose the widespread regulation of conduct through surveillance. The enforcement of socially acceptable forms of behavior, Foucault argues, became a widely dispersed function throughout society during the nineteenth century; individuals began to watch and regulate each other. No longer was physical torture an explicit check on deviance; rather, the more intangible and insidious process of being watched and thereby coerced into "normality" became common. Foucault's observations on the penal system have clear relevance to the rise of a middle-class mindset demanding sexual conformity during the same period. In his next major work, the introduction to *Herculine Barbin* (1978), the memoirs of a nineteenth-century hermaphrodite, Foucault probes similarly the policing function of medical discourses that attempt to fix "true" sexual identities, ones that deny the full range of human diversity. In such examinations of the nineteenth century, Foucault finds a new emphasis on and numerous new mechanisms for achieving social homogeneity and enforcing a narrow notion of propriety.

Even so, Foucault is acute in recognizing the impossibility of maintaining such control. In his three completed volumes of *The History of Sexuality* (1976–1984), Foucault explores the fluid nature of desire, which finds in its definition through metamorphosing discourses, new channels for expression, as well as new, challengeable boundaries. His most gay- and lesbian-relevant work here is his first volume, where he reflects on nineteenth-century repression, concluding that while the Victorians were explicitly concerned with regulating sexuality, they succeeded only in permeating social discourses with the sexual; they put sex into even greater cultural currency, rather than removing it from culture. Foucault thus advances our understanding of the birth of modern consciousness about sexual identity, finding in the concepts of the "heterosexual" and "homosexual" not only a construction of identity for the purposes of regulation, but also a starting point for subversion and resistance. As many theorists now argue, narrow notions of identity can be both confining and liberating.

Foucault's influence on gay and lesbian studies, as well as on the recent trend of "queer theory," has been immense. Eve Kosofsky Sedgwick's *Epistemology of the Closet,* Judith Butler's *Gender Trouble,* and Jonathan Dollimore's *Sexual Dissidence* are just a few of the many works that draw on and respond to

Foucault. And as his work has become increasingly central to theories of sexual identity, Foucault's tumultuous life has also come under scrutiny. Although his sexual orientation was well known, and his death from AIDS in 1984 was covered widely in the press, the specific resonance of Foucault's own sexuality in his work was barely considered until James Miller's critical biography, *The Passion of Michel Foucault,* was published in 1993. Although it has been condemned by some individuals as scandal-mongering and even homophobic, Miller's work does explore the tortured sense of self that resulted in Foucault's experimentations with hallucinogenic drugs and highly unsafe forms of sex, activities that continued even after his health was impaired and AIDS transmission routes were suspected. Although far from perfect, *The Passion of Michel Foucault* attempts to make sense of a life and philosophical legacy in ways that previous critics had nervously avoided.

There is no more important body of philosophical work within the gay and lesbian literary heritage than that of Michel Foucault. Although he is often (and rightly) criticized for being insensitive to women's issues and for being overly quick to pinpoint precise dates for dramatic alterations in human consciousness, Foucault himself was responsible for one such major change: in the way we perceive power and its use by and against individuals. While evincing his own blindspots, he helped call attention to those that in fact define the political, medical, and literary establishments still working to categorize and condemn individuals today. (See also IDENTITY and LITERARY THEORY: GAY, LESBIAN, AND QUEER.)

—Donald E. Hall

BIBLIOGRAPHY

Butler, Judith. *Gender Trouble: Feminism and the Subversion of Identity.* New York: Routledge, 1990. ■ Dollimore, Jonathan. *Sexual Dissidence: Augustine to Wilde, Freud to Foucault.* New York: Oxford University Press, 1991. ■ Eribon, Didier. *Michel Foucault.* Trans. Betsy Wing. Cambridge, Mass.: Harvard University Press, 1991. ■ Miller, James. *The Passion of Michel Foucault.* New York: Simon & Schuster, 1993. ■ Sedgwick, Eve Kosofsky. *Epistemology of the Closet.* Berkeley: University of California Press, 1990.

Frederics, Diana
(pseudonym, dates unknown)

"Diana Frederics" is the pseudonym for an author whose real identity remains a mystery. Her only known book is *Diana: A Strange Autobiography,* published in 1939 by the Dial Press. Though the autobiography would seem to provide clues about the writer's life, the book was published in France in 1946 under the title *Diana; roman,* which translates as *Diana; a novel.* Thus, not only is the author's identity a mystery, but the authenticity of her "autobiography" is even more uncertain than that of other autobiographies. *Diana* went out of print in the 1940s, and was reprinted in the 1975 Arno Series on Homosexuality. Few historians or literary critics have paid *Diana* any attention, notable exceptions being Jeannette Foster and Lillian Faderman. Although the printing history of *Diana* is relatively inconsistent, and it has received little attention by scholars of gay and lesbian studies, it seems to have had a rather international appeal. In addition to the French edition of 1946, there was an edition published under the English title in India in 1939.

Diana: A Strange Autobiography is the story of a young woman who, after reading a medical text on sexuality, begins to suspect that she is a lesbian. She decides to put aside this new information until she is strong enough to deal with it and, while at college, avoids intimate contact with those women to whom she is attracted. She lives in a "trial marriage" with a young man until she decides that she has been living a lie. The narrative follows her involvement in several relationships with women. In the concluding chapter, entitled "Fulfillment," Diana and her lover, Leslie, decide to stay together, remarking that "there's such a thing as vows meaning more just because they are secret."

The book is significant for several reasons. Diana is a self-identified lesbian who, though initially ashamed, develops into a politically aware and self-validated woman who is happy and fulfilled at the end of the book. Written in the late 1930s, a period often considered a "wasteland" for lesbian literature, *Diana* is, as Lillian Faderman suggests, an "oasis." But *Diana* is also significant because of the complicated issues it raises about the relationship of autobiography to truth, and the relationship between lesbian writers and the male-dominated medical profession, especially sexology. The book contains an introduction by Victor Robinson, a prominent sexologist, and the autobiographical narrator also uses sexological language. Despite this medical context for the book, the narrator uses sexological language and the case history model in complicated ways that occasionally serve to validate lesbian self-representation over medical representation and to naturalize lesbianism as one possibility along a spectrum of equally valid identities.

Of course, the mystery of the real identity—and especially the gender and sexual identity—of the author complicates readings of the text. Is "Diana Frederics" a lesbian writer who appropriates medical language for her own validation and self-representation? Or is "she" really a male physician, well-versed in sexological theory, validating lesbian identity while also maintaining the control of the male physician over what gets said about lesbians? Regardless of the answers to these questions, *Diana* is an interesting book that chronicles the relationship between lesbians and the larger culture, and between lesbians and the medical profession, in a narrative many will find far more satisfying than RADCLYFFE HALL's *The Well of Loneliness*.

—*Marylynne Diggs*

BIBLIOGRAPHY

Faderman, Lillian. *Odd Girls and Twilight Lovers: A History of Lesbian Life in Twentieth-Century America*. New York: Columbia University Press, 1991. ■ Foster, Jeannette. *Sex Variant Women in Literature*. 1956. Baltimore: Diana, 1975.

Freeman, Mary Eleanor Wilkins
(1853–1930)

Mary Eleanor Wilkins Freeman, after an adolescence unsettled by increasing financial hardship, moved with her family from her birthplace, Randolph, Massachusetts, to Brattleboro, Vermont. There, attempts to recoup economic stability ended with the successive deaths of her only sibling, her younger sister, Nan, in 1876, her mother in 1880, and her father in 1883. Mary was alone, with neither income nor profession, a history of indifference to conventional social activities, a passion for literature, no important social connections, and no prospects for or recorded interest in marriage. She returned to Randolph to live with the family of her lifelong friend, Mary Wales. The two Marys lived together through the years of Wilkins's literary apprenticeship and her greatest literary success until her often-postponed marriage to Charles Freeman, a New Jersey physician turned businessman, in 1902. The marriage was disrupted by Charles's increasing alcoholism and its associated disorders. After several years, the couple separated.

Freeman belonged to the network of literary women whose hub was Annie Adams Fields, wife of Henry Fields, publisher of the *Atlantic Monthly*. Among those women was SARAH ORNE JEWETT, who had been the young Wilkins's literary inspiration and model. Many of these women never married. Mary E. Wilkins, at least until her disastrous marriage, lived as a woman-oriented woman, her life centered on her writing and her relationship with Mary Wales.

Her first literary success came with the publication in 1883 by *Harper's Bazaar* of her story "Two Old Lovers." By 1887, enough stories had been published there and in *Harper's New Monthly Magazine* to compile her first collection: *A Humble Romance*. Four years later, *A New England Nun* followed. She received the Howells Medal of the American Academy of Arts and Letters and was elected to the National Institute of Arts and Letters in 1926.

Freeman's genius lay in her ability to penetrate and illuminate the conjunction between necessity and desire in a woman's life. Her stories often focus on that moment in a woman's life when she must act in the face of conflict between her personal values and the demands made by the "real" world— whether social, natural, or material—or between her ethics and her happiness, comfort, or even safety. Many of her stories are characterized by intense love and passionate devotion between women. In particular, "Two Friends" and "The Long Arm" illustrate the climate of the time and place in which lifelong partnerships between women were lived publicly and with community acceptance and support. These two stories, among the most important nineteenth-century U.S. lesbian stories, explore the extremes of devotion. However, whether Wilkins Freeman's stories are explicitly lesbian, as are these two, or about women whose daily lives, emotional, and often financial commitments are focused on women who are friends, neighbors, or family members, her fictional world is primarily women centered. Called a genius by peers and by those whom she influenced, she has long been recognized as one of the most important and influential practitioners of U.S. literary realism.

—*Susan Koppelman*

BIBLIOGRAPHY

Foster, Edward, ed. *Mary E. Wilkins Freeman*. New York: Hendricks House, 1956. ■ Freeman, Mary Wilkins. "Two Friends" and "The Long Arm." *"Two Friends" and Other Nineteenth Century Lesbian Stories by U.S. Women Writers*. Susan Koppelman, ed. New York: Meridian, 1994. ■ Marchalonis, Shirley, ed. *Critical Essays on Mary Wilkins Freeman*. New York: Macmillan, 1991. ■ Reichardt, Mary R., ed. *A Web of Relationships: Women in the Short Fiction of Mary Wilkins Freeman*. Jackson: University Press of Mississippi, 1992. ■ ———. *The Uncollected Stories of Mary Wilkins Freeman*. Jackson: University Press of Mississippi, 1992. ■ ———. *The Wind in the Rosebush & Other Stories of the Supernatural*. New York: Doubleday, Page and Company, 1903. ■ Westbrook, Perry. *Mary Wilkins Freeman*. Twayne's United States Authors Series. Rev. ed. New York: Macmillan, 1988.

French, Alice
(1850–1934)

Alice French, born in Andover, Massachusetts, moved with her family in 1856 to Davenport, Iowa, where her mother continued her staunch advocacy of Elizabeth Cady Stanton and her father became a wealthy manufacturer. The oldest of six children from a financially and academically privileged background, a member of the Davenport Unitarian Church's founding family, Alice French's interest in club work led to the presidency of the Iowa Society of Colonial Dames. She is described by George McMichael, her only biographer, as embracing conservative political views to protect traditional American values. He describes her as antilabor union, a xenophobe who portrayed foreigners as sinister figures, and a racist caricaturist. She also allegedly opposed prohibition and helped organize against the suffragists. This view of French contradicts the writer who satirized snobbery, class pride, and piously embraced martyrdoms of women to abusive husbands in her 1906 collection of stories, *A Slave to Duty and Other Women*. She promoted images of emotionally independent, financially self-sufficient, and women-centered women in her 1911 collection *Stories That End Well*, and embraced with enthusiasm the early writer and advocate of feminism, Lady Mary Wortley Montague, whose letters French edited and published. The tie that Alice French shared with Mary Wortley was that love for a woman was central to each of their lives.

By the time she was forty, French, publishing as "Octave Thanet," with nineteen years of increasing popular and financial success as an essayist and short story writer behind her, was working on her first novel, *We All*. She wrote six more books in the new century.

Her pseudonym combines the first name of her beloved school roommate Octavia Putman, with whom she shared a twelve-by-twelve room and a double bed during their year at Andover Academy, with a word she had seen painted on the side of a freight train car. McMichael writes that she adopted the androgynous pen name "to avoid the bias of anti-feminist magazine editors."

By 1890, she had been settled in her comfortable lifelong partnership with Jane Allen Crawford for close to a decade, dividing their year between their home in Davenport, Iowa, and their plantation in Arkansas. The two women shared their lives, except for Jane's four-year marriage (the ending of which is mysterious) and Jane's European tour. French/Thanet remains a mysterious figure because of the apparent conflict between her recorded opinions and her literary portrayals. The mystery will be solved only with more basic research on primary French materials to develop an integrated vision of this woman.

Alice French has been remembered as the first regionalist to write realistically about the two areas in which she lived (Iowa and Arkansas). As a consummate local color artist, she achieved great *fin de siècle* popularity and consequent prosperity. Contemporary critics such as Lillian Faderman, Paula Bennett, and Susan Koppelman, in unraveling the coded writings of nineteenth-century lesbians, have sparked new interest in her women-loving stories, which have been revealed as women-loving stories only as a result of the new readings. French's subtle, almost sly portrayals of ties between women who love each other are now being appreciated.

—*Susan Koppelman*

BIBLIOGRAPHY

McMichael, George. *Journey to Obscurity: The Life of Octave Thanet*. Lincoln: University of Nebraska Press, 1965. ■ Thanet, Octave. "My Lorelei—A Heidleberg Romance" and "Max—or His Picture." *"Two Friends" and Other Nineteenth Century Lesbian Stories by U.S. Women Writers*. Susan Koppelman, ed. New York: Meridian, 1994.

FRENCH LITERATURE

French Literature Before the Nineteenth Century

The number of gay and lesbian French writers living before 1800 for whom we have documented evidence of their sexual orientation is small indeed. This fact reflects in part an ignorance that time and fear have imposed on us. Not only has little of substance survived concerning the lives of the authors who wrote in the earliest centuries, but in all periods, even our own, many homosexuals have had good reason not to commit to paper any record of their thoughts or actions. Sodomy, it must be remembered, was an offense for which as late as 1750 the French authorities could and did order that a man be burned alive.

When we enter the sixteenth century and documents become more numerous, additional factors complicate the problem of identifying gay and lesbian figures. With some frequency, strident accusations of pederastic or lesbian behavior begin to be heard, and they will be repeated in ensuing periods. More temperate musings about the behavior of pre-nineteenth-century Frenchmen and women have emerged from modern authors who continue to sift through the leavings of the past. Yet do any of these voices speak the truth? Did Henry III have sexual relations with his mignons? Did Molière's interest in a boy called Baron include wanting to bed him? There is no simple way to arrive at a definitive response to such questions. The quantity of evidence available is very limited; the quality of the evidence, highly suspect. The attacks against Henry III (and similar ones made later against Voltaire) come from their enemies who, moreover, never maintain that they were eyewitnesses to the acts of which the accused stands charged.

One case where we may feel rather confident about the charge of buggery is that of Marc-Antoine Muret (1526–1585). During the early 1550s, Muret taught some of the finest literary minds in Paris. He befriended Pierre de Ronsard for whose *Amours* he wrote a commentary, explaining by means of his extensive classical learning the more recondite allusions in Ronsard's love poetry. In the very year that the commentary appeared (1553), he was obliged to quit Paris after, according to one source, having been imprisoned for a time. He fled to Toulouse, where in 1554 the law pursued him again. When Muret escaped, the city authorities ordered him burned in effigy "for being a Huguenot and a sodomite." Not one of Muret's Parisian friends defended him against the accusation, which soon resurfaced and brought his stay in Padua to an end (1558). Muret's apparent inability to quell the rumors about his sexual behavior or to exonerate himself has convinced most scholars that the humanist was in all likelihood guilty.

Nevertheless, the charge did not prevent him from securing a post at the University of Rome, where he taught for twenty years (1563–1584). In 1572, the Pope accorded him the highly coveted title of Roman citizen. Muret published annotated editions of many of the major Latin writers. He wrote commentaries on Cicero and Aristotle; his orations cover nineteen volumes. All these writings are in Latin, and Muret's command of that language was exceptional enough for contemporaries to consider his style a model to be imitated. Other humanists surpassed his editions of Tacitus and HORACE, but of Aristotle he had a profound grasp and dared to defend Greek letters against those who did not appreciate their significance.

French sixteenth-century humanists must be credited also with introducing the modern world to Anacreon and SAPPHO. In 1554, Henry Estienne (1531–1598) produced the first printed edition of the occasionally pederastic *Anacreontea*. Rémy Belleau (1528–1577) used Estienne's edition to render some of these happy poems of wine and love into French. Notable are his "Ha vrayment je vous puniray" (Ah, I shall punish you indeed) and "Fay moy d'une façon gentille" (Paint for me with a fine hand) where Belleau preserves uncensored the Greek poet's amorous words about his beloved Bathyllus.

Estienne's 1554 volume also included two works by Sappho. (One, already printed in 1546 by his father, Robert, is still counted among Sappho's writings; the authenticity of the other has been questioned.) Belleau appended to his translations from the *Anacreontea* the first French version of any work by Sappho, and here, too, Belleau retains the givens of the original. He makes clear that the speaker is female but keeps the fact unstated until late in the poem, well after the reader has heard about a woman's sweet voice that arouses intense emotion in the speaker.

Although the depiction of lesbian feelings appears very rarely in French love poetry of the sixteenth century, Pierre de Ronsard (1524–1585) and Pontus de Tyard (1521–1605) both composed love poems in which a woman speaks of her love for another female. Ronsard's "Pour vous montrer que j'ay parfaitte envie" (To show you that I desire you absolutely) and Pontus's "J'avois tousjours pensé que d'Amour et d'honneur" (I had always believed that through Love and honor) are remarkable not only for their subject but also for the treatment the subject receives. The sentiments expressed belong resolutely to the storehouse of commonplaces repeated over and over during the Renaissance in verse addressed to women by men, thus lending no little support to the contention that the portrayal of women loving women would enter an entirely new phase when the author was herself a woman.

Few French writers of the sixteenth century have enjoyed the fame of Michel de Montaigne (1533–1592), whose *Essays* intrigued such diverse minds as Pascal, Emerson, and GIDE. His "On Friendship" contains a moving account of the bond he formed with Etienne de La Boétie, a fellow public servant fated, unfortunately, to die when still a young man. The depths to which Montaigne was touched by La Boétie are evident: "And at our first meeting, which just happened to occur during a great feast and city gathering, we discovered that we were so taken with each other, so known to each other, so beholden to each other that from that time nothing was as close to us as each was to the other." Consequently, many modern readers have speculated that this was a homosexual relationship.

No evidence has ever come to light to support this hypothesis, however, and we may not overlook that in the same essay Montaigne establishes a firm distance between friendship (especially the kind he felt for La Boétie) and sexual passion. On the other hand, when Montaigne has finished enumerating the various bonds that cannot meet his definition of friendship, including pederasty and family ties, we are confronted by the realization that such friendship exists exclusively between adult males. Only their relationship rests on the melding of like personalities that Montaigne exalts in his essay.

Although no extant document allows us to trace the impact of this discussion of friendship on Montaigne's readers, it must be noted that the next century greatly admired his pages, referring to the essays as the "gentleman's breviary," that is, as a handbook of appropriate conduct. More intriguing still is the reappearance of certain attitudes expressed by Montaigne in the writings of a group of early seventeenth-century free thinkers. To be sure, these men adopted a far more radical stance, and their break with conventional morality rested above all on a questioning of philosophical and religious principles; yet some appear to have violated sexual taboos as well.

Prominent among the libertines are the poets DENIS SANGUIN DE SAINT-PAVIN (1595–1670), dubbed "the King of Sodom," and THÉOPHILE DE VIAU (1590–1626), whose alleged atheism and sexual activity with other males involved him in a protracted lawsuit. His friend François de Métel, seigneur de Boisrobert (1592?–1662), fared better. Numerous contemporary jibes alluding to his interest in young pages have survived and suggest that his proclivities were common knowledge. However, to the degree that Boisrobert felt the ignominy of disgrace, it was always for impolicy, not buggery. He enjoyed the protection of Cardinals Richelieu and Mazarin and played a critical role in the founding of the French Academy. His poetry could, like that of Théophile, escape the heaviness of the praises routinely sung to the king and his court. Often it did not, and more often still it sought only to be amusing. Nevertheless, as his early reflections on nature please today because of the freshness that the libertines brought momentarily to French poetry, so Boisrobert's witty lines delighted his own world and ensured him success even after the authorities had silenced the radical voices of his early friends.

Regarding their reception, it is pertinent to note that opposition to libertine thinking appeared very early in the century. A work first printed in 1605 shows that as of that date conservative minds were already outraged and alarmed. Entitled *Les Hermaphrodites* and attributed to one Thomas Artus, a classical scholar of some repute, this fascinating book describes an all-male society and its governing statutes. Internal evidence implies that the Hermaphrodite world was meant to mirror the court of Henry III and his mignons, whose indisputable penchant for jewels and elegant attire reappears in Artus's pages as a grotesque desire by males to ape the dress (and sexual role?) of the female. Even more interesting is the author's willingness to equate deviation from sexual norms with the dismissal of all established political, religious, and cultural values. Whereas the sodomite had previously been branded for his unnatural and monstrous behavior, Artus's book invites the reader to believe that such a man is both outside the divinely instituted order and actively committed to overturning that order.

Little wonder then, perhaps, that although the memoirs and correspondence left us by Tallemant des Réaux, Saint-Simon, and the Princess Palatine (Elizabeth, Duchess of Orléans) insinuate that many court figures of the seventeenth century practiced sodomy and lesbianism, no comparable material exists for any of the major writers of the classical period. Granted, some in the twentieth century have read the relationship between Orgon and Tartuffe in Molière's play (1664) about the pious hypocrite as arising out of homosexual feelings. The text, however, lends no support to such a reading. Tartuffe's ability to abet in Orgon his irascible and dictatorial nature and, at the same time, to create in him a sense of religious peace constitutes Molière's own justification for Orgon's attraction to the unprincipled opportunist.

Certain modern-day French homosexuals have clearly been made uneasy by the absence of a gay and lesbian presence in one of the great moments in their literature. Listen to Marc Daniel in his *Hommes du Grand Siècle:* "That the great classical writers of the second half of the seventeenth century passed over every form of homosexuality is further proof . . . that despite all the admirable qualities that make them the representatives of the 'Grand Siècle,' they lacked the fundamental *curiosity* and *critical sense* . . . that we quite rightly consider indispensable." Daniel does not seem to consider that there could be any relationship between a broad discussion of human society and sexuality and more enlightened reflection on the subject of homosexuality. Can it be that Racine's portrait of the irresistible urges of desire or Molière's comic demolition of the fatuousness of prejudiced minds brought no one to reexamine prevailing views on sodomy and its punishment? At least we may be certain that the eighteenth century had no difficulty understanding the political importance of such revelations about humankind.

Rousseau's *Confessions* (1782) relate an encounter between Jean-Jacques and a pederastic, predatory Moor. Voltaire's stay at the court of Frederick II apparently included a single same-sex adventure. These events exhaust the evidence that we possess for any personal involvement of the *philosophes* with homosexuality. (It is true that after coming to the defense of an abbé Desfontaines, incarcerated for sodomy, Voltaire was accused of having had homosexual relations in his youth. Although this remains, of course, a possibility, no conclusive proof has ever been discovered, and as René Pomeau reminds us, defending a friend cannot be transformed into the acceptance of a practice that, on several occasions, Voltaire condemned. Of, for example, the notion that in antiquity pederasty had once been formally estab-

lished, he quipped: "How can we possibly imagine that men had made a law which, if put into effect, would have destroyed the human race?")

Although neither Rousseau (1712–1778) nor Voltaire (1694–1778) reacted positively to his brush with buggery, both must be credited with sharing with the best minds of the period the realization that "the reevaluation of society necessitated a corresponding reevaluation of human nature." (The phrase belongs to Jacob Stockinger, whose article on eighteenth-century France gives multiple examples of this point.)

A novel by Denis Diderot (1713–1784) provides one such example. Written in 1760, but published only in 1796, *La Religieuse* uses the attempted seduction of a young nun by her mother superior to raise questions pertinent to the reevaluation Diderot sought. His aim: to attack the monastic vows that have put these women in dangerous proximity. Such vows are contrary to the "basic inclination of nature." "God made man a social creature. Can He be happy that he is locking himself away?" The ceremony and routine of the cloistered life, Diderot suggests, cannot refashion human instincts. Unnatural, that life will only cause what is natural to seek satisfaction through the means at hand and to erupt with a violence "unknown to those who live in the world." Thus, although *La Religieuse* portrays lesbianism as a perversion, the novel also roundly defends human sexuality against any effort, however culturally sanctioned, to deny its full expression.

The ability of the *philosophes* to influence Western liberal thought cannot be questioned, but in scope and daring these writers do not begin to equal the pages penned by DONATIEN-ALPHONSE-FRANÇOIS DE SADE (1740–1814), the famous Marquis de Sade. Of course, through the words this man has given to modern languages, one facet of that daring is well known, but there are others.

Whether Sade was homosexual or not remains in dispute. It was his adventures with women, not men, that brought scandal and prosecution into his life. Yet, in her essay *Must Sade Be Burned?* Simone de Beauvoir gives the impression that any man who spoke with such fervor (and so often) about sodomy had to have been a committed practitioner of the act. Equally intriguing are the remarks by Sade's model libertine in *Philosophy in the Bedroom* (1795). He admits that sodomy is his greatest pleasure, adding, "I adore doing it with both sexes; but a young boy's ass gives me, I confess, more enjoyment than does a girl's." Veiled autobiography or a writer's determined desire to shock and awaken? Much in Sade underscores the validity of both possibilities.

Before 1949, when Gilbert Lely began to publish a sizable archive of Sade material offered to him by the writer's family, public knowledge of the marquis derived primarily from distorted accounts and a mere handful of his extensive writings. Lely's biography of the author has at last set straight the facts of his life. Still, even when stripped of its mythic dimensions, it is an extraordinary biography, replete with great debauchery and even greater confinement. Between 1778 and 1814, Sade spent nearly twenty-seven years in prison.

Most of Sade's writings were composed during his long incarceration. They include plays, novels, and political and philosophical essays. Taken together, they show to what degree Sade's discussion of sex belongs to a much broader spectrum of concerns. Sade, for example, follows in the footsteps of the *philosophes* in denouncing the Church and "the pride, tyranny and despotism of the priests." He calls for a new moral order that ensures equality of the sexes and forbids the death penalty. Nature replaces God as the arbiter of acceptable behavior: "If nature forbad the joys of sodomy, incest, defilement, etc. would she allow us to take so much pleasure in performing such acts?" Moreover, discovering destruction to be one of the primary laws of nature, Sade overturns the Christian link between sex and procreation: "We have believed that nature would perish if our wonderful species came to an end on this globe, whereas, by handing back to nature the creative right that she grants to us, the complete destruction of the species would return to nature the power that we take away from her when we propagate." It is in this context that Sade situates his extended defense of sodomy. Indifferent to where man places his sperm, nature cannot be offended by sodomy and least of all by sodomy between males, since that act exists at the greatest possible distance from procreative coupling.

The liberation from Christian morality that Sade advocates is meant to affect the inner as well as the outer life of humanity. A character in *Philosophy in the Bedroom* asks: "Is it not through [the imagination] that we experience pleasure? Is that not the source of our most exciting sensual delights?" One interpretation of Sade's frequently graphic accounts of sexual perversion (such as *The 120 Days of Sodom*) would make of those pages the fruits of just such a liberated imagination.

However we choose to read and judge his books, Sade's contribution to our modern world is impressive. His unfettered entry into the repressed corners of human desire inspired fellow writers. (Flaubert, BAUDELAIRE, Lautréamont, SWINBURNE, and Dostoevski all acknowledged their debt to the marquis.) That voyage anticipated as well both the discipline and discoveries of psychoanalysis. Like the subconscious world he willingly plumbed, Sade's writings contain many disturbing elements; yet no author before him and few since have so thoroughly freed the sexual sphere from the binds of the Judeo-Christian yoke.

—*Donald Stone*

BIBLIOGRAPHY

Daniel, Marc. *Hommes du Grand Siècle: Etudes sur l'homosexualité sous les règnes de Louis XIII et de Louis XIV.* Paris: Arcadie, n. d. ■ Dejob, Charles. *Marc-Antione Muret: un professeur français en Italie dans la seconde moitié du XVIe siècle.* Paris: E. Thorin, 1881; rpt. Geneva: Slatkine, 1970. ■ Lely, Gilbert. *Vie du Marquis de Sade.* Paris: Garnier, 1982. ■ Lever, Maurice. *Sade: A Biography.* New York: Farrar, Straus and Giroux, 1993. ■ Pomeau, René. "Voltaire, du côté de Sodome." *Revue d'Histoire Littéraire de la France* 86 (1986): 235–247. ■ Stockinger, Jacob. "Homosexuality and the French Enlightenment." *Homosexualities and French Literature.* George Stambolian and Elaine Marks, eds. Ithaca, N.Y.: Cornell University Press, 1978. 352–377. ■ Stone, Donald. "The Sexual Outlaw in France, 1605." *Journal of the History of Sexuality* 2 (1992): 597–608.

French Literature: Nineteenth Century

The nineteenth century in France witnessed a dramatic increase in literary representations of same-sex eroticism, a development that can be traced both to literary trends and to historical change. Although the first half of the century is relatively poor in such depictions, after 1850, with the birth of literary movements such as symbolism, DECADENCE, realism, and naturalism, gay and lesbian sexuality becomes a significant subject in the national literature. One might say that, constituting more than simply a new "theme," these new representations changed the course of literary history.

In 1791, revolutionary penal codes did away with laws that had criminalized homosexuality, a reform that was maintained in the Napoleonic Code of 1804. Yet it was not until the 1830s, at the height of romanticism, that lesbian and gay male characters began to appear in French literature in significant numbers.

Most romantic writers were largely silent about non-heterosexual relationships, but others, in their first flirtations with homoeroticism, turned their attentions to the fluidity of sexuality, to a whole gamut of sexual deviance, rather than to "homosexuality" *per se*. This period witnessed an interest in ambiguous gender and mobile sexuality that included androgyny, transvestism, and hermaphroditism. The most significant contributions to this literature came from the authors Théophile Gautier, George Sand, and HONORÉ DE BALZAC.

Mademoiselle de Maupin (1835), by Gautier (1811–1872), gave birth to a heroine whose transvestism makes possible several transgressions of the heterosexual imperative. Mlle de Maupin, who dresses as a man and calls herself Théodore in order to move freely in male social spheres, combines delicate features with masculine attire and seduces both the male narrator, Albert, and his mistress, Rosette. Albert confesses his love for the consummately androgynous, and therefore irresistible, Théodore: "What I feel for this young man is truly incredible; never has a woman troubled me in this way." At the same time, Rosette manages to lure Théodore into her bed, and the discovery she makes there does nothing to cool her passions. *Mademoiselle de Maupin,* then, is less about lesbianism or gay male sexuality than about a questioning of gender boundaries (through dress and social interaction) that permits the exploration of unconventional sexualities.

Although *Mademoiselle de Maupin* is the most striking example of literary interest in indeterminate gender and sexuality, it is by no means the only one during this period. Balzac's short story, "Sarrasine" (1830), turns on the protagonist's attraction to a beautiful singer who is not a woman, as he believes, but a cross-dressing castrato. Somewhat later, Gautier's poem, "Contralto" (in *Emaux et camees,* 1852), compares the indeterminately sexed beauty of a Greek statue to that of a singer with a contralto voice. Similarly, Theodore de Banville's "Hermaphrodite" (in *Les Exiles,* 1867) relishes the uncertainty of a "beautiful being" whose torso resembles that of a heroic young man and whose breasts are like those of a pale virgin.

The androgyne, the transvestite, and the hermaphrodite are all figures who represent not the effacement of sexuality, but its doubling. In George Sand's literary circle, her transvestism did not hide her gender, but allowed her to avoid contemporary obstacles confining women. Moving in both social worlds like Gautier's Maupin, Sand was also notorious for moving in both sexual worlds: Her affairs with Alfred de Musset, Frédéric Chopin, and other men were no less talked about than her liaison with the actress Marie Dorval. Sand challenged traditional gender roles in several of her early works, but only in her third novel, *Lélia* (1833), does she allude, briefly, to a lesbian attraction with overtones of incest. At a masked ball the courtesan Pulcherie confesses to her cross-dressing sister, Lélia, that she first learned of desire while asleep in her arms.

The historical woman Aurore Dudevant (1804–1876), who fashioned herself into the writer and personality George Sand, influenced her contemporaries as much with her own life as with her writing. "Gamiani" (1833), an anonymous pornographic short story attributed to Musset, is said to be modeled after Sand. The countess Gamiani suffers from "the sad condition of having divorced with nature," and yet her sexuality is less defined in terms of a preferred object than of an insatiability of desire and a multiplication of partners—including, among others, Alcide, who participates as narrator and voyeur; depraved monks, countless nuns, and a particularly perverse mother superior; an innocent virgin; and even a well-endowed donkey. Similarly, Balzac's *Séraphîta* (1835) is said to be based on the Sand legend. This mystical novel, indebted to the Swedish philosopher Swedenborg's notion of divine androgyny, tells the story of the idealized double-sexed creature, Séraphîta, who also appears in masculine clothing as Séraphîtüs. Sand would later echo *Séraphîta* with her play *Gabriel* (1843), whose title character is raised and educated as a boy in order to preserve the family inheritance, only to be informed of her "true" sex when she reaches the threshold of adulthood. Tormented by this revelation, Gabriel flees to find the rightful heir, her cousin Astolphe. In the intrigue that follows, Astolphe falls in love with "Gabriel," whose secret is eventually revealed, to Astolphe's great relief. The protagonist passes back and forth between male and female personae, alternately called Gabriel and Gabrielle, but her search for happiness is frustrated in both guises by societal expectations of gender roles.

Balzac (1799–1850), whose voluminous *Comédie humaine* (1842–1848), a network of more than a hundred novels with recurring characters and intertwining plots, turned his gift for description and character analysis toward questions of sexuality and gender with greater insistence than his contemporaries. He created Vautrin, perhaps the first gay male literary figure of the modern period. A master criminal nicknamed "Trompe-la-mort," Vautrin finds himself in the masculine world of prison in *Splendeurs et misères des courtisanes* (1838–1847). His character also appears in *Le père Goriot* (1833) and *Illusions perdues* (1837–1845), among other novels.

A few of Balzac's texts include lesbian characters, most notably *La fille aux yeux d'or* (1835), where the young and beautiful Paquita is kept cloistered by her lesbian lover, a rich marquise. Paquita deceives her with a man, the marquise's own brother, Henri de Marsay, but not before he accedes to Paquita's wishes by donning female attire. Paquita addresses him as Mariquita in a moment of passion, and the novella ends in a bloodbath when the marquise learns of Paquita's betrayal. Latent lesbian themes also appear in *Béatrix* (1839) and *La cousine Bette* (1846).

The work of Balzac marks a moment of transition when representations of indeterminate gender coexisted with newly forming literary identities that separated the lesbian from the gay male character. French literature of the period seems to confirm historian MICHEL FOUCAULT's assertion in *The History of Sexuality* that homosexuality as a specific identity emerged in the second half of the nineteenth century. He attributed the "discovery" of the homosexual to the medical community. Defined largely in terms of perversion or degeneration, often allied with criminality and prostitution by sexologists, gay male and lesbian sexuality came of age in literature at a time when the European medical profession was subjecting it to close and largely unsympathetic scrutiny. Sexologists also helped to establish a new vocabulary—including such terms as "homosexuality," "Uranism," "inversion," "lesbian" as a noun, and "the third sex," all of which entered the French language during the second half of the nineteenth century.

After Balzac's death, a literary tradition that highlighted lesbian sexuality developed. In 1850, two plays were published that marked the birth of a literary fad focusing on the figure of SAPPHO: Arsène Houssaye's *Sapho, drame antique* and Philoxène Boyer's very popular *Sapho*. Although these Sapphos were heterosexual, they were among the first in a tradition that sexualized the Greek poet and subsequently identified her as the prototypic lesbian. But the sapphic literary craze was not limited to depictions of the ancient poet; indeed, the modern lesbian who flourished in symbolist poetry ranged from the virginal schoolgirl to the depraved nymphomaniac.

In the late 1840s, CHARLES BAUDELAIRE (1821–1867) publicized a collection called *Les Lesbiennes* that never appeared. In 1857, however, he published *Les Fleurs du mal* in which the lesbian is a central figure, represented above all in three poems entitled "Femmes damnées: Delphine et Hippolyte," "Femmes damnées," and "Lesbos." On publication, "Femmes damnées: Delphine et Hippolyte" and "Lesbos" (along with four other poems) were condemned as immoral by the Second Empire court and censored

from the work; they were not restored until 1949. "Lesbos," originally published in a literary review in 1850, was one of the first works identifying sapphism with lesbianism. An apologia for the ancient homeland of Sappho, the poem celebrates the isle of Lesbos as a sensual feminine world and a place of poetic creation. On the island, kisses are "languid or joyous, warm as suns and fresh as watermelons"; judgments disparaging lesbianism are repudiated. The two poems entitled "Femmes damnées" place lesbians in a modern setting. As their titles suggest, these poems have a more condemnatory tone than "Lesbos." "Femmes damnées: Delphine et Hippolyte" begins with portraits of two women embarking on a sexual relationship and has at its center the attempt of the self-assured Delphine to comfort and sway the uncertain and fearful Hippolyte. The poem ends with a biting condemnation of these "damned women" and their "bitter sterility." Similarly, the shorter "Femmes damnées" describes a nameless group of lesbians as a miserable lot doomed to exile. Still, both poems betray more than a hint of admiration for these social outcasts.

Théodore de Banville (1823–1891) contributed to the Sapphic tradition by including "Erinna" in his collection, *Les Exilés* (1867). Dedicated to Boyer, this poem contrasts with Baudelaire's torrid representation of Lesbos. Banville has Erinna, both Sappho's student and her successor, address a group of chaste young women poets, admonishing them to remain virginal in the pursuit of poetic perfection.

PAUL VERLAINE's sonnet series, *Amies* (first published in 1868, in Belgium, to avoid the censorship of the Second Empire), offers six erotic poems depicting lesbian sexuality. Although the final sonnet, "Sappho," is named after the Greek poet, the first five represent the sexual initiation of modern adolescent girls in a number of settings. Pierre Louÿs also wrote numerous poems focusing on lesbian coupling, seemingly directed to a male audience. Although authored by Louÿs himself, *Les Chansons de Bilitis* (1894) was presented as Louÿs's translations of recently found ancient Greek texts. His *Chansons secrètes de Bilitis*, a more explicitly erotic collection of poems, followed four years later. Louÿs was one of the most prolific pornographic writers of the period; his work, including both poems and fiction (such as *Les aventures du Roi Pausole*, 1901), explicitly depicts both heterosexual and lesbian lovemaking.

In the realm of prose fiction, popular novelists and avant-garde writers alike followed the poets' lead by creating lesbian characters. Adolphe Belot's novel, *Mademoiselle Giraud, ma femme* (1870), though practically unknown today, was a best-seller; in it, the protagonist discovers his wife to be involved with another woman. Emile Zola (1840–1902), one of the founders of the naturalist movement, represents lesbianism in several novels, most notably in *La Curée* (1871) and *Nana* (1879). A lesbian couple, the marquise d'Espanet and Suzanne Haffner, appears in the former, whereas Nana experiences several sapphic adventures in the latter. In the short story "La Femme de Paul" (1881) by Guy de Maupassant (1850–1893), Paul, the devoted and rather effeminate lover of Madeleine, loses sight of his mistress during a boating excursion when a raucous band of lesbians arrives. When he discovers Madeleine in the embrace of the mannish Pauline, he drowns himself in the river, moved by despair.

During the 1880s and 1890s, several more novels explored "degenerate" female sexuality. For example, Catulle Mendès's *Méphistophéla* (1890) traces the life of la baronne Sophor d'Hermelinge, who grows from an innocent young virgin into an obsessed, evil lesbian. Her degeneracy is attributed to a family curse, passed down from the father she never knew who was "raped" by her conniving and indecent mother in order to secure an inheritance. The plot of the novel, like its language, is ornate, and the tone hesitates between fascination and disapproval.

These and other texts of the period focusing on lesbians were authored nearly exclusively by men who betrayed no interest in gay male sexuality, either in their lives or their works. The tone and characterization of their writings varied widely. The works were often condemnatory or moralizing, but this did not prevent them from also being titillating, even pornographic. Whether ancient or modern, lesbian love was sometimes depicted as naively innocent, sometimes as lasciviously excessive. Some authors, like Baudelaire, turned the lesbian into a highly aestheticized figure who mirrored the artist's outcast and misunderstood existence. What these disparate representations had in common was their objectification of lesbianism. Written for a male audience, the works tended to be voyeuristic. Given the considerable number of allusions that these texts make to one another, one has the impression that they were often written in a spirit of rivalry, with other male writers specifically in mind. Prose texts in particular show the influence of the medical discourse on deviant female sexuality.

This overwhelming interest in lesbians by male authors seemed to wane by the end of the century, or at least to be overshadowed by a new lesbian visibility and self-expression. Works by a group of women belonging to NATALIE BARNEY's lesbian salon, later given the name Sappho 1900, explored lesbian sexuality from a subjective point of view. The works of RENÉE VIVIEN (1877–1909), Barney's lover and a pro-

lific poet, include the first lesbian translation of Sappho as well as countless poems that speak of love between women. Among the early works of COLETTE (1873–1954) are her series of novels focusing on the bisexual character Claudine (published 1900–1903).

The birth of modern gay male literature in France can be attributed to two symbolist poets who were notorious lovers, Paul Verlaine (1844–1896) and ARTHUR RIMBAUD (1854–1891). The mark they left on the traditions of the lyric and of gay male literature is stunning. As we have seen, the older Verlaine's first attempts at erotic verse produced *Les Amies;* he was one of the only poets of the period to cross over from portraying lesbianism to depicting gay male sexuality, a much more daring undertaking at the time because not yet condoned by literary tradition. When Rimbaud went to Paris and encountered Verlaine in 1871, their physical and literary relationship soon produced poems that pushed French verse to new extremes. They penned audacious poems on gay sexuality, the most renowned of which is the collaborative "Le sonnet du trou du cul." (Verlaine wrote the quatrains, Rimbaud the tercets.) But most of the gay pieces that they composed during their two years together were less graphic, more subtle in their symbolism. Verlaine wrote a number of poems that appear to be inspired by his relationship with Rimbaud, moving and often melancholic poems depicting a lover sometimes vulnerable in sleep ("Vers pour être calomnié" and "L'espoir luit comme un brin de paille dans l'étable") and others, particularly the magnificent "Crimen Amoris," describing the triumph of a graceful young prince. Much later, Verlaine returned to explicitly erotic verse, writing *Hombres* in 1891. This collection includes fifteen often explicit poems celebrating gay male sexuality.

Owing to his shorter career, Rimbaud left behind fewer gay poems, but his works are nonetheless marked by his sexuality, as well as by Verlaine's literary and affective influence. The elliptical "Le Coeur du pitre" seems to recount the humiliation of a rape. "O saisons, ô châteaux" alludes to the poet's passion for his male lover, an allusion later effaced by prudish editors. In *Une Saison en enfer* (written in 1873), Rimbaud offers his most direct and seemingly autobiographical reference to a gay couple. "Délires I" presents the confession of the "vierge folle" (resembling Verlaine) who recounts his seduction by the young "époux infernal."

A lesser-known poet, Albert Glatigny (1839–1873) published several explicitly erotic poems under the pseudonym "Sire de la Glotte." Comte de Lautréamont (pseudonym of Isidore Ducasse, 1846–1870), later claimed by surrealists as a precursor, included many dark and forbidden tales in his hallucinatory *Les Chants du Maldoror* (1868). These "songs," written in lyrical prose and containing representations of sadism, hermaphroditism, pederasty, and so on, were read widely by gay decadent authors at the end of the century.

The decadent movement of the 1880s was named after a poem by Verlaine ("Je suis l'Empire à la fin de la décadance"). This movement, an outgrowth of symbolism, was characterized by an interest in neurosis, the refinement of sensations, baroque language and decors; its authors focused on nonconformist sensibilities and sexualities of all kinds. Decadent sensibility and gay male sexuality are therefore intimately related, with gay authors and themes at the heart of the movement that initiated a fin-de-siècle renaissance of gay literature. JORIS-KARL HUYSMANS (1848–1907) wrote the prototypical decadent novel, *A Rebours* (1884), modeling his effete character Des Esseintes after Robert de Montesquiou, a gay symbolist poet famous for his extravagant personality and manners. Better known as a dandy than a writer, Montesquiou (1855–1921) also served as a model for PROUST's Baron de Charlus, but his sexuality is nearly invisible in his poetry. He reveals his homosexuality most clearly in his three-volume autobiography, *Les Pas effacés* (1923).

Symbolist and decadent circles included many other gay poets, most of whom are not well-known today. The work of Jean Lorrain (pseudonym of Paul Duval, 1856–1906) was only slightly less discreet than that of Montesquiou. Although openly gay, this symbolist poet only hints at his sexuality in such poems as "Narcissus," whose speaker calls himself a "blond ephebe." *The Poèmes aristophanesques* (1904) of Laurent Tailhade (1854–1919) includes a piece entitled "Le Troisième sexe," and many other rather sarcastic references to homosexuality; only in his posthumously published erotic poetry, *La Quintessence satyrique* (1926), did he write joyously of gay sexuality. Albert Samain (1858–1900) and Marc-André Raffalovich (1864–1934) also wrote gay poetry. (See also DECADENCE.)

In his essay, "Conseils familiers à un jeune écrivain" (1896), the symbolist critic Rémy de Gourmont (1858–1915) pointed to the proliferation of gay writers at the end of the century. He advises heterosexuals to adopt the mannerisms of "inverts" in order to enhance their literary reputation, but counsels gay writers to maintain a certain reserve since too much openness might be damaging to their careers.

The realist movement (ca 1850–1865) and its successor, naturalism (ca 1865–1895), though fascinated by lesbianism, avoided depictions of male homosexuality. The aim of realist authors was ostensibly to describe all phenomena in scientific detail, and naturalism pushed this aesthetic even further by documenting even the "basest" and heretofore most hidden aspects of the human character, including criminality and sexual deviance. So it is surprising that realist and naturalist fiction failed to turn its characteristically unflinching gaze to male homosexuality. Yet nonfictional texts by the mostly heterosexual-identified male authors associated with these movements suggest that it was not entirely foreign to them. For example, in the highly ironic *Dictionnaire des idées reçues* by Gustave Flaubert (1821–1880), "Pederasty" is defined as follows: "Sickness that affects all men at a certain age." Indeed, in his correspondence, Flaubert graphically describes his sexual encounters with young men, whereas in his fiction one finds only a passing allusion to "strange loves" that are "obscene unions as serious as marriage" (in his novel of ancient Carthage, *Salammbô*, 1862).

Similarly, the *Journal* of the brothers Goncourt, Edmond (1822–1896) and Jules (1830–1870), contains numerous reflections on the homoerotic activities of their contemporaries. This gossipy journal speculates on the sexuality of several authors who took pains to identify themselves as exclusively heterosexual (including Gautier, Barbey D'Aurevilly, and Maupassant), and relates stories about openly gay authors (Lorrain and Montesquiou, for example). In his novel *Les Frères Zemganno* (1879), Edmond evokes the more than familial love shared by the brothers.

Zola not only created no gay male characters, he deliberately avoided a literary study of male homosexuality when offered the opportunity. In 1889, he received a letter and accompanying diary from a self-loathing young Italian homosexual, who wrote that "I could have been a delightful and adored woman, a mother and wife beyond reproach, but I am only an incomplete and monstrous being, desiring the impermissible." This anonymous gay man exhorted Zola to turn his literary talent to a study of homosexuality. Zola declined to use these confessions as the basis of a literary portrait; instead, he presented them to a medical doctor, Saint-Paul, who was working on a study of "inversion." Under the pseudonym of Laupts, Saint-Paul subsequently published the document as *Le Roman d'un inverti-né* in *Archives d'Anthropologie criminelle et de psychologie normale et pathologique* (1894–95), with a preface by Zola.

Like Zola, Raffalovich also collaborated with psychiatrists and sexologists in new studies of sexual deviance. Unlike Zola, he was himself gay and has been called a homosexual militant. Raffalovich contributed numerous articles to the same medical review that published *Le Roman d'un inverti-né*. Grouped together in his volume *Uranisme et unisexualité* (1896), these articles set forth his theories on the différence between acquired and innate inversion. Similarly, the novelist and essayist Joséphin Péladan (1859–1918), who was obsessed by androgyny, explores this theme in his nineteen-volume *La décadence latine* (1886–1907).

Although gay male literature flourished more openly in the poetry of the period, there were several important gay novelists at the end of the century, including especially Pierre Loti (pseudonym of Julien Viaud, 1850–1923) and the Belgian Georges Eekhoud (1854–1927). Loti, a naval officer, wrote numerous travel novels, many characterized by their oriental setting. His *Aziyadé* (1879) tells the story of a sea captain who falls in love with a harem woman who, quite likely, is really a man in female dress; the character of Aziyadé returns in *Fantôme d'Orient* (1891), where her gender is again ambiguous. In *Aziyadé*, as well as in *Mon frère Yves* (1883), the author also writes of passionate friendships between men. Eekhoud's *Escal-Vigor* (1900) is perhaps the most daring gay novel of the period. Banned as pornographic, it is among the first to focus unapologetically on gay relationships. In *L'Autre vue* (1904),

Eekhoud's protagonist becomes a prison guard in order to seduce adolescent delinquents.

—*Gretchen Schultz*

BIBLIOGRAPHY

Berthier, Philippe. "Balzac du côté de Sodome." *Homosexual Themes in Literary Studies*. Wayne Dynes, ed. New York: Garland, 1992. 1–31. ■ Courouve, Claude. *Dictionnaire de l'homosexualitémasculine*. Paris: Payot, 1985. ■ De Jean, Joan. *Fictions of Sappho, 1546–1937*. Chicago: University of Chicago Press, 1989. ■ Faderman, Lillian. *Surpassing the love of Men: Romantic Friendship and Love between Women from the Renaissance to the Present*. New York: Morrow, 1981. ■ Foster, Jeannette. *Sex Variant Women in Literature*. 1956. Tallahassee, Fla.: Naiad Press, 1985. ■ Foucault, Michel. *The History of Sexuality; Volume I: An Introduction*. Trans. Robert Hurley. New York: Random House, 1978. ■ Groupe de Recherches et d'Études sur l'Homosocialité et les Homosexualités (GREH). *Actes du colloque international "Homosexualité et lesbianisme: mythes, mémoires, historiographies."* 3 vols. Lille: Cahiers Gai-Kitsch-Camp, 1989–1991. ■ Larivière, Michel, ed. *Les Amours masculines*. Paris: Lieu commun, 1984. ■ Lejeune, Philippe. "Autobiographie et homosexualité en France au 19e siècle." *Romantisme* 17:56 (1987): 79–94. ■ Mendès-Leite, Rommel, and Pierre-Olivier de Busscher, eds. *Studies from the French Cultures*. New York: Haworth Press, 1993. ■ Nye, Robert. *Masculinity and Male Codes of Honor in Modern France*. New York: Oxford University Press, 1993. ■ Stambolian, George, and Elaine Marks, eds. *Homosexualities and French Literature: Cultural Contexts, Critical Texts*. Ithaca, N.Y.: Cornell University Press, 1979. ■ Weil, Kari. *Androgyny and the Denial of Difference*. Charlottesville: University Press of Virginia, 1992.

French Literature: Twentieth Century

The contributions of gay men and lesbians to twentieth-century French literature have been closely intertwined with the course of mainstream literature. A general survey of twentieth-century French literature would surely mention MARCEL PROUST, ANDRÉ GIDE, and COLETTE, and it might very well also include JEAN COCTEAU, JEAN GENÊT, VIOLETTE LEDUC, and MARGUERITE YOURCENAR (to name but a few gay men and lesbians whose works are now part of the canon), while any overview of literary theory and continental thought would have to include ROLAND BARTHES, MICHEL FOUCAULT, and MONIQUE WITTIG. The contributions of these figures are outstanding: Marguerite Yourcenar, for example, was the first woman ever to be elected to the prestigious Académie Française, and André Gide, the author of *Corydon*, was awarded the Nobel prize for literature. But although these figures may stand out, their work did not take place

in a vacuum. It is part of a continuous tradition of gay and lesbian literature in twentieth-century France.

Twentieth-century France has for the most part displayed a permissive attitude toward sexual behavior in certain contexts though it should be remembered that the cosmopolitan capital city, Paris, provided a very different environment from the rest of the country, many parts of which remained (and remain today) quite conservative. In addition, social class played a role in how much sexual freedom an individual was permitted: Those with more wealth and social power generally enjoyed greater latitude. Although not always fully accepting of homosexuality, which has sometimes been construed as a German or British phenomenon, French society nevertheless allowed a certain degree of personal freedom to gay and lesbian people. Despite the general permissiveness, however, periods of social tolerance have alter-

nated with periods of greater repression in the twentieth century.

During the "belle époque" before World War I, there was a widespread perception of tolerance though there were different attitudes toward male and female homosexuality. In some circles, female homosexuality was considered practically *de rigueur* though arguably this posture may actually reflect a refusal to take female sexuality altogether seriously. Pierre Louÿs's famous book *Les chansons de Bilitis* (1894) may illustrate the point. Purportedly a translation from Greek of the works of a companion of SAPPHO, the book is primarily soft-core pornography directed toward heterosexual men (as is the 1970s film *Bilitis* by David Hamilton). Still, the name of Bilitis was widely adopted as a code word in the gay subcultures of Europe and the United States. It was even incorporated into the name of the American lesbian post–World War II homophile society, The Daughters of Bilitis.

The 1920s was also a particularly liberal decade. In 1924, the first gay newspaper, *Inversions,* appeared in Paris. A number of literary publications also drew widespread attention to homosexual issues. The most important of these were, of course, Proust's *Sodome et Gomorrhe* (1921) and Gide's *Corydon* (first widely available in the 1924 edition), but there were also other works by heterosexual writers that dealt with gay themes. These include Victor Margueritte's *La garçonne* ([1922]; trans. as *The Bachelor Girl,* 1923), Edouard Bourdet's play *La prisonnière* ([1926]; trans. as *The Captive,* 1926), and Rachilde's novelistic response *Le prisonnier* (1928). Some might argue that these heterosexual writers merely exploited gay and lesbian sexuality, but the popularity of their work and the debate they aroused made homosexuality more visible and contributed to the era's permissive atmosphere. *La garçonne,* for example, gave its name to a German lesbian magazine of the 1930s.

After this period of liberalism, the 1930s saw a conservative swing, beginning with the repressive Code de la Famille (1930), which gay historian and theorist Daniel Guérin sees as the origin of the Vichy legislation that later made homosexual behavior criminal in France for the first time since 1791. In 1942, during World War II, the Vichy government made homosexual relations with anyone under twenty-one illegal as part of its conservative (some would say fascist) family agenda. In the post–World War II period, there was some relaxation in social attitudes, and homophile movements such as André Baudry's Arcadie were founded, but there was no change in the law. On the contrary, the prohibition against homosexual activity by and with persons under twenty-one was reaffirmed in Article 331 of the Code Pénal that took effect after the Liberation; and in 1961, legal sanctions were toughened by automatically doubling the sentence of a homosexual convicted of "outrage public à la pudeur."

The social and political upheavals known as May '68 accelerated social change toward a liberalization of sexual mores. The May '68 uprising led to a reinvigorated feminist movement and also to a gay liberation movement. The Front Homosexuel d'Action Révolutionnaire (FHAR) was founded by, among others, the philosopher and novelist GUY HOCQUENGHEM in 1971. There was support from the socialist government of the 1980s for repeal of Article 331, and in 1982 this was accomplished; but consensual sex with minors between fifteen and eighteen years old was once again recriminalized—for homosexuals, not heterosexuals—in 1991, thanks to the conservative swing in recent French politics. The overhaul of the Code Napoléon in 1994 will no doubt raise further legal questions.

Despite the relative legal and social freedom extended to gay men and lesbians, open homosexuality has never been fully accepted in France. Consequently, many gay and lesbian writers experienced various degrees of marginalization. Nevertheless, they wrote and published, and there is a vital tradition of gay writing beyond the works offered by the best-known authors. The lesbian tradition, for example, includes the semiautobiographical works of Jeanne Galzy, Eveline Mayhère, and Jocelyne François, whereas gay male literature includes the varied writings of Henry de Montherlant, Roger Peyrefitte, and Julien Green.

In addition to writers who identified themselves as gay or lesbian, representations of gay and lesbian characters in the work of heterosexual authors have also added to gay visibility. Jean-Paul Sartre's gay characters—the autodidact of *La nausée* (1938), the lesbian Inès in *Huis-clos* (1944), Daniel of *Les chemins de la liberté* (1945–1949)—are not particularly attractive, yet Sartre unhesitatingly placed gay and lesbian figures squarely in the mainstream of literature. Another example of a work by a heterosexual writer to feature gay or lesbian subjects is Françoise Mallet-Joris's *Le rempart des béguines* ([1951]; trans. as *The Illusionist,* 1952), an account of the fifteen-year-old protagonist Hélène's affair with her father's mistress Tamara, based, it was claimed, on a story told to Mallet-Joris (the pseudonym of Françoise Lilar, b. 1930) by a schoolfriend. The novel was made into a film directed by Guy Casaril in 1972. There is also a strong female homoerotic element in the work of Marguerite Duras (b. 1914). In *L'amant* ([1984]; trans. as *The Lover,* 1985), for example, the autobiographical first-person narrator writes "My memory of men is never lit up and illuminated like my memory of women," echoing VIRGINIA WOOLF's much-quoted "women alone stir my imagination." The narrator of *The Lover* proceeds to offer an erotic meditation on the body of her fellow schoolgirl, Hélène Lagonelle.

A significant trend in gay and lesbian studies has been the recovery of work by writers who, for whatever reason, kept their sexual identity hidden. The recent publication of the diaries and letters of Simone de Beauvoir (1908–1986), for example, reveals that although her relationship with Sartre remained primary throughout her life, she also had several affairs with women, including her students Natalie (Natasha) Sorokine and Bianca Bienenfeld. (Referred to in Beauvoir's autobiographical works by the pseudonym "Louise Védrine," Bianca Lamblin, née Bienenfeld, published her own memoirs of Sartre and Beauvoir entitled *Mémoires d'une jeune fille dérangée* in 1983.) It is clear, however, that Beauvoir did not identify as a bisexual writer, either publicly or privately. How to evaluate such cases remains a lively topic of debate since it involves questions of identity politics, the social construction of sexuality as a heterosexual–homosexual binary, and the problem of defining and interpreting sexual behavior.

In addition to works by native French writers, the French gay and lesbian literary tradition includes works by writers who wrote as exiles in France. Gay and lesbian writers sought refuge in France partly because of the relative social freedom there, especially in Paris, but also because France was a relatively inexpensive place to live in the early part of the twentieth century. These expatriates include well-known figures such as GERTRUDE STEIN and DJUNA BARNES (whose *Ladies Almanack* [1928] is a virtual *roman à clef* of the expatriate lesbian community), as well as JAMES BALDWIN, whose *Giovanni's Room* (1956) was written in France, where he had come to escape American racism, and most recently, the novelist EDMUND WHITE, author of an important biography of Genêt. In addition, one should mention such writers as RENÉE VIVIEN (Pauline Tarn), NATALIE CLIFFORD BARNEY, JANET FLANNER, H.D. (HILDA DOOLITTLE), and numerous others treated elsewhere in this volume. The lesbian circle of Natalie Barney has been depicted by one of its French members, Lucie Delarue-Mardrus (1874–1945), whose brief affair with Barney was recorded in *Nos secrètes amours* (1951). In Delarue-Mardrus's *L'ange et les pervers* (1930), Barney is represented as Laurette Wells, the center of a Parisian group of lesbians. Many of the expatriate women who moved in Barney's circle wrote only in English, but some, including Barney herself and Vivien, wrote in French, and

thus exercised an influence on the course of French literature. Anglophones were not the only ones to seek refuge in France, however. CHRISTA WINSLOE (1888–1944), the author of the play that served as the basis for the classic German lesbian film *Mädchen in Uniform* (1931), for which Colette wrote the French subtitles, also sought exile in France during World War II and died there in 1944 in mysterious circumstances.

The tradition of gay and lesbian writing is in the process of both being rediscovered in the past and being created in the present. One recently rediscovered writer is Jeanne Galzy (1885–1980), whose works were well received in the 1920s and 1930s. They include *Jeunes filles en serre chaude* (1934), a semiautobiographical novel about the female students of the Ecole Normale Supérieure de Sèvres and the love affair between one student, Isabelle, and an English teacher Gladys Benz. Later, Galzy also published a series of four books under the title *La surprise de vivre* (*La surprise de vivre* [1969], *Les sources vives* [1971], *La cavalière* [1974], and *Le rossignol aveugle* [1976]). The series traces the life of a Protestant banking family, the Deshandrès, of the Languedoc from the turn of the century, focusing on the sentimental life of Eva, who falls in love with an English teacher (here named Hilda). Galzy's case is interesting not only for the merit of her work and the portrait it offers of lesbian life outside the capital, but because it suggests that a lesbian writer could be accepted during her lifetime by mainstream society. Galzy's novels were published by mainstream publishers such as Gallimard, and her work was widely appreciated. She received the Prix Fémina in 1923 and went on to serve on the jury that awarded this prize until her death. As testimony to her popularity, one of her novels, *L'initiatrice aux mains vides* (1929) was promptly translated into English as *Burnt Offering* (1930).

A similar phenomenon occurs in the case of Eveline Mayhère (1925–1957), author of *Je jure de m'éblouir* ([1958]; trans. as *I Will Not Serve*, 1959). In this autobiographical novel, the heroine Sylvie Ceyvenole struggles with her idealized feelings for her convent teacher Julienne Blessner, a struggle that ends in suicide, just as Mahyère committed suicide in 1957. The novel was published posthumously and received wide critical attention. It was reviewed for example by Claude Mauriac in *Le figaro* and had a full-page review in *Le figaro littéraire*. Although reviewers tended to dismiss the lesbian aspects of the relationship, preferring to see the plot as a theological allegory, that the novel received such attention at all suggests that gay and lesbian literature could find an audience and was not entirely ignored by the mainstream establishment in the 1950s.

Another figure who has won popular success for her lesbian writings is Jocelyne François (b. 1933). She is the author of a number of works, including *Les bonheurs* (1970; rpt. 1982), *Les amantes* (1978), and *Joue-nous "Espana"* (1980), which won the Prix Fémina. All three novels are autobiographical and focus on the relationship between two women: *Joue-nous "Espana"* recounts the narrator's childhood and love for her schoolfriend Marie-Claire. *Les Bonheurs* describes a seven-year hiatus in their relationship, during which time "Anne" marries and has children and is separated from Sarah (Marie-Claire). In *Les Amantes*, they are reunited and live together in Provence. The novels, whose main themes are love, nature, motherhood, and children, have been compared to prose poems because of Francois's highly poetic writing style.

A contemporary lesbian writer who has received critical acclaim is Hélène de Monferrand (b. 1947), a hospital administrator in Paris. Her first novel *Les amies d'Héloise* (1990) received the Prix Goncourt for best first novel. She followed up with *Journal de Suzanne* in 1991. Both novels concern the same characters: Héloise and her diplomat family (in which everyone's name begins with "H"); her teacher Suzanne (a concentration camp survivor); and her fellow student Manuela, her sister Erika, and their German industrialist family. *Les amies d'Héloise* is an epistolary novel, whereas in *Journal de Suzanne,* Monferrand adopts the format of a diary. Although there is much in Monferrand's novels that contemporary American readers would recognize, there are also several distinctly French elements: Monferrand explores the fate of lesbians during World War II, a theme that has been overlooked in other accounts, both fictional and historical, of the period; she underscores the recurring theme of what Elaine Marks has called "the gynaeceum," that is, the importance of the school as an erotically charged site for lesbian writers; and she participates in a larger French movement of coming to terms with the legacy of World War II in the present. Monferrand's characters are also conservative in their politics and lifestyle, preferring good manners and breeding over political correctness. Monferrand's works constitute an interesting reminder that gay and lesbian literature is not monolithic. Her characters' attitudes toward May '68, for example, suggests that not all gay and lesbian writers share radical or even leftist politics.

This point is illustrated more generally by the variety of gay and lesbian literature in twentieth-century France. Although some gay and lesbian writing may be identified with feminist, socialist, and other liberal or progressive political causes (as in the case of Monique Wittig and Daniel Guérin, for example), not all gay and lesbian writing fits this mold. In the case of Natalie Barney's expatriate circle, for example, the fascist sympathies of Barney and others are clear and puzzling. Barney's male contemporaries were not exempt from fascist sympathies, as the case of the novelist, dramatist, and essayist Henry de Montherlant (1896–1972) illustrates. Although bisexual, Montherlant was an unabashed misogynist and antifeminist (as Beauvoir argues in *Le deuxième sexe* [*The Second Sex*]) and espoused fascist causes in France.

During his lifetime, Montherlant, who was elected to the Académie Francaise in 1961, was known as a moralist for his novels about pure, self-sacrificing, and patriotic characters. But after his suicide in 1972, a different side of him emerged. Montherlant's correspondence with the career diplomat Roger Peyrefitte (b. 1907), whom he met in 1938, was published, revealing their mutual interest in casual affairs with boys. Montherlant's *Les garcons* (1969; trans. as *The Boys,* 1974), published late in his life, describes the affairs between boys at an elite French school, based on the author's own experiences, which echo those recounted in Peyrefitte's novel with a similar theme, *Les amitiés particulières* (1943; trans. as *Special Friendships,* 1950). (The latter was the basis of a film directed by Fred Surin.) Peyrefitte also wrote *L'exilé de Capri* (1959; trans. as *The Exile of Capri,* 1961), a fictionalized account of the life of the notorious belle-époque pederast, Baron Jacques d'Adelswärd Fersen (1880–1923).

Less reactionary, Julien Green (b. 1900) is nevertheless associated with the Catholic literary revival, a generally conservative movement. Green's parents were American, and Green attended the University of Virginia from 1919 to 1922 and subsequently set some of his work in the American South. His ambivalent portrayal of homosexual characters—in *Le malfaiteur* (1955; trans. as *The Transgressor,* 1957), for example—is testimony to his lifelong struggle with his own sexuality and the conflict between flesh and spirit. In a similar vein, Marcel Jouhandeau (1888–1979) explores the conflict between homosexual love, heterosexual marriage, and religious mysticism in his novels. *La Jeunesse de Théophile* (1921)—the name Théophile meaning, of course, "lover of God"—was the first in a series of novels set in the fictional town of Chamindour, and *Chronique d'une passion* (1949) describes the triangle between the narrator Marcel, his wife, Elise (Jouhandeau's wife's real name was Elizabeth), and his homosexual lover Jacques. Jouhandeau also addressed these themes in his diary and essays.

Among gay male writers, an important post-war presence has been that of Daniel Guérin (1904–1988).

Although he wrote in the inter-war years, too, it was in the post–World War II period that he became openly involved in gay liberation. His autobiographical writings include *Autobiographie de jeunesse* (1965), *Le feu du sang: autobiographie politique et charnelle* (1977), and *Son testament* (1979). His writings touch on, among other things, the class inflections of gay politics. He illustrates the problem of the rift between the gay liberation movement and the feminist movement in France. On the one hand, he was sensitive to the effects of Islamic fundamentalism on Arab women, but on the other, he could not understand the importance of rape as a feminist issue, seeing it merely as a problem of bourgeois repression.

Not surprisingly, given the spread of the epidemic, AIDS has become an important subject of recent gay literature in France, especially among men. Among the writers who have treated this theme is Hervé Guibert (1955–1991), best known for *A l'ami qui ne m'a pas sauvé la vie* (1990; trans. as *To the Friend Who Did Not Save My life*, 1991). In this autobiographical account of his battle with AIDS, Guibert uses a loose, diarylike format to describe his denial, diagnosis, and treatment. The novel also includes an account of the death of Michel Foucault (Guibert's friend, here represented under the pseudonym Muzil), which anticipates the course of the narrator's own illness. The narrator learns about a possible vaccine and anxiously charts his T-cell count as it slowly drops toward the level where he would no longer be eligible to take part in the French trial of the vaccine, a role promised him by an influential friend, Bill. But any sense of optimism fades as he learns that the miracle vaccine is not performing as well as anticipated in the United States and that the cure on which he had pinned his hopes will not materialize, not the least because he is aban-

doned by Bill (hence the novel's title). Hervé Guibert's other books include *La mort propagande, Des aveugles, Mes parents, L'image fantôme,* and *Le protocole compassionnel.* AIDS is also the theme of Cyril Collard's novel *Les nuits fauves* (1989), recently translated and made into a prize-winning film. Collard also died of AIDS, in 1993.

This overview of twentieth-century gay and lesbian French literature has attempted to show something of the background that produced the major figures discussed elsewhere. It is far from being an exhaustive account, omitting, for example, such writers as Renaud Camus, Eric Jourdan, Yves Navarre, and Michel Tournier, to name but a few who have also contributed to the twentieth-century French gay and lesbian literary tradition. But the very impossibility of offering a complete survey itself testifies to the richness of this tradition. (See also READING ACROSS ORIENTATIONS.)

—Melanie Hawthorne

BIBLIOGRAPHY

Aldrich, Robert. "Homosexuality in France." *Contemporary French Civilization* 7.1 (1982): 1–19. ■ Copley, Antony. *Sexual Moralities in France, 1780–1980: New Ideas on the Family, Divorce and Homosexuality.* New York: Routledge, 1989. ■ Foster, Jeannette H. *Sex Variant Women in Literature.* 1956; rpt. Tallahassee, Fla.: Naiad, 1985. ■ Huas, Jeanine. *L'homosexualité au temps de Proust.* Dinard: Editions Danclau, 1992. ■ Povert, Lionel. *Dictionnaire gay.* Paris: Jacques Grancher, 1994. ■ Schehr, Lawrence, ed. "Discourses and Sex." *Contemporary French Civilization* 16.2 (Summer–Fall 1992). ■ Shaw, Nannette. "Jocelyn François: An Introduction." *13th Moon* 8.1–2 (1984): 39–49. ■ Stambolian, George, and Elaine Marks, ed. *Homosexualities and French Literature: Cultural Contexts/Critical Texts.* Ithaca, N.Y.: Cornell, 1979. ■ Van Casselaer, Catherine. *Lot's Wife: Lesbian Paris, 1890–1914.* Liverpool: Janus Press, 1986.

Gale, Patrick
(*b.* 1962)

Patrick Gale has quickly established himself as one of England's most talented comic novelists. His novels have given the reader a Shakespearean variety of intertwined, intersecting plot lines, a zany world peopled by gays and lesbians existing in fairly easy relationships with the straight society, and a gritty London often hostile to relationships and existence alike. Chance and coincidence rule this world, but his characters hope for more. As Seth Peake, the young, talented violinist in *The Aerodynamics of Pork,* says, "It's fairly

hard to be a fag without nursing some hope that the social structure will change."

Gale's background is as varied and as colorful as those of his characters. Born in 1962 on the Isle of Wight, he was educated at Winchester and Oxford. Between 1979 and 1985, he worked as a waiter, a cook, a temporary typist, a singer with the London Philharmonic Choir, and a bone sorter for an archaeological team. He describes writing as both "an addiction and a livelihood."

At once tightly structured and loosely episodic in its survey of comic characters, *Ease* (1985) tells the story of Domina Tey, a successful playwright who has reached an impasse in her work and her life. Leaving Randy, her lover of some years, she takes a room in a rundown Bayswater boardinghouse. As she enters the lives of her fellow boarders—a "houseful of faggots, morticians, tarts and Trappist monks," she calls them—Domina gathers material for a new play and attempts to experience new depths of being. She learns that it is more difficult and more tragic to manipulate the lives of real people than the lives of characters.

The Aerodynamics of Pork (1985) deftly weaves together several story lines, the main threads of which involve searches for love. Seth Peake is eagerly anticipating his first serious lover, whom he finds in a twenty-one-year-old sculptor in Cornwall; Venetia, his older, still virgin sister, is experiencing a hysterical pregnancy; Huw Peake, their theologian father, suffering from "DeQuincey headaches," has collapsed into near madness and is raiding the houses of astrologers and stealing their current working notes and forecasts; and Mo Faithe, a lesbian police inspector, is searching for both the astrology thief and someone to love, since Maggie, her first lover, has died in an accident. By its final pages, the novel has woven all these threads together into a clear affirmation of gay and lesbian loves.

In *Kansas in August* (1987), Hilary and Henrietta (Henry) Metcalfe, brother and sister, find themselves involved with the same man, Rufus Barbour, a cheery bisexual, and with a baby boy Hilary finds abandoned outside a subway station. The cross-cutting between plots may have been artificial at times in the earlier novels, but here Gale has fully mastered the cuts, juxtapositions, and simultaneities. And, like the first two novels, *Kansas in August* fully exploits the mistaken and misrepresented identities, coincidences, and festivities, though it turns darker in tone as the characters are stripped of dreams and illusions. Indeed, from this point on, Gale's novels move into darker, less festive comedy, more bizarre characters, and less hopeful resolutions.

—*David Leon Higdon*

BIBLIOGRAPHY

Gale, Patrick. *The Aerodynamics of Pork*. London: Abacus, 1985. ■ ———. *The Cat Sanctuary*. London: Chalto & Windus, 1990. ■ ———. *Ease*. London: Abacus, 1985. ■ ———. *Facing the Tank*. London: Hutchinson, 1988. ■ ———. *Kansas in August*. London: Century, 1987. ■ ———. *Little Bits of Baby*. London: Chatto & Windus, 1989.

García Lorca, Federico
(1898–1936)

Born in Fuente Vaqueros, province of Granada, on June 5, 1898, Federico García Lorca is internationally recognized as Spain's most prominent lyric poet and dramatist of the twentieth century. His poetry and plays have been translated into dozens of languages and have been the object of study by critics all over the world. His books continue to sell, and his plays are staged and applauded every year. Since his murder in 1936 at the hands of Spanish fascist forces, Lorca has become a legendary tragic hero.

One cannot help speculating about Lorca's unfulfilled projects, the many more works he had planned to write and would have written had he not been the victim of a death that to this day is still clouded with controversy. Equally controversial are the thinly veiled homosexual motifs and themes present in Lorca's work that have long been intentionally silenced and overlooked by those wishing not to "soil" the reputation of one of Spain's most respected bards; among them, the Franco regime, the Lorca family, and homophobic Lorquian scholars who have dedicated their lives and careers to Lorca's work yet refuse to acknowledge a line of criticism that takes into account homoerotic desire.

The son of a wealthy landowner, Lorca grew up very comfortably. As a child, he demonstrated an affinity for music, painting, and puppetry. In 1909, the Lorca family moved to Granada, where the young Lorca studied music with Don Antonio Segura Mesa, a former disciple of Verdi. Indeed, prior to turning his creative urges to poetry, the young Lorca intended to pursue a musical career. In Granada, Lorca blossomed, and in future years, Granada's Arabic culture—a rich legacy of poetry, astronomy, and architecture—would become the subject of many of his poems. In addition, the city's population of gypsies, who since the fourteenth century had been living in the caves of the Sacromonte, would be the inspiration for the poet's *Gypsy Ballads* (written in 1924–1927 and published in 1928) and *Poem of the Deep Song* (written in 1921 and published in 1931).

In 1919, Lorca went to study at the University of Madrid and lived at the *Residencia de Estudiantes*—a student residence founded in 1910 as a center of intellectual life for gifted students. Among the students at the "Resi," as it was familiarly known, were Spain's most talented young artists and writers. The surrealist painter Salvador Dalí, with whom Lorca fell deeply in love, and Luis Buñuel, later famous as a filmmaker, became close friends with Lorca, whose room soon became a popular meeting place for intellectuals around Madrid. After what has been generally described as a "mysterious emotional crisis" (in fact, a depression brought on by Dalí's sexual rejection as well as by a stormy relationship with a young sculptor, Emilio Aladrén Perojo), Lorca traveled to New York City in 1927. This trip inspired some of his most singular poetic pieces, later collected under the title *Poet in New York* (1940).

After leaving New York City, Lorca spent three months in Cuba, a place he had dreamed of visiting ever since he was a child and where he spent, according to his own account, the happiest days of his life. Following his stay in New York City and Cuba, Lorca began to be more daring in the representation of homosexuality. Far away from his family and conservative Spanish values, he was able to conceive and begin writing his most openly homosexual work: "Ode to Walt Whitman," the dramatic piece *The Public,* and the unfinished *The Destruction of Sodom.* "Ode to Walt Whitman," published in Mexico in 1934 in a limited edition of fifty copies, but never published in Spain during Lorca's lifetime, reveals the poet's own contradictions concerning homosexuality. The ode takes on a moralistic tone by marking a clear distinction between a pure and desexualized homosexual love, epitomized by WHITMAN the lover of nature, and a debased sexuality, associated with the "maricas" or faggots (effeminate homosexuals). *The Public,* which with the exception of two scenes published in a Spanish magazine during Lorca's life was not published until 1978, and even then in an incomplete version, presents an examination of repressed homosexual desire as well as a defense of the individual's right to erotic liberty. Lorca categorized *The Public,* his most experimental play, as belonging to his "impossible theater." Also belonging to the impossible theater is *The Destruction of Sodom,* of which Lorca apparently wrote one act, although today only the first page of the piece survives. The theme of this play, according to Ian Gibson, was to be "the pleasures of the homosexual confraternity, who have made such a contribution to world culture."

In 1930, Lorca returned to Spain during a time of political tension and unrest. From 1930 to 1936, he wrote prodigiously, completing some of his better-known works: *Blood Wedding, Lament for Ignacio Sánchez Mejías, Yerma,* and *The House of Bernarda Alba.* On July 18, 1936, generals Francisco Franco and Yoldi Orgaz seized control of Las Palmas in the Canary Islands, an event that marked the beginning of the bloody Civil War that would last until 1939. Days before this event, Lorca, who was living in Madrid and becoming more and more alarmed by the increasing violence and chaos gripping the capital, decided to return to Granada to be with his family. But safety was not to be found there. On the afternoon of August 16, he was arrested by fascist extremists, and two or three days later, without formal accusation or trial, he was shot at dawn and buried in an unmarked grave near the village of Víznar.

To this day, exact details concerning Lorca's death are unclear. For close to forty years, the Franco regime efficiently silenced information concerning the writer's death. Why such an extraordinary writer and human being endowed with genuine charm, wit, and inventiveness would be brutally assassinated can only be explained by a militant fascist mentality hostile to the fame and recognition that the liberal homosexual poet from Granada was receiving nationally and internationally. In his well-documented biography of Lorca, Ian Gibson writes: "Among the assassins . . . was Juan Luis Trescastro . . . who boasted later that morning in Granada that he had just helped to shoot Lorca, firing, for good measure, two bullets into his arse for being a queer." Although many reasons have been cited for Lorca's assassination (among them, his liberalism, his rebellion against traditional values, his communist leanings), it is evident that his homosexuality was not absent from the motives of those who tortured and killed him. Spain's traditional inquisitorial Catholicism refused to permit the expression of a sexuality at variance with the dominant Christian morality. This intolerant environment well explains Lorca's fears and deliberate concealment of his homosexuality both in his personal life and in his work.

Lorca avoided ever using the word *homosexual* in his public life or in his writing; his texts and letters speak only of silences and guarded secrets. Yet his silences, half-sayings, and innuendoes speak volumes to the reader who carefully listens. In his famous "Ode to Walt Whitman," for example, the poetic voice alludes to the silencing of homosexual desire: "men with green gazes / who love men and burn their lips in silence" (my translation). In life, Lorca was forced to censure and speak only indirectly of homosexual desire. Even after his death, his homosexuality remained severely closeted in Spain. Although this silence may have been understandable during Franco's conservative regime, even after Franco's death in 1975 many critics were still reluctant to mention Lorca's

homosexuality and its relevance to his works. The first studies to do so were Paul Binding's *Lorca: The Gay Imagination,* published in London in 1985, and Angel Sahuquillo's *Federico García Lorca y la cultura de la homosexualidad masculina,* a doctoral dissertation that was completed in 1986 and finally published in Spain in 1991. Whereas Binding's work is elementary in its scholarship and suffers from a great number of inaccuracies, Sahuquillo's work has academic rigor and for the most part has been well received by Lorquian scholars. Yet, as Sahuquillo himself attests in his study, for over fifty years anyone attempting to study homosexuality in Lorca's work was accused of being "irresponsible, ignoble, envious, and vile." Among Sahuquillo's many contributions to and insights into this theme are his analyses of five poems that illustrate how the Andalusian poet encoded homosexual themes in his texts. Sahuquillo's thesis is that Lorca's obscure poetry, which has been described by its haunting lyrical beauty and ambiguity, encodes, through the use of mythological references and recurrent symbols, homoerotic desire. Sahuquillo also presents letters from Lorca's archives in which it is not uncommon to hear the poet express his pain at not being able to demonstrate his emotions and feelings openly: "Everything in my poetry strikes me as pitiful in that I have not expressed nor can I express my thoughts" (my translation). Such statements are indicative of an individual suffering as a result of having to live under the values of a society that morally rejected him.

Lorca's *Sonnets of Dark Love,* written in November 1935 and long suppressed by Lorca's family, were first published in a clandestine edition of 250 numbered copies in December 1983. As a result of this mysterious printing, Lorca's family was apparently pressured to finally officially publish the eleven sonnets in March 1984 in the Spanish newspaper *ABC.* Curiously, what was most controversial were not the poems themselves, in which the beloved's sex or gender is never explicitly identified, but rather the title of the cycle of poems. The Lorca family wished to entitle the cycle *Sonetos* (*Sonnets*) or *Sonetos de amor* (*Love Sonnets*), the latter being the title under which they finally appeared in *ABC* and in the new 1986 Aguilar edition of Lorca's complete works. Apparently, the title *Sonetos del amor oscuro* (*Sonnets of Dark Love*) had obvious homosexual overtones that had to be suppressed. Although it is true that Lorca left no document corroborating the title *Sonetos del amor oscuro,* a number of individuals who knew the poet well claim that this was the title he used to refer to them.

As a poet and dramatist, Lorca demonstrated an enormous thematic breadth and technical virtuosity. Although there is no denying that his early childhood in Andalusia left a mark on his artistic sensibility, perhaps his greatest achievement was his ability to avoid the trappings of a superficial folksy style by skillfully combining traditional popular motifs (Andalusian gypsies, flamenco music, bullfighters, the *Guardia Civil,* among others) with a brilliant modern sensibility that stylized and elevated the motifs onto a universal plane. Lorca's account of gypsies persecuted by the sinister *Guardia Civil* (*Gypsy Ballads* and *Poem of the Deep Song*), the oppression of blacks in Harlem (section II of *Poet in New York*), and the sexual repression of Andalusian women (*Blood Wedding* and *The House of Bernarda Alba*) portray marginalized figures who, like the homosexual, are persecuted by a dominant morality hostile to the open expression of difference. (See also DRAMATIC LITERATURE: MODERN DRAMA and SPANISH LITERATURE.)

—*Francisco Soto*

BIBLIOGRAPHY

Anderson, Andrew. *Lorca's Late Poetry: A Critical Study.* Leeds: Francis Cairns Publications, 1990. ■ Binding, Paul. *Lorca: The Gay Imagination.* London: Gay Men's Press, 1985. ■ Eisenberg, Daniel. "Reaction to the Publication of the *Sonetos de amor oscuro.*" *Bulletin of Hispanic Studies* 65 (1988): 261–271. ■ Gibson, Ian. *Federico García Lorca: A Life.* New York: Pantheon Books, 1989. ■ Harris, Derek. *García Lorca: Poeta en Nueva York.* London: Grant and Cutler, 1978. ■ Londré, Felicia Hardison. *Federico García Lorca.* New York: Ungar, 1984. ■ Sahuquillo, Angel. *Federico García Lorca y la cultura de la homosexualidad masculina.* Alicante: Instituto de Cultura "Juan Gil-Albert," 1991.

Gender

Traditionally, the division of human beings into two genders based on the biological differences between males and females has been viewed as one of the most natural, commonsense categories of identity. In this binary model, "sex," "gender," and "sexuality" constitute a unified whole. Thus a biologically sexed male is assumed to be innately masculine, with appropriately masculine appearance, character traits, and behaviors, including feelings of sexual attraction to people of the "opposite" sex—that is, to biologically sexed females, who—just as "naturally"—display appropriately feminine appearance, character traits, behaviors, and (hetero)sexual preference. By positing an irreducible difference between male and female genders, this polarized binary system reinforces the belief that men and women exist in a complementary yet mutually exclusive relationship to one other.

Since the 1970s, however, this commonsense view of human identity has come under increasingly sophisticated analyses as feminists began distinguishing between "sex"—which refers to an individual's biological (chromosomal) classification as male or female—and "gender," or the social and psychic meanings cultures assign to these biological differences. Together, sex and gender constitute what Gayle Rubin describes in her influential 1975 essay, "The Traffic in Women," as the sex–gender system, in which "raw biological sex" is transformed into nonsymmetrical, binary gender relations where the masculine occupies the privileged position. Based on biological capabilities (or "sex"), each human being is at birth appointed to one of two gender categories; this gender identity is continually reinforced and naturalized through language and social structures, such as kinship relationships, religion, education, and the media. According to Rubin and other contemporary theorists, then, masculinity and femininity are not innate, essential categories of human existence; they are, rather, social inventions, constructed categories with specific meanings that vary across cultures and historical periods. This distinction between anatomical sex-based male–female differences and the gendered, socially determined meanings ascribed to these biological categories provided feminists with an important tool in their theoretical and political analyses of the relations between women and men. By refuting the commonly held belief that masculinity and femininity are innate categories, the sex–gender system enabled feminists to argue that, because male dominance was not based on biology but on culturally imposed and enforced norms, it could be changed.

Despite the importance of this theoretical breakthrough, the resulting emphasis on binary gender relations could not fully account for twentieth-century Western concepts of identity, and in the late 1980s, this dualistic model was challenged both by self-identified feminists of color and by theorists working from an antihomophobic perspective. Norma Alarcón's argument in "The Theoretical Subject(s) of *This Bridge Called My Back* and Anglo-American Feminism" (1990) summarizes objections made by GLORIA ANZALDÚA, AUDRE LORDE, CHERRÍE MORAGA, and others. She maintains that Euro-American feminists' continued reliance on gender as the central axis of analysis limits their work in two ways: First, their emphasis on gender-based oppression prevents Anglo feminists from recognizing the complex, multiple ways ethnic, cultural, and class divisions make any description of female identity inadequate; second, their attempts to delineate specifically feminine forms of consciousness reinscribe conventional male–female configurations of identity. According to Alarcón, even when Anglo feminists began exploring the differences among women, these women were still defined primarily in opposition to men, thus reinforcing the heterosexist structure underlying Western cultures. Similarly, Rubin and other theorists interested in challenging twentieth-century Western cultures' heterosexism and homophobia argued that, given the relational nature of male–female gender categories, analyses focusing exclusively on gender support the presumed naturalness of heterosexuality. As Rubin asserts in another highly influential essay, "Thinking Sex" (1984), although gender and sexuality are intricately related, they are not interchangeable. Instead, they represent different axes of analysis and must be treated as such.

These objections to feminism's restrictive concepts of gender, coupled with MICHEL FOUCAULT's historicization of sexuality, have had a significant impact on the development of lesbian, gay, and queer theory as distinct fields of study. Whereas women's studies and feminist theory generally focus on gender itself and analyze gendered social relations—as well as the ways socially imposed and regulated gender norms shape Western categories of thought by establishing a series of hierarchically ordered binarisms—lesbian, gay, and queer theory shift the focus to sexuality and use gender as an analytical tool in their explorations of modern conceptualizations of sexual identities. Building on Foucault's work in *The History of Sexuality* (1978)—where he argued that sexuality is not a permanent, transhistorical human essence but rather a modern invention produced by discourse, or language systems such as religion, science, literature, and medicine—lesbian, gay, and queer theorists attempt to denaturalize the heterosexual matrix underlying Western cultures. Although Foucault himself ignores gender almost entirely, his description of the shift that occurred in the late nineteenth century as sexual acts were reconceived to indicate distinct sexual identities has greatly influenced contemporary theory in several ways. First, by positing the emergence of the homosexual and the heterosexual as distinct types of people, theorists can explore the interdependency between hetero- and homosexuality.

Second, by demonstrating that modern sexual identities are constructed through religion, science, and other discursive systems, theorists can examine the ways textual representations of gender and sexuality either reinforce or destabilize social meanings. Third, by distinguishing between gender and sexual identity, theorists can posit a spectrum of sexualities.

It is, however, important to emphasize that there is little agreement concerning the relationship between gender and sexuality. Because twentieth-century Western cultures have defined sexuality according to gender, the two concepts are intricately related. More specifically, in the popular imagination, sexuality is defined by the gender of an individual's preferred sexual partner, or sexual object-choice, so that a woman is defined as heterosexual if she is sexually attracted to men, and lesbian if her primary attraction is to women. Although the diversity in post-Foucauldian gender theory makes any summary far too reductive, there are at least three general trends that could be said to indicate the primary ways gender functions in lesbian, gay, and queer studies: the use of the already existing binary gender categories to define homosexuality; intragender investigations of a spectrum of male or female sexualities; and attempts to go beyond gender entirely and define sexuality in new ways. Whereas the first strategy equates gender with sexuality and thus reinforces the dichotomy between heterosexual and homosexual identities, the second and third methods distinguish gender from sexuality and use the former to destabilize the heterosexual–homosexual binary.

The first approach, which underscores the gendered difference between lesbians and gay men, equates sexuality with gender. In "Compulsory Heterosexuality and Lesbian Existence" (1980), for example, ADRIENNE RICH adopts the already existing binary gender system and locates all women along a lesbian continuum, ranging from female friendships to same-sex desire. Although Rich's lesbian continuum served an important political purpose by dispelling the homophobia in the mainstream U.S. women's movement, it did so by desexualizing lesbianism and downplaying the many ethnic, sexual, and class differences among women. For Joseph Bristow as well, the gendered difference between lesbians' and gay men's sexual object-choices assumes primary importance. As he asserts in his introduction to *Sexual Sameness* (1992), because gender is quite possibly the most important distinction imposed on lesbians and gay men, the gendered differences between them should assume greater theoretical weight. Thus Rich, Bristow, and other theorists of gendered difference illustrate what Eve Kosofsky Sedgwick describes as a "gender separatist" viewpoint, a bipolar model of gendered sexuality that reinforces the existing male–female binarism and heightens the differences between gay males and lesbians.

Whereas this polarization of gay male and female identities inadvertently reinstates the heterosexual coupling that structures Western social systems, the second approach attempts to destabilize gender-specific heterosexual identities—and, by extension, the oppressive nonsymmetrical hetero–homo opposition—by demonstrating their interconnections with gendered homosexual identities. Eve Sedgwick has played a major role in this undertaking. In *Between Men: English Literature and Male Homosocial Desire* (1985), she examines triangular romantic relationships between women and men to demonstrate that normative descriptions of heterosexual masculinity are shaped by homophobia and male homosexuality. Similarly, in *Epistemology of the Closet* (1990), Sedgwick attempts to denaturalize modern conceptions of male-gendered sexualities by exposing the unstable, dynamic yet interdependent relationship between male heterosexual and homosexual identities. In addition, she argues that the inconsistencies in conventional oppositions between male heterosexuality and homosexuality significantly shape twentieth-century Western knowledge systems. Sedgwick's innovative explorations of male bonding have established the theoretical basis for a number of important studies in gay male theory. Ed Cohen, for example, analyzes Victorian literary texts in order to denaturalize male heterosexual identities. In *Talk on the Wilde Side* (1993), he analyzes newspaper accounts of the OSCAR WILDE trials and other nineteenth-century popular writings to demonstrate that heterosexual masculinity developed in reaction to the invention of "the homosexual." In *Homographesis* (1994), Lee Edelman takes this trajectory even further and examines what he calls the "homosexual difference," or the arbitrary division between heterosexual and homosexual masculinities. Drawing on Wilde's *The Importance of Being Earnest*, PROUST's *Cities of the Plain*, and other male-authored literary and filmic texts, Edelman demonstrates that this arbitrary division is created through a system of external markings that defines as gay the mannerisms and dress of particular male bodies. These external inscriptions work to contain the threat of male homosexuality. According to Edelman, by severing the presumed connection between anatomy and sexual desire, male homosexuality destabilizes male heterosexual self-identity. Gay men function as a disavowed, intolerable masculinity, or as what Edelman calls "the other face of gender."

Given the restrictive descriptions of female sexuality and feminine desire, it is perhaps not surprising that less work has been done on lesbian sexualities. Indeed, according to Teresa de Lauretis and other women-feminists of sexual difference, in patriarchal cultures there is no adequate representation of female-gendered desire. Thus in "Sexual Indifference and Lesbian Representation" (1988), she draws on Luce Irigaray's description of "hommo-sexuality" and critiques the lack of gender differentiation in theories of male homosexuality and lesbianism. And in "Film and the Visible" (1991), she calls for the development of autonomous representations of lesbian sexuality that go beyond binary male–female gender categories. However, by positing an irreducible difference between male and female, she inadvertently reinstates the heterosexual presumption she attempts to escape. Similarly, in *A Lure of Knowledge: Lesbian Sexuality and Theory* (1991), Judith Roof examines the intersection between gender and sexuality and argues that filmic and literary representations of lesbian sexuality create an uncertainty that undermines the stability of rigid male-female binary gender systems.

The final approach, which attempts to complicate male–female gender categories by blurring the boundaries between them, is most fully illustrated by Judith Butler's theory of gender performativity. In *Gender Trouble* (1989), Butler maintains that because male–female gender categories inevitably reinforce Western cultures' heterosexual social contract, theorists should attempt to go beyond this binary meaning system. By positing "woman" and "man" as stable categories of identity, gender representations naturalize heterosexuality and support conservative constructions of normative masculinity and femininity. Butler's theory of gender performativity destabilizes this heterosexist binary by redefining gender as a process, a series of discontinuous acts that must be repeatedly performed. Drag, for example, creates a disjunction between sex and gender that denaturalizes heterosexist norms and suggests that sexual identities are far more fluid than generally assumed. In *Bodies That Matter* (1993), Butler both clarifies and extends this notion of gender performance to claim that sexed bodies, like gender, are created and regulated by social norms. This examination of the ways language structures our understanding of material bodies allows her to suggest that bodies are simultaneously engendered and racialized.

As this brief survey indicates, the recognition that gender relations are socially constructed categories of meaning has opened up a number of new areas in lesbian, gay, and queer studies. Although—or, perhaps, because—the relationship between gender and sexuality is quite slippery, the distinction between them has led to a number of important theoretical breakthroughs. By exposing the arbitrary nature of the rigid division between homosexuality and heterosexuality, recent gender theories complicate contemporary descriptions of human identity. (See also IDENTITY and LITERARY THEORY: GAY, LESBIAN, AND QUEER.)

—AnnLouise Keating

BIBLIOGRAPHY

Alarcón, Norma. "The Theoretical Subject(s) of *This Bridge Called My Back* and Anglo-American Feminism." *Haciendo Caros/Making Face, Making Soul: Creative and Critical Perspectives by Women of Color*. Gloria Anzaldúa, ed. San Francisco: Aunt Lute Foundation, 1990. 356–369. ■ Bristow, Joseph, ed. *Sexual Sameness: Textual Differences in Lesbian and Gay Writing*. New York: Routledge, 1992. ■ Butler, Judith. *Bodies That Matter: On the Discursive Limits of "Sex."* New York: Routledge, 1993. ■ ———. *Gender Trouble: Feminism and the Subversion of Identity*. New York: Routledge, 1989. ■ Cohen, Ed. *Talk on the Wilde Side: Toward a Genealogy of a Discourse on Male Sexualities*. New York: Routledge, 1993. ■ de Lauretis, Teresa. "Film and the Visible." *How Do I Look? Queer Film and Video*. Bad Object-Choices, eds. Seattle: Bay Press, 1991. 223–263. ■ ———. "Sexual Indifference and Lesbian Representation." *Theatre Journal* 40 (1988): 155–177. ■ Edelman, Lee. *Homographesis: Essays in Gay Literary and Cultural Theory*. New York: Routledge, 1994. ■ Foucault, Michel. *The History of Sexuality: An Introduction*. Vol. I. Trans. Robert Hurley. New York: Random House, 1978. ■ Rich, Adrienne. "Compulsory Heterosexuality and Lesbian Existence." *Signs* 5 (1980): 631–660. ■ Roof, Judith. *A Lure of Knowledge: Lesbian Sexuality and Theory*. New York: Columbia University Press, 1991. ■ Rubin, Gayle. "Thinking Sex: Notes for a Radical Theory of the Politics of Sexuality." *Pleasure and Danger; Exploring Female Sexuality*. Carole S. Vance, ed. 1984. New York: Pandora, 1992. 267–319. ■ ———. "The Traffic in Women: Notes on the 'Political Economy' of Sex." *Toward an Anthropology of Women*. Rayna R. Reiter, ed. New York: Monthly Review, 1975. 157–210. ■ Sedgwick, Eve Kosofsky. *Between Men: English Literature and Male Homosocial Desire*. New York: Columbia University Press, 1985. ■ ———. *Epistemology of the Closet*. Berkeley: University of California Press, 1990. ■ ———. *Tendencies*. Chapel Hill: University of North Carolina Press, 1993.

Genet, Jean
(1910–1986)

Jean Genet's work has left a powerful legacy to post-modernity and remains a provocation to questions of gay identity. Genet's fidelity to outcasts and the socially marginal, his simultaneous criticism of *and* participation in radical politics, his obsession with role-playing and identity, and his stylized violence and obscenity anticipate post-modern apprehensions and techniques. His commitment to the extremes of revolt contributed to the myth of "Jean Genet." Beginning with his first novel, *Our Lady of the Flowers* (1942), Genet openly embraced and affirmed his homosexuality, constantly recreating and manipulating his own identity throughout his career as a novelist, playwright, activist for the Black Panthers in the late 1960s, defender of the Palestine Liberation Organization, and friend of the French literati, especially Jean-Paul Sartre and JEAN COCTEAU (who aided in securing his official free pardon for criminal offenses in l948). Genet's homosexuality and his awareness of his sexual "marginality" encouraged the empathy he felt toward oppressed groups in his later career. Although Genet's revolt is deeply rooted in his awareness of his "deviant" sexuality, his political work was not predicated on his personal identity; instead, Genet worked on surmounting a simple affirmation of identity and forging a general coalition of socially disaffected groups. Scrupulously careful in how he represented others, as his dealings with the Black Panthers and the PLO attest, Genet's affirmation of his dissident status was, in effect, universalist: It led to a generalized concern for all those who were excluded from political power.

Born the illegitimate son of parents he never knew, Genet, abandoned by his mother at birth, brought up by Public Assistance, was finally sent to live with foster parents at the age of seven. His life as a thief began early; he was sent to Mettray, a French "reform" school for boys, at the age of fifteen. Much of his young adulthood was spent in prison for crimes such as theft and prostitution. Pronounced an unreformable criminal in 1948, Genet was nearly incarcerated for life until Sartre, Cocteau, and others convinced French authorities that his literary career was far too important. Most of Genet's work incorporates themes related to prison life: the inversion of bourgeois morals, prostitution, murder, theft, betrayal, and the complex formation of identities associated with criminal subcultures.

A writer who extolled individual treachery and betrayal as a virtue, Genet's novels and plays illuminate the possibilities of survival among men, and sometimes women, bound together by fierce, unrelenting erotic desire that illuminated and transfigured the "margins." Genet realized early the possibilities of refusal; his work is obsessed with transforming everyday objects—the vaseline confiscated by prison guards, the pin-ups of criminals placed on prison walls—into minitheaters of insurrection staged with minimal means. As a chronicler of outcasts, lost causes, and the underworld, Genet carefully scrutinizes the very notion of "stable identities," whether French, homosexual, black, or Palestinian. Though his novels are intricate explorations of the question of identity, primarily of Genet and the men he loves, his plays become ritualized means for staging and demolishing identity.

Genet's first novel, *Our Lady of the Flowers* (1942), was written in prison over an extended time since his manuscripts were constantly confiscated by prison officials. The very circumstances of the story highlight Genet's sexual identity: *Our Lady* is narrated by a masturbating prisoner who tells us that the characters he describes are products of his erotic fantasies conceived under the hot wool blanket of his bed. The narrator, Genet, most closely identifies with the "hero" of the novel, Louis Culafroy, known throughout the novel as Divine. Divine's experiences as a prostitute in Paris lead him to several erotic relationships: Darling Daintyfoot the thief and pimp, Gabriel the soldier, Our Lady of the Flowers the murderer, and Gorgui, another brutal killer. A story filled with sexually explicit descriptions of male prostitution, Genet's scatological language is a provocation to the reader's bourgeois sensibility. Genet states that all the characters created here are masturbatory fantasies, characters "chosen for that evening's delight." He tries to define throughout *Our Lady* the psychological nature of fantasy; the characters themselves often "dream" their sexual encounters with each other. At one point, Divine does not know "whether she is already dreaming or merely reminiscing." Usually referring to Divine as "she," Genet highlights the dual role of the queen and the complex relationships she/he has with her lovers. *Our Lady of the Flowers* is an exaltation of erotic passion and the triumph of Genet's imagination to overcome his dehumanized existence as a prisoner.

The Thief's Journal (1948), one of Genet's most accessible novels, deals in picaresque fashion with his travels through Spain, Yugoslavia, Germany, and Belgium in the 1930s. An important referent point for Jean-Paul Sartre's mammoth study, *Saint Genet* (1963), *The Thief's Journal* deals with the problem of sanctity and the inversion of values that Genet's work repeatedly examines. In speaking of his experiences as a thief, the book is filled with portrayals of his lovers and their strengths and foibles. Genet is certainly interested in the "truth" of his lovers, but the poetic transfiguration of his subculture is Genet's primary concern. In his portrayal of a criminal milieu and its survival tactics, Genet explores the possibilities of "camp" and outlines the parameters of a criminal subculture that is openly gay. *The Thief's Journal* is a loving recreation of criminal style and language, specifically the charm of the men he loves. He admires Stiltano for achieving "a harmony in bad taste"; for

Genet, Stiltano's own fashion sense, his "pair of green and tan crocodile shoes, a brown suit, a white silk shirt, a pink tie, a multicolored scarf and a green hat" become a means of empowerment. *The Thief's Journal* deals with coping mechanisms and how style can create identity and facilitate revolt.

The difficulty Genet's representation of homosexuality in *The Thief's Journal* presents for homophile readers today, however, remains a constant difficulty in his work. Genet's glorification of homosexuality as revolt leads him to equate it with crime in a manner that the bourgeois world he vilifies understands all too readily. In his description of the French Gestapo and his fascination with their treason and theft, he notes, "With homosexuality added, it would be sparkling, unassimilable." A difficulty that Genet's book presents to contemporary gay readers is one that besets much of his early novels; he is unwilling to consider specific differences between sexuality and crime, instead focusing obsessively on the links between them. *The Thief's Journal* offers a reason for this oversight of Genet's: "Excluded by my birth and tastes from the social order, I was not aware of its diversity. I wondered at its perfect coherence, which rejected me." Despite his minute exploration of a milieu excluded from the social order, Genet neglects to define his sexuality in terms other than those provided by the dominant class: as monstrous, criminal, and deviant.

Miracle of the Rose (1951), a complex, often mystical novel, is structured around the development of Genet's gay passions. In fact, as Tom Driver suggested, the book's scrutiny of prison life is plotted as a "bildung of gay passion" in which Genet moves from passive relations with prisoners to assuming butch roles. The novel explores the tendency of lovers to leave men for more "masculine" prisoners; it also explores the nuances of sexual relations between older men and young boys. The biographical development of *Miracle of the Rose* is born out of Genet's own experience of male–male relations; Genet plots his development from Mettray to Fontevrault as a growth from passive, "feminized" relations to relations where he plays the role of "masculine" older man to younger boys. Along with this subtle examination of relationships, the novel charts mystical states of awareness; Genet attempts to meld gay sensuality to mysticism. Harcamone is represented as a divinity in the novel, an unseen presence who hallows the prison of Fontevrault. In a climactic scene, Genet describes joining Harcamone during his martyrdom after the killing of a guard. Genet imaginatively links himself with Harcamone at the moment of his exaltation, his walk to the guillotine. None of the relations between men in Fontevrault are depicted as idyllic: *Miracle of the Rose* is about the failure of all relations in a prison system, and the mystical solution, the sacralization of Harcamone, is the only panacea to brutalized social conditions.

Genet explores further these themes of prison life and the relationships between prisoners in his first drama, *Deathwatch* (1946). Though not produced until 1949, two years after his first successful drama *The Maids* was produced, *Deathwatch* centers on three prison inmates and the homosocial and homoerotic ties that bind them together. The three characters, Green Eyes, Lefranc, and Maurice, are entangled in a jealous web, each scrambling to secure his position with the other two. Both Lefranc and Maurice desire Green Eyes, who, as the most brutal murderer of the three, is the undisputed leader of the pack. Green Eyes, in jail for murdering a young girl, observes the two men vying for his attention throughout the play, taunting each other's sexual prowess. The characters themselves are difficult to assess since none of them is reliable about the truth of his own emotions or intentions. Much of the dialogue in the play points toward the characters' pasts, yet no one ever reveals more about his life before prison besides the crime that put him there.

The final crime of the play is Lefranc's murder of Maurice. Intending to impress Green Eyes and to finally win his attention away from Maurice, Lefranc finds he is the victim of Green Eyes's betrayal—Green Eyes turns him in to the guard. This highly symbolic climax reemphasizes Genet's preoccupation with betrayal and martyrdom. The play investigates the relationship between the three inmates as well as the "outside" relationship with Green Eyes's unseen girlfriend. Convinced that both Lefranc and Maurice desire his girlfriend, Green Eyes finally "gives" her to the guard. The absurdity of *Deathwatch* is quite similar in tone to the "Theater of the Absurd," traditionally equated with dramatists such as Samuel Beckett, Harold Pinter, and Eugene Ionesco.

The Balcony (1956) is perhaps the best known of Genet's dramatic works. A brilliant and provocative play, *The Balcony* is set in a brothel, or the "house of illusions," in an undisclosed country. Madame Irma's house of illusions is a place where plumbers, bank clerks, and chiefs of police come to act out their sexual fantasies as judges, bishops, generals, and so on. The illusions must be erotic, complete, and undisturbed. When the illusion is broken, when one of the prostitutes breaks his or her role as criminal or penitent, the illusion is destroyed. The "bishop" notes that, "So long as we were in a room in a brothel, we belonged to our fantasies, but once having exposed them, we're now tied up with human beings, tied to you and forced to go on with this adventure according to the laws of visibility."

The most important event in *The Balcony* is the bloody "Revolution" occurring in the city. The play complicates the reality of this revolution, constantly questioning which is the more real, the sexual fantasies or the revolution. In fact, in Richard Schechner's 1979 New York production, the revolution was portrayed as yet another fantasy created for the erotic pleasure of Madame Irma's clients. The figure of Chantal, an ex-prostitute turned revolutionary, is the key link between the house of illusions and the revolution; she is a symbol of purity and inspiration for the revolutionaries, yet her death near the end of the play represents a victory for the counter-revolutionaries. In both cases, it is the nationalistic symbol that Genet implies is false, no more than a role. *The Balcony* is a stunning spectacle on stage. With scenes of sadomasochism, erotic fantasies, self-castration, and role-playing, the drama invites the audience to participate visually in many of the situations and fantasies Genet foregrounds in his novels.

Genet's dramatic works remain faithful to the playwright's interest in gender identity and sexual orientation. His other plays, including *The Maids* (1947, revised 1954), *The Blacks* (1958), and *The Screens* (1961), question the social roles people are assigned as a result of their race, class status, sexual orientation, or ethnicity. *The Maids* explores the relationship of two young servants and their wealthy mistress. Though Genet originally intended male actors to play the female roles, *The Maids* is usually staged by actresses. Highly stylized and ritualistic, *The Maids* was a huge success in Europe and remains a staple of continental drama. *The Blacks*, written as a vehicle for an all-black cast, is similar to the ritualistic theater of Antonin Artaud. The play consists of three complex stories all centering on the murder of a white woman, whose coffin remains in the center of the stage as a symbol of the Blacks' reaction to white domination. *The Screens*, Genet's response to the Algerian war (1954–1963), is literally a play of epic proportions containing nearly 100 characters on an enormous multileveled set. The play details both the war and the relationship between an Arab mother and son, one of the most sophisticated characterizations of a woman in all of Genet's works. As a dramatist, Genet has been both a delight and a terror for modern directors. Although his plays incorporate much of the richness inherent in the novels, many directors, including Peter Brook, have had enormous difficulty staging Genet's plays due in part to their surrealist qualities and cryptic characterizations.

After *The Screens* and its autodestruction of drama, Genet turned to perhaps the most fascinating and complex of the roles he assumed. From inverted saint to heir of Artaud, Genet then became a public intellectual eager to give whatever cultural weight he had accrued to marginal positions and groups, aiding their collective struggle. The search for revolt moved from an exploration of mystical reverie in *Miracle of the Rose* to more concrete collective actions. During a time of relative quiescence in writing, Genet became openly involved with militant politics in the late 1960s and early 1970s. He defended Mao's Red Guard, supported the Black Panthers during the turbulent years when they were subject to police harassment and brutality, and expressed his solidarity with the Palestine Liberation Organization after Israel took the West Bank in 1967. Interviewed by prestigious European newspapers, Genet would refuse to speak of his work; instead, he would use these interviews as an occasion for political activism. Genet disdained the word *intellectual*, but it was as a critical intellectual that he worked to sustain support from youth audiences and literary intellectuals for these causes. He toured U.S. college campuses in support of Panther Bobby Seale after Seale's arrest; he took credit for the recognition of gay rights in the Panther organization, mitigating the homophobia and sexism that touched many militant groups in the 1960s.

Genet's political commitments were pure and intransigent; despite his constant affirmation of treachery and betrayal in his novels, his work as an espouser of activist politics illustrates his commitment to any struggle where identities are in the process of formation, whether these identities be "black" or "Palestinian." Edward Said notes in his discussion in *Grand Street*: "Genet, therefore, is the traveler across identities, the tourist whose purpose is marriage with a foreign cause, so long as that cause is both revolutionary and in constant agitation." Success in the quotidian sense that usually constitutes political action Genet often suggested was beside the point. Edmund White, in his preface to *Prisoner of Love*, cites Genet as saying, "The day the Palestinians become institutionalized, I will no longer be on their side."

The complexities of Genet's relations to the Palestinian cause are charted in his last work, *Prisoner of Love* (published in 1986 as *Un Captif Amoureux*). Occasioned by Genet's return to Palestine after the 1982 massacres in Sara and Shatila, *Prisoner of Love* was completed the year of his death. In its effort to represent subordinated groups, the book reveals how much self-scrutiny was part of Genet's attempts to represent others. Part travelogue, cultural commentary, and psychological analysis of Genet's own motivations toward political commitment, the work is a provocation to current thinking on Arab–European relations. As Edward Said observed, Genet never simply goes "native": rather, he carefully examines the differences between his position as a Westerner and the position of indigenous Arabs. His cultural criticism and political analysis firmly reveals Genet as a critical intellectual in the general French tradition exemplified by Sartre: Yet one cannot imagine a less "nationalist" intellectual. Cosmopolitan in his willingness to be moved by causes vilified by dominant interests, Genet's intellectual allegiances are global.

Prisoner of Love also analyzes, in ways that the novels only suggested, how eroticism could lead to a radical politics. In the case of the Panthers, Genet admitted his erotic attraction to black men; likewise, he was aware of the libidinal charge that hedged his fascination with the young soldiers of the PLO. However, erotic attraction leads to the clearer articulation of what Genet's work had always promised to do: establish a new ethic. Rather than ostracize and eroticize these new attractions, Genet attempts to use them as an incitement to dialogue and self-scrutiny. Despite its focus on the male bonds of the military, *Prisoner*

of Love also led to Genet's most sustained meditation on women.

Genet died in 1986, leaving behind not only a striking body of work, but a powerful example, pure in its commitments and obsessions. (See also EROTICA AND PORNOGRAPHY.)

—*Amy Farmer*

BIBLIOGRAPHY

Brooks, Peter and Joseph Halpern, eds. *Genet: A Collection of Critical Essays.* Englewood Cliffs, N.J.: Prentice Hall, 1979. ■ Chaudhuri, Una. "The Politics of Theater: Play, Deceit, and Threat in Genet's *The Blacks.*" *Modern Drama* 28 (1985): 362–376. ■ Driver, Tom. "An Exaltation of Evil." *Saturday Review* (11 March 1967): 36–37, 113. ■ Said, Edward. "On Jean Genet's Late Works." *Grand Street* 9.4 (1990): 27–42. ■ Sartre, Jean-Paul. *Saint Genet.* Trans. Bernard Frechtman. New York: Pantheon Books, 1963. ■ Thody, Philip. *Jean Genet: A Study of His Novels and Plays.* New York: Stein and Day, 1970. ■ White, Edmund. *Genet.* London: Chatto and Windus, Ltd., 1993.

George, Stefan
(1868–1933)

Stefan Anton George, one of the foremost German poets of the turn of the century and considered a prophet of the early-twentieth-century "conservative revolution," was born on July 12, 1868, in Rüdesheim, the son of a wealthy Rhineland wine merchant. At an early age, he exhibited a gift for learning languages that later led to his many linguistic innovations in German and to his superb translations into German of the works of the French Symbolists, DANTE, and SHAKESPEARE, among others. Inspired by Mallarmé's coterie of writers and artists in Paris, George formed his own circle that was known as the Georgekreis (George-Circle). Indicative of George's elitism, he founded a literary journal, *Blätter für die Kunst (Pages for Art)*, which was available only to the members of his circle. A strong authoritarian personality, he founded his circle on the master–disciple relationship. His devotion to the artistic paradigm of "art for art's sake" manifested itself in his desire to shape his reality according to his aesthetic ideals rather than to society.

George's homosexuality is an open secret in the scholarship about him; that is, it is a commonplace that almost no one will admit. George, however, is as responsible for this closetedness as anyone since he strove in his work to create a private space that would

be accessible only to those "like-minded" individuals who possessed the code. Therefore, his poems allow themselves to be easily construed as "metaphorical" or "platonic," even if they most immediately appear to be about burning gay passion. George accomplishes this effect by addressing a genderless "you" in his poems and by personifying such terms as "love," "soul," and "heart."

Two works, *Algabal* (1892) and *Maximin* (1906), especially embody a gay sensibility. Algabal is a young king who builds himself a subterranean kingdom, the artificiality of which surpasses the natural beauty of the world above. The significance of the embrace of the Unnatural, the Barren, and the nonetheless Beautiful in this work cannot be missed by the reader aware of the stereotypes of gay love, but is simply readable as DECADENCE to one who is not. The poem's dedication to the memory of the Bavarian king, Ludwig II, a homosexual icon at the turn of the century, is also a signal to its gay meaning. *Maximin* was inspired by the Munich high school student, Maximilian Kronberger, whose early death served as an excuse to mythologize his memory. Although the youth's poetry was the overt excuse for his relationship to George, the poetry's mediocrity suggests that George encouraged Kronberger mainly because of his physical beauty. Heavily employing biblical imagery, the work depicts Maximin as the long-awaited savior. Although the first-person narrator speaks of spiritual fulfillment, in the climactic poem of the series, "Incarnation," the spiritual becomes indistinguishable from the erotic. Spiritual union is described with the language of sexual union.

After the National Socialist State offered him high honors which he rejected simply by not replying, George left Germany for Locarno, Switzerland, where he died on December 4, 1933.

—*Craig B. Palmer*

BIBLIOGRAPHY

Goldsmith, Ulrich K. *Stefan George*. New York: Columbia University Press, 1970. ∎ Keilson-Lauritz, Marita. *Von der Liebe die Freundschaft heißt*. Berlin: Verlag rosa Winkel, 1987. ∎ Metzger, Michael M., and Erika A. Metzger. *Stefan George*. New York: Twayne Publishers, 1972.

GERMAN AND AUSTRIAN LITERATURE

German and Austrian Literature Before the Nineteenth Century

The literary history of homosexuality in Germany and Austria before the nineteenth century is, to a great extent, still in its infancy. The following remarks must therefore be regarded as tentative and in need of supplementation. German scholarship is just beginning to learn to read for homosexuality.

Generally speaking, the periods of the Middle Ages, the Reformation, and the Baroque conceived of homosexuality in theological terms as one form of "Sodomiterey" (sodomy). Since definitions of sodomy typically insisted on penetration (male–male, anal, or with an animal), lesbian sexuality was virtually invisible. During the Middle Ages, the law codes of the various Germanic peoples did not proscribe homosexual acts. However, in 1532, Charles V promulgated the *Constitutio Criminalis Carolina*, which was binding for the Holy Roman Empire until it was abolished by Napoleon in 1806. The *Carolina* stated that "If any person should commit unchaste acts with an animal, a man with a man, a woman with a woman, then they have forfeited their lives, and they should be executed by fire according to common custom." Extant court records from the entire period, including the eighteenth century, show that this law was for the most part sparingly enforced. Nonetheless, the theologico-legal climate prohibited any direct and positive literary expressions of homosexuality.

A decisive change in the representation of homosexuality occurred during the eighteenth century, a change that can be attributed to the impulses of the Enlightenment. The enthusiastic reception of classical texts of antiquity allowed a forum for discussion. Philosophers, psychologists, and statesmen debated the appropriateness of Caroline law. Many argued against the death penalty even though it was not revoked in Austria until 1787 and in Prussia until 1794. Individual figures emerged, who despite their reputed inclination to "Greek love" or "Knabenliebe" (pederasty), were accepted and even celebrated in upper-class and intellectual circles. The eighteenth century was arguably the first period in German history that allowed for the construction of a homosexual identity, a period that came to an end in the first decade of the nineteenth century, when the conservative, romantic, and nationalistic backlash (re-)instituted a monogamous and heterosexual family morality.

The Middle Ages. The only direct allusions to homosexuality in medieval German literature are negative in nature and occur in didactic, critical, and humorous works. To this date, no literary treatment of lesbian homosexuality has been found. However, literature produced within homosocial settings, both male and female, religious and secular, did allow for the indirect representation of homosexuality.

In the *Eneit* (1170–1189) of Heinrich von Veldeke, based on French versions of the Aeneas story, the mother of Lavinia attempts to dissuade her daughter from marrying the hero by casting him as a cowardly homosexual. Although the stratagem is ineffective, the text gives evidence of the Christian prejudice against pagan homosexuality. A similar phenomenon can be encountered in the anonymously authored *Moriz von Craun* (ca 1200) in which Nero figures as the antipode of the ideal knight. Not only does he engage in active and passive homosexual relations, he actually becomes pregnant with a toad through medical intervention.

The anonymous comic tale *The Pregnant Monk* (ca 1300) involves an excessively naive monk who, in his first sexual encounter, is forced by his ineptitude to take the passive position. Believing that this necessarily results in pregnancy, he begs a monastery farmer to beat him to the point of abortion. The farmer obliges, even as he inquires about the father. The monk believes that a rabbit is his aborted child and develops strong feelings of remorse and maternal desire. He is ruled to be insane, and steps are taken to exorcise his demon. The story is amusing, but it also reveals the assumed connection between homosexuality and insanity.

In another comic tale, *Der Borte* by Dietrich von der Glezze (second half of the thirteenth century), an unfaithful wife seeks to regain her husband by manipulating him into an even more compromising situation. She disguises herself as a man with whom her husband promptly falls in love. Her husband's demand may well amount to the only suggestion of a homosexual scene in medieval German literature: He plans to enjoy every imaginable embrace with her/him, and to perform "that which men do with their women when they lie with them at night."

Ulrich von Lichtenstein's narrative poem *Frauendienst* (*Service of Ladies*) (1257) may or may not be autobiographical; in any event, it recounts the story of one Ulrich, a knight, who journeyed throughout northern Italy and Bohemia cross-dressed as Venus in order to honor his lady and all women. In discussions regarding the moral decay of their world,

a lady suggests that the knights are at fault for preferring homosexuality to the service of ladies. Another thirteenth-century poet known as the "Stricker" inveighs more strenuously against the moral depravity of his time. He accuses homosexuals of murder insofar as they plant their seed in infertile soil.

More positive, if indirect, representations of medieval homosexuality may be found embedded in accounts of homosocial cultural formations. *Tristan und Isold* (1205–1215) by Gottfried von Strassburg, for instance, is by no means unique in its depiction of the courtly ethos of intimate male friendship. An erotically laden discourse was cultivated that can be neither equated with nor separated from homosexuality. Indeed, some have argued that Gottfried subtly implies the homosexuality of King Mark in order to explain and partially legitimize Isolde's unfaithfulness with Tristan.

The same careful attention must be paid to the religious outpourings of celibate men and women. For instance, the twelfth-century Beguines, an officially unrecognized religious order of women who chose to be independent of male authority not only in the family but also in the church, included the mystic woman writer Mechthild von Magdeburg. The strong erotic cast of her exchanges with God must be seen in the context of her rejection of male authority. Male mystics typically eschewed the discourse of second-person erotic encounter, preferring the distance afforded by the third person. But there is one exception: Heinrich Seuse (1295–1366). His erotic yearning for union with God can only be described as homoerotic.

Reformation and Baroque. The largely negative representation of homosexuality continued in the Reformation and Baroque periods. The Renaissance that fostered a homosexual sensibility in Italy was decisively interrupted by Martin Luther and the concerns of the Reformation. The split between the Catholic and Protestant church fueled mutual charges of homosexuality; the traditions of celibacy and monastic life made the Catholic church the easier target.

Although the *History of Dr. Johann Faustus* (1587) by Johann Spies is clearly a work written on the threshold of modernity, it continues the connection between homosexuality and the devil. Every day Faust is entitled to select the woman he desires, and at night Mephisto submits to him in her guise. Goethe later thematized Mephisto's homosexuality in *Faust, Part Two*.

Interesting anecdotal evidence concerning Baroque homosexuality can be found in connection with the composer Johannes Rosenmüller (1619–1684). Active in Leipzig during the period between Schütz and Bach, he and some boys were investigated by the city for engaging in "coarse excess." The official documents declined to name the charge, but rumor spoke of sodomy. Though Rosenmüller was hounded by the reputation of a sodomite, he was never prosecuted; the boys, however, underwent inquisitional examination. His hymns and other musical compositions proved a dilemma to both the church and music history. Already in his lifetime, the practice emerged of including his songs but neglecting to name the composer.

The Adventurous Simplicissimus (1669) by Hans Jakob Christoffel von Grimmelshausen (1625?–1676), a picaresque novel set during the Thirty Years War, includes a telling transvestite episode depicted with an unusual measure of realism. The hero, cross-dressed as a young woman, awakens the desire of his cavalry captain, the captain's wife, and his servants. Although his disguise affords him the heterosexual pleasure of groping the captain's wife, she yields to the lesbian pleasure of affections with a young woman; there is no indication that she sees through his disguise.

One last Baroque poet to be mentioned is Daniel Casper von Lohenstein (1635–1683). Traditionally thought of as the epitome of excessively ornamental German Baroque poetry (*Schwulst*), Lohenstein was rediscovered as a quintessentially gay (and German) poet by HUBERT FICHTE in 1978. Fichte's sensitive reading of Lohenstein's *Agrippina* (1665), a treatment of the Nero story replete with incest, pederasty, male and female homosexuality, necrophilia, sadism, and masochism, brings an "amoral cheerfulness" to light. He provocatively and appropriately sets Lohenstein at the beginning of a tradition that will lead to the Enlightenment: "Was this Lohenstein's utopia? A republic without racial discrimination, with equal rights for women, and no sexual limits—before Sade, before Freud? . . . Lohenstein formulates this sexual liberty as a utopia of reason."

The Eighteenth Century. The extreme androcentrism of eighteenth-century Germany in conjunction with a lively (not to say erotically charged) preoccupation with Greek and Roman antiquity, a relatively open-minded commitment to scientific investigation of human behavior, and a determined break from Christian orthodoxy provided the basis for the development of a positive homosexual identity, at least among the educated classes (still a distinct minority). The court of Frederick the Great at Sans Souci, a male preserve where political, military, philosophical, and aesthetic interests were mingled in the intimate circles of male friends, may be taken as a hallmark of eighteenth-century German homosocialism. Frederick and his brother Henry were almost certainly gay. Nor was homosexuality restricted to the court; the *Letters on the Gallantries of Berlin* (1782), published anony-

mously by Johann Fiedel, depict the gay underworld of Berlin in lurid and sensational detail.

Practically no effort has been made to uncover lesbian relations in eighteenth-century Germany. Excluded from most, if not all, public institutions, considered incapable of male friendship, women were both "invisible" as well as forced to rely on one another for friendship and affection. Female social interactions regularly extended to the bedroom and permitted kissing and other intimate behaviors. We can assume that lesbian friendship and activity existed. The correspondence between literate women such as Luisa Gottsched (1713–1762) and her close friend Dorothea Henrietta von Runckel may begin to yield insights into its specific forms.

The possibilities for the expression of male homosexuality were greatly enriched by the translation and discussion of ancient texts of poetry, philosophy, and history. The Greek phenomenon of "Knabenliebe" [pederasty] and the debate concerning Socrates' sexuality (as intimated in the *Phaedrus* and *Symposium*) supplied new terms for homosexual inclinations. Individuals like JOHANN JOACHIM WINCKELMANN and Johannes von Müller were reputed to indulge in "Greek" or "Socratic," and even "Platonic," love. Prostitutes in boy bordellos were known as Ganymedes. In 1775, Christoph Meiners published *On the Male Love of the Greeks*.

Johann Joachim Winckelmann (1717–1768) was the central figure of homosexual self-identification. In a series of shorter and longer works of art history, including *Reflections on the Imitation of Greek Art* (1755) and the *History of the Art of Antiquity* (1764), Winckelmann not only conveyed an intoxicating vision of a culture of homoerotic beauty and sexual license, he also spoke in semicoded language to like-minded men and youths, inviting them to imitate his example. Like so many who would follow him, Winckelmann emigrated to Italy, partially because of the sexual freedom it afforded. Within eighteen years of his death, five separate correspondences with friends were published, including some unabashed love letters, a circumstance that testifies to the deep interest of many to connect with his homoerotic friendship. In 1805, Goethe published a biographical essay in *Winckelmann and His Age,* in which he discreetly refers to Winckelmann's homosexuality. Goethe's words became a touchstone for gay sensibility.

The other major homosexual figure of the period was Johannes von Müller (1752–1809). Born in Schaffhausen, Switzerland, Müller was an astonishingly erudite historian and admirer of Winckelmann. He was respected and liked by many major intellectuals, including Goethe, Herder, Gleim, and Bonnet.

Friedrich Schiller relied on his *History of the Swiss Confederation* for the writing of *William Tell*. In 1773, Müller fell in love with the Swiss nobleman Karl Viktor von Bonstetten, with whom he remained friends until Müller's death. A mutual friend, Friederike Brun, indiscreetly published Müller's early love letters to Bonstetten in 1798. The letters thematize friendship, document a literary tradition of male–male love, and indicate an awareness of their imitation of Winckelmann. Later in life, Müller was the dupe of an elaborate scheme to defraud him by exploiting his homosexuality. One of his former pupils (and perhaps lovers) invented a Hungarian Count Louis von Batthyani and penned letters to Müller in which the Count expressed his love and inclination. Müller responded with letters of unfettered passion and an awareness that this friendship and its depiction in letters far exceeded his earlier relationship with Bonstetten, possibly the purest expression of eighteenth-century homosocial desire that exists. After a year and more than a hundred letters, when the fiction could no longer be sustained, Müller was financially and psychologically destroyed. Goethe was one of several friends who helped him recover.

A continual challenge for gay and lesbian studies is to negotiate the overlap between homosocial friendship and homosexuality. Traditional scholarship has coined such concepts as the "discourse of sensibility" and the "cult of friendship" in order to defuse the homoerotic charge in the literature and letters of the period. Homosexuality is vigorously denied. However, both Winckelmann and Müller were members of extensive friendship networks. The impossibility of "drawing the line" emerges in an exemplary fashion in the case of one of Müller's older friends, a contemporary of Winckelmann, Johann Wilhelm Ludwig Gleim (1719–1803).

Literary history recognizes Gleim as a midcentury anacreontic poet and celebrator of Frederick the Great in his *Prussian Soldier Songs*. He lost the friend of his youth, Ewald von Kleist, also an anacreontic poet, in one of Frederick's wars. Of greater relevance, however, are his letters and the historical record of his cultivation of friendship as a way of life. As a bachelor with a comfortable salary, the mature Gleim sought out promising young men whom he supported in various ways. Some lived with him in his comfortable Halberstadt home, where he encouraged them in their poetic endeavors; for others he found positions as tutors in private homes. He maintained a lively correspondence with more than a hundred persons. In 1778, he published the *Briefe von den Herren Gleim und Jacobi* (*The Letters of Gleim and Jacobi*). The excessive tenderness displayed in these letters (over 13,000 epistolary "kisses") was an embarrassment even to the "age of sensibility." In his living quarters, he established what he called the "temple of friendship," actually two rooms containing approximately 120 portraits of his friends and some family members. (The Gleimhaus museum has preserved these rooms.) Pride of place went to portraits of Gleim himself and his youthful friend Kleist. Bookcases contained bound sets of correspondence that were available for casual reading by house guests. Was Gleim gay? Although there is no evidence of a specific homosexual act, the impression of an overwhelmingly homosocial culture could only be denied by a determined homophobia.

If this is true for Gleim, it certainly also holds for many others. Christian Fürchtegott Gellert was another bachelor poet. His popular novel *The Life of the Swedish Countess of G**** (1750) recounts the ordeals of a count and countess who are separated soon after marriage. While she undergoes an education in reason, he is removed to Russia and Siberia, where he is "educated" in feeling and the body. His tender love for a British fellow prisoner is most accurately described as latently homosexual. As for the countess, she unwittingly commits bigamy when she marries her husband's friend, a sensitive and distinctly unmanly type. At the conclusion of the novel, the countess is twice widowed, and the only married couple still alive consists of an "Amazon" and the count's sensitive British friend. Gellert has, in every respect, undermined the traditional heterosexual relationship.

No account of eighteenth-century Germany is complete without consideration of Johann Wolfgang von Goethe (1749–1832). His connection with Winckelmann and Müller has already been mentioned. On the strength of his theoretical writings, it is possible to argue that Goethe believed in a basic human bisexuality; it may be the case that this word best describes Goethe as well. Homosexual phenomena occur frequently in his literary works. The planned prehistory of *Werther* strongly suggests the protagonist's homoerotic desire. The Storm and Stress poem "Ganymede" evokes a passive homosexuality. The *Roman Elegies*, product of Goethe's yearlong sojourn in Italy, have been interpreted as the veiled account of a gay love affair. In the diaries and letters that were the basis for his *Italian Journey* (translated into English by W. H. AUDEN), he describes the homoerotic subculture with interest and approval; in a letter to his patron Karl August, he praises homosexuality as a solution to prostitutes and venereal disease. In *Faust*, the homosexuality of Mephisto becomes increasingly evident, and insofar as the devil is no longer unequivocally condemned, homosexuality is not demonized. At the play's conclusion, Mephisto is distracted at the decisive moment when Faust's soul is "saved." The distraction: naked angels whose buttocks draw his gaze irresistibly away from Faust's corpse.

During his Roman sojourn, Goethe became acquainted with Karl Philipp Moritz (1757–1793), yet another bachelor, whom he dubbed "my unfortunate twin brother." Moritz's autobiographical novel *Anton Reiser* (1785–1790) tells the story of a young man who suffers physical deprivation and psychological turmoil, never expresses any interest in women, cross-dresses for the stage (his best role ever), and longs to meet Goethe in order to "serve him." The record of their intense and unusual relationship in Rome (Goethe tended to Moritz as he recovered from a broken arm) gives evidence of Moritz's tormented love for Goethe. Although Moritz died young, he wrote prolifically, as well as edited a remarkable journal of psychology, the *Magazin zur Erfahrungsseelenkunde* (1783–1793), which published a stream of first- and third-person accounts of psychological anomalies, among them homosexuality.

Historians of German literature, culture, and sexuality agree that the period of eighteenth-century tolerance concluded in the first decade of the nineteenth century. They call attention to the irony that this coincides with the abolition of Caroline law and the death penalty for sodomy. Johannes von Müller found no sympathy with the male Romantics (Friedrich and August Schlegel, Clemens Brentano, and Achim von Arnim), though the women poets (Carolina Schlegel and Bettina Brentano, for example) responded warmly to his work. Possible causes for the shift in attitude include the internalization of moral codes, the collapse of cosmopolitanism and the rise of nationalism, the return to Christian orthodoxy and the rejection of antiquity, and finally, the attraction of irrationalism. Lesbians and gays know that human reason is one of their best allies.

—*Simon Richter*

BIBLIOGRAPHY

Brall, Helmut. "Geschlechtlichkeit, Homosexualität, Freundesliebe: Über mannmännliche Liebe in mittelalterlicher Literatur." *Forum Homosexualität und Literatur* 13 (1991): 5–27. ■ Crompton, Louis. "The Myth of Lesbian Impunity: Capital Laws from 1270 to 1791." *Journal of Homosexuality* 6 (1980–1981): 11–25. ■ Derks, Paul. *Die Schande der heiligen Päderastie: Homosexualität und Öffentlichkeit in der deutschen Literatur 1750–1850.* Berlin: Rosa Winkel, 1990. ■ Fichte, Hubert. *Homosexualität und Literatur 1.* Frankfurt a/M: S. Fischer, 1987. ■ Jaeger, C. Stephen. "Mark and Tristan: The Love of Medieval Kings and their Courts." *In Hohem Prise: A Festschrift in Honor of Ernst S. Dick.* Winder McConnel, ed. Göppingen: Kümmerle, 1989. ■ Mohr, Heinrich. "Freundschaftliche Briefe–Literatur oder Privatsache? Der Streit um Wilhelm Gleims Nachlaß." *Jahrbuch des Freien Deutschen Hochstifts.* Detlev Lüders, ed. Tübingen: Max Niemeyer, 1973. ■ Neel, Caro. "The Origins of the Beguines." *Signs* 14 (1989): 321–341. ■ Richter, Simon. *Laocoon's Body and the Aesthetics of Pain: Winckelmann, Lessing, Herder, Moritz and Goethe.* Detroit: Wayne State University Press, 1992. ■ Spreitzer, Brigitte. *Die stumme Sünde: Homo-sexualität im Mittelalter.* Göppingen: Kümmerle, 1988. ■ Steakley, James D. "Sodomy in Enlightenment Prussia: From Execution to Suicide." *Journal of Homosexuality* 16 (1989): 163–175. ■ Strauch, Gabriele. "Mechthild von Magdeburg and the Category of *Frauenmystik*." *Die Frau als Protagonistin und Dichterin im Mittelalter.* Albrecht Classen, ed. Göppingen: Kümmerle, 1991.

German and Austrian Literature: Nineteenth and Twentieth Centuries

The story of gay and lesbian literature in the German-speaking countries during the nineteenth and twentieth centuries reflects the changing cultural definitions of "homosexual" and the differing meanings of homosexual identity over the decades. An evolving discourse around homosexuality gives rise to a broad multiplicity of literary representations of homosexual figures and conceptions of homosexuality. The examples that follow are largely from German literature because it has produced more works on the topic than have Austrian or Swiss literatures.

With the rise of industrial capitalism in central Europe during the first half of the nineteenth century, gender roles became ever more rigidly defined. Masculine and feminine were seen as natural opposites that would seek their complement in each other. These positions carried over into the bedroom, where sexual practices not aimed at reproduction were increasingly defined as signs of illness, rather than exclusively as indications of immorality, as was previously the case. One such illness was homosexuality, a desire that received this name only much later, in 1869. Terms such as sodomy, pederasty, boy-love, Uranian love, and others preceded it. Homosexuality was defined as a crossing of gender borders; thus, the homosexual was assigned the characteristics (dress, personality, preferences) of the opposite sex.

The perceived "effeminacy" of male homosexual authors and characters is a central feature of early nineteenth-century German literature. The best illustration of this phenomenon is the poet AUGUST VON PLATEN (1796–1835), who was attacked by his critics, especially by his rival poet Heinrich Heine, for being "effeminate." To these critics, his poetry seemed not only unmasculine but also offensive in its excessive praise of male beauty.

An early work evokes the theme of crossing gender borders while integrating another motif common to this literature: seeing ancient Greece as a utopia of male–male love. In the pastoral story, *Ein Jahr in Arkadien* (*A Year in Arcadia* [1805]) by August, Duke of Saxony-Gotha (1772–1822), a tender love grows between two young men in ancient Greece. The Romantic cult of Duke August's time allowed men to express deep affection for each other, but even some of the author's contemporaries felt that his characters (and Duke August himself) stepped over the bounds of manly affection into unseemly eroticism.

The Enlightenment philosophy that saw homosexuality as counter to the procreative demands of reason and nature could also be used to defend same-sex desire. Heinrich Hößli, an educated Swiss homosexual, recognized this possibility and turned to his countryman Heinrich Zschokke (1771–1848), a renowned author and political liberal, in the hope of providing such a defense in fiction. Hößli, not a professional author, supplied Zschokke with information, much of it otherwise unavailable to the public, about an infamous 1817 court case in which a thirty-two-year-old lawyer in Berlin murdered his younger lover when the latter tried to end their relationship. Zschokke transformed the case into a novella, *Der Eros oder Über die Liebe* (*Eros or Concerning Love* [1821]), turning it into the object of heterosexual debate. A group of middle-class family and friends discusses the murder of Walter by Lukasson, "the most abhorrent oddity of the day," and declare it to be the act of an insane person. The son of one of Lukasson's judges, Holmar, provides the countervoice. For him, the abhorrent character of the day lies in the execution of Lukasson. Lukasson was driven insane, Holmar believes, by a society that has debased the noble love of the Greeks. Unable to express his inner yearnings freely and naturally, poor Lukasson was, according to Holmar's reasoning, destroyed by the society that seeks to confine male–male erotic desire to avenues of aberrance. His listeners reject this thesis, and their judgment carries the most weight in the text. Extremely disappointed in the story, Hößli later wrote his own two-volume nonfiction defense of homosexual love, *Eros: Die Männerliebe der Griechen* (*Eros: The Male Love of the Greeks* [1836 and 1838]).

Similar themes appear in the stories and novels of Alexander von Sternberg (1806–1868), prolific au-

thor for a liberal middle-class audience. His novella *Jena und Leipzig* (*Jena and Leipzig* [1844]) tells of the love of one Prussian officer, Franz von Selbitz, for another, Andreas Walt. Andreas welcomes Franz's friendship but cannot answer his love because he is heterosexual. When Andreas falls in love with a woman, Franz breaks off their friendship, renounces love, and immerses himself in his military career.

Lesbians are not evident in the literary discourse of this era in texts, as objects or subjects, but most probably did participate via literary salons, which often formed around a woman who drew together like-minded friends of both genders. Letters, diaries, and poetry often provide evidence of lesbian life at the time, since in them women writers could voice the heartfelt sentiments and yearnings they felt for other women. Romanticism's focus on feeling and the inner life allowed same-sex desire a certain, although limited, expression. Realism and the literature of the *Gründerzeit* (1870–1885) closed off that safe space in which women could write about loving women, at least as far as literary historians have so far uncovered.

The Wilhelmine period, the era from about 1870 to 1918, saw sexologists and psychiatrists displace theologians and priests as arbiters of normality. The medical profession at this time concluded that in most cases homosexuality represented an inborn condition. Sexologists and psychiatrists, however, differed on whether that condition was to be interpreted as an illness or as a natural, healthy occurrence. Perhaps the most important figure in the early years of this medical discourse is Karl Heinrich Ulrichs (1825–1895), who was a philosopher (and tax assessor), but not a physician. He proposed that some people are born with the "soul" (character) of the opposite gender; therefore, their desire for someone of the same sex is natural. For them heterosexuality would be an unnatural state.

The creation of a homosexual identity and the extensive public discussion of the topic in journals and newspapers led to the development of a homosexual liberation movement aimed at abolishing the legal prohibition of sexual acts between males in Germany (Paragraph 175 of the Penal Code, the German sodomy law). All these factors influenced the portrayal of homosexual characters in German-language fiction during this period.

Adolf von Wilbrandt (1837–1911) wrote the first novel in German to present male–male desire as a phenomenon deserving of acceptance because it is natural for the person involved, *Fridolins heimliche Ehe* (*Fridolin's Secret Marriage* [1875]). A forty-year-old art history professor, Fridolin, explains himself to a young scientist friend as a man born with two natures, one feminine and one masculine. This dual nature Fridolin calls his "secret marriage," believing he can never love just one person because the two natures alternate in dominance. He is for a time attracted to women and then, when his feminine nature asserts itself, to men. However, he does indeed find fulfillment (love, not sex) with Ferdinand, the brother of Ottilie, to whom Fridolin had briefly been attracted, and the novel ends happily.

This work contains motifs that those that follow will employ again and again: the masculine–feminine duality of the homosexual, the role of medical opinion, the use of ancient Greek society as a kind of "Golden Age," a trip to Italy in search of love. Unlike the works to follow, however, here the man who loves a man does not have to die, nor is the relationship condemned.

As the medical model for homosexuality grew in strength, homosexual characters appeared in increasing numbers within German literature. Magnus Hirschfeld (1868–1935), whose theory of homosexuals as a "Third Sex" between the heterosexual male and heterosexual female was based on Ulrichs's ideas, became the most articulate voice in the debate about homosexuality. This Berlin physician founded the "Scientific-Humanitarian Committee," the most influential of the homosexual emancipation groups between 1896 and 1933, and he led the fight for social tolerance and the abolition of sodomy laws on the basis of the "naturalness" of homosexuality.

Employing Hirschfeld's concepts, some works argue vehemently for legal and social change so that homosexual love may be accepted within mainstream society. A typical example of this literature is Aimée Duc's (b. 1867) short novel Sind es Frauen? (Are These Women? [1901]). Subtitled "Roman über das dritte Geschlecht" ("Novel about the Third Sex"), the work makes no apologies for women taking up careers and loving one another. Instead, it proselytizes for the naturalness of such sexual preference and for the need of social change in order to accommodate the new roles women are creating for themselves. The novel follows the lives of a group of women college students in Geneva and traces in particular the sentimentalized love between two of them.

Perhaps the best known lesbian character in German literature of the time is the Gräfin Geschwitz in Frank Wedekind's (1864–1918) "Lulu" plays, Erdgeist (Earth Spirit [1895]) and Die Büchse der Pandora (Pandora's Box [1904]). The countess gives herself over so completely to her obsessive love for Lulu that Geschwitz, like all the men involved with the prostitute-temptress, loses her life. She sacrifices herself while trying to save her beloved from Jack the Ripper.

Hirschfeld's was not the only medical theory to influence literary portrayals. The Freudian view of homosexuality as a stage within adolescent development also became a significant theme although it never shaped works to the extraordinary degree that the Third Sex theory did. The main character of Robert Musil's (1880–1942) novella Die Verwirrungen des Zöglings Törleß (The Confusions of Young Törleß [1906]) experiences a homosexual episode at a boys' military school. One of the other boys, weaker and seemingly effeminate, is forced to submit to the sadistic sexual fantasies of two pupils. Törleß becomes at first a voyeur of their sexual acts, then a desirous participant. Finally, however, he rejects such activities, presumably having outgrown them.

In the Wilhelmine period, the fictional presentation of homosexuality in German literature gradually evolved via a literary (as opposed to a purely medico-scientific) discourse centered on characters who love individuals of their own gender. Some writers, like JOHN HENRY MACKAY, used literature to defend homosexual love against the condemnation of a hostile society. Others, like THOMAS MANN, employed homosexuality as a literary metaphor for the precarious position of those whom society deems "different." No matter the author's intent, several characteristics are shared by this body of literature. Physicians appear in many works and function most often as mouthpieces for the defense of homosexuality as a natural phenomenon. Even when he does not speak very loudly, the doctor serves to set the limits of social acceptance. No portrayal of sexual activity between members of the same sex is permitted. A kiss or an embrace is as far as the characters go, and they are satisfied with such brief tenderness. This desexualized love led, almost of necessity, to portraying the homosexual character as a tragic figure. This role of tragic outsider, the unjustly persecuted, was designed to evoke the sympathies of the heterosexual majority, just as the nonerotic relationship aimed not to offend the majority's sensibility. The tragedy of persecution was underscored by the death of almost every homosexual character during this period.

Some of these features may be found in the poetry of the time, but the freedom of the genre to avoid becoming trapped in meanings assigned from outside allows the expression of sentiments that would be decried if they were expressed with the clarity of prose. STEFAN GEORGE's (1856–1933) poems mask the homoerotic love that often motivates them, but that desire still speaks, usually to a genderless "You." In such works as Maximin, Ein Gedenkbuch (Maximin, A Memorial Book [1907]) and Der Stern des Bundes (The Star of the Union [1914]), George employs a hermetic, often symbolic language whose meaning was to be interpreted by an artistic, male elite, the "George-Circle."

The tentative and ambiguous homosexual identities of the Wilhelmine period grew into more complete and artistically successful characters during the increased freedoms that accompanied the Weimar years. During the Weimar Republic (1918–1933), the depiction of homosexual characters in German literature moved away from strict conformity to the medical model and explored other conceptions of the lives of people who love individuals of the same sex. The medico-scientific discourse on homosexuality never disappeared completely, but its power waxed and waned. Between the world wars, the dominant discourse influencing literary portrayals of homosexuality shifted from Hirschfeld to Freud.

Homosexual acts figure as a kind of substitute for the lack of female company in Peter Martin Lampel's (1894–1965) play *Revolte im Erziehungshaus (Revolts in the Educational Home* [1928]) and his novel *Verratene Jungen (Betrayed Boys* [1929]). This kind of psychological discourse about homosexuality still compelled the erasure of homosexual desire and still necessitated the destruction of the character who could not grow out of homosexuality, as in *Dr. Angelo* (1924) by Erich Ebermayer (1900–1970).

Between 1918 and 1933, the creation of homosexual identity, often in the face of opposition and condemnation by the majority, becomes the central theme in prose works and in dramas centering on homosexuality. Certainly, poets also dealt with the question of identity, but no significant volumes of poetry by openly homosexual authors were produced during the Weimar era. Nor were significant poems about homosexual love by nonhomosexual authors produced.

In the novels of the period, the homosexual often takes the identity of the sexual-social outsider, as, for example, in KLAUS MANN's works. The orientation itself is no longer the "problem" of the literary work, but the homosexual figure cannot find a place within his or her society to survive, much less flourish. The attempts of the majority society to punish homosexuals who transgress the narrow confines of a socially allotted space are depicted in John Henry Mackay's (1864–1933) *Puppenjunge (The Hustler* [1926]) and Hans Siemsen's (1891–1969) *Verbotene Liebe (Forbidden Love* [1927]).

Whereas these two novels were directed mostly at a homosexual readership, Ferdinand Bruckner's (pseud. of Theodor Tagger, 1891–1958) plays *Krankheit der Jugend (Disease of Youth* [1926]) and *Die Verbrecher (The Criminals* [1928]) sought to rouse liberal, heterosexual sympathies for the plight of the unjustly persecuted homosexual. Were this persecu-

tion to continue, Bruckner implied, the homosexual might become a psychopathic outlaw, as he is indeed depicted in Arnolt Bronnen's (1845–1959) *Die Septembernovelle (September Novella* [1923]).

Lesbians, in particular, fared poorly in the fiction of this period, although they, too, appeared in greater numbers. The lesbian as an antisocial, unnatural, destructive force fuels Hans Kaltneker's (1895–1919) moral drama, *Die Schwester (The Sister* [written 1919, premiered 1922]). Women who are abused in marriages to men turn to each other for love and then for revenge on one of the husbands in Alfred Döblin's (1878–1957) novella, *Die beiden Freundinnen und ihr Giftmord (The Two Girlfriends and Their Murder by Poison* [1924]), based on an actual court trial.

By far the more aesthetically successful works of the Weimar period, and ones that resonated more deeply among lesbian readers, were written by the two best-known lesbian authors of the era, CHRISTA WINSLOE (1888–1944) and ANNA ELISABET WEIRAUCH (1887–1970). Winsloe told the story of Manuela Meinhardis, a girl who commits suicide when her love for her teacher is crushed by the authoritarian school that traps them both: *Mädchen in Uniform (Girls in Uniform* [1931]), best known in the film version. Weirauch's trilogy, *Der Skorpion (The Scorpion* [1919, 1920, 1931]), traces the path Mette Rudloff takes toward a lesbian identity of her own, not one modeled on the futile or misleading identities she encounters in the women she loves along the way.

Germany's greatest dramatist of the twentieth century, BERTOLT BRECHT (1895–1956), wrote quite often about male homosexual desire in his early works. There it is something amoral, even immoral, that upsets or destroys the normal order of things, whether that be heterosexual affairs (*Baal* [1918–1922]), the so-called rules of life aboard a pirates' ship ("Bargan läßt es sein," ["Bargan Lets Things Be"], 1921), the "friendship" of two gangsters (*Im Dickicht der Städte [In the Jungle of the Cities]*, 1924), or a political system (*Leben Eduards II [Life of Edward II]*, 1924).

The burgeoning homosexual subculture of the Weimar period produced a "Trivialliteratur" (popular literature) aimed specifically at a homosexual readership. Gay and lesbian newspapers and magazines printed stories and poems; small publishing houses brought out novellas, short story collections, and novels. All these works shared a belief that homosexual love was natural although bound to be persecuted by a homophobic society. In its naturalness lay its beauty (often heavily romanticized); in its persecution lay its tragedy (often steeped in bathos). In Erich Ernst's novel *Symphonie des Eros (Symphony of Eros* [1925]), a typical example, a high school teacher falls in love with one of his students. Despite the resistance of family and school authorities, homosexual love triumphs in this novel, as it also does in Max Schneider's *Glück* (*Happiness* [1927]).

By the late Weimar years, most works took a liberal, generally tolerant attitude toward homosexuality, as illustrated by the gay secondary characters in *Esch oder die Anarchie* (*Esch or Anarchy* [1931]) by Hermann Broch (1886–1951) and *Die Wandlung der Susanne Dasseldorf* (*The Transformation of Susanne Dasseldorf* [1932]) by Joseph Breitbach (1903–1980). Nonetheless, the place allotted to homosexuals generally remained that of outsider. Either the nature of same-sex desire remained fundamentally unacceptable or the character was unable to express that desire. Arnold Zweig's (1887–1968) novel *De Vriendt kehrt heim* (*De Vriendt Returns Home* [1932]), based on the life of the Jewish poet Jacob Israel de Haan, describes a lawyer and professor who becomes a political leader in Jerusalem. He falls from power when his love for an Arab boy becomes public knowledge. In the novella *Verwirrung der Gefühle* (*Confusion of Feelings* [1927]), Stefan Zweig (1881–1942) depicts a character who is tragically unable to build a homosexual identity. His story is sympathetically narrated by his former student, who rejected the professor's desire but never his mentor.

For the most part, the literary discourse on homosexuality between the wars did not search for identities that violated the norms of a bourgeois moral code. (BRUNO VOGEL's [1898–1987] works, especially *Alf* [1929], are exceptions; they refuse to concede the right to control males who love other males to any authority.) The development of the homosexual character moves not toward opposition but quite emphatically toward integration. By the late Weimar years, homosexual characters who had so often given up the ghost under the heel of heterosexual condemnation now refuse to die and begin to fight back. Yet the promise that the literary presentation of homosexuality seemed about to fulfill—namely, the erasure of the stigma of difference—remained a distant dream. The stamp of difference was reapplied in German society with a vengeance in the Nazi era.

During the Third Reich (1933–1945), homosexuality quickly became an unspeakable theme within acceptable National Socialist literature. It was considered an attribute of Jewish or decadent (that is, non-Aryan) lifestyles, aimed at undermining the natural divisions between masculine and feminine. Prior to 1933, however, this was not always the case in proto-fascist or right-wing fiction, which sometimes included homosexual characters, as, for example, in *Partenau* by Max René Hesse (1885–1952).

Some authors who went into exile in the Hitler years did continue to depict homosexuals, but difference remains their hallmark, as in Klaus Mann's novels from exile. Hans Siemsen's antifascist novel *Die Geschichte des Hitlerjungen Adolf Goers* (*The Story of the Hitler Youth Adolf Goers*, written in 1938, first published in English in 1940) tries to differentiate between the true homosexual love felt by two of its characters and the situational homosexuality involving forced sex between some Hitler Youth leaders and their charges. A similar attempt to rescue male–male love from its National Socialist perversions occurs in Ludwig Renn's (1889–1979) *Vor großen Wandlungen* (*Before Great Changes* [1936]).

In the post-war world of rebuilding infrastructure and restoring social order, gay and lesbian characters returned mostly to the closet. They functioned as secondary figures bearing the meanings assigned by stereotype. In Wolfgang Koeppen's (b. 1906) novel about Germany's failure to come to terms with its Nazi past, *Der Tod in Rom* (*Death in Rome* [1954]), the nephew of a former SS-general is gay. He is a composer, is attracted to boys, and the locale is Italy; in short, it incorporates many of the old stereotypes.

The "Trivialliteratur" produced by the homophile movement continued the Weimar tradition of magazine fiction and poetry. The Swiss journal *Der Kreis* (*The Circle*) gave voice to a variety of male homosexual experiences. Published from 1939 to 1967, the magazine reached an international audience and often printed stories in German, French, and English.

Weimar traditions are also continued in the prose works of Hans Henny Jahnn (1894–1959). His lengthy, often monumental novels, some of which were published in their unfinished form after his death, center on male friendships that often are erotic, excessive, and incapable of union (*Perrudja*, vol. 1 1929, vol. 2 1968; *Fluß ohne Ufer* [*River without Shore*], 3 vols. 1949 and 1961; *Jeden ereilt es* [*Each One Is Overtaken*], 1968).

A great admirer of Jahnn, HUBERT FICHTE (1935–1986) stands alone as the one post-war author who presents homosexuality without apology, graphically, and with a challenging, modernist language. Taken together, his novels, published between 1965 and 1974, construct a gay identity: *Das Waisenhaus* (*The Orphanage* [1965]), *Die Palette* (*The Palette* [1968]), and *Versuch über die Pubertät* (*Treatise Concerning Puberty* [1974]).

The gay liberation movement came slowly to the German-speaking countries, so a sharp increase in production by and about gay and lesbian people first appears in the 1980s. Prior to that, individual works appeared, but no general liberationist trend can be discerned. In Ingeborg Bachmann's (1926–1973) story "Ein Schritt nach Gomorrah" ("A Step towards Gomorrah," in the collection *Das dreißigste Jahr [The Thirtieth Year]* [1961]), a lesbian offers another woman the chance to break out of her unfulfilling marriage, but she cannot take it. In Martin Sperr's (b. 1944) drama *Jagdszenen aus Niederbayern (Hunting Scenes from Lower Bavaria* [1966]), a homosexual man becomes the latest victim of a fascist mentality still alive in German society.

Influenced by the American gay liberation movement of the 1970s, the new consciousness of an affirmative, politicized gay identity finally produced a new kind of German literature: *Verständigungstexte* (roughly: communicative texts). Mostly nonprofessional, these authors wrote autobiographical sketches, poems, and short stories about their own experiences, using literature as a means toward emancipation. Through this kind of writing, gays talked to each other, created their own identities, and found their voices. Anthologies such as *Schwule schreiben (Gays Write* [1977]) and *Andere Verhältnisse (Other Relationships* [1984]) were common.

Two books from 1975 spoke directly to the experiences and desires of lesbians and gay men. Verena Stefan's (b. 1947) *Häutungen (Sheddings* [1975]) narrates the growth of Cloe, the main character, from a naive young woman who defines herself through relationships with men to a strong, independent female in control of her life. Crucial in shedding these skins of tradition and oppression are the love relationships she forms with other women. Alexander Ziegler's (1944–1987) *Die Konsequenz (The Consequence* [1975]) reached enormous audiences when Wolfgang Petersen's 1977 film adaptation was shown on national television in all the German-speaking countries. The autobiographical story of a love destroyed because society deems it unacceptable and illegal, *Die Konsequenz* renders this love understandable and sympathetic. The film's romantic tone underscored the novel's plea for tolerance and resonated so deeply that Petersen brought out a volume of letters he had received from viewers, *Die Resonanz (The Resonance* [1980]).

Another book that voiced experiences common to gays and lesbians and that achieved much critical attention is Ronald Schernikau's (1960–1991) *kleinstadtnovelle (small town story* [1980]), published when its author was only nineteen years old. Its unique style (a mixture of first- and third-person perspectives, lack of capitalization, minimal punctuation) helped make the novella more than the usual coming-out story, especially by connecting the personal narrative to the political context in which all desire lives. With the support of his mother, the main character (identi-

fied only as "b") refuses to capitulate to institutionalized homophobia and ultimately escapes the confines of the small-town mentality that would silence him.

The number of lesbian characters in German literature increased enormously in the 1980s. (One critic has found only five works in which lesbians appeared between 1950 and 1969, but 130 in the 1980s.) The women's movement of the 1970s produced new kinds of literature and opened space for lesbian experience to be included in ways never before possible. An example is Marlene Stenten's (b. 1935) *Albina* (1986), which describes the dissolution of a lesbian relationship without laying blame for its demise on society or even on the partners. These qualities are new in lesbian fiction and bear the positive influence of feminist philosophies.

A few male authors have made careers by writing about gay topics for a largely gay audience. Detlev Meyer (b. 1950) is a gifted poet, satirical cultural critic, and successful novelist. His works present a portrait of gay life painted with both humor and affection. He is equally well known for poems about love and desire (*Heute nacht im Dschungel [Tonight in the Jungle]*, 1981; *Stehen Männer an den Grachten [When Men Are Standing at the Canals]*, 1990) and for the trilogy of novels under the title *Biographie der Bestürzung (Biography of Dismay)*: *Im Dampfbad greift nach mir ein Engel (In the Sauna an Angel Reaches out to Me* [1985]); *David steigt aufs Riesenrad (David Climbs upon the Ferris Wheel* [1987]); and *Ein letzter Dank den Leichtathleten (A Final Thanks to the Track Athletes* [1989]). The trilogy tells the story of two lovers, Dorn and Viktor, and their female friend Todora.

These late twentieth-century authors are connected to much earlier gay writers. For example, Ziegler, Schernikau, and Meyer, each in his own way, take up the theme of the gay man yearning for one man with whom to share his love. Like earlier writers, they also depict the difficulties, from without or within, of living and loving in an intolerant society.

Two Swiss novelists take up those themes and the larger tradition in slightly different ways. Guido Bachmann (b. 1940) connects the love between men to mythic homosexual archetypes in his trilogy *Zeit und Ewigkeit (Time and Eternity)*: *Gilgamesh*, 1967; *Die Parabel (The Parable)*, 1978; and *Echnaton*, 1982. Christoph Geiser (b. 1949) explores the presence of the past in gay life today. *Das geheime Fieber (Secret Fever* [1987]) is a novel about a man who becomes obsessed with the painter Caravaggio. In *Das Gefängnis der Wünsche (The Prison of Wishes* [1992]), the German poet Goethe and the MARQUIS DE SADE return to life in present-day Berlin.

The 1980s and 1990s in German gay literature have shown many similar developments to those in other Western countries. Genre fiction (such as detective novels) and photo books have increased in popularity. Probably the most widely read German gay author today is Ralf König (b. 1960), who writes and illustrates comic novels. AIDS has begun to appear as a theme in gay fiction while taking its toll among writers, critics, and readers. (Schernikau died of AIDS in 1991.) Meyer's *Ein letzter Dank den Leichtathleten* was one of the first works of fiction to grapple with the difficulty of writing about AIDS. The interior monologue of a man frozen by fear when diagnosed as HIV-positive is featured in Christoph Klimke's (b. 1959) story *Der Test* (1992) and in Mario Wirz's (b. 1956) autobiographical "report" *Es ist spät, ich kann nicht atmen* (*It Is Late, I Cannot Breathe* [1992]). The interiority of autobiographical fiction also characterizes Napoleon Seyfarth's (b. 1953) *Scwheine müssen nackt sein* (*Pigs Have to Be Naked* [1991]).

As with gay and lesbian literature itself, literary criticism of that fiction has been slow in developing. There has as yet been no outpouring of articles and books on this diverse literature. One academic journal (*FORUM*) exists, one publishing house is devoted exclusively to gay literature (Verlag rosa Winkel in Berlin), and one university offers courses in gay and lesbian studies (Siegen). But interest from all sides has increased—from the literary establishment, from the general public, from gay and lesbian critics and readers. Recent scholarly publications and the careers of some of the authors mentioned here indicate a promising future.

—*James W. Jones*

BIBLIOGRAPHY

Campe, Joachim, ed. *Andere Lieben. Homosexualität in der deutschen Literatur. Ein Lesebuch*. Frankfurt am Main: Suhrkamp, 1988. ■ Derks, Paul. *Die Schande der heiligen Päderastie. Homosexualität und Öffentlichkeit in der deutschen Literatur 1750-1850*. Berlin: Verlag rosa Winkel, 1990. ■ Faderman, Lillian and Brigitte Eriksson, ed. *Lesbians in Germany: 1890's-1920's*. 2d ed. [Original title: Lesbianism-Feminism in Turn-of-the-Century Germany (1980)] Tallahassee, Fla.: Naiad Press, 1990. ■ Hohmann, Joachim S., ed. *Der heimliche Sexus. Homosexuelle Belletristik in Deutschland von 1900 bis heute*. Frankfurt am Main: Foerster, 1979. ■ Jones, James W. *"We of the Third Sex": Literary Representations of Homosexuality in Wilhelmine Germany*. New York: Peter Lang, 1990. ■ Marti, Madeleine. *Hinterlegte Botschaften. Die Darstellung lesbischer Frauen in der deutschsprachigen Literatur seit 1945*. 2d ed. Stuttgart: J.B. Metzler, 1992. ■ Popp, Wolfgang. *Männerliebe. Homosexualität und Literatur*. Stuttgart: J.B. Metzler, 1992. ■ Vollhaber, Tomas. *Das Nichts. Die Angst. Die Erfahrung. Untersuchung zur zeitgenössischen schwulen Literatur*. Berlin: Verlag rosa Winkel, 1987.

Ghazali, Mehemmed
(d. 1535)

Ottoman erotic literature imitates Arabic and Persian. Most of it was composed for sultans and other dignitaries and frequently stresses the therapeutic value of pederasty. Most of this literature is tasteless and boring. The one major exception is the work of Mehemmed Ghazali, known as Deli Birader or "Stupid Brother." Ghazali was a scholar and poet born in the second half of the fifteenth century in Bursa, where he later became professor of Sufism, although soon afterward he joined the court of Crown Prince Qorqud, son of Sultan Bayezid II (d. 1512), in Manisa near the Aegean coast of Turkey.

At the court of Crown Prince Qorqud, Ghazali composed a pornographic allegorical work in seven chapters called "The Repellers of Troubles and the Remover of Anxieties," which he dedicated to Piyale Pasha, who belonged to the Crown Prince's inner circle. The style of the work is terse prose, punctuated here and there by witty poems composed according to the strictest rules of Muslim poetics. Linguistically, the book is very important because it contains vocabulary not found in ordinary literature. It was coldly received, however. Nevertheless, Ghazali remained at court until the Crown Prince was executed in 1512 by his brother Selim I. Having returned to Bursa with the intention of settling down to a quiet life, his restlessness caused him to travel. His scholarship and poetry made him popular and he returned to teaching. At some point, he moved to Istanbul, where he built a compound containing a garden, a mosque, a convent, and a bathhouse, which he turned into a pleasure house. The heavy traffic of boys made the neighbors uncomfortable, and city officials finally destroyed the compound. The next time we hear of Ghazali he is in Mecca, where he rebuilt his compound, but no further information about him survives save that he died in 1535.

The main topic of "The Repeller of Troubles and the Remover of Anxieties" is sex. One of the poems extols the therapeutic value of intercourse, especially for gay men, for whom God created the anus to provide immeasurable pleasure. The second chapter contains the description of a contest between boy-lovers and woman-lovers, which at one point turns into a bloody battle. "When the boy-lovers heard the woman-lovers disparage the asshole they gathered in flocks from near and far," and the conflict rages on, with penises as standards and testicles as maces. Needless to say, the boy-lovers carry the day! At the end of the contest, the leader of the woman-lovers is over-come and converts to the other camp. The account of the contest ends with a praise of the anus: "Sometimes it opens up like a thousand roses and laughs, sometimes it closes like a rosebud and falls silent. . . ."

—*Shinasi Tekin*

BIBLIOGRAPHY

Alpay, G. "Ghazali, Mehmed." *The Encyclopaedia of Islam: New Edition*. 4 vols. Leiden: Brill, 1965. 2: 1042–1043.

Ghost and Horror Fiction

Fear of the "other" has provoked fantasies and stories of the occult and supernatural for centuries. Behavior that appears to be contrary to society's norms has traditionally been regarded as unconventional, perverse, antireligious, or taboo. Throughout literature, but particularly since the nineteenth century, ghosts and goblins, witches and vampires, and other demonic creatures are evoked to symbolize the radically different and are ascribed thoughts and deeds that are marginalized or suppressed in daily life. It is no wonder that homosexuality appears so often in the context of the supernatural since it transgresses the conventional imaginations and violates the religious practices of average readers. Homosexuality is not, however, the only "other" to be found in ghost and horror fiction. Members of minority racial, ethnic, and religious groups, the emotionally disturbed or physically disabled, and the cloistered religious all also lead lives beyond the narrow scope of everyday life for most readers. In ghost and horror fiction, they too are evoked—alongside homosexuals—as the feared and despised but nonetheless fascinating "other."

Ghost and horror fiction is an umbrella term for stories of the occult, of terrifying acts of antisocial behavior, of physical and psychological horror, as well as of witchcraft, vampirism, and the demonic. The category encompasses elements of the Gothic tradition, such as dark castles, sadistic monks, ruined maidens, and bloody vampires, while its more contemporary examples add such horror fixtures as homicidal psychopaths, voodoo cults, pastoral evil, and science experiments gone wrong. Heathen rituals, blasphemous practices, and ghostly figures appear throughout the category's long history, but quite apart from its external features, the genre's primary and defining focus is the element of evil itself. Horror allows us to confront the issue of evil in our everyday lives by vicariously confronting unknown creatures and events, or, even more alarmingly, by exploring the evil within our neighbors and inside ourselves. Unlike fantasy or SCIENCE FICTION, most of the events in horror fiction take place in the natural world as we know it, instead of in constructed futures or on planets beyond the galaxy.

Homosexuality or homosexual elements appear throughout the broad scope of horror fiction beginning with the early Gothic tradition. WILLIAM BECKFORD's enormously popular *History of the Caliph Vathek* (1786) helped set the terms in which homosexuality was to be incorporated into the Gothic tradition. Since Beckford was widely rumored to be a homosexual, his tale was regarded as loosely autobiographical; indeed, the beautiful male prince who is the romance's protagonist may have been patterned on Beckford's lover. If the story is autobiographical, however, it reveals a great deal of self-loathing and perhaps a desire for punishment. It concerns a greedy Arabic hero who will do anything for money and power. His adventures take him through every conceivable vice and crime until he is finally doomed to everlasting misery. Another early work with lesbian elements is Denis Diderot's *La Religieuse* (1796), which tells the story of a young woman placed in a convent by her parents. She is lustfully pursued by the evil mother superior and assaulted by other demonic nuns. This work clearly views the cloistered religious environment as the source of "unnatural" desire, a frequent motif in gothic fiction.

OSCAR WILDE's *The Portrait of Dorian Gray* (1890) pivots on a gothic plot device by which a narcissistic young man makes a Faustian bargain to preserve his youthful beauty. The novel depicts a triangular relationship between the beautiful Dorian Gray and two older men, the painter Basil Hallward and the cynical aristocrat Lord Henry Wotton. The diabolism of the plot—as epitomized in Dorian's exchange of his soul for a portrait that grows old in his stead—culminates in the protagonist's murder of Basil. Finally, in an attempt to destroy his conscience altogether, he stabs the portrait, only to kill himself. The novel can be read as an allegory of homosexual ambivalence in which homosexuality is guilt-inducing and dangerous, yet also creative and alluring.

The nineteenth century's preoccupation with death found an outlet in its popular fiction, which reflects the attraction of spiritualism. Horror stories of the period frequently concentrate on the interaction between the living and the dead. Dead children, ancestral ghosts, vampires, mediums, and seances all regularly appear as characters or plot elements. Spirits walk among the living, spreading evil and influencing behavior. They have the most effect on women and their sexuality. Two poetic examples of female interaction with unearthly creatures are Samuel Taylor Coleridge's "Christabel" (1816) and CHRISTINA ROSSETTI's "Goblin Market" (1859). In each poem, the consequence of a young female protagonist's encounters with a supernatural being is an initiation into lesbian experience.

Reflecting the period's general ambivalence toward female sexuality, nineteenth-century horror fiction presents it as a force to be feared and suppressed, lest it "devour" innocent men and women. This is the point of one of the early lesbian vampire stories, Sheridan LeFanu's *Carmilla* (1872). In this tale, the heroine sleeps under the same roof as the beautiful vampire Carmilla, which sets the stage for lesbian interaction between the living and the dead. Same-sex sexual interaction between the dead and the living is, indeed, a staple of vampire stories generally. *The Vampyre* (1819) by John Polidori, a companion of LORD BYRON, recounts the relationship between a mortal and a noble vampire; it may be loosely based on Polidori's own relationship with Byron. The most famous vampire story of all, Bram Stoker's *Dracula* (1897), features same-sex interaction between the characters Lucy and Mina. Both women are asexual and submissive until Lucy begins to evolve into a vampire. As in Le Fanu's *Carmilla*, it takes a male hero to desex the female vampire by the use of a stake or sword and religion. Homosexual attachments are also found in *Sardia: A Story of Love* (1891) by Cora Lynn Daniels and in *True Story of a Vampire* (1894) by Count Stanislaus Stenbock. The latter story, which self-consciously revels in decadence, is a tale of fulfilled love between the hero and the vampire.

In the twentieth century, several authors have drawn sympathetic portraits of gay, lesbian, and bisexual vampires. George Viereck, who from all accounts was himself pansexual, created a bisexual vampire heroine on a quest for true love in *Gloria* (1952). His earlier novel, *The House of the Vampire* (1907), which features "psychic vampirism," is also notably homoerotic. In *Interview with a Vampire* (1976), the first novel of her enormously popular vampire series, Anne Rice introduces the likable vampire lovers, Louis and Lestat. As a young man, Louis is turned into a vampire by Lestat, who is older, more experienced, and irresistibly beautiful. The two live together, sleep and travel together, and eventually create a family with the child-turned-vampire Claudia. In *Hotel Transylvania* (1978) and *Blood Games* (1979), Chelsea Quinn Yarbro's bisexual vampire St. Germain becomes involved in complex human relationships. In *The Hunger* (1981), Whitley Strieber creates the beautiful bisexual Miriam, who possesses an elegant lifestyle and an attic full of the remains of dead lovers. Until her fateful encounter with Sarah, a sleep researcher, she has managed to pass as human for centuries.

One of the distinctions of Anne Rice's vampire world is that it features homosexual relationships between vampires as well as between the living and the dead, an innovation that other writers have adopted. In his Lambda-Award-winning stories "Hell Is for Children" (1989) and "Somewhere in the Night" (1989), Jeffrey McMahan features Andres, an out-of-the-closet vampire who cruises for a mate. In *The Gilda Stories* (1991), Jewelle Gomez presents the first African-American lesbian vampire, Gilda, who struggles to preserve herself in the years after slavery. Her relationship with the Native-American vampire, Bird, is central to the novel. Anna Livia's recent novel *Minimax* (1992) features legendary lesbians NATALIE BARNEY and RENÉE VIVIEN in a comic portrayal of vampire life. In *Lost Souls* (1992), horror writer Poppy Z. Brite combines evil, parapsychology, and an unforgettable trio of vampires. Not only does the novel feature homosexual relations between the vampires themselves and their human victims, but Brite introduces Ghost, the half-vampire teenager who has an intense homosexual encounter with a vampire who turns out to be his father.

Homosexual and bisexual vampires are not the only creatures with alternative lifestyles to appear in the pages of horror stories. Openly lesbian writer Natalie Clifford Barney features a hermaphrodite in her novel *The One Who Is Legion; or, A.D.'s After-Life* (1930). Here the spirit of the hermaphrodite, who resembles her former lover Renée Vivien, is assumed by the living body of a young woman. The more sinister *Lay of Maldoror* (1924), written by Comte de Lautréamont (pseudonym of Isidore Ducasse), presents a horrific environment in which demons and hermaphrodites are involved in a variety of homosexual and sadomasochistic acts. In this macabre work, male homosexuality is presented positively. What little tenderness there is in the *Lay of Maldoror* is directed toward beautiful boys, though they are tortured and sacrificed.

In the first third of this century, several novels were published with transsexual characters. These works include Barry Pain's *Exchange of Souls* (1911), Isador Schneider's *Dr. Transit* (1925), and Thorne Smith's *Turnabout* (1931). Since transsexuality is a subject that falls beyond the scope of the average reader and evokes a wide range of responses, some similar to but others quite different from those evoked by homosexuality, it is not surprising that it too became a thematic element in many horror and science-fiction works.

Both early and recent ghost tales include homosexual elements. HENRY JAMES's *The Turn of the Screw* (1898) presents both male and female ghosts and contains both male homosexual and lesbian overtones. The story hinges on a young governess's belief that her deceased predecessor and the dead valet Peter Quint have returned to possess the children—a boy and girl—in her charge. Several critics have commented on the homosexual elements in the plot, especially relative to the former governess's relations with the young girl and the valet's possible corruption of the boy. Another of James's ghost stories, "The Jolly Corner" (1908), is susceptible to a gay reading as an allegory in which the ghost represents the narrator's (and author's) repressed homosexuality. Two of E. F. BENSON's supernatural tales include homosexual elements: *The Inheritor* (1930) is a story about a supernatural curse, and *Raven's Brood* (1934), the account of a family in Cornwall and their experiences with evil rituals and demons, features a son who is involved in a homosexual relationship.

Shirley Jackson's celebrated *Haunting of Hill House* (1959) is strongly woman identified, as the character of Eleanor struggles with her feelings toward Theodora and her dead mother. *A Ghost Story* by Ada Trevanian (1858) is a romantic ghost tale of a teacher and a young girl, while the more recent "Ghost of Champ McQuest" (1988) by Ethan Mordden has gay men being harassed by a ghost on Fire Island. MAUREEN DUFFY's *The Microcosm* (1966) is a lesbian novel involving the ghosts of many women who visited the same bar. Stephen King, the prolific modern horror writer, links ghosts and homosexuality in his novel *The Shining* (1977). Vincent Varga's *Gaywick* (1980), a gothic romance set in Long Island at the turn of the century, is an entertaining adaptation of the genre. Featuring many gay characters, including a hero who is as attractive as he is wealthy, *Gaywick* self-consciously attempts to reclaim for gay readers a genre in which gay men and lesbians are often portrayed as villainous.

Even without ghosts, vampires, and demons, nasty things can happen to homosexual people in fiction. Numerous short stories and novels depict homosexual or bisexual people as victims of evil-doers. Clive Barker, for example, includes many positive homosexual images in his writing, and some gay villains as well. Gay characters can be found in *In the Hills, the Cities* (1984), where a vacationing gay couple becomes involved in gory rituals; in *Age of Desire* (1986), where gays are the victims of sexual assault; and in *Human Remains* (1984), which involves evil bisexuals and a young male prostitute. A particularly nasty villain is the evil lesbian Tascela of Robert Howard's *Red Nails* (1936), who kidnaps and tortures another woman. A gay man bent on revenge is the main character in Jeffrey McMahan's short story, "Dark Red Day" (1989), where the villain tries to wreak revenge on his first lover back in their hometown.

Although some openly gay contemporary horror writers such as Vincent Varga, Felice Picano, and Michael McDowell have pioneered by targeting a gay audience for their work and employing homosexuality as a central element of their fiction, they have done so by building on a long tradition rather than creating a new one. In addition to the classic titles mentioned in this essay, such as Bram Stoker's *Dracula* or Wilde's *The Picture of Dorian Gray*, tales published in specialized horror magazines also contributed to the linkage of homoeroticism and horror. These magazines, which flourished during the 1920s and 1930s and bore such titles as *Weird Tales* and *Strange Tales*, were aimed at adolescent boys and often contained subtle homosexual elements. (See also ENGLISH LITERATURE: ROMANTICISM and GOTHICISM.)

—*Catherine Geddis*

BIBLIOGRAPHY

Barron, Neil, ed. *Horror Literature: A Reader's Guide.* New York: Garland, 1990. ■ Carpenter, Lynette, and Wendy Kolmar. *Haunting the House of Fiction.* Knoxville: University of Tennessee Press, 1993. ■ Carter, Margaret. *The Vampire in Literature: A Critical Bibliography.* Ann Arbor: University Microfilms, 1989. ■ Castle, Terry. *The Apparitional Lesbian: Female Homosexuality and Modern Culture.* New York: Columbia University Press, 1993. ■ Garber, Eric, and Palio, Lynn. *Uranian Worlds: A Guide to Alternative Sexuality in Science Fiction, Fantasy and Horror.* Boston: G.K. Hall, 1990.

Gide, André
(1869–1951)

André Paul Guillaume Gide was born in Paris on November 22, 1869, at what he later termed a "crossroads," the intersection of his father Paul's southern, Huguenot, and modest upbringing, and his mother Juliette Rondeaux's Norman, bourgeois, and wealthy background. After the death of his father—an eminent professor of law in Paris—on October 28, 1880, the young André was surrounded during his early years almost exclusively by women: his mother, his Rondeaux aunts, his mother's English domestic Anna Shakelton, and his Rouen cousins. Because of several changes of domicile after his father's death, he received a rather fragmented education, attending the École Alsacienne, the École Henri IV, and the Lycée Montpellier. Yet despite these various uprootings, the females in his life instilled in him a sense of strict Protestant morality, modesty, obedience, social conformity, and duty—values against which Gide struggled and revolted his entire life. His early years were thus frustrating and unsettling. In his autobiography *Si le grain ne meurt* (*If It Die*, 1921); Gide describes a possible early revelation of a homosexual orientation. The young André, in tears in his mother's arms, declares that he is unlike the other schoolboys. As a youth, Gide suffered from fits, headaches, insomnia, unexplainable fatigue, and feelings of insecurity, the physical and mental manifestations of an unsettling and confused childhood.

Writing offered Gide a means of stabilization and the opportunity to put his life's experiences in order. By meticulously recording and reordering his feelings, experiences, and desires, Gide was able, as he remarked in *Si le grain ne meurt,* to "give form to a confused inner agitation." His philosophy evolved slowly as his own life experiences broadened. The major sources of inspiration of his writing were his relationships, friendships, and travels. Gide wove these experiences into his texts, and yet they represent more than mere sources of subject matter. As recorded in print, they are essential fragments that together compose the vast Gidian intertextual mosaic, where each work helps illuminate, and at times complicate, the reading of another. Through writing, Gide attempted to repair his childhood and his guilt. His diverse oeuvre, which numbers more than sixty titles and in which are represented nearly all literary genres, is remarkable not only on a personal level, but also on a cultural and historical one, for it gives the modern reader insights into the social and political issues of the time. Gide's style is precise, sensitive, refined, and subtle. Two important themes recur in his texts: the conflict between individual and social desires and rights, and the rebellion against traditional values and morals.

Attracted by the symbolist poet Mallarmé and his circle, Gide wrote early works such as *Les Cahiers d'André Walter* (*The Notebooks of André Walter,* published anonymously in 1891), *Le Traité de Narcisse* (*The Treatise on Narcissus,* 1891), and *Le Voyage d'Urien* (*Urien's Voyage,* 1893) that are somewhat more impersonal than his later ones. His literary career began with *Les Cahiers d'André Walter,* which is the story of a young man's love for his orphaned cousin Emmanuèle—a relationship enriched through books and religion. Walter struggles against his own corporal desires (the beast within him) and aspires to achieve a pure and idyllic love, untainted by physical contact. Then on her deathbed, Walter's mother asks her son to end this relationship. André envisions a plan that will cause Emmanuèle to disapprove of him and thus in this way he will merit her even more for having sacrificed his love. As with many of his works, *Les Cahiers* is loosely autobiographical, and in fact Gide draws many passages directly from his personal journal.

Around 1892, inspired by his readings of Goethe and Nietzsche, and influenced in part by OSCAR WILDE, whom he had met in Paris in 1891, Gide left behind symbolist influences and began to realize that he could express without hesitancy his true thoughts and desires. He adopted a more romantic style, one that more freely expressed his growing feeling of individualism, but that continued nonetheless to be restrained by an inescapable sense of obedience to conventional morality. At the age of twenty-four, however, Gide embarked for North Africa with his painter friend Paul A. Laurens. This trip was a rebirth for André, for in North Africa he discovered sexual feelings and desires that were formerly repressed. He participated in his first homosexual encounter with Ali, an Arab youth, as related in the pages of his autobiography *Si le grain ne meurt.*

Three important events took place in Gide's life in 1895. He returned to North Africa where he met up with Oscar Wilde and ALFRED DOUGLAS, and had further adventures with young Arab boys. Then his mother died in May, an event that marked Gide's further liberation from his inhibitions and constraints. Finally, in anticipation of his impending marriage to his cousin Madeleine Rondeaux in October, he consulted a doctor, for despite his newly found sexual freedom, he feared that his promiscuity in Algeria and Tunisia had not properly prepared him for marriage. The doctor, however, declared that Gide would forget his immoral penchants once wed.

Having found while a youth his cousin and future wife, Madeleine Rondeaux, in tears at the discovery of her mother's adultery, Gide developed an almost mystical dedication to the alleviation of her anguish. Madeleine occupies an important position in many of his writings. She is Emmanuèle in *Les Cahiers d'André Walter* and in his *Journal*, Alissa in *La Porte étroite* (*Strait is the Gate*, 1909) and Marceline in *L'Immoraliste* (*The Immoralist*, 1902). Gide saw in her both the hurt child of his own youth and a substitute for his own departed maternal figure, for Madeleine was two years older and more mature than he. He never consummated the marriage; his love for her was pure, and he felt that physical intimacy would have tarnished this ideal. The two developed, however, a deep moral and spiritual dependence on each other. By maintaining this pure idyllic relationship, Gide was able to cleanse his own sins. His *La Porte étroite* is a largely autobiographical account of their relationship. In it, Gide describes with precision the feelings of the Protestant milieu in which he was raised. Jérôme and Alissa are cousins. As austerely religious Protestants, they fervently follow the teachings of pastor Vautier, who preaches from Luke 13:24: "Strive to enter by the narrow door." Alissa, however, who has an intense need to do penance for her mother's adulterous actions, refuses Jérôme's proposal of marriage. Her saintlike conduct leads her to loneliness and eventual death.

Gide's *L'Immoraliste* is a psychological novel and thus the perfect format to give voice to his inner conflicts and torments. The novel touches on two major questions of the twentieth century: Is liberation from former traditions possible, and if so, what should be done with the freedoms newly gained? The homosexual orientation of Michel, the novel's protagonist, is thus an emblem of rebellion and freedom of choice. Michel rejects both traditional values (he squanders his inheritance, possessions, and land) and the ideal heterosexual relationship (he marries Marceline without love and disguises his indifference as an illness on their honeymoon). Moreover, he begins to partake in the discovery of homosexual desires, being attracted by the nakedness of Arab boys and the strength and beauty of male workers on his Norman property. Michel's homoerotic observations serve, according to

Emily Apter, as a means of tearing away at the acceptable Protestant ethic. He continues to ignore and abandon his fragile wife, who later dies on a trip to North Africa. Her passing, like that of Gide's mother Juliette, represents the ultimate moment of liberation from a morally repressive society. Michel's actions serve to attack the dominant social ideology, especially the Protestant ethic of duty and bourgeois morality. But whereas the excess in *La Porte étroite* lies in self-sacrifice and purity, Michel's excess is one of glorification of a self released from all moral constraint.

Troubled by marital difficulties and horrified by the events of World War I, Gide concentrated his efforts after 1914 on a critique of bourgeois society. In 1916, he began a friendship with the young Marc Allégret and the two spent time together in Switzerland. Their short relationship, according to Wallace Fowlie, was the only union that for Gide successfully combined a sexual love and a loving companionship. On his return to France, Gide received a blow; he learned that his wife, in reaction to his infidelities, had burned all of his letters to her. This event shattered the illusion of his idyllic love and devotion to her, for he considered these letters his best work. Seemingly in response to this shock, he published *Les Faux-Monnayeurs* (*The Counterfeiters*) in 1926, the only one of his works that he called a "novel." Like many of his other texts, *Les Faux-Monnayeurs* presents the failure of heterosexual unions and the substitution of homosexual relationships. The families Molinier and Profitendieu are guilty of infidelities past and present. The only relationship that ultimately succeeds is that of Edouard and his young nephew Olivier Molinier, who are clearly based on Gide and Marc Allégret. "It was for him [Allégret], to win his attention, his esteem, that I wrote *Les Faux-Monnayeurs,* just as all my preceding books were written under the influence of Em., or in the vain hope of convincing her," Gide wrote in his *Journal 1889-39*. The relationship between Edouard and Olivier also furnished Gide with an opportunity to make a case for pederasty, which Gide saw as permissible because it had been honored in ancient Greece and Rome.

That case is further elaborated in *Corydon* (1924). Written in the form of four Socratic dialogues between a narrator and Corydon—a former doctor preparing a text entitled *Défense de la péderastie* (*In Defense of Pederasty*)—the work is a witty and ironic treatise in defense of homosexuality. In it, Gide rethinks Western hegemonic culture by examining homosexuality's civilizing influence on ancient Greek society. Corydon points out, for example, that historical periods in which homosexuality was socially acceptable were not decadent, but rather saw great artistic achievements. Corydon's defense of homosexuality is further strengthened by an examination of homosexual practices among certain animals, and by a discussion of such ancient texts as PLUTARCH's *La vie de Pélopidas*—which proposes the strength of an army composed of homosexual lovers—and the fifth book of Diodore de Sicile—which outlines certain homosexual tendencies among the ancient Saxons.

The limited publication of *Corydon* was not well received, but the republication of Gide's autobiography *Si le grain ne meurt* in 1926 (only thirteen copies had been printed in 1921) caused a scandal, largely because of its frank and intimate revelations concerning his homosexual orientation and experiences. In many of his other works, the author's homosexuality was alluded to, but through rather ambiguous and subtle means, such as a certain indifference toward women and an intense curiosity about the masculine sex. In Gide's novels, notes Philippe Lejeune, "It is left up to the reader to either venture to the conclusion, or to not really understand at all." In his autobiography, however, Gide attempted to recount more clearly and explicitly his homosexual awakenings and his coming out. The inner conflict that Gide attempted to describe was not the acceptance of his homosexual orientation but the struggle against the strict social codes that had been ingrained in him from an early age. His masked homosexual orientation and the nonconsummation of his marriage were not Gide's only secrets. He had also engaged in an affair with Elisabeth Van Rysselberghe, the daughter of long-time friends; a union that resulted in the birth of Catherine in 1923, Gide's only offspring, whom he eventually adopted.

Although he refused a nomination to the French Academy, Gide accepted an honorary doctorate from Oxford University in 1947. That same year, he was awarded the Nobel Prize for literature. Gide's last major work, *Thésée* (*Theseus*, 1946), perhaps best gives voice to his feelings concerning his art. Theseus, pondering his life, feels that it has been lived in the service of mankind. He regrets none of his actions and hopes that his work will serve future generations.

> "C'est consentant que j'approche la mort solitaire. J'ai goûté des biens de la terre. Il m'est doux de penser qu'après moi, grâce à moi, les hommes se reconnaîtront plus heureux, meilleurs et plus libres. Pour le bien de l'humanité future, j'ai fait mon œuvre. J'ai vécu." ("I face death alone willingly. I've tasted the best of life. It is pleasing to me to think that after I'm gone, thanks to me, mankind will be happier, better and freer. For the benefit of future man, I created my work. I lived.")

Just as Theseus courageously battled the Minotaur, so Gide courageously used his homosexuality as a means of defying and challenging his suffocatingly strict moral and religious upbringing, the "monsters" of repressive traditions. The impressive body of scholarly writing that has been devoted to the study of Gide and his works clearly illustrates that he now occupies an important place in twentieth-century literature.

—Scott Fish

BIBLIOGRAPHY

Apter, Emily S. *André Gide and the Codes of Homosexuality*. Saratoga, Calif.: ANMA Libri & Co., 1987. ■ Bois-deffre, Pierre de. *Vie d'André Gide*. Paris: Hachette, 1970. ■ Brée, Germaine. *André Gide, l'insaisissable protée: Etude critique de l'œuvre d'André Gide*. Paris: Les Belles Lettres, 1953, 1970. ■ Brosman, Catharine S. *An Annotated Bibliography of Criticism on André Gide 1973-88*. New York: Garland, 1990. ■ Cordle, Thomas. *André Gide, Updated Edition*. New York: Twayne Publishers, 1993. ■ Delay, Jean. *La Jeunesse d'André Gide*. 2 vols. Paris: Gallimard, 1956–1957. ■ Fowlie, Wallace. *André Gide: His Life and His Art*. New York: Macmillan, 1965. ■ Howard, Richard. "From Exoticism to Homosexuality." *A New History of French Literature*. Denis Hollier, ed. Cambridge, Mass.: Harvard University Press, 1989. 836–842. ■ Lejeune, Philippe. *Exercices d'ambiguïté. Lectures de* Si le grain ne meurt *d'André Gide*. Paris: Lettres Modernes, 1974. ■ ———. "Gide et l'autobiographie." *La Revue des Lettres Modernes* 374–379 (1973): 31–69. ■ Ljungquist, Gary. "*Les Faux-Monnayeurs* as a Radical Statement on Homosexuality." *Selected Proceedings: 32nd Mountain Interstate Foreign Language Conference*. Georgorio C. Martin, ed. Winston-Salem, N.C.: Wake Forest University, 1984. 199–205. ■ Lucey, Michael. "The Consequence of Being Explicit: Watching Sex in Gide's *Si le grain ne meurt*." *Yale Journal of Criticism* 4.1 (1990): 174–192. ■ Martin, Claude, ed. *André Gide 9*. Paris: Lettres Modernes, 1991. ■ Mengay, Donald H. "The Distant Self: Unexpressed Homosexuality in André Gide's *L'Immoraliste*." *Journal of Homosexuality* 19.1 (1990): 1–22. ■ Moutote, Daniel. *Index des idées, images, et formules du Journal 1889-1939 d'Andé Gide*. Lyon: Université Lyon II, 1985. ■ Nettelbeck, Colin W. "*L'Immoraliste* turns ninety—or what more can be said about André Gide? An essay on cultural change." *Australian Journal of French Studies* 29.1 (1992): 102–124. ■ Pollard, Patrick. *André Gide: Homosexual Moralist*. New Haven, Conn.: Yale University Press, 1991. ■ Schlumberger, Jean. *Madeleine and André Gide*. Paris: Gallimard, 1956. ■ Stambolian, George and Elaine Marks, eds. *Homosexualities and French Literature*. Ithaca, N.Y.: Cornell University Press, 1979. ■ Watson-Williams, Helen. *André Gide and the Greek Myth: A Critical Study*. Oxford: Clarendon Press, 1967.

Gilgamesh

The historical Gilgamesh ruled in Uruk, a city in ancient Mesopotamia, around 2700 B.C.E. Sumerian traditions of his story existed from around 2000 B.C.E., and a Babylonian attempt to recast the diverse ancient materials into a connected narrative was made around 1600 B.C.E. His story, thus, predates both the Hebrew Bible and the Homeric epics by more than one thousand years and is arguably the world's oldest surviving work of narrative literature. The Standard Version of the text, which was established between 668 and 627 B.C.E. as part of the extraordinary library of Assyrian ruler Assurbanipal, had been lost until archeologists excavating mounds at ancient Nineveh and Nimrud in the mid-nineteenth century recovered and transliterated the cuneiform letters inscribed on clay tablets.

The poem is structured around Gilgamesh's love for Enkidu, a man created by the gods specifically to contain Gilgamesh's disturbing assertion of his kingly prerogative to sexually enjoy any woman in the community. Before their fated meeting, Enkidu pined in the countryside "for a comrade . . . who would understand his heart" (Sanders ed.). In the city, meanwhile, Gilgamesh dreams about mysterious objects whose attraction to him "was like the love of a woman," which his priestess-mother explains prophesy the imminent arrival of "the strong comrade, the one who brings help to his friend in his need . . . ; when you see him you will be glad; you will love him as a woman and he will never forsake you." Their decisive encounter occurs when Enkidu prevents Gilgamesh from entering a bridal house, intent on despoiling the bride. They fight like wild oxen but conclude by sealing their friendship in an embrace.

The heroic couple's exploits culminate in Gilgamesh's refusal to become the consort of Ishtar, goddess of love and war, and in Enkidu's defiantly throwing the "thigh" (a euphemism for the genitals) of the newly slaughtered Bull of Heaven in her face after she resentfully unleashed it on the heroic couple. To punish this effrontery, the gods cause Enkidu to sicken and die. In his last moments, Enkidu laments that he will never again be able to look on "my dear brother," whom he calls the very "water of life." Gilgamesh's response to the death of his friend is sublime in its excess: After watching over the corpse for seven days and nights, he finally dresses the lifeless body for burial "as one veils the bride" and orders that a statue of precious metals be raised in the likeness of Enkidu. He then sets out on the search for everlasting life and the secret of rejuvenation that dominates the last part of the poem. Gilgamesh confesses to everyone he meets that "since [Enkidu] went, my life is nothing." His search proves fruitless, however, and he returns to his kingly city where he reputedly composes the epic of his own adventures and carves them on the wall of the temple.

Although the poem refers repeatedly to Gilgamesh's love for Enkidu as the central event of his life without specifying the nature of that love or what form its expression might have taken, the relationship between the two men obviously arouses far more authentic and intense emotions than either feels able to experience with a woman. Indeed, *The Epic of Gilgamesh* may be considered the archetype for the great heroic couples of antiquity. The funeral elegy that Gilgamesh recites at the loss of Enkidu rivals both biblical David's much-praised lament for Jonathan, and Achilles's speeches protesting the death of Patroclus. Enkidu's willingness in one version of the poem to go down alive to the underworld in order to bring back two of Gilgamesh's best-loved possessions, only to be held there after breaking one of its taboos, provides a homosexual version of mythic love that braves the threat of death, rivaling the stories of Orpheus and Eurydice, or of Alcestis and Admetus. Gilgamesh's erection of a statue to memorialize his beloved anticipates the emperor Hadrian's deification of Antinous. Gilgamesh's story is particularly open to Jungian interpretation: By wrestling with and finally embracing the wild man Enkidu, Gilgamesh is able to contain his own dangerously lawless heterosexual impulses and channel his superhuman energies in heroic endeavors, his love for Enkidu allowing him a psychological completeness unavailable in any other relationship. (See also BIBLE and GREEK LITERATURE, ANCIENT.)

—*Raymond-Jean Frontain*

BIBLIOGRAPHY

Dynes, Wayne R., and Stephen Donaldson, eds. *Homosexuality in the Ancient World*. New York: Garland, 1992. ■ *The Epic of Gilgamesh*. Trans. N. K. Sanders. Rev. ed. Harmondsworth: Penguin, 1966. ■ *Gilgamesh: Translated from the Sin-leqi-unninni Version*. Trans. and eds. John Gardner and John Maier, with the assistance of Richard A. Henshaw. New York: Knopf, 1984. ■ Halperin, David M. "Heroes and Their Pals." *One Hundred Years of Homosexuality and Other Essays on Greek Love*. New York: Routledge, 1990. 75–87. ■ Speiser, E. A., trans. and section ed. "Akkadian Myths and Epics." *Ancient Near Eastern Texts Relating to the Old Testament*. James B. Pritchard, ed. 2nd ed. Princeton, N.J.: Princeton University Press, 1955. 60–119.

Ginsberg, Allen
(b. 1926)

Probably the best-known U.S. poet to emerge in the post–World War II period, Allen Ginsberg entered public awareness with the controversy over his first book, *Howl and Other Poems* (1956). A sharp denunciation of America's cultural temper during the Cold War, the volume included extremely frank celebration of the libido in all its manifestations, including the homoerotic. Throughout numerous later works, Ginsberg has embodied varied aspects of the counterculture: pacifism, drug experimentation, sexual liberation, hostility to bureaucracy (both capitalist and Communist), and openness to Eastern religions.

In his earliest writing, Ginsberg imitated the metaphysical poetry of Andrew Marvell and JOHN DONNE. Through romantic relationships with fellow BEAT GENERATION figures JACK KEROUAC and WILLIAM S. BURROUGHS—and with the help of a therapist who encouraged Ginsberg to accept his sexuality—the poet began to draw on personal experience in his work. He abandoned strict verse forms, instead producing rapidly written, uncensored compositions. These poems somewhat resemble the work of WALT WHITMAN with their use of anaphora and their extensive catalogues; but their diction probably owes more to the "spontaneous bop prosody" of Kerouac's novels.

Ginsberg's exploration of open forms culminated in *Howl and Other Poems*. The long title piece is a jeremiad in which the poet recalls how "the best minds of my generation" refused, and were "destroyed" by, the norms of middle-class society. Through the juxtaposition of images ("the crack of doom on the hydrogen jukebox") and an incantatory blend of Biblical cadences and jazz slang, "Howl" evoked extreme states of mind. But the volume also spoke of a feeling of solidarity and community among the dispossessed.

Howl's forthright treatment of gay life—sometimes with a dramatic coarseness of expression ("who let themselves be fucked in the ass by saintly motorcyclists, and screamed with joy")—contributed to the book's seizure by the San Francisco police and U.S. customs in 1956. Thanks to court testimony defending the book's literary merits by prominent writers and academics, *Howl* was declared not obscene. The book has sold more than 300,000 copies. (See also CENSORSHIP.)

Ginsberg's subsequent work shares with *Howl* a distinctive interweaving of the confessional mode with a prophetic or admonitory address to the public. The poet's "Kaddish" (1959) for his mother is a powerful, sometimes excruciating account of growing up with a schizophrenic parent. (The *kaddish* is a traditional Hebrew prayer of mourning.) Later poems recount Ginsberg's worldwide travels; his involvement with the hippy, antiwar, and antinuclear movements; his decades-long marriage to Peter Orlovsky; and his devotion to Buddhism.

Ginsberg's *Gay Sunshine Interview* (1974) is an important recollection of the poet's role as a pre-Stonewall gay spokesperson. The lectures and discussions collected in *Composed on the Tongue* (1980) provide an indispensable account of Ginsberg's politics and poetics. Ginsberg's *Collected Poems* (1984) is a kind of spiritual autobiography. With its extensive annotations, the volume also provides a remarkable document of the author's life as activist and public figure. Few contemporary writers have taken Shelley's definition of poets as "unacknowledged legislators of the world" quite so literally.
—*Scott McLemee*

BIBLIOGRAPHY

Avi-Ram, Amitai. "Free Verse in Whitman and Ginsberg: The Body and the Simulacrum." *The Continuing Presence of Walt Whitman: The Life After the Life.* Robert K. Martin, ed. Iowa City: University of Iowa Press, 1992. 93–113. ■ Berman, Paul. "Intimations of Mortality." *Parnassus* 8.1 (1979): 283–293. ■ Kramer, Jane. *Allen Ginsberg in America.* New York: Random House, 1969. ■ Martin, Robert K. *The Homosexual Tradition in American Poetry.* Austin: University of Texas Press, 1979. 165–170. ■ Portuges, Paul. *The Visionary Poetics of Allen Ginsberg.* Santa Barbara, Calif.: Ross-Erikson, 1978.

Gogol, Nikolai
(1809–1852)

Playwright, humorist, and novelist, Gogol was born on April 1, 1809, in Sorochintsy, Ukraine. His father was a dreamy country squire, proprietor of 200 serfs and author of pseudo-folkloric Ukrainian comedies in verse. His mother, née Maria Kosiarowska, instilled in Gogol a morbid religiosity that emphasized hellfire and retribution rather than Christian virtues. The future writer's greatest attachment in his early childhood was to his younger brother Ivan, who died when Nikolai was ten. His closeness to Ivan haunted Gogol's memory as a lost paradise, which he strove to regain with his lifelong search for an equally ideal male friend and companion.

Between the ages of twelve and nineteen, Gogol stayed at an all-male boarding school in the town of Nezhin. There, he began to write prose and poetry for the school's literary journal, had great success in school theatricals, especially in the parts of comical old women, and formed a sentimental attachment to his older fellow student, Gerasim Vysotsky. Vysotsky graduated two years before Gogol and departed for St. Petersburg. During the two years Gogol had to wait for his own graduation, he yearned to join his friend and wrote him a series of amorous letters. But their reunion in 1828, when Gogol, too, moved to St. Petersburg, came to naught—the first instance of Gogol's later infatuations with heterosexual men unable to respond.

Gogol brought to St. Petersburg a book-length narrative poem, *Hanz (sic) Kuechelgarten,* the result of his reading of the German Romantics. He published it at his own expense in 1829, and it was a total failure. Apart from some uncanny passages of surrealistic fantasy, the poem is indeed inept. Then came an odd work, "Woman," part story, part parable, which was meant to be a paean to women's beauty, but ended up as an incoherent dream about man's longing for spiritual and physical union with other male entities. With the publication in 1830 of the Ukrainian folk tale "Bisavriuk," an early version of "St. John's Eve," Gogol found his path to recognition and success.

Not initially interested in his Ukrainian heritage, Gogol understood after coming to St. Petersburg that this was a valuable literary asset. Through the efforts of Russian romantic poets and fiction writers, Ukraine had assumed in the Russian imagination the same position that Scotland had taken in English literature because of the popularity of Robert Burns and Sir Walter Scott. Here was an area and a nation, exotic yet familiar at the same time, with colorful customs, music, costumes, and folklore. Gogol's questioning of his mother and of her older female relatives gave him the material for his novellas about a fairy-tale-like Ukraine of olden times, novellas that were collected in two volumes (1831 and 1833), with the general title *Evenings on a Farm Near Dikanka.* This book made Gogol a national celebrity by the time he was twenty-four.

The first of these eight novellas, "St. John's Eve," launched Gogol's cardinal theme, which was to reverberate through his writings until the very end. Love,

marriage, or desire for a woman always leads to death or assorted dangers for the male protagonists. A happy end in a tale or play by Gogol consists of a man's escape from impending matrimony. The women in his tales are not villains (except in "Viy"), and in his later work live women may be replaced by feminine-gender objects—a carriage, an overcoat, or a deck of cards. The fatal law of retribution invariably becomes operative when the male fails to escape the female sway. The illogicality of this pattern was wrapped up in colorful operatic merriment in Gogol's early tales and in absurdist or surrealistic comedy in later ones—like Lautréamont (Isidore Ducasse) and Lewis Carroll, Gogol was an absurdist and a surrealist before these categories were invented.

Gogol's next cycle of tales, *Mirgorod* (1834), consists of a rural idyll ("Old World Landowners"), a comic social satire ("The Tale of How Ivan Ivanovich Quarelled with Ivan Nikiforovich"), a military romance ("Taras Bulba"), and a supernatural horror story ("Viy"). Despite their generic and thematic variety, these four tales are variations on the same framework: the happy existence of one man, two men, or a group of men is wrecked when one of them comes under the sway of a sexually emancipated female. The females are a pet cat in the first tale, an ugly battle-ax in the second, a loving and kindly Polish noblewoman in the third, and a beautiful but lethal witch in the fourth. Gogol's fear of his own homosexual desires, involuntarily revealed in *Mirgorod,* somehow led him to view *all* sexuality as fraught with danger.

The apex of Gogol's narrative art was reached in his cycle of St. Petersburg tales, written in 1835–1841 and comprising "The Portrait," "Nevsky Prospect," "Diary of a Madman," "The Nose," and "The Overcoat." In these tales, Gogol renounced the Ukrainian background and the supernatural forces of his earlier work and launched two myths that dominated Russian literature through the nineteenth and early twentieth centuries: the image of St. Petersburg as a ghostly, unreal, and fantastic place (later to be found in the novels of Feodor Dostoevsky and the poetry of Alexander Blok, Anna Akhmatova, and Osip Mandelstam) and the great myth of a single, powerless man face to face with the impersonal, inhuman metropolis, a theme that HONORÉ DE BALZAC and Charles Dickens were independently developing at the same time as Gogol.

Simultaneously with *Mirgorod* and the St. Petersburg cycle, Gogol undertook the writing of several comedies, of which the first to be completed was *The Inspector General* (1836). A comedy of misunderstanding, the play pits an inspired, flighty young liar against a group of ursine and corrupt municipal officials who mistake him for a government inspector.

The difference in their respective specific gravities keeps them on separate levels of existence. Gogol parodied the love interest, obligatory in drama, in the young man's lunatic offer to marry both the wife and the daughter of the town's mayor. Once they seem to consent, he gallops off in a troika, happily escaping the Gogolian matrimonial trap.

The play was liked by Tsar Nicholas I and the public. But to Gogol's horror, it was read by many as a sweeping indictment of all the social institutions of the Russian empire. The politically conservative writer was puzzled and stunned. In his panic, he fled Russia and eventually settled in Rome, where he was to reside for the next twelve years. In Italy, Gogol's inhibitions were loosened to the point where he allowed himself to love openly a young nobleman, Iosif Vielhorsky. It was a reciprocated love, but the young Iosif died of consumption less than a year after he and Gogol met. Two years later, Gogol became hopelessly infatuated with the poet Nikolai Yazykov, whose verse was mostly about women's beauty and his attraction to it. After trying for months to win Yazykov and addressing passionate letters to him, Gogol understood the futility of this undertaking.

During his Italian period, Gogol completed the two comedies he had begun in Russia. *Marriage* (1842), seen by his contemporaries as a satire on social climbing and on matchmaking customs, is actually a headlong attack on the entire institution of matrimony. *The Gamblers* (1843) is a play that could be properly understood only after the appearance of JEAN GENET and Vladimir Nabokov. Like Genet, Gogol shows in this play an all-male criminal subculture (cardsharps) who casually betray one another; and as in Nabokov's novel *Despair,* their criminal endeavors are an allegory for artistic creation. The "heroine" of the play is a specially marked deck of cards named Adelaida Ivanovna, with whom (or with which) the protagonist is in love, which assures his downfall.

The novel *Dead Souls* (1841) uses the formula of earlier Spanish, French, and English picaresque novels (for example, *Tom Jones* by Henry Fielding), but with one crucial difference: The *picaro,* Chichikov, has no interest in the sexual adventures so usual for the genre. His clever scheme for fleecing the landowners of a small provincial town and the government almost succeeds, but the subject of matrimony comes up near the end, and Chichikov has to abandon his loot and flee the town. Gogol imagined the central Russian provinces (which he had never seen) in this novel with such vividness that the critics and readers of his time believed he was offering a slice of life he had observed.

Like *The Inspector General* earlier, *Dead Souls* was read by many as a call to reform society and free the serfs. Outraged, Gogol responded by publishing a volume of essays, *Selected Passages from Correspondence with Friends* (1846), where he spoke his political mind openly: Slavery was justified in the Bible and must not be abolished; social stratification had been decreed by God; and any reform or political change is an offense against Christianity. This brought down on Gogol the wrath of almost every political faction in Russia. The rest of his life was devoted to efforts to write a sequel to *Dead Souls,* where his *picaro* would be morally uplifted by associating with virtuous aristocrats and saintly millionaires.

In January 1852, Gogol confessed his sexual orientation to a bigoted priest, Father Matthew Konstantinovsky, who prescribed abstinence from sleep and food, so as to cleanse Gogol's "inner filth." Gogol obeyed. He died of starvation on February 21, despite the ministrations of his friends. His death at the age of forty-three was hastened by doctors, who in order to help him, bled him profusely and subjected him to treatments that were physical tortures.

Much of Gogol's work was misread in the nineteenth century, when he was regarded as a photographic realist, the originator of the humanitarian and realistic trend in Russian literature. His complexity and originality were first noticed by the writers (rather than the critics) of the early and mid-twentieth century, such as Andrei Bely, Aleksei Remizov, and Vladimir Nabokov. Although his influence on Dostoevsky was enormous, Gogol's genuine impact on Russian writers came in the twentieth century, after his powerful imagination and unique perception of reality were truly understood.

—Simon Karlinsky

BIBLIOGRAPHY

Fanger, Donald. *Dostoevsky and Romantic Realism. A Study of Dostoevsky in Relation to Balzac, Dickens and Gogol.* Cambridge, Mass.: Harvard University Press, 1965. ■ Gippius, V. V. *Gogol.* Robert A. Maguire, ed. and trans. Ann Arbor: Ardis, 1981. ■ Karlinsky, Simon. "The Alogical and Absurdist Aspects of Russian Realist Drama." *Comparative Drama* 3 (Fall 1969): 147–155. ■ ———. *The Sexual Labyrinth of Nikolai Gogol.* Cambridge, Mass.: Harvard University Press, 1976; rpt. Chicago: University of Chicago Press, 1992. ■ Maguire, Robert A., ed. and trans. *Gogol from the Twentieth Century. Eleven Essays.* Princeton: Princeton University Press, 1974. ■ McLean, Hugh. "Gogol's Retreat from Love: Toward an Interpretation of *Mirgorod.*" *Russian Literature and Psychoanalysis.* Daniel Rancour-Laferriere, ed. *Linguistic and Literary Studies in Eastern Europe,* Vol. 31. Amsterdam: John Benjamin Publishing Co., 1989: 101–122. ■ Nabokov, Vladimir. *Nikolai Gogol.* Norfolk, Conn.: New Directions, 1944. ■ Setchkarev, Vsevolod. *Gogol: His Life and Works.* Robert Kramer, trans. New York: New York University Press, 1965.

Goodman, Paul
(1911–1972)

Novelist, poet, playwright, literary critic—Paul Goodman was, in his own preferred term, a "Man of Letters." He was also an intellectual polymath, the author of more than a dozen volumes on urban planning, psychological theory, and social commentary. A variety of outspoken commitments—to experimentalism in his literary practice; to anarchism and pacifism in his political activity; and to the frank acknowledgment of his bisexuality in his public life—often placed in jeopardy Goodman's career as a teacher and a writer. "I have been fired three times because of my queer behavior or my claim to the right of it," Goodman wrote late in life, "and these are the only times I have been fired." As an author, Goodman was both prolific (writing the equivalent of more than a book per year for over three decades) and highly eclectic. Few modern writers have worked in so many forms or ranged so widely in the subjects they treated.

Goodman's literary work is distinguished by a combination of classical learning and avant garde experimentation. His fiction, verse, and drama often incorporate stories and characters from Greek, Hebrew, and Roman literature and mythologies. But Goodman was also drawn to a kind of aesthetic abstraction, which he sometimes called "literary cubism": such components of a work as prose rhythm, narrative voice, or dialogue would be handled as purely formal elements. In his poems, traditional verse forms (such as sonnets and haiku) and elevated diction are frequently mixed with colloquial dialect, street scenes, or descriptions of "cruising" and casual sexual encounters. His short fiction includes naturalistic stories, fantasies, retellings of myths, and deeply introspective texts in a form Goodman called "the dialectical lyric," a term he borrowed from Kierkegaard.

Goodman's several novels may be divided into two broad categories: the realistic novels of community life, and the works of social and psychological allegory. *Parents' Day* (1951) and *Making Do* (1963), two autobiographical fictions, are written in a realistic mode. In each, a first-person narrator describes incidents and characters from his life in a small community (a progressive school and a bohemian circle, respectively); he mentions his own homosexuality matter-of-factly. Likewise, sexual issues and the problems of community are explicitly addressed in Goodman's more experimental narratives, including the four novels that make up *The Empire City* (1959),

his *magnum opus*. But in this tetralogy—as in *Don Juan; or, The Continuum of the Libido* (written 1941–1942, published 1979)—Goodman abandons realism in favor of complex (and sometimes highly mannered) allegories of alienation, desire, and antiauthoritarian radicalism.

Intellectually, Goodman was a stubborn anti-specialist. With his brother Percival Goodman, he wrote *Communitas* (1947), a now-classic volume on urban design. He also contributed the theoretical section of a collaborative work on *Gestalt Therapy* (1951). Goodman's neo-Aristotelian book on critical theory, *The Structure of Literature* (1954), is quite different in method from *Kafka's Prayer* (1947), which interprets the author through both psychoanalytic and theological approaches. "A man of letters finds that the nature of things is not easily divided into disciplines," as Goodman explained in his last book, *Little Prayers and Finite Experience* (1972).

In the early 1960s, after decades of marginality, Goodman was discovered by a generation of young readers who found that his work expressed their own sense of alienation. A pacifist and an anarchist in the tradition of HENRY DAVID THOREAU, Goodman's radicalism bore little resemblance either to orthodox Marxism or to the anti-Communist liberalism of the day. *Growing Up Absurd* (1960), his book on "problems of youth in the organized system," was particularly influential within the early New Left. In numerous books, lectures, and essays from the last dozen years of his life, Goodman addressed the problems of finding happiness, meaningful work, and a sense of community within bureaucratic society.

The candor with which he wrote about homosexual libido in his poetry and fiction—and in the notebook jottings published as *Five Years* (1966)—made Goodman an important and highly visible advocate of gay liberation. A particularly important document in this regard is "The Politics of Being Queer" (1969), an essay of personal as well as political reflection, published in *Nature Heals: The Psychological Essays of Paul Goodman* (1977).

—Scott McLemee

BIBLIOGRAPHY

Horowitz, Stephen P. "An Investigation of Paul Goodman and Black Mountain." *American Poetry* 7.1 (1989): 2–30. ■ Morton, Donald. "The Cultural Politics of (Sexual) Knowledge: On the Margins with Goodman." *Social Text* 25–26 (1990): 227–

241. ■ Nicely, Tom. *Adam and His Work: A Bibliography of Sources By and About Paul Goodman (1911-1972)*. Metuchen, N.J.: Scarecrow Press, 1979. ■ Parisi, Peter and Nicely, Tom. *Artist of the Actual: Essays on Paul Goodman*. Metuchen, N.J.: Scarecrow Press, 1986. ■ Stoehr, Taylor. "Paul Goodman and the New York Jews." *Salmagundi* 66 (1988): 50–103. ■ Widmer, Kingsley. *Paul Goodman*. Boston: Twayne Publishers, 1980.

Gothicism

§

Imagine this: Before you a lonely castle perched on a cliff top high above a rushing torrent across which a narrow and dilapidated footbridge is suspended. Behind you a darkly threatening forest glowers with menace, and the bridge is your only escape. But it leads to the castle in which you know you are not safe: If you are female, the castle houses a wicked aunt who has conspired with her malevolent husband to have you raped, murdered, and cast from the precipice in the dead of night; if you are male, the castle houses a bitter rival for the hand of your beloved, who will stop at nothing to have you destroyed: He has tried more than once to sneak up behind you and run you through with his stubby but fatal stiletto. Then imagine that you are in the castle itself, not up on the airy parapets and lofty towers, but down in a secret underground chamber; you hear a door creak in the distance, and you panic; peeking outside your chamber, you see the shimmering shadows of a candle approaching. You feel the floor and find a trapdoor; you open it carefully, and gaze into the darkness below. You have no choice but to descend, and as you do, you hear the door of your chamber open and the cry of frenzied desire in the man or woman who pursues you. Down the stairs you run, down and down, into the innermost reaches of the castle bowels. Your heart is racing as you reach the floor and find yourself in another closed room. You try to make out the shapes in the room. You cannot see, and so you feel your way along the walls. What you feel quickly horrifies you, for these are moldering corpses; you back away in disgust, but you cannot scream. In your rush, however, you knock over one of the corpses and something shiny rolls to your feet. You pick it up, and in the gloom you can just make out the features of a portrait. You recognize the portrait and realize suddenly that the decaying corpse you have just toppled was that of your own mother (or father). Just then the light approaches, and your pursuer reaches you with a scream of delight. And then you realize that that is your mother or father too! If you are lucky, you are dreaming, and you wake up now. If you are not lucky,

you are reading a Gothic novel and you cannot wake up. The situation is all too real.

The Gothic has always offered writers and readers the chance to experience the excitement of transgressive sexuality of various kinds. In the earliest examples of the Gothic novel, for instance, same-sex desire, incest, sado-masochistic ritual, fantasies of imprisonment, and other kinds of erotic violence are commonplace. My opening paragraph may sound like an exaggeration, but its details are taken from actual novels written between 1764, the date of HORACE WALPOLE's *The Castle of Otranto*, and 1818, the year of Mary Shelley's *Frankenstein*. After that initial vogue, the Gothic has flourished at the margins of respectable literature throughout the nineteenth and twentieth centuries, producing occasional masterpieces, such as Bram Stoker's *Dracula* (1897) and Shirley Jackson's *The Haunting of Hill House* (1959), and frequent popularizations, such as the films of *Frankenstein* and *Dracula* and the novels of Clive Barker and Anne Rice. But whatever permutations Gothic has taken since its origins in the eighteenth century, it has never strayed far from its interest in transgressive sexualities and its portrayal of illicit desires.

It is perhaps then no surprise that a large number of Gothic writers have been themselves outside the cultural norm for sexual behavior. Horace Walpole may not have been "homosexual" in any way we would understand, but he did devote himself to one male friend, a cousin, throughout his life; and although he never talked about problematic sexual desires, it was in his fevered dreams that the Gothic plot first presented itself for the thrill and delight of his readers. WILLIAM BECKFORD, who shaped the Gothic tale to an exotic eastern dimension in *Vathek* (1786), was himself hounded out of the country because of a romantic attachment to a younger male cousin, and MATTHEW G. LEWIS, the author of the infamous *The Monk* (1795), was famous for the all-male dinner parties at which Byron and others took part. It is no wonder that OSCAR WILDE turned to the Gothic in *The*

Picture of Dorian Gray (1891), or that after his imprisonment, he used as his pseudonym Sebastian Melmoth. Melmoth was the delectable hero of Charles Robert Maturin's *Melmoth the Wanderer* (1820), an exotically pansexual novel that tells the tale of a lost soul who must try to seduce every healthy person he meets.

Female authors were no less interested in the implications of same-sex love, and if they are not always as devoted to the violence of sexual frenzy—though in some cases they are, as in Charlotte Dacre's *Zofloya; or The Moor* (1806) and Mary Anne Radcliffe's *Manfroné; or The One-Handed Monk* (1809)—they often create female ROMANTIC FRIEND-SHIPS that are so convincing that their erotic implications are largely ignored. In Ann Radcliffe's novels, for instance, a "female" context is created in which even the romantic hero must be feminized before he can become acceptable to the heroine. No male heroics are acceptable: The hero is wounded and given up for dead; he suffers and cries; he shows himself to be more interested in domestic space than in the heroic landscape of battle; and so on. He treats the heroine like a sister. Of far more importance to the heroine, it seems, is the female friend or maternal accomplice who sees the heroine through her darkest hours and offers her the true solace that a female–female relation can. The emotional strength of these bonds has an erotics all their own, and when in vampire tales, such as Sheridan LeFanu's *Carmilla* (1872) and NATALIE BARNEY's *The One Who Is Legion* (1930), they are realized as the erotic complement to the male–male erotic rivalry that animates so much Gothic fiction.

The vampire motif has been particularly rich in exploring unconventional sexual desire. Stoker's *Dracula* was not the first such tale, but its sexual power was so compelling that vampire fiction has enjoyed an especially lively twentieth-century popularity. Anne Rice's *Vampire Chronicles,* written throughout the 1980s and still continuing, articulates a version of male–male desire that taps a genuine undercurrent in the earliest versions of the vampire lore and brings it into touch literally with the gay men of Castro Street in San Francisco, who step into her works with uncanny ease. Shirley Jackson's *The Haunting of Hill House,* on the other hand, brings us from the "romantic friendship" between women in early Gothic works to a sexualized relation that is more harrowing because of what it implies about its participants themselves than about their situation.

Three classic Gothic tales are essential to our gay and lesbian literary heritage. Mary Wollstonecraft's *The Wrongs of Woman* (1798) tells the story of a woman who is wrongly incarcerated in a mental asylum by a husband who wants to control her inheritance. The institution feels like a remote Gothic castle to those inside it, and the "patients" are treated with the contempt that Gothic heroines usually suffer. This heroine's story is complicated, and there is one man who seems to understand and sympathize. Far more compelling in the novel, however, are her attachments both to her infant daughter and to one of her attendants, the nearly silent Jemima. In this novel, Wollstonecraft describes what is Gothic not about the nightmare world of a woman's private imagination, but about the everyday world of sexual politics. With the women in her life, Maria finds solace, and the attachments she forms, if they are not erotic, suggest a source of power that can defy the abuse that women suffer. Maria is doomed not to succeed, just as Wollstonecraft herself died (in childbirth) before she could finish her project. In the text, however, she suggests ways in which women who find love in one another might escape their cultural victimization.

In *Frankenstein* (1818), Mary Shelley's masterpiece, male–male relations are rendered seriously problematic, but they are also memorably celebrated. Feminist critics have read Victor Frankenstein's monstrous creature as analogous to a female in early nineteenth-century society, and I find their readings persuasive. It would also be possible, it seems to me, to see the attachment between this mad scientist and the creature to whom he gives "birth," and who peeps through the curtain of his bed chamber and haunts him through frozen landscapes of the north, as something more than accidental. The creature is Frankenstein's real mate, and the fury with which he destroys the female creature he was constructing (and the vindictive fury with which the creature destroys Victor's own Elizabeth) only underlines their devotion to one another. Eve Kosofsky Sedgwick talks about "homosocial" relations between men and how often they are eroticized, especially in the Gothic. *Frankenstein* seems to me an ideal case of what she describes, and the lonely creature especially, haunting "normal" society and hoping for a place within it, might remind us of the positions that gays and lesbians were always forced to assume until they defied society's attempts to force them into a closet.

HENRY JAMES's *The Jolly Corner* (1908) tells the story of a man who returns from an ineffectual life in Europe to confront the ghost of the man he would have been had he stayed in America. The ghost has an eerie attraction for the hero, Spencer Brydon, and he wanders through the lonely house of his childhood in search of the seductive double. When he finally confronts him, of course, it is almost more than he can bear: The object of his desire is rough looking, pol-

luted somehow by the city, and disfigured. This subtle use of what Freud would call the "uncanny" is enough to mark Brydon with the knowledge of his own darker, less socially presentable side. When Alice Staverton, his New York friend, tells him that she accepts this darker truth, he can only bury his face in her bosom in profound thanks and relief. This sense of relief after a hideous disclosure is so close to what gay men and lesbians anticipate before coming out that it might seem that James is speaking to us. The details of James's biography, which suggests a deeply problematic sexual life centering on homosexual desire, support such a reading, as do the chords it strikes in those of us who have been there.

An important question to ask is this: Why do we read Gothic fictions? As violent and at times abusive as they are, what do we find in them to sustain us? To answer that question, we would have to turn to our own psychological makeups, as critics like Tania Modleski have done, and consider what it is that we process in these encounters with the grotesque. As gay and lesbian readers, it seems to me, we process the horror at the situation society places us in and the demands to conform that we constantly face. Gothic reading is not just an escape; it reminds us of what the stakes really are. If our own sexuality is transgressive, Gothic allows us the chance to break with the norm in our imaginations, which is so important to do before we decide to defy convention in fact. Gay and

lesbian critics are drawn to Gothic for just this reason: Before they knew why, Gothic appealed to them. Now that they know, they can hardly give it up. (See also ENGLISH LITERATURE: ROMANTICISM and GHOST AND HORROR FICTION.)

—*George E. Haggerty*

BIBLIOGRAPHY

Ellis, Kate Ferguson. *The Contested Castle: Gothic Novels and the Subversion of Domestic Ideology.* Urbana: University of Chicago Press, 1989. ■ Foucault, Michel. *The History of Sexuality, Volume I: An Introduction.* Trans. Robert Hurley. New York: Vintage-Random House, 1980. ■ Gilbert, Sandra M. and Susan Gubar. *The Madwoman in the Attic: The Woman Writer and the Nineteenth-Century Literary Imagination.* New Haven: Yale University Press, 1979. ■ Haggerty, George E. *Gothic Fiction/Gothic Form.* University Park: Pennsylvania State University Press, 1989. ■ Johnson, Barbara. "My Monster/My Self." *Diacritics* 12 (1982): 2–10. ■ Kahane, Claire. "The Gothic Mirror," in *The (M)other Tongue: Essays in Feminist Psychoanalytic Interpretation.* Shirley Nelson Garner, Claire Kahane, and Madelon Springnether, eds. Ithaca: Cornell University Press, 1985. ■ Keily, Robert. *The Romantic Novel in England.* Cambridge, Mass.: Harvard University Press, 1972. ■ Massé, Michelle A. *In the Name of Love: Women, Masochism, and the Gothic.* Ithaca, New York: Cornell University Press, 1992. ■ Modleski, Tania. *Loving With a Vengeance: Mass Produced Fantasies for Women.* New York: Routledge, 1982. ■ Sedgwick, Eve Kosofsky. *Between Men: English Literature and Male Homosexual Desire.* New York: Columbia University Press, 1985.

Goytisolo, Juan
(*b.* 1931)

Juan Goytisolo was born in Barcelona in 1931. He is today one of the most prominent literary figures of Spain. Although he is quite prolific, his critical acclaim is mostly due to his trilogy: *Señas de identidad* (*Marks of Identity*, 1966), *Reivindicación del conde don Julián* (*Count Julian*, 1970), and *Juan sin tierra* (*John the Landless*, 1975). Besides novels and an autobiography, he has published some literary criticism. Two of his brothers (José Agustín and Luis) are also writers.

Goytisolo's biography is, in a sense, recorded throughout his writings. He frequently uses autobiographical material in his novels. Certain incidents and people important to his personal development reappear in different forms throughout the body of his work, giving it a subjective interrelatedness. The author accepts this subjectivity in a conscious attempt to bind his work and his life. Many of his characters

(most notably, Álvaro Mendiola, who reappears in several novels) function as doubles of the author who is on the same internal voyage in search of the authentic self.

In his autobiographical work, *Coto vedado* (*Forbidden Territory*, 1985), Goytisolo reveals the decisive moments in his psychological and sexual development. The author claims it was French writer JEAN GENET who first helped him overcome his personal taboos and come to terms with his sexual orientation. He has had sexual relations with both men and women, but admits to feeling reservations in his dealings with the opposite sex.

Sexuality itself is a major component of his literature and his ethics. He relates sexual freedom directly to personal and political freedom. His own sexuality becomes a vehicle for channeling his moral opposition to Spain, the country he rejects and that he feels has rejected him. The author identifies his work with eroticism, equating the act of writing with masturbation, and describing his entry into the world of literature as a sort of copulation. He claims to be "procreating" himself and "impregnating" his reader through his writing. His work contains much phallic imagery and much vivid sexuality. When sexual acts are portrayed, they tend to be aggressive and often sadomasochistic.

In *Reivindicación del conde don Julián* and *Juan sin tierra,* two ideologically aggressive novels with profound psychological, historical, religious, and sexual implications, Goytisolo seems to come to terms with his true being, removing all inhibitions and false identities. The novels represent efforts to destroy his personal past and to establish the connection between political and sexual power. In *Juan sin tierra,* positive and negative social values are reversed. Heterosexuality and homosexuality conflict. Although society relates heterosexuality with reproduction, cleanliness, and clarity, and homosexuality with the anus, darkness, and uncleanness, the author inverts these values. He associates heterosexuality with capitalism and slavery, and homosexuality with rebellion against prohibition. In *Reivindicación,* he expresses his obsessive hatred of traditional Spain, attempting to critique the country through its literature, openly using the great writers of the Spanish canon as literary models in order to violate them and overcome them. He wants to show how the country has become petrified and how the individual, in order to be free, must free himself of stultified traditions. The aggression culminates with the symbolic rape and murder of the "motherland." The Álvaro of his earlier novel, *Señas de identidad,* becomes Count Julian, the legendary traitor of Spain, in his attack on the stale culture of his homeland. Goytisolo believes that to create a new self (through authorship), one must first destroy the old self. By embracing the figure of the exiled Count, he assumes the role of a rebellious deviant.

Goytisolo is an iconoclast in every sense of the word. His defiance is political, sexual, and literary. He takes great pride in being different and uses this difference to attack the status quo though his attacks can also be read as attempts at self-justification in confronting a world that is hostile to him. He is most staunchly opposed to the Catholic, middle-class morality that surrounded him from birth, believing that the prominent social values he has been taught have failed him. Instead, Goytisolo seeks to align himself with outcasts who, like him, are disconnected from the social order that surrounds them and threatens to obliterate them. The theme of alienation is repeated constantly. His works deal forcefully with the issue of finding one's self within a society that divorces us from our authentic nature. This seems, in part, an effort to purge himself of his own sense of alienation.

Goytisolo's rebellion is against the norms of his own social class; against his own family's reactionary position (particularly the values espoused by his father); against the brutality and demoralization of the society in which he was born; against ethnocentrism, consumerism, and repressed sexuality—issues that are all tied together in Goytisolo's world. Static cultural institutions, he claims, keep us from truly knowing our genuine selves. His preoccupation is with inventing a self beyond the external social data that he finds oppressive. Because of the defiant position he assumes, many of his books were originally banned in Francoist Spain.

Goytisolo eventually rejects Spain altogether, associating it with decadence, sterility, and death. He sees Spain as a sexually repressed country whose problems are directly related to this repression. He is in voluntary exile from Spain on ethical grounds, embracing, instead, the Arab world, which he associates with sexuality, fertility, and life. Currently, he resides in Marrakesh. His acceptance of Arab culture is related to its acceptance of homosexuality (particularly in contrast to Spanish ideology).

Goytisolo's novels have become progressively less realistic and more demanding of the reader, who must participate actively in deciphering the text. His literary techniques are innovative and experimental. Through such devices as interior monologues, chronological and spatial juxtapositions and discontinuities, the contrasting of different voices, sudden shifts in perspective, linguistic experimentation, characters with multiple personalities, and the rupture of grammatical coherence, Goytisolo has created a unique and personal voice within Spanish letters. His style is profoundly critical, darkly cynical, and often humorous. (See also SPANISH LITERATURE.)

—*María Dolores Costa*

BIBLIOGRAPHY

Burunat, Silvia. "El monólogo interior en Juan Goytisolo." *El monólogo interior como forma narrativa en la novela española.* Madrid: Ediciones José Porrúa Turanzas, 1980. 113–157. ■ Ilie, Paul. *Literature and Inner Exile.* Baltimore: Johns Hopkins University Press, 1980. ■ Levine, Linda Gould. "La odisea por el sexo en *La reivindicación del conde don Julián.*" *The Analysis of Hispanic Texts: Current Trends in Methodology.* New York: Bilingual Press, 1976. 90–108. ■ ———. "*Makbara:* Entre la espada y la pared—¿Política marxista o política sexual?" *Revista Iberoamericana* 116–117 (July–December 1981): 123–135. ■ Pérez, Genaro. *Formalist Elements in the Novels of Juan Goytisolo.* Madrid: Editorial Porrúa, 1979. ■ Romero, Hector R. *La evolución literaria de Juan Goytisolo.* Miami: Ediciones

Universal, 1979. ■ Schwartz, Kessel. "Stylistic and Psychosexual Constants in the Novels of Juan Goytisolo." *Norte* 4–6 (1972): 119–128. ■ Sobejano, G., et al. *Juan Goytisolo*. Madrid: Espiral, 1975. ■ Spires, Robert. "Process as Product: *Juan sin tierra*." *Beyond the Metafictional Mode: Directions in the Modern Spanish Novel*. Lexington: University Press of Kentucky, 1984. 72–88. ■ Ugarte, Michael. *Trilogy of Treason: An Intertextual Study of Juan Goytisolo*. Columbia: University of Missouri Press, 1982.

Grahn, Judy
(b. 1940)

Considering herself part of a generation that "began wresting poetry from the exclusive clutches of the sons and daughters of the American upperclass and returning it to the basic groups from which it seeped and sprung," Judy Grahn—lesbian feminist poet, gay cultural theorist, archeologist, critic, autobiographer, historian, archivist, publisher, biographer, activist, editor, anthropologist, and teacher who picketed the White House in 1963 with the Mattachine Society—has been one of the most effective leaders of the gay rights movement both pre- and post-Stonewall. In cogently and eloquently displaying ways in which sexuality is related to other economies in our culture like gender, race, and class, she is perhaps the most successful of our contemporary writers. Thus her latest book, *Blood, Bread, and Roses: How Menstruation Created the World* (1993), is dedicated "To poets." Though it argues that the female body is the origin for all knowledge, even for scientific measure, this is not an exclusionary book written exclusively for women, for inclusivity is at the heart of Judy Grahn's vision.

Born on July 28, 1940, in Chicago, Judy Grahn grew up in what she describes in *Another Mother Tongue: Gay Words, Gay Worlds* (1984) as "an economically poor and spiritually depressed" New Mexico town "near the hellish border of West Texas." Her father was a cook and her mother a photographer's assistant. Grahn has said that she knew she was a poet by the time she was nine, but it wasn't until she was twenty-five that she consciously committed herself to her work. She put herself through trade school working nights as a sandwich maker and then worked as a medical secretary in the daytime while attending college at night. In 1984, after attending six different colleges, she received her B.A. from San Francisco State. At twenty-five, she became seriously ill and went into a coma. In a public dialogue recorded in *Women Writers of the West Coast* (1983), Grahn remarked that when she came out of the coma, "I realized that if I was going to do what I had set out to do in my life, I would have to go all the way with it and take every single risk you could take. . . . I decided I would not do anything I didn't want to do that would keep me from my art." In 1969, then, with artist Wendy Cadden, Grahn founded her own press, the Women's Press Collective. Inspired in part by the fact that her first work, "The Psychoanalysis of Edward the Dyke" (1964), was considered unpublishable, this press began with only a mimeograph machine and was dedicated to publishing "work of women that we thought no one else would do." Grahn was also part of the first lesbian feminist collective, the Gay Women's Liberation Group, and was one of the founders of "A Woman's Place," the first U.S. women's bookstore.

Grahn's identity as a lesbian and a feminist infuses all of her work. Her writing is explicitly political, asserting the presence and strength of women and lesbian culture and critiquing the patriarchal and heterosexist social biases that shape our individual perceptions. In some of her early writings, this critique takes the form of satire, combining anger and humor. In "Edward the Dyke," for example, Grahn creates a satiric portrait of the medical profession's attempt to "cure" a lesbian of her "disease" and "depravity." In "A Woman Is Talking to Death" (1973), an angry poem articulating the sense of powerlessness and voicelessness of two women who feel they do not count in society, especially as lesbians, Grahn portrays lesbian life within the context of what she describes as "the criss-cross oppressions which people use against each other and which continually divide us." This long poem deals with racism and class oppression as well as misogyny and homophobia, and features a segment in which Grahn recounts her own experience of having been thrown out of the Air Force with a less-than-honorable discharge because she admitted to being a lesbian.

Grahn also uses her poetry to empower and reestablish possession of words and signs of lesbian culture that are often used as derogatory by outsiders. For example, a short poem in the *She Who* collection (1971–1972) confidently asserts, "I am the dyke in the matter, the other / I am the wall with the womanly swagger / I am the dragon, the dangerous dagger / I am the bulldyke, the bulldagger." Her portrait of "Carol" in the same collection concludes "Carol is another / queer / chickadee / like me, but Carol does / everything / better / if you let her." In these lines, readers can hear how conscientiously Grahn incorporates rhythm and meter into poetic meaning, implicitly reminding readers how much lesbian and gay history, like Native-American or other "vanished" histories, has been orally passed from generation to generation and queer to queer via storytelling.

At the same time, Grahn reverses conventional expectations to disempower negative attitudes toward lesbians that have become encoded into our language. In "A Mock Interrogation," a segment of "A Woman Is Talking to Death," a woman responds affirmatively to the question, "Have you ever committed any indecent acts with women?" by listing the times she failed to help a woman who needed her. This project of empowering language is made explicit in *Another Mother Tongue*, a text that defies generic category, combining autobiography and poetry with extensive research into the origin and evolution of words and symbols of lesbian and gay culture.

Although lesbian identity is always central in Grahn's work, her poetry also speaks of the importance of all women defining themselves according to what they have "in common" with other women, and not by what makes them different from men. In what is probably her best known group of poems, *The Common Woman* (1969), Grahn creates portraits of seven women, only one of whom is explicitly defined as having "taken a woman lover." Significantly, however, this poem appears fourth, making it the literal "center" of the collection. These poems, says Grahn, were written because she wanted "to read something which described regular, everyday women without making us look either superhuman or pathetic." The details of each woman's life are linked with powers in nature—a rattlesnake, a thunderstorm, the new moon, a crow, and so forth.

This connection between women's power and the power of the earth is one that Grahn repeatedly and frequently makes. The opening poem in *She Who* simply repeats, in various formations and with different emphases, the title phrase, until it becomes an endless and endlessly varying chant that seems to be at once the call of an owl and the sound of the wind itself. In "A Geology Lesson," the land, wind, and sea are forever transformed because "a woman of strong purpose" passed through. By the end of *She Who*, "She Who" has become a mythic goddess of natural power, a step toward what poet and critic Alicia

Ostriker calls "taking back the myths" from patriarchal culture. Indeed, at the conclusion of *Blood, Bread, and Roses*, Grahn even reclaims the fundamentally human quality of shame, which is not only "consciousness of ability to do evil," but "is also acknowledgment of something unfinished, raw, and is therefore the doorway to creativity and finding solutions."

In her poetry, Grahn continued this project of creating a "neomythology" in *The Queen of Wands* (1982) and *The Queen of Swords* (1987), the first two volumes of what Grahn envisions as a four-part series corresponding to the four suits of the Tarot. Both texts elaborate the story of Helen: In *Wands*, she travels around the world and through history, from ancient Greece to a factory and to Hollywood; in *Swords*, subtitled "A Play with Poetic Myth" and written explicitly for performance, Helen descends into "the underworld," which has been reconceptualized as a lesbian bar.

The phrase "Common Woman" has another dimension for Grahn, a self-defined working-class writer who believes that unique characteristics inhere in working-class writing: ". . . we often pile up many events within a small amount of space. . . . This means both that our lives are chock full of action and also that we are bursting with stories which haven't been printed, made into novels, dictionaries, philosophies." In "The Common Woman" poems, Grahn breaks stereotypes about working-class women, aiming for honest descriptions of the work women do, including waitressing, fixing a car, working in an office, and bartending. But perhaps Grahn's most powerful statement on working-class writing appears in her introduction to the collection *True to Life Adventure Stories* (Vol. 1; 1978). In the essay "Murdering the King's English," Grahn explains her decision, as an editor, not to standardize the language of the women whose stories she collected, but to "express workingclass writing as workingclass people do it," a form of expression that has been labeled "illiterate." Changing their language would be "saying that the occupation of writer belongs only to the upper class and those who can *pass* by using its standards."

Grahn's project of imbuing all of our work and culture with healthy doses of common sense is perhaps nowhere more evident than in her recuperative literary criticism. As a critic and historian, she has delineated a "Lesbian Poetic Tradition" in *The Highest Apple* (1985), a book dedicated "To All Lovers" (not only lesbians) and examining the work of nine poets— EMILY DICKINSON, AMY LOWELL, H.D., GERTRUDE STEIN, ADRIENNE RICH, AUDRE LORDE, OLGA BROUMAS, PAULA GUNN ALLEN, and herself—by linking them "in a tradition with Sappho." Her *Really Reading Gertrude*

Stein (1989) not only recovers little-known works by this lesbian writer but, as a map of rereading, energetically and profoundly urges readers beyond fascination with her celebrity and into appreciation of Stein's widely admired but little-read texts. One of the most important lesbian writers of this century, Judy Grahn continues to make vital contributions to audience development and literary production as she beckons each and every reader into a world exhilaratingly rich with common sense.

—*Martha Nell Smith and Stacy Steinberg*

BIBLIOGRAPHY

Avi-ram, Amitai F. "The Politics of the Refrain in Judy Grahn's *A Woman is Talking to Death*." *Women and Language* 10.2 (Spring 1987): 38–43. ■ Carruthers, Mary J. "The Re-Vision of the Muse: Adrienne Rich, Audre Lorde, Judy Grahn, Olga Broumas." *The Hudson Review* 36 (Summer 1983): 293–322. ■ Case, Sue-Ellen. "Judy Grahn's Gynopoetics: *The Queen of Swords*." *Studies in the Literary Imagination* 21.2 (Fall 1988): 47–67. ■ Montefiore, Jan, "'What words say': Three Women Poets Reading H.D." *Agenda* 25.3–4 (Autumn–Winter 1987–1988): 172–190. ■ Ostriker, Alicia. *Stealing the Language: The Emergence of Women's Poetry in America*. Boston: Beacon Press, 1986.

Gray, Thomas
(1716–1771)

Thomas Gray, the best-loved poet of the eighteenth century, was born to a distinctly middle-class family of shop owners, the only surviving child of twelve. His mother was a sweet-tempered woman who ran a millinery business with her sister; and his father was a violently jealous man who beat his wife and abused her with vile language. He was a lonely, bookish boy, and until two of his uncles, who were masters at Eton, arranged for his matriculation there, he had no friends his own age. At Eton, where he went in 1725, he eventually made a few close friends who shared his interest in literature and writing. Chief among these were HORACE WALPOLE, Richard West, and Thomas Ashton. All these boys had literary aspirations, and they dubbed themselves the Quadruple Alliance. Together they read VIRGIL, wrote poetry, and avoided the athletic field. Their mutual friendships became deeply romantic as the years progressed, and Gray grew to feel love for both the flamboyant and worldly Walpole and the shy and poetic West. When the latter died in 1742, Gray wrote one of his most touching sonnets, and later in life, after a break that has never been adequately explained, Walpole encouraged him in his work and himself published Gray's most famous poem, "Elegy Written in a Country Churchyard."

Gray went on to Cambridge after Eton, and it was there that he returned as a fellow some years after his undergraduate tenure. The quiet life of a teacher and scholar followed. Indeed, if he had not written a few of the most enduring poems in the language, his life would be of little interest. What becomes clear as one looks at Gray's experience, however, was that he for the most part suppressed his deeply emotional attachment to members of his own sex, and only in later life did he actually express the love he felt for another man. This man was Charles-Victor de Bonstettin, who came to Cambridge from Switzerland to study with the famous poet when Gray was in his early fifties. Gray fell for the young man in a devastating way and professed his love openly. Bonstettin was embarrassed by Gray's exuberance and declined his attentions. Soon, he returned to Switzerland to leave Gray only with the memory of sitting with him during the long Cambridge evenings. Of course, we cannot be sure that Gray did not consummate his love for Bonstettin, or that there were not others with whom he had sexual adventures. It seems to me, however, that the only place he realized the power of his emotional attachments fully was in his poetry.

Gray's "Sonnet on the Death of Richard West" (1742), his "Ode on a Distant Prospect of Eton College" (1742), and his "Elegy Written in a Country Churchyard" (1751) are memorials to the love he felt for other young men: In the first, he mourns the loss of a friend; in the second, he imagines the world of boys at school and warns them of ill to come; and in the third, he imagines his own almost friendless end. In the "Elegy," in fact, Gray talks about his own death in intimate terms, looks at his own corpse as it is carried to its grave, and even contemplates the grave itself. The poem ends with his own epitaph, in which he sees himself as a simply melancholy man, whose one wish was for a friend who could share that melancholy with him; he lies in hope of paternal forgiveness, and in fear of the hidden truths of his own soul. These few lines are a part of our heritage, to be sure:

Here rests his head upon the lap of Earth
A Youth to Fortune and to Fame unknown.

Fair Science frown'd not on his humble birth,
And Melancholy marked him for her own.

Large was his bounty, and his soul sincere,
Heav'n did a recompence as largely send:
He gave to Mis'ry all he had, a tear,
He gain'd from Heav'n ('twas all he wish'd)
    a friend.

No farther seek his merits to disclose,
Or draw his frailties from their dread abode,
(There they alike in trembling hope repose,)
The bosom of his Father and his God.

(See also ELEGY.)

—*George E. Haggerty*

BIBLIOGRAPHY

Bentman, Raymond. "Thomas Gray and the Poetry of Hapless Love." *Journal of the History of Sexuality* 3 (1992): 203–222. ■ Haggerty, George E. "'The Voice of Nature' in Gray's *Elegy*." *Homosexuality in Renaissance and Enlightenment England: Literary Representations in Historical Context*. Claude J. Summers. ed. New York: Haworth Press, 1992. 199–214. ■ Hagstrum, Jean. "Gray's Sensibility." *Fearful Joy: Papers from the Thomas Gray Bicentenary Conference at Carleton University*. J. Downey and B. Jones, eds. Montreal: McGill-Queens University, 1974. 6–19. ■ Rousseau, G. S. "The Pursuit of Homosexuality in the Eighteenth Century: 'Utterly Confused Category' and/or Rich Respository." *Eighteenth-Century Life* 9 (1985): 132–168. ■ Trumbach, Randolph. "London's Sodomites: Homosexual Behavior and Western Culture in the 18th Century." *Journal of Social History* 11 (1977): 171–174. ■ Watson-Smyth, Peter. "On Gray's *Elegy*." *The Spectator* 31 July 1971: 171–174.

GREEK LITERATURE

Greek Literature, Ancient

In the heritage of homosexual literature, ancient Greece holds a unique place. Here was a society relatively hospitable to the love of boys and youths, and, on occasion, to love between older men, in which poetry and prose that celebrated such affections formed a significant part of its culture. Nor was this phenomenon, as some have assumed, limited to a relatively short period in the classical age. Explicitly homoerotic themes are an important part of Greek literature from at least 600 B.C. till as late as 400 A.D. They appear in myths, lyric poetry, epic, tragedy, comedy, epigrams, philosophical debates, biography, and literary discussions. The influence of this literary tradition was immense. Its first impact was on the Romans, who absorbed and imitated the verse of SAPPHO, Alcaeus, Callimachus, THEOCRITUS, and the Greek Anthology, and who, through Ovid, became thoroughly familiar with homoerotic myths associated with the Olympian gods. Via Latin literature, these traditions reached medieval Christendom, primarily through its reading of Ovid, but also through the poetry of VIRGIL and HORACE. With the coming of the Renaissance, western Europe reimmersed itself directly in Greek culture, and this aspect of it found echoes in the vernacular literatures of Italy, France, and England. Until WHITMAN, most of the homosexual poetry of the West can be related to some Greek source, or to its reflection in classical Latin.

Archaic Greece. We know from historical accounts of ancient Greece that various forms of institutionalized pederasty were part of Greek life from early times. It was most highly developed in Crete, where ritualized abductions were part of the culture and conferred honorific status on the boy. In Spartan military society, men and boys were expected to form close bonds as "inspirers" and "hearers"; to emphasize the importance of these attachments, the Spartans sacrificed to Eros before giving battle. Opinion was keenly divided in classical times on whether such relations were sexual. PLUTARCH held that Spartan loves were not physical, but PLATO in his *Laws* implies the contrary, and Xenophon admitted that skepticism about their chastity was widespread. Male love was freely accepted and institutionalized in Thebes, where men pledged their vows at the shrine of Iolaüs, the lover of Heracles, the patron god of the city. Elis, the town in the Peloponnesus that presided over the games at Olympus, was ranked with Thebes in this regard. It held an annual beauty contest for boys. In Theognis' city, Megara, boys competed in a civic kissing competition. Plutarch tells a dramatic story about how Chalcis, on the island of Euboea, came to endorse male love enthusiastically after seeing its positive effect on military morale. In Athens, Solon was reputed to have been the lover of Pisistratus, who was in turn the lover of Charmus, who set up the first altar to Eros in the city.

In Greek love affairs, an older man, or *erastes,* became the mentor of a young boy, or *eromenos.* On the one side was age, wisdom, and accomplishment; on the other, youth, beauty, and a desire to emulate and excel. Male love was very much part of the communal life of Greek cities that had its center in the gymnasium. There men met, exercised in the nude, discoursed on politics and (if we may believe Plato) on philosophy, and in addition found lovers. Love between men, it was argued, inspired courage in war and prepared youths for careers as statesmen or philosophers. In late archaic times, many elegantly painted scenes on Greek vases show men courting boys or engaging in specifically sexual behavior. By 600 B.C. or shortly after, this culture was finding eloquent expression in Greek lyric poetry: Alcaeus and Solon were celebrating the love of boys, and Sappho was writing love poems to young women.

The case of Homer, on the other hand, was, and still is, the subject of much debate. The *Iliad* (ca 800–750 B.C.) was the undisputed masterpiece of Greek epic poetry and a kind of bible for the Greek world as a repository of myths, history, and exemplary tales of military valor. Central to its plot is the passionate attachment of Achilles and Patroclus. But did Homer mean us to perceive them as lovers? There is no doubt that later writers of the classical age such as Aeschylus and Aeschines thought so, and believed the lack of explicitness about an erotic element in their friendship was merely a sign of Homer's literary tact. But the *Iliad* does not fit the archetypal *erastes–eromenos* pattern. Achilles is the younger and more beautiful, but he is also the dominant personality. And in the *Iliad,* both men sleep with slave women. Critics who support the theory that Achilles and Patroclus are lovers (in the emotional, if not necessarily in the sexual sense) most often cite the passage in the *Iliad* where Achilles wishes all the other Greek warriors dead so "we two alone" might win glory in fighting the Trojans. They also note the wild intensity of Achilles' grief when Patroclus is killed fighting the Trojans. How puzzling the matter was to the Greeks is indicated by

the view of a leading Alexandrian editor of Homer, Aristarchus. Aristarchus held that Achilles and Patroclus were not lovers but that the "we two alone" passage implied they were. Therefore, he argued, the passage must be an interpolation. Whatever Homer's intent, Achilles, because he chose to sacrifice his life to avenge his comrade, was popularly seen in later times not just as the greatest warrior, but also as the heroic lover par excellence.

With Sappho of Lesbos (born ca 612), we are left with no doubt about the erotic feeling that imbues her lyrics addressed to young women. Love for her is an overwhelming, all-consuming passion. In her famous "Ode," she speaks of breaking into a cold sweat and standing tongue-tied in the presence of her beloved, who sits beside a man Sappho envies. Her prayer to Aphrodite recalls how the goddess once promised to make another woman fall in love with Sappho, who once more invokes her aid. Biographers in the late classical period looked askance at these passionate affairs, but Sappho during her lifetime seems to have retained a respected place in the society of Lesbos. After her death, her face appeared on the coins of her native city, Mytilene, and paintings and statues representing her were common throughout the classical world. Wealthy families from distant places sent their daughters to be trained by her in singing and dancing. Some of her poems are addressed to her pupils Anactoria and Atthis and recall the delights of their life together. Others bitterly reproach girls who she thinks have forgotten her. Her circle formed an aesthetic cult devoted to beauty and the arts, and probably performed at civic religious festivals. Sappho was married, had a daughter, and composed songs for weddings. However, the story that she fell in love with a ferryman named Phaon and committed suicide on his account is a later, unsubstantiated, legend.

Sappho's passionate lyrics were much admired in antiquity. Plato called her the "Tenth Muse." Unfortunately, fewer than half a dozen of her sparklingly brilliant poems have survived in anything like complete form; most of what we have are fragments. Sappho's influence on modern lesbian poetry in the late nineteenth and early twentieth century was of prime importance. Her elegant aestheticism and exotic remoteness piqued the imagination of male poets like BAUDELAIRE (see his "Lesbos") and inspired tributes by RENÉE VIVIEN and NATALIE BARNEY, American expatriates in Paris, and the poems in which AMY LOWELL celebrated her lover Ada Russell. HILDA DOOLITTLE (H. D.) fell under her spell, and WILLA CATHER wrote a review that is a kind of prose poem extolling Sappho's love poetry. The word *lesbian* in its modern sense was not, however, used by the ancient Greeks.

Plato speaks of the "female companions" and the common (derogatory) term was "tribade." "Lesbian" with its present meaning first appears in seventeenth-century France, which also coined the term *Sapphist.*

By coincidence, the first identifiable Greek male poet to write love poems to boys was also a native of Lesbos. Alcaeus was Sappho's contemporary and addressed poems to her, to which, Aristotle tells us, she wrote cool replies. He was an ardent partisan of the aristocratic faction on Lesbos to which Sappho's own family was allied. His love poems have disappeared, and we know of them only from references in Cicero and Horace. Horace tells us Alcaeus sang of Lycus "with his black eyes and black hair" (Odes, 1.32). Solon of Athens (ca 640–558) won fame as a democratic statesman and lawgiver; he ranked as one of the "Seven Sages" of the ancient world. In his youth, he wrote poems on the love of boys, praising their kisses and thighs. The law code he drew up for Athens forbade slaves to be the lovers of freeborn boys. Plutarch thought this measure was meant to "incite the worthy to that which he forbade the unworthy."

The poetry of Ibycus of Rhegium (in southern Italy) resembles Sappho's in treating love as an overpowering tempest of emotion. Lauded by the Alexandrian critics as one of the "Nine Lyric Poets" of Greece, he lived at the luxurious court of the tyrant Polycrates of Samos. Only fragments of his poems remain; some are pederastic. His epitaph calls him a "lover of the lyre" and a "lover of boys." Anacreon, born ca 570 at Teos on the coast of Asia Minor, was also a dependent of Polycrates, whose court was a major literary center where erotic verse was much favored. We know the names of three of the youths to whom Anacreon addressed love poems: Smerdies, Bathyllus, and Cleobolus. His poems are playful and pleasure-loving, their themes wine, women, song—and boys. A pretty story tells how, drunk, he stumbled against a nurse and child and abused them. The nurse expressed the pious wish that he might one day praise the child. Anacreon, we are told, later fell in love with the boy. When Polycrates was killed by Persian treachery, Anacreon had the good fortune to win the patronage of Hipparchus, the co-tyrant (with his brother Hippias) of Athens. After the fall of these rulers, democratic Athens raised a statue to him on the Acropolis where he stood, wine cup in hand, next to Pericles.

In contrast to the lighthearted poetry of the Samian tradition stand the *Elegies* of Theognis of Megara (fl ca 540). Theognis takes his role as mentor to youth seriously, and his gnomic verse became a Greek school classic. A conservative who faced exile and poverty after a popular revolt in his native city, he attempts in his poems to teach his *eromenos* Kurnos the ways of aristocratic tradition. One of his most impressive poems promises immortality to Kurnos in a style that adumbrates SHAKESPEARE's sonnets. His moods are many—bitter, chiding, idyllically happy. Finally he admits that the love of boys is an exasperating mixture of pain and joy, all the more charming for this uncertainty. About 1,000 A.D. a Byzantine editor divided the *Elegies* into two books, segregating the pederastic poems (about forty in number) in the shorter second book.

Theognis sought through his love poetry to transmit aristocratic mores. In later Greek literary tradition, however, male homosexual love was exalted as a safeguard against tyranny, and in Athens, two male lovers came to be perceived as the heroic patrons of democracy as the result of a dramatic episode that took place in 514. Thucydides tells the story, which appears in a slightly different version in Aristotle. Harmodius, the younger man, was the *eromenos* of Aristogiton. When the tyrant Hipparchus made advances, Harmodius repulsed him. Hipparchus revenged himself by publicly insulting Harmodius' sister. The lovers then conspired to assassinate both tyrants. They struck down Hipparchus in the Agora, but Hippias survived the attempt. Harmodius was killed on the spot; Aristogiton was captured and tortured to death. Though their quarrel was private rather than political, their efforts led finally to the overthrow of the tyranny and the reestablishment of Athenian democracy. In gratitude, the Athenians granted the lovers semi-divine honors and made them the center of a civic cult. Their statues in the Agora became Athens' chief secular monument, and a much quoted ritual drinking song (in effect the city's anthem) celebrated them for inaugurating "equal laws" through their revolt. In later Greek literature, such as Plato's *Symposium* and Plutarch's *Eroticos,* the "tyrannicides" stand beside Achilles and Patroclus as emblems of heroic love.

The Classical Period. The classical age in Greek culture is usually dated from the defeat of the Persians at the battle of Marathon (490) to the triumph of Philip of Macedon over the other Greek states at Chaeronea (338). It encompasses the greatest achievements of Greek architecture, sculpture, philosophy, and drama. Pindar of Thebes (who was about thirty at the time of Marathon) stands with Sappho as the greatest of Greek lyric poets. When Alexander later razed Thebes to punish it for a revolt he left only the house of Pindar standing. His noble sublimity contrasts with the graceful informality of Ibycus and Anacreon, but Athenaeus likened him to the earlier poets in his "immoderate" eroticism. His surviving odes all praise athletes who were winners of the Olympic and other panhellenic games. They make much of homoerotic myths. In his tenth Olympian ode, he retells the story of Zeus's abduction of the beautiful Trojan boy, Ganymede. His first Olympian ode even invents a new myth; in it he makes Poseidon the lover of Pelops, the founder of Elis, as a way of flattering the city. He shows a keen appreciation for the looks and personalities of the athletes he celebrates. As an old man, he fell in love with Theoxenus, to whom he wrote a glowing love poem still extant. He is said to have died, at eighty, leaning on the shoulder of the younger man in a theater.

The most impressive literary achievement of the classical period was Greek tragedy. None of the thirty-three extant plays by Aeschylus, Sophocles, and Euripides deals with homosexual love affairs. We know, however, from the writings of Athenaeus (ca 200 A.D.) that such plays existed and we are told that "the audience gladly accepted such stories." Athenaeus names as the first famous play on this theme Aeschylus' *Myrmidons*. The text has vanished, but enough fragments remain for us to guess at the plot. The play takes its title from Achilles' armed Thessalian followers at Troy, who presumably made up its chorus; its subject is Achilles' love for Patroclus. The climax was the death of Patroclus, who had died fighting in Achilles' armor, and its most quoted speech was Achilles' lament over the body of his dead lover. In it, he referred to their "many kisses" and to "the holy union of our thighs," a phrase that must have startled the Athenians. The other play mentioned by Athenaeus as notable for its treatment of same-sex love is Sophocles' *Niobe*. Niobe was the boastful mother whose six sons and six daughters were slain by Apollo and Artemis. It may seem strange that a play on such a topic should have had a homosexual emphasis. But Athenaeus tells us that the play was also known as the *Paiderastria* ("Love of Youths"), and Plutarch quotes a line in which one of the dying sons calls on his lover to protect him from Apollo's arrows. The disappearance of these plays, along with the seven books of Sappho, is probably the greatest loss the gay and lesbian literary heritage has known.

Sophocles' passion for young men was well known, and several anecdotes (some of them scandalous) survive, along with the name of one of his lovers—Demophon. One story tells of his rivalry with Euripides for the favors of a boy prostitute. Euripides himself wrote at least one play on a homosexual liaison, his *Chrysippus*. Chrysippus was the son of Pelops, who was abducted against his will by King Laius, Oedipus's father; in the Theban legend it is this crime that brings about the curse on Laius's family. The dramatist who in classical times was regarded as ranking next after Aeschylus, Sophocles, and Euripi-

des as a writer of tragedies was Agathon; unfortunately, all of his plays have vanished. It is in honor of his winning the prize for tragedy in 416 that the celebration described in Plato's *Symposium* is supposed to take place. In the dialogue, it is hinted that Agathon, who was remarkable for his beauty, is the lover of Pausanias, another of the speakers. The fact that they are an unusual, adult couple leads Pausanias to defend such relationships. About the year 406, Agathon emigrated to the court of King Archelaus of Macedon, who was a patron of drama. Euripides, who was now over seventy, joined him there and became his lover. Agathon would have been about forty. When queried by Archelaus about his love, Euripides is said to have replied that Agathon's beauty was impressive even in its autumn. Plutarch, in his *Eroticos,* takes this love affair between the two greatest poets of their age as the archetype of same-sex love between mature men.

If we lack Greek tragedies treating of homosexuality, there is no dearth of references to the subject in Aristophanes, whose comedies first appeared in 427. Since his works are farcical extravaganzas that deliberately border on the outrageous, most of the comments are satirical. Aristophanes has sometimes been regarded as homophobic but to take this view is to fail to understand Greek culture. The man who assumed the active role with boys or men did not compromise his masculinity. But as in modern Mediterranean and Latin American societies, a passive adult male was always liable to ridicule for playing what was perceived as a feminine role. Thus Aristophanes makes fun of Agathon in the *Thesmophoriazusae* for dressing in women's clothes—purportedly to throw himself into the mood of the heroine in a play he is writing. He repeatedly mocks Cleisthenes, the Athenian politician, as an Oriental eunuch. In the *Lysistrata* the tumescent husbands, desperate because of their wives' sex strike, propose him as a substitute.

But this mocking of male effeminacy, unpleasant as it often is, is not to be confused with simple anti-homosexualism. The uncultivated working-class Athenians who are the heroes of Aristophanes' comedies are quite willing to find satisfaction with male partners provided they take the active role. Thus Philocleon in the *Wasps* relishes examining nude boys as part of his jury assignment. At the end of the *Knights*, its hero is awarded both a woman and a boy as his prizes. In the *Birds*, Pisthetairos imagines a utopia where fathers of good-looking boys will scold him for not being aggressive enough in seducing their sons. But Aristophanes' comedies also have a serious side. Strongly conservative in his social views, he vigorously championed the plays of Aeschylus and attacked Euripides. The tragedy of Aeschylus he most admired seems to have been the *Myrmidons*; he quotes it more often than any other play. In the *Frogs,* he introduces Aeschylus as a character and makes him boast that his plays were in the true heroic style of Homer because they depicted "men of valor, lion-hearted heroes like Patroclus" who would inspire the audience to imitate them when they were called to battle. In the *Symposium,* Plato has Aristophanes speak in defense of male love. There he appears as a kind of "gay chauvinist" who claims that lovers of males are superior to the lovers of women since they are "more masculine" and most often provided political leadership.

Plato's *Symposium* and *Phaedrus* are the most brilliant and best known writings on Greek homosexuality to come down to us from the classical era. Plato records with dramatic vividness informal scenes where flirtations take place, lighthearted banter is exchanged, and current attitudes to male love are seriously discussed or implicitly revealed. Plato shares the popular enthusiasm for these affairs as the source of inspiring emotional bonds while arguing that they should remain unconsummated. The *Symposium* reveals popular Greek attitudes, the *Phaedrus* presents an ultra-romantic ideal of (chaste) male love, and a late work, the *Laws,* argues for punitive measures against physical acts. (See also PLATO.)

Edmund Spenser noted that English scholars of the Renaissance were much more likely to have read Xenophon than Plato. Xenophon's *Symposium* parallels Plato's and makes reference to it. It purports to be an account of a feast given by Callias to honor his young lover Autolycus, who had won a prize in the Panathenaic games. (This victory took place in 422 at which date, however, Xenophon would have been only eight years old.) During the evening, leading citizens of Athens discuss—and demonstrate by their present behavior—the power of male beauty to entrance other males. However, this is no special coterie: Callias' guests speak freely of the ubiquitousness of such infatuations in their society. Socrates delivers a definitive speech rhapsodically extolling male love but deprecating any sexual expression. He argues that Zeus's love for Ganymede and Achilles' for Patroclus was free from carnality, and that male love in Sparta is similarly nonphysical. At the same time, he strongly commends Callias' love for Autolycus and names approvingly a number of other prominent Athenians whose (Platonic) love affairs with other males were widely recognized. Xenophon's dialogue, though hardly of Platonic caliber, has substance, charm, and eloquence, and deserves to be better known. His other works—*The Constitution of Sparta,* the *Economist,*

and the *Anabasis* are also important for what they reveal of Greek attitudes; Xenophon's own view of male homosexuality is sometimes matter-of-fact, sometimes romantic, but it lacks Socrates' puritanism.

Another prose work that contains important information on Athenian law and throws much light on popular attitudes toward male love is Aeschines' speech, *Against Timarchus* (345). Demosthenes had accused Aeschines of betraying the city's interests in its negotiations with Philip of Macedon, and a popular demagogue named Timarchus had joined him in the indictment. Aeschines' defense was to accuse Timarchus of having led the life of a male courtesan: Athens had a law that men who prostituted themselves lost their civic rights and could not bring charges in the courts. What is striking about Aeschines' speech, however, is the pains he takes to make it clear that he is not opposed to male love affairs generally. He imagines that some Athenian general will appear in Timarchus' defense and attack Aeschines as an opponent of "honorable love" and a threat to traditional Athenian culture. Wanting to appear on the popular side of a long-standing debate, Aeschines quotes lengthy passages from the *Iliad* to argue for the view that Achilles and Patroclus were indeed lovers. He names approvingly various young Athenians well known for having attracted lovers through their beauty. He confesses, moreover, that he too has made a nuisance of himself by pursuing young men in the gymnasia and has written erotic verse. Aeschines' rhetoric throughout his speech demonstrates how strongly Athenian sentiment in the late classical period favored male love, provided it was not tainted by mercenary motives.

The Hellenistic Age. After the victories of Macedon and Rome, Greece lost its political independence but retained and, indeed, widened its cultural influence. Athens remained a major educational center for the Mediterranean world. In this age, Alexandria was founded and played a vital part in promoting scholarship and literature. About 280, Callimachus founded a new "Alexandrian" school of poetry that was fastidious and erudite. Though he inaugurated a revolution in style, Callimachus was a conservative in his amorous verse—a dozen of his epigrams on boy love appear in the Greek Anthology. One of these love poems is addressed to Theocritus. It would appear that once again the two leading Greek poets of their age were lovers.

Theocritus' poems reflect the internationalism of the Alexandrians; they are set in Italy and Sicily, on Aegean islands, and in Alexandria itself. As the inventor of "pastoral" poetry—in which the poet pretends to be a simple shepherd, he initiated a lasting genre and made a path for later homosexual poets. (See also

PASTORAL.) Theocritus' Idylls, or "short poems," attest to the way earlier traditions of Greek love persisted and flourished in Hellenistic times. Seven of the thirty Idylls ascribed to him touch on homosexual themes. In Idyll V ("Goatherd and Shepherd"), Comatas boasts of the girls who favor him, Lacon of the boys he enjoys. In Idyll VII ("The Harvest Festival"), Lycidas grieves over the departure of his lover for Mytilene; and Simichidas, who loves a girl, sings not of her but of the love of his friend Aratus for a boy. Idyll XXIII ("Erastes") is probably not by Theocritus; it tells the story of a boy whose lover kisses his doorpost and hangs himself in despair. The boy treats the corpse with cold disdain; when he goes to the gymnasium to swim, a statue of Eros falls and kills him, staining the water with his blood. Three of the Idylls (XII, XXIX, and XXX) are lover's complaints in which Theocritus addresses boys he has fallen in love with and chides them for their fickleness. In XII, he invokes the traditions of ancient Sparta and Thessaly, in XXIX, the love of Achilles for Patroclus: "Then there were men of gold, when the *eromenos* reflected the love of the *erastes*." In the former poem, he tells the boy their love will be known "two hundred generations" hence. Perhaps the most poignant and beautiful of the Idylls is XIII, which dramatizes Heracles' grief over the loss of young Hylas, accidentally drowned when the Argonauts break their journey at the Hellespont.

The most comprehensive collection of Greek poems to come down to us is the so-called Greek Anthology, a compilation based on earlier collections and given its final form by Cephalus, a Byzantine scholar of the tenth century. Two of its fifteen books consist of erotic epigrams—Book V (with 309 poems) is devoted to the love of women, Book XII (with 258) to the love of boys. Book XII derives in part from a collection called the "Garland of Meleager," put together about 50 B.C. by Meleager of Gadara, which contained his own poems and those of earlier writers. Meleager's thirty-one epigrams are the liveliest in Book XII. Wildly exuberant, he moves giddily, as he puts it, through a "sea of boys," registering every mood of the delighted or frustrated or fearful lover. The poet who contributes the most poems (about 100) to Book XII, however, is Straton of Sardis, who lived in the age of Hadrian. He may be credited as the first person known to have compiled a gay anthology. His collection, generally known by its Latin title as the *Musa Puerilis* (ca 140 A.D.), differed from Meleager's "Garland" in that it contained only homosexual poems, mainly his own. In essence, it formed the nucleus for Cephalus' Book XII. In its final form, Book XII of the Greek Anthology preserves poems by thirty poets from five centuries. They are short and pithy, lyrical or satirical, delicate protestations of devotion or coarse jests, lovers' boasts, laments or revenges, confessions of rapture, dementia, or despair.

That Straton's anthology should have appeared in the second century is appropriate, for the age of the Antonines produced a Hellenic revival that influenced the whole Greco-Roman world. There was a renewed interest in the classical legacy, including the historical and literary traditions of male love. We may say that in a sense, gay studies begin in this century with the writings of Plutarch, Straton, Athenaeus, and Aelian. The panculturalism of the era is symbolized in literature by Plutarch's *Parallel Lives* of famous Greeks and Romans and in life by the love of the Roman Emperor Hadrian for the Greek boy Antinous. (Unfortunately, Hadrian's own love poems to boys have been lost, though fragments of a poem in Greek describing a lion hunt with Antinous are extant.)

Plutarch put special emphasis on male love affairs in his biographies of Lycurgus, Solon, Agesilaus, Alexander, and Pelopidas. The "Life of Pelopidas" is of particular importance. In it, Plutarch gives a unique account of the Sacred Band of Thebes (378–38 B.C.), a regiment made up of three hundred lovers who fought as couples. Plutarch admiringly celebrates the unique discipline, high morale, and remarkable victories of this "army of lovers," which made it possible for the Thebans to defeat Sparta and become the leading military power in Greece for forty years. Plutarch's most striking contribution to gay literary history, however, is not his *Lives* but his philosophical dialogue, the *Eroticos*, or "Dialogue on Love" (ca 110 A.D.). The dialogue is of great interest for the light it throws on attitudes to male love in late classical times. It takes the form of a debate on which is better, the love of males or the love of women. The debate has a lively and entertaining dramatic frame—it is sparked by a vehement quarrel among his friends and admirers about whether a favored youth should marry. It represents opinion in Plutarch's day as fairly evenly divided, though Plutarch himself argues in favor of married love. Plutarch takes a high Platonic line on love, praises it as a kind of "erotic madness" (he quotes Sappho's "Ode" to establish this), and enumerates its personal and social benefits. But in order to defend conjugal love, he feels he must first defend love in general. To do this, he draws on Greek myth, history, and literature. Such traditions were abundant but almost exclusively homoerotic. The result is that Plutarch prefaces his defense of marriage with a long panegyric on *male* love extremely rich in historical anecdotes and literary material, an encyclopedia of (mainly positive) Greek ideas on the subject with much information that does not appear elsewhere. The paradoxical result is that though conjugal love gets Plutarch's special approval, the *Eroticos* ranks closely after the *Symposium* and the *Phaedrus* as a document in the gay literary heritage.

Rivaling Plutarch as a contribution to gay history, with a special emphasis on literature, is Book XIII of *The Deipnosophists,* or *The Savants at Dinner,* an enormous compilation of erudition by Athenaeus, who wrote at Naucratis, a Greek city in Egypt, at the end of the first century. Casual, sprawling, and chaotic, this marathon conversation makes reference to a wealth of stories and preserves much information about gay literary themes that would otherwise have been lost.

In the comedies of Menander and later Greek and Latin playwrights, the "boy-meets-girl" pattern established itself as the conventional love plot. It is also standard in the Greek novels that have come down to us. Some of them, however, have homosexual subplots. This is the case in the *Ephesian Tale* of Xenophon of Ephesus and the *Leucippe and Clitophon* of Achilles Tatius. (Greek novels are hard to date; it is possible that both works belong to the third century A.D.) The first tells the story of Hippothoos and Hyperanthes, the second that of Clinias and Charicles. Both episodes are treated romantically and sympathetically and strike a note of tragic pathos. Tatius' novel also contains a short discussion on which gender makes the more enjoyable partner in an amorous affair: each is commended. This question, a popular subject for debate in late antiquity, is central to the last full-length philosophical dialogue on homosexuality that has survived. The dialogue, entitled *Erotes,* or *The Loves,* in many ways parallels Plutarch's *Eroticos* and reads like a response to it. Once more we have a highly passionate debate between a homosexual and a heterosexual on the merits of their respective lifestyles. Originally ascribed to LUCIAN, it is written in his lively, not to say racy, style, but dates from after his death, perhaps from around 230 A.D. The setting for the debate is a visit by three men to the temple of Aphrodite at Cnidus to view Praxiteles' famous statue. Its arguments in favor of male love are very much in the mode of the *Symposium* and the *Eroticos.* Callicratidas, the homosexual speaker, makes the traditional claim for the ennobling influence of male love with some eloquence. There are, however, a few novelties. Callicratidas, when invoking the heroic side of Greek love, chooses as his exemplary lovers a new couple, Orestes and Pylades. He points to their self-sacrificing behavior in Euripides' *Iphigenia in Tauris,* where each is represented as willing to die to save the other. And, in contrast to the *Eroticos,* this time the debate is adjudicated in favor of the homosexual

speaker, a result that demonstrates how long the classical Greek view endured in antiquity.

Classical civilization may be said to have come to an end with the abolition of the Olympic Games, in 393, by the Christian Emperor Theodosius. Theodosius launched a determined campaign against paganism and passed a law that made homosexual acts punishable by burning. The last substantial work of ancient Greek literature to celebrate male love is the *Dionysiaca* of Nonnus. Apart from his authorship of the *Dionysiaca,* nothing is known of Nonnus, except that he lived at Panopolis in Egypt and (presumably later) produced a verse paraphrase of the gospel of St. John. Nonnus' dates are very uncertain. The composition of the *Dionysiaca* has been dated as early as the period 390–405 and as late as the end of the fifth century. Given the strong official reaction against paganism and the repeated attacks by the Fathers of the Church on the pederastic element in Greek religion and literature, the earlier dates seem more likely. Nonnus' vast epic in forty-eight books describes Dionysus' conquest of India; books ten through twelve recount, in baroque detail, his love for the boy Ampelus, who after his death is transformed into the vine sacred to the god. It also tells of the love of two boys, Carpus and Calamus. Carpus is drowned, and the grieving Calamus is turned into a water reed. It has been suggested that this myth may have inspired the title for Whitman's "Calamus" poems in his *Leaves of Grass.* Whether or not such a link exists between ancient Greek and modern American gay poetry, the *Dionysiaca* is a final, and remarkable, swan song to a literary tradition that existed for more than a millennium. (See also MYTH and ROMAN LITERATURE.)

—Louis Crompton

BIBLIOGRAPHY

Buffière, Félix. *Éros adolescent: la pédérastie dans la Grèce antique.* Paris: Les Belles Lettres, 1980. ■ Clarke, W. M. "Achilles and Patroclus in Love." *Hermes* 106(1978): 381–396. ■ Dover, Kenneth. *Greek Homosexuality.* Cambridge: Harvard University Press, 1978. ■ Dynes, Wayne, ed. *Encyclopedia of Homosexuality.* 2 vols. New York: Garland, 1990. ■ Foucault, Michel. *The Use of Pleasure.* Trans. R. Hurley. New York: Random House, 1985. ■ Flacelière, Robert. *Love in Ancient Greece.* Trans. J. Cleugh. New York: Crown, 1962. ■ Halperin, David. *One Hundred Years of Homosexuality and Other Essays on Greek Love.* New York: Routledge, 1990. ■ Licht, Hans. *Sexual Life in Ancient Greece.* London: Routledge, 1932. ■ Page, Dennis. *Sappho and Alcaeus.* Oxford: Oxford University Press, 1955. ■ Sergent, Bernard. *Homosexuality in Greek Myth.* Trans. A. Goldhammmer. Boston: Beacon, 1984.

Translations of most of the works cited will be found in the Loeb Classical Library; for the dialogues discussed, see *Lucian* (vol. 8); Plutarch, *Moralia* (vol. 9); and Xenophon, *Scriptora Minora* in the Loeb editions.

Greek Literature, Modern

Classical Greece has traditionally been viewed as the fertile field from which homosexual culture in the West has been nurtured. The modern state of Greece, however, seems somewhat reticent to accept homosexuality as a principal aspect of its culture. One might assume that extended foreign domination, the imposition of a military state, followed by a less than liberal socialist government, along with the Mediterranean focus on the traditional family as the primary social unit, nearly universal Christian orthodoxy, and a tendency toward machismo, have all contributed to rendering homosexuality almost invisible in contemporary Greek society. This is not to say that homosexuality is absent in modern Greece. One need only travel to Mykonos during the summer months to realize a gay presence, and Western women still pilgrimage to the Mytilene mecca in search of Sapphic sisters. Nor is it true that homosexuality never appears in contemporary Greek literature. In fact, one of Greece's greatest modern poets, CONSTANTINE CAVAFY, has included homosexuality as a fundamental element of his poetics.

Greece is a country of poets, and Constantine Petrou Cavafy (1863–1933) has been called, by the esteemed Greek literary historian C. A. Trypanis, "the most original of all the modern Greek poets." A shy and reclusive man whose poetry was never commercially published during his lifetime, Cavafy spent most of his life in the Greek community of Alexandria, employed as a petty bureaucrat. The major themes of Cavafy's work are philosophy, history, and hedonism, yet his disillusioned, ironically humane approach discounted Christianity, patriotism, and heterosexuality. E. M. FORSTER brilliantly described him as a poet at a "slight angle to the universe," and that peculiar perspective was the result of his gayness. Cavafy lived in a time well before liberation; he himself regarded his sexuality as at best a liability, at worst a perversion.

The poem "Walls" expresses perfectly Cavafy's feelings of isolation. Society "without a scrap of guilt" has built great, high walls around the poet who "can do nothing else, my brain deep gnawed by fate" "unwittingly shut off from all the world around." In "The Windows," whose title ironically evokes traditional symbols of freedom and truth, the poet is living in "dark chambers," fearful of exposure to light that could bring to him "another form of tyranny." "The City" mournfully describes the futility of attempting to escape one's past by geographic change. In "Awaiting the Barbarians," Cavafy exposes traditional societies' implicit need for outcasts, "who serve a solution of some sort." Even though Cavafy was tormented by his particular sexuality, there was no way he could squelch his natural desires. In "He Vows," the persona, after a night of debauchery, resolves "to lead a better life," but when night comes again, "quite helpless, there he goes again."

Cavafy was in love with the youthful male body at the height of its prime. He wrote many poems to fictitious, contemporary and historical men, sketching their desirable attributes: "blue eyes," "exquisite limbs," and "sweet lips." But with the poet's atheism came a fear of time. Cavafy describes life in "Candles" as "a row of candles brightly lit"; he is fearful of turning to see "how fast the darkened line grows long, / how fast the burnt-down candles multiply." In "An Old Man," Cavafy depicts an aged man, alone in a coffeeshop, regretting "all the urges he repressed . . . and all the splendid joys he sacrificed." "Now mocked by all the chances he has lost," he "falls asleep / leant up against the coffeeshop's hard tabletop." Only the artist can erase the pain of time; when the old man's poems are read by young "Ephebes," they are moved "by his depictions of the beautiful."

Dinos Christianopoulos (born Costandinos Dhimitriou in 1931) found his lyrical voice through Cavafy. Like his mentor, Christianopoulos has spent most of his life in his native surroundings, Thessaloniki, traveling only when absolutely necessary and only for the briefest periods. Christianopoulos used Cavafy as a model for the poetic expression of his homosexuality, often imitating the older poet's use of historical scenes and personages to convey contemporary ideas and sensations, thereby making universal the emotions expressed. Like Cavafy's, Christianopoulos's work is devoid of references to contemporary politics. The younger poet, however, as exemplified in his poem "The Splinter," expresses guilt at his "indifference about political matters." The poem documents the assassination of Gregory Lambrakis (1963), which our poet learns about, quite by accident, "returning from a date." Throughout contemporary Greece, men are being "clubbed down for their ideals," while Christianopoulos is still "mindlessly running off to make love in the meadows." The poet is distressed by his ennui, his inability to participate in social causes, which "disturbs me / like an imperceptible splinter that won't come out."

Guilt concerning sexual preference is present in the works of both poets. Unlike Cavafy, Christianopoulos's regret is magnified in his early works by his religious feelings (his chosen pseudonym, Christianopoulos, means son of Christ), and later by the pain his lifestyle generates in the people he loves. "Remorse" is a tender confessional of the poet's continual slide into nightly debauchery, made all the more personally agonizing by "my mother's face / when I return late at night and find her / waiting for me with a book in her hand, / silent, sleepless, pale . . ."

Christianopoulos's collection, *Small Poems* (1975), strips his poetry to its bare essence, removing all decoration, extended descriptors, punctuation, and capitalization, leaving the briefest epigrammatic images to surface and leap from the expansive white of the pages, like concentrated kernels of thought, into the mind of the reader. These poems are startling, sometimes brutal, yet unapologetic, sketching in bold simple strokes the onerous life of the gay man in contemporary Greece. The poet has moved from personifying a sexual seeker to a serious sexual outlaw: the prostitute. He has become limited to "the night below the navel," where even the smallest request for tenderness, a kiss, is refused, for "you won't entrust your lips to a cesspool." The life of a hustler is a sorry one, despised by others who "can't possibly know / how much i struggled / before i gave in," where even other groups of oppressed people "persecute us too." Christianopoulos's *Small Poems* are energized by isolation, repression, negation, and the fantasy of the quest. The poet warns his reader, "do not unbutton your flap / the poem will fall to pieces."

In the early part of this century, the movement known as The Cosmopolitan Poets (1915–1925) arose in Greece, primarily as a reaction against the Symbolists. The Cosmopolitans were escapists, seeking travel and exotic voyages to faraway places; they recorded the odd, exotic, different, and amazing (whether real or imagined). The first of these poets was Kóstas Ouránis (born Níarhos) who lived from 1890 to 1953. His works, especially *Spleen* (1911), exhibit the influence of BAUDELAIRE. The most celebrated of the Cosmopolitan Poets is Níkos Kavadhías (1910–1975) who took to sea as a cabin boy at nineteen and remained in that milieu for most of his life. Kavadhías's poetry brings alive the exotic, tough, marginal world of sailors, with its rough bars, whores, tattooed mariners, drugs, and the occasional gay tryst. In "A Midshipman on the Bridge in an Hour of Peril" (1931), a boy-sailor, fearful for his life during "cyclones and hurricanes," sweetly asks God for forgiveness for his sins, which include the knifing of a stranger over a young Arab girl, the stealing of "a roll of bills" from a poor prostitute, "And still more Lord . . . I blush with shame to think of it, / (ah but his lips were so rose-red and moist . . .) / I slept with a young Jewish boy one night in Seville."

Not all the Cosmopolitans took to sea. Some were armchair travelers, vicarious voyagers who revered the works of Cavafy, concocting their wild adventures in the smoke-filled coffeeshops of Athens. Alexander Baras, born in 1906 (named Menélaos Anaghnostópoulos) produced poetry that spanned the globe, from South America to Ethiopia, from Trieste to Asia. Cavafy's influence is clearly visible in his magnificent images of the male form. In "The Asiatics Pass" (1930), the poet describes "the Grandees of Asia," who pass by him, mounted on pachyderms, as they "kept in balance their sunburnt, / their voluptuous, indolent / and handsome bodies." "Centaur" (1935) is truly an encomium to male beauty. In one long and one short stanza, Baras envisions the playful ride of a nude man-boy on the bare back of a stallion. The boy is described in details worthy of Phidian sculpture: "supple body . . . overbrimming health . . . lightning in his eyes . . . desire on his lips . . . head high . . . muscles tight and well-knit . . . exquisite folds of his ribs . . . sleek thighs . . . smoothly shaped knees . . . perfectly cast calves . . . delicate ankles . . . his sex not deliberately hidden." The horse remains undescribed, whereas the boy, as the title suggests, is granted mythical perfection.

Elias Petropoulos (b. 1928) has been called the *enfant terrible* of contemporary Greek letters by the French critic Jacques Lacarrière. Petropoulos is a writer consumed with an unquenchable concern for those groups that have been deliberately excluded from acceptable society. He has become the anthropologist of the demimonde, recording the folktales and folksongs of neglected drug addicts, rejected whores, and scorned homosexuals. For his efforts, in particular for the works *The Good Robber's Manual* and the *Homosexuals' Lexicon*, Petropoulos was labeled a pornographer and imprisoned. After his release, he found it preferable to live in the more liberal atmospheres of Paris and Berlin. To date, none of his writings has been translated into English.

Costas Taktsis (b. 1927) is one of the few narrative writers to incorporate homosexuality in his prose. His novel *The Third Wedding* depicts the harsh realities of life experienced by Greece's lower classes before, during, and after World War II. Taktsis's unromantic prose, written in a colloquial idiom, is reminiscent of the Naturalism of Zola and the Verismo of Verga. The story is told through the eyes of two women, Nina and Hecuba. As their tales unfold, the reader quickly realizes that these women could survive the hardships of poverty, hunger, provincial prejudice, cultural constraints, and foreign occupation only through assertiveness, cunning, sarcasm, and heroism, which is related sometimes brutally, sometimes hilariously. Nina's tale incorporates a series of homosexual episodes. Her first love, Aryiris, was denied to her because he was a known homosexual. Her brother, Dino, suffers from "abnormal tendencies," which she witnesses one early morning as she happens upon him coupling on the veranda with her merchant marine husband, Fotis. Afterward she exclaims, "will any kind of hole satisfy these beasts?" Homosexuality is never depicted in a positive light, but its persistent appearances, despite the most adverse cultural restrictions, attest to its ubiquitousness.

Recently, Rae Dalven published an anthology, entitled *Daughters of Sappho* (1994), presenting, for the first time in English, twenty-five of the most prominent modern Greek women poets. Although the poems selected and the introductory remarks to each poet are not specifically concerned with lesbian issues, these poets introduce a women's perspective into the traditionally male-dominated world of modern Greek literature. By producing works concerned with women's consciousness, sensuality, and sexuality,

they expand the canon. They also propose a Hellenic feminism and feminize classical myth and contemporary history. To this chorus of Sapphic sisters, one must add the name of OLGA BROUMAS (b. 1949), a Greek-born woman whose American lyric is "steeped in the light of Greek myth." With her powerful songs of women loving women, Broumas has lit the lamp for lesbian lyricists from her motherland to follow. She warns her sisters, "we must find words or burn."

—*Joseph P. Consoli*

BIBLIOGRAPHY

Bien, Peter. *Constantine Cavafy.* New York: Columbia University Press, 1964. ■ Cavafy, Constantine P. *The Greek Poems of C.P. Cavafy: As Translated by Memas Kolaitis.* New Rochelle, N.Y.: Caratzas, 1989. ■ Dalven, Rae, ed. and trans. *Daughters of Sappho: Contemporary Greek Women Poets.* Rutherford, N.J.: Fairleigh University Press, 1994. ■ Friar, Kimon. *Modern Greek Poetry: From Caváfis to Elytis.* New York: Simon & Schuster, 1973. ■ ———. "The Poetry of Dinos Christianopoulos: An Introduction." *Journal of the Hellenic Diaspora* 6 (1969): 59–84. ■ Keeley, Edmund. *Cavafy's Alexandria: Study of a Myth in Progress.* Cambridge, Mass.: Harvard University Press, 1976. ■ Petropoulos, Elias. *Corps.* Trans. Frédéric Faure. Boulogne: Griot, 1991. ■ Trypanis, C. A. *Greek Poetry: From Homer to Seferis.* Chicago: University of Chicago Press, 1981.

Grumbach, Doris
(*b.* 1918)

Doris Grumbach was born on July 12, 1918, in New York City, the daughter of Helen and Leonard Isaac. She was educated at Washington Square College of New York University and holds a master's degree in English from Cornell University (1940). In 1941, she married Leonard Grumbach, whom she divorced in 1972. During World War II, she served two years in the Navy. Grumbach, who has four daughters, has taught both at the secondary and college level. The author of six novels, a biography, and two volumes of memoirs, Grumbach has written reviews for *The New York Times Book Review* and *The New Republic,* and is a frequent contributor to National Public Radio's "Morning Edition." She and her life partner, Sybil Pike, now reside in Sargentville, Maine, after having lived for a number of years in Washington, D.C.

Grumbach's first two novels, *The Spoil of the Flowers* (1962) and *The Short Throat, The Tender Mouth* (1964), were followed by her biography of Mary McCarthy, *The Company She Kept* (1967), which generated considerable controversy primarily

because of Grumbach's use of personal material McCarthy had given her but neither wanted nor expected to see in print. After a twelve-year hiatus, Grumbach returned to fiction, basing her next four novels on the lives of actual persons, including the American composer Edward MacDowell and his wife Marian (*Chamber Music,* 1979); Marilyn Monroe (*The Missing Person,* 1981); ELEANOR BUTLER AND SARAH PONSONBY (*The Ladies,* 1984); and Sylvia Plath and Diane Arbus (*The Magician's Girl,* 1987). In 1991, Grumbach published a memoir, *Coming into the End Zone,* inspired by the deaths from AIDS of many gay male friends. Grumbach seems obsessed with old age in this work, as she reluctantly celebrates her seventieth birthday, and makes plans to move from Washington, D.C., to Maine with her partner, Sibyl Pike. Grumbach followed *End Zone* with a second memoir, *Extra Innings* (1993), partly in response to criticism of *End Zone*'s representation of aging.

Gay and lesbian readers should find especially interesting those fictional works that have a major homosexual component. In *Chamber Music,* the ninety-year-old Caroline Maclaren retraces the course of her famous composer-husband Robert's career, revealing his incestuous relationship with his mother prior to their marriage, his homosexual affair with another young composer, and his death from syphilis (Grumbach's graphic description is unforgettable). At first, Caroline appears frustratingly self-effacing, practically a nonperson in the great man's light, but she comes alive the moment she begins a passionate liaison with Robert's nurse Anna. A well-placed metaphor concisely reflects this radical change in Caroline's existence: Anna's "glowing flesh" melts the "ice age" of Caroline's heart.

In *The Ladies,* Grumbach portrays the famous Ladies of Llangollen, whose story is one of the more remarkable in lesbian history. Their perfect devotion to each other never once diminished over fifty years. Grumbach's contribution to this story is to embellish historical fact with an imaginative recreation of their meeting, elopement, and daily life together in the Welsh village of Llangollen: The lesbian nature of the relationship is explored at length in Grumbach's text.

The Magician's Girl follows the lives of three women who remained lifelong friends after their student days at Barnard. Each gains recognition in her profession; two of the three die prematurely. Maud, overweight and unattractive, becomes a famous poet (having studied with and idolized an Ezra Pound-like figure) and eventually commits suicide; Minna, a professor of history, having left her husband, is killed by a car after finding bliss with a twenty-two-year-old male student. The third woman, Liz, a photographer celebrated for her portraits of "freaks," enjoys a fulfilling relationship with another woman. It seems not coincidental that the lesbian is the only one of the three friends not to die tragically and prematurely.

Reviews of Grumbach's work have been mixed. Praised by some readers for her imaginative portrayal of fictional characters modeled on real persons, she is castigated by others for her "dispassionate" or "reserved" representation of these same characters. Many critics note the propensity of Grumbach's characters for extensive self-reflection. Perhaps her most important contribution to gay and lesbian literature is the manner in which she consistently represents homosexual relationships matter-of-factly, as an integral part of the human landscape. Grumbach depicts lesbianism as a positive, life-giving force in women's lives.

—*Ann Cothran*

BIBLIOGRAPHY

Grumbach, Doris. *The Spoils of Flowers.* Garden City, N.Y.: Doubleday, 1962. ■ ———. *The Short Throat, the Tender Mouth.* Garden City, N.Y.: Doubleday, 1964. ■ ———. *The Company She Kept.* New York: Coward, 1967. ■ ———. *Chamber Music.* New York: Dutton, 1979. ■ ———. *The Missing Person.* New York: Putnam, 1981. ■ ———. *The Ladies.* New York: Dutton, 1984. ■ ———. *The Magician's Girl.* New York: Macmillan, 1987. ■ ———. *Coming Into the End Zone.* New York: Norton, 1991. ■ ———. *Extra Innings.* New York, Norton: 1993.

Gunn, Thom
(*b.* 1929)

Thom Gunn was born in Gravesend, Kent, and educated at University College School, Bedales, and Trinity College, Cambridge. Since coming to the United States in 1954, he has studied at Stanford and taught at the University of California, Berkeley. He has won a number of prestigious awards, including a Guggenheim Fellowship, the W. H. Smith Award, the Forward Press Award, and the MacArthur Prize.

Gunn's poetry has a popular reputation for sex and drugs and leather. This comes largely from the repeated anthologizing of his early poems from the collections *Fighting Terms* (1954) and *The Sense of Movement* (1956). In both books, a heroic masculine posing is celebrated as preferable, existentially, to the dull passivity of conformity. His leather boys in the poem "On the Move" are "always nearer by not keeping still." The voice of "Carnal Knowledge" admits that "even in bed I pose."

Posing does not disappear entirely from Gunn's later poems; there is often the sense of looking at looking at looking. And this perspective is exacerbated in the collections after *Moly* (1971) by hallucinogenic drugs' revelation of a self that can no longer be hidden in a costume. Probably his greatest poem is the title work of the collection *Jack Straw's Castle* (1976), a poem in which his poetic ego descends into the maelstrom of dream worlds and nightmare visions: "But night makes me uneasy: floor by floor / Rooms never guessed at." In this maelstrom, Charles Manson (Gunn's one-time neighbor) says to him,

"dreams don't come from nowhere: it's your dream / He says, you dreamt it."

Gunn comes back to this experience of nightmare vision with more sense of irony in another long poem, "The Menace," in the next collection, *The Passages of Joy* (1992). There "the one who wants to get me" turns out to be the reflection of himself in a store window and leads to a comic reflection on our construction of ourselves.

Constant in Gunn's poems from *Touch* (1967) onward, however, is what one critic has called "imaginative naturalness and greater openness of feeling." This increased naturalness entails both a loosening of the traditional poetic forms with which he began to write and a greater freedom with the life of the senses and with feeling. In the title poem, "Touch," a warmth surfaces from "the restraint of habits" and "the black frost / Of outsideness." And twenty-five years later, this warmth reappears, in his latest collection, as he sleeps with his more-than-forty-years lover in "the stay of your secure firm dry embrace."

From his embrace of the physical comes both an ability to risk and some of the finest gay elegies ever written: the poems that give the title to *The Man With Night Sweats* (1992). Once again, these poems are characterized by the contemplation of AIDS sufferers contemplating the bodies that they thought they knew. Here the bodily shields are now cracked and the pleasures "the hedonistic body basks within / And takes for granted" have gone away. But so have we who are left:

dizzy from a sense
Of being ejected with some violence
From vigil in some white and distant spot.

The loss is not simply personal but also of a community that Gunn describes as having been a "supple entwinement of the living mass." We are the Holocaust survivors filing past what leaves us "less defined," "unconfined," and "abandoned incomplete." And yet the greatness of these poems, as works of art, contradicts their ostensible theme of loss.

As a major gay poet, Gunn's influence can be seen on such other gay poets as Edgar Bowers, Michael Vince, Jim Powell, Robert Wells, and Gregory Woods. But he is also a prose writer and critic of great distinction who has written some of the most intelligent criticism of such gay poets as WHITMAN, GINSBERG, JAMES MERRILL, and ROBERT DUNCAN. *Collected Poems* and a new collection of prose, *Shelf Life*, were published in 1994. (See also ENGLISH LITERATURE: TWENTIETH CENTURY.)

—*Douglas Chambers*

BIBLIOGRAPHY

"Experience and Ideas: An Interview with Thom Gunn," *Quarto* 8 (1980): 9–11. ■ Parini, Jay. "Rule and Energy: The Poetry of Thom Gunn." *The Massachusetts Review* 13 (1982): 134–151. ■ "Thom Gunn at Sixty." Supplement to *PN Review* 16 (1989). ■ Wilmer, Clive. "Definition and Flow: A Personal Reading of Thom Gunn." *PN Review* 5 (1978): 51–57. ■ *Articulate Flesh: Male Homo-Eroticism in Modern Poetry*. New Haven: Yale University Press, 1987.

Hall, Radclyffe
(1880–1943)

Born Marguerite Radclyffe Hall, John, as she preferred to be known except as an author, was the miserably unhappy child of a miserably unhappy and very brief marriage. Her mother Marie Diehl, an American widow, married the extravagant and roaming Radclyffe Radclyffe Hall, grandson of a wealthy and knighted Lancashire physician. Unsuited to the demands of domestic life, he left his new wife months before John was born. John was, thus, from infancy in the care of a mother desperate to redress her grievances and to mold her daughter into an asset to recoup her fortunes. With no formal schooling and a restlessness that was to remain throughout her life, John developed an interest in the piano, at which she would compose lyrics and music

(later collected in five volumes of poetry), and in horses, riding, and motorcars, all the while pursuing attachments to girls and young women, none of which suited her socially ambitious mother. At age twenty-one, she inherited $10,000,000 (in 1993 dollars) from her paternal grandfather and left the stifling confines of her home. She began her lifelong travel to France and Italy and, at age twenty-eight, met Mabel Veronica Batten, "Ladye," with whom she lived, at first with Ladye's husband as well, until Ladye's death in 1915. Under Ladye's influence, she converted to Catholicism with a wholeheartedness that was to last all of her life and to color much of her life and writing. Ladye was instrumental in developing John's writing talents, through encouraging her first to publish her poetry and later to write fiction. Through Ladye, John also met Ladye's cousin, Una Lady Troubridge, the young wife of the aging Admiral Ernest Troubridge. Shortly before Ladye's death in 1915, John and Una became lovers, a lifelong commitment for both women. Hall spent the next thirteen years writing, publishing four novels, three of them highly successful in commercial and critical terms. She and Una socialized with many of the literary and lesbian notables in London and Paris, while living in Mayfair and vacationing for long periods in France and Italy. She also spent long serious hours studying psychic phenomena, joining and writing for the Society for Psychical Research, and devouring all she could find about the current scientific explorations of lesbianism, or inversion, as same-sex erotic desire was then called. In 1928, she published *The Well of Loneliness,* the novel for which she is best known. The next six years were less productive. She published only one novel and one collection of short stories. In 1934, John met Evguenia Souline, a thirty-year-old White Russian emigre without citizenship, who was to become her lover and in some senses her tormentor, as well as Una's. The relationship was stormy and ultimately destructive to John's health and to her work (she published only one more novel). In 1938, John and Una made plans to live permanently in Florence, Italy, only to have those plans disrupted by World War II. Beset by physical problems, John retired with Una to Devon, having obtained Souline's admission into England. The relationship with Souline deteriorated, while John's health was too poor to permit writing. She died in London of stomach cancer on October 7, 1943, and is buried with Ladye in Highgate Cemetery, London.

Hall lived her lesbianism openly and proudly, convinced that her inversion was "congenital," to use the categories of her mentor Havelock Ellis. In her forties, she began to dress in a style appropriate to her self-identification with "the third sex." She was instantly recognizable by her close-cropped hair, tailored jackets, flamboyant shirts and blouses, wide-brimmed hats, and often stocks and ties. She and Una were important figures in the lesbian circles of London, Rye, and Paris. But her importance to lesbian literature lies primarily in her most famous book, *The Well of Loneliness,* arguably the most important lesbian novel of the twentieth century.

Ironically, Hall never set out to be a consciously identified lesbian writer. All but four of her published works have no lesbian content, however disguised and covert, and of these four only *The Well* is explicitly lesbian. Her earliest works are the five volumes of poetry published between 1906 and 1915. Most of the poems are highly derivative Edwardian nature verses,

with only an occasional love poem hinting at ambiguous erotic attraction. The last volume, *The Forgotten Island,* is much more complex, a series of poems detailing erotic desire, the culmination of passion, and nostalgia for passion spent, accompanied by a desire to leave "The Island" behind. The gender of the beloved is never specified, a common enough practice for much love poetry, gay or straight, but it is possible to read in the sequence a veiled poetic treatment of a fleeting affair with Phoebe Hoare in 1913–1914.

Hall's first published novel, *The Forge* (1924), is of specific interest in lesbian literature only because it provides a fictionalized portrait of the American artist Romaine Brooks, NATALIE BARNEY's lover of fifty years. Similarly, *A Saturday Life* (1925) contains an interesting portrait of an older never-married woman, who produces desires in the protagonist Sidonie for a greater closeness, desires that she can never quite place or incorporate into her ever-changing ambitions. Most of the other novels, *Adam's Breed* (1926), *The Master of the House* (1932), and *The Sixth Beatitude* (1936) share common concerns in Hall's fiction—the exploration of the lives of humble people and the search for spiritual unity and wholeness that transcend time, place, and circumstance. As John once explained in a letter to Souline, she wrote about the poor and the outcast, the misfits as she called them, because she too shared some of their sufferings. The search for transcendence and spiritual wholeness is also tied to her sexual identity, at least insofar as she sought spiritual solace in an unshakable belief that God made her and all other inverts as part of a whole plan of Nature. Thus, although neither overtly nor covertly lesbian, these novels are part of the entire fabric of Hall's life and of her thinking about that life.

She once told Souline that *The Well of Loneliness* summed up all she had to say about inversion. *The Well,* however, is only the last of the works dealing with inversion, though it is the only work to do so explicitly. Hall's first completed novel (though the second to be published) was *The Unlit Lamp,* which many critics regard as her finest novel. The lesbian theme here is muted but nevertheless powerfully present. Joan Ogden, a troubled adolescent misfit who realizes that she is not at all interested in young men or marriage, is trapped by parental needs and provincial aspirations, particularly her mother's emotional reliance on Joan. Her tutor, the singular, angular, intellectually powerful "New Woman," Elizabeth Rodney, encourages Joan to escape both her mother's needs and provincial conventionality by going to college and setting up shared housing together. Joan ultimately lacks both the courage and means to carry through these plans and ends her days as a pinched,

drawn, and defeated companion to an elderly relative, her life sacrificed to an entrapping mother and to her own lack of courage.

The short story "Miss Ogilvy Finds Herself," written in 1926, though not published until 1934, was for Hall an experiment that would lead to the writing of *The Well*. Miss Ogilvy is another misfit, a woman with no interest in conventional romance or marriage, but with a talent for managing the business of life, running an estate, making financial decisions of importance and potential risk, settling disputes, taking charge of situations and the people involved in them—all activities gendered as masculine in that time. World War I gives Miss Ogilvy the opportunity to put these talents to patriotic use leading an ambulance corps on the front lines in France. After the war, she realizes she is more a misfit than ever. She ends her days in a quasi-mystical search for herself, one whose ultimate discovery is an atavistic return to her primitive self as the competent defender of "his" island, and especially of "his" lover. The inner circle is completed; Miss Ogilvy "fits" though twentieth-century life is impossible for her. She is found dead the next morning. This is by no means simply a bleak portrait nor a bleak assessment of lesbian possibility. It is not a portrait of a failed woman, nor of a failed invert, but rather of a failed culture, one that can accommodate its inverts only in times of national crisis without ever acknowledging their deepest, most primitive, and most natural sources. This is the theme that Hall took up again in her most famous novel *The Well of Loneliness*.

After the success of *The Unlit Lamp*, which won the Prix Femina, and *Adam's Breed*, which won the James Tait Black prize for the best literary novel of 1926, Hall felt confident enough to enlist Una's support for a novel about inversion. Her stated purpose was to present a sympathetic portrait of the "congenital invert," one that would show the full humanity and suffering of women like herself. The protagonist, Stephen Gordon, is not a veiled self-portrait, but rather a fictionalized version of Havelock Ellis's description of the true or born invert, pushed almost to the extreme. Stephen's childhood and adolescence are marked by difference, both in her "boyish" pursuits and in her attraction to women and aversion to romantic and sexual intimacy with men. Loathed by her mother, understood but unprotected by her father, Stephen is ultimately exiled from her beloved country estate and flees to Paris and the relative acceptance of the lesbian circles there (modeled after Natalie Barney and her salon). Like Miss Ogilvy, Stephen is temporarily fulfilled by the demands of World War I and her role as ambulance driver and by her love for another driver, Mary Llewellyn. This love sustains Stephen and Mary for several years but founders on Mary's attraction to Martin Hallam. Stephen orchestrates her own martyrdom to free Mary for a union with Martin.

The public outcry came swiftly. Hall's effectiveness in engaging the reader's sympathy and understanding alarmed the conservative moralists who succeeded in bringing the publisher before the Home Office in a highly publicized obscenity trial. Hall's own defense of the book's morality cited Ellis and Magnus Hirschfeld, another noted sexologist, claiming that inverts are a part of Nature, made that way by God, and then punished by a cruel and uncomprehending world. Their suffering cries out for redress and an end to persecution. She claimed also that *The Well* upholds conventional heterosexual morality. Only true inverts should live as Stephen cannot help living. No matter how much Mary Llewellyn may have loved Stephen, she is not a true invert and must therefore follow her own true (heterosexual) nature. This was a bold and powerful message in the literary world of the 1920s.

Nevertheless, the book was banned, though printed in France and thus widely available. The attempt to ban it in the United States having failed, American readers were able to purchase it freely. From these sources alone, *The Well* sold over 10,000 copies in its first year. Over the years, Hall claimed to have received more than 10,000 letters about the novel, many from grateful lesbians, but also many from nonlesbian supporters. By 1943, at Hall's death, the book had been translated into fourteen languages and was selling at over 100,000 copies year after year. It has never gone out of print. Despite the shifting critical reactions over three-quarters of a century, and despite Hall's "essentialist" turn-of-the-century views on sexology, *The Well of Loneliness* remains the one book most likely to have been read by lesbians and by those interested in a portrayal of lesbianism. Indeed it is one of the books most widely identified with lesbian literature the world over. (See also BUTCH/FEMME RELATIONS, ENGLISH LITERATURE: TWENTIETH CENTURY, and NOVEL: LESBIAN.)

—*Joanne Glasgow*

BIBLIOGRAPHY

Baker, Michael. *Our Three Selves: The Life of Radclyffe Hall.* New York: Morrow, 1985. ■ Brittain, Vera. *Radclyffe Hall: A Case of Obscenity?* New York: Barnes, 1969. ■ Dickson, Lovat. *Radclyffe Hall at the Well of Loneliness: A Sapphic Chronicle.* London: Collins, 1975. ■ Ormrod, Richard. *Una Troubridge: The Friend of Radclyffe Hall.* London: Cape, 1984. ■ Troubridge, Una. *The Life and Death of Radclyffe Hall.* London: Hammond, 1961.

Hall, Richard
(1926–1992)

Richard Hall was born Richard Hirshfeld in New York City on November 26, 1926, into an extended family of transplanted Southern Jews. In 1934, his immediate family moved to the New York suburb of White Plains, where his mother became active in the Episcopal Church and he and his sister were baptized. In 1938, after an antisemitic incident involving his sister's admission to a church-affiliated camp, Hall's mother changed their name and moved the family to another suburb. Hall matriculated at Harvard in 1943 and graduated *cum laude* in January 1948. In the 1950s, he underwent deep-Freudian analysis in an attempt to change his sexual orientation but abandoned psychiatric treatment in 1960 when he fell in love with a young Texan named Dan Allen, whom he described as the greatest influence on his life. After a career in advertising and publishing, Hall entered New York University to earn an M.A. in English Education. On graduation in 1970, he accepted a job at Inter American University in San Juan, Puerto Rico, where he served as acting director of the University Press until 1974. During the 1970s, he established a long-lasting relationship with Arthur Marceau (who died of AIDS in 1989) and began publishing fiction and nonfiction in the newly vital gay and lesbian media. From 1976 to 1982, Hall was contributing editor for books of the gay news magazine *The Advocate*. He died of complications from AIDS on October 29, 1992.

Although he is the author of a popular mystery (*The Butterscotch Prince*, 1975), a fine autobiographical novel (*Family Fictions*, 1991), and several plays, Hall's claim to lasting literary fame rests on his short fiction. Varied in their settings, their characters, and their modes, the stories collected in *Couplings* (1981), *Letters from a Great Uncle* (1985), and *Fidelities* (1992) demonstrate Hall's ability to encompass a wide range of character types and situations within a vision that can span the comic and the satiric as well as the tragic and the mythic. Typified by epiphanic moments, an empathetic approach to character, and an awareness of the complexities of truth, these works constitute a significant contribution to the post-Stonewall renaissance of gay literature.

Even though Hall's themes are both varied and universal, his subject matter is unabashedly and almost exclusively gay. His stories focus on issues of gay identity and community, on the problems of intimacy and commitment between men, and on the intersection of the public and the private in the process of self-fashioning. Hall's work features a wide variety of gay men who are captured at moments of crisis, grappling with the legacies of hurtful pasts as they struggle to achieve authenticity. "The Jilting of Tim Weatherall," an unsentimental yet extraordinarily moving account of a man dying of AIDS, may be his most powerful story.

Hall deserves recognition as an important chronicler of the post-Stonewall gay male experience and as an accomplished master of the short story. In carefully shaped fictions, distinguished by resonant prose, psychological penetration, and deeply imagined characters, Hall explores crucial issues of American gay life in the aftermath of liberation with empathy, clarity, and insight. As Michael Lynch observed in 1985, "the straight literary world has resisted recognizing Hall's fictional and critical achievements because of his material—our lives." Nevertheless, he remains "one of our prime cultural resources."

—*Claude J. Summers*

BIBLIOGRAPHY

Clark, J. Michael. *Liberation and Disillusionment: The Development of Gay Male Criticism and Popular Fiction a Decade After Stonewall.* Los Colines, Tex.: Liberal Press, 1987. ■ Lynch, Michael. "Reflections at Middle Age." *Body Politic,* August 1985, 36.

Hansberry, Lorraine
(1930–1965)

Lorraine Hansberry was born May 19, 1930, in Chicago, Illinois, to upper-middle-class African-American parents who had a family history of dedication to political and social reform. She studied painting at the Art Institute of Chicago and attended the University of Wisconsin, Roosevelt

College, and the University of Guadalajara in Mexico. Deciding that her future did not lie in the visual arts, in 1950 she went to New York City where she studied at the New School and in 1951 joined the staff of *Freedom,* a radical African-American journal. There she wrote articles and became associate editor in 1952. During this time, she met Robert Nemiroff, whom she married in 1953. Her attendance at the International Peace Congress in Uruguay and her association there with women from other countries heightened her awareness of many issues, among them feminism. By 1957, she was coming out, privately though not publicly, as a lesbian. She and Nemiroff quietly separated in 1957 and were divorced in 1964, but maintained a close personal and professional relationship until her death from cancer in January 1965.

Hansberry's first complete play, *A Raisin in the Sun* (1959), won the New York Drama Critics' Circle Award, a first for an African American. It also marked the first time a black woman had a play produced on Broadway. Her second play, *The Sign in Sidney Brustein's Window* (1964), challenged the idea that African Americans should deal exclusively with black subjects. Hansberry was terminally ill with cancer when this play went into rehearsal but was able intermittently to continue the political activism in which she was engaged her entire life. She also discussed her unfinished work at length with Nemiroff so that he might handle its appearance.

Lorraine Hansberry's life and work were distinguished by a commitment to ameliorating social injustice. Although she prioritized her attention in favor of black freedom and world peace, she also addressed the issue of gay liberation. In August 1957, she wrote two letters to the fledgling lesbian periodical, *The Ladder,* in which she supported the emerging American lesbian liberation movement. She endorsed women's need for their own publications and praised *The Ladder.* Most interesting, she connected homophobia and antifeminism, calling for analyses of ethical questions implicit in the social and moral inequities produced by patriarchal culture. In these letters, she condemned homosexual persecution as having its roots in social ignorance but also speculated that it owed something to "a philosophically active anti-feminist dogma." In *The Sign in Sidney Brustein's Window,* she links sexuality and creativity. Some critics have misread David, the homosexual character who is a dramatist, as a negative portrayal. However, in spite of his immaturity, he is a positive image of commitment, artistic creativity, and meaningful sexuality. He is humanly complex, and the play makes a plea for maturity in sexuality, whatever form it takes.

For Lorraine Hansberry, theater was a means of exploring inner conflicts and of demanding broader opportunities for the expression of human potential. Homosexuality was a subject about which she wrote and thought. When Margaret Wilkerson's biography, currently being written, appears, more will be known of the place of homosexuality in the dramatist's life. In any case, Hansberry's work gives evidence of her significant breaking away from stereotypical characterizations and of her willingness to take homosexuality seriously.

—*Dorothy H. Lee*

BIBLIOGRAPHY

Bond, Jean Caron, ed. *Lorraine Hansberry: Art of Thunder, Vision of Light.* A special issue of *Freedomways Magazine* 19.4 (1969). ■ Chene, Anne. *Lorraine Hansberry.* Boston: Twayne, 1984. ■ Hansberry, Lorraine. Letters to *The Ladder* 1.11 (August 1957): 26–30. Signed "LNN." Quoted in Jonathan Katz. *Gay American History: Lesbians and Gay Men in the U.S.A.* New York: Thomas Y. Crowell, 1976. ■ ———. *"A Raisin in the Sun" and "The Sign in Sidney Brustein's" Window.* New York: New American Library, 1966. ■ ———. *To Be Young, Gifted and Black: Lorraine Hansberry in Her Own Words.* Adapted by Robert Nemiroff. New York: New American Library, 1970. ■ Marre, Diana. "Lorraine Hansberry." *Notable Black American Women.* Jessie Carney Smith, ed. Detroit: Gale Research, 1992. 452–457. ■ Wilkerson, Margaret B. "Excavating Our History: The Importance of Biographies of Women of Color." *Black American Literature Forum* 24 (1990): 73–84.

Hansen, Joseph
(*b.* 1923)

Best known as the author of the Dave Brandstetter mystery series, Joseph Hansen has also published a considerable body of nonmystery fiction and poetry. Born in Aberdeen, South Dakota, on July 19, 1923, he moved with his family to Minneapolis in 1933 and in 1936 to southern California, where he has lived ever since. He attended Pasadena City College, and in 1943 married Jane Bancroft, with whom he had a daughter. He has made a career of writing, editing, and teaching.

Hansen's fiction, which is dominated by homosexual characters and themes, began to appear in the pre-Stonewall 1960s, when he was forced, for lack of any viable alternative, to publish under a pseudonym (James Colton) with small West Coast publishers who specialized in erotica. Notable among his early novels are *Lost on Twilight Road* (1964) and *Strange Marriage* (1965). The latter is an especially good example of gay pulp fiction of the mid-1960s. Internalizing much of the homophobia of its era, it chronicles the experience of a homosexual, Randy Hale, who marries in order to lead a "normal" life, but is irresistibly drawn back into gay sex by a sensitive young man. Reflecting the medically oriented dialogue of the 1950s and 1960s, it is a doctor who explains homosexuality to Hale's wife and makes possible the compromise "strange marriage" that allows the couple to continue their lives together.

In the post-Stonewall Brandstetter mystery series, some of Hansen's characters are able to achieve happiness and stability in gay relationships, but in his two "mainstream" novels of the 1980s, *A Smile in His Lifetime* (1981) and *Job's Year* (1983), the gay protagonists are plagued with loss and loneliness. Although powerfully written and guardedly optimistic in their conclusions, both novels are almost unrelentingly painful and show little of the positive aspects of the gay experience. Their depressing darkness seems imposed from without rather than naturally residing within the characters and situations.

In the 1990s, Hansen has turned from the Brandstetter series to writing novels that are intended to chronicle gay life on the West Coast during the 1940s and 1950s. The first of these, *Living Upstairs* (1993), is a moving account of young love in Hollywood during World War II. Beautifully written and featuring completely realized characters, *Living Upstairs* not only vividly evokes a particular time and place, it also tells a story that is haunting and tragic but not depressing. Unlike the novels of the 1980s, it captures the joys as well as the pain of gay life before Stonewall. An earnest of more works to come, *Living Upstairs* testifies to Hansen's continuing vitality.

A self-avowed conservative in the liberation movement, Hansen calls himself "homosexual" rather than "gay"; but in his own fashion, he has worked through his novels and short stories to help create a climate of acceptance for all homosexuals in the mainstream of American life. (See also MYSTERY FICTION: GAY MALE.)

—*Ted-Larry Pebworth*

BIBLIOGRAPHY

Jones, James. "Joseph Hansen." *Contemporary Gay American Novelists: A Bio-Bibliographical Critical Sourcebook.* Emmanuel S. Nelson, ed. Westport, Conn.: Greenwood, 1993. 189–196.
■ Kepner, Jim, "Hansen, Joseph." *Gay and Lesbian Literature.* Sharon Malinowski, ed. Detroit: St. James Press, 1994. 177–180.

The Harlem Renaissance

In African-American literary history, the 1920s and 1930s have been variously labeled the Jazz Age, the era of the New Negro, and most commonly, the Harlem Renaissance. Scholars debate the beginning and ending of the period; others question whether a "renaissance" occurred at all. Although most commentators agree that this period saw an unparalleled outpouring of artistic achievement and claim that this "movement" was successful in creating foundational steps in the long African-American arts tradition, still others hold that the renaissance was a failure. In recent years, the reading public has welcomed the recuperated literary reputations of many Harlem Renaissance figures as their works have been republished, researched, and studied. The Black Feminist movement has been a major force in validating and cementing canonical spaces for Jessie Fauset, NELLA LARSEN, Zora Neale Hurston, Angelina Grimké, Alice Dunbar-Nelson, Georgia Douglas Johnson, and others. Black feminist scholars have also been forthright in foregrounding the sexualities of these women as a prominent feature of their creative energies. For example, Gloria T. Hull has written honestly and intelligently on black lesbianism as critical to understanding the works of Grimké and Dunbar-Nelson. Studies of the male artists of the period, however, have, so far, only flirted with issues of sexuality in general and have ignored, denied, or dismissed homosexuality as an artistic influence.

It is indeed surprising that discussions of the Harlem Renaissance have not involved in-depth investigations of homosexuality when, in fact, the major male figures of the period were gay or bisexual: Alain Locke, COUNTEE CULLEN, LANGSTON HUGHES, Claude McKay, Wallace Thurman, Richard Bruce Nugent, and even the famous white sponsor CARL VAN VECHTEN. With the burgeoning interest in gay studies, however, scholars are beginning to research the lives and works of these artists in order to evaluate the ways in which homosexuality functioned as a liberating and constricting force.

Eric Garber's study creates a picturesque montage of Harlem gay life during this period when many African Americans tolerated, indulged in, and even celebrated homosexuality. Garber's is a cinematic look at gay life, art, and culture that pauses here and there to capture the details of the night club scene, art work, personalities, and so on. Painting Harlem as a gay liberated capital, Garber shows how homosexuality, among intellectuals especially, was accepted as a personal matter that did not interfere with the larger, more important work in racial and cultural advancement. Gays were oppressed during the period, but a thriving black gay subculture ensured that open secrets were kept. Bessie Smith, Ma Rainey, "Moms" Mabley, Mabel Hampton, Alberta Hunter, Gladys Bentley, and other lesbian or bisexual women found employment in show business, and many sang the blues about gay lives and loves. Drag balls, commonplace during the period, were called "spectacles of color" by Langston Hughes in *The Big Sea* (1945); such balls were frequented often by the Harlem bohemians who wrote candidly about them in their correspondence. Speakeasies and buffet flats (rental units notorious for cafeteria-style opportunities for a variety of sex) were spaces in which gays were granted generous liberation. Wallace Thurman, in *Infants of the Spring* (1932), gives a realistic rendering of the buffet flat that he, Langston Hughes, and Richard Bruce Nugent shared from time to time. This artistic community was a complex one with an intricate network of members that cut across all sectors of the art world. At a time when New York still had laws banning homosexuality and when baths and gay bars were raided frequently, it is noteworthy that the Harlem Renaissance was moved along, in great measure, by gay men and women who led amazing double lives.

The function of the closet during this period is complex. Although the closet has typically been seen as oppressive, many of these gay artists subverted the stultifying power of the closet by forming an artistic coalition grounded in secrecy and loyalty. Thus, the closet was reconstructed to form a protective shield against discrimination from publishers, patrons, and the media. The closet enabled many writers to blend into the mainstream and to publish without the fear of exposure.

Alain Locke (1886–1954), who has been credited with ushering in the New Negro movement, has been justly criticized for advancing the careers of young black males to the obvious neglect of such writers as Grimké, Dunbar-Nelson, and Georgia Douglas Johnson. Locke, a Harvard Ph.D. and professor at Howard University, promoted the careers of Wallace Thurman, Richard Bruce Nugent, Countee Cullen, and Langston Hughes. To crown only Locke with the accolade of inspiring the Harlem Renaissance is to deny the seminal positions held by W. E. B. DuBois, Jessie Fauset, James Weldon Johnson, and the *Opportunity* and *Crisis* organizations in fostering the careers of many of the period's artists. Without question a misogynist, Locke's contribution to the development of a gay male literary heritage was formidable and certainly deliberate. He was at the center of the Harlem gay coterie and very early on gave impetus to the careers of Cullen and, especially, Hughes.

Through frequent letters, Locke urged Countee Cullen (1903–1946) to write poetry aimed at bettering the race. Urging Cullen to read EDWARD CARPENTER's anthology of male–male friendship *Ioläus,* Locke helped the young writer find comfort in realizing his gay self. Thus, Locke was also, in part, responsible for Cullen's maturing gay sensibilities. Cullen learned the importance of the closet and wrote poetry that promoted the image and idea of the New Negro while also subtly expressing his gay self. Scholars are beginning to investigate the coded language in Cullen's poetry in order to establish him as a leading figure in the black gay male literary heritage. Many of the lyrics in *The Black Christ and Other Poems* (1929) and *The Medea and Some Poems* (1935) lend themselves to gay readings. Yet, in as early a work as *Color* (1925), Cullen wrote gay verses, such as "Tableau," "Fruit of the Flower," and "For a Poet"— a poem written at a time when Cullen was embroiled in unrequited love for Langston Hughes.

Before he had finished college at Lincoln University in Pennsylvania and during his many travels, Langston Hughes (1902–1967) was pursued by Locke, with Cullen mediating. Although sexual relationships never materialized, the intimate friendships of these three gay men were concretized in their commitment to their literary careers and shared racial ideologies. Although there were regular philosophical disagreements regarding the bewildering vocation of poets who were also deemed "race men," still a tight bond developed that knit these writers together for their entire lives. Hughes, arguably the most closeted of the renaissance gay males, had many close associations with homosexuals and lesbians throughout his life. And, as with Cullen, scholars are beginning to decipher the codification of his gayness in his poetry, drama, and fiction. Commentators have cited many poems as candidates for gay readings, among them "Young Sailor," "Waterfront Streets," "Desire," "Trumpet Player," "Café 3 A. M.," and the sequence of poems in *Montage of a Dream Deferred* (1951).

Angelina Weld Grimké (1880–1958) made her contribution to the lesbian literary heritage as a poet during the Harlem Renaissance. She was published in Locke's *The New Negro* (1925) and in Cullen's *Caroling Dusk* (1927). Grimké's love lyrics, many as yet unpublished, are mostly addressed to women and describe love that is hidden, unrequited, or otherwise unrealized. The honesty of the lesbian passion in these beautiful lyrics secures for Grimké a place in African-American gay literature. Poems such as "Rosalie," "If," "To Her of the Cruel Lips," "El Beso," "Autumn," "Give Me Your Eyes," "Caprichosa," and "My Shrine" are all testimony to the unrealized lesbian love for which Grimké longed.

Alice Dunbar-Nelson (1875–1935) was married several times, most notably to the poet Paul Laurence Dunbar. All of her marriages were troublesome for one reason or another, but despite her personal problems, she managed to write and publish fiction and poetry. The lesbian relationships that checkered her life had a significant influence on her creativity. For example, Gloria T. Hull suggests that, in the unpublished novel *This Lofty Oak,* Dunbar-Nelson chronicles the life of Edwina B. Kruse, one of her lovers. Dunbar-Nelson's literary reputation during the Harlem Renaissance is assessed largely (and Hull contends erroneously) on her achievement as a poet. She published "Violets" in *Crisis* in 1917, a work that exemplifies the polish and lucidity that typify her poetry, especially her sonnets. Hull documents other lesbian affairs with Fay Jackson Robinson, a Los Angeles journalist, and Helene Ricks London, a Bermuda artist. Dunbar-Nelson wrote poetry for these women, most of which does not survive except in diary fragments. Dunbar-Nelson's diary reveals her prominent place in an active network of African-American lesbians.

In *Home to Harlem* (1927), Jamaican-born Claude McKay (1899–1948) openly discusses Harlem's black experience with lesbianism and even has a significant black gay male character. Following Wayne F. Cooper's fine biography of McKay (which discusses honestly the writer's homosexuality), scholars are beginning to make connections between the writer's sexuality and his writing. Yet, as is the case with many of the renaissance writers, McKay's homosexuality as an influence on his creativity must be traced by reading between the lines. Some poems seem to be perfect candidates for such readings, among them "Bennie's Departure," "To Inspector W. E. Clark," "Alfonso, Dressing to Wait at Table," "The Barrier," "Courage," "Adolescence," "Home Thoughts," and "On Broadway." Other poems, such as "Desolate" and "Absence," can easily be given gay readings, inasmuch as gays often write on the themes of isolation, dreams deferred, unrequited or secret love, and alienation.

The short life of Wallace Thurman (1902–1934) gave to the African-American gay and lesbian tradition two novels—*The Blacker the Berry* (1929) and *Infants of the Spring* (1932)—which are unmatched as clear and honest depictions of black gay and lesbian life. The long life of Richard Bruce Nugent (1906–1989) produced very few literary monuments, but like Thurman, Nugent had a penchant for shocking readers and producing works with a decidedly foreign and provocative voice. Locke included Nugent's gay story "Sahdji" in *The New Negro* and encouraged the young writer to work at narrative. In 1926, the one and only issue of *Fire!!* (a quarterly "Devoted to the Younger Negro Artists"), carried Nugent's more developed homosexual story "Smoke, Lilies, and Jade"—now praised as the first published African-American gay short story. The story is the fictionalization of an evening Nugent spent walking and talking with Langston Hughes. The story is a major achievement in gay literary history because it can be read as a defense of homosexuality while it also poignantly thematizes male–male love as beautifully natural and wholesome. Even in his later years, Nugent continued to write openly about the gay experience: In 1970, *Crisis* published a Christmas story, "Beyond Where the Star Stood Still," in which Herod's catamite offers a remarkable gift to the infant Jesus. Again, Nugent—embracing the mushrooming gay rights movement—aimed at forcing the safe African-American world, shaped largely by the fundamentalist church, to face the reality of a black gay presence.

Although Harlem was awash with gay literary production during the renaissance, it would be overstating reality to say that there was a deliberate gay movement afoot. Homosexuality might have found toleration in the privacy of speakeasies and salon parties, but the boardrooms at major publishing companies were far less inviting. Couple that fact with the conservatism that underlined the very notion of a "Talented Tenth," and it is easy to conclude that any gay literary production (with the clear exception of Thurman and Nugent, who were severely criticized) would have to subvert, in rather creative ways, the mainstream white and black power establishments. The recurring themes, issues, and ideas in the gay and lesbian writing of the period underscore the endurance of those writers who strove to express their gay selves.

A recurrent motif in the writings of the period is the presence of a forbidden, unnamed, and genderless love. Also common is the use of nature to express the budding forth of an unquestionable though unutterable beauty that is often unappreciated and wasted. Most writers stutter through expressions of a kind of passion so noble yet so unattainable that it must be enacted secretly or abandoned.

Because sexuality is inextricably wound up in the very experience of being human, it often shares turf with deep religious experience or political conviction. Cullen's "The Black Christ," for example, is on the surface a narrative poem of salvation. Yet the poet weaves the salvation experience neatly into the somewhat veiled story of Jim's questionable sexuality. The homoeroticism of the poem pictures the lynched black boy as a beauty of nature who is raped and sacrificed because he goes unappreciated. Ironically, he is falsely accused and killed for attempting to rape a beautiful white girl whom he understands as the embodiment of Spring. The poem, like many of the period, can be read on a deeper, less apparent level as a diatribe against sexual repression.

Perhaps the most prevalent theme among gay writers of the period is that of the unrealized or displaced dream. One cannot read Grimké, Hughes, McKay, or Cullen without confronting the unachievable, unnamed, and haunting dream. From the most closeted to the most liberated, the writers of the gay Harlem Renaissance form an unquestionable tradition through which contemporary gay and lesbian readers can see the depth and range of experiences that, in many cases, mirror theirs. If these mirrored images have the power to transform and liberate, perhaps the new renaissance currently underway by African-American gay and lesbian writers will produce a literature that represents more realized and fulfilling dreams. (See also AFRICAN-AMERICAN LITERATURE, GAY MALE and AFRICAN-AMERICAN LITERATURE, LESBIAN.)
—*Alden Reimonenq*

BIBLIOGRAPHY

Anderson, Jervis. *This Was Harlem: A Cultural Portrait, 1900–1950.* New York: Farrar, Straus, Giroux, 1981. ■ Avi-Ram, Amitai F. "The Unreadable Black Body: 'Conventional' Poetic Form in the Harlem Renaissance." *Genders* 7 (1990): 32–45. ■ Baker, Houston A. *Afro-American Poetics: Revisions of Harlem and the Black Aesthetic.* Madison: University of Wisconsin Press, 1988. ■ ———. *Modernism and the Harlem Renaissance.* Chicago: University of Chicago Press, 1987. ■ Bell, Bernard W. *The Afro-American Novel and Its Tradition.* Amherst: University of Massachusetts Press, 1987. ■ Bontemps, Arna, ed. *The Harlem Renaissance Remembered.* New York: Dodd, Mead and Company, 1972. ■ Chapman, Abraham. "The Harlem Renaissance in Literary History." *College Language Association* 2 (September 1967): 38–58. ■ Cooper, Wayne F. *Claude McKay: Rebel Sojourner in the Harlem Renaissance, A Biography.* Baton Rouge: Louisiana State University Press, 1987. ■ Dunbar-Nelson, Alice. *Give Us Each Day: The Diary of Alice Dunbar-Nelson.* Gloria T. Hull, ed. New York: W. W. Norton, 1984. ■ Fabre, Michel. *From Harlem to Paris: Black American Writers in France, 1840–1980.* Urbana: University of Illinois Press, 1991. ■ Garber, Eric. "A Spectacle in Color: The Lesbian and Gay Subculture of Jazz Age Harlem." *Hidden from History: Reclaiming the Gay and Lesbian Past.* Martin Duberman, Martha Vicinus, and George Chauncey, Jr., eds. New York: New American Library, 1989. 318–331. ■ Huggins, Nathan. *Harlem Renaissance.* New York: Oxford University Press, 1971. ■ Hughes, Langston. *The Big Sea: An Autobiography.* New York: Knopf, 1945. ■ Hull, Gloria T. *Color, Sex, and Poetry: Three Women Writers of the Harlem Renaissance.* Bloomington: Indiana University Press, 1987. ■ Kramer, Victor A., ed. *The Harlem Renaissance Re-Examined.* New York: AMS, 1987. ■ Kellner, Bruce, ed. *The Harlem Renaissance: A Historical Dictionary for the Era.* New York: Methuen, 1984. ■ Lewis, David Levering. *When Harlem Was in Vogue.* New York: Knopf, 1981. ■ Rampersad, Arnold. *The Life of Langston Hughes, Volume I: 1902–1941, I Too, Sing America.* New York: Oxford University Press, 1986. ■ ———*The Life of Langston Hughes, Volume II: 1941–1967, I Dream a World.* New York: Oxford University Press, 1988. ■ Reimonenq, Alden. "Countee Cullen's Uranian 'Soul Windows.'" *Journal of Homosexuality* 26:2/3 (Fall 1993):143–165. ■ Singh, Amritjit, S. William Shiver, and Stanley Brodwin, eds. *The Harlem Renaissance: Revaluations.* New York: Garland, 1989. ■ Story, Ralph D. "Patronage and the Harlem Renaissance: You Get What You Pay For." *College Language Association Journal* 32/3 (1989): 284–295. ■ Wagner, Jean. *Black Poets of the United States.* Trans. Kenneth Douglas. Urbana: University of Illinois Press, 1973.

Harris, Bertha
(b. 1937)

Bertha Harris is one of the most stylishly innovative American fiction writers to emerge since Stonewall. Possessing a fine aesthetic sensibility and a gargantuan sense of fantasy, her experiments with the form of the novel are unlike any other examples of "new lesbian fiction" that have been published since 1969.

Harris was born in Fayetteville, North Carolina, and was educated at the University of North Carolina at Greensboro. Her roots are firmly planted in the South, and its voices and ambiance run firmly through her works. She has stated that she came to New York "to find lesbians," but, swept up in the social unrest of the early 1960s, she married briefly and had a daughter. To support her daughter, she edited and proof-read for a time, then returned to North Carolina, where she received her M.F.A. She wrote *Catching Saradove* (1969), her first novel, as part of her degree requirements.

The semiautobiographical *Saradove* is probably the closest Harris has come to writing a conventional work of fiction. But the themes of fantasy and character play that were to be developed and refined in her later works were already present in this early novel. Saradove herself, while having the trappings of a conventional fictional character, is also, according to Harris, "trying to break through the warped rituals of love and hate that her parents have taught her, through the means of magic, fantasy, play, sex." The novel shifts back and forth between the Lower East Side of Manhattan and Saradove's childhood South, and both worlds are populated by the lovers, waifs, antic Southerners, and sexually ambiguous types that became familiar in her later works.

Harris has said that she is obsessed by two things: music (particularly opera) and the South. These two obsessions define her second novel, *Confessions of Cherubino* (1972), which *The New Yorker* called an "ultra-violent comedy." Its theme seems to be the tyranny of sexual passion in all its various forms, but putting a fence around any of Harris's works is always a mistake. The novel tells of the emotional turmoils of a darkly comic group of characters (including Ellen and Margaret, who may be lovers or different aspects of the same person), but—as in most of Harris's work—the development of conventional plot and narrative is secondary to her inventive manipulation of the shifting psyches of her characters, who are always more than they seem to be.

Lover (first published in 1976, and reissued, with a new introduction by the author, in 1993) is Harris's most ambitious work; it has been compared to DJUNA BARNES's *Nightwood* and the eccentric stories of JANE BOWLES. It was written, as Harris has said, "straight from the libido, while I was madly in love, and liberated by the lesbian cultural movement of the mid-1970s." In her 1993 introduction, Harris says, "*Lover* should be absorbed as if it were a theatrical performance. There's tap dancing and singing, disguise, sleights of hand, mirror illusions, quick-change acts, and drag." The minds of the "sexual subversives" she writes about seem to meet on an interior plane, in which conventional storytelling gives way to brilliant imagery and electric verbal wordplay. Harris has expressed her hope that lesbian fiction will develop into an entirely new and elegant genre, far from the restrictions of nineteenth-century style that seem to typify the romances and detective fiction of the 1990s. With *Lover* she shows us what this genre might be like.

In 1977, Harris collaborated with Emily Sisley to produce *The Joy of Lesbian Sex,* a straightforward and often humorous guide to the methods and politics of lesbian lovemaking. She has written a book for young adults entitled (tentatively) *Gertrude and Alice Were Lovers,* which will be published in 1995, and is working on a new novel.

—*Ann Wadsworth*

BIBLIOGRAPHY

Koestenbaum, Wayne. "The Purple Reign of Bertha Harris." *Village Voice Literary Supplement* (October 1993): 18–19.

Hemingway, Ernest
(1899–1961)

The hunting-shooting-fishing (and writing) life of Ernest Hemingway begins with a little boy who was dressed in girl's clothing by his mother during his early years, a point Hemingway would later avoid when mythologizing his youth. He preferred to concentrate on roaming teenage adventures (apparently invented) in which his only problems were the sexual advances of adult hoboes, which he bravely resisted by carrying a knife wherever he went.

During his famous post–World War I sojourn in Paris (as recollected in the memoir *A Moveable Feast,* 1964), he encountered homosexual people of both sexes but always had greater difficulty dealing with

the men than with the women. Lesbians with whom he was capable of being relatively charming included GERTRUDE STEIN and Alice B. Toklas. Stein, who had many conversations with him about homosexuality, seemed to think he was hiding something about himself. This belief has developed into a critical cliché that avers that Hemingway must have been repressing his own homosexuality because of the amount of time he spent abusing other people's.

His favorite insults for other men were accusations of impotence, sterility, and homosexuality. He himself was often accused of being queer—notably by Zelda Fitzgerald, who said he and Scott Fitzgerald behaved like lovers—but such accusations were generally mischievous, made by people who knew how angrily Hemingway would defend his manly, heterosexual virtue.

There are several homosexual characters in Hemingway's fiction; there are also frank homophobes. Jake Barnes, the castrated heterosexual narrator of *The Sun Also Rises* (1926), is severely affronted when a group of homosexual men clusters around the woman he desires but cannot have. His first inclination is to attack the lot of them with his fists; but it is part of his heroic restraint that he refrains from doing so.

The short story "The Mother of a Queen" is about a rich homosexual bullfighter who begrudges the $20 he must spend on his mother's funeral. In "A Simple Enquiry," an Italian major unsuccessfully tries to seduce his young orderly. There is a "pederaste" painter in *Across the River and into the Trees* (1950) who paints in a saccharine style and hides his sexuality by keeping the company of women. A boy in *Islands in the Stream* (1932) has to give up his backgammon lessons with an older man when a discussion of ANDRÉ GIDE's homosexuality comes too close to a practical proposition. All these representations are more or less negative, some virtually abusive. Although the most characteristic of Hemingway's book titles is that of the 1927 collection of stories, *Men without Women,* his fervent admiration for masculine pursuits and the men who pursued them strictly excluded any man who seemed even a little bit queer.

Above all, Hemingway is known for his "masculine" voice which, at its best, shapes an exquisitely terse prose style. Underlying his portrayals of the men he respects is the concept of masculinity responding to all potential attacks, or resisting all potential signs of weakness, by exhibiting "grace under pressure." This is the central point of his books about bullfighting, and it is a point that he has to make with frequent homophobic utterances. Mixed in with all the bluster about bulls is the concept of *cojones,* or balls.

His last book, *The Garden of Eden,* published posthumously in 1986, is an extraordinary rhapsody on male sexual passivity, with a central character who needs to be penetrated by a woman more boyish than himself. It offers a kind of solution to the conundrum of the macho man who wants to take the "passive role" in intercourse with another man, but without losing his own masculine status: Let the other boy be a girl.

—*Gregory Woods*

BIBLIOGRAPHY

Baker, Carlos. *Ernest Hemingway: A Life Story.* New York: Scribner's, 1969. ■ Spilka, Mark. *Hemingway's Quarrel with Androgyny.* Lincoln: University of Nebraska Press, 1990. ■ Woods, Gregory. "The Injured Sex: Hemingway's Voice of Masculine Anxiety." *Textuality and Sexuality: Reading Theories and Practices.* Judith Still and Michael Worton, eds. Manchester: Manchester University Press, 1993. 160–172.

Highsmith, Patricia
(1921–1995)

Patricia Highsmith was born in Fort Worth, Texas, on January 19, 1921. Her father was of German and her mother of British descent. She was educated at Barnard College, New York, and became a freelance writer a year after she left college. She lived alternately in Europe and the United States, residing mostly in Switzerland. Among her hobbies were "carpentering, snail-watching, [and] travelling by train" (*Who's Who 1992*).

Crime fiction historian Julian Symons called Highsmith "the most important crime novelist at present in practice." Although now twenty years old, the citation exhibits the respect that Highsmith's writing still commonly commands. Her first novel *Strangers on a Train* (1949), later a film directed by Alfred Hitchcock, depicts that pattern of peculiar psychological imprisonment between two people that she was

to continue as her personal motif. Instead of an absolutely moral Holmes/Watson type of reassurance at the center of the novel, there is the subversive, explicitly homoerotic and tortured obsession of two murderers for each other. Although Bruno is the acknowledged "psychopath," the careerist and misogynistic Guy is hardly an attractive hero. Bruno's erotic possessiveness over his mother, his vicious hate of any of her lovers, especially of his father whom he has Guy murder, is suggestively oedipal. The novel is also concerned with the crisis of individuation between Guy and Bruno: "And Bruno, he and Bruno. Each was what the other had not chosen to be, the cast off self, what he thought he hated, but perhaps in reality loved." One disturbing and radical aspect of Highsmith's writing is her firm integration of good with evil, no longer cast out as other, but slipping, undifferentiated, into the totality of human behavior. This is not literature for those who desire positive images; it makes the reader very uncomfortable.

Critic Kathleen Gregory Klein argues that Highsmith has gone as far as creating a new fictional form, citing her introduction of the cult-figure serial killer Tom Ripley as a new type of criminal superhero, prefiguring similar cultural icons that appeared in the 1990s. (*The Talented Mr. Ripley* was awarded the Edgar Allan Poe Scroll by the Mystery Writers of America in 1955.) The Ripley books are generically akin to a series. Characters reappear in subsequent titles and undergo development, and Ripley himself inspires readerly identification, at least because he is so amorally fascinating. Highsmith's deliberate violations of realism foreground the claustrophobic and violent world of the mind, where simple Manichean moralities break down. Lesbian and gay readers, themselves positioned in an uneasy relation to the law and its regulation of permissible behavior, find in Ripley the antithesis to state-sanctioned Christian virtue. He pushes transgression to the limit.

Carol, first published in 1952 as *The Price of Salt,* under the pseudonym Claire Morgan, is Highsmith's only explicitly lesbian novel. It sold nearly one million copies in the United States in 1953 alone. Lesbian readers' response was one of gratitude—finally they were offered a novel that did not end in death, despair, or debasement. *Carol* is an erotic love story that retains the Highsmith taste for a tightly fought psychodrama. The two central characters, Therese and Carol, are strapped together by a desire tabulated by the intense hold the ordinary, daily exchanges of romance can exert over the self. Ostensibly Carol is the adored, and Therese does the adoring, but Highsmith suggests depths in their relationship, often conveyed by an apparently casual remark, which belie this simple structure. *Carol* has the flavor of a psychological thriller in the sense that it maintains narrative anxiety and suspense while exploring the emotional implications of desire and dependency. Its reissue by Penguin Books in 1991 is a testament to its subtly wrought portrait of a relationship.

Patricia Highsmith is not an author who offers predictable, comforting role models to lesbian or gay readers but one who provides narrative absorption through psychological subtlety. Her novels interrogate what constitutes personhood and what motivations drive the self: two pertinent and enduring questions for modern lesbian and gay identity. (See also MYSTERY FICTION, GAY MALE and NOVEL: LESBIAN.)

—*Sally R. Munt*

BIBLIOGRAPHY

Klein, Kathleen Gregory. "Patricia Highsmith." *And Then There Were Nine . . . More Women of Mystery.* Jane S. Bakeman, ed. Bowling Green, Ohio: Bowling Green State University Popular Press, 1985. 170–197. ■ Munt, Sally R. *Murder by the Book: Feminism and the Crime Novel.* London and New York: Routledge, 1994. ■ Phillips, Deborah. "Mystery Woman—Patricia Highsmith." *Women's Review* (London) No. 6 (April 1986): 14–15. ■ Symons, Julian. *Bloody Murder.* London: Viking, 1972.

Hine, Daryl
(b. 1936)

Although he has lived in the United States since 1967, the poet Daryl Hine was born in British Columbia, Canada, and attended McGill University in Montreal, where his poetic career began with the publication of two highly praised short volumes, *Five Poems* (1955) and *The Carnal and the Crane* (1957). Between Montreal and arrival at the University of Chicago in 1967, Hine traveled extensively in Europe, experience that resulted in a novel (*The Prince of Darkness & Co.,* 1961) and a travel account (*Polish Subtitles,* 1962). Having gained the Ph.D. degree, Hine taught classics at the University of Chicago for several years and edited the prestigious *Poetry* magazine from 1968 to 1978. His early work culminated in the poetry volumes *The Wooden Horse* (1965) and *Minutes* (1968). His reputation was firmly secured by the praise of the eminent Canadian critic Northrop Frye, who "doubt[ed] if any Canadian poet [had] potentially greater talents," and of American poet RICHARD HOWARD, who drew attention to Hine's "special status as a *Wunderkind.*" As an intensely literary poet with enviable classical learnedness, Hine's affiliations are with the gay American formalists Richard Howard and JAMES MERRILL, rather than with any Canadian school of poets.

Hine's homosexuality was largely a matter of insider knowledge during the first phase of his career, but in 1975 he published an autobiography of his early years in verse, *In & Out,* in which he chronicled two romances of his McGill career that framed his attempt to escape his sexuality by converting to Catholicism and spending a summer in a Vermont Benedictine monastery. *In & Out* is both witty and painfully moving, and clarifies how Hine's intellectual engagement with both classicism and Catholicism provided the confused young poet with a way of articulating homosexual experience and a way of coming out. Harold Bloom praised *In & Out* (available at that time only in a privately printed and circulated version) as "amazingly good verse" that authoritatively documented the "quasi-identity of sexual and religious experience."

Since 1975, Hine's volumes of poetry have dealt more explicitly with the pain of growing up gay during the 1940s and 1950s and—along with the work of poets like Howard Moss, Richard Howard, and James Merrill—have given serious homosexual poetry a place in the mainstream of American poetry. This process gained public recognition with the publication of *In & Out* by Knopf in 1989. (See also CANADIAN LITERATURE IN ENGLISH.)

—*Patrick Holland*

BIBLIOGRAPHY

Bloom, Harold. "The Year's Books: Harold Bloom on Poetry, Part I." *The New Republic,* November 20, 1976, p. 21. ■ Frye, Northrop. *The Bush Garden: Essays on the Canadian Imagination.* Toronto: Anansi, 1971. ■ Howard, Richard. *Alone with America: Essays on the Art of Poetry in the United States Since 1950.* New York: Atheneum, 1969.

Hocquenghem, Guy
(1946–1988)

Guy Hocquenghem was born in the suburbs of Paris in 1946 and was educated at the École Normale Supérieure. His participation in the 1968 student rebellion in France formed his allegiance to the Communist Party, which later expelled him because of his homosexuality. Hocquenghem later became one of the first gay men to join the Front Homosexuel d'Action Révolutionnaire, originally formed by Lesbian separatists who split from the Mouvement Homophile de France in 1971.

Before his death from AIDS in 1988, Hocquenghem produced a considerable canon of theoretical and creative writings; he also wrote and produced a documentary film about gay history, *Race d'Ep! Un siècle d'image de l'homosexualité.* His primary importance, however, rests in a trilogy of theoretical tracts he wrote, only one of which is available in an English translation. *Le désir homosexuel* (1972), *L'Après-Mai des faunes* (1974), and *Le dérive homosexuelle* (1977) form a radical critique of Freudian psychological theory and liberal social theory from a Marxist perspective. Forging a theory of the privatized anus, Hocquenghem attempts to use devalued sexualities and devalued body parts to form a link between the construction of the libido in psychoanalysis and the sustenance of class structures in capitalistic culture.

In the wake of the rebellion, which radically altered the academic structure of France, Hocquenghem received an appointment as professor of philosophy at the University of Vincennes-Saint Denis. With another professor, René Schérer, he wrote two important though often overlooked tracts, *Co-ire, album systématique de l'enfance* (1976), which examines the construction of childhood sexuality from a Marxist perspective, and *L'ame atomique, pour une esthétique d'ère nucléaire* (1986), which argues for a new epicureanism that would liberate play and frivolity as positions of agency within postmodern politics.

Hocquenghem's career as an experimental fiction writer began in the 1980s, when, partly as a response to his deteriorating health, he adopted gnosticism as a philosophy and faith. His first collection of stories, *Fin de section* (1976), led the way to his most famous novel, *L'Amour en relief* (1982), which tells the story of a blind foreign boy who circulates through French society. The story explores the ways in which pleasure can form a resistance to totalitarianism, and in many ways is a fictional counterpart to *L'ame atomique*. *La colère de l'agneau* (1986) is a fictional retelling of the vision of St. John the Evangelist. *Eve* (1987) combines the story of Genesis with Hocquenghem's reflections on his own body decaying from AIDS. His last novel, *Les Voyages et aventures extraordinaires du frère Angelo* (1988), is the tale of an Italian monk's travels in America.

Although Hocquenghem had a major impact on leftist thinking in France, his reputation has not grown to international prominence. Indeed, only the first of his theoretical tracts and his first novel have been translated into English, and though *Race d'Ep!* has been released in America as *The Homosexual Century,* it is virtually unknown. Hocquenghem remains, in effect, a major queer theorist awaiting discovery by the world he sought to liberate and guide. (See also LITERARY THEORY: GAY, LESBIAN, AND QUEER.)

—*Gregory W. Bredbeck*

BIBLIOGRAPHY

Hocquenghem, Guy. *Eve.* Paris: Editions Albin Michel, 1987. ■ ———. *Fin de section.* Paris: Editions Albin Michel, 1976. ■ ———. *Homosexual Desire.* Trans. Danielle Dangoor. London: Allison and Busby, 1978. ■ ———. *La colère de l'agneau.* Paris: Editions Albin Michel, 1986. ■ ———. *La dérive homo-sex-uelle.* Paris: Editions Universitaires, 1977. ■ ———. *L'Amour en relief.* Paris: Editions Albin Michel, 1982. ■ ———. *L'Après-Mai des faunes.* Paris: Editions Universitaires, 1974. ■ ———. *Le désir homosexuel.* Paris: Editions Universitaires, 1972. ■ ———. *Les Voyages et aventures extraordinaires du frère Angelo.* Paris: Editions Albin Michel, 1988. ■ ———. *Love in Relief.* Trans. Michael Whistler. New York: Seahorse Press, 1986. ■ ———, with René Schérer. *Co-ire, album systématique de l'enfance.* Paris: Editions Universitaires, 1976. ■ ———, with René Schérer *L'ame atomique, pour une esthétique d'ère nucléaire.* Paris: Editions Universitaires, 1986.

Holleran, Andrew
(*b.* 1943)

"Andrew Holleran" is the pseudonym of an author who has tenaciously guarded his anonymity, which makes it difficult to determine precise biographical details. He was probably born around 1943 and more than likely comes from an upper-middle-class background. In an interview granted to *Publisher's Weekly* in 1983, Holleran admitted that the relatively affluent white characters depicted in his two novels *Dancer from the Dance* (1978) and *Nights in Aruba* (1983) largely reflect his own life. Holleran was educated at a private prep school, and later attended Harvard, served in West Germany with the Army, and afterward began studying law, which he abandoned in favor of studying writing at the University of Iowa. In 1971, he moved to New York.

Holleran's first novel, *Dancer from the Dance,* one of the first major breakthrough novels of the early 1980s, chronicles the life of "that tiny subspecies of homosexual, the doomed queen, who puts the car in gear and drives *right* off the cliff!" The novel documents the life of an enigmatic and beautiful man, Malone, who becomes subsumed by the frenetic gay social circuit of Manhattan and Fire Island. Holleran is regularly lauded as a great prose stylist, and this somewhat trite plot line becomes an occasion for weaving a poetic myth of identity around and within the bars, discos, and house parties that typified a certain segment of the gay world in the late 1970s. This is a gay *Great Gatsby,* with East and West Egg replaced by Fire Island and the Pines.

Nights in Aruba, Holleran's second novel, moves away from Manhattan and tells the life of one gay man: his childhood on Aruba, where his father worked as an executive at a refinery; his service in the military in Germany and the bonding with other gay men he met there; his relocation to New York and his frequent visits to Florida where his parents have retired. The tension between an openly gay life in New York and a closeted family life in Florida becomes the central topic of the novel, and in his interview in *Publisher's Weekly* Holleran called this split "absolutely and completely" reflective of his own life and further calls it a problem "with no resolution, finally."

Nights in Aruba was published in 1983, only two years after *The New York Times* published its first story about a mysterious cancer found in forty-one homosexuals. Yet the impact of AIDS is already felt strongly in the novel. At one point, the narrator tells us that "by this time I was wary of disease," and later laments that "celebrities of our sexual demimonde were dying of bizarre cancers." The impact of AIDS on Holleran as a writer has been tremendous, and his third book, *Ground Zero,* is a collection of vignettes and essays that outline his responses to the plague. Holleran's intellect shows forth clearly in the essays, which range from ruminations on physical anguish in the writings of GEORGE SANTAYANA, to a poetic tribute to the theatrical magic of CHARLES LUDLUM, to an essay on "My Last Trick" that seems to form a eulogy for the world he so lovingly painted in *Dancer from the Dance.* (See also THE VIOLET QUILL.)

—*Gregory W. Bredbeck*

BIBLIOGRAPHY

Lahr, John. "Camp Tales." *New York Times Book Review* January 14, 1979: 15, 39–40. ■ "PW Interviews Andrew Holleran." *Publisher's Weekly* 224 (July 29, 1983): 72–73. ■ Robinson, Paul. "Dancer from the Dance by Andrew Holleran." *The New Republic* 179 (September 30, 1978): 33–34. ■ Seebohm, Caroline. "Husbands, Lovers and Parents." *New York Times Book Review* 88 (September 25, 1983): 14, 30.

Hopkins, Gerard Manley
(1844–1889)

Born into a financially comfortable family of marine insurance adjustors, the oldest of nine children, Hopkins was small of stature and extremely lively of mind. Acceptance into Balliol College, Oxford, on a classics scholarship allowed him to study with Benjamin Jowett, the influential translator of Plato and discreet commentator on "Greek love," and WALTER PATER, who would later become the center of a cult of young men dedicated to Greek beauty, Renaissance intensity, and modern AESTHETICISM. But it was the lingering shadow of John Henry Newman that most influenced Hopkins at Oxford. At age twenty-two, Hopkins not only converted to Roman Catholicism but, on the advice of Newman, shortly afterward entered the Jesuit order where he was ordained a priest in 1877 after years of rigorous study. He taught at various Jesuit schools until 1885, when he was elected professor of classics at University College, Dublin, in whose cold, damp climate Hopkins's ever-weak constitution gradually failed. He died only four years later, of typhoid fever, after a period of somewhat questionable emotional stability.

It is unlikely that Hopkins would have considered himself a homosexual. Recently reproduced diaries from his Oxford years, however, reveal an obsessive concern with male beauty complemented by a fear of what seem coded references to masturbatory fantasizing. (He felt enormous guilt, for example, over being distracted from a religious service by a choirboy's beauty, and had repeatedly to resolve to avoid "imprudent looking" at fellow students, at a roommate when naked, and even at men playing public sports.) The closest he seems to have come to indulging his feelings was during his years at Oxford in his crush on Digby Mackworth Dolben, a religiously flamboyant, emotionally immature youth three years his junior. Dolben encouraged Hopkins's Anglo-Catholicism, whose emphasis on baroque ritual, brocaded vestments, ornate church fixtures, and Latin chant offered many homoerotically oriented men of the period a pious channel for their sensual impulses, and in whose idealization of male chastity many found a fortuitous alternative to the Victorian idealization of marriage and family. Indeed, Hopkins's later choice of the rigorous, mortifying rule of the Jesuits seems to have been a deliberate attempt to discipline what he feared were his dangerously sensuous preoccupations. Hopkins's personal relations seem never to have recovered from the shock of Dolben's drowning in 1867, aged only nineteen; he became increasingly withdrawn in his relations, allowing friendly feelings to emerge only from a safe distance in his extraordinary correspondences with future poet-laureate Robert Bridges and fellow religious poets Coventry Patmore and Canon Dixon.

What Hopkins suppressed in his emotional and sexual relations, however, he was free to express in some of the most original poetry of the Victorian period. His poems depend on a sensuous rush of words restrained by the most rigorous of meters, creating an explosive world of sensual fullness whose expression is carefully controlled. Hopkins's insistence that all natural beauty is the revelation of an inhering godhead sacramentalizes but cannot obscure the fundamentally deep sensuousness of Hopkins's nature. And as Michael Lynch points out, male beauty proved for Hopkins to be one of the most splendid witnesses to the divine. For example, writing ecstatically of a young "bugler boy" making his first communion, Hopkins praises "Christ's darling" as the "breathing bloom of a chastity in mansexfine," concluding that "it does my heart good" to see "limber liquid youth . . . yield . . . tender as a pushed peach" to his catechetical instruction. A more telling instance of Hopkins's sublimated homoeroticism, however, is the "Epithalamion" that he began as a wedding gift for a younger brother and his fiancée. Its initial description of a rural paradisal setting in which the young heterosexual lovers may roam as a prelapsarian Adam and Eve is quickly overtaken by the poet's homoerotic fantasy of "a listless stranger" who is restored to joy by the sight of naked boys frolicking in a secluded pool. "Here [the stranger] feasts: lovely is all," the poet exclaims, and no amount of pious commentary can recover the poem from its unintended digression from the celebration of "spousal love." (See also ENGLISH LITERATURE: NINETEENTH CENTURY.)

—*Raymond-Jean Frontain*

BIBLIOGRAPHY

Bristow, Joseph. "'Churlsgrace': Gerard Manley Hopkins and the Working-Class Male Body." *ELH* 59(1992): 693–711. ■ Dellamora, Richard. *Masculine Desire: The Sexual Politics of Victorian Aestheticism.* Chapel Hill: University of North Carolina Press, 1990. ■ Hilliard, David. "UnEnglish and Unmanly: Anglo-Catholicism and Homosexuality." *Victorian Studies* 25 (Winter 1982): 181–210. ■ Lynch, Michael. "Recovering Hopkins, Recovering Ourselves." *Hopkins Quarterly* 6 (1979): 107–117. ∎ Martin, Robert Bernard. *Gerard Manley Hopkins: A Very Private Life*. New York: G. P. Putnam's Sons, 1991. ∎

Overholser, Renée O. "'Looking with Terrible Temptation': Gerard Manley Hopkins and Beautiful Bodies." *Victorian Literature and Culture* 19(1991): 25–53.

Horace

(65–8 B.C.)

Quintus Horatius Flaccus, or Horace, as he is usually known among English speakers, was the son of a freed slave of Venusia in southeastern Italy. His father was sufficiently successful in business, and sufficiently ambitious for his son, to afford him a literary education. Accomplishment in literature could give access to a career in the Roman civil service or, in the case of a budding poet, to the networks of aristocratic patronage. In addition, at about the age of twenty, Horace was sent to Athens to study philosophy. Such training was common for the sons of established and upwardly mobile families. He would have been exposed at least to the lineaments of several philosophical traditions, and his later writings suggest that he achieved some depth, as well as breadth, in his philosophical studies. During his years in Athens, Horace also began to establish "friendships": relationships with young Roman aristocrats that were not only social but also political and professional.

With the outbreak of civil war, triggered by the conflicts between Octavian, Mark Antony, and their supporters on the one hand, and Brutus, Cassius, and their supporters on the other, Horace's student career abruptly ended. Brutus was received with great enthusiasm by the Romans in Athens, many of whom favored the established order that he represented. Horace undertook an appointment as a junior officer (*tribunus militum*) in Brutus' army, a rather exalted position for a freedman's son. However, Horace's military career, which was spent chiefly in plundering the eastern provinces to finance the war, was cut short by the defeat of Brutus and Cassius at Phillipi, Macedonia, in 42 B.C., a battle in which Horace took part.

On his return to Italy, Horace found that his estates in Venusia had been confiscated for distribution to Octavian's veterans. He had enough money, however, to purchase a lucrative position as a civil servant (*scriba quaestorius*) in the Roman government. Although eligible by age thirty to stand for public office, he declined to do so. Playing political hardball was uncongenial, and he decided that he was satisfied with a middling social rank. He did, however, enter enthusiastically on the social life of Rome. His observations of the follies, pretensions, and social aspirations, not only of his fellow citizens, but also of himself, form the basis for his earliest published work, two volumes of *Satires,* which appeared in 35 and 30 B.C. These paint an unforgettable picture of Roman society as Horace knew it during his twenties and early thirties, reflecting both high and low life, elegance and vulgarity, and showing the poet in an environment of dinner parties, social climbing, literary study, warm friendships, and apparently uncomplicated erotic adventures.

Two of the most important relationships of Horace's life were established by the time he produced his *Satires*. One was with the poet VIRGIL, for whom he appears to have entertained feelings of sincere tenderness: He refers to him as "one half of my soul" (*Odes* 1.3). The other was with Maecenas, five or ten years older than Horace, a fabulously wealthy aristocrat of Etruscan origin who flouted the self-consciously earnest morality of respectable Roman society. Although an intimate member of Octavian's inner circle of power, he refused to enter the Senate or behave like a typical Roman statesman. He wore jewelry, loose, flowing garments and liked to conduct business *deshabillé*. He had numerous love affairs with persons of both sexes, maintained a stormy relationship with his beautiful wife, and ignored criticism. Maecenas took Horace under his protection and gave him a farm near Tibur, some miles east of Rome. This "Sabine" farm, celebrated in several passages in his works, was the source of great happiness to the poet. Suetonius (*De Vita Horatii*) reports that Maecenas claimed to love Horace "more than my own bowels" and asked Augustus to remember the poet "as being dear to me" (*Horati Flacci ut mei esto memor*).

Horace's greatest poetic achievement is normally identified with his four books of *Odes* (*Carmina*), the first three of which were published in 23 B.C., the fourth about eight years later. His program in the *Odes*, from a metrical point of view, was to apply the rhythms of the Greek lyric poets, especially of SAPPHO and Alcaeus, to Latin poetry, a project that, he claims, he was the first poet to undertake. The *Odes* are an astonishing technical and poetic achievement. They are characterized by an extremely careful organization of words in brilliant rhetorical patterns (impossible to

reproduce in English translation), as well as a masterly handling of verbal sonority, imagery, and theme. Notable, too, is the extreme subtlety of thought and feeling that pervades these poems, the humor that is often missed on first reading, and the ingenious allusiveness that is simultaneously literary and autobiographical.

Finally, among his later works are to be found two books of *Epistles,* dealing principally with philosophical and personal subjects, especially the subject of friendship (again in its extended sense), and with literary criticism (especially the epistle known as the *Ars Poetica,* or "Art of Poetry"). The *Epistles* also reflect Horace's weariness of the politics and careerism of the Roman scene, and express his desire for a life of rural retirement and solitary contemplation.

Horace lived and died a bachelor. He was short and fat and complained of premature baldness. After his death on November 27, 8 B.C., he was buried beside the tomb of Maecenas.

The erotic environment assumed in Horace's poetry is characterized by an easygoing, matter-of-fact bisexuality. Love affairs are frequently visualized as being light, transitory, and not very serious though a deeper emotional disturbance is often suggested and sometimes explicitly described. Horace often appears indifferent to the sex of a love partner, whether his own or a friend's. He refers to his own "thousand passions for girls, thousand passions for boys" (*Sat.* 2.3.325). He asks a friend why he would burst with sexual frustration when a slave girl or a slave boy is at hand to provide instant gratification (*Sat.* 1.2.116–118). He warns another friend of the trouble that might arise should he develop a strong passion for a slave girl or a boy (*Ep.* 18.72). In referring to these bisexual attractions, Horace almost invariably mentions the female partner first and then the male. In a series of three, the male appearing last seems to hold a climactic position, as in *Odes* 2.5, where Horace, describing a friend's amatory history, refers first to Chloris, then to Pholoe, and finally to the boy Gyges.

Horace normally describes the object of homosexual love as a pubescent boy, frequently (perhaps always) a slave. In *Odes* 1.4, he assumes that so young a male will be of interest chiefly to other males, women generally preferring older boys. Encouraging his friend Sestius to enjoy the pleasures of life while there is yet opportunity, Horace reminds him that, after death, he shall not be able to admire the beautiful Lycidas, "for whom all the young men are hot, and to whom the girls too will soon warm up." Ligurinus is described as having the long hair and beardless cheeks of a young adolescent (*Odes* 4.10). A sexually ambiguous appearance is prized in the slave Gyges, whose

sex cannot be determined even by the most experienced observers (*Odes* 2.5). Whether or not there is an explicit erotic interest, the handsome slave boy, especially when employed, like Zeus's Ganymede, as a wine steward, frequently symbolizes the good life. Thus *Odes* 1.38, Horace's subtle comment on life, death, and Epicurean joy, is addressed to his young male slave. An athletic, royal youth with oiled hair represents money and success for the upwardly mobile Iccius in *Odes* 1.29. The loss of such a slave is the occasion for a consolatory poem to his friend Valgius Rufus (*Odes* 2.9).

Horace's poetry evinces as strong a sensitivity to male as to female beauty. He commemorates his lyric predecessor Alcaeus's celebration of his lover Lycus, "beautiful with his dark eyes and black hair" (*Odes* 1.32). Sometimes the youth in question is involved in a heterosexual relationship, in which case Horace's comments seem to take on a voyeuristic character. Pyrrha is being courted by a "slender boy, his hair steeped in fragrant oils" (*Odes* 1.5). Neobule is in love with Hebrus, who bathes his oil-glistening shoulders in the Tiber and is an admirable athlete (*Odes* 3.12). Telephus, who is being pursued by the girl Rhode, is addressed as "radiant with thick hair and as bright as the evening star" (*Odes* 3.19). Sometimes these heterosexual affairs are complicated by a little extracurricular homosexuality on the part of the male partner. Thus in *Odes* 3.20, Nearchus has been seduced away from his female paramour by another male, Pyrrhus, whom Horace warns against his rival's vengeance.

In Horace's poetry, effeminacy is not a quality to be attributed only to pubescent slave boys. The lovestruck heterosexual male can also be described as departing from Roman standards of virility. In *Sat.* 2.3.254–255, the poet asks the lovelorn if he will give up the effeminate tokens of romantic passion (garters, elbow cushion, neck wrap). In *Odes* 1.8, Horace presents another description of the baleful effects of heterosexual passion: Sybaris, who has fallen in love with Lydia, has abandoned the manly pursuits of the gymnasium and military camp. His sudden effeminacy is further emphasized by comparison with Achilles' boyhood transvestism. In fact, the notion of the effeminate heterosexual lover was commonplace in ancient literature. For instance, in the Pseudo-Lucianic dialogue *Erotes,* the heterosexual is depicted as "womanish" (he wears makeup) and morally inferior, whereas the homosexual is described as manly, athletic, and high-minded.

It is debatable to what extent, if any, Horace conceives of same-sex friendship in homoerotic terms. Friendship was a central theme in Epicurean philosophy but was not understood as amatory. Nevertheless, the ardent tone in which the bond between friends is described by Horace and other ancient writers tends to convey to modern Western readers a romantic impression that may be illusory. Numida, returning from abroad, greets all of his friends with kisses but reserves the lion's share for his "sweet" Lamia. Horace's own expressions of affection for his friends are quite passionate by modern, Western standards. Virgil is described as "one half of my soul"(*Odes* 1.3). Maecenas is "beloved" (*dilecte, Odes* 2.20). He is "part" of Horace's "soul"(*Odes* 2.17), and Horace forecasts that he cannot long survive Maecenas' death. (His projection proved true: The poet died only a few months after his patron.) He visualizes friends as placing one another before all other relations and sticking together through thick and thin (*Odes* 2.6 and 2.17). Whatever the character of such references, there is little doubt that Horace's treatment of friendship inspired homosexuals in later ages. Certainly A. E. HOUSMAN, when he translated *Odes* 4.7 (*More Poems* 5), interpreted Horace's mention of the love between Theseus and Perithous as homoerotic.

Horace's love poetry, whether addressed to females or males, draws much of its drama from the delicate tension between the pretense of transient pleasure and the suggestion of real emotional disturbance. It is interesting that one of the rare occasions when the latter is explicitly stated occurs in *Odes* 4.1 (published and probably composed in middle age). Although this poem begins with an expression of disillusionment with life and love, it ends with an expostulation to a slave boy:

> Then why, alas, does the unwonted tear run down my cheeks, Ligurinus? Why does my eloquent tongue falter indecorously in silence in the midst of my words? In my dreams I am at one moment holding you close, at another moment I pursue you through the grasses of Mars' Field, or through the swift waters, hard-hearted one.

(See also ROMAN LITERATURE.)

—*Brad Walton*

BIBLIOGRAPHY

Armstrong, David. *Horace.* New Haven: Yale University Press, 1989. ■ Commager, Steel. *The Odes of Horace.* New Haven: Yale University Press, 1962. ■ Connor, Peter. *Horace's Lyric Poetry: The Force of Humour.* Berwick: Aureal, 1987. ■ Griffin, Jasper. *Augustan Poetry and Roman Life.* Oxford: Oxford University Press, 1985. ■ Kilpatrick, Ross. *The Poetry of Friendship: Horace, Epistles I.* Edmonton: University of Alberta Press, 1986. ■ Lee, Owen. *Word, Sound and Image in the Odes of Horace.* Ann Arbor: University of Michigan Press, 1969. ■ Putnam, Michael J. *The Artifices of Eternity: Horace's Fourth Book of Odes.* Ithaca, N.Y.: Cornell University Press, 1986. ■ Rudd, Niall. *The Satires of Horace.* Cambridge: Cambridge University Press, 1966. ■ Santirocco, Matthew. *Unity and Design in Horace's Odes.* Chapel Hill: University of North Carolina Press, 1986. ■ Wilkinson, L. P. *Horace and His Lyric Poetry.* Cambridge: Cambridge University Press, 1946.

Housman, A. E.
(1859–1936)

To mainstream readers of his time, A. E. Housman was the admired author of two best-selling collections, *A Shropshire Lad* (1896) and *Last Poems* (1922), whose texts were taken as universal statements. Some became staples of English verse (for example, "When I was one-and-twenty"), and others contributed catch phrases to the language ("a world I never made"). Esteemed professionally as well, Housman was ultimately regarded as the leading Latinist in the English-speaking world. He held the Chair of Latin at Cambridge from 1911, and for nineteen years before that had been Professor of Latin at University College, London. Housman's eventual scholarly eminence was a particular personal triumph since he surprisingly had failed his examination in Greats at Oxford in 1881, qualifying only for a minimal Pass degree. He had to pursue his classical scholarship independently while working for ten years as a clerk in the London Patent Office before winning the University College post.

For all its universality, however, Housman's poetry is inextricably rooted in homosexual experience and consciousness and is also a significant reflector of gay history. These facts were sensed by knowing readers from the two books Housman published in his lifetime, and they are obvious from his *More Poems* (1936) and *Additional Poems* (1937), the two more candid posthumous volumes that Housman's brother Laurence, his literary executor and also homosexual, assembled from Housman's unpublished manuscripts. Indeed, in the history of post-classical homosexual literature, Housman is the first homosexual poet to have left an indisputable body of private homosexual work paralleling his more coded public writing, though other homosexual writers from the late eighteenth century on had also left frank homosexual documents to be published posthumously. His work is also the first in the aftermath of the WILDE scandal to show how fully the prosecution of Wilde failed at its intended purpose of silencing homosexuality: As Housman's verse testifies, the prosecution actually spurred homosexual writers to even greater expressiveness, though their work necessarily had to be coded or kept hidden. Among similar private work by contemporaries are Goldsworthy Lowes Dickinson's 1896 love poems to Ferdinand Schiller, A. C. Benson's diary, begun in 1897, and, most famously, E. M. FORSTER's *Maurice* (1914).

The initial impetus for Housman's poetic career was an unreciprocated homosexual attachment—his profound attraction to Moses Jackson, the heterosexual Oxford classmate who remained the love of his life and whom Housman is said to have told, "You are largely responsible for my writing poetry." The chief subject of Housman's most autobiographical poems, Jackson was also, for example, the primary reason Housman composed his long-awaited *Last Poems* when he did. Jackson was dying in Canada at the time, and Housman wanted to finish the volume in time for him to have it. Housman met Jackson when he went up to St. John's College, Oxford, in 1877, and shared rooms with him and another classmate in their last year. Housman's failure at Greats has been attributed in part to shock at his growing realization of his homosexuality through his love for Jackson, as well as to his inadequate preparation because of intellectual stubbornness and to his distress at the illness and bankruptcy of his father, a genial but spendthrift country solicitor. The attraction of the Patent Office job for Housman was that Jackson was already working there in a higher post. For three years, Housman shared London lodgings with Jackson and his younger brother Adalbert. Adalbert, unlike Moses, may have shared Housman's sexuality; he and Housman seem to have had an affair, and Housman wrote two moving tributes to him—*More Poems* 41 and 42—after his sudden death from typhoid in 1892.

In late 1885, a breach occurred between Housman and Jackson, apparently over Jackson's conclusive rejection of Housman's overtures. Housman disappeared for a week, and when he returned he moved out of the Jacksons' flat, taking up the solitary mode of living he would maintain until his death. Housman and Jackson remained friends, however, though Jackson apparently blocked any further opportunities for intense displays between them. For example, until Jackson moved to India to teach in 1887, Housman still saw him at the Patent Office every day, but when

Jackson returned briefly to England in 1889 to marry, Housman not only was not invited to the wedding but knew nothing about it until the couple had left the country. Jackson lived abroad for the rest of his life, and, except for a few short visits to England, his and Housman's later relationship was entirely by letter. Housman seems to have continued seeing Adalbert Jackson in London until his death, however, and in his later life the only portraits on display in his Cambridge rooms were two photographs of the Jackson brothers over the fireplace.

Contemporary homosexual readers sensed a kinship in Housman's verse. Oscar Wilde's friend Robert Ross, for example, learned some of *A Shropshire Lad* by heart to recite to him in prison. And after the posthumous books mainstream critics became more vocal—one reviewer of *More Poems* proposed that "intense love came to him in the guise of 'the love that dares not speak its name.'" But Housman's sexual orientation did not become indisputable public knowledge until 1967, with the appearance of Laurence Housman's "A. E. Housman's 'De Amicitia,'" an essay he wrote around 1940 and had deposited in 1942 with the British Museum, stipulating that it not be published for twenty-five years. There Laurence discusses Alfred frankly as homosexual and, through his own recollections and evidence like Housman's till-then unpublished diary for 1888 through 1890, chronicles Housman's lifelong love for Jackson and his briefer relationship with Adalbert; he also identifies the Housman poems he believes most autobiographical. (Little primary documentation of the Housman–Jackson relationship survives: All of their letters were destroyed, except for their last to each other, and Housman's to Jackson is in private hands and cannot be printed or quoted.)

The other homosexual root to Housman's poetic career was his anger at homosexual suffering and persecution. Part of the "continuous excitement" that Housman said led him to compose most of the poems of *A Shropshire Lad* quickly in 1894–1895 was his agitation at Oscar Wilde's conviction in May 1895 and at the suicide of a young homosexual Woolwich naval cadet described in the newspaper in August of the same year. He wrote intense, ironic poems about each (*Additional Poems* 18, *A Shropshire Lad* 44 and 45) and sent Wilde an autographed copy of *A Shropshire Lad* on his release from prison. Relatedly, despite the universal application traditionally given to his poems, Housman seems to have written chiefly to support and encourage a beleaguered male homosexual community of readers. This intention is clearly implied by the fact that he did not destroy his franker unpublished poems but left them to Laurence's disposal; he also conveys it metaphorically in *A Shropshire Lad* 63 ("up and down I sow them / For lads like me to find") and states it more bluntly in the introductory poem to *More Poems* ("This is for all ill-treated fellows / . . . For them to read when they're in trouble / And I am not"). As mentioned, some contemporary homosexual readers recognized this dimension of Housman, and, continuing the pattern, in subsequent years his work provided a catch term for homosexual identity among British male homosexuals. In his 1968 autobiography, *My Father and Myself*, J. R. ACKERLEY, for example, refers to the continental countries where "one was not in danger of arrest and imprisonment for the colour of one's hair," alluding to the metaphor Housman used for homosexuality in his Oscar Wilde poem.

In his poems published in his lifetime, Housman understandably presents his homosexual feelings and consciousness in coded ways, though sometimes he punctures those codes daringly. In *A Shropshire Lad*, only eight of the sixty-three poems clearly depict heterosexual situations, and of the other personal lyrics, five leave the gender of the beloved unspecified (a common device in earlier homosexual writing), and seventeen fasten on "lads," "friends," or other male figures. Particularly intense examples of the latter tactic are the classic "To an Athlete Dying Young" (19) and poems 23, 35, and 42. Some of the book's more assertively homosexual poems stretch the "lad" or "friend" frames to make near-blatant romantic statements—for example, 24 and, especially, 33 ("I think the love I bear you / Should make you not to die"). The speaker's legacy of his "flowers" to "luckless lads . . . like me" in the book's final poem (63) also seems, as mentioned, a metaphorical statement of Housman's underlying homosexual intention in his work as a whole. Three other homosexually based *A Shropshire Lad* poems could only be certified as such by readers with inside knowledge—44 and 45, the two Woolwich cadet poems (Laurence found the newspaper clipping about the suicide inserted next to the poems in Alfred's personal copy of *A Shropshire Lad*), and 22, in which the speaker makes eye contact with a "single redcoat" of the Royal Guards, which was known at the time to be a common source of male prostitution. Laurence Housman also cites the well-known 30, in which "Fear contended with desire" and "fire and ice within me fight," as rooted in Alfred's homosexual conflicts.

Suggesting Housman's increasing defiance of the taboo of homosexual "unspeakableness" with age, the same patterns recur more pointedly in *Last Poems*. Here only three poems (of forty-two) clearly recount heterosexual situations, three leave the gender of the beloved unspecified (though biographical knowledge would identify 26's "wide apart lie we, my love" as for Jackson), and thirteen are preoccupied with "lads," "friends," and "comrades." Some of these give themselves away even more glaringly than their *A Shropshire Lad* counterparts. The speaker of 32 declares that "in boyhood / . . . It was not . . . sweethearts to be kind, / But . . . friends to die for / That I would seek"; and in 24, the retrospective epithalamium Housman wrote for Jackson's wedding (all the more poignant since Housman was excluded from it entirely), he describes himself as the "Friend and comrade [who] yield[s] you o'er / To her that hardly loves you more." But the most blatant of the *Last Poems* is the unusually long "Hell Gate" (31), an allegory of homosexual resistance in which two warrior-comrades defeat Sin and Death at the gate of hell and go off together on "the homeward track": "Tyranny and terror flown / Left a pair of friends alone, / . . . All that stirred was he and I." In addition, Laurence Housman has identified number 12, perhaps *Last Poems'* most famous poem ("Keep we must, if keep we can, / These foreign laws of God and man"), as a record of Alfred's struggle as a homosexual with his dominant heterosexual society.

Housman's posthumous volumes contain some protective poems he could have published in his lifetime (indeed, *More Poems* 18 and 23, two of the book's three heterosexual pieces, are rejects from *Last Poems*), but they are notable chiefly for their unprecedentedly frank depictions of Housman's homosexual experience and concerns. *More Poems* has forthright poems about Jackson—12, 30, and the famous 31 ("Because I liked you better / Than suits a man to say")—as well as Housman's romantic elegies for Adalbert (41, 42) and his declaration of the end of his affair with the Venetian gondolier, Andrea (44). (From the little evidence that exists about it now, Housman's later active erotic life seems to have taken place entirely during his annual summer trips to the continent. In addition to letting slip references to Andrea, Housman mentioned a young Frenchman traveling companion and the Paris "bains de vapeur"—turkish baths—to English friends.) Moreover, as suggested above, *More Poems'* introductory poem—"This is for all ill-treated fellows"—seems Housman's clearest statement that his primary intended audience was other male homosexuals.

Fittingly, the shorter *Additional Poems* has no heterosexual texts at all. Further frank poems about Jackson appear—2 ("Oh were he and I together") and 7 ("He would not stay for me")—plus the threat to break homosexual silence implied in 6 ("Ask me no more, for fear I should reply"). *Additional Poems'* most notable work is arguably "Oh who is that young sinner" (18), Housman's fiercely empathetic poem about Wilde, written shortly after Wilde's conviction and one of the most important texts in the history of gay literature. Besides showing Housman's awareness of the history and language of gay oppression ("In the good old time 'twas hanging," "'Tis a shame to human nature"), Housman's ironic method in the poem offers the fullest demonstration in his work that his occasionally depressive statements about homosexuality should not be taken at face value. Here—as in *A Shropshire Lad* 45's "your sickness is your soul," *More Poems* 12's "unlucky love," and *More Poems* 21's "cursed trouble"—Housman's deliberate and repeated use of the homophobic language of society ("He can curse the God that made him for the colour

of his hair") is his means of stirring his readers to oppose that society.

—*Joseph Cady*

BIBLIOGRAPHY

Bayley, John. *Housman's Poems.* Oxford: Clarendon Press, 1992. ■ Graves, Richard Perceval. *A. E. Housman: The Scholar-Poet.* New York: Scribner's, 1980. ■ Housman, A. E. *Collected Poems.* New York: Holt, Rinehart and Winston, 1965. ■ Housman, Laurence. "A. E. Housman's 'De Amicitia' (Annotated by John Carter)." *Encounter* 30.4 (October 1967): 33–41. ■ Page, Norman. *A. E. Housman: A Critical Biography.* New York: Schocken, 1983. ■ Ricks, Christopher, ed. *A. E. Housman: A Collection of Critical Essays.* Englewood Cliffs, N.J.: Prentice-Hall, 1968.

Howard, Richard
(*b.* 1929)

Among the most accomplished of contemporary American poets, Richard Howard worries the subtleties of language and life in poems that are at once elegant and vigorous. He was born in Cleveland and educated at Columbia University and the Sorbonne. Currently University Professor of English at the University of Houston and poetry editor of *The Paris Review,* he is also a distinguished translator and critic. He has translated more than 150 books by French authors—including CHARLES BAUDELAIRE, ANDRÉ GIDE, JEAN COCTEAU, and ROLAND BARTHES—and he has written incisive accounts of contemporary American poets, collected in *Alone with America: Essays on the Art of Poetry in the United States Since 1950* (1969). But his own searching and witty poetry is his most significant contribution to the gay and lesbian literary heritage.

Howard's first two books, *Quantities* (1962) and *The Damages* (1967), composed of original lyrics in several forms, translations, and imitations, are the work of a sophisticated and introspective young man, prematurely old and preoccupied with aging. In these poems, which evince the influence of W. H. AUDEN and MARCEL PROUST, Howard is obsessed with personal loss and public malaise, themes that also recur in the more ambitious later works.

Howard's third volume, the Pulitzer Prize–winning *Untitled Subjects* (1969), marks an important turning point in his career. A collection of fifteen dramatic monologues, letters, and journal entries whose subjects are nineteenth- and early-twentieth-century personages, actual and imaginary, famous and obscure,

Untitled Subjects established Howard's reputation as an authentic successor to Robert Browning in his understanding of character and in his evocation of the past to illuminate the present. Although manipulating the voices of others, his concerns are not merely historical, but contemporary and personal.

Howard's fourth book, *Findings* (1971), consists of dramatic monologues and more obviously personal poems in which he continues to speak as a poet of "otherness." In his fifth collection, *Two-Part Inventions* (1974), he expands the dramatic monologue into dialogue and returns to the nineteenth and the early twentieth centuries for his subjects. *Fellow Feelings* (1976) is a miscellaneous collection of lyrics, some in Howard's own voice and some in the personae of fellow feelers, poets and painters, many of whom are gay. *Misgivings* (1979), *Lining Up* (1984), *No Traveller* (1989), and *Like Most Revelations* (1994) similarly combine poems spoken in Howard's own voice with poems spoken by historical personages, though in these later collections, the figures are more apt to be French or Greek than English.

Howard's persistent themes are those of identity, existential loneliness, and the losses exacted by time. Homosexuality, which he defines as not a problem but a solution, is a significant and continuing thread that runs through all the books. Whether expressed in the more intimate early poems, such as "DO IT AGAIN: Didactic Stanzas" from *The Damages,* or in the historical dialogues such as "Wildflowers" from *Two-Part Inventions,* which stunningly recreates the meeting between WALT WHITMAN and OSCAR WILDE in

Camden in 1882, homosexuality is a recurrent motif. In "Decades," from *Fellow Feelings,* Howard locates himself within a tradition of homosexual poetry in America, clasping hands with Whitman and HART CRANE. In other poems, he pays tribute to Auden, who functioned for him as a poetic father and prior ego. Other noteworthy poems with gay subject matter include "The Giant on Giant-Killing" from *Fellow Feelings,* which retells the David and Goliath story from the perspective of a love-smitten giant; the meditation "On Hearing Your Lover Is Going to the Baths Tonight" from *Lining Up;* and, from *Like Most Revelations,* "What Word Did the Greeks Have for It" and the extraordinary contrapuntal dialogue, "Man Who Beat Up Homosexuals Reported to Have AIDS Virus." Howard's identification with fellow feelers, especially gay artists, enables him simultaneously to affirm and escape the self.

—*Claude J. Summers*

BIBLIOGRAPHY

Bergman, David. *Gaiety Transfigured: Gay Self-Representation in American Literature.* Madison: University of Wisconsin Press, 1991. ■ Lynch, Michael. "The Life Below the Life." *The Gay Academic.* Louie Crew, ed. Palo Alto, Calif.: ETC. Publications, 1978. 178–192. ■ Sloss, Henry. "*Cleaving and Burning:* An Essay on Richard Howard's Poetry." *Shenandoah* 29.1 (Fall 1977): 85–103. ■ Summers, Claude J., and Ted-Larry Pebworth. "'We Join the Fathers': Time and the Maturing of Richard Howard." *Contemporary Poetry: A Journal of Criticism* 3.4 (1978): 13–35.

§ *Hughes, Langston*
(1902–1967)

James Mercer Langston Hughes, born February 1, 1902, in Joplin, Missouri, began life in poverty and frequently moved from city to city as his parents tried unsuccessfully to escape racism and economic hardship. Hughes's father, an attorney, gave up on the United States and, in 1903, left his family to live and work in Mexico. The young Hughes lived alternately with his maternal grandmother in Lawrence, Kansas, and his mother in whatever city she could find work.

Hughes, as a seventh grader, worked cleaning the lobby and toilets of a hotel near his school. These impoverished conditions made indelible impressions on the young boy. He would never forget his place as a poor black in America. In the early 1920s, Hughes contemplated his place in the world as a poor "Negro" and as a poet. Writing his famous "A Negro Speaks of Rivers," he expressed the silent viewpoint of many black Americans who looked to spiritual growth as they faced racism and economic stagnation.

Hughes attended Columbia University from 1921 to 1922 but left to travel (most often working to pay his passage) extensively in Europe and Africa before deciding to enter Lincoln University of Pennsylvania, where he studied from 1926 to 1929. Even before graduating from college, Hughes had published *The Weary Blues* (1926) and *Fine Clothes to the Jew* (1927). From this point on, he wrote in virtually every genre and published nonstop until his death in New York on May 22, 1967. Hughes's literary legacy is enormous and varied. He holds an undisputed and honored place in American letters. Hughes always claimed that he was committed to writing simply about the black experience in a language the masses could understand, learn from, and enjoy. He embraced jazz, spirituals, and the blues in his works and, thus, became the people's poet.

One of the greatest ironies in the life of the people's poet was his own understandable silence regarding the oppression of gays. As a gay man, Hughes lived that secret life silently in the confines of a very narrow, but well-constructed closet—one that still shelters him today.

On June 13, 1991, *The Los Angeles Times* ran an article entitled "Battle Lines" reporting on the controversy that erupted over the use of his poem "Tell Me" for a poster ushering in Lesbian and Gay History Month. The five-line poem asks a question Hughes posed often in his work: Why must my dreams be deferred? The poem is a kind of gestalt in which the phrase "Why should it be *my*" is used three times to emphasize personal anguish over loneliness and the unattainability of dreams. The "it" of the poem can be taken to be racism, poverty, homosexuality, or a host of other reasons that dreams are not achieved. Thus, the poem is an appropriate expression of outrage against heterosexism. Using Hughes's own words to express this sentiment, however, had the additional power of reclamation: The poster's gay designers boldly claimed Hughes as one of their own.

Hughes's biographers do little to settle definitely the question of the poet's sexuality: Faith Berry holds that Hughes was gay, whereas Arnold Rampersad—though he documents Hughes's admission of a homosexual encounter with a seaman in 1926— asserts that he could not find incontrovertible evidence that the writer was gay. It should not be surprising to anyone who has tried to recapitulate the lives of literary figures during pre-Stonewall America that finding physical traces of overt homosexuality is rare indeed. The closet, by the turn of the century, had been so firmly erected by heterosexism that the fear of coming out could last a lifetime, especially for public figures.

For Rampersad and others who refuse to read between the lines in order to elucidate the facts of Hughes's life, it is clear that a political agenda is operative. These scholars are unwilling to associate an African-American cultural and literary hero, one of America's most celebrated black writers, with a perceived "abnormality." Unless this attitude is transcended, a better understanding of Hughes, the man and artist, will be difficult to effect. There is ample evidence in Rampersad's biography to indicate that Hughes was gay, especially his close alliances with such gay men as Alain Locke, Noël Sullivan, Richard Bruce Nugent, COUNTEE CULLEN, Claude McKay, and Wallace Thurman. That Hughes managed his closet so closely is testimony to the oppression he endured.

Recently, scholars have started to pay attention to the influence of homosexuality on Hughes's literary imagination. Many of Hughes's poems invite gay readings. Such poems enable scholars to theorize on the poet's use of the male–male gaze as a common feature in his writings. Focusing on such poems as "Joy," "Desire," "Café: 3 A. M.," "Waterfront Streets," "Young Sailor," "Trumpet Player," "Tell Me," and many poems in *Montage of a Dream Deferred* (1951), we can identify homoeroticism and other gay markings. As this kind of scholarship continues, as the reading public is made more aware that sexuality has great consequences for artistic creativity, and as the homosexual closet is deconstructed, surely then Hughes will take his place in literary history not just as a race and folk poet, but as one whose complex achievement includes battling oppression through his veiled homosexual expressivity. Then we will see that Hughes was not silent about his gayness after all. (See also THE HARLEM RENAISSANCE and AFRICAN-AMERICAN LITERATURE, GAY MALE.)

—*Alden Reimonenq*

BIBLIOGRAPHY

Berry, Faith. *Langston Hughes: Before and Beyond Harlem.* Westport, Conn.: Lawrence Hill & Co., 1983. ■ Emmanuel, James A. *Langston Hughes.* Boston: Twayne, 1967. ■ Hemphill, Essex. "*Looking for Langston:* An Interview with Isaac Julien." *Brother to Brother.* Essex Hemphill, ed. Boston: Alyson, 1991. 174–180. ■ ———. "Undressing Icons." *Brother to Brother.* Essex Hemphill, ed. Boston: Alyson, 1991. 181–183. ■ Lewis, David L. *When Harlem Was in Vogue.* New York: Oxford University Press, 1989. ■ Prowle, Allen D. "Langston Hughes." *The Black American Writer, Volume II: Poetry and Drama.* Chris Bigsby, ed. DeLand, Fl.: Everett/Edwards, 1969. 77–87. ■ Rampersad, Arnold. *The Life of Langston Hughes, Volume I: 1902-1941, I, Too, Sing America.* New York: Oxford University Press, 1986. ■ ———. *The Life of Langston Hughes, Volume II: 1941-1967, I Dream a World.* New York: Oxford University Press, 1988. ■ Smith, Raymond. "Langston Hughes: Evolution of the Poetic Persona." *The Harlem Renaissance Re-Examined.* Victor A. Kramer, ed. New York: AMS, 1987. 235–251. ■ Story, Ralph D. "Patronage and the Harlem Renaissance: You Get What You Pay For." *College Language Association Journal* 32/3 (1989). 284–295. ■ Tracy, Steven C. *Langston Hughes & the Blues.* Urbana: University of Illinois Press, 1988. ■ Williams, Sherley Anne. "Langston Hughes and the Negro Renaissance: 'Harlem Literati in the Twenties.'" *The Langston Hughes Review* (Spring 1985):37–39. ■ Woods, Gregory. "Gay Re-readings of the Harlem Renaissance Poets." *Journal of Homosexuality* 26:2/3 (Fall 1994):127–142.

Humor

§ The Mattachine Society, a "homophile" organization founded in 1950, took its name from the court jester, whose job it was to express political observations and social insights cleverly veiled with acerbic humor, so the king would not grow angry and have him beheaded. In Western civilization, this has been the traditional posture of homosexual and lesbian commentators on cultural mores. Like other minority groups, gay men and lesbians have had to develop a particular sense of humor among themselves in order to make their marginal social status endurable, and a defensive awareness toward the rest of the world in order to disarm their adversaries with laughter. The outsider who moves in society but is not an acknowledged part of it has a unique insight to offer, an objective view from the periphery, but there is always the danger of becoming too confident and overstepping the limit, as OSCAR WILDE, the greatest wit of them all, learned when he defied his lover's father too boldly and landed in prison, a broken man.

The success of lesbian and gay humor long rested on the fact that the humorist was invisible, at first as a member of an undefined social group, and later as a person with a self-acknowledged but publicly closeted identity. Much of the social satire of the closeted humorist is suffused with a rage caused by the forced disguise of strong feelings. That anger is the basis of much of the outrageous mockery of society's taste and manners that characterizes the peculiarly gay humor known as CAMP. But with the recent opening of the closet door and the emergence of gay men and lesbians as a visible minority group, gay and lesbian humorists have now been able to turn their social satire on themselves and generate laughter at the foibles of the new community as it struggles to define itself and establish its own mores within a wider social tradition.

In different times and places, gay and lesbian humor has necessarily taken different forms. What is uproariously funny in one cultural context may not be even mildly amusing in another. Effective humor relies on the recognition of references to common experience or knowledge against a background of shared values. For these reasons, it is difficult to pin down a universal definition of gay and lesbian humor. Is it limited to humor by gay men and lesbians about themselves and the society they live in? Can it include the work of nongay or nonlesbian writers who depict funny gay or lesbian characters and situations without condescension? Is it material that amuses gay men and lesbians regardless of its source? That is, is it defined by audience response rather than by author's intent? Do gay men and lesbians, transvestites and leatherfolk all find the same things funny, or are there several separate traditions?

Whether it is engendered by visibly or invisibly homosexual writers, the humor we are examining is the product of a quality called "gay sensibility," whose very existence is arguable and which is nearly impossible to define because even within the limits of one era and one culture, there is such a complex diversity of gay and lesbian consciousness based on categorical differences such as ethnicity, age, education, geography, and manners. Gay sensibility may be the result of a sharpened aesthetic taste intensified by the experience of oppression, or it may be a celebration of the special perspective granted to those who are different from the sexual norm. At a panel discussion called "Is There a Gay Sensibility, and If So, What Effect Does It Have on the Arts?" Jeff Weinstein gave the most insightful response: "No, there is no such thing as a gay sensibility, and yes, it has an immense impact on the arts."

In fiction, poetry and plays, in essays, and more recently, in stand-up comedy routines and cartoons, the literature of lesbian and gay humor appears in various guises, such as the urbane (often snide) epi-gram, the limerick, the farcical escapade, the exaggerated stereotype, and the social satire. Its tones range from gentle self-mockery to bitter sarcasm, from ingenious irony to the black humor that allows subjects as grim as bigotry and death to be confronted with apparent insouciance.

Frequently, especially in work composed before the late twentieth century, gay and lesbian humor is contained within some larger social and thematic context; that is, it is not about gay lives. The gay or lesbian sensibility may be connected to the larger society by one of several means. The use of a surrogate (usually an ostensibly heterosexual character who secretly represents the homosexual point of view) is at its most complex in MARCEL PROUST's *Remembrance of Things Past* (1913–1927). Much of the obvious humor in this long work is based on pointed observations of French society's romantic pursuits, hypocrisy, and gossip. The narrator, Marcel, has a keen but intolerant interest in characters who seem homosexual, like the Baron de Charlus, about whom he makes jokes, but there is another, more secretive level of humor encoded in the book if the reader agrees with Gregory Woods's controversial contention that Marcel is intended to be understood, at least by gay male readers, as a closeted homosexual like himself. This reading, though it is unorthodox, is a good illustration of the specialized nature of closeted humor as a sort of dirty joke to be shared only by those in the know, turning a lengthy literary work into one extended double entendre.

RONALD FIRBANK becomes his own surrogate in a much lighter way when he has his characters comment on his own writing in order to lampoon both them and himself in *The Flower beneath the Foot* (1923): "I suppose I'm getting squeamish! But this Ronald Firbank I can't take to at all. *Valmouth!* Was there ever a novel more coarse? I assure you I hadn't gone very far when I had to put it down." GERTRUDE STEIN became her own lover's surrogate when she turned one of her whole books into a sort of joke by calling it *The Autobiography of Alice B. Toklas* (1933). In *Breakfast at Tiffany's* (1950) TRUMAN CAPOTE still felt it necessary to use a surrogate—this time a female—to represent his own gay sensibility in the charmingly fraudulent Holly Golightly, who like many a gay man exchanges her dull backwater youth for a glamorous Manhattan charade. GORE VIDAL's comic surrogate looks at life from both sides. In *Myra Breckenridge* (1968), his confused character Myron has a sex change that turns him into the eponymous heroine who wields a wicked dildo in her war against gender roles.

Now that there is a self-defined gay and lesbian audience, and now that writers can publicly identify their sexuality, comic novels do not need a surrogate to connect openly gay or lesbian characters to a larger society. Instead they may allow their characters' lives to express a universal theme, such as coming of age. In RITA MAE BROWN's modern picaresque classic, *Rubyfruit Jungle* (1973), the roguish Molly Bolt confronts the hypocrisies of both heterosexual and homosexual societies. Alternatively, gay and lesbian characters may be part of a spectrum of character types in a mixed social setting, such as Michael among his tolerant friends in ARMISTEAD MAUPIN's comic paean to a lovably zany San Francisco, the *Tales of the City* series (1978–1991). Stephen McCauley directly involves his gay character George Mullen in the social and sexual lives of his heterosexual friends in *The Object of My Affection* (1987), as does Joe Keenan with his gay lovers in the farcical *Blue Heaven* (1988). Robert Rodi ridicules the efforts of his character Lionel Frank to hide his homosexuality from the straight world in *Closet Case* (1994).

For those who are "twice-blessed" and belong to two minority groups, a character's ethnic identity may be used to connect him or her to a larger society. A Jewish lesbian feminist reporter explores the demimonde of New York's Lower East Side in SARAH SCHULMAN's *The Sophie Horowitz Story* (1984). Joseph Torchia suffuses *The Kryptonite Kid* (1979) with Italian-American sensibility. Douglas Sadownick ranges from New York to Los Angeles with his state-of-the-art gay vision as he explores the cultures of both his Jewish grandmother and his Latino boyfriend (with a healthy smattering of African-American therapist and Anglo-Saxon lover) in *Sacred Lips of the Bronx* (1994). And Larry Duplechan's *Blackbird* (1986) uses gentle humor to trace the growing gay awareness of Johnny Ray Russeau, a black gay man in a straight white world.

Larger social issues may underlie the comic connection between the gay character and society. The underworld of narcotics users is the setting for WILLIAM S. BURROUGHS's savagely funny, surrealistic *Naked Lunch* (1959). In James Kirkwood's *P.S. Your Cat is Dead* (1972), the tables are turned when the narrator seduces the man who has come to burglarize his apartment, and the criminal is drawn into the gay world. And AIDS, normally a deadly serious topic, links David B. Feinberg's character B. J. Rosenthal to the world at large in the scathingly witty novel *Eighty-Sixed* (1989).

Some modern gay and lesbian novelists may choose to write about gay and lesbian characters in their own social milieu, but they run the risk of being "ghettoized," or limited to a gay or lesbian readership. John Preston's *Franny, The Queen of Provincetown* (1983) places a charmingly effeminate man in one of the few resorts where at certain moments gays may seem to be the majority. Jane DeLynn's *Don Juan in the Village* (1990) takes its narrator on a far-ranging quest for lesbian love, whose discouragements are reported with bitingly ironic wit. LARRY KRAMER's *Faggots* (1978) is a comic assault on the promiscuous sexual mores of the fledgling gay community. Ethan Mordden's *I've a Feeling We're Not in Kansas Anymore* (1983) is subtitled "Tales of Gay Manhattan."

The humor in gay poetry is usually a very individual matter, ranging from the mildly amusing to the raucously ribald to the bitterly sarcastic, sometimes suffusing entire poems and other times appearing in just a small section, even just a single line or comparison. Stephen Coote in his *Penguin Book of Homosexual Verse* (1983) has collected some (mercifully) anonymous limericks:

A young Harvard man, sweet and tender,
Went out with some queers on a bender.
 He came back in two days
 In a sexual haze,
No longer quite sure of his gender.

W. H. AUDEN writes contemptuously of "Uncle Henry":

Weady for some fun,
visit yearly Wome, Damascus,
in Mowocco look for fwesh a-
 musin' places.

Such humor seems quaint compared to more contemporary lesbian and gay verse, whose mockery ranges from gentle to savage. FRANK O'HARA's "Homosexuality" has a candor that is somewhat unrefreshing when he evaluates the "tearooms" where men had sex on Manhattan's Lexington Avenue subway line:

14th Street is drunken and credulous,
53rd tries to tremble but is too at rest. The
good love a park and the inept a railway
station.

Marilyn Hacker's humor in "Sonnet Ending with a Film Subtitle" has an angry edge:

Some day we women all will break our fetters
And raise our daughters to be Lesbians.
(I wonder if the bastard kept my letters?)
Here follow untranslatable French puns.

But ALLEN GINSBERG clearly had a twinkle in his eye when he imagined his poetic ancestor in "A Supermarket in California":

> I saw you, Walt Whitman, childless, lonely old
>   grubber, poking
> among the meats in the refrigerator and eyeing the
>   grocery boys.

EDWARD FIELD pretends to be self-pitying as he stands next to a wanted poster hoping to be recognized in "Unwanted":

> I was unwanted then and I'm unwanted now
> Ah guess ah'll go up echo mountain and crah.

And DARYL HINE wistfully recalls a social encounter with a boy who earlier had been part of a gang that attacked him in "March," a section from the book-length narrative of his school days, *Academic Festival Overtures* (1985):

> If dancing with girls had always felt like a duty,
> Dancing with my own sex was a pleasant
>   surprise.
> Being older, more masculine-looking and bigger,
> My impetuous partner masterfully led,
> While servile but inefficient I tried to follow,
> Two beats behind the music or two steps
>   ahead.

Carl Morse's humor is used as a weapon against heterosexual oppression in "Dream of the Artfairy," in which all the art and music made by fairies becomes invisible to straights:

> And then in the classroom of our days
> the fairy voices died—in mid-pronunciation.
> So:

> —I taste a liquor never brewed
>   from tankards __ __ __,
> —The mass of men lead lives __ ___ _____,
> —A rose is a rose __ __ __,
> —They told me to take a streetcar ____ ____,
> —Out of the cradle _____ _____,
> —Call me _____ . . . *

> *If you filled in any of the above, even in your head,
> you may be a gifted fairy.

JANE CHAMBERS uses black humor to describe the widespread horrors of child abuse in "Why are Daddies So Mean":

In the South there is a saying,
that a virgin is a six year old who can outrun her
    Pappy and her brothers.

Jewelle L. Gomez attacks the strictures of political correctness when she parodies Catholic confession in "Our Feminist Who Art in Heaven":

> Bless me sister
> for I have sinned . . .
> I swore three times
> (saying God
> instead of Goddess).
> But the most mortal
> sin of all:
> politically incorrect sex.

Alfred Corn speaks a volume in the first line of his poem, "Older Men": "I used to prefer them and now I'm one of them—." And RICHARD HOWARD, perhaps our most erudite contemporary poet, turns a steamy Italian seduction into a bedroom farce with layers of meaning when a Doberman Pinscher, Deucie (whose name evokes the actress Eleanora Duse), jumps on the bed and interrupts the coitus in "Poem Beginning with a Line by Isadora Duncan":

> But could a dog deter
> that lover at that point? It was my own
>   screams of "Deucie, down!"
> which shrivelled my assailant to his doom
>   as only memory can:
> Deucie—Duse: mine as much as his
>   the disgrace awakened,
> in a sacred name consigned to comedy,
>   the fiasco of farce
> laughter has no erectile tendencies:
>   Deucie and I were saved . . .

When gay humor takes to the stage, it may be overtly or covertly homosexual, according to the tastes of the audience and the time in which it is performed. In the pre-Stonewall years, the laughter was usually generated by the commentaries on heterosexual social manners, cleverly mimicked and informed by the gay outsider's sensibility. Oscar Wilde's memorable comedies, such as *The Importance of Being Earnest* (1895) and *Lady Windermere's Fan* (1892), are full of his well-honed wit. NOEL COWARD, whose sexual preferences were widely known but not openly discussed, wrote ostensibly straight sophisticated comedies of manners, such as *Private Lives* (1930) and *Design for Living* (1933), which contained implicit or oblique allusions to homosexuality, yet regaled English audiences, who treasured his insight into their lives. Wilde's and Coward's literary descendant was JOE ORTON, whose farces, such as *Entertaining Mister Sloane* (1964) and *Loot* (1965), have an angry undertone. One notable exception to writing about heterosexual society is MART CROWLEY's *The Boys in the Band* (1968), which presents a birthday party attended by an array of stereotypical, self-hating gay men, whose bitterly funny humor allowed straight audiences to laugh *at* them rather than *with* them: "Who was it that always used to say, 'You show me a happy homosexual, and I'll show you a gay corpse.'"

After the great emergence from the closet, gay theater with self-affirming characters began to crop up like wildflowers in spring. Now gay patrons could not only laugh at secret jokes in straight plays, they could be directly addressed. Holly Hughes's *The Well of Horniness* (1983) turns an allusion to a classic novel of lesbian despair into a celebration of freedom onstage. Many Off-Off-Off Broadway productions, seen by small but enthusiastic audiences, featured same-sex domestic comedies or bathhouse farces, often focused on the sexual exploits of the newly liberated lifestyles, with laughter imposed by the ironies of the closet. This grass roots tradition produced a strong comic literature in the plays of ROBERT PATRICK (*The Haunted Host* [1975], *Untold Decades* [1988]), Doric Wilson (*Street Theater* [1981]), Robert Chesley (*Stray Dog Story* [1982]), and Terrence McNally (*The Lisbon Traviata* [1985]). The sexual anxiety imposed by AIDS is treated with comic relief in Paul Rudnick's *Jeffrey* (1992). CHARLES LUDLAM's brilliantly campy Theater of the Ridiculous offered transvestite parodies of classic plays, famous stars, and literary guises, and Christopher Durang parodied TENNESSEE WILLIAMS in *For Whom the Southern Belle Tolls.*

As the audiences grew to include nongays, the awareness level dropped. Drag playwright Charles Busch says that his audience is predominantly gay for about three months, and after that he loses about one-quarter of his laughs. Nonetheless, the small theater success of some plays made it clear to producers that general audiences wanted to see a new kind of sensibility onstage, and gay comedy moved to Broadway in the Tony-winning works of HARVEY FIERSTEIN. *Torch Song Trilogy* (1981) features a sharp-witted drag performer whose heart is sorely tested by his relationships with his mother, his lovers, and his adopted son, but who keeps his audience laughing. William Finn's *Falsettos* (1992), which deals with the restructuring of a family with a gay father and husband, along with AIDS, baseball, bar mitzvahs, and everything else a cast of seven can handle, also moved

from Off-Broadway to Tony-winning success in the legitimate theater.

Eventually, gay-themed comic plays were written directly for Broadway. Fierstein's *La Cage aux Folles* (1983)—like *Torch Song Trilogy* the story of a stage transvestite with a straight son—based on the film of the same name, was mounted as a successful major musical. And Tony Kushner's two-part *Angels in America* (1992, 1993), which deals with romance, loyalty, politics, mysticism, race relations, Ethel Rosenberg, and AIDS, evinced a healthy dose of humor and was the recipient of many awards, including the Pulitzer Prize.

Hollywood screenplays, with a few exceptions like the film version of *Torch Song Trilogy,* lag far behind the stage in the production of comedies made from a gay or lesbian point of view, perhaps because of the huge sums of money required to produce major films, but also because of the homophobic fear that audiences (who are willing to pay to see everything from Ninja mystics to Mexican magical realism) will not buy tickets to see funny homosexual films. Gay characters have appeared as amusingly unthreatening friends and neighbors of the major heterosexual characters, but the only studio-backed films made by gay filmmakers have not been comic. However, gay and lesbian filmmakers have been able to film their comic vision in an ever-growing number of less expensive independent films such as John Greyson's *Zero Patience,* an AIDS musical, and Rose Troche's *Go Fish,* a Generation X lesbian romantic comedy.

The gay and lesbian comic essay has long been a means of disseminating humor within the community. Clark Henley's *The Butch Manual* (1982) is a satire teaching the inherently effeminate male how to adopt the masculinized "clone" image that became de rigeur in the 1970s: "Smiles are considered socially acceptable on babies. Smiles on gay people are considered desperate. A smile is an open invitation for rejection. The Butch safeguard against an accidental smile is a large moustache and a beard." Boyd McDonald's humor is based on a shocking honesty about matters sexual. His film reviews have more to do with the actors' underwear than with their acting, but his opinions make his readers laugh with self-recognition. Penny Perkins also satirizes gay and lesbian sensibility when she asks, "What is a Lesbian Date?": "A Lesbian Date is Something that Takes Place with Reservations." Fran Lebowitz writes for a larger audience, both homosexual and heterosexual. In "The Primary Cause of Heterosexuality Among Males in Urban Areas: Yet Another Crackpot Theory" from *Metropolitan Life* (1974), she turns the usual complaint inside out and depicts the heterosexual woman in a bar in Manhattan's

SoHo wondering where all the gay men are: "Why, she may ask, is this quarter of the city so heavily populated by young men to whom the name Ronald Firbank means nothing? To this query there can be only one reply—heterosexuality among males in urban areas is caused by overcrowding in artist colonies."

A newer form of gay humor are the cartoons, comic strips, and illustrated stories by artists such as Rick Fiala, Donelan, Jennifer Camper, Alison Bechdel, Donna DeMassa, and Howard Cruse. Some of these appear in general-interest gay and lesbian magazines, such as *The Advocate,* and others appear in magazines devoted to same-sex cartoon humor, such as *Gay Comix*. Although some of the material deals with the tribulations of being gay in a straight world, much of it is aimed at the foibles within the community, covering issues such as clothing, dating, domesticity, and gay male and lesbian political relations.

The witty epigram, or one-liner, has long been a staple of the expression of humorous gay sensibility, as in Oscar Wilde's, "I can resist anything but temptation!" During Manhattan's "pansy craze" of the 1920s and 1930s, gay performers like Gene Malin emceed nightclub shows, at first in Greenwich Village but later in less bohemian midtown, acting like straight men imitating gay men. Malin boasted, "I wear a rose in my lapel because it won't stay in my hair!" In *The Queens' Vernacular* (1972), Bruce Rodgers accompanies most of his definitions of gay terms with witty examples.

Today, the epigram has reached the stage and the airwaves with a host of gay and lesbian stand-up comedians, like Robin Tyler, Tom Ammiano, Sara Cytron, Frank Maya, Jaffe Cohen, Kate Clinton, and Reno. Speaking to their homosexual audience, they can discuss the social issues of the moment and comment on family relations from a gay and lesbian perspective. Some of them, however, will go on to reach a general audience, which will necessarily dilute the gay and lesbian content of their material. There are famous gay and lesbian performers, who must remain unnamed here because they are closeted, who began with a general audience and have kept their humor general while winking about issues of sexual identity. But with the passage of time, that strategy is becoming less necessary.

Having been refined in the crucible of minority oppression, lesbian and gay consciousness continues to evolve away from its once ghettoized sensibility. Gay and lesbian humor has grown less secretively angry and more openly celebratory, and it is becoming recognized beyond the borders of the world that gave birth to it. As it enters the mainstream in its various forms, it is increasingly being seen as a cultural treasure, not only for gay men and lesbians, but for all people who appreciate laughter. (See also FOLKLORE.)

—*Arnie Kantrowitz*

BIBLIOGRAPHY

Austen, Roger. *Playing the Game: The Homosexual Novel in America*. Indianapolis: Bobbs-Merrill, 1977. ■ Chauncey, George. *Gay New York: Gender, Urban Culture, and the Making of the Gay Male World 1890–1940*. New York: Basic Books, 1994. ■ Stevens, Robin, ed. *Girlfriend Number One: Lesbian Life in the Nineties*. Pittsburgh: Cleis Press, 1994. ■ Woods, Gregory. "High Culture and High Camp: The Case of Marcel Proust." *Camp Grounds*. David Bergman, ed. Amherst: University of Massachusetts Press, 1993. 121–133.

Huysmans, Joris-Karl
(1848–1907)

J.K. Huysmans was born Charles-Marie-Georges Huysmans on February 5, 1848, in Paris, the only child of a French mother and a Dutch father. He earned his degree under a private tutor, studied law at the University of Paris, and worked as a civil servant in the Ministry of the Interior, where he remained for thirty-two years. A cosmopolitan man of refined taste and sensibility, Huysmans admired the descriptive writing of Charles Dickens, but practiced a poetic novel, a form known in France as the prose poem. This genre, which typically emphasized sensation and an elaborate or exotic setting, was perfectly suited to his elegant style and rich vocabulary.

Huysmans was a prolific writer of novels, art criticism, essays, short stories, and prose poems. His most renowned work, *Against the Grain* or *Against Nature* (*À Rebour,* 1884), celebrated the decadent movement in European art and literature, later to be embraced by OSCAR WILDE, Aubrey Beardsley, and others. In this novel, the protagonist, Duke Jean Floresas des Esseintes, embodies the AESTHETICISM found in Wilde. A wealthy aesthete living a life of pleasure in his country house, Des Esseintes is characterized by his addiction to exquisite sensations, exoticism, flowers, decoration, perfume, and art. *Against the Grain* ranks with Wilde's *Picture of Dorian Gray* and Moore's *Confessions of a Young Man* as important examples of the decadent movement.

Huysmans's other significant novel is *Down There* (*Là-bas,* 1891), which describes the world of the occult of the 1880s, a world of Satanism, demonology, magic rites, and black masses, both imagined and actual in Paris and Lyon of the day, a subject matter also appearing in BAUDELAIRE, RIMBAUD, and others. Another novel, *Marthe* (1876), explores the world of prostitution. Since Huysmans was one of the first to describe or record the major impressionist painters, his *Art Criticism* (*L'Art Moderne,* 1883), particularly the section on "The Impressionist Salons of 1880, 1881, 1882," is valuable because it provides insights on such luminaries as Whistler, Degas, and Renoir. The artistic creed of impressionism, which stresses the importance of capturing the moment, is somewhat analogous to the emphasis on sensation in Huysmans's novels.

Huysmans maintained a correspondence with numerous writers of his day, including the homosexual symbolist poet Jean Lorrain and the novelist ANDRÉ GIDE. Huysmans met PAUL VERLAINE in the summer of 1884, and in 1904, he edited and prefaced Verlaine's *Religious Poetry.* Although Wilde was a more notorious figure than Huysmans, Huysmans influenced several of Wilde's artistic principles, especially those associated with "art for art's sake," "Art Nouveau," "DECADENCE," and "impressionism."

Huysmans exemplified a style of homosexuality at a pivotal moment in the emergence of a gay identity. He was an inveterate collector of antiques and an art reviewer who praised the fine arts. He surrounded himself with male companions, the artistic and poetic circle of his day; and in his novels, he depicted an ornate, sumptuous world of beauty and sensation. His fictitious characters resemble certain members of French society, a class of rich, aristocratic, decadent aesthetes, whom Wilde and PROUST also later cultivated as central characters in their novels.

—*Clarence McClanahan*

BIBLIOGRAPHY

Baldick, Robert. *The Life of J.K. Huysmans.* Oxford: Clarendon Press, 1955. ■ Banks, Brian R. *The Image of Huysmans.* New York: AMS Press, 1990. ■ Brombert, Victor. *The Romantic Prison: The French Tradition.* Princeton: Princeton University Press, 1978. ■ Cevasco, George A. *J.K. Huysmans in England and America: A Bibliography.* Charlottesville: Bibliographical Society of the University of Virginia, 1962. ■ Garber, Frederick. *The Anatomy of the Self from Richardson to Huysmans.* Princeton: Princeton University Press, 1982. ■ Kahn, Annette. *J.K. Huysmans: Novelist, Poet, and Art Critic.* Ann Arbor: UMI Research Press, 1987. ■ Laver, James. *The First Decadent: Being the Strange Life of J.K. Huysmans.* London: Faber & Faber, 1954. ■ Ridge, George Ross. *Joris-Karl Huysmans.* New York: Twayne Publishers, 1968.

Identity

Although the topic of homosexual identity is a complex one, it has polarized activists, theorists, and literary critics into two primary camps: essentialists and constructionists. The former (usually labeled "essentialist" by their detractors rather than embracing the term themselves) believe that the lesbian and gay sense of "self" is natural, fundamental, and historically constant. Often arguing from a biological, psychological, or other scientific basis, the essentialists emphasize the transhistorical similarities in the experiences of men and women attracted to members of the same sex. Constructionists, on the other hand, often utilizing methodologies of critical theory, philosophy, economics, and historicism, argue that constructions of identity, whether heterosexual or homosexual, are historically contingent, that homosexuality as it is understood today came into being only in the late nineteenth century, and that prior manifestations of same-sex desire were vastly different from what we today call the gay and lesbian experience of self-hood. Constructionists constitute a much more self-conscious movement than do the essentialists. Nevertheless, the two camps, with few exceptions, share a common desire: to demonstrate the fundamental amorality of sexual orientation and sexual identity. Although drawing on vastly different traditions and theories and beginning with very distinct assumptions, proponents of both constructionist and essentialist theories have produced valuable insights into gay and lesbian lives, ones that can contribute usefully to our understanding of the gay and lesbian literary heritage.

Chief among the cultural critics whose writing has been termed essentialist are JUDY GRAHN, author of *Another Mother Tongue,* and Robert K. Martin, author of *The Homosexual Tradition in American Poetry.* Grahn examines cultural documents, myths, and traditions from around the world, whereas Martin focuses specifically on poetic works from American literature, to emphasize a shared experience that helps us understand the oppression of homosexuals today by looking at contrasts and roots in the past. For such scholars, gay identity stretches back through time, and though it has always reflected historical circumstances, it has nevertheless hinged upon a sense of difference that has invariably separated the identity of same-sex loving individuals from their opposite-sex loving contemporaries. Using such an interpretive model, critics examining the homoerotic works of SAPPHO or SHAKESPEARE would invariably emphasize the commonality between modern gay and lesbian lives and those of men and women from centuries past, as Joseph Pequigney does in *Such is My Love: A Study of Shakespeare's Sonnets*. Working from similar presuppositions, the French feminist theorist MONIQUE WITTIG, in *The Lesbian Body* and other works, argues forcefully that lesbian identity in particular has an immutable, antipatriarchal core that finally transcends historical situation and cultural context.

Considerable support has been given to the essentialist position by scientists examining biological bases for homosexuality. Researchers such as Simon LeVay have worked to isolate genetic and physiological differences between homosexuals and heterosexuals. Though still inconclusive, preliminary results from examinations of brain matter of lesbians and gays indicate that there may be essential differences in physiology. Similarly, scientific examinations of DNA have revealed possible genetic distinctions in chromosomal patterns in lesbians and gays. In fact, compelling work on homosexuality in families suggests that sexual orientation may be inherited; the most convincing research has focused on identical twins who, though separated at birth, nevertheless share a homosexual identity in adulthood. Conclusive proof of biologically based homosexuality would certainly allow lesbian and gay activists to argue effectively that full civil rights are in order for a group of individuals who are as "natural" as their heterosexual counterparts. Some worry, however, that effective genetic testing might lead to selective abortion or genetic engineering in attempts to eradicate homosexuality.

But proof of an essential homosexual identity would clearly affect how we perceive and interpret the works of writers such as APHRA BEHN, CHRISTOPHER MARLOWE, CHRISTINA ROSSETTI, WALT WHITMAN, and others who lived before the late nineteenth-century origins of the term *homosexual*. In many ways, an essentialist paradigm mandates a clear designation of orientation, thus encouraging the reader or critic to fix the sexuality of a given writer through evidence from texts and biographical material. If Whitman is approached from an essentialist perspective and labeled "homosexual," as he is by Robert K. Martin, then much of his poetry appears immediately to engage in oppositional work, reflecting a sense of oppression and difference that may be historically specific, but that is nevertheless accessible to the modern reader. Similarly, Christina Rossetti's *Goblin Market* (1862), when the writer is categorized as "homosexual," becomes a clear statement of lesbian subversion of a male-centered sexual economy. The mention of heterosexual marriage at the end of the poem can then be interpreted as either a capitulation to heterosexism in the publishing industry or a renunciation of the characters' true "selves" in the face of a pervasive social and internalized homophobia.

Constructionists would find such analysis reductive and historically suspect. Broadly influenced by the work of MICHEL FOUCAULT, constructionists look askance at any work that attempts to impose the categories of "homosexual" and "heterosexual" on texts predating the creation of those terms in the late nineteenth century. Although there can be no doubt that individuals engaged in same-sex erotic acts before the late nineteenth century, constructionists would argue that such individuals did not necessarily assume an oppositional stance to society that resulted in a clear sense of sexual identity. Rather, such activity would have fallen under a category of proscribed acts that included theft, forgery, adultery, and other legal or religious transgressions. In Volume I of *The History of Sexuality*, Foucault traces the metamorphosis of the social discourse on sexuality in the nineteenth century that he feels results in the creation of specifically sexual identities; before Havelock Ellis and other researchers of the period branded the "homosexual" as a "type," there were no discursive means by which sexual activity alone could lead to an identification of the self that would be socially uniform enough to allow us to responsibly analyze it as "homosexuality." Lesbian- and gay-relevant themes may resonate throughout the history of literature, and modern readers may find that they share emotions or experiences with past authors, but constructionists would argue that we cannot impose ourselves and our categories onto vastly different and potentially unknowable sets of discourses and desires. Constructionists thus account clearly for the explosion in gay- and lesbian-themed works near the end of the nineteenth century. The new psycho-medical designation of "homosexual" allowed for a categorization of feelings and encounters that resulted in literary expressions of a well-defined homosexual identity, as is evinced in the erotic novel *Teleny* (1893), usually attributed to OSCAR WILDE. In this work, the main character, Des Grieux, feels incomplete and unfulfilled until he realizes that he is sexually drawn to men. That realization allows for an assumption of a lifestyle that is both erotically and aesthetically satisfying, since it is based on certain high-cultural values. According to constructionists, such a homosexual identity should be understood as a direct result of late-nineteenth century elitism and Francophilia. In a similar way, RADCLYFFE HALL's *The Well of Loneliness* (1928) can be read as an expression of a specific time and place, Paris in the 1920s, rather than an evocation of a transhistorical lesbian identity or set of experiences.

Two prominent literary critics who work from a constructionist model are Eve Kosofsky Sedgwick and Lillian Faderman. Sedgwick's work focuses specifically on literature written by men and traces changing representations of social and emotional ties between men. In her first work of gay-relevant criticism, aptly titled *Between Men,* she delineates homosociality from homosexuality, exploring the use of women in literature to mediate diverse forms of desire between male characters. In doing so, she carefully avoids terming all such desire "homosexual" or even "sexual." Her study moves from the erotic sonnets of Shakespeare through the seventeenth, eighteenth, and nineteenth centuries as she traces the historical contexts that have variously allowed and limited expressions of male–male desire. She expands this analysis in *Epistemology of the Closet,* which explores the creation and effects of closeted homosexual life as it is reflected in literature from MELVILLE through PROUST. In this work, as elsewhere, Sedgwick argues that the construction of homosexual identity in the 1880s and 1890s resulted from intersecting class, gender, medical, and social discourses, ones that mandated control over reproduction and the uses of the male body, but that also operate to expose and identify homosexual desire in ways that continue to subvert moves toward its suppression.

The same complex awareness of historical contexts that Sedgwick brings to discussions of desire between men, Faderman reveals in her classic study of ROMANTIC FRIENDSHIP between women, *Surpassing the Love of Men.* Although occasionally using the anachronistic term *lesbian* to describe women's experiences from early periods in English history, Faderman argues that there is no transhistorical essence that constitutes lesbian identity or experience, rather the spectacle of female–female sexual contact has been used variously to arouse men as well as incite anxiety about feminist threats to male hegemony, even as the possibility of bonding, both sexual and nonsexual, between women has offered to some individuals an opportunity for a construction of a safe space away from domineering men. She, like others, pinpoints the end of the nineteenth century as the time when sexologists constructed a pathological lesbian identity that served diverse regulatory needs but that also formed a new concept through which women-loving-women could identify themselves. Although not deploying Foucault's theories, Faderman's work clearly lends support to the French theorist's statements that discourse, in this case fiction, works as both a tool of oppression and as a mechanism for identification that subverts oppression.

For both constructionists and essentialists, their perspectives on homosexual identity become points of departure for specific political demands concerning the decriminalization of expressions of same-sex love, fairness in employment and housing, and the right to accurate representation in the media, fiction, and nonfiction. Thus the term "identity politics" has become popular as lesbians and gays, as well as other oppressed groups, have come to use a fixed sense of primary identity as a basis for social activism. But many would argue that inherent in identity politics is a disturbing process of limitation and reduction, for all human beings have many identities, reflecting not only sexual orientation, but also sex, class, ethnicity, region, profession, religion, and so on. To claim an identity such as "lesbian" or "gay" is necessarily to obscure the importance of other factors that would fracture any sense of unity with other people in the group to which one claims affiliation. Most troubling in such a process is the possibility that persistent social prejudices and hierarchies will continue to be replicated; thus many African-American women have felt marginalized in predominantly white lesbian groups, as have some lower-class men among groups of gays who embrace a narrow notion of identity built on AESTHETICISM and elitism. In JAMES BALDWIN's *Giovanni's Room,* we see the difficulty of arriving at a common sense of identity when class status and cultural heritage so clearly differentiate the perceptions of the two main characters, David and Giovanni. Likewise, AUDRE LORDE in *Zami: A New Spelling of My Name* (1982), as well as other works, deals openly with the problems of interracial affairs between women who may similarly embrace an explicitly lesbian identity, but whose different life experiences and encounters with oppression make common ground difficult to find.

Further undermining narrow notions of gay and lesbian identity is the continuing presence of self-identifying bisexuals, as well as bisexual desire and experiences among individuals identifying themselves as homosexual. Identity politics seems to mandate a continued binarism, whereby individuals attracted to members of their own sex are pressed to identify themselves in clear opposition to heterosexuality as well as heterosexism. But as Kinsey found in the famous sex surveys of the 1940s and 1950s, the overwhelming majority of individuals fall somewhere in between absolute hetero- or homosexuality. Narrow categories may make sense as a basis for political activism, but they also have the potential for confining individuals in ways that limit self-expression. Thus DAVID LEAVITT in *The Lost Language of Cranes* (1986), as well as several short stories, explores the plight of men who are under pressure to choose an identity, either gay or straight, when in actuality they love members of both sexes. Rosa Guy's title character in *Ruby* (1976) must also come to terms with conflicting desires in a world that limits one to relationships with members of the opposite sex. In both writers' works, desire does not necessarily seek or need an encounter with a member of a particular sex for fulfillment; characters look instead for other individuals who can offer companionship and support in a hostile world.

Thus one is left with the paradox of identity being both liberating and oppressive, both necessary for action and necessarily limiting that action. Some contemporary critical theorists such as Judith Butler argue that we have embraced notions of identity that are far too narrow and unnecessarily rigid. In *Gender Trouble*, Butler argues that social change can be effected through destabilizing identity, causing "gender trouble," by disrupting the performative aspects of gender: dress, mannerisms, voice, and the like. Similarly, the notion of a vaguely defined "queer" identity has been embraced by some individuals as a less restrictive, yet still oppositional, strategy for self-identification. Such "queerness" would allow social and political ties between lesbians, gays, bisexuals, and transgressive heterosexuals, all of whom reject narrow notions of sexual conventionality. But these attempts to move beyond a binary system of gender and orientational identification will inevitably trouble many, for seemingly basic to humanness is the need to claim affiliation as we shift to some larger group at least some of

the responsibility for determining the parameters of self-representation, patterns of behavior, and beliefs. Although VIRGINIA WOOLF's title character in *Orlando* (1928) may alter sexual identities in a relatively effortless way, few individuals seem capable of such transition. In fact, lesbians and gays may need to define themselves, whether through constructionist or essentialist models, in order to feel positive and healthy about desires that are still reviled and stigmatized by much of society. In *Woman on the Edge of Time* (1976), Marge Piercy envisions a future society that has moved beyond strict notions of gender and orientation, but such freedom seems very distant from our politicized world of restrictive rules and narrow strategies for countering those rules. (See also GENDER and POST-MODERNISM.)

—Donald E. Hall

BIBLIOGRAPHY

Boswell, John. *Christianity, Social Tolerance, and Homosexuality*. Chicago: University of Chicago Press, 1980. ■ Burr, Chandler. "Homosexuality and Biology." *The Atlantic* 271.3 (1993): 47–65. ■ Butler, Judith. *Gender Trouble: Feminism and the Subversion of Identity*. New York: Routledge, 1990. ■ Cady, Joseph. "'Masculine Love,' Renaissance Writing, and the 'New Invention' of Homosexuality." *Homosexuality in Renaissance and Enlightenment England*. Claude J. Summers, ed. New York: Haworth, 1992. 9–40. ■ Faderman, Lillian. *Surpassing the Love of Men: Romantic Friendship between Women from the Renaissance to the Present*. New York: Morrow, 1981. ■ Foucault, Michel. *The History of Sexuality*. Vol. I. Trans. Robert Hurley. New York: Random, 1978. ■ Grahn, Judy. *Another Mother Tongue: Gay Words, Gay Worlds*. Boston: Beacon Press, 1984. ■ LeVay, Simon. *The Sexual Brain*. Cambridge, Mass.: MIT Press, 1993. ■ Martin, Robert K. *The Homosexual Tradition in American Poetry*. Austin: University of Texas Press, 1979. ■ Pequigney, Joseph. *Such is My Love: A Study of Shakespeare's Sonnets*. Chicago: University of Chicago Press, 1985. ■ Sedgwick, Eve Kosofsky. *Between Men: English Literature and Male Homosocial Desire*. New York: Columbia University Press, 1985. ■ ———. *Epistemology of the Closet*. Berkeley: University of California Press, 1990. ■ Summers, Claude. "Homosexuality and Renaissance Literature, or the Anxieties of Anachronism." *South Central Review* 9(1992): 2–23. ■ Wittig, Monique. *The Lesbian Body*. Trans. David Le Vay. Boston: Beacon, 1986.

Inge, William
(1913–1973)

William Inge is perhaps most renowned for his four successful Broadway plays, *Come Back, Little Sheba* (1950), *Picnic* (1953), *Bus Stop* (1955), *The Dark at the Top of the Stairs* (1957), and

the Hollywood films based upon them. Set in the American heartland of his native Kansas, each drama portrays the domestic tensions, repressed sexuality, and conservative societal norms that Inge associated with life in small, Midwestern towns. It was a lifestyle Inge had experienced first hand, having been born, raised, and educated primarily in Kansas, and having spent his early career as a teacher in small towns in Kansas and Missouri.

A lifelong bachelor, Inge kept careful guard over his personal life, seeking to suppress any information that might adversely affect his careers as a high school teacher, newspaper arts critic, and college professor. Later, his difficulties with alcohol, his homosexuality, and his extensive psychoanalytic therapy were cloaked in secrecy so that he might maintain his well-crafted public image as one of the most successful and highly respected dramatists of the 1950s. Winner of the Pulitzer Prize for Drama in 1953 for *Picnic* and the 1961 Academy Award for Best Original Screenplay for *Splendor in the Grass,* Inge remained closeted throughout his career as a playwright, screenwriter, and novelist. He took his own life in 1973.

The Boy in the Basement, a one-act play written in the early 1950s, but not published until 1962, is Inge's only play that addresses homosexuality overtly. This well-sketched portrait of a middle-aged mortician who must come to grips with both his aging mother's discovery of his homosexuality and the senseless drowning of an attractive youth is a concise, hauntingly effective view of closeted homosexual desire and the trauma of "coming out."

Inge included openly homosexual characters in two other plays, both written late in his career when homosexuality was more openly addressed societally and when his success as a dramatist was waning. Most significant is Pinky in *Where's Daddy?* (1966), Inge's final full-length play, who eludes many gay stereo-

types in Inge's presentation of him as the male protagonist's surrogate father and the play's moral center. The other is Archie, an effeminate intellectual awaiting execution for the murder of his mother and grandmother, who appears in *The Disposal* (1967). Elsewhere Inge often leaves the sexual orientation of characters in question, for example, Virgil in *Bus Stop,* Bobby in *A Loss of Roses* (1960), and Vince in *Natural Affection* (1963).

Despite creating relatively few homosexual literary characters, Inge frequently acknowledged the existence of gay culture and desire in both his dramatic dialogue and prose, often reflecting the status of the culture at the time the works were written. Inge's work has been virtually untouched by recent scholarly criticism and could potentially benefit from careful gay analysis. Even Inge's four early successes could be tapped in such an endeavor for his overt celebration and foregrounding of both male and female sexuality, his championing of athleticism and muscle culture, his incisive critique of heterosexual domesticity and desire, and his close examination of parent–child relationships.

—*Jay Scott Chipman*

BIBLIOGRAPHY

Brustein, Robert. "The Men-Taming Women of William Inge." *Seasons of Discontent: Dramatic Opinions 1959–1965.* New York: Simon & Schuster, 1965. 83–93. ■ McClure, Arthur F. *A Bibliographic Guide to the Works of William Inge.* Lewiston, New York: E. Mellen Press, 1991. ■ Shuman, R. Baird. *William Inge.* Rev. ed. Boston: Twayne, 1989. ■ "The Works of William Inge" Issue. *Kansas Quarterly* 18 (Fall 1986). ■ Voss, Ralph F. *A Life of William Inge: The Strains of Triumph.* Lawrence: University Press of Kansas, 1989.

Interrelations of Gay and Lesbian Literature

A history of interrelations in the gay and lesbian literary heritage has not yet appeared. The purpose of this entry is less to sketch it than to point to a few writers, from Juvenal to JUDY GRAHN, who can introduce a subject that has received limited attention. The histories of gay men and lesbians are radically different, and the models used to describe one cannot be assumed to describe the other. I highlight what may be an obvious point because the pairing of "gay and lesbian" in terms like "gay and lesbian studies" implies that the two terms are directly comparable. Nevertheless, although the two terms are often joined in titles of organizations or programs,

they are rarely linked in most recent literary scholarship on homosexuality. The challenge is to describe interrelations in the gay and lesbian literary heritages without blurring them into each other.

Patriarchal systems of oppression have continually troubled such interrelations. ADRIENNE RICH writes in "The Meaning of Our Love For Women Is What We Have Constantly to Expand" that "lesbians have never had the economic and cultural power of homosexual men." If gay men have been oppressed because of their sexuality, they have had opportunities in education and writing that have been systematically denied to lesbians as women. Although many might argue that the concept of a distinctively gay or lesbian identity is of relatively recent date, literary texts going back to the classics implicitly or explicitly compare erotic relations between women and erotic relations between men. Looking at these past episodes in the history of interrelations of gay and lesbian texts and authors is interesting in part because it suggests both origins for and possible alternatives to the "odd couple" model that now seems so unsatisfying.

In this history, two general areas can be distinguished: (1) representations of desire between men and desire between women; (2) biographical connections between male and female artists. In terms of the first category, the paralleling of gays and lesbians might seem to go back to the Sodom and Gomorrah narrative in Genesis 18. In one interpretation of this narrative, Sodom is supposed to stand for male homosexuality; Gomorrah, for female. Yet, although the association of Sodom with male homosexuality derives from the Christian fathers, it is difficult to find evidence of the association of lesbianism with Gomorrah before the nineteenth-century French poet Alfred de Vigny, whom MARCEL PROUST quotes in his epigraph to *Cities of the Plain* in *Remembrance of Things Past.* This absence underscores that a history of male and female homosexuality cannot treat them as two versions of the same thing. For reasons that shift with time and culture, they have generally, though not always, been represented as radically different activities.

This difference is evident as early as the writers of classical Rome. For both Juvenal and Ovid, sexual relations between males, usually the passion of an older man for a younger one, are so ordinary that they can be assumed to be normative. Lesbian relations appear in contrast as far more dangerous or imaginatively intriguing as a mode of sexual behavior. Juvenal's misogynistic Satire VI sustains a tirade against the evils of women and includes a vivid portrayal of the sexual relations between two female characters, Maura and Tullia. Given what he perceives as the depraved status of women, Juvenal recommends that men find not a chaste and virtuous woman but a pretty boy. Although he considers lesbianism revolting, he suggests that male pederasty is the ideal. Ovid at the end of Book IX of the *Metamorphoses,* however, gives a female character, Iphis, a searching speech describing her passion for another woman, Ianthe. Iphis at last mysteriously turns into a man so that she can marry her beloved. Ovid does not condemn sexual relations between men, but he describes Jupiter's infatuation with Ganymede in only a few lines, as if it were far less imaginatively compelling than love between women. This distinction suggests that love between women is a more interesting poetic topic than love between men.

The English Renaissance offers a sharp contrast to these classical authors. Whereas WILLIAM SHAKESPEARE's comedies, such as *As You Like It,* notoriously flirt with same-sex desire both between men and between women (see Traub), his tragedies may be even more intriguing in contrasting bonds between men and those between women. Although these bonds are not overtly sexual, as in Juvenal and Ovid, more can hinge on them than on relations that are. *Othello,* for example, prefigures the familiar gendered split of public and private spheres whereby men came to dominate the public sphere and women the private one. This division invites the comparison of homosocial bonds within the different spheres (that is, friendships between members of the same sex) versus the heterosexual ones that bridge them. Female friendship seems to be the only haven in the play from male power struggles. When Emilia gives Desdemona's handkerchief to Iago, her action seems not a sign of Desdemona's unfaithfulness to Othello, but of Emilia's to Desdemona. Relations between men, in contrast, acquire the horrific fascination that relations between women held for Juvenal. Iago's devious seduction of Othello and Othello's abandonment of Desdemona for Iago combine to form the play's most erotically charged relationship. Homosocial relationships between women appear nurturing and stable, whereas those between men are racked with deceit, suspicion, and destructive contests for power. Relations between women become more positive as they become more emotional, and relations between men become worse as they do the same.

By the end of the eighteenth century in England, the possible interrelations of desire between men and desire between women had altered when the division of public and private had become routine for the British middle classes. Eve Kosofsky Sedgwick in *Between Men* has argued that this division intensified anxiety about relations between men in the public sphere. Samuel Taylor Coleridge's poem "Christabel" (ca 1798–1800) suggests that this anxiety may have been even more intense regarding women in the private one. The poem describes the possession of Christabel's spirit by the mysterious Geraldine. In a scene that some contemporaries interpreted as a representation of lesbian sexuality, Geraldine puts a spell on Christabel when, after the two have disrobed, she touches her with her bosom. The poem's first part ends abruptly after Geraldine's curse on Christabel, so the activities between the two women in the bed are left to the reader's imagination. In the second part, Geraldine turns her attention to Christabel's father, Sir Leoline. She mesmerizes him by pretending to be the daughter of his long-lost friend, Lord Roland. The poem's most famous passage describes the painful decay of the friendship between the two men; his love for his lost friend leads Sir Leoline to vow to help Geraldine. The poem ends abruptly after Christabel's futile attempts to stop their union.

Relations between men in this poem seem to follow Sedgwick's paradigm of a triangle in which a female figure (Geraldine) mediates homosocial desire between two men (Sir Leoline and Lord Roland). But the prior relations between daughters complicate this paradigm: Homosocial desire between men in this poem becomes apparent only because of a prior, far more dangerous coupling between women. Although many of Coleridge's contemporaries greeted "Christabel" with incomprehension or disgust, it eventually became a cult poem for the Aesthetic movement in England. WALTER PATER, for example, praised it highly and singled out the passage describing friendship between men for special praise.

If nineteenth-century male writers emphasized male friendship in "Christabel," twentieth-century women writers reappropriated the poem to emphasize its lesbian aspects. Rosamond Lehmann, for example, in *Dusty Answer* (1927), names the novel's lesbian seductress "Geraldine Manners." Likewise, in "The Gipsy's Baby" (1946), she describes the peculiar understandings and tensions that exist between a child, "Chrissy," and her nurse "Isabel." Toni McNaron in her lesbian-feminist memoir *I Dwell in Possibility* (1992) describes how one stepping-stone on her way toward self-awareness of her lesbian identity occurred when, after reading "Christabel," she and her college roommate nicknamed one another "Chris" and "Gere."

By the end of the nineteenth century, sexual definitions had been codified to the extent that gay men and lesbians began to appear in literature as codes for one another. Sedgwick argues that WILLA CATHER in "Paul's Case" (1905) represented her own lesbian sexuality through the figure of an effeminate boy. Similarly, in Marcel Proust's *Remembrance of Things Past* (1913–1927), the suspected lesbianism of Albertine functions partly as a code for Proust's own gay desires. Such coding should not be taken to mean that gay male characters and lesbians simply became interchangeable, but that these two forms of sexuality were treated as more directly comparable than they had been in the past.

Thus far, I have discussed only interrelations between literary portrayals of desire between men and desire between women. The other side of this history involves actual writers and how they understood one another. Personal documents from the beginning of the nineteenth century suggest that male and female homosexuality had begun to function as codes for one

another in life in a way that they did not until the end of the century in fiction. LORD BYRON, in writing of his love for the choirboy John Edlestone, compared it to the love of the Ladies of Llangollen (LADY ELEANOR BUTLER AND SARAH PONSONBY), a lesbian couple living in Wales who became famous as an example of "ROMANTIC FRIENDSHIP"; he boasted that he and Edlestone would outdo even the ladies. Later, after he had become a successful author, he sent his works to them. Although Byron scholars have rarely noted this fact, it suggests that he viewed their same-sex relationship as a model for his own.

Interestingly, just as lesbian relationships became a model for Byron's gay ones, so Byron's sexuality became a model for lesbians. Anne Lister, a lesbian whose diaries have recently been decoded and published, was an ardent fan of Byron's and contemplated using his poetry to further possible lesbian affairs. When she visited the ladies of Llangollen, she chatted with one of them about Byron, VIRGIL, and Tasso. Each of these male writers represented either actual desire between males, as in Virgil's second eclogue, or cross-dressing that flirted with the possibility, as in the Tancredi and Clorinda episode of Tasso's *Gerusalemme Liberata* and in the relations between Lara and Kaled in Byron's *Lara*. Although Lister does not explicitly mention Byron's sexual relations with other males, her discussions of him hint that she either knew or intuited that Byron was no exemplar of normative masculinity. Furthermore, as Terry Castle has noted, the Byronic hero became an icon in the later lesbian tradition in the case of such writers as George Sand, RADCLYFFE HALL, and VITA SACKVILLE-WEST.

By the twentieth century, the image of gay and lesbian artists as "odd couples" became more frequent. The Parisian circles associated with American high MODERNISM contain several examples of such collaborations. Perhaps the most famous was the association between the author GERTRUDE STEIN and the composer Virgil Thomson, which produced *Four Saints in Three Acts* (first performed 1934) and *The Mother of Us All* (first performed 1947). In the entertainment industry, a series of "lavender" marriages and romances allowed homosexual artists to maintain a conventional cover for the edification of the public, as in the marriage of the actress Katherine Cornell and the director Guthrie McClintic. Similarly, gay men chose the lesbian Greta Garbo as one of their most prized cult images, whereas lesbians chose a gay man, James Dean, as a comparable figure.

Adrienne Rich's essay, cited earlier, was written in 1977 and warns lesbians about the dangers of losing a feminist identity in a larger gay liberation movement. Without endorsing a simple separatism, she argues eloquently for the need to maintain a distinctive lesbian feminist movement. A more recent work, Judy Grahn's updated *Another Mother Tongue* (1984), offers a more positive view of the possibilities for a coalition between gay men and lesbians. Grahn notes that the 1980s were an important time for such a coalition both because of AIDS and because lesbians involved in what mainstream feminism perceived to be "deviant" sexualities often found a more positive reception among gay men than among straight women. Her inspiring account glosses over the tensions that Rich's essay reveals and that continue today (see Berlant and Freeman). These tensions partly reflect the discourse of the radical Right and the mainstream media, in which gays and lesbians are either paired as if they were interchangeable or lesbians are reduced to invisibility. Given the perceptions that such discourse creates, it is all the more pressing to envision a history of the relations between gay men and lesbians that, instead of swamping one at the expense of the other or reducing them to an "odd couple," could provide a groundwork for future transformations.

—Andrew Elfenbein

BIBLIOGRAPHY

Berlant, Lauren, and Elizabeth Freeman. "Queer Nationality." *boundary* 2 19 (1992): 149–180. ■ Boswell, John. *Christianity, Social Tolerance, and Homosexuality: Gay People in Western Europe from the Beginning of the Christian Era to the Fourteenth Century*. Chicago: University of Chicago Press, 1980. ■ Bowers, Jane. "The Writer in the Theater: Gertrude Stein's *Four Saints in Three Acts*." *Critical Essays on Gertrude Stein*. Michael J. Hoffman, ed. Boston: G.K. Hall, 1988. 210–224. ■ Castle, Terry. *The Apparitional Lesbian: Female Homosexuality and Modern Culture*. New York: Columbia University Press, 1993. ■ Grahn, Judy. *Another Mother Tongue: Gay Words, Gay Worlds*. Updated and expanded edition. Boston: Beacon Press, 1984. ■ Rich, Adrienne. "The Meaning of Our Love For Women is What We Have to Expand Constantly." *On Lies, Secrets, and Silence: Selected Prose, 1966–1978*. New York and London: Norton, 1979. 223–230. ■ Sedgwick, Eve Kosofsky. *Between Men: English Literature and Male Homosocial Desire*. New York: Columbia University Press, 1985. ■ ———. "Willa Cather and Others." *Tendencies*. Durham, N.C.: Duke University Press, 1993. 167–176. ■ Traub, Valerie. "Desire and the Difference It Makes." *The Matter of Difference: Materialist Feminist Criticism of Shakespeare*. Valerie Wayne, ed. New York: Harvester/Wheatsheaf, 1991. 81–114.

Isherwood, Christopher
(1904–1986)

Born into a distinguished Cheshire family on August 20, 1904, Christopher Isherwood was educated at Repton School and Corpus Christi, Cambridge. After leaving Cambridge without a degree in 1925, he renewed his friendship with W. H. AUDEN, his former classmate at St. Edmund's preparatory school. For over ten years, the two shared an unromantic relationship in which sex gave their friendship an added dimension. Two years his junior, Auden cast Isherwood in the role of literary mentor and soon introduced him to a fellow Oxford undergraduate, STEPHEN SPENDER. The trio formed the nucleus of what would later be called The Auden Gang, the angry young writers who dominated the English literary scene of the 1930s. From 1930 to 1933, Isherwood lived in Berlin, where he felt released from the social and sexual inhibitions that stifled his development in England. Immersing himself in the bohemian world of male prostitutes, he lived almost anonymously in shabbily genteel and working-class areas of the city and began translating his experience of the demimonde into what would eventually become the unsurpassed portrait of pre-Hitler Germany, the Berlin stories. By collaborating with Auden on three avant-garde plays and by supporting various left-wing causes, Isherwood gained a reputation for ideological commitment. But partly because of his growing awareness of himself as a homosexual, he deeply distrusted communism, and he became more and more dissatisfied with the emptiness of left-wing rhetoric. In 1939, he and Auden emigrated to the United States. Settling permanently in Los Angeles, Isherwood began writing film scripts, and in 1940, under the influence of a Hindu monk and surrogate father, converted to Vedantism, a philosophy that would influence all of his later work. He became a U.S. citizen in 1946. In 1953, he fell in love with an eighteen-year-old college student, Don Bachardy, who was to achieve independent success as an artist. The relationship proved to be the most enduring union of Isherwood's life. In his 1971 biography of his parents, *Kathleen and Frank*, he explicitly revealed his homosexuality, which was more fully explored in his 1976 autobiography *Christopher and His Kind*. During the 1970s, Isherwood was an active participant in the burgeoning American gay liberation movement. By the time of his death on January 4, 1986, he had become a deeply revered icon of contemporary

Anglo-American gay culture, a courage-teacher who vigorously protested the "heterosexual dictatorship" and unashamedly expressed solidarity with his "kind."

Isherwood's homosexuality had a major influence on his art. His interest in certain psychological predicaments and in recurring character types and themes, especially such mythopoeic types as the Truly Weak Man, the Truly Strong Man, and the Evil Mother, and such obsessions as war, The Test, the struggle toward maturity, and the search for a father, may all be directly or indirectly related to his homosexuality. Certainly, Isherwood's fascination with the antiheroic hero, his rebellion against bourgeois respectability, his empathy with the alienated and the excluded, and his ironic perspective are all intertwined with his awareness of himself as a homosexual. Moreover, homosexuality, even when suppressed or disguised for legal or artistic reasons, is a crucial presence in the novels, an indispensable aspect of the myth of the outsider that Isherwood cultivated so assiduously. Isherwood sees the homosexual as a faithful mirror of the human condition and a symbol both of individuality and of the variousness of human possibilities.

Homosexuality features in the early novels in many guises, from the repressed passions of *All the Conspirators* (1928) to the fuller depictions of homosexual characters and situations in *The Memorial* (1932), where Edward Blake is never able to escape the impact of the loss in World War I of his best friend; and from the coyly comic portrait of Baron Kuno von Pregnitz, whose secret fantasies revolve around English schoolboy adventure stories, in *The Last of Mr. Norris* (1935) to the spoiled homosexual idyll of Peter Wilkinson and Otto Nowak in *Goodbye to Berlin* (1939). In these early works, Isherwood presents homosexuality unapologetically and without the self-consciousness and melodrama that mark contemporaneous treatments of the issue. He refrains from sensationalizing the gay subculture; he deftly defuses and domesticates aspects of gay life that lesser writers might have rendered as decadence or depravity; and he reveals considerable insight into the dynamics of gay relationships. Moreover, what is faulted in the early fiction is the repression rather than the expression of homosexuality, a repression that underlines the isolation of the narrator of *Goodbye to Berlin*, who is attracted to Otto Nowak's "naked brown body so sleek with health," but whose inability to connect meaningfully even with the characters with whom he is in most intimate contact mirrors the essential loneliness of Berlin itself. In the early fiction, Isherwood depicts his gay characters as infected (along with many others) with the soul sickness that denies life and distorts reality. They manifest symptoms of the obscure dread that pervades post-World War I England and pre-Hitler Germany. For example, Edward Blake of *The Memorial* is a version of a recurrent character type in Isherwood's early work, the Truly Weak Man; he constantly needs to test himself and is unable to combine love and sex. But Blake's unhappiness (which leads to a suicide attempt) is due not to his homosexuality but to his predicament as a casualty of the first world war. Similarly, the unhappiness that plagues the gay characters in *The Last of Mr. Norris* and *Goodbye to Berlin* is attributed not to their homosexuality but to their failure of commitment to life, a failure that they share with everyone else in the novels. In the early works, the gay characters are juxtaposed with the heterosexual ones to reveal beneath their apparent polarities a shared reality of the deadened spirit. As one character in *Goodbye to Berlin* remarks, "Eventually we're all queer."

Isherwood's later novels, beginning with *The World in the Evening* (1954), probe more deeply and focus more intently on the plight of the homosexual in a homophobic society. In these works, gay characters are both more numerous and their homosexuality defined more sharply in terms of their social roles and the obstacles they face than is the case in the earlier fiction. The dilemma faced by the gay characters of the later novels is epitomized by their apparently incompatible needs to assert their individuality and to feel a sense of community. This conundrum is felt by Bob Wood, the Quaker artist of *The World in the Evening,* one of the earliest sympathetic portraits of a gay activist in Anglo-American literature. The angriest of Isherwood's gay characters, Wood bitterly attacks the heterosexual majority for its failure to accept the gay minority. Sick of futile discussions of the etiology of homosexuality, he would like to "march down the street with a banner saying, 'We're queer because we're queer because we're queer,'" but even this protest, wildly unlikely in the early 1940s, when the action of the novel takes place, is impossible: His lover, Charles, a Jew who has changed his name, "is sick of belonging to these whining, militant minorities." At the end of the novel, Wood joins the Navy. His motives are not conventionally patriotic, but he refuses to accept exemption from military service on the basis of his sexual orientation "because what they're claiming is that us queers are unfit for their beautiful pure Army and Navy—when they ought to be glad to have us." The solidarity that Wood feels with his fellow homosexuals is extremely rare in the literature of the period, as is Isherwood's conception of homosexuals as a legitimate minority with real grievances.

In the "Ambrose" section of *Down There on a Visit* (1962), Isherwood creates a haunting portrait of the homosexual as persecuted victim. The title character is an expatriate Englishman who has created a self-sufficient anarchic community on the Greek island of St. Gregory. Described in terms suggesting saintliness and otherworldly absorption, Ambrose retreats to his island, where he reigns over a disorderly menagerie like "one of Shakespeare's exiled kings." On St. Gregory, he attempts to create a brave new world of his own imagining. His fantasy of a homosexual kingdom is revealing as a parody of the unjust reality that provokes his alienation. In this fantasy, it is heterosexuality that is illegal: "meanwhile it'll be winked at, of course, as long as it's practiced in decent privacy. I think we shall even allow a few bars to be opened for people with those unfortunate tendencies, in certain quarters of the larger cities." This comic riff embodies the homosexual's bitterness at being excluded from the larger society, but it also betrays Ambrose's hidden desire for involvement in the world. Ambrose, no less than Bob Wood, suffers from the absence of community.

The need for community is also an issue in *A Single Man* (1964), Isherwood's masterpiece. The protagonist, George, a late-middle-aged and lonely expatriate Briton grieving at the death of his lover of many years, is the most fully human of all Isherwood's gay characters. He shares the alienation and anger of Bob Wood and Ambrose, but he is more central and rounded than they. Indeed, George emerges in the novel as an Everyman figure, with whom anyone can identify. In addition, *A Single Man* more fully develops the context of gay oppression than do the earlier novels and places it within a still larger context of spiritual transcendence. Dealing with universal themes of commitment and grief, alienation and isolation, the book concretely explores the gay sensibility and masterfully balances worldly and religious points of view. It regards the assertions of individual uniqueness and of minority consciousness as indispensable worldly and political goals, but it finally subsumes them in the Vedantic idea of the oneness of life. In making concrete this resolution, the novel presents a sustained and moving portrait of male homosexual love. The minority consciousness of *A Single Man* helps make possible the balance the novel strikes between assertions of tribal identity and a wider view in which differences are merely circumstantial and insignificant. But another reason for Isherwood's minority consciousness is clearly political. To portray homosexuals as simply another tribe in a nation comprising many different tribes is both to soften the stigma linked to homosexuality and to encourage solidarity among gay people. And by associating the mistreatment of homosexuals with the discrimination suffered by other minorities in America, Isherwood legitimizes the grievances of gay people at a time when homosexuals were not recognized either as a genuine minority or as valuable members of the human community. Presaging the gay liberation movement, *A Single Man* presents homosexuality as simply a human variation that should be accorded value and respect and depicts homosexuals as a group whose grievances should be redressed.

Isherwood's last novel, *A Meeting by the River* (1967), is set in a Hindu monastery on the banks of the Ganges and incorporates most directly the religious values that more obliquely inform *A Single Man* and the other late novels. The slight plot pivots on the unsuccessful attempt of a bisexual movie producer to dissuade his younger brother from taking final vows as a swami. The producer, Patrick, is among the most unpleasant characters in all of Isherwood's fiction; he is attracted toward a vision of homosexual union "in which two men learn to trust each other so completely that there's no fear left and they experience and share everything together in the flesh and in the spirit," but he retreats to a cowardly and hypocritical conformity. Still, there is hope for Patrick. The union of the brothers at the end of the book is the consummation of their long searches for symbolic brotherhood. These quests lead one to the glimpse of a Whitmanesque ideal of gay love and the other to the achievement of spiritual brotherhood in a monastery. Finally revealing the commonality within the two very different siblings, the novel offers the concept of brotherhood as a means of escaping the imprisoning ego.

More forthrightly than any other major writer of his generation, Isherwood embraced the contemporary gay liberation movement. That allegiance was altogether appropriate, for his novels—all written before the Stonewall riots that traditionally date the beginning of the movement—incorporate gay liberation perspectives, especially the need for solidarity among homosexuals and the recognition of homosexuals as an aggrieved minority. Isherwood's greatest achievement, however, is in creating gay characters—preeminently George in *A Single Man*—whose homosexuality is a simple given, an integral part of the wholeness of personality, and in placing those characters in situations and contexts where their homosexuality functions as an emblem of their common humanity. (See also ENGLISH LITERATURE: TWENTIETH CENTURY and NOVEL: GAY MALE.)

—*Claude J. Summers*

BIBLIOGRAPHY

Finney, Brian. *Christopher Isherwood: A Critical Biography.* New York: Oxford University Press, 1979. ■ Fryer, Jonathan. *Isherwood: A Biography of Christopher Isherwood.* London: New English Library, 1977. ■ Funk, Robert W. *Christopher Isherwood: A Reference Guide.* Boston: G.K. Hall, 1979. ■ Heilbrun, Carolyn C. *Christopher Isherwood.* Columbia Essays on Modern Literature 53. New York: Columbia University Press, 1970. ■ Hynes, Samuel L. *The Auden Generation: Literature and Politics in England in the 1930s.* London: Bodley Head, 1976. ■ King, Francis. *Christopher Isherwood.* Writers and Their Work 240. Harlow, Essex: Longman, 1979. ■ Lehmann, John. *Isherwood: A Personal Memoir.* New York: Henry Holt, 1987. ■ Piazza, Paul. *Christopher Isherwood: Myth and Anti-Myth.* New York: Columbia University Press, 1978. ■ Schwerdt, Lisa M. *Isherwood's Fiction: The Self and Technique.* London: Macmillan, 1989. ■ Summers, Claude J. *Christopher Isherwood.* New York: Ungar, 1980. ■ ———. *Gay Fictions: Wilde to Stonewall.* New York: Continuum, 1990. ■ Wilde, Alan. *Christopher Isherwood.* Twayne's United States Authors Series 173. New York: Twayne, 1971.

Italian Literature

Italy figures large in the Western homoerotic imagination: The novels of HENRY JAMES, E. M. FORSTER, THOMAS MANN, and more recently EDMUND WHITE testify to the persuasive romance of Italy as a favored location for the gay writer. External perceptions of Italy, however, continue to oscillate between two contrasting mythical poles. It is either seen as the prehistoric land of sexually available nymphs and shepherds or is condemned to remain the cenotaph of high culture in which homosexual aesthetes can vent their artistic sensibility. Both versions have probably played a part in the varied constructions of gay identity but say little about the historical realities and cultural representations of homosexuality in Italy itself.

The discussion of homosexuality in Italy is complicated also because it is difficult to view the peninsula as a single historical or geographical unit before Unification in 1870, and even today Italy is marked by enormous social and cultural diversity. Although many similarities between individual towns and states could obtain, there were also countless variations due to the type of government, the nature of foreign influences that may have held sway, the religious climate, and the very great differences that existed between urban and rural communities. It should therefore be remembered that there is a certain artificiality in establishing links of continuity between writers whose national allegiances can be considered sometimes tenuous. Moreover, political division and economic underdevelopment led to Italy largely missing out on the bourgeois cultural revolution of the eighteenth and nineteenth centuries. Perhaps the most significant loss to the country and to this project is that Italy had little part in the great novel explosion of the period. As a result, Italy did not until more recently have a strong tradition in the very genre that has as its fundamental motivation the negotiation between the individual subject and society. If homosexuality itself has had a discontinuous, fragmented history and a precarious inscription in literature, perhaps for this reason alone the Italian experience with its frayed edges, silences, and contradictions can somehow stand as emblematic of that shattered past and tradition.

The complexities of representing homosexuality in literature and locating it in its social context have been most tellingly explored in recent years in a novel that only with a great effort of the imagination would normally be classified as gay, Umberto Eco's *Il nome della rosa (The Name of the Rose).* Published in 1980, the work operates on a number of levels. It is a compelling detective story, a historical novel set in the Middle Ages, a compendium of arcane period detail, a fictional exemplification of semiotic theory, a metaphorical exploration of the troubled Italian political situation of the 1970s, and much more besides. What unites these disparate threads is that they all in some manner relate to the intimate bonds between men that structure the ways in which society functions. Such bonds have been referred to as "homosocial," a term that uneasily brings together the political and erotic aspects of relationships between men. The main character in the novel is William of Baskerville, a Franciscan monk who has been invited to a monastery in the north of Italy to take part in talks aimed at reconciling the warring factions of the church, itself the archetypal bastion of male authority. He is accompanied by a young German novice, Adso, who is the story's narrator and who acts as William's scribe and assistant throughout the course of the events related. They are bound together by the type of affection that has long been thought to characterize relations between an older and younger man. William is the teacher, Adso the disciple. The erotic nature of these bonds is made more explicit on their arrival at the monastery. The monastic community has been torn asunder by homicide and it is soon apparent that one of the possible motives is (homo)sexual jealousy among the monks. The novel is about power and about the ways in which power between men operates. It is finally revealed that in this monastery supposedly devoted to celibate learning, unauthorized access to the library shelves is often most expediently gained through the exchange of illicit sexual favors, which of course must remain secret. The homosocial community of men is defined in terms of its uncanny potential for homosexuality: homosexuality in the guise of criminality. The homosexual as outlaw haunts this community.

In the novel's other main plot, the negotiations between the different factions of the church, the charge of homosexual behavior is used to discredit the various dissenting (often non-Italian) groups classified as heretical. What is interesting about the accusation is not its accuracy as an index to actual behavior but its acknowledgment of the threat that homosexuality poses to communities of men bound by common interest. The heresy lies in the betrayal of the homoerotic possibilities of men's relations with each other. Conversely, dissident groups call into question the moral rectitude of the ecclesiastical court by drawing attention to its wanton dedication to sodomy. Again, these accusations should not necessarily be read as evidence of historical fact (although they may also be read as such) but rather as indicators of the metaphorical power of homosexual behavior to destabilize the social body. It is the uncertain relativism of sexual behavior that contributes to the social meaning of homosexuality.

The main reason for looking initially at *Il nome della rosa* as in some senses exemplary in the representation of homosexuality in Italian literature is the emphasis it gives to the function of homosexuality in society as opposed to viewing homosexual behavior as the expression of an individual identity. Until recently, Italian literature has produced few attempts at homosexual self-inscription, and the bulk of literature on the topic has come from men and women not themselves homosexual. Although this is limiting in that it denies us insight into the lived and felt experiences of homosexuals, it does provide an interesting perspective on the meanings that homosexuality had at given historical moments. *Il nome della rosa* is also typical in that it omits almost totally the experience of women in history. The only female character in the book is an unnamed peasant girl with whom Adso has his allegedly only sexual encounter, an encounter that takes place in silence since neither speaks the other's language. The girl had entered the abbey in order to trade her flesh for some leftover offal. The expendability of her only currency is demonstrated as she is later burned as a heretic, a sacrifice to the homosocial order.

Nowhere is the patriarchal nature of Italian society more clearly revealed than in the realm of literature. In the past, few women wrote, and the manner in which women were represented in literature by men tended to reinforce masculinist stereotypes. The relative absence of a thriving novel tradition in Italy exacerbated this lack. In addition, lesbians are poorly represented even in contemporary literature. It is pointless to speculate too much on the reasons for this and more fruitful to interrogate how this lack functions. Judith Brown in her introduction to *Immodest Acts: The Life of a Lesbian Nun in Renaissance History* demonstrates that in the Middle Ages and the Renaissance the sexual desire of women for each other, though recognized, was only rarely taken seriously and was viewed as a much less grave aberration than male homosexuality. Brown suggests that this might be on account of the fact that it posed little challenge to the homosocial order and that the possibilities for women actually to set up home together, for example, would have been slight indeed. The fantasy of lesbian nuns, Brown points out, belongs to a later era, for convents in the earlier period were judged more as centers of heterosexually oriented license. The desire to write women who desire other women out of existence is aptly shown by the Enlightenment writer Alessandro Verri who, in his novel of 1789, *Le avventure di Saffo (The Adventures of Sappho)*, takes pains to deny that the great female poet was anything other than a lover of men. More regularly, lesbian experience is simply not represented, or, if it is, it is—like much of the writing on male homosexuality—invoked in order to stand metaphorically for something else. In recent years, the only novel by a woman to have been called "lesbian" is Silvia Castelli's *Pitonessa* (1978). However, this work does not recount the desire of women for each other but attacks phallocentric discourse through the use of asyntactical, unpunctuated language. Otherwise woman-centered experience finds expression in the work of novelists such as Matilde Serao (1856–1927) and Anna Banti (1895–1985), although neither explore the erotic possibilities of such experience. Neither Sibilla Aleramo (1876–1960), who had a relationship with Lina Poletti, nor the leading contemporary writer, Dacia Maraini, who has openly declared her bisexuality, inscribe this experience in writing.

One of the most common metaphorical uses of homosexuality is as an indicator of the moral and political corruption of the state. DANTE in his depiction of the sodomites in the seventh circle of Hell in cantos

15 and 16 of the *Inferno* explicitly links the allegedly widespread practice of homosexuality in Florence to the political decline of the city and to the moral decadence of the Florentine people. From a theological point of view, the sinners are already damned, but in these cantos Dante's respect for the individuals he meets and interest in the politics of his native city appear to override his condemnation of their vice. The sodomites he encounters are all from Florence, and Dante makes the most of his conversations with them to expound his views on the city's decline. Florence in this period was riven by factional infighting. Dante's criticism relates more particularly to the fact that the city's increased prosperity had led to a general slackening of moral standards especially among the newly enriched classes. Homosexuality is associated with unnerving social change. This perceived relation is one that will be taken up by a number of later writers.

Sodomy in the Middle Ages and the Renaissance periods was often referred to as the "Florentine vice." In 1494, when the Medici regime in Florence fell, one of the main charges leveled against it as an indicator of its depravity by its leading opponent, the revolutionary, fanatical priest Girolamo Savonarola (1452–1498), was that it was excessively given over to the practice of sodomy. An intimate connection was adduced between homosexual acts and political turpitude. Some centuries later, the Enlightenment thinker, Cesare Beccaria, argued in *Dei delitti e delle pene* (*On Crimes and Punishments* [1764]) that "la greca libidine" ought to be discouraged since its occurrence did indeed signify the waning of civilization; he placed it on a par with infanticide and adultery. Unlike Savonarola, however, Beccaria advocated prevention rather than immolation as the correct response.

That the association of homosexuality and social decline does not belong solely to the past is amply demonstrated in twentieth-century literature. It is a fairly common topos among left-wing writers attempting to portray the decadence and moral bankruptcy of the bourgeoisie. In her short novel *Valentino* (1957) and later in *Caro Michele* (*Dear Michele* [1973]), Natalia Ginzburg uses the figure of the male homosexual to symbolize the cruel indifference of men to women in a society where human relations are essentially sterile.

A more overtly political note is given to this theme by antifascist writers for whom the struggle against tyranny is often represented as the prerogative of a virile working class. In novels such as Ignazio Silone's *Fontamara* (1933) and *Le terre del Sacramento* (*The Estate in Abruzzi* [1950]) by Francesco Jovine, the antifascist hero is big, muscular, and morally upright. His normative heterosexuality forms an essential part of his political credentials. Conversely, supporters of the Fascist regime are invariably sexually suspect. Their sexual ambivalence is inseparable from their political misallegiance. The most overt example of this occurs in Alberto Moravia's novel *Il conformista* (*The Conformist* [1951]). Marcello, the main character, is shown to be a supporter of Mussolini on account of the absence of a strong father figure in his life. As a child, he is seen as effeminate by his school friends. He is almost seduced by an older man who promises to give the boy a gun in exchange for what he, the man, wants. There is a brief struggle in which the gun goes off and Marcello flees, leaving the man for dead. Indelibly marked by these experiences, Marcello is portrayed as a cold and repressed figure, a homosexual. As an adult anxious to feel part of society, he imitates its values and is prepared to kill for them. He marries a woman he does not love to prove his normality yet later learns that she has had a lesbian affair in the past. In this novel, the malfunction of middle-class Italian society is represented through the metaphor of sexual aberration. Moravia's thesis is that Mussolini's attraction for this class lay in his ability to compensate on some level for its lack of manliness. In this way, Moravia avoids any substantial political critique of the system.

In the work of Cesare Pavese and Vasco Pratolini, it is the figure of the lesbian that is used to suggest the moral emptiness or absolute wickedness of the regime. In his two short novels, *Tra donne sole* (*Among Women Only* [1949]) and *La bella estate* (*The Beautiful Summer* [1940]), Pavese portrays the life of the decadent, bohemian bourgeoisie of Turin in the 1930s. In the first of these, two of the numerous minor characters are revealed to have had a lesbian relationship, but its significance is trivialized as merely the result of boredom or emotional immaturity, the sign of the moral stagnation of their class. Similarly, in *La bella estate,* Amalia contracts syphilis after a sexual encounter with a female artist. Again the idea of a relationship between women is used simply to underline male political, sexual, and emotional impotence and the extent of moral apathy in a particular class. A more disturbing picture emerges in Pratolini's *Cronache dei poveri amanti* (*A Tale of Poor Lovers* [1947]), which offers a panoramic vision of the lives of the inhabitants of one Florentine street. These simple folk are dominated by the figure of the elderly, bedridden Signora, who controls the affairs of the street from her top floor apartment through a network of informants dependent on her in a number of ways. Beautiful in her youth, she exploited her charms to lead men to their destruction, but now she is grossly disfigured, and her physical deformity directly expresses her evil nature. Moreover, she forces her young female attendants to submit to her lascivious caresses. Pratolini makes explicit the parallel between her manipulation of those around her and the tyranny of Fascism. Physically and morally, she is likened to Mussolini. Fascism is a lesbian. There can be no greater condemnation.

The theme of homosexuality and Fascism receives a different treatment by Giorgio Bassani in *Gli occhiali d'oro* (*The Gold-Rimmed Spectacles* [1958]). The novel is set in Ferrara during the 1930s and focuses on the disgrace of Athos Fadigati, a well-established doctor in the city. Fadigati is known to be homosexual yet initially his position—and especially his discretion—protects him from public disapproval. Finally, however, the Ferrarese bourgeoisie can no longer turn a blind eye once he begins to flaunt his relationship with a good-looking younger man by whom he is shamelessly exploited and humiliated. Public derision is compounded by the criminal behavior of his companion, and the story ends in Fadigati's suicide. The novel is told from the perspective of a young Jewish boy and becomes a kind of parable of the alienation of the formerly integrated Jewish community in Italy after the introduction of the Race Laws in 1938.

Bassani adds a new dimension to the familiar topos that Italian homosexual relations have tended to follow the Greek intergenerational model. In Italy, the pedagogical rather than the erotic nature of relations between men of widely differing ages has often been stressed. This tension between purity of intent and carnal longing is at the heart of the poetry of MICHELANGELO BUONARROTI (1475–1564). The tension is worked out through the use of typical Petrarchan conceits such as the inaccessibility of the loved one and the idealization of physical beauty, or through characteristic imagery such as the icy fire. As a poet, Michelangelo is perhaps best known for the sonnets and madrigals inspired by Tommaso de' Cavalieri whom Michelangelo met in 1532 when Tommaso was twenty-three. Michelangelo's poetic innovation lies in his reworking of a set of conventions that previously had been employed solely to express heterosexual love. The innovation required only the alteration of pronouns revealing the gender of the beloved, but in doing so, the poet is able to make a personal statement within a rigidly coded poetic form. The conventional nature of his poetry is indicated when later he deploys similar imagery and conceits to address Vittoria Colonna, a female poet whom he greatly admired. James Saslow in his book *The Poetry of Michelangelo* notes that the Petrarchan tradition provided Michelangelo with a ready framework in terms of which to express

his unrequited love. In addition, a form so dependent on the structure of paradox could well convey the poet's own apparent anxiety toward homosexual feelings and the extent to which they came into conflict with his Christian faith.

It should not be supposed, however, that the anguished tone of Michelangelo's lyric poetry exhausts the ways in which homosexual desire was experienced in the Italian Renaissance. Other writers offer a more accepting view of the place of homosexuality in society. Pietro Aretino's play *Il marescalco* (*The Stablemaster*) is a case in point. First produced in 1533 for the court of Mantua, which provided a haven for Aretino after he had encountered problems with the official censors in the less liberal Papal States, the play has as its central character a man whose erotic preferences are unambiguously homosexual. That this preference is a definite aspect of his personality rather than simply a vice among others is clear. The comedy is structured around a very simple "beffa" or trick. The homosexual stablemaster is mischievously informed that his master has decided to have him marry a wealthy young bride. The stablemaster is appalled, and the play consists largely of his frantic attempts to be absolved of the marriage. He is the butt of much humor, yet in the end has the last laugh when he discovers at the wedding ceremony that his bride to be is in fact the willing page, Carlo, in drag. Particularly interesting are the arguments used to persuade the stablemaster that he ought to marry. The religious argument is never invoked, and criticisms of his reluctance to marry are couched purely in social terms. The arguments put forward suggest that marriage is about social control and procreation. Unruly young men settle down once they are married, and of course the state needs children in order to prosper. In exchange, the man will receive all the domestic comforts a wife can provide. The exact benefits to her are unclear. Ironically, it is left to the stable master, all too often and simplistically deemed a misogynist, to expose the fact that these domestic duties are those normally carried out by a servant, prompting the obvious conclusion that for women marriage is a veiled form of servitude.

A similar plot can be found in a short story by Matteo Bandello (1485–1561), No. IV of his *Novelle* (collected short stories), which tells the tale of Porciello, a poet and notorious homosexual, who has been forced to marry in order to conceal, at least in part, his unnatural vice. He subsequently falls ill, so his wife attempts to persuade him to confess and atone for this particular sin. A succession of priests fail to elicit the confession that he has ever performed any act "contra natura." In the end, he confesses to his preference but claims that this desire is so much part of him that it could never be classified as against nature. Although this causes great public scandal, he recovers and lives to pursue his own pleasure. Again homosexuality is barely censured, and the character in the story clearly asserts the right to enjoy a homosexual identity.

The exact force of religious injunction in these texts remains uncertain. In the anonymous play from Siena, *Gli ingannati* (*The Deceived* [1538]), the homosexual pedant is threatened by one of the other characters with burning at the stake, the traditional penalty for those convicted of sodomy. Yet the jocular tone of the exchange may question whether such punishment is likely.

In contrast also to the elevated and highly stylized tone of Michelangelo, the language of these writers is explicit and often bawdy in describing sex and the human body. There existed too a large vocabulary of euphemistic terms to convey such matters. Alan Smith has recently proposed in his exploration of the scurrilous nonsense poetry of Burchiello (1404–1449) that this rhetoric could be employed to produce veiled critiques of the political regimes of the period, underlining the extent to which the body and its regulation are fundamental to practices of state.

The politics of the body and of homoerotic desire can however be variously manifest. The beauty of the effete youth Medoro in Ariosto's *Orlando furioso* (1532) is tenderly described, yet he is also presented as an improbable lover for the beautiful Angelica, the much sought after heroine of the epic: The desirability of boys is often seen as interchangeable with that of women. In Torquato Tasso's *Gerusalemme liberata* (*Jerusalem Delivered* [1581]), written later in the sixteenth century in the more repressive climate of the Catholic Counter-Reformation, the homoerotic element does not disappear but is tellingly displaced onto the infidel. The death of the page Lesbino and the lament of his lord Solimano are movingly evoked, yet the taint of their love does not infect the Christian encampment. Tasso is thus able to incorporate an element of homoeroticism into his narrative while representing homosexual relations as essentially a pagan vice.

Sexual relationships between males of different ages as an ideal form of communion is believed to have had particular currency during the Renaissance when the rediscovery of and enthusiasm for classical culture provided a means of justifying practices subject to religious interdict. In this vein, Ariosto in his *Satires* (1517–1525) alleged that the sexual pursuit of boys was the particular vice of Humanists. Conversely, it could be argued that the ability to appreciate manly beauty was itself the fruit of a good classical education. Homoeroticism and high culture were intimately linked. POLIZIANO in his verse fabula-drama *Orfeo* (*Orpheus* [1480]) cites classical precedents such as Ganymede, Hercules, and Jupiter to explicate the attachments of Orpheus. Yet Poliziano himself in his earlier Greek and Latin epigrams alludes to the possibility of love between boys of the same age. Guido Ruggiero in his research on Venice demonstrates that the nature of homosexual attachments was more varied than often supposed.

In more recent times, however, the adoration of young boys has been associated with a desire for the primitive, the natural. The work of PIER PAOLO PASOLINI is perhaps most characteristic of this tendency. For Pasolini, the connection is primarily a political one, for the youths he worshipped came inevitably from the peasant or working class. In this context, he is probably best known for his portrayal of the "ragazzi di vita," the poor Roman boys whom he befriended. Their apparent amorality and thus their refusal to live by bourgeois values held a strong attraction for the writer. On an individual level, however, these boys are only fleetingly represented in Pasolini's work. His most sustained and most idyllic portrayal of homosexual love occurs in one of his earliest works, *Amado mio* (1948), which is set in the countryside of the northern region of Friuli. The central focus of this unfinished novel is on the relationship between the well-educated and sophisticated Desiderio and Benito/Iasìs, the poor peasant whom he meets at a country ball. The opening scenes are infused with a lyrical homoeroticism in which the pastoral setting and the receptiveness of the young boys to each other's kisses in the absence of female partners represent the apex of happiness for Desiderio. Unfortunately, Benito, the boy he falls in love with, is the most reluctant in recognizing and acting on his desire. The novel is largely occupied with the frustrations of Desiderio's courtship of the boy he renames Iasìs. Finally, Iasìs swoons into his lover's arms under the sway of Rita Hayworth, whose captivating presence in *Gilda* enables him to embrace his heart's desire. The novel ends on the promise of love. Unashamedly sentimental, it contrasts with Pasolini's better-known later works, particularly in the portrayal of class difference. Desiderio and his bourgeois companion, Gilberto, are not objects of contempt like those members of the bourgeoisie found in *Ragazzi di vita* (1955), for example. The peasant boys too are impeccably virtuous and ennobled by love although they do tend to be easily impressed. Gilberto's lover Mario coyly declines his suggestion that they visit the seaside because he cannot afford to go. This provides a sharp contrast with Pasolini's later representation of inter-class relationships where sex is inseparable from money and love is out of the question. It is at odds also with the images of homosexuality normally associated with Pasolini, whose reputation based on public scandal and the brutal nature of his death too often cancels out the lyricism of his homoerotic imagination.

Amado mio offers an interesting correlation with Pasolini's early dialect poetry in which masturbating youths symbolize the possibility of escape and freedom from a repressive society. This image is also one that inhabits the poetry of SANDRO PENNA (1906–1977). Penna's youths are commonly sailors or athletes, the glimpse of whose beauty allows the poet to transcend, however briefly, the travails of the everyday. Penna never attempts to transform these intuitions into narrative; for him, the erotic remains part of an aesthetic or metaphysical dimension of remembered experience.

In most of the literature so far mentioned, there is little attempt to articulate homosexual subjectivity or experience. In the twentieth century when this has occurred, it has most often been in terms of a very crude Freudian framework. Male homosexuality is the almost inevitable result of a weak or absent father and a domineering mother. This is the case, for example, in the novels by Bassani and Moravia already mentioned and of the more complex, although unfinished, novel *Ernesto* by UMBERTO SABA (1883–1957). In *Ernesto,* published posthumously in 1975, the Triestine writer, better known as a poet, charts the early homosexual experiences of an adolescent boy at the turn of the century. *Ernesto* is one of the rare examples of the coming-out novel in Italian literature. Saba explores the boy's conflicting feelings of shame and desire as he is initiated into homosexuality by a slightly older, working-class man in awe of Ernesto's education and social status. Particularly interesting is the way in which Saba charts Ernesto's dissatisfaction with the passive role automatically assigned to him. His longing to be the more active partner is largely responsible for the breakup of the affair. At the end of the novel, Ernesto meets a boy only slightly younger than himself and seems to be on the point of embarking on a more equitable relationship. However, Saba's notes explaining how he intended to complete the text indicate that the two would end up in a sordid heterosexual love triangle. In a novel that is full of commonplace assumptions concerning the nature of homosexual relations, Saba seems incapable of imagining homosexuality as anything more than a very temporary rupture of the dominant social order. This limitation is reflected also in the assumption of Ernesto's lover that Ernesto, like most teenage boys who engage temporarily in homosexual activity, will eventually marry even though he knows that he himself never will. He sees his sexuality as a part of his social identity.

The emergence in Italy in the 1980s of two highly successful and openly gay writers has begun to compensate in part for the spectral presence of homosexuality in Italian literature in the past. Although neither Aldo Busi (born 1948) nor Pier Vittorio Tondelli (1955–1991) can be regarded as gay activists, both have brought homosexuality firmly into the public domain. Busi's first novel *Seminario sulla gioventù* (*Seminar on Youth* [1984]) set the tone for his subsequent work. It is a loosely plotted adventure story set mainly in Paris in the late 1960s. The gay protagonist stumbles through a number of sexual and emotional encounters remaining completely unchanged in the process. The writing is humorous, linguistically inventive, and focuses primarily on the confrontation of the self and a chaotic and confusing world. Homosexuality is seen as another means of overthrowing the preconceptions of a repressed society. It has little value beyond this although its presence is constantly proclaimed. Busi's second and third novels, *Vita standard di un venditore provvisorio di collant* (*The Standard Life of a Temporary Pantyhose Salesman* [1985]) and *La delfina bizantina* (*The Byzantine Dolphin* [1986]), accentuate his iconoclastic attitude toward plot and language, involving the reader in increasingly complex narrative games. The more recent works of this most prolific writer consist largely of autobiographical meditations on literature, travel, and numerous other aspects of contemporary life, including sex, which for Busi remains primarily an enormously enjoyable adventure, a heretical aside in a stultifying world.

Tondelli's first novel, the episodic *Altri libertini* (*Other Libertines*), caused him to be prosecuted for obscenity subsequent to its publication in 1980. The novel deals with moments from the lives of a group of loosely associated individuals who all live somehow on the margins of society. Fluidity of sexual identity is a typical characteristic. For Tondelli, as for Busi, homosexuality is essentially a signifier of marginality, of dissidence. Linguistically, Tondelli attacks the codes of conventional writing by disrupting syntax and by using the language of those he writes about; the novel is full of slang and foreign terms. Tondelli's later works appear less dismissive of convention and are increasingly reflective in nature. *Pao pao* (*Guard Duty* [1982]) is a largely autobiographical piece on the homoerotic possibilities offered by compulsory national service in Italy. In *Rimini* (1985), he moves away from an explicitly gay theme before returning to a specifically gay context in order to explore the themes of illness, loss, and isolation in *Camere sepa-*

rate (*Separate Rooms* [1989]), the last novel to be published before his death. Italian critics—in a characteristic gesture that seeks to deny the specificity and value of gay experience—tend to insist that in this text Tondelli uses the figure of the homosexual and his existential solitude to investigate the universals of human nature. This in itself is perhaps indicative of a culture that has tended to view male homosexuality as an activity rather than as an identity while refusing to recognize the desire of women for each other as a significant option. Homosexuality is always a social phenomenon.

—*Derek Duncan*

BIBLIOGRAPHY

Andrews, Richard. *Scripts and Scenarios: The Performance of Comedy in Renaissance Italy.* Cambridge: Cambridge University Press, 1993. ■ Baranski, Zygmunt G., and Lino Pertile, eds. *The New Italian Novel.* Edinburgh: Edinburgh University Press, 1993. ■ Brown, Judith C. *Immodest Acts: The Life of a Lesbian Nun In Renaissance Italy.* Oxford: Oxford University Press, 1986. ■ Cicioni, Maria. "'Insiders and Outsiders' in Giorgio Bassani's *Gli occhiali d'oro." Italian Studies* 41 (1986): 101–115. ■ de Lauretis, Teresa. "Gaudy Rose: Eco and Narcissism." *Technologies of Gender: Essays on Theory, Film, and Fiction.* London: Macmillan, 1987. 51–69. ■ Günsberg, Maggie. "'Donna Liberata'?: The Portrayal of Women in the Italian Renaissance Epic." *The Italianist* 7 (1987): 7–35. ■ Lazzaro-Weiss, Carol. *From Margins to Mainstream: Feminism and Fictional Modes in Italian Women's Writing, 1968-1990.* Philadelphia: University of Pennsylvania Press, 1993. ■ Ruggiero, Guido. *The Boundaries of Eros: Sex Crime and Sexuality in Renaissance Venice.* Oxford: Oxford University Press, 1985. ■ Saslow, James M. *Ganymede in the Renaissance: Homosexuality in Art and Society.* New Haven, Conn.: Yale University Press, 1986. ■ ———, ed. *The Poetry of Michelangelo: An Annotated Translation.* New Haven, Conn.: Yale University Press, 1991. ■ ———. "Homosexuality in the Renaissance: Behavior, Identity, and Artistic Expression." *Hidden from History: Reclaiming the Gay and Lesbian Past.* Martin Bauml Duberman, Martha Vicinus, and George Chauncey, Jr., eds. New York: New American Library, 1989. 90–105. ■ Smith Alan K. "Fraudomy: Reading Sexuality and Politics in Burchiello." *Queering the Renaissance.* Jonathan Goldberg, ed. Durham, N.C.: Duke University Press, 1994. 84–106. ■ Wood, Sharon. *Woman as Object: Language and Gender in the Work of Alberto Moravia.* London: Pluto Press, 1990.

James VI and I
(1566–1625)

In 1567, at one year of age and during a civil war, James Stewart, son of Mary, Queen of Scots, was crowned King of Scots. Though his early years were lived amid political strife, his education, begun when he was three, was intended to fashion him into an exemplary Renaissance prince. His tutors included the fearsome George Buchanan, a scholar and political theorist of European reputation, who believed that a king should be the most learned man in his dominions. Though James rejected Buchanan's political ideas, he did develop a love of learning (especially of the Bible and theology) and an intellectual curiosity that later made him a considerable scholar and intellectual in his own right.

The 1580s saw James's cultivation of a brilliant group of court poets and musicians. He himself published two collections of verse in 1584 and 1591. The most interesting poem is "Ane metaphoricall invention of a tragedy called Phoenix," an allegorical account of a disastrous adventure involving the Duke of Lennox, a Catholic kinsman who came from France and, winning the thirteen-year-old king's love, gained short-lived political ascendancy along with the hatred of the Kirk and the Protestant lords. James's writing often sprang from personal involvement in a situation: *Daemonologie* (1597), which was written to prove witches' devilish powers, followed an outbreak of witch hunting; and *Basilikon Doron* (1599), an advice manual for his eldest son Prince Henry, registered the political pressures of the moment. Even his obsession with the Apocalypse, reflected in two books interpreting the obscure images of the Book of Revelation as prophecies for Christendom, sprang from his hoped-for participation in these events as a Christian prince.

In 1603, James succeeded Queen Elizabeth I to became King of England. In the years that followed, he delivered cogent speeches to Parliament developing ideas about the nature of kingship; entered pamphlet controversies over the Papacy's temporal powers; and sponsored lavishly produced masques that celebrated the court hierarchy. Political advancement at court was extended to handsome young favorites, notably Robert Carr, Earl of Somerset, and then George Villiers, Duke of Buckingham, whose charm, intelligence and beauty earned spectacular reward. James's homosexuality was obscure neither to contemporaries nor to later historians, and he himself seemed unconcerned that his most passionate attachments were to men. A remarkable letter of 1615, written in reproach to Somerset, analyzes in passionate terms the complex relations between king and favorite in which dependency, power, and desire are commingled. Surprisingly perhaps, James always expressed hatred of sodomy, mentioning it in *Basilikon Doron* as an offense not to be pardoned by a king, and in 1610 refusing to pardon those convicted of it.

In his last years, James published little, but continued to write letters to Buckingham that give fascinating insights into his subjectivity and their relationship. The literary enterprise for which James has been remembered is his long-cherished project to sponsor a new translation of the BIBLE, undertaken by a team of scholars at his direction, published in 1611, and known since as the King James Version.

—*Lawrence Normand*

BIBLIOGRAPHY

Akrigg, G. P. V. "The Literary Achievement of King James I." *University of Toronto Quarterly* 44 (1975): 115–129. ■ Bingham, Caroline. *The Making of a King: The Early Years of James VI and I*. London: Collins, 1968. ■ ———. *James I of England*. London: Weidenfeld and Nicholson, 1981. ■ Shire, Helena M. *Song, Dance and Poetry of the Court of Scotland under King James VI*. Cambridge: Cambridge University Press, 1969.

James, Henry
(1843–1916)

Henry James was born in New York City, on April 15, 1843. He belonged to a prominent American family, whose cultural milieu consisted of the intelligentsia of New England, and whose scholarly and social connections extended throughout Europe. His father, Henry James, Sr., was a noted Swedenborgian philosopher and man of letters, a friend of Ralph Waldo Emerson and Thomas Carlyle. Because Henry Sr. favored frequent changes of scenery, the James children spent their childhood divided between the United States and Europe, and were educated on both continents. The family returned to New England before war broke out between the states, and while helping to extinguish a fire in Newport, Henry Jr. sustained what he later called "an obscure hurt." This injury became the source of much biographical and critical speculation about the cause of the author's lack of sexual interest in women.

Henry's eldest brother, William, who went on to become an acclaimed philosopher and psychologist, showed early artistic and academic promise. Henry Jr. attempted to define a space for himself distinct from both his brother and his father. In the early 1860s, Henry began to write short stories and reviews for the *Atlantic Monthly, The Nation,* and the *North American Review.* Attracted by the European cultural environment, Henry traveled throughout Europe for fifteen months but was forced to return to the United States in April 1870, because of financial difficulties. James then managed to secure a position as the *New York Tribune* correspondent in Paris and sailed again for Europe in 1875. He decided to make England his permanent home and resided in London until 1897, when he retired to Lamb House, in Rye. In 1914, on the outbreak of World War I, the author became involved in the war effort, and devoted much time and energy to the support of British troops. Disturbed by the U.S. government's reluctance to enter the war, James became a British citizen in 1915. He received one of England's highest honors in 1916, an Order of Merit; shortly thereafter, his health deteriorating, James died of a stroke in Lamb House on February 28, 1916.

James's writing career was long and productive. He published nearly thirty novels and novellas, in addition to a myriad of short stories, travel sketches, and critical essays. With the advent of *Daisy Miller,* in 1878, he claimed a place in London's distinguished writing circle, boasting, at one point, that he had accepted more than 107 dinner invitations in one social season. James won literary acclaim for his artistic devotion to the form of the novel, innovating the dramatic presentation of character and perfecting the technique of narrative "point of view." By the 1890s, however, his writings had begun to lose their popular appeal. As one commentator noted, James was the most famous novelist in Europe who was never read. In an effort to reestablish his popularity (and to bolster his finances), James turned to drama. His efforts met with minimal success, and when he was booed off the stage at the London opening of *Guy Domville* in January 1895, he decided to restrict his literary endeavors to writing short stories and novels. Although James's later fiction was never to meet with the popularity of his earlier writings, it always elicited favorable critical reviews. Indeed, at the turn of the century, the author produced the three novels of the "Major Phase"—*The Ambassadors* (1903), *The Wings of the*

Dove (1902), and *The Golden Bowl* (1904)—which are generally regarded as his literary masterpieces.

James's many close friendships with women have received a great deal of critical and biographical attention. Following the author's lead in his autobiographical *Notes of a Son and Brother* (1914), critics concentrated on James's early involvement with his cousin Minny Temple, whose death in 1870 was thought to be one of the reasons behind his decision to remain single. James maintained a warm friendship with Constance Fenimore Woolson, and some biographers have speculated that her suicide in 1894 was due to her inability to establish a reciprocal romantic relationship with James. Yet, despite (or perhaps, because of) the scholarly scrutiny focused on James's friendships with women, his sexuality and sexual preferences remained shrouded until the 1980s and 1990s. RICHARD HALL has claimed that heterosexual critics of James have been unable to decipher the signs of his homosexuality, and although some pioneering critics, like Robert K. Martin, argued in the 1970s that James's sexual orientation imbued his fiction, the bulk of Jamesian scholarship remained under the influence of the "official" biographical data. Since the 1980s, however, interest in James's sexuality has led to a reappraisal of his life and writings. A number of insightful analyses of his novels have been produced, leading to a reassessment of James as a gay literary figure, and lending his novels' famous ambiguity a different hue. Whether James's homosexuality was active remains an open question (Hugh Walpole told a story of how he propositioned James, only to meet with a horrified, "I can't! I can't!"), but, as Fred Kaplan demonstrates in his 1992 biography, *The Imagination of Genius,* the author had a number of intimate relationships with young men. In 1876, James met and fell in love with Paul Joukowsky, a young Russian painter and intellectual. Although his association with Joukowsky was short-lived, the friendships he established with men like Jonathan Sturges and Morton Fullerton were to endure for many years. These friendships appear to have been primarily spiritual and asexual, but his attachment to Hendrik Andersen, a young sculptor, generated an intensely erotic correspondence. James treasured his relationship with Andersen, and this relationship was to provide him with a source of joy throughout his later life.

James was ambivalent about his own sexuality, and his ambivalence is perhaps most apparent in his response to OSCAR WILDE. James was by no means an advocate of gay rights, and was, in fact, horrified by Wilde's flamboyant sexuality (as well as jealous of Wilde's popularity). In letters to intimate friends, he spoke of the Wilde trial in no uncertain terms, drawing attention to his view that Wilde's fate was

> hideously, atrociously dramatic & really interesting. . . . It is the squalid gratuitousness of it all . . . of the mere exposure—that blurs the spectacle. But the *fall* . . . to that sordid prison-cell & this gulf of obscenity over which the ghoulish public hangs & gloats—it is beyond any utterance of irony or any pang of compassion! He was never in the smallest degree interesting to me—but this hideous human history has made him so—in a manner.

James also refused to sign the petition circulated in 1896 requesting a pardon for Wilde. Of course, one can speculate that Wilde's fate made no small impression on James, and strengthened his desire to keep his own relationships private and hidden from public view.

Although James was praised for his innovative portrayals of women (particularly of the "American girl," whom he made famous), many of his novels also focus on relationships between men. As Leland S. Person, Jr. has demonstrated, James's writings often construct, deconstruct, and reconstruct masculinity in a number of intriguing ways. The author's first acknowledged novel, *Roderick Hudson* (1876), traces the development of a friendship between an older and wealthy art connoisseur, Rowland Mallett, and his protégé, the brilliant sculptor, Roderick Hudson. The passages devoted to the budding friendship between the two men are among the most powerful in the novel; and though the friendship is doomed and, indeed, the novel concludes with Hudson's suicide, the young sculptor's impact on Mallett's life provides the focal point of the text.

In *The Bostonians,* published in 1885, James shifts his literary focus and dramatizes a relationship between two Boston women. The latent lesbianism in the novel has received a great deal of critical attention, and in 1978, Judith Fetterley contested conventional views of the relationship between Olive Chancellor and Verena Tarrant as "deranged" and "abnormal." Fetterley points out that the novel was inspired by Henry's sister, Alice, and her longtime companion, Katherine Loring, and argues that "James's understanding of their relationship, though at times critical, is imbued by a genuine sympathy. Thus, if one looks to the external context surrounding the conception of *The Bostonians,* one can find only support for the love between Olive and Verena." Fetterley's analysis engenders a different reading of Olive and Verena's association, but this association, much like the male homoerotic relationships in James's literary oeuvre, is doomed within the text. *The Bostonians* details how a Southern macho hero, Basil Ransom, intrudes into the women's friendship, ultimately "winning" Verena, and leaving Olive bereft. The portrayal of Ransom's virility, and the problems exposed therein, however, also work to undercut and subvert traditional representations of masculinity.

The critique of normative role-playing, which is an important aspect of *The Bostonians* and of a number of James's later fictions, often underpins the construction of the famous Jamesian observer. The observer—a man outside the social circle represented in the texts, who records the foibles of those whom he is watching—is frequently in a position to analyze and comment on the structure of normative heterosexual relations. In *The Sacred Fount* (1901), for example, the observer-figure narrates the story, and hypothesizes that, in the heterosexual relationships he is evaluating, the elder partner draws energy from the younger, who weakens as a result. In *The Ambassadors,* traditionally hailed as James's masterpiece, Lambert Strether, an aging male character, performs the role of the observer. Strether travels to Paris, on behalf of his fiancée, to watch over and return to her her errant son, Chad Newsome. Through Chad and his paramour, Marie de Vionnet, Strether learns to embrace life and to "live all you can." Repudiating his fiancée and his female confidante in Paris, he embarks on a new life, alone, but rejuvenated. The seemingly disinterested position of the observer, therefore, often gives way to a friendship with a younger man, which empowers the observer to repudiate conventional restrictions.

James's short stories frequently focus on the theme of male friendship. Texts like "The Pupil" (1890) portray homoerotic relationships between older men and their protégés, and trace enriching, if short-lived, associations. In "The Author of Beltraffio" (1884), a young critic attempts to resolve the domestic difficulties of his literary hero, Mark Ambient, only to find that his intervention into Ambient's marriage indirectly causes the death of Ambient's son. In "The Middle Years" (1893), a relationship develops between a dying author and a young doctor at a resort. This relationship enriches the doctor's cultural existence, but also results in his poverty, since his attention to the author enrages his female patron, who cuts the doctor out of her will. As Eve Kosofsky Sedgwick has argued, *The Beast in the Jungle* (1903) comprises a case study of "homosexual panic." Moreover, stories like "The Jolly Corner" (1908), which involves a protagonist who confronts himself as he might have been had he not left America for a solitary existence in Europe, dramatize the ways in which the protagonist comes to embrace heterosexual love. Even though the above might suggest that James's portrayals of

women suffer as a result of the privileged male relationships in his short stories, and to a certain extent this is so, at the same time, James's treatment of women is also deft and skillful, and has led many feminist critics to applaud his representations of femininity. James, a man of his time, did not support women's rights (and was frequently quite dismissive of female writers), but his female characters are among the most positively represented in British and American literature.

In turn, although James's ambivalence toward gay love and lifestyles propels his fiction, his portrayals of male friendships are provocative and powerful. Indeed, the fated nature of these relationships testifies not only to James's inability to conceive of a space wherein homosexual love might be dramatized in fruition, it also points to the pall cast by the Wilde trials, wherein the specter of Oscar shadowed the comportment of many gay men of his age. James, caught within a myriad of conflicting cultural positions—an American living in Europe, a gay man living in a normative heterosexual world—was able to channel his own marginality into literary texts that document the anxieties of his age, be they social, sexual, or cultural. In so doing, this closeted gay man was able to transform his personal difficulties into novels that represent and document a crucial stage in the development of homotextual traditions.

—*Priscilla L. Walton*

BIBLIOGRAPHY

Allen, Elizabeth. *A Woman's Place in the Novels of Henry James.* London: Macmillan, 1984. ■ Bersani, Leo. "The Jamesian Lie." *A Future for Astyanax: Character and Desire in Literature.* Boston: Little Brown, 1976. ■ Edel, Leon. *Henry James: A Life.* New York: Harper & Row, 1985. ■ Fetterley, Judith. *The Resisting Reader: A Feminist Approach to American Fiction.* Bloomington: Indiana University Press, 1981. ■ Hall, Richard. "Henry James: Interpreting an Obsessive Memory." *Literary Visions of Homosexuality.* Stuart Kellogg, ed. New York: Haworth Press, 1983. ■ Kaplan, Fred. *Henry James: The Imagination of Genius.* New York: William Morrow, 1992. ■ Martin, Robert K. "'The High Felicity' of Comradeship: A New Reading of *Roderick Hudson.*" *American Literary Realism* 2 (1978): 100–108. ■ Moon, Michael. "Sexuality and Visual Terrorism in *The Wings of the Dove.*" *Criticism* 28.4 (1986): 427–443. ■ Person, Leland S. "Henry James, George Sand, and the Suspense of Masculinity." *PMLA* 106 (1991): 515–528. ■ ——. "Strether's 'Penal Form': The Pleasure of Imaginative Surrender." *Papers on Language & Literature* 23 (1987): 27–40. ■ Savoy, Eric. "Hypocrite Lecteur: Walter Pater, Henry James and Homotextual Politics." *Dalhousie Review* 72.1 (1992): 12–36. ■ Sedgwick, Eve Kosofsky. *Epistemology of the Closet.* Berkeley: University of California Press, 1990. ■ Seltzer, Mark. *Henry James and the Art of Power.* Ithaca, N.Y.: Cornell University Press, 1984. ■ Walton, Priscilla L. *The Disruption of the Feminine in Henry James.* Toronto: University of Toronto Press, 1992. ■ Winner, Viola Hopkins. "The Artist and the Man in 'The Author of Beltraffio.'" *PMLA* 83 (1968): 102–108.

Japanese Literature

The trajectory of Japanese literature and its treatment of same-sex love differs radically from that of Western literatures, thus bringing into question the very notion of a Japanese "gay and lesbian literary tradition." Nevertheless, there are numerous literary works dating from the classical court culture of the Heian Period (794–1185) up to modern times that will be of interest to anyone concerned with understanding the various meanings ascribed to sexual and emotional relations between members of the same sex in Japan. This essay will guide the modern reader through Japanese literary texts with an eye to placing depictions of same-sex love within their proper literary historical context, thereby allowing modern readers to read with a minimum of distortion. What emerges will be a non-Western image of same-sex love that can enrich and expand the horizons of the contemporary gay and lesbian reader.

But first, several general characteristics of Japanese literary history need to be clarified. Literacy in Japan began with the emerging imperial court's official encounters with Chinese literary culture beginning in the fifth century. Literature was thus at first the concern of a small elite—consisting of courtiers, Buddhist priests and nuns, and later, high-ranking warriors and rich merchants—that adopted Chinese literature wholesale as its literary and cultural heritage. Except for poetry composed in vernacular Japanese, Chinese was the literate language of the elite until the ninth century. From the tenth century, a vernacular literature came into being at the hands of court women who were largely excluded from the benefits of Chinese literacy but who were deeply influenced by Buddhist thought. Writing in vernacular Japanese gradually came to be practiced also by men. Late in the twelfth century, the collapse of the centralized court led to a diaspora effect in which the literate elite scattered across Japan, spreading its courtly culture to provincial warlords and their samurai warriors. Though warlords held the reigns of political power at this time, they hungered for the cultural legitimacy that only the court elite could provide. This period represented the first major transferral of court culture outside the court. After a period of prolonged political instability and civil war, Japan was unified in 1600 under the powerful Tokugawa shoguns, whose base of power was in Edo. Unification led to the dramatic growth of urban centers in Kyoto, Osaka, and Edo in the seventeenth century and to the emergence of a population of artisans and merchants who amassed great wealth but who were despised as unproductive members within the social hierarchy. The urban classes nevertheless were able to build a vibrant popular literary culture by drawing on the traditions of court poetry and prose that had been passed on to the samurai. This popular culture was created in almost total isolation from the rest of the world, imposed by an official government policy of isolation from the West. Tokugawa hegemony lasted uninterrupted until 1868 when foreign pressure led to the samurai system being abolished and the Emperor Meiji was elevated to the position of monarch within a constitutional monarchy. The decision by Japan's leaders to integrate Japan with the West militarily, socially, and to some extent culturally brought with it a huge influx of European literary ideas that altered permanently the way Japanese would read and write sexuality.

Within this movement of literary history—initially turned toward the continental culture of China, then inward, and finally toward Europe and the United States—the depiction of same-sex love ebbs and flows in interesting ways. Throughout the entire tradition, depictions of male–male love (nanshoku) predominate overwhelmingly. In the premodern period, these depictions came out of three major cultural structures that privileged male–male sexuality: the temple culture of monks and priests, the samurai culture of the warrior, and the urban townsman's culture of the kabuki theater, each of which took its position in turn as the dominant form of male love from approximately the twelfth century into the nineteenth century. With Japan's entry into the world as a modern nation-state in 1868, the Japanese elite began the conscious introduction of new discourses of sexuality, including the discourses of law and medical science then prevalent in Europe that labeled homosexuality as criminal or abnormal. (Interestingly, Christian religious discourse was largely ignored.) It was the medical discourse of the Taisho Era (1912–1925) that first problematized female homosexuality and brought it to the attention of writers in a way that traditional Buddhist-based discourses had failed to do. Although difficult to characterize briefly, contemporary discourses of sexuality in Japan can be said to blend elements of medical discourse with popular conceptions of homosexuality in a way similar to but ultimately distinct from most contemporary Western societies.

Several interesting depictions of same-sex love date from the period when women writers at court were first developing a vernacular literature. The eleventh-century *Tale of Genji* (*Genji monogatari*; tr. Seidensticker, 1976), by Lady Murasaki Shikibu, is widely acclaimed as the great masterpiece of Japanese literature and is an uncommonly rich source for understanding what sexuality might have meant to Heian courtiers within their polygamous society. It contains no obvious depictions of same-sex love, but male friendships are repeatedly eroticized through competition for women. In one instance, the tale's hero, Genji, is depicted as spending the night with the younger brother of a woman who spurned him. The most complex exploration of a same-sex relationship, however, is in the character of Kaoru, known as Genji's son. Kaoru is introspective, does not respond erotically to women, and in general goes against all conventions of the amorous Heian male courtier. Kaoru learns in the course of the story that his birth was the result of an illicit love between Genji's young wife, the Third Princess, and another man. This fact establishes in Kaoru a father-complex that resolves itself somewhat when he apprentices himself to study Buddhist scripture under the tutelage of a saintly man known as the Eighth Prince, half-brother to Genji, who lives in a remote town outside the capital in self-imposed exile with his daughters. Kaoru finds stability and fulfillment as the spiritual student of the Eighth Prince, but three years later, the Prince dies and leaves Kaoru bereft. The final chapters of the *Tale of Genji* record Kaoru's attempt to ease his loss by forming relationships, none of them sexual, with the Prince's three daughters. The first daughter commits suicide by starvation rather than make herself vulnerable to Kaoru; the second marries his amorous rival, Niou; and the third is so torn between Kaoru and Niou that she attempts suicide and ultimately renounces the world to live in seclusion as a Buddhist nun. None of the sisters can serve Kaoru successfully as a surrogate for their father, and at the tale's end, Kaoru is still ensnared in his desire to recapture his love for the Eighth Prince. It is a powerful portrait of a man unable to achieve Buddhist enlightenment because of his bonds to another man.

Another interesting portrait explicitly inspired by elements of Kaoru's characterization in the *Tale of Genji* appears late in the Heian Period in a tale called *The Changelings* (*Torikaebaya monogatari*; tr. Willig, 1983), whose author is unknown but who is thought to have been a woman at court. It tells the story of a female who is raised in her brother's role as a boy and passes in court society as a man, and her brother who conversely assumes his sister's female role at court.

The switch is depicted as an odd situation arising, in Buddhist terms, from the special workings of cause and effect that dictate the karmic fates of the siblings. The female "man" takes a wife, who is unaware that anything is amiss in the marriage until she has a sexual experience with her husband's friend, Saisho. When the "husband" hears that his wife is pregnant, he feels betrayed by his wife and suspects his friend. Saisho has indeed discovered the deception and eventually ends up impregnating the "husband," whose beauty he has always admired, thus forcing the whole unstable situation to a crisis. After both "husband" and wife bear their children by Saisho, the "husband" reverts to the woman's role previously filled by her brother and soon achieves the enviable position of being named consort to the emperor, while her brother takes over his sister's role as a man, including wife and court rank. Saisho is kept in the dark about the switch, however, and his resultant confusion gives the otherwise tormented tale a wonderfully humorous touch. The narrative is a sophisticated exploration of love relations across gender and sex lines and addresses the seemingly modern question of discrepancies between biological sex and acquired gender identities, and their relation to individual human personality.

With the emergence after the twelfth century of a temple culture informed by courtly tradition, literary activity shifted into the hands of the Buddhist clergy; depictions of male–male love changed accordingly. Members of the male Buddhist clergy generally took vows to avoid sexual contact with women, but sexual and romantic relationships with boy acolytes (*chigo*) seem to have flourished in the temples as what was often described as a natural "outlet" for the men's emotional and sexual needs. A widely known popular legend in fact attributes the introduction of male love to the great spiritual leader Kukai (Kobo Daishi, 774–835), who studied esoteric "True Words" Buddhism in China where he first encountered it and then brought the custom back with him when he established the center of esoteric Buddhism at Mt. Koya in Japan. Numerous love poems by Buddhist priests addressed to their beloved acolytes are preserved in the imperial poetic anthologies dating from the tenth to the thirteenth centuries, attesting to how thoroughly male love between priests and acolytes was integrated into classical court culture. Subsequently, a group of popular prose narratives called acolyte tales (*chigo monogatari*) appeared in the fourteenth and fifteenth centuries and were circulated and reprinted well into the Edo Period (1600–1868). Acolyte tales derived from a tradition of Buddhist enlightenment tales (*hosshin mono*) or confessional tales (*zange mono*), and typically told of a monk's love for a boy and how loss of the beloved led to the monk's realization of Buddhist truth. Youthful male beauty symbolically serves in these tales both to attract (delude, in Buddhist terms) the monk and to dispel the attraction (delusion). Inevitably, the acolyte is revealed to be an incarnation of a Bodhisattva, such as Jizo (Sanskrit: *Ksitigarbha*) or Kannon (Sanskrit: *Avalokitesvara*), who transformed itself into a beautiful boy in order to bring a monk to salvation.

Male love relationships between adult samurai and adolescent samurai youths (*wakashu*) in which an age difference and a sexual and emotional hierarchy existed between lover and beloved became a prominent feature of samurai society from this period, especially among the elite. Such relationships were so unproblematic that few contemporary stories record the phenomenon. One rare example was the powerful Ashikaga shogun Yoshimitsu's (1358–1408) patronage of the future Noh actor and playwright Zeami (1363–1443). Yoshimitsu observed him in a performance in 1374 when Zeami was just twelve and was so smitten with his beauty and genius that he took him into his retinue and nurtured his talent for several decades. Their relationship caused something of a scandal because of the difference in class and rank between Zeami and the young shogun, which may explain why the relationship is relatively well documented. Zeami's critical essays on Noh reveal an aesthetic explicitly based on the appreciation of youthful male beauty, and state that a young actor achieves full "flower" when he learns to interiorize his youthful physical beauty and convert it into lifelong theatrical skill.

Ironically, the model of male love as practiced by samurai was first given literary expression by a merchant-class writer, IHARA SAIKAKU (1642–1693), in a collection of stories titled *The Great Mirror of Male Love* (*Nanshoku okagami* [1687]; tr. Schalow, 1990). This happened because urban society's contact with the samurai class in the early years of the seventeenth century led to the adoption of certain features of samurai life, including the practice of male love, and Saikaku's merchant-class readers were eager to read about how such relations were practiced by their social superiors. Thus, Saikaku's rendering of male love relations between a samurai man and youth was idealized from the merchant's perspective. The merchant class's own version of male love was fundamentally different from the samurai model in that it was based on a commercial transaction and involved boy prostitution between youthful kabuki actors (*kabuki wakashu*) and their patrons. Whether the youths were samurai or kabuki actors, Saikaku's narratives always depict the beloved youth as a paragon ("mirror") of

male love. Among their adult male lovers, however, there are two distinct types. One group is made up of "connoisseurs of boys" (*shojin zuki*) who nevertheless marry, support families, and have sexual relations with their wives or courtesans. The other group is made up of "woman haters" (*onna girai*) whose feelings for boys are exclusive and preclude marriage or maintaining a household. The two groups find their rough equivalent in the modern dichotomy between bisexuality and exclusive homosexuality. Interestingly, Saikaku did not structure *The Great Mirror of Male Love* around the "bisexual" ethos of the connoisseur but around the exclusively "homosexual" ethos of the woman hater because of the latter's clearly superior devotion to the "Way of the Youth" (*wakashudo*). Saikaku's adoption of the woman hater's viewpoint gives the opening and closing sections of the book a misogynistic tone that modern readers will find offensive, but Saikaku's misogyny must be understood as employed strategically for literary purposes since he wrote so differently about women elsewhere in his oeuvre. Another interesting feature of Saikaku's depiction in *The Great Mirror of Male Love* is that it makes clear that the strict formulation of male love as a relationship between an adult man and a youth is frequently maintained only in the form of fictive role-playing. Thus, in "The ABCs of Boy Love," the samurai youth and his male lover are both nine-year-old boys (eight by Western count) who affect the style of a man-youth relationship. In "Two Old Cherry Trees Still in Bloom," the samurai couple consists of a sixty-six-year-old man and his companion, age sixty-three, who still sports the hairstyle of a "youth." And in "Bamboo Clappers Strike the Hateful Number," the "youth" in the text is a youthful-looking thirty-eight-year-old kabuki actor. In each case, Saikaku shows how the literal age-based hierarchy between a man and a youth has been replaced by a fictive hierarchy no longer based on age but maintained through role-play.

In addition to Saikaku, another Edo Period writer who wrote about male love was Ueda Akinari (1734–1809). He included stories about both the samurai and monk-acolyte traditions of male love in his collection of didactic narratives, *Tales of Moonlight and Rain* (*Ugetsu monogatari* [1776]; tr. Zolbrod, 1974). "Chrysanthemum Tryst" details the miraculous tale of a dead samurai whose spirit returns to visit his beloved in order to fulfill a vow made when they parted; when the beloved learns that his lover was tortured and killed because of a false accusation, he avenges the treachery. The point of the story, typical in tales of samurai male love, is to impress the reader with the admirable loyalty of the two men's mutual devotion. In "The Blue Hood," the tradition of acolyte tales from the fifteenth century is revived and given a new twist by Akinari. Here, a monk in a mountain temple is confronted with the death of his beloved acolyte but, rather than it leading to his realization of Buddhist truth in a manner typical of stories in the genre, the monk shows the extent of his love and delusion by refusing to accept the boy's death. Instead, he goes on making love to the boy's corpse until the dead flesh could no longer sustain love-making, at which point he ate it, bones and all. The monk's inability to accept the boy's death turns him into a ghoul who comes down from the mountain temple to terrorize villagers in the valley below, which he visits in order to search the graveyards for bodies to eat. The monk becomes enlightened only after the villagers beg an itinerant priest to confront him with a powerful Zen phrase that releases him from his attachment. The moral of the narrative, typical of Buddhist enlightenment stories, is the power of Buddhist spirituality to dispell even the most deeply rooted attachments, here symbolized by the love of a monk for a boy.

The Buddhist and samurai traditions of male love, and their commercial counterpart in the kabuki theater, virtually disappeared from literature in the modern era under the influence of Western legal and medical discourses introduced in the Meiji Era (1868–1912). Traditional *nanshoku* (male love) was gradually refigured at this time as *doseiai* ("same-sex love" = homosexuality) and became a taboo subject. The Japanese were determined that Europeans view them as civilized, and depictions of homosexuality had no place in the newly civilized society the Meiji rulers were intent on creating. The transition was not without its problems, however, and one writer who dealt sensitively with the question of how male intimacy was to be reconfigured for modern Japanese men was Natsume Soseki (1867–1916). His novel *Kokoro* (1914; tr. McClellan, 1957) is a story about a male student and his mentor, and about the mentor's secret feelings of love and remorse toward his male friend "K," which are revealed to the student during the narrative. The work can be read, at one level, as a moving farewell to the Edo Period traditions of intimacy and love between males. By the 1920s, the influence of Marxist thought and ideas of human liberation led to a certain amount of writing that equated same-sex love with personal liberty. Notable among these were poems by the great modern woman poet Yosano Akiko (1878–1942), inspired by her love for another woman, Yamakawa Tomiko; and the autobiographical writings of Miyamoto Yuriko (1899–1951) in which she treats her seven-year relationship with the self-identified lesbian journalist and

scholar of Russian literature, Yuasa Yoshiko. Both writers believed that modern industrialized societies devalued women, and for them woman's love for woman was part of a political and personal stance regarding women's equality and worth.

The modern Japanese writer best known for depicting homosexual love is surely MISHIMA YUKIO (1925–1970), who created memorable portraits of male homosexuality in *Confessions of a Mask* (*Kamen no kokuhaku* [1949]; tr. Weatherby, 1958) and *Forbidden Colors* (*Kinjiki* [1951–1953]; tr. Marks, 1968), and of female homosexuality in *Temple of Dawn* (*Akatsuki no tera* [1968–1970]; tr. Saunders and Seigle, 1973). *Confessions of a Mask* recounts the young male protagonist's growing awareness of homosexual feelings pivoting around certain intense sadomasochistic images that are inspired by, for example, the sight of the dirty naked legs of a night-soil man or a painting by Italian artist Guido Reni of ST. SEBASTIAN writhing in agony. These images haunt the college-age protagonist as he attempts to develop a "normal" relationship with a girlfriend. It is in some ways a typical gay "coming out" (or coming of age) story and is often read as autobiographical, though Mishima vehemently denied that he was trying to reveal anything about himself in it. *Forbidden Colors* is a more abstract depiction of a male homosexual relationship, again problematized by a failed relationship with a woman, in which a rich older man buys the love of a young man who is stunningly handsome but who lacks the ability to love. As in MANN's *Death in Venice,* the older man's longing for the beauty of youth is associated with aestheticism and death. In *Temple of Dawn,* Mishima depicts lesbian lovers in the slightly artificial context of a Buddhist belief in reincarnation; one of the women is characterized as the reincarnation of a young man once loved by the aging protagonist of the story, who spies on the women while they are making love in order to ascertain by a birthmark that she is indeed the youth reborn. The women's lesbian relationship per se is not central to the story, seeming more like a mechanical literary device, and the depiction thus lacks the personal intensity and literary power Mishima could muster when writing about male homosexuality, which was closer to his heart. Mishima is said to have boasted that *Confessions of a Mask* was the first important Japanese homosexual narrative since Saikaku's *The Great Mirror of Male Love,* but a major difference exists between Mishima and the tradition he admired: Mishima wrote in an environment in which homosexuality was stigmatized. The title *Confessions of a Mask* can be understood as an attempt to speak through the stigma ("mask") about the truth ("confession") of homosexual feelings. Mishima's literary homosexuality is always struggling to emerge from the shadow of deviance in which medical and popular discourses placed it, into the sunlight of an unstigmatized tradition. He was acutely aware of the samurai tradition of male love and wrote extensively about his responses to that tradition in *Yukio Mishima on Hagakure* (*Hagakure nyumon* [1968]; tr. Sparling, 1977). When Mishima and his college-age male lover, Morita Masakatsu, died in a spectacular double-suicide by sword in 1970, it may have been Mishima's ultimate attempt to recreate in nonliterary form the tradition of samurai male love.

A modern writer befriended by Mishima who has achieved acclaim for his recognizably "gay" aesthetic is the poet TAKAHASHI MUTSUO (b. 1937). His English language *Poems of a Penisist* (tr. Sato, 1975) has been compared to GINSBERG's *Howl* in its wild power, and a subsequent collection in English titled *A Bunch of Keys* (tr. Sato, 1984) established Takahashi as the spokesman for a generation of self-identified gay Japanese men seeking a sense of liberation and pride. Oddly enough, Takahashi calls himself a Catholic and draws on the imagery and form of Catholic prayer in many of his poems. "Ode" (1971; revised 1980), for example, begins "In the name of / man, member, / and the holy fluid / AMEN," and then proceeds to devise a virtual theology of homosexuality in which the phallus is God, and the mouth is the great Void in man's soul that only God can fill. Needless to say, Takahashi's brand of Catholicism is not likely to be endorsed by the Pope.

A distinctly Japanese "gay male literature" has come into being in recent years, drawing more on the literary spirit of Takahashi than Mishima. Several widely read contemporary gay novels, such as Hiruma Hisao's English-titled works *Yes, Yes, Yes* (1989) and *Happy Birthday* (1990), resemble the work of modern Western gay writers: tentatively exploring what it means to be gay in a sometimes unfriendly world. Perhaps the major hint that the narratives are by and about Japanese men is in the recurring pattern of relations between an older and younger man, following the tradition of *nanshoku*. Hiruma's *Yes, Yes, Yes*, for example, concludes with the younger protagonist's involvement with a middle-aged man. Their relationship is not unlike that of the boy actors of the kabuki theater and their patrons as depicted 300 years earlier in Saikaku's narratives.

—*Paul Gordon Schalow*

BIBLIOGRAPHY

Childs, Margaret H. "*Chigo Monogatari*: Love Stories or Buddhist Sermons?" *Monumenta Nipponica* 35.2 (Summer 1980): 127–151. ■ ———. *Rethinking Sorrow: Revelatory Tales of Late Medieval Japan*. Ann Arbor: Center for Japanese Studies, The University of Michigan, 1991. ■ Pflugfelder, Gregory. "Strange Fates: Sex, Gender, and Sexuality in *Torikaebaya Monogatari*." *Monumenta Nipponica* 47.3 (Autumn 1992): 347–368. ■ Schalow, Paul Gordon. "The Invention of a Literary Tradition of Male Love: Kitamura Kigin's *Iwatsutsuji*." *Monumenta Nipponica* 48.1 (Spring 1993): 1–31. ■ ———. "Male Love in Early Modern Japan: A Literary Depiction of the 'Youth.'" *Hidden From History: Reclaiming the Gay and Lesbian Past*. Martin Duberman, Martha Vicinus, and George Chauncey, Jr., eds. New York: New American Library, 1989. 118–128. ■ Willig, Rosette F. *The Changelings: A Classical Japanese Court Tale*. Stanford, Calif.: Stanford University Press, 1983.

Jarman, Derek
(1942–1994)

Derek Jarman was born in Northwood, England, into a middle-class, Royal Air Force family, and his early life was spent on military bases and at public school. At his father's insistence, he took a degree at King's College, London, before going to art school. Arriving at the Slade in 1963, he found an exciting milieu, including openly gay artists such as David Hockney and Patrick Procktor, and he showed his paintings in several exhibitions. During this period, he enjoyed to the full the sexual and artistic freedoms of the 1960s in London.

With the acquisition of a Super 8 camera in 1970, Jarman began recording the details of his own life and discovered the autobiographical subject that was to become the driving force of all of his subsequent films and books. His creative work always criss-crossed the boundaries of established artistic media: painting, filming, writing, gay activism, and even gardening all reinforced one another to form part of an increasingly explicit project to celebrate gay sexuality and imagine a place for it in English culture. He began his career as a painter and stage designer, including designing the sets for Ken Russell's film *The Devils* (1971). His own first feature film *Sebastiane* (1975) became an unexpected hit due to its open homoeroticism and helped inspire the growing gay liberation movement.

In *Dancing Ledge* (1984), Jarman began writing autobiography that combined material from his own life with a sense of English history and the mythic past. In 1986, he discovered he was HIV-positive and decided to make that knowledge public: Without intending to, he was to become an exemplar of living creatively with AIDS. *Modern Nature* (1992) is his most substantial literary achievement. It records in journal form his life in London and Dungeness (where he owned a cottage by the sea), his friends, his film projects, his past life, his present reading and thinking, and his efforts to see his garden flourish on the exposed, rocky beach. In the next book, *At Your Own Risk* (1992), the awareness of AIDS is greater, and so is the anger and sexual frankness. Queer politics informs his struggles against disease and against the persistent homophobia of his society. These books precisely evoke English cultural life over a thirty-year period.

From canonical literary texts, Jarman made brilliantly reimagined versions of Shakespeare's *The Tempest* (1979) and Marlowe's *Edward II* (1991). *The Tempest* is full of spectacle and wit. *Edward II* modernizes Marlowe's analysis of sex and politics to apply it to contemporary England and to expose the centuries-long oppression of homosexuals by the English ruling class. The books that came out of the making of particular films stand as significant works in their own right.

His last film, *Blue* (1993), shows a pure blue screen with a complex soundtrack of music, sounds, and words (some from Jarman's own hospital notes) to represent the approach of blindness. Jarman said the screen was blue because you can't see the virus. In the grim atmosphere of the late 1980s and early 1990s, Jarman became a fierce fighter for—and celebrator of—queer sexuality.

—*Lawrence Normand*

BIBLIOGRAPHY

Jarman, Derek. *Dancing Ledge*. Shaun Allen, ed. London: Quartet, 1984. 2nd. ed. 1991. ■ ———. *The Last of England*. David L Hirst, ed. London: Constable, 1987. ■ ———. *Caravaggio*. London: Thames and Hudson, 1986. ■ ———. *Modern Nature: The Journals of Derek Jarman*. London: Century, 1991. ■ ———. *At Your Own Risk: A Saint's Testament*. Michael Christie, ed. London: Hutchinson, 1992. ■ ———. *Queer Edward II*. London: British Film Institute Publications, 1991. ■ ———. *Chroma: A Meditation on the Nature of Colour*. London: Century, 1994. ■ MacCabe, Colin. Obituary of Derek Jarman. *The Independent* (London), February 21, 1994. p. 14.

Jarry, Alfred
(1873–1907)

Alfred-Henry Jarry was born in Laval (Mayenne) on September 8, 1873. His mother, an eccentric, headstrong woman who strongly influenced her son, left her husband when Jarry was six, taking her children with her and moving first to Saint-Brieuc (1879) and then to Rennes (1888). Images and material from Jarry's Breton childhood would later appear throughout his work. He moved to Paris in 1891 to attend Lycée Henri IV and began publishing in 1893, when two of his works were awarded prizes. His success gained him entrance the following year to the group of writers affiliated with the newly founded *Mercure de France*. From 1893 to 1895, he enjoyed a brief but intense friendship with his reputed literary collaborator, the future poet Léon-Paul Fargue, a fellow student at Henri IV. Though Jarry jested often about his homosexuality, this is his only known relationship, and it provided the material for his semiautobiographical play, *Haldernablou* (1894). Jarry, at twenty-three, reached the height of his literary fame in December 1896, when the premier of *Ubu roi* (*King Ubu*) at Lugné-Poe's Théâtre de l'Oeuvre caused a riot with its opening word, *merdre* (loosely translated as "shee-it"). The play closed after the second performance. Jarry continued to write over the next eleven years, but he gained little or no recognition. A heavy drinker given to eccentric extremes of behavior, he died on November 1, 1907, at the age of thirty-four. Credited with having invented the Theater of the Absurd with *Ubu roi* and his theories of staging, Jarry was also a novelist, poet, and journalist. His work is characterized by a love of paradox and by bizarre juxtapositions of images, qualities that led the surrealists to claim him as one of their precursors. His quick wit and keen sense of the absurd came together in pataphysics, his science of imaginary solutions.

Sexuality in all its excess and perversity provides the material for much of Jarry's work. But even his most outrageous novels reveal a curiosity marked more by innocence than by prurience. Although the semiautobiographical *Haldernablou* (in *Les Minutes de sable mémorial* [*Minutes of Memorial Sand*, 1894]) is his only work to deal exclusively with homosexuality, homosexual characters and themes appear in other works, particularly *Les Jours et les nuits* (*Days and Nights,* 1897), *L'Amour en visites* (*Love Goes Visiting,* 1898), *Messaline* (*The Garden of Priapus,* 1899), and *Le Surmâle* (*The Supermale,* 1902). In 1903, Baron Jacques d'Adelsward-Fersen, a second-rate poet and minor aristocrat, was charged with recruiting lycée students to participate in black masses and orgies "in the greek style." Jarry wrote about the affair in three articles ("L'Ame ouverte à l'art antique" ["Opening the Soul to Ancient Art"], "Littérature," and "Héliogabale à travers les âges" ["Heliogabalus Through the Centuries"], all collected in *La Chandelle verte* [*The Green Candle,* 1969]), which, though not directly supportive of the Baron, satirize the bourgeois perception of homosexuality's threat to family values by relocating the threat from the supposed pederast to the legal system itself.

Like Jarry himself, his characters are often eccentrics, struggling to maintain a sense of their own identity in a world that refuses to understand them. Though these struggles invariably end in destruction, we find in them representations of the homosexual actively attempting to assert and to create himself at a time when homosexuality was becoming increasingly pathologized.

—*A. Mitchell Brown*

BIBLIOGRAPHY

Apollinaire, Guillaume. "Feu Alfred Jarry." *Oeuvres en prose complètes.* vol. II. Pierre Caizergues and Michel Décaudin, eds. Paris: Gallimard, Bibliothèque de la Pléiade, 1991. ■ Arnaud, Noël. *Alfred Jarry d'Ubu roi au Docteur Faustroll.* Paris: La Table Ronde, 1974. ■ Beaumont, Keith. *Alfred Jarry: A Critical and Biographical Study.* New York: St. Martin's Press, 1984. ■ Rachilde. *Alfred Jarry ou le Surmâle des lettres.* Paris: Grasset, 1928. ■ Shattuck, Roger. *The Banquet Years. The Arts in France, 1885–1918.* London: Faber & Faber, Ltd., 1958. ■ Stillman, Linda Klieger. *Alfred Jarry.* Boston: Twayne Publishers, 1983.

Jewett, Sarah Orne
(1849–1909)

For the most part, fortune was kind to Sarah Orne Jewett. Born on September 3, 1849, into a prosperous and stable family in South Berwick, Maine, she was the second of three daughters of Theodore H. Jewett, a country physician, and Caroline F. Perry. She adored her father, who guided her through the family's large library and frequently allowed her to accompany him on his rounds throughout the coastal countryside because ill health made regular attendance at school difficult for her. In the course of these rambles, Jewett acquired the habits of empathy and observation that would serve her so well as a writer of sketches and narratives of New England village life.

Jewett demonstrated an early inclination toward writing; she published her first story in 1868 when she was just eighteen, and she enjoyed a long and productive career. Championed by such influential editors as William Dean Howells and Horace Scudder, Jewett's work was regularly featured in *The Atlantic Monthly* and shrewdly marketed by the publisher Houghton Mifflin for three and a half decades. She produced fifteen novels or collections for adults as well as several works for children and carved out a comfortable niche for herself in the competitive literary marketplace of post–Civil War America. Claiming to have no talent for plot, Jewett perfected the art of the short story as a nondramatic exploration of what she called the "romance" of "every-day life." Women were consistently the focus of Jewett's imaginative energies, from her portrait of young female friendship in *Deephaven* (1877) and her study of a talented girl's search for vocation in *A Country Doctor* (1884) to the tale of an elderly woman's fantasy friendship with Queen Victoria featured in *The Queen's Twin and Other Stories* (1899). Clearly, however, the highlight of Jewett's career was *The Country of the Pointed Firs* (1896), a delicate yet tightly crafted narrative of a summer visit to a small town on the coast of Maine. The narrator is a writer who comes to Dunnet Landing in search of solitude but instead finds herself drawn deeply into the life of the town and into a friendship with her landlady, the herbalist Almira Todd. In its loving attention to the details of women's lives and its lack of self-consciousness in exploring powerful bonds between women, *Pointed Firs* ranks as a classic not just of American regionalism but of the proto-lesbian literature that emerged out of what historian Carroll Smith-Rosenberg has described as "the female world of love and ritual," a pre-Freudian world in which women's romantic friendships were objects chiefly of veneration rather than suspicion.

Annie Adams Fields was a primary feature in Jewett's personal experience of that world since the two women maintained a "Boston marriage" from early in the 1880s until Jewett's death. The widow of

Boston publisher James T. Fields, the gracious, vivacious Annie provided Jewett with companionship and emotional support and introduced her to a galaxy of literary and cultural stars that included ALFRED LORD TENNYSON, Matthew Arnold, HENRY JAMES, Rudyard Kipling, and CHRISTINA ROSSETTI. An indefatigable traveler and dazzling hostess, Annie was also fifteen years older than Jewett and likely served as the model for the older women who so frequently guide younger women in Jewett's fiction. Jewett's letters to Fields (compiled by Fields and published after Jewett's death) suggest that the relationship was marked by intense feelings as well as shifting moods and roles. She alternately expresses daughterly dependence, playful childishness, and physical longing: "I shall be with you tomorrow, your dear birthday. . . . I am tired of writing things. I want now to paint things, and drive things, and *kiss* things."

Jewett's limpid prose style often evokes comparisons to her predecessor, Nathaniel Hawthorne, though compassion and a keen sense of social comedy make her New England look considerably less gloomy than his. From the standpoint of gay and lesbian literary history, however, Jewett's most important connection is to novelist WILLA CATHER (1873–1947), whom Jewett met and mentored in the last year of her life. In letters from this period (also published by Fields), she advised the future Pulitzer Prize winner first to abandon journalism and devote herself full time to writing fiction and secondly to give up the "masquerade" of male narrators, which Cather was then deploying as a means of disguising her affection for women. For Jewett, whose sexual and literary identities were formed against the backdrop of culturally sanctioned romantic friendships, such disguises were unnecessary and distracting. In her world, a woman could write openly of her love for another woman, could, as she suggested to Cather in response to one of her stories, "even care enough to wish to take [a beloved endangered woman] away from such a life, by some means or other." Jewett died in 1909 of a cerebral hemorrhage, and with her, it seems, died the imaginative possibilities of that premodern, relatively less sex-conscious world. Though Cather took her advice and left journalism, even dedicating her breakthrough novel of 1913, *O Pioneers!*, to Jewett's memory, she wrestled throughout her career with the problem of representing desire in a culture that by then regarded intimacy between women as "unnatural." Jewett was a crucial precursor and role model, but the feelings she explores in stories like "Martha's Lady" (1897), in which the protagonist harbors a love for another woman that is "half a pain and half a golden joy," signified something different to the readers of Cather's generation. Thus, she clung to her "masquerade" as a historical and occupational necessity, feeling forced to conceal what her literary foremother openly celebrated. Jewett's serene insistence that "a woman could love her in that same protecting way" poignantly yet clearly marks the cultural gulf that fell between these two prominent American women writers. (See also ROMANTIC FRIENDSHIP, FEMALE.)

—*Marilee Lindemann*

BIBLIOGRAPHY

Cary, Richard, ed. *An Appreciation of Sarah Orne Jewett.* Waterville, Me.: Colby College Press, 1973. ■ Donovan, Josephine. *Sarah Orne Jewett.* New York: Frederick Ungar, 1981. ■ Lindemann, Marilee. "Sarah Orne Jewett." *Modern American Women Writers.* Elaine Showalter, ed. New York: Scribner's, 1991. 235–250. ■ Nagel, Gwen L., ed. *Critical Essays on Sarah Orne Jewett.* Boston: G.K. Hall, 1984. ■ Roman, Judith A. *Annie Adams Fields: The Spirit of Charles Street.* Bloomington: Indiana University Press, 1990. ■ Sherman, Sarah Way. *Sarah Orne Jewett: An American Persephone.* Hanover, N.H.: University Press of New England, 1989. ■ Smith-Rosenberg, Carroll. "The Female World of Love and Ritual: Relations between Women in Nineteenth-Century America," *Signs* 1 (Autumn 1975): 1–29. ■ Toth, Susan Allen. "Sarah Orne Jewett and Friends: A Community of Interest." *Studies in Short Fiction* 9 (Summer 1972): 233–241. ■ Zagarell, Sandra A. "Narrative of Community: The Identification of a Genre." *Signs* 13 (Spring 1988): 498–527.

Jewish-American Literature

With some notable exceptions, American Jewish gay and lesbian writers have tended to be secularists; for them "Jewish" is not necessarily an indicator of a particular religious position or sensibility but an affirmation of ethnic and cultural identity. One reason for this lack of religious content may be the Mosaic code as expressed in the book of Leviticus. But there is division within Judaism on how Leviticus should be interpreted. Conservative and Orthodox Jewish circles argue that the Torah explicitly forbids and condemns homosexuality, whereas the Reform and Reconstructionist branches argue for a new reading. The latter also argue for a complete acceptance of gays and lesbians into their ranks based on the history of Jewish liberal thought. The Reform and Reconstructionist branches of Judaism in America have been among the first religious groups—in any of the major faiths in this country—to accept gays as part of their synagogues, ordaining gay clergy and, more recently, permitting gay commitment ceremonies. The Conservative and Orthodox branches have been less forthcoming, as was evident by the argument over whether members of the New York gay synagogue, Beth Simchat Torah, affiliated with the Reform movement, were to be allowed to march in the 1993 New York Salute to Israel parade.

The first significant gay character to appear in American Jewish writing is Harry Singermann in Myron Brinig's family saga, *Singermann* (1929) and *This Man Is My Brother* (1932). Although Brinig was not gay, his characterization of Harry goes beyond the stereotypes of the era and is compassionate and sympathetic. Even though Harry Singermann is described as "too flushed and effeminate," with an unfortunate infatuation for his adopted nephew that leads to his eventual suicide, he is also the competent head of the family's department store to whom all other family members respectfully defer in financial and artistic matters. He is certainly not ostracized, either by family or by community, which may be a result of the fact that the Singermann household perceives its Jewishness more in terms of cultural than religious identity.

For GERTURDE STEIN, to be a Jewish lesbian indeed meant to be "doubly other" since she considered both her gender and her religion to disqualify her for the definition of "genius" to which she aspired. In her 1941 novel *Ida,* however, Stein imagined a character who finds empowerment only through doubling herself, by constructing a "twin" through whom she may risk the troubling elements of sexuality and freedom. The novel explores the degree to which heterosexual relations are silencing so that only the same-sex self-multiplication she envisions permits the voice she seeks. Although in her own life Stein could not fully come to an acceptance of her own double identity as a lesbian and a Jew, she here creatively imagines doubling her identity as a way to find her voice.

The earliest lesbian character in American Jewish writing is Rivkele, the daughter of a Jewish brothel keeper, in Sholem Asch's play *God of Vengeance* (1922), who falls in love with one of her father's prostitutes. Not surprisingly, this relationship created such an uproar that the play was briefly shut down, and its star spent a night in jail.

The distinction of having created the first fully developed lesbian character goes to Jo Sinclair and her 1946 novel, *Wasteland.* Jo Sinclair is the pseudonym for Ruth Seid; *Wasteland,* her partly autobiographical first novel, won the Harper Prize in 1946 and remained on the best-seller lists for months. Although most reviewers of the novel considered Jake Brown, a man undergoing psychotherapy because of his problematic relationship to his family's Jewishness, the protagonist, one can easily also argue that Debbie Brown, Jake's sister, is the real main character. Before the novel's action even begins, the psychotherapist Debbie recommends to her brother has helped her appreciate her value as a human being and accept herself as a lesbian. *Wasteland* became one of the first full and loving portraits of a lesbian in twentieth-century American fiction. The importance of the novel rests on two points. First of all, Debbie is instrumental in helping her brother come to terms with himself as a Jew. As such, the novel represents a celebration of ethnicity; such an act of cultural identification spoke to many different kinds of minority readers and writers at the time. In addition, *Wasteland* provided lesbians with a role model both in the protagonist and in the author who had created her. Its celebration of the interconnectedness of ethnicity, religion, and sexual orientation makes *Wasteland* an important forerunner of the contemporary anthology *Twice Blessed: On Being Lesbian or Gay and Jewish* (1989). Sinclair would not again broach the subject of lesbianism that boldly; only during the tolerant war years did she feel comfortable enough to create an openly lesbian protagonist. The problem of being a butch Jewish lesbian in the conformist 1950s, a subject Sinclair chose not to confront in her fiction, has been brilliantly evoked recently by Leslie Feinberg in *Stone Butch Blues* (1993).

It would take almost another twenty years before an American Jewish gay male author would create a protagonist to stand side by side with Debbie Brown. PAUL GOODMAN's novels *Parents' Day* (1951) and *Making Do* (1963) are significant stepping-stones in that direction, but the first Jewish gay main character is Stephen Wolfe of Sanford Friedman's 1965 novel *Totempole.* The novel follows Stephen's life, from a privileged youth growing up on New York's Riverside Drive during the Depression, through his college years, to his tour of duty in Korea where he finally learns to accept his homosexuality through the thoughtful and compassionate help of a Korean prisoner of war. Stephen's psychological problems clearly derive from his upbringing as a Jew. At summer camp, he develops his first infatuation with one of the male camp counselors. At the same time, his Hebrew lessons emphasize the concept of "uncleanness," which the adolescent associates with masturbation. Friedman carefully explores the repressiveness of Stephen's upbringing and the repercussions it has on him through his college years. Although he commences a sexual relationship with his uninhibited roommate, his deeply seated religious fears die hard; he reads ST. AUGUSTINE and does penance. Finally, in Korea where Stephen is completing his military tour of duty in a prisoner of war camp, the psychological barriers he has erected around himself break down with the help of Pak Sun Bo, who teaches Stephen not to despise his own body. At the end of the novel, Stephen has liberated himself from his childhood terrors and is ready to return to the United States with a clear sexual identity. The novel is a gay Bildungsroman; Stephen renounces that part of his Jewish heritage that has been psychologically maiming him. In this respect, the novel presents a much more pessimistic outlook about the possibilities of reconciling ethnic and religious traditions and sexual orientation than Jo Sinclair offered in 1946.

In contrast to Stephen Wolfe, the characters of *Privates* (1986), a novel by Gene Horowitz, do not experience any guilt. Although the main scenes of the novel also take place during the Korean war, they are flashbacks framed by scenes of contemporary life. It is possible that Horowitz's contemporary setting has affected his characters' memories. Certainly such easy reconciliation between Jewishness and gay identity was not conceivable for Friedman writing in pre-Stonewall days, though poet ALLEN GINSBERG was able to incorporate both aspects of his identity even in his works that antedate Stonewall.

Not surprisingly, however, most openly gay and lesbian American Jewish writing has appeared in the post-Stonewall era. The sheer number of fiction writers, poets, and playwrights who have achieved recognition is astounding. One of the trends of the literature of the past twenty-five years is that gay male writers usually treat Jewishness as an ethnic and cultural identity, whereas lesbian authors also explore the religious dimensions of Judaism. Geoffrey Linden's novel *Jigsaw* (1974) is an early post-Stonewall attempt to reconcile ethnicity and sexual orientation. The narrative structure artfully juxtaposes first-person diary entries with a third-person narrative. The pattern is random to reflect the novel's title; the reader is thus challenged to create a full psychological portrait of Steven Tucker, the protagonist. In the absence of positive Jewish gay role models, Steven feels an overbearing sense of guilt that he only slowly overcomes with the help of a psychiatrist.

Such seriousness is not the intent of S. Steinberg's *A Fairy Tale* (1980). The novel plays on many American Jewish stereotypes, especially the overbearing female who is a consummate matchmaker; it is always outrageously funny. Once Aunt Sylvia, the narrator's busybody aunt, accepts her nephew as a gay man, she uses all of her talents to find him the right mate. Instead of being alienated from family and ethnic culture, the hero of this lightweight romance wins his family's wholehearted approval along with the man of his dreams.

Years from Now (1987), Gary Glickman's first novel, is also indebted to the tradition of Jewish family sagas. Interestingly, David, the main character, decides both to be a father and to assert his gay identity. For him, the continuity of the tribe is as important as gay self-realization. The novel emphasizes the possibility of reconciliation between David and his family and its religious traditions.

With his 1978 novel *Faggots,* LARRY KRAMER introduced a distinctly moralistic voice into American Jewish gay writing. In contrast to other novelists at the time who were celebrating a newly emerging gay sensibility, Kramer depicts a group of men whose use of drugs, sadomasochism, and lack of serious or lasting relationships he greatly opposes. Although many of the novel's characters are Jewish, the novel's Jewish content rests less in these individual characters than in Kramer's relentless jeremiad, predicting doom for gay men if they do not mend their promiscuous ways and bring a moral content back into their lives. Largely attacked at the time of publication for its extreme position, the novel is a precursor of Kramer's subsequent career as an enraged moralist.

Some of the finest American Jewish gay male literature so far has been produced by Lev Raphael, who—along with Judith Katz—is at the forefront of exploring what it means to be Jewish and queer. Raphael articulates this dilemma for the gay Jewish male in his short story collection *Dancing on Tisha B'Av* (1990). In the title story, Nat and Mark, devout Orthodox Jews, fall in love, establishing an ideal relationship as they share the same devotion to both Judaism and their gay selves. Yet Raphael also convincingly conveys the paradox for the observant Jew: the devotion to a faith that will deny him a place in its sanctuary. Nevertheless, Raphael examines how one can walk the fine line between personal devotion and ethnic exclusion. He arrives at a tentative but loving reconciliation of the conflict of sexual orientation and religious affiliation. *Winter Eyes* (1992), Raphael's first novel, intertwines the account of a sensitive boy's coming to terms with his sexuality with the story of his Holocaust survivor parents who have tried to erase the past completely from their lives. Yet no matter how much the parents attempt to shield their son from the events of the past, the Holocaust is the all-pervading subtext of the family's problems. The novel's subject significantly broadens the focus of gay male writing.

Sacred Lips of the Bronx (1994), Douglas Sadownick's first novel, combines questions of Jewish identity with the subject of AIDS. His protagonist, Michael Kaplan, a Los Angeles-based journalist covering AIDS issues, experiences anxiety about his deteriorating relationship with his lover of ten years. This volatile situation forces him, through a reexamination of unresolved issues of his adolescence, to confront his present life. While the AIDS crisis permeates the fabric of the book, so does Michael's long-dead grandmother who has begun to appear to him as she did right after her death. These elements of the fantastic, which are indebted to a long tradition of such writing in Jewish literature (and has also influenced Tony Kushner and Judith Katz but has otherwise been ignored so far in American Jewish gay and lesbian writing), open up new vistas for Jewish gay writing. Finally, the grandmother's unequivocal approval of Michael's life signifies not only personal but also tribal acceptance.

Of course, incorporating Jewish subject matter into their works is not a concern for all Jewish gay writers. DAVID LEAVITT's characters are devoid of a particular ethnicity. One can read his novel *The Lost Language of Cranes* (1986) as a Jewish family saga, but such a reading is strained. David Feinberg's two AIDS novels, *Eighty-Sixed* (1989) and *Spontaneous Combustion* (1991), have a Jewish protagonist, Benjamin Rosenthal, whose Jewishness has little relevance in his life, with the possible exception of visits to his mother's upstate New York home, which he characterizes as being full of Jewish guilt trips. In the same category, we find Martin Schecter's novel *Two Halves of New Haven* (1992), which is a coming-out novel with a relatively minor Jewish angle; Paul, the narrator, sees his Jewishness as an ethnic, but not as a potentially guilt-inducing religious identity. Other recent fiction includes Harlan Greene's *Why We Never Danced the Charleston* (1984), Stan Leventhal's *Mountain Climbing in Sheridan Square* (1988), RICHARD HALL's *Family Fictions* (1991), Bernard Cooper's *A Year of Rhymes,* Stuart Edelson's *Black Glass* (1993), and Eugene Stein's *Straitjacket & Tie* (1994).

Jewish gay playwrights such as HARVEY FIERSTEIN, William Finn, William Hoffman, Larry Kramer, and Tony Kushner have become household names. While all of them use Jewish gay characters, Kramer and Kushner are particularly imbued with a deep sense of Jewish history in the twentieth century. Their dramatizations of the AIDS crisis are informed by their awareness of the Holocaust. Indeed, as Kramer demonstrates in *Reports from the Holocaust* (1989), the AIDS crisis—with suggestions of quarantines, identifying tattoos, and "camps"—is immersed in the language of the Shoah. For Kramer and Kushner, both of whom are writing with an obvious awareness of their doubly marginalized status as gay men and as Jews, the Holocaust is less a metaphor than it is part of their immediate past and present consciousness.

Apart from making direct comparisons between the Holocaust and the AIDS crisis, Kramer's two autobiographical AIDS plays, *The Normal Heart* (1985) and its sequel *The Destiny of Me* (1993), also delineate the makings of a Jewish gay radical, very much in the tradition of twentieth-century progressive Jewish thought. Ned Weeks, the plays' major character, and Larry Kramer, his creator, are Jewish activists and moralists who have taken their lessons from the Jewish past and apply them to the pressing concerns of contemporary life.

Tony Kushner's evocation of Jewish history and the Holocaust in reference to AIDS in both parts of *Angels in America—Millennium Approaches* (1993) and *Perestroika* (1994)—is more complex and subtle than Kramer's. Kushner does not refer to the Shoah by name, but the awareness of it permeates the entire play. In addition, the struggle of the two central characters, Louis and Roy Cohn, with their Jewish identity, indicates that Kushner, much like Kramer, has woven an awareness of ancestral and cultural heritage into the fabric of the play itself. William Hoffman's *As Is* (1985) and Paul Rudnick's *Jeffrey* (1994) also confront the AIDS crisis. Less specifically Jewish than Kramer's and Kushner's evocations, they are powerful plays that have been hailed both for their compassion and humor.

Before the AIDS crisis mobilized the best writing by American Jewish playwrights, Martin Sherman had already produced his shattering play *Bent* (1979). Set in Nazi Germany, it follows the persecution of Max, a Berlin gay man who, having survived the brutal murder of his lover, and being interned in Dachau as a Jew because he proved to his tormentors that he was not "bent," gradually begins to accept the love that Horst, another gay prisoner, offers him. When Horst is executed, Max discards his yellow Jewish star, retrieves Horst's jacket with its pink triangle and commits suicide by hurling himself into the camp's electric fence.

A much lighter play, *If This Isn't Love* (1982), by Sidney Morris depicts the often stormy, but ultimately enduring, relationship between a Jewish actor and an Irish-American teacher. Probably the strongest comedy with American Jewish subject matter is Harvey Fierstein's *Torch Song Trilogy* (1979), which follows the life of Arnold Beckoff, the protagonist, over a period of six years, from self-centeredness to committed involvement with other people.

Among Jewish lesbian fiction writers, the tension between sexual orientation and ethnic and religious concerns is even more palpable than among their male colleagues. What most Jewish lesbian writers have in common is their ability to create a new commentary on Jewish life in America. Taken collectively, their works represent an emerging poetics of American Jewish lesbian writing, presenting readers with tales of deliverance from heterosexual norms and patriarchal control, so often the dominant force in American Jewish culture and literature.

No reinterpretation of Jewish life is an easy task. Emerging from a position of almost absolute invisibility within a community that itself is marginal requires considerable perseverance. In fact, to assume a lesbian identity within the Jewish community, a woman must overcome not only the image of asexuality but also that of invisibility. The theoretical underpinnings of such a position have been thoroughly and fruitfully explored by ADRIENNE RICH, in both her poetry and essays, and by Irena Klepfisz, especially in her collection *Dreams of an Insomniac: Jewish Feminist Essays, Speeches and Diatribes* (1990).

At the most basic level is a return to a symbolic ethnicity, an ethnicity paradoxically based on a secure Americanism, defined by eating certain foods, observing selected religious rites, or wearing T-shirts that proclaim one ethnic allegiance or another. Such a concept of ethnicity is embraced by Lesléa Newman in her novel *In Every Laugh a Tear* (1992). The protagonist, Linda Steinblatt, is a thoroughly secular Jewish lesbian, who nevertheless has changed her first name to Shayna to affirm her Jewishness more publicly. The relationship between Shayna and her Puerto Rican lover, Luz Borghes, is Newman's attempt at bringing about a multicultural awareness and cross-cultural fertilization and reconciliation. Of course, this emphasis on heritage and ethnic reconciliation is very timely. In her introduction to the ground-breaking anthology, *Nice Jewish Girls* (1989), Evelyn Torton Beck provides a damning sketch of antisemitism in the lesbian community. Newman's novel, or at least that part of the plot involving Shayna and Luz, is an attempt to bridge cross-ethnic racism.

Although it is relatively easy to present ethnicity symbolically, a more daring and complex task for a writer is the creative reinterpretation of the culture as it has developed in America. This is exactly what Judith Katz achieves in *Running Fiercely Toward a High Thin Sound* (1992). All of her main characters are Jewish, and the themes of Jewish identity and of lesbian self-assertion are inextricably intertwined. Katz does not attempt to construct new Jewish feminist ceremonies, but she creates a dream world in which strong Jewish women of the past and present work together as healers. By injecting this dream world into an otherwise realistic narrative, Katz reinterprets Jewish culture and identity, connecting the contemporary world of American Jews with that of the European past, especially that of the Warsaw Ghetto during the Holocaust. The role of women as healers, as the saviors of cultures, forms the all-important background. Lesbians and heterosexual women work together, creating a vision of sisterhood in which the domestic problems of the characters do not necessarily become irrelevant but certainly diminish. Katz creates a rich synthesis between religious and lesbian mythmaking.

Between symbolic ethnicity on the one hand and fundamental reinterpretation of Jewish history to encompass the history of Jewish women and lesbians on the other, we find a middle ground that is best represented by Jyl Lynn Felman's short stories, collected under the title *Hot Chicken Wings* (1992). In her programmatic manifesto, "The Forbidden, or What Makes Me a Jewish Lesbian Writer," Felman maps out her approach to the question of identity. As to her Jewishness, Felman comments, that what "makes me a Jewish writer is the fact that my parents kept kosher, and longed for their progeny to do the same." This statement may sound like one of involuntary identification with the concept of symbolic ethnicity, but Felman avoids such easy categorization. She goes on to say that keeping kosher

> means eating only that food which is permitted according to Jewish law and avoiding all else— that which is forbidden, is treyf. So the very act of eating that [i.e., the forbidden] makes my stories Jewish. Lurking in the background of every scene I write is a sense of the forbidden.

Here the sense of otherness is projected onto that which is non-Jewish. Felman concludes this passage by tying together her identity as a Jew with her identity as a lesbian: "But what makes my stories lesbian with the emphasis on Jewish is the fact that my characters don't just imagine what eating pussy is like, they actually eat it. And eating pussy for me is just like eating treyf." The argument that Felman presents here is complex and perhaps unresolved. Even though there seems to be some deep-seated ambivalence, both about being a Jew and being a lesbian, in such a remark, it points to Felman's ultimate goal of reconciliation: to make the forbidden kosher, that is to say, to integrate as fully as possible Jewish and lesbian identity.

SARAH SCHULMAN's works are not always specifically Jewish in content, but both *The Sophie Horowitz Story* (1984) and *Girls, Visions and Everything* (1986) have Jewish main characters. Her most recent novel, *Empathy* (1992), successfully blends psychoanalysis and Jewish identity. Anna, the novel's protagonist, is psychologically so bruised that she has developed a split personality. The narrative ends with the restoration of her sanity and her reconciliation with her family, an event that significantly takes place during a Passover Seder. Schulman is also the one Jewish lesbian fiction writer whose work directly deals with AIDS; thus there exist strong links between her and the writings of Jewish gay male authors.

There are, of course, other Jewish lesbian novels with similar thematics, including ELANA NACHMAN/DYKEWOMON's *Riverfinger Women* (1974), Alice Bloch's *The Law of Return* (1983), Ruth Geller's *Triangles* (1984), Edith Konecky's *A Place at the Table* (1989), Melanie Kay/Kantrowitz's *My Jewish Face & Other Stories* (1990), and Andrea Freud Loewenstein's *The Worry Girl* (1992). These writers relate both to Jewish and lesbian literary traditions and to the concerns of contemporary American culture. For these authors, being Jewish lesbians or lesbian Jews and writing about that experience—that is, going public—has been empowering and liberating, personally as well as collectively.

Although American Jewish literature in general has been pronounced moribund for more than twenty years, no such pronouncements can be made for American Jewish gay and lesbian literature. A new collection of short fiction, *Writing Our Way Home* (1992), edited by Ted Solotaroff and Nessa Rapoport, was consciously designed to point to new directions for American Jewish literature. In her introduction, Rapoport envisions new kinds of Jews—"children and grandchildren of Holocaust survivors, converts to Judaism, Sephardim, descendants of conversos in the American Southwest, lesbians, and gay men"—who will revitalize American Jewish fiction. American Jewish gay and lesbian literature with its rich heritage, diverse subject matter, and thriving vitality has indeed imbued American Jewish literature with new life.

—Ludger Brinker

BIBLIOGRAPHY

Balka, Christie, and Andy Rose, eds. *Twice Blessed: On Being Lesbian or Gay and Jewish.* Boston: Beacon, 1989. ■ Beck, Evelyn Tornton, ed. *Nice Jewish Girls: A Lesbian Anthology.* Rev. ed. Boston: Beacon, 1989. ■ Kaye/Kantrowitz, Melanie. *The Issue is Power: Essays on Women, Jews, Violence and Resistance.* San Francisco: Aunt Lute Books, 1992. ■ Klepfisz, Irena. *Dreams of an Insomniac: Jewish Feminist Essays, Speeches and Diatribes.* Portland, Oreg.: Eighth Mountain Press, 1990. ■ Solotaroff, Ted, and Nessa Rapoport, eds. *Writing Our Way Home: Contemporary Stories by American Jewish Writers.* New York: Schocken, 1992. ■ Zahava, Irene, ed. *Speaking for Ourselves: Short Stories by Jewish Lesbians.* Freedom: Calif.: Crossing Press, 1990.

Jordan, June
(*b.* 1936)

Born on July 9, 1936, in Harlem to Jamaican immigrants, June Jordan grew up in Brooklyn's Bedford-Stuyvesant neighborhood. Her childhood in one of the largest black urban areas in the country, coupled with her three high school years at a predominantly white preparatory school, gave Jordan an early understanding of racial conflicts. She attended Barnard College, where she met and married Michael Meyer, a white Columbia University student who shared her political beliefs. Divorced after eleven years, Jordan continued studying architectural design and working as a freelance political journalist to support herself and her son. Her broad-based inclusive politics were significantly influenced by her work in 1964 with visionary architect Buckminster Fuller, her mother's suicide in 1966, her meetings with Fannie Lou Hamer in 1969, and her travels to Nicaragua in the 1980s. She began her teaching career in 1967 at the City College of New York and has also taught at Connecticut College, Sarah Lawrence, and Yale; in 1989, she became a professor of African-American studies at the University of California, Berkeley, and began writing a political column for *The Progressive* magazine. Since 1969, she has received a number of awards and fellowships, including a Rockefeller Grant, the Prix de Rome in Environmental Design, a National Endowment for the Arts Fellowship, and a National Association of Black Journalists Award.

Although primarily known for her poetry, Jordan has written essays, plays, novels, and musicals. The title of her 1989 collection of new and previously published poems, *Naming Our Destiny*, succinctly describes her ethical vision, as well as a central theme in her work: the importance of individual and collective self-determination. This dual emphasis on personal and communal autonomy, coupled with the belief that her own self-determination entails recognizing and affirming the interconnections between herself and apparently dissimilar peoples, gives Jordan's work an aggressive optimism and a diversity that grow increasingly complex in her later writings. Throughout her work, she explores multiple personal, national, and international issues, including her relationships with female and male lovers, homophobia, Black English, racial violence in Atlanta, South African apartheid, and the Palestinian crisis.

Given the opposition bisexuals have received from both heterosexual and lesbian and gay communities, Jordan's willingness to identify herself openly as bisexual establishes an extremely important precedent. Her most radical statement can be found in "A New Politics of Sexuality" (in *Technical Difficulties,* 1993), where she calls for a "new, bisexual politics of sexuality." In addition to rejecting the stereotypical views of bisexuals, she associates sexual independence with political commitment and maintains that homopho-

bia and heterosexism do not represent "special interest" concerns or secondary forms of oppression less important than racism or sexism. Indeed, she suggests that sexual oppression is perhaps the most deeply seated form of human conflict. Jordan enacts her bisexual politics in "A Short Note to My Very Critical Friends and Well-Beloved Comrades," "Meta-Rhetoric," "Poem for Buddy," and other poems in *Naming Our Destiny,* where she rejects restrictive labels and exclusionary political positions based on sexuality, color, class, or nationality.

—*AnnLouise Keating*

BIBLIOGRAPHY

Erickson, Peter. "The Love Poetry of June Jordan." *Callaloo* 9 (1986): 221–234. ■ ———. "State of the Union." *Transition* 59 (1992): 104–109. ■ Harjo, Joy. "An Interview with June Jordan." *High Plains Literary Review* 3 (1988): 60–76. ■ Parmar, Prathiba. "Black Feminism: the Politics of Articulation." *Identity: Community, Culture, Difference.* Jonathan Rutherford, ed. London: Lawrence & Wishart, 1990. 101–127.

Journalism and Publishing

For many gay men and lesbians, the printed page is one of the chief builders of identity and community. Hence, the gay and lesbian press is of prime importance in sustaining a frequently embattled minority. Newspapers and periodicals directed to the gay and lesbian community not only distribute information about local events and national and world news of interest to its audience, but they also function as the principal link many readers have with other gay men and lesbians. They typically document the local gay and lesbian scene while also serving as a vital lifeline connecting isolated readers to the larger gay and lesbian social and political movement. Those gay men and lesbians who lack easy access to major cities or other centers of community depend especially on gay and lesbian journalists for a necessary link with others of a like identity.

Before Stonewall, gay men and lesbians found little material readily available from people who shared their identity. The mainstream media rarely presented work of gay and lesbian interest, and when they did, they invariably approached the subject from a heterosexual viewpoint, contributing to the presumption that there was no substantial lesbian and gay male population. Moreover, on the infrequent occasions

when gay men and lesbians received attention in the mass media, they tended to be portrayed in stereotypical and sensationalistic terms. The invisibility of gay men and lesbians in newspapers and other media fostered their isolation and oppression. Indeed, the development of viable gay and lesbian communities, to say nothing of a mass movement for social justice, was made possible only by the creation of a gay and lesbian press, which helped transform an illicit, almost exclusively sexually oriented subculture into a broadly based mainstream movement.

Among the earliest stirrings of an alternative media addressing gay and lesbian issues occurred in Prussia in the 1890s. Magnus Hirschfeld founded his Wissenschaftlich-humanitare Kommittee (Scientific Humanitarian Committee) to awaken thought about German laws on homosexuality. From this group in 1899 came *Jarhbuch für sexuelle Zwischenstufen,* the first scholarly journal for the study of concerns of interest to homosexuals. Other German publications proliferated throughout the early decades of the twentieth century; among them was one directed toward lesbians, *Freundin.* Two French journals also appeared quite early, *Akademos,* which was published monthly during 1909 by Count Adelswärd Fersen, and *Inversions,* which appeared briefly in 1925 before being suppressed by the police. Hitler's regime likewise suppressed the publications of the German gay and lesbian movement and destroyed much of Hirschfeld's research; nevertheless, other European groups dedicated to understanding homosexuality and to increasing tolerance for gay men and lesbians arose, and they frequently published newsletters and other periodicals. The journal *Der Kreis* (*The Circle*) began publishing in 1932 in Zurich, and, after World War II, *Vriendschap* (*Friendship*) and *Lesbos* were established in Holland.

In the United States, communication was spread through sporadic leaflets and short-lived newspapers such as *Friendship and Freedom,* which Henry Gerber distributed in Chicago in 1925. Gerber, who served in the American army of occupation in the Rhineland after World War I, was deeply influenced by the German homosexual emancipation movement. On December 10, 1924, the state of Illinois granted a charter to his Society for Human Rights, the first documented gay rights organization in the United States. The Society managed to publish two issues of its periodical before Gerber and several of his associates were arrested and charged with spurious crimes. In 1925, advocacy of gay rights was dangerous, and a gay press was subject to persecution and suppression, a state of affairs that continued for some time.

An American gay and lesbian press did not materialize until after World War II, when conditions for the growth of a gay and lesbian community were somewhat improved. Nine issues of a newsletter called *Vice Versa* appeared in Los Angeles in 1947 and 1948. Edited and mostly written by the pseudonymous Lisa Ben (an anagram for Lesbian) and intended to provide an opportunity for lesbians to express their thoughts and feelings, *Vice Versa* featured film, music, and book reviews, occasional stories and articles, and editorials on various aspects of lesbian life.

In the 1950s, the establishment of the Mattachine Society and the Daughters of Bilitis led to the proliferation of other publications. The Mattachine Society was the most important pre-Stonewall gay organization in the United States. It was founded in Los Angeles in 1951 by Henry Hay and other radical leftists, but it was soon to evolve into a moderate, accommodationist organization. Its evolution was itself a defensive reaction to the virulent homophobia that characterized the 1950s, when homosexuals and other "deviants" were often scapegoated by the McCarthyite crusade against communism.

ONE magazine was the most provocative and most significant of the early homophile publications. Established in 1953 as a forum for gay men and lesbians to speak to one another, it outspokenly challenged the dominant views and stereotypes of homosexuals and homosexual behavior. Although formally independent of the Mattachine Society, its first editor, Dale Jennings, and most of its editorial board were members. *ONE* was especially courageous in challenging the infringement of the civil rights of homosexuals and publicizing "witch hunts" around the country. Perhaps not coincidentally, it soon found itself at the center of a major battle for homosexual civil rights. In 1954, the Los Angeles postmaster seized copies of *ONE* and refused to mail them on the grounds that the magazine was "obscene, lewd, lascivious and filthy." The seizure set the stage for a protracted court battle with significant consequences for the gay and lesbian movement. In 1956, a federal district court upheld the postmaster's action; the next year so did an appeals court, which characterized the magazine as "cheap pornography" simply because it discussed homosexuality. In January 1958, however, the United States Supreme Court unanimously reversed the findings of the lower courts. This major victory was crucial to the growth of the homophile movement. *ONE* continued publication until 1972.

In 1955, the Mattachine Society, now grown more conservative, launched its own magazine, the *Mattachine Review,* which was published by the Society's San Francisco chapter. Less confrontational than *ONE,* the *Review* tended to focus on gay history and culture and to urge a moderate rather than radical approach to civil rights issues. The *Review* was printed by a small business owned by its editors Hal Call and Don Lucas, the Pan-Graphic Press, which published other work of interest to gay and lesbian readers, including Bob Damron's *Address Book,* a directory of gay bars and meeting places that is still periodically updated and reissued. *Mattachine Review* ceased publication in 1966.

The Daughters of Bilitis, which was founded in 1955 by eight women, including Phyllis Lyon and Del Martin, launched the *Ladder* in 1956. Although closely allied with the Mattachine Society, the Daughters of Bilitis was especially attuned to the distinctive problems and particular situations of lesbians. The *Ladder* self-consciously attempted to reach out to lesbians away from the large cities and avoided an overtly political stance, concentrating instead on poetry, fiction, history, and biography. One of its most valuable features was a column by Barbara Grier entitled "Lesbiana" that contained succinct summaries of current lesbian literature. The magazine was transformed in 1968, when Grier became editor and made it into a more polemical, lesbian-feminist journal. Torn apart by the tensions between old-time moderates and new radicals, the Daughters of Bilitis dissolved in 1970, and the *Ladder* ceased publication a short time later.

These early homophile journals were published under enormously difficult conditions. The organizations that sponsored them were themselves tiny and constantly embattled, endangered from without by vicious homophobia and from within by personality conflicts and differing visions. Deprived of advertising revenues and ordinary distribution channels, these magazines were subsidized by their editors, writers, and sponsoring organizations, and they heavily depended on subscriptions and gifts from readers. Although their circulation figures remained very small (probably no more than 5,000 subscribers for *ONE* in its heyday, and many less for the others), the homophile journals nevertheless made crucial contributions toward the development of a national mass movement for gay rights. By facilitating dialogue among gay men and lesbians, these publications created a sense of minority identity, even as they also performed a crucially important educational activity. They informed their readers of gay and lesbian history and literature as well as of police raids and civil rights abuses across the country.

Gay journalism and publishing in the 1960s grew out of the early homophile organizations and publications. The Mattachine Society spread from the West Coast. A newsletter called *The Gazette* was issued by activist Frank Kameny who established the Mattachine Society of Washington, D.C. The *Eastern Mattachine Review* was also published in Washington in the mid-1960s, and SIR (the Society for Individual Rights), a San Francisco homophile organization, began *Vector,* a monthly, in 1965. Sometimes publications were associated with bars, which were one of the few places where gays and lesbians could discover information about activities pertaining to their community. The practice of bar guilds publishing or facilitating give-away publications continues to this day in many areas of the country. A marked increase in underground or alternative publications of all kinds during the 1960s, coupled with the heterosexual sexual revolution and an emerging feminism, also contributed to the creation of a climate that made possible the creation of a national gay and lesbian press.

The watershed year for gay and lesbian publishing was 1967, when *The Advocate* was founded in California and the Oscar Wilde Memorial Bookstore opened in New York City's Greenwich Village. Founded by gay activist Craig Rodwell, the Oscar Wilde Bookstore was the first bookstore (and perhaps the first business that was neither sexually nor alcoholically oriented) to cater specifically to gay men and lesbians. At first, the bookstore sold only a handful of titles, the scarcity of material exacerbated by Rodwell's refusal to stock pornography. Soon afterward, bookstores that concentrated on gay and lesbian literature opened in other cities, including San Francisco where the Walt Whitman Bookshop thrived for many years. Today, most major cities boast at least one bookstore catering to gay and lesbian readers. These bookstores tend to be community centers as well as places of business and frequently sponsor readings and other activities. Among the leading gay and lesbian bookstores are A Different Light in San Francisco, Los Angeles, and New York; Three Lives Bookstore in New York; Giovanni's Room in Philadelphia; Lambda Rising in Washington, D.C.; Glad Day Bookshop in Toronto and Boston; People Like Us Books and Unabridged Bookstore in Chicago; Liberty Books in Austin, Texas; Category Six Books in Denver; and Unicorn Bookstore in West Hollywood. Several gay and lesbian bookstores issue catalogues and conduct mail-order business, thereby reaching readers far beyond their geographic locations. Almost all large general bookstores in urban areas in most parts of the country now feature sections devoted to gay and lesbian literature, but the specialized bookstores continue to serve an important purpose in fostering a sense of community.

When established in Los Angeles in 1967, *The Advocate* was a local newspaper concentrating largely on local events and issues, such as police brutality and city council elections. It soon broadened its scope, however, and became a national newsmagazine, attempting to cover news from around the country. For many years, it was by far the most influential—if sometimes controversial—journal of gay liberation. Under the editorship of RICHARD HALL and others, its book review section was especially strong, frequently featuring interviews with important writers. Today, claiming a circulation in excess of 75,000 copies, *The Advocate* remains the gay and lesbian newsmagazine of record though its early emphasis on books has given way to a much greater emphasis on mass entertainment. Slickly designed and executed, it stresses national and international news and features. Although for many years the only advertisers it could attract were for sexually oriented products, it now advertises a wide variety of mainstream items. It continues to publish personal and classified advertisements of an explicitly sexual nature though now they are segregated into a separate publication. Having achieved an unprecedented level of journalistic respectability, *The Advocate* is now sold in shopping malls and quoted in the national media.

The Advocate's transformation from a radical, underground newspaper to a respectable, mainstream

publication is itself a kind of parable of the relative success of the gay and lesbian liberation movement and, perhaps, of its cooptation by middle-class consumerism. Gay liberation newspapers proliferated throughout the continent (and abroad) in the 1970s, most of them concentrating on local news and events and featuring sexually explicit advertising and a liberationist rather than homophile editorial stance. Practically every major city in the United States, Canada, and Western Europe spawned at least one gay liberation newspaper in the 1970s. Particularly notable because they often adopted radical or confrontational stances that countered the gradually increasing conservatism of *The Advocate* were *Gay Community News* in Boston and *The Body Politic* in Toronto, both of which are now defunct. From the West Coast, *Gay Sunshine,* founded by Winston Leyland, combined a Berkeley-style radicalism with a passion for literature. *Gay Sunshine* frequently featured in-depth interviews with gay writers and spawned publication ventures such as the *Manroot* poetry series and Gay Sunshine Press. On the East Coast, Boston's *Fag Rag* also specialized in radicalism and confrontation and published creative work by gay men, especially through its affiliated press, Good Gay Poets. Gay male poetry was also featured in *Mouth of the Dragon,* which published many of the most interesting gay poets of the 1970s. Another journal founded in the 1970s is *RFD* ("a journal for country faggots"), which gives the lie to the myth that the gay and lesbian liberation movement has been exclusively urban. *RFD* publishes a wide variety of work, including poetry, recipes, essays on gay spirituality, and news of interest to rural gay men.

Two lesbian journals founded in the 1970s also deserve note. *Lesbian Tide* began in 1973 after the *Ladder* ceased publication. It embraced the radical stance that Barbara Grier attempted to impose on the *Ladder,* but without the organizational sponsorship of the Daughters of Bilitis, which, by the early 1970s, seemed to many to be outdated. A strong lesbian-feminist slant also characterizes *Sinister Wisdom,* which was founded in Berkeley in 1976 and is still publishing. A quarterly that presents creative and analytical work from lesbians of many different backgrounds and experiences, *Sinister Wisdom* has been a very influential forum for the past two decades.

Equally influential has been *Christopher Street,* perhaps the most sophisticated of gay publications. It was founded in May 1976 in New York as a kind of gay *New Yorker.* Its early imitations of the *New Yorker* extended into featuring a large number of intelligent and often hilarious cartoons. With its glossy covers and handsome design, it reaches a large and literate audience. Specializing in fiction and essays, the magazine has published some of the leading gay and lesbian writers of our time, including especially ANDREW HOLLERAN and Quentin Crisp. It is affiliated with New York's leading gay newspaper, the *Native.*

Another innovation in gay and lesbian publishing during the 1970s was the establishment of newsletters sponsored by political, religious, and professional organizations or caucuses, and the appearance of scholarly journals devoted to the study of homosexuality. The newsletters, which number in the hundreds, were chiefly means of communication and of building solidarity around common interests. The scholarly journals, which included *Gai Saber* (1977–1978), *Gay Books Bulletin / Cabirion* (1979–1985), and *Gay Literature* (1976), were responses to the beginnings of the gay studies movement. They were attempts to provide outlets for a burgeoning scholarly interest in homosexuality at a time when established scholarly journals and presses were leery of the subject, though by the end of the decade some university presses, such as the University of Chicago Press, had declared themselves open to gay studies. The most substantial of these new journals of the 1970s, and the only one of them that survives, is the *Journal of Homosexuality,* founded by John DeCecco at San Francisco State University in 1974. Although originally heavily slanted toward the quantitative social sciences, in more recent years it has broadened its scope by including essays in the humanities, including literary studies. Published by Haworth Press, which frequently publishes special issues of the journal as separate books, the *Journal of Homosexuality* has been an important venue for the dissemination of scholarly information about homosexuality and about gay men and lesbians.

The 1970s also saw the proliferation of presses dedicated to publishing work that mainstream publishers evinced no interest in. These include many women's presses, several with a lesbian-feminist ethos. Five presses founded in the 1970s are of special interest to gay and lesbian readers. In 1973, Daughters Inc. was founded by novelist June Arnold and her lover-attorney Parke Bowman, political theorist Charlotte Bunch, and novelist BERTHA HARRIS. It published five titles annually from 1973 through 1978, including work by the founders. Also in 1973, Barbara Grier and Donna McBride, with the assistance of two backers, established the lesbian-feminist publishing house, Naiad Press. Naiad Press's first book was *Latecomer* by Sarah Aldridge (1974). Its titles include important work by JANE RULE, Sheila Ortiz Taylor, and Katherine V. Forrest. Although it is especially noted for its lesbian mysteries and romances, Naiad Press has also published nonfiction such as Rosemary Curb and

Nancy Manahan's *Lesbian Nuns: Breaking Silence* (1985) and Barbara Grier's *The Lesbian in Literature: A Bibliography* (1981). In 1977, novelist and poet Felice Picano founded SeaHorse Press in New York City, which has published work by such authors as Dennis Cooper, Martin Duberman, Brad Gooch, and Doric Wilson. Subsequently, Picano collaborated with two other small gay presses to form the Gay Presses of New York, which has published among other notable titles HARVEY FIERSTEIN's *Torch Song Trilogy* (1981) and Picano's own fictionalized memoir *Ambidextrous* (1985). Also in 1977, Sasha Alyson founded Alyson Press in Boston. Alyson has published a large list of gay and lesbian formula fiction and nonfiction, including works specifically targeted to young adults, as well as reprints of gay and lesbian classics, such as Richard Meeker's *Better Angel,* which was originally published in 1933. Alyson has recently begun a line of books for children: Alyson Wonderland.

The 1980s and 1990s have seen continued growth in gay and lesbian publishing. In *Putting Out 1991: A Publishing Resource for Lesbian & Gay Writers,* Edisol W. Dotson identified approximately 450 publishing outlets for gay and lesbian work. The acceptance of gay and lesbian writers and themes in the mainstream media is one of the most significant developments of our time. The most prominent of the openly gay journalists, RANDY SHILTS in San Francisco and Jeffrey Schmalz in New York, made gay issues the center of their reporting and writing. Shilts's *And the Band Played On* (1987) and Schmalz's AIDS reporting for *The New York Times* are landmarks in journalistic accounts of the AIDS epidemic. Other breakthrough journalists include Deb Price, whose syndicated column focusing on lesbian and gay issues appears in such newspapers as the *Detroit News*, the *San Jose Mercury,* the *Chicago Sun-Times*, and the *San Francisco Chronicle*; and David Sedaris, who appears regularly on National Public Radio's Morning Edition. Among other significant works of gay journalism must be counted Shilts's *The Mayor of Castro Street: The Life and Times of Harvey Milk* (1982) and *Conduct Unbecoming: Lesbians and Gays in the U.S. Military: Vietnam to the Persian Gulf* (1993), as well as EDMUND WHITE's *States of Desire: Travels in Gay America* (1980), Frank Browning's *The Culture of Desire: Paradox and Perversity in Gay Lives Today* (1993) and Bruce Bawer's *A Place at the Table: The Gay Individual in American Society* (1993).

Spurred on by openly gay and lesbian editors such as Bill Whitehead, Michael Denneny, and Carole DeSanti, some major publishing houses such as Crown, Dutton, and St. Martin's Press have been particularly open to gay and lesbian writers. Similarly, university presses have aggressively sought manuscripts on gay and lesbian subjects, and new scholarly journals that welcome gay and lesbian studies have proliferated, including *GLQ: A Journal of Lesbian and Gay Studies, Journal of the History of Sexuality, Genders,* and *differences: A Journal of Feminist Cultural Studies.* Professional organizations in the publishing field have also been formed. The Publishing Triangle, with a membership of more than 600, is a group of lesbian and gay men in the publishing industry; whereas the National Lesbian and Gay Journalists Association comprises twelve chapters with a combined membership in excess of 800 members. Both groups are dedicated to bringing gay and lesbian issues to the public's attention.

One phenomenon of gay and lesbian publishing in the 1980s and 1990s has been its encroachment into the American heartland. Among the significant literary journals founded in the 1980s, for example, a number were published on neither coast. *Common Lives/Lesbian Lives* began publishing in Iowa City, Iowa, in 1981; *The James White Review* was founded in Minneapolis in 1983; *The Evergreen Chronicles* in Minneapolis in 1985; and *Tribe* in Baltimore in 1987. *Tribe* and *James White Review* concentrate on gay male creative writing, whereas *Common Lives/Lesbian Lives* focuses on lesbian creative writing, and *The Evergreen Chronicles* publishes both lesbian and gay male work. Other important developments of the era include the founding of Kitchen Table/Women of Color Press by writers AUDRE LORDE, Barbara Smith, and CHERRÍE MORAGA in 1981 and the brief efflorescence of *Out/Look*, a serious quarterly that was published from San Francisco at the end of the 1980s and attempted to appeal to both lesbians and gay men and to reflect the racial and ethnic diversity of the gay and lesbian communities.

Another phenomenon of gay and lesbian publishing in the 1990s, at least on the fringes, was the emergence of the "'zines," cheaply printed, often confrontational, frequently semipornographic magazines directed toward young gay and lesbian readers. Some are produced through desktop publishing and distributed haphazardly through bookstores in urban centers. Among these 'zines are *My Comrade/Sister!, Shrimp,* and *Lavender Godzilla. Backspace,* founded in 1992 and published from Somerville, Massachusetts, describes itself as "An Alternative Zine for the Lesbian, Gay & Bisexual Community." A good example of desktop publishing, *Backspace* includes poetry, fiction, and commentary from lesbian, gay, and bisexual writers. Bar 'zines like New York's *Homo Xtra* and *Next* and Los Angeles's *Planet Homo* have achieved significant popularity.

At the other end of the publishing spectrum, glossy magazines such as *Genre*, *10 Percent*, and *Out* have recently emerged. *Genre* focuses on interests and trends important to gay men, whereas *10 Percent* and *Out* attempt to appeal to both gay men and lesbians. All three magazines target affluent consumers and feature profiles of successful and uncloseted gay men and lesbians, book reviews, and articles on fashion, travel, and politics. They attract advertisers as diverse as American Express, Absolut Vodka, Diesel Jeans, and Apple Computers. As gays and lesbians have become more visible, their buying power has also gained more notice. The new willingness of advertisers to support gay and lesbian magazines may be a tangible sign of the increased acceptability of homosexuality in American life. Another new glossy publication is also a sign of the times: *POZ*, a literate and lively magazine about life with AIDS, directed toward all people who have been affected by the epidemic, which is, in fact, just about everybody. (See also AMERICAN LITERATURE: LESBIAN, 1900–1969; AMERICAN LITERATURE: GAY MALE LITERATURE, POST-STONEWALL; AMERICAN LITERATURE: LESBIAN LITERATURE, POST-STONEWALL; and CANADIAN LITERATURE IN ENGLISH.)

—*Kenneth Pobo*

BIBLIOGRAPHY

D'Emilio, John. *Sexual Politics: Sexual Communities: The Making of a Homosexual Minority in the United States, 1940–1970.* Chicago: University of Chicago Press, 1983. ■ Faderman, Lillian. *Odd Girls & Twilight Lovers: A History of Lesbian Life in Twentieth Century America.* New York: Penguin, 1992. ■ Groff, David. "Queer Publishing: Between the Covers." *Poets & Writers* 21.3 (1993): 48–55. ■ Marcus, Eric. *Making History.* New York: HarperCollins, 1992. ■ Robert B. Marks Ridinger. "So's Your Old Lady: Naming Patterns in the Gay and Lesbian Press." *Journal of Homosexuality* 28.4 (1994). ■ Rosenkrantz, H. Glenn. "Welcome to the Gay '90s." *Washington Journalism Review* (December 1992): 31–35.

Kenny, Maurice
(*b.* 1929)

Maurice Kenny was born in upstate New York, his father a Mohawk Indian and his mother part Seneca. At the age of nine, when his parents separated, he went to live with his mother in New York City. After a flirtation with juvenile delinquency, Kenny returned to upstate New York to live with his father. As a result, Kenny identifies most strongly with his father's Mohawk heritage.

Kenny began writing poetry as a teenager. At seventeen, he discovered WALT WHITMAN and was deeply drawn to his natural language and rhythm, qualities Kenny later discovered in Native oral traditions. Kenny attended Butler University in Indiana and St. Lawrence University in New York, and he studied with Louise Bogan at New York University. He was twenty-eight when he issued his first poetry collection and did not publish again until he settled in Brooklyn in 1967.

Kenny credits his poem, "First Rule," written in the late 1960s, with leading him back to the oral traditions of his Native heritage. The incantatory quality of his poems have led some to describe them as "chants." Kenny prefers to call his works "pieces," reserving the term *chant* for works of a more ritual nature, in which "I mean certain things to take place in your heads."

Two collections, *North: Poems of Home* (1977) and *Dancing Back Strong the Nation* (1979), reflect Kenny's consciousness of his Native cultural heritage. In 1976, Kenny claimed his gay identity with the publication of "Tinselled Bucks: An Historical Study in Indian Homosexuality" and the poem "*Winkte*" in *Gay Sunshine*. Drawing on diverse sources, Kenny boldly reclaimed Native two-spirit traditions for contemporary gay Indians. Gay and Indian consciousness come together in his 1979 anthology, *Only As Far As Brooklyn*, where, as Rochelle Ratner argues, Kenny's mature and distinctive voice fully emerges. The process of reclaiming his past continued in the 1984 collection, *The Mama Poems* (for which he received an American Book Award), in which Kenny writes for the first time about his childhood and family.

In the 1980s, Kenny turned to narrative poetry. In *Blackrobe* (1982), he relates the story of a Jesuit missionary martyred by the Mohawks in 1646. In *Tekonwatonti/Molly Brant* (1992), Kenny recovers the voice of Molly Brant, sister of Mohawk Chief Joseph Brant, who married Sir William Johnson. A common trait of these characters, and of Kenny's own persona, is that they are multiply located. They are figures who cross (and often transgress) boundaries between cultures and ways of being: Indians in a white world, gay men in a heterosexual world, missionaries among Indians, and Indian women married to white men. Kenny's identification with all these positions reflects his own complex history. At the same time, his use of multiple voices creates nuanced portrayals of characters and events in which the mixed motives of both oppressors and oppressed are acknowledged. This is subjective, revisionist history, but not mythologizing and not "politically correct" rhetoric. Kenny's interest in historically grounded characters distinguishes his work from the mythico-poetics of feminist Native writers like PAULA GUNN ALLEN.

The search for the historical voice of Native people led Kenny to reevaluate the legacy of Walt Whitman. In "Whitman's Indifference to Indians," Kenny criticizes the poet's silence concerning the policies of the U.S. government toward Indians, and he concludes, "It is regrettable, tragic, a great loss that the American Indian did not prove a fit subject for Whitman's powerful poetics. . . . Sitting-Bull, Rain-in-the-face, Black Kettle, Roman Nose and their brothers and sisters await still a courageous poet to recreate their lives and deeds. . . . Perhaps their own sons and daughters will take up the pen. Whitman's indifference failed them."

Kenny has published over twenty-five collections of poetry, fiction, and essays. His work has appeared in over forty-five anthologies, magazines, and journals in several languages, and radio and film productions. In the words of Joseph Bruchac, he ranks among "the four or five significant Native American poets." He currently lives in upstate New York, where he is poet-in-residence at North Country Community College at Saranac Lake and visiting professor at Paul Smith College. (See also NATIVE NORTH AMERICAN LITERATURE.)

—*Will Roscoe*

BIBLIOGRAPHY

Bruchac, Joseph. *Survival This Way: Interviews with American Indian Poets.* Tucson: Sun Tracks/University of Arizona Press, 1987. ■ Kenny, Maurice. "Whitman's Indifference to Indians." *The Continuing Presence of Walt Whitman: The Life after the Life.* Robert K. Martin, ed. Iowa City: University of Iowa Press, 1992. ■ Ratner, Rochelle. "Brooklyn and Beyond: Maurice Kenny and the Legacy of Walt Whitman." *Poetry East* (New York), forthcoming. ■ Swann, Brian and Arnold Krupat, eds. *I Tell You Now: Autobiographical Essays by Native American Writers.* Lincoln: University of Nebraska Press, 1987, 1989.

Kerouac, Jack
(1922–1969)

Jack Kerouac, born Jean-Louis Kerouac in Lowell, Massachusetts, on March 12, 1922, was the third child of a working-class, French-Canadian family. Kerouac did not speak English until he attended parochial school at the age of six, the French-Canadian dialect Joual being his primary language. In 1926, Kerouac's older brother Gerard died of rheumatic fever. Gerard's death had a profound effect on the young Kerouac, initiating his lifelong search for the meaning of life and death, which would become the main theme of his writing. Kerouac moved to New York City in 1939, where he attended Horace Mann Prep School for a year before going on to Columbia University via a football scholarship. Leaving Columbia in 1942, Kerouac joined the merchant marines and sailed to Greenland. He then enlisted in the U.S. Navy but was discharged on psychiatric grounds. Through his first wife, Edie Parker, Kerouac met ALLEN GINSBERG and WILLIAM BURROUGHS in 1944. In 1946, Neal Cassady became involved with their group, and the nucleus of the BEAT GENERATION was created. It was with Cassady that Kerouac took to the road. They in effect created the lifestyle that would become the model for the "Beat way of life." It combined a rejection of responsibility and of what they saw as bankrupt bourgeois American culture with a search for a life-affirming spirituality. In 1950, one year after his marriage to Parker was legally annulled, Kerouac married Joan Haverty. Kerouac left Haverty after seven months when she announced her pregnancy. On February 16, 1952, Haverty gave birth to a daughter, Jan, whom Kerouac, consistent with his lifelong avoidance of responsibility, never acknowledged. He died in 1969, from complications of alcoholism.

Kerouac's misogynistic tendencies and Catholic guilt made lasting relationships with men and women impossible, as evidenced by his short-term marriages and his casual attitude toward his male lovers (among whom were Allen Ginsberg, William Burroughs, Alan Ansen, and GORE VIDAL). Kerouac's uneasiness toward his homosexuality led to his practice of omitting his own homosexual experiences from his books. For example, *The Subterraneans* (1958) alters his real-life affair with Gore Vidal into a platonic night spent in a hotel room. Despite this reticence and ambivalence, many of his early works authentically depict gay culture at a time when such portrayals were rare in popular literature.

Seen as the authentic voice of the Beat Generation, Kerouac is best known for his novel *On the Road*

(1957), which he wrote in three weeks, employing a writing method he would come to call "spontaneous prose." In 1958, in "Essentials of Spontaneous Prose," Kerouac likened his writing method to that of a jazz musician. Kerouac felt that if he relied on spontaneity and improvisation and less on revision, he would achieve a deeper connection between author and audience. This style led to an incredible output by Kerouac. Between the publication of his first novel, *The Town and the City* (1950), and *On the Road,* Kerouac wrote the manuscripts of eight novels and two future books of poetry. Kerouac envisioned his novels as one connecting story (modeled after BALZAC's *La Comedie Humaine*), which he called "Legend of Dulouz," Dulouz being the fictional name he gave himself. Although known mainly for his novels depicting Beat life, Kerouac's experimental writings (including *Visions of Cody* [1972], *Book of Dreams,* [1961], and *Old Angel Midnight,* [1959]), most of which were widely circulated in manuscript, were sources of inspiration for several writers by virtue of their inventiveness and their unique use of sound. Kerouac was also one of the first American writers to embrace Buddhism and incorporate its philosophy into his work. The Buddhist influence is especially prominent in *The Dharma Bums* (1958), *Tristessa* (1960), and *Visions of Gerard* (1963). In 1956, at the urging of Gary Snyder, Kerouac wrote his first and only published sutra, *The Scripture of the Golden Eternity* (1960).

—*Carmine Esposito*

BIBLIOGRAPHY

Charters, Ann. *Kerouac: A Biography.* New York: St. Martin, 1987. ■ Clark, Tom. *Jack Kerouac.* San Diego: Harcourt Brace Jovanovich, 1984. ■ ———. *Kerouac's Last Word: Jack Kerouac in Escapade.* Sudbury, Mass.: Water Row, 1987. ■ French, Warren. *Jack Kerouac.* Boston: Twayne Publishers, 1986. ■ Hunt, Tim. *Kerouac's Crooked Road: Development of Fiction.* Hamden, Conn.: Archon Books, 1981. ■ Jones, James T. *Map of Mexico City Blues: Jack Kerouac as Poet.* Carbondale: Southern Illinois University Press, 1992. ■ Nicosia, Gerald. *Memory Babe: A Critical Biography of Jack Kerouac.* New York: Grove Press, 1983. ■ Walsh, Joy. *Kerouac: Statement in Brown.* Clarence Center, N.Y.: Textile Bridge, 1984. ■ Weinreich, Regina. *The Spontaneous Poetics of Jack Kerouac: A Study of the Fiction.* Carbondale, Ill.: Paragon House, 1990.

Kleist, Heinrich von
(1777–1811)

Heinrich von Kleist emerges from the hands of critics and biographers as a complex and dynamic figure, at once a romantic, realist, Rousseauist, Prussian nationalist, social critic, existentialist, and more recently, modernist. During the almost ten years of his creative life, Kleist was enormously productive, writing seven plays, one uncompleted; eight novellas published in two volumes of *Erzählungen* (1810–1811); and essays on art and literature, as well as journalism and verse. His oeuvre is unfailingly paradoxical and provocative, reflecting the conflicts between individual consciousness and society, struggles often indirectly expressed in his treatment of sexual themes. Kleist's personal associations are marked by similar ambiguities: fervent though physically unconsummated attachments to several women and close, turbulent relationships with male companions.

Born in Frankfurt an der Oder, the oldest son of a Prussian army captain, Kleist survived the early death of both father (1788) and mother (1793). Entering the army at Potsdam at age fifteen, he attempted to follow the family tradition of a military career and participated in the campaign against the French Revolutionary armies in the Rhineland. Recent biographical criticism suggests that Kleist first formed gay relationships in the military, beginning lifelong associations with Ernst von Pfuel and Rühle von Lilienstern. In 1799, Kleist resigned his commission in order to study at the University of Frankfurt. He became engaged to Wilhelmine von Zenge and shortly thereafter embarked for Würzburg in search of a treatment for what appears to have been a sexual disorder. Unsuccessful in his quest, Kleist was plagued by moral and emotional upheavals, including the famous "Kant crisis," which undermined his faith in truth and knowledge and inaugurated a period of despondency and personal anguish. Shortly after breaking his engagement, he completed his first tragic drama, later entitled *Die Familie Schroffenstein (Family Schroffenstein,* 1804), and destroyed the manuscript of the drama *Robert Guiskard* (1803) while fighting against despair and a desire for death. After protracted illnesses and a complete physical breakdown, Kleist left government work to complete the play *Der Zebrochne Krug (The Broken Jug,* 1806), as well as the dramas *Amphitryon* and *Penthesilea* (1807), while also working on his novellas and later writing and editing the periodical *Phöbus* and the *Berliner Abend-*

blätter. In November 1811, he and Henriette Vogel formed a suicide pact; Kleist shot Vogel and then himself.

There is hardly a work in which Kleist did not yield to the lure of self-destruction, often through the yoking of illicit sex and death, as in the novellas *Die Verlobung in St. Domingo* (*The Engagement in St. Domingo*) and *Das Erdbeben in Chili* (*The Earthquake in Chili*). *Die Familien Schroffenstein,* a play that was criticized for its salaciousness, further explores societal ramifications of transgressive sexuality. Scenes of the grotesque and the absurd are hallmarks of Kleist's style; they throw into sharp relief the chasm between individual consciousness and an illusory world. The shocking scenes of dismemberment and cannibalism in *Penthesilea* examine more pointedly the problems of identity, placing the unisexual societies of the AMAZONS and the Greeks against a backdrop of startling brutality. With its overtones of rape and father-daughter incest, the novella *The Marquise von O . . .* adds guilt and repression to an already ambiguous moral order that marks it as characteristically Kleistian. Although Kleist has long been claimed by critics as "ahead of his time," the sexual tensions underscoring his work have yet to be adequately explored.

—*Anna Sonser*

BIBLIOGRAPHY

Angress, Ruth. "Kleist's Nation of Amazons." *Beyond the Eternal Feminine: Critical Essays on Women and German Literature.* Susan L. Cocalis and Kay Goodman, eds. Stuttgart: Heinz, 1982. 99–134. ■ Brown, H. M. *Kleist and the Tragic Ideal: A Study of Penthesilea and its Relationship to Kleist's Personal and Literary Development 1806–1808.* Bern: Lang, 1977. ■ Cixous, Hélène, and Catharine Clément. *La jeune née.* Paris: Union Générale d'Editions, 1975. ■ Maass, Joachim. *Kleist: A Biography.* Trans. Ralph Manheim. London: Secker and Warburg, 1983. ■ McGlathery, James M. *Desire's Sway: The Plays and Stories of Heinrich von Kleist.* Detroit: Wayne State University Press, 1983. ■ Prandi, Julie D. *Spirited Women Heroes: Major Female Characters in the Dramas of Goethe, Schiller and Kleist.* Bern: Lang, 1983. ■ Sembdner, Helmut, ed. *Heinrich von Kleists Lebensspuren: Dokumente und Berichte der Zeitgenossen.* Zweite, veränderte and erweiterte Auflage. Bremen: Schunemann, 1964. ■ Silz, Walter. *Heinrich von Kleist: Studies in his Works and Literary Character.* Philadelphia: University of Pennsylvania Press, 1961. ■ Wilson, Jean. *The Challenge of Belatedness: Goethe, Kleist, Hoffmannstahl.* Lanham: University Press of America, Inc., 1991. ■ Zimmermann, Hans Dieter. *Kleist, die Liebe und der Tod.* Frankfurt am Main: Athenaum, 1989.

Kramer, Larry
(*b.* 1935)

Larry Kramer was born into a well-to-do professional family in Bridgeport, Connecticut, in 1935. He completed a B.A. at Yale in 1957 and served in the army for a year after graduating. In 1958, he began a career in the entertainment industry, working first for the William Morris Agency and then for Columbia Pictures. His first professional writing was the screenplay for the 1969 movie adaptation of D. H. LAWRENCE's *Women in Love,* which he also produced and for which he received an Academy Award nomination.

Kramer gained prominence in the world of gay writing in 1978, when his novel *Faggots* was published. A scathing satire of the gay circuit in Manhattan and on Fire Island, the novel traces the life and neuroses of Fred Lemish, a middle-aged Jewish gay man looking for love in a world that only wants to have sex. The world of fast-lane gay New York becomes the real subject of the book, and Kramer's narrative focuses on the drug and alcohol abuse, the sado-masochism and the promiscuity that he sees as both typical and reprehensible. The novel met with immediate hostility from reviewers in both the gay and straight press, yet ironically went on to become a best-seller. In 1987, when the novel was reissued, politics and disease had forced many changes in the community Kramer lampooned, and both gay and straight readers were considerably more laudatory of the book.

Although *Faggots* marked an important breakthrough novel for gay publishing, Kramer himself will most likely be remembered as an AIDS activist. In 1981, he cofounded Gay Men's Health Crisis in New York, the first community-based AIDS service organization in America. Disenchanted with what he perceived to be the lethal dangers of an uncontrollable AIDS bureaucracy, he founded AIDS Coalition to Unleash Power (ACT UP) in 1988, which became and remains one of the most powerful direct action political groups in America.

Spurred by his own HIV positivity and his work in the AIDS field, Kramer wrote *The Normal Heart* in 1986, one of the first artistic responses to the AIDS crisis. The play, which established Kramer as a dramatist, received the Dramatists Guild Marton Award, the City Lights Award, the Sarah Siddons Award for the best play of the year, and a nomination for an

Olivier Award. *The Normal Heart* tells the story of Ned Weeks, an AIDS activist who defies the AIDS service establishment and preaches for an extreme response to AIDS, including sexual abstinence. Like *Faggots*, *The Normal Heart* polarized the gay community, but unlike *Faggots*, it has been universally received as a major work of art.

Kramer's most recent writings have been direct political polemics, all of which have been gathered in *Reports from the Holocaust: The Making of an AIDS Activist* (1989). He continues to produce theatrical pieces, such as "The Destiny of Me" (1992), which extends the story of Ned Weeks, and some short fiction; however, at this point, there is little doubt that he will be best remembered as the man who almost single-handedly began the gay political response to AIDS in America. (See also DRAMATIC LITERATURE: CONTEMPORARY DRAMA.)

—*Gregory W. Bredbeck*

BIBLIOGRAPHY

Bergman, David. *Gaiety Transfigured: Gay Self-Representation in American Literature*. Madison: University of Wisconsin Press, 1991. ■ Duberman, Martin. Review of *Faggots*. *The New Republic* 180.1 (January 6, 1979): 30–32. ■ Lahr, John. "Camp Tales." *The New York Times Book Review*, January 14, 1979, 39–40. ■ McCracken, Samuel. Review of *Faggots*. *Commentary* 67.1 (January 1979): 19–29.

Kuzmin, Mikhail Alekseyevich
(187?–1936)

The Russian writer Mikhail Kuzmin was initially attracted to theater and music. He developed his interest in theater early in life, attending operettas in Saratov, near Yaroslavl, where he was born. Kuzmin became a member of Nikolai Rimsky-Korsakov's music composition class at the St. Petersburg Conservatory in 1891, completing three years of the seven-year program, while also learning German and Italian. During his life, Kuzmin translated writing not only from German and Italian, but also from English, French, Greek, and Latin, including works by Apuleius, Aubrey Beardsley, LORD BYRON, and Johann Goethe, as well as 110 of WILLIAM SHAKESPEARE's sonnets and 9 of his plays.

In 1904, the homosexual Georgy Vasilevich Chicherin (1872–1936) introduced Kuzmin to *Mir iskoustva* (The World of Art), an artistic circle centered primarily on Sergei Diaghilev (1872–1929), best known for making the Ballets Russes a major influence in the European art world, and for his relationship with the dancer Vaslav Nijinsky. The group attracted Kuzmin because of its theatrical concerns, its Art Nouveau aesthetic, and its relation to Symbolism. *Mir iskoustva* also appealed to Kuzmin because of its large homosexual membership and its penchant for dandyism.

At this time, Kuzmin was often a resident at the "Tower," Vyacheslav Ivanov's apartment, the major literary center of St. Petersburg from approximately 1905 to 1907. Kuzmin's first publications appeared in 1905 in *Zelenyi sbornik* (*Green Miscellany*), including the homosexual and idealist play *Istoriia rytsaria d'Alessio* (*The History of the Knight d'Alessio*). His literary career gained noticeable momentum when the Moscow Decadent and Symbolist Valeri Bryusov (1873–1924) published twelve of Kuzmin's "Aleksandriiskie pesni" ("Alexandrian Songs") and his novel *Kril'ya* (*Wings*, 1906) in the journal *Vesy* (*The Scales*, 1904–1909). *Wings* was published separately in 1907.

Vladimir Markov claims that the Alexandrian poems constitute the first major corpus of Russian free verse to be published. They contain lush descriptions of male beauty and a steady flow of mystical, orientalist imagery reflecting the author's travels in Egypt and Italy in the mid-1890s. Dealing with love for young men, as described by various male and female narrators, the Alexandrian songs make up the last section of Kuzmin's first published collection of verse, *Seti* (*Nets*, 1908), which was compiled on Bryusov's request and which Alexander Blok (1880–1921) claimed to be in love with. *Wings* is Kuzmin's most popular prose work, having been published in numerous editions. A sympathetic depiction of gayness, the novel narrates the relationship between the adolescent Vanya and the older, urbane Larion Dmitrievich Stroop, who helps the younger man acknowledge and accept his homosexuality.

In the ten years following the initial success of *Wings*, Kuzmin wrote a number of literary and theatrical works, including the plays *Opasnaia predostorozhnost'* (*Dangerous Precaution*, 1907), complete with gender transgressions and a concluding affirmation of homosexual love, and *Venetsianskie bezumtsy* (*The Venetian Madcaps*, 1915), which, like many of Kuzmin's works, depicts a woman interfering in male–male affections. The publication of Kuzmin's essay "O prekrasnoi yasnosti" ("On Beautiful Clarity") in 1910 led many of Kuzmin's contemporaries to affiliate the author with the newly formulated poetic movement of Acmeism, which countered Symbolist obscurity with clarity, economy, and precision. Though this connection is reinforced by Kuzmin's support for Anna Akhmatova (1889–1966) and by his membership in the short-lived school of Clarism, he states in his personal writings that he saw Acmeism to be an obtuse and passing fad.

In 1910, Kuzmin met his first major love, the poet Vsevolod Knyazev. In the same year, he published *Kuranty lyubvi* (*The Carillon of Love*), a collection of poems written in the style of eighteenth-century pastorals and set to music by Kuzmin himself. Two years later, he published *Osennie ozera* (*Lakes in Autumn*), possibly the work by him that most idealizes homosexuality. Knyazev committed suicide in 1913, and Kuzmin met Yury Yurkun, also a poet, soon after. The two men lived together with Yurkun's mother, and they were joined, for a short while, by Yurkun's wife, Olga Arbenina. Kuzmin and Yurkun's relationship lasted until Kuzmin's death.

After the Communist government came to power in 1917, Kuzmin sat on the Praesidium of the Association of Artists in Petrograd, along with such authors as Blok and Vladimir Mayakovsky (1893–1930), and worked as an official translator under Maxim Gorky (1868–1936). He also helped found the daily *Zhizn iskuostva* (*The Life of Art*) in 1918 and, along with Viktor Skhlovsky (1893–1984), worked as one of its editors. He published two more collections of verse at this time, *Ekho* (*Echo,* 1921) and *Paraboly* (*Parabolas,* 1922), as well as two chapters of *Roman Wonders* (1922), which is set in the reign of Marcus Aurelius and which he felt was his finest work of prose. Ultimately, however, Kuzmin's writing fell into political disfavor, with Lev Trotsky (1879–1940) stating, in his *Literature and Revolution* (1924), that Kuzmin's books were disreputable and useless.

Kuzmin's final great work was *Forel' razbivaet led* (*The Trout Breaks the Ice,* 1929), a poem sequence in often highly imagistic and symbolic form that focuses predominantly on one man's idealized, and ultimately reciprocated, love for another. The sequence is also characterized by an economy of language, an aesthetic sensitivity, and decadent characters. When Kuzmin read sections of the sequence in his last public performance in 1928, the gate-crashing crowd of homosexuals and other supporters showered the writer with flowers. Knyazev appears in the sequence as the "stripling with a bullet through his brain," and Yurkun appears as Mister Dorian, an allusion to OSCAR WILDE's novel, *The Picture of Dorian Gray.*

Kuzmin died in 1936 of pneumonia, two years before Yurkun and many other writers were arrested under the Stalinist regime and shot. Respected by many of his contemporaries, including Blok, Mayakovsky, and Velemir Khlebnikov (1885–1922), Kuzmin's work is currently experiencing renewed attention in Russia and elsewhere. (See also RUSSIAN LITERATURE.)

—Dennis Denisoff

BIBLIOGRAPHY

Green, Michael. "Mikhail Kuzmin and the Theatre." *Russian Literature Triquarterly* 7 (1973): 243–267. ■ Kuzmin, Mikhail. *Proza.* Vladimir Markov, ed. and intro. 3 vols. Berkeley: Berkeley Slavic Specialties, 1984. ■ ———. *Selected Prose and Poetry.* Michael Green, ed. and trans. Ann Arbor: Ardis, 1979. ■ ———. *Sobranie stikhov.* John E. Malmstad and Vladimir Markov, eds. 3 vols. Munich: Fink Verlag, 1977–1978. ■ ———. *Wings, Prose and Poetry.* Neil Granoien and Michael Green, ed. and trans. Ann Arbor: Ardis, 1972. ■ Malmstad, John E. "Mixail Kuzmin. A Chronicle of His Life and Times." *Sobranie stikhov.* vol. 3. Munich: Fink Verlag, 1977–1978. 9–319. ■ Markov, Vladimir. "Poeziya Mikhaila Kuzmina." *Sobranie stikhov.* vol. 3. Munich: Fink Verlag, 1977–1978. 321–426. ■ Moreva, G. A., ed. *Mikhail Kuzmin i russkaia kultura dvatsatova veka: tezusi i materiali konferentsii 15–17 maia 1990 g.* Leningrad: Sovet no istorii mirovoi kulturi an sssr, 1990.

Larsen, Nella
(1891–1964)

Nella Larsen was born April 13, 1891, in Chicago, Illinois, to a Danish mother and a West Indian father. Throughout her life, her attitude toward the dual heritage of her racially mixed parentage shifted. After studying at Fisk University and the University of Copenhagen, she became a nurse and worked, first, at Tuskegee, Alabama, and then, New York City hospitals. She also did social work and, after a training course, became a librarian for the New York Public Library. In 1919, Larsen married Elmer S. Imes, a physicist, and they became active members of the Harlem social and intellectual elite. Meanwhile, she began to write children's literature.

In the late 1920s, she published two major novels: *Quicksand* (1928), for which she received the Harmon Foundation Bronze Award, and *Passing* (1929). A series of wounding events then occurred. She was accused of plagiarism in her short story "Sanctuary," a charge that she denied. After becoming the first African American to receive a Guggenheim fellowship, which she used to write for a year in Europe, she returned to the United States to face increased marital difficulties, a divorce (1933), and sensational press accounts of the plagiarism controversy. No further evidence of her writing exists.

During the final thirty years of her life, Larsen had a series of nursing jobs in New York City. Forgotten by the literary world, she was found dead in her apartment in 1964. Her life, which presents a pattern of continual futile attempts alternately to separate and to connect the worlds of her experience, is reflected in her fiction, which depicts characters who do the same.

In recent years, new interest has emerged in Nella Larsen's novels as a result of increased awareness of African-American women writers and of feminist criticism. The latter commentary has focused on her treatment of female sexuality and the constraints imposed on her handling of this subject by social conventions. As public, critical, and authorial silencing took place, her use of stylistic indirection often masked her thematic intent. The protagonists of her novels are characterized by an acute sense of double consciousness in their quests for selfhood. Their ambivalence regarding racial identity, class, and gender roles is pervasive. With respect to gender, Larsen depicts traditional domestic roles as constricting and the repression of sexual desire as damaging. In her novels, inhibition leads to sterile lives. Moreover, as seen in *Quicksand,* deprivation of sensual expression can lead conversely to a compensatory or reactive overdependence on sexual passion for fulfillment. This behavior ends in emotional and physical entrapment, that is, the figurative quicksand of repeated pregnancy and domestic toil. On lesbianism, Larsen is more covert. In *Passing*, the relationship between the two central women characters is presented on the surface as inexplicably mesmerizing. The diction's consistently erotic overtones, however, suggest unacknowledged repressed impulses. This novel ends in one woman's ambiguous death and questions about the culpability of the other. Complex motivation is suggested, but not clarified. The most compelling explanation is that this character's fear of her own sexual desire causes her to kill the other. In this case, denial is literally death-giving.

Nella Larsen's novels implicitly indict a society that causes alienation from self by its prejudices. Her characters are at a loss to bridge constructively their conflicting desires. That Larsen could not push her craftsmanship to less puzzling, more explicit statement is further evidence of the strangling effects of conventional fictional treatments of sexuality.

—*Dorothy H. Lee*

BIBLIOGRAPHY

Ammons, Elizabeth. "Jumping Out the Window: Nella Larsen's *Passing* and the End of an Era." *Conflicting Stories: American Women Writers at the Turn into the Twentieth Century.* New York: Oxford University Press, 1992. 183–200. ■ Bone, Robert A. *The Negro Novel in America.* Rev. ed. New Haven: Yale University Press, 1965. ■ Christian, Barbara. *Black Women Novelists: The Development of a Tradition 1892–1976.* Westport, Conn.: Greenwood Press, 1980. ■ Gayle, Addison, Jr. *The Way of the New World: The Black Novel in America.* Garden City, N.Y.: Anchor, 1975. ■ Larsen, Nella. *The Collected Fiction of Nella Larsen,* ed. Charles R. Larson. Garden City, N.Y.: Anchor/Doubleday, 1992. ■ McDowell, Deborah E. "Introduction." *Nella Larsen: "Quicksand" and "Passing."* New Brunswick: Rutgers University Press, 1986. ■ ———. "That nameless . . . shameless impulse: Sexuality in Nella Larsen's *Quicksand* and *Passing.*" *Black Feminist Criticism and Literary Theory.* Joe Weixlmann and Houston Baker, eds. Greenwood, Fla.: Penkevill, 1988. 139–167. ■ Shockley, Ann Allen. "Nella Larsen." *Afro-American Women Writers 1746–1933: An Anthology and Critical Guide.* New York: Meridian, 1989. 432–440. ■ Thornton, Hortense. "Sexism as Quagmire: Nella Larsen's *Quicksand.*" *CLA Journal* 16.3(1973): 285–301. ■ Wall, Cheryl. "Passing for What? Aspects of Identity in Nella Larsen's Novels." *Black American Literature Forum* 20 (1986): 97–111.

Latin American Literature

Any attempt to discuss a lesbian and gay heritage for Latin America must inevitably confront the problem of the impact of dominant cultures, such as those of major world centers (usually European or North American) and recognized establishment groups (typically white, middle-class, and male), on a cluster of societies that might at one time have been characterized as Third World or dependent and perhaps now could profitably be examined from the perspective of marginality. Both the medico-criminal concept of homosexuality (homosexuality defined as either an illness or a crime or as both) and the agenda whereby homosexuality is affirmed as a legitimate sexual identity (today often called queer theory, as a term to cover both gay and lesbian sensibilities) are dominant-society ideas that have only an imperfect and even a distorting applicability to Latin America. The misapplication of these concepts to Latin America especially distorts if we fail to take into account the region's enormous diversity, with its different geographies, cultures, linguistic traditions, classes, and ethnic and racial traditions. If one speaks globally about Latin America, it is difficult to avoid being superficial, and if one speaks about specific Latin American societies, there is the risk of partializing phenomena, in the sense that the range of data may not be extensive enough to allow for persuasive conclusions.

To be sure, Brazil is virtually a continent of its own, and its homoerotic traditions evince considerable complexity. Adolfo Caminha's *O Bom-Crioulo* (1895; *The Good Nigger,* but published in English with its original Portugese title) is the first Latin American novel to deal with homosexuality as a theme, whereas Aluísio Azevedo's *O cortiço* (1890; *The Tenement*) contains the first scenes of lesbian seduction and sexual acts. Caminha, while not eschewing the tragic mode of homosexuality as a psychological problem, attracts attention today for dwelling on the sincerity of the black seaman's passion and on the way in which his homoeroticism is persecuted by agents of patriarchal order: military discipline, compulsory heterosexuality, and white racism. Caminha introduces into Latin American sociocultural thought a view of homosexuality as tied to larger issues of patriarchal social order. This view continues to the present and contrasts with the North American emphasis on questions of personal identity and internal psychological processes. Notwithstanding some exceptions, from *O Bom-Crioulo* on, homoeroticism in Latin American literature is repeatedly linked to collective history. Thus, it is no coincidence that the emergence of homosexuality as a frequent subject in Latin American writing goes hand in hand with resistance to authoritarian military dictatorships that brand anything other than monogamous heterosexual procreative matrimony as a threat to the social fabric. Concomitantly, by attributing homosexual identity only to the insertee in sexual relations, these writings implicitly question the legitimacy of femininity in its various "natural" and "imitated" versions. This is one reason the carnival, with its strong (though contained) element of male-to-female cross-dressing, especially in Brazil, and transvestism in general may be more out-rageous in Latin America than it is in Europe or the United States.

Although Azevedo's *O cortiço* establishes a tradition for the recognition of lesbian sexuality in Brazil and Latin America, it is written from a masculinist point of view and depicts the seduction of a local girl by a French courtesan. Yet Azevedo is quite forthright in describing the details of lesbian passion, and the experience unleashes the young girl's blocked menstrual development in a way that is subsequently received with joy. Here, then, lesbian passion is, if only left-handedly, legitimated as a threshold experience that leads to procreative normalcy. Thanks to the agency of the foreign rouée, French sexual practices, like French culture in general, proves beneficial to native flowerings, all within a context of the harshest facts of life as economic transaction. Neither denouncing nor glorifying homosexuality, Azevedo treats lesbianism as part of the maturational process of his modest Brazilian protagonists on their way out of the tenement.

Both "homosexuality" and "gay sensibility" are improper terms to describe same-sex sexuality in Latin America to the extent that these terms describe a configuration of the social order that may correspond to British or North American society, but not to Latin American. In Latin America, homosocialism and the division between private and public life have always included opportunities for same-sex relations that do not necessarily provide for anything like the construction of a homosexual identity. The indigenous cultures of Latin America furnish traces of both ritual homosexuality and pansexual eroticism, traces of a sexuality that both complements procreative heterosexuality and resists five hundred years of an imposed Judeo-Christian sexual morality. Moreover, some of the most diverse societies in Latin America offer examples of the macho who makes it with both men and women without ever yielding an iota of his masculine persona. The figure of the *maricón* (the fag or the queer in the most stereotypic terms) is reserved exclusively for the insertee though there may well be a disjunction between the ideology of the macho insertor and the maricón insertee and what may in fact be the intimate details of their sexual practices.

Thus, Latin American culture may define homosexuality in two ways: either in terms of the Euro-American medico-criminal discourse, where any sexual commerce between individuals of the same sex makes them both homosexual or, more paradigmatically, in terms of a distinction between the insertor, who never loses his alignment with establishment masculinity, and the insertee, to whom alone a deviant sexual persona is attributed. In MANUEL PUIG's *El beso de la mujer araña* (1976; *Kiss of the Spider Woman*), it is clear that the queer is Molina. Even when Valentín has sex with Molina, there is never any question about Valentín's masculinity. Babenco's film version for the American and international audience is disconcerting because Valentín is never "gayified," even when he and Molina exchange commitments. Valentín recognizes the justice of nonheterosexuality, whereas Molina assumes Valentín's revolutionary political activism. Still, it is an unavoidable fact of Latin American fiction that the figure of the insertee, aside from any characterization as morally, emotionally, and psychologically disadvantaged, is routinely portrayed as the victim of macho exploitation, whether in terms of male rage, power politics, personal and social revenge, or opportunistic randiness. This is a point that REINALDO ARENAS makes about the concentration camps for gay men in the early years of the Castro government in Cuba. In the case of the Chilean José Donoso's *El lugar sin límites* (1966; *Hell Has No Limits*), the figure of the transvestite maricón serves only to reaffirm the masculinist code. Yet the macho who turns on the maricón is as much a victim of the social structure as the latter is, losing in the process the object of his erotic attachment. Only when the macho is challenged over his masculinity in a public fashion does there appear to be any questioning of the division of sexual roles; when the macho's preferences are challenged, the violent—and murderous—reaffirmation of the male code must take place. But until that point, the separation of the public and the private—everything is permitted, but nothing is discussed—allows for a fluid sexual satisfaction that does not gibe with the Euro-American discourse on homosexuality.

Of course, there are examples in Latin American literature of the endorsement of rigid demarcations between heterosexuality and homosexuality, with the latter looming large with any transgression of the former and affecting equally both partners in the transaction. LUIS ZAPATA is the most prominent gay writer in Mexico at the moment, but his half-dozen novels—even though they include dimensions of sexual liberation and the Latin American conflation of the personal and the political—have routinely been criticized for reproducing older European stereotypes and a typically American model of homosexual tragedy. Zapata may not subscribe to any proposition concerning the inherent wrongness of homosexuality, but many of his Mexican characters, moving in what is often alleged to be the gayest of Latin American societies, certainly do not come close to anything like erotic fulfillment. One can understand the terrible fate of characters whose sexuality collides with tyranny, as in novels set in Puig's Argentina or Arenas's Cuba, but Zapata's characters exist within the confines of relatively open and noncoercive social contracts in contemporary Mexico. Alternatively, one could argue that the passive liberalism of Mexico, which reflects the North American pattern of assimilating its uncomfortable minorities on the margins of society, provides Zapata with a model of even greater human aggression than military tyranny. The latter is so explicit as to make clear what the battle lines are, whereas the former is ambiguous enough to make it impossible to define the question in concrete terms of human rights violations. This greater tragedy emerges in Zapata's Mexican novels and in texts from similar "liberal" societies like Isaac Chocrón's Venezuela, Luis Rafael Sánchez's Puerto Rico, or João Trevisan's Brazil.

As thorny an issue as homosexual identity is, gay sensibility presents an even greater problem. There continues to be resistance in Latin America to simply making "gay" a nonbiased synonym for the negatively charged "homosexual," especially since, as a foreign-sounding word in Spanish and Portuguese, it is viewed as representative of a foreign ideology. The notion of gayness has two fundamental problems in the Latin American context. The first is that it tends to be associated with a middle class that is privileged in terms of its economic status, its professionalism, and its opportunities to consume foreign culture—either in the original or in translation—and to travel abroad in order to assimilate an international style. This association of gayness with middle-class privilege is evident in Jaime Humberto Hermosillo's 1984 film, now virtually a gay classic, *Doña Herlinda y su hijo* (*Doña Herlinda and Her Son*); it is the only Latin American film, discounting Babenco's English-language *Kiss of the Spider Woman,* to be included in the revised edition of Vito Russo's *The Celluloid Closet.* The film is a brilliant utopian vision of the restructuring of the patriarchal family, whereby bisexuality allows a young doctor to have both a wife (herself a professional) and a child by her and to have his male lover, all of them living happily ever after together, literally, with his mother in a house that she has built for them.

The displacement of a rigid heterosexist patriarchal order by a more open matriarchal one is undoubtedly meaningful for Mexican and Latin American audiences, particularly since the resistant matriarchy in the private sphere has traditionally been accommodating toward gayness, even when the matriarchy is also complicitous with the patriarchy in wanting sons to produce grandsons, as Doña Herlinda clearly also desires. But Doña Herlinda is a well-to-do widow, and her son belongs to one of the most prestigious and well-paying professions in his society; there is little fear that the insulated cocoon they inhabit—surrounded by the international trappings of their class and behind the protective walls, hedges, and grills of their estate—will ever be disturbed by the police who harass less advantaged gays in the public spaces that are all they can afford to inhabit. Part of the meaning of Hermosillo's film for Mexicans is that it is set in Guadalajara, not only one of Mexico's most traditionally Catholic cities (the opening shot is of the 450-year-old cathedral) but also one where homoeroticism is very much on display and frequently and vigorously repressed, at least in its many public manifestations. Several major gay novels like Brazil's *Nivaldo e Jerônimo* (1981) by Darcy Penteado, Mexico's *En jirones* (1985; *In Tatters*) by Zapata or *Utopía gay* (1983; *Gay Utopia*) by José Rafael Calva, Argentina's *La otra mejilla* (1986; *The Other Cheek*) by Oscar Hermes Villordo, or Venezuela's *Toda una dama* (1988; *A Real Lady*) by Isaac Chocrón all involve members of the middle class, especially professionals, who are able to construct their lives in accordance with international models. Indeed, these characters view both their conflict with their society and their opportunities for an alternate sensibility as the consequence of their access to extranational perspectives. The point is not that there is somehow something amiss with these texts, but that they must be read with an awareness of their participation in the controversies of national versus international culture in Latin American artistic and critical circles.

The second problem associated with a gay identity as it has been promulgated within Euro-American culture is the danger of indiscriminately including homoerotic practices among social groups excluded from the Euro-American model. In the United States, the pursuit of marginalized identities has resulted in the recovery of a submerged homoeroticism in some Native American societies (whether tagged as berdache clans, ritual practices, or quotidian behavior) and an interest in exploring similar phenomena in other marginalized groups. For example, CHERRÍE MORAGA, in both her play *Giving Up the Ghost* (1986) and in her personal ethnic memoir *Loving in the War Years* (1983), discriminates between what she sees as a destructive lesbianism in Anglo society (because it allegedly duplicates macho stereotypes) and a productive lesbianism in Chicano society (where the Hispanic emphasis on the dignity and sensitivity of interpersonal relations counters the violence of the Anglo world). She affirms a strong and vibrant lesbian continuum in Hispanic culture that affords her a way of coming to terms with her own personhood. Terri de la Peña's novel *Margins* (1992) details a similar pattern. Indeed, one of the sustaining themes of anthologies of Chicana lesbianism like *Compañeras; Latina Lesbians (an Anthology)* (1987), *Chicano Lesbians: The Girls Our Mothers Warned Us About* (1991), and the Chicana material in *The Bridge Called My Back: Writings by Radical Women of Color* (1981, of which Cherríe Moraga is the first editor) is the coordination of Chicana-Latina culture and a profoundly spiritual lesbian identity that is disconsonant with white, middle-class, leisure-society images.

The existence, and the sustained survival, of a homoerotics among large segments of the socially disadvantaged, or at least among those who only sporadically accede to positions of public privilege, may have escaped recognition because this homoerotics cannot be captured within the parameters of an internationalist gay sensibility. Carlos Monsiváis's magnificent cultural critiques have underscored the deep homoeroticism of the poets of the internationalist Contemporáneos group in Mexico (late 1920s to mid-1940s), but have also delved into a wide array of popular culture practices that can be said to be marked by alternate sexuality, including homoerotics. Manuel Puig was also interested in sexual modalities among subordinate groups, among individuals who did not recognize themselves as homosexuals not because they denied their "true nature," but because what their society called homosexuality or a gay sensibility failed to match the business of their lives. This was one of the reasons that Puig on several occasions energetically repudiated any validity for the concept of homosexuality. His first—and for many his best—novel, *La traición de Rita Hayworth* (1968; *Betrayed by Rita Hayworth*), establishes a pattern of interest in erotic feelings and practices that match poorly both the medico-criminal concept of homosexuality and the politics of gay identity. Puig pursued this pattern throughout his career. His last novel, *Cae la noche tropical* (1988; *Tropical Night Falling*), although superficially dealing with marginalized older women, may be read as a homoerotic text where gender roles have yet to be carefully distributed. Many working-class men populate the pages of Puig's novels, with their machismo tinged with emotions and experiences that do not conform to the conventional stereotypes of the heterosexual Latin lover. The same is also true of novels by Mexico's José Joaquín Blanco, the narrative essays by Brazil's Glauco Mattoso (one of which also has a comic book version), and the social anthropological narratives of Néstor Perlongher, an Argentine working in Brazil. There has yet to be an adequate analysis of homoeroticism among the socially marginal figures in the Cuban Severo Sarduy's fiction, especially texts like *Cobra* (1972), *Maitreya* (1978), and *Colibrí* (1984), and one suspects that this is so because they cannot be dealt with conveniently by the models of an internationalist gay sensibility. Moreover, discussions of Sarduy's poetry always seem to stop short of his remarkably explicit homoerotic writing in *El Cristo de la rue Jacob* (1987; *The Christ of the Rue Jacob*) and *Un testigo fugaz y disfrazado* (1985; *A Fleeting and Masked Witness*). Similarly, criticism on JOSÉ LEZAMA LIMA's dense novel *Paradiso* (1966) has been unable to decide definitively as to the presence of homoeroticism in the text, a question whose interest is compounded by the fact that the novel was published in Cuba at a time when those accused of homosexuality suffered draconian persecutions. Virgilio Piñera's expressionist-surrealist narratives have also been resistant to transparent gay readings though Piñera was himself a victim of Cuba's revolutionary morality.

A gay sensibility or gay aesthetic may be detected in several prominent Latin American writers, even when homosexual themes are not present. These writers, whose texts do, of course, sometimes incorporate explicitly homosexual themes, include, in addition to Puig and Sarduy, the following: Brazil's Aguinaldo Silva, João Trevisan, and Silviano Santiago; Colombia's Fernando Vallejo and Gustavo Alvarez Gardeazábal; Mexico's Luis González del Alba; Puerto Rico's Luis Rafael Sánchez; and Argentina's Juan José Hernández. Yet there has been nothing like a systematic critical exploration of the topic, in part, one hypothesizes, because of the absence of adequate models that take into account the general configurations of Latin American society and the specific circumstances of individual national cultures. Such circumstances include, for example, the crossed paternity of Puerto Rico, caught between the U.S. and Hispanic social practices; the particular structural violence that characterizes life in Colombia for Alvarez Gardeazábal (and also for his acclaimed compatriot, Gabriel García Márquez, who has attained fame and fortune without ever having so much as hinted at a homoerotic dimension in his narrative world); the repression of the social outcasts and the uncontained urban specter in Blanco's Mexico City. In most of these writers, the personal is correlated with the political, and questions of sexual politics are inevitably related to larger issues of social construction. Such relationships are emphatically evident in Alvarez Gardeazábal's novel *El divino* (1986; *The Divine One*), in which a favorably portrayed gay man is also a drug trafficker. Any minimally satisfactory critical exegesis of this novel must work through the challenging correlations the author establishes, beginning with the questions of whether the character's homoeroti-cism is compromised by what is usually understood as a criminal activity or whether the depictions of both homoeroticism and drug trafficking are indicative of the author's revised interpretation of what is "good" and "bad" in Colombian society.

Lesbian culture in Latin America is different from gay male culture and also from North American lesbian culture though it bears some similarity to the lesbianism to be observed among marginalized women of color in the United States. As in the case of male homosexuality, a distinction must be made between international cultural models and models peculiar to each society. Sylvia Molloy is the author of one of the only two Latin American lesbian novels to be translated into English, *En breve cárcel* (1981; published in English as *Certificate of Absence*). Molloy, a Paris-educated Argentine who has been a professor at several ivy league universities in the United States and currently holds an Albert Schweitzer chair at New York University, has written a novel in which lesbianism and First World feminism intersect. The protagonist's background is Argentine, but her experiences are set in France and the United States and her recording of them reflects the private struggle of the writer to find an authentic self-expression. Clearly, these factors are all privileged, white, middle-class dimensions that make the novel immediately accessible to foreign readers. In contrast is the performance theater of Mexico City's Jesusa Rodríguez, where the limited-access space of a private bar (Teatro La Capilla/Bar El Hábito, which experiences repeated police harassment), the lack of published texts, and the enactment of female proletarian subjectivities, as well as the distaste that her work has provoked among more establishment feminists, all point to a lesbian framing that escapes customary international definitions, even when it may be coextensive with the Chicana-Latina lesbian identity described earlier.

Lesbian writing remains very much a minority voice in Latin America even though published writing by women, including lost and forgotten texts, has increased dramatically in the past two decades. One suspects that a combination of factors account for the paucity of lesbian publications, including a reluctance, in the face of opposition to feminist writing in general, to use literature as a vehicle for lesbian issues. The apparent silence of lesbian voices may, however, be more apparent than real and may involve a serious matter of critical optics, whereby it has not yet been possible for us to see a sustained lesbian tradition among women writers. Octavio Paz's book on the seventeenth-century Mexican nun Sor Juana Inés de la Cruz, for example, is profoundly ambiguous and ultimately contradictory in its handling of the poems

Sor Juana addressed to one of her patronesses, the Marquesa de La Laguina. At times Paz recognizes homoerotic sentiments, whereas at other moments he seems to dismiss such details as part of the conventional amatory rhetoric of the period. This ambiguous response parallels the division in Shakespearean criticism concerning the love sonnets addressed to a young man. Yet, it is now generally agreed, supported by research in the area of lesbian nuns, that Sor Juana's poetry must be taken as the point of departure for a lesbian literary tradition in Mexico and Latin America, both in terms of the tenor of much of her writing, which is now enthusiastically endorsed as central to a Hispanic feminist descendence, and in terms of her personal biography, despite all the shadowy factual areas that render it so perplexing.

But if Sor Juana is a lesbian foremother for Mexican writers, it will require much intensive literary historiography and some powerful analytical models to fill in the gaps between her death in 1695 and the publication of the first lesbian novel in Mexico, Rosamaría Roffiel's *Amora* (1989). Roffiel had already written some excellent homoerotic poetry before the publication of *Amora,* joining the ranks of such figures as Sabina Berman in affirming poetry as a privileged space of lesbian expression. But as a narrative *Amora* allows for a full play of social concerns in the way in which it introduces intersecting lines between a generalized feminism that resists the overwhelming machismo of Mexican patriarchal society and a specifically lesbian sensibility that characterizes the intimacies between women who are brought together because of their shared sense of marginalization, repression, and oppression. One could argue that Roffiel reenacts in Spanish and in a narrative framework a dominant-society perspective like ADRIENNE RICH's notion of a lesbian continuum. Roffiel's stance may be the result of the urban internationalization of Mexico City or it may be part of a postmodern position that must necessarily transcend local ideologies, whether those of Mexican machismo or those of Mexican *marianismo* (woman's compulsory adherence to demure sacrifice as modeled by the Virgin Mary).

Sara Levi Calderón's *Dos mujeres* (1990; published in English as *The Two Mujeres* [that is, Women]) is quite a different story, beginning with the added dimension of the Jewish minority status in Mexico City and the fact that the author uses a pseudonym, in order, one suspects, to protect the honor of her family. *Dos mujeres* is a novel of feminine rage in the face of a constellation of abusive forces that engage in every strategy possible to coerce—physically and psychologically—the protagonist into sub-

mission and subservience. Not surprisingly, and as part of an imperative to break with the (essentially gay male) prototype of homosexual tragedy, Levi Calderón's novel is a chronicle of triumphant liberation; however, the cost is a tremendous one, as successive layers of conventional feminine identity are stripped away. The protagonist loses her identity as a good Jewish daughter, her identity as a loyal wife, her identity as an omnipresent soothing mother, and her overall identity as a dedicated guardian of the patriarchal order. Moreover, she violates the stern imperative to uphold a social pact of exemplary respectability in order not to occasion *shande far di goyim* (shame in front of non-Jews). Levi Calderón's novel is, of course, the occasion for multiple levels of shame in its rewriting of the social text, for a sense of shame and outrage is essential to the lesbian critique of an implacable heterosexist order. *Dos mujeres* reinterprets the matriarchal model, both in terms of Jewish culture, as epitomized by the Sarah of the Tanakh on whom the author slyly bases her pseudonym, and in terms of the Guadalupan myth, the figure of the mother as the servant of Mexico's patron saint, the Virgin of Guadalupe. The immigrant daughter's rejection of Guadalupan motherhood is as scandalous as her separation from traditional Jewish family life, a conjunction of elements that has ensured the novel an important place in contemporary Mexican fiction—much to the consternation of heterosexist feminists whose affinities lie within a Christian Mexican tradition that Levi Calderón appears to spurn. The reaction of heterosexist feminists to *Dos mujeres* may explain why Mexico's most important contemporary woman writer, Elena Poniatowska, herself an immigrant daughter, has studiously avoided any lesbian resonances in her own impressive oeuvre. It may, however, be possible to deploy a reading strategy by which the female protagonist of the documentary narrative *Hasta no verte, Jesús mío* (1969; *Until We Meet Again*) transcends patriarchal authority and her relationship with the author-narrator becomes sexually problematical in ways that challenge heterosexist feminist interpretations.

When dealing with Latin American literature, one needs to seek out homoeroticism in areas not immediately apparent when reading either as a foreigner or as a Latin American inscribed within a patriarchal order that denies the possibility of public discourse about alternate sexuality. One must look for materials that escape privileged generic or conceptual categories. In Mexico, for example, this means attention to the song lyrics of Chavela Vargas, texts that are really quite stunning in their unabashed lesbian positioning, including a same-sex marking in the narrator—narratee relationship that is unique in female-voiced compositions in Hispanic society, where for either male or female singers a potentially homoerotic relationship (as in the ballads of FEDERICO GARCÍA LORCA or the love songs of the Mexican gay popular singer Juan Gabriel) requires either conventionally distributed sex roles or, at best, common gender ambiguities. The children's songs of Argentina's María Elena Walsh and her fiction addressed to children probably cannot be demonstrated categorically to be marked by a lesbian consciousness. But there must be some point to be made about a woman publicly identified as a lesbian who devotes virtually the bulk of her creative writing to the production of literature for children. One of Walsh's songs is the leitmotif for Luis Puenzo's Academy Award winning *The Official Story* (1985), a movie about women's consciousness and feminist solidarity in the face of a masculinist military dictatorship, concentrated in the figure of a little girl who is the tragic victim of an anarchy provoked not by rebellious women but by tyrannical men.

Finally, one needs to examine even the commercially motivated popular art of someone like the Brazilian novelist Cassandra Rios. Her novels may be unabashedly written to be read on the beach during the lazy days of summer, but their audacious sexual transgressions, including nonchalant lesbianism, are as much indexes of shifting erotic sensibilities as they are of the commercial advantages associated with the exotic and outrageous behavior of her socioeconomically privileged characters. Rios surely sells the bulk of her novels to bored philistines who enjoy the jolts of deviant sexuality that her unmistakable potboilers provide. But the very fact that middle-class popular culture texts in Brazil are transgressive in a way that is not true in the United States cannot be overlooked. Such texts may offer a potentially productive opportunity to articulate a lesbian identity within the popular culture enjoyed by the dominant social classes.

Concluding comments regarding possible avenues of future research on lesbian and gay motifs in Latin America follow clearly from what has been discussed up to this point. On the one hand, there is the need to recognize that a way of talking about homosexuality as illness and crime has been incorporated into Latin American social consciousness as a consequence of international influences. The same is true of the concept of gay sensibility. Yet both gay male and lesbian issues and identities in Latin America not only reflect the parameters of the internationalizing Euro-American models but also manifest a unique Latin American experience, including the remnants of pre-Hispanic homoeroticism. Perhaps the most abiding and cohesive characteristic of Latin American homoerotics,

one that crosses gender and ideological lines, is the imperative to make the personal political.

—*David William Foster*

BIBLIOGRAPHY

Acevedo, Zelmar. *Homosexualidad: hacia la destrucción de los mitos.* Buenos Aires: Ediciones del Ser, 1985. ■ Almaguer, Tomás. "Chicano Men: A Cartography of Homosexual Identity and Behavior." *différences* 3.2 (Summer 1991): 75–100. ■ Bruce-Novoa, Juan. "Homosexuality and the Chicano Novel." *Confluencia; revista hispánica de cultura y literatura* 2.1 (1986): 69–87. Also in *European Perspectives on Hispanic Literature of the United States.* Genvieve Fabre, ed. Houston: Arte Público Press, 1988. 98–106. ■ *Chicana Lesbians: The Girls Our Mothers Warned Us about.* Carla Trujillo, ed. San Francisco: Aunt Lute Books, 1991. ■ *Compañeras: Latina Lesbians (an Anthology).* Juanita Ramos, ed. New York: Latina Lesbian History Project, 1987. ■ Foster, David William. *Gay and Lesbian Themes in Latin American Literature.* Austin: University of Texas Press, 1991. ■ Fry, Peter. "Da hierarquia á igualdade: a construção histórica da homossexualidade." *Para inglês ver; identidade e política na cultura brasileira.* Rio de Janeiro: Zahar, 1982. 87–115. ■ ———. "Léonie, Pompinha, Amaro e Aleixo, prostituição, homossexualidade e raça em dois romances naturalistas." *Caminhos cruzados; linguagem, antropncias naturais.* São Paulo, 1982. 33–51. ■ Howes, Robert. "The Literature of Outsiders: the Literature of the Gay Community in Latin America." *Latin American Masses and Minorities: Their Images and Realities.* Dan C. Hazen, ed. SALALM no. 30. Madison: SALALM Secretariat, Memorial Library, University of Wisconsin, 1985. 1:288–304; 580–591. ■ Jáuregui, Carlos Luis. *La homosexual-idad en la Argentina.* Buenos Aires: Ediciones Tarso, 1978. ■ Jockl, Alejandro. *Ahora, los gay.* Buenos Aires: Ediciones de la Pluma, 1984. ■ Leyland, Winston, ed. *My Deep Dark Pain Is Love; a Collection of Latin American Gay Fiction.* San Francisco: Gay Sunshine Press, 1983. ■ ———. *Now the Volcano; an Anthology of Latin American Gay Literature.* Trans. by Erskine Lane, Franklin D. Blanton, and Simon Karlinsky. San Francisco: Gay Sunshine Press, 1979. ■ Lumsden, Ian. *Homosexualidad: sociedad y estado en México.* México, D.F.: Solediciones; Toronto: Canadian Gay Archives, 1991. ■ Moraga, Cherríe. *Loving in the War Years: lo que nunca pasó por sus labios.* Boston: South End, 1983. ■ Mott, Luiz. *Escravidáo, homossexualidade e demonologia.* São Paulo: Icone, 1988. ■ Murray, Stephen O., ed. *Male Homosexuality in Central and South America.* San Francisco: Instituto Obregón; New York: GAU-NY, 1987. ■ Parker, Richard G. *Bodies, Pleasures, and Passions; Sexual Culture in Contemporary Brazil.* Boston: Beacon Press, 1990. ■ Paz, Octavio. *Sor Juana Inés de la Cruz o las trampas de la fe.* México, D.F.: Fondo de Cultura Económica, 1982. ■ Schaefer-Rodríguez, Claudia. "The Power of Subversive Imagination: Homosexual Utopian Discourse in Contemporary Mexican Literature." *Latin American Literary Review* 33 (1989): 29–41. ■ Schwartz, Kessel. "Homosexuality as a Theme in Representative Contemporary Spanish American Novels." *Kentucky Romance Quarterly* 22 (1975): 247–257. ■ *This Bridge Called My Back: Writings by Radical Women of Color.* Cherríe Moraga and Gloria Anzaldúa, eds. New York: Kitchen Table: Women of Color Press, 1981. ■ Trevisan, João S. *Perverts in Paradise.* Trans. Martin Foreman. London: GMP Publications, 1986. Originally published as *Devassos no paraíso* (1986). ■ Young, Allen. *Gays under the Cuban Revolution.* San Francisco: Grey Fox Press, 1981.

LATINA/O LITERATURE

Latina Literature

Latina lesbian literature is a fast-growing, vibrant literary tradition with a diversity that resists easy classification. Until the mid-1980s, the relative shortage of publications by and about Latina lesbians made it difficult to delineate a specific body of texts and a single set of shared characteristics that could be defined as "Latina lesbian." The many cultures, colors, immigration patterns, and languages included under the umbrella term "Latina" indicate a multiplicity that makes attempts to describe this field even more problematic. Yet this variety, coupled with the highly political challenges to restrictive descriptions of sexuality found in late-twentieth-century Latina lesbian writings, gives this emergent body of literature a complexity and a visionary perspective that significantly enrich twentieth-century U.S. literature. In addition to expanding conventional literary genres and redefining previously established conceptions of lesbian identity, Latina lesbian literature offers readers innovative models for creating alliances among diverse peoples.

Before the 1980s, Latina writing of any type received little critical attention, and the homophobia in academic and Latino communities made it even less likely that Latina writings with explicit lesbian content would be published, taught, or explored in literary scholarship. Because sexuality has been seen as one of the most taboo topics in Latino discourse, the Latina writer who breaks this culturally imposed silence generally has been condemned for violating her community's mores. Consequently, many Latina lesbians felt compelled to choose between their sexual and cultural identities, and those writers who identified publicly as lesbian often did so outside their ethnic communities. However, the widespread acceptance of openly lesbian writings by GLORIA ANZALDÚA and CHERRÍE MORAGA, in conjunction with a growing lesbian, gay, and feminist readership, has reduced this need for self-imposed secrecy. By the late 1980s, a number of writers had begun including explorations of Latina same-sex desire into their works. Sheila Ortiz Taylor's publishing career illustrates this recent shift. Designed and marketed to appeal to a main-stream lesbian audience, her first two novels, *Faultline* (1982) and *Spring Forward, Fall Back* (1985), contain no overt references to Chicana cultures or identities. Yet in *Southbound, Faultline*'s 1990 sequel, Taylor explores her Chicana protagonist's ethnic heritage.

As Taylor's increased willingness to incorporate representations of Chicana lesbian identity into her work implies, U.S. Latina lesbian literature has made remarkable progress since the mid-1980s. Although it is premature to offer definitive descriptions, several general trends can be said to characterize this emergent literary field: the use of autobiographical material to construct complex identities; the production of hybrid texts that challenge conventional literary genres; the analysis of interlocking forms of oppression; a bisexual inflection; and the development of alliances between people of diverse sexualities, cultures, genders, and classes. As an increasing number of Latina lesbians reject culturally imposed sanctions and attempt to synthesize their sexuality with their ethnic identities, they often engage in a twofold self-naming process that combines political critique with the invention of empowering individual and collective self-definitions. By integrating their personal experiences into their poetry, fiction, and prose, they create multilayered texts that explore a diverse range of interconnected issues.

The two earliest anthologies of Latina lesbian writings, Juanita Ramos's 1987 *Compañeras: Latina Lesbians* and Carla Trujillo's 1991 *Chicana Lesbians: The Girls Our Mothers Warned Us About,* illustrate the linguistic, thematic, and cultural diversity characterizing this literature. *Compañeras* contains a wide range of genres—including oral histories, coming out narratives, letters, journal entries, poetry, interviews, stories, and art work—by forty-seven Latinas of Puerto Rican, Mexican, Cuban, Chilean, Honduran, Brazilian, Columbian, Argentinian, Peruvian, and Nicaraguan descent. *Chicana Lesbians* encompasses a similar variety. Composed of theoretical and creative writings and art work by twenty-four Chicanas, this collection indicates the many differences in class, region, education, color, and language found even within a particular subgroup of Latina lesbian literature. These bilingual anthologies include a number of distinctive styles and topics, ranging from fictional explorations of interracial relationships, to stringent critiques of sexism and homophobia in Latino and dominant U.S. cultures, to playful, erotic celebrations of women's same-sex desire.

As writings by Gloria Anzaldúa and Cherríe Moraga indicate, this diversity characterizes single-authored Latina lesbian texts as well. In *Borderlands/La Frontera: The New Mestiza* (1987), a hybrid collection of poetry, essays, and personal narrative, Anzaldúa transgresses conventional literary genres and creates cultural autobiography. She combines personal experience with history and revisionist myth to construct self-affirmative individual and collective identities. Even her linguistic style, or "code switching,"—her transitions from standard to working-class English to Chicano Spanish to Tex-Mex to Nahuatl-Aztec furthers this attempt to integrate personal and communal self-definition. Like many of the writers in *Compañeras* and *Chicana Lesbians,* Anzaldúa constructs a highly affirmative identity in the context of multiple forms of oppression. By interweaving accounts of the racism, sexism, and classism she experienced growing up in south Texas with historical and mythic analyses of the successive Aztec and Spanish conquests of indigenous gynecentric Indian tribes, she simultaneously reclaims her political, cultural, and spiritual Mexican and Nahuatl roots and constructs a mestizaje identity, a new concept of personhood that synergistically combines apparently contradictory Euro-American and indigenous traditions. Similarly, in *Prieta* (1994), Anzaldúa defies Western literary conventions and creates a short story cycle that blends autobiography, allegory, fiction, and myth with realistic Tex-Mex dialogue, settings, and characters.

Like *Borderlands/La Frontera,* Moraga's *Loving in the War Years* (1983) and *The Last Generation* (1993) could be described as cultural autobiographies, for Moraga unites autobiographical narrative with history and social protest with self-definition to develop empowering individual and collective identities. Like Anzaldúa and many other self-identified Latina lesbians, she explores a wide range of issues, including indigenous spiritualities; the dilemmas of light-skinned, biracial people; conventional gender roles; U.S. imperialism; the sexism and racism within Latino communities; and lesbian sexualities. However, whereas Anzaldúa depicts her sexuality as a conscious choice and the ultimate rebellion against her ethnic community's restrictive mores, Moraga does not. Instead, she simultaneously naturalizes her same-sex desire and associates it with her decision to adopt a politicized Chicana identity. In her work, lesbianism becomes the vehicle enabling her to overcome her light-skin privileges and comprehend the oppression experienced by dark-skinned peoples of all ethnic backgrounds.

As these distinctions between Moraga's and Anzaldúa's self-definitions suggest, representations of Latina lesbian identity, like Latina lesbian literature itself, resist simplistic classification. Even the use of culturally specific same-sex images takes a variety of forms, including a bisexual inflection, or an oscillation between homosexual and heterosexual representations that destabilizes the binary system structuring sex-gender categories. For example, *Singing Softly/Cantando Bajito* (1989), the first novel by self-identified Puerto Rican lesbian Carmen de Monteflores, does not explore explicitly lesbian issues or portray lesbian-identified characters. However, de Monteflores's depiction of female friendships provocatively undermines the assumed "naturalness" of the heterosexual relationships she describes. Similarly, Amalia's ambivalent attraction to Marisa in Moraga's 1986 two-act play, *Giving Up the Ghost,* and Anzaldúa's depiction of Prieta's heterosexual relationship with a Latino, as well as her sexualized attraction to a gay Anglo male, in *Prieta* challenge the (apparent) permanence and stability of the dichotomy between heterosexuality and homosexuality. This bisexual inflection also occurs in apparently nonlesbian texts, like those by Denise Chávez and Ana Castillo. Although these Latina writers do not identify as lesbian, the representations of female desire in Chávez's *The Last of the Menu Girls* (1986) and in Castillo's *The Mixquiahuala Letters* (1986) and *Sapagonia* (1990), as well as the latter's publications in *Chicana Lesbians,* complicate facile definitions of Latina lesbian literature.

Unlike many Euro-American lesbian texts, which focus almost exclusively on the construction of gendered, sexualized identities, Latina lesbian texts generally depict sexuality and gender as aspects of multifaceted identities that, depending on the particular writer, also include ethnicity, color, class, language, and cultural and religious traditions. In *The Margarita Poems* (1987), for instance, Luz María Umpierre combines literary and regional allusions to Puerto Rico with sexually explicit language and highly erotic imagery to simultaneously affirm and construct her identity as a Latina lesbian, a Puerto Rican, and a woman. Throughout the nine Spanish and English poems in this volume, she associates her desire for an Amazonian island homeland and her quest for "Julia"—who represents, among other things, Julia de Burgos, one of Puerto Rico's most famous poets—

with her search for a new Latina lesbian identity. Terri de la Peña employs similar strategies in her mainstream fiction. Like Umpierre and Moraga, she associates lesbianism with the adoption of an ethnic-specific identity. In "La Maya" (1989) and *Margins* (1992), for example, she downplays the homophobia and heterosexism found in many Latino communities and emphasizes the parallels between her Chicana protagonists' quests for their Mexican-Indian spiritual and cultural heritage and their sexual relationships with dark-skinned Chicanas or Mexicanas. Although Anzaldúa is more critical of Latino restrictions against same-sex desire, she too associates her sexuality with her cultural background. In both her creative and theoretical writings, she rejects the ethnocentrism implied by the words *lesbian* and *homosexual* and adopts culturally specific terms like "mita' y mita'" ("half and half") to describe her sexual preference. By acknowledging the terms' derogatory implications, she simultaneously challenges conventional Eurocentric sexual and gender categories and exposes Mexican Americans' heterosexism, homophobia, and sexism.

By associating physical desire with the desire to reclaim their cultural roots, self-identified Latina lesbian writers expand conventional Western notions of lesbian identity in three ways. First, by identifying their sexuality with non-Western cultural traditions, they counter the commonly held Latino belief that Latinas' same-sex desire indicates ethnic betrayal or assimilation into the dominant Anglo culture. Second, their simultaneous focus on sexuality and ethnicity complicates conventional Eurocentric descriptions of lesbian identity formation, thus providing an important corrective to the monolithic images of lesbian identity found in much twentieth-century Euro-American lesbian literature. Third, this dual focus on sexual and ethnic identities indicates Latina lesbians' ability to make complex negotiations between two or more apparently disparate communities.

Juanita Ramos's coming out narrative, "Bayamón, Brooklyn y yo" (1987), provides a striking example of this mediational complexity. Whereas the majority of Euro-American coming out stories focus primarily on the growing acceptance of a stigmatized sexual identity, Ramos associates coming out as a lesbian with coming out as a Puerto Rican. As she describes her attempts to synthesize her sexual, ethnic, and gender identities, she explores a diverse set of issues—including her desire to create self-empowering communities of women; her bicultural ambivalence and struggles against U.S. racism and color prejudice; her alienation from the homophobic radical left Puerto Rican liberation movement; and the subsequent diffi-culties she experienced in attempting to integrate her lesbianism with her political activism. Ramos's ability to shift between "mainstream" lesbian-feminist groups, specific Latino political and familial communities, and the dominant North American culture gives her work a visionary, ethical perspective most readily seen in her urgent call for mestizaje coalitions that work to end all forms of oppression.

As Ramos's narrative indicates, self-identified Latina lesbians' willingness to acknowledge their own complexity allows them to develop alliances among people from diverse groups. Indeed, the cross-cultural communities Ramos and others create represent one of Latina lesbian literature's most notable contributions to contemporary literature. *This Bridge Called My Back*—the groundbreaking 1981 anthology of writings by self-identified radical women of color edited by Anzaldúa and Moraga—illustrates the importance of this mediational role. By compelling feminists of all genders, sexualities, and ethnic backgrounds to participate in the formation of a more inclusive feminist movement, this anthology has significantly altered U.S. feminist theory.

Anzaldúa's *Making Face, Making Soul: Haciendo Caras* indicates a further extension of this desire to create alliances and dialogues among diverse peoples. In this 1990 anthology of creative and theoretical pieces by self-identified women of color, Anzaldúa attempts to develop coalitions between nonacademic and academic social activists. In the preface, she rejects the inaccessible, elitist nature of academic "high" theory and underscores the importance of inventing new theorizing methods, "*mestizaje* theories," that "create new categories for those of us left out or pushed out of the existing ones."

It is this ability to create expansive new categories that makes the emerging field of Latina lesbian literature so vital to twentieth-century U.S. literary studies. By destabilizing apparently fixed classifications and provocatively crossing sexual, cultural, gender, and genre boundaries, Latina lesbian writing breaks down the categories that lead to stereotyping, overgeneralizations, and arbitrary divisions between apparently dissimilar groups. In so doing, it opens up new spaces where mestizaje connections—alliances between people from diverse sexualities, cultures, genders, and classes—can occur.

—*AnnLouise Keating*

BIBLIOGRAPHY

Alarcón, Norma, Ana Castillo, and Cherríe Moraga, eds. *The Sexuality of Latinas*. Berkeley: Third Woman Press, 1989. ■ Anzaldúa, Gloria. *Borderlands/La Frontera: The New Mestiza*. San Francisco: Spinsters/Aunt Lute, 1987. ■ ———. *Prieta*. San

Francisco: Spinsters/Aunt Lute, 1994. ■ ———, ed. *Haciendo Caras/Making Face, Making Soul: Creative and Critical Perspectives by Women of Color.* San Francisco: Aunt Lute Foundation, 1990. ■ Castillo, Ana. "La Macha: Toward a Beautiful Whole Self." Trujillo 24–48. ■ ———. *The Mixquiahuala Letters.* Binghamton, N.Y.: Bilingual Press, 1986. ■ ———. *Sapagonia (An Anti-Romance in 3/8 Meter).* Tempe, Ariz.: Bilingual Press, 1990. ■ ———. "What Only Lovers." Trujillo 60–61. ■ Chávez, Denise. *The Last of the Menu Girls.* Houston: Arte Público Press, 1986. ■ de la Peña, Terri. "Beyond El Camino Real." Trujillo 85–94. ■ ———. "Desert Quartet." *Lesbian Love Stories.* Vol. 2. Irene Zahava, ed. Freedom, Calif.: Crossing Press, 1991. ■ ———. "Good-Bye Ricky Ricardo; Hello Lesbianism." *The Original Coming Out Stories,* Expanded ed. Julia Penelope and Susan Wolfe, eds. Freedom, Calif.: Crossing Press, 1989. ■ ———. "La Maya." *Intricate Passions: A Collection of Erotic Short Fiction.* Tee Corinne, ed. Austin: Banned Books, 1989. ■ ———. *Margins.* Seattle: Seal Press, 1992. ■ ———. "Mujeres Morenas." *Lesbian Love Stories.* Vol. 2. Irene Zahava, ed.

Freedom, Calif.: Crossing Press, 1991. ■ de Monteflores, Carmen. *Singing Softly/Cantando Bajito.* San Francisco: Spinsters/Aunt Lute, 1989. ■ Moraga, Cherríe. *Giving Up the Ghost.* Los Angeles: West End Press, 1986. ■ ———. *The Last Generation.* Boston: South End Press, 1993. ■ ———. *Loving in the War Years: lo que nunca pasó por sus labios.* Boston: South End Press, 1983. ■ Moraga, Cherríe and Gloria Anzaldúa, eds. *This Bridge Called My Back: Writings by Radical Women of Color.* New York: Kitchen Table: Women of Color Press, 1983. ■ Navarro, Marta A. "Interview with Ana Castillo." Trujillo 113–132. ■ Ramos, Janita, ed. *Compañeras: Latina Lesbians (An Anthology).* New York: Latina Lesbian History Project, 1987. ■ ———. "Baya-món, Brooklyn y yo." Ramos 89–96. ■ Taylor, Sheila Ortiz. *Faultline.* Tallahassee, Fla.: Naiad, 1982. ■ ———. *Southbound.* Tallahassee, Fla.: Naiad, 1990. ■ ———. *Spring Forward/Fall Back.* Tallahassee, Fla.: Naiad, 1985. ■ Trujillo, Carla, ed. *Chicana Lesbians: The Girls Our Mothers Warned Us About.* Berkeley: Third Woman Press, 1991. ■ Umpierre, María Luz. *The Margarita Poems.* Berkeley: Third Woman Press, 1987.

Latino Literature

Despite the proliferation of a Chicano and Latino literary renaissance in the wake of the Chicano movement of the 1960s, few Chicano and Latino gay men have been published to date. Although the early 1980s produced a distinct and influential tradition of Chicana and Latina lesbian writings, Chicano and Latino gay male writers have yet to approach such a degree of visibility. Such invisibility inevitably raises the question, why are there so few published works by Latino gay men? One way to approach this question is to recognize the omnipresence of machismo in Latino cultures. Machismo—the hyperinvestment in traditional masculinity and the consequent limited conceptions of gender and sexuality—contributes to the refusal of many Latino men who engage in same-sex activity to identify themselves as "gay." Moreover, the monumental influence of Catholicism on Latinos also increases the difficulty of proclaiming themselves "gay." Certainly the cultural forces of machismo and Catholicism among Latinos have combined to undervalue—if not foreclose—a Latino gay identity.

Another factor contributing to the paucity of writings by Latinos is located on the other side of the border. If Latino cultures are homophobic, U.S. culture exercises various forms of racism. Chicano literary theorist José David Saldívar has noted, for instance, that the writings of various Latinos—including Chicano gay novelist Arturo Islas who died of AIDS complications in 1991—were rejected by various publishers and agents because the work was assumed to be either too limited or not "ethnic" enough. Self-identifying Latino gay male writers must therefore combat the dual forces of homophobia and racism. Unlike Chicana and Latina lesbian writers who were able to form coalitions with other lesbians of color, with white lesbians, and with the multiracial nonlesbians within the feminist movement of the 1970s in order to facilitate the process of establishing their own publishing venues and opportunities, Latino gay men have neither experienced an overt politicization around a Latino gay identity nor had access to support from Latino and white gay male publishing institutions. Finally, the AIDS pandemic has decimated the Latino gay male population in the United States. Homophobia, racism, and AIDS are, then, the major factors that begin to account for the lack of a Latino gay male literary heritage.

Yet Latino gay writers do publish books. Whether or not their writings participate in the construction of a North American gay literary tradition—let alone a Latino gay tradition—remains to be seen. The question points to the vexed and perhaps futile business of establishing criteria (themes, forms, subject-positions) that can be classified and contained within the rubric "gay." Moreover, attempts to identify a distinct Latino literary tradition remain problematic since Latino must be understood as a diverse people living in the United States who trace their ethnicity to any of the countries of South America, Central America, the Caribbean, or Mexico, regardless of race. In many cases, the writings of Latino gay men are more accurately linked to the literary traditions of their country of origin or North American and European movements and trends rather than to a U.S. gay movement. Nonetheless, Latino gay men have published novels, poetry, drama, and essays that deal directly with gay themes and issues. Certain characteristic themes and recurring motifs can be identified as central to Latino gay men. The role of the Latino gay man within the traditional Latino family, the experience of a border identity and its ramifications within two distinct cultures, the attempts to assimilate into U.S. gay culture, and the efforts to cultivate a Latino gay culture in the United States are the most prevalent topics in Latino gay literature. Although Latino gay men employ various literary methods and traditions to tell their stories, social realism remains the primary mode of expression.

JOHN RECHY, the most renowned Latino gay male writer, has written about gay issues since the publication of his enormously successful and influential novel *City of Night* in 1963. Rechy's canon, which includes nine novels, one nonfiction "documentary," a play, and numerous essays, varies in its focus on homosexuality. It is a topic that he writes about frequently but not exclusively. Rechy's early works establish a pattern among Latino gay male writers that is typical of much of North American gay literature. His first gay novels concentrate on autobiographical aspects and speculate on the possibilities of a gay identity both before and after Stonewall. This exploration often involves a candid discussion of sexual practices and fantasies that have led many of his earliest critics to label his work pornographic. In the novels that attempt to foreground questions of sexuality, Rechy places the interrogation of ethnicity on the sidelines. Conversely, in the novels that focus on Latino experiences, homosexuality is not a major subject. In all of his work, Rechy relies on realist techniques to depict the experiences of ethnic and sexual minorities. Rechy is best understood as a writer who emerged from a specific historical moment in gay history, a time before gay men of color were politically organized. His writings—including his nongay work—chart the history of a gay culture that continues to ask many gay men of color to choose between their ethnic or racial identities and their sexual identities. For Rechy, these categories have remained discrete in his work. And yet, to understand his *oeuvre* and its seemingly inherent contradictions, it is necessary to recognize the social forces of racism and homophobia that have historically positioned Latino gay men and lesbians to choose between these categories in the first place.

Other Latino gay men have faced this dual oppression and have made their simultaneous experience of racism and homophobia the focus of their writing. The poetic novels of Chicano writer Arturo Islas, *The Rain God* (1984) and *Migrant Souls* (1990), describe the life and times of Miguel Chico, a closeted Chicano gay man. The two novels—the first and second parts of an unfinished trilogy—focus on Chico's struggles to form an identity that will resolve the tensions of his conservative Southwest Latino heritage and his new life in the gay urban culture of San Francisco. Yet rather than focusing exclusively on the perspective of Miguel Chico, Islas provides snapshots of the various members of his extended family. These stories of other family members are told in third-person narratives that move backward and forward in time and provide multiple perspectives on various intratextual events. Such narratives demonstrate the sociohistorical forces that combine to produce Miguel Chico's crisis of identity. Like William Faulkner and Gabriel Garcia Marquez, Islas combines elements of social realism with magical and psychological realism to engage the reader in a complex poetic network of associative images and events. Islas is most interested in exploring the concept of a border identity: How does one reconcile sexuality with ethnicity? What are the effects of this dilemma in the traditional and conservative Latino kinship structure? What possible spiritual growth can stem from this crisis? Islas poses these questions effectively in the domain of tragedy where individuals struggle in defeat against the social forces that undo them.

If Islas describes Latino gay identity as fundamentally tragic, Colombian born writer Jaime Manrique, in his successful cross-over novel *Latin Moon in Manhattan* (1992), offers the comic antidote to Islas's tragic novels. Manrique's novel describes the adventures of Santiago Martínez, a Colombian gay male immigrant living in New York City. Manrique also provides his readers with a wide-ranging portrait of his protagonist's extended family and friends, including a boyhood friend who dies of AIDS complications and a Latina lesbian motorcyclist whom his family plans for him to marry. In place of Islas's tragic approach, however, Manrique traces Santiago's madcap journey from Bogota to Times Square with full comic flair. Unlike the protagonists in the novels of Rechy and Islas, Manrique's central character is able to reconcile the various configurations of his identity. Rather than focusing on the formation of his character's pysche, Manrique chooses to concentrate on his character's multifaceted experiences as a Latino gay immigrant. By the end of the novel, when all the various plots and subplots are resolved, Manrique's protagonist is shown in the midst of his newly fashioned community, which includes family members, other nongay Latino neighbors, and non-Latino gays. The novel concludes with the central character, surrounded by his loved ones, aware finally that his life in New York, though always quirky and complicated, is joyful. Manrique's entertaining humor, reminiscent of that of the Spanish filmmaker Pedro Almodovar, marks a turning point in Latino gay fiction. When read in the context of the earlier Latino gay fiction of Rechy and Islas, Manrique's novel demonstrates the diversity of styles and approaches available to Latino gay male writers who write about similar themes. Significantly, *Latin Moon in Manhattan* is unequivocally a comedy. It is the first novel by a Latino gay male writer to address issues of identity and culture with irony.

Although the novels of Rechy, Islas, and Manrique illustrate some of the shared themes of Latino gay writers and the divergent means writers choose to employ these issues in their fictions, other Latino gay men writing in different genres have made considerable contributions that must not be overlooked or underestimated. *Hunger of Memory* (1983), the controversial essayist Richard Rodriguez's conservative memoir, for example, has helped shape—for bettter or worse—the debates facing all Latinos in the United States around issues of bilingual education and affirmative action. The instant success of *Hunger of Memory* positioned Rodriguez as one of the most widely read Latino writers. In *Days of Obligation* (1992), his more recent collection of essays, Rodriguez is more forthcoming about his homosexuality—an issue he sidesteps in his earlier memoir—and begins to address gay-related issues more explicitly, albeit within a very limited and often frustrating scope. Still, such disclosures position him as the most recognizable Latino gay man in contemporary literature. Even though Rodriguez lacks the gay and lesbian readership of his contemporaries, no other Latino gay male writer has had consecutive best-sellers among mainstream readers. Other successful Latino gay male writers include the gifted mystery writer Michael Nava, whose Latino gay detective Henry Rios has emerged as one of the most interesting recurring characters in contemporary gay male fiction (see also MYSTERY FICTION, GAY MALE); the poet Francisco Alarcon whose award-winning work ranges from the erotics of contemporary life to the indigenous heritage of the Americas; and the playwright Joe Dante (aka Conrado Morales), who was one of the co-authors of the Broadway megahit *A Chorus Line* (1975) and who died of AIDS complications in 1991.

There are also a number of Latino gay male writers whose works have yet to appear in separate editions. Their writings are available only in small press anthologies; lesbian and gay periodicals; or, in the case of performers, on video. The current proliferation of performance art in lesbian and gay culture has enabled many talented Latinos to stage their work across the country. Los Angeles-based writers such as Luis Alfaro, who in his lyrical solo piece *Downtown* (1991) describes his childhood and upbringing in the impoverished and gang-infested Pico-Union neighborhood, and Alberto Antonio Araiza, whose solo piece about testing HIV-positive, *Meet My Beat* (1991), has been performed throughout the United States and Europe, are perhaps the most interesting and successful Latino gay male performance artists currently at work. Araiza and Alfaro are also instrumental forces behind *VIVA!*, an organization for Latino lesbian and gay artists in Los Angeles. Alfaro's unpublished comedy about a dysfunctional Latino family, *Bitter Homes and Gardens*, has been staged in workshops throughout the country. Other talented writers include the Texas writer and performer, Paul Bonin-Rodriguez; Colombian-American poet and activist, David Acosta; Alberto Sandoval, the Puerto Rican playwright and AIDS theorist; and Chicano writer Gil Cuadros, whose fiction and poetry appear regularly in gay and lesbian journals. All these writers invoke distinct literary styles in order to address any number of issues relevant to Latino gay men.

—*David Román*

BIBLIOGRAPHY

Bredbeck, Gregory. "John Rechy." *Contemporary Gay American Novelists: A Bio-Bibliographical Critical Sourcebook.* Emmanuel S. Nelson, ed. Westport, Conn.: Greenwood Press, 1993. 340–351. ■ Bruce-Novoa, Juan. "Homosexuality and the Chicano Novel." *Confluencia* 2:1 (Fall 1986): 69–77. ■ Klawitter, George. "Michael Nava." *Contemporary Gay American Novelists: A Bio-Bibliographical Critical Sourcebook.* Emmanuel S. Nelson, ed. Westport, Conn.: Greenwood Press, 1993. 291–297. ■ Ortiz, Ricardo. "Sexuality Degree Zero: Pleasure and Power in the Novels of John Rechy, Arturo Islas, and Michael Nava." *Critical Essays: Gay and Lesbian Writers of Color.* Emmanuel S. Nelson, ed. New York: Haworth Press, forthcoming. ■ Román, David. "Teatro Viva! Latino Performance and the Politics of AIDS in Los Angeles," *Lesbian and Gay Issues in Hispanic Literature.* Emilie Bergmann and Paul Julien Smith, eds. Durham, N.C.: Duke University Press, forthcoming. ■ ———. "Arturo Islas." *Contemporary Gay American Novelists: A Bio-Bibliographical Critical Sourcebook.* Emmanuel S. Nelson, ed. Westport, Conn.: Greenwood Press, 1993. 221–225. ■ Saldívar, José David. *The Dialectics of Our America: Genealogy, Cultural Critique, and Literary History.* Durham, N.C.: Duke University Press, 1991.

Lawrence, D. H.
(1885–1930)

Born the son of a Nottingham coal miner and a strong-willed mother on September 11, 1885, D. H. Lawrence grew up amid considerable poverty in the Eastwood section of Nottingham in northern England. The fourth of five children, Lawrence was exceptionally close to his mother, who encouraged his early interest in painting and his pursuit of a university education. Success on an examination won him a full scholarship (of those taking the examination, he was among the first eleven candidates in the whole of England), allowing him to attend Nottingham University. His fitful high-school romance with Jessie Chambers, two years younger than Lawrence and the model for Emily in Lawrence's first novel, *The White Peacock* (1911), and for Miriam in *Sons and Lovers* (1913), continued while he attended the university. Lawrence subsequently became romantically involved with Alice Dax, a married woman seven years his senior, a militant socialist and suffragist, who was the model for Clara Dawes of *Sons and Lovers*. After she ended their affair, Lawrence eloped with Frieda Weekley. From an aristocratic German family (and the cousin of Baron von Richthofen, the "Red Baron"), Frieda was the wife of one of Lawrence's former professors and the mother of three children. The Lawrences' marriage was notoriously stormy, involving violent verbal battles culminating in cutlery throwing and fist-fighting in the presence of friends.

Although *Sons and Lovers* achieved critical acclaim, the publication of *The Rainbow* (1915) brought Lawrence unwanted notoriety when the book was suppressed by a court order. During the war, he and Frieda were further harassed by police officials because of Lawrence's pacifism and suspicions generated by a German-born wife. The Lawrences were ordered to leave their residence in Cornwall by military authorities who suspected them of spying. Much of the bitterness of the war years, along with Lawrence's disenchantment with English narrow-mindedness, can be found in what is perhaps the novelist's greatest exploration of homosexual subject matter, *Women in Love* (1920). Here Lawrence and Frieda are depicted as Rupert Birkin and Ursula Brangwen in a tale based partly on Lawrence's clamorous relationship with the writer KATHERINE MANSFIELD, her husband, the literary critic John Middleton Murry (Gudrun and Gerald of the novel), and Lady Ottoline Morrell (Hermione Roddice). It was during the composition of *Women in Love* that Lawrence, frustrated by his failure to forge a deeper bond with Murray, evidently had a sexual relationship with a Cornish farmer named William Henry Hocking in the town of Tregerthen.

The short-lived affair was the culmination of a long-standing struggle with homosexual feelings. "I would like to know why nearly every man that approaches greatness tends to homosexuality, whether he admits it or not," Lawrence wrote to a friend in 1913. Lawrence told another acquaintance, "I believe the nearest I've come to perfect love was with a coal-miner when I was about sixteen." Yet Lawrence's inability to intensify his relationships with either Murry or Hocking generated his most forthright fictional examinations of homosexual desire, an intense five-year absorption in the subject that included not only *Women in Love* and *Aaron's Rod* (1922) but the treatise "Goats and Compasses" (1917) and the self-suppressed Prologue to *Women In Love*. Lawrence destroyed "Goats and Compasses," and though no pages survive, both Ottoline Morrell and Lawrence's friend Cecil Gray read it and found it to be shrilly dogmatic. Its argument remains unknown, although the essay's title suggests a struggle between panlike homoerotics and scientific rationalism.

Lawrence spent the last part of his short life traveling with Frieda to Italy, America, and Mexico, the last the setting for *The Plumed Serpent* (1926). In addition to his fiction, Lawrence published several volumes of poetry, critical essays, and travel narratives. Lawrence's last novel, *Lady Chatterly's Lover* (1928), won him his greatest fame but was not published in an unexpurgated English edition until after a groundbreaking censorship trial in 1961. Always frail in health, Lawrence died of tuberculosis in 1930 in Vence, France, while traveling with Frieda in the company of Aldous and Maria Huxley.

Lawrence was a twentieth-century maverick in his open and formally adventurous discussion of all sexual issues and especially homosexuality. Perhaps no other major modernist author was so continually absorbed in the subject of homosexual desire, a theme that continually informs Lawrence's work, beginning with the swimming idyll sequence of his first novel, *The White Peacock* (1911), and continuing with the initiation ritual in *The Plumed Serpent*, Lawrence's penultimate novel. Throughout the fiction, poetry, and even plays (his 1926 *David* in part depicted the story of the Biblical David's friendship with Jonathan), Lawrence explored homosexual love in both male and female relations. *The Rainbow,* for example, includes a character of obvious lesbian inclinations, Winifred Inger, and her emotional hold on Ursula Brangwen, and the novella *The Fox* explores the intimate friendship between two women as it is shattered by a male intruder to their farm. Like FORSTER and GIDE, Lawrence was fascinated by the mystique of sexual relations with working-class men; unlike them, however, he expounded this fascination from the perspective of the working-class artist. Deeply suspicious of the effects of industrialization—he had himself witnessed it destroy the English landscape and the vestiges of communal culture—Lawrence grew to love primitive civilizations and all he imagined they offered in the way of expansive love. Although he proselytized on behalf of the unconscious, Lawrence repudiated psychoanalysis's attempt at thoroughly calibrating human sexuality and criticized Freud's project as fomenting mere "sex in the head." Psychoanalysis, he believed, robbed modern man of the dark, mythic power inherent in true eros. This belief in the mythopoetic value of the darkly erotic led him to stress nonverbalized expressions of homoerotic feeling, often with a violent, primitivist undercurrent. The much-anthologized story "The Prussian Officer" (1914), for example, portrays the masochistic yearning of an officer for the youthful soldier under his command in a tightly wrought narrative containing virtually no dialogue and ending with a dual death in an eerily peaceful forest.

Lawrence's writing dealing with homosexuality poses unusual problems, for the novelist was highly conflicted in his attitude toward homosexual desire and was, in many ways, a social conservative of a markedly puritan temperament. Many readers, moreover, have been troubled by Lawrence's glorification of what has been characterized as his misogynistic "cult of the phallus" as well as by the fascistic implications of his philosophy of "blood consciousness." Others have found Lawrence's often febrile, repetitive prose style to be an obstacle to a full appreciation of his work. In addition, Lawrence's fictional endorsement of homosexual desire is generally represented as existing in conflict with either a fearful sexual domination by women or a repellently effete homosexual coterie. Thus Gudrun and the memorably malevolent bisexual German artist Loerke in *Women in Love* come to represent a deadly alliance that defeats Gerald in his unrealized love for Birkin. Lawrence's own experiences with homosexual men were acrimonious; he once claimed that BLOOMSBURY homosexuals such as the painter Duncan Grant and the economist John Maynard Keynes made him "mad with misery and hostility and rage" and reminded him of "black beetles" (an apparent reference to the beetle's mating habit of climbing onto the back of the host).

Still, Lawrence's torment over his own homosexual inclinations gives his work an extraordinary, unsentimental force that is lacking in the fiction of more inwardly resolved writers of the day and that renders much of the period's homosexual writing restrained by comparison. In rejecting homosexual AESTHETICISM for a more masculine credo and a devotion to savage nature, Lawrence is close in spirit to the English and American writers EDWARD CARPENTER and WALT WHITMAN. A great admirer of the American poet, Lawrence claimed to find in Whitman's *Calamus* poems "one of the clues to a real solution—a new adjustment. I believe in what he calls 'manly love', the real implicit reliance of one man on another . . . only it must be deeper, more ultimate than emotion and personality, cool separateness and yet the ultimate reliance."

Women in Love, a masterpiece of modernist fiction, is the novelist's most daring exploration of homosexuality through its hero Birkin's search for a bisexual ethic as a way of transcending what Lawrence considered a crisis in English culture. The twin poles of Birkin's agonized erotic consciousness and his search for "two kinds of love," wedded to the novel's heightened sense of cultural fragmentation, lend *Women in Love* an exceptional tensile strength and apocalyptic magnitude. In the novel's preface, Lawrence claimed the catastrophe of the Great War required that men form a bond lest "new life" be "strangled unborn within them." This statement is a more poetic expression of what the novel itself makes implicit and the Prologue rendered emphatic: Heterosexual marriage must acknowledge man's need to have the love of another man or else all will suffer a spiritual death.

Excised from the final text by Lawrence himself, the Prologue reveals in great detail Rupert Birkin's struggle against overwhelming homosexual longings. It was not published until 1965 and was not included in an edition of *Women in Love* until 1987. Hocking himself is probably twice alluded to in the Prologue in the description of the "strange Cornish type of man, with dark eyes likes holes in his head" who powerfully attracts Birkin as well as in the minor character of William Hosken. The Rupert of the Prologue is torn not only between females and males, but between "two classes of men," the "white-skinned, keen limbed men with eyes like blue-flashing ice and hair like crystals of winter sunshine" and "men with dark eyes that one can enter and plunge into, bathe in as in liquid darkness." Although Rupert wants to "cast out these desires," he senses that a "man can no more slay a living desire in him" than "he can prevent his body from feeling heat and cold."

Despite the potential for true passion and tenderness between men—glimpsed in the famous wrestling sequence in the novel's "Gladiatorial" chapter and in Gerald's nursing of Rupert in the chapter "Man to Man"—real devotion between men is stymied by a failure of nerve. Nonetheless, the tragedy of Gerald's death is undercut by *Women in Love*'s extraordinary concluding endorsement of bisexuality. "You can't have two kinds of love," Ursula insists to Birkin after Gerald's body has been buried, as she dismisses Birkin's ideas as "an obstinacy, a theory, a perversity." Rupert's response and *Women in Love*'s final sentence is a refusal to accept a delimited heterosexual arrangement: "I don't believe that."

In affirming same-sex friendship, Lawrence typically contrasted his all-male idylls with effete homosexual men, while portraying women as upholders of suffocating marital convention. In *Aaron's Rod*, a coal miner leaves his fatuous wife, takes up the flute, and travels to Italy to join the free-spirited Rawdon Lily. There he encounters a group of vacationing English exiles, whose homosexuality is implied in their doting interest in the working-class Aaron as well as in their social cattiness. (WILDE's friend Reggie Turner appears in the biting portrait of Algy Constable, "flapping his eyelids like some crazy owl.") The novel concludes with Rawdon beseeching Aaron to submit to the demands of his own soul. Lawrence returned to homosexual themes in episodes in later works, among them the "Nightmare" chapter of *Kangaroo* (1923), as well in several short stories. His tales "The Blind Man" (1924) and "Jimmy and the Desperate Woman" (1928) both powerfully recast the familiar Lawrentian scenario in which homoerotic affection threatens—yet also complements—an unsatisfying marital relationship.

Lawrence's genius consists in his emphasis on the barely articulated, unconscious dynamics of homoerotic relations as they move in a state of crisis, flux, and cathartic confrontation. His willingness to transcend the conventions of the nineteenth-century novel, subverting what he once characterized as the "old, stable ego," and, in turn, the stable sexual self, enabled him at his best to depict the experimental excitement of same-sex relations. Alone among writers of the period, he brought to the theme of homosexuality a genuine working-class perspective. A self-proclaimed enemy of the hyperarticulated sexuality of forward-thinking individuals, he was, paradoxically, himself the great novelist of the painfully unsayable. It was a gift that rendered Lawrence exceptionally adept at apprehending the "unspeakable" promptings of same-sex desire. A ferociously brilliant artist, he remains one of the most forcefully imaginative, complicated, and least understood navigators of homosexual consciousness in this century.

—*Richard Kaye*

BIBLIOGRAPHY

Aldington, Richard. *D.H. Lawrence: Portrait of a Genius, But . . .* New York: Collier Books, 1950. ■ Delaney, Paul. *D.H. Lawrence's Nightmare: The Writer and His Circle in the Years of the Great War.* New York: The Free Press, 1978. ■ Delavenay, Emile. *D.H. Lawrence and Edward Carpenter: A Study in Edwardian Transition.* London: Heinmann, 1971. ■ Kermode, Frank. *D.H. Lawrence.* New York: Viking Press, 1973. ■ Lawrence, Frieda. *Not I, But the Wind. . . .* London: Heinmann, 1935. ■ Meyers, Jeffrey. *D.H. Lawrence.* New York: Alfred Knopf, 1960. ■ Moore, Harry T. *The Priest of Love.* New York: Penguin, 1976. ■ Sagar, Keith. *D.H. Lawrence: Life Into Art.* Athens: University of Georgia Press, 1985. ■ Stevens, C. J. *Lawrence at Tregerthen (D.H. Lawrence in Cornwall).* Troy, New York: Whitson Publishing Co., 1988. ■ Worthen, John. *D.H. Lawrence: The Early Years, 1885–1912.* Cambridge: Cambridge University Press, 1991.

Lawrence, T. E.
(1888–1935)

Thomas Edward Lawrence, or "Lawrence of Arabia," is best known as the author of *Seven Pillars of Wisdom* (1935), a brilliant account of his role in the revolt of the Arabs during the latter half of World War I, a revolt instigated by the British in order to drive the Turks out of Syria and Palestine. Lawrence chose Emir Feisal to lead the campaign and masterminded the guerrilla tactics that would contain and cripple the Turkish garrisons, especially at Medina, by cutting railways and telegraphs in surprise raids. But Lawrence labored under a sense of duplicity, knowing that the British had no genuine interest in Arab independence and were simply using the Arabs in the war against Germany. Though he mourned the brutality into which the campaign gradually sank, the contrast is striking between Lawrence's tidy and effective raids on the Eastern Front and the appalling waste of "human ammunition" on the Western.

Although homosexuality is the subject of only a tiny portion of this epic narrative, it plays a pivotal role in the psychological background. Chapter 80 tells how Lawrence was captured while on reconnaissance in Deraa and how he rejected the sexual advances of the Turkish Bey who held him. It then describes vividly the torture he received from the Bey's guards and, more obliquely, their brutal sodomizing of him. Lawrence, who maintained complete celibacy and hated even to be touched, never recovered from this trauma; he believed that he had been robbed of his "integrity" and his spirit had been broken, apparently forever.

Lawrence largely hides from view a later and equally discouraging event, namely, news of the death of Salim Ahmed, the young man who was the "S.A." to whom the book is dedicated. Lawrence had met Ahmed while working on an archeological dig in Carchemish, Syria, several years before the war. At this time, Ahmed (or Dahoum as Lawrence called him) was only fourteen, but they established a close friendship. *Seven Pillars* opens with a cryptic dedicatory poem, which hints that it was for the sake of "S.A." that he worked and suffered for the cause of Arab independence. When Dahoum died of typhoid behind Turkish lines in September 1918, the revolt had nearly reached its goal at Damascus. In *Seven Pillars,* and more explicitly in his correspondence, Lawrence suggests that his distaste for the entire exploit in its last triumphant days was owing largely to news of his friend's death.

The authorized biography attempts to defend Lawrence against "charges" of homosexuality, and indeed anyone seeking proof of his orientation in sexual acts will find little evidence of any sexuality at all. But there is no doubt that Lawrence was able to form closer attachments to young men (such as Dahoum, R. A. M. Guy, and Jock Chambers) than to women. Meyers (*Homosexuality and Literature*) produces strong evidence from the letters that Lawrence was tormented by the knowledge that he had surrendered to the rapists at Deraa and had experienced a masochistic sexual pleasure.

Lawrence was the illegitimate child of Sir Thomas Chapman and Sarah Lawrence who, after eloping in Ireland, changed their name by deed poll in England. Lawrence himself would change his name to John Hume Ross, when he joined the Royal Air Force in 1922, and again to T. E. Shaw when he joined the Tank Corps a year later. His experiences as a recruit are the subject of *The Mint,* a sequel to *Seven Pillars of Wisdom* published posthumously in 1955. On May 13, 1935, he suffered severe injuries in a motorcycle accident and died six days later. David Lean's 1962 film, *Lawrence of Arabia,* and Terence Rattigan's play of the same year, *Ross,* have helped shape the myth that surrounds this complicated and enigmatic figure. But well before these dramatic portrayals, Lawrence served as a model for the neurotic hero—the "Truly Weak Man" who must continually prove himself by acts of heroism—in the works of the angry young gay men of the 1930s, W. H. AUDEN and CHRISTOPHER ISHERWOOD. (See also ENGLISH LITERATURE: TWENTIETH CENTURY.)

—Matthew Parfitt

BIBLIOGRAPHY

Aldington, Richard. *Lawrence of Arabia: A Biographical Enquiry.* London: Collins, 1955. ■ Meyers, Jeffrey. *Homosexuality and Literature, 1890–1930.* Montreal: McGill-Queen's University Press, 1977. ■ ———. *The Wounded Spirit: T.E. Lawrence's Seven Pillars of Wisdom.* Preface by Sir Alec Kirkbride. New York: St. Martin's Press, 1989. ■ ———. *T. E. Lawrence: A Bibliography.* New York: Garland Publishing, 1974. ■ Rattigan, Terence. *Ross, A Dramatic Portrait.* New York: Random House, 1962. ■ Wilson, Jeremy. *Lawrence of Arabia: The Authorized Biography of T.E. Lawrence.* New York: Atheneum, 1989.

Leavitt, David
(b. 1961)

David Leavitt was born on June 23, 1961, in Pittsburgh, the son of Harold Jack Leavitt, a professor who later taught at Stanford University, and Gloria Rosenthal Leavitt, a housewife and liberal political activist. He grew up in Palo Alto, California, and attended Yale University, graduating Phi Beta Kappa in 1983 with a B.A. in English.

Leavitt achieved early notice. While still a student at Yale, he published a short story, "Territory," in *The New Yorker;* another *New Yorker* story, "Out Here," followed shortly. These two stories along with seven others formed his first collection, *Family Dancing* (1984), which was nominated for the National Book Critics Circle Award and for the PEN-Faulkner Award. *Family Dancing* is particularly interesting for the way in which Leavitt is able to integrate gay issues into the fabric of contemporary American life and for his skill in depicting middle-aged women. His first novel, *The Lost Language of Cranes* (1986), tells a double "coming out" story, that of a young New Yorker whose increasing openness about his homosexuality forces his middle-aged father finally to confront his own sexuality.

His next novel, *Equal Affections* (1989), is another story with intergenerational concerns. Its main character, a gay lawyer, must deal with his remarkable mother's two-decade-long fight with cancer. The novel also features a lesbian sister and a father who, like Leavitt's own, is a professor at a California university. *Equal Affections* is often read as an autobiographical book, but Leavitt himself dismisses such approaches. In 1989, Leavitt received a Guggenheim fellowship and was foreign writer-in-residence in Barcelona at the Institute of Catalan Letters.

With his second short story collection, *A Place I've Never Been* (1990), Leavitt breaks new ground. Leavitt's stories of Americans in Europe invite comparison with HENRY JAMES. In these tales, Leavitt leaves the world of urban American gay life for other territory. His most recent novel, *While England Sleeps* (1993), goes even farther away from the milieu of his early work, tracing the politically charged homosexual romance between an upper-class writer and a working-class Communist in 1930s England. The novel was the center of a scandal when STEPHEN SPENDER filed suit, alleging that the novel's plot was taken directly from his memoir, *World within World* (1951). The suit was settled when Leavitt's publisher agreed to withdraw the novel and reissue it with minor changes made to distance it from Spender's work; Leavitt himself has charged that Spender's objections are motivated by homophobia, an allegation that Spender has denied.

Leavitt has overcome the problems attendant on early success. Though his recent books have received decidedly mixed reviews, he has continued to produce new work regularly. His reputation is greater in Europe than in America, witness the BBC production of a film based on *The Lost Language of Cranes*. He has been involved actively in the contemporary literary world, editing a special issue of *Mississippi Quarterly* devoted to the work of younger writers and serving as coeditor of *The Penguin Book of Gay Short Stories*. Still a young man, Leavitt has produced fiction of quality and intelligence. He is one of the brightest stars of the gay literary world today. (See also NOVEL: GAY MALE.)

—*D. S. Lawson*

BIBLIOGRAPHY

Iannone, Carol. "Post-Counterculture Tristesse." *Commentary* 85.5 (February 1987): 57–61. ■ Lawson, D. S. "David Leavitt." *Contemporary Gay American Novelists: A Bio-Bibliographical Critical Sourcebook.* Emmanuel S. Nelson, ed. Westport, Conn.: Greenwood, 1993. 248–253. ■ Leavitt, David. "Did I Plagiarize His Life?" *New York Times Magazine* (April 3, 1994): 36–37. ■ Lilly, Mark. *Gay Men's Literature in the Twentieth Century.* New York: New York University Press, 1993. ■ Spender, Stephen. "My Life Is Mine; It Is Not David Leavitt's." *New York Times Book Review* (Sept. 4, 1994): 10–12. ■ Weir, John. "Fleeing the Fame Factory." *Advocate* (October 19, 1993): 50–55.

Leduc, Violette
(1907–1972)

Despite the rediscovery of women writers and the gay and lesbian literary tradition, few writers continue to be as underappreciated by both critics and the public as Violette Leduc. Is it because of her untimely death and her unstable, neurotic personality? Or is it the unevenness of her work coupled with its predominantly female subject matter? The irony is that Leduc is arguably a stronger stylist and more candid erotic explorer than Marguerite Duras; a more astute psychological observer than Nathalie Sarraute; and a more dramatic chronicler of the woman's condition than Simone de Beauvoir.

Leduc was born April 7, 1907, in Arras, where her mother Berthe had gone to give birth to her illegitimate daughter fathered by the son of a couple she worked for. In Valenciennes, the young Violette spent most of her childhood suffering from an ugly self-image and from her mother's hostility and overprotectiveness. Her two most tender friendships were with her grandmother Fideline and her maternal aunt Laure. Her formal education, begun in 1913, was interrupted by World War I. After the war, she went to a boarding school, the College de Duoai, where she experienced lesbian affairs with a classmate and a music instructor who was fired over the incident. In the meantime, her mother married, bringing an unwelcome end to the all-female family.

In 1926, Leduc moved to Paris and enrolled in the Lycée Racine. That same year, she failed her baccalaureate exam and ended up working as a telephone operator and secretary at Plon publishers, where she eventually became a proofreader and publicity writer.

In 1932, she made the acquaintance of the writer Maurice Sachs, who urged her to write professionally. She then began her career as a freelance journalist whose stories, features, and editorials were published in various magazines. In 1939, she married Gabriel Mercier, who was soon drafted; she divorced him after World War II. During the war, Leduc hid out in a small town in Normandy with Sachs, a homosexual with whom she grew infatuated but who never reciprocated her sexual attraction. (Similar incidents of "impossible love" occurred after the war with Simone de Beauvoir and JEAN GENET, and are recounted in detail by EDMUND WHITE in his biography of Genet.) Leduc herself used her thinly disguised infatuation with Beauvoir in *L'Affamée* (*Starved*). When Sachs left, she took up black marketing and made a small fortune. But when the war ended, she lost her money and was imprisoned briefly.

Leduc's one stroke of post-war good fortune was that de Beauvoir read the manuscript of her first novel, *L'Asphyxie* (*In the Prison of Her Skin*) and became her mentor, helping her get the novel published in 1946. It received critical raves from Albert Camus, Jean Genet, and Marcel Jouhandeau among others. Leduc continued to write and publish other works, including *L'Affamée* in 1948, *Ravages* in 1955, and *La Vieille Fille et le mort* (*The Old Maid and the Dead Man*) in 1958. But popular and commercial success eluded her until 1964 when *La Batarde* (*The Bastard*) was published—minus the *Therese et Isabelle* section, which her publisher deemed too explicit in its depiction of lesbian lovemaking. (*Therese et Isabelle* was finally published in 1966 and made into a film in 1968.) *La Batarde* nearly won the prestigious Prix Goncourt and became a best-seller, and its success enabled Leduc to buy a house in the town of Faucon in the Vaucluse region. She settled there and completed the second and third installments of her projected four-volume autobiography—*La Folie en tete* (*Mad in Pursuit*, 1970) and *La Chasse a l'amour* (*The Hunt for Love*, 1972)—neither of which approached the mastery of *La Batarde*. Leduc developed breast cancer and, after two operations, died on May 28, 1972.

One reason success and esteem may have escaped Leduc for so long is because so much of her work is autobiographical and blurs the distinctions between fact and fiction. Her life was indeed a history of calamities, each of which became grist for her fiction. Many critics accused her of writing self-indulgent confessions, even though her "in extremis" characters and controversial subject matter should have made her seem a natural part of the post-war flowering of French existentialism.

As their titles often suggest, Leduc's books are filled with images of deprivation and defeat. Yet her work is never merely documentary or therapeutic. To read the best of her novels and memoirs—*In the Prison of Her Skin*, *Ravages*, *La Batarde*, and *Therese and Isabelle*—is to see how Leduc reworks and revises each character and each incident for purely literary purposes. The subtlety of her work lies both in its stylistic originality—as in the metaphorically charged language of the talking Metro steps scene in *La Batarde* and the powerfully lyrical lovemaking scene in *Therese and Isabelle*—and in its ability to transform friends, family members, and even Leduc herself into absurdist parables of female identity and the social conditions that women of her generation faced. If any writer can be described as the female Kafka that writer is surely Violette Leduc.

—*Jacob Stockinger*

BIBLIOGRAPHY

Benkov, Edith J. "Violette Leduc." *Gay and Lesbian Literature.* Sharon Malinowski, ed. Detroit: St. James Press, 1994. 220–223. ■ Bree, Germaine. *Women Writers in France.* New Brunswick: Rutgers University Press, 1973. ■ De Courtivron, Isabelle. *Violette Leduc.* Boston: Twayne Publishers, 1985. ■ Flanner, Janet. *Paris Journal: Volume 2, 1965–1971.* William Shawn, ed. New York: Atheneum, 1971. ■ Marks, Elaine. "Lesbian Intertextuality." *Homosexualities and French Literature.* George Stambolian and Elaine Marks, eds. Ithaca, N.Y.: Cornell University Press, 1979. 353–377. ■ White, Edmund. *Genet: A Biography.* New York: Knopf, 1993.

Lee, Vernon
(1856–1935)

Born Violet Paget at Château Saint-Léonard near Boulogne, France, on October 14, 1856, into a privileged and cosmopolitan family, Lee was educated by her mother, half brother, and governesses. Her travels in Europe with her family aroused her interest in learning new cultures, aesthetics, and art. By the age of fourteen, she had written *Biographie d'une monnaie* (*Biography of Money*, 1879) in French, in which she used a narrative frame to weave portraits of a coin's owners from the Roman civilization of Hadrian to her own time. She also wrote in Italian, German, and English. She published in *Frazer's Magazine* in 1878 and 1879 on art and aesthetics, adopting the pseudonym Vernon Lee, believing that a masculine name would lend greater credence to her writings. Along with her male pseudonym, she also adopted male attire.

Lee was a prolific essayist, critic, novelist, biographer, dramatist, travel and short story writer, publishing some forty-five major works. She understood the Victorians' love of travel and created a genre called "genius loci" or "spirit of places." These works are impressionistic travel sketches, which delineate the spirit of a particular region. From 1897 to 1925, she produced seven volumes of this genre, most notably, *Genius Loci: Notes on Places* (1899).

Her *Studies of the Eighteenth Century in Italy* (1880), which describes the characters and lives of musicians and singers, catapulted her writing career to the literary and artistic circles of London. Her collection of essays on art, *Belcaro* (1881), and her collection of essays on the Renaissance, *Euphorion* (1884), were also highly acclaimed. Her drama *Ariadne in Mantua* (1903) featured a cross-dressing heroine. Her collection of aesthetic essays on *Beauty and Ugliness and Other Studies in Psychological Aesthetics* (1912) initiated the theory of "empathy" or the German concept "Einfühlung" into English aesthetic discourse, while *The Beautiful* (1913) continued her exploration of aesthetic theory.

Lee's first "ROMANTIC FRIENDSHIPS" may have begun in the 1870s. Her relationship with her companion Annie Meyers ended in 1881. From 1881 to 1887, her traveling companion was Mary Robinson, whom she met at a drawing-room party. Mary's eventual marriage to James Darmsteter, which was probably not consummated, ended Lee's passionate attachment. Devastated by Mary's marriage, Lee was comforted by her new friend Clementina (Kit) Anstruther-Thomson, who was to have a profound effect on her work. Lee described her friendship with Kit Thomson as a "new love and new life." This friendship lasted from 1887 to 1897. Kit was a "Venus figure" for Lee; she described her in her correspon-

dence as a "Venus de Milo," a woman of beauty, a friend, and a spiritual lover. This relationship inspired Lee's creativity, and during this time, Lee wrote and perfected her writings on aesthetics.

Lee's involvement with the aesthetic movement of the nineteenth century brought her close to such prominent people as Dante Gabriel Rosetti, WALTER PATER, William Morris, Edward Burne-Jones, John Singer Sargent, and OSCAR WILDE. Mrs. Sargent encouraged Lee to develop her creative potential. Robert Browning, a lifelong friend, acknowledged her in his poem "Inapprehensiveness," collected in *Asolando* (1889). Lee's pacifist manifesto, *Satan the Waster,* (1920), which explored the ruinous psychological effects of World War I, was attacked in the *Times Literary Supplement* in 1920, but George Bernard Shaw responded in a review in the *Nation* by praising Lee's intellectual acumen. Edith Wharton's "Life and Letters" in *A Backward Glance* (1934) is also a complimentary reminiscence. Although Lee does not explore lesbian themes directly in her literary or aesthetic works, she is a significant figure who successfully pursued a literary life at a time when women faced serious obstacles in doing so. Perhaps her most enduring legacy is the example she left of a woman who was committed, both intellectually and emotionally, to other women. Her correspondence with Anstruther-Thomson is especially intriguing as a passionate and animated commentary on women's friendships, while her creative writings reveal a fertile lesbian imagination.

—*Clarence McClanahan*

BIBLIOGRAPHY

Cary, Richard. "Vernon Lee's Vignettes of Literary Acquaintances." *Colby Library Quarterly* 9 (September 1970): 179–199. ■ Gardner, Burdett. *Lesbian Imagination (Victorian Style): A Psychological and Critical Study of Vernon Lee.* New York: Garland, 1987. ■ Gunn, Peter. *Vernon Lee/Violet Paget, 1856-1935.* London: Oxford University Press, 1964. ■ Mannocchi, Phyllis A. "Vernon Lee and Kit Anstruther-Thomson: A Study of Love and Collaboration between Romantic Friends." *Women's Studies* 12.2 (1986): 129–148. ■ Ormond, Richard. "John Singer Sargent and Vernon Lee." *Colby Library Quarterly* 9 (September 1970): 154–178.

Le Guin, Ursula K.
(*b.* 1929)

Ursula K. Le Guin was born October 21, 1929, in Berkeley, California, the daughter of the anthropologist Alfred Kroeber and the writer The-

odora Kroeber. Le Guin was educated at Radcliffe and Columbia, married the historian Charles Le Guin, and now lives in Portland, Oregon. She has been considered one of the so-called New Wave of science fiction writers who arose in the 1960s though her work is by no means confined to that genre. Informed partly by her interest in Taoism, her fiction is notable for the purity and directness of its style, for the originality of its concepts, and for its air of solid wisdom. She has won a number of Hugo and Nebula Awards and a National Book Award.

Le Guin has written poetry, criticism, several volumes of short stories, and some sixteen novels, but she rarely deals directly with issues of homosexuality. (An exception is the short story "Quoits" in the collection *Searoads,* 1991, in which a middle-aged woman copes with the death of her lesbian partner.) In Le Guin's fiction, male beauty receives its due tribute, minor characters who happen to be homosexual are not unknown, and male rapacity and female uselessness figure in several imperfect societies. But Le Guin deals with sexuality itself in her best-known novel, *The Left Hand of Darkness* (1969), whereas her more recent work, such as *Tehanu: The Last Book of Earthsea* (1990), evinces a subtly articulated feminism. *The Left Hand of Darkness* posits a world, Gethen, whose natives are human in every respect except that they are androgynous and mostly sexually neuter; for a few days each month, they enter a period of intense sexual activity during which they can become either male or female. This potentiality forces Earth-bound readers to reexamine their assumptions about sex roles and stereotypes, achievement of sexual fulfillment, modes of parenting, and structures of family life. The frigid climate of Gethen only enriches these complexities: Whether shaped by its holistic sexuality or by the need to survive, Gethenian society has never known war.

The story is told largely by a young black man from Terra, serving as first envoy of an interplanetary union that Gethen has been invited to join. His mission becomes a cause of conflict among Gethenian nations, and he is forced to flee for his life across a great ice sheet, accompanied by a Gethenian friend. The envoy has to learn first to deal with his friend's sexuality as the latter comes inevitably into estrus, and beyond that he has to learn to see his friend not as a sexual oddity but as an individual and a fellow human being.

Le Guin herself has several times discussed the problems of her *tour de force.* She notes the male bias of English pronouns and her failure to dramatize fully the feminine side of her Gethenians. In her collection of criticism, *The Language of the Night,* she also admits to a kind of shortfall of imagination in *The Left Hand of Darkness* whereby she "quite unnecessarily locked the Gethenians into heterosexuality . . . the omission [of the homosexual option] implies that sexuality is heterosexuality. I regret this very much."

In 1969, Le Guin was less consciously a feminist than she later became. Her evolving feminism eventually presented her with *Tehanu,* the fourth book of the classic Earthsea fantasy series. Ged the archmage-hero of the earlier books has returned home shorn of his power, but the heart of the novel is with Tenar, once the priestess of Atuan, now a farmer's widow, and the disfigured girl-child Therru. *Tehanu* is a novel about pain and learning, about what one does when the great male fantasy, the heroic quest, is over and it is time to start living within a merely human community.

Le Guin's work is not addressed specifically to gay or lesbian matters, but to the need to prize human individuality in every form. Her subjects are various, but her themes are strongly continuous: Against the value of uniqueness is set the need for community—what binds these seeming polarities is the enabling power of love. (See also SCIENCE FICTION AND FANTASY.)

—*Michael N. Stanton*

BIBLIOGRAPHY

Bucknall, Barbara. *Ursula K. Le Guin.* New York: Ungar, 1981. ■ Cummins, Elizabeth. *Understanding Ursula K. Le Guin.* Rev. ed. Columbia: University of South Carolina Press, 1993. ■ Olander, Joseph D. and Martin H. Greenberg, eds. *Ursula K. Le Guin.* New York: Taplinger, 1979. ■ Selinger, Bernard. *Le Guin and Identity in Contemporary Fiction.* Ann Arbor: UMI Research Press, 1988. ■ Spivak, Charlotte. *Ursula K. Le Guin.* Boston: Twayne Publishers, 1984.

Lewis, Matthew G.
(1775–1818)

Matthew "Monk" Lewis was born to a fairly prosperous family of some distinction. His father, who deeply loved his son, was England's Deputy Secretary at War; and his mother, also deeply loving, was literary, musical, and in all things encour-aging to her son. Lewis's parents divorced when the boy was six years old, and throughout his life he acted as emissary between them. He was educated at Westminster School and Christ Church, Oxford, and after leaving university, at eighteen, he went to The Hague to pursue a diplomatic career, at the same time convinced that he had a future as a writer. During his six months in The Hague, he composed his scandalous masterpiece *The Monk* (1795), which earned him the nickname that lasted until his death. After that "succès du scandale," Lewis was appointed to Parliament, and he served as a member of the House of Commons from 1796 to 1802. As a member of Parliament, he received special censure for his novel, but his heart was not in politics, and he spent most of the time after the publication of *The Monk* working on other literary products, one of which, *The Castle Spectre* (1797), was a huge success on the stage.

Chief among his attachments was his love for William Kelly, the ne'er-do-well son of Mrs. Kelly, an author with whom he corresponded, and to whom he offered various kinds of financial aid, among them the cost of educating her son. Lewis was involved with William for fifteen years, and though there is no proof of sexual involvement, Lewis did include the younger man in his will and speak of him always in affectionate, if frustrated, terms. The question of Lewis's "homosexuality" has been debated by his biographers, such as Summers and Peck, but surely they have been asking the wrong questions. That Lewis was of an unconventional sexual makeup is clear in his life as well as his works.

But whether or not anything about Lewis's own sexual behavior can be proved, *The Monk* is one of the great works in the gay and lesbian literary tradition. It is the story of frustrated desire expressed, at first anyway, as male–male love. Ambrosio, the hero of the novel, is a handsome monk above reproach in his private affairs. Then suddenly he finds himself involved with the emotions of a young (male) novice, whom he befriends and who becomes more and more tormenting to his solace. When this young man comes out to Ambrosio as a woman, Lewis has solved a dilemma of representation (male–male desire would have made his work even more notorious than it was), but he has not suppressed the same-sex desire of the work or made it less accessible to a gay reading. (See also GOTHICISM.)

—*George E. Haggerty*

BIBLIOGRAPHY

Byron, George Gordon, Lord. *Byron's Letters and Journals.* Leslie Marchand, ed. 12 vols. London: John Murray, 1973–1982. ■ Crompton, Louis. *Byron and Greek Love: Homophobia in Nineteenth-Century England.* Berkeley: University of California Press, 1985. ■ Haggerty, George E. "Literature and Homosexuality in the Late Eighteenth Century: Walpole, Beckford, and Lewis." *Studies in the Novel* 18 (1986): 341–352. ■ Marchand, Leslie. *Byron: A Biography.* 3 vols. New York: Knopf, 1957. ■ Peck, Louis F. *A Life of Matthew G. Lewis.* Cambridge, Mass.: Harvard University Press, 1961. ■ Rousseau, G. S. "The Pursuit of Homosexuality in the Eighteenth Century: 'Utterly Confused Category' and/or Rich Respository." *Eighteenth-Century Life* 9 (1985): 132–168. ■ Summers, Montague. *The Gothic Quest: A History of the Gothic Novel.* London: Fortune, 1938.

Lezama Lima, José
(1910–1976)

Born in Havana, Cuba, on December 19, 1910, José Lezama Lima is a major Latin-American literary figure. Although he received a law degree from the University of Havana in 1938, and indeed practiced law for some time, Lezama's true passion was literature. Apart from two brief trips—one to Mexico in 1949 and another to Jamaica in 1950—the "immobile traveler," as Lezama identified himself, never left Havana, dedicating himself entirely to writing and exploring the cultures of the world through his readings. Lezama's house at Trocadero 162 was filled with over ten thousand books and was the site of countless literary meetings with young writers who would stop by to engage the maestro in dialogue. A voracious but undisciplined reader, Lezama, as Emir Rodríguez Monegal observed, "absorbed everything pell-mell, unsystematically, with no clear chronology, . . . [giving] him a highly personal, synchronic perspective of Western culture." Lezama's eccentric erudition and extensive range of (mis)readings account for his singular poetic insights, his intoxicating, excessive, and encyclopedic style.

Until the publication of his novel *Paradiso* (1966), which brought him instant international fame and notoriety, Lezama was primarily known as a poet. In 1937, at the age of twenty-seven, his first poetic composition, *Muerte de Narciso* (*Death of Narcissus*), was published. The linguistic exuberance and ornamental erudition of this long, mythological poem sent shock waves through the Cuban literary establishment. Here was a difficult, yet highly bewitching and extravagant new style of baroque poetry—in the tradition of the great seventeenth-century Spanish baroque master Luis de Góngora—that translated reality into a dense labyrinth of verbal allusions. *Muerte de Narciso* provided a radical alternative to the folkloric and politically committed poetry of Nicolas Guillén who until that time dominated the Cuban literary establishment. Lezama soon became the intellectual leader of a new generation of Cuban writers who were not afraid to assimilate and experiment with new avant-garde theories. Lezama soon published other collections of poetry and books of essays, all highly provocative with their textured imagery and allegorical symbols. In addition, he founded and edited several important literary journals, among them *Orígenes* (1944–1956), considered by Latin-American scholars to have been one of the most significant literary magazines of this century.

For Lezama, literature was the expression of a dynamic and vital search for truth. It was this search for a lost, unitary principle, the process in itself rather than the end result, that motivated him most. His writing is marked by a constant probing of the boundaries of knowledge and artistic expression.

The publication of *Paradiso* in 1966 marked an important turning point in Lezama's career. Internationally, the novel was immediately recognized as a masterpiece. However, the novel's total lack of political commitment to the Cuban Revolution, as well as its explicit descriptions of male homosexual relations, was met with resistance in Cuba and placed Lezama in a precarious situation. As early as 1965, the new Cuban socialist regime had been conducting systematic purges of homosexuals whose conduct was considered to be at variance with revolutionary morals. Forced labor camps under the name of UMAP (an acronym for Unidades Militares de Ayuda a la Producción or Military Units for Aid to Production) were constructed in the province of Camagüey, Cuba, with the purpose of correcting so-called antisocial and deviant behaviors that, according to the government, threatened the creation of a true revolutionary consciousness. In actuality, the publication of *Paradiso* encountered numerous obstacles and government censorship before it was finally published in a limited edition of four thousand copies. (In 1968, it was republished simultaneously in larger print runs in Mexico and Argentina; the English translation appeared in 1974.) It was obviously a question of what type of literature the Cuban state chose to support since the new editorial houses were publishing other novels that clearly reflected a "revolutionary consciousness" in large print runs of fifteen to twenty thousand copies. That *Paradiso* was published at all is a testament to Lezama's reputation as an important literary figure that the Castro regime could not simply silence altogether if it wanted to preserve any form of credibility internationally.

Paradiso—a vast creative space that combines autobiography, fiction, and poetry in an endless proliferation of language—does not examine the specificity of homosexual desire, but rather homosexuality as part of an aesthetic view of existence. Lezama's novel is a work of pure aestheticism in which the richness of language is the true protagonist. The task of reading (deciphering) this monumental text, a novel that Rodríguez Monegal calls "the prose equivalent of Lezama's arduous volumes of poetry and criticism," may be too difficult for most readers. The story's constant digressions, ambiguities, conceptual and linguistic exuberance, and general refusal to say anything in a straightforward fashion will surely frustrate the reader who is searching for referential clarity. Lezama's famous dictum, "Only the difficult is stimulating," sums up his poetic system and should serve as a forewarning of *Paradiso*'s elaborate and complex style. The word's ability to astonish, to dazzle with its acoustic resonances, was what most interested Lezama, who, although venturing into the limitless possibilities of the novel genre, in the end was still a poet. Nonetheless, beneath *Paradiso*'s marvelous difficulties there are many stories, among them, a Bildungsroman, or novel of education, much in the same tradition as James Joyce's *Portrait of the Artist as a Young Man*.

The first seven chapters of *Paradiso* take the reader through the family life and childhood experiences of Jose Cemí, Lezama's poetic double. A pampered and sickly child suffering from asthma, Cemí ultimately emerges as the main subject in the novel. The death of his father, a military officer in the Cuban army and a symbol of masculine rectitude, is the impetus for the young boy's poetical destiny and search for salvation through the "Image" and the poetic word. As Cemí's mother tells him midway though the novel: "Your father's death was a profound event, I know that my children and I will give it depth while we are alive, because it left me with a dream that one of us would be a witness to our transfiguration in order to fill that absence." This lofty and erudite way of talking is typical of how the characters, be they children, grandmothers, or illiterate servants, express themselves in *Paradiso*.

The second half of *Paradiso* (Chapters 8–14) deals with Cemí's adolescence, sexual discovery, and special friendships with Fronesis and Foción. This triangular relationship structures the second half of the novel as a world of ideas in which the three friends engage in endless discussions about the meaning of the universe. Many critics have seen Cemí, Fronesis, and Foción as aspects of one personality, that is, a composite protagonist. More than corporeality, throughout the novel, Fronesis (whose name in Greek means "prudence") and Foción (who embodies chaos and a lack of reason) appear as dramatic functions or ideological options for the young Cemí who is seeking his vocation and personal destiny. In the end, Cemí synthesizes what he has learned from his friends and is ready to fulfill his artistic vocation.

In Chapter 8, a number of homosexual interludes are explicitly described that lead Cemí, Fronesis, and Foción to engage in lengthy philosophical discussions about the nature and origin of homosexuality in Chapters 9 and 10. These chapters, as well as the role that Fronesis and Foción play in the novel, have elicited varied interpretations among critics. Some scholars (Gustavo Pellón and Enrique Lihn, among others) believe that Lezama assigns a negative value to homosexuality, associating it with madness, the loss of reason, sterility, and a dangerous detour faced by Cemí in his years of poetic apprenticeship. Other critics see the frank discussions of homosexuality more positively: Gustavo Pérez Firmat postulates that Cemí's spiritual development entails a concomitant affirmation of his homosexuality, whereas Emilio Bejel sees homosexuality in *Paradiso* as an emblem of poetry, a creative surplus that goes beyond the permitted limits.

Regardless of the different interpretations that have been posited, on a simple plot level the reader cannot help reacting to what happens to the characters at the end of *Paradiso*: Foción, openly homosexual, goes mad as a result of his frustrated desire for Fronesis; Fronesis is sent to Paris by his father to protect him from Foción's homosexual advances; and Cemí, who rises above the carnal trappings of the flesh, manages to maintain his reason and equilibrium and can finally begin to write (the novel ends with the words "now we can begin").

Prior to his death on August 9, 1976, Lezama had been working on another novel that was to have been the continuation and culmination of *Paradiso*. The unfinished manuscript was published posthumously in 1977 under the title *Oppiano Licario*. (The title refers to a character who appears in both *Paradiso* and *Oppiano Licario* as Cemí's spiritual guide and protector.) Although most of the principal characters of the first novel reappear, the story is mostly centered on Fronesis, now living in Paris. Fronesis, whose reckless and carefree sensuality is described on various occa-

sions, attracts a number of individuals, both male and female, who cannot resist his physical and spiritual beauty. In a study of *Oppiano Licario*, Benito Pelegrín provides a close reading of Fronesis's sensual and homoerotic dream presented in Chapter 3, in which he finally is able to accept Foción's (homosexual) friendship: "The reality of the dream was to show [Fronesis] the secret closeness and sensuality of his friendship with Foción" (my translation). In *Oppiano Licario,* according to Pelegrín, "we no longer have the good heterosexual in opposition to the depraved homosexual, a *Paradiso* opposed to an *Inferno,* but rather the homosexual object is split in pairs of opposites between the friend and the enemy, the good and the bad, the individual that can be accepted and the individual that should be rejected" (my translation).

The reader should not be quick to judge Lezama's portrayal of homosexuality harshly. In both *Paradiso* and *Oppiano Licario,* homosexual interludes occupy a considerable portion of the texts. The mere fact that the author dared to express detailed sexual relations between men, at a time when such expressions were generally looked down on in Latin-American literature and severely censored by the Cuban revolutionary establishment, represents an important turning point in Latin-American letters that paved the way for a greater representation of homosexual desire.

—*Francisco Soto*

BIBLIOGRAPHY

Bejel, Emilio. *Jose Lezama Lima, Poet of the Image.* Gainesville: University of Florida Press, 1990. ■ Lihn, Enrique. "*Paradiso,* novela y homosexualidad." *Hispamérica* 8.22 (1979): 3–21. ■ Pelegrín, Benito. "Espejo, doble, homologo y homosexualidad en *Oppiano Licario* de José Lezama Lima." *Coloquio internacional: escritura y sexualidad en la literatura hispanoamericana.* Madrid: Editorial Fundamentos, 1990: 129–154. ■ Pellón, Gustavo. *José Lezama Lima's Joyful Vision.* Austin: University of Texas Press, 1989. ■ Pereira, Manuel. "El curso délfico." *Quimera* no. 110 (mayo 1992): 28–39. ■ Pérez Firmat, Gustavo. "Descent into *Paradiso*: A Study of Heaven and Homosexuality." *Hispania* 59.2 (1976): 247–257. ■ Rodríguez Monegal, Emir. *The Borzoi Anthology of Latin American Litereature.* Vol 2. New York: Knopf, 1977. ■ Souza, Raymond D. *Major Cuban Novelists.* Columbia: University of Missouri Press, 1976. ■ ———. *The Poetic Fiction of José Lezama Lima.* Columbia: University of Missouri Press, 1983.

Literary Theory: Gay, Lesbian, and Queer

Readers, generally speaking, are familiar with a type of writing about texts that has been called *literary criticism*. Criticism explicates facts about texts, analyzes them, and in the broadest sense, instructs a reader in *what* a text means. Literary criticism has also been a practice of valuation and

evaluation. Through demonstrating what a text means, literary criticism also determines whether or not what a text means is worth consideration. Literary theory, in contradistinction, attempts to examine *how* a text means. Russian critic Mikhail Bakhtin has been responsible for establishing the groundwork of literary theory through his formulation of *heteroglossia*. As Bakhtin sees it, at any given time, a number of cultural determinants allow a text, phrase, or word to have meaning. These may be social, historical, physiological, political, even personal. But a text or word must have relevance in relation to these contextual codes in order to make a meaning. Reading a word, then, presupposes these conditions; theory, in response, attempts to *delimit* or expose for view these grounding assumptions that allow meaning to happen.

Gay and lesbian criticism has had a brief but astounding history. Works such as Bonnie Zimmerman's *The Safe Sea of Women* (1990), Robert K. Martin's *The Homosexual Tradition in American Poetry* (1979), and John Boswell's *Christianity, Social Tolerance and Homosexuality* (1980) have looked at history, either in its "true" form or in the form of texts, and have elaborated how homosexuality has been a topic or theme within it. The political importance of such work is undeniable, but gay, lesbian, and queer theory by and large eschew the assumptions that motivate it. Gay, lesbian, and queer theory examine the ways in which sexuality and sexual difference play with, within, and against the very conditions of meaning that allow a word to be uttered. As such, any text, even one as "factual" and "nonsexual" as a parking ticket or a recipe for a casserole, can become the object of gay, lesbian, and queer theorization.

Although gay, lesbian, and queer theory are related practices, the three terms delineate separate emphases marked by different assumptions about the relationship between gender and sexuality. In two germinal essays, "The Traffic in Women: Notes on the 'Political Economy' of Sex" (1975) and "Thinking Sex: Notes for a Radical Theory of the Politics of Sexuality" (1975), Gayle Rubin elaborates a theory that has become central: that gender difference and sexual difference are related but are not the same. Gender difference refers to those spectrums of meaning governed by the binary terms *man/woman*, whereas sexual difference refers to those governed by the binary terms *heterosexual/homosexual*. Typically, sexual difference is expressed *through* gender difference; hence the common stereotypes of the feminine gay man and the masculine lesbian, wherein a deviance in relation to sexuality is made meaningful through a deviance in gender identification. Although sexual difference and gender difference are almost inextricable from each other in Western cultures, it should theoretically be possible to separate them and to examine the interplays between and within them. Moreover, how gender and sexual difference interact in any given text can provide clues about the ways in which power operates in the culture producing that text. Reading these clues, by and large, has been the goal of gay, lesbian, and queer theory.

With Rubin's distinction in mind, gay, lesbian, and queer theory can be roughly defined: Gay theory examines sexual difference as it is applicable to the male gender; lesbian theory examines sexual difference as it is applicable to the female gender; queer theory attempts to examine sexual difference separate from gender altogether, or with a radical depriviliging of the status of gender in traditional discourses. In practice, these categories seldom remain intact, and gay, lesbian, and queer theory exist as interdependent discourses that both facilitate and contest each other. Moreover, all three types of theory are eclectic and draw on other theoretical discourses such as psychoanalysis, cultural materialism, Marxism, semiotics, structuralism, and feminism. This plurality of practices makes it difficult to trace "genealogies" for any of the three fields, but it is nonetheless possible to outline certain works and principles that have been exceptionally influential within each area.

Lesbian theory has the most difficult history to sketch, primarily because its development has been so intimately connected with the history of feminism. In the early feminist movement, the identification of the lesbian as the "woman-identified-woman" that surfaced in numerous pamphlets of the 1960s seemed to allow her to function as a metaphor for an identity entirely separate from the male economy of power. Yet in feminist critical practice, this notion of separatism was frequently redirected to a consideration of relations between the sexes. Kate Millet's *Sexual Politics* (1969), arguably the most important early feminist tract, bears out this point. Her literary analyses focus on the representation of women in the writings of four males: D. H. LAWRENCE, Henry Miller, Norman Mailer, and JEAN GENET. Although the critique powerfully exposes the sexist assumptions that underpin the representation of women in these texts, it also silences the possibilities for the lesbian to emerge by necessarily grounding itself in a cross-gendered dynamic; which is to say, because the critique assumes the presence of the female subject and the male writer, the man–woman dichotomy that makes heterosexuality meaningful is always the precondition for analysis.

As feminism moved onward from Millet's groundbreaking work, it also moved into a more woman-identified space. Works such as Ellen Moer's

Literary Women (1976), Elaine Showalter's *A Literature of Their Own* (1977), and Sandra Gilbert's and Susan Gubar's *The Madwoman in the Attic* (1979) all examine writing by women from a woman's perspective. This approach in many ways enables a privileging and decentering of the male gender, yet despite this move, it still does not allow the emergence of a lesbian practice. The primary assumption governing this second phase of feminist inquiry is a unity of gender experience, and as such, differences between women become effaced. That is, by grouping literature around the category of "woman," this "gynocritics," as Showalter later called it, also ignores the axis of sexual difference that is necessary to define the lesbian as different from the heterosexual woman.

Lesbianism has emerged most forcefully as a theoretical dialogue in the work of several French feminists. In the late 1970s, a group of French feminists loosely aligned with the Mouvement de libération des femmes (MLF) began to forge a theoretical practice around the notion of a *féminité* that opposed the masculine bias present in Western modes of thought. Writers such as Luce Irigiray, Marguerite Duras, Claudia Hermann, and especially, HÉLÈNE CIXOUS created what has become known as *l'écriture féminine*, or writing from/of woman. In contradistinction to masculine writing, which champions a unitary vision of meaningful language structured by the phallus, woman's writing would, theoretically, break up that unity and provide a plural and fragmented vision based on the unboundedness of female desire. Because the theoretical impulse behind *l'écriture féminine* is to articulate a system of meaning absolutely noncontingent on masculine parameters, the lesbian again provides a productive theoretical trope for these theorists. Cixous, for example, in her manifesto "The Laugh of the Medusa," implores women to remember the early American feminist slogan that "we are all lesbians," which she interprets as meaning that women should not denigrate one another as they have been denigrated by men. Although *l'écriture féminine* provides a more visible articulation of lesbianism than most other feminist practices, it again treats lesbianism as a metaphor or trope that can be strategically used to destabilize the relationship between the terms *man* and *woman*, which again places lesbianism within a program governed by a heterosexual gender division.

The vexed relationship between gender difference and sexual difference that erases the lesbian in these previous theories is precisely what separatist lesbian theory has reacted against in both the American and French critical scenes. In America, this resistance is perhaps best embodied in the pioneering work of poet ADRIENNE RICH. Rich's essay "Compulsory Heterosexuality and Lesbian Existence" (1980) outlines two ideas central to lesbian theory: first, that lesbian desire exists as a continuum of desiring possibilities between women that range from friendship to sexual involvement; second, that culture presupposes heterosexuality as an inevitability, and hence the multiple manifestations of lesbian desire in culture become either erased or distorted. For Rich, then, lesbianism exists as both a disrupter of male power and a genuine bond of meaning between women. It plays within the relations of gender difference but is also a distinct form of sexual difference.

French feminist MONIQUE WITTIG has carried the separatism of Rich a step further. Reacting against the French feminism that amalgamates lesbianism within a broader metaphoric schema, Wittig argues that the very concept of woman is a political category constructed by men for their use. Therefore, lesbians, who refuse to participate in this economy of masculine use, defy gender. In her most famous essay, "The Straight Mind" (1980), Wittig ends with the bold pronouncement, "Lesbians are not women." Wittig's strident claims have infuriated many critics, but they nonetheless can be seen as an important step in liberating the axis of sexual difference from that of gender difference.

This admittedly brief sketch of the emergence of lesbian theory needs also to recognize an important and complementary movement, the development of a lesbian practice within film studies. Film studies, perhaps more than any other academic area, has been responsible for interrogating the construction of the psychoanalytic subject, and lesbian intervention into this field has led to substantial innovations in Freudian and Lacanian theory. The first intervention in this field, Laura Mulvey's "Visual Pleasure and Narrative Cinema" (1975), appropriates psychoanalytic theory to explain how traditional Hollywood cinema constructs woman in order to embody and contain threats of castration, and to thereby posit a unitary and solidified masculine spectator position for the audience. Mulvey's argument does not engage lesbianism directly, but her recognition that the very form of looking inherent in film encodes strategies of gender and power has enabled the formation of a lesbian critique. Teresa de Lauretis's *Technologies of Gender* (1987) and, especially, her recent article "Sexual Indifference and Lesbian Representation" (1990), expand Mulvey's notion of a gendered power within the *form* of cinema (as opposed to the thematic *content* of cinema) in order to demonstrate how the cinematic apparatus subsumes differences such as lesbianism in order to construct a male, patriarchal form of representation.

Precisely because lesbian theory has been both empowered and disempowered by its relationship to feminist theory—which itself bears both an empowered and disempowered relationship to feminism itself, that is, to the politics of women in the world—it has also typically and understandably been concerned with the lesbian subject, that is, with the politics of lesbians in the world. Such a statement may seem to go without saying, were it not for the ways in which gay male theory has worked in an opposite direction. The initial stages of gay male theory seem to derive predominantly from the social constructionist precepts of MICHEL FOUCAULT, whose influential *The History of Sexuality* (1978) sketches the construction of sexuality as a technology of social control, an effort to construct an identifiable meaning for people in Western societies. As such, gay male theory emerged, ironically enough, with a notion of ignoring the gay male altogether and looking instead at the category of "the homosexual" as a disembodied social construct.

The intersection of gay theory and social constructionism had its canonical moment in British sociological writings of the early 1970s. In 1968, Mary McIntosh published an article, "The Homosexual Role," that both predated and anticipated Foucault's work in arguing that "the homosexual" was a social role that emerged in England in the seventeenth century. A number of important early essays spurred by this work are collected in the anthology *The Making of the Modern Homosexual* (1981). McIntosh's stance, along with the emerging work of Foucault, resulted in a number of sociological studies of sexuality that examined sexual roles as effects of the configurations of power in culture; most notable among these are Jeffrey Weeks's *Sex, Politics and Society* (1981) and *Sexuality and Its Discontents* (1985), and Dennis Altman's *The Homosexualization of America* (1982), which focuses on the construction of gay male culture in contemporary America. One problem implicit in much of the social constructionist work is, again, the issue of subsuming the lesbian. Work such as that of Foucault seems to avoid an undue attention to gender difference by examining the categories of heterosexuality/homosexuality in cultural formations; yet, in practice, the terms *homosexual* and *gay*—unless specified as female—generally connote male homosexuality. And with only a few exceptions, social constructionist work has done little to undermine this territorializing gender assumption.

The social constructionist movement also highlights the strong current of Marxism underpinning much gay theory. One central but often overlooked voice in this respect is that of GUY HOCQUENGHEM. In 1968, Hocquenghem published his book *Homosexual Desire*, which is a radical Marxist revision of Freudian analysis. Strongly influenced by the French leftist rebellions of 1968, and also deeply indebted to the theory of "schizoanalysis" proposed by Gilles Deleuze and Félix Guattari in *Anti-Oedipus*, Hocquenghem's theory examines the historical and psychological construction of "the homosexual" as a displacement and repression of society's own homosexual desire. Arguing that desire is an unbroken and polyvocal phenomenon, *Homosexual Desire* suggests that the establishment of exclusive homosexuality is a way of isolating and expelling those segments of desire that do not imitate the productive and reproductive goals of capitalism. Sexuality, therefore, is not a "natural" phenomenon but is the effect of the economic relations of a given culture.

Hocquenghem's tract shares much with the social constructionists, but by stressing a divide between desire and identity, it also presages the concerns that have constellated around the relatively new practices of queer theory. Unlike gay and lesbian theory, which focus on the intersections of desire and identity, queer theory typically disembodies desire and examines how homoeroticism and heteroeroticism function, intermingling and mutually confusing modes of expression within the constructions of cultures and identities. The text that has been most responsible for initiating the tenets of queer theory is Eve Kosofsky Sedgwick's *Between Men: English Literature and Male Homosocial Desire* (1985). Sedgwick eschews an analysis of homosexuality and heterosexuality in favor of an examination of homosexuality and "homosociality." Homosociality represents the various bonds between men that are necessary to maintain a society, especially those that involve the transmission of status and property through women—marriage, birth, and so on. These bonds between men *through* women are posited by Western cultures as being antithetical to pure homosexual bonds, which do not need to process women as mediating figures, but Sedgwick proceeds to demonstrate how the two antithetical terms continually collapse into each other in practice and in literature. Hence Sedgwick finds the origin and reflection of homoeroticism within heteroerotic practices themselves. Sedgwick's analysis bears a striking similarity to that of Hocquenghem and also to Luce Irigiray's conception of "hom(m)o-sexuality" in the important essay "Women on the Market" (1978). Yet more than any other single work, Sedgwick's analysis has focused an awareness that desire and identity are neither coterminous nor congruous; hence the analysis of desire becomes a potent means of destabilizing the assumptions that underpin the construction of both gay and straight identities.

As this description implies, queer theory is a plural and diffuse set of practices, not a unified field of theory. A brief description of two important texts can begin to suggest the polymorphousness of the topic. Judith Butler's *Gender Trouble* (1990) begins by reading a number of contemporary theorists, including Jacques Lacan, Foucault, Wittig, Julia Kristeva, and Irigiray, in order to demonstrate how gender functions as both a solidifying and unintentionally destabilizing assumption within their arguments. Her own theory then proposes that a number of subversive "performative" strategies, including parody and drag, can be used to "overplay" the codes of gender and thereby foreground identity in its most subversive and denaturalized forms. Jonathan Dollimore's *Sexual Dissidence* (1991) begins by contrasting the homosexual writings of ANDRÉ GIDE and OSCAR WILDE. Gide symbolizes for Dollimore a sort of acceptance of identity troubled or altered by sexual difference, whereas Wilde symbolizes a full embrace of difference that, in its extremity, calls into question the very possibility of identity. These two positions become theoretical polarities that Dollimore traces through both the Renaissance and contemporary culture. What should be apparent from these unavoidably reductive summaries is that though gay and lesbian theory attempt to examine different identities, queer theory examines differences in order to undermine the very notion of identity.

Although the representative authors mentioned here can be seen as exemplifying certain key ideas in the formation of gay, lesbian, and queer theoretical practices, it is also true that a multitude of other theorists could have as easily been invoked; moreover, the practices that have crystalized around the terms *gay, lesbian,* and *queer* have a history, and a thorough examination of this history would have to include SAPPHO and PLATO, RADCLYFFE HALL and Havelock Ellis, Lady Mary Wroth and WILLIAM SHAKESPEARE, and many others. The problematic inevitably involved in summarizing gay, lesbian, and queer theory is that the common but misplaced notion that "theory" is solely a postmodern phenomenon forces a disengagement of the history that has enabled the very articulation of the words *gay, lesbian,* and *queer* themselves. Moreover, any survey such as this is happily destined to become quickly antiquated, for gay, lesbian, and queer theory are at such a tremendous level of production and accomplishment that all three fields are being continuously rewritten and redefined. Yet the form sketched here—the inevitable tension involved in writing with and against concepts of identity—is

one that will likely remain central to all three fields for some time to come; thus, though the content of this survey may change, the general tensions it maps out may serve as a helpful and reliable outline for readers approaching these theoretical fields for the first time. (See also FEMINIST LITERARY THEORY, GENDER, and IDENTITY.)

—*Gregory W. Bredbeck*

BIBLIOGRAPHY

Abelove, Henry, Michèle Aina Barale, and David M. Halperin, eds. *The Gay and Lesbian Studies Reader.* New York: Routledge, 1993. ■ Altman, Dennis. *The Homosexualization of America.* Boston: Beacon Press, 1982. ■ Butler, Judith. *Gender Trouble: Feminism and the Subversion of Identity.* New York: Routledge, 1990. ■ Cixous, Hélène. "The Laugh of the Medusa." *The Signs Reader: Women, Gender and Scholarship.* Elizabeth Abel and Emily K. Abel, eds. Chicago: University of Chicago Press, 1983. 279–297. ■ de Lauretis, Teresa. *Technologies of Gender: Essays on Theory, Film, and Fiction.* Bloomington: Indiana University Press, 1987. ■ ———. "Sexual Indifference and Lesbian Representation." *Performing Feminisms: Feminist Critical Theory and Theatre.* Sue-Ellen Case, ed. Baltimore: Johns Hopkins University Press, 1990. 17–39. ■ Deleuze, Gilles and Félix Guattari. *Anti-Oedipus: Capitalism and Schizophrenia.* Trans. Robert Hurley, Mark Seem, and Helen R. Lane. Minneapolis: University of Minnesota Press, 1983. ■ Dollimore, Jonathan. *Sexual Dissidence: Augustine to Wilde, Freud to Foucault.* Oxford: Clarendon Press, 1991. ■ Foucault, Michel. *The History of Sexuality: An Introduction, Volume I,* New York: Random House, 1978. ■ Fuss, Diana. *Inside/Out: Lesbian Theories, Gay Theories.* New York: Routledge, 1991. ■ Hocquenghem, Guy. *Homosexual Desire.* Trans. Danielle Dangoor. London: Allison and Busby, 1978. ■ Irigaray, Luce. "Women on the Market." *This Sex Which Is Not One.* Trans. Catherine Porter with Carolyn Burke. Ithaca, N.Y.: Cornell University Press, 1985. 170–191. ■ McIntosh, Mary. "The Homosexual Role." *The Making of the Modern Homosexual.* Kenneth Plummer, ed. London: Hutchinson, 1981. 30–44. ■ Millett, Kate. *Sexual Politics.* New York: Simon & Schuster, 1969. ■ Mulvey, Laura. "Visual Pleasure and Narrative Cinema." *Visual and Other Pleasures.* Bloomington: Indiana University Press, 1989. 14–26. ■ Plummer, Kenneth, ed. *The Making of the Modern Homosexual.* London: Hutchinson, 1981. ■ Rich, Adrienne. "Compulsory Heterosexuality and Lesbian Existence." *Women, Sex and Sexuality.* Catharine R. Stimpson and Ethel Spector Person, eds. Chicago: University of Chicago Press, 1980. 62–91. ■ Sedgwick, Eve Kosofsky. *Between Men: English Literature and Male Homosocial Desire.* New York: Columbia University Press, 1985. ■ Showalter, Elaine. "Feminist Criticism in the Wilderness." *The New Feminist Criticism: Essays on Women, Literature and Theory.* Elaine Showalter, ed. New York: Pantheon, 1985. 243–270. ■ ———. "Toward a Feminist Poetic." *The New Feminist Criticism: Essays on Women, Literature and Theory.* Elaine Showalter, ed. New York: Pantheon, 1985. 125–143. ■ Weeks, Jeffrey. *Sex, Politics and Society: The Regulation of Sexuality Since 1800.* London: Longman, 1981. ■ ———. *Sexuality and Its Discontents.* London: Routledge and Kegan Paul, 1985. ■ Wittig, Monique. *The Straight Mind and Other Essays.* Boston: Beacon Press, 1992.

Lorde, Audre
(1934–1992)

Born on February 18, 1934, in New York City of West Indian parents, Audre Lorde was educated at Hunter College and Columbia University. On completing a master's degree in library studies in 1961 at Columbia University, she initially worked as a librarian in New York. From 1968 onward, she held various academic positions: first, as a lecturer in creative writing at City College and in the Education Department at Herbert H. Lehman College, later as an Associate Professor of English at John Jay College of Criminal Justice, where she fought for a Black Studies Department. Lorde also taught English at Hunter College, was a poet in residence at Tougaloo College, and a visiting lecturer throughout the United States. In 1962, she married Edwon Ashley Rollins and had two children, Elizabeth and Jonathan. Ultimately, the marriage failed. After her divorce from Rollins in 1970, Lorde began to have long-term relationships with women. She died in 1992 after a long battle with cancer.

Throughout her life, Lorde fought for African Americans' rights both as an activist and as a writer. The political nature of her work is obvious in essays such as "Apartheid U.S.A" and "I am your Sister," where, while stressing the need for women to organize across sexualities, she examines the way that black lesbians are stereotyped by whites as well as by blacks.

Lorde's lesbianism had a major influence on her work. *Zami: A New Spelling of My Name* (1982), considered by the writer as a "biomythography," a synthesis of history, biography, and mythology, is a lesbian text. Lesbianism for Lorde had a broad definition. While using the term to describe women who have sexual relations with other women, she expanded its scope to include women whose emotional connectedness is centered on women regardless of sexual intimacy. Emotional bonding among women is at the center of *Zami*. So is the celebration of women's power and figures of ancestral African mothers. From its beginning, the book explores the physical and emotional aspects of Audre, a black poet, and her relationships with other women—Eudora, Gennie, Muriel, and Afrekete, among others. Lorde examines the significance of these relationships to her life as an artist. Rather than presenting a rupture between the sexual and emotional life of the black woman poet and her creative work, the text raises the possibility of integrating both aspects of the life experience.

Lorde, self-identified as a black feminist lesbian poet warrior, started writing poetry when she was twelve and never stopped. Even her prose work is marked by a lyrical sensibility. In *Zami: A New Spelling of My Name*, lesbian unions are poetically presented: "her hips moved like surf upon the water's edge" and "sweat-slippery dark bodies, sacred as the ocean at high tide." Even in *The Cancer Journals* (1980), we find a poetic quality. Written as an affirmation of survival, the book documents the experiences of living with cancer and dealing with pain.

Permeated by a strong social and political consciousness, Lorde's work gives special attention to the dynamics of being a black woman. In "A Woman Speaks," from *The Black Unicorn* collection (1978), the poetic voice states: "I am woman and not white," while in another poem the same voice identifies being black with a unicorn: "The black unicorn is restless / the black unicorn is unrelenting / the black unicorn is not free." "Sisters in Arms" from *Our Dead Behind Us* (1986) explores solidarity among black women, and the theme of the black woman artist, central to all of Lorde's work, is presented in "To the Poet Who Happens to Be Black and the Black Poet Who Happens to be a Woman" of *Our Dead Behind Us*. The affirmations of her identities as a black woman and a lesbian are paramount motifs in her work.

Intertwined with the affirmations of racial and sexual identities, love remains a constant theme in Lorde's work. Various forms of love—both lesbian and heterosexual—appear at the center of her texts, particularly her first collections of poetry: *The First Cities* (1968), *The New York Head Shop and Museum* (1974), and *The Black Unicorn*. In her essay "Uses of the Erotic: The Erotic as Power," she examines the question of loving and the tremendous power of the erotic. For her, the erotic was a deep enlightening force within women's lives, a source of power and knowledge.

In general, the voices in Lorde's work challenge the conventions and norms of a racist, heterosexist, and homophobic society and stress the urgency of fighting against inequality. From her first texts, the poet reiterates her sexual identity and reaffirms her literary as well as social space. In her poetry, essays, interviews, and fiction, she articulates a political discourse that underscores the oppression suffered by black lesbians. By inscribing her own experiences and stressing the responsibility of identifying herself as black and lesbian, Lorde avoids blanket generalizations and rigid essentialism. Most important, she bespeaks the specificity of the situation of black lesbians in the United States. By recognizing that her blackness and her lesbianism were not separate, she unified both struggles. (See also AFRICAN-AMERICAN LITERATURE, LESBIAN and POETRY, LESBIAN.)

—Elena M. Martínez

BIBLIOGRAPHY

"Audre Lorde." *Callaloo*. A Special Section. 14:1 (1991): 39–95. ■ Evans, Mari. *Black Women Writers: (1950–1980) A Critical Evaluation*. New York: Doubleday, 1984. ■ Metzger, Linda, ed. *Black Writers. A Selection of Sketches from Contemporary Authors*. Detroit: Gale Research, 1989. 364–366. ■ Tate, Claudia. *Black Women Writers at Work*. New York: Continuum, 1983.

Lowell, Amy
(1874–1925)

Amy Lowell was a poet, translator, essayist, literary biographer, and public speaker. She was born February 9, 1874, in Brookline, Massachusetts, to Augustus and Katherine Lawrence Lowell. She was much younger than her siblings and so grew up lonely in the company of literate and socially sophisticated adults on the ten-acre family estate, Sevenels. She was a precocious child even among a prominent family of high achievers and important New England personages, James Russell Lowell, a great-cousin, among them. Throughout her life, Lowell would struggle to distinguish herself on her own merits and accomplishments, apart from her family fortune and famous relatives. She attended private girls' schools until age seventeen when she left school to care for her elderly parents. At home, she undertook a rigorous self-education, reading widely among the several thousand books in the library of Sevenels. She became an ardent student of poetry, especially Keats's. After her parents' deaths, Lowell purchased Sevenels from her father's estate, transforming the house and stables into a compound almost totally devoted to her two great endeavors: creating and promoting modern American poetry and breeding dogs. After a decade of poor health and painful operations brought on by an injury suffered while lifting a buggy out of a ditch, Lowell died of a stroke on May 12, 1925. She was survived by Ada (Dwyer) Russell, the woman with whom she had shared her home and her passions for thirteen years.

Lowell's first poem was published at age thirty-six in *Atlantic Monthly,* but subsequently her poetry production was as prolific as her reading was voracious. She published on average a volume a year even during the most debilitating periods of her illness. Her last book of poems, *What's O'Clock* (1925), published posthumously, received the Pulitzer Prize in 1926. Much of Lowell's poetry was inspired by her two great muses, Ada Russell, also her fairest and most reliable critic, and Eleonora Duse, a popular stage actress for whom Lowell's infatuation was powerful and lifelong, though they met only twice. Lowell wrote dozens of sonnets and lyrics to and for Duse, some of which were so intimate they were suppressed until the deaths of both women. But much of Lowell's published poetry is extremely frank, forthrightly sensual, and often overtly lesbian.

The effectiveness of Lowell's best work derives from its startling detail and provocative imagery. Her favorite images are water, bathing, and fountains; flowers and gardens; nature and natural phenomena. She employs these figures again and again in passionate lyrics, often addressed to "Beloved" (Ada Russell). In *Sword Blades and Poppy Seed* (1914), the lesbian poetry is highly coded, as in "Aubade." Others of the poems veil lesberoticism beneath stylistic convention, as in the last stanzas of "In a Garden":

> And I wished for night and you.
> I wanted to see you in the swimming-pool,
> White and shining in the silver-flecked water.
> While the moon rode over the garden,
> High in the arch of night,
> And the scent of the lilacs was heavy with
> stillness.
> Night, and the water, and you in your
> whiteness, bathing!

But in *Pictures of the Floating World* (1919), Lowell's lesbian lyrics and conceits become more explicit even as they also grow more tender and nostalgic, the result of her maturing relationship with Russell and her chronic ill health, as in "A Decade":

> When you came, you were like red wine and
> honey,
> And the taste of you burnt my mouth with its
> sweetness.

Now you are like morning bread,
Smooth and pleasant.
I hardly taste you at all for I know your savour,
But I am completely nourished.

Lowell was exceptionally obese all of her life, and though easily hurt by insults and ridicule, she was quite unselfconscious about representing her body as sexual, sensual, and pleasurable in her poetry. Lowell was in this respect and in all things disarming, famous for smoking cigars and wearing men's shirts, and for these predilections she was the target of numerous humiliations and personal attacks from critics more intent on mocking her appearance and habits than assessing seriously her work.

Lowell was, in addition, a tireless promoter and patron of poetry. She wished to be thought of as an "activist" of American poetry. Her fame and generosity introduced her to many of America's most promising poets: Robert Frost, Edwin Arlington Robinson, SARA TEASDALE, Elinor Wylie, and others. She was a good booster and did much to enlarge their reading publics and enhance their critical esteem. Most notable in this capacity, Lowell brought Imagism from England to the United States. In 1913, Lowell read some poetry by "H.D., Imagiste" in Harriet Monroe's little magazine, *Poetry,* and immediately recognized in it an affinity with her own work: "direct treatment of the thing," no superfluous language, the rhythm of music rather than traditional poetic meter—the defining traits of Imagism. HILDA DOOLITTLE's appearance in *Poetry* had been the project of another poet, promoter, and strong personality, Ezra Pound. Later in 1913, Lowell traveled to England to meet H.D. and to learn more about what she could do in the service of Imagism, which she thought of as the very future of poetry.

As Lowell's reputation and success as champion of Imagism in the United States grew, publishing three volumes of *Some Imagist Poets* from 1915 to 1917, Ezra Pound grew more furious, believing he had been deposed as head of a movement he considered his rightful domain. He withdrew his participation, moving on to Vorticism and hoping to defame Lowell by scoffing "Amygisme" and supporting spoofs and jibes directed at her. Still, Imagism under the promotion and practice of Lowell represents a major development in American poetry. Eventually, though, Lowell came to believe less and less in the principles of any particular school of poetic expression and committed her energies to writing her two-volume biography of John Keats, which she dedicated to Ada Russell, and to developing "polyphonic prose," a style of lyric prose marked by crafted patterns of sound and imagery. Her *Keats* was a great success in the United States, but critics received it poorly in England, where they viewed her work as presumptuous and an affront to British literary history. Yet again, it seems, her work was dismissed on personal bases—her gender, her size, her sexuality, her personal style, and in the case of *Keats,* her nationality. Still, her permanent contributions to literature and American poetry are undeniable.

—Carolyn Leste Law

BIBLIOGRAPHY

Benvenuto, Richard. *Amy Lowell.* Boston: Twayne Publishers, 1985. ■ Faderman, Lillian. "Warding off the Watch and Ward Society: Amy Lowell's Treatment of the Lesbian Theme." *Gay Books Bulletin* 1.2 (Summer 1979): 23–27. ■ Gould, Jean. "Amy Lowell: Imagism and Surrealism." *American Women Poets: Pioneers of Modern Poetry.* New York: Dodd, Mead, 1980. 29–65. ■ ———. *Amy: The World of Amy Lowell and the Imagist Movement.* New York: Dodd, Mead, 1975. ■ Lowell, Amy. *Complete Poetical Works.* Intro. Louis Untermeyer. Boston: Houghton Mifflin, 1955.

Lucian
(ca 120–ca 185)

Lucian was born at Samosata, a town on the Euphrates. He is best known as a satirical author of seventy to eighty prose pieces in Greek, including essays, speeches, letters, dialogues, and stories influenced by Attic old comedy, Homeric myth, Platonic dialogue, and Menippean satire. Only incidentally engaged with the details of contemporary history, Lucian's works deploy stock types such as the misanthrope, tyrant, debauchee, and sycophant and do not advance a consistent philosophical position.

Homosexuality in Lucian is not the root of individual identity. It is instead treated as one of a related series of personal traits that characterize villainy, pretension, and ignorance. The titular character of *The Mistaken Critic,* for instance, is deplored, as a part of his general iniquity, for his effeminacy and prostitution, and for two incidents of fellatio, one of which the critic performed at a public banquet on a hired man with a penis so enormous that his jaw is hyperbolically described as having been dislocated. *A Pro-*

fessor of Public Speaking, Alexander the False Prophet, The Passing of Peregrinus, and The Ignorant Book-Collector similarly present homosexuality in connection with other forms of apparent profligacy and cultural uncouthness.

In "Zeus and Ganymede," part of Lucian's *Dialogues of the Gods,* Zeus's pederastic infatuation with the lunkheaded Ganymede is in keeping with the sensuality of the heterosexual gods. The novel *Lucius, or the Ass* includes a rollicking tale of priests who capture a village youth and force him to have sex with them, thus making a minor point on moral hypocrisy. The ironically titled *A True Story* is an account of a voyage to the moon, a land where there are no women and where marriage and procreation is between men under 25, who act as wives, and older men, who act as husbands, an obvious glance at classical male–male pederasty. Because moonmen do not possess anuses, intercourse is through an opening above the calf, and new men are thus conceived in the thigh. Alternately, "tree people" emerge from acorns that grow on enormous penis-shaped trees of flesh produced by the planting of right testicles in the ground.

The nonsatirical *Erôtes,* or *Amores,* written by pseudo-Lucian, is a third- or fourth-century dialogue within a dialogue that advocates male–male love. In the *Erôtes,* Lycinus recounts a debate between Charicles of Corinth, who advocated love for women, and Callicratidas of Athens, who favored men. Callicratidas carries the day by arguing three main points: Marriage to women was invented out of reproductive necessity, whereas love for men was cultivated for its beauty and is therefore more honorable and a sign of social progress; though animals do not engage in homosexual love neither do they know anything of philosophy or friendship; women are vain and trite, whereas young men are sober, brave, and intelligent, and therefore, to love a young man is to express one's own wisdom and virtue. In his defense, Callicratidas departs from normative hierarchical pederasty by envisioning an Aristotelian friendship between equals that also includes sexual relations. (See also GREEK LITERATURE, ANCIENT.)

—*M. Morgan Holmes*

BIBLIOGRAPHY

Anderson, Graham. *Studies in Lucian's Comic Fiction.* Leiden: E. J. Brill, 1976. ■ Branham, Robert Bracht. *Unruly Eloquence: Lucian and the Comedy of Traditions.* Cambridge, Mass.: Harvard University Press, 1989. ■ Cantarella, Eva. *Bisexuality in the Ancient World.* 1988. Trans. Cormac Cuilleanain. New Haven: Yale University Press, 1992. ■ Halperin, David M. "Historicizing the Sexual Body: Sexual Preferences and Erotic Identities in the Pseudo-Lucianic Erotes." *Discourses of Sexuality: From Aristotle to AIDS.* Domna C. Stanton, ed. Ann Arbor: University of Michigan Press, 1992. 236–261. ■ Jones, C. P. *Culture and Society in Lucian.* Cambridge, Mass.: Harvard University Press, 1986. ■ Lucian. *Lucian.* Trans. A. D. Harmon, K. Kilburn and M. D. Macleod. 8 vols. Loeb Classical Library. Cambridge, Mass.: Harvard University Press, 1913–1967. ■ Robinson, Christopher. *Lucian and His Influence in Europe.* London: Duckworth, 1979.

Mackay, John Henry
(1864–1933)

Mackay was born in Scotland on February 6, 1864, the son of a marine insurance broker who died when Mackay was only nineteen months old. His mother, of a well-to-do Hamburg family, then returned with him to Germany, where he grew up with German as his mother tongue. He first gained recognition as a lyric poet and his novellas were early examples of naturalism, but it was his presentation of individualist anarchism in the semifictional *Die Anarchisten* (*The Anarchists*) that made him famous overnight. It was published in German and in English translation in 1891 and was later translated into eight other languages.

Mackay's *Der Schwimmer* (*The Swimmer*), one of the first literary sports novels, appeared in 1901. He was at the height of his fame, but the death of his mother the following year brought on a depression from which he recovered only by dedicating himself to the cause of gaining sympathetic recognition of man-boy love. (Mackay himself was most attracted to boys fourteen to seventeen years old.) He planned a literary campaign, using the pseudonym Sagitta. He intended to publish six books in a variety of literary forms, but his project had hardly begun when the first books were confiscated and charges brought against Mackay's publisher, who never revealed the identity of Sagitta. After a nineteen-month trial, the books were legally declared obscene in 1909, and the publisher was required to pay a fine and court costs. Mackay bore all this financial burden, yet continued the project and, in 1913, published a one-volume edition of *Die Buecher der namelosen Liebe von*

Sagitta (*Sagitta's Books of the Nameless Love*), which he sold underground. Most notable in the collection is the autobiographical novel *Fenny Skaller*, a moving "coming-out" story of a boy-lover.

During World War I, Mackay worked on *Der Freiheitsucher* (*The Freedom Seeker*), a sequel to *Die Anarchisten*, which he published in 1920. Its reception was disappointing, but a real financial blow came in 1923 when the runaway inflation wiped out the value of a lifetime annuity he had purchased with his inheritance from his mother. Despite the hardships, Mackay returned as Sagitta in 1926 with his seventh Book of the Nameless Love, *Der Puppenjunge* (*The Hustler*), a classic boy-love novel set in the contemporary milieu of boy prostitutes in Berlin. In a note to the American publisher of this book, CHRISTOPHER ISHERWOOD said, "It gives a picture of the Berlin sexual underworld early in this century which I know, from my own experience, to be authentic." Although *Der Puppenjunge* could be sold in bookstores in the Weimar Republic, all writings of Sagitta were banned by the Nazis.

Although Mackay wrote about homosexuality most explicitly as Sagitta, the subject can also be found in his other writings. In an early short story and in many lyric poems, the absence of personal pronouns permits a heterosexual reading of what were undoubtedly homosexual situations. Only in 1931 did he include obvious homosexual characters in the novella *Der Unschuldige* (*The Innocent*), a work almost unique at the time for its inclusion of homosexuality as a matter of fact and not as a sickness or a symbolic evil.

By the time of Mackay's death on May 16, 1933, it had long been an open secret that he was Sagitta, and he wrote in his will that any future publications were to bear his real name. This was done in 1979; since then, there has been a return of interest in this unique writer.

—Hubert Kennedy

BIBLIOGRAPHY

Kennedy, Hubert. *Anarchist der Liebe: John Henry Mackay als Sagitta*. Trans. Almuth Carstens. Berlin: Edition Aurora, 1988. ■ Mackay, John Henry. *Die Buecher der namenlosen Liebe von Sagitta*. 2 vols. Berlin: Verlag rosa Winkel, 1979. ■ ———. *Fenny Skaller and Other Prose Writings from the Books of the Nameless Love*. Trans. Hubert Kennedy. Amsterdam: Southernwood Press, 1988. ■ ———. *The Hustler: The Story of a Nameless Love from Friedrich Street*. Trans. Hubert Kennedy. Boston: Alyson, 1985. ■ Mornin, Edward. *Kunst und Anarchismus: "innere Zusammen-hänge" in den Schriften John Henry Mackays*. Freiburg/Br.: Verlag der Mackay-Gesellschaft, 1983. ■ Riley, Thomas A. *Germany's Post-Anarchist John Henry Mackay: A Contribution to the History of German Literature at the Turn of the Century, 1880-1920*. New York: Revisionist Press, 1972. ■ Solneman, K. H. Z. [Kurt Helmut Zube]. *Der Bahn-brecher John Henry Mackay: Sein Leben und sein Werk*. Freiburg/Br.: Verlag der Mackay-Gesellschaft, 1979.

Mann, Klaus
(1906–1949)

The oldest son of THOMAS MANN's six children, Klaus Mann received an education in alternative schools and began writing fiction at an early age. In the 1920s, he became a well-known representative, as author and anthologist, of the new German writers describing a generation adrift in metropolitan life. In the 1930s, he became a leader in the cultural resistance to fascism.

His relationship with his father was difficult, in part due to the father's greater talent and in part due to the son's greater ability to accept and live out his homosexual desires. But Klaus Mann's vision of homosexuality is marked by loneliness and alienation. In his autobiography, *The Turning Point* (1942), Mann wrote: "To be an outsider is the one unbearable humiliation." That belief shaped his portrayal of male and female homosexual characters. In his fiction, same-sex love ends or bears no hope of success, for those involved switch their affections to a heterosexual love object (*Anja und Esther* [*Anja and Esther*, 1925]), literally succumb to the futility of such relationships and die (*Alexander*, 1930), or continue to suffer a lonely existence (*Vor dem Leben* [*Before Life*, 1925]).

His most hopeful novel, *Der fromme Tanz* (*The Pious Dance*, 1926), promotes a utopian vision of platonic male friendship, hard work, and unrealized homoeroticism. Often, homosexuality functions as a symbol of the decadence Mann saw within his own generation and time. In *Der Vulkan* (*The Volcano*, 1939), a budding love is destroyed by the drug addiction of one of the young men. His most openly homosexual novel, *Windy Night, Rainy Morrow* (also called *Peter and Paul*, 1947), remained unfinished at his death.

Trapped within the possibilities allowed by his day, his homosexual characters cannot break the bonds of being always the Other. These figures often bear the stamp of Magnus Hirschfeld's "Third Sex" theory: Male homosexuals are usually rather effeminate artistic types, and lesbians are masculinized females. They may revel in their position beyond the reach of bourgeois society, but they go to pieces because of it. This is also true of Klaus Mann's heterosexual characters, but their demise into the demimonde of drugs and desire or their otherwise tragic existence is not due to their sexuality or sexual identity.

The melancholic hopelessness in his fiction stands in contrast to Mann's nonfiction works (for example, *Andre Gide and the Crisis of Modern Thought,* 1943) and to his involvement with the U.S. Army (as a journalist and translator) in working toward the defeat of Nazism and toward a more egalitarian future. His essay on the homophobic attacks used by the left in an attempt to discredit the Nazis—"Homosexualität und Faschismus" ("Homosexuality and Fascism," 1934)—is often cited as one of the key gay texts of the early 1930s. In exile after 1933, he turned to the past, specifically to the homosexual past for inspiration for his novels: *Alexander, Symphonie Pathétique (Pathetic Symphony,* 1935), *Vergittertes Fenster (Barred Window,* 1937). These great men from the homosexual pantheon—Alexander the Great, Tchaikovsky, and King Ludwig II of Bavaria—function as lonely figures whose love separates them from their societies.

His fictional view seems to reveal his own personal truth, for Klaus Mann chose to commit suicide.

Klaus Mann has long been seen as the son of Germany's most famous twentieth-century author, as someone who wrote too quickly and superficially, and as a homosexual whose suicide fit the script for literary homosexuals. In recent decades, critics—mostly gay critics in Germany—have found much more than the tragic, but talented, homosexual son. Through new studies, a biography, and the publication of his diaries, a truer picture has developed. Klaus Mann stands now on his own, as gay German author, critic, and activist.

—*James W. Jones*

BIBLIOGRAPHY

Dirschauer, Wilfried, ed. *Klaus Mann und das Exil.* Worms: Georg Heintz, 1973. ■ Grünewald, Michael. *Klaus Mann, 1906–1949: Eine Bibliographie.* Munich: Edition Spangenberg, 1984. ■ Härle, Gerhard. *Männerweiblichkeit. Zur Homosexualität bei Klaus und Thomas Mann.* Frankfurt a.M.: Athenäum, 1988. ■ Kröhnke, Friedrich. *Propaganda für Klaus Mann.* Frankfurt a.M.: Materialis, 1981. ■ Kroll, Frederic, ed. *Klaus-Mann-Schriftenreihe.* Vols. 1–5. Wiesbaden: Edition Klaus Blahak, 1976–1986. ■ Wolfram, Suzanne. *Die tödliche Wunde: Über die Untrennbarkeit von Tod und Eros im Werk von Klaus Mann.* Frankfurt a.M.: Peter Lang, 1986. ■ Zynda, Stefan. *Sexualität bei Klaus Mann.* Bonn: Bouvier Verlag Herbert Grundmann, 1986.

§ Mann, Thomas
(1875–1955)

One of Germany's greatest authors of this century and winner of the 1929 Nobel Prize for literature, Mann bridges nineteenth-century realist fiction and the twentieth-century modernist style in his novels, short stories, and essays. Thomas Mann was born the second of five children to parents who embodied the duality that would become the central theme of his writing. Thomas Johann Heinrich Mann, his father, was a very successful businessman as well as an influential and respected citizen of the North German port of Lübeck. His mother, Julia da Silva-Bruhns, was the daughter of a German businessman and a Brazilian mother. Through her, Thomas became interested in music, literature, and art, which, because of his mother's parentage, Mann always associated with Southern cultures and climates. His pragmatism and work ethic derived from the Northern influence of his father, he believed. When his father died in 1891, at the age of fifty-one, the family business was sold. His father had realized that neither Thomas nor

his older brother Heinrich would become his successor, as both had shown more interest in literature than in business.

Mann chafed under the rigid order of the college preparatory school he attended in Lübeck and failed two years. Because of this, he completed six of the nine years that comprise the educational sequence in a German *Gymnasium* and received the lesser diploma of "Mittlere Reife" in 1894. Between 1894 and 1896, he did attend lectures on history, art, and literature at the Technical University in Munich, the city to which his mother had moved in 1892.

Thomas Mann married Katja Pringsheim in 1905, and they had six children, three daughters and three sons. The Mann family contained several extremely gifted members. His brother Heinrich wrote many novels and dramas, the best-known of which is the novel *Professor Unrat* from which the film *The Blue Angel* was made. His daughter Erika was a stage actress, married W. H. AUDEN (in order to get British citizenship) and became the caretaker of her father's literary heritage after his death. His first son KLAUS wrote novels, short stories, plays, and essays depicting life for Germany's disaffected bohemian youth in the interwar period. His open homosexuality led to some conflict with his father, who chose to express his homosexual desires in a very different manner. Golo, the second son, became a respected German historian.

For many in the German-speaking world, Mann was the epitome of the "educated burgher," that man of the upper middle class whose comfortable economic status allowed him to acquire not only possessions but a cultural education, a spirit of refinement and good taste. Indeed, his works and his interests reflect such a status. Many of his stories and novels (for example, *Buddenbrooks*, 1901) depict an upper-middle-class milieu and the concerns of that family life.

Yet Mann struggled against a complete identification with bourgeois society. Indeed, he believed the source of his artistic inspiration lay in a realm antithetical to the bourgeois one he achieved in reality, namely, in the erotic, the sexual, and in particular, within homosexual desire. Many of Mann's chief works pursue the struggle to maintain a balance between the spheres of the artist and of the everyday, family man. Often at the core of that struggle is one male's urge to love another, an urge that teeters between expression and repression.

In the letter to his friend Count Hermann Keyserling, published as "Über die Ehe" ("About Marriage," 1925), Mann tries to separate the creative and enduring institution of marriage, which creates families and, ultimately, states, from the artistically necessary, but eventually destructive force of homoeroticism. "There is no blessing in it save that of beauty, and that is the blessing of death," he wrote about same-sex desire. The essay is a defense against the author's own homoerotic feelings. Mann was the solid burgher of his generation, celebrated author, and family father. Mann admits, if one reads carefully, that homosexual desire may have inspired his art, but homosexual identity had to be rejected since it threatened not only "society" but his own preeminent status.

These themes of homosexuality leading to the destruction of social institutions and to the death of the individual homosexual are woven into several of Mann's best works. In *Der Tod in Venedig* (*Death in Venice,* 1912), the famous author Gustav Aschenbach has kept his life under tight control. On a trip to Venice, he drops those reins and unleashes emotions that eventually overpower him. The immediate catalyst is a beautiful Polish boy of fourteen. Aschenbach spies him with his sisters and governess at the hotel they share and is enraptured by the blond youth's beauty, which reminds him of a masterpiece of Greek sculpture. He learns the boy's name—Tadzio—but never speaks to him. Instead, he watches him play on the beach or spend time with his family at meals or on strolls through the city. A cholera epidemic strikes Venice. Aschenbach remains to be near his beloved, even though he is fully aware of the danger of this fatal disease. The reserved, restrained German author all but disappears in the passion he develops for this youth. He writes only a few pages; he puts on makeup and colorful clothing to appear younger than his years; finally, he falls ill and dies while watching Tadzio, who seems to beckon him "into an immensity of richest expectation."

Mann's own interests and experiences clearly inspired and shaped the novella. In 1911, Thomas Mann vacationed in Venice and became very attracted to a fourteen-year-old Polish boy whom he saw. Like Aschenbach, Mann never met the boy. Thomas Mann's diaries and letters, along with several essays and prose works, provide evidence of the author's erotic attraction to his own sex, particularly to handsome young men. Of particular interest to literary historians have been the relationships he formed with Paul Ehrenburg (which lasted from approximately 1899 to 1903) and with Klaus Heuser (which began in 1927 when Heuser was sixteen and which lasted for several years). Such friendships and the passages Mann devoted to this topic both in fiction and nonfiction works provide conclusive proof that the author did indeed experience—and value—homosexual feelings. Unfortunately, many critics over the years have chosen to deny this fact. The publication of Mann's diaries over the past decades has made further such denials impossible.

In the story *Tonio Kröger* (1903), Mann uses the homoerotic feelings that the title character has as a boy for his friend Hans Hansen to indicate that Tonio, from childhood on, is separated from normal, bourgeois life. Homoeroticism becomes a metaphor for difference, for *Außenseitertum* (being an outsider). He yearns to belong to those "blond and blue-eyed, the brightly living, the happy, those worthy of love, the ordinary people." But to join them he would have to relinquish his identity as an artist. And crucial to that identity is the position outside their realm of everyday existence, the place from which the artist creates, a place that borders on the homoerotic.

In the division between art and bourgeois life, Mann found a forebear in the nineteenth-century poet AUGUST VON PLATEN. Platen's poems and diaries revealed his homosexuality, which had even become the basis of a famous literary feud when Heinrich Heine, whose literary reputation has since eclipsed that of

Platen, tried to disparage the man and his work as being unworthy of attention, much less greatness, due to Platen's sexual nature. In his essay "Über Platen" ("About Platen," 1926), Mann separates the poet's life from his literary creations. Platen, Mann felt, channeled his sexual desires into his art. The repression he exercised in his bourgeois life provided him with the inspiration necessary to create poetry although even Mann admits that Platen may have bestowed some sensual love on "unworthy boys."

It should also be noted that Mann described his affinity with another nineteenth-century poet, the American WALT WHITMAN. In his speech "Von deutscher Republik" ("On the German Republic," 1922), Mann called on Whitman's vision of democracy as an ideal that Germany might pursue. In the process, he did not want to allow conservative German forces to usurp the "spiritual love of comrades" for their own nationalist purposes. He spoke of "the queerly sympathetic response one feels upon touching with one's own hand the naked flesh of the body," wanting to reclaim that emotion in building the first German republic that was only then being born. But Mann distanced himself from embracing that flesh too openly in his essay about marriage a few years later.

Mann's unresolved attitude toward homoeroticism (his fear of secret desire becoming public identity and thus destroying the stability of his life) expresses itself in his 1924 novel, *Der Zauberberg* (*The Magic Mountain*). The main character, Hans Castorp, comes to visit his cousin at Berghof, a sanatorium for tuberculosis patients. Instead of staying three weeks, he remains for seven years, high in the Swiss Alps where time moves quite differently from the way it does in the "flatland" Castorp has left. In the world below, European civilization is descending into the chaos that will become World War I.

In this *Bildungsroman* (novel of education), the simple, young engineer becomes a patient at the sanatorium and a pupil of two men representing opposing views of the world as well as philosophical traditions, Settembrini and Naptha. Crucial to Castorp's physical rejuvenation and spiritual renewal is Clavdia Chauchat, a Russian emigree staying at Berghof. She uncannily resembles Pribislav Hippe, a boy whom Hans had loved when they were fourteen-year-old schoolmates. Through his relationship, emotional and sexual, with Chauchat, Castorp resolves his homosexuality in favor of, as Karl Werner Böhm argues, bisexuality. Freud's influence on Thomas Mann was significant and may certainly have played a role in Mann's conception of how homosexual desire might be integrated, rather than repressed or destroyed. Nonetheless, illness remains ineluctably attached to it.

Typically, Mann does not describe homosexual desire overtly or bluntly. Instead, he makes its appearance evident through symbols and metaphors. The "pencil-lending" episodes of *Der Zauberberg* exemplify this practice and have become iconic examples of writing about homosexual desire without naming it explicitly. Years ago, Hans had secretly "borrowed" a pencil from his classmate Pribislav. When Mann describes the reawakened memory of that moment, it becomes clear that the pencil symbolizes Pribislav's penis. Hans yearned to express his love for his friend sexually, but all he could bring himself to do was to take one of his friend's possessions, as a token of him. The deeply symbolic value of that token becomes evident when Chauchat offers Hans a pencil and triggers that memory, thus enabling him to resolve his homosexual past, to "get well."

In the 1929 novella *Mario und der Zauberer* (*Mario and the Magician*), Italy again serves as the intersection of culture and the banal, of art devolved into eroticism. Cipolla, the "magician" of the title, performs in the resort city of Torre di Venere. He is a hypnotist who uses no swaying watches or mesmerizing devices, but instead simply forces his will on his subjects. Cipolla's act of power is all the more compelling since his appearance would suggest a weak soul: He is a hunchback. After various scenaria with unwilling townfolk doing his bidding, his fancy lights upon an attractive young waiter, Mario, whom he seems more to entice than to request to join him on stage. After referring to Mario as "Ganymede," it quickly becomes apparent that Cipolla wants to play the role of Zeus. The magician weaves his dark magic by speaking about Mario's "troubles" with his girlfriend, offering himself as the more understanding, more deserving love object. Obeying the supplication Cipolla utters as a spell—"Trust me, I love you"— Mario kisses him. That moment of artistic triumph— "a momentous moment, grotesque and thrilling, the moment of Mario's bliss"—marks Cipolla's destruction, for he has crossed that line Mann described in *Death in Venice* as separating the realm of artistic inspiration from overt homoeroticism and, ultimately, death. Immediately when the spell is broken, Mario pulls a gun and kills Cipolla, avenging himself for the magician's public humiliation of him. In addition to the work's relation to themes Mann developed in other stories, it should be noted that the author who would leave Germany for exile in 1933 already here begins to depict the links between fascism, homoeroticism, and homophobia.

Doktor Faustus (1947), Mann's great parable about Germany's descent into fascism, also contains an artist figure who is homosexual. Using the Faust myth, the novel traces the decay of bourgeois culture in Germany from the late nineteenth century to the present. The composer Adrian Leverkühn makes a pact with the devil in order to be able to create masterpieces of music for a few years. In exchange, he grants the devil his soul. One of the musicians in Leverkühn's circle of friends is Rudi Schwerdtfeger, with whom Leverkühn has, for a time, a sexual relationship. Again, homosexual desire is, in Mann's conception, antithetical to those forces and institutions that maintain and advance society.

Several critics believe that in some of Mann's later works, for example, *Die Betrogene* (*The Deceived*, 1953) and *Bekenntnisse des Hochstaplers Felix Krull* (*Confessions of Felix Krull, Confidence Man*, 1954), he purposely disguised his own homosexual feelings and gave them a heterosexual guise by having female characters experience what he himself had felt for a younger man.

Thomas Mann's depiction of homosexual desire can be seen as an attempt to encode homosexuality in a manner that would allow him to speak what at the time was unspeakable for him, namely, his own homosexual feelings. This dual Otherness, that of the artist and that of the homosexual, found private expression in his diaries. As it became the major theme of his works, it took on other forms in language (metaphor, allusion, topoi), character, and plot. Mann's fictional works have proved of enormous interest to gay scholars recently because so much "about" homosexual desire in fiction prior to Stonewall has to be read between the lines. It remains encoded, yet open to the interpretation of a generation of readers whose experiences and indeed definitions of homosexuality are quite different from Mann's own.

—*James W. Jones*

BIBLIOGRAPHY

Baumgart, Reinhard. "Thomas Mann als erotischer Schriftsteller." *Forum. Homosexualität und Literatur* 4 (1988): 5–22. ■ Böhm, Karl Werner. "Die homosexuellen Elemente in Thomas Manns 'Der Zauberberg.'" *Stationen der Thomas-Mann-Forschung. Aufsätze seit 1970.* Hermann Kurzke, ed. Würzburg: Königshausen und Neumann, 1985. 145–65. ■ Bravermann, Albert and Larry David Nachman. "The Dialectic of Decadence: An Analysis of Thomas Mann's *Death in Venice*." *Germanic Review* 45 (1970): 289–298. ■ Detering, Heinrich. "Der Literat als Abenteurer: 'Tonio Kröger' zwischen 'Dorian Gray' und 'Der Tod in Venedig.'" *Forum. Homosexualität und Literatur* 14 (1992): 5–22. ■ Feuerlicht, Ignace. "Thomas Mann and Homoeroticism." *Germanic Review* 57 (1982): 89–97. ■ Härle, Gerhard. *Die Gestalt des Schönen. Untersuchung zur Homosexualitätsthematik in Thomas Manns Roman 'Der Zauberberg.'* Königstein: Hain Verlag bei Athenäum, 1986. ■ Härle, Gerhard, ed. *"Heimsuchung und süßes Gift:" Erotik und Poetik bei Thomas Mann.* Frankfurt am Main: Fischer Taschenbuch, 1992. ■ Härle, Gerhard. *Männerweiblichkeit: Zur Homosexualität bei Klaus und Thomas Mann.* Frankfurt am Main: Athenäum, 1988. ■ Jones, James W. *"We of the Third Sex:" Literary Representations of Homosexuality in Wilhelmine Germany.* New York: Peter Lang, 1990. ■ Lubich, Frederick Alfred. "Die Entfaltung der Dialektik von Logos und Eros in Thomas Manns 'Der Tod in Venedig.'" *Colloquia Germanica* 18/2 (1985): 140–159. ■ Mann, Erika, ed. *Thomas Mann. Briefe 1889-1936.* Frankfurt am Main: S. Fischer, 1961. ■ Martin, Robert K. "Walt Whitman and Thomas Mann." *Quarterly Review* 4 (1986): 1–6. ■ Mayer, Hans. "Der Tod in Venedig. Ein Thema mit Variationen." *Literaturwissenschaft und Geistesgeschichte. Festschrift für Richard Brinkmann.* Jürgen Brummack et al. eds. Tübingen: Max Niemeyer, 1981: 711–724. ■ Noble, C. A. M. *Krankheit, Verbrechen und künstlerisches Schaffen bei Thomas Mann.* Bern: Herbert Lang & Cie, 1970. ■ Ott, Volker. *Homotropie und die Figur des Homotropen in der Literatur des zwanzigsten Jahrhunderts.* Bern: Peter Lang, 1979. ■ Reed, T. J. *Thomas Mann. "Der Tod in Venedig." Text, Materialien, Kommentar.* Munich, Vienna: Carl Hanser Verlag, 1983. ■ Wanner, Hans. *Individualität, Identität und Rolle. Das frühe Werk Heinrich Manns und Thomas Erzählungen "Gladius Dei" und "Der Tod in Venedig."* Munich: tuduv-Verlagsgesellschaft, 1976. ■ Winston, Richard and Clara, eds. *Thomas Mann Diaries: 1918–1921, 1933–1939.* New York: Abrams, 1982.

Mansfield, Katherine
(1888–1923)

Katherine Mansfield was born Kathleen Mansfield Beauchamp in Wellington, New Zealand. Her closest relationship was with her grandmother, who figures as the most sympathetic figure in her "New Zealand" stories. A chronological arrangement of those stories by Ian Gordon, entitled *Undiscovered Country* (1974), provides an insight into her own perspective on her childhood. After attending Wellington Girls' High School, she was sent to Queen's College, London, as a finishing school. Back in Wellington, she became disenchanted with its intellectual life. Though her father helped her get some of her early stories published, she pined for London. She was allowed to return in 1908, with an annual allowance to supplement any income from her writing.

In London, she found her way into the literary scene, working principally with John Middleton Murry. Her personal life often got in the way of her writing career. Married hastily to an acquaintance, she was pregnant by another man. The marriage lasted barely days. Her mother sailed at once for London (after cutting Kathleen out of her will), hustled her off to a spa in Germany, then left her alone to go through the suffering of a miscarriage. Although this episode has usually been seen as an attempt to conceal her pregnancy, it has been suggested plausibly by both Antony Alpers and Gillian Boddy that her mother was seeking the then fashionable water cure for lesbian tendencies. That young Katherine had many close female friendships is beyond doubt. Some mystery still surrounds her relationship with Maata Matapuhu, a Maori princess and fellow schoolgirl. An interesting account of this bond is provided by Witi Ihimaera in his novella "Maata," part of his centennial volume, *Dear Miss Mansfield* (1989), in which he investigates the missing manuscript of an early novel. Mansfield's own unfinished manuscript "Maata," however, seems to record her close friendship with Ida Baker.

Separated from her husband, she lived with John Middleton Murry, whom she eventually married after her divorce. They traveled widely, mostly in the hope of improving her health, and much of her writing was done in Mentone, France. It seems clear that she suffered from syphilis as well as tuberculosis. At Gurdjieff's health center at Fontainebleau, she finally succumbed to the disease that had ravaged her for years.

Her fiction is best read in company with her journals and letters, which throw light on the way her ideas for subjects formed and matured. A crucial episode was the death of her brother Leslie in World War I, which seems to have unblocked her New Zealand experiences, leading to some of her finest writing.

Although there is little openly lesbian writing, there is always a deep concern with the status of women.

Most of her characters are women, and the few men are seen through unsympathetic eyes. "Frau Brechenmayer Attends a Wedding" has been cited by C. A. Hankin as an undisguised attack on male sexual dominance. In the later New Zealand stories, Mansfield explores the world of feminine friendship and female sexuality. The only extant writing that is clearly lesbian is the vignette "Leves Amores," now published as an appendix to Clair Tomalin's critical study.

Mansfield employs a feminist approach to life and literature. She reveals with cruel clarity how male sexual and economic dominance has denied women an independent role. Only too often in her stories women reject the possibility of independence or are unable to take advantage of it, as, for example, in "The Colonel's Daughters." Mansfield was clearly critical of women's assigned role but unable to suggest a satisfactory alternative.

Although VIRGINIA WOOLF, with whom Katherine Mansfield had a close but uncertain relationship, dismissed her stories as minor, later critics agree that Mansfield played a critical role in redirecting the modern short story toward psychological exploration. She acknowledged her debt to Chekhov but made her own way, creating the first slice-of-life stories in English.

—*Murray S. Martin*

BIBLIOGRAPHY

Alpers, Antony. *The Life of Katherine Mansfield*. New York: Viking, 1980. ■ Boddy, Gillian. *Katherine Mansfield: The Woman and the Writer*. Ringwood, VIC.: Penguin, 1988. ■ Hankin, Cherry A. *Katherine Mansfield and her Confessional Stories*. London: Macmillan, 1983. ■ Ihimaera, Witi. *Dear Miss Mansfield: A Tribute to Kathleen Mansfield Beauchamp*. New York: Viking, 1989. ■ Tomalin, Claire. *Katherine Mansfield: A Secret Life*. New York: St. Martin's Press, 1987.

Marchessault, Jovette
(*b.* 1938)

Jovette Marchessault was born on February 9, 1938, in Montreal but spent her earliest years in the nearby countryside where her father was employed as a munitions worker during World War II. In her autobiographical novel, *La Mère des herbes* (1980; translated as *Mother of the Grass,* 1989), she recounts the devastation she felt when the family was forced to move to one of the poorest districts in the center of Montreal after the munitions plant closed. The sense of a lost paradise is one that appears frequently in her prose fiction where she frequently laments the disappearance of paradises of all sorts— sexual, spiritual, natural—crushed by the heavy weight of religious and social sanction.

The strongest influence on Marchessault's early life was her grandmother, a half-Indian herbalist, gifted pianist, and inspired painter of hen portraits. This formidable creativity served, she said, as a kind of "alibi" that relieved her of the necessity to create in her own right. Instead, she spent the years between thirteen (when she left school) and thirty-one in a series of jobs that ranged from washing diapers to operating a machine in a garment factory, to clerking in a bookstore and, finally, to a four-year stint pursuing delinquent accounts for the Grolier encyclopedia firm. These jobs were punctuated by long Greyhound bus trips to Mexico and the West Coast and visits to the bars and cafes frequented by gays and intellectuals in the heavily repressive atmosphere of Duplessis's Quebec. Through this whole period, she read voraciously, becoming almost wholly self-educated.

To the horror of her family, she quit her job at Grolier after her grandmother's death, determined on an artistic career. Initially, she became a painter, and within two years achieved a one-woman show at a Montreal gallery, followed by other exhibitions in New York, Paris, and Brussels. In 1975, she published *Le crachat solaire* (The Solar Spit; translated in 1988 as *Like a Child of the Earth*), the first volume of a three-volume autobiographical work with the overall title *Comme une enfant de la terre*, which won the Prix France-Québec in 1976. Far from straightforward working-class autobiography or confessional, these volumes, which include *La Mère des herbes* (1980; translated as *Mother of the Grass*, 1989) and *Des cailloux blancs pour les forêts obscures* (1987; translated as *White Pebbles for the Dark Forests*, 1990), are lyrical and impassioned attempts to reclaim myth and experience for women in general and lesbians in particular.

In 1980, with the publication of *Tryptique lesbienne*, Marchessault risked her developing career by becoming the first Quebec novelist unequivocally to declare her lesbianism. The longest piece in the book, "A Lesbian Chronicle from Medieval Quebec," is a poetic and visionary account of growing up and coming out in the context of traditional, closed, and Roman Catholic Quebec. Filled with puns and informed by an uncompromising fury at the devastation wrought by the Church's misogyny and sexual repression, the piece concludes on a note of hope as its narrator is redeemed from spiritual death by the love of another woman. The other two pieces in the volume, "Night Cows" and "The Angel Makers," are incantatory celebrations of a nonpatriarchal universe in which sisters embrace beyond the stars, and abortion in the hands of the mother-midwife is seen as a means of reclaiming procreation from patriarchal control and a way of "interrupting the cycle of reincarnation."

In the last decade, Marchessault has devoted most of her attention to the theater. Characteristically, her plays, all successfully produced in Montreal and a number of which have also been staged in English, are inventive invocations of women writers and artists, often lesbian, which aim to supplant a dominant male literary tradition with another, female and lesbian, past. (See also QUÉBÉCOIS LITERATURE.)

—*Yvonne Mathews Klein*

BIBLIOGRAPHY

Gaboriau, Linda. "Jovette Marchessault: A Luminous Wake in Space." *Canada Theatre Review* 43 (Spring 1985): 91–99. ■ Marchessault, Jovette. *Lesbian Triptych*. Trans. Yvonne M. Klein. With an Introduction and Bibliography by Barbara Goddard and a Postface by Gloria Feman Orenstein. Toronto: Women's Press, 1985. ■ Rosenfeld, Martha. "The Development of a Lesbian Sensibility in the Work of Jovette Marchessault and Nicole Brossard." Paula Gilbert Lewis, ed. *Traditionalism, Nationalism and Feminism: Women Writers of Quebec*. Westport, Conn.: Greenwood Press, 1985: 227–239.

Marlowe, Christopher
(1564–1593)

Born in Canterbury in the same year as SHAKESPEARE, Marlowe was his most significant predecessor as an English playwright who was also a great poet. The son of a cobbler, who earned a scholarship to Cambridge, where he received a B.A. in 1584 and an M.A. in 1587, Marlowe pursued a course of study that was designed to culminate in holy orders, yet the most profound result of his education may have been his love of classical literature, especially Ovid, whom he was to translate and whose comic ironies and worldly sophistication were to influence him greatly. A writer deeply immersed in both religion and classics, Marlowe reflects in his work the tension between Christian culture's condemnation and classical culture's acceptance of homoerotics. He was probably an agent in the Elizabethan spy network run by Sir Francis Walsingham, yet he was frequently in trouble with authorities. In 1593, he was accused by Elizabeth's Privy Council of heresy and blasphemy, but before he could answer the indictment he was murdered in a tavern in Deptford.

Two documents about Marlowe, both produced shortly after his death, testify to his heterodoxy and iconoclasm, the so-called "Baines libel" and a report by the playwright Thomas Kyd, with whom Marlowe shared lodgings in 1591. These documents were probably devised to exonerate their authors from serious charges by blaming the dramatist, but they nevertheless seem to capture the voice of the poet, and their sentiments are not inconsistent with those expressed or implied in his work. In both cases, Marlowe is accused of espousing a variety of dangerous beliefs, of which homoerotic sentiments are simply part of a continuum of blasphemous ideas. The notorious statements attributed to Marlowe in the Baines libel that "St John the Evangelist was bedfellow to Christ and leaned alwaies in his bosome, that he used him as the sinners of Sodoma" and "That all they that love not Tobacco & Boies were fooles" are tellingly interspersed with atheistic and seditious claims. The outrageousness of the cheeky denunciation of those who are not attracted to boys and tobacco resides less in the notion that they are fools than in the blithe equation of pederasty and pipe smoking. Such an equivalence serves to reduce sodomy from a grave offense to a merely personal predilection and thereby rebukes the hysteria of the Renaissance's moral and legal discourse on homosexuality.

Marlowe represents homoerotic situations and incidents in his plays and poems more frequently and more variously than any other major writer of his day. His representations range from the lyrical idealization of youthful male beauty in *Hero and Leander* to the literally sodomitic murder of the king in *Edward II*. As Gregory Woods observes, the Marlovian world is one in which most desirers are mature men in the prime of manhood, whereas most of the desired are adolescent boys or very young men, a pattern that suggests the age asymmetrical *paederastia* of classical homosexuality and that contributes to Marlowe's characteristic association of eroticism and power. But what is most noteworthy about Marlowe's depiction of same-sex relations is that his posture is consistently oppositional vis-à-vis his culture's official condemnation of homosexuality even as that condemnation inevitably and powerfully shapes his varied representations.

Marlowe's famous lyric beginning "Come live with me, and be my love" is a brilliant recital of the pastoral delights with which Corydon attempts to woo Alexis in VIRGIL's homoerotic second eclogue. Marlowe's seductive poem economically imagines an idyllic, self-contained golden age far removed from the demands and constraints of Elizabethan society. Yet what is most striking about it as an adaptation of the second eclogue is not that it contains homoerotic innuendoes but, quite to the contrary, that it suppresses the unapologetic homoeroticism of its source. By failing to specify the gender of the passionate shepherd's love, Marlowe may hint at the possibility of homosexual bliss, and thereby query the dominant assumptions of his society, but he never makes that teasing hint concrete or explicit. The poem is not entitled "Corydon to Alexis." In fact, the nonspecificity of its most common title, "The Passionate Shepherd to His Love," leaves open the door for the explicit heterosexualizing of Ralegh's "Nymph's Reply to the Shepherd." Marlowe's suppression of the overt homosexuality of Virgil's text testifies to the restraints of Elizabethan society. (See also PASTORAL.)

In *Hero and Leander,* his version of the classical story of star-crossed heterosexual passion, Marlowe presents both an extraordinary homoerotic description of Leander and an extended homoerotic encounter between the youth and a love-smitten Neptune. These comic scenes derive their power to shock and titillate from the satiric view of homosexuality that they delightfully flout. For example, the enthusiastic celebration of Leander's beauty, figured forth in a proliferation of classical myths, itself constitutes a challenge to the Christian strictures against homoeroticism. In describing "Amorous *Leander,* beautifull and yoong," whose "bodie was as straight as *Circes* wand, / *Jove* might have sipt out *Nectar* from his hand," Marlowe not only compares Leander with Ganymede (who in the Renaissance was the most pervasive symbol of homosexuality) but also calls particular attention to "That heavenly path, with many a curious dint, / That runs along his backe" (1.51, 61–62, 68–69), only to confess the inability of his "rude pen" to do justice to the shapeliness of the youth's buttocks. Clearly, this homoerotic blazon that culminates in the very site of sodomy is exuberantly defiant. Moreover, Marlowe's assumption of a universal homoerotic impulse in *Hero and Leander* contradicts his age's assumption of an exclusively heterosexual desire. Leander's beauty is "all that men desire" (1.84); it moves alike both the "rudest paisant" and the "barbarous *Thratian soldier*" (1.79, 81). The very playfulness of Marlowe's subversiveness here and throughout the epyllion destabilizes the seriousness of dominant constructions of gender and sexuality.

Resistance to the massive condemnation of homosexuality in Renaissance England is also at the heart of Marlowe's Ovidian account of Neptune's infatuation with Leander. When the "saphir visag'd god" spies Leander in the sea, Neptune concludes that he must be Ganymede. He pulls the youth down to the splendors of the pearl-strewn, gold-heaped sea bottom. In this spectacular setting, "The lustie god imbr-

ast him, cald him love, / And swore he never should returne to Jove" (2.167–168). Only when the mortal youth is almost drowned does Neptune realize that he is not Jove's cupbearer. He releases Leander and gives him safe passage through the sea, but not before caressing and attempting to seduce him:

> He clapt his plumpe cheekes, with his tresses
> playd,
> And smiling wantonly, his love bewrayd.
> He watcht his armes, and as they opend wide,
> At every stroke, betwixt them would he slide,
> And steale a kisse, and then run out and
> daunce,
> And as he turnd, cast many a lustfull glaunce,–
> And threw him gawdie toies to please his eie,–
> And dive into the water, and there prie
> Upon his brest, his thighs, and everie lim,
> And up againe, and close beside him swim,
> And talke of love. (2.181–191)

When the shocked Leander protests in exasperation, "You are deceav'd, I am no woman I" (2.192), Neptune merely smiles and begins to tell him a homoerotic tale of shepherds and satyrs, evocative of THEOCRITUS's *Idylls*.

Marlowe's joke in this farcical episode is not only on the passionate god, who mistakes a beautiful mortal for Ganymede, but also—and more trenchantly—on the naive youth, who can imagine only heterosexual desire. As Gregory Bredbeck points out, the tale that Neptune begins reciting is designed to suggest "an alternative world existing beyond the limits of Leander's narrow perspective." Significantly, the point of the episode—quite apart from its considerable titillation value and its foregrounding of the awkward heterosexual lovemaking of Hero and Leander—is the essential likeness of same-sex and other-sex attraction. Neptune, realizing that Leander is also smitten by love, generously returns to the rich ocean bed for gifts for the youth to bring to Hero; reconciled, the deity and the mortal are united in their common emotional state despite their difference in sexual object choices. As the narrator concludes, "In gentle brests, / Relenting thoughts, remorse and pittie rests. / And who have hard hearts, and obdurat minds, / But vicious, harebraind, and illit'rat hinds?" (2.215–218). Surely, the hard-hearted hinds indicted here include those censorious souls in Marlowe's society who were unable to conceive of homoeroticism as other than shameful.

The depictions of homoeroticism in Marlowe's plays include Henry III's obsession with his minions in *The Massacre at Paris* and the startling scene that opens *Dido, Queen of Carthage,* in which Jupiter is discovered "dandling *Ganimed* upon his knee" (s.d.), as well as other less clear-cut scenes and characterizations in the *Tamburlaine* plays and *Doctor Faustus,* and most prominently, the full exploration of homosexual love in *Edward II.* What these dramatic depictions share are Marlowe's characteristic association of eroticism with issues of power and his equally characteristic resistance to his society's attitudes toward homoerotics.

The comic scene that opens *Dido,* for example, appears at first glance to confirm the satirical view of homosexuality in its depiction of a lecherous old man besotted with a "female wanton boy" (l.51) who barters his embraces for feathers and gems. But, as Bruce Smith observes, "With the actual Ganymede of *Dido,* as with all the figurative 'Ganymedes' of his later plays and poems, we can never quite tell whether Marlowe is *playing* the satirist or *taunting* the satirists." The ambiguity that informs this opening scene of *Dido* is, in fact, paradigmatic of the work as a whole. In contrasting the amorous dalliance of Ovidian comedy in the first scene with the momentous events of Virgilian seriousness that constitute the main plot of the play, Marlowe creates a vantage point from which all the principals in the drama are viewed and tested, but it is by no means clear that Jupiter's amorous toying with Ganymede is to be judged more harshly than the steadfast indifference of Aeneas to the love of Dido. Indeed, the very frivolity of the opening scene signals Marlowe's intention to reinterpret his Virgilian source from a perspective that values destiny less than love. Presenting pederasty as the sport of gods, *Dido* subverts received ideas about homosexuality as well as about Virgilian destiny.

The conflict of love and duty is also at issue in *Edward II,* Marlowe's great tragedy of a man torn between his hereditary role as king and his personal proclivities as expressed most fully in his love for another man. The play is the Renaissance's greatest dramatization of homoerotic love, a love centered in the complete identification of Edward and Gaveston, despite their crucial differences of rank and class. Locating in homosexual love the world well lost, the play pivots on Edward's choice of love "Despite of time, despite of enemies" (l.1456) and on Gaveston's matching declaration of love for "The king, upon whose bosome let me die, / And with the world be still at enmitie" (ll.14–15). In *Edward II,* Marlowe depicts homoeroticism in casual, occasionally elevated, frequently moving, and always human terms; and in appending the names of Edward and Gaveston to a roll call of famous homosexual lovers—Alexander and Hephaestion, Hercules and Hylas, Patroclus and

Achilles, Cicero and Octavius, Socrates and Alcibiades, Jove and Ganymede—the play counters its Christian context with a classical locus in which homosexuality is a mark of distinction, associated with mighty kings and great philosophers. By humanizing homosexuality, Marlowe implicitly attacks the prevalent religious, legal, and popular attitudes of his day. Indeed, the hypocrisy of morality mongering of all kinds is systematically exposed and unmercifully parodied in the play. In its refusal to moralize either sex or politics, *Edward II* is seditious and radical.

It is difficult to overstate the significance of *Edward II* in the history of literary depictions of homosexuality, yet it is equally important not to regard the play as simply a liberal defense of sexual freedom. Although Marlowe refuses to condemn homosexuality, he complicates the relationships of Edward and his lovers, presenting them ambiguously rather than merely sympathetically; they are tainted with the self-seeking that characterizes everyone in the play, including the reactionary, class-conscious barons. The king's willful attachment to his lovers clearly accounts for his failure as a monarch and culminates in his gruesome murder, making him finally a martyr to his passion. Ultimately, *Edward II* is a tragedy of existential loneliness, in which the protagonist's conflicting identities are reconciled only in his brutal death.

The murder of the king by Lightborn, the sadistic assassin armed with a "red hote" poker (l.2479) who approaches Edward as intimately and solicitously as a lover, is not, however, simply retribution, as it might have been in a work by someone less committed than Marlowe to resisting his society's prejudices. The unmistakably allegorical action meaningfully joins the opposed worlds of eroticism and political violence. It combines elements of sexual desire and violent "policy" and juxtaposes the world of erotic freedom represented by Edward's love for Gaveston with the cynical world of power politics symbolized by the union of Mortimer and Isabella, whose love "hatcheth death and hate" (l.1801). The sodomitical murder is not merely gratuitous violence or simply a grotesque parody of homosexual lovemaking; still less is it the embodiment of a moralistic justice, as homophobic critics have alleged. Rather, the fatal rape at once exposes the brutality of a corrupt society that values power above all else, mocks the moralists who would justify a ruthless competition of wills with preachments, and reveals the suffering king as the bare, forked animal, unaccommodated man, an emblem of shared humanity. (See also PASTORAL and ENGLISH LITERATURE: RENAISSANCE.)

—Claude J. Summers

BIBLIOGRAPHY

Boyette, Purvis. "Wanton Humour and Wanton Poets: Homosexuality in Marlowe's Edward II." *Tulane Studies in English* 12 (1977): 33–50. ■ Bredbeck, Gregory W. *Sodomy and Interpretation: Marlowe to Milton.* Ithaca, N.Y.: Cornell University Press, 1991. ■ Goldberg, Jonathan. *Sodometries: Renaissance Texts, Modern Sexualities.* Stanford, Calif.: Stanford University Press, 1992. ■ ———. "Sodomy and Society: The Case of Christopher Marlowe." *Southwest Review* 69 (1984): 371–378. ■ Kocher, Paul H. *Christopher Marlowe: A Study of His Thought, Learning, and Character.* Chapel Hill, N.C.: University of North Carolina Press, 1946; New York: Russell & Russell, 1962. ■ Shepherd, Simon. *Marlowe and the Politics of Elizabethan Theatre.* New York: St. Martin's, 1986. ■ Smith, Bruce R. *Homosexual Desire in Shakespeare's England: A Cultural Poetics.* Chicago: University of Chicago Press, 1991. ■ Summers, Claude J. "Homosexuality and Renaissance Literature, or the Anxieties of Anachronism." *South Central Review* 9 (1992): 2–23. ■ ———. "Marlowe and Constructions of Renaissance Homosexuality." *Canadian Review of Comparative Literature* 21 (1994): 27–44. ■ ———. "Sex, Politics, and Self-Realization in *Edward II.*" *"A Poet and a Filthy Play-maker": New Essays on Christopher Marlowe.* Kenneth Friedenreich, Roma Gill, and Constance B. Kuriyama, eds. New York: AMS, 1988. 221–240. ■ Woods, Gregory. "Body, Costume, and Desire in Christopher Marlowe." *Homosexuality in Renaissance and Enlightenment England: Literary Representations in Historical Context.* Claude J. Summers, ed. New York: Haworth, 1992. 69–84.

Mars-Jones, Adam
(*b.* 1954)

Born in 1954 into an upper-middle-class legal family in London—his father was a judge, his mother a lawyer—Mars-Jones was educated at Westminster School and Cambridge University. He is now film critic of the London *Independent.*

Mars-Jones won considerable praise for his first book, *Lantern Lectures* (1981), a set of three novellas written in a postmodern mode. "Hoosh-Mi" is a grotesque story of the British Queen's contracting rabies from a pet corgi's bite, and continuing to fulfill royal functions under increasingly adverse conditions. Told by various narrators, it combines dark humor with sharp analysis of royalty's contemporary futility. A similar mixture of fiction and documentary is also evident in "Bathpool Park," which takes Harry Hawkes's *The Capture of the Black Panther,* about a notorious murderer, as a starting point to show a criminal's construction of a crime. The story goes on to show the police, the press and the judiciary—social institutions specifically designed to find out and publicly narrate the truth—failing to discover it. *Lantern Lecture*'s technical qualities were noted in a review by Galen Strawson, who cited the "emotionally deadpanned style of delivery, the technical impassivity of the allusive, *cloisonné* construction."

Mars-Jones's critical skills are evident in his 1983 selection of lesbian and gay fiction, *Mae West is Dead*. The stories by young American and British writers give an impression of the very different ways it had become possible to live as gay people in the 1980s. Mars-Jones selected them to counter mainstream gay fiction's connivance with commercialized gay lifestyles.

Mars-Jones has been writing stories about AIDS since 1986, first in a collection with EDMUND WHITE, *The Darker Proof: Stories from a Crisis* (1987); then in a collection of his own, *Monopolies of Loss* (1992). It was after acting as "buddy" for two AIDS sufferers that he realized that he could write about the subject. Postmodern techniques are dropped in favor of a precise, deliberately restricted realism and first-person narration in the later stories. "A Small Spade" concerns two young men's trip to the seaside and the difficulties caused by one of them (who is HIV-positive) having a splinter in his finger. "The Changes of Those Terrible Years" is told by a man who has turned his large house into a hospice, benefitting the ill but

also himself as he acquires power and purpose from others' misfortune. Mars-Jones recognizes the irony of a writer discovering in a disease, which is so fearful for those who suffer from it, a subject that benefits him so much as a writer. The stories he has written about AIDS have sought to diminish attention due to the virus so that it becomes, in his own words, "neither ignored nor holding centre stage."

Mars-Jones's only novel, *The Waters of Thirst* (1993), uses the first-person narration and authorial irony developed in the AIDS stories to present a man waiting for a kidney-replacement operation, and so denied the gustatory pleasures of the healthy, and developing a fastidious imaginary relationship with a porn star. The novel, using the techniques of the stories but without the subject of AIDS, has baffled many readers, though most have seen it as a metaphor for denial in a world with HIV.

—*Lawrence Normand*

BIBLIOGRAPHY

Mars-Jones, Adam. *Lantern Lecture, and Other Stories.* London: Faber, 1981. ■ ———, ed. *Mae West is Dead: Recent Lesbian and Gay Fiction.* London: Faber, 1983. ■ ———, and White, Edmund. *The Darker Proof: Stories from a Crisis.* London: Faber, 1987. ■ ———. *Venus Envy.* London: Chatto and Windus [Chatto Counterblasts No. 14], 1990. ■ ———. *Monopolies of Loss.* London: Faber, 1992. ■ ———. *The Waters of Thirst.* London: Faber, 1993. ■ Strawson, Galen. Review of *Lantern Lecture.* *Times Literary Supplement* (October 9, 1981).

Matthiessen, F.O.
(1902–1950)

Francis Otto Matthiessen, one of the most prominent literary critics of the twentieth century, was born to William Frederick and Lucy Orne Matthiessen on February 19, 1902, in Pasadena, California. After his parents' divorce in 1915, Matthiessen lived on his grandfather's farm in Illinois, later attended boarding school in Tarrytown, New York, and then, toward the end of World War I, joined the Canadian Air Force. He entered Yale in 1919, graduated in 1923 with many honors, and then became a Rhodes Scholar at Oxford, receiving a B. Litt. in 1925. While sailing for Oxford, he met the painter Russell Cheney; they would be lovers until Cheney's death in 1945. Cheney, though closeted in many ways, was a profoundly positive influence on Matthiessen, encouraging his interest in gay and lesbian literary figures like WALT WHITMAN and SARAH

ORNE JEWETT. Indeed, their relationship was modeled on that of Sarah Orne Jewett and Annie Fields. Matthiessen entered Harvard Graduate School in 1925 and received his A.M. in 1926 and Ph.D. in 1927. He became an instructor in English at Yale in 1927, leaving in 1929 for Harvard, where he stayed until his death. In a series of remembrances published just after his death, *F.O. Matthiessen: A Collective Portrait,* students at Harvard described him as quick-tempered but generous with his time. A committed socialist, he founded the Harvard Teachers' Union and worked in the Progressive Party for Henry Wallace's 1948 presidential campaign. Increasingly depressed after Cheney's death and threatened by the witch hunts of the cold war, Matthiessen committed suicide in 1950, jumping from a tenth-floor hotel-room window.

Matthiessen's numerous critical works concentrate mostly on American literature. Most notable are *Sarah Orne Jewett* (1929), *Translation: An Elizabethan Art* (1931), *The Achievement of T.S. Eliot: An Essay on the Nature of Poetry* (1935, 1947), his masterpiece *American Renaissance: Art and Expression in the Age of Emerson and Whitman* (1941), and books on HENRY JAMES, the James family, and Theodore Dreiser. Matthiessen's work bears little obvious mark of his homosexuality, but his interests carry a subtext of homosexuality: Most of his book-length works deal exclusively with or favor subjects who were lesbian or gay or whose sexuality was in question—Jewett, Henry James, T. S. ELIOT, MELVILLE, and Whitman. Though discussions of homosexuality seem absent from these writings, or—in the case of Whitman—homophobic, careful reading reveals a subversive and favorable approach to these writers' sexualities. His devotion to Cheney led him to publish a catalogue of Cheney's work, *Russell Cheney, 1881–1945: A Record of His Work*, in 1947. *Rat and the Devil: Journal Letters of F.O. Matthiessen and Russell Cheney*, edited and published by Matthiessen's friend Louis Hyde in 1978, provides selections from over twenty years of correspondence between Matthiessen and Cheney, chronicles their relationship, and demonstrates how these two men, without a sense of gay community, constructed their identities from reading and writing.

Matthiessen coined the phrase "American Renaissance" for the 1850s flowering of American literature. Though *American Renaissance* encouraged a view of American literature that excluded women and minority writers, Matthiessen's work continues to be a topic of critical study. He integrated his radical political and sexual outlook into his writings during repressive times in interesting and controversial ways. David Bergman, in his 1991 book *Gaiety Transfigured,* argues that Matthiessen's *American Renaissance* was an expression of his love for Cheney, who kindled Matthiessen's interest in Whitman, and a covert celebration of the homosexual artist. However, Michael Cadden, in the 1990 essay "Engendering F.O.M.: The Private Life of *American Renaissance*," expresses disappointment over the gap between the sexual Whitman presented in Matthiessen's correspondence with Cheney and the almost disembodied Whitman of *American Renaissance*. Even though Matthiessen's critical works provoke both enthusiasm and disappointment, he was undeniably instrumental in including the subversive presence of gay writers in American literature.

—*Alan E. Kozlowski*

BIBLIOGRAPHY

Barber, C. L. "A Preliminary Bibliography of F.O. Matthiessen." *Monthly Review* 2 (1950): 316–322. ■ ———. "A Supplementary Bibliography of F.O. Matthiessen." *Monthly Review* 4 (1952): 174–175. ■ Bergman, David. *Gaiety Transfigured: Gay Self-Representation in American Literature*. Madison: University of Wisconsin Press, 1991. ■ Cadden, Michael. "Engendering F.O.M.: The Private Life of *American Renaissance*." *Engendering Men: The Question of Male Feminist Criticism*. Joseph A. Boone and Michael Cadden, eds. New York: Routledge, 1990. 26–35. ■ Cain, William E. *F.O. Matthiessen and the Politics of Criticism*. Madison: University of Wisconsin Press, 1988. ■ Gunn, Giles B. *F.O. Matthiessen: The Critical Achievement*. Seattle: University of Washington Press, 1975. ■ Hyde, Louis, ed. *Rat and the Devil: Journal Letters of F.O. Matthiessen and Russell Cheney*. Hamden, Conn.: Archon, 1978. ■ Marx, Leo. "Double Consciousness and the Cultural Politics of F.O. Matthiessen." *Monthly Review* 34 (1983): 34–56. ■ Sweezy, Paul M., and Leo Huberman. *F.O. Matthiessen (1902–1950): A Collective Portrait*. New York: Schuman, 1950.

Maugham, W. Somerset
(1874–1965)

Maugham was an extremely productive writer who gained popular success with novels, short stories, and plays. In 1908, he had four plays running simultaneously on the London stage; before he died, his novel *Of Human Bondage* (1915) had sold over ten million copies; and from *Orientations* (1899) to *Creatures of Circumstances* (1947), he was regarded as a master of the well-made short story, especially for stories such as "Rain" and "The Colonel's Lady." Nevertheless, when assessing his long career, Maugham declared that he was "in the very first row of the second-rate."

Maugham was born in Paris, the son of the solicitor and legal adviser to the British embassy. Orphaned by the age of ten, he was sent to Whitstable, Kent, to be cared for by his uncle. He was educated at King's School, Canterbury, which later received his books, some manuscripts, an endowment, and his ashes; at Heidelberg University, where he did not take a degree; and at St. Thomas's Hospital, London. In 1897, he received his medical MRCS and LRCP, but the success of his first novel, *Liza of Lambeth* (1897), a realistic depiction of conditions in the London slums and the inadequacy of medical attention, turned him from medicine to literature.

Except for *Liza,* Maugham's early novels are largely forgotten. He began writing for the stage in 1903 and achieved considerable success with his light comedy, *Lady Frederic* (1907). He continued his stage success with *Our Betters* (1917), *The Circle* (1921), and *For Services Rendered* (1932). In 1933, he retired from the theater, largely because the topics he wished to treat were not welcomed by theater managers and sponsors.

In 1915, he fathered a daughter, and in 1916, he married her mother, Syrie Wellcome. He and his wife were frequently apart, and the marriage ended in divorce in 1927. During this period, Maugham achieved success as a novelist. *Of Human Bondage* fictionalized his own early years in the life of Philip Carey, and *The Moon and Sixpence* (1919) used the life of Gaugin as the basis for the story of Charles Strickland, a stockbroker who goes to Tahiti to paint and to escape conventional norms of society. *Cakes and Ale* (1930), famous for its fictionalization of Thomas Hardy, and *The Razor's Edge* (1945), which turns to the asceticism and mysticism of India in tracing its protagonist's search for self-perfection, are his best-known later works. *Ashenden* (1928) grew out of his service as an intelligence agent in World War I.

In 1914, Maugham met Gerald Haxton, a young American who would be his companion until his death in 1944, and in 1926, Maugham bought Villa Mauresque, at St. Jaen, Cap Ferrat, on the French Riviera, where he would live, when not traveling, for most of the rest of his life. In 1940, Maugham fled France on a coal boat and lived out the war in America. In 1946, with a generosity surprising those who had experienced his caustic wit, Maugham founded the Somerset Maugham Award, which enabled young writers to travel. Maugham carefully avoided treating homosexual themes and depicting homosexual characters in his works, possibly because, as the American novelist, Glenway Wescott, pointed out, "Willie's generation lived in mortal terror of the OSCAR WILDE trial."

—*David Leon Higdon*

BIBLIOGRAPHY

Calder, Robert. *Maugham and the Quest for Freedom.* New York: Doubleday, 1973. ■ ———. *Willie: The Life of W. Somerset Maugham.* New York: St. Martin's Press, 1990. ■ Morgan, Ted. *Maugham: A Biography.* New York: Simon & Schuster, 1980. ■ Raphael, Frederic. *Maugham and His World.* New York: Scribner's, 1976.

Maupin, Armistead
(*b.* 1944)

Novelist Armistead Maupin is often compared to Charles Dickens: Each wrote originally for serial publication, each frames his art for a popular audience, and each examines critically the social array of his chosen city. Like Dickens's London, Maupin's San Francisco is populated by all sorts and conditions of humankind: waifs and scoundrels, high-society hypocrites and burghers complacent in their middle-class ways, and, at the center, a group of earnest seekers after a happy life.

That Maupin's gay and lesbian characters are seeded in this larger social milieu is no accident; Maupin speaks of his intention to "create a large framework of humanity and to place gay characters within that framework." The community is Maupin's theme: His San Francisco is home to interlocking networks of friends, lovers, and enemies. As these groups develop and evolve, some become supportive and nurturing, others hypocritical and stifling. This social awareness marks Maupin's emergence as a political spokesperson and critic of the Far Right and of the entertainment industry.

Armistead Jones Maupin, Jr. was born to be a Young Republican: Raised in a conservative North Carolina family, he wrote for the *Daily Tar Heel* while a student at the University of North Carolina at Chapel Hill. After dropping out of law school, he worked at a Raleigh television station where the manager, Jesse Helms, was already gaining notoriety for his conservative television commentaries. Several tours of duty with the Navy (one in Vietnam) and work on a Charleston newspaper landed him eventually in California, where in 1976 the San Francisco *Chronicle* began publishing his *Tales of the City*.

Later revised for book publication (in five separate volumes), these daily columns followed several young residents of 28 Barbary Lane, a house on San Francisco's Russian Hill. (The series' sixth and final novel, *Sure of You* [1989], appeared only in book form.) A woman of eccentric tastes and a mysterious past, Anna Madrigal is both landlady and surrogate parent, supporting her "children" through their searches for happiness. Mary Ann Singleton, whose arrival in San Francisco inaugurates the series, struggles to balance professional ambitions with commitments to family and friends. Woman-chasing Brian Hawkins and gay Everyman Michael Tolliver pursue parallel quests for love—from the sexual liberation of the late 1970s to the quiet hard-won joys of domesticity in the 1980s. A sharp social critic, Maupin narrates the interwoven tales of these city dwellers with a wealth of detail and gentle satire that illuminates the boundaries and beliefs of various communities, most notably in the contrasting descriptions of a womyn's music festival and the exclusive Bohemian Grove encampment in *Significant Others* (1987). The series in effect constitutes a social history of two tumultuous decades.

Mirroring the communities it depicts, the series turns bleaker when AIDS enters its characters' lives.

Sharp divisions develop between those who demonstrate "bravery and conspicuous beauty" in battling the disease and those who retreat into piety or indifference. The diverse Barbary Lane "family," forged through tears and joy, breaks apart, reflecting Maupin's sense of real-life betrayals of the gay community. *Maybe the Moon* (1992), his first post-*Tales* novel, builds on these themes of community and hypocrisy; its screenwriters, actors, and Hollywood executives struggle for happiness, nurture and betray each other, and find love in the most unexpected places.

—*Randal Woodland*

BIBLIOGRAPHY

Bass, Barbara Kaplan. "Armistead Maupin." *Contemporary Gay American Novelists.* Emmanuel Nelson, ed. Westport, Conn.: Greenwood, 1993. 254–259. ■ Ross, Jean W. Interview. *Contemporary Authors.* Vol. 130. Detroit: Gale, 1990. 308–311

McCullers, Carson
(1917–1967)

When her first novel, *The Heart is a Lonely Hunter,* was published to acclaim in 1940, Carson McCullers, at only twenty-three, seemed set for a lifetime of literary glory. In fact, some believe that, in a life beset by illness, she never realized her full potential. Still, her corpus, though short, is impressive and spans a variety of genres from novel and short story to plays, the odd magazine article, and even some poetry. A number of her novels have also been brought to film.

Born in Columbus, Georgia, McCullers is characterized as one of the chief exponents of the so-called Southern gothic. Accordingly, she is renowned for her depiction of lonely, festering townships and her careful cataloging of the sexual and social alienation of their desolate occupants. Certainly her novels reflect both the bleakness and the strange beauty of the genre. Momentarily, love triumphs. Thus the affecting, yet strangely unaccountable, love of the deaf mute Singer for his friend Antonapoulos in *The Heart is a Lonely Hunter* serves as a focus and a catalyst for the other relations depicted in the novel. However, as befits the type, Singer's subsequent suicide projects the book onto another level of despair, its message of hope rendered ambiguous if not totally muted. The other novels seem similarly hard to place and range from the tense antebellum tragedy of *Reflections in a Golden Eye* (1941) to the carnival hysteria of *The Ballad of the Sad Café* (1943). Although never obviously either lesbian or gay, however, characters like the independent Miss Amelia, the belligerent tomboys Mick and Frankie, the sensitive Biff Brannon, and the tortured Captain Penderton offer uncomfortable resistance to the social ideal of neat heterosexuality. It is in this tendency to disrupt obvious categorization that McCullers's corpus holds an interest.

McCullers' own life is as ambiguous as her novels. She was married twice to the same man, Reeves McCullers; both declared their attraction for their own sex and in later life often pursued each other's amours. This complicated ménage ended with Reeves's suicide in 1953. Carson's great love alongside Reeves was for fellow writer Annemarie Clarac-Schwarzenbach. This relation was unfortunately cut short by the latter's unexpected death in 1942. Always delightfully indiscreet about her love interests, there are numerous stories linking McCullers romantically with Gypsy Rose Lee, Greta Garbo, and (the extremely reluctant) Katherine Anne Porter, before whose door she allegedly mounted guard. Inevitably, much of this information is confined to rumor and speculation since Virginia Spencer Carr's biography *The Lonely Hunter,* though otherwise excellent, gives only the most discreet coverage to affairs of the flesh.

McCullers never came out as a lesbian, nor did she as a rule employ the term *bisexual*. She was renowned for her cheeky play on sex, delighting in claiming at inappropriate moments, "I was born a man." Like her novels, however, her life provokes a questioning of obvious categories. It is in this ability to provoke debate in both her life and work that McCullers is most useful to the lesbian and gay heritage.

—*Clare Whatling*

BIBLIOGRAPHY

Bloom, Harold, ed. *Carson McCullers.* New York: Chelsea, 1986. ■ Carr, Virginia Spencer. *The Lonely Hunter: A Biography of Carson McCullers.* New York: Doubleday, 1975. ■ Shapiro, Adrian et al. *Carson McCullers: A Descriptive Listing and Annotated Bibliography.* New York: Garland, 1980. ■ Westling, Louise. *Sacred Groves and Ravaged Gardens: The Fiction of Eudora Welty, Carson McCullers and Flannery O'Connor.* Athens: University of Georgia Press, 1985.

Melville, Herman
(1819–1891)

Novelist and poet Herman Melville was born in New York City to a prosperous and distinguished family. In 1830, his father's bankruptcy and subsequent madness brought a radical alteration in the young man's life. The sense of a patrician past, of a dark secret, and of a radical loss of social status remained with him forever. Although Maria Melville's family aided their now poor relations, further disasters followed quickly. Herman Melville thus became the impoverished but genteel man who is sent off to sea, a career for which he had in no way been prepared. In 1839, after his brother's bankruptcy, Herman shipped to Liverpool as a cabin boy, an experience that is recorded in his novel *Redburn* (1849). After his return, and a trip west, Melville sailed on a whaling ship in the South Seas, where he jumped ship in the Marquesas (an experience that inspired *Typee* [1846]) and returned via Tahiti and Hawaii. Melville was married in 1847 and lived in New York until 1850, when he moved to Pittsfield, where he wrote *Moby-Dick* (1851).

Although it is now above all *Moby-Dick* that establishes his reputation as the most important novelist of the American nineteenth century, Melville in his lifetime was known for his travel books, especially *Typee* and *Omoo* (1847). It is somewhat naive to think of these works, especially *Typee,* as simply travel books since they represent the trying out of many of the themes that are central to Melville's more mature work. Moreover, the travel narrative offers an opportunity for distance from one's own culture and the exploration of alternative *mores.* One of *Typee*'s principal concerns is the role of racism and its links to colonialism. The travel narrative provided opportunity for a dark satire although it always ran the risk of participating in the very colonial strategies that it sought to expose. This risk of replication amid opposition derives from the need to possess the "other" culture sufficiently to speak on its behalf. This situation is complicated when, as here, the affiliation with the "other" is heightened by a sense of desire.

Melville inherited a tradition of writing about the exotic South Pacific as a primitive utopia and an erotic paradise. He introduced a variation into that debate by focusing particularly on male beauty and same-sex male relationships, even as his work with its depiction of the "naked houris" drew on long-established patterns of representation that tried to come to terms with a society that apparently offered a free circulation of sexual bodies of both sexes. Trying to render this scene, Melville fell back on both the French tradition of the Tahitian sexual paradise and the Greek idealization of the young male body. In many ways, the scene was unreadable by Western observers, especially since the acts of invasion, conversion, and colonization had already transformed that which was being observed. Melville imagines himself as a first visitor to an unknown kingdom, when in fact he was following in the (intellectual) footsteps of a hundred years. The unreadability of the scene, the need to interpret and hence transform, was represented concretely by the tattooing that covers the Polynesian bodies—making them at first unattractive to European eyes—and that suggests their ultimate difference. At the same time, the prevalence of tattooing challenges the assumption of the primitive or natural "other" since the tattooing itself suggests instead an opaque language of the body that is fully inscribed in and on every part of the body politic. Melville would return to the figure of tattooing in *Moby-Dick,* the first part of which in many ways rewrites *Typee.* For the moment, however, the tattooed bodies of the Polynesians are part of a structure of fear of the unknown or unfamiliar that terrorizes Tom and Toby (while fascinating them). Leaving the ship means leaving all cultural assumptions behind, venturing perhaps into the land of the cannibals, the eaters of human flesh.

Melville's fascination with the Marquesans was increased by the fact that they repeatedly demanded interpretation. The two rival tribes were seen as good and bad, friendly and dangerous; but which was which? The dilemma was partly concrete: A misreading could be fatal. But it also suggested the larger problem of cultural epistemology, as well as that of systems of value. How can the anthropologist record his or her experiences without making use of models and expectations that come from his or her own culture and training? Is "bad" anything more than the name ascribed to those we disagree with? The accusation of cannibalism was one of the principal means of condemning the Marquesans, but was it (perhaps fatally) naive to believe that this accusation was purely the product of discourse, that there was no experience lying behind it? Melville tries to use his book as a means of exploring these problems, even if they remain ultimately insoluble. He also seeks to explore social organization, in particular the operation of systems of sexuality and gender that radically differ from his own.

Melville's particular site for the exploration of these social issues is the figure of Marnoo, arising out of a tradition of the Noble Savage. Unlike the other natives, Marnoo has no facial tattoos and so can plausibly be seen as a "Polynesian Apollo." He is able to move between the two cultures of Typee and the West, just as he is able to join male and female beauty in a perfect androgynous whole. Although Marnoo becomes the means of Tom's escape, he is not the special friend of Polynesian custom: That role is played by Kory-Kory. Although he is an "attached follower" and "faithful valet," he is also "a hideous object." When writing *Typee*, Melville was unable to join the two sides of his experience of the Polynesian male: one side that ethnocentrically saw the other as grotesque and disfigured, and another side that located in Polynesia a physical perfection of the body unknown since Greece. In *Moby-Dick*, this distinction would break down. Although the erotic is still tentative in *Typee* (except for wonderfully comic scenes such as Kory-Kory's masturbatory striking of a light), the social is clearly depicted as part of a critique of Western culture. Melville notices that the usual marital unit of the island is composed of two men and one woman, and speculates that this organization may contribute to the general peacefulness of the society. It also, of course, contributes to homosocial if not homosexual relations.

Melville's next major work, *Redburn,* draws on autobiographical material, including Melville's journey to Liverpool ten years earlier. The first sections of the book depict Wellingborough Redburn's misadventures as the innocent of good family suddenly introduced into the crueler world of the ship. These scenes are then paralleled in the latter part of the book when the British dandy Harry Bolton is subject to scorn on the return journey. The subject of the novel is America's (and Melville's) relationship to the past, whether represented by the distinguished family or by the mother country England. That relationship, apparently idyllic, is finally revealed to have been already corrupted. Along with that political theme, there is the related subject of masculinity, for the revolutionary nation invents itself in part through its claim to masculinity. Melville here, as in other works, notably *Pierre* (1852), struggles with the heritage of a too-loving mother who may have rendered her son unfit for success in a new competitive world. *Redburn* wonders about the viability of those who are "other," about their ability to survive in the masculine world of the ship (or the new America).

The dominant figure of the first part of the book is the sailor Jackson, who serves as a partial sketch for Ahab as well as for Claggart in "Billy Budd" (published 1924). The name illustrates Melville's political theme; by alluding to General Jackson, he invokes the figure most clearly associated with the democratization and masculinization of America, as well as with the near-extermination of the native peoples. Jackson's presence on board a ship sailing to the slave port of Liverpool emphasizes Melville's view, expressed in "Benito Cereno" (1856) as well, that racism lies at the heart of the American experience. The novel's Jackson is devoured by hatred, including the hatred of those healthier, younger, and more attractive. His "malevolence" toward Redburn has its source in envy of the fact that he is "young and handsome." Melville sees such hatred as a response to the absence of love, and he increasingly posits love between men as a response to isolation. Redburn worries that his own loneliness might turn him into a Jackson, and thus is ready for his encounter with Harry that can offer a saving friendship in a world run by an unfeeling and deceitful captain.

Harry Bolton represents a more traditional and civilized culture, but his feminine and aristocratic nature makes him not only doomed to failure but also an inadequate model for Melville, who seeks a balance between the sexes, neither too masculine nor too feminine, as he sought a balance between the cultures of imperialism and those of the colonized. Redburn greets Harry with enthusiasm, finding in him the

European version of the *tayo* or ideal friend. The physical description of Harry emphasizes his "womanly" qualities and gives him an androgynous beauty. Although Redburn exclaims, "I now had a comrade. . . . Harry . . . shared with me his purse and his heart," he resists giving his "whole soul" to Harry, even as he insists that he is still searching for "the unbounded bosom of some immaculate friend." Harry takes Redburn to Aladdin's Palace, a mysterious den of unspecified iniquity that is probably meant to suggest a male brothel as well as a gambling den. Redburn's naiveté is such that he cannot grasp the nature of the "Palace" (ironically named) or indeed of Harry's place as a prostitute in a world of "molly houses." Melville no longer seems content to depict the ideal world of the South Seas; he must locate his male friends in a real social space. But where will that be? And how will they inhabit it? These questions were almost impossible to answer in the 1840s. The marginalization of the homosexual, which as FOUCAULT suggests, follows on the creation of a homosexual identity, makes all friendship suspect.

Harry is also a figure of the artist, another marginal figure in the new social structure. His Orphic voice has the power of undermining the authority of the ship, of returning his listeners to a pastoral world of untrammeled desire. In that pastoral, there is another musician, the young Carlo, who is described as a young wine god, Caravaggio's Bacchus, perhaps. As the beautiful adolescent, Carlo is permitted a degree of gender ambiguity that would be impossible even for Harry. He offers a long paean of praise to his hand organ, a remarkable celebration of masturbation that would later be echoed in the sperm-squeezing scene in *Moby-Dick*. Carlo's music has extraordinary power to "make, unmake me; build me up; to pieces take me." Even as he celebrates this remarkable music and its creator, Redburn the narrator must sacrifice his friend Harry, described as a "hunted . . . zebra . . . pursued from bowsprit to mainmast." Harry's refusal to climb the mast a second time marks his cowardice and lack of masculinity for the crew. The "girlish youth" is too much like the epicene LORD BYRON to be able to survive in the new world of New York. Redburn returns home, apparently finding no place in his life for his friend Harry, just as Melville could not write a text in which the two friends could find a life together. The world of Byron was over, replaced by a new American democratic reality of economic competition and masculine energy.

Moby-Dick, Melville's greatest work, brings together almost all the themes of his earlier work. The character of Queequeg takes on many of the qualities of the Polynesian figures, whereas the captain, Ahab, is a culmination of all the versions of evil captains abusing power, even as he is pitied in his loneliness and isolation. The incisive political commentary on American imperialism and the failure of democracy is given an ever sharper edge, as Melville imagines an America driven by a madman toward destruction, just retribution for racial crimes. Once again male friendship offers an opportunity for resistance, and here that opportunity comes closest to realization.

The first sections of the novel concern the preparation for a whaling trip. On the way to Nantucket, Ishmael, the narrator, has to spend a night in New Bedford. Since the inn is crowded, he has to share accommodations in the landlord's wedding bed with a harpooner, Queequeg. The thought of spending the night with a cannibal arouses comically inflated fears in Ishmael. Finally reluctantly going to bed, Ishmael awakens the next morning to find "Queequeg's arm thrown over me in the most loving and affectionate manner. You had almost thought I had been his wife." Their friendship is maintained throughout, until Queequeg's coffin becomes the means of Ishmael's survival from the wreck of the *Pequod*. The language of the first scenes featuring the two men is filled with imagery of marriage as well as with a sense of sexual and racial transgression. Ishamel remembers a crime for which he had been punished by his stepmother, and he finds "hugging a fellow male in that matrimonial sort of way" "unbecoming." The male domestic idyll is interrupted by chapters that depict the chapel and the sermon of Father Mapple, reminders of the source of the fear of otherness and particularly of male friendship in Christianity. Ishmael concludes, "I'll try a pagan friend . . . since Christian kindness has proved but hollow courtesy."

In their "hearts' honeymoon," Queequeg and Ishmael unwrite many of the cultural fears that prevent communication across the boundaries of race and culture. Although presented in a tone of comic exaggeration, the wedding of Ishmael and Queequeg as a symbolic miscegenation that strikes at the heart of American and Western history possesses real potential to undercut a system of authority. One of Melville's most daring insights in *Moby-Dick* is the recognition of homophobia as a force linked to racism and required by patriarchal society just as much as the suppression of women. Male friendship, as Melville presents it, has the capacity of interrupting an economy of production. Like his contemporary WHITMAN, Melville sees in male friendship a social potential that is linked to the democratic mission of America. But Melville's view is much darker than Whitman's, for he places the scene of racial and sexual harmony *prior to* the death-driven journey of the *Pequod*. For Melville, the democratic potential is threatened not so much by a reassertion of traditional political authority as by the persistence of structures of hierarchy and abuse in a democratic culture or by the capacity of democratic culture to spawn monsters like Ahab, demagogues who play upon the weakness of the mob.

Language use varies radically in the text of *Moby-Dick,* from Queequeg's simple "pidgin" to Ishmael's matter-of-fact everyday speech to Ahab's grandiloquent speeches that echo their Renaissance sources. The "elevated" language of Ahab's soliloquies is the most dangerous since it operates by a kind of mesmerism, demanding participation and assent by the listener. In the chapter "The Doubloon," Melville has almost all of his characters read the coin nailed to the masthead. Although there is but "one text," there are many "rendering[s]." Queequeg is not only a reader of these signs, but a porter of them; language and body are one. Unlike the others, who establish a radical distance between self and world, between subject and object, Queequeg represents an unbroken unity of experience. The nature of that body-consciousness is then turned comically into a discussion of what Queequeg discovers in looking at his own body, "something there in the vicinity of his thigh—I guess it's Sagittarius or the Archer." Such bawdy humor in Melville always signals a release of repression. By identifying his own body as a double of the inscribed coin, Queequeg asserts his own reclaimed phallus.

As the Etymology section of the novel hints, the *baleine* or whale is also the *phallena* or phallus. Faced with a culture that he perceived as increasingly removed from the body and from pleasure, Melville calls repeatedly for a reclamation of pleasure. Nowhere is this more evident than in the chapter, "A Squeeze of the Hand." In an amazing progression of images, Melville moves from Pip's isolation and madness to the possibility of social harmony in mutual masturbation. The passage derives its transgressive power in part from the moral purity campaign of the mid-nineteenth century that sought to suppress all eroticism, including masturbation, seen in economic terms as a "spending" or wasting of sperm. But its power to trouble does not depend entirely on its historical context. In the middle of a factory scene of alienated labor, Melville imagines a scene of reclaimed fraternity. The "sperm" of the whale becomes the shared sperm of the men who are able to return in imagination at least to a "musky meadow." This pastoral vision cannot last, of course, but its potential is enormous. It is a brief interlude in the drive of the novel toward its apocalyptic conclusion. The chapters following "A Squeeze of the Hand" remind us of the role played by the church and industry in the suppression

of desire. (Melville would return to this theme in "A Tartarus of Maids.") Against the pagan celebration of fertility in the worship of the phallus by a matriarchal culture, Melville sets the antibody culture of the Jewish and Christian traditions, with their emphasis on ritual mutilation or circumcision. Against a culture of work, Melville imagines a culture of play, just as he opposes a world of linguistic play to one of fixed meaning, or of compulsory reproduction to polymorphous pleasure. Melville imagines the possibility of individual change—Ishmael is altered by his contact with Queequeg—but it is hard to see how larger social change can take place. All he can do is warn of the consequences of a will to power that apparently knows no bounds.

Although *Moby-Dick* is now generally regarded as the most important of Melville's works, it received a baffled if not hostile response (the *Athenaeum* called it "so much trash"), and Melville sought to reclaim his reputation with a new novel that he called "calculated for popularity," *Pierre.* It is hard to imagine what he was thinking. Only recently has psychoanalytic theory begun to offer ways of dealing with the unresolved impulses of this strange text, at once classical tragedy, domestic romance, and urban narrative. Pierre is divided in his love between two women, his intended bride Lucy and the darker Isabel, his illegitimate half-sister. As Newton Arvin noticed almost 50 years ago, Pierre's desire is "to preserve the incestuous bond with his father by uniting himself to this mysterious girl who . . . strongly resembles that parent." That the heterosexual drama is in fact a disguised or unrecognized homosexual one is confirmed by the allusion to SHAKESPEARE's Sonnet 144 at the end of the book: The Good Angel and the Bad Angel are to be understood not only as innocence and experience but even more as homosexual and heterosexual. By choosing Isabel, Pierre also loses his friendship with his cousin Glen Stanley, which is described in the ideal terms of male friendship. The boys' love-friendship gives way to the claims of heterosexuality and paternity. How much of this content was conscious remains uncertain, but James Creech has recently seen *Pierre* as concealing a conscious homosexuality that is conveyed to knowing readers by what amounts to a series of winks. Whatever the importance of such a subplot, *Pierre* failed to win Melville many new readers, and he increasingly withdrew into a dark sense of dejection and failure.

Melville's final sustained treatment of power and desire comes in the novella "Billy Budd," left in manuscript at his death. It has often been taken as a kind of testament since it would seem to represent Melville's last thoughts, but many readings (including that of Benjamin Britten's opera) have been far too willing to see a final reconciliation to the world. The novella recapitulates many of the themes of the earlier works, such as the injustice of power on shipboard, but it is much darker about the possibility of resistance. It is also far less optimistic about the possibility for affection. In part, these shifts may be due to Melville's increasing age and isolation, but they also reflect a shift in the conceptualization of homosexuality. What was seen in the 1840s as a characteristic of non-Western societies, or as a set of forbidden acts, was seen by the 1890s as an object of medical scrutiny. Writing now as a contemporary of the early Freud, Melville sees his villain Claggart as a repressed homosexual whose desires for Billy can only be translated into a false accusation against him. Claggart's evil (or "depravity" by nature) is the product of a failure to acknowledge his own desires.

Unlike the love that threatens to disrupt order in *Moby-Dick,* the emotions here do not include love, except in its parodic version of paternal love in the figure of Captain Vere. Billy is accused of spreading mutiny on shipboard; his inability to speak leads him to strike out against Claggart and inadvertently kill him. Although the men on board the *Bellipotent* are fond of Billy, they are not moved to rebellion by his execution. The only tribute they offer Billy is the sentimental ballad, "Bristol Mary," which serves to safely heterosexualize the story. All the accounts, Melville insists, amount to falsifications. The surgeon's scientific observation of the absence of ejaculation at the moment of the hanging illustrates the failure to understand the emotional and erotic roots of the story. Billy Budd, the "new" homosexual, is a victim of everyone around him. Too beautiful, too "rosy," too androgynous, he cannot offer an effective alternative to the masculine authority of the ship. Billy's illiteracy is both real and symbolic. Unable to read, he cannot understand the social text that surrounds him or see the signs of hatred that he provokes. It is Vere, the apparently kind man who is willing to sacrifice Billy for his own advancement, who remains the dominant figure of the tale. Such genteel fathers collaborate with the more directly violent police figures such as Claggart. Together they rule in the name of masculinity. Even at the end of his career, Melville was searching for a way out of the patriarchy. But he no longer believed that he could find it. The powerful would always prevail, using whatever they could to further their own interests and to conceal the homoerotic bonds that threaten to implicate them as well.

Although almost forgotten by the end of his life, Melville enjoyed a considerable revival beginning in the 1920s. He was appreciated by many gay readers, including E. M. FORSTER, who wrote the libretto for Britten's *Billy Budd* (1951), and WILLIAM PLOMER, who wrote introductions to British editions of *Billy Budd, Redburn,* and *White-Jacket.* HART CRANE was one of Melville's early admirers and wrote "At Melville's Tomb" (1925). Melville's status as husband and father probably delayed wider recognition of his homosexuality, but more recently critics have come to recognize the unmistakable evidence of the texts.

The political activism of the 1960s helped produce a much more activist view of Melville, in response to an earlier view of him as largely conservative. His concern with meaning has made him a perfect object of deconstruction. And his sexual politics have been brought to light partly in terms of his own utopian desires, partly in terms of a complex pattern of desires. In death, as in life, Melville remains a dark, ungraspable figure.

—*Robert K. Martin*

BIBLIOGRAPHY

Arvin, Newton. *Herman Melville. A Critical Biography.* New York: Sloane, 1950. ■ Chase, Richard. *Herman Melville. A Critical Study.* New York: Macmillan, 1949. ■ Creech, James. *Closet Writing/Gay Reading. The Case of Melville's Pierre.* Chicago: University of Chicago Press, 1993. ■ Martin, Robert K. *Hero, Stranger, and Captain. Male Friendship, Social Critique, and Literary Form in the Sea Novels of Herman Melville.* Chapel Hill: University of North Carolina Press, 1986. ■ Miller, Edwin Haviland. *Melville.* New York: Braziller, 1975. ■ Rogin, Michael. *Subversive Genealogy. The Politics and Art of Herman Melville.* New York: Knopf, 1983. ■ Sedgwick, Eve Kosofsky. *Epistemology of the Closet.* Berkeley: University of California Press, 1990.

Merrill, James
(1926–1995)

Born on March 3, 1926, to Charles Merrill, the stockbroker-founder of Merrill/Lynch, and Helen Ingram, James Merrill enjoyed the blessings of wealth and the culture of leisure. His Prussian–English nanny, whose sister was decorated for playing duets with the Queen Mother of Belgium, taught him French and German. His parents divorced when he was twelve, and his nanny was let go. When Merrill was a senior in high school, his father collected some of his poems and short stories in a volume and had it printed under the title *Jim's Book*. After graduating from the Lawrenceville School, Merrill matriculated at Amherst College but interrupted his studies to serve in the army in World War II. He graduated in 1947, and four years later, having published *First Poems*, he suffered from writer's block and sought psychiatric help in Rome. Settling in Stonington, Connecticut, on Water Street, he spent half of each year in Greece until 1979. From then until his death he divided his residence between Stonington and Key West, where his lover David Jackson kept a home.

Homosexual themes surface in early Merrill poems, but they are sometimes buried in metaphor, as in "A Renewal," a short lyric in *The Country of a Thousand Years of Peace* (1959). Since Merrill was never secretive about his sexual preference, his poems do not need excessive decoding: Anyone who knows the basic facts of his life can understand the personae of his poems. For example, there is an undercurrent of his relationship with David Jackson as early as "David's Night in Velihs," a lyric in *The Fire Screen* (1969).

The most notorious of Merrill's books are the trilogy in which Jackson appears as a co-medium using a Ouija board in an exciting foray into the occult. The two call up various dead poets (AUDEN, Yeats), four archangels, and assorted figures from Merrill's past. Dialogue from the spirits appears in uppercase letters. The Ouija board experiments began in an August 23, 1955, session with Jackson's wife, Doris; within a week, Merrill had composed "Voices from the Other World," the first of the poems using material from the board. The first part of the trilogy was published as "The Book of Ephraim" in *Divine Comedies*. *Mirabell: Books of Number* followed two years later, and *Scripts for the Pageant* appeared in 1980. The three were combined into *The Changing Light at Sandover* in 1982, with a coda, "The Higher Keys," in which twenty-six spirits return for a final visit. Merrill is asked to read the entire trilogy aloud, and the book ends with the word *Admittedly*, the first word of "The Book of Ephraim."

In addition to his volumes of poetry, Merrill published two novels. *The Seraglio* (1957), written in traditional novel style, concerns a young man named Francis Tanning who, unlike his rich father, is not interested in women. In a grisly scene, Francis, confused over his sexual identity, tries to castrate himself. The protagonist has been read as a thinly disguised portrait of Merrill himself: Midway in the novel, Francis begins to use a Ouija board. *The (Diblos) Notebook* (1965) is a radically different kind of experimental novel. Conceived as a notebook, the novel attempts to simulate the act of writing, employing false plots, shifts in point of view, and crossed-out words.

Although Merrill's chief work, his trilogy, may read at times as a tedious voyage into the esoteric, it is significant in its ever-present endorsement of a gay relationship. Under the drama of the Ouija board and bursts of poetic color, the playful use of terza rima and other traditional verse forms, there are touches of ordinary solicitude for the author's lover: David's toothache, David's operation. Merrill's significance as a gay writer lies in his deliberate use of a personal relationship to fuel his poetry. He contends, in *Mirabell,* that gay love actuates the creation of poetry and music. Merrill had one of the most musical ears in modern poetry: His beautiful turns of rhyme are anomalous in an age that privileges free verse.

—George Klawitter

BIBLIOGRAPHY

Humphries, Jefferson. "James Merrill's Voice within the Mirror." *Losing the Text: Readings in Literary Desire.* Athens: University of Georgia Press, 1986. 21–54. ■ Kalstone, David. *Five Temperaments.* New York: Oxford University Press, 1977. ■ Lehman, David and Charles Berger, eds. *James Merrill: Essays in Criticism.* Ithaca, New York: Cornell University Press, 1983. ■ McClatchy, J. D. "The Art of Poetry XXXI: James Merrill." *Paris Review* 84 (Summer 1982): 184–219. ■ Moffett, Judith. *James Merrill: An Introduction to the Poetry.* New York: Columbia University Press, 1984. ■ White, Edmund. "The Inverted Type: Homosexuality as a Theme in James Merrill's Prophetic Books." *Literary Visions of Homosexuality.* Stuart Kellogg, ed. New York: Haworth, 1983. 47–52.

Mew, Charlotte
(1869–1928)

Charlotte Mary Mew was born in London on November 15, 1869. Her father, Frederick Mew, was an architect. Her mother, Anna Maria Kendall Mew, was the daughter of the head of her husband's firm. Mew was strictly brought up by her nurse, Elizabeth Goodman, whom she was later to describe in the memoir "An Old Servant." The family was often struck by hardship; three of Mew's siblings died in childhood, and two others went insane in their twenties.

Mew wrote stories and verses in her teens. Her first published work was the story "Passed," accepted by Henry Harland for the 1894 number of *The Yellow Book*. Harland praised but rejected her next offering, "The China Bowl," and for the next decade and a half Mew published only the occasional story or essay, mostly in order to supplement the family's dwindling income. Mew wrote most of her poems between 1909 and 1916. In 1912, she gained notice when Henry Massingham's radical paper *The Nation* published her poem "The Farmer's Bride." Mew was soon taken up by the hostess Catherine Scott, at whose teas she read and thereby gained some literary attention. Introduced to Alida Klementaski and Harold Monro of the Poetry Bookshop, she published a chapbook, "The Farmer's Bride," under its imprint in 1916. The volume did not sell well, but Sidney Cockerell, the director of the Fitzwilliam Museum, noticed it and sent copies to his literary friends, including Siegfried Sassoon and Thomas Hardy. Hardy was particularly impressed by her work. A second edition of "The Farmer's Bride" with additional poems was published in 1921. Cockerell's patronage enabled Mew to receive a small Civil List pension in 1923.

Mew's personal life was a series of setbacks. Two serious love affairs, with the writer Ella D'Arcy in 1898 and with the popular novelist May Sinclair nine years later, came to nothing when the women did not return her affection. Sinclair cruelly publicized Mew's attraction to her and Mew became the butt of ridicule. Mew's poetry does not explicitly mention her lesbianism but encodes the emotional pain of hiding her sexuality in complex dramatic monologues on themes of loss and isolation. In "The Farmer's Bride," a young farmer recounts the story of his wife, who was so frightened by him that she fled from the marriage and into the woods. Quickly recaptured by a posse of men, she quietly does her housework: "Happy enough to chat and play . . . / So long as men-folk keep away." Though the poem ends by concentrating on the farmer's thwarted erotic longing for his bride, it also exhibits a strong subtext of compulsory heterosexuality. "Saturday Market" instructs the reader: "Bury your heart in some deep hollow." The poem might be read as an allegory of Mew's denied desires since it places desire in the context of shame.

Mew's last years were difficult. She was no longer writing verse, and a series of deaths affected her greatly. Her beloved mother died in 1923. Her sister Anne, with whom she had lived all of her life, died in 1927 after a painful battle with liver cancer. In February 1928, Mew was beginning to show evidence of mental strain and was put in a nursing home. On March 24 of that year, she committed suicide by drinking a bottle of disinfectant. A posthumous volume, *The Rambling Sailor,* edited by Alida Klementaski Monro, was published in 1929.

—*James Najarian*

BIBLIOGRAPHY

Boll, T. E. M. "The Mystery of Charlotte Mew and May Sinclair: An Inquiry." *Bulletin of the New York Public Library* 75 (September 1970): 445–453. ■ Davidow, Mary C. "The Charlotte Mew–May Sinclair Relationship: A Reply." *Bulletin of the New York Public Library* 75 (March 1971): 295–300. ■ Fitzgerald, Penelope. *Charlotte Mew and Her Friends.* London: Collins, 1984. ■ Mew, Charlotte. *Collected Poems and Prose.* Val Warner, ed. Manchester: Carcanet, 1981. ■ Mizejewski, Linda. "Charlotte Mew and the Unrepentant Magdalene: A Myth in Transition." *Texas Studies in Literature and Language* 26 (Fall 1984): 282–302.

Michelangelo
(1475–1564)

The son of a magistrate, Michelangelo was born in Caprese, a village near Florence. At the age of thirteen, he became an apprentice in the painter Domenico Ghirlandaio's workshop, where his precocious talent was recognized almost immediately. Soon he attracted the attention of Lorenzo de' Medici ("the Magnificent"), the powerful Florentine patron, who invited the promising young man into the elite inner sanctum of the Medici household, which was then at the center of a flourishing artistic circle. It was there that Michelangelo was exposed to the ideas of the outstanding artists, intellectuals, and noblemen of his day, a group of whom would regularly gather for meals and conversation. Michelangelo's talents were nurtured at the Medici Court, where he was allowed to study the fine collection of statuary in the family's renowned garden, a virtual museum of antiquities, and from this time forward he began to produce the works of art that have made him the most celebrated figure of the Italian Renaissance in the eyes of popular culture. The colossal statue of David, the frescoes of the Sistine Chapel, and the dome of St. Peter's Cathedral are among the many masterpieces of his long career that are rightly acknowledged as essential landmarks in the history of art, and they have elicited strong responses from the moment of their first exhibition to the present day.

Michelangelo's poetry has not consistently elicited the same enthusiasm even though the artist spent considerable time creating over three hundred poems in the Italian vernacular over a period spanning six decades (ca 1501–1560, with the vast majority of the extant verse written ca 1530–1550). Although some of his contemporaries did commend his poetic gifts, modern scholars have been slow to grant Michelangelo status as an eminent literary figure. The poetry has sometimes been trivialized as a second-class adjunct to the artwork, useful primarily for explaining the imagery of the paintings, statues, and drawings. Perhaps the most judicious view is that the poetry and art are worthy of mutual respect, and that, though not attaining the artwork's sustained level of stellar achievement, the verse contains moments of indisputable genius. At any rate, the verbal and visual modes were commonly viewed as interrelated in Renaissance aesthetic theory, and profoundly aware of the philosophical rapprochement between poetry and the plastic arts, Michelangelo himself paid both literary and artistic homage to select people whom he loved dearly.

Both verbal and visual craftsmanship are brilliantly combined in the series of poems and drawings intended for Tommaso Cavalieri, a handsome Roman aristocrat. At the age of fifty-seven, Michelangelo became smitten in 1532 with the "infinitely lovely" Cavalieri, who at the age of twenty-three seemed to embody all the ideals of masculine beauty that the aging artist had searched for throughout his career. As a result, we are fortunate to have a trove of artistic evidence that seems to record, under the guise of subtly encoded symbolism, the emotions that Michelangelo felt for the cultivated young man.

Of particular interest to gay studies has been the imagery of flight that permeates various items created (or, in some cases, assumed to be created) for Cavalieri. The drawing of Ganymede, which we are told was expressly made for the beloved Tommaso, portrays the nude Trojan prince Ganymede being swept aloft by a giant bird that is actually Jupiter in disguise. The iconography of the drawing can be read as an allegory of Michelangelo's own conflicted sexual responsiveness to the youthful Cavalieri. On the one hand, Ganymede's abduction by Jupiter in the form of a giant bird was frequently explicated as an archetypal myth of the soul's rapt transportation to the heavenly spheres, a transcendent aerial journey away from the carnality of earthly desires. On the other hand, Ganymede, a young man of exceptional beauty, and the metamorphosed Jupiter could also be interpreted as flying into sensual rapture, entering the highest realm of unabashed erotic ecstasy with one another. Both readings of the Ganymede myth—spiritual versus sexual flight—appear to be present in an uneasy, irreconcilable alliance that seems intentional on Michelangelo's part. The fact that this homoerotically charged drawing was made specifically for Cavalieri, to whom Michelangelo wrote passionately suggestive letters, implies that the artist was trying to convey a message of ardent desire that included a physical, as well as a metaphysical, aspect. The tensions of seductive sensuousness versus Platonic idealism that permeate the drawing can also be found in the allusions to flight in the poetry composed for Cavalieri during this period (the early to mid-1530s). For example, in "Veggio co' bei vostr' occhi" ("I see with your beautiful eyes"), Michelangelo the poet celebrates Cavalieri as a source of inspiration and airborne rapture: "Though I am featherless, I take flight upon your wings, . . . and my words begin to breathe upon your breath." The bristling energies of homoeroticism are impossible to erase from the ecstatic images of flight in both verbal and visual contexts.

Michelangelo's images of earthbound captivity and servitude bristle with homoerotic energies as well. Two of his sonnets, "D'altrui pietoso" and "A che più debb' io" (nicknamed, respectively, "The Silkworm" and "Love's Lordship" by the Victorian translator JOHN ADDINGTON SYMONDS), are among the greatest lyrics of same-sex desire in world literature. These poems, memorable for their evocation of masochistic fetishism and grotesque self-loathing, reinvigorate what had become, during the Cinquecento, the rather moribund imitative tradition of the courtly love lyric. Michelangelo takes the commonplaces of hyperbolic romantic discourse and infuses them with the dramatic dynamism of his own repressed desires for the male body.

In "The Silkworm," the poetic speaker, as usual a thinly veiled authorial mask for Michelangelo himself, longs for his skin to be flayed, thus becoming the raw material that will be transformed into garments to clothe the exquisite body of the fair beloved (probably Cavalieri):

Kind to the world, but to itself unkind,
  A worm is born, that dying noiselessly
  Despoils itself to clothe fair limbs, and be
In its true worth by death alone divined.
Would I might die thus for my lord to find
  Raiment in my outworn mortality:
  That, changing like the snake, I might be free
To cast off flesh wherein I dwell confined!
Oh, were it mine, that shaggy fleece that stays,
  Woven and wrought into a vestment fair,
  Around his breast so beauteous in such bliss!
All through the day he'd clasp me! Would I were
  The shoes that bear his burden; when the ways
  Were wet with rain, his feet I then should kiss!
      (adapted from Symonds's translation)

The image of being flayed alive is thematically relevant to Michelangelo's self-portrait as the flayed martyr St. Bartholomew in the Sistine Chapel's *Last Judgment* fresco. In both the poem (1535) and the fresco (1534–1541), Michelangelo portrays himself as an annihilated piece of flesh that yearns to be transmogrified into a different form in order to accord with the superior status of the male beloved: The Christ of the *Last Judgment,* awe-inspiring as His wrath is, holds out the blissful possibility of eternal life in a state of grace, while Cavalieri in the sonnet offers a vaguely similar possibility of a fanciful kind of life after death. The poem, however, foregrounds the idea of physical proximity and sensual infatuation that, in effect, undermines its own hypothetical denials of the living flesh. The fantasy of corporeal oneness with the beloved seems foremost in the mind of the poem's speaker. In the cosmos of Michelangelo's poetry, the fascination with male physical splendor, despite superficial disclaimers to the contrary, is almost always imbued with the urgency of erotic appetite and sensual craving.

In "Love's Lordship," sensual craving for the sumptuous Cavalieri causes Michelangelo, as the poem's speaker, to become a slave of passion:

Why should I seek to ease intense desire
  With still more tears and windy words of grief,
  When heaven, or late or soon, sends no relief
To souls whom love hath robed around with fire?
Why need my aching heart to death aspire,
  When all must die? Nay, death beyond belief
  Unto these eyes would be both sweet and brief,
Since in my sum of woes all joys expire!

Therefore because I cannot shun the blow
  I rather seek, say who must rule my breast,
  Gliding between his gladness and his woe?
If only chains and bands can make me blest,
  No marvel if alone and nude I go
  An armed Cavalier's captive and slave confessed.
      (adapted from Symonds's translation)

Michelangelo, like his great literary forefathers DANTE and Petrarch, makes suffering supremely artful. And yet one feels that the mournful grief represented here is a source of delight, insofar as the naked speaker's imprisonment by the armed "cavalier," a deliberate pun on the name Cavalieri, can ultimately bring about felicity. Giving in to the bondage of total obsession with Tommaso, for whom Michelangelo created one of the few portrait drawings of his long artistic career, is a paradoxical kind of erotic liberation, a strange kind of permission to drop sexual inhibitions, on an imaginative level, by having the beloved enforce restrictions.

In the late 1530s and 1540s, Michelangelo began to turn his attention away from Tommaso Cavalieri to Vittoria Colonna, a distinguished poet and woman of letters in her own right. Although Cavalieri and Michelangelo remained friends, the young man went on to marry and apparently did not reciprocate the artist's libidinal overtures. Michelangelo, by contrast, never married, and his occasional exercises in heteroerotic Petrarchan verse seldom attain the fervent amorous immediacy that characterizes his homoerotic lyrics. The poetry dedicated to attractive men—not only Cavalieri, but also Febo di Poggio, Cecchino Bracci, and other figures who are either fictional or difficult to identify with precision—is a testament to the artist's intense fascination with male beauty, a fascination that is overwhelmingly dominant in the artwork. And yet no documentation indicates beyond reasonable doubt that Michelangelo ever physically consummated a relationship with anyone. The closest relationship that he ever had with a woman was with Vittoria Colonna, Marchioness of Pescara, a devout widow who seemed to fulfill his need for a nonsexualized friendship with a female of remarkable talent and theological conviction.

In the final phase of Michelangelo's poetic career (ca 1540–1560), the embodiment of male perfection is typically represented as having passed into the afterlife or in meditative religious contexts. In addition to a small group of elegiac lamentations written for deceased friends, the artist writes an extraordinary series of fifty funerary poems for the ill-fated Cecchino Bracci, a handsome adolescent who died prematurely at the age of fifteen, and a moving series of lyric prayers to Christ, the Savior who, according to Christian belief, sacrificed His perfect body for the salvation of humankind. Hence, the poetry of male beauty and masculine belovedness becomes increasingly preoccupied with death, spiritual mysticism, divine judgment, and redemption. In what may be his last poem, "Non più per altro" ("No longer by any other means"), Michelangelo invokes Christ's blood as the healer of "innumerable sins and human urges," and the reader seems asked to ponder exactly how homoerotic desire figures into the artist's own lifelong struggle with the very human urges of "love, that passion dangerous and vain."

In the first printed edition of the poetry, which was not published until almost sixty years after the author's death, the editor was obviously troubled by the haunting homoerotic inflections of Michelangelo's verse. Therefore, in the original volume of the collected poems (1623), which was edited by the artist's grandnephew "Michelangelo the Younger," genders were changed in some instances and certain references were falsified in order to be more palatable to orthodox tastes. This "corrected" version of Michelangelo's manuscripts was the standard text until the unexpurgated versions of the poetic canon began to appear in the latter half of the nineteenth century. Several important editions have appeared since World War II, making Michelangelo's literary efforts available to a broader audience and improving scholarly comprehension of textual issues that bear upon representations of gender (Michelangelo himself sometimes revised gender designations during the drafting process or elected not to specify the sex of the addressee of his poems). The relatively recent edition by James Saslow prints the Italian texts along with literal English translations that are helpful to students whose Italian is in need of assistance. With the rise of lesbian and gay studies in the 1980s and 1990s, it seems certain that Michelangelo's poetic canon will continue to provoke interest and remain a point of contention for debates about how the self was sexually constructed in Renaissance discourse.

If a gay male author is defined loosely as someone whose erotic drives and fantasies are directed principally toward members of his own sex, then Michelangelo should be deemed an appropriate figure to be understood as participating in the evolution of the gay literary tradition. The poems—perhaps our most meaningful evidence for Michelangelo's construction of sexual selfhood—teem with homoerotic dynamism and an attendant ethic of sublimation. Although Michelangelo wrote in a variety of verse forms and literary modes, the sonnets that address appealing male beloveds are, at their best, his most intriguing contribution to the literary history of same-sex desire. The poet's lack of formal education and training in classical languages did not impede his ability to write verse that surpassed that of many of his more learned contemporaries. Innovative, obscure, elliptical, at times metrically and ideologically unorthodox—Michelangelo's poetic legacy deserves the full attention of the academy. Indeed, not until SHAKESPEARE would another sonneteer represent same-sex desire with such sensuous complexity, emotional resonance, and linguistic artfulness. (See also CENSORSHIP and ITALIAN LITERATURE.)

—Stedman Mays

BIBLIOGRAPHY

Barkan, Leonard. *Transuming Passion: Ganymede and the Erotics of Humanism.* Stanford: Stanford University Press, 1991. ■ Barricelli, Jean-Pierre. "Michelangelo's *Finito*: In the Self, the Later Sonnets, and the Last *Pietà*." *New Literary History* 24 (1993): 597–616. ■ Buonarroti, Michelangelo. *Complete Poems and Selected Letters of Michelangelo.* Trans. Creighton Gilbert. Robert N. Linscott, ed. 3d ed. Princeton: Princeton University Press, 1980. ■ ———. *Michelangelo Buonarroti: Rime.* Enzo Noè Girardi, ed. Bari: Laterza, 1960. ■ ———. *The Poetry of Michelangelo.* Trans. James M. Saslow. New Haven: Yale University Press, 1991. ■ ———, and Campanella, Tommaso. *The Sonnets of Michael Angelo Buonarroti and Tommaso Campanella.* Trans. John Addington Symonds. London: Smith, Elder, & Co., 1878. Rev. ed. New York: G.P. Putnam's Sons, 1902. ■ Cambon, Glauco. *Michelangelo's Poetry: Fury of Form.* Princeton: Princeton University Press, 1985. ■ Clements, Robert J. *The Poetry of Michelangelo.* New York: New York University Press, 1965. ■ Dall'Orto, Giovanni. "'Socratic Love' as a Disguise for Same-Sex Love in the Italian Renaissance." *The Pursuit of Sodomy: Male Homosexuality in Renaissance and Enlightenment Europe.* Kent Gerard and Gert Hekma, eds. New York: Harrington Park Press, 1989. 33–65. ■ Hibbard, Howard. *Michelangelo.* 2nd ed. New York: Harper & Row, 1985. ■ Liebert, Robert S. *Michelangelo: A Psychoanalytic Study of His Life and Images.* New Haven: Yale University Press, 1983. ■ Pater, Walter. "The Poetry of Michelangelo." *The Renaissance: Studies in Art and Poetry.* Adam Phillips, ed. Oxford: Oxford University Press, 1986. 47–62. ■ Kennedy, William J. "Petrarchan Authority and Gender Revisions in Michelangelo's *Rime*." *Interpreting the Italian Renaissance: Literary Perspectives.* Antonio Toscano, ed. Stony Brook, N.Y.: Filibrary, 1991. 55–66. ■ Saslow, James M. *Ganymede in the Renaissance: Homosexuality in Art and Society.* New Haven: Yale University Press, 1986. ■ ———. "'A Veil of Ice between My Heart and the Fire': Michelangelo's Sexual Identity and Early Modern Constructs of Homosexuality." *Genders* 2 (1988): 77–90. ■ Summers, David. *Michelangelo and the Language of Art.* Princeton: Princeton University Press, 1981.

MIDDLE EASTERN LITERATURE

Middle Eastern Literature: Arabic

The expression of male homoerotic sentiment is one of the dominant themes in classical Arabic literature from the ninth century to the nineteenth. In poetry, traditionally considered the supreme art among the Arabs, love lyrics by male poets about males were almost as popular as those about females, and in certain times and places even more popular. But in prose literature as well, including such varied genres as anecdotal collections, vignettes in rhymed prose known as *maqamat*, shadowplays, and explicit erotica, homoerotic themes, mostly male but also female, are anything but rare. Even though homosexual behavior is condemned in the strongest terms by Islamic law, a position reiterated by numerous legal and pietistic works devoted to the subject, homoerotic love generally appears in poetry and belles lettres as a phenomenon every bit as natural as heteroerotic love and subject to the same range of treatments, from humorous to passionate.

This striking affirmation of homosexuality does not, however, go back to the earliest period of Arabic literature. In the extant poetry from the sixth, seventh, and early eighth centuries—from a generation or two before the advent of Islam through its first century—there are virtually no references to homosexuality at all. It was during this period that love poetry developed into an independent genre, or rather two, one playful and teasing, the other, known as *udhri* verse, passionate and even despairing; but both were initially uniformly heteroerotic. Then, quite abruptly in the late eighth century, in the cosmopolitan atmosphere of the newly founded capital at Baghdad, a generation of poets began to celebrate the illicit joys of wine and boys, in verses whose sparkle and charm have made the most famous of them, Abu Nuwas (died ca 815), one of the glories of Arabic literature.

The pederastic love celebrated by Abu Nuwas is of a type familiar from ancient Greece. The objects of his affection are adolescent boys, whose charms are conventionally described in terms virtually identical to those for women: wide hips, a narrow waist, languid eyes, and so forth. The sexual goal, implicitly understood in his chaster poems but graphically described in the more licentious ones, is anal intercourse, with the poet taking the active role. The boy is presumed to submit, if he does, out of mercenary rather than sexual motives, while the poet, as penetrator in the sexual act, retains his masculinity intact. An interest in boys was fully compatible with an interest in women, and even Abu Nuwas wrote a number of love poems directed at the latter. Besides their physical attractions, boys and women also shared a subordinate status in society; in poetry about boys this subordination is often further emphasized by making the boy a member of the lower classes, or a slave, or a Christian. Since drinking wine is forbidden by Islam, taverns were normally run by Christians, and one of Abu Nuwas's favorite themes is the seduction of a Christian boy serving as cupbearer during a night of revelry in one of these taverns.

Convention stated that a boy lost his allure once he became adult, the transition being marked by the growth of his beard. The first down on the cheeks was universally considered an enhancement of the boy's beauty, but also heralded its imminent termination. This crucial transition became an extremely popular topos for poetry and soon enough generated a response defending the unspoilt beauty of a fully bearded young man. Both points of view continued to find advocates for centuries, resulting eventually in anthologies of "beard poetry" devoted exclusively to this debate. Nevertheless, the age differential between active and passive partners in a male homosexual relation remained crucial since the sexual submission of one adult male to another was considered a repugnant idea in this society and assumed to be the result of a pathological desire to be penetrated. The adult passive homosexual was an object of derision, and not normally a subject for poetry, an exception proving the rule being the licentious poet Jahshawayh (ninth century), who flaunted his passive homosexuality and wrote panegyrics on the penis.

Explicitly sexual poetry such as Jahshawayh's fell under the generic rubric "licentious" (*mujun*) and was distinguished from the chaster love lyric (*ghazal*). From the time of Abu Nuwas, both of these genres were cultivated in both heteroerotic and homoerotic varieties, and the speed with which the homoerotic love lyric, in particular, became established in the normal poetic repertoire is astonishing. Such famous ninth-century poets as Abu Tammam, al-Buhturi, and Ibn al-Mu'tazz composed both homoerotic and heteroerotic love poems, but far more of the former. Homoerotic poetry was certainly not unwelcome at the caliphal court, and some caliphs actively encouraged it. The libertine caliph al-Amin (reigned 809–813), in particular, who patronized Abu Nuwas, was notorious for his fondness for the court eunuchs, and in particular the black eunuch Kawthar. According to a famous story, his mother attempted to lure him away from the eunuchs by dressing up the court slave girls in boys' clothing, bobbing their hair, and painting artificial mustaches on their faces. The ploy succeeded in deflecting al-Amin's attention but also initiated an extraordinary vogue among the aristocracy for these "boy-girls" (ghulamiyat) that was to persist for several generations.

There is no evidence that these ghulamiyat were identified in any way with lesbianism—they were, after all, meant to appeal to men. A few of them, however, were said to have had lesbian affairs, as were some of the slave girls in general, particularly some of those who were trained in poetry and song and commanded high prices—and considerable prestige—among the upper classes. A certain amount of lesbian love poetry is preserved, but though the anthologists, uniformly male, evince little bias against lesbianism, they also display strikingly little interest in it, and most of the female poets we know of are represented as fully heterosexual in both their lives and their art.

Some years after al-Amin, under the caliph al-Mutawakkil (reigned 847–861), homoerotic poetry again found favor at court, amid an atmosphere of general hedonism and libertinism. Al-Mutawakkil also offered encouragement to the mukhannaths, passive homosexual male transvestites who served as musicians and court jesters, and particularly the celebrated Abbada, whose witticisms were faithfully reported by anthologists for centuries. Other court wits devoted their talents to composing scandalous essays with titles such as Lesbians and Passive Male Homosexuals, The Superiority of the Rectum over the Mouth, and Rare Anecdotes about Eunuchs. All these works are unfortunately lost, but we find extensive quotations from them in later Arabic works of erotica, the earliest surviving of which dates from the late tenth century.

Extant prose discussions of homosexuality are in any case not lacking for the ninth century, most notably in the works of al-Jahiz (died 868), one of the greatest prose writers in the history of Arabic litera-ture. In his role of objective observer of the human scene, al-Jahiz broaches the topic frequently, remarking, for example, that "you will find among women some who prefer women, others who prefer men, others who prefer eunuchs, and yet others who like them all without distinction, and the same holds true with men's preferences for men, women, or eunuchs." Elsewhere, however, he shows himself quite hostile to homosexuality in either sex, declaring it unnatural and shameful. He also remarks on the abruptness with which male homoeroticism has become a public, and literary, phenomenon, and offers an interesting, if not entirely convincing, explanation. The revolutionary troops from eastern Iran who installed the Abbasid dynasty of caliphs in 750, he tells us, were forbidden to take their wives with them on campaign and resorted for sexual satisfaction to their pages; they then brought this newly acquired taste to Baghdad, where it has since flourished.

Besides its inherent implausibility, this explanation fails to account for an obvious continuity with both sexual and literary patterns known from the pre-Islamic eastern Mediterranean, and one that is deducible, although evidence is largely lacking, for the pre-Islamic Iranian world as well. Al-Jahiz would not have known much about these earlier traditions, but, ironically, his own work reflects them. Certainly his most extended discussion of male homosexuality is to be found in his well-known Maids and Youths, a debate between proponents of the love of boys and the love of women (won by the latter, which is not surprising, given al-Jahiz's own views). The advocate of boys lists such advantages as their not menstruating or getting pregnant and their generally greater availability, whereas the advocate of women points out that boys are attractive for only a very short period—until their beard grows—but women can retain their allure into their forties. What is striking is that the form of this debate, as well as many of its arguments, parallels similar debates in the Greek literature of late antiquity. Similarly, poems on the beard topos look almost like—but are not—translations of Greek poems preserved in the sixth-century Greek Anthology. How these apparent continuities are to be reconciled with the discontinuity we find in Arabic literature is a puzzle that remains unexplained.

One of the arguments put forth by the advocate of women in al-Jahiz's debate is that sex with boys is forbidden by Islamic law, whereas sex with women is licit under conditions of marriage or concubinage. In fact, Islamic sanctions against anal intercourse, considered the male homosexual act, are extremely harsh. In contrast to the societal attitudes that are reflected in literature, both the active and passive partners are in law considered equally culpable. The various legal schools differ on the appropriate punishment, some of them making sodomy a capital crime, others reducing the sentence to one hundred lashes for the unmarried offender, in analogy with the penalty for heterosexual fornication, and even the most lenient prescribing a discretionary punishment by the judge for which a reduced number of lashes and imprisonment are suggested. As with heterosexual fornication, however, the rules of evidence are made almost impossibly stringent: Conviction is permitted only on the basis of repeated confession or the eyewitnessing of the act of penetration by four (in some schools two) male witnesses of established probity. In general, the jurists treat (active) homosexuality in a manner strictly analogous to heterosexual fornication—as a natural temptation but a grievous (if apparently seldom prosecuted) offense. This conception is echoed not only in al-Jahiz's debate (in which the advocate of boys retorts to the advocate of women that heterosexual fornication is more harshly and explicitly condemned by the law than homosexual sodomy), but also in the numerous later debates composed in the same spirit over the following centuries (one of which turns up in the *Arabian Nights*).

Another argument advanced by the advocate of girls in al-Jahiz's debate is that no one is known ever to have died of love for a boy, whereas the famous lovers who have perished from unfulfilled passion for their unobtainable female beloveds are legion. The reference here is to the *udhri* tradition of poet-lovers, whose equally devoted beloveds were married off to another man or otherwise separated from them, and who either went mad or died from their frustrated, chaste passion. In al-Jahiz's day, there was indeed no homoerotic poetry that took itself this seriously; but this deficiency was soon to be remedied. Already in al-Jahiz's own old age, a bureaucrat named Khalid al-Katib was producing a long series of plaintive laments on an unobtainable boy, and in the following generation a prominent jurist was to codify a form of chaste homoerotic passion just as intense as that of the heteroerotic *udhri* tradition.

Muhammad ibn Dawud al-Zahiri, the son and successor of the founder of a conservative Islamic law school which has not survived, is best known for his anthology of poetry, *The Book of the Flower,* whose first half deals with love poetry and is considered the prototype of the "theory of love" genre in Arabic literature, of which we have dozens of exemplars extending into at least the eighteenth century. Ibn Dawud's book tracks the progress of the stereotypical love affair, illustrating each stage with both heteroerotic and homoerotic verses, the latter mostly from his own pen. Central to his idealizing view is a statement transmitted from the Prophet Muhammad that "He who loves passionately, remains chaste, hides his love, and then dies, dies a martyr," and thus enters Paradise directly, without awaiting the Last Judgment. According to several accounts of dubious historicity, Ibn Dawud cited this tradition on his deathbed, explaining that he was dying from his chaste passion for a younger man named Ibn Jami'. The transmitter of these anecdotes, Ibn Dawud's friend and colleague Niftawayh, himself composed chaste homoerotic love lyrics, and numerous later poets also pursued this genre.

Also particularly associated with the name of Ibn Dawud, although not explicitly attested to in his book, was the doctrine of the "permitted gaze," according to which looking on a boy's beauty, without physical relations, was allowed under Islamic law. The primary advocates of this doctrine, however, were not legal experts such as Ibn Dawud, but Sufi mystics, who began sometime in the ninth century to practice such "gazing" as a religious exercise, seeing in the beautiful boy a "witness" to God's beauty and creative power. Such exercises were often associated with spiritual "concerts," and songs and verses celebrating the beauty of and love for a boy as a metaphor for God's beauty became a significant subgenre of mystical Arabic poetry, though it was to achieve far greater popularity in Persian. Religious conservatives, however, continued for centuries to attack both the "permitted gaze" and the martyr tradition.

In the century following Ibn Dawud, two poets stand out for their particular contributions to the homoerotic lyric. The first, al-Khubza'aruzzi (died ca 938), was an illiterate baker of rice bread in Basra, in lower Iraq, whose delicate lyrics on the beautiful young men of the city attracted the admiring attention of the aristocratic court poets, who would visit his bakery in order to hear him declaim his verses. Two generations later, in the city of Tinnis in Egypt, Ibn Waki'al-Tinnisi (died 1003) charmed his contemporaries with his poetic evocations of gardens, wine, and boys, recalling both the waggishness of Abu Nuwas and the elegance of Ibn al-Mu'tazz. Extensive selections from the poetry of both al-Khubza'aruzzi and Ibn Waki' are preserved in several works by the indefatigable anthologist al-Tha'alibi (died 1038). Among al-Tha'alibi's collections the one entitled *The Book of Boys* is unfortunately lost, but it was of considerable influence in later centuries, when a series of literary figures compiled similar "beauty" anthologies, beginning with al-'Adili's (mid-thirteenth century) *A Thousand and One Boys* and its heteroerotic companion *A Thousand and One Girls.*

The parallel popularity of heteroerotic and male homoerotic love poetry (with lesbian poetry a rare anomaly) was as true of Islamic Spain as of elsewhere in the Arabic-speaking world. Of particular interest in Andalusian literature is the best known of the "love theory" books, *The Ring of the Dove* by the jurist Ibn Hazm (died 1064), which eschews the anthology form, previously standard, for a mixture of the author's own verse with prose anecdotes about his contemporaries and their affairs, both heterosexual and homosexual. Aside from its final moralizing chapters condemning the evils of heterosexual fornication and sodomy, this work offers in its matter-of-fact way a valuable picture of love among the aristocracy and in the Andalusian courts.

The classical period in Arabic literature closes with the twelfth century. The subsequent post-classical period is much less well known but remained at least as rich in homoerotic literature as the preceding centuries. The increasing domination of Turks and Circassians in Arabic-speaking lands resulted in a perceptible shift in the canons of beauty, narrow "Turkish" eyes, for example, coming into fashion for both sexes. The increasingly prevalent system of military slavery, which culminated in the Mamluk (slave) sultanate in late medieval Egypt, seems to have encouraged the cultivation of homosexual attachments in the barracks, and the young Turkish slave soldier, perhaps a bit older than his classical counterpart, became the ideal love object. These developments are reflected in the encyclopedias and anthologies that this age of literary systematization produced in prodigious quantities, including regular series of "beard" books, "beauty" books, and general erotica, the best known example of the last of these being *The Perfumed Garden* by al-Nafzawi (fifteenth century).

The range of homoerotic literature produced in the late medieval period, much of which remains to be discovered, is perhaps best illustrated by two works from fourteenth-century Egypt. The Cairene eye physician and poet Ibn Daniyal (died 1310) exploited the popular art of the shadow play (in which translucent figures held against a backlighted screen served as characters for a kind of Punch and Judy show) to produce three extraordinary scripts virtuosic in style and licentious in genre. The third of these plays, *The Lovelorn (al-Mutayyam)* mocks romantic convention by portraying an affair between the sex-obsessed title character and a standoffish Turkish slaveboy, which degenerates into an orgiastic banquet at which a series of characters representing a variety of sexual tastes declaim poetry before passing out from intoxication. At the opposite extreme, al-Safadi (died 1363) composed a romantic *maqama*, comprising some seventy-five pages in elegant rhymed prose, in which a narrator tells of his falling in love with a young Turkish soldier whom he encountered hunting in a pleasure park, and of their subsequent tryst, whose physical consummation is left tantalizingly ambiguous.

The expression of homoerotic sentiment, in various forms, remained a constant of Arabic literature into the nineteenth century. In modern times, and in particular with the impact of the Victorian mores of colonizing Europeans, respectable society in the Arab world has on the whole become hostile to homosexuality and embarrassed by its prominence in the literary tradition. Recent conservative religious movements have only reinforced this negative stance. Nevertheless, a few writers have broached the topic in their fiction, and though they tend to treat it more as a psychological and societal problem than as a cause for celebration, they do depict the survival of traditional attitudes alongside the more recent puritanism in their societies. Particularly noteworthy are two novels with homosexual subplots by the Egyptian Nobelist Naguib Mahfouz, *Midaq Alley* and *Sugar Street*. Instances of homosexual themes in the extensive Arab Francophone literature include *The Seven-Headed Serpent* by Ali Ghanem and *The Great Repudiation* by Rachid Boudjedra, both Algerians, and *Proud Beggars* by the Egyptian Albert Cossery.

—*Everett K. Rowson*

BIBLIOGRAPHY

Ahmad al-Tifashi. *Les délices des coeurs*. Trans. René R. Khawam. Paris: Phoebus, 1981. Sections dealing with homosexuality trans. from French by Edward A. Lacey as *The Delight of Hearts*. San Francisco: Gay Sunshine Press, 1988. ■ Arazi, Albert. *Amour divin et amour profane dans l'Islam médiéval à travers le Diwan de Khalid al-Katib*. Paris: Maisonneuve, 1990. ■ Bell, Joseph Norman. *Love Theory in Later Hanbalite Islam*. Albany: State University of New York Press, 1979. ■ Dunne, Bruce W. "Homosexuality in the Middle East: An Agenda for Historical Research." *Arab Studies Quarterly* 12/3 and 4 (1990): 55–82. ■ Giffen, Lois Anita. *Theory of Profane Love among the Arabs: The Development of the Genre*. New York: New York University Press, 1971. ■ Hutchins, William Maynard, trans. *Nine Essays of Al-Jahiz*. New York: 1989. ■ Ibn Hazm. *The Ring of the Dove*. Trans. A. J. Arberry. London: Luzac, 1953. ■ Lane, Erskine, trans. *In Praise of Boys: Moorish Poems from Al-Andalus*. San Francisco: Gay Sunshine Press, 1975. ■ Marsot, Afaf Lutfi al-Sayyid, ed. *Society and the Sexes in Medieval Islam*. Malibu, Calif.: Undena Press, 1979. ■ Matar, Nabil I. "Homosexuality in the Early Novels of Nageeb Mahfouz." *Journal of Homosexuality* 26 (1994): 77–90. ■ Monteil, V., trans. *Abu Nuwas, Le Vin, le vent, la vie*. Paris: 1979. ■ Mouhammad al-Nawadji. *La prairie des gazelles: éloge des beaux adolescents*. Trans. René R. Khawam. Paris: Phoebus, 1989. ■ Raven, Willem. *Ibn Dawud al-Isbahani and His Kitab al-Zahra*. Amsterdam: 1989. ■ Rowson, Everett K. "The Categorization of Gender and Sexual Irregularity in Medieval Arabic Vice Lists." *Body*

Guards: The Cultural Politics of Gender Ambiguity. Julia Epstein and Kristina Straub, eds. New York: Routledge, 1991. 50–79. ■ ———. "The Effeminates of Early Medina." Journal of the American Oriental Society 111 (1991): 671–693. ■ ———. "Two Homoerotic Narratives from Mamluk Literature: al-Safadi's Law'at al-shaki and Ibn Daniyal's al-Mutayyam." For the Beauty of a Fawn: Reinterpreting Homoerotic Imagery in the Arabo-Islamic Tradition. J. W. Wright, Jr., ed. Forthcoming. ■ Shaykh Nafzawi. The Glory of the Perfumed Garden. London: Granada Publishing, 1978.

Middle Eastern Literature: Persian

Iran, or Persia, possesses a religious literature reaching back to the second millennium B.C.E. The Avesta, or the holy book of the Zoroastrians, is written in an old Iranian language related to Farsi, or modern Persian. The greater part of the Avesta, including hymns to deities (the Yashts), some of epic dimensions, and a corpus of religious rules and regulations (Videvdad), was composed in the first millennium B.C.E. During the first millennium of our era until well into the Islamic period (from 651 in Iran), a large body of indigenous literature, mostly on religious subjects, was added to the earlier compilations.

According to Zoroastrianism, the religion allegedly founded by Zarathustra, the universe is divided into two warring camps, those of the Good and Evil Spirits. Homosexuality is assigned to the latter. Indeed, the Evil Spirit instituted it during the early history of the universe by performing sodomy on himself to create "demons, lies, and other abortions." In the Avesta, homosexuality is mentioned only a few times, but it is literally demonized. For example, in the Videvdad, both the active and passive partners in sodomy are described as demons, demon worshippers, and incubi and succubi of demons. The punishment for a man who is sodomized against his will is specified as 800 strokes of the horse whip, which is the same punishment for killing a sheepdog; but if he commits sodomy willingly his sin is inexpiable. In another text, sodomites are said to be the only offenders who can be executed without the permission of high priests or kings.

Somewhat reminiscent of DANTE's Divine Comedy, The Book of Arda Wiraz, written in the ninth century C.E., describes a journey into the afterlife by the soul of Arda Wiraz, who is shown the rewards and punishments of men and women in hell. The first sin he encounters in hell is that of passive sodomy; all other sins, including heterosexual sodomy, are further down—that is, considered more severe. This distinction between homosexual and heterosexual sodomy may owe something to Muslim culture.

The theme of homosexuality is relatively common in Persian literature of the Islamic period. It is most often expressed in poetry as idealized love of young, hairless boys, but it is also found in rough pornographic prose and poetry, including satire. Homosexuality also appears in wisdom literature. Commonly it is coupled with disparaging remarks about women and heterosexual love and intercourse, an attitude not alien to Muslim culture in general.

Homosexuality is a topic in the Qabusname (1083), a book of advice from a father to his son. The advice of the father is that one should exclude neither form of sexuality but try both. Sometimes one is better than the other. For instance, intercourse with women is deemed healthier in winter, with young men in summer. On the whole, intelligence is seen as a more important criterion than gender for choosing a lover.

The most important Persian poet to explore the love of young men by men is Sa'di of Shiraz. He was born before 1189 and wrote his masterpieces, including the Golestan (Rose Garden), near the middle of the thirteenth century. Chapter 5 of the Golestan is wholly devoted to the love of youths, most of them male, some female, and some impossible to determine since Persian grammar is not gendered. In Sa'di's poetry, as in most Persian poetry, the love of a beautiful boy, the shahid or "witness [of beauty]," is the means by which the poet focuses on the Divine Beloved. This spirituality does not, however, make the poetic expression less sensuous. Sa'di also wrote a number of pornographic poems, in which he exhibits the same artful skill as in his more spiritual work.

The greatest practitioner of erotic satire is 'Obeid-e Zakani (Nezam al-din 'Obeid Allah Zakini), who died around 1370. Much of his work, which is partly in prose and partly in verse, has considerable literary merit. It frequently takes the form of short anecdotes or jokes, some of them quite coarse and of a type still repeated everywhere. For example: "A sodomite says to a young boy, 'If you let me fuck you, I promise I will use only half my dick.' The boy consents. The sodomite rams it in to the hilt. The boy reminds him of his promise. The sodomite replies that he meant the second half of his dick."

Of more literary significance is 'Obeid-e Zakani's parody of the Persian national epic poem, *The Book of Kings*, which was written by Ferdousi (Abu l-Qasem Mansur) in the second half of the tenth century. One of the main figures in this voluminous composition is Rostam, who performs numerous heroic deeds and becomes a national hero. 'Obeid-e Zakani gives an interesting twist to Rostam's duels with his opponent Human, turning one of them into an erotic tryst. This poem thereby provides one of the few examples of adult male reciprocal sex in which mutuality is emphasized. When the heroes put aside their martial weapons and attack each other with their impressive natural equipment, they alternate being top and bottom. The poet concludes: "Know that eternal bliss is in intercourse, but only he obtains bliss who also gives."

Under the Turkish Ghaznavid, Seljuq, and Khawarazmshah rulers of Iran in the eleventh and twelfth centuries, pederasty was quite common in courtly circles. Ayaz, a slave boy of Sultan Mahmud of Ghazna achieved fame in literature as a model lover. Mahmud and Ayaz eventually gained a place among the favorite pairs of lovers in Persian literature, and Ayaz himself becomes a model of purity in Sufi literature.

A modern poet who explores pederasty in his verse is Iradj Mirza (1874–1926), who was official court poet before becoming a civil servant. His poetry remains popular. Some of his poems describe his infatuation with young men. In one, he recounts sodomizing the son of one of his friends after getting him drunk. The upset boy eventually promises to keep quiet for ten packs of cigarettes.

Descriptions of lesbians and lesbian love are absent from Persian literature though the seclusion of women from men fostered female relationships, as frequently observed by Western travelers in the East.

—*Prods Oktor Skjærvø*

BIBLIOGRAPHY

Matini, J. "Ayaz." *Encylopaedia Iranica*. London: Routledge & Kegan Paul, 1987. ■ Müller, F. Max, ed. *The Sacred Books of the East*. Oxford: Oxford University Press, vols. 4 (1880) and 24 (1885). ■ Southgate, M. S. "Men, Women, and Boys: Love and Sex in the Works of SA'DI." *Iranian Studies* 17.4 (1984): 413–452.

Millay, Edna Saint Vincent
(1892–1950)

Like all persons heavily scrutinized by the public eye, Edna Saint Vincent Millay always had to pay some deference to the reputation that preceded her. She achieved fame early on in life as the pretty, petite "It Girl" of poetry, a characterization that always followed her. Her turn toward politics and social criticism in the 1930s was unpalatable to many—some critics accused her of prostituting her talent—as if that move was inappropriate for her. The irony of that resistance is that Millay's work and life was about playing but also transcending prescribed social roles; she habitually complicated set norms and stereotypes, and confronted and embraced supposedly contradictory positions. Millay is a poet well known to a wide reading audience: Our understanding of her personality has no doubt been limited by her fame and by a public unwillingness to allow her the complexity we demand of literary figures who have not achieved her popular appeal. Part of her complexity includes her sexual orientation; she expressed her bisexuality in her work and life, but her homosexuality has not been fully explored either critically or biographically.

She was born on February 22, 1892. In her childhood and adult life, those close to her called her Vincent. At an early age, Millay learned a self-sufficiency and independence more typical of males of the time, but also enjoyed an interdependence with the females of her household. Millay grew up in an unconventional family from which her father Henry had been asked to leave when she was seven by her mother Cora Buzelle Millay, at least in part because of his gambling. According to biographer Joan Dash, Millay's first known lover, Floyd Dell, reported that "'Her mother had expected a son, and when the child was a girl, she brought her up, she told me, like a son—to be self-reliant and fearless and ambitious.'" Cora worked as a district nurse and often left Millay and her two younger sisters to play and fend for themselves for extended periods. However, she was said to be a very dedicated mother who fostered the girls' talents and creativity in music and literature (she boasted the best library in Camden, Maine). They were a tightly knit family and Millay remained highly devoted to her mother and sisters into her adult life. Cora's determination to see her daughters succeed led to Millay's first real notice, as she urged Millay to enter a poetry contest in which her poem "Renascence" placed fourth. Publication of the poem that many thought should have taken first prize brought her introductions to the New York literary scene and in turn a scholarship to Vassar at age twenty-one. Millay balked at Vassar's control over her personal life and its exclusion of men from campus, probably not because she felt deprived of male companionship (she had shown no interest in the many boys attracted to the Millay household) but because her sex meant containment for the first time. Rebellious at school, she nevertheless took advantage of the Vassar years to form intense female friendships and reinforce the feminist views ingrained in much of her verse.

Although best-known for her lyrical poetry written often in traditional forms like the sonnet (she won a Pulitzer Prize in 1922 for *The Harp Weaver*), Millay was involved also in the theater—writing, directing, and performing in plays at Vassar and as a member of the Provincetown Players in Greenwich Village in her years right after college. While playing the lead in her own *The Princess Marries the Page* at Vassar, she was approached by the British actress Edith Wynne Matthison, who, excited by the performance, came backstage to kiss Millay and invite her to her summer home. Millay felt great passion in the kiss and the two exchanged letters, providing one of her few known straightforward pronouncements of lesbian love. "You wrote me a beautiful letter,—I wonder if you meant it to be as beautiful as it was.—I think you did; for somehow I know that your feeling for me, however slight it is, is of the nature of love. . . . When you tell me to come, I will come, by the next train, just as I am. This is not meekness, be assured; I do not come naturally by meekness; know that it is a proud surrender to You."

After finishing *A Few Figs from Thistles* (1920), the volume of poetry that brought Millay much attention for her descriptions of free and cavalier female sexuality, Millay began working on a five-act verse play Vassar had commissioned for the fiftieth anniversary of its Alumnae Association. In an Elizabethan set, *The Lamp and the Bell* (1921) unfolds around the characters Bianca and Beatrice, step-sisters (a relationship that allows fierce female attachment without an incestuous blood tie) who remain devoted primarily to each other even while Bianca is manipulated into marrying Beatrice's suitor. Easily read as thwarting homosexual desire, the male character serves to distract the attentions of the sisters from each other

until he is accidentally killed by Bianca. The two women are reunited just prior to Bianca's death. Although certainly not Millay's *chef d'oeuvre*, the play is an interesting reflection on the poet's own conflicted sexuality.

The sonnets Millay penned certainly reveal much more readily the poet's talent, conveying in even and controlled verse the tensions and conflicts not so containable in real life. In these a reader will find much of Millay's inner struggle with heterosexuality and her own sexual desire, as, for example, in the sonnet from *Huntsman, What Quarry* (1939) that begins "I too beneath your moon, almighty Sex." Coming to grips with erotic desire seemingly inappropriate for a lady, Millay in bitter tones hints at the difficulty of owning that "shadowy" part of herself both teased out and critically judged by curious women, boys, and girls. A woman is the object of her sexual yearnings in the sonnet from *Fatal Interview* (1931) that opens "Night is my sister, and how deep in love." Unconventional and headstrong in her wants and needs, Millay felt uncomfortable in a heterosexual world of female passivity, yet she was also unwilling to embrace an alternative, lesbian reality of different or less defined roles.

Millay is better known for her philandering with men during her Greenwich Village years than for her relationships with women. She refused a proposal from Dell, who wanted to cure her of her "Sapphic tendencies," believing that marriage would confine her to traditional female roles. She had a series of love affairs, expressing not only her belief that love was temporary but also her unwillingness to commit to a man. But in 1923 she married Eugen Boissevain, a businessman and self-proclaimed feminist. Boissevain expected their relationship to be open though the number and sexual orientation of Millay's affairs are unrecorded. Once at a cocktail party, Millay discussed her recurrent headaches with a psychologist who asked her about her attraction to women. Millay exclaimed, "'Oh, you mean I'm homosexual! Of course I am, and heterosexual too, but what's that got to do with my headache?'"

Biographers have speculated that Millay found in Boissevain the mother she had yearned for since childhood; however, Boissevain, though attending to Millay's needs, did not foster the independent spirit typical of her younger years. Millay continued through her life to write prolifically, publishing about thirty books in all, and Boissevain managed her personal life and career with an almost suffocating devotion, nursing her during frequent illnesses and arranging for her numerous readings and public appearances. She remained with him until his death in 1949. She died at home of heart failure on October 19, 1950.

The importance of Millay to lesbian and gay literary studies still needs to be assessed and the lesbian content of her work further explored. As a well known and respected poet, Millay is an important figure whose self-acknowledged bisexuality is highly significant for positioning homosexuality as part of the mainstream. Moreover, a full appreciation of her work necessitates seeing her lesbianism in it.

—*Jennifer S. Wilson*

BIBLIOGRAPHY

Brittin, Norman A. *Edna St. Vincent Millay*. Boston: Twayne Publishers, 1982. ■ Cheney, Anne. *Millay in Greenwich Village*. University: University of Alabama Press, 1975. ■ Dash, Joan. *A Life of One's Own: Three Gifted Women and the Men They Married*. New York: Harper & Row, 1973. ■ Thesing, William B., ed. *Critical Essays on Edna St. Vincent Millay*. New York: G.K. Hall, 1993. ■ Walker, Cheryl. *Masks Outrageous and Austere: Culture, Psyche, and Persona in Modern Women Poets*. Bloomington: Indiana University Press, 1991.

Miller, Isabel
(b. 1924)

Isabel Miller was born Alma Routsong on November 26, 1924, in Traverse City, Michigan. She began college in 1942 and received an honors B.A. in art from Michigan State University in 1949. In the interim, she served two years in the U.S. Navy and married Bruce Brodie, with whom she remained fifteen years. Routsong, who came out under the pen name Isabel Miller, a combination of an anagram for "lesbia" and her mother's birth name, is a lesbian fiction writer, whose works explore, often across class divides, relationships among women.

Although Routsong published two novels under her own name (*A Gradual Joy* and *Round Shape*) in the 1950s, her best-known work is *A Place for Us*, with which she introduced herself as a lesbian writer using the pseudonym Isabel Miller. Completed in 1967 and printed two years later in a 1,000-copy Bleeker Street edition that Miller financed herself, the novel was first sold on Village street corners and at meetings of the New York chapter of the Daughters of Bilitis. In 1971, it received the American Library Association's first annual Gay Book Award. McGraw-Hill's release of the novel as *Patience and Sarah* one year later brought it to mainstream bookstores across the country.

Inspired by the companionship of Mary Ann Wilson and Miss Brundidge, who lived in Greene County, New York, in the 1820s, *Patience and Sarah* is a historical romance, which typically celebrates the present by projecting its prohibitions and desires onto an idealized past. A literary touchstone for the activism of the late 1960s and early 1970s, *Patience and Sarah* recounts the joyous trials of saucy, educated painter Patience White and cross-dressing farmer Sarah Dowling, who leave their native Connecticut in order to set up house together in upstate New York. There they tackle the conflict between conventional gender and sex prescriptions and unconventional behavior: Greene County becomes their green world. Miller subsequently complicates this vision in *Patience and Sarah*'s never completed sequel; "A Dooryard Full of Flowers," published in a 1993 collection of stories of the same name, frames the lovers' utopia not as an actual landscape but as an imaginative exercise. Miller's writings celebrate the lesbian experiences they help define. More particularly, the lesbian representation in *Patience and Sarah* provides a way of reading lesbian culture. So where Miller's first novel fictionalizes history, her third historicizes that fiction. In *Side by Side* (1990) artist Patricia and herbalist Sharon resemble in both name and occupation Miller's nineteenth-century heroines. Patricia attends Brundidge-Willson College. The two women belong to a lesbian group called "A Place for Us." For Miller, fiction and lesbianism are "side by side" experiences.

One of Miller's contributions to lesbian literature is her readiness to envision lesbian characters able to lead fulfilling lives. These characters may not encompass the diversity of the lesbian community. Their concerns and experiences may tend only to address white middle-class expectations. Still, to paraphrase the title of Miller's 1986 novel, for the love of good women her works are worth reading. (See also CROSS-DRESSING.)

—*Margaret Breen and Elsa A. Bruguier*

BIBLIOGRAPHY

Katz, Jonathan. Interview: "1962–1972: Alma Routsong, Writing and Publishing *Patience and Sarah*, 'I Felt I Had Found My People.'" *Gay American History: Lesbians and Gay Men in the U.S.A.; A Documentary*. Jonathan Katz, ed. New York: Crowell, 1976: 433–443. ■ Minurdi, Regina. Rev. of *Patience and Sarah. Library Journal* 97 (1972): 2,492–2,495. ■ Ridinger, Robert B. Marks. "Alma Routsong." *Gay and Lesbian Literature*. Sharon Malinowski, ed. Detroit: St. James Press, 1994.

330–331. ■ Wavle, Elizabeth M. "Isabel Miller, pseud." *Contemporary Lesbian Writers of the U.S.: A Bio-Bibliographical Critical Sourcebook*. Sandra Pollack and Denise D. Knight, eds. Westport, Conn.: Greenwood Press, 1993. ■ Zimmerman, Bonnie. *The Safe Sea of Women, Lesbian Fiction, 1969-1989*. Boston: Beacon Press, 1990.

Milton, John
(1608–1674)

Milton may be the greatest poet in the English language. A political activist and fierce controversialist, he is at once the voice of revolutionary idealism and the icon of Christian humanism, as monumentalized in *Paradise Lost* (1667). Although he has often been accused of misogyny, his attitude toward women was advanced for his day. Similarly, though there is no doubt that he accepted the biblical condemnation of sodomy, there is reason to think that his attitude toward same-sex relations was enlightened for his age.

In a psychoanalytic study, John Shawcross analyzed Milton's intense relationship with his boyhood friend Charles Diodati, concluding that "The total view of Diodati seen from the extant evidence certainly points to a homosexual nature; of Milton, to a latent homosexualism which was probably repressed consciously (as well as subconsciously) from becoming overt except with Diodati." There is no evidence that Milton was ever again so attached to another male after Diodati's early death in 1638. In 1642, the poet married the seventeen-year-old Mary Powell and subsequently remarried twice following the deaths of his wives. Still, his attachment to Diodati may help explain his attitudes toward homosexuality in *Paradise Regained* (1670) and other works. The homosexual allusions of Elegy VII (1627), the epigraphs on the title pages of the *Masque* (1637) and *Poems* (1645), which are from VIRGIL's homoerotic second eclogue, and the highly charged homoeroticism and homosexual allusions of his elegy for Diodati, *Epitaphium Damonis* (1638), all suggest both Milton's deep familiarity with the classical literature of homosexuality and his capacity for discovering in it emotions correlative to his own.

In various prose works, Milton unremarkably lists sodomy among the numerous offenses against chastity and evokes Sodom as a precedent of God's anger with the ungodly. More interesting are the notes recorded in the Trinity manuscript for a proposed dramatization of the Sodom story. In "Cupids funeral pile. Sodom burning," Milton planned to depict the residents of the city "every one with mistresse, or Ganymed," and to feature an angelic debate about "love & how it differs from lust." What is clear from these notes is that though Milton recognized homosexuals and heterosexuals as distinct classes, he did not conceive of the Sodom story as referring exclusively to homosexuality. God's destruction of Sodom signified to Milton the generalized issue of lust, as is also clear from the citation of "that bituminous Lake where *Sodom* flam'd" in *Paradise Lost* (10.562) in association with the bitter ashes tasted by the fallen angels after the fall of Adam and Eve. In *Paradise Lost* (1.502–506), Milton juxtaposes the Sodom episode with the grisly tale recounted in Judges 19 of the Levite concubine who is gang-raped to death. He seems to have interpreted both biblical stories as warnings against rape and inhospitality.

Milton's most significant literary engagement with homosexuality occurs in *Paradise Regained*. There he tactfully incorporates a homosexual temptation into the famous banquet scene by means of significant allusions to Alexander the Great, Scipio Africanus, Ganymede, and Hylas. After citing Alexander and Scipio as examples of individuals unsusceptible to heterosexual temptations, Satan tempts Christ with a seductive *tableau vivant* that includes "Tall stripling youths rich clad, of fairer hew / Then *Ganymed* or *Hylas*" (2.352–53). Milton's carefully modulated homoerotic temptation thus reaches its culmination in the alluring presence of beautiful youths who symbolize the power of homosexual love to attract figures as stalwart as Jove and Hercules and as restrained as Alexander and Scipio. (See also ELEGY.)

—*Claude J. Summers*

BIBLIOGRAPHY

Bredbeck, Gregory W. *Sodomy and Interpretation: Marlowe to Milton*. Ithaca, N.Y.: Cornell University Press, 1991 ■ Shawcross, John T. "Milton and Diodati: An Essay in Psychodynamic Meaning." *Milton Studies* 7 (1977): 127–63. ■ Summers, Claude J. "The (Homo)Sexual Temptation in *Paradise Regained*." "*Grateful Vicissitude*": *Essays in Honor of J. Max Patrick*. Harrison T. Meserole and Michael A. Mikolajczak, eds. (forthcoming).

Mishima, Yukio
(1925–1970)

On November 25, 1970, Yukio Mishima attempted a military coup d'état at the Ichigaya, Tokyo, headquarters of the Japanese Self-Defense Forces aided by four young men, selected "cadets" of his "private army." Mishima expected the Self-Defense Forces to support his belief in the need to revise the Japanese constitution; they would unite with his private military group, the "Shield Society" (whose constituents were right-wing young men), in order to establish a mobilized National Army. He tried to appeal to their nationalism, saying that the coup would "restore Japan to her true form" and bring back the Imperial reign and military system, both of which had been abolished after World War II. The members of the Self-Defense Forces simply laughed at him. Failing in this coup attempt, he killed himself on the spot.

This incident consequently puzzled the world not only because an internationally renowned writer committed suicide but because he employed seppuku (or harakiri, disemboweling himself), which was difficult to associate with modern democratic Japan. How could such an intelligent and perspicacious man like Mishima be unaware of the anachronism of a military coup d'état? His actions generated a furor of interpretation. Some suspected this incident was in reality a pretext to attain his lifelong desire to live and die by the code of the samurai, for whom male bonding and death had the most value. In this interpretation, the Shield Society was merely a vehicle to this end. However, the intent of Mishima's seppuku still resists explanation. He consciously and constantly kept mythologizing himself throughout his life. The manner of his death gave a final flourish to his myth.

Mishima was born to a family dominated by his petulant and oppressive paternal grandmother, Natsu. Less than a couple of months after his birth, he was snatched away by Natsu from his mother, Shizue, who was allowed to see her infant son only when she was summoned to breast-feed him under her mother-in-law's supervision. Natsu seldom allowed him to be taken out of her room. Since she disliked boys' roughness, she forbade him to associate with other boys, and his companions were limited to women or girls. As a consequence, he picked up (in Japanese male chauvinistic terms) feminine patterns of speech, as well as women's taste and sensitivity. Mishima's father was said to be extremely callous and egotistic; he was indifferent to his son's well-being and egotistic; he was indifferent to his son's well-being and let Mishima become a hostage to Natsu to pacify his temperamental mother. Whether Mishima's homosexuality was innate or acquired, his early experiences led him to misogyny compounded with misanthropy. The lack of a male role model in his household steered him toward an obsession for masculinity.

As a young man, Mishima was "feminine"—thin and weak. At thirty, he launched on his quest for masculinizing himself and sought occasions for performing heroic masculine roles: He started weight-lifting; he learned martial arts and boxing; he wore overtly "masculine" costumes (leather, loincloths, uniforms, sports shirts with fronts widely open); he married and fathered two children; he organized his Shield Society, collaborated in designing their uniforms, and participated with them in the practice sessions of the Self-Defense Army; and, finally, he killed himself in the traditional ritual of the heroic Japanese warrior.

His homoerotic interests are manifested in his works in several ways: for instance, narcissism in his photoerotic book *Ba-ra-kei: Ordeal by Roses* (1963); praise of a female impersonating Kabuki actor in "Onnagata" (1957); critical writings on JEAN GENET and OSCAR WILDE; and extensive allusions to Western writers of male-homoerotic inclination (ANDRÉ GIDE, WALTER PATER, MARCEL PROUST, THOMAS MANN, to name only a few).

With *Confessions of a Mask* (1949), Mishima bared his suppressed homosexuality. *Confessions* was the first novel dealing with male homosexuality in modern Japanese literature that gained both artistic recognition and wide popularity. The story abounds with references to Western figures of homosexual tendency: Heliogabalus, MICHELANGELO, DE SADE, WINCKELMANN, HUYSMANS, Wilde, and Proust.

The protagonist, at the age of four, is awakened to his sexuality; he recognizes his preference for young blue-collar workers. His first object of love is a night-soil man, a ladler of excrement. He feels "a kind of desire like stinging pain" for this man. His gaze is riveted to his close-fitting work trousers, which outline "the lower half of his body, which move[s] lithely and seem[s] to be walking directly toward [him]." "Choked with desire," he longs to be this man—desires to identify and unite with him. Watching the young man, the protagonist realizes that his sensuous attraction originates from both the "feeling of tragedy" and the "feeling of intimacy with danger," which the man emanates. Obviously, this is the narrator's subjective reading of this young man; he projects his imagination onto the object of his love.

To the narrator, homoerotic sensuousness should be accompanied by tragedy or danger. In extreme cases, tragedy and danger should take the form of violence, blood, and death. As a result, *Confessions* proliferates with bloody sadomasochism and death linked with homoeroticism. Guido Reni's painting of SAINT SEBASTIAN represents all these facets and incites the protagonist at the age of twelve to experience his first masturbatory ejaculation. In correlation to this emphasis in *Confessions,* a couple of months before his coup d'état, Mishima had his photograph taken posing as Saint Sebastian, bound to a tree and pierced by arrows—a harbinger of his seppuku, or martyrdom. In addition, his necrophilic predilections linked with eroticism surface in many of his later works: "Patriotism" (1960), *The Sailor Who Fell from Grace with the Sea* (1963), *Sun and Steel* (1968), and *Runaway Horses* (1969), whose heroes incarnated Mishima's ideal types.

As its title suggests, *Confessions of a Mask* is narrated by the protagonist wearing a "mask," or conversely, by the mask wearing a human face—a mask without a face behind it. The reader is put in an ambivalent position: whether to take this confession as a lie or fiction by a masked person, or as an autobiography craftily disguised as fiction by the use of the "mask," or as truth inseparably intertwined with imagination. According to some Mishima critics, *Confessions* is a faithful documentation of the author and his family. In any case, the title and style of the book indubitably attains Mishima's intention of puzzling the reader about his sexuality.

Another of Mishima's stories that shocked the public with its homosexual theme was *Forbidden Colors* (1951–1953). Before writing this novel, Mishima openly frequented a Tokyo gay bar under the pretext of doing research for this work. According to Mishima, he wanted to eradicate the generalized Japanese correlation of the homosexual relationship between two men with that of two heterosexuals, in which male (active) and female (passive) roles are played. He therefore set forth the premise that male love was no more than the love between two men, surpassing such role-playing as masculine or feminine. This novel has a more sociological approach to homosexuality than *Confessions*. In *Confessions,* Mishima described a solitary young gay man, who uses his "confessions" as the means for an abrupt "coming out," but within the story remains closeted. In contrast, the hero of *Forbidden Colors,* Yuichi, comes out of his solitary closet into a wider one—Tokyo's ho-

mosexual society. Yuichi is amazed at "the unexpected scope of [the homosexual] world" and the ubiquitous existence of gays, who are, in appearance and professions, indistinguishable from "normal" men. He identifies with them in longing for the time when "the truth that man loves man would overthrow the old truth that man loves woman." He realizes that fraternal relationships such as "friendship, the love of comrades, philanthropy, the love of master and protégé" are in fact variants of homosexual love. By today's standards, these ideas sound naive, but in Mishima's day, they were epoch-making statements. In fact, one of the merits of this novel lies in Mishima's vivid depiction of Tokyo's gay underground society soon after World War II. Further, his iconoclastic approach to the prescribed Japanese masculine ideas of the early 1950s—though not extensively pursued—makes this book a harbinger of contemporary gay studies.

In *Forbidden Colors,* while displaying his misanthropy and misogyny, Mishima was also interested in describing the demonic nature of a beautiful young man, Yuichi, and the interaction with his contrasting double, an old hideous-looking writer, Shunsuke. Through this contrast, Mishima exemplified the supremacy of physical beauty over spiritual maturity or intelligence, making Yuichi his unapproachable ideal. Soon after finishing this novel, he accordingly decided to make himself into a "Yuichi" through body-building.

The motive and process of remaking himself into his ideal is depicted in *Sun and Steel* (1968). This book manifested Mishima's abhorrence of Japanese intellectuals (like Shunsuke), whose overvaluation of intelligence made them conceited, physically unattractive armchair theorists. He praised muscular beauty, which became synonymous with action in his aestheticism. Muscle and action were the antitheses of what a sedentary and meditative writer would embody. Thus, by placing muscle, action, and beauty (and by extension, warrior and masculinity) in the same category, he emphasized their superiority to intelligence and language (writer and femininity). Gazing at his Greek-godlike body, Mishima felt his transition from man of language to man of muscle to be a rebirth of himself, who used to be a "grotesque old man of twenty-five years of age," as he wrote in "Watashi no henreki jidai" ("My Wandering Years") in 1964.

Mishima now turned exhibitionistic—modeling for nude photographs, appearing on stage and in movies, recording songs, and indulging in masquerades and pageantry as the general of his private army. But his obsession with action, acting, and exhibitionism resulted in a paradox—although he loathed language, which he identified with femininity, he nevertheless remained a writer. He tried to justify this paradox by resorting to an old notion of the harmonious blend of "sword and chrysanthemum" or warrior and writer. This resolution, however, contradicted what he repeatedly asserted: his wish to die as a warrior.

Mishima developed an intriguing paradox about his muscled body. He found that the construction of a body required pain; for if one had a beautifully sculpted body and yet needed to feel life within it, the surest way to affirm its life was pain, or more exactly, bleeding. To him, the untrained body was not a body: It was a symbol of unmanliness; it was dead from the start. Hence, the paradox: A body worthy of being called masculine required pain and blood. Naturally, the most appropriate profession for this type of "bleeding" was that of a military man: His profession was ideally to die; and being a man of action, he was liberated from "language." At the same time, Mishima developed a unique theory about the military uniform: It required a sculpturelike body; it was exposed to danger—to being "pierced by a bullet and stained with blood" (*Sun and Steel*). All these theories then prompted a notion that the moment he started pumping up his body, he started preparing for self-willed death.

Mishima provides a fascinating study of a writer obsessed with the quest for masculinity. It led him to homosexual interests, masculine cults, male bonding, militaristic activities, and finally to the most masculine form of death. As a result, in his scheme of aesthetics, homoeroticism became inseparable from suicide. He is unique among the world's writers in that he linked homoeroticism with self-willed death and put this theory into action. In so doing, he kept masking and unmasking his sexual orientation by overexposing it in massive pageantry. Of course, to put people in ambiguity about his sexuality was what the mask was always intended to achieve. (See also JAPANESE LITERATURE.)

—*Seigo Nakao*

BIBLIOGRAPHY

Boardman, Gwenn R. "Greek Hero and Japanese Samurai: Mishima's New Aesthetic." *Critique* 12 (1971): 103–115. ■ Hijiya-Kirschnereit, Irmela. "Thomas Mann's Short Novel *Der Tod in Venedig* and Mishima Yukio's Novel *Kinjiki*: A Comparison." *European Studies on Japan*. Ian Nish and Charles Dunn, eds. Tenterden, Kent: Norbury, 1979. 312–317. ■ Hosoe, Eikoh, photographer. *Ba-ra-kei = Ordeal by Roses: Photographs of Mishima Yukio*. New York: Aperture, 1985. ■ Jackson, Earl, Jr. "Kabuki Narratives of Male Homoerotic Desire in Saikaku and Mishima." *Theater Journal* 41 (1989): 459–477. ■ Nathan, John. *Mishima: A Biography*. Boston: Little, Brown, 1974. ■ Petersen, Gwenn Boardman. *The Moon in the Water*. Honolulu: University of Hawaii Press, 1979. ■ Shrader, Paul, dir. *Mishima: A Life in Four Chapters*. With Ken Ogata and Toshiyuki Mizushima. Zoetrope Lucas Film, 1985. ■ Stokes, Henry Scott. *The Life and Death of Yukio Mishima*. New York: Farrar, Straus and Giroux, 1974. ■ Wolfe, Peter. *Yukio Mishima*. New York: Continuum, 1989.

Modernism

A major cultural and artistic movement dominating the Western world from approximately 1890 to 1940, depending on the country, modernism is now recognized as one of the most creative periods in human history, worthy of being discussed alongside Periclean Athens and the European Renaissance. No art was left untouched, and most were transformed by this international movement. It is generally agreed that the movement was cross-disciplinary, dominated by its own myth of discontinuity, fully urban and technological in nature, extremely self-conscious in its avant-garde and experimental facets, and characterized by both an elitist sensibility and an egotistical valuing of the self, two features that offended many at the time and others ever since, even more so than did its insistent questioning of received values and conventions, its revolutionary manifestos, and its outright rejection of the weight of conservative conventions and mores that had been gathering force in Europe since the Congress of Vienna in 1815. Moreover, as with Classical Athens and Renaissance Europe, much of the dynamism of modernism came from a deep pessimism and a fascination with irrational forces. As early as 1891, Thomas Hardy had labeled the new cultural restiveness "the ache of modernism," a label that became more and more appropriate as modernism reached its heights during the 1920s.

In music, the pounding rhythms of Igor Stravinsky and the atonalities of Arnold Schoenberg displaced the swelling melodies of Pyotr Ilyich Tchaikovsky. In painting, the cubism of Pablo Picasso and the abstractions of Wassily Kandinsky displaced the perspectivism, representationalism, and impressionism of Gustave Courbet, Pierre Auguste Renoir, Hilaire-Germain-Edgar Degas, and Edouard Manet. In sculpture, the polished forms of Constantin Brancusi and the emaciated figures of Alberto Giacometti displaced the public monumentalism and realism of works such as George Grey Barnard's *Struggle of the Two Natures in Man* (1888–1894) and Sir Edwin Landseer's Trafalgar Square lions (1858–1863). In literature, the experimentalism of James Joyce, GERTRUDE STEIN, and ERNEST HEMINGWAY, the temporal fragmentations of Joseph Conrad, Ford Madox Ford, and T. S. ELIOT, the interiority of the characters of VIRGINIA WOOLF, MARCEL PROUST, and THOMAS MANN emphatically displaced the chronologically organized, plot-driven, social novels of the nineteenth century. Whatever the actualities, modernism perceived itself as warring against continuity, tradition, and a sense of the past. In many ways, modernism styled itself as an arrogant repudiation of the past: Filippio Marinetti, the leading Italian futurist, for instance, proposed that museums be utterly destroyed so that the new century could escape the burden of the past. These displacements, however, did not occur without battles of one kind or another. The premiere of Stravinsky's *Rite of Spring* in Paris in 1912 quite literally led to a riot in the theater.

At first, modernism as a historical period does not appear friendly to either homosexuals or lesbians. After all, modernism is bounded by the 1895 London trial of OSCAR WILDE, with one London newspaper reporting that Wilde had been "charged with one of the most heinous crimes that can be alleged against a man—a crime too horrible and too revolting to be spoken of even by man," and ended with homosexuals wearing pink triangles joining millions of others who had been marked for extermination in the Nazi death camps. And although lesbian behavior was not proscribed in numerous countries at this time, the obscenity trial of RADCLYFFE HALL's *The Well of Loneliness* in London in 1928 came as a public condemnation of lesbianism. These actions, moreover, were not merely retrograde battles mounted by the old culture; modernism itself had an ugly subtext of sexism, homophobia, antisemitism, and at times, fascism. A number of modernist voices condemned homosexuals and lesbians. Ezra Pound placed a coarse homophobic statement in the twelfth of his *Cantos,* and Wyndham Lewis savagely caricatured the homosexuality of the BLOOMSBURY GROUP in his novel *The Apes of God* (1930). Numerous painters and writers, among them Marinetti, Pablo Picasso, and Marcel Duchamp, were hostile to homosexuality. Among the English, conflicts between the heterosexual and the homosexual worlds may best be seen in D. H. LAWRENCE's *Women in Love* (1922), especially in the nude wrestling scene between Rupert Birkin and Gerald Crich, mirroring Lawrence's own troubled sexuality. Even in Virginia

Woolf's novels, one finds unfavorable portraits of lesbians, especially Doris Kilman in *Mrs. Dalloway* (1925); however, the homoeroticism in the same novel makes a much more complex statement about human sexuality than the mere presence of Miss Kilman indicates.

Despite modernist homophobia, however, a number of events established the ground on which later twentieth-century gays and lesbians would begin to demand liberation. At first, these came in the form of books: Richard von Kraff-Ebing's *Psychopathia Sexualis* (1886), which openly discussed homosexuality, and Havelock Ellis's *Sexual Inversion* (1897), which was one of the first books to treat homosexuality as "neither a disease nor a crime." In 1899, Magnus Hirschfeld founded *Der Eigene,* a journal devoted to issues of human sexuality, and in 1911, he established the Institute for Sexual Science, described in CHRISTOPHER ISHERWOOD's *Christopher and His Kind* (1976), which remained the best-known center for the study of sexuality until it was destroyed by Nazi troops May 6, 1933. During the twenty years of its existence, it and other groups worked in Germany to repeal the notorious Paragraph 175, which criminalized homosexual behavior. In 1921, Berlin hosted the First Congress of the World League for Sexual Science; this initial meeting was followed with meetings in Copenhagen (1928), London (1929), and Vienna (1930). In the Soviet Union, homosexuality was briefly decriminalized between 1917 and 1920 and not subjected to Stalinist repressions until 1934. In 1924, the Society for Human Rights was founded in America, the first of several slight advances continuing until Alfred Kinsey was assigned to teach a sex education class at Indiana University in 1937, research for which started Kinsey on his way to his monumental publications on human sexuality in 1948 and 1953.

If one looks to modernist literature, one is struck more by the number of significant writers who were homosexual or lesbian than by the number of works addressing same-sex themes, depicting gay and lesbian characters, or exploring the relationships between these individuals and their societies. In France, there were COLETTE, JEAN COCTEAU, ANDRÉ GIDE, and Marcel Proust. In England, there were E. M. FORSTER, LYTTON STRACHEY, Virginia Woolf, W. SOMERSET MAUGHAM, NOEL COWARD, and a host of lesser writers such as E. F. BENSON, NORMAN DOUGLAS, RONALD FIRBANK, Hector Hugh Munro (Saki), and FREDERICK WILLIAM ROLFE (Baron Corvo). From America, came Gertrude Stein, EDNA ST. VINCENT MILLAY, AMY LOWELL, and WILLA CATHER, as well as HART CRANE. Elsewhere, CONSTANTINE CAVAFY was boldly recording the urban gay man's world in his poems.

The homosexual and lesbian worlds of modernism also accomplished much outside fiction, drama, and poetry. Margaret Anderson founded *The Little Review* (1915–1917), one of the most forward-looking and experimental journals of the period, and in Paris SYLVIA BEACH established perhaps the best-known bookstore of the period, Shakespeare and Company. Both women were instrumental in bringing James Joyce's *Ulysses* to readers. EDWARD CARPENTER edited *Ioläus* (1902), the first anthology of gay literature, one that stressed positive self-images, and other writers such as Hans Blucher in Germany and L. S. A. M. Romer in Holland brought balanced views of the homosexual to the attention of society in their *The Role of the Erotic in Male Society* (1917–1919) and *Unknown People: The Physiological Development of the Sexes in Connection with Homosexuality* (1904).

Modernism saw a considerable outpouring of homosexual writing, especially in the short story and the novel, to a lesser extent in poetry, drama, and film. Although Radclyffe Hall's *The Well of Loneliness* (1928) achieved notoriety because of its pornography trial and the official destruction of its first edition, it was certainly not the only nor the best of the lesbian novels. Among the others are DJUNA BARNES's *Ladies Almanack* (1928) and *Nightwood* (1936), which depicts gay life in Paris and Berlin, Colette's many stories about the tomboyish Claudine, VITA SACKVILLE-WEST's *Challenge* (1924), which fictionalized her affair with Violet Keppel, Gertrude Stein's *Q. E. D.,* with its explicit lesbian relationship, and Virginia Woolf's *Orlando* (1928), which made perhaps the key statement on androgyny through having Orlando metamorphose from an Elizabethan male into a neoclassical female.

Male novelists, though, were more recognized and more rewarded, two of them being honored with the Nobel Prize for Literature. Some, like W. Somerset Maugham, remained rigorously closeted though his affair with Gerald Haxton and his inversion of one of his early homosexual affairs to a heterosexual affair in *Of Human Bondage* (1915) were well known. Hector Hugh Munro, better known by his pen name "Saki," was equally guarded except in stories such as "Gabriel-Ernest" and "Quail Seed," and most of his readers would probably have been shocked had they known that his pen name refers to a cupbearer or beautiful boy and carries esoteric homoerotic connotations. Even E. M. Forster, who in 1914 in *Maurice,* wrote one of the frankest and most romantic explorations of same-sex love, suppressed his work. His novel reached print only in 1971, the year following his death. Others boldly, sometimes recklessly, pushed subject matter well into previously forbidden areas: Xavier Mayne (the pen name of EDWARD IRENAEUS

PRIME-STEVENSON) published *Imre* (1908), which chronicles Oswald's affair in Hungary with Imre, a cavalry officer. Under the pen name "Sagitta," JOHN HENRY MACKAY's *Der Puppenjungen* (1926) explored the milieu of boy prostitutes in Berlin and espoused an agenda of "equal freedom for all," topics also addressed by Aleister Crowley in *White Stains* (1898), one of the earliest English homosexual novels. Near the end of the modernist period, GEORGE SANTAYANA, an American better known as a philosopher, published *The Last Puritan* (1935), which treated a sailor in the Royal Navy caught up in a homosexual scandal aboard ship.

To these, however, must be added names indisputably central to modernist fiction: André Gide, Thomas Mann, and Marcel Proust. Proust's *A la recherche du temps perdu* (1913–1927) depicts numerous homosexuals—Robert de Saint-Loup-en-Bray, Charles Morel, Prince Gilbert de Guermantes, Jupien, Legandin, Nissim Bernard, and of course, Baron de Charlus, one of the most memorable characters in the novel and yet one more fictionalization of Count Robert de Montesquiou (1855–1921), who had already appeared as Jean des Esseintes in JORIS-KARL HUYSMANS's *A rebours* (1884) and as the peacock in Edmond Rostand's *Chantecler* (1910). The title of Proust's fourth volume, *Sodome et Gomorrhe* (1922, translated as *Cities of the Plain*) foregrounded homosexuality firmly and openly, but readers expecting moral condemnation figured in the title's biblical allusion found more of Proust's attack on social snobbery and the affectations of Parisian society and were treated to an essay on the nature of homosexual love and ultimately, in the seventh volume, to the spectacle of Charlus chained to a bed in Jupien's male brothel, being whipped by a soldier. The German author, Thomas Mann, offered an equally broad canvas liberally populated by gays, ranging from his now classic depiction of boy-man love in *Death in Venice* (1912) to male adolescent love in *Tonio Kröger* (1903) and *The Magic Mountain* (1924). His *Doctor Faustus* (1947) linked homosexuality to artistic creativity. Mann's son, KLAUS MANN, built his own literary career on tales of same-sex love, first with a collection of short stories, *Before Life* (1925), in which the lovers have little chance of success, and then with historical novels about three famous homosexuals: Alexander the Great (1930), Tchaikovsky (1935), and Ludwig II (1937). Beside the works of Proust and Mann, Gide's *Corydon* (1924), a Socratic dialogue on sexuality, seems a slight accomplishment. Minor accomplishments can be seen in the other genres. Mauritz Stiller, the Swedish director, created what is often called the first gay film with *The Wings* in 1916.

Gay and lesbian literature had indeed made major steps in subject matter, tone, and theme in the years since *Teleny; or, The Reverse of the Medal* (1893) had defined suicide by the protagonist as appropriate closure. Having been written and published between 1890 and 1940, however, does not necessarily mark a book as being "modernist." A book needs to partake of the modernist temper and ethos before it can be so marked. But since most of the gay and lesbian fiction written during these fifty years is part of the modernist reaction against standards of both past and present and since any number of these works are also experimental in their handling of narrative, they can validly be considered a significant part of the modernist movement.

Modernism gradually saw authority begin to shift from religion, which considered homosexuality a sin, to psychology, which early saw homosexuality as an illness. Ironically, the arts and their cultures were moving in opposite directions. The literature of modernism moved boldly, occasionally stridently, and at most times favorably toward serious treatment of homosexuals and homosexual cultures, striking out against sexual repressions in many forms while the cultures were preparing the way for suppression, even destruction, of the same individuals and subcultures. The socially conscious, activist authors began to displace modernism as early as the 1930s, and in their agendas for reshaping civilization and making the world anew gays and lesbians and their literature were once more emphatically marginalized and, in some countries, silenced.

—*David Leon Higdon*

BIBLIOGRAPHY

Bergman, David. *Gaiety Transfigured: Gay Self-Representation in American Literature.* Madison: University of Wisconsin Press, 1991. ■ Calinescu, Matei. *Five Faces of Modernity: Modernism, Avant-Garde, Decadence, Kitsch, Postmodernism.* Durham: Duke University Press, 1987. ■ Chefdor, Monique, Ricardo Quinones, and Albert Wachtel, eds. *Modernism: Challenges and Perspectives.* Urbana: University of Illinois Press, 1986. ■ Eysteinsson, Astradur. *The Concept of Modernism.* Ithaca, N.Y.: Cornell University Press, 1990. ■ Greenberg, David F. *The Construction of Homosexuality.* Chicago: University of Chicago Press, 1988. ■ Levin, James. *The Gay Novel: The Male Homosexual Image in America.* New York: Irvington, 1983. ■ Martin, Robert K. *The Homosexual Tradition in American Poetry.* Austin: University of Texas Press, 1979. ■ Sedgwick, Eve Kosofsky. *Between Men: English Literature and Male Homosocial Desire.* New York: Columbia University Press, 1983. ■ Stambolian, George and Elaine Marks, eds. *Homosexualities and French Literature: Cultural Contexts/Critical Texts.* Ithaca, N.Y.: Cornell University Press, 1979. ■ Summers, Claude. *Gay Fictions: Wilde to Stonewall: Studies in a Male Homosexual Literary Tradition.* New York: Continuum, 1990. ■ Weeks, Jeffrey. *Coming Out: Homosexual Politics in Britain, from the Nineteenth Century to the Present.* London: Quartet Books, 1977.

Monette, Paul
(1945–1995)

Paul Monette was born in Lawrence, Massachusetts, in 1945. He was educated at prestigious schools in New England: Phillips Andover Academy and Yale University, where he received his B.A. in 1967. He began his prolific writing career soon after graduating from Yale. For eight years, he wrote poetry exclusively. After coming out in his late twenties, he met Roger Horwitz, who was to be his lover for over twenty years. Also during his late twenties, he grew disillusioned with poetry and shifted his interest to the novel, not to return to poetry until the 1980s. In 1977, Monette and Horwitz moved to Los Angeles. Once in Hollywood, Monette wrote a number of screenplays that, though never produced, provided him the means to be a writer. Monette published four novels between 1978 and 1982. These novels were enormously successful and established his career as a writer of popular fiction. He also wrote several novelizations of films.

Monette's life changed dramatically when Roger Horwitz was diagnosed with AIDS in the early 1980s. After Horwitz's death in 1986, Monette wrote extensively about the years of their battles with AIDS (*Borrowed Time,* 1988) and how he himself coped with losing a lover to AIDS (*Love Alone,* 1988). These works are two of the most powerful accounts written about AIDS thus far. Their publication catapulted Monette into the national arena as a spokesperson for AIDS. Along with fellow writer LARRY KRAMER, he emerged as one of the most familiar and outspoken AIDS activists of our time. Since very few out gay men have had the opportunity to address national issues in mainstream venues at any previous time in U.S. history, Monette's high-visibility profile was one of his most significant achievements. He went on to write two important novels about AIDS, *Afterlife* (1990) and *Halfway Home* (1991).

In his fiction, Monette unabashedly depicts gay men who strive to fashion personal identities that lead them to love, friendship, and self-fulfillment. His early novels generally begin where most coming-out novels end; his protagonists have already come to terms with their sexuality long before the novels' projected time frames. Monette has his characters negotiate family relations, societal expectations, and personal desires in light of their decisions to lead lives as openly gay men. Two major motifs emerge in these novels: the spark of gay male relations and the dynamic alternative family structures that gay men create for themselves within a homophobic society. These themes are placed in literary forms that rely on the structures of romance, melodrama, and fantasy. Monette's finest novel, *Afterlife*, combines the elements of traditional comedy and the resistance novel; it is the first gay novel written about AIDS that fuses personal love interests with political activism. Monette's harrowing collection of deeply personal poems, *Love Alone: 18 Elegies for Rog*, conveys both the horrors of AIDS and the inconsolable pain of love lost. The elegies are an invaluable companion to *Borrowed Time*.

Before the publication and success of his memoir, *Becoming a Man*, it seemed inevitable that Monette would be remembered most for his writings on AIDS. *Becoming a Man*, however, focuses on the dilemmas of growing up gay. It provides at once an unsparing account of the nightmare of the closet and a moving and often humorous depiction of the struggle to come out. *Becoming a Man* won the 1992 National Book Award for nonfiction, a historical moment in the history of lesbian and gay literature and culture in the United States. (See also AIDS LITERATURE.)

—David Román

BIBLIOGRAPHY

Cady, Joseph. "Immersive and Counterimmersive Writing About AIDS: The Achievement of Paul Monette's *Love Alone*." *Writing AIDS: Gay Literature, Language and Analysis*. Timothy Murphy and Suzanne Poirier, eds. New York: Columbia University Press, 1993. 244–264. ■ Clum, John M. "'The Time Before the War': AIDS, Memory, and Desire." *American Literature* 62:2 (1990): 648–667. ■ Edelman, Lee. "The Mirror and the Tank: 'AIDS,' Subjectivity and the Rhetoric of Activism." *Writing AIDS: Gay Literature, Language and Analysis*. Timothy Murphy and Suzanne Poirier, eds. New York: Columbia University Press, 1993. 9–38. ■ Román, David. "Tropical Fruit?: Latino 'Gay' Men in Three Resistance Novels of the Americas." *Tropicalizations*. Francis Aparicio and Susana Chávez-Silverman. eds. Berkeley: University of California Press, forthcoming. ■ ———. "Paul Monette." *Contemporary Gay American Novelists: A Bio-Bibliographical Source-book*. Emmanuel S. Nelson, ed. Westport Conn.: Greenwood Press, 1993. 272–281.

Moraga, Cherríe
(b. 1952)

Born in Whitter, California, on September 25, 1952, Moraga is the daughter of an Anglo, Joseph Lawrence, and a Chicana, Elvira Moraga. She credits a childhood spent in the kitchen listening to the stories told by her mother with her profound appreciation for language. Despite the privileges of her light skin and college degree, Moraga claims that she lacked knowledge and language to express herself as a Chicana until she came out as a lesbian. In order to write as a lesbian, Moraga left Los Angeles and the security of her teaching position and her extended family. Discovering that only white women were represented in lesbian literature and challenged by the heterosexism of her writing group, Moraga began to define her experience as a lesbian, a Chicana, and a Chicana lesbian with a distinct blend of Spanish and English, of traditional narrative and poetic forms.

While pursuing graduate work in Feminist Writings at San Francisco State University, she met GLORIA ANZALDÚA who convinced her to co-edit a collection of writings by women of color. Published in 1981, *This Bridge Called My Back: Writings by Radical Women of Color* provided a forum for these women to articulate their rage at the racism and oppression they encountered, even within the women's movement. In the preface, Moraga declares that Women of Color are revolutionary forces, bridges who straddle the divisions within society. Her own contributions—an essay, "La Guera," and two poems, "The Welder" and "For the Color of My Mother"—recognize the emotional and sexual ties between Chicanas.

Loving in the War Years: (lo que nunca paso por sus labios) (1983), the first book of poetry published by an openly lesbian Chicana, interweaves celebratory poems of lesbian passion with two essays that examine how the myth of "La Malichina," Cortez's consort, distorts and oppresses the Chicana's exploration of her sexuality. Moraga argues that the male-identified Chicano culture silences Chicanas, sexually and verbally. Her collage of poems and narratives in both Spanish and English recreates "la familia" as an intricate web of emotional and sexual ties between women.

In 1984, a Minneapolis women's theater, Foot of the Mountain, staged a reading of Moraga's drama *Giving Up the Ghost*, perhaps the first explicitly lesbian play by a Chicana. The three characters, Marissa, Corky

(Marissa's younger self), and Amalia, break dramatic tradition as they break the silences surrounding women's sexuality, Chicana oppression, and lesbian invisibility. Their monologues compose a disturbing narrative of sexual confusion and isolation. In particular, Corky's painfully bleak story of her rape enrages and empowers female audiences. Moraga's two plays in progress, *The Shadow of Man* and *La extranjero*, continue to examine gender identities and sexuality within "la familia."

As a founder of the publishing house The Kitchen Table/Women of Color Press and a part-time lecturer in Chicano Studies at the University of California, Berkeley, Moraga calls into question basic assumptions about Chicana identity by articulating the voices of the silenced. (See also LATINA LESBIAN LITERATURE.)

—*Amy Gilley*

BIBLIOGRAPHY

Alacorn, Norma. "Making Families from Scratch: Split Subjectivities in the Work of Hemelna Maria Viramontes and Cherríe Moraga." *The Americas Review: A Review of Hispanic Literature and Art of the USA* 15:3–4 (Fall/Winter 1987): 147–159. ■ Sternbach, Nancy Spaorta. "'A Deep Racial Memory of Love': The Chicana Feminism of Cherríe Moraga." *Breaking Boundaries: Latina Writing and Critical Readings.* Asuncion Horno-Delgado, ed. Amherst: University of Massachusetts Press, 1989. 48–61. ■ Umpierre, Luz-Marie. "Interview with Cherríe Moraga." *The Americas Review: A Review of Hispanic Literature and Art of the USA* 14:2 (Summer 1986): 54–67. ■ Yarbo-Bejarano, Yvonne. "Cherríe Moraga." *Chicano Writers: First Series in Dictionary of Literary Biography.* Francisco A Lomeli and Carl R. Shirley, eds. Detroit: Gale Research Inc, 1989. 165–177. ■ ———. "Cherríe Moraga's Giving Up the Ghost: The Representation of Female Desire." *Third Woman* 3:1–2 (1986): 113–120.

Musical Theater

As William Goldman notes in his book on Broadway, *The Season,* the Broadway musical would not exist without homosexual involvement. Goldman speculates that homosexuals, like other marginalized groups, tend to congregate in areas where they feel safest, and theater has long been a homosexual stronghold. Although Goldman's study of one Broadway season is more than twenty-five years old, his chapter on "Homosexuals" remains one of the best discussions of gay men and the commercial theater. Still, it does not explain completely the attachment many gay men have to the musical theater or the fact that in the popular imagination a passion for showtunes is practically a marker for homosexuality.

The musical theater is, of course, by no means exclusively homosexual in its creators, performers, or audiences. Many of the best and most famous composing teams—Richard Rodgers and Oscar Hammerstein II, Alan Jay Lerner and Frederick Loewe, George and Ira Gershwin, for example—were apparently quite straight, though other accomplished Broadway composers, notably Cole Porter, Leonard Bernstein, and Jerry Herman, were and are at least predominantly homosexual. The number of other homosexual men and women involved in the creation and performance of Broadway musicals is difficult to estimate, but surely it is very high. So great is homosexual participation in musical theater, for example, that Martin Gottfried in his biography of choreographer and director Bob Fosse speculates on several occasions

how (and if) Fosse's heterosexuality made his choreography and direction different from the work of his peers. Homosexual choreographers, designers, writers, actors, dancers, singers, costumers, and so on have contributed enormously to the creation and sustenance of the Broadway musical. But that does not necessarily explain why so many gay men enjoy the musical theater, collect recordings of the shows, savor Broadway lore, and follow the careers of particular musical theater stars. Surely these gay fans are aligned spiritually with their more frequently noted brothers, the "opera queens." Lesbians have also been involved in the musical theater, but there has not developed among lesbians the same cultic response to Broadway musicals as there has among gay men.

Musical theater during its peak in the first two-thirds of this century served gay men in several ways. Perhaps most important, it provided a safe place for gay men and straights to meet on a culturally neutral, although closeted, playing field. The musical theater made male participation in song and dance—activities identified with highbrow effeminacy in many parts of American society—acceptable in a popular entertainment form that reinforced the validity of heterosexual romance. Thus, gay (as well as straight) men could engage in culturally suspect behavior and win approval for doing so. Unlike OPERA, the Broadway musical made it a point to attract large audiences, becoming even more accessible to small-town gays and straights alike through national touring companies, amateur productions, cast albums, and movie adaptations. Broadway shows and their associated lore and products also provided a connection with New York, a mecca for many gays trapped in repressive places leading what they felt were boring lives. No doubt many straight fans felt the same, but gay men learned quickly of the high gay involvement on Broadway in important creative and performing roles, a fact that made musicals additionally appealing to gay men.

Furthermore, artistic gay men could engage in "show" or "performance"—public display of *their* interests—in what was at once a particularly American and gay context. Opera and ballet, until very recently, were tainted with a strongly European and classist aura, but the Broadway book musical from its earliest days—as in the Jerome Kern, Oscar Hammerstein musical *Show Boat* (1927)—was centered in American history and culture, presenting the country's energy and myths of exploration, settlement, success, and happiness. In taking part in the musical's mythic display, gay men participated, at least vicariously, in a culture and history that otherwise tended to be silent about their own lives.

Although most Broadway musicals feature homosexual involvement in their creation and performance, some shows more than others may be said to have a "homosexual sensibility." For instance, Herman's *Mame* (1966) may be said to be a "gay" musical with its fanciful period costumes, elaborate wigs, and bitchy dialogue (which found its way into at least one song, "Bosom Buddies"), and friendship between two women, Mame and Vera. Mame and Vera are less the drag queens they are sometimes accused of being than women who speak their minds. The beauty of *Mame* is that the show is at once about assertive women *and* about gay male fantasies of being rich, living in New York, and dressing in ways that are strong declarations of personality. Another gay subtext to *Mame* is the relationship between Mame and her orphaned nephew, Patrick. The story can be taken as is or "straight," but *Mame* also plays into the recurrent gay scenario of having an older, wiser man initiate a younger one into the ways of a sophisticated, urban life. The genius of *Mame* as popular entertainment is that the show works so well as a straight and a gay musical without giving offense to either group.

Similarly, more complex musicals than *Mame* also have homoerotic elements: for example, the beefcake in "There is Nothing Like a Dame" (irony piling upon irony) from Rodgers and Hammerstein's *South Pacific* (1949) and the ambiguity in the name and character of Reno Sweeney in Porter's *Anything Goes* (1934),

to say nothing of the gay double entendres that a knowing audience would discern in Porter's lyrics. More complex is the identification with and worship of women musical comedy stars. Such Broadway stars as Helen Morgan, who sang the torch song "Bill" in the original *Show Boat,* Ethel Merman, Mary Martin, Gwen Verdon, Julie Andrews, Chita Rivera, Bernadette Peters, and Patti Lupone have been the object of intense gay male interest. Although these women also have large heterosexual followings, their cult status in the gay male community has extended to their being impersonated by drag queens. Accounting for that cult following is difficult, but it seems to be made up of equal parts of admiration for talent and admiration for the ways these women remake themselves as musical comedy stars, defying conventional notions about what constitutes power and beauty. Because they frequently present themselves as larger than—or at least different from—everyday life, they inspire admiration from others outside the norm.

An important element of gay male interest in the Broadway musical and its heroines is CAMP. Everything from the dream ballets of early musicals to the outsized performances and self-presentations of such stars as Carol Channing are fodder for camp followers. If we accept CHRISTOPHER ISHERWOOD's definition of high camp as a mockery or satire of something we take very seriously, then the gay male cultic response, one that celebrates the Broadway musical and its divas even as it also makes fun of them, is surely a version of camp. This camp informs such diverse, even inbred, works as revues sending up the musical as a genre, television parodies of musicals (especially "The Carol Burnett Show"), and the Off-Broadway show *Forbidden Broadway* with its ever-changing mockeries of Broadway shows and its stars, especially women.

Even though some musicals, such as, for example, Rodgers and Hammerstein's *Carousel* (1945) and *The King and I* (1951) and Lerner and Loewe's *Brigadoon* (1947) and *My Fair Lady* (1956), are straighter than others, like Bernstein's *West Side Story* (1957), Herman's *Mame* (1965), Cy Coleman and Dorothy Fields's *Sweet Charity* (1966), and John Kander and Fred Ebb's *Cabaret* (1966), in theme or presentation, homosexual code is often discernible in most of them. But although some Off-Broadway musicals had dealt with gay themes, the Broadway musical did not "come out" until Herman's *La Cage aux Folles* (1983), based on the popular French film of the same name. Although much was made of the fact that the two male leads never kissed, the work was nonetheless a measure of how acceptable open homosexuality had become by the early 1980s. The show followed typical

Broadway musicals in that its libretto was based on another source; it had two pairs of romantic leads (the gay owners of a nightclub, one of whom was a drag queen, and two juvenile lovers, one of whom was the son of the "straighter" club owner); and it featured an obstacle to romantic love, which was overcome in the course of the play. *La Cage aux Folles* also featured other staples of Broadway musicals: lavish sets and costumes, as well as show-stopping dance numbers and touching ballads by a Broadway favorite, gay composer and lyricist Jerry Herman. The musical followed the tradition of the "straight" musical by being conservative, respectful of traditional family values, and blatantly commercial.

La Cage aux Folles is a lot less antiseptic in its presentation of its gay romance than, for example, *My Fair Lady* and *The King and I* are in presenting the straight equivalent. The show is also gay-influenced in its outlandish costumes, especially those worn by Albin in drag, and its privileging of performance and spectacle as means of self-expression and assertion of place in the world. *La Cage aux Folles* is a huge success with straights and gays alike because it embodies at once gay values and those of the Broadway musical itself.

Broadway's other openly gay musicals, William Finn's *Falsettos* (1992) and Kander and Ebb's *Kiss of the Spider Woman* (1993), use conventions of the genre in far different ways. *Falsettos,* the combination of two of Finn's "Marvin" musicals, tells the story of Marvin, who leaves his wife and son for a gay life with a lover; Marvin's ex-wife becomes involved with Marvin's therapist; and Marvin's lover is diagnosed with AIDS and dies at the end of the show. *Falsettos* is the opposite of *La Cage* in presentation: It relies on suggestive sets and costumes rather than spectacle, and unlike most Broadway musicals that feature equal song and dialogue, it is mostly sung. (*Falsettos* is not the first Broadway musical in which singing dominates: Others include Frank Loesser's *The Most Happy Fella* [1956] and Stephen Sondheim's *Sweeney Todd* [1979].) Nor does it feature songs clearly written to be hits, like *La Cage aux Folles*'s "I Am What I Am" and "The Best of Times."

Falsettos emphasizes the concept of family, not only through the depiction of Marvin's traditional family but also his new one with his lover and his friends, "the lesbians next door." At the heart of *Falsettos* is the need for love, community, and stability, prerequisites for happiness that can also provide a hedge against disaster. *Falsettos* is a little musical that was as much a commercial success on its small terms as *La Cage aux Folles* was on its larger level. Deserving praise for its original and clever music and

lyrics, *Falsettos* follows in the footsteps of its illustrious, straight-themed predecessors in celebrating romance, family, and community.

La Cage aux Folles is a big musical that tells an uncomplicated, simple love story whose purpose is only to entertain, and *Falsettos* is a small, almost chamber musical that tells a serious story with wit and sadness. Their successor, *Kiss of the Spider Woman,* combines the showmanship of *La Cage aux Folles* with the seriousness of purpose of *Falsettos.* Based on MANUEL PUIG's novel and the subsequent film by Hector Babenco, the musical is what the film should have been. It combines gay appreciation of the conventions of the Broadway musical with an overtly gay story. In prison in an unnamed South American country, a gay window dresser, arrested for sex with a minor, shares a cell with a straight, overserious, political activist. During their confinement, the gay man shares his memories of the lavish production numbers of his favorite film star while the political activist slowly politicizes him. The play's musical numbers not only feature Aurora, the film star, in dances and songs reminiscent of 1930s and 1940s film musicals (another cult favorite of gay men), but also features the prisoners in monologues and dream sequences that explore their thoughts and explain plot action. At the end of the play, the gay man, released from prison, carries a message for the activist, and is assassinated; the finale shows him united finally with Aurora in the musical of his dreams.

One of the most brilliant artistic strategies of *Kiss of the Spider Woman* is to use the Broadway gay sensibility, also embraced by straights, to tell a gay story. Many of Aurora's numbers are self-consciously campy and intended to be recognized as such and to be associated particularly with the contributions of gay men to popular entertainment. *Kiss of the Spider Woman* shows how such images function as survival tactics as dear to Molina as the political ones are to his straight, puritanical cellmate.

At its best, the Broadway musical is the antithesis of puritanism and oppression. Its celebration of play may well account for its significance to many gay men. From its early days, through its closeted but coded works such as *Mame,* to the recent triumphs of *La Cage aux Folles, Falsettos,* and *Kiss of the Spider Woman,* the Broadway musical has celebrated performance and play, two areas that at least one part of the gay community prizes. Now threatened by daunting economic factors and its abandonment by talented people to other venues, the musical nonetheless remains an important part of American gay culture and history. (See also DRAMATIC LITERATURE.)

—*Thomas Dukes*

BIBLIOGRAPHY

Goldman, William. *The Season.* New York: Harcourt, 1969. ■ Gottfried, Martin. *All That Jazz: The Life and Death of Bob Fosse.* New York: New York: Bantam, 1990. ■ Laufe, Abe. *Broadway's Greatest Musicals.* New York: Funk and Wagnalls, 1973. ■ Mates, Julian. *America's Musical Stage: Two Hundred Years of Musical Theatre.* Westport, Conn.: Greenwood, 1985. ■ Suskin, Steven. *Opening Night on Broadway: A Critical Quotebook of the Golden Era of the Musical Theater.* New York: Schirmer, 1990.

MYSTERY FICTION

Mystery Fiction, Gay Male

Between the 1930s and the 1960s, gay males occasionally appeared in British and American mystery fiction, but they were largely relegated to minor roles as either villains or victims, and their lives were invariably pictured as bleak and unfulfilled. Typical early examples of villainous gays are the effeminate hood in Dashiell Hammett's *The Maltese Falcon* (1930) and the transvestite Nazi spy in Ross Macdonald's *The Dark Tunnel* (1944, published under the name Kenneth Millar). In Britain, with its deep-seated and prevalent homophobia, even among gays, relatively little has changed in the last two decades. With some notable exceptions, British mystery writers still portray gays as unnatural and tormented. But beginning in 1952, with *Death in the Fifth Position* by GORE VIDAL writing as Edgar Box, the American mystery novel has progressively opened itself to the portrayal of gay males as admirable characters, even to the point of accepting them as detectives. Significantly, this change had its impetus primarily within that most macho of subgenres, the hard-boiled detective novel. And unlike lesbian mystery novels, which are much more numerous but which have largely been published by small specialized presses, the gay male mystery novel has been welcomed by such mainstream publishers as Avon, St. Martin's, and Holt.

Although some gay mystery fiction seems to have been written primarily to exploit the more flamboyant elements of gay male life and to provide a kind of freak-show tour of the gay subculture, the main impetus of post-Stonewall gay mystery novels has been the normalization of gay life. In these works, gay individuals and the gay subculture tend to be demystified and robbed of their sensationalism. Shortly after Stonewall, the mystery novel featuring major gay characters found a strong and sure voice in JOSEPH HANSEN, and it has swelled to a significant corpus in the 1980s and 1990s. And although a few political conservatives among mainstream straight mystery writers still portray gays as degenerates, many more of their less bigoted fellows now include admirable and likable gay men as minor characters.

Important in opening the mainstream mystery novel to gay characters and themes is the influential and long-running Tom Ripley series by an acknowledged master of suspense novels, PATRICIA HIGHSMITH: *The Talented Mr. Ripley* (1955), *Ripley Under Ground* (1970), *Ripley's Game* (1974), *The Boy Who Followed Ripley* (1980), and *Ripley Under Water* (1992). Ripley is a charming and cultured bisexual who, in the course of the five novels, commits several murders and other serious criminal offenses. But Highsmith manages to make Ripley such an appealing character that the reader is manipulated, however unwillingly, into siding with him against the forces of retribution and into hoping for his success in eluding capture and prosecution. Ironically, it is only because Tom is a criminal that the first Ripley novel could be published by a mainstream press in the homophobic 1950s, yet the sympathy he evokes in the reader is ultimately gay positive. Given Highsmith's extraordinary insight into the complexity and ambiguity of moral issues, it is not surprising that gay male readers have helped make the Ripley novels cult classics.

The first appearance of a gay detective in a mystery novel published by a mainstream press occurred in 1966, when George Baxt, then at the beginning of what was to become a prolific career in the crime novel, published *A Queer Kind of Death,* inaugurating a trilogy that was completed with *Swing Low, Sweet Harriet* (1967) and *Topsy and Evil* (1968).

During the investigation of the death of a hustler, the flashy African-American New York homicide detective Pharoah Love becomes intrigued by one of the chief suspects, the bisexual writer Seth Piro, and decides that since he has not been especially gratified in heterosexual affairs of the heart, he will try a homosexual union. Realizing that Seth is the murderer, he pressures the writer into an affair by less than subtle threats of exposure and then falsifies evidence to protect him. In the second book of the series, centering on aging movie queens, Seth finally balks at the arrangement and is killed by Love in the same way that he himself had killed the hustler. In the third and last installment, Love has left the police department under a cloud of suspicion and has undergone a sex change operation, reappearing on the scene as Ocelot, an exotic cabaret entertainer who is doomed to die in the closing chapter.

Anthony Boucher, doyen of crime fiction critics, hailed *A Queer Kind of Death* in *The New York Times Book Review* as "beautifully plotted and written with elegance and wit" and exclaimed (to his presumably straight readers), "you must under no circumstances miss it." And at the time, even gay readers, starved for anything in popular fiction that reflected—however perversely and sensationally—a bit of their own experience, welcomed the trilogy. But with the self-awareness and pride triggered by Stonewall, a gay reader is now hard pressed to find any virtues beyond campy wit (for example, "A thing of beauty is a boy forever") in these three books. The gay men in Baxt's trilogy have either "chosen" or been "indoctrinated into" their homosexual behavior; they are invariably pictured as "misfits"; and their actions are self-destructive, devious, and unethical in the extreme. What we now realize is that the only reason that these books were allowed to be published in the 1960s was that they are fundamentally homophobic.

Shortly after Stonewall, a new kind of gay detective novel appeared in Joseph Hansen's *Fadeout* (1970), the first in a series of twelve novels and two short stories—including *Death Claims* (1973), *Troublemaker* (1975), *The Man Everybody Was Afraid of* (1978), *Skinflick* (1979), *Gravedigger* (1982), *Nightwork* (1984), *Brandstetter and Others* (short stories, 1984), *The Little Dog Laughed* (1986), *Early Graves* (1987), *Obedience* (1988), *The Boy Who Was Buried This Morning* (1990)—that ostensibly concluded in 1991 with *A Country of Old Men*. For the first time in the crime genre, Hansen presented gay men and lesbians in all of their variety, without sensation, as simply men and women with understandable desires, triumphs, and frustrations.

Hansen's detective is Dave Brandstetter, a handsome gay male who in the course of the twenty-one-year series progresses naturally from middle to old age. In the first four novels, he is a claims investigator for a large West Coast insurance company run by his father, and in the last eight, he is a free-lance detective. Although Brandstetter is cast somewhat in the mold of Ross Macdonald's Lew Archer, a determined, largely humorless but compassionate solver of human puzzles, Hansen frames the mysteries he investigates with much more of the detective's private life than we are ever afforded in the Archer series. At the beginning of *Fadeout*, we see Brandstetter mourning the death of Rod Fleming, the interior decorator who had been his lover for twenty-five years. As the series progresses, we follow the uneasy and ultimately doomed relationship of Brandstetter with Doug Sawyer, a middle-aged artist who is himself mourning the death of a longtime lover; in the last several novels, we experience the sometimes rocky but fulfilling relationship between Brandstetter and Cecil Harris, a young African-American television newsman who woos Dave relentlessly until he wins his heart. Also important to the texture of the books are recurring minor characters who are Dave's constant friends: the restaurateur Max Romano, the lesbian designer Madge Dunstan, the gay telephone executive whom Dave has known since high school, his father's young widow Amanda, and several more. With them, Hansen creates a believable world that is at once interesting and inviting.

At the commencement of the series, Hansen also owes much to Ross Macdonald in the area of plotting. Current violence stems from dark secrets in the past, and it is the detective's task to uncover the details of former relationships and actions in order to solve present crimes. Further, the earlier Brandstetter novels deal almost exclusively with gay or bisexual characters and themes. As the series progresses, however, the plots become less formulaic, and Dave investigates mysteries that have little or nothing to do with homosexuality (such as the dumping of toxic waste, religious cults, and drug dealing). In this progression, Hansen performs a valuable service by showing that gays constantly interact with the straight world in important, meaningful ways. He does this without compromising the integrity of his gay characters, however, and some of the later novels also deal with important issues directly related to being gay, such as homophobia and AIDS.

Finally, in the area of setting, Hansen equals if not surpasses his master Macdonald in capturing the feel of Los Angeles and the small towns and cities up and down the Southern California coast. He obviously realizes that many people read mystery fiction primarily for its sense of place and people, and his descriptions of both are masterful.

A Country of Old Men is labeled "The Last Dave Brandstetter Mystery" on both its dust cover and its title page, and Hansen is currently working on a series of novels based on his own life and times. Thousands of his fans sincerely hope, however, that they have not seen the last of Dave and Cecil and the other characters who make up their world. Hansen has wryly (and wisely) left himself a loophole at the end of the book, and if Sherlock Holmes—at the insistence of his fans—could survive the Reichenbach Falls, surely there is the possibility that sometime in the future we may applaud *The Return of Dave Brandstetter*.

The critical and commercial success of Hansen's Brandstetter novels paved the way for mainstream gay-positive detective fiction, and in the last twenty years several single novels and series of novels that feature gay male detectives have been issued by major publishers. Most of the series fail to measure up to the high standard of the Hansen novels, but most provide considerable entertainment, and one—by Michael Nava—is a major achievement, consisting of four excellent mysteries that are in fact excellent novels regardless of genre.

A series of four novels has been published under the name of Nathan Aldyne, the joint pseudonym of Michael McDowell and Axel Young: *Vermilion* (1980), *Cobalt* (1982), *Slate* (1984), and *Canary* (1986). Set in Boston and Provincetown, they feature as amateur detectives Daniel Valentine, a gay social worker turned bartender, and his straight female best friend Clarisse Lovelace, who moves from working in a real estate office to attending law school. Set entirely within the milieus of gay bars and summer resorts, they deal with the murder of gay men against backdrops of hustling, drug dealing, and sado-masochistic activities. The books are often witty and breezy, but they lack any real depth, and one gets the impression that they exist primarily to exploit the pre-AIDS gay bar scene. Moreover, as the series progresses, the books become more and more focused on Clarisse, who is undoubtedly a colorful character, and the less interesting Valentine fades into the background. Although a fifth novel was promised in the late 1980s, it has failed to appear, and it now seems safe to assume that the series will not continue.

A much better series was begun about the same time by Richard Lipez writing as Richard Stevenson: *Death Trick* (1981), *On the Other Hand, Death* (1984), *Ice Blues* (1986), and *Third Man Out* (1992). Although it begins with some of the campiness, wit, and exploitation that mark the Aldyne novels, the Stevenson series is ultimately more serious and more satisfying. Set in Albany, New York, it centers on Don Strachey, a gay private detective approaching middle age, and Timothy Callahan, his Jesuit-educated lover who works in an office of the state government. As the series opens, Strachey is recently divorced, living alone, and casually promiscuous, which threatens his future with the conservative and monogamous Timmy. As the novels progress, the two make a home and life together and Strachey—faced with such serious issues as widespread and deadly homophobia, the gay rights movement, political corruption, AIDS, outing, and the sexual hypocrisy of the Roman Catholic Church—has his gay consciousness raised. Stevenson is adept at creating believable and sympathetic characters, and though some of the situations strain credulity, the writing is always good.

The late Samuel Steward, legendary author of picaresque pornographic works under the name of Phil Andros, wrote two quasi-autobiographical novels featuring himself, GERTRUDE STEIN, and Alice B. Toklas: *Murder Is Murder Is Murder* (1985) and *The Caravaggio Shawl* (1989). Set in France in the 1930s, the series is most interesting for its evocation of time and place and for its account of the relationship between the principals. Although Steward's presence in the novels as "Johnny" gives the series a strong gay male interest, the detection is done by the redoubtable Gertrude, with valuable aid from her devoted Alice.

The most exploitative series in gay detective fiction since Baxt's Pharoah Love trilogy is authored by a woman, the Matt Sinclair mysteries by Tony Fennelly: *The Glory Hole Murders* (1985) and *The Closet Hanging* (1987). Set in New Orleans, they offer little more than bitchily camp tours of the sleazier elements of the gay worlds of the French Quarter and the Creole haute monde. Of an old New Orleans family, Sinclair, formerly an assistant district attorney and now the owner of a shop specializing in expensive reproductions of antiques, is coercively deputized by an African-American police detective to help solve murders involving gays. Sinclair is himself mostly gay (though Fennelly manages to bed him with females in both novels) and lives with a nelly but loving young man named Robin, whom he treats very badly. Most of the situations in both novels are unbelievable, and most of the characters—including Sinclair himself—are unsympathetic.

A native of the Chicago area, Mark Richard Zubro has published four detective novels in one series and two in a second. The first series consists, so far, of *A Simple Suburban Murder* (1989), *Why Isn't Becky Twitchell Dead?* (1990), *The Only Good Priest* (1991), and *The Principal Cause of Death* (1992). In these novels, the amateur detectives are a pair of lovers: Tom Mason, an ex-Marine English teacher in a suburban high school (as is Zubro himself), and

Scott Carpenter, "one of the highest paid pitchers in the Major Leagues." The two divide their lives between Tom's home, "a farmhouse in the middle of one of the last cornfields in southwestern Cook County" and Scott's luxury penthouse on Lake Shore Drive in Chicago, where they work out and make love (but rarely cook). If the reader can accept this highly unlikely premise, straight out of gay fantasy, the novels are entertaining and suspenseful, if somewhat awkwardly written. Three of the mysteries arise out of Tom's teaching job and involve such serious matters as drug dealing in schools and underaged prostitution and pornography. The fourth deals with the murder of a Catholic priest who, against orders from the chancery, ministers to a gay-supportive Dignity-like organization in the Chicago archdiocese. Part of the charm of the series is the interaction of Tom and Scott with their families and straight colleagues and their obvious joy in their own relationship.

The two novels so far in Zubro's second series, *Sorry Now?* (1991) and *Political Poison* (1993), are police procedurals and feature Paul Turner, an openly gay homicide detective in the Chicago Police Department. A widower, Paul must balance caring for two sons, one of whom has spina bifida, and his love life with the frequently long hours demanded by his job. The two cases involve the murder of the daughter of a prominent right-wing televangelist and politician and the murder of a Chicago alderman. Neither crime is gay-centered, but both novels include important gay characters. Although Paul is more believable than Tom and Scott, the unreserved support he gets from his colleagues in the police department and from the straight world in general seems wishful thinking. These two novels draw authentic Chicago locales and present an interesting portrait of a gay father, but the writing is often clumsy and the mysteries themselves are solved arbitrarily.

Steve Johnson's *Final Atonement* (1992) and *False Confessions* (1993) have begun what promises to be a fine police procedural series. Doug Orlando is an openly gay homicide detective based in Brooklyn. He has been ostracized by his department because he has broken the rule against testifying against a fellow officer, and the spite of his colleagues finds expression in antigay remarks and actions. In the first novel, Doug investigates the murder of a renegade Hassidic rabbi against a backdrop of racial and political tensions. In the second, the murder of a priest leads him into the dark world of S&M clubs and tattoo parlors. The supporting characters, including Doug's Italian immigrant mother and his Jewish lover who teaches English at NYU, are well drawn; the plots are intricate and interesting; and the writing is excellent.

Boston is the scene of a recently emerging series by Grant Michaels: *A Body to Die For* (1990), *Love You to Death* (1993), and *Dead on Your Feet* (1993). His detective is an amateur, an ex-psychologist hairdresser of Czech descent named Stanislav Kraychic but known professionally as Vannos. In the first novel, Stan is drawn into detecting when he is suspected of killing a young gay park ranger; in the second, he agrees to help the former receptionist at his salon when she is accused of poisoning her boyfriend; in the third, he investigates a murder in a ballet company. Often frustrated in love but always plucky, Stan is the sassiest protagonist in gay detective fiction, and much of the appeal of these three novels is the sexually tense relationship between Stan and his would-be nemesis, the presumably straight and definitely handsome Boston homicide detective Vito Branco.

By far the best recent series of gay mystery novels is that by Michael Nava, consisting, as yet, of *The Little Death* (1986), *Goldenboy* (1988), *How Town* (1990), and *The Hidden Law* (1992). Nava's protagonist is Henry Rios, a young gay Hispanic lawyer who practices first in the San Francisco Bay area and then in Los Angeles. Although the cases Rios pursues are intriguing, the novels work less well as mysteries than as explorations of character. Rios is haunted by his dead father, whom he could never please, and he immerses himself in work and alcohol. In the second novel, he meets and falls in love with a young man who is HIV-positive, and in the third and fourth novels, he watches helplessly as his lover gradually succumbs to the ravages of AIDS. Matching Nava's insight into character and relationships, moreover, is his skill with language. The books are powerfully and beautifully written, the last two especially so as the poems that inform them and provide their titles (by e. e. cummings and W. H. AUDEN, respectively) subtly reverberate throughout, adding texture and depth and connecting the books to significant literary and cultural traditions. In this brief series, Nava grows into a first-rate novelist. Still a young man, he is definitely a writer to follow.

Another writer to follow is Steven Saylor, who has recently begun a series of mysteries set in ancient Rome: *Roman Blood* (1991), *Arms of Nemesis* (1992), and *Catilina's Riddle* (1993). Although his detective—Gordianus the Finder—is not himself gay, Saylor (who has published gay erotica under the pseudonym Aaron Travis) includes a number of sympathetic gay characters in these novels. Meticulously researched and strongly written, they provide fascinating portraits of such historical figures as Cicero, Sulla, Crassus, and Catiline; and they vividly recreate the tumultuous beginnings of the Roman Empire.

Not all gay mysteries are parts of series, of course, and there have been several good independent novels published in the last twenty-five years. Notable among them are three non-Brandstetter mysteries by Joseph Hansen: *Known Homosexual* (published under the pseudonym James Colton in 1968, reissued under Hansen's name as *Stranger to Himself* in 1977, and reprinted in 1984 as *Pretty Boy Dead*), *Backtrack* (1982), and *Steps Going Down* (1985). Three other mysteries well worth reading are RICHARD HALL's *Butterscotch Prince* (1975, revised 1983), Stephen Lewis's *Cowboy Blues* (1985), and Jack Ricardo's *The Night G.A.A. Died* (1992). Hall's novel, set in New York, has its protagonist coming to terms with his own gayness as he pursues the killer of his lover; it is the first gay liberationist mystery novel. Although written and published only recently, Ricardo's novel also deals with the early struggle of the liberation movement heralded by Stonewall. Archie Cain, a private detective who was forced out of the New York Police Department when he openly declared his gayness, investigates the murder of an officer of the Gay Activists Alliance in 1971. Lewis's finely crafted novel is set in Los Angeles and features an appealing gay private detective, Jake Lieberman, who investigates the disappearance of a gay rodeo performer and would-be country singer. It was obviously intended as the first of a series, which unfortunately has failed to materialize. Also of interest are Robert Bentley's *Here There Be Dragons* (1972), an excellent espionage thriller; Terry Miller's *Standing By* (1984), a mystery set in the New York theater world; and Russell A. Brown's *Sherlock Holmes and the Mysterious Friend of Oscar Wilde* (1988), a clever pastiche set in Victorian London. Finally, Michael Nava has edited a fine collection of gay mystery short stories, *Finale* (1989).

The mystery novel is a logical and appropriate vehicle for gay writers, especially in the United States. Beginning with the hard-boiled school in the 1920s, its politics have often been radical, and it has been a mirror of social change. It has a tradition of pitting the outlaw against the establishment and, eventually, of redefining society in such a way that the outsider can find a useful and secure place within it. The gay mystery novel, like its straight counterpart, is multi-faceted and varied, ranging from often bumbling amateur sleuthing to shrewdly observed police procedurals, from light escapism to the serious study of character. But in all its manifestations and sub-genres, gay mystery fiction at once reflects and helps effect the integration of gays into the American social fabric as human beings worthy of interest, compassion, and respect.

—*Ted-Larry Pebworth*

BIBLIOGRAPHY

Baird, Newton. "Joseph Hansen." *Twentieth-Century Crime and Mystery Writers*. John M. Reilly, ed. 2nd ed. New York: St. Martin's, 1985. 419–421. ■ Geherin, David. "Dave Brandstetter." *The American Private Eye*. New York: Ungar, 1985. 176–183. ■ Hansen, Joseph. "Matters Grave and Gay." *Colloquium on Crime*. Robin W. Winks, ed. New York: Scribner's, 1986. 111–126. ■ Hastings, Solomon. "Homosexuals in the Mystery: Victims or Victimizers?" *Murder Ink*. Dilys Winn, ed. New York: Workman, 1977. 494–495. ■ Jones, James W. "Joseph Hansen" *Contemporary Gay American Novelists: A Bio-Bibliographical Critical Sourcebook*. Emmanuel S. Nelson, ed. Westport, Conn.: Greenwood, 1993. 189–196. ■ Klawitter, George. "Michael Nava." *Contemporary Gay American Novelists: A Bio-Bibliographical Critical Sourcebook*. Emmanuel S. Nelson, ed. Westport, Conn.: Greenwood, 1993. 291–297. ■ Levin, James B. "Mystery and Detective Fiction." *Encyclopedia of Homosexuality*. Wayne R. Dynes et al., eds. 2 vols. New York: Garland, 1990. 2:864–866.

Mystery Fiction, Lesbian

The lesbian mystery novel has its origins in the ubiquitous lesbian pulp fictions of the 1950s and early 1960s. A paradigm of deviance, drugs, and urban decay located these literary lesbians in lonely antithesis to the security of the law-abiding suburban American dream. Such popular potboilers constituted a plethora of splendidly sordid sensationals blessed with such titles as *Strange Sisters*, *The Shadowy Sex*, and *Lesbians in Black Lace*. These books were primarily about sex, supposedly written for prurient heterosexual males, but lesbian readers loved them. The thrilling glimpse into an underworld of intrigue and suspense is redelivered in the lesbian crime novels of the present, which allow us to step into, relish, and then render safe a quagmire of sex, violence, and death.

The first lesbian feminist crime novel was M. F. Beal's *Angel Dance* (1977). Its angry, complex, visionary indictment of heterosexual and patriarchal capitalism is steaming with the peculiar energy of 1970s protest culture. The Chicana detective and first-person narrator Kat Guerrera is a subversive. The character embodies the way class, race, gender, and sexuality interface to uphold the hegemonic order of law. The corrupt power of the state is represented as being so extensive that concepts of "justice" can no longer be invoked.

This figure of the lesbian guerrilla was an icon of 1970s resistance culture, as distilled by French materialist philosopher MONIQUE WITTIG in her 1971 novel *Les Guérillères*. This invention of a new, militant category of lesbian, inspired by the myth of the AMAZON, invigorated a whole community of women to declare war on the political institution of heterosexuality. The lesbian detectives reproduced this figure in the 1980s and 1990s.

The traditional crime novel is a site for the expression of anxieties about society in which the enemy is named and destroyed. In the lesbian and feminist crime novel, the terms often become inverted so that the state is identified as the corrupt enemy, and the lesbian sleuth, normally the feared and hated Other, is the victor. The narrative resolution of the mystery is resolved in two stages: First, by using the process of individuation intrinsic to the thriller mode, the lesbian hero achieves self-determination; second, she becomes integrated into a community. The first phase is often represented by coming out, the second frequently by finding love or discovering the lesbian community, in a movement toward politicized integration.

These structures are to be found in other lesbian literary genres, but in mystery novels the formation of an identity happens through the solution of a crime. The central narrative device and locus of readerly pleasure is discovery. For example, in an early feminist best-seller, *Murder in the Collective* by Barbara Wilson (1984), we meet Pam Nilsen, thinly disguised Proto-Dyke. Her hands sweat and her body is wracked by erotic fevers as she gulps and swallows in the presence of Hadley. They eventually manage to consummate their lust; however, the romantic tension is yoked to the crime fiction hermeneutic of alternate disclosure and disappointment. Pam's new identity gives her individuality through a sense of difference, not just from her (heterosexual) twin, but in the series of dialectical oppositions set up by the text around race, class, gender, and sexuality. "Identity" is seen as a transitional process of discovery involving contradictory states of desire—for sex and for a new "self."

The new identities offered to the reader of the lesbian mystery novel are dependent upon the possible political alternatives presented by any given cultural period or context. Thus, texts of the 1970s offer different models of sexuality from texts of the 1980s or 1990s. Early lesbian feminist crime novels of the 1980s tended to be inflected by the specific counter-cultural discourses of that time, structuring men as the enemy and making lesbian feminism a heroic principle. The signposts of lesbian feminism—sisterhood, collectivism, "wimmin's" energy, and "wombyn's" anger—are scattered throughout these texts. By the mid- and late-1980s, however, the prerogative of identity politics had seemingly superseded the earlier lesbian feminism, and consequently, a complex critique of diverse social forces began to emerge.

A British attempt to disrupt racial and gender stereotypes can be found in Claire Macquet's *Looking for Ammu* (1992). The cover-blurb promises "A film noir world where distinctions between saints and sinners become devastatingly uncertain," thus invoking the urban dystopian tradition of the hard-boiled crime novel in which perception itself, intrinsic to investigation, is at best unstable, at worst morally flawed. *Looking for Ammu* breaks with feminist crime convention by rejecting the model of a super-sleuth. White nursing tutor Harriet Weston, a prissy, conceited, repressed, self-righteous narrator, pursues her mythologized mentor, Black Dr. Ammu Bai. As Harriet tries to find the missing Ammu, the investigative trajectory incisively deconstructs the sign of Black-Woman-As-Mystical-Enigma, signaling how sexualized and racist this dominant narrative construction is. Thus, a formally noble act of discovery is revealed—through some viciously satiric writing—as self-interest. That the narrator is in love with her idol is plain from the first chapter. Evoking the classic way White Westerners have fantasized the Black Other, the text lays bare the eroticism in this White gaze. The text manipulates the generic certainties of both detective and romance fiction to leave the reader questioning the representation of desire.

Lesbian mystery fiction has consistently problematized the use of the heroic in the crime novel. A swathe of novels predominant in the mid-1980s self-consciously appropriated the image of the avenging knight, proferring a sexy superdyke striding the city streets in her steel-capped Doc Martins, swinging her double-headed axe, dispensing slayed patriarchs in her wake. This was one form of transgressing the genre. Later manifestations made more explicit the legacy of BUTCH-FEMME roles in this image. These literary figures made more acceptable pre-Women's Liberation lesbian sexual identities, which were becoming reintegrated and reformed for the new sexual cultures of the 1980s and 1990s. However, is the fact that so many dyke detectives appeared as *butch* fantasies due to the regrettably intransigent masculine conventions of the genre? Or is the effect on the representation of the heroic rather more destabilizing, more parodic? The figure of the detective is crucially a fantasy of agency, which is culturally conflated with masculinity in both the dominant culture and within feminism itself. Could a femme detective focus our desires so effectively?

As a subcultural stereotype, the butch detective works at two levels of identification for the reader. Not only does the reader desire the butch, she also wants to *be* the butch. In her outlaw status, the butch detective promises a romantic, forbidden fantasy and the incarnation of a felt alienation that is fictionally empowered. The convention of the detective hero is appropriated and destabilized by the parodic acknowledgment that the complex sign "butch" can encapsulate a field of contradictions, primarily dependent on readerly projections.

In genre theory, detective fiction has been most likened to satire. Menippean satire, in its simplest form, consists of a dialogue between stylized characters who merely mouth ideas. The two speakers are an eiron, the hero, and an alazon, someone usually revealed to be a deluded and pompous fool. The alazon's self-delusion is continually confirmed in inverse relation to the eiron's discernment. The lesbian crime fiction detective's dramatic function is to expose alazons using her ratiocinative powers, thus leading the reader into a changed and enlightened consciousness. The feminist ideological project presents patriarchy and heterosexism as synonymous with alazony, thus "false consciousness" is revealed by an investigation into gender relations. It is a persuasive structure that artfully seduces the proto-feminist reader. The protagonist or eiron is able to scrutinize the hysterical excesses of masculinity with a deflationary gaze. Masculinity, in these narratives, usually ends up shooting itself in the foot.

The novels that achieve the most convincing critique of patriarchy, heterosexism, and masculinity have not done it through "political correctness" or even through the simple moral dualism that lesbian equals good and patriarch equals bad. The most effective lesbian crime novels have been those that have most enthusiastically embraced the need to entertain the reader, to interweave suspense with pleasure. Those, such as *She Came Too Late* (1986) and *She Came in a Flash* (1988) by Mary Wings, which reproduce most faithfully the classic element of satire succeed most as popular novels. The defining glance of the detective is to reveal the real and sordid nature of the world, but this revelation is achieved obliquely, through the sideways glance of satire. Novels that are consciously satiric employ a heroine who tends to undermine her own transcendence. Sarah Dreher's serial antihero Stoner is a case in point: She humorously incarnates the misfit motif pandemic to lesbian identity; she is a detective outlaw who can reassuredly exorcise the reader's internalized homophobia. Like the classical fool, she attracts the laughter of self-recognition; she is the awkward, soft-hearted butch who parodies back to ourselves our inflated desires for a heroine.

Urban sexual identities during the 1980s were inflected with a self-conscious irony expressed through the parodic reinvention of roles for sexual interaction. Lesbians as a group are highly self-conscious and ironically self-referential; along with other minority cultures, they have recognized the destabilizing potential of parody. Having a sense of humor is an essential survival tool for lesbians, necessary to deflect some of the damage dominant homophobic and misogynistic discourses inflict on us. Thus lesbian crime novels, by their double deflationary gaze—at the sex–gender system and at ourselves—swing the two-headed axe liberally not just to destroy, but also to carve out and recombine new kinds of identities for us to inhabit.

For example, Barbara Wilson's *Gaudi Afternoon* (1990) is symptomatic of the shifting debates that see gender and sexual identities as, in the words of Judith Butler, "performative strategies of insubordination." Seeing gayness as being a "necessary drag," Butler regards the sense of play and pleasure so prevalent in the production of homosexuality as fundamentally destabilizing the seriousness and "naturalness" of heterosexuality. *Gaudi Afternoon* concerns Cassandra Reilly, a translator who is hired by Frankie from San Francisco to find her gay husband in Barcelona in order that he might sign some family papers. But the novel soon degenerates into comic gender picaresque. Cassandra's task is to chase a circling chaos of individuals involved in a custody contest where each claims to be the real mother. Frankie, the "wife," is actually a male–female transsexual; Ben, the "husband," is a radical feminist bulldagger; April, her New Age cultural feminist "girl"friend, is an Earth Mother who dislikes children and a male–female transsexual, but Ben doesn't know it; April's "friend" is her gay closet-cross-dressing stepbrother with whom she shares "shame issues." In this world where there is no grounding real of the physical, there is no final recourse to the body either, as in the nature–culture opposition. All is "up for grabs," and the only conclusion to draw from this parodic cacophony is the rejection of "true sexualities" in favor of the hilarious creativity of inventing new ones. The fun is in the performance—the process—not the end result.

The more literary of the lesbian crime novels have experimented with a kind of parodic inventiveness infused by postmodernist aesthetics. SARAH

SCHULMAN's works most clearly exhibit this confluence of interest. Every literary form evolves, and even during the short period of time in which this subgenre has developed, identifiable trends toward a more metafictional awareness can be detected. Many of the earlier novels such as Vicki P. McConnell's *Mrs. Porter's Letter* (1982), *The Burnton Widows* (1984), and *Double Daughter* (1988) were little more than pulp romances, published by the highly popular Naiad Press, renowned for producing the lesbian sentimental "quickie"; but the form also soon diversified into the various permutations to be found in the mainstream and traditional detective genre. For example, the classic Golden Age format of the country house murder exemplified by Dorothy L. Sayers and Agatha Christie structures *Something Shady* (1986) by Sarah Dreher, and a North American interpretation of the small town mystery is the format of Dreher's later novel *A Captive in Time* (1990). A related British subgenre—one that allows for the inclusion of lesbian "teenage crushes"—is the girl's school mystery, such as *Report for Murder* (1987) by Val McDermid and *Hallowed Murder* (1989) by Ellen Hart. The police procedural that has been popular in mainstream U.S. crime fiction since the 1960s is rewritten with a lesbian cop-hero in *Amateur City* (1984), *Murder at the Nightwood Bar* (1987), and *The Beverly Malibu* (1989), all by established lesbian genre author Katherine Forrest. *Lessons in Murder* (1988), *Fatal Reunion* (1989), and *Death Down Under* (1990) are Australian versions by Claire McNab.

The urban dystopia allows the exploration of gender and sexuality in the city and particularly stresses themes of the urban oppression of women; examples are *Death Strip* (1986) by Benita Kirkland, *Sisters of the Road* (1986) by Barbara Wilson, and *Jumping the Cracks* (1987) by Rebecca O'Rourke. The hard-boiled private eye is the essence of the American form; a masculinized hero alienated from the urban jungle is turned into a lesbian in *She Came Too Late* (1986) and *She Came in a Flash* (1988) by Mary Wings and *A Reason to Kill* (1978), *Work for a Million* (1986), and *Beyond Hope* (1987) by the Canadian writer Eve Zaremba. The supernatural chiller, such as *The Crystal Curtain* (1988) by Sandy Bayer, improvises themes of spirituality from cultural feminism—indeed almost all of Camarin Grae's novels contain these mysterious elements.

Crime fiction has a long tradition of female investigators, but the lesbian mystery novels that proffer an amateur investigator are unimaginable without the kinds of interventions into the workplace that feminism made in the 1970s. *Cass and the Stone Butch* (1987) and *Skiptrace* (1988) by Antoinette Azolakov

and *In the Game* (1991) by Nikki Baker all offer ironic versions of the lone woman supersleuth. In the British novels *Report for Murder* (1987), *Common Murder* (1989), and *Final Edition* (1991), she is dressed as the journalist-investigator. Finally, lesbian mystery fiction has also appropriated the political thriller in *Blood Sisters* (1981) by Valerie Miner and *The Providence File* (1991) by Amanda Kyle Williams. Both works deal with terrorism, but from opposite ends of the political spectrum. Lesbian mystery fiction has exploited a variety of formula fictions, and a diversity of ideological belief is represented in them.

Many of these books are enjoyable as pulp fictions. They exploded into the new markets created by gay consumerism during the 1980s. Gay and lesbian publishing enterprises have flourished in the post-Stonewall era in "out and proud" purchasing communities. In creating our own popular culture, we have inevitably drawn on the mainstream models offered to us, and the resultant combinations vary in form and content. The crime novel, with its legacy of socialist critique (Dashiell Hammett, for example, was a communist), its formal relationship to parody, and its tendency to produce antiheroic narratives, contains elements favorable to countercultural appropriation. But the lesbian crime novel had its heyday under the individualistic era of Reaganism and Thatcherism. It often posed answers to crime and social problems in the form of personal rather than structural acts of justice. Its *modus operandi,* in a decade when television was inundating us with programs that fictionalized the upholding of—rather than the resistance to—hegemonic versions of the law, must cause us to consider what readerly needs were being satisfied.

Popular narratives are never wholly reactionary nor wholly radical because despite their offering us dominant reading positions to occupy, readers will always find a way to read "other-wise," to put their own particular needs and interpretations into the text. This is how we can read Hitchcock's film *Rebecca* (1940) as a lesbian thriller. With the lesbian crime novel, we can speculate why it proliferated during a decade of individualistic identity politics, in the aftermath of the liberation movements of the 1970s. We can observe that lesbian feminist science fiction—the literature of utopian vision, of hope and social possibilities—was the favorite form of the 1970s but became passé by the 1980s. Crime fiction allows us to express anxieties about a period of conformity, conventionalism, and crackdown, but did it give us any impetus for new formulations of the law? (See also SCIENCE FICTION.)

—*Sally R. Munt*

BIBLIOGRAPHY

Butler, Judith. *Gender Trouble*. New York: Routledge, 1990. ■ ———. "Imitation and Gender Insubordination." *Inside/Out: Lesbian Theories, Gay Theories*. Diana Fuss, ed. New York: Routledge, 1991. 13–31. ■ Munt, Sally R. "The Investigators: Lesbian Crime Fiction." *Sweet Dreams: Gender, Sexuality and Popular Fiction*. Susannah Radstone, ed. London: Lawrence & Wishart, 1988. 91–120. ■ ———. *Murder by the Book: Feminism and the Crime Novel*. London and New York: Routledge, 1994. ■ Palmer, Paulina. "The Lesbian Feminist Thriller and Detective Novel." *What Lesbians Do in Books*. Elaine Hobby and Chris White, eds. London: Women's Press, 1991. 9–27. ■ Reddy, Maureen T. *Sisters in Crime*. New York: Continuum, 1988. ■ Wittig, Monique. *Les Guérillères*. New York: Viking, 1971.

Myth

Myth and literature are deeply interdependent and often indistinguishable. Being, in essence, the traditional tales told about gods and about human or semidivine heroes, myths generally take a narrative though sometimes a dramatic form. Usually they are first recorded in poetry, as Homer and Hesiod demonstrate with respect to the classical mythology that is to be focused on here. The *Iliad* and *Odyssey*, from the eighth century, and *Theogony*, from around 700 B.C., are our prime and richest sources of the Greek myths, but the poems are themselves mythic, that is, they belong equally in the fields of the mythologist and of the literary scholar. Aristotle ranks plot—or *muthos*, the source of our word *myth*—as the first element of tragedy and epic. In the *Poetics* (Chap. 6) *muthos* refers to "the combination of the incidents, or things done in the story," but the Greek tragedies and Homeric epics that Aristotle has in mind are mythic also in the sense of being "imitations"—or representations—of the legendary actions of divine and heroic agents. Thus Aristotelian poetics enables us to equate myth with the plot that is the "life and soul" of the poems in the two highest literary genres. Pindar uses a lyric form, the ode, to draw upon and contribute to the treasures of Hellenic mythology. The Latin works that are most remarkable for being at once literature as (Greco-Roman) myth and myth as literature are VIRGIL's *Aeneid* and Ovid's *Metamorphoses*.

The literariness of myth, however, is but part of the story. Mythological scholarship has discerned many additional features and functions. Myths explain origins; the genesis of everything from the cosmos, the gods, or mankind to the emergence of a species of flower. They can accomplish in a non-abstractive mode some explanatory functions of philosophy or science; yet the physical sciences and philosophy tend to refute and reject myths, the literary and other arts to adopt, adapt, and invent them. Variant versions are rather the rule than the exception. Myths may combine with rituals and cults to compose the religious experience of a community. Anonymous for the most part, myths are as if communal dreams emanating from the unconscious of a people. The truth value varies, with myths believable as literally true within the orbit of the culture that spawns them and deemed erroneous or fictitious elsewhere; yet elsewhere they may also be viewed as imparters of archetypal and psychological verities. Finally, they may mirror, account for, and validate social institutions, such as, for example, the male pederasty that prevailed in ancient Greece.

Of all the myths from Greco-Roman antiquity that treat of male homoeroticism, the rape of Ganymede deserves first place. The youngest son of Tros, eponymous king of Troy, he excelled in physical beauty, and that determined his fate. He was tending flocks or else hunting game one day when Zeus, having fallen in love with him, swooped down in the form of an eagle (or, in a variant, sent an eagle), seized him, bore him to Mount Olympus, and there made him the cupbearer of the gods—in place of Hebe—and his own ever-youthful beloved.

Tros was grief-stricken at his loss, until Zeus sent him some superlative horses as a compensatory gift and the message that his son would never age or die, whereupon his sorrow turned into joy. Hera (the Romans' Juno) was doubly offended, as mother of the displaced Hebe, also goddess of youth, and as the chief god's ever jealous wife. Zeus was an inveterate womanizer, and "goddessizer," but his way with female partners was to impregnate them and leave; he had never brought any of his women to live on Olympus nor granted any of them divine immortality. Ganymede may have been his only masculine love, but he was special. Eventually he was celestialized as the constellation Aquarius, the "water bearer."

The Ganymede legend goes all the way back to the *Iliad*, where, however, it differs significantly from the more familiar later version. The boy was already the son of a Tros recompensed with horses (5.265–269), but no eagle abducts him. Some unnamed gods, finding him "the loveliest born of the race of mortals," do so instead, and they take him up to dwell with them and to be the wine-pourer of Zeus (20.230–235). He is not said to be enamored of the youth, to whom the divinities apparently respond aesthetically rather than erotically. Neither Homer nor Hesiod ever explicitly ascribes homosexual experiences to the gods or to heroes. The sexualization of Zeus's role in the myth came later, possibly not before the sixth century.

The exaltation of Ganymede as inamorato of Zeus gives male homosexuality its most celebrated myth—and one of far-reaching effects. This myth particularly, if not uniquely, has proved a godsend to gay artists and writers ever since the Italian Renaissance. That the supreme god exemplifies and sanctions homoerotic love has been taken as classic paganism's answer, alternative, and antidote to the harsh, vindictive, and, in the usual exegesis, antihomosexual story of Sodom and Gomorrah at Genesis 19 (whence "sodomy" and "sodomite"), which is all that Judeo-Christian mythology has to offer lesbian and gay culture. And in the area of ordinary language, from the Middle Ages until well into the seventeenth century a ganymede—the name turned into a common noun—was a "sexually submissive or kept boy" or a "catamite," a sixteenth-century synonym from the Latin *catamitus,* which in turn is said to derive from the Greek name Ganymedes.

During the seventh century, the male pederastic practices characteristic of Hellenic civilization took root. In following the received code of conduct, a citizen of the polis, a man who had or could have a beard, was in his twenties or older, and either single or married, would amorously consort with a freeborn adolescent who was still without facial hair and might have been as young as twelve and was rarely over eighteen. Each partner took—or at least was expected to take—a prescribed role: The man was to be active, the initiator, impassioned, the wooer with words and with gifts, a strong pedagogical influence, and the recipient of orgasmic pleasure by means of penile insertion from a frontal position between the closed thighs of the youth; he, in turn, was supposed to be passive, reluctant, unaroused, educationally benefited, and if he chose to grant his sexual favors, to do so standing, staring straight ahead, and without an erection or delectation. Later, though the loverly aspect of the association faded when hair defaced the younger countenance, the two were likely to remain joined in friendship. The lover was the *erastes,* the beloved the *eromenos.* It was these conventions that governed the behaviors imputed to the deities and heroes in the post–Homeric and post–Hesiodic myths.

When the gods in classical mythology fall homoerotically in love, they never do so with other gods or with adult human males; rather they always do so with a mortal youth. They enter into liaisons in which they, like Zeus, act the part of the erastes to an adolescent who, like Ganymede, serves as the eromenos. The sexual acts imagined to be performed by the divine–human lovers, though not described in detail, can be assumed to conform, just as the structure of the relationship does, to the cultural ideal of pederastic unions.

Poseidon desired the young Pelops, ivory-shouldered and the son of Zeus's son Tantalus. The sea god came to him by chariot, took him off to Olympus, and made him his beloved. That was before the arrival of Ganymede, who, however, remained there, whereas Pelops after a time was returned to the world of mortals. In adulthood, he wished to wed Hippodamia, but her kingly father would give her only to the suitor who could defeat him in a chariot race. None had. So Pelops sought help from his powerful friend, reminding Poseidon of the joy he had found in their love, and obtained from him, also the god of horses, a chariot of gold drawn by winged steeds with which to win the race and bride. (In a variant, he wins by trickery.) Here the divine erastes is impassioned at first and takes the initiative, then keeps the beloved only during his adolescence, and afterward proves to be an amicable and dependable benefactor. Pindar created this homoerotic myth in an ode, *Olympian I,* to substitute for another myth, wherein Pelops is cannibalized by a deity, which the poet disapproved of as impious.

Phoebus Apollo—with his eternally smooth and splendid body the very model of the ephebe—had many male loves, more than any other god, but the two of his romances we know most about are those with Hyacinthus and Admetus. Hyacinthus was, like Ganymede, preeminently handsome and the teenaged youngest son of a king—here king of Sparta. At least two gods sought his affection, as did a man, Thamyris, a legendary bard of Thrace. He boasted that he could outdo the Muses in song, and when they heard about that—some say from Apollo with malice toward a rival—they punished him by depriving him of his sight, voice, and art. Zephyrus, the West Wind, was another who desired Hyacinthus. This rivalry of gods for the love of a youth may be singular. Hyacinthus chose Apollo. One day they stripped and oiled themselves and the divine erastes demonstrated how to throw a discus, but it somehow miscarried and struck his eromenos a fatal blow on the head. In some versions, Zephyrus was so smitten with jealousy that he blew the discus on its killing way. The death, whether or not accidental, was devastating to Apollo.

He was unable to save the boy but caused a flower to spring from his blood—the hyacinth, and traced on its petals were letters, whether his Greek initial *Y* or else *AI AI* to signify his lover's cry of "woe."

Apollo's loves tended to wind up plants. Daphne became the laurel, for another example, and the cypress came from Cyparissus, a boy dear to the god. This eromenos, having accidentally killed a favorite stag, was so distraught that he wished to mourn forever. The gods obliged by changing him into the mourning tree.

As a punishment for slaying the Cyclopes, Apollo once had to spend a year in servitude to Admetus in Thessaly. He burned with desire for the fair young king and made him his beloved. During that year of love, the royal livestock increased phenomenally. Later Phoebus exerted his supernatural powers on behalf of Admetus, as an ex-lover should, for example, in enabling him to perform an impossible task set by Alcestis's father as a condition for marrying her, or in inducing the Fates to spare his life if someone would agree to die in his stead. But a problem arises over whether the erastes-eromenos relationship can be compatible with that of servant and master. Would the god have been conceived of as socially inferior while sexually on top? Some mythologists recently have doubted that Apollo could have been the erastes. But with no ancient evidence to the contrary, the mythic anomaly remains intact.

The first love of Dionysus (the Latin Bacchus), according to a myth from the fifth century A.D., was a boy named Ampelus. The two wrestled, swam, and hunted together. Ampelus befriended animals, and one day encountering a bull, he mounted it, only to be thrown from it, gored, and killed. The god was heartbroken and shed his first tears, and was comforted only on learning that the beloved body would turn into the vine. This metamorphic consequence of male-male love both gave the world wine and enabled Dionysus to fulfill his destiny to be its god.

A truly eccentric theistic myth is another one, likewise late, concerning Dionysus; we cannot tell how old it was when Clement of Alexandria recorded it in the second century A.D. Dionysus wanted to go to Hades to rescue his mother Semele but did not know the way. He asked someone called Polymnus for help. The man agreed to direct him there if on his return he would submit to him sexually. The god swore to do so, but when he came back he could not find Polymnus, who meanwhile had died. Dionysus located his grave, there carved the branch of a fig tree into the shape of a phallus, and sat upon it to keep his promise. Here the god is decidedly not an erastes, and he breaches the classical Greek pederastic ethic in two

ways: by the willingness both to accept anal penetration and to give his body to pay a debt. The tale is no doubt for purists an instance of Hellenistic decadence.

Fellatio was just not Greek, except when done by female prostitutes in the social order and by male satyrs in the mythic. The latter were part-human and part-animal figures, with equine tails, ears, sometimes legs, and genitals, which were massive in a culture where the model human physique was graced with a small penis. Satyrs were polymorphous in their sensuality, and their diverse lascivious activities pictured on vases include, besides fellatio, masturbation. Pan, the pastoral and nature god, with his pipes and the horns, legs, and tail of a goat, would indulge in autoeroticism too; and though a compulsive nymph-chaser, he also liked shepherd boys—in particular Daphnis.

The boyfriends of heroes generally have the same qualities as those of gods—adolescence and astonishing pulchritude, along with royal blood or divine forebears. Hylas, whose parents were a king and a nymph, had these properties; and Heracles (the Roman Hercules), after slaying his father Thiodamas in a dispute, took him away and became his surrogate father and erastes, teaching him all that a hero should know. Master and pupil were mutually devoted and inseparable. They joined Jason, in quest of the golden fleece, aboard the Argo. At Chios, the Argonauts disembarked and began to prepare a meal. Hylas wandered off by himself to fetch water for his lover, and as he bent over a spring to fill his pitcher, the nymph of the water was dazzled by his beauty and grace and pulled him into her element to be her paramour. He cried out, but to no avail. Heracles frantically sought his lost eromenos and got the local inhabitants to join in the fruitless search. While it was going on, the Argonauts, with the winds favorable, set sail and left the bereft hero behind.

Iolaus, Heracles's nephew, the son of his half or twin brother Iphicles, was initially his eromenos and afterward continued as a lifelong companion who shared in many of the hero's exploits and adventures. Here the pederastic eros of uncle for nephew grew into deep and abiding philia, in contrast to the love between Heracles and Hylas that was aborted when the love was still in an erotic phase.

Orpheus, the Thracian singer and classical pattern of the poet-musician, was woebegone after failing at the very last moment to regain his wife Eurydice from Hades. Thereafter, whether from a continuing commitment to her or from the pain of losing her twice, he resolved to shun women (and was later butchered for so doing by resentful maenads). Instead, he gave "his love to tender boys . . . enjoying the springtime and first flower of their youth." He introduced pederastic behavior into Thrace, but his mode of conduct as represented in Ovid's *Metamorphoses* (10.83–85) may be criticizable from an Hellenic viewpoint for being rather promiscuous and nonpedagogical.

Mythology is obsessed with origins; hence the focus on the provenance of same-sex love. A number of originators are designated in myths, either with respect to a particular locale, as Orpheus in the case of Thrace, or as radical innovators. Another Thracian bard, Thamyris, is regarded by some as the first to love another male, with Hyacinthus or Hymenaeus (both of whom Apollo loved too) and perhaps Narcissus as the objects of his passion; but he seems not to have won any of them, or at least we are never informed that he did. Although other scattered and peripheral stories may deal with the initiation of homosexuality, the most widespread Hellenic traditions were that it arose in Crete or, alternatively, that Laius, the king of Thebes and the father killed by his son Oedipus, deserves credit for its invention.

When the Theban throne was usurped for a time, Laius was exiled to the court of Pelops in Pisa, where he was hospitably received. Of Pelops's many sons, the youngest and favorite was Chrysippus, whose mother was not the queen Hippodamia but a nymph. He was a young beauty, and Laius, when teaching him to drive a chariot, fell passionately in love with him, thus bringing pederastic eros into being. Later when Laius was recalled by his subjects, he abducted the youth, who was the great love of his life, and returned with him to Thebes. The aftermaths vary considerably. In one version, Chrysippus killed himself for shame; in another, Hippodamia killed him sleeping in Laius's bed and used Laius's sword to pin the crime on him, but the dying boy cleared his lover of suspicion. Or else was he murdered by his half brothers Atreus and Thyestes? The Sphinx may have been sent to Thebes by Hera as a punishment for the king's abduction of Chrysippus.

Laius as founder of the *paiderasteia*, as the Greek institution of pederasty is called, is especially interesting in connection with the psychoanalytic theory of the Oedipus complex. The informing and defining myth of this psychosexual process details the relations of the eponymous hero with his parents, Laius and Jocasta. According to Freud, the father (the Laius ectype) has crucial functions in the sexual development of the son (the Oedipus ectype), and if he performs them successfully, the boy can move along a libidinal path toward the goal, reached at puberty, of choosing a female love object (a Jocasta substitute figure). Now what happens to this theory when the grand passion of the archetypal father turns out to be an adolescent boy? Could that paternal figure be effectual in helping to bring the conflict with the son to a heterosexual resolution? Discussions of the Oedipus complex in either its positive or negative forms rarely take into account Laius's pederastic libido.

Does Achilles make love with Patroclus in the *Iliad*? The text does not expressly say so, and that settles the matter for most classicists and mythologists. Yet there are dissenting voices, some holding that the love of the heroes is tacitly sexual, and others persuasively arguing that their attachment is homophilic in the sense of loverlike feelings without carnal intimacy. For nearly all Hellenic writers and commentators, however, the question was not were they lovers—they were; rather it was which one took which sexual role. Achilles, the younger but dominant one, was commonly deemed the erastes. In *Myrmidones,* a lost play by Aeschylus that survives only in two brief fragments, Achilles, contemplating Patroclus dead, recalls "our frequent kisses" and dotes on the eromenos's thighs, for it would have been between them that he derived his genital pleasure. In the *Symposium,* PLATO has Phaedrus disagree with Aeschylus and contend that Patroclus, as the older one and less fair, should be the erastes. The Greeks of the classical period had to assimilate the relationship of the archaic heroes to their own pederastic categories, however inappropriate these were when the lovers were both past adolescence.

The exquisite Narcissus was the desired of many, male and female alike, but was sexually unmoved by one and all. In a Greek myth, he sent a sword as a gift to Ameinias, a young man who wooed him and was spurned. The would-be erastes plunged the blade into himself outside the house of the cruel Narcissus and died cursing him. A little later Narcissus looked into water and was captivated, at last, by the person he found therein. But it was, alas, himself, and so in frustration he committed suicide. Out of the bloodshed, the first narcissus bloomed.

In Ovid's later and far better known version, (*Metamorphoses* 3.341–510), Narcissus, at sixteen, was again indifferent to suitors of both sexes. His most pathetic victim was the nymph Echo who, on being repudiated, wasted away to a mere voice. When Narcissus lay beside the pool and, looking in, fell in love with the face he beheld, he thought it was someone else's, that of a youth of his own age who appeared to be returning the love. He could not comprehend why the two of them, though they stretched out their arms to each other, could not embrace. Then all at once it dawned on him that he and the other were one and the same. This recognition made him so despondent that he pined away with thwarted desire and succumbed. His corpse metamorphosed into the narcissus.

It is a pity that Narcissus, when self-infatuated, never found the obvious outlet of autoeroticism. Was it because male masturbation was too grossly satyric to be tolerable to Ovid and his Roman readers? Then again, when Narcissus says, "What I desire I have" (*quod cupio mecum est*), the words would seem to denote satisfaction, which is what he should attain, if one listens to Freud. He makes narcissism a major factor in homosexual orientation. Accordingly, inverts "are plainly seeking *themselves* as a love-object," and a narcissist may love "what he himself is (i.e. himself)." Just so with Narcissus; he does in fact have the male love object he seeks, does possess what he loves (himself). But that possession of the loved self does not bring the fruition anticipated in the theory, bringing instead despair and self-repudiation: "O that I might be parted from my own body." Narcissus, then, at best but partially exemplifies Freudian narcissism.

This survey, though not exhaustive, covers most of the homoerotic myths of antiquity and the principal ones. Among some notable omissions are Virgil's mythoheroic young lovers Nisus and Euryalis in the *Aeneid* (9.176–449) and his mythopastoral Corydon whose love complaint fills the second Eclogue. Yet what may surprise, in light of the ubiquity of boy loving among the Hellenes, is not how many but how relatively few of the myths tell of same-sex love. About half of the major gods of the Greek pantheon have no intermale involvements, these being Ares, Hephaestus, Hades, and apparently Hermes, even though one obscure myth does suggest otherwise. Moreover, the heterosexual love stories of gods and heroes are far more numerous and on the whole better known than the mythic homosexual stories. None of the extant Greek tragedies with their mythological plots dramatizes single-sex loves although some lost ones did, including Euripides's *Chrysippus* as well as Aeschylus's *Myrmidones*. If we had no other evidence than the myths themselves to go on, we would have quite an inadequate sense of how extensive the practice and approval of pederastic erotics really were.

Nevertheless, the gay heritage from this great body of Western mythology is rich, and much richer, sad to say, than the lesbian heritage. Lesbianism hardly exists in the myths. No goddess ever has sexual relations with another goddess, or with a nymph, or with a girl. Nor, at the human level, do women fall in love with women. Not even the AMAZONS, through living in an exclusively female society and warriors in a female army, did so. They had sexual unions once a year with men of neighboring tribes for the purpose of breeding daughters (sons they destroyed), but they did not become lovers to one another. Ovid writes of a girl-loving girl, but in a narrative that views lesbian feelings with abhorrence. Iphis was brought up as a boy because her Cretan father would have killed a daughter at her birth. At thirteen, she was betrothed to Ianthe, whom she loved passionately but with the sense that such same-sex love was unnatural and monstrous. On the eve of the wedding, a merciful goddess solved her desperate dilemma with a miraculous sex change, turning her actually into the boy she had always seemed (*Metamorphoses* 9.666–797).

Between SAPPHO in the early sixth century and PLATO two centuries later, Hellenic writing was silent on the subject of lesbian sexuality. Sappho of Lesbos, the island that yielded our elegant term for the love between women that she wrote about, was so highly regarded as a poet as to be dubbed "the tenth muse"; she habitually appeals to Aphrodite in her amatory lyrics, thereby establishing the goddess as the patroness of lesbian as she is of other types of love.

Plato composed for the *Symposium* and assigned to Aristophanes a myth to account for sexual orientations. Once upon a time the human race consisted of people whose shape was round and whose bodily parts were like ours but doubled and somewhat rearranged; and each person was a member of one of three sexes: male, female, and male-female. They were so powerful that the gods felt threatened, and Zeus hit upon the expedient of weakening them by cutting them in half. The result was that each thereafter sought to unite with the missing half through love. The homosexual desired his other male half, the lesbian her other female half, and the formerly androgynous one desired his or her counterpart of the other sex. This myth is truly remarkable. It shows that the notion of a sexual IDENTITY innate to the human personality is very old, and thus it roundly refutes the contention of those gay theorists who insist that homosexual identity is a concept that could not possibly have predated the invention of the word *homosexual* in the later nineteenth century. Besides, this myth legitimates lesbian love by putting it on the same level as male-male and opposite-sex love—a radical move in the Athens of that time.

Society as organized within the Greek polis was indeed phallocentric. The virile member was highly privileged—if, that is, it belonged to a freeborn adult, for his sexual hegemony extended over eromenoi and wife, as also over slaves and prostitutes. However honorable their *paiderasteia* may have been to the Greeks, they were severely homophobic when it came to lesbianism, Sappho and the *Symposium* notwithstanding. The Romans had a different erotics of pederasty. The boys they made love with were slaves, but they were just as averse to romances between women.

The classical myths manifest cultural biases in their ignoring and ignorance of lesbian love.

Though reflecting the mores and religious beliefs as well as biases of the Greek and Roman ancients, these myths transcend their native civilizations to play a crucial role in the gay and lesbian literary heritage. They do so in several ways: by bearing witness to awesome societies of the past wherein at least some forms of homosexuality were naturalized and exalted; by making a rich vein of positive images, tropes, and allusions available for textualizations of same-sex love; and by enabling Western writers of later periods to read and represent their lived experience of homoeroticism in the timeless light of classical mythology. (See also GREEK LITERATURE, ANCIENT and ROMAN LITERATURE.)

—Joseph Pequigney

BIBLIOGRAPHY

Aristotle. *Poetics.* Trans. Ingram Bywater. *Basic Works.* Richard McKeon, ed. New York: Random House, 1941. ■ Bonnefoy, Yves, comp. and ed. *Mythologies.* Wendy Doniger, dir. of trans. 2 vols. Chicago: University of Chicago Press, 1991. ■ Calasso, Roberto. *The Marriage of Cadmus and Harmony.* Trans. Tim Parks. New York: Knopf, 1993. ■ Cantarella, Eva. *Bisexuality in the Ancient World.* Trans. Cormac O'Cuilleanain. New Haven, Conn.: Yale University Press, 1992. ■ Clarke, W. M. "Achilles and Patroclus in Love." *Hermes* 106 (1978): 381–396. ■ Dover, K. J. *Greek Homosexuality.* New York: Vintage Books, 1980. ■ Downing, Christine. *Myths and Mysteries of Same-Sex Love.* New York: Continuum, 1989. ■ Foucault, Michel. *The Care of the Self.* Vol. 3 of *The History of Sexuality.* New York: Vintage Books, 1988. ■ ———. *The Use of Pleasure.* Vol. 2 of *The History of Sexuality.* New York: Vintage Books, 1976. ■ Freud, Sigmund. "On Narcissism: An Introduction." *The Standard Edition of the Complete Psychological Works.* James Strachey, ed. 24 vols. London: Hogarth Press, 1966–1974. 14:67–102. ■ ———. *Three Essays on the Theory of Sexuality.* SE. 7:125–230. ■ Graves, Robert. *The Greek Myths.* 2 vols. Baltimore: Penguin Books, 1955. ■ Halperin, David M., John J. Winkler, Froma I. Zeitlin, eds. *Before Sexuality: The Construction of Erotic Experience in the Ancient Greek World.* Princeton: Princeton University Press, 1990. ■ Halperin, David M. *One Hundred Years of Homosexuality: And Other Essays on Greek Love.* London: Routledge, 1990. ■ Homer. *The Iliad.* Trans. Richmond Lattimore. Chicago: University of Chicago Press, 1951. ■ Ovid. *Metamorphoses.* Loeb Classical Library. 2 vols. Cambridge, Mass.: Harvard University Press, 1946. ■ *The Oxford Classical Dictionary.* N. G. L. Hammond and H. H. Scullard, eds. Oxford: Clarendon Press, 1970. ■ Plato. *The Symposium. Works.* Trans. Benjamin Jowett. Irwin Edman, ed. New York: Modern Library, 1928. ■ Saslow, James M. *Ganymede in the Renaissance: Homosexuality in Art and Society.* New Haven, Conn.: Yale University Press, 1986. ■ Sergent, Bernard. *Homosexuality in Greek Myth.* Trans. Arthur Goldhammer. Boston: Beacon Press, 1986.

Native North American Literature

It is a singular fact that we can speak of a Native lesbian and gay literary heritage at all, for the percentage of gays and lesbians in the larger population—modest by anyone's measure—would seem to reach the vanishing point when applied to those who can trace their ancestry to North America's original inhabitants. (The term *Native* is meant here to include those who identify as Native American, American Indian, Canadian Indian, and Alaskan Native [Eskimo, Inuit, and Aleut].) This was not always the case, however. At the time of Columbus's arrival, a thousand or more societies flourished in every reach of the continent, speaking hundreds of distinct languages. And in most of these societies, one could find representatives of the third gender tradition of the "berdache" (an unfortunate European misnomer) or "two-spirit" (the preferred term of contemporary Indians), individuals who combined male and female activities, particularly in the areas of work roles and religion. In fact, Native North America was arguably one of the most gay-positive regions of the globe before European contact.

One legacy of conquest is that the production of works by Native people that meet Western criteria of "literary" remains a recent phenomenon. Arlene Hirschfelder's 1973 bibliography, *American Indian and Eskimo Authors,* identified only a dozen novels by Indians, the oldest dating to 1899. The first collection of Native poetry did not appear until 1918. It was not until N. Scott Momaday's *House Made of Dawn,* which received the 1968 Pulitzer Prize for fiction, that creative writing by Native people emerged as a genre in its own right. Given this history, it may seem ambitious to attempt to identify a specifically lesbian and gay Native tradition, and, in fact, many Native people would object to this kind of separate treatment as typically Western and alien to the Native spirit of inclusiveness. But as is the case with all matters of lesbian and gay history and culture, a closer look is warranted. The reader who is willing to seek out works published outside the mainstream will find that lesbian and gay Indians have made unique contributions to Native literature, past and present. For convenience sake, I will describe these contributions in terms of three nonexclusive phases: traditional, transitional, and contemporary.

The "traditional" period, which should not be considered over as long as tribes continue to maintain and produce historical literary forms, includes what is usually termed "oral literature"—myths, folk tales, poems, songs, and ritual texts—although, I would argue (with Dennis Tedlock) that the distinction between written and oral, literate and nonliterate is of little value when we consider how Native use of literary formulas and mnemonic systems achieve the purpose of fixing texts no less effectively than writing. Berdaches or two-spirits were certainly active contributors to these tribal literatures, although we have few examples of traditional literature that we can attribute to specific individuals. Similarly, none of the standard folklore indexes includes entries on "berdache" motifs or characters. (My "Bibliography of Berdache and Alternative Gender Roles among North American Indians" corrects this to an extent.)

One exception is the famous Zuni "man-woman," We'wha (d. 1896), who recited numerous myths and tales to the anthropologist Matilda Coxe Stevenson. Stevenson's exhaustive monograph on the Zunis (1904) includes one tale specifically credited to We'wha, and it is clear that We'wha was also a key source for the versions of the Zuni origin myths Stevenson published. This is evident in the greater amount of detail they offer concerning the supernatural two-spirit, Ko'lhamana (*ko-*, supernatural + *lhamana*, "berdache"). In other words, We'wha was able to use traditional tribal literature to construct and express his identity as a two-spirit.

The "transitional" period of Native lesbian and gay literature begins, roughly speaking, with the generation that followed We'wha. This period is characterized by extensive Indian-white cultural interaction and major changes in two-spirit roles. At government boarding schools and on closely supervised reservations, cross-dressing and homosexuality were ruthlessly suppressed, as were the use of Native languages and customs in general. On the other hand, for better or worse, it was in government schools and from missionaries that many Native people learned how to read and write in English, and where they first encountered such forms as novels, poetry, and autobiography.

The exemplary figure from this period is the Navajo two-spirit, Hastíín Klah (1867–1937). In the course of his training as a medicine man and *nádleehé* (two-spirit), Hastíín Klah mastered a vast store of mythology, folklore, prayers, and songs. Because he did not cross-dress, except for certain ceremonial occasions, the many non-Indians he befriended were unaware (or able to overlook) his special third-gender status. These included Franc Newcomb, who ran a trading post with her husband and later wrote Hastíín Klah's biography; Mary Cabot Wheelwright, a wealthy, amateur scholar of Navajo religion; and anthropologist Gladys Reichard, all of whom helped record Hastíín Klah's ceremonial knowledge in the 1920s and 1930s. An analysis of this literature reveals that Hastíín Klah not only elaborated but also rationalized and synthesized the role of the two-spirit figure known as Begochídíín. In other accounts, Begochídíín appears primarily as a trickster figure, but in myths told by Hastíín Klah, he emerges as a transcendental culture bearer who unites the opposites of male and female, young and old, good and evil to become a savior figure for the Navajo people.

Another individual representative of the transitional period was the Mescalero Apache singer and religious leader, Bernard Second (d. 1988), who worked closely with anthropologist Claire Farrer. Like Hastíín Klah, he did not cross-dress, but he still fulfilled traditional social and religious expectations for a "man-woman." (Elmer Gage, a Mohave interviewed in a 1965 issue of *One Magazine,* is yet another example.) No doubt other individuals from this period will be identified in the future, including Indian writers before the 1960s whose lesbian or gay sexual identity has not been previously known and such gay writers as LANGSTON HUGHES, whose Indian heritage has been overlooked.

While still involved in producing and maintaining traditional literary forms, the process of working with anthropologists and others to document their repertoire exposed Klah and others to Western techniques of inscription. In the case of religious material, this involved a significant break from tradition. At the same time, it laid the groundwork for the development of an independent artistic identity in a more Western sense and the use of writing for the inscription of original works as well as the preservation of more traditional forms.

The "contemporary" period of lesbian and gay Native writing begins in 1976 with the publication by Gay Sunshine of MAURICE KENNY's (Mohawk) "Tinselled Bucks: An Historical Study of Indian Homosexuality" and his poem "*Winkte*" (the Sioux term for two-spirits; both works are reprinted in *Living the Spirit,* ed. Will Roscoe). Clearly influenced by 1960s Native revivalism, Kenny's essay cites a wide range of ethnographic and literary references to two-spirit roles and male homosexuality in traditional times and concludes with an optimistic prediction of their restoration. "We were special!," he boldly declares in *"Winkte,"* "We had power with the people!"

The next important moment in lesbian and gay Native writing came with the 1981 publication of PAULA GUNN ALLEN's (Laguna Pueblo/Sioux) essay "Beloved Women: Lesbians in American Indian Cultures" (reprinted in her collection of essays, *Sacred Hoop*). Although she had been publishing woman-identified poetry since the 1970s, Allen debated a year before placing her landmark essay on Native lesbians, aware of the extremely hostile reception that many Native feminists (let alone lesbian-feminists) had received in Indian communities. "Under the reign of the patriarchy, the medicine-dyke has become anathema; her presence has been hidden under the power-destroying blanket of complete silence," she wrote. "We must not allow this silence to prevent us from discovering and reclaiming who we have been and who we are."

The decision to come out publicly in their writing was a consequential one for both Kenny and Allen. Born in 1929 and 1939 respectively, they saw tribal homophobia, fostered by government and church-directed campaigns of assimilation, reach a peak in their generations. Until the 1970s, lesbian and gay Indians found it necessary to migrate to urban areas to act on their desires, maintaining uneasy relationships with their families and reservation communities. As Kenny writes in his poem "Apache":

> in the night of smoke
> safe from reservation
> eyes and rules
> gentle fingers
> turned back the sheets

But coming out has not appeared to have hindered the careers of either Allen or Kenny, and their stature continues to grow, as evidenced by their inclusion (along with Daniel David Moses) in such canonical collections as *Harper's Anthology of 20th Century Native Poetry,* edited by Duane Niatum (1988).

Two Native lesbians—Barbara Cameron (Hunkpapa), cofounder of Gay American Indians, and Chrystos (Menominee)—appeared in CHERRÍE MORAGA's and GLORIA ANZALDÚA's anthology *This Bridge Called My Back: Writings by Radical Women of Color,* published in 1981. Two years later eleven Native lesbians appeared in Beth Brant's (Bay of Quinte Mohawk) landmark collection, *A Gathering of Spirit: Writing and Art by North American Indian Women* (1983; 1984). This was the first anthology of Native writing edited entirely by a Native person. The collection included poems and short prose from Cam-

eron, Chrystos, Allen, Janice Gould (Koyangk'auwi Maidu), Terri Meyette (Yaqui), Mary Moran (Métis), Kateri Sardella (Micmac), Vickie Sears (Cherokee), Anita Valerio (Blood/Chicana), and Midnight Sun (Anishnawbe).

The first specifically gay and lesbian collection of Native writing was *Living the Spirit: A Gay American Indian Anthology,* edited by Will Roscoe in 1988. Contents ranged from traditional myths and tales to contemporary poetry, short stories, essays, interviews, and an excerpt from Allen's novel-in-progress, *Raven's Road.* Contributors included Brant, Chrystos, Kenny, Midnight Sun, Gould, Randy Burns (Northern Paiute), Clyde Hall/M. Owlfeather (Shoshone-Métis/Cree), Erna Pahe (Navajo), Debra S. O'Gara (Tlingit), Lawrence William O'Connor (Winnebago), Ben the Dancer (Yankton Sioux), Daniel-Harry Steward (Wintu), Anne Waters (Seminole/Choctaw/Chickasaw/Cherokee), Daniel Little Hawk (Lakota/Southern Cheyenne/Aztec), Tala Sanning (Oglala Sioux), Nola M. Hadley (Appalachian/Cherokee), Carole LaFavor (Ojibwa), Joe Dale Tate Nevaquaya (Comanche/Yuchi), and Richard La Fortune (Yupik Eskimo).

Chrystos is one of the most popular lesbian Native writers today, having published three books of poems and contributed to numerous literary magazines. Denouncing white rip-offs of Native culture is a recurring theme of her work. As she writes in "Winter Count," "Now we are rare & occasionally cherished as Eagles / though not by farmers who still potshot us for sport." But when it comes to her love life, Chrystos can switch emotional registers to write poems of exquisite tenderness and eroticism.

Beth Brant continues to publish both stories and poems, while tirelessly promoting the work of other Native writers. She typically draws on personal experiences and is at her best when recounting with wry humor the foibles of her Mohawk relatives or giving a lesbian twist to the traditional Coyote story. She has received an Ontario Arts Council Award and a National Endowment for the Arts Literature Fellowship. Other Native lesbian authors who have published book-length works include Vickie Sears and Janice Gould.

Of the contemporary gay male Native writers, Clyde Hall (M. Owlfeather) is one of the more active. His poetry, short stories, and essays have appeared in numerous venues, including *Living the Spirit.* Maintaining a wide network of literary contacts, Hall has influenced such non-Indian writers as Tom Spanbauer and Winfred Blevins. Another active writer is Terry Tafoya (Taos/Warm Springs), who has published both traditional and contemporary stories as well as poetry and essays. His play, *Good Medicine,* received an award at the 1985 Minority Playwrights' Festival for the Group Theatre in Seattle. Canadian Daniel David Moses (Delaware) has had several plays produced and published, along with collections of his poetry. His play, *The Dreaming Beauty,* was a winner in the 1990 Theatre Canada National Playwriting Competition. William Merasty (Cree) has also produced a play in Canada.

Native lesbian and gay writers share with other Indian writers a sense of belonging to both the natural world and a close-knit community, of survival against enormous odds, and of a proud (sometimes idealized) past. Irony and self-mocking humor are common. Also typical is a path of development that includes both alienation from and a return to the tribal community. At the same time, lesbian and gay Native writing is striking in its celebration of eroticism. One finds this especially in the work of Paula Gunn Allen; Chrystos, who has published a volume of erotic poetry, *In Her I Am* (1993); and Judith Mountain-Leaf Volborth (Blackfoot/Comanche), who is currently working on a collection of lesbian sensual verse. At the same time, one is also likely to find a heightened sense of the internal problems of Native communities—whether alcoholism, violence, sexism, or homophobia. But the bicultural experience of lesbian and gay Native authors can also be the source of powerful connections. In "A Long Story," Beth Brant juxtaposes an account of Indian mothers at the end of the nineteenth century whose children are forcibly taken to boarding schools with that of a contemporary lesbian mother who loses her children in a custody battle.

Long before the emergence of lesbian and gay Native writing, the two-spirit tradition captured the imagination of non-Indian writers. Two of the most frequently cited passages from the genre of "contact literature" include George Catlin's account of the "Dance to the Berdashe" (in *Letters and Notes on the Manners, Customs, and Conditions of the North American Indians* [1841]) and John Tanner's description of the two-spirit Ozaw-wen-dib's attempt to seduce him in his *A Narrative of the Captivity and Adventures of John Tanner* (1830). The influence of accounts like these is apparent in the portrayal of Little Horse, a Cheyenne *hemaneh*, in Thomas Berger's *Little Big Man* (1964) and in its subsequent screenplay (1970). (By contrast, over 20 years later, Kevin Costner's film epic, *Dances with Wolves*, although acclaimed for its authenticity, made no mention of the Lakota *winkte* tradition.) In a somewhat different genre is Richard Amory's *Song of the Loon* series. These highly romanticized erotic Westerns are fondly remembered by gay men who discovered them in the 1960s. More recently, male two-spirit characters appear in Tom Spanbauer's *The Man Who Fell in Love with the Moon* (1991) and William Henderson's *Native* (1993). At least two nongay Native writers have also included two-spirit or gay characters in their work, Gerald Vizenor (*Heirs of Columbus* [1991]) and Leslie Marmon Silko (*Almanac of the Dead* [1991]).

Whereas male two-spirits evoked dismay and disgust on the part of most white frontiersmen, the desire of females to enter the roles and occupations of men struck them as both romantic and tragic. Portrayals of female two-spirits appear in American literature as early as the 1840s with the novels of Emerson Bennett (*The Prairie Flower; or, Adventures in the Far West* [ca 1850] and *Leni Leoti; or, Adventures in the Far West* [1851]). Other treatments include James Beckwourth's account of "Pine Leaf" (1931), probably based on the true story of Woman Chief; James Willard Schultz's *Running Eagle* (1919), based on an actual Blackfoot female warrior; and Frederick Manfred's torrid *The Manly-Hearted Woman* (1975).

The future of Native North American lesbian and gay writing is a bright one. The writers mentioned here appear in anthologies and collections with growing frequency. The first full-length autobiography, by Canadian Kevin White, was published in 1993, and the first novel by a lesbian or gay Native author with gay characters is likely to appear soon. Already a second anthology by and about lesbian and gay Native people, *The Basket and the Bow,* edited by Sheila Wahsquonaikezhik and Gilbert Deschamps, is scheduled for publication.

Unlike so many contemporary lesbian and gay writers, white and nonwhite, Native gay writers are not haunted by the sense of having no past and no social contribution to make. By connecting to the heritage of the two-spirit tradition, an important part of the development of most of the writers discussed here, lesbian and gay Native writers are forging a unique vision of what it means to be gay. In contrast to Euro-American gay literature where the themes of alienation and marginalization are so common, gay and lesbian Native writers promise a literature of affirmation, grounded in a visionary tradition with deep historical roots.

—*Will Roscoe*

BIBLIOGRAPHY

Allen, Paula Gunn. *The Sacred Hoop: Recovering the Feminine in American Indian Traditions.* Boston: Beacon Press, 1986. ∎ Brant, Beth, ed. *A Gathering of Spirit: Writing and Art by North American Indian Women.* 2d ed. Montpelier, Vt.: Sinister Wisdom, 1984; Vancouver, BC and Ithaca, N.Y.: Press Gang/Firebrand Books, 1991. ∎ ———. *Mohawk Trail.* Ithaca, N.Y.:

Firebrand, 1985. ■ ———. *Food and Spirits*. Ithaca, N.Y. and Vancouver, BC: Firebrand Books and Press Gang, 1991. ■ Chrystos. *Dream On*. Vancouver, BC: Press Gang, 1991. ■ ———. *Not Vanishing*. Vancouver, BC: Press Gang, 1988. ■ Corinne, Tee A., ed. *Riding Desire: An Anthology of Erotic Writing*. Austin, Tex.: Banned Books, 1991. ■ Farrer, Claire R. *Kaledioscopic Vision and the Rope of Experience*, forthcoming. ■ Fife, Connie, ed. *The Colour of Resistance: A Native Women's Anthology*. Toronto: Sister Vision Press, 1993. ■ Gould, Janice. *Beneath My Heart*. Ithaca, N.Y.: Firebrand Books, 1990. ■ Kenny, Maurice. *Only as Far as Brooklyn*. New York: Good Gay Poets, 1979, 1981. ■ [Klah, Hastíín]. *The Story of the Navajo Hail Chant*. Trans. Gladys A. Reichard. New York: Gladys A. Reichard, 1944. ■ Klah, Hasteen. *Navajo Creation Myth: The Story of the Emergence*. Navajo Religion Series, vol. 1. Santa Fe: Museum of Navaho Ceremonial Art, 1942. ■ Lesley, Craig and Katheryn Stavrakis. *Talking Leaves: Contemporary Native American Short Stories*. New York: Laurel, 1991. ■ Morse, Carl, and Joan Larkin, eds. *Gay and Lesbian Poetry in Our Time: An Anthology*. New York: St. Martin's Press, 1988. ■ Moses, Daniel D., and Terry Goldie, eds. *An Anthology of Native Canadian Literature in English*. Toronto: Oxford University Press, 1992. ■ Roscoe, Will. "Bibliography of Berdache and Alternative Gender Roles among North American Indians." *Journal of Homosexuality* 14(3/4) (1987): 81–171. ■ ———, ed. *Living the Spirit: A Gay American Indian Anthology*. New York: St. Martin's Press, 1988. ■ ———. "Living the Tradition: Gay American Indians." *Gay Spirit: Myth and Meaning*, Mark Thompson, ed. New York: St. Martin's Press, 1987. 69–77. ■ ———. "We'wha and Klah: The American Indian Berdache as Artist and Priest." *American Indian Quarterly* 12.2 (1988): 127–150. ■ ———. *The Zuni Man-Woman*. Albuquerque: University of New Mexico Press, 1991. ■ Sears, Vickie L. *Simple Songs*. Ithaca, N.Y.: Firebrand Books, 1990. ■ Tafoya, Terry. *Change!: Northwest Native American Legends*. Acoma, N.Mex.: Pueblo of Acoma Press, 1984. ■ ———. "Why Ant Has A Small Waist" and "Dancing with Dash-Kayah." *I Become Part of It: Sacred Dimensions in Native American Life*. D. M. Dooling and Paul Jordan-Smith, eds. New York: Parabola Books, 1989. 89–91, 92–100. ■ Tedlock, Dennis. "The Spoken Word and the Work of Interpretation in American Indian Religion." *Traditional American Indian Literatures: Texts and Interpretations*. Karl Kroeber, ed. Lincoln: University of Nebraska Press, 1981. 45–64. ■ White, Kevin. *Where Eagles Dare to Soar: Indians, Politics and AIDS*. Kahnawake, Quebec: Owera Books, 1993.

Nin, Anaïs
(1903–1977)

Anaïs Nin was born in Neuilly-sur-Seine, a suburb of Paris, on February 21, 1903, the only daughter and oldest child of Joaquin Nin, a Spanish composer and pianist who abandoned his family when she was ten years old, and Rosa Culmell, an operatic singer and daughter of a well-to-do Cuban family. Rosa took her three children to New York when Anais was eleven years old. On board ship, she began a diary that would grow to 150 volumes in more than 50 years. Though the first volume would not be published until 1966, Nin began publishing poetic fiction based on her diary in 1936.

Nin's most prolific period of creativity was during the time that she lived with her husband, Hugh Guiler, in Paris from 1923 to 1939, especially after she met Henry Miller at the end of 1931. Her first book, just completed when she met Miller, was *D.H. Lawrence: an Unprofessional Study* (1932). Out of the frenzied writing of her diary during this period of her sexual awakening—when she fell in love with first June and then Henry Miller—came a brief poetic novelette (*The House of Incest*, 1936) and a book of short fiction (*The Winter of Artifice*, 1939). These are still among her best fiction. Though a severely censored and altered version of the diaries of this period became her *Diary I* (1966), the unexpurgated portions of this period appeared long after her death as *Henry and June* (1986) and *Incest* (1992).

The title of the latter volume, like the impetus for her diary writing, came from sexual violation and abandonment by her beloved, narcissistic father. She began her diary not only to win him back but to create the "good" girl whom he could love. Though she saw him on various occasions when she first moved to France, she reconciled with him in 1932. Then they began a sexual affair propelled both by his continued exploitation of her need for love and by her recent sexual awakening. Eventually, after psychoanalysis, she abandoned her father, who died in Cuba in 1949.

In the 1940s in New York City, Nin felt rejected by the literary establishment, which valued the literature of political engagement above interior, poetic character studies such as hers. She set up her own printing press in Greenwich Village; here she republished her Paris books and a collection of short fiction, *Under a Glass Bell* (1944). She also wrote erotica—admitted hack work—for a dollar a page, money she gave to the youthful and needy artists in her circle. Her first mainstream publisher, Dutton, was secured for her by GORE VIDAL, one of her growing group of gay and bisexual male friends (several of whom became her lovers).

After mining her diary for six novels—*Ladders to Fire* (1946), *Children of the Albatross* (1947), *The Four Chambered Heart* (1950), *A Spy in the House of Love* (1954), *Seduction of the Minotaur* (1961), and *Collages* (1964)—Nin began publishing the diaries. Six volumes of the diary appeared before her death and made her a cult figure of the feminist movement, with audiences in the thousands on college campuses. Though radical feminists criticized her for her lack of interest in political and economic issues, many lesbians sensed her commitment to openness and freedom of expression for women. She often stated her acceptance of any kind of love, saying that only the failure to love was wrong.

Before diary publication and fame, however, she had developed her own woman-identified consciousness. She loved emotionally and physically both men and women. Though she denies lesbianism in *Seduction of the Minotaur,* unpublished portions of her diary suggest otherwise. During the last nearly thirty years of her life, she divided her time alternately between two husbands, Hugh Guiler in New York City and Rupert Pole in Los Angeles.

Though her fame is based on the erotica published after her death and on her mysterious bisexual femininity, her enormous diary is her principal contribution to literature. The four volumes entitled *The Early Diary of Anaïs Nin* (1978–1985), only slightly edited, give us the best published portrait of the artist as a young girl. If we ever see a reunification of the distorted—expurgated and unexpurgated—diaries of her adult years, we might better be able to judge the validity of Miller's prediction that her diary would "take its place beside the revelations of ST. AUGUSTINE, PETRONIUS, Abelard, Rousseau, [and] PROUST."

—*Noel Riley Fitch*

BIBLIOGRAPHY

Cutting, Rose Marie. *Anaïs Nin: A Reference Guide*. Boston: G.K. Hall, 1978. ■ Fitch, Noel Riley. *Anaïs: The Erotic Life of Anaïs Nin*. Boston: Little Brown, 1993. ■ ———. "The Literary Passion of Anaïs Nin & Henry Miller." *Significant Others: Creativity & Intimate Partnership*. Whitney Chadwick and Isabelle de Courtivron, eds. London: Thames & Hudson, 1993. 155–171. ■ Franklin, Benjamin V. *Anaïs Nin: A Bibliography*. Kent, Ohio: Kent State University Press, 1973. ■ ———, and Duane Schneider. *Anaïs Nin: An Introduction*. Athens: Ohio University Press, 1979. ■ Hinz, Evelyn J. *The Mirror and the Garden: Realism and Reality in the Writings of Anaïs Nin*. Columbus: Ohio State University Libraries, 1971. ■ Jason, Philip K. *Anaïs Nin and Her Critics*. Columbia, S.C.: Camden House, 1993. ■ Nin, Anaïs and Henry Miller. *A Literate Passion: Letters of Anaïs Nin and Henry Miller, 1932–1953*. Gunther Stuhlmann, ed. San Diego: Harcourt Brace Jovanovich, 1987. ■ Scholar, Nancy. *Anaïs Nin*. Boston: Twayne Publishers, 1984. ■ Spencer, Sharon. *Collage of Dreams: The Writings of Anaïs Nin*. Rev. ed. New York: Harcourt Brace Jovanovich, 1981. ■ Stuhlmann, Gunther, ed. *Anaïs: An International Journal*. Vols. 1–11 (1983–1993).

THE NOVEL

The Novel: Gay Male

The gay male novel is a form of fiction in which male homosexuality is central—not always a central problem but certainly a central concern. That said, few other absolute statements are possible. The protagonist of such a novel is likely to be gay, as are at least some of the lesser characters. Feelings of love arise; sexual acts occur; conflicts with the straight world—parents, teachers, friends, employers—happen. One way to trace the emergence of the gay male novel is to measure the frankness with which such things are described. Common topics include discovery and acceptance of sexual orientation, coming of age, coming out (especially to family), relationships, and the pursuit of happiness; these topics can be handled positively or negatively. It would logically follow that writers of gay novels are themselves gay, but even this cannot be taken for granted.

Novels in which male homosexuality occurs are almost as old as the form itself; novels in which male homosexuality is central are a relatively recent phenomenon. Early in the history of English-language novels, JOHN CLELAND's *Fanny Hill* or *Memoirs of a Woman of Pleasure* (1749) finds Fanny watching through a peephole in fascinated disgust as two men cavort in an adjacent room. Cleland's bit of erotica is a good example of male homosexuality treated incidentally, and (at least ostensibly) disapprovingly; similarly, Tobias Smollett's *Roderick Random* (1748) bemoans in passing the increase in sodomitic activities among the English.

Later in the eighteenth century, the appearance of various exotic subgenres of the novel provided opportunities to approach gay sex at least obliquely. WILLIAM BECKFORD's Oriental tale *Vathek* (1786), for example, contains ambiguous erotic fantasies and visions. In M. G. LEWIS's Gothic novel *The Monk* (1795), the title character feels strongly attracted to the young postulant Rosario and is smitten with his boyish beauty. Rosario, however, turns out to be a female in disguise, and the monk's lust obligingly becomes heterosexual. Both Beckford and Lewis were themselves homosexual and could, by removing their fiction to distant times and places, speak in a veiled fashion of desires forbidden in more conventional "realistic" fiction.

With the growth of middle-class prudishness even before the Victorian Age, nothing like these fictions appeared in respectable literature for many decades. It has been suggested that in *Oliver Twist* (1838) Fagin taught his boys more ways of earning their keep than just stealing handkerchiefs. It may be so; Dickens surely knew the ways of the London underworld as well as any man, but in the spirit of the age even the most indirect allusion was impermissible.

The thriving Victorian pornography industry, however, included male-male sex, in narrations like *My Secret Life* (1890) or collections like *The Pearl*. Depraved elderly noblemen and eager teenage servant boys were a common motif: These are a heterosexual's dream of naughty gay sex, and again they are only incidental, bubbles on a tide of heterosexual escapades. Indeed, they seem to have as much to do with Britain's eternal preoccupation with class as with sex: The titillation is that a lord and a page boy are in bed together, not that two males are.

The precursor of modern gay fiction is widely acknowledged to be the 1890s novel *Teleny*. René Teleny is a concert pianist and is adored by Camille de Grieux, whom he instructs in homosexual love, the acts of which are carefully described. After a melodramatic number of misunderstandings and betrayals, each attempts suicide. De Grieux is saved, but Teleny dies, surviving just long enough for a reconciliation to occur. This novel is often associated with the name of OSCAR WILDE, either as author or editor, but the attribution is speculative. Richard Ellmann's magisterial biography of Wilde does not even mention *Teleny*. Nonetheless it stands as an early example of romantic gay fiction.

Oscar Wilde was, however, responsible for a much more subversive book: *The Picture of Dorian Gray* (1891). Although homosexual acts are not alluded to in the novel, an alert reading yields the underlying ideas: Physically, Dorian is extremely beautiful, he seems perpetually young, and he clearly despises women. Basil Hallward, the artist who painted the titular portrait, idolizes him (as passages found only in the serial version emphasize). Gray has caused certain young men to leave England in disgrace and appears to be blackmailing others. He becomes a world-weary aesthete about whose fair self hovers a faint air of corruption. Wilde underlines the kinds of sins Dorian commits, or causes others to commit, by the character's very name: An alternative form of "Doric," it alludes to the homosexual-warrior society of ancient Greece.

Wilde's novel, written some time before he met his lover and nemesis, LORD ALFRED DOUGLAS, was a *succès de scandale*. If *The Picture of Dorian Gray* did not influence ANDRÉ GIDE, THOMAS MANN, and others, it at least set a precedent for their treatment of homosexuality as at once alluring and fatal, in works like Gide's *The Immoralist* (1902) and Mann's *Death in Venice* (1912); Mann's son KLAUS wrote a gay novel, *Mephisto*, in 1936. Wilde the man provided still another opening. With an irony he no doubt appreciated, it was Wilde's life, not his art, that brought issues of homosexuality before the public in his famous trial of 1895 and his subsequent imprisonment and exile.

Meanwhile, on the American side of the Atlantic, mainstream fiction and homoerotic fiction were by some accounts nearly congruent. In *Love and Death in the American Novel,* Leslie Fiedler has identified a recurrent pattern of the friendship of two men, usually of contrasting ethnicity, outside the normal bounds of society: Natty Bumppo and Chingachgook in Fenimore Cooper's *The Last of the Mohicans* (1826), Huck and Jim in Mark Twain's *Huckleberry Finn* (1885), and most notably, Ishmael and Queequeg in HERMAN MELVILLE's *Moby-Dick* (1851). The picture of the New England "isolato," Ishmael, and Queequeg, the denizen of Rokovoko, cozily in bed together at the Spouter Inn is thought provoking.

But Melville's plainest tale of fatal love between men is his novella *Billy Budd,* left in manuscript at Melville's death in 1891. Impressed aboard the *Bellipotent,* the handsome sailor Billy is the object of the repressed emotions of the master-at-arms, Claggart, who, Melville tells us, could have loved Billy "but for fate and ban." The repressed feelings transmute into hatred and jealousy, and Claggart brings Billy up on charges; Billy, speechless with rage and surprise, strikes out, killing Claggart. Captain Vere, who also loves Billy in his own strait-laced way, observes that Claggart was "struck dead by an angel of God—and yet the angel must hang." And so he does. Melville's novella concentrates many issues—innocence versus experience, authority versus freedom, justice versus law—but the cause of them all is sexual attraction; Melville pointedly emphasizes Billy's physical beauty and Claggart's sensitivity to it. Behind the novella's action is Melville's own experience in the all-male world of a ship. (The novella is dedicated to Jack Chase, one of Melville's real-life sailor heroes).

A key mediating figure in the development of gay literature on either side of the Atlantic was not a novelist but a poet, WALT WHITMAN. He met Oscar Wilde on the latter's visit to the United States in 1882 and was an influence on EDWARD CARPENTER, who in turn later became a major influence on E. M. FORSTER and *Maurice*. Whitman's quite frank celebrations of male-male love and camaraderie (more acceptable, it seems, in free verse than in prose fiction) provided both a touchstone and an encouragement to many later writers. Carpenter was a Cambridge don who gave up his academic post and moved to the north of England where he practiced a communal life, vegetarianism, and the values of craftsmanship and simplicity as celebrated by writers like THOREAU and William Morris. His justification of homosexuality, or a Uranian way of life, as he called it, was considerably influenced in expression by Whitman.

When E. M. Forster visited Carpenter and his working-class lover George Merrill in late 1913, he was inspired to write a homosexual novel and set to work at once on *Maurice,* as he explains in the "Terminal Note" to that novel. Forster did not intend to publish the book, at least not during his mother's lifetime, and it was not in fact published until the year after his own death in 1970. Despite its publication date, *Maurice* is very much a novel of turn-of-the-century England: pastoral in quality, leisurely in pace, reticent in expression. Forster's protagonist, Maurice Hall, is presented as normal in every respect except the crucial one of sexual orientation. When his first lover, Clive Durham, somewhat improbably turns straight at the age of twenty-four, Maurice is devastated, but eventually finds happiness in the arms of one of Durham's gamekeepers, Alec Scudder. *Maurice* critiques an English educational system that seems to encourage male-male love up to a point, but not to the point at which it might become rewarding; and a class system that discourages love among those who are not social equals. That Maurice finds fulfillment suggests that the novel has elements of fantasy; indeed, it is dedicated "To a Happier Year": not the year in which it might be publish-

able, but the year in which the relationship it depicts might become acceptable.

Maurice aside, the first half of the century in England was comparatively fallow. There were the elegant arabesques of RONALD FIRBANK, so drenched in homoeroticism as to have become CAMP; there was E. F. BENSON's odd *Ravens' Blood* (1934), and there was D. H. LAWRENCE. The homoerotic undertones of much of Lawrence's fiction, *Women in Love* (1920) for example, are well known; he himself told KATHERINE MANSFIELD, "I believe tremendously in friendship between man and man, a pledging of men to each other inviolably," and added, "But I have not ever met or formed such a friendship." Other exceptions might include Alec Waugh's *The Loom of Youth* (1917), which created a scandal with its suggestions of schoolboy homosexuality, parts of his brother EVELYN's *Brideshead Revisited* (1945), J. R. ACKERLEY's *Hindoo Holiday* (1932), which had to be tamed in revision before publication, and DENTON WELCH's lyrical work.

In both England and America, the vast historical upheaval of World War II did much to unseat traditional structures of value and patterns of behavior. In England, the Wolfenden Report (1957) and consequent legislation legalizing homosexuality were influential events. So in America were the Kinsey Report of 1948, which revealed that three-eighths of American men had had at least some homosexual experience, and the legendary Stonewall Riots of 1969, in which for the first time police harassment of gay men met with widespread and determined resistance. These events and many others repositioned social attitudes toward gay men and gay men's attitudes toward themselves.

In England, one of the first writers to take advantage of new possibilities in gay male fiction was a woman. After writing several novels about young nurses in which submerged lesbian themes were present, MARY RENAULT, an Englishwoman who spent much of her adult life in South Africa, made a breakthrough in 1953 with *The Charioteer,* her first fiction dealing with male homosexuality. Laurie, a young soldier wounded at Dunkirk and evacuated to hospital, meets again the older man he had adored at school. After many vicissitudes, they manage to establish a firm relationship. Marred by its scorn for certain kinds of homosexual men (the effete, the effeminate), *The Charioteer* nonetheless represents a new candor in dealing with male-male sexual desire.

The more she distanced herself from her material, the more feelingly Renault seemed able to write. *The Charioteer* dealt with the sex not her own; when she combined that with a removal into the past, into the Hellenic and Hellenistic worlds of Periclean Athens and the empire of Alexander the Great, she found her true moment. Little in historical fiction, or in gay fiction, is as finely realized as *The Mask of Apollo* (1966) or *The Persian Boy* (1972). Similarly, the French novelist MARGUERITE YOURCENAR found history a safe haven in which to discuss male love, in her classic *Memoirs of Hadrian* (1951).

In the United States, too, serious gay fiction could now reach a wider public although its tone reflected both the public's presumed hostility and the gay man's perplexity. GORE VIDAL's *The City and the Pillar* (1948, revised 1965) and JAMES BALDWIN's *Giovanni's Room* (1956) may stand as typical examples of gay male fiction—nearly the only examples, except perhaps TRUMAN CAPOTE's hauntingly Gothic *Other Voices, Other Rooms* (1948)—in the years immediately after World War II. Each in its own way demonstrates the impossibility of a favorable resolution of the homosexual's plight, not least because in each case the protagonist refuses to admit even to himself that he is gay. In their public aspect, both novels are about gay men's relations to society, or lack thereof, and about the milieus in which homosexuality can, if not thrive, at least be tolerated. In their private aspects, the novels are about knowing oneself and about how dishonesty breeds dishonesty.

Something close to despair pervades each novel: Both are obsessed with liquor and death. *The City and the Pillar* opens with twenty-five-year-old Jim Willard getting blind drunk in a bar; the second chapter goes back to his adolescence and his one moment of supreme sexual joy with his best friend, Bob Ford; subsequent chapters lead back to the opening scene. We learn that Jim is getting drunk because he has just killed Ford, who, meeting Jim after many years, now contemptuously spurns Jim's love. The novel is not just about failure to deal with one's own sexual nature, but is also about the fatal consequences of remaking a memory of the past into a dream of the future. This account is of the first version of the novel; it was a pioneering work and as such has historical as well as literary interest. (We learn, for instance, that the word *gay* was in common use at that time— 1948—as self-description among New York homosexuals.)

In *Giovanni's Room,* the first-person narrator, an American in Paris by the name of David (also known as Butch) is a confused and unpleasant young man. He first meets Giovanni in a gay club where the boy tends bar. David believes he has been in but not of the homosexual subculture of Paris; when he meets Giovanni, both are instantly smitten. But David cannot accept the implications of his feelings; he tells himself that the relationship with Giovanni, the time spent in Giovanni's room, is just an interlude until his girlfriend returns from Spain. When she does, David's self-imposed heterosexuality fails him, and they are driven to mutual loathing. Meanwhile, Giovanni has been convicted of the murder of Guillaume, the bar owner, who wants Giovanni as his kept boy. The novel opens on the day of Giovanni's execution, but we are to see David as a tragic victim too: a victim of his own fear of commitment and of his bottomless capacity for fooling himself.

A gay reader might take up Vidal or Baldwin, glad that a major fact of his being could now be discussed in fiction, and put them down, angered and saddened by their portrayals of inevitable misery. A different novel entirely is CHRISTOPHER ISHERWOOD's *A Single Man* (1964). Written by a transplanted Englishman living in California about a transplanted Englishman living in California, it shows a man well-adjusted within himself and capable of functioning in ordinary (straight) society. Fully cognizant of his nature, George does not fall into fantasies about himself (although he can fantasize vividly about boys he sees); capable of self-mockery, he is not drenched in self-contempt. He is even amused at the pedestrianism of the heterosexual world around him. George's lover has died some time since, and thus he is a single man in the most literal way. He is a college teacher, and when, toward the end of the novel, he meets one of his students in the bar where he and his lover first met, it seems that a new relationship or at least an adventure is in the offing. But it passes away. George appears to die at the end of the novel (the passage is rendered in conditional terms), but even so, *A Single Man* is a highly positive work, a portrait of a day in the life of a gay man who is unimpaired in his dignity and self-esteem.

Another novel that caused some stir in 1964 was JOHN RECHY's *City of Night,* which throws us back into the demimonde of "deviant" sex. As the title suggests, it portrays a dark world of hustlers, drag queens, impersonal furtive sex, and lovelessness. Written in a tone and style that clearly show the influence of Beat writers like JACK KEROUAC, *City of Night* has the quality of a documentary or exposé. Certainly it was then the fullest exploration of that mostly urban sexual subculture that is its subject although the work of Hubert Selby, Jr. (*Last Exit to Brooklyn* [1964] and later titles) has a similar grittiness. Likewise, the even earlier work of WILLIAM S. BURROUGHS such as *Naked Lunch* (1959), with its kaleidoscopic presentation and its hallucinogenic mixture of drugs, sex, and death, hit like a shock wave. For all its impact, Burroughs's fiction suggested that the world of the homosexual was a fairly weird, very much a foreign, place.

The American 1960s were notoriously years of upheaval and new freedom, or permissiveness, in society, politics, pharmaceuticals, and no less in gay literature. Thanks to new translations the work of two remarkable Frenchmen began to make its mark: that of the MARQUIS DE SADE, in which homosexual activity was only one item in a complete catalogue of revolutionary libertinage, as in *The 120 Days of Sodom* (1785), and that of JEAN GENET (*Our Lady of the Flowers* [1943] and the autobiographical *The Thief's Journal* [1949]). Separated by almost a century and a half, both these men wrote largely from prison, both celebrated sexual outlawry as freedom and consecration, both detested middle-class morality. Both were congenial to the temper of the 1960s. Representative American novels of the early 1970s include Daniel Curzon's gloomy *Something You Do in the Dark* (1971), Terry Andrews's disturbing *The Story of Harold* (1974), and PATRICIA NELL WARREN's popular melodrama, *The Front Runner* (1974).

Writing in 1977, Roger Austen made the suggestion that there is a kind of Gresham's Law of gay fiction: Bad writing drives out good, or more precisely, gay porn drives out serious gay art:

> as a result [of the influx of hard-core gay porn] the more serious and literate gay writer has found himself the victim of a paradox: with the wide-open acceptance of frankly homosexual fiction, the future of his sort of novel is threatened by its lurid competition.

His fears were unfounded, as it turned out. Already in 1976 ARMISTEAD MAUPIN had published the first of his series, *Tales of the City,* which nearly achieved bestseller status. And in 1978 appeared three remarkable, and quite different, gay novels: ANDREW HOLLERAN's *Dancer from the Dance,* LARRY KRAMER's *Faggots,* and EDMUND WHITE's *Nocturnes for the King of Naples.* In the same year, DAVID PLANTE began his series of Francoeur novels (*The Family,* followed by *The Country* [1981] and *The Woods* [1982]). For the moment, gay fiction seemed to be in very good health.

Plante's spare prose deals with an adolescent boy's coming to terms with his sexuality within a Franco-American culture. Of the three others, Holleran's is the most lyrical, a whirlwind tour of New York gay life featuring the unquenchable monologist, Sutherland. As the title (from Yeats's "Among School Children") suggests, the novel asks, how can you tell the gay man from the world he moves in? Does it totally define him? Kramer's novel is far earthier, as the obnoxious title makes clear, a subterranean tour of some of the same territory as *Dancer.* White's *Noc-*

turnes is the most interesting technically, a meditative series of images in the vocative case, an apologia addressed by a young man to the older lover he has left.

Plante is an expatriate New Englander; the other three writers were then very much identified with the New York scene. Holleran and White were among the seven members of a short-lived but productive literary group in the early 1980s called the VIOLET QUILL. Other novelists in the Violet Quill included Felice Picano, ROBERT FERRO, and George Whitmore.

The situation in England from roughly 1950 to 1980 seems less defined, more diffuse. There was no crystallizing moment such as Stonewall there, and the nation had grudgingly legalized homosexuality in 1967. The novels of ANGUS WILSON (*Hemlock and After* [1952] and others) and Iris Murdoch (*The Bell* [1955] and others) are rife with homosexual characters, but there is little inwardness of presentation. The homosexuality seems a construct, a way of investigating the social and ethical behavior of other characters, or of creating revealing situations.

In English novels of the period, homosexuality seems linked to certain institutions, particularly—and unsurprisingly—the school and the army. Such places demand uniformity in more than just garb, and in them the fate of the different or sensitive individual is highlighted. Examples (besides *The Charioteer,* already mentioned) include Simon Raven's *Fielding Gray* (1967) and Michael Campbell's *Lord Dismiss Us* (1967), both school novels; Susan Hill's *Strange Meeting* (1971) and Jennifer Johnston's *How Many Miles to Babylon?* (1971), both set in World War I; and Robin Maugham's account of the military and sexual struggles of General Gordon at Khartoum, *The Last Encounter* (1974). Also set in World War I, and carrying strange homosexual undertones, is *The Wars* (1977) by the Canadian writer Timothy Findley.

Then came AIDS. "The paradox is," Edmund White wrote in 1991,

> that AIDS which destroyed so many of these distinguished writers [in the Violet Quill circle], has also, as a phenomenon, made homosexuality a much more familiar part of the American landscape. The grotesque irony is that at the very moment so many writers are threatened with extinction, gay literature is healthy and flourishing as never before.

The tragic impact of AIDS on a generation and more of artists can hardly be overestimated; no writer can practice his craft today without taking account of it, whether in acceptance or in defiance, in sorrow or in anger. Yet White is correct in asserting the health of gay literature: He himself has published two more novels, *A Boy's Own Story* (1982) and *The Beautiful Room Is Empty* (1988) along with a considerable body of criticism; Maupin continued the *Tales* series; Andrew Holleran published a second novel, *Nights in Aruba* (1985). Given the uniquely personal nature of the AIDS crisis, it is not surprising to find works that hover between fiction and memoir, as in the writing of PAUL MONETTE.

New talents also emerged in the 1980s. DAVID LEAVITT, to take only one luminous example, published a collection of short stories, *Family Dancing,* in 1985, and a novel, *The Lost Language of Cranes,* in 1986. *Cranes* is an exemplary work because it deals with so many aspects of gay life: a father and son, Owen and Philip Benjamin, are both gay; Owen, closeted, guilty, seeking only anonymous sex in movie houses, seems to belong in a novel of the 1950s; his son is a young man of the 1980s, comfortable in his sexuality but as the novel opens uncomfortable at not having come out to his parents. Rose Benjamin, wife and mother, feels that she has been living in a travesty of a family when the various truths do emerge. The novel handles the well-worn theme of failure to communicate in fresh and perceptive ways, as well as portraying strategies gay men adopt for living in straight society.

Other writers of distinction who have emerged since about 1980 include Charles Nelson (*The Boy Who Picked the Bullets Up* [1981]), Robert Glück (*Jack the Modernist* [1985]), Michael Cunningham (*A Home at the End of the World* [1990]), Melvin Dixon (*Trouble the Waters* [1989] and *Vanishing Rooms* [1991]), Stephen McCauley (*The Easy Way Out* [1993]), and Louis Begley (*As Max Saw It* [1994]). English writers include David Rees (*In the Tent* [1979] and other titles), PATRICK GALE (*Kansas in August* [1988]), Alan Hollinghurst (*The Swimming-Pool Library* [1988]), NEIL BARTLETT (*Ready to Catch Him Should He Fall* [1990]), and ADAM MARS-JONES (*The Waters of Thirst* [1994]).

Gay novels, like many other novels, are about a search for identity. Just as Tom Jones and Tristram Shandy need to discover who they are in order to live and function in their society, so do protagonists of gay novels. The difference is that early gay fiction presents situations in which the protagonist refuses to admit who or what he is, or, having acknowledged his sexuality, finds that his IDENTITY is repugnant to society at large.

Not until Stonewall and the gay liberation movement of the 1970s did gays achieve sufficient critical mass to establish, in urban centers like San Francisco, New York, and London, islands of gay culture (gay ghettos, in a less favorable view) where gay art might thrive. In such art, a gay identity, whether defined by exclusion or as related to the larger culture, might be realized. Then came AIDS to attack the entire effort; once more homosexuality and death became identified, in tragic, not symbolic, terms.

Gay identity has other implications for the writers. Many dislike being identified as "gay writers"; some accept the label with greater or lesser reluctance; others sidestep it. The Australian Nobelist PATRICK WHITE, with becoming modesty, attributed all the insights that made him a great writer to his homosexuality, yet until his last novel, *The Twyborn Affair* (1979), any possibly homosexual themes or characters in his fiction were artfully camouflaged. Still, now is an exciting time to be a gay writer. A widespread acceptance of homosexuality coexists with manifest homophobia. How the gay novel will deal with this condition is a question continually being answered.

—*Michael N. Stanton*

BIBLIOGRAPHY

Adams, Stephen. *The Homosexual Hero in Contemporary Fiction.* New York: Harper & Row, 1980. ■ Austen, Roger. *Playing the Game: The Homosexual Novel in America.* Indianapolis: Bobbs, Merrill, 1977. ■ Levin, James. *The Gay Novel in America.* New York: Garland, 1991. ■ Lilly, Mark. *Gay Men's Literature in the Twentieth Century.* New York: New York University Press, 1993. ■ Summers, Claude. *Gay Fictions: Wilde to Stonewall.* New York: Continuum, 1990. ■ White, Edmund. "Out of the Closet, Onto the Bookshelf," *New York Times Book Review* (June 16, 1991): 22, 24, 35.

§ *The Novel: Lesbian*

From the great modernist writers of the 1920s and 1930s to the pulp writers of the 1950s to the lesbian writers of today, lesbian novelists have had a powerful impact on the lesbian community. Not only do lesbian novels define and redefine what it means to be a lesbian in our society, they provide an important record of changing cultural attitudes toward lesbianism. By depicting different versions of the lesbian experience, the lesbian novel enriches and enhances lesbian culture. More broadly, lesbian novels, by questioning gender norms, debating what it means to be a woman in our society, and questioning dominant values, have not only depicted the lesbian community but also helped to constitute it.

Exactly what features make a novel "lesbian" are difficult to specify. Critics have different ideas about how to define the lesbian novel, but most agree on two points: The author must be a lesbian, and the central character or characters must be lesbians. Using this definition, novels that contain central lesbian characters but were written by men, such as HENRY JAMES's *The Bostonians* (1886) or Compton Mackenzie's *Extraordinary Women* (1928), fail to qualify as lesbian novels. Moreover, novels with a significant lesbian content but written by heterosexual women, such as Mary McCarthy's *The Group* (1963), do not qualify as lesbian novels. As important as authorship in defining the lesbian novel is audience reception; although the audience does not have to be exclusively lesbian, the book should have particular appeal for lesbians. Numerous lesbian novels, such as VIRGINIA WOOLF's *Orlando* (1928), RITA MAE BROWN's *Rubyfruit Jungle* (1973), and JEANETTE WINTERSON's *Oranges Are Not the Only Fruit* (1987), attract many heterosexual as well as homosexual readers. The lesbian novel may contain lesbianism in either an overt or covert fashion. A number of important lesbian writers, such as WILLA CATHER, GERTRUDE STEIN, and Virginia Woolf, do not explicitly refer to lesbianism in their novels; still, these writers do create lesbian subtexts in their work. Ultimately, all that can be said with certainty about the lesbian novel is that it is a genre that resists firm categorization since there is no single definition.

A thorough discussion of all important lesbian novels is beyond the scope of this brief essay, but I shall at least mention many of the most significant lesbian novels of the twentieth century. No study of the lesbian novel can be complete without citing RADCLYFFE HALL's *The Well of Loneliness* (1928), a novel that, as Bonnie Zimmerman has noted, has helped define lesbianism in this century. It was the first novel written by a lesbian that talked openly about homosexuality. Stephen Gordon, the novel's handsome, aristocratic lesbian heroine, was a role model that lesbians strove to emulate for over fifty years. Countless women identified with Stephen's struggle to be a lesbian during a period when homosexuals were considered abnormal and mentally disturbed. When it was published, Hall's book, which was banned as obscene in England, caused a scandal because it endorsed the view that lesbians should have a place in society and not be shunned as social pariahs. Despite Hall's positive portrayal of lesbianism, her work has had ambivalent responses from lesbian readers. Although some of them praise Hall's novel for its unconcealed depiction of lesbian relationships, others condemn it for Hall's adherence to an essentialist belief—first made popular by the late nineteenth-century sexologist Richard von Krafft-Ebing—that lesbians and lesbian mannerisms are the products of congenital "inversion." Some lesbian readers are critical of Hall's angst-filled narrative and of her masculinist bias; they argue that *The Well of Loneliness* does not present lesbianism positively. Whether or not we accept Hall's ideology, however, we can still respect Hall's courage in depicting lesbianism openly. We can also appreciate that Hall's novel helped innumerable lesbians discover that they were not alone. Even today, we can admire the characterization of Stephen Gordon, who remains one of the most fully developed heroines in lesbian fiction.

Not all lesbian novelists in the interwar period felt comfortable talking openly about lesbianism in their writing, particularly since blatant lesbianism could result in getting a novel banned or discouraging its publication. These writers frequently disguised the lesbian content of their work. Instead of the straightforward realistic depiction of lesbianism in Radclyffe Hall's novel, DJUNA BARNES's *Nightwood* (1936), for example, presents a very different image of lesbianism. Throughout this surreal modernist novel, lesbianism is a topic just below the surface. One of the characters, Frau Mann, is called "the property of no man." Two other characters, Nora Flood and Robin Vote, fall in love, and their tumultuous relationship is the focus of much of the convoluted narrative. Like *Nightwood*, Virginia Woolf's *Orlando: A Biography* (1928) also explores gender and sexual identification, but in a text that revolves around the adventures of Orlando, a thinly disguised version of Woolf's lover VITA SACK-VILLE-WEST. Orlando transforms from male to female throughout a number of centuries. Although less phantasmagorical than *Orlando*, Gertrude Stein's *The Autobiography of Alice B. Toklas* (1933) is also a fantastic tale, wherein Stein, under the alias of Toklas, writes the supposed autobiography of her lover, describing her life with Stein. These three novels show how modern writers resorted to nonrealistic, often fantastic, story lines in order to make lesbianism a more acceptable subject to discuss.

By the 1950s, PATRICIA HIGHSMITH had returned to the realism of Radclyffe Hall. In *The Price of Salt*, published under the pseudonym "Claire Morgan" in 1952, Highsmith shows lesbians not as mannish women or helpless neurotics—as they were commonly portrayed—but as women who can easily blend into a heterosexual crowd. Therese Belivet, a young artist living in New York City, falls in love with Carol Aird, a wealthy woman separated from her husband and living with her daughter. Throughout the novel, the two women gradually become closer and ultimately begin a sexual relationship, which is fulfilling for both of them. Their blossoming relationship, however, seems destined to end when the women learn that Carol's former husband has had them followed and threatens to use his information about his ex-wife's new affair to gain custody of their daughter. Faced with the need to choose between her daughter and her new lover, Carol decides to go to her lover—a truly radical decision for the 1950s. What is even more unusual about *The Price of Salt* is that insanity and suicide, which were the necessary complements of lesbianism in most 1950s popular fiction, never appear. Indeed, the lesbian relationship in this novel actually appears to be superior to the heterosexual relationships in the text; as Carol comments, "the rapport between two men or two women can be absolute and perfect, as it can never be between man and woman." Because of Highsmith's sensitivity to lesbianism and her creation of a lesbian novel in which lesbianism is not doomed to failure, her work continues to be read in the 1990s.

In sharp contrast to the portrayal of lesbianism in Highsmith's novel, the hundreds of lesbian pulp novels published in the 1950s and early 1960s, the "Golden Age" of the pulps, typically are chock-full of madness, suicide, adultery, and even incest. Despite their sensationalistic contents, these novels, sold at bus stops and drugstores and directed largely at a heterosexual audience, also gained wide popularity with lesbians. Bonnie Zimmerman writes, "These pulp paperbacks were crucial to the lesbian culture of the 1950s because they offered proof of lesbian existence." For many lesbians, the pulps were one of the few sources of affirmation. Although some of the novels read more like a male fantasy of what it means to be a lesbian, the better ones, particularly those written by ANN BANNON, provide a sensitive and tolerant image of the difficulties confronting lesbian women in the 1950s and early 1960s. Lesbian pulp writers, such as Ann Aldrich, Ann Bannon, Randy Salem, and Valerie Taylor, showed in their fiction that social prejudice against lesbians was morally wrong. They also suggested that lesbians were driven to insanity or death because of the society around them that condemned them as abnormal, not because they were inherently psychologically disturbed. For the period, this was an unusual and refreshing message.

Along with the prevalent pulps, there were also some notable lesbian novels written in the 1960s. JANE RULE published *Desert of the Heart* in 1964. Critic Gillian Spraggs calls Rule's novel "a book that challenged a wilderness of silence and malice." Set in Reno, Nevada, the story focuses on the relationship between Evelyn, a professor of English literature, and Ann, a change girl at a Reno casino, who is also a successful cartoonist. Evelyn is just getting a divorce from her husband of many years because of their incompatibility; in this fashion, Rule points out that heterosexual relationships are not always superior to homosexual ones. Surprisingly enough, at the end of the novel, Evelyn and Ann are still together and planning to establish a life with each other. Rule refuses to accept the commonly held assumption that homosexual relationships are doomed to be fleeting. Other writers in the 1960s, like ISABEL MILLER in *A Place for Us* (1969; later renamed *Patience and Sarah*) and MAY SARTON in *Mrs. Stevens Hears the Mermaids Singing* (1965), also explored lesbian relationships and the social forces that made them difficult to maintain for long periods. In her historical novel set in Calvinist New England, Miller attempts to imagine a lesbian relationship in the absence of a lesbian subculture.

Like Rule, Miller, and Sarton, MAUREEN DUFFY, a British author whose writing reflects a working-class sensibility, was one of the novelists of the 1960s who tried to portray lesbian experience in her work, which includes novels, plays, nonfiction, and poetry. She is the first contemporary British lesbian novelist publicly to announce her sexual identification. *The Microcosm* (1966), which is one of Duffy's most important works, centers on lesbianism. Like other lesbian novels that focus on the community found at a lesbian bar (for instance, Nisa Donnelly's *The Bar Stories* [1989] and Katherine Forrest's *Murder at the Nightwood Bar* [1987]), Duffy's work describes the bar microcosm that has played such a significant role in the lives of many lesbians. Like writers such as Djuna Barnes and Gertrude Stein, Duffy experiments with language and tries out different points of view. Like Barnes, Duffy also plays with gender; we are not sure, for instance, whether "he" refers to an anatomical male or to a butch lesbian. Criticized by some lesbian critics for her Freudian views of lesbianism, Duffy nevertheless deserves serious attention since her depictions of lesbian life go far beyond what is contained in Freud's theories.

In the early 1970s, a novel was published that had a profound and lasting effect on future lesbian literature. Without a doubt, Rita Mae Brown's *Rubyfruit Jungle* (1973) is one of the most influential and best-known of all lesbian novels. Brown's popular *Bildungsroman*, which was first published by the feminist press Daughters Inc. and then by Bantam Books, has remained in print for over twenty years. *Rubyfruit Jungle* caused a sensation because of its positively portrayed lesbian heroine, Molly Bolt. Despite her illegitimate birth and her impoverished background, Molly, thanks to her superior intelligence and strength of character, wins a full scholarship to the University of Florida. Even when she is a child, Molly knows that she never wants to get married and assumes that she is a lesbian. In college, she begins to experience lesbian life and has an affair with another woman student. When she is expelled from school because she is a lesbian, Molly heads to New York City where she studies to be a film director. This novel is a coming out story that traces Molly's maturation as an individual and, particularly, as a lesbian. Brown's ebullient, often farcical, picaresque account of a lesbian coming of age showed that lesbianism did not mean that a woman would necessarily be confined to an insane asylum or commit suicide. Instead, Molly is a survivor who manages to overcome tremendous obstacles.

The remarkable success of *Rubyfruit Jungle* spawned an explosion of lesbian novels. A number of feminist publishers, including Naiad Press, Daughters Press, Diana Press, and the Women's Press Collective, jumped onto the bandwagon, as did publishers such as Crossing Press and Seal Press that were not solely lesbian publishers but did publish lesbian literature. These feminist presses were particularly important because they published nontraditional or experimental narratives, such as June Arnold's *Sister Gin* (1975), BERTHA HARRIS's *Lover* (1976), and ELANA DYKEWOMON's *Riverfinger Women* (1974), that were not acceptable to the major publishing companies. Even more presses publishing lesbian novels sprang up in the 1980s, and it became more common for the mainstream publishing houses to produce lesbian novels. For example, Dutton published SARAH SCHULMAN's *After Delores,* Knopf published LISA ALTHER's *Other Women* (1984), and St. Martin's Press published Nisa Donnelly's *The Bar Stories: A Novel After All* (1989). Today, in the 1990s, the increasing number of publishers willing to produce lesbian novels has resulted in far greater diversity, the new offerings ranging from murder mysteries to romances to more experimental genres. (See also JOURNALISM AND PUBLISHING.)

Unfortunately, even these more recent novels have only rarely addressed the complex concerns of lesbians of color. Finding lesbian novels that address the concerns of nonwhite lesbians is difficult, and always has been so, particularly before the 1980s. ANN ALLEN SHOCKLEY is the only novelist who focused on black lesbian lives and reached a broad audience before the 1980s. In *Loving Her* (1974), an account of an interracial love affair, and her other novels, Shockley explores with sensitivity the difficulties facing African-American lesbians. A few other writers, the most notable being AUDRE LORDE, also explored the situation of African-American lesbians. In her "biomythography" *Zami: A New Spelling of My Name* (1982), Lorde wrote one of the most memorable accounts of what it means to be black and lesbian in the United States. Lesbian writers with a Native-American background are even less common than African-American writers. An important exception is PAULA GUNN ALLEN. In her novel *The Woman Who Owned the Shadows* (1983), Gunn describes the experience of a Native-American lesbian. Her myth-laden, symbolic writing places Gunn among the many contemporary lesbian novelists who are trying to stretch language's meaning.

While some authors have explored the present or past in order to discuss lesbians' experiences, other novelists have looked into the mythical future in order to understand lesbian lives. Since some writers would argue that lesbian experience can never be portrayed in the context of a patriarchal society, they have tried in their fiction to redesign the world. Certainly the best-known novels to reenvision a different lesbian future are MONIQUE WITTIG's. In *The Lesbian Body* (1975), the author explores how a phallocentric society has limited the ways in which we view lesbianism. Using experimental prose that works to redefine the way we perceive the lesbian subject, Wittig creates a lesbian world in which the conventions of a patriarchal society no longer apply. Other novels depicting alternative lesbian realities followed Wittig's work, most notably JOANNA RUSS's *The Female Man* (1975) and Sally Gearhart's *The Wanderground* (1978). These texts help reenvision how lesbian (and heterosexual) society should be constructed. By showing communities where lesbianism is central rather than marginal, these novels suggest that society need not be based on heterosexuality.

Contemporary lesbian writers frequently explore more conventional genres than the utopian novel, revitalizing formula fiction like the romance, mystery, and detective novel to make it reflect the realities of lesbian life. In the 1980s and 1990s, one of the most popular genres of the lesbian novel has been the detective story. Authors as diverse as Katherine Forrest, Camarin Grae, Vicki McConnell, Claire McNab, Diana McRae, Jaye Maiman, Mary Morell, Sarah Schulman, Pat Welch, Barbara Wilson, and Mary Wings, as well as many others, have written detective stories that focus on lesbians and lesbian culture. The detective genre has obtained wide popularity in the lesbian community because it explores notions, such as passing for heterosexual, that are essential features of the lesbian world. The lesbian detectives in these novels, whether they are as official as Kate Delafield, a member of the LAPD homicide squad or as unofficial as Emma Victor, who works for a women's hotline, explore what it means to negotiate the division between heterosexual and homosexual. The novels themselves often explore the meaning of lesbian experience as much as they dwell on the mystery that needs to be solved. Delafield, for instance, in *Murder at the Nightwood Bar,* must deal with how she is perceived as heterosexual at her job, but as homosexual when she enters a lesbian bar: "She felt stripped of her gray gabardine pants and jacket, her conservative cloak of invisibility in the conventional world. In here she was fully exposed against her natural background."

As well as being an arena to explore lesbian identity, the detective novel has also been a space to explore variations in style. Mary Wings, for instance, in *She Came Too Late* (1987) uses the hard-boiled style made famous by Raymond Chandler. Sarah Schulman, influenced by post-modern theories, is only one of many contemporary lesbian writers who attempted to create a more experimental lesbian prose in the 1980s. On the surface, many of Schulman's novels, such as *The Sophie Horowitz Story* (1984) and *After Delores* (1988), are detective stories, but they are also texts that are just as concerned about exploring the meaning of identity as they are in solving a crime. Schulman's *Girls, Visions and Everything* (1986), although not a crime novel, still has the gritty, urban background of Shulman's other stories. In this book, Schulman explores the streets and alleys of New York City through the character of Lila Futuransky, a poor Jewish lesbian. Although the story focuses on Lila's romance with Emily, it also explores what it means to view culture from a lesbian perspective, as does Schulman's most recent novel, *Empathy* (1992). (See also MYSTERY FICTION, LESBIAN.)

Like Schulman, Jeanette Winterson tries to expand the limits of the traditional lesbian novel. Winterson's first novel, *Oranges Are Not the Only Fruit* (1985), is definitely a lesbian success story; the book even became a BBC television production in 1990.

Winterson's hilarious but poignant work focuses on the coming of age of a young lesbian, Jeanette, in an evangelical household in the industrial midlands of England. Artistically, the novel is a brilliant success. Critic Hilary Hinds especially notes its "fluidity, its ability to cut across so many critical and cultural categories and positions, its refusal to be pigeonholed as one sort of text or another . . . ." In her later novels, *The Passion* (1987), *Sexing the Cherry* (1989), and *Written on the Body* (1992), Winterson continues to show that she is what critic Terry Castle calls "the reigning mistress of postmodern lesbian drollery."

There are many other important lesbian novelists in the 1990s, including Paula Martinac and DOROTHY ALLISON. In *Home Movies* (1993), Martinac explores how a lesbian understands the death of her uncle from AIDS. Allison, too, is concerned with addressing social issues in her novel *Bastard Out of Carolina* (1992), which discusses poverty and child abuse in the South. Martinac and Allison are only two of the many contemporary lesbian novelists who use the novel as a forum for social critique. Schulman, Winterson, Martinac, Allison, and other lesbian writers seek to redefine the lesbian novel in the 1990s and beyond. We can await the results with great anticipation.

—*Sherrie A. Inness*

BIBLIOGRAPHY

Castle, Terry. *The Apparitional Lesbian: Female Homosexuality and Modern Culture.* New York: Columbia University Press, 1993. ■ Hinds, Hilary. "Oranges Are Not the Only Fruit: Reaching Audiences Other Lesbian Texts Cannot Reach." *New Lesbian Criticism: Literary and Cultural Readings.* Sally Munt, ed. New York: Columbia University Press, 1992. 153–172. ■ Jay, Karla and Joanne Glasgow, eds. *Lesbian Texts and Contexts: Radical Revisions.* New York: New York University Press, 1990. ■ Spraggs, Gillian. "Hell and the Mirror: A Reading of *Desert of the Heart.*" *New Lesbian Criticism: Literary and Cultural Readings.* Sally Munt, ed. New York: Columbia University Press, 1992. 115–131. ■ Stimpson, Catharine. "Zero Degree Deviancy: The Lesbian Novel in English." *Critical Inquiry* 8.2 (Winter 1981): 363–379. ■ Zimmerman, Bonnie. *The Safe Sea of Women: Lesbian Fiction 1969-1989.* Boston: Beacon, 1990.

O'Hara, Frank
(1926–1966)

Frank O'Hara was born in Baltimore on June 27, 1926. In 1927, his family moved to Grafton, Massachusetts, and O'Hara was educated in private schools until 1944. He served a two-year tour of duty in the Navy before beginning college at Harvard as a music major. He eventually changed his major to English and graduated with a B.A. in 1950; he completed an M.A. from the University of Michigan in 1951. O'Hara began writing in earnest while at Michigan; he won the university's Hopwood Award in Creative Writing and wrote two plays, *Try! Try!* and *Change Your Bedding,* that were mounted at the Poet's Theatre in Cambridge.

On graduation, O'Hara assumed a position at the Museum of Modern Art (MOMA) in New York. He left for a two-year period in 1953 to 1955 to assume an associate editorship of *Art News* and then returned to MOMA as a special assistant to the International Program. In 1960, he was promoted to curator of paintings and sculptures. O'Hara's career as a poet is intricately interwoven with his life in the art world; indeed, O'Hara is often thought of as one of the major art critics of the late 1950s and early 1960s. In 1959, he published a study of Jackson Pollock for George Braziller's Great American Artists Series, which is frequently considered to be *the* canonical study of Pollock. O'Hara also published studies of contemporary Spanish art, Robert Motherwell, David Smith, and Nakian.

The influence of art is everywhere in O'Hara's writings. His first major volume of poetry, *A City Winter and Other Poems* (1952), was published by the Tibor de Nagy Gallery. Its poems demonstrate a preoccupation with surrealism and with dadaist collage and montage techniques. Two of O'Hara's texts specifically work as collaboration with artists: *Stones* (1958) is a series of lithographs by Larry Rivers combined with poems by O'Hara; *Odes* (1960) was illustrated by serigraphs by Mike Goldberg. O'Hara also participated in the growing avant-garde film culture of New York, and coproduced two experimental films with Al Leslie, *The Last Clean Shirt* (1963) and *Philosophy in the Bedroom* (1965).

One of O'Hara's most important poetic innovations was an allegiance to popular culture. Although his poems are structured by the elite concerns of art, his subjects and images are frequently drawn from the world of urban gay male culture. "The Day Lady Died," one of O'Hara's most famous poems, tells of the moment he heard that Billie Holiday had passed away. The title itself puns on Holiday's popular nickname, Lady Day. "Biotherm (For Bill Berkson)," one of the major collage poems of O'Hara, combines, among other things, images of Fire Island, classic Hollywood cinema, and restaurant menus. Biotherm itself was the brand name of a popular sunscreen.

O'Hara died on July 25, 1966, when he was struck by a dune buggy on Fire Island. His death was untimely, but his influence on gay poetry is undeniable. Among the poets who acknowledge a direct debt to O'Hara's stylistic innovations are JOHN ASHBERY, Kenneth Koch, NED ROREM, ROBERT DUNCAN, and ALLEN GINSBERG.

—*Gregory W. Bredbeck*

BIBLIOGRAPHY

Altieri, Charles. "The Significance of Frank O'Hara." *Iowa Review,* 4 (Winter 1973): 90–104. ■ Berkson, Bill and Joe LeSueur, eds. *Homage to Frank O'Hara.* Bolinas, Calif.: Big Sky, 1988. ■ Bredbeck, Gregory W. "B/O ---- Barthes's Text/O'Hara's Trick." *PMLA* 108 (1993): 268–282. ■ Elledge, Jim, ed. *Frank O'Hara: To Be True to a City.* Ann Arbor: University of Michigan Press, 1990. ■ Gooch, Brad. *City Poet: The Life and Times of Frank O'Hara.* New York: Knopf, 1993. ■ Holahan, Susan. "Frank O'Hara's Poetry." *American Poetry Since 1960: Some Critical Perspectives.* Robert B. Shaw, ed. Cheadle Hulme: Carcanet Press, 1973. 109–122. ■ Perloff, Marjorie. *Frank O'Hara: Poet Among Painters.* Austin: University of Texas Press, 1977.

Opera

Although Hildegard of Bingen (1098–1179) and her community of nuns are now thought to have created the first musical drama, *Ordo Virtutum (The Play of the Virtues,* 1158), the art form we know today as opera developed in seventeenth-century Venice, where a large public audience and the patronage of wealthy aristocratic families encouraged its popular proliferation. We cannot know with certainty whether individual members of l'Accademia degli Incogniti (the Academy of the Anonymous) who worked behind the scenes to promote this new genre were in fact homosexuals, but their artistic and intel-lectual presuppositions made opera a particularly friendly forum for homoerotic representations. The members of the Accademia were anticlerical, pro-Aristotelean, and devoted to cultural debate; they challenged the prevailing dogma that a single point of view was applicable to the multifaceted society of Venice. Opera, therefore, dramatized for them a multiplicity of perspectives, the superiority of the here and now, and the centrality of human love and passion. Accordingly, operas such as Francesco Cavalli's *La Callisto* (1651), Giacomo Castoreo's *Pericle Effeminato (Pericles Effeminate,* 1653), and Aurelio Aureli's *Alcibiade*

(1680), all denounced by the enemies of the Accademia as "decadent," presented Greco-Roman narratives of male and female homosexual desire and gender role subversion, often thinly disguised as tales for moral "edification," through the means of cross-dressed performers.

Claudio Monteverdi (1567–1643), the most famous member of the Accademia, was responsible, through the development of *stile rappresentativo* (representative style), for operatic constructions of madness and desire. Accordingly, both male and female characters could be portrayed as losing control of reason through anger, passion, grief, or love, as the titles of such operas as Monteverdi's *La Finta Pazza Licori* (*Licori, the False Madwoman*), Vivaldi's *Orlando Furioso* (*Orlando Enraged*), Cavalli's *Amore Innamorato* (*Eros Enamoured*), and Ferrari's *La Maga Fulminata* (*The Fulminating Sorceress*) indicate. Such earlier operas, which have recently enjoyed revival in the wake of contemporary feminist, gay, and lesbian movements, are notable for the sexual and gender ambiguity of their casting. For example, the title role of Monteverdi's *La Favola d'Orfeo* (*The Fable of Orpheus*, 1607) can be sung either by a tenor or a soprano. His even more daring *L'incoronazione di Poppea* (*The Coronation of Poppea*, 1643) portrays Poppea, a highly skilled Roman courtesan, employing her vocal eloquence and rhetorical prowess to scheme her way into power as Empress. The characters of Ottone, her former lover, and Nero are soprano roles for male *castrato* or female soprano. Arnalta, Poppea's nurse, has traditionally been sung by a male tenor *en travesti* (in drag); "her" moment of glory in the opera comes with Poppea's marriage to Nero, an aria in which the nurse triumphs in having been born a slave but dying a lady, the recipient of society's flattery and praise.

As opera grew in popularity throughout the eighteenth century, many of the heroic leading roles were composed for *castrati*. At that time, boys with outstanding voices were often surgically castrated prior to puberty in order to retain their soprano or contralto *tessaturas,* and the *castrato* voice became famous for its power and otherworldly beauty. Although of dubious legality, this practice was tolerated and even encouraged by the Roman Catholic Church in light of St. Paul's injunction that women should remain silent in church. Many of the *castrati,* who adopted exotic stage names such as Senesino, Farinelli, and Caffarelli, were extremely popular figures capable of inciting audiences to heights of feverish rapture and abandon. George Frederic Handel (1685–1759), himself probably homosexual, not only created many roles for *castrati* but also developed the Venetian opera's preoccupations with gender ambiguity. Throughout an intrigue-filled, dramatic career in opera replete with spectacular successes and abject failures, Handel composed such works as *Giulio Cesare* (1724), whose lead role, as well as three others for both male and female characters, were composed for *castrati,* and *Alcina* (1735), which concerns the attempts of the pagan sorceress Alcina to subvert the virtue of the exemplary Christian knight Orlando. *Serse* (1738), one of Handel's finest operas, dramatizes, through an elaborate series of star-crossed and cross-dressed loves, the immensely complicated plottings of the rivalries of King Xerxes and his brother Arsemenes (sung by a female mezzo-soprano) for the love of Romilda, whose sister Atalanta is secretly in love with Arsemenes.

Although the *castrati* remained an important factor in opera until the early nineteenth century, the gradual suppression of the practice for humane reasons caused a shift in the casting of heroic male roles, as well as those of adolescent boys, to female mezzo-sopranos, resulting in what has become known as *travesti* or "trouser" roles. For example, Christoph Willibald Gluck (1714–1787) originally wrote the male lead of *Orfeo ed Euridice* (1762) for the famous *castrato* Gaetano Guadagni; when the opera was revived by Hector Berlioz in 1859, however, Orfeo was sung by the mezzo-soprano Pauline Viardot, one of the most acclaimed singers of her day. Moreover, subsequent opera composers such as Wolfgang Amadeus Mozart (1756–1791), Gioacchino Antonio Rossini (1792–1868), and Vincenzo Bellini (1801–1835) made further artistic developments in the portrayal of *travesti* roles as well as, in the case of Bellini, the representation of female ROMANTIC FRIENDSHIP. Mozart's famous opera *Le Nozze di Figaro* (*The Marriage of Figaro*, 1786), takes the occasion of the passing away of the *droit du seigneur* (the feudal right of the lord to spend the wedding night with the bride of any man under his rule) to explore the subversive pleasures of female–female love. Cherubino, played by a mezzo-soprano, is the womanizing page of Countess Almaviva; while madly in love with the Countess, "he" seduces Barbarina, the gardener's daughter. Cherubino sings an impassioned aria, "Non so piu," in which he proclaims "Every woman makes me change color, every woman makes me tremble." This character type later reappears as Oktavian in Richard Strauss's *fin-de-siècle* opera *Der Rosenkavalier* (1911), which makes the lesbian eroticism implicit in *Le Nozze* even more apparent. Other Mozart operas, notably *La Finta Giardiniera* (*The Fake Garden Girl*, 1774) and *La Clemenza di Tito* (*The Clemency of Titus,* 1791) feature *travesti* roles for women, which became particularly popular in French opera. Subsequent trouser roles of note include Siebel in Charles Gounod's *Faust* (1859), Count Orlovsky in Johann Strauss's *Die Fledermaus* (1874), and Nicklausse in Jacques Offenbach's *Les Contes d'Hoffmann* (1881).

In contrast to Mozart's operas, however, in which the female *travesti* roles are comic, Rossini's female trouser roles (or, more accurately, armor roles) are typically heroic and serious figures. This development indicates Rossini's purposeful reassignment of roles (for example, the title role in *Tancredi* [1813], Malcolm in *La Donna del Lago* [*The Lady of the Lake*, 1819], and Calbo in *Maometto II* [1820]) once the exclusive property of *castrati*, to women, who perform such actions as fighting duels, leading armies to victory, and rescuing and romancing the soprano heroines. The "armor role" reaches its most spectacular development, however, in *Semiramide* (1823), the plot of which would defy even the most ingenious Freudian interpretation. The soprano, Queen Semiramide, falls madly in love with the mezzo-soprano Arsace, commander of her army and, unknown to her, her long-lost son. At the same time, Arsace is in love with the soprano, Princess Azema, and seeks vengeance for the murder of "his" father, who was killed, not coincidentally, by Semiramide. Bellini, however, deployed his far more developed *travesti* roles to more romantic ends. His *I Capuleti e I Montecchi* (1830) features a mezzo in the role of Romeo in this moving adaptation of the story of SHAKESPEARE's star-crossed lovers. Moreover, in *Norma* (1831), romantic friendship between two women is given one of opera's most eloquent and impassioned expressions. In the rapturous duet "Mira, o Norma" ("Look, Norma"), Adalgisa and Norma, who had once been rivals for the love of the same man, swear their eternal loyalty and love to each other, concluding "With you I shall set my face firmly against the shame which fate may bring, as long as I feel your heart beating next to mine."

Nineteenth-century opera witnessed an emphasis on heterosexual and family romance, as well as extensive development of distinctive national traditions. Giuseppi Verdi (1813–1901), whose operas consistently link the realms of private romance and public politics, can be seen as combining the strengths of both eighteenth- and nineteenth-century opera. Through this juxtaposition, male homoerotic subtexts can be discerned in works such as *Un Ballo in Maschera* (*A Masked Ball,* 1859) and *Don Carlo* (1867). *Un Ballo in Maschera* is based on a historical event, the assassination of King Gustavus III of Sweden, but due to political censorship that forbade the representation of regicide on stage, Verdi set the opera in the improba-

ble location of colonial Boston. Although Gustavus was, in fact, homosexual and assassinated for purely political reasons, the opera presents him as involved in a clandestine, albeit ostensibly chaste, liaison with the wife of one of his ministers and posits this affair as the motive for his murder. Although the King's sexuality is thus erased, homosexuality reappears obliquely through one of the more unique uses of a trouser role. The King enjoys a playful camaraderie, presented as a flirtation in some productions, with his page Oscar; but since this role is played by a coloratura soprano, the relationship between them is rendered ambiguous. *Don Carlo* (1867) is likewise based on historical characters, particularly Don Carlos, the Crown Prince of Spain, and his father King Philip II. The only purely fictional character in the plot is the Prince's friend, Roderigo, who selflessly sacrifices his life for the other man. Both men are involved in a political plot against the King, but Roderigo is clearly motivated by his unrequited love for Don Carlos. Their duet, "Dio, che nell'alma infondere" (God, who has filled our souls), is a vow of mutual fealty and love comparable to that of Norma and Adalgisa.

Richard Wagner's *Parsifal* (1882) represents an elaborate development of the themes of male homosocial bonding and homosexual desire, couched in a complex Christian and mythological allegory of sin and redemption. In the opera, Amfortas, King of the Holy Grail, suffers from a wound that will not heal, inflicted when he succumbs to the temptations of Kundry, who has been urged on by the jealous and self-castrated Klingsor. Gurnemanz, the wise elder of the all-male community of knights, prophesies that only a "pure fool" can heal the King, and such a figure enters in the character of Parsifal. By overcoming Kundry's attempted seduction, he regains the sacred spear, which caused Amfortas's wound and was lost to the brotherhood, from Klingsor. The spear transmutes from an instrument of war to a symbol of reconciliation and healing. Parsifal baptizes Kundry, who then dies, and the opera ends with the circle of men united in brotherhood and equality.

The early twentieth century witnessed the creation of new modes of gay and lesbian representation, beginning with the antibourgeois *fin-de-siècle* aesthetics evident in Richard Strauss's *Salomé* (1905) and *Elektra* (1909), and Alban Berg's *Lulu* (1937), all of which deal quite explicitly with sexuality in a manner openly defiant of censorship and societal norms. *Salomé,* the libretto of which is a German translation of OSCAR WILDE's play, pits Judeo-Christian morality against unbridled "pagan" lust in the confrontation between the prophet Jokanaan (John the Baptist) and Salomé, who demands his head after he spurns her advances.

Lulu, based on Frank Wedekind's plays, features opera's first openly lesbian character, Countess Geschwitz, who dies as the result of her unrequited love for the amoral protagonist Lulu and emerges as perhaps the only sympathetic and genuinely humane character in the opera.

By contrast, gay modernist composers, such as Maurice Ravel (1875–1937) and Virgil Thomson (1896–1989), eschewed traditional heterosexual plots and developed nonexploitative and nonsensational modes that explore the psychological, metaphysical, and social parameters of individuality and community, and are simultaneously whimsical and meditative in tone. Ravel's *L'Enfant et les Sortilèges (The Child and the Enchantments,* 1925), with libretto by CO-LETTE, is a profound consideration of the relationships among mother identification, destructiveness, creativity, and ethical responsibility, set in a magical child's world in which injured animals and objects become speaking subjects. The American composer Thomson collaborated with his librettist GERTRUDE STEIN to produce two highly original works. *Four Saints in Three Acts* (1934), which has traditionally featured an all-black cast, takes place in Spain and portrays both actual and fictional, male and female Catholic saints, who work together harmoniously to achieve collective sainthood. *The Mother of Us All* (1947) is a stirring paean to the nineteenth-century American suffragist Susan B. Anthony, and presents the struggles of the feminist movement through a series of anachronistic tableaux of Americana.

The early twentieth century, moreover, marks the beginning of opera as a significant force in gay and lesbian subculture. Sopranos and mezzo-sopranos such as Mary Garden, Emma Calvé, Geraldine Ferrar, and Kathleen Ferrier became cultural icons to lesbian opera fans. Indeed, the American lesbian novelist WILLA CATHER, herself a devotee of opera, wrote *The Song of the Lark* (1915), a fictionalized biography of the great Wagnerian soprano Olive Fremstad. Concurrently, this period witnesses the flourishing of the popular gay cult of the "opera queen," which perhaps reached its zenith in the worship of the American-born dramatic coloratura soprano Maria Callas (1923–1977). This often obsessive admiration is based on a complex identification with the diva as a spectacular, larger-than-life female figure who displays proud defiance and stylistic bravura in a life nonetheless characterized, both on and off the stage, by being "undone" by faithless men, unsympathetic reviewers, gossip mongers, and ambitious rivals. The diva thus becomes a suffering surrogate in an allegory of the love that may not dare to *speak* its name but certainly may be *sung,* particularly in a foreign language.

Although opera has thus served as a vehicle for CAMP masquerade, diva identification, and obsessive fandom, more recent works by gay composers, such as Francis Poulenc's *Dialogues des Carmélites* (1957) and Sir Benjamin Britten's *Peter Grimes* (1945), *Billy Budd* (1951), and *Death in Venice* (1973), deal quite seriously with gay- and lesbian-related themes such as social exclusion, shame, persecution, and the price of being different in a conformist world, all of which gained particular urgency in the wake of the holocaust of World War II and the subsequent emergence of gay and lesbian identity politics. In his compelling *Dialogues des Carmélites,* Poulenc returns to the scene of the French Revolution to explore how a community of women, the Carmelite nuns of Compiègne, respond to their scapegoating and martyrdom at the hands of the all-male revolutionary authorities. *Peter Grimes* deals with an uncompromising and fiercely proud iconoclast, implicated in the deaths of his young apprentices and suspected of "perversion" by his neighbors, whose unwillingness to accept help finally causes his destruction. Britten and his lifelong lover, the lyric tenor Sir Peter Pears (1910–1986), were pacifists who were firmly committed to human rights; concerns that are reflected not only in *Peter Grimes* but in virtually all of Britten's operas. *Billy Budd,* with libretto by E. M. FORSTER and Eric Crozier after HERMAN MELVILLE's novella, explores the persecution of the beautiful, Christ-like sailor Billy Budd in a setting of male homosocial conflict during war. Britten's final opera, *Death in Venice,* based on THOMAS MANN's novella, contrasts the Apollonian self-repression of the German writer Aschenbach with the Dionysian sensuality of the youthful Tadzio, and represents the older man's death in the face of this conflict between mind and body, culture and desire, and authority and freedom.

The increasing presence and visibility of gay and lesbian artists and audiences in opera in recent years has not only contributed to the revival of earlier Baroque works but also to productions of mainstream operas that explore the homoerotic possibilities of familiar and ostensibly heterosexual plots. Newer compositions, notably John Corigliano's *The Ghosts of Versailles* (1991), combine the pleasures of camp masquerade with serious considerations of the issues of personal liberty, sexuality, scapegoating, and misogyny, thus indicating the direction that future operatic plots may pursue. (See also MUSICAL THEATER.)

—*Corinne E. Blackmer and Patricia Juliana Smith*

BIBLIOGRAPHY

Clément, Catherine. *Opera, or the Undoing of Women.* Minneapolis: University of Minnesota Press, 1988. ■ Heriot, Angus. *The Castrati in Opera.* New York: Da Capo Press, 1974. ■

Koestenbaum, Wayne. *The Queen's Throat: Opera, Homosexuality, and the Mystery of Desire.* New York: Poseidon Press, 1993. ■ Matheopoulos, Helena. *Diva: Great Sopranos and Mezzos Discuss Their Art.* Boston: Northeastern University Press, 1991. ■ McClary, Susan. *Feminine Endings: Music, Gender, and Sexuality.* Minneapolis: University of Minnesota Press, 1991. ■ Mohr, Richard D. *Gay Ideas: Outing and Other Controversies.* Boston: Beacon Press, 1992. ■ Pendle, Karin, ed. *Women & Music: A History.* Bloomington and Indianapolis: Indiana University Press, 1991. ■ Rosand, Ellen. *Opera in Seventeenth Century Venice: The Creation of a Genre.* Berkeley: University of California Press, 1991.

Orton, Joe
(1933–1967)

John Kingsley Orton was born in Leicester, England, on January 1, 1933, the son of William and Elsie Orton. He was the oldest of five children and grew up in a working-class neighborhood where his father was a gardener for the city of Leicester. As a student, he was mediocre at best. There were no hints in his unremarkable youth of the witty, sophisticated, controversial, and successful man of the theater Orton would become.

After joining several local theatrical companies, mostly playing insignificant roles, Orton took elocution lessons to get rid of both a slight lisp and his Leicester accent. He had for a time been a student at a business college but was admitted to the Royal Academy of Dramatic Arts after auditioning in 1951. His move to London was a pivotal moment in his life, serving as the beginning of his real career as a performer and writer and as his introduction to fellow RADA student Kenneth Halliwell, who would become his mentor and lover. Halliwell encouraged Orton to read and study literature and had a great impact on the development of Orton's creative abilities.

Orton worked variously as an actor and stage manager for several years. He and Halliwell collaborated on an unpublished novel, *The Boy Hairdresser* (1960). They were arrested and charged with defacing books borrowed from public libraries. They used plates from art books to decorate their flat and altered a number of books to make them obscene. They were sent to prison for six months in 1962.

After their release from jail, Orton began to write in earnest, working on his own novel, *Head to Toe* (published in 1971), and writing plays. As Orton became a famous, though controversial, figure in London theatrical circles, Halliwell grew increasingly alienated and distraught, largely as a result of the continuing rejection he faced as both a writer and a visual artist and of his poor self-image as an older, heavier, and balding companion to the boyish Orton. In probably the best known event of Orton's life, on August 9, 1967, he was bludgeoned to death in his sleep by Halliwell, who subsequently took a lethal dose of Nembutals. Orton's life and death have been the subject of three plays: Simon Moss's *Cock-Ups* (1981); Lanie Robertson's *Nasty Little Secrets* (1983); and John Lahr's *Diary of a Somebody* (1987). Stephen Frears directed a film, *Prick Up Your Ears* (1987), based on John Lahr's superb biography of Orton. The screenplay of the film, by Alan Bennett, was published as well.

At the time of his death, Orton was on the verge of worldwide fame. *Loot* had been named the *Evening Standard*'s best play of 1966. He had been commissioned to write a script for a movie to star The Beatles—*Up Against It* (unproduced, though posthumously published, 1979). He was in the final stages of revising *What the Butler Saw* (1967), often regarded as his best play.

Orton's plays can be read as twisted, exaggerated autobiography. Like the title character in *Entertaining Mr. Sloane* (1963), Orton was capable of using his physical attractiveness and cheeky charm to get what he wanted from people. The ineffectual Kemp in *Sloane*—and Buchanan in *The Good and Faithful Servant* (1964)—seem based on Orton's father. Like Ray in *Servant,* Orton had been raised with the expectation that he would enter commerce as a clerk.

Orton's first play, *The Ruffian on the Stair* (1963), is based in rather obvious ways on Harold Pinter's early work, though seen through a decidedly queer consciousness. The play features a number of jokes about sexual encounters in public bathrooms, for example. An incestuous, homosexual relationship between brothers forms the background for the plot.

The unique dramatic style that has come to be called "Ortonesque" is clearly seen in Orton's next play, *Entertaining Mr. Sloane.* The handsome young drifter Sloane has slept with men and women, modeled for pornographic pictures, and eventually is shared sexually by a middle-aged brother and sister after he murders their father. The lurid events of the play are undercut by the deadpan reactions the characters have to what happens. Rarely does the dialogue veer away from meaningless, polite, bourgeois conversation, even when sex or violence is imminent. The juxtaposition of outrageous events with mundane language is at the heart of Orton's comedic style. His characters strive to maintain social poses while seducing, destroying, deceiving, or murdering each other.

In *Loot* (1966), Orton focuses on the homosexual character Hal, who robs banks and even uses his own dead mother's corpse as a vehicle for his underhanded, criminal enterprises. *What the Butler Saw* (1967, posthumously produced in 1969) is Orton's most Wildean play, a savage farce with underlying social commentary. The play features cross-dressing, outrageous sexual innuendo, and the debunking of cherished British national myths such as the heroism of Winston Churchill.

Surely Orton is rightly seen as an important precursor by the contemporary queer literary movement. His work is remarkably open in its sexuality. But Orton is important not only for his role in queer theater, but also as perhaps the finest writer of farce in the twentieth century.

—*D. S. Lawson*

BIBLIOGRAPHY

Bigsby, C. W. E. *Joe Orton*. London: Methuen, 1982. ■ Charney, Maurice. *Joe Orton*. New York: Grove, 1984. ■ Clum, John. *Acting Gay: Male Homosexuality in Modern Drama*. New York: Columbia University Press, 1992. ■ Curtis, David. "Those Awful Orton Diaries." *Sacred Heart University Review* 7.1–2 (Fall–Spring 1986–1987): 40–51. ■ de Jongh, Nicholas. *Not in Front of the Audience: Homosexuality on Stage*. London: Routledge, 1992. ■ Esslin, Martin. "Joe Orton: The Comedy of (Ill) Manners." *Contemporary English Drama*. C. W. E. Bigsby, ed. New York: Holmes and Meier, 1981. 95–107. ■ Gallix, Andrew. *Joe Orton's Comedy of the Last Laugh*. New York: Garland, 1993. ■ Lahr, John. *Prick Up Your Ears: The Biography of Joe Orton*. New York: Knopf, 1978. ■ Lilly, Mark. *Gay Men's Literature in the Twentieth Century*. New York: New York University Press, 1993. ■ Nakayama, Randall S. "Domesticating Mr. Orton." *Theatre Journal* 45.2 (May 1993): 185–195. ■ Page, Adrian. "An Age of Surfaces: Joe Orton's Drama and Post-Modernism." *The Death of the Playwright? Modern British Drama and Literary Theory*. Adrian Page, ed. New York: St. Martin's, 1992. 142–159. ■ Shepherd, Simon. *Because We're Queers: The Life and Crimes of Kenneth Halliwell and Joe Orton*. London: Gay Men's Press, 1989. ■ Sinfield, Alan. "Who Was Afraid of Joe Orton?" *Textual Practice* 4.2 (Summer 1990): 259–277. Rpt. *Sexual Sameness: Textual Differences in Lesbian and Gay Writing*. Joseph Bristow, ed. London: Routledge, 1992. 170–186. ■ Worth, Katharine J. "Form and Style in the Plays of Joe Orton." *Modern British Dramatists*. John Russell Brown, ed. Englewood Cliffs, N.J.: Prentice-Hall, 1984. 75–84.

Owen, Wilfred
(1893–1918)

Wilfred Owen was born and brought up chiefly in Shropshire, England. After failing to get into university, he worked for a vicar and then in France as an English teacher before enlisting at the beginning of World War I at the age of 21. Much of Owen's earliest poetry is in the homoerotic tradition that includes Shelley's "Adonais," TENNYSON's *In Memoriam*, and A. E. HOUSMAN's *A Shropshire Lad*: poems that simultaneously celebrate and mourn the beauty of a dead young man. Owen tried initially to combine this tradition with the religiosity of his upbringing: In "The Time was Aeon," Jesus Christ is depicted as a beautiful, suffering boy. As he grew older, Owen cared less and less for organized religion. "Maundy Thursday" describes churchgoers kissing the cross during a service; the narrator kisses the hands of the boy who holds the cross. Ultimately, it was war poetry that was to give him a socially acceptable way to express his erotic feelings for other men.

Owen went to France as an officer at the end of 1916. In June 1917, he was sent back to England suffering from shellshock. He went to a hospital near Edinburgh, where he met the bisexual poet Siegfried Sassoon. Sassoon encouraged Owen to think of himself as a poet. It was perhaps at Sassoon's suggestion that Owen reread "Adonais" and read the Greek elegies. Sassoon also gave Owen an introduction to homosexual literary circles in London: Through him, Owen met OSCAR WILDE's friend Robbie Ross, the poet Osbert Sitwell, and Charles Scott Moncrieff, the translator of PROUST.

Owen's use of consonance and near-rhymes, possibly adapted from GERARD MANLEY HOPKINS's experiments in technique, had been one of the distinctive features of his poetry since well before the meeting with Sassoon. Furthermore, Owen had already begun to combine the homoeroticism latent in ELEGY with precise observation of the horror of trench warfare. Poems like "Anthem for Doomed Youth," "Greater Love," "Strange Meeting," "Dulce et Decorum Est," "Arms and the Boy," and "Disabled" are written in the elegiac mode but also contain details that ground the poetry in the daily experience of the poet and of his comrades. Just as Owen's prosody and diction are based on traditional models that they then subvert, so Owen's best poetry takes the elegy as its point of departure only to finish by being both more personal and more political than the traditional elegy. Owen never forgot that he was writing about real boys and men dying all around him every day. He tried to write in a poetic language that would retain the Keatsian style he admired while it vividly expressed violence, sorrow, and rage; in his best poems, he succeeds brilliantly.

In the end, Owen became one of the boys he wrote about. He returned to France at the end of August 1918. In early October, he participated in an attack for which he received the Military Cross. Wilfred Owen was killed on November 4, 1918; the news reached his parents as the bells rang to celebrate the Armistice. Owen published only five poems in his lifetime. Within a few years of his death, he had come to be regarded as one of the best of the war poets; he has only recently begun to be discussed as a homosexual poet. At the end of World War II, Benjamin Britten used some of Owen's poems in his *War Requiem;* the requiem was filmed in 1988 by DEREK JARMAN. (See also WAR LITERATURE.)

—Stephen Guy-Bray

BIBLIOGRAPHY

Backman, Sven. *Tradition Transformed*. Lund: CWK Gleerup, 1979. ■ Fussell, Paul. *The Great War and Modern Memory*. New York and London: Oxford University Press, 1975. ■ Gilbert, Sandra M. "Soldier's Heart: Literary Men, Literary Women, and the Great War." *Signs* 8 (1982–83): 422–450. ■ Hibberd, Dominic. *Owen the Poet*. London: MacMillan, 1986. ■ ——. *Wilfred Owen: The Last Year 1917–1918*. London: Constable, 1992. ■ Kerr, Douglas. "The Disciplines of the Wars: Army Training and the Language of Wilfred Owen." *Modern Language Review* 87 (1992): 286–299. ■ Larkin, Philip. "The Real Wilfred." *Encounter* 44 3 (1975): 73–74. ■ Musil, Caryn McTighe. "Wilfred Owen and Abram." *Women's Studies* 13 1–2 (1986): 49–61. ■ Owen, Harold. *Journey from Obscurity*. 3 vols. London: Oxford University Press, 1963–1965. ■ Parfitt, George. *English Poetry of the First World War*. Hemel Hempstead: Harvester Wheatsheaf, 1990. ■ Silkin, Jon. *Out of Battle*. London: Oxford University Press, 1972. ■ Stallworthy, Jon. *Wilfred Owen*. London: Oxford University Press and Chatto and Windus, 1974. ■ Taylor, Martin, ed. *Lads: Love Poetry of the Trenches*. London: Constable, 1989.

Parnok, Sophia
(1885–1933)

Sophia Yakovlevna Parnok, Russia's only openly lesbian poet, was born in Taganrog, Russia, on August 11, 1885, the first child of a physician who died when Sophia was six years old. Parnok's father, a pharmacist, remarried shortly after his first wife's death. Friction with her stepmother and, later, with her father, who strongly disapproved of her lesbianism, cast a shadow over Parnok's youth, but tempered her in moral courage and independence. From the age of six she took refuge in writing, and during her last two years at the gymnasium (1901–1903) wrote extensively, especially about her lesbian sexuality and first love affairs. Her creativity would remain closely linked with her lesbian experience throughout her poetic life as she struggled to make her unique voice heard in her antilesbian literary culture.

In 1905, Parnok left home with an actress lover and spent a year in Europe. For a time, she studied at the Geneva Conservatory, but a lack of funds forced her to return to her hated father's house. To become independent of him, she married a close friend and fellow poet and settled in St. Petersburg. She began publishing her poems in journals, but marriage soon stifled her creativity and also hampered her personal life. In January 1909, she braved social censure and financial ruin and decided to leave her husband in order to make what she termed "a new start." After her divorce, Parnok settled in Moscow, became marginally self-supporting, and made a modest career as a journalist, translator, opera librettist, and poet. At the beginning of World War I, she met the young poet MARINA TSVETAEVA, with whom she became involved in a passionate love affair that left important traces in the poetry of both women. Parnok's belated first book of verse, *Poems,* appeared shortly before she and Tsvetaeva broke up in 1916. The lyrics in *Poems* presented the first, revolutionarily nondecadent, lesbian desiring subject ever to be heard in a book of Russian poetry.

Parnok and her new lover, Lyudmila Erarskaya, an actress, left Moscow in late summer 1917 and spent the Civil War years in the Crimean town of Sudak. There Parnok was inspired by her love for Erarskaya to write one of her masterpieces, the dramatic poem and libretto for Alexander Spendiarov's opera *Almast.* The physical deprivations of the Sudak years took their toll on Parnok's precarious health (she was a lifelong sufferer from Grave's disease), but the time she spent in the Crimea was a period of spiritual ferment and creative rebirth. Under the aegis of her poetic "sister" SAPPHO and her "Sugdalian sibyl" Eugenia Gertsyk (an intimate, platonic friend), the seeds of Parnok's mature lesbian lyricism were sown and yielded a first harvest in the collections *Roses of Pieria*

(1922) and *The Vine* (1923), which she published on her return to Moscow. Shortly after the appearance of *The Vine*, she met Olga Tsuberbiller, a mathematician at Moscow University, with whom she lived in a permanent relationship from 1925 until her (Parnok's) death in 1933.

The Soviet censorship soon decided that Parnok's poetic voice was "unlawful," and she was unable to publish after 1928. Nor did her work find favor with her similarly repressed fellow poets, who were embarrassed by her personal politics of the poet's soul and her straightforward, nonmetaphoric expression of lesbian love and experience. Parnok's last two collections, *Music* (1926) and *Half-voiced* (1928), attracted no notice from the official literary establishment.

During the last five years of her life, Parnok eked out a living doing translations. She was frequently bedridden and wrote poetry exclusively for "the secret drawer." Her isolation from readers and her status as an "invisible woman" in Russian poetry became constant themes in her late and best verse. In late 1931, she met Nina Vedeneyeva, a physicist. The two middle-aged women fell impossibly in love, and their affair inspired Parnok's greatest lesbian work, the cycles "Ursa Major" and "Useless Goods." Parnok's health collapsed under the "passionate burden" of her love affair, and she died after a heart attack in a village outside Moscow on August 26, 1933.

—*Diana L. Burgin*

BIBLIOGRAPHY

Burgin, Diana Lewis. "After the Ball Is Over: Sophia Parnok's Creative Relationship with Marina Tsvetaeva." *The Russian Review* 47 (1988): 425–444. ■ ———. "Laid Out in Lavender: Perceptions of Lesbian Love in Russian Literature and Criticism of the Silver Age, 1893–1917." *Sexuality and the Body in Russian Culture.* Jane Costlow, Stephanie Sandler, and Judith Vowles, eds. Stanford: Stanford University Press, 1993. 177–203. ■ ———. "Signs of a Response: Two Possible Parnok Replies to Her *Podruga.*" *Slavic and East European Journal* 35.2 (1992): 214–227. ■ ———. "Sophia Parnok and the Writing of a Lesbian Poet's Life." *Slavic Review* 51.2 (Summer 1992): 214–231. ■ ———. *Sophia Parnok: The Life and Work of Russia's Sappho.* New York: New York University Press, 1994. [Includes English verse translations of ninety-two Parnok lyrics]. ■ Parnok, Sophia. *Sobranie stikhotvorenii* [Collected Poems]. Ann Arbor, Mich.: Ardis, 1979. ■ Poliakova, Sophia. *[Ne]zakatnye ony dni: Tsvetaeva i Parnok.* Ann Arbor, Mich.: Ardis, 1983.

Pasolini, Pier Paolo
(1922–1975)

Pier Paolo Pasolini was one of the great Marxist homosexual artists of our time. As such, he met trouble throughout his career as both a writer and a filmmaker. His sexuality—or rather, that he was not closeted about it—consistently offended not only the Roman Catholic orthodoxy of post-war Italy but also the Marxist establishment. His Marxism offended Catholics, while his interest in Christian culture irritated Communists. Rather than feeling despondent, Pasolini thrived on the controversy he stirred wherever he turned. His was a dialectical genius that did not create work out of thin air: It depended on a process of provocation and response.

Born in Bologna in 1922, Pasolini was brought up in his mother's birthplace in rural Friuli. There, when he was sixteen, one of his teachers introduced him to the works of ARTHUR RIMBAUD; his response was to begin to see poetry's potential for cultural opposition to Fascism, not to mention its capacity to give voice to sexual unorthodoxy. Pasolini's own first poems, written in Friulian dialect, were published in 1942 and well received. During the war, he started working as a teacher in a local school. Even though his brother Guido had been shot by Communist partisans in 1945, Pasolini soon joined the regional branch of the Party.

On September 30, 1949, he met up with three local boys and went into the bushes with them. The outcome of this uncomplicated—and not isolated—event was that he was subsequently arrested for "corruption of minors and obscene acts in a public place." He was immediately suspended from his job and expelled from the Communist Party. His notebooks and diaries from this period—*Atti impure* and *Amado mio*—as well as the novel that he drafted at this time but published later, *Il sogno di una cosa* (1962; *A Dream of Something,* 1988), capture the atmosphere of the region and the era in their representations of the political activities and loves—homo- and heterosexual—of Friulian boys.

Most of Pasolini's fiction and much of his poetry is shaped by his fascination with the lives of subproletarian youths, first in Friuli and then in the sprawling outskirts of Rome. His political stances were, likewise, often based on what he knew of the lives of the "*ragazzi di vita.*"

Largely as a result of the 1949 scandal, Pasolini moved to Rome early in 1950. He soon began writing about the Roman boys, many of them the kinds of hustlers and small-time crooks whose company both frightened and delighted him and whom he would later give bit parts in his films. Stories from this period appear in *Ali dagli occhi azzuri* (1965; selections in *Roman Nights,* 1986). Both of his major novels appeared during this same burst of activity: *Ragazzi di vita* (1955; *The Ragazzi,* 1968) and *Una vita violenta* (1959; *A Violent Life,* 1968). The former caused a scandal on the grounds of its supposed obscenity; both scandalized commentators on the left who were unused to such unsentimental, neo-realist representations of the working class. Pasolini's celebrations of young masculinity in all its cruelty, scatology, and eroticism were clearly out of step with the idealizing mythologies that emanated from both the Vatican and Moscow.

As Pasolini was gradually drawn into the intellectual community of Rome in the 1950s, he inevitably met and began to collaborate with some of the new-wave Italian filmmakers as well as writers. From working on screenplays, he soon graduated to directing his own films. The first, *Accattone,* appeared in 1961. Although he went on writing for the rest of his life, he devoted more and more attention to the cinema. Occasionally, both processes were combined: *Teorema,* for instance, appeared simultaneously as both film and novel (1968; *Theorem,* 1992). The film provoked another obscenity scandal in its account of a young male guest who systematically bewitches and seduces all the members of a bourgeois family, female and male alike.

As a filmmaker, Pasolini had a particularly literary talent. Certainly, many of his greatest films are adaptations of written texts, from the "proletarian" account of *The Gospel According to St Matthew* (1964),

through the "Trilogy of Life" based on *The Decameron* (1971), *The Canterbury Tales* (1972), and *The Arabian Nights* (1973), to his extraordinary last film *Salò* (1975), in which he set the dying days of Italian Fascism in a graphic version of the MARQUIS DE SADE's pornographic divine comedy, *The 120 Days of Sodom.* Even the most popular of these works have a strong thematic continuity with Pasolini's poetry and his critical and theoretical writings. The intensity of his erotic interests informs them all.

Despite his reputation for sexual radicalism, Pasolini's attitudes were in many respects downright reactionary, led by nostalgia. He regretted the increasing independence of young Italian girls on the grounds that, once they ceased to be confined to their family homes in a state of purdah, boys would become less available for homosexual encounters. He opposed both contraception and abortion because they, too, facilitated heterosexual relations among the young and undermined the traditional Italian tolerance of casual sexual encounters between unmarried young men. It may be that in his admiration for Saint Paul as a writer-revolutionary, Pasolini allowed himself to be too readily persuaded by Pauline misogyny.

Although there are plenty of conspiracy theories to argue otherwise, Pasolini was murdered in 1975 by a hustler he had picked up at Rome's central station and driven out to the beach at Ostia. His detractors, and even some of his admirers, see this as an appropriate end to his career. (See also ITALIAN LITERATURE.)

—*Gregory Woods*

BIBLIOGRAPHY

Siciliano, Enzo. *Pasolini.* London: Bloomsbury, 1987.

Pastoral

Pastoral derives from the Latin word *pastoralis,* which denotes things connected to shepherding and other types of animal husbandry. The setting of literary pastorals is usually a rustic *locus amoenus* where shepherd-poets sing of their lives and loves. Generally written for a sophisticated, urbane audience, pastorals often possess a gently ironic naiveté combined with a nostalgia for what are perceived to have been simpler, more straightforward times.

The ancient Greek poet THEOCRITUS is taken as the originator of the pastoral genre. Homoeroticism fig-

ures prominently in his pastoral and nonpastoral *Idylls,* as it does in the *Eclogues* (43–37 B.C.) of his most famous classical successor, the Roman poet VIRGIL. Theocritus' and Virgil's poems present male-male desire as part and parcel of a broad economy of desire, as debauched and as refined as any examples of heterosexual passion. The profound and eloquent representations of homoerotic love found in these two authors have been continuing sources of inspiration for writers concerned with representing the plurality of human affection, as well as contesting a heterosexist normalization of desire in literary and social domains.

Theocritus' *Idylls* makes the prototypical division of pastoral literature into elegiac and romantic or erotic modes. Idyll I is a pastoral elegy sung by Thyrsis for Daphnis, a shepherd who will not love a maiden and who therefore dies to spite love. The *Lament for Bion,* attributed improbably to the Syracusan Greek poet Moschus (fl ca 150 B.C.), follows in this elegiac tradition. The speaker of this poem bewails the death of his dear friend, a grief shared by the homoerotic figures of Apollo, Priapus, satyrs, and nameless young men. Virgil's Eclogue V is an elegy on the death of Daphnis sung by the shepherds Mopsus and Menalcas, whose profound attachment to Daphnis conveys a sense of homoerotic affection similar to that found in Theocritus' first idyll.

Francesco Petrarch's (1304–1374) *Bucolicum Carmen* (1346–1352), a series of Virgilian eclogues, offers variations on classical elegy. Eclogue II is a lament for Argus by the shepherds Pythias and Silvius in which Petrarch allegorically explores and recounts his own sense of personal loss at the death of his close friend, Robert of Naples. Eclogue XI is Petrarch's only all-female eclogue. Its lesbian eroticism is conveyed by the expression of passionate love and sorrow for the dead Galatea by the nymphs Niobe, Fusca, and Fulgida. As projections of Petrarch's own grief over his beloved Laura's death, the mourners figure an unusual androgyny in the poet and confound a simple reading of a putative "heterosexual" orientation.

The best known of English pastoral elegies based on Theocritean and Virgilian models is JOHN MILTON's (1608–1674) *Lycidas* (1638), a heartfelt lament that commemorates the death of the author's friend, Edward King. Not as insistently pastoral as Milton's work, Percy Bysshe Shelley's (1792–1822) *Adonais* (1821) mourns the death of John Keats through the expression of deep, sexually ambiguous yearning for a departed male friend described as "a portion of the loveliness / Which once he made more lovely." Matthew Arnold's (1822–1888) *Thyrsis* (1866) commemorates the death of his friend Arthur Hugh Clough. Its vision of a homoerotic, unspoiled innocence is reinforced by reading the companion pastoral *The Scholar-Gipsy* (1853), in which Arnold evokes a sexually charged image of a sturdy youth (Clough) uncorrupted by modern decay.

Theocritus and Virgil provide the major models for pastoral explorations of romantic and erotic yearning and celebration. In Theocritus' Idyll V, Comatas and Lacon engage in a ribald verbal spat that blatantly conveys the heated erotic fascination between the two young men through references to buggery and sexual temptation. A singing contest in Idyll VI between two handsome adolescents, Amoetas and Daphnis, is matched in its sweetness by Idyll VII's presentation of Lycidas' fond dream to have whiled away his years with Comatas, minding his goats and listening to his music. Unrequited pederastic love also forms a part of this poem in the account of Aratus, who yearns for the hard-hearted Philinus. Similar to his nonpastoral homoerotic idylls, Theocritus' pastoral poems typically counsel that love ought to be seized when it appears because, just like the seasons, human life is a fleeting thing.

Virgil's second eclogue depicts the shepherd Corydon's lament for the unrequited love of handsome Alexis. Even though Corydon recognizes the folly of his ardor, he cannot resist love. Though BYRON pretended to think this poem "horrid" (*Don Juan* 1.42) because of its depiction of homoerotic love, Corydon's complaint, at once comic and profound, inspired numerous literary imitators. Calpurnius Siculus (fl A.D. 50–60) imitated Theocritus' fifth idyll in his sixth eclogue, which figures a debate full of homoerotic jokes and connotations between the shepherds Astylus and Lycidas. Nemesianus (late third century A.D.) followed in Virgil's footsteps with a tender eclogue that registers the equivalency of hetero- and homoerotic desire through a series of alternating speeches by Mopsus, whom the maiden Meroe shuns, and by Lycidas, whose love the young man Iollas spurns. As with numerous other pastorals about male-male attraction, the emphasis in Lycidas' speech is on the shortness of time and Iollas' physical maturation, a central concern of classical pederastic relations.

Post-classical pastoral works generally avoid direct expressions of homoerotic passion and experience; they do, however, often maintain a homoerotic undercurrent through imitation of Greek and Roman prototypes. From 1318 to 1321, DANTE (1265–1321) and a young scholar at Bologna, Giovanni del Virgilio, exchanged a brief series of Latin epistles in the form of pastoral eclogues that were instrumental in establishing the importance of pastoral for later European authors. Virgilio began by writing to Dante, who was in exile at Ravenna, asking him to come live with him at Bologna. Eclogue I is Dante's reply. Styling himself as the shepherd Tityrus and his companion Dino Perini as Meliboeus, he refuses Virgilio's (Mopsus) suggestion by detailing the simple pastoral delights he and Perini possess: a humble cottage, a shared bed, and a warm meal. Virgilio's Responsive Eclogue asks Dante not to afflict one who loves him, but to come and share his cavern. He invokes the homoerotic power of Virgil's second eclogue by saying he will have Corydon call Alexis to strew Dante's couch with fragrant thyme. In his concluding Eclogue II, Dante gives his final refusal of his admirer's entreaties, a predictable end to their Virgilian exchange.

Eclogue VIII of Petrarch's *Bucolicum Carmen* is a dialogue between two shepherds, Amyclas and Ganymede. The poem consists of an argument in which Ganymede attempts to persuade Amyclas, who has lived with Ganymede for twenty years, to remain in their pleasant valley. Allegorically, Amyclas represents Petrarch and Ganymede figures Cardinal Giovanni Colonna, whom Petrarch left at Vaucluse when he returned to Italy in November of 1347. Ganymede's traditionally homoerotic identity underwrites his principal argument that Amyclas' departure would be an unjust abandonment of his loving shepherd comrades, and invites speculation on one of Petrarch's significant male relations.

In the January eclogue of Edmund Spenser's (ca 1552–1599) *Shepheardes Calendar* (1579)—itself a foundational pastoral text for the English Renaissance—the shepherd Colin Clout is enamored of a woman named Rosalind who will not return his devotion. As it turns out, the gifts Colin gives to Rosalind had been given to him by his own rejected male suitor, Hobbinol. The gloss to this provided by the enigmatic E. K. troubles any heterosexist reading of the text by explaining that Hobbinol's relationship with Colin is not an example of "disorderly" pederastic love, but of a variety of pederasty that the ancients deemed moral and above "gynerastice," the love of men for women.

CHRISTOPHER MARLOWE's (1564–1593) poem "The Passionate Shepherd to His Love," an Ovidian plea to revel in love, also follows in the tradition of Virgil's second eclogue. The speaker of this poem has generally been assumed to be male and the auditor a woman. However, Marlowe's poem undermines these gender ascriptions by refusing a definitive gender to either of the characters. (The title was not added until it was anthologized in *The Passionate Pilgrim* in 1599, six years after Marlowe's death.) Based on its self-conscious imitation of a homoerotic Virgilian original, and in the context of Marlowe's other works, this pastoral poem warrants a rereading attentive to its homoerotic potential. Related in spirit to Marlowe's work is *The Teares of an Affectionate Shepheard Sicke for Love* (1594), also titled *The Complaint of Daphnis for the Love of Ganimede,* by RICHARD BARNFIELD (1574–1627), a rapturous account of the shepherd Daphnis' unrequited love for the amber-locked Ganimede. While his rival Guendolena desires Ganimede only for his beauty and her own pleasure, Daphnis' love conforms to the classical ideal of worshipping a male beloved's inner virtue.

Pastoral romance, which flourished especially during the Renaissance, constitutes a particular branch of romantic and erotic pastoral expression. Although the form derives some of its motivation from Theocritus and Virgil, its primary influence comes from late classical novels, most importantly Longus' (third century A.D.) *Daphnis and Chloe.* Set on the utopian island of Lesbos, this urbane and witty story recounts the love—and the obstacles to that love—between Daphnis and Chloe. At the end of Book III, lovesick Daphnis fetches a perfect apple for his beloved Chloe, a gift that recalls the Sapphic love poetry admired by Longus' sophisticated readers. In addition, the comic buffoonery, in Book IV, of the gross pederast Gnathon's attempts to get the handsome Daphnis for his sexual pleasure is ironically juxtaposed against the eloquent self-defense that Gnathon makes by claiming only to be following the precedent set by the illustrious gods.

Homoeroticism is not condemned in Longus, so much as it is deployed as a cultured and witty adornment to a primarily heteroerotic narrative. This is also partly true for later pastoral romances that engage homoerotic desire through the trope of transvestism, which draws on the importance of disguise in classical romance fiction. In Honoré d'Urfé's (1567–1625) French romance, *L'Astrée* (1627), cross-dressing is always temporary though it can lead to confusions of sexual and gender identity as it does with Adamas, Silvandre, and especially Celadon. In d'Urfé's text and numerous other romances, homoeroticism questions the supposed universality of heterosexual desire. Love between the sexes in these texts is often tortured and incoherent; "friendship" between persons of the same sex, however, is generally tranquil and honest. Such is the case in Sir Philip Sidney's (1554–1586) *Arcadia* (1590; 1593), where the powerful bond between Pyrocles and Musidorus suggests a latent nostalgia for the former homoerotic liberty of male-male friendship.

Lesbian eroticism emerges in conjunction with transvestism in another pastoral romance, *La Diana* (1559) of Jorge de Montemayor (1519–1561). *La Diana* explores lesbian eroticism as subtly and tenderly as heterosexual attachments. As in *L'Astrée,* same-sex groupings provide the opportunity for homoerotic desire to flourish, for it is during a women-only night of worshipping at the temple of Minerva in Book I that the shepherdess Selvagia falls in love with Ysmenia, who is in fact a cross-dressed man. In Book II, Felismena's rival, Celia, believing her to be a man, falls in love with her and dies of unrequited love. Lesbian eroticism reaches a high pitch in WILLIAM SHAKESPEARE's (1564–1616) pastoral play *As You Like It* (1599), where the shepherdess Phebe loves "at first sight" the cross-dressed Rosalind, primarily for her feminine aspects. In the same work, Rosalind's costuming as Ganymede and subsequent playful wooing by the love-sick Orlando also invoke a homoerotic tension that is not annulled by the closure of marriage at the end.

The tradition of elegiac lament is fused with romance in chapter 5 of Jacopo Sannazaro's (1458–1530) *Arcadia* (1504), where ten cowherds dance around the tomb of the shepherd Androgeo. The barely concealed homoeroticism of this scene is fully realized in the following eclogue when Ergasto sings of Androgeo sitting in heaven between Daphnis and Meliboeus, and describes Androgeo's relation to the cowherds as having been like that of a bull to its herd.

In the twentieth century, pastoral has disappeared as a pure genre; yet, the image of a blissful, natural space apart from the turmoils and repressions of society has remained important in much of gay literature. In E. M. FORSTER's (1879–1970) *A Room with a View* (1908), the Reverend Beebe swims naked with the young, handsome George and Freddy in a secluded forest pool. *Maurice* (1913; 1971), also by Forster, presents the idyllic union of Maurice and his lover Alec, a literary descendant of Virgil's Alexis. Aschenbach's pederastic infatuation with the beautiful and unattainable youth Tadzio in THOMAS MANN's (1875–1955) *Death in Venice* (1912) also occurs in a setting of Arcadian beauty. In a short piece entitled "Idyll" (1981), Guy Davenport parodies Theocritus' boisterous, erotic dialogue between the shepherds Komatas and Lakon, and has WALT WHITMAN make an appearance as a beneficent father figure for young gay men, thereby expressing the importance of continuity and community for homosexual literary and social existence.

—*M. Morgan Holmes*

BIBLIOGRAPHY

Alpers, Paul. "What is Pastoral?" *Critical Inquiry* 8 (1982): 437–460. ■ Bredbeck, Gregory W. *Sodomy and Interpretation: Marlowe to Milton.* Ithaca, N.Y.: Cornell University Press, 1991. ■ Fone, Byrne R. S. "This Other Eden: Arcadia and the Homosexual Imagination," *Literary Visions of Homosexuality.* 1983. Rpt. as *Essays on Gay Literature.* Stuart Kellogg, ed. New York: Harrington Park Press, 1985. 13–34. ■ Giantvalley, Scott. "Barnfield, Drayton, and Marlowe: Homoeroticism and Homosexuality in Elizabethan Literature." *Pacific Coast Philology* 16 (1981): 9–24. ■ Gregorio, Laurence A. *The Pastoral Masquerade: Disguise and Identity in L'Astrée.* Stanford French and Italian Studies 73. Saratoga, Calif.: ANMA, 1992. ■ Halperin, David M. *Before Pastoral: Theocritus and the Ancient Tradition of Bucolic Poetry.* New Haven: Yale University Press, 1983. ■ Kennedy, William J. *Jacopo Sannazaro and the Uses of Pastoral.* Hanover, N.H.: University Press of New England, 1983. ■ Marinelli, Peter V. *Pastoral.* London: Methuen, 1971. ■ Rhodes, Elizabeth. "Skirting the Men: Gender Roles in Sixteenth-century Pastoral Books," *Journal of Hispanic Philology* 11 (1988): 131–149. ■ Sannazaro, Jacopo. *Arcadia and the Piscatory Eclogues.* Trans. Ralph Nash. Detroit: Wayne State University Press, 1966. ■ Zeitlin, Froma I. "The Poetics of Eros: Nature, Art, and Imitation in Longus's *Daphnis and Chloe.*" *Before Sexuality; The Construction of Erotic Experience in the Ancient Greek World.* David M. Halperin et al., eds. Princeton: Princeton University Press, 1990. 417–464.

Pater, Walter
(1839–1894)

Among British prose writers of the Victorian era, Walter Pater stands as the embodiment of stylistic elegance. His critical essays—ranging widely over Classical, Renaissance, Romantic, and contemporary artists and writers—are themselves literary works of the first order. William Butler Yeats called Pater's novel *Marius the Epicurean* (1885, rev. 1892) "the only great prose in modern English." A close student of German philosophy (particularly the work of Hegel) and well read in the French writers of the period, Pater's criticism and fiction were highly cerebral, yet embraced the purely sensuous dimensions of art and life. From the 1870s through the 1890s, he was regarded by the reading public as a major theorist and practitioner of AESTHETICISM and DECADENCE. (Pater himself regarded this identification with some perplexity, though his influence on OSCAR WILDE, for instance, was clear). His stylistic elegance and his dangerous ideas about art's autonomy from morality, combined with rumors of homosexuality at Oxford, where he taught, made Pater's name virtually synonymous with gay sensibility during the late nineteenth century. In 1876, speaking as a guardian of public morals, W. T. Courthope announced: "we repudiate the effeminate desires which Mr. Pater, the mouthpiece of our artistic 'culture,' would encourage in society." In recent decades, Pater has been rediscovered by critics as one of the most important English sources of literary MODERNISM.

Pater began contributing reviews and essays to the *Westminster* and the *Fortnightly Reviews* during the late 1860s, including pieces on the poetry of William Morris and the prose of Coleridge. In a remarkably candid paper on the great German classicist, JOHANN

JOACHIM WINCKELMANN, published in 1867, Pater noted: "That his affinity with Hellenism was not merely intellectual, that the subtler threads of temperament were interwoven in it, is proved by his romantic, fervid friendships with young men." A number of Pater's essays were assembled in *Studies in the History of the Renaissance* (1873)—including the study of Winckelmann, who, as Pater explained in the preface, "coming in the eighteenth century, really belongs in spirit to an earlier age." But *The Renaissance,* as the book is usually called, was more than a collection of magazine pieces. For in assembling them for republication, Pater elaborated on the aesthetic doctrine running throughout the essays.

In the preface, Pater dismissed efforts "to define beauty in the abstract." Rather, when discussing a given work of art, literature, or music, the critic must answer the question: "How is my nature modified by its presence, and under its influence?" This demands of the critic "the power of being deeply moved by the presence of beautiful objects." Such critical impressionism doubtless appeared self-indulgent, even solipsistic, in itself; but Pater's "Conclusion" carried it still further. Writing in a philosophical vein, he insisted that the universe's flux of life, death, and constant change made the passionate enjoyment of each moment the greatest human good:

> Not the fruit of experience, but experience itself, is the end. A counted number of pulses only is given to us of a variegated, dramatic life. . . . With this sense of the splendor of our experience and of its awful brevity, gathering all we are into one desperate effort to see and touch, we shall hardly have time to make theories about the things we see and touch.

As Pater concludes, art will serve best "to give nothing but the highest quality to your moments as they pass, and simply for those moments' sake."

This radically amoral vision of privately cultivated sensibility quickly became notorious. In the second edition (1877), Pater suppressed the "Conclusion" on the grounds that "it might possibly mislead some of those young men into whose hands it might fall"—as he put it when restoring a version of the essay in the book's third edition (1888).

Pater's hedonistic doctrine lent itself to caricature. In W. H. Mallock's satirical novel *The New Republic* (1876), Pater appears as "Mr. Rose, the pre-Raphaelite," a character whose "two topics are self-indulgence and art." Rose finds modern city life dreary except for "the shops of certain of our upholsterers and dealers in works of art." Mallock's portrait hints at other proclivities beyond a taste for fine upholstery: Rose gazes "upon life as a chamber, which we decorate as we would decorate the chamber of the woman or the youth that we love," and is described as showing a special interest in young men. There were also allusions to Pater in Charles Edward Hutchinson's pamphlet *Boy Worship* (1880), an exposé of homosexuals at Oxford.

Morally upsetting though some readers found *The Renaissance,* the book found its audience: By the 1880s, Pater's criticism was well established among younger writers as exemplary of avant garde aesthetic attitudes. His historical novel *Marius the Epicurean,* set in Rome during the era of emperor Marcus Aurelius, was warmly received. Marius's personal journey—from the revival of old paganism, to the literary influence of his friend Flavian, followed by the consolations of Greek philosophy after Flavian's death, through Stoicism during his service in Aurelius's court, to the verge of conversion to the new religion, Christianity, before his death—is presented through an intricate web of narrative, essayistic passages, and translations and paraphrases from literary and philosophical works. Marius's passionate friendships with the poet Flavian and with Cornelius, a Christian, weave a homophile dimension into the book, which is often read as Pater's spiritual autobiography. Besides its poetic prose, the novel revealed subtleties of Pater's vision belied by the caricatures of his earlier work—including a close interest in the varieties of religious experience. Subsequent critics have seen in *Marius* a prototype of the novels of James Joyce and THOMAS MANN.

Pater continued writing fiction in this hybrid form—part short story, part essay, part memoir—after completing *Marius.* His *Imaginary Portraits* (1887) gathered fictional texts that drew on mythological and historical sources, developing *personae* that (as in the "imaginary portrait" of Marius) served in part as figures of psychological allegory. And with *Gaston de Latour,* set in sixteenth-century France, Pater sought to extend *Marius* by projecting a trilogy of historical novels. The book, which remained uncompleted when Pater died in 1894, was published with the subtitle "An Unfinished Romance" in 1896.

The last volume Pater saw through the press, *Plato and Platonism* (1893), is now often regarded purely as prose poetry, though it was greeted respectfully by Plato scholars on its publication. Other papers reflecting Pater's serious interest in Hellenic culture were assembled in the posthumous *Greek Studies* (1895). But it is primarily for his commentary on English literature that Pater's reputation as critic survives. The essays on diverse topics collected in *Appreciations* (1889) include writings on SHAKESPEARE, Browne,

Coleridge, Wordsworth, Lamb, and Rossetti—as well as an essay on "Style" that serves as an important statement of Pater's aesthetic theory both as critic and as prose artist.

Running throughout Pater's work is a sustained engagement with the idea of culture as both a means and an end to life: The art object serves as a tool for increased enjoyment of our limited run of years, while the *bildung* of the artist's own personality and creative powers can be exemplary for our conduct, like the lives of the saints for the faithful. What his contemporaries took to be a shocking, even perverse license for self-indulgence, in fact was a doctrine that demanded a studious, even somewhat ascetic cultivation of the receptiveness to beauty. And as *Marius the Epicurean* puts it, in the most characteristically Paterian way, this is "an art in some degree peculiar to each individual character; with the modifications, that is, due to its special constitution, and the peculiar circumstances of its growth, inasmuch as no one of us is 'like another, all in all.'" (See also ENGLISH LITERATURE: NINETEENTH CENTURY.)

—*Scott McLemee*

BIBLIOGRAPHY

Adams, James Eli. "Gentleman, Dandy, Priest: Manliness and Social Authority in Pater's Aestheticism." *ELH* 59 (1992): 441–466. ■ Bendz, Ernst Paulus. *Influence of Pater and Matthew Arnold in the Prose Writings of Oscar Wilde.* Gothenberg: Wettergren and Kerber, 1914. ■ Bloom, Harold, ed. *Walter Pater: Modern Critical Views.* New York: Chelsea House, 1985. ■ Buckler, William E. *Walter Pater: The Critic as Artist of Ideas.* New York: New York University Press, 1987. ■ Fletcher, Ian. *Walter Pater.* London: Longmans Green, 1959. ■ Inman, Billie Andrew. "Estrangement and Connection: Walter Pater, Benjamin Jowett and William Hardinge." *Pater in the 1990s.* Laurel Drake and Ian Small, eds. Greensboro, N.C.: ELT Press, 1991. 1–20. ■ Iser, Wolfgang. *Walter Pater: The Aesthetic Moment.* Trans. Henry David Wilson. Cambridge: Cambridge University Press, 1987. ■ Levey, Michael. *The Case of Walter Pater.* London: Thames and Hudson, 1978. ■ McGowan, John. "From Pater to Wilde to Joyce: Modernist Epiphany and the Soulful Self." *Texas Studies in Language and Literature* 32 (1990): 417–445. ■ Monsman, Gerald. *Walter Pater's Art of Autobiography.* New Haven, Conn.: Yale University Press, 1980. ■ Seiler, R. M., ed. *Walter Pater: The Critical Heritage.* London: Routledge and Kegan Paul, 1980. ■ Williams, Carolyn. *Transfigured World: Walter Pater's Aesthetic Historicism.* Ithaca, N.Y.: Cornell University Press, 1989.

Patrick, Robert
(*b.* 1937)

Mainstream critics and historians often ignore his work, but Robert Patrick is a founding father of gay drama in America and an influence in the development of gay drama in England. A number of his contemporary and younger playwrights have been touched and influenced by his work.

Born in Texas in 1937, raised in various places in the South and Southwest, Robert Patrick's real life began when he arrived in New York in the mid-1960s and found his way to the Caffe Cino, where both Off-Off-Broadway and gay theater in America were born. Patrick, then known to his friends as Una O'Connor, worked by day as a typist in the city morgue but after dark threw himself body and soul into the Cino, as actor, stagehand, publicist, co-manager, and playwright. His first play, *The Haunted Host,* was produced at the Cino in 1964. After Joe Cino's death in 1967, Patrick, who had already written dozens of plays, moved his base of operation to the Old Reliable Tavern Theatre in the East Village and, occasionally, to La Mama, the center of downtown theatrical experimentation. By the late 1960s, he was produced Off-Broadway and once, with *Kennedy's Children,* briefly on Broadway. When London's Gay Sweatshop began presenting plays in 1975, two of Patrick's plays, *One Person* and *The Haunted Host,* were included in the first season. (*Kennedy's Children* had been produced in London in 1974.)

Patrick's early work reflects the restless experimentation with theatrical form of the late 1960s. Monologues, musical extravaganzas, television parodies, nudity, drag, and camp humor fill his varied early work. Yet Patrick is at his best in his more conventional plays, which satirize the many ways gay men, trained to hate themselves, avoid the possibility of love. Patrick's best work offers the most hilarious, savage satires we have of gay life in New York in the 1960s and 1970s. He was, in his heyday, Greenwich Village's Ben Jonson. *T-Shirts* (1978) pictures the sexual marketplace of gay society as "a conglomerate as heartless as Con Ed," in which youth and beauty are the only currency. In *T-Shirts,* Patrick dramatizes a conflict between a handsome hunk and a cynical, flamboyant queen that results in a tie in which both learn about the compromises they have made. In *The Haunted Host* (1964), a playwright, determined to avoid repeating a disastrous past relationship, is visited by the spitting image of his beautiful ex-lover and realizes that he has shut himself off from the possibility of love. Patrick can also, as he does in the one-act plays contained in *Untold Decades* (1988), celebrate the ways in which gay men have managed to love in times of repression and, recently, epidemic.

Patrick's self-portraits appear throughout his work, never more poignantly than in his best-known play, *Kennedy's Children* (1973), in which, in alternating monologues, five denizens of a bar recollect where they were the night John F. Kennedy was murdered. Sparger, a sometime drag queen and gay actor in a welter of experimental theater events, recounts the history of a thinly disguised Caffe Cino, which for him represented the 1960s.

Patrick now lives in California and still writes constantly. His latest work is a novel, *Temple Slave* (1994), which chronicles the years of Caffe Cino. (See also DRAMATIC LITERATURE: MODERN DRAMA.)

—*John M. Clum*

BIBLIOGRAPHY

Patrick, Robert. *The Haunted Host. Homosexual Acts: A Volume of Gay Plays.* Ed Berman, ed. London: Inter-Action, 1975. ■ ———. *Kennedy's Children.* New York: Random House, 1976. ■ ———. *Mercy Drop and Other Plays.* New York: Calamus Books, 1979. ■ ———. *Robert Patrick's Cheap Theatricks.* New York: Winter House, 1972. ■ ———. *T-Shirts. Gay Plays: The First Collection.* William M. Hoffman, ed. New York: Avon, 1979. ■ ———. *Untold Decades: Seven Comedies of Gay Romance.* New York: St. Martins, 1988.

Penna, Sandro
(1906–1977)

Sandro Penna was born in Perugia, but after the age of sixteen, spent most of his life in Rome. By some standards, his life was uneventful, unambitious, lonely, scruffy, and sordid. One does not have to endorse this view. Penna made firm choices about the two things in life that interested him most: poetry and boys. He did not live a public life, even if his private life was generally conducted in public places. Furthermore, his poetry never developed beyond its earliest forms and topics; he was content to spend his life perfecting the narrowness of his craft.

Penna's friend, the bisexual poet UMBERTO SABA, helped him get published. He gradually accumulated a distinguished collection of friends and admirers, including the novelists Elsa Morante and Alberto Moravia. For several years, he had a competition with PIER PAOLO PASOLINI to see who could make love with the greater number of boys along the overgrown banks of the Tiber and in the scattered urinals of Rome's ugly urban landscape. It was Pasolini who most consistently championed Penna's poetry.

Boyhood was Penna's inspiration and his topic. In his verse, the figure of the boy is a personification of love. Boyhood itself is Eros demythologized, the embodiment of desire. The words *ragazzo* and *fanciullo* become even more resonant than *lad* had been to homosexual English poets at the turn of the century. Boys exert a uniquely transformative power not only on the landscapes they inhabit but also on the lesser mortals with whom they come into contact. Penna identifies with them in their adolescent loneliness, envies their camaraderie, and joins them in erotic solidarity on hot Roman evenings.

Each poem is as fleeting as the encounter it records. Each constitutes a moment of intense feeling, often a concentrated mixture of past loves and present desires. Penna does not write with the intellect but with the focus of emotions that are physically based. His poetry takes pleasure in pleasure, reestablishing the shock of joy. In a particularly expressive phrase, "L'amore era con me nella mia mano" (literally, "love was with me in my hand"), he articulates both a sense of loss and a crucially ambiguous association of mutual and solitary masturbation.

One poem sums up Penna's attitude to criticism of his thematic narrowness. Responding to the complaint that there are always young men in his poems, the poet replies: "Ma io non so parlare d'altre cose. / Le altre cose son tutte noiose" ("But I don't know how to write about anything else. Everything else is just boring"). If his sexual interest is a limitation, it is one he accepts with cheerful equanimity.

—*Gregory Woods*

BIBLIOGRAPHY

di Fonzo, Giulio. *Sandro Penna: La luce e il silenzio.* Roma: Edizioni dell'Ateneo, 1981. ■ Garboli, Cesare. *Penna Papers.* Milano: Garzanti, 1984. ■ Pecora, Elio. *Sandro Penna: Una cheta follia.* Milano: Frasinelli, 1984.

Pessoa, Fernando
(1888–1935)

Pessoa is the greatest Portuguese poet since Vaz de Camoes in the Renaissance. He established MODERNISM in Portugal and deeply influenced the language. It is said that even Lisbon chamber maids speak differently from their grandparents because of him. He was born (on June 13, 1888) and died (on November 30, 1935) in Lisbon, but grew up in Natal, South Africa, where he had an English education, attending the University of Cape of Good Hope, Capetown. At fifteen, he published a number of virtuosic English sonnets modeled on SHAKESPEARE's. In 1905, he returned to Portugal, where for the rest of his life he earned his living as a business correspondent (writing letters for export companies in foreign languages) and was also a habitue of literary cafes. He was briefly connected with the nationalist movement in poetry called *saudosismo* and edited two short-lived journals. Like his near contemporary LANGSTON HUGHES in the United States, he was essentially a reclusive, though dandyish, person. His sexuality is at best a guess, for no certain relationship with man or woman has been documented, but homoerotocism is important to his poetry.

Like CAVAFY, another near contemporary, he developed a style based on multiple voices and distinct personae. He wrote and published under a great number of names, each of whose work grew from competing traditions, and some of whom engaged in literary rivalries with one another in journals and had biographies and even horoscopes attached to their publications. For these distinct personalities, he invented the term *heteronym*; the most important are Alberto Caeiro, Alvaro de Campos, Ricardo Reis, and the writer of his English poetry, published under his own name. Each has received intense critical scrutiny; each is acclaimed to have established specific developments in modern Portuguese writing. The English poetry exhibits the best of a high Edwardian style, steeped in Elizabethanisms, similar to but perhaps better than the poetry of Rupert Brooke or Sacherville Sitwell. Many of the English poems have a homoerotic explicitness that Pessoa's post-WILDE English counterparts scarcely dared. The long poem "Antinous," published with *35 Sonnets* (1918), is singled out as the finest of his English style. It also has provoked speculation about his sexuality, for it luxuriates over the Hadrian-Antinous story in the grand style of an Elizabethan erotic mock epic.

In contrast, Alvaro de Campos writes in the tradition of WHITMAN. His work founded a Whitmanesque school in Portuguese, much as Pablo Neruda's did in Spanish. Campos's "Salutation to Walt Whitman" is an ecstatic love song across time, with lines like these:

> . . . And just as you felt everything, so I feel
> everything, and so here we are clasping hands
> Clasping hands, Walt, clasping hands, with
>   the universe
> doing a dance in our soul. (16–17)

It ends with de Campos embracing Whitman as mentor/father/lover, imagining a psychic insemination of the spirit:

> Goodbye, bless you, live forever, O Great
>   Bastard of Apollo,
> Impotent and ardent lover of the nine muses
>   and of the graces,
> Cable-car from Olympus to us and from us to
>   Olympus. (219–221)

One is reminded of HART CRANE's similar stance in *The Bridge*.

Pessoa's *heteronyms* have provided a field day for psychoanalytically inclined critics, such as Roditi, Hamburger, and Paz, who see them as the work of a schizophrenic uniquely articulated as art. Recent trends in queer theory, especially interrogations into performativity, might, however, inspire a new generation of readers to discover in Pessoa's unprecedented virtuosity not a psychosis of failed identity but a powerful expression of a ventriloquistic "poetic drag" that destructs the very notion of straight adult unitary self.

—*Donald N. Mager*

BIBLIOGRAPHY

Hamburger, Michael. "Multiple Personalities." *The Truth of Poetry*. New York: Methuen, 1982. ■ Monteiro, George, ed. *The Man Who Never Was: Essays on Fernando Pessoa*. Providence, R.I.: Gavea-Brown, 1982. ■ Pessoa, Fernando. *Selected Poems*. Trans. Edwin Honig. Intro. Octavio Paz. Chicago: Swallow Press, 1971. ■ Roditi, Edouard. "Fernando Pessoa: Outsider Among English Poets." *The Literary Review* 6.3 (1963): 372–385.

Petronius
(ca 27–66)

The author of *The Satyricon* is traditionally identified with the Gaius (or Titus) Petronius described in Tacitus's *Annals* as a sensualist "who made luxury a fine art," and whose suicide in 66, after being falsely betrayed by a rival and dismissed by the emperor Nero as his "arbiter" of elegance and sensual pleasure, is described by Tacitus as the ultimate act of refined self-control. Only fragments survive of *The Satyricon,* Petronius's brilliant satire of excesses in Nero's Rome, but they remain both the best evidence for homosexual behavior at the height of the Roman Empire and one of the most bumptious homoerotic picaresque narratives ever written.

The world of *The Satyricon* at times resembles a sexual carnival. Encolpius (whose name, translator Arrowsmith concludes, means "crotch") is a student with an exceptional phallic endowment, but whose offenses against the god Priapus result in a sequence of painful but generally comic misadventures, including the humiliation of sexual impotence and the loss of his teenaged boyfriend Giton to his equally impressively endowed friend and rival Asclytus. In the world through which they move, genders are happily interchangeable when pleasure is at stake. Thus, although the *nouveau riche* Trimalchio was named his former master's heir because of the sexual favors he provided well past the age when it was seemly for him to act in a passive role, he boasts how faithfully he serviced his mistress as well; his own wife is angry, not that he keeps a stable of beautiful male slaves, but that he kisses his favorite boy publicly in her presence. Encolpius is driven to suicidal despair by his jealous love of Giton but is happy to try to satisfy beautiful, sexually voracious Circe. Poetaster Eumolpus leches after every handsome younger man that he sees, but when given the choice of a legacy-hunter's son or daughter, he happily chooses the girl, leaving the boy to Encolpius, whom he had just been attempting to seduce. The only crime in Petronius's imagined universe, as the paired tales of the Widow of Ephesus and of the Boy of Pergamon suggest, is denying one's sexual appetites; such hypocrisy is punished, generally through comic ridicule.

The Satyricon is the prototype for such contemporary gay novels as JOHN RECHY's *City of Night* (1963), Daniel Curzon's *The Misadventures of Tim McPick* (1975), and LUIS ZAPATA's *Adonis Garcia* (1979) in which travel licenses sexual experimentation as well as indulgence. An English translation of *The Satyricon* first published in Paris in 1902 and purported to be by "Sebastian Melmoth," a well-known pseudonym of OSCAR WILDE, suggests a second important influence that Petronius's narrative has had on gay letters. Although clearly not Wilde's work, the anonymous translator's attempt to promote the underground classic by linking it to the refined AESTHETICISM, sexual self-indulgence, and satiric sharpness of the Victorian Age's most famous homosexual, implicitly defines a gay tradition of arbitrating elegance and of disrupting conventional sexual values that might include, additionally, CHRISTOPHER MARLOWE, JOE ORTON, and Quentin Crisp. The controversial 1968 film version of *Satyricon* by Federico Fellini captures Petronius's satiric grotesquerie and powerful homoeroticism, while losing most of its campy humor.

—*Raymond-Jean Frontain*

BIBLIOGRAPHY

Haig, Thomas. *The Novel in Antiquity.* Berkeley: University of California Press, 1983. ■ Petronius. *The Satyricon.* Trans. William Arrowsmith. New York: New American Library, 1960. ■ ———. *The Satyricon and the Fragments.* Trans. J. P. Sullivan. Rev. ed. Harmondsworth: Penguin, 1974. ■ Richardson, T. Wade. "Homosexuality in the *Satyricon.*" *Classica et Mediaevalia* 35 (1984): 105–127. ■ Slater, Niall W. *Reading Petronius.* Baltimore: Johns Hopkins University Press, 1990. ■ Sullivan, J. P. *The Satyricon of Petronius: A Literary Study.* Bloomington: Indiana University Press, 1968.

Philips, Katherine
(1632–1664)

Katherine Philips, called "The Matchless Orinda" and considered "The English SAPPHO" of her day, was born into the London merchant class and educated at boarding school. When her father, John Fowler, died, Katherine's mother remarried and moved to Wales, taking her daughter with her. In August 1648, when she was sixteen years old, Katherine married a wealthy Welsh Puritan, James Philips, who was thirty-eight years her senior. They had two children, a boy, Hector, who died in infancy, and a girl, who outlived her mother.

During her marriage, Katherine frequently managed her husband's business affairs, but more commonly she devoted herself to literature and the pursuit of female friendships. Through her "Society of Friendship," a formally organized unit whose members took classical pseudonyms, Philips maintained a social network of women-identified women, whose relationships with each other she documented in her poetry. These poems were circulated in manuscript to great acclaim during Philips's life, but not printed until 1664, the year of her death from smallpox at age thirty-two. Also known in her lifetime for her translations from the French of several plays by Corneille, Philips is best known today for her poems, authoritatively printed in one short posthumous volume in 1667.

About two thirds of Philips's printed poems are about erotic relationships among women. Although the female lovers she addresses were married, as was Philips, their marriages were the conventional domestic arrangements of the period, implying neither love nor sexual attraction. Philips writes poems using the adopted names "Orinda" for herself, "Rosania" for Mary Aubrey, and "Lucasia" for Anne Owen. She also writes openly to them and others using their full names or initials. Several of her poems are to other women in their circle, namely "Pastora" and "Phillis," whose joyous relationship is modeled as a contrast to Orinda's solitude when she is no longer with Lucasia.

Until 1652, "Rosania" (Mary Aubrey) and Philips were lovers. Poem #68, "on Rosania's Apostacy and Lucasia's friendship," presents Orinda's justification for leaving Rosania in favor of Lucasia. From 1652 until 1662, Philips and Anne Owen were lovers. The first poem in Philips's short volume is "To The Truly Noble Mrs Anne Owen, on my first Approaches." In later poems, Owen as Lucasia is welcomed into the society of friendship, praised, loved, and courted by Orinda. When Owen's husband died, Philips, in poem #92, consoled her. When Owen remarried in 1651 and went to live in Ireland, Philips went also. She stayed for a year until her own husband recalled her. Her ten-year relationship with Anne Owen was at the center of Philips's short life. Over half of her poems, such as "Orinda to Lucasia," "To My Excellent Lucasia, on Our Friendship," and "To my Lucasia, in defence of declared Friendship," celebrate that relationship. "Parting with Lucasia" details Orinda's grief at their separation, as does "Orinda to Lucasia parting October 1661 at London."

"Orinda to Lucasia," in a traditional pastoral mode, illustrates the importance of the female beloved. Lucasia is the sun who will restore the light and energy of day (life) to Orinda, who cries for her "friend" to appear as the birds, flowers, and brooks call for their own renewal at a delayed sunrise. The "sun" is "tardy," so that the "weary birds" must "court their glorious planet to appear." The "drooping flowers . . . languish down into their beds: / While brooks . . . Openly murmer and demand" that the sun come. But Lucasia means *more* to Orinda than the sun to the world, and if Lucasia delays too long, she will come in time not to save Orinda, but to see her die. Traditional lovesickness unto death from a cruel mistress becomes transformed in this poem to an urgent request for the presence of the willing beloved who will grant life if she comes speedily, but will be the speaker's chief mourner should she die.

The conventional terminology of opposites as an indication of lovesickness appears—light versus dark, day versus night, presence and absence, life and death—while the elements of nature that reflect the lover's state of being are microcosmic in relation to the magnitude of Orinda's feelings. Through the lens of customary literary metaphors, the relationship of the two women is erotically presented in a clever reworking of the romance tradition and idealized classical friendship that highlights the sexual reality inherent in the concrete, physical terminology of the poem.

The relationship between Lucasia and Orinda is further developed and clarified in "To My Excellent Lucasia, on Our Friendship," for which the traditional soul–body dichotomy is the metaphorical basis. In this poem, Orinda's soul is not only given life by Lucasia, but Lucasia's soul actually becomes the animating force of her lover's body: "never had Orinda found / A soul till she found thine" (11–12). The lovers are united in one immortal soul, and their relationship grants to the speaker attributes similar to those of a "bridegroom" or "crown-conquerer." Philips presents the metaphor in an overstatement that extends the cosmic aspects of their loving: "They have but pieces of the earth, / I've all the world in thee." The lovers' relationship is one of traditional courtly desire transformed into a union with a soul mate through whom one may participate in heaven. Their love also remains "innocent" because they are both women. Given their mutually female design, the speaker can "say without a crime, / I am not thine, but thee" and encourage their "flames" to "light and shine" without "false fear" since they are "innocent as our design, / Immortal as our soul."

The speaker invokes both spirituality and innocent design as justifications for such language of excess, even though convention would allow her the license to claim another's soul as her own because of their affection alone. But, as female lovers, they need more than a mere statement rejecting the ordinary. So Orinda's argument is that she and Lucasia are "innocent" because as women they do not have the necessary equipment to fulfill society's notion of "the sex act." In a phallocentric culture that defines sexual behavior according to penile instrumentality, sex exclusive of men is not merely unthinkable, it is impossible. Therefore, to address the question of relationship in these poems is to redefine conventional definitions of eroticism and sexuality.

During her lifetime, Philips's literary reputation was enhanced by the praise of important English writers who considered Orinda "Matchless." Known to be a "Sapphist" in both art and life, she was a model lesbian poet. Although she has been reclaimed by twentieth-century feminist literary critics, the sexual aspect of Philips's poetry has sometimes been denied.

An informed reading of her work, however, demonstrates clearly the sensibility that prioritizes erotic attraction between women, acts on it, and celebrates it, not merely as an idea but in fact.

—*Arlene M. Stiebel*

BIBLIOGRAPHY

Andreadis, Harriette. "The Sapphic-Platonics of Katherine Philips, 1632-1664." *Signs: Journal of Women in Culture and Society* 15.1 (1989): 34–60. ■ Mermin, Dorothy. "Women Becoming Poets: Katherine Philips, Aphra Behn, Anne Finch." *ELH* 57.2 (1990): 335–356. ■ Souers, Philip Webster. *The Matchless Orinda.* Cambridge: Harvard University Press, 1931. ■ Stiebel, Arlene. "Not Since Sappho: The Erotic in Poems of Katherine Philips and Aphra Behn." *Homosexuality in Renaissance and Enlightenment England.* Claude J. Summers, ed. Binghamton, N.Y.: Haworth, 1992. 153–171. ■ ———. "Subversive Sexuality: Masking the Erotic in Poems by Katherine Philips and Aphra Behn." *Renaissance Discourses of Desire.* Claude J. Summers and Ted-Larry Pebworth, eds. Columbia: University of Missouri Press, 1993. 223–236.

Plante, David
(*b.* 1940)

David Robert Plante was born in Providence, Rhode Island, on March 4, 1940, of French-Canadian and Indian descent. After several early, short-lived jobs, Plante went to London on what was to be a short visit, only to spend much of his life to date there. Since the publication of his first novel, *The Ghost of Henry James* in 1970, Plante has proved to be one of the most prolific and experimental of contemporary writers, with twelve other novels, as well as many reviews, essays, and a nonfiction book, *Difficult Women* (1983), to his credit. Plante's work is as wide-ranging in subject, style, and content as it is voluminous; he is one of today's most exciting writers.

Gay male characters and men who seem sexually ambiguous feature in a variety of ways in such early Plante novels as *The Ghost of Henry James, Slides* (1971), *Relatives* (1972), and *The Darkness of the Body* (1974). Although these novels show gay characters in differing degrees of specificity, even more overtly homosexual men can be found in *Figures in Bright Air* (1976), *The Foreigner* (1984), and *The Catholic* (1986). Plante is most noted for *The Family* (1978), *The Country* (1981), and *The Woods* (1982), his highly acclaimed Francoeur "trilogy." (*The Foreigner* and *The Catholic* have rather specific links to the trilogy but are set "away" from the family of the novels.) While these novels vary in their presentation

of overtly gay characters or sex scenes, they do suggest other coming-of-age works by gay writers such as TENNESSEE WILLIAMS, CARSON McCULLERS, and TRUMAN CAPOTE. However, Plante's novels lack the gothic extravagances often associated with those other writers. Plante's low-key approach allows the other family members and characters to emerge as clearly as his narrator, Daniel, who seems sexually ambiguous in the trilogy. Such ambiguity as found in life is a hallmark of Plante's writing, sexuality included.

Plante's approach to homosexuality ranges from the explicit and emotionally violent, as in *The Catholic,* to the quietly transcending, as in his earlier novels. In the novels of the trilogy, as well as *The Foreigner* and *The Accident* (1991), Plante's leading male characters suggest sexualities unacknowledged. Plante focuses not only on the varieties of love and sexuality but on the different expressions love and sexuality may take. For example, some characters engage enthusiastically in a variety of sexual practices, some seem to be bisexual or inclined that way, and some appear to be determining their sexuality or sexualities. Thus, his novels—as well as his nonfiction account of his encounters with three *Difficult Women*—may be said to examine a variety of homosexualities as well as heterosexual ones. Plante refuses clearly to be locked in as a writer, and this refusal makes his gay characters, and his work generally, complex and remarkable, as does his often experimental style. Plante's conviction that he himself has many identities and different sexualities shows in his writing.

Those who call for a more integrated approach to homosexuality in literature, and in life for that matter, would do well to read Plante's novels. Perhaps most important, his experimentation with prose style is bound up in the different ways he presents homosexuality in his novels and stories. Plante sometimes challenges the use of linear narrative and our expectations of what narrative should be. For example, in one novel he uses short chapters to represent photographic slides, and in others he dispenses with the background information and certain identification of time and place we often expect from narrative. Simi-

larly, he explores sexuality of all kinds as being equally undefined, unsure, and changing. As a result, Plante's work demands much from the reader, and gives much in return.

—*Thomas Dukes*

BIBLIOGRAPHY

Baker, John F. "David Plante." *Publishers Weekly.* December 24, 1982. 12–13. ■ Dukes, Thomas. "David Plante." *Contemporary Gay American Novelists.* Emmanuel S. Nelson, ed. Westport, Conn.: Greenwood, 1993. 309–315. ■ Gordon, Mary. "David Plante." *Good Boys and Dead Girls.* New York: Viking, 1991. 108–111. ■ Kaiser, John R. "David Plante." *Dictionary of Literary Biography Yearbook 1983.* Detroit: Gale, 1983. 298–304. ■ Nye, Robert. "David Plante." *Contemporary Novelists.* James Vinson, ed. New York: St. Martin's, 1976. 1088–1089.

von Platen, August
(1796–1835)

Count August von Platen was born on October 24, 1796, in Ansbach, Bavaria, the son of an impoverished nobleman. He attended the Military Academy at Munich (1806–1810) and the Royal Institute of Pages (1810–1814), resulting in his commission as a lieutenant in 1815 in a regiment against France during the time of Napoleon; he, however, engaged in no action. After a leave of absence in 1818, Platen studied at the University of Würzburg, transferring a year later to Erlangen, where he studied under the idealist philosopher of Romanticism, Friedrich Schelling, and made the acquaintance of many of the leading writers of the time, including Goethe. Platen was extremely erudite, mastering a dozen languages, including literary Greek and Latin, French for social status, Persian for poetic reasons, and even English.

In 1821, Platen published *Ghaselen,* his first major collection of poems. In this work, he adopted the "ghasel," modeled after the Persian poet Hafiz's (1326–1390) verse. In 1824, Platen traveled to Italy and in Venice created *Sonnets from Venice* (*Sonette aus Venedig,* 1825), which are Petrarchan in form. His *Songs of the Poles* (*Polenlieder,* 1831), expressing sympathy for the Poles in their rebellion against tyranny, are among the great classical poems of their time. His drama *The Glass Slipper* (*Der gläserne Pantoffel,* 1824) is a comedy with fairy tale elements.

An admirer of MICHELANGELO and Italian art, Platen visited Florence, Rome, Naples, Syracuse, and

Sicily. While in Naples in the 1820s, he formed a friendship with the poet and painter August Kopisch, all the while perfecting the content and form of his poetry. By 1826, he had moved permanently to Italy, supported by a pension from his friend King Ludwig I of Bavaria. Focusing his sexual urges into the artistic and creative realms, Platen transformed his passion for same-sex relations from the physical to the intellectual. On occasion, a friendship lasted only a year or so—for example, his intense relationship with a young painter, Rühl—but it nevertheless served to heighten his creative powers. His controversial, multilingual, autobiographical narrative, which contains an explicitly erotic homosexual theme, was not published until the end of the nineteenth century, under the title *Diary* (*Die Tagebücher,* 1896–1900).

In his poetry, Platen employs a recurrent homoerotic image borrowed from Persian poetry, the tulip, which is a spiritual symbol for masculine love. Platen's longing for love and friendship is a persistent motif in his work. He addressed seven sonnets to "Cardenio," an Erlangen student, who is described as a young, tall, dark, and handsome man with full lips. Platen addressed an additional twenty-one sonnets to another Erlangen student, "Karl Theodor German." Embodying themes of Platonic love, friendship, longing, idealism, and beauty, Platen's sonnets express unrequited love for men.

Platen's homosexuality is the subject of a vicious attack by Heinrich Heine in *The Baths of Lucca* (*Die*

Bäder von Lucca, 1829). EDWARD CARPENTER, however, expressed his appreciation for Platen in his *Ioälus, An Anthology of Friendship* (1902). Among German writers who admired Platen is THOMAS MANN, who praised him in a lecture in 1930; Platen's poem "Tristan" (1825) inspired Mann's novella *Tristan and Isolde* (1903). In 1985, the homosexual, avant-garde writer HUBERT FICHTE published a noteworthy tribute to Platen, describing the poet as a "creative master like Whitman, Rimbaud, and Genêt." Although no biography of Platen has yet been written in English, his life is engaging while his art is captivating.

—*Clarence McClanahan*

BIBLIOGRAPHY

Atkins, Stuart. "A Humanistic Approach to Literature: Critical Interpretations of Two Sonnets by Platen." *German Quarterly* 25 (1952): 258–276. ∎ Bumm, Peter. *August Graf von Platen: Eine Biographie*. Paderborn: Ferdinand Schöningh, 1990. ∎ Carpenter, Edward. *Ioälus, An Anthology of Friendship*. New York: Pagan Press, 1982. ∎ Dove, Richard. *The "Individualität" of August von Platen*. Bern: Peter Lang, 1983. ∎ Fichte, Hubert. "Deiner Umarmungen süsse Sehnsucht." *Die Geschichte der Empfindungen am Beispiel der französischen Schriften des Grafen August von Platen-Hallermünde*. Tübingen: Konkursbuchverlag, 1985. ∎ Heine, Heinrich. "The Baths of Lucca." *The Works of Heinrich Heine*. Trans. Charles G. Leland. New York: AMS, 1990. ∎ Mann, Thomas. "August von Platen." *Leiden und Grösse der Meister*. Neue Aufsätze. Berlin: Fischer, 1933. ∎ Sammons, Jeffrey L. "Platen's Tulip Image." *Monatshefte* 52 (1960): 293–301.

Plato
(427–327 B.C.)

Among Greek writers on homosexual themes, Plato is preeminent not only as a major philosopher but also as the greatest master of Greek prose. The *Symposium* and the *Phaedrus,* dialogues that deal directly with the subject of male love, stand among Plato's finest literary achievements. Plato was born into an aristocratic Athenian family that claimed descent from Solon and ancient kings. His relatives led the antidemocratic reaction of 404; when democracy was restored five years later, Plato's teacher Socrates was put to death on a charge of undermining Athenian faith and morals through his critical teachings. The disillusioned Plato then left Greece to travel abroad; in Sicily, he met Dion, brother-in-law of the powerful tyrant, Dionysus. The two men appear to have been drawn to each other by shared philosophical and political interests and a strong personal bond.

Plato's amorous susceptibility seems to have centered principally on young men. Unlike most Greek males, Plato never married. Diogenes Laertius in his *Lives and Opinions of Eminent Philosophers* (ca 250 A.D.) gives considerable attention to his subjects' erotic interests, partly because he enjoyed gossip but also because he realized how profound a role same-sex love affairs played in the careers of Greek thinkers. He speaks of Plato's "passionate attachment for males." He quotes three poems to women ascribed to Plato, and five to men. Of the latter, one is on the pleasure of kissing Agathon, another acknowledges the attraction of his pupil Aster, and a third hesitates to praise

the beauty of Alexis for fear of alerting rivals. But Plato's most fully documented relation was with Dion.

Plato traveled to Syracuse at Dion's request in 387 hoping to mitigate the harsh rule of the tyrannical Dionysus, but the mission was not a success. Two years afterward Dion helped Plato found his famous school, the Academy, in a grove near Athens. It survived as a pedagogical center until Justinian closed it (for religious reasons) nine centuries later. In 367, Dion persuaded Plato once more to visit Sicily, this time aspiring to influence Dionysus' heir, but the second Dionysus proved as intractable as the first. Finally, Dion overthrew him and seized power, only to be himself assassinated. Plato wrote his epitaph: "[Now] in your wide-wayed city, honored at last you rest, / O Dion, whose love once maddened the heart within this breast."

It is hardly too much to say that Plato's dialogues are suffused with a homoerotic ambience. At the opening of the *Charmides*, Socrates, returning from the battle of Potidaea, comes to the wrestling school of Taureus and inquires who are the new beauties among the boys. Though Socrates qualifies his query by explaining he is interested in intellect as well as appearance, he and the others are constantly aware of the power of youthful male beauty to excite and inspire. The young Charmides is recommended as the cream of the crop, and his entry is duly dramatized. A crowd of admirers attends him. Those present—including the young boys—grow silent with awe at his good looks and compete to have him sit beside them. Socrates, when he catches a glimpse of the "inside of his garment" feels a surge of desire, which he dutifully suppresses. Similarly, at the start of the *Protagoras,* Socrates is teased for chasing the "fair Alcibiades," now showing his first trace of beard; later in the dialogue Pausanias and Agathon are introduced as a male couple. Phaedo, after whom Plato named the dialogue that records Socrates' last words, had been discovered by the philosopher serving in a male brothel. He had been captured in a war between Elis and Sparta, and sold as slave to the keeper of the house in Athens.

Plato's principal writings on homosexuality are the *Symposium,* the *Phaedrus,* and the *Laws.* The first, which was composed when Plato was about 43, is of prime importance in giving us the varied views of a group of Athenian intellectuals on Greek love. It represents a compendium of popular ideas on the subject, and introduces us to Socrates' criticism of them. This critique is developed more fully in the *Phaedrus* with its rhapsodic poetry and exalted myths. The *Laws,* which Plato completed shortly before his death at eighty, is a very different work, both in style and tone. Here a harsh puritanism discards poetry for an emphasis on social control.

The *Symposium,* with its seven different speakers, gives a wide-lens perspective on the theme of love in fifth-century Athens. It is symptomatic of Greek society that these men assume that love as a serious emotion will ordinarily mean love between males. Their views should not be regarded as those of a narrow coterie. A host of other writers (see also GREEK LITERATURE, ANCIENT) amply demonstrate that much of what they say was common coin not just in Athens but throughout the Greek world.

The dialogue is organized not as a debate, but as a series of panegyrics on love. The first speaker, Phaedrus, is naively enthusiastic and routinely utters the clichés of popular opinion. Love is inspirational—as an incentive to honorable conduct, it is a more potent force than family, social position, or wealth. It encourages bravery in war since no lover would want to disgrace himself in his lover's eyes by running away in battle. Here Phaedrus makes his famous boast that "an army of lovers" might defeat the whole world. We may note that what gave love its prestige in the Hellenic world was the idea that lovers would, on occasion, sacrifice their lives for one another. This is the crucial idea that was to remain central to discussions of love among Greeks throughout antiquity. Lovers who were comrades in battle or allies in opposing political oppression were regarded as most likely to manifest this supreme virtue. These had

perforcedly to be men. On this account, Phaedrus downgrades the love of Orpheus and Eurydice, the Romeo and Juliet of classical mythology. He gives as his reason that Orpheus does not die for his bride, but sneaks into Hades alive; moreover, as a musician, he does not measure up to the masculine ideals of a military society. Nevertheless, Alcestis, who was willing to die for her husband Admetus, demonstrates that on occasion women are capable of love in its most heroic form. But the great exemplar of this tradition is Achilles, who died to avenge Patroclus.

During his speech, Phaedrus leaves us in the dark about whether he is speaking of "Platonic" love or consummated affairs, though a reference to Aeschylus' play shows that he was familiar with the view that Achilles and Patroclus were lovers in the physical sense. (The only objection Phaedrus has to the *Myrmidons* is that Aeschylus made Achilles the *erastes,* or lover, whereas in Homer he is the more beautiful of the two men, and therefore more eligible for the role of *eromenos,* or beloved.) Pausanias, the next speaker, tackles the ethical question that Phaedrus had ignored. He does this by introducing a famous distinction that has haunted Western moral thought for more than two thousand years: the distinction between "higher" and "lower" forms of love. To this end, he has recourse to an inconsistency in Greek mythology. Traditional myths had two different accounts of the birth of Aphrodite, the goddess of love. In one, she was the daughter of Uranus (whose name meant "Heaven"), sprung from the foam when his son Cronos castrated him and threw his member into the sea. In the other, she was the daughter of Cronos' son Zeus by the Titaness Dione. Pausanias connects these myths with the fact that Aphrodite was also worshipped under different names—Aphrodite Urania (the "Heavenly" Aphrodite, daughter of Uranus) and Aphrodite Pandemos (the "Common," that is, promiscuous, Aphrodite). The second kind of love is purely physical and includes the desire for women as well as boys. The higher love, on the other hand, has an ideal, spiritual component and is directed only to young men who are beginning to develop beards and intellect. In making this claim, Pausanias was going directly against popular Greek opinion that held that boys were suitable love objects only until their beards grew since they then lost their feminine beauty. Pausanias counters this widespread prejudice with an appeal to the moral ideal of fidelity since only those who love mature males will be capable of forming lasting attachments that will endure throughout a lifetime. (At the time of the *Symposium,* Pausanias' affair with Agathon, the host at the banquet, had lasted at least a decade.)

So far it is not apparent whether Pausanias' higher love involves a sexual element. He clarifies this point in the second part of his speech when he looks at the subject geographically. In Thebes, Elis, and Sparta, he claims, there is no restraint on physical relations, and youths may freely gratify their lovers. In Asiatic Ionia, on the other hand, the absolute rule of the Persians discourages love affairs among their Greek subjects since such relations might lead to political revolt. (To establish this, Pausanias invokes the examples of the Athenian tyrannicides, Aristogiton and Harmodius.) In Athens, by contrast, opinion is neither totally for nor against male love. There, extravagant behavior by lovesick male adults is condoned but boys are teased by their peers if they have lovers. Pausanias approves of this system since it guarantees that boys will be chary of granting their favors and will not yield for venal reasons, but only when they can claim that their lover is a man of virtue and wisdom who will inculcate these virtues. Pausanias argues that young males should gratify only such lovers, thus establishing the fact that his higher love is, in effect, mixed—that is, it combines the physical with the spiritual.

Aristophanes makes a similar assumption. Sexual acts exist, he thinks, both for procreation and for the physical satisfaction of male couples. His argument is set in a fantastic framework, the kind of comic myth one might expect to find in his theatrical extravaganzas. Human beings were once, he tells us, double creatures made up of double males, double females, or two genders united. He uses this myth to "explain" the origin of differing sexual orientations. For when Zeus, as a punishment, severed these double beings, the halves tried to recombine: hence male homosexuality, lesbianism, and heterosexuality. But Aristophanes' fable is by no means neutral in its values. He concludes that homosexuality is superior to heterosexuality since anything that involves two males must be nobler than that which mixes genders. Thus lovers of males are "more manly" than lovers of women. The boys who surrender themselves to men are not shameless but models of spirited virility who later become the principal leaders in public life. In classical Greece, "homosexism" might, as on this occasion, predominate over "heterosexism."

The speech on love of the physician Eryximachus does not touch on homosexuality since it is couched in general physiological terms. Nor does Agathon's speech take up the social and ethical themes broached by his lover Pausanias. It is a flowery exercise in rhetoric that Socrates punctures with ironic questions. Socrates, in developing his own theory of love, pursues a wholly different line from the preceding speakers. He confirms the homoerotic bias of the others by

assuming that love will first be inspired by the beauty of boys, but argues that love for the beauty of an individual should give way to love for beauty generally. Love should, indeed, ultimately be directed not to persons at all but to abstract ideals such as beauty, justice, and truth. In its highest manifestation, it will take the form of love for the constitutions and laws of utopian states. In the end, Socrates sublimates erotics into politics, leaving personal relations behind entirely. The final speech, by Alcibiades, who has burst in drunk upon the party, is a detailed account of how the handsome young Athenian tried in vain to seduce Socrates in order to make him his mentor. He expresses astonishment, which he expects the others to share, that Socrates should have resisted his charms.

The dialectic of the *Symposium* leaves an important question unanswered. Though Socrates obviously regards the love of beautiful boys as the lowest step on the ladder of love, it is not clear if its physical manifestation is simply given a lower place in his moral scheme of things or is entirely forbidden. The *Phaedrus* focuses on this issue. Phaedrus begins by showing Socrates a clever speech by the orator Lysias. It argues that a young man ought to yield his favors not to someone who is in love with him but to a nonlover since the latter will be less jealous and less likely to betray him by boasting of the affair. After some typical irony, Socrates reveals that he regards such an idea as a kind of blasphemy against the sacred idea of love, which for him is a form of "divine madness." He then presents the myth of the soul as a charioteer driving two horses. The ugly black horse is passion, the noble white horse reason and self-control. Though the beauty of the male beloved may lead the black horse to assault him, the lover must do everything he can to subdue and tame the animal. Only then will he grow the wings that will take the pair to heaven. The lover may touch, kiss, and embrace the beloved, but they must remain chaste. The passage in which Plato sets forth this fantasy is one of the most eloquent, imaginative, and beautiful in Greek prose. Never has anyone praised love between males in more exalted terms, or worked harder to make frustration sound seductive.

At the end of the *Phaedrus,* Plato relaxes his strictness slightly by admitting that those who momentarily "accomplish that desire of their hearts which to the many is bliss" may, if they later learn control, also soar to the skies as winged beings. Again, in the *Republic,* Plato goes so far as to allow the man who has demonstrated unusual courage in battle to kiss the boy or girl of his choice as a reward, though no more than this. When we come to Plato's last work, the *Laws,* however, all tolerance has vanished. The book, though cast in the form of a dialogue between an Athenian, a Cretan, and a Spartan, lacks the drama, wit, and poetry of the earlier dialogues; it is primarily a dry setting forth of a detailed law code for an ideal city. Love as an inspirational value has all but disappeared. Plato's spokesman, the Athenian, argues that all physical expressions of love between men should be rigorously repressed. To support this view, he maintains that homosexual relations are not procreative, that they are unnatural since male animals do not engage in them, and that they do not promote courage in battle since the passive partner assumes a feminine role unworthy of a soldier and the active partner is seeking pleasure instead of inuring himself to pain.

Plato wishes to introduce a law prohibiting male relations. He admits that this will be exceedingly difficult since most virile young Greeks will reject the proposal as absurd and impossible. He notes in response that some athletes do practice continence as part of their training. Most likely, however, such behavior can only be effectively banned through the introduction of some religious taboo such as exists in the case of incest. Here we have a chilling prophecy of what was to happen four centuries later with the advent of Christianity. But one cannot credit the *Laws* with much appeal; liberals and conservatives alike have been repelled by this repressive society which forbade foreign travel, commerce, or religious dissent, and subjected all citizens to a discipline akin to that of a military barracks. Modern critics have, indeed, found in it a prototype of twentieth-century fascism.

Plato thus stands in the paradoxical position of having written some of the most enthusiastic pages on homosexuality in all literature and some of the most negative. After his death, the Platonic Academy in Athens carried on his pedagogical traditions. Plato's first successor was his nephew. After him, the headship passed to Xenocrates. The young Polemo came to Xenocrates' class to mock, was enchanted, shed a wife, and becoming the older man's lover, inherited his post. He, in turn, loved Crates, who lived with him, succeeded him, and shared his tomb. The Platonic pair entertained another Academic couple at their table, Crantor and his *eromenos,* Arcesilaus. So for a full century, from 339 to 240, leadership in the Academy passed from lover to beloved.

Plato's doctrine of love had great influence on later Greek thought, most notably on PLUTARCH, a devoted Platonist who celebrated male love in his *Lives* and followed Plato closely in his own panegyric on love in the *Eroticus*. His authorship of "On Education," the only essay on this topic to come down to us from antiquity, has been disputed. But the essay, which was widely admired in the Renaissance, is thoroughly Plutarchan (and Platonic) in its endorsement of the pedagogic eros. After noting that some severe fathers may disapprove of their sons' having lovers, the author commends the practice, citing the examples of Socrates, Plato, Xenophon, Aeschines, and a multitude of others who approved of chaste male loves as a way of "guiding adolescents towards culture and political leadership and excellence of character." Less original than Plutarch is Maximus of Tyre, a rhetorician who lectured in Rome about 180 A.D. Of his forty orations, four (18–21) extol the Socratic eros as a path to honor and virtue. But Maximus not only echoes the *Laws* by decrying intercourse between men as sterile and unnatural, he consistently denies that there was anything physical in any of the loves of those he invokes as models. Thus the love of Achilles for Patroclus was not carnal, and the loves of even such poets as SAPPHO and Anacreon were, he maintains, as pure as Socrates'.

Though the impact of Plato's erotic dialogues on later Greek culture was very great, they seem to have had little influence on Latin writers, and they remained unknown in the West in the Middle Ages. Their rediscovery was a major event in Renaissance literature. Ficino's epochal *Commentary on the Symposium* (1475) and his translation of the dialogue made "Platonic" love fashionable throughout literary Europe, but he minimized the homoerotic element. Castiglione's *The Courtier* (1518), a highly influential work, completely "heterosexualized" Platonic love, thus obscuring its real origins. Even though Plato opposed giving physical expression to homosexual desires, many Christian writers, from the church fathers onward, regarded it as scandalous that he had gone so far as to portray a society where such feelings were openly recognized, discussed, and approved. Some learned authors of the English Renaissance, such as Sir Philip Sidney, revealed a (disapproving) knowledge of the original texts, but awareness of the role male love played in Plato's teachings remained, in England at least, a secret reserved to scolars versed in Greek literature. The first English translation of the *Symposium,* published by Floyd Sydenham in 1767, was outrageously bowdlerized. Male references and pronouns were changed to female and Plato's "army of lovers" transformed into an army of knights and ladies. Alcibiades' speech was omitted as contrary to English morals. To counter this travesty, Percy Bysshe Shelley prepared an accurate translation, but when it was finally published after his death, it too was bowdlerized so as to obliterate any homosexual details. The first candid English version to reveal Plato's world in uncensored form was the Bohn Library edition of 1849.

—*Louis Crompton*

BIBLIOGRAPHY

Dover, Kenneth. *Greek Homosexuality*. London: Duckworth, 1978. ■ Foucault, Michel. *The Use of Pleasure*. Trans. R. Hurley. New York: Random House, 1985. ■ Halperin, David. "Why is Diotima a Woman?" *One Hundred Years of Homosexuality and Other Essays on Greek Love*. New York: Routledge, 1990. ■ Marrou, H. I. *A History of Education in Antiquity*. Trans. G. Lamb. New York: Sheed and Ward, 1956. ■ Plato. *Laws*. Trans. T. L. Pangle. New York: Basic Books, 1980. ■ ———. *Phaedrus*. Trans. R. Hackworth. Cambridge: Cambridge University Press, 1952. ■ ———. *Symposium*. Trans. W. Hamilton. Harmondsworth: Penguin, 1951.

Plomer, William
(1903–1973)

Novelist and poet William Plomer was born in South Africa, in Pietersburg, Transvaal, where his father was a civil servant, on December 10, 1903. Plomer entered an Anglican school, St. John's College in Johannesburg, in 1912. Both parents were English. His mother, with no love for South Africa, took him to England, where he spent three miserable years at a small private school in Kent and one happier year at Rugby. Back in South Africa, he chose not to continue his education. Instead, he used experience garnered during a farm apprenticeship and a period assisting his parents at a native trading station in his first novel, *Turbott Wolfe,* published by Leonard and VIRGINIA WOOLF's Hogarth Press in 1925. As the book was going to press, Plomer got to know Roy Campbell and Laurens van der Post, two rebel white South Africans, and together they worked on a radical periodical, *Voorslag* ("whiplash"). All three withdrew after publication of the second issue, angered by attempts to muzzle their writing. This was the turning point in Plomer's career; he knew that the Woolfs would provide him entrance to London literary circles so, following three happy years teaching in Japan, he went to England to make his permanent home.

Although discreet about his homosexuality, Plomer accepted it. He enjoyed his first affair when he was eleven years old, with a steward on board ship. He always felt himself to be an outsider, and thereafter most of his short-term affairs were with other outsiders. He was attracted to black South African men, to students he taught in Japan from 1926 to 1929, and in England, to working-class boys and men in uniform. Overt homosexuality is absent from his novels and poems, but he confided to the editor of his revised, posthumously published autobiography that he expected his biographer to take his sexual orientation seriously because it was important to his work. The relevance of Plomer's sexuality to his work is evident in *Turbott Wolfe,* for example, which was ahead of its time in telling a story of miscegenation in South Africa. A reader who knows something about Plomer can see how specific homosexual impulses are transferred to the story of a love affair between a white woman and a black man; additionally, the white woman clearly stands in for a male figure. This kind of transference occurs throughout Plomer's writing.

In England, where he settled in 1929, Plomer moved in interconnected and influential literary circles energized by homosexual bonds. He mixed with AUDEN and ISHERWOOD, E. M. FORSTER and Virginia Woolf, Harold Nicolson, John Lehmann, and J. R. ACKERLEY, among others. Here he could count on warm support for his chosen lifestyle, as when he came close to public disgrace during World War II: A serviceman whom he solicited for sex turned him over to the police, but friends successfully intervened. On the other hand, his friend Roy Campbell (with Plomer, the most distinguished white South African writer of his generation) broke with him in 1933 and issued veiled attacks motivated by deep-rooted homophobia in his satirical verse.

After *Turbott Wolfe,* Plomer developed as a modernist novelist and poet. He invented a comic-macabre form of ballad, which W. H. Auden used as a model. He collaborated with composer Benjamin Britten as librettist for several operas, and for the last thirty years of his life, as a respected "person of letters," had an unassuming and devoted companion in Charles Erdmann.

—*Patrick Holland*

BIBLIOGRAPHY

Alexander, Peter F. *William Plomer: A Biography*. Oxford: Oxford University Press, 1989. ■ Doyle, J. R. *William Plomer*. New York: Twayne Publishers, 1969. ■ Van der Post, Laurens. *A Walk with a White Bushman*. London: Chatto & Windus, 1986.

Plutarch
(ca 46–ca 120)

No ancient is more instructive about pederasty than Plutarch. Educated in Athens by the Platonic philosopher Ammonius, Plutarch was also influenced by the Peripatetics and Stoics, but he rejected Epicureanism. Traveling throughout Hellas and to Rome as ambassador of his native city, he associated with prominent political and literary figures and proclaimed that Greeks and Romans should be partners in the Roman Empire. In Chaeronea, he maintained a sort of private academy for his friends and pupils, remaining active into old age.

Plutarch's *Moralia* and his *Parallel Lives,* our main biographical source for Greek and Roman military or political leaders, take up twenty-six volumes in the Loeb Classical Library. This makes him the most published Greek author there, excelling even Aristotle's twenty-three volumes and rivaling the Roman Cicero's thirty.

Plutarch's works provide crucial information about ancient sexualities. In the *Parallel Lives,* he recorded much about the homoerotic proclivities of the Romans, while three-fourths of his twenty-three Greek heroes had eromenoi (beloved boys) or helped to institutionalize pederasty. His "Pelopidas," for example, is our best source for Epaminondas, the leader of the Sacred Band of 150 pairs of lovers who so inspired the Greeks. In "Lycurgus," one of our very few sources about Greek lesbianism, Plutarch depicts the Spartan system that produced courageous tyrannicidal couples and also avers that Spartan ladies loved girls. Plutarch makes Theseus the beloved of the Cretan king Minos and attributes pederastic laws in Athens to Solon. He portrays Themistocles and Aristides, the victors in the Persian wars, as rivals for a beautiful youth and depicts Socrates' favorite Alcibiades as having stolen husbands from women when he was a youth and, as a man, wives from their husbands. According to the *Lives,* the Hellenistic king Demetrius and Alexander the Great were, like the poets of the *Greek Anthology,* also promiscuous.

Plutarch's charming dialogue the "Eroticus" is a debate on whether love of women or of youths should be preferred. The author relies heavily on PLATO's *Phaedrus* and *Symposium* for erotic theory but unlike Plato allows that love of females could be as inspiring as love of boys. However, like other Greeks, he mostly describes the love of upper-class men for noble youths. One of the speakers in the "Eroticus" proclaims that "it is not gentlemanly or urbane to make love to slave boys: such love is mere copulation, like the love of women." Plutarch depicts the love of Euripides for Agathon as the archetype of androphile homosexuality, that is, of love between adult males.

In "On the Education of Children," Plutarch expressly condemns the grossly sensual pederasty practiced by Thebans, Elians, and Cretans (including the *harpagmos,* the ritual kidnapping of the beloved) but praises the more civically oriented and decorous Athenian and Spartan varieties, as had Xenophon and Plato. In Plutarch's "Gryllus," the chief speaker is a pig that insists that animals conform solely to nature: "to this very day the lusts of animals have encompassed no intercourse of male with male or of female with female. But you have a good deal of this sort of thing among your high and virtuous nobility, to say nothing of the lesser breeds." This appears to be Plutarch's clever rejoinder to the speaker in Plato's *Laws* who declares homosexuality to be against nature. Here nature is equated with the behavior of animals; pederasty, with humans, especially the "high and virtuous nobility." Thus Plutarch attests the millennium-long contribution of *paiderasteia* to Hellenism but reflects (or deflects) the moralizing criticism of it, whose beginning MICHEL FOUCAULT aptly traced to the Socratic circle, but whose prevalence during the Imperial period the French scholar vastly overemphasized.

Virtually unknown in the West during the Middle Ages, Plutarch's legacy to Western culture was revived in the Renaissance. Translated into English by Sir Thomas North in the Elizabethan era, his *Parallel Lives* furnished the material for SHAKESPEARE's Roman plays, while the *Moralia* were translated by Philemon Holland as *The Philosophy* (1603). Both translators relied on Jacques Amyot's pathbreaking French translation, which Montaigne also used.

—*William A. Percy*

BIBLIOGRAPHY

Hirschfeld, Magnus. *Die Homosexualität des Mannes und des Weibes.* Berlin: Louis Marcus Verlagsbuchhandlung, 1914. ∎ Licht, Hans. *Sexual Life in Ancient Greece.* New York: Barnes and Noble, 1963. ∎ Martin, Hubert. "Plutarch, Plato, and Eros." *Classical Bulletin* 60 (1984): 82–88. ∎ Smith, Bruce R. *Homosexual Desire in Shakespeare's England: A Cultural Poetics.* Chicago: The University of Chicago Press, 1991. ∎ Symonds, John Addington. *A Problem in Greek Ethics.* In *Male Love: A Problem in Greek Ethics and Other Writings.* John Lauritsen, ed. New York: Pagan Press, 1983.

POETRY

Poetry, Gay Male

§ If we are to speak of a "gay tradition" in literature—and every gay theorist warns us to be careful if we wish to do so—it would be primarily a tradition not of novels but of verse, something like, but even broader than, the contents list of Stephen Coote's *Penguin Book of Homosexual Verse*, beginning in the ancient world and progressing with great vitality—considering how widely stigmatized male-male love has been at various points in history—through the Middle Ages and Renaissance, beyond the modern world into the era of the post-modern; from pederasty to sodomy, from homosexuality to gayness, and beyond. More inclusive than Coote, it might include the epic of GILGAMESH, Hispano-Arabic love poetry, the *Chanson de Roland*, Turkish *divan* poetry, and so forth.

Certain forms (the sonnet) and genres (the funeral elegy) have proved particularly fruitful, as have particular periods (the Renaissance) and cultures (Arabic). One can also draw broad conclusions about the homoerotic outcomes of verse written for specific purposes. In this context, one thinks of dramatic verse in which the modulations of the gendered voice so frequently faltered: In most dramatic traditions, the words of the two genders were spoken only by males, men and boys, on either side of the defining moment of maturation. The inevitable outcome was an undercurrent of implication that one man might desire another. Elsewhere, one can see retrospectively that certain poetic movements have enabled their successor movements to voice the homoerotic impulse. For instance, the "DECADENCE" of the *fin de siècle* (CHARLES BAUDELAIRE, PAUL VERLAINE, ARTHUR RIMBAUD) offered a conduit into MODERNISM (T.S. ELIOT, HART CRANE).

We are not thinking of mere by-ways, obscure deviations from the mainstream. Male poets who loved boys do not always materialize as radical subverters of conservative traditions or as isolated eccentrics. Gay poetry does not always go against the grain; indeed, there have been many times when it *was* the grain. Again and again, if one examines the most deep-rooted traditions of love poetry, with the most strongly established conventions of both form and topic, not to mention etiquette, one comes across love poems addressed by men to boys.

Such poems are often to be found nestling happily in the midst of heterosexual love poems. For instance, there is an anthology of 656 poems by Chinese court poets of the Southern Dynasties, entitled *New Songs from a Jade Terrace*. It was compiled by the poet Hsu Ling in about 545 A.D. As you work your way through the collection, you occasionally encounter a poem which, although as conventional in its imagery and formality as any of the others, is about a desired boy rather than a woman. Yet these homoerotic poems are not simply formal exercises, allowed into the very public space of the anthology because the "friendship" they express is "platonic" or "chaste." On the contrary, a poem like Wu Chun's "A Boy" is explicitly dismissive of "virtue." A man invites a boy to bed—nothing could be less equivocal.

One factor that helps explain why some cultures produce a proliferation of love poems addressed to boys by men is, quite simply, male privilege. The sheer availability of boys makes their concrete presence amenable to transposition into erotic imagery. The poetry of the Ottoman Empire, for instance, is shaped by the fact of a society in which women's clothing and their segregation rendered them all but invisible to men; boys, on the other hand, might be seen in all their glory at the public baths.

The problem for us today is to conceive of how the mind of a poet might work in a society with completely different sexual rules from our own. Consider the erotic range of a poet like CATULLUS (ca 84–54), the scabrous laureate of the late Roman republic. His verse includes tender and vibrant love poems addressed to Clodia Metelli ("Lesbia"), a married woman; enthusiastic epithalamia on matrimony; insulting epigrams accusing a man called Gellius of all manner of sexual transgressions, including incest and cock-sucking; what we might now (inaccurately) call "homophobic" tirades against men who loved men instead of boys, or against men who took the "wrong" part in oral or anal intercourse with boys; and so on. However, it is also clear that Catullus, true not only to the conventions of his society but also to the promptings of his own heart and genitals, loved sex with young men and loved one man, Juventius, with greater ardor than the feeling was returned. Perhaps this is not the work of a "gay poet" in the contemporary sense; yet it offers the gay reader a broad range of interest, both in terms of identifiably shared emotions and as a documentary glimpse of "our" sexual history. The two great virtues of Catullus' view of sexuality are his sense of humor—which leads him to laugh at himself as often as at others—and his seriousness, the depth of his commitment to his own desires. The tension between the two moods brings him close, at times, to a tone that we might recognize in certain types of modern gay irony.

However, gay literature is not simply a matter of the emotional records of individual writers. Gay poets do not, on their own, "make" gay poetry. There are processes of selection, production, and evaluation to be taken into account. Our canons of literature of quality are no more eternal than any other. Indeed, gay literary critics have been fairly explicit about the intentional social purposes behind their reevaluations of past texts and canons. The contingencies behind the heralding of gay classics need to be acknowledged and made manifest.

The canon of gay literature has been constructed by bookish homosexuals, most explicitly since the debates on sexuality and identity that flourished in the last third of the nineteenth century. The clearest canonizations have been effected not only by critical appraisal but also by the assembling of anthologies. Anthologists have clearly hoped to create a sense of cultural continuity and an international community of shared sexual interest. Yet it is worth bearing in mind that, terminology apart, the notion of a subsector of literature devoted to homoeroticism is not particularly new. History is littered with patrons who had specific erotic interests and tailored their commissions accordingly. At other times, artists took it on themselves to make entrepreneurial choices that affected the subsequent availability of specific types or art work.

Strato of Sardis, who lived in the second century A.D. and wrote lively epigrams expressing an interest in both women and boys, nevertheless edited a narrowly specific collection called *Mousa Paidiké* (*Pederastic Poems*). Almost one hundred of Strato's poems have come down to us because this anthology was absorbed into the so-called Palatine Anthology, which, combined with the collection by Maximum Planudes, became that magnificent resource of 4,000 epigrams, *The Greek Anthology*. Whether one calls the *Mousa Paidiké* a gay anthology depends on the purity of the individual reader's sense of history.

Regardless of their definitional elisions and inaccuracies, anthologies have played a central role in establishing canons of homosexual literature. Furthermore, since the late nineteenth century, they have actually provided homosexual readers with a broad kind of gay cultural education that would not have been on offer even in the English "public" schools and Oxbridge colleges whose curricula were so heavily based on the Graeco-Roman classics. The "anthology of friendship" furnished extracts from a complete curriculum for the diligent, homosexual autodidact.

The ground had been prepared in the researches of men like Sir Richard Burton and JOHN ADDINGTON SYMONDS. The latter's essay *A Problem in Modern Ethics* (1891), for instance, included useful sections on "Literature—Historical Anthropological" (summarizing Burton's 1885 theory of the existence of a pederastic "Sotadic Zone" encircling the Earth); "Literature—Polemical" (summarizing and commenting on the sexological work of K. H. Ulrichs); and, more to the present point, "Literature—Idealistic" (a short essay on WALT WHITMAN, naming some of the main homoerotic poems and quoting the whole of "For You 0 Democracy").

Perhaps the most significant and original of the subsequent anthologies was EDWARD CARPENTER's *Ioläus* (1902), supposedly an "anthology of friendship" but actually an attempt to map out the cultural and historical roots of the people Symonds had called "the third sex" and whom Carpenter called "the intermediate sex." It consisted of five chapters. The first of these, "Friendship-customs in the Pagan and Early World," gathers together extracts of anthropological prose about the customs of "primitive peoples" (extracts from HERMAN MELVILLE's *Omoo* and *Typee,* for instance), followed by historical accounts of "comradeship," mainly from ancient Greek culture (the Theban band, Harmodius and Aristogeiton, Orestes and Pylades, Damon and Pythias). In the second chapter, "The Place of Friendship in Greek Life and Thought," Carpenter provides extracts from PLATO (*Symposium* and the *Phaedrus*) and PLUTARCH. The third chapter, "Poetry of Friendship among Greeks and Romans," turns to "literary" texts, offering selections from Homer (Achilles and Patroclus), Theognis, Anacreon, Meleager, THEOCRITUS, Bion, Ovid, VIRGIL, Catullus, and Martial.

Turning from the ancient world, Carpenter compiled a fourth chapter on "Friendship in Early Christian and Medieval Times." Here, alongside selections from ST. AUGUSTINE's *Confessions,* one finds brief examples of "Eastern" love poetry by the likes of Hafiz of Shiraz, together with fragments of J. S. Buckingham's travel writing. Chapter five, "The Renaissance and Modern Times," moves from Montaigne's essays to MICHELANGELO's sonnets; from RICHARD BARNFIELD through SIR FRANCIS BACON to SHAKESPEARE (sonnets 18, 20, 104, and 108 plus brief extracts from *The Merchant of Venice* and *Henry V*). The rest of this chapter is a haphazard mixture of items, ranging from WINCKELMANN's letters to the poetry of AUGUST VON PLATEN; from Wagner's letters to poems by the pioneering sexologist K. H. Ulrichs; and from BYRON and Shelley, through ALFRED TENNYSON's *In Memoriam* (five sections: 13, 18, 59, 127, and 128), to Walt Whitman ("Recorders Ages Hence," "When I Heard at the Close of the Day," and "I Hear It Was Charged Against Me").

The enlarged edition of *Ioläus* that Carpenter published in 1926 contained an appendix covering the same breadth as that of the body of the book, from Aristotle to Edward Fitzgerald, via Prussia and Ceylon. In the preface to the first edition, Carpenter had acknowledged that the collection was "only incomplete, and a small contribution, at best, towards a large subject." Knowing as well as anyone how very large the subject was indeed, Carpenter left the apology to stand even in the enlarged edition.

By the time Patrick Anderson and Alistair Sutherland had come to publish their book *Eros* (1961)— again an "anthology of friendship," again named after a boy in Greek myth—the canon had greatly expanded. The ten chapters of this new collection were as follows. "The Great Originals" lays the ground rules with the stories of David and Jonathan, and Achilles and Patroclus, and Zeus and Ganymede. Interestingly, the chapter ends with OSCAR WILDE's famous courtroom plea on behalf of "the love that dare not speak its name," a decision by which Anderson and Sutherland clearly intend to link their ancient material not only with modern instances of "friendship" but also with criminalized homosexuality. (Remember that *Eros* came out between the publication of the Wolfenden Report of 1957, which proposed the legalization of private, consensual homosexual acts in England, and the Sexual Offences Act of 1967, which effected the reforms.)

The second chapter, "The Greeks," gives a much fuller account than Carpenter's of Greek customs, thought, and literature; and its poetic selections are arranged under thematic subheadings such as "Boyflowers," "Eyes of Fire and Virtue," "The Variety of Loves—and of Love," and "Jokes about Effeminacy." The last named, containing an extract from Aristophanes's *Thesmophoriazusae*, is useful as a reminder that our heritage includes not only celebrations of same-sex love, but also expressions of what has come to be called homophobia.

There follows a chapter on "The Romans," primarily consisting of prose essays (Cicero) and fiction (PETRONIUS), but also, of course, containing Virgil's second eclogue and other poetry by HORACE, Tibullus, Catullus, and Juvenal. Like the passage from Aristophanes, the items from Juvenal's *Satires* mock effeminacy. Chapter four, "The Dark and Middle Ages," turns to the Christian world via the new proliferation of penalties for sodomy—again, clearly broadening the scope of the anthology beyond mere "friendship." Included thereafter are several of Helen Waddell's famous translations of medieval love poems and a number of love letters between monks. As in *Ioläus,* this chapter shifts its focus to the Islamic world with extensive selections from Hafiz, followed by poems of boy-love by a number of "Moors."

"The Renaissance" follows, with letters and sonnets by Michelangelo and essays by Montaigne. Sir Philip Sidney opens the account, and Shakespeare is represented by twenty-six sonnets (12, 13, 17, 18, 19, 20, 22, 27, 29, 41, 42, 53, 54, 62, 67, 73, 79, 80, 98, 99, 104, 106, 110, 116, 135, and 114). Long extracts from CHRISTOPHER MARLOWE's *Hero and Leander* and Richard Barnfield's pastorals lead into essays by Sir Francis Bacon and Sir Thomas Browne. Chapter six, "Eighteenth Century and Romantics," begins with an account of the loves of THOMAS GRAY; continues with sizable extracts from WILLIAM BECKFORD's short novel *Vathek* and ten poems by BYRON; and ends with an extract from *Endymion,* which the editors say, "for all the normality of Keats," establishes that "the spirit of Eros" nevertheless flourishes in his verse.

A relatively short chapter on "The Nineteenth Century" (twenty-one pages) includes thirteen sections of Tennyson's *In Memoriam* (6, 7, 12, 13, 18, 22, 27, 49, 69, 78, 90, 125, and 128); single items by Edward Fitzgerald, Robert Browning, and William Morris; and, finally, poems by the Uranians William Johnson Cory and Rev. E. E. Bradford. This is one of the collection's key (but low-key) moments, as the editors shift from major writers in the general canon to minor, all-but-forgotten writers whose poetry is of interest for only thematic rather than aesthetic and qualitative reasons. Not to put too fine a point on it, Cory and Bradford are here because they were queer.

The eighth chapter, on "The Moderns," is 138 pages long and divided by Western nation: France (poetry by Arthur Rimbaud and Paul Verlaine, fiction by JORIS-KARL HUYSMANS and MARCEL PROUST, nonfiction by ANDRÉ GIDE), the United States of America (Walt Whitman and Hart Crane; Herman Melville, HENRY THOREAU, and Sherwood Anderson), Germany (only STEFAN GEORGE), Greece (nine poems by CONSTANTINE CAVAFY), and Britain. The twelve chosen

Whitman poems are "In Paths Untrodden," "For You O Democracy," "The Base of All Metaphysics," "Recorders Ages Hence," "When I Heard at the Close of the Day," "Behold This Swarthy Face," "I Saw in Louisiana a Live-oak Growing," "We Two Boys Together Clinging," "Here the Frailest Leaves of Me," "A Glimpse," "What Think You I Take My Pen in Hand," and "O You Whom I Often and Silently Come."

The British subsection starts with Edward Carpenter, quoting his poetry but not mentioning *Ioläus*. There follows a small pantheon of homophile writers from the turn of the century: John Addington Symonds, Oscar Wilde, and ALFRED DOUGLAS, A. E. HOUSMAN, and FREDERICK ROLFE ("Baron Corvo"). Modernism's first representative is D. H. LAWRENCE, with fifteen pages of extracts from his fiction, but no poetry. Forrest Reid is granted nine pages, but CHRISTOPHER ISHERWOOD less than one. STEPHEN SPENDER is represented by five poems, George Barker by three, and DENTON WELCH by almost seven pages from his journals. However, W. H. AUDEN is briefly mentioned but never quoted. The chapter ends with single poems from F. T. Prince, WILLIAM PLOMER, John Lehmann, and editor Patrick Anderson himself.

The ninth chapter is a peculiar confection called "Exotic Encounters," a rather narrow anthology of fictional and factual prose accounts of European or white American travelers' encounters with the other, the foreigner. Finally, chapter ten presents "The School Story" as if it were a significant and major subsection of our culture. (The chapter is only one page shorter than chapter seven, on the nineteenth century.) Apart from one Frenchman, Roger Peyrefitte, this section cites only British writers. Thus, the anthology as a whole ends in eccentric anticlimax, giving little sense of a vibrant future for homosexual writing. It offers no inkling, for instance, of any poet in the United States after Hart Crane.

The first major attempt at a cross-cultural and trans-historical survey of poetry alone was *The Penguin Book of Homosexual Verse*, edited by Stephen Coote and published in 1983. In his introduction, Coote sets out his parameters—or rather, their lack—with blithe unconcern for the problems he is raising with every sentence. He begins: "This is a collection of poems by and about gay people. It ranges in time and place from classical Athens to contemporary New York." He would like his book to be read primarily for pleasure, but also as "a history of the different ways in which homosexual people have been seen and have seen themselves." The introduction's subsections follow a now fairly familiar historical path: "Ancient Greece," "Rome," "Lesbians in Classical Poetry," "The Making of Prejudice" (this covering the territory equivalent to Anderson and Sutherland's fourth chapter, "The Dark and Middle Ages"), "Renaissance and Enlightenment," "The Making of the 'Homosexual,'" and "Gay Today." The body of the anthology itself is not subdivided.

Of the main English-language poets who, by now, simply could not be left out of such a collection, Coote made the following selections: Shakespeare (sonnets 20, 29, 35, 36, 53, 55, 57, 60, 67, 87, 94, 104, 110, 116, and 144), Tennyson (*In Memoriam*, sections 7, 9, 13, 27, and 80), Whitman ("We Two Boys Together Clinging," "A Glimpse," "Vigil Strange I Kept on the Field One Night," "O Tan-Faced Prairie-Boy," and "The Beautiful Swimmer"). On the other hand, there are problematic major omissions from the collection. Of these, the most glaring is Hart Crane. Also compromising is the fact that of W. H. Auden's poems, Coote includes only the relatively trivial "Uncle Henry."

Coote's collection was widely reviewed because of its "Penguin Book of..." status. More often than not, it was criticized for its inclusiveness, particularly for its inclusion of sexually celebratory verse of the post-Stonewall era. The problem is, of course, in the nature of canons: Do we make our choices of gay culture according to aesthetic or sociohistorical criteria? Clearly, any book that unapologetically places the likes of OLGA BROUMAS and Chuck Ortleb next to Homer and Shakespeare is likely to cause aesthetes to shudder, particularly if it appears to include the latter pair for thematic reasons rather than for the fact that they were "great" poets. But how else can a gay anthologist operate at all?

The main defense available to the compiler of such a broad survey must be located in the pleasure of the reader; and the reader in question should be assumed to be lesbian or gay. The gay anthology is addressed to the gay reader, both to induce enjoyment and to convey a sense of cultural solidarity.

Given these functions of the "pleasure principle" in the compilation of anthologies, academic-historical and academic-aesthetic complaints may prove irrelevant to the success or failure of the enterprise. In a nutshell, it may be completely beside the point whether William Shakespeare was "gay" or "queer" or a "homosexual" or a "sodomite"; or if he and the male addressee of his sonnets were "just good friends"; or even if no such friend ever existed and the sonnets in question were—as so many heterosexually identified critics have claimed—mere poetic exercises, common to their time. All this is irrelevant if any of the sonnets are amenable to being read by a gay reader *as if they were* "gay poems." If they work as if they were, they *are*. The reader's pleasure is paramount.

To this extent, anthologies like Coote's function well as capacious lucky dips, in which any page one turns to will offer a potential gay text. And in the present context, at least, a potential gay text *is* a gay text. It is in their educational roles, on the other hand, that such collections really do raise problems. For instance, Coote's hope that his book will be treated as "a record, a history" of representations of "homosexual people" is obviously compromised by the editor's—and therefore the book's—willingness to assume a trans-historical and cross-cultural unifying definition of gay culture. This slippage has already occurred between the title's "homosexual verse" and the first sentence of the introduction's "poems by and about gay people." Add to this the fact that Coote's own translations of the gay classics incorporate such culturally and historically specific epithets as "faggot," "queer," and "queen," and one must reluctantly conclude that the academic uses of the book are limited; or, at least, that the book needs to be shelved next to a more skeptical volume of sexual history.

Of course, Coote's strategies are determined—or, to some extent, sanctioned—by the moment of their conception. *The Penguin Book of Homosexual Verse* was a response to a marketing need created by the growing currency of gay culture during the previous decade. In some sense, for all its faults, it represented the culmination of what some writers and readers had been working toward: the establishing of a canon; the continuation of a tradition. Although published in 1983, the book had its origins in possibilities raised by Gay Liberation. Although in some respects already a rather dated concept in 1983, this anthology of "homosexual verse" nevertheless bore the stamp of 1969.

The latter date is the point in cultural history after which, at last, we can unproblematically speak about a certain kind of text as "gay poetry": that is to say, poetry about being gay, by men who identify themselves as being gay. It was then—in the industrialized West at the end of the 1960s—that a systematic renaming occurred, and "queers" and "homosexuals" became "gay." In much the same way as, shortly beforehand, "negroes" had become "black." Such redefinition at street level, of course, cannot fail to have its impact on the cultural forms that use language as their primary matter. "Gay liberation" spawned "gay literature." Winston Leyland was not exaggerating in his introduction to *Orgasms of Light* when he spoke of a "Gay Cultural Renaissance."

Consider the following sequence of events in the United States. Each may be, on its own, relatively trivial; but taken together they constitute a significant, even major, development. *E pluribus unum.* In 1969, the poet Paul Mariah founded *ManRoot* magazine

and the *ManRoot* press in San Francisco. In 1970, also in San Francisco, Winston Leyland founded *Gay Sunshine* magazine. In 1971, the Boston Gay Liberation Front established *Fag Rag* magazine, and then, in 1972, the Good Gay Poets publishing house. In 1973, Ian Young's pioneering gay poetry anthology *The Male Muse* was published. In 1974, Andrew Bifrost founded *Mouth of the Dragon* ("A Poetry Journal of Male Love") in New York. In the same year *RFD* ("A Country Journal for Gay Men Everywhere") was established in Tennessee. New York's *Christopher Street* followed in 1976. In 1977, the novelist Felice Picano started the Sea Horse Press. Meanwhile, back in 1975, Winston Leyland had published the poetry anthology *Angels of the Lyre* under the new imprint of the Gay Sunshine Press; it was followed by a second anthology, *Orgasms of Light,* in 1977. In 1983, Ian Young followed up *The Male Muse* with *Son of the Male Muse,* a collection of much younger writers than had appeared in the earlier book.

For the most part, these ventures involved white gay men. It was not until 1986 that the African-American Blackheart Collective started *Other Countries* magazine. In the same year, Joseph Beam's anthology *In the Life* was published. Essex Hemphill's sequel to the latter, *Brother to Brother,* appeared in 1991, the same year as Assoto [sic] Saint's *The Road Before Us,* a collection of work by no fewer than one hundred gay black poets; ten of the same poets were represented in the later collection *Here to Dare* (1992). In 1992, Vega Studios published *A Warm December,* a collection of poems by, and photographs of, gay black men. In 1988, Will Roscoe's *Living the Spirit* became the first major anthology of gay American Indian texts, but its inclusion of verse was limited.

Although it prematurely ended the careers of many of the poets who had appeared in the journals and anthologies listed above, the AIDS epidemic also energized artists as well as activists. In its way, the crisis provided the impetus for a new "Gay Cultural Renaissance" like the one that had occurred after—or had been occurring ever since—the Stonewall riots. AIDS has spawned its own magazines—a notable example being *Art and Understanding,* the rather pompously named "Journal of literature and art about AIDS"—and its own anthologies. Of the latter, the most substantial is Michael Klein's *Poets for Life* (1989).

In 1979, the pre-Stonewall American gay canon was more authoritatively established than before with the publication of Robert K. Martin's *The Homosexual Tradition in American Poetry,* a book that, despite the wave of homophobic reviews it received, set a high critical standard for gay academics in English studies to follow. Martin begins his account by establishing in great detail the textual evidence of Walt Whitman's homoerotic concerns. Thus, as ever in gay reevaluations of American literature, Whitman stands as the presiding and defining "father" of the tradition. A second chapter discusses the "Academic Tradition" of Fitz-Greene Halleck, BAYARD TAYLOR, and GEORGE SANTAYANA. Chapter three is entirely devoted to Hart Crane, the "bridge" between Whitman and Modernism. Chapter four offers brief analyses of the work of ALLEN GINSBERG, ROBERT DUNCAN, THOM GUNN, EDWARD FIELD, RICHARD HOWARD, JAMES MERRILL, and Alfred Corn. Finally, an endnote discusses "The Future," in relation to which Martin speaks of "a tradition that seems certain to grow, confident in its readers and lovers."

The subsequent establishment and expansion of gay studies in the American academic world and elsewhere has encouraged young academics to embark on increasingly sophisticated appraisals of gay culture that, far from feeding parasitically on that culture (as antiacademic myth might have it) serve in fact to strengthen and affirm it.

The United States does not have the monopoly on such developments. Similar patterns have been repeated, on a smaller scale, throughout the industrialized world. Magazines having established the existence of both gay writers and a gay readership, small presses either were established to publish both poetry anthologies and collections by individual poets or were initially set up as general gay publishers, but later, given confidence and cash flow, were able to start publishing poetry titles—which are generally loss-makers relying on subsidy from a company's more popular titles. An example of the latter type of operation is the "Gay Verse" series produced by the Gay Men's Press in London. Although the press was founded in 1979, it did not publish verse until Martin Humphries's anthology Not Love Alone in 1985. Humphries went on to act as poetry editor to a series of titles, most of which used the work of two or three writers. Humphries and Steve Cranfield had reached an advanced stage in the editing of an AIDS-related poetry anthology in 1992 when the directors of the press decided to close down the verse series. Poetry had flourished in the epidemic, only to catch its death in a recession. More committed to the promotion of poetry, the lesbian and gay Oscars Press appeared to be in a good position to take over where the Gay Men's Press had left off. Oscars had started early in 1986 as a reading group involving poets who had appeared in Not Love Alone; they published the first of a series of chapbooks in 1987 and the first of their paperback anthologies in 1990.

By the time one arrives at an event like the publication of Carl Morse and Joan Larkin's Gay and Lesbian Poetry in Our Time (1988), it is clear that the culture of homosexuality has been established for long enough to be able to sustain, not only the replacement of one canon with another, but also the simultaneous implication that many younger writers are strongly placed to invade the new canon in due course. The book's dust jacket claims that it includes poetry written between 1950 and the time of publication—though, in fact, two of the three Auden poems included date from 1937 and 1938, and at least two of the LANGSTON HUGHES poems are from earlier than 1950. Be that as it may, the book balances canonical homosexual (W. H. Auden), gay (Allen Ginsberg), and lesbian writers (ADRIENNE RICH) with the new wave of much younger poets (Mark Ameen, Dennis Cooper, Alexis De Veaux, Kitty Tsui, and so on). Thematically, it moves from quietly affirmative voices of the McCarthyite era to the more flamboyant celebrations of Gay liberation—though this historical progression is obscured by the editors' decision to arrange the poets not chronologically but alphabetically—and it incorporates poetry of the AIDS epidemic seamlessly into its cross-section of cultural development. Its portentous title clearly expresses the seriousness of its canonizing intent.

Even given the effects of homophobia on the production, distribution, and evaluation of texts, we are in charge of our own culture. We have our own requirements, and set our own standards thereby. It is the gay reader who decides what is a good gay poem. This is why gay-edited anthologies and gay-authored critical works are at the crux of the development of gay reading practices. As important as the poem itself are the ways in which we come to hear of it, find a copy of it, read it, and keep it to ourselves or pass it on to others. Gay poetry emerges from a network of readers as much as from poets themselves. The book you are reading continues the process.

—Gregory Woods

BIBLIOGRAPHY

Andersen, Patrick, and Alistair Sutherland, eds. Eros: An Anthology of Male Friendship. London: Anthony Blond, 1961. ■ Carpenter, Edward. Anthology of Friendship: Ioläus. London: George Allen & Unwin, 1902; enlarged, 1906. ■ Coote, Stephen, ed. The Penguin Book of Homosexual Verse. London: Penguin, 1983. ■ d'Arch Smith, Timothy. Love in Earnest: Some Notes on the Lives and Writings of English "Uranian" Poets from 1889 to 1930. London: Routledge & Kegan Paul, 1970. ■ Edwinson, Edmund. Men and Boys: An Anthology. New York: privately printed, 1924. ■ Humphries, Martin, ed. Not Love Alone: A Modern Gay Anthology. London: GMP, 1985. ■ Jay, Peter, ed. The Greek Anthology. New York: Penguin, 1981. ■ Klein, Michael, ed. Poets for Life: Seventy-Six Poets Respond to AIDS. New York: Crown, 1989. ■ Leyland,

Winston, ed. *Angels of the Lyre: A Gay Poetry Anthology.* San Francisco: Gay Sunshine, 1975. ■ ———. *Orgasms of Light. The Gay Sunshine Anthology.* San Francisco: Gay Sunshine, 1977. ■ Martin, Robert K. *The Homosexual Tradition in American Poetry.* Austin: University of Texas Press, 1979. ■ Morse, Carl, and Joan Larkin, eds. *Gay and Lesbian Poetry in Our Time: An Anthology.* New York: St. Martin's Press, 1988. ■ *New Songs from a Jade Terrace.* New York: Penguin, 1986. ■ Paris, Renzo, and Antonio Veneziani, eds. *L'amicizia amorosa: antologia della poesia omosessuale italiana dal XIII secolo a oggi.* Milano: Gammalibri, 1982. ■ Reade, Brian, ed. *Sexual Heretics: Male Homosexuality in English Literature from 1850 to 1900: An Anthology.* London: Routledge & Kegan Paul, 1970. ■ Saint, Assotto. *Here to Dare: 10 Gay Black Poets.* New York: Galiens Press, 1992. ■ Saint, Assoto [sic], ed. *The Road Before Us: 100 Gay Black Poets.* New York: Galiens Press, 1991. ■ Woods, Gregory. *Articulate Flesh: Male-Homoeroticism and Modern Poetry.* New Haven: Yale University Press, 1987. ■ ———. "'Absurd! Ridiculous! Disgusting!' Paradox in Poetry by Gay Men." *Lesbian and Gay Writing.* Mark Lilly, ed. London: Macmillan, 1990. 175–198. ■ Young, Ian, ed. *The Male Muse: A Gay Anthology.* Trumansburg, N.Y.: Crossing Press, 1973. ■ ———. *Son of the Male Muse: New Gay Poetry.* Trumansburg, N.Y.: Crossing Press, 1983.

Poetry, Lesbian

Does "lesbian poetry" refer to poetry by lesbians or poetry with a certain eroticized woman-identified sensibility? Both of these definitions and more are included in the term. To meet the terms of that second definition, must such poetry have been written by a "real" lesbian? Or does poetry by Pierre Louÿs, PAUL VERLAINE, and CHARLES BAUDELAIRE, poetry that, as Lillian Faderman suggests, might be categorized as "lesbian exoticism," count as "lesbian poetry"? Apparently the organizers of the "Daughters of Bilitis," a contemporary group of visible lesbians hoping to dispel myths of sexual pathology who cryptically named themselves after Pierre Louÿs's lesbian work *Chansons de Bilitis,* considered his work lesbian poetry. Although scholars quibble over whether applying the term *lesbian* to EMILY DICKINSON is anachronistic, artists, musicians, dramatists, and poets, lesbian and otherwise, have recognized this premier woman poet as an "American SAPPHO." Of sapphic poets writing from the sixteenth century to 1950, Louise Bernikow argued:

> Whether all the woman-to-woman relationships that exist in the lives of these poets were explicitly sexual or not is difficult to know, for taboo was always in the way and evidence that might have told the true nature of those relationships is missing. Yet what matters most is not who did what to whom in what bed, but the direction of emotional attention.

From these nineteenth-century examples of poetic production and twentieth-century examples of poetic consumption, readers can see that they might do well to formulate principles for defining poetry as lesbian from the archaic architectural definition for "lesbian" rules—from a mason's rule of lead, which bends to fit the curves of a molding (OED); hence, figuratively, lesbian rules are pliant and accommodating principles for judgment. The primary principles for judging poetry as lesbian, then, are flexible and include both poetry written by lesbians and poetry exploring *and celebrating* lesbian eroticism and sexuality from a variety of perspectives. And "lesbian" refers to eroticized emotional attachment as well as to literal flesh-and-blood experience.

Lesbian theorist Katie King could have been talking about all lesbian poetry, lesbian poets, as well as critics and readers who want to identify certain poetry as lesbian when she described her objectives in a close reading of the poetry of AUDRE LORDE: that she wants to appropriate academic "forms of authority" and thereby "empower Lorde's texts; in short to enable their literary canonisation." As King points out, poetry has long been a valorized genre in which Lorde and many other lesbian poets have a political investment, and as Alicia Ostriker makes plain in her critical history of contemporary women's poetry, the "extraordinary tide of poetry by American women in our own time" is "challenging and transforming the history of poetry . . . the self and culture" by producing new knowledge about "explicitly female experience." Of the "long-hidden, long-repressed feelings" and thoughts of women, none has been rendered more invisible and inaudible than those of lesbians. Thus contemporary lesbian and bisexual poets like Lorde, JUDY GRAHN, Ai, Alta, Joy Harjo, Susan Griffin, Pat Parker, ADRIENNE RICH, and many others have championed poetry for its ability "to release imprisoned strata of experience into the daylight of language."

The history of lesbian poetry might be divided into several eras or phases, but for our purposes we shall consider two. First, there are centuries of poetry prior to the late 1950s and early 1960s in which women

poets were scarce and, with the exception of Sappho, lesbian poets were practically invisible (and readers should be aware that Sappho's lesbianism was frequently obscured and, by many critics, denied); second are the recent decades in which women's poetry has achieved prominence and lesbian poetry has been key in moving audiences beyond aesthetic appreciation and into political action. Surveys of anthologies, which make works available and begin to formulate canons, and critical studies, which direct readers' attentions and significantly contribute to canon formation, recount these histories of lesbian poetry and time and again highlight the distinct break between recent highly politicized lesbian poetry and a tradition of lesbian forerunners. The primary objective of canon formation has not been to establish an exclusionary immutable pantheon of great lesbian poets in The Great Tradition of Lesbian Poetry but rather to recover erotic writings and authors lost to traditional literary histories through neglect, ascription of minority status to lesbian writers and their expressions, "objective" aesthetic evaluations resulting in a diminution of lesbian poets' talents, and even censorship that erases or denies the lesbianism of a particular woman or lesbianism in poetic expression.

Even now lesbian poetry is often obscured by the most commonly used bibliographic tools. Searching the Library of Congress catalog in 1994 for items pertaining to the subject "lesbian poetry," for example, users will find only one entry, Elly Bulkin and Joan Larkin's Lesbian Poetry (1981). Names of self-identified lesbian poets like OLGA BROUMAS, Minnie Bruce Pratt, MURIEL RUKEYSER, Susan Sherman, Chrystos, Cheryl Clarke, MAY SARTON, MAY SWENSON, Marilyn Hacker, Adrienne Rich, Audre Lorde, and Judy Grahn do not appear, nor do those of AMY LOWELL, ELIZABETH BISHOP, Bessie Smith, Elsa Gidlow, Angelina Grimké, Emily Dickinson, GERTRUDE STEIN, or H.D.. Of vital importance for the accessibility and distribution of lesbian poetry are women's and gay and lesbian bookstores that thrive as a direct result of the recent women's and gay liberation movements, the hundreds of alternative presses (for example, Shameless Hussy, Poets' Press, Out & Out Books, Crossing Press, Diana Press, Naiad Press, Women's Press Collective, Firebrand Books) and journals (for example, The Ladder, Heresies, Vice Versa, Sinister Wisdom, Conditions, off our backs) started and supported by feminist and lesbian poets and writers like Grahn, Lorde, Wendy Cadden, Diane Di Prima, Barbara Grier, and others; anthologies like Fran Winant's We Are All Lesbians (1973), Bulkin and Larkin's Lesbian Poetry (1981; first published as Amazon Poetry: An Anthology of Lesbian Poetry, 1975), CHERRÍE

MORAGA and GLORIA ANZALDÚA's This Bridge Called My Back (1981), Evelyn Torton Beck's Nice Jewish Girls: A Lesbian Anthology (1982), Barbara Smith's Home Girls (1983), Lilian Mohin's Beautiful Barbarians: Lesbian Feminist Poetry (1986), Carl Morse and Larkin's Gay and Lesbian Poetry in Our Time (1988), Christian McEwen's Naming the Waves: Contemporary Lesbian Poetry (1988), and Stephen Coote's The Penguin Book of Homosexual Verse (1983); and literary histories like Jan Clausen's A Movement of Poets: Thoughts on Poetry and Feminism (1982), Ostriker's Stealing the Language: The Emergence of Women's Poetry in America (1986), and Grahn's The Highest Apple: Sappho and the Lesbian Poetic Tradition (1985).

At once erotic and intellectual but not in conventional, expected senses, lesbian poetry makes visible an even "queerer" lot than the poetic foremothers— "We women who write poetry"—whom Amy Lowell appreciates in "The Sisters," in which "Sapho—not Miss or Mrs.," "Mrs. Browning, aloof and delicate," and "Miss Dickinson . . . Emily," the "lonely brainchild of a gaunt maturity" with whom "you're really here, or never anywhere at all / In range of mind," serve as exemplars of the women writers, the "spiritual relations" with whom Lowell proudly claims to be "in love." Lowell was herself a lesbian, and lesbian poets have been instrumental in making lesbian forerunners visible. In The Highest Apple (1985), Judy Grahn offers a perpetually delectable tradition of nine modern poets linked to Sappho: Dickinson, Lowell, H.D., Stein, Rich, Lorde, Broumas, PAULA GUNN ALLEN, and Grahn herself. Dedicating her study "To All Lovers" (not exclusively lesbian lovers), Grahn clearly states her objective: "The story I am telling is of the re-emergence of the public Lesbian voice." Claiming that poetry is especially important to women, Grahn makes the even more controversial claim that it is a vital "tool for survival" for lesbians and says that "more than one Lesbian has been kept from floundering on the rocks of alienation from her own culture, her own center, by having access, at least, to Lesbian poetry." Immediately she remarks the indisputable fact that "We owe a great deal to poetry; two of our most important names, for instance: Lesbian and Sapphic," effectively arguing the case for a study focused on lesbian poetry.

So along with essayists who have been especially influential (such as Mary J. Carruthers, Elly Bulkin, Catharine Stimpson, Rich, Lorde, and Pratt), Grahn shores up the production of a new genre, lesbian poetry. In "'Kissing/Against the Light': A Look at Lesbian Poetry," her 1978 (rev. 1981, 1982) essay that serves as an important historical marker in the first decades' evolution of politically conscious lesbian poetry, Bulkin reiterates the heart of an important lesbian vision:

> Uncovering a poetic tradition representative of lesbians of color and poor and working-class lesbians of all races involves, as Barbara Noda has written, reexamining "the words 'lesbian,' 'historical,' and even 'poet.'" A beginning problem is definitional, as Paula Gunn Allen makes clear in her exploration of her own American Indian culture:

> > It is not known if those
> > who warred and hunted on the plains
> > chanted and hexed in the hills
> > divined and healed in the mountains
> > gazed and walked beneath the seas
> > were Lesbians
> > It is never known
> > if any woman was a lesbian

> The search is further compounded when the goal is finding not just a lesbian, but a lesbian *poet*, especially among those groups . . . without a way to get their written or oral poetry reproduced and distributed.

Ostriker characterizes Rich as a poet of ideas. Concomitantly, many lesbian poets hold dear and share profound ideas about transforming cultural, personal, social, familial values, and in ways that ask more, not less, caretaking and consideration between and among individuals.

Recently Judith Roof plumbed the significance of the fact that the "emergence of activist gay and lesbian groups and the naming of the postmodern occur at about the same time. Del Martin, Phyllis Lyon, and others founded the Daughters of Bilitis in the autumn of 1955, a year after" the first use of "the term *postmodern*." Before Stonewall, both usages marked "rejection of legitimating metanarratives that form the basis for deciding what is true," and

> by the mid-eighties some critics . . . see the lesbian and the postmodern as categories that challenge centered logic and identity, the lesbian confronting heterosexuality and gender, the postmodern questioning subjectivity, knowledge, and truth. . . . Different phenomena brought together in the suggestion of a shared context, the lesbian and the post-modern are less an equation than a very contemporary comparison generated finally not by

any postmodern intellectual practice but rather by a very traditional drive for identity, certainty, and legitimation.

Lesbian poetry, then, poses many a previously unimagined question about language, its possibilities and limitations, and is sometimes as radically experimental exploiting language and form as it is sometimes radically political.

Of Grahn's "A Woman Is Talking to Death," Bulkin wrote:

> "That's a fact," Grahn keeps observing as she builds image after image of women ignored, derided, abused. The central "fact" of the poem is finally the poet's own lesbianism. In a society that perceives lesbians as committing "indecent acts" and that leers at women who kiss each other, who call each other "lovers," who admit to "wanting" another woman, Grahn forces a rethinking of both language and the assumptions behind it.

Remarking that the "rhetorical drive" of Grahn's poetry draws on biblical and protesting oral traditions, Bulkin concludes that "this oral quality" underscores the "sense that the poem should be heard with others, not read by oneself." This is not a poetry for private pleasure only but a poetry of motivation meant to act as a force to change the world. As lesbian and gay activists have worked to make public awareness of sexualities that have been mystified, oppressed, and punished through cultural conventions and legal systems of privatization and domestication, so many contemporary lesbian poets create works especially conducive for public discourse and education. Describing Rich's role as poet/prophet in 1985, Catharine Stimpson might have been describing a score of other lesbian poets:

> Because patriarchal culture has been silent about lesbians and "all women who are not defined by the men in their lives," the prophet/witness must give speech to experience for the first time. This is one meaning of writing a whole new poetry. However, patriarchal culture has not been consistently silent. Sometimes, it has lied about lesbians. The prophet/witness must then use and affirm ". . . a vocabulary that has been used negatively and pejoratively."

Stimpson continues, ". . . she must transvalue language" to tell "stories that matter," that give "images from the mind and of the body, for the relief of the body and the reconstruction of the mind."

Some lesbian poets like Angelina Grimké or H.D. have written in forms readily embraced by the white male literary definition of poetry, whereas others, like blues singer Bessie Smith, have worked in forms traditionally regarded as of a lower artistic order. Like Grahn and many other lesbian poets, Minnie Bruce Pratt consciously composes a prosy kind of poetry, the primary objective of which is straightforward explicit expression, knowing that some will deny that it is art. Stimpson astutely apprises the import of this generic "miscegenation," and again her comments about Rich pertain to many lesbian poets:

> . . . Rich, a sophisticated student of the genetics of the text, coherently crossed autobiography with biography; polemic with scholarship; political theory with literary criticism. In part, her transgressions of generic conventions are the deconstructive gestures of post-modernism—without much manic play or ludic romps. In greater part, her mingling of "subjective" and "objective" genres, advocacy and argument, demonstrates her belief in their inseparability. Her style also emblemizes the position of contemporary, educated women. No longer forced to choose between public or private lives, women can lead both—at once. No longer forced to choose between writing about public or private concerns, women can take on both—at once.

And enjoy success at doing so. Witness changes in Florence Howe's "Introduction" to *No More Masks! An Anthology of Twentieth-Century American Women Poets: Newly Revised and Expanded* (1993). Bulkin notes the minimizing commentary of Howe's introduction to the 1973 version of *No More Masks!*: "In her long introduction . . . Florence Howe recognized the existence of lesbian poetry—at least *recent* lesbian poetry—but seemed to regard lesbianism as just one more theme women can write about; its political significance—and history—seemed lost." By 1993, however, Howe describes lesbianism as identity and directly links her change in consciousness as one of the effects of women's and lesbian poetry:

> What has altered in poetry during these two decades of rapid change and discovery for all areas of women's life and history? . . . the specificity of identity has become especially important, in life and in art. Some poets identify themselves as lesbian, as working-class, as

ethnically Jewish or Slavic, Chinese or Chicana, or some combination of these and other elements.

Audre Lorde wrote extensively on the importance of poetry that is "not sterile word play" but is "revelatory distillation of experience" and of the erotic that does not emphasize "sensation without feeling" but acts as a "measure between the beginnings of our sense of self and the chaos of our strongest feelings." In "Poetry Is Not a Luxury," she flatly declares that

> Poetry is not only dream and vision; it is the skeleton architecture of our lives. It lays the foundations for a future of change, a bridge across our fears of what has never been before. . . . Our poems formulate the implications of ourselves, what we feel within and dare make real (or bring action into accordance with), our fears, our hopes, our most cherished terrors.

Persuaded that "moving into sunlight against the body of a woman I love" is as profound a statement as "writing a good poem," Lorde insisted that the lesbian poet's responsibility is to embrace the political implications and effects of the actions brought forth by her writing. She is far from alone, for effecting political, social, and cultural change is characteristic of lesbian poetry today.

Indeed, Minnie Bruce Pratt assumes the mantle of poet/prophet when asked as a participant in a poetry series to respond to its theme, Shelley's "Poets are the unacknowledged legislators of the world," and plainly describes the vulnerable outlaw status of the *lesbian poet*:

> As a lesbian poet, I have been contemplating Shelley's words. To be a poet who is a lesbian is to be a potential felon in half the states of this country and the District of Columbia, where I live. In some countries of the world, to be a lesbian poet is to be subject, by law, to imprisonment or even execution. How I love is outside the law. And when I write and speak of my life as a lesbian, my poems have also been seen as outside the bounds of poetry.

The very word *lesbian* is intensely charged, evoking some of the nastiest responses to and assumptions made about any group. Lesbians are women without men, so are by the very fact of their existence threatening to patriarchal social arrangements. Not surprisingly, lesbians have been seen as dangerous and as sexually wild and out of control. Grahn satirically caricatures the tradition-bound response of a homophobic aggressive doctor in "Edward the Dyke":

> Your disease has gotten completely out of control. We scientists know of course that it's a highly pleasurable experience to take someone's penis or vagina into your mouth— it's pleasurable and enjoyable. Everyone knows that. But after you've taken a thousand pleasurable penises or vaginas into your mouth and had a thousand people take your pleasurable penis or vagina into their mouth, what have you accomplished? What have you got to show for it? . . . Do you see how you're missing the meaning of life? . . .

Yet this response to homoerotic love misses the point, pornographically dismembering lesbians and gay men into sexually driven body parts. Not only by decrying social injustices and institutionally reinforced prejudice, but also through graphically beautiful love poetry, lesbian poet/prophets expound the profundities of lesbian physical love. Perhaps the most famous example besides Rich's "Floating Poem" is Lorde's "Love Poem":

> And I knew when I entered her I was
> high wind in her forests hollow
> fingers whispering sound
> honey flowed
> from the split cups
> impaled on a lance of tongues
> on the tips of her breast on her navel
> and my breath
> howling into her entrances
> through lungs of pain.

Her lover's body is the promised land flowing with milk and honey, a sheltering forest and a wilderness in which lesbian lovers freely revel in one another and their mutual delight.

The genre "lesbian poetry" was recognized not first by scholars or booksellers but by women who needed to give voice to such experience, and by women who needed to be reassured of a lesbian literary history. Politics, sexuality, lyric, epic, history, autobiography, biography, polemics, aesthetics, and gentle persuasion intersect in lesbian poetry and affect teaching (both formally in the academy and informally among general readers) and thus effect cultural change. A sense of separation and disenfranchisement has characterized the work and reception of many a lesbian poet. But with the burgeoning of alternative curricula and the visibility and information proffered by the literary history you are presently reading, lesbian poetry will, let us hope, to borrow a phrase from Gertrude Stein, become *everybody's poetry and proud heritage* not just that of those who imaginatively inhabit the separate isle of Lesbos. After all, lesbian poetry is, as that white patriarch Robert Frost remarked of poetry itself, "the stuff of life." (See also POST-MODERNISM.)

—*Martha Nell Smith*

BIBLIOGRAPHY

Barrington, Judith. *An Intimate Wilderness: Lesbian Writers on Sexuality*. Portland, Oreg.: Eighth Mountain Press, 1991. ■ Bernikow, Louise, ed. *The World Split Open 1552–1950*. New York: Vintage, 1974. ■ Brandt, Kate. *Happy Endings: Lesbian Writers Talk about their Lives and Work*. Tallahassee, Fla.: Naiad Press, 1993. ■ Bristow, Joseph, ed. *Sexual Sameness: Textual Differences in Lesbian and Gay Writing*. London: Routledge, 1992. ■ Bulkin, Elly. "'Kissing/Against the Light': A Look at Lesbian Poetry." *Lesbian Studies: Present and Future*. Margaret Cruikshank, ed. Old Westbury, N.Y.: Feminist Press, 1982. ■ Carruthers, Mary J. "The Re-Vision of the Muse: Adrienne Rich, Audre Lorde, Judy Grahn, Olga Broumas." *Hudson Review* 36.2 (Summer 1983): 293–322. ■ Clausen, Jan. *A Movement of Poets: Thoughts on Poetry and Feminism*. Brooklyn: Long Haul, 1982. ■ Corinne, Tee, ed. *The Poetry of Sex: Lesbians Write the Erotic*. Austin, Tex.: Banned Books, 1992. ■ Covino, Gina, and Laurel Galana. *The Lesbian Reader: An Amazon Quarterly Anthology*. Oakland, Calif.: Amazon Press, 1975. ■ Cruikshank, Margaret, ed. *New Lesbian Writing: An Anthology*. San Francisco: Grey Fox Press, 1984. ■ Doan, Laura L. *The Lesbian Postmodern*. New York: Columbia University Press, 1994. ■ Grahn, Judy. *The Highest Apple: Sappho and the Lesbian Poetic Tradition*. San Francisco: Spinsters, Ink, 1985. ■ Gubar, Susan. "Sapphistries." *Signs* 10.1 (Autumn 1984): 43–62. ■ King, Katie. "Audre Lorde's Lacquered Layerings: The Lesbian Bar as a Site of Literary Production." *Cultural Studies* 2.3 (October 1988): 321–342. Rpt. *New Lesbian Criticism: Literary and Cultural Readings*. Sally Munt, ed. New York: Columbia University Press, 1992. 51–74. ■ Lorde, Audre. *Sister Outsider: Essays and Speeches*. Freedom, Calif.: Crossing Press, 1984. ■ Luczak, Raymond, ed. *Eyes of Desire: A Deaf Gay & Lesbian Reader*. Boston: Alyson, 1993. ■ Meese, Elizabeth A. *(Sem)erotics: Theorizing Lesbian Writing*. New York: New York University Press, 1992. ■ Munt, Sally, ed. *New Lesbian Criticism: Literary and Cultural Readings*. New York: Columbia University Press, 1992. ■ Ostriker, Alicia. *Stealing the Language: The Emergence of Women's Poetry in America*. Boston: Beacon Press, 1986. ■ Picano, Felice. *A True Likeness: Lesbian and Gay Writing Today*. New York: Sea Horse Press, 1980. ■ Pratt, Minnie Bruce. *Rebellion: Essays 1980–1991*. Ithaca, N.Y.: Firebrand Books, 1991. ■ Ramas, Juanita, ed. *Compañeras: Latina Lesbians (An Anthology)*. New York: Latina Lesbian History Project, 1987. ■ Roscoe, Will, coordinator. *Living the Spirit: A Gay American Indian Anthology*. Gay American Indians History Project. New York: St. Martin's Press, 1988. ■ Sheba Collective. *More Serious Pleasure: Lesbian Erotic Stories and Poetry*. Pittsburgh: Cleis Press, 1990. ■ ———. *Serious Pleasure: Lesbian Erotic Stories and Poetry*. Pittsburgh: Cleis Press, 1989. ■ Stimpson, Catharine. "Adrienne Rich and Lesbian/Feminist Poetry." *Parnassus* 12.2/13.1 (Spring/Summer/Fall/Winter 1985): 249–268. ■ Weathers, Carolyn, and Wrenn, Jenny. *In a Different Light: An Anthology of Lesbian Writers*. Los Angeles: Clothespin Fever Press, 1989.

Poliziano
(1454–1494)

Angelo Ambrogini, called Poliziano from his birthplace, Montepulciano, and sometimes referred to as Politian in English, distinguished himself equally in scholarship and poetry. His teachers included Marsilio Ficino, John Argyropulos, and Christoforo Landino, while Linacre, Grocyn, and Reuchlin were among his pupils. His scholarly and literary talents were manifested as early as 1470, when his Latin translation of Homer's *Iliad* began to appear. At nineteen, he was engaged by Lorenzo de' Medici as a tutor to his sons Piero and Giovanni (later Pope Leo X), and two years later, he became Lorenzo's personal secretary. A rupture with Lorenzo's wife, Clarice, in 1478 was the occasion of Poliziano's removal to Mantua under the protection of Cardinal Francesco Gonzaga. In 1480, he was permitted to return to Florence where he became Professor of Greek and Latin literature at the Academy. His eloquence, his profound knowledge of the classics, and his abilities as a teacher made him famous throughout Europe. His later years were principally devoted to philology. The story related by Paolo Giovio (1483–1552), attributing Poliziano's early death to an amorous paroxysm for a beautiful young man, though often repeated, is viewed with skepticism by current scholars.

Poliziano's poetic genius was exercised in no fewer than three languages: Latin, Greek, and Italian. His corpus of Greek poetry consists of about sixty epigrams. In Latin, he produced numerous epigrams, odes, and elegies, as well as his famous *Silvae*, hexameter introductions to his lectures in literature, considered stylistic ideals throughout the Renaissance. Poliziano's Latin poetry is remarkable not only for its exquisite polish, but also for its distinct individuality of voice. His Italian poetry, equally accomplished, fuses diverse forms. The *stanze*, written in honor of Giuliano de' Medici, mixes narrative and mythological allegory. The *Orfeo*, a "pastoral fable" containing elements of sacred drama and eclogue, foreshadowed Italian secular theater and influenced Ariosto and Tasso. Poliziano also wrote a history of the Pazzi conspiracy in Latin prose, as well as two influential collections of scholarly *Miscellanea*.

Poliziano's homoerotic poetry is found mainly in his Greek and Latin epigrams, published when he was seventeen. In one he describes his love for two youths dissimilar in every respect except their antipathy toward him. Another contains a remarkably frank celebration of the physical pleasures he enjoys with his lover. Another describes his susceptibility to the "vertiginous" glances of a beautiful boy. In one he describes himself as being in the habit of kissing the "redolent lips of youths" although he declines to kiss one who drinks urine. He shows a preference for blonds. He complains of an inveterate tease. He refers to the homosexuality of VIRGIL and Anacreon. With apparent hypocrisy, Poliziano sometimes uses homosexuality as the basis of reproaches—rather implausible ones—against his literary rival, Marullo (1453–1500).

—*Brad Walton*

BIBLIOGRAPHY

Bigi, Emilio. *La Cultura del Poliziano e altri studi umanistici.* Pisa: Nistri Lischi, 1967. ■ Branca, Vittore. *Poliziano e l'umanesimo della parola.* Torino: Giulio Einandi, 1983. ■ Cascio, Renzo lo. *Poliziano.* Palermo: Palumbo, 1970. ■ Maier, Ida. *Ange Politien.* Geneva: Droz, 1966. ■ Poliziano, Angelo Ambrogini. *Prose volgari inedite e poesie latine e greche edite e inedite.* Hildesheim: George Olms, 1976.

Post-modernism

In literary studies, the stance of post-modern critics and writers is characterized by a rejection of the values of eighteenth-century Enlightenment thought, most particularly by a rejection of the notions of rationality and objectivity and of the understanding of the self as a rational, unitary entity. Instead, post-modern thought emphasizes a form of subjectivity that is multiple rather than singular and fluid rather than static. Subjectivity, as used by postmodern thinkers, refers to a subjective sense of self that includes agency—the capacity for action—as distinguished from the condition of an obliterated selfhood that results when an individual is objectified, made into an object to be possessed sexually, materially, or imaginatively by those who are culturally dominant. For the post-modernist, subjectivities (since subjectivity is not singular or fixed) are always in process; post-modernism therefore argues against the privileging of naturalized or essentialized positions and points of view. Reality, or "the real," is constructed and contingent on such constraints as time, place, race, class, gender, and sexuality; consequently, attempts to establish transhistorical or transcultural validity for ideas or points of view is seen as futile, with the result that all universalizing notions are obviated.

The post-modern critic, creative writer, filmmaker or artist is distinguished by her or his concerted efforts to situate particular subjects in their exact times and places, to contextualize those subjects as precisely as possible, maintaining always the awareness that all representations are inevitably, irreducibly ideological in nature and complicit with dominant ideologies, even as they attempt to subvert them. For this reason, the stance of the self-consciously post-modern author is almost inevitably self-reflexive and ironic, always aware that even the post-modernist is unavoidably compromised.

Post-modernism both grows out of and subverts MODERNISM. These two intellectual movements, historically dominating roughly the first and second halves of the twentieth century, have in common their often playful use of self-referentiality, irony, indeterminacy (or ambiguity), parody, and the exploration of language. Both also share a persistent challenging of traditional, realistic forms of representation. Post-modern art and criticism, however, challenge modernism's adherence to an ideology of artistic autonomy, individual expression, and the elitist splitting off of art from mass culture and everyday life. The concern of post-modern art and criticism is to "decenter" and to unfix these rationalist, humanist assumptions about what is "natural" or essential. As the notion of an autonomous individuality is "decentered," both humanist and capitalist notions of selfhood and subjectivity are called into question.

A consequence of this decentering is that one of the primary post-modern projects is the problematizing of the marginal, the liminal, and the "Other," that have been traditionally overlooked. This has entailed a shifting of attention from the study of European-American white males and their cultural productions to an examination of the complex contexts of the lives of, for instance, women, ethnic, and racial minorities, gay/lesbian/bisexual/transgendered individuals, and inhabitants of the so-called Third World. Linda Hutcheon describes the intellectual goal of post-modernism as being to erode our assumptions by examining them, "to de-naturalize some of the dominant features of our way of life; to point out that those entities that we unthinkingly experience as 'natural' (they might even include capitalism, patriarchy, liberal humanism) are in fact 'cultural'; made by us, not given to us," so that post-modernism "provokes an investigation of how we make meaning in culture."

The post-modern emphasis on problematizing marginalized and "other" peoples, cultures, and experiences has helped develop gay and lesbian studies and move them into new areas of criticism and theoretical sophistication. In seeking to be inclusive of all gender deviancies and all gender deviant or transgendered persons, many post-modern gay and lesbian writers have chosen to describe themselves as "queer" and to reconfigure gay and lesbian studies as "queer theory." The post-modern perspective has served to propel queer theory, itself originally marginalized, into an avant-garde position with respect to the academic mainstream, an irony very much in keeping with the post-modern commitment to doubleness and duplicity, and with the penchant of post-modernism for appropriating, installing, and reinforcing, as much as for undermining and subverting, the conventions and assumptions it appears to challenge.

The most important ways in which post-modern thought has shaped queer theory are (1) in distinguishing between sex and sexuality; (2) in describing the tension between social construction (that is, culturally produced meaning) and essentialism (that is, biological determinism) as they apply to sex and gender; (3) in bringing to consciousness in the gay/lesbian/bisexual/transgendered communities crucial issues concerning identity and identity politics; and (4) in exploring, in both life and the arts, modes of gender-bending and gender-performativity, understandings of gender that grow out of post-modern self-reflexivity.

David Halperin has stated most clearly the crucial distinction between sex and sexuality: "Unlike sex, sexuality is a cultural production: it represents the appropriation of the human body and of its physiological capacities by an ideological discourse. Sexuality is not a somatic fact; it is a cultural effect." Given this distinction, and the presumed essence of sex (or biology), a primary emphasis of queer theory has been an understanding and a recovery of the historical construction of sexuality. Through such a recovery, we have begun to identify and define the full range of homosexual behaviors and identities in their historical and geographical particularity. Historians of sexuality are attempting to locate the relatively recent (probably in sixteenth- or seventeenth-century Europe) emergence of homosexuality as an identity inscribed within a subculture. As Edward Stein notes, "the categories of sexual orientation that we use in twentieth-century North America are culturally-bound categories" we must not extend without great caution to other times or places because "in other cultures people do not see the gender or biological sex of a person's sexual object choice as revealing significant information about his or her erotic preferences." The example most often used to demonstrate this point is that of ancient Greece, where social status rather than object choice determined appropriate sexual behavior so that a power differential was maintained between sexual partners; thus, for male citizens, appropriate partners were noncitizens, male or female slaves, and women and boys, *not* other male citizens. Before the emergence, then, of homosexual identity as we know it in sixteenth- and seventeenth-century Europe, it was particular behaviors between members of the same sex—most often males—that were proscribed. It was considered sinful, or criminal, to participate in certain behaviors, but the persons so participating were not thought of as having identities coterminous with those behaviors. That is, they continued to be identified primarily as persons of a particular sex, class, race, occupation, and so on. Though the information available about English women before the nineteenth century is more scarce than that about men, it is possible to name some of the cultural constructions that governed female-female erotic relations. Terms like "tribades," "tommies," romantic friends, and Boston marriages denote some of the cultural constructs antedating the more recent "lesbians."

Tensions between the (post-modern) adherents of social construction and the (more traditionalist) advocates of essentialism became acute in the late 1980s and have led to an ongoing discussion of the relative influences of environment and biology in shaping homosexual identity. This discussion is a version of the more traditional dialogue about nurture and nature, now driven by the tools and methodologies of modern historiography and by sophisticated scientific studies of genes and DNA. The extent to which sexual identity is shaped by culture and variable from time to time and place to place and the degree to which it is biologically determined and therefore universal (or transhistorical and transcultural) continue to be central to issues of identity politics within the gay/lesbian/bisexual/transgendered communities, as well as in gay and lesbian imaginative literature and in queer theory. There is an increasing awareness among theorists of social construction that political essentialism—that is, the argument that there is a fixed gay or lesbian identity—has important utility in the real-world recognition of gays and lesbians as individuals in quest of equal rights and in the advancement of their status as responsible citizens of larger political communities. Alternatively, the impetus to find a "gay gene" and to establish a fixed, stable gay identity has yielded with increasing frequency to a more nuanced comprehension of the convergence of environmental and biological influences. It has become apparent that there are considerable political dangers involved in the assertion of a genetic etiology for sexual orientation insofar as homophobic groups and individuals might be encouraged to "fix" what might be regarded as a genetic malfunction. The respective proponents of social construction and essentialism are thus more frequently coming to value the utility of each other's perspectives.

Gay and lesbian writers and creative artists have begun seriously to explore the possibilities inherent in a post-modern understanding of gender and gender roles. Judith Butler argues in *Gender Trouble* that gender and gender roles are manifested as self-conscious performances. For Butler, gender roles are performances through which we negotiate social and sexual relations; they have meaning only within particular cultural contexts, and they are learned and articulated as part of the cultural production of meaning. We see this understanding of gender as performance explored in director Jennie Livingston's poignant film portrait of amateur black and Hispanic drag artists, *Paris is Burning* (1992), in which gender performance is the focus of a subset of contemporary gay subculture in New York. A literary example of self-conscious gender play is the manipulation of first-person narrative voice by JEANETTE WINTERSON in *Written on the Body* (1992). In this novel, the author sets out deliberately to problematize the sex-gender dialectic by teasing the reader with the narrator's fluid gender identity; though the narrator is in all likelihood female, Winterson is careful not to provide clear gender markings, in fact naming her Lothario, so that the nature and significance of gender identity are repeatedly interrogated.

Even as much contemporary literature by gay men, such as DAVID LEAVITT's *The Lost Language of Cranes* (1986), attempts a realistic portrayal of the emotional complexities of gay life in a heterosexual world, films by gay men have often proved to be more technically daring and intellectually exploratory. Films like *Queer Edward II* (1991) by the late DEREK JARMAN and Gregg Araki's *The Living End* (1992) are notable examples of the current flourishing of a gay post-modern cinema, perhaps a late-century development following the earlier work of PIER PAOLO PASOLINI and Werner Maria Fassbinder in Europe.

A few younger gay writers use post-modern techniques to explore unorthodox subjects, as does the minimalist Dennis Cooper in his novels *Closer* (1990) and *Frisk* (1991), in which he uses a fragmented consciousness to explore the connections between self-destruction, death, and desire. Literature by lesbians, however, has more self-consciously adopted a post-modern and assertively transgressive stance in its representation of lesbian culture and erotic life. MONIQUE WITTIG's novels, especially *Les Guerillères* (1985), SARAH SCHULMAN's novels *After Dolores* (1989) and *Empathy* (1992), the fiction of Jeanette Winterson, the poetry of OLGA BROUMAS, and the mixed-genre work of GLORIA ANZALDÚA and CHERRÍE MORAGA, for instance, may all be said to exemplify the formal experimentation and complex mixture of tones characteristic of post-modern culture.

It is, of course, impossible to predict the future course of literary and artistic production by gay men and lesbians. But it is apparent that the coming of age of queer theory and queer politics and the maturation of a self-conscious artistic and literary enterprise have been enabled by and have contributed meaningfully to post-modern culture. (See also GENDER, IDENTITY, and LITERARY THEORY: GAY, LESBIAN, AND QUEER.)

—*Harriette Andreadis*

BIBLIOGRAPHY

Abelove, Henry, Michèle Barale, and David Halpern, eds. *The Lesbian and Gay Studies Reader*. London: Routledge, 1993. ■ Altman, Dennis, et al., eds. *Homosexuality, Which Homosexuality?: International Conference on Gay and Lesbian Studies*. London and Amsterdam: GMP Publishers and Uitgeverij An Dekker/Schorer, 1989. ■ Butler, Judith. *Gender Trouble: Feminism and the Subversion of Identity*. London: Routledge, 1990. ■ ———. *Bodies That Matter: On the Discursive Limits of "Sex."* London: Routledge, 1993. ■ Doan, Laura, ed. *The Lesbian Post-modern*. New York: Columbia University Press, 1994. ■ Dollimore, Jonathan. *Sexual Dissidence: Augustine to Wilde, Freud to Foucault*. Oxford: Clarendon Press, 1991. ■ Foucault, Michel. *The History of Sexuality, Volume 1: An Introduction*. Trans. Robert Hurley. New York: Pantheon, 1978. ■ Fuss, Diana. *Essentially Speaking: Feminism, Nature & Difference*. London: Routledge, 1989. ■ Greenberg, David. *The Construction of Homosexuality*. Chicago: University of Chicago Press, 1988. ■ Halperin, David M. *One Hundred Years of Homosexuality and Other Essays on Greek Love*. London: Routledge, 1990. ■ Hutcheon, Linda. *The Politics of Post-modernism*. London: Routledge, 1989. ■ Levay, Simon. *The Sexual Brain*. Cambridge, Mass.: MIT Press, 1993. ■ Stein, Edward, ed. *Forms of Desire: Sexual Orientation and the Social Constructionist Controversy*. London: Routledge, 1992.

Price, Reynolds
(*b*. 1933)

A native of eastern North Carolina, Reynolds Price has rarely strayed far from home. After attending Oxford University on a Rhodes scholarship, he returned to Duke University where he has taught ever since. Though most acclaimed for his fiction, Price has also published drama, poetry, and essays. His abiding interest in narrative yielded a volume of biblical retellings and two memoirs: a collection of childhood memories and an account of his life since the 1984 diagnosis of a spinal tumor that left him unable to walk.

Price's contribution to the gay literary heritage must be read indirectly since he does not treat gay themes at great length (though his novel *The Promise of Rest* [1994] focuses on the return home of a man with AIDS) nor has he spoken explicitly about his own sexual identity. Particularly in Price's poetry, the careful reader may note a particular idealization in describing the male body, a special attentiveness to a graceful stance or a muscular profile, as when the sight of his young friend Straw sprawled across the hood of a car unearths a buried memory for Hutch Mayfield, the central character in *The Source of Light* (1981): "Now the different place which Straw constituted, in

power and need, demanded homage. The sight of the stripped boy asleep in his arms last Saturday dawn stood clear in Hutch's mind. He watched it gladly with no regret."

Yet other characters are equally obsessed with female bodies; Price returns again and again to the workings of Eros in shaping relationships. Gay relationships most often blossom as one manifestation of this deeply human urge toward connectedness: Hutch Mayfield's sexual relationships with men are sources of grace and comfort, and his eventual decision to marry his fiancée Ann constitutes choosing a life's course rather than rejecting homosexuality. Price's noteworthy ability to create deep and complex women marks a treatment of gender distinctive among male authors; Price himself describes human experience as a "vast common room" that authors should use more fully.

Another distinctive concern is male friendship. For men of all ages, classes, and sexual orientations, a long conversation with a trusted male friend is a source of refuge from the demands of family and work, as when in the novel *Good Hearts* (1988) Wesley Beavers, escaping from both a marriage and a heterosexual affair, takes refuge with a gay male acquaintance. The unrealized sexual possibilities in their evening together offer Wesley a perspective from which to assess his life. Such homosocial bonds burn most brightly in the novel *The Tongues of Angels* (1990), based on Price's experience as a summer camp counselor. The intense friendship between Bridge Boatner and Rafe Noren, though never expressed sexually, shimmers with erotic heat. Bridge gains from Rafe's angelic life and tragic death a glimpse of another realm of existence that will forever affect him. Yet this friendship echoes across Price's fiction with countless other relationships, particularly those among family members. In the intricate dances of human bonding between parent and child, between lovers, between friends, Price traces the surprising epiphanies, harsh realities, and ineffable joys of the workings of grace.

—*Randal Woodland*

BIBLIOGRAPHY

Conversations with Reynolds Price. Jefferson Humphries, ed. Jackson: University Press of Mississippi, 1991.

Proust, Marcel
(1871–1922)

Marcel Proust was born in 1871. His Jewish mother was highly educated; his father was a distinguished professor of hygiene. Proust had a comfortable and protected bourgeois childhood—all the more cosseted after the age of nine when he had the first in a lifelong sequence of debilitating asthma attacks. Three years later, he began to masturbate, usually locking himself away in the lavatory at the top of his parents' house. At school, his interests were focused mainly in the areas of literature, philosophy, botany, and history—subjects that would all exert a strong influence on his fiction. At the age of eighteen, he did a year's military service at Orléans, an experience that would also significantly shape the fiction.

After taking degrees in law (1893) and philosophy (1895) at the Sorbonne, he embarked on a relatively leisurely existence consisting of social visits, neurotic illnesses, and the writing of belles lettres. In 1895, he also started trying to write a massive autobiographical novel, *Jean Santeuil* (unpublished until 1952; English translation, 1955). This book is marred by a basic structural weakness that the author never managed to resolve. The result is a rambling and episodic narrative with insufficient thematic unity to make it cohere. After working on it for four years, Proust abandoned it.

His emotional and sexual life, meanwhile, took on a distinct pattern. Although he conducted a series of chivalrous romantic affairs with prominent society hostesses, his closest encounters were with men. With his social equals or betters, he formed intense romantic friendships that may, on occasion, have been sexual; but his main love affairs were with servants—the most important of these being his chauffeur Alfred Agostinelli, whom he met in 1907. Proust also had encounters that were purely sexual, these invariably with men of a lower social class. The deaths of his father (1903) and mother (1905), though causing him intense and lasting pain, left him freer to organize his life around his erotic needs.

In about 1909, Proust began his second large-scale attempt at autobiographical fiction. He spent the rest of his life writing *A la recherche du temps perdu* and never completed it to his own satisfaction. Yet the novel is one of the major documents of Modernist subjectivity (particularly regarding its concern with the nature of time and involuntary memory). Furthermore, by any standard, it is a great gay novel. The present essay cites the English translation by C. K. Scott Moncrieff, which has itself attained a classic status: What with all its eccentricities and errors, it can now be seen as a CAMP *tour de force*.

The key characters around whom Proust teases out the topic of homosexuality are Robert de Saint-Loup, the Baron Palamède ("mémé") de Charlus, Albertine Simonet, and the narrator himself. Saint-Loup first appears to Marcel, and therefore to the reader, as a lover of women: His affair with Rachel is protracted and intense. But later in life, even though he marries Gilberte Swann, Saint-Loup develops his interest in men, and his last great love is Charles Morel. Little information reaches us about his affairs with men because Marcel hears only rumors of them, often at third hand. More visible is the Baron de Charlus, the great comic character Proust based on the poet Robert de Montesquiou, among others. He, too, appears first as if heterosexual—he is reputed, early on, to be the lover of Odette de Crécy—but he becomes Proust's most detailed representation of a man-loving man. His loves are many and varied, but the affair to which the narrator has clearest access is the one with Charles Morel (prior to Saint-Loup's liaison with the same).

Charlus is vain and snobbish, by turns demonstratively masculine and abjectly effeminate, both silly and profound. His life spans the whole period of the novel, and his intimacies bridge the social spectrum from palace to gutter. His erotic interests are especially varied as he grows older toward the end of the novel, when he develops a taste for small boys (XII, 95) and pays working-class men in Jupien's brothel to whip and humiliate him. In his relations with Marcel, he is both generous and haughty, and always unpredictable.

ANDRÉ GIDE had turned the novel down for publication by the Nouvelle Revue Francaise, on the spurious grounds that Proust was a socialite whose book was probably just fictionalized gossip about the *beau monde*. He lived to regret this careless decision when he discovered what the book was really like. However, he never approved of its representations of what he regarded as the negative aspects of homosexuality. The Baron de Charlus represented most of the things from which, in both his writings and his own life, Gide was at pains to distance himself. As he said in a letter to Proust (June 14, 1914), he was worried that readers would take the complex individual Charlus as a representative of a type. It seems he did not want to be tarred with that brush.

Because Marcel, the narrator, is fascinated by those who do not fit into strictly heterosexual patterns of social and sexual intercourse, *A la recherche du temps perdu* returns to the topic of homosexuality again and again. Lesbianism is raised, chiefly as a phantom, when for hundreds of pages Marcel fusses about whether his beloved Albertine has had affairs with other young women. As suspicion turns to paranoia, lesbianism is thus defined in a context of heterosexual jealousy. (Similarly, Charles Swann lengthily interrogates Odette, when she is still his mistress, about whether she has had affairs with other women. She has. II, 200–215) As it turns out after her accidental death, Albertine was indeed predominantly lesbian (XI, 179–183); but by this time, for Marcel, the heat has gone out of the matter. The book's most haunting lesbian scene occurs in the first volume but echoes throughout the next eleven: this is the occasion that Marcel witnesses at Montjouvain—characteristically prying through the window of a private house—when Mlle Vinteuil makes love with her girlfriend whilst desecrating a photograph of her own father (I, 218–227). The scene gives Marcel a crucial insight into the cruel side of the human heart.

In truth, the account of the relationship between Albertine and Marcel is far less about a woman's sexuality than about a man's obsession with it. His suspicions turn him into something of an expert—at least, to his own satisfaction—on the culture and customs of Gomorrah. Likewise, his abiding interest in the Baron de Charlus gives him an education in the customs of the Sodomites. As a consequence, the novel contains several long essays on homosexuality, which display a fascinating combination of speculation, invention, ignorance, and solid information. Whether one should blame the ignorance on Marcel or Proust is a moot point. The generous view is to regard many of Marcel's utterances as being written by Proust at a considerable ironic distance.

Among the views expressed at various points in the novel are the following. Homosexual people—or rather, "inverts," the term with which Proust is happier—constitute not only a race apart, like the Jews, but a cursed race (*la race maudite*) who often support one another by the secretive means of a kind of international freemasonry. Inversion should not be categorized as a vice, even if there are plenty of inverts who are vicious. Some remain solitary; others socialize and organize with their own kind. Inversion has extensive parallels, both literal and symbolic, within the world of botany. It is possible to detect such people by observing details of behavior and physique; they are adept at recognizing one another. A distinction should be made between people who are homosexual by convention, as in ancient Greece, and those of the modern world whose homosexuality is involuntary. Male inverts make good husbands. Above all, however, the narrative keeps coming back to the figure of the homosexual man who is attracted only to heterosexual men and can therefore never find a partner who is able or willing to return his love. Charlus is the embodiment of this conundrum.

As André Gide noticed, the major problem with Proust's representations of homosexuality is that he used his own most abiding and precious memories of love to flesh out the novel's picture of heterosexual relations and was inadvertently left, in the case of homosexuality, with predominantly negative themes and events. This is where the *Recherche* may be said to reveal the gaping flaw in its construction. It is a flaw imposed on the artist by the homophobia of his times. By the time Proust was aware of the consequences of his initial decision to heterosexualize his narrator, it was too late to adjust the disproportionately negative view the book conveys of its homosexual characters and the relationships they form.

In order to restore one's complete respect for the book, it may be useful both to approach Proust *du coté de chez* ROLAND BARTHES, and to look out for signs of the ironic distance between Proust and his self-portrait, Marcel. Barthes makes some particularly revealing comments on the scene in *La Prisonnière* when Albertine accidentally lets slip the first half of an obscene expression. She covers her mouth, as if to cram the obscenity back into the silence of her body, but she cannot hope to hide her always very expressive blushes or to censor the eloquence of her sudden speechlessness. Marcel, her lover and captor and—inasmuch as he keeps confiding in *us* his doubts about her fidelity and virtue—her betrayer, is at first puzzled by her half-utterance; and when she refuses to complete her sentence, he mentally tries out several possible endings, none of them making sense. When he finally understands what she said, he deduces from it proof that she is lesbian (X, 185–188). Roland Barthes comments that Marcel is horrified, "for it is the dreaded ghetto of female homosexuality, of crude cruising, which is suddenly revealed thereby: a whole scene through the keyhole of language."

One has to assume that Barthes is taking a characteristically ironic step beyond the common view of *A la recherche* as a *roman à clef*. If there is a key to this novel, we are invited not to turn it, but to remove it and peek through the hole. This phrase, "the keyhole of language" (*le trou de serrure du langage*), is what impresses one as going straight to the heart of Proust's method. Of course, Barthes is preparing the ground for a conventional post-structuralist reading of the book as an unstable text open to an infinity of subjective readings, based on a free discourse between writer and reader. His point about the "keyhole of language" has a general application, in so far as when we read fiction and "see images" of fictional characters, we are not looking through the author's eyes or the narrator's eyes at an existing and complete reality; we are not holding up a mirror to an already detailed scene, nor are we looking into a mirror held by author or narrator. What flashes and fragments we "see," or imagine we see, we see through and in the medium of the language in which they are presented to us. This may be mildly interesting as a general proposition; but, applied to Proust, it has more particular and literal reference to narrative technique and our readings of it. To understand and enjoy the *Recherche,* one must have an ear for gossip—not merely in order to follow up the real-life equivalencies of Proust's characters and events—that is, not to treat the book as autobiography and biography, a grand Soap Opera based on a true story. The book is that, to be sure; and, as such, it is *actually* an act of gossip. (It is clear from Proust's letters that he held a gossip's view of the upper reaches of French society. Samuel Beckett called the Proust of the letters a "garrulous old dowager.") But that may be its least compelling aspect. More interesting are the technical aspects of the matter, the way the book is narrated: For it is here that Proust really innovates as a gay writer.

The usual narrative mode in Proust involves the relaying—with rhetorical flourishes and personal opinions of varying relevance—of information gained either by hearsay and eavesdropping, or by the visual observation of a partially obstructed scene (between figures across the distances of a drawing room; through peepholes; between the curtain and the window frame; and so on). Most of Marcel's information comes to him *incomplete.* His inferences and inventions fill the gaps, in the best tradition of gossip.

Marcel is an obsessive detective of secrets, a follower of the minutest clues. (In a sense, since he learns everything piecemeal, all the information he absorbs functions as a clue to the final picture.) He is most consistently involved in the great Gay Soap Opera quandary of wondering *Is-he-or-isn't-he?* and *Is-she-or-isn't-she?* That is to say, which of the other characters are homosexual? Although he wishes to be known as a heterosexual, innocent of such affairs, Marcel claims to know all the little secret signs that mean "perversion." He finds visible, physical signs of homosexuality, generally based around the loins. One thinks, in particular, of the muscular wave that ripples over Legrandin's hips outside Combray church, a "wholly carnal fluency" that draws Marcel's attention to "the possibility of a Legrandin altogether different to the one whom we knew" (I, 169). And we must not forget the "almost symbolical behind" of Charlus (VIII, 10).

Tones of speech, also, lead Marcel into sexual conjecture. On the very day when he first finds out about Charlus, he hears behind him the voice of Vaugoubert and decides at once, "He is a Charlus." Indeed, he already has the confidence to speak of his own "trained ear" in this connection (VII, 89). There seem to be other points at which his ear responds in this way, not to voice alone, but to language. Could this be why he consistently misunderstands the gay lift-boy in the hotel at Balbec (IV, 137–138); or why he says Jupien uses "the most ingenious turns of speech" (V, 18)? There can be no doubt as to why, during the War, Saint-Loup learns the slang of as many servicemen as possible, regardless of nationality and rank (XII, 122).

There are two types of clue in operation throughout the book: those to which Marcel responds (or fails to respond) when analyzing other characters and those that he leaves as clues for us readers, rather than state the facts outright. One of his stated reasons for merely hinting at character in this way is that "the truth has no need to be uttered to be made apparent, and that one may perhaps gather it with more certainty, without waiting for words, from a thousand outward signs, even from certain invisible phenomena, analogous in the sphere of human character to what in nature are atmospheric changes" (V, 82).

So, as we have seen, Marcel can draw profound deductions from a movement in a man's hips. And we are expected to read such clues as he does, unprompted, when, for instance, one man greets another "with a smile which it was hard to *intercept,* harder still to interpret" (XI, 344, my emphasis); or when Saint-Loup darts at a waiter a glance that "in its limpid penetration seemed to indicate a kind of curiosity and investigation entirely different" from that of an "ordinary" diner (XI, 360). In such cases, Marcel simultaneously infers and implies a sexual situation, without any certainty whatsoever, in his mind or in ours.

Marcel's hints to the reader often take shape as unspecific promises, accompanied by an "as we shall see," that sometimes, perhaps deliberately, gets lost in his other plans and never comes to pass. We are promised certain "quarrels" between Charlus and "people wholly unlike Mme. de Villeparisis" (V, 369–370); a vision of "Highnesses and Majesties" not of the Blood Royal but "of another sort altogether," again in connection with Charlus (VI, 162); proof that homosexuality is curable (VII, 35); Charlus "doing things which would have stupefied the members of his family and his friends" (X, 13) and appeasing "his vicious cravings" (X, 49); and troubles brewing for the Saint-Loup marriage, not in a social but "in another connection" (XI, 350). Even if such promises do come to fruition (as some of them do), given the book's length, the reader has often forgotten the promise by the time it is fulfilled. Perhaps its original suggestiveness is sufficient on its own; no further evidence is required. Whether or not the book dutifully delivers, the reader's suspicious imagination will already have done the trick.

The whole book is packed with errors of conjecture, particularly in the matters of sexual status and event. Consider a few examples, all with reference to Charlus. The Marquis de Saint-Loup, himself bisexual, keeps referring to Charlus, his uncle, as a great womanizer, a petticoat-chaser (V, 228; VII, 127, 135); and so, on one occasion, does Swann (VII, 150). Part of Charlus's reputation for evil is based on a general public confusion, whereby he is associated with another Charlus who was arrested in a disreputable house (VIII, 68). Charlus himself fondly imagines that only a handful of close intimates is aware he is homosexual, whereas, in fact, this is very widely known (VIII, 259). In *Sodome et Gomorrhe,* there is a running joke at Charlus's expense, whereby, whenever anyone says, in a perfectly innocent context, that he is "one of them" or "one of us," Charlus immediately bristles with defensive indignation, under the mistaken impression that it is his sexuality that is being referred to (VIII, 120, 159, 263). In the same volume, Charlus wrongly imagines that Cottard is making eyes at him (VIII, 90). Finally, Marcel tells us that Charlus's whole lifestyle is in error since the Baron confuses his "mania" (his homosexuality) with sentimental friendship (X, 1). The issue seems much more complicated than Marcel realizes, and this may well be a mistake on his part rather than the Baron's. If so, the logical outcome would be that Marcel has consistently misjudged Charlus throughout the book in his efforts to portray him as a personification of vice.

In any case, the important thing about the book's great network of mistakes is that conjecture—which leads as often into error as to truth, and does so purely by chance—is shown to be, in its way, far more creatively functional than the self-consciously "scientific" or "objective" approaches Marcel often dutifully adopts in deference to the twentieth century.

In speaking of the "creative" aspect of gossip, one should not include the kind to be found in the *Divina Commedia,* a dead gossip about dead people, which DANTE presents as a *fait accompli,* a last judgment against which there can be no arguing. In Proust—and this is where the whole technique takes its place among the preoccupations of MODERNISM—the process of weaving a character out of more or less unrelated fragments of suggestion and suspicion evolves in front of our eyes, as the fortuitous result of opinion and luck, resulting in a literature of subjectivity and contingency.

No characters ever achieve that monolithic certainty of definition that any self-respecting omniscient narrator could have granted them. Take the relatively solid heterosexuality of Swann. Although it remains the dominant impression, it is not the whole story. One of the most consistently homoerotic set pieces in the whole novel is narrated (by Marcel) from Swann's point of view. This is when he enters the Sainte-Euverte household and, heading upstairs with leisurely reluctance, appraises the lavish and ornamental display of servants on the staircase. There are "enormous footmen" with "greyhound profiles" drowsing on benches; a statuesque, "strapping great lad in livery," who seems useless, "purely decorative," with hair like that of a Greek statue painted by Mantegna; colossal men whose "decorative presence and marmorean immobility" suggest to Swann that this should be named the "Staircase of the Giants"; and a young footman who resembles an "angel or sentinel" by the bisexual Cellini. Finally, he recovers "his sense of the general ugliness of the human male" when this spectacle of monumental attendants gives way to that of his fellow guests (II, 147–151). Swann's dreams, too, are revealing. In one, a young man weeps to be losing him as he departs on a train (II, 189); and in another, he has to console another tearful youth, who turns out to be himself (II, 223–225). Swann tells Marcel that the friendships of Charlus are "purely platonic" (VII, 150); but, some time after Swann's death, while discussing with Brichot whether or not Swann was homosexual, Charlus says, "I don't deny that long ago in our schooldays, once by accident"—at which point, discretion interrupts, and Charlus merely reveals that Swann had "a peach-like complexion" as a boy, "as beautiful as Cupid himself" (X, 126). That is all. What remains is a cluster of suggestions, as substantial as rumor, that Marcel is always glad to repeat but often reluctant to substantiate.

Even Marcel's "scientific" pronouncements, far from being objective and detached, actually tend to be opinionated and explicitly reactionary. For instance, the dull and ignorant lecture he gives on homosexuality at the start of *Sodome et Gomorrhe* was evidently designed as Proust's gay-conservative reply to André Gide's much more radical (and more convincingly scientific) book *Corydon*, which had been published in the previous year (1920). Marcel's warning "against the lamentable error of proposing . . . to create a Sodomist movement and to rebuild Sodom" presupposes a Sodom modeled on the aristocratic Faubourg Saint-Germain (VII, 45). The whole passage really only makes sense if we read it as being historically and personally specific to Marcel in his time. In this case, it throws some very useful light on Marcel's own closeted yearning for teenage boys.

Although he is forever trying to provide one, Marcel seems temperamentally unsuited to giving a complete overview of the people and events he describes. It seems quite wrong, therefore, to speak of this as a "panoramic" novel. On the contrary, it is a narrowly specific *peephole* novel (or, as Barthes might put it, a *keyhole* novel), whose narrator is a spy. Marcel's habit of *looking-through* becomes a narrative mannerism. Observations made from his windows in the hotel at Balbec or in the Hotel de Guermantes may seem natural enough, and unforced. But when, as the psychological climax to *Le Temps Retrouvé*, he peeks through a hole in a brothel door to watch Charlus being whipped by a male whore, Marcel's powerful imagination provides us with a wealth of details he could only have seen if the peephole had been moveable and equipped with a zoom lens. For once, his account is impossibly complete (XII, 155–156).

Throughout the book, amorous and sexual processes (such as flirtation and cruising) are associated with espionage. The cruising eyes of Charlus are occasionally "shot through by a look of intense activity such as the sight of a person whom they do not know excites only in men to whom . . . it suggests thoughts that would not occur to anyone else—madmen, for instance, or spies" (IV, 69). When Marcel sees Saint-Loup leaving Jupien's brothel in a suspiciously quick and covert manner, he asks himself, "Was this hotel being used as a meeting-place of spies?" (XII, 150) The idea is mistaken but not inappropriate. As Roland Barthes says, the novel is "a tremendous *intrigue,* a *farce* network;" in which all characters (particularly, of course, Marcel himself) are informants, stool pigeons, definitively indiscreet.

What this does to our position as readers, in our "discoursing with the text," is the novel's real *tour de force* since we are involved in the intrigue as its principal beneficiaries. We are the point to which all the gossip flows, and it is our presence that attracts it. However, we do not get away with this lightly: We press our eye to the keyhole and see a keyhole-shaped reflection of our own eye staring back—assuming we are healthily self-conscious. The point is that, in order to appreciate the full quality and resonance of Marcel's gossip, we ourselves have to become fully involved *as gossips* in the process of drawing conclusions from his clues. We are ourselves implicated in the intrigue.

Proust's trick of turning all of his readers into inveterate gossips is closely linked to one of his main themes, of the relation between aesthetic creativity and homosexual intercourse. One of the book's longest running jokes persistently nudges the arts into a realm suggestive of sexual irregularity. The liaison between Charlus and the violinist Morel gives rise to a barely straight-faced equation of music and sodomy. "I should like to listen to a little music this evening," says Charlus when he first picks Morel up; "I pay five hundred francs for the evening" (VIII, 11). Later, when Charlus and Morel play together for the Verdurins and their guests, Marcel comments that the Baron's keyboard style has its "equivalent" in his "nervous defects," by which is meant his homosexuality (VIII, 137). When Mme. Verdurin puts the two lovers in communicating bedrooms, she cannot resist this innuendo: "If you want to have a little music, don't worry about us, the walls are as thick as a fortress" (VIII, 261). (See, also, X, 15.) At times the equation broadens to include artistic activities in general. Something of the kind seems to occur when a woman says she loves "artistic" men because "there is no one like them for understanding women" (I, 104). The whole issue of Bergotte's apparent "vices" is concerned with "a literary solution" to the moral problems raised by "really vicious lives" (III, 185–186).

By obsessing us with the *Is-he-isn't-he?* question, in the end, Marcel forces us to ask it of *him*. (The usual line on this matter of their sexualities has been that Proust was homosexual, his narrator heterosexual; but one is not obliged to follow it.) We may feel the need to ask such questions as the following. Why does Marcel find Albertine most sexy when she is sleeping? Why does he keep accusing her of being a lesbian? Why does he become the most accomplished homosexual spotter in the book? Why does he keep spying on the flirtations of homosexual men? Why, in his only general pronouncement on the appearance of the male body, when he says it is "marred as though by an iron clamp left sticking in a statue that has been taken down from its niche" (IX, 98), why is he so clearly thinking of men as being in a perpetual state of erection? Finally, and perhaps most revealingly, why does he have no name? (Calling him Marcel, after the author, is a mere convenience.)

Marcel is certainly not beyond reacting positively to male beauty. He shows us a young servant with "a bold manner and a charming face" (V, 271); a pageboy "as beautiful as Endymion, with incredibly perfect features" (VII, 268); and a "handsome angel" of a butcher, up to his elbows in gore (IX, 180). Young men on the beach at Balbec are "demigods" (III, 366), while the Comte d'Argencourt and the Duc de Chatellerault—both tall, blond, young, and homosexual—look "like a condensation of the light of the spring evening" in which they appear (V, 289). The two sons of Mme. de Surgis, to whom Charlus will later take a fancy, are described by Marcel as possessing "great and dissimilar beauty," inherited from their mother (VII, 119). Marcel, rather lamely, excuses this tendency to admire good-looking boys and men as "the mania which leads people who are innocent of inversion to speak of masculine beauty" (VIII, 283).

Furthermore, there are equivocal moments in all of Marcel's infatuations with beautiful women. There is the occasion, for instance, when he dreams of Gilberte as a treacherous young man (III, 289–290). He sees something of Mme. Swann "in the masculine gender and the calling of a bathing superintendent" at Balbec (III, 369); and, conversely, he sees in a portrait of the same woman, at first, "a somewhat boyish girl," then "an effeminate youth, vicious and pensive" (IV, 206). Saint-Loup reminds him of his beloved Mme. de Guermantes (V, 101). And the relationship with Albertine fails (if it tries) to resist the intrusion of the author's autobiography: Whatever one's theoretical principles, it is as difficult to separate Albertine from Alfred Agostinelli as Marcel from Proust.

Certain nonexplicit remarks seem comprehensible to Proust, rather than to the Marcel who makes them, unless the latter has the former's inside knowledge of a relatively hidden homosexual culture. One should include among these a description of Legrandin as "a Saint Sebastian of snobbery" (I, 175); and of the Emperor William II as a green carnation (VI, 298).

It may be that, as André Maurois once said, Marcel's love for Albertine is "nothing but a morbid curiosity." He loves her in order to get close enough to observe her, to find out about her; and he does so in order to spy on himself. He is testing his own heterosexual resolve. Furthermore, it is hard not to conclude that he is testing it in a manner that prejudges the issue. The imprisoned Albertine (the *prisonnière* Marcel hides in his most private sanctum in order to contemplate her dormancy at his leisure) calls to mind the metaphor with which that era made a kind of sense of the homosexual male: the female soul *imprisoned in* a male physique. The monstrous act of appropriation whereby he incorporates her into his own domain—ostensibly an expression of desire—seems more clearly a sign of Marcel's homosexuality: he steals and keeps her precisely because he *does not* desire her. (Whether or not he knows this is another matter.)

As soon as we have established the *Is-he-isn't-he?* doubt about Marcel—with whom, remember, we are in conspiracy to inform/misinform ourselves about the other characters—we have to understand that exactly the same doubt arises about *us,* and directly affects our competence to participate in the text. It appears that Proust is consistently aware of, and plays with, the fact that the book is openly, ostensibly chattering with *hetero*sexuals from a *hetero*sexual (Marcel's) point of view, *but* that it has a closeted *homo*sexual subtext of exchanges between a sexually equivocal Marcel and his *homo*sexual readers. This gives *A la recherche du temps perdu* a preeminent position in the as-yet-unwritten history of literary Camp and in the history of homosexual culture. Its place in straight male Modernism may be a red herring.

—*Gregory Woods*

BIBLIOGRAPHY

Barthes, Roland. *A Lover's Discourse.* London: Cape, 1979. ■ Bersani, Leo. *Marcel Proust: The Fictions of Life and Art.* New York: Oxford University Press, 1965. ■ Hayman, Ronald. *Proust: A Biography.* London: Heinemann, 1990. ■ Meyers, Jeffrey. *Homosexuality and Literature 1890–1930.* London: Athlone Press, 1977. ■ Painter, George D. *Marcel Proust: A Biography.* Volume One, London: Chatto & Windus, 1959; Volume Two, London: Chatto & Windus, 1965. ■ Rivers, J. E. *Proust ant the Art of Love: The Aesthetics of Sexuality in the Life, Times, and Art of Marcel Proust.* New York: Columbia University Press, 1980. ■ Sedgwick, Eve Kosofsky. *Epistemology of the Closet.* Berkeley: University of California Press, 1991.

Puig, Manuel
(1932–1990)

Manuel Puig was born in General Villegas, an isolated town in Buenos Aires Province, Argentina, on December 28, 1932. As a child, bored by the provincialism of his surroundings, the young Puig would go to the local moviehouse five nights a week to be entertained by the glamour of Hollywood movies. After completing his elementary education, Puig was sent to boarding school in Buenos Aires. In 1950, he entered the University of Buenos Aires, first studying philosophy then architecture, but never obtained a degree. In 1956, he was awarded a scholarship to study film at the Centro Sperimentale di Cinematografia and from 1956 to 1962 he moved back and forth between Rome, London, and Argentina attempting, unsuccessfully, to get his film career off the ground. In 1963, abandoning hope of a career in cinema, he moved to New York City where he began to work on his first novel, *La traición de Rita Hayworth (Betrayed by Rita Hayworth)*. The novel was published in Argentina in 1968 but not after first running into censorship problems as a result of the portrayal of the protagonist Toto as effeminate and sexually ambivalent. In 1969, the prestigious French publisher Gallimard issued the French translation of *La traición de Rita Hayworth,* and in June of that year the work was selected by *Le Monde* as one of the best novels of 1968–1969. After this recognition, Puig became one of the most admired and popular authors in Latin America.

Although Puig also published plays and film scripts, he is most recognized in Latin-American letters today for the innovative techniques of his novels. The Argentine writer can perhaps be classified as one of Latin America's first post-modern authors. He is responsible for breaking through to a post-modern, unpretentious literary space where so-called low-brow culture is considered as valid an indicator of personal and collective truths as high-brow art. His use of popular mass culture (for example, Hollywood movie stars, tragic plot lines, popular radio serials, sentimental and commercialized melodramas) made such an impact on Latin-American letters that soon other writers—Julio Cortázar, Mario Vargas Llosa, and José Donoso, among others—began to write novels and plays based on mass-entertainment products. (See also POST-MODERNISM.)

In addition to *La traición de Rita Hayworth,* Puig wrote seven other novels, each carefully crafted and fascinating to both the general reader and the profes-sional critic: *Boquitas pintadas: Folletín (Heartbreak Tango: A Serial,* 1969); *The Buenos Aires Affair: Novela policial (The Buenos Aires Affair: A Detective Novel,* 1973); *El beso de la mujer araña (Kiss of the Spider Woman,* 1976); *Pubis angelical (Pubis Angelical,* 1979); *Maldición eterna a quien lea estas páginas (Eternal Curse on the Reader of These Pages,* 1980); *Sangre de amor correspondido (Blood of Requited Love,* 1982); and *Cae la noche tropical (Tropical Night Falling,* 1988).

In 1973, while living in Greenwich Village, Puig began to write his fourth novel, the story of two cellmates in a Buenos Aires prison during Argentina's military dictatorship of the 1970s. Luis Alberto Molina, an aging homosexual convicted of "corrupting minors," is a modern-day Scheherazade who recounts and recreates filmed stories to seduce a young Marxist political activist, Valentín Arregui Paz. The novel is the now classic *El beso de la mujer araña (Kiss of the Spider Woman),* which was made into a commercially successful Hollywood film in 1985, and has also been adapted for the stage, both as a drama (in Spanish and in English) and as a Tony Award–winning musical. (See also MUSICAL THEATER.)

Although homosexual themes and motifs are suggested in a number of Puig's novels, in *El beso de la mujer araña* explicit homosexual desire is central to the fiction. The text unfolds chronologically as a dialogue between the two prisoners who share a small cell. In this reduced space, movies, recounted by the effeminate homosexual Molina, provide a temporary escape from the narrow spatial (and psychological) limits imposed by imprisonment. The movies that Molina retells are far from realistic; they are melodramatic stories of love and self-sacrifice. Through Molina's nostalgic retelling and Valentín's comments, the reader discerns the gradual changes and transformations that begin to take place in each character. Eventually, each changes (that is, seduces) the other. Through his talks with Valentín, the apolitical and frivolous Molina begins to care about the problems of the socially outcast and in the end sacrifices his life for Valentín's political cause. In turn, the doctrinaire Marxist guerrilla Valentín learns from Molina that fantasies can also be liberating, even revolutionary. As their relationship deepens, Valentín agrees to have sex with Molina. While their lovemaking conforms to the stereotypical passive and active roles found in traditional Hispanic society, and Molina sees himself as a woman trapped in a male body who wants to have sex with a "real" man, sex is nevertheless presented as an oasis outside history and politics where individuals can find a liberating space for intimate communion.

In *El beso de la mujer araña,* the reader hears the words of the two protagonists without intervention from a third-person narrator. The only authorial intervention is a series of eight erudite footnotes dispersed throughout the chapters whose purpose is primarily to inform the (Hispanic) reader about various theories concerning the origins and nature of homosexuality. The last note, however, presents the work of a so-called Danish scholar, Dr. Anneli Taub (an invented figure) who summarizes all the theoretical models previously presented and, in addition, proposes a political and revolutionary theory of homosexuality. Dr. Taub urges homosexuals to organize and to participate in the political process.

When it first appeared, the open portrayal of homosexuality in *El beso de la mujer araña* was unsettling for many members of the Hispanic literary establishment who found it difficult to accept an openly gay novel. Yet, though it was considered a flop with intellectuals and critics, the novel, nonetheless, gained popularity and eventually became a best-seller. By portraying the gay Molina as sympathetically complex, Puig counteracted the Hispanic world's intolerance toward homosexuality. In the end, *El beso de la mujer araña* is perhaps the most popular politically incorrect gay love story ever written. Despite its stereotypical notions of femininity and traditional pas-sive-active sex roles, *El beso de la mujer araña* clearly articulates the triumph of the redemptive force of love.

When Manuel Puig died in 1990 at the age of fifty-seven, *The New York Times* obituary claimed that he had suffered cardiac arrest following a routine gall bladder operation. What was most puzzling, however, was that the obituary mentioned Puig's two "sons," thus making him appear to have been heterosexual. In 1993, the Colombian writer Jaime Manrique wrote an excellent article for *Christopher Street* ("Manuel Puig: The Writer as Diva"), in which he recounts a number of personal encounters with Puig, whom he describes as openly homosexual. Manrique's article reads like a detective story in which he searches for answers concerning the "mysterious" death of the Argentine writer. Manrique reveals certain details that lead him to believe that Puig died of AIDS. If this was so, why then the coverup? Manrique suggests: "After all, if homosexuality is the greatest taboo in Hispanic culture, AIDS is the unspeakable." (See also CROSS-DRESSING.)

—Francisco Soto

BIBLIOGRAPHY

Christ, Ronald. "A Last Interview with Manuel Puig." *World Literature Today* 65.4 (1991): 571–578. ■ Clark, David Draper. "Manuel Puig: Selected Bibliography." *World Literature Today* 65 (1991): 655–662. ■ Kerr, Lucille. *Suspended Fictions: Reading Novels by Manuel Puig.* Urbana: University of Illinois Press, 1987. ■ Lavers, Norman. *Pop Culture into Art: The Novels of Manuel Puig.* Columbia: University of Missouri Press, 1988. ■ Manrique, Jaime. "Manuel Puig: The Writer as Diva." *Christopher Street* 203 (July 1993): 14–27. ■ Tittler, Jonathan. *Manuel Puig.* New York: Twayne Publishers, 1993.

Purdy, James
(b. 1923)

James Purdy was born in Ohio and moved to Chicago when he was still in his teens. He attended the University of Chicago and the University of Puebla in Mexico. From 1949 to 1953, he taught at Lawrence College in Wisconsin and then lived abroad for some years. He now lives in Brooklyn, New York. Purdy began to publish stories in magazines in the 1940s. In the 1950s, he tried without success to find an American publisher. His first book was published privately in his own country and then by a major publisher in England, where he had many supporters in the literary world, most notably DAME EDITH SITWELL and ANGUS WILSON.

Purdy has always been isolated from the literary establishment, largely because his works are unusual thematically and stylistically and because he has been a savage social critic. He has concentrated on topics that book reviewers have preferred to ignore. His first novel, *63:Dream Palace* (1956), dealt with obsessive love, homosexuality, and urban alienation, and ended with fratricide. These are typical themes in Purdy's works, which often describe obsessive love between men. Purdy writes about men who are unable to express their love for other men because homosexuality is unthinkable to them. The result of this failure can be horrifying violence, as in *Eustace Chisholm and the Works* (1967) and *Narrow Rooms* (1978). The love need not be sexual, as *In a Shallow Grave* (1975) shows. Purdy's protagonists are usually people who have not found love in their families and who can find no home in the cities in which they live. The happiness of love is temporary and is usually the means by which the protagonist is led to his fate. In some of Purdy's recent work, AIDS has been one of the many kinds of fate awaiting those who search for love.

In addition to novels of urban alienation, Purdy has written novels such as *The Nephew* (1960), which deals with small-town life in the Midwest. His later books of this kind, like *Jeremy's Version* (1970) or *In the Hollow of his Hand* (1986), are increasingly Gothic, in the tradition of Sherwood Anderson and CARSON McCULLERS. His rural characters, like his urban ones and like the protagonists of Greek drama, are pursued by a malevolent destiny. Purdy's gloom and pessimism are tempered to some extent by his humor, especially in black comedies like *Cabot Wright Begins* (1964). Purdy's most recent novel, *Out With the Stars* (1992), presents his usual themes in a high camp manner reminiscent of RONALD FIRBANK.

Purdy's style is one of his most distinctive qualities. Like Mark Twain and Sinclair Lewis, Purdy attempts to reproduce everyday American speech both in his dialogue and in his narration. The flatness and simplicity of this style form an effective background for his stories of obsession. At times, as in *In a Shallow Grave* and many of his short stories, this simplicity takes on a biblical grandeur that is the perfect vehicle to present his characters, who are simultaneously exalted and tormented by larger-than-life emotions.

Although Purdy has published excellent novels, short stories, poems, and plays for almost forty years, he has never achieved the popular fame or the critical attention he deserves. He has, however, always been highly regarded by other writers and has had a great influence on such younger gay writers as Dennis Cooper and Paul Russell.

—*Stephen Guy-Bray*

BIBLIOGRAPHY

Adams, Stephen. *The Homosexual as Hero in Contemporary Fiction.* London: Vision Press, 1980. ■ Baldanza, Frank. "Northern Gothic." *Southern Review* 10 (1974): 566–582. ■ Brantlinger, Patrick. "Missing Corpses: The Deconstructive Mysteries of James Purdy and Franz Kafka." *Novel* 20 (1986): 27–40. ■ Pease, Donald. "False Starts and Wounded Allegories in the Abandoned House of Fiction of James Purdy." *Twentieth Century Literature* 28 (1982): 335–349. ■ Schwarzschild, Bettina. *The Not Right House: Essays on James Purdy.* Columbia: University of Missouri Press, 1969. ■ Tanner, Tony. *City of Words.* New York: Harper and Row, 1971.

Québécois Literature

Québécois literature is relatively young. First linked to French literary movements and trends, it slowly became distinct during the late nineteenth and early twentieth centuries. Until the 1950s, most of Québécois literature conformed to a strict religious and moral order and tended to valorize rural and traditional values. In pre-1950s literature, the city, where a lesbian and gay subculture will soon emerge, is usually pictured as sinful and dangerous.

In the late 1950s and early 1960s, however, an in-depth transformation of Québec society occurred. This so-called Quiet Revolution brought changes to many aspects of life, including politics, religion, language, and literature. French Canadians became Québécois or Acadiens, and became proud of who they were. Tired of being treated as second-class citizens, they finally asserted themselves as a minority group and expressed pride in the originality and distinctness of their culture. Changes in Québécois literature inevitably paralleled this cultural transformation. Various linguistic experiments were attempted, including the literary use of an artificially constructed dialect, the *joual*, and forms of syntactical destabilization. The city—often Montréal—was depicted positively, as a place of potential happiness and self-realization. Finally, sexuality also came to be portrayed affirmatively, and sexually suggestive scenes became a recurring motif in Québécois literature.

Gay and lesbian characters suddenly appeared in mainstream novels and drama. In the 1960s, Jean Basile (1932–1992) wrote a trilogy set in Montréal. In the second book, *Le Grand Khan* (The Great Khan [1967]), Adolphe, a gay character, openly discusses with the narrator, Jonathan, his vision of homosexuality. A dramatic scene also takes place in a gay bar. Gay characters also people the plays of MICHEL TREMBLAY (b. 1942) during this period. Hosanna, Cuirette, la Duchesse de Langeais, and Sandra are transvestites or bikers and are presented as the nocturnal inhabitants of the city, as metaphorical sisters of the main characters of the play, *Les Belles-Soeurs* (*The Guid Sisters* [1968]). They appear in many works of Tremblay, but play determinant roles in *La Duchesse de Langeais* (1969), *Demain matin*

Montréal m'attend (*Tomorrow Morning, Montréal Will Be Mine* [1970]), *Hosanna* (1973), and *Damnée Manon, Sacrée Sandra* (*Darn Mandy, Holy Sandy* [1977]).

During the Quiet Revolution, MARIE-CLAIRE BLAIS (b. 1939) came into prominence. Her work from the very beginning featured gay and lesbian characters. In *Le Loup* (*The Wolf*, 1972) and *Les Nuits de l'Underground* (*Nights in the Underground: An Exploration of Love* [1978]), lesbians and gay men are at the center of the plots. In *Le Loup,* which features psychological introspection, tormented characters, and experimental writing, the author offers a very personal and even mythical vision of life. In *Les Nuits de l'Underground*, Blais organizes her plot around a landmark lesbian bar called *L'Underground.* Obviously inspired by the dynamics of the love relationships between women in a lesbian milieu, she follows—from a distance—the various personal transformations of Geneviève, a French sculptor who slowly discovers two realities: the French Canadian society and her lesbian feelings. Blais's experimental writing, especially her use of the sentence and of the dense paragraph, attempts to imitate the underground subculture that Geneviève slowly discovers.

In the last part of Blais's *Nuits de l'Underground,* the reader can discern a liberation discourse making its way through the imaginations of the various characters. In many works of the 1970s and early 1980s, the gay liberation movement is indeed the main source of inspiration. Once again literature and history parallel each other, for in 1977 the Québec government introduced a sexual orientation amendment into its antidiscrimination charter. This liberal legislation probably helped speed up the emergence of an organized lesbian and gay community in Québec.

A watershed publication of the new era of liberation is a collective work that appeared in 1978, *Sortir*—which may be translated as two expressions: coming out or going out. In this work artists, psychologists, and writers such as Paul Chamberland, Michel Tremblay, Jean Basile, and Denis Vanier gave their own views of homosexuality and discussed how the situation of sexual minorities could be improved. Lesbian and gay writers also participated openly in public events. One such public meeting devoted to gay writers is recorded in the November 1979 special issue of the lesbian and gay periodical *Le Berdache.* At the same time, the new feelings and emotions of openly gay men and out lesbians were given expression in many other venues, perhaps especially in poetry.

One of the principal writers to emerge in this era of liberation is NICOLE BROSSARD (b. 1943). One of the leaders of the formalist movement, she explores in her work how the body and the text (the *corps-texte*) interact and influence each other. *French Kiss* (1974), one of her major works of the 1970s, creates a renewed poetical language through the interaction of body and text. Although the energy of the French kiss is definitely owned by women, in the book's final chapter the text opens up on an urban vision. In *L'Amèr* (*These Our Mothers* [1977]), Brossard links her lyricism to the mythical construction of the mother's body and womb. Finally, with *Amantes* (*Lovhers* [1980]), Brossard explores a new love discourse centered on the love between women.

Other women writers attempted various ways to break the silence of the body and the woman's mind, and tried to create a new literature that could express the needs and desires of women in general and lesbians in particular. In *L'Euguélionne* (*The Euguelionne: A Triptych Novel* [1976]), for example, Louky Bersianik (b. 1930) writes a new genesis of the Woman as seen through a Lacanian optic. In *Pique-nique sur l'Acropole* (Picnic on the Acropolis [1979]), she creates a new version of PLATO's *Symposium* in which, this time, women participate in the dialogue. In the second part of the book, different aspects of women's sexuality and oppression are discussed, including masturbation and sexual intercourse with women and men.

Other writers push further their interest in the new language needed by lesbians to express themselves freely. The concern with language dominates JOVETTE MARCHESSAULT's (b. 1938) *Tryptique lesbien* (*Lesbian Triptych* [1980]) and Yolande Villemaire's (b. 1949) *Adrénaline* (1982) and *Fidèles d'amour* (Faithful Companions of Love [1981]). For them, history has to be rewritten to create new feminine myths, and language must be transformed. Josée Yvon (b. 1950), in books that are half prose and half poetry, creates powerful images that are comparable to science fiction comic strips. In *Travesties-Kamikaze* (Kamikaze Transvestites [1980]), *Danseuses-mamelouk* (Mameluke Dancers [1982]), and *Maîtresses-Cherokees* (Cherokee Mistresses [1986]), a marginal world that resists the dominant culture is vividly realized. In many ways, these poets do not distinguish the lesbian liberation movement from women's liberation.

In the liberation era, a few male poets, also linked to the formalist movement, published works that include aspects of the gay lifestyle. André Roy's (b. 1944) poetical work of this period is quite interesting in this regard. In *Les Passions du samedi* (1979), Roy offers a catalogue of erotic parts of the body (muscles, hair), of sensations (tiredness, night fever, pleasure, anxiety), and, finally, of places and objects linked to gay courtship (bar, bedroom, bed, movies). At the end of his work, the reader can find an index to the feelings and behaviors of habitués of the gay nightlife. The codification aspect is interesting and original enough to form a model of a particular kind of gay discourse. Roy also published other poetical works dealing with similar topics; critics usually refer to these works as the "Passions cycle"—*Petit Supplément aux Passions* (1980), *Monsieur Désir* (1981), *Les Lits de l'Amérique* (1983). These books, along with *Les Passions du samedi* have been translated as *The Passions of Mister Desire: Selected Poems*. In his subsequent works, Roy moves toward a more symbolic approach to lyricism, drifting away from specifically gay themes.

Jean-Paul Daoust (b. 1946) also integrates homoeroticism in his poetry. The images and poetical language that he uses are quite original, as he alternates literary references and cinematographic flashes, producing an urban rhythm composed of allusions to Dracula, Dorian Gray, Marilyn Monroe, and others. This technique dominates such works as *Oui, Cher* (Yes, Dear [1976]), *Portraits d'intérieur* (Interior Portraits [1981]), and *Poèmes de Babylone* (Poems of Babylonia [1982]). In *Soleils d'Acajou* (Mahogany Suns [1984]) and *Les Garçons magiques* (The Magical Boys [1986]), Daoust gives less importance to his search for a renewed poetic language but emphasizes more the way he expresses emotions. In *Les Garçons magiques,* he states that he wants to write his own story, as a guy who loves guys, and that he will also tell about the lives of other young men, the magical ones.

Paul Chamberland is also an important contributor to Québécois gay literature of the liberation era. In *Le Prince de Sexamour* (Sex-love Prince [1976]), Chamberland states that we should liberate sexuality and in the process free ourselves of the capitalist world. He also sees homosexuality as a means through which human beings can come to understand themselves. He posits the creation of a new, essentially gay figure: the "hommenfant" (the childman or adultchild). The same theme is also explored in the *Émergence de l'Adultenfant* (The Birth of the Adultchild [1983]). Finally, in *Marcher dans Outremont ou ailleurs* (To Walk in Outremont or Elsewhere [1987]), young men are portrayed in a variety of brief scenes as the initiators of a revolution of love.

Just as Chamberland's work was written in order to affect society, so Jean Basile, in his book *Iconostase pour Pier Paolo Pasolini* (Iconstasis for Pier Paolo Pasolini [1983]), had the same goal in mind. As the title indicates, the book, written after the death of PASOLINI, is a poetical discourse about gays, feminism, and men. In it, Basile tries to use the traditional condemnatory discourse of homosexuality to praise the birth of a new gay person. As a somewhat carnavalesque work, it makes gold from the base metal of scorn and condemnation.

It was not accidental that gay writers turned to poetry in order to express a new vision of homosexuality and a new pride in gayness. Québécois poets had used poetry for similar purposes with respect to the nationalism issue. Poetry helped in a way to create the imaginary of a land from which politicians and materialism were excluded. Lesbian and gay poets rewrote our history, expressed our emotions without censorship, and gave their vision of a new world in which power, moral standards, and homosexuality itself were transformed. These writers did not express the same views about the gay and lesbian subculture. For some, discotheques and movies were the source of their images of the gay life. For others, the subculture was rejected in favor of a new world in which lesbians and gay men would function as shamanic figures who transform society.

In the 1980s and 1990s, gay issues are also prominent on the stage and in novels but with distinct differences from their earlier manifestations. The recent works of Michel Tremblay, for example, center on less exotic characters than the transvestites who peopled his earlier works. In *Les Anciennes odeurs* (*Remember Me* [1981]), two gay men, a French teacher and his ex-lover, now a TV star, revisit their relationship. What brings them together has less to do with their sexual orientation, however, than with a tragedy in the actor's life: the death of his father. In two recently published novels, *Le Coeur découvert* (*Heart Laid Bare* [1989]) and *Le Coeur éclaté* (The Burst Heart [1993]), Tremblay's descriptions of the intimate lives of gay characters are framed in the concerns of the postmodern Québécois novel and society: the extended family, urban life in Montréal, and travel beyond the province. Two other novels published in the 1980s also reflect the common themes of the Québécois novel of the period: Stephen Schecter's *T'es beau en écoeurant* (You Are Such a Cutie [1984]) explores the different aspects of a love affair between a Jewish anglophone and a French Canadian man in Montréal, whereas Guy Ménard's *L'Accent aigu* (Acute Accent [1983]) tells the story of a Québécois student in Paris who falls in love.

In the early 1990s, while new writers reveal their own visions of the lesbian and gay world, one can sense the emergence of new trends. Lyricism, suspense, and art forms like photography replace realism. In Francois Brunet's *L'Acte de Folie* (Act of Madness or Folly [1993]), these techniques are used to describe the fight against AIDS; in Michel Butler's *L'Homme de mon lit* (The Man Who Shared My Bed [1992]), they are employed to describe the tragic ending of a relationship; and in André Martin's *Darlinghurst Heroes,* they are used to recount the adventures of a gay character in Australia.

The transformations of the novel have their parallel in drama. In recent plays emphasizing the intensity of love, gay characters are featured in tragic situations. René-Daniel Dubois's (b. 1955) *Being at Home with Claude* (1986) is the story of a male prostitute who turns himself in to the police, telling them that he killed a young man. The play focuses on the dialogue between the police inspector and the prostitute, who slowly puts together his feelings and discovers his love for the man he killed. This very popular play has also had a second life; in 1991, the director Jean Beaudin made a movie of it with the same title. Finally, two other plays, *Les Feluettes (Lilies, or The Revival of a Romantic Dream* [1988]) by Michel Marc Bouchard (b. 1958) and *Provincetown Playhouse, juillet 1919, j'avais 19 ans (Provincetown Playhouse, July 1919* [1981]) by Normand Chaurette (b. 1954), should be acknowledged. In both plays, part of the action takes place at the beginning of the century, the first in Roberval, where two teenagers are deeply in love, and the other in Provincetown, where gay actors symbolically kill a child on stage.

It is difficult to predict with any certainty the future of Québécois gay and lesbian literature. AIDS, a conspicuous topic in recent books, will certainly continue to be a major concern of gay male writers, but not the only one. Lesbian writers are likely to continue to be deeply influenced by the powerful works of Nicole Brossard, Louky Bersianik, or Josée Yvon. Lesbian and gay male literature seems destined to merge into mainstream Québécois literature. This process, in fact, has already begun. Indeed, most of the recent lesbian and gay literary works discussed here have been published by prominent Québécois publishers. What is certain is that however it evolves Québécois gay and lesbian literature will continue to illuminate our lives.

—*Guy Poirier*

BIBLIOGRAPHY

Basile, Jean. *Le Grand Khan.* Montréal: Éditions de l'Estérel, 1967. ■ ———. *Iconostase pour Pier Paolo Pasolini; Discours poétique sur les gays, le féminisme et les nouveaux mâles.* Montréal: VLB éditeur, 1983. ■ Bersianik, Louky. *L'Euguélionne.* Montréal: La Presse, 1976. ■ ———. *Le Piquenique sur l'Acropole.* Montréal: VLB éditeur, 1979. ■ Blais, Marie-Claire. *Le Loup.* Montréal, éditions du Jour, 1972. ■ ———. *Les Nuits de l'Underground.* Montréal: Stanké, 1978. ■ Bouchard, Michel Marc. *Les Feluettes.* Montréal: Leméac, 1988. ■ Brossard Nicole. *Amantes.* Montréal: Quinze, 1980. ■ ———. *L'Amèr.* Montréal: Quinze, 1977. ■ ———. *French Kiss.* Montréal: Quinze, 1974. ■ Brunet, François. *L'Acte de folie.* Montréal: éditions Les Entretiens, 1992. ■ Butler, Michel. *L'Homme de mon lit.* Montréal: VLB éditeur, 1992. ■ Chamberland, Paul. *Émergence de l'Adultenfant.* Montréal: Jean Basile éditeur, 1983. ■ ———. *Marcher dans Outremont ou ailleurs.* Montréal: VLB éditeur, 1987. ■ ———. *Le Prince de Sexamour.* Montréal: L'Hexagone, 1976. ■ Chaurette, Normand. *Provincetown Playhouse, juillet 1919, j'avais 19 ans.* Montréal: Leméac, 1981. ■ Daoust, Jean-Paul. *Les Garçons magiques.* Montréal: VLB éditeur, 1986. ■ ———. *Oui, Cher.* Montréal: Éd. Cul Q, 1976. ■ ———. *Poèmes de Babylone.* Trois-Rivières: Écrits des Forges, 1982. ■ ———. *Portrait d'intérieur.* Trois-Rivières, A.P.L.M., 1981. ■ ———. *Soleils d'Acajou.* Montréal: Nouvelle Optique, 1984. ■ Dubois, René-Daniel. *Being at home with Claude.* Montréal: Leméac, 1986. ■ Marchessault, Jovette. *Tryptique lesbien.* Montréal: Pleine Lune, 1980. ■ Martin, André. *Darlinghurst Heroes.* Montréal: Les Herbes rouges, 1993. ■ Ménard, Guy. *L'Accent aigu.* Leméac, 1983. ■ Roy, André. *Les Lits de l'Amérique.* Montréal: *Les Herbes rouges,* no 116–117, 1983. ■ ———. *Monsieur Désir.* Montréal: *Les Herbes rouges,* no 88–89, 1981. ■ ———. *Les Passions du samedi.* Montréal: Les Herbes rouges, 1979. ■ ———. *Petit Supplément aux Passions.* Montréal: *Les Herbes rouges,* no 79–80, 1980. ■ Schecter, Stephen. *T'es beau en écoeurant.* Montréal: Nouvelle Optique, 1984. ■ *Sortir.* Montréal: Les Éditions de l'Aurore, 1978. ■ Tremblay, Michel. *Les Anciennes odeurs.* Montréal: Leméac, 1981. ■ ———. *Le Coeur découvert.* Montréal: Leméac, 1986. ■ ———. *Le Coeur éclaté.* Montréal: Leméac, 1993. ■ ———. *Damnée Manon, Sacrée Sandra.* Montréal: Leméac, 1977. ■ ———. *Demain matin Montréal m'attend.* Montréal: Leméac, 1972 (1970). ■ ———. *La Duchesse de Langeais.* Montréal: Leméac, 1970. ■ ———. *Hosanna.* Montréal: Leméac, 1973. ■ Villemaire, Yolande. *Adrénaline.* Montréal: Noroît, 1982. ■ ———. *Fidèles d'Amour.* Paris: Mai Hors saison 7, 1981. ■ Yvon, Josée. *Danseuses-mamelouk.* Montréal: VLB éditeur, 1982. ■ ———. *Maîtresses-Cherokees.* Montréal: VLB éditeur, 1986. ■ ———. *Travesties-Kamikaze.* Montréal: Les Herbes rouges, 1980.

Reading Across Orientations

To start to read is to anticipate having an encounter, literal or symbolic, with oneself. That is why the best reading is not a simple act but requires creativity and imagination from the reader who becomes a co-author by making sense of the text, who changes the text and is changed by it. Such is the power of reading to carry us across distinctions, definitions, and orientations that the process can be described as "cross-reading." Consciously or unconsciously and in varying degrees, we all become cross-readers whenever we read books, no less than all of us—women and men, blacks and whites, gays and straights—become cross-viewers whenever we look at photographs or watch films, videos, and television. Whether I am a heterosexual reading JEAN GENET or a homosexual reading Norman Mailer, I read the book and the book reads me.

The essential act of reading is a careful and disciplined "misreading" through which we orient ourselves by the text and the text by ourselves. We transform the suggestive symbolism of a parable into the explicit realism of a chronicle, and vice-versa, so that the distinctions between fact and fiction, belief and disbelief, become blurred and allow one character to represent many kinds of readers. The best reading, like the best writing, takes place on a metaphorical rather than literal plane and relies more on connotation than denotation. To cross-read is to clothe the text in difference, to violate boundaries, and to substitute orientations in order to broaden both one's own horizon and the text's. Even among nineteenth-century classics, that is how Simon Karlinksy uncovers the gay GOGOL, how Eve Kosofsky Sedgwick discerns homosexual silence and panic in HENRY JAMES, how James Creech reveals MELVILLE's *Pierre, or The Ambiguities* (1852) as a tale not of incest but of unfulfilled homosexual desire. That is also why reading, more than any other single activity, continues to remain at the core of education in so many diverse cultures around the world. In the arguments over a nontraditional, multicultural, and minority-centered canon versus a body of more traditional majority-centered masterpieces, both sides share one deeply held belief: The power of reading to shape an individual's sensibility and reinvent reality is so strong that control of the process must be either seized or retained.

How do gay readers read straight writers? Not very differently, one suspects, from how straight readers read gay writers with the crucial exception, of course, that the majority-minority power dynamic is reversed, which means that a heterosexual reading usually pushes the text toward conformism whereas a homosexual reading pushes it toward rebellion. But no matter how strict a methodology is adopted—and many contemporary gay critics diminish their own impact by relying on an esoteric and pseudoscientific jargon that is impenetrable to most nonspecialists—reading is ultimately a selfish, not altruistic, act. We read primarily for our own sake, only secondarily for the text's or author's. We declare our own personal masterpieces and define our own private canon. "Reading is transformational," declared master deconstructionist

Jacques Derrida, but long before deconstruction became a critical ideal it proved a practical necessity for many gay and lesbian readers. Throughout history, those readers have turned to themes, characters, structure, language, social-historical context, and the author's biography, all the time reading between the lines to determine whether the text is friend or foe—and to find out how to convert the latter to the former.

Most young readers—gay, lesbian, and bisexual as well as heterosexual—first turn to texts chosen for them. By necessity, they read what parents, teachers, and critics say or at least imply is "straight" literature, only to find out later that many of those authors and works are far from straight and that "coming out" brings these same homosexual readers closer to the texts, not further away from them. The irony is that, in the end, so many gay and lesbian readers have managed to "homosexualize" straight literature much more successfully than the literature has managed to "heterosexualize" them. Perhaps that explains why so much contemporary criticism of gay and lesbian literature is written, almost to the point of self-parody, from a first-person, quasi-confessional point of view that emphasizes the quality of reading over the kind of text.

Many signs point to the mid-twentieth-century French existentialists and their structuralist heirs as the pioneers who gathered momentum for modern gay and lesbian cross-readings. Probably the greatest testament to a heterosexual's ability to read a gay writer is Jean-Paul Sartre's massive 1952 study of Jean Genet, *Saint Genet: Actor and Martyr*. Indeed, Sartre, an exemplary cross-writer as well as cross-reader, also used gay themes and characters in his own works, notably the philosophical treatise *Being and Nothingness* (1943), the trilogy of novels *The Roads to Freedom* (1945–1950), the story "Childhood of a Leader" in *The Wall and Other Stories* (1939), and the play *No Exit* (1944). For her part, his companion Simone de Beauvoir wrote insightfully about lesbians in *The Second Sex* (1949) and helped champion VIOLETTE LEDUC, a novelist whose neurotic but strong lesbian voice paved the way for a generation of lesbian-feminists from the late 1960s onward.

This attention to sexual nonconformism did not come about by chance. The existentialists' exploration of gays and lesbians took place within their larger project to portray minorities and marginals (women, blacks, Third-World societies, Arabs, Jews, and communists) in their relationship to issues such as choice, freedom, authenticity, and political action. The commitment of the existentialists to minority sexuality also suggests that tolerance, empathy, and curiosity can be more important than personal experience as conditions for successful cross-reading. Even the more absurdist writers who never incorporated explicitly gay and lesbian themes or sociopolitical commentary—Albert Camus, Samuel Beckett, and Eugene Ionesco—helped set the stage in Europe, much as the Beat movement did in the United States and the Angry Young Men did in England, for a rejection of the middle-class morality, including heterosexual assumptions, that accompanied so much reading and literary analysis. It was a time when various expressions of "otherness" became metaphors for "self" and produced an era especially conducive to cross-reading. Male or female, white or black, straight or gay—for a while everyone dwelled in JAMES BALDWIN's "another county," shared the public inconsequentiality of Ralph Ellison's "invisible man," and mourned LANGSTON HUGHES's "dream deferred." And it is no mere coincidence that the power of this generation of cross-readers informed the Stonewall generation, which in 1969 began the movement for gay liberation. The irony is that for all their exemplary cross-readings, Sartre's and Beauvoir's allegiance to Marxist materialist theory, which dictated that culture follows social, political, and economic realities, got it wrong; the cultural stirrings of gay liberation came before the political ones did. Before it took to the streets, political activism was first rehearsed on the pages of novels and essays, poems and plays.

The quintessential action of bending the text—of "unstraightening" it, if you will—remains the way that many gays and lesbians first approach a consciousness of themselves and their minority sexuality. It is the way they make great writing great for them. The difference now is that criticism has finally begun to catch up, to the point of acknowledging the importance of the reader's "subject position." Certainly, the abundant insights of one of this century's most famous and pioneering readers, French critic ROLAND BARTHES—the intellectual successor to Sartre who emphasized text over context—are linked directly to his homosexuality, to his early awareness of marginality and transgression, and especially to a lifelong questioning of his own reading habits, as exemplified by such analyses as *Mythologies* (1957), *S/Z* (1970), *The Pleasure of the Text* (1973), and *A Lover's Discourse* (1977). If we read experimentally, sooner or later we read as Barthes does, eclectically and across categories, blending the historical with the contemporary, the factual with the fictitious.

What kind of works most give rise to cross-reading? Transgression of all kinds always seems one of the hallmarks of writers who challenge received notions of social order and personal identity. Like a bearded cheek receiving a bearded kiss, the grammatical transgressions of American poet Wallace Ste-
vens—his "extremest book by the wisest man"—strike an immediately sympathetic note and appeal in the same odd way as the precious street slang spoken by fart-sniffing convicts in Genet or the profane patois and massacred sentences of the adventurers in Celine's grimly picaresque novels. The synesthetic correspondences that CHARLES BAUDELAIRE discerned, the parallelisms that ARTHUR RIMBAUD found between vowels and colors, the "exquisite hour" of PAUL VERLAINE—such nineteenth-century poetic expressions of DECADENCE and symbolism seemed preciously effeminate, a kind of linguistic or imagistic cross-dressing. Such vocabularies and image repertoires also represented a way to transform illegitimacy into legitimacy and the exotic into the mainstream if one was but original, subversive, and creative enough.

A certain kind of interpretive open-endedness, of floating meaning, also allows one to cross-read. That is why Franz Kafka's novels and short stories so easily lend themselves to cross-reading. You don't have to stretch the text very far to read "The Hunger Artist" (1924) as a tale of unrequited secret desires, *The Trial* (1925) as a cautionary tale of social oppression and self-defeating "passing," and "The Metamorphosis" (1915) as a parable of closeted denial and coming out. "I was Gregor Samsa," confesses American novelist PAUL MONETTE in his prize-winning memoir *Becoming a Man* (1992). He speaks for many gay men and lesbians when he adds, "It was not the last time I would take my life out of a book."

Cultural exoticism—the North Africa of PAUL BOWLES and ANDRÉ GIDE, the Italy of E. M. FORSTER—often appeals to cross-readers because it is easy to substitute equivalencies for exactitude. That is why it is harder, though not impossible, to cross-read the stories of Raymond Carver or Anton Chekhov. Indeed, if you seek the closest equivalent of a sexual Kafka—and it is the absence of sex in Kafka's world that speaks to closeted gays as much as it is the suggestiveness of nonconformity and alienation—then look to the post-war French novelist, Marguerite Duras. Though almost exclusively heterosexual on their surface, her works convey the kind of amoral sensuality and antibourgeois impulses that speak of bisexuality and a world where lover-loved is really a metaphor for all kinds of forbidden exchanges and alliances. The older-younger and Chinese-French dichotomies of the main characters in her best-seller *The Lover* (1984) are more pertinent than the male-female difference. Treat the protagonists as two women or two men, and you will add a layer of marginality without much changing the narrative since Duras's deepest sense of erotic romance is her distinctive style with its richly confusing and sensually androgynous prose.

The same transgressive combination of eroticism and exoticism lies at the heart of the nineteenth-century Romantic sensibility. Much more than men, women embodied "sexual outlaws" and, as prostitutes and adulterers, linked romanticism to realism and naturalism. In her self-destructiveness, Flaubert's Emma Bovary speaks to all cross-reading sexual nonconformists as do BALZAC's Esther Gobseck, Tolstoy's Anna Karenina, and Zola's Nana. These nineteenth-century women are larger than life in the same way that leading women in grand opera—another product of the same age—seem culturally heroic. In their sense of tragic love, sexual repression, and sociopolitical oppression, such women speak to gay men who share their sensibility and out-of-power circumstances if not their actual fates.

Probably the most common denominator in cross-reading is dangerous desire. Each era defines its own notion of erotic subversion, and that very notion appeals to gays and lesbians who know first-hand the tragedy, both literary and real-life, engendered by unsafe sexual identity. Consider Sherwood Anderson's story "Hands" in *Winesburg, Ohio* (1920), in which a teacher's reputation is ruined by false accusations of boy love. Some gay readers would no doubt see the tale as more realistic if irony did not become the *deus ex machina* to affirm a heterosexual social order; if the allegations had proved true so that the protagonist were condemned, as the readers would have been, for fact instead of fantasy. Similarly, perhaps attenuated transgression also explains why even though the MARQUIS DE SADE openly described the desires and actions that better writers left unnamed, he did not help affirm a gay identity. His pretentious philosophical works contain no real characters but torsos attached to oversized and obscenely nicknamed genitals.

Same-sex bonding, a sharing of "homosocial" space, is another way to discern "homotextuality" and "homographesis." For example, a particular poignancy marks the bonding and subsequent splitting up of Falstaff and Prince Hal in SHAKESPEARE's *Henry IV* plays, and also of Montaigne's syntactically intimate homage to his friendship with La Boetie ("Because it was he, because it was I"). It turned out just as many gays suspected all along—there was indeed much more to the camaraderie of soldiers and road travelers in WALT WHITMAN's *Leaves of Grass* (1855–1860) than the vaguely cosmic and asexual brotherhood emphasized by traditional critics. From a gay viewpoint, it is not surprising that a Hermann Hesse revival took place in the androgynous hippie culture of the late 1960s. Many gay and bisexual men must have felt liberated by the unapologetically close male bonding in *Narcissus and Goldmund* (1930) and

attracted to the master-apprentice relationship in *Magister Ludi* (1943). The point is not that these characters are gay—they aren't—but that they could be. In Hesse, men are placed close, physically and emotionally, to other men without the inevitable conflict and competition arising, and without a woman coming between them. Lesbians feel much the same way when they find a text in which women, even straight women, are allowed to negotiate the world without men.

HUMOR, particularly the irreverent verbal jousting that minority groups often use as a destigmatizing or desensitizing strategy, is also at the heart of some cross-reading. Indeed, the verbal pyrotechnics of Falstaff, especially when he mocks Hal's king-father, amounts to mocking the patriarchal structure of both the family and the monarchy. Of course, the plays and witticisms of OSCAR WILDE remain the quintessential examples of serious CAMP and popular culture that would eventually find its way into modern literature and criticism. Does anyone discern something pejoratively homosexual in Moliere's Tartuffe, the kind of slippery righteousness and smoothly articulate hypocrisy—made more oily by rhymed couplets—that you find among some gay right-wingers and fundamentalists? Apparently so, judging by even mainstream productions where the stagecraft reads between the lines of the text and brings to the surface the implications of Tartuffe's exploitative use of women, his foppish effeminacy, and his bonding with men. The stage, not the page, ends up "outing" one of the most famous characters in Western drama.

Texts, too, exhibit "tendencies." That is how we come to suspect WILLA CATHER's and MARGUERITE YOURCENAR's lesbianism through their gay male characters long before we know the biographical facts. Cross-reading is one of the best ways to penetrate the camouflage and transform those tendencies into a full-fledged interpretation.

Given the growing pressure to censor adult art by the uneasy coalition of religious fundamentalists on the right and children's advocates on the left, perhaps the most pertinent lesson of cross-reading provides a defense against would-be censors: Gay writing does not influence the reader's orientation so much as the reader's identity affects the text's. Gay reading precedes gay writing and, in many cases, even gay behavior if we believe memoirs of writers such as Paul Monette and JAMES MERRILL. Censors may take away a gay text, but cross-reading remains. An equally provocative conclusion is that the reality of explicit sex acts remains largely irrelevant to the establishment of gay and lesbian literary traditions, which depend much more on attributes such as character, theme, language, and structure. Cross-reading relies much more on potentiality, including the silence of self-repression, than on precision.

Cross-reading also calls into question much of the best of past criticism and literary history. Until relatively recently, critics did not recognize gay writers as part of the mainstream of modern literature, let alone as perhaps the strongest current in that mainstream. Whether those past critics were homophobic is beside the point; they were, at least in part, simply wrong. It is those critics, not gay or lesbian cross-readers, who stand most guilty of misreading individual works and misrepresenting their collective history.

It is difficult today to look at almost any literature and not see gay and lesbian writers squarely at the center of twentieth-century writing. In French literature, one can cite PROUST, Gide, Genet, COCTEAU, COLETTE, Leduc, Yourcenar, and MONIQUE WITTIG; in English and American literature, the names are Whitman, Wilde, Forster, VIRGINIA WOOLF, James Baldwin, Langston Hughes, GERTRUDE STEIN, HART CRANE, TENNESSEE WILLIAMS, CHRISTOPHER ISHERWOOD, WILLIAM BURROUGHS, and ALLEN GINSBERG; in Russian, MIKHAIL KUZMIN, Sergei Esenin, SOPHIA PARNOK, Anna Akhmatova, MARINA TSVETAEVA, and Zinaida Gippius; in Japanese, YUKIO MISHIMA and Yasunari Kawabata; in Spanish, GARCIA LORCA and MANUEL PUIG. Even these few names show the closeness of the gay and lesbian literary tradition to the modern literary tradition, even as the list also shows how the modern gay and lesbian literary tradition has itself been established by gay and lesbian interpretations of apparently straight authors.

Finally, a momentous historical and aesthetic shift seems to be taking place. Gay readers have given rise to gay writers, and the historical necessity of distorting so-called straight literature and heterosexual sensibilities may be becoming outmoded as literature falls increasingly prey to niche marketing. Will the new explicitness cost us irony, subtlety, and empathy as we strive to "read"—that is, to make sense of—the world and the text, others and ourselves? Less cross-reading may need to be done, but what the act of cross-reading loses to necessity it will gain back from openness and explicitness. More, not fewer, cross-reading analyses

seem to be appearing in gay and lesbian studies, an academic discipline that is no longer just outing and uncloseting the gay and lesbian but also militantly appropriating the straight. The relevance of an exchange between gay readers and straight texts, like that which occurs between homosexual writers and the heterosexual public, can no longer be discounted or dismissed. Cross-reading, at last, is out of the closet.

—*Jacob Stockinger*

BIBLIOGRAPHY

Bergman, David. *Gaiety Transfigured: Gay Self-Representation in American Literature.* Madison: University of Wisconsin Press, 1991. ■ Creech, James. *Closet Writing, Gay Reading.* Chicago: University of Chicago Press, 1993. ■ Doty, Alexander. *Making Things Perfectly Queer: Interpreting Mass Culture.* Minneapolis: University of Minnesota Press, 1992. ■ Iser, Wolfgang. *The Act of Reading: A Theory of Aesthetic Response.* Baltimore: Johns Hopkins University Press, 1978. ■ Karlinsky, Simon. *The Sexual Labyrinth of Nikolai Gogol.* Cambridge, Mass.: Harvard University Press, 1976. ■ Koestenbaum, Wayne. *The Queen's Voice: Opera, Homosexuality and the Mystery of Desire.* New York: Poseidon Press, 1993. ■ Martin, Robert K. *The Homosexual Tradition in American Poetry.* Austin: University of Texas Press, 1979. ■ Miller, D. A. *Bringing Out Roland Barthes.* Berkeley: University of California Press, 1992. ■ Scholes, Robert. *Protocols of Reading.* New Haven: Yale University Press, 1989. ■ Sedgwick, Eve Kosofsky. *Between Men: English Literature and Male Homosocial Desire.* New York: Columbia University Press, 1985. ■ ———. *Epistemology of the Closet.* Berkeley: University of California Press, 1990. ■ ———. *Tendencies.* Durham: Duke University Press, 1993. ■ Stockinger, Jacob. "The Gay Mishima." *Gay Roots: 20 Years of Gay Sunshine.* Winston Leyland, ed. Gay Sunshine Press, 1991. 450–462. ■ ———. "Homosexuality and the French Enlightenment." *Homosexualities and French Literature.* Elaine Marks and George Stambolian, eds. Ithaca, N.Y.: Cornell University Press, 1979. 161–185. ■ ———. "Homotextuality: A Proposal." *The Gay Academic.* Louie Crew, ed. Palm Springs: Etc. Publications, 1979. 135–151. ■ ———. "Impurity and Sexual Politics in the Provinces: Colette's Anti-Idyll in 'The Patriarch.'" *Women's Studies* 8 (1981): 356–369. ■ ———. "The Test of Love and Nature: Colette and Lesbians." *Colette: The Woman, The Writer.* Erica Eisinger and Mari McCarty, eds. University Park: Penn State University Press, 1981. 75–94. ■ Summers, Claude J. *Gay Fictions: Wilde to Stonewall: Studies in a Male Homosexual Literary Tradition.* New York: Continuum, 1990. ■ Tompkins, Jane. *Reader-Response Criticism: From Formalism to Post-Structuralism.* Baltimore: Johns Hopkins University Press, 1980. ■ White, Edmund. *Genet: A Biography.* New York: Knopf, 1993.

Rechy, John
(*b.* 1934)

John Rechy was born in El Paso, Texas, in 1934. His parents, Mexican aristocrats, fled to avoid persecution during the purges of Pancho Villa. Rechy studied journalism at Texas Western College and the New School for Social Research in New York before serving in Germany in the U.S.

Army. Afterward, Rechy relocated to New York and began a period of hustling and drifting that inspired much of his early writing. Rechy's first novel, *City of Night* (1963), began as a letter to a friend about his experiences at Mardi Gras and was then reworked into a short story for *Evergreen Review*.

Rechy's reputation as a gay writer rests primarily on *City of Night,* which documents the wanderings of a nameless male hustler from El Paso to New York, Los Angeles, and New Orleans. This narrative is punctuated by recollections of the narrator's childhood in El Paso. The novel is structured by two types of chapters, accounts of the narrator's wanderings and character sketches of people he meets as a hustler. Each character sketch builds for the reader a knowable person, but then each narrative chapter immediately pulls the reader away and moves him or her onward. This technique in many ways forces the reader into the position of hustler: "knowing" someone, but only transiently and temporarily. This impermanence of human contact is mockingly displayed in the fact that the novel never provides a name for its narrator.

Sex in *City of Night* is a job, not an identity. Rechy's later novels, however, move more directly into the world of gay male writing. *Numbers* (1967) tells the story of Johnny Rio, a former hustler who now pursues only free sex and exclusively with men. Johnny's pursuit of "numbers" in Los Angeles's Griffith Park is a ritual of purgation. He explains to a gay man who has befriended him that he intends to trick with thirty "numbers" in the park, and that this will then allow him to attempt other types of encounters: "It'll be only with people with identity . . . that's what the park was about . . . and the numbers. Losing control and losing identity. But I'm in control again, and that's what I won." If the narrator of *City of Night* hustles to avoid an identity, Johnny attempts to hustle *toward* an identity: And with this movement, Rechy's

canon moves from the world of homosexual behavior into the world of gay identity.

Although almost all of Rechy's novels contain gay characters and themes, his only two other novels to deal primarily with them are *This Days's Death* (1969), which tells the story of a man caught in a police vice raid in Griffith Park, and *Rushes* (1979), which tells the bleak story of a group of friends in an urban leather bar. Rechy also has written a nonfiction "documentary" about three days in the life of a gay hustler, *The Sexual Outlaw* (1977). Yet despite these obvious examinations of gay male identity, Rechy himself has consistently derided the label of "gay writer"; indeed, his most recent novels, *Marilyn's Daughter* (1988) and *The Miraculous Day of Amalia Gomez* (1991), adopt heterosexual women as their protagonists. Rechy will most likely be remembered in the tradition of gay male writing as a brutal and lyrical chronicler of the pre-Stonewall sexual underworld. (See also EROTICA AND PORNOGRAPHY and LATINO LITERATURE.)

—*Gregory W. Bredbeck*

BIBLIOGRAPHY

Bruce-Novoa, Juan. "In Search of the Honest Outlaw: John Rechy." *Minority Voices* 3 (1979): 37–45. ■ ———. "Homosexuality and the Chicano Novel." *Confluencia* 2:1 (Fall 1986): 69–77. ■ Giles, James R., and Wanda Giles. "An Interview with John Rechy." *Chicago Review* 25 (1973): 19–31. ■ Heifetz, Henry. "The Anti-Social Act of Writing." *Studies on the Left* 4 (Spring 1964): 6–9. ■ Hoffman, Stanton. "The Cities of Night: John Rechy's *City of Night* and the American Literature of Homosexuality." *Chicago Review* 17:2/3 (1964): 195–206. ■ Satterfield, Ben. "John Rechy's Tormented World." *Southwest Review* 67:1 (Winter 1982): 78–85. ■ Tatum, Charles M. "The Sexual Underworlds of John Rechy." *Minority Voices* 3 (1979): 47–52. ■ Zamora, Carlos. "Odysseus in John Rechy's *City of Night:* The Epistemological Journey." *Minority Voices* 3 (1979): 53–62.

§*Renault, Mary*
(1905–1983)

Mary Renault was born Eileen Mary Challans in London, September 4, 1905, daughter of Frank Challans, a physician, and Clementine (Baxter) Challans. (Her pen name, which she used throughout her career, was taken from Otway's *Venice Preserved*.) Although she wrote short stories, radio plays, and nonfiction, Renault is best known as a novelist. The last eight of her fourteen novels, histor-

ical fictions set in ancient Greece, are the most highly regarded. All of her novels, however, deal at some level of explicitness with homosexuality: a diffused or suggested lesbianism in the first five and an openly presented male homosexuality in the last nine.

Educated in London and Bristol, Renault read English at St. Hugh's College, Oxford, from which she graduated in 1928. In 1933, having rejected most of the conventional options available to women, Renault entered nurses' training. At Radcliffe Infirmary, Oxford, she met Julie Mullard, a fellow nurse who became her lifelong companion.

Renault's first novel, *Purposes of Love,* was published in 1939 and like the next five was based more or less directly on her nursing and hospital experience. Her fourth novel, *Return to Night* (1947), won the MGM Prize of $150,000. The money provided a financial base for Renault and Mullard, and in 1948, they emigrated to South Africa where they lived, first in Durban and, after 1960, in Cape Town, until Renault's death.

Renault's first five novels have the trappings of "nurse romances" but go beyond the norm of that formulaic genre in their shrewdness of observation and their submerged hints of lesbian relationships. Renault subsequently repudiated them; in an afterword to a reissue of *The Friendly Young Ladies,* she called its ending silly— silly in that the tomboyish Leo (Leonora) after a two-year relationship with Helen leaves for the kindly (and thoroughly heterosexual) Joe: "more . . . impossible unions happen in real life every day," Renault writes, "but it is naïve to present them as happy endings."

Three things mark Renault's progress from a competent popular novelist to a master of her craft: first, the change of emphasis from female to male homosexuality with *The Charioteer* in 1953; second, the move from contemporary to ancient setting in *The Last of the Wine* (1956) and after—her choosing, that is, to become a historical novelist; and third, her adoption of a first-person narrative point of view. By moving into the distant past, specifically a past where homosexual relationships were not just accepted but in some contexts celebrated, Renault could show the integrity and fitness of such bonds. Adopting a first-person narrator allowed Renault to imagine her way more deeply into Hellenic culture, just as Hellenic culture itself allowed her to imagine her characters' sexuality more liberally. Of course not all Renault's historical novels are written in the first person (*Fire from Heaven* and *Funeral Games* are not) and not all of her major characters are homosexual (Theseus in *The King Must Die* and *The Bull from the Sea* and Simonides in *The Praise Singer* are not), but their world accepts male-male ties without compunction.

Such acceptance is not found in the modern world of *The Charioteer.* A young soldier wounded in the Dunkirk withdrawal confronts his emerging homosexual feelings and discovers that an adored older schoolmate had been—and still is—equally drawn. The novel is a courageous treatment of a vexed subject, but it is still constrained by being set in the 1940s and by having been written in the 1950s. The repres-

sive power of a homophobic society can be seen not only in character behavior but also in authorial strategies.

In ancient Greece, Renault could stop disguising youths as tomboys, could finesse modern shame, and could simply omit the heartlessly incompetent mothers who litter her earlier books. Still, however dramatic a shift of twenty-five centuries is, the change is less a break than a revelation—Renault had been, as Bernard Dick has shown, a secret Hellenist all along.

Renault's first classical novel, *The Last of the Wine,* illustrates well enough her postulates about sexuality in ancient Hellas. There is first the union of two young men or youths of equal station, a friendship or comradeship-in-arms like that of Lysis and the narrator Alexias, a tie that also has a strong sexual element. Then there is the relationship of older to younger males (such as Polymedes' unsuccessful courtship of Alexias), possibly mentorial in character but also a sexual pursuit of the younger male. Third in importance and sequence is the marriage vow, a responsibility to be taken up in later life: Lysis marries Thalia amid general approval. These patterns are governed by two assumptions—one that men are capable of both homosexual and heterosexual responses, the other that (since this is the Athens of Socrates) the relationship seeks to evoke and exalt what is highest and most excellent in each partner.

In later novels, Renault moves to Hellenistic times to chronicle the career of Alexander the Great. The first of this series, *The Mask of Apollo* (1966), brings to imaginative life a body of careful research into the nature of Greek theater. Its protagonist-narrator, Nikeratos, has had his successes and failures as an actor, but he has achieved a firm union with the younger actor Thettalos. At the end of the novel, the boy Alexander comes backstage after a performance in the provinces, and Nikeratos is struck by his beauty, presence, and power. *Fire from Heaven* (1970) goes back to recreate the young hero's childhood and boyhood. *The Persian Boy* (1972) is told by Bagoas, a beautiful young Persian eunuch who becomes Alexander's lover. *The Persian Boy* ends with the death of Alexander, and the ironically titled *Funeral Games* (1981) relates the bloodshed and power struggles that follow his death.

What distinguishes Renault's historical fiction is her ability to interweave seamlessly the fictive and the factual (the invented Nikeratos and the historical Thettalos, the effects of Socrates' teaching on imaginary young men); to expand mere hints in the historical record (Bagoas, for example) into plausible and circumstantially complex events or characters; and to create realistic and believable psychologies for her characters: not modern sensibilities in period costumes, but minds evidently molded by the culture out of which they spring and that they in turn influence. Above all, Renault's work depicts with love and care an age and a culture in which homosexual love was neither deviance nor norm but part of experience. (See also NOVEL: GAY MALE.)

—*Michael N. Stanton*

BIBLIOGRAPHY

Dick, Bernard F. *The Hellenism of Mary Renault.* Carbondale: Southern Illinois University Press, 1972. ■ Summers, Claude J. *Gay Fictions: Wilde to Stonewall.* New York: Continuum, 1990. ■ Sweetman, David. *Mary Renault: A Biography.* New York: Harcourt Brace, 1993.

Reve, Gerard
(*b.* 1923)

Gerard Kornelis van het Reve was born on December 14, 1923, in Amsterdam and attended school there at the Vossius-gymnasium. During the war years, Reve studied graphic design, and from 1945 to 1947, was a reporter for the national daily newspaper *Het Parool.* His first novel, *De avonden (The Evenings,* 1947) met with critical acclaim and was awarded the Reina Prinsen Geerligs Prize, granted annually to the best young writer in The Netherlands. Considered now to be a classic of modern Dutch literature, the novel initially met with much controversy, fueled in part by its frank depiction of the aimless life of its main character. Reve was embroiled in more controversy when references to masturbation in an early novella were considered pornographic by the Minister of State who ruled against providing Reve with a travel stipend. Reve publicly announced his intention to immigrate to England in protest, and he spent a number of years there working as a hospital attendant, reading the Bible, studying drama, and writing plays. When his first publication in English, *The Acrobat and Other Stories* (1956), was a financial failure, Reve returned to The Netherlands to work as an editor and writer for the literary periodical *Tirade.* Reve received wide acclaim when he single-handedly broke a post-war taboo against openly treating homosexuality in Dutch literature with two publications, each a cross between letter writing and fiction: *Op Weg naar het Einde (Approaching the End,* 1963) and *Nader tot U (Nearer to Thee,* 1966). The controversies surrounding his increasingly explicit treatment of homosexuality culminated in 1967, when, after his much-publicized conversion to Roman Catholicism, he was officially charged with blasphemy for writing an article in the journal *Dialoog* that characterized Christ as a donkey with whom he wanted to have sexual intercourse. The closely followed case, which was eventually dismissed, ensured for Reve lasting celebrity status in The Netherlands. In 1968, Reve was awarded the prestigious P.C. Hooft Prize for Literature. Since 1969, he has lived in France.

Although his lasting literary fame rests on the classic post-war novel *De avonden,* Reve's enduring influence as a writer rests largely on the innovations he brought to Dutch literature in both style and subject matter. A largely plotless account of the last ten nights of 1946 from the perspective of an aimless young office worker, *De avonden* is typical of Reve's early work in that it captures the gloomy mood of the post-war years from the perspective of a solitary, often sardonic and funny, male antihero. Reve's early protagonists, though not explicitly gay, are often described as isolated and in danger; they feel vulnerable without knowing why and remain anxiously observant, experiencing a generalized fear of being found out.

Although much of Reve's early work focuses on very broad themes of life and death, fear and despair, his mature writing is preoccupied with the search for homosexual love and for God. In a wide variety of genres, Reve has made significant inquiries into the nature of pleasure and pain and the relationship between fact and fantasy. In an important group of books, most notably in *Lieve Jongens (Dear Boys,* 1973), Reve frames stories within stories in order to explore the enjoyment derived from fantasy.

Reve has long been acknowledged for his profound influence on the post-War Dutch novel, but his role in pioneering European gay writing and his contribution to the liberalization of attitudes toward homosexuality in The Netherlands has only recently begun to be fully appreciated.

—*Robert Nashak*

BIBLIOGRAPHY

Meijer, Mia. *Gerard Reve.* Brugge: Orion, 1973. ■ Snapper, J. P. *De Spiegel der verlossing in het wek van Gerard Reve (The Mirror of Redemption in the Work Gerard Reve).* Utrecht: Veen, 1990.

Rich, Adrienne
(b. 1929)

Adrienne Rich's unflinching moral vision, constant and courageous interrogations of her selves, and of her own and other writers' philosophical positions and artistic responsibilities, make her, as poet and critic Alicia Ostriker has observed, "a poet of ideas" who "cannot accept either a public or private life not motivated by the will to change oneself, to change others, to change the world," and who "asks us," therefore, "to think that we need to give birth to ourselves." In a national poetry industry where creative writing programs pledge allegiance to honing technique and to the commonplace that form is content, Rich, a master of craft and form, unfashionably refuses to identify poetry with skillful design and insists that it must be forceful enough to change lives. Indeed, David Kalstone pronounced Rich's *The Will to Change* (1971) "an extraordinary book of poems and something else as well." Readers may agree or disagree with Rich, but no one can read her work and think "oh, it is only poetry" or "oh, here is yet another pretty prose piece by a well-known poet." Her aestheticization of politics and politicization of aesthetics gently yet fiercely urge every reader continually to ask and honestly answer the question doubly posed in "The Spirit of Place," her 1980 poem for Michelle Cliff: "*With whom do you believe your lot is cast?*"; "(with whom do you believe your lot is cast?)."

Born May 16, 1929, into an intellectual and affluent household in Baltimore, Maryland, Adrienne Rich began writing poetry as a child, encouraged by her father and his "very Victorian, pre-Raphaelite" library. In 1951 she took her A.B. from Radcliffe College and published *A Change of World,* which W. H. AUDEN selected for the Yale Younger Poets Award. In 1953, Rich married Alfred Conrad, an economist at Harvard; she gave birth to three sons between 1955 and 1959, and resided with her family in Cambridge, Massachusetts, until 1966, when they moved to New York City. Both she and her husband became increasingly active in Vietnam War protests. Rich, drawn by her "swirling wants" ("A Valediction Forbidding Mourning," 1970), left her marriage in 1970. Later in that year, Conrad committed suicide. Since 1976, Rich has lived with Michelle Cliff. They moved to Montague, Massachusetts, in 1979 and relocated in 1984 to Santa Cruz, California, where they presently reside.

In what can only be called the most distinguished of careers, Adrienne Rich has, from her earliest to latest publications, garnered awards and fellowship support. Besides the Yale prize in 1951, her twenty volumes of poetry (including five volumes of reprinted selected poems) and four collections of prose have been honored by awards from the Poetry Society of America (1955, 1971, 1992), the National Institute for Arts and Letters (1960), *Poetry* magazine (1963, 1968), the Ruth Lilly Poetry Prize (1986), Brandeis Creative Arts Medal (1987), New York University (1989), the National Poetry Association for Distinguished Service to the Art of Poetry (1989), the Bay Area Book Reviewers (1990), the Common Wealth Award in Literature (1991), the *Los Angeles Times* and *Nation* (1992), and the Poet's Prize (1993). In 1974, she won the National Book Award for *Diving into the Wreck* (an honor shared with ALLEN GINSBERG). In 1990, Rich became a member of the department of literature of the American Academy and Institute of Arts and Letters, and in 1991, a member of the American Academy of Arts and Sciences. She has taught in a wide range of settings, from the SEEK program at City College of New York (1968) to Douglass College of Rutgers University (1976–1979), Cornell (1981–1987), and Stanford (1986–1993). She has received honorary doctorates from Wheaton College (1967), Smith College (1979), College of Wooster, Ohio (1987), Brandeis (1987), City College of New York (1990), Harvard (1990), and Swarthmore (1992). Her writing has been supported by two Guggenheim Fellowships (1952–1953, 1961–1962), a Bollingen Foundation grant (1962), and an Amy Lowell Travelling Fellowship (1962–1963); and she has been a fellow at Bryn Mawr (1975) and the University of Chicago (1989). In 1981, the National Gay Task Force recognized her accomplishments with the Fund for Human Dignity Award; in 1992, she received the William Whitehead Award of the Publishing Triangle for lifetime achievement in letters; and in 1994, she was awarded a MacArthur Fellowship. Awareness of the extraordinary number of distinguished awards she has received and the teaching positions she has held is important for appreciating, contextualizing, and assessing Rich's position as America's most widely read lesbian poet. It also underscores the courage she has shown in assuming responsibility toward the vast majority of women, lesbians, and gay men who struggle in anonymity. What she said of Minnie Bruce Pratt, Chrystos, and AUDRE LORDE's winning NEA grants is also true of her own numerous honors: They "are signs of the power not only of [her] work, but of the current of resistance running beneath the inertia and pseudo events that have constituted public life in the United States for two decades" (1993).

Rich dedicated *Of Woman Born: Motherhood as Experience and Institution* (1976) "*To my grandmothers* / Mary Gravely [and] Hattie Rice / *whose lives I begin to imagine*" and concluded her "Acknowledgments" by saluting other members of her family:

> Finally, I cannot imagine having written this book without the presence in my life of my mother, who offers a continuing example of transformation and rebirth; and of my sister, with and from whom I go on learning about sisterhood, daughterhood, motherhood, and the struggle of women toward a shared, irreversible, liberation.

Indeed, Rich's role as a public figure, as an immensely respected and popular poet, has seen important transformations. The first is that from the polite, "good girl" poetry of the early 1950s to the poems of the still-evolving feminist activist and theorist that she began writing in the late 1950s and early 1960s with her breakthrough volume *Snapshots of a Daughter-In-Law* (1954–1962). In the title poem of this volume, Rich observes, "A thinking woman sleeps with monsters." When she won the National Book Award, she rejected the recognition as an individual but, in a statement written with Audre Lorde and ALICE WALKER, accepted the honor on behalf of all women.

By the mid-1970s, Rich began to assume another mantle of responsibility as a lesbian-feminist public poet. Following the publication of her most controversial, still-debated theoretical essay, "Compulsory Heterosexuality and Lesbian Existence" (1980), Rich co-edited the lesbian-feminist journal *Sinister Wisdom* (1981–1983). This involvement with a "marginalized" journal is in keeping with her practice of contributing work to smaller feminist presses and journals, even as she is also published by W.W. Norton, one of the most prestigious commercial publishing houses. For example, "Twenty-One Love Poems" (1974–1976), the most famous and widely admired sequence of American lesbian love poetry published to date, first appeared in a limited edition, "designed and hand-printed by Bonnie Carpenter at Effie's Press" (1977) before its inclusion in *The Dream of a Common Language* (1978), published by Norton. Similarly, "Poetry III" and "Upcountry" were first published as broadsides and "Sources" as a chapbook by Heyeck Press (1983–1985) before their inclusion in Norton's *Your Native Land, Your Life* (1986). Thus, Rich's support of women and lesbians has been material as well as philosophical. In "Adrienne Rich and Lesbian/Feminist Poetry," Catharine Stimpson observed:

> 'Lesbian.' For many, heterosexual or homosexual, the word still constricts the throat. Those 'slimy' sibilants; those 'nasty' nasalities. 'Lesbian' makes even 'feminist' sound lissome, decent, sane. In 1975, Adrienne Rich's reputation was secure. She might have eased up and toyed with honors. Yet, she was doing nothing less than seizing and caressing that word: 'lesbian.' She was working hard for 'a whole new poetry' that was to begin in two women's 'limitless desire.'

In the early 1980s, Rich began to explore her Jewishness and to claim her Jewish father, "to break his silence, his taboos" in "Sources" (August 1981–August 1982) and the essay "Split at the Root" (1982). In keeping with her habit of providing practical support for work she deems important, Rich recently devoted her time and energy to serving as a member of the founding editorial group of *Bridges: A Journal for Jewish Feminists and Our Friends* (1990).

Two of the most quoted lines of lesbian poetry, and of contemporary love poetry, are those from poem XIX of "Twenty-One Love Poems": "two women together is a work / nothing in civilization has made simple." The poem remarks the miracle of any couple staying together, remaining and growing more dedicated in love, and the special miracle of a long-committed couple whose union is routinely disdained by those who fear homosexual difference. Between poems XIV and XV of this sequence appears "(THE FLOATING POEM, UNNUMBERED)," widely received as the most beautiful iteration of cunnilingus as physical love:

> . . . Your traveled, generous thighs
> between which my whole face has come and
>   come—
> the innocence and wisdom of the place my
>   tongue has found there—
> the live, insatiate dance of your nipples in my
>   mouth—
> your touch on me, firm, protective, searching
> me out, your strong tongue and slender fingers
> reaching where I had been waiting years for
>   you
> in my rose-wet cave—whatever happens, this is.

In the mid-1980s, Rich's fusing of the personal and political is poignantly voiced in "In Memoriam: D.K." (1986), her tribute to one of her ablest critics and supporters, David Kalstone:

A man walking on the street
feels unwell has felt unwell
all week, a little. . . Give me your living hand
   If I could take the hour
death moved into you undeclared, unnamed
—even if sweet, if I could take that hour.

Rich mourns this sensitive, invaluable poetic interpreter and teacher who died of AIDS.

Committed to plumbing her various heritages, Rich's poetry contains depths and breadths of psychological and social meanings that resonate to and from identities, subjectivities, rationalities, and emotions. Rich has, as Olga Broumas notes, "extraordinary powers—of perception, eloquence, rhythm, courage, the rare fusion of vision and action, the ability to suggest not only to others but to herself a course of action in the mind and follow it in the next breath in the world," and thus many are "drawn by the mind of [this] woman whose work and life have been an act of becoming conscious against the established order." As Gloria Bowles observed more than a decade ago, Adrienne Rich has time and again exhorted feminist scholars to remain "dedicated to the process of discussion and reformulation," always remaining open to the previously unimaginable possibilities of reconceptualization.

In "Voices from the air" (1993), Rich recently declared of her medium that

A poem can't free us from the struggle for existence, but it can uncover desires and appetites buried under the accumulating emergencies of our lives, the fabricated wants and needs we have had urged on us, have accepted as our own. It's not a philosophical or psychological blueprint; it's an instrument for embodied experience. But we seek that experience, or recognize it when it is offered to us, because it reminds us in some way of our need. After that rearousal of desire, the task of acting on that truth, or making love, or meeting other needs, is ours.

Adrienne Rich lends new meaning to Ralph Waldo Emerson's nineteenth-century proclamation that the poet is no mere versifier but a seer and sayer, for this American lesbian feminist poet utters truths denied or previously unrealized so plainly, memorably, and for-cibly that they demand to be reckoned with. Indeed, the vast number of books, articles, and papers published on Rich testify to the generative nature of her work. Nearly two decades ago, Rich answered her own repeatedly reiterated query in "Natural Resources" (1977): "I have to cast my lot with those / who age after age, perversely, / with no extraordinary power, / reconstitute the world." Through her monumental gift of poetry and her activism on behalf of lesbian and gay liberation and civil rights for everyone, she has indeed cast her lot with those who reconstitute the world. Her poems, her essays, interviews, and speeches are all a call to action, for they each remind us, as she remarked in 1991, that "Experience is always larger than language." (See also FEMINIST LITERARY THEORY and POETRY, LESBIAN.)

—*Martha Nell Smith*

BIBLIOGRAPHY

Alkalay-Gut, Karen. "The Lesbian Imperative in Poetry." *Contemporary Review* 24 (1983): 209–211. ■ Bennett, Paula. *My Life a Loaded Gun: Female Creativity and Feminist Poetics.* Boston: Beacon, 1986; rpt. *My Life a Loaded Gun: Dickinson, Plath, Rich and Female Creativity.* Urbana: University of Illinois Press, 1990. ■ Bulkin, Elly. "An Interview with Adrienne Rich." *Conditions: One: A Magazine of Writing by Women with an Emphasis on Writing by Lesbians* 1.1 (April 1977); and "An Interview with Adrienne Rich." *Conditions: Two* 1.2 (October 1977). ■ Carruthers, Mary J. "The Re-Vision of the Muse: Adrienne Rich, Audre Lorde, Judy Grahn, Olga Broumas." *The Hudson Review* 36.2 (Summer 1983): 293–322. ■ Cooper, Jane Roberta, ed. *Reading Adrienne Rich: Reviews and Re-Visions, 1951–1981.* Ann Arbor: University of Michigan Press, 1984. ■ DeShazer, Mary K. *Inspiring Women: Reimagining the Muse.* New York: Pergamon Press, 1986. ■ Diehl, Joanne Feit. *Women Poets and the American Sublime.* Bloomington: Indiana University Press, 1990. ■ DuPlessis, Rachel Blau. "The Critique of Consciousness and Myth in Levertov, Rich and Rukeyser." *Feminist Studies* 3.1–2 (1975): 199–221. ■ Erkkila, Betsy. *The Wicked Sisters: Women Poets, Literary History & Discord.* New York: Oxford University Press, 1992. ■ Farwell, Marilyn R. "Adrienne Rich and an Organic Feminist Criticism." *College English* 39.2 (1977): 191–203. ■ Ferguson, Ann, Jaquelyn N. Zita, and Kathryn Pyne Addelson. "Viewpoint: On 'Compulsory Heterosexuality and Lesbian Existence': Defining the Issues." *Signs* 7.1 (Autumn 1981): 158–199. ■ Friedman, Susan Stanford. "'I Go Where I Love': An Intertextual Study of H.D. and Adrienne Rich." *Signs* 9.2 (Winter 1983): 228–245. ■ Gelpi, Barbara Charlesworth, and Albert Gelpi, eds. *Adrienne Rich's Poetry: Texts of the Poems; The Poet on Her Work; Reviews and Criticism.* New York: W.W. Norton, 1975. ■ Hedley, Jane. "Surviving to Speak New Language: Mary Daly and Adrienne Rich." *Hypatia* 7.2 (Spring 1992): 40–62. ■ Kalstone, David. *Five Temperaments: Elizabeth Bishop, Robert Lowell, James Merrill, Adrienne Rich, John Ashbery.* New York: Oxford University Press, 1977. ■ McDaniel, Judith. *Reconstructing the World: The Poetry and Visions of Adrienne Rich.* Argyle, N.Y.: Spinsters Ink, 1979. ■ Ostriker, Alicia. "Her Cargo: Adrienne Rich and the Common Language." *American Poetry Review* 6.4 (1979): 6–10; rpt. *Writing Like a Woman.* Ann Arbor: University of Michigan Press, 1983. ■ Schwarz, Judith. "Questionnaire on Issues in Lesbian History." *Frontiers: A Journal of Women's Studies* 4.3 (1979): 1–12. ■ Stimpson, Catharine. "Adrienne Rich and Lesbian/Feminist Poetry." *Parnassus: Poetry in Review* 12–13 (1985): 249–268. ■ Strine, Mary S. "The Politics of Asking Women's Questions: Voice and Value in the Poetry of Adrienne Rich." *Text and Performance Quarterly* 9.1 (January 1989): 24–41.

Rimbaud, Arthur
(1854–1891)

Jean-Nicolas-Arthur Rimbaud was born on October 20, 1854, in Charleville in northern France. Born of rural parents, Rimbaud enrolled in Charleville's Institution Rossat and then, in the spring of 1865, attended the Collège de Charleville where he earned his degree. He was an exceptional child who excelled in academic work by mastering two levels in one year.

Rimbaud began writing very early, first in Latin, then in French. His first French poem was "The Orphans' Gifts" ("Les Étrennes des orphelins") of 1869. With the encouragement of his young professor-mentor Georges Izambard, he had written twenty-two poems by 1870. By the age of sixteen, he had published several poems in the journal *Le Parnasse Contemporain*.

In 1870, Rimbaud first traveled to Paris. His first sexual experience may have occurred there in 1871 in a barracks with a group of soldiers; his poem "The Stolen Heart" ("Le Coeur volé") may describe such an experience and may be interpreted in terms of sexual seduction or initiation.

Rimbaud met PAUL VERLAINE on his trip to Paris in 1870 and received an invitation to come to Paris in September 1871. Although Verlaine was married and ten years Rimbaud's senior, a homosexual relationship between the two men ensued. For the next year and a half, they were together in Paris in the Latin Quarter, in the cafes, and in the literary salons. They traveled together to Brussels and London and acknowledged each other in their writing. Rimbaud, for example, playfully refers to Verlaine's eyes in his famous poem "Vowels" (1871). The couple may appear masked in the section of *A Season in Hell* (1873) entitled "Délire I": "Foolish Virgin, The Infernal Bridegroom." Nearly all of Rimbaud's mature poetry was written during his love affair with Verlaine. The latter encouraged him in the creation of *The Illuminations* in London in 1872 and *A Season in Hell* in 1873. When the affair ended in July of 1873, when Verlaine shot him in the wrist during a violent quarrel, Rimbaud essentially abandoned his career as a poet.

After a Brussels printer published *A Season in Hell* in October 1873, providing a way for Rimbaud to send a few copies to his friends in Paris, Rimbaud's interest in his own work declined. During 1874 and 1875, he traveled widely in Europe. In the spring of 1876, he enlisted in the Dutch army, but soon abandoned that, preferring to travel to Sweden, Denmark, Greece, and Egypt, where in 1880 he was a coffee buyer and in 1887 sold guns. Rimbaud died on November 10, 1891, at the age of thirty-seven. He is often regarded as the exemplar of the genius who abandoned poetry for a life of action.

Rimbaud's best-known poem *The Drunken Boat* (*Le Bateau ivre*) was created in 1871 before his seventeenth birthday; it celebrates liberation, especially Rimbaud's liberation of the senses, and apparently evolved from the beginning of his relationship with Verlaine. Rimbaud's artistic world is a world of symbols, hallucinations, dreams, and visions, exemplified especially in *A Season in Hell* and *The Illuminations*. One of his professed techniques was a "derangement of all the senses." Rimbaud's two letters (*Lettres du Voyant*) of May 1871 constitute a literary manifesto in which the poet is assigned the role of "clairvoyant," "magician," and "artist."

In his art, Rimbaud assumes the mask of diverse personalities, both male and female. In his letter to Izambard of May 13, 1871, appears a novel concept, "I is someone else" ("Je est un autre"). Is the "someone else" creative artist, persona, or another? Is it a mask for his sexual identity? Rimbaud enhances his writing with motifs of love, music, fantasy, memory, myth, and adolescent visions. The section "Alchemy of the Word" ("L'alchimie du verbe," 1873) in *A Season in Hell* embodies Rimbaud's doctrine of "alchemy," "witchcraft," or "magic" since the section shows a preponderance of "poetic" words and creates an incantatory effect.

The Illuminations—a psychological autobiography in free verse and prose poems—depicts a myriad of settings, a fairy world of time, place, history, fiction, and beauty. Rimbaud concludes The Illuminations with the "genie": a being both human and supernatural, embodying affection, love, reason, and optimism. Written in the nineteenth-century French symbolist style, rich in poetic diction, the work employs symbols to represent ideas, objects, and states.

Although Rimbaud gave up poetry before he was nineteen, he can be described as a boy-poet-emperor, whose palace is his imagination, where he takes his friends on a fantastic voyage to an imaginary realm of magicians, faeries, gods, angels, and genies. In some respects, Rimbaud redefines art and reinvents love by means of a liberation of art and self. Because Rimbaud's writing stresses liberation, he is a progenitor of modern gay poetics, influencing such poets and prose writers as ANDRÉ GIDE, JEAN COCTEAU, FEDERICO GARCÍA LORCA, HART CRANE, and JEAN GENÊT. Several artists have sketched Rimbaud, but Verlaine's Rimbaud (1872) most memorably portrays the young poet as a genius, an example of the modern creative spirit, the boy-poet whose art is based solely on his individual creativity.

—Clarence McClanahan

BIBLIOGRAPHY

Bonnefoy, Yves. Rimbaud. Trans. Paul Schmidt. New York: Harper Colophon, 1973. ■ Dillman, Karin J. The Subject of Rimbaud: From Self to 'Je.' New York: Peter Lang, 1984. ■ Fowlie, Wallace. Rimbaud. Chicago: University of Chicago Press, 1966. ■ Hare, Humphrey. Sketch for a Portrait of Rimbaud. New York: Haskell House, 1974. ■ Lawler, James. Rimbaud's Theatre of the Self. Cambridge, Mass.: Harvard University Press, 1992. ■ Morrissette, Bruce. The Great Rimbaud Forgery: The Affair of "La chasse spirituelle." St. Louis: Washington University Studies, 1956. ■ Petitfils, Pierre. Rimbaud. Trans. Alan Sheridan. Charlottesville: University Press of Virginia, 1987. ■ Rickword, Edgell. Rimbaud: The Boy and The Poet. New York: Haskell House, 1971. ■ Starkie, Enid. Arthur Rimbaud. New York: New Directions, 1961.

Rochester, John Wilmot, Earl of (1647–1680)

Since his alleged "death-bed repentance" in 1680, John Wilmot, the Second Earl of Rochester, has been the stuff of which legends are made. One of the most notorious rakes in Restoration England, Rochester is primarily remembered for his devilish pranks, sexual conquests, bawdy jokes, and drunken escapades. Born at Ditchley in Oxfordshire, the son of Henry Wilmot, First Earl of Rochester, and Anne St. John, Countess of Rochester, John was educated primarily at Oxford. His travels took him to Italy and France, but his notoriety as a sexually mischievous aristocrat came mostly from his years in the entourage at Whitehall during the reign of Charles II. One of Charles's favorites, Rochester was nevertheless exiled numerous times by the king for libelous poetry and scandalous behavior at court. Rochester frequently attacked the king and his multiple mistresses in poems like "A Satyr on Charles II."

Although many readers have focused on Rochester's scathing satires on the upper class, as well as the "Satyr Against Reason and Mankind" (one of his "cleanest" poems) as the most intellectually challenging of his body of work, it is in his satires against sexuality, particularly heterosexuality, that Rochester's poetic voice finds its most powerful expression.

The focus of heterosexual marriage, or at least of a monogamous relationship in Rochester's poetry, is intercourse. Rochester describes, often in highly misogynistic terms, heterosexual intercourse as a key grotesque event. In poems like "By All Love's Soft, Yet Mighty Pow'rs," distinctions between bodily functions—copulation, menstruation, and defecation—are effectively collapsed. Rochester uses the common term for menstruation, "Flowers," in this poem to evoke the unsavory effects of making love while a woman is menstruating. (In juxtaposing this image with a "smock" which is "beshit," Rochester forms a troublesome alliance between two kinds of "waste," both of which are produced by his mistress.) This mixture of blood, sperm, and feces is certainly meant to shock and offend his Restoration audience in that it gives a less attractive "body" to courtly love poetry.

Rochester constructs heterosexual love as imperfect or incomplete in his poetry. Poems such as "The Imperfect Enjoyment," a poem dealing with premature ejaculation, and his widely anthologized "A Ramble in St. James's Park," the latter narrated by an angry lover cursing his overflirtatious mistress, both describe the heterosexual experience as unproductive. The recurrent imagery of waste, "wasted" sperm and

squandered attempts at pleasure, highlights the speaker's frustration in the aforementioned poems, but this "refuse" is often set against the relatively clean and waste-free love between men.

In Rochester's "Love A Woman? You're an Ass!," the narrator reduces the womb to a place of drudgery, a space fit only for servants forced to obey commands. The misogyny of the poem clearly offers the occasion to enter homosocial ties; the speaker refers to both his male friendship, his "lewd well-natur'd friend," and his "sweet soft page" as natural alternatives to intercourse with his mistress. "Wit" in fact is considered a product of homosocial exchange and revelry: It is produced when women are banished from the scene. In a poem like "The Disabled Debauchee," Rochester's persona is so wrapped up in sexual ecstasy that in recalling a ménage à trois with his mistress and a page boy, he cannot remember which sexual roles each of the participants played.

The infamous farce *Sodom: The Quintessence of Debauchery* has been credited to Rochester. In *Sodom,* King Bolloxinion declares "buggery" to be the intercourse of choice throughout the land since heterosexuality is so abhorrent and unclean. The play consists of one explicit sex scene after another as the king's subjects, both men and women, find other ways to satisfy themselves sexually than normative heterosexuality.

Rochester's poems participate in the libertine ethic of bisexuality so prevalent during the Restoration. Being part of the court culture not only gave Rochester his infamous reputation but access to the aristocratic privilege of sexual liberty and experimentation. His poetic persona explores all the available avenues of sexual activity open to men of his class in the Restoration. (See also ENGLISH LIERATURE: RESTORATION & EIGHTEENTH CENTURY.)

—Amy Farmer

BIBLIOGRAPHY

Holton, Robert. "Sexuality and Social Hierarchy in Sidney and Rochester." *Mosaic: A Journal for the Interdisciplinary Study of Literature* 24 (1991): 47–65. ■ Rawson, Claude. "System of Excess." *Times Literary Supplement,* 29 March 1985: 335–336. ■ Treglown, Jeremy, ed. *Spirit of Wit: Reconsiderations of Rochester.* Hamden, Conn.: Shoe String, 1982. ■ Vieth, David. *Attribution in Restoration Poetry: A Study of Rochester's Poems 1680.* New Haven: Yale University Press, 1963. ■ ———. *John Wilmot, Earl of Rochester: Critical Essays.* New York: Garland, Vol. VIII, 1988. ■ Weber, Harold. "'Drudging in Fair Aurelia's Womb': Constructing Homosexual Economies in Rochester's Poetry." *The Eighteenth Century: Theory and Interpretation* 33 (1992): 99–117.

Rolfe, Frederick William
(1860–1913)

Frederick William Serafino Austin Lewis Mary Rolfe, who also used the name Baron Corvo, is important for the gay literary heritage because of his distinctive decadent prose style, his outrageous decadent lifestyle, and his unashamed celebration of eroticized male friendships in his works. Although his formal schooling was never completed, he acquired a strong intellectual training in classics, theology, and history. At age fifteen, he converted to Roman Catholicism. Thereafter, although asked to leave more than one seminary, he pursued the dream of becoming a priest. He supported himself after a fashion as a photographer and painter, as a teacher and tutor, and finally as a writer. In 1910, at the end of a twenty-year period of self-imposed celibacy intended to prove his vocation, he found himself in Venice. He fell in love with the city and its erotic license and refused to leave although this made it almost impossible for him to manage his business affairs. In addition, he alienated himself from one friend after another with malicious letters. Turned out of his hotel for failure to pay the bill, he died of exposure, killed by the treacherous climate of the Venice he loved.

Perhaps more than his work, Rolfe's curious mismanagement of his life has brought him cult status, beginning in A. J. A. Symons's *Quest for Corvo* (1934), a work highlighting the excitement of a scholarly investigation. Rolfe appears as a distinctive presence in the nonfiction and sometimes the fiction of many writers who knew him. He is satirized as *The Unspeakable Skipton* (1959) by Pamela Hansford Johnson. Frequently described with considerable justification as a paranoid personality, Rolfe is also frequently described without any justification whatsoever as a corrupter of youth. As *The Venice Letters* (written 1909–1910, published 1974) make clear, he was interested only in boys in their late teens, and these boys were characteristically worldly and aggressive sensualists.

Stories Toto Told Me (1898) and *In His Own Image* (1901), Rolfe's first books, are saints' lives narrated in dialect by a precocious servant. These collections earned Rolfe a certain early reputation as a stylist. They are now of gay interest because of their erotic, phallic imagery, which turn-of-the-century readers may not have been consciously aware of.

The particular frustration Rolfe felt in his futile pursuit of ordination is recreated in perhaps his masterpiece, *Hadrian the Seventh* (1904). In self-consciously exquisite prose, George Rose, the hero of this novel, is translated from expelled seminarian to Pope and then sets about reforming the world only to be assassinated by a socialist incorrigible. The prose of *Chronicles of the House of Borgia* (1901) is perhaps even more self-indulgent, but this less accessible book has helped make Rolfe a major exemplar of decadent style.

Apart from some poetry, the novels *Nicholas Crabbe* (written 1904, published 1958) and *The Desire and Pursuit of the Whole* (written 1909–1910, published 1934) express most clearly Rolfe's admiration for adolescent beauty. Not this subject matter but venomous caricatures and Rolfe's business troubles kept the books from being published in his own day. Both works are structured as romances of androgynous obsession somewhat in the manner of Théophile Gautier's *Mademoiselle de Maupin* (1835–1836). Crabbe's beloved in the novel that bears his name is based on Rolfe's sometime poetic collaborator Sholto Douglas. The sad conclusion of the novel suggests that Rolfe believed that such relationships could not succeed, at least among Englishmen.

In *The Desire and Pursuit of the Whole,* however, Rolfe contrives to give his story a happy ending. In this book, Crabbe rescues an apparent boy from an earthquake and, although ostensibly pleased to discover that the one he has saved is really a girl, brings his beloved back to Venice outfitted as the fascinating gondolier Zildo (modeled on Rolfe's special friend of the time, Ermenegildo Vianello). But Crabbe loses his ability to sustain the relationship and is finally tempted to suicide when illness reduces him to feminine passivity and leaves him unable to sort out disagreements with publishers or to circumvent the enmity of inconstant friends. However, in masculine guise, Zildo, having recovered the patrimony lost in the earthquake, rescues Crabbe through creative business management and a timely blood transfusion. By reversing the sexual dynamics normally prescribed for man and woman (or man and boy), this parable ends with the two about to complete their romance in marriage, a naked and improbable wish fulfillment.

—*Edmund Miller*

BIBLIOGRAPHY

Benkovitz, Miriam J. *Frederick Rolfe, Baron Corvo.* New York: Putnam, 1977. ■ Gilsdorf, Jeanette W., and Nicholas A. Salerno. "Frederick W. Rolfe, Baron Corvo: An Annotated Bibliography of Writings about Him." *English Literature in Transition* 23 (1980): 3–83. ■ Symons, A. J. A. *Quest for Corvo: An Experiment in Biography.* Intro. Julian Symons, 1934. Harmondsworth: Penguin, 1966. ■ Woolf, Cecil, and Brocard Sewell, eds. *New Quests for Corvo: A Collection of Essays by Various Hands.* Intro. Pamela Hansford Johnson. London: Icon, 1961.

Roman Literature

For the most part, classical Latin poetry on homosexual themes closely follows Greek models. Nevertheless, the cultures held sharply differing attitudes toward male love. In ancient Greece, the mentorship associated with pederasty was intended to prepare youths for active citizenship; consequently, love affairs with male slaves were disparaged as inappropriate and undignified. Rome reversed this pattern. A nation of conquerors, the Romans condoned sex with captured or purchased slaves of either sex. Since slaves formed a large part of the population in late republican and imperial times, young male bedmates were available in abundance and freely enjoyed without censure. Cato the Censor complained about 200 B.C. that a handsome slave boy cost as much as a farm. On the other hand, because of the association of homosexuality with slavery, relations with freeborn youth were frowned on as compromising the boy's manhood and civic status. It was the generally accepted view that submission to another male was a "necessity for a slave" and a "disgrace for a freeborn boy." For this reason, a common assumption among modern literary historians is that the boys about whom Latin poets wrote poems were slaves; but this assumption is often open to question. A typical pattern in CATULLUS, Tibullus, VIRGIL, and HORACE is a courtship followed by rejection. Neither of these suggests a master-slave relation where the power of the owner was absolute.

Because the records are fragmentary and confusing, there has been much debate about whether sex with freeborn youth was against the law; the scope and nature of the *Lex Scantinia,* presumed to punish the seduction of boys under seventeen, is much in doubt. Quite possibly, it corresponds to a law mentioned by Quintilian that imposed a substantial fine, but this is not certain. Whatever the law, it seems to have been all but totally ignored. More significant from a literary perspective is the negative view Romans of the classical age generally took toward love as a form of human experience. Though five substantial Greek dialogues extolling the value of love have survived and we have records of about a dozen books now lost, the only significant treatment of the subject in Latin philosophy is to be found in Cicero's *Tusculan Disputations.* Books 32 to 35, which fill barely four or five pages, treat of love under the heading of undesirable perturbations of the soul. Derisively dismissive of Platonic idealizations, and ignoring the traditions of Zeno and the early Stoics that condoned boy-love as morally blameless, Cicero follows Epicurus in denouncing love for either gender as a disturbing emotion to be avoided at all costs. The Greeks' cult of love, he thinks, sprang from the shameless nudity of the Greek gymnasium. Cicero deplores the love poetry of Anacreon and Ibycus, and is shocked that Alcaeus, whom he otherwise admires, should have devoted lines to the subject. He does not distinguish between the love of women and the love of youths; both are equally dangerous. In taking this stand, Cicero comes close to the view of the greatest of Latin philosophical poets. In *On the Nature of Things,* Lucretius warns against the wounding shafts of Venus whether they proceed from a woman or from "a boy with womanish limbs." He urges the afflicted man to plunge into promiscuity as a remedy for love; Cicero, on the contrary, affects a disdain for all forms of sexual experience.

Given this cultural bias, it is not surprising that homosexuality in Latin political oratory is always treated unfavorably. Especially damaging was any hint that a man had taken a passive role in male relations or entered into them for the purpose of mercenary or political gain. Rhetorical accusations of this kind abounded in the politic arena in late republican times. Cataline, Pompey, Caesar, Clodius, Antony, and Octavius were all subject to them. Cicero himself develops attacks along this line unsparingly in his orations against Verres, Gabinius, Cataline, and most notably, Mark Antony. For example, Antony is accused of having played the catamite to Curio as a teenager for venial reasons in an affair Cicero claims first-hand knowledge of. This is taken to establish Antony's inherent slavishness and to explain psychologically his willingness to submit to the political tyranny of Caesar.

Yet in spite of this cultural prejudice, homoerotic poems are part of the repertory of nearly all the major Latin love poets. This schizophrenia is undoubtedly due to the influence of Greek culture. Rome's attitude to Greece was profoundly ambivalent. Triumphing over the Greeks militarily, the Romans were nevertheless quickly forced to recognize their superiority in art, philosophy, and literature. Greece was on the one hand the land of luxury and decadence, but it was also the fountainhead of all that was highest in intellectual and aesthetic culture. The first important Latin comic writer, Plautus, borrowed plots from the Athenian stage. However, the treatment of homosexuality in Plautus' comedies probably reflects Roman manners of his own time, that is ca 200 B.C.; all the sexual encounters are between masters and slaves. Intrigues or joking banter based on homosexuality occur in the *Casina, Asinaria, Captivi,* and *Mostellaria.* Plautus' braggart soldier in the *Miles Gloriosus* has an eye for both genders.

These plays were popular entertainment for unlettered crowds. Among cultivated Romans, ambivalence about erotic poetry in the Greek tradition is dramatically highlighted in Aulus Gellius' *Attic Nights* (ca 140 A.D.). Here Greek and Latin literati meet in Athens to argue in favor of their own languages. The Greeks point out that Latin poetry lacks the charms of Aphrodite. In response, the Latin rhetorician Julianus covers his head (like Socrates when he repeats the libertine ideas of Lysias in the *Phaedrus*) and recites in "exceedingly tender tones" four love poems, two addressed to males. The homoerotic poems, which show a strong Greek influence, are by Quintus Catulus, a Hellenized Roman general who was consul with Marius in 102 B.C., and his contemporary, Valerius Aeditus.

Roman inconsistency in matters of love is amusingly demonstrable in the case of Cicero himself. Despite his public posture in the Senate and his philosophical writings, in which he attacks Greek love and erotic poetry, we have evidence, in the letters of Pliny the Younger, that Cicero in private life was less austere. Pliny, wondering whether it might be respectable for a Roman official to write erotic verse, plucks up courage from the example of Cicero, who, he tells us, wrote poems about kissing his freedman, Tiro. Tiro, who began life as a slave, became Cicero's secretary and literary executor. After his mentor's death, he wrote his biography and had a distinguished literary career of his own. The relation thus provides a parallel in Roman life with the Greek *erastes-eromenos* bond and the traditions of the Platonic Academy.

Roman literature in the last days of the republic and the reign of Augustus exhibits a deep cultural conflict. Livy, in his history, had painted a picture of early Rome as a society of unpolished, hard-working farmers who despised luxury and dissipation. Catullus reacted violently against such a lifestyle. "Let us live and love," he tells Lesbia, and ignore the criticism of "crabbed old men." Catullus is most famous for his passionate poems to his mistress, but his poems to a boy named Juventius go even further in breaking taboos. "Lesbia" was a pseudonym for Clodia; Catullus calls Juventius the "flower of the Juventii," thus violating the convention that had made pseudonyms in love poems *de rigueur* by revealing that his beloved was not a slave but a youth from a distinguished family. Catullus' aggressive machismo finds expression in the abuse he repeatedly heaps on *cinaedi* (sexually passive males), whom he threatens with anal and oral rape. Nevertheless, in his longest poem, "Atthis," he shows a strange fascination—almost an identification—with this mythological figure who, as part of the ritual of the cult of "great Mother" is feminized by his self-emasculation.

The poetry of Catullus is passionate, vivid, and often brutal. Tibullus is a gentler soul. But in his own way, he is also in revolt against the *mos maiorum*, the ancient Roman code, especially that part of it that glorified conquest and domination. He prefers love to war, which he denounces as mere spoliation. Tibullus, in his love elegies, contributes something unique to Latin poetry, a verse essay on how to court a boy. In a sense this elegy (1.4) prefigures Ovid's *Art of Love* as a treatise on seduction. But it lacks Ovid's sophisticated, detached, man-of-the-world tone; instead, the poem is suffused with what can only be described as a kind of tender wistfulness as Tibullus describes his susceptibility to the touching mixture of shyness and self-assurance he finds in male adolescents. It is also hard to imagine, as he describes these elaborate, devoted wooings, that he is writing about slaves. At the end of the poem, he reveals his own passion for the unresponsive Marathus. In elegy nine, we find that Marathus, who had sworn devotion, has now deserted him for a wealthier suitor; the wounded Tibullus hopes this rival's wife will be just as unfaithful. These vicissitudes are a standard part of Latin love elegies, and identical with the complications we find in the heterosexual affairs they usually describe, as, for instance, in Tibullus' poems about his mistress Delia.

Even poets who do not write about their own involvements with boys take bisexuality for granted. When Propertius' affair with Cynthia goes awry, he makes an exasperated wish: If my enemy is in love, may it be with a girl, if my friend, with a boy. He provides sympathetic counsel to his fellow poet Gallus who loves a boy, warning him to keep the youth away from women. To make his point, he retells at length THEOCRITUS' tale of Hercules' love for Hylas, whom he lost to the nymphs of the pool.

Though bisexuality is all but ubiquitous in Latin love poetry, it was mainly three poets who transmitted knowledge of this tradition to medieval Europe: Horace, Virgil, and, above all, Ovid. Since awareness of Greek literature was largely lost in the west after the fall of Rome, they were unique conduits for the gay literary heritage to later times.

Horace himself had a first-hand knowledge of Greece, having been a student at Athens. He felt sufficiently at ease with its ancient literature to experiment with the archaic meters of Archilochus, SAPPHO, and Alcaeus, poets as remote in his time as CHAUCER is in ours. He sings of Anacreon's love for Bathyllus, perhaps hinting at his friend Maecenas' love for a handsome contemporary actor of that name. He tells us that his protective father always chaperoned him on the way to school to preserve him from "infamy." This reminds us that male "chastity" in Roman culture meant not abstinence from affairs with women (these did not count) but only with males, and then only from participation in a passive role. But Horace had no compunction about sex with boys when he matured. In the second poem of his third book of satires, he imagines a dour Stoic philosopher named Damasippus scolding him for his "thousand boys" and "thousand girls," a rebuke Horace shrugs off. In his eleventh epode, he complains (or boasts?) that "love sets me as it sets no other man, / Yearning for soft lads or tender girls." His attitude to sex is that of Diogenes and the Greek Cynics; such urges should be satisfied with the least possible fuss. Again, slavery made such easy gratification possible. He is an Epicurean not in the style of Epicurus, who was wary of sexual pleasure, but of Lucretius, though he does not manifest Lucretius' specific fear of emotional involvement. Only once in his many poems about women and boys do we feel a real poignancy. In the first poem of his fourth book of odes, published when he was fifty-two, Horace laments that he can no longer hope for the reciprocal love of "woman or boy," and mourns the indifference of Ligurinus, who haunts his frustrated dreams.

In the eleventh century, Norman clerical poets, writing medieval Latin verse, harked back to Horace, referring pointedly to his love poems to boys. In a later age, BYRON used Latin phrases from Horace's poems to communicate his own homosexual interests in letters to knowledgeable friends and made the adjective "Horatian" a code word for "bisexual."

Virgil, as the author of Rome's national epic the *Aeneid*, ranks as Rome's greatest poet. He is of importance for the gay literary heritage for two reasons. He wrote the most famous of Latin homoerotic poems (his second, or Corydon, eclogue) and he also made a serious attempt to introduce the heroic tradition of Greek love into Latin literature.

Virgil found a place at the center of Roman political culture. This set him apart from poets like Catullus, who had mocked his elders; Tibullus, who renounced war for peace on his farm; and Propertius, who, hearing of a new law that might separate him from his mistress, wondered why he should be expected to supply sons for the battlefield. In effect, much classical Latin poetry belongs to what we would today call a counterculture. Ovid was just as little interested in the heroic as a theme, and rejected it for love and romantic myths. In this, he took his place with the poets of the erotic revolt, but at a cost. He was exiled by the irate Augustus, ostensibly for publishing the *Art of Love,* a treatise that made no careful distinction between the seduction of citizen's wives and more conventionally accessible Roman demimondaines.

Ovid's treatment of homosexuality was less inflammatory. He writes no poems to boys himself but, like his fellow poets, he assumes the universality of bisexuality. At the beginning of his *Loves,* he laments that he has "no boy to sing of" or "long-haired girl," these being equally acceptable subjects for the erotic poet. Unlike most Romans he does, however, state a clear preference. In the *Art of Love,* he says he favors the embraces of a woman because boys get less pleasure from sexual encounters. But this lack of personal involvement did not prevent him from exploiting the homoerotic elements in Greek myth to the full when he came to write the *Metamorphoses.* Such myths were to evoke the special wrath of the Fathers of the Church as evincing the immorality of Greco-Roman paganism. For Ovid, however, stories of the loves of the gods for beautiful boys were simply raw material to be exploited poetically. As a result, Ovid was the main source for such myths in the Middle Ages, when he became, somewhat surprisingly, the favorite poet of Christian Europe, much admired and widely quoted and imitated in what has been called "the Age of Ovid."

Ovid sets the homoerotic stories of the *Metamorphoses* within a particular narrative frame. The Greek poet Phanocles, writing in the third century B.C., had produced a poem called *The Loves, or Beautiful Boys* in which he anthologized the legends of gods (such as Dionysus) and heroes (such as Tantalus and Agamemnon) who had loved youths. Among these stories was the tale of Orpheus who, after the death of his wife Eurydice, had turned from the love of women to the love of boys. Ovid adopts this version

of the Orpheus legend in book ten of the *Metamorphoses*. He speculates philosophically about the causes of the change in Orpheus' erotic interests: Perhaps, he conjectures, this was Orpheus' way of remaining faithful to his dead wife. The women of Thrace, however, are jealous and insulted by his neglect. To make matters worse, the Thracian men, who had not experienced such loves before, imitate Orpheus' example. Because of this myth, Orpheus was sometimes identified as the "inventor" of pederasty. For this distinction, he competed with several other figures in Greek legend—Zeus, King Minos of Crete, Thamyris (another Thracian bard of early times), and Laius of Thebes. Ovid has Orpheus, in this new phase of his life, sing of "pretty boys whom gods desire." We hear the story of Jupiter, who turns himself into an eagle to carry off the Trojan prince Ganymede. Through Ovid's tale, and a plenitude of Hellenistic works of art, Ganymede entered the literature of the Middle Ages and the Renaissance as the archetypal beloved boy.

Orpheus' stories make book ten the preeminently gay book of the *Metamorphoses.* Two of Orpheus' tales involve boys beloved of Apollo who die pathetically in early youth, Cyparissus and Hyacinth. Cyparissus dies of grief over the death of a pet deer and is turned into a tree. Hyacinth is killed when Apollo throws a discus that accidentally strikes him; from his blood springs the "sanguine flower inscribed with woe" of MILTON's "Lycidas." Ganymede and the eagle and Apollo and Hyacinth both inspired sculpture in the Renaissance by the bisexual Benvenuto Cellini. The death of Hyacinth at the hands of his lover is a common theme in early medieval poetry. Byron, on the eve of his departure from England in 1809, looked forward to finding "hyacinths" and other exotic flowers in Greece.

Orpheus' own death is equally tragic but more brutal. The angry Thracian women, in the guise of fierce Maenads, kill him with spears and stones, and dismember his body. Their master Bacchus, incensed at the death of the poet, punishes them by turning them into oak trees. The fable made a strong impression on the Middle Ages. The unknown author of the *Ovide Moralizé,* writing in the early fourteenth century, blamed Orpheus for having invented a love "against nature and against the law." In that part of the *Romance of the Rose* assigned to Jean de Meun, the allegorical figure of "Genius" declares that Orpheus deserved hanging for having led men to abandon heterosexuality. After 1600, the Orpheus story, as in the libretti for famous operas by Peri, Monteverdi, and Gluck, almost always centers on the poet's love for Eurydice, and the homosexual coda to his story is suppressed. However, the Renaissance humanist, ANGELO POLIZIANO, used the Ovidian ending in the finale of a play he wrote for the court of Mantua about 1480. In *La favola di Orfeo,* Poliziano has Orpheus "pluck the new flowers, the springtime of the better (!) sex, when men are all lithe and slender." A decade later Albrecht Dürer made an impressive drawing of the scene from Ovid. It shows Orpheus on his knees as two Maenads club him to death; the drawing bears a revealing inscription in German, "Orfeus, der erst puseran"—"Orpheus, the first sodomite."

Not all the homoerotic stories of the *Metamorphosis* are in book ten. Book three tells the tale of Narcissus. In Ovid's version, Narcissus is loved by girls *and* boys, but it is specifically a boy he scorns who sets the curse on him; he falls fatally in love with another "lovely boy" when he sees his image reflected in a pool. Lesbianism is a theme rarely treated in Latin literature, but one story in book nine describes the love of two girls. Iphis, who has been raised as a boy, falls in love with Ianthe. But though Ovid regards the love of boys as commonplace, love between females is unthinkable in his world. Ovid represents Iphis as shocked and horrified when she discovers her feelings; a benevolent goddess resolves the impasse by changing her into a boy. An unknown medieval author borrowed this last detail for the parallel episode of Princess Ide and Olive in the Huon of Bordeaux romance, probably written in the early fourteenth century. Here the Virgin Mary performs a similar miracle to save the lesbian lovers, who have done no more than kiss and embrace, from being burned at the stake. (See also MYTH.)

Latin writers produced little prose fiction; by far the most significant achievement in this genre is the *Satyricon* of PETRONIUS, which has been acclaimed as the first gay novel. The main plot involves homosexual intrigues, as the low-life protagonist Encolpius ("the crotch") fights to keep possession of the effeminate Giton. The novel is a masterwork of satirical realism, probably written for the court of Nero. The nouveau riche ex-slave Trimalchio admits to having served his former master in bed; he fondles his own handsome slave boy at the most monstrously extravagant feast in literature.

The poet Statius was a younger contemporary of Petronius; one of the poems in a collection he entitled *Silvae* is unique in Latin poetry (2.6). It is an elegy in which Statius expresses his sympathy for his friend Flavius Ursus, who has suffered the loss of a beloved slave boy. It shows that such slaves were not always pretty darlings, for the fifteen-year-old Philetus is compared, not to Ganymede but to Theseus and Achilles, and his love for his master is assimilated to the heroic tradition of Greek pederasty; Statius characterizes Ursus' love as Cecropian, that is, Athenian. With Virgil's Nisus and Euryalus, this poem stands alone as an instance of this kind of idealistic Hellenizing in Latin literature.

Both Statius and Martial flattered the tyrannical emperor Domitian (r. 81–96), but this is all they have in common. Martial's fourteen books of *Epigrams* are a veritable sexual encyclopedia, which throw a flood of light on popular attitudes in imperial Rome. Martial is unabashedly bisexual and represents himself as defending his pederastic escapades to his wife, citing the examples of Jupiter, Hercules, Apollo, and Achilles. He writes many poems about kissing boys in the style of Catullus' poems to Juventius. He professes to like effeminate youths but also fantasizes an affair with an exotic blond Egyptian who is "a man to others" but a girl to him. Although astonishingly candid about his own tastes, he is also relentless in exposing, in poems in which the victim is safely pseudonymous, what he perceives to be transgressions against the Latin code of sexual behavior on the part of others. In these epigrams, Martial excoriates adult male passives, stereotypical lesbians, and women or men who perform oral sex with either gender, but admits to enjoying fellation by women. His epigrams are the equivalent of a modern scandal sheet, reporting spicy vignettes from contemporary Roman life, for example, the shocking news of a mock marriage between "brawny Callistratus" and "bearded Afer."

Like his friend Martial, Juvenal is a satirist. His second satire attacks effeminate adult male homosexuals. Indeed, its 170 lines make it the longest pronouncement on homosexuality by any Latin writer in any genre. Where Martial does not profess to be a moralist but merely reflects the everyday prejudices of the man in the street, Juvenal presents himself, in his much more elaborate essays, as an austere defender of traditional Roman values in a degenerate age. Juvenal begins by attacking men who appear and act masculine, and assume airs of moral superiority, but are secretly *cinaedi.* He professes to prefer open effeminacy but immediately afterward ridicules men who wear see-through robes in public, or necklaces, or ribbons, or "bright blue checks." He singles out, as an alarming development of his times, the appearance of effeminate homosexuality in ancient Roman families who at one time exemplified the city's masculine military might, as in the case of a Gracchus who had appeared as a bride at a homosexual wedding.

On the basis of Juvenal's loud vituperations, one might be tempted simply to classify him as a rabid homophobe. But this would be to overlook the difference between Roman perceptions in such matters and our own. For example, in his sixth satire, Juvenal attacks women, in one of the most vehemently misogynist works of all time, as moral monsters no sane man would think of marrying. He then advocates that a man, to spare himself the trials of heterosexual marriage, should prefer as a bedfellow some undemanding boy who will not nag or quarrel or try to wheedle gifts.

This may seem contradictory to modern readers who recollect the vitriol of Juvenal's second satire, but in Rome it was not felt as inconsistent to denounce one kind of homosexuality while condoning another. The crucial point was not the gender of a man's sexual companion but the role he played; so long as a man was the active partner his masculinity went unimpugned. Apparently Juvenal's proposal in satire six was more than a mere rhetorical gambit. There is other evidence that he had a sexual preference for males. A poem by Martial inviting Juvenal to his country home recommends a young huntsman with whom, he says, Juvenal will enjoy consorting "in some secret woods." Since some of the fiercest literary attacks on *cinaedi* come from writers who themselves show marked homosexual or bisexual interests, one may speculate that they were inspired by an anxiety to establish that their liking for male partners was of the "right" sort.

When we look at the treatment of homosexuality in Latin biography, we are struck by the contrast with comparable works in Greek. Suetonius was a younger contemporary of PLUTARCH; the date of the *Lives of the Caesars* (ca 140 A.D.) is not much later than the *Parallel Lives,* but the way in which male love enters the picture is strikingly different. Plutarch regards it as natural and even honorific that a ruler like Pisistratus might have an *erastes* like Solon. Agesilaus, whom Plutarch presents as the most admirable of Sparta's kings, is identified as the *eromenos,* or beloved, of Lysander and as a fatherly and benign patron of young men who are lovers. Alexander's love for the beautiful Persian youth Bagoas is portrayed sympathetically. Epaminondas' male loves are cited as examples of heroic devotion, and the Theban approval of same-sex ties that made possible the victories of the city's Sacred Band is extolled as wise civic policy.

In contrast, although Suetonius ascribes homosexual relations to all but two of the twelve emperors he writes of, there is not a single instance in which these references are not used to impute something shameful about the ruler's character. Caesar was Nicomedes' passive partner, Tiberius exploited children, Caligula allowed himself to be mounted, Nero castrated his lover Sporus and played the shrinking virgin in the arms of another man, and so on. Clearly Suetonius is continuing in his imperial biographies the same tradition we find in the speeches of Cicero and other republican orators; male relations are a part of Latin political discourse only when the leader whose life is under scrutiny is indicted as a *cinaedus* or a seducer of freeborn boys.

Claudius and Vespasian are the only emperors to escape such accusations in Suetonius. In Roman biography, it is hard to find any reference to a distinguished citizen's male affairs that is even neutral in tone, let alone laudatory. The life of Virgil by Donatus (or Suetonius) would be one rare example. Another would be Dio Cassius' comments on the emperor Trajan. Trajan was a successful, humane, and popular prince for whom the Senate voted the title "Optimus," the "best" of rulers. Dio remarks that Trajan had a passion for boys and wine, but that he was never anything but sober, and "in his relation with boys he harmed no one."

In Suetonius and in the satire of Martial and Juvenal, we find a clear contrast between Greek and Latin traditions at the beginning of the second century A.D. Nevertheless, other evidence shows that the Hellenic renaissance that marked the age of the Antonines also influenced Latin literature on love. We have noted the poem Statius wrote to his friend to console him for the death of a loved slave boy in which the heroic Greek ideal is pervasive. This confluence of the two cultures is also notable in a speech of Apuleius'. The author of the *The Golden Ass* had been arraigned on a charge of sorcery in a Roman court in North Africa about 150; his accuser made use of Apuleius' love poems to boys to argue against his claim that he was a serious philosopher. To defend himself, Apuleius cites Greek poets like Anacreon and Alcman, and to demonstrate that serious men might also write homoerotic lyrics, quotes verse by Solon and PLATO. But he adds to this tradition Latin poems by Valerius Aeditus and Quintus Catulus—though not, surprisingly, the Juventius poems of the more famous Gaius Catullus— and even poems by the emperor Hadrian, who had died a few years previously. Since Apuleius' use of pseudonyms in his poems had been represented as a sinister detail, Apuleius is at pains to show that this was accepted as proper, and that those poets (like the early satirist Lucilius) who had used real names had been strongly criticized. But the most striking touch in his oration is his appeal in the peroration to the Platonic ideal of Uranian love as set forth in Pausanias' speech in the *Symposium*. This is very far from Cicero's contemptuous ridicule of such ideas two centuries earlier.

This confluence of the two cultures manifests itself also in the literary movement known as the Second

Sophistic, which came to fruition near the end of the second century. It included rhetoricians like Maximus of Tyre, who delivered speeches on Socratic love in Rome in the reign of Commodus (ca 190), and Philostratus, another Greek rhetorician at the court of the Severan empress Julia Domna. Philostratus' works include a collection of *Love Letters* by imaginary characters; almost half of his sixty letters are addressed to boys. His Latin contemporary Aelian, writing in Greek for a Roman audience, included a significant number of anecdotes about Greek love relations from Sparta, Thebes, Athens, and Macedonia in his popular *Historical Miscellanies*.

Nothing in the second century, however, so well symbolized the convergence of Greek and Latin traditions as the love of the emperor Hadrian for the Greek boy Antinous. Perhaps the most brilliant of all the emperors, Hadrian was an ardent student of Greek literature, religion, and history. He commemorated Epaminondas and the Sacred Band by raising a monument with a laudatory poem on the battlefield of Leuctra where the Theban hero had died and been buried with his lover. Hadrian had lived in Athens as its archon under his predecessor Trajan, and added to the city a new suburb, a magnificent temple of Jupiter, a library, and a gymnasium. At Thespiae in Boeotia, site of a famous temple of Eros, Hadrian inscribed a poem to the God of Love and the Uranian Aphrodite. Apuleius, as we have seen, claimed to have read Hadrian's own love poems to boys, which have, unfortunately, been lost. However, fragments of a poem by the Alexandrian poet Pancrates on a dramatic episode in the life of Hadrian have survived; they tell how the emperor saved the life of Antinous in a lion hunt in Libya. When Antinous, still in his early youth, drowned in the Nile, Hadrian mourned his death extravagantly, built a majestic new city on the site in his honor, had him deified as the founder of a new mystery religion, and filled the empire with statues of the beautiful youth, some of which rank among the greatest masterpieces of the Hellenistic period. In modern literature, the love affair of the emperor and his favorite is acutely and sympathetically analyzed in MARGUERITE YOURCENAR's historical novel, *Memoirs of Hadrian* (1951), which purports to reconstruct Hadrian's lost autobiography. It was this work, equally impressive for its literary quality and for its historical erudition, that led to Yourcenar's election to the French Academy as its first woman member. (See also GREEK LITERATURE, ANCIENT.)

—Louis Crompton

BIBLIOGRAPHY

Cantarella, Eva. *Bisexuality in the Ancient World.* Trans. C. Ó Cuilleánáin. New Haven: Yale University Press, 1992. ■ Cody, Jane. "The *Senex Amator* in Plautus' *Casina.*" *Hermes* 104(1976): 453–474. ■ Dynes, Wayne. "Orpheus without Eurydice." *Gai Saber* 1(1978): 268–273. ■ *Encyclopedia of Homosexuality.* Wayne Dynes, ed. 2 vols. New York: Garland, 1990. ■ Lambert, Royston. *Beloved and God: The Story of Hadrian and Antinous.* New York: Viking, 1984. ■ Lilja, Saara. *Homosexuality in Republican and Augustan Rome.* Helsinki: Societas Scientificarum Fennica, 1983. ■ MacMullen, Ramsay. "Roman Attitudes to Greek Love." *Historia* 31(1982): 484–502. ■ Richardson, T. Wade. "Homosexuality in the *Satyricon.*" *Classica et Mediaevalia* 35(1984): 104–127. ■ Verstraete, Beert. "Slavery and the Social Dynamics of Male Homosexuality in Ancient Rome." *Journal of Homosexuality* 5(1980): 227–236.

ROMANTIC FRIENDSHIP

Romantic Friendship, Female

§ Many historians believe that, until the late nineteenth and early twentieth centuries, intimate, exclusive, and often erotic relations between white women of the middle and upper classes were perceived as normal and compatible with heterosexuality in Anglo-European culture. A variety of terms have emerged for communicating the rich history of these relationships while preserving the distinctions between them and contemporary homosexual relations. Today the most commonly used term for such relationships between women is "Romantic Friendship."

Elizabeth Mavor, in *The Ladies of Llangollen: A Study of Romantic Friendship* (1971), addresses the apparent social acceptability of love between women in eighteenth-century England. In her study of ELEA-NOR BUTLER AND SARAH PONSONBY, two women who eloped together, she notes that Ponsonby's family, though concerned, was relieved that she had not eloped with a man. *The Hamwood Papers of the Ladies of Llangollen and Caroline Hamilton* notes that one relative, apparently believing that "improprieties" occurred only between the sexes, remarked of Sarah's conduct: "'though it has an appearance of imprudence, is I am sure void of serious impropriety. There were no gentlemen concerned, nor does it appear to be anything more than a scheme of Romantic Friendship.'"

Although Elizabeth Mavor uses the eighteenth-century phrase *Romantic Friendship* in her study of the "Ladies of Llangollen," it did not achieve wide usage in historical and literary scholarship until the publication of Lillian Faderman's *Surpassing the Love of Men: Romantic Friendship and Love Between Women from the Renaissance to the Present* (1981). Faderman applies the term to a wide range of women's emotional, passionate, and occasionally erotic relationships with each other before World War I in the United States, Great Britain, and other countries in Western Europe, most notably France. But more important than the history of the phrase is the history of the idea—an idea defined by historians and literary scholars—and its implications for gay and lesbian studies in general.

William R. Taylor and Christopher Lasch offer an early discussion of the phenomena of what they called "sororial relations" in nineteenth-century American culture. They were among the first historians to acknowledge the presence of such relationships, to recognize the element of social acceptance surrounding them, and to contend that calling them "lesbian" was historically inaccurate. Historian Carroll Smith-Rosenberg applauds Taylor and Lasch's attention to a phenomenon which, she says, "consciously or unconsciously we have chosen to ignore." But rather than seeing this "female world of love and ritual" as an effect of the disintegration of familial bonds, as Taylor and Lasch did, Smith-Rosenberg sees it as emerging during a period of intense concern about the dangers of heterosexual relations in which separate homosocial spheres of interaction became safe places in which intimate relations between women were "socially acceptable and fully compatible with heterosexual marriage." Lillian Faderman's study of Romantic Friendship, mentioned earlier, is the most exhaustive and influential to date. She suggests that Romantic Friendship was celebrated, even fashionable, until the twentieth century. Although cross-dressing and other signs of usurping male power and privilege were often met with punitive measures, intimacy and erotic expressions between women rarely were. She contends that women were often innocent of the sexual implications of their exclusive and passionate bonds with one another, having internalized the view that women were sexually passionless. Only in a post-Freudian era, she claims, were women generally aware of their sexual potential. Faderman locates the great transformation in public perception of same-sex intimacy at the end of the nineteenth and beginning of the twentieth century, when sexologists began to define such relations as both "lesbian" and "perverse." Until then, they were innocently, and ambiguously, defined as Romantic Friendships and held a socially acceptable position in Anglo-European culture.

This idea of Romantic Friendship provided literary scholars with a new way to read passionate expressions exchanged between women in literature written before the twentieth century. Faderman's own study evolved from an interest in the poetry and letters of EMILY DICKINSON, a nineteenth-century American poet whose letters to future sister-in-law Sue Gilbert contained profuse articulations of love and longing. Faderman and others have noted the license taken by many twentieth-century biographers who omitted the more passionate language between women or made great efforts to explain such language as symptomatic of a more sentimental era in history. One biography of Mary Wollstonecraft typifies the circumspect attitude with which biographers approached the subject. The biographer remarked that it was a "relief" to discover that Wollstonecraft had "a certain secret disloyalty" to Fanny Blood, to whom she wrote many professions of love; apparently the biographer invoked such disloyalty as evidence that Wollstonecraft was not lesbian.

Nineteenth-century British writer George Eliot apparently patterned many of the close female friendships in her early novels on her Romantic Friendship with Sara Sophia Hennell, but later became concerned about the lesbian implications of her writing. Fluent in German and traveling in international intellectual circles, Eliot was undoubtedly aware of the growing interest among German scientists in sexual pathology, something that may have contributed to her abandoning lesbian themes. Faderman suggests that literature specifically linking lesbian love with evil and pathology was well-developed in France and Germany several years before it became the paradigmatic form of representation in the United States and Great Britain. She cites many examples of lesbian evil and exoticism in the work of French writers Gautier, BALZAC, Zola, and BAUDELAIRE.

Nineteenth-century American literature is not without its own share of pathological lesbian representation, however. Margaret J. M. Sweat's *Ethel's Love-Life: A Novel* (1859) presents Leonora as an "organism" whose peculiar pathology is related to her love for other women. Louisa May Alcott, best known for her contributions to children's literature, wrote two novels that, though typical of the Romantic Friendship model in some ways, also hint at something less "innocent." In *Work: A Story of Experience* (1873), Christie and Rachel's romantic friendship is destroyed by Rachel's attraction for a vaguely described sin. In *An Old-Fashioned Girl* (1870), Rebecca and Lizzie, though idealized as feminist artists, are also expected to be "mannish and rough" by the conventional Fanny, who ultimately describes them as a "different race of creatures."

HENRY JAMES and MARY WILKINS FREEMAN have come to be read as transitional figures whose writings represent a shift from the social acceptance of Romantic Friendship in nineteenth-century American culture to the redefinition of same-sex intimacies as pathological or perverse in the twentieth century. In *The Bostonians* (1886) James depicts the "Boston marriage" between Olive and Verena as a wholly conventional aspect of New England life. But he also represents Olive's role in the relationship as manipulative and vampiric. Mary Wilkins Freeman's short piece of detective fiction, "The Long Arm" (1895), represents the culture's growing distrust of relations between women but also gives voice to those who feel their Romantic Friendships are under siege from a culture that does not understand a broader definition of family and home.

The writing of SARAH ORNE JEWETT and WILLA CATHER, appearing a generation apart, indicates the swiftness of this transition from social acceptability to outcast identity. Jewett, writing at the end of the nineteenth century, is able to depict Romantic Friendships between women rather openly, as in "Martha's Lady." But, as Sharon O'Brien has demonstrated, Cather employs a more encoded language. Critics have interpreted Cather's use of male narrators as a rhetorical strategy that enabled her to articulate a lesbian sensibility without appearing lesbian to a culture increasingly uncomfortable with same-sex intimacy. Jewett, Cather's mentor in many ways, objected to Cather's literary cross-dressing, seeing it as a disingenuous "masquerade" for her true feelings. But Jewett did not understand the new sexual culture in which Cather was writing. Jewett probably would have been surprised to find that her own posthumously published letters were censored, four fifths of them being omitted altogether.

The Romantic Friendship hypothesis provided a nonthreatening context for discovering and writing about literary foremothers, an important project in lesbian literary studies in the 1970s. For a culture whose existence had been made invisible and whose history had been erased, finding historical role models, literary foremothers to whom we could look for validation and representation, was empowering. In this respect, the idea of Romantic Friendship has provided both a history and an education about historical accuracy. We now have a sense of the variety of forms that homosocial arrangements have taken in Anglo-European cultures over the last 400 years. We also have learned that what looks familiar to a contemporary gay or lesbian reader may have meant something entirely different to the author of an earlier text, an idea that was theorized more completely by MICHEL FOUCAULT. This idea of homosexuality as a recently socially constructed domain of identity has encouraged long overdue reconsiderations of what constitutes "lesbian literature": Is it writing by self-identified lesbians, writing about lesbians, or writing with which the contemporary lesbian reader identifies? Or, is lesbian a metaphor for resistance? Is lesbian literature writing that disobeys more generally the male and heterosexual conventions of language and narrative?

Although the Romantic Friendship hypothesis provided lesbian readers with a host of foremothers and a more complicated notion of lesbian history and literature, it also, according to some, understated the element of sexuality. *Surpassing the Love of Men* seems comfortable with dismissing the issue of genital sexuality between women, seeing it as a relatively insignificant aspect of lesbian identity. Whereas the "woman-identified-woman" of the 1970s and early 1980s celebrated the notion of Romantic Friendship, "queers" of the 1990s, perhaps informed by the feminist "sex wars," often see the whole concept as conspicuously asexual, a reduction of lesbian genealogy to a continuous history of feminists who like to cuddle. Some contemporary critics, like Lisa Moore, feel that the model, though enlarging the canon of lesbian literary history, has created a "prohibition against reading sex between women in history." The erasure of the sexual potential of homosocial relations in the Romantic Friendship hypothesis is itself an indication of the fact that the idea emerged at a particular moment in the recent history of lesbian-feminist politics. Informed by ADRIENNE RICH's idea of a "lesbian continuum" and the concept of the "woman-identified-woman," the Romantic Friendship hypothesis, as an invention of historians and literary scholars, was an expression of the lesbian-feminist values of the late 1970s and early 1980s. Faderman admits that she found a "contemporary analog to romantic friendship" in lesbian-feminism, and that "in a sense female same-sex love had come full circle."

Although Faderman's most recent book, *Odd Girls and Twilight Lovers*, claims that "women's intimate relationships were universally encouraged in centuries outside of our own," thus more firmly inscribing the distinction between the nineteenth and twentieth centuries, the assumptions underlying the Romantic Friendship hypothesis continue to be reconsidered. Lisa Moore has argued that the ideology of romantic friendship coexisted with a "wariness" of women's sexual relations with each other. She reads English writer Maria Edgeworth's novel *Belinda* (1801) and the Pirie and Woods trial of two Scottish teachers accused of having sex with a pupil as illustrating the fear of lesbian sexuality and the attempt to dissociate it from white, middle-class women by blaming it on foreign and servant-class women. Mary E. Wood also departs from the Romantic Friendship hypothesis and the focus on sexological discourse, seeing the ideology of separate homosocial spheres as providing a model that nineteenth-century American women like Margaret Fuller appropriated and manipulated for the creation of a subversive form of lesbian identification.

The idea of Romantic Friendship thus remains a contested category in the history of same-sex relations, a category that ultimately represents the tricky relationship between history and the historian's own contemporary moment. Despite the quibbles over the meaning of intimate and erotic relationships between women prior to the emergence of modern lesbian identity, the Romantic Friendship concept has deepened our understanding of women's relationships in distant and not so distant history. As a part of the idiom of our gay and lesbian literary heritage, Romantic Friendship continues to raise issues about the place of sexuality in lesbian identity and in lesbian literary and social history.

—*Marylynne Diggs*

BIBLIOGRAPHY

Bell, Mrs. G. H. *The Hamwood Papers of the Ladies of Llangollen and Caroline Hamilton*. London: Macmillan, 1930. ■ Bennett, Paula. *Emily Dickinson*. London: Harvester, 1990. ■ Faderman, Lillian. *Odd Girls and Twilight Lovers: A History of Lesbian Life in Twentieth-Century America*. New York: Columbia University Press, 1991. ■ ———. *Surpassing the Love of Men: Romantic Friendship and Love Between Women from the Renaissance to the Present*. New York: William Morrow, 1981. ■ Farwell, Marilyn R. "Heterosexual Plots and Lesbian Subtexts: Toward a Theory of Lesbian Narrative Space." *Lesbian Texts and Contexts: Radical Revisions*. Karla Jay and Joanne Glasgow, eds. New York: New York University Press, 1990. 91–103. ■ Fetterley, Judith. "*My Antonia*, Jim Burden, and the Dilemma of the Lesbian Writer." *Lesbian Texts and Contexts: Radical Revisions*. Karla Jay and Joanne Glasgow, eds. New York: New York University Press, 1990. 145–163. ■ Foucault, Michel. *The History of Sexuality: Volume 1, An Introduction*. 1978. Trans. Robert Hurley. New York: Vintage, 1980. ■ Mavor, Elizabeth. *The Ladies of Llangollen: A Study of Romantic Friendship*. New York: Penguin, 1973. ■ Moore, Lisa. "'Something More Tender Still than Friendship': Romantic Friendship in Early Nineteenth-Century England." *Feminist Studies* 18 (1992): 499–520. ■ O'Brien, Sharon. "'The Thing Not Named': Willa Cather as a Lesbian Writer." *The Lesbian Issue: Essays from Signs*. Estelle B. Freedman et al., eds. Chicago: University of Chicago Press, 1985. 67–90. ■ Rich, Adrienne. "Compulsory Heterosexuality and Lesbian Existence." *Signs* 5 (1980): 631–660. ■ Russ, Joanna. "To Write 'Like a Woman': Transformations of Identity in the Work of Willa Cather." *Historical, Literary, and Erotic Aspects of Lesbianism*. Monika Kehoe, ed. New York: Harrington-Haworth, 1986. 77–87. ■ Smith-Rosenberg, Carroll. "The Female World of Love and Ritual: Relations Between Women in Nineteenth-Century America." *Signs* 1 (1975): 1–29. ■ Stimpson, Catharine R. "Afterword: Lesbian Studies in the 1990s." *Lesbian Texts and Contexts: Radical Revisions*. Karla Jay and Joanne Glasgow, eds. New York: New York University Press, 1990. 377–382. ■ Taylor, William R. and Christopher Lasch. "Two 'Kindred Spirits': Sorority and Family in New England, 1839–1846." *New England Quarterly* 36 (1963): 23–41. ■ Wood, Mary E. "'With Ready Eye': Margaret Fuller and Lesbianism in Nineteenth-Century American Literature." *American Literature* 65 (1993): 1–18. ■ Zimmerman, Bonnie. "'The Dark Eye Beaming': Female Friendship in George Eliot's Fictions." *Lesbian Texts and Contexts: Radical Revisions*. Karla Jay and Joanne Glasgow, eds. New York: New York University Press, 1990. 126–144.

Romantic Friendship, Male

Critics use the term *male romantic friendship* to describe strong attachments between men in works ranging from ancient epics and medieval romances to Renaissance plays, Gothic novels, westerns, and war movies. In traditional scholarship, the term is potentially homophobic: By distinguishing "normal," nonerotic relationships between men from "abnormal," overtly sexual ones, it allays suspicions that literary masterpieces might condone homosexuality. Whenever one critic questions the intensity of Antonio's love for Sebastian in WILLIAM SHAKESPEARE's *Twelfth Night* (1601), for example, another reassures readers that the play merely illustrates a long-standing Renaissance convention of friendship.

By arguing that earlier cultures expressed the least carnal affections in the most impassioned language, such critics ignore the embarrassing possibility that such cultures might have tolerated actual homoeroticism.

Recent work in gender studies exposes the opposition between romantic friendship and homosexuality as a theoretical red herring. In societies that located homosocial relationships along a continuum between the extremes of nonsexual affection and genital contact, distinctions between romantic friendships and homoerotic attachments were less absolute. As critics and historians have come to recognize, earlier cultures accepted the possibility that erotic attraction colored all significant relationships between men. But as norms of "proper" sexual conduct became more codified in the early modern period, readers found the literary records of less homophobic centuries increasingly disturbing. The same-sex couples upheld by previous generations as models of friendship occasioned heated debates. Whereas readers sympathetic to homosexuality hailed Alcibiades's love for Socrates in PLATO's *Symposium* (ca 380 B.C.E.) as proof that the Greeks championed homoeroticism, homophobes glossed it over as a literary convention.

The ancient world proved particularly resistant to the homophobic goal of denying an erotic aspect to romantic friendships in literature and history. Writers in Palestine, Greece, and Rome highly praised such friendships. In the Hebrew Scriptures, David proclaims that Jonathan's love for him "was wonderful, passing the love of women" (II Samuel 1:26). Throughout the *Iliad* (ca 750 B.C.E.), heterosexual desire leads to disaster: Paris's abduction of Helen is the immediate cause of the Trojan War. When Agamemnon steals the maiden Briseis from Achilles, the latter avenges himself by withdrawing from battle and letting the Trojans advance against the Greek camp. But when Achilles learns that Hector has killed his beloved friend Patroclus, he forgets Briseis and resumes the fight against Troy with a ferocity that assures the Greeks of final victory.

The *Iliad* held an obvious moral for later writers: Whereas Achilles's love for a woman led to dangerous divisions among the Greek soldiers, his love for a man inspired decisive military action. The Greek idealization of friendship—further exemplified by such mythical pairings as Damon and Pythias, Pylades and Orestes, Pirithous and Theseus, Hylas and Hercules, Apollo and Hyacinthus—had a strong impact on Roman culture. Cicero's essay "De Amicitia" ("Of Friendship," 44 B.C.E.) evokes the language of erotic union in hailing the mixture of two friends' souls in a single consciousness. Book IX of VIRGIL's *Aeneid* (19 B.C.E.) offers the ancient world's most poignant image of romantic friendship. When Nisus volunteers for the dangerous mission of crossing the enemy camp at night, his comrade Euryalus insists on accompanying him. By testifying to their commitment both to each other and to their country, their tragic death establishes same-sex love as a basis for Roman patriotism. Aeneas himself must renounce the Carthaginian Queen Dido as a distraction from his destiny. But his devotion to a male comrade inspires his last heroic action. Just as Achilles slays Hector to avenge Patroclus, Aeneas kills his arch-antagonist Turnus specifically to avenge the death of his beloved Pallas.

During the Middle Ages, the classical cult of friendship merged with two other traditions of same-sex bonding: the Germanic *comitatus,* or bond of reciprocal obligations between lord and thanes, and Christian monasticism. For centuries Christ's affection for the Apostle John inspired devoted friendships between bishops, priests, monks, scholars, and laity. As John Boswell has noted, Saint Paulinus wrote passionate poetry to Ausonius, Gottschalk expressed tender affection to a younger monk, and Saint Anselm praised Lanfranc and Gilbert in the most extravagant hyperboles.

Medieval works written outside clerical circles often thematize a conflict between same-sex friendship and heterosexual attachment. In the *Decameron* (ca 1351), Boccaccio tells the story of Titus and Gisippus, two friends whose mutual devotion is threatened when Titus falls in love with Gisippus's fiancée. But friendship triumphs when Gisippus offers the girl to Titus to prevent him from dying of unrequited desire. When Gisippus is later condemned for a murder that he did not commit, Titus offers to die in his place. This display of perfect friendship compels the real murderer to confess his crime. The Emperor Octavius then pardons all three men, and Titus returns Gisippus's earlier favor by offering him his sister in marriage. In the *Teseida* (1340–1342), Boccaccio depicts a conflict between same-sex friendship and heterosexual love that has more tragic consequences. Palemone and Arcita are not only cousins but "sworn brothers" who have vowed to defend each other in war and peace. But when they both fall in love with Emilia, they forget their vows and pursue each other's destruction.

The Renaissance revival of classical antiquity went hand-in-hand with a revival of interest in classical friendship. Montaigne's essay "De l'amitié" (1580) praises friendship along Ciceronian lines as a condition superior to all other human relationships. In a misogynistic turn typical of Renaissance discourses on the subject, Montaigne insists that friendship surpasses heterosexual attachment because women are fundamentally incapable of such complete spiritual communion. Writers more skeptical toward classical authority sometimes objected to this exclusion of women. When Ariosto recast Nisus and Euryalus's tragedy as the Cloridano and Medoro episode of *Orlando Furioso* (1516), he drastically altered the ending to privilege heterosexual attraction over homosocial bonds. Unlike Euryalus, Medoro does not die with his beloved comrade. When the beautiful Angelica revives him, he forgets Cloridano, falls passionately in love with her, and elopes.

The Reformation's opposition to monasticism eradicated medieval and Renaissance Europe's principal institutional support for the cult of male same-sex friendship. Since Protestantism championed marriage as the fundamental basis of society, writers in early modern England anxiously weighed the claims of romantic friendship against those of matrimony. Book IV of Spenser's *Faerie Queene* (1596) purports to be a celebration of friendship. But for Spenser, "friendship" loses its association with same-sex love and becomes a more general force of cosmic harmony. Book IV's titular heroes, Cambel and Telamond, end up marrying each other's sister in an episode that reconciles homosocial and heterosexual inclinations.

Shakespeare's *Sonnets* (ca 1596) present a particularly tortured clash between antithetical codes of same-sex friendship and heterosexual desire. As in the *Decameron,* the love of two men, the poet-speaker and the Fair Young Man, for the same woman tests friendship's limits. In this case, both men end up sleeping with the Dark Lady in a complex erotic triangle grounded in mutual betrayal and perversely displaced desire. A potentially similar triangle emerges in *The Merchant of Venice* (ca 1596) when Bassanio informs his friend Antonio that he intends to court the wealthy and beautiful Portia. But unlike the speaker of the *Sonnets,* Antonio shows no interest in women. After the play's comic resolutions have created multiple pairs of heterosexual lovers, Antonio stands alone in his uncompromised devotion to Bassanio.

Although some critics have seen Antonio as a prototype of the isolated homosexual, a more historically informed interpretation presents him as the final representative of a classical tradition undermined by the Reformation's compulsory heterosexuality. Perhaps the last testament to the older tradition is JOHN MILTON's Sixth Neo-Latin Elegy (1639), a lament for the death of his friend Charles Diodati. By the time Milton wrote *Paradise Lost* (1667), with Book IV's paean to "wedded love," he had followed Ariosto's Medoro in abandoning romantic same-sex friendships for marriage, the institution that was soon to become the basis of the bourgeois family.

As Sedgwick argues in *Between Men,* the eighteenth and nineteenth centuries witnessed a drastic shift in the dynamics of homosocial bonding. A developing context of homophobia and paranoia about sexual definition necessitated the increasing mediation of intense same-sex friendships through a female third party. By falling in love with women, one and sometimes both friends dispel fears that their affection for each other might constitute actual homosexual desire. This triangulation of homosocial desire often reduces the friends to rivals for the same girl or to panders helping each other achieve sexual conquests. In Charles Dickens's *Our Mutual Friend* (1864–1865), for instance, Charley Hexam's friendship with his teacher Bradley Headstone becomes more complicated when Headstone meets Hexam's sister Lizzie and falls in love with her. In William Makepeace Thackeray's *Henry Esmond* (1852), Lord Castlewood virtually thrusts his wife Rachel onto the rakish Lord Mohun, with whom he has cultivated a passionate friendship. But after playing pander, Castlewood must also play the enraged rival: He loses his life dueling against Mohun over Rachel's honor.

Nineteenth-century poets also introduced complicated strategies to dissociate male friendships from suspicions of homosexuality. Although LORD BYRON sometimes presented his attachments to boys and youths as the recovery of a noble classical past, his contemporaries characterized it in less exalted terms as aristocratic decadence. In "A Discourse on the Manners of the Ancient Greeks Relative to the Subject of Love" (1818), Percy Bysshe Shelley nervously explains the intensity of Greek same-sex affection as a consequence of the debased status of Greek women: Since friendship depended on the full parity of moral excellence, Greek men could not experience it with uneducated women. At first, ALFRED LORD TENNYSON's *In Memoriam: A.H.H.* (1850), an elegiac sequence lamenting the death of his friend Arthur Hallam, appears to be the nineteenth-century's least paranoid expression of male romantic friendship. But by elegiac definition, Hallam is dead: Although Tennyson imagines him in one poem as his own bridegroom, his death prevents that quasi-conjugal passion from ever achieving a physical consummation.

The triangulation that neutralized the threat of homosexuality in nineteenth-century British experience did not necessarily apply to American representations of same-sex friendship on the frontiers of white civilization. In the figure of Natty Bumpo, James Fenimore Cooper introduced a recurrent American character type, the white man who exchanges domestic stability with a wife and children for a friendship with another man who embodies the freedom of uncivilized nature. While Natty Bumpo finds his most intense personal commitment in his friendship with the Indian Chingachgook, HERMAN MELVILLE's Ishmael finds it with Queequeg, and Mark Twain's Huckleberry Finn with the runaway slave Joe. As Leslie Fiedler has argued, American literature repeatedly posits an Eden devoid of women, a Paradise in which same-sex friendships take the place of heterosexual marriage.

In *Democratic Vistas* (1871), WALT WHITMAN hails male romantic friendship as the basis for a revitalized American democracy. Adopting two terms from nineteenth-century phrenology, Whitman distinguishes between a spiritualized bonding between men, "adhesiveness," and a more crudely material attraction between men and women, "amativeness." Classical phrenologists did not present the two categories as either antithetical or specifically gendered: For them, "amativeness" referred to sexual attraction and "adhesiveness" to intense, but not essentially erotic, friendship. As Michael Lynch argues, Whitman anticipates the modern distinction between heterosexuality and homosexuality by setting the terms in strictly gendered opposition. For Whitman, amativeness refers only to opposite-sex attraction and adhesiveness only to same-sex attraction.

Since the emergence of "homosexuality" as a specific psychological category, Western culture has posited even sharper divisions between divergent experiences of affection. In current discourse, "male friendship" suggests an "innocent," "normal," fundamentally nonerotic bond between members of the same sex. Friendship so conceived opposes "homosexuality," a "deviant," "abnormal," and preeminently erotic bond between men. Sex education manuals typically reassure adolescent boys that they can harbor intense affection for members of the same sex without being "homosexuals."

But clear distinctions between erotic and nonerotic affections rarely hold up in practice. Wherever the dream of an all-male Eden persists—in westerns, science fiction, sports stories, detective movies, or prison narratives—romantic friendship retains its unmistakably erotic dimensions. In EVELYN WAUGH's *Brides-head Revisited* (1944), all-male Oxford colleges foster a passionate devotion between Sebastian Flyte and Charles Ryder. The mountains and trout streams of Spain form the backdrop for Jake and Bill's friendship in HEMINGWAY's *The Sun Also Rises* (1926). A particular subset of male romantic friendships that dates at least to Virgil's Nisus and Euryalus, the attachment between a boy or youth and an older man, dominates Hollywood westerns like *Red River* (1948) and *Shane* (1953). By emphasizing the older man's role as mentor and surrogate father, such films only partially dispel anxieties about pedophilia. Given the intensity of post–World War II homophobia, it is not surprising that the entertainment industry has increasingly restricted its representation of romantic male friendships to those between prepubescent boys safely destined for heterosexual marriage.

—*John Watkins*

BIBLIOGRAPHY

Boswell, John. *Christianity, Social Tolerance, and Homosexuality: Gay People in Western Europe from the Beginning of the Christian Era to the Fourteenth Century.* Chicago: University of Chicago Press, 1980. ■ Bray, Alan. *Homosexuality in Renaissance England.* London: Gay Men's Press, 1982. ■ ———. "Homosexuality and the Signs of Male Friendship in Elizabethan England." *Queering the Renaissance.* Jonathan Goldberg, ed. Durham, N.C.: Duke University Press, 1994. 40–61. ■ Carpenter, Edward. *Ioläus: An Anthology of Friendship.* 1917. Rpt. New York: Pagan Press, 1982. ■ Dellamora, Richard. *Masculine Desire: The Politics of Victorian Aestheticism.* Chapel Hill: University of North Carolina Press, 1990. ■ Fiedler, Leslie A. *Love and Death in the American Novel.* 1960. Rpt. New York: Stein and Day, 1975. ■ Goldberg, Jonathan. *Sodometries: Renaissance Texts, Modern Sexualities.* Stanford: Stanford University Press, 1992. ■ Lynch, Michael. "'Here is Adhesiveness': From Friendship to Homosexuality." *Victorian Studies* 29 (1985): 67–96. ■ Martin, Robert K. *Hero Captain, and Stranger: Male Friendship, Social Critique, and Literary Form in the Sea Novels of Herman Melville.* Chapel Hill: University of North Carolina Press, 1986. ■ Mills, Lauren Joseph. *One Soul in Bodies Twain.* Bloomington, Indiana: Principia Press, 1937. ■ Sedgwick, Eve Kosofsky. *Between Men: English Literature and Male Homosocial Desire.* New York: Columbia University Press, 1985. ■ Smith, Bruce R. *Homosexual Desire in Shakespeare's England.* Chicago: University of Chicago Press, 1991.

Rorem, Ned
(*b.* 1923)

Born in Richmond, Indiana, on October 23, 1923, and raised in a childhood Quaker environment that emphasized exposure to the fine arts resources available in Chicago, Ned Rorem exhibited musical and literary talents by the age of nine. Following a varied education in both contemporary and classical music, and an introduction to French culture that was to have permanent consequences for his later contributions to gay literature, Rorem received the Gershwin Memorial Award in 1948, which permitted him to make a long-planned visit to Paris. His planned three months were to stretch into a residence of some nine years.

The impact of the varied artistic, political, and literary currents composing Parisian culture prompted Rorem to record his thoughts and observations in the first of what would eventually become a series of personal chronicles. His inclusion in this account—published in 1966 as *The Paris Diary of Ned Rorem*—of unprecedentedly candid descriptions of homosexual love affairs and relationships at a time when such subjects were considered either ludicrous or unmentionable created a mild sensation and helped make him a cult figure among gay readers who were not necessarily interested in his music. Rorem's witty, often surprisingly deep, and occasionally profound ruminations, delivered in an apparently unselfconscious but wonderfully literate style, marked him as a significant observer of the Parisian cultural scene. *The Paris Diary* also helped establish the diary as a literary form of gay and lesbian writing and as a vehicle for social analysis and self-expression. Although Rorem would later disavow any intent of being an early gay liberationist (saying simply that he was too lazy to bother lying about his sexual orientation), through his diaries readers were offered a deeply drawn portrait of an individual who accepted his desires as merely one part of an integrated, stable personality. It would be two years before any comparably open account appeared again, in the form of Quentin Crisp's tartly humorous work *The Naked Civil Servant*.

Rorem's diaries, including the *New York Diary* (1967), *The Final Diary: 1961-1972* (1974; reprinted as *The Later Diaries of Ned Rorem*, 1983), and *An Absolute Gift: A New Diary* (1974), trace his return to the United States, his establishment as a major American composer—particularly of art songs, of which he is considered the contemporary master—and the maturation of his philosophies of musical composition. Public displays of very private introspection, his musings in the *Diaries*, complemented by his essays on music, such as those collected in *Pure Contraption: A Composer's Essays* (1974), permit readers to achieve a depth of understanding of the human being within the art usually reserved for long-established figures whose works have been subjected to intense critical scrutiny. *Knowing When to Stop*, his formal memoirs completed in early 1994, continues this tradition while synthesizing later creative insights and experiences.

Rorem's homosexuality influences his music in a number of ways, including the fact that the most important source of lyrics for his music is WALT WHITMAN. Rorem adapted the homoerotic "Calamus" section of Whitman's *Leaves of Grass* into a song cycle, and Whitman's homoerotic verse also provided the background for the oratorio "Goodbye My Fancy." A commission for a choral work from the Gay Men's Chorus of New York in 1988 sparked the weaving of seven poems into "The Whitman Cantata." Rorem has also adapted texts by such gay and lesbian writers as GERTRUDE STEIN, ADRIENNE RICH, JOHN ASHBERY, FRANK O'HARA, PAUL MONETTE, and THOM GUNN. Rorem's regular columns for New York's *Christopher Street* magazine in the late 1970s and early 1980s also maintained his presence in the post-Stonewall gay and lesbian literary scene.

—*Robert B. Marks Ridinger*

BIBLIOGRAPHY

Greco, Stephen. "In Prose, In Music—A Master Of Composition." *Advocate*, October 4, 1979, pp. 35–37. ■ Oestreich, James R. "At 70, An Enfant Terrible As Elder . . . Statesman." *New York Times*, January 6, 1994, section 2, pp. 1, 30.

Rossetti, Christina
(1830–1894)

Christina Rossetti was born on December 5, 1830, to Gabriele and Frances Polidori Rossetti. Her father was Italian, her mother half English and half Italian, and Rossetti grew up speaking both languages. Her family was skilled in literature and the arts. Her sister Maria was to write a study of DANTE and eventually become an Anglican nun, her brother Dante Gabriel was to become a famous painter and poet, and her brother William a literary critic and the family's chronicler.

Rossetti seems to have been a bright, happy child, but her temperament mysteriously changed in her early teens, and she became serious and introspective. The Rossetti household had always been a religious one of an Evangelical cast. In the 1840s, the family turned to Anglo-Catholicism. The rituals and beliefs of Christina's religion were to influence the direction of the rest of her life very deeply. From ages eighteen to twenty, she was often ill; one doctor diagnosed her illness as "religious mania." Just before she turned seventeen, she accepted a proposal of marriage from a minor artist of her brother's circle, James Collinson, a recent convert from Catholicism. She broke off the engagement when he converted back. To break off an engagement on religious grounds was not unusual for a devout woman of the nineteenth century, but the experience was to become emblematic of the life of renunciation that she would lead.

Rossetti was a precocious versifier, though she had some trouble publishing her work. She published verses in the Pre-Raphaelite brotherhood's short-lived publication *The Germ* in 1850. Later in the decade, her brother Dante Gabriel tried to get John Ruskin to promote her verse, but he demurred. Public attention did not come until *Macmillan's* published her short lyric "Up-Hill" in 1861. Alexander Macmillan was to publish her first volume of verse, *Goblin Market and Other Poems,* in the following year. *The Prince's Progress* followed in 1866, and other volumes were published on a regular basis. Rossetti's poetry is marked by its euphony of sound and mastery of technique. In her later volumes, Rossetti concentrated on religious verse, and she published her works with the Society for the Propagation of Christian Knowledge. These works included a commentary on the Apocalypse, *The Face of the Deep* (1892). Her religious verse exhibits the same technical skill as her secular writing and exhibits an unusual combination of intensity and sincerity.

Rossetti's personal life was not happy. She was often ill and was misdiagnosed with tuberculosis twice. In the 1860s, she again refused a suitor on religious grounds. This time the man was Charles Cayley, an absent-minded scholar who seems to have proposed to Rossetti in the middle of the decade. Though she may have loved Cayley and remained friends with him, he was an agnostic. In 1871, Rossetti developed Graves' disease. She lost much of her hair and her skin turned brown, and the illness rendered her a near-invalid for the rest of her life.

Rossetti's poetry has a sexual element resulting from the repressions her religion engendered and from her lifelong interest in "fallen women" and their redemption. Rossetti worked for ten years in the House of Charity, a penitentiary for unwed mothers and other "fallen women" run by Anglican nuns. Her most powerful sustained work, *Goblin Market,* exhibits an interest in redemption in vigorous female terms.

In the poem, the sisters Lizzie and Laura, who live together in a house on the moors, are tempted each night by the cries of goblins selling fruit. One evening Laura walks out of the house and purchases some fruit with a lock of her blond hair. She eats her fill in front of the goblins and returns. On the following evenings, Laura is struck by an immense craving for the fruit, yet she can no longer hear the goblins selling their wares, even though her sister still can. She begins to pine away. Lizzie approaches the goblins hoping to purchase some more fruit to restore her sister's life. Though she offers them money, she refuses to part with her hair. The goblins pelt her with their fruit in disgust and run off. Laura is restored to health by licking the fruit juices off Lizzie's face and body.

Though the poem has been variously described as an allegory of Christian redemption and as a warning against the temptation of sexuality, it creates a powerful, erotically charged version of female-to-female affection. The language of the poem is resolutely sexual. The sisters walk "With clasping arms and cautioning lips / With tingling cheeks and finger tips." When Lizzie returns covered in the pulp of the goblin fruit, she says to Laura: "Hug me, kiss me, suck my juices." Laura in return kisses her with a "hungry mouth." In other poems, Rossetti imagines female sexuality in deep detail. The "Babylon the Great" section of *The World* delineates the Woman of Revelation as a sexualized Medusa figure. A sonnet, also entitled "The World," figures the secular world as a sexual temptress: "By day she woos me, soft, exceeding fair."

Rossetti's last years were marked by the deaths of her mother and sister and by her increasing devotion to her religion, of which she always felt somewhat unworthy. Her final months were spent in great physical pain. She died of cancer on December 29, 1894.

—*James Najarian*

BIBLIOGRAPHY

Battiscombe, Georgina. *Christina Rossetti: A Divided Life.* London: Constable, 1981. ■ Homans, Margaret. "'Syllables of Velvet': Dickinson, Rossetti, and the Rhetorics of Sexuality." *Feminist Studies* 11 (Fall 1983): 569–593. ■ Jones, Kathleen. *Learning Not To Be First: The Life of Christina Rossetti.* Gloucestershire: Windrush Press, 1991. ■ Mermin, Dorothy. "Heroic Sisterhood in *Goblin Market.*" *Victorian Poetry* 21 (Summer 1983): 107–118. ■ Rosenblum, Dolores. "Christina Rossetti: The Inward Pose." *Shakespeare's Sisters: Feminist Essays on Women Poets.* Sandra M. Gilbert and Susan Gubar, eds. Bloomington: Indiana University Press, 1979. 82–98.

Rukeyser, Muriel
(1913–1980)

Muriel Rukeyser was born and lived most of her life in New York City. The elder of two daughters, she grew up in an upper-middle-class family of Midwestern and German-Jewish descent. Accustomed to both chauffeurs and nursemaids during her childhood, Rukeyser was educated at the Ethical Culture School in New York City, followed by two years at Vassar College. Writer and activist, she attended the 1933 trial of the Scottsboro Nine in Alabama, covered the antifascist Olympics in Barcelona in 1936 as correspondent for London's *Life and Letters Today*, taught at the California Labor School in 1945, traveled to Hanoi in 1972 as a peace ambassador, and stood in silent protest outside South Korean political prisoner and poet Kim Chi-Ha's jail cell in 1975. Her poems engage with much of twentieth-century, Left history in the United States, yet are also personal and autobiographical. Her work reflects an integrated political-aesthetic vision that refused the conventional separation of private and public spheres. Author of eighteen books of poetry, four of prose, children's books, and numerous translations, Rukeyser won many prestigious awards during her lifetime, including the Yale Younger Poets Prize (1935) and election to the National Institute of Arts and Letters (1967).

Details of Rukeyser's personal life remain a matter of speculation. Rukeyser herself never wrote or spoke publicly about her sexual identity. She was briefly married in 1945 and gave birth to her only child, William Rukeyser, in 1947. (Her son's father was not her former husband.) She also had lesbian relationships. In 1978, she accepted an invitation to participate in a Lesbian Poetry Reading at the annual conference of the Modern Language Association, a decision that seems to reflect her intention to assume a more public lesbian identity. Unfortunately, she suffered a stroke prior to this event and was unable to attend.

There is no doubt that her work has been enormously important to many feminist and lesbian readers. Her poems constantly break silence around previously unwritten areas of female experience, for example, sex, menstruation, breast-feeding, mother-daughter relationships, and female aging. As she wrote in her well-known tribute to the sculptor Käthe Kollwitz, "What would happen if one woman told the truth about her life? / The world would split open." Significantly, she was always particularly attuned to the power of silencing. She wrote of being "unable to speak, in exile from myself" ("The Poem as Mask") and regularly asked her students to write about what they "could not say." She states pointedly in "The Speed of Darkness": "I am working out the vocabulary of my silence." In "The Transgress," she describes herself "thundering on tabu," and alludes to the "bed of forbidden things finally known." In "Letter to the Front," she enjoins her readers not to "fear the hidden." Such lines can be read as a direct response to the cultural silences surrounding homosexuality.

Rukeyser's poetics and politics were never separatist. She was an extraordinarily inclusive, democratic poet whose work affirms "the faces of all love" ("Private Life of the Sphinx"). Her poems address a broadly conceived audience, including men and women: "A people various as life / whose strength is in our many voices and our hope / of a future of many" ("Speech of the Mother").

—*Anne F. Herzog*

BIBLIOGRAPHY

Daniels, Kate, and Richard Jones. *Poetry East: a special double issue on Muriel Rukeyser* 16–17 (Spring–Summer 1985). ■ Gardinier, Suzanne. "'A World that Will Hold All the People': On Muriel Rukeyser." *Kenyon Review* 14.3 (1992): 88–105. ■ Kertesz, Louise. *Poetic Vision of Muriel Rukeyser*. Baton Rouge: Louisiana State University Press, 1980. ■ McDaniel, Judith. "A Conversation with Muriel Rukeyser." *New Women's Times Feminist Review* (April 25–May 8, 1980): 4+. ■ Rukeyser, Muriel. *The Collected Poems of Muriel Rukeyser*. New York: McGraw-Hill, 1978. ■ ———. *A Muriel Rukeyser Reader*. Jan Heller Levi, ed. New York: Norton, 1994. ■ ———. *Out of Silence: Selected Poems*. Kate Daniels, ed. Evanston: TriQuarterly, 1992.

Rule, Jane
(b. 1931)

Jane Rule was born in Plainfield, New Jersey, on March 28, 1931, the daughter of Arthur Richard and Carlotta Jane Rule. In 1952, she earned a B.A. in English from Mills College and then, for a year, studied at University College, London. In 1956, she moved to Vancouver, British Columbia; she now lives on Galiano Island. Teacher, author, and out lesbian, Rule is best known as a fiction writer. Her awards include the Canadian Authors' Association Award for Best Novel (1978), the Benson and Hedges Award for Best Short Stories (1978), the Literary Award of the Gay Academic Union (1978), and the Fund for Human Dignity's Award of Merit (1983).

Rule's book of criticism, seven novels, and numerous short stories and essays address lesbian and gay issues to varying degrees, most often by presenting them as universal concerns. Though typically outcasts, her characters do not belong to a subculture; whether queer or straight, they participate in what she calls the human family, whose members' task it is to learn to get along with one another. The cultivation of nurturing relationships and communities in the wake of obtrusive social "systems" is a predominant theme in her work, as is the appreciation for landscape and nature, which some critics have called a particularly Canadian motif.

Rule's first novel, *Desert of the Heart* (1964), recounts a lesbian love story via conventional Christian images and narrative strategies. By invoking and subverting representations of gender and sexual taboos from such canonical texts as the Bible, *The Divine Comedy,* and *The Pilgrim's Progress,* the two protagonists of this coming-out novel explore the significance of their involvement. Self-consciously literary, *Desert of the Heart* offers an affirming, insightful, and optimistic depiction of lesbian love, one rare indeed in pre-Stonewall fiction. Dedicated to Rule's life partner Helen Sonthoff, the novel was made into the 1986 lesbian cult film *Desert Hearts,* directed by Donna Deitch.

Although interested in renegotiating mainstream literary paradigms, Rule sees her writing as free of any overt ideology; she does not align herself firmly with either lesbian feminist or separatist platforms. Her successful recent novel *Memory Board* (1987), for example, examines aging and AIDS, not as political but as personal concerns to be dealt with in a matter-of-fact manner that nourishes human intimacy. For Rule, politics has no place in art; the literary work arrives at its own truth or set of truths through the particular vision of the artist. This position, which also informs *Lesbian Images* (1975), a pioneering discussion of women writers and their treatment of love between women, risks being labeled naive and complacent: It neither acknowledges the ideological power of language (whereby the structures of thought used actually determine what is said) nor the inevitably political nature of proclaiming a nonpartisan stance. Still, her fiction, especially in its delineation of character and theme, expresses a large-spirited commitment to diverse communities and a range of experiences. Rule's novels and collections of short stories are all available from lesbian feminist publishers, having all been reprinted by Naiad Press in the United States and by Pandora Press in London.

—*Margaret Soenser Breen*

BIBLIOGRAPHY

Hancock, Geoffrey. "An Interview with Jane Rule." *Canadian Fiction Magazine.* 23 (Autumn 1976): 57–112. ■ Schuster, Marilyn R. "Strategies for Survival: The Subtle Subversion of Jane Rule." *Feminist Studies* 7.3 (Fall 1991): 431–450. ■ Sonthoff, Helen. "A Bibliography." *Canadian Fiction Magazine* 23 (Autumn 1976): 133–138. ■ ———. "Celebration: Jane Rule's Fiction." *Canadian Fiction Magazine* 23 (Autumn 1976): 121–132. ■ Spraggs, Gillian. "Hell and the Mirror: A Reading of *Desert of the Heart.*" *New Lesbian Criticism: Literary and Cultural Readings.* Sally Munt, ed. New York: Columbia University Press, 1992. 115–131. ■ Zimmerman, Bonnie. *The Safe Sea of Women in Lesbian Fiction, 1969-1988.* Boston: Beacon Press, 1990.

Russ, Joanna
(b. 1937)

§

Science fiction writer and critic Joanna Russ was born February 22, 1937, to Bertha Zinner and Everett I. Russ, and grew up in the Bronx. She claims, "I spent my childhood half in the Bronx Zoo and half in the Botanical Gardens." In 1953 in high school, she was one of the top ten Westinghouse Science Talent Search Winners. Russ received her B.A. with High Honors in English from Cornell University in June 1957, and her M.F.A. at Yale University School of Drama in June 1960. Russ came out about 1969, the subject of her only nonscience fiction novel *On Strike Against God* (1980). After teaching at Cornell University, SUNY at Binghampton, and the University of Colorado at Boulder, Russ is Professor of English at the University of Washington (Seattle). Russ suffers from back problems and writes standing up.

Russ's science fiction began to be published in 1959. According to Russ, her 1967 Alyx story marked a change: "I had turned from writing love stories . . . to writing stories about women in which the woman won." Russ continued the Alyx series with *Picnic on Paradise* (1968) and *The Adventures of Alyx* (1986). Her friendship with the gay science fiction writer Samuel Delany has influenced her writing throughout her career.

Two of Russ's science fictions changed the genre and created controversy. Her 1969 short story, "When It Changed," appeared in 1972 and won a Nebula Award. In first person, the story depicts a human with a wife and daughters on a colonized planet, living through the first hours of regaining contact with earthmen. After several pages, readers realize that the narrator is female, that all the people on this planet are lesbians. Russ uses role-reversal (a woman as husband and narrator) and the misogyny and homophobia of the spacemen to call into question the necessity of gender roles. Her novel *The Female Man* (1975) opened new possibilities of form as well as content for science fiction. Russ magnified the sf convention of parallel histories by bringing together the same woman as she exists in four different lives—oppressed heterosexual Jeannine from a United States in which the Depression never ended; Joanna (note the author's name), an unmarried university professor from a culture like ours; Jael, an assassin from a world where the sexes are literally at war; and Janet Evason from a utopian lesbian planet. Written in a "lyric" stream of consciousness style that Russ discusses in her essay "What Can a Heroine Do?" *The Female Man* is a funny and serious book about what is wrong with patriarchy and how to fix it. Russ links her anger at inequality and her humor: "wit is a kind of rage, a form of hostility" ("Joanna Russ," 209). The anti-colonizing fiction *We Who Are About To . . .* (1977) continues Russ's experimental lyric feminism: A space-ship crashes, the survivors try to start a colony and fail, and the older woman protagonist, who resists, kills the others and finds her own meditative way to die. During the 1970s, Russ also published *And Chaos Died* (1970) and *The Two of Them* (1978). Russ has mainly worked in the sf short story during the last decade, publishing three collections: *Extraordinary People* (1984), *The Zanzibar Cat* (1984), and *The Hidden Side of the Moon* (1987). Striving for compression, Russ's short stories are dense and delightfully perverse twistings of generic conventions: a lesbian gothic tale, for example, and a ghost story in which a daughter learns to mother herself.

Russ's criticism began in the general aesthetics of science fiction and moved to passionate feminist critiques of science fiction and other literatures. Her essays "What Can a Heroine Do?" "Images of Women" (both in Susan Cornillon's *Images of Women,* 1972) and "Amor Vincit" (*Science Fiction Studies,* 1980) are central to feminist sf criticism. Her book *How to Suppress Women's Writing* (1983) is a witty catalogue of reasons why literary history denies the existence of women's writing: her husband wrote it, she wrote it but it wasn't really art, and so on. In *Magic Mommas,* Russ treats broad issues of women's and gay and lesbian liberation, returning to science fiction in the essay on Kirk-Spock pornography. (See also SCIENCE FICTION AND FANTASY.)

—*Jane L. Donawerth*

BIBLIOGRAPHY

"Joanna Russ." *Across the Wounded Galaxies: Interviews with Contemporary American Science Fiction Writers.* Larry McCaffery, ed. Urbana: University of Illinois Press, 1990. ∎ Moyan, Tom. *Dream the Impossible.* New York: Methuen, 1986.

Russian Literature

Like Russian history, Russian literature can be conveniently divided into three periods: the Kievan (tenth to thirteenth centuries A.D.), the Muscovite (fourteenth to seventeenth centuries), and modern (eighteenth century and later). Kievan history began with the unification in the 860s of twelve East Slavic tribes (ancestors of the modern Russians, Ukrainians, and Belarussians) into a nation with its capital in Kiev. The country's rulers were converted to Christianity in 988. The new religion, which came from Byzantium, brought with it the Slavic alphabet, devised earlier by Byzantine missionaries. The earliest Russian literature, which was also the literature of other East and South Slavic peoples, consisted mainly of historical (chronicles) and religious (prayer books, sermons, lives of saints) genres.

As Vasily Rozanov pointed out in 1913, instances of homosexual love can be found in certain lives of saints (*vitae*) that date from the Kievan period. For example, "The Legend of Boris and Gleb," written by an anonymous monk at the turn of the eleventh century, enjoyed a wide circulation not only in Russia, but also in other Eastern Orthodox countries, such as Bulgaria, Serbia, and even the non-Slavic-speaking

Rumania. (Religious literature was written in all these countries in Old Church Slavic, a medieval South Slavic dialect that had the same function in Orthodox countries that Latin had in Catholic ones.) Combining features of history, hagiography, and lyric poetry, "The Legend" told of the assassination of two young Kievan princes for dynastic reasons. Prince Boris had a favorite squire, George the Hungarian. He had a magnificent golden necklace made for George because "he was loved by Boris beyond all reckoning." When the four assassins pierced Boris with their swords, George flung himself on the body of his prince, exclaiming: "I will not be left behind, my precious lord! Ere the beauty of thy body begins to wilt, let it be granted that my life may end!" Through the standard life-of-saint format, imported from Byzantium, the author's sympathy for the mutual love of Boris and George comes unmistakably through.

George's brother Moses, later canonized by the Orthodox Church as St. Moses the Hungarian, was the only member of Boris's retinue to survive the massacre. His later fate is told in a section devoted to him in *The Kievan Paterikon,* a compilation of monastic lives dating from the 1220s. Moses was taken prisoner and sold as a slave to a Polish noblewoman who became enamored of his powerful physique. For a year, she tried to seduce him, offering him his freedom and even her own hand in marriage, but Moses preferred the company of her other male slaves. Finally, his mocking refusals exasperated the noblewoman and she ordered that Moses be given one hundred lashes and castrated. He found his way to the Kievan Crypt Monastery, where he lived for another ten years. The story of Moses the Hungarian is clearly influenced by the biblical account of Joseph and Potiphar's wife. But it can still be read (as Vasily Rozanov maintained) as a tale of a Russian medieval homosexual, punished because he would not enter a heterosexual marriage.

The culturally rich Kievan period ended in 1240, when Kiev was occupied and virtually destroyed by an army of nomadic Mongol invaders. The invasion was followed by 250 years of Mongol captivity. When Russia regained its independence, it had a new capital in Moscow. The Muscovite period may have been the era of the greatest visibility and tolerance for male homosexuality that the world had seen since the days of ancient Greece and Rome. During the fifteenth, sixteenth, and seventeenth centuries, foreign travelers and ambassadors, coming from countries where "sodomites" were subjected to torture, burning at the stake, and life-long incarcerations, repeatedly registered their amazement and shock at the unconcealed manifestations of homosexual behavior by Russian men of every social class. Among the numerous testimonies to this visibility in travel and memoir literature are the books by Sigismund von Herberstein and Adam Olearius and an amusing poem by the Englishman George Turberville, "To Dancie." Turberville visited Moscow with a diplomatic mission in 1568, the time of one of Ivan the Terrible's worst political purges. The poet was struck not by the carnage, however, but by the open homosexuality of the Russian peasants.

But homosexuality existed not only among the lower classes; it also extended to the ruling monarchs as well. Grand Prince Vasily III of Moscow (reigned from 1505 to 1533) was homosexual throughout his life. He went to the extent of announcing this fact to other gay men of his time by shaving off his beard when his twenty-year marriage to his first wife was terminated—being beardless was a sort of gay password at the time. During Vasily's second marriage, he was able to perform his conjugal duties only when an officer of his guard joined him and his wife in bed in the nude. The son of Vasily III's second marriage, Ivan IV, better known as Ivan the Terrible, was married no less than seven times. But he was also attracted to young men in female attire. One of the most ruthless chieftains of Ivan's political police, Feodor Basmanov, rose to his high position through performing seductive dances in women's clothes at the tsar's court. The nineteenth-century poet A. K. Tolstoy (1817–1875) wrote a historical novel, *Prince Serebriany* (1862), set during the reign of Ivan the Terrible, where he described with great frankness the paradoxical character of Feodor: a capable military commander; the scheming initiator of murderous political purges; the tsar's bed partner; and an effeminate homosexual who discussed in public the cosmetics he used to improve his complexion and hair.

Also bisexual was the False Dmitri, the runaway monk who claimed to be the youngest son of Ivan the Terrible and who overthrew Tsar Boris Godunov to reign for less than a year in Moscow. During the pretender's wedding to the aristocratic Pole Marina Mniszech in 1606, he was waited upon by his lover, the eighteen-year-old Prince Ivan Khvorostinin. The latter, a scion of a noble family of ancient lineage, was attired for the occasion in a dazzling brocaded outfit, which he managed to change to two other equally dazzling ones in the course of the festivities. In his later life, Khvorostinin repeatedly got into trouble with the authorities, not because of his homosexuality or his involvement with the pretender, but because of his satirical writings in prose and in verse (doggerel, really). His satire was aimed at Russian backwardness and lack of culture. He repeatedly asserted the superiority of Western Protestant countries, their fashions and their high intellectual level. Such praise for the West was considered the height of heresy. The young prince was repeatedly denounced by his friends and servants. But he was quite good at talking his way out of incarceration or confiscation of his property. He never got to realize his great dream of going to live in Holland or Italy; he died of natural causes at the age of thirty-seven.

The main reflection of homosexuality in the literature of Muscovite Russia survives in the writings of Orthodox churchmen who denounced the practice. "Sermon No. 12" by Metropolitan Daniel, a popular Moscow preacher of the 1530s, offers an extended panorama of various homosexual types of his time, both effeminate and not. Archpriest Avvakum was the leader of the Old Believers during the religious schism of the 1650s. (The Old Believers broke away from the Orthodox Church because of the reforms in the ritual and in corrected spelling of biblical names instituted by the Patriarch Nikon; in the eighteenth and nineteenth centuries, Old Believer communities gave rise to numerous lesser religious dissenter sects.) In his *Autobiography* (1673), much admired for its style by later writers, Avvakum states that he refused to hear confession of any man who shaved off his beard. On one occasion, Avvakum enraged a provincial governor by refusing to bless his son, who, by shaving his beard, must have tried to look seductive to other men. The father responded by having the churchman thrown into the river Volga. Apart from clerical admonitions, nothing else restrained the homosexual behavior among the men of Kievan and Muscovite Russia.

Beginning with the earliest known Russian legal code, *Russkaia pravda* (*Russian Justice*), promulgated during the reign of Iaroslav the Wise (who ruled from 1019 to 1054) and up to the military regulations of Peter the Great early in the eighteenth century, no Russian legislation prohibited "the sin of Sodom" or any other homosexual practice. As Eve Levin has shown in her book *Sex and Society in the World of Orthodox Slavs, 900–1700,* unlike Western Europe, which often had laws based on Old Testament interdictions, Eastern Orthodox Christianity considered various forms of sexual deviance not as crimes, but as sins, subject to religious jurisdiction. What Eve Levin established was that in this area the main concern was not so much the sex of the participants or the organs involved, but the *relative position* of the partners during the sex act. The woman below and the man above was permitted as the "natural" way; reversal of this position was "unnatural" and a sin. Homosexual and lesbian contacts were thus sinful, the sin being of the same magnitude as the reversal of positions in heterosexual intercourse. It was of no concern to civil authorities and it could be expiated by going to confession, doing an assigned number of prostrations, and abstaining from meat and milk products for several months. Summing up the testimony of foreign and native observers of Muscovite Russia, the authoritative nineteenth-century historian Sergei Soloviov wrote: "Nowhere, either in the Orient or in the West, was [homosexuality] taken as lightly as in Russia."

Only after the increase in travel of Russians abroad during the reign of Peter the Great was it understood that the practices the Russians had taken for granted for almost a millennium were regarded with horror or with fury by those who lived in the supposedly more civilized countries in the West. In the eighteenth century, the open homosexuality of the Muscovite period had to go underground. Yet, at the same time, it made a renewed appearance in the religious dissenter sects that split from the Old Believers during that same century. Two of these sects, Khlysty (a distorted plural form of Christ) and Skoptsy (Castrates) had recognizable homosexual and bisexual strains in their culture, folklore, and religious rituals. The major gay poet of the early twentieth century, Nikolai Kliuev, incorporated much of these sects' lore into his visionary poetry.

By the middle of the eighteenth century, Russian literature caught up with the current West European literary forms. The end of that century was in Russia, as elsewhere, the Age of Sentimentalism. The leading Russian Sentimentalist poet was Ivan Dmitriev (1760–1837). He wrote clever satires, saccharine love songs, and didactic fables. Dmitriev was a government official who eventually rose to the position of Minister of Justice in the reign of Alexander I. In his government career, he was nepotistic, surrounding himself with handsome young assistants, some of whom owed their advancement to the fact that they were Dmitriev's lovers. In his poetry, however, he wore a heterosexual mask, pretending to pine for some neoclassical Chloe or Phyllis. The exceptions are his adaptations of La Fontaine's fables "The Two Pidgeons" and "The Two Friends," which he turned into unequivocal depictions of love affairs between males.

With Alexander Pushkin (1799–1837), Russian literature acquired its first major figure of international significance. A happily adjusted heterosexual, Pushkin viewed alternative forms of sexuality with an amused tolerance that was not otherwise typical of Russian nineteenth-century writers. In the fall of 1823, while Pushkin was in exile in the south of Russia, he addressed a remarkable letter to the memoirist Philip Vigel (whose subsequently published memoirs described Vigel's orientation and the homosexual circles of his time). In this letter and an attached witty poem, Pushkin commiserated with Vigel for having to live in Kishinev (now the capital of Moldova) rather than in the civilized city of Sodom, "that Paris of the Old Testament." He mentioned three handsome brothers in Kishinev who might be receptive to Vigel's advances, and invited him for a visit in Odessa, but with the proviso: "To serve you I'll be all too happy / With all my soul, my verse, my prose, / But Vigel, you must spare my rear!" In his poems that imitated the Greek Anthology or Muslim poets, Pushkin assumed the persona of a man attracted to adolescent boys, a literary strategem that had no correlates in his life.

Pushkin's younger contemporary Mikhail Lermontov (1814–1841) wrote of homosexual love in the cycle of poems known as his "Hussar" or "Cadet" poems. Written when he was twenty and a student at a military academy, two of the five poems of this cycle depict the sexual encounters between other cadets. Though the theme is treated with clear distaste, the details are so concrete that Lermontov must have personally witnessed the incidents he described. NIKOLAI GOGOL (1809–1852), only ten years younger than Pushkin, was one of the most harrowing cases of sexual self-repression to be found in the annals of literature. Totally and exclusively gay, Gogol spent his life denying this fact to himself and to others, mainly for religious reasons. His stories and plays are permeated with fear of marriage and other forms of sexual contact with women, but Gogol enveloped this theme in such a cloud of symbols and surrealistic fantasies that his contemporary readers failed to discern its presence. A sketch for his second play, *Marriage* (a headlong attack on the entire institution of matrimony), mentioned an official who so loved his subordinate that he slept in the same bed with him, a passage that was removed from the finished version of the play. This brilliant writer committed suicide at the age of forty-three, after confessing his true sexuality to a bigoted priest who ordered him to fast and pray day and night if he wanted to escape hellfire and brimstone.

The two giants of Russian nineteenth-century literature, Tolstoy and Dostoevsky, were men of the Victorian age who regarded all forms of sexuality as impure, distasteful, and dangerous. The theme of homosexuality in the life of Leo Tolstoy (1828–1910) deserves a special study that will undoubtedly be written one day. In his childhood, Tolstoy kept falling in love with both boys and girls, and recorded such experiences in the first two novels of his early autobiographical trilogy *Childhood* (1852), *Boyhood* (1854), and *Youth* (1857). While serving in the army in the 1850s, Tolstoy was strongly attracted to several of his fellow soldiers. But he noted in his diaries that he rejected same-sex love because his attraction to men was purely physical—he was drawn only to very handsome men whose characters were usually not admirable—while his love for women was based on their personalities and good qualities and not exclusively on their looks. In his later novels, Tolstoy showed male homosexuality in a negative light.

Anna Karenina (1877) contains a brief vignette of two inseparable army officers, whom Anna's lover Alexei Vronsky and his friends avoid, suspecting them, not without reason, of having an affair with each other (Part Two, Chapter XIX). In *Resurrection* (1899), the aged Tolstoy wanted to indict the inequities and corruption of Tsarist Russia. The novel contains an episode about a high government official who gets convicted for violating paragraph 995 of the criminal code. (Criminalization of male homosexuality for the entire population was enacted in the code of 1832–1845, promulgated during the reign of the most repressive of the Romanovs, Nicholas I. The law was hard to enforce and was very rarely applied.) The convicted homosexual arouses the warm sympathy of St. Petersburg high society and, since his sentence calls for resettlement in Siberia, he arranges a transfer to one of the major Siberian cities, keeping the same rank. Later in the novel, a reptilian government-employed lawman (who spitefully railroads the novel's heroine, Maslova, to a Siberian penal colony) defends equal rights for homosexuals and proposes that marriage between men be legalized. Both of these characters were meant to suggest the country's moral decay.

Feodor Dostoevsky (1821–1881) was far less interested in homosexuality than Tolstoy. In an early novel, *Netochka Nezvanova* (1849), Dostoevsky depicted a passionate lesbian infatuation between two adolescent girls. In *Notes from the House of the Dead* (1862), a semifictionalized account of Dostoevsky's own experiences in a Siberian hard-labor camp, there are veiled indications that homosexuality was practiced by some of the convicts. But in the curious episode that involves the violent and hardened professional criminal Petrov, the narrator seems perplexed about the reasons for Petrov's fondness for his own person. Petrov seeks the narrator out, plies him with meaningless questions just to be in his presence, and constantly does him favors. In recompense, all Petrov wants is to undress the narrator at the communal baths and to soap and wash his body while seated at his feet. The narrator (who clearly stands for Dostoevsky) offers several tentative psychological explanations for Petrov's behavior but finds them all unsatisfactory. The most obvious explanation of all, which is that Petrov found the narrator physically attractive and desirable, just did not occur to Dostoevsky.

Some of the less-known Russian writers of the second half of the nineteenth century also touched on homosexual themes. Ivan Kushchevsky (1847–1876) was a radical writer who lived only long enough to write a volume of stories and the satirical novel *Nikolai Negorev, or The Prosperous Russian* (1871). The title character belongs to a coterie of idealistic young revolutionaries, all of whom he eventually betrays to the authorities. At the end of the novel, looking for opportunities to start a new career, Negorev encounters an apparent homosexual named Stern, who has "prohibited relationships with several young men." Through Stern, Negorev meets a group of aristocratic young men, who refer to each other as "countess" or "princess," brag of their conquests of other men, and are much given to shrieking. Negorev decides to investigate this group, hoping to blackmail one of them—for homosexuality, the modern reader expects. However, the author becomes confused: The fellow does get blackmailed, but for having gotten pregnant the daughter of a powerful official and trying to obtain an illegal abortion for her. By denouncing the couple to the young woman's father and offering to marry her himself so as to cover up her condition, Negorev sets himself up for a major career in the government bureaucracy. (Unlike in Germany or England of the time, blackmail for homosexuality seems to have been unknown in nineteenth-century Russia.)

Homosexuality became somewhat more visible in Russian life and literature after the momentous reforms initiated by Tsar Alexander II in the early 1860s, which abolished serfdom, replaced an archaic legal system with trials by jury open to press and public, and reduced the censorship of books and periodicals. Konstantin Leontiev (1831–1891) was an ultraconservative political philosopher, a literary critic, and novelist, who spent much of his life in consular service in the countries of the Near East. Bisexuality was a theme he often treated in his fiction. In his early novel *A Husband's Confession* (1867), the husband loves his young wife, but he also falls in love with a mustachioed Turk taken captive during the Crimean War. To give expression to this second love, he encourages his wife to become the Turk's mistress and to run away with him to Turkey. Such simultaneous infatuation of a man with a well-bred but drab female and with a robust and colorful male is also the situation in Leontiev's best-known novel, *The Egyptian Dove* (1881). His story "Hamid and Manoli," published in 1869, is an account of a love affair between two men, a Turk and a Cretan, which ends in a bloody tragedy because of the prejudices of the Cretan's Christian family. It is the only piece of Russian literature of the nineteenth century that denounces the ugliness of homophobia.

One of the greatest Russian celebrities in the second half of the nineteenth century, both at home and abroad, was the explorer and author of travel books Nikolai Przhevalsky (1839–1888). His accounts of his travels and adventures (such as his famous discovery of the undomesticated horse, *Equus przevalskii*) were best-sellers in Russia and were widely popular in translation in England and America. A recent biography by Donald Rayfield showed that each of Przhevalsky's expeditions was planned to include a young male lover-companion. The great love of his life was Piotr Kozlov, who spent Przhevalsky's last years with him and who later became a noted explorer in his own right. The literary qualities of Przhevalsky's books were greatly admired by Anton Chekhov, who in his obituary of the explorer called him "a hero as vital as the sun." Vladimir Nabokov, in the most personal and perfect of his Russian novels, *The Gift*, based the character of the protagonist's father on Przhevalsky (minus his homosexuality). Nabokov's description of the father's expeditions to the remote regions of Central Asia is a set of variations on themes from Przhevalsky's writings.

The decade of the 1890s saw a mass emergence of lesbians and gay men on the Russian cultural scene. There were several quite visible gay grand dukes (brothers, uncles, or nephews of the last three tsars). The most overt of them was the Grand Duke Sergei Alexandrovich, brother of Alexander III and uncle of Nicholas II, who appeared with his current lover at official functions and at the theater and opera. Close to the tsar's court was the reactionary publisher Prince Vladimir Meshchersky. When the latter got involved in a scandal because of his affair with a bugle boy from the imperial marching band in the late 1880s, Tsar Alexander III ordered the case to be quashed and the witnesses silenced. An associate of the Grand Duke Sergei and of Meshchersky was the poet Alexei Apukhtin (1841–1893), author of flashy salon lyrics and a classmate and one-time lover of Peter Tchaikovsky. Apukhtin's and Tchaikovsky's orientation was generally known, as was that of the liberal lesbian publisher Anna Yevreinova (1844–1919) and the poet and editor Polyxena Soloviova (1867–1924). Both of these women lived openly with their female partners, arrangements that were accepted by their families and by society. The association of critics and artists, "The World of Art," headed by Sergei Diaghilev, which in 1898 launched their epochal journal of the same name, was predominantly gay. It was on the pages of that journal that the Symbolist poet Zinaida Gippius (1869–1945) published in 1899 her travelogue "On the Shores of the Ionian Sea," where she described in detail the homosexual colony at Taormina in Sicily, which was grouped around Baron Wilhelm von Gloeden, the pioneer photographer of male nudes. Elsewhere, Gippius published an extended account of a gay and lesbian bar that she had visited in Paris.

The massive, nationwide uprising known as the Revolution of 1905 forced Nicholas II to issue his October Manifesto, which authorized a parliamentary system, legalized all political parties, and virtually abolished preliminary censorship of books and periodicals. From 1906 onward, there appeared in Russia lesbian and gay poets, fiction writers, and artists who saw in the new freedom of expression a chance to describe their lifestyles in an honest and affirmative manner. MIKHAIL KUZMIN (1872–1936), the most outspoken, prolific and well-known of Russia's gay writers, made his literary debut in 1906, when the prestigious art journal *Vesy* (Libra) serialized his autobiographical novel *Wings*.

Published in book form one year later, *Wings* used the format of the *Bildungsroman* (novel of self-education), following the example of such Western classics as Goethe's *Wilhelm Meister* and Flaubert's *Sentimental Education*. The young Ivan (Vanya) Smurov's growing attraction to his older friend Larion turns to fear and revulsion when he learns that Larion moves in St. Petersburg's gay circles and patronizes a gay bathhouse. Vanya learns to accept his own feelings after he stays with an Old Believer family on the Volga who tell him that any form of love is better than repression and hatred. Vanya discovers that he cannot respond sexually to women; then he takes an eye-opening trip to Italy. The novel ends with Vanya accepting Larion's offer to live and travel together, a decision that makes him feel as if he had grown wings.

On its first appearance, *Wings* was attacked as pornographic by both the conservative and left-wing publications. But the novel's acclaim by the leading poets and critics of the day soon put Kuzmin beyond the reach of journalistic sniping. It was as a poet that Kuzmin soon acquired the stature of a major figure. Despite the themes of gay love and gay sex that permeated his poetry, it was extolled by the greatest poets of the age, from Alexander Blok to Vladimir Mayakovsky. Between 1906 and the early 1920s, Kuzmin wrote and published several other novels, many short stories, plays, and a great deal of poetry. His plays on gay themes, such as *Dangerous Precaution* (1907) and *The Venetian Madcaps* (1914) were performed at professional theaters and at amateur theatricals. A whole generation of Russian gay men in the decade before the October Revolution saw

Kuzmin as their spokesman. His poetry and *Wings* became their catechism.

Much gay literature was published in Russia during the first two decades of our century. The leading Symbolist poet Viacheslav Ivanov (1866–1945) brought out in 1911 his much-acclaimed book of verse *Cor Ardens,* which contained a section called "Eros" about the married poet's homosexual experiences. Ivanov's wife, Lydia Zinovieva-Annibal (1866–1907), specialized in the topic of lesbian love. Her short novel *Thirty-Three Freaks* and her collection of stories *The Tragic Zoo* (both 1907) were much discussed in the press and made lesbian love a better-known phenomenon. Around 1910, there appeared in Russia a group of poets called "peasant," not so much because of their origins, but because the survival of the peasant way of life in the twentieth century and a sort of peasant separatism from the rest of society were their central concerns. The undisputed leader of this group was Nikolai Kliuev (1887–1937). Born in a peasant family that belonged to the Khlysty sect, Kliuev learned (and taught his followers) how to combine his native village folklore with the modernist style and versification developed by the Russian Symbolist poets. Kliuev's undisguised homosexuality did not prevent most critics and intellectuals of the time from considering him the leading literary spokesman for the whole of Russian peasantry.

Kliuev's poetry, with its crowded imagery and a tone akin to magic spells and incantations, served as a model for a whole school of poets and fiction writers. The most notable of his disciples was Sergei Esenin (1895–1925), much better known in the West because of his brief marriage to the dancer Isadora Duncan. For about two years (1915–1917), Kliuev and Esenin lived together as lovers and wrote about it in their poetry. Although married during his short life to three women, Esenin could write meaningful love poetry only when it was addressed to other men.

His last poem, which was also his suicide note, was addressed to a young Jewish poet who had spent the night with him a few days earlier. Because Esenin's poetry was an object of a veritable cult in the last decades of the Soviet system, all references to his homosexuality, in his poetry and in memoirs about him, were banned. Most Russians today respond with stupefaction or rage when this aspect of his life and writings is mentioned.

The February Revolution of 1917 brought to power moderate democrats and libertarian Socialists and it turned the country into a democracy for the next eight months. But the seizure of power by Lenin and Trotsky in October led to the negation and reversal of all the rights that homosexual and lesbian writers and artists had gained through the revolutions of 1905 and February 1917. Because the most visible homosexuals of the prerevolutionary decades belonged to royalty or aristocracy (the grand dukes, Meshchersky) or were politically ultraconservative (Leontiev, Przhevalsky, Tchaikovsky), the Bolshevik government assumed from the start that homosexuality was the vice of upper-class exploiters. Lenin himself, who had set out to create the Soviet Union in his own image, was a blue-nosed Puritan in sexual and cultural matters. Lenin was shocked that in Germany women were allowed to read Freud and he declared unequivocally that he saw *any* kind of sexual liberation as antisocial and non-Marxist.

Much has been written in Germany and England in the 1920s and in America from the 1970s on about the supposed abrogation by the Bolsheviks of all antihomosexual laws after they came to power. What they actually abrogated was the entire Criminal Code of the Russian Empire, of which paragraphs 995 and 996 were a very small portion. A new criminal code was promulgated in 1922 and amended in 1926. This new code did not mention sexual contacts between consenting adults, which meant that male homosexuality was legal. (Lesbianism was never criminalized in Russia.) But as discovered recently, there were two show trials staged right after the appearance of the 1922 code. One trial was of a group of Baltic Fleet sailors who had rented a large apartment in which to receive their gay lovers and friends. The other one involved a lesbian couple, one of whom had changed her name to its masculine form and took to wearing male clothes so that she and her lover could be seen as spouses. The trials were publicized only locally; internationally, the Soviet Union pretended to have the most liberal legislation on sexuality in the world until the late 1920s. The local press accounts recognized that homosexuality did not violate any Soviet law, but stressed that overt homosexual behavior should be punished because the condition is contagious and might lead young people to imitate the behavior of the gay sailors or the lesbian couple.

The flowering of gay and lesbian poetry, fiction, drama, and art that existed during the decade that preceded the October Revolution was gradually stifled in the 1920s. The right to print gay-affirmative works, won after the Revolution of 1905, did not become extinct until the late 1920s. Such acclaimed figures of earlier times as Kuzmin and Kliuev were doing their best work during that decade. But their books could no longer be advertised or receive favorable reviews in the Soviet press. One of the worst casualties of these new conditions was the fine lesbian poet SOPHIA PARNOK (1885–1933). Her two most important books of verse, *Music* (1926) and *In a Hushed Voice* (1928), were greeted by total silence in the press, and no one but the poet's friends knew that these books were published. (In the 1970s, the Soviet scholar Sophia Poliakova wrote the biography of Parnok and prepared an edition of her poetry, which she sent abroad to be published. This brought Parnok the recognition she was denied in her lifetime.)

Among the numerous talented poets and fiction writers who made their debuts in the 1920s, there was not a single openly lesbian or gay figure. By 1922, numerous noted writers had immigrated to the West, among them the great bisexual poet MARINA TSVETAEVA (1892–1941), who did her most important writing while in exile; also, the openly gay critic Georgy Adamovich (1894–1972) and gay poet Anatoly Steiger (1907–1944). The most important novelist produced by the Russian emigration, Vladimir Nabokov (1899–1977), later an American writer, had homosexual characters in many of his fictions, though he usually wrote of them in a sarcastic tone.

Of the gay writers who stayed in Russia, Kuzmin and Parnok could no longer publish their work after the late 1920s. Esenin was driven to suicide in 1925, and Kliuev was sent to a gulag camp, where he died. Stalin's criminalization of male homosexuality in 1933 led to the worst stigmatization and persecution of homosexuals in Russia's history. The mass arrests in 1934 and periodic crackdowns since that time led to the virtual invisibility of gay men and lesbians in Russian life and literature for the next four decades. Only in the 1970s did there appear underground gay writers, such as the poet Gennady Trifonov (b. 1945), who served a hard labor sentence from 1976 to 1980 for privately circulating gay poetry in manuscript; and the fiction writer Yevgeny Kharitonov, who died at the age of forty in 1981, but was published to great acclaim in 1993. With the coming of *glasnost*, gay figures of the past, such as Leontiev and Kuzmin, have been reprinted; a number of gay periodicals have appeared; and foreign gay novels by MARCEL PROUST and JAMES BALDWIN have been translated. Despite the present chaotic conditions in Russia, the recent decriminalization of homosexuality by Boris Yeltsin's government suggests that the future of Russian gay literature might well turn out to be promising.

—*Simon Karlinsky*

BIBLIOGRAPHY

Burgin, Diana Lewis. "Laid Out in Lavender: Perception of Lesbian Love in Russian Literature and Criticism of the Silver Age, 1893-1917." *Sexuality and the Body in Russian Culture.* Jane T. Costlow, Stephanie Sandler, and Judith Vowles, eds. Stanford: Stanford University Press, 1993: 177–203. ■ G. R.

"Protsessy gomoseksualistov" [Legal proceedings against homosexuals]. *Ezhenedel'nik sovetskoi iustitsii* [*Soviet Justice Weekly*] 33 (1922): 16–17. ■ Herberstein, Sigismund von. *Description of Moscow and Muscovy*. Bertold Picard, ed. J. B. C. Grundy, trans. London: Dent, 1966. ■ Hopkins, William. "Lermontov's Hussar Poems." *Russian Literature Triquarterly* 14 (1976): 36–47. ■ Karlinsky, Simon. *Marina Tsvetaeva. The Woman, Her World and Her Poetry*. Cambridge: Cambridge University Press, 1987 or 1988. ■ ———. "Russia's Gay Literature and Culture: The Impact of the October Revolution." *Hidden from History. Reclaiming the Gay and Lesbian Past*. Martin Bauml Duberman, Martha Vicinus, and George Chauncey, Jr., eds. New York: New American Library, 1989: 348–364. ■ ———. "Russia's Gay History and Literature. (11th-20th Centuries)." *Gay Sunshine* 29/30 (1976): 1–7. Reprinted in *Gay Roots. Twenty Years of Gay Sunshine*. Winston Leyland, ed. San Francisco: Gay Sunshine Press, 1991: 81–104. ■ ———. *The Sexual Labyrinth of Nikolai Gogol*. Cambridge: Harvard University Press, 1976. Paperback reissue, Chicago: University of Chicago Press, 1992. ■ Kozlovskii, Vladimir. *Argo russkoi gomosek-sual'noi subku'ltury* [*The Slang of Russian Homosexual Subculture*]. Benson, Vt.: Chalidze Publications, 1986. ■ Levin, Eve. *Sex and Society in the World of Orthodox Slavs, 900–1700*. Ithaca, N.Y.: Cornell University Press, 1989. ■ Olearius, Adam. *The Travels of Olearius in Seventeenth-Century Russia*. Samuel Baron, ed. Stanford: Stanford University Press, 1967. ■ Poznansky, Alexander. *Tchaikovsky. The Quest for the Inner Man*. Boston: Schirmer, 1991. ■ Rayfield, Donald. *The Dream of Lhasa: The Life of Nikolai Przhevalsky, Explorer of Central Asia*. Athens: Ohio University Press, 1976. ■ Rozanov, Vasilii. *Liudi lunnogo sveta* [*People of lunar light*]. 2d ed. St. Petersburg: Ivan Mitiurnikov, 1913. ■ Turberville, George. "To Dancie." *Rude and Barbarous Kingdom*. Lloyd E. Berry and Robert O. Crommey, eds. Madison: University of Wisconsin Press, 1968. ■ Zen'kovskii, Sergei. "Drug Samozvantsa, eretik i stikhotvorets. Kniaz' Ivan Khvorostinin" [The Pretender's friend, heretic and poet. Prince Ivan Khvorostinin]. *Opyty* 6 (1956): 77–88. ■ Zlobin, Vladimir. *A Difficult Soul. Zinaida Gippius*. Simon Karlinsky, ed. Berkeley: University of California Press, 1980.

Saba, Umberto
(1883–1957)

Umberto Saba's real name was Umberto Poli. His Christian father abandoned his Jewish mother while she was pregnant, so Saba was brought up by his mother and some aunts in the Jewish quarter of Trieste. (He did not meet his father until the age of twenty.) He received very little formal education, a fact that probably contributes to the limpid quality of his verse.

In 1902, he gave up business to devote himself to poetry; he made his living by freelancing for newspapers. In 1908, he did a year's military service in Salerno and then returned to Trieste to get married. In 1919, he bought a bookstore in Trieste, and in 1921, published a collection of his poems under his own imprint. He gave them the title *Il canzoniere* (*The Songbook*). With the poems arranged as if in a narrative order, the book derived its unity from being read as a continuous lyric autobiography. Saba gradually added to the volume, and new editions appeared in 1945, 1951, and 1961. Eventually it contained more than four hundred poems, written over a fifty-year period.

Being of mixed race, Saba had to leave Trieste during the Nazi occupation. He fled to Florence and spent the duration moving from house to house to keep one step ahead of possible deportation. This period apart, his life was uneventful, and the poetic autobiography is less concerned with events than with people—often with people he had loved. He spoke of his life as being "relatively poor in external events but rich in emotions and inner resonances."

Much of Saba's fame rests on poems he wrote about or to his wife Carolina (Lina) and his daughter Lina (Linuccia), who was born in 1910. But *Il canzoniere* is also full of boys. Saba once said that a poet is "a child who marvels at what happens to him when he grows up"; and, indeed, the spirit of the book is very close to adolescence. A nostalgic aura of male puberty, whether the poet's own or that of boys his roving eye admires in later life, hangs over many poems. In "Un ricordo" ("A Memory"), Saba recalls a friendship that he now, in adulthood, recognizes as having been his first love affair. Nor does age diminish his capacity for "loving friendship" ("amicizia amorosa"), as he demonstrates in the poem "Vecchio e giovane," which begins with the words "An old man loved a boy." The mood of the book is often melancholic but never depressive. It is true that each beautiful boy proves the older poet's mortality; but each also enables him to reacquaint himself with joys he first encountered when he, too, was young.

Late in his life, a few weeks after his seventieth birthday in 1953, when he had virtually given up writing poetry, Saba began the short novel *Ernesto* in which he revisited not only the scenes but also the moods of his puberty. Autobiographical at least in part—but to what extent is not clear—the novel chronicles a boy's sexual awakening, starting when he loses his virginity to a man he works with. Subsequently, he has his first heterosexual experience with a prostitute, forms a loving friendship with another boy, and in the end, meets the girl who will eventually become his wife.

Saba died in 1957. *Ernesto* was published posthumously in 1975 and subsequently filmed. Saba is generally ranked alongside the greatest of modern Italian poets, Eugenio Montale and Giuseppe Ungaretti. He should also be included in the canon of significant gay writers of the modernist period. (See also ITALIAN LITERATURE.)

—*Gregory Woods*

BIBLIOGRAPHY

Saba, Umberto. *Il Canzoniere*. Torino: Einaudi, 1961. ■ ———. *Ernesto*. Manchester: Carcanet, 1987. ■ ———. *Thirty-one Poems*. Manchester: Carcanet, 1980.

Sackville-West, Vita
(1892–1962)

Most readers know Vita Sackville-West, if they know her at all, for her love affair with VIRGINIA WOOLF, and for Woolf's brilliant depiction of her as the alluring hero-heroine of *Orlando* (1928). But Sackville-West was a prolific author in her own right. Her fifty-five books include seven collections of poems and stories, twelve novels, and twenty-two works of nonfiction. Yet these works reveal only in veiled and muted ways the woman who captivated Virginia Woolf and inspired *Orlando,* whose affairs (mostly with women) precipitated international scandals and provoked threats of murder and suicide from lovers and husbands of lovers. Although her letters make frequent—usually cryptic—allusions to her sexual relationships with women (and Victoria Glendinning fills out the story with rich detail in her 1983 biography), Vita wrote directly and at length about her sexual identity only once, in a secret journal in 1920, discovered after her death from cancer in 1962 by her son Nigel Nicolson and published as part of *Portrait of a Marriage* in 1973.

Nicolson intended *Portrait of a Marriage* as a "panegyric" of the flexible and enduring relationship between Sackville-West and Harold Nicolson—in a marriage of nearly fifty years that provided social and emotional security for both partners, while allowing freedom for numerous affairs, almost entirely lesbian and homosexual. Nicolson was a young career diplomat when Vita met him in 1910. She was a self-conscious aristocrat, descended on her father's side from Thomas Sackville (1536–1608), Earl of Dorset, Lord High Treasurer of England, poet, courtier, and cousin to the Queen. But she was equally fascinated by her maternal grandmother— a Spanish gypsy dancer who called herself Pepita and appeared on stage as "The Star of Andalusia."

Writing was Vita's passion. By the time she met Nicolson, she had already authored two novels, two plays in French, and a verse drama about the suicide of the unappreciated poet Thomas Chatterton. She was also "in love" with her girlhood friend, Rosamund Grosvenor. "Oh, I dare say I realized vaguely that I had no business to sleep with Rosamund, and I should certainly never have allowed anyone to find it out," she admits in the secret journal, but she saw no conflict between the two relationships: "I really was innocent." Her first son, Ben, was born in 1914, the second, Nigel, in 1917.

In 1918, when another girlhood friendship, with Violet Keppel, blazed into sexual passion, conflict careened toward public scandal. The two women traveled together to Cornwall, Paris, southern France, and Monte Carlo, with Vita dressing in men's clothes and calling herself "Julian." Keppel's marriage to Denys Trefusis in 1919 only heightened the passion between them, and in 1920, when the two women "eloped" to France, the two husbands pursued in a private plane and catapulted all four into international headlines. Sackville-West wrote a fictional account of the affair in her novel *Challenge* (1923), but she moved the action to a Greek island and depicted the relationship (between "Julian" and "Eve") as heterosexual. The more revealing document is the secret journal she began in 1920 in an effort to understand her "Dr. Jekyll and Mr. Hyde personality"—a "brutal and hard and savage" side of herself that reveled in amorous adventures with female lovers, and a "seraphic and childlike" side content with marriage to Nicolson. Nor did she write only for private catharsis. Rather, by analyzing her attractions to women "in an impersonal and scientific spirit," she hoped to create a useful record for the day she saw coming when "the psychology of people like myself will be a matter of interest, and . . . it will be recognized that many more people of my type do exist than under the present-day system of hypocrisy is commonly admitted."

The psychology of people like herself was not something Sackville-West explored publicly in poems and novels. Nevertheless, her works do invite readings as highly coded and carefully veiled expressions of her values and experiences. Cultural and temperamental dualities in novels like *Heritage* (1919), *The Dragon in Shallow Waters* (1921), *Grey Wethers* (1923), and *The Devil at Westease* (1947) mirror the duality she imagined inheriting from the Sackvilles and her Spanish grandmother, and that duality mirrors the psychosexual one described in the secret journal. Portrayals of marriage and sexual relationships between men and women in *The Edwardians* (1930), *All Passion Spent* (1931), and *Family History* (1932), hint at the psychological balancing act that enabled her own marriage to Nicolson. Critic Suzanne Raitt, moreover, calls attention to the almost invisible homosexual subplot in *The Edwardians* and points out that the charged use of the word *queer* in a dialogue between the explorer Anquetil and the main character—a dialogue in which Anquetil urges Sebastian to abandon his proposed marriage and "Come away with me"— predates by two years the OED's first recorded use of the word to mean "homosexual." If *Challenge* (1923) is a *roman à clef* about the affair with Violet Keppel, *Dark Island* (1934) is another, about her relationship with Gwen St. Aubyn. Sackville-West here projects herself into both the jealous husband, Venn, and the devoted secretary, Cristina, who battle each other for possession of Shirin (Vita's real-life Persian pet name for St. Aubyn), and the erotic quality of the relationship between Shirin and Cristina, though not explicit, is unmistakably suggested. Only in her last novel, *No Signposts in the Sea* (1961), does Sackville-West make any explicit reference to lesbian love, however, and there she carefully distances herself from it. "Perhaps a relationship between two women must always be incomplete," the main character, Laura, speculates to a male friend, "—unless, I suppose, they have Lesbian inclinations which I don't happen to share. Then, or so I have been given to understand, the concord may approach perfection."

Sackville-West was not the great writer she longed to be. Her poetry and prose fiction were conservative compared to the new modes being forged by T. S. ELIOT, STEPHEN SPENDER, W. H. AUDEN, Virginia Woolf, and James Joyce. But her long poem, *The Land,* won the Hawthornden Prize in 1927, *The Edwardians* was a best-seller, and her works consistently made money for Leonard and Virginia Woolf's Hogarth Press, which published them between 1924 and 1940. More important, her works, her letters, and her life provide a glimpse into a period when something identifiable as "lesbian consciousness" can first be seen coming into existence, and they document the struggle of one passionate, intelligent, upper-class woman to articulate what it might mean.

—*Sherron E. Knopp*

BIBLIOGRAPHY

DeSalvo, Louise. "Lighting the Cave: The Relationship between Vita Sackville-West and Virginia Woolf." *Signs* 4 (1979): 718–739. ■ Glendinning, Victoria. *Vita: The Life of V. Sackville-West.* New York: Knopf, 1983. ■ Jullian, Philippe, and John Phillips. *The Other Woman: A Life of Violet Trefusis.* Boston: Houghton Mifflin, 1976. ■ Knopp, Sherron E. "'If I Saw You Would You Kiss Me?': Sapphism and the Subversiveness of Virginia Woolf's *Orlando.*" *PMLA* 103 (1988): 24–34. ■ Nicolson, Nigel. *Portrait of a Marriage: V. Sackville-West & Harold Nicolson.* New York: Atheneum, 1973. ■ Raitt, Suzanne. *Vita and Virginia: The Work and Friendship of V. Sackville-West and Virginia Woolf.* Oxford: Clarendon Press, 1993. ■ Stevens, Michael. *V. Sackville-West: A Critical Biography.* New York: Charles Scribner's Sons, 1973. ■ Trautmann, Joanne. *The Jessamy Brides: The Friendship of Virginia Woolf and V. Sackville West.* University Park: Pennsylvania State University, 1973. ■ Watson, Sara Ruth. *V. Sackville-West.* New York: Twayne Publishers, 1972.

Sade, Marquis de
(1740–1814)

The Comte Donatien-Alphonse-Francois de Sade, more often called the Marquis de Sade, lent his name to the complex psychosexual phenomenon of sadism—that is, the derivation of pleasure from cruelty through inflicting physical pain, mental suffering, or both. A prolific author of plays, stories, essays, novellas, and letters, Sade's most lasting works have been such pornographic fictions as *Justine, ou Les Infortunes de la Vertu* (1791) and *Philosophie dans le boudoir* (1795). In them, as in numerous other erotic texts, the pleasures of torture figure prominently among the varied (indeed, polymorphous) sexual activities enjoyed by the libertine characters. Yet there is more to Sade's writings than sadism, in the clinical sense Krafft-Ebing gave that term in his *Psychopathia sexualis* (1876). For running throughout the Sadean *oeuvre*—and often overlapping with the most calculated outrages of his obscene novels—is a philosophical discourse on freedom, power, evil, and desire.

In one of the great ironies of world literature, the Marquis de Sade was descended from the Laura to whom Petrarch devoted his sonnets of romantic love. An altogether less sublimated approach to sexuality prevailed among the French aristocracy into which the Marquis was born, however. Sade's father, for instance, was arrested while "cruising" the Tuileries Gardens for male prostitutes. Bisexual in orientation—and early disposed to a taste for inflicting pain on his sexual partners—Sade was, from his late twenties onward, embroiled in numerous scandals leading to jail and exile. In 1772, he was sentenced to death as a "sodomite." Though the sentence was lifted in 1776, he was imprisoned for many years. Early in July 1789, from his cell window in the Bastille, he yelled that the prisoners were being slaughtered by the guards. Freed during the Revolution, he was a supporter of the Republic—though as a noble, Sade and his family were suspect by the government. His books denounced for immorality, Sade was again jailed in 1801 and died in the insane asylum at Charenton in 1814.

If sexual license made Sade a criminal, imprisonment made him an author: Most of his sizable literary output was produced during incarceration. In his first important writing, "Dialogue entre un pretre et un moribond" (1782), the priest who arrives to take a deathbed confession is shocked to find that the dying man regrets only his restraint in satisfying his urges. Desire, argues the "moribond," is created by nature and ought to be satisfied; all codes of restraint, social and religious, are manmade. This text—reminiscent of other "philosophical tales" by French Enlightenment thinkers such as Voltaire and Diderot—contains the gist of Sade's atheist and "immoralist" creed, elaborated in greater detail throughout subsequent essays and stories.

With his most ambitious work, *Les Cint Vingt Journees de Sodome* (*The Hundred Twenty Days of Sodom*), composed the same year, Sade created a world in which every erotic desire might be systematically gratified. Isolated in a chateau for four months, the noblemen in Sade's pornographic epic are furnished with sufficient provisions and sexual partners to indulge every libidinous possibility they can imagine. The result is an exhaustive, somewhat bewildering work of erotic algebra. Besides every permutation of hetero- and homosexual interaction, Sade's libertines enjoy blasphemy, coprophilia, and necrophilia; and the narrative includes descriptions of torture, mutilation, and murder so brutally graphic that the book is a test of readerly endurance. The book was unfinished; large portions of it exist only as notes describing the sexual acts to be narrated. (Late in the text, one finds numbered passages such as this: "137. A notorious sodomist, in order to combine that crime with those of incest, murder, rape, sacrilege, and adultery, first inserts a Host in his ass, then has himself embuggered by his own son, rapes his married daughter, and kills his niece.") Sade believed the manuscript had been destroyed, and it was only discovered and published in 1904.

Precisely through their grandiose, credibility-defying visions of unrestrained indulgence, Sade's fictions attempt to subvert all religious and social codes proscribing sexual desire. Besides depicting countless sexual tableaux of great vividness—and sometimes gravity-defying complexity—Sade makes his characters representatives of different philosophical positions. This conjunction of pornography and theory reaches perhaps its most successful expression in *Philosophie dans le boudoir* (*Philosophy in the Bedroom*), in which a group of libertines initiates a young woman into the techniques and ideology of Sadean eroticism. In the midst of their orgy, the characters stop to rest and listen to the reading of a pamphlet calling for the abolition of Christianity as ultimately the enemy of republican institutions. In an amusing use of slang, Sade fuses the philosophical and the erotic by employing the verb *socratiser*—"to socratize"—a term referring to the practice of inserting a finger in the anus.

The prohibition against homosexuality forms only one target of Sade's delirious yet systematic efforts to outrage all morality, whether religious or secular. Yet Simone de Beauvoir has compellingly argued that homosexual libido is central to Sade's own personality as it emerges from his fiction—focusing particularly on the character of Dolmance, the senior libertine and master of ceremonies in *Philosophie dans le boudoir,* who Beauvoir, like many other readers, takes as representative of Sade himself. One of the women in the dialogue calls Dolmance "a sodomite out of principle [who] not only worships his own sex but never yields to ours save when we consent to put at his disposal those so well beloved charms of which he habitually makes use when consorting with men." Dolmance—who Sade depicts as a kind of erotic superman, tireless and inventive—announces that the ideal sexual position is to be, simultaneously, the active and the passive partner of anal intercourse.

For well over a century, Sade's writings were suppressed—a fate that helped create his reputation as an apostle of liberty. Advocacy of his work by the surrealists and the work of a few devoted scholars have led to a greater appreciation of his transgressive vision, which has deeply influenced writers including Georges Bataille and MICHEL FOUCAULT. Enacting a perverse fusion of desire and ideology, Sade pursues the idea of sexual freedom with a ruthlessness that is often genuinely unnerving. Alternating between pornographic and theoretical discourses—composed in a prose that shifts with astonishing ease between eloquence and vulgarity, combining humor and the most nightmarelike brutality—Sade's novels are among the most disturbing literary works ever written. (See also FRENCH LITERATURE BEFORE THE NINETEENTH CENTURY and EROTICA AND PORNOGRAPHY.)

—Scott McLemee

BIBLIOGRAPHY

Beauvoir, Simone de. "Must We Burn Sade?" Trans. Annette Michelson. *The Marquis de Sade: The 120 Days of Sodom and Other Writings.* Ed. and trans. Austryn Wainhouse and Richard Seaver. New York: Grove Press, 1966. 3–64. ■ Ferguson, Francis. "Sade and the Pornographic Legacy." *Representations* 36 (1991): 1–21. ■ Gallop, Jane. *Intersections: A Reading of Sade with Bataille, Blanchot, and Klossowski.* Lincoln: University of Nebraska Press, 1981. ■ Harari, Josue. "Sade's Discourse on Method: Rudiments for a Theory of Fantasy." *Modern Language Notes* 99.5 (1984): 1057–1071. ■ Lacan, Jacques. "Kant with Sade." Trans. James B. Swenson, Jr. *October* 51 (1989): 55–75. ■ Lever, Maurice. *Sade: A Biography.* Trans. Arthur Goldhammer. New York: Farrar, Straus and Giroux, 1993. ■ Lyly, Gilbert. *The Marquis de Sade: A Biography.* Trans. Alec Brown. New York: Grove Press, 1970. ■ Michael, Colette Verger. *The Marquis de Sade: The Man, His Works, and His Critics: An Annotated Bibliography.* New York: Garland, 1986. ■ Saylor, Douglas B. *The Sadomasochistic Homotext: Readings in Sade, Balzac, and Proust.* New York: Peter Lang, 1993. 39–63.

Sadomasochistic Literature

Over the past two decades, sadomasochistic literature has emerged as one of the most controversial and vibrant forms of lesbian and gay writing. A fantasy space of leather, sex, power, and performance, S/M is increasingly becoming a privileged arena in the lesbian and gay community for debating the nature of gender identification and sex. The theatricality at the heart of S/M practice has prompted the production of an enormous body of S/M writing, a literature whose breadth and quality has helped make S/M more visible, if not more tolerated, in America and abroad. Authors of such pioneering books as *The Leatherman's Handbook, II* (1989) and the lesbian S/M anthology *Coming to Power* (1981) have made revolutionary claims for S/M literature as a force of liberation. Others in the lesbian and gay community have regarded S/M as an embarrassing cousin, a negative force that, at best, has no real liberating influence and, at worst, actually reinforces oppressive behaviors and attitudes. Undoubtedly, the subculture of S/M remains so central to gay and lesbian life because it speaks not only to the binary oppositions of public-private, male-female that help shape sexuality, but also to the vexing issues of domination, submission, uniformity, and humiliation. S/M literature as a genre confronts these aspects of gay and lesbian experience and, for better or worse, poses a constant challenge to them.

Lesbian and gay S/M literature abounds in variety and resists overarching definitions. In part, this reflects the difficulty of defining S/M sexuality in general. To say that sadomasochism is simply the giving and receiving of pain for erotic gratification belies the complexity of the behavior, let alone its representation in literature. Although S/M, like homosexuality, is generally considered to be a transhistorical and transcultural phenomenon, the term *sadomasochism* was first used in the late nineteenth century by the medical forensic specialist Richard von Krafft-Ebing. Mark Thompson, among other S/M advocates, has found significance in the fact that in an effort to pathologize certain behaviors and to some extent control them, "sadomasochism" and "homosexuality" became categories in the medical community at roughly the same historical period.

Sadomasochism is a performative, fantasmatic practice, and so it is fitting that it receives its name from literary sources. The term *sadism* derives from the MARQUIS DE SADE (1740–1814), a French nobleman imprisoned for his libertinism and for writing fantastic novels such as *Justine* and *Juliette* (1797) that equated sexual pleasure with the inflicting of pain, humiliation, and cruelty. The term *masochism* derives from Leopold von Sacher-Masoch (1836–1895), whose novels, such as *Venus in Furs,* are classic tales of submissive males and cruel mistresses. Following Krafft-Ebing's lead, Freudian psychoanalysis has had much to say about sadomasochism, generally regarding S/M behavior as a narcissistic attachment that directs both aggressive and libidinal (erotic) energies against the self through the partner who is a representation of the self.

For most people, however, S/M has the less subtle connotations of whips and chains and pleasure in pain. But for many of the people who produce and read S/M literature and who practice S/M as part of a dissenting subcultural tradition, S/M is believed to be a means of radically contesting the sexual assumptions of the majority culture. Generally speaking, these self-proclaimed radicals choose to define gay and lesbian S/M as a consensual exchange of power involving physical pleasure and eroticism among two or more homosexuals who play the roles of sadist/top/dominant and masochist/bottom/passive. Consensual S/M partners are said to disavow cruelty, coercion, and force in favor of a heightened sense of the kinds of boundary breaking, trust building, and creativity that is part of all erotic life.

More than anything else, S/M literature has depended on the S/M subculture for its existence and vitality. This is not to say, however, that S/M motifs have not played an important part in the literary traditions of many cultures throughout time. Ancient Greece, Rome, Persia, and Asia, for example, produced a considerable amount of prose, drama, and poetry with homosexual sadomasochistic themes. Euripides' Greek tragedy *Chrissippus* is lost but PETRONIUS's *Satyricon,* with its scenes of dissolute sex in the Roman Empire, still exerts an influence on the S/M imagination today. Both the medieval traditions of Christian asceticism and Renaissance erotic writings, such as Antonio Rocco's *Alcibiades the Schoolboy,* were often permeated with sadomasochistic motifs. Although the French Enlightenment produced the writings of the Marquis de Sade, Victorian London one hundred years later produced the notorious novel *Teleny.* Twentieth-century French writers, such as Georges Bataille and JEAN GENET, explored homosexual S/M themes in influential ways. Pauline Reage's *The Story of O* (1954) made a great impact on lesbian erotic writing, and in fact, today's most influential lesbian S/M organization, Samois, gets its name from the estate of Anne-Marie, the lesbian dominatrix who pierces O and brands her. The American writer WILLIAM S. BURROUGHS in works such as *Naked Lunch* (1959) crafted a style that combines fantasy and chronicle to document the male and drug cultures of the 1950s. Burroughs gained a lasting literary reputation and made a marked impact on the style of S/M literature in the following decades.

The history of what may be properly termed lesbian and gay sadomasochistic literature is inextricably linked to the history of the American leather scene. The first male leather bar opened in New York in 1955, and the scene grew in fits and starts until around 1970, when the explosion of the bar scene meant that S/M could become a lasting component of gay and lesbian cultural practices. As readers of Denis Medoc, GERARD REVE, Aldo Busi, and YUKIO MISHIMA can attest, S/M practice and its literature is very much an international phenomenon. Its roots, however, and its most influential manifestations have been American. Although S/M writing includes drama and poetry, it is as fiction, erotic fiction in particular, that S/M literature has had its greatest success and impact.

Gay male writers have been extraordinarily prolific in S/M literature especially since the 1970s, which saw a veritable boom in underground and aboveground S/M publishing, much of it having to do with the emerging leather scene. Eliot George's *The Leather Boys* (1961), William Carney's *The Real Thing* (1968), and Terry Andrews's *The Story of Harold* (1974) were three of the earliest novels to explore the lifestyles of the first generations of leathermen. Dirk Vanden's *I Want It All* (1969) was the first book in a series to document the emerging leather community in San Francisco. These works helped pave the way for an entire industry of leatherman fiction and erotica. JOHN RECHY's *Rushes* (1979) is one of the most serious and tough-minded attempts to examine the New York leather scene of the 1970s. More recently, Bill Lee has followed in the tradition of Dirk Vanden by charting San Francisco's leatherman scene in *Rogues of San Francisco* (1993) and other books. Some of the best pornographic fiction to come out of the leatherman tradition is by Tim Barrus, whose *Mineshaft* (1984), like Leo Cardini's *Mineshaft Nights* (1970) before it, describes the sexual exploits of the infamous New York S/M palace of the same name. Phil Andros's *Different Strokes* (1986) and Jack Fritscher's *Leather Blues* (1984) and *Stand By Your Man* (1987) are three of the best erotic short story collections in this vein. Larry Townsend is perhaps the most widely read writer of leatherman erotica. His landmark *The Leatherman's Handbook, II* (1989) has received wide circulation and interest. Townsend is considered to be one of the most reliable sources for leatherman fiction. Helping to bring S/M out from the underground, Townsend founded his own publishing company that met with success with *Dream Master and Other SM Stories* (1992).

With scenes of bondage and discipline, submission and dominance, leather fiction is a theater of high risk, mastery, and triumph. From pulp porn to the sophisticated novel, the actions most often depicted include whipping, body piercing, tattooing, scarification, hanging, electric shocking, stretching on racks, mouth gagging, imprisonment, suffocation, shaving, burning, clamping, fisting, and bootlicking. More so than pain, it is suffering that provides the drama for these behaviors that serve as expressions of powerlessness for the player in the bottom role and of power for the top. The role-playing that is so fundamental to S/M sexual life makes its way into gay S/M fiction as well. Familiar "scenes" have traditionally included warrior-captive, sergeant-private, executive-employee, horse-rider, parent-child, teacher-student, priest-penitent, and doctor-patient. Historical settings and stories of war are popular in gay male S/M fiction. For example, Aaron Travis's *Slaves of the Empire* (1992) charts the exploits of a fugitiye gladiator and his slave boys. Charles Nelson's *The Boy Who Picked the Bullets Up* (1981) follows a medical corpsman in Vietnam. Christ-like persecution themes, as in Paul Binding's *Kingfisher Weather* (1989) and Joseph Caldwell's *In Such Dark Places* (1978), are common, as are prison narratives such as Robert N. Boyd's *Sex Behind Bars* (1984). The best scatological writing includes *Tides of Lust* (1973) by the sci-fi writer Samuel R. Delany.

One of the most frequently depicted dimensions of S/M sexuality explored in gay fiction is the master-slave relationship. For example, in John Preston's notable novel *His Entertainment for His Master* (1986), an erotic theater is assembled for a select audience. Preston's *Mister Benson* (1980), whose success was followed with a collection of energetic short stories *I Once Had a Master* (1984), is a classic of modern S/M fiction. The book was first serialized in *Drummer* magazine in the mid-1970s to great appeal and, unlike so much of underground S/M writing, is still available in print. It charts a master-slave relationship between Aristotle Benson, a wealthy, educated topman and his younger slave Jamie, whose youth and inexperience literally enslave him to his master. The novel illustrates the ways in which S/M practice, as a theatrical force, can permeate the aesthetics of the novel. The link between pleasure and pain and the eroticism associated with delayed gratification inform the narrative structure of the novel. The novel opens with Jamie waiting around in a disappointingly "pseudo" leather bar for the "five longest minutes in [his] life." The reader is slavishly forced to join him as he impatiently waits for Mr. Benson, an authentic S/M master, to show interest in him. At the end of the novel, Mister Benson celebrates the transformative power of performance in S/M and the performative nature of S/M identity:

> It seems to me that I've had a hand in creating this man who is now my slave/lover/brother/possession/recruit/masochist. He wasn't this person before me. He is something more since me. And there, as far as I'm concerned, is the magic of SM. The kid that was Jamie *knew* he had to change and he decided to trust me to change him.

As Mr. Benson and Jamie, top and bottom, become implicated in each other's sexual identity, the novel form finds itself aptly suited to describe the complex interrelationship between their S/M identities and desires. Jamie's sexual identity is dependent on the role he plays in Mr. Benson's dramatic scenarios. It remains, in short, a kind of fiction.

The complex nature of S/M fantasy life has given rise to some remarkable experimental fiction such as Tim Barrus's novel *Genocide* (1988) and Aaron Travis's short story collection *The Flesh Fables* (1990). Like Preston, Travis explores the construction of sexual identity, but he does so in a sophisticated mixture of naturalistic chronicle and gothic fantasy that confuses the master-slave power dynamic. In stories such as "Blue Night," the polarized identities of sadist and masochist break down as the slave's submission becomes a way of asserting his power and masculinity. As in much recent gay male S/M literature, masochism in "Blue Night" becomes the locus not of weakness but of power. By emphasizing the mutuality and interdependence of the S/M dynamic, masculinity is preserved for all participants as a sign of individual power and autonomy.

Of course, not all literature dealing with S/M celebrates its cathartic and redemptive powers. In many gay novels, sadistic pleasure is had at the expense of reciprocity, and masochism is viewed as a form of gay self-hatred and powerlessness. Gay murder mysteries, such as Tony Fennelly's *Glory Hole Murders* (1985), often associate sadomasochism with deadly risk. Dennis Cooper's *Frisk* (1991) comes at S/M from a critical standpoint, exploring the permeable boundary between fantasy and reality, ecstasy and horror. In Steve Abbot's *Holy Terror* (1989), a kind of gothic romance with some S/M themes, masochistic submission is linked to romantic love when the main character falls for eyes that say: "We know what you want even more than you do." A cross between Nabokov's *Lolita* and MANN's *Death in Venice,* Gilbert Adair's *Love and Death on Long Island* (1980) is a witty expression of the impossibility of fulfillment and the humiliations associated with passions for young boys.

Sadistic erotic relationships between sons and real or imagined fathers permeate the gay novel. In Will Aitken's *Terre Haute* (1989), Jared McCarthy's father punishes him for masturbating to *Physique* magazine. This association of older men and pain is a frequent theme in European novels. *Neons,* by the French writer Denis Belloc, tells the story of a young man whose father's death and his subsequent life with an abusive stepfather pattern his adult masochism. Several well-known Spanish novels have also associated youth and masochism, including JUAN GOYTISOLO's

Forbidden Territory (1985) and Realms of Strife (1986) and Terenci Moix's The Weight of Straw (1990). In Confessions of a Mask (1958), the well-known Japanese writer YUKIO MISHIMA autobiographically depicts his youthful identification with ST. SEBASTIAN. As one of the few American playwrights to write about S/M for the stage, Robert Chesley has devoted much of his work to criticizing S/M for reinforcing gay self-hatred. Night Sweat (1984), for example, is a frank argument against the masochistic thrust of much of gay life.

Nowhere has the ideological content of S/M literature been more rigorously scrutinized than in the debates within radical feminism concerning the ascendancy of lesbian S/M. With the founding in the late 1970s of Samois, a lesbian feminist S/M advocacy group, lesbian S/M has been on the defensive to distinguish its practices from the kinds of misogyny associated with male violence. In volumes such as Against Sadomasochism (1982) and Unleashing Feminism (1993), radical feminists associated with the antipornography movement have argued that sadomasochistic activity among lesbians stems from and perpetuates violence against women. In this context, lesbian S/M literature is seen to recapitulate and reinforce the oppressive structures of patriarchal society. The volume of lesbian S/M writing Coming to Power (1981) was a pioneering attempt to make a case for consensual S/M. The anti-S/M movement has consistently denied the possibility that consent between partners legitimizes acts that would otherwise be oppressive. It has argued that the kind of distance from patriarchy that true consent requires is unavailable to those who practice S/M. Lesbian S/M literature, in its effort to combat the impression of false consciousness, has been extraordinarily innovative in finding ways of understanding S/M that are compatible with feminism.

The most important lesbian S/M author is Pat Califia, who has established herself as one of the most innovative of all S/M writers. The very act of writing S/M literature is, for Califia, a political gesture, a commitment to fighting onslaughts from both the right-wing and from antipornography feminists. An attack against those who try to ban or control knowledge of S/M, her fiction attempts to break the rules and stretch the boundaries of lesbian aesthetic practice. Her short story collection Macho Sluts (1988), which includes the much-acclaimed story "The Calyx of Isis," includes nonlesbian scenarios as well as vanilla (non-S/M) sex. Her novel Doc and Fluff (1990), which tells "the distopian tale of a girl and her biker," is a witty exploration of the difference between S/M practice and misogyny. Unlike much of gay male S/M literature, Califia's fiction has responded to the AIDS crisis in positive and imaginative ways. Seeing herself as a kind of "tribal storyteller" intent on shattering S/M's reliance on well-worn "scenes," Califia never hesitates to make didactic statements concerning the role of trust, consent, honesty, and above all, imagination in lesbian sexuality. Literature, for Califia, is the best way for S/M to exert its own radical potential.

As it does in much lesbian S/M fiction, goddess worship makes its way into the light-hearted Doc and Fluff in the form of the High Priestess Raven. The goddess is a key figure in the notable novels of Artemis Oakgrove, the author of the trilogy The Raging Peace, Dreams of Vengeance, and Throne of Council (1984). An eccentric piece of fantasy literature, Oakgrove's Throne trilogy contrasts sharply with her Nighthawk, a novel about "dangerous inner-city women" featuring a gang of black butches and a white slave girl. S/M-themed lesbian short fiction can also be found in DOROTHY ALLISON's Trash (1988) and Cappy Kotz's The First Stroke (1988). The Dog-Collar Murders by the successful "vanilla" novelist Barbara Wilson defends S/M against the charge that it is internalized male hatred that inevitably leads to violence. Lesbian S/M literature has been at the forefront of recognizing the legitimacy of consensual S/M practice while criticizing the real social structures that S/M practice in part reflects and contests.

Although critics of S/M fiction continue to claim that it reinforces gay self-hatred, they also level the more serious charge that it advances conservative social and sexual ideologies. Since the majority of S/M literature is produced by and for white males, critics have tried to show the ways in which S/M culture replicates race, class, and gender hierarchies. It is true that S/M literature too often eroticizes racial and ethnic difference. And in its less rigorous forms, it also depicts positions of power and dominance based on class position and misogynistic notions of masculinity. Perhaps these tendencies are rooted in the origins of S/M culture in America. Scholars have argued that it arose out of the biker culture of the 1950s, which is often seen as a reaction against the domestic stability and white-collar positions offered to white males in post–World War II America. The association of male homosexuality with S/M imagery such as leather, piercing, and tatoos is sometimes seen as a reaction against the widespread belief that homosexuality was a form of gender deviance and effeminacy. If S/M has become a prominent mode of gay life and gay style, some critics have argued that it is only imitating the rise of a new form of masculinity associated with the rising conservatism of the 1980s and 1990s. But to call S/M, especially in its most radical and dissenting forms, politically conservative is clearly too simplistic.

There is reason to believe, for example, that the politics of confrontation and outrage that have come to be associated with the ascendancy of queer politics owes a significant debt to S/M. Not surprisingly, some S/M writers lament the increased visibility and cultural mainstreaming of S/M practice as a watering down of its empowering potential.

The heated wars over lesbian S/M, like the attempts in America and abroad to ban consensual S/M sex and to censor its representation, attest to the fact that S/M continues to be a site of extraordinary controversy and fascination. S/M writing, as Mark Thompson's spirited nonfiction anthology *Leatherfolk* (1991) demonstrates, has constructed itself as a form of emancipation for all lesbians and gays. As a crucial site of S/M performance, sadomasochistic literature continues to stake a claim for S/M's radical potential. (See also EROTICA AND PORNOGRAPHY.)

—*Robert Nashak*

BIBLIOGRAPHY

Preston, John, ed. *Flesh and the Word: An Anthology of Erotic Writing*. New York: Plume, 1992. ■ Samois, eds. *Coming to Power*. 3d ed. Boston: Alyson Publications, 1987. ■ Thompson, Mark, ed. *Leatherfolk: Radical Sex, People, Politics, and Practice*. Boston: Alyson, 1991. ■ Townsend, Larry. *The Leatherman's Handbook II*. 3d ed. New York: Carlyle Communications, 1993.

Saikaku, Ihara
(1642–1693)

Saikaku's primary appeal to modern readers interested in a gay and lesbian literary tradition is his collection of forty short stories called *The Great Mirror of Male Love* (*Nanshoku okagami* [1687]; tr. Schalow, 1990), which depicted male homosexual love (*nanshoku*) as it was practiced in seventeenth-century Japan. The issue of female homosexuality is notable for its absence from the discourse of the day and is likewise missing from Saikaku's works, with the one exception of a scene in *The Life of an Amorous Woman* (*Koshoku ichidai onna* [1684]; tr. Morris, 1963) in which the female protagonist is forced to make love with the mistress who hired her as a maid.

Virtually nothing is known of the man behind the pen name Saikaku ("western crane") apart from the several dozen poetic anthologies and collections of short stories that were published under this and another pen name of his, Kakuei ("crane eternal"). From all accounts, the man's first love was *haikai* poetry (comic linked verse), which he practiced from an early age and with an eccentric ardor that earned him the sobriquet "Dutch Saikaku" (*oranda Saikaku*) after the outlandish Europeans allowed to trade with Japan during the Edo Period (1600–1868). In 1682, he turned to writing prose fiction, and in little more than a decade until his death in 1693, he managed to create a literary legacy in prose that placed him firmly among the major writers of narrative fiction in Japan. The man's real name may have been Hirayama Togo; he was possibly the scion of a sword-making family from the town of Ibara who had settled in the castle town of Osaka as members of the urban merchant class, manufacturing, selling, and maintaining the swords that were so vital to the samurai and urban classes. (Samurai traditionally sported two swords, one long and one short, and merchants were allowed to carry a single short sword, whereas farmers were forbidden to own swords at all.) His status as son of a wealthy merchant family meant that he was a man of means, able to afford the urban pleasures of attending theater performances and visiting the pleasure quarters that would appear later in his fictional creations. The fact that he came from a family of sword makers may have given him special access to the world of the samurai class, to which the average merchant or urban dweller would have had limited entry, and this may explain his detailed knowledge of samurai manners and mores. His lifelong composition of comic linked verse was also a leisurely pursuit indicative of wealth, but he took it further than expected of the average well-to-do young merchant and in fact became a respected teacher of *haikai*, widely sought by potential students and ultimately master to a large group of direct disciples.

The equilibrium between the merchant activities he was born into and the poetic avocation he cultivated was shattered in 1675 upon the death of his young wife in an epidemic, after which he retired from business and devoted himself completely to *haikai* composition and his poetry students. He composed long sequences of verse in so-called "arrow counting" (*yakazu*) contests in which the aim was to spontaneously release as many verses as possible within a prescribed time limit, and became so adept at the form that rivals no longer dared challenge him. He then tried his hand at writing plays for the kabuki and puppet (*joruri*) theaters, but they failed. More successfully, he wrote an actor-evaluation book (*yakusha hyobanki*) critiquing the acting and sexual skills of youthful male actors on the kabuki stage who doubled as boy prostitutes. These activities reveal an active literary mind that was engaged with the newly emergent popular urban culture of Osaka and Kyoto. When he wrote his first collection of short stories, *The Life of an Amorous Man* (*Koshoku ichidai otoko* [1682]; tr. Hamada, 1964), it was for private circulation among his students and friends in Osaka, but the work so captured the imagination of its readers that he attempted further publishing efforts. Gradually he developed a sense of himself as a writer and created the literary persona whom we refer to today as "Saikaku."

Saikaku's writing career took him through three discernible though not entirely distinct periods based on the themes he chose to address: These were his books on love (*koshoku bon*), books on samurai life (*buke bon*), and books on merchant life (*chonin bon*). The work of Saikaku's that had perhaps the broadest appeal was *The Great Mirror of Male Love*, for it contained all three thematic elements, and it is this book that is most relevant to placing Saikaku in an ongoing tradition of gay and lesbian literature. Saikaku shows great familiarity with the way vernacular narratives (*kana zoshi*) from earlier in the seventeenth century discussed male homosexual love. The volume is framed as an antifemale polemic in the opening and closing sections, directed primarily at the men who prefer women as sexual partners. Along the lines of *kana zoshi* discussions, Saikaku treats the issue of preference for women or boys as an aesthetic issue and proceeds on the assumption that boys are superior as lovers on aesthetic grounds. Each narrative within the collection focuses on a specific youth whose relationship with an adult man shows him to be a paragon of the ideals of male love, ideals such as loyalty, honor, and faithfulness to one's "brotherly troth." The stories thus valorize the youth in a distinctly new formulation of male love called *wakashudo* ("the way of the youth"), commonly abbreviated to *shudo*.

The first twenty stories of *The Great Mirror of Male Love* treat samurai man–youth relations. Death is prominent as the means whereby the youth proves his faithfulness to the ideals of *shudo*. Typically, youths and their adult male lovers battle interlopers and, after successfully defending the honor of their relationship, manfully take their own lives. The second twenty stories treat youths in the kabuki theater and their merchant-class patrons. There, the means of upholding the ideals of *shudo* are necessarily different. Typically, the kabuki youth proves that he has mastered the ideals of *shudo* by attracting and satisfying many men; in some cases, he defends his relationship with a specific man by renouncing the stage to devote himself to him or, in most cases, to his memory since the man usually disappears or is deceased.

Where Saikaku breaks new ground and goes beyond what was done in earlier vernacular texts on male love is in his division of the adult men who love youths into two groups, woman-haters (*onna girai*) and connoisseurs of boys (*shojin zuki*). The woman-hater is exclusive in his preference for the love of youths, whereas the connoisseur of boys enjoys their love along with the love of women. The two groups are in some ways parallel to the categories in many modern societies of the (exclusively) homosexual and the bisexual. Saikaku builds *The Great Mirror of Male Love* around the exclusive ethos of the woman-hater since it is the "homosexual" woman-hater's extreme stance that best suits Saikaku's artistic goals for the book, namely, that it depict paragons of male love.

It should be remembered that Saikaku wrote very differently about women and about male love in his other works, a result of his different artistic goals in those works. In *The Life of an Amorous Man*, for example, male love appears as a playful variation to loving women, very much in the mode of the "bisexual" connoisseur of boys. The sequel to that work, *The Great Mirror of Loves* (*Shoen okagami* [1684]) depicted an exclusively "heterosexual" interest in women by the hero, identified as the son of the original "amorous man." All this serves to prove that the stance taken in *The Great Mirror of Male Love* is just that: a stance, taken by a writer for artistic reasons to entertain an urban readership in the closing decades of the seventeenth century in Edo Period Japan.

The theme of male love moved Saikaku from his books on love into his later books on, first, samurai life and, later, merchant life. In the same year that *The Great Mirror of Male Love* was published, Saikaku also wrote a collection of stories about samurai vendettas, *The Transmission of the Martial Arts* (*Budo denrai ki* [1687]), some of which were to avenge wrongs motivated by male love. In the following year, Saikaku came out with another collection called *Tales of Samurai Honor* (*Buke giri monogatari* [1688]; tr. Callahan, 1981), which similarly contained stories about the role of honor in male love. In the last stage of his career, Saikaku focused on the concerns of merchant life, primarily advice in business and making money, structured around biographical success stories that conveyed the ethical principles of merchant society. (See also JAPANESE LITERATURE.)

—*Paul Gordon Schalow*

BIBLIOGRAPHY

Danly, Robert Lyons. *In the Shade of Spring Leaves, The Life and Writings of Higuchi Ichiyo, a Woman of Letters in Meiji Japan.* New Haven: Yale University Press, 1981. ■ Drake, Christopher. "Saikaku's Haikai Requiem: *A Thousand Haikai Alone in a Single Day,* The First Hundred Verses." *Harvard Journal of Asiatic Studies* 52.2 (December 1992): 481–588. ■ Hibbett, Howard S. *The Floating World in Japanese Fiction.* London: Oxford University Press, 1959. ■ ———. "Saikaku as a Realist." *Harvard Journal of Asiatic Studies* 15 (December 1952): 408–418. ■ Ihara Saikaku. *The Great Mirror of Male Love.* Trans. by Paul Gordon Schalow. Stanford: Stanford University Press, 1990. ■ Lane, Richard. "Postwar Japanese Studies of the Novelist Saikaku." *Harvard Journal of Asiatic Studies* 18 (June 1955): 181–199. ■ Schalow, Paul G. "Male Love in Early Modern Japan: A Literary Depiction of the 'Youth.'" *Hidden From History: Reclaiming the Gay and Lesbian Past.* Martin Duberman, Martha Vicinus, and George Chauncey, Jr., eds. New York: New American Library, 1989, 118–128.

Saint-Pavin, Denis Sanguin de
(1595–1670)

Saint-Pavin was born to Marie du Mesnil and Jacques II Sanguin, Lord of Livry, who served three terms as Prévot des marchands (mayor) of Paris (1606–1612). The Sanguins served both King and Church in many illustrious capacities and were related by marriage to such powerful families as the Séguier and de Thou. During Saint-Pavin's years at the Jesuit College, La Flèche, he met René Descartes and Jacques La Vallée Des Barreaux, the latter of whom would become THÉOPHILE DE VIAU's lover and, subsequently, Saint-Pavin's. Shortly after leaving La Flèche, Saint-Pavin acquired the first of a series of religious benefices as commendatory abbot. He also took his place among the generation of 1620, as Antoine Adam called the group of young aristocrats and poets gathered around Théophile de Viau in Paris. Théophile, reflecting the libertine, Epicurean thinking of the Italian philosopher Giulio Vanini, stated "We should follow Nature's dictates; her Empire is pleasant and her laws are not strict." This notion informs many of Saint-Pavin's poems as well. A consummate gentleman and libertine, Saint-Pavin spurned the important secular and sacred posts that his family connections might have afforded him and instead devoted his time to poetry and to friendships. The following partial list of his friends includes several whose homosexual escapades appear in contemporary memoirs: the illustrious general, Louis, Prince de Condé; the musician, Jean Baptiste Lully; the playwright, François le Metel Boisrobert; and the poet, Des Barreaux. Saint-Pavin's intimate friendship with the last is confirmed both by records of the Paris Parliament as well as by contemporary letters. Saint-Pavin frequented the salons of his great friend, Madame de Sévigné, and those of the Marquise de Rambouillet, Madame des Houlières, and Ninon de Lenclos as well. This sophisticated audience for Saint-Pavin's primarily occasional, epigrammatic verse would have appreciated both its sly interweaving of literary allusions and its fundamental understanding of human psychology and social dynamics.

In the largest body of his verse, the gallant sonnets, Saint-Pavin explores the dynamics of heterosexual love by playing with and against traditional themes and tropes. The libertine sonnets and epigrams, however, though displaying similar textual strategies, posit the superiority of sodomy, especially with male partners. The self-portrait that emerges from his work is that of a man who was acutely self-conscious and fully cognizant of his own homosexual identity. Only one untitled lyric poem and three verse letters discuss homosexual love and desire with a serious tone; more typically, Saint-Pavin treats this topic with a brittle wit calculated to provoke a male coterie audience to laughter. In the epigrams of Martial, he finds topoi and structures that he seasons with contemporary elements. His brilliantly crafted poems reflect an aesthetics and sense of community not often recognized as part of the age of grandeur.

The following poem, "Cher Tircis tu tiens bonne table," with its sly wit and urbanity, is an excellent example of Saint-Pavin's conflation of social values and physical pleasure:

> Dear Tircis, what a host you are!
> The groaning board, the wine beyond
>   compare!
> But even better than all that
> is the manner of your invitation. That
> little messenger, this morning,
> while performing his office,
> calling me to the feast,
> was such a delight!
> Again and again, concoct for me such
>   banquets,
> Tircis. Or, by that same messenger,
> just send a note and tell me not to come.

Both Saint-Pavin's lifestyle and his libertine verse won him the sobriquet King of Sodom. Yet even in an age when many less flagrant sodomites were burnt at the stake, his rank and social connections guaranteed his safety. The audacity of his libertine poems was made palatable by their urbane language, literary sophistication, and finesse. Indeed, in 1668, Louis XIV appointed Saint-Pavin his honorary chaplain and advisor.

Since Saint-Pavin's status as gentleman precluded his publishing, his poetry circulated in manuscript. Although disparate manuscript collections contain examples of Saint-Pavin's verse, the most complete collection is that compiled by Valentin Conrart, held at the Bibliothèque de l'Arsenal in Paris. Saint-Pavin's gallant and occasional poems have been frequently anthologized since 1652, but the most frankly libertine poems were only first published in a separate, limited edition in 1911 by Frédéric Lachèvre. A decade later, Félix Gaiffe cited several sonnets about Louis XIV and his brother "Monsieur" (Phillipe of Orleans), the leading homosexual of the day, noting only their urbane sophistication, not their author. In 1934, Louis Perceau reproduced fifty-nine "vers libres" according to their sequence in the Conrart manuscripts. Although this volume remains the major published source of Saint-Pavin's erotic poems, Perceau, like more recent editors of erotica, omits any discussion of the literary merit of the works.

Widely acknowledged as the last master of the French sonnet by literary critics, Saint-Pavin is representative of the age and class in which he flourished. His intellectual, witty verse, arguing for enjoying love and physical pleasure while satisfying those of the mind, plays on the eternal complexities of the social environment. Mirroring a specific moment in time as well as an unchanging human condition, his accessible poems continue to delight while they also express a particular homosexual sensibility.

—*Kathleen Collins-Clark*

BIBLIOGRAPHY

Béalu, Marcel, ed. *La Poésie érotique de langue française*. Paris: Editions Seghers, 1971. ■ Collins, Kathleen. *A Libertine in the Salons: the Poetry of Denis Sanguin de Saint-Pavin (1595–1670)*. University Microfilms, 1986. ■ ———. "Pleasure's Artful Garb: Saint-Pavin's Poetic Strategies." *Continuum* 3 (1991): 171–189. ■ *Disciples et Successeurs de Théophile de Viau: Les Vies et les poésies libertines inédites de Des Barreaux et de Saint-Pavin*. Vol 2 of *Le Libertinage au XVIIe siècle*. 11 vols. Paris: Honoré Champion, 1911. ■ Lever, Maurice. *Les Buchers de Sodome*. Paris: Fayard, 1985. ■ Perceau, Louis. *Cabinet secret du Parnasse*. Vol. 4. Paris: 1934. ■ *Recueil des plus belles pièces des Poètes françois, tant anciens que modernes, depuis Villon jusqu'à M. de Benserade*. Fontenelle, ed. Paris: Barbin, 1692. ■ Tillet, Titon du. *Le Parnasse Français*. Paris: J.B. Coignard fils, 1732. ■ Turquéty, Edouard. "Analecta-Biblion." *Bulletin du bibliophile*. Paris: J. Techener, 1862.

Santayana, George
(1863–1952)

Remembered now chiefly as an American philosopher from the age of William James and Josiah Royce, George Santayana was a poet, novelist, and literary critic as well as a speculative thinker. Born in Spain, Santayana moved to the United States at age nine with his mother, settling in Boston, where, as student and later instructor at Harvard, he began his career as poet and philosopher. (His students there included T. S. ELIOT and Wallace Stevens; and sometime in 1895 or 1896, he met GERTRUDE STEIN). Santayana spent the last four decades of his life traveling throughout Europe, living by his pen. It was during this period as *belles lettrist* that he wrote his novel *The Last Puritan* (1935), as well as such major philosophical works as *Skepticism and Animal Faith* (1923) and the four-volume *Realms of Being* (1927–1940).

Santayana's place in the gay literary tradition derives perhaps less directly from his writings (though the subtle homoeroticism of *The Last Puritan* is a significant contribution) than from the impact of anti-gay bigotry on his professional life at Harvard. Although regarded as brilliant by his peers (including William James), Santayana's status as a bachelor met with the university administration's clear disapproval. Harvard president Charles Eliot remarked that Santayana's literary activities might prove "something futile, or even harmful, because unnatural and untimely"—darkly hinting at additional irregularities beyond his AESTHETICISM. From 1889 through 1907, Santayana remained an instructor, and was only promoted to professor in 1907, following publication of *The Life of Reason* (1905–1906), a quasi-Hegelian work in five volumes. Almost immediately after his mother's death in 1912, Santayana resigned his professorship and spent the rest of his life as writer and wandering scholar.

By his own account, Santayana did not really understand his own sexual preference until fairly late in life. During a 1929 conversation about A. E. HOUSMAN, a favorite poet, Santayana told his secretary Daniel Cory that Housman "was really what people nowadays call 'homosexual'; the sentiment of his poems is unmistakable." Santayana then added: "I think I must have been that way in my Harvard days, though I was unconscious of it at the time."

One finds Santayana's clearest homophile expression in a set of four elegiac sonnets for Warwick Potter, a young man Santayana called his "last real friend," who died of cholera following a boating accident in 1893. The sequence, "To W.P." (1894) inevitably recalls MILTON's "Lycidas," though Santayana's poem is much less an exercise in literary and mythological allusion than Milton's. More than "Lycidas," it seems a genuine outpouring of grief—though the sense of loss is transformed by the poet into resignation and even acceptance: "For time a sadder mask may spread / Over the face that ever should be young." The sequence ends on a note of transcendence, with his grieving friends vowing to

Potter to "Keep you in whatsoe'er things are good, and rear / In our weak virtues monuments to you." Even so, Santayana's most powerful lines convey the wounding permanence of loss: "And I scarce know which part may greater be— / What I keep of you, or you rob from me."

The audience for Santayana's work declined precipitously following his death. His literary talent as a prose artist has only made him suspect among philosophers. During recent years, however, there has been a revival of interest in his life and work, and 1986 saw publication of the first of twenty volumes in a critical edition of *The Works of George Santayana*.

—*Scott McLemee*

BIBLIOGRAPHY

Conner, Frederick W. "'To Dream With One Eye Open': The Wit, Wisdom, and Present Standing of George Santayana." *Soundings* 74.1–2 (1991): 159–178. ■ Cory, Daniel. *Santayana: The Later Years: A Portrait with Letters.* New York: Braziller, 1963. ■ Martin, Robert K. *The Homosexual Tradition in American Poetry.* Austin: University of Texas Press, 1979. 108–114. ■ McCormick, John. *George Santayana: A Biography.* New York: Knopf, 1987. ■ Posnock, Ross. "Genteel Androgyny: Santayana, Henry James, Howard Sturgis." *Raritan* 10.3 (1991): 58–84.

Sappho
(ca 630? B.C.)

The earliest woman writer whose work survives and the most famous, Sappho has been admired throughout the ages. To the ancients, she needed no introduction: She was known simply as *the* poetess, the female equivalent to Homer, *the* poet. She was so esteemed by her compatriots that her portrait graced the coins of her native Lesbos. She was admired by male poets such as BAUDELAIRE, A. C. SWINBURNE, and Ezra Pound as the greatest of lyric poets; by female poets like NATALIE BARNEY, AMY LOWELL, and H.D. as the font of their poetic tradition. To lesbians around the world today, she is the archetypal lesbian and their symbolic mother. Although Sappho was the sole woman to be admitted to the canon of the nine great lyric poets in antiquity, she was the only one of them to attain mythic status when PLATO first elevated her to the rank of the Muses. She is the only ancient author to have become the stuff of legend. She was a popular subject for Greek art from the sixth and fifth century B.C. onward, she was presumably the subject of the six different Greek comedies entitled *Sappho* (none of

which survive), and she became a tragic romantic heroine based on Ovid's use of the legend of her love for the ferryman Phaeon. Lesbians owe their two most important names to her: Lesbian and Sapphic. As JUDY GRAHN so aptly asks in *The Highest Apple,* "When has a larger group of humans, more pervasive behavior, and much more than this, the tradition of women's secret powers that such names imply, ever been named for a single poet?"

Despite Sappho's fame, almost nothing can be said about her with any degree of certainty. She was born in the town of Eresus on the west shore of the island of Lesbos, the third largest island in the Aegean Sea situated a few miles off the coast of ancient Lydia (modern Turkey), possibly as early as 630 B.C. or as late as 609 B.C. She spent most of her life in Mytilene, the principal town of Lesbos, and was exiled to Sicily from 604/3 B.C. to 596/5 B.C. because of her family's political activities. She was of aristocratic birth. Her father's name is given variously as either Simon, Eunomius, Eurygyus, Eurytus, Semus, Scamon, Euarchus, or Scamandronymus; her mother's name was Cleis. She had three brothers, Larichus, Eurygyus or Erigyus, and Charaxus, whom she is said to have berated in her poetry for his expensive affair with the notorious courtesan Rhodopis. She was married and had a daughter named Cleis. She was a Lesbian by birth and by inclination.

In antiquity, the word *Lesbian* meant simply "native of Lesbos." So, we refer to Sappho and her male contemporary Alcaeus as Lesbian poets much as one might speak of H.D. and Amy Lowell as American poets. The denotation of female homosexuality for the word *Lesbian* is relatively recent. In the English language, it is first attested in the 1890 *Billing's Medical Dictionary* and moved quickly into medical, literary, and underground use. The word *Lesbian* did have special connotations in antiquity. Lesbos was the center of Aeolian culture, and its natives were perceived by the rest of the Greek world (namely, Dorian and Ionian Greeks, who were far more pragmatic and ascetic in temperament) as passionate, intense, and sensual people with a great love of nature and of physical beauty. As Denys Page states in *Sappho and Alcaeus,* the poets of Lesbos created "the most exquisite lyrical poetry the world has known." It is perhaps due to this exquisiteness and sensuality that Lesbos was to become "a byword for corruption" and "decadent sensuality" comparable to the reputation of the Provençal troubadours and their erotic literature in later times. In antiquity, "Lesbian woman" did not denote a female homosexual, but a licentious woman who freely indulged in shameful sexual behavior. Hence the Greek verb *lesbiazein,* "to act the lesbian," meant "to fellate" or otherwise "play the whore." After the second century A.D., the common term for a homosexual woman was *tribas* (from the verb meaning "to rub" or "massage"), which the Liddell and Scott *Greek-English Lexicon* defines as "A woman who practices unnatural vice with herself or other women." The specific term applied to Sappho's relations by the Hellenistic biographers (third century B.C.) is *gynerastia,* the "erotic love of women."

It is supposed that Sappho was the teacher of a group of young, unmarried aristocratic girls who came to her from all over the Greek world for instruction in the arts of beauty, music, poetry, and dance. From Sappho's poetry, we infer that there were other such women's circles on Lesbos during her time, for she directed witty invective poetry against her rivals, Gorgo and Andromeda. For example, Fragment 57 insults Andromeda's taste in girls (all translations are my own):

What witch, Andromeda, addled your wits?
Some farm-girl with her faded calico

Dragging the dust. This season,
Hemlines skim slim ankle-bones
And we wear silk
In the city.

Atthis, to whom Sappho directed tender verse, apparently became a defector and is chastised accordingly in Fragment 49:

I did love you once, Atthis
But that was long ago.
I thought you were a little thing:
A girl without grace.

But what Sappho is primarily known for is her impassioned love poetry toward young women.

Of Sappho's nine books of lyric poetry, approximately 200 fragments survive, many of them consisting of only one or two words or a few isolated characters. Many of the surviving fragments are in the same poetic meter, a meter that appears to have been Sappho's favorite (if not her invention) and so is called after her, the sapphic stanza. We have only one complete poem and forty fragments that are long enough to offer a degree of sense. What happened to the prodigious volumes of her work? Legend has it that after the church father Tatian branded Sappho a whore in 140 A.D., presumably due to her "unnatural" love for young women, her books were burned by the Christians. One version of the legend claims that this occurred under Gregory Nazianzen about 380 A.D. Other sources set the burning in Constantinople and Rome in 1073 A.D. Whether the stories are true, or whether her work disappeared through neglect (as with many ancient authors), no manuscript survived in Europe. Still, as Meleager, the compiler of the ancient anthology (ca 90 B.C.) said, the remains of Sappho are "few, but roses."

The surviving fragments of Sappho focus on the sensual world. Gardens, varieties of flowers and blossoming herbs, smoking incense, and perfumed oils provide a riot of scent and color. The poems express delight in the look and feel of fine fabrics, in floral garlands set about flowing hair, the soft bed, a companion's tender flesh, the music of the lyre, the thrill of a girl's singing, the joyful dance, the pleasures of love, and the sadness of the inevitable parting. Aphrodite, the goddess of love and sexuality, is ever present. In the poems of Sappho, she is not portrayed as a fearsome deity, but as a mentor and confidante. We see this special relationship in the two summoning hymns to Aphrodite. In poem 1, Sappho, the rejected lover, calls upon Aphrodite for aid. In Fragment 2, Sappho invokes Aphrodite, the Cyprian goddess,

to attend upon her and her companions in an idyllic
setting:

Come to me from Crete
To this, your sacred temple.
Here, to this gracious glade of apples
And altars thick with incense.

Here, cool water bubbles up
Through broken apple-boughs
In a clearing shaded all with roses
And quivering leaves drip enchantment.

Here, meadow grass that feeds strong horses
Concedes to a riot of spring flowers
And soft honeyed breezes blow.

* * *

Here, then, Cyprian, bring garlands
And gods' nectar in golden cups.
Be our gentle serving maid:
Let divinity mingle with our feast.

A major component of Sappho's verse (and of Greek
poetry in general) is its aurality. The modern *reader*
of poetry forgets that the ancients were not readers at
all, but auditors. Consequently, the sound of a poem
was of extreme importance. Sappho was an acknowledged master of poetic sound effects, meter, and euphony. Unfortunately, because the Greek language
and its verse are innately incompatible with English,
this aural component is almost impossible to convey
in translation. Such is the case, too, with Sappho's
skillful use of hidden metaphor, ambiguity, wordplay,
wit, irony, and allusion. Her poetry is deeply engaged
with the Homeric tradition, subtly applying the epithets and formulaic phrases of heroic epic verse to
women's erotic experience. In so doing, she implicitly
sets women's private experience of love on a par with
men's public performance in war. She says, in effect,
"This is different, but this, too, is heroic."

In the face of her erotic poetry, it is hard to believe
that scholars continue to argue that Sappho was not
a lesbian in the modern sense of the word. From the
first extant comments on Sappho's erotic relations
with young women in the Hellenistic period to the
present day, critics (predominantly male), appalled at
the thought of women engaging in lesbian sexual
activity, have tried to deny Sappho's homosexuality.
Their attempts range from deliberately mistranslating
words that indicate that the beloved is female to
forcing a heterosexual context on poems depicting
lesbian desire. For example, the famous Fragment 31
has been described as a marriage-song in which
Sappho relates the girl's desirability for the groom's

benefit. Her feelings in the poem continue to be hotly
disputed. They have been described as anything ranging from jealousy, love, fear, wonder, and terror to an
anxiety attack brought on by penis-envy. Had this
poem been written by a man, there would be little
dispute. Nor has there been in the many translations
penned by men. Of course, the gender dynamics of the
poem are significantly altered when it becomes a male
voice describing his response to a woman. Such translations are an insidious (if unintentional) way of
heterosexualizing Sappho. In the poem, Sappho
watches a man's reaction to her beloved and marvels
at his composure, so different from her own response.
To anyone who has ever been a lover, the symptoms
of infatuation are unmistakable:

Fragment 31
To me, he seems like a God, that man,
Who can sit at ease in your presence
Who can hear your melodic voice
Strumming close in his ear,
Your provocative laughter:

Ample cause for cardiac arrest.
You spied, I swallow all voice
And my tongue lies crippled.
A lyric fire sweeps my flesh
And my eyes stare blindly.
Rhombs crash close in my ear,
A chilling sweat fingers my spine,
Trembling invades my every part
And I am greener than grass.
To myself, I seem like a corpse, or near.

There is a whole tradition of "defenders" of Sappho.
David Robinson is typical: "Villainous stories arose
about her and gathered vileness till they reached a
climax in the licentious Latin of Ovid." The most
famous of Sappho's "defenders" was the German
Ulrich von Wilamowitz-Moellendorff who in his classic *Sappho und Simonides* depicted Sappho as a chaste
haus frau, a virtuous pillar of the community and
moral instructor of young girls. As Page describes it,
Wilamowitz "gave new and lasting dignity to the old
theory that Sappho was a paragon of moral and social
virtues and that her poetry was grossly misunderstood
in antiquity." Wilamovitz explained Sappho's relationship with her charges by depicting her as a cult
priestess in the service of an "honest" (that is, nonsexual) Aphrodite. As Page points out, there is absolutely
no evidence for this theory. Nevertheless, much scholarly ink has been spilled trying to prove that despite
her professed love of women, despite her poetic genius, Sappho was still a "good" woman.

Historically, male critics have been extremely uncomfortable when faced with women of poetic genius. This discomfort stems from the tradition that "good" women are silent women, seeking not fame in the public world, but to nurture their families and foster the worldly ambitions of their husbands and male relations. This unease is sometimes assuaged by belittling the poet's accomplishment, or, if this cannot be done, by denying that the author was female. It is for this reason that although the poets Sappho (Greek 630? B.C.), Erinna (Greek, ca 612? B.C.), Sulpicia (Roman, ca 30? B.C.), and EMILY DICKINSON (American, 1830–1886) could not be more historically distant and culturally different, the criticism on them is almost interchangeable. For example, critics maintain that their lyrics are not crafted, but unstudied emotional outpourings; their poems are not the work of imagination, but a biographical record set in verse; their work is not intended for publication, but for the private amusement of a few chosen friends. More recent criticism has acknowledged the poetic merits of Sulpicia: It has also given birth to the idea that the poet was male. So, too, with Erinna, a woman who died virgin at age nineteen and whom the ancients praised as the equal of Homer. In *The Woman and the Lyre,* Jane McIntosh Snyder notes that the one surviving fragment of Erinna has been interpreted in various ways, ranging from "a genuine cry of grief" ("genuine" and thus unstudied) to "a 'brilliant' forgery by a male writer from Cos or Rhodes." The underlying assumption behind such critical gender switching is that women cannot write good poetry. What, then, is such a critic to do with Sappho? The historical tradition is too strong to deny her femininity, and her literary reputation is too powerful for her poetic skills to be denied. Still, these prejudices influence her commentators, as we can see in David M. Robinson's summary of her work in *Sappho and Her Influence:* "Sappho then, was a pure and good woman. . . . If she ever collected her verse it was only to promote the idealization of marriage pageants, and not with the purpose of publishing a full edition of her songs." Note that, as with Fragment 31, Sappho's homoerotic lyrics have been placed in the service of heterosexuality. The denial of Sappho's intent to publish, and the interest in eternal fame that such an intent implies, is especially curious since it was Sappho who, as far as we know, invented the literary motif of the poet achieving immortality through verse.

The issue of Sappho's status as a poet is complicated by her homosexuality. It is, indeed, her homosexuality—not her verse—that is the focus of scholarship: what critics call "the moral question." As Judith Hallett explains in "Sappho and Her Social Context: Sense and Sensuality," "Modern criticism of supposedly homosexual or at least bisexual Greek male lyric poets . . . does not reflect the same obsession with their sexual preferences to the neglect of their poetry." She notes that commentators of the poet Anacreon make few remarks on his homosexual poetry, yet in the one fragment that seems to refer to female homosexuality, many scholars have taken pains to prove that Anacreon is not characterizing the woman in his poem as homosexual. Ultimately, though, even Hallett seems to reject Sappho's homosexuality, concluding that "there are no references in Sappho's lyrics to any physiological details of female homoerotic involvement." This conclusion, however, ignores the fact that the Greeks would have considered physiological details of erotic involvement—heterosexual *or* homosexual— completely inappropriate for the higher genres of poetry in which Sappho wrote.

What is the evidence for Sappho's homosexuality? The erotic nature of her poems where both lover and beloved are clearly female implies lesbian interest although many scholars vehemently maintain that this interest was never consummated. There is, however, one fragmentary poem that implies lesbian practice. Sappho and another woman, possibly one of her charges, say a tearful final goodbye. The girl stresses that she leaves Sappho against her will. Presumably, she is going to get married. Sappho consoles the girl by reminding her of the pleasures they shared when she lay at Sappho's side. There are fragmentary references to garlands hung about a soft neck, to anointing skin with fragrant ointments, to lying on a soft bed where, according to the particular verb form, the girl satisfies someone else's erotic desire. Since there are only two people depicted in the scene—the girl and Sappho—this would seem to be a clear description of lesbian activity, yet some scholars have mistranslated *pothos,* the word normally used of sexual passion, and taken the verb *exies* "you expelled (by satisfying)" as reflexive to translate the phrase as "you satisfied your desire (for rest)," that is, after too much dancing.

Despite the strong evidence to the contrary, serious attempts have been made to heterosexualize Sappho. In antiquity, a legend was created that, in the end, Sappho renounced the love of women and fell in love with the ferryman Phaeon. Too ugly to get her man, she leapt off of the Leucadian Cliff to her death. This legend is so incongruous with the authorial voice in Sappho's verse that the ancient biographers themselves were confused: They list *two* Sapphos of Lesbos. The second Sappho is described as either a lyre player or courtesan, but specifically not the poetess. It is this second Sappho who committed suicide for love of Phaeon. Ovid, in his Epistles, conflates the two

Sapphos: It is the great poet Sappho who renounces girls and longs for Phaeon. It is this Sappho that writers, artists, and composers have focused on ever after.

Some commentators cite as proof of Sappho's heterosexuality the fact that she was married and had a daughter. Curiously, her husband is cited as Kerkylas from Andros. The name Kerkylas is based on the word for "penis." Andros comes from the word for "men." If we translate, then, we find that the most famous lesbian of all was married to Penis of the city of Men. Too good to be true? In any event, it is likely that she *was* married, but this has no bearing on her sexual orientation. Greek society was very different from our own: Marriage was seen as a civic responsibility and familial obligation. It was not designed—nor expected—to fulfill one's erotic or romantic needs. For that, men looked elsewhere. And marriage did not interfere with their homosexual affairs. Marital relations were known as a *ponos* or "labor," *ergon* "work," or *kamnos,* "toil." In contrast, erotic affairs were called *paidia* or "play." Men were so unenthusiastic about participating in sexual intercourse with their wives that they had to be reminded. PLUTARCH in his life of Solon suggests that a man should make love to his wife three times a month in order to ease marital tensions. Foreplay was actively discouraged: Too much pleasure might give a woman power over her husband and, thus, undermine his authority.

Clearly, women could not expect sexual fulfillment within marriage. But for a woman to remain unmarried in this society was unthinkable. According to Eva Cantarella in her book *Pandora's Daughters,* girls were betrothed as young as five years old and, by thirteen or fourteen, they were subjected to arranged marriages to men who were aged thirty or older. Before and after marriage, women were completely segregated in the internal part of the house to which men had no access. Women did not come into contact with men outside their immediate family except occasionally at public festivals and funerals. On Lesbos, aristocratic women like Sappho got an education, albeit a "female" one emphasizing music, singing, and dancing. But as Cantarella points out, at least this education helped form their individual personalities and offered them a means to express it. If we take Sappho as a model teacher, it would appear that an appreciation of sensual expression, including lesbian affairs, was part of a girl's education. When a girl moved from maiden to married woman (at about fourteen), her time for play was over. She would have only memories of what must have been the happiest time of her life. It is no wonder that she wept on graduation. Women were segregated with other women, and socialized and trained by them. What would be more natural than for romantic attractions and rivalries to occur among them, as occurred among their menfolk? Who is to say if Greek women had homosexual affairs of their own? Sappho does, but, unfortunately, she is our only direct source for love between women; as Cantarella states, "Unlike male homosexuality, female homosexuality was not an instrument for the training of citizens. It therefore by definition interested only women."

What is astonishing about Sappho is that in the face of one of the more rigid cultures in history, through generations of patriarchal misogyny and homophobia, she broke through the silence imposed on female homosexuality. By the extraordinary power of her verse, Sappho forces the critic and the reader to reckon with her as a woman and as a lesbian. As Susan Gubar states in her article "Sapphistries," Sappho represents "all the lost women of genius in literary history, especially all the lesbian artists whose work has been destroyed, sanitized or heterosexualized." The drive to recover the lesbian Sappho in the twentieth century began with the poets Natalie Barney, Renée Vivien, H.D., and Amy Lowell in their search for their poetic roots. In *Surpassing the Love of Men,* Lillian Faderman describes Barney's and Vivien's 1904 trip to Lesbos in the hopes of forming a poetic colony of women in Sappho's honor. Although this dream was not realized, the two poets did create a new Lesbos of sorts in their famous Paris salon. Sappho's literary influence continues to be felt among lesbians: We see it in the work of PAULA GUNN ALLEN, JUDY GRAHN, ADRIENNE RICH, AUDRE LORDE, OLGA BROUMAS, and many others.

When lesbians in the twentieth century struggled to find their voice, they heard the clear tones of Sappho drowning out centuries of patriarchal grumbling to speak proudly and openly of her love. As Judy Grahn explains, the lesbian has traditionally been a figure for the outcast who is despised by mainstream (heterosexual) society, yet Sappho was not only accepted by her society, she was one of its heroes. Grahn notes that even though "There is a great deal of lamentation in the work of modern Lesbians," this lamentation is completely absent in the work of Sappho. In fact, it is expressly rejected in Fragment 150:

> It is not right to raise a dirge
> In a house the Muses roam.
> This wailing is unworthy
> Of women like us.

To perhaps overenthusiastic lesbians and feminists, Sappho represents a utopian dream: a socially prominent woman of influence and genius dwelling in a matriarchal society where, as Dolores Klaich has it in *Woman + Woman: Attitudes Toward Lesbianism,* "Women of the day were free to be educated in the same manner as their brothers, they were free to participate in politics, they could own property and conduct legal business, they were not bound solely to domestic duties, and could love whom they pleased." Klaich goes on to say that though Sappho "has been portrayed as a rebellious feminist who screamed out at strictures that circumscribed the lives of Greek women," this is not so, "for there were no strictures at which to scream."

Although I understand and sympathize with the impulse of Klaich and others to create such utopian myths, I believe that, ultimately, such mythologizing seriously undermines Sappho's very real accomplishment: namely, that she lived proudly as a lesbian and achieved everlasting fame as a poet in spite of the severe obstacles posed by her society. If we deny the existence of these historical obstacles, we effectively deny the strength of character, will, and sheer genius that Sappho displayed in overcoming them. And the evidence overwhelmingly indicates that, though the utopian dream is compelling, it is simply not true. As Cantarella explains, there is no proof that a matriarchal society ever existed and much to suggest the contrary. Even those who subscribe to the myth of matriarchy place it in the Neolithic Period, between 12,000 and 6,000 B.C. and, thus, some 11,400 to 5,400 years before the birth of Sappho. Bonnie Zimmerman's re-creation in *The Safe Sea of Women: Lesbian Fiction 1969–1989* is more probable. In her discussion of what she calls "The third formative myth in lesbian literature, and the keystone of lesbian feminist culture," she explains that "The lesbian community functions as an alternative reality to heterosexual society, providing the individual quest hero with validation, pride, joy and self-affirmation." It is "an environment in which woman-loving women find freedom and wholeness as well as sanctuary from a threatening world." It is the Lesbian Nation, that symbolic space where the lesbian feels welcome and at home. Zimmerman states that "mythically," Lesbian Nation existed on Sappho's Lesbos, but her description of Lesbian Nation, to some degree, fits in realistically with what we can infer from Sappho's poems. Namely, that there existed within this extremely rigid Greek culture a community of women who, even if just for a little while, loved one another and supported one another. This, they would always remember. And they could draw strength from Sappho's assurance that they would live on in memory. For her prediction to her female companions has come true many times over now: "I tell you, someone will remember us, even in another time."

—Anita George

BIBLIOGRAPHY

Burnett, Anne Pippin. *Three Archaic Poets.* London: Gerald Duckworth, 1983. ■ Cantarella, Eva. *Pandora's Daughters: The Role and Status of Women in Greek and Roman Antiquity.* Baltimore: John Hopkins, 1987. ■ De Jean, Joan. *Fictions of Sappho 1546-1937.* Chicago: University of Chicago Press, 1989. ■ Dover, Kenneth J. *Greek Homosexuality.* Cambridge, Mass.: Harvard University Press, 1978. ■ Faderman, Lillian. *Surpassing the Love of Men.* New York: William Morrow, 1981. ■ Grahn, Judy. *The Highest Apple: Sappho and the Lesbian Poetic Tradition.* San Francisco: Spinsters, Ink, 1985. ■ Hallett, Judith. "Sappho and Her Social Context," *Signs* 4 (1979): 447–464. ■ Klaich, Dolores. *Woman + Woman: Attitudes Toward Lesbianism.* New York: Simon & Schuster, 1974. ■ Lefkowitz, Mary R. "Critical Stereotypes and the Poetry of Sappho." *Greek, Roman & Byzantine Studies* 14 (1973): 113–123. ■ Page, Denys. *Sappho and Alcaeus.* Oxford: Clarendon Press, 1965. ■ Rissman, Leah. *Love as War: Homeric Allusion in the Poetry of Sappho.* Konigstein: Verlag Anton Hain, 1983. ■ Robinson, David M. *Sappho and Her Influence.* Boston: Marshall Jones, 1924. ■ Snyder, Jane McIntosh. *The Woman and the Lyre: Women Writers in Classical Greece and Rome.* Carbondale: Southern Illinois University Press, 1989. ■ Winkler, John J. "Double Consciousness in Sappho's Lyrics." *The Constraints of Desire.* New York: Routledge, 1990. 162–187. ■ Zimmerman, Bonnie. *The Safe Sea of Women: Lesbian Fiction 1969–1989.* Boston: Beacon Press, 1990.

Sargeson, Frank
(1903–1982)

Frank Sargeson was born Norris Frank Davey in the then small country town of Hamilton, in the Waikato district of New Zealand. He trained to be a solicitor. After a brief stint in an office, he took off on a tour of Europe and began to experiment with writing. After some time on his uncle's farm, he retired to his family's holiday cottage at Takapuna on Auckland's North Shore and settled down to write. Those were the lean years of the Great Depression, but he kept doggedly to his task. His first short story, "Conversation with My Uncle," appeared in 1935 and presaged what was to come—terse, vernacular tales of ordinary men in ordinary circumstances.

He has discussed his upbringing extensively in the first installment of his memoirs, *Once Is Enough* (1973). His strongly Methodist family may well have conditioned him both to accept social norms and to rebel, covertly, against them. Although he spent most of his adult years in a homosexual relationship with Harry Doyle (an ex-jockey), he never came out publicly. The nearest he came to such a move was to resign as president of the New Zealand Branch of P.E.N., after a public breach with A. R. D. Fairburn over the influence of homosexuals on New Zealand literature.

His short stories came to be regarded as the epitome of New Zealand writing. They were about regular blokes whose laconic utterances were far from the pretensions of most previous writers. They spoke to those who yearned for a genuine New Zealand literature, and critics developed the phrase "the world of Frank Sargeson" to describe what they saw as a genuine representation of the New Zealand of the settler. Sargeson himself disputed the myth that had grown around him, claiming simply to have written about what he saw as he saw it. His stories continued through the early 1950s until he decided to take a break while reconsidering his objectives. From the early 1970s onward, he produced a series of novels, accompanied and followed by several autobiographical pieces.

Most critics have failed to see the connection between his earlier stories and his later novels, and few have recognized that sexual problems and antagonisms form the basis of his plots. "That Summer," for example, written in the late 1930s, and often regarded as his most perfect story, recounts the experience of two mates in the depression. Perhaps its most poignant moment is Terry's farewell to his dying mate. He is unable to voice his affection, but the understatement comes through, for those with the needed understanding, as a complete statement of love and of the problems that result. By contrast, *A Game of Hide and Seek* (1972) treats openly of a gay union between a New Zealand Pakeha [white] and a Samoan at much more length without, however, reaching the same level of emotion.

In a society that conspires to devalue and suppress the expression of emotion by males, it is not unusual for violence to substitute for love, and this aspect of Sargeson's stories has been explored by Joost Daalder. Kai Jensen, in an exploration of "The Hole that Jack Dug," exposes the sexual polarization common to New Zealand literature in the 1930s. He points out that the hole is indeed a parable of essential male wholeness. Few critics, however, have been willing to explore the effect of homosexuality on Frank Sargeson's writing. An exception is Bruce King, who comments on the paradox that "Sargeson's homosexual stories should be seen as the quintessence of New Zealandism."

—*Murray S. Martin*

BIBLIOGRAPHY

Daalder, Joost. "Violence in the Stories of Frank Sargeson." *Journal of New Zealand Literature* 4 (1986): 56–80. ■ Jensen, Kai. "Holes, Wholeness, and Holiness in Frank Sargeson's Writing." *Landfall* 44 (1991): 32–49. ■ King, Bruce. *The New English Literatures: Cultural Nationalism in a Changing World.* New York: St. Martin's Press, 1980. ■ McEldowney, Dennis. *Frank Sargeson in His Time.* Dunedin: McIndoe, 1976. ■ Sargeson, Frank. "Conversation with Frank Sargeson." *Landfall* 24 (March 1970): 4–27; (June 1970): 142–160.

Sarton, May
(*b.* 1912)

A writer who has worked successfully in many forms of expression, including poetry, the novel, essays, and the journal, May Sarton was born in Belgium on May 3, 1912. Her father, George Sarton, was a historian of science. Her mother, Mabel Sarton, was a designer and an artist. The family moved to America when Sarton was two years old.

Sarton first published poetry when she was still a teenager. As a young woman, she joined Eva Le Gallienne's Civic Repertory Theatre Company. Subsequently, she created her own theater company, which failed in the Great Depression. Sarton feels that this failure helped steer her toward a literary career. *Encounter in April,* her first book of poems, was published in 1937. Over forty more books in various genres have followed.

Sarton's achievements in any of her chosen genres would assure her a place of respect in American letters. For example, women's groups all over the world study her ten journals for their insights into women and the creative process. She writes often about her work as a writer and the tasks of shaping everyday life. Perhaps the most famous of such books is *Journal of a Solitude* (1977) in which Sarton explores both the joys and terrors of living alone. Her poetry often invites the same kind of intimacy with a reader that her journals do. Many of the settings and characters in the poems are those of her journals.

In the journals, Sarton sometimes examines her lesbian relationships. The most recent journals are also the most open about her lesbianism. The subject, however, has been central to her work throughout her career. For many years, she lived with Judith Matlack, and she remembers this relationship in *Honey in the Hive* (1988). Sarton writes with great honesty and charm about this and other relationships as well. The persona who emerges from the journals is feisty, joyous (particularly in Nature's changes and beauty), and dedicated to keeping her craft alive, often despite hostile critics.

Of twentieth-century poets, Sarton is somewhat of an outsider in that she often prefers metered, rhymed verse to free verse. Her last three collections, however, suggest a greater interest in free verse. Sound, for her, is not a minor consideration as she builds a poem; it largely determines the line. Her *Selected Poems* was published in 1978, arranged by theme rather than chronology. In 1993, a new collected poems appeared, including many poems that have been out of print for many years.

Sarton says that for her the Muse is always female. In her tale *The Poet and the Donkey,* her main character Andy Lightfoot becomes inspired only through the presence of a female Muse. The donkey becomes the missing Muse; Nature brings a Muse to the poet when the poet is ready (perhaps without knowing it) to write.

The poem is not the only element of experience illumined by the presence of a creature. One of Sarton's most beloved books, *The Fur Person* (1957), portrays two women who live with a cat who, essentially, adopts them as his owner. While the owners are referred to as "old maids," this book suggests a subtle reevaluation of the role of the spinster in society. As Andy Lightfoot needs the donkey, these two women need their "fur person" to complete their family. Sarton never patronizes the animal world; such a world gives beauty and definition to the lives of her characters.

Sarton's fiction, like her poetry and journals, has become more lesbian identified with the passing years. Of her nineteen novels, perhaps *The Education of Harriet Hatfield* (1989) and *Mrs. Stevens Hears The Mermaids Singing* (1965) most closely focus on the awakening of a lesbian identity. *The Education Of Harriet Hatfield* is particularly frightening; the open-

ing of a woman-centered bookstore leads to violence—and difficult questions for the protagonist. Here Sarton confronts homophobia dead-on. In interviews, Sarton has expressed anger at critics who derided her novel *A Reckoning* (1978), which contains a memorable portrait of a gay male son, by marginalizing it as a "lesbian novel." Sarton's work in nonfiction extends from her journals to twelve portraits of significant figures in her life in *A World of Light* (1976). Subtitled "Portraits and Celebrations," this book gives a glimpse into the lives of her father, her mother, some friends, and some literary figures such as ELIZABETH BOWEN and Louise Bogan. The anecdotal style creates an intimacy, as if one is listening to Sarton speak personally with the reader about these people. The settings and milieu in which she met or knew these people emerge as she probes their characters.

Works such as *Writings on Writing* (1980) collect essays and interviews Sarton has given over the years. In the film *May Sarton: A Self-Portrait* (1982), Sarton discusses issues such as poetry, romantic love, Nature, her parents, and "inner space." In this film, Sarton discusses aging and its effects on her as a woman and as a writer. She reads "Gestalt at Sixty," a poem that evokes the hard struggles of a watershed year. The house becomes, for the poet, a sanctuary, a safe space where questions are both welcome and scary. Another film, *May Sarton: Writing in the Upward Years* (1991), further explores her feelings about aging.

In both films and in her writing as well, the symbol of the phoenix shapes and centers the work. The bird that rose out of its own ashes parallels Sarton's own career. The journals inform us of a woman who often had to fight for publication, let alone recognition. To this day, she claims she wants an inclusive readership, one that is not limited to any group, but to which she is free to speak and to give an honest reflection of her life.

Her poetry, fiction, and nonfiction have one word in common: courage. One of her best journals, entitled *Plant Dreaming Deep* (1968), may be as much of a reminder for its writer as for its readers: Dreams need time to clarify and grow. In the deep places, the seed emerges.

—*Kenneth Pobo*

BIBLIOGRAPHY

Kallet, Marilyn. *A House of Gathering.* Knoxville, Tenn.: University of Tennessee Press, 1993. ■ Saum, Karen. "The Art of Poetry XXXII; May Sarton." *Paris Review* 25 (Fall 1983): 80–110. ■ Sibley, Agnes Marie. *May Sarton.* New York: Twayne Publishers, 1972.

Schulman, Sarah
(b. 1958)

Sarah Schulman, author and playwright, was born into a second-generation immigrant European Jewish family in Mount Sinai Hospital, New York City, on July 28, 1958. She still lives in Manhattan, on the Lower East Side, which forms a backdrop to all of her writing. A lifelong political activist, Schulman has been involved in a number of strategic social movements, including Abortion Rights, ACT-UP, and most recently, the Lesbian Avengers. She is the cofounder of the Lesbian and Gay Experimental Film Festival and is a prodigious contributor to the mainstream and progressive press, including *The New York Times, The Guardian, Interview, The Face, Mother Jones, Ms. Magazine, The Village Voice, The Advocate, Cineaste,* and *Jump-Cut.*

Schulman's writing blends narrative experimentation with political critique. She constructs lesbian identity around the landscape of the modern, taking New York as the archetypal literary site. Changing, fluid, complex, and fragmented, the lesbian fights for a space juxtaposed with, and superimposed on, other cultural identities, such as Jewish, working class, or black. These "ethnocentricities" then force the reader, by a process of narrative investigation, to question the construction of identity itself.

The Sophie Horowitz Story (1984), Schulman's first novel, reveals a cornucopia of literary and political conventions skewered by a sharp satiric wit. Sophie is an early feminist sleuth-reporter parodying the Search for Woman, which has so preoccupied previous dicks. Tracing her feminist mentors proves both a hopeless and revelatory task, for in the novel icons fall from their pedestals, and the message clearly berates the tendency of subcultures to put their trust in heroes.

The hero of *Girls, Visions and Everything* (1986) is New York, "the most beautiful woman [she] had ever known." This city is mapped out with emotional happenings, and as Lila Futuransky, female flâneuse, walks the streets, these locations stand for symbols of connection, an antithesis to Reagan's America. Modeling herself on the JACK KEROUAC of *On the Road,* Lila is similarly self-exploratory on her adventure, but hers is based on a female erotic aesthetic.

After Delores (1988), by contrast, is an excruciatingly painful narrative of loss, of being left by your lover for another woman. The unnamed narrator occupies what Schulman described in an interview as such "a place of sadness that [it] pushes people into a hallucinatory relationship to the world." The combat zones in this novel are drawn with knives. It won the American Library Association's Gay and Lesbian Book Award and was recently optioned for the screen.

People in Trouble (1990) comes closer to realism than previous works and is the novel most focused on political imperatives. Three central characters work out their sexual identities; each is confronted by the emergence of an AIDS activist organization, Justice. The novel rejects the ironic disengagement symptomatic of postmodernist aesthetics in favor of a voluntary compulsion to act, to change. *People in Trouble* is a warning not to confuse style with political transformations. It won the 1990 Gregory Kolovakos Memorial Prize.

Empathy (1992) takes on the Freudian accusations that lesbians hate men or want to be men. In challenging this relational identity, Schulman rejects the social realist linear narrative in favor of a variety of literary styles: plays, a movie, a short story, a college essay, a poem, personal ads, and recipes. All these genres combine to refute the traditional "coming-out" narrative form. Lesbian identity thus becomes a clash of systems, a traveling implosion. "With *Empathy,* the lesbian novel comes of age," comments Fay Weldon. Schulman is an incisive author whose work will have a rare quality of longevity.

—Sally R. Munt

BIBLIOGRAPHY

Munt, Sally R. "What Does it Mean to Sing 'Somewhere Over the Rainbow...' and Release Balloons?: Postmodernism and the Fiction of Sarah Schulman." *New Lesbian Criticism: Literary and Cultural Readings.* Sally R. Munt, ed. New York: Columbia University Press, 1992. 33–49.

Science Fiction and Fantasy

Readers who turn to science fiction and fantasy for depictions of alternative sexuality find two features of these literary genres in opposition. On the one hand, as genres of popular literature, science fiction and fantasy often seem even more constrained than nongenre literature by their conventions of characterization and the effects that these conventions have on depictions of sexuality and gender. On the other hand, science fiction and fantasy seem also to promise more freedom than do nongenre literatures to imagine alternatives to the privileged assumptions of heterosexuality and masculinity that suffuse our culture. In science fiction, these conventions originated in the boys' adventure stories of the late nineteenth century, a time when technology was transforming industry and promising to transform life for the better. Writers like Garett Serviss, for example, turned Thomas Edison into a technological wizard whose genius was to devise weaponry that would enable Earth to conquer Mars. In fantasy, a nostalgic romanticism pursued its own spirit of marvelous adventure although it rejected technology in favor of magical or superhuman powers. Writers like Edgar Rice Burroughs, for instance, achieved popularity with heroes who did not require help from advanced technology: Tarzan in the jungle or John Carter on Mars. By promoting their popularity through enriched action and superhuman abilities, such early works of science fiction and fantasy instituted conventions for characterization that shifted away from individual complexity toward more easily accessible stereotypes. Such conventions do not promote intense considerations of sexuality in general or innovative considerations of alternative sexuality in particular.

Eventually, however, the two genres did learn how to free their characters from the limitations of their conventions. Science fiction freed them through extrapolation, a narrative trope that is particularly well suited for considering sexuality and gender as social constructions. In contrast, fantasy freed them through schemes of magic, which are better suited for considering sexuality and gender as essential features of identity.

In science fiction, extrapolation allows writers to focus not on the way things are, as fantasy and nongenre literature do, but on the way things can change. It provides science fiction with a quality that Darko Suvin has called, "cognitive estrangement," the recognition that what we are reading is not the world as we know it, but a world whose change forces us to reconsider our own with an outsider's perspective. When the extrapolation involves sexuality or gender, it can force us to reconsider the most basic heterosexist assumptions in our culture. In *Ethan of Athos* (1986), for example, Lois McMaster Bujold extends the present array of reproductive technologies to create an all-male world in which imported ova are fertilized, gestated, and brought to term in carefully monitored artificial wombs. On Athos, cosexual male partnerings to rear children are the norm. In *Walk to the End of the World* (1974), Suzy McKee Charnas extrapolates from the familiar opposition of the sexes to a post-holocaust Earth in which women are kept as slaves for breeding and men are the normative sexual partners for other men. A culture of escaped female slaves has developed an equivalent norm for female sexual partners. Thus, science fiction, by extrapolating fundamental changes in our culture, enables writers like Bujold or Charnas to challenge basic assumptions in our social construction of sexuality and gender.

In fantasy, the equivalent to science fiction's use of extrapolation comes from schemes of magic. Such schemes provide fantasy with its own version of cognitive estrangement because they displace our materially based, scientifically shaped understanding of the world's dynamics with powers that are nonmaterial. Often, such powers are spiritual or psionic (parapsychological powers, such as mind reading or mental manipulation of the physical world). The displacement asks us to reconsider the nature of being.

Applied to sexuality and gender, such displacement in the nature of being enables fantasy to reinterpret the nature of sexual and gender identities. Some works do so by taking the disposition of sexual desire and transforming it with paranormal psychology. In such works, the ability to do magic emerges through an intense same-sex bonding or a sexual coming of age. Thus, Marion Zimmer Bradley and Mercedes Lackey have both developed series in which telepathy, telekinesis, and other psionic powers emerge with puberty. In Bradley's *The Heritage of Hastur* (1975), for example, Regis Hastur's effort to repress a homosexual affair also impedes the awakening of his psionic "laran" ability. In Lackey's *Magic's Pawn* (1989), Vanyel's homoerotic bond with another student of magic enables the student to open him telepathically and unleash Vanyel's powerful but latent psionic skills.

In addition, magic enables fantasy to enhance the value attributed to alternative sexuality and gender. The magic is already an alternative to ordinary power, particularly in such power's masculine guise as brute force or military muscle. Wielders of magic, who are not usually distinguished by their ordinary power, become superior beings through their extraordinary power. When these figures also embody alternative sexualities or gender identities, their extraordinary power revalues these alternatives positively. For example, once Vanyel's latent psionic powers are released through his homoerotic relationship, he becomes the leading protector of Valdemar, with his homoeroticism accepted as an essential feature of his character. In Diane Duane's *The Door into Fire* (1979) and its sequels, the central protagonists are two lovers, Prince Freelorn and the sorcerer Herewiss. It is Herewiss's love for the prince that drives Herewiss to discover his innermost magic, a power using elemental fire, so that the two men can work together for the good of their kingdom. With these lovers in the lead, gay and lesbian relationships are depicted with approval throughout the series.

As such examples from the two genres indicate, when we consider how science fiction and fantasy tell their stories of sexuality and gender, we need to pay at least as much attention to extrapolation and magic in the narrative as we do to the conventions of characterization. Once we have perceived the tension in these genres between freedom in the narrative and constraint in the characterization, we can refine this perception along two additional dimensions: how science fiction and fantasy balance the socially mimetic and nonmimetic, and how they have exploited more recent developments in narratology.

In addition to extrapolation and magic, science fiction and fantasy use several features that reflect the social context in which they are written, such as the degree of explicitness with which the genres depict sexuality and the degree to which gender stereotyping is incorporated into their depictions of character. In addition, both genres use features that contrast more sharply with their social context. In science fiction, such features include several technologies that reconfigure sex or reproduction. In fantasy, such features include iconographic figures, such as mythological deities and worthies of alternative history, who allow for further reinterpretations of human sexuality and gender.

Prior to the 1960s, explicit sexuality of any kind was not characteristic of science fiction and fantasy. Although the covers of some 1930s pulp magazines showed scantily clad women menaced by tentacled aliens, the covers were more lurid than the magazines' contents. For many years, the editors who controlled what was published felt that they had to protect the adolescent male readership that they identified as their principal market. In such a context, writers like Forrest Reid (1875–1947), Edgar Pangborn (1909–1976), or Thomas Burnett Swann (1928–1976), who featured passionate male friendships in their work, were exceptional; almost until the end of their careers, including so much as a kiss would have been too much.

As the readership for science fiction and fantasy began to age in the 1950s, however, writers like Philip Jose Farmer and Theodore Sturgeon were able to introduce more explicit sexuality into their work. Farmer's "The Lovers" (1952) depicted human-alien miscegenation. Not only did Sturgeon make homosexuality an explicit element of science fiction in "The World Well Lost" (1953), he depicted it sympatheti-

cally, by making a pair of homosexual aliens refugees from a planetary culture as repressive as Senator Joseph McCarthy's America. And in *Venus Plus X* (1960), he depicted humanity as gender-neutral beings while pointedly satirizing the gender stereotyping of the period. Although not usually identified as a genre writer like Farmer or Sturgeon, WILLIAM S. BURROUGHS in 1959 published *Naked Lunch,* the first of many works in which he linked drug use and homosexuality as antiauthoritarian activities. The result was a surreal narrative that estranged the action from the ordinary world as science fiction and fantasy do.

Until the late 1960s, however, few other writers depicted alternative sexuality or revised gender roles with Sturgeon's tolerance for the alternative or Burroughs's intolerance for the ordinary. Images of homosexual male societies, for example, remained strongly negative in the eyes of most science fiction and fantasy authors. When overpopulation drives the world away from heterosexuality in Charles Beaumont's *The Crooked Man* (1955), inhumane homosexuals begin to oppress their heterosexual minority. In *False Fatherland* (1968) by A. Bertram Chandler, an all-male culture collapses when women arrive, as the men spontaneously recover both chivalry and rape. And in "The Crime and Glory of Commander Suzdal" (1964) by Cordwainer Smith [Paul M. A. Linebarger], the title character destroys an entire planet of jaded homosexuals, who lured him there with a false distress signal.

By the late 1960s, however, science fiction and fantasy began to reflect the changes prompted by the civil rights movement and the emergence of a counterculture. Within the genres, these changes were incorporated into a movement called "the new wave," a movement more skeptical of technology, more liberated socially, and more interested in stylistic experimentation. New wave writers were more likely to claim an interest in "inner space" instead of outer space and to call their work "speculative fiction" instead of fantasy or science fiction. They were less shy about explicit sexuality and more sympathetic to reconsiderations of gender roles and the social status of sexual minorities.

As rising expectations for social equity rippled from race to gender to sexual orientation, women writers sympathetic to these expectations took up both genres in increasing numbers—among others, Alice Sheldon (1915–1987), URSULA K. LE GUIN (b. 1929), Sally Miller Gearhart (b. 1931), Marge Piercy (b. 1936), JOANNA RUSS (b. 1937), Suzy McKee Charnas (b. 1939), Elizabeth A. Lynn (b. 1947), and Diane Duane (b. 1952). These women were joined by a smaller number of male writers with comparable sympathies, notably Thomas M. Disch (b. 1940) and Samuel R. Delany (b. 1942). Under their collective influence, sympathetic depictions of alternative sexuality and gender multiplied in science fiction and fantasy.

In "When It Changed" (1972), for example, Russ takes science fiction's customary treatment of an all-female planet visited by men and turns it inside out; instead of experiencing a reflexive transformation into an eager heterosexual, the female narrator precisely identifies the men as a profound threat to her culture and lesbian identity. In Piercy's *Woman on the Edge of Time* (1976), an abused woman in a mental institution time travels to a future that is feminist, ecologically sensitive, and accepting of homosexuality. In Gearhart's *The Wanderground, Stories of the Hill Women* (1978), women have been driven to the hills by male violence; these assertively feminist women incorporate psychic awareness and nature worship in their culture.

More sympathetic depictions of alternative sexuality and gender also increased among writers whose work was identified less completely with such concerns. These writers often reshape the more traditional features of the genres into figurative devices that illuminate essential problems experienced by women and sexual minorities. Thus, John Varley made the protagonist of his Gaean Trilogy (1979–1984) a bisexual female space pilot, Sirocco (Rocky) Jones. At the climax of the trilogy, Jones displaces an otherwise superior alien being through the self-sacrificing love of the female astrogator in her crew. In another three-volume work, *Cyteen* (1988), C. J. Cherryh places the discrimination experienced by a male scientist and his male-android lover at the center of the complications of her plot. And in *Unicorn Mountain* (1988), Michael Bishop includes a gay male AIDS patient among the sensitively drawn central characters who must respond to an irruption of dying unicorns at their Colorado ranch.

Just as writers in science fiction and fantasy learned to use more explicit depictions of sex and revised concepts of gender to convey a greater sensitivity and tolerance, they also learned to use features that were less reflective of their social context. In science fiction, such features include technologies that reconfigure sex or reproduction. In fantasy, they include deities from classical mythology, characters from fairy tales, and figures from a sexually revisionist history.

Among the technologies that reconfigure sex or reproduction, science fiction has used transsexuality, cloning, and artificial gestation. Unlike the procedures currently available to transsexuals, sexual reassignment in science fiction allows the altered individual to reproduce sexually after the change. In two notable instances, Robert Heinlein's "All You Zombies" (1959) and David Gerrold's *The Man Who Folded Himself* (1973), the changes are effected through time travel, producing multiple individuals who become their own parents or siblings across the branching time lines. Both writers seem more concerned with the temporal paradoxes in the situation than with the consequences for gender or sexual identity. Even so, Gerrold develops the potential for homosexual relations between the multiple individuals, for they are narcissistically attracted to one another.

In *Triton* (1976), Samuel R. Delany looks even more closely than Gerrold at the motivations and consequences of changing sex. In the world of *Triton* (where changing sex is easy), Delany's protagonist, Bron, starts as a sexist male, pursues an impossible relationship with a woman who will not accede to his sexist demands, and ends as a woman searching unhappily for the kind of man he(?) had been. Dissatisfied as a man and as a woman, Bron provides an innovative study of the interaction between sexual and gender identity.

As a device for exploring these identities, a number of other writers have found cloning more apt than sex changes. Cloning does not involve the temporal paradoxes that claim the reader's attention in "All You Zombies" and *The Man Who Folded Himself,* and clones allow for a greater range of interpersonal relationships than the reader finds in *Triton.* When such interpersonal relationships occur among the clones themselves, the interactions are highly narcissistic. In "Nine Lives" (1969), for example, Ursula K. Le Guin traces the grief that overwhelms the survivor of a ten-clone team when the other nine members are killed. Bisexual relations among the clones intensify the sense of loss. In "Flowering Narcissus" (1973), Thomas Scortia resolves the problem that Bron faces in *Triton* by providing a rough-and-tumble female clone for a rough-and-tumble male biker. In contrast, the protagonist Lilo in John Varley's *The Ophiuchi Hotline* (1977) pursues her bisexual interests outside her clone sisters.

Writers interested in all-female or all-male societies have used cloning for reproduction, focusing more attention on its contribution to social than to personal identity. In "Houston, Houston, Do You Read?" James Tiptree, Jr. [Alice Sheldon] makes cloning a reproductive strategy for the world once men have died out. The natural affinity of clone sisters provides a genetic foundation for the communal spirit that permeates this world's demasculinized culture. In *Hatching Stones* (1991), Anna Wilson suggests that men might find cloning a form of reproduction preferable to heterosexual relations.

Through a variety of technologies that reconfigure sex or reproduction, then, science fiction writers have been able to tell stories with a greater tolerance and sensitivity for alternative sexuality and gender. Fantasy writers, who would find such technologies inappropriate in their stories, have turned to iconographic characters more suited to the magic that informs their worlds. Such characters include mythological deities, fairy-tale characters, and a few revisionist historical personages. Often, the stories work best for promoting tolerance when the more grandly scaled deities from mythology are refracted through a prism of humor. Thus, in *An Asian Minor: The True Story of Ganymede* (1981), Felice Picano works up a rollicking rendition of the relationship between Zeus and his cup-bearer, one of the classical prototypes for pederastic love. In another humorous rendition of a divine liaison, Meredith More in *October Obsession* (1988) tells how Aunt Josie ran off with the moon goddess, Selene. In a similar spirit, Wendy Hays makes up her own fairy tale about a very, very big lesbian and her enchanted dog in "The Giant Person and Her Hell-Hound" (1974).

For fantasy writers working with more historical figures, sexually revisionist accounts provide a refracting prism less humorous in tone but no less useful in effect. In *Gloriana: Or the Unfulfilled Queen: Being a Romance* (1979), for instance, Michael Moorcock recasts Elizabeth I as an erotically unsatisfied bisexual. In *Armor of Light* (1988), Melissa Scott and Lisa Barnett send the homosexual poet-dramatist CHRISTOPHER MARLOWE on an unhistorical mission to rescue the homosexual KING JAMES VI of Scotland, the heir to Elizabeth I, from sorcerous treachery. And in *Strange Devices of the Sun and Moon* (1993), Lisa Scott recasts Marlowe's desire for men and the reports of his mysteriously violent death as details in another sorcerous plot to unsettle Elizabeth's throne as well as the throne of faerie.

Since the new wave, writers using features like cloning or mythological deities have addressed more fully questions of gender and sexual identity. Furthermore, many of these writers have depicted sympathetic lesbian, gay, bisexual, transsexual, or transgendered characters in much greater numbers than anyone might have anticipated in the late 1960s. Nevertheless, only a few writers have developed skills of narrative and style that earn them serious consideration as artists as well as social commentators. On the short list of writers whose technical skills are as great as their concern with alternative sexuality and gender, we can include William S. Burroughs, Joanna Russ, Thomas M. Disch, and Samuel R. Delany.

Of the four, Burroughs is the least likely to be regarded as a genre writer. His work is not marketed as science fiction or fantasy, and his concerns with narrative innovation precede the new wave. By the time he was writing *The Soft Machine* (1961), Burroughs had developed the use of "cut-ups," in which narrative passages were cut apart and randomly reassembled. This fragmentation of the narrative line suited the drug-saturated sensibility and anarchic sexuality characteristic of his work. His earlier books, from *Naked Lunch* (1959) through *Nova Express* (1964), are nightmarish visions of a repressive NOVA gang and the efforts of homosexual junkies to evade and impair the gang's control. Having developed the cut-up technique in *Nova Express* to a staccato rhythm of great poetic power but conceptual opacity, he made varying use of it in subsequent volumes, like *The Wild Boys: A Book of the Dead* (1971), *Port of Saints* (1975), and the series, *Cities of the Red Night* (1981–1987). In these later works, he further mythologizes the embattled homosexual junkies as an anarchic gang, the wild boys.

Joanna Russ has established herself as the most powerful feminist voice in science fiction. With the revival of American feminism in the late 1960s, Russ's work introduced sharply delineated renditions of women's antipathy to a male-dominated world. Even in an early story like "When It Changed" (1972), she cast the alternative to male domination as antiauthoritarian and lesbian. Within this stance, Russ has included sensitive depictions of lesbians and gay males in many of her works: *And Chaos Died* (1970), "Corruption" (1976), *The Two of Them* (1978), and "Bodies" (1984). In "The Clichés from Outer Space" (1985), she provides a devastating commentary on the ways in which science fiction has devalued women. Russ's masterwork remains *The Female Man* (1975). In it, Russ deploys multiple points of view to convey the varied, often conflicting responses that women develop in a sexist culture. Its protagonists are four women from alternative realities, ranging from the husband-seeking Jeannine to the murderously anti-male Jael. Each seems to incorporate a significant dimension of Russ's own complex identity as a contemporary woman. As the four women interact, the book develops an astute, unsparing perspective on the difficulty they have in supporting one another and the potential for lesbian intimacy to overcome their conflicting self-images and objectives.

Thomas M. Disch established a formidable reputation as a leading American writer in the new wave. A versatile literary craftsman, Disch has pursued his writing beyond the boundaries of science fiction with several volumes of poetry, two plays, nongenre fiction and history, and literary criticism and reviews. Even in the earlier years of his career, when his work was primarily science fiction, its tone was characterized by a sharp intelligence and a dry wit. To the discomfort of many science fiction readers, he also wrote with an unusually cool indifference regarding the value of humanity. As his career developed, he moved away from the genre, putting less emphasis on technology and extrapolation and more on the precise and subtle delineation of his characters. At the same time, he began to focus more intently on the figure of the artist and the difficulties for the creative imagination in an unresponsive culture.

In many stories, Disch includes gay and lesbian characters, but in only a few does he give them leading roles. In *334* (1974), Disch's most accomplished work, he links a set of stories by giving the characters a common residence, a massive, state-run housing project in a dystopian New York of 2025. Two of the featured residents are an interracial pair of lesbian lovers. Despite a greater acceptance of homosexuality in their society, they—like most characters in the book—struggle to survive amid repressive police and a failed economy. As characters reappear in each other's stories, the book develops a multiple perspective comparable to that of *The Female Man*. In a later book, *On Wings of Song* (1979), Disch reworks several of *334*'s concepts with elements of magic realism. His protagonist is a naive bisexual, Daniel Weinreb, whose culture suffers from the repression of a revived, fundamentalist Christianity. Amid this repression, people have begun to escape their bodies through a form of astral projection that can be triggered by exquisite operatic singing. Daniel aspires to achieve such an escape, but his efforts to develop his singing ability lead him into a humiliating experience in blackface and chastity belt as the flunky of his castrati voice teacher.

Like Disch, Samuel R. Delany became a leading American practitioner in the new wave. Black and bisexual, Delany frequently features socially marginalized outsiders as protagonists in his work. Their eroticism often involves elements of sadomasochism. Gifted and intense, Delaney also incorporates a wide range of mythic allusion into his narrative texture and probes deeply into the nature of science fiction's language and the protocols required to read it. Throughout the 1960s, the conceptual texture in his work grew increasingly dense. In the 1970s, as he produced more literary analysis and his ideas about science fiction's language matured, the linguistic texture in his narratives also became increasingly dense. With the Neveryon series (1976–1987), his work has become more and more like genre meta-fiction, very self-aware of heroic fantasy's conventions, even as it sets them up to subvert them. Whereas Disch has

redirected his work toward a nongenre audience, Delany has done so toward a more academically inclined one.

Notable works by Delany include shorter pieces like "Aye, and Gomorrah . . ." (1967) and "Time Considered as a Helix of Semi-Precious Stones" (1969) and longer works like *The Einstein Intersection* (1967), *Dahlgren* (1975), *Triton* (1976), and the four volumes in his Neveryon series: *Tales of Neveryon* (1976), *Neveryona* (1979), *Flight from Neveryon* (1985), and *The Bridge of Lost Desire* (1987).

In "Aye, and Gomorrah . . ." neutered spacemen become the objects of erotic desire for perverted humans called "frelks." In "Time . . . Stones," a confidence man escapes the police with the help of a former, masochistic lover. In *The Einstein Intersection,* aliens try to decipher humanity after it has disappeared from earth. Taking on human bodies, the aliens reenact a colliding set of stories from mythology and popular culture. Their understanding remains unresolved. *Dahlgren,* Delany's longest single book, divided his readership. Those who regarded his earlier work as precocious and exciting science fiction found *Dahlgren* undisciplined, unfocused, and unreadable. Others who were more tolerant of his increasing preoccupation with language theory found it an ambitious, challenging masterwork by a mature literary artist. In its narrative, an allegorical protagonist, the Kid, comes to Bellona, where the violent urban culture is comparable to the near-future dystopia of Disch's *334*. In Bellona, the Kid loves, lives, and leaves, having written a book about his experience that might be *Dahlgren*.

The Neveryon series pursues *Dahlgren*'s concern with the construction of literary fiction in a setting reminiscent of heroic fantasy in its barbarian mode. At first glance, Robert E. Howard's Conan might feel at home here, but Delany subverts the elements of heroic fantasy by fragmenting the narrative and rearranging its temporal order. He fills the fragments with explicit erotic details of mastery and enslavement that his models would have left implicit. And he frames it all with a pseudo-academic critical apparatus of commentary and notes. The result is a post-structural fiction that would be more at home with Umberto Eco or Italo Calvino than with Conan.

In the Neveryon series, Delany has pushed his genre far beyond the boundaries of its conventions. In doing so, he demonstrates as fully as anyone that science fiction and fantasy can transcend the limits of their traditional conventions, explore innovative depictions of gender and alternative sexuality, and convey this freedom and innovation with an ambitious technical sophistication. Although it is true that his work—like that of Burroughs, Russ, and Disch—remains atypical, such work does assure us that readers concerned with alternative sexuality in literature will find worthwhile texts in science fiction and fantasy.

—Joseph Marchesani

BIBLIOGRAPHY

Barron, Neil, ed. *Anatomy of Wonder, A Critical Guide to Science Fiction.* 3d ed. New York: R.R. Bowker, 1987. ■ Clute, John, and Peter Nichols, eds. *The Encyclopedia of Science Fiction.* London: Orbit, 1993. ■ Decarnin, Camilla, Eric Garber, and Lyn Paleo, eds. *Worlds Apart: An Anthology of Lesbian and Gay Science Fiction and Fantasy.* Boston: Alyson, 1986. ■ Elliot, Jeffrey, ed. *Kindred Spirits: An Anthology of Gay and Lesbian Science Fiction Stories.* Boston: Alyson, 1984. ■ Garber, Eric, and Lyn Paleo, eds. *Uranian Worlds: A Guide to Alternative Sexuality in Science Fiction, Fantasy, and Horror.* 2d ed. Boston: G.K. Hall, 1990. ■ Riemer, James D. "Homosexuality in Science Fiction and Fantasy." *Erotic Universe.* David Palumbo, ed. Westport, Conn.: Greenwood Press, 1986. ■ Sturgis, Susanna J., ed. *Memories and Visions: Women's Fantasy & Science Fiction.* Freedom, Calif.: Crossing Press, 1989. ■ Suvin, Darko. *The Metamorphoses of Science Fiction.* New Haven, Conn.: Yale University Press, 1979.

Scott, Sarah
(1723–1795)

The details of Sarah (Robinson) Scott's private life are becoming increasingly familiar. Born in 1723 to an established Yorkshire family, Sarah Robinson began writing at an early age; her sister, with whom she was close, was the famous "bluestocking" Elizabeth Montague; in 1748, she met Lady Barbara Montague (no relation to her sister), the daughter of the first earl of Halifax and his wife, Lady Mary Lumley, with whom she maintained an intimate relation until Lady Barbara's death in 1765. In 1751, Sarah Robinson married George Lewis Scott, and she separated from him in 1752. Her first novel, *The History of Cornelia*, appeared in 1750. Between 1750 and her death in 1795, Sarah Scott published four more novels and three histories. *Millenium Hall* (1762) was her most popular work. *Millenium Hall* attempts to challenge the "sex-gender system" by working within the structure of exemplary narratives, such as were popular in midcentury, to offer an alternative to male-oriented interpretations of female sexual power. In doing so, Scott challenges as well our conceptions of female sexuality in the eighteenth century and our preconceptions concerning female-female relations within that extraordinarily imprecise category of "ROMANTIC FRIENDSHIP," which flourished throughout the later eighteenth century.

In *Millenium Hall*, Scott offers a narrative form that challenges patriarchy with the tales of a group of women who remain at the end of their romantic adventures "happily unmarried." Although nominally written as a letter from "a gentleman on his travels," the novel establishes an elaborate strategy to resist the authority of the patriarchal narrative voice. Scott's seemingly crude arrangement of internal narration—the novel consists of a series of tales told by or about the inhabitants of Millenium Hall—represents the most obvious of her techniques: The tales create a female subject position within the text in order to undermine the "romance plot" that was already strong enough to determine popular expectation. By challenging the conventions of romantic narrative, Scott is able to reconceive their ideological range. In her personal life, Sarah Scott found an alternative to the ruthlessly limited possibilities available to women in the eighteenth century. In this novel, she dramatizes this discovery in a way that claims narrative authority for women loving women and offers women in general an escape from the prison-house of patriarchal narrative.

—George E. Haggerty

BIBLIOGRAPHY

De Lauretis, Teresa. *Alice Doesn't: Feminism, Semiotics, Cinema.* Bloomington: Indiana University Press, 1984. ■ DuPlessis, Rachel Blau. *Writing Beyond the Ending: Narrative Strategies of Twentieth-Century Women Writers.* Bloomington: Indiana University Press, 1985. ■ Faderman, Lillian. *Surpassing the Love of Men: Romantic Friendship and Love Between Women from the Renaissance to the Present.* New York: Morrow, 1981. ■ Farwell, Marilyn R. "Heterosexual Plots and Lesbian Subtexts: Toward a Theory of Lesbian Narrative Space." *Lesbian Texts and Contexts.* Karla Jay and Joanne Glasgow, eds. New York: New York University Press, 1990. 91–103. ■ Mavor, Elizabeth. *The Ladies of Llangollen: A Study in Romantic Friendship.* London: Michael Joseph, 1971. ■ Spencer, Jane. *The Rise of the Woman Novelist, From Aphra Behn to Jane Austen.* Oxford: Blackwell, 1986. ■ Todd, Janet. *Female Friendship in Literature.* New York: Columbia University Press, 1980. ■ ———. *The Sign of Angellica: Women, Writing and Fiction, 1660-1800.* London: Virago, 1989.

Scriblerians

The "Scriblerians," an all-male club flourishing in the early eighteenth century, remains among the most thoroughly homosocial literary groups to be found in modern history. However, the club's origin, development, and demise, as well as the colorful personalities of its original six members, and the sense in which it can be considered a "club," is so complex that any monolithic explanation of its formation based on homosocial affinity is inadequate. Male social clubs and literary societies were commonplace in the eighteenth century, but the Scriblerians, in addition to unprecedented literary brilliance, were distinguished by the individual members' homosocial needs, which formed a conscious *raison d'etre* for coming together in the first place. From the start, the group intended to be more than a gathering place for "like-minded wits," and hoped to create a symbolic space where politico-literary collaboration could combine with heightened friendship amounting to less than romantic attachment. VIRGINIA WOOLF captures an essential aspect of its fiber in *Orlando* in the episode where Pope and Addison take tea.

The original six members were John Arbuthnot, Queen Anne's Scottish physician and a scientist of some distinction; John Gay, the poet and playwright of the *Beggar's Opera* (1728); Robert Harley, the Earl of Oxford and a man who felt comfortable when surrounded by "the wits"; Thomas Parnell, the Irish poet; Alexander Pope, the greatest poet of his generation; and Jonathan Swift, the churchman-writer and brilliant author of *Gulliver's Travels* (1726). All were bachelors except Oxford and Parnell, and Parnell's marriage was troubled by his chronic depression and less than heterosexual temperament. The original club was the result of an amalgam of two groups: one led by Swift, the other by Pope. Swift's group was a generation older than Pope's and four of the men—Swift, Harley, Arbuthnot, Parnell—were old enough to have been the fathers of Pope and Gay. The older members were Tory in their politics and brought prestige, authority, and experience; the younger, wit, youth, and ambition. Nevertheless, the deep homoerotic underpinnings of the group—old and young—were intrinsic to its existence.

The club's *raison d'etre* was as psychosexual as politico-literary, in Swift's words in a letter dated September 20, 1723, to Pope: "I have often endeavored to establish a friendship among all men of genius, and would fain have done it. They are seldom above three or four contemporaries, and, if they could be united, would

drive the world before them." It may be true that genius steers the world's ship, but Swift's vision of "friendship" brimmed over with romantic and sexual overtones. Furthermore, Swift was at this time isolated and deeply alienated, and the all-male friendship he idealizes is driven as vigorously by psychosexual urges as by any magnanimous desire to unite genius. Swift's isolation was caused, in part, by his rift with two rival Whigs, the essayists Joseph Addison and Richard Steele, as homosocial in their own liaisons as the proto-Scriblerians were; so much so that years later Pope told Joseph Spence, a memoirist who copied down whatever Pope dictated, that Addison and Steele "had been a couple of h--s," that is, hermaphrodites. It is impossible to know precisely what Pope meant and whether his remark has any veracity, the point being rather the homosocial rivalry that fed into the stream that had created the Scriblerians in the first place.

The first group of six called itself "the Saturday club" but soon gave way to a larger fellowship of about twenty men who grasped on to "the Brothers Club," intending to rival the famous Whig Kit-Cat club, a group often loud and vulgar when convened. Swift's vision was of a few men, bound together by their "love" for each other, as well as their learning, wit, and genius. Into this group, Swift drew Dr. Arbuthnot, Matthew Prior—a bachelor whose politics were deeply conservative and who may have been homosexual in our modern sense—and Dr. Friend, a scholar at Christ Church in Oxford. But Swift also had a literary protégé in Thomas Parnell, like himself an Irishman of English descent who was also a member of the Church of Ireland and who was young enough to be his son. The group met almost weekly in 1711–1712, but it was not until the young Pope—then nearing twenty-five—approached Swift in October 1713 that the idea of a "Scriblerian club" became reality. Pope's plan was that the "scribbling friends" would collaborate on a burlesque monthly periodical poised to satirize hack writing and pretentious erudition, but it is also plain that a complex web of emotional needs of older and younger men influenced their decisions.

Pope's role was the most problematic, if only because he remained the club's most loyal member—the glue cementing them—and he was their only Catholic who kept his ties with the Protestant Whig wits, Addison and Steele, a stance placing him in an ambiguous, middle political position. Moreover, his relation to his protégé John Gay was deeply homoerotic. Three years older than Pope, Gay was confused about his professional and personal course and revered Pope as an ultimate authority. To reciprocate, Pope submitted the drafts of his poems to Gay for commentary. The symmetry of Swift and Parnell, Pope and Gay, parallel groups of leaders and disciples, was unavoidable and noted by the Scriblerians themselves in their prolific letters. Arbuthnot and Oxford were less patterned, but there was genial irony in Pope's affection for Arbuthnot who, though old enough to be Pope's father, deferred to him on all literary matters. The disparity of the members was also preeminent: Swift's isolation from the London literary world contrasted with Pope's meteoric rise there, and whereas Parnell was gloomy, Gay was sunny. Within these differences, the abundant Scriblerian correspondences confirm that Swift was vigorous in winning over Pope: to extract him from the Whig wits and permanently remove him from the camp of Addison and Steele. A "Pope–Addison–Steele triumvirate," with a Whig rather than Tory Pope at its center, was too painful for Swift to contemplate. To complicate matters, Pope had yet to learn that intimacy with Swift inevitably elicited enmity from the rival Addisonians.

Swift insisted the club remain small so that it could meet frequently and in modest accommodations, Harley being the only member of means, the one figure from another social class who exuded prestige. When Harley attended, the fare was grand; otherwise, modest in menu and drink. Any public venue, such as an inn or coffeehouse, was unacceptable given the group's secret political agenda. Secrecy was doubly necessary when Harley attended in view of his post as England's Lord Treasurer, despite the club's urge to publicize his glamour and prestige. When the Court was in London, the club often met in Arbuthnot's room in St. James's Palace to accommodate him if the Queen summoned; on other occasions, in the various member's lodgings, taking turns and always without the presence of women. Gatherings included walking parties as well as nocturnal excursions to country estates, suggesting the degree to which their intimacy extended beyond the familiar although there is no extant evidence whatever of overt homosexual (genital) activity.

The group shared an agenda: collaboration on a massive prose *Works of the Learned* exposing corruption in art and learning. This took the form of highly allusive prose "Memoirs of Martinus Scriblerus," named for a fictional post-Lutheran Germanic family from Munster, whose pedantic hero-son "Martinus" epitomized all they despised. Begun in 1714, the work took fifteen years to publish (1729), but the original club of six survived only a few months, from the autumn of 1713 to the summer of 1714, its members

suffering ill fortune and rocked by the death of Queen Anne in August 1714. Gay, Arbuthnot, and Harley all lost their posts at Court; broken and bitter over his treatment by the Whigs, Swift retired to Ireland, as did Parnell, though for different reasons. Only Pope remained dedicated to "Scriblerus"; as a Catholic without rights at Court, he was unaffected by the Queen's death and the Tory party's demise. But the nation's political shift to Whig supremacy meant the club could not continue as it had; if it did, it would have to go even further underground. Only the intimate friendship of Gay, Pope, and Arbuthnot kept its Scriblerian spirit alive despite Parnell's sudden death in 1717 and Harley's in 1724. Even so, by the mid-1720s, it was clear that the original club had unraveled.

It was Swift's remarkable visit to England in 1726, after an eleven-year absence, together with the collaborative literary projects of the three surviving members, which revived the group. Even if Swift generously encouraged their literary projects (for example, Pope's *Dunciad* [1728] and Gay's *Beggar's Opera*), both his visits had unfortunate consequences, especially his cooling off with Pope in a sequence of events that remains nebulous. To unravel it, one must backtrack and consult the original Scriblerian groups: youngers and elders, Whigs and Tories, and especially Pope's concept of an epicene, all-male friendship.

From his earliest youth, Pope craved older, male literary advisors who could help fashion himself as an original poet. Congreve and Wycherley the playwrights, Swift, Arbuthnot, and many others were to fill this role. With them, he pursued a calling for "friendship" that always entailed some *je ne sais quois* quality beyond platonic male camaraderie, and in return for this "friendship," he immortalized them in poetry. For example, he composed his devastating poetic *Epistle to Dr. Arbuthnot* (1734), containing the famous attack on the notoriously homosexual Lord Hervey (ringing with such lines as Hervey, "that curd of Asses' milk, that stings and stinks"), to symbolize their granitic friendship. Pope's accident with the cow when he was eight years old, which caused him to shrink into dwarfdom rather than grow tall as a healthy boy, and which rendered dysfunctional his genital apparatus, thwarted his fundamentally romantic temperament, as any reader of *Eloisa to Abelard* (1717) quickly grasped. Among the Scriblerians, Gay was temperamentally so devoted to Pope that he virtually adopted him as his perpetual mentor, but Pope relied on older, more established, men than Gay. The entangled homoerotic friendships of these figures were suffused with psychosexual implications, even if explicitly unacknowledged, and nowhere more evident than in their literary collaborations. *Collabora-*

tion is the preeminent feature: And it remains the least understood aspect by their biographers.

Over many years, letters exchanged between Pope and Swift had been emotionally charged, but Pope's mood was especially strained during the summer of 1726, when Swift visited London and remained with him in Twickenham for three weeks. Pope was by now the most famous poet of his era, and Swift could no longer pretend Pope was just another Scriblerian or even just another intimate friend to be cultivated. Before arriving, Swift wrote to him on August 4: "I love and esteem you for reasons that most others have little to do with, and would be the same although you had never touched a pen, further than writing to me." This admission of unconditional "love" apart from intellectual achievement ("never touched a pen") is perhaps less erotic than appears on the surface—especially Swift's unrelenting concern for Pope's health and sense of Pope's integrity and the dignity of his human character. Almost twenty years later, Swift imagined Pope mourning him longer than the other Scriblerians in his *Verses on the Death of Dr. Swift* (1739). Nevertheless, Swift complained that Pope had treated him almost sadistically that summer, revealing his emotional discontent specifically as a form of sadism: "I know no body [who] has dealt with me so *cruelly* as you, the consequences of which usage I fear will last as long as my life, for so long shall I be (in spite of my heart) entirely yours." These and other letters show the disappointed father-figure feeling abandoned by his symbolically powerful young son.

Nevertheless, their biographers have devalued their homoerotic enmeshment while cohabiting in Twickenham. They were together day and night, spending hours in conversation, perhaps of an intimate kind, but Swift left well before the date of his prearranged departure, exacerbating the symbolic son's anxiety and consequent guilt. "Many a short sigh," Pope wrote on August 22, "you cost me the day I left you, and many more you will cost me, till the day you return." The sincere and sensuous language evokes the image of an abandoned lover (Pope) discovering himself practically homeless without his "friend." Swift feigned stoic disaffection and wounded pride; Pope, the abandoned female, insisted to Swift, "you left me a softer man," his villa at Twickenham no longer the symbolic retreat he had created: "I really walk'd about like a man banish'd, and when I came home, found it no home." Pope's language after Swift's departure is so extreme in its images of mutancy and amputation that one wonders how he symbolically construed their friendship. "'Tis a sensation like that of a limb lopp'd off, one is trying every minute unawares to use it, and finds it is not." But Pope could not refrain. "I may say," he protested to Swift, that "you

have used me more cruelly than you have done any other man." This "cruelty," Pope plaintively wrote, is abandonment of a "love" once given, even if only verbally. "You have made it more impossible for me to live at ease without you: Habitude itself would have done that, if I had less friendship in my nature than I have."

The warm, homoerotic Pope, forever solicitous of male friendship, unabashedly mourned Swift's departure, his pain deriving, he confided to Swift, "from a warm uneasy desire after you." In Pope's case, it was the first time he had actually lived with any man, other than his faithful servant John Serle, under the same roof. Pope could not extinguish the memory of his ecstasy, some part of it nostalgically anchored to earlier Scriblerian activity: "I wish I could think no more of it, but lye down and sleep till we meet again, and let that day (how far off soever it will be) be the morrow." Pope's romantic heart had been starved over many years, long before Swift returned to England, but it continued to pump heroically when he concluded his homoerotic letter of August 22: "Indeed you are engraved elsewhere than on the Cups you sent me."

As the summer of 1726 faded, their epistolary confessions of intimacy, despite difference, continued. "I can only swear," Swift confided to Pope while rehashing their time spent together, "that you have taught me to dream." Six weeks later, Pope lamented to Swift, now back in Ireland, that "I see no sunshine but in the face of a friend." Again, erotic desire is camouflaged in Scriblerian friendship, and the younger man (Pope) forever courting the older (Swift) was Pope's lifelong habit. By October 1727, Pope was again addressing Swift in the persona of a *woman,* this time as the giddy girl his poetic voice had pretended to be ten years earlier in *Eloisa to Abelard,* where the male poet-narrator assumes the mask of his female protagonist Eloisa. Pope's letter to Swift dated October 2, 1727, links heterosexual attraction to images of potency and the bubbling over of love:

> It is a perfect trouble to me to write to you, and your kind letter left for me at Mr. Gay's [John Gay's] affected me so much, that it made me feel like a girl. I can't tell what to say to you; I only feel that I wish you well in every circumstance of life: that 'tis almost as good to be hated, as to be loved, considering the pain it is to minds of any tender turn, to find themselves so utterly impotent to do any good, or give ease to those who deserve most from us.

However, it was the loss of "domestic bliss" with the other, older man (perhaps of "the softer variety" Pope had described earlier to Swift) that pained him most.

Pope ends his plaintive epistolary song to Swift by yoking domesticity and emotional tenderness in a confessional tone he had never used before. "I was sorry to find you could think yourself easier in any house than in mine, tho' at the same time I can allow for a tenderness in your way of thinking, even when it seem'd to want that tenderness. I can't explain my meaning, perhaps you know it." Perhaps Swift did, but the confession surpassed any iterated Scriblerian homosocial fraternity and continued to dwell on hearth and home. "I will not leave your room," Pope protested, "if I am ill." But the agony in Twickenham ultimately transformed both men, who were now (in the summer of 1726) altered from the turks they had been when first assembled in 1712. Swift was bleaker, less persuaded that any collaboration, other than epistolary, had value in such a leaden world; Pope less in need of the father figures he had ardently cultivated throughout "this long Disease, my life." To heighten his sense of loss, Gay's death on December 4, 1732, crushed Pope, but in a different way than it would have when the club of six was flourishing.

Pope's craving for epicene male friendships lies at the center of Scriblerian sensibility in the decades after 1714. Despite his romantic exhortations to women (the Blount sisters, Lady Mary Wortley Montagu), his correspondence with *men* is suffused with a blend of unctuous endearment and homoerotic fire, and it amounts to nonsense to conclude from it that his erotically charged language ("I dream of you" or "you have taught me what love is") is arbitrary or a product of the epistolary conventions of his Georgian sensibility. His commentary involves abundant conceit and artifice, to be sure; but it also pinpoints the brand of all-male friendship the club cultivated. Their collaborative letters (written by two, three, and sometimes four men, each passing the letter to the next for comments and additions) brim with desire and sexual innuendo, and Swift's "double letters" to "Pope-Gay" are particularly revelatory as the seemingly distant patriarch writes symbolically from Ireland to his "two Scriblerian sons." An ideal of erotic friendship is no chimera in these multiple epistles circulating through the posts. The Scriblerus club and its politico-literary

agenda was their conscious pretext and was, no doubt, a common ground. It could not have started, let alone flourished as it did, without the interdependence each man felt on another. When scrutinized from our contemporary perspective, and without the sin of anachronism, it must be interpreted as a different enterprise from the milieu of, for example, HORACE WALPOLE and his all-male correspondents. They too were homoerotic, but their networks anticipate Victorian arrangements of all-male attachment rather than the unique blend of friendship and literary collaboration fostered by the Scriblerians. Collaboration is the key ingredient.

The Scriblerians were the first organized group in English literature to initiate a form of literary collaboration with clearly homosocial resonances. Later in the eighteenth century, the "Dilettanti" (young connoisseurs taking the Grand Tour who collected "marbles" abroad and retrieved them to England) followed in their footsteps. The Scriblerian enterprise represents an activity lying somewhere between the purely hedonistic pleasures of the Augustan clubs (the dissipated Beefstakes, Macaronis, and Medmenham Monks) and the formal "colleges of authors" populated by "scheming projectors" of the type Swift ridiculed in *Gulliver's Travels*.

—*G. S. Rousseau*

BIBLIOGRAPHY

Ehrenpreis, Irvin. *Swift: the Man, His Works, and the Age.* Cambridge, Mass.: Harvard University Press, 1962–1983. 2 vols. ■ Foxe, Christopher. *Locke and the Scriblerians: Identity and Consciousness in early eighteenth-century Britain.* Berkeley: University of California Press, 1989. ■ Kerby-Miller, Charles, ed. *Memoirs of the Extraordinary Life, Works, and Discoveries of Martinus Scriblerus.* New Haven, Conn.: Yale University Press, 1950. ■ Koesten-baum, Wayne. *Double Talk: The Erotics of Male Literary Collaboration.* New York: Routledge, 1989. ■ Mack, Maynard. *Alexander Pope: A Life.* New York: Norton, 1986. ■ Nicolson, M. H., and G. S. Rousseau. *This Long Disease, My Life: Alexander Pope and the Sciences.* Princeton: Princeton University Press, 1968. ■ Rousseau, G. S., and Pat Rogers, eds. *The Enduring Legacy: Alexander Pope Tercentenary Essays.* Cambridge: Cambridge University Press, 1988. ■ Sherburn, George, ed. *The Correspondence of Alexander Pope.* Oxford: Clarendon Press, 1956. 5 vols. ■ Williams, Carolyn D. *Pope, Homer and Manliness.* London: Routledge, 1992.

Sebastian, St.
(d. 287)

Although he has had various embodiments throughout history—plague saint in the Middle Ages, shimmering youth of Apollonian beauty throughout the Renaissance, "decadent" androgyne in the late nineteenth century—Sebastian (d. 287) has long been known as the homosexual's saint. Precisely when and how this role evolved may be related to details of St. Sebastian's life, the earliest reference to which can be found in the *Martyrology* of 354 A.D., which refers to him as a young nobleman from either Milan or Narbonne, whose official capacity was commander of a company of archers of the imperial bodyguard. According to the Church's official *Acta Sanctorum,* Sebastian, serving under the emperors Diocletian and Maximian, came to the rescue of Christian soldiers, Marcellinus and Mark, and thereby confessed his own Christianity. Diocletian insisted that Sebastian be shot to death by his fellow archers; these orders were followed, and Sebastian was left for dead. What is often neglected in later accounts is that Sebastian survived this initial attack after having been nursed by a "pious woman," Irene. Diocletian was required to order a second execution, and this time Sebastian was beaten to death by soldiers in the Hippodrome.

These details—based on accounts written centuries after Sebastian's death and therefore largely apocryphal—may have helped form Sebastian's subsequent reputation as a homosexual martyr since his story constitutes a kind of "coming out" tale followed by his survival of an execution that may be read symbolically as a penetration. Possibly his role as a plague saint may have generated associations between Sebastian and what, in a nineteenth-century medical context, was represented as a disease, homosexuality. In the Renaissance, Sebastian emerged as an extraordinarily popular subject for painters, perhaps rivaled only by Jesus and Mary; he was especially prized by artists who saw in the young saint a figure of Hellenic loveliness. Numerous painters—Tintoretto, Mantegna, Titian, Guido Reni, Giorgione, Perugino, Botticelli, Bazzi ("Il Sodoma")—recast Sebastian as a martyr beatifically receptive to his arrow-ridden fate. There is some evidence to suggest that St. Sebastian fostered homoerotic implications in the Renaissance; in SHAKESPEARE's *Twelfth Night* (1600), for example, the character of Sebastian, saved from a shipwreck by Antonio, is the intense focus of Antonio's love: "And to his image, which methought did promise / Most venerable worth, did I devotion." It was primarily the Renaissance depiction of Sebastian that served a later, explicitly homosexual cult of St. Sebastian that took hold with remarkable force beginning in the nineteenth century.

Visiting Rome in 1844, Charles Dickens expressed bewilderment that St. Sebastian should have been such a pervasive subject for Italian artists, bemoaning the "indiscriminate and determined raptures" of certain critics as "incompatible with the true appreciation of the really great and transcendent works of art." In-creasingly, Sebastian in the nineteenth century is fought over by Victorian traditionalists and mischief-minded aesthetes attempting to sustain competing conceptions of the martyr's identity. In his religiously inspired 1847 *Sketches in the History of Christian Art,* Lord Lindsay praised a series of fourteenth-century frescoes by noting that "their peculiar merit consists in the conception of the character of St. Sebastian, not as hot, enthusiastic youth, the fond fancy of later painters, but as a mature man, circumspect and wary while caution will suit his purpose, but resolute as a lion when it becomes necessary to throw off disguise." Lord Lindsay traces Sebastian's status as feminized male to the misguided conceptions of Renaissance painters. The godfather of English AESTHETICISM, WALTER PATER, devotes a fictional "imaginary portrait" to the tale of "Sebastian van Storck" (1886) in which one can observe a new transmutation of the martyr, this time as a death-courting passive youth. No longer representing stalwart Christian courage, Pater's Sebastian is "in flight from all that was positive," who seemed "in love with death, preferring winter to summer." Increasingly, he became a sado-masochistic icon of deliberate perversity. "What is religious about that St. Sebastian, brilliant in his youthfulness, like the suffering Bacchus of Christianity?" asks a character in Anatole France's novel *The Red Lily* (1894).

OSCAR WILDE, who adopted the pseudonym "Sebastian Melmoth" on his release from prison, invokes Sebastian in his 1881 poem to Keats, "The Grave of Keats," whom he describes as "fair Sebastian, and as foully slain." For Wilde, the Roman martyr becomes a self-consciously deployed subcultural emblem. FREDERICK ROLFE's novel, *The Desire and Pursuit of the Whole* (written in 1909 but published in 1934), features a hero who is himself writing a novel with a character named Sebastian Archer as its protagonist. Rolfe's 1891 sonnets dedicated to a Reni Sebastian in Rome's Capitoline gallery were considered so scandalous on their publication in *The Artist* magazine that they helped in the ousting of Charles Kains-Jackson as editor. St. Sebastian appeared centrally in the innovative work of the French painters Odilon Redon and Gustave Moreau, while in 1906 the American photographer F. Holland Day welcomed Sebastian to the epoch of the photograph by executing a sequence of images of the martyr modeled on working-class youths.

With the 1911 performance of Debussy's *Le Martyre de St. Sébastien* at Paris's Châtelet Theater, an eclectic amalgam of orchestral music, mime, and dance based on a play by Gabriele d'Annunzio and starring the dancer Ida Rubinstein, Sebastian stood at the controversial center of a stylized pageant. "Encore! Encore! Encore!" proclaimed Rubinstein's androgyne-saint as the arrows were tossed at her svelte body. That a woman and a Jew was cast as a Christian martyr only intensified the cultural backlash against Sebastian's recent adherents, persuading the Catholic Church to blacklist the performance. The soldier Sebastian became a popular subject in homoerotic poems of World War I, while the martyr's very name frequently stood for a Europe in a crisis of spiritual paralysis, notably in EVELYN WAUGH's *Brideshead Revisited* (1945), whose Sebastian Flyte, scion of an aristocratic Catholic family, stands for an entire generation, as Waugh wrote, "doomed to decay and spoliation." A resilient "decadent" motif in the work of such diverse literary artists as COCTEAU, T. S. ELIOT, Wallace Stevens, MISHIMA, Kafka, Rilke, AUDEN, and THOMAS MANN (whose Aschenbach in Mann's 1911 *Death in Venice* worships Sebastian as a "new type of hero"), Sebastian has also engaged numerous contemporary artists. Robert Wilson revived the Debussy work at the Paris Opera in 1989, and DEREK JARMAN directed a film on the martyr's life, *Sebastiane* (1976), scripted entirely in Latin. Jarman's film rekindled an embellishment of the saint's legend by suggesting that Sebastian had been the object of Diocletian's unrequited love.

Sebastian's extraordinary success as a "gay saint" is related to his status as an updated replacement for other culturally resonant "homosexual legends"—Hadrian and Antinous, Jonathan and David, Ganymede—whose myths were reducible to narratives of love. But the essence of Sebastian's tale resists such sentimentalization, standing as a modern emblem of radical isolationism, both a homoerotically charged object of desire and a source of solace for the rejected homosexual. Since the advent of AIDS, St. Sebastian's historical position as a saint with the power to ward off the plague has been given a new sustenance, inspiring artists, such as the late David Wojnarowicz, to incorporate the martyr into their works. In painting, literature, film, music, theater, performance art, and recently, a video for the rock group R.E.M., St. Sebastian remains the most frequently renewed archetype of modern gay identity.

—Richard Kaye

BIBLIOGRAPHY

Acta Sanctorum. Brussels: J. Reiter, 1863. (Januarii), Volume 2, 629. ■ Del Castillo, Michel et al., *Saint Sébastien: Adonis et Martyr.* Paris: Album Persona, 1983. ■ Dynes, Wayne. "Reply to James Saslow." *Gai Saber: Journal of the Gay Academic Union* 1:2 (Summer 1977): 150–151. ■ Forestier, Sylvie. *Saint Sébastien: Rituels et Figures.* Paris: Musée des arts et traditions populaires, 1984. ■ Kraehling, Victor. *Saint Sébastien dans l'Art.* Paris: Editions Alsatia, 1938. ■ Réau, Louis. *L'iconographie de l'Art Chrétien.* Paris: Presses Universitaires de France, 1959. ■ Saslow, James M. "The Tenderest Lover: Saint Sebastian in Renaissance Painting. A Proposed Homoerotic Iconology for North Italian Art 1450–1550." *Gai Saber: Journal of the Gay Academic Union.* 1:1 (Spring 1977): 58–66.

Seward, Anna
(1742–1809)

Dubbed the "Swan of Lichfield," Anna Seward was eldest daughter of Thomas Seward, canon residentiary of Lichfield Cathedral. Encouraged to write by Erasmus Darwin, Seward became one of the best-known English women poets of her time. She also published in the *Gentleman's Magazine,* sometimes under the pseudonym "Benvolio," and engaged in debates with other critics. Widely connected to writers and clergy, Seward lived her entire life at Lichfield and never married. She seems to have been liked and admired for her liveliness and generosity though criticized for self-importance, outspokenness, and unconventionality.

Although most of Seward's intense attachments were to women, scholars have focused on her deep involvement with John Saville, vicar choral at Lichfield and a renowned vocalist who was separated from his wife. Their relationship subjected them to censure though Seward insisted it was "pure and disinterested." She was grief-stricken by Saville's sudden death in 1803.

Biographers have also noted Seward's passion for her foster sister Honora Sneyd, who came to live in the Seward household at the age of five when Anna was thirteen. After the death of Anna's sister Sarah in 1763, Honora became her closest companion, and the attachment grew more intense. Seward expressed her passionate devotion through her involvement in Honora's romantic life as well as in poetry dedicated to her. She was devastated and outraged by Honora's marriage to Richard Lovell Edgeworth in 1773 and literally went into mourning. Even after her death in 1780, Honora remained an important figure in Seward's interior life.

It appears, however, that this relationship was not Seward's sole experience of romantic female friendship. She had charged relationships with at least three other women, Penelope Weston (later Mrs. Pennington), a Miss Mompesson, and Elizabeth Cornwallis, whom Seward named "Clarissa." Of these three, the relationship with Cornwallis, which Seward refers to as the "unpartaken and secret treasure of my soul," is the most interesting: It was conducted through secret correspondence and surreptitious meetings because Cornwallis's father abhorred female friendships and controlled his daughter's contacts with women.

In addition to these ROMANTIC FRIENDSHIPS, Seward was associated with circles of literary and intellectual women. She regularly attended Lady Anna Miller's gatherings at Bath Easton. ELEANOR BUTLER AND SARAH PONSONBY, the famous "Ladies of Llangollen" who had eloped together and settled in Wales, were her dear friends and correspondents. She wrote several poems in their honor, the longest and best known of which, *Llangollen Vale*, was published in 1796.

Seward's poetry is often sentimental and ornate, but some poems are quite powerful. Much of

Llangollen Vale, for example, could be described as mythic pastoral verse, but the poem also includes a surprisingly forthright celebration of the "sisters in love" and places the two women in a heroic lineage. The poems dedicated to Honora are marked by a similar excess, but they testify to Seward's deep attachment. Seward memorializes their "plighted love" at first joyously and then later, after Honora's marriage, with deep lament. Additional poems dedicated to other women might also lend themselves to lesbian reading. Seward's public and private writings, as well as her extensive connections with women, make her a fruitful figure for further study.

—*Marian Urquilla and Susan S. Lanser*

BIBLIOGRAPHY

Ashmun, Margaret Eliza. *The Singing Swan: An Account of Anna Seward and Her Acquaintance with Dr. Johnson, Boswell, & Others of Their Time.* New Haven, Conn.: Yale University Press, 1931. ■ Lucas, E. V. *A Swan and Her Friends.* London: Methuen, 1907. ■ Scott, Walter. *Biographical Memoirs of Eminent Novelists, and Other Distinguished Persons.* Vol. 2. Edinburgh: R. Cadell, 1834. Rpt. New York: Books for Libraries Press, 1972.

Shakespeare, William
(1564–1616)

As one of the key figures that Western civilization has used to define itself, William Shakespeare stands in a complicated, fiercely contested relationship to homosexuality. The subject of Shakespeare and homosexuality is really four subjects: *it* (homosexuality), *he* (Shakespeare), *they* (Shakespeare's contemporaries), and *we* (actors, audiences, readers, and cultural pundits across the four centuries since Shakespeare's death).

It: Like "sexuality" in general, "*homo*sexuality" did not exist as a conceptual category in sixteenth-century Europe. That does not mean, of course, that feelings we today would describe as homoerotic did not exist, any less than behavior we would describe as homosexual. The closest that early modern English comes to a word for homosexuality is "sodomy." But "sodomy" was a short-hand term for socially taboo acts that we today would put in very different categories from sexual acts. Even in the law books, "sodomy" spilled over into heresy, witchcraft, and treason.

These conceptual differences remind us that sexuality is not a natural given but something that changes as social and political circumstances change.

He: Concerning the sexuality of William Shakespeare the man, we are in a position to say almost nothing. No private documents of any kind survive. What we have instead are a handful of public documents—entries in the parish register of his baptism and burial, conveyances of real estate, his testimony in a court case involving the dowry of his London landlord's daughter, his last will and testament—plus a few snide remarks, mostly by rival playwrights, on his facile talents as a scriptwriter and several testimonials to his geniality. None of these documents and comments makes any specifically sexual references. In this respect, Shakespeare differs from his near-contemporary CHRISTOPHER MARLOWE, who was accused (after he was safely dead) of having said such things as "all they that love not Tobacco & Boies [are] fooles." It is worth noting, however, that Shakespeare's domestic arrangements were, by early modern standards, not exactly ideal. With the help of other people's money, he negotiated the ecclesiastical hurdles necessary to marry in a hurry a woman who was eight years his senior. His first child was born six months after the event. He apparently spent most of his career living in London while his wife and children stayed behind in Stratford. Shortly before his death, he dictated a will that is unusual in making his elder daughter, not his wife, the primary beneficiary of his estate.

They: Concerning the sexuality of William Shakespeare's contemporaries, we are in a position to say a great deal more, thanks in no small part to Shakespeare's plays and poems. The general picture looks radically contradictory. If all we had to go on were law books, we would have to conclude that early modern England was a virulently homophobic society. The sodomy statute 5 Elizabeth, chapter 17, passed by Parliament in 1562–1563, made acts of sexual penetration between males a felony that was punishable by death. Listening to certain speeches in Shakespeare's plays, however, we are astonished to hear expressions of homoerotic feeling that seem by today's standards remarkably direct and, more to the point, remarkably uncomplicated. In *Coriolanus* (1608), for example, the warrior Aufidius welcomes his erstwhile enemy by casting his feelings in the erotic terms of marriage:

> O, let me clip ye
> In arms as sound as when I wooed, in heart
> As merry as when our nuptial day was done,
> And tapers burnt to bedward! Know thou first,
> I loved the maid I married; never man
> Sighed truer breath. But that I see thee here,
> Thou noble thing, more dances my rapt heart
> Than when I first my wedded mistress saw
> Bestride my threshold.
> (4.5.113–118, Oxford edition)

What Aufidius felt on his wedding night was nothing to what he feels in the presence of his arch enemy. Just what are we to make of such a disparity between the courtroom and the theater? We might, first, stress the differences between the two places as venues. In the courtroom, attention is centered on certain specific sexual acts; in the theater, the focus widens to include desires and fears, to what it feels on the inside to say and do things that the law considers only from the outside. We may begin to suspect also that same-sex relationships were positioned vis-à-vis marriage in rather different ways than they are today. Finally, we should confront the fact that erotic attachments between people of the same gender constituted a major "fault line" in the culture of early modern England. On the one hand, 5 Elizabeth, chapter 17, proclaims an intense homophobia; on the other hand, speeches like Aufidius's imply an equally intense homoeroticism. Shakespeare's works are situated along this crack in the social edifice.

Aufidius's language bespeaks a social structure that privileged the bonds of men with men over all other social ties. In political terms, all the key social institutions in early modern England were male. Sir William Segar's *Honor Military, and Civill* (1602) distinguishes two "arenas of action" open to men, "business" and "honor":

> The principall markes whereat every mans endevour in this life aimeth, are either Profit, or Honor, Th'one proper to vulgar people, and men of inferior Fortune; The other due to persons of better birth, and generous disposition. For as the former by paines, and parsimony do onely labour to become rich; so th'other by Military skil, or knowledge in Civill government, aspire to Honor, and humane glory.

A boy who was thrust by his parents into the arena of "honor" would start off in an all-male school. He then might proceed to one of the all-male colleges of Oxford or Cambridge or take up the study of law at one of the all-male inns-of-court in London. This was the course pursued by Christopher Marlowe. A boy who entered the arena of "business" might also start off in an all-male school. He then would join a group of other adolescent males as an apprentice to a craftsman or a merchant. In effect, this was the course pursued by William Shakespeare. Professional acting companies in London may not have enjoyed the same social status as the guilds of goldsmiths, tailors, grocers, and other trades, but troupes like the one Shakespeare joined were set up as joint-stock ventures and operated like trade guilds, with boy actors in the position of apprentices. Since putting on plays was not a recognized way of making a living, a legal fiction was maintained that actors were "servants" attached to a member of the nobility. Hence the successive names by which Shakespeare's troupe was known: first the Lord Chamberlain's Men, later the King's Men. The problematic status of professional theater—it professed to be an arena of "honor" but in fact functioned as an arena of "business"—made it a perfect setting for playing out the problematic place of homoeroticism in early modern culture. In the theater, it was possible to act out conflicts and contradictions that would have been glossed over elsewhere.

Like Oxford and Cambridge colleges, like the inns of court, like trade guilds, professional acting companies were all-male institutions. Some witnesses, not all of them hostile Puritans, imply that homosexual behavior was fostered by these economic and social circumstances. In Ben Jonson's play *Poetaster* (acted by the Children of the Chapel Royal, 1600) a father hears that his son has decided to become an actor and exclaims, "What? Shall I have my son a stager now? An ingle for players?" (1.2.13–14). (Through the eighteenth century, "ingle" remained a slang term for what the *The Oxford English Dictionary* terms "a boy-favourite (in bad sense).") If Puritan extremists can be trusted, actions that were rumored to go on in the tiring house among the players went on also among the audience after they had left the theater. In the *Anatomie of Abuses* (1583), Philip Stubbes fulminates over

> the flocking and running to Theaters and curtens, daylie and hourely, night and daye, tyme and tyde, to see Playes and Enterludes; where such wanton gestures, such bawdie speaches, such laughing and fleering, such kissing and bussing, such clipping and culling, Suche winckinge and glancinge of wanton eyes, and the like, is used, as is wonderfull to behold. Than, these goodly pageants being done, every mate sorts to his mate, every one bringes another homeward of their way verye freendly, and in their secret conclaves (covertly) they play *the Sodomits,* or worse. And these be the fruits of Playes and Enterluds for the most part.

The primary focus of erotic attention in Shakespeare's theater, or so Stubbes and other detractors imply, was boy actors dressed up as women. Certainly there are instances in Shakespeare's plays where boy actors are scripted to tease the audience about their gender. In *The Two Gentlemen of Verona* (1594), for example, Julia decides to disguise herself as a page and follow her lover Proteus, who is leaving her behind while he travels with his friend Valentine. "What fashion, madam, shall I make your breeches?" asks the boy actor playing Julia's maid. Whatever you like, replies the boy actor playing Julia. "You must needs have them with a cod-piece, madam," warns the boy/maid. "Out, out, Lucetta," exclaims the boy/lady. "That will be ill-favoured" (2.6.49–54). Even before "Julia" puts on "her" male disguise, "Lucetta" calls attention to the very thing that makes "Julia" no more than a

theatrical illusion. The Epilogue to *As You Like It* (1598), scripted to be spoken by the boy actor who has played Rosalind, is perhaps the most famous occasion in Shakespeare's scripts when illusion cancels illusion to reveal the boy's body beneath. Since "Rosalind" has spent much of the play disguised as "Ganymede" (in early modern English, a slang term synonymous with "ingle"), it is not clear just *who* is speaking—"Rosalind," "Ganymede," or the boy actor who has played them both—when the speaker of the Epilogue offers to kiss the male members of the audience:

> If I were a woman I would kiss as many of you as had beards that pleased me, complexions that liked me, and breaths that I defied not. And I am sure, as many as have good beards, or good faces, or sweet breaths will for my kind offer, when I make curtsy, bid me farewell (Epi. 16–21).

In *Twelfth Night* (1601), probably the latest of Shakespeare's comedies, the confusions about gender are greatest of all. When shipwrecked Viola disguises herself as "Cesario," he/she/he manages to excite the desires of both Duke Orsino and Lady Olivia. Orsino prolongs the confusion to the very end by insisting on calling Viola "Cesario" until he/she/he changes back into female clothes and becomes his wife. Against the suggestiveness of such situations, we must weigh the evidence, scanty though it may be, of eyewitnesses who saw Shakespeare's plays in their original performances. Not a single one of these eyewitnesses registers any erotic interest whatsoever in the boy actors he saw perform. Instead, each witness writes about the fictional female characters he saw on stage as if they were actual female persons. In Shakespeare's scripts at least, erotic teasing about cross-dressing seems to be confined to comedy and specifically to those episodes in which a boy playing a girl dresses up as a boy. Cross-dressing, as Marjorie Garber argues in *Vested Interests,* may in fact be the basis of all theatrical illusion making. Instead of trying to decide whether a cross-dressed figure in a Shakespeare play is "really" male or "really" female, we should perhaps try to see him/her/it as *both*.

In any event, boy actors in female garb are far from being the only focus of homoerotic attention in Shakespeare's scripts. Achilles and Patroclus in *Troilus and Cressida* (1603) are the most blatantly sexual in a series of male companions who populate Shakespeare's plays from beginning to end and who express their bonds with one another in erotic terms. As with Achilles and Patroclus, it is often war that brings out the erotic subtext in male friendship. In *Henry V* (1599), for example, Suffolk and York die in the embrace of man and wife. After kissing Suffolk's wounds, York, a witness reports, turned

> and over Suffolk's neck
> He threw his wounded arm, and kissed his lips,
> And so espoused to death, with blood he
> sealed
> A testament of noble-ending love. (4.5.24–27)

Moments like this, when love finds its consummation on the battlefield, help explain why Iago should be so jealous of Othello after Othello has married Desdemona, or why Mercutio should thrust such crude sexual jokes at Romeo after his friend has fallen in love with Juliet—and then rush off to a violent death. Aufidius and Coriolanus, Achilles and Patroclus, Suffolk and York, Iago and Othello, Mercutio and Romeo: In every case, the erotic charge is generated, not by differences in gender, not by differences in age, but by differences in power. In different ways, each of these scripts is set amid political circumstances that compel men to be, simultaneously, each other's comrade and each other's enemy. Those conflicted circumstances explain, perhaps, why homoerotic desire on the early modern stage so often ends in violence. Coriolanus finishes his political career by practically begging Aufidius and his men to chop him to pieces with their swords; Patroclus is brutally murdered by Hector; Achilles takes his revenge by butchering Hector; Suffolk and York are martyred by the French; Othello is tricked by Iago into destroying himself; Mercutio is thrust through with a sword. In the eroticized politics of plays like these, we witness in a particularly extreme form the conflict between homophobia and homoeroticism that characterized early modern England. Christian dogma may have condemned sodomy, but in a rigidly patriarchal society, male homoeroticism had a certain political utility. It strengthened and solidified male bonds.

From the frequency with which such plots of male bonding are played out in Shakespeare's scripts, we might easily conclude that early modern theater was an exclusively male concern and that any erotic interplay in that theater occurred solely among males. In plays written by men and acted by men in a culture dominated by men, what place could there possibly be for the erotic experience of women? Such a place does exist, Valerie Traub argues in *Desire and Anxiety,* but it exists apart from men, and it is all the more interesting for its separateness. In a patriarchal society like "Elizabethan" England, female eroticism was deemed important only insofar as it concerned men. Hence the huge value placed on female virginity before marriage and on chastity afterward. It was not so much moral considerations that compelled a woman to allow no man but her husband into her body but economic and political considerations. On the legitimacy of a man's offspring depended the whole legal system of transferring property in the arena of business and transferring title in the arena of honor. Female eroticism that was not directly concerned with men—that is, female eroticism that we would label "lesbian"—was another matter entirely. As far as early modern men were concerned, out of presence was out of mind. The sodomy statutes reflect this male myopia. Interpreting the laws for would-be prosecutors, Sir Edward Coke in his *Institutes of the Laws of England* (Part 3, 1644) catalogs all the possible variations in sexual crime: "Buggery is a detestable and abominable sin, amongst Christians not to be named, committed by carnall knowledge against the ordinance of the Creator and order of nature, by mankind with mankind, or with brute beast, or by womankind with brute beast." Womankind with womankind seems not to have struck Coke as a possibility—or at least as a possibility in which the law would be interested. The case of womankind with beast was another matter, precisely because the beast in question was assumed to be male. Women as well as men are covered by the sodomy statutes, Coke explains, because the wording is

> *if any person, &c.* which extend as well to a woman as to a man, and therefore if she commit Buggery with a beast, she is a person that commits Buggery with a beast, to which end this word [*person*] was used. And the rather, for that somewhat before the making of this Act, a great Lady had committed Buggery with a Baboon, and conceived by it, &c.

Of all the *et ceteras* in the world, this is one we would most like to have filled in.

The autonomy of female eroticism was, in a way, enhanced by the all-male composition of Shakespeare's company. One effect of having boy actors play women's parts was to separate *gender* roles from *sexual* roles. In the circumstances of Shakespeare's theater, the differences that make characters desire one another sexually are played out within the same gender. Physically, that is the case with males; imaginatively, it is also the case with females. Julia and her maid Lucetta in *The Two Gentlemen of Verona* are the earliest in a series of closely bonded female pairs who sometimes speak of their affection for one another in terms that are graphically physical. When Helena and Hermia in *A Mid-*

summer Night's Dream (1594–1595) have fallen out with one another over men, Helena reminds her friend how they once enjoyed such intimacy that they seemed joined in body:

> We, Hermia, like two artificial gods
> Have with our needles created one flower,
> Both on one sampler, sitting on one cushion,
> Both warbling of one song, both in one key,
> As if our hands, our sides, voices, and minds
> Had been incoporate. So we grew together,
> Like to a double cherry: seeming parted,
> But yet an union in partition,
> Two lovely berries moulded on one stem.
> (3.2.204–212)

If the corporeal images here seem merely sentimental, the erotic implications are much stronger when Titania explains to Oberon why she insists on keeping her Indian page and so provokes the quarrel that occasions all the midsummer night confusions. The Indian page sounds very much like a child conceived without the intervention of men:

> His mother was a vot'ress of my order,
> And in the spicèd Indian air by night
> Full often hath she gossiped by my side,
> And sat with me on Neptune's yellow sands,
> Marking th'embarkèd traders on the flood,
> When we have laughed to see the sails conceive
> And grow big-bellied with the wanton wind,
> Which she with pretty and with swimming gait
> Following, her womb then rich with my young
>   squire,
> Would imitate. . . . (2.1.122–132)

The celebrations of female separateness spoken by Helena and by Titania seem all the more resonant in a play that opens with the forced marriage of the queen of the Amazons. Similar mutualities couple Portia and Nerissa in *The Merchant of Venice* (1596–1597), Rosalind and Celia in *As You Like It* (1598), Desdemona and Emilia in *Othello* (1603–1604), Cleopatra and Iris in *Antony and Cleopatra* (1606), Hermione and Paulina in *The Winter's Tale* (1609–1610), and Emilia and Flavina in *The Two Noble Kinsmen* (1613). To all these female pairs, relationships with men come as interruptions, often as violent interruptions. As Emilia says of Flavina, "The true love 'tween maid and maid may be/ More than in sex dividual" (*TNK* 1.3.81–82).

The same scenario is played out among men. Again and again, the plots in Shakespeare's plays turn on the situation of two male friends set apart by a woman.

At the end of *The Two Gentlemen of Verona*, Valentine entertains the hope that he and his friend Proteus, both now betrothed to be married, will nonetheless enjoy "One feast, one house, one mutual happiness" (5.4.171). That likelihood seems slight, if we take into account Shakespeare's later experiments with the same situation. Mercutio's death in *Romeo and Juliet* poses a brusque reply to Valentine's optimism. So does Othello's self-destruction. So do Macbeth's murder of Banquo, Antony's political suicide, Leontes's falling out with Polixines in *The Winter's Tale,* and Palemon and Arcite's disastrous rivalry over Emilia in *The Two Noble Kinsmen.* Even in comedy, even short of death, the results are never entirely happy. The strange melancholy that plagues Antonio in *The Merchant of Venice* seems to be explained when Bassanio, the friend for whom Antonio has risked all, tells Antonio in front of the Venetian court, in front of Shylock— and in front of his disguised wife:

> Antonio, I am married to a wife
> Which is as dear to me as life itself,
> But life itself, my wife, and all the world
> Are not with me esteemed above thy life.
> I would lose all, ay, sacrifice them all
> Here to this devil, to deliver you.
> (4.1.279–284)

Nonetheless, at the end of the play, Antonio is left standing alone amid the newly married couples. If "homosexual" and "heterosexual" were not separate categories in early modern England, if male privilege took precedence over moral scruples about marital fidelity, *The Merchant of Venice* may in fact be depicting not an either/or choice but a both/and compromise. For Bassanio, if not for Antonio, there may have been no contradiction in being married to a woman and enjoying erotic friendship with a man at the same time. The situation of Shakespeare's other homoerotic Antonio, the ship's captain who saves Sebastian's life in *Twelfth Night,* looks much less auspicious. Far from suffering from an inarticulate melancholy, this Antonio is Shakespeare's most forthright character in speaking about his homoerotic desires. When Sebastian tries to thank Antonio for all the pains he has taken in rescuing him, Antonio cuts him short:

> I could not stay behind you. My desire,
> More sharp than filèd steel, did spur me forth,
> And not all love to see you—though so much
> As might have drawn one to a longer voyage—
> But jealousy might befall your travel. . . .
> (3.4.4–8)

The reward for such forthrightness, however, is isolation. In the play's final scene, once Sebastian has been betrothed to Lady Olivia, Antonio is scripted to say not a word. In a society that both nurtured homoerotic bonds and yet denied them, what indeed *could* he say?

From different perspectives, Shakespeare addresses the same erotic conflicts in his nondramatic works. Unlike the plays, which were acted before large and diverse audiences, Shakespeare's narrative poems *Venus and Adonis* (1593) and *The Rape of Lucrece* (1594) were directed at a distinct coterie of readers. Unlike the plays, which failed to qualify as serious literature by Renaissance standards, both of these narrative poems boast classical pedigrees. Unlike the plays, which were marketed as capitalist commodities, both poems are set forth in the trappings of aristocratic patronage. Dedicated to Henry Wriothesley, Earl of Southampton, both *Venus and Adonis* and *The Rape of Lucrece* are witty retellings of classical myths, a literary genre that had special in-group appeal to the university-educated young gentlemen of the inns of court.

With other exercises in the genre like Marlowe's *Hero and Leander* (printed 1598) and Francis Beaumont's *Salmacis and Hermaphroditus* (1602), Shakespeare's *Venus and Adonis* shares a homoerotic interest that this particular coterie of male readers clearly found appealing. That interest shows up not in the plot situation (it is, after all, the goddess Venus who falls in love with the adolescent Adonis) but in the perspective that male readers are invited to take toward that situation. Erotic desire in the poem is all on Venus's side; the center of erotic attention is not Venus's body but Adonis's. Looking at Adonis through Venus's eyes, the reader discovers a hermaphroditic charm not unlike that radiated by the cross-dressed heroines of Shakespeare's comedies. Wooed by Venus, Adonis blushes like a maiden (l.50). His voice is like a mermaid's (l.429). His face is hairless (l.487). When, in desperation, Venus wrestles this paragon of beauty to the ground, the reader joins Venus in the active role of ravishing him:

> Now quick desire hath caught the yielding prey,
> And glutton-like she feeds, yet never filleth.
> Her lips are conquerors, his lips obey,
> Paying what ransom the insulter willeth,
> Whose vulture thought doth pitch the price so high
> That she will draw his lips' rich treasure dry.
> (ll.547– 552)

Adonis, alas, is not interested. He would rather go hunting with his friends. Seen from the perspective shared by Venus and the reader, the goring of Adonis by a wild boar looks very much like an act of rape:

> 'Tis true, 'tis true; thus was Adonis slain;
> He ran upon the boar with his sharp spear,
> Who did not whet his teeth at him again,
> But by a kiss thought to persuade him there,
> And, nuzzling in his flank, the loving swine
> Sheathed unaware the tusk in his soft groin.
> (ll.1111–1116)

Published the next year, dedicated to the same noble patron, and addressed to the same coterie readership, *The Rape of Lucrece* reenacts the archetypal plot, familiar from Shakespeare's plays, of two male allies set apart by a woman. Tarquin's rape of his friend's wife, Lucrece, may occasion some brilliant speeches from Lucrece, but ultimately it serves the political end of changing Rome from a monarchy that harbors such peremptory power as Tarquin's to a republic that honors the integrity of such patriots as Tarquin's betrayed friend Collatine. In effect, Lucrece figures as a token of erotic exchange in the political alliances that men make with men.

The both/and possibilities of erotic experience in early modern England receive their most searching exploration in Shakespeare's 154 sonnets. First printed as a group in 1609, Shakespeare's sonnets belonged originally not to the public culture of print but to the private culture of manuscript poetry that circulated among friends. In a catalog of England's great writers, made eleven years before the sonnets saw print, Francis Meres speaks of Shakespeare's "sugred Sonnets among his private friends." Just who these friends were is not known. Only twelve of Shakespeare's sonnets show up in any surviving seventeenth-century manuscripts; in only two of these manuscripts does more than a single sonnet appear. By every indication, Shakespeare had nothing to do with the volume of *Shakespeares Sonnets, Never before Imprinted* that the printer Thomas Thorpe put on the market in 1609. With its title alone, the book communicates a sense of privacy breached, of secrets made public—an effect enhanced by the poems' first-person perspective. To watch a play is to observe other people's actions. To read a story like *Venus and Adonis* is to find out about someone else's experience. To read a poem that begins with "I . . ." is to establish terms of intimacy with that "I," to make *his* experience *your* experience. The results of these circumstances have been two: (1) a small library of books that try to sleuth out who the people mentioned in the sonnets "really" are and (2) a still-continuing culture war over the homoerotic desires articulated by the speaking "I."

As they were printed by Thorpe in 1609, Shakespeare's sonnets imply a definite cast of characters if not an agreed-upon plot line. The first 126 poems seemed to be addressed to a fair-complexioned man, possibly a nobleman, who is younger than the speaker; the final 28, to a dark-complexioned woman who is the speaker's mistress. Centuries of hours, acres of trees, and vats of ink have been consumed since the eighteenth century in the quest to prove just who these people are. The most frequently mentioned candidate for the young man is Henry Wriothesley, the dedicatee of *Venus and Adonis* and *The Rape of Lucrece.* Outside the sonnets themselves, however, not a single piece of evidence survives to prove or to disprove such claims. Rather than assuming that the first-person of the sonnets speaks for William Shakespeare, we should perhaps note the ways in which these three characters—the speaking "I," the young man, the woman—depend on one another for their identities. At least in this book of poems, none of them ever stands alone, not even the speaking "I." He may be talking about himself, but he does so only by also talking about the young man or the woman. He needs both of them, as sonnet 144 confesses:

> Two loves have I, of comfort and despair,
> Which like two spirits do suggest me still.
> The better angel is a man right fair,
> The worser spirit a woman colored ill.

The controversy centers on whether he needs both of these people sexually. "Therefore I lie with her, and she with me,/ And in our faults by lies we flattered be" (138.13–14): The cynical sensuality of the sonnets addressed to "the dark lady" have never been in question. The speaker's erotic attachment to the young man is much less direct: It emerges only gradually in the course of the sonnets, it is communicated through puns, it is fundamentally implicated in the speaker's sexual relations with the lady. Taken altogether, the sonnets to the "man right fair" seem to tell the story of a failed love affair—but a love affair in which "a woman colored ill" is very much a factor.

The first nineteen poems urge the young man to preserve his beauty by getting married and begetting children. By sonnet 16 ("But wherefore do not you a mightier way/ Make war upon the bloody tyrant, time"), the speaker has begun, however, to insinuate his own designs on the young man, first by promising to preserve the young man's beauty in the medium of verse, then by speaking more and more openly about the erotic desires that he himself feels toward the young man. The pair formed by sonnets 20 ("A woman's face with nature's own hand painted/ Hast thou, the master-mistress of my passion") and 21 ("So is it not with me as with that muse/ Stirred by a painted beauty to his verse") conjoin the two things that preoccupy the speaker in all the ensuing sonnets to the young man: making love and making verse. The graphically physical lovemaking in these poems is playfully encoded in puns, many of which are sustained throughout the entire sequence: "have" (52.14, 87.13, 110.9–12, 129.6), "use" (2.9, 4.7, 6.5, 20.14, 40.6, 48.3, 78.3, 134.10), "will" for male and female sexual organs as well as for sexual desire in general (57.13, 112.3, 134.2, 135, 136, 143.13, 154.9), "pride" for penis (64.2, 52.12, 151.9–11), and "all" (sounds like "awl") for penis (looks like an awl) (26.8, 75.9–14, 109.13–14). Several times the young man is cryptically referred to as the speaker's "rose" (1.2, 54.11–13, 67.8, 95.2–3, 98.10–11, 109.13–14). The difficulty that modern readers have had with the sexuality of Shakespeare's sonnets has been less a problem with decoding these puns than with assuming that the speaker cannot be erotically involved with a man and a woman at the same time. Either he is homosexual, or he is heterosexual—or so modern ideas about sexuality would insist. In the sonnets, as in the comedies, it is both/and, not either/or that makes better sense of the textual evidence. By accepting that the speaker is erotically involved both with the young man and with the mistress, we find ourselves in a position to see how the two relationships are like each other and how they are different. It is the differences that are the more remarkable. The sonnets to the young man communicate idealistic expectations that stand in the sharpest possible contrast to the sexual cynicism of the sonnets to the mistress. Gender in Shakespeare's sonnets has more to do with the speaker's feelings than it does with his lovers' bodies.

Shakespeare speaks about homoerotic desire in a variety of modes: across the broad expanse of public theater, among the coterie readership of *Venus and Adonis* and *The Rape of Lucrece,* within the circle of friends who read his sonnets in manuscript. Despite the absence of any truly private documents from the hand of Shakespeare, these three angles of vision converge to give us an extraordinarily rounded view of sexual experience at the very beginning of the modern era. Homosexuality as an *it* may not have existed in early modern England, Shakespeare as a *he* may remain elusive, but the *they* set in place by Shakespeare's works constitute a major body of evidence in the history of sexuality.

We: One index of how quickly and decisively the history of sexuality was changing is the second printed edition of the sonnets, published in 1640, twenty-four years after Shakespeare's death. John Benson, the publisher of *Poems written by Wil. Shakespeare Gent.*, went to extraordinary lengths to disguise the homoeroticism of the original poems. He rearranged the order so as to obliterate any suggestion of a plot line, he combined individual sonnets into longer wholes so as to play up formal artifice at the expense of personal reference, he even supplied titles that specify the object of the poets' desires to have been exclusively female, not male as well as female. That thirty-one years had elapsed without a second edition of the sonnets (by 1640, *Venus and Adonis* had gone through no fewer than sixteen editions) may indicate that Shakespeare's sonnets were thought to be strange, idiosyncratic poems even in 1609, but Benson's edition of 1640 sets the wave of the future. By the end of the seventeenth century "sodomy," once a catch-all category for deviant behavior of all sorts, had solidified in the public mind into a distinct sexual act. The sodomite had emerged as a recognizable social type. During the same years, Shakespeare's sonnets had ceased to be read.

This great category shift is the culmination of a series of events: separation of sodomy from witchcraft in the Elizabethan sodomy law, open comment on the homosexuality of JAMES I, the temporary hegemony of Puritan ideology during the interregnum, the counterreaction of libertine French culture with the restoration of Charles II, the rise of middle-class propriety, the first solid evidence of a homosexual subculture in London. All these changes in social context made for changes in the way Shakespeare's plays and poems were read by individuals, acted in the theater, and codified by culture makers. When George Granville adapted *The Merchant of Venice* for a production in 1701, he supplied a prologue in which the ghost of Shakespeare, talking with the ghost of the Restoration playwright John Dryden, makes a point of disowning any suspicion of homosexuality. First the ghost of Dryden berates modern audiences who prefer "*French Grimace, Buffoons, and Mimics*" to British drama:

> 'Thro Perspectives revers'd they Nature view,
> Which gives the Passions Images, not true.
> *Strephon* for *Strephon* sighs; and *Sapho* dies,
> Shot to the Soul by brighter *Sapho*'s Eyes. . . .

The ghost of Shakespeare is horrified:

> These Crimes unknown, in our less polish'd Age,
> Now seem above Correction of the Stage. . . .

The message here hardly needs restating: Shakespeare is a British hero, and as a British hero he most certainly is not a sodomite. In the cultural language of the eighteenth century, the homoeroticism in Shakespeare's works became unreadable and unspeakable.

To this campaign of cultural imperialism, Shakespeare's sonnets proved stubbornly resistant. Benson's decorous version of 1640 kept readers of the sonnets—such readers as there were—out of harm's way until 1766, when new editorial principles demanded an edition based on the original text of 1609. Suddenly there was some explaining to be done. Concerning sonnet 20 ("A woman's face with nature's own hand painted/ Hast thou, the master-mistress of my passion") the editor George Steevens felt compelled to append this note: "It is impossible to read this fulsome panegyrick, addressed to a male object, without an equal mixture of disgust and indignation." Edmund Malone, the first great Shakespeare scholar, saved the day by explaining that "such addresses to men, however indelicate, were customary in our author's time, and neither imported criminality nor were esteemed indecorous." The history of Shakespeare criticism in the nineteenth and twentieth centuries has been the history of one desperate attempt after another to prove Malone right. Attempts to reclaim the sonnets in works like OSCAR WILDE's "Portrait of Mr W. H." (1889) have been written off by the Guardians of Culture as anachronistic fantasies.

Unwillingness to acknowledge homoeroticism in works by the paragon of British literature persists even in the public remarks of W. H. AUDEN. Making a play on bed-secrets and Red-secrets, Auden told friends in the early 1960s that "it won't do just yet to admit that the top Bard was in the homintern"—and stood by that conviction when he wrote a preface to the New American Library paperback of the sonnets the same year. Homosexual readers, he complains in this preface, have ignored the fact that the sonnets to "the dark lady" are unmistakably sexual and that Shakespeare, after all, was a married man and a father.

> That we are confronted in the sonnets by a mystery rather than by an aberration is evidenced for me by the fact that men and women whose sexual tastes are perfectly normal, but who enjoy and understand poetry, have always been able to read them as expressions of what they understand by the word *love*, without finding the masculine pronoun an obstacle.

That may be true. "Obstacles," on the other hand, often provide the key to significant historical differences. It is precisely the masculine pronoun in the sonnets, like all the other markers of homoerotic experience in the plays and poems, that accounts for William Shakespeare's importance in the history of sexuality. His importance in the *politics* of sexuality is clear enough in Auden's attempt to explain it all away. (See also ENGLISH LITERATURE: RENAISSANCE.)

—*Bruce R. Smith*

BIBLIOGRAPHY

Auden, W. H. Introduction to William Shakespeare, *The Sonnets*. William Burto, ed. New York: New American Library, 1964. ■ Bergeron, David M., and Geraldo U. DeSousa. *Shakespeare: A Study and Research Guide*. 2nd ed. rev. Lawrence: University of Kansas Press, 1987. ■ Bray, Alan. *Homosexuality in Renaissance England*. London: Gay Men's Press, 1982. ■ Bredbeck, Gregory W. *Sodomy and Interpretation: Marlowe to Milton*. Ithaca, New York: Cornell University Press, 1991. ■ de Grazia, Margreta. *Shakespeare "Verbatim": The Reproduction of Authenticity and the 1790 Apparatus*. Oxford: Clarendon Press, 1990. ■ Dobson, Michael. *The Making of the National Poet: Shakespeare, Adaptation and Authorship, 1660-1769*. Oxford: Clarendon Press, 1992. ■ Dollimore, Jonathan. *Sexual Dissidence: Augustine to Wilde, Freud to Foucault*. Oxford: Clarendon Press, 1991. ■ Garber, Marjorie. *Vested Interests: Cross-Dressing and Cultural Anxiety*. London and New York: Routledge, 1992. ■ Goldberg, Jonathan. *Sodometries: Renaissance Texts, Modern Sexualities*. Stanford, Calif.: Stanford University Press, 1993. ■ Green, Martin. *Wriostheley's Roses in Shakespeare's Sonnets, Poems, and Plays*. Baltimore: Clevedon Press, 1993. ■ Pequigney, Joseph. *Such is My Love: A Study of Shakespeare's Sonnets*. Chicago: University of Chicago Press, 1985. ■ Schoenbaum, Samuel. *William Shakespeare: A Documentary Life*. Oxford: Clarendon Press, 1975. ■ Shakespeare, William. *The Complete Works*. Stanley Wells and Gary Taylor, eds. Oxford: Clarendon Press, 1986. ■ Sinfield, Alan. *Faultlines: Cultural Materialism and the Politics of Dissident Reading*. Berkeley: University of California Press, 1992. ■ Smith, Bruce R. *Homosexual Desire in Shakespeare's England: A Cultural Poetics*. Chicago: University of Chicago Press, 1991. ■ Stallybrass, Peter. "Editing as Cultural Formation: The Sexing of Shakespeare's Sonnets." *Modern Language Quarterly* 54.1 (1993): 91–103. ■ Summers, Claude J., ed. *Homosexuality in Renaissance and Enlightenment England: Literary Representations in Historical Context*. New York: Haworth Press, 1992. ■ Traub, Valerie. *Desire and Anxiety: Circulations of Sexuality in Shakespearean Drama*. London and New York: Routledge, 1992. ■ Zimmerman, Susan, ed. *Erotic Politics: Desire on the Renaissance Stage*. London and New York: Routledge, 1992.

Shilts, Randy
(1951–1994)

Randy Shilts pioneered as an openly gay journalist, working in both the newly emerging gay press of the 1970s and then as a reporter assigned to cover the gay and lesbian community of San Francisco for mainstream newspapers and television stations. Born in Davenport, Iowa, on August 8, 1951, he was educated at the University of Oregon, where he received a B.S. in 1975. After a stint with the gay newsmagazine *The Advocate*, he worked as a correspondent for several San Francisco television stations and newspapers. By the time of his death of complications from AIDS on February 17, 1994, he had become by far the most successful openly gay journalist in the nation, an astute interpreter of the various issues affecting American gay men and lesbians, especially gay and lesbian politics, the AIDS epidemic, and discrimination in the military, the subjects of his three highly acclaimed books.

Shilts's first book, *The Mayor of Castro Street: The Life and Times of Harvey Milk* (1982), is a biography of the first openly gay elected official in the country, the charismatic San Francisco Supervisor, who was assassinated in 1978 and became a martyr for the burgeoning gay rights movement. As the title indicates, the book is a history of a turbulent era as well as a chronicle of a particular life. Shilts tells the story of how San Francisco became the vortex of the national gay rights movement and how Milk came to personify the aspirations of a diverse constituency. The book analyzes San Francisco city politics in illuminating detail; provides fascinating accounts of the various political campaigns waged by Milk, including the successful struggle to defeat a statewide initiative that would have banned gay men and lesbians from teaching school in California; and recounts the aftermath of Milk's murder, including the trial of his assassin, Dan White, and the riots that flared after White's so-called Twinkie defense allowed him to escape conviction for first-degree murder.

In *And the Band Played on: Politics, People, and the AIDS Epidemic* (1987), Shilts tells the always fascinating, frequently depressing, and sometimes exhilarating story of the emergence of the disease that decimated gay communities throughout the country as it spread almost unchecked for the first five years after its appearance. Gripping and richly detailed, the book is an extraordinary work of investigative journalism. Seeking to explain why American medical and political institutions did so little for so long, Shilts documents the petty bickerings, turf disputes, scientific rivalries, and failures of political vision that exacerbated the crisis, even as he also chronicles the heroism of individuals who struggled mightily to contain it.

Shilts's final book is another massive work that combines history and investigative journalism, *Conduct Unbecoming: Gays and Lesbians in the U.S. Military: Vietnam to the Persian Gulf* (1993). Influenced by Allan Bérubé's account of gays in World War II, *Coming Out Under Fire* (1990), *Conduct Unbecoming* brilliantly uncovers the scandalous mistreatment suffered by gay men and lesbians in the military. While documenting the fact that many of the most celebrated American soldiers have been gay, the book also traces the development of a gay subculture within the ranks. Like Shilts's other two books, *Conduct Unbecoming* focuses on the stories of a host of individuals. These stories, many of which are as compel- ling as finely crafted suspense fiction, function to humanize and render personal an important public issue. Beyond that, the stories mirror the homophobia that gay men and lesbians encounter in all sectors of society.

Perhaps Shilts's greatest achievement as a writer was that he brought novelistic skills to the practice of journalism. All three of his books are distinguished by compelling narratives and vividly detailed character portrayals. (See also JOURNALISM AND PUBLISHING.)

—Claude J. Summers

BIBLIOGRAPHY

Shilts, Randy. *And the Band Played on: Politics, People, and the AIDS Epidemic.* New York: St. Martin's, 1987. ■ ———. *Conduct Unbecoming: Gays and Lesbians in the U.S. Military: Vietnam to the Persian Gulf.* New York: St. Martin's, 1993. ■ ———. *The Mayor of Castro Street: The Life and Times of Harvey Milk.* New York: St. Martin's, 1982.

Shockley, Ann Allen
(b. 1927)

Popular short story writer and novelist, as well as librarian, critic, and editor, Ann Allen Shockley was born June 21, 1927, in Louisville, Kentucky. The daughter of social workers Bessie Lucas and Henry Allen, Shockley received her B.A. in 1948 from Fisk University, where she currently works as archivist, librarian, and professor, and her M.S.L.S. in 1959 from Western Reserve, now Case Western Reserve. In 1949, she married teacher William Shockley, whom she later divorced. She is best known for her groundbreaking lesbian fiction: *Loving Her* (1974) is arguably the first novel to offer a black lesbian as its primary character.

Loving Her centers on an interracial relationship between Renay, who is black, and Terry, who is white, and equates that relationship with a journey into self-discovery. A novel of development, *Loving Her* moves inward. It opens with the breakup of Renay's marriage and subsequently focuses on her inner awakening: the recovery of her dream of becoming an accomplished pianist and the discovery of her lesbianism. Reflecting a sensibility that predates the black, lesbian, and women's liberation movements, Renay's empowering bond with Terry frames racial difference as a secondary issue: a skin-deep phenomenon within the relationship, a vehicle for homophobia without. In a reworking of *The Well of Loneliness*, with which it invites comparison, *Loving Her* casts lesbianism as the nourisher and heterosexuality as the violator of female, familial, and racial integrity.

Shockley, who has named herself a "social[ly] conscious writer," extends her fictional treatment of interracial and lesbian experiences with her collection of short stories, *The Black and White of It* (1980), which celebrates the gains women have made in the wake of racial and sexual oppression. In "A Birthday Remembered," Tobie, the biological daughter of the protagonist's deceased lover, embodies those gains. She is a confident, well-adjusted adolescent who considers "Aunt El" family, recognizes the importance of personal independence and economic self-reliance, and identifies her deceased mother's relationship as having been loving, legitimate, and a model to emulate.

Shockley's stories are scenarios of survival much more than of living. In "One More Saturday Night Around," principal character Marcia endures stolen moments in motel rooms with her former college lover, now married. Far from ideal, these trysts represent a determination and resourcefulness complicated by tangible obstacles.

Shockley consistently explores possibilities for social transformation across sexual and racial divides. Challenging the homophobia that, according to her 1979 essay "The Black Lesbian in American Literature: An Overview," pervades the black community, her second novel, *Say Jesus and Come to Me* (1982), situates its lesbian love story amid feminist meetings and religious revivals. The juxtaposition of evangelicalism and lesbianism is surprising and subversive.

Shockley's works offer complex, wide-ranging portrayals of lesbian experience. Though at times character and plot development are inconsistent, and though awkward phrasings tend to reduce descriptions of lovemaking to hilarious detail, her fiction constitutes a brave contribution to lesbian literature. (See also AFRICAN-AMERICAN LITERATURE, LESBIAN.)

—Margaret Breen and Elsa A. Bruguier

BIBLIOGRAPHY

Bogus, S. Diane. "Ann Allen Shockley." *Gay and Lesbian Literature.* Sharon Malinowski, ed. Detroit: St. James Press, 1994. 349–351. ■ Dandridge, Rita B. *Ann Allen Shockley: An Annotated Primary and Secondary Bibliography.* New York: Greenwood Press, 1987. ■ Gomez, Jewelle L. "A Cultural Legacy Denied and Discovered: Black Lesbians and Fiction by Women." *Home Girls.* Barbara Smith, ed. New York: Kitchen Table Press, 1983. 110–123. ■ Zimmerman, Bonnie. *The Safe Sea of Women, Lesbian Fiction, 1969–1989.* Boston: Beacon Press, 1990.

Sitwell, Edith
(1887–1964)

Edith Sitwell was born on September 7, 1887, the daughter of Sir George and Lady Ida Sitwell. Like most young women of her class, she was educated at home. In 1903, Helen Rootham, an aspiring poet who translated the works of ARTHUR RIMBAUD into English, was engaged as her governess. Under Rootham's tutelage, Sitwell was introduced to the French symbolist poets whose influence is evident in her work, and, in 1913, the two women left the Sitwell family home and set up lodgings in London. Freed from parental restrictions, Sitwell embarked on a literary career and published her first volume of poetry, *The Mother and Other Poems,* in 1915. The following year, as the center of a literary circle that included Rootham and her brothers Osbert (1892–1969) and Satcheverell Sitwell (1897–1988), she initiated *Wheels,* an avant-garde literary anthology issued in yearly "cycles" until 1921.

Sitwell disdained what she deemed the traditional "weakness" of female-authored poetry, believing that SAPPHO, CHRISTINA ROSSETTI, and EMILY DICKINSON were the only women poets worthy of emulation. Her own growing fame and notoriety as an experimental artist culminated in 1923 with the first public performance of *Façade,* an "entertainment" in which she recited her cycle of poems from behind a screen and through a megaphone to the accompaniment of music composed and conducted by William Walton. The poems comprising *Façade* emphasize the sounds of individual words and employ eccentric diction, all placed in the rhythms of contemporary popular dance music (for example, waltz and fox-trot). In overall effect, this pioneering work of performance art deflates entrenched Victorian mores. Although her artistic activities drew much critical derision, they also propelled her to the forefront of MODERNISM; she became friends with VIRGINIA WOOLF and GERTRUDE STEIN, the latter of whom she introduced to the British public. The 1930s, by contrast, brought Sitwell personal and professional sorrow as well as severe financial exigency. She moved to Paris in 1932 with the terminally ill Rootham and remained there until her companion's death in 1938. During this sojourn, she concentrated on prose works, including her fantastic historical novel *I Live Under a Black Sun,* and participated in various literary salons that included Stein, NATALIE BARNEY, SYLVIA BEACH, and Adrienne Monnier. She also formed a close friendship with Bryher Ellerman, the wealthy lesbian author who served as a generous benefactress for the rest of Sitwell's life.

Her growing cultural pessimism, which became evident in her ambitious narrative poem *Gold Coast Customs* (1929), was deepened by World War II. "Still Falls the Rain" (1942), later set to music by Benjamin Britten and originally performed by Britten's lover Peter Pears, juxtaposes the bombing of London with the crucifixion of Christ and indicates Sitwell's desire for personal and cosmic spiritual healing. Her post-war poetry is almost entirely concerned with human suffering on a global scale. The fear of nuclear annihilation produced by the Cold War and the infirmities of age led to her conversion to Catholicism in 1955, with EVELYN WAUGH serving as her sponsor.

Both personally and professionally, Sitwell surrounded herself throughout her life with gay men, including her brother Osbert. She was emotionally attached for many years to the painter Pavel Tchelitchew. Additionally, she formed artistic collaborations and friendships with RONALD FIRBANK, WILFRED OWEN, Cecil Beaton, Alvaro Guevara, STEPHEN

SPENDER, W. H. AUDEN, and JAMES PURDY. Her last poem, "The Outcasts" (1962), was a gesture of support for the reform of British antihomosexuality laws.

Edith Sitwell was named Dame Commander of the British Empire in 1954. She died December 11, 1964. Her autobiography, *Taken Care Of*, was published the following year.

—*Patricia Juliana Smith*

BIBLIOGRAPHY

Elborn, Geoffrey. *Edith Sitwell: A Biography*. Garden City, N.Y.: Doubleday, 1981. ■ Glendinning, Victoria. *Edith Sitwell: A Unicorn Among Lions*. New York: Knopf, 1981. ■ Lehmann, John. *A Nest of Tigers: The Sitwells in Their Times*. London: Macmillan, 1968. ■ Pearson, John. *The Sitwells: A Family's Biography*. New York: Harcourt Brace Jovanovich, 1980. ■ Salter, Elizabeth and Allanah Harper. *Edith Sitwell: Fire of the Mind*. London: Michael Joseph, 1976.

Somerville, Edith (1858–1949) and Violet Martin (1862–1915)

Authors of numerous hunting sketches, short stories, and novels, Edith Somerville and Violet Martin were second cousins and members of the Anglo-Irish ascendancy. Somerville was born May 2, 1858, in Corfu and died October 8, 1949, at Castle Townshend, Ireland. She was raised in her family's West Cork eighteenth-century "big house." This upbringing provided material for her writings, most of which she co-authored with her companion Violet Martin, who was born at Ross House, County Galway, on June 11, 1862, and died on December 21, 1915, in the home she shared with Somerville in Drishane, County Cork. The collaborative works of the two women explore, often comically and with particular attention to Irish idiom, relations between the landed classes and the peasantry. A keen huntswoman and suffragist, Somerville was also in later life a close friend of lesbian composer Ethel Smythe.

Trained as an illustrator, Somerville met Martin in 1886. The encounter was pivotal: As Somerville recalled in *Irish Memories* (1917), the meeting "proved the hinge of my life, the place where my fate, and hers, turned over. . . ." Somerville's is the language of ROMANTIC FRIENDSHIP. The two women became life and literary partners. Their families were initially shocked by the latter relationship: Writing seemed a vulgar occupation. Although both women took pseudonyms—Martin was "Martin Ross," Somerville was "Guilles Herring"—only Martin's endured. The cousins' collaboration yielded a highly successful partnership that lasted nearly three decades and, arguably, even longer. Although Martin died in 1915, Somerville believed that communication with her continued via automatic writing; Somerville's later works were published under both their names.

Somerville and Ross are best known for *Some Experiences of an Irish R.M.* (1899), a collection of comic short stories, but the early novel *The Real Charlotte* (1894) is their most important literary achievement. Like the authors themselves, the two principal characters of the novel are cousins; and Charlotte can best be understood in terms of her cousin Francie, her physical, emotional, and economic counterpoint. Where Charlotte is plain and middle-aged, Francie is beautiful and young; where Charlotte is a ruthless schemer, Francie is a good-hearted blunderer; and where Charlotte steadily gains wealth and land, Francie refuses the marriage proposal that would afford her the same. In these respects opposites, the women are nonetheless both placed in plots of frustrated desire. Not even Francie's marriage to the man whom Charlotte loves and the latter's consequent attempts to ruin the couple financially can disrupt the powerful kinship between the two women. The romantic aspirations of each are thwarted because the woman lacks either one or both of those conventional ingredients of female mobility, looks and wealth. Charlotte and Francie constitute the real couple of the novel.

Criticism of *The Real Charlotte*, perhaps the finest Irish novel of the nineteenth century, includes uneasy speculation concerning the authors' private lives, which serves to discount Somerville and Ross's achievements. The partners have been called "eccentric" and their literary productions "unlikely." Although Somerville never spoke of her relationship with Ross as lesbian, her memoirs indicate clearly that it was passionate and primary. To judge from the authors' thirteen published volumes, it was also nourishing.

—*Margaret Breen*

BIBLIOGRAPHY

Cronin, Anthony. "Edith Somerville and Martin Ross: Women Fighting Back." *Heritage Now*. New York: St. Martin's, 1983.

■ Faderman, Lillian. *Surpassing the Love of Men: Romantic Friendship and Love between Women from the Renaissance to the Present.* New York: Morrow, 1981. ■ Mooney, Shawn R.

"'Colliding Stars': Heterosexism in Biographical Representations of Somerville and Ross." *Canadian Journal of Irish Studies* 18.1 (July 1992): 157–175.

Sontag, Susan
(b. 1933)

Best known as a cultural critic, Susan Sontag has long been preoccupied with European modernist aesthetics and thought—a set of influences strongly marking her fiction and filmmaking as well as her essays. Her landmark study "Notes on 'Camp'" (1964) was the first detailed account of this variety of gay sensibility. In a number of other essays—on Jack Smith's film *Flaming Creatures,* WILLIAM BURROUGHS, PAUL GOODMAN, ROLAND BARTHES, and Robert Mapplethorpe—she has focused on gay figures, though without much attention to their sexual identity as such. Sontag rarely writes in an autobiographical mode; she has treated her own lesbian sexuality as a strictly private matter. But a complex engagement with gay male culture runs throughout Sontag's work, often intersecting with her concern for twentieth-century literary and artistic avant-gardes.

Trained academically in philosophy and comparative literature, Sontag began her literary career with two novels, *The Benefactor* (1963) and *Death Kit* (1967); critics have noticed in them echoes of ANDRÉ GIDE and Nathalie Sarraute, respectively. In essays published throughout the 1960s and 1970s, Sontag introduced Anglophone readers to the work of such figures as Antonin Artaud, Roland Barthes, Claude Levi-Strauss, Jean-Luc Godard, Walter Benjamin, and E. M. Cioran. Two rather Bergmanesque films, *Duet for Cannibals* (1969) and *Brother Carl* (1971), were written and directed by Sontag in Sweden; her documentary, *Promised Lands* (1974), concerned the aftermath of the 1973 Arab-Israeli war. Both her criticism—gathered in *Against Interpretation* (1966), *Styles of Radical Will* (1969), and *Under the Sign of Saturn* (1980)—and the short fiction collected in *I, Etcetra* (1978) display aphoristic and densely allusive qualities, more reminiscent of Friedrich Nietzsche or Jorge Luis Borges than of any contemporary writer in English.

Just this combination of historical consciousness and philosophical reflection distinguishes "Notes on 'Camp,'" a central text in her *ouevre*. Sontag's awareness of the paradox involved in bringing high seriousness to bear on the humorous and marginal discourse of CAMP makes this an exceptionally complex essay. She interprets camp as "a victory of 'style' over 'content,' . . . of irony over tragedy," reading it as a variant of Wildean dandyism "in the age of mass culture."

Sontag returns to the question of moralistic versus aestheticist responses to "the age of mass culture" in a controversial essay on German director Leni Riefenstahl and in *On Photography* (1977). But what made the essay on camp particularly important when published in the mid-1960s was its prescient critical attention to a gay subculture. "Homosexuals have pinned their integration into society on promoting the aesthetic sense," she argued. "Camp is a solvent of morality. It neutralizes moral indignation, sponsors playfulness."

In remission from a cancer initially diagnosed as fatal, Sontag penned *Illness as Metaphor* (1978) as a critique of the cultural mythologies surrounding tuberculosis, syphilis, and cancer. "Nothing is more punitive than to give a disease a meaning—that meaning invariably being a moralistic one," she wrote. "Any important disease whose causality is murky, and for which treatment is ineffectual, tends to be awash in significance." With *AIDS and Its Metaphors* (1989), she extends the historical and cultural analysis of the earlier volume. A short story "The Way We Live Now" (1986) depicts the impact on a group of friends of the news that one in their circle has AIDS. Her third novel, *The Volcano Lover: A Historical Romance* (1992), returns to many of the questions of taste and sensibility first sketched in "Notes on 'Camp.'"

—*Scott McLemee*

BIBLIOGRAPHY

Frank, Marcie. "The Critic as Performance Artist: Susan Sontag's Writing and Gay Cultures." *Camp Grounds: Style and Homosexuality.* David Bergman, ed. Amherst: University of Massachusetts Press, 1993. 173–184. ■ Kennedy, Liam. "Precocious Archaeology: Susan Sontag and the Criticism of Culture." *Journal of American Studies* 24.1 (1990): 23–39. ■ McLemee, Scott. "On Demythologizing AIDS: Susan Sontag's *AIDS and Its Metaphors.*" *New Politics,* new series 7 (1989): 170–176. ■ Nelson, Cary. "Soliciting Self-Knowledge: The Rhetoric of Susan Sontag's Criticism." *Critical Inquiry* 6.4 (1980): 707–726. ■ Sayres, Sohnya. *Susan Sontag: The Elegiac Modernist.* New York: Routledge, 1990.

South Asian Literatures

South Asia, or the Indian subcontinent, is a spectacular mosaic of many cultures, ethnicities, religions, languages, and traditions. It is home to over one billion people, and the nearly fifteen million South Asians who live abroad constitute one of the largest twentieth-century diasporas. Inheritors of some of the oldest literary traditions in the world, contemporary South Asian writers build on a rich classical past. A consistent and articulate homosexual discourse, however, is largely absent in the classical as well as contemporary South Asian writing. It is in the literature of the South Asian diaspora, especially since the mid-1980s, that a visible and vocal gay and lesbian tradition has begun to emerge.

Some historical evidence suggests considerable social acceptance of sexual diversity in ancient South Asia: In parts of the subcontinent, for example, centuries-old erotic sculptures depict men and women engaged in a variety of homosexual as well as heterosexual activities; some classical Hindu myths recognize, even affirm, the fluidity of gender as well as sexual identities. But the written works produced in ancient South Asia, generally speaking, either remain silent on the subject of homosexuality or merely allude to it. For example, the Vedic texts, thought to be nearly 4,000 years old, do not mention homosexuality, whereas Valmiki's *Ramayana* and Vyasa's *Mahabharata*—the two great Indian epics—make only fleeting references to it. The notable exception to this trend, however, is Vatsyayana's *The Kama Sutra*. Arguably the world's oldest sex manual, it devotes an entire chapter to homosexuality. Here Vatsyayana, a Hindu sage, offers explicitly detailed instructions on how to perform homosexual acts. Among the medieval texts only two engage homosexual themes: Emperor Babur's autobiographical *Tuzuki-i-Babri* contains a sentimental recollection of his erotic love for a teenage boy; Dargah Quli Khan's personal diary *Muraqqa-e-Delhi: The Moghal Capital in Muhammad Shaw's Time* briefly documents his foray into the pederastic circles of Islamic Delhi.

There is even greater reticence on homosexuality in contemporary South Asian literatures—a reticence that perhaps reflects the generally conservative sexual mores of the people. In the voluminous body of literature that is produced in South Asian countries, in English as well as in about twenty indigenous languages, there is hardly an imaginative text that sympathetically explores the theme of male homosexuality. Only a few women writers—none of whom is identified as a lesbian—have published works that deal with sexual love between women. Ismat Chughatai's "Lihaf" ("The Quilt"), written in Urdu, was first published in 1942. Narrated from the point of view of a ten-year-old girl, the story focuses on the sexual relationship between an aristocratic Indian woman and her female servant. Shortly after its publication, the author appeared in court to defend herself against charges of obscenity. She won. When Kamala Das, a well-known poet in South Asia, published *My Story* in 1976, she created a minor scandal: The candid autobiography not only revealed her extramarital heterosexual affairs but also her adolescent crush on a female teacher and a brief lesbian encounter with an older student. More controversial is Shobha De's *Strange Obsession* (1993), a rambunctious novel about lesbian love published by the prestigious Penguin Books of India. Though Shobha De—the wife of a very wealthy Bombay businessman and mother of six children—has been dismissed by the literary establishment as a mere purveyor of filth, her novel has become a national best-seller. Her commercial success certainly indicates widespread interest among Indian readers in works that explicitly deal with nontraditional sexualities; however, the interest, to some extent, may simply be prurient curiosity.

Although self-identified gay and lesbian artists are yet to break into the South Asian literary scene, a few writers of the South Asian diaspora have begun to explore gay, lesbian, and bisexual themes with some candor. The relative openness of this small group of writers is perhaps largely due to their diasporic locations: They live in either the United States or Britain—countries that have well-established gay and lesbian communities with a tradition of organized resistance—and therefore have greater sexual and artistic freedom and wider publishing opportunities. Further, their physical separation from family and community probably gives them relative privacy and greater freedom from culturally imposed constraints. Except for Hanif Kureishi, who was born in England, all the other writers in this group were born in South Asia and emigrated to the West as young adults. But even these writers, with a few exceptions, tend to be cautious about sexual self-disclosure; some even seem uncertain about the role of their sexuality in their literary projects. Very few writers openly explore the personal conflicts and political contradictions generated by their interacting ethnocultural, post-colonial, and homosexual subjectivities.

Among the more cautious writers is Prafulla Mohanti, a gay South Asian artist who lives in London. An acclaimed writer and distinguished painter, Mohanti recalls in his autobiographical *Through Brown Eyes* (1985) his childhood in a small Indian village and his adult life as an immigrant in an increasingly racist and violent England. Although the autobiography spans the first forty-five years of his life, Mohanti meticulously avoids any references to his sexuality; instead, he foregrounds ethnic issues and immigrant concerns. But the conspicuous sexual silence that characterizes his autobiography is in itself a subtle strategy: It is a way of speaking the unspeakable. This silence, in addition to a casual remark that many art critics have commented on the preponderance of phallic symbols in his paintings, remains the only textual marker of his homosexuality.

Whereas Mohanti resolutely maintains his sexual silence in his immigrant autobiography, Agha Shahid Ali engages in cautious self-disclosure. In some of his earlier poems—such as "Leaving Your City," "Beyond the Ash Rains," and "A Rehearsal of Loss"—the poet reveals his pain over lost love, but the gender of the lover remains unspecified. A common tactic among precontemporary homosexual poets in the West, this deliberate elision of gender specificity makes gay readings of the poems possible. In his more recent work, however, Ali appears less anxious to conceal his sexuality. "A Nostalgist's Map of America," written after learning about a close friend's AIDS diagnosis, is an exceptionally powerful rendering of personal anguish. Homoerotic overtones are even more evident in "In Search of Evanescence," a hauntingly eloquent meditation on the poet's relationship with Phil, the friend dying of AIDS.

A bit more candid than Ali is Vikram Seth, one of the most celebrated South Asian novelists. His highly praised *The Golden Gate* (1986), a novel in verse, has an all-American cast of characters and offers a bemused look at the 1980s yuppie lifestyle in northern California. Young and prosperous but bored and lonely, the characters in the novel search for meaning and happiness. Bisexual Phil falls in love with gay Ed, but Ed, a devout Catholic, is tormented by sexual guilt. While he gradually learns to understand and accept his sexuality, Phil falls in love with Liz, Ed's sister, and they marry. Lurking beneath the novel's gentle satire on the Californian ethos is Seth's message that sexual self-acceptance, meaningful commitment, and genuine love are the bases of an authentic life. In his most recent work, *A Suitable Boy* (1993), Seth projects an epic vision of Indian life during the 1950s.

Here homosexuality is merely hinted at: In one of the novel's numerous subplots, there is a suggestion that two male characters—Maan Kapoor and Firoz Khan—were once lovers.

Unlike Mohanti, Ali, and Seth, Andrew Harvey deals with homosexual themes explicitly, elaborately, and consistently in all three of his novels, but his place in South Asian gay literature is problematic. By birth an Anglo-Indian—a term used in India to refer to people of racially mixed background—Harvey was born in Nagpur and grew up in Old Delhi. At age nine, he moved to England to live with his English grandparents. Though India continues to dominate his consciousness—he is profoundly influenced by Buddhist spirituality and Hindu mysticism—he feels no ethnic identification with India. A blurb on the cover of his recent spiritual autobiography, *Hidden Journey* (1991), for example, calls him a "native" of India, but in the text itself Harvey stresses his "Englishness" and views Indians as vaguely familiar but largely exotic Others.

Absence of any overt ethnic consciousness marks all three of Harvey's gay novels. In each of them the main characters frantically search for heightened self-knowledge, for love that often remains elusive, and for mystical insight into the puzzle of their lives. At the center of *One Last Mirror* (1985), Harvey's first novel, is the relationship between an elderly widow and a young bisexual male. *Burning Houses* (1986), Harvey's best-known novel, is a work that focuses on the complex relationship between Charles, a young English writer, and Adolphe, an aging queen, and their mutual attempt to narrate Charles's troubled relationship with Mark, a married man. *The Web* (1987), a sequel to *Burning Houses,* deals with Charles's struggle to understand Mark's emotional collapse and subsequent disappearance. Charles is clearly an autobiographical character, but he is consistently presented as an "Englishman."

In contrast to Harvey, Hanif Kureishi explores the many ambivalences and complexities of his problematic identity as a diasporic post-colonial who is simultaneously an ethnic and sexual outsider in a troubled England. *My Beautiful Laundrette* (1986), Kureishi's brilliant screenplay, deals with the gay romance between Omar, a young British-born Pakistani, and Johnny, a working-class Englishman. Through the tensions and conflicts inherent in their relationship, Kureishi traces the interconnections among race, class, and sexuality in contemporary multicultural England. As much a critique of post-imperial Britain as it is an incisive commentary on the Indo-Pakistani immigrant culture in London, *My Beautiful Laundrette* is the first text by an openly gay South Asian writer to create a South Asian gay male character. And

Kureishi accomplishes it gracefully and unapologetically. In *The Buddha of Suburbia* (1990), his first and only novel to date, Kureishi once again explores the interconnections among race, class, and sexuality. A comic-satirical *bildungsroman*, the novel tracks the picaresque misadventures of Karim, its bisexual, British-born Pakistani protagonist. But at the heart of the narrative lies a more serious project: Kureishi's systematic attempt to collapse national, racial, and sexual boundaries in order to reimagine the meaning of each.

Suniti Namjoshi is the only openly lesbian South Asian writer with significant publications. She began to publish poetry in India during the late 1960s, but her early work can hardly be characterized as "lesbian." She spent much of the following decade in the United States, Canada, and England and became increasingly involved in feminist and lesbian political activism. Her works published during the 1980s reveal her politicization: a radical lesbian-feminist consciousness informs each of them. Her *Feminist Fables* (1981), a collection of poems and prose narratives, offers a subversive perspective on patriarchal assumptions. *The Conversations of Cow* (1985), an innovative mixture of fiction, fantasy, and fable, is a hilarious novella that examines the relationship between Suniti, a feminist lesbian separatist, and Bhadravati, a lesbian brahmin cow. What Namjoshi calls "the bloodier aspects of gay and women's liberation" provides the content for her 1984 collection of poems titled *From the Bedside Book of Nightmares*. Here again she injects her satiric wit and subversive humor into her intensely political musings. *Flesh and Paper* (1986)—a poetic dialogue between Namjoshi and her lover, the Australian-born poet Gillian Hanscombe—reveals how profoundly her poetic imagination is shaped by her lesbian-feminist politics. Her most recent work, *The Mothers of Maya Diip* (1989), is a novel that is set in a mythical South Asian nation with only female inhabitants. The matriarchal arrangement provides Namjoshi with an opportunity to satirize a wide range of contemporary human institutions and ideologies, including Western feminism and lesbian separatism.

Since the mid-1980s, hundreds of young gay and lesbian South Asians living in the metropolitan centers of Europe and North America have begun to assert their presence by forming support groups. Begun partly in response to the racism they encounter in the predominantly white queer communities of the West but also in an effort to counter their sense of alienation from the heterosexist South Asian diasporic cultures, these groups provide their members with a sense of community and create safe spaces for them to focus on their individual dilemmas and collective concerns. Many of the groups regularly publish newsletters, such as *Shakti Khabar* (London), *Trikone* (San Jose), *Shamakami* (San Francisco), and *Khush Kayal* (Toronto), which have subscribers in many countries. These publications seek to link South Asian gay and lesbian individuals as well as communities scattered around the world and to help forge a global South Asian queer identity. These newsletters also serve as forums for creative self-expression. Many of them regularly include art work, poems, short stories, and autobiographical narratives by members.

The emergence of an international South Asian gay and lesbian community is most clearly reflected in the pioneering anthology *A Lotus of Another Color: An Unfolding of the South Asian Gay and Lesbian Experience* (1993). Edited by Rakesh Ratti, this volume consists of coming-out narratives, poetry, fiction, biography, and formal essays by thirty-two gay, lesbian, and bisexual contributors from around the world. Some of the entries in the volume attempt to document gay and lesbian presence in the histories, mythologies, and religious traditions of South Asia; others articulate the lived and imagined experiences of contemporary South Asian gay men and lesbians. Some of the most compelling pieces in the anthology are the autobiographical narratives that reveal the complex intersections of ethnicity, migrancy, post-coloniality, and (homo)sexuality in the lives of diasporic South Asians. The individual voices in the volume suggest the heterogeneity of the South Asian queer experience; yet their voices, collectively, succeed eminently in defining and articulating a singular South Asian queer identity. A landmark event in the history of South Asian gay and lesbian writing, the publication of *A Lotus of a Different Color* will no doubt give impetus to the growth of this fledgling literary tradition.

—*Emmanuel S. Nelson*

BIBLIOGRAPHY

Brooks, Brenda. "Words Invent the World: An Interview with Gillian Hanscombe & Suniti Namjoshi." *Trikone* 2.4 (November 1987): 1,4. ■ Chughtai, Ismat. "Lihaf." Trans. Surjit Singh Dulai and Carlo Coppola. *Trikone* 5.2 (March–April 1990): 1–3. ■ Knippling, Alpana Sharma. "Hanif Kureishi." *Writers of the Indian Diaspora: A Bio-Bibliographical Critical Sourcebook.* Emmanuel S. Nelson, ed. Westport, Conn.: Greenwood Press, 1993. 159–168. ■ McGifford, Diane. "Suniti Namjoshi." *Writers of the Indian Diaspora: A Bio-Bibliographical Critical Sourcebook.* Emmanuel S. Nelson, ed. Westport, Conn.: Greenwood Press, 1993. 291–297. ■ Parmar, Pratibha. "The Conversations of Cow: Suniti Namjoshi's Thoughts on Being a Woman, Lesbian, and Indian." *Trikone* 4.4 (July–August 1989): 1–4. ■ Rashid, Ian. *Black Markets, White Boyfriends and Other Acts of Elision.* Toronto: Toronto South Asian Review Press, 1991. ■ Ratti, Rakesh, ed. *A Lotus of Another Color: An Unfolding of the South Asian Gay and Lesbian Experience.* Boston: Alyson, 1993.

Spanish Literature

The tradition of representing homosexuality in Spanish literature is neither as extensive nor as progressive as in the other major Western European literatures. It is, indeed, largely a twentieth-century phenomenon, with the great bulk of frank discussions of homosexuality emerging in the liberal post-Franco decades. Medieval allusions to homosexuality, for example, tend to be more legalistic than literary. The thirteenth-century code of law, compiled under the supervision of King Alfonso X and known as *Las siete partidas* (*The Seven Laws*), specifies the death penalty for what it terms "sins against nature." The statute appears in the seventh section of the inventory, which also deals with the presence of Jews on Spanish territory, tellingly associating same-sex sexual relationships with heresy and alienness. *Las siete partidas* does not mention female-female sexuality; the compilers probably found lesbianism either inconceivable or insignificant. It is not clear to what extent the medieval laws were enforced, but there is no doubt that the religious and civil prohibitions against homosexuality have for centuries both reflected and helped perpetuate prejudice against gay men and lesbians in Spanish life and literature.

One of the first significant Spanish portrayals of homosexuality occurs in Francisco Delicado's *La lozana andaluza* (*The Lusty Andalusian Woman* [1528]), a dialogued novel, with the author's personal commentary and explanations interspersed throughout the text. The "lozana" of the title is a sexual libertine who, along with her cohorts, preaches a philosophy of free love. The characters exhibit no inhibitions in their sexual exploits. Their desire is for a world in which everyone can act sexually in the manner of his or her choosing. Hence, it is not surprising that both lesbianism and male homosexuality appear in the text. Delicado's intentions have been debated. The author presents himself as a friend of the protagonist and frequently interrupts the action to justify her conduct. Some critics have simply dismissed the work as obscenity, whereas others have read it as a condemnation of the moral and social corruption during the age of Charles V. Little is known of Delicado's life, but he may have come from a family of converted Jews. If so, this background may have led him to identify strongly with other marginalized people during the Spanish Inquisition.

In the pastoral novels of the Spanish Renaissance, homosexual love is hinted at via the confusions of cross-dressing and androgyny. However, the cross-dressing and androgyny presented in these novels are usually subsumed in apparently innocent, adolescent games. Playing with gender roles facilitates the awakening and exploration of sexual desires, but those desires are invariably heterosexual in the end. Hence, the implied homosexuality of these texts is merely a phase through which the characters pass on their way to "mature" heterosexuality. Curiously, however, this configuration privileges homosexuality as the original sexual orientation. Many moralists of the era found these games less than innocent, charging that they signaled the coming decadence and effeminacy of Spanish society.

The literature of the Renaissance is also filled with pseudo-androgynes. One popular form is that of the female transvestite who recurrently makes her way onto the stage of Golden Age drama. Although some of the portrayals harbor lesbian undertones, this character type usually dresses like a man not to express her sexual nature, but to obtain privileges denied to her because she is female.

Homosexuality is an important presence in the nineteenth-century naturalist classic, *La Regenta* (*The Regent* [1884]), but in a very unpleasant way. In this novel, Leopoldo Alas (also known as Clarín) conducts a scathing critique of the ethical, social, and sexual perversions of the fictional town of Vetusta. The narrative revolves around Ana Ozores, known to all the townspeople as "la Regenta" because of her husband's previous political position. Through the collusion of the hypocritical members of her upper-crust circle, Ana, the pinnacle of moral righteousness, succumbs to the depravity that Vetusta fosters and celebrates by having an affair with the local Don Juan—one Álvaro Mesía, a superficial libertine and dandy. When her confessor, Fermín de Pas, falls in love with her, the affair becomes a tragic love triangle, ending with the death of Ana's husband, Víctor, in a duel with Mesía that the jealous and manipulative de Pas partially orchestrates. The heterosexual transgressions of the main plot are, however, placed in perspective by Celedonio, one of the most famous gay male characters in Spanish literature. He has the dubious distinction of opening and closing the door to this Asturian town. The character barely exists in the text, appearing rather as an almost subterranean presence that constantly threatens to resurface. This presentation and the fact that his homosexuality is not pertinent to the plot suggest that his function is predominantly symbolic. If Celedonio is the messenger boy, the message is that Vetusta is a depraved and miserable place.

Ambiguous sexuality is a prominent theme throughout Alas's novel, which also contains hints of latent lesbian feelings among the women. Much female attention is focused on Ana. Obdulia, the would-be femme fatale of the town, though heterosexual in orientation, appears captivated by Ana. Her desire to possess the men in her life seems motivated by her desire to vicariously possess Ana. Tellingly, Obdulia's feelings for Ana are entirely sensual. Like Celedonio, Obdulia is a sexual aggressor. The narrator does not express the same disgust for her feelings toward Ana as he does for Celedonio's "bestial" inclinations, but he animalizes both of them. The characterization of homosexuals as predatory and bestial in *La Regenta* is paradigmatic of representations of homosexuality in much Spanish literature.

A more positive, though also disturbing, portrayal of male homosexuality occurs in an early twentieth-century novella by Ramón del Valle-Inclán, an eccentric dandy who wrote four novellas (one representing each season) that he entitled *Sonatas* (1902–1905). These *Sonatas* are written as diaries that chronicle the sexual and romantic exploits of the Marquis of Bradomín, a dapper and decadent Don Juan. In a scene of the *Sonata* dedicated to summer, a fair-haired adolescent approaches a mulatto cabin boy and inspires only partially sublimated desires in Bradomín, who is observing alongside his latest conquest, la Niña Chloe. The scene is decidedly homoerotic since the two young men openly embrace. These "happy" and "abhorred" homosexual characters—"shadows," as Bradomín refers to them—momentarily beckon to the Marquis, but he is incapable of following. Although there is an indication that Bradomín might be inclined to act on these impulses, he denies that this is so, claiming that, despite having given in to all the other "satanic" pleasures, this one will remain foreign to him.

Here the quintessential heterosexual, a celebrated seducer of women, admits to homoerotic feelings and bemoans the constrictions of his faith that prevent him from acting. The heavens (that is, Catholic dogma) are against him, inclining him exclusively toward females. Bradomín is deeply saddened by his incapacity to act on his impulses, believing that Christianity has destroyed the sheer joy of ancient pagan societies. The scene, in fact, inspires classical associations in Bradomin's imagination. For him, the homosexual act, at least between men, is a sacred mystery in which only a few chosen ones now participate, reliving the ancient Greek and Roman tradition. This is the reli-

gion he would like to recuperate to counter the restrictive Catholic faith. There is a clear suggestion in the text that, as he gets older, these homosexual impulses become stronger, thus evoking the intergenerational coupling of a Roman emperor.

Although the protagonist's tendencies are frustrated by learned inhibitions and not acted on, still the depiction of homosexuality in the summer *Sonata* is positive, especially since it conveys the idea that homoeroticism is aesthetically and emotionally uplifting. This type of love is perverse from Bradomín's perspective, but it is authentically love. It must be borne in mind, however, that the protagonist is a sexual degenerate. Valle-Inclán clearly views homosexuality as decadent. The twist, however, is that this author has a more positive opinion of DECADENCE than is the norm. Moreover, of all the sensual pleasures that the world offers, both mundane and deviant, homosexuality is the only one that remains alien to the protagonist. This indicates the strength of the prohibition against homosexuality in Valle-Inclán's day even among dandies and libertines.

Valle-Inclán may be regarded as forerunner of the Vanguard movement, often referred to in Spain as the Generation of 27, which embraced a novel, antibourgeois morality. Two gay authors who are grouped with the Generation of 27 are LUIS CERNUDA and FEDERICO GARCÍA LORCA. Although they did not enjoy the freedom of expression afforded their successor JUAN GOYTISOLO, the two can be seen as predecessors to the Catalan author who later in the century uses homosexuality, among other weapons, to defy Spanish tradition.

Of the two, Cernuda is probably the one who most regularly incorporates homoerotic motifs. The very titles of his collections of poetry—*La realidad y el deseo* (*Reality and Desire* [1936]), *Poemas para un cuerpo* (*Poems for a Body* [1957])—indicate the sexually charged nature of his work. Another of his recurrent themes is that of marginalization or ostracism, which relates to his position as outsider and to the oppression he experienced. Far from silencing him, however, his exclusion became the catalyst for his poetic expression.

The second author, Federico García Lorca, is the more universally renowned. His homosexuality is also very well known, but it is habitually disregarded or camouflaged in critical circles. Lorca's play, *El público* (*The Public* [1930]) and the poems collected in the volume *Poeta en Nueva York* (*Poet in New York* [1940]), both written at about the same time, are the works in which the author most seriously delves into questions of homosexuality. Like Cernuda in his early period, he does so in surrealist fashion, although the issues of sexuality, passion, love, and prejudice are expressed quite clearly. True love, Lorca tells us in *El público*, surpasses any notion of gender. Critics traditionally have found the work problematic, seeing in it a perverse, tortured sexual preoccupation. Recently, however, the play has been deemed key to an understanding of Lorca's ideology and aesthetics. Many of the violent images that appear in the play foreshadow Goytisolo's later aggressive stance toward social norms. The poems included in *Poeta en Nueva York* are also surrealistic. In the "Ode to Walt Whitman," Lorca reconstrues some of the same images that Alas had used in *La Regenta* to animalize and disfigure Celedonio—namely, that of the toad. Many critics read Lorca's tragic trilogy (three plays that deal with the sexual and social frustrations of women in conservative, rural Spain—*Bodas de sangre* [*Blood Wedding,* 1933], *Yerma* [1934], and *La casa de Bernarda Alba* [*The House of Bernardo Alba,* 1936]) allegorically, and see in it aspects of the playwright's own sexuality, particularly his defiance, rage, and ultimate frustration.

Another member of the Generation of 27, surrealist film director and author Luis Buñuel, also used homosexual themes in his cinematic and literary work. In "El arco iris y la cataplasma" ("The Rainbow and the Poultice," 1927), a poem he intended to include in his book *El perro andaluz* (*The Andalusian Dog*), Buñuel deliberately provokes the prudish reader. The poem is essentially a series of gratuitous, indecorous questions, including comments that graphically describe homosexual acts. Throughout all of his work, Buñuel shows an intense preoccupation with sex, religion, and the defiance of authority.

Given the extraordinary proliferation of homosexual characters in period pieces chronicling the years of the Spanish Civil War (1936–1939), one might think that homosexual activity was at least partially responsible for the conflict. The works in question are post–Civil War novels, and, as in their nineteenth-century counterpart, *La Regenta,* these characters pop into the text not for their own sake or to allow the authors to explore homosexuality seriously, but to represent depravity and imminent doom.

Nobel Prize–winner Camilo José Cela narrates the beginning of the Spanish Civil War by tracing the impact of the mounting historical events on the lives of several Madrid residents in his 1969 work, *San Camilo, 1936.* The novel includes two important gay characters who never meet each other. The first is Pepito la Zubiela, the so-called "faggot from Cádiz." The other is Matiítas Serrano, who plays a more prominent role. Both are ridiculous, pathetic, simple-minded, puerile, and utterly devoid of political opinions, despite the social turmoil that surrounds them, as if being homosexual precluded a person from participating in any aspect of life other than the sexual.

Cela returns to the gay theme in *Mazurca para dos muertos* (*Mazurca for Two Dead Men* [1983]), a novel that also chronicles the war years although this time within the confines of a small, Nationalist-occupied town in the region of Galicia. In *Mazurca,* the author again intertwines sex, violence, and death—constants throughout his work. In this case, however, the primary gay (or bisexual) character is a woman—la señorita Ramona, a somewhat wealthy eccentric. Ramona is an arrogant spinster who has an almost flippant acquaintance with death. Sexually, she is an impetuous instigator who manipulates the women and men around her into meaningless encounters.

Ana María Matute's novel *Los soldados lloran de noche* (*Soldiers Cry at Night* [1964]) depicts a sordid sexual relationship between two women, Dionisia and Elena. The nature of the connection between Elena and Dionisia is suggested rather than stated overtly, thus giving the impression that it is considered too awful to be mentioned explicitly (though it may be that General Franco's censors compelled the reticence). The relationship, viewed retrospectively through the eyes of Elena's daughter, Marta, takes place in the pre–Civil War years (1933–1934), and the setting is a dusty, dingy hotel run by the two women. In exploring the fragments of her childhood memories in order to recuperate some significance from them, Marta remembers her home as a cold, dark, dirty jail filled with lies and sin. The novelist Esther Tusquets will later employ a similar quest motif in *El mismo mar de todos los veranos* (*The Same Sea as Every Summer* [1978]), though she will invert Matute's practice by valorizing a lesbian relationship as truly authentic. In Matute's depiction, however, lesbianism is unattractive. The portrait of Dionisia is particularly ugly. Not unlike Cela's Ramona, she is a frightening, domineering, and manipulative woman. Everything about her seems dark, savage, and perverse. Matute provides little insight into her feelings or motivations.

Matute's treatment of homosexual attraction is no more flattering in her 1952 novel, *Fiesta al Noroeste* (*Fiesta in the Northwest*). In this work, the Cain and Abel opposition, frequent in her writing, reflects the emotions unleashed during the Spanish Civil War. Most of the novel consists of the confessions of Juan Medinao, the deformed, legitimate son of a wealthy landowner. He comes to represent the aristocracy, capitalism, the Church, and caciquismo—the forces that sustained Francisco Franco during the war. He also, not incidentally, experiences homosexual attraction toward his handsome, illegitimate half-brother, Pablo. As in *Los soldados,* the homoerotic attraction is portrayed as an obsessive need to control its object. Juan eventually rapes Pablo's mother in order to symbolically possess him.

Miguel Delibes also incorporates the homosexual theme into his narration of the Civil War period. The gay character in his semiautobiographical work, *377A, madera de héroe (The Stuff of Heroes* [1987]), is Jairo, an attractive, middle-aged bachelor who walks into the childhood of Gervasio, the would-be hero of the title. There is some mystery surrounding Jairo from the moment he first appears in the novel. He proves to be a man of few words and unknown habits who hangs engravings of flagellated saints and naked boys in his hotel room. Jairo becomes interested in Crucita, Gervasio's adolescent and physically underdeveloped sister, eventually marrying her. The breakup of this marriage due to Jairo's obsession with the girl's androgynous figure and the grotesque manner in which he is murdered by his homosexual lover eventually reveal his perverse and disturbing sexuality to the conservative, Catholic family.

Several other works of the post-war period incorporate homosexuality in one form or another. Carmen Laforet's novel *La insolación (Sunstroke),* published in 1963, focuses on the life of Martin, its narrator-protagonist, during his post-war adolescence. Martin's father, a macho military man obsessed with virility, finds his son sleeping with a neighbor, Carlos. Incorrectly suspecting the two of homosexual behavior, the father beats the boy, inducing him to leave the house and pursue his artistic vocation.

Another woman writer of this period is Ana María Moix, the younger sister of gay novelist Terençi Moix (who predominantly writes in his native Catalan tongue). Moix's first novel, *Julia* (1970), written as an interior monologue, depicts the Catalan bourgeoisie in the post-war period. When first published, the novel suffered some forty-five cuts at the hands of the censor. The title character in this novel embarks on a relationship with Eva, her literature teacher. Though the novel suggests a sexual dimension to the relationship, it never makes the sexual dynamics patently clear, and Julia never becomes fully aware of her sexuality. For her, Eva represents mother, friend, and lover. Significantly, however, Moix indicts traditional values and institutions from a distinctly feminine viewpoint. In one sleepless night, Julia relives the events of the previous years in what appears to be an emotional purging. She was raised in a decadent and repressive environment. One of her two brothers (Rafael) died in adolescence. The other (Ernesto, autobiographically representing Terençi) is a homosexual. At the age of six, Julia was raped by Víctor, a family friend. From this event, she develops a growing aversion to men and a striking need for a strong female figure in her life. Moix unwittingly regenerates the notion that lesbians are not women who love women, but women who hate men. This configuration allows men to remain the central force in female sexuality.

In a later novel, *¿Walter, por qué te fuiste? (Walter, Why Did You Leave?* [1973]), Moix reinstates some of the same characters who appeared in *Julia.* Here, again, she treats the subject of homosexuality in both serious and farcical ways. The plot of the novel—ostensibly a search for the Walter of the title—is allegorically an inquiry into the meaning of life. The title of Teresa Barbero's *El último verano en el espejo (The Last Summer in the Mirror* [1967]) evokes Tusquets's later novel, *El mismo mar de todos los veranos.* The work explores the sexual feelings between Elena and Marta—quite interestingly, the same names given to the mother and daughter in Matute's *Los soldados lloran de noche.*

Francisco Umbral, a Spanish journalist, essayist, and literary critic, addresses homosexuality and feminism in literature in *Tratado de perversiones (Treaty on Perversions* [1977]). He associates both phenomena with decadence. The text is so plagued with internal contradictions that it becomes a boon for feminists and gay activists. Concerning gays, the book is a rather fanciful apologia for homophobia and heterosexism, and provides little insight. His interpretation of feminist criticism is equally misguided.

Antonio D. Olano wrote his book on homosexuality, *Carta abierta a un muchacho "diferente" (Open Letter to a "Different" Young Man* [1974]), at about the same time as Umbral, but the two works diverge greatly. Olano's purpose is to illustrate homosexuality by using concrete examples. The author observes heterogeneity in the gay community and attacks one-dimensional stereotypes about it. Olano's essay is colloquial and conversational, which is why "letter" surfaces as the most appropriate category for his writing. It is likewise appropriate because the tone of the work is far more lyrical than analytic. Presumably he is writing this letter to the (male) homosexuals of Spain whose cases he has studied, but the complacent, bourgeois, heterosexual reader is always present in the text. While looking at the cases of these homosexuals, he keeps one eye on those who disdain them in the name of morality. Olano becomes the voyeur eavesdropping on the intimacy of his supposedly generic "Manolo," the name he uses to protect the privacy of the men whose lives he evokes. By identifying Manolo as every man (or every gay man), then relating his secrets, Olano establishes a delicate balance between revelation and concealment.

Another post-war author, Juan Goytisolo, uses homosexuality as an emblem of bravado. In three of his novels, *Señas de identidad* (*Marks of Identity* [1966]), *Reivindicación del conde don Julián* (*Count Julian* [1970]), and *Juan sin tierra* (*John the Landless* [1975]), he exalts homosexuality for rejecting Hispanic social norms. The sexual and scatological themes in the trilogy are often extreme and grotesque. In the last two books, he metaphorically sodomizes the values of bourgeois, heterosexual, Catholic Spain—the very Spain that, once internalized, prevented Bradomín from acting on his sexual impulses.

Goytisolo renounces the oppressive and repressed heterosexual culture of his homeland to embrace a more sensual, festive alternative culture, which he associates with homosexuality. There is much cruelty in this simultaneously joyous and brutal celebration. He attempts to recuperate the virility (associated with violence) that has been denied to homosexuals. But his recuperated virility is more like coarse contempt; hence, he may reestablish the cultural definition of homosexuality in the very act of subverting it. He is also somewhat misogynistic in directing his attack specifically against women (quite graphically against the female genitalia, and, by extension, against female sexuality). The Manichean construction of sexuality that associates heterosexuality with the good and the spiritual, and homosexuality with evil and the body, is reiterated by Goytisolo, only this time it is conscious and freely chosen. His theatrically ardent opposition turns out to be a parody of heterosexual paranoia. Goytisolo understands society's fear of the homosexual, and turns it against that very society, aggressively and vindictively using it to destroy its repressive underpinnings. Violence here is seen as an act of self-assertion and self-expression, as it is in much of the imagery found in García Lorca's *Poeta en Nueva York*.

Post-Franco Spain (the late 1970s, 1980s, and 1990s) experienced intense liberalizations that allowed a new crop of daring and innovative writers to come to the forefront. As a consequence, homosexuality gained a far more prominent position in the literature of Post-Franco Spain than it had at any other period in Spanish history. Here we find the most sympathetic portrayals of gays to date although it would be naive to assume that homosexuality is now generally accepted as a viable alternative in Spain. In some of these texts, homosexuals are still secondary characters. In most cases, they are also still used as symbols. But rather than symbolizing decadence and depravity, in post-Franco literature homosexuals frequently signify insubordination against the oppressive morality imposed for four decades by the Franco regime.

It is perhaps natural, and certainly noteworthy, that Spain's women writers are in the forefront of making homosexuality more palatable to the common reader. Women have greater cause to rebel against the patriarchal tradition than male writers. The insurrection in these new works is directed against the silence imposed by censorship and a reactionary adherence to Catholic dogma during the earlier Franco years. In the Franco era, there were many things that women were expected to keep silent about and much knowledge that was off-limits to them. Sexuality was definitely a taboo subject, as were political attitudes that strayed from the official one. By tackling the theme of homosexuality, the new women writers can confront both political and sexual issues simultaneously. In many of the texts written by Spain's new women authors, we can also detect the subtle influence of a strand of feminist criticism that views lesbianism as the ultimate expression of the female subject. Perhaps it is because of this that lesbians have fared better in recent literary treatment than have gay males.

One of the most significant of the cadre of post-Franco women writers is Esther Tusquets, known for her trilogy on the themes of female attachments (not always lesbian in the strictest sense of the word) and the dissatisfaction and disintegration of heterosexual relationships. When lesbianism appears in her fiction, it is graphic, sensual, and erotically charged. Despite this sexual explicitness, Tusquets has enjoyed, for the most part, the advantage of not being marginalized as a lesbian author. Her first novel, *El mismo mar de todos los veranos* (*The Same Sea as Every Summer*), was published in 1978. Its middle-aged female narrator-protagonist (known only as E), experiences a midlife crisis that leads her to seek fulfillment outside traditional bounds. Having experienced a lonely childhood and two failed heterosexual relationships, she begins a painful search for authenticity that will include a rejection of the values and traditions of her social class and a search for self-realization and self-expression. At this level, numerous parallels can be drawn between this novel and that of another Catalan author, Juan Goytisolo. His novel, *Señas de identidad*, reflects many of the same themes, only from a male point of view. Central to Tusquets's novel is the love affair with Clara, a young Colombian student. The relationship with Clara is carefully poised against the decadent society that has annihilated the narrator's will and that will, acting through the protagonist's family, eventually destroy the relationship. Nevertheless, authentic homosexual love in Tusquets's work leads to renewal of the self. Those who truly love experience a rebirth, whereas those who cannot love experience a form of death. The relationship with Clara is the most meaningful one that the narrator has had—the one that brings her the closest to self-awareness and self-realization. Both Clara and the protagonist overcome the traditional boundaries of the self through their relationship. Tusquets endows her characters with individuality. There is no prototypical homosexual within her text. Clara is utterly different from the narrator, and lesbianism becomes a dynamic that is defined collaboratively between the two.

Tusquets's second novel, *El amor es un juego solitario* (*Love Is a Solitary Game* [1973]), deals with a conjectural love triangle among three characters—Elia, Clara, and Ricardo. It provides a psychoanalysis of the motives and emotions of the three as they approach their intended threesome. Clara (not the same as in the earlier novel) is a naïve lesbian who gives in to her desires. She eventually agrees to the threesome out of authentic feelings of love for Elia and is ultimately the only one of the three who feels love more strongly than lust. Although it is true that her feelings allow her to be used by the other two, they also provide her with the strength and courage to reject them.

In 1979, Rosa Montero published *Crónica del desamor* (*Chronicle of Disaffection*). Through a staunchly feminist perspective, the novel examines many themes that in the Franco era were strictly taboo: unwed mothers, contraception, abortion, and homosexuality, among them. The protagonist, Ana, has a gay friend named Cecilio who suffers a "tortured" homosexuality. There is a faint echo of *La Regenta* in the similarity of names in the two works. For Ana, Cecilio comes to symbolize a collapse of faith in heterosexual coupling. Here "couple" is plainly a heterosexual term since the homosexual, as usual, is isolated. Both in *Crónica del desamor* and in Montero's later novel, *La función delta* (*The Delta Function* [1981]), homosexuality—male in both cases—represents the ultimate impossibility of heterosexual relationships.

Two additional Spanish novelists who take up the theme of homosexuality are Carmen Riera and Marta Portal. Riera, like other writers who emerged in the post-Franco period, uses homosexuality as one tool among many to attack the repression of the former regime. Her *Palabra de mujer* (*A Woman's Word* [1980]) is a tale of love told through remembrances. The name of the remembered lover is withheld until the very end so that the reader is shocked to suddenly discover that she was a woman. Portal turns to lesbianism in her 1983 novel, *Un espacio erótico* (*An Erotic Space*). The work revolves around Elvira, who has an erotic experience with her female cousin, Elena. This experience, like that of Tusquets's protagonist-narrator in *El mismo mar*, Martín in Laforet's *Insolación*, and Cernuda's poetic voice, has the effect of freeing the protagonist so that she can express herself as a writer.

Despite the liberalization of attitudes toward homosexuality that marks post-Franco Spain, gay men and lesbians are by no means fully accepted, either in real life or in literature. It is important to emphasize that even in the works of recent gay or sympathetic authors, the homosexual is still rejected and marginalized by Spanish society. Complete, satisfactory integration remains an impossibility in both literature and life, but at least gay men and lesbians in these texts are given the option of change and growth. The message seems to be that if redemption is to be found for the homosexual, it will come from within the self, and not from the surrounding community. The homosexual will be saved, not by being demarginalized and assimilated, but by consciously assuming his or her existence as outcast.

—*María Dolores Costa*

BIBLIOGRAPHY

Bellver, Catherine G. "The Language of Eroticism in the Novels of Esther Tusquets." *Anales de la Literatura Española Contemporánea* 9.1–3 (1984): 13–27. ■ Brown, Joan Lipman. "Men by Women in the Contemporary Spanish Novel." *Hispanic Review* 60 (1992): 55–70. ■ ———, ed. *Women Writers of Contemporary Spain: Exiles in the Homeland.* Newark: University of Delaware Press, 1991. ■ Cull, John T. "Androgyny in the Spanish Pastoral Novel." *Hispanic Review* 57 (1989): 317–334. ■ Lee-Bonanno, Lucy. "The Renewal of the Quest in Esther Tusquets's *El mismo mar de todos los veranos.*" *Feminine Concerns in Contemporary Spanish Fiction by Women.* Roberto C. Manteiga, Carolyn Galerstein, and Kathleen McNerney, eds. Potomoc, Md.: Scripta Humanistica, 1988. 134–151. ■ Miller, Beth. *Women in Hispanic Literature: Icons and Fallen Idols.* Berkeley: University of California Press, 1983. ■ Ordóñez, Elizabeth. *Voices of Their Own: Contemporary Spanish Narrative by Women.* Lewisburg: Bucknell University Press, 1991. ■ Pérez, Janet. *Contemporary Women Writers of Spain.* Boston: Twayne Publishers, 1988. ■ Smith, Paul Julian. *The Body Hispanic: Gender and Sexuality in Spanish and Spanish American Narrative.* Oxford: Clarendon Press, 1992. ■ Ugarte, Michael. "Luis Cernuda and the Poetics of Exile." *Monographic Review* 2 (1986): 84–100.

Spender, Sir Stephen
(b. 1909)

Born February 28, 1909, in London, Stephen Spender has devoted his career of over sixty years to writing poems, essays, novels, and dramas, as well as to translating and teaching. In recognition of his contribution to literature, he was knighted in 1983, and he has received numerous awards for his writing. Despite the occasional frank discussion of his early homosexual attractions and experiences, his writings are much more concerned with liberal political causes and aesthetic issues such as the relationship between literature and society than with homosexuality.

Orphaned in his teens, Spender recounts in his memoir *World within World* (1951) that he was taught from childhood to "be ashamed of his body." In a passage that helps explain the title, Spender characterizes his father as a "Puritan decadent" who taught him that the human body "is a nameless horror of nameless desires which isolate him within a world of his own." The liberation from this attitude figures prominently in Spender's autobiographical novel *The Temple,* written in 1929 but not published until 1988.

The reworked novel traces many of the lines drawn in *World within World*. Set in 1929 near the end of the Weimar Republic, it celebrates the innocence and hedonism of a group of young men in Germany. Conflicted by puritanical images of sin and guilt, Paul Schoner nonetheless discovers that he can experience his physical body as a "source of joy" and can see it as a "temple." Little of this newfound freedom, however, characterizes Paul's first homosexual encounter: He engages in mutual masturbation with Ernst, whom he finds physically repulsive, reaches orgasm quickly, then feels obligated to see Ernst achieve an "arid climax." Immediately afterward, Paul goes swimming, as if to wash away any traces of this experience. Just as abruptly, he meets a woman named Irmi, with whom he has exhilarating sex on the beach. Although noted for its open discussion of sexuality, the novel may disappoint readers who are searching for evidence of Spender's orientation: Such scenes of sexual awakening in the novel are few, and they are fully subordinated to the central theme of creative and intellectual freedom in Germany before the advent of Nazism.

As a student at University College, Oxford, in 1928, Spender came under the influence of W. H. AUDEN, whom he regarded with fear and trembling. Determined to be a poet, he submitted drafts of his poems for criticism and received instruction on the few contemporary poets Auden admired. More important, however, Auden taught him that "guilt and inhibition stood between oneself and the satisfaction of one's needs." Also in 1928, he began a friendship with CHRISTOPHER ISHERWOOD, whose criticism and support he found invaluable. Their relationship was initially that of mentor and disciple, but it eventually evolved into mutual friendship and respect.

Writing in his journal for 1939, as Europe prepared for war, Spender reviewed the heady days of 1929 and defined his ideal as *Freundschaft,* the "friendship" of two young men who experienced life together and "were happy in each other's company." This friendship was not necessarily exclusively homosexual; indeed, many young Germans Spender knew were bisexual. Having left Oxford in 1931 without completing his degree, he traveled extensively and lived for a time in Barcelona with Hellmut, the apparent subject of a notably erotic poem entitled "Helmut." (Originally published in the 1934 edition of *Poems* as "Alas when he laughs it is not he," the poem was not included in *Collected Poems 1928–1953* though it is reprinted in *Collected Poems 1928–1985*.)

In September 1933, Spender met Tony Hyndman ("Jimmy Younger" of *World*), with whom he lived for the next three years. Their relationship was stormy and ultimately unsatisfying for Spender, who felt an emotional and intellectual imbalance, as suggested by his giving the name "Younger" to his friend, despite his claim that characters in this autobiography have "their real names and attributes." Suddenly in 1936, he announced their breakup and his plans to marry Inez Pearn, to whom he was engaged for only three weeks. (Many details of Spender's relationship with Hyndman, as recounted in the autobiography, were adapted by DAVID LEAVITT in his novel *While England Sleeps* [1993]. Charging unlawful use, Spender sued Leavitt and his publisher, Viking Press, but in February 1994, the case was resolved out of court. The settlement specifies that the "pornographic" material be deleted from subsequent editions of the novel, much to the dismay of Leavitt, who sees latent homophobia in the charges, an allegation Spender denies.)

In the late 1930s, Spender directed his energies to leftist political causes, joining the Communist Party in 1937, serving as a journalist in the Spanish Civil War, and writing left-wing essays, including *Forward from Liberalism* (1937) and *The New Realism* (1939). Announcing his decision to become a Communist, Spender wrote that "the most important political aim of our time should be the United–Front," aligning the communist movements in the Soviet Union, Spain, and France. The same image—a "united front"—informs the description in *Journals 1939-1983* of the *Freundschaft* ideal, in which two men "face the world together."

Spender divorced in 1939, and two years later married Natasha Litvin, a concert pianist; two children, Matthew and Lizzie, were born in 1945 and 1951. Some critics have concluded that he repudiated his homosexuality when he rejected Tony Hyndman in 1936 and opted for a life as husband and father; others, however, see him as a complex man who resists easy labeling. Two of Spender's poems selected for inclusion in the *Penguin Book of Homosexual Verse*—"How strangely this sun reminds me of my love!" and "To T.A.R.H. [Tony Hyndman]"—were both printed in *Collected Poems 1928–1953*, but

removed from the latest and presumably final edition of *Collected Poems 1928–1985*. It hardly needs to be said that conditions in the 1930s—whether in Berlin, Barcelona, or London—were dangerous for homosexuals. That Spender writes as openly as he does about his relationship with his "German friend" Hellmut, or about his "agonized" concern for Tony's well-being during the Spanish Civil War, whether that concern was motivated by a sense of guilt or responsibility, demonstrates courage that few writers of Spender's generation and reputation can claim.

—*G. Patton Wright*

BIBLIOGRAPHY

Kulkarni, H. B. *Stephen Spender: Works and Criticism: An Annotated Bibliography.* New York: Garland, 1976. ■ Leavitt, David. "Did I Plagiarize His Life?" *New York Times Magazine* (April 3, 1994): 36–37. ■ Spender, Stephen. "My Life Is Mine; It Is Not David Leavitt's." *New York Times Book Review* (Sept. 4, 1994): 10–12.

Spicer, Jack
(1925–1965)

On January 30, 1925, Jack Spicer was born John Lester Spicer in Hollywood, California, where his parents managed a small hotel. Migrating north in 1945, he arrived on the campus of the University of California, Berkeley, a gay if virginal male, a poet for life. He formed enduring connections with two other students, the poets Robin Blaser and ROBERT DUNCAN, and studied Old Norse, Anglo-Saxon, and German to prepare for a career in linguistics. This putative career was blighted by Spicer's refusal to sign the "Loyalty Oath," a provision of the Sloan-Levering Act that required all California state employees (including graduate teaching assistants at Berkeley) to swear loyalty to the United States. He left the university and embarked on a number of low-paying, short-lived jobs in Minnesota, New York, and Boston. In 1957, he returned to San Francisco and began his mature career as a poet with the "dictated" poems of *After Lorca* (1957) and the eleven books that followed. Spicer's controversial theories of dictation metaphorically reduce the poet to a "radio," picking up signals from the "invisible world," and indeed he sometimes joked that his poetry was really written by "Martians." The personality of the poet, he argued, should be kept out of the poem as much as possible. Such an argument ran directly counter to prevailing American poetic practice, then (as now) largely a

poetry of voice. "If you want to write opinions, write a letter to the editor, don't write a poem," he insisted.

The lyric beauty, intellectual power, and formal invention of Spicer's poetry attracted a core of disciples who met in the North Beach bars and the San Francisco parks he favored. The open homosexuality of his core group, the "Spicer Circle," resulted in the marginalization of some of the most moving love poetry produced in this century. Spicer's "Several Years' Love," for example, commemorates his tumultuous love affairs of the period with a nod toward Shakespeare's Sonnet 144: "Two loves I had. One rang a bell / Connected on both sides with hell / The other'd written me a letter / In which he said I've written better / They pushed their cocks in many places / And I'm not certain of their faces / Or which I kissed or which I didn't / Or which of both of them I hadn't" (*The Heads of the Town Up to the Aether*, 1960–1961).

Although writing and living in the middle of the Beat movement, Spicer and Duncan stood oddly set apart from it, maintaining an approach to poetry and art that wedded aesthetics to intellect. Spicer's relations with his gay contemporaries ALLEN GINSBERG and FRANK O'HARA remained antagonistic: Ginsberg was too "populist"; O'Hara a superficial versifier. Indeed, Spicer quarreled with almost everyone he knew, and as he reached his thirties, his incipient alcoholism became widely known and feared. Sober he could be the most gracious and loving of men, but he was an unpleasant drunk. Still, his "derangement of the senses" provided a fertile field for the outside forces that, he claimed, wrote his poetry for him.

After forty years of allegiance to California, Spicer decided to leave San Francisco and emigrate to Vancouver, British Columbia, in the summer of 1965. But before he could leave, he collapsed into a prehepatic coma in his building elevator and died several weeks later in the poverty ward of San Francisco General Hospital on August 17. During his lifetime, his books were reissued in small editions by a variety of local presses; a natural anarchist, Spicer viewed copyright askance. All of his work has since been reissued or newly published to meet the rising interest in this brilliantly original gay poet.

—*Kevin Killian*

BIBLIOGRAPHY

Davidson, Michael. *The San Francisco Renaissance: Poetics and Community at Mid-Century.* Cambridge: Cambridge University Press, 1989. ■ Dorbin, Sanford. "A Checklist of the Published Writings of Jack Spicer." *California Librarian* (Sacramento) (October 1970), 251–261. ■ Foster, Edward Halsey. *Jack Spicer.* Boise, Idaho: Boise State University Western Writers Series, 1991.

SPORTS LITERATURE

Sports Literature: Gay Male

The male athlete is an important gay icon. The literary significance of the athlete and sports changes, however, with the shifting history of sexual culture. Moreover, the cultural significance of the athlete depends not only on the historical construction of gender and sexuality, but also of sports itself.

In Ancient Greece, male homosexuality, especially pederasty, was celebrated as the highest form of love, as PLATO writes in the *Symposium*. This valorization of pederasty, of course, reflects the particular form of patriarchy that was at work in Greek culture of the time. The connection between athletics and pederastic sexuality was facilitated by the importance of the gymnasium in Greek social and cultural life; it was a gathering place both for young men (ephebes) who exercised naked and older men, such as the famed Socrates, who while admiring the young athletes would hold forth on the politics and philosophy of the time. Greek men were devoted to the *kouros* (beautiful young men) who distinguished themselves in athletics. The great poet from Thebes, Pindar (518–438 B.C.), wrote many odes celebrating the beauty and accomplishments of athletes, the most famous being the *Olympian Odes.* These poems revered the paradigm of young Greek manhood, *kalokagathia,* meaning the mixture of physical beauty (*kalon*) and valor (*to agathon*). Pindar's odes show that for the Greeks homosexual attractiveness and athleticism were one and the same. The great athletic competitions—the Olympian, Pythian, Nemean, and Isthmian Games—were religious festivals in which naked young men competed for immortality, a feat accomplished by becoming famous in athletic victory. For the Greeks, immortality depended on being remembered. Pindar's veneration of athletes, therefore, also had a religious dimension.

A notable and long-standing literary heritage surrounds swimming and bathing. This has been amply documented by Charles Sprawson in *Haunts of the Black Masseur: The Swimmer as Hero* (1992). He offers numerous literary references to the baths and the myriad pleasures of swimming and being naked with other men through the ages. The homosexual baths of the twentieth century seem rather ordinary compared to Classical Roman pleasures, where, for example, Tiberius is reported to have swum among rose petals while specially trained naked boys would swim up between his legs and nibble. But bathing scenes are familiar in much homoerotic literature, ranging from the *Idylls* of THEOCRITUS to WHITMAN's "Song of Myself" to E. M. FORSTER's *A Room with a View* (1905).

From the late nineteenth century on, the literary connection between homosexuality and sports has reflected the social discourses that have shaped both historically. Several trends can be noted. In fiction, athleticism has been portrayed as a personal proclivity that indicates the masculine "normality" of homosexual characters. In other works, homosexuality is symbolic of a youthful, ambiguous sexual naivete that is eventually transcended. And in others, athleticism is sexually fetishized as indicative of a particularly "hot" male body, promising the eroticism of an especially robust sexual scene. The nonfiction of gay male sports literature includes several biographies and autobiographies of noted homosexual athletes. There is also a nascent scholarly literature that crosses the bridge between gay studies and sports studies, documenting the social phenomenon of homosexuality in contemporary sports culture.

GORE VIDAL, in *The City and the Pillar* (1948), describes the experience of a young professional tennis player, Jim Willard, coming to accept himself as homosexual. Vidal's choice of tennis was probably inspired by the homosexuality of the great tennis star Bill Tilden. Jim's athleticism and that of the men to whom he is attracted is an emblem of normal masculinity, which Vidal contrasts with the perverted effeminacy characteristic of the homosexual stereotype. This equation of athleticism, masculinity, and normality is attributable to the cultural significance of twentieth-century North American sports. The growing importance of athleticism in North American society was the product of a deliberate attempt to assert a masculine influence on the lives of young men. As America changed from being a rural agrarian to an urban industrial society, fathers were increasingly absent. It was thought that boys' masculine development was endangered by too much feminine influence, at home with the women and in school where the majority of teachers were women. Organizations, such as the YMCA, promoted sports as part of the proper education of young males. Athleticism thus became associated in the American consciousness with normal masculinity. Casting his homosexual protagonist as an athlete, Vidal attempts to address homophobia by appealing to the cultural equation of athletics, masculinity, and normality.

Vidal's embrace of the athlete as the sign of the acceptability of homosexuality is at odds with his homosexual literary predecessor, OSCAR WILDE. Explaining the unacceptablity of athletics for young homosexual men, Wilde is reported to have said "football is all very well as a game for rough girls; but it is hardly suitable for delicate boys." Reflecting the dandyism of his time, Wilde is here giving tongue-in-cheek expression to the positive nature of effeminacy among men. Indeed, it is to that historical image of homosexual men as effeminate that Vidal is responding in his invocation of athleticism in *The City and the Pillar.*

PATRICIA NELL WARREN's *The Front Runner* (1974) is the tragic homosexual love story of a coach and his athlete striving for normal life in a homophobic world. Like *The City and the Pillar,* this novel attempts to cast homosexuality as normal by appealing to the North American cultural significance of athletics as a sign of normality—a significance that is currently being eroded by the many scandals associated with the professional sports entertainment industry. Warren's appeal is not so much to the masculinity of athleticism as it is to its relevance as a healthy pursuit. The novel was well attuned to the emerging gay liberation movement of the 1970s, which combatted the medicalization of homosexuality as a psychopathology, trumpeting it as a normal, healthy sexual alternative. The book was so successful at appealing to such gay sensibilities that it spawned a large international organization of gay running clubs called "The Front Runners," which has member clubs in most large North American cities.

Gay coming-of-age fiction also exploits the symbolism of athletics. In *The Boys on the Rock* (1984) by John Fox, for instance, the young protagonist, a swimmer named Billy, is attracted to twins, who are also swimmers. Athleticism here has an ephebophilic appeal. The young male athlete is a boy poised on the brink of manhood, having much of the physical prowess and strength of an older man, but not yet mature. Here is an appeal that young athletes often embody, a mixture of power and naivete which inevitably must pass. Although central to any coming-of-age story, because it brings such liberation, loss of innocence is especially delightful for gay adolescents. Billy's desire for the athletic twins is a desire for this adolescent transformation.

Brad Walton's satirical baroque opera, *The Loves of Wayne Gretsky,* first performed in Toronto in 1990 (the libretto of the first act was published in *The Village Voice,* March 9, 1993), is the fictional account of the love affair between the great hockey stars Wayne Gretsky and Mario Lemieux, and explores the struggle between Nature and Nurture in homosexual desire. From a formal perspective, it is a meticulous neo-baroque work, orchestrated for baroque ensemble, with traditional baroque vocalizations and dramatic structure. But its marriage of baroque form with late twentieth-century concerns about the construction of homosexuality and its evocation of popular sports figures make it a gay post-modern work.

The homoerotic desirability of athletes and the masculine world of sports is important to the gay literary heritage. The "hot jock" has become a staple of gay erotic literature. Because the composition of the objects of homoerotic desire, such as the "hot jock," gives expression to trends in the social construction of homosexuality itself, these are indicative of the nature of homosexuality in a particular historical setting. Sports and the athletic body appeal to several influential aspects of late twentieth-century "mainstream" gay male culture: (1) a preoccupation with masculinity and the gay eroticization of it; (2) the broader cultural fetishization of youth, the athlete being typically youthful; and (3) the body understood as a plastic, malleable object that can be made to conform to erotic ideals—athletic training is the means by which bodies are made into hyperreal objects of homoerotic desire. Gay literature, therefore, that invokes athletic bodies and settings also invokes such gay sensibilities surrounding masculinity and the body.

A plethora of gay pornographic magazines feature pictures and stories of athletes, sports settings, and athletic paraphernalia. This includes magazines with titles such as *Jock, Drummer,* and *Inches.* There are also collections of "one-handed" short stories that will often feature the "hot jock"—with titles such as *Flesh, Guys,* and *First Hand.* (Boyd McDonald was very influential in the development of this genre). Often the characters in the stories are athletes: football players, bodybuilders, and swimmers being among the most popular. Favorite settings are locker rooms, showers, gymnasia, sports camps, and wilderness. The most important athletic equipment to be featured is the jock strap, often portrayed as the quintessential homoerotic garment. The importance of the jock strap stems from the fact that it enshrines the twin centers of homoerotic desire, the phallus as the epitome of masculinity and the anus as the cherished place in which masculinity meets its undoing.

Certainly an important part of the heritage is the gay liberation magazine. Attempting to sell sometimes dry political messages to an erotically oriented market, gay journals frequently use athletic imagery. And if the classified advertisements in gay liberation journals can be read as literature, then many literary evocations of athleticism are to be found there, with references to athletic body types: swimmer's body, bodybuilder, runner's build, and so on. Men seek "workout partners" and sometimes wrestling bouts.

Appealing in a more coy, but nevertheless gay, fashion to the homoerotic desirability of athletes are body-building magazines such as *Men's Fitness* and workout "textbooks" such as *Working Out* (1983) by Charles Hix. Here, barely submerged homoerotic subtexts permeate advice on how to transform one's body into the paradigmatic gay athletic body. In these publications, fairly scanty technical texts are amply supplemented with photographs of athletic men exercising or just sitting around looking beautiful. For instance, *Working Out* has a chapter entitled "The locker room: Alone/together," with a picture of men lounging in a locker room, others removing their shirts, while a naked man towels himself dry. The men's muscle and fitness literature has replaced an earlier homoerotic genre: books and magazines about dance, such as *After Dark Magazine,* which in turn was the successor to the earlier twentieth-century physical culture magazines. This form allows the homoerotic content of a publication to be masked by the ostensible "legitimacy" of exercise, art, or culture. In such publications, the function of the text is to mask the homoerotic import of the soft-core visual images.

The world of professional sports has been an extremely hostile environment for gay men. Although this hostility has prevented many gay men from pursuing athletic careers, those who have done so have felt it important to keep their sexuality a secret. A few professional athletes, however, have come out and written about their homosexuality. David Kopay is probably the most famous case in point. He was a National Football League player who publicly revealed his homosexuality and subsequently never worked in professional football again. His book, *The David Kopay Story,* was written with Perry Deane Young (1977, 1988). Olympic medalist and world-champion diver Greg Louganis revealed his homosexuality and affliction with HIV/AIDS in the best-seller *Breaking the Surface* (1995). A bodybuilder and former Mr. Universe, Bob Paris and his spouse, Rod Jackson, have published the story of their coming out and attempts at becoming officially married: *Straight from the Heart: A Love Story* (1994). The major league baseball umpire Dave Pallone chronicles his difficulties as a gay man in professional baseball in *Behind the Mask: My Double Life in Baseball* (1990). Jim Perrin's biography of the writer and mountaineer John Menlove Edwards, *Menlove: The Life of John Menlove Edwards* (1985), is also well worth reading. And the life of the great tennis star, Bill Tilden, twice jailed for his sexual involvement with adolescent boys, and whose desperation over his life ended in suicide, is recounted in *Big Bill Tilden: The Triumphs and the Tragedy* (1975) by *Sports Illustrated* journalist Frank Deford.

In the wake of gay liberation, with the flourishing of scholarly work on many facets of homosexuality, it is remarkable that so little has been written about the phenomenon of homosexuality in sports culture in general. Brian Pronger's *The Arena of Masculinity: Sports, Homosexuality and the Meaning of Sex* (1990) is the only work so far to examine the interplay of gay and sports cultures. The Gay Games, a lesbian and gay athletic and cultural festival that originated in 1982 in San Francisco and has been held quadrennially since has been documented by Roy Coe in *A Sense of Pride: The Story of Gay Games II* (1986). Lesbian and gay newspapers, both local and national, regularly report lesbian and gay community sports events and organizations.

—Brian Pronger

BIBLIOGRAPHY

Coe, Roy. *A Sense of Pride: The Story of Gay Games II.* San Francisco: Pride Publications, 1986. ■ Deford, Frank. *Big Bill Tilden: The Triumphs and the Tragedy.* New York: Simon & Schuster, 1975. ■ Jackson-Paris, Rod and Bob. *Straight from the Heart: A Love Story.* New York: Warner, 1994. ■ Kopay, Dave, and Perry Deane Young. *The David Kopay Story.* New York: Primus, 1988. ■ Louganis, Greg, with Eric Marcus. *Breaking the Surface.* New York: Random House, 1995. ■ Pallone, Dave. *Behind the Mask: My Double Life in Baseball.* New York: Viking, 1990. ■ Perrin, Jim. *Menlove: The Life of John Menlove Edwards.* London: Gollancz, 1985. ■ Pronger, Brian. *The Arena of Masculinity: Sports, Homosexuality and the Meaning of Sex.* New York: St. Martin's, 1990. ■ ———. "Gay Jocks: A Phenomenology of Gay Men in Athletics." *Men, Masculinity and the Gender Order: Critical Feminist Perspectives.* Michael Messner and Don Sabo, eds. Champaign, Ill.: Human Kinetics, 1990. ■ Sprawson, Charles. *Haunts of the Black Masseur: The Swimmer as Hero.* London: Vintage, 1992.

Sports Literature: Lesbian

Given the high representation of lesbians in women's sports and the fact that athletes and gym teachers are virtual lesbian icons, it is remarkable that sports and sportswomen have played so minor a role in lesbian literature. Perhaps the paucity of attention to athletes and sports in lesbian literature is a reflection of the larger society's ambivalence toward female athleticism. Whereas male athleticism symbolizes mainstream culture's construction of masculinity, the female counterpart does not signify society's conception of femininity. Gay male authors often portray their gay male characters as athletes in order to demonstrate the normality of homosexuality, but such an option is not available to lesbian writers, for in the popular imagination, female athleticism is often regarded as a sign of confused gender identity. If the gay male athlete defies the stereotype of male homosexuals as effeminate, the lesbian athlete tends to confirm the stereotype of the mannish lesbian.

When lesbian athletes and coaches appear in literature, they are frequently depicted as having stereotypically "masculine" athletic interests and values. For example, they tend to be fiercely competitive; for them, winning is the only thing. Such portrayals reflect the period when equal opportunity was the top priority for women's sports advocates. However, more radical feminist challenges to mainstream sports have influenced some recent novels. These works present multidimensional lesbian characters who compete for reasons of personal fulfillment rather than to beat their opponents. Feminist influence is also evident in the celebration of the physical strength and muscularity of lesbian athletes and in the challenges to heterosexist definitions of female sexual attractiveness. At the same time, however, a new stereotype emerges in some recent literature, where the lesbian athlete is portrayed as totally apolitical, in contrast to her feminist (and nonathletic) partner. More thoughtful approaches explore the tensions and contradictions experienced by various lesbian characters in relation to women's sports. Whatever their perspective, most contemporary novelists acknowledge that the mere fact of being lesbian in sports is itself a political issue.

The explicit association of sports with lesbians, although not a strongly developed theme in fiction, has a long history. RADCLYFFE HALL's influential novel *The Well of Loneliness* (1928), for example, emphasizes the athleticism of its protagonist. As a young girl, Stephen Gordon is portrayed as strong and muscular, more adept at playing cricket and climbing trees than some of her male peers. She is contemptuous of girls of her age who have been raised to be fragile and delicate, and she dislikes traditional girls' play activities. At a young age, Stephen accompanies her father on horseback on the foxhunt, riding astride when "proper" girls and women were expected to ride sidesaddle. This early portrayal of a lesbian character with so-called masculine athletic interests and talents helped create the figure of the mythic mannish lesbian and foreshadowed many later fictional lesbian characters.

Another genre of fiction in the early decades of the century—the "schoolgirl stories" of novelists such as Elsie Oxenham and Angela Brazil—makes a connection between sports and intimate female friendships. The team sports and country dancing of the English private girls' school are central to many of these novels. In the United States, to a lesser extent, women's college athletics inspired some juvenile fiction, such as the 1899 novels *Vassar Stories* by Grace Gallaher and *Vassar Studies* by Julia Schwartze. At the turn of the century, these all-female school and college contexts commonly gave rise to intense and intimate female relationships.

Such relationships are at the heart of *Miss Pym Disposes,* a 1946 novel by Josephine Tey, a British author of psychological mysteries. The main character is Miss Lucy Pym, and the setting is 1940s England, at the Leys Physical Training College, a women-only institution dedicated to training physical education teachers. Only two of Tey's numerous female characters express romantic interest in men, and the notion of "crushes" or "raves" among the young women (or between the young women and their older instructors) is virtually taken for granted. In contrast, by the 1940s, many authors of British "schoolgirl stories" had succumbed to public pressure to downplay intimate female friendships and to introduce heterosexual romances.

In *Miss Pym Disposes,* Teresa, a Brazilian student and an "outsider" to the British boarding school scene, is the only character who is openly critical of "raves." Commenting on the relationship between Pamela Nash (nicknamed Beau) and Mary Innes, Teresa claims that this kind of friendship is not quite normal: "nice, of course . . . quite irreproachable. But normal, no. That David and Jonathan relationship. It is a very happy one, no doubt, but it . . . excludes so much." However, Beau and Mary are openly affectionate and make no attempt to hide their relationship. In her somewhat gushing style, Tey develops a picture of attractive young female physical education students in the prime of youth, glowing with health and energy. There is no attempt to downplay the young women's joyous physicality, open affection, and playful spirits. Although Teresa dismisses their interaction as childish, Miss Pym finds the entire scene exciting and engaging. However, the novel ends on a tragic note, with a murder and the subsequent breakup of the relationship between Beau and Mary. This kind of melodramatic device for dissolving the lesbian relationship is familiar in novels of the era.

By the 1970s, however, the influence of the women's movements on feminist and lesbian fiction is apparent. Marge Piercy's *The High Cost of Living* (1978) provides an interesting commentary on sexual politics in 1970s urban North America. The main character is Leslie, a twenty-three-year-old lesbian living in a working-class Detroit neighborhood. Karate, for Leslie, is a means of bodily empowerment, a physical activity that she does for herself. She is proud of her muscles, because "every muscle represents years of effort." Practicing karate reassures her that her body is strong and graceful—good "the way a good race horse was good." After she gains her black belt, she decides to volunteer to teach a self-defense course for a women's collective. At the end of the first class, deeply moved by the needs of these women, Leslie makes a symbolic gesture of reconciling her two worlds, the lesbian feminist community and the mainstream. Instead of the traditional opening ritual of bowing, she suggests that the women form a circle and hold hands.

RITA MAE BROWN's *Sudden Death* (1983) is set in the world of professional tennis, a world in which lesbians have been both spectacularly successful and a potential embarrassment to the public-relations conscious management. The fact that Brown wrote the novel after the breakup of her widely publicized affair with tennis legend Martina Navratilova encouraged readers and critics to approach the novel as a *roman a clef*. Carmen, a twenty-four-year-old professional tennis player from Argentina, is in a lesbian relationship with Harriet, a thirty-six-year-old professor of religion. Carmen is portrayed as a totally self-absorbed and overindulged "love-junkie," whereas Harriet is virtually flawless: patient, witty, sexy, intelligent, loyal. One critic described the book as prose "worthy of the National Enquirer." However, despite Brown's nasty characterization of most female professional tennis players, both straight and gay, she does confront the issue of homophobia on the tennis circuit with no holds barred. Especially noteworthy in this regard are the debates between women's tennis officials and potential sponsors over various players' marketability. Clearly, a player's talent is less significant than her heterosexual attractiveness. Soon after the scandal about Carmen's lesbian relationship, the Women's Tennis Guild initiates a rigid dress code. This issue of "compulsory heterosexuality" as enforced in and through women's sport is the central thesis of Helen Lenskyj's *Out of Bounds: Women, Sport and Sexuality* (1986), which analyzes trends in North American women's sports throughout the twentieth century.

The influence of feminism is evident in Jenifer Levin's 1982 novel *Water Dancer,* which poses a challenge to the mainstream "heroic quest" genre of sports fiction. The main lesbian character is Dorey, a young marathon swimmer who is determined to swim the dangerous waters of San Antonio Straits. Rather than viewing herself as a "giant" who dominates the water and her opponents, Dorey has reached the point of surrendering to the water and now sees herself as a "water dancer." During the course of the novel, Dorey has sexual encounters with her coach, Sarge, and also with his wife, Ilana, who has long played the role of nurturer to the young male swimmers who train with Sarge. Ilana also seems to see herself primarily as a nurturer to Dorey, but the novel leaves most details of their emotional and sexual ties unexplored, and in the end, it is unclear which relationship Dorey is willing to sacrifice—Ilana's or Sarge's.

The characters in this novel, male and female, lesbian and straight, are multidimensional, and Levin's thoughtful portrayals of a wide spectrum of friendships and relationships are rare in sports fiction. However, apart from Dorey's symbiotic relationship to the water, it is difficult to see how her obsession with marathon swimming and her brutal self-discipline differ significantly from Sarge's or from that of any of her male counterparts.

In Levin's second lesbian sports novel, *The Sea of Light* (1993), there are three major lesbian characters: Bren, a university swimming coach, whose partner, Kay, is an English professor; Babe, a former competitive swimmer who is recovering from an airplane crash; and Ellie, the team captain. The literary device of multiple narrators is used, thus facilitating an intimacy between the reader and several characters. Bren is firmly closeted, and puts considerable energy into maintaining a professional distance between herself and her athletes, especially the lesbian swimmers. She is totally committed to competitive swimming and refuses to deal with Kay's critique of competitive sports. Bren is clearly an advocate of the "no pain no gain" school of coaching. In a stereotypical portrayal of campus politics, it is Kay, the nonathlete, who is interested in women's studies and critical of competitive sports, whereas all the athletes are too immersed in sporting competition to concern themselves with political issues.

Both Babe and Ellie, young women in their early twenties, are struggling with their sexual identities but soon become lovers. Unlike many sports novels with lesbian characters, these women are not portrayed as physically perfect. Having survived a plane crash, as well as surgery for sports-related injuries, Babe's body is a mass of scars. When Ellie initiates their first sexual encounter, she begins by caressing the scars on Babe's back. Ellie finds Babe's strength erotic in itself: "a big, smooth, firm, fleshy strength that I love, that I want, have loved and have wanted all my life."

Judith Alguire's 1988 novel, *All Out,* is a lesbian romance, with women's marathon running as a central focus. The main characters are Kay, a successful distance runner, and Tab, her roommate, best friend, and occasional lover, who is a university teacher and political lesbian. Like many of the primary characters in lesbian sports fiction, Kay is portrayed as an apolitical lesbian in single-minded pursuit of sporting victory, whereas her nonathlete partner, Tab, is the voice of a lesbian-feminist analysis of society in general and sports in particular. "What do sports really do to advance women?" she asks. "They benefit only the elite, those few women at the top, particularly those who fit the male notion of what a female athlete should look like." And she concludes, "Sport fosters competition rather than cooperation. Cooperation is the key to advancement."

Conflict between Kay and Tab is both political and personal—their housekeeping standards are worlds apart, as are their stances on lesbian visibility. For example, Tab is outraged when the coach asks Kay to make sure that one of her more outspoken lesbian teammates is dressed "appropriately" for a reception (that is, not in her usual butch attire). By the end of the novel, however, Kay is prepared to take a more radical stance, as indicated by her decision to wear a button stating "Mother Nature is a Lesbian" when she receives her medal for winning the women's marathon. By the end, too, Kay and Tab agree to a monogamous relationship.

Joyce Bright's novel, *Sunday's Child* (1988), also has marathon running as its sports focus. Like Kay in *All Out,* Kate, the main character, has her sights set on the Olympics. Initially, Kate is in a heterosexual relationship. Her running partner and closest friend, Angie, is lesbian. Predictably, the two become lovers. A compelling subplot is the mystery of the serial rapist whose assaults are deeply disturbing to both women—Angie as a burnt-out rape crisis counselor and Kate as a survivor of child sexual abuse. The novel has a clear feminist message in its treatment of sexual violence, women's friendships, and female sexualities. Unlike many other novels reviewed here, it does not set up the lesbian "jock" as apathetic to political or feminist issues.

Novelist R. R. Knudson also deserves to be mentioned in this overview. None of her characters is explicitly lesbian, but her work has an important place in women's sports literature. Her main character in her juvenile fiction, dating from 1972 to 1984, is Zan, a gifted all-round high school athlete. Zan's (unofficial) coach and best friend (but not boyfriend) is a completely unathletic boy called Arthur Rinehart. Zan is single-minded in her sporting endeavors and scathing in her assessment of girls who have no interest in the rough and tumble of sports. The characterization in *Zanbanger* (1977) of the overweight female coach as a "giant, red-faced dimwit" borders on cruel. Knudson juxtaposes the philosophy of the female physical education teacher, who is more intent on promoting "ladylike" play than athletic skills, with Zan's and Rinehart's emphasis on "serious" training, aggressive play, and winning at all costs.

Knudson has been criticized for her books' liberal agenda. The overall message is that women must act like men, play men's sports, and gain male approval in order to be taken seriously. The male world of sports thus remains unchanged, and only a few exceptional girls and women can enter it. However, had she been writing in a later era, Knudson may have had more safety and freedom both to develop openly lesbian characters and to challenge the dominant sports ethos.

Lady Lobo (1993), by Kristen Garrett, represents a new wave of lesbian sports fiction, which might be termed contemporary lesbian "pulp," where the main character spends all of her time either on the basketball court or in bed. Most of the book's action is conveyed through "in-your-face" vernacular, making it fast-paced but often superficial. However, the novel presents a realistic view of the brutal world of American college basketball. For example, the players' love-hate relationship with the coach (a straight woman) speaks for itself. Using the senior players as informants and disciplinarians, the coach polices every aspect of the young women's lives: what they eat and drink, whom they date, whether they meet the curfew. In women's competitive sports, as this novel portrays, the goal is to win, no matter what the cost.

Casey, the main lesbian character, is a young woman recruited from high school for a college team. Her two loves are basketball and sex, and her high profile on the college team produces endless opportunities for the latter. Casual sex is Casey's style; serious relationships might interfere with her basketball career. In both basketball and sex, Casey is used to being in control, and her relationship with Sharika, an older black women who is a former professional tennis player, challenges her on many levels.

In light of the central place of softball in the North American lesbian communities, it has a surprisingly low profile in lesbian sports fiction. Yvonne Zipter's entertaining history of lesbian softball, *Diamonds are a Dyke's Best Friend* (1988), should inspire future authors to use softball in sports fiction. As Zipter points out, softball has for decades served as an unofficial but widely recognized meeting place for lesbians, both players and spectators. It also provides an appropriate context for feminist challenges to highly competitive sport, as leagues experiment with more woman-friendly rules and organizing structures.

Women's sports has provided a home for many lesbians—not always a totally safe place, but an appropriate context for the celebration of women's strength, physicality, and friendships. It remains largely untapped as a topic or setting in lesbian literature. But recent novels and the publication of Susan Fox Rogers's anthology *Sportsdykes: Stories from on and off the Field* (1994), which features both fiction and nonfiction, are signs of a new sophistication and thoughtfulness in approaching the role of sports in lesbian lives.

—*Helen Lenskyj*

BIBLIOGRAPHY

Auchmuty, Rosemary. "You're a dyke, Angela! Elsie J. Oxenham and the Rise and Fall of the Schoolgirl Story." *Not a Passing Phase: Reclaiming Lesbians in History, 1840-1985.* Lesbian History Group, ed. London: Women's Press, 1989. ■ Foster, Jeannette. *Sex Variant Women in Literature.* Tallahassee, Fla.: Naiad Press, 1985. ■ Griffin, Patricia. "R. R. Knudson's Sport Fiction: A Feminist Critique." *Arete* 3.1 (1985): 3–10. ■ Lesnkyj, Helen. *Out of Bounds: Women, Sport and Sexuality.* Toronto: Women's Press, 1986. ■ Rogers, Susan Fox, ed. *Sportsdykes: Stories from on and off the Field.* New York: St. Martin's Press, 1994. ■ Zipter, Yvonne. *Diamonds are a Dyke's Best Friend.* Ithaca, N.Y.: Firebrand, 1988.

Stein, Gertrude
(1874–1946)

Gertrude Stein, who later delighted in teasing officials with the difficult spelling of her birthplace, was born in Allegheny, Pennsylvania, on February 3, 1874, the youngest child of a prosperous family of German-Jewish descent. During her childhood, Stein's family resided temporarily in Europe and later moved to Oakland, California, where she was educated both privately and in public school. The deaths during her adolescence of her overbearing father and her self-effacing mother left Stein in the care of her older brother Michael, who became the benevolent patriarch of the family. In 1893, Stein accompanied her brother Leo, with whom she was very close, to Harvard. There she studied psychology at Harvard Annex (Radcliffe College) under William James, the author of *Varieties of Religious Experience* (1902) and the older brother of HENRY JAMES. Stein excelled under James's enthusiastic mentoring, and she published two articles in *Harvard Psychological Review* that represented the beginning of her lifelong interest in character typology. She later remarked in *The Autobiography of Alice B. Toklas* that her second article, "Cultivated Motor Automatism: A Study of Character in Its Relation to Attention" (1896), represented the beginning of the "method of writing to be afterwards developed in Three Lives and The Making of Americans [sic]." In this experiment, subjects made marks on paper while overhearing conversation or daydreaming. Based on the capacities of these subjects to concentrate under these conditions, Stein derived a theory of the "bottom nature" or "bottom rhythm" of her subjects. She classified character according to two basic types: Type I was "high-strung, imaginative, and nervous" whereas Type II was "blond, pale, and phlegmatic." On the advice of William James, who told her that knowledge of medicine was necessary to the study of psychology, Stein enrolled in Johns Hopkins Medical School, which had recently begun to admit women students.

For the first two years, Stein continued her laboratory work and therefore enjoyed medical school, but during her final years her grades suffered. In an early indication of her rebellion against maternal roles and medical views of the female body, Stein particularly disliked obstetrics although her experience of delivering babies in the African-American community in Baltimore served as the basis for "Melanctha," a story in her first published work, *Three Lives*. Most significant, however, her increasing difficulties in medical school paralleled her growing awareness of her lesbianism. Her sexuality placed her in conflict not only with the bourgeois morality she espoused but also with the views of feminist theorists such as Charlotte Perkins Gilman, who argued in *Women and Economics* (1898) that the unfettered expression of sexuality would jeopardize women's capacity to succeed in the professions and gain economic independence from men. While in Baltimore, Stein became involved in a group of college women led by Mabel Haynes and Grace Lounsbury, who were, unlike Stein, experts at disguising the reality of lesbian passion behind the respectable cover of female ROMANTIC FRIENDSHIP. Stein had little idea of these social dynamics when Mabel Haynes suddenly dropped her "friendship" with Lounsbury and began an affair with another student, May Bookstaver. In the meantime, Stein herself, despite her professed horror of "passion in its many disguised forms," fell precipitously in love with Bookstaver. Confronted by an experienced and formidable rival, as well as by her own moral crises and sexual naivete, Stein found herself excluded from the Bookstaver-Haynes romance. Indeed, May stayed

temporarily with Mabel, and both women subsequently ended their college affair and, obedient to societal and familial dictates, married men.

During travels to New York, London, and Paris after leaving Johns Hopkins, Stein transmuted the drama of this relationship into her first novel, *Q. E. D.* (1903), which stands for *quod erat demonstrandum* ("what is to be proved") and which was first posthumously published as *Things As They Are* (1950). Like her other early unpublished work *Fernhurst* (1904), which concerns the conflicted three-way relationship between the lesbian dean of Bryn Mawr, Miss Carey Thomas, and two professors, Mary Gwinn and Alfred Hodder, *Q. E. D.* is uncharacteristic of Stein's later work because it employs conventional, linear narration and treats the subject of lesbianism in literal, unencoded language. The story is narrated in three parts, each devoted to the "bottom nature" or ruling characteristic of one person in the triangle. Adele, the character based on Stein, is a hearty and sincere young woman who recognizes only two varieties of feeling, a Whitmanesque "affectionate comradeship" and a Wildean cultivation of "physical passion." Ironically, Adele's programmatic rejection of the latter coincides with her growing attraction to Helen, an ambivalent and seductive woman based on May Bookstaver. The two potential lovers are jealously watched over by the worldly and cynical Mabel, who treats her lover Helen as a possession. Later, this trio of female companions returns from Europe to the United States, and Adele and Helen arrange for a clandestine meeting in New York that culminates in an embrace and a declaration of love. Mabel, her jealousy fiercely aroused, reveals to her rival Adele the precise sexual and financial nature of her relationship with Helen. Adele oscillates between sympathy for Helen's dependency and revulsion at her willingness to "prostitute" herself. By the time Adele has finally decided to dispense with her moral scruples, Helen has become exhausted by Adele's dithering and rejects her advances. *Q. E. D.* thus ends with Adele, thrust back into the role of the romantic friend, recognizing that the dynamics of the relationship are "very near being a dead-lock."

Writing *Q. E. D.* gave Stein a way of understanding her unsuccessful relationship to Bookstaver as well as her failure in medical school. She once again followed her brother Leo, this time to Paris, where he had found an apartment on 27 Rue de Fleurus. After enduring a period of despondency and lethargy, Stein, with Leo, began to collect the works of such modernist painters as Picasso, Cezanne, and Matisse. During the same period that she sat for Picasso's famous portrait of her, Stein wrote her first mature work, *Three Lives* (pub. 1909). These stories were, according to Stein, influenced by Cezanne, whom she said had revolutionized painting by giving equal emphasis to all the elements in a composition. This democratic mode of composition is evident in both the style and subject matter of *Three Lives*. The work, written in a repetitive or "insistent" style that employs simple diction and limited vocabulary to great effect, examines three working-class female outsiders ("The Good Anna," "Melanctha," and "The Gentle Lena") living in Baltimore ("Bridgepoint" in the text) who are crushed by circumstances beyond their control and who die young from bad luck, childbirth, or the inability to form meaningful and lasting human bonds. The text also provides an implicit analysis of Stein's dissatisfaction with medical school, for the illicit and unsuccessful practice of medicine lurks in the background of each of these stories and shows "science" to be ineffectual in ameliorating the condition of these women's lives.

The inadequacy of nineteenth-century notions of scientific and moral progress is particularly evident in "Melanctha," the longest and most stylistically ambitious of the stories. Although "Melanctha" has been interpreted as a transposition of the lesbian drama of *Q. E. D.* into heterosexual and African-American terms, the relationship between these two texts is, in fact, more complex than such an argument would suggest. The story retains an important lesbian element in the teacher-student relationship between Melanctha and Jane Harden, a reckless seductress who initiates the younger woman into the mysteries of lesbian sexuality and who shows her "what everybody wanted, and what one did with power when one had it." Reflecting Stein's unhappy experiences at that point in her life, however, the relationship between Jane and Melanctha is a "passing phase" from which Melanctha "graduates" into her heterosexual romance with Jeff Campbell. Even at this juncture, however, the heterosexualization of the narrative is incomplete, for Stein projects a masculinized version of herself in the character of Jeff Campbell, a naively moralistic African-American doctor who wants his people to "live regular" and avoid "excitements." Crucial aspects of the characters of Stein and Bookstaver are also apparent in Melanctha herself, a woman who "feels blue about all the way her world is made" and who wanders disconsolately from relationship to relationship. Significantly, this story, as well as "The Good Lena" and "The Gentle Anna," shows bonds between women as tenuous and problematic, reflecting both Stein's relationship with her "shadowy" mother and her inability to form a lasting, mature bond with another woman.

Stein next turned her attention to *The Making of Americans* (pub. 1925), a massive project begun in 1903 that chronicles, through the dual histories of the Hersland and Dehning families, her efforts to understand the dynamics and liberate herself from the influence of her paternalistic family and the constraints of the Victorian novel. In the course of the text, Stein uses an exhaustive analysis of the manifold components of character in the context of intergenerational conflict to define herself as an outsider, an original lesbian author who finally rejects the confines of the traditional family. The people in the text are not unified subjects but rather conflicting aggregates of forces, encountering others whom they either repel, besiege, or submit to in an intricate field of gendered power relations. Although she rarely depicts lesbianism openly in *The Making of Americans,* she places her narrative voice outside the family frame and addresses herself to the "Brothers Singular" who, like the author, are rejected by American society and who "flee before the disapproval of . . . all them who never any way can understand why such ways and not the others are so dear to us."

Stein thus indicates that her "singularity" as a lesbian impelled her voluntary expatriation to Paris, "an older world accustomed to take all manner of strange forms into its bosom." At this stage of her career, however, her decision to present herself as a "singular" reveals her self-definition as an ungendered "original" and a possibly tainted anomaly. Her self-masculinization also corresponds to her reading of Otto Weininger's misogynistic and antisemitic treatise, *Sex and Character* (1906). Weininger, a self-loathing Jewish homosexual who subsequently committed suicide, characterizes Jews as "effeminate" men, proclaims women incapable of selfhood and male genius but, significantly, argues that "female homosexuals," unlike other women, could achieve a quasi-masculine transcendence. Obliged by necessity to define the meaning of modernist lesbian authorship in relative isolation, Stein found temporary consolation and self-affirmation in these dubious arguments. Hence, the early phase of her writing dramatizes the conflicts of a lesbian writer with strong bourgeois and male identification who gradually, over the course of her career, discovers the means to affirm both her sexuality and her gender.

This process of mature self-acceptance was facilitated by Alice B. Toklas, who first met Stein in 1907 while on a visit to Paris from her San Francisco home. Like Stein, Toklas was from a prosperous Jewish family and had had an unsuccessful romance with another woman. During a three-year transition period, Toklas gradually exerted her predominance in

Gertrude and Leo's domestic arrangements. This power struggle is explored in *Two* (1908–1912), a long early portrait of the conflict between sister and brother that chronicles Stein's liberation from Leo's censorious contempt for her writing and sexual orientation. By 1913, Leo had moved from the apartment in 27 Rue de Fleurus and the two women had established themselves in what Stein referred to as the "daily island living" of an independent lesbian couple. In Toklas, Stein not only found a loving and loyal domestic partner, but also a secretary (Toklas learned to type in order to transcribe the manuscript of *The Making of Americans*) and an audience who agreed with Stein's assessment of her own genius. Accordingly, Stein gradually abandoned schematized character typology for verbal portraits that sought to free their subjects from larger systems of association as well as the constraints of temporal narration and conventional syntax and grammar.

Stein's early verbal portraits tend to focus on dynamic relations among groups, trios, or pairs of individuals, organized conceptually according to nationality ("Italians"), gender ("Many, Many Women"), or a dominant activity or trait. For example, "Ada," included in *Geography and Plays* (1922), is Stein's early tribute to Alice Toklas. The portrait briefly recapitulates the story of Ada's "tender" separation from her paternal family and ends on a note of unqualified domestic felicity involving both the listening to and the telling of stories to "the other one," namely, Stein. Here, as elsewhere in her work, Toklas serves as audience, muse, and collaborator in an artistic project that allows Stein to explore fully her creative identity. The use of incremental repetition, the ungendered subject "one," and limited vocabulary characterize the portraits of this period, including the famous "Miss Furr and Miss Skeene" (1922), which was based on a lesbian couple, Maud Hunt Squire and Ethel Mars, who visited Stein and Toklas in Paris. Through repetition-within-variation of the dominant verbal motifs "being gay," "regularly," and "cultivating their voices," the portrait associates (perhaps for the first time in print) the appellation "gay" with a homosexual couple. Furthermore, the text also indicates that such bonds are "regular" ("normal" and "habitual") and something to be artistically "cultivated" ("socially constructed"). Stein's less well known portrait of homosexual men, simply and tellingly titled "Men," makes the erotic content of such "gay" alliances clear and opens with the statement: "Sometimes men are kissing." The remainder of this evocative portrait explores the interpersonal dynamics of erotic longing and fulfillment, communication and estrangement, and winning and losing among gay men.

A marked shift from character typology and repetition to visuality and object-description accompanies the more complex modes of verbal play in *Tender Buttons* (1914), one of the outstanding achievements of modernist literature. Although written in 1912, *Tender Buttons* anticipates many of the theoretical premises of post-modernism regarding linguistic indeterminacy and post-Freudian psychoanalytic theory; hence, an informed appreciation of Stein's work has in great measure depended on the development of such analytic tools. Divided into three sections ("Objects," "Food," and "Rooms"), the work dismantles conventional syntax and semantics to uncover the embodied mystery, erotic power, and surrealistic "thing-ness" of the common entities that surround, sustain, and shelter human life. Although each interpretation of this challenging and playful text must, in some measure, be unique, the condensed verbal encodings of *Tender Buttons* also represent Stein's effort to create a metaphorical sexual vernacular of lesbianism that accurately reflects the richness of lived experience. Hence, rather than a literal or "scientific" use of language in which each word corresponds to a single referent outside the text, there is elaborate punning so that terms hover at the boundary between paraphrasable sense and opacity. Words such as "pencil" not only mean "writing implement" but also connote "phallic object" and "dildo." Similarly, "box" means "container" and also "female genitalia" and "interiority." Such highly condensed layers of public and private meanings, embedded in a context of unabashed lesbian eroticism, inform the structure of *Tender Buttons*.

From 1912 to 1925, Stein turned her attention to shorter forms she termed "poems," in which a major theme is established then elaborated in the body of the text, much as a piece of music develops the themes set out in the opening bars. These poems are, for the most part, accounts in dialogue form (between Stein and Toklas) of various domestic and erotic adventures. "Lifting Belly" (pub. 1953), a *tour de force* of lesbian lovemaking, equates the joys of lesbian sex with those of female creativity. The "body" of the poem elaborates on the multiple meanings of the title: the "lifting up" of the body in response to sexual arousal; the "swelling" of the abdomen as a metaphorical state of "pregnancy" or creativity; and, finally, the "enlarging" of the significance of lesbianism in a world in which lesbians are often rendered both insignificant and invisible. The final lines of the poem (spoken, perhaps, in unison by both partners), "In the midst of writing there is merriment," is the joyous sexual context that gives "birth" to the poem as well as the triumphant coda of this poetic fugue for two collaborative female voices. Other works of this period are similarly ebullient and celebratory. "Pink Melon Joy" elaborates on the delights of female sexuality; "Didn't Nelly and Lilly Love You" heals Alice Toklas of the pain of earlier failed romances; and "A Book Concluding With As a Wife Has a Cow A Love Story" tells the story of a "wife" (Alice) having a "cow" (an orgasm).

Throughout this period of intense literary innovation, Stein encountered great difficulties getting her writing published, although her lifelong friend, the American critic and novelist CARL VAN VECHTEN, tirelessly promoted her work, and many of her other literary contemporaries also recognized her importance. Although she remained outwardly indifferent to the scorn and disapproval that greeted her work, she also began writing accessible explanations of her poetics for the public. In "Composition as Explanation" (1926), which remains one of the most cogent analyses of her writing practices, Stein explains her apparent nonsense as an attempt to represent a "continuous present" and to elucidate new awarenesses of time generated by post-war experience. She also takes issue with nineteenth-century conceptions of linear time, progress, and representation. For Stein, things in themselves remain the same, whereas compositions, or the way those things are assembled and arranged, change. Geniuses, like herself, are essentially people outside time because they are ahead of their times. Hence, Stein must wait for the public to catch up with her: "The creator of the new composition in arts is an outlaw until he is a classic . . . For a very long time everybody refuses and then almost without a pause almost everybody accepts." According to Stein, the transition between refusal and acceptance is never gradual, but rather abrupt and startling.

Although *The Autobiography of Alice B. Toklas* (1933) began as a joke, this stylistically uncharacteristic work was responsible for suddenly transforming her from an "eccentric" personality into a best-selling author and "household name." By assuming the voice of her lover Toklas, and thereby playfully dramatizing the problematic relations between her private identity as a lesbian and her public perception by her audience, Stein was able to position herself in the center of the narrative of MODERNISM. This entertaining and deceptively transparent book is filled with spirited gossip and portraits of many of the important artistic figures of the time (for example, Cezanne, Matisse, Picasso, HEMINGWAY, Pound, ELIOT, Joyce, Fitzgerald, Sherwood Anderson, and Margaret Anderson). The early narrative recounts the years before Stein and Toklas met, then describes their encounters with various celebrated people, their alliances and rivalries, and their experiences of driving an ambulance during World War I. Toklas's voice as narrator allowed Stein to make several important claims, the most famous of which became the bells that rang each time Toklas met a genius. There had been three of them: the philosopher Alfred North Whitehead, the painter Pablo Picasso, and, of course, the writer Gertrude Stein.

The success of the *Autobiography* launched Stein on a highly publicized lecture tour through England and the United States. Yet, having at last secured the broad recognition she had long sought, Stein nevertheless was dismayed that audiences seemed much more interested in her personality than her writing. Hence, she became increasingly preoccupied with problems of identity and audience, and how knowledge of identity can or cannot be described, transmitted, or understood. *The Geographical History of America* (1936), *Everybody's Autobiography* (1937), and *Ida: A Novel* (1941), explore the difference between "writing," the kind of work customers were willing to pay for, and "really writing," the intellectually challenging and hermetic sort she had labored at for more than thirty years. *The Geographical History of America*, a formidable instance of "really writing," explores the meanings of literature, geography, and autobiography, and the loss of self under the sway of such influences as time, audience awareness, and money. Her often quoted phrase, "I am I because my little dog knows me," is a paradox. Self-recognition can become distorted when it identifies outside itself, but since her "little dog" possesses no sense of human nature, human mind, or human time, it "entifies" rather than "identifies" Stein. Such reflections are, in part, motivated by Stein's understandable refusal to be reduced to her contemporary audience's limited understanding of the meanings of lesbian authorship, as well as their prejudice against perceiving lesbians as transformers of culture. In *What Are Masterpieces* (1940), Stein endeavors both to transcend history and meaning, and to explain the historical relevance and significance of her work. Masterpieces deal with matters of human nature, but their authors, in the act of writing, are paradoxically free of human nature's restraints and therefore create timeless work. By contrast, *Everybody's Autobiography* is, as the title suggests, audience-friendly "writing" that not only narrates Stein's childhood and her subsequent lecture tour in her native land but also contains some of her most quotable material. For example, of the influence of Roosevelt, Hitler, and Mussolini, she writes: "There is too much fathering going on just now and there is no doubt about it fathers are depressing."

Regardless of how ambivalently Stein regarded her public, she continued her interest in audience-centered "writing" both before and after World War II. During the war, Stein and Toklas lived mostly in their country house in Bilignin and in the nearby town of Culoz. During this time, Stein wrote *Paris France* (1940), a tribute to her adopted homeland, *Wars I Have Seen* (1945), a meditation on the relation of modernity, war, and nationalism to historical contingency and coincidence, and *Mrs. Reynolds* (pub. 1952), an allegorical novel about Hitler and Stalin. With the liberation of France, Stein and Toklas returned to Paris in 1944, where she surrounded herself with American military personnel and even toured with the Army in Germany. In *Brewsie and Willie* (1946), Stein returns to the dialogue style of her earliest published work, *Three Lives,* and records, with evident appreciation, the contours of GI speech. The book not only discusses everything from anxieties over post-war industrialism to renewed hopes for women's rights but also subtly delineates the development of a distinct gay subculture in the homosocial camaraderie fostered by World War II.

During the mid-point of her career, Stein had also become interested in saints and landscapes, a preoccupation that not only resulted in her fanciful novel *Lucy Church Amiably,* which Stein and Toklas published as the first title in their Plain Edition in 1930, but also in her first opera libretto, *Four Saints in Three Acts* (pub. 1934), for which the American gay composer Virgil Thomson composed the music. A modernist version of a long-standing gay and lesbian interest in saints' lives, the opera recounts, in a whimsical and meditative fashion, the harmonious efforts of a group of male and female Spanish Carmelite mystics to achieve sainthood. In her final work, Stein once again returned to opera. Her libretto for Thomson's *The Mother of Us All* (1947) is her most explicitly feminist work, a moving paean to the American suffragist Susan B. Anthony. Alice Toklas appears thinly disguised as Anna Howard Shaw, Anthony's loyal compatriot, and Anthony often seems to speak for Stein herself. Stein implicitly links her literary revolutions to Anthony's revolutionary political struggle to secure the vote for women and encourage people to live as individuals. Even as Anthony did not live to see her goals accomplished, so does Stein herself seem to realize that she may not live to see her revolution in letters brought to fruition. In its evocative epilogue, *The Mother of Us All* enshrines Susan B. Anthony and Gertrude Stein as monuments to which the other women in the cast pay homage, "Not to what I won but to what was done."

Gertrude Stein's death from cancer on July 27, 1946, made front-page headlines although she was, at that time, largely out of print and unread, at least in academia. Only with the advent of the second wave of the women's movement, as well as the development of post-structuralist, feminist, and lesbian and gay literary criticism, has the full extent of Stein's importance as an innovator and transformer of the English language become apparent.

—*Corinne E. Blackmer*

BIBLIOGRAPHY

Bloom, Harold, ed. *Modern Critical Views: Gertrude Stein.* New York: Chelsea House, 1986. ■ Brinnin, John Malcolm. *The Third Rose: Gertrude Stein and Her World.* Boston: Little, Brown, 1959. ■ Grahn, Judy. *Really Reading Gertrude Stein: A Selected Anthology with Essays by Judy Grahn.* Freedom, Calif.: The Crossing Press, 1989. ■ Hoffman, Michael J., ed. *Critical Essays on Gertrude Stein.* Boston: G.K. Hall, 1986. ■ Kellner, Bruce, ed. *A Gertrude Stein Companion: Content with the Example.* New York: Greenwood Press, 1988. ■ Ruddick, Lisa. *Reading Gertrude Stein: Body, Text, Gnosis.* Ithaca, N.Y.: Cornell University Press, 1990.

Stevenson, Edward Irenaeus Prime-
(1868–1942)

The man who might well be styled the first modern American gay author, Stevenson was born in New Jersey to a literary family. Although admitted to the bar, he never practiced, becoming instead a professional writer, publishing short fiction, poetry, and musical criticism as an editor for popular magazines such as *Harper's* and *The New York Independent.* He also wrote boys' books, two of which were later admitted by the author as couching an underlying homoerotic dynamic: *White Cockades: An Incident of the 'Forty-Five'* (1887) and *Left to Themselves: Being the Ordeal of Gerald and Philip* (1891). These Horatio Alger-like novels extolled adolescent romantic friendship, giving form simultaneously to the American dream and at least one type of homosexual teen fantasy.

More important, at the same time his public literary career was in full swing, Stevenson was also covertly publishing (through an English press in Italy) a series of gay-themed works under the pseudonym

Xavier Mayne. In *The Intersexes* (1908), Stevenson presented a passionately constructed history and defense of European and American homosexuality that was less "scientific" than his models Krafft-Ebing and Havelock Ellis but more anecdotal, personal, and polemic. This massive volume, severely limited in circulation, stood for many years as the single major rebuttal by an American gay author to the pathologizing of the homosexual by the growing psychological establishment.

Stevenson's chef-d'oeuvre, however, is the cerebral but fascinating novel that owes a great deal to the style of HENRY JAMES, *Imre: A Memorandum* (1906). Styled "a little psychological romance" by its author, *Imre* recounts the developing love between a thirty-something British aristocrat and a twenty-five-year-old Magyar military officer, exploring the wary psychological dynamics of the coming-out of the two main characters. Both men are insistently masculine types tempered by a love of art. The story's ending is unprecedented—the first in American gay writing where homosexuals are united and happy as the tale closes.

In 1913, Stevenson published, again at his own expense, a collection titled *Her Enemy, Some Friends—And Other Personages,* which contains several homoerotic stories delineating "passional friendships between adults—in accents chiefly tragic." "Aquæ Multæ Non—," "A Great Patience," and "Weed and Flower: An Art Theory" are moving tales of gay love among the upper class, and "Once—But Not Twice" shows Stevenson at his melancholy best, displaying a deep understanding of homosexual middle age, the irrecoverability of the past, and regret for the Life-Not-Lived (a gay theme common in this period). "Out of the Sun" recounts a gay man's last hours, reminding us that in those days youthful suicides were often the sad markers of homosexuality to those "in the know." This story additionally provides a fascinating and detailed glimpse into a homosexual's library at the turn of the century, and tells what music, operas, and great bachelor-composers (Beethoven, Schubert, Brahms, Tchaikovsky) had been coded lavender by an earlier generation.

Stevenson moved to Europe in the first decade of the century, gradually publishing less and less until his death in Lausanne, Switzerland, on July 23, 1942.

—*James J. Gifford*

BIBLIOGRAPHY

Austen, Roger. *Playing the Game: The Homosexual Novel in America.* Indianapolis: Bobbs-Merrill, 1977. ■ Fone, Byrne R. S. "This Other Eden: Arcadia and the Homosexual Imagination." *Essays on Gay Literature.* Stuart Kellogg, ed. New York: Harrington Park Press, 1985. 13–34. ■ Garde, Noel I. "The First Native American 'Gay' Novel: A Study." *One Institute Quarterly: Homophile Studies* (Spring 1960): 185–190. ■ ———. "The Mysterious Father of American Homophile Literature: A Historical Study." *One Institute Quarterly: Homophile Studies* (Fall 1958): 94–98. ■ Katz, Jonathan Ned. *Gay American History: Lesbians and Gay Men in the U.S.A.* New York: Avon, 1976.

Stoddard, Charles Warren
(1843–1909)

Charles Warren Stoddard was born in Rochester, New York, on August 7, 1843, third of five children and second son to Sarah Freeman and Samuel Burr Stoddard, a paper merchant. As their fortunes declined during the next decade, the family moved about upstate New York and then left for San Francisco in 1854. Although Stoddard subsequently returned East for two years to live with his grandparents, he regarded himself as a Californian, and his first poems were published, under the pseudonym "Pip Pepperpod," in the *Golden Era.*

During the 1860s, after he had quit school and dedicated himself to a literary career, Stoddard joined San Francisco's journalistic and Bohemian circles, and he established enduring relationships with Ambrose Bierce, Ina Coolbrith, Bret Harte, and Samuel Clemens. Beloved for his wit and amiability, Stoddard had a genius for friendship; his large literary acquaintance ultimately included both contemporary and younger writers, such as Robert Louis Stevenson, W. D. Howells, Henry Adams, Joaquin Miller, Jack London, George Sterling, Bliss Carman, Yone Noguchi, and George Cabot Lodge. Stoddard was also connected to the developing gay networks of the nineteenth century through his friendships with Theodore F. Dwight and Dewitt Miller.

Raised a Protestant, Stoddard converted to Roman Catholicism soon after the appearance of his *Poems* in 1867. Stoddard remained devout in his faith—among his most popular books was a spiritual autobiography, *A Troubled Heart* (1885)—and he cherished the companionship of priests, including Father Damien, missionary to the lepers of Molokai. As a respected man of letters, Stoddard was recruited to academic positions at prominent Catholic institutions: Notre Dame, where he clashed with colleagues over his attentions to the students and resigned after three semesters; the Catholic University of America, where he taught from 1889 to 1901.

Inspired to sexual self-awareness by reading WHITMAN's "Calamus" poems, Stoddard gained his first experience with the natives of Hawaii and Tahiti, about whom he wrote his best stories, those collected in *South-Sea Idyls* (1874, 1892) and *The Island of Tranquil Delights* (1904). The subtle eroticism of Stoddard's tropical tales was evidently lost on his audience—except for "Xavier Mayne" (EDWARD PRIME-STEVENSON), who noted their significance in *The Intersexes* (1908). Readers were also mystified by Stoddard's only novel, *For the Pleasure of His Company* (1903), an (unsuccessfully) experimental work of gay fiction.

Stoddard fell in love with the painter Frank Millet during the 1870s and lived with him in Venice. But he usually favored youthful companions. Of his several "kids," as he called them, the most important was Kenneth O'Connor, aged fifteen in 1895, when Stoddard unofficially adopted him and took him home to his Washington "Bungalow." In 1903, his health

failing and his relationship with Kenneth deteriorating, Stoddard returned to California. After a triumphal visit to San Francisco, where he was feted as a pioneering California writer, he settled in Monterey, where he died of a heart attack on April 23, 1909. Stoddard's modest literary reputation had already faded before his collected *Poems* appeared posthumously in 1917. The gayest of the island stories have recently been collected in *Cruising the South Seas* (1987).

—*John W. Crowley*

BIBLIOGRAPHY

Austen, Roger. *Genteel Pagan: The Double Life of Charles Warren Stoddard.* John W. Crowley, ed. Amherst: University of Massachusetts Press, 1991. ■ ———. *Playing the Game: The Homosexual Novel in America.* Indianapolis: Bobbs-Merrill, 1977. ■ Crowley, John W. "Howells, Stoddard, and Male Homosocial Attachment." *The Mask of Fiction: Essays on W. D. Howells.* Amherst: University of Massachusetts Press, 1989. ■ Gale, Robert L. *Charles Warren Stoddard.* Western Writers Series No. 30. Boise, Idaho: Boise State University Press, 1977. ■ Longton, Ray C. *Three Writers of the Far West: A Reference Guide.* Boston: G. K. Hall, 1980. ■ Stroven, Carl G. "A Life of Charles Warren Stoddard." Ph.D. Diss. Duke, 1939. ■ Walker, Franklin. *San Francisco's Literary Frontier.* New York: Knopf, 1939.

Strachey, Lytton
(1880–1932)

Giles Lytton Strachey was born in London on March 1, 1880, one of thirteen children of Richard Strachey and Jane Maria Grant. The large discrepancy in his parents' ages (thirty years) resulted in Lytton being much closer to his mother than his father. At Cambridge, he found his niche and made lasting friends, including those who would later form the nucleus of the BLOOMSBURY GROUP. It was in this milieu that Strachey wrote about and spoke openly of his homosexuality.

Two essays, not published during his lifetime, are explicitly homosexual. The first is an *Arabian Nights* inspired tale titled (appropriately) "An Arabian Night." It is a very light king-falls-in-love-with-shepherd-boy story (reprinted in *The Really Interesting Question*). The other essay is a thinly veiled defense of homosexuality probably inspired by the OSCAR WILDE trial; here Strachey remarks:

> but I perpetually wonder what an immoral act is . . . whether it is immoral to embrace, whether it is immoral to make a seminal dis-

charge, and whether it is immoral to copulate in a somewhat unusual manner . . . Why, I wish to know, is it perfectly moral for me to copulate with a personage whose sexual organs are different from my own, and perfectly immoral for me to copulate with a personage whose sexual organs are not different? (reprinted in *The Really Interesting Question*)

But Strachey is noted most for being a biographer and critic. He had a Dorothy Parker-like wit, sharp tongue, irreverent sense of humor, and did not suffer fools gently. It was this new approach to writing biography (as evidenced in *Eminent Victorians, Queen Victoria,* and *Elizabeth and Essex*), which is considered—almost universally—as "revolutionary." His goal was to shatter the myths set up by Victorian society, expose the hypocrisy, and end the hagiography. This he did. Aspects of *Queen Victoria* read like a dish article in any current gay publication. In an essay on the Cambridge master John North, Strachey leaves the reader with an image of this once prim and proper professor (who after an illness takes up the bottle and a penchant for naughty stories) with an apparent moral about-face (reprinted in *The Shorter Strachey*). His sharp tongue is evidenced in his review of Elizabeth Lee's translation of La Bruyere and Vauvenargues. "And if Miss Lee has failed with Vauvenargues it was not to be expected that she would succeed with La Bruyere. This would have required a special talent, a fine instinct, and a reverent mind . . ." (reprinted in *Literary Essays*). In his diary, Strachey writes about the loneliness of the Liverpool years, the desire for love, and of the unhappiness with his looks—thinking his face too oddly shaped. He grew his trademark beard for added character.

Lasting love proved elusive for Strachey. He did, however, have one person totally devoted to him, the painter Dora Carrington. Carrington knew Strachey was gay but was still hopelessly in love with him—even to the exclusion of several well-meaning suitors. She committed suicide after Strachey's death from cancer in 1932.

—*Lee Arnold*

BIBLIOGRAPHY

Strachey, Giles Lytton. *Elizabeth and Essex: A Tragic History.* London: Chatto & Windus, 1928. ■ ———. *Eminent Victorians: Cardinal Manning, Florence Nightingale, Dr. Arnold, General Gordon.* London: Chatto & Windus, 1918. ■ ———. *Literary Essays.* New York: Harcourt, Brace & World, 1949. ■ ———. *Queen Victoria.* London: Chatto & Windus, 1921. ■ ———. *The Really Interesting Question and Other Papers.* Paul Levy, ed. London: Weidenfeld and Nicolson, 1972. ■ ———. *The Shorter Strachey.* Oxford: Oxford University Press, 1980.

Sturgis, Howard Overing
(1855–1920)

The son of wealthy expatriate Americans, Howard Overing Sturgis spent his life in England surrounded by privilege and ease. Affable and witty, he was a favorite with HENRY JAMES, Edith Wharton, and A. C. Benson, and the subject of a memorable sketch by E. M. FORSTER. Sturgis was a popular host known for his biting tongue and gift for mimicry. James, a frequent guest at Qu'Acre, Sturgis's estate, once gushed to "Howdie," "You are indeed as a missing mother to me, & I, babi-like, . . . gurgle back my gratitude." Sturgis maintained a lifelong relationship with a much younger man, William Haynes-Smith, familiarly known as "the Babe." GEORGE SANTAYANA, distantly related, said that:

> [Sturgis] became, save for the accident of sex, which was not yet a serious encumbrance, a perfect young lady of the Victorian type. He . . . instinctively embraced the proper liberal humanitarian principles in politics and history. . . . He learned to sew, to embroider, to knit, and to do crochet. . . . He would emit little frightened cries, if the cab he was in turned too fast round a corner; and in crossing a muddy road he would pick up the edge of his short covert-coat, as the ladies in those days picked up their trailing skirts. . . . Howard attracted affection, and however astonished one might be at first, or even scornful, one was always won over in the end.

Sturgis wrote three novels: *Tim: A Story of Eton* (1891), *All That Was Possible* (1894), and *Belchamber* (1904). The first and last betray a clear homosexual dynamic. *Tim* was published anonymously, dedicated to the "love that surpasses the love of women." EDWARD PRIME-STEVENSON labeled *Tim* "a minute study of psychic Uranianism between two school-lads," a sympathetic but tragic depiction of a sensitive child in British public school. *Belchamber,* dedicated to Haynes-Smith, is a drama of family, duty, and marriage among the British upper classes. The heir to a powerful estate managed in his minority by his strong-willed widowed mother, Sainty abhors sports and boys' play, preferring embroidery and books. He marries from a sense of duty rather than passionate attachment and soon discovers that his wife finds him repugnant. When she later presents him with a son, he gradually comes to accept the child as his own, becoming an enthusiastic parent in contrast to his wife's near-abandonment of the boy. The baby's sudden death allows Sainty a chance for hollow revenge on his wife.

Tim had sold well, but the lukewarm reception of *Belchamber,* along with withering criticism from Henry James, caused Sturgis to abandon writing altogether except for a few unpublished short stories. Elmer Borklund notes recurrent themes—the plight of the sensitive outsider and the revenge that society takes on anyone who fails to "fit in." Sturgis deliberately overturns the gender codes of his day in presenting a domestic model of homosexuality—the sensitive male whose sexuality is submerged in social dynamics and family duty. According to Leon Edel, *Belchamber* records "with great accuracy the natural history of a passive male," although Fred Kaplan exasperatedly notes that "it is difficult to tell whether the homoerotic elements are the result of innocent, unconscious confusions or are self-consciously subversive." It is Sturgis's gift as a writer that he simultaneously accomplishes both.

—*James Gifford*

BIBLIOGRAPHY

Austen, Roger. *Playing the Game: The Homosexual Novel in America*. Indianapolis: Bobbs-Merrill, 1977. ■ Benson, A. C. *Memories and Friends*. London: John Murray, 1924. ■ Borklund, Elmer. "Howard Sturgis, Henry James, and Belchamber." *Modern Philology* 58 (1961): 255–269. ■ Edel, Leon. *Henry James: The Master: 1901–1916*. New York: Avon, 1972. ■ Forster, E. M. "Howard Overing Sturgis." *Abinger Harvest*. London: Edward Arnold, 1936. 121–129. ■ Harris, Alan. Introduction. *Belchamber*. By Howard Overing Sturgis. London: Duckworth, 1965. v–xvii. ■ Kaplan, Fred. *Henry James: The Imagination of Genius*. New York: William Morrow, 1992. ■ Mayne, Xavier [Edward Irenaeus Prime-Stevenson]. *The Intersexes*. 1908. New York: Arno Press, 1975. ■ Santayana, George. *Persons and Places: Fragments of Autobiography*. William G. Holzberger and Herman J Saatkamp, Jr., eds. Cambridge: MIT Press, 1986. ■ Seymour, Miranda. *A Ring of Conspirators: Henry James and His Literary Circle 1895–1915*. Boston: Houghton Mifflin, 1988. ■ Wharton, Edith. *A Backward Glance*. New York: Scribner, 1985.

Swenson, May
(1913–1989)

Born in Logan, Utah, on May 28, 1913, May Swenson became one of America's most inventive and incisive poets. English was actually her second language since Swedish was spoken in her childhood home. Beginning in 1954, she published ten collections of poetry during her lifetime and one book of translations of the poems of Swedish poet Tomas Transtromer. These include works such as *Another Animal* (1954), *To Mix With Time* (1963), *Iconographs* (1970), *New And Selected Things Taking Place* (1978), and *In Other Words* (1987). Swenson died in Ocean View, Delaware, on December 4, 1989.

Swenson's work is wide and varied. Many of her poems delight in the natural world. Others incorporate scientific research, particularly that having to do with space exploration. Others root themselves in love and eroticism, especially lesbian sexuality. Many of her love poems were published as a single collection in 1991 as *The Love Poems of May Swenson*.

Nature and sexuality are not separate categories in her work; to be a part of Nature, as we all are, joins us to a common sexual energy. Her strongest love poems, such as "Fireflies," "Dark Wild Honey," and "Wednesday at The Waldorf," rely on Nature imagery for much of their vitality and beauty. The couple in "Wednesday at The Walforf," for example, sits in the hotel restaurant under whales that cavort overhead. When the couple goes to their hotel room, the whales are still playing. The poem ends with a hush, a descending peace. The erotic transforms even a busy and anonymous place into one of joy and desire.

Windows and Stones, her translations of Transtromer's poetry, helped introduce English-speaking audiences to his work. Transtromer is a psychologist as well as a poet; his interest in human perception and in our relationship with the landscape and place suggests Swenson's own interest in these areas.

Perception, for a poet like Swenson, is also a matter of how a poem looks to the eye. How a poem shapes the page (and vice versa) helps determine our perception of subject and sound. In "A Trellis for R" the design of Swenson's poem suggests a trellis. The reader sees the trellis both pictorially and emotionally. Landscape and place are not decorative so much as they are atlases, maps to lead us inward and outward.

An amusing poem from her last collection, *In Other Words,* is called "The Gay Life." Here Swenson rearranges the traditional family's building blocks: mommy, daddy, and baby. One slips into the others' roles. In this poem, people desire a more fluid response to their assigned roles: Mommies don't always want to be mommies, and daddies don't always want to be daddies. In this fluidity, joy can sneak in. Life can become "gay" in more than one way.

For Swenson, desire bursts free in such fluidity the way rain bolts free from clouds. It is liberating. What we see and feel isn't rain alone; it's language, urgent and dynamic.

—*Kenneth Pobo*

BIBLIOGRAPHY

Collier, Michael. "Poetic Voices." *Partisan Review* 58 (Summer 1991): 565–569. ■ Packard, William. *The Poet's Craft*. New

York: Paragon House, 1987. ■ Swenson, Paul. "May In October." *Weber Studies* 8 (1991): 18–31. ■ Transtromer, Tomas. *Windows and Stones: Selected Poems of Tomas Transtromer.*
Trans. May Swenson. Pittsburgh: University of Pittsburgh Press, 1972. ■ Van Duyn, Mona. "Important Witness to the World." *Parnassus: Poetry In Review* 16.1. (1990): 154–156.

Swinburne, Algernon Charles
(1837–1909)

Algernon Charles Swinburne was born on April 5, 1837, to Charles and Jane Swinburne. The Swinburnes were an old and wealthy family, and Swinburne grew up in comfort on the Isle of Wight. A sickly child, he was educated for four years at Eton but was removed by his parents before he had completed his studies. He continued his education under a series of private tutors and went up to Oxford in 1856. Though he was a talented scholar, he was sent down for a disciplinary infraction and never sat the examinations for his degree.

Swinburne had a striking appearance; he was very short and thin, with a huge head and large quantities of flame-red hair. He had a nervous temperament, could behave erratically, and was subject to tremors. His early talent was apparent; he wrote plays in a Jacobean style in his early teens and grew up speaking both French and Italian. He also had a lively interest in flagellation—a taste probably acquired at Eton, and he shared his sexual interests with, among others, Lord Houghton, who had amassed a large library of erotica. For his own entertainment, Swinburne composed flagellation sketches, farcical novels, and reviews of nonexistent French poets. He tried to publish some of these works, but primarily he circulated them among his friends—who included Dante Gabriel Rossetti, his brother William Rossetti, and Edward Burne-Jones of the Pre-Raphaelite brotherhood. Swinburne was known as a great republican and had a particular hatred of Napoleon III.

For Swinburne, critical success and controversy came in quick succession. His drama *Atalanta in Calydon,* which combined Swinburne's felicitous effects of sound with an attention to Greek dramatic structure, was published to great acclaim in 1865. The next year his *Poems and Ballads* scandalized Victorian critical and moral opinion and was withdrawn from circulation by its publisher. The volume included "Dolores," which glorified masochism, "Hermaphroditus," which exhibited Swinburne's lasting interest in bisexuality, and "Anactoria," which glorified lesbianism in an address of SAPPHO to her lover. Swinburne was a masochist and a flagellant who enjoyed visits to the flagellation brothels of London, particularly an establishment named "Verbena Lodge." He was fascinated by lesbianism and bisexuality not only for their erotics but because he interpreted them as gestures of social and cultural rebellion. His friendships with George Powell and Simeon Solomon encouraged his interest in same-sex sexuality, though he was at times ambivalent about what he called Solomon's "Platonism." Swinburne was staunchly antitheistic and saw in sadomasochistic and same-sex sexuality possible extensions of Shelleyan revolt.

Swinburne wrote in every genre with varying success. His works include two novels, *Love's Cross-Currents* and *Lesbia Brandon,* long verse plays, and many collections of verse. By the late 1860s, Swinburne had become addicted to alcohol, and it quickly undermined his health. His alcoholic sprees also began to lose him friends. In 1879, Theodore Watts (later Watts-Dunton), a solicitor and minor writer, established Swinburne in his house in Putney outside London. Watts tactfully weaned Swinburne from alcohol and from those of his friends who had encouraged him to drink. Though the household treatment at Putney might be thought stifling, Watts undoubtedly saved Swinburne's life. Swinburne continued to write until his death thirty years later.

Swinburne remained devoted to the romantic ideal of the supremacy of the imagination even as his political beliefs turned sharply to the right in his old age. Swinburne's death occurred when Watts himself was ill in bed and could not supervise him; Swinburne walked outside in bad weather and contracted pneumonia. He died on April 10, 1909. As he had requested, the Christian burial service was not read over him. (See also DECADENCE and ENGLISH LITERATURE: NINETEENTH CENTURY.)

—*James Najarian*

BIBLIOGRAPHY

Dellamora, Richard. *Masculine Desire: The Sexual Politics of Victorian Aestheticism.* Chapel Hill: University of North Carolina Press, 1990. ■ Harrison, Antony H. "The Aesthetics of Androgyny in Swinburne's Early Poetry." *Tennessee Studies in Literature* 23 (1978): 87–99. ■ McGann, Jerome J. *Swinburne: An Experiment in Criticism.* Chicago: University of Chicago

Press, 1972. ■ Riede, David G. *Swinburne: A Study of Romantic Mythmaking*. Charlottesville: University of Virginia Press, 1978. ■ Rooksby, Ricky and Nicholas Shrimpton. *The Whole Music of Passion: New Essays on Swinburne*. Aldershot: Scolar Press, 1993. ■ Thomas, Donald. *Swinburne: The Poet in His World*. London: Weidenfeld and Nicolson, 1979.

Symonds, John Addington
(1840–1893)

John Addington Symonds was the most daring innovator in the history of nineteenth-century British homosexual writing and consciousness though some of his work was not entirely unprecedented and was also part of a more widespread movement in the earlier modern West toward greater homosexual frankness. Because of homosexuality's official "unspeakableness" in his time, Symonds's plainest homosexual work had to remain private, and within that realm he produced some pioneering work, including several firsts. The poems that poured from him in the 1860s and 1870s and that he distributed to friends in private pamphlets of the mid- and late-1870s and the early 1880s—such as *Lyra Viginti Chordarum, The Lotos Garland of Antinous and Diego, Pantarkes, Rhaetica, Tales of Ancient Greece, Crocuses and Soldanellas, Old and New, Fragilia Labilia*—are some of the frankest Victorian homosexual writing, if not always distinguished as literature. He also wrote what he and his audiences thought were the first essays in defense of homosexuality in English, the privately printed and distributed *A Problem in Greek Ethics* (written in 1873, published 1883), based in the proficiency in the classics he gained at Oxford, and *A Problem in Modern Ethics* (1891), which focuses on later history as well as on the new sexology and ends with proposals for legal reform. (They could not have known of JEREMY BENTHAM's unpublished work.)

Perhaps most important, between 1889 and 1893 Symonds composed his unprecedented *Memoirs*, the first self-conscious homosexual autobiography known to us now, which remained unpublished until 1984 and which is an indispensable text in gay studies (and from which most of the personal quotations by him here are taken). Moreover, the many letters Symonds wrote to other homosexuals—starting in 1863 with his friend Graham Dakyns and continuing with Horatio Brown, WALT WHITMAN, Edmund Gosse, Charles Kains-Jackson, and EDWARD CARPENTER—though certainly not the first frank homosexual letters by a Western writer are the first surviving examples in history of extensive and candid homosexual correspondence. They are a goldmine of Victorian homosexual experience and consciousness. Furthermore, the private circulation of Symonds's work, especially

of *A Problem in Modern Ethics,* whose fifty original copies were passed to many more hands, helped create toward the end of his life a confidential network of informed homosexuals who regarded him as a liberationist leader, "the Gladstone of the affair" as HENRY JAMES, one of that network's most interested members, dubbed him in an 1893 letter.

Symonds also included homosexual implication or direct content in his published work from relatively early in his career and increasingly in his final years. In his 1876 *Studies of the Greek Poets, Second Series,* Symonds's effusive praise of Greek "friendship" and his brief remark that in ancient Greece "even paiderastia had its honourable aspects" led to a withering 1877 review essay, "The Greek Spirit in Modern Literature" by Richard St. John Tyrwhitt. The critic's persistent use of coded language suggests that Symonds's homosexuality was already known to some resourceful Victorian readers: Tyrwhitt refers to Symonds's praise of "phallic ecstasy," to his "palpitations at male beauty," and to "the divine youths whose beauties he appreciates so thoroughly." Symonds's complete translation of MICHELANGELO's sonnets in 1878 was the first in English and the first based on the accurate 1863 Gausti text, which corrected Michelangelo the Younger's heterosexualizing of the poems in his 1623 edition. Although not blunt about the sonnets' homosexuality, Symonds comes closer to divulging it than ever before by mentioning the earlier bowdlerizing of the poems about "masculine beauty" and by translating the sonnets to Tommaso Cavalieri in their true, male-male, form for the first time.

In addition, the four books of poems Symonds published publicly—*Many Moods* (1878), *New and Old* (1880), *Animi Figura* (1882), and *Vagabunduli Libellus* (1884)—have some protective heterosexual or sexually undifferentiated pieces, but also contain enough frankly ardent male-male declarations that it is difficult to see how readers could not have been startled by them. For example, in "The Meeting of David and Jonathan" (*Many Moods*), Jonathan takes David "In his arms of strength / [and] in that kiss / Soul into soul was knit and bliss to bliss"; and in "The Ponte di Paradiso" (*New and Old*), a male speaker in contemporary Venice frankly evokes a lost male love:

"Once more, a living god, he stands, / . . . what electric thrill, / 'Twixt me and him, / Shot with a sudden ache that still / Makes daylight dim." Many of these poems are taken from Symonds's private pamphlets, and, correspondingly, Symonds admitted in letters and his *Memoirs* that the most heterosexual of them (such as the sonnet sequence "Stella Maris" in *Vagabunduli Libellus*) "were mutilated [from their manuscript form] to adapt them to the female sex" and actually refer to other men.

In 1891, Symonds began publishing poems in journals that interested contemporaries knew were associated with homosexuality, first *The Artist*, which had taken on a definite homosexual aspect after Charles Kains-Jackson became editor in 1888, and later *The Spirit Lamp*, edited at Oxford by LORD ALFRED DOUGLAS. In addition, Symonds's last three books, all for wider audiences and all published in 1893, contain degrees of homosexual assertiveness. Three essays in the collection *In the Key of Blue*—"The Dantesque and Platonic Ideals of Love," "Edward Cracroft Lefroy," and "Clifton and a Lad's Love"—raise the subjects of "Hellenic instincts" and "the affection of a man for a man." In his biography of Michelangelo, he maintains a transparent level of euphemism while working to dismantle the myth of Michelangelo's attachment to Vittoria Colonna and discussing in extensive detail Michelangelo's passionate poems and letters to Cavalieri and other men; he also reports his own discovery in the Buonarroti archives that earlier scholars had suppressed and distorted Michelangelo's letters, just as earlier editors had falsified his poems. In his *Walt Whitman: A Study,* Symonds's contradictory discussion of the *Calamus* poems is the most blatant example in his widely available criticism of the strain he felt at his culture's insistence on homosexuality's "unspeakableness." Together with his reading of the *Phaedrus* and the *Symposium* in his last year at Harrow, which gave him "the true *liber amoris* at last, . . . the sanction of the love which had been ruling me from childhood," Symonds's discovery of Whitman and his "love of comrades" in 1865 transformed his life, and from 1871 he pursued Whitman in correspondence about the homosexual meaning of *Calamus,* finally receiving in August 1890 Whitman's apparently conclusive disavowal of Symonds's "morbid inferences." While acknowledging this letter in his study of Whitman, and stating that "an impartial critic will [conclude] that what he calls the 'adhesiveness' of comradeship is meant to have no interblending with . . . sexual love," Symonds also persists in raising homosexual possibilities, declaring, for example, that "I am not certain whether his own feelings upon this delicate topic may not have altered since the time when 'Calamus' was first composed"

and that "Whitman recognises among the sacred emotions . . . an intense, jealous, throbbing, sensitive, expectant love of man for man, . . . a love that finds honest delight in hand-touch, meeting lips, hours of privacy, close personal contact."

This strand of Symonds's widely available work, together with the confidential knowledge circulating as a result of his private writings, made Symonds's homosexuality an open secret in Victorian literary and cultural circles by the time of his death. For example, in an 1894 essay, SWINBURNE castigated "the cult of the calamus, as expounded by Mr. Addington Symonds and his fellow-calamites" and dubbed Symonds "The Platonic amorist of blue-breeched gondoliers who is now in Aretino's bosom." Contrastingly, in May 1893, *The Artist* published a strikingly frank memorial poem, calling Symonds "comrade dear" and proclaiming "'Let men be lovers,' your voice rang clear, / 'Let men be lovers, and Truth be Truth.'"

The same mixture of information spurred Havelock Ellis to inquire in a July 1891 letter about Symonds's work on "this question of Greek love in modern life." The query led ultimately to Symonds's final, posthumous, and briefly acknowledged publication, his collaboration with Ellis on *Sexual Inversion.* Symonds died ten months into the project, but he had contributed the literary and historical discussions to the manuscript, as well as several of the case histories, gleaned from the many private letters he had received in response to *A Problem in Modern Ethics.* When *Sexual Inversion* appeared, first in German translation in 1896 and then in England in 1897, Symonds was listed as coauthor. *A Problem in Greek Ethics* saw public print for the first time as Appendix A, and Symonds also contributed Appendix C, "Ulrichs's Views" (originally Chapter IX of *A Problem in Modern Ethics*). Horrified at the book's frankness, Horatio Brown, Symonds's literary executor, withdrew his permission for Ellis to cite Symonds and attempted to buy up the entire printing for destruction. Consequently, in the second British printing later in 1897, Symonds was removed as coauthor and identified in the text only as "Z" (a "friend" to whom Ellis is "more especially indebted"), the appendix on Ulrichs was retained (but now authored by "Z"), and *A Problem in Greek Ethics* was deleted. Symonds was never listed again on the title page of *Sexual Inversion,* which eventually became Part Two of Volume II of Ellis's collected *Studies in the Psychology of Sex.* These events could be a parable of Symonds's reputation in the decades after his death. Surreptitious reprints of *A Problem in Modern Ethics* and *A Problem in Greek Ethics* appeared in England in 1901 and 1896, respectively, and a reprint of *A Problem in*

Greek Ethics appeared in Holland in 1908, suggesting continued interest in Symonds's work among an underground of homosexual readers. Discreet biographies by Horatio Brown (1895) and Van Wyck Brooks (1914) were also published. But Symonds's standing faded in the first half of the twentieth century. Interest in him began to revive only in the 1960s, with Phyllis Grosskurth's then pathbreaking biography (1964), the first to discuss any Victorian homosexual frankly, and with Herbert M. Schueller and Robert L. Peters's invaluable three-volume collection of Symonds's letters (1967–1969). It has swelled with the emergence of gay studies.

Symonds was aware of his "persistent passion for the male sex" from his earliest erotic recollections, but his pioneering homosexual work was not accomplished without considerable strain against, and concession to, the "social law" of his time, which "regarded this love as abominable and unnatural." Among these strains and concessions were his unwitting precipitation of the homosexual scandal that drove Charles John Vaughan from the headmastership of Harrow in 1859; his 1864 marriage and eventual fathering of four children; his persistent health crises, leading to a diagnosis of tuberculosis in 1865 and a move to the Swiss Alps in 1877; and his 1868 mental breakdown and contemplation of suicide. But those developments must be seen together with positive milestones like his mettle in writing to William Johnson (later Cory) in 1859 after reading *Ionica* and "exposing the state of my feelings and asking his advice"; his relationships with Willie Dyer, Alfred Brooke, Norman Moor (with whom he had his first experience of sexual intercourse with another male, at the age of twenty-nine), and Angelo Fusato; and his monumental, seven-volume, *Renaissance in Italy* (1875–1886), the first full-scale study of the subject in English, which gained him his greatest professional recognition.

Symonds's work poses a sharp challenge to the currently dominant argument in gay studies that homosexuality and homosexuals are late nineteenth-century "inventions," functions chiefly of that period's new "medicalization of homosexuality," with its coining of the actual terminology of "homosexuality." In his *Memoirs*, Symonds clearly presents himself as someone with a de facto homosexual orientation and a definite sense of social difference because of it long before the new sexological literature started to burgeon in the late 1880s. That literature was available at the time of his *Memoirs*, however, so Symonds could have been influenced by it as he wrote the book. But in the *Memoirs* chapters concerned most analytically with his sexual development and awareness, Symonds inserted statements in the manuscript indicating that he had not yet read the new sexologists when he wrote them. Perhaps even more significant, the new terminology of "homosexuality" is completely absent from Symonds's self-portrait in the *Memoirs*. His favorite terms for his orientation there are either earlier categorical language like "masculine love" or extended descriptive phrases that amount to direct de facto denotations of the subject, like "passion between males" or "a man's love for a man." We need to look elsewhere to explain Symonds's early and persistent search for "men constituted like me" and for positive images of homosexuality and his status as the first and foremost nineteenth-century British homosexual writer to "put the facts on record . . . so that fellow-sufferers . . . should feel that they are not alone." (See also ENGLISH LITERATURE: NINETEENTH CENTURY.)

—*Joseph Cady*

BIBLIOGRAPHY

Cady, Joseph. "'What Cannot Be': John Addington Symonds's *Memoirs* and Official Mappings of Victorian Homosexuality." *Victorian Newsletter* 81 (Spring 1992): 47–51. ■ Ellis, Havelock, and John Addington Symonds. *Sexual Inversion*. London: Wilson and Macmillan, 1897. Reprint. New York: Arno Press, 1975. ■ Grosskurth, Phyllis. *The Woeful Victorian: A Biography of John Addington Symonds*. New York: Holt, Rinehart and Winston, 1964. ■ Reade, Brian, ed. *Sexual Heretics: Male Homosexuality in English Literature from 1850 to 1900*. New York: Coward-McCann, 1971. ■ Schueller, Herbert M., and Robert L. Peters, eds. *The Letters of John Addington Symonds*. 3 vols. Detroit: Wayne State University Press, 1967–1969.

§ *Takahashi, Mutsuo*
(*b.* 1937)

Japanese writer Mutsuo Takahashi was born in Japan on December 15, 1937, and educated at Fukuoka University of Education. His poetry and work in the drama are internationally recognized.

Takahashi has published several volumes of poetry, including *You Dirty Ones, Do Dirtier Things* (1966), *Poems Of A Penisist* (1975), *The Structure Of The Kingdom* (1982), *A Bunch Of Keys* (1984), *Prac-*

tice/Drinking Eating (1988), *The Garden Of Rabbits* (1988), and *Sleeping Sinning Falling* (1992). Few poets bring as much skill and passion to their poems, especially those that consider homosexual desire, as does Takahashi. He has received many prestigious awards for his work, including the Reketei Prize, the Yomiuri Prize, and the Takami Jun Prize.

His work in drama has also earned acclaim. He won the Yamamoto Kenkichi Prize in 1987 for his stage script called *Princess Medea*. Other works in drama include an adaptation of W. B. Yeats's play *At The Hawk's Well* and a noh play inspired by Georges Bataille's *Le Proces de Gil de Rais*.

Even in his earliest work, Takahashi writes with vitality and precision about homosexual desire. Although Japan does not outlaw homosexual relations, the homosexual there remains an outcast because often he does not engage in the rituals and practices of Japanese family life. The "okama" ("queen") is laughed at and ostracized. The more he is ostracized, the easier it is to keep the laughter going—at the okama's expense. Takahashi's poems give dignity to the okama, celebrating both his sexual desires and his outcast status.

Moreover, most of Takahashi's explicitly gay work celebrates desire, finding joy in the male body much as WALT WHITMAN's poems do. The poems eagerly name body parts as they probe desire and longing. The speaker of Takahashi's masterful poem "Ode" celebrates his erotic and promiscuous life much as a priest celebrates the Eucharist. This 1,000-line poem begins with a parody of the Mass: "In the name of / Man, member, / and the holy fluid, / AMEN." As the speaker seeks out sex in the places most frowned on by his society, he is reborn, saved by each new encounter. The glory hole, for example, takes on spiritual significance. Only what is "made flesh" satisfies.

Poems Of A Penisist is one of the most important collections of poetry on homosexual desire and sex written in this century. The personae in these poems do not compromise—they see the world as outsiders ("a faggot that fingers point at") but being outsiders brings them joy and meaning. As the majority society mocks and condemns them, their joy in their identity as gay men, as individuals who enjoy pleasure with other men, gives them strength. In this collection, the speakers consider both their present and their past, sometimes by exploring family memories, such as the uncle who died at age twenty-two and will be forever remembered by one speaker as "this young god." The implication is that even as a very young boy, the speaker was preparing for his future erotic life—both in the flesh and on the page. (See also JAPANESE LITERATURE.)

—*Kenneth Pobo*

BIBLIOGRAPHY

Takahashi, Mutsuo. *Poems Of A Penisist*. Trans. Heroaki Sato. Chicago: Chicago Review Press, 1975. ■ ———. *A Bunch Of Keys*. Trans. Heroaki Sato. Trumansburg, N.Y.: Crossing Press, 1984. ■ ———. *Sleeping Sinning Falling*. Trans. Heroaki Sato. San Francisco: City Lights Books, 1992.

Teasdale, Sara
(1884–1933)

Sara Teasdale might be viewed as a casualty of the struggle between propriety and passion that marked late Victorian social mores. Born in St. Louis into a genteel middle-class family, she was overprotected by her mother, who instilled in her young daughter an anxiety about her own body—its physical inadequacy and its ailments—that was to affect both her work and her personal relationships for most of her brief life. Because of her mother's fears, Teasdale was educated at home until she was nine, and, left to herself, she retreated into her own dreamy world; she spent hours fantasizing about the romantic possibilities of her own life. Keeping reality at a tasteful distance became a habit of her life and of her art.

Although she cultivated romantic obsessions about men, the strongest relationships in her life were with women. After completing her college education at Hosmer Hall in St. Louis, she and several other young women formed a literary association called The Potters, which published a monthly magazine, *The Potter's Wheel*, in which Teasdale's early poems appeared. Many of her early works were addressed to particular women, whose identities were disguised. Her first major work was a set of effusive sonnets in praise of Eleonora Duse, which was included in her first collection, *Sonnets to Duse and Other Poems* (1907).

In 1908, Teasdale formed an intense friendship with Marion Cummings Stanley, with whom she was able for the first time to discuss matters such as her own ill health and her curiosity about sex. Their friendship temporarily released Teasdale from the constrictions of her rigid upbringing, and she commemorated it in a poem entitled "Song," which concludes "For all my world is in your arms, / My sun and stars are you" (from *Helen of Troy and Other Poems,* 1911). At the same time, Teasdale was also carrying on a correspondence that mixed flirtation and serious poetic debate with John Myers O'Hara, a young poet living in New York. This was the first of a series of passionate relationships with men that were conducted by Teasdale almost entirely from afar. They corresponded for over three years before they finally met face to face, and the meeting was a disappointment for both of them.

Teasdale traveled widely, although while abroad she spent much of her time abed with one illness or another. When she settled in New York, she formed friendships with Jessie Rittenhouse (a founder of the Poetry Society) and John Hall Wheelock, another young poet, with whom she fell seriously in love. His unwillingness to commit himself to her seems to have been part of the attraction, but despite that handicap, they remained friends for the remainder of her life. Her poetry was becoming more widely known, and generally praised, and with the publication of *Rivers to the Sea* (1915), she was acknowledged as a significant American writer.

Teasdale's physical and emotional health, however, remained frail. As she approached the age of thirty, she became almost frantic to be married, and indeed at one point she had several suitors to choose from. The poet Vachel Lindsay pursued her with passion and ardent verse, but he was too wild for her, and she settled for the businessman Ernst Filsinger, a fellow St. Louisan. She was full of hope about this union, but in the end she was unable to reconcile her romantic fantasies with the realities of married life. "I am not yours, not lost in you," she wrote in a poem composed just before their wedding in 1914. And afterward, "why . . . alone for me / is there no ecstasy?" ("Midnight Rain," 1915). She sued Filsinger for divorce in 1929.

Teasdale's emotional life became more and more unstable, and she fell into deep depressions from which she gradually lost the will to extract herself. The poems in *Flame and Shadow* (1920) and *Dark of the Moon* (1926) are darker than her earlier, simpler lyrics, and many of them deal with her lifelong preoccupation with death. The last great friendship of her life was with Margaret Conklin, a young student who came into Teasdale's life in 1926 and wooed her almost like a lover. Teasdale saw in Conklin the reincarnation of herself as a child, and their relationship was profound and complex. If there was a lesbian component to it, however, it was probably unacknowledged. In January 1933, at the age of forty-eight, weighed down by despair, Teasdale ingested a large number of sedatives and was found dead in her bathtub the following morning. *Strange Victory,* including a poem to Conklin, was published later that year.

— *Ann Wadsworth*

BIBLIOGRAPHY

Carpenter, Margaret H. *Sara Teasdale: A Biography.* New York: Schulte, 1960. ■ Drake, William. *Sara Teasdale: Woman & Poet.* San Francisco: Harper & Row, 1979. ■ Schoen, Carol B. *Sara Teasdale.* Boston: Twayne Publishers, 1986.

Tennyson, Alfred Lord
(1809–1892)

Surely few literary figures so directly challenge reductive notions of sexual identity as does the Victorian poet Alfred Lord Tennyson. *In Memoriam* is both Tennyson's greatest work and the most beautiful homoerotic ELEGY in the English language, yet there is little doubt that Tennyson himself was sexually attracted to women. Androgynous male characters and homoeroticism abound throughout Tennyson's poetry, particularly from his early years, but he is often considered one of the stuffiest and most prudish of his generation of writers. So, one might ask, what does one do with Tennyson? Rather than dismissing him as an anomaly, it seems much more productive to allow Tennyson to disrupt our overly easy classifications of writers and to recognize through his work that transgression is much more common than rigid adherence to narrow, though convenient, literary and sexual categories.

Tennyson's life and career spans the nineteenth century, capturing the Victorian age in many of its complexities. Born on August 6, 1809, in Somersby, England, to an Anglican minister, George Clayton Tennyson, and his wife, Elizabeth Fytche Tennyson, Alfred demonstrated his considerable poetic talents at a very early age, composing his first lines of verse at age five and his first poem at age eight. He and his brothers Frederick and Charles produced a full book of poetry in 1827, when Alfred was barely eighteen. After studying at Cambridge University and benefiting from the added intellectual stimulation of a literary society there called the "Apostles," his creative activity accelerated, and he published increasingly successful volumes of poetry in 1830, 1832, and 1842. But these were also turbulent years for Tennyson; his father died in 1831, his beloved friend Hallam (for whom *In Memoriam* was later written) died in Vienna in 1833, he had a series of painful, unrequited romantic attachments to women during his twenties and thirties, and in 1843 he finally entered a mental hospital to recover from a nervous collapse. But Tennyson continued writing and revising his poetry, and he recovered to receive the highest acclaim possible for his efforts. In 1845, he was granted a permanent government stipend to support his work, and by 1850, when *In Memoriam* was published, he had become the favorite of Queen Victoria, who named him Poet Laureate in that year, filling the vacancy left by the death of William Wordsworth. In 1850, he also married the woman he had loved for many years, Emily Sellwood, with whom he later had two children. His successes continued, as Tennyson produced new volumes of poetry and plays (although the latter have been practically forgotten) every two or three years for the remainder of his life. Tennyson was again honored in 1883 by being named the first Lord Tennyson, and even though his reputation among critics waned somewhat as the years passed, he continued to be widely loved and respected until his death from influenza on October 6, 1892.

What helps make all this remarkable and Tennyson's work of immediate relevance for gay audiences is that Tennyson's extraordinary success and wide following were built on poetry that included numerous homoerotic situations and allusions. However, it is clearly erroneous to call Tennyson a "gay" poet; the term is anachronistic when discussing the Victorian age and it is doubtful that Tennyson ever had sexual contact with another man. Yet Tennyson's work is important to include in any consideration of a larger gay literary heritage because of its profound emotional content and stunning beauty, which can still speak to audiences today, even though it was written during a period often considered sexually and emotionally sterile.

Expressions of love between men and intriguingly androgynous characters are found throughout Tennyson's early poetry. His "Mort d'Arthur" (1842) portrays the passing of the great medieval king as he is attended by his loving, though somewhat wavering, attendant Sir Bedivere; the latter cradles his dying companion in his arms and sheds numerous tears over Arthur's death and the passing of an entire age of heroism. Similarly, "Sir Galahad" (1842) is an evocation of a period and mindset far removed from that of narrow Victorian definitions of masculinity. Calling himself a "maiden knight," Galahad describes his earnest search for the Holy Grail after seeing it once in a vision; Tennyson uses Galahad effectively and transgressively as a symbol of purity in body and spirit, a man whose "virgin heart" is given to his God. Such androgyny abounds as well in "The Princess" (1847), which concerns the exploits of an effeminate, tender-hearted Prince who loves a feminist, separatist woman; they are finally united after the Prince cross-dresses in order to enter her private university for women. The androgynous Prince continues to challenge Victorian gender stereotypes even after his somewhat predictable conquest of the Princess, by imagining a future when the sexes will become increasingly similar to one another. Finally, Tennyson portrays chaste but tenderly expressed love between men in a later poem entitled "The Holy Grail" (1869). Again set at the time of King Arthur, the poem begins with the knight Sir Percivale telling of his exploits to the adoring monk Ambrosius, who "loved him much beyond the rest, / And honor'd him, and wrought into his heart / A way by love that waken'd love within" (9–11). Here we meet once more Sir Galahad, whom King Arthur calls "beautiful" and who is chaste enough to see the Grail. But such is denied Percivale, who is good but humanly fallible; he is tempted by visions that include a lovely woman beckoning to him but also a splendid knight who "Open'd his arms to embrace me as he came, / And up I went and touch'd him, and he too / Fell to dust, and I was left alone / And wearying in a land of sand and thorns" (417–420). Percivale fails in his mission to find the Grail but ends up living with the monk, who peevishly tries to elicit an admission of love from Percivale. But like his beloved, Ambrosius too is denied that which he most desires.

Such portrayals of chaste male love during a bygone era are juxtaposed with other visions of sensual indulgence that clearly cause Tennyson considerable anxiety. A severe critic of his own age, Tennyson used carefully drawn images of "debauchery" between men as a sign of social and moral degeneration. This practice is seen most clearly in "The Vision of Sin" (1842), where the narrator tells of a drunken, cynical man, a failed poet, who has squandered his youth and energies in pleasure seeking. The poet is first shown as a chaste youth approaching a palace, into which "a child of sin" leads him "by the curls" (5–6); there he encounters a "company" whose sex remains unrevealed, but who engage in orgiastic behavior, panting "hand-in-hand with faces pale" (19), catching each other "with wild grimaces" (35), twisting "hard in fierce embraces" (40), and finally collapsing in "luxurious agony" (43). That Tennyson is hinting at homosexual activity here is given support later in the poem when the aged, unsuccessful poet calls over a degenerate waiter, one who has been "a sinner too" (92), saying "We are men of ruin'd blood" (99) and suggesting that they join in "Friendship!—to be two in one" (107). They drink to "Frantic love and frantic hate" (150). The poet later cries drunkenly "Buss [kiss] me thou rough sketch of man, / Far too naked to be shamed!" (189–190). Throughout the poem, images of transgressive, even horrific, sensuality are mingled with ones of violence and death to portray the spiritual agony of a lost soul, one who may represent an age of abandon and indulgence that stands in stark contrast to that of the pure love shared by the men of King Arthur's court.

But even if Tennyson viewed erotic contact between men with some alarm, he cannot be termed simplistically "homophobic," for his greatest achievement was a monumental poem professing his profound emotional attachment to another man. *In Memoriam* (first published 1850, revised repeatedly thereafter) is a testament to the marriage of souls and lasting emotional ties between Alfred and his friend Hallam, even after the latter's tragically early demise. *In Memoriam* is both long and difficult, containing 131 separate groups of stanzas, arranged broadly around three Christmas celebrations following Hallam's death. The poem as a whole moves from despair to reconciliation to hope as Tennyson learns to accept the passing of his beloved and even rejoice in another person's wedding celebration. But the journey to such acceptance is long and arduous, and the poem's early stanzas express the poet's agonizing loneliness. Tennyson questions God over the senseless death of one "whom I found so fair" (Prologue 38). Referring to himself often as "widow'd" and Hallam as his "love," Tennyson speaks powerfully to any reader who has endured the death of a close friend or lover, describing accurately the sense of physical loss: "A void where heart on heart reposed; / And, where warm hands have prest and closed" (XIII 5–6). Such physicality gives the poem a consistently romantic, if not always sexual, texture, as Tennyson imagines "falling on [Hallam's] faithful heart" and "breathing thro' his lips" to revive the dying man (XVIII 14–15). But ending this first section is a note of hope, for Tennyson makes the now famous claim that "'Tis better to have loved and lost / Than never to have loved at all" (XXVII 15–16).

Moving slowly through despair and doubt, Tennyson states mournfully that "I shall be thy mate no more" (XLI 20), as he constantly battles depression and feelings of hopelessness. But Tennyson repeatedly proclaims that his love will endure, and making reference to SHAKESPEARE's homoerotic sonnets, implies that his poem will itself immortalize his friend (LXI 9–12). Throughout, Tennyson indicates that he and Hallam are linked forever, as he refers to the two as "a single soul" (LXXXIV 44). But the sense of physical loss takes years to diminish, as Tennyson cries long after Hallam's death "Descend, and touch, and enter; here / The wish too strong for words to name, / That in this blindness of the frame / My Ghost may feel that thine is near" (XCIII 13–16). Something of a supernatural reunion does take place as Tennyson finds some comfort in two of Hallam's remaining letters, "So word by word, and line by line, / The dead man touch'd me from the past, / And all at once it seem'd at last / His living soul was flash'd on mine, / And mine in his was wound" (XCV 33–37). This section comes closest to an expression of something approaching sexual contact, and Tennyson revised it in 1878 to read "*The* living soul . . ." and "mine in *this* . . ." reacting perhaps to a new consciousness near the end of the century concerning the implications of physical contact between men and the seemingly erotic content of the original description.

In any case, the poem thereafter moves toward its close, as if the quasi-physical reunion was enough to assure Tennyson that he and his friend would reunite after death: "Dear friend, far off, my lost desire, / So far, so near in woe and weal, / O loved the most, when most I feel / There is a lower and a higher; / Known and unknown, human, divine; / Sweet human hand and lips and eye; / Dear heavenly friend that canst not die, / Mine, mine for ever, ever mine" (CXXIX 1–8). As Tennyson watches the marriage of his sister at the end of the poem, he imagines "A stiller guest, / Perchance, perchance, among the rest, / And, tho' in silence, wishing joy" (Epilogue 86–88). In the course of the elegy, Tennyson has moved through stages of denial, anger, and acceptance, as he comes to view the world again with hope, infused with the memories of his beloved comrade and full of expectation of a tender reunion. That he and Hallam probably never had sexual contact is practically irrelevant given the profound beauty of the emotions expressed in the poem and the enduring power of Tennyson's recovery of joy after long despair.

The changes that Tennyson made in the preceding lines, ones that work to erase some of the most obvious sexual energy in the poem, augered yet another indication that late in his life and late in the century, Tennyson felt a degree of self-consciousness about his early effusions over androgyny and male-male emotional attachment. In 1889, just three years before his death, Tennyson wrote the short poem "On One Who Affected an Effeminate Manner": "While man and woman still are incomplete, / I prize that soul where man and woman meet, / Which types all Nature's male and female plan / But, friend, man-woman is not woman-man." This epigram condemns "effeminate" men for inverting the "natural" gender order and placing "feminine" or "womanly" characteristics above "masculine," "manly" ones. Such condemnation of inversion no doubt relates to the late nineteenth-century medical denunciation of sexual and gender nonconformity as unnatural and indicative of a stunted or warped IDENTITY. Tennyson's own son Hallam (named after Tennyson's beloved, of course) seemed particularly uncomfortable with the homoeroticism of some of his father's poetry and as an adult expended considerable anxious energy on refuting any "perverse" readings of *In Memoriam* and earlier works.

Given Tennyson's own clear interest in specifically male experience and emotional attachment (though he did write many poems about beautiful, ethereal women), it is not surprising that there is little to be found in his poetry that relates to lesbian desire or romantic attachments between women. In fact, the only passing reference is found in *The Princess* when the young feminist states that she and a fellow student are "faster welded in one love / Than pairs of wedlock" (IV 236–237); in hinting at romantic involvement between transgressive women, Tennyson participates in a tendency among the Victorians to portray rebellious women as sexually nonconformist, even homosexual. This allowed patriarchal Victorian men to claim that the women's movement threatened the very cornerstone of Victorian society: the nuclear, heterosexual family. Certainly it provided one of many excuses contained within the context of the poem for the harsh treatment that the rebellious women receive as they are conquered and reintegrated into Victorian heterosexual culture.

Thus Tennyson clearly does not fit into convenient categories such as "radical" or even "progressive"; rather, he, like so many of his contemporaries, was an eager participant in the ongoing debates on gender roles and the place of emotion and commitment in a society that seemed obsessed with technological progress and the accumulation of wealth. As part of his explorations of alternative forms for social organization and moral engagement, he looked to homosocial bonding as one source for positive (in the case of men) or negative (in the case of women) emotional ties that might have an effect upon the fragmentation that he saw around him. But homosocial and homosexual desire are not always easily distinguishable, and certainly in *In Memoriam* the boundary between platonic and actively erotic forms of love seems fuzzy. In this way, Tennyson challenges our own ability to classify writers as "gay" and "straight." Though heterosexual, Tennyson wrote poetry dealing with love between men that is still capable of evoking a profound response from gay audiences today and that has an important place in any consideration of gay literary history. (See also ENGLISH LITERATURE: NINETEENTH CENTURY.)

—Donald E. Hall

BIBLIOGRAPHY

Dellamora, Richard. *Masculine Desire: The Sexual Politics of Victorian Aestheticism.* Chapel Hill: University of North Carolina Press, 1990. ■ Faderman, Lillian. *Surpassing the Love of Men: Romantic Friendship and Love between Women from the Renaissance to the Present.* New York: Morrow, 1981. ■ Hoeveler, Diane. "Manly-Women and Womanly-Men: Tennyson's Androgynous Ideal in *The Princess* and *In Memoriam*." *Michigan Occasional Papers in Women's Studies.* No. 19. Ann Arbor: University of Michigan, 1982. ■ Martin, Robert Bernard. *Tennyson: The Unquiet Heart.* Oxford: Oxford University Press, 1980. ■ Nunokawa, Jeff. "In Memoriam and the Extinction of the Homosexual." *ELH* 58 (1991): 427–448. ■ Ricks, Christopher. *Tennyson.* 2d ed. Berkeley: University of California Press, 1989. ■ Sedgwick, Eve Kosofsky. *Between Men: English Literature and Male Homosocial Desire.* New York: Columbia University Press, 1985. ■ Shaw, Marion. *Alfred Lord Tennyson.* Atlantic Highlands, N.J.: Humanities Press International, 1988. ■ Sinfield, Alan. *Alfred Tennyson.* Oxford: Basil Blackwell, 1986. ■ Tennyson, Alfred Lord. *The Works of Alfred Lord Tennyson.* 6 vols. New York: Macmillan, 1903.

Theocritus
(ca 308–240 B.C.E.)

Little is known of Theocritus, the first great voice in the homoerotic pastoral tradition. He appears to have been born in Sicily in the late fourth century B.C.E., and to have lived both at the court of Ptolemy Philadelphius (patron of the great poetic school of Alexandria) and in Syracuse, where he is reputed to have died around 240 B.C.E. His significance for gay literary history resides in the fact that five of his thirty *Idylls* map the emotional and poetic terrains of intense—especially frustrated—homosexual desire that later poets would explore in greater detail.

Theocritus' pastoral idylls figure the naturalness of homoerotic desire through nature itself. "The Beloved Boy" (Idyll 12), for example, compares the delight that the speaker feels at his lover's return after a two-day absence to the exuberance one experiences when spring begins budding after a long winter. After referring to Diocles, an Athenian who died saving the life of the boy he loved and in whose honor kissing contests are held every spring at his tomb, the speaker says that he hopes likewise to be remembered 200 years after his death as a faithful lover of beautiful boys.

But if nature figures the possibility of emotional and sensual bliss, it also threatens the possibility of tempest and wintry sterility. Theocritus' other homoerotic idylls focus largely on the pain of frustrated or lost love. "Hylas" (Idyll 13)—one of the most famous homosexual lyrics of the ancient world—subverts the traditionally heroic values of Greek poetry by noting how even Hercules could not resist loving a beautiful boy, "golden-haired Hylas," who drowned when, trying to fetch water for his lover, he was pulled down by the nymphs of the stream who fell in love with him and wanted to keep him as their own. "The struggles and frustrations of love stand in for the mortal peril of heroic combat," notes David Halperin, as Hercules, unable to save his lover, lapses into madness in his grief. For Theocritus, love's power is stronger than the physical might of even the greatest hero.

Dominated by seasonal change, the natural world makes Theocritus' remaining pastoral speakers acutely conscious of both the transience of human affection and of the aging process that must inevitably destroy the sweet bloom of youth. "The Lover" (Idyll 23), a dramatic lament spoken by a man moments before he kills himself for unrequited love, warns the heartless boy that as he ages his beauty will harden and he will himself "burn" and "weep" for a cruel boy. Similarly, "For a Boy" (Idyll 29) warns a beautiful young man who scorns the speaker's love that he too will age and his beauty lose its freshness. Thus, if he does not "show more kindness" and "return the love of a man who is true" now when he is young and lovable, no one will show him any affection later when he himself is old and desperate for a beautiful young

man's attention. As this poem in particular demonstrates, the poignancy of Theocritus' *Idylls* lies in their assumption that no matter how painful it is to lose the boy whom one loves, or not to have one's love returned, it is impossible *not* to fall madly in love with a beautiful boy. The speaker of "For Another Boy" (Idyll 30), who finds himself falling in love again after a particularly painful experience, knows full well that "as a man grows old, / he should steer himself clear of the love of young boys." Love, however, answers him that the only alternative to loving a boy is simply ceasing to exist.

Few classical poets have explored the natural realm of passion with as much psychological penetration as Theocritus, or with as lasting an influence. His *Idylls* are the source of a homoerotic pastoral tradition that includes VIRGIL's second eclogue, Spenser's *Shepherd's Calendar,* and BARNFIELD's *Affectionate Shepherd,* as well as anticipates the homoerotic confusion in the Forest of Arden in SHAKESPEARE's *As You Like It,* MILTON's "Lycidas," and possibly even WHITMAN's *Calamus* poems. With the biblical Song of Songs, Theocritus' *Idylls* provided a model that allows for the configuration of the male body with the natural landscape, Nature herself permitting the unleashing of homoerotic desire. But unfortunately, as so many of Theocritus' speakers learn, if homoerotic desire is as simple and effortless as Nature herself, it is just as easily disrupted or frustrated by the naturalness of aging or of changing affections. (See also PASTORAL.)

—*Raymond-Jean Frontain*

BIBLIOGRAPHY

Dover, K. J. *Greek Homosexuality.* Cambridge: Harvard University Press, 1978. ■ Frontain, Raymond-Jean. "Mad about the Boy: Review Essay." *The James White Review* 9 (Spring 1992): 18–19. ■ Halperin, David M. *Before Pastoral: Theocritus and the Ancient Tradition of Bucolic Poetry.* New Haven: Yale University Press, 1983. ■ Mastronarde, Donald J. "Theocritus' Idyll 13: Love and the Hero." *Transactions of the American Philosophical Association* 99 (1968): 273–290. ■ Segal, Charles. *Poetry and Myth in Ancient Pastoral: Essays on Theocritus and Virgil.* Princeton: Princeton University Press, 1981. ■ Sergent, Bernard. *Homosexuality in Greek Myth.* Trans. Arthur Goldhammer. Boston: Beacon Press, 1986. ■ Theocritus. *The Idylls. Greek Pastoral Poetry.* Trans. Anthony Holden. Baltimore: Penguin, 1974. 43–153.

Thoreau, Henry David

(1817–1862)

Henry David Thoreau was born in Concord, Massachusetts, on July 12, 1817. He attended the newly founded Concord Academy and,

after taking several leaves from his studies to earn money and to regain his health after his first attack of tuberculosis, went on to graduate from Harvard with the class of 1837. Thoreau is perhaps best known for his stay at Walden Pond, chronicled in *Walden* (1854), and his night in jail after refusing to pay a poll tax to a government that supported the Mexican War and endorsed slavery. He wrote about this latter act of protest in "Resistance to Civil Government," popularly known as "Civil Disobedience," an essay that has inspired many, including Gandhi and Martin Luther King, Jr. In addition to *Walden* and his well-known speeches and essays on antebellum social concerns, he wrote *A Week on the Concord and Merrimack Rivers* (1849), based on a canoe trip he took with his brother, John. Thoreau kept voluminous journals and wrote essays about nature, perception, and science, many of which were published posthumously. These include *The Maine Woods, Cape Cod,* and the recently compiled *Natural History Essays* and *Faith in a Seed.* Thoreau died May 6, 1862, of tuberculosis, the same disease that had earlier killed both his brother and father.

Biographers remain undecided about Thoreau's sexuality. He never married. He proposed to Ellen Sewall in 1840, but she rejected his offer. Some believe he was a "repressed" homosexual and others that he was asexual and remained celibate all of his life. But his *Journals,* his essay "Chastity and Sensuality," and the long discourse on "Friendship" in *A Week* are prolific expressions of the beauty, and the agony, of love between men. Some of these discussions are said to refer to his brother or to Ralph Waldo Emerson. Others clearly refer to two men whom Thoreau found particularly attractive: Tom Fowler, whom Thoreau chose as a guide on a trip to the Maine woods; and Alek Therien, the Canadian woodchopper who visited Thoreau at Walden Pond.

The passion evident in his discourses on love and friendship, and the utter lack of reference to women in his writings, has made Thoreau of great interest to scholars of gay and lesbian literature. Jonathan Katz included a section on Thoreau in his *Gay American History.* Walter Harding, the distinguished Thoreau scholar, argued quite convincingly in 1991 that Thoreau's "actions and words . . . indicate a specific sexual interest in members of his own sex." Complicating matters concerning Thoreau's sexuality is historical research suggesting that homosexual IDENTITY is a late nineteenth-century phenomenon. But, as Michael Warner suggests, Thoreau's writing resists normalization even within nineteenth-century "rhetorics of romance and sexuality." Although Thoreau may not have identified as "homosexual" in the way a twentieth-century gay man might, his rhetoric of sexual difference strikes a chord with gay readers and anticipates an emerging homosexual identity: "I love man with the same distinction that I love woman—as if my friend were of some third sex—some other or some stranger and still my friend" (*Journal* 2:245). Given the complexity of Thoreau's meditations on relationships between men, and the historical complexity of homosexual identity, Thoreau's writing will be a source of great interest to gay and lesbian literary studies for many years to come.

—*Marylynne Diggs*

BIBLIOGRAPHY

Gozzi, Raymond, ed. *Thoreau's Psychology: Eight Essays.* Lanham, Md.: University Press of America, 1983. ∎ Harding, Walter. *The Days of Henry Thoreau: A Biography.* Princeton: Princeton University Press, 1982. ∎ ———. "Thoreau's Sexuality." *Journal of Homosexuality* 21.3 (1991): 23–45. ∎ Katz, Jonathan. *Gay American History: Lesbians and Gay Men in the U.S.A.* New York: Avon-Discus, 1978. ∎ Wagenknecht, Edward. *Henry David Thoreau: What Manner of Man?* Amherst, Mass.: University of Massachusetts Press, 1981. ∎ Warner, Michael. "Walden's Erotic Economy." *Comparative American Identities: Race, Sex and Nationality in the Modern Text.* Hortense J. Spillers, ed. New York: Routledge, 1991. 157–174.

Travel Literature

The development of travel literature in relation to gay and lesbian sensibility has been one of the least understood areas of modern cultural history and anthropology. Before approximately 1800, the development has been even less clear, especially the degree to which travel was a means of coping with homosexual desire, rather than indulging or satisfying it. Scholars have assumed that travelers in history harbored no erotic or sexual curiosity: Thus even the much discussed Grand Tour of the Enlightenment was shorn of its significant erotic components. The old model was that travelers voyaged to other countries to inspect foreign customs and practices, antiquities and shrines, for purely educational purposes, a view that omitted the traveler's erotic curiosity because such a topic was considered impolite for public discussion until our generation. Travelers to Greece and Rome offer perfect examples of the "polite school" of interpretation of the Grand Tour, one in which all discussion was couched in the terms of neoclassical retrieval, archaeological marbles, and cultural enrichment; yet the record shows that travelers were as impressed with the sexual customs of the natives. Richard Payne Knight's discovery in the 1780s of priapic fertility cults in Sicily demonstrates the point. When the English Society of Dilettanti privately published Knight's *Discourse on the Worship of Priapus* (1786) there was near hysteria among educated circles in London because neoclassical retrieval had been discussed in these terms. Nevertheless, at home it became clear to what degree eros and travel commingled.

The essence of travel over the Alps was the discovery of landscapes and customs at variance with practices at home. In the sexual domain, these new images—couples, partners, lovers, arrangements of social classes—combined to provide an entirely new education for the traveler. Italy and the Italians stimulated the northern European imagination most: Here in the sunny Mediterranean south, amid the ruins of a Roman past, social relations between men and women appeared to flourish in another realm than anything known at home. Seymour Conway, one of the travelers in HORACE WALPOLE's circle, wrote on departing Florence in 1752, "there are but two things at all thought of here—love and antiquities, of which the former predominates . . . ." Conway's sentiment continued to be echoed down through the eighteenth and nineteenth centuries, as travelers returning from Italy publicized the erotic liaisons they had seen there, prompting those who had never traveled south to construe Italy and points farther east as the home of homosexual relations. The anonymous author of *Reasons for the Growth of Sodomy in England* (1729) reiterated the point, and Daniel Defoe even claimed that boys could be bought there for almost nothing. The variety of homo- and heterosexual arrangements—the Italian institutions of the lover, mistress, gigolo, and cisisbeo, in which a married woman takes a male lover—differed from patterns in northern Europe. As WILLIAM BECKFORD commented, the Mediterranean was "the place for sinners of a certain sort." Travelers on the Grand Tour personally witnessed sodomitical networks clustered around the great villas in Florence (Earl of Tylney), Rome (Cardinal Albani), and Naples (Sir William Hamilton and his erotic wife "Emma" were the subject, for example, of many paintings depicting nubile female beauty). Conway's perception about "love and antiquity" crystallized into a paradigm of "eros and retrieval" that informed every aspect of the neoclassical movement, about which so much has been written and which has such significant implications for the history of collecting and connoisseurship.

Northern Europeans' travel beyond Italy to the Balkans and Greece was rare before 1800. Both locales had rich associations with homosexuality, however. In ancient Greece, of course, men and boys had been institutionally encouraged to become "lovers" (erastes and eromenos), and by 1760, dictionaries explained that "buggery" derived from the Bulgarian "bouger" or "bugger," pushing farther east than Italy the home of sodomy and birth of man-boy love. Those, such as Jesuit missionaries, who traveled still farther east returned with vivid accounts of homosexuality in Turkey and the Levant, and even points farther east in the Orient. By approximately 1800, an Orientalism developed that linked turqueries to all-male harems, and Turkish spies to cults of oriental pederasty. One nineteenth-century account described English travelers as having been bathed by boys in lemon oil under the moonlight in Persepolis. Travelers to the "New World" across the Atlantic also claimed to have witnessed homosexual rites in Florida, Mexico, Brazil, and points farther south, but these were allegedly more primitive than the civilized customs of the Orient. In the New World flourished cannibal rituals and voodoo ceremonies, as well as sodomy of a cruder version than anything found in the Orient. Captain Cook and his cohorts filled pages of their logs with accounts of their erotic dalliances on Pacific beaches, often among naked young males who made no distinction between the genders. Predictably, a notion of the "sexual Other," remote from anything known to exist in Europe, developed. It was unnecessary to await a HERMAN MELVILLE or WALT WHITMAN before the construction of this new sexual type who was the product of the traveler's imagination and desire more than anything anyone had actually seen.

Closer to home, parents and their sons (women did not undertake the Grand Tour) faced the practical hurdles involved in such dangerous travel. In England, the average age was sixteen to twenty, but some males postponed travel to twenty-five or even thirty. The youth was customarily accompanied by a tutor or governor and one or more servants. Families funded the trip, which varied from a month to several years on a route normally proceeding through Belgium and Paris over the Alps and ending in Rome or one of the other Italian cities. The travelers kept copious notes and diaries, returning with handwritten records of everything they had seen, including exotic sexual customs and practices. Their experience altered their sensibility and shaped a new moral sense in which sex and sexuality were expanded to encompass new possibilities and arrangements. As one traveler said, "never again will I be the same."

The role of the tutor or governor was seminal. Parents advertised and interviewed for the position, carefully screening the candidates for their moral and religious views. To the governors or tutors were entrusted the allocation of funds, as well as an all-embracing pastoral role. Problems of ill health on the road or at sea required swift judgments, and conditions of living abroad could be fraught with peril. Trouble lurked everywhere—inclement weather, robbery, pestilence, even murder—for life on the road was fundamentally unpredictable. The entourage of travelers, tutor, and servants proceeded in close quarters, as travelogues and fiction show, often sleeping in one room and even in the same beds. The tutor regulated the itinerary and sites that could be seen (for example, the opera in Italy), as well as the amorous life of his travelers. Few if any English parents would have approved of life in Horace Mann's Casa Manetti in Florence in the middle of the eighteenth century if they could have witnessed its activities. In Horace Walpole's version, they drank through the night, were amorous until sunrise, and slept through the hot afternoons. Homosexual tutors and governors often made pacts of secrecy, each promising not to expose the other. Some governors had genital sex with their tutees while abroad, a more common practice than has been conceded by the polite school of cultural historians. Even if genital activity was infrequent, the degree of homosociality among these governors was high, as is clear from the activities of the "little club" formed in Leiden, Holland, that included the pre-Romantic English poet Mark Akenside and his lawyer-lover Jeremiah Dyson, and the group of European university students they fell in with.

The diaries of tutors or governors were commonly edited on return home, often morally expurgated, and published as part of the biographical record of the travelers. Even the letters of the travelers are permeated with these erotic accounts, as in the writings of THOMAS GRAY and Horace Walpole (in our sense lovers as young men), some of which constitute important imaginative literature in their own right and describe the travelers' erotic curiosity and attachments.

The "Quadruple Alliance"—Horace Walpole, Thomas Gray, Richard West, and Thomas Ashton—serves as a perfect example of how the homoeroticism of travelers could affect the Grand Tour. The four had met at Eton, where they formed the deepest affections in the way schoolboys often do. Later, they took the Grand Tour together, staying away for several years, primarily in the environs of Florence. Walpole and Gray traveled as a pair: Walpole, the richer man, paying for the more modest Gray, and traveling with a caravan of servants and governors. But after two years, they fell out in Florence for reasons that have never been understood, and Gray returned to England alone, but not before they had indulged every facet of their erotic curiosity.

Two generations later, BYRON's school group followed a similar pattern, also having met at school and traveling together in pairs. Others, like the Baron Poellnitz, moved around from court to court, grasping hospitality and homosexual romance where they could, "having fallen in love with all the Princes . . . on the earth." These were real-life travels; the developing novel—narratives such as Tobias Smollett's *Peregrine Pickle* (1751)—fictionalized such exotic travels and narrated them in minute detail because they intrigued the reading public.

The variations on these forms of travel are noteworthy for the specific way they delineate the rise of idealized homosexual types. For example, JOHANN WINCKELMANN, the great German aesthetician who was probably homosexual, traveled less out of curiosity than out of exotic, almost lurid, fascination with Italy. His southern haunts included Adriatic villas surrounding Venice and Cardinal Albani's sprawling villa in Rome, where he gathered with other homosocial figures such as the bisexual painter Mengs. Others from the north gathered around the extensive collections of the Comte Caylus, the fabulously wealthy antiquarian collector and connoisseur who kissed the head of a fawn each night before going to bed and who nearly worshipped homoerotic marbles such as the heads and coins of Antinous he collected by the hundreds. Someday the travels of these figures will be chronicled in the detail they deserve without omission of the erotic component.

More generally, erotic life in Italy was remote from the firsthand experience of any northern traveler, but even Italy seemed familiar compared to the exoticism William Beckford, England's wealthiest man as he has been called, craved. Beckford was the homosexual traveler par excellence in search of exotic males: brown, brawny, hairless, deep-eyed. He made several "grand tours" on the Continent, each time dreaming of pushing farther eastward, erotically idealizing the young men he met, sometimes drawing them, and almost always rewarding them financially for their services. Eventually, his heart and mind were captured by the young Portugese Gregorio Franchi, whose wife and children Beckford subsidized. Still, he yearned to push eastward, to sail down the Adriatic to Ottoman palaces and the Levant, and his best-known Gothic tale, *Vathek* (1786), idealizes the dreamy and still hairless young man whose common tongue speaks the universal language of love. Beckford's Portugese diaries depict the new homosexual type: the remote "sexual Other" whose anatomical body, native tongue, dietary and other local customs radically differ from the traveler's.

Byron, Shelley, and their circle also traveled extensively, to Switzerland, Italy, and Greece, where Byron died fighting for Greek independence. Byron indulged Albanian and Turkish fantasies of the "northerner," just as Englishmen had indulged those from the south, cross-dressing in the costume of the sexual other—a symbolic act suggesting sexual transfer—and engaging in overt genital acts. The importance of travel for Byron's homoerotic imagination, as for the affluent writer of Gothic fiction MATTHEW LEWIS's, has only recently been understood and remains an undervalued component of his version of "Greek love."

Costume also looms large in the conceptualizations of these travelers, especially cross-dressing in the garb of the other, as the portraits of Byron in Albanian drag reveal: A very different type of cross-dressing from the vocational version practiced at home—for example—by Defoe's Roxana and the eighteenth-century lesbian writer Charlotte Charke, both of whom cross-dressed as men. Their version is more akin to Lady Mary Wortley Montagu's donning of male garb, and in her *Memoirs* (1775), Charke claims that if it was scandalous to dress as a woman, it was much less so to dress as a man. It is as if the purchase of a costume were a substitution for the sexual transference itself. The implication for homosexual transfer was apparent to Beckford: Arabian nights passed in the harem were desirable; in the company of dark-skinned, hairless boys even more exotic and pleasurable; but with Beckford cross-dressed as a Turk, still more hedonistic. By the time of his last trip abroad, Beckford had transcended the mindset, even the erotic mental landscape, associated with the Grand Tour.

Travel has always circumscribed the domain of the erotic, but the retrieval of artifacts is a relatively recent development in history, and the link of the Grand Tour and homosexual sensibility has not been dwelled on. By the nineteenth century, though, the erotic dimension of travel was taken for granted, even if rarely discussed in public. Cities like Paris, Rome, and Naples abounded with homosexual activity, and northern travelers knew where to find the action. The Victorian Grand Tour differed from its predecessors to the extent that homosexual travelers formally networked and made use of homosexual contacts abroad. JOHN ADDINGTON SYMONDS, for example, acted as an international homosexual clearinghouse, coordinating gay correspondence and keeping people

in touch. But Symonds is also exemplary in another way: as the archetype of the Romantic homosexual exile. A distinguished historian of the Renaissance, he fled England to Italy and eventually settled with his Italian lover in Davos, Switzerland, refusing to return to his native England on the grounds that it was oppressive to homosexuals like himself. Instead, he offered hospitality to hundreds of men passing through. Exchanging one's country for sexual reasons was risky, with serious consequences whether one remained abroad (clear evidence of being a sodomite) or returned (evidence the traveler had fled, like Beckford, from scandal).

Walt Whitman captured some of the potency of homosexual fantasy among travelers in poems like "We two boys together clinging," in which the metaphors of traveling together, in groups, arm in arm, breast on breast, are potent. The liberating potentiality of travel is also apparent to novelists like E. M. FORSTER, whose Italian novels feature the transformations of Englishmen by their experiences abroad. For English writers in the 1930s, it was Weimar Germany that seemed to offer the greatest prospect of liberation, as witnessed by the work and experiences of CHRISTOPHER ISHERWOOD, STEPHEN SPENDER, and W. H. AUDEN. Isherwood's autobiographical *Christopher and His Kind* (1980) is particularly interesting as a travel book, for it is in large part the saga of Christopher and his German working-class lover Heinz, who in the late 1930s move restlessly from one European city to another in search of a haven where they can live together. EDMUND WHITE has also inscribed the dynamics of the gay travel experience in his fiction, as well as in his nonfiction *States of Desire: Travels in Gay America* (1980). *States of Desire* and gay guides like the periodically issued *Spartacus,* to say nothing of the organized tours for gay men and lesbians led by Hans Ebenstein and others, now seem highly efficient means of exploring places, but they are not entirely new inventions. The paradigm of the mother country has altered, as has remaining abroad. And it can no longer be said, as it was in the nineteenth century: "Be suspicious of any Englishman who exchanges England for Italy even for purely political reasons."

Perhaps NORMAN DOUGLAS, the twentieth-century English poet and novelist, has uttered the last word about homosexual travel and its significations when providing reasons for going abroad the first time: "Norman Douglas of Capri, and of Naples and Florence, was formerly of England, which he fled during the war to avoid persecution for kissing a boy and giving him some cakes and a shilling."

—*G. S. Rousseau*

BIBLIOGRAPHY

Beckford, William. *Dreams, Waking Thoughts, and Incidents: in a Series of Letters, from Various Parts of Europe.* London: J. Johnson, 1783. ■ Chaney, Edward. *The Grand Tour and Beyond: British and American Travellers in Southern Italy, 1545-1960.* London: Oxford University Press, 1974. ■ Fussell, Paul. *Abroad: British Literary Traveling between the Wars.* New York: Oxford University Press, 1980. ■ ———, ed. *The Norton Book of Travel.* New York: Norton, 1986. ■ Massie, Allan. *Byron's Travels.* London: Sidgwick and Jackson, 1988. ■ Porter, Dennis. *Haunted Journeys: Desire and Transgression in European Travel Writing.* Princeton: Princeton University Press, 1991. ■ Rousseau, G. S. "In the House of Madame van der Tasse: Homosocial Desire and a University Club during the Enlightenment." *The Pursuit of Sodomy: Male Homosexuality in Renaissance and Enlightenment Europe.* Kent Gerard, ed. New York: Haworth Press, 1987. 311–348. ■ ———. *Perilous Enlightenment: Pre- and Post-modern Discourses: Sexual, Historical.* Manchester: Manchester University Press, 1990. ■ ———. "The Sorrows of Priapus: Anticlericalism, Homosocial Desire, and Richard Payne Knight." *Sexual Underworlds of the Enlightenment.* G. S. Rousseau, ed. Chapel Hill: University of North Carolina Press, 1987. 101–153. ■ ———, and Roy Porter, eds. *Exoticism in the Enlightenment.* Manchester: Manchester University Press, 1989. ■ Stoye, John. *English Travellers in the Renaissance.* London: Routledge and Kegan Paul, 1954.

Tremblay, Michel
(b. 1942)

Montreal-born playwright and novelist Tremblay draws on his own Catholic working-class background in his presentation of bar culture characters and their relatives. He is notably prolific and versatile, having produced librettos, screenplays, musicals, short stories, novels, and memoirs. In his work, he weaves together high-brow and pop culture, otherworldly and mundane visions. He constantly thematizes the interplay of fantasy and realism, dreams and pragmatism.

Most remarkable of Tremblay's realist devices is his use of *joual*, idiomatic French as spoken by working-class Québécois. The status-signifying power of *joual* in Québec is akin to that of black English in the United States. Tremblay's gesture is more than truthfulness to his roots, for his attention to language and class is paired with a focus on gender and human relations: mothers and their complexes, the antics of divas of either gender, gay male couples involved in parenting. His fictional universe thrives on places deemed feminine, places of both nurture and spectacle.

Featuring an all-woman cast and employing *joual* throughout, the 1968 production of *Les Belles-Soeurs* (*The Sisters-in-Law*) launched a cycle of interlocking plays and novels. Ensnared in familial entanglements, sanctimonious and outrageous types from Montreal's east end struggle against themselves, each other, and the pasts of their parents. Fantasy is intrinsic to Tremblay's work. In *La Maison Suspendue* (*The Hanging House*, 1991), multiple time planes intersect in a single setting to depict the forces that shape the very different homosexualities displayed by Jean-Marc and his uncle Édouard. In each generation, contention over the uses of imagination recurs. The bitter struggle between Albertine and her brother Édouard, the drag queen known as La Duchesse, is replayed in various guises and tones between Hosanna and Cuirette (*Hosanna*, 1974), Jean-Marc and Luc (*Remember Me*, 1984), Sandra and Manon (*Damnée Manon, Sacrée Sandra* [*Darn Mandy, Holy Sandy*], 1981).

The recurring question is whether it is better to cede to escapist dreams or to remain determined, if accommodating, pragmatists. Tremblay's heroes turn the either-or question toward a position where the real winners are those who shatter and rebuild dreams. These winners are often his gayest creatures. Be it Hosanna's Halloween fiasco in posing as Elizabeth Taylor's Cleopatra, Sandra's wild orgy of green lipstick and nail polish capped by posing as a swish Virgin Mary, or La Duchesse's intoxicated rap on life, the queens drop masks only to extend their repertoires in more masterly performances.

In the 1990s, Tremblay has himself taken on a new mask to tell old tales. In his autobiographical stories, the touchstones continue to be films (*Les Vues animées* [*The Moving Pictures*], 1990) and theater (*Douze coups de théâtre* [*A Dozen Dramatic Twists*], 1992) and the setting is still Montréal's east end, but the manner is more intimate. Perhaps because he was never out to his mother, who died in 1963, Tremblay's constant return to particular locales evokes a persistent and pervasive mixture of suffering, homosexuality, and creativity. With such themes, his writing inflects gayness with multiple marginalities that are at once personal and universal. (See also QUÉBÉCOIS LITERATURE.)

—François Lachance

BIBLIOGRAPHY

Wallace, Robert. "Homo création: pour une poétique du théâtre gai." *Jeu* 54 (1990): 24–42. ■ ———. *Producing Marginality: Theatre and Criticism in Canada.* Saskatoon: Fifth House, 1990.

Tsvetaeva, Marina Ivanovna
(1892–1941)

Widely considered one of the four greatest twentieth-century Russian poets, and an innovative prose writer and dramatist, Marina Tsvetaeva was born in Moscow on October 8, 1892. Her father was an art professor and her mother a gifted pianist of Polish descent, whose father had forbidden her a concert career. Although Tsvetaeva's mother wanted her daughter to become a pianist, Marina herself was drawn to words and began writing poetry at the age of six. Her first volume of poems, *Evening Album,* was published in 1910 and consisted of verse written between the ages of fifteen and seventeen. Aside from her youthful love affair with the poet SOPHIA PARNOK, Tsvetaeva's self-acknowledged bisexuality, her lesbianism, and the lesbian theme that runs throughout her poetry, prose, letters, and journals have all been ignored or, at best, mentioned in passing by most of her Western biographers. Most Russian Tsvetaeva scholars try to deny the poet's lesbianism and its significance in her work.

Tsvetaeva revealed an attraction to her own sex from childhood, both in her reading and in her relationships with other children. She tells the story of her childhood love for another girl in her prose work, "The House at Old Pimen." Despite her lesbian inclinations, or perhaps in an effort to neutralize the anxiety they clearly caused her, Tsvetaeva married young and immediately had a daughter. Then, at the beginning of World War I, she met Sophia Parnok and fell in love at first sight. This passionate affair was fraught with ambivalence for Tsvetaeva, but it inspired the most artistically mature work of her early period, the lyrical cycle "Girlfriend" (1914–1915), a masterpiece of lesbian love poetry that was published only in the 1970s and has not yet been translated into English in its entirety. Although both Parnok and Tsvetaeva predicted that their love was doomed almost from the start, Tsvetaeva was traumatized by their breakup in early 1916. She called the loss of Parnok the "first catastrophe" of her life and nurtured vengeful feelings toward Parnok for the rest of her life. In the aftermath of the affair, Tsvetaeva returned to her husband and immediately became pregnant. Her second daughter was born in early 1917.

Tsvetaeva spent the 1917 Revolution and ensuing Civil War in Moscow, alone with her two young daughters; her husband was an officer in the White army. She was forced to put her infant daughter in an orphanage where the little girl died of starvation.

Tsvetaeva's work from 1918 to 1920 with the Third Stage, an avant-garde Moscow theater group, led to her intimacy with Sonya Holliday, an actress. Their apparently platonic, but intensely erotic love affair was described by Tsvetaeva much later in the prose work "The Tale of Sonechka" (which has yet to be translated into English) and in a cycle of lyrics, "Poems to Sonechka." "The Tale of Sonechka" must also be read in part as the third rewriting of Tsvetaeva's affair with her first Sonya (Sophia Parnok).

Just after the publication of her most famous collection of poems, *Mileposts I* (1922), Tsvetaeva left the Soviet Union and was finally reunited with her husband in Prague. In early 1925, their son was born and later that year the family moved to Paris where Tsvetaeva lived for the next fourteen years. At first, she was welcomed into Russian émigré literary life in Paris, but during the 1930s, when most of her prose works were written, she was increasingly isolated and criticized. Eventually, she was treated as an outcast because of her husband's pro-Soviet political activities, which included espionage for the Soviet secret police.

In the early 1930s, Tsvetaeva met NATALIE CLIFFORD BARNEY, the famous expatriate American lesbian writer, the "Amazon of Letters," and gave a poetry reading at Barney's Rue Jacob salon. But neither she nor her work was given an enthusiastic reception. Feeling rejected, Tsvetaeva wrote (in French) her "Lettre à l'Amazone" (1932, rev. 1934), a highly encoded, autobiographical and polemical work with two addressees: Barney and Tsvetaeva's former lover—and other lesbian rejector—Sophia Parnok. In "Lettre's" story of a lesbian love affair between a young girl and an older woman, Tsvetaeva rewrote her and Parnok's affair for the second time. Simultaneously, she composed an ambiguous, intensely personal and moving epitaph to her lost "girlfriend" (Parnok), the only lover who made it possible for her to have an orgasm and to like her sexual self. "Lettre à l'Amazone" also gives expression to Tsvetaeva's struggle with her own lesbianism. Her internalized homophobia leads her to defend lesbian relationships against the censure of society, God, and the state, while striking out at them as an offense to nature and Mother. The first English translation of "Lettre" is now being prepared for publication.

At the end of the 1930s, Tsvetaeva returned to Soviet Russia where tragedy awaited her. First, her daughter was arrested in August 1939 and sent to a concentration camp; then her husband was arrested and executed as an enemy of the people. Shunned by her poet colleagues in Moscow, she was sent to live outside the city in Golitsyno. Despite her desperate situation during the year after her return, she became involved in a relationship with Tatyana Kvanina, the wife of a minor writer. Part of their intimate correspondence has recently appeared in a Russian journal.

After the German offensive began in earnest, Tsvetaeva and her teenage son were evacuated to Yelabuga in the Tatar Autonomous Republic. There, the beleaguered poet could find no work or assistance. On August 31, 1941, finding herself alone in the house for a few hours, she hung herself from a beam in the ceiling. She was buried in an unmarked grave in the Yelabuga cemetery.

—Diana L. Burgin

BIBLIOGRAPHY

Feinstein, Elaine. *A Captive Lion: The Life of Marina Tsvetaeva.* New York: Dutton, 1987. ■ Feiler, Lily. *Marina Tsvetaeva: The Double Beat of Heaven and Hell.* Durham, N.C.: Duke University Press, 1994. ■ Gove, Antonina. "The Feminine Stereotype and Beyond: Role Conflict and Resolution in the Poetics of Marina Tsvetaeva." *Slavic Review* 36.2 (1977). ■ Karlinsky, Simon. *Marina Tsvetaeva: The Woman, Her World, and Her Poetry.* Cambridge: Cambridge University Press, 1985. ■ Kroth, Anya M. "Androgyny as an Exemplary Feature of Marina Tsvetaeva's Dichotomous Poetic Vision." *Slavic Review* 38.4 (1979). ■ Poliakova, Sophia. *[Ne]zakatnye ony dni: Tsvetaeva i Parnok.* Ann Arbor: Ardis, 1983. ■ Sandler, Stephanie. "Embodied Words: Gender in Cvetaeva's Reading of Pushkin." *Slavic and East European Journal* 34.2 (1990). ■ Schweitzer, Viktoria. *Tsvetaeva.* Trans. Robert Chandler and H. T. Willetts; poetry trans. Peter Norman. Angela Livingstone, ed. London: Harper and Collins, 1992. ■ Taubman, Jane A. *A Life through Poetry: Marina Tsvetaeva's Lyric Diary.* Columbus: Slavica, 1989.

Uranian Poets

The term *Uranian* derives from PLATO's *Symposium,* in which Pausanias distinguishes between Heavenly Aphrodite (Aphrodite Urania) and Common Aphrodite (Aphrodite Pandeumia). According to Pausanias, men who are inspired by Heavenly Love "are attracted towards the male sex, and value it as being naturally the stronger and more intelligent . . . their intention is to form a lasting attachment and partnership for life." The term *Urning* was popularized by the Austrian legal official Karl Heinrich Ulrichs in the late 1860s and 1870s and was soon adapted in England as *Uranian,* used by such leaders of the early English homosexual emancipation movement as JOHN ADDINGTON SYMONDS and EDWARD CARPENTER. As employed by them, the term embraces homosexuals generally. More narrowly, however, *Uranianism* designates a movement in English poetry, from the close of the Victorian era to the middle of the interwar period, whose theme is love for the adolescent boy. Inspired by feelings akin to the *paiderasteia* of the ancient Greeks, but far more circumspect and clandestine because of the prevailing cultural attitudes of their time, the Uranian poets left a minor legacy to the gay and lesbian literary heritage.

The object of the Uranian poets' love was the youth between 12 and 17, not the adult male, the concern of modern androphile homosexuality. In their lifetimes, the two orientations were not clearly distinguished; J. Z. Eglinton (pseudonym of Walter Breen, 1928–1993) drew the line of demarcation between them clearly and correctly in his epoch-making *Greek Love* (1964). Pederasty was the predominant form of male homosexuality in Greco-Roman antiquity, but in the twentieth century the proportions have been reversed so that the prevalent type is the androphile. Hence the Uranians were a "minority within a minority" and their poems often have the quality of pieces written for a small clique of critics and admirers who knew the earlier works in the same recondite genre.

The Uranians turned for inspiration first of all to the pederastic literature in Greek and Latin, which Christian intolerance had obscured but not obliterated. Steeped as they were in classical education at the British public schools of the late Victorian and Edwardian eras, they found and appreciated poetry that was not part of the canon approved for class reading. In particular the twelfth book of the *Greek Anthology,* the *Musa paidik* of Strato of Sardis, in modern times first published in full only in 1764, was for them a gold mine of themes and images, especially the superiority of male adolescent beauty. But throughout classical literature, the Uranians could discover what their heterosexual contemporaries often missed: unabashed erotic fascination with the androgynous but fleeting charm of youth.

The characteristic themes of Uranian verse reflect the special relationship between the pederast and his beloved boy. The brevity of the *anthos,* the "pride" of the adolescent, is a recurrent subject, because its passing spells the end of the boy's charm and of the adult's fascination with him. The growth of hair on the boy's body, and the need for the razor, repelled the modern quite as much as the ancient boy lover.

Often all that the pederast could do was engage in voyeurism, in gazing at an opportune moment on the nude bodies in the locker room or stripped for swimming. Even so, the erotic thrill was perhaps intensified by the futility of the desire. And the imperfections of the real boy were offset by fantasies of the ideal youth, the quintessence of boyhood that emerged in dreams and visions, the *puer aeternus* who would never age, would never lose the androgynous beauty prized by the lover.

The superiority of the male bonding inspired by boy love to marriage and procreation is another commonplace in the Uranians' lore. This had been an argument of Greek philosophers, living as they did in a society where *paiderasteia* was the recognized and approved initiatory-pedagogical form of homosexuality and where they had the love affairs of the gods as exempla, but in modern times it was overshadowed by the religious taboo.

Understandably, an aesthetic paganism runs through the verses of the Uranian poets, even though some of them were clergymen of the Church of England. The legends of Zeus and Ganymede, Heracles and Hylas, Achilles and Patroclus, and the history of Hadrian and Antinous, however denatured they may have been in the popular mind, served poets of boy love perfectly for the voicing of their unorthodox passions. Still, an occasional author voiced the hope that pederasty was inspired and protected by the Christian God as well.

The erotic side of the relationship, explicit enough in the classical models, had to be kept to the subtlest minimum in the Uranians. They could not allow their readers (or the police) to suspect that their love was ever tainted by "gross sensuality." Curiously enough, their verse attains the apogee of indecency when it mingles eroticism with religion. The fatal allure of the acolyte for the priest who is inclined toward boy love motivated a story, "The Priest and the Acolyte," that figured in the trial of OSCAR WILDE in 1895.

Among the negative themes in their writing is the lack of reciprocity from the boy, who in his early teens is simply unable to respond to what an intellectually gifted and mature adult is trying to offer him. This had been a motif of ancient pederastic writing as well, but now it was compounded by the guilt in which Christian morality had enveloped every shade of homoerotic feeling and action. The passion is judged fruitless, dangerous, frustrating, and the poet casti-

gates himself for yielding to the boy's evanescent charms in full knowledge of its "immorality." The chasm between the boy lover's inner self and the beliefs of an intolerant society could never be bridged.

The most significant Uranian poets were the following: John Leslie Barford (1886–1937), who wrote *Ladslove Lyrics* (1918), *Young Things* (1921), *Fantasies* (1923), and *Whimsies* (1934); Edwin Emmanuel Bradford (1860–1944), who wrote a series of books of verse, from *Sonnets Songs & Ballads* (1908) and *Passing the Love of Women and Other Poems* (1913) to *Boyhood* (1930); Ralph Nicholas Chubb (1892–1960), who was also a gifted lithographer, and who wrote *Manhood* (1924), followed by a long series of deluxe illustrated volumes in which the art stood in an inverse relationship to the quality of the poetry, the last entitled *The Golden City with Idylls and Allegories* (1961); George Cecil Ives (1867–1950), who authored two volumes, *Book of Chains* (1897) and *Eros' Throne* (1900), as well as several articles rashly defending the "new hedonism"; Charles Philip Castle Kains Jackson (1857–1933), who composed *Finibus Cantat Amor* (1922) and *Lysis* (1924); Edmund John (1883–1917), who produced *The Flute of Sardonyx* (1913), *The Wind in the Temple* (1915), and *Symphonie Symbolique* (1919); Edward Cracroft Lefroy (1855–1891), who published *Echoes from Theocritus* (1883), followed by other volumes; Francis Edwin Murray (1854–1932), who composed *Rondeaux of Boyhood* (1923) and *From a Lover's Garden* (1924); John Gambril Francis Nicholson (1886–1931), who issued *Love in Earnest: Sonnets, Ballads, and Lyrics* (1892), followed by *A Chaplet of Southernwood* (1896), *A Garland of Ladslove* (1911), and "*Opals and Pebbles*" (1928); the Russian Jew Marc-André Raffalovich (1864–1934), who was a pioneer writer on homosexuality in French and who wrote several volumes of poetry in English, beginning with *Cyril and Lionel and other Poems: a Volume of Sentimental Studies* (1884); Charles Edward Sayle (1864–1924), whose works include *Bertha: a Story of Love* (1885), *Erotidia* (1889), *Musa Consolatrix* (1893), and *Private Music* (1911); Stanislaus Eric, Count Stenbock (1860–1895), who wrote *Love, Sleep and Dreams* (ca 1881) and two further volumes of poetry; Montague Summers (1880–1948), who later acquired an international reputation as a somewhat credulous Roman Catholic authority on witchcraft, the miraculous, and the supernatural and who wrote *Antinous and Other Poems* (1907); and John Moray Stuart-Young (1881–1939), who composed *Fairy Gold* (1904), followed by *Osrac, the Self-Sufficient, and Other Poems. With a Memoir of the Late Oscar Wilde* (1905), *An Urning's Love (Being a Poetic Study of Morbidity)* (1905), and

Who Buys My Dreams? (1923). All these poets are discussed in Timothy d'Arch Smith's excellent study, *Love in Earnest: Some Notes on the Lives and Writings of English 'Uranian' Poets from 1889 to 1930* (1970).

Some thirty-seven Americans figure among the Uranians whose works were collected in *Men and Boys: An Anthology,* edited by Edmund Edwinson (pseudonym of Edward M. Slocum) and published in 1924. Of these, by far the most important is William Alexander Percy (1885–1942), who published several volumes of verse with Yale University Press, later collected in an edition issued by Knopf in 1943. He achieved lasting fame, however, with his autobiography *Lanterns on the Levee* (1941), the classic depiction of the world of the plantation-owning class in the Mississippi delta, where he subtly reveals his pederastic interests. Although members of his family, including the late novelist Walker Percy, have tried to deny his homosexuality, he was one in spirit with his British contemporaries. Another American who belongs in this set is Edward Perry Warren (1860–1928), the Boston art connoisseur who spent most of his life in England. Besides *Itamos* (1903) and *The Wild Rose* (1909), he published (under the pseudonym Arthur Lyon Raile) a *Defence of Uranian Love* in three volumes (1926–1928). He is responsible for major holdings by American museums of Greek erotic vases depicting pederastic themes—a treasure long withheld from the general public.

Although Uranianism received its initial impetus from Ulrichs and the German movement, it was an indigenous phenomenon that owed nothing to German predecessors or models. It was an afterglow of the great poetic tradition of nineteenth-century England and remained firmly in a post-Tennysonian style. The Uranian poets made little impression on English letters. The authors belonged to a self-conscious, unconventional elite who shunned the prying gaze of their contemporaries. Their work was often privately printed, in small editions meant solely for initiated readers. None of the Uranian poets ever rose to the level of an A. E. HOUSMAN, whose work shares their paganism and sexual unconventionality, but whose orientation was ephebo- or androphilic, and whose great love affair had been with a college undergraduate of his own age, not with an adolescent.

—*Warren Johansson*

BIBLIOGRAPHY

Eglinton, J. Z. (pseudonym of Walter Breen). *Greek Love.* New York: Oliver Layton Press, 1964. ■ Hilliard, David. "Unenglish and Unmanly: Anglo-Catholicism and Homosexuality." *Victorian Studies* 25 (1982): 181–210. ■ Rahman, Tariq. "Ephebophilia and the Creation of a Spiritual Myth in the Works of Ralph Nicholas Chubb." *Journal of Homosexuality* 20.1–2 (1990): 103–127. ■ Smith, Timothy d'Arch. *Love in Earnest: Some Notes on the Lives and Writings of English 'Uranian' Poets from 1889 to 1930.* London: Routledge & Kegan Paul, 1970.

Van Vechten, Carl
(1880–1964)

Carl Van Vechten is best known for his interest in African-American culture. Carlo, as he was known by friends, was in the 1920s Harlem's "most enthusiastic and ubiquitous Nordic." His articles on music and literature in *Vanity Fair* and *The New York Times* are often credited for discovering the New Negro Movement for whites. Not only did he write about the music, drama, and literature of the New Negro Movement, he also befriended many of its important artists and organizers, and was himself an influential patron. Van Vechten donated money for literary prizes and supported many of the younger generation of black writers, including LANGSTON HUGHES and COUNTEE CULLEN. Van Vechten's efforts to promote African-American culture also echoed in his photography.

His provocative photographs taken from 1932 until his death document important African-American figures in the arts.

Van Vechten's philanthropic pursuits in African-American culture were inspired by his father, who cofounded a school for African-American children in rural Mississippi. Like his father, Van Vechten had an interest in African-American culture. Unlike his father, however, he could not stay in Cedar Rapids, Iowa, where he was born on June 17, 1880; Van Vechten fled to Chicago. While attending the University of Chicago from 1899 to 1903, he developed his interest in black music. His passion for the ragtime he heard in Chicago inspired the eight books of music and other arts criticism he wrote after he moved to New York City in 1906.

After his books of criticism, Van Vechten wrote seven novels. His most controversial is *Nigger Heaven* (1926), whose title and depiction of Harlem life sent shock waves throughout the African-American community. His novels are more than provocative, however; they weave romantic relationships between men and reflect his own life and the people he admired.

His first novel, *Peter Whiffle: His Life and Works* (1922), is as much a memoir as it is fiction. It is a tongue-in-cheek roman à clef that starts with a preface in which Van Vechten explains the purpose of the novel and introduces himself as our guide. Whiffle, a flamboyant author who never completed a book and a close friend of Van Vechten's, writes a letter just before his death requesting Van Vechten to write a book about his life so that he may live on past his death. The novel furnishes guideposts to Whiffle's and Van Vechten's intimate relationship and mythologizes Whiffle. *Peter Whiffle* is a nod and a wink to those readers who recognize the title character as a particular type, "the gay, faun-like Peter of Paris"; to those who do not, he is a mystery.

Van Vechten's second novel, *The Blind Bow-Boy* (1923), celebrates 1920s bohemian culture in New York City. The novel tells the story of young Harold Prewett, fresh from college, who is sent to New York by his father to reject the temptations of an uninhib-ited New York society revolving around its queen, Campaspe Lorillard. Prewett soon learns of his father's plans and rebels by leaving his wife of two weeks; he sails to Europe with the Duke of Middlebottom, whose stationery reads "A thing of beauty is a boy forever."

Van Vechten's five subsequent novels, including *The Tattooed Countess* (1924), *Firecrackers* (1925), *Spider Boy* (1928), and *Parties* (1930), return to the characters and places of his first two, connecting them to each other as well as to other new characters. With his novels, Van Vechten creates a gay, bohemian society not unlike the one he lived in and the one he depicts in *The Blind Bow-Boy,* but with himself as its queen.

—*Seth Clark Silberman*

BIBLIOGRAPHY

Byrd, Rudolph P. *Generations in Black & White: Photographs by Carl Van Vechten.* Athens: University of Georgia Press, 1993. ■ Kellner, Bruce. *Carl Van Vechten and the Irreverent Decades.* Norman: University of Oklahoma Press, 1968. ■ ——, ed. *Letters of Carl Van Vechten.* New Haven, Conn.: Yale University Press, 1987. ■ Lewis, David Levering. *When Harlem Was in Vogue.* New York: Oxford University Press, 1979. ■ Lueders, Edward. *Carl Van Vechten and the Twenties.* Albuquerque: University of New Mexico Press, 1955.

Verlaine, Paul
(1844–1896)

Born into a bourgeois family in Metz, France, Paul Verlaine was the pampered only child of a military father and doting mother. As a young boy, he moved with his parents to the outskirts of Paris, later the city of departure and return for an errant poet; and yet his calm early years did not presage the tempestuous and disorderly adulthood that was to follow. Leaving the refuge of the familial bosom, this "fearful and spoiled child" grew mischievous and bold, and devoted himself to his Parisian education, one both literary and erotic. When Verlaine described the early period of his life in his *Confessions* (1895), he characteristically minimized his homosexual attractions and interactions while nonetheless relating pubescent gropings with younger classmates.

Verlaine recounted more straightforwardly his blossoming literary interests. By the time he received his baccalauréat in 1862, he was an avid reader of the contemporary poets he would soon befriend in literary salons and cafes. After abandoning law school, he became a civil servant for the city of Paris, all the while continuing to write poetry and literary criticism. His first collection of poetry, *Poèmes saturniens* (1866), was strongly marked by the influence of the Parnassian movement and the poetry of one of his idols, CHARLES BAUDELAIRE.

Verlaine's first erotic work, *Les Amies* (1868), described lesbian sexuality. Inserting himself in a tradition of sapphic poetry that Baudelaire helped inaugurate, he published this collection pseudonymously in Brussels in order to escape French censorship. The first five of the six sonnets, all written in feminine rhymes, evoke rather innocently the couplings of adolescent girls. In darkly warm, perfumed, and languorous settings, naive and delicious young creatures speak of and make love, wearing thin robes of cotton and surrounded by muslin drapes. "Sappho," the final, inverted, sonnet, describes the suicide of this ancient mistress of lesbians and patron of poetry. She devotes her last thoughts to sleeping virgins before jumping into the sea.

Fêtes galantes (1869) followed, a more original collection of delicate, pastoral poems inspired by the eighteenth-century painter Watteau. This work made evident some of the contradictions that characterized Verlaine, a sensitive writer of refined and musical poems who was also prone to alcoholic excess and bouts of violence. These contradictions served to diminish Verlaine's reputation relative to the other great symbolist poets, Baudelaire, Mallarmé, and RIMBAUD. On one hand, some critics saw him as an almost effeminate poet of light verse unequal to the profundity of Baudelaire or the obscurity of Mallarmé. On the other, the "vulgarity" of his life and some of his subsequent works were deemed unseemly. Paul Valéry, for example, later wrote of his fascination at seeing the aging Verlaine saunter from one cafe to the next, but also of his distaste that prevented him from greeting a poet he deeply admired.

Verlaine's conflicted sexuality also became manifest in the late 1860s. Although taken with a friend and literary collaborator, Lucien Viotti, whose "ephebic body's exquisite proportions" he later described, Verlaine pursued a relationship with Mathilde Mauté, whom he married in 1870. *La Bonne chanson* (1870), dedicated to his new wife, sang with chaste sensitivity of her youthful beauty and of the marriage of their souls. He was nonetheless deeply distraught when Viotti died in combat the same year.

With his early publications, Verlaine gained renown and respect from other writers, including a young schoolboy and aspiring poet, Arthur Rimbaud, who wrote him admiring letters from the provinces. The convergence of Verlaine's marriage to Mathilde and the arrival of Rimbaud in Paris the following year exacerbated the conflict within Verlaine between bourgeois respectability and scandalous rebellion. The bond between the two poets was nearly instantaneous. Verlaine spent less and less time at home with his pregnant wife and disapproving in-laws, and more and more time with Rimbaud, whose aesthetic project was to "discover the unknown through the unsettling of all the senses." The younger, more audacious poet found a pliable and willing partner in Verlaine; together they scandalized their literary colleagues and the Mauté family. Often coming home drunk and occasionally abusing his wife, now the mother of the infant Georges, Verlaine was also experiencing new sensual delights with Rimbaud, and writing some of his most original poetry, which would later be collected in *Romances sans paroles* (1874). In his article, "Visions of Violence: Rimbaud and Verlaine," Paul Schmidt describes their sometimes sadomasochistic relationship as at once a laboratory for "new loves" and new poetry.

Verlaine's Rimbaud years were turbulent and impassioned. With other poets, they formed a group called the "vilains bonshommes"; and in cafes, they filled a notebook with bawdy poems that survived as the *Album zutique*. "Le sonnet du trou du cul" was penned by both of them, with Verlaine contributing the quatrains and Rimbaud the tercets. This poem in praise of the anus begins, "Dark and puckered like a violet carnation, it breathes, humbly hidden among the froth, still humid from love that follows the soft slope of a white ass down to its deepest rim."

After leaving Mathilde to travel with Rimbaud in Belgium, Verlaine lived with his lover for a while in London. Enamored of Rimbaud but determined to preserve his marriage, Verlaine was torn between the two. His relationship with Rimbaud ended violently when Verlaine shot him during a quarrel in Brussels. Although the wound was not serious, Verlaine was sentenced to two years in a Belgian prison, after having been forced to undergo a humiliating rectal examination that determined the nature of his sexual relationship with Rimbaud.

The months spent in prison allowed Verlaine time for reflection and time to write. While composing poems for a collection to be entitled *Cellulairement* (1875, but not published intact until 1992), he also underwent a religious conversion. His post-prison years, although no less disorderly, were nonetheless punctuated with bouts of piety and mysticism. Verlaine met with Rimbaud only once after his release from prison. The meeting proved frustrating, for his attempt to effect his former lover's religious conversion met with mockery. In many ways, the "scandalous" relationship between Verlaine and Rimbaud has overshadowed Verlaine's contributions as a poet who helped revolutionize French verse.

Verlaine's attempts to reconcile with Mathilde failed, and on returning to Paris, he was greeted as a pariah by his former literary colleagues. Unable to find a publisher for *Cellulairement,* he began again to wander, teaching for a while in France and in England. In 1878, he met and fell in love with a student, Lucien Létinois, and this relationship stabilized him for a time. The two men traveled to England and then settled with Lucien's parents on a farm in the Ardennes, where Verlaine continued to write. He published *Sagesse* in 1881, the first in a series of religious collections.

Verlaine's periods of serenity and sobriety were always short-lived. When he returned to Paris in 1882, where he began to attract attention from the younger generation of poets, he was nearly destitute and relied on his mother, Stéphanie, for financial as well as emotional support. After Lucien's death in 1883, Verlaine and his mother returned to the country, where he scandalized their small community with his drunkenness, violence, and seductions of farm boys. Writing all the while, he gradually reestablished his name in Paris, with his notoriety now actually enhancing rather than sullying his reputation. *Jadis et naguère* (1884), a heterogeneous collection of old and new poems, did not have much success, but his *Poètes maudits* (1884), a series of literary portraits that introduced Rimbaud's work to the new generation of symbolists and decadents, was well received. A second series of *Poètes maudits* followed in 1888, including the portrait of "Pauvre Lélian." With this anagram of his name, Verlaine concretized a sense of self that he projected in future writings as a poor, misunderstood, occasionally guilty but essentially naive and well-meaning person.

In the Ardennes, Verlaine was arrested for violence against his mother and sentenced to a month in a country prison. On his release, he returned definitively to Paris where he lived in a small and dank apartment. Confined there for months, immobilized by a rheumatic leg that would plague him for the rest of his life, he composed poems destined for future collections, including two more religious works, *Amour* (1888) and *Bonheur* (1891), as well as the quite lusty *Parallèlement* (1889). After their reconciliation, his mother joined him in this tenement only to die there the following year, a loss that Verlaine suffered deeply.

The last ten years of Verlaine's life were also arduous yet productive. He spent this time in and out of hospitals, ever short of money, often dragging his stiff leg from one cafe to the next, or propped up in a booth, glassy-eyed, an absinthe before him. His preference for younger men continued, and in 1888 he fell in love with an elegant painter named Frédéric-Auguste Cazals who left Verlaine when the relationship began to endanger the younger man's reputation. At the end of his life, Verlaine's sexual and emotional needs were satisfied by two women, Philomène Boudin and Eugénie Krantz. Verlaine's frequent stays in the hospital, punctuated by visits from loyal friends and devoted young admirers (including Rachilde, J.-K. HUYSMANS, and ANDRÉ GIDE), were not entirely unpleasant. In fact, these hospitals gave him a place to sleep and favored his productivity. He published eleven collections of poetry during the last six years of his life, and four more posthumously. These later poems, alternately religious and erotic (evocative of Boudin and Krantz), are little read today. Verlaine's most notable works during his last years were autobiographical texts that parceled his life into periods of

incarceration: *Mes hôpitaux* (1891) and *Mes prisons* (1893). In his *Confessions,* he returned to his youth, tracing his life from birth to his marriage with Mathilde. His prose works often whitewash his sexuality, but in real life Verlaine never abstained from following his pleasures.

Such pleasures and the relationships that provided them are not absent from Verlaine's poetry. Indeed, Viotti, Rimbaud, Létinois, and Cazals, as well as less personal references to gay love, figure in much of his work. Inevitably associated with Rimbaud, Verlaine was in fact not only his lover and literary colleague, but also his chronicler and publisher. It was thanks to Verlaine's insistence and vigilance that Rimbaud's unpublished poetry came to light. The portrait in *Poètes maudits* reintroduced Rimbaud to a contemporary audience in 1884, and the first edition of the *Illuminations,* prefaced by Verlaine, followed two years later. Verlaine also prefaced Rimbaud's posthumous *Poésies complètes* in 1895 and wrote a number of articles on him that helped assure Rimbaud's reputation as one of the most original poets of the century.

Romances sans paroles and *Cellulairement* are among Verlaine's collections most marked by his partnership with Rimbaud. Although *Romances sans paroles* does not evoke their relationship explicitly, its poems chart the poets' wanderings in Belgium and England, and show Verlaine coming into his own as an original writer. *Cellulairement* (whose poems Verlaine later dispersed in *Sagesse, Jadis et naguère,* and *Parallèlement*) contains some of Verlaine's most magnificent poems and evokes his lover in "L'espoir luit" as a fragile sleeper menaced by an intrusive woman. "Vers pour être calomnié," from *Jadis et naguère,* returns to this tableau, representing the speaker watching anxiously over a young sleeper whose body resembles his own. The masterpiece of Verlaine's Rimbaud cycle, the long hendecasyllabic "Crimen amoris," although nestled among a series of religious epics, describes a lovely adolescent demon with admiration and tenderness.

Parallèlement is an unapologetic exaltation of the flesh. In addition to the previously published lesbian cycle and some heteroerotic poems, this collection contains two poems entitled "Explication" that refer to his relationship with Rimbaud. "Sur une statue de Ganymède," "Pierrot Gamin," "Ces passions," "Laeti et errabundi," among others, also evoke the author's homosexual desire. *Amour,* in contrast, contains a cycle of twenty-five poems dedicated to his "spiritual son," Lucien Létinois, that insists on the purity of Lucien and of Verlaine's relationship with him. Similarly, the very Catholic *Bonheur,* composed during Verlaine's relationship with Cazals, includes a prayer to this young friend who arrives, like Christ, to save the speaker from his debauchery (XV: "Mon ami, ma plus belle amitié . . .").

Aside from his contribution to the *Album zutique,* only in a posthumously published collection did Verlaine give unchecked erotic expressions of his homosexuality. *Hombrès* (1904) contains fifteen jubilant poems (including the "Sonnet du trou du cul") that praise the male body and gay male love in explicit language. Although the editor Le Dantec refused to include this collection in the modern critical edition of Verlaine's complete works, it is available both in a French edition edited by J.-P. Corsetti and J.-P. Giusto and in an English translation by Alan Stone (*Royal Tastes, Erotic Writings,* 1980).

Verlaine was a brilliant poet who preferred to see his sensuality and mysticism, refinement and crudity, naivete and shrewdness, as parallel elements. His poetry, like his life, was often determined by an aesthetics of opposition that united precision with dispersal. "Crimen amoris" closes with these images of dispersal that urge toward coherence: "La forme molle au loin monte des collines / Comme un amour encore mal défini, / Et le brouillard qui s'essore des ravines / Semble un effort vers quelque but réuni" ("The vague form climbs the hills in the distance / Like a love still poorly defined, / And the fog that leaps up from ravines / Resembles an effort toward some unified destination"). Although Verlaine's own life was at times errant, his bewilderment was matched with a keenness that focused unremittingly from beginning to end on his two great and inseparable enthusiasms, poetry and sensuality. (See also FRENCH LITERATURE: NINETEENTH CENTURY.)

—*Gretchen Schultz*

BIBLIOGRAPHY

Petitfils, Pierre. *Verlaine.* Paris: Julliard, 1981. ■ Peyre, Henri. *Rimbaud vu par Verlaine.* Paris: Nizet, 1975. ■ Schmidt, Paul. "Visions of Violence: Rimbaud and Verlaine." *Homosexualities and French Literature.* Elaine Marks and George Stambolian, eds. Ithaca, N.Y.: Cornell University Press, 1979. ■ Stephan, Philip. *Paul Verlaine and the Decadence: 1882–1890.* Totowa, N.J.: Rowman and Littlefield, 1974. ■ Troyat, Henri. *Verlaine.* Paris: Flammarion, 1993.

Viau, Théophile de
(1590–1626)

The French poet Théophile de Viau was born in 1590 in Clairac into a Huguenot family that had recently been promoted to the ranks of the lesser nobility. During his youth, he studied medicine in Bordeaux and Holland; he also joined a troupe of traveling actors for whom he wrote plays. During Théophile's short life, he suffered attacks—often politically motivated—for his libertine morals and scandalous poetry. Banished from Paris in 1619, he retreated to his family estate at Boussères where he wrote a free verse and prose translation of PLATO's *Treatise on the immortality of the soul or the death of Socrates,* considered at the time to be a libertine text. Accused by the Jesuit priest Father Garasse and various judges of filling his work with impious and dangerous libertine ideas, Théophile should nonetheless be understood not as a philosopher, but as a remarkable, albeit free-thinking, poet. Brought back to Paris by the King at the request of his favorite, the Duke de Luynes, he gained fame as a major court poet. In 1621, he published the first volume of his *Works,* which established him as the leading poet of his day.

Although Théophile converted to Catholicism in 1622 for political reasons, Father Garasse accused him of leading a band of atheists and called him the king of libertines. Convicted in August 1623 of the crime of *lèse-majesté divine,* Théophile was condemned to the stake but only burned in effigy. Then in September 1623, he was arrested and imprisoned in the Conciergerie where he would remain for almost two years until finally cleared of the charges against him. Théophile was nonetheless banished forever from the kingdom of France, as was the Jesuit father Voisin, one of his chief adversaries. This judgment, while almost constituting an absolution for the poet, nevertheless marks the end of the flamboyant libertine movement. On his release, Théophile went into hiding, staying with one friend and then another; in December, he left Paris with the Duke of Montmorency, who was rejoining his regiment near La Rochelle. Then, on September 25, 1626, at the age of thirty-six, Théophile died in Paris at the home of his influential protector, the Duke of Montmorency.

Although his penchant for male lovers is generally acknowledged, Théophile's homosexuality and indeed all of his intimate relationships remain largely a matter of inference drawn from his highly personal poetry. His contemporary Tallement des Réaux refers to Jacques la Vallée des Barreaux as Théophile's widow, thus indicating that their physical relationship was common knowledge at the time. Father Garasse labels the group of writers, young noblemen, and bourgeois gathered around Théophile "beaux esprits," to suggest their free sexual mores as well as their free thinking.

Théophile's verse is a poetry of ideas, inspired by Montaigne, Epicurus, Lucretius, Giulio Vanini, HORACE, Pliny, and Seneca, all of whom were considered libertine thinkers. His credo, "follow Nature's law," takes on added resonance when natural inclination leads the lover outside relationships condoned by the Church. Advocating "the total enjoyment of one's limited time on earth in a spirit of generosity," Théophile gives full rein to sexual passion, seeing it as a major source of pleasure. Equally important is his conviction that poetry should be the sincere, personal expression of the poet's own experience and feelings, a belief that informs all of his work.

Théophile's poetry is noted for its rich imagery, vivid representation of nature, mythological allusions, and powerful evocations of sensuality. His verse frequently celebrates physical beauty and pleasure in ways that transgress gender boundaries. Among his cabaret poems, for example, "Par ce doux appétit des vices," addressed to the Duke of Buckingham, and "Marquis, comment te portes du?" posit sexual contact between men with a spirit of camaraderie and urbanity. Homosexual love is also occasionally the subject of witty and intense epigrams, such as "Philandre sur la maladie de Thyrsis." With some eighty-eight editions of his work appearing between 1621 and 1696, he was the most frequently published poet in seventeenth-century France. At once conscious of both his common humanity and his own distinct individuality, Théophile is a major seventeenth-century French poet. The critical role he played in the libertine movement, the surprisingly modern esthetic of his work, and its vast generic range mark him as a particularly rich figure in the patrimony of gay writers.

—*Kathleen Collins-Clark*

BIBLIOGRAPHY

Adam, Antoine. *Théophile de Viau et la libre pensée française en 1620*. Paris: Droz, 1935. ■ Collins-Clark, Kathleen. "Théophile de Viau and the Echo of Distant Voices." *Les Actes de Las Vegas*. Tuebingen: Biblio 17, 1991. ■ Duchêne, Roger, ed. *Théophile de Viau, Actes du Colloque du CMR 17: Papers on French Seventeenth Century Literature*. Tuebingen: Biblio 17, 1991. ■ Gaudiani, Claire. *The Cabaret Poetry of Théophile de Viau*. Tuebingen: Gunter Narr Verlag, 1981. ■ Gautier, Théophile. *Les Grotesques*. Paris: Desessatt, 1844. ■ Lachèvre, Frédéric. *Le libertinage au XVIIe siécle*, vol 1. Paris: Champion, 1909. ■ ———. *Le Procès du poète Théophile de Viau. Publication intégrale des pièces inédites des Archives natinales*. 2 vols. Geneva: Slatkine, 1968. ■ Rizza, Cecilia. "Place et fonction de la mythologie dans l'univers poétiqe de Théophile de Viau." *La Metamorphose dans la poésie baroue française et anglaise: Variations et resurgences*. Tuebingen: Gunter Narr, 1980. ■ Viau, Théophile de. *Oeuvres Complètes*. Guido Saba, ed. 4 vols. Paris: Librairie A.G. Nizet, 1979–1987.

Vidal, Gore
(b. 1925)

The multifaceted [Eugene] Gore Vidal [Jr.] is a novelist, playwright, essayist, mystery writer (under the pseudonym Edgar Box), screenwriter, social critic, literary critic, congressional candidate, political activist, and actor. Entering the army during World War II while in his teens and rising to the rank of sergeant, Vidal has had no formal higher education. He is important for the gay literary heritage because of the straightforwardness with which he has pursued gay themes and included gay characters in his work, beginning in his teens when we wrote his first novel, *Williwaw* (1946). He has also steadily upped the ante about what sorts of gay material could be included in his mainstream works and as a result has made it easier for a wide range of other writers to find public acknowledgment of their material. Although the grandson of a United States Senator, Vidal feels uncomfortable in America because of his sexuality and has lived mostly in Italy since the mid-1960s, sharing his life with his companion Howard Austen.

The City and the Pillar (1948), Vidal's third novel, is the story of professional tennis player Jim Willard, a man who never outgrows a boyhood crush on his best friend, Bob Ford. The idea that men who enjoy sex with other men circulate among ordinary people undetected is implicit everywhere in this novel and outraged some original readers. Although Vidal argues here and in many places in his nonfiction that there is no homosexual identity and everyone is bisexual, the plot of the book proves the contrary. For *The City and the Pillar* is, despite itself, the first mainstream coming-out novel. At the insistence of the publisher, the original book ended with a violent death, although Vidal had gone against tradition by having his protagonist kill his boyhood love rather than expiate his own supposed transgressions through death. Claude Summers notes that the ending originally published is unsatisfactory not merely because it is "melodramatic and unbelievable. It is also as falsely romanticized as the modes of thought the novel criticizes with such cool clarity." In 1968, in light of changed social values, Vidal was able to publish *The City and the Pillar Revised,* a substantially altered version of the book with a different ending. The revision is more shocking because in it Bob is sodomized, not murdered. But the violence of this revised ending is better justified since Bob does not simply reject Jim as "queer," precipitating Jim's retaliation; he initiates the violence. There is a strong statement of how inflammatory such name-calling can be.

Most of Vidal's works have more or less prominent gay characters, and he is important for the consistency with which he has continually expanded gay visibility in mainstream fiction and, to some extent, drama, for example, in *The Best Man* (1960), where the plot turns on a question of blackmail about an episode of homosexuality in the life of an essentially straight man. In his plays and novels with modern settings, Vidal's ear for contemporary idiom is so perfect and his understanding of current fads and obsessions so sure that he is always readable and often an incisive critic of modern life as well. His stylistic experiments indicate both by their virtues and by their failings that when he controls his art he has the stylistic powers of a major craftsman.

In one such stylistic experiment, *Myra Breckinridge* (1968), Vidal returned to the public eye at the center of a major controversy. Going VIRGINIA WOOLF's *Orlando* one better, Vidal's *Myra Breckinridge* is the first instance of a novel in which the main character undergoes a clinical sex change, a brilliantly chosen image for satire of contemporary mores. *Myra Breckinridge* alternates first-person narrators (one as if transcribed from unedited tape recordings) very effectively. Regarded as scandalous and even dangerous when first published, the sexual content is fairly tame by the standard of what is discussed regularly on television nowadays. The sequel *Myron* (1974) uses filmmaking effectively as a metaphor for time travel to contrast the present unfavorably to the past; the book is also highly successful in manipulating euphemisms to mock Nixon-decade politicians. But even with all this and a raunchy sexuality, the book was neither a critical nor a popular success; because of changing standards of taste, although appearing only six years after *Myra Breckinridge* but five years after Stonewall, it was not even a *succès de scandale.*

Two Sisters (1970) is, however, Vidal's most successful tour de force both in experimental point of view and in realistic representation of homosexual identity. A silly screenplay for an unmade film is the centerpiece of this work. There are again alternating first-person narrators from past and present who have very different perspectives on the nature of this curious piece of writing. The work is something of a *roman à clef* satirizing Jacqueline Kennedy Onassis, ANAÏS NIN, Norman Mailer, and other celebrities— and perhaps Vidal, who has written himself into the book as one of the two main narrators. This self-projection is in the tradition of W. SOMERSET MAUGHAM or CHRISTOPHER ISHERWOOD, but Vidal writes with much more forthrightness about his sexuality, thus taking the nonfiction novel to a new plane of self-revelation. He shows himself exploring sexual as well as artistic freedom in Europe away from the conservatism of America.

Early in his career Vidal wrote occasional short stories. Kiernan credits the stories collected in *A Thirsty Evil* (1956) with bringing Vidal's style to maturity by enabling him to develop a feel for a variety of narrators. And these stories include Vidal's most focused attention on gay milieux before *Myra Breckinridge.* "Three Strategems," for example, uses two narrators in the manner of several of Vidal's most technically proficient novels to bring insight to an encounter between an epileptic hustler and a prospective client. And "The Zenner Trophy," with a third-person restrictive point of view, shows a teacher gaining respect for a boy being expelled from school for homosexual activity by the clear certainty with which the boy apparently understands himself.

In addition to fiction and drama, Vidal has written a large number of essays, often disputatious ones. He has a broad range of insightful but usually not very comforting comments to make about American politics and the American character in general. In an analysis unfortunately still apt today, the essay "Pink Triangle and Yellow Star" (1981), for example, describes how Jewish intellectuals have been undermining their own minority rights by their conventional stereotyping of practitioners of what Vidal calls "same-sex sex." (See also CROSS-DRESSING and NOVEL: GAY MALE.)
—*Edmund Miller*

BIBLIOGRAPHY

Dick, Bernard F. *The Apostate Angel: A Critical Study of Gore Vidal.* New York: Random House, 1974. ■ Kiernan, Robert F. *Gore Vidal.* New York: Ungar, 1982. ■ Parini, Jay, ed. *Gore Vidal: Writer Against the Grain.* New York: Columbia University Press, 1992. ■ Summers, Claude J. *Gay Fictions: Wilde to Stonewall. Studies in a Gay Male Literary Tradition.* New York: Ungar, 1990. ■ White, Ray Lewis. *Gore Vidal.* Boston: Twayne Publishers, 1968.

The Violet Quill

In its narrowest sense, the Violet (or Lavender) Quill was simply a circle of gay male writers in Manhattan who met a few times in 1980 and 1981 to read to one another from their works in progress. In a much larger sense, however, the Violet Quill commands interest because this group of friends and rivals—Christopher Cox, ROBERT FERRO, Michael Grumley, ANDREW HOLLERAN, Felice Picano, EDMUND WHITE, and George Whitmore—helped create the post-Stonewall renaissance of American gay male writing. The members of the Violet Quill were quite different from one another and did not consciously constitute a "school," but collectively and individually they placed homosexuality at the very center of their literary visions. As David Bergman has observed, they "shared several impulses: a desire to write works that reflected their gay experiences, and specifically, autobiographical fiction; a desire to write for gay readers without having to explain their point of view to shocked and unknowing heterosexual readers; and finally, a desire to write . . . in a selection of the language really used by gay men." In retrospect, they may be seen as pioneers in the struggle to create a literature that reflected the social revolution wrought by the Stonewall uprising. Their works chronicle both the headiness of the early years of gay liberation and the tragedy of the AIDS epidemic, to which four of the seven have succumbed.

Of the writers of the Violet Quill, the ones who have achieved the greatest renown are the novelists Edmund White, Andrew Holleran, and Robert Ferro. These three writers have had an enormous impact on the development of contemporary gay literature. Holleran's *Dancer from the Dance* (1978), Ferro's *The Family of Max Desir* (1983), and White's *The Beautiful Room Is Empty* (1988) surely rank among the most influential accounts of American gay life yet written. White and Holleran continue to be important figures in the gay literary world; Ferro died of AIDS in 1988.

At the time of the Violet Quill's formation, probably the best known member of the group (at least to the general public) was Felice Picano, who had already published some commercially successful heterosexual formula fiction, including the thriller *Eyes* (1976). The most prolific member of the Violet Quill, he has produced a number of gay novels, poems, stories, and memoirs; in 1977, he founded SeaHorse Press, New York's first gay publishing house. His works include *The Deformity Lover and Other Poems* (1978), *The Lure* (1979), *Late in the Season* (1981), *Slashed to Ribbons in Defense of Love and Other Stories* (1983), and *Men Who Loved Me: A Memoir in the Form of a Novel* (1989).

George Whitmore, author of two autobiographical novels, *The Confessions of Danny Slocum, or Gay Life in the Big City* (1980) and *Nebraska* (1987), also wrote memorable essays focusing on individuals affected by the AIDS epidemic. Two of the essays were originally published in *The New York Times Magazine*; they were published in book form as *Someone Was Here: Profiles in the AIDS Epidemic* (1988). He died of the disease in 1989.

Michael Grumley, the lover of Robert Ferro, collaborated with him on a nonfiction book, *Atlantis: The Autobiography of a Search* (1970). His other works include two other books of nonfiction—*Hard Corps: Studies in Leather and Sadomasochism* (1977) and *After Midnight* (1978)—and a novel, *Life Drawings* (1991), which was published after his death from AIDS in 1988.

Christopher Cox, sometime lover of Edmund White, wrote only one book, the nonfiction guide, *A Key West Companion* (1983). However, his recently published short story, "Aunt Persia and the Jesus Man," included in Bergman's anthology, *The Violet Quill Reader* (1994), amply testifies to his talent as a creative writer. He eventually entered publishing, first as an assistant to Bill Whitehead, who edited White and Ferro, and then as an editor in his own right. He died of AIDS in 1988.

Bergman's *The Violet Quill Reader* collects a generous selection of the writings of this group, including heretofore unpublished work such as some correspondence of Holleran and Ferro, excerpts from the journals of Picano and Grumley, stories by Cox and Picano, and a lecture on gay literature by Ferro.

—*Claude J. Summers*

BIBLIOGRAPHY

Bergman, David, ed. *The Violet Quill Reader*. New York: St. Martin's, 1994.

Virgil
(70–19 B.C.)

The pastoral setting of so many of Virgil's shorter poems was not merely a literary convention; he was in fact born on a farm near Mantua and throughout his life struck his contemporaries as shy, awkward, and countrified. Of sturdy build, Virgil, nevertheless, suffered from poor health and was often ill from headaches and hemorrhaging lungs; his modesty and lack of aggressiveness earned him a nickname—"the Virgin." His earliest patron, Asinius Pollio, encouraged him to write of rural life in his first important poems, the *Eclogues,* completed when Virgil was about thirty. Pollio, a former general, had retired from public affairs to devote himself to authorship and the encouragement of literature. He had known CATULLUS and was a friend of HORACE. He also owned a slave named Alexander, with whom Virgil, who never married, fell in love.

We know this last detail from a biography of Virgil appended to the *Commentary* of Donatus, a fourth-century critic. (It is possible that this *Life* is by Suetonius rather than Donatus; scholarship has been unable to decide the issue.) Virgil is characterized as "inclined to passions for boys," an unusual instance of a man's being assigned a specific preference by a Latin biographer. We are also told that Virgil "especially favored" two boys named Cebes and Alexander, that the boys were educated by him, and that Cebes even became a poet. We also learn that Alexander was a slave given to Virgil by Pollio and that he was, in fact, the "Alexis" of Virgil's second eclogue. Both of the boys had, presumably, been slaves, but apart from this, Virgil's relation to them seems to have approximated to the Greek ideal, according to which the older man became the protector and mentor of the younger. One other ancient document also seems to attest to Virgil's homosexuality. The collection of epigrams and short poems called the *Catalepton* has two poems that are probably by Virgil, the fifth and seventh. In the first, the poet says farewell to a friend in Rome and to all the city's "beautiful boys"; in the second, he confesses to Varius that he is in love with a boy.

Five of Virgil's ten pastoral *Eclogues* make at least some incidental reference to homosexuality. By far the most famous of these is the second or Corydon eclogue. Though Romans were theoretically supposed to limit their male amours to slave boys, this is one of the few poems in which the boy's slave status is explicitly mentioned. He is introduced as Alexis, "the darling of the master" (*delicias domini*). The poem invites reflection on the paradoxes involved in "courting" a slave. By custom and by Roman law, a master might simply command any slave's sexual compliance. Yet the literary conventions of homoerotic verse, which the Romans took over from the Greeks, required that the poet should express frustration, be at the mercy of the boy's refusal, and even suffer his disdain. Arab rulers, in love with male slaves in tenth-century Spain, relished the piquancy of the situation in poems that declared frankly, "You are my slave, I am yours." Roman poets, less given to paradox, stuck to the Greek convention, so that we are, in fact, often in doubt about the boy's status.

Ancient writers (such as the Donatian biographer, Martial, Apuleius, and Servius) all assume that Corydon is simply a persona assumed by the modest Virgil, and equate the two. Corydon is described in the poem as a simple shepherd (whether free or slave is not made clear), presumably also the servant of "the master." Though he is wealthy enough to own a thousand sheep, he has no proprietary rights over Alexis. Corydon wants them "to live together" a life devoted to hunting and herding, and risks sunstroke to pursue the youth, who is indifferent to his suffering despair. We may find in all this a kind of humorous self-deprecation. Corydon reminds himself, "You are only a rustic," as if he fears Alexis may prefer some sophisticated city dweller. At the end, he judges himself a lunatic for neglecting the homely tasks of the farm for this mad passion.

The Corydon eclogue became the most famous poem on male love in Latin literature. It is Corydon's love for Alexis, not Catullus' passion for Juventius or Tibullus' for Marathus, that is cited by later Latin poets and critics when they discuss the poetry of male love. It is noteworthy, however, that, whatever Virgil's own sexual preference, Corydon represents himself as bisexual. He complains that Alexis is so cruel that he (Corydon) would have been better off with the temperamental Amaryllis (a woman) or swarthy Menalcas (another male). Later eclogues maintain this democratic balance. In the third eclogue, Menalcas scolds the goatherd Damoetas, who evens the score by alleging that Menalcas was once possessed by another male in a shrine while tittering nymphs looked on. When their rivalry takes the form of a singing contest, Damoetas sings of his love for Galatea and Amaryllis, while Menalcas salutes the boy Amyntas as his "flame." In eclogue five, Menalcas asks Mopsus to sing a song about Phyllis or, alternatively, about the boy Alcon. In eclogue seven, another singing match finds Corydon still lamenting the "handsome Alexis" but also enraptured of the sea nymph Galatea. Gallus, in the tenth eclogue, shows the same lack of prejudice as to gender; he bemoans the loss of his mistress Lycoris but envies the Arcadians—if he had their musical skill, he might win any "Phyllis or Amyntas." These figures are, of course, not real characters but shadowy names; what is striking is that their sex is equally immaterial.

Up to this point, Virgil might have seemed to rank with Catullus, Tibullus, Propertius, and other poets of the "erotic revolt" who sang of dalliance and derided traditional Roman values. (See also ROMAN LITERATURE.) But Virgil now turned from the artificialities of Theocritaean pastoral to write another set of poems, the Georgics, which dealt more realistically with the practical techniques, trials, and delights of farm life. The poems pleased Augustus, who wanted to repopulate the Italian countryside by settling his veterans on the land. Augustus now enlisted Virgil to write a Roman epic to rival Greece's Iliad. The Aeneid was intended to celebrate Rome's roots in myth and legend, the glories of its conquests, and the divine nature of the imperial mission, which was to impose its own version of law and order on the Mediterranean world. The emphasis in the Aeneid is on pious duty, not personal relationships. Consequently, Aeneas leaves Dido, the Queen of Carthage, after their brief love affair, to fulfill his destiny by leading the Trojans to Italy, where they become the progenitors of the Roman race.

Virgil's epic appears to downplay love as a value. But in fact, it offered him an opportunity to elevate the Roman view of male love from amorous play with a pretty slave to the heroic ideal of the Greeks. Virgil does this by incorporating into the Aeneid the story of Nisus and Euryalus. Euryalus is a handsome soldier in the bloom of youth, Nisus a mature warrior who is bound to him by what Virgil calls an "amor pius." Their love—Virgil uses the word several times—is clearly meant to mirror the bond that unites Achilles and Patroclus in the Iliad. Indeed, Virgil has so managed that they more nearly fulfill the classical pattern of the Greek "lover" (erastes) and "beloved" (eromenos) than do Homer's heroes. (See also GREEK LITERATURE, ANCIENT.) Their story seems very closely tailored to match the ideal set forth by Phaedrus in PLATO's Symposium, the ideal of two comrades in arms whose love leads to heroic self-sacrifice. To this end, Virgil repeatedly emphasizes Euryalus' beauty and Nisus' protective leadership.

In the fifth book of the Aeneid, the men take part in a footrace. Nisus stumbles and brings down with him another runner to make Euryalus the winner. The young man's good looks lead Aeneas' soldiers to condone this trick and award him the prize. In book nine, the pair are on guard duty at night, together. Nisus plans to make a dangerous foray to take a vital message to Aeneas. Euryalus begs to join him, and the pair slaughter many sleeping enemy soldiers. However, the younger man is separated from his lover in the dark and surrounded by vengeful Rutulians. Nisus tries heroically to save him but is cut down and expires on the dead boy's body in a kind of Liebestod. (This is not quite the only example of Greek love in the Aeneid; in book ten, the valiant Cydon is briefly introduced as the lover of the handsome Clytius and characterized as a pederast.) After their deaths, Virgil salutes Nisus and Euryalus as "Fortunate both" and prophecies that their fame will last as long as Rome's. Obviously, he hoped they would become to the Latins what Achilles and Patroclus were to the Greeks. But this was not to be: Virgil's effort to engraft the Greek ideal of heroic pederasty onto Latin culture is of great interest, but he did not succeed in influencing later writers.

The Middle Ages held Virgil in high regard, esteeming him as a prophet and seer as well as a poet. DANTE, who apparently knew the Donatian biography, made him his guide through Hell and Purgatory, and the unusual courtesy he shows to sodomites in both domains may stem partly from his knowledge of his mentor's tastes. Nevertheless, an unamiable medieval legend (traceable to the thirteenth century) held that all sodomites had died at the moment of Christ's birth, and some ecclesiastics who were confused about the date of Virgil's death maintained that he too had died in the holocaust. In the Renaissance, CHRISTOPHER MARLOWE appears to have been inspired by the Corydon eclogue to issue his own seductive invitation to the pastoral life—"Come live with me and be my love." No doubt Marlowe's own homosexuality drew him to the poem. RICHARD BARNFIELD published in 1594 a work called The Affectionate Shepherd, which bore the inflammatory subtitle "The Complaint of Daphnis for the Love of Ganymede." When he found himself attacked by unsympathetic English readers for the homoeroticism of his verses, his rather disingenuous defense was to maintain that his poem was only "an imitation of Virgil, in the second eclogue of Alexis."

In English translations, references to homosexual love in Greek and Latin classics were typically handled in one of three ways. Passages were omitted (as with Ovid's account of Orpheus' turning to the love of boys in George Sandys's 1626 translation of the Metamorphoses), pronouns were changed to disguise genders (as in renderings of SAPPHO and Plato), or more rarely, the translator added some editorial moralizing. This was the case with the lines on Cydon as they appeared in Dryden's famous rhymed version of the *Aeneid* (1698). Where Virgil had simply called Clytius Cydon's "latest joy" and remarked that Cydon's amorous life was almost ended on the battlefield, Dryden saw fit to interpolate a very un-Virgilian comment: "The wretched Cydon had received his doom, / Who courted Clytius in his beardless bloom, / And sought with lust obscene polluted joys." Byron, in search of literature that would validate his own youthful homosexual feelings, found inspiration in the episode of Nisus and Euryalus, and published his own translation while he was still in his teens. His contemporary JEREMY BENTHAM, arguing for the reform of England's lethal sodomy law, cited the episode as proof that the Romans tolerated male love. The anonymous author of *Don Leon* (a poem that purported to be BYRON's own account of his homosexual experiences) included

a list of famous homosexuals that began with Virgil: "When young Alexis claimed a Virgil's sigh, / He told the world his choice, and may not I?" In 1924, ANDRÉ GIDE published four dialogues in defense of homosexuality under the title *Corydon*.(See also PASTORAL and ROMAN LITERATURE.)

—*Louis Crompton*

BIBLIOGRAPHY

"Life of Vergil." *Suetonius.* Vol. 2. Trans. J. C. Rolfe. Cambridge, Mass.: Harvard University Press, 1965. ■ Lilja, Saara. *Homosexuality in Republican and Augustan Rome.* Helsinki: Societas Scientificarum Fennica, 1982. ■ Makowski, John F. "Nisus and Euryalus: A Platonic Relationship." *Classical Journal* 85(1989): 1–15. ■ Virgil. *The Eclogues and Georgics.* Trans. C. Day Lewis. Garden City, N.Y.: Anchor Books, 1964. ■ ———. *The Aeneid.* Trans. R. Fitzgerald. New York: Random House, 1983.

Vivien, Renée
(1877–1909)

Renée Vivien was born Pauline Mary Tarn on June 11, 1877, in Paddington, England, into a prosperous family of merchants. Pauline and her sister, Antoinette, attended school in Paris until their father, John, died when Pauline was nine. Their mother, Mary Gillet Bennett, decided to return to England, the prospect of which dismayed Pauline since she already identified herself as French, a fact that would influence her writing and thinking.

Her life in England was not pleasant. Her mother tried to have Pauline declared insane in order to acquire the money left directly to her daughter. The magistrates sided with Pauline, who was made a ward of the court until she reached her majority in 1898 and returned to Paris.

Once there, Pauline changed her name, first to René or R. Vivien, to signify her "rebirth." Though she had begun writing in English at the age of six, as an adult she wrote only in French, and at first pretended that the romantic sonnets contained in *Etudes et Préludes* (*Etudes and Preludes,* 1901), and *Cendres et Poussières* (*Ashes and Dust,* 1902), were written by a man. In 1903, she altered her first name slightly to the feminine Renée on the cover of *Evocations* (1903), a transformation that initially took her readers by surprise but that did not diminish the reputation she had already garnered as one of the best second-generation Symbolist poets.

At the end of 1899, Vivien's childhood friend, Violet Shilleto, introduced her to NATALIE CLIFFORD BARNEY, the wealthy and beautiful American, who was already leading an active lesbian life in Paris. As Vivien recounted in her novel, *Une Femme m'apparut* (*A Woman Appeared to Me,* 1904), she was almost instantly fixated by the magnetic personality of Barney: "I would evoke over and over again the faraway hour when I saw her for the first time, and the shudder which ran down my spine when my eyes met her eyes of mortal steel. . . . I had a dim premonition that this woman would determine the pattern of my destiny, and that her face was the fearful face of my Future." Much of Vivien's work was inspired by their relationship.

In the summer of 1900, Vivien and Barney traveled together to Bar Harbor, Maine, to visit Barney's family, after which they studied classical Greek for several weeks in the early fall at Bryn Mawr. On their return to Paris, Barney and Vivien continued to study classical Greek and French prosody with Professor Charles-Brun, a classical scholar. Vivien, the apter pupil, was soon writing verse imitative of SAPPHO's. Charles-Brun drew the attention of the publisher Alphonse Lemerre to Vivien's poetry, and her first book, *Etudes and Préludes,* was published in 1901. The volume set the tone for her subsequent work since it alternated melancholy love sonnets addressed to women with decadent longings for the embrace of death.

Vivien's personal life was less harmonious than her poetry. Vivien was tormented by Barney's infidelities and by the death in 1901 of Violet Shilleto, who was one of the major inspirations for Vivien's poetry, which is filled with images of the purple flower, so much so that she is often called "the muse of the violets." While Barney was away in Bar Harbor, Vivien, on hearing false rumors of Barney's impending marriage, broke with Barney and then tried, for the second or third time in her life, to commit suicide. At the end of 1901, Vivien met the Baroness Hélène de Zuylen de Nyevelt, a Rothschild, with whom she would spend the next several years.

The Baroness offered Vivien emotional and perhaps financial security, under which her poetry flourished. Most of Vivien's work is dedicated to "H.L.C.B.," the initials of the Baroness's first names. But Barney briefly reignited her affair with Vivien in 1904 when the two ran off together to Lesbos, where they hoped to establish a Sapphic circle of artists. The project was abandoned when Vivien decided to rekindle her relationship with the Baroness.

In 1906, the Baroness ended her relationship with Vivien, who went on to have affairs with a singer and at least two members of the demimonde. Eventually, she spent most of her time shut up in her apartment at 23, Avenue Bois du Boulogne. There she nailed the windows closed and filled the rooms with Buddhas and incense. At other times, she traveled widely, including to many parts of Europe and Asia as well as to Turkey, Mytilene, and Hawaii.

Despite her erratic lifestyle, which seemed to embrace both the encloistered, decadent urges of the Symbolists and the restless wandering of RIMBAUD, she continued to write prolifically. She published four volumes of poetry between 1906 and 1908, including *A l'Heure des Mains jointes* (*At the Hour of Joined Hands,* 1906); *Sillages* (*Wakes,* 1908); and *Flambeaux éteints* (*Extinguished Torches,* 1908). She also completed a novel, *Anne Boleyn* (which was not published until 1982), about the second wife of Henry VIII. She became increasingly alcoholic and anorexic and, after making a deathbed conversion to Catholicism, she died of those two diseases on November 18, 1909. Three volumes of poetry were published posthumously: *Dans un Coin de Violettes* (*In a Corner of Violets*), *Les Vents des Vaisseaux* (*The Winds in the Sails*), and *Haillons* (*Rags*).

Although Vivien is often remembered for her dramatic life and turbulent affair with Natalie Barney, she was an astoundingly prolific writer. Between 1901 and 1909, she wrote fourteen volumes of poetry, three volumes of short stories and prose poems, two novels, and translated Sappho into modern French. In addition, most critics believe she collaborated with the Baroness de Zuylen de Nyevelt under the name of "Paule Riversdale" in writing two volumes of verse and two novels: *Vers l'Amour* (*Towards Love*), *Echos et Reflets* (*Echos and Reflections*), *L'Etre double* (*Double Being*), and *Netsuké.* She also contributed to many journals, including the feminist *La Fronde,* edited by Marguerite Durand.

Her poems openly celebrated lesboerotic love twenty years before RADCLYFFE HALL published *The Well of Loneliness.* Although she often portrayed herself as someone who was in mourning for the loss of Violet Shilleto or who was abandoned by the faithless Natalie Barney, still she was completely unapologetic about the homosexual nature of her emotional longings. As she said in "Psappha revit," "Our caresses are melodious poems / Our love is greater than all other loves." She knew that most of her contemporaries would scorn her because "my look sought out your tender look." As a result, like her beloved Sappho, she wrote for an imagined audience of contemporary and future lesbians who would share her adoration of other women.

She imagined lesbians as the prototype for what she idealized as gynandromorphs. In *A Woman Appeared to Me, Double Being,* and other works, she created a superior, sexless (but essentially female) entity who was complete unto herself and powerfully endowed with poetic talent. Like many of her contemporaries, including Rachilde, Lucie Delarue-Mardrus, and Natalie Barney, she was fascinated by the idea of androgyny. A revival of Greek culture at the turn of the century had brought Plato's myth of the androgyne to the public's attention, but Vivien subverted that myth by prioritizing the female element of the dyad instead of incorporating female elements into a male entity as most classical authors were wont to do.

Unhappy with the course of literary history, Vivien set out to rewrite it, starting with Sappho, whom she almost single-handedly reclaimed as a lesbian. Nineteenth-century literature had generally portrayed Sappho as the mother of Cleis and the woman so betrayed by the ferryman Phaon that she leapt to her death over the Leucadian cliff. Vivien anonymously translated the fragments of Sappho into modern French for the first time in her *Sapho* (1909). She rewrote Sappho's life, starting with the reclamation of the uncorrupted form of her name, "Psappha." In a series of meditations and expansions on Sapphic fragments, entitled *Sapho* (1903), Vivien recreated Sappho's school of followers on Mytilene and gave them a voice. In later works, she raised Sappho to the level of a muse or even to that of a goddess of lesbian love.

Vivien also turned her attention to reestablishing other figures who, to her mind, were neglected or misrepresented by history. One of these was Lilith, the apocryphal first wife of Adam, whom Vivien saw as a heroine who would rather sleep with snakes than submit to Adam's will. In *La Dame à la Louve* (*The Woman of the Wolf,* 1904), Vivien turned her attention to the biblical Vashti, the first wife of King Ahasuerus. Instead of depicting her as the wife who was cast out in favor of Queen Esther, Vivien portrayed her as a heroine who defied the king's scandalous demand that she appear before his courtiers without her veil.

Vivien's attempt to rewrite literary history was quite broad-ranging. Some of the tales in *The Woman of the Wolf* are set in the American wilderness. Invariably, the female protagonists are braver than their male peers. Inevitably, they die rather than submit to the powers of nature or of men. Vivien even tackled the genre of the fairy tale. In "Prince Charming," the prince and princess have a fabulous wedding, after which the astounded family of the bride discovers that the groom is the prince's sister disguised in male clothing.

Vivien also rewrote and reimagined elements of her own life. In numerous poems, prose poems, and in her novel *A Woman Appeared to Me,* Vivien obsessively recreated her relationship with Natalie Barney. Barney is repeatedly portrayed as the femme fatale who seduces and betrays the poor poet. One of Vivien's favorite images was to recreate Barney as the faithless Atthis, who drives the talented poet Sappho to suicide. However, recent scholarship by Jean-Paul Goujon and Agnès Théveniault suggests that Vivien was far less of a victim than she liked to portray herself. For example, amid her emotional drama with Barney and the Baroness, Vivien was carrying on a torrid correspondence with Kérimé Turkhan-Pacha, a highly cultivated Turkish woman living in Constantinople, to whom she wrote in 1905: "I love you, I love only you, and I suffer, because one suffers from every love." Yet in her lyrics, she portrays herself as the hapless victim of others' infidelities.

The literary reputation of Renée Vivien has changed dramatically in the course of the twentieth century. In the first two decades after Vivien's death, Charles Maurras attempted to tie Vivien to other late Romantic writers, such as Anna de Noailles. Others, such as Yves-Gérard Le Dantec in *Renée Vivien: Femme damnée, Femme sauvée,* focused on her conversion to Catholicism, which placed Vivien in a tradition of reformed Decadent writers, such as BAUDELAIRE, who had also repented on his deathbed. In an attempt to preserve her reputation as a writer and to keep her lesbian secrets away from public scrutiny, scholar Salomon Reinarch reportedly locked up Vivien's private papers in the Bibliothèque Nationale until the year 2000. Natalie Barney attempted to keep Vivien's name alive by establishing a literary prize in her honor.

Despite these efforts, Renée Vivien lapsed into obscurity as a writer, in part because her Symbolist techniques were already dated while she was still writing, the movement having hit a peak in the final decades of the preceding century. Her rhymes and sonnets were considered unadventurous and passé in contrast to the experimental poetry and blank verse of the early decades of the twentieth century. Vivien's radical ideas were often overlooked beneath the traditional forms in which they were cloaked.

The blatantly lesboerotic nature of her work made it unpublishable in England and the United States so that in fact nothing appeared in English until Jeannette H. Foster's stilted translation of *A Woman Appeared to Me* was published by Naiad in 1976. But Vivien's Symbolist roman à clef did not stir the imaginations of readers so much as her real-life romance with Natalie Barney. And Vivien's poetry, filled as it is with violets and lilies, made Vivien seem more of a garden poet than a revolutionary thinker. Like her aborted plan to turn Mytilene into a lesbian artists' colony, Vivien's ideas were often more wonderful in conception than execution. But her stories of powerful women who fearlessly faced every type of risk and her dreams of woman-controlled spaces in an era when most women were still domestically enclosed make her worthy of the attention of "the women of the future" for whom she wrote.

—*Karla Jay*

BIBLIOGRAPHY

Barney, Natalie Clifford. *Adventures of the Mind.* New York: New York University Press, 1992. ■ ———. *A Perilous Advantage: The Best of Natalie Clifford Barney.* Norwich, Vt.: New Victoria, 1992. ■ Colette. *The Pure and the Impure.* New York: Farrar Straus, 1967. ■ Goujon, Jean-Paul. *Tes Blessures sont plus douces que leurs Caresses: Vie de Renée Vivien.* Paris: Régine Desforges, 1986. ■ Germain, André. *Renée Vivien.* Paris: Crès, 1917. ■ Jay, Karla. *The Amazon and the Page: Natalie Clifford Barney and Renée Vivien.* Bloomington: Indiana University Press, 1988. ■ LeDantec, Yves-Gérard. *Renée Vivien: Femme damnée, Femme sauvée.* Aix-en-Provence: Editions du Feu, 1930. ■ Lorenz, Paul. *Sapho, 1900: Renée Vivien.* Paris: Julliard, 1977. ■ Maurras, Charles. *Le Romantisme féminin.* Paris: Cité des Livres, 1926. ■ Théveniault, Agnès. "Un leger Murmure": Vie et Oeuvre de Renée Vivien (1877-1909), Master's Thesis, Université de Paris VII, 1991. ■ Tinayre, Marcelle. *Une Soirée chez Renée Vivien, (2 Nov. 1908).* Gouy: Mesidor, 1981.

Vogel, Bruno
(1898–1983)

Vogel's experiences as a soldier during World War I and as a homosexual in a society hostile to any open expression of same-sex love shaped his political and aesthetic vision. Shortly after the war, he cofounded the "Gemeinschaft Wir" ("We, the Community"), a local chapter of the Scientific-Humanitarian Committee in Leipzig, his hometown. This Committee was the largest group working for homosexual emancipation in Germany from 1896 to 1933. Its founder, Dr. Magnus Hirschfeld, arranged a job for Vogel at the Committee's Berlin headquarters in the Institute for Sexual Research. In November 1929, Vogel was elected to the Committee's board of directors.

By that time, Vogel had made a name for himself as a writer. In 1924, he published the antiwar *Es lebe der Krieg!* (*Long Live War!*), which caused him to be tried (and later acquitted) for blasphemy. A passionate socialist and pacifist, Vogel recognized early the danger of National Socialism. From 1931 to 1937, he lived in various European cities. As was the case with many of Germany's left-wing intellectuals, writers, and artists, the exile became permanent. For the next sixteen years, Vogel lived in Capetown, South Africa, where his involvement with the black community eventually led to difficulties with the white government. In late 1952, he moved to London, where he remained until his death in 1983.

Vogel's two chief prose works deal with the themes of anti-militarism and anti-imperialism. Three of the seven stories that make up *Ein Gulasch und andere Skizzen* (*A Gulash and Other Sketches,* 1928) delineate male homosexual characters as the voices of humanity, reason, and love. They point the way out of the economic hardship and moral decay around them by refusing to be separated from their fellow-sufferers, who are all nongay. A striking example of this expression of solidarity is a man's explanation of why he and his friends must work against the new wave of militarism in Germany: "I love a young man."

That love of a young man forms the center of Vogel's best-known work, the novel *Alf* (1929). Told in Vogel's spare, ironic style, the novel focuses on two high-school-age boys, Alf and Felix, who fall in love, innocently, naively. When Felix learns that male homosexual acts are forbidden by law (the infamous Paragraph 175, Germany's sodomy law), he breaks off their relationship. He does not tell Alf the reason, wanting to preserve his beloved's innocence. Felix volunteers for the trenches of World War I. Soon, the boys renew their friendship through letters, and the truth comes out. Each discovers the ways in which society has lied to them about sexuality, patriotism, and religion. Felix plans to rejoin Alf, but is killed in battle. The novel ends with Alf's pledge to his lover to "fight against evil and stupidity . . . so that no one will have to go through what we did."

Bruno Vogel's novel develops a central theme in gay and lesbian literature (as in gay and lesbian life): the challenge of creating an identity from sexual difference in a society bent on erasing difference. Vogel's gift as an author lies in his ability to state, simply and directly, the bond between private emotion and public life. He makes clear that no separation can exist between these two, or the so-called private life will fall victim to the forces seeking to dominate the public arena. Other authors who described the lives of homosexual characters had recognized this dilemma, but none defined it as sharply and immediately as Vogel did.

—*James W. Jones*

BIBLIOGRAPHY

Vogel, Bruno. *Alf. Eine Skizze.* Berlin: ASY-Verlag, 1929; rpt. Lollar am Lahn: Verlag Andreas Achenbach, 1977. ■ ———. *Ein Gulasch und andere Skizzen.* Rudolstadt: Greifenverlag, 1928. ■ ———. *Alf.* Trans. Samuel Johnson. Intro. Michael Gilbert. London: GMP Publishers, 1992.

Walker, Alice
(b. 1944)

Alice Malsenior Walker was born February 9, 1944, in Eatonton, Georgia, to an African-American sharecropper family. She attended Spelman College from 1961 to 1963, and graduated from Sarah Lawrence College in 1965. In 1964, she traveled to Africa and began to write poetry, some of it published in the 1968 collection, *Once.* After college, she worked for New York City's welfare department and for the civil rights movement in Mississippi. In 1967, she married Melvyn R. Levanthal, a civil rights lawyer, and they had a daughter, Rebecca, in 1969. In 1976, they were amicably divorced. In the 1970s, Walker's writing career began to blossom. By 1974, she was a contributing editor at *Ms. Magazine*.

Walker has received many writing fellowships from, for example, the MacDowell Colony, the Radcliffe Institute, and the Guggenheim Foundation. She has taught at several universities and has published numerous volumes of poetry, fiction, and essays. Among the prestigious awards she has received are the Lillian Smith Award for *Revolutionary Petunias* (1973), which was also nominated for a National Book Award; the Rosenthal Foundation Award from the American Academy of Arts and Letters (1974); and the 1983 Pulitzer Prize for *The Color Purple* (1982). In 1981, she moved to California, where she continues to live and write.

Alice Walker's work speaks to such universal themes as spiritual survival; the achievement of individual identity, freedom, and power; and the interconnectedness of self and community. Her concern with these issues is effectively cast within the framework of black female experience. She explores the damage to the individual self wrought by racism and sexism, which she sees as related consequences of patriarchal cultures. As she depicts racial and sexual taboos, she diagnoses abusive behavior as an expression of self-hatred and the fragmentation of female wholeness as effected by conformity. Walker's recurrent argument is that healthy self-definition stems from self-knowledge and self-love. Within these contexts, she treats lesbianism as natural and freeing, notably in *The Color Purple*. Here Celie, the protagonist, is figuratively reborn from a death of the spirit through her sister/friend/lover's teaching. She is sexually and spiritually awakened to both the beauty of her body and the possibility of personal autonomy within a shared and reciprocal relationship. It is clear from Walker's entire work that there are no forbidden loves or themes. She demands that conventions be questioned. Her most recent novel, *Possessing the Secret of Joy* (1992), is about the practice of performing clitoridectomies on African women. She forces the reader to share her character's physical pain but even more to empathize with the mutilation of her spirit. Fact and metaphor join.

Alice Walker sees women as scarred by rigid, constricting gender categories. As her last novel announces, the "secret of joy" is resistance. Her entire work says that society must change to enable personal transformation and wholeness. Resistance to inhibiting taboos is potentially redemptive, and affective bonding, of which lesbianism is an example, can be curative and liberating. Walker is important both for her expression of these themes and for her fictional representation of characters who break conventional stereotypes.

—*Dorothy H. Lee*

BIBLIOGRAPHY

Bloom, Harold, ed. *Alice Walker: Modern Critical Views.* New York: Chelsea House Publishers, 1989. ■ Christian, Barbara. "Alice Walker: The Black Woman Artist as Wayward." *Black Women Writers (1950–1980).* Mari Evans, ed. New York: Anchor, 1984. 457–477. ■ ———. "No More Buried Lives: The Theme of Lesbianism in Lorde, Naylor, Shange, Walker." *Feminist Issues* 5.1 (Spring 1985): 3–20. ■ McDowell, Deborah. "The Changing Same: Generational Connections and Black Women Novelists." *New Literary History* 18.2 (Winter 1987): 281–302.

Walpole, Horace
(1717–1797)

Horace Walpole was the youngest child of one of the most powerful political figures of the eighteenth century and his wealthy and beautiful wife. The great Sir Robert Walpole, considered by many to be the first "prime" minister, ran English government for a generation. Horace hated him as much as he loved the mother whom he saw offended by his father's infidelities. His parentage, nevertheless, gave him a certain stature and sense of self-importance that never left him.

At ten, Walpole was sent to Eton College, where he became part of the "Quadruple Alliance" of sensitive literary friends, which included THOMAS GRAY, the most popular poet of the century, and Richard West, a sensitive and inverted young writer who died in his twenties and was the cause of a deeply moving series of letters and poems between Walpole and Gray. These two men remained friends throughout the latter's life, and Walpole continued to champion his poetry and defend him personally in the forty years he survived him. The two traveled on the continent together after university—they both went to Cambridge—and after several months together on the "Grand Tour," they had a bitter falling out that took years to put behind them. Walpole shared Gray's devotion to other men, and though he is as little likely to have actually had sexual experiences with men, he did love several in his long life, for a great portion of it devoting himself to one cousin, Henry Conway.

Walpole is famous for such literary productions as *The Castle of Otranto* (1764), which almost single-handedly instituted the Gothic novel vogue. *The Castle of Otranto* tells the story of a jealous and ambitious prince, Manfred, who exercises power through abuse of the men and women around him. Early on in the work, he is responsible for his "puny" son's death, and later he murders his daughter. Between these two events, he torments his wife and attempts to rape his son's fiancée. This may not sound very "gay," but Walpole is chronicling the virulence of paternal control and exhibiting various ways in which a family can be dysfunctional. It may take the sexual outsider, after all, to point out the destructiveness of a father. In another important work, this time a play, *The Mysterious Mother* (1768), Walpole problematizes the family in other ways. His Gothic enterprise seems intent on exposing the horrors of domestic life. He claimed to come to the Gothic material in his dreams. These are dreams that some of us probably know quite well.

The other side of his life of writing is that found in the forty-four volumes of his *Correspondence*. Walpole was one of the most famous letter writers of the century, and his delightful effusions are filled with a connoisseur's knowledge of literature and the arts, a gossip's familiarity with scandal, and a fop's attention to the details of dress, family, and social position.

—*George E. Haggerty*

BIBLIOGRAPHY

Graham, Kenneth, ed. *Gothic Fictions: Prohibition/Transgression*. New York: AMS, 1989. ■ Haggerty, George E. "Literature and Homosexuality in the Late Eighteenth Century: Walpole, Beckford, and Lewis." *Studies in the Novel* 18 (1986): 341–352. ■ Ketton-Cremer, R. W. *Horace Walpole: A Biography*. Ithaca, New York: Cornell University Press, 1964

War Literature

The unique conditions of wartime create multiple possibilities for homoerotic writing, for while the military at once nurtures intense same-sex friendships and prohibits their expression in sexual acts, the tribulations of war itself can often work to dismantle inhibitions. Although love between comrades is a constant theme in war literature, descriptions of the homosexual act are comparatively rare, especially prior to the twentieth century, and the relationships that war literature frequently celebrates are sometimes ill-suited to categories like "homosexual" or "heterosexual."

War literature with clear homoerotic content falls roughly into three categories, each associated with a historical period. Ever since Homer's *Iliad*, heroic poetry has celebrated the friendship between an inseparable pair of comrades in erotic terms, finding in the death of one the occasion for eulogizing the love that bound them. This heroic mode dominates until the nineteenth century, when the war ELEGY comes to prominence (as, for example, in WHITMAN's *Drum Taps*). The war elegy, frequently written from first-hand experience, flourishes especially in the poetry of World War I. From the turn of the century, prose fiction begins to explore homosexuality, usually as a problem between military men, and perhaps more often warning of dangers than singing love's praises. Though homoerotic war fiction resists generalizations, this form may be most characteristic of World War II.

At the fountainhead of Western literature, Homer's *Iliad* (late eighth century B.C.) provides the archetype of comrade-love in the friendship between Achilles and Patroclus. Achilles forgets his great anger against Agamemnon when his servant Patroclus joins the battle wearing the armor of his master, and is killed by Hector. Achilles' grief now drives the action, for his wrath turns away from the Greeks toward the Trojan hero Hector as the murderer of his beloved friend. David Halperin has remarked the "conjugal" qualities of their friendship, qualities that belong also to warrior pairs such as David and Jonathan in the Books of Samuel and between GILGAMESH and Enkidu. Though Achilles' love for Patroclus is barely sexualized in Homer, later Greeks took for granted that their relationship was pederastic—though there was disagreement about which of them was the beloved and which the lover. Achilles seemed both the more senior of the two and the more desirable. Aeschylus gave their friendship an explicitly erotic coloring in his lost tragedy *Achilleis,* but in PLATO's *Symposium,* Phaedrus argues that the playwright was wrong to give the role of beloved to Patroclus, for Achilles was the most beautiful of all heroes and Patroclus much the older of the two.

In VIRGIL's *Aeneid* (19 B.C.), the friendship between warriors is still not explicitly homoerotic, but the kind of pederastic devotion between soldier pairs that made the Sacred Band of Thebes so formidable (as described by PLUTARCH and Xenophon) is one that Virgil, during the reign of Augustus, still sees as possible and praiseworthy. The episode in Book IX, celebrating the devotion of Nisus to the boy Euryalus, is the most memorable account of homoerotic comrade-love in Western literature. The pair volunteer to carry a message through enemy territory to Aeneas; after Euryalus is captured, Nisus attempts a rescue but both perish, with Nisus sacrificing himself to repay his friend's death. In John Dryden's translation (1697): "Dying, he [Nisus] slew; and, stagg'ring on the plain, / With swimming eyes he sought his lover slain; / Then quiet on his bleeding bosom fell, / Content, in death, to be reveng'd so well." Yet the entire epic is colored by a homoeroticism only slightly less explicit, for heterosexual relations are always treated with some suspicion, whereas male friendship is idealized.

The heroic mode of Homer and Virgil remained the model for homoerotic war literature until the middle of the nineteenth century. Thus in the twelfth-century *Song of Roland*, Roland may be betrothed to Aude, but his warm friendship with her brother Oliver overshadows this relation, and when Oliver is killed, Roland's grief and thirst for revenge rival those of Achilles. In Abraham Cowley's *Davideis* (1656), David is portrayed as a young warrior so beautiful that his distracting looks even play a part in slaying Goliath. Virgil's precedent allows Cowley richly to amplify the Bible's single line of praise for David's beauty, and, as Raymond Frontain suggests, to defend Charles II's proclivities with a Biblical sanction. A century later, the young BYRON published a sensuous translation of the Nisus-Euryalus episode, and a prose-poem, "The Death of Calmar and Orla" in *Hours of Idleness.* Byron clearly found on the battlefield a convenient setting for Virgilian homoeroticism: "No maid was the sigh of [Calmar's] soul: his thoughts were given to friendship—to dark-haired Orla, destroyer of heroes." The text ends with the slain Orla still clasping the hand of Calmar, who lies across his bosom: "Theirs is one stream of blood." Calmar asks to be buried with his friend rather than to live on in grief.

By no means are all homoerotically charged war poems elegies, but in the poem on the death of a comrade the poet is usually most free to express passion and sensuality. *Drum Taps* (1865), Walt Whitman's sequence of poems on the Civil War that reflects his experience as a hospital volunteer, includes several poems that appreciate soldiers in more or less homoerotic terms (for example, "First O Songs for a Prelude" and "O Tan-Faced Prairie-Boy"). But it is elegies such as "Vigil Strange I Kept on the Field One Night," "Reconciliation," and "As I Lay with My Head in Your Lap Camerado" that allow Whitman to express himself unrestrainedly. In "Reconciliation," the speaker's tenderness for the fallen soldier overpowers the enmity between armies, in terms that anticipate WILFRED OWEN's "Strange Meeting": "my enemy is dead, a man divine as myself is dead, / I look where he lies white-faced and still in the coffin—I draw near, / Bend down and touch lightly with my lips the white face in the coffin." But Whitman's war poems lack the bitterness that suffuses the poetry of World War I. Even when Whitman has an occasion to mention official deceit, as in "Come up from the Fields Father," he does not suggest that every death is a waste and the war a mere sham.

A sudden eruption of homoeroticism, sometimes explicitly thematized as "sexual inversion," is one of the most remarkable features of the literature of World War I, and the literature is vast. The crumbling of Europe's dream of the steady march of civilization and the disillusionment brought on by the interminable horror of trench warfare represented an inversion of the old world that made it possible to explore sexual inversion and seek tolerance: If the old era's complacencies could be torn away, why not its shibboleths too?

Most of the war poets were of the officer class (David Jones being an exception) and had acquired a classical education at a school for boys; a large number of their poems express a tenderness for the enlisted soldier that is at once sensuous and paternalistic. It is not simply that the dead youth is lamented, but his beauty is praised and his camaraderie prized above every other attachment, dividing the society of the trenches from the home front. Wilfred Owen, often considered the finest poet of the Great War, made "the pity of war" his theme (he himself was killed only a week before the armistice), but the term *pity* conveys a rich meaning here, involving not only compassion but outrage, committing the poet to an unflinching realism and an appreciation for beauty in depicting the nightmare: "'My Love!' one moaned. Love-languid seemed his mood, / Till, slowly lowered, his whole face kissed the mud. / And the Bayonets' long teeth grinned; / Rabbles of Shells hooted and groaned; / And the Gas hissed" ("The Last Laugh").

Owen's poems suggest that the sense of detachment from civilians of either sex and intimacy only with other soldiers of the front—whether allies or enemies—is not Owen's alone but expresses a philosophy common to all in the trenches. (See "Smile, Smile, Smile"; "Arms and the Boy"; "Anthem for Doomed Youth"; "A Terre.") And indeed, soldier poets such as Siegfried Sassoon ("To His Dead Body"), Ivor Gurney ("To His Love"), Edmund Blunden ("1916 Seen from 1921"), Herbert Read ("My Company"), Robert Graves ("Not Dead"), Jones, and Isaac Rosenberg, each in his own way convey the same sense that the unspeakable horrors of trench warfare can enter poetry only when tempered by love for and among the men. The poems of Robert Nichols are less imaginative and original than Owen's, but in them the homoerotic element is particularly pronounced; see "The Burial in Flanders (H. S. G., Ypres, 1916)" and "Plaint of Friendship by Death Broken." Paul Fussell's chapter entitled "Soldier Boys" in *The Great War and Modern Memory* is an indispensable essay on the motifs that characterize the homoeroticism in World War I poetry and their relation to the work of Victorians such as the Uranians and HOUSMAN. However, the homoerotic content in these war elegies is invariably platonic, a muted delight in physical qualities suggesting youth, innocence, and nobility and never tainted by acts of sex beyond the poetic kiss. STEPHEN SPENDER, among others, carried on the tradition of war elegies during the Spanish Civil War.

Homosexuality is also a fleeting presence—often somewhat veiled, but hardly more so than heterosexuality—in the memoirs of the Great War, including the most enduring: Siegfried Sassoon's lightly fictionalized *Memoirs of an Infantry Officer* (1930), T. E. LAWRENCE's *Seven Pillars of Wisdom* (1935), and Robert Graves's *Goodbye To All That* (1929).

Homoerotic war fiction has its early exemplars in HERMAN MELVILLE's *Billy Budd, Foretopman* (written 1891, published 1924) and D. H. LAWRENCE's "The Prussian Officer," published just two months after the beginning of World War I. *Billy Budd* is typical in that the repression of homosexuality in a military setting expresses itself destructively, and its villain John Claggart anticipates a long tradition of "sick" homosexual superior officers in the novels of the two world wars. Set during Britain's wars with France, and based on a mutiny at Spithead in 1797, Billy Budd is the "Handsome Sailor" who arouses the envy of Claggart, the master-at-arms of the warship *Bellipotent*. When Claggart fails to entrap Budd in a mutiny plot,

he accuses Billy before the captain. Horrified and rendered mute by his speech impediment, Budd strikes Claggart and fells him with a single blow to the head. Captain Vere believes in Budd's innocence, and is just as conscious of Budd's charms as Claggart, but he adheres to military regulations and sentences Budd to be hanged for having killed a superior officer. Billy's last words, "God bless Captain Vere!," and the Christ imagery in his death scene, confirm his alignment with Good and Claggart's with Evil. Vere himself will soon die in a battle near Gibraltar, murmuring the name of Billy Budd as he expires. The need to control and repress sexual desire drives the plot; as Robert K. Martin points out, Billy's stammer emblematizes the stifled protest that can only be expressed in violence: "In this homosocial world, charged with sexual potential, only strict control of the homosexual within can prevent a mutiny."

In Lawrence's "The Prussian Officer," the homoerotic impulses of Captain Hauptmann remain wholly unspoken and even largely unconscious; instead they manifest themselves sadistically in torments that the captain inflicts on his defenseless young orderly. When at last the orderly murders the captain, it seems almost the inevitable consequence of his victimization. As in *Billy Budd*, then, the military provides circumstances in which sexual "pathology" can only lead to tragedy.

The repressed homosexual, usually in authority and so able to inflict harm on underlings, is particularly prominent in the novels written about World War II or the years immediately preceding it, as in Günter Grass's *The Tin Drum* (1962), KLAUS MANN's *Mephisto* (1936), and Norman Mailer's *The Naked and the Dead* (1948). Many novels written in the McCarthyist 1950s express that period's fear and suspicion of homosexuals. (See Tuthill in Ralph Leveridge's *Walk on the Water* [1951], Ensign Edge in Martin Dibner's *The Deep Six* [1953], and Sergeant Callan in Dennis Murphy's *The Sergeant* [1958].) For a few writers of the World War I era, on the other hand, the Uranian movement, the OSCAR WILDE trials, and the theories of Havelock Ellis and Freud (who refused to consider homosexuality a disease), made it possible to write sympathetically about "sexual inversion" and through their novels to appeal for tolerance and understanding.

An exceptional work of this kind is A. J. Fitzroy's *Despised and Rejected* (1918). Fitzroy (the pseudonym of Rose Allatini, ca 1890–ca 1980) links the persecution suffered by homosexuals with that suffered by conscientious objectors. Belatedly, its bisexual heroine falls in love with its homosexual hero, but the latter has fallen profoundly in love with an ardent young pacifist. Both men go to prison, but through the dialogue of pacifists and civilian militarists, the novel indicts, with insight amounting to clairvoyance, the mentality that fuels both war and sexual conformism. It was well received but quickly banned. But while more famous and sophisticated writers such as E. M. FORSTER and VIRGINIA WOOLF took comparatively equivocal stands on homosexuality, Fitzroy's novel is unwavering.

On the German side, BRUNO VOGEL's *Alf* (1929; banned by the Nazis in 1933) made a similarly wide-ranging critique through two students who fall in love but are separated by a misunderstanding that leads to Alf's enlistment. The bulk of the novel consists of their letters; however, these give a thin picture of wartime conditions both at the front and the rear.

The Great War plays a significant role in RADCLYFFE HALL's *The Well of Loneliness* (1928). In Book Four, its heroine, Stephen Gordon, joins the ambulance unit of the significantly named Mrs. Breakspeare and meets Mary Llewelyn, with whom she falls deeply in love. Hall attaches great significance to the role of women at the front: "a battalion was formed in those terrible years that would never again be completely disbanded. War and death had given them a right to life, and life tasted sweet, very sweet to their palates." (Likewise, GERTRUDE STEIN and Alice B. Toklas traveled around France by car as members of the American Fund for French Wounded.) *The Well of Loneliness* was banned following a famous obscenity trial at which Forster, Woolf, Bennett, and other writers attempted to testify in its favor. Although Virginia Woolf's *Mrs. Dalloway* (1925) is "about" neither homosexuality nor war, both figure heavily in the margins of Mrs. Dalloway's consciousness. Here too, the suggestion that unthinking conventionality has fueled the war creates a link between pacifism and sexual nonconformism.

MARCEL PROUST took a highly sympathetic view of sexual inversion in *Sodome et Gomorrhe* (1921), the fourth book of *A la Recherche de Temps Perdu*. The homosexuality of the fictional Marcel's friend, Robert de Saint Loup, and Robert's uncle, the Baron de Charlus, appear well before war breaks out, but in the climactic seventh volume the prevalence of sexual inversion in Paris comes to be associated with the moral and social upheavals effected by the war's brutality. When Marcel returns from a sanitarium in 1916, he finds that Charlus is able to see through the militaristic cant of the historical moment, but his own darker side is witnessed by Marcel when he stumbles across Jupien's hotel in a backstreet where Charlus is being brutally flagellated by a young sailor. As the enemy's bombs explode round about, Charlus himself explicitly associates the fate of Paris with the destruction of Sodom by fire from heaven, and Marcel reflects at some length upon the analogy.

Though the literature of World War II tends to portray homosexuality as depraved, there are some noteworthy exceptions. MARY RENAULT's *The Charioteer* (1954) concerns the search for true and honorable love among soldiers in a military hospital in France just after Dunkirk; it draws its title and basic theme from Plato's allegory of the soul as a charioteer pulled by two horses, one virtuous, the other vicious, who respond oppositely to the vision of beauty. Laurie Odell falls in love with Andrew Raynes, a Quaker conscientious objector, but he is also drawn to an openly homosexual former schoolmate who has saved his life, and the plot turns on Laurie's quest for a worthy lover. Although envisioning this as a possibility distinguishes it from many novels of the era, the depiction of the culture and etiology of homosexuality is stereotypical. Andrew's innocence derives both from his principles as an objector and from his naivete about homosexuality.

The wartime setting in Italy toward the end of World War II is more crucial in Loren Wahl's *The Invisible Glass* (1950); Steve, a white officer, and Chick, a black enlisted man, connect briefly but are unable to overcome the forces arraigned against them, and the novel ends in tragedy. Several other novels of the late 1940s and the 1950s deserve to be mentioned. Also set in wartime Italy is the "Momma" episode in *The Gallery* (1947) by JOHN HORNE BURNS, where a gay bar that caters to an international cast of military men is portrayed through the eyes of its proprietor in strikingly positive terms. In Lonnie Coleman's novel *Ship's Company* (1955), the vignette entitled "The Theban Warriors" concerns the seduction of the ostensibly straight narrator by Montgomery, an unusually self-assured and unapologetically gay shipmate. But aside from the naval setting, the story is hardly concerned with war. Russell Thacher's *The Captain* (1951) is set during the war in the Pacific, but the relatively positive presentation of the homosexual affair between Esposito and Gilchrist plays a secondary role in the novel as a whole.

In the 1960s, a handful of plays and novels dealt with the relationship between homosexuality and war in intriguing ways that escape the categories so far discussed here. Sanford Friedman's *Totempole* (1965) features an army love affair between its protagonist and a North Korean doctor war prisoner. Homosexuality has a profound if somewhat implausible connection to the motivation behind war in Norman Mailer's *Why Are We in Vietnam?* (1967). The novel associates the homosexual desire that enters into the friendship between its all-American main characters, D. J. and Tex, with the need to exert power over others, and so suggests that the title's question can be answered with reference to the difficulty that heterosexual men have in dealing with latent homosexuality.

Equally original and even more distressing, Anthony Burgess's *The Wanting Seed* (1962) is a dystopian vision of England in some unspecified, amoral future as it moves through the phases of a cycle driven by a perpetual overpopulation crisis. At first, homosexuality is officially encouraged and heterosexuals suffer persecution, but a strange sterility soon blights the world and leads to an anarchic phase of cannibalism and indiscriminate heterosexual copulation. A new government restores order and addresses the crisis by declaring war on an unnamed (in fact, nonexistent) enemy and massacring its own armies in staged trench battles strongly reminiscent of World War I. Burgess presents homosexuality and war as equally disturbing solutions to overpopulation.

John Osborne's play *A Patriot for Me* (1965) is set in Eastern Europe in 1890 and concerns an ambitious officer in the Austro-Hungarian army, Redl, who insists on being careless with his homosexual affairs, even though his superiors have arranged a marriage for him. The theme is familiar: Homosexuality is tolerated by the military only as long as it remains hidden.

In Martin Sherman's 1979 play *Bent*, the Nazi program to exterminate homosexuals and Jews works first to debase but ultimately to embolden its gay hero. After an unsuccessful attempt to elude the authorities, a Nazi officer forces Max to participate in the torture of his lover, Rudi. Max is sent to a concentration camp where he pretends to be Jewish rather than wear the pink triangle, but he falls in love with Horst, a prisoner who does wear it. When Horst is killed, Max touches him for the first time, puts on his jacket emblazoned with the pink triangle, and commits suicide by walking into the electrified fence.

The most important fictional account of homoeroticism in the Vietnam War is the epistolary novel by Charles Nelson, *The Boy Who Picked the Bullets Up* (1981). This lively work offers a picaresque, though finally shattering, account of the sexual adventures of a young medic who is sent to Vietnam. (See also ROMANTIC FRIENDSHIP, MALE.)

—*Matthew Parfitt*

BIBLIOGRAPHY

Cady, Joseph. "Drum Taps and Nineteenth-Century Male Homosexual Literature." *Walt Whitman: Here and Now.* Joann P. Krieg, ed. Westport, Conn.: Greenwood, 1985. ■ Frontain, Raymond Jean. "Ruddy and Goodly to Look at Withal: Drayton, Cowley and the Biblical Model for Renaissance Hom(m)osexuality." *Cahiers Elizabethains* 36 (1989): 11–24. ■ Fussell, Paul. "Soldier Boys." *The Great War and Modern Memory.* New York: Oxford University Press, 1975. ■ Gilbert, Sandra and Susan Gubar. *No Man's Land: The Place of the Woman Writer in the Twentieth Century.* 2 vols. New Haven: Yale University Press, 1988. ■ Halperin, David M. "Heroes and Their Pals." *One Hundred Years of Homosexuality: And Other Essays On Greek Love.* New York: Routledge, 1990. ■ Martin, Robert K. *Hero, Captain, and Stranger: Male Friendship, Social Critique, and Literary Form in the Sea Novels of Herman Melville.* Chapel Hill: University of North Carolina Press, 1986. ■ Meyers, Jeffrey. "T. E. Lawrence: *Seven Pillars of Wisdom.*" *Homosexuality and Literature, 1890–1930.* Montreal: McGill-Queen's University Press, 1977. 114–130. ■ Silkin, Jon. *Out of Battle: The Poetry of the Great War.* London: Oxford University Press, 1972. ■ Stambolian, George and Elaine Marks, ed. *Homosexualities and French Literature: Cultural Contexts/Critical Texts.* Ithaca, N.Y.: Cornell University Press, 1979. ■ Summers, Claude J. *Gay Fictions: Wilde to Stonewall: Studies in a Male Homosexual Literary Tradition.* New York: Continuum, 1990. ■ Woods, Gregory. *Articulate Flesh: Male Homo-Eroticism and Modern Poetry.* New Haven: Yale University Press, 1987.

Warner, Sylvia Townsend
(1893–1978)

Sylvia Townsend Warner was born on December 6, 1893, at Harrow School, Middlesex, where her father, George Townsend Warner, was a history master. She was educated privately by her parents. Initially attracted to a musical career, she planned to study composition in Vienna with Arnold Schoenberg but was prevented from doing so by the outbreak of World War I. After her father's death in 1916, she moved to London, where she was engaged for ten years as one of the editors of the comprehensive *Tudor Church Music* (ten volumes, 1922–1929) for Oxford University Press. In the mid-1920s, she turned her attention to literature, and within five years published two popular volumes of poetry, a collection of short stories, and three novels, including the highly successful *Lolly Willowes* (1926) and *Mr. Fortune's Maggot* (1927). Her first novel, a gently subversive call for female self-determination, is the narrative of a prototypical spinster aunt who eschews the oppressive protection and comforts of the patriarchal extended family and finds fulfillment as a witch. Chosen as the first selection of the newly founded Book-of-the-

Month Club, *Lolly Willowes* established Warner's literary fame in the United States, and her popularity with American audiences was sustained for nearly four decades through more than a hundred short stories originally published in the *New Yorker. Mr. Fortune's Maggot*, a subtle psychological study of repressed homosexual desire in the context of colonialism, relates the misadventure of a "fatally sodomitical" Anglican missionary who falls in love with his only convert on a South Seas isle, only to lose his own faith.

In 1926, Warner met Valentine Ackland (1906–1969), a young poet given to dressing in male attire. The two women gradually fell in love and lived together from 1930 until Ackland's death. Ackland's traumatic youth, her struggles with alcohol, her family's rejection of her lesbianism, and her early years with Warner are recorded in the posthumously published *For Sylvia: An Honest Account* (1985). After establishing their household at East Chaldon in Dorset, Warner and Ackland produced a joint volume of verse, *Whether a Dove or a Seagull* (1934), and, in response to the growing threat of fascism in Europe, became active in the Communist Party of Great Britain. In support of the Loyalist cause in the Spanish Civil War, they visited Spain in 1937 and 1938. The theme of political revolution is central in Warner's two novels of this period, *Summer Will Show* (1936) and *After the Death of Don Juan* (1938). Set in the Paris Commune of 1848, *Summer Will Show* incorporates lesbianism and the breakdown of class and social barriers through Communism in its representation of the love between its protagonists, Sophia Willoughby, an English gentlewoman, and Minna Lemuel, the Jewish former mistress of Sophia's estranged husband. The complex dynamics of relationships between women also provide the impetus for *The Corner that Held Them* (1948), a novel depicting life in a fourteenth-century convent.

After World War II, during which their home in East Chaldon was destroyed by a bomb dropped by a German warplane, Warner and Ackland settled at Frome Vauchurch, Dorset, where they spent the remainder of their lives. Although deeply bereaved by Ackland's death from breast cancer in 1969, Warner continued to write poems and short stories until her own death on May 1, 1978. Although Warner's works had slipped from popularity and had gone out of print during the post-war period (possibly as a response to her political activism), feminist presses, particularly Virago, have reissued many of her novels in recent years, and lesbian and feminist critics are increasingly recognizing her as an important lesbian voice of the early twentieth century. (See also ENGLISH LITERATURE: TWENTIETH CENTURY.)

—*Patricia Juliana Smith*

BIBLIOGRAPHY

Ackland, Valentine. *For Sylvia: An Honest Account*. New York: Norton, 1985. ■ Brothers, Barbara. "Flying the Nets at Forty: *Lolly Willowes* as Female Bildungsroman." *Old Maids to Radical Spinsters: Unmarried Women in the Twentieth-Century Novel*. Laura Doan, ed. Urbana: University of Illinois Press, 1991. 195–212. ■ Castle, Terry. "Sylvia Townsend Warner and the Counterplot of Lesbian Fiction." *Sexual Sameness: Texual Difference in Lesbian and Gay Writing*. Joseph Bristow, ed. London: Routledge, 1992. 128–147. ■ Harman, Claire. *Sylvia Townsend Warner*. London: Chatto & Windus, 1989. ■ Marcus, Jane. "A Wilderness of One's Own: Feminist Fantasy Novels of the Twenties: Rebecca West and Sylvia Townsend Warner." *Women Writers and the City: Essays in Feminist Literary Criticism*. Susan Merrill Squier, ed. Knoxville: University of Tennessee Press, 1984. 134–160. ■ Mulford, Wendy. *This Narrow Place: Sylvia Townsend Warner and Valentine Ackland: Life, Letters and Politics, 1930-1951*. London: Pandora, 1988. ■ Spraggs, Gillian. "Exiled to Home: The Poetry of Sylvia Townsend Warner and Valentine Ackland." *Lesbian and Gay Writing: An Anthology of Critical Essays*. Mark Lilly, ed. London: Macmillan, 1990. 109–125.

Warren, Patricia Nell
(b. 1936)

Winner of the 1978 Walt Whitman Award for Excellence in Gay Literature, Patricia Nell Warren is the author of three successful novels about American gay culture that exemplify post-Stonewall, pre-AIDS, popular adult mainstream fiction. Warner's well-crafted narratives center on stalwart gay protagonists who must deal with the personal and political ramifications of mid-1970s American society confronting a burgeoning gay liberation movement. Downplaying graphic sex and exoticism in favor of challenging stereotypes and demystifying gay lifestyles, Warren's gay-affirmative novels held appeal for both gay and nongay readers.

In *The Front Runner* (1974), Warren explores the often-denied issue of the presence of gays in athletics. Primarily the story of a love that develops between a closeted ex-Marine track coach and an "out" gay college distance runner who has set his sights on participation in the Olympic Games, *The Front Runner* documents the characters' struggles and victories in the parallel challenges encountered while training for and participating in Olympic competition and building and maintaining a gay partnership. In addition to calling attention to heterosexist politics dominant in amateur athletics and resistance to intergenerational gay relationships, Warren foreshadows contemporary issues of gay parenting, media "outing," gay marriages, tabloid journalism, and legal battles to attain gay civil rights.

Warren extends her foray into the explication of same-sex love in *The Fancy Dancer* (1976). Set in Warren's native Montana, *The Fancy Dancer* charts the complications that arise when a young Catholic priest and a troubled but freewheeling biracial mechanic residing among the priest's parishioners seduce and mentor each other. By tracing the process of the pair's discovery, acknowledgment, and acceptance of their gayness, Warren is able to address the clash between gay identity and spirituality and the restrictiveness of church dogma and small-town conservatism. Simultaneously, however, she fosters an appreciation for cultural differences and celebrates the diversity of urban and rural gay lifestyles.

An Anita Bryant-like born-again political crusader running on an antigay platform is the strong antagonistic force in *The Beauty Queen* (1978). In this work, Warren tackles the impact of antigay political rhetoric as well as continues her exploration of homophobic religious fervor and the backlash against demands for gay civil rights. Warren creates a trio of diverse gay characters standing in opposition to the ex-beauty queen turned state senator, including two gay police officers who are her first major lesbian character and first major gay exotic character. Told from four points of view, *The Beauty Queen* also addresses issues of gay bashing, gay political activism, discrimination in employment and housing, and the psychological strains of closetedness.

As an independent author, Warren published eight books (five under the pseudonym Patricia Kilina) while working for twenty-two years as a book editor for *Reader's Digest*. Now a full-time freelance writer and artist, she contributes to periodicals, and in 1991, published *One is the Sun*, a novel about the courage, determination, and spirituality of Native-American and European-immigrant women.

—*Jay Scott Chipman*

BIBLIOGRAPHY

Kilina, Patricia. *The Last Centennial*. New York: Dial Press, 1971. ■ Steuernagel, Trudy. "Contemporary Homosexual Fiction and the Gay Rights Movement." *Journal of Popular Culture* 20 (Winter 1986): 125–134. ■ Warren, Patricia Nell. *The Beauty Queen*. New York: William Morrow, 1978. ■ ———. *The Fancy Dancer*. New York: William Morrow, 1976. ■ ———. *The Front Runner*. New York: William Morrow, 1974. ■ ———. *One is the Sun*. New York: Ballantine, 1991.

Waugh, Evelyn
(1903–1966)

Evelyn Waugh poses a paradox for gay readers. He moved somewhat freely in homosexual circles while having at least three affairs at Oxford in the early 1920s, then married, fathered six children, and apparently remained heterosexual. He created in Charles Ryder and Sebastian Flyte of *Brideshead Revisited* (1945) a moving tribute to homoeroticism yet subjected other figures in his works to archly homophobic contempt. His conversion to a deeply felt, ardently held Catholicism and his inability to be other than nostalgic about his youth explain much of this paradox.

Arthur Waugh, his father, was a minor literary figure in London who eventually became managing director of the Chapman & Hall publishing firm. Evelyn spent most of his childhood in Hampstead, progressing through school at Heath Mount, Lancing—a school "designed . . . to inculcate High churchmanship"—and Hertford College, Oxford, where he so neglected academic work that he received only a third-class degree. In 1928, he married Evelyn Gardiner and after a Mediterranean cruise, settled in London to write. They divorced in 1930, and their marriage was annulled in 1936, the year before he married Laura Herbert and settled first in Gloucestershire, then in Somerset.

Between 1928 and 1942, Waugh established himself as one of the most trenchant and able satirists of the world of the "Bright Young Things," as the British called their "Lost Generation." He savaged this world in *Decline and Fall* (1928), *Vile Bodies* (1930), *Black Mischief* (1932), *A Handful of Dust* (1934), *Scoop* (1938), and *Put Out More Flags* (1942).

Waugh depicted a wide range of homosexuals, all of them apparently based on men he had known, but his two queens—Ambrose Silk in *Put Out More Flags* and Anthony Blanche in *Brideshead Revisited*—are perhaps the most memorable. An intellectual aesthete, author, and head of the atheism section of the Ministry of Information, Silk has had many affairs and eventually moves from one country to another after fleeing England under accusations that he is a Fascist. It is obvious from *The Ivory Tower*, Silk's ill-founded periodical, that Waugh is attacking modernist extremes more than human sexuality. Anthony Blanche, who recites T. S. ELIOT's "The Waste Land" through a megaphone from a Christ Church balcony at Oxford, is even more affected in his stutter, his avant-garde views, his acquaintances with COCTEAU, Diaghilev, FIRBANK, GIDE, and PROUST. Without question, he is Waugh's most worldly homosexual and also one of the most insightful characters in *Brideshead Revisited*.

The obviously homoerotic, undoubtedly homosexual relationship between Sebastian Flyte, second son of the Marquis of Marchmain, and Charles Ryder during the Oxford episodes in *Brideshead Revisited* is handled frankly and openly, with several of the characters recognizing it as "an English habit" that is a phase of sexual development in the all-male university world. Sebastian, however, is sent down from university; drifts aimlessly into alcoholism; travels to Morocco; tries to rescue Kurt, his German companion, from Nazi authorities in Greece; and returns to Morocco where he works as a kind of handyman for a monastery. Charles becomes a successful artist; marries the sister of a classmate; has an affair with Sebastian's sister, at least in part because she so strikingly resembles Sebastian; and converts to Catholicism sometime after the death of the Marquis.

Waugh's later novels honed his satiric wit and trenchant observations. *The Loved One* (1948), set in Hollywood, mordantly satirizes American burial practices, here particularly pet burials; and *Sword of Honour* (1965), a trilogy consisting of *Men at Arms* (1952), *Officers and Gentlemen* (1955), and *Unconditional Surrender* (1961), documents masculine army life during World War II. Waugh's final work, *The Ordeal of Gilbert Pinfold* (1957), an autobiographical novel, treats an author's crisis and hallucinations brought on during a ship's voyage by drugs and alcohol.

—*David Leon Higdon*

BIBLIOGRAPHY

Blayac, Alain. *Evelyn Waugh*. New York: St. Martin's Press, 1991. ■ Carpenter, Humphrey. *The Brideshead Generation: Evelyn Waugh and His Friends*. Boston: Houghton Mifflin, 1990. ■ Davis, Robert Murray. *Evelyn Waugh and the Forms of His Time*. Washington, D.C.: Catholic University of America Press, 1989. ■ McDonnell, Jacqueline. *Evelyn Waugh*. New York: St. Martin's Press, 1988. ■ Stannard, Martin. *Evelyn Waugh: The Early Years 1903–1939*. New York: W.W. Norton, 1987. ■ ———. *Evelyn Waugh: The Late Years 1939-1966*. New York: W.W. Norton, 1987. ■ Sykes, Christopher. *Evelyn Waugh: A Biography*. Boston: Little Brown, 1975.

Weirauch, Anna Elisabet
(1887–1970)

Born in Galatz, Rumania, Weirauch was moved, along with her sister, by her mother to Germany upon their father's death in 1891. By the turn of the century, they were living in Berlin, where Anna Elisabet studied acting. From 1906 to 1914, she was a member of Max Reinhardt's prestigious ensemble at the Deutsches Theater.

Although she had written plays, she discovered after the war that her real talent lay in writing prose. Clearly, she had been writing for some time already since four novels and three novellas all appeared in 1919, the beginning of her long career. One of these was the first volume of *Der Skorpion* (*The Scorpion*, 1919, 1921, 1931), the work for which Weirauch is remembered today.

This three-volume lesbian *Entwicklungsroman* (a novel that traces the development of its main character from childhood into young adulthood) follows Mette Rudloff from her troubled childhood, in search of love and of answers about her "different" sexuality, to her acceptance of her nature and the possibility that she can now find the love she has sought. The first volume portrays her from childhood through her early twenties. Olga, the first woman she loves, succumbs to the view of homosexual love as decadent and futile. After breaking off their relationship, she commits suicide.

Mette's family hires a psychiatrist to "cure" her, but Mette refuses to accept a medical view of lesbians as aberrant and diseased.

Over the course of the next two volumes, Mette experiences the lesbian and homosexual subcultures, mostly in Berlin, but never finds a home there. Each woman with whom she falls in love proves flawed, or scarred, by the outcast status of lesbians (and bisexuals) within this culture. Alcohol and drug use, promiscuity and psychological role-playing characterize the lives of most of the women she meets in Berlin's lesbian underground. By the end of the third novel, Mette has discarded the false choices of the metropolis—heterosexuality, suicide, "decadent" lesbianism—as being contrary to her nature. Having moved to the country, she learns to live alone and to accept herself. There, she realizes, she is ready to share her future with another woman.

This work stands out from the multitude of fiction depicting lesbian or homosexual characters during the Weimar Republic. It does not apply a medical theory to the origin and appearance of same-sex love, nor does Weirauch deem it necessary to supply "scientific" evidence to defend her characters. These aspects explain the enormous resonance of this work. The first edition of the initial volume quickly sold out. Readers, especially lesbians, praised the novels' sympathetic and true-to-life depictions of lesbian characters. They begged Weirauch to tell more of Mette's story, a request she gladly granted. The novels have been translated into several languages. In English alone, they have had seven editions in various forms.

Weirauch was gifted with a talent for writing prose and plots that afforded easy accessibility to and strong identification with readers. Her career spanned some of the most politically turbulent years in German history. Yet that reality makes only brief appearances in her stories. Much among her *oeuvre* can perhaps justly be labeled "trivial," but her trilogy *Der Skorpion* has found a secure place within the canon of literature that depicts homosexual characters with veracity and skill.

—*James W. Jones*

BIBLIOGRAPHY

Foster, Jeannette H. *Sex Variant Women in Literature.* Tallahassee, Fla.: Naiad Press, 1985. ■ Katz, Jonathan. *Gay/Lesbian Almanac.* New York: Harper and Row, 1983. ■ Schoppmann, Claudia. *Der Roman 'Der Skorpion' von Anna Elisabet Weirauch.* Berlin: Frühlings Erwachen, 1986.

Welch, Denton
(1915–1948)

Maurice Denton Welch was born on March 29, 1915, in Shanghai, China, where both sides of the family were established in business. He was largely educated, unhappily, in England. His life took a major turn for the better when he began art school since his natural aptitude seemed to lie with painting. In one of those cruel twists in which disaster hurts the writer and helps art, Welch, while riding a bicycle, was run over by a car when he was twenty. Paralyzing, crippling injuries made him largely an invalid—and a fine writer. Those injuries led to Welch's premature death on December 30, 1948.

Welch wrote poems, mostly immature, and stories, some good, and Michael De-la-Noy believes that Welch's mature canvases mark him as a skillful and significant painter. Yet, Welch's reputation rests largely on three highly autobiographical novels: *Maiden Voyage* (1943), *In Youth Is Pleasure* (1945), the posthumously published *A Voice Through a Cloud* (1950) (almost but not quite completed by Welch before his death), as well as *The Journals of Denton Welch* (1984), edited skillfully by De-la-Noy. (An earlier, very abridged version of the journals was edited by Jocelyn Brooke. Welch also left behind unfinished works.) What is clear from Welch's writing is that his chief limitation is also his chief virtue: his focus on himself. For his time and place, Welch's novels are surprisingly suffused with homosexuality. More important, they have what might be called a "queenly aura"; that is, Welch's writing possesses a sensibility at once queenly, yet hardly campy or superficial. Nor does he go for the cheap laugh. His examination of the people around him, very thinly disguised in the novels, and his exploration of his own homosexual feelings and responses to the world show Welch to be a writer of consequence.

If Welch essentially repeated one story in his novels, he refined that story to perfection with his last. As important as the homosexual nature of Welch's books is his writing about his crippling accident and his life as a disabled person in his masterpiece *A Voice Through a Cloud.* Here Welch turns his life into art by the depth and distance of his writing about his personal experiences as an odd man out in his culture; few have described physical suffering any better. Unlike his earlier novels, which can have an almost adolescent self-centeredness about them, *A Voice Through a Cloud* manages to connect the individual's situation to that of everyone.

Welch's literary art is constrained by his focus on himself and, one may conclude, by his lack of worldly experience as an adult. Unlike another writer, Flannery O'Connor, who was also confined by illness for much of her writing life, Welch never developed greatly the ability to see outside his own world view (although his view can be highly entertaining) or to take the lives of others as raw material for his work. That he had the natural writer's ability to observe the world carefully is shown most obviously in the *Journals* and in his last novel. All of Welch's work makes clear what gay literature, and modern literature generally, lost when the accident that made him a fine writer finally took his life. (See also ENGLISH LITERATURE: TWENTIETH CENTURY.)

—*Thomas Dukes*

BIBLIOGRAPHY

De-la-Noy, Michael. *Denton Welch: The Making of a Writer.* New York: Viking, 1984. ■ Phillips, Robert. *Denton Welch.* New York: Twayne Publishers, 1974.

White, Edmund
(b. 1940)

One of the most prominent and highly acclaimed figures of contemporary gay literature, Edmund White works in many distinct categories of fiction and nonfiction. First gaining critical attention for his experimental fiction from such critics as Vladimir Nabokov, White has continued to explore the intersections of art and life. That the lives he treats are often those of gay men is not incidental to his work, yet he is not easily comprehended within the stereotypical bounds of "gay literature."

His first novel, *Forgetting Elena* (1973), offers an amnesiac's view of a mysterious place much like Fire Island, with, as Simon Karlinsky observed, "its highly stylized rites, charades, and inbred snobberies." White cast his next novel, *Nocturnes for the King of Naples* (1978), in the form of a lament of a young man for his older lover, mixing mythic allusion and baroque description; a *tour de force,* this novel achieves the "impossible" goal of sustained second-person narrative. *Caracole* (1985), though with a stronger narrative thread, occupies a similar fantastical kingdom of desire as two lovers, male and female, find themselves and each other in the social networks of a large city. The novel's nineteenth-century setting fits its elaborate plotting: the rich sensuality of a costume drama becomes the occasion for a morality play.

White also excels as reporter and social critic. Coauthor of the groundbreaking volume *The Joy of Gay Sex* (1977), White contributed to the sumptuous how-to manual a sense of the social and cultural dimensions of gay male sexuality. Broadening his focus with *States of Desire: Travels in Gay America* (1980), White wrote about gay Americans in fifteen major cities, producing a mosaic of gay life in the late 1970s. These two books made White a de facto gay spokesperson, a role that he has neither refused nor totally accepted. The dilemma of the gay writer, White told William Goldstein in 1982, is that "the novelist's first obligation is to be true to his own vision, not to be some sort of common denominator of public relations man to all gay people." His 1993 biography of JEAN GENET, together with an edition of Genet's work, provides an in-depth look at one particular gay life, one whose experiments in narrative form and literary treatments of gay life influenced White's own work.

Bridging his fantastic imaginative creations and his cannily realistic social observations, White's series of semiautobiographical novels (*A Boy's Own Story* [1982] and *The Beautiful Room Is Empty* [1988]) attempts, as White said in a *Paris Review* interview "to show one gay life in particular depth." Tracing the quest for self-identity against the expectations of family and friends in *A Boy's Own Story,* White remarkably mixes the cosmic and the commonplace, as when the unnamed narrator and his friend Kevin explore the outer boundaries of their common masculinity:

> When he turned his face my way it was dark, indistinguishable; his back and shoulders were carving up strips of light, carving them this way and that as he twisted and bobbed. The water was dark, opaque, but it caught the sun's gold light, the wavy dragon scales writhing under a sainted knight's halo. At last Kevin swam up beside me; his submerged body looked small, boneless. He said we should go down to the store and buy some Vaseline.

Such grappling with male bodies, both physical and mental, propels *A Boy's Own Story* onward against the backdrop of Midwestern family life. *The Beautiful Room Is Empty* traces the narrator's experiments with desire and romance as he moves through an exclusive prep school, sessions with a psychotherapist, and the Stonewall riots. The narrator's swings between joyful acceptance and critical self-loathing reflect the emerging national gay consciousness.

The events of these novels mirror the shape of White's own early life: growing up in Cincinnati, dealing with a demanding father, attending the exclusive Cranbrook Academy. As an undergraduate at the University of Michigan, White twice won the prestigious Hopwood award, the first of numerous awards for his writing. He worked for a while at Time-Life Books until his writing brought him teaching jobs at Yale, Columbia, and Johns Hopkins. Since 1983, he has lived in both New York and Paris.

His two autobiographical novels, conceived as part of a tetralogy, are generally acknowledged as White's most successful work. His nonfiction has often been read through a moralistic or sociological lens. *States of Desire,* for example, was broadly criticized for the promiscuity of its subjects. Though some of these critics, including some in the gay press, focused on White's principle of selection, reviews were more often occasion for social comment, as in Paul Cowan's dismissal of the book as "a journey through promiscuous all-male America—a desolate place to live."

The changing lives of gay men, particularly as they are devastated by AIDS, continue to shape White's work. His collection of stories with ADAM MARS-JONES, *The Darker Proof: Stories from a Crisis* (1988), was one of the first works of serious fiction to treat the impact of AIDS. In a 1987 essay in *Artforum,* White summarizes his obligation to gay culture in these words: "To have been oppressed in the '50s, freed in the '60s, exalted in the '70s, and wiped out in the '80s is a quick itinerary for a whole culture to follow. For we are witnessing not just the death of individuals but a menace to an entire culture. All the more reason to bear witness to the cultural moment." All of White's work can be seen as intimately bound to gay culture, simultaneously reflecting its shifting contours and shaping its most provocative edges.

—*Randal Woodland*

BIBLIOGRAPHY

Bergman, David. "Edmund White." *Contemporary Gay American Novelists.* Emmanuel Nelson, ed. Westport, Conn.: Greenwood, 1993. 386–394. ■ Cowan, Paul. "The Pursuit of Happiness." *New York Times Book Review* (February 3, 1980): 12–13. ■ Goldstein, William. "Edmund White." *Publishers Weekly* (September 24, 1982): 6–8. ■ "An Interview with Edmund White." *Paris Review* (Fall 1988): 47–80. ■ Karlinsky, Simon. "America, Texas, and Fire Island." *The Nation* 218 (1974): 23–24. ■ Wilson, Carter. "Remembering Desire." *The Nation* 235 (1982): 503–505.

White, Patrick
(1912–1990)

By the end of his life, Patrick White ranked as Australia's greatest novelist and, as winner of the Nobel Prize for Literature in 1973, among the greatest fiction writers of the modern period. His major achievement was the production of twelve novels between 1939 and 1986, including *The Aunt's Story* (1948), *Voss* (1957), *The Vivisector* (1970), and *The Twyborn Affair* (1979). Homosexuality is an explicit interest only in the last-named of these novels, but in *Flaws in the Glass,* the "self-portrait" he published in 1981, White publicly declared his homosexuality in an extraordinarily candid and laconic record of his life and opinions.

In Australian terms, White was born with a silver spoon in his mouth. His parents were members of the wealthy Hunter Valley grazier society of New South Wales, a tightly knit conservative clan that exerted considerable—if indirect—influence on the state government. Whereas his father was quiet and mild-mannered, his mother Ruth was socially ambitious, a determined woman whose predatory qualities both fascinated and horrified her son. He was to remark that a good many of the intimidating women characters of his novels were modeled from his mother, with whom he carried on a lifelong feud. But the wider society itself, dividing its time between the rich Hunter Valley estates and the social season in Sydney, provided material for novels that simultaneously analyzed the life of this class sharply and celebrated the New South Wales landscape with sensual bravura.

Patrick White's attitude to his native Australia was always markedly conflicted—as was Australian response to his novels.

Until he was thirty-three, much of White's life was spent in England and Europe, for his mother insisted on placing him at Cheltenham, an English public school, for his high school years. Experiencing the double humiliation there of being both a colonial and an (unconfessed) homosexual, he was utterly miserable and never forgave Ruth White for abandoning him. The ensuing years at Cambridge University were happier, but it took him a while to discover that academic pursuits held no interest. After leaving university, he lived for some years in London, mixing with artists and actors and experiencing a number of homosexual liaisons. It was in North Africa and Greece, however, that his mature life began to take shape. He was part of a British Army Intelligence Unit when he met the soldier Manoly Lascaris, who became his lover and lifelong companion. In *Flaws in the Glass*, White pays tribute to him as "this small Greek of immense moral strength, who became the central mandala in my life's hitherto messy design." They set up household in New South Wales soon after the end of World War II and were together when White died. Probably because of Lascaris, Greece and its people became significant for White and his writing.

The two decades following White's return to his native Australia, with which he began an intense love-hate relationship, saw the publication of his long, major novels. One of them, *Voss* (1957), earned the respect of his fellow Australians since it was based on the doomed journey into the Australian desert of the legendary German explorer Leichardt. But White himself discounted *Voss*; he was only mildly excited to see it performed as an opera at the end of his life and was dismayed by unsuccessful projects to make a film of it. Like his other novels of the period, though, it probed the quest of its central character against the surrounding materialism, banality, and snobbery of Australian society. White was not conventionally religious but had a deeply religious, even visionary, sense of life; his major characters, like the artist figure of *The Vivisector* (1970), are ultimately interested in the meaning of existence, which they will know only in death.

Until the 1960s, White spurned politics. He voted automatically for the conservative parties in federal and state elections, and espoused personally conservative values. This changed abruptly on December 9, 1969, when he participated very publicly in an anti-Vietnam War demonstration. After that, he was politically active, witnessing against censorship, environmental destruction, colonialist politics, and the nuclear industry. By the end of his life, he was an ardent advocate for Australia as a republic. He protested against the form of the Australian bicentennial celebrations in 1988, and—although he had accepted the Nobel Prize—consistently refused to accept official Australian awards.

White never supported the gay liberation movement, though his attitude toward his own homosexuality, and that of others, changed as he aged. In his "self-portrait," he disavowed interest in homosexual society. He was bored by people who discussed their homosexuality as though it was a condition they had discovered: "I see myself not so much a homosexual as a mind possessed by the spirit of man or woman according to actual situations or the characters I become in my writing." That situation is the one explored in *The Twyborn Affair* (1979), where the central character appears in the different guises of a homosexual man, a woman, and a transvestite male who runs a (heterosexual) brothel. Nevertheless, homosexuality was a significant theme of this novel, for the first time in White's writing. Immediately on completion of *The Twyborn Affair*, he wrote *Flaws in the Glass*, an autobiography that was a coming-out story designed to shock. During the last decade of his life, White conceded that there was a gay cause, putting his own sexual orientation on the line in an Australia that was still highly resistant to avowals of homosexuality.

Patrick White's last decade was an accomplished, happy one. He renounced his affiliations with the polite Sydney society into which he had been born and mixed with younger artists and theater people. Producers and directors staged his plays in Sydney and Adelaide. These distinctive and eccentric plays failed to attract large or enthusiastic audiences, and they have not yet received the critical attention of the novels, yet White regarded their productions as the high point of his life and career; through them, he finally established contact with an Australia in which he might feel somewhat at home.

David Marr's 1991 biography, *Patrick White: A Life*, is exemplary in placing its subject's sexuality at the very center and accounting for the richness of a life and body of work in terms of a particular gay sensibility.

—*Patrick Holland*

BIBLIOGRAPHY

Marr, David. *Patrick White: A Life*. London: Jonathan Cape, 1991.

Whitman, Walt

(1819–1892)

Born in West Hills, Long Island, Whitman was the first author of working-class origins to reach prominence in the United States. Although he was in many ways a disciple of poet Ralph Waldo Emerson, he lacked Emerson's financial assurance and Harvard education. Whitman was a product of the unsettled and mobile life of the poor and largely self-taught. In his early years, he worked variously as a carpenter, printer, and country schoolteacher. His first published work was completely undistinguished—mediocre formal verse and moral reform tracts, including the temperance novel *Franklin Evans* (1842).

One of Whitman's earliest publications was the short story "The Child's Champion" (1841), later reprinted as "The Child and the Profligate." The twelve-year-old Charles is dragged into a tavern and an attempt is made to force him to drink. Charles, who has sworn a temperance oath to his mother, resists and is saved by Lankton, a dissipated but prosperous client, who takes Charles into his bed and a union blessed by a hovering angel. Whitman's later revisions play down the homosexual associations of this tale, creating a second bed and changing "close knit love" to "friendship." The story highlights several of the concerns that would run throughout Whitman's career, including the affiliation to moral reform, which was, in the American 1840s, an integral part of political reform. But we may also note the willingness to censor himself and the insistence on love between males that is pederastic in terms of age and class difference but that is cast in realistic terms that violate the tradition of idealized Greek love. At the same time the moral purity tract allowed, as it always does, for a disguised presentation of a transgressive subtext. By situating the love story between men in the context of a warning about the dangers of drink, Whitman not only enables the publication of his material, but indeed identifies homosexuality not *with* vice but against it.

In 1841, Whitman went to New York, working first as a printer and then as a writer for the *Aurora,* the Brooklyn *Daily Eagle,* and other papers. In 1848, Whitman traveled to New Orleans, a journey that was to mark a turning point in his life. Although Whitman was working for the *Crescent,* he found time to explore the city and record its impressions. Whitman came directly into contact with slavery and with a culture vastly different from that of New York. There has been much discussion of Whitman's experiences during the New Orleans visit, fed in particular by Whitman's boast to JOHN ADDINGTON SYMONDS at the end of his life that he had sired six children and had "one living southern grand-child." More concrete evidence may be found in the fact that "Once I pass'd through a populous city," a poem recalling New Orleans, originally read "of all that city I remember only the man who wandered with me, there, for love of me" before Whitman's emendation in the manuscript to "I remember only a woman I casually met there who detain'd me for love of me." Despite such evidence, the story of a heterosexual New Orleans romance has had a long life, thanks to its power to "normalize" the national poet.

Whatever happened in Louisiana, it had an important impact on Whitman's conception of male love. Although not, apparently, written until 1859, the sequence "Live Oak with Moss," which was later dispersed in the "Calamus" section of *Leaves of Grass,* is obviously indebted to the New Orleans trip. The second of the poems in the original sequence specifically identifies Louisiana as its site. The twig that the poet breaks off is "twined around [with] a little moss," bringing him to thoughts of isolation and love. More directly, the twig "remains to me a curious token—it makes me think of manly love" and of his own inability to live "without a friend, a lover, near." What seems to have prompted Whitman's return to this material was a rupture with a lover, probably Fred Vaughan. The "Calamus" poems record both the joy of their relationship and Whitman's despair at its loss.

Whitman's major work was *Leaves of Grass;* although it began as a slim volume of less than 150 pages, it had become by Whitman's death a hefty volume of almost 600 pages. Whitman added to, removed, revised, restored; but he never wrote another book. It was also an organic process of growth and decay. Although the last, or Death-Bed, edition represents Whitman's last thoughts, it cannot give us a sense of the growth of the work nor of Whitman's thought at any given time. For that we must turn to some of the most important of the editions.

The original edition was published in 1855. It includes an eighteen-page preface and twelve poems. The preface defines the American purpose of the volume, by rendering the experience of America to create a great poem. Whitman's America is open, expansive, and adventurous. "Here," he declares, "are the roughs and the beards and space and ruggedness and nonchalance that the soul loves." Borrowing from Emerson's call for a national poet, Whitman places that poet in rebellion against a European heritage that was still strong seventy years after the revolution. He must also give himself a role that will break with the tradition of the learned poet like Longfellow (only twelve years older than Whitman) and situate the new poet outdoors, with the working class. Whitman's evocation of "the roughs and the beards" is inscribed in a tradition that identifies revolution with masculinity, whereas to be learned or cultured is to be "feminine" and hence colonized. In "Song of Myself," the most important of the poems in the first edition, Whitman picks up his reference to beards from the preface, and proclaims, "Washes and razors for foofoos .... for me freckles and a bristling beard" (l. 468). The foofoo, or dandy, is rejected in favor of the freckled outdoorsman, whose beard signals his unlimited masculinity. In terms of the politics of self-presentation of his time, Whitman is making an argument of class as much as anything, but he needs to link class to gender and so unwittingly sets in process an identification of the gay man with the masculine. At the same time, Whitman's own self-presentation, including his frontispiece portrait as a casual worker with his hand on his hip, indicates a sense of gender as performance.

While creating a figure of masculinity that could free him from association with the European aesthete, Whitman was also insisting on the equality of the sexes. Among the American qualities to be included in the poem of America, after "the noble character of the young mechanics," there is "the perfect equality of the female with the male." Whitman was undoubtedly sincere in this commitment, as his support for such reformers as Frances Wright would testify, and as his own literary practice of gender inclusiveness demonstrates. At the same time, whatever his intentions, the unconscious of his language worked in other ways. The poets of America were to be "begotten" of the "fatherstuff" of science and practical experience and to form "sinewy races of bards." And the new America was envisioned as a place for "the evergrowing communes of brothers and lovers." Whitman's ardent homosociality placed certain limitations on his vision of equality for women.

Occasionally, he could find a way to bring together his own concerns as a homosexual and his insight into the suffering of women, just as he could write movingly of the plight of the American slave. One particularly striking instance of the intersection of male homoerotic and female desire occurs in section 11 of "Song of Myself." The bathing scene involving "twenty-eight young men, and all so friendly" is a celebration of men together, enjoying a freedom refused in mid-nineteenth century America to women. But the scene is also observed by the woman who looks from "aft the blinds of the window" before entering into the celebration and "splash[ing] in the water." The perspective then shifts to the young men, who feel "an unseen hand" passing over their bodies, as someone whom they do not see "seizes fast to them ... puffs and declines with pendant and bending arch" until they ejaculate, sousing their partners with spray. The repressed desires of the woman and the young men come together, in a scene that derives its power from its violation of convention. The sexuality is hetero, homo, auto, perhaps truly queer, that is, lacking fixed definition.

Such moments in Whitman characteristically give way, as here, to celebrations of the male working-class body. These men are celebrated not only for their professions or trades, but just as important for their physical presence. We see the "hairy chests" of the blacksmiths and "the lithe sheer of their waists" as well as the "polish'd and perfect limbs" of the black driver. Whitman's is a world of diversity and repeated pleasures. It is decidedly urban, capturing the rapidly changing life of the street and its multiple activities. The pleasure Whitman takes in observing other men's bodies is heightened by the transitory nature of the experience: The city is a place for cruising. This theme is made explicit in the "Calamus" poem, "City of Orgies," which concludes, "O Manhattan, your frequent and swift flash of eyes offering me love, / Offering response to my own." The city of Whitman, unlike that of the sensation novels of the mid-nineteenth century, is not frightening but inviting. It contains within it a world of male desire that often goes unnoticed by others, a world of constantly repeated flirtations and erotic possibilities.

If Whitman took his nationalism and his optimism from Emerson, he was not satisfied with the Transcendentalist version of neo-Platonism. Such a philosophy saw the body merely as a means toward a higher, purely spiritual existence. Whitman's task in *Leaves of Grass* is to reclaim the body, to counter Western idealism with a new idea of a balance between body and soul. This tactic was essential for the creation of a view of homosexuality that did not privilege the "ideal" or nonphysical relationship over an embodied experience. Whitman locates the divine in the individual, not in a spirit outside the self, only rarely glimpsed. This sense of the divinity of the self is indebted to Whitman's Quaker background, but he was also similar to many of the utopian reformers of the 1840s in claiming not only a radical political equality but an equality within the hierarchy of the body.

Thus in section 24 of "Song of Myself," Whitman celebrates himself not as an isolated, superior being, but instead as "the son" of Manhattan, "turbulent, fleshy, sensual, eating drinking and breeding": as he put it in the first version, "an American, one of the roughs." The new urban poet marks off his distance from the rural and village world of Emerson. Whereas Emerson fears any intoxication as a false stimulant, Whitman revels in the appetites of the body. What is at stake is not merely philosophical, but social as well: There will be no more standing aloof from the issues of the day. Implicitly recalling Emerson's reticence to join in the abolitionist campaign (as in the women's rights campaign), Whitman gives himself a role of speaking for the excluded: "Through me many long-dumb voices, / Voices of the interminable generations of prisoners and slaves." These "forbidden voices" lose their indecency in Whitman's mouth, as he seeks a new vocabulary of democratic inclusiveness. In one of his most provocative lines he writes, "The scent of these arm-pits is aroma finer than prayer."

The male body and the male genitals are for Whitman a prime example of the act of suppression in the name of propriety. He will name them and praise them, locating them directly in the landscape of nature poetry:

> Root of washed sweet-flag, timorous pond-
>   snipe, nest of guarded duplicate eggs,
>   it shall be you,
> Mixed tussled hay of head and beard and
>   brawn it shall be you;
> Trickling sap of maple, fibre of manly wheat,
>   it shall be you . . .
> Winds whose soft-tickling genitals rub against
>   me it shall be you,
> Broad muscular fields, branches of liveoak,
>   loving lounger in my winding paths, it
>   shall be you,
> Hands I have taken, face I have kissed, mortal
>   I have ever touched, it shall be you.
>   ("Song of Myself," ll. 535–543)

By locating the celebration of the body outdoors, Whitman works directly against the association of "corruption" with urban life; he makes nature itself the site of erotic play.

Although Whitman has often been charged with displaying too much facile optimism, the poems reveal his awareness of limitations and pain. The limitations were those that dominated American civil discourse in the 1850s: the problem of slavery and the de-mand for equal rights for women. Among the poet's many manifestations in "Song of Myself" is that of "the hounded slave," whose suffering is rendered graphically:

> I wince at the bite of the dogs,
> Hell and despair are upon me, crack and again
>   crack the marksmen,
> I clutch the rails of the fence, my gore dribs,
>   thinn'd with the ooze of my skin,
> I fall on the weeds and stones,
> The riders spur their unwilling horses, haul
>   close,
> Taunt my dizzy ears and beat me violently over
>   the head with whip-stocks. (ll. 838–843)

Another is "the mother of old, condemned for a witch." To these national issues must be added the dramas of personal identity. Whitman's sense of himself drawn physically to other men and his belief in the power of male love to work against patriarchal authority were countered by a strong feeling of unspeakability. How render a love that seemed to Whitman to have so few precedents? How evoke that love without inviting condemnation for immorality? In the 1855 edition, Whitman could only begin a cautious exploration of these issues. He acknowledged the need to go beyond the surface and to reveal himself but felt unable to do so:

> Man or woman, I might tell how I like you,
>   but cannot,
> And might tell what is in me, and what it is in
>   you, but cannot,
> And might tell that pining I have, that pulse of
>   my nights and days. (ll. 991–993)

Here Whitman's nonsexist "man or woman" serves also to disguise his subject. What is there that he "cannot" tell if the beloved is a woman? It is in fact Whitman's homosexuality that must still leave him speechless, able only to speak through the voices of others who have suffered, to become a general voice of the outcast and forbidden.

Whitman's homosexual identity had to wait until the 1860 "Calamus" poems that are derived directly from these lines, as Whitman announces in the first poem that his new mission is "To tell the secret of my nights and days, / To celebrate the need of comrades." Still, even before "Calamus" he was nonetheless able to identify passionate love, implicitly homosexual, as the source of vision. Section 5 of "Song of Myself" presents an idyllic moment of sexuality, "How you settled your head athwart my hips and gently turn'd over upon me," as the source of a vision of a redeemed world that has gone beyond a system of relative values. There is a long tradition, of course, of the use of an erotic vocabulary to present a mystical experience, but also an equally long one that does the reverse. We can probably never know which is the vehicle and which the tenor. In other sections of the poem, Whitman is bolder in his presentation of the sexual. In section 21, for instance, the poet sees himself as the lover of the earth in terms that are strikingly frank: "Thruster holding tight and that I hold tight! / We hurt each other as the bridegroom and the bride hurt each other" (1860, ll. 449–450). Whitman eliminated these lines in later editions, but they were part of his original conception, and they still speak eloquently about his power to employ the sexual as part of a larger social and philosophical program. Whitman loves the earth and penetrates it (a traditional metaphor for the male), but he is also in his turn penetrated *by* the earth, thus reversing the human-earth hierarchy and challenging fixed gender roles.

Whitman's first edition is thus highly erotic but largely lacking in the sense of identity or community. It is revolutionary in its frank treatment of sexuality and particularly in its use of sexuality as a means to spiritual insight and vision. In his second edition in 1856, Whitman added a crucial poem, later called "Song of the Open Road," that enabled him to deal at once with his mission as a national poet and as a lover of men. Interspersed with the poem's dominant narrative of freedom ("I ordain myself loos'd of limits and imaginary lines / Going where I list, my own master total and absolute" [ll. 53–4]) is another narrative, at first attributed to the highway itself, of a love that will "adhere to me." The word *adhere* takes on particular significance here, for it is linked to the phrenologists' term *adhesiveness,* which Whitman appropriated and made into a term for homosexuality. Whitman's first use of the term makes its meaning for him clear:

> Here is adhesiveness—it is not previously
> fashion'd, it is apropos;
> Do you know what it is as you pass to be loved
> by strangers?
> Do you know the talk of those turning
> eye-balls? (ll. 91–93)

For Emerson the eyeball was transparent, offering no physical barrier between mind and pure idea; for Whitman the eyeball was restored to its physical being, and made into an organ of desire. This scene of cruising clarifies the meaning of Whitman's city: It is the place of multiple sexual invitations. If the city offers a confirmation of the widespread nature of male desire, it still offers for Whitman no sense of identity. He proposes "adhesiveness," the unfashioned word, to fill that gap.

Beginning with section 9, Whitman begins all but one of the remaining sections of the poem with the French revolutionary call, "Allons!" The exhortation and the plural subject indicate a sense of shared urgency. The road that leads to individual freedom also leads to self-discovery and self-identification. Marching through the streets, he calls forth his fellow "adhesives," urging them to take their place in the great Enlightenment parade of released subjectivity. He recognizes the price paid for concealment, the price of the closet. "Out of the dark confinement! out from behind the screen!" he exclaims. Those being called on to join the procession have led lives of self-hatred, filled with the internalization of social judgments. Their double lives hide "a secret silent loathing and despair," the despair of those who can reveal their truth to no one. Such people are everywhere, Whitman insists, married, in public life, apparently conventional citizens, but always unable to speak of themselves. It is the desperate lives of such people that give rise to the revolutionary fervor of "Song of the Open Road." Asking for "active rebellion," Whitman reassures his readers that he himself has "tried" the "open road" of resistance to sexual orthodoxy. As if to demonstrate his own experience, and his willingness to speak on their behalf, he closes the poem with a gesture of friendship and love that breaks down social barriers.

> Camerado, I give you my hand!
> I give you my love more precious than money,
> I give you myself before preaching or law;
> Will you give me yourself? will you come
> travel with me?
> Shall we stick by each other as long as we live?
> (ll. 220–224)

The most important poem of this period is the work composed in 1856, originally called "Proto-Leaf" and placed first in the 1860 *Leaves of Grass:* It is known now as "Starting from Paumanok." Beginning autobiographically, and thus locating himself as part of a specifically American heritage (even to the North American Indian name and sense of precolonial history), Whitman moves to a justification of his art. As in so many of the 1860 poems, Whitman sees his purpose as the foundation of an "ideal of manly love." The need for an inherently egalitarian form of affection, intricately tied as it is to the democratic mission of the United States, is not merely social, but deeply personal. Whitman recognizes the need to write out of his experience of frustration and denied love, to "let flame from me the burning fires that were threatening to consume me" by writing "the evangel-poem of comrades and of love." Human love and divine love are celebrated as equals; it is no longer a matter of using the world as a means to a higher state of being. Whitman celebrates the history and the future of America (unfortunately leaving "the red aborigines" as little more than the "names" after their "depart[ure]"). At the end of the poem, Whitman constructs one of his marvelous catalogues, or paratactic structures of parallelism that celebrate diversity of vision, each of the lines beginning "See." The cities, technology, nature, work are all hailed as part of a triumphant vision of the future. The last two sections make it clear that that utopian vision can be achieved by the poet and his comrade and the "adhesiveness" they share. The poem ends in an ecstatic call to "one more desirer and lover" to "haste, haste on, with me."

Whitman's fullest exploration of his homosexual identity and its place in culture is to be found in the forty-five poems of the "Calamus" sequence. In some sense, Whitman's version of VIRGIL's "Bucolics," these poems are a sustained engagement with the history of homosexual representation as well as an account of a threatened love. The first poem of the sequence locates the poet outside normal social space (in the space of the pastoral, in other words). His escape there is born not only out of a desire to escape the corrupt world of city or court (although there is some of that feeling, despite the poetry's earlier celebration of the city's erotic life) but also out of a need to find a place of meditation and self-recognition. The poem, like many of Whitman's, is structured around two times: before and after awareness. In order to "escape" the conventional world and its values, the poet must follow "paths untrodden" that can lead to the "margins." He must, in other words, acknowledge his difference and hence his freedom from "standards hitherto published." In this place of seclusion, he escapes the meaningless talk ("the clank of the world") to find instead the "tongues aromatic" of the calamus plant and ultimately of a sensual bliss of comrade love. His offering to the world, indeed his child in the imagery of the poem brought forth in the ninth month, is a new kind of song, one that, by revealing his own "secret" will offer to others the models or "types of athletic love."

Many other poems in this sequence develop and vary these themes. The second poem ("Scented herbage of my breast"), for instance, states the need to escape from the appearance of heterosexuality: "I will escape from the sham that was proposed to me, / I will sound myself and comrades only." The eighth poem, "Long I thought that knowledge alone would suffice me" once again deals with the conversion pattern, from ignorance to understanding. In this case, the structure is autobiographical. The poet sees himself as devoted first to knowledge, then to the land, then to heroes, and finally to the New World (in other words, the dominant missions of the earlier editions of *Leaves of Grass*). But he resolves to ignore these social missions for a personal one:

> I heed knowledge, and the grandeur of
> The States, and the example of heroes,
>   no more,
> I am indifferent to my own songs—I will go
>   with him I love,
> It is to be enough for us that we are together—
>   We never separate again. (1860, 11. 10–12)

The spirit of many of the love poems in "Calamus" is a kind of "All for Love"; nothing can stand up against the value of personal affection. This view would be sorely tested within a very short time after the publication of "Calamus" by the outbreak of the Civil War.

In preparing the 1860 edition, however, Whitman was an optimist. The fifth "Calamus" poem, "States!," saw "a new friendship" as the basis of social unity. Whitman was applying to the nation the ideas of the social reformers and their search for a new community based on equality and love. "Manly affection" will be visible everywhere, Whitman announces, and will link the states. This is to be the true continuation of the French revolution: "The dependence of Liberty shall be lovers, / The continuance of Equality shall be comrades." The new land, joined by a new social order, would be "indissoluble."

The "Calamus" poems lack much of the frank sexuality of "Song of Myself." They insist, not on homosexual *acts,* but on homosexual being in the world. At the same time, joyous as they are, there is a boyish exuberance about them that suggests a relative innocence about the realities of social conflict. The slave whose suffering is so visible in the 1855 edition is now almost invisible even on the eve of the war. The poems attempt to locate a homosexual republic, a paradise of men who are freed from evil (like the parallel heterosexual collection, "Children of Adam," the new regenerate race, in which Whitman found room for poems that had once been in "Calamus").

Darkness is evoked in "Calamus" primarily in personal terms. It is the product of isolation as well as the failure of personal love. Whitman wonders whether his love for other men is actually shared by others; he seeks community. He is tempted to repress his feelings, but, as he puts it in the ninth "Calamus" poem, "Hours continuing long," "it is useless—I am what I am." Recent theory has argued against the existence of a "natural" or "essential" homosexuality, pointing out, correctly, that the social meanings of sexual acts vary from one culture to another. But Whitman's portrayal of his emotional life is based on the acknowledgment of a fundamental self, shaped by experience, that is not to be denied. In his loneliness, Whitman asks "Is there even one other like me?" The question is posed in a moment of suffering and loss; for the isolation is all the greater when there is no one to share the pain. His response can only be one of rendering public the troubled self, as in the fifteenth poem, "O drops of me!" Here the poet recognizes the connection between pain and freedom, recognizes that the suffering of acknowledgment may lead to a reduction of repression. The imagery of the poem joins blood and semen (as frequently in nineteenth-century thought), and sets up a paradox that the "wounds" of the body "free" the blood from its prison. It must of course be remembered that Whitman is writing amid a moral purity campaign that condemns masturbation as severely as homosexuality. These drops of blood or semen offer the candor of self-revelation, of "confession" (Whitman is thus placed in the discourse of confession as self-creation and subjectification, in FOUCAULT's terms). These painful drops are not incidentals, nor are they confined to certain moments only, they "stain every page"; but they also "saturate" and "glow" as the sense of shame is driven out.

Although Whitman's symbol of a new love, the calamus, can be found only in the forest pond, the realization of its consequences extends far beyond that sheltered site. The nineteenth poem, "Mind you the timid models of the rest," deals with the result of the acknowledgment of a new identity that enables him to question the "majority." Whitman portrays himself here as a simple man, a workman with "swarthy and unrefined face," "white wool, unclipt upon [his] neck," a man, he says, "without charm." Yet he receives and returns the kisses of another man, a Manhattanese, a product of the new social freedom of the city in the mid-nineteenth century. Whitman insists on the public nature of their affection, of a kiss at a streetcorner or "in the public room." Whitman's demand for social space is still not granted in America, but he made a major contribution to the claim upon it. What is more, he does not situate that claim for open affection, for a part in the large social world, upon toleration of a minority, but indeed upon its specifically American quality. If America is to be the home of the free, to be the new society divorced from its European origins, then it must find a place for such "natural" affection. Whitman's claim for homosexual space is thus conducted in the same spirit as the abolitionist or women's rights campaigns of his time: It is a call to fulfill the opportunity of the revolution. The two men in Whitman's poem "observe that salute of American comrades," the kiss that replaces the bowed head.

The Civil War made such claims for an American identity difficult to sustain. Whitman, who had been involved with a Free-Soil newspaper much earlier, was at first an ardent supporter of the Union, but the experience of suffering and the repeated fratricide soon cast a darker shadow over his work. Although he devoted himself personally to caring for the wounded, his poems sought a way of integrating his affection for men into an art that needed to reflect the sense of loss. There was, of course, a natural form available to him—the ELEGY—which had often served to mourn the dead beloved and which offered a "safe" way of expressing love for another man, now that he was dead. (TENNYSON's "In Memoriam" was published in 1850, offering a contemporary example, but the model of MILTON's "Lycidas" was also there.) Some of the "Drum Taps" poems were sentimental, such as that Victorian narrative, "Come up from the fields father." Others were more successful in integrating Whitman's concerns, notably "Vigil strange I kept on the field one night." Here the exchange of looks precedes the battle, so that the speaker returns to find the "dear comrade" "in death so cold." This personal loss is absorbed into a ritual of mourning, in which the two act out a consummation of their love. The comrade is then buried, as the "boy of responding kisses, (never again on earth responding.)" The poem traces the night spent together and the morning that brings the poet new life in the ability to care for the dead soldier and an acceptance of death, enacted in the loving burial. Whitman's mission in the "Drum Taps" poems, as in his life, becomes caring for the sick and wounded, bringing them loving affection and asking for love in return. The letters that he later received over many years from soldiers he had met testify movingly to the power of that friendship. The dream of a united America, and the search for a personal friend, give way in the later poems to a desire for fulfillment in death. The "cries of anguish" of the battlefield give rise to a tempered optimism and a pervasive affection that does not depend on personal sexual identity.

The many losses of the Civil War were echoed in the loss of President Lincoln. Whitman's elegy for Lincoln, "When Lilacs Last in the Dooryard Bloom'd," expresses the national sense of loss in terms of personal love. The lilac, sign of early spring, becomes a token of affection, replacing the calamus of the earlier poems without losing many of its associations. The poet's flowery offering to the coffin of Lincoln becomes an offering to all coffins, to all those dead in the war. The poem seeks adequate forms of mourning, ways to integrate the solitary voice of the griever into the national sense of loss and the universal, mythic sense of renewal through death. Consolation can be found in the peace to which the dead have passed and in the world of nature. The poem's dominant symbols come together, preserving the memory of his comrades, "the dead I loved so well," now brought together "in the fragrant pines and the cedars dusk and dim" (11. 203–206).

Whitman's work quickly established a sense of gay community among his readers. Writers such as Bayard Taylor, Bram Stoker, and CHARLES WARREN STODDARD wrote to express their gratitude and received encouragement from Whitman. An 1868 edition of poems in England brought him many new readers. Among them were socialists such as EDWARD CARPENTER, who in repeated essays and Whitman-like poems sought to continue Whitman's heritage in its radical implications for the reorganization of society and sexuality. It was this radical Whitman, mediated through Carpenter, who reached E. M. FORSTER, leading him to create his memorable bathing scene in *A Room with a View* (1908) and to respond to Whitman's "Passage to India" (1871), a late poem seeking a completion of the spiritual mission in the embrace of the "Comrade perfect," with his novel *A Passage to India* (1924). Later gay poets have also responded to Whitman, notably HART CRANE, who tried in *The Bridge* (1930) to create a modernist myth of America, and Beats such as ALLEN GINSBERG who were dubious about Whitman's vision, even as they adopted his free verse and his apparent authorization of a freedom of subject matter and an openness about homosexuality. For many of these readers, what remained essential about Whitman was his search for an adequate language and form. Like twentieth-century French feminists, Whitman made his poetics an integral part of his politics. His long, loose, inclusive lines were inherently democratic and capable of giving expression to the realities of homosexual life. Instead of the sentence of fixed form, structure, and meaning, he offers a polymorphous field of pleasure and a political program that demands a reconsideration of the American dream and its potential.

—*Robert K. Martin*

BIBLIOGRAPHY

Allen, Gay Wilson. *The New Walt Whitman Handbook.* New York: New York University Press, 1985. ■ ———. *The Solitary Singer. A Critical Biography of Walt Whitman.* New York: Macmillan, 1955. ■ Arvin, Newton. *Whitman.* New York: Macmillan, 1938. ■ Asselineau, Roger. *The Evolution of Walt Whitman.* 2 vols. Cambridge, Mass.: Harvard University Press, 1960. ■ Bowers, Fredson. *Whitman's Manuscripts. Leaves of Grass (1860).* Chicago: University of Chicago Press, 1955. ■ Fone, Byrne R. S. *Masculine Landscapes. Walt Whitman and the Homoerotic Text.* Carbondale: Southern Illinois University Press, 1992. ■ Kaplan, Justin. *Walt Whitman. A Life.* New York: Simon & Schuster, 1980. ■ Killingsworth, M. Jimmie. *Whitman's Poetry of the Body. Sexuality, Politics, and the Text.* Chapel Hill: University of North Carolina Press, 1989. ■ Martin, Robert K. *The Homosexual Tradition in American Poetry.* Austin: University of Texas Press, 1979. ■ ———, ed. *The Continuing Presence of Walt Whitman. The Life after the Life.* Iowa City: University of Iowa Press, 1992. ■ Miller, Edwin H. *Walt Whitman's Poetry. A Psychological Journey.* Boston: Beacon, 1968. ■ ———. *Walt Whitman's "Song of Myself". A Mosaic of Interpretations.* Iowa City: University of Iowa Press, 1989. ■ Miller, James E., Jr. *A Critical Guide to Leaves of Grass.* Chicago: University of Chicago Press, 1957. ■ Moon, Michael. *Disseminating Whitman. Revision and Corporeality in Leaves of Grass.* Cambridge, Mass.: Harvard University Press, 1991. ■ Shively, Charley, ed. *Calamus Leaves. Walt Whitman's Working Class Camerados.* San Francisco: Gay Sunshine, 1987. ■ ———. *Drum Beats. Walt Whitman's Civil War Boy Lovers.* San Francisco: Gay Sunshine, 1989. ■ Zweig, Paul. *Walt Whitman: The Making of the Poet.* New York: Basic, 1984.

Wilde, Oscar
(1854–1900)

The importance of Oscar Wilde resides both in his art and in his personality. He is one of the most accomplished writers of his generation, but quite apart from his actual literary achievement, he is significant as a symbolic figure who exemplified a way of being homosexual at a pivotal moment in the emergence of gay consciousness, the crucial final decade of the nineteenth century. Actually, however, Wilde's literary significance is inseparable from his function as a symbolic figure. Although he frequently asserted the impersonality of art, his own art is irreparably bound to his personality. In fact, his greatest artistic creation is the complex and contradictory persona reflected in his work and in his life. Ultimately, that persona became transfigured from a witty aesthete into a figure as poignant as it was unpredictable, Saint Oscar, the homosexual martyr.

Born to accomplished but eccentric parents in Ireland in 1854, Wilde was educated at Trinity College, Dublin, and Magdalen College, Oxford, where he was almost equally influenced by the practically incompatible artistic doctrines of the moralistic John Ruskin and the epicurean WALTER PATER. Leaving Oxford in 1878, he declared prophetically, "Somehow or other I'll be famous, and if not famous, I'll be notorious." A master of drawing attention to himself, he quickly became known as the high priest of AESTHETICISM, the intimate of artists, and the companion of actresses. A superb conversationalist and a flamboyant dandy, he became a celebrity by virtue of his outrageousness as much as through his actual accomplishments.

Wilde's penchant for self-advertisement and for audacious posing ought not to obscure the seriousness behind his apparent flippancy, however. The apostle of aestheticism and decadence, the dandy addicted to gold-tipped cigarettes and exquisite *objets d'arts,* the social butterfly who cultivated the lords and ladies of the aristocracy, and the witty epigrammatist who delighted in deflating Victorian pomposity while celebrating the trivial at the expense of the earnest was also a penetrating social critic who defended individualism and pluralism and attacked economic and social exploitation and injustice. In *The Soul of Man under Socialism* (1891), for example, he enunciated a doctrine of libertarian socialism quite at variance with his mask of frivolity. For all its utopian idealism and arch wit, the pamphlet acutely dissects the harmful effects of private property on rich and poor alike. It is also filled with subtle insights into the nature of oppression, as when it redefines selfishness in terms of authoritarian morality: "Selfishness is not living as one wishes to live, it is asking others to live as one wishes to live. And unselfishness is letting other people's lives alone, not interfering with them." Wilde's antiauthoritarianism and his scorn for the philistinism of his late Victorian age are particularly important aspects of his persona and of his emergence as a symbolic figure, even as they are qualified by his almost equally strong need for social acceptance.

Wilde's need for social acceptance may have been a factor in his 1884 marriage to a young, somewhat conventional and naive socialite, Constance Lloyd, a union that quickly produced two sons. Although he had flirted with homosexuality for many years and had aroused the suspicions and gossip of many (and later came to regard himself as having always been homosexual), he seems to have begun the sustained practice of homosexuality in 1886, when he met a young Canadian, Robbie Ross, who was to be his lifelong and faithful friend and eventually his literary executor. In 1891, Wilde met LORD ALFRED DOUGLAS, the twenty-one-year-old son of the ninth Marquess of Queensbury, who was to hound Wilde to his spectacular fall. Douglas apparently introduced Wilde to the Victorian homosexual underground of male brothels and procurers and prostitutes who were to figure prominently in the sensational trials of 1895. Although Douglas appears to have been a thoroughly undisciplined young man, utterly unworthy of Wilde's devotion, the writer became so infatuated as to lose all sense of proportion and finally to embark on the course of action that was to culminate in his sentence to two years' penal servitude at hard labor. In hindsight, Wilde's association with Douglas seems a disaster. At the same time, however, the tumultuous affair may have inspired Wilde to some of his best work. Unquestionably, the discovery of his homosexuality liberated his art and marks a major breakthrough in his artistic maturity.

Indeed, Wilde's brief period of serious achievement, which began in 1888 with the publication of his collection of fairy tales, *The Happy Prince,* coincides with his period of homosexual activity. Over the next seven years, he was to produce important prose works such as *The Picture of Dorian Gray* (1890, 1891), *The Soul of Man under Socialism, Intentions* (1891), *Lord Arthur Savile's Crime and Other Stories* (1891), and *House of Pomegranates* (1891), as well as the five successful plays: *Salomé* (1893), *Lady Windermere's Fan* (1892), *A Woman of No Importance* (1893), *An Ideal Husband* (1895), and *The Importance of Being Earnest* (1895). This brief period of genuine accomplishment ended abruptly on February 18, 1895, only four days after the triumphant opening of *The Importance of Being Earnest,* when the Marquess of Queensberry left a card for Wilde at his club: "To Oscar Wilde, posing somdomite [*sic*]." Encouraged by Douglas, who loathed his father, Wilde sued Queensberry for criminal libel: a suit that was won by the bitter and unstable Marquess and that was to culminate in Wilde's own prosecutions for "gross indecency between males."

The severity of Wilde's sentence—which contributed to his premature death in exile in Paris in 1900—and the extremity of his suffering rendered him a martyr in the struggle for homosexual emancipation. Yet Wilde is, it must be acknowledged, an unlikely martyr and an ambiguous one. His martyrdom, after all, resulted as much from his own folly as from the viciousness of his persecutors, who were not eager to prosecute him or other homosexuals of high social standing or artistic prominence. Indeed, his trials and conviction may fairly be blamed on his (and Alfred Douglas's) willed stupidity and penchant for self-dramatization, and perhaps as well on his unconscious need for exposure and punishment. The theme of martyrdom runs through much of his work, early and late, and probably reflects the strong masochistic element in his personality, even as it also mirrors his sense of alienation. Moreover, his disastrous decision to prosecute Queensberry for alleging that he posed as a sodomite was itself reactionary rather than defiant.

Even after the debacle of his libel suit against Queensberry, Wilde could have escaped his own prosecution by fleeing to the Continent, a solution tacitly suggested by the magistrate, who apparently delayed issuing the warrant for his arrest in order to permit him to go abroad. That he did not go into exile, as so many prominent Victorian homosexuals had done when faced with the prospect of scandal and prison, is a measure less of his rebelliousness than of his felt need to maintain his position in society. Even the eloquent defense in his second trial of "the Love that dare not speak its name"—"a great affection of an elder for a younger man as there was between David and Jonathan, such as PLATO made the very basis of his philosophy, and such as you will find in the sonnets of Michael Angelo and Shakespeare. . . . that deep, spiritual affection which is as pure as it is perfect"—is sharply undercut by the fact that the speech, largely untrue and certainly misleading, was designed to deny the physical expression of his homosexuality rather than to defend it. The only hero of the Wilde trials was the procurer Alfred Taylor, who loyally refused to testify against his client and consequently shared his harsh punishment.

Wilde's own folly and masochism may have brought him into the prisoner's dock at Old Bailey, but once there he was victimized by the bigotry and hypocrisy of a society that he had ridiculed and exposed and yet could never completely reject. He became the scapegoat for his society's sexual and moral insecurities. Not surprisingly, however, those insecurities were also Wilde's own, as indicated by the reticence and coyness of his depictions of homosexuality in texts such as "The Portrait of Mr. W.H." and *The Picture of Dorian Gray.* Although Wilde deserves enormous credit for bravery in even broaching gay themes at a time when it was dangerous to do so, his gay texts before his fall tend to be divided against themselves. Heir to a homosexual aesthetic tradition that stretches from WINCKELMANN to Pater and the center in England of *fin de siècle* dandyism and DECADENCE, Wilde still remains surprisingly moralistic in these works.

Wilde's homosexuality leaves its mark on most of his canon, usually expressed indirectly in the form of a recurrent interest in scandalous secrets, mysterious pasts, and divided lives, though he may have contributed to the explicitly homosexual erotic novel *Teleny, or The Reverse of the Medal* (1893), which was apparently written by several members of his circle. In a play like *The Importance of Being Earnest,* Wilde translates the ambivalence he felt toward his homosexuality—epitomized by the very notion of "Bunburying," the need to lead a double life—into a complex parody of both himself and his society and thereby creates a masterpiece, perhaps the greatest comedy in the language. Without ever mentioning homosexuality, Wilde in *Importance* creates the quintessentially gay play. He turns Victorian values on their heads and discovers in the comedy of CAMP a means of covertly attacking his society's prejudices and discreetly defending his own nonconformity. The farce brilliantly depicts the liminal position that Wilde occupied in relation to his homophobic society, *in* it, yet not *of* it. Perhaps the most poignant aspect of *Importance* is the fact that its comedy is fueled by Wilde's desperate desire to be accepted by the very society he lampoons. In his earlier works that approach the homosexual theme more directly, however, the author's ambivalence fails to achieve resolution, and the result is a kind of imaginative paralysis: a rueful suspension between idealism and realism in "The Portrait of Mr. W.H." and a melodramatic moralism in *The Picture of Dorian Gray.* Only after his dizzying fall, in the painful but sly *De Profundis* does Wilde achieve a vision at once unified and capacious enough to contain his contradictoriness.

"The Portrait of Mr. W.H." is a work on which Wilde expended great time and effort, and it is one of the most revealing of his stories. The original version was published as an article of 12,000 words in 1889, but Wilde became more and more obsessed with the subject of SHAKESPEARE's *Sonnets,* and during the next four years, he revised and augmented the story, in the process more than doubling its length. The manuscript of the revised story, actually a novelette, was thought to have been lost in the chaos that accompanied the sale of Wilde's property after his arrest; many years later, it was discovered in the offices of Wilde's publisher, John Lane, and the revised version finally achieved print in 1921. On one level, the story is merely a pleasant speculation on the identity of the young man of Shakespeare's *Sonnets,* whom Wilde identifies as a boy actor named Willie Hughes, and a detailed interpretation of the sequence and its relationship to Shakespeare's plays. But on another level, the work is also a meditation on homosexuality and a foiled coming out story, Nabokovian in its complexity and irony.

"The Portrait of Mr. W.H." is divided into five sections, the middle three of which are devoted almost entirely to analyses of Shakespeare's poems and his relationship with the young man of the *Sonnets,* whereas the first and final sections are devoted to the contemporary frame story. Significantly, both the middle and the framing sections are self-consciously homosexual in tone. Whereas the Shakespeare material deals specifically with the poet's attachment to a young man, Willie Hughes, who becomes the symbol of an idealized homosexuality, the framing sections are concerned with characters who are sketched in terms of an easily recognizable homosexual style—one that Wilde more than anyone else helped establish in the popular imagination. Cyril Graham, Erskine, and the unnamed narrator are effete connoisseurs who interpret high culture to the middle classes. Central to both sections is the association of homosexual Eros and creativity and the motif of an older man inspired by the beauty of a younger one.

"The Portrait of Mr. W.H." can be read as a cautious defense of homosexuality in terms very similar to the defense that Wilde would later offer for "the Love that dare not speak its name." Associating Willie Hughes with Gaveston in MARLOWE's *Edward II* and linking the love of the *Sonnets* with the neoplatonism of Ficino and MICHELANGELO and the Hellenism of Winckelmann, the story presents homosexual passion as transcending but not denying the physical. At the same time, however, the narrator frankly acknowledges that the idealistic sixteenth-century philosophy that explains Shakespeare's attachment to Willie Hughes would be denounced as immoral and criminal in his own age. In answer to critics who see in the *Sonnets* "something dangerous, something unlawful even," he defiantly asserts the superiority of the soul's affections to man-made law. Most tellingly, he recognizes both peril and potential in the kind of love that Shakespeare felt for Willie Hughes: "It is no doubt true that to be filled with an absorbing passion is to surrender the security of one's lower life, and yet in such surrender there may be gain." This notion that there may be gain in embracing a higher truth than the security of everyday reality reverberates throughout the story, finally mocking the narrator himself when he rejects his own soul's truth, his homosexuality.

Perhaps even more important than its idealization and cautious defense of homosexuality is the novelette's emphasis on the continuity of homosexual feeling from the past to the present, even as that recognition culminates in an acknowledgment of the dangers of self-discovery and an awareness of gay oppression. This continuity, rather than the identity of Mr. W.H., is the real secret of the *Sonnets* and the real connection between the frame-story and the critical sections. In "The Portrait of Mr. W.H.," to study the *Sonnets* is to recognize a personal affinity with the homoerotic passion of Shakespeare and Willie Hughes. As a result of his absorption with Shakespeare's poems, Cyril, Erskine, and the narrator each finds reflected in the *Sonnets* an image of his own homosexuality. More accurately, they project onto their reading of Shakespeare's sequence their own homosexual sensibilities, discovering in the text the mirror of their own desire. Thus, the search for the solution "to the greatest mystery of modern literature" finally reveals less about the *Sonnets* than about Cyril, Erskine, and especially the narrator.

The narrator's ultimate repudiation of the Willie Hughes hypothesis is usually regarded merely as a witty Wildean narrative twist, illustrating the paradox "that in convincing someone else of a belief you lose the belief yourself." But the narrator's repudiation is also a response to the dangers of self-discovery. More specifically, it symbolizes his sublimation of his homosexual nature, reflecting his awareness and fear of gay oppression. In "The Portrait of Mr. W.H.," Wilde enacts a parable about the difficulty of maintaining homosexual idealism in the late nineteenth century (particularly in contrast to the Renaissance, which is presented as a romantic, Hellenistic era), illustrating how the age was—in Cyril's words—"afraid to turn the key that unlocked the mystery of the poet's heart." Although implicated in Cyril's forgery and Erskine's fraud, this idealism nevertheless represents a higher truth than the security of the life of everyday consciousness. But the narrator, prizing safety above honesty, chooses to live in the mundane reality of a philistine world rather than accept his own deepest nature. Thus, "The Portrait of Mr. W.H." both defends homosexuality and regretfully—perhaps prophetically—rejects it.

"The Portrait of Mr. W.H." and Wilde's flawed yet haunting experiment in the gothic novel, *The Picture of Dorian Gray,* share a number of similarities, including an ambivalence toward homosexuality. The similarities may be because Wilde probably revised the story at the same time as he revised the novel, which was originally published in *Lippincott's Monthly Magazine* in July 1890, then expanded and reissued as a book in 1891. In a real sense, however, *The Picture of Dorian Gray* is even more ambivalent about homosexuality than "The Portrait of Mr. W.H." Whereas the novelette depicts regretfully the failure to attempt a potentially liberating self-realization, the novel risks satirizing the very notion of self-realization by (perhaps unintentionally) equating it with mere dissipation and self-indulgence.

The novel's fascination resides in the discrepancy between its obvious moral and its contradictory tone. The moralism of the novel is apparent from its plot structure, which emphasizes the fall and punishment of a narcissistic young man who makes a Faustian bargain to preserve his youthful beauty. Wilde himself explained the story as a condemnation of excess. But such moralism is undercut by the fact that the good characters in the novel are weak and passive, whereas the corrupt ones are glamorous and strong. In addition, the ambiguous narrator makes the hedonistic doctrine enunciated by Sir Henry Wotton and embraced by Dorian Gray seductive indeed. Notwithstanding the retributive ending of the book, the Faustian dream of an escape from human limitations and moral strictures is rendered more appealingly than the superimposed morals condemning narcissism and excess. It is no wonder that in the popular imagination, the name Dorian Gray conjures not an image of evil but of supernaturally extended youth bought at the trivial price of a disfigured portrait.

Homosexuality is an important aspect of *The Picture of Dorian Gray,* and the novel deserves credit as a pioneering depiction of homosexual relationships in serious English fiction. But it is important to emphasize that Wilde hints at homosexuality rather than expresses it directly. Homosexual readers would certainly have responded to the book's undercurrent of gay feeling and may have found the very name "Dorian" suggestive of Greek homosexuality since it was Dorian tribesmen who allegedly introduced homosexuality into Greece. But Wilde purposely leaves the exact nature of the sins of Dorian Gray mysterious and vague; his dissipations are by no means exclusively or even primarily homosexual. More clearly homoerotic, however, is the competition of Basil Hallward and Lord Henry Wotton for the attentions of Dorian.

Wilde's attitude toward homosexuality in the novel may best be seen in his portrayal of Basil. The character most clearly defined as homosexual, Hallward is also the most morally sensitive character. He represents an idealized, platonized homosexuality, linked to a long tradition of art and philosophy. Tellingly, however, Basil's love for Dorian is presented ambiguously. On the one hand, its power is confirmed by the transformation of Basil's art that it effects. On the other hand, it is the source of guilt and fear, and the very art that it inspires is ominous, for that art culminates in the sinister portrait. By presenting the naive and unformed Dorian with an image of himself (the artist's own image of him), by awakening him to his beauty and thereby encouraging his vanity, Basil may even be said to initiate the entire tragedy. The

diabolism of the painting may be dismissed as a gothic plot device, but Wilde's serious purpose in implicating Basil in the corruption of Dorian Gray is to underline the major theme of the work, the wickedness of using others. This theme is clearest in Dorian's heartless exploitation of others and in the amused, detached voyeurism of Lord Henry, but it is involved as well in Basil's reduction of Dorian to "simply a motive in art" found "in the curves of certain lines, in the loveliness and subtleties of certain colours."

If Basil is to blame for objectifying Dorian, so too is Lord Henry. Although Basil and Henry are at first glance extremely dissimilar—the one earnest and idealistic, the other cynical and disillusioned—the rivals share an artistic impulse. They both want to transform and re-present reality, a desire that may be a psychological compensation for their essential passivity. Basil's artistry finds expression in painting, Henry's in the exercise of influence. Tellingly, Henry's homoerotic attraction to Dorian is whetted voyeuristically by Basil's worship of the young man, and Henry is thereby roused from his characteristic languor to a desire to influence Dorian, a process that is itself a sublimated expression of homosexuality. The worldly cynic undertakes as his goal the "making" of Dorian much as a poet or sculptor might shape a work of art.

The central irony of *The Picture of Dorian Gray* is that the Hellenic ideal of "the harmony of soul and body" pursued by Basil and Henry alike, and localized in their separate visions of Dorian, is not realized largely because they project onto the young man their own unbalanced and fragmentary images. Moreover, in the corrupt and materialistic world of late-nineteenth-century London, Dorian's project of self-realization amounts simply to a self-indulgence that mocks both Basil's idealism and Henry's tendentious (mis)interpretation of Pateresque epicureanism. Rather than harmonizing, in the course of the novel, Dorian's soul and body become increasingly disconnected and finally separated entirely, as symbolized in the increasing disjunction between the unaging beauty of Dorian's body and the hideous representation of his soul (that is, the picture). This irony suggests that the Faustian theme is by no means confined to the gothic diabolism of Dorian's supernatural bargain for a youthful appearance. By assuming godlike powers of creation, Basil and Henry also partake in the Faustian desire to escape human limitations.

But if Basil and Henry are finally condemned for their objectification of Dorian and for their Faustian aspirations, the romantic dream of an idealized harmony of body and soul nevertheless survives the moralistic conclusion to protest against an unsatisfactory reality and a tragic history. *The Picture of Dorian*

Gray is a text divided against itself, but its creative tensions yield both a poignant sense of loss that the world cannot be recreated and made whole and an implied vision of a world at ease with homosexuality, a world in which sensual enjoyment has been made an element of "a new spirituality, of which a fine instinct for beauty was to be the dominant characteristic." Perhaps more responsible than any other single English work in forging the stereotypical link between art, decadence, and homosexuality, *The Picture of Dorian Gray*—for all its moralistic posturing—mourns the loss of a golden age and art's inability to recreate that homoerotic harmony of flesh and spirit nostalgically associated with Hellenism.

Wilde's most important and least ambivalent contribution to gay literature is the remarkable letter written in prison, *De Profundis,* a work that creatively transmutes the disaster of his prosecution and imprisonment into a ludic triumph. Written over a period of three months in 1897, after he had been imprisoned for some eighteen months, and addressed to Lord Alfred Douglas, *De Profundis* is far more than the recriminatory attack of a disenchanted lover or a self-serving, self-pitying tract. It might best be described as Wilde's attempt to create and present a complex and contradictory but nevertheless authentic self, one to displace or qualify the masks he had himself created earlier and the ugly images attributed to him in the popular press. The importance of Wilde's prison letter for gay literature is that in it the writer breaks out of the bourgeois mold he had so frequently attacked yet to which he so tenaciously clung. As a result of his imprisonment, he discovers a new freedom and emerges as Saint Oscar, the victim of gay oppression who finally triumphs over a philistine society.

The key faculty of the authentic self that Wilde creates in *De Profundis* is *imagination.* Imagination, as used in the work, is a preexistentialist term for the individual's attentiveness to received ideas and relationships; it indicates a liveliness of the spirit, an awareness of the meaning of experience, a critical alertness to the nature of one's relationships both to others and to social institutions, and a constant questioning of established social codes. In *De Profundis,* imagination is Wilde's means of liberating himself from his problematic relationship to society.

The most daring aspect of *De Profundis* is Wilde's simultaneous depictions of Christ in his image and himself in Christ's image. Christ is presented not as a supernatural being but as a fascinating artist whose power of imagination "makes him the palpitating centre of romance." The embodiment of *agape,* Christ understands the sufferings of others. He is also the proponent of radical individualism, and rather than consisting of moralistic prohibitions, Christ's "morality is all sympathy." Wilde also depicts Christ as an imaginative social critic, alert to the injustices of society and waging a war against social tyranny. Christ's antagonists are the philistines, who never question the dehumanizing and limiting social codes that they enforce, codes that have created a thoroughly inhumane prison system, incarcerated Wilde for his homosexuality, and robbed him of his children. The portrait of Christ as the romantic artist martyred by a philistine society functions for Wilde not merely as self-aggrandizement but also as a means of attacking the religious base of philistine morality.

In *De Profundis,* Wilde defends his homosexuality, or Uranianism, obliquely but strongly, and the work deserves a prominent place in the literature of homosexual apologias. Wilde's frank admission of his homosexuality as "a fact about me" translates his sexual identity into an element of the new self-knowledge he has gained in the crucible of suffering and one that he will not willingly deny or surrender. Skeptical of the medical model of homosexuality emerging in the late nineteenth century, he refers dismissively to Cesare Lomboroso, an Italian criminologist who believed homosexuality was a congenital dysfunction, to be treated in insane asylums rather than prisons. Although open to a theoretical connection between homosexuality and artistic creativity, as implied by homosexual apologists like JOHN ADDINGTON SYMONDS and EDWARD CARPENTER and endorsed in "The Portrait of Mr. W.H." and *The Picture of Dorian Gray,* Wilde observes laconically that "the pathological phenomenon in question is also found among those who have not genius." Rather than belaboring the causes of homosexuality, he is defiant of those who would condemn him. He resolutely denounces the "wrong and unjust laws" of the "wrong and unjust system" that convicted him, and confesses that "The one disgraceful, unpardonable, and to all time contemptible action of my life was my allowing myself to be forced into appealing to Society for help and protection. . . ." This new awareness of his relation to a society whose code he violated yet naively looked to for protection is an important measure of his growth in imagination as a result of his experience.

The most moving aspect of *De Profundis* is Wilde's graphic account of the mental and physical pain he has undergone in prison. Deserted by Douglas, humiliated by a vengeful public, branded and cast out from society, he describes his life as a veritable "Symphony of Sorrow." But the supreme theme of the work is the meaningfulness of suffering. Wilde declares that suffering "is really a revelation. One discerns things that one never discerned before." He concludes that "to have become a *deeper* man is the privilege of those who have suffered." It is this deeper man who triumphs in *De Profundis*. As a result of seeing the world differently, he is able to accept himself and his plight without bitterness. He emerges as a kind of Harlequin Christ figure, a martyred clown who enjoys the last laugh. He exercises his imagination to translate his martyrdom into a triumph analogous to the Christian comedy implicit in Good Friday and the Resurrection.

The new self that triumphs at the end of *De Profundis* revels defiantly in his exclusion from society, his marginality as homosexual pariah. Thus, Wilde rejects the artificial society that has condemned him and looks to nature for comfort and consolation:

> Society, as we have constituted it, will have no place for me, has none to offer; but Nature, whose sweet rains fall on unjust and just alike, will have clefts in the rocks where I may hide and secret valleys in whose silence I may weep undisturbed. She will hang the night with stars so that I may walk abroad in the darkness without stumbling, and send the wind over my footprints so that none may track me to my hurt: she will cleanse me in great waters, and with bitter herbs make me whole.

This passage, with its defiant assertion of Wilde's status as a child of nature, its criticism of a shallow society, its yearning for an Arcadian retreat, its faint but deliberate echoes of Ecclesiastes, and its self-dramatization that approaches parody, is at once slyly comic and deeply moving, expressing in little the complex comic tone of the whole, where tragedy and comedy not only coexist but deepen each other.

It may be true, as W. H. AUDEN observed, that the Wilde scandal had a disastrous effect on the arts "because it allowed the philistine man to identify himself with the decent man," but it is also true, as John Cowper Powys remarked, that Wilde consequently became "a sort of rallying cry to all those writers and artists who suffer, in one degree or other, from the persecution of the mob." For homosexuals, he became a martyr figure, a haunting symbol of gay vulnerability and gay resistance. Responsible more than anyone else for forming the popular stereotype of the homosexual as a dandiacal wit who flaunts middle-class mores, he is also most responsible for exemplifying the political realities of gay oppression. He is a symbolic figure not only because his imprisonment is the political reality that all subsequent considerations of homosexuality must confront, but also because his defiance and his painfully earned self-realization are important lessons in the struggle for gay liberation. (See also ENGLISH LITERATURE: NINETEENTH CENTURY.)

—*Claude J. Summers*

BIBLIOGRAPHY

Auden, W. H. "An Improbable Life." *Forewords and Afterwords.* Edward Mendelson, ed. New York: Random House, 1973. 302–324. ■ Cohen, Ed. *Talk on the Wilde Side: Toward a Genealogy of Discourse on Male Sexualities.* New York: Routledge, 1993. ■ ———. "Writing Gone Wilde: Homoerotic Desire in the Closet of Representation." *PMLA* 102 (1987): 801–813. ■ Cohen, Philip K. *The Moral Vision of Oscar Wilde.* Rutherford, N.J.: Fairleigh Dickinson University Press, 1978. ■ Cohen, William A. "Willie and Wilde: Reading *The Portrait of Mr. W.H.*" *South Atlantic Quarterly* 88 (1989): 219–245. ■ Ellmann, Richard. *Oscar Wilde.* New York: Viking, 1987. ■ ———, ed. *Oscar Wilde: A Collection of Critical Essays.* Englewood Cliffs, N.J.: Prentice-Hall, 1969. ■ Gagnier, Reginia. *Idylls of the Marketplace: Oscar Wilde and the Victorian Public.* Stanford: Stanford University Press, 1986. ■ Hyde, H. Montgomery. *Oscar Wilde.* London: Eyre Methuen, 1975. ■ Nassaar, Christopher S. *Into the Demon Universe: A Literary Exploration of Oscar Wilde.* New Haven: Yale University Press, 1974. ■ Oates, Joyce Carol. "The Picture of Dorian Gray: Wilde's Parable of the Fall." *Critical Inquiry* 7 (1980): 419–428. ■ Powys, John Cowper. "Wilde as a Symbolic Figure." *Oscar Wilde: The Critical Heritage.* Karl Beckson, ed. London: Routledge & Kegan Paul, 1970. 357. ■ Shewan, Rodney. *Oscar Wilde: Art and Egotism.* London: Macmillan, 1977. ■ Summers, Claude J. *Gay Fictions: Wilde to Stonewall.* New York: Continuum, 1990.

Wilhelm, Gale
(1908–1991)

Gale Wilhelm was born April 26, 1908, in Eugene, Oregon, the daughter of Ethel Gale Brewer and Wilson Price Wilhelm. She was educated in Oregon, Idaho, and Washington, and—except for 1935 when she lived in New York City and worked as associate editor of *Literary America*—lived on the West Coast, primarily in the San Francisco Bay area. Wilhelm lived for ten years with Helen Hope Rudolph Page, a great-grandniece of Stephen A. Douglas, who was associated with Carl Sandburg's four-volume biography of Abraham Lincoln and had literary connections. From 1948 on, for the last forty-three years of her life, Wilhelm had a happy relationship with a second lover, who has chosen to remain anonymous, with whom she lived in Berkeley. Wilhelm died on July 11, 1991, at age eighty-three, having lived most of her life in some comfort on an independent income.

In the ten years between 1935 and 1945, Wilhelm published a few poems, several short stories, and six brief novels; however, she spent the last forty-six years of her life without further literary production, perhaps because she was too content to write, as has been suggested, or because reviews of her work had become increasingly unappreciative. Early reviews of Wilhelm's work celebrate her as a talented, promising writer, comparing her with HEMINGWAY and WOOLF, but later commentaries suggest that she had not realized the potential of her early novels. The lesbian subject matter of two of her novels elicited some negative responses, but there was also a good deal of positive reinforcement in the reception of this work.

We Too Are Drifting (1935) tells the story of woodcut artist Jan Morale's struggle to extricate herself from a destructive sexual attachment to bisexual Madeline and of her delicately conducted romance with the younger and more innocent Victoria. The tone is bittersweet, for in the end Jan must watch as Victoria goes away with her family and the young man they have chosen for her. The triangle is complicated by Kletkin, a sculptor whose feeling for Jan inspires, before his tragic death, an award-winning statue of Hermaphroditus. Wilhelm suggests a genetic etiology for homosexuality when she portrays Jan's disgraced, dead twin brother as effeminate. Wilhelm's writing is characterized by what Jeannette Foster has called "meticulous restraint," a minimalist style of understated yet powerfully felt emotions, accentuated by the absence of quotation marks and the sparseness of other punctuation.

Wilhelm's second novelette, *No Letters for the Dead* (1936), again addresses unconventional, even sensational, subject matter in the tragic story of Paula, who becomes a prostitute to support herself while her lover is in prison, writing him cheerful letters to disguise her plight. *Torchlight to Valhalla* (1938) returns to the subject of love between women in the coming-out story of Morgen, a twenty-one-year-old novelist who loses the artist father who has raised her, is unsuccessfully courted by a suitable young man, and finally finds herself in her love for seventeen-year-old Toni. This ending, by implying the possibility of happiness in lesbian relations, stands in clear contrast to the poignancy with which *We Too Are Drifting* concludes.

Wilhelm's final three books abandon the subject of lesbian sexuality. *Bring Home the Bride* (1940), *Time Between* (1943), and *Never Let Me Go* (1945) have been described as mannered and precious. This later work disappointed those who expected her earlier efforts to result in a more considerable accomplishment. Her last novel was described, not unfairly, as shallow.

Despite a disappointing career, Wilhelm contributed significantly to the lesbian literary heritage in *We Too Are Drifting* and *Torchlight to Valhalla* by presenting lesbian relations unapologetically. In these works, she makes no effort to explain or justify or plead a cause (as had done RADCLYFFE HALL so recently) but presents her characters enmeshed in very human, often confused relations, attached to each other through not always the most admirable of emotions or motivations. For this, Wilhelm has always been treasured by a small group of loyal readers.

—*Harriette Andreadis*

BIBLIOGRAPHY

Foster, Jeannette H. *Sex Variant Women in Literature.* 1956. Tallahassee: Naiad Press, 1985. ■ Warfel, Harry R. *American Novelists of Today.* New York: American Book Company, 1951.

Williams, Jonathan
(b. 1929)

Jonathan Williams was born in Asheville, North Carolina, and educated at St. Alban's School in Washington and at Princeton University. His real education, however, began at Black Mountain College (1951–1956), where he met Charles Olson and, in company with another gay poet, ROBERT DUNCAN, took on Ezra Pound's lesson of compact speech and William Carlos Williams's maxim "no ideas but in things."

Jonathan Williams has been described as a cross "between Richard Pryor and the Roman poet Martial." Indeed, his poetic reception has suffered from his refusal to keep the flesh and the spirit separate. Either he is criticized by the traditional straight world for lowering poetic tone or ignored by the gay world, both for seeing the raunchiness of our world in classical terms and for having a sense of history. For him Zeus is a randy old-goat tourist snatching up the local Ganymede trade, and Catullus is familiar with jock straps. His old friend, the writer and classical scholar Guy Davenport (who has also written the best criticism on him), offers him such a vision: "he suggests Socrates sat on a bench in the gym, / the lovers came flocking / for the simple reason he was the best talker in town."

"I haven't seen the territory yet that can't be sexualized or examined for its poetic cuisine, or its birds, or for its dialects," Williams has written. In one of his recent collections, *Quantulumcumque* (1991) (the word means "as much as can be said in a small space"), is an epigram of a modern hustler that reappropriates classical epigram form:

> Donnie
> pocket full of green
> bottom full of cum

But he has also been concerned with feeling—with getting beyond what he calls the verbal and imaginative penury of "hardcornponeography." What he imagines best is the hard-on longing for it of country boys wild for passion. He has also written a fine sequence based on the fears and failings of the men interviewed by Havelock Ellis and a beautiful love poem ("Lexington Nocturne"), in which he lets his hand hang for a moment in the hair of his as-yet-unseduced bedmate and concludes "let that be all / for then."

Words are always squirming away from Williams as he attempts to see (not say) what is out there. (He talks about making poems *out* not *up*.) Often his titles (the lens of his poetic camera) are longer than the poems themselves. Believing, like William Blake, that

to generalize is to be an idiot, he has been described as a "poet of the complex actual." Williams is a pathologist of the ordinary, listening to the quirks and privacies of speech as they reveal character. Many of his poems sound like (and are) overheards:

> i hear you do
> not care greatly for
> the fair sex the
> fair sex he snapped
> back which is that

Along with his lover, the accomplished poet, Tom Meyer, Williams has been busy running Jargon Press, which has been responsible for publishing a number of gay poets—James Broughton, Robert Duncan, Harold Norse, and Paul Metcalf among them. Some of his essays and reviews have been collected in *The Magpie's Bagpipe* (1982), but much of his liveliest work still remains uncollected in the annual collections of squibs and ripostes that he sends out to friends.

If he has failings they are the result of his being too large, of embracing multitudes, as WHITMAN would put it. His bibliography extends to more than a hundred books and booklets as well as many other publications. It would be hard to think of any one person who has done more for poetry, gay and straight, in America.

—*Douglas Chambers*

BIBLIOGRAPHY

Davenport, Guy. *Jonathan Williams, Poet.* Cleveland: Asphodel Book Shop, 1969. ■ Fielding Dawson / Jonathan Williams Number. *Vort* 4 (Fall 1973). ■ Interview with Jonathan Williams. *Gay Sunshine* 28 (Spring 1976). ■ Irby, Kenneth. "America's Largest Openair Museum." *Parnassus* (Spring 1981): 307–328. ■ Marks, Jim. "A Jargon of their Own Making." *The Advocate* 24 (Nov. 1987).

Williams, Tennessee
(1911–1983)

Like many twentieth-century writers who were celebrities as well as artists, particularly writers whose work is often autobiographical, Williams's life is almost as well known as his work. Born Thomas Lanier Williams in 1911, his mother was a prim minister's daughter, his father a tough shoe salesman who called his son "Miss Nancy." In the autobiographical *The Glass Menagerie* (1945), Williams includes his father only as a smiling photograph

on the wall, a case of artistic wishful thinking. Williams's deepest attachment was to his sister, Rose, institutionalized in the 1930s and lobotomized after accusing her father of sexual abuse. A published writer of fiction and poetry since he was a teenager, Williams studied writing at the University of Iowa and, after some initial failures, became the best known playwright of the 1940s and 1950s. The last twenty years of his life were spent trying to recapture the success of his early plays, but substance abuse and a loss of self- and artistic control are evident in his later work. He died from choking on the cap of a medicine container.

Williams's gayness was an open secret he neither publicly confirmed nor denied until the post-Stonewall era when gay critics took him to task for not coming out, which he did in a series of public utterances, his *Memoirs* (1975), self-portraits in some of the later plays, and the novel, *Moishe and the World of Reason* (1975), all of which document, often pathetically, Williams's sense of himself as a gay man. There are several volumes of witty, confessional letters to friends DONALD WINDHAM and Maria St. Just and a raft of cynical, exploitative kiss-and-tell books by men who claimed to know Williams well in his later, declining years. However, anyone who had read his stories and poems, in which Williams could be more candid than he could be in works written for a Broadway audience, had ample evidence of his homosexuality.

Tennessee Williams's work poses fascinating problems for the gay reader. At his best, Williams wrote some of the greatest American plays, but though homosexuals are sometimes mentioned, they are dead, closeted safely in the exposition but never appearing on stage. In his post-Stonewall plays, in which openly homosexual characters appear, they serve only to dramatize Williams's negative feelings about his own homosexuality. In the 1940s and 1950s, Williams presented in his finest stories poetic renderings of homosexual desire, but homoeroticism was always linked to death. Only in his lyric poetry does one find positive expression of homoerotic desire.

These contradictions are not presented to damn Williams for not having a contemporary gay sensibility but to say that his attitude toward his own homosexuality reflected the era in which he lived. In the late 1940s and early 1950s, the McCarthy era, during which Williams wrote his best work, homosexuality branded one a traitor as well as a "degenerate." Williams's best work was an expression of his homosexuality combined with the intense neuroses that fueled his imagination and crippled his life. Gay critics have debated in recent years whether Williams's work is marked by "internalized homophobia" (Clum) or whether he is a subversive artist whose work can be best interpreted through the lens of leftist French theorists like ROLAND BARTHES and MICHEL FOUCAULT (Savran). David Bergman sees Williams's characteristic linking of homosexuality and cannibalism as both religious (the homosexual as martyr) and Freudian (homosexuality as accommodation to and rebellion against the father figure), as well as part of a central American gay literary tradition that has its roots in the work of HERMAN MELVILLE. The diverse but complementary work of these critics can be read as necessary counters to the heterosexist critics of the past who either ignored Williams's homosexuality altogether or saw it as the root of his personal and artistic failings. As is the case with many gay artists, the gay critical discussion of Williams, however lively, is just beginning.

A starting point for gay readers of Williams is not the plays but the short stories, particularly the two set in the decaying Joy Rio movie theater, "Hard Candy" and "The Mysteries of the Joy Rio." The Joy Rio is a once opulent opera house with horseshoe tiers of boxes above the orchestra and balcony level. Now the theater shows westerns, mass-produced myths of conventional American masculinity, while in the dark, roped-off upper boxes, various combinations of people engage in furtive sex. There lonely watchmaker Emil Kroger spent many hours before he fell in love with Pablo Gonzalez and succumbed to cancer of the bowels. There lonely Pablo, dying of the same disease, looks for brief moments of joy. There fat old Mr. Krupper, with his bag of hard candy and pocketful of quarters to bribe boys for sexual favors, succumbs to a heart attack while kneeling before the most beautiful boy he had ever seen. Theater in these stories is not only the place for the display of conventional heterosexual myths. In its dark corners, furtive homosexual dramas are also played out, dramas of transient joy, of aging, ugly people coming into contact with youth and beauty. In these moments of ecstasy and worship that the theater offers, it becomes a cathedral to those alliteratively linked religious concepts in Williams's work, desire and death. In these stories, one sees some of Williams's basic connections: sodomy with malignancy of the bowels, and sex as simultaneous confrontation with beauty and death. One also sees Williams's typical sex object, the young, dark, down-and-out hustler who is sometimes an angel of death, sometimes (as in "One Arm") a GENET-like punk saint. The stories open a theatrical space for the acting out of homosexual desire that is also disease and death. The most revolutionary aspect of these stories is contained in the narrative voice, both deadpan and playful, valorizing the activity at the Joy Rio while describing it as a prim outsider would see it—Williams is always aware of the prejudices of his audience. The double entendre of the title "Hard Candy" is typical of the sly humor with which Williams deflates the pathos of the situations he creates. The same playfulness is contained in Williams's wittier gay poems, like "San Sebastiano de Sodoma," in which "Mary from Her tower / of heaven" watches arrows pierce the throat and thigh of the martyr who was "an emperor's concubine," or his best-known poem, "Life Story," a hilarious depiction of post-coital attempts at communication. Blanche DuBois demonstrates the same playfulness while flirting with the young paperboy in *A Streetcar Named Desire,* transforming the event into grand theater while understanding its more banal premise, "You make my mouth water."

One sees Williams's darker connections in two of his major plays, *Cat On a Hot Tin Roof* (1955) and *Suddenly Last Summer* (1958). In *Cat On a Hot Tin Roof,* Brick Pollitt and his wife are living in the room once occupied by Jack Straw and Peter Ochello, the founders of the plantation now run by Big Daddy. Straw and Ochello are dead, but the bed they shared dominates the setting. Homosexual love is both dead and central to the play. The omnisexual, phallic Big Daddy, who hints at a sexual relationship with his former bosses, who left him their plantation, is dying of cancer of the bowels. Big Daddy's son, Brick, a former football star, is drinking himself to death, following in the footsteps of his beloved friend, Skipper. Brick is trapped by the sexual categories he has been taught: Men are for friendship, women are for sex. Unfortunately for him, those categories have become blurred: His best friend was sexually attracted to him, and his wife wants their marriage to have, in addition to sex, the honesty of a friendship. Brick hung up on his friend's admission of desire and has shut out his wife sexually and emotionally. Unable to endure any kind of intimacy, Brick drinks himself into detachment.

Brick's real problem is that he cannot face the complexity of his own emotions and sexual desires. He needs to see his feelings for Skipper as pure because the thought of being branded as a queer terrifies him. Like all deeply closeted people, Brick is obsessed with what his audience will think. The central scene of *Cat On a Hot Tin Roof* is a reversal of the usual father-son confrontation over homosexuality. Here son Brick is horrified that Big Daddy is not shocked at the thought of homosexuality while Big Daddy sees Brick's rejection of Skipper as a profound betrayal.

Throughout the play, Williams privileges the troubled closeted homosexual over the fertile heterosexuals. The heterosexual is Brick's awkward, nerdy brother, Gooper, trapped in a loveless marriage with the crass, hyperfertile Mae. Both Gooper and Mae see the plantation as rightfully theirs, for they have done all the right things. Gooper is a successful lawyer and family man. To him, it is outrageous that Big Daddy would favor the drunken wastrel whose marriage is a lie. Fertility of the land and the womb is crucial to the future of the Pollitt plantation, but that plantation was the offspring of a gay couple and will go to Brick and his determined wife, Maggie. *Cat On a Hot Tin Roof* comes as close to valorizing homosexuality as Williams got in his plays.

Suddenly Last Summer is one of Williams's more poetic dramas, a meditation on desire and cannibalism, which combines many of Williams's more common themes and images. A young woman, Catherine, has been institutionalized and threatened with the possibility of lobotomy for telling the truth about the death of her cousin, Sebastian Venable. Catherine is one of the many women in Williams's work (one thinks particularly of Laura in *The Glass Menagerie* and Blanche DuBois) whose fate (institutionalization and the threat of lobotomy) is that of his sister, Rose. Catherine has been brought to the conservatory of the splendid New Orleans home of Sebastian's powerful mother to face her family and a psychiatrist. The conservatory is filled with carnivorous plants and filled with the sounds of the jungle. It is Sebastian's garden, representing his vision of nature, that he tried to capture in his poetry but was most vividly depicted in his death as he was torn apart and eaten by the poor Mexican boys whose sexual favors he sought.

Sebastian saw the world as variations on cannibalism, but the ultimate violence is threatened by his mother: "Cut this hideous story out of her brain." Mrs. Venable, intent on protecting her son's image as an asexual visionary primarily devoted to his poetry and to her as his muse, will mutilate Catherine's mind rather than have the truth known about her son's homosexual activity. However, the psychiatrist will not order the lobotomy and Catherine's narrative, the truth about Sebastian, will take precedence over his privately published poetry. On one level, *Suddenly Last Summer* can be seen and read as Williams's depiction of the relationship between homosexual life and art, about the price paid for revealing the policed secret of homosexuality. Yet once again, the homosexual is dead, never seen but only discussed, like Skipper in *Cat On a Hot Tin Roof* and Blanche's first husband who shot himself when Blanche publicly confronted him with his homosexuality. Only Baron de Charlus in the more fantastic *Camino Real* (1953) appears on stage. When in the 1970s Williams could actually depict homosexuality more candidly, he created, in *Small Craft Warnings* (1970), a self-hating homosexual artist who laments the "deadening coarseness" in the lives of most homosexuals.

However, this literal reading of Williams's plays neglects the ways he brilliantly codes his plays so that gay readings are possible. *A Streetcar Named Desire,* in particular, can be seen and read as a gay play. Its theatrical transformations, CAMP, and careful use of gay slang (less known by a general audience in 1947) allow gay audiences to read their own transgressive text. This is not to say that Blanche is literally a gay man in drag but can be read as male and/or female, gay and/or straight. Certainly the focus on the animal magnetism of the macho Stanley Kowalski, treating him as the object of characters' and audience's gaze and desire and—in his silly, sometime brutal masculine posturing—also of their ridicule, can be given a gay reading. *Belle Reprieve,* the recent gender-inverted deconstruction of *Streetcar* performed by the gay troupe Bloolips and the lesbian troupe Split Britches, offered a hilarious but cogent gay interpretation of Williams's classic.

—*John M. Clum*

BIBLIOGRAPHY

Bergman, David. *Gaiety Transfigured: Gay Self-Representation in American Literature.* Madison, Wis.: University of Wisconsin Press, 1991. ■ Bigsby, C. W. E. *A Critical Introduction to Twentieth Century American Drama, II: Williams, Miller, Albee.* Cambridge: Cambridge, 1984. ■ Clum, John M. *Acting Gay: Male Homosexuality in Modern Drama.* New York: Columbia, 1992. ■ ———. "Something Cloudy, Something Clear: Homophobia in Tennessee Williams." *Displacing Homophobia: Studies in Gay Male Literature and Culture.* Ronald Butters, John M. Clum, Michael Moon, eds. Durham, N.C.: Duke University Press, 1989. ■ Savran, David. *Communists, Cowboys and Queers: The Politics of Masculinity in the Work of Arthur Miller and Tennessee Williams.* Minneapolis: University of Minnesota Press, 1992. ■ Spoto, Donald. *The Kindness of Strangers: The Life of Tennessee Williams.* New York: Ballantine, 1986. ■ St. Just, Maria. *Five O'Clock Angel: Letters of Tennessee Williams to Maria St. Just, 1948–1982.* New York: Knopf, 1990. ■ Summers, Claude J. *Gay Fictions: Wilde to Stonewall: Studies in a Male Homosexual Literary Tradition.* New York: Continuum, 1990.

Wilson, Sir Angus
(1913–1991)

Whereas one can accurately predict a number of things about a new novel by certain authors, one has never been able to predict what kind of novel Sir Angus Wilson would write or where his career would take him. He was a true man of letters, following a path quite unusual for a British writer. On the one hand, he published studies of Charles Dickens, Emile Zola, Rudyard Kipling, and technique in fiction, held visiting appointments at fifteen American universities, and was active in the Arts Council of Great Britain and the Royal Society of Literature, activities that helped earn him a knighthood in 1980. On the other hand, he authored eight novels and numerous short stories, treating subjects as varied as scholarly fraud in Anglo-Saxon archaeology, the non-human milieu of the New Towns, the London zoo as futurist fable, a sweeping anti-Galsworthian survey of an English family, and a terrorist attempt to blow up Parliament. Scattered throughout these works are a number of gay characters, presented from a decidedly nonapologetic gay viewpoint. Indeed, describing his work, Wilson singled out his "open statement of the possibility of homosexual happiness within a conventional framework" as a defining feature of his fiction.

Wilson, whose satire and wit led Kingsley Amis later to call him "our Thackeray," was born Frank Johnstone, and was educated at Westminster and Merton College, Oxford, where he took an honors degree in history in 1936. He worked for the British Museum (1937–1955), where he became deputy superintendent of the Reading Room (1949–1955) and was also responsible for replacing the books destroyed in World War II. In 1966, he was appointed professor at the University of East Anglia.

Between his first novel, *Hemlock and After* (1952), published when he was thirty-nine, not an unusual age for a British novelist to debut, and his last, *Setting the World on Fire* (1980), Wilson gradually moved from realistic social satire done within a traditional form to modernist myth and literary pastiche, all the while trenchantly critiquing liberal humanism. He was driven, he admitted, by "deep distrust of money, property, and the sort of responsibility that goes with them." In many ways, his 1952 book on Zola taught him how to write a novel.

In *Hemlock and After,* Bernard Sands, a famous and gay novelist, confronts the problems of exercising authority in both private and public worlds—the recurrent Wilson problem—as he attempts to found a haven for young writers and to deal with his paranoid wife. Sands's affair with Eric causes him to begin to question his motivation in both areas. Similar questioning of motivation also informs *Anglo-Saxon Attitudes* (1952), in which Gerald Middleton, a retired history professor, confronts the possibility that a key discovery relating to Anglo-Saxon culture may well have been faked by his mentor; and in *The Middle Age of Mrs. Eliot* (1958), Meg Eliot's husband is killed by an assassin in an Oriental airport, and she attempts to piece together a life while living with her brother and his companion. These novels are enriched by the secondary characters, often the keenly observed butts of satire, depicted with Dickensian laughter and censure. Indeed, wit and satire join with Wilson's general pessimism and rigorous depiction of themes as he delineates an individual's capacity for self-delusion and those rare moments of enlightenment, as when the Mosson family in *Setting the World on Fire* confronts the intrusion of terrorists into their seventeenth-century mansion with its famed Phaeton ceiling in an attempt to light a fire that will destroy a world through the immediate destruction of Parliament and its members. (See also ENGLISH LITERATURE: TWENTIETH CENTURY.)

—*David Leon Higdon*

BIBLIOGRAPHY

Cox, C. B. *The Free Spirit*. London: Oxford University Press, 1963. ■ Faulkner, Peter. *Angus Wilson: Mimic and Moralist*. New York: Viking, 1980. ■ Gardner, Averil. *Angus Wilson*. Boston: Twayne Publishers, 1985. ■ Gransden, K. W. *Angus Wilson*. London: Longmans, 1969.

Wilson, Lanford
(b. 1937)

Lanford Wilson was born in Lebanon, Missouri, on April 13, 1937, the son of Ralph Eugene and Violetta Tate Wilson. His childhood home of Lebanon serves as the locale for the plays comprising the Talley trilogy. His parents divorced when Wilson was five; he then moved with his mother to Springfield, Missouri, where she found work in a garment factory. His mother remarried when he was eleven and the new family moved to a farm near Ozark, where Wilson attended high school, graduating in 1955. He went to San Diego to visit his father and step-family in 1956, a trip that forms the basis of the autobiographical play, *Lemon Sky* (1970). Wilson briefly attended San Diego State, but as the play would indicate, the reunion was not a successful one, so Wilson left, moving to Chicago, where he lived for six years, working as an artist for an advertising agency and taking a playwrighting course at a University of Chicago extension. In 1962, Wilson moved to New York, where he quickly became associated with the burgeoning avant-garde theater movement in Greenwich Village. His early plays were produced at Caffe Cino and the La Mama Experimental Theater Club.

In 1969, Wilson, Marshall Mason, Rob Thirkield, and Tanya Berezin founded the Circle Repertory Company. Wilson has continued to be associated with Circle Rep, and Mason has directed the premieres of his productions ever since. Wilson first reached Broadway in 1968 with *The Gingham Dog* and has since achieved many successes there; he won the Pulitzer Prize in 1980 for *Talley's Folly* and remains one of America's most frequently produced and widely respected playwrights.

Wilson has taken on a variety of subjects in his work; thus overt portrayals of gay men and their lives make up only a portion of his dramatic opus. His early one-act play "The Madness of Lady Bright" (1964) depicts the demise of a lonely, disturbed drag queen. *Balm in Gilead* (1965) includes several identifiably gay characters among its enormous cast. It would be difficult to imagine not portraying Robert in *The Gingham Dog* (1968) as a gay character; although there are no direct descriptions of him as such, he plays a parallel role to that of Larry in *Burn This* (1987), who is identified as a gay man. Tom in the one-act "A Portrait of the Cosmos" (1987) is interrogated by an off-stage policeman for having murdered a gay lover.

One of Wilson's most successful portrayals of gay themes occurs in *Lemon Sky*, in which the main character, Alan (whose situation is based on Wilson's own life after high school), is forced to come to grips with his homosexuality when he attempts a reconciliation with his estranged father. The play is obviously influenced by TENNESSEE WILLIAMS's *The Glass Menagerie*, in which Wilson performed in a high school production. One sees the pain Alan experiences in *Lemon Sky* as being a primary force in the development of an artist, one who creates order and beauty out of himself, his past, and his imagination.

Wilson's other major "gay play" is *Fifth of July* (1978), chronologically the last of the Talley trilogy. Just as *Lemon Sky* owes a debt to Williams, *Fifth of July* is influenced by Anton Chekhov. Kenneth Talley, the play's main character, having lost both his legs in Vietnam, is trying to sell the Talley home in Lebanon to avoid having to live under the microscope of a small town as both a handicapped person and an openly gay man. His lover Jed, on the other hand, is busy on the property planting a formal garden that will take decades to mature. The play ends with the tentative creation of an alternative kind of family with Ken and Jed at the center, but Ken's Aunt Sally (the same Sally

Talley of *Talley's Folly* now widowed and grown old), his sister June, and his niece Shirley are all part of the extended clan as well. Though their future is uncertain at the play's end, these characters have a chance to be happy and productive together.

It is certainly possible to read some of the heterosexual couples in Wilson's plays as representative of gay people as well. Matt and Sally in *Talley's Folly,* for example, face much familial opposition resulting from bigotry and prejudice (Matt is a Jew) and are depicted as sterile, unable to produce children. The interracial couple at the heart of *The Gingham Dog,* likewise, face enormous societal opposition to their marriage. Moreover, Wilson frequently creates characters who must operate at the borders of society (the homeless Vietnam veteran Lyman Fellers in *Redwood Curtain,* for example) or who openly violate societal norms (for example, Pale in *Burn This*). These characters, too, can be seen as having significant parallels to the experience of gay people.

Wilson is still an actively producing playwright, apparently at the height of his creative powers. As an openly gay man who is successful in mainstream theater, Wilson is a model for many aspiring writers. In his occasional depictions of gay subjects, he proves himself to be a powerful voice speaking of the lives of gay men today.

—D. S. Lawson

BIBLIOGRAPHY

Barnett, Gene A. *Lanford Wilson.* Boston: Twayne Publishers, 1987. ■ Bryer, Jackson R. *Lanford Wilson: A Casebook.* New York: Garland, 1993. ■ Busby, Mark. *Lanford Wilson.* Boise: Boise State University Press, 1987. ■ Cohn, Ruby. *New American Dramatists: 1960–1980.* London: Macmillan, 1982. ■ Robertson, C. Warren. "Lanford Wilson." *American Playwrights Since 1945: A Guide to Scholarship, Criticism, and Performance.* Philip C. Kolin, ed. New York: Greenwood, 1989. 528–539. ■ Ryzuk, Mary S. *The Circle Repertory Company: The First Fifteen Years.* Ames: Iowa State University Press, 1989. ■ Schevy, Henry I. "Images of the Past in the Plays of Lanford Wilson." *Essays on Contemporary American Drama.* Hedwig Bock and Albert Wertheim, eds. Munich: Huber, 1981. 225–240. ■ Schlatter, James F. "Some Kind of Future: The War for Inheritance in the Work of Three American Playwrights of the 1970s." *South Central Review* 7.1 (Spring 1990): 56–75. ■ Witham, Barry. "Images of America: Wilson, Weller, Horovitz." *Theatre Journal* 34 (1982): 223–232.

Winckelmann, Johann Joachim
(1717–1768)

Winckelmann, the first German to have been publicly acknowledged as a homosexual, was born in Stendal, the son of a cobbler. His family's modest financial situation limited his career choices. After two years of studying theology in Halle, where he also heard lectures on aesthetics by Alexander Gottlieb Baumgarten, he briefly assumed a position as tutor in a private household. One year later, he studied medicine in Jena; his knowledge of anatomy and his documented interest in hermaphrodites and other sexual anomalies would stand him in good stead during the composition of his *History of the Art of Antiquity.* Lack of other opportunities compelled him to accept a position as tutor to the Lamprecht family. His sole pupil, Peter Lamprecht, was his first love, and soon thereafter lived with him in Seehausen where Winckelmann was deputy headmaster of the Latin School (1743–1748). It was during this time that he systematically read his way through the entire Greek and Latin corpus insofar as it was available.

In 1748, Winckelmann was appointed librarian to Count von Bünau in Nöthniz near Dresden where he enjoyed not only greater access to works of antiquity, but also the cultural milieu of the court of Dresden. Dresden was known for its outstanding collection of art and plaster casts (the Laocoön among them), as well as its culture of sexual freedom, not to say excess. In Dresden, Winckelmann became acquainted with several diplomatic representatives of Rome and eventually decided to convert to Catholicism in 1754 in order to profit from Roman patronage. Although his conversion is common knowledge, few are aware that his emigration was nearly prevented because of his reluctance to part from the young Lamprecht.

In 1755, several months before his departure for Rome, his first book, *Reflections on the Imitation of Greek Works in Painting and Sculpture,* was published. Germany and Europe were suddenly presented with an inspired and distinctly aesthetic vision of Greek antiquity, dominated by the figure of the unabashed and beautiful male nude. In the fall of 1755, Winckelmann left Germany.

Winckelmann lived in Rome and Italy for thirteen years. He began modestly. Befriended by the German painter Anton Rafael Mengs, he went regularly to galleries and museums, and planned a monumental work of art history. In 1757, he was appointed librarian to Cardinal Archinto, whose death two years later allowed him to transfer to the patronage of Cardinal Albani, a man who shared Winckelmann's aesthetic and erotic proclivities. The association with Albani afforded Winckelmann unusual freedom and protection: He moved in the best social circles, acquired art and antiquities for both the cardinal and himself, and was entitled to the use of Albani's summer home for occasional trysts and more prolonged affairs.

The evidence of Winckelmann's homosexuality is substantial. His correspondence alone (over a thousand letters, many to confidantes) allows the scholar to document a life rich in friendship and love, supplemented by sexual encounters with Italian youths. Winckelmann repeatedly acknowledges that he was never attracted to women. His sole affair with a woman occurred late in his life and under the most peculiar circumstances: The woman in question was Mengs's wife, the initiator Mengs himself. Third-person accounts confirm the homosexual contours of Winckelmann's life. Perhaps the most interesting is that of Casanova, who claims to have caught Winckelmann in the act.

After Lamprecht, Winckelmann's second great love was a young nobleman from the Baltics whom he met in 1762 and for whom he served as *cicerone,* as he did for so many. Although his love was unrequited, Winckelmann published a monument to their friendship, entitled *Abhandlung von der Fähigkeit der Empfindung des Schönen in der Kunst* (1763), a text that evocatively links homoerotic friendship with aesthetic education.

In 1764, Winckelmann's magnum opus, the *History of the Art of Antiquity,* was published. In this first modern work of art history, Winckelmann engages in detailed discussion of artworks and styles, setting them in a political and historical context, and organizing the whole according to a model of organic growth and decay. Winckelmann himself was most proud of the aesthetic section of the *History,* a philosophical treatment of beauty that is distinctly gay. Ideal beauty is realized within a homosexual and desiring gaze trained on the bodies of eunuchs and castrati. Winckelmann attempts to argue that eunuchs populated the gymnasia and artists' studios of ancient Athens, but it is clear that he is referring to his own considerable experience with castrati dating back to the opera in Dresden and continuing as a part of daily life in Rome.

In 1768, his European reputation established, Winckelmann responded to long-standing invitations from the courts of Vienna and Berlin. North of the Alps, however, he was overcome by an irrational panic, and though he did enjoy an audience with Maria-Theresa, he canceled the visit to Berlin and headed south. In Trieste, he was forced to wait on a ship, and it is during this delay that he became acquainted with his murderer, Francesco Arcangeli. Although the official police documents have been published, the true motive has never been determined. The rumor that his death was the result of a shady homosexual liaison persists.

After his death, Winckelmann continued to be a figure of homosexual identification. Even as the German infatuation with Greek antiquity grew stronger, circles of male friends shared and distributed their copies of Winckelmann's letters. Within eighteen years of his death, five separate correspondences had been published, including the complete set of his love letters to the Baltic nobleman. At the turn of the century, Goethe reread Winckelmann's works, his published correspondence, and the letters that Dietrich Berendis, Winckelmann's boyhood friend, had brought to Weimar, and decided to memorialize him. The result was a book aptly called *Winckelmann und sein Jahrhundert* (1805), which included the Berendis letters, essays by an art historian and a classicist, as well as Goethe's own biographical essay. In sections entitled "Friendship" and "Beauty," which would become touchstones of homosexual sensibility, Goethe obliquely if unmistakably evoked the deep connection between Winckelmann's aesthetics and homosexuality. The only account that comes close to rivaling Goethe's is the English-language essay on Winckelmann by WALTER PATER. (See also AESTHETICISM and GERMAN AND AUSTRIAN LITERATURE BEFORE THE NINETEENTH CENTURY.)

—Simon Richter

BIBLIOGRAPHY

Derks, Paul. *Die Schande der heiligen Päderastie: Homosexualität und Öffentlichkeit in der deutschen Literatur 1750-1850.* Berlin: Rosa Winkel, 1990. ■ Leppmann, Wolfgang. *Winckelmann.* New York: Knopf, 1970. ■ Pater, Walter. *The Renaissance: Studies in Art and Poetry.* Berkeley, Los Angeles, London: University of California Press, 1980. ■ Richter, Simon. *Laocoön's Body and the Aesthetics of Pain: Winckelmann, Lessing, Herder, Moritz and Goethe.* Detroit: Wayne State University Press, 1992. ■ Sweet, Denis. "The Personal, the Political and the Aesthetic: Johann Winckelmann's Enlightenment Life." *Journal of Homosexuality* 16 (1988/89): 147–162. ■ ———. "Winckelmann—welcher Winckelmann? Etappen der Winckelmann-Rezeption." *Forum Homosexualität und Literatur* 5 (1988): 5–15. ■ Wangenheim, Wolfgang von. "Casanova trifft Winckelmann oder Die Kunst des Begehrens." *Merkur* 39 (1985): 106–120. ■ ———. "Winckelmann als Held." *Forum Homosexualität und Literatur* 5 (1988): 17–43.

Windham, Donald

(b. 1920)

Born in Atlanta, Georgia, on July 2, 1920, Donald Windham moved with his partner, Fred Melton, a graphic artist, to New York City in 1939, where he soon became friends with TENNESSEE WILLIAMS, Paul Cadmus, TRUMAN CAPOTE, and Lincoln Kirstein. During World War II, Windham contributed to and edited Kirstein's *Dance Index* and collaborated with Williams on a stage adaptation of D. H. LAWRENCE's, *You Touched Me*. In 1943, after Melton had married, Windham met Sandy Montgomery Campbell, a Princeton freshman, who became his lifelong partner. An actor and publisher of handsome limited editions, Campbell saw through his press, the Stamperia Valdonega in Verona, many of the first editions of Windham's works until his death in 1988.

Beginning in 1947, Windham began to place short stories in *Horizon, The Listener, Botteghe Oscure,* and *New Directions*. He has published five novels, one short story collection, and two memoirs. In addition, he has contributed essays on artists such as Pavel Tchelitchev, edited Campbell's memoirs, and written unpublished stage adaptations of MELVILLE's *Billy Budd,* Isak Dinesen's *The Angelic Avengers,* and his own "The Starless Air."

Windham has made his major contribution to gay life as a memoirist and editor. In addition to editing his letters from E. M. FORSTER and Alice B. Toklas, Windham has used his diaries to write on Tennessee Williams and Truman Capote. Windham's *The Hero Continues,* although not intended as a *roman à clef,* has a protagonist who shares various traits with Williams. Struck by the inaccuracy of Williams's *Memoirs,* Windham published Williams's letters to him. However, Williams falsely claimed that Windham had not been granted permission by him and trashed the volume. Windham's *Lost Friendships: A Memoir of Truman Capote, Tennessee Williams, and Others* (1987), his best book, not only tells a moving story of the emotional difficulties of two famous writers but

also offers insights into the way imagination can be used by artists both to foster their productivity and distort their personal lives. It shows the price demanded by success of two gay men who sought to please a heterosexual public.

In his fiction, Windham has treated homosexuality both openly and as a subtext; however, it never becomes his main topic. He has published five stories with gay themes: "The Kelly Boys," "The Hitchhiker," "Rome," "The Warm Country," and "Servants with Torches." *The Dog Star* (1950) tells of a teenager who, still haunted by the suicide of his best friend, kills himself. The protagonist of *The Hero Continues* (1960) has a drunken one-night stand with a teenaged boy. The openly gay-oriented *Two People* (1965) centers on a married American businessman and the Italian teenager he picks up. *Tanaquil* (1972), set in the art world of the 1940s, has as a character a bisexual photographer based on George Platt Lynes. *Stone in the Hourglass* (1981), a story of art forgery and murder, includes two amusing same-sex bedroom scenes. Windham remains provocative in his refusal to make simple correlations between same-sex attraction, sexual activity, IDENTITY, and self-definition.

—*Peter G. Christensen*

BIBLIOGRAPHY

Kellner, Bruce. "Donald Windham." *Contemporary Gay American Novelists: A Bio-Bibliographical Critical Sourcebook.* Emmanuel S. Nelson, ed. Westport, Conn.: Greenwood Press, 1993. 401–407. ■ ———. *Donald Windham: A Bio-Bibliography.* Westport, Conn.: Greenwood Press, 1991. ■ Rader, Dotson. "The Private Letters of Tennessee Williams." *London Magazine* 18.4 (July 1978): 18–28. ■ Willingham, Robert M., Jr. "Donald Windham." *Dictionary of Literary Biography, Vol. 6: American Novelists Since World War II.* Second Series. James E. Kibler, Jr., ed. Detroit: Gale, 1980. 380–386. ■ Windham, Donald. "Donald Windham Replies to Dotson Rader." *London Magazine* 20.11–12 (February–March 1981): 80–88.

Winsloe, Christa

(1888–1944)

Winsloe led a life in opposition to the expectations of her family and her society and created from it a body of fiction that portrays the

difficulties felt by a woman who does not wish to conform. Her role was to have been that of an army officer's wife; instead, she pursued a career as a sculptress. In 1913, however, she did fulfill her family's desire by marrying the Hungarian Baron Ludwig Hatvany. Her first literary effort, *Das schwarze Schaf* (*The Black Sheep*), dates from the early years of her marriage. The unpublished novel portrays a girl who is a social outsider, both at school and in her career as an artist. She gains acceptance only through marriage to the right man.

Her real life took a different turn. Owing to her husband's numerous affairs, Winsloe went to Munich where she returned to sculpting and also began to write professionally. Her novella *Männer kehren heim* (*Men Return Home;* date unknown) voices the concern that would motivate her fiction, namely, the question of sexual identity within a society stratified according to gender roles. During World War I, a girl is attacked by several soldiers and, to maintain her safety, she dresses in her brother's clothes for the rest of the war.

In 1930, her drama, *Ritter Nérestan* (*Knight Nérestan*), premiered in Leipzig. Retitled *Gestern und heute* (*Yesterday and Today*) for its Berlin premiere, this play made Winsloe's career as an author. The work became most famous in its film adaptation, *Mädchen in Uniform* (*Girls in Uniform*, 1931; directed by Leontine Sagan). The play tells of the schoolgirl Manuela von Meinhardis, who is forced into the strict confines of a Prussian girls' school. She finds solace and love in her relationship with one of her teachers, Fräulein von Bernburg. After performing the lead male role in the school play, Manuela has too much to drink and openly declares her love for her teacher. The headmistress views such feelings as "sinful" and "morbid" and decides Manuela must be expelled. Unable to face separation from her beloved, Manuela commits suicide. Two conclusions were created for the film version. In one, Manuela dies, but in the other she is saved by her classmates. The latter version was deemed unacceptable by American censors; therefore, the former was for decades the only version available in the United States.

Winsloe was involved in a lesbian relationship with the American journalist Dorothy Thompson in the early 1930s, but it ended by 1935. Thompson seems to have been uncomfortable with living as or identifying herself as a lesbian, and Winsloe could not find work in the United States. Winsloe's novel *Life Begins* (1935), published only in English, describes a young sculptress who gains the courage to live openly with the woman she loves. The heroine of her last novel, *Passagiera* (*Passengers*, 1938), however, has lost that confidence. Her identity as a woman and even as an individual disappears as she submerges herself in the mass of people on board an ocean liner. Winsloe continued writing, turning to film scripts. One of these films, *Aiono* (1943), returns to her earlier theme by depicting a Finnish refugee who dresses in male clothing in order to survive.

Winsloe was active in the antifascist movement in France, even hiding refugees in the home she shared with her lover, the Swiss author Simone Gentet. Under circumstances that have never been completely clarified, both women were murdered in early June 1944.

—*James W. Jones*

BIBLIOGRAPHY

Dyer, Richard. *Now You See It: Studies on Lesbian and Gay Film.* New York: Routledge, 1990. ■ Foster, Jeannette H. *Sex Variant Women in Literature.* Tallahassee, Fla.: Naiad Press, 1985. ■ Katz, Jonathan. *Gay American History.* New York: Thomas Y. Crowell, 1976. ■ ———. *Gay/Lesbian Almanac.* New York: Harper and Row, 1983. ■ Reinig, Christa. "Christa Reinig über Christa Winsloe." *Mädchen in Uniform.* Christa Winsloe. Munich: Frauenoffensive, 1983: 241–248. ■ Rich, B. Ruby. "*Mädchen in Uniform:* From Repressive Tolerance to Erotic Liberation." Mary Ann Doane, Patricia Mellencamp, and Linda Williams, eds. *Re-Vision.* Los Angeles: American Film Institute, 1984. ■ Russo, Vito. *The Celluloid Closet.* New York: Harper and Row, 1981. ■ Sanders, Marion K. *Dorothy Thompson: A Legend in Her Time.* New York: Avon, 1974: 188–193. ■ Sheehan, Vincent. *Dorothy and Red.* Boston: Houghton Mifflin, 1963.

Winterson, Jeanette
(*b.* 1959)

Jeanette Winterson was born in Manchester, England, and adopted as an infant by Constance and John William Winterson, both Pentecostalists. Raised in an evangelical atmosphere, Winterson began preaching and writing sermons at the age of eight. Given her talent for winning converts,

she seemed destined for a career as a missionary; but, as she explains, "this didn't work out." Her inclination toward "Unnatural Passion" lead to irreconcilable differences with the church congregation, and, as a consequence, she left home at fifteen. She subsequently attended Accrington College of Further Education and supported herself through a variety of odd jobs, including driving an ice cream van, doing janitorial work in a mental hospital, and preparing corpses in a funeral home, experiences to which she makes wry reference in various novels. Winterson was eventually admitted to St. Catherine's College, Oxford, from which she received a Bachelor of Arts degree in 1981. After graduating, she moved to London, where she worked at the Roundhouse Theatre and in the publishing business.

In 1985, while living "a life of poverty," she published her first novel, *Oranges Are Not the Only Fruit,* a fictionalized autobiography that vividly, painfully, and humorously portrays the absolutist mindset of Christian fundamentalism and the intense homophobia of the basically homosocial female members of the congregation. This witty inversion of the traditional religious conversion narrative, with the titles of its seven chapters corresponding with the first seven books of the Old Testament, provides a new twist to the by-now traditional lesbian coming-out narrative. Although written in two months for financial reward, the novel brought Winterson critical acclaim and the Whitbread Prize for best first fiction. She later wrote the screenplay for the 1990 British television film version of *Oranges Are Not the Only Fruit,* which won the British Academy of Film and Television Arts award for best drama. A now-disowned work, *Boating for Beginners* was also published in 1985. This broad satirical farce utilizes the biblical tale of Noah's Ark to lampoon both organized religion and commercial hucksterism, representing them as barely separable from one another. Winterson has devoted herself to writing full-time since publishing *The Passion* (1987), a novel set during the Napoleonic Wars. Through the medium of magic realism, the author presents the narrative of Henri, a young man of ambivalent sexuality conscripted as a cook into Napoleon's army, crossed with that of the androgynous, bisexual Villanelle, the web-footed daughter of a Venetian boatman. *The Passion* won the John Llewelyn Rhys Memorial Prize for best writer under thirty-five years of age and firmly established Winterson's literary reputation.

Her most ambitious novel, *Sexing the Cherry* (1989), further elaborates the magic realism of *The Passion* in the digressive tale of Jordan and his giantess mother, the Dog Woman. Set initially in Restoration London against a backdrop of wondrous discoveries from the New World, the narrative follows the travels and travails of its characters as they transcend time, place, and gender, thus questioning the reality of any central, unified truth or, indeed, reality itself. With the publication of *Sexing the Cherry,* Winterson received the E. M. FORSTER Award from the American Academy of Arts and Letters. *Written on the Body* (1992), the erotically charged account of the love of the unnamed, ambiguously gendered narrator for the captivating and terminally ill Louise, has brought Winterson favorable attention from diverse audiences.

In addition to her novels, she has written a fitness guide for women and has edited anthologies of short stories. A writer of great intelligence and imagination, Jeanette Winterson has gained a following not only among lesbian and gay readers but mainstream ones as well. She promises to be an influential force in shaping the future of English-language letters.

—*Patricia Juliana Smith*

BIBLIOGRAPHY

Hinds, Hilary. "*Oranges Are Not the Only Fruit*: Reaching Audiences Other Lesbian Texts Cannot Reach." *New Lesbian Criticism: Literary and Cultural Readings.* Sally Munt, ed. New York: Columbia University Press, 1992. 153–172. ■ O'Rourke, Rebecca. "Fingers in the Fruit Basket: A Feminist Reading of Jeanette Winterson's *Oranges Are Not the Only Fruit.*" *Feminist Criticism: Theory and Practice.* Susan Sellers, Linda Hutcheon, and Paul Perron, eds. Toronto: University of Toronto Press, 1991. ■ Suleiman, Susan Rubin. "Mothers and the Avant-Garde: A Case of Mistaken Identity?" *Femmes Frauen Women.* Francoise van Rossum-Guyon, ed. Amsterdam: Rodopi, 1990. 135–146.

Wittig, Monique
(*b.* 1935)

Monique Wittig startled her audience at the Modern Language Association Convention in 1978 when she announced with conviction, "I am a lesbian, not a woman." Controversial and brilliant, Wittig has produced some of the most challenging fictional and theoretical work of second-wave feminism. Internationally recognized as a talented experimentalist, Wittig's goal is to "pulverize the old forms and formal conventions." "It is quite possible for a work of literature to operate as a war machine upon its epoch," she says, not by direct political intervention, but rather by linguistically "universalizing" a particular point of view.

Monique Wittig was born in 1935 in Alsace, France; her father was Henri Dubois, a poet. She attended the Sorbonne in Paris and studied with some of the great French intellectuals of the time. Her first book *L'Opoponax*, published in Paris in 1964 when she was 28, won the prestigious Prix Médicis and garnered high praise from well-established French writers Marguerite Duras and Nathalie Sarraute and, in America, from Mary McCarthy. The book, about childhood, was purely descriptive and objective, relentlessly in the present and subversively inclusive. Its universalizing point of view provoked readers to enter its world. "I see, I breathe, I chew, I feel through her eyes, her mouth, her hands, her skin . . . I become childhood," wrote Claude Simone in his review. Translated into English two years later, it was favorably reviewed in the most prestigious literary publications—*The Times Literary Supplement, The New York Review of Books,* and *The New Yorker*—as a virtuoso work of avant-garde writing.

Les Guérillères, published five years after Wittig's first book, is a structured series of prose poems, again revolutionary in form and language, but this time revolutionary in politics also. In this chronicle of epic warfare, *elles* are the sovereign presence, conquerors of the world and the word. *Elles* are not "the women"—a mistranslation that often surfaces in David Le Vay's English rendition—but rather the universal "they," a linguistic assault on the masculine collective pronoun *ils.* For Wittig, gender in language is the "fictive sex." Linguistic gender marks social convention, she says in an essay entitled "The Mark of Gender," "cast[ing] sheaves of reality upon the social body, stamping it and violently shaping it." Thus, as women are marked by gender in language (particularly French), so are they marked in the social world, always particular, never universal as is "man." Other masculine conventions, such as the power of the phallus, are refused and examined for absurdity: "They do not say that vulvas with their elliptical shape are to be compared to suns, planets, innumerable galaxies. . . . They do not say that the vulva is the primal form which as such describes the world in all its extent, in all its movement. They do not in their discourses create conventional figures derived from these symbols." Seen as a book emerging from Women's Liberation, *Les Guérillères* was not as enthusiastically received as *L'Opoponax.* Nevertheless, it is probably the most widely read of any of Wittig's books to date.

A progression in Wittig's work toward lesbian subjectivity reached its explicit statement in her third and most controversial book, *Le Corps Lesbien* (1973). Appropriating sources as varied as Greek mythology and the Christian mass, Wittig "lesbianizes" familiar figures: Ulyssea returns from her long voyage to the Amazon islands; the veil of Christa "the much-crucified" illuminates the anguished body; and Sappho, a lesbian legend in her own right, is elevated to the stature of a goddess. In the title itself, the linguistic difficulty surfaces—the masculine body (*le corps*) is lesbian. Although in English the title, *The Lesbian Body,* presents no contradiction, the book is introduced with an author's note that explains the pronoun manipulations that were, in effect, the subject of each of her books—the "motors for which functioning parts had to be designed."

The form of *Le Corps Lesbien* is a cycle of poems rather than a narrative. In almost every poem, the characters, *j/e* (I) and *tu* (you) violently tear each other to pieces in the process of love. The violence of this book—which one reviewer called "misanthropic"—is disturbing on a number of levels. The slashed pronoun *j/e* embodies the violence of women's entry into language. The dismembering and devouring of the characters are performed with passionate precision: "M/y most delectable one *I* set about eating you. . . . Having absorbed the external part of your ear *I* burst the tympanum, I feel the rounded hammerbone rolling between m/y lips, m/y teeth crush it, I find the anvil and the stirrup-bone, I crunch them. . . ." But perhaps most disturbing for general readers—and some lesbian readers—is the book's powerful eroticism and intimacy.

In 1976, *Brouillon pour un dictionnaire des amantes* was published in France. Written in collaboration with Sande Zeig, it was translated by the authors as *Lesbian Peoples: Material for a Dictionary.* In contrast to *The Lesbian Body, Lesbian Peoples* has a light touch. It is an imaginative take on history that chronicles by keywords, sometimes in strange juxtaposition, the passage of a mythic people to the utopian "Glorious Age." As much a period piece as a rewriting of historical periodization, key figures of lesbian feminism make cameo appearances. Jill Johnston's "Lesbian Nation" is cited as the last nation to exist before the beginning of the Glorious Age.

Wittig's most recent book of fiction was published in France in 1985 as *Virgile, Non,* and two years later in English as *Across the Acheron.* Elements of all of her previous writing are present: parody—of DANTE's *Divine Comedy*; revolutionary utopia—paradise is across the Golden Gate Bridge; and Wittig's unconventional namings—the central character is none other than "Wittig." This book is the least well-known of her published works, perhaps because the idea that lesbians (and women) existing in the "straight" world are living in a kind of purgatory is not as popular as it once was or, perhaps, because this is the least "universal" of her books.

Monique Wittig immigrated to the United States in 1976. Once in North America, she turned her pen to theoretical essays on feminism, language, and literature. In these essays, mostly written in English and published in *Feminist Issues,* Wittig developed her ideas about what she described as "materialist lesbianism," where lesbians represent the possibility of escaping the category of "woman" by refusing her "role" and rejecting the "economic, ideological, and political power of a man." In these essays, Wittig also finally began to explain the linguistic manipulations in her complex fictions, with which many readers struggled. Some of these essays, including "One is Not Born a Woman," "The Category of Sex," and "The Mark of Gender," have become canonical in Women's Studies; in the emergent field of Lesbian and Gay Studies, "The Straight Mind" has particular significance. Her essays have recently been collected and published under this title.

Monique Wittig's linguistic brilliance and political courage make her truly one of the avant-garde. To date, only one book-length study of her work has been published, but the importance of her books and essays for several generations of thinkers in the areas of gender and sexuality will make her the subject of many more. And who knows what new "subjects" Wittig has yet to invent. (See also LITERARY THEORY: GAY, LESBIAN, AND QUEER.)

—*Julia Creet*

BIBLIOGRAPHY

Ostrovsky, Erika. *A Constant Journey: The Fiction of Monique Wittig.* Carbondale and Edwardsville: Southern Illinois University Press, 1991. ■ Shaktini, Namascar. "Displacing the Phallic Subject: Wittig's Lesbian Writing." *Signs* 8 (1982): 29–44. ■ "Special Monique Wittig." *Vlasta* 4 (1985). ■ Stambolian, George and Elaine Marks, eds. *Homosexualities and French Literature.* Ithaca, N.Y.: Cornell University Press, 1979. 353–377. ■ Wenzel, Hélène Vivienne. "The Text as Body/Politics: An Appreciation of Monique Wittig's Writings in Context." *Feminist Studies* 7 (1981): 264–287.

Woolf, Virginia
(1882–1941)

Virginia Woolf was born Adeline Virginia Stephen on January 25, 1882, in Hyde Park Gate, London, the daughter of Leslie Stephen, a man of letters, who in the same year began editing the *Dictionary of National Biography,* and Julia Pattle Duckworth, a Victorian beauty immortalized in the photographs of Julia Margaret Cameron. Virginia's mother's first marriage ended with the death of her husband, leaving her with three children, one of whom, Gerald Duckworth, is known to have sexually molested Woolf as an adolescent. Her adolescence was marked as well by a sequence of deaths and the first bout of a mental illness that would haunt her for the rest of her life: Her mother died in 1895; her half-sister Stella, who served as mother-substitute, in 1897; her father in 1904 and her brother Thoby in 1906. She experienced her first mental breakdown following her mother's death at the age of thirteen, while the final one ended with her suicide when she walked into the river Ouse on March 28, 1941.

Woolf developed her closest attachment to her sister Vanessa, what she called "a very close conspiracy." The two sisters functioned as co-conspirators in their alliance as women artists, on the one hand, against the tyranny of the father who repeatedly sought to enlist their services as surrogate wives; on the other hand, against Victorian mores that considered marriage the only suitable profession for middle-class daughters. Vanessa likewise served as surrogate mother by taking over the maternal function after Stella's death, and by eventually becoming herself a mother, in contrast to the younger Virginia. As women artists, the two sisters recognized a clear division of labor: Virginia the writer in her study, Vanessa the painter in her studio. All the children were educated at home, in the father's library and with private tutors, although the two brothers eventually attended Cambridge University.

Following Leslie Stephen's death, the four siblings moved to BLOOMSBURY, a section of London that would eventually give name to a group of artists and intellectuals, the Bloomsbury Group. This group began when Thoby and his Cambridge friends moved back to London and met every Thursday evening to discuss art and literature, as well as pressing political issues such as pacifism and socialism. Initially, Virginia and Vanessa were the only two women present, as Thoby's sisters but also as intellectuals and artists.

Several of the male participants were avowed homosexuals, including LYTTON STRACHEY, who proposed to Virginia in 1909, although the engagement was almost immediately broken off. Woolf's relationship to gay men remained an ambivalent one. On the one hand, she appreciated a lack of sexual interest that made it possible for her to have access to an intellectual environment based on an indifference to her gender; on the other hand, the absence of women meant a lacking female eroticism that for her prohibited creativity. Much later, on August 19, 1930, she wrote in a letter to Ethel Smyth: "It is true that I only want to show off to women. Women alone stir my imagination." In 1912, she married Leonard Woolf, "a penniless Jew," also a member of the Bloomsbury Group, a political writer who had recently returned from service in India. This marriage is considered to have been a supportive although passionless one. In 1917, the Woolfs established Hogarth Press as an attempt to engage Virginia in more practical work in the hope of keeping at bay further bouts of mental illness. The Press published the works of several lesbian and gay writers, including E. M. FORSTER, CHRISTOPHER ISHERWOOD, and VITA SACKVILLE-WEST.

The move to Bloomsbury also marked Woolf's initiation as a writer. Her first publication took the form of an unsigned review in the newspaper *Guardian*, facilitated by Violet Dickinson. The relationship with Dickinson was one of several intense friendships Woolf had with women throughout her life. These affairs of the heart left their traces in passionate letters and diary entries characterized by a mutual attraction and a desire for emotional intimacy expressed in highly eroticized language. They often resulted in literary works, not always published, written as tribute to friendships that greatly fostered—but were ultimately confined to—writing. Often these women were older, unmarried, more masculine in appearance, and highly successful artists; often they offered Woolf some form of maternal protection as she struggled with another incident of physical or mental illness. All of them shared with Woolf an interest in art and provided critical readings of her work. None of these relationships are known to have had a sexual component.

Woolf's first passionate friendship was with Madge Vaughan, the daughter of the well-known writer and sexologist, JOHN ADDINGTON SYMONDS, whom Woolf met at the age of sixteen and was to serve as a model for Sally Seton in *Mrs. Dalloway* (1925). Violet Dickinson, almost twice Woolf's age when she nursed her during the mental breakdown following the death of her father, was an unmarried Quaker for whom she wrote "Friendship Gallery" (1907), a spoof

biography that anticipates *Orlando* (1928). It describes a utopian community of women inspired and led by Dickinson with Woolf as the artist figure, a model for other women writers and recorder of the community's development. Much later Woolf looked back on this friendship as the one that enabled her to say for the first time with confidence, "I am a writer." The final of such friendships was with Ethel Smyth, a well-known composer, whom Virginia met in 1930, when Woolf was forty-eight and Smyth seventy years old. Woolf named her in the original draft of her essay "Professions for Women" as the model for the professional woman but also, once again, as the artist who engages in a different artistic medium, a more public and therefore more ambitious one for women than that of the writer. Their friendship was also based on a bond over the loss of the mother; Smyth wrote in a 1930 letter to Woolf: "Now you can imagine how much sexual feeling has to do with an emotion for one's mother."

Woolf met VITA SACKVILLE-WEST, with whom she had the only intense friendship to include a physical relationship, in 1922. In this case, the age difference was reversed, Virginia was forty and Vita thirty years old and Virginia was the more confident and recognized of the two writers. But Vita was the experienced "Sapphist." The affair began in 1925, the point at which Woolf wrote in her *Diary*, "These Sapphists *love* women; friendship is never untinged with amorosity" (December 21), and is thought to have lasted until 1928. During that time, Vita took two trips to Persia to visit her husband, who was working in the British embassy in Tehran. The second time she traveled in the company of another woman, which began to create a rift as Woolf became less and less tolerant of Vita's other affairs. In 1928, Woolf and E. M. Forster wrote a letter defending RADCLYFFE HALL's *The Well of Loneliness*, not as a good novel or because of its lesbian content, but in the name of free speech. Various members of Bloomsbury appeared at the obscenity trial prepared to testify as expert witnesses, including Woolf, who described her presence as a way of also defending Vita's Sapphism. At the end of the same year, Woolf delivered the lectures at Newnham and Girton Colleges, which were to become *A Room of One's Own* (1929), accompanied by Vita, to whom she had dedicated *Orlando*, which had appeared just a few months earlier. By then, the affair had ended but a strong friendship continued until 1934. These ten years were the most productive in the lives of both writers. Their emotional attachment to each other was completely severed only by Woolf's death.

Woolf has been named "the Invalid Lady of Bloomsbury" (E. M. Forster), a "sexless Sappho" (nephew and biographer Quentin Bell), and "a gue-rilla fighter in a Victorian skirt" (Jane Marcus, femi-nist literary critic). Most recently, she has been described, in conjunction with Vita, as a "married lesbian" (Suzanne Raitt), someone for whom lesbian-ism was an emotional, even a sexual orientation, but not a political identity necessarily incompatible with or even disruptive of marriage. Nor do any of her works contain explicitly lesbian characters who are not somehow deficient of a femininity associated with social respectability. And yet as the most revered modernist woman writer, Woolf is also considered to be the author of the first positive "Sapphic" portrait in the form of "the longest and most charming love letter in literature," *Orlando*. Same-sex desire in the form of eroticized relationships between women re-mains fundamental to Woolf's thinking about the connection between women and creativity. Female homoeroticism most often takes the form either of mourning for a lost maternal femininity or of a con-flation between female artist, spinster, and lesbian. On the one hand, a sexually charged but always elusive relationship to the mother; on the other hand, a nonsexualized female artist—unmarried, celibate, childless, but independent. The female artist has ac-cess to an artistic medium that allows her to put into question a compulsory heterosexuality that leaves the attractions between women unrealized, both sexually and aesthetically. At the same time, the figure of the lesbian as unmarried woman threatens to politicize the erotic, thereby producing the "mannish lesbian" as sexual and thus social outcast.

Woolf repeatedly describes the nature of female homoeroticism in terms of "that vast chamber where nobody has yet been," as in this passage from *A Room of One's Own*. In what is considered the first example of feminist history and literary criticism, she makes her most explicit statement about the relations be-tween women as both existing in real life and nonex-istent in literature. By introducing "Chloe and Olivia," characters in a novel authored by the ficti-tious Mary Carmichael, she suggests that women exist not only in relation to men but also in relation to each other (these two share a laboratory). They can even like each other, a liking that has served as a sign for many readers of the possibility of love, and therefore lesbian desire.

The first and only novel to explicitly deal with both female eroticism and the figure of the lesbian is *Mrs. Dalloway,* a novel about a day in the life of Clarissa Dalloway, the wife of an M.P., a day spent preparing for a party she will host. This ostensibly meager plot is meant to focus attention on both a subplot, Clarissa's memories of Sally Seton, with whom she fell in love as a young girl, and a parallel plot, that of Septimus Smith, a shell-shocked veteran who commits suicide during Clarissa's party. Although Clarissa and Septimus never meet, they are connected by the im-portance of and yet impossibility of same-sex desire, for Clarissa because she and Sally both chose marriage to rich, respectable men, for Septimus because his love object was killed during the war. By choosing Richard Dalloway over Peter Walsh, who intercepted the kiss from Sally that marks "the most exquisite moment of her whole life," Clarissa is allowed to retreat to the virginal bed in the attic that preserves the memory of a pastoral and premarital homoeroticism. Sally repre-sents the beautiful adolescent given to self-abandon-ment who has a way with flowers and a passion for envisioning the abolition of private property and the attainment of equal rights for women. She is the one through whom Woolf represents lesbianism as an erotic attachment brought to a close by marriage but also as the occasion for a highly eroticized language. Mrs. Dalloway's love for Sally is described as follows: "Then, for that moment, she had seen an illumination; a match burning in a crocus; an inner meaning almost expressed. But the close withdrew; the hard softened. It was over—the moment." Although Sally inspires in Clarissa an identification with the desire men must feel for women, she herself remains at a far remove from the masculinized lesbian, Miss Killman, the tutor of Mrs. Dalloway's daughter, Elizabeth. Miss Killman is described as poor, clumsy, over forty; she works for a living, is prone to religious fervor and pro-German sympathies, and always wears the same mackintosh. At the same time, she is a highly knowledgeable historian and economically independent. Her attrac-tion to Elizabeth is presented as a sexual orientation rather than a passing phase, and thus unlike the eroticized language used to elicit Sally, Miss Killman's lesbianism is described in terms of an authoritarian politics:

> For it was not her one hated but the idea of her, which undoubtedly had gathered in to itself a great deal that was not Miss Killman; had become one of those spectres with which one battles in the night; one of those spectres who stand astride us and suck up half our life-blood, dominators and tyrants; for no doubt with another throw of the dice, had the black been uppermost and not the white, she would have loved Miss Killman! But not in this world. No.

In this world, such a politicized identity, embodied by the masculinized woman, evokes the familial patriarch.

In *To the Lighthouse* (1927), the Miss Killman figure is more positively portrayed via Lily Briscoe, who is also poor and unmarried, yet nevertheless an artist. Like Elizabeth Dalloway, she has "little Chinese eyes," connoting an exoticism associated with a younger generation of independent women. This novel also recounts a day and another day ten years later in the life of a family, the Ramsays with their six children, in the Hebrides. The homoerotic content takes the form of the relationship between Lily, a guest at the summer house, and Mrs. Ramsay, who both is and isn't a figure for the mother. Mrs. Ramsay once again represents the hostess who views Lily in terms of an inferior version of femininity, not beautiful, not marriageable, whose paintings hold no interest for her, or potentially anyone else. Lily needs Mrs. Ramsay as the lost maternal figure whose recovery remains essential to the production of art and yet whose renunciation must be complete if a woman is to actually become an artist. Again the language is highly eroticized:

> Could loving, as people called it, make her and Mrs. Ramsay one? for it was not knowledge but unity she desired, not inscriptions on tablets, nothing that could be written in any language known to men, but intimacy itself, which is knowledge, she had thought, leaning her head on Mrs. Ramsay's knee.

The novel also contains two minor characters, two of the Ramsay's children, a daughter who imagines Constantinople when another woman about to become engaged holds her hand, and a son who becomes the mourned love object of the poet Mr. Carmichael, when he receives news of his death on the battlefield.

In her final novel, *Between the Acts* (1941), Woolf represents her protagonist, Miss La Trobe, as not only a more successful artist than Lily Briscoe but also as an avowed lesbian:

> Since the row with the actress who had shared her bed and her purse the need of drink had grown on her. And the horror and the terror of being alone. One of these days she would break—which of the village laws? Sobriety? Chastity? Or take something that did not properly belong to her?

Reminiscent of Miss Killman, the more openly lesbian, the more socially deviant the character becomes. And yet she is also the author and producer of a literary historical pageant held yearly at a country house, where it remains unclear whether the audience or the actors are those enacting a performance, and where every person is simply an assumed part, the most worn-out being that of the heterosexual couple.

A similar retelling of literary history as parody structures *Orlando,* the work that has most contributed to Woolf's reputation as a lesbian writer. Subtitled "A Biography," it attempts to revolutionize the genre by telling the life of Orlando, who lives for three hundred years—from Queen Elizabeth I's reign to the present day (October 11, 1928). Sometime during the eighteenth century, while ambassador to Turkey, Orlando changes from a man into a woman, although the sex of the original love object, Sasha, remains unchanged:

> though she herself was a woman, it was still a woman she loved; and if the consciousness of being of the same sex had any effect at all, it was to quicken and deepen those feelings which she had had as a man. For now a thousand hints and mysteries became plain to her that were then dark.

As a woman, the character continues to cross-dress although she eventually marries and bears a child. Yet the most important relationship in the novel remains the one between Orlando and the biographer, who frequently enters the text to discuss how difficult it is to adhere to the conventions of biography. One such convention assumes that the person being written about is dead. Vita, who posed for several of the photographs that accompany the text, was delighted with what Woolf had written. On her first reading, she writes in a letter, "you have invented a new form of Narcissism,—I confess,—I am in love with Orlando—this is a complication I had not foreseen" (October 11, 1928).

Not only does the novel make Vita immortal, Woolf in addition is able to grant her several wishes: having the best of both sexes and the most of each one, sexually. Woolf enables her to inherit the family estate, Knole, which Vita had been disinherited of due to her gender. She makes her an accomplished writer, rather than giving her the "pen of brass" she thought she really had. And finally she bestows on her beauty through Orlando's stately legs, thereby representing her as a "real woman," in contrast to her own sense of herself as a "eunuch." And yet Woolf's one venture into female eroticism ended with *Orlando,* capturing in print what she wasn't able to have in life due to Vita's infidelity and her own stifled sexuality. Originally entitled "The Jessamy Brides" ("Jessamy" referring to a dandy or fop), *Orlando* represents both what Woolf could never be or have except through her art. (See also ENGLISH LITERATURE: TWENTIETH CENTURY.)

—Anne Herrmann

BIBLIOGRAPHY

Bell, Quentin. *Virginia Woolf: A Biography.* New York: Harcourt Brace Jovanovich, 1972. ■ DeSalvo, Louise A. "Lighting the Cave: The Relationship between Vita Sackville-West and Virginia Woolf." *Signs* 8:2 (Winter 1982): 195–214. ■ Hawkes, Ellen. "Woolf's 'Magical Garden of Woman.'" *New Feminist Essays on Virginia Woolf.* Jane Marcus, ed. Lincoln: University of Nebraska Press, 1981. ■ Herrmann, Anne. *The Dialogic and Difference: "An/Other Woman" in Virginia Woolf and Christa Wolf.* New York: Columbia University Press, 1989. ■ Jensen, Emily. "Clarissa Dalloway's Respectable Suicide." *Virginia Woolf: A Feminist Slant.* Jane Marcus, ed. Lincoln: University of Nebraska Press, 1983. ■ Knopp, Sherron E. "'If I saw you would you kiss me?': Sapphism and the Subversiveness of Virginia Woolf's *Orlando.*" *Sexual Sameness: Textual Differences in Lesbian and Gay Writing.* Joseph Bristow, ed. London: Routledge, 1992. ■ Love, Jean O. "*Orlando* and Its Genesis: Venturing and Experimenting in Art, Love, and Sex." *Virginia Woolf: Revaluation and Continuity.* Ralph Freedman, ed. Berkeley: University of California Press, 1980. ■ Marcus, Jane. *Virginia Woolf and the Languages of Patriarchy.* Bloomington: Indiana University Press, 1987. ■ Meese, Elizabeth. "When Virginia Looked at Vita, What Did She See; or Lesbian : Feminist : Woman—What's the Differ(e/a)nce?" *Feminist Studies* 18:1 (Spring 1992): 99–118. ■ Raitt, Suzanne. *Vita and Virginia: The World and Friendship of V. Sackville-West and Virginia Woolf.* Oxford: Oxford University Press, 1993. ■ Rose, Phyllis. *Woman of Letters: A Life of Virginia Woolf.* New York: Oxford University Press, 1978. ■ Rosenman, Ellen Bayuk. "Sexual Identity and *A Room of One's Own:* 'Secret Economies' in Virginia Woolf's Feminist Discourse." *Signs* 14:3 (Spring 1989): 634–650.

Young Adult Literature

Gay and lesbian young adult literature—books targeted at readers aged twelve and up—ranges widely in sensitivity, topic, quality, and political and social insight. The field includes works as various as John Donovan's pioneering and intelligent *I'll Get There. It Better Be Worth the Trip,* (1969), Larry Hulse's homophobic *Just the Right Amount of Wrong* (1982), and Ron Koertge's extremely optimistic and affirming *The Arizona Kid* (1988). The market for children's and young adult literature has expanded greatly in the last twenty-five years, and now a proliferation of materials is available to gay and lesbian adolescents, including comic books with gay characters and after-school television specials focused on gay issues. Since 1969, more than seventy young adult fiction titles featuring gay or lesbian themes or characters have appeared, more than half of them since 1985.

Although the focus and tone of this fiction have changed over these twenty-five years, the field continues to be dominated by male characters and white, middle-class settings. African-American, Asian-American, Native-American, and Hispanic authors and characters are dramatically underrepresented. Perhaps not surprisingly, this literature is shaped by and reinforces the dominant social values and prejudices of American society. Homosexuality is too often simply a plot device or "problem" to be overcome; only rarely does it occasion penetrating social criticism.

In 1976, Frances Hanckel and John Cunningham asked in the *Wilson Library Bulletin,* "Can Young Gays Find Happiness in YA Books?" At that time, a distinctive literary genre defined as young adult lesbian and gay fiction barely existed. From 1969 to 1976, only five novels were published with gay and lesbian themes: Donovan's *I'll Get There. It Better Be Worth the Trip,* Isabelle Holland's *The Man without a Face* (1970), Sandra Scoppettone's *Trying Hard to Hear You* (1974), Rosa Guy's *Ruby* (1976), and Mary W. Sullivan's *What's This About, Pete?* (1976). In their review article, Hanckel and Cunningham noted that, apart from filling a gap, most of these titles offered little accuracy or reassurance for straight and gay young readers. The situation has since improved somewhat, but as a field, young adult gay and lesbian literature remains enmeshed in stereotypes.

In 1983, Jan Goodman summarized several assumptions that, in spite of the best intentions of the authors of young adult gay and lesbian literature, marred this fiction. For example, the assumption that being a lesbian or a gay man is physically dangerous and sometimes life-threatening pervades these books. More than half of the lesbian and gay protagonists in young adult literature meet with physical harm or tragedy. Even in a work like Scoppettone's *Happy Endings Are All Alike* (1978), which features two lesbian characters who enjoy mutual solace in their relationship, a horrifying subplot undermines the positive message, though it also effectively exposes the violence that often accompanies bigotry: After a disturbed male classmate sees the two women kissing, the lesbian protagonist is raped. In one of the most disturbing novels of the genre, Hulse's *Just the Right Amount of Wrong*, fear of the consequences of being exposed as homosexual is strong enough to motivate murder. Set in Farleigh, Kentucky, the local sheriff, Nate Lemur, kills Mr. Wilkes, the new bachelor high school principal, to protect the secret of their relationship. Before the murder, the central character, Jerry Blankenship, and some friends observe Wilkes and Lemur at Wilkes's house. Although the boys never speak of their discovery, untrue rumors begin to spread that Wilkes is sexually interested in young boys. Thus, an adult gay character in a position of responsibility and respect is first compromised by untrue allegations and is ultimately destroyed by homophobia, as embodied in the person of the sheriff. Aidan Chambers's *Dance On My Grave* (1982) ends in a fatal automobile accident, and Paul, a protagonist in Frank Mosca's *All-American Boys* (1983), is badly beaten by male classmates in a particularly violent fag-bashing story line.

The tendency for physical harm and death to come to gay and lesbian characters appears to have subsided somewhat in the past several years. Of the eleven novels in this genre published in the last four years, including Penny Raife Durant's *When Heroes Die* (1992), Diana Wieler's *Bad Boy* (1992), Rik Isensee's *We're Not Alone* (1992), and Liza Ketchum Murrow's *Twelve Days in August* (1993), none of the primary or secondary lesbian and gay characters face the horrible fates that befell characters in earlier works.

Another stereotypical assumption that young adult fiction tends to reflect is that lesbian and gay characters, youths and adults, live lonely, bleak, deprived, and unhappy lives; so much so that the message seems to be that children and young people should by no means fall under the influence of gay and lesbian adults. In young adult fiction, the homosexuality of characters (or its revelation) often results in loss of friends, loss of career, loss of family, and loss of community. Although two teachers in Nancy Garden's *Annie on My Mind* (1982) act as positive lesbian role models in a stable, loving relationship, they both lose their jobs. Jinx, a character in Jane Futcher's *Crush* (1981), is expelled from an exclusive girls' boarding school during the mid-1960s. Gary Bargar's *What Ever Happened to Mr. Forster?* (1981) is set in Kansas City in 1958. Although Mr. Forster is represented as a mentor and hero for sixth-grader Louis Lamb, he ultimately loses his job as a direct result of the disclosure of his gayness. These and many other early examples of lesbian and gay young adult literature are set in the 1950s and 1960s, during more repressive and homophobic eras. But the message of gay loneliness is also repeated in more recent works

with contemporary settings. In Ann Rinaldi's *The Good Side of My Heart* (1987), for example, a handsome, mysterious new boy in town, Josh, finds himself the object of narrator Brie's considerable romantic admiration. When Josh explains that he is gay, Brie's sadness over his "wasted" masculinity and her pity for him result in his social isolation.

A particularly disturbing set of homophobic and misogynist assumptions are contained in Judith St. George's *Just Call Me Margo* (1981). Margo discovers the nature of the relationship between her tennis coach, Miss Frye, and her English teacher, Miss Durrett. Miss Durrett is physically disabled, personally unappealing, and socially unpleasant. As Christine Jenkins points out, Miss Durrett embodies the myth of the lesbian who simply cannot attract a man. The representation of Miss Durrett as physically disabled and personally unpleasant also confirms cultural myths about disabled people as unappealing and about lesbians as willing to accept those people who have been judged inadequate for a "real" relationship with men.

More subtly, as Goodman notes, when gay and lesbian characters are shown in happy relationships, they have no friends or support outside those relationships. In Garden's *Annie on My Mind,* a warm, sensitive, and positive story, the adult women who are depicted in a loving alliance have no extended support system, nor any group of friends, gay or not. The successful lesbian or gay relationship is a self-contained unit, continuing without social acceptance or grounding. An exception is found in Scott Bunn's *Just Hold On* (1982). Although this story recapitulates some potentially destructive stereotypes, the characters Stephen and Rolf are ensconced within a warm circle of friends.

Even in young adult literature in which gay and lesbian adults act as positive role models for teens, lesbian and gay adults—particularly those who are teachers—are frequently indicted and punished for their alleged influence on the emerging homosexuality of teen characters. Community distrust of gay teachers surfaces in many works. Rarely is there any basis for the claim that an actual romantic relationship exists between students and teachers, although in David Rees's *The Milkman's on His Way* (1982) a teacher does initiate a student into his first homosexual experience. Far more common in this literature are students' crushes on teachers and intense homosocial bonds between teachers and students. Among works that depict such crushes and bonds are Holland's *The Man without a Face*, Barger's *What Ever Happened to Mr. Forster?*, and Garden's *Annie on My Mind.*

The greatest failure of gay and lesbian young adult fiction as a genre is that the works are generally plotted around the "problem" of homosexuality. Consequently, the lives of the gay and lesbian teen and adult characters revolve almost exclusively around the issue of their homosexuality; and gay and lesbian characters are included simply because of their gayness rather than because of their intrinsic interest or complexity. These tendencies are legacies of the category's origins in the "problem novel" genre that became popular in young adult fiction in the late 1960s. In the best works, however, homosexuality is presented as simply part of the lives of the characters rather than the central issue, and the "problem" is not homosexuality per se. For example, Norma Klein's *My Life as a Body* (1987) treats the lesbianism of a major character, Claudia, merely as an important aspect of her existence.

Young adult literature has only begun to meet the challenge of educating its audience to the dangers and problems associated with AIDS. In an important article on this subject, Alan Teasley uncovered only eight young adult titles in which AIDS is a major theme. Most of these books do not associate AIDS exclusively with gay men, although the first, M. E. Kerr's well-written and affecting *Night Kites* (1986), features the protagonist's brother as a gay man with AIDS. In Alice Hoffman's *At Risk* (1988), however, Amanda Ferrell has contracted AIDS from contaminated blood, as has the protagonist's uncle in Alida Young's *I Never Got to Say Goodbye* (1988). In Koertge's *The Arizona Kid*, the main character, Billy, is not gay, but his Uncle Wes is. Wes and his circle of gay friends (many with AIDS) are secondary to the major action, but Wes provides safer sex education for Billy in his romance with Cara. Michael Bishop's *Unicorn Mountain* (1988) is set in Colorado, where unicorns appear to a group of young people living in the mountains. One character, Bo, is a young man with AIDS; in a subplot, he discovers that the unicorns are dying of a rare disease.

The world available to young adult audiences is overwhelmingly white, middle class, and male. Working-class characters appear in only five of the seventy titles that feature gay and lesbian characters and themes. These include Guy's *Ruby*, Garden's *Annie on My Mind*, and Rees's *In the Tent* (1979). Only three titles feature African-American characters: Guy's *Ruby*, Jacqueline Woodson's *The Dear One* (1992), and Rees's *The Milkman's on His Way*. In the field of young adult lesbian and gay fiction, there are apparently only three authors of color, Alice Childress, Rosa Guy, and Jacqueline Woodson.

Despite the limitations of young adult fiction (including its failure to offer realistic settings and to create well-developed characters) and its tendency to perpetuate stereotypes about gay men and lesbians, the field contains several titles that are well worth reading and sharing with young people. These offer constructive and reassuring images and address sensitively and engagingly a number of important issues of interest to gay and lesbian youth, including homophobia, coming out, and accepting the sexuality of parents, siblings, teachers, and friends. For example, Koertge's *The Arizona Kid*, which is distinguished by humor and warmth, presents gay characters in a relatively stable and interesting community. Deborah Hautzig's *Hey, Dollface* (1978) is the classic crush novel, and Barbara Wersba's *Crazy Vanilla* (1986) compellingly depicts a younger brother's coming to terms with his elder sibling's gayness. Woodson's *The Dear One* (1991) features a lesbian couple, Marion and Bernadette, who are strong and productive individuals. Some recent novels, such as Francesca Lia Block's *Weetzie Bat* (1989) and Klein's *My Life as a Body*, have begun to deproblematize the gayness of gay characters. Still others, such as Joyce Sweeney's *Face the Dragon* (1990), Jackie Calhoun's *Sticks and Stones* (1992), and Rik Isensee's *We're Not Alone*, have begun to explore the larger social and personal implications of sexual identity. Taken in the aggregate, young adult gay and lesbian literature can be best regarded as a world of promise and possibility with a huge agenda ahead. (See also CHILDREN'S LITERATURE.)

—*Melinda Kanner*

BIBLIOGRAPHY

Connor, Matt. "Flight from the Closet: Gay Characters Come Out." *Genre* 2 (December 1992): 58–61, 84. ■ Cuseo, Allan A. *Homosexual Characters in YA Novels: A Literary Analysis, 1969–1982.* Metuchen, N.J.: Scarecrow Press, 1992. ■ Garden, Nancy. "Dick and Jane Grow up Gay." *Lambda Book Report* 3.7 (1992): 7–10. ■ Goodman, Jan. "Out of the Closet but Paying the Price: Lesbian and Gay Characters in Children's Literature." *Interracial Books for Children Bulletin* 14.3–4 (1983): 13–15. ■ Hanckel, Frances, and John Cunningham. "Can Young Gays Find Happiness in YA books?" *Wilson Library Bulletin* 50.7 (1976): 528–534. ■ Jenkins, Christine. "Gay and Lesbian Books for Young Adults." *Feminist Bookstore News* 9.3 (1987): 24–25. ■ ———. "Heartthrobs and Heartbreaks: A Guide to Young Adult Books with Gay Themes." *Out/Look* 1.3 (Fall 1988): 82–92. ■ ———. "Young Adult Novels with Gay/Lesbian Characters and Themes 1969–1992: A Historical Reading of Content, Gender, and Narrative Distance." *Youth Services in Libraries* 7 (1993): 43–55. ■ ———, and Julie Morris. *A Look at Gayness: An Annotated Bibliography of Gay Materials for Young People.* Ann Arbor, Mich.: Kindred Spirit Press, 1982. ■ ———, and Julie Morris. "Recommended Books on Gay/Lesbian Themes." *Interracial Books for Children* 14.3–4 (1983): 16–19. ■ MacDonald, Stephen. "Young, Gay, and the Problem of Self-identity: An Annotated Bibliography." *Kids and Libraries.* Ken Hycock and Carol-Ann Haycock, eds. Vancouver, BC: Dyad Services, 1984. 87–90. ■ Olson, Ray. "Almost Grown and Gay." *Voice of Youth Advocates* 3 (April 1980):

1923. ■ Paolella, Edward C. "Resources for and about Lesbian and Gay Youth: An Annotated Survey." *References Services Review* 12 (1984): 72–92. ■ Sumara, Dennis. "Gay and Lesbian Voices in Literature: Making Room on the Shelf." *English Quarterly* 28.1 (1993): 30–34. ■ Teasley, Alan. "YA Literature about AIDS: Encountering the Unimaginable." *The ALAN Review* 20.3 (1993): 18–23. ■ Tillapaugh, Meg. "AIDS: A Problem for Today's YA Problem Novel." *School Library Journal.* 39 (1993): 22–25. ■ Wilson, David E. "The Open Library: YA Books for Gay Teens." *English Journal* 73.7 (1984): 60–63.

Yourcenar, Marguerite
(1903–1987)

On January 22, 1981, Marguerite Yourcenar took her place in literary history when she became the first female "immortal" admitted to the French Academy since its founding in 1635. She was an ideal choice—and a much more suitable candidate than the more sensual COLETTE or the more political Simone de Beauvoir—because her career embodied exactly the kind of classical humanism the conservative Academy liked to honor. Her writings are marked by measured, aphoristic sentences; by quietly reflective characters; by restrained lyricism; by thorough research and highly literate allusions to history and culture; and by attempts to adapt classical literature to contemporary concerns.

Yet Yourcenar's life and career are filled with paradoxes. The philosopher-king narrator of *Memoirs of Hadrian* (1951) and the alchemist protagonist of *The Abyss* (1968) suggest that Yourcenar admired the heroics of knowing; yet she seemed to live the self-examined life by examining the lives of others. Her many meditations on the meaning of love and pleasure often had their roots in personal crisis; yet they were always filtered through historical, mythological or fictitious characters. As a stylist, she was self-consciously French; yet she spent the largest part of her productive life in self-imposed exile from France. She was a product of an education that emphasized ancient and classic European culture; yet she translated Negro spirituals, blues, and gospel tunes as well as Japanese Noh plays. She lacked direct contact and intimacy with family; yet she devoted the last part of her career to reconstructing a long and exhaustively detailed account of her family's origins. She was a lesbian who spent forty-two years with the same woman; yet she spoke of homosexuality in her work almost exclusively through male characters, including a volume-length study of YUKIO MISHIMA (*Mishima; ou, La Vision du vide* [*Mishima: A Vision of the Void*], 1981), while only two lesbians (SAPPHO in *Fires* [1936] and Marguerite of Austria in *The Abyss*) make cameo

appearances. And she was a fiercely proud, independent, and resourceful woman who has often been accused of depicting only weak women in her writings, especially Sophie in *Coup de Grace* (1939).

Even the facts of Yourcenar's life are hard to ascertain. Yourcenar drew up a chronology in the Pleiade edition of her works, but biographer Josyane Savigneau takes exception to many dates and argues persuasively that Yourcenar forged her own persona just as she created, and then revised, her historical fictions.

Yourcenar was born Marguerite Antoinette Jeanne Marie Ghislaine Cleenewerck de Crayencour in Brussels on June 8, 1903. Her mother died shortly after her birth, and the young Marguerite spent her childhood traveling with her wealthy father, Michel, who was almost fifty years her senior. She was educated privately. The outbreak of World War I exiled her in England, where she studied English and Latin. Later, she studied Greek in Paris and learned Italian on her own. Her literary aspirations manifested themselves early, and while still in her teens, Yourcenar published two books privately—*The Garden of Chimeras* and *The Gods Are Not Dead*—and she chose Yourcenar, an anagram of her birth name, as her pen name. She also undertook two ambitious projects, "Death Drives the Cart" and "Crosscurrents," that started as short stories but eventually led to the fictional masterpieces of her maturity: *Memoirs of Hadrian, The Abyss,* and *Two Lives and a Dream* (1982).

In 1929, in the wake of the Wall Street crash and mismanagement by her half-brother, Yourcenar lost her inheritance from her mother; and her father, who had remarried two years earlier, died in poverty. But that same year, her first major work, *Alexis,* was published. Without mentioning the word *homosexuality,* which Yourcenar considered too clinical, this Gidean novel purports to be the letter written by a married man who must leave his wife and small child to come to terms with transgressive pleasure and his new identity. *Alexis* sets the pattern for much of Yourcenar's work, which tempers scandalous passion with a classical literary treatment that relies on restraint and eloquence rather than explicitness and melodrama, and that seeks validating precedents in history and mythology.

After the critical success of *Alexis,* Yourcenar decided to spend her remaining money on a decade of the "luxurious freedom" of travel and writing. In the 1930s, according to Savigneau's biography, Yourcenar seduced many women and fell into desperate, unreciprocated love with two men. The outcome was *Fires,* a series of prose poems meant to express her passions and philosophy of love through monologues by figures from ancient Greek and, in one case, Christian myths.

In 1937, Yourcenar met Grace Frick, an American college professor who remained her lifelong collaborator and translator until Frick's death in 1979. Observers have often seen this as a somewhat abusive marriage of convenience in which Frick took charge of the daily business while Yourcenar steeped herself in history and literature.

A Coin in Nine Hands (*Denier du Reve*) first appeared in 1934, then was drastically revised in 1959. Along with *La Nouvelle Eurydice* (*The New Eurydice,* 1931), it is perhaps the least successful of her prose works, even though the novel is also the closest she ever came to writing fiction with a contemporary setting. The work takes place in Fascist Rome and centers on a plot to assassinate Mussolini, with characters and events tied together by a coin that changes hands. Yourcenar drastically revised the text in the 1950s to eliminate any sympathy for the Italian fascists.

In 1938, Yourcenar published *Oriental Stories,* which draws on myths of the Balkans, India, and China as well as the Japanese novelist Lady Murasaki to create almost Kafkaesque parables of excessive love and artistic creation. These miniatures may well be the most underrated part of Yourcenar's fiction.

In 1939, she published *Coup de Grace,* a melodramatic novel of politics and love in revolutionary Eastern Europe that became a best-seller in English twenty years later. In 1977, it was made into a film by the German director Volker Schlondorff, though Yourcenar objected to the elimination of Erick's repressed homosexuality and to a leftist revision of its politics. In the misogyny and militarylike hardness of its main character, some critics discerned a reactionary side to the author.

Also in 1939, Yourcenar came to the United States to visit Frick and ended up exiled in the United States by the outbreak of World War II. From New York City, the couple moved to Hartford, Connecticut, where Frick had found a job. In the summer of 1942, the couple spent their first vacation at Mount Desert Island, off the coast of Maine, where in 1950, they moved permanently into the house they nicknamed "Petit Plaisance." Yourcenar taught comparative literature at Sarah Lawrence College from 1942 to 1953, and in 1947, became a naturalized U.S. citizen.

In 1951, *Memoirs of Hadrian* brought Yourcenar both critical acclaim and commercial success; it won the Prix Femina Vacaresco, and by 1989, had sold almost a million copies. Couched as a farewell letter from the Emperor Hadrian to his successor, Marcus Aurelius, this "voice portrait" and "passionate reconstitution," as Yourcenar described her historical novels, seems typical for its lyrical style, extensive research, and restrained eroticism, expressed though Hadrian's love for the Greek teenager Antinous. Adding perhaps to the novel's appeal in the years after World War II and in the early days of the Cold War were the parallels it captured between the "pax romana" and the "pax americana." The novel is a long meditation on the idea of empire, on conquest and rule—whether of a political or military nature, whether of a loved one or of one's self. Rome's Hellenism, its ready acceptance of a superior culture's influence, also embodied the allure that history and foreign cultures seemed to hold for Yourcenar.

Honors followed. In 1955, Yourcenar won the Page One award of the Newspaper Guild of New York, and in 1963, the Prix Combat. But in 1959, Frick was diagnosed with the breast cancer that would eventually kill her. In 1966, Plon publishers sued Gallimard for the rights to issue Yourcenar's *The Abyss* [*L'Oeuvre au noir* in French or *The Work in the Black Phase*]. The court decision allowed Yourcenar to choose her publisher. She decided on Gallimard, the biggest and most prestigious house in France, which thereafter began to reissue her complete works. The critical reassessment that would culminate in her election to the Academy soon began.

In 1968, *The Abyss* was finally published, also to great critical acclaim and popular interest. It won the Prix Femina and helped get Yourcenar elected to the Royal Belgian Academy in 1969. The novel, chronicling the life of a sixteenth-century alchemist, Zeno, represented a major departure for Yourcenar and seems a mirrorlike complement of *Memoirs of Hadrian,* a comparison Yourcenar herself often discussed in interviews and in her essay on the historical novel. Hadrian's life is recounted in the first person, Zeno's in the third person; Hadrian's tale takes place in sunny Mediterranean climes, whereas Zeno's unfolds in the pre-Renaissance darkness of the Low Countries; Hadrian recounts the subjective world of ruling other men, whereas Zeno's story concerns a misanthropic scholar who seeks objective, scientific truth. If *Memoirs of Hadrian* coincided with its historical setting, *The Abyss,* as a novel of protest, seemed perfectly timed to the student rebellions of 1968 and the countercultural movement of the late 1960s. Its terrain, meant to embody the artist Dürer, is a border zone between the ancient Ptolemaic world view and the new scientific outlook pioneered by modern astronomy. Alchemy becomes a metaphor for the transformations of people and civilizations, and the persecuted Zeno, born in 1510, is seen as an intellectual bridge from the world before the Scientific Revolution to the revolutionary empiricism of Copernicus and Galileo. Zeno is also a sexual dissenter whose homosexual episodes epitomize his moral heresy.

In 1971, two volumes of Yourcenar's collected plays were published. Closet dramas like *Electra, or The Fall of Masks* and *Dialogue in the Swamp* remain more valuable for their poetry than their stagecraft. Still, her plays helped Yourcenar win the Prix Monaco in 1973. In 1974, *Dear Departed (Souvenirs Pieux),* the first volume of *The Labyrinth of the World*—a large-scale genealogical biography written much like a historical romance—was published, and brought Yourcenar the Grand Prix des Lettres of the French Ministry of Culture in 1975. The second volume, *Archives of the North (Archives du Nord),* appeared in 1977.

In 1980, her French citizenship was restored, and Yourcenar agreed to be nominated for the French Academy after winning the Academy's Grand Prix de la Litterature. Though accused of being antisemitic by some opponents, she was finally received into the French Academy on January 22, 1981—only months after Frick had died.

The following year saw Yourcenar's last major work of fiction, *Two Lives and a Dream (Comme l'eau qui coule* or *Like Water That Flows),* which included three novellas. "An Obscure Man," the longest story, is an emotionally subdued and Rembrandt-like portrait of Nathaniel, a lower-class, uneducated Renaissance Dutch Everyman who wanders from Europe to an an island off the coast of Canada and back again. "A Lovely Morning" continues the first tale by tracking Nathaniel's son in a Jacobean acting troupe. Unrelated to the first two, "Anna Soror" is a tale of adult, consensual brother-sister incest in a court of baroque Naples done in a "nervous and agitated" style meant to mimic that of the painter El Greco.

Yourcenar died on December 17, 1987, at Petit Plaisance. The next year, the concluding volume of the "Labyrinth" triptych, *What? Eternity (Quoi? L'Eternite),* appeared posthumously.

Except for documenting a taste for travel and different cultures, biographical information on Yourcenar is of limited use. What emerges from a close reading of Yourcenar's life is really her determination to keep her life separate from her art and to root her work in her imagination. In the way she fused fact and fiction, Western and non-Western culture, history and contemporary life, Yourcenar could be characterized as postmodern, even though many critics continue to see her as pre-modern, as an anomaly set apart from her time. Yet it is also possible to see Yourcenar's work as a different expression of the same existentialism that preoccupied other famous writers of her generation such as Sartre, Camus, and Beauvoir. Much of her work, like theirs, stresses the issues of choice, commitment, ethics, and historical circumstances. Her vast historical re-creations have much in common, for example, with the existentialist psychological studies that Sartre undertook of the writers JEAN GENET, Gustave Flaubert, and CHARLES BAUDELAIRE. And her frequent use of transgressive eroticism, expressed through "in extremis" characters and situations, underscores certain similarities to Colette, Marguerite Duras, and VIOLETTE LEDUC. Marguerite Yourcenar dwelled in history, to be sure, but she also resided in her own age.

As her many prefaces and postscripts attest, Yourcenar remained one of her best critics. "Every literary work," she wrote in an afterword to "An Obscure Man," "is fashioned thus out of a mixture of vision, memory and act, of ideas and information received in the course of a lifetime from conversations or books, and the sharing of our own existence."

—*Jacob Stockinger*

BIBLIOGRAPHY

Auchincloss, Louis. "On Power and History: What Marguerite Yourcenar Knew." *New York Times Book Review,* Jan. 10, 1988, 9. ■ Bree, Germaine. *Women Writers in France.* New Brunswick: Rutgers University Press, 1973. ■ DeRosbo, Patrick. *Entretiens radiophoniques avec Marguerite Yourcenar.* Paris: Mercure de France, 1972. ■ Farrell, C. Frederic and Edith R. Farrell. "Marguerite Yourcenar." *Gay and Lesbian Literature.* Sharon Malinowski, ed. Detroit: St. James Press, 1994. 429–432. ■ Horn, Pierre L. *Marguerite Yourcenar.* Boston: Twayne Publishers, 1985. ■ Howard, Joan E. *From Violence to Vision: Sacrifice in the Works of Marguerite Yourcenar.* Carbondale: Southern Illinois University Press, 1992. ■ Savigneau, Josyane. *Marguerite Yourcenar: Inventing a Life.* Chicago: University of Chicago Press, 1993. ■ Shurr, Georgia Hooks. *A Reader's Guide to Marguerite Yourcenar.* Lanham: University Press of America, 1987.

Zapata, Luis
(b. 1951)

Luis Zapata is Mexico's most successful and productive gay writer. Between 1975 and 1990, he published four novels and a novelette in which the main character is either denotatively or connotatively gay. In 1981, his critically acclaimed *Las aventuras, desventuras y sueños de Adonis García, el vampiro de la colonia Roma* became the first Latin-American gay novel to be translated into English. Two years later, his short story "De amor es mi negra pena" gave the title to Winston Leyland's collection of Latin-American gay fiction, *My Deep Dark Pain is Love*. Zapata has used a wide array of writing styles and techniques to present a variety of homosexual types and situations; taken together they offer a broad look into Mexican gay culture.

Born and raised in an upper-middle-class family in provincial Chilpancingo, Zapata's childhood, like Alvaro's in *La hermana secreta de Angélica María* (*The Secret Sister of Angelica María*), revolved around going to the movies. His adolescent writings were screenplays, often comedies about recent newlyweds. These details, taken from his autobiographical *De cuerpo entero* (*Looking Back*), explain several elements of his work: the prominent function of cinema and popular culture, the application of humor, and his tendency both to mock and relish and finally to co-opt traditional heterosexual fantasies. In 1975, he published his first work, *Hasta en las mejores familias* (*Even in the Best Families*), which traces the relationship between an alienated, sexually ambivalent youth and his father, a closeted homosexual. Four years later, Zapata published *Las aventuras. . . .* The work is presented as a transcript of a taped monologue recounting the adventures of a local hustler, Adonis García, a sexy and highly sexed, often wasted, street kid. In 1983, Zapata published *Melodrama*, a camp novelette about a love-conquers-all relationship between a dynamic and athletic youth and a handsome, married detective. Two years later, *En jirones* (*In Shreds*) appeared. The novel is a narrative in the form of a diary of an obsessive relationship between two young professionals: one gay-identified and the other straight-identified and eventually married. Zapata's most recent novel, *La hermana secreta . . .* (1989), is the story of Alvaro, a hermaphrodite in love with the cinema. He has also written several short stories with a gay theme, included in his 1983 and 1989 collections.

Traits common in his works include a linguistic and stylistic playfulness and a democratic presentation of homosexual types. Zapata indulges the gay reader through his use of CAMP, narrative tease, and sexual explicitness. His subject matter tends toward the melodramatic, romantic, or marginal. Heterosexuality appears almost exclusively in terms of families, and these are often presented as clichés. Hypocrisy revealed and accepted is a common resolution to the conundrum of homosexual pleasure versus heterosexual family duties. There are no lesbians in his literature, and the few female characters are generally mothers or sisters. In writing about a marginal and repressed culture, his fiction also has some qualities of protest literature. (See also LATIN AMERICAN LITERATURE.)

—*Maurice Westmoreland*

BIBLIOGRAPHY

Foster, David William. *Gay and Lesbian Themes in Latin American Writing*. Austin: University of Texas Press, 1991. ■ ———. Review of Luis Zapata, *Adonis García: A Picaresque Novel*. Trans. E. A. Lacey, and Winston Leyland, ed. *My Deep Dark Pain is Love: A Collection of Latin American Gay Fiction*. *Chasqui* 13:1 (November 1983): 90–92. ■ Jaén, Didier T. "La Neo-Picaresca en México: Elena Poniatowska y Luis Zapata." *Tinta* 1.5 (Spring 1987): 23–29. ■ Leyland, Winston, ed. *My Deep Dark Pain Is Love: A Collection of Latin American Gay Fiction*. Trans. E. A. Lacey. San Francisco: Gay Sunshine Press, 1983. ■ Schaefer-Rodriguez, Claudia. "The Power of Subversive Imagination: Homosexual Utopian Discourse in Contemporary Mexican Literature." *Latin American Literary Review* 33 (1989): 29–41. ■ Schneider, Luis Mario. "El tema homosexual en la nueva narrativa mexicana." *Casa del tiempo* [Mexico] 49–50 (1985): 82–86. ■ Torres-Rosado, Santos. "Canon and Innovation in *Adonis García: A Picaresque Novel*." *Revista monográfica* 7(1991): 276–283. ■ Westmoreland, Maurice. *Luis Zapata: Camp, Machismo, and the Family* (manuscript in progress).

Notes on Contributors

Harriette Andreadis is Associate Professor of English at Texas A&M University, where she was the founding Director of the Women's Studies Program and where she has established courses in lesbian and gay literature.

Lee Arnold is Library Director of the Historical Society of Pennsylvania.

Ian Barnard teaches in the Department of English and Comparative Literature at San Diego State University. He has written on antihomophobic pedagogy and on gay men in feminism.

David Bergman, Professor of English at Towson State University, is author of *Gaiety Transfigured: Gay Self-Representation in American Literature* and editor of *Camp Grounds* and *The Violet Quill Reader*. His volume of poetry, *Cracking the Code*, won the George Elliston Poetry Prize.

Corinne E. Blackmer is Assistant Professor of English at Southern Connecticut State University. With Patricia Juliana Smith, she has edited a collection of essays on opera.

David Lorenzo Boyd is Assistant Professor of English at the University of Pennsylvania and author of *Sodomy, Silence, and Social Control in Middle English Literature*.

Gregory Bredbeck is Associate Professor of English at the University of California, Riverside. He is author of *Sodomy and Interpretation: Marlowe to Milton*, among other studies of gay literature and culture.

Margaret Breen received her Ph.D. from Rutgers University in 1993. She is Visiting Assistant Professor of English at the University of Connecticut and has published essays on Bunyan and Yeats.

Ludger Brinker is an instructor in English at Macomb Community College and an associate member of the graduate faculty at Wayne State University. He is author of a forthcoming study entitled *Alfred Kazin's Autobiographies*.

A. Mitchell Brown is a Ph.D. candidate at Cornell University, where he is completing his thesis on represen-

tations of homosexuality and the development of homosexual subjectivity in French literature.

Elsa A. Bruguier is associated with the Mabel Smith Douglass Library at Rutgers University.

Diana L. Burgin is Professor of Russian at the University of Massachusetts-Boston. She has published widely on Russian literature.

Joseph Cady teaches at the University of Rochester Medical School. He is author of several studies of gay literature in the Renaissance and in the nineteenth and twentieth centuries, as well as of essays on AIDS literature.

Robert L. Caserio, Associate Professor of English at Temple University, is at work on a book entitled *Citizen Queer: Gay Representations and Democratic Dogma in Twentieth-Century Fiction*.

Max Cavitch is a graduate student at Rutgers University.

Douglas Chambers is Professor of English at the University of Toronto. He is author of numerous books and essays on subjects ranging from Renaissance literature to contemporary poetry.

Jay Scott Chipman is an actor, director, playwright, and theater historian. He is completing a Ph.D. in theater history and performance studies at the University of Pittsburgh.

Peter Christensen teaches English at Marquette University and the University of Wisconsin at Milwaukee. He has published articles on Thornton Wilder, Jean Cocteau, Vernon Lee, and Marguerite Yourcenar.

John M. Clum is Professor of English and Professor of the Practice of Theater at Duke University. His most recent book is *Acting Gay: Male Homosexuality in Modern Drama*.

Kathleen Collins-Clark is Assistant Professor of French at the University of Michigan-Dearborn. Her critical edition of the poetry of Saint-Pavin is in progress.

Joseph P. Consoli is Humanities Bibliographer at Rutgers University. He is author of *Giovanni Boccaccio:*

An Annotated Bibliography and of articles and essays on Pasolini, Busi, and Eco.

Maria Dolores Costa received her Ph.D. in Spanish literature from the University of Massachusetts. She is Assistant Professor of Spanish at California State University, Los Angeles.

Ann Cothran is Associate Professor of French at Wittenberg University. Her current research involves lesbian representation in Colette's works.

Julia Creet is a doctoral student in the History of Consciousness program at the University of California at Santa Cruz. She has published in *differences, Out/Look,* and *Resources for Feminist Research.*

Louis Crompton is Professor Emeritus of English at the University of Nebraska. Cofounder of the Gay and Lesbian Caucus of the Modern Language Association, he is author of the highly acclaimed *Byron and Greek Love,* among numerous other works.

Diane Griffin Crowder is Professor of French and Women's Studies at Cornell College. She has published on lesbian pedagogy, semiotics, and the lesbian body as social text, as well as on the works of Colette and of Monique Wittig.

John W. Crowley, Professor of English at Syracuse University, is author of numerous books and essays on American writers, and editor of Roger Austen's *Genteel Pagan: The Double Life of Charles Warren Stoddard.*

Stuart Curran is Professor of English at the University of Pennsylvania. He has written extensively on Shelley and other English Romantics and from 1980 to 1993 was editor of the *Keats-Shelley Journal.*

Dennis Denisoff, a doctoral candidate in English literature at McGill University in Montréal, is also a novelist and poet, as well as editor of *Queeries,* a collection of Canadian gay male prose.

Marylynne Diggs recently completed her Ph.D. at the University of Oregon, where she wrote a dissertation entitled "Sex, Race, and Resistance: Scientific Authority and the Politics of Identity in American Literature."

Jane Donawerth is Associate Professor of English at the University of Maryland at College Park, where she teaches Renaissance literature, history of rhetorical theory, and science fiction and utopias by women.

Thomas Dukes is Associate Professor of English at the University of Akron. The single father of two cats, he has published in *Poetry, Women's Studies,* and *War, Literature, and the Arts,* among other journals.

Derek Duncan lectures in the Italian Department at the University of Bristol, England. He obtained his doctorate in modern Italian fiction from the University of Edinburgh and researches and publishes in that field, while also working on a study of the representations of AIDS in France, the United Kingdom, and the United States.

Andrew Elfenbein is Assistant Professor of English at the University of Minnesota. He is author of *Byron and the Victorians,* which is forthcoming from Cambridge University Press.

David L. Eng, a doctoral student in Comparative Literature at the University of California, Berkeley, specializes in Asian-American literatures as well as Chinese and American film.

Carmine Esposito is a graduate student in English at City University of New York.

Amy Farmer is a Ph.D. candidate at the University of Illinois at Urbana-Champaign. She is the editor of *Voices/Writing,* an anthology of student essays published by HarperCollins. Her dissertation topic is feminist theology in seventeenth-century prose and fiction.

Scott Fish, a doctoral candidate at the University of Wisconsin-Madison, is writing his dissertation on André Gide.

Noel Riley Fitch is the author of such critically acclaimed books as *Sylvia Beach and the Lost Generation* and *Anaïs: The Erotic Life of Anaïs Nin.* She teaches nonfiction writing at the University of Southern California and expatriate literature at the American University of Paris.

David William Foster is Regents' Professor of Spanish at Arizona State University, where he is Director of Spanish Graduate Studies. He has published extensively on Hispanic literature, including *Gay and Lesbian Themes in Latin American Writing.*

Raymond-Jean Frontain is Associate Professor of English at the University of Central Arkansas. He has published widely on seventeenth-century English literature and on English adaptations of Biblical literature.

Candace Fujikane, a doctoral student in English at the University of California, Berkeley, works with Asian-American literatures and the local literatures of Hawaii.

Catherine Geddis is a librarian at the Mabel S. Douglass Library of Rutgers University. She is currently working on an annotated bibliography of material related to lesbian and bisexual women of color.

Anita George specializes in comparative study of English and Classical Greek and Roman literature and is particularly interested in feminist theory. She is currently working on a poetic translation of Sappho.

James Gifford is Professor of Humanities at Mohawk Valley Community College in New York. He holds degrees from Fordham, Columbia, and Syracuse Universities.

Amy Gilley holds a Ph.D. in Dramatic Art from the University of California, Santa Barbara.

Joanne Glasgow is Professor of English and Women's Studies at Bergen Community College and coeditor of *Lesbian Texts and Contexts: Radical Revisions.* A former president of the Women's Caucus for the Modern Languages, she is a member of the editorial board of the New York University Press lesbian series, The Cutting Edge.

Joseph P. Goodwin is Assistant Director of Career Services at Ball State University. He is author of *More Man Than You'll Ever Be: Gay Folklore and Acculturation in Middle America.*

Mark Graves is an instructor at Bowling Green State University, where he teaches courses in modern literature, war literature, and rhetoric and writing.

Stephen Guy-Bray teaches English at Trent University. He has published on Marlowe, who was the subject of his doctoral dissertation at the University of Toronto.

George E. Haggerty, Professor of English at the University of California, Riverside, is author of *Gothic Fiction/Gothic Form* and a variety of essays on the literature of the eighteenth century. He is also coeditor of *The Profession of Desire.*

Donald E. Hall is Assistant Professor of English at California State University, Northridge. He is editor of *Muscular Christianity: Embodying the Victorian Age.* His book *Fixing Patriarchy: Feminism and Mid-Victorian Male Novelists* is in progress.

Melanie Hawthorne is Associate Professor of French and an affiliate of the Women's Studies Program at Texas A&M University. She works primarily on French nineteenth-century literature, especially on the decadent writer Rachilde, about whom she is writing a book.

Anne Herrmann is Associate Professor of English and Women's Studies at the University of Michigan-Ann Arbor. She is the author of *The Dialogic and Difference: "An/Other Woman" in Virginia Woolf and Christa Wolf.*

Anne F. Herzog is Assistant Professor of English at West Chester University. She is working on a book-length study of Muriel Rukeyser.

David Leon Higdon is the Paul Whitfield Horn Professor of English at Texas Tech University. He has published widely on Conrad and other figures associated with Modernism.

Patrick Holland is Associate Professor of English at the University of Guelph in Ontario.

M. Morgan Holmes is a doctoral candidate in English literature at McGill University in Montréal. His dissertation concerns the interface of sexual and religious discourse and the applicability of "queer theory" to early modern literature.

Nancy Hurrelbrinck recently received her doctorate from the University of Virginia. She is currently writing a book about Emily Dickinson's relationship with her sister-in-law.

Ann Imbrie is Professor of English at Vassar College. She is a specialist in seventeenth-century English literature

Sherrie A. Inness is Assistant Professor of English at Miami University of Ohio. She received her Ph.D. from the University of California, San Diego, where she wrote a thesis on the representation of student life at American women's colleges during the Progressive Era.

Karla Jay is Professor of English at Pace University. A pioneer in the field of gay and lesbian studies, she has published widely, including such titles as *Out of the Closets: Voices of Gay Liberation* (with Allen Young), *The Amazon and the Page: Natalie Clifford Barney and Renée Vivien,* and *Lesbian Texts and Contexts: Radical Revisions* (with Joanne Glasgow).

Warren Johansson, who died in 1994, was a founding member of the Scholarship Committee of the Gay Academic Union. An Associate Editor of *Encyclopedia of Homosexuality,* he coauthored *Outing: Shattering the Conspiracy of Silence.*

Terrence Johnson holds a Ph.D. in English from the University of California, Los Angeles.

James W. Jones, Associate Professor of German at Central Michigan University, is author of *"We of the Third Sex": Literary Representations of Homosexuality in Wilhelmine Germany* and of several essays on AIDS discourse in Germany and the United States.

Melinda Kanner is a cultural anthropologist and Assistant Professor of Psychology at Antioch College. She regularly teaches courses in human sexuality and lesbian and gay studies.

Arnie Kantrowitz is Associate Professor of English at the College of Staten Island, City University of New York. He is author of *Under the Rainbow: Growing up Gay* and of numerous essays, poems, and stories. He was a founding member of the Gay and Lesbian Alliance Against Defamation (GLAAD).

Simon Karlinsky is Professor Emeritus of Russian at the University of California, Berkeley. His books include *The Sexual Labyrinth of Nikolai Gogol, Russian Drama from Its Beginnings to the Age of Pushkin,* and *Marina Tsvetaeva: The Woman, Her World, and Her Poetry.*

Beth A. Kattelman is pursuing her doctorate in theater at Ohio State University, where she serves as editor of *Theatre Studies.* Cofounder of the New Venture Theatre, she has written numerous children's theater pieces that have been performed throughout the United States.

Richard Kaye is a Ph.D. candidate in English at Princeton University, where he is completing a dissertation on flirtation in the Victorian and Edwardian novel. He is also working on a book-length study of St. Sebastian in nineteenth-century art and literature.

AnnLouise Keating is Assistant Professor of English and Women's Studies at Eastern New Mexico University. She has published on "(Re)Visionary Techniques in the Works of Paula Gunn Allen, Gloria Anzaldúa, and Audre Lorde," as well as on contemporary Chicana writers, Melville, and Emerson.

Hubert Kennedy has published in several fields and several languages. Among his books is a biography of the German pioneer of gay liberation, Karl Heinrich Ulrichs. He has also translated the gay novels of John Henry Mackay.

Kevin Killian, author of *Shy* and *Bedrooms Have Windows,* is a poet, playwright, and novelist. He is currently collaborating on a biography of Jack Spicer.

George Klawitter is Associate Professor of English at St. Edward's University in Austin, Texas. He is editor of *The Poetry of Richard Barnfield* and author of *The Enigmatic Narrator: Same-Sex Love in the Poetry of John Donne.*

Yvonne M. Klein teaches English Literature and women's studies courses at Dawson College in Montréal. A frequent translator of lesbian and feminist fiction, she was awarded the Canadian Governor General's prize for best

English translation in 1986 for her translation of Jovette Marchessault's *Lesbian Triptych*.

Sherron E. Knopp is Professor of English at Williams College. Her primary focus for teaching and research is medieval and Renaissance literature, but her 1988 essay on Virginia Woolf's *Orlando* won the Crompton-Noll Award of the Gay and Lesbian Caucus of the Modern Language Association.

Kevin Kopelson is Assistant Professor of English at the University of Iowa and author of *Love's Litany: The Writing of Modern Homoerotics*.

Susan Koppelman is the editor of groundbreaking critical collections of American women's short stories. She also edited the first anthology of feminist literary criticism.

Alan Kozlowski is a Ph.D. candidate in English at Loyola University of Chicago. His dissertation is entitled "Whitman's Readers and the Politics of the Canon."

Francois Lachance is a graduate student in comparative literature at the University of Toronto.

Susan S. Lanser is Professor of Comparative Literature and English at the University of Maryland at College Park. She is author of *The Narrative Act* and *Fictions of Authority: Women Writers and Narrative Voice*, as well as numerous essays on feminist criticism and lesbian writing. She has recently coedited *Women Critics: An Anthology*.

Carolyn Leste Law is a doctoral candidate in English at the University of Minnesota. She is coeditor of *This Fine Place So Far from Home: Voices of Academics from the Working Class* and an associate editor of *Hurricane Alice: A Feminist Quarterly*.

D. S. Lawson is Assistant Professor of English at Lander University, Greenwood, South Carolina. He has published essays on AIDS theater, David Leavitt, Paul Russell, and James Merrill. His poetry has appeared in such journals as *The James White Review, Bay Windows, Amethyst*, and *Five Fingers Review*.

Dorothy H. Lee is Professor of English and Comparative Literature Emerita at the University of Michigan-Dearborn. She has published on African-American, English, and European literature.

Helen Jefferson Lenskji teaches Women's Studies at the Ontario Institute for Studies in Education, Toronto.

Maurice van Lieshout is guest researcher in gay literary studies in the Department of Comparative Literature at the University of Amsterdam. He has published books on homosexual identity, gay youth, and the early history of gay emancipation.

Marilee Lindemann is Assistant Professor of English at the University of Maryland. She has published on Cather, Jewett, and contemporary women's fiction.

Anna Livia, who is currently writing her dissertation on gender and cohesion in modern French literature at the University of California, Berkeley, is author of four novels, two collections of short stories, and *A Perilous Advantage,* an edited translation of the work of Natalie Clifford Barney.

Donald N. Mager is Assistant Professor of English at Johnson C. Smith University in Charlotte, North Carolina.

Joseph Marchesani is Assistant Professor of English at Pennsylvania State University, McKeesport, where he teaches science fiction and fantasy literature.

Murray S. Martin, a native of New Zealand, has published widely in library science as well as on gay and lesbian literature. He is University Librarian and Professor of Library Science Emeritus at Tufts University.

Robert K. Martin, Professor of English at the Université de Montréal, is author of *The Homosexual Tradition in American Poetry* and *Hero, Captain and Stranger: Male Friendship, Social Critique and Literary Form in the Sea Novels of Herman Melville,* and editor of *The Continuing Presence of Walt Whitman: The Life after the Life*.

Elena M. Martinez is Assistant Professor of Latin American literature at Baruch College, City University of New York. She is author of two books on Latin-American literature and is currently working on one entitled *Lesbian Voices from Latin America*.

Stedman Mays is currently working on a study of male beauty and the evolution of Renaissance lyric poetry, *The Embodiment and Disembodiment of the Male Beloved: The Same-Sex Sonnet Tradition, Michaelangelo to Shakespeare*.

Clarence McClanahan holds a Ph.D. in Comparative Literature from New York University. He is the author of *European Romanticism: Literary Societies, Poets, and Poetry*. He works in administration at Stanford University.

Scott McLemee, a critic and essayist with a special interest in the intellectual history of American radical and countercultural groups, has contributed to such publications as *The New York Times, Washington Post, The Village Voice,* and *In These Times*. He is editor or coeditor of four books by and about the Caribbean writer C. L. R. James.

Toni A. H. McNaron is Professor of English at the University of Minnesota. She has published widely on Renaissance literature and on lesbian and feminist issues.

Edmund Miller is Professor of English and Chair of the English Department at the C.W. Post Campus of Long Island University. He is author of erotic stories and of several books of poetry, as well as of scholarly books about seventeenth-century British literature.

David J. Moriarity, a Vietnam veteran, is Assistant Professor of English at the C.W. Post Campus of Long Island University. He has written on William Cullen Bryant, John Cheever, Toni Morrison, and John Todhunter.

Lianne Moyes is Assistant Professor of English Studies at the Université de Montréal. She works in the fields of twentieth-century women's writing and Canadian literature.

Sally R. Munt is Senior Lecturer in English and Cultural Studies at the Nottingham Trent University in England. She is editor of *New Lesbian Criticism: Literary and Cultural Readings* and author of *Murder by the Book: Feminism and the Crime Novel.*

James Najarian is writing a dissertation at Yale University on the poetic influence of Keats and its relationship to male-male desire in the nineteenth century.

Seigo Nakao is Assistant Professor of Japanese Language, Culture, and Literature at Oakland University. His Ph.D. is from New York University.

Robert Nashak is a doctoral candidate in English at UCLA. He is the recipient of a Mellon Fellowship in the Humanities and of a Fulbright grant for study in The Netherlands.

Emmanuel S. Nelson is Professor of English at the State University of New York at Cortland. He is editor of *AIDS: The Literary Response* and of *Critical Essays: Gay and Lesbian Writers of Color* and author of essays on ethnic and gay literatures.

Lawrence Normand teaches English at the University of Wales, Lampeter. He has published on Elizabethan drama and twentieth-century poetry and is coauthor (with Gareth Roberts) of *Witch-hunting in Early Modern Scotland.*

Craig B. Palmer is a graduate student in German at Washington University.

Matthew Parfitt is Assistant Professor in the Division of Rhetoric and Humanities at Boston University. His scholarly projects include studies of Frost, Chaucer, and hermeneutic theory.

Alice A. Parker directs the Women's Studies Program at the University of Alabama, where she is Associate Professor of French and Humanities. Her work includes articles on eighteenth-century French women writers, contemporary francophone lesbian writers, and feminist and lesbian theory.

Ted-Larry Pebworth, William E. Stirton Professor of English at the University of Michigan-Dearborn, has published numerous books and essays, especially on seventeenth-century literature.

Joseph Pequigney is Professor of English at the State University of New York at Stony Brook. Author of *Such Is My Love: A Study of Shakespeare's Sonnets*, he has published widely on Renaissance subjects.

William A. Percy is Professor of History at the University of Massachusetts, Boston. Among his many publications is *Outing: Shattering the Conspiracy of Silence*, which he coauthored with the late Warren Johansson.

Kenneth Pobo teaches at Widener University. His essays appear in *A House of Gathering: Poets on May Sarton's Poetry, Asylum*, and *Poet & Critic*. His most recent poetry chapbook, *Yes: Irises*, appeared in 1992.

Guy Poirier is Assistant Professor of French at Simon Fraser University, where he teaches French Renaissance and Québécois literature.

Brian Pronger teaches philosophy at the School of Physical and Health Education at the University of Toronto. An avid swimmer, runner, and cyclist, he is author of *The Arena of Masculinity: Sports, Homosexuality and the Meaning of Sex.*

Alden Reimonenq is Associate Professor of English at St. Mary's College of California. He is working on a biographical and critical study of Countee Cullen. His poetry and reviews have appeared in *James White Review* and in the anthology *Milking Black Bull: 12 Black Gay Poets.*

Simon Richter is Assistant Professor of German Literature at the University of Maryland. He is author of *Laocoön's Body and the Aesthetics of Pain: Winckelmann, Lessing, Herder, Moritz and Goethe.*

Robert B. Marks Ridinger is Chair of the Humanities and Behavioral Sciences Department, University Libraries, Northern Illinois University. He created the *Index to The Advocate, 1967-1982*, compiled *The Homosexual and Society: An Annotated Bibliography*, and contributed to *Gay and Lesbian Literature.*

David Román is Assistant Professor of English at the University of Pennsylvania. He is author of *Acts of Intervention: Contemporary U.S. Theatre and Performance, Gay Men, and AIDS.*

Will Roscoe is the author of *The Zuni Man-Woman* and *Queer Spirits: A Gay Men's Myth Book*. He edited *Living the Spirit: A Gay American Indian Anthology.*

George S. Rousseau is Professor of English and Eighteenth-Century Studies at UCLA. He has published widely in the areas of eighteenth-century literature, history, science, and the history of sexuality.

Everett K. Rowson is Associate Professor of Arabic and Islamic Studies at the University of Pennsylvania. He has published several essays on homosexuality in medieval Arabic literature and society, and is currently engaged in a study of homosexuality in Islamic law.

Paul G. Schalow is Associate Professor of Japanese at Rutgers University. He received his doctorate from Harvard in 1985. His most recent research project is a study of how male love was debated in seventeenth-century vernacular Japanese texts.

Meg Schoerke is Assistant Professor of English at San Francisco State University. She has published poetry and reviews in *Triquarterly, American Scholar*, and other journals.

Gretchen Schultz is Assistant Professor of French Studies at Brown University. She specializes in nineteenth-century literature and poetics, French feminism, and gender and sexuality studies.

Charles Shively is Professor of American Studies at the University of Massachusetts, Boston. He has published widely in both gay and academic presses, including *Calamus Lovers: Walt Whitman's Working Class Camerados.*

Seth Clark Silberman is a Ph.D. candidate in Comparative Literature at the University of Maryland at College Park. He is finishing a study of black gay writer Richard Nugent and working on an investigation of American "drag queen narratives."

Prods Oktor Skjaervo is Aga Khan Professor of Iranian at Harvard University. He specializes in ancient Iranian languages and religions.

Bruce R. Smith, Professor of English at Georgetown University, is the author of the highly acclaimed *Homosexual Desire in Shakespeare's England: A Cultural Poetics.* In 1993, he was elected President of the Shakespeare Association of America.

Martha Nell Smith is Associate Director of the Graduate Program in English at the University of Maryland. She is author of *Rowing in Eden: Rereading Emily Dickinson.*

Patricia Juliana Smith is Lecturer in English and Women's Studies at the University of Connecticut at Stamford. With Corinne Blackmer she has edited a collection of essays on opera.

Anna Sonser is a doctoral candidate in English at the University of Toronto. Her research interests include the contemporary gothic novel.

Francisco Soto is Assistant Professor of Spanish and Latin American Literature at the College of Staten Island, City University of New York. He is author of *Reinaldo Arenas: The Pentagonia.*

Michael N. Stanton is Associate Professor of English at the University of Vermont. He has written on English literary journalism and on such figures as Charles Dickens and Stephen King.

Stacy Steinberg is a Ph.D. candidate at the University of Maryland.

Arlene Stiebel received her Ph.D. from Columbia University with a specialization in Renaissance English and Comparative Literature. She is Professor of English at California State University, Northridge, where she also teaches Women's Studies.

Jacob Stockinger is features editor of *The Capital Times* newspaper in Madison, Wisconsin. He received his Ph.D. in French from the University of Wisconsin-Madison, where he teaches in the Department of Agricultural Journalism. He has published widely on gay and lesbian literature.

Donald Stone is Professor Emeritus of Romance Languages and Literatures at Harvard University. He is the author of books on Ronsard and French humanist tragedy and of numerous articles and editions dealing with Renaissance literature.

Claude J. Summers is William E. Stirton Professor in the Humanities and Professor of English at the University of Michigan-Dearborn. He has published widely on seventeenth- and twentieth-century English literature, including book-length studies of Forster and Isherwood, as well as *Gay Fictions: Wilde to Stonewall* and *Homosexuality in Renaissance and Enlightenment England: Literary Representations in Historical Context.*

Shinasi Tekin is Senior Lecturer in Turkish at Harvard University, where he edits the *Journal of Turkish Studies.*

Marian Urquilla is a graduate student at the University of Maryland.

Giovanni Vitiello recently completed his Ph.D. in Chinese Literature at the University of California, Berkeley. His thesis was a study of homosexuality in seventeenth-century Chinese literature.

Ann Wadsworth is a writer and editor who has published stories in *Christopher Street* and elsewhere. She is currently Publications Coordinator of the Boston Athenaeum.

Alan Wald is Professor in the English Department and Program in American Culture at the University of Michigan. He is the author of five books about culture and radical politics, the most recent of which is *Writing from the Left.*

Brad Walton is a Toronto writer, translator, librettist, and composer. As an undergraduate, he specialized in classics. His graduate work has been devoted to theology and church history.

Priscilla L. Walton is Assistant Professor of English at Carleton University. She is author of *The Disruption of the Feminine in Henry James.*

John Watkins is Assistant Professor of English at the University of Minnesota. He is author of *The Specter of Dido: Spenser and Virgilian Epic* and of essays on Chaucer, the *Pearl*-Poet, and Byron.

Maurice Westmoreland is Assistant Professor of Hispanic Studies at the State University of New York-Albany.

Clare Whatling teaches at the Nottingham Trent University in England. She has published articles on Joan Nestle, Pat Califia, Julia Kristeva, and Jodie Foster.

Jennifer Wilson is an instructor in English and composition at the University of Minnesota, where she is writing a Ph.D. thesis on modern American poetry.

Randal Woodland received his Ph.D. from the University of North Carolina at Chapel Hill. He has taught at UCLA and at the University of Michigan-Dearborn, where he serves as Director of the Writing Program.

Gregory Woods teaches in the Department of English and Media Studies at the Nottingham Trent University in England. He is the author of *Articulate Flesh: Male Homo-eroticism in Modern Poetry* and of a collection of poems, *We Have the Melon.* His essays and reviews on gay culture and on the AIDS epidemic have appeared in books and journals in Britain, Italy, and the United States.

G. Patton Wright is assistant editor of *College English* and the founder of The Dipylon Press in Cambridge, Massachusetts. He is the editor of the definitive edition of Virginia Woolf's *Mrs. Dalloway.*

Index   TO ENTRIES AND WRITERS